Making Literature Matter

AN ANTHOLOGY

FOR READERS AND WRITERS

FIFTH EDITION

John Schilb
Indiana University

John Clifford
University of North Carolina at Wilmington

*Kirsten
(personal copy)*

BEDFORD / ST. MARTIN'S   Boston ▪ New York

For Bedford/St. Martin's
Senior Executive Editor: Stephen A. Scipione
Production Editor: Katherine Caruana
Senior Production Supervisor: Dennis Conroy
Senior Marketing Manager: Adrienne Petsick
Associate Editor: Shannon Walsh
Editorial Assistant: Alyssa Demirjian
Copyeditor: Linda McLatchie
Indexer: Mary White
Photo Researcher: Linda Finigan
Permissions Manager: Kalina K. Ingham
Senior Art Director: Anna Palchik
Text Design: Jean Hammond
Cover Design: Donna L. Dennison
Cover Art: Boat Race Jazz © Jill Hoy, www.jillhoy.com
Composition: NK Graphics
Printing and Binding: Quad/Graphics Taunton

President: Joan E. Feinberg
Editorial Director: Denise B. Wydra
Editor in Chief: Karen S. Henry
Director of Marketing: Karen R. Soeltz
Director of Production: Susan W. Brown
Associate Director, Editorial Production: Elise S. Kaiser
Managing Editor: Elizabeth M. Schaaf

Library of Congress Control Number: 2011924034

6 5 4 3 2

f e d c b

For information, write: Bedford/St. Martin's, 75 Arlington Street, Boston, MA 02116
(617-399-4000)

ISBN: 978-0-312-65354-5

Preface for Instructors

A host of compelling literary works; plentiful advice on how to read them closely; and detailed suggestions for writing about them: many an instructor has valued these elements of *Making Literature Matter*, and so they remain central in its fifth edition. As usual, the book reflects our decades of teaching both literature and composition. Always we strive to make this volume a resource especially for classes that blend the two subjects. Indeed, we believe that literature can benefit all sorts of composition courses, including those that prepare first-year or second-year students to write in various fields. After all, most disciplines emphasize careful interpretation, passionate engagement, and keen awareness of human complexity — the sort of analysis that literary texts invite. For students who might otherwise grope for things to say in their papers, literature often sparks insights. It gives them questions to pursue and ideas to mine.

As before, Part One spends much time identifying not only ways to read but also ways to write. Our recommendations for writing are grounded in rhetoric, a set of principles and practices that, from ancient times to the present, has guided the art of persuasion. In particular, we show how to construct *arguments* about literature. We stress that argument is, at its best, not crude verbal combat, but instead a calm, self-reflective attempt to gain support for one's views. We explain that this process involves choosing an issue, forming a claim, and mustering evidence for it, so that even audiences initially skeptical will come to see the claim's logic. Whenever we offer strategies for reading or for writing, we model them with examples, often from papers or informal jottings in which students use these techniques.

Then, as usual, the bulk of our literary selections come in the theme-based chapters that comprise Part Two. The chapters' main topics remain unchanged from the fourth edition, for plainly they remain relevant to students' lives. Specifically, the subjects are families; love; freedom and confinement; doing justice; and journeys. And again, each chapter is divided into small clusters, an arrangement that encourages study of texts' similarities and differences. While a class can learn much by focusing on works in isolation, juxtaposing them can sharpen awareness of their nuances, so that students are more apt to write perceptively about them. Each chapter still includes four kinds of clusters that classes have found distinctly illuminating: a set of works by a single author; a single work together with critics' interpretations of it; a single work joined by documents that put it into a larger cultural context; and a work accompanied by one or more transformations ("re-visions") of it.

New to the Fifth Edition

Many new and diverse selections. For the book's literary contents, naturally we have kept selections that instructors report to be perennial favorites. As you would expect, however, we have made numerous replacements, bringing in texts that we think will engage students as readers, promote lively discussion, and generate thoughtful writing. In Chapter 4's treatment of the writing process, for instance, the sample comparative paper deals with literary works more recent than before: contemporary poems by Don Paterson and Luisa A. Igloria. In Chapter 10 ("Families"), the cluster dealing with a single author's works now focuses on poet Sharon Olds, and Chapter 11's cultural context unit centers on a story by Jhumpa Lahiri. Throughout the book, readers will find new examples of literature's multicultural range. With this edition, our scope has grown to include not only canonical writers like Keats and Thoreau but also ethnically diverse modern voices like Lorna Dee Cervantes, Audre Lorde, Barry Lopez, Nelly Sachs, Atul Gawande, Ha Jin, Linh Dinh, and Toi Derricotte.

"In the News" clusters. To each chapter in Part Two, we have made a significant addition: a cluster that reflects Ezra Pound's definition of literature as "news that stays news." Each of these groupings encourages students to draw parallels between literature and contemporary events. We stress that a text from years ago — even from the distant past — can have enduring import. For example, in Chapter 11 ("Love"), we follow canonical elegies with accounts of new memorial practices: those emerging on the World Wide Web. Next, in Chapter 12 ("Freedom and Confinement"), a Karen Russell story about vampires is accompanied by a number of articles about their current popularity in American culture. In Chapter 13 ("Doing Justice"), we put the ancient drama *Antigone* together with articles about modern counterparts of its heroine, women fighting dictators in Iran and Myanmar. In Chapter 14 ("Journeys"), we again present Tim O'Brien's classic Vietnam War story "The Things They Carried," but now it appears with Valerie Seiling Jacobs's recent piece on the things her stepson carried to war in Iraq.

New guidance on thinking, reading, and writing critically about literature. We have revised the book's first chapter so that it gives students a better sense of what *literature* is in the first place. To elaborate the term, we trace differences between Maxine Kumin's poem "Woodchucks" and a news article about hunters of these creatures. As always, Part One emphasizes methods for reading and writing critically, but through various additions we provide even greater guidance for these crucial activities. The extra help includes discussion in Chapter 2 of how to analyze literary characters by identifying their emotions and by naming their speech acts. We not only explain these two new strategies but also model them, by applying the first to a poem by Edward Hirsch and the second to a story by Paul Lisicky. To demonstrate all the techniques we suggest for reading, we have incorporated into the same chapter a student's annotation of an X. J. Kennedy poem.

More sample student research papers.   In the concluding chapter of Part One, whose subject is how to write to research papers, we have increased the number of sample student essays. Once more, all of them demonstrate research-based approaches to Charlotte Perkins Gilman's story "The Yellow Wallpaper," but we have added an essay that shows how to study literature through a particular theorist's lens. In this case, the theorist is Michel Foucault, whose concept of "discipline" serves as a tool for analyzing Gilman's themes. Furthermore, we have updated the sample paper that illustrates how literary works can help advance arguments about contemporary social issues. The new essay uses Gilman's story as a springboard for critiquing recent studies of postpartum depression.

A new full-color portfolio pairing images and poems.   Finally, and most conspicuously, we have added a series of color plates. Each touches on one of the broad themes in the book. More precisely, each plate combines a picture with a poem, helping students develop a fresh, thought-provoking perspective on both works. Overall, this new section acknowledges a current academic trend: increasingly, the fields of literary studies and composition are interested not only in verbal rhetoric but also in *visual* rhetoric. Moreover, today's students are already immersed in a constant stream of images, many of which they gaze at merely by switching on their phones. They are likely to be comfortable with, even relish, studying literature in this context, especially because the process can help them generate more original and nuanced claims. The first plate displays Edward Hopper's painting *Office at Night* with a poem about it by Rolando Perez, who interprets Hopper as telling a certain story. In some of the other plates, image and text are not so directly linked. Their subject is roughly the same, but how best to compare the two works is quite open to debate. For instance, students might have various notions of how to relate Michael Sebastian's photo of a suburban neighborhood to the poem we place it with, Philip Levine's tale of a single house. To be sure, not all classes will know exactly how to examine visual art. Therefore, we introduce the section by explaining what details to look for in a picture, drawing examples from Hopper's office scene. Then, to show how writers might interpret literary and visual works together, we present a sample student paper, which compares Hopper's painting and Perez's poem.

Acknowledgments

The terrific staff at Bedford/St. Martin's continue to be wise and generous collaborators in our efforts. Once again, we have relied especially on two people who are wonderful guides and true friends: senior executive editor Steve

Scipione and company president Joan Feinberg. In the editorial department, we want to express thanks in particular to the thoughtful and incisive editorial director Denise Wydra, the indispensable editor in chief Karen Henry, and three hardworking editorial assistants: Kate Mayhew, Alyssa Demirjian, and especially Shannon Walsh. In production, we are grateful to the director, Susan W. Brown, and the associate director, Elise Kaiser; to managing editor Elizabeth Schaaf, to assistant managing editor John Amburg, and to copyeditor Linda McLatchie; and especially to our gracious and resilient production editor Katie Caruana, who was able to keep this complicated project on track and on schedule. In the permissions department, manager Kalina Ingham, editor Caryn Burtt, photo researcher Linda Finigan, and photo research manager Martha Friedman expertly and efficiently negotiated and obtained reprint rights. In marketing, we are most grateful to director Karen Soeltz, senior marketing manager Jenna Bookin Barry, and marketing manager Adrienne Petsick.

Once more, we thank Janet E. Gardner, formerly of the University of Massachusetts at Dartmouth, for her contributions to the chapter on research, as well as Joyce Hollingsworth of the University of North Carolina at Wilmington for her ample work on the Instructor's Manual. As always, John Schilb is indebted to his former University of Maryland colleague Jeanne Fahnestock and his current colleagues at Indiana University, especially Christine Farris, Kathy Smith, and Lisa Ottum. He also thanks Gary Weissman from the University of Cincinnati for calling his attention to Ira Sher's story "The Man in the Well." John Clifford thanks poet Daniel Terry for his help.

Of course, we remain grateful as well to the instructors who have commented on various editions over the years — especially to those who have adopted the book, some for many editions. For their extremely helpful responses, we thank Julie Aipperspach Anderson, Texas A&M University; Jonathan Alexander, University of Southern Colorado; Donna Allen, Erie Community College; Virginia Anderson, University of Texas at Austin; Liana Andreasen, South Texas College; Sonja L. Andrus, Collin County Community College; Andrew Armond, Belmont Abbey College; Carolyn Baker, San Antonio College; Rance G. Baker, San Antonio College; Barbara Barnard, Hunter College; Charles Bateman, Essex County College; Linda Bensel-Meyers, University of Tennessee, Knoxville; Elaine Boothby, South River High School; Colleen Brooks-Edgar, South Texas College; Elizabeth L. Cobb, Chapman University; Chauna Craig, Indiana University of Pennsylvania; Timothy R. Cramer, Santa Monica College; Michael A. Cronin, Northern Oklahoma College; Rosemary B. Day, Central New Mexico Community College–Montoya Campus; Thomas Deans, Kansas State University; Kevin J. H. Dettmar, Pomona College; Jennifer Dorfield, Westfield State College; Michael Doyle, Blue Ridge Community College; Penelope Dugan, Richard Stockton College of New Jersey; Thomas Dukes, University of Akron; Mary Dutterer, Howard Community College; Kelly Edmisten, University of North Carolina at Wilmington; Irene R. Fairley, Northeastern University; Joli Furnari, Montclair State University; Selma Goldstein, Rider University; Martha K. Goodman, Central Virginia Community College;

Christopher Gould, University of North Carolina at Wilmington; Maureen Groome, Brevard Community College; Chad Hammett, Texas State University; Martin Harris, Belmont Abbey College; William Harrison, Northern Virginia Community College; Iris Rose Hart, Santa Fe Community College; Carol Peterson Haviland, California State University, San Bernardino; Ana Hernandez, Miami-Dade College–Wolfson; John Heyda, Miami University–Middletown; Jeff Hoogeveen, Lincoln University; Richard Dean Hovey, Pima Community College; Karen Howard, Volunteer State Community College; Clark Hutton, Volunteer State Community College; Joan Kellerman, University of Massachusetts–Dartmouth; Sabine A. Klein, Purdue University; Sonya Lancaster, University of Kansas; Kasee Clifton Laster, Ashland University; Marianne Layer, Armstrong Atlantic State University; Margaret Lindgren, University of Cincinnati; Betty Mandeville, Volunteer State Community College; Kelly Martin, Collin County Community College; Phillip Mayfield, Fullerton College; Miles S. McCrimmon, J. Sargeant Reynolds Community College; Christopher McDermott, University of Georgia; Mandy McDougal, Volunteer State Community College; Steven Newman, University of Nebraska–Omaha; Dana Nichols, Gainesville State College; Jim O'Loughlin, University of Northern Iowa; Gordon O'Neal, Collin County Community College; Christine Peter, University of Massachusetts–Dartmouth; Brenton Phillips, Cloud County Community College; Nancy Lawson Remler, Armstrong Atlantic State University; David Rollison, College of Marin; Jane Rosecrans, J. Sargeant Reynolds Community College; Teri Rosen, Hunter College; Lisa Roy-Davis, Collin County Community College; Donna Samet, Broward Community College; Jamie Sanchez, Volunteer State Community College; Daniel Schierenbeck, University of Central Missouri; Meryl F. Schwartz, Lakeland Community College; Pauline Scott, Alabama State University; Julie Segedy, Chabot College; Lucia Seranyan, Northern Virginia Community College, Woodbridge Campus; Kimberly Alford Singh, Northern Virginia Community College; Jason Skipper, Miami University at Oxford; Jennifer Smith, Miami University at Oxford; Debra L. Snyder, Livingstone College; Jamieson Spencer, St. Louis Community College; Pam Stinson, Northern Oklahoma College; Jonathan Taylor, Ferris State University; Julie Tilton, San Bernardino Valley College; Larry A. VanMeter, Texas A&M University; William Verrone, University of North Carolina at Wilmington; Phillippe (Phil) West, Concordia University; Sharon Winn, Northeastern State University; Bertha Wise, Oklahoma City Community College; Pauline G. Woodward, Endicott College.

Always, new editions feature changes, but this we must repeat: what matters most to John Schilb is Wendy Elliot; what matters most to John Clifford is Janet Ellerby, and we dedicate this book to them.

John Schilb, Indiana University
John Clifford, University of North Carolina at Wilmington

You Get More Digital Choices for *Making Literature Matter*

Making Literature Matter doesn't stop with a book. Online, you'll find both free and affordable premium resources to help students get even more out of the book and your course. You'll also find convenient instructor resources and even a nationwide community of teachers. To learn more about or to order any of the following products, contact your Bedford/St. Martin's sales representative, e-mail sales support (**sales_support@bfwpub.com**), or visit the Web site at **bedfordstmartins.com/catalog/makinglitmatter**.

Re:Writing for Literature
bedfordstmartins.com/rewritinglit

Send students to free and open resources, choose flexible premium resources to supplement your print text, or upgrade to an expanding collection of innovative digital content.

Free and open resources at *Re:Writing for Literature* provide students with easy-to-access visual tutorials, reference materials, and support for working with sources.

- **VirtuaLit** Tutorials for Close Reading (Fiction, Poetry, and Drama)
- **AuthorLinks** Annotated research links for more than 800 authors
- **VideoCentral: Literature Sampler** A peek into our growing collection of video interviews with today's authors
- **LitQuiz** A database of self-tests on literary works and elements
- **LitGloss** A glossary of literary terms
- **Sample Papers** MLA-style models for literature
- **Research and Documentation Online**, by Diana Hacker, for finding and citing sources
- **The Bedford Bibliographer**, by Mike Palmquist, for building a bibliography

VideoCentral: Literature — a Bedford/St. Martin's production created with writer and teacher Peter Berkow — is a growing collection of video interviews with today's writers, talking about their craft. Your students can hear from Ha Jin on how he uses humor and tension in his writing, Anne Rice on how she advances plot through dialogue, Chitra Banerjee Divakaruni on how she writes from experience, and Frank McCourt on how he created memorable voices.

For a list of authors and topics and a sample video, visit **bedfordstmartins .com/videolit**. *VideoCentral: Literature* can be packaged with new student editions of the book. An activation code is required and must be purchased. To order *VideoCentral: Literature* with the print book, use ISBN 978-1-4576-0710-3.

Consider upgrading to *Re:Writing Plus*, our collection of premium materials for literature and writing. As subscribers, you and your students can access hundreds of additional readings — including public domain short stories, poems, and plays — as well as the most innovative and interactive help with writing; the first ever peer-review game; and hundreds of models of writing.

Subscriptions also include access to *VideoCentral: Literature*, described on the previous page. An activation code is required and must be purchased. For more information, visit **bedfordstmartins.com/rewritingplus**.

Instructor Resources
bedfordstmartins.com/catalog/makinglitmatter

You have a lot to do in your course. Bedford/St. Martin's wants to make it easy for you to find the support you need — and to get it quickly.

Resources for Teaching Making Literature Matter: An Anthology for Readers and Writers, **Fifth Edition, prepared by John Schilb, John Clifford, and Joyce Hollingsworth**, includes sample syllabi; additional commentaries on the literary selections, in particular those in the anthology, "Literature and Its Issues," with many suggestions for teaching them; and an annotated list of scholarly works that link the teaching of literature with composition instruction. For the PDF, go to **bedfordstmartins.com/catalog/ makinglitmatter**. To order the print edition, use ISBN 978-0-312-68044-2.

Teaching Central offers the entire list of Bedford/St. Martin's print and online professional resources in one place. You'll find landmark reference works, sourcebooks on pedagogical issues, award-winning collections, and practical advice for the classroom — all free for instructors and available through the student center or at **bedfordstmartins.com/catalog/teachingcentral**.

The Bedford/St. Martin's Video & DVD Library offers selected videos and DVDs of plays and stories included in *Making Literature Matter* and is available to qualified adopters of the anthology. To learn more, contact your Bedford/ St. Martin's sales representative or e-mail sales support (**sales_support@ bfwpub.com**).

Literary Reprints. Titles in the Case Studies in Contemporary Criticism series, Bedford Cultural Edition series, and the Bedford Shakespeare series can be shrink-wrapped with *Making Literature Matter* for instructors who want to teach longer works in conjunction with the anthology. (For a complete list of available titles, visit **bedfordstmartins.com/catalog/literaryreprints**.)

TradeUp: Get 50 percent off all trade titles when packaged with your textbook! Add more value and choice to your students' learning experiences by packaging their Bedford/St. Martin's textbook with one of a thousand titles from our sister publishers such as Farrar, Straus and Giroux and St. Martin's Press — at a discount of 50 percent off the regular price.

Brief Contents

Contents

6. How to Write about Poems   143

≡ PART TWO   Literature and Its Issues

10. Families   247

Contents by Genre

Stories

Poems

Plays

Essays/Nonfiction

Critical Commentaries

Cultural Contexts

News Stories and Editorials

Images: Paintings and Photographs

Working with Literature

CHAPTER 1

What Is Literature? How and Why Does It Matter?

The title of this book, *Making Literature Matter*, may seem curious to you. Presumably your school assumes that literature already matters, for otherwise it would hardly offer courses in the subject. Quite possibly you are taking this course because you think literature is important or hope it will become so for you. But with our title, we want to emphasize that literature does not exist in a social vacuum. Rather, literature is part of human relationships; people *make* literature matter to other people. We are especially concerned with how you can make literature matter to others as well as to yourself. Above all, we point out ways you can argue about literature, both in class discussions and in your own writing.

Here is a poem that has engaged many readers, judging by how often it has appeared in literature anthologies since its first publication in 1963. The author is James Wright (1927–1980), who was born and raised in the industrial town of Martin's Ferry, Ohio, and won the Pulitzer Prize for poetry in 1972. Many of Wright's poems deal with the working-class life he experienced. Early in his career as a poet, he wrote in conventional forms, but later he became much more experimental. The following poem, perhaps Wright's most famous, is a case in point. The poem's speaker, you will see, comes to a judgment about whether he's managed to make his very existence matter.

JAMES WRIGHT

Lying in a Hammock at William Duffy's Farm in Pine Island, Minnesota

Over my head, I see the bronze butterfly,
Asleep on the black trunk,
Blowing like a leaf in green shadow.
Down the ravine behind the empty house,
The cowbells follow one another
Into the distances of the afternoon.
To my right,
In a field of sunlight between two pines,
The droppings of last year's horses

5

Blaze up into golden stones.   10
I lean back, as the evening darkens and comes on.
A chicken hawk floats over, looking for home.
I have wasted my life.   *[1963]*

Did the last line startle you? For many readers, Wright's poem is memorable because its conclusion is unexpected, even jarring. At first glance, nothing in the speaker's description of his surroundings justifies his blunt self-condemnation at the end. If anything, the previous lines evoke rural tranquility, so that a more predictable finish would be "I am now at peace." Instead, the speaker suddenly criticizes himself. Intrigued by this mysterious move, readers usually look at the whole poem again, studying it for signs of growing despair. Often they debate with one another how the ending does relate to preceding lines. Thus, although the poem's speaker implies his life hasn't mattered, the poem itself has mattered to readers, plunging them into lively exchanges over how to interpret Wright's text.

We present Wright's poem to begin pointing out how literature can matter to people. We will keep referring to the poem in this introduction. But now we turn to three big questions:

- How have people defined *literature?*
- Why study literature in a college writing course?
- What can *you* do to make literature matter to others?

How Have People Defined *Literature?*

Asked to define *literature,* most people would include Wright's text, along with other poems. In addition to poetry, they would say *literature* encompasses fiction (novels as well as short stories) and drama. But limiting the term's scope to these genres can be misleading, for they are rooted in everyday life. Often they employ ordinary forms of talk, although they may play with such expressions and blend them with less common ones. Someone lying in a hammock may, in fact, recite details of the landscape — especially if he or she is talking to someone else on a cell phone, as is common nowadays. And quite possibly you have heard someone proclaim "I have wasted my life" or make a similar declaration. In any case, surely much of Wright's language is familiar to you, even if you haven't seen it arranged into these particular phrases and lines.

The genres regarded as literary are tied in other ways to everyday behavior. For instance, things function as symbols not only in poems but also in daily conversation. Even people who aren't poets have little trouble associating shadows, evening, darkness, and hawks with death. (In the case of Wright's poem, the issue then becomes whether the text supports or complicates this association.) Hammocks, too, are often treated as meaningful images. They are familiar symbols of "taking it easy." (With Wright's poem, the issue again becomes whether the speaker's hammock signifies *more* than just leisure.)

Throughout the day, then, it can be said that people put literary genres into practice. Perhaps you have commented on certain situations by quoting a song lyric or citing words from a poem, story, or play. Surely you are poetic in the sense that you use metaphors in your everyday conversations. After all, most of us are capable, as Wright's speaker is, of comparing a butterfly to a leaf (even if we aren't apt to compare horse droppings to "golden stones"). Probably you are often theatrical as well, carrying out various kinds of scripts and performing any number of roles. Furthermore, probably you are engaged in storytelling no matter how little fiction you actually write. Imagine this familiar situation: you are late for a meeting with friends because you got stuck in traffic, and now you must explain to them your delay. Your explanation may well become a tale of suspense, with you the hero racing against time to escape the bumper-to-bumper horde. As writer Joan Didion has observed, "We tell ourselves stories in order to live." Almost all of us spin narratives day after day because doing so helps us meaningfully frame our lives. (Unfortunately, the story that Wright's speaker tells is "I have wasted my life." Nevertheless, it's a means for interpreting his existence, and maybe somehow it helps him keep on living.)

You may admit that literature is grounded in real life and yet still tend to apply the term only to written texts of fiction, poetry, and drama. But this tendency is distinctly modern, for the term *literature* has not always been applied so restrictively. *Literature* was at first a characteristic of *readers*. From the term's emergence in the fourteenth century to the middle of the eighteenth, *literature* was more or less a synonym for *literacy*. People of literature were assumed to be well read.

In the late eighteenth century, however, the term's meaning changed. Increasingly it referred to books and other printed texts rather than to people who read them. At the beginning of this shift, the scope of literature was broad, encompassing nearly all public writing. But as the nineteenth century proceeded, the term's range shrank. More and more people considered literature to be imaginative or creative writing, which they distinguished from nonfiction. This trend did take years to build; in the early 1900s, literature anthologies still featured essays as well as excerpts from histories and biographies. By the mid-1900s, though, the narrower definition of literature prevailed.

This limited definition has become vulnerable. From the early 1970s, a number of literature faculty have called for widening it. In 1979, for instance, a National Endowment for the Humanities–Modern Language Association institute entitled "Women's Nontraditional Literature" applied the term *literature* to genres that had not been thought of as such. Participants studied essays, letters, diaries, autobiographies, and oral testimonies. To each of these genres, women have contributed much; in fact, the institute's participants concluded that a literature curriculum slights many works by women if it focuses on fiction, poetry, and drama alone.

Of course, even within these three categories, the term *literature* has been selectively applied. Take the case of novelist and short-story writer Stephen King, whose books have sold millions of copies. Despite his commercial success, a lot of readers — including some of his fans — refuse to call King's writing literature. They assume that to call something literature is to say that it has artistic merit, and for them King's tales of horror fall short.

Yet people who use the term *literature* as a compliment may still disagree about whether a certain text deserves it. Plenty of readers do praise King's writing as literature, even as others deem it simply entertainment. In short, artistic standards differ. To be sure, some works have been constantly admired through the years; regarded as classics, they are frequently taught in literature classes. *Hamlet* and other plays by William Shakespeare are obvious examples. But in the last twenty years, much controversy has arisen over the *literary canon*, those works taught again and again. Are there good reasons why the canon has consisted mostly of works by white men? Or have the principles of selection been skewed by sexism and racism? Should the canon be changed to accommodate a greater range of authors? Or should literary studies resist having any canon at all? These questions have provoked various answers and continued debate.

Also in question are attempts to separate literature from *nonfiction*. Much nonfiction shows imagination and relies on devices found in novels, short stories, poems, and plays. The last few years have seen the emergence of the term *creative nonfiction* as a synonym for essays, autobiographies, histories, and journalistic accounts that use evocative language and strong narratives. Conversely, works of fiction, poetry, and drama may center on real-life events. For example, beginning with James Wright's "Lying in a Hammock," several of the poems in our book can easily be seen as autobiographical. Perhaps you have suspected already that the speaker in Wright's poem is Wright himself. In numerous interviews, Wright admitted as much. He acknowledged that he based the poem on his own experience of lying in a hammock, which really did lead him to think "I have wasted my life."

A note of caution is in order. While testimony such as Wright's can be illuminating, it should be used prudently. In crucial respects, Wright's poem still differs from Wright's life. The text is a representation of his experience, not the experience itself. His particular choice and arrangement of words continue to merit study, especially because he could have depicted his experience in plenty of other ways. As critic Charles Altieri notes, important to specify are the ways in which a poem is "binding the forms of syntax to the possibilities of feeling." Keep in mind, too, that the author of a work is not always the ideal guide to it. After all, the work may matter to its readers by raising for them issues and ideas that the author did not foresee. Besides, often the author's comments about the text leave certain aspects of it unexplained. Though Wright disclosed his poem's origins, readers must still decide how to connect its various images to its final line. Even so, "Lying in a Hammock" confirms that a literary work can stem from actual circumstances, whatever use the reader makes of facts about them.

Some people argue, however, that literature about real events is still "literary" because it inspires contemplation rather than action. This view of literature has traditionally been summed up as "art for art's sake." This notion brushes aside, however, all the poems, novels, short stories, and plays that encourage audiences to undertake certain acts. Included in our book, for example, is Sherman Alexie's "Capital Punishment," a poem designed to spark resistance to the death penalty. True, not every poem is so conspicuously action-oriented. Wright's "Lying in a Hammock" seems more geared toward reflection, especially because the speaker is physically reclining while he observes nature and ponders his life. But readers may take even this poem as an incitement to change their behavior, so that they can feel they have not wasted their own lives.

In our book, we resist endorsing a single definition of *literature*. Rather, we encourage you to review and perhaps rethink what the term means to you. At the same time, to expand the realm of literature, we include several essays in addition to short stories, poems, and plays. We also present numerous critical commentaries as well as various historical documents. Throughout the book, we invite you to make connections among these different kinds of texts. You need not treat them as altogether separate species.

What Makes Literature "Literature"?
Comparing a News Story and a Poem

We have suggested that, in some respects, literature can resemble other writing. So, too, can it resemble ordinary speech. Still, literature can be viewed as a distinct category, even if controversies arise over what specific texts belong to it. Usually, works classified as literature permit the reader to treat their characters as imaginary. Just as often, these works' use of language is especially skillful and challenging. Through their style, they dramatically depict people, situations, and settings, emotionally drawing their readers in. At the same time, many of the words in such texts can have more than one meaning. They might be ambiguous, symbolic, or metaphorical. Furthermore, the main characters are often complicated, even mysterious. Their acts, relationships, and motives defy simple diagnosis. Typically, just as complex is any "lesson" these works teach. They illuminate life, but they do so by showing how it resists reduction to clichés or other slogans. Furthermore, the basic design of these works may not be immediately clear. Their patterns may be detectable only after repeated reading. Overall, a literary work tends to make its readers *analyze* it, *interpret* it. They may then disagree about its meaning and impact. Indeed, we hope that our own literary selections will spark debates in your class.

A literary work's special features can be more apparent if you compare it with another kind of text on the same topic. Consider the following pair of examples. Each of these pieces of writing deals with the ways humans react when wildlife invades their home turf. In particular, each dramatizes the exasperation that many people feel when woodchucks destroy their farms or gardens. But while one text is a newspaper article, the other is a poem, and the differences are striking.

■ **BEFORE YOU READ**

Take ten minutes or so to freewrite a response to one or more of the following questions, all of which are related to the two texts you are about to read.

1. What species of wildlife do you think people are justified in fearing or despising?

2. What experiences, if any, have you had with animals encroaching on your property?

3. When woodchucks, moles, mice, rabbits, deer, or other animals feast on a farm or garden, does its owner have a right to destroy them? Why, or why not?

4. To what extent do you believe in the concept of "animal rights"? In what sorts of cases, if any, do you think it applies? In what sorts of cases, if any, do you think it is misapplied?

Here is the newspaper article, Joyce Wadler's "Peter Rabbit Must Die," which appeared in the June 5, 2008, issue of the *New York Times*.

JOYCE WADLER

Peter Rabbit Must Die

The homeowner, a city-boy artist and illustrator who had moved to rural Pennsylvania, never wanted to kill the woodchucks. Sure, they were ruining the garden and digging up the foundations of outbuildings, but it was a moral issue: the artist, who is still so uncomfortable about what transpired — and so concerned about how his New York clients would feel about it that he is not willing to be identified — did not want to take a life.

Given the size of the property — a 12-acre former horse farm — fencing was out of the question. He bought a Havahart live animal trap but did not catch a thing. And he worried that releasing woodchucks down the road would only be dumping the problem on a neighbor. So he moved on to that tried-and-true landlord's tactic: harassment. He attached a hose to the exhaust pipe of his old pickup truck and stuffed it into a burrow — not to kill the woodchucks, just to encourage them to move on. That didn't work, either.

Finally, the artist decided he would have to shoot the animals. First, though, he went to each hole and made an announcement.

"I said: 'I intend to kill you. You have 24 hours to get out,'" he recalls. "I wanted to give them fair warning. I said, 'If I were you, I would find another place to live.' I also promised them I would not take a shot unless I knew it would be fatal."

He is making this into a funny story, he says, but when he killed his first woodchuck he "literally felt sick."

5

"I went outside and knelt down to it and said a little prayer to whatever the powers that be that when my turn comes, I will do it as gracefully and uncomplainingly."

Eventually, though, he embraced his mission and grew so obsessed with it that an aunt began to call him Woodchuck Johnny. How many did he kill that summer?

"I stopped at 19," he says. "One was a suicide. It realized its days were numbered and ran in front of a car."

The artist's story is not as unusual as some would like to believe. As summer closes in, gardeners around the country are starting to worry about the animals that may end up enjoying their roses and cucumbers more than they do. Any day now, they know, they may come upon a carrot patch ravaged by groundhogs, lettuce ransacked by rabbits and squirrels, or a massacre in the koi pond.

But for many gardeners—the tenderhearted ones, who pride themselves   10
on their decency and compassion—killing pests, particularly those with big eyes, fluffy tails, and cousins who work for Disney, could never be a solution of first resort.

"People who garden have an obvious love of life, a reverence for life, and to kill something in order to garden is very rough," says Liz Krieg, who runs the Rising Sun Greenhouses and Landscape Company in Bethel, Vermont, and who dispatches only the scarlet lily beetle.

City people tend to take up gardening in their yards or at their summer houses with a generous attitude toward summer's bounty, ready to live and let live. The woodchucks want a few zucchini? No problem, there are enough to go around. The rabbits are decimating the lettuce? Get a humane trap and move them elsewhere.

Soon enough, though, they realize it's not that simple. The animals do not take one or two tomatoes as if they're in a greenmarket in the Hamptons; they go down the row sampling, so that everything is ruined. Or they uproot and destroy a crop, without eating a thing, in their search for insects and grubs. There is, in fact, a sameness to the stories the gardeners tell: "If they just had taken one head of lettuce, or a few strawberries—but they decimated the whole thing!" After a season of grueling labor and multiple attempts at benign deterrence, the sight of a trashed garden is often the last straw: the moment when a gentle gardener will suddenly go Rambo.

Such was the case with Susanne Williams, a retired supply officer for the Alaska Department of Transportation, who lives with her husband in Douglas, near Juneau. Gardening is a struggle in southeast Alaska, she says; there is not a lot of sun. But she and her husband have two gardens, one at their home overlooking the Gastineau Channel, the other at the local community garden near the Mendenhall Glacier. They give much of their produce to charity and put up mesh at home in an unsuccessful attempt to keep out porcupines.

Five years ago there were serious animal problems at the community gar-   15
den — black bear, deer, beaver — but "the worst pest of all was the porcupine,"

Ms. Williams says. "The kindhearted would trap them and drive them 10 or 15 miles away, until one of the forest people said they just came back."

It reached a point, Ms. Williams says, when gardeners were so frustrated that at least 30 of the 150 plots were empty.

"So finally, four years ago, we put an electric fence all around this big field, but the porcupines then decide to burrow under the fence," she says. "They're ingenious. So we had to put rocks down and pour cement."

Even then, a porcupine managed to get in. And when she saw it, "strolling along, munching away," she could stand no more.

"He was after my carrot crop," she explains. "I said, I just cannot handle this anymore. He sees me and tries to wander off, but they can't run very fast. I got him with the sledgehammer. He tried to dodge me, but I got him on the head."

And no, she hasn't lost any sleep over it.   20

"It was sad, but I am tired of being the fancy kitchen for critters," she says. She has a friend in the area who has "just given up" on being kind to the animals: "He goes after them with a pitchfork and puts them in his compost pile. I don't think the PETA people would like him much."

She adds: "Doesn't the spinach scream when it boils? I think probably all living things have some scream going on. We're all predators, no matter whether we're animals, mineral, birds, or fish, and that's part of it."

Taking pest control into your own hands, of course, is no simple matter. There are the ethical and emotional issues, and while it is often legal to kill a pest, there are innumerable federal, state, and municipal laws and regulations that may make it illegal.

There would seem, at first, to be many alternatives to killing. Besides mesh and electric fences, there are nets to cast over trees and gardens; foul scents with names like Not Tonight, Deer; and home remedies like sprinkling cayenne pepper around the tomatoes and dumping used cat litter into woodchuck holes. There are scarecrows in the north and fake alligators in the south, and household pets to scare predators away or to do the gardeners' dirty work. There are capture-and-release traps.

But none of these methods work all the time, and some, depending on   25
the species you are trying to catch and the area in which you live, may not even be legal. The New York State Environmental Protection Law, for example, forbids anyone but a state Nuisance Wildlife Control Operator from transporting a wild animal, which puts the kibosh on the use of capture-and-release traps.

Trapping and moving animals may not be in their best interests, either: a backyard suburban squirrel, transported to a forest, is easy prey for hawks and foxes, said John Hadidian, the director of urban wildlife programs for the Humane Society of the United States and the primary author of *Wild Neighbors: The Humane Approach to Living with Wildlife.* (The book suggests tolerance as its first choice for everything from bats to rats.)

And releasing an animal in a more familiar setting may not be in your neighbors' best interests.

"We have yet to find anyone in outlying areas who says, 'We love raccoons, please bring your humanely trapped critters here and let them go,'" says Wendell Martin, a retired engineer who has a five-acre garden in Meridian, Idaho, near Boise. Raccoons have uprooted and upended his water lilies to find snails. Mr. Martin finally borrowed a .22 and shot them. It was not an ethical problem for him, he says — the animals are overpopulated in his area — but it was not easy emotionally. (This year there seem to be fewer of them, and he has been trying to protect his plants with wire mesh.)

Then there are the difficulties that can arise when transporting a wild animal.

Jessica DuLong, a Brooklyn writer and marine engineer, managed to grow   30
a fruit-bearing cherry tree on her roof, but even in the wake of what she calls the Great Cherry Massacre of 2007 she was not interested in punishing the squirrels who preyed on it. She trapped one in a live animal trap and set out to Prospect Park with good intentions.

Unfortunately, the squirrel had no way of knowing this. It threw itself against the walls of the cage with such ferocity it cut itself; it defecated; it ran back and forth inside the long cage in a frenzy so that the cage flipped up and down like a manic miniature seesaw. New Yorkers, seeing a fluffy tail in distress, yelled at the human involved.

"This entire class of preschool kids was out in one of their little preschool wagons, and the squirrel is looking rabid and bleeding at the mouth," she says. "It was not what I had in mind when I started this humanitarian project."

Not all city people, of course, are so sweetly disposed to cute rodents. Joanna Lennig is an executive headhunter who lives in Brooklyn but grew up in Maine and New Hampshire. As a 10-year-old she was stunned to see her mother, "an incredibly polite, retiring, WASP lady," attacking a woodchuck in the vegetable garden with a shovel.

"You know that body posture someone has when they're using a pickax," Ms. Lennig says. "She was just enraged. We just talked about this recently — being WASPs, we'd never talked about it. We were a family who canned the corn and canned the beans and really put food aside for the winter, so having an animal go through the green beans, she was furious. She said she'd had it."

Ms. Lennig herself has no sentimental attachment to squirrels. About   35
three years ago she saw signs of digging in the rooftop garden of her brownstone, which has pots of blueberry bushes, grape vines, tomatoes, and peppers as well as flowering plants, and is a regular stop on garden tours. She was unconcerned by this evidence of squirrel interlopers until the day she went up to find the garden destroyed, the blueberry bush razed, the tomato plants eaten through.

"There was a wow factor," Ms. Lennig says. "Like when one looks out at the aftermath of a really, really, really destructive thunderstorm and says, 'Look at that tree branch on the Volvo.'" Ms. Lennig went "straight to rage." She and her husband bought a Havahart trap and captured a squirrel, then realized they did not have a plan. Transporting it to a nearby park didn't seem an effective solution. Squirrels, they had heard, were territorial; it would only come back.

They did, however, as conscientious environmentalists, have a large rain barrel on the roof, which they used to water the garden. Who first came up with the idea of drowning, Ms. Lennig cannot recall, but it was her husband who handled the first executions. The trap, which was long and narrow, fit perfectly in the barrel.

Ms. Lennig has yet to be able to deal with the removal of the corpse, which is then thrown into the garbage. But she and her husband are now so comfortable with this form of pest control that when they visited Ms. Lennig's in-laws at their lakefront property last year, where squirrels were climbing on the deck and ravaging the planters, they offered to drown them.

"My husband and I said, 'We'll take them to the lake,'" she says, "but our in-laws were having none of that. We had to get in the car and drive them five miles away. I spent the entire weekend like a soccer mom, driving squirrels around."

Isn't drowning cruel?   40

No, Ms. Lennig says. She recalls reading that you lose consciousness and then your heart stops; it's actually one of the nicer ways to go.

A reporter remembers reading just the opposite (and the Humane Society agrees that drowning is inhumane).

"Listen," Ms. Lennig says. "I'm a former attorney. What do I know?"

Few who have made the leap from pacifism to search-and-destroy missions are this open on the subject. Who, after all, wants to risk being labeled a hardened animal killer? There are, however, those willing to take the heat. Boldest are those who admit to killing garden pests simply because they are annoying.

Dan Rattiner is the founder of *Dan's Papers* and the author of *In the Hamp-*   45
tons: My Fifty Years with Farmers, Fishermen, Artists, Billionaires, and Celebrities.
He has a house in East Hampton, and for the last three years he has hired exterminators to get rid of the carpenter bees, which, he is well aware, do not sting.

So what do they do?

"They sort of follow you around," Mr. Rattiner says. "They're curious, like Curious George bees."

That sounds sort of sweet.

No, Mr. Rattiner says.

"You can't sit outside — the carpenter bees come over to see what you're   50
eating," he says. "They don't land on you, it's not like menacing, it's like having small children that aren't yours. You just want them gone. There's no other way to do it, and I feel very badly about it. I don't know why they keep coming back. You'd think they'd talk to each other about what happened last year."

Many gardeners are able to kill only one species.

"If I see a spider, I would never kill it," says Jessica Melville, a nurse in Woodstock, Vermont. "We have woodchucks in the yard; they don't bother me at all."

But Ms. Melville, who lives with her husband, Hunter, and two sons, is terrified of snakes. Unfortunately, her home, an 1850 farmhouse, is built into a stone wall that the local milk snakes and garter snakes love. Ms. Melville's husband, who co-founded cyberrentals.com, explained to her that those snakes are harmful only to the insects they catch, but no matter. Before kneeling down in the perennial bed, Ms. Melville used to do what her family called her snake dance, jumping up and down, because when those snakes heard the pounding, they slithered away. If she happened to see a snake, she'd retreat into the house, and that would be it for that day's gardening.

The Melvilles tried a granulated repellent called Snake Away. It didn't work, so Mr. Melville, who occasionally hunts birds, bought his wife a 20-gauge shotgun. Although some might think a snake would be a difficult target, it is not. Often, when a predator is near, a snake will freeze.

"I just went up really close," Ms. Melville says. "I was probably five feet 55
from it. The first shot I missed. The second time I got it and then it was: 'Oh, this is great! One less snake I have to deal with.'"

Ms. Melville has been shooting snakes for the last three years and estimates that she has killed about 15. But she's killing snakes that are eating bugs? Doesn't that distress her?

"No," Ms. Melville says. "I'm just a happier gardener."

Second thoughts? Regrets? Nightmares?

"Nope, never," Ms. Melville says. "I'm just glad they're gone."

Regrets are even rarer among those whose livelihoods are threatened by 60
pests.

Oskian Yaziciyan lives in Homestead, Florida, about a 20-minute drive north of Key Largo, where he runs Goldfish & Koi U.S.A., a two-and-a-half-acre ornamental fish and water lily farm. He has great feelings of affection for some of the animals other people detest. He had a pet squirrel as a boy and loves to watch squirrels. He finds them charming.

On the other hand, when he first began his business 12 years ago, and an equally adorable raccoon figured out how to depress a pipe to let the water out of a tank and ate about $6,000 worth of koi, it did not end well.

So what did Mr. Yaziciyan do?

"I'm not going to tell you," Mr. Yaziciyan said. "I told my wife I took it to the Everglades."

Mr. Yaziciyan has since made a practice of covering the ponds with shade 65
cloth, netting, or wire. It is not an aesthetic solution. And it doesn't always get rid of his biggest problem: birds. Herons, which are a protected species, are a problem, as are crows, Mr. Yaziciyan wrote in an e-mail message, because they eat the eyes out of fish and snatch surface swimmers. Heron, with their rapier-like beaks, are adept killing machines.

"Koi are very expensive fish — you have a 14- or 15-inch koi, depending on the grade, it could be $50 or $2,000," says Mr. Yaziciyan, whose own stock ranges from a more modest $5 to $500. "They go for the larger fish, your prize fish. They even kill fish they are unable to swallow. They pull it out of the water, eat its guts out."

This eating-the-eyes-out part is casting a new light on the bucolic animal kingdom, Mr. Yaziciyan is told.

"I got a lot of blind fish," Mr. Yaziciyan says.

Mr. Yaziciyan says he does not touch the heron. But he has gone after ravens, blue birds, and crows with a net, banging their heads against a concrete or wood surface. It's a quick death.

One visualizes a chirping cartoon bird, advising Snow White on an available share in the woods. We're talking the bluebird of happiness, Mr. Yaziciyan. Isn't it difficult to slam it against the concrete?   70

"Not really," Mr. Yaziciyan says. "It's a small bird. It may be a blue jay, maybe a blue bird with gray on it. I've seen them poke the eyes out of the fish. You gotta do what you gotta do. You got a $50 fish that is totally useless. No one will buy a fish with one eye. I got dozens of fish with one eye."

The food chain is a brutal business. Or a natural one. Which brings us back to the artist with the groundhog problem. He was finally able to make a little bit of peace with shooting the woodchucks on his property by cooking and eating them. "It was a way of taking full responsibility for taking a life," he says. "Almost like a spiritual journey."

"Any number of local people offered up recipes," the artist adds. "The guy who was doing some roofing work was Italian, and he described this wonderful recipe: essentially shallots, red wine, cured green olives, black pepper, and rosemary. My father-in-law had a big helping. He declared it the best woodchuck he'd ever eaten."   *[2008]*

Many readers would, with reason, call certain aspects of this piece literary:

- It features various people telling stories, about their campaigns to eliminate pests.
- Some of the stories seem at least semifictional, an example being the tale of the woodchuck who deliberately committed suicide.
- Overall, the article is vivid in style. It helps you imagine, for instance, the "frenzy" of a squirrel encaged, and it makes crisp use of metaphor when it refers to "the moment when a gentle gardener will suddenly go Rambo."
- Further, the reporter presents her interviewees as colorful characters. Often, their dialogue is snappy and thought-provoking: for instance, "Doesn't the spinach scream when it boils? I think probably all living things have some scream going on."
- Literature is often associated with psychological and philosophical complexity, and a few of the people that Wadler talked with display some of this. They brood over whether it is ever acceptable to harm animals.

Now let's turn to the poem. Entitled "Woodchucks," it is by Maxine Kumin (b. 1925) and appears in her 1982 collection *Our Ground Time Here Will Be Brief.*

Narrator Possibly Psychotic?

MAXINE KUMIN

Woodchucks

mercy

Gassing the woodchucks didn't turn out right.
The knockout bomb from the Feed and Grain Exchange
was featured as merciful, quick at the bone   *gas vs. cyanide*
and the case we had against them was airtight,
both exits shoehorned shut with puddingstone,°   5
but they had a sub-sub-basement out of range.

Next morning they turned up again, no worse
for the cyanide than we for our cigarettes
and state-store Scotch, all of us up to scratch.
They brought down the marigolds as a matter of course   *revenge*   10
and then took over the vegetable patch
nipping the broccoli shoots, beheading the carrots.

The food from our mouths, I said, righteously thrilling
to the feel of the .22, the bullets' neat noses.
I, a lapsed pacifist fallen from grace   15
puffed with Darwinian° pieties for killing,   *repeating imagery*
now drew a bead on the littlest woodchuck's face.
He died down in the everbearing roses.

merciless

Ten minutes later I dropped the mother. She
flipflopped in the air and fell, her needle teeth   20
still hooked in a leaf of early Swiss chard.
Another baby next. O one-two-three
the murderer inside me rose up hard,
the hawkeye killer came on stage forthwith.

odd rhyme scheme...

There's one chuck left. Old wily fellow, he keeps   25
me cocked and ready day after day after day.   *obsession*
All night I hunt his humped-up form. I dream
I sight along the barrel in my sleep.
If only they'd all consented to die unseen   *Former Nazi?*
gassed underground the quiet Nazi way.   *Nazi comparison?*   [1972]   30

5 **puddingstone:** Cement mixed with pebbles.   16 **Darwinian:** Charles Darwin (1809–1882), an English naturalist who first theorized about evolution and natural selection.

Although, like the news article, the poem deals with woodchucks, it differs from the article in ways that for many readers would establish it as more literary:

- While "Peter Rabbit Must Die" is arranged in paragraphs, "Woodchucks" proceeds through stanzas. This kind of structure, common in poetry, draws attention to words that begin and end lines.

- Like many poems, Kumin's also includes words that stand out because they rhyme (e.g., "scratch" and "patch," "grace" and "face"), virtually echo (e.g., "Gassing" and "gassed"), or begin with the same sound, a pattern known as alliteration (e.g., "bomb" and "bone," "food" and "feel," "neat" and "noses").
- In addition, some words in this poem seem to have multiple meanings. For example, "right" in the first line can mean not only "efficient" but also "ethical," just as "airtight" can mean "perfect" in a *practical* sense as well as "indisputable" in a *philosophical* sense.
- Overall, whereas Wadler makes readers chiefly aware of her *content*, Kumin's readers are at least as concerned with *form*. Most of them would linger over the language of "Woodchucks" more than they would over the news report's style. Noteworthy, for instance, is how the speaker looks back ironically on her own language ("The food from our mouths, I said, righteously thrilling"), thereby casting doubt on its logic. And of course, her concluding analogy to the Nazis jolts; it pushes readers to wonder how much the entire poem has been about Hitler's genocidal regime.
- In general, the speaker's mind seems to go through a whole series of stages, making the speaker's thought processes appear more intricate than those of anyone described in the news report.
- Kumin's speaker, like many characters in literature, is hard to pigeonhole. Wadler identifies her interview subjects as particular individuals, but like many reporters she ultimately seems more interested in them as examples of basic human types. For instance, she says that the artist's tale "is not as unusual as some would like to believe," suggesting that he is a common sort of person afflicted by pests: the sensitive soul driven to lash back. Given the words that Kumin's speaker uses and the various patterns they take, she requires more figuring out.
- Whereas the news writer surely expects you to assume that her interviewees are real, you do not have to take Kumin's speaker as such. This figure may reflect the poet's own experience to some extent, for Kumin has operated a farm in New Hampshire and so perhaps has hunted pests herself. Still, you are free to see her central character as fictive. This possibility enables you to speculate long and broadly about the speaker's psyche — including ideas and feelings of hers that she may not be quite aware of. Notice that after referring to "we," she eventually shifts to "I," a change that may be unconscious but that nonetheless implies she has become personally obsessed. Because you can see the poem's speaker as imaginary, you are also free to entertain various responses to her. If she were an actual person — someone you knew or might someday meet — you might feel compelled to make a single, fast judgment about her. The poem, however, lets you access her thinking while not pressuring you to decide quickly how ethical she is. Your attitudes toward her can shift,

clash, and blend more than if her acts had real-life effects. In this respect, "Woodchucks" is a thought experiment, as are most literary works. Still, in exercising your interpretive powers, such texts help you cope with the world. They heighten your awareness of the ways in which it, too, demands careful study.

We are *not* saying that poems are always superior to news reports. That would be an excessive claim. Besides, we find "Peter Rabbit Must Die" both charming and instructive. But, as "Woodchucks" demonstrates, literary works often lead you to grapple with more extensive and trickier questions — thereby offering you much to address in your own writing.

Meanwhile, you might better sense the challenges and pleasures of literature by performing the sort of comparison we have just done. Reading "Woodchucks" along with "Peter Rabbit Must Die" can alert you to intriguing things in the poem you might otherwise miss. To encourage this kind of inquiry, each chapter of Part Two contains a cluster that pairs literature and journalism on a current "hot" topic, one related to the chapter's theme.

▤ THINKING ABOUT THE TEXT

Below are just a few of the questions that "Woodchucks" provokes. Choose one of them. Then, take ten minutes or so and freewrite an answer to it, supporting your statements with specific words from the poem.

1. In line 4, the word *case* evidently refers to a method of entrapping the woodchucks, but probably it also refers to the speaker's reasons for hunting them. How good are her reasons? What might be the "case" for *not* killing these animals?

2. What key changes — psychological as well as physical — does the speaker go through in her campaign to get rid of the woodchucks?

3. To what extent does the speaker suggest that her feelings are mixed and even in conflict?

4. Presumably the last line alludes to the mass exterminations of the Holocaust. What would you say to someone who argues that this is an inappropriate, even tasteless, way to end a poem about woodchucks?

Why Study Literature in a College Writing Course?

We assume you are reading this book in a course aimed at helping you write. Quite likely the course is meant to prepare you for writing assignments throughout college, including papers in fields beyond English. It's natural to wonder how reading literature serves this purpose.

Much academic writing is, in fact, based on reading. You'll find the two interconnected in course after course. Many classes will ask you to produce essays that analyze published texts. To *analyze* means going beyond your first impressions, carefully noting a text's ideas, techniques, and effects. You'll also find yourself needing to *synthesize*: that is, to trace how the text is patterned, as well as how it relates to other works. Together, these acts of analysis and synthesis have been called reading *closely*, a process we explain and model in Chapter 2. We encourage you to practice this method with the selections in our book.

Often, college courses will ask you to write about some text that isn't easily understood. The purpose of your paper will be to help other readers of the text grasp its meanings and, perhaps, judge its worth. Literature is a good training ground for these skills of interpretation and evaluation. The poems, stories, plays, and essays in this book repeatedly invite inquiry. They don't settle for delivering simple straightforward messages. Rather, they offer puzzles, complications, metaphors, symbols, and mysteries, thereby recognizing that life is complex. In particular, literary works encourage you to ponder the multiple dimensions of language: how, for example, a word's meaning can vary depending on context. Furthermore, much literature can help you understand your own life and conduct it better. In this capacity, literature serves as "equipment for living," scholar-critic Kenneth Burke's description of its function.

Some people *dislike* literature because they find it too vague and indirect. They resent that it often forces them to figure out symbols and implications when they would rather have ideas presented outright. Perhaps you wish the speaker in Wright's poem had made clear why his observations prompted him to criticize himself. But in life, truth can be complicated and elusive. In many ways, literature is most realistic when it suggests the same. Besides, many readers — perhaps including you — appreciate literature most when it resists simple decoding, forcing them to adopt new assumptions and learn new methods of analysis. Indeed, throughout this book we suggest that the most interesting and profitable conversations about literature are those in which the issues are not easily resolved. One of the best things your course can provide you and your classmates is the chance to exchange insights about texts such as Wright's.

We have been suggesting that one value of studying literature in a writing class is that it often engages not just thought but feeling. The two interweave so that readers find themselves engaging in interpretation and evaluation because they *care* about lives depicted in the text. Most of the works in this book appeal to your emotions, encouraging you to identify with certain characters, to be disturbed by others, and to wonder what happens next in the plot. Indeed, many readers of literature prize the moments when it makes them laugh or cry or gasp as well as think. To be sure, it can be argued that the most worthwhile literature gets us to comprehend, and perhaps even appreciate, certain kinds of people who would normally confuse or disturb us. Perhaps you would never say to yourself "I have wasted my life"; all the same, you may find it valuable to analyze how Wright's speaker reaches this conclusion. "When it's the real thing," critic Frank Lentricchia suggests, "literature enlarges us, strips the film of familiarity from the world; creates bonds of sympathy with all kinds, even with evil characters, who we learn are all in the family." This "enlargement" is both intellectual *and* emotional.

Finally, writing about literature is good training for other fields because literary analysis often involves taking an interdisciplinary perspective. A typical interpretation of James Wright's poem, for example, will bring in principles of psychology to explain the speaker's frame of mind. Similarly, to evaluate his statement "I have wasted my life," readers find themselves grappling with the philosophical question of what constitutes a "productive" or "good" life. Moreover, the poem's farm setting has economic, political, historical, and sociological significance, for much less of the world's population performs agricultural labor than was the case a century ago. Wright's brief text can even play a role in studies of cross-cultural relationships, for as Sven Birkerts has pointed out, the poem is one of several experiments the poet tried with Chinese literary forms.

What Can *You* Do to Make Literature Matter to Others?

In an 1895 essay called "The Art of Fiction," the American novelist, short-story writer, and critic Henry James wrote, "Art lives upon discussion, upon experiment, upon curiosity, upon variety of attempt, upon the exchange of views and the comparison of standpoints." Certainly James was suggesting that the creators of literature play a big role in making it matter. But he was suggesting, too, that plenty of other people contribute to literature's impact. Today, these people include publishers, printers, agents, advertisers, librarians, professional reviewers, bookstore staff, Internet chat groups, and even show-business figures such as Oprah Winfrey, who has interested millions of viewers in participating in her "book club." Teachers of literature also make it matter—or at least they try to. Perhaps your parents or other family members have contributed to your appreciation of certain literary texts; many adults introduce their children and grandchildren to books they loved when young. Moreover, friends often recommend works of literature to one another.

Again, we concede that some people think of literature negatively, believing that it matters in a way they don't like. The ancient Greek philosopher Plato wanted to ban poets from his ideal republic because he thought they merely imitated truth. Throughout subsequent history, various groups have tried to abolish or censor much literature. In communities across the contemporary United States, pressure groups have succeeded in removing particular novels from library shelves, including classics such as Mark Twain's *Adventures of Huckleberry Finn* and J. D. Salinger's *The Catcher in the Rye*. History has also seen many writers killed, jailed, or harassed for their work. In recent years, the most conspicuous example of such persecution has been the Ayatollah Khomeini's indictment of author Salman Rushdie. In 1989, the ayatollah was so enraged by the portrayal of Islam in Rushdie's novel *The Satanic Verses* that he commanded his followers to hunt Rushdie down and slay him. Even after the ayatollah died, Rushdie was in danger, for the *fatwa* against him remained in effect. Not until eight years after the original edict did the Iranian government back away from it. At present, Rushdie still enjoys only a limited measure of safety, and the affair stands as a reminder that some writers risk their lives.

Ironically, the ayatollah's execution order was a sort of homage to literature, a fearsome way of crediting it with the power to shape thinking.

Our book aims to help you join the conversations that Henry James saw as nourishing literature. More specifically, our book focuses on helping you argue about literature, whether your audience is your classmates, your teacher, or other people. While arguments involve real or potential disagreement, they need not be waged like wars. When we use the term *argument* in this book, we have in mind civilized efforts through which people try to make their views persuasive. When you argue about literature, you are carefully reasoning with others, helping them see how a certain text should matter to them.

In particular, we have much to say about you as a writer. A key goal of your course, we assume, is to help you compose more effective texts of your own. By writing arguments about literature, you make it matter to others. Moreover, you learn about yourself as you analyze a literary text and negotiate other readers' views of it. We emphasize that, at its best, arguing is a process of inquiry for everyone involved. Both you and your audience may wind up changing your minds.

☰ WRITING ASSIGNMENTS

1. Write a brief essay in which you explain what you value in literature by focusing on why you like a particular literary work. Don't worry about whether you are defining *literature* correctly. This exercise will help you begin to review the values you hold as you read a work that you regard as literary.

2. Sometimes a literary work matters to you in one way when you first read it and in another way when you read it again. Write a brief essay in which you discuss a work that you interpreted differently when you reread it. What significance did it have for you the first time? What was its significance later? What about your life changed between the two readings? If you cannot think of a literary work, choose a film you have seen.

3. Write a brief essay in which you identify the values that a previous literature teacher of yours seemed to hold. Be sure to identify, too, ways in which the teacher expressed these values. You may want to bring up one or more specific events that took place in the teacher's classroom.

4. Many bookstores sell computer-instruction manuals. Examine one of these. Do you consider it literature? Write a brief essay answering this question. Be sure to explain how you are defining *literature* and to refer to the manual's specific features.

5. Visit a bookstore at your school or in your town. Spend at least half an hour looking at books in various sections of the store, noting how the publishers of these works try to make them matter. Look at such things as the books' physical formats, the language on their covers, and any introductory material they include. Write a brief essay in which you identify and evaluate the strategies for "mattering" used by at least three of these books.

6. Visit a Web site that includes readers' comments about particular works of fiction. A good example is www.amazon.com, a commercial online "bookstore." Another good site is Oprah Winfrey's, www.oprah.com, which features extensive exchanges about novels she has chosen for her "book club." At whatever site you visit, choose a novel or short-story collection that has attracted many reader comments. Write a brief essay in which you identify the values that seem reflected in the comments. In what respects does literature seem to matter to these readers? What do they evidently hope to find in it?

≡ SUMMING UP

- **Literature encompasses poetry, fiction, and plays — but may also encompass other genres, such as nonfiction essays.** This book does not endorse a single definition of *literature* but encourages you to review and perhaps rethink what the term means to you. (pp. 4–7)

- **Literary texts tend to show certain characteristics more than other texts, such as news articles, do.** For example, they call attention to their form; they explore the multiple meanings of words; they present psychological complexity; and they require interpretation. (pp. 7–8)

- **Studying literature in a college writing course makes sense for several reasons.** Many other courses require you to write about reading; literature offers you ground for developing skills of interpretation and evaluation that many college writing assignments demand; literature serves as "equipment for living"; reading it engages both thought and feeling; and literary analysis is often interdisciplinary. (pp. 17–19)

- **The *literary canon* — works taught again and again as great art — is nowadays being reevaluated.** (p. 6)

- **Understanding literature involves collaboration with other readers and comparison with other texts.** (pp. 17–19)

- **Thinking about literature is enhanced and clarified by writing about it.** (p. 18)

- **The most effective arguments about literature involve inquiry, not rancor and battle.** (p. 20)

CHAPTER 2

How to Read Closely

Courses in many disciplines ask for *close reading*. But literature classes strongly emphasize it — one reason they are good preparation for other fields. Nevertheless, the steps involved in close reading are not always clear to students. Perhaps you have been told to engage in this process without knowing what it entails. Because close reading is central to literary studies, plays a big role in other courses, and yet remains murky for many students, this chapter both explains it and models it.

If you are taking a course that asks you to *write* about the literary works you study, close reading of them will help you form ideas about them worth spreading to *your* audiences. Such reading will also help you decide what details of these texts will best support your points about them. So, as we proceed to explain close reading, we treat it mainly as what some would call a method of invention. It's a way for you, as a *writer*, to discover things to say about literature.

Basic Strategies for Close Reading

Actually, close reading consists of not one strategy but several. All of them can help you gain insights into a literary work, which you might then convey through your writing. You need not follow these strategies in the order we list them here, but try each of them.

1. Make predictions as you read. That is, guess what will happen and how the text will turn out. If you wind up being surprised, fine. You may get a richer understanding of the text as you reflect on how it *defies* your expectations.

2. Reread the text. Reread the text several times, focusing each time on a different element of the text and using at least one of these occasions to read aloud. Few readers of a literary work can immediately see everything important and interesting in it. You greatly increase your chances of getting ideas about a text if you read it again and again. At first, you may be preoccupied with following the plot or with figuring out the text's main theme. Only by examining the text repeatedly may you notice several of its other aspects, including features that really stir your thoughts. But don't try to study everything in the text each time you look at it. Use each reading of it to study just one characteristic. In an early stage, for example, you might trace the text's repetitions, and then you might use a later reading to pinpoint its ambiguous words. This division of labor can, in the end, generate many insights that a less focused approach would not.

Reading all of the text or portions of it out loud gives you a better sense of how the text is manipulating language. Reading aloud is especially useful in the case of poems, for you may detect rhymes or soundalike words that you would not notice when reading silently.

3. Test the text against your own experiences.   Keep in mind your experiences, beliefs, assumptions, and values as you read the text, but note ways that it challenges or complicates these things. When you first read a particular literary work, your interpretations and judgments are bound to be influenced by your personal background. This includes your beliefs, assumptions, and values, as well as things that have happened to you. Indeed, many people read a literary work hoping they can personally identify with the characters, situations, and views it presents. Moreover, this is an understandable goal. Pay attention, though, to details of the text that do *not* match your life and current thinking. After all, the author may be deliberately challenging or complicating readers' habitual attitudes. In any case, parts of the text that are hard to identify with will often provide you with great subjects when you write about the work. Bear in mind, though, that you will not interest your readers if you simply criticize characters in the work or sneer at other elements of it. In particular, try not to sum up characters with negative labels such as *immoral, weird,* or *sick.* These terms often strike readers as reflecting mere prejudice — a poor substitute for careful analysis of human complexity.

4. Look for patterns in the text and disruptions of them.   Many a literary work is organized by various patterns, which may not be evident on first reading. In fact, you might not detect a number of these patterns until you read the text several times. You may even see these better if you move back and forth in the text instead of just reading it straight through. Typically, a literary work's patterns include repetitions of words and of actions; oppositions; words similar or related in meaning; and technical methods of organization (such as rhyme schemes or frequent use of flashbacks). Just as important to note are moments in the text that are inconsistent with one or more of its patterns. Locate and think about places where the work makes a significant shift, in meaning, imagery, tone, plot, a character's behavior, narrative point of view, or even physical format (for example, a change in rhyme scheme).

5. Note ambiguities.   These are places where the text's meaning is not crystal clear and therefore calls for interpretation: for example, words that can have more than one definition; symbols that have multiple implications; and actions that suggest various things about a character.

6. Consider the author's alternatives.   That is, think about what the author *could* have done and yet did not do. The author of a literary work faces all sorts of decisions in composing it. And as you study the work, you will have more to say about it if you think about those choices. Try, then, to compare the author's handling of particular passages to other possible treatments of them. By considering, for example, why the author chose a certain word over others, you may better detect implications and effects of the author's actual language. Similarly, by reflecting on how the author *might* have portrayed a certain character more simplistically, you strengthen your ability to analyze the character's variety of traits.

7. Ask questions.   As you read, generate questions that have more than one possible answer. When we first read a literary work, most of us try to get comfortable with it. We search for passages that are clear; we groan when we encounter ones that are mysterious or confusing. Sooner or later, though, we must confront puzzles in the text if we are to analyze it in depth. Furthermore, if we plan to *write* about the text, we are more likely to come up with ideas worth communicating to our readers if we present ourselves as helping them deal with matters *not* immediately clear. After all, our audience will not need our analysis if it centers on what's obvious. Therefore, list multiple questions that the work raises for you, especially ones that have various possible answers. Then, if you focus on addressing one of these questions in your writing—providing and supporting your own particular answer to it—your readers will find value in turning to *your* text. Furthermore, when you come across literary passages that seem easy to understand, consider how they might actually involve more than one possible meaning. Even little words may prove ambiguous and, therefore, worth analyzing in your writing. Of course, you may have to consult a dictionary in order to see the different meanings that a word can have.

The questions you come up with need hardly be restricted to matters of the work's "theme." After all, most any literary text worth studying can't be reduced to a single message. Often, such texts play with multiple ideas, perhaps emphasizing tensions among them. Therefore, it may make more sense for you to refer to a work's *themes*. Actually, as we have been suggesting throughout our catalog of reading strategies, any literary text has several other features. As a writer, you may wind up with much more to say about a literary work if you consider one or more of these other elements: for example, facts obscured or absent in the text; possible definitions of key words; symbols; patterns; evaluations to be made of the characters or the overall work; the text's historical and cultural context; the text's genre; its relevance to current political debates; and cause-effect relationships. In the next chapter, we explain these elements at greater length, identifying them as *issues* you might write about.

8. Jot down possible answers.   Even while reading the text, begin developing and pulling together your thoughts by informally writing about it. See if you can generate not only good questions but also tentative answers to them. Writing need not be the final outcome of your reflections on a literary work. You can jot down ideas about the text even as you first encounter it. Such informal, preliminary writing can actually help you generate insights into the text that you would not have achieved simply by scanning it. The following are some of the specific things you might do:

- *Make notes in the text itself.* A common method is to mark key passages, either by underlining these passages or by running a highlighter over them. Both ways of marking are popular because they help readers recall main features of the text. But use these techniques moderately if you use them at all, for marking lots of passages will leave you unable to distinguish the really important parts of the text. Also, try "talking back" to the text in its margins. Next to particular passages, you might jot down words of your own, indicating any feelings and questions you have about those parts. On any page of the text, you might circle related words and then draw lines between these words to emphasize their connection. If a word or an idea shows up on numerous pages, you might circle it each time. Furthermore, try cross-referencing, by listing on at least one page the numbers of all those pages where the word or idea appears.

- *As you read the text, occasionally look away from it, and jot down anything in it you recall.* This memory exercise lets you review your developing impressions of the text. When you turn back to its actual words, you may find that you have distorted or overlooked aspects of it that you should take into account.

- *At various moments in your reading, freewrite about the text for ten minutes or so.* Spontaneously explore your preliminary thoughts and feelings about it, as well as any personal experiences the text leads you to recall. One logical moment to do freewriting is when you have finished reading the text. But you do not have to wait until then; as you read, you might pause occasionally to freewrite. This way, you give yourself an opportunity to develop and review your thoughts about the text early on.

- *Create a "dialectical notebook."* So named by composition theorist Ann Berthoff, it involves using pages of your regular notebook in a particular way. On each page, draw a line down the middle to create two columns. In the left column, list various details of the text: specifically, words, images, characters, and events that strike you. In the right column, jot down for each detail one or more sentences indicating *why* you were drawn to it. Take as many pages as you need to record and reflect on your observations. You can also use the two-column format to carry out a dialogue with yourself about the text. This is an especially good way to ponder aspects of the text that you find confusing, mysterious, or complex.

- *Play with the text by revising it.* Doing so will make you more aware of options that the author rejected and will give you a better sense of the moves that the author chose to make. Specifically, you might rearrange parts of the text, add to it, change some of its words, or shift its narrative point of view. After you revise the text, compare your alternative version with the original, considering especially differences in their effects.

CLOSE READINGS OF A POEM

To demonstrate what it means to read closely, we present observations that various students made about a poem. Even before you look at the students' comments, try doing what they did. We asked each of them to read the poem several times (step 2, pp. 22–23). More specifically, they devoted each of their readings to a particular element of the poem:

- First, they focused on how it fulfilled or defied their predictions.
- Then, they considered how the poem matched and diverged from their personal backgrounds.
- They then traced the poem's patterns, as well as breaks from these.
- They noted places where the poem is puzzling, ambiguous, or unclear.
- Next, they identified at least one choice that the poem's author faced.
- They then settled on questions that have more than one possible answer and that therefore might be worth addressing in a formal essay about the poem.
- Finally, pulling their thoughts together, they came up with tentative answers to these questions, which they might then have developed in a formal essay.

Again, the order of these stages is not the only one possible; the important thing is to go through them all. At each stage of their reading, the students also did a few minutes of freewriting, using this strategy to develop thoughts about whatever element was their focus. Following the poem are excerpts from these informal reflections.

The poem is by Sharon Olds (b. 1942), who teaches at New York University and has produced many volumes of verse. "Summer Solstice, New York City" appears in her 1987 book, *The Gold Cell*. Again, like most of the other literature we include in Part One, the poem deals with work — in this case, efforts by New York City police to prevent a suicide.

SHARON OLDS

Summer Solstice, New York City

By the end of the longest day of the year he could not stand it,
he went up the iron stairs through the roof of the building
and over the soft, tarry surface
to the edge, put one leg over the complex green tin cornice
and said if they came a step closer that was it.   5
Then the huge machinery of the earth began to work for his life,
the cops came in their suits blue-gray as the sky on a cloudy evening,
and one put on a bullet-proof vest, a
black shell around his own life,
life of his children's father, in case   10
the man was armed, and one, slung with a

rope like the sign of his bounden duty,
came up out of a hole in the top of the neighboring building
- like the gold hole they say is in the top of the head, - ⇒ halo?
and began to lurk toward the man who wanted to die.   15
The tallest cop approached him directly,
softly, slowly, talking to him, talking, talking,
while the man's leg hung over the lip of the next world
and the crowd gathered in the street, silent, and the
hairy net with its implacable grid was   20
unfolded near the curb and spread out and
stretched as the sheet is prepared to receive at birth.
Then they all came a little closer
where he squatted next to his death, his shirt
glowing its milky glow like something   25
growing in a dish at night in the dark in a lab and then
everything stopped
as his body jerked and he
stepped down from the parapet and went toward them
and they closed on him, I thought they were going to   30
beat him up, as a mother whose child has been
lost will scream at the child when it's found, they
took him by the arms and held him up and
leaned him against the wall of the chimney and the
tall cop lit a cigarette   35
in his own mouth, and gave it to him, and
then they all lit cigarettes, and the
red, glowing ends burned like the
tiny campfires we lit at night
back at the beginning of the world.   [1987]   40

Making Predictions

KATHERINE: I was really tense as I read this poem because I thought the man
would jump at the end and then we would get a horrible description of him
splattering on the sidewalk. I didn't predict the cops would succeed in
talking him out of it. When the poet says he "jerked," that could easily have
been the start of his jumping, but thank God he is instead stepping back.
I'm glad that they persuaded him to remain alive.

MARIA: I was like the poem's speaker expecting that they would physically grab
him and treat him roughly, and so I was surprised when they were nice to
him and even offered him a cigarette.

TREVOR: I predicted that the poem would end with the man still on the edge of
the building deciding whether or not to jump off, because I think that in a
way it would be neat to leave us guessing whether he's really going to do it.
I wasn't all that surprised when he pulled back and joined the cops, because
that was certainly one possible outcome. However, I was surprised when the

author had them smoking cigarettes at the end like "at the beginning of the world." I didn't expect that image of prehistoric people to show up here at the end.

Reflecting on One's Personal Background

JAMES: It's hard for me to sympathize with someone who commits suicide, especially because someone at my high school killed himself and all of his friends and family were terribly saddened by what he did. I think that no matter how bad things get for you, there's a way out if only you look for it. Suicide is no answer, and it hurts the people you leave behind. So I'm glad that the man in this poem winds up not committing suicide. If he had, I would have thought less of him.

CARLA: I vaguely remember seeing some movies in which a character stands on a ledge and thinks about jumping off it. In real life, I've never seen something like that. What this poem most brings to my mind are reports I heard about people jumping off the World Trade Towers to escape being killed by fire. Of course, they died anyway. As I recall, TV didn't show these people jumping, out of respect for them I guess, and I'm glad that I didn't have to see this happen. Still, I'm aware that it did. Anyway, the man thinking about suicide in this poem isn't facing the same situation. He can easily live if he wants to.

BOB: I guess the police are obligated to try rescuing the man even if they have to risk their own lives. I've never been in this position, so I'm not sure how I'd feel if I'd been assigned to save the man in this poem. Though I disapprove of suicide, maybe I wouldn't have the guts to try confronting him on the edge of the building, and I'm not sure I could talk to him calmly, because if he did jump he might take me down with him. I admire the ability of these cops to stay cool and talk him into joining them. I'm also impressed that they then treat him like a friend instead of like a potentially violent nut case that they have to get under control through force. If it were me, I think I might want to throw him to the ground and pin his arms so that he wouldn't try something like that again.

Reading for Patterns and for Breaks in Patterns

DOMINICK: This may be too little a thing to think about, but I notice that the word "it" is repeated in the beginning section of the poem. The first line ends with "it," and line 5 does also. I'm not sure what is meant by "it" in "he could not stand it." Obviously on one level "it" here means his life, but he seems to have something specific about his life in mind when he says this, but we don't learn what he's specifically thinking of. The second "it" seems to refer to the fact that he will kill himself if they come closer. But that reference too isn't as clear as it might be. I see that later on "it" comes up again as a word for the cigarette that the cop gives to the man (after lighting it in his own mouth, yuk!). Maybe we're supposed to connect this "it" to the "its" at the start.

BOB: After the middle of the poem we start to get a lot of birth imagery. The word "birth" is even stated, and a little later there's the image of something "growing" in a lab dish.

JARED: "World" is repeated. In the middle of the poem, there's a reference to "the next world," and the very last word of the poem is "world," meaning the world where we currently live.

COURTNEY: I found a number of references to children. There are the words "his children's father," and then toward the end the word "child" is repeated, though this time it's a mother's child. And then the last line refers to "the beginning of the world," as if the world is a child that has just been born.

FRANK: It's funny that the word "end" is one of the first words of the poem, and then the word "beginning" is one of its last words. I can more easily imagine the reverse. Anyway, "end" and "beginning" are opposites that the poet seems to want us to think about. Come to think of it, there is mention of "ends" near the conclusion, but these are the "ends" of the men's cigarettes and not the end of the world.

ALEX: The word "day" appears in the first line (it's "the longest day of the year"), but later there is the word "night" ("growing in a dish at night"), and then "night" is in the next-to-last line. Ironically, things get brighter (the man decides to live) as the poem moves from "day" to "night."

PAUL: As the poem moves along, there's a shift in pronouns. In the first half or so, we get forms of "he" and "they." Then the word "I" suddenly appears, and then the next-to-last line has the word "we."

Reading for Puzzles, Ambiguities, and Unclear Moments

KATHERINE: I just don't learn enough about this man's thinking to know why he's even planning to kill himself. This is something the poem doesn't make clear. But I guess the "I" of the poem doesn't know the man's thinking either, and meanwhile she's in the position of possibly witnessing the man falling to the pavement! Maybe the author doesn't tell us exactly why the man wants to commit suicide because we can then identify more easily with him. We can think about moments when we were incredibly unhappy, whether or not we were depressed by the same things he is.

TIM: We're told that the cop approaching the man is doing a lot of talking, but we don't find out what he specifically says, even though this may have played a big role in getting the man to step back and live.

HILLARY: The gold hole sounds like something from folklore, but I don't know the background.

RACHEL: I'm wondering how much we're supposed to focus on the speaker's reactions to what's going on, or whether we should think more about the man and the policemen.

Reading for the Author's Choices

KATHERINE: Olds could have had the man jump and die. Even if this poem is based on a real incident where the man decided to live, she could have changed what happened. Also, if she still went with the rescue version, she could have had the policemen treat the man roughly after they rescued him.

PAUL: The word "I" could have appeared more often throughout the poem, especially because the poem is written from the point of view of someone observing this suicide attempt.

TIM: We might have been told why the man was thinking of killing himself and what the cops said to him. I realize this information would be hard for the speaker of the poem to give us, since she's just observing the whole business from the street below. Still, maybe Olds could have found a way of telling us at least a little more about what the men on the roof were saying and thinking.

BOB: The author didn't have to use birth images. She could have described this event without them. In fact, death imagery seems more appropriate when a poem is about a possible suicide.

Generating Questions That Have More Than One Possible Answer

JENNIFER: What might the poet be trying to convey when she ends the poem with the image of "the beginning of the world"? The last line really captures my attention.

PAUL: What should we conclude when the pronouns shift from "he" and "they" to "I" and finally "we"?

VICTORIA: How should we interpret the poem's repeated references to children and to parents (both father and mother)?

BOB: How important are the cops as characters in this poem?

Stating Tentative Answers

JENNIFER: Maybe the poet is telling us that each time you overcome depression and decide to go on living, it's like the rebirth of the world, and you're rejoining a "we" in the sense of rejoining the rest of humanity.

PAUL: I believe that the speaker comes to identify with the man and his rescuers and then sees herself and them as all part of a common humanity, as if we all have to decide when to risk our lives and when to preserve them.

VICTORIA: In a paper, I could argue that these child and parent references are used by Olds to suggest that even as adults, we sometimes act like children and sometimes have to act like a parent, but Olds evidently prefers that we not act like a very stern parent.

BOB: The cops are very important in this poem. So much of it is about what they do and how they maybe feel. They're required to save the guy, they're part of "huge machinery," and one of them might end up sacrificing the "life of his children's father" just in order to rescue someone who wants to kill himself anyway, but then the cops turn out to be quite sympathetic toward the guy. There's even this odd religious-type moment with the sharing of a cigarette and then all the men lighting up. I think I would focus my paper on how the cops do their duty to preserve life even when they probably didn't want to, and then something spiritual happens because they didn't give up on the job they were assigned.

DAN: If I'm remembering correctly, the summer solstice is a turning point in the year, and you could say that there's a turning point in this poem when the man steps down from the ledge and chooses not to die. After the summer solstice we're heading toward winter, which is associated with death, but psychologically the poem goes in the opposite direction.

Think about your own developing understanding of Olds's poem. What aspect of it might you focus on in a formal essay? What's a claim that you might make? To us, the students' claims we have quoted seem promising topics for papers. Nevertheless, they could probably stand some polishing and further reflection. After all, they are the outcome of freewriting — an exploratory phase. In any case, what we want to stress is that you are more likely to get ideas about a literary work if you use the reading strategies that this group of students applied.

Reading Closely by Annotating

When you use such strategies, you may come up with several observations about the literary work you are reading. You may even find it helpful to record them directly on the text. Then, by reviewing the points you have annotated and connecting them to one another, you will provide yourself with a solid foundation for a paper. Here we demonstrate this process by showing how student Kara Lundquist annotated a poem by the noted writer and editor X. J. Kennedy (b. 1929) and then composed a possible opening paragraph for an essay about it.

X. J. KENNEDY
Death of a Window Washer

(He) dropped the way you'd slam an obstinate sash, — *Window washer is given no name.*

His (split) belt like a shade unrolling, flapping. — *Did his body "split" when he hit the ground? Poem avoids gruesome details to focus mostly on bystanders.*

Forgotten on his account, the mindless copying

Machine ran scores of memos no one wanted.

Heads stared from every floor, noon traffic halted   5

As though transformed to stone. Cops sealed the block

> Alliteration: What do "c" words suggest?

With sawhorse barricades, laid canvas cover.

Nuns crossed themselves, flies went on being alive,

> Nuns' reaction different from insects'. But are the humans here much more sensitive?

A broker counted ten shares sold as five,

> Echoes "account" in line 3. Did the dead man count (matter)?

And by coincidence a digital clock   10

Stopped in front of a second it couldn't leap over.

> Do people prefer to "leap over" deaths like this?

Struck wordless by his tumble from the sky

To their feet, two lovers held fast to each other

Uttering cries. But he had made no cry.

He'd made the city pause briefly to suffer   15

> At first seems to mean "experience pain," then seems to mean "put up with."

His taking ample room for once. In rather

A tedious while the rinsed street, left to dry,

> "Tedious" to whom? People soon get impatient for the body to go.

Unlatched its gates that passersby might pass.

> Unusual to ask why he lived in the first place.

Why did he live and die? His legacy

> Relates to "wordless" in line 12 and "no cry" in line 14.

Is mute: one final gleaming pane of glass.   20

> "Pane of glass " (clear vision) seems opposite of "mute." Connect "pane" to "pain"?

[2007]

Here is the paragraph that Kara composed, based on her annotations.

> X. J. Kennedy's poem "Death of a Window Washer" emphasizes not the title character's horrible accident, but rather how bystanders react to it. The poem suggests that although people may be *momentarily* affected by the death of an ordinary person whom they do not know, eventually they want to resume their own lives and pay him little attention. The specific situation that the poem dramatizes is the accidental plunge of a window washer from a city building. Certainly this incident shocks, at first, the passersby who witness it. Even though "flies went on being alive," various human beings are disturbed by the man's sudden death. But as the poem proceeds, the city's inhabitants

want to go back to their personal pursuits. A turning point in the poem is the word "suffer," which the speaker uses to describe the city dwellers at the end of line 15. This word might, at first, lead the reader to believe that they are tormented by the window washer's accident. But in the next line, it becomes clear that they are "suffering" in the sense that they are impatiently waiting for his corpse to be removed. Rather than permanently grieve over his having "passed" (i.e., died), they want to "pass" his body (line 18) and take up their daily existence once again. Therefore, although his death has been highly visible to them, they don't really bother to learn anything about him. His life is *not* revealed to them like the reality behind a "gleaming pane of glass." The speaker's concluding use of this image is, in fact, ironic.

Further Strategies for Close Reading

IDENTIFY CHARACTERS' EMOTIONS

Your feelings about the characters in a literary work can help you write a paper about it. Especially useful to consider is *why* you view these people as you do. What specific aspects of their thinking and conduct affect your attitudes toward them? You will have more material for the paper, though, if you also examine how the characters feel. With this strategy of close reading, you patiently and carefully identify *their* emotions, not simply your own. This analysis can even wind up giving you your paper's key idea — what, in our next chapter, we will call its *main claim*.

As you pinpoint the characters' passions and moods, try not to judge these right away. Emotions that may at first seem obnoxious or odd can have interesting roots. Also, they may be stages in complex mental journeys. A character may display numerous feelings, including ones that conflict, and undergo major changes of heart. Bear in mind, too, that many people in literature repress or mask their real desires, so the reader must infer their true inner states. Identify as well any emotions that characters significantly *lack*. Noting what feelings they *might* have had helps you pinpoint those they express.

We invite you to practice this method of analysis with the following poem. "Execution" is by the veteran poet Edward Hirsch (b. 1950) and appeared in his 1989 book *The Night Parade* as well as in a 2010 retrospective on his career, *The Living Fire: New and Selected Poems*. As you read the text, try to specify the emotions of the speaker and his main subject, his former coach. We follow up the poem with specific questions about their feelings. Then, to demonstrate the potential benefit of this approach to literature, we present a few ideas that student Courtney Reeves came up with when she applied it to "Execution." The insights she gained helped her eventually construct the introduction to an essay she wrote on the poem.

EDWARD HIRSCH

Execution

The last time I saw my high school football coach
He had cancer stenciled into his face
Like pencil marks from the sun, like intricate
Drawings on the chalkboard, small x's and o's
That he copied down in a neat numerical hand   5
Before practice in the morning. By day's end
The board was a spiderweb of options and counters,
Blasts and sweeps, a constellation of players
Shining under his favorite word, *Execution*,
Underlined in the upper right-hand corner of things.   10
He believed in football like a new religion
And had perfect unquestioning faith in the fundamentals
Of blocking and tackling, the idea of warfare
Without suffering or death, the concept of teammates
Moving in harmony like the planets — and yet   15
Our awkward adolescent bodies were always canceling
The flawless beauty of Saturday afternoons in September,
Falling away from the particular grace of autumn,
The clear weather, the ideal game he imagined.
And so he drove us through punishing drills   20
On weekday afternoons, and doubled our practice time,
And challenged us to hammer him with forearms,
And devised elaborate, last-second plays — a flea-
Flicker, a triple reverse — to save us from defeat.
Almost always they worked. He despised losing   25
And loved winning more than his own body, maybe even
More than himself. But the last time I saw him
He looked wobbly and stunned by illness,
And I remembered the game in my senior year
When we met a downstate team who loved hitting   30
More than we did, who battered us all afternoon
With a vengeance, who destroyed us with timing
And power, with deadly, impersonal authority,
Machine-like fury, perfect execution.   [1989]

▤ THINKING ABOUT THE TEXT

1. To what extent does the speaker seem grief-stricken about his coach's
   mortal illness? Point to specific words in the text that influence your
   answer.

2. In line 11, the speaker says of the coach, "He believed in football like a
   new religion." What values would someone like the coach need to have
   in order to feel so passionately about this sport? Why might someone

who regards "football like a new religion" not necessarily feel the same way about baseball or basketball?

3. In line 25, the speaker says that the coach "despised losing." How, if at all, did he reveal this attitude to his players? Identify specific words that help you address this question.

4. What other words in the poem indicate to you how the coach, during the speaker's youth, felt about high school football?

5. Where, if anywhere, does the speaker indicate how the players felt about the coach back then? Where, if anywhere, is the speaker evasive about what the players' attitudes toward the coach were?

6. In line 28, the speaker says that the coach now "looked wobbly and stunned by illness." What, evidently, was the coach feeling about his misfortune?

7. How does the speaker seem to feel about the football game he recalls at the end of the poem?

8. The title word, "execution," appears twice in the poem. Do these two appearances reflect the same emotion, or different ones? Explain.

9. If the title of this poem were the name of an emotion, what emotion would you think appropriate?

After examining the characters' emotions, Courtney Reeves formed these ideas for her paper on the poem. We italicize her references to emotions.

> The speaker does not openly express *sorrow* for his former coach when he finds him both *physically and mentally suffering* from cancer. Nor is it clear that the speaker was ever extremely *fond* of the coach, although probably he *respected* him when he played for him. In general, the poem is not a blatant *sympathy* card for the coach. Instead, it seems chiefly a philosophical reflection, carried out with some *sadness*. The speaker seems mostly to *brood* about the ironies of the coach's present situation, including how these ironies apply to the speaker himself. Noticing that the coach now looks *"wobbly and stunned,"* the speaker obviously thinks that a big reason he appears this way is that cancer has physically attacked him. The speaker also seems to believe that the disease has *psychologically thrown the coach off balance,* in at least two respects. First, although the coach is surely aware that his cancer may kill him, he cannot know for certain how long he actually has to live. The title of the poem, "Execution," refers in one sense to killing that is swift and scheduled, but the coach has now entered a period of *scary* unpredictability about his fate. Second, the coach's look of *unsteadiness and confusion* results from his lifelong belief that people can overcome their limits through skillful physical performances, another sense of the word "execution." This was a goal that the coach *strived for* when he pushed the speaker and his fellow

players to achieve a perfect "execution" of plays that would enable
them to defeat all opposing teams. Having cancer *shocks* the coach by
showing him that he was naive in making football "a new religion" in
which proper training of the body would mean success not only on the
field but throughout life. He discovers that even though the game of
football usually lacks real "suffering and death," these things strike all
of us eventually, and that even though he "loved winning more than his
own body," he depended on his body's health. The speaker, on the
other hand, does not seem "wobbly and stunned" by what has happened to the coach. He suggests that during his boyhood he himself
saw the reality of human limits with greater clarity and *detachment*
than the coach did. Perhaps, though, the speaker is with *at least a bit
of desperation* trying to ward off death by writing this well-"executed"
poem about it, just as the coach *frenziedly* wrote marks on the blackboard to help the team "execute" plays.

IDENTIFY SPEECH ACTS

Another way to read a literary text closely and get ideas about it is to identify
the **speech acts** in it. Speech acts are things that the characters *do* with words.
Try to specify what types of behavior characters engage in as they talk, as well
as the effects they aim to have on their listeners. These performances often reveal key aspects of their personalities, features you might overlook if you focus
just on their physical acts. When you study their verbal expressions as dramatic
gestures, you also provide yourself with more material for a paper — including,
perhaps, for its main claim.

Of course, for many speech acts in literature — and for many in real
life — there is no single, clearly correct label. How best to describe them is a
matter of interpretation. When you read about one of these acts, several terms
for it may occur to you, leaving you to decide which fits best.

For examples of speech acts, let's return briefly to Sharon Olds's poem
"Summer Solstice, New York City." In line 5, the man on the roof who contem-
plates suicide tells the people attempting to stop him that "if they came a step
closer that was it." You can easily call his words a *warning*. Later, the poem's
speaker admits that she wondered whether the police officers would react angrily to the man,

... as a mother whose child has been
lost will scream at the child when it's found ... (lines 31-32)

You might say that she envisions their strongly *scolding* him. Actually, though,
their behavior toward him is gentler from the start. Early on, the poem's speaker
observes that

The tallest cop approached him directly,
softly, slowly, talking to him, talking, talking (lines 16-17)

Although neither you nor the poem's speaker knows what exactly the officer is
saying, you can guess what he is *doing* as he talks to the man. What label

would you apply to this speech act? What does he evidently hope to achieve through it?

Theorists of speech acts have compiled long lists of them, and probably you can think of plenty on your own. Below, we list just a few kinds. For clarity's sake, all of our sample sentences begin with "I," but each of these acts can take other forms.

- The speaker maintains that something is in fact the case.

  Claiming: I *claim* that Brad and Angelina are on the brink of splitting up.

  Concluding: I *conclude* from the data that gender differences are trivial.

  Arguing: I *argue* that victim impact statements deserve more attention in trials.

- The speaker tries to make the hearer carry out the speaker's wish.

  Requesting: I *request* that you turn off your cell phones.

  Demanding: I *demand* that you stop seeing him.

  Recommending: I *recommend* that you drive us home by taking the shortcut.

- The speaker states an intention to do something.

  Promising: I *promise* to get home by 5:00 p.m.

  Guaranteeing: I *guarantee* that I will fix your car by tomorrow.

  Warning: I *warn* you I will call the police if you do not leave right now.

- The speaker establishes a new state of affairs.

  Declaring: I *declare* you the winner of the race.

  Firing: I hereby *fire* you from this company.

  Approving: I hereby *approve* your application for a driver's license.

- The speaker acknowledges that he or she holds a particular attitude toward something.

  Apologizing: I *apologize* to you for my behavior last night.

  Congratulating: I *congratulate* you on your promotion.

  Protesting: I *protest* your decision to extend the school year.

In addition, many speech acts are best identified by their actual effect on the listener, whether or not it is the impact that the speaker was striving for. Here are some examples: *humiliation, intimidation, scaring, harassment, persuading,* and *misleading.*

A few other things are important to bear in mind:

- Someone may pretend to engage in a particular kind of speech act and yet not fulfill one of its normal conditions: for example, an *apology* may not be sincere; the speaker may not really have the authority to *fire* workers.

- A speech act may not be the kind that it first appears to be: for example, when the head of a corporation seems to make a *suggestion*, the staff might take it as an *order*.
- Often you can better grasp the nature of a particular speech act if you identify options that the speaker rejected — things that the speaker *might* have done but decided not to. For instance, the police officers in Olds's poem *might* have scolded the man on the roof; instead, they chose to talk with him in a friendlier way.
- Most scholars who study "speech acts" extend this term to cover *various* media (not just speech) and *various* communicative signs (not just words). For examples of how broadly the term can be applied, look at photographs that you and other people have posted on Facebook or similar sites. Which of these images strike you as performing the following acts? (Note that an image can have more than one function.)

commemorating	advertising
mourning	denying
announcing	protesting
arguing	bragging
joking	warning

To practice analyzing speech acts in literature, read the following story, "What Might Life Be Like in the 21st Century?" Originally it appeared in the fall 2009 issue of the literary journal *Prairie Schooner*, the special topic of which was baby boomers. The author, Paul Lisicky, is from that generation. He has written several stories as brief as this one, all of them being examples of what many literary critics today call "microfiction," "sudden fiction," or "flash fiction." In an interview, Lisicky has acknowledged that the story is somewhat autobiographical, but he encourages his readers to regard it as largely a work of imagination. As you read it, try to come up with names for the speech acts you find in it. Afterward, we will pose some questions that help you do this. Then, to demonstrate the potential benefit of this approach, we present a few ideas that student Lauren Hollinger came up with when she applied it to Lisicky's story. The insights she gained helped her eventually construct the introduction to an essay she wrote on it.

PAUL LISICKY
What Might Life Be Like in the 21st Century?

My mother probably didn't expect him to have black hair and blue, blue eyes. Parent-teacher night: no other reason she'd have talked to Mr. Science, who would have looked past her to the other mothers, even if I'd built an atom smasher behind the school. The topic of discussion was my science fair project, "What Might Life Be Like in the 21st Century." I'd waited until the night before to throw it all together, as I'd done with every homework assignment that year, out of some protest I couldn't put a name to. What was the point of saying the here-and-now was good for us? My protest must have shown up in everything I did, from my matted hair, refusal to speak a word in class, to my walking off the field whenever I saw a fly ball coming in my direction. I was ready to go to sleep, though I hadn't even started my day. So no surprise Mr. Science led my mother to the corner of the cafeteria, sat her down away from the other mothers, and told her in a slow, deep voice that he saw no future for the likes of me.

I think of how it must have felt to take in those words. Did it hurt to hear them? Did they excite her? Or did she relax into the hot scratchy wool of her skirt as a patient might take to the gravest diagnosis? No wonder my perfected city didn't look like the other projects on the table. No wonder she couldn't take in the sleek shiny houses I'd drawn without wanting to head for the door. And in that moment, when it was still possible to turn back, she might have wanted to touch Mr. Science's face. Instead, he turned his head and saved her from that apology. She looked out toward the other mothers moving around the cafeteria tables, tried to picture herself among them, happy and glistening, and listened to what she could of his words.

"Science fair projects," he said, with an easy, cruel smile curving his mouth, "are about proving what's already known and finding the evidence to support those claims. I have to be honest with you. That's not what I'm seeing in your son's project."

"And his grade?" she said, with hope, as if she hadn't even heard the half of it.

"Well," he said, and held up two hands, letting them hang in the air. "If I gave him an F, maybe it'll teach him a thing or two." 5

"Thank you," she said and stood up. She gathered her scarf and gloves. And drove home, calming herself by counting the trees along the way, as if she'd finally found the key to help me live.

What could I say to her delivery, her looking around the living room — chair to table to desk to chair — as if its dimensions had become more spacious in her absence? She sat down across from me, face shining, eyes deadly cool, in the hopes I'd finally get it. I couldn't tell her I didn't care about proof and evidence. I couldn't say that the world didn't want us in it because who among us even had the words to make those claims? That world? That world was a funhouse, full of mirrors reflecting nothing but my tossed-off homework, my drowsing shoulders, the thick, drab poison of me, me, me, me, me. I wanted to be more than that sad little nothing. I wanted to roll in the grass with the animals. The future? So what if it ended up letting us down? I was ready to get there. I was ready to rattle its gates, even if I couldn't see past the houses, parks, and boulevards I'd drawn on that smudged sheet of posterboard.

The future arrived: that much I was sure of. And though it didn't have the fires and punishments that transfigured their dreams, it did have all those other things, and more. The human touch? She ached for it, starved for it. Why shouldn't she eat the sweet rind she'd been wanting for herself? That must have crossed her mind every time she saw me walking down the street, past the orange trees, away from her. We knew exactly what it was she deserved, but the city was already ruined.   *[2009]*

▤ THINKING ABOUT THE TEXT

1. What term best describes what the narrator is doing when he refers to the teacher as "Mr. Science"? (Think about the attitude he seems to express.)
2. What specific actions of his does the narrator himself call a "protest"?
3. With what word does the narrator indicate that even his silence in class was a kind of speech act?
4. What speech act would you say the teacher performed when he told the narrator's mother "that he saw no future for the likes of me"? (Think about the attitude that the teacher seemed to express.) The narrator does not put quote marks around these words, suggesting that he may be paraphrasing what the teacher really said. What may have been this teacher's actual words?
5. At the beginning of the second paragraph, the narrator wonders how the teacher's statement affected his mother. Notice his specific questions about her feelings. What do you call the speech acts that would stir these emotions?
6. The narrator suggests that if his mother had touched the teacher's face, this would have been an "apology." How so?
7. What speech act did the teacher expect science fair projects to perform? That is, what did he believe to be their proper function?
8. What speech act was the mother performing when she asked the teacher about her son's grade? What speech act was the teacher performing with his response? The mother then thanked the teacher. Why do you think she did so?
9. What do you suppose the mother told her son when she returned home? What speech act do you imagine she performed in talking to him?
10. In a sense, the narrator performs a number of speech acts as he tells this story about his past. What are some of the things he does as he recalls the episode?

After examining the characters' speech acts, Lauren Hollinger formed these ideas for her paper on the story. We italicize her references to verbal behavior.

> The narrator is *reviewing* and *evaluating* his self as a youth. He has arrived at some point in the future, in the sense that he is speaking

from a time beyond the main events of the story, although we readers cannot know how many years have passed or whether he is in better shape now than he was then. In telling us about his experience with the science fair, he appears to be on the verge of *apologizing* for depriving his mother of a "human touch" and for waging "some protest I couldn't put a name to." He even sounds as if he's *accusing* himself of selfishness when he refers to "the thick, drab poison of me, me, me, me, me" and when he *declares*, "We knew exactly what it was she deserved" (that is, a better son than he was being then). Yet he does not come right out and *confess* that he was completely wrong in his assumptions and conduct. In fact, he still seems to *sneer* with contempt at the science teacher, *mocking* him with the name "Mr. Science" and evidently *criticizing* him for *intimidating* the narrator's mother rather than treating her more sensitively. Moreover, he still seems to *reject* the teacher's view that "science fair projects . . . are about *proving* what's already known and finding the evidence to support those *claims.*" In addition, he gives the impression that he is *gently scolding* his mother for being naive when the teacher left her believing that "she'd finally found the key to help me live." When the narrator ends the story with the *pronouncement* that "the city was already ruined," he is apparently *admitting* that he was not living the kind of life that his mother and the teacher wanted him to. But when he *recalls* that "I didn't care about proof and evidence" and when he *remembers* that although the future was vague to him he was "ready to rattle its gates," he comes across as *continuing to defend* the boy he was. In general, therefore, the narrator *expresses some guilt* over his conduct toward his mother and *acknowledges* he was obnoxiously self-centered back then, but he nevertheless *accepts as valid* that younger self's wish for a future other than the one that his mother and the teacher *prescribed*.

Using Topics of Literary Studies to Get Ideas

You can also get ideas about the text if, as you read it, you consider how it deals with **topics** that have preoccupied literary studies as a profession. Some of these topics have interested the discipline for many years. One example is work, a common subject of the literature in Part One. Traditionally, literary studies has also been concerned with the chapter topics in Part Two: family relations, love, freedom and confinement, justice, and journeys. Moreover, the discipline has long called attention to topics that are essentially classic conflicts: for example, innocence versus experience, free will versus fate or determinism, the individual versus society, nature versus culture, and eternity versus the passing time.

Over the last few years, however, literary studies has turned to several new concerns. For instance, quite a few literary critics now consider the ways in which literary texts are often *about* reading, writing, interpretation, and evaluation. Critics increasingly refer to some of the following subjects in their analysis of literature:

- Traits that significantly shape human identity, including gender, race, ethnic background, social class, sexual orientation, cultural background, nationality, and historical context
- Representations of groups, including stereotypes held by others
- Acknowledgments — or denials — of differences among human beings
- Divisions, conflicts, and multiple forces *within* the self
- Boundaries, including the processes through which these are created, preserved, and challenged
- Politics and ideology, including the various forms that power and authority can take; acts of domination, oppression, exclusion, and appropriation; and acts of subversion, resistance, and parody
- Ways that carnivals and other festivities challenge or preserve social order
- Distinctions between what's universal and what's historically or culturally specific
- Relations between the public and the private, the social and the personal
- Relations between the apparently central and the apparently marginal
- Relations between what's supposedly normal and what's supposedly abnormal
- Relations between "high" culture and "low" (that is, mass or popular) culture
- Economic and technological developments, as well as their effects
- The role of performance in everyday life
- Values — ethical, aesthetic, religious, professional, and institutional
- Desire and pleasure
- The body
- The unconscious
- Memory, including public commemorations as well as personal memory

If you find that a literary text touches on one of these topics, try next to determine how the work specifically addresses that topic. Perhaps you will consider the topic an element of the text's themes. In any case, remember that, by itself, a topic is not the same as a theme. While a topic can usually be expressed in a word or a short phrase, a theme is a whole claim or assertion that you believe the text makes.

Actually, the topics we have identified may be most worth consulting when you have just begun analyzing a literary text and are far from establishing a theme. By using these topics, you can generate preliminary questions about the text, various issues you can then explore.

To demonstrate how these topics can stimulate inquiry, we apply some of them to the following poem, "Night Waitress." It is from the 1986 book

Ghost Memory, by the late American poet Lynda Hull (1954–1994). Hull had been developing an impressive career in literature when she died in a car accident. This poem is also about work, the speaker being the night waitress of the title.

LYNDA HULL

Night Waitress

Reflected in the plate glass, the pies
look like clouds drifting off my shoulder.
I'm telling myself my face has character,
not beauty. It's my mother's Slavic face.
She washed the floor on hands and knees   5
below the Black Madonna, praying
to her god of sorrows and visions
who's not here tonight when I lay out the plates,
small planets, the cups and moons of saucers.
At this hour the men all look   10
as if they'd never had mothers.
They do not see me. I bring the cups.
I bring the silver. There's the man
who leans over the jukebox nightly
pressing the combinations   15
of numbers. I would not stop him
if he touched me, but it's only songs
of risky love he leans into. The cook sings
with the jukebox, a moan and sizzle
into the grill. On his forehead   20
a tattooed cross furrows,
diminished when he frowns. He sings words
dragged up from the bottom of his lungs.
I want a song that rolls
through the night like a big Cadillac   25
past factories to the refineries
squatting on the bay, round and shiny
as the coffee urn warming my palm.
Sometimes when coffee cruises my mind
visiting the most remote way stations,   30
I think of my room as a calm arrival
each book and lamp in its place. The calendar
on my wall predicts no disaster
only another white square waiting
to be filled like the desire that fills   35
jail cells, the old arrest
that makes me stare out the window or want

to try every bar down the street.
When I walk out of here in the morning
my mouth is bitter with sleeplessness.   40
Men surge to the factories and I'm too tired
to look. Fingers grip lunch box handles,
belt buckles gleam, wind riffles my uniform
and it's not romantic when the sun unlids
the end of the avenue. I'm fading   45
in the morning's insinuations
collecting in the crevices of buildings,
in wrinkles, in every fault
of this frail machinery.   *[1986]*

≡ A WRITING EXERCISE

After you read "Night Waitress," do a ten-minute freewrite in which you try
to identify how the poem relates to one or more of the topics mentioned on
page 42.

We think that several of the topics now popular in literary studies are relevant to Hull's poem. Here are a few possibilities, along with questions that
these topics can generate.

Gender.   The speaker alludes to conventional roles through which men and
women relate to each other. When the speaker declares that "at this hour the
men all look / as if they'd never had mothers," she indicates that women have
often played a maternal role for men. Furthermore, she implies that often
women have been the primary caretaker of their sons. (Notice that she makes
no reference to fathers.) What is the effect of this attention to women as mothers of men? In most of the poem, the speaker refers to men as potential lovers.
Yet even as she suggests she would like a sexual relationship with a man, she
suggests as well that she has had trouble establishing worthwhile attachments.
Why has she had such difficulty, do you think? Does the problem seem due to
her personality alone, or do you sense larger forces shaping her situation? Notice, too, that the poem refers to the factory workers as male, while the woman
who speaks is a waitress. To what extent does American society perpetuate a
gendered division of labor?

Ethnic background.   Near the start of the poem, the speaker refers to her
"mother's Slavic face" and points out that her mother served "the Black Madonna," a religious icon popular in Central European countries such as the
Czech Republic and Poland. What is the effect of these particular ethnic references? To pursue this line of inquiry, probably you will need to do research into
the Black Madonna, whether in a library or on the Internet.

Social class.   In part, considering social class means thinking about people's
ability to obtain material goods. When the speaker compares her ideal song to

"a big Cadillac," she implies that she doesn't currently possess such a luxurious car. At the same time, she is expressing her desire for the song, not the car. Why might the song be more important to her right now? Social class is also a matter of how various workplaces are related to one another. This poem evokes a restaurant, factories, refineries, and bars. How are these settings connected as parts of American society? Think, too, about how you would label the social class of the various occupations the poem mentions. What would you say is the social class of a waitress? To what classes would you assign people who work in factories and refineries? Who, for the most part, are the social classes that have to work at night?

Sexual orientation.   The speaker of "Night Waitress" seems heterosexual, an orientation often regarded as the only legitimate one. Because almost all societies have made heterosexuality the norm, a lot of people forget that it is a particular orientation and that not everyone identifies with it. Within literary studies, gay and lesbian critics have pointed out that a literary work may seem to deal with sexuality in general but may actually refer just to heterosexuality. Perhaps "Night Waitress" is examining heterosexuality as a specific social force. If so, how might the speaker's discontent be related to heterosexuality's influence as a particular institution? Keep in mind that you don't have to assume anything about the author's sexuality as you pursue such a question. In fact, heterosexuality may be a more important topic in Hull's poem than she intended.

Divisions, conflicts, and multiple forces within the self.   The poem's beginning indicates that the speaker experiences herself as divided. The first four lines reveal that she feels pride and disappointment in her mirror image: "I'm telling myself my face has character, / not beauty." Later she indicates that within her mind are "remote way stations" that she visits only on occasion. Furthermore, she seems to contradict herself. Although she initially refers to her room as "a calm arrival," she goes on to describe that place negatively, as empty and confined. Early in the evening, she seems sexually attracted to the man playing the jukebox ("I would not stop him / if he touched me"), but by morning her mood is "not romantic" and she is "too tired / to look" at the male factory workers. What may be the significance of these paradoxes?

Boundaries.   In the first line, the speaker is apparently looking at a window, and later she reveals that at times she feels driven to "stare out the window" of her room. What should a reader make of these two references to such a common boundary? When the speaker observes that the men in the restaurant "do not see me," she indicates that a boundary exists between them and her. Do you think she is merely being paranoid, or do you suspect that the men are indeed ignoring her? If they *are* oblivious to her, how do you explain their behavior? Still another boundary explored in the poem is the line between night and day. What happens when the speaker crosses this line? What can night, day, and the boundary between them signify? You might also consider what the author of a literary work does with its technical boundaries. Often a poem creates boundaries in its breaks between stanzas. Yet "Night Waitress" is a continuous, unbroken text; what is the effect of Hull's making it so? At the same time, Hull doesn't always respect sentence boundaries in her lines. At several points in the poem, sentences spill over from one line to another. This poetic technique is called **enjambment**; what is its effect here?

Politics and ideology.   When, in referring to the jukebox man, the speaker declares that "I would not stop him / if he touched me," she can be taken to imply that male customers often flirt with waitresses. How might flirtation be seen as involving power, authority, and even outright domination? Do you see the poem as commenting on such things? Earlier we raised issues of social class; these can be seen as political issues, too. How would you describe a society in which some people have "a big Cadillac" and others do not?

Carnivals and other festivities.   Although the poem does not refer to a "carnival" in any sense of that word, it does mention bars, which today are regarded by many people as places of festive retreat from work. What adjectives would you use to describe the speaker when she says that sometimes she wants "to try every bar down the street"?

Distinctions between what is universal and what is historically or culturally specific.   Try to identify anything that is historically or culturally specific about this poem's setting. Certainly the word *Slavic* and the reference to the Black Madonna indicate that the speaker has a particular background. You might also note her description of the restaurant, her use of the Cadillac as a metaphor, and her mention of the "factories" and the "refineries" that are "squatting on the bay." Although a wide range of places might fit these details, the poem's setting does not seem universal. Indeed, many readers are attracted to literature *because* it deals with specific landscapes, people, and plots. Nevertheless, these same readers usually expect to get some larger, more widely applicable meanings out of literature even as they are engaged by its specific details. Are you inclined to draw general conclusions from "Night Waitress"? If so, what general meanings do you find in it? What sorts of people do you think might learn something about themselves from reading this poem?

Relations between the public and the private, the social and the personal.   The speaker of "Night Waitress" works in a very public place, a restaurant. Yet she seems to feel isolated there, trapped in her own private world. How did she come to experience public life this way, do you think? Later, she initially seems to value her room as a private retreat, calling it "a calm arrival," but then she describes it as a place so lonely that it leads her to "stare out the window or want / to try every bar down the street." How, then, would you ultimately describe the relations between the speaker's public life and her private one? In addressing this issue, probably you need to consider whether the speaker's difficulties are merely personal or reflect a larger social disorder. When, at the end of the poem, she refers to "this frail machinery," is she referring just to herself, or is she suggesting that this phrase applies to her society in general? If she is indeed making a social observation, what do you sense are the "faults" in her society? Who else might be "fading"?

Relations between "high" culture and "low" culture.   Although the speaker does not identify the "songs / of risky love" playing on the jukebox, surely they are examples of what is called low, mass, or popular culture. Just as a lot of us are moved by such music when we hear it, so the jukebox player and the cook are engaged by it. In contrast, the poem itself can be considered an example of high culture. Often poetry is regarded as a serious art even by people who don't read it. In what ways, if any, does this poem conceivably resemble the songs it mentions? Given that author Lynda Hull is in essence playing with combinations of words, can we compare her with "the man / who leans over the jukebox nightly / pressing the combinations / of numbers"? (Actually, *numbers* has been a poetic term; centuries ago, it was commonly used as a synonym for the rhythms of poems.)

The role of performance in everyday life.   The most conspicuous performer in this poem is the cook, who "sings words / dragged up from the bottom of his lungs." But in everyday life, people often perform in the sense of taking on certain roles, even disguising their real personalities. Do you see such instances of performing in this poem? If so, where? Notice that the speaker wears a uniform; can that be considered a costume she wears while performing as a waitress?

Religious values.   The speaker clearly refers to religion when she recalls her mother's devotion to the Black Madonna, behavior that involved "praying / to her god of sorrows and visions." And although that god is "not here tonight," the speaker's description of waitressing has ritualistic overtones reminiscent of religious ceremonies. When she says, "I bring the cups. / I bring the silver," she could almost be describing preparations for Communion. In fact, she depicts the cook as wearing a religious emblem: "On his forehead / a tattooed cross furrows, / diminished when he frowns." What do you make of all this religious imagery? Might the speaker be trying to pursue certain religious values? Can she be reasonably described as looking for salvation?

Desire and pleasure.   The speaker explicitly mentions the word *desire* when she describes the emptiness she feels in her room, a feeling of desolation "that makes me stare out the window or want / to try every bar down the street." These lines may lead you to believe that her desire is basically sexual. Yet when the speaker uses the words *I want* earlier in the poem, she expresses her wish for "a song that rolls / through the night like a big Cadillac." Here, her longing does not appear sexual in nature. Is the speaker referring to at least two kinds of desire, then? Or do you see her as afflicted with basically one kind?

The body.   A notable feature of this poem is its attention to body parts. The speaker mentions her "shoulder," her "face," her mother's "face," her mother's "hands and knees," the cook's "forehead," his "lungs," her "palm," the "way stations" of her "mind," her "mouth," the factory workers' "fingers," and their "belt buckles." At the same time, the speaker never describes any particular body as a whole. What is the effect of this emphasis on mere parts? Does it connect in any way to the speaker's ultimate "fading"?

Memory.   Already we have noted the speaker's reference to her mother at the start of the poem. In what way, if any, is it significant that she engages in recollection? What circumstances in her life might have prompted the speaker to look back at the past?

■ A WRITING EXERCISE

We have applied several topics from our list to Lynda Hull's poem "Night Waitress." Now see how you can apply topics from the list to another poem about work in Part One. Try to come up with several questions about the poem you choose, referring to topics on our list. Then select one of the questions you have formulated, and freewrite for ten minutes in response to it.

■ SUMMING UP

- *Close reading* is a process that consists of several strategies, all of which can help you get ideas about a literary work for an essay you will write. These strategies include making predictions as you read; rereading the text with a different focus each time; reading aloud; comparing the text with your personal experience; tracing patterns and breaks from them; noting ambiguities; considering the author's alternatives; generating questions; and formulating a tentative claim. (pp. 22–25)

- Close reading is aided by several *writing* strategies. These include commenting in the text's margins; note-taking; freewriting; creating a "dialectical notebook"; and playfully revising the text. (pp. 26–31)

- To generate ideas about a literary text, consider its characters' emotions and speech acts, as well as how the text deals with topics that have preoccupied literary studies. (pp. 33–48)

CHAPTER 3

How to Make Arguments about Literature

Our writing assignments are designed to help you reflect on the literature you read. Although these assignments are varied, mostly we encourage you to argue about literature. We do so for three reasons. First, the term **argument** refers to a kind of talk as well as a kind of writing; thus, focusing on this term can help you relate your own written work to discussions in class. Second, you will read a work of literature with greater direction and purpose if you are working toward the goal of constructing arguments about it. Finally, when you argue, you learn a lot, because you have to ponder things you may have taken for granted as well as things unfamiliar to you.

Specifically, *arguing* is a process in which you identify a subject of current or possible debate; you take a position on that subject; you analyze why you view the subject the way you do; and you try to persuade others that your view is worth sharing or is at least reasonable. Often the process of arguing is not straightforward. Just when you think you have decided how you feel about a subject, class discussion may lead you to change your position or shift to a completely different topic. Whatever the case, to argue well means to engage in self-examination. Also, it means attending to the world around you, especially to the ways that other people think differently than you.

For many, *argument* is a negative term. Perhaps it makes you think of unpleasant shouting matches you have been in or witnessed—times when people have bitterly disagreed with one another and refused to compromise. Almost everyone has experienced arguments of this sort. Moreover, they are a kind of argument that the media promote. On talk radio, hosts as well as callers are often brutally argumentative, mixing strong opinion with outright insult. Similarly, television's political talk shows regularly become sheer quarrels; panelists fall again and again into nasty, noisy debate. Spats are even more spectacular on daytime talk shows, which invite friends and family members to clash in public on such high-voltage topics as "You Stole Him from Me and I Want Him Back!" On occasion, the participants turn from words to fists. No wonder many people see argument as fierce competition, even as a form of war.

Although many people view argument as war, we encourage you to argue in a more positive sense. In any meaning of the term, to *argue* is to disagree with others or to set forth a view that you suspect not everyone holds. But argument need not be a competition in which you aim to prove that only you are right. At times you might collaborate with someone else in arguing a position. You also can concede that several views on the subject are possible, even as you develop your own position. In fact, your audience is more likely to be persuaded if you treat other people's opinions fairly. Furthermore, successful arguers establish common ground with their audience; they identify and honor at least some of the beliefs that their readers or listeners hold.

Keep in mind, too, that participants in an argument ought to learn from one another. If you take seriously other people's responses to your position, you will find yourself reexamining why and how you express that view. As we have already noted, you may even change your mind. Above all, we hope you will see argument as *inquiry*, a process in which you think hard about your beliefs rather than just declare them.

As we discuss the process of arguing about literature, we mention arguments that might be made about the following pair of stories. Each features a speaker who is introducing someone else to certain kinds of work. It is useful to compare these texts. Indeed, we emphasize comparison throughout this book. As you read each story, take a few moments to reflect on the questions we ask after each one, perhaps jotting down your responses to keep them in your mind as you read the rest of the chapter.

The first story, "Orientation," originally appeared in a 1994 issue of *Seattle Review* and was subsequently selected for *The Best American Short Stories 1995*.

DANIEL OROZCO

Orientation

The son of Nicaraguan immigrants, California-born Daniel Orozco (b. 1957) currently teaches at the University of Idaho. His award-winning short fiction has appeared in a variety of magazines, including Harper's *and* Zoetrope, *and has been collected in* Orientation and Other Stories *(2011). He received a B.A. from Stanford University, an M.A. from San Francisco State University, and an M.F.A. from the University of Washington. He has also held a writing fellowship at Stanford.*

Those are the offices and these are the cubicles. That's my cubicle there, and this is your cubicle. This is your phone. Never answer your phone. Let the Voicemail System answer it. This is your Voicemail System Manual. There are no personal phone calls allowed. We do, however, allow for emergencies. If you must make an emergency phone call, ask your supervisor first. If you can't find your supervisor, ask Phillip Spiers, who sits over there. He'll check with Clarissa Nicks, who sits over there. If you make an emergency phone call without asking, you may be let go.

These are your IN and OUT boxes. All the forms in your IN box must be logged in by the date shown in the upper left-hand corner, initialed by you in the upper right-hand corner, and distributed to the Processing Analyst whose name is numerically coded in the lower left-hand corner. The lower right-hand corner is left blank. Here's your Processing Analyst Numerical Code Index. And here's your Forms Processing Procedures Manual.

You must pace your work. What do I mean? I'm glad you asked that. We pace our work according to the eight-hour workday. If you have twelve hours of work in your IN box, for example, you must compress that work into the eight-hour day. If you have one hour of work in your IN box, you must expand that work to fill the eight-hour day. That was a good question. Feel free to ask questions. Ask too many questions, however, and you may be let go.

That is our receptionist. She is a temp. We go through receptionists here. They quit with alarming frequency. Be polite and civil to the temps. Learn their names, and invite them to lunch occasionally. But don't get close to them, as it only makes it more difficult when they leave. And they always leave. You can be sure of that.

The men's room is over there. The women's room is over there. John   5
LaFountaine, who sits over there, uses the women's room occasionally. He says it is accidental. We know better, but we let it pass. John LaFountaine is harmless, his forays into the forbidden territory of the women's room simply a benign thrill, a faint blip on the dull flat line of his life.

Russell Nash, who sits in the cubicle to your left, is in love with Amanda Pierce, who sits in the cubicle to your right. They ride the same bus together after work. For Amanda Pierce, it is just a tedious bus ride made less tedious by the idle nattering of Russell Nash. But for Russell Nash, it is the highlight of his day. It is the highlight of his life. Russell Nash has put on forty pounds, and grows fatter with each passing month, nibbling on chips and cookies while peeking glumly over the partitions at Amanda Pierce, and gorging himself at home on cold pizza and ice cream while watching adult videos on TV.

Amanda Pierce, in the cubicle to your right, has a six-year-old son named Jamie, who is autistic. Her cubicle is plastered from top to bottom with the boy's crayon artwork — sheet after sheet of precisely drawn concentric circles and ellipses, in black and yellow. She rotates them every other Friday. Be sure to comment on them. Amanda Pierce also has a husband, who is a lawyer. He subjects her to an escalating array of painful and humiliating sex games, to which Amanda Pierce reluctantly submits. She comes to work exhausted and freshly wounded each morning, wincing from the abrasions on her breasts, or the bruises on her abdomen, or the second-degree burns on the backs of her thighs.

But we're not supposed to know any of this. Do not let on. If you let on, you may be let go.

Amanda Pierce, who tolerates Russell Nash, is in love with Albert Bosch, whose office is over there. Albert Bosch, who only dimly registers Amanda Pierce's existence, has eyes only for Ellie Tapper, who sits over there. Ellie Tapper, who hates Albert Bosch, would walk through fire for Curtis Lance. But Curtis Lance hates Ellie Tapper. Isn't the world a funny place? Not in the ha-ha sense, of course.

Anika Bloom sits in that cubicle. Last year, while reviewing quarterly re-   10
ports in a meeting with Barry Hacker, Anika Bloom's left palm began to bleed.

She fell into a trance, stared into her hand, and told Barry Hacker when and how his wife would die. We laughed it off. She was, after all, a new employee. But Barry Hacker's wife is dead. So unless you want to know exactly when and how you'll die, never talk to Anika Bloom.

Colin Heavey sits in that cubicle over there. He was new once, just like you. We warned him about Anika Bloom. But at last year's Christmas Potluck, he felt sorry for her when he saw that no one was talking to her. Colin Heavey brought her a drink. He hasn't been himself since. Colin Heavey is doomed. There's nothing he can do about it, and we are powerless to help him. Stay away from Colin Heavey. Never give any of your work to him. If he asks to do something, tell him you have to check with me. If he asks again, tell him I haven't gotten back to you.

This is the Fire Exit. There are several on this floor, and they are marked accordingly. We have a Floor Evacuation Review every three months, and an Escape Route Quiz once a month. We have our Biannual Fire Drill twice a year, and our Annual Earthquake Drill once a year. These are precautions only. These things never happen.

For your information, we have a comprehensive health plan. Any catastrophic illness, any unforeseen tragedy is completely covered. All dependents are completely covered. Larry Bagdikian, who sits over there, has six daughters. If anything were to happen to any of his girls, or to all of them, if all six were to simultaneously fall victim to illness or injury — stricken with a hideous degenerative muscle disease or some rare toxic blood disorder, sprayed with semiautomatic gunfire while on a class field trip, or attacked in their bunk beds by some prowling nocturnal lunatic — if any of this were to pass, Larry's girls would all be taken care of. Larry Bagdikian would not have to pay one dime. He would have nothing to worry about.

We also have a generous vacation and sick leave policy. We have an excellent disability insurance plan. We have a stable and profitable pension fund. We get group discounts for the symphony, and block seating at the ballpark. We get commuter ticket books for the bridge. We have Direct Deposit. We are all members of Costco.

This is our kitchenette. And this, this is our Mr. Coffee. We have a coffee   15
pool, into which we each pay two dollars a week for coffee, filters, sugar, and CoffeeMate. If you prefer Cremora or half-and-half to CoffeeMate, there is a special pool for three dollars a week. If you prefer Sweet 'n Low to sugar, there is a special pool for two-fifty a week. We do not do decaf. You are allowed to join the coffee pool of your choice, but you are not allowed to touch the Mr. Coffee.

This is the microwave oven. You are allowed to *heat* food in the microwave oven. You are not, however, allowed to *cook* food in the microwave oven.

We get one hour for lunch. We also get one fifteen-minute break in the morning, and one fifteen-minute break in the afternoon. Always take your breaks. If you skip a break, it is gone forever. For your information, your break is a privilege, not a right. If you abuse the break policy, we are authorized to rescind your breaks. Lunch, however, is a right, not a privilege. If you abuse the lunch policy, our hands will be tied, and we will be forced to look the other way. We will not enjoy that.

This is the refrigerator. You may put your lunch in it. Barry Hacker, who sits over there, steals food from this refrigerator. His petty theft is an outlet for his grief. Last New Year's Eve, while kissing his wife, a blood vessel burst in her brain. Barry Hacker's wife was two months pregnant at the time, and lingered in a coma for half a year before dying. It was a tragic loss for Barry Hacker. He hasn't been himself since. Barry Hacker's wife was a beautiful woman. She was also completely covered. Barry Hacker did not have to pay one dime. But his dead wife haunts him. She haunts all of us. We have seen her, reflected in the monitors of our computers, moving past our cubicles. We have seen the dim shadow of her face in our photocopies. She pencils herself in in the receptionist's appointment book, with the notation: To see Barry Hacker. She has left messages in the receptionist's Voicemail box, messages garbled by the electronic chirrups and buzzes in the phone line, her voice echoing from an immense distance within the ambient hum. But the voice is hers. And beneath her voice, beneath the tidal *whoosh* of static and hiss, the gurgling and crying of a baby can be heard.

In any case, if you bring a lunch, put a little something extra in the bag for Barry Hacker. We have four Barrys in this office. Isn't that a coincidence?

This is Matthew Payne's office. He is our Unit Manager, and his door is always closed. We have never seen him, and you will never see him. But he is here. You can be sure of that. He is all around us.

This is the Custodian's Closet. You have no business in the Custodian's Closet.

And this, this is our Supplies Cabinet. If you need supplies, see Curtis Lance. He will log you in on the Supplies Cabinet Authorization Log, then give you a Supplies Authorization Slip. Present your pink copy of the Supplies Authorization Slip to Ellie Tapper. She will log you in on the Supplies Cabinet Key Log, then give you the key. Because the Supplies Cabinet is located outside the Unit Manager's office, you must be very quiet. Gather your supplies quietly. The Supplies Cabinet is divided into four sections. Section One contains letterhead stationery, blank paper and envelopes, memo and note pads, and so on. Section Two contains pens and pencils and typewriter and printer ribbons, and the like. In Section Three we have erasers, correction fluids, transparent tapes, glue sticks, et cetera. And in Section Four we have paper clips and push pins and scissors and razor blades. And here are the spare blades for the shredder. Do not touch the shredder, which is located over there. The shredder is of no concern to you.

Gwendolyn Stich sits in that office there. She is crazy about penguins, and collects penguin knickknacks: penguin posters and coffee mugs and stationery, penguin stuffed animals, penguin jewelry, penguin sweaters and T-shirts and socks. She has a pair of penguin fuzzy slippers she wears when working late at the office. She has a tape cassette of penguin sounds which she listens to for relaxation. Her favorite colors are black and white. She has personalized license plates that read PEN GWEN. Every morning, she passes through all the cubicles to wish each of us a *good* morning. She brings Danish on Wednesdays for Hump Day morning break, and doughnuts on Fridays for TGIF afternoon break. She organizes the Annual Christmas Potluck, and is in charge of the Birthday List. Gwendolyn Stich's door is always open to all of us. She will always lend an ear, and put in a good word for you; she will always give you a hand, or the shirt off her back, or a shoulder to cry on. Because her door is always open, she hides and cries in a stall in the women's room. And John LaFountaine — who, enthralled when a woman enters, sits quietly in his stall with his knees to his chest — John LaFountaine has heard her vomiting in there. We have come upon Gwendolyn Stich huddled in the stairwell, shivering in the updraft, sipping a Diet Mr. Pibb and hugging her knees. She does not let any of this interfere with her work. If it interfered with her work, she might have to be let go.

Kevin Howard sits in that cubicle over there. He is a serial killer, the one they call the Carpet Cutter, responsible for the mutilations across town. We're not supposed to know that, so do not let on. Don't worry. His compulsion inflicts itself on strangers only, and the routine established is elaborate and unwavering. The victim must be a white male, a young adult no older than thirty, heavyset, with dark hair and eyes, and the like. The victim must be chosen at random, before sunset, from a public place; the victim is followed home, and must put up a struggle; et cetera. The carnage inflicted is precise: the angle and direction of the incisions; the layering of skin and muscle tissue; the rearrangement of the visceral organs; and so on. Kevin Howard does not let any of this interfere with his work. He is, in fact, our fastest typist. He types as if he were on fire. He has a secret crush on Gwendolyn Stich, and leaves a red-foil-wrapped Hershey's Kiss on her desk every afternoon. But he hates Anika Bloom, and keeps well away from her. In his presence, she has uncontrollable fits of shaking and trembling. Her left palm does not stop bleeding.

In any case, when Kevin Howard gets caught, act surprised. Say that he   25
seemed like a nice person, a bit of a loner, perhaps, but always quiet and polite.

This is the photocopier room. And this, this is our view. It faces southwest. West is down there, toward the water. North is back there. Because we are on the seventeenth floor, we are afforded a magnificent view. Isn't it beautiful? It overlooks the park, where the tops of those trees are. You can see a segment of the bay between those two buildings there. You can see the sun set in the gap between those two buildings over there. You can see this building reflected in the glass panels of that building across the way. There. See? That's you, waving. And look there. There's Anika Bloom in the kitchenette, waving back.

Enjoy this view while photocopying. If you have problems with the photocopier, see Russell Nash. If you have any questions, ask your supervisor. If you can't find your supervisor, ask Phillip Spiers. He sits over there. He'll check with Clarissa Nicks. She sits over there. If you can't find them, feel free to ask me. That's my cubicle. I sit in there.   *[1994]*

■ **THINKING ABOUT THE TEXT**

1. Orozco reports that since his story was published, "it has even been included in an employee orientation manual, which is either very funny or very disturbing." What is *your* reaction to this news? Does this orientation resemble other orientations with which you are familiar? In what ways? Consider the kinds of advice given and language used.

2. Does the office described here resemble other offices with which you are familiar? In what ways? At what points in the story does this office seem unusual?

3. List at least three adjectives that describe Orozco's narrator. What influences your evaluation of this narrator? What would you say to someone who claims that the story is more about the narrator than about the office?

4. What assumptions do you make about the narrator's audience, that is, the listener being oriented? Write a page or two from this person's point of view, stating his or her response to the orientation.

5. Does the order of the narrator's statements matter? Explain.

The next story, Jamaica Kincaid's "Girl," first appeared in *The New Yorker* in 1978 and was later reprinted in her first book, a 1984 collection of short stories entitled *At the Bottom of the River.*

JAMAICA KINCAID

Girl

Originally named Elaine Potter Richardson, Jamaica Kincaid (b. 1949) was born on the island of Antigua in the West Indies. At the time, Antigua was a British colony. Kincaid lived there until she was seventeen, when she emigrated to the United States. Soon she became a nanny for the family of Michael Arlen, television critic for The New Yorker. *Eventually, the magazine published her own short stories and during the early 1990s her gardening columns. Although she continues to live in the United States, almost all of her writing deals with her native land. In particular, she has written about Antiguan women growing up under British domination. She has published the novels* Annie John *(1985),* Lucy *(1990),* Autobiography of My Mother *(1996), and* Mr. Potter *(2002). Her books of nonfiction include* A Small Place, *an analysis of Antigua (1988); a memoir,* My Brother *(1997);* My Garden (Book) *(1999); and* Talk Stories *(2001), a collection of brief observations that she originally wrote for* The New Yorker. *In 2009, she was inducted into the American Academy of Arts and Sciences and is currently a professor of literature at Claremont McKenna College in California.*

Wash the white clothes on Monday and put them on the stone heap; wash the color clothes on Tuesday and put them on the clothesline to dry; don't walk barehead in the hot sun; cook pumpkin fritters in very hot sweet oil; soak your little cloths right after you take them off; when buying cotton to make yourself a nice blouse, be sure that it doesn't have gum on it, because that way it won't   5
hold up well after a wash; soak salt fish overnight before you cook it; is it true that you sing benna° in Sunday school?; always eat your food in such a way that it won't turn someone else's stomach; on Sundays try to walk like a lady and not like the slut you are so bent on becoming; don't sing benna in Sunday school; you mustn't speak to wharf-rat boys, not even to give directions; don't   10
eat fruits on the street — flies will follow you; *but I don't sing benna on Sundays at all and never in Sunday school*; this is how to sew on a button; this is how to make a button-hole for the button you have just sewed on; this is how to hem a dress when you see the hem coming down and so to prevent yourself from looking like the slut I know you are so bent on becoming; this is how you iron your fa-   15
ther's khaki shirt so that it doesn't have a crease; this is how you iron your father's khaki pants so that they don't have a crease; this is how you grow okra — far from the house, because okra tree harbors red ants; when you are growing dasheen, make sure it gets plenty of water or else it makes your throat itch when you are eating it; this is how you sweep a corner; this is how you   20
sweep a whole house; this is how you sweep a yard; this is how you smile to someone you don't like too much; this is how you smile to someone you don't like at all; this is how you smile to someone you like completely; this is how you set a table for tea; this is how you set a table for dinner; this is how you set a table for dinner with an important guest; this is how you set a table for lunch;   25
this is how you set a table for breakfast; this is how to behave in the presence of men who don't know you very well, and this way they won't recognize immediately the slut I have warned you against becoming; be sure to wash every day, even if it is with your own spit; don't squat down to play marbles — you are not a boy, you know; don't pick people's flowers — you might catch something;   30
don't throw stones at blackbirds, because it might not be a blackbird at all; this is how to make a bread pudding; this is how to make doukona;° this is how to make pepper pot; this is how to make a good medicine for a cold; this is how to make a good medicine to throw away a child before it even becomes a child; this is how to catch a fish; this is how to throw back a fish you don't like, and that   35
way something bad won't fall on you; this is how to bully a man; this is how a man bullies you; this is how to love a man, and if this doesn't work there are other ways, and if they don't work don't feel too bad about giving up; this is how to spit up in the air if you feel like it, and this is how to move quick so that it doesn't fall on you; this is how to make ends meet; always squeeze bread to   40
make sure it's fresh; *but what if the baker won't let me feel the bread?*; you mean to say that after all you are really going to be the kind of woman who the baker won't let near the bread?   *[1978]*

---

benna: Calypso music.   **doukona:** A spicy plantain pudding.

■ THINKING ABOUT THE TEXT

1. Is "Girl" really a story? What characteristics of a story come to mind as you consider this issue?

2. Describe the culture depicted in "Girl" as well as the role of females in that culture. Is either the culture or the role of females in it different from what you are familiar with? Explain.

3. Do you think that the instructions to this girl are all given on the same occasion? Why, or why not? Who do you suppose is giving the instructions? Would you say that the instructor is oppressive or domineering? Identify some of the assumptions behind your position.

4. What effect does Kincaid achieve by making this text a single long sentence? By having the girl speak at only two brief moments?

5. At one point, the girl is shown "how to make a good medicine to throw away a child before it even becomes a child" (lines 33–34). What do you think of the instructor's willingness to give such advice? What do you conclude from its position in the text between "how to make a good medicine for a cold" (line 33) and "how to catch a fish" (line 35)? Does the order of the various pieces of advice matter? Could Kincaid have presented them in a different order without changing their effects?

■ A WRITING EXERCISE

Once you have read both stories, write brief responses to each. You might jot down things you especially notice about them, feelings they evoke in you, and questions you have about them. You might also note your own work experiences that they lead you to recall. With each story, freewrite for ten minutes without stopping.

Strategies for Making Arguments about Literature

We turn now to specific elements of argument. An argument involves six basic elements. When you argue, you attempt to persuade an audience to accept your claims regarding an issue by presenting evidence and relying on warrants. The boldfaced words are key to this book; we mention them often. Here we explain what we mean by each, beginning with *issue* and then moving to *claims, persuasion, audience, evidence,* and *warrants*. Throughout our discussion, we refer to the stories by Orozco and Kincaid.

▌.IDENTIFY ISSUES

An issue is something about which people have disagreed or might disagree. Even as you read a text, you can try to guess what features of it will lead to disagreements in class. You may sense that your own reaction to certain aspects of the text is heavily influenced by your background and values, which other students may not share. Some parts of the text may leave you with conflicting ideas or mixed feelings, as if half of you disagrees with the other half. At moments like these, you come to realize what topics are issues for you, and next you can urge the rest of your class to see these topics as issues, too.

An issue is best defined as a question with no obvious, immediate answer. Thus, you can start identifying issues by noting questions that occur to you as you read. Perhaps this question-posing approach to texts is new for you. Often readers demand that a text be clear, and they get annoyed if it leaves them puzzled. Certain writing ought to be immediately clear in meaning; think of operating instructions on a plane's emergency doors. But the value of a literary work often lies in the work's complexities, which can lead readers to reexamine their own ways of perceiving the world. Also, your discussions and papers about literature are likely to be most useful when they go beyond the obvious to deal with more challenging matters. When your class begins talking about a work, you may feel obliged to stay quiet if you have no firm statements to make. But you can contribute a lot by bringing up questions that occurred to you as you read. Especially worth raising are questions that continue to haunt you.

In the case of Daniel Orozco's "Orientation," one possible issue concerns the reliability of the narrator. Should we accept as true everything the narrator says, or should we be suspicious of the orientation this person gives? A possible issue with Jamaica Kincaid's "Girl" concerns how much affection the main speaker has for the girl she addresses. A logical hypothesis is that these two are mother and daughter, but to what degree is the speaker showing motherly love? In fact, people may disagree over how to define this term. What does it mean to *you*?

You may feel unable to answer questions like these. But again, you achieve much when you simply formulate questions and bring them up in class. As other students help you ponder them, you will grow better able to explore issues through writing as well as through conversation.

You are more likely to come up with questions about a text if you assume that for every decision the writer made, alternatives existed. In "Orientation," Orozco might have had the many characters speak, but instead he chose to write the story as a mostly uninterrupted monologue. Similarly, Kincaid might have given the girl of her title more of a speaking voice. When you begin to explore why authors made the choices they did, you also begin to examine the effects of those choices.

You will recognize writers' options more easily if you compare their texts with others. For instance, with "Orientation" you cannot be sure how old the narrator and new employee are, but Kincaid's story is pointedly entitled "Girl," and its speaker is clearly a female adult. Although both stories are about education, Kincaid's is concerned with the transition from youth to adulthood. She shows how a girl's transition to womanhood involves learning certain gender "rules" of her sex. Thinking of Kincaid's focus can strengthen your awareness that Orozco has chosen not to reveal whether his story's two characters are male or female.

Next we identify ten kinds of issues that arise in literature courses. Our list will help you detect the issues that come up in your class and discover others to bring up in discussions or in your writing. The list does not include every kind of issue; you may think of others. Moreover, you may find that an issue can fit into more than one of the categories we name. But when you do have an issue that seems hard to classify, try to assign it to a single category, if only for the time being. You will then have some initial guidance for your reading, class discussions, and writing. If you later feel that the issue belongs to another category, you can shift your focus.

▶1. Issues of fact. Rarely does a work of literature provide complete information about its characters and events. Rather, literature is usually marked by what literary theorist Wolfgang Iser calls "gaps," moments when certain facts are omitted or obscured. At such times, readers may give various answers to the question, What is happening in this text? Readers tackle questions of fact only if they suspect that the answers will affect their overall view of a text. It may not matter, for example, that we fail to learn the exact product or service of the company described in Orozco's "Orientation." More consequential seems the question of whether Barry Hacker's dead wife is really sending messages to the office. Imagine a reader who believes that Orozco's narrator is merely fantasizing a ghost. Imagine a second reader who thinks the wife is truly haunting the office. How might these two readers see the whole story differently because of their different assumptions?

▶2. Issues of theme. You may be familiar with the term **theme** from other literature courses. By *theme* critics usually mean the main claim that an author seems to be making with his or her text. Sometimes a theme is defined in terms of a single word — for example, *work* or *love*. But such words are really mere topics. Identifying the topics addressed by a text can be a useful way of starting to analyze that text, and earlier in Part One we list several topics that currently preoccupy literary studies. A text's theme, however, is best seen as an assertion that you need at least one whole sentence to express.

With many texts, an issue of theme arises because readers can easily disagree about the text's main idea. In literature classes, such disagreements often occur, in part because literary works tend to express their themes indirectly. This is especially the case with stories like "Orientation" and "Girl," in which the main speaker's views are not necessarily the same as the author's. Readers of these two stories may give various answers to the question, What is the author ultimately saying? Perhaps some readers will take Kincaid to imply that mothers always know best. Other readers may conclude that Kincaid thinks that excessively controlling mothers are damaging to children.

If you try to express a text's theme, avoid making a statement that is so general that it could apply to many other works. Arguing that Kincaid's theme is "Girls are pressured to fit stereotyped roles" does not get at her story's details. On the other hand, do not let a text's details restrict you so much that you make the theme seem relevant only to a small group. If you argue that Kincaid's theme is "Antiguan women are domineering," then the many readers who are *not* from Antigua will wonder why they should care. In short, try to express themes as *midlevel generalizations.* With Kincaid's story, one possible theme is "In some cultures, women prepare girls for adulthood by teaching them to follow conventions *and* to assert themselves." A statement like this seems both attentive to Kincaid's specific text and applicable to a large portion of humanity. You are free to challenge this version of Kincaid's theme by proposing an alternative. Moreover, even if you do accept this statement as her theme, you are then free to decide whether it is a sound observation. Identifying a theme is one thing; evaluating it is another.

Keep in mind that a theme ties together various parts of a text. Focusing on a single passage, even if it seems thematic, may lead you to ignore other passages that a statement of theme should encompass. For instance, the last words of "Girl" may tempt you to believe that its theme is "be the kind of woman who feels the bread." Yet in other parts of the story, the main speaker seems to be calling for a compliant attitude. You need to take these moments into account as well.

Often you will sense a work's theme but still have to decide whether to state it as an **observation** or as a **recommendation.** You would be doing the first, for example, if you expressed Kincaid's theme as we did above: "In some cultures, women prepare girls for adulthood by teaching them to follow conventions *and* to assert themselves." You would be doing the second if you said Kincaid's theme is "Women should teach girls to follow conventions *and* to assert themselves." Indeed, people who depict a theme as a recommendation often use a word like *should.* Neither way of expressing a theme is necessarily better than the other. But notice that each way conjures up a particular image of the author. Reporting Kincaid's theme as an observation suggests that she is writing as a psychologist, a philosopher, or some other analyst of human nature. Reporting her theme as a recommendation suggests that she is writing as a teacher, preacher, manager, or coach: someone who is telling her readers what to do. Your decision about how to phrase a theme will depend in part on which image of the author you think is appropriate.

You risk obscuring the intellectual, emotional, and stylistic richness of a text if you insist on reducing it to a single message. Try stating the text's theme as a problem for which there is no easy solution, which suggests that the text is complex. For instance, if you say that Kincaid's theme is "In some cultures, women who prepare girls for adulthood are caught in a contradiction between wanting to empower them and wanting to keep them safe," you position yourself to address various elements of the story.

Also weigh the possibility that a text is conveying more than one theme. If you plan to associate the text with any theme at all, you might refer to *a* theme of the text rather than *the* theme of the text. Your use of the term *theme* would still have implications. Above all, you would still be suggesting that you have identified one of the text's major points. Subsequently, you might have to defend this claim, showing how the point you have identified is indeed central to the text.

Issues of theme have loomed large in literary studies. We hope that you will find them useful to pursue. But because references to theme are so common in literary studies, students sometimes forget that there are other kinds of issues. As you move through this list, you may find some that interest you more.

3. Issues of definition. In arguments about literature, issues of definition arise most often when readers try to decide what an author means by a particular word. The titles of Orozco's and Kincaid's stories are puzzling. In the first case, what does "orientation" mean, given that the narrator's description of life in this office might easily disorient someone? In the second case, what does it mean to be a "girl" in this kind of culture? Notice that an issue of definition can arise even with ordinary language. Look at how the narrator of "Orientation" uses the word *free* in the story's third paragraph: "Feel free to ask questions. Ask too many questions, however, and you may be let go." To what extent, and in what sense, do the characters in the story seem "free"? Answering this question involves, we think, considering how much the office workers are able to assert themselves through their eccentric behavior.

4. Issues of symbolism. In literary studies, an issue of symbolism usually centers on a particular image. In question are the image's meaning and purpose, including whether the image is more than just a detail. In "Orientation," the artwork of Amanda Pierce's autistic son is "sheet after sheet of precisely drawn concentric circles and ellipses, in black and yellow" (para. 7). Some readers may argue that the boy's art is one of many indications that life in this office is bizarre. Other readers may contend that the drawings have greater significance but may differ about what their significance is — that the narrator's thinking is circular, in the sense that the narrator is obsessed with describing the employees' eccentricities, or that the employees' actions are circular, in the sense that they are stuck repeating their strange conduct.

5. Issues of pattern. With issues of pattern, you observe how a text is organized and try to determine how certain parts of the text relate to other parts. But think, too, about the meaning and purpose of any pattern you find, especially since readers may disagree about the pattern's significance. Also ponder the implications of any moment when a text *breaks* with a pattern it has been following. Disruptions of a pattern may be as important as the pattern itself.

A conspicuous pattern in "Girl" is the main speaker's series of commands, which includes repeated use of the words *this is how*. Indeed, **repetition** is a common pattern in literature. Yet at two points in Kincaid's story, the speaker is interrupted by italicized protests from the girl: "*but I don't sing benna on Sundays at all and never in Sunday school*" (lines 11–12) and "*but what if the baker won't let me feel the bread?*" (line 41). What should we conclude about the main speaker from her string of orders? What should we conclude about the girl from her two disruptions? Readers may have various answers to these questions.

A text's apparent oppositions are also patterns that may be debated. An example in "Orientation" is the distinction that the narrator makes between the majority of the office workers and those who should be avoided (Anika Bloom and Colin Heavey). Does this distinction make sense, or do the two groups seem more similar than the narrator admits? Again, different answers are possible.

6. Issues of evaluation. Consciously or unconsciously, **evaluation** always plays a central role in reading. When you read a work of literature, you evaluate its ideas and the actions of its characters. You judge, too, the views you assume the author is promoting. Moreover, you gauge the artistic quality of the text.

Specifically, you engage in three kinds of evaluation as you read. One kind is *philosophical*: you decide whether a particular idea or action is wise. Another kind is *ethical*: you decide whether an idea or action is morally good. The third kind is *aesthetic*: you decide whether the work as a whole or parts of the text succeed as art. Another reader may disagree with your criteria for wisdom, morality, and art; people's standards often differ. It is not surprising, then, that in the study of literature issues of evaluation come up frequently.

Sometimes you may have trouble distinguishing the three types of judgment from each other. Philosophical evaluation, ethical evaluation, and aesthetic evaluation can overlap. Probably the first two operate in the mind of a reader who is judging the advice given by the main speaker in "Girl." This reader may, for instance, find the speaker insensitive: that is, neither smart nor humane. Moreover, if this reader thinks Kincaid sympathizes with the speaker, then he or she may consider "Girl" flawed as a work of art. Keep in mind, however, that you can admire many aspects of a literary work even if you disagree with the ideas you see the author promoting. Someone may relish Kincaid's colorful language regardless of the views presented in the story.

But whose works should be taught? Many scholars argue that literary studies have focused too much on white male authors, and some refuse to assume that the works of these authors are great and universally relevant. They criticize the long neglect of female and minority writers like Kincaid, a black woman born and raised in the West Indies. In part because of these scholars' arguments, "Girl" now appears in many literature anthologies. Yet other people continue to prize "classics" by William Shakespeare, John Milton, and William Blake. This ongoing debate about the literature curriculum includes disagreements about the worth of recent texts. After all, contemporary literature has yet to pass a "test of time." Does Orozco's 1994 story deserve to be anthologized and taught? We think so and have included "Orientation" in our own book. What, though, is *your* evaluation of it? Also, what particular standards have you used to judge it?

7. Issues of historical and cultural context. Plenty of literary works have engaged readers who are quite unlike their authors. These readers may include much-later generations and inhabitants of distant lands. Nevertheless, an author's own **historical and cultural context** may significantly shape his or her text. Although "Orientation" has elements that probably strike you as strange, many details of this story no doubt remind you of life in offices throughout the present-day United States. Still, readers may disagree over exactly which features of the story are typical of the contemporary American workplace. Consider as well Jamaica Kincaid's use of her past in "Girl." Though she has lived in the United States since she was seventeen, she evidently tapped memories of her childhood on Antigua to write this story and to represent the island's culture. Since many of the story's readers would be unfamiliar with Antigua, she had to decide what aspects of it to acquaint them with. What features of it does she emphasize, and what features does she downplay or omit? When Kincaid was born, Antiguans were under British control, and many labored hard for little money. Do these historical facts matter in "Girl"? If so, in what conceivable ways? Notice that answering such political and economic questions usually requires research. Even then, answers may be complicated. Indeed, rarely does a literary text straightforwardly reflect its author's background. Debate arises over how text and context relate.

We provide some background for each literary work we present to help you begin to situate it historically and culturally. In Chapter 9, we explain how to put literature in context, especially by doing research in the library and on the Internet. For now, we want to emphasize that contextualizing a work involves more than just piling up facts about its origin. In the study of literature, issues of historical and cultural context are often issues of *relevance*: which facts about a work's creation are important for readers to know, and *how* would awareness of these facts help readers better understand the work? Readers can inform themselves about a particular author's life, for instance, but they may disagree about the extent to which a given text is autobiographical.

Perhaps you like to connect a literary work with its author's own life. The authors of the two stories we have been discussing apparently drew to some extent on their personal experiences. Orozco has worked in an office, and Kincaid was a girl on Antigua. Of course, it is unlikely that Orozco's coworkers included a serial killer and a woman whose palms bled. You may be tempted, though, to think that "Girl" consists of advice Kincaid herself received. Yet when you assert that a work is thoroughly autobiographical, you risk overlooking aspects of the text that depart from the author's own experiences, impressions, and beliefs. We are not urging you to refrain from ever connecting the author's text to the author's life. Rather, we are pointing out that whatever links you forge may be the subject of debate.

Even the term *history* can be defined in various ways. When you refer to a work's historical context, you need to clarify whether you are examining (1) the life of the work's author; (2) the time period in which it was written; (3) any time period mentioned within the text; (4) its subsequent reception, including responses to it by later generations; or (5) the forms in which the work has been published, which may involve changes in its spelling, punctuation, wording, and overall appearance.

8. Issues of genre. So far we have been identifying categories of issues. Issues of **genre** are *about* categorization, for they involve determining what *kind* of text a particular work is. You might categorize the works by Orozco and Kincaid as belonging to the short-story genre, but someone might disagree because they do not seem to have a conventional plot. This debate would involve deciding what the essential characteristics of a "short story" are. Even if you argue that Orozco's and Kincaid's texts belong to this genre, you could attempt to classify them more precisely by aiming for terms that better sum up their specific content and form. Issues of genre often arise with such further classification.

A literary text may relate in some way to a characteristic of ordinary, real-life interactions. Orozco's title — "Orientation" — signals that he is having fun with the guided tour that many offices give their new workers. Similarly, Kincaid's story "Girl" belongs to the parental-advice genre. Try, though, to distinguish between text genre and real-life genre. Orozco's story can be labeled a *parody* (a comic imitation) or *satire* (an ironic critique) of an orientation, and Kincaid's story can be categorized as *an exploration of how gender roles are reinforced.* In any case, you may find that two or more labels are appropriate for a particular text. For instance, perhaps you see Orozco's "Orientation" as both a *parody* and a *horror story.* If so, you must decide whether these labels are equally helpful. Much of the time, issues of genre are issues of priority. Readers debate not whether a certain label for a work is appropriate but whether that label is the best.

9. Issues of social policy. In many works of literature, writers have attempted to instigate social reform by exposing defects in their cultures and encouraging specific cures. A famous example is Upton Sinclair's 1906 novel, *The Jungle*, which vividly depicts horrible conditions in Chicago's stockyards and thereby led the meat-processing plant owners to adopt more humane and hygienic practices. Even a work of literature that is not blatantly political or that seems rooted in the distant past may make you conscious of your own society's problems and possible solutions to them. Yet you and your classmates may propose different definitions of and solutions for cultural problems. The result is what we call issues of **social policy.**

Sometimes your position on a current issue of social policy will affect how you read a certain literary work. If you have worked in a highly regimented office, you may empathize with some of the employees described in Orozco's story. Similarly, your view on how girls and boys should be educated may affect your response to Kincaid's text. Even if current issues of social policy do not influence your original reading of a work, you can still use the work to raise such issues in your writing or in class discussion. Imagine discussing Orozco's story at a labor union's convention. What social policies might the story be used to promote there?

10. Issues of cause and effect. Issues of **causality** are common in literary studies. Often they arise as readers present different explanations for a character's behavior. What causes Orozco's character Gwendolyn Stich to cry in the women's room? Why does the girl in Kincaid's story protest at two particular moments? Remember that even a work's narrator or main speaker is a character with motives worth analyzing. What personal reasons, for example, might lead Orozco's narrator to present the orientation in this way?

Such questions can be rephrased to center on the author. For instance, you can ask why Kincaid ends her story by having the characters speak about feeling the bread. If you look back at our discussion of these ten types of issues, you may see that most issues can be phrased as questions about the author's purposes. But remember your options. Focusing on authorial intent in a given case may not be as useful as sticking with another type of issue. Or you may turn a question about authorial intent into a question about authorial **effect**. How should readers react when Kincaid ends her story the way she does? You can address questions like this without sounding as if you know exactly what the author intended.

MAKE A CLAIM

You may not be used to calling things you say or write *claims*. But even when you utter a simple observation about the weather — for instance, "It's beginning to rain" — you are making a claim. Basically, a **claim** is a statement that is spoken or written so that others will consider it to be true. With this definition in mind, you may start noticing claims everywhere. Most of us make lots of them every day. Furthermore, most of our claims are accepted as true by the people to whom we make them. Imagine how difficult life would be if the opposite were the case; human beings would be perpetually anxious if they distrusted almost everything they were told.

At times, though, claims do conflict with other claims. In a literature course, disagreements inevitably arise. Again, try not to let disagreements scare you. You can learn a lot from encountering views other than yours and from having to support your own. Moreover, exciting talk can occur as your class negotiates differences of opinion.

Recall that we defined an *issue* as a question with various debatable answers. *Claims*, as we use the term, are the debatable answers. For examples of claims in literary studies, look at our explanations of ten kinds of issues. In that discussion, we mentioned a host of claims: that Orozco's narrator is merely fantasizing a ghost, that Kincaid's theme is "Women should teach girls to follow conventions *and* to assert themselves," that the autistic boy's circles symbolize the circular thinking of Orozco's narrator, that the main speaker in "Girl" is insensitive, and that "Orientation" is a horror story. These claims are debatable because in each case at least one other position is possible.

Not every claim is a firm, sweeping generalization. In some instances, you may want to *qualify* a claim of yours, which involves expressing the claim in words that make it less than absolute. The terms available for qualifying a claim are numerous. You might use words such as *perhaps, maybe, seems, appears, probably*, and *most likely* to indicate that you are not reporting a definite fact. Similarly, words such as *some, many, most*, and *several* allow you to acknowledge that your claim is limited in scope, applicable to just a portion of whatever you are discussing.

In literature classes, two types of claims are especially common. To criticize Kincaid's main speaker is to engage in **evaluation**. To identify themes of "Girl" is to engage in **interpretation**. Conventionally, interpretation is the kind of analysis that depends on hypotheses rather than simple observation of plain fact. Throughout this book, we refer to the practice of interpreting a work or certain aspects of it. Admittedly, sometimes you may have trouble distinguishing interpretation from evaluation. When you evaluate some feature of a work or make an overall judgment of that work, probably you are operating with a certain interpretation as well, even if you do not make that interpretation explicit. Similarly, when you interpret part of a work or the text as a whole, probably you have already decided whether the text is worth figuring out. Nevertheless, the two types of claims differ in their emphases. When you attempt to interpret a work, you are mostly analyzing it; when you attempt to evaluate the work, you are mostly judging it.

In class discussions, other students may resist a claim you make about a literary work. Naturally, you may choose to defend your view at length. But remain open to the possibility of changing your mind, either by modifying your claim somehow or by shifting completely to another one. Also, entertain the possibility that a view different from yours is just as reasonable, even if you do not share it.

In much of your writing for your course, you will be identifying an issue and making one main claim about it, which can be called your **thesis**. As you attempt to support your main claim, you will make a number of smaller claims. In drafts of your paper, welcome opportunities to test the claims you make in it. Review your claims with classmates to help you determine how persuasive your thinking is. You will be left with a stronger sense of what you must do to make your paper credible.

AIM TO PERSUADE

As we have noted, argument is often associated with arrogant insistence. Many assume that if two people are arguing, they are each demanding to be seen as correct. At its best, however, argument involves careful efforts to persuade. When you make such an effort, you indicate that you believe your claims, even if you remain open to revising them. You indicate as well that you would like others to agree with you. Yet to attempt **persuasion** is to concede that you must support your claims if others are to value them.

The art of persuasion has been studied for centuries under the name of **rhetoric**. Today, the term *rhetoric* is often used negatively: politicians accuse one another of indulging in "mere rhetoric," as if the term meant deceptive exaggeration. But human beings habitually resort to persuasion; hence, rhetoric deserves more esteem. Besides, only in modern times has rhetoric not been regarded as a central part of education. In ancient Greece and Rome as well as in Renaissance Europe, rhetoric was an important academic subject. It was viewed, too, as a body of thought that people could actually put to use, especially in the realm of public affairs. Much of the advice we give you about writing looks back to this history. Over and over, we convey to you principles drawn from the rhetorical tradition.

As you have probably discovered on many occasions, swaying people who hold views different from yours can be difficult. You will not always be able to change their minds, yet you may still convince them that your claims are at least reasonable. Moreover, the process of trying to persuade others will compel you to clarify your ideas, to review why you hold them, and to analyze the people you aim to affect. Again, your effort to influence them may even involve making various **qualifications** of your claims as well as various **concessions**. A qualification is a word like *probably, possibly, maybe,* or *perhaps,* which writers use when they are willing to admit that their claim cannot be absolutely proven. A concession is an acknowledgment that a claim other than yours — even one that disagrees with yours — is at least somewhat reasonable.

CONSIDER YOUR AUDIENCE

When you hear the word **audience**, perhaps you think first of people attending plays, concerts, movies, or lectures. Yet *audience* also describes readers, including the people who read your writing. Not everything you write is for other people's eyes; in this course, you may produce notes, journal entries, and even full-length drafts that only you will see. From time to time in the course, however, you will do public writing. On these occasions, you will be trying to persuade your audience to accept whatever claims you make.

These occasions will require you to consider more than just your subject matter. If you are truly to persuade your readers, you must take them into account. Unfortunately, you will not be able to find out everything about your audience beforehand. Moreover, you will have to study the ways in which your readers differ from one another. Usually, though, you will be able to identify some of their common values, experiences, and assumptions. Having this knowledge will strengthen your ability to make a case they appreciate.

In analyzing a work of literature, you may try to identify its *implied reader*: that is, the type of person that the work seems to address. Remember, too, that people may have read the work in manuscript or when it was first published. Finally, the work may have had innumerable readers since. Often we ask you to write about a text's effect on you and to compare your reaction with your classmates'.

GATHER AND PRESENT EVIDENCE

Evidence is the support that you give your claims so that others will accept them. What sort of evidence you must provide depends on what your audience requires to be persuaded. When you make claims during class discussions, your classmates and instructor might ask you follow-up questions, thereby suggesting what you must do to convince them. As a writer, you might often find yourself having to guess your readers' standards of evidence. Naturally, your guesses will be influenced by any prior experiences you have had with your audience. Moreover, you may have opportunities to review drafts with some of its members.

When you make an argument about literature, the evidence most valued by your audience is likely to be details from the work itself. Direct quotations from the text are powerful indications that your claims are well grounded. But when you quote, you need to avoid willful selectivity. If, when writing about Kincaid's story, you quote the girl's question "*but what if the baker won't let me feel the bread?*" without acknowledging the main speaker's response, you may come across as misrepresenting the text. In general, quoting from various parts of a text will help you give your readers the impression that you are being accurate.

If you make claims about the historical or cultural context of a work, your evidence may include facts about its original circumstances. You may be drawn to the author's own experiences and statements, believing these shed light on the text. But again, use such materials cautiously, for they are not always strong evidence for your claims. People are not obliged to accept the author's declaration of his or her intent as a guide to the finished work. Some people may feel that the author's statement of intention was deliberately misleading, while others may claim that the author failed to understand his or her own achievement.

Another kind of evidence for your arguments about literature is your ethos. This is a traditional term in rhetoric; it refers to the image of you that your audience gets as you attempt to persuade. Actually, there are two kinds of ethos. One is the image of you that your audience holds even before you present your analysis. Often your audience will not know much about you beforehand. In general, this kind of ethos plays a role when the speaker or writer has a prior reputation. When Colin Powell gives a speech, he can expect much of his audience to start off trusting him, since millions of Americans admire him for his achievements as an army general and as a former secretary of state.

Even if you are not well known, the second kind of ethos may greatly influence how people respond to your argument. This is the image of you that your audience develops in hearing or reading your actual words. To secure your audience's trust, you ought to give the impression that you are calmly and methodically laying out your claims as well as your reasons for them. Making concessions to views different from yours is also a good strategy, indicating that you aim to be fair. On the other hand, if your presentation is disorganized or your tone self-righteous, your audience may see you as someone not committed to serious inquiry.

UNDERSTAND THE WARRANTS

Of all the elements of argument, warrants may be the least familiar to you. You have heard of search warrants and arrest warrants, documents that indicate the police are justified in searching a place or jailing a person. More generally, warrants are the beliefs that lead people to call certain things evidence for their claims. Imagine that you have just made a claim to your classmates and are now trying to support it. Imagine further that your listeners are reluctant to call your supporting information *evidence*; they want you to explain why you do so. In effect, your audience is asking you to identify your warrants: that is, the assumptions that make you think the information you have given reinforces your case. Throughout this book, we use the terms *warrants* and *assumptions* interchangeably.

Let's say you claim that when the narrator of "Orientation" remarks that "this building [is] reflected in the glass panels of that building across the way," author Orozco is suggesting that this office is closed in on itself and not open enough to other kinds of living. As evidence for your claim, you might point out the following things: (1) at this moment in the story a window acts as a mirror, (2) mirrors are sometimes associated with a fixation on the self, and (3) the narrator has already provided many examples of the employees' being stuck in their own routines. But then you may be asked for your warrants — your reasons for presenting this evidence as support for your claim. Some of your assumptions might be about literature: for instance, the transformation of an image (for example, a window into a mirror) is often symbolically significant, and images are often related to how characters in the text behave. Some of your assumptions might be about human nature: for example, if people are trapped in routines, they have trouble seeing how others live in the world at large. Some of your assumptions might be about historical periods and cultures: for instance, many contemporary American offices seem self-enclosed. Often literature classes are most enlightening when students discuss their assumptions about literature, about human nature, and about particular times and places. Your classmates may differ in their assumptions because they differ in the ways they grew up, the experiences they have had, the reading they have done, and the authorities that have influenced them.

Once you state your warrants for a claim you are making, your audience may go further, asking you to identify assumptions supporting the warrants themselves. But more frequently you will have to decide how much you should mention your warrants in the first place. In class discussion, usually your classmates' and instructor's responses to your claims will indicate how much you have to spell out your assumptions. When you write, you have to rely more on your own judgment of what your audience requires. If you suspect that your readers will find your evidence unusual, you should identify your warrants at length. If, however, your readers are bound to accept your evidence, then a presentation of warrants may simply distract them. Again, reviewing drafts of your paper with potential readers will help you determine what to do.

Looking at Literature as Argument

Much of this book concerns arguing *about* literature. But many works of literature can be said to present arguments themselves. Admittedly, not all of literature can be seen as containing or making arguments, but occasionally you will find that associating a literary text with argument opens up productive lines of inquiry. Moreover, as you argue about literature, arguments *within* literature can help you see how you might persuade others.

Some works lay out an argument that the author obviously approves of. For an example, let us turn to the following poem. It was written around 1652, by John Milton (1608–1674), a poet who played a leading role in England's Puritan revolution. Seeking to make dominant their own version of Christianity, the Puritans executed King Charles I and installed their leader, Oliver Cromwell, as head of state. Milton wrote "When I Consider How My Light Is Spent" while working as an official in Cromwell's government. This is an autobiographical poem and refers to Milton's growing blindness, which threatened to prevent him from serving both his political leader and his religious one, God.

JOHN MILTON

When I Consider How My Light Is Spent

When I consider how my light is spent,
   Ere half my days in this dark world and wide,
   And that one talent which is death to hide
Lodged with me useless, though my soul more bent
To serve therewith my Maker, and present   5
   My true account, lest He returning chide;
   "Doth God exact day-labor, light denied?"
I fondly ask. But Patience, to prevent
That murmur, soon replies, "God doth not need
   Either man's work or His own gifts. Who best   10
   Bear His mild yoke, they serve Him best. His state
Is kingly: thousands at His bidding speed,
   And post o'er land and ocean without rest;
   They also serve who only stand and wait."   *[c. 1652]*

The speaker does not actually spell out his warrants. Consider, however, his reference to Christ's parable of the talents (Luke 19:12–27). In the ancient Middle East, a *talent* was a unit of money. In the parable, a servant is scolded by his master for hoarding the one talent that his master had given him. By telling this story, Christ implies that people should make use of the gifts afforded them by God. For the speaker in Milton's poem, the parable has a lot of authority. Evidently he feels that he should carry out its lesson. In effect, then, the parable has indeed become a warrant for him: that is, a basis for finding his blindness cause for lament.

Who, exactly, is the speaker's audience? Perhaps he is not addressing anyone in particular. Or perhaps the speaker's mind is divided and one side of it is addressing the other. Or perhaps the speaker is addressing God, even though he refers to God in the third person. Given that the speaker is answered by Patience, perhaps he means to address *that* figure, although Patience may actually be just a part of him rather than an altogether separate being.

At any rate, Patience takes the speaker for an audience in responding. And while Patience does not provide evidence, let alone warrants, Patience does make claims about God and his followers. Furthermore, Milton as author seems to endorse Patience's claims; apparently he is using the poem to advance them. Besides pointing out *how* God is served, Milton suggests that God *ought* to be served, even if God lets bad things happen to good people like Milton.

Every author can be considered an audience for his or her own writing, but some authors write expressly to engage in a dialogue with themselves. Perhaps Milton wrote his poem partly to convince himself that his religion was still valid and his life still worth living. Significantly, he did not publish the poem until about twenty years later. Yet because he did publish it eventually, at some point he must have contemplated a larger audience for it. The first readers of the poem would have been a relatively small segment of the English population: those literate and prosperous enough to have access to books of poetry. In addition, a number of the poem's first readers would have shared Milton's religious beliefs. Perhaps, however, Milton felt that even the faith of this band had to be bolstered. For one thing, not every Protestant of the time would have shared Milton's enthusiasm for the Puritan government. Recall that this regime executed the king, supposedly replacing him with the rule of God. Milton's words "His state / Is kingly" can be seen as an effort to persuade readers that the Puritans did put God on England's throne.

Other literary works, though, present an argument that the author is unlikely to endorse. In such cases, we might describe the work as *ironic*, because we sense a distance between the position being expressed and the author's own view. An example is a poem from 1940, "The Unknown Citizen," by W. H. Auden (1907–1973). Though born in England and widely regarded as the finest English poet of the twentieth century, Auden moved to the United States in 1953, became an American citizen, and spent his remaining years living alternately in the United States and Austria. This poem supposedly presents us with the words on a memorial to an anonymous worker. In essence, the poem makes an argument for celebrating his life. Yet, as you read, note places where Auden is inviting you to question whether the honoree really deserves admiration.

W. H. AUDEN

The Unknown Citizen

(To JS/07 M 378
This Marble Monument*
Is Erected by the State)

He was found by the Bureau of Statistics to be
One against whom there was no official complaint,
And all the reports on his conduct agree
That, in the modern sense of an old-fashioned word, he was a saint,
For in everything he did he served the Greater Community.   5

Except for the War till the day he retired,
He worked in a factory and never got fired,
But satisfied his employers, Fudge Motors Inc.
Yet he wasn't a scab or odd in his views.
For his Union reports that he paid his dues,   10
(Our report on his Union shows it was sound)
And our Social Psychology workers found
That he was popular with his mates and liked a drink.
The Press are convinced that he bought a paper every day
And that his reactions to advertisements were normal in every way.   15
Policies taken out in his name prove that he was fully insured,
And his Health-card shows he was once in a hospital but left it cured.
Both Producers Research and High-Grade Living declare
He was fully sensible to the advantages of the Instalment Plan
And had everything necessary to the Modern Man,   20
A phonograph, a radio, a car and a frigidaire.
Our researchers into Public Opinion are content
That he held the proper opinions for the time of year;
When there was peace, he was for peace: when there was war, he went.
He was married and added five children to the population,   25
Which our Eugenist says was the right number for a parent of his
    generation.
And our teachers report that he never interfered with their education.
Was he free? Was he happy? The question is absurd:
Had anything been wrong, we should certainly have heard.   [1940]

Certain arguments made in literary texts may or may not have the author's endorsement. Faced with a conflict of ideas, readers must engage in interpretation, forced to decide which position is apt to be the author's own view.
A classic example is "Mending Wall," a famous poem by Robert Frost (1874–
1963), from his 1914 book, *North of Boston.* Troubled by his neighbor's desire
to repair the wall between their farms, the poem's speaker argues against its
necessity, but literary critics have long debated whether Frost agrees with the
speaker's claims and reasons. How persuasive do you find them?

ROBERT FROST

Mending Wall

Something there is that doesn't love a wall,
That sends the frozen-ground-swell under it,
And spills the upper boulders in the sun;
And makes gaps even two can pass abreast.
The work of hunters is another thing: 5
I have come after them and made repair
Where they have left not one stone on a stone,

But they would have the rabbit out of hiding,
To please the yelping dogs. The gaps I mean,
No one has seen them made or heard them made,   10
But at spring mending-time we find them there.
I let my neighbor know beyond the hill;
And on a day we meet to walk the line
And set the wall between us once again.
We keep the wall between us as we go.   15
To each the boulders that have fallen to each.
And some are loaves and some so nearly balls
We have to use a spell to make them balance:
"Stay where you are until our backs are turned!"
We wear our fingers rough with handling them.   20
Oh, just another kind of outdoor game,
One on a side. It comes to little more:
There where it is we do not need the wall:
He is all pine and I am apple orchard.
My apple trees will never get across   25
And eat the cones under his pines, I tell him.
He only says, "Good fences make good neighbors."
Spring is the mischief in me, and I wonder
If I could put a notion in his head:
"Why do they make good neighbors? Isn't it   30
Where there are cows? But here there are no cows.
Before I built a wall I'd ask to know
What I was walling in or walling out,
And to whom I was like to give offense.
Something there is that doesn't love a wall,   35
That wants it down." I could say "Elves" to him,
But it's not elves exactly, and I'd rather
He said it for himself. I see him there
Bringing a stone grasped firmly by the top
In each hand, like an old-stone savage armed.   40
He moves in darkness as it seems to me,
Not of woods only and the shade of trees.
He will not go behind his father's saying,
And he likes having thought of it so well
He says again, "Good fences make good neighbors." [1914] 45

Broken Friendship?

Getting along well...

& neither will cross the boundary of friends.

↗ ¶3 – repetition

The neighbor feels he must remove himself from personal attachment → He is trying to justify it

Most works of literature do not incorporate each element of argument we
have discussed. Rarely do they feature arguments that do everything: acknowledge an audience, specify an issue, articulate claims, and carefully support
these claims with substantial evidence and identified warrants. When characters argue, typically they do so in dramatic situations, not the sort of circumstances that permit elaborate debate. Also, literature has traditionally been a
way for authors to make their own arguments indirectly: that is, to persuade

with characterization, plot, and image rather than with straightforward development of claims. Do register the "gaps" as well as the strengths of any argument you find in a literary work. If the argument seems incomplete, however, bear in mind that a more drawn-out argument may have made the work less compelling.

≣ SUMMING UP

- When you argue, you attempt to *persuade* an *audience* to accept your *claims* regarding an *issue* by presenting *evidence* and relying on *warrants*.

- An *issue* is something about which people have disagreed or might disagree. Defined as questions with no obvious, immediate answers, ten kinds of issues that arise in literature courses are those of (1) fact, (2) theme, (3) definition, (4) symbolism, (5) pattern, (6) evaluation, (7) historical and cultural context, (8) genre, (9) social policy, and (10) cause and effect. (pp. 57–65)

- *Claims* are the debatable answers to an issue. In literature classes, two common types of claims are those of interpretation and those of evaluation. (pp. 65–66)

- The art of *persuasion* — changing people's minds, convincing them that claims are reasonable — has been studied for centuries under the term *rhetoric*. Effective persuasion may involve making *qualifications* and *concessions*. (pp. 66–67)

- The term *audience* applies to the people who read your writing. If you are to persuade them, you must take into account their common values, experiences, and assumptions, not just focus on your subject matter. (p. 67)

- *Evidence* is the support that you give your claims so that others will accept them. When you make an argument about a literary work, your readers expect you to support your case with details in the text and to convince them by methodically laying out your claims as well as your reasons for them. (pp. 67–68)

- *Warrants* are the beliefs that lead people to call certain things evidence for their claims. The terms *warrants* and *assumptions* are more or less interchangeable. (pp. 68–69)

- Some literary works can be said to present arguments themselves. Certain characters make claims, often in debate with one another, through characterization, plot, and image, and other works indicate that the author is arguing for a certain position. (pp. 69–74)

CHAPTER 4

The Writing Process

In Chapters 5–8, we discuss how to write about each of the four literary genres featured in this book. Here, however, we suggest how to write about a literary work of any genre. To make our advice concrete, we mostly trace what one student did as she worked on a writing assignment for a course much like yours. The assignment was given to a class that had been reading and discussing several poems about work, including the poems we included in Chapter 2. Each student chose a single poem from the syllabus and wrote a 600-word argument paper on it for a general audience. We focus on the writing process of a student named Abby Hazelton.

Ultimately, Abby chose to write about William Wordsworth's "The Solitary Reaper." In his own day, Wordsworth (1770–1850) was poet laureate of England, and he continues to be regarded as a major British Romantic poet. He and fellow poet Samuel Taylor Coleridge collaborated on *Lyrical Ballads* (1798), a collection of verse that became a landmark of Romantic poetry. In his preface to the second edition two years later, Wordsworth famously defined *poetry* as "emotion recollected in tranquillity," contended that it should draw on "common life," and called for it to incorporate "language really used by men." Like many other Romantics, Wordsworth celebrated scenes of nature and country life, while deploring the increasing spread of cities. "The Solitary Reaper" appeared in his 1807 *Poems in Two Volumes*.

Before examining Abby's writing process, read Wordsworth's poem.

WILLIAM WORDSWORTH
The Solitary Reaper

Behold her, single in the field,
   Yon solitary Highland Lass!
Reaping and singing by herself;
   Stop here, or gently pass!
Alone she cuts and binds the grain,
And sings a melancholy strain;
O listen! for the Vale profound
Is overflowing with the sound.

No Nightingale did ever chaunt
   More welcome notes to weary bands   10

[Handwritten marginal notes:]
Is an actual author experience, BUT, could be taken metaphorically for two reapers, one of grain, one of death.
> reaper of the grain
maiden is lonely? is speaker longing?
she is not truly alone

5

Of travellers in some shady haunt,
   Among Arabian sands:
A voice so thrilling ne'er was heard
In spring-time from the Cuckoo-bird,
Breaking the silence of the seas   15
Among the farthest Hebrides.

Will no one tell me what she sings? —
   Perhaps the plaintive numbers flow
For old, unhappy, far-off things,
   And battles long ago: 20
Or is it some more humble lay,
   Familiar matter of to-day?
Some natural sorrow, loss, or pain,   *→ death*
That has been, and may be again?

Whate'er the theme, the Maiden sang   25
   As if her song could have no ending;
I saw her singing at her work,
   And o'er the sickle bending; —
I listen'd, motionless and still;
   And, as I mounted up the hill,   30
The music in my heart I bore,
Long after it was heard no more.

narrator is the reader?

we went to take her into the next life

[1807]

Once she chose to write about Wordsworth's poem for her paper, Abby engaged in four sorts of activities: (1) exploring, (2) planning, (3) composing, and (4) revising. As we describe each, keep in mind that these activities need not be consecutive. Abby moved back and forth among them as she worked on her assignment.

Strategies for Exploring

As you read a literary work, you are bound to interpret and judge it. Yet not all reading is close reading, which can also be called **critical reading**. This process involves carefully and self-consciously analyzing various aspects of a text, including its meanings, its effects, and its treatment of typical elements of its genre. When you read a work closely and critically, you also note questions it raises for you — issues you might explore further in class discussion and writing. Indeed, close reading is a process of self-reflection. During this process, you monitor your own response to the text and try to identify why you see the text the way you do.

Exploring, the first stage of writing an essay about literature, is this particular process of reading. As we explain in Chapter 2, it specifically involves the following:

- Making predictions as you read
- Rereading the text with a different focus each time, including at least one stage in which you read aloud

- Comparing the text with your personal experience
- Tracing patterns and breaks from these patterns
- Noting ambiguities
- Considering the author's alternatives
- Generating questions
- Considering how the text deals with topics that have preoccupied literary studies
- Formulating a tentative claim
- Using informal writing to move through all these steps, including commenting in the text's margins; note-taking; freewriting; creating a "dialectical notebook"; and playfully revising the text

☰ A WRITING EXERCISE

Do at least ten minutes of freewriting about Wordsworth's poem, keeping it nearby so that you can consult it if you need to. In particular, try to raise questions about the poem, and consider which of these may be worth addressing in a more formal paper.

Here is an excerpt from Abby's freewriting.

> I see that this poem consists of four stanzas, each of which is eight lines long. But these stanzas have different emphases. The first stanza is a series of commands. The speaker tells people to "Behold," "Stop here, or gently pass," and "listen." The second stanza mainly describes the reaper. The third stanza is basically a bunch of questions. The fourth is the speaker's recollection of his experience in general. So I could write a paper about how this poem changes as it moves along and why the stanzas shift in emphasis. But one problem with a paper like that is that it might get me bogged down in mechanically moving from stanza to stanza. I don't want that to happen. Another thing I could do is answer one of the speaker's own questions, which are about what kind of song the reaper is singing. Evidently this "Highland Lass" is using a Scottish dialect that he doesn't understand. But I'm just as ignorant as he is about the song. I guess I'm more likely to contribute some analysis of my own if I come up with a question myself. I'm struck by the fact that he doesn't give us much sense of the reaper's song. There's no way that a printed poem could convey the reaper's tune, but still. And the words are foreign to the speaker. But I'm surprised that he doesn't make a little effort to convey at least some of the song's lyrics even if they're foreign words that he might hear wrong or misspell. How can I as a reader join him in experiencing the beauty of her song if I don't learn any of its words? I wonder if we're supposed to see the poem as being more about the speaker than about the reaper. More specifically, maybe we're supposed to be a little disturbed that he's a British intellectual who is making a spectacle out of a foreign

woman from the working class. At any rate, he seems bent on controlling this experience even as he invites us to share it. Another question
for me is, Why does he shift from present tense to past tense in the last
stanza? This change is really curious to me. I don't see anything earlier
on that prepares me for it. First, we're led to believe that the speaker is
observing the reaper right then and there, but at the end he speaks as
if this occurred in the past, though maybe the recent past. This
inconsistency in the time frame makes me think that in some important
way the overall poem is about time. At any rate, I'm drawn to the inconsistency because it's so blatant. If I wrote about it, I might still devote
a paragraph to each stanza, but I'd be starting with the last one and
referring back to the others in order to explain that stanza. What I still
have to figure out, though, is what exactly the poem is saying about
time when it makes the shift of tense.

Freewriting enabled Abby to raise several questions. At the same time, she
realized that her paper could not deal with everything that puzzled her. When
you first get an assignment like hers, you may fear that you will have nothing
to say. But you will come up with a lot of material if, like Abby, you take time for
exploration. As we have suggested, it's a process of examining potential subjects through writing, discussion, and just plain thinking. One of your challenges will be to choose among the various issues you have formulated. At the
end of this excerpt from her freewriting, Abby is on the verge of choosing to
analyze the poem's shift of tense in its final stanza. For her, this shift is an interesting change from a pattern, the poem's previous uses of present tense. Abby
has not yet decided how to explain this shift; at the moment, it remains for her
a mystery. But her paper would achieve little if it focused just on aspects of the
poem that are easy to interpret. Though Abby has more thinking to do about
the poem's shift of tense, it seems a promising subject for her precisely because
it puzzles her.

Strategies for Planning

Planning for an assignment like Abby's involves five main activities:

1. Choosing the text you will analyze
2. Identifying your audience
3. Identifying the main issue, claim, and evidence you will present
4. Identifying the warrants you will use
5. Determining how you will organize your argument

CHOOSE A TEXT

Abby considered several poems before choosing one for her paper. She settled
on Wordsworth's for five reasons. First, it was a text that left her with plenty of
questions. Second, she believed that these questions could be issues for other

readers. Third, she felt increasingly able to *argue* about the poem — that is, to make and support claims about it. Fourth, she believed that she could adequately analyze the poem within the assignment's word limit. Finally, Wordsworth's poem drew her because she had heard about the Romantic movement in English literature and was curious to study an example of it.

Faced with the same assignment, you might choose a different poem than Abby did. Still, the principles that she followed are useful. Think about them whenever you are free to decide which texts you will write about. With some assignments, of course, you may need a while to decide which text is best for you. And later, after you have made your decision, you may want to make a switch. For example, you may find yourself changing your mind once you have done a complete draft. Frustrated by the text you have chosen, you may realize that another inspires you more. If so, consider making a substitution. Naturally, you will feel more able to switch if you have ample time left to write the paper, so avoid waiting to start your paper just before it is due.

IDENTIFY YOUR AUDIENCE

To determine what your readers will see as an issue and to make your claims about it persuasive to them, you need to develop an audience profile. Perhaps your instructor will specify your audience. You may be asked, for example, to imagine yourself writing for a particular group in a particular situation. If you were Abby, how would you analyze "The Solitary Reaper" for an orchestra wanting to know what this poem implies about music? Even when not required of you, such an exercise can be fun and thought-provoking for you as you plan a paper.

Most often, though, instructors ask students to write for a "general" audience, the readership that Abby was asked to address. Assume that a general audience is one that will want evidence for your claims. While this audience will include your instructor, let it also include your classmates, since in class discussions they will be an audience for you whenever you speak. Besides, your class may engage in peer review, with students giving one another feedback on their drafts.

If your audience is indeed supposed to be a general group of readers, what can you assume about their prior knowledge? You may not be sure. Above all, you may wonder how familiar your readers already are with the text you are analyzing. Perhaps your teacher will resolve your uncertainty, telling you exactly how much your audience knows about the text. Then again, you may be left to guess. Should you presume that your audience is totally unfamiliar with the text? This approach is risky, for it may lead you to spend a lot of your paper merely summarizing the text rather than analyzing it. A better move is to write as if your audience is at least a bit more knowledgeable. Here is a good rule of thumb: *assume that your audience has, in fact, read the text but that you need to recall for this group any features of the text that are crucial to your argument*. Although probably your paper will still include summary, the amount you provide will be limited, and your own ideas will be more prominent.

IDENTIFY YOUR ISSUE, CLAIM, AND EVIDENCE

When you have written papers for previous classes, you may have been most concerned with coming up with a thesis. Maybe you did not encounter the term *issue* at all. But good planning for a paper does entail identifying the main issue you will address. Once you have sensed what that issue is, try phrasing it as a question. If the answer would be obvious to your readers, be cautious, for you really do not have an issue if the problem you are raising can be easily resolved.

Also, try to identify what *kind* of issue you will focus on. For help, look at our list of various types (pp. 57–65). Within "The Solitary Reaper," the speaker raises an issue of fact: he wants to know what sort of song the reaper is singing. But as someone writing about Wordsworth's poem, Abby wanted to focus on another kind of issue, which she decided is best regarded as an issue of pattern. More precisely, she thought her main question might be, What should we conclude from the inconsistency in pattern that occurs when the final stanza shifts to past tense? To be sure, Abby recognized that addressing this issue would lead to issues of theme and of cause and effect, for she would have to consider why Wordsworth shifts tenses and how the shift relates to his overall subject.

Now that she had identified her main issue, Abby had to determine her main claim. Perhaps you have grown comfortable with the term *thesis* and want to keep using it. Fine. Bear in mind, though, that your thesis is the main *claim* you will make and proceed to support. And when, as Abby did, you put your main issue as a question, then your main claim is your answer to that question. Sometimes you will come up with question and answer simultaneously. Once in a while, you may even settle on your answer first, not being certain yet how to word the question. Whatever the case, planning for your paper involves articulating both the question (the issue) and the answer (your main claim). Try actually writing both down, making sure to phrase your main issue as a question and your main claim as the answer. Again, Abby's main issue was, What should we conclude from the inconsistency in pattern that occurs when the final stanza shifts to past tense? After much thought, she expressed her main claim this way:

> One possible justification for the shift to past tense is that it reminds us of the speaker's inability to halt the passage of time. He would like to freeze his encounter with the reaper, keeping it always in the present. But as the shift in tense indicates, time goes on, making the encounter part of the speaker's past. Perhaps, therefore, the poem's real subject is the idea that time is always in flux.

Audiences usually want evidence, and as we noted earlier, most arguments you write about literature will need to cite details of the work itself. Because direct quotation is usually an effective move, Abby planned to elaborate her claim by citing several of Wordsworth's references to time. Remember, though, that you need to avoid seeming willfully selective when you quote. While Abby expected to quote from Wordsworth's last stanza, she also knew she had to relate it to earlier lines so that her readers would see her as illuminating the basic subject of the whole poem. In particular, she looked for language in the first three stanzas that might hint at the speaker's lack of control over time, thereby previewing the last stanza's emphasis.

IDENTIFY YOUR WARRANTS

Often, to think about particular challenges of your paper is to think about your warrants. Remember that warrants are assumptions; they are what lead you to call certain things evidence for your claims. Abby knew that one of her warrants was an assumption about Wordsworth himself — that he was not being sloppy when he shifted tenses in his last stanza. Rarely will your paper need to admit all the warrants on which it relies. Most of the time, your task will be to guess which warrants your readers do want stated. Abby felt there was at least one warrant she would have to spell out — her belief that the poem's verb tenses reveal something about the speaker's state of mind.

DETERMINE YOUR ORGANIZATION

To make sure their texts seem organized, most writers first do an **outline**, a list of their key points in the order they will appear. Outlines are indeed a good idea, but bear in mind that there are various kinds. One popular type, which you may already know, is the **sentence outline**. As the name implies, it lists the writer's key points in sentence form. Its advantages are obvious: this kind of outline forces you to develop a detailed picture of your argument's major steps, and it leaves you with sentences you can then incorporate into your paper. Unfortunately, sentence outlines tend to discourage flexibility. Because they demand much thought and energy, you may hesitate to revise them, even if you come to feel your paper would work better with a new structure.

A second, equally familiar outline is the **topic outline**, a list in which the writer uses a few words to signify the main subjects that he or she will discuss. Because it is sketchy, this kind of outline allows writers to go back and change plans if necessary. Nevertheless, a topic outline may fail to provide all the guidance a writer needs.

We find a third type useful: a **rhetorical purpose outline**. As with the first two, you list the major sections of your paper. Next, you briefly indicate two things for each section: the effect you want it to have on your audience, and how you will achieve that effect. Here is the rhetorical purpose outline that Abby devised for her paper.

INTRODUCTION

The audience needs to know the text I'll discuss.	I'll identify Wordsworth's poem.
The audience must know my main issue.	I'll point out that the poem is puzzling in its shift of tenses at the end.

| The audience must know my main claim. | I'll argue that the shift to past tense suggests that the poem's real subject is the inability of human beings to halt the passage of time. |

ANALYSIS OF THE POEM'S FINAL STANZA

| The audience needs to see in detail how the final stanza's shift to past tense signals the speaker's inability to control the passage of time. | I will point out not only the shift of tense but also other words in the last stanza that imply time moves on. I will note as well that music is an especially fleeting medium, so the reaper's song was bound to fade. |

ANALYSIS OF THE PRECEDING STANZAS

| To accept that the passage of time is the poem's real concern, the audience must see that the preceding stanzas hint at this subject. | I will analyze the first three stanzas in turn, showing how each implies the speaker is frustrated over his inability to control time. |

CONCLUSION

| The audience may need to be clearer about what I consider the ultimate *tone* of the poem. | I will say that although the poem can be thought of as a warm tribute to the singing reaper, the final emphasis on the passage of time is pessimistic in tone, and the speaker winds up as "solitary" as the reaper. |

For your own rhetorical purpose outlines, you may want to use phrases rather than sentences. If you do use sentences, as Abby did, you do not have to write all that many. Note that Abby wrote relatively few as she stated the effects she would aim for and her strategies for achieving those effects. Thus, she was not tremendously invested in preserving her original outline. She felt free to change it if it failed to prove helpful.

Strategies for Composing

Composing is not always distinguishable from exploring, planning, and revising. As you prepare for your paper, you may jot down words or whole sentences. Once you begin a draft, you may alter that draft in several ways before you complete it. You may be especially prone to making changes in drafts if you use a computer, for word processing enables you to jump around in your text, revisiting and revising what you have written.

Still, most writers feel that doing a draft is an activity in its own right, and a major one at that. The next four chapters present various tips for writing about specific genres, and Chapter 9 discusses writing research papers. Meanwhile, here are some tips to help you with composing in general.

DECIDE ON A TITLE

You may be inclined to let your **title** be the same as that of the text you discuss. Were you to write about Wordsworth's poem, then, you would be calling your own paper "The Solitary Reaper." But often such mimicry backfires. For one thing, it may lead your readers to think that you are unoriginal and perhaps even lazy. Also, you risk confusing your audience, since your paper would actually be about Wordsworth's poem rather than being the poem itself. So take the time to come up with a title of your own. Certainly it may announce the text you will focus on, but let it do more. In particular, use your title to indicate the main claim you will be making. With just a few words, you can preview the argument to come.

MAKE CHOICES ABOUT YOUR STYLE

Perhaps you have been told to "sound like yourself" when you write. Yet that can be a difficult demand (especially if you are not sure what your "self" is really like). Above all, the style you choose depends on your audience and purpose. In writing an argument for a general audience, probably you would do best to avoid the extremes of pomposity and breezy informality. Try to stick with words you know well, and if you do want to use some that are only hazily familiar to you, check their dictionary definitions first.

At some point in our lives, probably all of us have been warned not to use *I* in our writing. In the course you are taking, however, you may be asked to write about your experiences. If so, you will find *I* hard to avoid. Whether to use it does become a real question when you get assignments like Abby's, which require you chiefly to make an argument about a text. Since you are supposed to focus on that text, your readers may be disconcerted if you keep referring to yourself. Even so, you need not assume that your personal life is irrelevant to the task. Your opening paragraph might refer to your personal encounters with the text, as a way of establishing the issue you will discuss. A personal anecdote might serve as a forceful conclusion to your paper. Moreover, before you reach the conclusion, you might orient your readers to the structure of your paper by using certain expressions that feature the word *I*: for example, *As I suggested earlier, As I have noted, As I argue later.* In general, you may be justified in saying *I* at certain moments. When tempted to use this pronoun, though, consider whether it really is your best move.

In a paper, the expressions *I think* and *I feel* are rarely effective. Often writers resort to such phrasing because they sense they are offering nothing more than their own opinion. The audience may view such expressions as indications of a weak argument or limited evidence. You might make the claim more persuasive by avoiding *I think* and *I feel* and by qualifying it through words such as *probably, possibly, maybe,* and *perhaps.* If you believe that you have little evidence for a claim you want to make, take time out from writing and go back to exploring your ideas. If you can, come up with additional means of support.

Arguments about literature are most compelling when supported by quotations, but be careful not to quote excessively. If you constantly repeat other people's words, providing few of your own, your readers will hardly get a sense of you as an author. Moreover, a paper full of quotation marks is hard to read. Make sure to quote selectively, remembering that sometimes you can simply paraphrase. When you do quote, try to cite only the words you need. You do not have to reproduce a whole line or sentence if one word is enough to support your point.

When summarizing what happens in a literary work, be careful not to shift tenses as you go along. Your reader may be confused if you shift back and forth between past and present. We suggest that you stick primarily to the present tense, which is the tense that literary critics customarily employ. For example, instead of saying that the speaker *praised* the lass, say that he *praises* her.

DRAFT AN INTRODUCTION

As a general principle, use your introduction to identify as quickly and efficiently as possible

- the main text that you will analyze;
- the main issue about it that you will address; and
- the main claim that you will develop in response to that issue.

Don't waste time with grand philosophical statements such as "Society doesn't always appreciate the work that everyone does," or "Over the centuries, much literature has been about work," or "William Wordsworth was a great British Romantic poet."

Remember that your main issue should be a significant question with no obvious answer. Try using one or more of the following strategies to establish that issue at the start of your essay:

- **State the issue as, indeed, a question.** For example: "Why, conceivably, does Wordsworth shift to the past tense in his poem's final stanza?"
- **Apply a word like *puzzling, confusing, mysterious,* or *curious* to whatever feature your issue will be about.** For example: "Because Wordsworth uses present tense for much of the poem, it is puzzling that he turns to past tense at the very end."
- **Through personal reference, state that you were first puzzled by a particular feature of the work but are now able to interpret it.** For

Asking questions in essay is okay ✗

example: "At first, I was confused when Wordsworth shifted to the past tense, but now I have arrived at a possible explanation for this move."

- **Indicate that you aim to help other readers of the work, who may have trouble understanding the feature of it you will focus on.** For example: "Quite a few readers of Wordsworth's poem may have difficulty seeing why he shifts to the past tense at the end. There is, however, a possible explanation for this move."
- **Indicate that you will express disagreement with existing or possible interpretations.** For example: "While some readers of Wordsworth's poem may feel that his shift to the past tense shows a wonderful ability to preserve his experience with the reaper, a more plausible interpretation is that it shows his isolation after meeting her."

LIMIT PLOT SUMMARY

Short stories and plays spin tales. So do many poems and essays. But if you are writing about a literary text that is narrative in form, don't spend much of your paper just summarizing the narrative. Developing a genuine argument about the work involves more than recounting its plot. Here are strategies you can use to limit this:

- **Assume that your reader knows the basic plot and needs only a few brief reminders of its key elements.**
- **Keep in mind that your main purpose is to put forth, explain, and support a *claim* about the text — your answer to some question you raise about it.**
- **After your introduction, try to begin each new paragraph with a subclaim that helps you develop your main claim.** Use the rest of the paragraph to elaborate and provide evidence for this subclaim. *Don't begin a paragraph simply by recording a plot incident, for doing so is liable to bog you down in sheer summary.*
- **Instead of reciting plot details, write about how the work you are analyzing is *constructed*.** Make observations about specific methods that the author uses to present the story, including techniques of organization and characterization. For example, rather than say "The speaker in Wordsworth's poem wonders what the woman is singing," state and develop a point like "Wordsworth chooses not to translate the woman's song for us; instead, he depicts the speaker as not knowing her words, so that the poem becomes mostly about the effect of her song as sheer musical notes."
- **Instead of turning frequently to plot details, try to linger on some of the author's specific language, exploring possible definitions of particular words.** For example, rather than say "The speaker in Wordsworth's poem remembers the woman's music," examine possible meanings of the word *bore* in the poem's next-to-last line,

"The music in my heart I bore." *Bore* can simply mean "carried," and probably that is one meaning that Wordsworth has in mind here. But it can also mean "engraved, deeply inscribed," and perhaps Wordsworth wants us to think of this definition, too.

DECIDE HOW TO REFER TO THE AUTHOR'S LIFE AND INTENTIONS

Be cautious about relating the work to the author's life. Sometimes a certain character within the work may indeed express the author's own views, but don't simply assume that a character speaks for the author. Even the *I* of a first-person poem may differ significantly from its creator. True, many literary works are at least somewhat autobiographical, based on one or more aspects of the author's life. Nevertheless, even works that are largely autobiographical may not be entirely so. Besides, knowledge of the author's life won't always help you figure out his or her text. Wordsworth may have derived "The Solitary Reaper" from a personal encounter, but we must still interpret the particular poem he proceeded to write. So,

- **Be careful in linking a work to the author's own circumstances.** Such connections can be legitimate, but the more you push them, the more you may risk distorting the work's exact design. You also risk neglecting the author's artistic achievement. Not everyone who hears a reaper sing could turn this event into a poem!

Much of what you write about a literary work will reflect your understanding of its author's intentions. Needless to say, you can't peer into the author's mind. Rather, you'll make hypotheses about the author's aims. So,

- **Sometimes, at least, admit that you are guessing at what the author thought.** Often, your reader will assume that you are speculating about the author's aims, but your argument about them can be more persuasive if, at times, you acknowledge that you're trying to come up with the best hypothesis rather than stating an absolute fact. Take care, however, to explain why your guesses are logical.
- **If you suspect that the author might object to your view of the text, feel free to acknowledge such possible disagreements.** In fact, many theorists argue that a literary work may differ from how its author sees it. They refuse, therefore, to treat the author as an absolute authority on the work. D. H. Lawrence's advice was "Trust the tale, not the teller." Even if Lawrence is right, of course, you must show how *your* interpretation of a text manages to make sense of it.
- **Feel free to concede that your analysis of the work isn't the only reasonable one.** You can develop your main claim about a literary work partly by noting and addressing ways in which other readers may disagree with you about it. Bear in mind, though, that you will annoy your own audience if you come across as dogmatic.

Be as fair as you can to views different from yours. Actually, your readers will appreciate it if at times you concede that yours is not the only reasonable interpretation. You can even specify one or more alternatives. Of course, you would still try to make a case for *your* explanation, perhaps by saying why it is *more plausible* or *more helpful* than its rivals. But speak of these competitors with respect, instead of just dismissing them with scorn.

Flaw

RECOGNIZE AND AVOID LOGICAL FALLACIES   ☆ Recommended ☆

Although arguments presented in literary texts are often not logical, your arguments about these texts should be. Readers do not expect a poem's speaker, for example, to present cogently reasoned arguments to her lover, nor do they expect a lament for the lost passions of youth to be anything but subjective. But different kinds of writing have different conventions. What works in poetry may not be appropriate in an argument. The kinds of serious arguments you are expected to create cannot be successful using heartfelt emotion alone. When you write about literature, shaky thinking might cause your audience to dismiss your ideas. Your claims and the assumptions behind them should be clear and reasoned. If they are not, you might be committing a **fallacy**, a common term for unsound reasoning.

In the next several paragraphs, we discuss typical logical fallacies. Some of them are especially relevant to literary studies, and for all of them we provide examples related to "The Solitary Reaper." We do not want you to brood over this list, seeing it as a catalog of sins to which you might fall prey. If you constantly fear being accused of fallacies, you might be too paralyzed to make claims at all! In our discussion of fallacies, we also identify circumstances in which your audience might *not* object to a particular fallacy. In addition, we suggest how a writer might revise such claims to be more persuasive. Indeed, the main value in studying fallacies is to identify ways you might develop arguments more effectively.

One of the most common fallacies, ***ad hominem*** (Latin: "toward the man"), is probably the easiest to commit because it is the hardest to resist. Instead of doing the hard work of analyzing the claim and the evidence, we simply ignore them and attack the character of the person making the argument. Instead of trying to figure out what is going on in a complex work of literature, we say, "How can you take seriously a poem about love written by a manic depressive who commits suicide?" It is best to focus on the message, not the messenger.

A related fallacy, **begging the question** (a kind of circular reasoning in which the statement being argued is already assumed to have been decided) is also involved in this example since it is assumed (not proved) that unstable poets cannot have cogent insights about love.

In writing about "The Solitary Reaper," a classmate of Abby's ignored whatever argument the poem is making and focused on Wordsworth's credibility as an observer: "British intellectuals have been either romanticizing or degrading country people for centuries. Whatever Wordsworth thinks about the

Do not attack speaker!

'Highland Lass' is almost certainly wrong." First of all, the speaker of the poem should not be automatically equated with the poet. When they write, poets and fictional writers construct personae that may or may not reflect their own views. Second, attacking Wordsworth is a fallacy for several reasons. It first has to be demonstrated that the poet is a British intellectual, that intellectuals have consistently misrepresented rural people, and that the speaker has done so in this particular case. The classmate should revise her claim so that it deals with the words in the text, not her view of the poet's credibility.

Professional historians, mathematicians, and philosophers usually cite other professionals working in their field; that is, they **appeal to authority** to bolster their credibility. Disciplinary knowledge is created by a community of scholars who cite the ideas of its members as evidence for their claims. The warrant is that recognized authorities know what they are talking about. Quoting them is persuasive. But not completely: appeals to authority can also be fallacious. Literary critics, like other thinkers, often disagree. Just citing an expert does not conclusively prove your claim. A classmate of Abby's, for example, quoted a critic, Ian Lancashire, who says that the narrator "transcends the limitations of mortality," but the student did not give his own reasons or his own evidence for thinking this way. This appeal to critical authority without giving reasons or evidence is a fallacy because a sound argument would at least have to consider other critics. An argument is a reasoning process in which claims are supported, not simply asserted, even if they come from an expert.

A related fallacy involves using quotations from unreliable sources. Although the Internet is often a valuable tool, students sometimes use it uncritically. If you went to the search engine Google and entered Wordsworth's "The Solitary Reaper," you would quickly find Ian Lancashire's essay; and since he is a professor at the University of Toronto with many publications on this and other Romantic topics, citing him is appropriate. But some of the commentators noted by the Google search are students, perhaps English majors who have written a paper for a course on the Romantic poets. Using them as authorities would damage your judgment and credibility.

Equally harmful to the soundness of your argument is to rely too heavily on personal experience as evidence for your claim. Personal experience can sometimes be compelling and authoritative. Feminist and postcolonial critics (see the Appendix, pp. 1621–45) have successfully used their own experiences with discrimination to create cogent arguments. But they rarely rely exclusively on personal experience. Instead they blend relevant experience with textual and critical specifics. Telling your readers that "The Solitary Reaper" is factually flawed because you never saw harvesters work alone when you worked on your uncle's farm would be a fallacy.

Actually, the previous example of using personal experience as authority is also unsound because the personal sample is too small to warrant a reasonable conclusion. It is hard to convince your audience if you claim too much based on limited experience. A student arguing that "The Solitary

Reaper" demonstrates that field workers are melancholy would be committing a **hasty generalization** fallacy. Simply claiming less would improve the argument. In fact, this student might change the focus of her argument by doing research on other poems by Wordsworth, finding several that deal with young women in nature. Using "She Dwelt among Untrodden Ways" and "She Was a Phantom of Delight," the student might argue that Wordsworth is so enraptured by the natural world that he often blurs the boundaries between people and nature.

Another common fallacy is *post hoc, ergo propter hoc* (Latin: "because of this, then that"). Few of us escape this error in cause and effect. Many superstitions probably began because of this fallacy. A man breaks a mirror and bad luck follows. Did the mirror cause the bad luck? Logic says no, but the next day he breaks a leg, and a week later his car is stolen. The coincidence is often too tempting to resist. Does smoking marijuana lead to hard drugs? Logic says no, since you could argue just as plausibly that almost anything (carrots, beer, coffee) that comes before could be said to cause what comes after. Unless a clear, logical link between the two events is demonstrated, you might be accused of the *post hoc* fallacy.

In writing about "The Solitary Reaper," you might want to argue that the "melancholy strain" the traveler heard caused him to have a deeper appreciation for the beauty and mystery of rural people. But perhaps the narrator held such an opinion for a long time, or perhaps this is just one of dozens of such encounters that the poet remembers fondly. A sounder argument would focus on the cause and effect that does seem to be in the text: the mystery of the song's content adds to the emotional response the poet has.

Most of us commit a version of the **intentional fallacy** when we defend ourselves against someone we offended by saying, "That's not what I meant. It was just a joke." The problem arises because we are not always able to carry out our intentions. Perhaps our language is not precise enough, or perhaps our intention to be sincere or honest or witty gets mixed up with other intentions we have to sound intelligent, confident, or impressive. Students are often surprised when teachers tell them that a writer's stated intentions cannot be taken as the final word on a poem's meaning. "Wordsworth knows the poem better than anyone else" is an understandable retort. But that might not be the case. Wordsworth might not be the most astute reader of his own work. And he may not be fully aware of all that he intended. A student would be committing an intentional fallacy by arguing that "The Solitary Reaper" is written in the language used by the common man because Wordsworth says so in his preface to *Lyrical Ballads*. While this student should be commended for doing extra research, another student might point out that "Vale profound," "plaintive numbers," and "humble lay" seem conventionally poetic. Like others, this fallacy is easily revised by claiming less: "Most of 'The Solitary Reaper' is written in simple diction to approximate the language used by ordinary people."

When you try to destroy someone's argument by ignoring their main point and focusing on something marginal, you are attacking a **straw man**. The student who argues that we should dismiss Wordsworth's credibility as an observer because of "his absurd declaration that 'a voice so thrilling ne'er was heard'" is committing the straw man fallacy. While it is probably true that the song he hears is not the most thrilling in the history of the world, this is hardly Wordsworth's main point. Writers gain more credibility if they deal with a writer's strongest or main claim.

A favorite tactic of traditionalists trying to hold the line against change, the **slippery slope** fallacy is used to claim that if we allow one thing to happen, then slipping into catastrophe is just around the corner. If we do not prevent students from wearing gangsta rap fashions, gangs will eventually roam the hallways; if we allow the morning-after pill, sexual anarchy will follow. A small step is seen as precipitating an avalanche.

The following claim by a student anticipates something that simply is not logically called for: "Although Wordsworth probably means well, his praise for the 'Highland Lass' is a dangerous move since she is probably illiterate and full of rural biases and superstitions. His failure to discriminate will lead to loss of judgment and standards." Again, claiming less improves the argument: Wordsworth is less interested in the content ("Whate'er the theme") than in the "music in my heart," an emotional response that we hope does not carry over into his views on medicine, engineering, and economics.

We are all guilty at times of the fallacy of **oversimplification** — of not seeing the inevitable complexity of things. At the risk of committing a hasty generalization ourselves, it is probably the case that your instructor will be impressed if you look for complexity in literary texts and in your arguments. Seeing complexity is a consequence of hard thinking. There are rarely two sides to a question. More likely, there are a dozen plausible and reasonable perspectives. The cliché that the truth often appears in shades of gray rather than in black and white gets at the idea that simple solutions are often the result of shallow thinking.

Complexity is not what the following claim reveals: "'The Solitary Reaper' is a poem about a traveler who hears a young girl 'singing by herself,' and like a catchy ad, the tune stays with him." Being exposed to other viewpoints in class discussions and in peer-group revision can help this student avoid oversimplifying the experience Wordsworth has, one that touches on issues of mortality, the mysteries of emotional response, the purpose of poetry, and the power of the natural world. When Henry David Thoreau, the author of *Walden* (1854), urged his contemporaries to live simply, he was talking about their lifestyles, not their thinking.

Non sequitur is a general catchall fallacy that means "it does not follow." Some principle of logic has been violated when we make a claim that the evidence cannot support. In "The Solitary Reaper," it does not follow that because the Highland Lass "sings a melancholy strain," she herself is sad. She could be happy, absentminded, or simply bored. Perhaps the song is a conventional ballad typically sung by workers to pass the time. Revising this fallacy, like many of the others, involves setting aside time in the revision process to look again at your claims and the assumptions behind them, carefully and objectively making a clear connection between your claim and the evidence you say supports it.

First Draft of a Student Paper

The following is Abby's first complete draft of her paper. Eventually, she revised this draft after a group of her classmates reviewed it and after she reflected further on it herself. For the moment, though, read this first version, and decide what you would have said to her about it.

Abby Hazelton
Professor Ramsey
English 102
4 March - - - -

[handwritten annotation: ? (not good) assumptions]

The Passage of Time in
"The Solitary Reaper"

[handwritten marginal annotations: has evidence that should be used later / no focus; jumps around; long...]

William Wordsworth, one of the most famous writers in the movement known as British Romanticism, liked to write about beautiful features of the countryside. In his poem "The Solitary Reaper," the speaker enthuses over a girl who sings as she works in the fields. Yet although he is enraptured by her "melancholy strain," he is unsure what it is *about* because she is using a Scottish dialect that he cannot understand. By contrast, the subject of the poem itself seems much clearer. The very title of the poem refers to the singing girl, and the subsequent lines repeatedly praise her song as wonderfully haunting. Nevertheless, the poem has puzzling aspects. Many readers are likely to wonder if they are supposed to find the speaker guilty of cultural and class superiority when he, as a British intellectual, treats a Scottish peasant girl as a spectacle. Another issue, the one I focus on in my paper, arises when the final stanza shifts to past tense. In the first three stanzas, the speaker uses present tense, as if he is currently observing the singer whom he describes. In the concluding stanza, however, the speaker uses verbs such as "sang," "saw," and "listen'd," as if he is *recalling* his encounter with her. How can we explain this inconsistency? One possible justification for the final shift to past tense is that it reminds us of the speaker's inability to halt the passage of time. Even though he would like to freeze the encounter, time goes on. Perhaps, therefore, the poem's real subject is the idea that time is always in flux. Indeed, even before the final stanza, the speaker betrays an awareness that he can't bend time to his will.

Simply by virtue of the shift to past tense, the last stanza indicates that time goes on despite the speaker's wishes. But other elements of this stanza convey the same notion. Recalling his experience of the girl's singing, the speaker reports that he was "motionless and still," yet in the very next line he admits that he eventually moved: "I mounted up the hill." When the speaker says that "the Maiden sang / As if her song could have no ending," the words "As if" are significant, implying that the song did end for him in reality. Similarly, the poem itself has to end at some point. In fact, it concludes with the words "no more," which stress that the singer and her song now belong to the speaker's past. Only in his "heart," apparently, can he retain them. Furthermore, the medium of print can never convey the sound of music. In fact, prior to recording technology, music was the most fleeting of media, its notes fading with each new moment. By seeking to transmit music, the speaker ensures that he will wind up being frustrated by time.

Even if the final stanza's shift of tense is jarring, the first three stanzas give hints that the speaker will end up defeated by time. Significantly, the poem's very first word is "Behold." In issuing this command, the speaker evidently hopes that other people will abandon all motion and gaze at the singer, basking in her song. The speaker reinforces this call for paralysis with the command that begins line 4: "Stop here." Yet, as if acknowledging limits to his control, he adds "or gently pass!" Besides referring to other human beings, these commands seem directed at time itself. The speaker hopes that time, too, will "Stop" and "Behold." Even at this point in the poem, however, he realizes that time is inclined to "pass," in which case he hopes that it will at least move on "gently."

The second stanza is chiefly concerned with space. Comparing the girl's song to other sounds, the speaker ranges from "Arabian sands" to "the seas / Among the farthest Hebrides." In the third stanza, however, he focuses again on time. Trying to determine the subject of the song, he expresses uncertainty about its time frame. He wonders whether the song concerns "old, unhappy, far-off things / And battles long ago" or instead deals with "Familiar matter of to-day." Moreover, even if he suspects the song's subject is "Some natural sorrow, loss, or pain," he is unsure whether this experience of despair is confined to the past ("has been") or will reoccur ("may be again"). Whichever of the possibilities he raises is true, the speaker is clearly limited in his ability to figure out the song's relation to time. In other words, he cannot force time into a meaningful pattern, let alone prevent its passing.

By the end of the poem, the speaker seems as "solitary" as the reaper. In addition to losing his experience with her as time moves on, he is isolated in other ways. Throughout the poem, actually, we don't see him in the company of others. His opening "Behold" is directed at no one in particular. Furthermore, we can't be sure whether he is speaking to actual passersby or, rather, to the poem's hypothetical future readers. Nor, for all his praise of the singer, does he apparently talk to her. Rather, he gives the impression that he keeps at a distance. Even if he did try to converse with the reaper, he himself would still be "solitary" in the sense of failing to understand her language and failing to communicate her song to his readers. He does not even bother trying to reproduce some of the song's words. Therefore, despite the speaker's enchantment over the reaper, this poem is ultimately pessimistic. The speaker is left only with his memories of a wonderful experience. He has lost the experience itself.

Strategies for Revising

Most first drafts are far from perfect. Even experienced professional writers often have to revise their work. Besides making changes on their own, many of them solicit feedback from others. In various workplaces, writing is collaborative, with coauthors exchanging ideas as they try to improve a piece. Remain open to the possibility that your draft needs changes, perhaps several. Of course, you are more apt to revise extensively if you have given yourself enough time. Conversely, you will not feel able to change much of your paper if it is due the next day. You will also limit your ability to revise if you work only with your original manuscript, scribbling possible changes between the lines. This practice amounts to conservatism, for it encourages you to keep passages that really ought to be overhauled.

You may have trouble, however, improving a draft if you are checking many things in it at once. Therefore, read the draft repeatedly, looking at a different aspect of it each time. A good way to begin is to outline the paper you have written and then compare that outline with your original one. If the two outlines differ, your draft may or may not need adjusting; perhaps you were wise to swerve from your original plan. In any case, you should ponder your departures from that plan, considering whether they were for the best.

If, like Abby, you are writing an argument paper, our Checklist for Revising box has some topics and questions you might apply as you review your first draft. Some of these considerations overlap. Nevertheless, take them in turn rather than all at once.

▀ A CHECKLIST FOR REVISING

Logic

- Will my audience see that the issue I am focusing on is indeed an issue?

- Will the audience be able to follow the logic of my argument?

- Is the logic as persuasive as it might be? Is there more evidence I can provide? Do I need to identify more of my warrants?

- Have I addressed all of my audience's potential concerns?

Organization

- Does my introduction identify the issue that I will focus on? Does it state my main claim?

- Will my audience be able to detect and follow the stages of my argument?

(continued on next page)

≡ A CHECKLIST FOR REVISING

- Does the order of my paragraphs seem purposeful rather than arbitrary?
- Have I done all I can to signal connections within and between sentences? Within and between paragraphs?
- Have I avoided getting bogged down in mere summary?
- Will my conclusion satisfy readers? Does it leave any key questions dangling?

Clarity

- Does my title offer a good preview of my argument?
- Will each of my sentences be immediately clear?
- Am I sure how to define each word that I have used?

Emphasis

- Have I put key points in prominent places?
- Have I worded each sentence for maximum impact? In particular, is each sentence as concise as possible? Do I use active verbs whenever I can?

Style

- Are my tone and level of vocabulary appropriate?
- Will my audience think me fair-minded? Should I make any more concessions?
- Do I use any mannerisms that may distract my readers?
- Have I used any expressions that may annoy or offend?
- Is there anything else I can do to make my paper readable and interesting?

Grammar

- Is each of my sentences grammatically correct?
- Have I punctuated properly?

Physical Appearance

- Have I followed the proper format for quotations, notes, and bibliography?
- Are there any typographical errors?

We list these considerations from most to least important. When revising a draft, think first about matters of logic, organization, and clarity. There is little point in fixing the grammar of particular sentences if you are going to drop them later because they fail to advance your argument.

As we noted, a group of Abby's classmates discussed her draft. Most of these students seemed to like her overall argument, including her main issue and claim. Having been similarly confused by the poem's shift of tense, they appreciated the light that Abby shed on it. They were impressed by her willingness to examine the poem's specific words. They especially liked her closing analogy between the reaper and the speaker himself. Nevertheless, the group made several comments about Abby's paper that she took as suggestions for improvement. Ultimately, she decided that the following changes were in order.

1. She should make her introduction more concise.   The first draft is so long and dense that it may confuse readers instead of helping them sense the paper's main concerns. This problem is common to first drafts. In this preliminary phase, many writers worry that they will fail to generate *enough* words; they are hardly thinking about how to restrain themselves. Moreover, the writer of a first draft may still be unsure about the paper's whole argument, so the introduction often lacks a sharp focus. After Abby finished and reviewed her first draft, she saw ways of making her introduction tighter.

2. She should rearrange paragraphs.   After her introduction, Abby discussed the poem's last stanza in more detail. Then she moved back to stanza 1. Next, just before her paper's conclusion, she analyzed stanzas 2 and 3. Abby thought that the structure of her paper moved logically from the obvious to the hidden: the poem's last stanza emphasized the passage of time, and the earlier stanzas touched on this subject more subtly. Yet Abby's method of organization frustrated her classmates. They thought her paper would be easier to follow if, after the introduction, it moved chronologically through the poem. For them, her discussion of stanzas 2 and 3 seemed especially mislocated. Though she had positioned this discussion as her paper's climax, her classmates did not sense it to be her most significant and compelling moment of insight. Most important, they believed, were her comments on the *final* stanza, for that seemed to them the most important part of Wordsworth's poem. In other words, they thought the climax of the paper would be stronger if it focused on the climax of the poem. Abby hesitated to adopt her classmates' recommendation, but eventually she did so. When you read her final version, see if you like her rearrangement of paragraphs. Sometimes, though not always, a paper about a literary work seems more coherent if it does follow the work's chronological structure. And papers should indeed build to a climax, even if readers disagree about what its content should be.

3. She should reconsider her claim that "this poem is ultimately pessimistic."   Abby's classmates thought this claim did not fully account for the poem's last two lines: "The music in my heart I bore, / Long after it was heard no more." While they agreed with her that the words "no more" emphasize that the singer has faded into the past, they disagreed that her song is lost as well, for it remains in the speaker's "heart." They noted that Abby had acknowledged this fact, but they felt she had done so too briefly and dismissively. In addition, one student encouraged her to think about poetry and music as ways of keeping memories alive. More specifically, he suggested that the speaker of "The Solitary Reaper" is Wordsworth himself, who is using this poem to preserve his memory of an actual encounter. After studying the poem again, Abby decided that her classmates' ideas had merit, and she incorporated them into her revision. Of course, such advice is not always worth heeding. Still, writers should accept the invitation to look more closely at whatever text they are analyzing.

Revised Draft of a Student Paper

Here is the new version of the paper that Abby wrote. Attached to it are marginal comments by us that call your attention to her strategies.

Abby Hazelton
Professor Ramsey
English 102
11 March - - - -

not confident (open to interruption)

The Passage of Time in "The Solitary Reaper"

In William Wordsworth's poem "The Solitary Reaper," the speaker enthuses over a girl who sings as she works in the fields. Throughout the poem, his rapture is evident. Yet in the last stanza, he makes a puzzling move, shifting to past tense after using present tense in the previous three stanzas. No longer does he seem to be currently observing the singer he describes; rather, now he seems to be *recalling* his encounter with her. One possible justification for this shift in tense is that it reminds us of the speaker's inability to halt the passage of time. Even though he would like to freeze the encounter, time goes on. Perhaps, therefore, the poem's real theme is that time is always in flux. Indeed, even before the final stanza, the speaker betrays an awareness that he can't bend time to his will.

Shortly! to the point

Significantly, the poem's very first word is "Behold." In issuing this command, the speaker evidently hopes that other people will abandon all motion and gaze at the singer. The speaker reinforces this call for paralysis with the command that begins line 4: "Stop here." Yet, as if acknowledging limits to his control, he adds "or gently pass!" Besides referring to other human beings, these commands seem directed at time itself. The speaker hopes that time, too, will "Stop" and "Behold."

Title clearly indicates particular work being analyzed and aspect to be focused on.

Immediately refers to specific detail of text.

With "puzzling," signals issue to be addressed.

Identifies main claim.

Connects feature of poem to be focused on to other parts of it.

Analyzes implication of poem's particular language rather than just beginning with plot detail.

Develops point that even poem's early stanzas show concern about passage of time that final stanza emphasizes.

Even at this point in the poem, however, he realizes that time is inclined to "pass," in which case he hopes that it will at least move on "gently."

The second stanza is chiefly concerned with space. Comparing the girl's song to other sounds, the speaker ranges from "Arabian sands" to "the seas / Among the farthest Hebrides." In the third stanza, however, he focuses again on time. Trying to determine the subject of her song, he expresses uncertainty about its time frame. He wonders whether the song concerns "old, unhappy, far-off things / And battles long ago" or instead deals with "Familiar matter of to-day." Moreover, even if he suspects the song's subject is "Some natural sorrow, loss, or pain," he is unsure whether this experience of despair is confined to the past ("has been") or will reoccur ("may be again"). Whichever of the possibilities he raises is true, the speaker is clearly limited in his ability to figure out the song's relation to time. In other words, he cannot force time into a meaningful pattern, let alone prevent its passing.

Simply by virtue of the shift to past tense, the last stanza indicates that time goes on despite the speaker's wishes. But other elements of the stanza convey this same notion. Recalling his experience of the girl's singing, the speaker reports that he was "motionless and still," yet in the very next line he admits that he eventually moved: "I mounted up the hill." When the speaker says that "the Maiden sang / As if her song could have no ending," the words "As if" are significant, implying that the song did end for him in reality. Similarly, the poem itself has to end at some point. In fact, it concludes with the words "no more," which stress that the singer and her song now belong to the speaker's past. Only in his "heart," apparently, can he retain them.

This situation seems to leave the speaker as "solitary" as the reaper. Throughout the poem, actually, we don't see him in the company of others. His opening "Behold" is directed at no one in particular. Furthermore, we can't be sure he is speaking to actual passersby or, rather, to the poem's hypothetical future readers. Nor, for all his praise of the singer, does he apparently talk to her. Rather, he gives the impression that he keeps at a distance. Even if he did converse with the reaper, he himself would still be "solitary" in the sense of failing to understand her dialect and failing to communicate her words to his readers. As things stand, he is apparently unable or unwilling to reproduce any of the song's lyrics. Just as important, the medium of print can never convey the sounds of music. In fact, prior to recording technology, music was the most fleeting of media, its notes fading with each new moment.

Moves chronologically through poem, carefully pointing out how second stanza differs from first.

Makes distinctions among stanzas' topics. Returns to main claim of essay.

Refers to actual words of poem to support points.

Ends paragraph by reminding us what main claim is.

Directs attention to part of poem with which she is most concerned.

Traces implications of poem's words, especially as these are related to main issue and claim.

Connects last stanza to other parts of poem.

Several observations support idea that speaker is isolated.

By seeking to transmit music, the speaker ensures that he will wind up being frustrated by time.

Yet perhaps the singer and her song are preserved in more than just the speaker's "heart." It can be argued that they are also preserved by the poem, if only to a limited extent. More generally, we can say that literature is a means by which human beings partially succeed in perpetuating things. This idea seems quite relevant to "The Solitary Reaper" if we suppose that the speaker is the poet himself and that he actually witnessed the scene he describes. If we make such assumptions, we can see Wordsworth as analogous to the speaker. After all, both engage in commemorative verbal art. Because time passes, the "strains" that Wordsworth and the singer produce in their efforts to preserve time are bound to be "melancholy." Still, their art matters, for through it they can imaginatively "reap" experiences that would otherwise fade.

Concludes climactic paragraph with substantial analysis.

Signals that she is simply making a suggestion here, rather than asserting definite new point.

Concluding paragraph reminds us of main issue and claim but goes beyond sheer repetition to bring up some new suggestions.

To us, Abby's revision is more persuasive and compelling than her first draft. In particular, she has nicely complicated her claim about the poem's "pessimism." Nevertheless, we would hesitate to call this revision the definitive version of her paper. Maybe you have thought of things Abby could do to make it even more effective. In presenting her two drafts, we mainly want to emphasize the importance of revision. We hope, too, that you will remember our specific tips as you work on your own writing.

Strategies for Writing a Comparative Paper

Much writing about literature *compares* two or more texts. After all, you can gain many insights into a text by noting how it resembles and differs from others. Throughout this book, therefore, we cluster texts, encouraging you to trace similarities and differences within each set. For instance, the chapters in Part One repeatedly present clusters that treat various aspects of work. At the moment, we offer suggestions for writing a comparative paper, a task you may be assigned in your course.

To aid our discussion, we ask that you read the following two poems. The first, "Two Trees," appears in the 2009 verse collection *Rain* by Don Paterson (b. 1963), a Scottish writer who is also a jazz musician, a professor at the University of St. Andrews, and the poetry editor for the publisher Picador Macmillan. Next comes "Regarding History," a poem from the 2005 book *Trill & Mordent* by Luisa A. Igloria (b. 1961), a Filipina American writer who is a professor of English and creative writing at Old Dominion University in Norfolk, Virginia.

DON PATERSON
Two Trees

One morning, Don Miguel got out of bed
with one idea rooted in his head:
to graft his orange to his lemon tree.
It took him the whole day to work them free,
lay open their sides, and lash them tight.   5
For twelve months, from the shame or from the fright
they put forth nothing; but one day there appeared
two lights in the dark leaves. Over the years
the limbs would get themselves so tangled up
each bough looked like it gave a double crop,   10
and not one kid in the village didn't know
the magic tree in Miguel's patio.

The man who bought the house had had no dream
so who can say what dark malicious whim
led him to take his axe and split the bole   15
along its fused seam, and then dig two holes.
And no, they did not die from solitude;
nor did their branches bear a sterile fruit;
nor did their unhealed flanks weep every spring
for those four yards that lost them everything   20
as each strained on its shackled root to face
the other's empty, intricate embrace.
They were trees, and trees don't weep or ache or shout.
And trees are all this poem is about.   *[2009]*

LUISA A. IGLORIA
Regarding History

A pair of trees on one side of the walk, leaning
now into the wind in a stance we'd call involuntary —
I can see them from the kitchen window, as I take meat
out of the oven and hold my palms above the crust, darkened
with burnt sugar. Nailed with cloves, small earth of flesh   5
still smoldering from its furnace. In truth I want to take it
into the garden and bury it in soil. There are times
I grow weary of coaxing music from silence, silence
from the circularity of logic, logic from the artifact.
Then, the possibilities of sunlight are less attractive   10
than baying at the moon. I want to take your face
in my hands, grow sweet from what it tells, tend
how it leans and turns, trellis or vine of morning-glory.

I wish for limbs pared to muscle, to climb away from
chance and all its missed appointments, its half-drunk   15
cups of coffee. Tell me what I'll find, in this
early period at the beginning of a century.
Tell me what I'll find, stumbling into a boat
and pushing off into the year's last dark hours.   *[2005]*

LIST SIMILARITIES AND DIFFERENCES

A class like yours sensed value in comparing Paterson's poem with Igloria's. So
the students proceeded to brainstorm lists of specific similarities and differences — something you might do to start analyzing texts you bring together.
For these two poems, the class came up with the following comparisons:

SIMILARITIES

In both poems, a prominent role is played by a real pair of trees, and
their relation to each other seems important.

Both poems describe labor. In Paterson's, it's the labor of joining and
then separating the trees; in Igloria's, it's the labor of cooking,
burying, coaxing, climbing, and "pushing off."

The word *limbs* appears in both poems.

Both poems contain many words that have negative connotations.
Paterson's poem includes such words as *shame, fright, dark
malicious whim, die, sterile, unhealed, weep, strained, shackled,
empty,* and *ache,* while Igloria's poem includes such words as
darkened, burnt, Nailed, bury, weary, missed, and *dark.*

More specifically, both poems contain words associated with death.

Both poems refer to the time frame of a year, with Paterson's mentioning "twelve months" and Igloria's concluding with "the year's last
dark hours."

DIFFERENCES

The speaker in Igloria's poem uses first person, indicated by the
pronoun *I*, while the speaker in Paterson's poem is no specific,
identifiable person.

Paterson's poem does, however, name a particular character (Don
Miguel) and refers to several other people (kids in the village, the
man who chopped apart the trees), while the only people in
Igloria's poem seem to be "I" and "you."

Paterson's poem centers on a particular image, the two trees, whereas
Igloria's poem has other images besides the pair of trees.

Paterson's poem seems more like a narrative; it tells a story. Igloria's poem seems to be more the expression of the speaker's mood.

While Igloria's speaker is clearly interested in the pair of trees as metaphors for her relationship with "you," Paterson's poem leaves readers to interpret whether and how the two trees have meta-phorical implications.

"Two Trees" rhymes, but "Regarding History" does not.

"Regarding History" seems in many respects a love poem, but "Two Trees" is hard to see in that way.

"Two Trees" comments on the fact that it is a poem, but "Regarding History" does not.

"Regarding History" ends with its speaker wanting to know something ("Tell me what I'll find"), but "Two Trees" may leave its *readers* wanting to know something: whether we're supposed to accept its speaker's claim that "trees are all this poem is about."

As you plan your own comparative paper, lists such as these can help you organize your thoughts. To be sure, this class did not immediately think of all the similarities and differences it ended up noting. Usually, going beyond obvious points of comparison is a gradual process, for which you should give yourself plenty of time. Similarly, once you have made lists such as the one above, take time to decide which similarities and differences truly merit your attention. At most, only a few can be part of your paper's main issue and claim.

CONSIDER "WEIGHTING" YOUR COMPARISON

Unfortunately, many students writing a comparative analysis are content to put forth main claims such as these:

There are many similarities and differences between "Two Trees" and "Regarding History."

While "Two Trees" and "Regarding History" have many similarities, in many ways they are also different.

While "Two Trees" and "Regarding History" are different in many ways, they are similar in others.

Several problems arise with these common methods of introducing a comparative paper. For one thing, they give the reader no preview of the specific ideas to come. Indeed, they could have been written by someone who never bothered to read the two poems, for any two texts are similar in certain ways and different in others. Furthermore, these sorts of claims leave no meaningful and compelling way of organizing the paper. Rather, they encourage the writer to proceed arbitrarily, noting miscellaneous similarities and differences on impulse. More precisely, claims such as these fail to identify the *issue* driving the paper. Why compare Paterson's and Igloria's poems in the first place? Comparison is a means to an end, not an end in itself. What important question is the writer using these two texts to answer? In short, what's at stake?

A more fruitful approach, we think, is to write a *weighted* comparative analysis — that is, an argument chiefly concerned with *one* text more than others. When professional literary critics compare two texts, often they mainly want to answer a question about just one of them. They bring in the second text because they believe that doing so helps them address the issue they are raising about their key text. True, a good paper can result even when you treat equally all texts you discuss. But you might write a paper that seems more purposeful and coherent if you focus basically on one work, using comparisons to resolve some issue concerning it.

A Student Comparative Paper

The following paper by student Jeremy Cooper demonstrates weighted comparative analysis. The author refers to Igloria's "Regarding History" along with Paterson's "Two Trees," but he is mostly concerned with Paterson's poem. He brings up Igloria's poem not to do comparison for its own sake but to address a question he has about Paterson's text.

Jeremy Cooper

Professor Budnoy

English 102

15 October - - - -

Title does not merely repeat title of the poem to be analyzed. Moreover, title specifies what aspect of that poem he will examine.

Don Paterson's Criticism of Nature's Owners

Until its last two lines, Don Paterson's poem "Two Trees" tells a fairly straightforward story. The title refers to an orange tree and a lemon tree that stood next to each other on an estate. The speaker in the poem recalls how these trees were treated by two different owners of the property. The first owner, Don Miguel, successfully grafted the trees together. The next owner, a man unnamed by the speaker, separated them with an axe. Given the speaker's clear description of these events, most readers would probably have no trouble understanding what happened to the trees. But the poem's concluding pair of lines is puzzling:

First sentence refers to poem he will focus on, his primary text.

They were trees, and trees don't weep or ache or shout.
And trees are all this poem is about.

Signals issue that the paper will address.

On the surface, the word *all* seems equivalent to "merely." If this is the case, readers might feel that Paterson is encouraging them to take a limited view of his poem, seeing it as concerned with nothing more than trees. They would then feel *discouraged* from looking for additional significance or meaning in his text. But this interpretation of Paterson's focus risks making his poem appear relatively trivial, an impression that he surely does not want to create. A likelier possibility is that the speaker is being ironic in his final declaration, stating the word *all* sarcastically. Such a tone might then move readers to question whether the poem is simply about trees. They might feel compelled to consider how its real subject is something else. Indeed, the poem's actual main topic seems to be the regrettable attitudes that human beings take toward nature when they are able to own it.

Trees play a major role in Paterson's poem, as their presence in the title suggests. In the first of the poem's two stanzas, the speaker describes Don Miguel's effort to fuse the orange tree and the lemon tree together, something that he evidently managed to accomplish so well that the trees became hard to distinguish from each other: "the limbs would get themselves so tangled up / each bough looked like it gave a double crop." In the second stanza, the speaker turns to describing how the next owner of the trees did the opposite thing to them, splitting them apart. The poem presents no other scenic feature to compete with the two trees for the reader's attention. The speaker just briefly mentions a bed, a patio, a house, and an axe.

> *Introductory paragraph ends by stating the claim about the primary text that the paper will support and develop.*

That the focus is very much on the trees becomes even more apparent if we compare this poem with another in which two trees figure, Luisa A. Igloria's "Regarding History." Igloria's poem begins with "A pair of trees on one side of the walk, leaning / now into the wind in a stance we'd call involuntary." Later, the speaker seems to have these two trees still in mind when she says that she wants to hold her lover's face and feel "how it leans and turns, trellis or vine of morning-glory." The close relation of the word *leans* in this line to *leaning* in the earlier one implies that the trees remain a meaningful symbol for her throughout the poem. But, unlike Paterson's speaker, Igloria's turns her thoughts to a number of images other than trees. For example, besides her beloved's face, she thinks of food she has just prepared ("meat / out of the oven," which she has evidently "Nailed with cloves"), her garden, sunlight, the moon, muscles, coffee, and a boat. Basically, the two trees in this poem are just part of its many elements. By contrast, the pair of trees in Paterson's poem is much more prominent.

> *This is a secondary text, which he uses to reinforce the point he has just made about his primary text.*

The question then becomes what we as readers should make of their central role in that poem. Some of us may be inclined to see Paterson's trees as a metaphor, their physical existence being less significant than something else they represent. The pair of trees in "Regarding History" do seem metaphorical, functioning in the speaker's mind as stand-ins for a human relationship. When she observes that the trees are "leaning / now into the wind in a stance we'd call involuntary," she appears to be actually thinking of her relationship with her beloved. Specifically, she seems worried about pressures on their relationship that threaten their ability to keep it steady. This concern of hers comes up again later, when she expresses a desire "to take your face" and "tend / how it leans and turns." Here, too, she evidently feels that her connection to her loved one is challenged by outside forces. As in her earlier remark about the trees, she fears that she will not be able to protect her relationship from influences that will make her and her lover do "involuntary" things. In comparison, though, the two trees in Paterson's poem do not appear to have a metaphorical function. In the first place, the speaker of "Two Trees" lacks a distinct personality, so that the poem does not encourage readers to interpret the trees he mentions as representing thoughts or feelings of his. Whereas Igloria's speaker dominates "Regarding History" with her clearly marked hopes and concerns, Paterson's speaker writes largely like a reporter narrating news events. Moreover, when he tells what the two property owners did to the trees, he describes these actions so precisely and concretely that he makes it hard for readers to consider the trees as symbolic rather than physical. Also, in such lines as "they did not die from solitude" and "nor did their unhealed flanks weep every spring," the speaker seems to be reminding the reader that they are, in fact, basically vegetation rather than images of something in the human mind. If anything, these lines discourage the reader from interpreting the trees as metaphors.

He has identified a possible interpretation but now offers a different one, which he proceeds to argue for.

He uses comparison with his secondary text to support his argument about his primary text.

But if the two trees in Paterson's poem come across mainly as real elements of nature, the attitudes that their owners show toward them are nevertheless significant. Actually, the poem's main subject is not the trees of the title, but the intense and disturbing emotions that drove Don Miguel and the later owner to handle them roughly. The feelings that led the second owner to separate the trees seem villainous. The speaker suggests that this man "had had no dream" but instead acted on some mysterious "dark malicious whim" that compelled him to "split" them apart, leaving their flanks "unhealed" and their roots "shackled." This language gives the impression of a plantation owner in the pre–Civil War American South, the type of person who cruelly divided slave families and kept their members

He is working with the claim he put forth in his introduction.

separated in bondage. Because the poem ends with the physical stress inflicted upon the trees by their second owner, some readers may be more bothered by this man's behavior than they are by Don Miguel's. They might even appreciate Don Miguel's interest in uniting the trees, especially because his labor resulted in the heartening picture of "two lights in the dark leaves." But the language used to describe his actions, too, is mostly negative. The words *lay open, lash them tight, shame, fright,* and *tangled up* imply traumatic destruction, even rape, rather than blissful harmony. In his willingness to manipulate the trees, Don Miguel therefore seems no better than the man who replaced him. Furthermore, Don Miguel's behavior toward the trees did not have the excuse of being carefully thought out and planned. He simply awoke "with one idea rooted in his head: / to graft his orange to his lemon tree." Just as the word *Don* is an indication that he is a man of power in his community, so the repetition of the word *his* in this line suggests that he felt able to perform surgery on the trees merely because he owned them. Both of the men in the poem avoided thinking of what was best for the trees. Instead, both preferred to exercise the authority they had as possessors of the trees, no matter how abusive their handling of the trees might be. The speaker in Igloria's poem calls attention to what she currently *lacks* or is *unable* to do, through statements like "I want to take your face," "I wish for limbs pared to muscle," and "Tell me what I'll find." Furthermore, she does not possess the two trees that figure in "Regarding History." Rather, she is a mere observer of them: "I can see them from the kitchen window." In Paterson's poem, on the other hand, Don Miguel and the second man treat their trees violently and are able to do so because the trees are legally theirs.

Again, he acknowledges the possibility of an interpretation different from his, before advancing his view.

Once more, he uses comparison with his secondary text to reinforce his argument about his primary text.

Paterson does not end his poem by directly indicating what he thinks is the proper way of treating trees like those of his title. He does not clearly offer some sort of prescription for their care. Many readers may, nevertheless, come away from the poem concluding that human beings should avoid tampering with trees and, more generally, should leave nature alone as often as possible. In any case, Paterson's central purpose seems to be to make us more aware that when humans own some of nature, they may treat it arrogantly, whether in the pursuit of unity (Don Miguel's aim when he fuses the trees) or separation (the second man's goal when he breaks them apart).

He suggests that this interpretation is possible but that he is more interested in getting his readers to accept his main claim about the poem: the idea he returns to in his final sentence.

Jeremy gains much from comparing "Two Trees" with "Regarding History." In paragraph 3, the analysis of the modest role that trees play in Igloria's poem bolsters Jeremy's claim that they are the core of Paterson's poem. In paragraph 4, the discussion of how Igloria uses trees as metaphors strengthens Jeremy's point that Paterson's trees are literal. In paragraph 5, the observation that Igloria's speaker is *not* an owner of trees helps Jeremy stress that Paterson's men possess them. Obviously, though, Jeremy focuses his paper on Paterson's poem, not on both. By concentrating chiefly on "Two Trees," he enables himself to develop a tight and logical argument, whereas focusing on both poems would encourage him to roam through similarities and differences at random.

Perhaps you know the advice usually given about how to organize a comparative paper. Traditionally, writers aiming to compare two texts learn of two options: (1) discuss one text and then move to the other, comparing it with the first; (2) discuss the texts together, noting each of their similarities and differences in turn. Both of these alternatives make sense and provide a ready-made structure for your paper; either can result in a coherent essay. Still, a weighted analysis such as Jeremy's — an analysis that focuses on one text more than another — is more likely than either of the alternatives to seem the logical evolution of a pointed claim.

▤ SUMMING UP

- **Writing an argument about a literary work involves *exploring, planning, composing,* and *revising*.** (pp. 76–93)

- ***Exploring* requires you to read the work closely, noting questions it raises for you.** Does the text confirm your predictions about it? Does rereading it change your mind? How does it compare with your personal experience? What patterns, and breaks from these patterns, do you find? What ambiguities? What were the author's alternatives? How does the text deal with common topics in literary studies? What is a tentative claim you can make about it? (pp. 76–78)

- ***Planning* combines several activities.** These include selecting a text to write about; envisioning your audience; identifying your main issue, claim, and evidence as you anticipate challenges to them; deciding what warrants to use; and determining how you will organize your argument. (pp. 78–82)

- **Keep in mind the following tips when you are *composing* a draft.**

  Decide on a title that previews your main claim. (p. 83)

  Choose a style that fits your audience and purpose. (pp. 83–84)

  Draft an introduction that identifies as quickly and efficiently as possible the main text you will analyze, your main issue, and your main claim. (pp. 84–85)

≣ SUMMING UP

Limit plot summary. (pp. 85–86)

Decide how you will refer to the author's life and intentions. (pp. 86–87)

Recognize and avoid logical fallacies. (pp. 87–90)

- *Revising* **is a process.** Read your draft repeatedly, looking at a different aspect of it each time, in particular its logic, organization, clarity, emphases, style, grammar, and physical appearance. (pp. 93–96)

- **Be cautious about relating the work to its author's life, and be alert to fallacious reasoning in your arguments and those of others.** (pp. 86–90)

- **Feel free to concede that your analysis of a literary work is not the only reasonable interpretation of it.** (pp. 86–87)

- **Favor** *weighted* **comparison if you are writing a paper that compares two or more literary works.** (pp. 101–02)

CHAPTER 5

How to Write about Stories

Short stories can be said to resemble novels. Above all, both are works of fiction. Yet the difference in length matters. As William Trevor, a veteran writer of short stories, has observed, short fiction is "the art of the glimpse; it deals in echoes and reverberations; craftily it withholds information. Novels tell all. Short stories tell as little as they dare." Maybe Trevor overstates the situation when he claims that novels reveal everything. All sorts of texts feature what literary theorist Wolfgang Iser calls "gaps." Still, Trevor is right to emphasize that short stories usually tell much less than novels do. They demand that you understand and evaluate characters on the basis of just a few details and events. In this respect, short stories resemble poems. Both tend to rely on compression rather than expansion, seeking to affect their audience with a sharply limited number of words.

Short stories' focused use of language can make the experience of reading them wonderfully intense. Furthermore, you may end up considering important human issues as you try to interpret the "glimpses" they provide. Precisely because short stories "tell as little as they dare," they offer you much to ponder as you proceed to write about them.

In discussing the writing process, we refer often to the three stories that follow. The stories tell of the work that a person does or does not do to care for others. The first story, "The Use of Force," is by a writer more known for his poetry, William Carlos Williams (1883–1963). Even as he produced literature, Williams served as a doctor in his hometown of Rutherford, New Jersey, as well as in the nearby city of Paterson. The story presented here, which appeared in Williams's 1938 collection, *Life along the Passaic River*, is one of several based on his medical work during the Great Depression. The second selection, "A Visit of Charity," is by a pioneer of the modern American short story, Eudora Welty (1909–2001), who spent most of her life in her hometown of Jackson, Mississippi. The final story, "The Man in the Well," is the most recent, having first appeared in 1995 in the magazine *Chicago Review*. Its author, Ira Sher, is a novelist and Web designer as well as a writer of short fiction. He read the story aloud on the June 21, 1996, episode of the radio series *This American Life*; the broadcast is available on the Web.

WILLIAM CARLOS WILLIAMS
The Use of Force

They were new patients to me, all I had was the name, Olson. Please come down as soon as you can, my daughter is very sick. When I arrived I was met by the mother, a big startled looking woman, very clean and apologetic who merely said, Is this the doctor? and let me in. In the back, she added. You must excuse us, doctor, we have her in the kitchen where it is warm. It is very damp here sometimes.

The child was fully dressed and sitting on her father's lap near the kitchen table. He tried to get up, but I motioned for him not to bother, took off my overcoat and started to look things over. I could see that they were all very nervous, eyeing me up and down distrustfully. As often, in such cases, they weren't telling me more than they had to, it was up to me to tell them; that's why they were spending three dollars on me.

The child was fairly eating me up with her cold, steady eyes, and no expression to her face whatever. She did not move and seemed, inwardly, quiet; an unusually attractive little thing, and as strong as a heifer in appearance. But her face was flushed, she was breathing rapidly, and I realized that she had a high fever. She had magnificent blond hair, in profusion. One of those picture children often reproduced in advertising leaflets and the photogravure sections of the Sunday papers.

She's had a fever for three days, began the father and we don't know what it comes from. My wife has given her things, you know, like people do, but it don't do no good. And there's been a lot of sickness around. So we tho't you'd better look her over and tell us what is the matter.

As doctors often do I took a trial shot at it as a point of departure. Has she   5 had a sore throat?

Both parents answered me together, No . . . No, she says her throat don't hurt her.

Does your throat hurt you? added the mother to the child. But the little girl's expression didn't change nor did she move her eyes from my face.

Have you looked?

I tried to, said the mother, but I couldn't see.

As it happens we had been having a number of cases of diphtheria in the   10 school to which the child went during that month and we were all, quite apparently, thinking of that, though no one had as yet spoken of the thing.

Well, I said, suppose we take a look at the throat first. I smiled in my best professional manner and asking for the child's first name I said, come on, Mathilda, open your mouth and let's take a look at your throat.

Nothing doing.

Aw, come on, I coaxed, just open your mouth wide and let me take a look. Look, I said opening both hands wide, I haven't anything in my hands. Just open up and let me see.

Such a nice man, put in the mother. Look how kind he is to you. Come on, do what he tells you to, he won't hurt you.

At that I ground my teeth in disgust. If only they wouldn't use the word "hurt" I might be able to get somewhere. But I did not allow myself to be hurried or disturbed but speaking quietly and slowly I approached the child again. 15

As I moved my chair a little nearer suddenly with one catlike movement both her hands clawed instinctively for my eyes and she almost reached them too. In fact she knocked my glasses flying and they fell, though unbroken, several feet away from me on the kitchen floor.

Both the mother and father almost turned themselves inside out in embarrassment and apology. You bad girl, said the mother, taking her and shaking her by one arm. Look what you've done. The nice man . . .

For heaven's sake, I broke in. Don't call me a nice man to her. I'm here to look at her throat on the chance that she might have diphtheria and possibly die of it. But that's nothing to her. Look here, I said to the child, we're going to look at your throat. You're old enough to understand what I'm saying. Will you open it now by yourself or shall we have to open it for you?

Not a move. Even her expression hadn't changed. Her breaths however were coming faster and faster. Then the battle began. I had to do it. I had to have a throat culture for her own protection. But first I told the parents that it was entirely up to them. I explained the danger but said that I would not insist on a throat examination so long as they would take the responsibility.

If you don't do what the doctor says you'll have to go to the hospital, the mother admonished her severely. 20

Oh yeah? I had to smile to myself. After all, I had already fallen in love with the savage brat, the parents were contemptible to me. In the ensuing struggle they grew more and more abject, crushed, exhausted while she surely rose to magnificent heights of insane fury of effort bred of her terror of me.

The father tried his best, and he was a big man but the fact that she was his daughter, his shame at her behavior and his dread of hurting her made him release her just at the critical times when I had almost achieved success, till I wanted to kill him. But his dread also that she might have diphtheria made him tell me to go on, go on though he himself was almost fainting, while the mother moved back and forth behind us raising and lowering her hands in an agony of apprehension.

Put her in front of you on your lap, I ordered, and hold both her wrists.

But as soon as he did the child let out a scream. Don't, you're hurting me. Let go of my hands. Let them go I tell you. Then she shrieked terrifyingly, hysterically. Stop it! Stop it! You're killing me!

Do you think she can stand it, doctor! said the mother. 25

You get out, said the husband to his wife. Do you want her to die of diphtheria?

Come on now, hold her, I said.

Then I grasped the child's head with my left hand and tried to get the wooden tongue depressor between her teeth. She fought, with clenched teeth, desperately! But now I also had grown furious — at a child. I tried to hold myself down but I couldn't. I know how to expose a throat for inspection. And I did my best. When finally I got the wooden spatula behind the last teeth and just the point of it into the mouth cavity, she opened up for an instant but before I could see anything she came down again and gripped the wooden blade between her molars. She reduced it to splinters before I could get it out again.

Aren't you ashamed, the mother yelled at her. Aren't you ashamed to act like that in front of the doctor?

Get me a smooth-handled spoon of some sort, I told the mother. We're going through with this. The child's mouth was already bleeding. Her tongue was cut and she was screaming in wild hysterical shrieks. Perhaps I should have desisted and come back in an hour or more. No doubt it would have been better. But I have seen at least two children lying dead in bed of neglect in such cases, and feeling that I must get a diagnosis now or never I went at it again. But the worst of it was that I too had got beyond reason. I could have torn the child apart in my own fury and enjoyed it. It was a pleasure to attack her. My face was burning with it.

The damned little brat must be protected against her own idiocy, one says to one's self at such times. Others must be protected against her. It is a social necessity. And all these things are true. But a blind fury, a feeling of adult shame, bred of a longing for muscular release are the operatives. One goes on to the end.

In the final unreasoning assault I overpowered the child's neck and jaws. I forced the heavy silver spoon back of her teeth and down her throat till she gagged. And there it was—both tonsils covered with membrane. She had fought valiantly to keep me from knowing her secret. She had been hiding that sore throat for three days at least and lying to her parents in order to escape just such an outcome as this.

Now truly she was furious. She had been on the defensive before but now she attacked. Tried to get off her father's lap and fly at me while tears of defeat blinded her eyes.   *[1938]*

EUDORA WELTY
A Visit of Charity

It was mid-morning—a very cold, bright day. Holding a potted plant before her, a girl of fourteen jumped off the bus in front of the Old Ladies' Home, on the outskirts of town. She wore a red coat, and her straight yellow hair was hanging down loose from the pointed white cap all the little girls were wearing that year. She stopped for a moment beside one of the prickly dark shrubs with which the city had beautified the Home, and then proceeded slowly toward the building, which was of whitewashed brick and reflected the winter sunlight like a block of ice. As she walked vaguely up the steps she shifted the small pot from hand to hand; then she had to set it down and remove her mittens before she could open the heavy door.

"I'm a Campfire Girl. . . . I have to pay a visit to some old lady," she told the nurse at the desk. This was a woman in a white uniform who looked as if she were cold; she had close-cut hair which stood up on the very top of her head exactly like a sea wave. Marian, the little girl, did not tell her that this visit would give her a minimum of only three points in her score.

"Acquainted with any of our residents?" asked the nurse. She lifted one eyebrow and spoke like a man.

"With any old ladies? No—but—that is, any of them will do," Marian stammered. With her free hand she pushed her hair behind her ears, as she did when it was time to study Science.

The nurse shrugged and rose. "You have a nice _multiflora cineraria°_ there," 5 she remarked as she walked ahead down the hall of closed doors to pick out an old lady.

There was loose, bulging linoleum on the floor. Marian felt as if she were walking on the waves, but the nurse paid no attention to it. There was a smell in the hall like the interior of a clock. Everything was silent until, behind one of the doors, an old lady of some kind cleared her throat like a sheep bleating. This decided the nurse. Stopping in her tracks, she first extended her arm, bent her elbow, and leaned forward from the hips—all to examine the watch strapped to her wrist; then she gave a loud double-rap on the door.

"There are two in each room," the nurse remarked over her shoulder.

"Two what?" asked Marian without thinking. The sound like a sheep's bleating almost made her turn around and run back.

One old woman was pulling the door open in short, gradual jerks, and when she saw the nurse a strange smile forced her old face dangerously awry. Marian, suddenly propelled by the strong, impatient arm of the nurse, saw next the side-face of another old woman, even older, who was lying flat in bed with a cap on and a counterpane° drawn up to her chin.

"Visitor," said the nurse, and after one more shove she was off up the hall. 10

Marian stood tongue-tied; both hands held the potted plant. The old woman, still with that terrible, square smile (which was a smile of welcome) stamped on her bony face, was waiting. . . . Perhaps she said something. The old woman in bed said nothing at all, and she did not look around.

Suddenly Marian saw a hand, quick as a bird claw, reach up in the air and pluck the white cap off her head. At the same time, another claw to match drew her all the way into the room, and the next moment the door closed behind her.

"My, my, my," said the old lady at her side.

Marian stood enclosed by a bed, a washstand, and a chair; the tiny room had altogether too much furniture. Everything smelled wet—even the bare floor. She held on to the back of the chair, which was wicker and felt soft and damp. Her heart beat more and more slowly, her hands got colder and colder, and she could not hear whether the old women were saying anything or not.

multiflora cineraria: A houseplant with brightly colored flowers and heart-shaped leaves.
counterpane: Bedspread.

She could not see them very clearly. How dark it was! The window shade was down, and the only door was shut. Marian looked at the ceiling. . . . It was like being caught in a robbers' cave, just before one was murdered.

"Did you come to be our little girl for a while?" the first robber asked.   15

Then something was snatched from Marian's hand — the little potted plant.

"Flowers!" screamed the old woman. She stood holding the pot in an undecided way. "Pretty flowers," she added.

Then the old woman in bed cleared her throat and spoke. "They are not pretty," she said, still without looking around, but very distinctly.

Marian suddenly pitched against the chair and sat down in it.

"Pretty flowers," the first old woman insisted. "Pretty — pretty . . ."   20

Marian wished she had the little pot back for just a moment — she had forgotten to look at the plant herself before giving it away. What did it look like?

"Stinkweeds," said the other old woman sharply. She had a bunchy white forehead and red eyes like a sheep. Now she turned them toward Marian. The fogginess seemed to rise in her throat again, and she bleated, "Who — are — you?"

To her surprise, Marian could not remember her name. "I'm a Campfire Girl," she said finally.

"Watch out for the germs," said the old woman like a sheep, not addressing anyone.

"One came out last month to see us," said the first old woman.   25

A sheep or a germ? wondered Marian dreamily, holding on to the chair.

"Did not!" cried the other old woman.

"Did so! Read to us out of the Bible, and we enjoyed it!" screamed the first.

"Who enjoyed it!" said the woman in bed. Her mouth was unexpectedly small and sorrowful, like a pet's.

"We enjoyed it," insisted the other. "You enjoyed it — I enjoyed it."   30

"We all enjoyed it," said Marian, without realizing that she had said a word.

The first old woman had just finished putting the potted plant high, high on the top of the wardrobe, where it could hardly be seen from below. Marian wondered how she had ever succeeded in placing it there, how she could ever have reached so high.

"You mustn't pay any attention to old Addie," she now said to the little girl. "She's ailing today."

"Will you shut your mouth?" said the woman in bed. "I am not."

"You're a story."   35

"I can't stay but a minute — really, I can't," said Marian suddenly. She looked down at the wet floor and thought that if she were sick in here they would have to let her go.

With much to-do the first old woman sat down in a rocking chair — still another piece of furniture! — and began to rock. With the fingers of one hand she touched a very dirty cameo pin on her chest. "What do you do at school?" she asked.

"I don't know . . ." said Marian. She tried to think but she could not.

"Oh, but the flowers are beautiful," the old woman whispered. She seemed to rock faster and faster; Marian did not see how anyone could rock so fast.

"Ugly," said the woman in bed.   40

"If we bring flowers — " Marian began, and then fell silent. She had almost said that if Campfire Girls brought flowers to the Old Ladies' Home, the visit would count one extra point, and if they took a Bible with them on the bus and read it to the old ladies, it counted double. But the old woman had not listened, anyway; she was rocking and watching the other one, who watched back from the bed.

"Poor Addie is ailing. She has to take medicine — see?" she said, pointing a horny finger at a row of bottles on the table, and rocking so high that her black comfort shoes lifted off the floor like a little child's.

"I am no more sick than you are," said the woman in bed.

"Oh, yes you are!"

"I just got more sense than you have, that's all," said the other old woman,   45 nodding her head.

"That's only the contrary way she talks when *you all* come," said the first old lady with sudden intimacy. She stopped the rocker with a neat pat of her feet and leaned toward Marian. Her hand reached over — it felt like a petunia leaf, clinging and just a little sticky.

"Will you hush! Will you hush!" cried the other one.

Marian leaned back rigidly in her chair.

"When I was a little girl like you, I went to school and all," said the old woman in the same intimate, menacing voice. "Not here — another town . . ."

"Hush!" said the sick woman. "You never went to school. You never   50 came and you never went. You never were anything — only here. You never were born! You don't know anything. Your head is empty, your heart and hands and your old black purse are all empty, even that little old box that you brought with you you brought empty — you showed it to me. And yet you talk, talk, talk, talk, talk all the time until I think I'm losing my mind! Who are you? You're a stranger — a perfect stranger! Don't you know you're a stranger? Is it possible that they have actually done a thing like this to anyone — sent them in a stranger to talk, and rock, and tell away her whole long rigmarole? Do they seriously suppose that I'll be able to keep it up, day in, day out, night in, night out, living in the same room with a terrible old woman — forever?"

Marian saw the old woman's eyes grow bright and turn toward her. This old woman was looking at her with despair and calculation in her face. Her small lips suddenly dropped apart, and exposed a half circle of false teeth with tan gums.

"Come here, I want to tell you something," she whispered. "Come here!"

Marian was trembling, and her heart nearly stopped beating altogether for a moment.

"Now, now, Addie," said the first old woman. "That's not polite. Do you know what's really the matter with old Addie today?" She, too, looked at Marian; one of her eyelids dropped low.

"The matter?" the child repeated stupidly. "What's the matter with her?"   55

"Why, she's mad because it's her birthday!" said the first old woman, beginning to rock again and giving a little crow as though she had answered her own riddle.

"It is not, it is not!" screamed the old woman in bed. "It is not my birthday, no one knows when that is but myself, and will you please be quiet and say nothing more, or I'll go straight out of my mind!" She turned her eyes toward Marian again, and presently she said in the soft, foggy voice, "When the worst comes to the worst, I ring this bell, and the nurse comes." One of her hands was drawn out from under the patched counterpane — a thin little hand with enormous black freckles. With a finger which would not hold still she pointed to a little bell on the table among the bottles.

"How old are you?" Marian breathed. Now she could see the old woman in bed very closely and plainly, and very abruptly, from all sides, as in dreams. She wondered about her — she wondered for a moment as though there was nothing else in the world to wonder about. It was the first time such a thing had happened to Marian.

"I won't tell!"

The old face on the pillow, where Marian was bending over it, slowly gath-   60
ered and collapsed. Soft whimpers came out of the small open mouth. It was a sheep that she sounded like — a little lamb. Marian's face drew very close, the yellow hair hung forward.

"She's crying!" She turned a bright, burning face up to the first old woman.

"That's Addie for you," the old woman said spitefully.

Marian jumped up and moved toward the door. For the second time, the claw almost touched her hair, but it was not quick enough. The little girl put her cap on.

"Well, it was a real visit," said the old woman, following Marian through the doorway and all the way out into the hall. Then from behind she suddenly clutched the child with her sharp little fingers. In an affected, high-pitched whine she cried, "Oh, little girl, have you a penny to spare for a poor old woman that's not got anything of her own? We don't have a thing in the world — not a penny for candy — not a thing! Little girl, just a nickel — a penny —"

Marian pulled violently against the old hands for a moment before she was   65
free. Then she ran down the hall, without looking behind her and without looking at the nurse, who was reading *Field & Stream* at her desk. The nurse, after another triple motion to consult her wrist watch, asked automatically the question put to visitors in all institutions: "Won't you stay and have dinner with *us*?"

Marian never replied. She pushed the heavy door open into the cold air and ran down the steps.

Under the prickly shrub she stooped and quickly, without being seen, retrieved a red apple she had hidden there.

Her yellow hair under the white cap, her scarlet coat, her bare knees all flashed in the sunlight as she ran to meet the big bus rocketing through the street.

"Wait for me!" she shouted. As though at an imperial command, the bus ground to a stop.

She jumped on and took a big bite out of the apple.]   ⟨[1941]⟩   70

IRA SHER
The Man in the Well

I was nine when I discovered the man in the well in an abandoned farm-lot near my home. I was with a group of friends, playing hide and go seek or something when I found the well, and then I heard the voice of the man in the well calling out for help.

I think it's important that we decided not to help him. Everyone, like myself, was probably on the verge of fetching a rope, or asking where we could find a ladder, but then we looked around at each other and it was decided. I don't remember if we told ourselves a reason why we couldn't help him, but we had decided then. Because of this, I never went very close to the lip of the well, or I only came up on my hands and knees, so that he couldn't see me; and just as we wouldn't allow him to see us, I know that none of us ever saw the man in the well — the well was too dark for that, too deep, even when the sun was high up, angling light down the stone sides like golden hair.

I remember that we were still full of games and laughter when we called down to him. He had heard us shouting while we were playing, and he had been hollering for us to come; he was so relieved at that moment.

"God, get me out. I've been here for days." He must have known we were children, because he immediately instructed us to "go get a ladder, get help."

At first afraid to disobey the voice from the man in the well, we turned   5
around and actually began to walk toward the nearest house, which was Arthur's. But along the way we slowed down, and then we stopped, and after waiting what seemed like a good while, we quietly came back to the well.

We stood or lay around the lip, listening for maybe half an hour, and then Arthur, after some hesitation, called down, "What's your name?" This, after all, seemed like the most natural question.

The man answered back immediately, "Do you have the ladder?"

We all looked at Arthur, and he called back down, "No, we couldn't find one."

Now that we had established some sort of a dialogue, everyone had questions he or she wanted to ask the man in the well, but the man wouldn't stop speaking:

"Go tell your parents there's someone in this well. If they have a rope or a   10
ladder . . ." he trailed off. His voice was raw and sometimes he would cough. "Just tell your parents."

We were quiet, but this time no one stood up or moved. Someone, I think little Jason, called down, "Hello. Is it dark?" and then, after a moment, "Can you see the sky?"

He didn't answer but instead told us to go again.

When we were quiet for a bit, he called to see if we had gone.

After a pause, Wendy crawled right to the edge so that her hair lifted slightly in the updraft. "Is there any water down there?"

"Have they gone for help?" he asked.   15

She looked around at us, and then she called down, "Yes, they're all gone now. Isn't there any water down there?" I don't think anyone smiled at how easy it was to deceive him — this was too important. "Isn't there?" she said again.

"No," he said. "It's very dry." He cleared his throat. "Do you think it will rain?" She stood up and took in the whole sky with her blue eyes, making sure. "No, I don't think so." We heard him coughing in the well, and we waited for a while, thinking about him waiting in the well.

Resting on the grass and cement by the well, I tried to picture him. I tried to imagine the gesture of his hand reaching to cover his mouth, each time he coughed. Or perhaps he was too tired to make that gesture, each time. After an hour, he began calling again, but for some reason we didn't want to answer. We got up and began running, filling up with panic as we moved, until we were racing across the ruts of the old field. I kept turning, stumbling as I looked behind. Perhaps he had heard us getting up and running away from the well. Only Wendy stayed by the well for a while, watching us run as his calling grew louder and wilder, until finally she ran, too, and then we were all far away.

The next morning we came back, most of us carrying bread or fruit or something to eat in our pockets. Arthur brought a canvas bag from his house and a plastic jug of water.

When we got to the well we stood around quietly for a moment listening   20
for him.

"Maybe he's asleep," Wendy said.

We sat down around the mouth of the well on the old concrete slab, warming in the sun and coursing with ants and tiny insects. Aaron called down then, when everyone was comfortable, and the man answered right away, as if he had been listening to us the whole time.

"Did your parents get help?"

Arthur kneeled at the edge of the well and called "Watch out," and then he let the bag fall after holding it out for a moment, maybe for the man to see. It hit the ground more quickly than I had expected; that, combined with a feeling that he could hear everything we said, made him suddenly closer, as if he might be able to see us. I wanted to be very quiet, so that if he heard or saw anyone, he would not notice me. The man in the well started coughing, and Arthur volunteered, "There's some water in the bag. We all brought something."

We could hear him moving around down there. After a few minutes he   25
asked us, "When are they coming? What did your parents say?"

We all looked at each other, aware that he couldn't address anyone in particular. He must have understood this, because he called out in his thin, groping voice, "What are your names?"

No one answered until Aaron, who was the oldest, said, "My father said he's coming, with the police. And he knows what to do." We admired Aaron very much for coming up with this, on the spot.

"Are they on their way?" the man in the well asked. We could hear that he was eating.

"My father said don't worry, because he's coming with the police."

Little Jason came up next to Aaron and asked, "What's your name?" be-   30
cause we still didn't know what to call him. When we talked among ourselves, he had simply become "the man."

He didn't answer, so Jason asked him how old he was, and then Grace came up too and asked him something, I don't remember. We all asked such stupid questions, and he wouldn't answer anyone. Finally, we all stopped talking, and we lay down on the cement.

It was a hot day, so after a while, Grace got up, and then Little Jason and another young boy, Robert I think, and went to town to sit in the cool movie theater. That was what we did most afternoons back then. After an hour everyone had left except Wendy and myself, and I was beginning to think I would go, too.

He called up to us all of a sudden. "Are they coming now?"

"Yes," Wendy said, looking at me, and I nodded my head. She sounded certain: "I think they're almost here. Aaron said his dad is almost here."

As soon as she said it she was sorry, because she'd broken one of the rules.   35
I could see it on her face, eyes filling with space as she moved back from the well. Now he had one of our names. She said "They're going to come" to cover up the mistake, but there it was, and there was nothing to do about it.

The man in the well didn't say anything for a few minutes. Then he surprised us again by asking, "Is it going to rain?"

Wendy stood up and turned around like she had done the other day, but the sky was clear. "No," she said.

Then he asked again, "They're coming, you said. Aaron's dad," and he shouted, "Right?" so that we jumped, and stood up, and began running away, just as we had the day before. We could hear him shouting for a while, and we were afraid someone might hear. I thought that toward the end maybe he had said he was sorry. But I never asked Wendy what she thought he'd said.

Everyone was there again on the following morning. It was all I could think about during supper the night before, and then the anticipation in the morning over breakfast. My mother was very upset with something at the time. I could hear her weeping at night in her room downstairs, and the stubborn murmur of my father. There was a feeling to those days, months actually, that I can't describe without resorting to the man in the well, as if through a great whispering, like a gathering of clouds, or the long sound, the turbulent wreck of the ocean.

At the well we put together the things to eat we had smuggled out, but we   40
hadn't even gotten them all in the bag when the voice of the man in the well soared out sharply, "They're on their way, now?"

We stood very still, so that he couldn't hear us, but I knew what was coming and I couldn't do anything to soften or blur the words of the voice.

"Aaron," he pronounced, and I had imagined him practicing that voice all night long, and holding it in his mouth so that he wouldn't let it slip away in his sleep. Aaron lost all the color in his face, and he looked at us with suspicion, as if we had somehow taken on a part of the man in the well. I didn't even glance at Wendy. We were both too embarrassed — neither of us said anything; we were all quiet then. Arthur finished assembling the bag, and we could see his hands shaking as he dropped it into the well. We heard the man in the well moving around.

After ten minutes or so, Grace called down to him, "What's your name?" but someone pulled her back from the well, and we became silent again. Today the question humiliated us with its simplicity.

There was no sound for a while from the well, except for the cloth noises and the scraping the man in the well made as he moved around. Then he called out, in a pleasant voice, "Aaron, what do you think my name is?"

Aaron, who had been very still this whole time, looked around at all of us   45
again. We knew he was afraid; his fingers were pulling with a separate life at the collar of his shirt, and maybe because she felt badly for him, Wendy answered instead: "Is your name Charles?" It sounded inane, but the man in the well answered.

"No," the man said.

She thought for a moment. "Edgar."

"No, no."

Little Jason called out, "David?"

"No," the man in the well said.   50

Then Aaron, who had been absolutely quiet, said "Arthur" in a small, clear voice, and we all started. I could see Arthur was furious, but Aaron was older and bigger than he was, and nothing could be said or done without giving himself, his name, away; we knew the man in the well was listening for the changes in our breath, anything. Aaron didn't look at Arthur, or anyone, and then he began giving all of our names, one at a time. We all watched him, trembling, our faces the faces I had seen pasted on the spectators in the freak tent when the circus had come to town. We were watching such a deformity take place before our eyes; and I remember the spasm of anger when he said my name, and felt the man in the well soak it up — because the man in the well understood. The man in the well didn't say anything, now.

When Aaron was done, we all waited for the man in the well to speak up. I stood on one leg, then the other, and eventually I sat down. We had to wait for an hour, and today no one wanted to leave to lie in the shade or hide in the velvet movie seats.

At last, the man in the well said, "All right, then. Arthur. What do you think I look like?" We heard him cough a couple of times, and then a sound like the smacking of lips. Arthur, who was sitting on the ground with his chin propped on his fists, didn't say anything. How could he — I knew I couldn't answer, myself, if the man in the well called me by name. He called a few of us, and I watched the shudder move from face to face.

Then he was quiet for a while. It was afternoon now, and the light was changing, withdrawing from the well. It was as if the well was filling up with earth. The man in the well moved around a bit, and then he called Jason. He asked, "How old do you think I am, Jason?" He didn't seem to care that no one would answer, or he seemed to expect that no one would. He said, "Wendy. Are they coming now? Is Aaron's dad coming now?" He walked around a bit, we heard him rummage in the bag of food, and he said, "All right. What's my name?" He used everyone's name; he asked everyone. When he said my name, I felt the water clouding my eyes, and I wanted to throw stones, dirt down the well to crush out his voice. But we couldn't do anything, none of us did — because then he would know.

In the evening we could tell he was getting tired. He wasn't saying much,   55
and seemed to have lost interest in us. Before we left that day, as we were rising quietly and looking at the dark shadows of the trees we had to move through to reach our homes, he said, "Why didn't you tell anyone?" He coughed. "Didn't you want to tell anyone?" Perhaps he heard the hesitation in our breaths, but he wasn't going to help us now. It was almost night then, and we were spared the detail of having to see and read each other's faces.

That night it rained, and I listened to the rain on the roof and my mother sobbing, downstairs, until I fell asleep. After that we didn't play by the well anymore; even when we were much older, we didn't go back. I will never go back.   [1995]

▉ A WRITING EXERCISE

Once you have read the three stories, freewrite your reaction to them, spending at least ten minutes on each. For each story, note any personal experience affecting your response as well as one or more questions that you have about the story even after you have finished reading it. Remember that posing questions is a good way to prepare for a formal paper on the story, enabling you to identify issues worth writing about at length.

Students' Personal Responses to the Stories

Here is some freewriting that students did about the three stories you have just read.

Alison Caldwell on Williams's "The Use of Force":

> I can understand why the doctor got furious at the girl. He was
> asking her to open her mouth for her own good, and she started
> physically attacking him. On the other hand, I can sympathize with the
> girl. I can remember being scared of doctors when I was that young.
> I dreaded having to get various shots. The girl in the story is probably
> not used to seeing doctors in the first place, so this one is bound to

seem especially frightening to her. I can sympathize with her parents, too, because they only want what's best for their daughter and they're doing everything they can to assist the doctor. I was kind of shocked to see the doctor fuming with anger at them. Of course, his reaction to them is one of the interesting things about this story, along with the strange respect that he feels in a way for the girl. I guess the biggest issue for me is what we're to make of the doctor's sort of identification with the girl even as he gets mad at her and she strongly resists him. There's some connection between these two characters that I need to figure out. I notice that at the end her eyes are "blinded" and not long before he's possessed by a "blind fury." Probably I should explore this particular similarity more.

Monica Albertson on Welty's "A Visit of Charity":

I'm not sure which character I should be sympathizing with in Welty's story. Right away I disliked the girl because she wasn't really interested in seeing the old women. I don't know why the story is called "A Visit of Charity," since she just wanted to get more points. And yet I have to admit that when I was younger I was sort of like her. I remember one time when my church youth group had to sing Christmas carols at an old folks' home, and I was uneasy about having to meet all these ancient men and women I didn't know, some of whom could barely walk or talk. It's funny, because I was always comfortable around my grandparents, but I have to confess that being around all those old people at once spooked me a little. I smiled a lot at them and joined in the singing and helped hand out candy canes afterward. But I couldn't wait to leave. Once I did, I felt proud of myself for going there, but I guess I also felt a little guilty because I didn't really want to be there at all. So, maybe I'm being hypocritical when I criticize the girl in Welty's story for insensitivity. Anyway, I expected that Welty would present in a good light any old women that Marian encountered, just to emphasize that Marian was being unkind and that it's really sad for people to have to live in a retirement home (or senior citizens center or whatever they're calling such places nowadays). And yet the two old women she meets are cranky and unpleasant. Even the receptionist doesn't come off all that good. If I were Marian, I probably would have left even sooner than she did! Maybe Welty didn't want us to sympathize with anyone in the story, and maybe that's OK. I tend to want a story to make at least some of the characters sympathetic, but maybe it's unfair of me to demand that. Still, I'm wondering if I'm not appreciating Welty's characters enough. When the two old women argue, should we side with one of them, or are we supposed to be bothered by them both? Are we supposed to think any better of the girl by the time she leaves? The apple she eats immediately made me think of the Adam and Eve story, but I don't know what I'm supposed to do with that parallel.

Todd Mayes on Sher's "The Man in the Well":

> I found the situation in this story chilling. There's a mysterious man trapped in a well, the children mysteriously fail to go for help, and at the end of the story I'm not sure what exactly happens to the man, although I get the sense that he's died alone in the well. Because the other characters are children, I started off thinking they are pure and innocent, but gradually I wonder whether they are being cruel in not rescuing the man. Some of them even go off to the movies, which seems coldly indifferent to him. I think about the boys in the novel *Lord of the Flies*, which I read in high school. They turn on each other and do savage things. The children in this story, though, do not seem plainly evil toward the man, and in fact they even seem kind of frightened of him, especially when he learns their names. That's another disturbing thing about the story — why does Aaron give him the names of all the other children? Wendy blurted out a name almost by accident, but Aaron seems deliberate. But I wonder, too, if the man is all that innocent. At any rate, I learn hardly anything about him. He's never physically revealed. He's just a voice, and near the end he seems to taunt the children by speaking all their names. Maybe he needed to do more to convince them that he wasn't some kind of monster. Even so, I get the impression that the narrator of the story still feels guilty about the children's behavior. Why does he recall the story in the first place, especially if it happened many years ago? He says at the end that "I will never go back," but he does go back in the sense that he revisits the episode in his mind, as if he can't shake the feeling that he and the others should have treated the man better instead of letting him die.

Before any of these students could produce a full-length paper on the story they freewrote on, they had to do more writing and thinking. Yet simply by jotting down some observations and questions, they provided themselves with seeds of a paper. Compare your thoughts to theirs. To what extent did you react to the stories as they did? In what ways, if any, did your responses differ from theirs? What would you say to them if they were your classmates, especially as they proceeded to write more developed arguments?

The Elements of Short Fiction

Whether discussing them in class or writing about them, you will improve your ability to analyze stories like Williams's, Welty's, and Sher's if you grow familiar with typical elements of short fiction. These elements include plot and structure, point of view, characters, setting, imagery, language, and theme.

PLOT AND STRUCTURE

For many readers, the most important element in any work of fiction is plot. As they turn the pages of a short story, their main question is, What will happen next? In reading Williams's story, probably you were curious, as the narrator is, to know whether the girl is concealing an infected throat. In reading Welty's story, quite possibly you wanted to know how Marian's visit to the rest home would turn out. In reading Sher's story, most likely you hoped to learn whether the children would ever help rescue the man. Furthermore, if a friend unfamiliar with Williams's, Welty's, and Sher's stories asked you what each was about, you would probably begin by summarizing their plots.

■ A WRITING EXERCISE

In one or two sentences, summarize what you take to be the plot of Welty's story. Then read the following three summaries of her plot, which were written by three other students. Finally, list a few similarities and differences you notice as you compare the three summaries with one another and with yours.

> *Jerry's summary:* A girl visits an Old Ladies' Home just so she can add some points to her record as a Campfire Girl. Much to her dismay, she encounters two roommates who fight a lot with each other, and their unpleasantness eventually causes her to flee.

> *Carla's summary:* A young girl named Marian, who starts off basically interested in only herself, is forced to consider the suffering of old people when she spends time with two old women at a retirement home. Eventually she leaves in fear and disgust, but as she leaves she eats an apple, which implies that she is no longer as innocent as she was and that she is maybe a little more prepared to acknowledge what goes on in the wider world.

> *Matt's summary:* A really insensitive girl meets two old women, and though in many respects she is put off by both of them, she can't help being intrigued by the one who is sick in bed. Maybe she becomes more aware of mortality at this point, but if so, she has trouble facing it and in the end runs away.

To an extent, the students point out different things. For instance, only Carla mentions the apple, and only Matt observes that Marian is momentarily interested in the bedridden woman. Also, these two students are more willing than Jerry is to speculate about Marian's final state of mind. At the same time, Carla's summary ends on a slightly more upbeat note than Matt's. She emphasizes that Marian has perhaps become more open-minded, while Matt concludes by pointing out that Marian nevertheless flees.

Any summary of Welty's story will be somewhat personal. It is bound to reflect the reader's own sense of who the story's main characters are, which of their actions are significant, how these actions are connected, and what principles these actions illustrate. Were you to compare summaries with Jerry, Carla, and Matt in class, each of you might learn much from discussing experiences and beliefs that influenced your accounts.

Even so, you do not have to treat every summary of Welty's story as merely subjective. Probably some accounts of it are more attentive than others to actual details of Welty's text. If a reader declared that Marian loves visiting the Old Ladies' Home, many other readers would rightfully disagree, pointing out that Marian dashes off. If you discussed Welty's story with Jerry, Carla, and Matt, the four of you would probably consider which summary of it is best. Furthermore, each of you would probably argue for your respective candidates by pointing to specific passages in Welty's text. Ultimately, you might still prefer your own summary. On the other hand, you might wind up adopting someone else's, or you might want to combine aspects of various summaries you have read.

Jerry's, Carla's, and Matt's summaries do have some features in common, indicating that there are certain basic things for you to consider when you examine a short story's plot. For example, plots usually center on human beings, who can be seen as engaging in actions, as being acted upon, or both. In recounting the plot of Welty's story, each of the three students focuses on Marian. Furthermore, each describes her as acting (she "encounters," "flees," "spends time," "leaves," "eats," "meets," "runs away") *and* as being affected by other forces (the "unpleasantness" of the old women "causes her to flee"; she is "forced to consider" their pain; she is "put off" as well as "intrigued"). Also, most short stories put characters into a high-pressure situation, whether for dark or comic effect. To earn the merit points she desires, Marian has to contend with the feuding roommates.

Besides physical events, a short story may involve psychological developments. Each student here points to mental changes in Welty's heroine. According to Jerry, Marian experiences "dismay." According to Carla, she "starts off basically interested in only herself" but perhaps becomes "a little more prepared to acknowledge what goes on in the wider world." According to Matt, she starts off "really insensitive," perhaps grows "more aware of mortality," yet then "has trouble facing it." Many stories do show characters undergoing complete or partial conversions. Meanwhile, a number of stories include characters who stick to their beliefs but gain a new perspective on them.

Jerry, Carla, and Matt connect Marian's visit to the rest home with her subsequent behavior. Like most plot summaries, in other words, theirs bring up relations of cause and effect. The novelist and short-story writer E. M. Forster refers to cause and effect in his famous definition of plot. To Forster, a plot is not simply one incident after another, such as "the king died and then the queen died." Rather, it is a situation or a whole chain of events in which there are reasons *why* characters behave as they do. Forster's example: "The king died, and then the queen died of grief."

Writers of short stories do not always make cause and effect immediately clear. Another possible plot, Forster suggests, is "The queen died, no one knew why, until it was discovered that it was through grief at the death of the king." In this scenario, all of the characters lack information about the queen's true psychology for a while, and perhaps the reader is in the dark as well. Indeed, many short stories leave the reader ignorant for a spell. For instance, only near the conclusion of her story does Welty reveal that before entering the rest home, Marian had put an apple under the shrub. Why does the author withhold this key fact from you? Perhaps Welty was silent about the apple because, had she reported it right away, its echoes of Eve might have overshadowed your interpretation of the story as you read. Worth considering are issues of effect: what the characters' behavior makes you think of them and what impact the author's strategies have on you.

When you summarize a story's plot, you may be inclined to put events in chronological order. But remember that short stories are not always linear. Often they depart from strict chronology, moving back and forth in time. Consider the following opening sentences, both of which deal with a funeral ceremony. They come from two of the stories featured in this book, William Faulkner's "A Rose for Emily," reprinted in Chapter 11, and Andre Dubus's "Killings," reprinted in Chapter 13.

> When Miss Emily Grierson died, our whole town went to her funeral: the men through a sort of respectful affection for a fallen monument, the women mostly out of curiosity to see the inside of her house, which no one save an old manservant—a combined gardener and cook—had seen in at least ten years.

> On the August morning when Matt Fowler buried his youngest son, Frank, who had lived for twenty-one years, eight months, and four days, Matt's older son, Steve, turned to him as the family left the grave and walked between their friends, and said: "I should kill him."

Probably Faulkner's opening makes you wonder why Emily Grierson kept people out of her house. Probably Dubus's opening makes you wonder how Frank died and whom Steve means by "him." Eventually the authors do answer these questions by moving their stories back in time. Faulkner presents episodes in Emily's life, returning only at the end of the story to the time after her death. Dubus spends much of his story's first half on flashbacks that inform you about Frank's murder; then, Dubus returns to the present and shows Matt's effort to avenge his son. Many literary critics use the term discourse for a text's actual ordering of events. Chronologically, Emily Grierson's funeral comes near the end of Faulkner's short story. Yet it appears at the beginning of his discourse. Chronologically, Frank's funeral is sandwiched between several events. Yet it is the start of Dubus's discourse.

Alice Adams, author of many short stories, offers a more detailed outline of their typical **structure**. She has proposed the formula ABDCE: these letters stand for **action, background, development, climax**, and **ending**. More precisely, Adams has said that she sometimes begins a story with an action, follows that action with some background information, and then moves the plot forward in time through a major turning point and toward some sort of resolution. Not all writers of short stories follow this scheme. In fact, Adams does not always stick to it. Certainly a lot of short stories combine her background and development stages, moving the plot along while offering details of their characters' pasts. And sometimes a story will have several turning points rather than a single distinct climax. But by keeping Adams's formula in mind, if only as a common way to construct short stories, you will be better prepared to recognize how a story departs from chronological order.

The first paragraph of Welty's story seems to be centered on *action*. Marian arrives at the Old Ladies' Home and prepares to enter it. Even so, Welty provides some basic information in this paragraph, describing Marian and the rest home as if the reader is unfamiliar with both. Yet only in the second paragraph do you learn Marian's name and the purpose of her visit. Therefore, Welty can be said to obey Adams's formula, beginning with *action* and then moving to *background*. Note, however, that the second paragraph features *development* as well. By explaining to the receptionist who she is and why she is there, Marian takes a step closer to the central event, her meeting with the two roommates. The remainder of the story keeps moving forward in time.

Williams's story "The Use of Force" begins with a paragraph that establishes the *background* to the narrator's visit. Nevertheless, the paragraph is brief and the background slight, with the narrator acknowledging that "They were new patients to me, all I had was the name, Olson." Then we are quickly plunged into *action*, as the narrator starts to describe his experience at the Olson house. Even as the story proceeds, we continue to receive some background information, as when the narrator tells us of an outbreak of diphtheria at the child's school. Yet, for the most part, we sense *development* as the narrator wages an increasingly violent struggle to open the child's mouth.

Sher's story "The Man in the Well" begins by plunging you right into a scene of *action*, with the narrator and his friends discovering the title character. Although you learn that the narrator was nine years old at the time, the story provides only minimal *background* for its cast. Instead, it chiefly *develops* its plot, taking you through a day-by-day account of the children's interactions with the man.

What about *climax*, Adams's fourth term? Traditionally, the climax of a story has been defined as a peak moment of drama appearing near the end. Also, it is usually thought of as a point when at least one character commits a significant act, experiences a significant change, makes a significant discovery, learns a significant lesson, or perhaps does all these things. With Welty's story, you could argue that the climax is when Marian asks Addie her age, meets with refusal, sees Addie crying, and tries to bolt. Certainly this is a dramatic moment, involving intense display of emotion resulting in Marian's departure. But Welty indicates, too, that Marian here experiences inner change. When she looks on Addie "as though there was nothing else in the world to wonder about," this is "the first time such a thing had happened to Marian."

Adams's term *ending* may seem unnecessary. Why would anyone have to be reminded that stories end? Yet a story's climax may engage readers so much that they overlook whatever follows. If the climax of Welty's story is Marian's conversation with the tearful Addie, then the ending is basically in four parts: the plea that Addie's roommate makes to Marian as she is leaving; Marian's final encounter with the receptionist; Marian's retrieval of the apple; and her escape on the bus, where she bites into the apple. Keep in mind that the ending of a story may relate somehow to its beginning. The ending of Welty's "A Visit of Charity," for instance, brings the story full circle. Whereas at the start

Marian gets off a bus, hides the apple, and meets the receptionist, at the conclusion she rushes by the receptionist, recovers the apple, and boards another bus. However a story ends, ask yourself if any of the characters have changed at some point between start and finish. Does the conclusion of the story indicate that at least one person has developed in some way, or does it leave you with the feeling of lives frozen since the start? As Welty's story ends, readers may have various opinions about Marian. Some may find that she has not been changed all that much by her visit to the home, while others may feel that it has helped her mature.

A common organizational device in short stories is repetition. It takes various forms. First, a story may repeat various words; in Williams's story, for example, the word "look" appears again and again. Second, a story may repeatedly refer to a certain image. Third, a story may involve repeated actions. In Welty's "A Visit of Charity," the two roommates repeatedly argue; Marian travels by bus at the beginning and at the end; and the receptionist consults her wristwatch both when Marian arrives and when she leaves. Of course, even a story that features recurring events may eventually present something new. In Sher's story, the children's repeated encounters with the man — including their repeated unwillingness to help him escape — ends with his calling of their names and then their final departure from him.

POINT OF VIEW

A short story may be told from a particular character's perspective or **point of view**. Probably you have noticed that Williams's story is written in the **first person**; it is narrated by someone using the pronoun *I*. With every first-person story, you have to decide how much to accept the narrator's point of view, keeping in mind that the narrator may be psychologically complex. How objective does the narrator seem in depicting other people and events? In what ways, if any, do the narrator's perceptions seem influenced by his or her personal experiences, circumstances, feelings, values, and beliefs? Does the narrator seem to have changed in any way since the events recalled? How reasonable do the narrator's judgments seem? At what moments, if any, do you find yourself disagreeing with the narrator's view of things?

Not every short story is narrated by an identifiable person. Many of them are told by what has been traditionally called an **omniscient narrator**. The word *omniscient* means "all-knowing" and is often used as an adjective for God. An omniscient narrator is usually a seemingly all-knowing, objective voice. This is the kind of voice at work in Welty's story, right from the first paragraph. There, Marian is described in an authoritatively matter-of-fact tone that appears detached from her: "Holding a potted plant before her, a girl of fourteen jumped off the bus in front of the Old Ladies' Home." Keep in mind, though, that a story may rely primarily on an omniscient narrator and yet at some points seem immersed in a character's perspective. This, too, is the case with Welty's story. Consider the following passage about Marian:

> Everything smelled wet — even the bare floor. She held on to the back of the chair, which was wicker and felt soft and damp. Her heart beat more

and more slowly, her hands got colder and colder, and she could not hear whether the old women were saying anything or not. She could not see them very clearly. How dark it was! The window shade was down, and the only door was shut. Marian looked at the ceiling. . . . It was like being caught in a robbers' cave, just before one was murdered.

The passage remains in the third person, referring to "she" rather than to "I." Nevertheless, the passage seems intimately in touch with Marian's physical sensations. Indeed, the sentence "How dark it was!" seems something that Marian would say to herself. Similarly, the analogy to the robbers' cave may be Marian's own personal perception, and as such, the analogy may reveal more about her own state of mind than about the room. Many literary critics use the term free indirect style for moments like this, when a narrator otherwise omniscient conveys a particular character's viewpoint by resorting to the character's own language.

Throughout this book, we encourage you to analyze an author's strategies by considering the options that he or she faced. You may better understand a short story's point of view if you think about the available alternatives. For example, how would you have reacted to Welty's story if it had focused on Addie's perceptions more than on Marian's? How would the impact of Sher's story change if it were narrated by each of the children in turn? With Williams's story, how would you have felt if the narrator had been omniscient?

≣ A WRITING EXERCISE

Choose a passage from Williams's, Welty's, or Sher's story and rewrite it from another point of view. Then exchange your rewritten passage with a classmate's response to this assignment. Finally, write a paragraph analyzing your classmate's revision. Specifically, compare the revision with the original passage that your classmate chose, noting any differences in effect.

CHARACTERS

Although we have been discussing plots, we have also referred to the people caught up in them. Any analysis you do of a short story will reflect your understanding and evaluation of its **characters**. Rarely does the author of a story provide you with extended, enormously detailed biographies. Rather, you see the story's characters at select moments of their lives. To quote William Trevor again, the short story is "the art of the glimpse."

≣ A WRITING EXERCISE

Choose any character from the three stories featured here. Off the top of your head, jot down at least five adjectives you think apply to that character. Next, exchange lists with a classmate. When you look at your classmate's list, circle the adjective that surprises you most, even if it deals with another character. Finally, write a brief essay in which you consider how applicable that adjective is. Do you agree with your classmate that it suits the character he or she chose? Why, or why not?

You may want to judge characters according to how easily you can identify with them. Yet there is little reason for you to read works that merely reinforce your prejudices. Furthermore, you may overlook the potential richness of a story if you insist that its characters fit your usual standards of behavior. An author can teach you much by introducing you to the complexity of people you might automatically praise or condemn in real life. Many of us would immediately condemn someone who failed to help a man stuck in a well, but Sher encourages us to analyze carefully the children in his story rather than just denounce them. You may be tempted to dismiss the roommates in Welty's story as unpleasant, even "sick"; in any case, take the story as an opportunity to explore *why* women in a rest home may express discontent.

One thing to consider about the characters in a story is what each basically desires. At the beginning of Welty's story, for example, Marian is hardly visiting the Old Ladies' Home out of "charity," despite that word's presence in the story's title. Rather, Marian hopes to earn points as a Campfire Girl. Again, characters in a story may change, so consider whether the particular characters you are examining alter their thinking. Perhaps you feel that Marian's visit broadens her vision of life; then again, perhaps you conclude that she remains much the same.

Reading a short story involves relating its characters to one another. In part, you will be determining their relative importance in the story. When a particular character seems to be the story's focus, he or she is referred to as the story's **protagonist**. Many readers would say that the doctor is the protagonist of Williams's story, Marian is the protagonist of Welty's, and Sher's narrator is the protagonist of "The Man in the Well." When the protagonist is in notable conflict with another character, the latter is referred to as the **antagonist**. In Williams's story, the child seems to assume this role, since the narrator winds up fighting her. To be sure, the relationship between a protagonist and an antagonist may show nuances worth exploring. For example, Williams's narrator does not simply hate his patient. Rather, he wants to help her, and he grudgingly admires her stubbornness while harboring scorn for her parents.

Even a seemingly minor character can perform some noteworthy function in the story. Take Grace in "The Man in the Well." She is a girl the narrator identifies by name just twice, and her only specified physical action is to abandon the man for a trip to the movies. But the word *grace* has traditionally implied religious mercy, so when this character leaves the man just to pursue her own pleasure, the situation is darkly ironic.

In many short stories, characters are allies or enemies. But as the story proceeds, they may alter their relationships, forging new bonds or developing new conflicts. Although Welty's Marian initially finds both roommates unpleasant, she grows more conscious of the tension *between* them, and then for a moment she sympathizes with Addie. It is possible, too, for one character to be ambivalent about another, feeling both drawn and opposed to that person. We have already suggested that such is the case with Williams's narrator as he struggles with the child. One might argue, too, that the two roommates in Welty's story have a love-hate relationship, needing each other's company even as they bicker. As perhaps you have found in your own experience, human relationships are often far from simple. Works of literature can prove especially interesting when they suggest as much.

What power and influence people can achieve have often depended on particular traits of theirs. These include their gender, social class, race, ethnic background, nationality, sexual orientation, and the kind of work they do. Because these attributes can greatly affect a person's life, pay attention to them if an author gestures toward them in describing a character. For instance, in Williams's story, the family that the narrator visits is obviously poor, so much so that the parents call for a doctor only when they absolutely must.

Typically, characters express views of one another, and you have to decide how accurate these are. Some characters will seem wise observers of humanity. Others will strike you as making distorted statements about the world, revealing little more than their own biases and quirks. And some characters will seem to fall in the middle, coming across as partly objective and partly subjective. On occasion, you and your classmates may find yourselves debating which category a particular character fits. One interesting case is Welty's character Addie. Look again at the speech in which she berates her roommate:

> "Hush!" said the sick woman. "You never went to school. You never came and you never went. You never were anything — only here. You never were born! You don't know anything. Your head is empty, your heart and hands and your old black purse are all empty, even that little old box that you brought with you you brought empty — you showed it to me. And yet you talk, talk, talk, talk, talk all the time until I think I'm losing my mind! Who are you? You're a stranger — a perfect stranger! Don't you know you're a stranger? Is it possible that they have actually done a thing like this to anyone — sent them in a stranger to talk, and rock, and tell away her whole long rigmarole? Do they seriously suppose that I'll be able to keep it up, day in, day out, night in, night out, living in the same room with a terrible old woman — forever?"

Some may argue that this speech is merely an unreasonable rant, indicating Addie's dour mood rather than her roommate's true nature. (For one thing, contrary to Addie's declaration, the roommate must have been born!) Yet it can also be argued that Addie shrewdly diagnoses her situation. Perhaps statements like "you never were born," "your head is empty," and "you're a stranger" are true in a metaphorical sense.

SETTING

Usually a short story enables readers to examine how people behave in concrete circumstances. The characters are located in a particular place or **setting**. Moreover, they are shown at particular moments in their personal histories.

Sometimes the story goes further, referring to them as living at a certain point in world history.

As the word *sometimes* implies, short stories vary in the precision with which they identify their settings. At one extreme is Haruki Murakami's "Another Way to Die," featured in Chapter 12. The story's place and time are sharply defined: the action occurs in a Manchurian zoo in August 1945, when the Russian army was about to seize the region from its Japanese occupiers. On the other hand, the setting of Williams's "The Use of Force" is much less exact. Most of the action occurs in the Olsons' kitchen, but we get practically no details of it. Mainly we learn that "it is warm," while the rest of the house can be "very damp." And though the Olsons are evidently from the working class, the text does not situate them within a particular region or era. Even when a story's setting is rather vague, certain details may seem historically or geographically specific. For example, Ralph Ellison's "Battle Royal" (Chapter 14) takes place in an unidentified town, but one that is evidently in the segregationist South, sometime during the first half of the twentieth century.

Short stories differ as well in the importance of their setting. Sometimes, as with "The Use of Force," location serves as a mere backdrop for the plot. At other times, the setting can be a looming presence. When Welty's character Marian visits the Old Ladies' Home, we get her vivid impressions of it. Even when a story's setting seems ordinary, it may become filled with drama and meaning as the plot develops.

Stories may focus on one site and show it changing over time. This is the case with Faulkner's "A Rose for Emily" (Chapter 11), in which Emily's town comes to view her differently over the years. Of course, a story may take place in more than one setting, and when it does, the differences between its various sites may be notable. Nathaniel Hawthorne's story "Young Goodman Brown" (Chapter 13) draws a sharp symbolic contrast between town and forest.

One way of analyzing characters is to consider how they accommodate themselves — or fail to accommodate themselves — to their surroundings. The two roommates in Welty's story are evidently frustrated with living in the Old Ladies' Home, and they take out their frustration on each other.

≡ A WRITING EXERCISE

To become more aware of how setting may function in a short story, write a two- to three-page description of a setting you associate with someone you know. Choose a particular room, building, or landscape in which you have seen that person. In your description, use details of the setting to reveal something about his or her life.

IMAGERY

Just like poems, short stories often use **imagery** to convey meaning. Sometimes a character in the story may interpret a particular image just the way you do. Some stories, though, include images that you and the characters may analyze quite differently. One example is the apple in Welty's story. Whereas Marian probably views the apple as just something to eat, many readers would make other associations with it, thinking in particular of the apple that Adam and Eve ate from the tree of knowledge in the Garden of Eden. By the end of Welty's story, perhaps Marian has indeed become like Adam and Eve, in that she has lost her innocence and grown more aware that human beings age. At any rate, many readers would call Marian's apple a **symbol**. Traditionally, that is the term for an image seen as representing some concept or concepts. Again, Marian herself probably does not view her apple as symbolic; indeed, characters within stories rarely use the word *symbol* at all.

Images may appear in the form of metaphors or other figures of speech. For example, when Marian enters the Old Ladies' Home, she experiences "a smell in the hall like the interior of a clock." Welty soon builds on the clock image as she describes the receptionist checking her wristwatch, an action that this character repeats near the end. Welty's whole story can be said to deal with time and its effects, both on the old and on the young.

Images in short stories usually appeal to the reader's visual sense. Most often, they are things you can picture in your mind. Yet stories are not limited to rendering visual impressions. They may refer to other senses, too. In Sher's story, the children are affected by the man's voice, while Welty's young heroine notices the odor in the hall.

≡ A WRITING EXERCISE

Write a brief essay in which you analyze how a particular advertisement uses imagery. The ad may come from any medium, including a newspaper, a magazine, television, or radio. What specific associations do you make with the ad's imagery? Why do you think the advertiser used it? Would you say that this use of imagery is successful? Why, or why not?

LANGUAGE

Everything about short stories we have discussed so far concerns **language**. After all, works of literature are constructed entirely out of words. Here, however, we call your attention to three specific uses of language in stories: title, predominant style, and dialogue.

A story's **title** may be just as important as any words in the text. Not always will the relevance of the title be immediately clear to you. Usually you have to read a story all the way through before you can sense fully how its title applies. In any case, play with the title in your mind, considering its various possible meanings and implications.

≡ A WRITING EXERCISE

Write a brief essay in which you focus on Williams's, Welty's, or Sher's story and examine how the title relates to the actual text. Consider the writer's alternatives. If you choose to discuss Welty's "A Visit of Charity," you may find it helpful to think about this famous passage from the New Testament: "And now abideth faith, hope, charity, these three; but the greatest of these is charity" (I Corinthians 13:13). You may also want to look up the word *charity* in a dictionary.

Not all short stories have a uniform **style**. Some feature various tones, dialects, vocabularies, and levels of formality. Stories that do have a predominant style are often narrated in the first person, thus giving the impression of a presiding "voice." Williams's story "The Use of Force," with its matter-of-fact, conversational tone, comes across as an anecdote that someone is relating to a friend.

Dialogue may serve more than one purpose in a short story. By reporting various things, characters may provide you with necessary background for the plot. In Welty's story, it's only from the roommates' fragmentary remarks that Marian — and the reader — can learn anything about their lives up until now. Actually, dialogue can also be thought of as an action in itself, moving the plot along. Try to identify the particular kinds of acts that characters perform when they speak. For instance, the man in Sher's story repeatedly coaxes the children to get help. Moreover, the mother in "The Use of Force" makes a plea when she begs her daughter to open her mouth for the narrator: "Such a nice man. . . . Look how kind he is to you. Come on, do what he tells you to, he won't hurt you." Just a bit later, though, the narrator scolds the mother herself: "For heaven's sake, I broke in. Don't call me a nice man to her." To the narrator, no longer are the girl's parents his partners; instead, he feels contempt for them. Indeed, dialogue may function to reveal shifts in characters' relations with one another.

THEME

We have already discussed the term **theme** on pages 59 to 61. There, we identified issues of theme as one kind of issue that comes up in literary studies. At the same time, we suggested that the term *theme* applies to various literary genres, not just short stories. Later, in Chapters 6, 7, and 8, we examine theme in connection with poems, plays, and essays. Here, though, we consider theme as an element of short fiction. In doing so, we review some points from our earlier discussion, applying them now to the three stories you have just read.

Recall that we defined the theme of a work as the main claim it seems to make. Furthermore, we identified it as an assertion, a proposition, or a statement rather than as a single word. "Charity" is obviously a *topic* of Welty's story, but because it is just one word, it is not an adequate expression of the story's *theme*. The following exercise invites you to consider just what that theme may be.

▣ A WRITING EXERCISE

Here we list possible statements of theme for Williams's, Welty's, and Sher's stories. Choose one of these stories, and rank the statements listed for it, placing at the top whatever sentence you think most accurately expresses the story's theme. Then, in two or three pages, explain your reasoning, referring at least once to each statement you have ranked. Propose your own statement of the story's theme if none of those listed seem adequate to you.

Statements of Theme for Williams's "The Use of Force"

1. Force against people is justified when it is used to halt disease.
2. Though we like to think that doctors are kind, they may actually scorn us.
3. Doctors should be especially sensitive when their patient is a child.
4. Children are capable of stubborn fury.
5. The desire to help may be met with resistance.
6. Working-class life is different from the life of middle-class professionals.
7. We should cooperate with doctors, even if they seem threatening to us.
8. People may secretly admire those who resist them.
9. All of us are "blind" in one way or another.
10. The cure may be worse than the disease.

Statements of Theme for Welty's "A Visit of Charity"

1. Be nice to old people, for many of them have it tough.
2. None of us can escape the passage of time.
3. Searching for merit points is incompatible with a true spirit of charity.
4. Everyone has to give up dreams of innocence and paradise, just as Adam and Eve did.
5. Although we are tempted to repress our awareness of mortality, we should maintain that awareness.
6. We should all behave charitably toward one another.
7. We can tell how charitable we are by the way we treat people we find strange or irritable.
8. Old-age homes need to be made more pleasant, both for the residents and for their visitors.
9. Whenever we become strongly aware of mortality, we tend to repress that awareness, thus robbing ourselves of any benefit we may gain from it.
10. Young people are capable of showing interest in others, if only for a moment, but for better or worse they're basically self-centered.

Statements of Theme for Sher's "The Man in the Well"

1. We should be more compassionate toward people who are trapped.
2. Children may have difficulty sharing the perspective of another person.

3. Even in their later years, people may have trouble forgiving themselves for bad things they did when they were young.

4. Within groups, people may engage in conduct that is wilder, stranger, or more uncivilized than their usual behavior when alone.

5. People project their fears or suspicions onto others, even those who do not actually pose a threat to them.

6. People need to see one another's faces if they are to trust one another.

7. When dealing with an adult, even a helpless one, children may have in their minds images of parental authority that affect how they treat the person.

8. Children may fail to understand when an adult is in danger.

9. Children are capable of conspiring with one another against the adult world.

10. The psychological reality of children and adults is a deep well within themselves that they cannot see into.

Think about the other points we made when we discussed theme in Chapter 3. To see how these apply to short fiction, we can start by relating each point to the stories by Williams, Welty, and Sher.

1. Try to state a text's theme as a midlevel generalization. If you were to put it in very broad terms, your audience would see it as fitting a great many works besides the one you have read. If you went to the opposite extreme, tying the theme completely to specific details of the text, your audience might think the theme irrelevant to their own lives.

The phrase "the moral of the story" suggests that a story can usually be reduced to a single message, often a principle of ethics or religion. Plenty of examples can be cited to support this suggestion. In the New Testament, for instance, Jesus tells stories — they are called *parables* — to convey some of his key ideas. In any number of cultures today, stories are used to teach children elements of good conduct. Moreover, people often determine the significance of a real-life event by building a story from it and by drawing a moral from it at the same time. These two processes conspicuously dovetailed when England's Princess Diana was killed in a car crash. Given that she died fleeing photographers, many people saw her entire life story as that of a woman hounded by the media. The moral was simultaneous and clear: thou shalt honor the right to privacy.

It is possible to lose sight of a story's theme by placing too much emphasis on minor details of the text. The more common temptation, however, is to turn a story's theme into an all-too-general cliché. Actually, a story is often most interesting when it *complicates* some widely held idea that it seemed ready to endorse. Therefore, a useful exercise is to start with a general thematic statement about the story and then make it increasingly specific. With "The Man in the Well," for example, you might begin by supposing that a theme is "Children are not always as nice and innocent as adults like to assume." Your next step would be to identify the specific spin that Sher's story puts on this idea. How does his story differ from others on this theme? Note, for instance, that the narrator and his friends cannot see the title character and so are free to imagine him as a potential threat. Other stories might portray such a person as clearly pleasant and in need of help. With this observation in mind, try to rephrase our version of Sher's theme so that it seems more in touch with the specific details of his text.

2. A theme of a text may be related to its title.   It may also be expressed by some statement made within the text. But often various parts of the text merit consideration as you try to determine its theme.

In our discussion of a short story's language, we called attention to the potential significance of its title. The title may serve as a guide to the story's theme. What clues, if any, do you find in the three story titles in this chapter — "The Use of Force," "A Visit of Charity," and "The Man in the Well"? Of course, determining a story's theme entails going beyond the title. You have to read, and usually reread, the entire text. In doing so, you may come across a statement that seems a candidate for the theme because it is a philosophical generalization. Nevertheless, take the time to consider whether the story's essence is indeed captured by this statement alone.

3. You can state a text's theme either as an observation or as a recommendation.   Each way of putting it evokes a certain image of the text's author. When you state the theme as an **observation**, you depict the author as a psychologist, a philosopher, or some other kind of analyst. When you state the theme as a **recommendation** — which often involves your using the word *should* — you depict the author as a teacher, preacher, manager, or coach. That is, the author comes across as telling readers what to do.

As we have noted, stories are often used to teach lessons. Moreover, often the lessons are recommendations for action, capable of being phrased as "Do X" or "Do not do X." The alternative is to make a generalization about some state of affairs. When you try to express a particular story's theme, which of these two options should you follow? There are several things to consider in making your decision. First is your personal comfort: do you feel at ease with both ways of stating the theme, or is one of these ways more to your taste? Also worth pondering is the impression you want to give of the author: do you want to portray this person as a maker of recommendations, or do you want to assign the author a more modest role?

4. Consider stating a text's theme as a problem.   That way, you are more apt to convey the complexity and drama of the text.

We have suggested that short stories often pivot around conflicts between people and conflicts within people. Perhaps the most interesting stories are ones that pose conflicts not easily resolved. Probably you will be more faithful to such a text if you phrase its theme as a problem. In the case of Sher's story, for example, you might state the theme as follows: "People may normally be inclined to help someone else but may lack sufficient knowledge of the person to feel comfortable about rescuing him or her."

5. Rather than refer to *the* theme of a text, you might refer to *a* theme of the text, implying that the text has more than one. You would still be suggesting that you have identified a central idea of the text. Subsequently, you might have to defend your claim.

Unlike the average novel, the typical short story pivots around only a few ideas. Yet you need not insist that the story you are analyzing has a single theme; in fact, even the shortest piece of short fiction may have a number of them. Besides, your audience is apt to think you nicely open-minded if you suggest that the theme you have discovered is not the only one. We believe, for example, that Williams's story has at least two themes. One is that people who usually sympathize with the working class may have trouble understanding and appreciating particular members of it. A second theme, however, is that oppressed people — especially children — may misrecognize, so to speak, the efforts of somebody who is genuinely trying to help them. Although we are labeling each of these ideas *a* theme of Williams's story rather than *the* theme of it, we are still making strong claims. To use the term *theme* at all implies that we are identifying key principles of the text. You might disagree with our claims about Williams's themes, and if you do, we would have to support our position in order to change your mind.

Perhaps the biggest challenge you will face in writing about short stories is to avoid long stretches of plot summary. Selected details of the plot will often serve as key evidence for you. You will need to describe such moments from the story you are discussing, even if your audience has already read it. But your readers are apt to be frustrated if you just repeat plot at length. They will feel that they may as well turn back to the story itself rather than linger with your rehash. Your paper is worth your readers' time only if you provide insights of your own, *analyzing* the story rather than just *summarizing* it.

To understand what analysis of a short story involves, let's return to Alison Caldwell, whose freewriting on "The Use of Force" you read earlier. Assigned to write an argument paper about a short story, Alison decided to focus on Williams's. She realized that for her paper to be effective, she had to come up with an issue worth addressing, a claim about that issue, and evidence for that claim. Moreover, she had to be prepared to identify the warrants or assumptions behind her evidence.

For most writing assignments, settling on an issue will be your most important preliminary step. Without a driving question, you will have difficulty producing fresh, organized, and sustained analysis. For her paper on "The Use of Force," Alison chose to address an issue that she had raised in her freewriting: What's the most important connection between the narrator and the child? Ultimately, she saw this as an issue of pattern because she would have to identify, analyze, and rank in order of importance whatever sets of words link the two characters. Again, building on her freewriting, Alison thought in particular about the narrator's closing reference to the child's "blindness." In her paper, she came to argue that "blindness" was the most important similarity between these two people. She realized, of course, that she would have to explore various possible meanings of the term, especially since neither character was literally blind. To a certain extent, then, she would have to address an issue of definition, even as the issue of pattern remained her key concern. Moreover, she felt obliged to justify her emphasis on the narrator's final words. You will see that in her paper she states her warrant for taking them as evidence. The narrator's concluding reference to "blindness" is significant, she contends, because the last words of a character often are. To be sure, Alison also assumed that Williams was deliberate rather than arbitrary in having the narrator speak this way at the end.

A paper about a short story need not explicitly mention the elements of short fiction we have identified. Nevertheless, thinking of these elements can help you plan such a paper, providing you with some preliminary terms for your analysis. Alison perceived that her paper would be very much about two characters who on the surface are protagonist and antagonist but who actually have features in common. Also, the paper would attend much to the story's ending. It would deal as well with a particular symbol, blindness.

When you plan a paper about a short story, keep in mind that you are more apt to persuade readers if you include quotations from the text you discuss. Before you attempt a complete draft, copy in your notebook any words from the story that might figure in your analysis. Alison, for example, was pretty sure that her paper on "The Use of Force" would incorporate the narrator's final words, "tears of defeat blinded her eyes," as well as his interesting declaration that "I had already fallen in love with the savage brat, the parents were contemptible to me." Yet, as with plot summary, quoting should be limited, so that the paper seems to be an original argument about the story instead of a mere recycling of it. Alison sensed that practically every sentence of Williams's story could be quoted and then plumbed for meaning. At the same time, she realized that she should quote only some words rather than every word.

Final Draft of a Student Paper

Here is Alison's final draft of her paper about "The Use of Force." As you read it, keep in mind that it emerged only after she had done several preliminary drafts, in consultation with some of her classmates as well as her instructor. Although Alison's paper is a good example of how to write about a short story, most drafts can stand to be revised further. What do you think Alison has done well in her paper? If she planned to do yet another version, what suggestions would you make?

Alison Caldwell
Professor Stein
English 1A
3 November - - - -

Forms of Blindness in "The Use of Force"

In William Carlos Williams's story "The Use of Force," the narrator
is a doctor frustrated by one of his patients, a young girl who refuses to
let him determine if her throat is infected. After violently struggling
with the child, he finally manages to pry open her mouth and does
find her tonsils diseased. In an important sense, therefore, the child
is the narrator's antagonist, over whom he eventually triumphs. Yet
throughout the story, the narrator seems to identify with the child,
almost as if she is his secret self or double. At the same time, we
readers must decide which of her characteristics he shares most. To
answer this question, we should consider the narrator's very last
words, which seem significant just because they serve as his conclusion.
After his victory over the girl, he reports, "tears of defeat blinded her
eyes." These final words suggest that he, too, has been "blind," in
various senses of the term. Most important, his anger at the child has
obscured for him her humanity. Even at the end, perhaps, he does not
fully "see" the limits of his compassion.

To understand the narrator's identification with the child, we
should note his relationship with her parents. Though her mother and
father are allies in his fight against her, he feels increasing scorn for
them. When the mother says to the child "he won't hurt you," the
narrator must conceal his "disgust." Later, he openly snarls at the
mother: "For heaven's sake, I broke in. Don't call me a nice man."
Although the child accuses the narrator of "killing me," he is actually
homicidal toward her ineffective father: "I wanted to kill him."

With the child, the narrator has a different relationship. At several
moments, he is negative about her, too. When she resists his effort to
open her mouth with a wooden tongue depressor, he gets "furious,"
even though he realizes that he is angry at a mere girl. Eventually, his
wrath becomes so intense that "I could have torn the child apart in
my own fury and enjoyed it." Nevertheless, his anger is mixed with
admiration. The child's sheer force of resistance makes him think
highly of her. After he triumphs, he admits to himself that "She had
fought valiantly to keep me from knowing her secret." More important,
midway through the story he contrasts her quite favorably with her
parents: "I had already fallen in love with the savage brat, the parents
were contemptible to me. In the ensuing struggle they grew more and
more abject, crushed, exhausted while she surely rose to magnificent
heights of insane fury of effort bred of her terror of me."

The narrator's identification with the child is not simply one
person's respect for another. In various ways, he comes to resemble

her. For example, both find her parents unhelpful as allies. If she shows "insane fury of effort," he feels his "own fury." She violently resists him; he violently attacks her. If "her face was flushed," eventually he feels a "pleasure" in combat with her that leaves his face "burning." Perhaps the narrator finds the child compelling precisely because they mirror each other.

But which of their similarities is most important? By announcing at the end that the girl has been "blinded," the narrator invites us to suppose that he has been "blind" as well and to believe that this is their most noteworthy connection. Significantly, the narrator wears glasses, which the girl knocks off. Literally, he lacks clear vision. For much of the story, though, the narrator has been "blind" in that he lacks the opportunity to see what disease lurks behind the girl's mouth. His earnestly repeated use of the word "look" suggests what a struggle it is for him to view his patient's secret. After proposing to the parents that "we take a look at the throat first," he pleads with the girl to "open your mouth and let's take a look at your throat." When she refuses, he begs her to "let me take a look. . . . Just open up and let me see." He even resorts to the word "look" as he tries to reassure her: "Look, I said opening both hands wide, I haven't anything in my hands." Once he gets more exasperated with the child, he uses the word "look" more sternly: "Look here, I said to the child, we're going to look at your throat."

Yet the narrator seems "blind" in a psychological sense, too. As he intensifies his attack on the girl, he tells himself that he is doing so for her own and society's good: "The damned little brat must be protected against her own idiocy, one says to one's self at such times. Others must be protected against her." At some point, though, he realizes that his rationalizations protect *himself*. In reality, he comes to acknowledge, he has been driven by "a blind fury" that leads him to a "final unreasoning assault." Here, the word "blind" refers to obsession with victory, regardless of its human consequences. For the narrator, helping the girl becomes less crucial than conquering her.

Nevertheless, the narrator *doesn't* seem "blind" as he looks back on his own conduct. Notice that he tells the story in the past tense, which means that he is analyzing how he behaved on a previous occasion. As he reviews what he did and felt when he visited the Olsons, he comes across as remarkably candid about his own base motives. We readers do not have to infer that he acted mainly out of "a blind fury"; he himself informs us of this fact. If anything, we may conclude that he is now a man of vision, bursting with true insights about himself.

We need not accept all of his self-analysis, however. By acknowledging his more negative feelings, he may win points with us for honesty without really changing his behavior or mindset. Even as he notes his "blind fury," for example, he concludes that "One goes on to the end," as if humanity in general would inevitably have acted as he did. When he makes this fatalistic declaration, he may be protecting himself yet again by refusing to see ways in which he must still take personal responsibility.

Perhaps he is using a strategy that many middle-class professionals have used when confronted with lower-class suffering. Although Williams provides few details of the Olsons' life, clearly they belong at best to the working class. Their house can get "very damp," they seem unused to doctors, and the narrator points out that the mother is "clean," as if she might well have been living in filth. The narrator is not blatantly prejudiced against the lower classes. After all, he has responded when the Olsons summoned him. But he seems disposed to think of the parents as stupid, and his concern about their daughter stems in part from his effort to stop a diphtheria outbreak. His tone of ironic wisdom in telling the story is consistent with a basic detachment from such people. By summarizing his visit to the Olsons with the world-weary statement "One goes on to the end," he may still be "blinding" himself to the possibility of forming a genuine bond with this specific family.

≡ SUMMING UP

- **Short stories require you to understand and evaluate them on the basis of just a few details and events.**

- **Think carefully about the title and its possible meanings and implications.**

- The elements of short fiction include *plot* and *structure*, *point of view*, *characters*, *setting*, *imagery*, *language*, and *theme*.

- *Plot* and *structure* are related, but plots usually center on human beings and their actions, and structure often follows the ABDCE formula (action, background, development, climax, ending). (pp. 122–27)

- *Points of view* vary and include first person and omniscient. (pp. 127–28)

- As you analyze and evaluate the *characters* in a short story (pp. 128–30), **consider these questions:**

  What does each character desire?

  How do the characters, even minor characters, relate to one another?

  Can you identify a protagonist and an antagonist?

(continued on next page)

≣ SUMMING UP

How are the characters' lives affected by traits such as gender, class, race, ethnicity, nationality, sexual orientation, and occupation?

Can you trust the accuracy of the views the characters have of one another?

How does the characters' dialogue function — does it provide background, advance the plot, reveal shifts in characters' relations, or what?

- *Setting* provides a context for actions. One way of analyzing characters is to consider how they do or do not accommodate themselves to their surroundings. (pp. 130–31)

- *Images* appeal to the reader's senses — usually the visual sense — and may appear in the form of metaphors and other figures of speech. (pp. 131–32)

- The language of a short story may have various meanings and implications. Think about the potential significance not only of its title, but also of its style and dialogue. (pp. 132–33)

- A *theme* of a short story is a claim it seems to make, best identified as an assertion, a proposition, or a statement. In your writing, try to state the theme as a midlevel generalization, either as an observation, as a recommendation, or as a problem. (pp. 133–38)

- In writing an argument about a short story, remember to formulate an issue worth addressing. (pp. 137–38)

Comparing Poems and Pictures

Although literature and visual art may seem quite different media, they have often been closely connected. For one thing, any page of literature is a visual image, whether or not readers are always conscious of this fact. Also, most publishers of literature carefully design the covers of their books, aiming to lure readers in. Specific genres and authors, however, have forged even stronger relations between literature and art. Beginning in classical times and continuing today, many poems have precisely described existing paintings and sculptures; this tradition of verse is called **ekphrasis**. In the late eighteenth century, William Blake made highly ornamental engravings of his poems, so that they were striking works of art and not just written texts. In the nineteenth century, many novels included illustrations, a tradition evident today in children's picture books. At present, perhaps you are a fan of **graphic novels**: comic books that combine words and images to tell stories aimed at adults.

Aside from this history of connections, comparing a literary text with an image is a good mental exercise. The process can help you acquire more insights into each work. Given this possibility, we present several pairings of poems and works of art. Every pairing deals with one of the topics addressed in Parts One and Two of this book: work, family, love, freedom and confinement, justice, and journeys. In some cases, the literary text was written in response to its accompanying image. In other cases, we connect a poem and an image for the first time, inviting you to trace their similarities and differences. With any of these pairings, comparison can help you generate ideas for writing, a principle we stress throughout this book.

Analyzing Visual Art

You can better understand a work of visual art — and develop ideas for an essay about it — if you raise certain questions about it and try to answer them. These questions apply to various types of pictures. Bear in mind that even photographs are not mere reproductions of reality. People who create them are, consciously or not, choosing their subject and figuring out how best to represent it. Especially in the age of digital technologies such as Photoshop, images caught by the camera can be tweaked in all sorts of ways. Moreover, the scene depicted might be a staged fantasy in the first place.

Here are the questions to ask yourself as you examine a picture with an eye to analyzing it:

1. What details do you see in the picture? Besides recognizable objects and figures (human beings or animals), consider shapes, colors, lighting, and shading. Do not list just the picture's most prominent elements, for those that at first seem trivial may turn out to be important for you.

2. What are aspects of the picture's *style* — the artist's particular way of handling the subject? Among other things, consider what the artist does and does not allow the viewer to see; how realistic or abstract the work seems; and whether anyone in the picture looks directly at the viewer.

3. How has the artist organized the picture? Note especially patterns of resemblance and contrast. Think, too, about whether the picture's design directs the viewer's attention to a particular part of it.

4. What mood does the picture evoke? Consider emotions that you experience as a viewer, as well as those that seem to be felt by any living figures in the scene.

5. What is at least one detail of the picture that strikes you as puzzling (and therefore especially in need of interpretation)?

6. Does the picture seem to tell a story or appear to be part of a story that has already begun and will continue?

7. How does the picture relate to its title and (where applicable) to its caption?

8. What are some options that the artist could have explored but did not pursue?

Writing an Essay That Compares Literature and Art

Before you write an essay comparing a work of literature with a work of art, collect as many details as you can about each. The questions above can help you do this with the artwork. For aid in gathering observations about the literary text, see Chapter 2, How to Read Closely, especially the section on Strategies for Close Reading. Then, as you proceed to write, keep the following principles especially in mind:

- You do not have to give equal space to each work. Rather, you may prefer to come up with an issue and a main claim by focusing on interpreting *one* of the works: either the literary text *or* the visual image. Your secondary work will still play some role in the essay, but your primary one will receive greater attention. The result will be what in Chapter 4 we call a *weighted* comparison. (See that chapter for more tips.)

- Assume that your reader is at least somewhat familiar with both the literary work and the image but needs to be reminded of their basic details. In particular, help your audience *visualize* the art you discuss.

- Refer at least sometimes to the author of the literary work and to the artist who created the image. Doing so will help you analyze how their productions involve particular strategies of representation — attempts to affect audiences in particular ways.

A Sample Paper Comparing a Poem and a Picture

To give you a better idea of what an essay comparing literature and art looks like, we present a paper by student Karl Magnusson. He connects Edward Hopper's painting *Office at Night* to a prose poem of the same title by Rolando Perez. This pairing is the first in our color plates section. As you will see, Karl's essay is a weighted comparison; it focuses mostly on Perez's poem.

Karl Magnusson
Professor Kemper
English W350
May 16, ----

Lack of Motion and Speech in
Rolando Perez's "Office at Night"

Edward Hopper's painting *Office at Night* depicts a man and a woman working in the kind of setting indicated by the title. The man is apparently the boss of the woman, who seems to be his secretary. He sits at a desk by an open window, studying a document that he holds in front of him. She is positioned to the left and slightly to the rear of him. More precisely, she stands at a filing cabinet with her right hand resting on an open drawer. Their respective postures suggest that she is waiting to hear what he will say next. Perhaps she has just asked him a question and he is thinking about how to answer, or perhaps she is simply expecting him, as her superior, to issue her a new order. In any case, viewers of the painting are free to interpret their interaction, and different spectators might come up with different ideas about what these people really mean to each other. Indeed, not everyone would conceive their relationship to be what Rolando Perez imagines it as being in his poem about Hopper's artwork. Also entitled "Office at Night," Perez's poem speculates that the man and woman have a romantic interest in each other that neither he nor she can express. Furthermore, the poem conveys their reticence in terms that have often been used to describe the medium of painting in general.

The poem draws attention more to the self-repression of the boss. The secretary, too, evidently does not feel able to

Immediately refers to the painting and then proceeds to summarize its key details.

Now turns to the poem, which will be the primary work in this weighted comparison.

This is the essay's main claim, which is about the poem.

speak frankly about their emotions, perhaps because she is after all his employee. But the text tends to focus on *his* reluctance to reveal that he is enamored of her. This mixture of lust and hesitation is evident right near the start of the poem. There, just before describing the secretary's alluring clothes, the poem's speaker wonders, "How many times did he [the boss] dream of this very same scenario." The implication is that the boss has entertained sensual visions of his employee in his mind while doing nothing to bring them about. He merely fantasizes a romance with her, not actually helping it come to life. Soon after, the reader learns that *she* had to prompt *him* to "open the window" and let fresh air in. Evidently she wishes to stimulate their senses and admit their real feelings, but this is behavior that he apparently would never "have dared" to engage in on his own. Later, he resists actually inviting her to take their office working relationship in a romantic direction. Although he apparently considers the possibility that "he would do something, he would act, produce the right combination of words" to initiate a courtship, he remains silent and still. The implication is that he is restrained by the memory of his previous disappointments in love — "too many truths in the past." Whatever specific episodes in his past he is thinking of, the result is that "now history holds him back." Rather than "suggest[ing] that they lock up and go for a drink somewhere," he stays emotionally locked up, not letting his true attachment to her emerge.

Proceeds to support the main argument with specific lines from the poem.

In describing physical details of the office, the poem's speaker sums up the couple's inability to be emotionally open with each other. In part, the speaker does this by sometimes using images of motion that underscore by contrast how the man and woman fail to act on their feelings. The "patch of light" that "touches them both . . . lightly, very lightly . . . as with fingertips" is a reminder that these two people do not physically touch each other at all. The phrase "gently carried there by the wind" — used in reference to a piece of paper on the floor — indirectly emphasizes that the couple will not let themselves be carried away by passion. When, however, near the end of the poem, the speaker describes the paper as "timidly undisturbed," the symbolism is more direct: the word "timidly" seems to fit the couple as well, for they have been too scared to confess their emotional bond. Moreover, the speaker's observation that "he hasn't moved, and she hasn't moved" directly reinforces their *psychological* paralysis. The poem's final phrase, "wounded and frozen infinity," is not just an overview of this late-night office environment. The speaker is also indicating the basic state of the couple's relationship. They are "wounded" in the sense that they suffer unfulfilled desires for each other. They are "frozen" in the sense that they cannot reveal these desires. The word "infinity" implies that, given their inertia, their situation is unlikely to change.

Not every poem about Hopper's *Office at Night* painting would necessarily focus on its two human figures. Nor would every poem about the painting necessarily depict their relationship in the way that Perez's does. Indeed, a distinctive feature of his poem is that his portrait of the couple attributes to them characteristics often associated with the medium of painting itself. Aware, like most people, that figures in a painting do not move, Perez takes this fact and makes it an element of the couple's behavior. The static nature of painting in general is echoed in their paralytic inhibition. Furthermore, just as people in paintings do not speak aloud, so the couple in Perez's poem resist articulating what they really feel. Also, just as viewers of a painting have to guess the thoughts of anyone shown in it, so Perez's man and woman force themselves to guess what is on each other's mind.

Perez could be seen as tolerating and even encouraging affairs between bosses and their secretaries. In this respect, his text seems more in keeping with the world of 1940, the year Hopper painted *Office at Night*. Back then, expressions of love between a manager and a subordinate might have been smiled upon, perceived as what the poem's speaker calls "the correct combination of words" and "the correct series of reactions." The same expressions now, however, might be condemned as politically and even legally *in*correct. Certainly government and company policies on sexual harassment warn executives not to seduce the employees who serve them. Nevertheless, it would be unfair simply to dismiss Perez's poem or Hopper's painting as outdated, especially because the audiences for these works do not have to take them as being just about romance in the office. Both the poem and the painting allow for interpretations that see the couple as universal — as people who might exist anywhere. In this case, their reticence toward each other would be a widespread human problem: the difficulty of communicating the stirrings of one's heart.

The concluding paragraph does not simply repeat what has already been said. It touches on a new subject: changes in policies on office affairs.

Edward Hopper, *Office at Night*. 1940. Oil on canvas. 30-5/16 × 33-15/16 ×
2-3/4″ framed. Collection Walker Art Center, Minneapolis. Gift of the T. B.
Walker Foundation, Gilbert M. Walker Fund, 1948. Acc.#1948.21.

ROLANDO PEREZ
Office at Night

It is past nine o'clock, and she has stayed late to help him. How many times did he dream of this very same scenario: her standing there in her tight blue dress, with her black pumps and flesh-colored stockings. And now it has finally happened. Without him having to ask — not that he would have dared — she volunteered all on her own.

He had to "open the window."

"This office at night is a bit stuffy."

A sheet of paper that once lay on top of other papers on his desk, now lies on the green carpet — to his right — gently carried there by the wind. Standing at a black filing cabinet, searching for some old bills, she has noticed the paper lying on the floor. The desk lamp throws a shadow on the desk, and illuminates his hands. And a patch of light, reflected on the wall, touches them both . . . lightly, very lightly . . . as with finger tips.

Will she bend over to pick it up?   5

If only the phone beside him would ring, then he would do something, he would act, produce the correct combination of words that would elicit the correct series of reactions from her. He might even suggest that they lock up and go for a drink somewhere. But having heard too many truths in the past, now history holds him back. In his suit, with his shirt buttoned to the top, and his tie still on, he hasn't moved, and she hasn't moved; and the wind-swept paper will stay on the floor, halfway between his desk and her cabinet, timidly undisturbed, in this wounded and frozen infinity.   *[2002]*

From *Fortune* Magazine, October 1, 2001.
© 2001 Time Inc. Used under license.

DEBORAH GARRISON

I Saw You Walking

I saw you walking through Newark Penn Station
in your shoes of white ash. At the corner
of my nervous glance your dazed passage
first forced me away, tracing the crescent
berth you'd give a drunk, a lurcher, nuzzling   5
all corners with ill will and his stench, but
not this one, not today; one shirt arm's sheared
clean from the shoulder, the whole bare limb
wet with muscle and shining dimly pink,
the other full-sheathed in cotton, Brooks Bros.   10
type, the cuff yet buttoned at the wrist, a
parody of careful dress, preparedness—
so you had not rolled up your sleeves yet this
morning when your suit jacket (here are
the pants, dark gray, with subtle stripe, as worn   15
by men like you on ordinary days)
and briefcase (you've none, reverse commuter
come from the pit with nothing to carry
but your life) were torn from you, as your life
was not. Your face itself seemed to be walking,   20
leading your body north, though the age
of the face, blank and ashen, passing forth
and away from me, was unclear, the sandy
crown of hair powdered white like your feet, but
underneath not yet gray—forty-seven?   25

forty-eight? The age of someone's father—
and I trembled for your luck, for your broad,
dusted back, half shirted, walking away;
I should have dropped to my knees to thank God
you were alive, o my God, in whom I don't believe.   *[2001]*   30

PHILIP LEVINE
A Story

Everyone loves a story. Let's begin with a house.
We can fill it with careful rooms and fill the rooms
with things—tables, chairs, cupboards, drawers
closed to hide tiny beds where children once slept
or big drawers that yawn open to reveal   5
precisely folded garments washed half to death,
unsoiled, stale, and waiting to be worn out.
There must be a kitchen, and the kitchen
must have a stove, perhaps a big iron one
with a fat black pipe that vanishes into the ceiling   10
to reach the sky and exhale its smells and collusions.
This was the center of whatever family life
was here, this and the sink gone yellow
around the drain where the water, dirty or pure,
ran off with no explanation, somehow like the point   15
of this, the story we promised and may yet deliver.
Make no mistake, a family was here. You see
the path worn into the linoleum where the wood,
gray and certainly pine, shows through.
Father stood there in the middle of his life   20
to call to the heavens he imagined above the roof
must surely be listening. When no one answered
you can see where his heel came down again
and again, even though he'd been taught
never to demand. Not that life was especially cruel;   25
they had well water they pumped at first,
a stove that gave heat, a mother who stood
at the sink at all hours and gazed longingly
to where the woods once held the voices
of small bears—themselves a family—and the songs   30
of birds long fled once the deep woods surrendered
one tree at a time after the workmen arrived
with jugs of hot coffee. The worn spot on the sill
is where Mother rested her head when no one saw,
those two stained ridges were handholds   35

Michael Sebastian, *Big Wheel* (2010). © Michael Sebastian.

she relied on; they never let her down.
Where is she now? You think you have a right
to know everything? The children tiny enough
to inhabit cupboards, large enough to have rooms
of their own and to abandon them, the father   40
with his right hand raised against the sky?
If those questions are too personal, then tell us,
where are the woods? They had to have been
because the continent was clothed in trees.
We all read that in school and knew it to be true.   45
Yet all we see are houses, rows and rows
of houses as far as sight, and where sight vanishes
into nothing, into the new world no one has seen,
there has to be more than dust, wind-borne particles
of burning earth, the earth we lost, and nothing else.   *[2009]*   50

Gustav Klimt, *The Kiss.*
1907–1908. Oester-
reichische Galerie im
Belvedere, Vienna,
Austria. Photo Credit:
Erick Lessing / Art
Resource, NY.

LAWRENCE FERLINGHETTI

Short Story on a Painting of Gustav Klimt

They are kneeling upright on a flowered bed
    He
        has just caught her there
                and holds her still
    Her gown   5
           has slipped down
                  off her shoulder
He has an urgent hunger
        His dark head
            bends to hers   10
            hungrily
And the woman the woman
    turns her tangerine lips from his
        one hand like the head of a dead swan
           draped down over   15
                his heavy neck
        the fingers
           strangely crimped
              tightly together
    her other arm doubled up   20
        against her tight breast

her hand a languid claw
                    clutching his hand
          which would turn her mouth
                              to his   25
    her long dress made
              of multicolored blossoms
                    quilted on gold
    her Titian hair
          with blue stars in it   30
 And his gold
              harlequin robe
                    checkered with
                          dark squares
  Gold garlands   35
          stream down over
                    her bare calves &
                          tensed feet
Nearby there must be
          a jeweled tree   40
          with glass leaves aglitter
                in the gold air
It must be
          morning
                    in a faraway place somewhere   45
They
     are silent together
                    as in a flowered field
          upon the summer couch
                    which must be hers   50
  And he holds her still
                    so passionately
          holds her head to his
                    so gently so insistently
          to make her turn   55
                    her lips to his
Her eyes are closed
                like folded petals
She
     will not open   60
                He
                    is not the One   *[1976]*

Edvard Munch, *The Scream*. © 2011 The
Munch Museum / The Munch-Ellingsen
Group / Artists Rights Society (ARS), NY.
Photo credit: The Art Archive / Nasjonal
Galleriet Oslo.

MAY MILLER
The Scream

I am a woman controlled,
Remember this; I never scream,
Yet I stood a form apart
Watching my other frenzied self
Beaten by words and wounds   5
Make in silence a mighty scream—
A scream that the wind took up
And thrust through the bars of night
Beyond all reason's final rim.
Out where the sea's last murmur dies   10
And the gull's cry has no sound,
Out where city voices fade,
Stilled in a lyric sleep
Where silence is its own design,
My scream hovered a ghost denied   15
Wanting the shape of lips.   *[1975]*

Larry Rivers,
*Washington Crossing
the Delaware.* 1953.
Art © Estate of Larry
Rivers / Licensed by
VAGA, New York, NY.
The Museum of
Modern Art, New
York, NY. Photo credit:
The Museum of
Modern Art / Art
Resource, NY.

FRANK O'HARA

On Seeing Larry Rivers' "Washington Crossing the Delaware" at the Museum of Modern Art

Now that our hero has come back to us
in his white pants and we know his nose
trembling like a flag under fire,
we see the calm cold river is supporting
our forces, the beautiful history.   5

To be more revolutionary than a nun
is our desire, to be secular and intimate
as, when sighting a redcoat, you smile
and pull the trigger. Anxieties
and animosities, flaming and feeding   10

on theoretical considerations and
the jealous spiritualities of the abstract
the robot? they're smoke, billows above
the physical event. They have burned up.
See how free we are! as a nation of persons.   15

Dear father of our country, so alive
you must have lied incessantly to be
immediate, here are your bones crossed
on my breast like a rusty flintlock,
a pirate's flag, bravely specific   20

and ever so light in the misty glare
of a crossing by water in winter to a shore
other than that the bridge reaches for.
Don't shoot until, the white of freedom glinting
on your gun barrel, you see the general fear.   *[1955]*   25

Jeff Wall, "Dead Troops Talk (a vision after an ambush of a Red Army patrol, near Moqor, Afghanistan, winter 1986)." 1992. Transparency in lightbox, 229 × 417 cm. Courtesy of the artist.

WILFRED OWEN

Dulce Et Decorum Est

Bent double, like old beggars under sacks,
Knock-kneed, coughing like hags, we cursed through sludge,
Till on the haunting flares we turned our backs
And towards our distant rest began to trudge.
Men marched asleep. Many had lost their boots   5
But limped on, blood-shod. All went lame; all blind;
Drunk with fatigue; deaf even to the hoots
Of disappointed shells that dropped behind.

GAS! Gas! Quick, boys! — An ecstasy of fumbling,
Fitting the clumsy helmets just in time;   10
But someone still was yelling out and stumbling
And floundering like a man in fire or lime. —
Dim, through the misty panes and thick green light,
As under a green sea, I saw him drowning.

In all my dreams, before my helpless sight,   15
He plunges at me, guttering, choking, drowning.

If in some smothering dreams you too could pace
Behind the wagon that we flung him in,
And watch the white eyes writhing in his face,
His hanging face, like a devil's sick of sin;   20
If you could hear, at every jolt, the blood
Come gargling from the froth-corrupted lungs,
Obscene as cancer, bitter as the cud
Of vile, incurable sores on innocent tongues, —
My friend, you would not tell with such high zest   25
To children ardent for some desperate glory,
The old Lie: Dulce et decorum est
Pro patria mori.

[1920]

Rembrandt van Rijn, *Self Portrait at the Age of 63*. 1669. Oil on canvas, 86 × 70.5 cm. National Gallery, London. Photo Credit: © National Gallery, London / Art Resource, NY.

LINDA PASTAN

Ethics

In ethics class so many years ago
our teacher asked this question every fall:
if there were a fire in a museum
which would you save, a Rembrandt painting
or an old woman who hadn't many   5
years left anyhow? Restless on hard chairs
caring little for pictures or old age
we'd opt one year for life, the next for art
and always half-heartedly. Sometimes
the woman borrowed my grandmother's face   10
leaving her usual kitchen to wander
some drafty, half-imagined museum.
One year, feeling clever, I replied
why not let the woman decide herself?
Linda, the teacher would report, eschews   15
the burdens of responsibility.
This fall in a real museum I stand
before a real Rembrandt, old woman,
or nearly so, myself. The colors
within this frame are darker than autumn,   20
darker even than winter — the browns of earth,
though earth's most radiant elements burn
through the canvas. I know now that woman
and painting and season are almost one
and all beyond saving by children.   *[1980]*   25

Pieter Brueghel the Elder, *Landscape with the Fall of Icarus*. Musee d'Art Ancien, Musees Royaux des Beaux-Arts, Brussels, Belgium. Photo Credit: Scala / Art Resource, NY.

W. H. AUDEN

Musée des Beaux Arts

About suffering they were never wrong,
The old Masters: how well they understood
Its human position: how it takes place
While someone else is eating or opening a window or just walking dully along;
How, when the aged are reverently, passionately waiting   5
For the miraculous birth, there always must be
Children who did not specially want it to happen, skating
On a pond at the edge of the wood:
They never forgot
That even the dreadful martyrdom must run its course   10
Anyhow in a corner, some untidy spot
Where the dogs go on with their doggy life and the torturer's horse
Scratches its innocent behind on a tree.

In Brueghel's *Icarus*, for instance: how everything turns away
Quite leisurely from the disaster; the ploughman may   15
Have heard the splash, the forsaken cry,
But for him it was not an important failure; the sun shone
As it had to on the white legs disappearing into the green
Water, and the expensive delicate ship that must have seen
Something amazing, a boy falling out of the sky,   20
Had somewhere to get to and sailed calmly on.   *[1940]*

CHAPTER 6

How to Write about Poems

Some students are put off by poetry, perhaps because their early experiences with it were discouraging. They imagine that poems have deep hidden meanings they can't uncover. Maybe their high-school English teacher always had the right interpretation, and they rarely did. This need not be the case. Poetry can be accessible to all readers.

The problem is often a confusion about the nature of poetry, since poetry is more compressed than prose. Poetry focuses more on connotative, emotional, or associative meanings and conveys meaning more through suggestion, indirection, and the use of metaphor, symbol, and imagery than prose does. It seldom hands us a specific meaning. Poetic texts suggest certain possibilities, but the reader completes the transaction. Part of the meaning comes from the writer, part from the text itself, and part from the reader. Even students who are the same age, race, religion, and ethnicity are not duplicates of one another. Each has unique experiences, family histories, and emotional lives. If thirty people read a poem about conformity or responsibility, all thirty will have varying views about these concepts, even though they will probably have some commonalities. (Most societies are so saturated with shared cultural experiences that it is nearly impossible to avoid some overlap in responses.)

In a good class discussion, then, we should be aware that even though we might be members of the same culture, each of us reads from a unique perspective, a perspective that might also shift from time to time. If a woman reads a poem about childbirth, her identity as a female will seem more relevant than if she were reading a poem about death, a more universal experience. In other words, how we read a poem and how significant and meaningful the poem is for us depends both on the content of the poem and on our specific circumstances. Suppose you are fourteen when you first read a poem about dating; you would likely have very different responses rereading it at nineteen, twenty-five, and fifty. We read poems through our experiences. As we gain new experiences, our readings change.

One reason to respond in writing to your first reading is to be able to separate your first thoughts from those of your classmates. They too will bring their own experiences, values, and ideas to the discussion. In the give-and-take of open discussion, it may be difficult to remember what you first said. Of course, the point of a classroom discussion is not simply to defend your initial response, for then you would be denying yourself the benefit of other people's ideas.

A good discussion should open up the poem, allow you to see it from multiple viewpoints, and enable you to expand your perspective, to see how others make sense of the world.

This rich mixture of the poet's text, the reader's response, and discussion among several readers can create new possibilities of meaning. Even more than fiction or drama, poetry encourages creative readings that can be simultaneously true to the text and to the reader. A lively class discussion can uncover a dozen or more plausible interpretations of a poem, each backed up with valid evidence both from the poem and the reader's experience. You may try to persuade others that your views about the poem are correct; others may do the same to you. This negotiation is at the heart of a liberal, democratic education. In fact, maybe the most respected and repeated notion about being well-educated is the ability to empathize with another's point of view, to see as another sees. Reading, discussing, and writing about poetry can help you become a person who can both create meaning and understand and appreciate how others do. This is one important way literature matters.

The following nine poems are about work — about the joys and sorrows, the satisfactions and frustrations of physical labor. Some people might think of poets as intellectuals who are far removed from the experiences of the working class, but this is not the case. Indeed, many poets were themselves brought up in working-class homes and know firsthand the dignity and value of such work. Even among poets who do not toil with their hands, few lack the imaginative empathy that would allow them to write perceptively about firefighters and factory workers, cleaning women and mill workers. These nine poems are especially relevant today when physical work is becoming less and less a reality among middle-class Americans. Poems that matter are poems about real life — about love and death, about pain and loss, about beauty and hope. These nine poems about work are about all of these and more.

The first poem, "We Did Not Fear the Father," is by Charles Fort (b. 1951), an African American poet who grew up in New Britain, Connecticut, taught in the South for a number of years, and now lives and teaches in Nebraska. His poem first appeared in *The Georgia Review.* Philip Levine (b. 1928) grew up in Detroit. Much of his poetry, including "What Work Is," recalls his youth in his native city, where he worked as a laborer in Detroit factories. Mary Oliver's (b. 1935) "Singapore" appeared in *House of Light* (1992). She has won a Pulitzer Prize for her poetry. "Blackberries" is by Yusef Komunyakaa (b. 1947), who has become known for exploring various aspects of African American experience; the poem is from *Magic City* (1992). Edwin Arlington Robinson's "The Mill" is the oldest poem in the cluster. Robinson (1869–1935) is considered the first major poet of twentieth-century America. Jimmy Santiago Baca (b. 1952) was born in Santa Fe, New Mexico. He won the American Book Award for *Martin and Meditations on the South Valley* (1988). His poem here is from *Immigrants in Our Own Land* (1982). Louise Erdrich (b. 1954) is of mixed German, Chippewa, and French ancestry. Her novels *Love Medicine* and *Tracks* were best-sellers. "The Lady in the Pink Mustang" is from her poetry collection *Jacklight* (1984). Marge Piercy (b. 1936) was a child of the Depression, and her roots are thoroughly working class. She grew up Jewish in Detroit, a city that was "black and white by blocks." Piercy has worked as a secretary, a switchboard operator, a department-store clerk, an artist's model, and a low-paid part-time instructor. James Tate (b. 1943), writes: "'The Restaurant Business' seems to me to be very much a slice of life. . . . Some people say they hate their lives, and then will kill to defend them, because it's all they have, and they can't change." The poem appeared in *Best American Poetry 2003*.

CHARLES FORT
We Did Not Fear the Father

We did not fear the father as the barber who stood
like a general in a white jacket with a green visor cap.
For six long days he held a straight razor like a sword
until his porcelain-chrome chariot became a down-home chair.
The crop-eared son learned to see how the workingman's   5
day job after the night shift filled the son's small pockets
with licorice, filled the offering plate, and paid for the keeper
who clipped our grape vines under his own pageant.

We did not fear the father as landlord in our three-story tenement
who took charge of four apartments and the attic dwellers.   10
We searched each corner of the dirt cellar for a fuse box
while he broke out plasterboard upstairs with a sledgehammer.
We peeled out paper from wire mesh and read the headline news
a century old before he lifted us like birds into our bunk beds.

We did not fear the father until he entered the tomb of noise   15
for his night job, shaping molten steel into ball bearings
as we stared into the barbed grate where he stood
before the furnace sending smoke into the trees.
Fear became the eight-hour echo and glow inside his skull,
the high-pitched metal scraping our ears as our provider   20
left the factory floor with oil and sawdust inside his mouth
and punched out as fermented daylight burned his eyes.
We did not fear our father until he stooped in the dark.   *[1999]*

PHILIP LEVINE
What Work Is

We stand in the rain in a long line
waiting at Ford Highland Park. For work.
You know what work is — if you're
old enough to read this you know what
work is, although you may not do it.   5

Forget you. This is about waiting,
shifting from one foot to another.
Feeling the light rain falling like mist
into your hair, blurring your vision
until you think you see your own brother   10
ahead of you, maybe ten places.
You rub your glasses with your fingers,
and of course it's someone else's brother,
narrower across the shoulders than
yours but with the same sad slouch, the grin   15
that does not hide the stubbornness,
the sad refusal to give in to
rain, to the hours wasted waiting,
to the knowledge that somewhere ahead
a man is waiting who will say, "No,   20
we're not hiring today," for any
reason he wants. You love your brother,
now suddenly you can hardly stand
the love flooding you for your brother,
who's not beside you or behind or   25
ahead because he's home trying to
sleep off a miserable night shift
at Cadillac so he can get up
before noon to study his German.
Works eight hours a night so he can sing   30
Wagner, the opera you hate most,
the worst music ever invented.
How long has it been since you told him
you loved him, held his wide shoulders,
opened your eyes wide and said those words,   35
and maybe kissed his cheek? You've never
done something so simple, so obvious,
not because you're too young or too dumb,
not because you're jealous or even mean
or incapable of crying in   40
the presence of another man, no,
just because you don't know what work is.   *[1991]*

MARY OLIVER
Singapore

In Singapore, in the airport,
a darkness was ripped from my eyes.
In the women's restroom, one compartment stood open.

A woman knelt there, washing something
   in the white bowl.   5

Disgust argued in my stomach
and I felt, in my pocket, for my ticket.

A poem should always have birds in it.
Kingfishers, say, with their bold eyes and gaudy wings.
Rivers are pleasant, and of course trees.   10
A waterfall, or if that's not possible, a fountain
   rising and falling.
A person wants to stand in a happy place, in a poem.

When the woman turned I could not answer her face.
Her beauty and her embarrassment struggled together, and   15
   neither could win.
She smiled and I smiled. What kind of nonsense is this?
Everybody needs a job.
Yes, a person wants to stand in a happy place, in a poem.
But first we must watch her as she stares down at her labor,   20
   which is dull enough.
She is washing the tops of the airport ashtrays, as big as
   hubcaps, with a blue rag.
Her small hands turn the metal, scrubbing and rinsing.
She does not work slowly, nor quickly, but like a river.
Her dark hair is like the wing of a bird.   25

I don't doubt for a moment that she loves her life.
And I want her to rise up from the crust and the slop
   and fly down to the river.
This probably won't happen.   30
But maybe it will.
If the world were only pain and logic, who would want it?

Of course, it isn't.
Neither do I mean anything miraculous, but only
the light that can shine out of a life. I mean   35
the way she unfolded and refolded the blue cloth,
the way her smile was only for my sake; I mean
the way this poem is filled with trees, and birds.

[1992]

YUSEF KOMUNYAKAA

Blackberries

They left my hands like a printer's
Or thief's before a police blotter
& pulled me into early morning's

Terrestrial sweetness, so thick
The damp ground was consecrated   5
Where they fell among a garland of thorns.

Although I could smell old lime-covered
History, at ten I'd still hold out my hands
& berries fell into them. Eating from one
& filling a half gallon with the other,   10
I ate the mythology & dreamt
Of pies & cobbler, almost

Needful as forgiveness. My bird dog Spot
Eyed blue jays & thrashers. The mud frogs
In rich blackness, hid from daylight.   15
An hour later, beside City Limits Road
I balanced a gleaming can in each hand,
Limboed between worlds, repeating *one dollar.*
The big blue car made me sweat.
Wintertime crawled out of the windows.   20
When I leaned closer I saw the boy
& girl my age, in the wide back seat
Smirking, & it was then I remembered my fingers
Burning with thorns among berries too ripe to touch.   *[1992]*

EDWIN ARLINGTON ROBINSON

The Mill

The miller's wife had waited long,
      The tea was cold, the fire was dead;
And there might yet be nothing wrong
      In how he went and what he said;
"There are no millers any more,"   5
      Was all that she had heard him say;
And he had lingered at the door
      So long that it seemed yesterday.

Sick with fear that had no form
      She knew that she was there at last;   10
And in the mill there was a warm
      And mealy fragrance of the past.
What else there was would only seem
      To say again what he had meant;
And what was hanging from a beam   15
      Would not have heeded where she went.

And if she thought it followed her,
      She may have reasoned in the dark

That one way of the few there were
   Would hide her and would leave no mark: 20
Black water, smooth above the weir
   Like starry velvet in the night,
Though ruffled once, would soon appear
   The same as ever to the sight.   *[1920]*

JIMMY SANTIAGO BACA
So Mexicans Are Taking Jobs from Americans

O Yes? do they come on horses
with rifles, and say,
   Ese, gringo, gimmee your job?
And do you, gringo, take off your ring,
drop your wallet into a blanket   5
spread over the ground, and walk away?

I hear Mexicans are taking your jobs away.
Do they sneak into town at night,
and as you're walking home with a whore,
do they mug you, a knife at your throat,   10
saying, I want your job?

Even on TV, an asthmatic leader
crawls turtle heavy, leaning on an assistant,
and from a nest of wrinkles on his face,
a tongue paddles through flashing waves   15
of lightbulbs, of cameramen, rasping,
"They're taking our jobs away."

Well, I've gone about trying to find them,
asking just where the hell are these fighters.

The rifles I hear sound in the night   20
are white farmers shooting blacks and browns
whose ribs I see jutting out
and starving children,
I see the poor marching for a little work,
I see small white farmers selling out   25
to clean-suited farmers living in New York,
who've never been on a farm,
don't know the look of a hoof or the smell
of a woman's body bending all day long in fields.

I see this, and I hear only a few people   30
got all the money in this world, the rest
count their pennies to buy bread and butter.

Below that cool green sea of money,
millions and millions of people fight to live,
search for pearls in the darkest depths   35
of their dreams, hold their breath for years
trying to cross poverty to just having something.

The children are dead already. We are killing them,
that is what America should be saying;
on TV, in the streets, in offices, should be saying,   40
"We aren't giving the children a chance to live."

    Mexicans are taking our jobs, they say instead.
    What they really say is, let them die,
    and the children too.   *[1982]*

LOUISE ERDRICH
The Lady in the Pink Mustang

The sun goes down for hours, taking more of her along
than the night leaves her with.
A body moving in the dust
must shed its heavy parts in order to go on.

Perhaps you have heard of her, the Lady in the Pink Mustang,   5
whose bare lap is floodlit from under the dash,
who cruises beneath the high snouts of semis, reading
the blink of their lights. *Yes. Move Over. Now.*
or *How Much.* Her price shrinks into the dark.

She can't keep much trash in a Mustang,   10
and that's what she likes. Travel light. Don't keep
what does not have immediate uses. The road thinks ahead.
It thinks for her, a streamer from Bismarck to Fargo
bending through Minnesota to accommodate the land.

She won't carry things she can't use anymore.   15
Just a suit, sets of underwear, what you would expect
in a Pink Mustang. Things she could leave anywhere.

There is a point in the distance where the road meets itself,
where coming and going must kiss into one.
She is always at that place, seen from behind,   20
motionless, torn forward, living in a zone
all her own. It is like she has burned right through time,
the brand, the mark, owning the woman who bears it.

She owns them, not one will admit what they cannot
come close to must own them. She takes them along,   25

traveling light. It is what she must face every time
she is touched. The body disposable as cups.

To live, instead of turn, on a dime.
One light point that is so down in value.
Painting her nipples silver for a show, she is thinking,   30
You out there. What do you know.

Come out of the dark where you're safe. Kissing these
bits of change, stamped out, ground to a luster,
is to kiss yourself away piece by piece
until we're even. Until the last   35
coin is rubbed for luck and spent.
I don't sell for nothing less.   *[1984]*

MARGE PIERCY
The Secretary Chant

My hips are a desk.
From my ears hang
chains of paper clips.
Rubber bands form my hair.

My breasts are wells of mimeograph ink.   5
My feet bear casters.
Buzz. Click.
My head is a badly organized file.
My head is a switchboard

where crossed lines crackle.   10
Press my fingers
and in my eyes appear
credit and debit.
Zing. Tinkle.

My navel is a reject button.   15
From my mouth issue canceled reams.
Swollen, heavy, rectangular
I am about to be delivered
of a baby

Xerox machine.   20
File me under W
because I wonce
was
a woman.   *[1973]*

JAMES TATE

The Restaurant Business

Elsie and I were having a nice, little romantic
dinner at our favorite restaurant, when the owner of
the restaurant came over and sat down at our table.
We had always greeted one another in a friendly fashion,
but we had never had an actual conversation with him   5
before. "I have no life," he said. "I work nineteen
hours a day. I employ a hundred-and-twenty people.
There's more paper work than you could ever imagine.
This place is killing me," he said with tears in his
eyes. We had stopped eating and just stared at him   10
in dumbfoundment. "Everybody needs a life," I said.
"You could sell the place." "My customers would kill
me. I have customers who drive two-hundred-and-fifty
miles each week to eat here. What would I tell them?"
he said. "You could change your name and move far   15
away, live in the wilderness with lots of animals,"
I said. Our food was getting cold. Neither of us
had taken a bite since he joined us. "But my guilt,
I'd have to live with a terrible guilt. The thought
of taking away so much pleasure from so many fine   20
people would keep me from enjoying anything," he said.
"But you said that you have no life, didn't you?"
Elsie said. There was a note of exasperation in her
voice. "My wife would have left me long ago if it
weren't for the money. She's the one that gets to   25
enjoy that, I don't," he said. It's true, the place
was always packed. He was making a ton of money.
"I don't get to do anything. My children grew up
without me. I own a boat, but I've only been on it
once. I don't go to movies, I don't watch television.   30
I don't know anything about sports or politics. It's
a pathetic way to live," he said. I looked at Elsie.
She looked like she wanted to slap him, and not just
once. "I had always thought you were really something.
Boy, was I mistaken. Everybody has a life, everybody   35
but you. And what right do you think you have to
spoil our romantic meal with your contemptible story?"
I said. "In here, I'm God. This is my kingdom, and
you are my peasant serfs. You eat only what I'm willing
to give you. And when I talk, you must listen. Scum,"   40
he said, and walked off, erect, chest pushed out, proud,
possessed.   [2003]

▇ A WRITING EXERCISE

Look again at the topics of literary studies (pp. 41–43), selecting one that seems promising as an interpretive lens through which to view the nine work poems in this cluster. Freewrite for a few minutes on all nine, but don't worry if your topic doesn't seem to fit all the poems. A later exercise will eventually ask you to pick the three poems that work best.

A Student's Personal Responses to the Poems

The following are selections from the response journal of Michaela Fiorucci, a nineteen-year-old sophomore from Cape May, New Jersey, who chose to focus on boundaries — on the various divisions we set up between ourselves and other people, such as income, race, gender, sexual preference, and religion. It seemed to her an interesting way to talk about work since Michaela had observed barriers of all kinds between workers at her job at the university.

Using an explorative strategy, Michaela did some freewriting on the nine poems, hoping to discover an argument about boundaries that might fit at least three of the poems. The following are selections from her response journal.

In "We Did Not Fear the Father," the poet begins with a division between his father as a normal man and his own image of him as a general in a chariot. Mostly there is the father's separation from the family during his day job, his night job, and his landlord job. In the last stanza we can see the real separation that the poet has been leading up to — the separation of the father as he enters "the tomb of noise" where he might lose his health. The boundary the poet really fears is between a robust and a "stooped" father, between his protection and his loss.

Although the boundary in "What Work Is" seems to be between those who know what hard work is and those who don't, the narrator shifts his focus when he thinks he sees his brother in line, waiting for work. The most significant boundary in the poem is emotional intimacy or honesty. The poet laments our inability to cross that psychological boundary.

In "Singapore," there is a clear boundary between the middle-class American tourist and the cleaning lady, so much so that at first the narrator says, "Disgust argued in my stomach." The cleaning woman also seems to believe in a barrier and continues to work in a steady way. The narrator finally sees beauty in her dedication to her work. When the narrator does see beauty in her work habits, it helps close the barrier between them. There are also the issues of boundaries between fantasy and reality and between a world of pain and logic and one with birds and rivers. But at the end these boundaries also seem to be closing.

In "Blackberries," the young boy seems to be living in a rural paradise, beyond the city boundaries, outside the usual urban and suburban environment. He lives in a land of bird dogs, jays, thrashers, and mud frogs. He makes comparisons between blackness and light that seem to anticipate the economic boundary that appears in the last stanza, the one between the poor boy and the rich kids in the car. It is this division between the children in air-conditioned comfort and the narrator on the outside looking in that seems to be the main point of this poem. Some boundaries cause us pain.

"The Mill" tells the sad story of a miller who could not see a boundary between himself and his job. When he tells his wife "there are no millers any more," he is really saying that his life is over; he has no reason to live. And so he crosses the boundary between life and death. Tragically, his wife also has difficulty seeing herself outside her role as wife and housekeeper, and so she also crosses that ultimate boundary. She does so, however, in a completely different way: she drowns herself, so no one will know. She passes through life's boundary without leaving a trace.

In "So Mexicans Are Taking Jobs from Americans," the speaker reflects bitterly on two types of boundaries. The first is the illusory boundary between violent Mexicans who cross over into America and forcibly seize jobs from peaceful working-class Americans. The second is the actual boundary between the American and Mexican have-nots, who fight over hardscrabble jobs, and the American corporate farmers who control the jobs and pit the poor against each other as they grow rich from their labor. While the wealthy float on a "cool green sea of money," the poor drown beneath that sea, holding their breath for years as they try to cross a sea of poverty. Economic opportunity, not geography, is the real boundary that divides nations and separates the impoverished many from the wealthy few.

"The Lady in the Pink Mustang" exists in an in-between state. She is an outsider who is defined by the boundaries of what the law would call her: a prostitute. She is presented as somehow nonhuman, a commodity with a "body disposable as cups." Her lack of a core personal identity is emphasized by the fact that she has no name — she is referred to only as a "Lady." This lack of a core self gives her a kind of freedom, suggested by how lightly she travels (with a few disposable items, like a suit and some underwear) and the endless way she roams the broad empty Midwestern roads. But even this freedom is compromised: she must stay on the road because "It thinks for her" and is traveled by the truck drivers who provide her livelihood. At once free and not free, powerful and disempowered, bounded and without boundaries, she lives "in a zone / all her own."

Although "The Secretary Chant" is not meant to be subtle in equating a woman with desks, mimeograph ink, and a switchboard, Piercy's metaphors make a strong statement about how certain jobs can make you feel like a robot. This can happen even to high-paid workers; however, we know that women, especially secretaries, were expected to wait on their male bosses hand-and-foot without much pay or proper respect for the tedious low-paid work that they did. The actual boundary between the inanimate objects found in an office and a person is obviously significant, but the ending "I wonce / was / a woman" directly asserts that even that boundary can be crossed by work that dehumanizes.

"The Restaurant Business" is a funny poem, although it is surely meant to be taken seriously. The obvious boundary crossed is the one between the owner and his customers. This situation probably would never happen, but people do complain bitterly about work and school. Perhaps because of too much work, some people don't really have a life. But there still seems to be a lot of exaggeration here. The owner's life does seem bleak. He has erected a wall between work and the rest of his life, and at first he doesn't seem as if he can get over that wall to enjoy himself. But when he blows up at the end, it seems clear that he wants the life he has because he is in total control. He wouldn't change if he could.

After reading these nine brief freewrites to her response group, Michaela decided that "Blackberries," "Singapore," and "The Mill" were the most promising. Michaela still didn't have a focus, but she liked the idea that boundaries, like walls, sometimes serve a purpose and sometimes they don't. She remembered a discussion of Robert Frost's "Mending Wall" from another course that focused on negotiating the walls we build between us. Her professor liked this idea since it helped her considerably narrow the concept of boundaries.

After reviewing her freewriting, Michaela wrote the following first draft and read it to her response group. She then discussed with her instructor her plans for a revision. Her instructor made a number of specific and general comments. After reading her first draft, what feedback would you give Michaela? Her revision appears at the end of the chapter.

First Draft of a Student Paper

Michaela Fiorucci
Mr. Hardee
English 102
15 April - - - -

Boundaries in Robinson, Komunyakaa, and Oliver

Although most sophomores I know at school value their privacy, they also want to create intimate relationships. It is often hard to reconcile these two impulses. Most middle-class students are lucky enough to have their own rooms, private enclaves against annoying sisters and brothers, intrusive mothers and fathers. But a room is also more than a physical boundary; it is also a symbolic assertion of identity. It says, "I'm separate from others, even within the closeness of the family." Such a commitment to physical privacy might be innocent enough, but it does contain dangerous seeds, especially when extended beyond the home to neighborhoods. When different ethnic groups want boundaries between them, it is no longer innocent. When the upper classes need to be separated from workers because they see each other as radically different, a dangerous boundary has been erected.

It would be reductive, however, to say all boundaries need to be erased. Edwin Arlington Robinson's "The Mill" is a good example of the dangerous consequences of a missing boundary. The poem narrates the sad story of a farm couple who commit suicide — the husband because he feels useless, the wife because she can't imagine life without her husband. During my first few readings, I was struck by the lack of communication between the couple. He must have been depressed for a long time, but it seems they never discussed his feelings. Keeping an emotional distance from others was probably a typical part of the way men and women dealt with each other a hundred years ago. It was a boundary not to be crossed. Apparently he could not say, "I feel terrible that I am going to lose my job." And his wife accepts his reticence, even though he might have been having second thoughts as he "lingered at the door." Clearly this is a boundary that should have been breached. But after several readings I began to realize that the boundary that should have been established wasn't — the idea that a person's value or worth is synonymous with his or her identity is dehumanizing. And it probably isn't something that just happened in the past. Nor is the equally dehumanizing idea that a wife is nothing without her husband. When the miller's wife decides to "leave no mark" by jumping into the pond, she is admitting she is not a worthwhile person by herself. Both identify totally with a role that in my view should be only one aspect of a complex human life. The final barrier she crosses, from life to death, is symbolically represented in the poem as a feminine domestic gesture: she doesn't want to leave a mess. The boundaries of person and occupation should be made clear; the arbitrary boundaries between genders should not.

When the narrator in "Blackberries" claims that he is "Limboed between worlds," he means the rural paradise of "Terrestrial sweetness" and "rich blackness" he temporarily lives in versus the commercial, urban work that "made me sweat." He has constructed a boundary between the ancient picking of berries and the technology of automobiles, between a natural closeness with nature and the artificial "Wintertime crawled out of the windows." Even though the narrator is only ten, he senses the sensual joys of being one with nature. He seems to reject "old lime-covered / History" in favor of "mythology," which seems to suggest a conscious rejection or maybe repression of the contemporary world. But this boundary cannot stand. He needs the outside world to survive, and when the car approaches, it is the modern world and all its pluses and minuses that draw near. When he looks in, he sees "Smirking" children; he sees class prejudice, hierarchy, and economic reality. The smirkers of the world are in charge. This realization dissolves the protective boundary around his Garden of Eden, and he feels physical pain. But really he feels the pain of initiation, the pain of having to cross a boundary he wanted to delay as long as possible. Although we can sympathize with the young narrator, he would probably have fared better by not making his boundary so extreme.

The narrator in Mary Oliver's "Singapore" at first sees a significant boundary between herself as a middle-class traveler and a cleaning woman washing a toilet. It is a separation we might all make, given our socialization to see this kind of physical labor as degrading. College-educated people in America have a tendency to see themselves as distinct from workers. For most, a woman washing something in a compartment is beyond the pale, a clear indication that the woman is other. But Oliver does have some conflicting ideas since she says a "Disgust argued in my stomach." Since we are also socialized to be tolerant and open-minded, she knows she shouldn't think this way. And since she is also a writer with ideas about how a poem should "always have birds in it," she looks harder at the cleaning woman, finally seeing in her face, in her hair, and in the way she works slowly, "like a river," the positive aspects she probably wants to find. Oliver does not simply accept the boundaries that her culture constructs but negotiates with herself, eventually seeing that "light . . . can shine out of a life" even where we do not expect it. In the woman's careful folding and unfolding of her blue work cloth and in her smile, Oliver eclipses the social boundary and ends up with a life-affirming vision "filled with trees, and birds."

The Elements of Poetry

SPEAKER AND TONE

The voice we hear in a poem could be the poet's, but it is better to think of the speaker as an artistic construction — perhaps a **persona** (mask) for the poet or perhaps a character who does not resemble the poet at all. For example, the speaker in Robert Browning's poem "My Last Duchess" (see Chapter 13, "Doing Justice") is not Browning himself but instead a sinister duke. In large part, to describe any poem's speaker is to pinpoint the person's tone or attitude. Sometimes this is hard to discern. The tone could be ironic or sentimental, joyful or morose, or a combination of emotions. To get a precise sense of it, read the poem aloud, actually performing the speaker's role. Bear in mind that his or her tone may change over the course of the poem. For instance, as the speaker in Yusef Komunyakaa's "Blackberries" recalls a day in his childhood when he picked fruit and then tried to sell it on a highway, he shifts from nostalgia (remembering "Terrestrial sweetness") to bitter recognition of racism (the "Smirking" of the children, evidently white, who passed him in their car). Furthermore, some poems feature other voices besides the main speaker's, requiring you to compare various forms of talk. James Tate's "The Restaurant Business," for example, presents a conversation involving not only the "I" who narrates the poem but also his romantic partner Elsie as well as the restaurant owner. You, as a reader, are left to analyze and evaluate the statements that all three of these people make.

■ **A WRITING EXERCISE**

Each poem in this cluster has a distinctive tone. Sometimes the speaker speaks in the first person; sometimes, in the third person as an observer. Compare the tone of the speaker in Charles Fort's or Mary Oliver's poem with the tone of Edwin Arlington Robinson's "The Mill," noting if it is easier to sense the speaker's tone when *I* or *we* is used.

DICTION AND SYNTAX

With "We Did Not Fear the Father," we initially assume that "fear" in the first line carries the usual negative **denotation** of anxiety, but the image that follows — the "general in a white jacket with a green visor cap" — doesn't seem threatening. In line three, "razor" and "sword" might cause concern, but that quickly dissolves under the positive **connotations** of "chariot" and "downhome chair." Except for the similes and metaphors, throughout the first stanza the diction and syntax seem almost colloquial and straightforward, mostly with the usual subject-verb-object pattern. The second half of the first stanza is also filled with positive connotations ("licorice," "offering plate," and "grape vines") that continue to undercut the worrisome "fear" of the first line.

But Fort repeats "We did not fear the father," this time referring to him not as barber but as landlord. Again the speaker's syntax and diction undercut any threat. On the contrary, the poetic simile "lifted us like birds" suggests a gentle and strong provider.

In the last stanza, he again repeats the opening phrase but adds the simple but critical "until." Now we anticipate that there might actually be a reason for "fear" in its usual denotation. But again we see the father at work. Now as factory worker, "shaping molten steel into ball bearings." The diction becomes more menacing ("barbed grate," "glow inside his skull," "metal scraping our ears," "punched out," "burned his eyes"). Now we are prepared for the simple declarative sentence: "We did not fear our father until he stooped in the dark." The poignant image of the father "stooped" dramatically clarifies the meaning of the ambiguous "fear": the children fear that his hard work has seriously weakened their "general." The speaker is actually fearful for his father and, of course, by extension fearful that his protector will be taken from him.

▤ A WRITING EXERCISE

Compare the diction and syntax in "Singapore" and "Blackberries." How do the denotation and connotation of the words convey the speaker's attitude? How does the syntax?

FIGURES OF SPEECH

When we use figures of speech, we mean something other than the words' literal meaning. In the first sentence of "Singapore," Mary Oliver writes that "a darkness was ripped from my eyes." This direct comparison is a **metaphor**. Had she been more indirect, she might have written "it was like a darkness . . . ," a common literary device called a **simile**. Poets use metaphors and similes to help us see in a fresh perspective. Comparing love to a rose encourages us to think differently about love, helping us see its delicate beauty. Of course, today that comparison is no longer novel and can even be a cliché, suggesting that a writer is not trying to be original and is settling instead for an easy comparison. When Robert Burns wrote "my love is like a red, red rose" more than two hundred years ago, it was a fresh comparison that excited new ways of looking at love. Indeed, some theorists, like the contemporary American philosopher Richard Rorty, think that metaphors can change our ways of looking at the world. Our thinking about time, for example, might be different if we didn't think with linear metaphors about the past being behind us and the future up ahead. What if, as some American Indian languages do, ours used a circular metaphor, having just one day that constantly repeated itself? Would our perceptions of time change? And since Marge Piercy's poem "The Secretary Chant" was written in 1973, did her metaphors of a woman as a desk, rubber bands, paper clips, and a wastepaper basket help the culture see the widespread dehumanization of female workers?

What if Mary Oliver had begun her poem by saying that "a misunderstanding was corrected," instead of "a darkness was ripped from my eyes"? Her metaphor is not only more dramatic and memorable but also more suggestive. Darkness deepens the idea of lack of knowledge, suggesting not only intellectual blindness but also a host of negative connotations that readers might associate with the dark. Fresh metaphors can be expansive and illuminating. They help us understand the world differently.

Oliver creatively uses metaphors and similes throughout "Singapore." "Disgust argued" is an interesting metaphor or perhaps a personification, in which the speaker's stomach is given the ability to argue. She interrupts her observation of the cleaning woman in the third stanza to make a comment on the function of poetry itself, claiming that poems should have birds, rivers, and trees in them. Is she suggesting metaphorically that poems should be pleasant? Is that the only thing birds, rivers, and trees suggest to you?

She returns to the woman, and they exchange glances. Apparently the speaker is struggling with her own socialization that sees this kind of physical labor as demeaning. She directly describes the woman's "scrubbing and rinsing" but then returns to similes, describing her work as being "like a river" and her hair "like the wing of a bird." These comparisons seem for a moment to clarify the event for the speaker, helping her see this seemingly oppressive job positively. Amazingly, she wants the woman actually to become a bird and "rise up from the crust and the slop and fly."

But in the final stanza, she reminds us that she isn't really expecting that kind of physical miracle; instead, she wants to remind us that how we describe the woman working controls how we feel about her. If we see the folding and unfolding of her washcloth metaphorically, then we might see her differently; we might see her natural dignity, her beauty, and how her "light" was able to illuminate the speaker's "darkness."

Although students often seem perplexed when professors find hidden **symbols** in poems, writers rarely plant such puzzling images deep in the recesses of their texts. The best symbols grow naturally out of the meaning-making process that readers go through. In the context of a particular poem, symbols are usually objects that can stand for general ideas. And like metaphors and similes, they suggest different things to different readers. The whale in *Moby-Dick*, for example, can be read as a symbol for implacable evil or perhaps the mysteries of the universe. The glass unicorn in *The Glass Menagerie* is often read as a symbol for Laura's fragility, but it might also suggest her uniqueness or maybe her isolation from real life. In "Singapore," the specific event of the speaker watching a woman washing ashtrays in a toilet could be symbolic of anything we find unpleasant or strange or alien. And the whole event, including her eventual understanding, could easily be an **allegory** or extended symbol for the necessity for all of us to transcend our cultural socialization to understand other cultures and other attitudes toward working.

≡ A WRITING EXERCISE

Look at several of the poems in this cluster, noting the metaphors, similes, symbols, and allegories that you notice. Do they enhance the meaning of the poem? Do they help you see the situation in a fresh way?

SOUND

The English poet Alexander Pope hoped that poetry's **sound** could become "an echo to [its] sense," that what the ear hears would reinforce what the mind understands. To many people, **rhyme** is the most recognizable aspect of poetry. The matching of final vowel and consonant sounds can make a poem trite or interesting. The now-familiar rhyming of "moon" and "June" with "swoon" suggests a poet who will settle for a cliché rather than do the hard work of being fresh. Rhyme, of course, is pleasing to the ear and makes the poem easier to remember, but it also gives the poem psychological force. Most contemporary poets choose not to rhyme, preferring the flexibility and freedom of free verse. But sound is still a high priority.

In Philip Levine's "What Work Is," for example, sound is used in subtle ways to reinforce meaning. Poets use *alliteration*, for example, to connect words near each other by repeating the initial consonant sound. A variation, *asso-*

nance, repeats vowel sounds. Levine focuses on the shifting meaning of work, claiming first that "You know what work is" and then in the last line that "you don't know what work is." Levine begins by talking about the difficulties of physical labor and concludes by noting the difficult work of emotional intimacy. He creates patterns of sound that prepare us for this shift. A number of words are repeated: *work, stand, know, waiting, rain, long, love, sad, ahead, man, wide, not,* and *because,* as well as the phrase "You know what work is." And a number of words are alliteratively connected:

> forget, foot, feeling, falling, fingers
>
> someone, shoulders, same sad slouch, stubbornness, sad
>
> wasted waiting, wants, somewhere
>
> brother, beside, behind
>
> works, worst, wide, words
>
> never, not

Although these sounds probably affect readers unconsciously, they do prepare us for a shift from people waiting for a job to the job of brotherly love. The repeated sounds connect both halves of the poem. Note the way *stand* first means being in line but later ("you can hardly stand / the love") connects with a brotherly bond. Similarly, *shift* first describes restless behavior in line but later the night job of the sleeping brother. The word *long* also fits this pattern, as it initially means the length of the line and later refers to the duration of their relationship: "How long has it been since you told him / you loved him." In these and other ways, Levine uses sound to enhance meaning.

≡ A WRITING EXERCISE

Note the use of alliteration in "We Did Not Fear the Father." How might this and other sound devices enhance the poem's meaning?

RHYTHM AND METER

Many poets in the early twentieth century chose to have their poems rhyme. Edwin Arlington Robinson's "The Mill" employs a typical **rhyme scheme** in which in each stanza the last words in lines 1 and 3 sound the same and the last words in lines 2 and 4 sound the same. We indicate such a pattern with letters — *abab.* The second half of the first stanza would then be *cdcd* and so forth.

　　Rhythm in poetry refers to the beat, a series of stresses, pauses, and accents. We are powerfully attuned to rhythm, whether it is our own heartbeat or the throb of the bass guitar in a rock band. When we pronounce a word, we give more **stress** (breath, emphasis) to some syllables than to others. When these stresses occur at a regular interval over, say, a line of poetry, we refer to it as **meter.** When we scan a line of poetry, we try to mark its stresses and pauses. We use ´ to indicate a stressed syllable and ˘ for an unstressed one. The basic measuring unit for these stressed and unstressed syllables in English is the **foot**. There are four usual feet: *iambic, trochaic, anapestic,* and *dactylic.* An **iamb** is an unstressed syllable followed by a stressed one, as in "the woods." Reversed we have a **trochee**, as in "tiger." An **anapest** contains three syllables that are unstressed, then unstressed, then stressed, as in "When the blúe / wăve rŏlls nightly / ŏn deép Galilee." The reverse, the **dactyl**, can be heard in the Mother Goose rhyme, "Pússy cát, / pússy cát / whére have yŏu / beén?" If you look at the first four lines of "The Mill" again, you can hear a regular beat of iambs:

> The mĭll / er's wĭfe / hăd waĭt / ĕd lŏng.
>
> The tea / wăs cŏld, / the fire / wăs dead;
>
> Ănd there / mĭght yet / bĕ noth / ĭng wrong
>
> Ĭn hŏw / hĕ went / ănd what / hĕ said:

Depending on the number of feet, we give lines various names. If a line contains one foot, it is a **monometer**; two, a **dimeter**; three, a **trimeter**; four, a **tetrameter**; five, a **pentameter**; six, a **hexameter**; seven, a **heptameter**; and eight, an **octometer**. So Robinson's lines are iambic tetrameter. Most lines in Shakespeare's sonnets are iambic pentameter, or five iambs.

Note the punctuation in Robinson's poem. When a line ends with a comma, we are meant to pause very briefly; when a line ends with a period (end stop), we pause a bit longer. But when there is no punctuation (line 7), we are meant to continue on until the end of the next line. This is known as *enjambment.* These poetic techniques improve the sound and flow of the poem and enhance the thoughts and feelings that give poetry its memorable depth and meaningfulness.

▤ A WRITING EXERCISE

Finish marking the rhythm and meter of "The Mill." Why do you think the poet chose these patterns rather than free verse? Does the rhyme add to the poem's somber, rather grim conclusion?

THEME

Some readers are fond of extracting ideas from poems, claiming, for example, that the theme of "Blackberries" is the loss of innocence or that the theme of "What Work Is" is the emotional reticence of men. In a sense, these thematic observations are plausible enough, but they are limiting and misleading. "Blackberries" certainly seems to have something to do with the interruption of a certain view about physical labor, but the significance for each reader might be much more specific, having to do with the noble savage; the Garden of Eden; hierarchy in society; the arrogance of the rich; or sensitivity, cruelty, and dignity. Reducing a complex, ambiguous poem to a bald statement robs the poem of its evocative power, its mystery, and its art.

Some critics stress the response of readers; others care only for what the text itself says; still others are concerned with the social and cultural implications of the poem's meaning. Psychoanalytic readers may see poems as reflections of the psychological health or illness of the poet; source-hunting or intertextual readers want to find references and hints of other literary works hidden deep within the poem. Feminist readers may find sexism, Marxists may find economic injustice, and gay and lesbian readers may find heterosexual bias. Readers can and will find in texts a whole range of issues. Perhaps we find what we are looking for, or we find what matters most to us.

This does not mean that we should think of committed readers as biased or as distorting the text to fulfill their own agenda, although biased or distorted readings are not rare. In a literature course, readers are entitled to read poems according to their own interpretations as long as they follow the general convention of academic discourse. That is, it is possible to make a reasonable case that "Blackberries" is really about rejecting contemporary technology in favor of rural life. The reason that some themes sound more plausible than others is that these critics marshal their evidence from the text and their own experience. Usually the evidence that fits best wins: if you can persuade others that you have significant textual support for your theme and if you present a balanced and judicious persona, you can usually carry the day. Poems almost always have several reasonable themes. The critic's job is to argue for a theme that seems to make the most sense in relation to the support. Often the same evidence can be used to bolster different themes because themes are really just higher-level generalizations than the particulars found in the text. Critics use the concrete elements of a poem to make more general abstract statements. In "Blackberries," for example, the same textual support could be used to uphold a theme about the cruelty of children or the more general notion of an initiation in a class-conscious culture or the even more general idea of the inevitable loss of innocence.

▤ A WRITING EXERCISE

What are some possible themes introduced in "The Mill"? How might the theme change if read from the context of gender? Culture? Economics? Psychology?

Revised Draft of a Student Paper

Michaela Fiorucci
Mr. Hardee
English 102
25 April - - - -

Negotiating Boundaries

Although most college students value their privacy, they also want to create intimate relationships; it is often hard to reconcile these two impulses. Most middle-class students are lucky enough to have their own bedrooms, private enclaves against annoying sisters and brothers, intrusive mothers and fathers. But such boundaries are more than physical barriers; they are also a symbolic assertion of identity. They say, "I'm separate from you even within the closeness of our family." Such a commitment to physical privacy might be innocent enough, but it does contain dangerous seeds, especially when extended beyond the home to neighborhoods. When different ethnic groups want boundaries between them, it is no longer innocent. When the upper classes want to be separated from workers because they see each other as radically different, a dangerously undemocratic boundary has been erected. Boundaries clearly serve a protective function, but unneeded ones can also prevent us from helping and understanding each other. Writers like Edwin Arlington Robinson, Yusef Komunyakaa, and Mary Oliver understand that we must negotiate boundaries, building them when they increase privacy and self-worth and bridging them when human solidarity can be enhanced.

It would be reductive to say that boundaries are either good or bad, since their value depends so much on context. Robinson's "The Mill" is a good example of the dangerous consequences of a failure to cross a boundary that should not exist and then a failure to establish a boundary where one should exist. The poem narrates the sad story of a farm couple who commit suicide — the husband because he feels useless, the wife because she can't imagine life without her husband. A contemporary reader is struck by the lack of communication between the couple. He must have been depressed for a long time, but it seems they never discussed his feelings. Keeping such an emotional boundary between husband and wife was probably typical of the way men and women dealt with each other one hundred years ago. Apparently it was a constructed barrier that few could cross. He simply could not bare his heart by saying, "I feel terrible that I am going to lose my job." And his wife accepts his reticence, even though he might have been having second thoughts as he "lingered at the door." Clearly this is a boundary that should have been breached. The time for their solidarity was before he kills himself, not after.

After several readings it is clear that the boundary that should have been established wasn't. The miller is the victim of the demeaning idea that a person's worth is synonymous with his or her occupation. When his job disappears, so must he. Although Robinson's tone is flat, we sense his frustration with the inevitability of this grim tragedy, one that is compounded by the equally dehumanizing idea that a wife cannot exist without her husband. When the miller's wife decides to "leave no mark" by jumping into the pond, she is admitting that she is useless outside her matrimonial role. Both identify with a role that should be only one aspect of a complex human life. The final barrier she crosses, from life to death, is symbolically represented in the poem as a feminine domestic gesture: she doesn't want to leave a mess. She continues as a housewife even in death. The boundaries between a person and occupation should be clear, but the arbitrary boundaries between husbands and wives should continue to be eradicated.

When the ten-year-old narrator in "Blackberries" claims that he is "Limboed between worlds," he means the rural paradise of "Terrestrial sweetness" and "rich blackness" he temporarily lives in versus the commercial urban world that seems to make him anxious. He has constructed a boundary between the ancient task of picking berries and the modern technology of automobiles, between a closeness with nature and the artificial air-conditioning of the car. Although the narrator enjoys being one with nature, he seems to be cutting himself off from the realities of the world. He seems to reject "old lime-covered / History" in favor of "mythology," which seems to suggest a conscious rejection of the present. But this is a boundary that cannot stand. He needs the outside world to survive financially, and so when the car approaches, it is the modern world and all its complexity that draws near. When he looks into the car, he sees "Smirking" children; he sees class prejudice, hierarchy, and economic reality. The smirkers of the world are in charge. It is this realization that dissolves the protective boundary around his Garden of Eden; consequently, he feels physical pain, but it is really the pain of initiation into reality that he feels. He must now cross a boundary he tried to delay. Although we can sympathize with the young narrator, like the couple in "The Mill," he would have been better off not making his boundary so extreme.

The narrator in Mary Oliver's "Singapore" also imagines that she sees a significant boundary, here between herself as a middle-class traveler and a cleaning woman laboring over a toilet. It is a separation we might all make, given our socialization in America to consider this kind of physical labor as degrading. College-educated people have a tendency to see themselves as distinct from the working class. For many, a woman washing an ashtray in a toilet bowl is beyond the pale, a clear indication that the woman is Other. But Oliver does not simply give into her cultural conditioning; she contests the boundary, asserting that a "Disgust argued in my stomach." Since part of our democratic socialization is also to be tolerant and open-minded, Oliver knows that she shouldn't stereotype workers. And since she is also a writer with ideas about how a poem should "always have birds in it," she looks hard at the cleaning woman, finally seeing in her face, in her hair, and in the way she works, slowly "like a river," the positive aspects of the woman that most of us would probably miss.

Oliver does not simply accept the boundaries that her culture constructs. Instead, she negotiates internally, eventually seeing that a "light . . . can shine out of a life" even where we would not expect it. In the woman's careful folding and unfolding of her blue work cloth and in her smile, Oliver sees a beauty that helps her eclipse a social boundary, ending with a life-affirming vision "filled with trees, and birds." Such an insight does not come easily to us because we usually accept our given cultural boundaries. The miller and his wife are tragically unequipped to bridge the divide between them. Likewise, the boy in "Blackberries" is unable to sustain his fantasy boundaries. Oliver's traveler, however, struggles to negotiate boundaries and is thereby able to increase human solidarity even across class structures and cultures.

☰ SUMMING UP

- **The elements of poetry include *speaker* and *tone*, *diction* and *syntax*, *figures of speech*, *sound*, *rhythm* and *meter*, and *theme*.**

- **Identify the speaker and tone.** The voice we hear in a poem is often a *persona* — a "mask" that could be the poet's real voice or a complete fiction. Paying attention to the speaker's tone — his or her attitude — illuminates a poem's meaning. (pp. 157–58)

- **Be aware of the complexities of *diction* and *syntax*.** In poetry, the connotations or emotional and personal associations of the diction — word choice — often suggest more than the literal meaning of the words. Poetry is more compressed and indirect than prose, so meaning is often suggested through connotation, metaphor, and imagery and is seldom finite. The order of the words — syntax — can be varied and experimented with to amplify and complicate meaning. (pp. 158–59)

- **Major figures of speech include *metaphor* and *symbols*.** A metaphor is a dramatic direct comparison — "Love is a rose," "Faith is a sea" — that poets use to help readers see and think differently and creatively. Similes ("My love is like a red, red rose") are more indirect, but no less suggestive. Symbols suggest general ideas. They reinforce or extend the poem's possible meanings and rarely point in one direction. (pp. 159–60)

- ***Sound*, *rhythm*, and *meter* work together to give a poem psychological force.** How a poem sounds is often overlooked, perhaps because modern poems often do not rhyme. *Alliteration*, for example, connects words and enhances meaning. As in music, rhythm adds to the meaning of poetry, encircling the thoughts and feeling that give poetry depth and meaning. (pp. 160–62)

- **Don't expect a poem's theme to be straightforward or clear-cut.** Strong poems are rich, complex, and often ambiguous. Narrow theme statements such as "'What Work Is' is about the emotional reticence of men" are often misleading and limiting. Although this statement is plausible enough, a number of other ideas are certainly possible. Be wary of reducing a poem's theme to a bold statement that robs the poem of its subtlety and evocative power. (pp. 162–63)

≣ SUMMING UP

- **Arguing successfully that your interpretation is worth considering depends largely on the validity of your evidence.** Poems almost always have several reasonable themes. We can argue strongly for a theme, however, if we can support our claim. The critic who presents the best evidence for a particular theme in a balanced and judicious way is often the most persuasive. (pp. 162–63)

CHAPTER 7

═

═

How to Write about Plays

Most plays incorporate elements also found in short fiction, such as plot, characters, dialogue, setting, and theme. But unlike short fiction and other literary genres, plays are typically enacted live, in front of an audience. Theater professionals distinguish between the written *script* of a play and its actual *performances*. When you write about a play, you may wind up saying little or nothing about performances of it. When you first read and analyze a play, however, try to imagine ways of staging it. You might even research past productions of the play, noting how scenery, costumes, and lighting — as well as particular actors — were used.

Because a play is usually meant to be staged, its readers are rarely its only interpreters. Theater audiences also ponder its meanings. So, too, do cast members; no doubt you have heard of actors "interpreting" their parts. When a play is put on, even members of the backstage team are involved in interpreting it. The technical designers' choices of sets, costumes, and lighting reflect their ideas about the play, while the director works with cast and crew to implement a particular vision of it. No matter what the author of the script intended, theater is a collaborative art: all of the key figures involved in a play's production are active interpreters of the play in that they influence the audience's understanding and experience of it. Therefore, you can develop good ideas when you read a play if you imagine yourself directing a production of it. More specifically, think what you would say to the actors as you guided them through their parts. As you engage in this thought experiment, you will see that you have options, for even directors keen on staying faithful to the script know it can be staged in any number of ways. Perhaps your course will give you and other students the chance to perform a scene together; if so, you will be deciding what interpretation of the scene to set forth.

To help you understand how to write about plays, we refer often to the following two scenes, which come from plays later in the book. Each of these scenes involves a mother and her grown daughter, who reports frustrations with the world of work.

Our first scene is an early one in Tennessee Williams's *The Glass Menagerie*, a 1945 play about a family struggling to survive in St. Louis. (The complete play is presented in Chapter 10, "Families," where the scene appears on pp. 367–71.) Amanda Wingfield's husband fled years earlier, leaving her to raise their children, Laura and Tom, alone. The scene we present involves

Amanda and the now adult Laura. Laura is painfully shy, in part because she is physically disabled. Believing that Laura must eventually become self-supporting, Amanda has insisted that her daughter attend business school. At the beginning of this scene, however, Amanda returns home to report an embarrassing discovery: Laura has been skipping classes without telling her.

TENNESSEE WILLIAMS
From *The Glass Menagerie*

Scene 2

"Laura, Haven't You Ever Liked Some Boy?"

On the dark stage the screen is lighted with the image of blue roses.
    Gradually Laura's figure becomes apparent and the screen goes out.
    The music subsides.
    Laura is seated in the delicate ivory chair at the small clawfoot table.
    She wears a dress of soft violet material for a kimono — her hair tied back from her forehead with a ribbon.
    She is washing and polishing her collection of glass.
    Amanda appears on the fire-escape steps. At the sound of her ascent, Laura catches her breath, thrusts the bowl of ornaments away, and seats herself stiffly before the diagram of the typewriter keyboard as though it held her spellbound. Something has happened to Amanda. It is written in her face as she climbs to the landing: a look that is grim and hopeless and a little absurd.
    She has on one of those cheap or imitation velvety-looking cloth coats with imitation fur collar. Her hat is five or six years old, one of those dreadful cloche hats that were worn in the late twenties, and she is clasping an enormous black patent-leather pocketbook with nickel clasp and initials. This is her full-dress outfit, the one she usually wears to the D.A.R.°
    Before entering she looks through the door.
    She purses her lips, opens her eyes wide, rolls them upward, and shakes her head.
    Then she slowly lets herself in the door. Seeing her mother's expression Laura touches her lips with a nervous gesture.

LAURA: Hello, Mother, I was — *(She makes a nervous gesture toward the chart on the wall. Amanda leans against the shut door and stares at Laura with a martyred look.)*

AMANDA: Deception? Deception? *(She slowly removes her hat and gloves, continuing the swift suffering stare. She lets the hat and gloves fall on the floor — a bit of acting.)*

LAURA *(shakily)*: How was the D.A.R. meeting? *(Amanda slowly opens her purse and removes a dainty white handkerchief, which she shakes out delicately and*

D.A.R.: Daughters of the American Revolution; members must document that they have ancestors who served the patriots' cause in the Revolutionary War.

delicately touches to her lips and nostrils.) Didn't you go to the D.A.R. meeting, Mother?

AMANDA *(faintly, almost inaudibly):*   —No.—No. *(Then more forcibly.)* I did not have the strength—to go to the D.A.R. In fact, I did not have the courage! I wanted to find a hole in the ground and hide myself in it forever! *(She crosses slowly to the wall and removes the diagram of the typewriter keyboard. She holds it in front of her for a second, staring at it sweetly and sorrowfully—then bites her lips and tears it in two pieces.)*

LAURA *(faintly):*   Why did you do that, Mother? *(Amanda repeats the same procedure with the chart of the Gregg Alphabet.°)* Why are you —

AMANDA: Why? Why? How old are you, Laura?

LAURA: Mother, you know my age.

AMANDA: I thought that you were an adult; it seems that I was mistaken. *(She crosses slowly to the sofa and sinks down and stares at Laura.)*

LAURA: Please don't stare at me, Mother.

Amanda closes her eyes and lowers her head. Count ten.

AMANDA: What are we going to do, what is going to become of us, what is the future?

Count ten.

LAURA: Has something happened, Mother? *(Amanda draws a long breath and takes out the handkerchief again. Dabbing process.)* Mother, has—something happened?

AMANDA: I'll be all right in a minute. I'm just bewildered—*(count five)*—by life. . . .

LAURA: Mother, I wish that you would tell me what's happened.

AMANDA: As you know, I was supposed to be inducted into my office at the D.A.R. this afternoon. *(Image: A swarm of typewriters.)* But I stopped off at Rubicam's Business College to speak to your teachers about your having a cold and ask them what progress they thought you were making down there.

LAURA: Oh. . . .

AMANDA: I went to the typing instructor and introduced myself as your mother. She didn't know who you were. Wingfield, she said. We don't have any such student enrolled at the school! I assured her she did, that you had been going to classes since early in January. "I wonder," she said, "if you could be talking about that terribly shy little girl who dropped out of school after only a few days' attendance?" "No," I said, "Laura, my daughter, has been going to school every day for the past six weeks!" "Excuse me," she said. She took the attendance book out and there was your name, unmistakably printed, and all the dates you were absent until they decided that you had dropped out of school. I still said, "No, there must have been some mistake! There must have been some mix-up in the records!" And she said,

Gregg Alphabet: The system of shorthand symbols invented by John Robert Gregg (1867–1948).

"No — I remember her perfectly now. Her hand shook so that she couldn't hit the right keys! The first time we gave a speed-test, she broke down completely — was sick at the stomach and almost had to be carried into the wash-room! After that morning she never showed up any more. We phoned the house but never got any answer" — while I was working at Famous and Barr, I suppose, demonstrating those — Oh! I felt so weak I could barely keep on my feet. I had to sit down while they got me a glass of water! Fifty dollars' tuition, all of our plans — my hopes and ambitions for you — just gone up the spout, just gone up the spout like that. *(Laura draws a long breath and gets awkwardly to her feet. She crosses to the Victrola, and winds it up.)* What are you doing?

LAURA: Oh! *(She releases the handle and returns to her seat.)*

AMANDA: Laura, where have you been going when you've gone out pretending that you were going to business college?

LAURA: I've just been going out walking.

AMANDA: That's not true.

LAURA: It is. I just went walking.

AMANDA: Walking? Walking? In winter? Deliberately courting pneumonia in that light coat? Where did you walk to, Laura?

LAURA: It was the lesser of two evils, Mother. *(Image: Winter scene in park.)* I couldn't go back up. I — threw up — on the floor!

AMANDA: From half past seven till after five every day you mean to tell me you walked around in the park, because you wanted to make me think that you were still going to Rubicam's Business College?

LAURA: It wasn't as bad as it sounds. I went inside places to get warmed up.

AMANDA: Inside where?

LAURA: I went in the art museum and the bird-houses at the Zoo. I visited the penguins every day! Sometimes I did without lunch and went to the movies. Lately I've been spending most of my afternoons in the Jewel-box, that big glass house where they raise the tropical flowers.

AMANDA: You did all this to deceive me, just for the deception? *(Laura looks down.)* Why?

LAURA: Mother, when you're disappointed, you get that awful suffering look on your face, like the picture of Jesus' mother in the museum!

AMANDA: Hush!

LAURA: I couldn't face it.

Pause. A whisper of strings.

(Legend: "The Crust of Humility.")

AMANDA *(hopelessly fingering the huge pocketbook):*   So what are we going to do the rest of our lives? Stay home and watch the parades go by? Amuse ourselves with the glass menagerie, darling? Eternally play those worn-out phonograph records your father left as a painful reminder of him? We won't have a business career — we've given that up because it gave us nervous indigestion! *(Laughs wearily.)* What is there left but dependency all our lives? I know so well what becomes of unmarried women who aren't prepared to occupy a position. I've seen such pitiful cases in the South — barely tolerated spinsters living upon the grudging patronage of sister's husband or brother's wife! — stuck away in some little mousetrap of a room — encouraged by one in-law to visit another — little birdlike women without any nest — eating the crust of humility all their life! Is that the future that we've mapped out for ourselves? I swear it's the only alternative I can think of! It isn't a very pleasant alternative, is it? Of course — some girls *do marry. (Laura twists her hands nervously.)* Haven't you ever liked some boy?

LAURA: Yes. I liked one once. *(Rises.)* I came across his picture a while ago.

AMANDA *(with some interest):*   He gave you his picture?

LAURA: No, it's in the year-book.

AMANDA *(disappointed):*   Oh — a high-school boy.

(Screen image: Jim as a high-school hero bearing a silver cup.)

LAURA: Yes. His name was Jim. *(Laura lifts the heavy annual from the clawfoot table.)* Here he is in *The Pirates of Penzance.*

AMANDA *(absently):*   The what?

LAURA: The operetta the senior class put on. He had a wonderful voice and we sat across the aisle from each other Mondays, Wednesdays, and Fridays in the Aud. Here he is with the silver cup for debating! See his grin?

AMANDA *(absently):*   He must have had a jolly disposition.

LAURA: He used to call me — Blue Roses.

(Image: Blue roses.)

AMANDA: Why did he call you such a name as that?

LAURA: When I had that attack of pleurosis — he asked me what was the matter when I came back. I said pleurosis — he thought that I said Blue Roses! So that's what he always called me after that. Whenever he saw me, he'd holler, "Hello, Blue Roses!" I didn't care for the girl that he went out with. Emily Meisenbach. Emily was the best-dressed girl at Soldan. She never struck me, though, as being sincere. . . . It says in the Personal Section — they're engaged. That's — six years ago! They must be married by now.

AMANDA: Girls that aren't cut out for business careers usually wind up married to some nice man. *(Gets up with a spark of revival.)* Sister, that's what you'll do!

Laura utters a startled, doubtful laugh. She reaches quickly for a piece of glass.

LAURA: But, Mother —

AMANDA: Yes? *(Crossing to photograph.)*

LAURA *(in a tone of frightened apology):*   I'm — crippled!

(Image: Screen.)

AMANDA: Nonsense! Laura, I've told you never, never to use that word. Why, you're not crippled, you just have a little defect — hardly noticeable, even! When people have some slight disadvantage like that, they cultivate other things to make up for it — develop charm — and vivacity — and — *charm!*

That's all you have to do! *(She turns again to the photograph.)* One thing your father had *plenty of*—was *charm!*

Tom motions to the fiddle in the wings.
(The scene fades out with music.)   [1945]

■ **A WRITING EXERCISE**

In three to five sentences, write a summary of the scene from *The Glass Menagerie* that you have just read. Do not attempt to *evaluate* the two characters' behavior. Rather, focus on identifying the most important things they say and do.

Our second scene is from Marsha Norman's 1983 two-character play *'night, Mother.* (The complete play is presented in Chapter 14, "Journeys," where the scene appears on pp. 1578–80.) This drama is distinctive in two respects. One has to do with form: the play takes ninety minutes to perform, and what goes on *within* the play is a ninety-minute conversation at night between Thelma Cates and her adult daughter, Jessie. Indeed, in most evening performances of the play, the clocks on the set show the same time as the audience's own. Just as striking is the play's subject matter. Soon after their conversation begins, Jessie tells her mother that she intends to shoot herself at the end of the night. Jessie mentions several motives for committing suicide, including her epilepsy, the breakup of her marriage, the delinquency of her son, and her general despair. For much of the play, though, she bustles around, attempting to put her mother's house physically in order before she dies. Meanwhile, Thelma tries to talk her daughter out of ending her life. In the following excerpt, the two women discuss Jessie's inability to keep a job, though ironically Jessie is efficiently doing household work for her mother on this fateful night.

MARSHA NORMAN
From '*night, Mother*

JESSIE *(going back into the kitchen):*   I called this morning and canceled the papers, except for Sunday, for your puzzles; you'll still get that one.
MAMA: Let's get another dog, Jessie! You liked a big dog, now, didn't you? That King dog, didn't you?
JESSIE *(washing her hands):*   I did like that King dog, yes.
MAMA: I'm so dumb. He's the one run under the tractor.
JESSIE: That makes him dumb, not you.
MAMA: For bringing it up.
JESSIE: It's O.K. Handi-Wipes and sponges under the sink.
MAMA: We could get a new dog and keep him in the house. Dogs are cheap!
JESSIE *(getting big pill jars out of the cabinet):*   No.

MAMA: Something for you to take care of.

JESSIE: I've had you, Mama.

MAMA *(frantically starting to fill pill bottles):*   You do too much for me. I can fill pill bottles all day, Jessie, and change the shelf paper and wash the floor when I get through. You just watch me. You don't have to do another thing in this house if you don't want to. You don't have to take care of me, Jessie.

JESSIE: I know that. You've just been letting me do it so I'll have something to do, haven't you?

MAMA *(realizing this was a mistake):*   I don't do it as well as you. I just meant if it tires you out or makes you feel used . . .

JESSIE: Mama, I know you used to ride the bus. Riding the bus and it's hot and bumpy and crowded and too noisy and more than anything in the world you want to get off and the only reason in the world you don't get off is it's still fifty blocks from where you're going? Well, I can get off right now if I want to, because even if I ride fifty more years and get off then, it's the same place when I step down to it. Whenever I feel like it, I can get off. As soon as I've had enough, it's my stop. I've had enough.

MAMA: You're feeling sorry for yourself!

JESSIE: The plumber's helper is under the sink, too.

MAMA: You're not having a good time! Whoever promised you a good time? Do you think I've had a good time?

JESSIE: I think you're pretty happy, yeah. You have things you like to do.

MAMA: Like what?

JESSIE: Like crochet.

MAMA: I'll teach you to crochet.

JESSIE: I can't do any of that nice work, Mama.

MAMA: Good time don't come looking for you, Jessie. You could work some puzzles or put in a garden or go to the store. Let's call a taxi and go to the A&P!

JESSIE: I shopped you up for about two weeks already. You're not going to need toilet paper till Thanksgiving.

MAMA *(interrupting):*   You're acting like some little brat, Jessie. You're mad and everybody's boring and you don't have anything to do and you don't like me and you don't like going out and you don't like staying in and you never talk on the phone and you don't watch TV and you're miserable and it's your own sweet fault.

JESSIE: And it's time I did something about it.

MAMA: Not something like killing yourself. Something like . . . buying us all new dishes! I'd like that. Or maybe the doctor would let you get a driver's license now, or I know what let's do right this minute, let's rearrange the furniture.

JESSIE: I'll do that. If you want. I always thought if the TV was somewhere else, you wouldn't get such a glare on it during the day. I'll do whatever you want before I go.

MAMA *(badly frightened by those words):*   You could get a job!

JESSIE: I took that telephone sales job and I didn't even make enough money to pay the phone bill, and I tried to work at the gift shop at the hospital

and they said I made people real uncomfortable smiling at them the way
I did.

MAMA: You could keep books. You kept your dad's books.

JESSIE: But nobody ever checked them.

MAMA: When he died, they checked them.

JESSIE: And that's when they took the books away from me.

MAMA: That's because without him there wasn't any business, Jessie!

JESSIE *(putting the pill bottles away):*   You know I couldn't work. I can't do anything. I've never been around people my whole life except when I went to
the hospital. I could have a seizure any time. What good would a job do?
The kind of job I could get would make me feel worse.

MAMA: Jessie!

JESSIE: It's true!

MAMA: It's what you think is true!

JESSIE *(struck by the clarity of that):*   That's right. It's what I think is true.

MAMA *(hysterically):*   But I can't do anything about that!

JESSIE *(quietly):*   No. You can't. *(Mama slumps, if not physically, at least emotionally.)* And I can't do anything either, about my life, to change it, make it
better, make me feel better about it. Like it better, make it work. But I can
stop it. Shut it down, turn it off like the radio when there's nothing on I
want to listen to. It's all I really have that belongs to me and I'm going to
say what happens to it. And it's going to stop. And I'm going to stop it. So.
Let's just have a good time.

MAMA: Have a good time.

JESSIE: We can't go on fussing all night. I mean, I could ask you things I always
wanted to know and you could make me some hot chocolate. The old way.

MAMA *(in despair):*   It takes cocoa, Jessie.

JESSIE *(gets it out of the cabinet):*   I bought cocoa, Mama. And I'd like to have a
caramel apple and do your nails.

MAMA: You didn't eat a bite of supper.

JESSIE: Does that mean I can't have a caramel apple?

MAMA: Of course not. I mean . . . *(Smiling a little.)* Of course you can have a
caramel apple.

JESSIE: I thought I could.

MAMA: I make the best caramel apples in the world.

JESSIE: I know you do.

MAMA: Or used to. And you don't get cocoa like mine anywhere anymore.

JESSIE: It takes time, I know, but . . .

MAMA: The salt is the trick.

JESSIE: Trouble and everything.

MAMA *(backing away toward the stove):*   It's no trouble. What trouble? You put it
in the pan and stir it up. All right. Fine. Caramel apples. Cocoa. O.K.

*Jessie walks to the counter to retrieve her cigarettes as Mama looks for the right pan.
There are brief near-smiles, and maybe Mama clears her throat. We have a truce, for
the moment. A genuine but nevertheless uneasy one. Jessie, who has been in constant
motion since the beginning, now seems content to sit.*

Mama starts looking for a pan to make the cocoa, getting out all the pans in the cabinets in the process. It looks like she's making a mess on purpose so Jessie will have to put them all away again. Mama is buying time, or trying to, and entertaining.

[1983]

≡ A WRITING EXERCISE

In three to five sentences, write a summary of the scene from *'night, Mother* that you have just read. Do not attempt to *evaluate* the two characters' behavior. Rather, focus on identifying the most important things they say and do.

The Elements of Drama

You will strengthen your ability to write about plays like Williams's and Norman's if you grow familiar with typical elements of drama. These elements include plot and structure, characters, stage directions and setting, imagery, language, and theme.

PLOT AND STRUCTURE

After each of the two scenes you have read, we have asked you to write a summary because doing so moves you into considerations of **plot**. Most plays, like most short stories, do have a plot. When you read them, you find yourself following a **narrative**, a sequence of interrelated events. As with short fiction, the reader of a play is often anxious to know how events will turn out. Will *The Glass Menagerie*'s Laura Wingfield find a rewarding romantic relationship, especially now that she seems too scared to pursue a business career? Will *'night, Mother*'s Jessie Cates kill herself? In fact, there are various ways you can describe the plot; just bear in mind that your account should be grounded in details found in the text. Perhaps you will emphasize characters' emotional conflicts, for often a play's plot involves psychological tension as well as physical acts. If you focus on character, your summary of the play's **structure** will reflect your understanding of which people are central to it. As you may have guessed, we think the characters in our excerpts are major figures throughout their respective plays. Sometimes, though, a character's status is less immediately clear.

Summarizing the plot of a play can mean arranging its events chronologically. Yet bear in mind that some of the play's important events may have occurred in the characters' distant or immediate past. In the scene from *The Glass Menagerie*, for example, Amanda tells a long anecdote about her visit to the business school, where a teacher told her that Laura was no longer attending. Actually, many plays feature acts of recollection and revelation that lead characters to come to a new understanding of their history. When Jessie recalls her history of failed jobs, in the scene from *'night, Mother*, she draws a conclusion that perhaps she reached only recently: "I can't do anything." You may, like

Thelma, disagree with this judgment, but significantly it gives Jessie an incentive to end her life.

☰ A WRITING EXERCISE

Reread at least one of the scenes we have presented, noting moments when the characters are engaged basically in remembrance. Then write a paragraph in which you make and support a claim about the extent to which the scene is concerned with the past rather than with the present or future.

In discussing the structure of short stories, we said that many of them follow Alice Adams's formula ABDCE (**action, background, development, climax,** and **ending**). This scheme, however, does not fit many plays. In one sense, the average play is entirely action, for its performers constantly make physical movements of various sorts. Furthermore, as we have been suggesting, information about background can surface often as characters talk. Yet the terms *development, climax,* and *ending* do seem appropriate for many plays.

Certainly, each of the two scenes we have excerpted develop the play as a whole. The mother-daughter conversation from *The Glass Menagerie* reveals that Amanda is a Southern "lady" in two crucial respects: the scene begins with Amanda's social embarrassment on finding Laura a truant and ends with Amanda calling for Laura to rely on "charm." When the mother-daughter conversation from *'night, Mother* concludes with a truce, this moment of peace is temporary, for Jessie has declared that suicide is her only remaining means of power: though her life has been miserable, at least now she can "shut it down, turn it off." In other words, both scenes bring up important matters but leave them to be resolved in the rest of the play.

We will not reveal how the terms *climax* and *ending* fit the two dramas' overall plots, for you might prefer to discover on your own how both plays turn out. But in the case of *'night, Mother,* you probably can imagine that the climax is Thelma's final attempt to prevent her daughter's suicide. After all, their debate about this move has been the play's central conflict. Similarly, the play is bound to end with the success or failure of Thelma's effort, though the specific details of the final moment deserve close analysis. Always consider what, exactly, characters are doing when the curtain falls.

Like short stories, plays often use repetition as an organizational device. Characters may repeat certain words; for example, notice how Amanda ends *The Glass Menagerie* scene by using the word *charm* three times. Also, a play may show repeated actions, as *'night, Mother* does when it shows Jessie performing numerous household chores. In addition, a play may suggest that the onstage situation echoes previous events. On many an occasion, Amanda probably has pushed Laura to take charge of her own life. No doubt Jessie and Thelma have quarreled about subjects other than suicide.

Through the centuries, plays have been subdivided in all sorts of ways. Sophocles' ancient Greek drama *Antigone*, which appears in Chapter 13, "Doing

Justice," alternates choral sections with scenes that involve only two characters. All of Shakespeare's plays (such as *Othello* in Chapter 11, "Love") and most modern ones are divided into acts, which are often further divided into scenes. For example, *A Raisin in the Sun* (in Chapter 10, "Families") has three acts, which vary in their number of scenes: act 1 includes two, act 2 has three, and act 3 has one scene only. But not all modern plays feature multiple acts. *'Night, Mother* is a single act long, as is *The Table* (in Chapter 13, "Doing Justice"), while *The Glass Menagerie* consists of seven scenes. Of course, you may see a play as having other divisions than its official ones. In fact, a good exercise is to break a play down into segments that more precisely reflect the development of the plot.

CHARACTERS

As with short stories, a good step in analyzing a play's characters is to consider what each desires. The drama or comedy of many plays arises when the desires of one character conflict with those of another. A strong example can be found in the scene from *'night, Mother*, where Jessie seeks to end her life and Thelma tries to preserve it. Also important to analyze is whether and how characters eventually alter their desires, perhaps coming to share the values of people whom they have opposed.

■ A WRITING EXERCISE

Choose one of the scenes we have excerpted, and write a brief, informal essay in which you examine the scene for signs that either or both of the characters will eventually change.

The main character of a play is referred to as its **protagonist**, and a character who notably opposes this person is referred to as the **antagonist**. As you might guess even without reading Shakespeare's play, Othello is the protagonist of *Othello*, while his supposed friend Iago turns out to be his antagonist. Applying these terms may be tricky or impossible in some instances. In *The Glass Menagerie*, Amanda's son, Tom, repeatedly argues with her, but either character might be called the protagonist. A similar difficulty arises with the characters who argue in the scene from *'night, Mother.* Of course, a play may be interesting precisely because it makes the terms *protagonist* and *antagonist* hard to apply.

In discussing the elements of short fiction, we referred to point of view, the perspective from which a story is told. But very few plays are narrated. One of the rare cases is *The Glass Menagerie*, which is framed by monologues by Amanda's son, Tom. In general, the play supposedly presents his memories. Even in this instance, however, at plenty of moments the narrator is *not* observing or interpreting the action. Similarly, while it is possible to claim that much of Shakespeare's *Hamlet* reflects the title character's point of view, he is offstage for stretches, and the audience may focus on other characters even when he appears. In general, therefore, the term *point of view* fits plays less well than it does short fiction. In fact, worth thinking about is the possible significance of characters who are not physically present. A character may be important even if he or she never appears onstage. Such is the case with Amanda Wingfield's husband, whose physical presence is available to her now only as a photograph. Such, too, is the case with numerous people whom Jessie and Thelma refer to in *'night, Mother*, including Jessie's father, former husband, brother, and son.

In most plays, characters' lives are influenced by their social standing, which in turn is influenced by particular traits of theirs. These may include their gender, social class, race, ethnic background, nationality, and sexual orientation and the kind of work they do. For instance, *The Glass Menagerie's* Amanda Wingfield is still affected by her upbringing as a Southern lady, though now she must struggle to survive financially in St. Louis, a modern city in a Midwestern state.

■ A WRITING EXERCISE

In almost all productions of *The Glass Menagerie* and *'night, Mother*, the characters have been played by white performers. Choose either *The Glass Menagerie* scene we have excerpted or the *'night, Mother* scene. Do you think there would be significantly different effects and implications if the actors in the scene were of another race? Address this issue in a brief, informal essay.

STAGE DIRECTIONS AND SETTING

When analyzing a script, pay attention to the stage directions it gives. Through a slight physical movement, performers can indicate important developments in their characters' thoughts. Look, for example, at the conclusion of our scene from *'night, Mother.* Through stage directions, playwright Marsha Norman suggests how the mother and daughter may be seen as momentarily resting before resuming their conflict. Always, you can imagine additional ways that a play's performers might move around. What else, for instance, might you have the actors in Norman's play do at this point?

You can learn much about a play's characters by studying how they accommodate themselves — or fail to accommodate themselves — to the places in which you find them. Notice what Thelma does at the end of the scene we have excerpted from *'night, Mother: "Mama starts looking for a pan to make the cocoa, getting out all the pans in the cabinets in the process. It looks like she's making a mess on purpose so Jessie will have to put them all away again."* Is Thelma controlling the kitchen space in an effort to control Jessie — creating chaos so that her daughter will be distracted from thoughts of suicide?

To understand better how a play might be staged, you can research its actual production history. Granted, finding out about its previous stagings may be difficult. But at the very least, you can discover some of the theatrical conventions that must have shaped presentations of the play, even one that is centuries old. Take the case of Sophocles' *Antigone*, which appears in Chapter 13, "Doing Justice." While classical scholars would like to learn more about early performances of these dramas, they already know that ancient Greek plays were staged in open-air arenas. They know, too, that Sophocles' chorus turned in unison at particular moments and that cast members wore large masks.

Most of the modern plays we include in this book were first staged in a style most often called **realism**. Not every modern play fits this description, though. Introducing his script for *The Glass Menagerie*, Tennessee Williams calls for a different rendition of the Wingfield apartment: "The scene is memory and therefore nonrealistic. Memory takes a lot of poetic license. It omits some details; others are exaggerated, according to the emotional values of the articles it touches, for memory is seated predominantly in the heart. The interior is therefore rather dim and poetic." As you can tell from the particular scene we have excerpted, the nonrealistic atmosphere that Williams urges is reinforced by the highly theatrical use of slides. Realism, by contrast, is typified by the set for *'night, Mother* as author Marsha Norman envisions it. The Cates house, Norman writes, should be depicted as the home "of very specific real people who happen to live in a particular part of the country" (presumably an area of the South). To achieve this realistic impression, Norman calls for a set with various lifelike features. For example, "The living room is cluttered with magazines and needlework catalogues, ashtrays and candy dishes."

When a production is quite true to life, audiences may think it has no style at all. Nevertheless, even realism uses identifiable conventions. A common one is what theater professionals refer to as the *illusion of the fourth wall*, which is essentially what Norman recommends for *'night, Mother*. She suggests that the actors pretend the "house" is fully enclosed, whereas the set has just three walls, and the audience looks in.

Some plays can be staged in any number of styles and still work well. Shakespeare wrote *Othello* (in Chapter 11, "Love") in Renaissance England, but successful productions of it have been set in later times, such as late-nineteenth-century England. Indeed, few modern productions of *Othello* follow the Renaissance tradition of an all-male cast. Since the first production of *The Glass Menagerie*, the play has been successfully mounted with various degrees of realism. Some versions strictly follow Williams's guidelines, striving to be "nonrealistic" and "poetic," whereas others make the Wingfield apartment as lifelike as Thelma Cates's house. You may feel that any divergence from a playwright's directives is wrong; nevertheless, remember that productions of a play may be more diverse in style than the script indicates.

≡ A WRITING EXERCISE

A particular theater's architecture may affect a production team's decisions. Realism's illusion of the fourth wall works best on a **proscenium stage**, which is the kind probably most familiar to you. A proscenium stage is a boxlike space where the actors perform in front of the entire audience. In a proscenium production of 'night, Mother, the Cates home can be depicted in great detail. The performing spaces at some theaters, however, are "in the round" — that is, the audience completely encircles the stage. What would have to be done with the 'night, Mother setting then? List some items in it that an in-the-round staging could accommodate. Or, if you prefer, do this listing for The Glass Menagerie.

IMAGERY

When plays use images to convey meaning, sometimes they do so through a title. A clear example is The Glass Menagerie, whose title refers to Laura's collection of figurines but also signifies the fragility of her family's life and dreams. As you have seen, this image also comes up in the play's conversations; often, dialogue enables symbols to emerge and develop. Just as often, a play's meaningful images are physically presented in the staging — through gestures, costumes, lighting, and props. When Amanda Wingfield enters wearing "one of those cheap or imitation velvety-looking cloth coats with imitation fur collar," her clothes imply a futile effort to conceal her dire financial condition. When she proceeds to shred her daughter's typewriting charts, she dramatically acknowledges that her plan for Laura's schooling has been destroyed.

You may interpret an image differently than characters within the play do. Take the gesture that Jessie Cates makes as she tells her mother, "You know I couldn't work." At this moment, Jessie is putting pill bottles away, an action that mirrors her insistence that nothing will remedy her miserable life. Although Jessie herself probably does not make this connection, you may very well do so.

☰ A WRITING EXERCISE

Imagine that you have been asked to stage the scene from The Glass Menagerie or the one from 'night, Mother. List gestures not mentioned in the script that you would have the actors perform. Then compare lists with a classmate working with the same scene.

LANGUAGE

You can learn much about a play's meaning and impact from studying the language in its script. Try starting with the play's title. As we have already discussed, the title of The Glass Menagerie seems symbolically important, but even the apparently ordinary title of 'night, Mother carries weight. Although Jessie has commonly said these two words at the end of an evening, on this occasion they have chilling significance, since she intends to leave her mother for eternal rest.

In most plays, language is a matter of dialogue. The audience tries to figure out the play by focusing on how the characters address one another. A revealing use of language occurs, for example, near the end of our scene from *The Glass Menagerie*. Resisting Amanda's dream of marrying her off, Laura points out that "I'm — crippled!" But Amanda continues to show optimism, by objecting to Laura's self-description: "Nonsense! Laura, I've told you never, never to use that word. Why, you're not crippled, you just have a little defect — hardly noticeable, even!" To be sure, Amanda is not always so optimistic; earlier in the scene, she is frustrated by Laura's failure to attend business school. Her dismissal of Laura's term "crippled," however, reveals how capable she is of wishful thinking, too. Meanwhile, Laura's instant labeling of herself emphasizes her tendency to recoil from life.

A character's style of speaking can be revealing as well, often indicating something about the character's social background. Actors playing Amanda Wingfield usually adopt a Southern accent to emphasize how much her upbringing in that region has influenced her. It is also plausible for Thelma and Jessie in *'night, Mother* to speak with Southern inflections. Significantly, though, Marsha Norman's introduction to the script explicitly warns against making their accents "heavy," which Norman fears "would further distance the audience from [them]."

Remember that the pauses or silences within a play may be just as important as its dialogue. Notice that at the beginning of the scene from *The Glass Menagerie*, Amanda hesitates before she enters the apartment and speaks to Laura; evidently, she is pained at the prospect of confronting her daughter about Laura's absence from school. Actually, directors of plays often add moments of silence that the script does not explicitly demand, giving the performers another means of expressing their characters' feelings.

THEME

We have already discussed **theme** on pages 162–63, and here we build on some points from our earlier discussion. A theme is the main claim — an assertion, a proposition, or a statement — that a literary work seems to make. As with other literary genres, try to state a play's theme as a midlevel generalization. If expressed in broad terms, it will seem to fit many other works besides the one you have read. If narrowly tied to the play's characters and their particular situation, it will seem irrelevant to most other people's lives. With *'night, Mother*, an example of a broad theme would be "Mothers should try to understand their daughters better." At the opposite extreme, a narrow theme would be "Southern women who fail at their jobs and relationships might resolve to commit suicide, especially if they are also epileptic." If, after reading Marsha Norman's entire play, you want to identify one of its themes, you might start with the broad generalization we have cited and then try to narrow it down to a midlevel one. You might even think of ways that Norman's play *complicates* that broad generalization.

You can state a play's theme as an **observation** or as a **recommendation**. With Norman's play, an observation-type theme would be "Despair might drive someone to see suicide as a rational choice." A recommendation-type theme would be "People who want to commit suicide should be allowed to do so if their life will otherwise probably be bleak." Neither way of stating the theme is automatically preferable, but remain aware of the different tones and effects they may carry. Consider, too, the possibility of stating the theme as a problem, in this example: "People may seem to have strong justification for killing themselves, but their loved ones will understandably have difficulty letting them commit suicide." Furthermore, consider referring to *a* theme of the play rather than *the* theme, thereby acknowledging the possibility that the play is making several important claims.

When you write about a play, certainly you will refer to its text, or **script**. But probably the play was meant to be staged, and most likely it has been. Thus, you might refer to actual productions of it and to ways it can be performed. Remember, though, that different productions of the play may stress different meanings and create different effects. In your paper, you might discuss how much room for interpretation the script allows those who would stage it. For any paper you write about the play, look beyond the characters' dialogue and study whatever stage directions the script gives.

Undoubtedly, your paper will have to offer some plot summary, even if your audience has already read the play. After all, certain details of the plot will be important support for your points. But as with papers about short fiction, keep the amount of plot summary small, mentioning only events in the play that are crucial to your overall argument. Your reader should feel that you are analyzing the play rather than just recounting it.

To better show you what analysis of a play involves, we present the final draft of a paper by student Tim Kerwin. Required to write about a particular scene in a play read by his class, he chose the scene from *'night, Mother* that we have been examining. Tim realized that although he would be dealing with just one scene, he would have to be even more selective — identifying a particular issue, developing a particular claim, and referring to particular elements of the scene. After reading this scene several times, Tim grew especially interested in a moment that occurs during Jessie's debate with her mother, Thelma. The two women have been arguing about whether Jessie should abandon thoughts of suicide and seek employment. To Thelma's advice that "You could get a job!," Jessie replies, "The kind of job I could get would make me feel worse." Thelma tries to continue the argument by claiming that Jessie's belief is simply "what you think is true." Curiously, though, Jessie does not protest; instead, she says, "That's right. It's what I think is true." Tim wondered why mother and daughter are able to agree at this point. More specifically, he wondered whether they actually mean the same thing when each observes that Jessie goes by what she "think[s] is true." Tim saw that he could address an issue of definition by trying to identify each woman's meaning. In his final paper, his main claim is his position on this issue. He argues that whereas Thelma is accusing her daughter of ignoring reality, Jessie is asserting her power to decide the nature and direction of her own life.

Final Draft of a Student Paper

Here is Tim's final draft. It emerged after he had written several drafts and consulted classmates as well as his instructor. As you read this version of his paper, note its strengths, but also think of any suggestions that might help him make the paper even better.

Tim Kerwin

Professor Caswell

English 102

21 April - - - -

The Significance of What Jessie "Thinks"

Throughout Marsha Norman's play 'night, Mother, Jessie Cates plans to kill herself. In much of the play, though, her mother, Thelma, argues with her about whether this act is justified. In fact, most of the play's drama arises from the two women's conflict over the appropriateness of suicide. Yet at one moment, mother and daughter briefly seem to agree with each other. This point comes as they quarrel over whether Jessie should try to soothe her despair by working. When Thelma tells Jessie, "You could get a job!," Jessie claims that "The kind of job I could get would make me feel worse." This response does not stop Thelma, who argues back that what Jessie believes is nothing more than "what you think is true." But rather than keep their conflict going at this moment, Jessie says something surprising: "That's right. It's what I think is true." What should we make of the fact that the two women seem in accord here? A strong possibility is that they have different things in mind when each refers to Jessie's reliance on what she "think[s] is true." Most likely, Thelma is declaring that Jessie is imagining her own world instead of truly paying attention to reality. On the other hand, Jessie seems to be claiming that she has the right and ability to determine how her life will turn out.

To Thelma, Jessie's desire to kill herself cannot be defended at all. Basically, she charges her daughter with childish self-pity. Prior to declaring that Jessie's pessimism about a job is merely "what you think is true," Thelma describes Jessie as "acting like some little brat." Furthermore, she accuses her of "feeling sorry for yourself," even concluding that Jessie's mental suffering is "your own sweet fault." The simplicity of this diagnosis is matched by the simplicity of Thelma's proposed solutions. She thinks her daughter just needs to be occupied with adult activities. While acknowledging that she can probably get along without Jessie's housework ("You don't have to take care of me, Jessie"), Thelma does recommend concrete projects: for example, "You could work some puzzles or put in a garden or go to the store." Even though the two women spend extended time discussing jobs, seeking employment is just another suggestion on Thelma's hastily improvised list of things to do. Of course, by saying anything that pops into her head, she is trying to delay Jessie's suicide. If she can buy enough time, Thelma believes, she can persuade Jessie to change her mind. When, however, Thelma asserts that her daughter acts on the basis of "what you think is true," she is specifically arguing that Jessie is being willfully blind to the opportunities that the world offers her.

Although Jessie seemingly agrees with Thelma's statement, she clearly believes that she is more realistic than her mother. Certainly she is claiming greater insight when she declares that her epilepsy makes her unfit for a job: "You know I couldn't work." Indeed, the words "You know" imply that Thelma, not Jessie, is denying obvious facts. Jessie also proclaims her greater commitment to reality by referring to her concrete household labors even as Thelma talks at length. She may not be able to work for money, but she constantly reminds Thelma that she does everyday chores for free. She points out, for example, that she has canceled the newspaper except for Sunday's edition; that she has stored "Handi-Wipes and sponges under the sink"; that she has put the plumber's helper there; that she has bought cocoa; and that she is ready to give Thelma a manicure. She even removes pill bottles and cocoa from the kitchen cabinets as Thelma speaks. In other words, Jessie presents herself as highly attentive to the physical world and used to helping Thelma manage it. Agreeing with her mother's "what you think is true" comment, then, seems inconsistent.

We can explain this apparent inconsistency by considering how Jessie may be interpreting her mother's remark differently from Thelma. Quite possibly, Jessie is not agreeing that she just makes things up. Indeed, while Thelma is taking a position on which of the two is more realistic, Jessie may not be addressing this question at all. When she says "It's what I think is true," the words "I" and "think" take on another significance for her. With her use of the word "think" she is suggesting that the state of a person's mind deserves to be a key factor in his or her life decisions, whatever the physical world is actually like. The implication is that if Jessie is depressed, that is what matters, whether or not there are attractive places on this earth. Moreover, by emphasizing the first-person pronoun, Jessie may be chiefly asserting authority over how to describe and pursue her life, even if the world does exist objectively apart from her. Thus, when Thelma replies that "I can't do anything about that!," she is recognizing that for Jessie, their debate is ultimately not about who is more conscious of reality. Rather, the debate is about whether Jessie should be able to decide her destiny. Although these questions *can* be related to each other, they are nevertheless not the same.

When Marsha Norman wrote '*night, Mother*, probably she was aware that many members of the audience would be reluctant to approve Jessie's suicide plan. In this respect, they would be more like Thelma than like Jessie. Although they might find Thelma's responses to Jessie too simplistic, they would join her in assuming that suicide is fundamentally wrong. In fact, Norman does not make clear how much she herself sympathizes with Jessie's intention. The play does make plain, however, the kinds of debates that plans like Jessie's can prompt. In this respect, the moment of apparent agreement between Thelma and Jessie points toward two issues. One issue, which Thelma presses, is whether a suicidal person is being realistic. The other, which ultimately seems to occupy Jessie more, is whether a person should have the privilege of asserting herself through suicide. The first is an issue of knowledge; the second, an issue of rights. In the end, Norman leaves her audience having to figure out their own positions on both.

☰ SUMMING UP

- **Consider the differences between page and stage.** Theater professionals distinguish between a play's written script and its actual performances, so consider how any play you are analyzing has been or might be staged. Try to imagine yourself as its director, thinking about how you would guide the actors through their parts. (p. 168)

- **The elements of drama include** *plot* **and** *structure, characters, stage directions* **and** *setting, imagery, language,* **and** *theme.*

- **The** *plot* **and** *structure* **of plays often resemble those of stories.** Like short stories, plays often feature plot development, a climax, a significant ending, and repetitions of words and situations. (pp. 176–78)

- *Characters* **in plays function like characters in stories.** As such, they can often be analyzed by asking the same questions (see Summing Up on pp. 141–42). A difference is that most plays lack a narrator and even a central point of view; you have to figure out the characters' thoughts from dialogue and movement.

- **When analyzing a script, pay attention to its** *stage directions,* **and imagine other ways that the actors might move around.** (pp. 179–80)

- **While some plays do not describe their** *setting* **precisely, others stress that they are occurring in particular places or moments.** As with short stories, you can learn much about a play's characters by examining how they accommodate themselves — or fail to accommodate themselves — to their settings. (pp. 179–80)

■ SUMMING UP

- *Images* are often conveyed through words and stagecraft — through dialogue, gestures, costumes, lighting, and props. (p. 181)

- Most plays rely on dialogue as their most important *language*, making their audience figure things out from how the characters address one another. Pauses or silences may be important as well. (pp. 181–82)

- The *theme* of a play is the main claim — an assertion, a proposition, or a statement — that it seems to make. As when writing about short stories, try to state the theme as a midlevel generalization, either as an observation or as a recommendation. By specifically wording the theme as a problem, you may better convey the complexity and drama of the play. (pp. 182–83)

- When you write about a play, remember to formulate an issue worth addressing, a claim about that issue, and evidence for that claim, besides preparing to identify your warrants. Keep in mind that you will refer to its script, but you might also discuss how much room for interpretation the script allows those who would stage it.

CHAPTER 8

How to Write about Essays

Many readers do not realize that nonfiction is a literary genre. They believe that writing about information and facts, science and technology, history and biography, memories and arguments is far different from writing traditional literary works such as sonnets, short stories, and plays. But what counts as literature is often more a matter of tradition and perspective than a matter of content, language, or merit. Many contemporary critics have noticed that definitions of literature are quite subjective, even arbitrary. We are told that literature must move us emotionally; it must contain imaginative, extraordinary language; it must deal with profound, timeless, and universal themes. If these claims are true of poems, stories, and plays, they might also be true of essays, autobiographies, memoirs, and historical writing.

Essays demand as much of a reader's attention as fiction, drama, and poetry do. They also demand a reader's active participation. And as with more conventional literature, the intellectual, emotional, and aesthetic rewards of attentively reading essays are significant.

Writing about essays in college is best done as a process that begins with careful reading and a first response and ends with editing and proofreading. Author Henry David Thoreau once noted that books should be read with the same care and deliberation with which they were written. This is as true for essays as it is for complex modern poetry. Few people, even professionals, can read a text and write cogently about it the first time. Writing well about essays — actively participating in a cycle of reading, reflecting, and writing — takes as much energy and discipline as writing about other genres. And the results are always worth it.

The two essays presented here deal with women and work — more specifically, with the struggles of gifted African American women in a context of poverty and oppression. Both essays were originally speeches. "Many Rivers to Cross" by June Jordan (1936–2002) was the keynote address at a 1981 conference on "Women and Work" held at Barnard College in New York City. In the speech, Jordan recalls the suicide of her mother fifteen years earlier. Alice Walker's speech was given at a May 1973 conference on "The Black Woman: Myths and Realities" held at Radcliffe College in large part as a response to Daniel Moynihan's 1965 report, which emphasized the link between fatherless families and poverty among African Americans. Walker (b. 1944) made additions when it appeared in the May 1974 issue of *Ms.* and then in the essay collection *In Search of Our Mothers' Gardens: Womanist Prose* (1983).

JUNE JORDAN
Many Rivers to Cross

When my mother killed herself I was looking for a job. That was fifteen years ago. I had no money and no food. On the pleasure side I was down to my last pack of Pall Malls plus half a bottle of J and B. I needed to find work because I needed to be able fully to support myself and my eight-year-old son, very fast. My plan was to raise enough big bucks so that I could take an okay apartment inside an acceptable public school district, by September. That deadline left me less than three months to turn my fortunes right side up.

It seemed that I had everything to do at once. Somehow, I must move all of our things, mostly books and toys, out of the housing project before the rent fell due, again. I must do this without letting my neighbors know because destitution and divorce added up to personal shame, and failure. Those same neighbors had looked upon my husband and me as an ideal young couple, in many ways: inseparable, doting, ambitious. They had kept me busy and laughing in the hard weeks following my husband's departure for graduate school in Chicago; they had been the ones to remember him warmly through teasing remarks and questions all that long year that I remained alone, waiting for his return while I became the "temporary," sole breadwinner of our peculiar long-distance family by telephone. They had been the ones who kindly stopped the teasing and the queries when the year ended and my husband, the father of my child, did not come back. They never asked me and I never told them what that meant, altogether. I don't think I really knew.

I could see how my husband would proceed more or less naturally from graduate school to a professional occupation of his choice, just as he had shifted rather easily from me, his wife, to another man's wife — another woman. What I could not see was how I should go forward, now, in any natural, coherent way. As a mother without a husband, as a poet without a publisher, a freelance journalist without assignment, a city planner without a contract, it seemed to me that several incontestable and conflicting necessities had suddenly eliminated the whole realm of choice from my life.

My husband and I agreed that he would have the divorce that he wanted, and I would have the child. This ordinary settlement is, as millions of women will testify, as absurd as saying, "I'll give you a call, you handle everything else." At any rate, as my lawyer explained, the law then was the same as the law today; the courts would surely award me a reasonable amount of the father's income as child support, but the courts would also insist that they could not enforce their own decree. In other words, according to the law, what a father owes to his child is not serious compared to what a man owes to the bank for a car, or a vacation. Hence, as they say, it is extremely regrettable but none-theless true that the courts cannot garnish a father's salary, nor freeze his ac-count, nor seize his property on behalf of his children, in our society. Apparently this is because a child is not a car or a couch or a boat. (I would suppose this is the very best available definition of the difference between an American child and a car.)

Anyway, I wanted to get out of the projects as quickly as possible. But I was going to need help because I couldn't bend down and I couldn't carry anything heavy and I couldn't let my parents know about these problems because I didn't want to fight with them about the reasons behind the problems — which was the same reason I couldn't walk around or sit up straight to read or write with-out vomiting and acute abdominal pain. My parents would have evaluated that reason as a terrible secret compounded by a terrible crime; once again an un-married woman, I had, nevertheless, become pregnant. What's more I had tried to interrupt this pregnancy even though this particular effort required not only one but a total of three abortions — each of them illegal and amaz-ingly expensive, as well as, evidently, somewhat poorly executed.

My mother, against my father's furious rejections of me and what he viewed as my failure, offered what she could; she had no money herself but there was space in the old brownstone of my childhood. I would live with them during the summer while I pursued my crash schedule for cash, and she would spend as much time with Christopher, her only and beloved grandchild, as her worsening but partially undiagnosed illness allowed.

After she suffered a stroke, her serenely imposing figure had shrunk into an unevenly balanced, starved shell of chronic disorder. In the last two years, her physical condition had forced her retirement from nursing, and she spent most of her days on a makeshift cot pushed against the wall of the dining room next to the kitchen. She could do very few things for herself, besides snack on crackers, or pour ready-made juice into a cup and then drink it.

In June, 1966, I moved from the projects into my parents' house with the help of a woman named Mrs. Hazel Griffin. Since my teens, she had been my hairdresser. Every day, all day, she stood on her feet, washing and straightening hair in her crowded shop, the Arch of Beauty. Mrs. Griffin had never been mar-ried, had never finished high school, and she ran the Arch of Beauty with an imperturbable and contagious sense of success. She had a daughter as old as I who worked alongside her mother, coddling customer fantasy into confidence. Gradually, Mrs. Griffin and I became close; as my own mother became more and more bedridden and demoralized, Mrs. Griffin extended herself — drop-ping by my parents' house to make dinner for them, or calling me to wish me good luck on a special freelance venture, and so forth. It was Mrs. Griffin who closed her shop for a whole day and drove all the way from Brooklyn to my housing project apartment in Queens. It was Mrs. Griffin who packed me up, so to speak, and carried me and the boxes back to Brooklyn, back to the house of my parents. It was Mrs. Griffin who ignored my father standing hateful at the top of the stone steps of the house and not saying a word of thanks and not

5

once relieving her of a single load she wrestled up the stairs and past him. My father hated Mrs. Griffin because he was proud and because she was a stranger of mercy. My father hated Mrs. Griffin because he was like that sometimes: hateful and crazy.

My father alternated between weeping bouts of self-pity and storm explosions of wrath against the gods apparently determined to ruin him. These were his alternating reactions to my mother's increasing enfeeblement, her stoic depression. I think he was scared; who would take care of him? Would she get well again and make everything all right again?

This is how we organized the brownstone; I fixed a room for my son on the   10
top floor of the house. I slept on the parlor floor in the front room. My father slept on the same floor, in the back. My mother stayed downstairs.

About a week after moving in, my mother asked me about the progress of my plans. I told her things were not terrific but that there were two different planning jobs I hoped to secure within a few days. One of them involved a study of new towns in Sweden and the other one involved an analysis of the social consequences of a huge hydro-electric dam under construction in Ghana. My mother stared at me uncomprehendingly and then urged me to look for work in the local post office. We bitterly argued about what she dismissed as my "high-falutin" ideas and, I believe, that was the last substantial conversation between us.

From my first memory of him, my father had always worked at the post office. His favorite was the night shift, which brought him home usually between three and four o'clock in the morning.

It was hot. I finally fell asleep that night, a few nights after the argument between my mother and myself. She seemed to be rallying; that afternoon, she and my son had spent a long time in the backyard, oblivious to the heat and the mosquitoes. They were both tired but peaceful when they noisily re-entered the house, holding hands awkwardly.

But someone was knocking at the door to my room. Why should I wake up? It would be impossible to fall asleep again. It was so hot. The knocking continued. I switched on the light by the bed: 3:30 A.M. It must be my father. Furious, I pulled on a pair of shorts and a t-shirt. "What do you want? What's the matter?" I asked him, through the door. Had he gone berserk? What could he have to talk about at that ridiculous hour?

"OK, all right," I said, rubbing my eyes awake as I stepped to the door and   15
opened it. "What?"

To my surprise, my father stood there looking very uncertain.

"It's your mother," he told me, in a burly, formal voice. "I think she's dead, but I'm not sure." He was avoiding my eyes.

"What do you mean," I answered.

"I want you to go downstairs and figure it out."

I could not believe what he was saying to me. "You want me to figure out if   20
my mother is dead or alive?"

"I can't tell! I don't know!!" he shouted angrily.

"Jesus Christ," I muttered, angry and beside myself.

I turned and glanced about my room, wondering if I could find anything to carry with me on this mission; what do you use to determine a life or a death? I couldn't see anything obvious that might be useful.

"I'll wait up here," my father said. "You call up and let me know."

I could not believe it; a man married to a woman more than forty years and   25
he can't tell if she's alive or dead and he wakes up his kid and tells her, "You figure it out."

I was at the bottom of the stairs. I halted just outside the dining room where my mother slept. Suppose she really was dead? Suppose my father was not just being crazy and hateful? "Naw," I shook my head and confidently entered the room.

"Momma?!" I called, aloud. At the edge of the cot, my mother was leaning forward, one arm braced to hoist her body up. She was trying to stand up! I rushed over. "Wait. Here, I'll help you!" I said.

And I reached out my hands to give her a lift. The body of my mother was stiff. She was not yet cold, but she was stiff. Maybe I had come downstairs just in time! I tried to loosen her arms, to change her position, to ease her into lying down.

"Momma!" I kept saying. "Momma, listen to me! It's OK! I'm here and everything. Just relax. Relax! Give me a hand, now. I'm trying to help you lie down!"

Her body did not relax. She did not answer me. But she was not cold. Her   30
eyes were not shut.

From upstairs my father was yelling, "Is she dead? Is she dead?"

"No!" I screamed at him. "No! She's not dead!"

At this, my father tore down the stairs and into the room. Then he braked.

"Milly?" he called out, tentative. Then he shouted at me and banged around the walls. "You damn fool. Don't you see now she's gone. Now she's gone!" We began to argue.

"She's alive! Call the doctor!"   35

"No!"

"Yes!"

At last my father left the room to call the doctor.

I straightened up. I felt completely exhausted from trying to gain a response from my mother. There she was, stiff on the edge of her bed, just about to stand up. Her lips were set, determined. She would manage it, but by herself. I could not help. Her eyes fixed on some point below the floor.

"Momma!" I shook her hard as I could to rouse her into focus. Now she fell   40
back on the cot, but frozen and in the wrong position. It hit me that she might be dead. She might be dead.

My father reappeared at the door. He would not come any closer. "Dr. Davis says he will come. And he call the police."

The police? Would they know if my mother was dead or alive? Who would know?

I went to the phone and called my aunt. "Come quick," I said. "My father thinks Momma has died but she's here but she's stiff."

Soon the house was weird and ugly and crowded and I thought I was losing my mind.

Three white policemen stood around telling me my mother was dead.   45
"How do you know?" I asked, and they shrugged and then they repeated themselves. And the doctor never came. But my aunt came and my uncle and they said she was dead.

After a conference with the cops, my aunt disappeared and when she came back she held a bottle in one of her hands. She and the police whispered together some more. Then one of the cops said, "Don't worry about it. We won't say anything." My aunt signalled me to follow her into the hallway where she let me understand that, in fact, my mother had committed suicide.

I could not assimilate this information: suicide.

I broke away from my aunt and ran to the telephone. I called a friend of mine, a woman who talked back loud to me so that I could realize my growing hysteria, and check it. Then I called my cousin Valerie who lived in Harlem; she woke up instantly and urged me to come right away.

I hurried to the top floor and stood my sleeping son on his feet. I wanted to get him out of this house of death more than I ever wanted anything. He could not stand by himself so I carried him down the two flights to the street and laid him on the backseat and then took off.

At Valerie's, my son continued to sleep, so we put him to bed, closed the   50
door, and talked. My cousin made me eat eggs, drink whiskey, and shower. She would take care of Christopher, she said. I should go back and deal with the situation in Brooklyn.

When I arrived, the house was absolutely full of women from the church dressed as though they were going to Sunday communion. It seemed to me they were, every one of them, wearing hats and gloves and drinking coffee and solemnly addressing invitations to a funeral and I could not find my mother anywhere and I could not find an empty spot in the house where I could sit down and smoke a cigarette.

My mother was dead.

Feeling completely out of place, I headed for the front door, ready to leave. My father grabbed my shoulder from behind and forcibly spun me around.

"You see this?" he smiled, waving a large document in the air. "This am insurance paper for you!" He waved it into my face. "Your mother, she left you insurance, see?"

I watched him.   55

"But I gwine burn it in the furnace before I give it you to t'row away on trash!"

"Is that money?" I demanded. "Did my mother leave me money?"

"Eh-heh!" he laughed. "And you don't get it from me. Not today, not tomorrow. Not until I dead and buried!"

My father grabbed for my arm and I swung away from him. He hit me on my head and I hit back. We were fighting.

Suddenly, the ladies from the church bustled about and pushed, horrified,   60
between us. This was a sin, they said, for a father and a child to fight in the
house of the dead and the mother not yet in the ground! Such a good woman
she was, they said. She was a good woman, a good woman, they all agreed. Out
of respect for the memory of this good woman, in deference to my mother who
had committed suicide, the ladies shook their hats and insisted we should not
fight; I should not fight with my father.

Utterly disgusted and disoriented, I went back to Harlem. By the time
I reached my cousin's place I had begun to bleed, heavily. Valerie said I was
hemorrhaging so she called up her boyfriend and the two of them hobbled me
into Harlem Hospital.

I don't know how long I remained unconscious, but when I opened my
eyes I found myself on the women's ward, with an intravenous setup feeding
into my arm. After a while, Valerie showed up. Christopher was fine, she told
me; my friends were taking turns with him. Whatever I did, I should not admit
I'd had an abortion or I'd get her into trouble, and myself in trouble. Just play
dumb and rest. I'd have to stay on the ward for several days. My mother's funeral was tomorrow afternoon. What did I want her to tell people to explain
why I wouldn't be there? She meant, what lie?

I thought about it and I decided I had nothing to say; if I couldn't tell the
truth then the hell with it.

I lay in that bed at Harlem Hospital, thinking and sleeping. I wanted to
get well.

I wanted to be strong. I never wanted to be weak again as long as I lived. I   65
thought about my mother and her suicide and I thought about how my father
could not tell whether she was dead or alive.

I wanted to get well and what I wanted to do as soon as I was strong again,
actually, what I wanted to do was I wanted to live my life so that people would
know unmistakably that I am alive, so that when I finally die people will know
the difference for sure between my living and my death.

And I thought about the idea of my mother as a good woman and I rejected that, because I don't see why it's a good thing when you give up, or when
you cooperate with those who hate you or when you polish and iron and mend
and endlessly mollify for the sake of the people who love the way that you kill
yourself day by day silently.

And I think all of this is really about women and work. Certainly this is
all about me as a woman and my life work. I mean I am not sure my mother's
suicide was something extraordinary. Perhaps most women must deal with
a similar inheritance, the legacy of a woman whose death you cannot possibly
pinpoint because she died so many, many times and because, even before
she became your mother, the life of that woman was taken; I say it was taken
away.

And really it was to honor my mother that I did fight with my father, that
man who could not tell the living from the dead.

And really it is to honor Mrs. Hazel Griffin and my cousin Valerie and   70
all the women I love, including myself, that I am working for the courage to

admit the truth that Bertolt Brecht has written; he says, "It takes courage to say that the good were defeated not because they were good, but because they were weak."

I cherish the mercy and the grace of women's work. But I know there is new work that we must undertake as well: that new work will make defeat detestable to us. That new women's work will mean we will not die trying to stand up: we will live that way: standing up.

I came too late to help my mother to her feet.

By way of everlasting thanks to all of the women who have helped me to stay alive I am working never to be late again.   *[1985]*

ALICE WALKER

In Search of Our Mothers' Gardens

> I described her own nature and temperament. Told how they needed a larger life for their expression. . . . I pointed out that in lieu of proper channels, her emotions had overflowed into paths that dissipated them. I talked, beautifully I thought, about an art that would be born, an art that would open the way for women the likes of her. I asked her to hope, and build up an inner life against the coming of that day. . . . I sang, with a strange quiver in my voice, a promise song.
> — "Avey," JEAN TOOMER, *Cane*
> *The poet speaking to a prostitute who falls asleep while he's talking*

When the poet Jean Toomer walked through the South in the early twenties, he discovered a curious thing: black women whose spirituality was so intense, so deep, so *unconscious*, they were themselves unaware of the richness they held. They stumbled blindly through their lives: creatures so abused and mutilated in body, so dimmed and confused by pain, that they considered themselves unworthy even of hope. In the selfless abstractions their bodies became to the men who used them, they became more than "sexual objects," more even than mere women: they became "Saints." Instead of being perceived as whole persons, their bodies became shrines: what was thought to be their minds became temples suitable for worship. These crazy Saints stared out at the world, wildly, like lunatics — or quietly, like suicides; and the "God" that was in their gaze was as mute as a great stone.

Who were these Saints? These crazy, loony, pitiful women?

Some of them, without a doubt, were our mothers and grandmothers.

In the still heat of the post-Reconstruction South, this is how they seemed to Jean Toomer: exquisite butterflies trapped in an evil honey, toiling away their lives in an era, a century, that did not acknowledge them, except as "the *mule* of the world." They dreamed dreams that no one knew — not even themselves, in any coherent fashion — and saw visions no one could understand. They wandered or sat about the countryside crooning lullabies to ghosts, and drawing the mother of Christ in charcoal on courthouse walls.

They forced their minds to desert their bodies and their striving spirits   5
sought to rise, like frail whirlwinds from the hard red clay. And when those frail
whirlwinds fell, in scattered particles, upon the ground, no one mourned. Instead, men lit candles to celebrate the emptiness that remained, as people do
who enter a beautiful but vacant space to resurrect a God.

Our mothers and grandmothers, some of them: moving to music not yet
written. And they waited.

They waited for a day when the unknown thing that was in them would be
made known; but guessed, somehow in their darkness, that on the day of their
revelation they would be long dead. Therefore to Toomer they walked, and even
ran, in slow motion. For they were going nowhere immediate, and the future
was not yet within their grasp. And men took our mothers and grandmothers,
"but got no pleasure from it." So complex was their passion and their calm.

To Toomer, they lay vacant and fallow as autumn fields, with harvest time
never in sight: and he saw them enter loveless marriages, without joy; and become prostitutes, without resistance; and become mothers of children, without fulfillment.

For these grandmothers and mothers of ours were not Saints, but Artists;
driven to a numb and bleeding madness by the springs of creativity in them for
which there was no release. They were Creators, who lived lives of spiritual
waste, because they were so rich in spirituality — which is the basis of
Art — that the strain of enduring their unused and unwanted talent drove
them insane. Throwing away this spirituality was their pathetic attempt to
lighten the soul to a weight their work-worn, sexually abused bodies could bear.

What did it mean for a black woman to be an artist in our grandmothers'   10
time? In our great-grandmothers' day? It is a question with an answer cruel
enough to stop the blood.

Did you have a genius of a great-great-grandmother who died under some
ignorant and depraved white overseer's lash? Or was she required to bake bis-
cuits for a lazy backwater tramp, when she cried out in her soul to paint water-
colors of sunsets, or the rain falling on the green and peaceful pasturelands? Or
was her body broken and forced to bear children (who were more often than
not sold away from her) — eight, ten, fifteen, twenty children — when her one
joy was the thought of modeling heroic figures of rebellion, in stone or clay?

How was the creativity of the black woman kept alive, year after year and
century after century, when for most of the years black people have been in
America, it was a punishable crime for a black person to read or write? And the
freedom to paint, to sculpt, to expand the mind with action did not exist. Consider, if you can bear to imagine it, what might have been the result if singing,
too, had been forbidden by law. Listen to the voices of Bessie Smith, Billie
Holiday, Nina Simone, Roberta Flack, and Aretha Franklin, among others, and
imagine those voices muzzled for life. Then you may begin to comprehend the
lives of our "crazy," "Sainted" mothers and grandmothers. The agony of the
lives of women who might have been Poets, Novelists, Essayists, and Short-
Story Writers (over a period of centuries), who died with their real gifts stifled
within them.

And, if this were the end of the story, we would have cause to cry out in my paraphrase of Okot p'Bitek's great poem:

> O, my clanswoman
> Let us all cry together!
> Come,
> Let us mourn the death of our mother,
> The death of a Queen
> The ash that was produced
> By a great fire!
> O, this homestead is utterly dead
> Close the gates
> With *lacari* thorns,
> For our mother
> The creator of the Stool is lost!
> And all the young men
> Have perished in the wilderness!

But this is not the end of the story, for all the young women — our mothers and grandmothers, *ourselves* — have not perished in the wilderness. And if we ask ourselves why, and search for and find the answer, we will know beyond all efforts to erase it from our minds, just exactly who, and of what, we black American women are.

One example, perhaps the most pathetic, most misunderstood one, can provide a backdrop for our mothers' work: Phillis Wheatley, a slave in the 1700s.

15

Virginia Woolf, in her book *A Room of One's Own*, wrote that in order for a woman to write fiction she must have two things, certainly: a room of her own (with key and lock) and enough money to support herself.

What then are we to make of Phillis Wheatley, a slave, who owned not even herself? This sickly, frail black girl who required a servant of her own at times — her health was so precarious — and who, had she been white, would have been easily considered the intellectual superior of all the women and most of the men in the society of her day.

Virginia Woolf wrote further, speaking of course not of our Phillis, that "any woman born with a great gift in the sixteenth century [insert "eighteenth century," insert "black woman," insert "born or made a slave"] would certainly have gone crazed, shot herself, or ended her days in some lonely cottage outside the village, half witch, half wizard [insert "Saint"], feared and mocked at. For it needs little skill and psychology to be sure that a highly gifted girl who had tried to use her gift of poetry would have been so thwarted and hindered by contrary instincts [add "chains, guns, the lash, the ownership of one's body by someone else, submission to an alien religion"], that she must have lost her health and sanity to a certainty."

The key words, as they relate to Phillis, are "contrary instincts." For when we read the poetry of Phillis Wheatley — as when we read the novels of Nella Larsen or the oddly false-sounding autobiography of that freest of all black women writers, Zora Hurston — evidence of "contrary instincts" is everywhere. Her loyalties were completely divided, as was, without question, her mind.

But how could this be otherwise? Captured at seven, a slave of wealthy,   20
doting whites who instilled in her the "savagery" of the Africa they "rescued"
her from . . . one wonders if she was even able to remember her homeland as
she had known it, or as it really was.

Yet, because she did try to use her gift for poetry in a world that made her
a slave, she was "so thwarted and hindered by . . . contrary instincts, that
she . . . lost her health. . . ." In the last years of her brief life, burdened not only
with the need to express her gift but also with a penniless, friendless "freedom"
and several small children for whom she was forced to do strenuous work to
feed, she lost her health, certainly. Suffering from malnutrition and neglect and
who knows what mental agonies, Phillis Wheatley died.

So torn by "contrary instincts" was black, kidnapped, enslaved Phillis that
her description of "the Goddess" — as she poetically called the Liberty she did
not have — is ironically, cruelly humorous. And, in fact, has held Phillis up to
ridicule for more than a century. It is usually read prior to hanging Phillis's
memory as that of a fool. She wrote:

> The Goddess comes, she moves divinely fair,
> Olive and laurel binds her *golden* hair.
> Wherever shines this native of the skies,
> Unnumber'd charms and recent graces rise. [My italics]

It is obvious that Phillis, the slave, combed the "Goddess's" hair every
morning; prior, perhaps, to bringing in the milk, or fixing her mistress's lunch.
She took her imagery from the one thing she saw elevated above all others.

With the benefit of hindsight we ask, "How could she?"

But at last, Phillis, we understand. No more snickering when your stiff,   25
struggling, ambivalent lines are forced on us. We know now that you were not
an idiot or a traitor; only a sickly little black girl, snatched from your home and
country and made a slave; a woman who still struggled to sing the song that
was your gift, although in a land of barbarians who praised you for your bewildered tongue. It is not so much what you sang, as that you kept alive, in so
many of our ancestors, *the notion of song.*

Black women are called, in the folklore that so aptly identifies one's status in
society, "the *mule* of the world," because we have been handed the burdens that
everyone else — *everyone* else — refused to carry. We have also been called
"Matriarchs," "Superwomen," and "Mean and Evil Bitches." Not to mention
"Castraters" and "Sapphire's Mama." When we have pleaded for understanding, our character has been distorted; when we have asked for simple caring,
we have been handed empty inspirational appellations, then stuck in the farthest corner. When we have asked for love, we have been given children. In
short, even our plainer gifts, our labors of fidelity and love, have been knocked
down our throats. To be an artist and a black woman, even today, lowers our
status in many respects, rather than raises it; and yet, artists we will be.

Therefore we must fearlessly pull out of ourselves and look at and identify
with our lives the living creativity some of our great-grandmothers were not

allowed to know. I stress *some* of them because it is well known that the majority of our great-grandmothers knew, even without "knowing" it, the reality of their spirituality, even if they didn't recognize it beyond what happened in the singing at church — and they never had any intention of giving it up.

How they did it — those millions of black women who were not Phillis Wheatley, or Lucy Terry or Frances Harper or Zora Hurston or Nella Larsen or Bessie Smith; or Elizabeth Catlett, or Katherine Dunham, either — brings me to the title of this essay, "In Search of Our Mothers' Gardens," which is a personal account that is yet shared, in its theme and its meaning, by all of us. I found, while thinking about the far-reaching world of the creative black woman, that often the truest answer to a question that really matters can be found very close.

In the late 1920s my mother ran away from home to marry my father. Marriage, if not running away, was expected of seventeen-year-old girls. By the time she was twenty, she had two children and was pregnant with a third. Five children later, I was born. And this is how I came to know my mother: she seemed a large, soft, loving-eyed woman who was rarely impatient in our home. Her quick, violent temper was on view only a few times a year, when she battled with the white landlord who had the misfortune to suggest to her that her children did not need to go to school.

She made all the clothes we wore, even my brothers' overalls. She made all 30 the towels and sheets we used. She spent the summers canning vegetables and fruits. She spent the winter evenings making quilts enough to cover all our beds.

During the "working" day, she labored beside — not behind — my father in the fields. Her day began before sunup, and did not end until late at night. There was never a moment for her to sit down, undisturbed, to unravel her own private thoughts; never a time free from interruption — by work or the noisy inquiries of her many children. And yet, it is to my mother — and all our mothers who were not famous — that I went in search of the secret of what has fed that muzzled and often mutilated, but vibrant, creative spirit that the black woman has inherited, and that pops out in wild and unlikely places to this day.

But when, you will ask, did my overworked mother have time to know or care about feeding the creative spirit?

The answer is so simple that many of us have spent years discovering it. We have constantly looked high, when we should have looked high — and low.

For example: in the Smithsonian Institution in Washington, D.C., there hangs a quilt unlike any other in the world. In fanciful, inspired, and yet simple and identifiable figures, it portrays the story of the Crucifixion. It is considered rare, beyond price. Though it follows no known pattern of quiltmaking, and though it is made of bits and pieces of worthless rags, it is obviously the work of a person of powerful imagination and deep spiritual feeling. Below this quilt I saw a note that says it was made by "an anonymous Black woman in Alabama, a hundred years ago."

If we could locate this "anonymous" black woman from Alabama, she   35
would turn out to be one of our grandmothers—an artist who left her mark in
the only materials she could afford, and in the only medium her position in
society allowed her to use.

As Virginia Woolf wrote further, in *A Room of One's Own*:

> Yet genius of a sort must have existed among women as it must have ex-
> isted among the working class. [Change this to "slaves" and "the wives
> and daughters of sharecroppers."] Now and again an Emily Brontë or a
> Robert Burns [change this to "a Zora Hurston or a Richard Wright"]
> blazes out and proves its presence. But certainly it never got itself on to
> paper. When, however, one reads of a witch being ducked, of a woman
> possessed by devils [or "Sainthood"], of a wise woman selling herbs [or
> root workers], or even a very remarkable man who had a mother, then I
> think we are on the track of a lost novelist, a suppressed poet, or some
> mute and inglorious Jane Austen. . . . Indeed, I would venture to guess
> that Anon, who wrote so many poems without signing them, was often a
> woman. . . .

And so our mothers and grandmothers have, more often than not anony-
mously, handed on the creative spark, the seed of the flower they themselves
never hoped to see: or like a sealed letter they could not plainly read.

And so it is, certainly, with my own mother. Unlike "Ma" Rainey's songs,
which retained their creator's name even while blasting forth from Bessie
Smith's mouth, no song or poem will bear my mother's name. Yet so many of
the stories that I write, that we all write, are my mother's stories. Only recently
did I fully realize this: that through years of listening to my mother's stories of
her life, I have absorbed not only the stories themselves, but something of the
manner in which she spoke, something of the urgency that involves the knowledge that her stories—like her life—must be recorded. It is probably for this
reason that so much of what I have written is about characters whose counterparts in real life are so much older than I am.

But the telling of these stories, which came from my mother's lips as natu-
rally as breathing, was not the only way my mother showed herself as an artist.
For stories, too, were subject to being distracted, to dying without conclusion.
Dinners must be started, and cotton must be gathered before the big rains. The
artist that was and is my mother showed itself to me only after many years.
This is what I finally noticed:

Like Mem, a character in *The Third Life of Grange Copeland*, my mother   40
adorned with flowers whatever shabby house we were forced to live in. And not
just your typical straggly country stand of zinnias, either. She planted ambitious gardens—and still does—with over fifty different varieties of plants that
bloom profusely from early March until late November. Before she left home for
the fields, she watered her flowers, chopped up the grass, and laid out new beds.
When she returned from the fields she might divide clumps of bulbs, dig a cold
pit, uproot and replant roses, or prune branches from her taller bushes or
trees—until night came and it was too dark to see.

Whatever she planted grew as if by magic, and her fame as a grower of flowers spread over three counties. Because of her creativity with her flowers, even my memories of poverty are seen through a screen of blooms — sunflowers, petunias, roses, dahlias, forsythia, spirea, delphiniums, verbena . . . and so on.

And I remember people coming to my mother's yard to be given cuttings from her flowers; I hear again the praise showered on her because whatever rocky soil she landed on, she turned into a garden. A garden so brilliant with colors, so original in its design, so magnificent with life and creativity, that to this day people drive by our house in Georgia — perfect strangers and imperfect strangers — and ask to stand or walk among my mother's art.

I notice that it is only when my mother is working in her flowers that she is radiant, almost to the point of being invisible — except as Creator: hand and eye. She is involved in work her soul must have. Ordering the universe in the image of her personal conception of Beauty.

Her face, as she prepares the Art that is her gift, is a legacy of respect she leaves to me, for all that illuminates and cherishes life. She has handed down respect for the possibilities — and the will to grasp them.

For her, so hindered and intruded upon in so many ways, being an artist 45
has still been a daily part of her life. This ability to hold on, even in very simple ways, is work black women have done for a very long time.

This poem is not enough, but it is something, for the woman who literally covered the holes in our walls with sunflowers:

> They were women then
> My mama's generation
> Husky of voice — Stout of
> Step
> With fists as well as
> Hands
> How they battered down
> Doors
> And ironed
> Starched white
> Shirts
> How they led
> Armies
> Headragged Generals
> Across mined
> Fields
> Booby-trapped
> Kitchens
> To discover books
> Desks
> A place for us
> How they knew what we
> *Must* know
> Without knowing a page
> Of it
> Themselves.

Guided by my heritage of a love of beauty and a respect for strength — in search of my mother's garden, I found my own.

And perhaps in Africa over two hundred years ago, there was just such a mother; perhaps she painted vivid and daring decorations in oranges and yellows and greens on the walls of her hut; perhaps she sang — in a voice like Roberta Flack's — *sweetly* over the compounds of her village; perhaps she wove the most stunning mats or told the most ingenious stories of all the village storytellers. Perhaps she was herself a poet — though only her daughter's name is signed to the poems that we know.

Perhaps Phillis Wheatley's mother was also an artist.

Perhaps in more than Phillis Wheatley's biological life is her mother's signature made clear.   50

[1974]

≡ A WRITING EXERCISE

Read Jordan's "Many Rivers to Cross," jotting down your notes and comments in the margin. Consider your immediate reactions, and don't ignore personal associations. Then freewrite a response to her essay for ten minutes.

A Student's Personal Response

Isla Bravo wrote in her journal:

> It was shocking to read about Jordan's mother's suicide in the first sentence of "Many Rivers to Cross." I expected the rest of the essay to be about only that one event, but she went on to talk about everything else that was going on in her life around that time first. It is hard to understand how she managed everything in her life. She is out of money and needs to find a way to improve her financial status in just three months. My family may not have everything we've ever wanted, but we've always done pretty well, and I never worried about where we lived.
>
> Even though I have never had to struggle the way Jordan did, I can relate to her descriptions of her friends and neighbors. They all help her out the best they can when her husband leaves her and then when her mother dies. These are the people that she really appreciates in her life. They are the same kind of people that brought food to my parents when my grandmother died. These are the people that she loves, and she creates her own sort of family despite the fact that her father is so mean to her. These are people with whom she creates relationships that aren't defined by specific standards created by society.
>
> When Jordan says that her mother's death may not be extraordinary, that maybe every woman watches someone die over and over, she is really talking about all the little things that can wear a lot of

women down and cause their deaths a long time before they actually die. She can't even tell that her mother is dead because she's been wearing down for so long. The image of her mother looking as if she was "just about to stand up" made me think of my grandmother's funeral and how she looked like she was sleeping rather than dead. For Jordan the image of her mother in that sort of paralysis is also an image of her possible future. It is strange to think of someone whose life has been so hard on them that their death doesn't create a jarring difference.

Jordan seems to be trying to keep herself from wearing down just like her mother at the end. Women are given roles by society that prevent them from being able to really enjoy their lives. She uses her other friends and family as models for how to survive. She has a friend who calms her down on the phone, a cousin that gives her advice in the hospital, and more that take care of her son when she can't. Mrs. Griffin is a good example of the type of person she wants to be. She has to work hard to avoid becoming her mother. It seems as if she is motivated by guilt because she wasn't able to help her mother when she says, "I came too late to help my mother to her feet." Even though it wasn't her fault that her mother put up with so much, it certainly makes her determined to prevent her life from ending up the same way her mother's did.

The Elements of Essays

First impressions are valuable, but writing intelligently about essays should not be completely spontaneous. We can be personal and insightful, but persuading others about the validity of our reading takes a more focused and textually informed presentation. The following discussion of the basic elements of the essay is meant to increase your ability to analyze and write about essays. The elements include voice, style, structure, and ideas.

VOICE

When we read the first few sentences of an essay, we usually hear the narrator's **voice**: we hear a person speaking to us, and we begin to notice if he or she sounds friendly or hostile, stuffy or casual, self-assured or tentative. The voice might be austere and technical or personal and flamboyant. The voice may be intimate or remote. It may be sincere, hectoring, hysterical, meditative, or ironic. The possibilities are endless.

We usually get a sense of the writer's voice from the **tone** the writer projects. In the first paragraph of Walker's essay, we get a sense of the speaker's voice through the informed and serious tone that she takes. We also sense some irony and anger, especially when she asks, "Who were . . . these crazy, loony, pitiful women?" There also seems a note of lyrical sadness in her tone in paragraph 6: "Our mothers and grandmothers, some of them: moving to music not yet written. And they waited." Writing about such complex matters as racism and art, Walker's voice is equally complex. At times her tone is alternately angry ("When we have pleaded," para. 26); hopeful ("Therefore we must fearlessly pull out of ourselves," para. 27); thoughtful (para. 28); admiring (para. 29), and honestly self-reflective ("Only recently did I fully realize this," para. 38). And there are numerous examples of her employing a celebratory tone, especially when she discusses the matriarchal artists she so admires. The tone of her speculative conclusion is dramatic as she uses "perhaps" seven times, a rhetorically satisfying ending to an essay meant to be a moving argument about the ability of oppressed women to keep their artistic spirit alive. When we speak of a writer's persona, we mean a kind of performance mask or stance the writer assumes. Writers are trying to construct a persona that will serve their purposes. Voice and tone are techniques that help writers create a persona.

▤ A WRITING EXERCISE

Read June Jordan's essay "Many Rivers to Cross," and make some notes about the voice you hear. Like Walker, Jordan is also concerned with injustice and racism. Is her tone angrier? More determined? And like Walker, Jordan employs the rhetorical technique of repetition to conclude her essay. How would you compare the effectiveness of repeating "I" with Walker's "perhaps"?

STYLE

We all have stylish friends. They look good. Their shoes and pants and shirts seem to complement each other perfectly. It's not that they are color-coordinated — that would be too obvious for them — it's something more subtle. They seem to make just the right choices. When they go to a party, to the movies, or to school, they have a personal style that is their own.

Writers also have **style**. They make specific choices in words, in syntax and sentence length, in diction, in metaphors, even in sentence beginnings and endings. Writers use parallelism, balance, formal diction, poetic language, even sentence fragments to create their own styles.

Review each of the two essays with an eye to comparing the styles of Walker and Jordan. Notice the interesting use of the colon in Walker's first sentence and the dramatic repetition of "so intense, so deep, so *unconscious*." Actually, Walker's first paragraph makes creative use of the colon and dash. She writes sophisticated, complex sentences, varying the usual subject-verb-object pattern. In the second and third paragraphs, she varies the length of her sentences with short questions and statements before returning in the fourth, fifth, and sixth paragraphs to a literary style employing metaphors ("exquisite butterflies"), similes ("like frail whirlwinds"), and analogies ("moving to music"). It is an impassioned style, moving, evocative, and committed. Displaying

literary devices, rhetorical flourishes, and emotional honesty, Walker writes
her own rules for how a persuasive essay works.

≡ A WRITING EXERCISE

Note any literary techniques in Jordan's style. Focus especially on the last
dozen paragraphs or so. Are her sentences as complex as Walker's? Is her
style appropriate to her purpose? Explain.

STRUCTURE

The way essayists put their work together is not mysterious. The best writers
create a **structure** to fit their needs. Most do not have a prearranged structure
in mind or feel the need to obey the composition rules many students think
they have to follow: topic sentence first and three examples following. Writers
of essays aren't inclined to follow formulas. Essayists begin and end as they see
fit; they give explicit topic sentences or create narratives that imply themes;
they begin with an assertion and support it, or vice versa. Essayists are inven-
tors of structures that fit the occasion and their own way of seeing the world.
The thought of the essay significantly influences its structure. Like the relationship between mind and body, form and thought are inseparable.

Walker's essay is an argument, and its structure is part of her persuasive
intent. In "Looking at Literature as Argument" (pp. 69–70), we note that literary writers sometimes specify an issue, make claims, and then explicitly support these claims with substantial evidence, hoping to persuade a particular
audience. Most literary texts usually make arguments indirectly, but essays are
often more direct. Walker directly uses personal experience in the service of her
argument. Although students are sometimes taught that their own experiences are too subjective to persuade others, experienced writers like Walker
and Jordan use personal and literary experiences to call for certain changes in
the attitudes of their readers.

In her first paragraph, Walker reveals some of her **assumptions** or warrants, especially the idea that black women were not aware of their capabili-
ties, were "abused and mutilated," and were misread. After establishing
common ground with her audience — that these women are the mothers and
grandmothers of the speaker and her audience — Walker comes eventually to
her thesis in paragraph 9, in which she asserts that these women were "not
Saints, but Artists." After asking how these women kept their creativity from
disappearing, she notes that African American women of her mother's generation found a way through song and other strategies to keep an artistic heritage
alive in spite of the barriers they faced. Most of the essay then develops this idea
more concretely.

Walker's essay does not use a thesis statement and then a point-by-point
argument. Instead, she leads us into her main idea gradually, interweaving
examples, letting one idea lead to another, coming back to ideas mentioned

earlier, and developing them further. She ends by returning to her Phillis Wheatley example to make a connection to the deep past, as just one of the many ways she achieves coherence and unity in this quiltlike essay, sewn together with carefully crafted transitions.

≡ A WRITING EXERCISE

As you read through Jordan's essay, describe the structure or organizing strategies that she uses. How does her extended personal narrative support her main idea?

IDEAS

All writers have something on their minds when they write. That seems especially true when writers decide to put their **ideas** into a nonfictional form such as the essay. Of course, lots of ideas fill poems and short stories too, but they are usually expressed more indirectly. Although essays seem more idea-driven, this does not mean that as readers we have a responsibility to extract the precise idea or argument the writer had in mind. That may not even be possible since in the creative process of all writing, ideas get modified or changed. Sometimes a writer's original intention is significantly transformed; sometimes writers are not fully conscious of all their hidden intentions. Regardless, readers of essays are not simply miners unearthing hidden meanings; they are more like coproducers. And in creating that meaning, ideas are central.

"In Search of Our Mothers' Gardens" is an argument based on the idea that Walker's ancestors were not really the strange "crazy, loony, pitiful women" that Jean Toomer thought — not "exquisite butterflies" but artists "driven to a numb and bleeding madness by the springs of creativity in them for which there was no release." They could not do the work that was in their hearts and minds, and yet they managed to survive. They did so, Walker claims, through a psychological process Freud might call sublimation, by channeling their unacceptable creative drive into such acceptable ordinary paths as singing, quilting, and gardening. Phillis Wheatley is used as an example of an artist whose natural creativity was so thwarted that her health deteriorated as a result. And after reviewing her main ideas of heritage, love of beauty, and respect for the strength of her creative ancestors, Walker concludes with the speculation that perhaps the artistic tradition goes back even further than Wheatley, back to Wheatley's African mother and beyond.

≡ A WRITING EXERCISE

Ideas are often more powerful and more dramatic when they seem to evolve as a result of personal experience and not simply from political beliefs or ideological conviction. There seems to be a considerable difference between starkly asserting that black women were not able to live up to their potential and enveloping that idea, which Walker does here. What do you

think are some ideas that June Jordan develops? Comment on the effectiveness of her extended narrative in enhancing her ideas.

Final Draft of a Student Paper

After writing journal entries and a freewrite, Isla planned her essay and then
wrote a draft. She used responses from several students in a small-group workshop and from her instructor to help her revise her essay, sharpening her focus
and supporting her claims more explicitly. Here is Isla's final version.

Isla Bravo
Ms. Hollingsworth
English 201
21 April - - - -

Resisting Women's Roles

June Jordan takes a strongly feminist stance against the roles
women are forced to contend with in her essay "Many Rivers to
Cross." She begins the essay from her experience as a woman who has
conformed to the social expectations of a wife, daughter, and mother.
Her commitment to these roles has left her as a single mother who is
contending with an unwanted pregnancy, forced to care for a dying
mother and a belligerent father, and without a place of her own to live
or work. This essay is Jordan's own testimonial to why women need to
establish their independence and not allow society to control their
lives. She makes this statement by exploring her own defiance of
society's conventions regarding the roles for women as wife, daughter,
and mother in an attempt to preserve herself from the restrictions that
destroyed her mother.

Women are expected by society to place their families before their
careers, and part of this sacrifice includes aiding their husband's
careers in lieu of their own. Jordan portrays herself as an example of
how this convention is detrimental to a woman's ability to survive
on her own. Jordan sacrifices her own professional ambition to her
husband's pursuit of his career. The ensuing complications depict the
limitations and perils of the idea that women must always place their
own careers behind their husbands. Rather than specifically condemn
this social expectation, she provides an illustration of the destruction
it can cause. Her own career is a secondary priority, subjugated to her
roles as a supportive wife and mother, while her husband pursues
graduate school in another city and has an affair with another man's
wife. Jordan squanders a year of her life waiting for her husband's
return and becomes "a mother without a husband, . . . a poet without
a publisher, a freelance journalist without assignment, a city planner
without a contract." She abides by the social conventions that insist

she support her husband, and her life remains in stasis until he steps out of his own commitments. By living her life under the social guidelines for a wife, she allows herself to be exploited for her husband's convenience. Her needs are supplanted by her husband's, and his abandonment leaves her embarrassed and destitute.

Jordan's depiction of her parents' relationship illustrates the generational quality of these social conventions. Her parents' relationship foreshadows the potential outcome of her marriage if it continues. Her parents' relationship is wholly restricted to the typical gender roles they both inherit from society. Her mother subjugates her own life only to the needs of her husband, a sacrifice he expects from her. This historical relationship becomes clear when Jordan describes her father's response to her mother's fatal illness when she says, "I think he was scared; who would take care of him? Would she get well again and make everything all right again?" The fact that his concern was about his own life — "who would take care of him?" — makes it clear that their relationship revolved around only his own comfort. Jordan is desperate to prevent her own life from following this path.

Jordan's relationship with her father explores another aspect of the expectations placed on women by society, that of a daughter. Jordan's father's reliance on her mother for all of his comfort turns onto Jordan when her mother is no longer able to fulfill these duties. Jordan's role as his daughter, her most important function, is dynamically portrayed when her father forces her to check her mother's body to see if she is alive because he is incapable or unwilling to do it himself. He says to her, "I'll wait up here. . . . You call up and let me know," only to yell at her inaccurate determination. His anger appears to stem more from the disruption to his own life rather than from the loss of his wife; he is angry rather than sad. He appears almost offended by her death and his daughter's failure to provide him with the level of comfort he craves for his life. His own expectations for the superior role in the household have been created by a male-dominated society and have been enforced by the manner in which his wife seems to have fulfilled those expectations as well. The role of a dutiful child is not by itself destructive until it begins to take precedence in this destructive manner. His expectation is that Jordan should take on the role of caregiver, waiting on him despite any reluctance on her part and regardless of the animosity that exists between them.

Jordan also defies social conventions by her unwillingness to become a mother again to the new baby she's carrying. She attempts to abort the child several times until she finally does lose the baby. Jordan describes the advice she receives from a friend in the hospital: "Whatever I did, I should not admit I'd had an abortion or I'd get her into trouble, and myself in trouble." The possibility that Jordan does not want to be a mother to another child is abhorrent to the social standards that have formed her life and surroundings. Motherhood is the expected career for a woman, and her choice to not have another baby is a direct rejection of those standards.

As a woman in this particular culture, she has certain designated assignments of work that include being a daughter, wife, and mother. She rejects a caretaker role for her father, her marriage has dissolved, and she has an abortion. These portrayals do not suggest a rejection of these roles in their entirety; rather, they explicitly show how they can become harmful if they force women into situations they might have avoided if not for these societal pressures. From this point, she is able to look toward her own career and her own needs. The role society imposes on her as a woman puts her in a position that deemphasizes her own ambitions and preferences. The end of her mother's life is the catalyst that forces her to fully recognize the restrictions that she has been living with and that her mother succumbed to until her death. Jordan says, "I came too late to help my mother to her feet. . . . I am working never to be late again." She wants to free herself from the limiting standards for women in society and hopefully free other women as well.

▤ SUMMING UP

- **Essays (and nonfiction) use language as imaginatively and effectively as other genres of literature.** Essays should — like stories, poems, and plays — be read with care and deliberation and written about with energy and discipline. (p. 188)

- **The elements of essays include *voice, style, structure,* and *ideas.***

- **In essays, *voice* is important.** The writer's voice (which might be sincere, ironic, or meditative) can convey the tone a writer projects. But even in essays, writers might assume a persona that serves their purposes. (pp. 203–04)

- **The *style* and *structure* of essays often provide useful models for writers.** Noticing how essays are put together, how sentences and paragraphs follow one another logically, can lead to the writing of well-organized and stylish essays. (pp. 204–06)

- **As in all genres, *ideas* are crucial, but they seem especially prominent in essays.** (pp. 206–07)

- **Argumentative essays model effective ways to make arguments.** It is often valuable to analyze argumentative essays for the ways that writers make claims about issues, support their claims with evidence, and project a good image of themselves. (pp. 205–06)

CHAPTER 9

How to Write a Research Paper

At the conclusion of this chapter, we discuss four specific kinds of research papers, in each case providing a sample student essay on Charlotte Perkins Gilman's short story "The Yellow Wallpaper." (You will find the story in Chapter 12, "Freedom and Confinement.") But first we explain in general the research process and how it can lead to successful writing. You may imagine that writing a research paper for your English class is a significantly different, and perhaps more difficult, assignment than others you have had. Because more steps are involved in their writing (for example, additional reading and analysis of sources), research papers tend to be long-range projects. They also tend to be more formal than other kinds of papers because they involve integrating and documenting source material.

These differences, however, are essentially of magnitude and appearance, not of substance. Despite the common misconception (cause of much unnecessary anxiety) that writing a research paper requires a special set of knowledge and skills, it draws principally on the same kind of knowledge and skills needed to write other types of papers. A writer still needs to begin with an arguable **issue** and a **claim**, still needs to marshal **evidence** to defend that claim, and still needs to present that evidence persuasively to convince an audience that the claim has merit. The main difference between research papers and other papers that you will write for this course is that the evidence for a research paper comes from a wider variety of sources.

Writing about literature begins with a **primary research source** — the story, poem, play, or essay on which the paper is focused. In addition to this primary source, however, research papers call on **secondary research sources** — historical, biographical, cultural, and critical documents that writers use to support their claims. Moreover, writing a research paper requires you to **synthesize** your sources. That is, your paper must draw connections between them, not just bring them in randomly one by one. In a sense, synthesis is orchestration — you convey to your reader how your sources harmonize or clash. For example, you might show how various published essays on a literary work illustrate a *pattern* of interpretation, expressing basically the same idea about the text. Or you might emphasize how some published analyses of the text differ in significant ways. In any case, whether through comparison or contrast, you must make clear how your sources relate to one another and how they bear on your argument.

Strategies for Identifying an Issue and a Tentative Claim

Your first task in writing a research paper is to identify an issue that you genuinely want to think and to learn more about. The more interested you are in your issue, the better your paper will be. You may choose, for example, to write about issues of theme, symbolism, pattern, or genre, or you may prefer to explore contextual issues of social policy or of the author's biography, culture, or historical period. Any of the types of issues described on pages 57–65 are potentially suitable for research. The type of secondary research materials you use will depend largely on the issue you choose to pursue.

First, read your primary source carefully, taking notes as you do so. If you work with the texts in this book, you will want to read the biographical and contextual information about the author and any questions or commentaries that follow the texts. Then ask questions of your own to figure out what really interests you about the literature. Do not look for simple issues or questions that can be easily answered with a few factual statements; instead, try to discover a topic that will challenge you to perform serious research and do some hard thinking.

Before you begin looking for secondary research sources for your paper, formulate a tentative claim, much like a scientist who begins research with a hypothesis to be tested and affirmed or refuted. Since this tentative claim is unlikely to find its way into your final paper, do not worry if it seems a little vague or obvious. You will have plenty of opportunities to refine it as your research proceeds. Having a tentative claim in mind — or, better still, on paper — will prevent you from becoming overwhelmed by the multitude of potential secondary sources available to you.

Strategies for Finding and Using Secondary Sources

Once you have your topic in mind and have sketched a tentative claim, begin looking for secondary research sources. Many different types of sources for literary research are available, and the types you will need will depend largely on the type of claim you choose to defend. If your issue is primarily one of interpretation — about the theme, patterns, or symbolism of the text, for instance — you will most likely need to consult literary criticism to see what has been said in the past about the literature you are discussing. If your issue concerns historical or cultural context, including issues of social policy, you may need to consult newspapers, magazines, and similar sorts of cultural documents. Some topics might require several different types of sources.

Researching your project divides into two main activities. First, you will need to identify several secondary sources and construct a **working bibliography** — that is, a list of the materials you might use. Some researchers find it useful to record this working bibliography on a stack of note cards, with one entry per card containing all the pertinent information to help find the source and later to list it in the paper's bibliography, called the **Works Cited**. Nowadays, though, many researchers prefer to record their working bibliographies on a computer file. Once you have compiled a working bibliography, you will be ready to move on to the second stage: tracking down the materials you have identified, reading and evaluating them, and writing notes from (and about) them as a preliminary step to writing your own paper.

As you make note of potentially useful sources, it is important that you include in your working bibliography all of the information — including names, titles, publication information, and page numbers — that will eventually be needed for your Works Cited list. An explanation of the Works Cited format for each type of source (from books and articles to CD-ROMs and Web sites) begins on page 219. Acquaint yourself with this format before you begin compiling your working bibliography; otherwise, you may forget to record crucial information that you will need when you prepare the final version of your paper.

SEARCH FOR SOURCES IN THE LIBRARY AND ONLINE

Not many years ago, for most people the word *research* was synonymous with hours spent in the library hunting for books and articles. For many students today, *research* has become synonymous with the Internet. We have quickly come to believe that "everything" is available online. When it comes to scholarly research on literary topics, though, this is simply not true. Many of the best and most reliable sources are still available only in old-fashioned print media. If you restrict yourself to sources available electronically — on the Internet, say, or in full-text articles on CD-ROMs — you do yourself a serious disservice as a researcher. A good place to commence your research is your college or university library's computerized **catalog**. Be aware that scholarly books are often quite specialized and that you may want to start with one or two fairly general titles to orient you before venturing into more sharply focused scholarship.

Perhaps an even better place than the library catalog to begin research for your paper is the ***MLA International Bibliography***, published each year by the Modern Language Association. Most college and university libraries carry Internet, CD-ROM, and print versions of this work, which lists scholarly books and articles on a wide range of topics in literary criticism and history. The Internet and CD-ROM versions are powerful and flexible tools that allow a researcher to enter a topic or the name of an author or a work of literature and then to see on-screen a list of books and articles addressing that topic. These references can be copied by hand, printed out, or downloaded to your computer for your working bibliography.

Sources of cultural information other than literary criticism and history can be found by using other excellent options widely available in the print and electronic archives of college and university libraries. These include *InfoTrac*, a user-friendly electronic index of academic and general-interest periodicals including scholarly journals, magazines, and several prominent newspapers. Many researchers also like to use the *Readers' Guide to Periodical Literature* (available in print, CD-ROM, and online versions), *Newspaper Abstracts*, and the many specialized indexes devoted to particular fields of study, from science, to history, to education. Let your topic lead you to the information sources that will be most valuable to you. Your reference librarians will be happy to tell you what is available in your particular library as well as how to use any of these books and databases.

These days, reliable information is widely and conveniently available on CD-ROMs, many of which may be found in college and university libraries. These include texts of literary works (often with commentaries on these works), bibliographies and indexes to help you locate more traditional sources of information, and even the texts of historical and cultural documents. (For example, a CD-ROM about Robert Frost includes the texts of his poems, critical commentaries, relevant source materials, biographical and autobiographical passages, and recordings of Frost reading his own poetry.) In addition, standard reference works such as encyclopedias and dictionaries are often available on CD-ROM, where they can be efficiently searched for background information or factual corroboration (names, dates, spelling) for your paper. Keep in mind that you may need to rely on your librarian to tell you about your library's holdings because many CD-ROMs are not yet indexed in the same way as traditional books and magazines.

A wealth of information is available on the Internet as well, and, as with the information in the library, your goal is to find useful information efficiently, evaluate it carefully, and make effective use of it in your paper. Unfortunately, and unlike a library's sources, the information on the Internet is not indexed and organized to make it easily accessible to researchers. You will need to do a certain amount of "surfing" if you are to find appropriate materials for your project. A number of **search engines** (programs for finding information) are designed to help you track down documents on the Web, and if you are an old hand on the Internet, you can probably depend on search engines that have served you well in the past. Bear in mind, however, that relying on just one search engine (for example, Google) may not lead you to all the sources that would benefit you. Moreover, do not just settle for the first entries that a search engine turns up. Better sources may require a longer hunt with different key words.

Special care is needed to evaluate online sources, since anyone can put information on the Net. It will be up to you to determine if you are reading a piece of professional criticism or a middle-school term paper. When using online sources for serious research, look especially for work that has been signed by the author and is hosted by a respectable site, such as a university or a library.

EVALUATE THE SOURCES

Whatever method you use to locate your research materials, remember that not all sources are created equal. Be sure to allot some time for **evaluating** the materials you find. In general, the best and most reliable sources of information for academic papers are (1) books published by academic and university presses; (2) print or online articles appearing in scholarly and professional journals; and (3) print or online articles in prominent, reputable newspapers, such as the *New York Times* or the *Washington Post*. Many other types of sources — from CD-ROMs to popular magazines — may prove useful to you as well, but if you have any hesitation about the trustworthiness of a source, approach it with healthy skepticism. Also, the more recent your information, the better (unless, of course, you are doing historical research).

In general, you should ask the following basic questions of your sources: (1) Is the information recent, and if not, is the validity of the information likely to have changed significantly over time? (2) How credible is the author? Is he or she a recognized expert on the subject? (3) Is the source published by an established, respectable press, or does it appear in a well-respected journal or periodical (the *Los Angeles Times* has more credibility than the *National Enquirer*, for example) or Web site (one supported by a university or library, for instance)? (4) Based on what you've learned about responsible argument, do the arguments in your source seem sound, fair, and thoughtful? Is the evidence convincing? Is the development of the argument logical?

You increase your own credibility with your audience by using the most reliable research materials available to you, so do not just stick with whatever comes to hand if you have the opportunity to find a stronger source.

Strategies for Working with Sources

Once you have identified a number of sources for your paper and tracked down the books, periodicals, or other materials, it is time to begin reading, analyzing, and taking notes. At this point, it is especially important to keep yourself well organized and to write down *everything* that may be of use to you later. No matter how good your memory, do not count on remembering a few days (or even hours) later which notes or quotations come from which sources. Scrupulously write down page numbers and Web addresses, and double-check facts and spellings.

Many researchers find it easier to stay organized if they divide the notes they take into three basic categories: summaries, paraphrases, and quotations. (A fourth category is notes of your own ideas, prompted by your research. Write these down as well, keeping them separate and clearly labeled, as you would any other notes.)

Student researchers often rely too heavily on **quotations**, copying verbatim large sections from their research sources. Do not make this mistake. Instead, start your note-taking with a **summary** of the source in question — just one or two sentences indicating in your own words the author's main point. Such summaries guarantee that you understand the gist of an author's argument and (since they are your own words) can readily be incorporated in your paper. You might think of a summary as a restatement of the author's principal claim, perhaps with a brief indication of the types of supporting evidence he or she marshals. You can also write summaries of supporting points — subsections of an author's argument — if they seem applicable to your paper. A summary should not, however, include quotations, exhaustive detail about subpoints, or a list of all the evidence in a given source. A summary is meant to provide a succinct overview — to demonstrate that you have grasped a point and can convey it to your readers.

Chances are you will want to take more specific notes as well, ones that **paraphrase** the most germane passages in a particular source. Unlike a summary, a paraphrase does not condense an argument or leave out supporting evidence; instead it puts the information into new words. A paraphrase is generally no shorter than the material being paraphrased, but it still has two advantages over a quotation. First, as with a summary, an accurate paraphrase proves that you understand the material you've read. Second, again as with a summary, a paraphrase is easier to integrate into your paper than a quotation, since it is already written in your own words and style. When you include a paraphrase in your notes, indicate on the note the page numbers in the original source.

The rule of thumb about summarizing or paraphrasing is that you must always clearly indicate which ideas are yours and which are those of others. It is **plagiarism** — a serious violation of academic standards — to accept credit for another's ideas, even if you put them in your own words. Ideas in your paper that are not attributed to a source will be assumed to be your own, so to avoid plagiarism it is important to leave no doubt in your reader's mind about when you are summarizing or paraphrasing. Always cite the source.

An exception to the rule is **common knowledge** — factual information that the average reader can be expected to know or that is readily available in many easily accessible sources — which need not be referenced. For example, it is common knowledge that Kate Chopin was an American writer. It is also common knowledge that her original name was Katherine O'Flaherty and that she was born in St. Louis in 1851 and died there in 1904, even though most people would have to look that information up in an encyclopedia or a biographical dictionary to verify it.

Sometimes, of course, you will want to copy quotations directly from a source. Do so sparingly, copying quotations only when the author's own words are especially succinct and pertinent. When you write down a quotation, enclose it in quotation marks, and record the *exact* wording, right down to the punctuation. As with a paraphrase, make note of the original page numbers for the quotation, as you will need to indicate this in your final paper.

Each time you take a note, be it summary, paraphrase, or quotation, take a moment to think about why you wrote it down. Why is this particular note from this source important? Write a brief commentary about the note's importance, maybe just a sentence or a few words, perhaps on the back of a note card (if you are using note cards). When the time comes to draft your paper, such commentaries will help you remember why you bothered to take the note and may restart your train of thought if it gets stuck.

And do not forget: If something you read in a source sparks an original idea, write it down and label it clearly as your own. Keep these notes with your notes from the primary and secondary sources. Without your own ideas, your paper will be little more than a report, a record of what others have said. Your ideas will provide the framework for an argument that is your own.

Strategies for Integrating Sources

With your research completed (at least for the moment), it is time to get down to drafting the paper. At this point, many students find themselves overwhelmed with information and wonder if they are really in any better shape to begin writing than they were before starting their research. But having read and thought about a number of authors' ideas and arguments, you are almost certainly more prepared to construct an argument of your own. You can, of course, use any method that has worked for you in the past to devise a first draft of your paper. If you are having trouble getting started, though, you might look to Chapters 4 through 8 of this book, which discuss general strategies for exploring, planning, and drafting papers as well as more specific ideas for working with individual literary genres.

Start by revisiting your tentative claim. Refine it to take into account what you have learned during your research. With your revised and refined claim at hand, examine your assembled notes, and try to subdivide them into groups of related ideas, each of which can form a single section of your paper or even a single piece of supporting evidence for your claim. You can then arrange the groups of notes according to a logical developmental pattern — for example, from cause to effect or from weakest to strongest evidence — which may provide a structure for the body of your essay. As you write, avoid using your own comments as a kind of glue to hold together other people's ideas. Instead, you are constructing an argument of your own, using secondary sources to support your own structure of claims and evidence.

Anytime you summarize, paraphrase, or quote another author, it should be clear how this author's ideas or words relate to your own argument. Keep in mind that, in your final paper, it is quite unlikely that every note you took deserves a place. Be prepared to discard any notes that do not, in some fashion, support your claim and strengthen your argument. Remember also that direct quotations should be used sparingly for greatest effect; papers that rely too heavily on them make for choppy reading. By contrast, summaries and paraphrases are in your own words and should be a clean and easy fit with your prose style.

When you quote directly from either primary or secondary sources, you will need to follow special conventions of format and style. When quoting up to four lines of prose or three lines of poetry, integrate the quotation directly into your paragraph, enclosing the quoted material in double quotation marks and checking to make sure that the quotation accurately reflects the original. Longer quotations are set off from the text by starting a new line and indenting one inch on the left margin only; these are called **block quotations**. For these, quotation marks are omitted since the indention is enough to indicate that the material is a quotation. Examples of the correct format for both long and short quotations appear in Katie Johnson's paper (pp. 224–28).

When a short quotation is from a poem, line breaks in the poem are indicated by slash marks, with single spaces on either side. The following example demonstrates the format for a short quotation, in this case from William Shakespeare's sonnet "Let me not to the marriage of true minds." The number in parentheses is a page reference, and the format for citing page numbers is explained in the next section, "Strategies for Documenting Sources (MLA Format)."

> Shakespeare tells us that "Love is not love / Which alters
> when it alteration finds, / Or bends with the remover to
> remove" (345).

While it is essential to quote accurately, sometimes you may need to alter a quotation slightly, either by deleting text for brevity or by adding or changing text to incorporate it grammatically. If you delete words from a quotation, indicate the deletion by inserting an ellipsis (three periods with spaces between them), as demonstrated below with another quotation from the Shakespeare sonnet.

> Love, Shakespeare tells us, is "not Time's fool . . . But bears
> it out even to the edge of doom" (345–46).

If you need to change or add words for clarity or grammatical correctness, indicate the changes with square brackets. If, for instance, you wanted to clarify the meaning of "It" in Shakespeare's line "It is the star to every wandering bark," you could do so like this:

> Shakespeare claims that "[Love] is the star to every
> wandering bark" (345).

In addition to these format considerations, remember a few general rules of thumb as you deploy primary and secondary sources in your paper. First, without stinting on necessary information, keep quotations as short as possible — your argument will flow more smoothly if you do. Quotations long enough to be blocked should be relatively rare. Second, never assume that a quotation is self-sufficient or its meaning self-evident. Every time you put a quotation in your paper, take the time to introduce it clearly and comment on it to demonstrate why you chose to include it in the first place. Finally, quote fairly and accurately, and stick to a consistent format (such as the MLA style explained in the next section) when giving credit to your sources.

Strategies for Documenting Sources (MLA Format)

Documentation is the means by which you give credit to the authors of all primary and secondary sources cited within a research paper. It serves two principal purposes: (1) it allows your readers to find out more about the origin of the ideas you present, and (2) it protects you from charges of plagiarism. Every academic discipline follows slightly different conventions for documentation, but the method most commonly used for writing about literature is the format devised by the Modern Language Association (MLA). This documentation method encompasses **in-text citations**, which briefly identify within the body of your paper the source of a particular quotation, summary, or paraphrase, and a bibliography, called **Works Cited**, which gives more complete publication information.

While mastering the precise requirements of MLA punctuation and format can be time-consuming and even frustrating, getting it right adds immeasurably to the professionalism of a finished paper. More detailed information, including special circumstances and documentation styles for types of sources not covered here, will be found in the *MLA Handbook for Writers of Research Papers*, Seventh Edition (New York: Modern Language Association, 2009). Of course, if your instructor requests that you follow a different documentation method, you should follow his or her instructions instead.

MLA IN-TEXT CITATION

Each time you include information from any outside source — whether in the form of a summary, a paraphrase, or a quotation — you must provide your reader with a brief reference indicating the author and page number of the original. This reference directs the reader to the Works Cited list, where more complete information is available.

There are two basic methods for in-text citation. The first, and usually preferable, method is to include the author's name in the text of your essay and note the page number in parentheses at the end of the citation. The following paraphrase and quotation from James Joyce's "Araby" (p. 609) show the format to be followed for this method. Note that the page number (without the abbreviation "pg." or additional punctuation) is enclosed within parentheses and that the final punctuation for the sentence occurs after the parenthetical reference, effectively making the reference part of the preceding sentence. For a direct quotation, the closing quotation marks come before the page reference, but the final period is still saved until after the reference.

> Joyce's narrator recounts how he thought of Mangan's sister constantly, even at the most inappropriate times (610).

> Joyce's narrator claims that he thought of Mangan's sister "even in places the most hostile to romance" (610).

The method is similar for long quotations (those set off from the main text of your essay). The only differences are that the final punctuation mark comes before the parenthetical page reference, and that the quotation is not enclosed within quotation marks.

In those cases where citing the author's name in your text would be awkward or difficult, you may include both the author's last name and the page reference in the parenthetical citation. The following example draws a quotation from Victor Villanueva Jr.'s essay "Whose Voice Is It Anyway?," which comments on the ideas of Richard Rodriguez. (We juxtapose Villanueva's essay with Rodriguez's "Aria" in Chapter 12.)

According to one commentator, Rodriguez overlooks important distinctions among America's immigrants, failing in particular to acknowledge that "choice hardly entered into most minorities' decisions to become Americans" (Villanueva 993).

Knowing the last name of the author is enough to allow your reader to find out more about the reference in the Works Cited, and having the page number makes it easy to find the original of the quotation, summary, or paraphrase should your reader choose to. The only time more information is needed is if you cite more than one work by the same author. In this case, you will need to specify from which of the author's works a particular citation comes. Electronic sources, such as CD-ROMs and Internet sources, are generally not divided into numbered pages. If you cite from such a source, the parenthetical reference need include only the author's last name (or, if the work is anonymous, an identifying title).

MLA WORKS CITED

The second feature of the MLA format is the Works Cited list, or bibliography. This list should begin on a new page of your paper and should be double-spaced throughout and use hanging indention, which means that all lines except the first are indented one-half inch. The list is alphabetized by author's last name (or by the title in the case of anonymous works) and includes every primary and secondary source referred to in your paper. The format for the most common types of entries is given below. If any of the information called for is unavailable for a particular source, simply skip that element and keep the rest of the entry as close as possible to the given format. An anonymous work, for instance, skips the author's name and is alphabetized under the title.

Books

Entries in your Works Cited for books should contain as much of the following information as is available to you. Follow the order and format exactly as given, with a period after each numbered element below (between author and title, and so on). Not all of these elements will be needed for most books. Copy the information directly from the title and publication pages of the book, not from a library catalog or other reference, because these sources often leave out some information.

1. The name of the author (or editor, if no author is listed, or organization in the case of a corporate author), last name first.
2. The full title, in italics. If the book has a subtitle, put a colon between title and subtitle.
3. The name(s) of the editor(s), if the book has both an author and an editor, following the abbreviation "Ed."
4. The name(s) of the translator or compiler, following the abbreviation "Trans." or "Comp.," as appropriate.
5. The edition, if other than the first.

6. The volume(s) used, if the book is part of a multivolume set.
7. The city of publication (followed by a colon), name of the publisher (comma), and year.
8. The medium of publication (Print, Web, etc.), followed by a period.
9. The name of any series to which the book belongs.

The examples below cover the most common types of books you will encounter.

A book by a single author or editor.   Simply follow the elements and format as listed above. The first example below is for a book by a single author; note also the abbreviation "UP," for "University Press." The second example is a book by a single editor. The third is for a book with both an author (Conrad) and an editor (Murfin); note also that it is a third edition and a book in a series, so these facts are listed as well.

> Cima, Gay Gibson. *Performing Women: Female Characters, Male Play-wrights, and the Modern Stage*. Ithaca: Cornell UP, 1993. Print.
> Tucker, Robert C., ed. *The Marx-Engels Reader*. New York: Norton, 1972. Print.
> Conrad, Joseph. *Heart of Darkness*. Ed. Ross C Murfin. 3rd ed. Boston: Bedford, 2011. Print. Case Studies in Contemporary Criticism.

A book with multiple authors or editors.   If a book has two or three authors or editors, list all names, but note that only the first name is given last name first and the rest are in normal order. In cases where a book has four or more authors or editors, give only the first name listed on the title page, followed by a comma and the phrase "et al." (Latin for "and others").

> Leeming, David, and Jake Page. *God: Myths of the Male Divine*. New York: Oxford UP, 1996. Print.
> Arrow, Kenneth Joseph, et al., eds. *Education in a Research University*. Stanford: Stanford UP, 1996. Print.

A book with a corporate author.   When a book has a group, government agency, or other organization listed as its author, treat that organization in your Works Cited just as you would a single author.

> National Conference on Undergraduate Research. *Proceedings of the National Conference on Undergraduate Research*. Asheville: U of North Carolina, 1995. Print.

Short Works from Collections and Anthologies

Many scholarly books are collections of articles on a single topic by several different authors. When you cite an article from such a collection, include the information given below. The format is the same for works of literature that appear in an anthology, such as this one.

1. The name of the author(s) of the article or literary work.
2. The title of the short work, enclosed in quotation marks.

3. The title of the anthology, italicized.
4. The name(s) of the editor(s) of the collection or anthology.
5. All relevant publication information, in the same order and format as it would appear in a book citation.
6. The inclusive page numbers for the shorter work.
7. The medium of publication.

A single work from a collection or an anthology.   If you are citing only one article or literary work from any given collection or anthology, simply follow the format outlined above and demonstrated in the following examples.

> Kirk, Russell. "Eliot's Christian Imagination." *The Placing of T. S. Eliot.*
> Ed. Jewel Spears Brooker. Columbia: U of Missouri P, 1991. 136–44.
> Print.
> Silko, Leslie Marmon. "Yellow Woman." *Making Literature Matter: An*
> *Anthology for Readers and Writers.* 5th ed. Ed. John Schilb and John
> Clifford. Boston: Bedford, 2012. 602–09. Print.

Multiple works from the same collection or anthology.   If you are citing more than one short work from a single collection or anthology, it is often more efficient to set up a **cross-reference.** This means first writing a single general entry that provides full publication information for the collection or anthology as a whole. The entries for the shorter works then contain only the author and title of the shorter work, the names of the editors of the book, and the page numbers of the shorter work. The example below shows an entry for a short story cross-referenced with a general entry for this book; note that the entries remain in alphabetical order in your Works Cited, regardless of whether the general or specialized entry comes first.

> Faulkner, William. "A Rose for Emily." Schilb and Clifford 714–20.
> Schilb, John, and John Clifford, eds. *Making Literature Matter: An*
> *Anthology for Readers and Writers.* 5th ed. Boston: Bedford, 2012.
> Print.

Works in Periodicals

The following information should be included, in the given order and format, when you cite articles and other short works from journals, magazines, or newspapers.

1. The name(s) of the author(s) of the short work.
2. The title of the short work, in quotation marks.
3. The title of the periodical, italicized.
4. All relevant publication information as explained in the examples below.
5. The inclusive page numbers for the shorter work.
6. The medium of publication.

A work in a scholarly journal.   Publication information for works from scholarly and professional journals should include the volume number and the issue number, separated by a period; the year of publication in parentheses, followed by a colon; the page numbers of the shorter work; and the medium of publication.

> Charles, Casey. "Gender Trouble in *Twelfth Night.*" *Theatre Journal* 49.2
>   (1997): 121–41. Print.

An article in a magazine.   Publication information for articles in general-circulation magazines includes the month(s) of publication for a monthly (or bimonthly), or the date (day, abbreviated month, then year) for a weekly or bi-weekly, followed by a colon, the page numbers of the article, and the medium of publication.

> Cowley, Malcolm. "It Took a Village." *Utne Reader* Nov.–Dec. 1997:
>   48–49. Print.
> Levy, Steven. "On the Net, Anything Goes." *Newsweek* 7 July 1997:
>   28–30. Print.

An article in a newspaper.   When citing an article from a newspaper, in-clude the date (day, abbreviated month, year) and the edition if one is listed on the masthead, followed by a colon, the page numbers (including the section number or letter, if applicable), and the medium of publication.

> Cobb, Nathan. "How to Dig Up a Family Tree." *Boston Globe* 9 Mar. 1998:
>   C7. Print.

CD-ROMs

CD-ROMs come in two basic types: those published in a single edition — including major reference works like dictionaries and encyclopedias — and those published serially on a regular basis. In a Works Cited list, the first type is treated like a book and the second like a periodical. Details of citation appear in the following examples.

Single-edition CD-ROMs.   An entry for a single-edition CD-ROM is format-ted like one for a book, but with "CD-ROM" as the medium of publication. Most CD-ROMs are divided into smaller subsections, and these should be treated like short works from anthologies.

> "Realism." *The Oxford English Dictionary*. 2nd ed. Oxford: Oxford UP,
>   1992. CD-ROM.

Serial CD-ROMs.   Treat information published on periodically released CD-ROMs just as you would articles in print periodicals, but also include the title of the CD-ROM, italicized; the word *CD-ROM*; the name of the vendor dis-tributing the CD-ROM; and the date of electronic publication. Many such CD-ROMs contain reprints and abstracts of print works, and in these cases, the publisher and date for the print version should be listed as well, preceding the information for the electronic version.

> Brodie, James Michael, and Barbara K. Curry. *Sweet Words So Brave: The Story of African American Literature*. Madison: Knowledge Unlimited, 1996. CD-ROM. *ERIC*. SilverPlatter. 1997.

The Internet

Internet sources fall into several categories — World Wide Web documents and postings to newsgroups, listservs, and so on. Documentation for these sources should include as much of the following information as is available, in the order and format specified.

1. The name of the author(s), last name first (as for a print publication).
2. The title of the section of the work accessed (the subject line for e-mails and postings) in quotation marks.
3. The title of the Web site in italics.
4. The name of the sponsor or publisher of the Web site.
5. The date the material was published or updated.
6. The medium of publication.
7. The date you access a site.

The examples below show entries for a Web site and a newsgroup citation, two of the most common sorts of Internet sources.

> Brandes, Jay. "Maya Angelou: A Bibliography of Literary Criticism." Troy University, 20 Aug. 1997. Web. 10 June 2009.
> Broun, Mike. "Jane Austen Video Package Launched." *Google groups*. Google, 1 Mar. 1998. Web. 10 June 2009.

Personal Communication

In some cases you may get information directly from another person, either by conducting an interview or by receiving correspondence. In this case, include in your Works Cited the name of the person who gave you the information, the type of communication you had with that person, the date of the communication, and the medium if other than a personal interview.

> McCorkle, Patrick. Personal interview. 12 Mar. 2004.
> Aburrow, Clare. Message to the author. 15 Apr. 2004. E-mail.

Multiple Works by the Same Author

If you cite more than one work (in any medium) by a single author, the individual works are alphabetized by title. The author's full name is given only for the first citation in the Works Cited, after which it is replaced by three hyphens. The rest of the citation follows whatever format is appropriate for the medium of the source. The following two entries are for a work in an anthology and a book, both by the same author.

> Faulkner, William. "A Rose for Emily." *Making Literature Matter: An Anthology for Readers and Writers*. 5th ed. Ed. John Schilb and John Clifford. Boston: Bedford, 2012. 714–20. Print.
>
> - - - . *The Sound and the Fury*. New York: Modern Library, 1956. Print.

Occasionally, you may have an idea or find a piece of information that seems important to your paper but that you just cannot work in smoothly without interrupting the flow of ideas. Such information can be included in the form of **endnotes**. A small superscript number in your text signals a note, and the notes themselves appear on a separate page at the end of your paper, before the Works Cited.

Four Annotated Student Research Papers

A PAPER THAT DEALS WITH EXISTING INTERPRETATIONS OF A LITERARY WORK

A research paper assignment may require you to develop a claim about a literary work by relating your analysis to previous interpretations of the text. An example of a paper like this is the following essay, in which student Katie Johnson makes an argument about Charlotte Perkins Gilman's story "The Yellow Wallpaper" by incorporating statements made by people who have already written about it. To prepare for writing her paper, she especially consulted the *MLA International Bibliography*, through which she located several published articles about Gilman's tale. The bibliographies of these articles led her to still more interpretations of the story. The biggest challenge in writing a paper like this is to stay focused on developing an idea of your own, rather than just inserting and echoing opinions held by others. Katie ended up examining an element of Gilman's story that she felt had not been adequately noted, let alone properly interpreted, by literary critics. As her essay proceeds, therefore, she does not simply agree with all the interpreters she cites. She treats with respect, however, those she finds fault with, civilly pointing out how her own thoughts differ. In addition, she clearly takes seriously the specific language of the critics she mentions, pondering their actual words rather than superficially summarizing their views.

Katie Johnson
Professor Van Wyck
English L141
5 May - - - -

The Meaning of the Husband's Fainting
in "The Yellow Wallpaper"

   At the end of Charlotte Perkins Gilman's short story "The Yellow Wallpaper," the narrator is in a state that many people observing her would consider madness. She has torn off the wallpaper in her room and now seems proud of being able to "creep smoothly on the floor" (967). Her outwardly bizarre behavior at this point, along with her telling of the whole story beforehand, has led most literary critics to focus on analyzing her final conduct, as if it was the only really noteworthy feature of this concluding scene. Just as striking, however, is the final behavior of the narrator's husband, John. Up until the ending, he has acted as an authority on his wife's medical condition, and he has tried to assert power by always telling her what to do. At the conclusion, though, his mastery plainly vanishes. After finding the key to his wife's room, letting himself in, and beholding her crawling, he faints. Both the narrator and her husband end up on the floor. The narrator herself is highly aware of John's collapse, as she shows when she complains that "I had to creep over him every time!" (967). Because John's fainting is a dramatic reversal of his previous behavior and resembles the narrator's final physical position, it is surprising that only some literary critics have bothered to comment on John's breakdown, and even then the comments are relatively few. This neglect is a shame because, through John's fainting, Gilman seems to imply that he is left without any clear gender role to support him when his wife defies his manly effort to keep her what his society would consider sane.

Concisely summarizes the story's conclusion in first paragraph, which ends by stating main claim the essay will develop.

 Until the last scene, John has repeatedly attempted to control his wife in the way that his society would expect of a man. This effort of his is reinforced by the professional standing he has achieved as a doctor. His masculine authority is interconnected with his medical authority. As we readers are made aware, he does not succeed in thoroughly bending his wife's will to his. Much of her narration is about her secret rebellion against him, which takes the form of imagining women trapped in the wallpaper of her room. Despite her hidden thoughts, however, he is often issuing commands to her, and she finds it hard to resist his domination. She admits to us that "I take pains to control myself — before him, at least, and that makes me very tired" (957). His attempts at enforcing his power over her include shutting her up in an odd country house in the first place. When she expresses suspicion of the estate, he simply "laughs" and "scoffs" (956), as he seems to do whenever she reveals independent thinking. She also says that he "hardly lets me stir without special direction" and gives her "a schedule prescription for each hour in the day" (957). Furthermore, he discourages her from writing, does not want to let her have visitors, and refuses to leave the estate when she informs him that she is not getting any better. Actually, he treats her more like his child than his wife, which is revealed when he asks "What is it, little girl?" (962) one night when she wakes up bothered by the wallpaper. All in all, he fits the nineteenth-century image of the ideal man as someone who gives his wife orders and expects her to follow them, though John tries to disguise his bossiness by declaring that he loves her and is looking out for her best interests.

The literary critics who do write about John's fainting at the end of the story tend to see it as a moment of irony, because in their view this masculine authority figure winds up physically collapsing in a way that is stereotypically associated with women. For example, Carol Margaret Davison states that when John faints, he is "assuming the traditional role of frail female" (66). Greg Johnson describes John's fall as "Gilman's witty inversion of a conventional heroine's confrontation with Gothic terror" (529), and similarly, Beverly A. Hume says that what happens is that John is "altering his conventional role as a soothing, masculine figure to that of a stereotypically weak nineteenth-century female" (478). These comments are not unreasonable, because during the nineteenth century, fainting was indeed something that women were believed to do more often than men. But a pair of literary critics has made another observation that, even though it sounds like the ones I have just quoted, points in a different direction that seems worth pursuing. Sandra M. Gilbert and Susan Gubar refer to John's fainting as an "unmasculine swoon of surprise" (91). They sound as if they are saying that he now seems feminine, but actually the word "unmasculine" simply indicates that he is no longer acting like a stereotypical male, so that readers of the story have to wonder whether he has any kind of identity left to him now. In fact, John's fainting seems like a total falling apart, as if he has become incapable of performing any further role at all, whether it is stereotypically feminine or masculine. Though his wife is creeping, at least she is still able to move, whereas he lies paralyzed. Overall, he appears to suffer a complete loss of identity rather than take on a female identity. Because his wife has fallen into what he sees as madness despite his efforts to control her, he experiences a shattering of his male ego, the result being not that he is left with a "womanly" self but that he now lacks any sense of self at all. Just as he has only leased the estate instead of owning it, so too has his personhood proven impermanent because his ability to treat his wife as his property has apparently gone. At the very end of the story, the narrator even refers to her husband merely as "that man" (967), suggesting that he is no longer recognizable as an individual human being.

More than one literary critic has argued that John has suffered a loss of power only momentarily and that he will soon

Synthesizes comments from critics, combining them to indicate the pattern she finds in interpretations of the story.

Does not flatly declare critics "wrong" but will develop an idea they have not mentioned.

Carefully analyzes a particular word that this pair of critics uses. Rest of paragraph develops main claim.

dominate his wife just as much as he did before. Judith Fetterley contends that "when John recovers from his faint, he will put her in a prison from which there will be no escape" (164), and Paula Treichler claims that

> As the ending of her narrative, her madness will no doubt commit her to more intense medical treatment, perhaps to the dreaded Weir Mitchell of whom her husband has spoken. The surrender of patriarchy is only temporary; her husband has merely fainted, after all, not died, and will no doubt move swiftly and severely to deal with her. Her individual escape is temporary and compromised. (67)

Because quotation from Treichler is somewhat lengthy, Katie puts it in block form.

Unfortunately, Gilman did not write a sequel called "The Yellow Wallpaper: The Next Day" to let us know exactly what happens to the couple after the husband wakes up. Fetterley and Treichler might have been right if the events of this story had taken place in real life and involved a real married couple. Though it was based on Gilman's actual situation,[1] the story should be treated as a work of fiction, and Gilman has chosen to conclude it by showing John as physically overcome. If she had wanted to suggest that he will quickly regain power, presumably she would have done so. As the text stands, the final scene emphasizes his new weakness, not signs of a strength that will soon be restored to him.

Synthesizes two critics' observations, putting them together as examples of a view that she questions.

Directs readers to endnote.

Disagrees with two critics but carefully explains why and avoids using hostile tone.

Although both the husband and the wife are in a bad physical state at the end, we as readers do not have to sympathize with them equally. Especially by having the wife narrate the story, Gilman has designed it so that we are encouraged to care far more about her than about John. A lot of readers might even feel joy at his collapse, regarding it as the bringing down of a tyrant. In any case, his fainting is worth paying attention to as a sign that he has experienced a loss of masculine power that leaves him unable to function as any kind of self.

Uses final paragraph not only to restate main claim but also to add the point that readers of story do not have to feel as sorry for John as they do for his wife.

Endnote

[1] Gilman recalls the personal experience that motivated her to write her story in her essay "Why I Wrote 'The Yellow Wallpaper.'"

Endnote provides information that could not be easily integrated into main text of essay.

Works Cited

Davison, Carol Margaret. "Haunted House / Haunted Heroine: *Citation for article in* Female Gothic Closets in 'The Yellow Wallpaper.'" *Women's* *scholarly journal.* *Studies* 33.1 (2004): 47–75. Print.

Fetterley, Judith. "Reading about Reading: 'A Jury of Her Peers,' *Citation for work in* 'The Murders in the Rue Morgue,' and 'The Yellow Wall- *anthology.* paper.'" *Gender and Reading: Essays on Readers, Texts, and Contexts*. Ed. Elizabeth A. Flynn and Patrocinio P. Schweickart. Baltimore: John Hopkins UP, 1986. 147–64. Print.

Gilbert, Sandra M., and Susan Gubar. *The Madwoman in the* *Citation for book.* *Attic: The Woman Writer and the Nineteenth-Century Literary Imagination*. New Haven: Yale UP, 1979. Print.

Gilman, Charlotte Perkins. "Why I Wrote 'The Yellow Wall- *Note style for multiple* paper.'" 1913. Schilb and Clifford 968–69. *works by the same author.*
– – –. "The Yellow Wallpaper." 1892. Schilb and Clifford *Note, too, that when you* 956–67. *cite more than one work* *from the same book, you* Hume, Beverly A. "Gilman's 'Interminable Grotesque': The *give the book its own entry* Narrator of 'The Yellow Wallpaper.'" *Studies in Short Fiction* *and then cite each work* 28.4 (1991): 477–84. Print. *from it in the shorthand*

Johnson, Greg. "Gilman's Gothic Allegory: Rage and Redemp- *form you see here.* tion in 'The Yellow Wallpaper.'" *Studies in Short Fiction* 26.4 (1989): 521–30. Print.

Schilb, John, and John Clifford, eds. *Making Literature Matter:* *Citation for anthology.* *An Anthology for Readers and Writers*. 5th ed. Boston: Bedford, 2012. Print.

Treichler, Paula A. "Escaping the Sentence: Diagnosis and Discourse in 'The Yellow Wallpaper.'" *Tulsa Studies in Women's Literature* 3.1/2 (1984): 61–77. Print.

A PAPER THAT PLACES A LITERARY WORK IN HISTORICAL AND CULTURAL CONTEXT

When scholars do research on a literary work, often they are trying to place it in its original situation. They wish to identify how it relates to the historical and cultural context in which it emerged. If you write a research paper aiming to provide such background for a literary text, you will probably incorporate various sources. But your essay needs to focus on developing a claim of your own about the text. This is what the following paper by student Brittany Thomas does. Her essay connects Gilman's "The Yellow Wallpaper" to its original time. To prepare for the paper, Brittany examined autobiographical writings by Gilman as well as a lecture by S. Weir Mitchell, Gilman's own real-life doctor. She also investigated scholarship on nineteenth-century medical treatments of women. Becoming interested in the "rest cure" on which Gilman's story was based, Brittany realized that Gilman's plot leaves out the massages that were normally part of this therapy. In her paper, Brittany states and elaborates the claim that this omission was probably intentional — an effort by Gilman to emphasize the narrator's isolation from human touch.

Brittany Thomas
Professor Schneebaum
English L202
25 April ----

The Relative Absence of the Human Touch
in "The Yellow Wallpaper"

In her essay "Why I Wrote 'The Yellow Wallpaper,' " Charlotte Perkins Gilman reveals that her famous story was inspired by a personal depression that got worse when she underwent a "rest cure" prescribed to her by "a noted specialist in nervous diseases, the best known in the country" (968). Though she does not name this doctor in the essay, we are aware today that he was S. Weir Mitchell, a name that she actually brings up briefly in "The Yellow Wallpaper." The rest cure that the story's narrator goes through, however, does not seem to have all the features that Mitchell's did. Interestingly, neither by reading the essay nor by reading Gilman's story would you realize that Mitchell's treatment involved massage. The question for an interpreter of the story thus becomes, Why did Gilman leave massage out of "The Yellow Wallpaper"? Because we can only guess at her intentions, perhaps a better way of putting the question is this: What is the effect of omitting massage from the story? One important consequence is that there is less of a literal human touch in the story than there might have been, and so the heroine's alienation from others and her withdrawal into fantasy seem stronger than they might have been.

> *Immediately mentions one of her sources, but only to set up main claim about Gilman's story, which she states at end of paragraph.*

> *Using question form helps signal cause/effect issue that the essay will address.*

> *This is the essay's main claim.*

Mitchell himself seems to have regarded massage as a very big component of his rest cure. He gives it a lot of attention in his 1904 lecture "The Evolution of the Rest Treatment." There he describes at length two cases, one of a man and one of a woman, where he found out that rubbing the body helped the person overcome depression. He recalls arriving at the conclusion "that massage was a tonic of extraordinary value" (972), and he continues his lecture by giving a brief account of the larger world history of what he terms "this invaluable therapeutic measure" (973). Evidently Mitchell did not perform massage himself; in his lecture, he describes having others do it for him. Perhaps he thought that if he personally rubbed a patient's body, he would run the risk of being accused of a sexual advance. Despite his use of stand-ins for him, he clearly considered massage a necessary feature of his rest cure. One

> *Briefly summarizes Mitchell's lecture, focusing on his remarks about massage rather than spending additional time on other topics of his speech.*

reason was that he thought the depressed person's body needed some form of physical stimulation, which the person would not otherwise be getting by lying around so much of the time. He states in his lecture that massage was something that "enabled me to use rest in bed without causing the injurious effects of unassisted rest" (972). Probably this method also reflected a more general belief of his, which Jane F. Thrailkill describes as the assumption "that the efficacy of his cure lay in its treatment of a patient's material body, not in what we might now term the psychological effects of isolation or of his own charismatic presence" (532). Thrailkill goes on to point out that Mitchell was not alone in this belief: "[T]he medical wisdom of the day . . . conceived of a patient as a conceptually inert bundle of physiological processes" (552).[1] Massage was a means of helpfully manipulating the physique, which for Mitchell and other doctors of his era was the main source of difficulties that today might be seen as chiefly mental.

Analyzes at length one particular source, Mitchell's lecture.

Square brackets indicate alteration of text being quoted. Ellipses indicate words deleted from original text.

Given that massage was so important to Mitchell, it is significant that Gilman's references to it are not consistent. She does recall being massaged when she discusses how Mitchell treated her medically in her autobiography *The Living of Charlotte Perkins Gilman*. In that book, she says that besides being "put to bed and kept there," she was "fed, bathed, [and] rubbed" (96). She does not refer to massage, however, in "Why I Wrote 'The Yellow Wallpaper.'" More important for interpretations of the story, she does not make massage part of "The Yellow Wallpaper" itself. It plays no role at all in the plot. The elements of the rest cure that come up in the story are, instead, physical seclusion and forced abandonment of work.

Synthesis of three texts, comparing what they do with the topic of massage. More specifically, compares Gilman's autobiography; Gilman's essay on writing the story; and the story itself.

If massage were a major element of the rest cure that the narrator goes through in "The Yellow Wallpaper," the story would probably feature a lot more human touching than it presently does. The way the story is written, the heroine experiences relatively little physical contact with other people, or at least she does not tell us that she is having much of this. What is especially interesting is that we do not find many instances of her being physically touched by her husband, John. There are, in fact, a few places in the text where he does touch her. She says that when she informs him that she is disturbed by the wallpaper, "he took me in his arms and called me a blessed little goose" (958). When she weeps because he will not leave the house to visit relatives, "dear John gathered me up in his arms, and just carried me upstairs and laid me on the bed, and sat by me and read to me till it tired my head" (961). When she complains that he is wrong to think she is getting better, he gives her "a big hug" and says "'Bless her

In effect, admits it would be misleading to claim there are no instances of touching in the story. Proceeds to bring together (to synthesize) various examples of such contact.

little heart! . . . she shall be as sick as she pleases!' " (962). Yet his moments of touching her not only are very few but also reflect his insensitivity toward her. His folding her in his arms seems an effort to control her and trivialize her protests, not an expression of genuine love. Moreover, she takes no real comfort from his touch. If this amounts to rubbing her, then from her point of view, he is rubbing her the wrong way. Again, however, massage is significantly absent from this story, and because what touches there are seem so few and inhumane, readers are led to feel that the narrator is pretty much alone in her concerns. She has only the imaginary woman in the wallpaper to bond with, and she seems drawn to that woman in large part because her human companions have no true understanding of the distress that caused her to need some sort of cure in the first place.

Accounts for details of story that might seem to conflict with main claim.

In calling attention to the role of massage in S. Weir Mitchell's rest cure, I do not mean to minimize the importance of his treatment's other components. The physical rest he demanded of his patients was certainly a big element of the cure, so that we can easily see why Gilman made it central to her story. In his lecture, Mitchell also points out that he applied electrical charges to the patient's body. Historians of women's health Barbara Ehrenreich and Deirdre English argue that Mitchell relied heavily as well on "the technique of healing by *command*" (119, emphasis in original), constantly and firmly giving orders to his patients so that they felt obligated to obey his wishes and to get better on the precise schedule he had in mind. Massage certainly figured, however, in Mitchell's mode of treatment, including his handling of Gilman's own case, so that her omission of it from "The Yellow Wallpaper" seems a deliberate strategy for giving other things emphasis. Above all, the quite limited role of human touching in the story serves to make readers highly aware that the narrator is without the loving, intimate company she really needs to recover from her depression.

Heads off possible misunderstanding of argument; dealing with it enables her to write a concluding paragraph that does more than just repeat main claim.

Endnote

[1] Thrailkill spends much of her article tracing how an emphasis on treating depression through physical means (the approach taken by Mitchell) gave way late in the nineteenth century to a more psychological and verbal form of therapy (such as Sigmund Freud practiced).

Endnote provides information that could not be easily integrated into main text of the essay.

Works Cited

Ehrenreich, Barbara, and Deirdre English. *For Her Own Good: 150 Years of the Experts' Advice to Women*. Garden City: Doubleday-Anchor, 1978. Print.

Gilman, Charlotte Perkins. *The Living of Charlotte Perkins Gilman*. 1935. New York: Arno Press, 1972. Print.

- - -. "Why I Wrote 'The Yellow Wallpaper.' " 1913. Schilb and Clifford 968–69.

- - -. "The Yellow Wallpaper." 1892. Schilb and Clifford 956–67.

Mitchell, S. Weir. Excerpt from "The Evolution of the Rest Treatment." 1904. Schilb and Clifford 970–73.

Schilb, John, and John Clifford, eds. *Making Literature Matter: An Anthology for Readers and Writers*. 5th ed. Boston: Bedford, 2012. Print.

Thrailkill, Jane F. "Doctoring 'The Yellow Wallpaper.' " *ELH* 69.2 (2005): 525–66. Print.

Citation for book.

Note style for multiple works by same author.

When you cite more than one work from the same book, you give the book its own entry and cite each work from it in the shorthand form you see here.

Citation for anthology.

Citation for scholarly article.

A PAPER THAT ANALYZES A LITERARY WORK THROUGH THE FRAMEWORK OF A PARTICULAR THEORIST

In the appendix, we explain how to write a research paper that takes one of the critical approaches now popular in literary theory. Some research papers, however, make an argument about a literary work by applying to it the ideas of a single theorist. Often, this is someone whose concepts have already influenced many scholars. Perhaps this person has even pioneered an entire field of thought. Examples include the father of psychoanalysis, Sigmund Freud; the founder of Marxist theory, Karl Marx; leading voices of existentialism such as Friedrich Nietzsche and Martin Heidegger; and the modern feminist writer Virginia Woolf.

If you attempt a paper like this, the theorist you choose might not have read the literary work you discuss. Even so, his or her ideas can illuminate it. Of course, you need to summarize the theorist's thinking in a manner that is both helpful and concise. Instead of just offering scattered, random passages from this person's writing, try to provide an efficient overview of the theorist's basic *framework*: that is, the main ideas that this figure contributes. You will especially want to specify the ideas that are most helpful for interpreting your chosen literary text. In essence, you will be using these concepts as a *lens*. Your paper can, however, admit that the theorist's principles do not cover *everything* important in the text. Probably you will be more credible to your reader if you concede that while the theorist's framework is useful, it provides a less-than-exact explanation. In fact, you will be seen more as developing a claim of your own if you point out the *limits* of the theorist's ideas along with their strengths. This is what student Jacob Grobowicz does in the following paper. His essay applies to "The Yellow Wallpaper" the ideas of the late Michel Foucault, a French theorist whose writings about modern power relations have inspired scholars in the social sciences and humanities. But Jacob does not simply quote from Foucault's writings. Instead, he critically examines the lens he provides, arguing that it clarifies major parts of the story but does not account for them all.

Jacob Grobowicz
Professor Burke
English L202
10 May - - - -

Using Foucault to Understand Disciplinary Power
in Gilman's "The Yellow Wallpaper"

Michel Foucault provides a useful framework for understanding the narrator's experiences in Charlotte Perkins Gilman's 1892 short story "The Yellow Wallpaper." More specifically, the theory of power that Foucault puts forth in his book *Discipline and Punish*[1] sheds light on the narrator's frustration with the "rest cure" that her husband makes her undergo. Of course, any perspective on a literary work may neglect some aspects of it. As a slant on Gilman's story, Foucault's book does have limits. In particular, *Discipline and Punish* does not pay much attention to gender, a significant element of the narrator's life. Still, quite relevant to her situation is Foucault's central argument in the book, which is that "discipline" is the main form of power in the modern age.

> *Directs reader to an endnote.*
>
> *Immediately establishes what literary work the paper will focus on, as well as what theorist and what specific text by that theorist.*
>
> *The paper's main claim, which identifies which of the theorist's concepts the paper will apply to the story.*

When Foucault refers to "discipline" in his book, he has two meanings of the term in mind, though he sees them as closely related to each other. First, human beings have become "disciplined" in the sense that they feel pressured to follow the standards held by all sorts of authorities. According to his historical account, power was previously associated with the figure of the king. Judges were a narrow group of officials who carried out the will of the monarch by punishing blatant violators of the law. Foucault also points out that the punishment usually took the form of physical imprisonment. The emphasis was on confinement of the criminal's body, not on reform of the criminal's soul. Foucault views the modern era, however, as a major shift from this state of affairs. He declares that nowadays, the administrators of power are more widespread: "The judges of normality are everywhere. We are in the society of the teacher-judge, the doctor-judge, the educator-judge, the 'social-worker' judge" (304). Furthermore, these figures look beyond sheer criminals and try to control all humanity. In fact, they aim to mold human beings' basic thinking, a goal they pursue by getting people to adopt

> *Begins a two-paragraph section that summarizes relevant details of theorist's framework and defines a key term of his.*

conformist ideas and values promoted by various fields of expertise. Increasingly, Foucault claims, human beings are kept in place through forms of training, knowledge, and examination that are developed and advanced by academic and professional specialties — "disciplines" in the second sense of the word. Foucault argues that although these fields pose as benevolent "sciences of man," they actually participate in "the modern play of coercion over bodies, gestures and behavior" (191).

Discipline and Power stresses this idea by spending many pages on the image of the Panopticon. This is a model for a prison, proposed in the nineteenth century by British philosopher Jeremy Bentham. He envisioned a penitentiary with a central tower whose guards could observe all of the surrounding cells. The prisoners would feel constantly threatened by the tower's gaze, even though they could not be sure when the building was actually occupied. Eventually, their insecurity would drive them to monitor and restrict their conduct on their own, thereby doing the guards' work. Foucault brings up the Panopticon to argue that while institutions still engage in external surveillance — watching people in various ways — fields of expertise now serve dominant forces by leading people to engage in *self*-surveillance. In this respect, power can be said to *produce* the self rather than simply repress it.

Of all the experts that Foucault mentions in *Discipline and Power*, the one most significant to the narrator of "The Yellow Wallpaper" is "the doctor-judge." Suffering from a depression that seems related to her having recently given birth, she is in the hands of a physician named John who is also her husband. His diagnosis of her is reinforced by her brother, who is a doctor as well. Moreover, when the narrator fails to get physically better as fast as John would like, he threatens to deliver her over to S. Weir Mitchell, the real-life medical expert whose rest cure proved unendurable to Gilman herself. By linking three physicians to each other — John, the brother, and Mitchell — Gilman suggests that her heroine must cope with principles and values imposed on her by the field of medicine in general, which Foucault calls attention to as a discipline that manipulates people's identities in the name of health. In John's view, his spouse is not experiencing any serious discontentment with her life, even though the reader senses that she is, in fact, distressed at having to accommodate herself to the roles of wife and mother as defined by the field of medicine specifically and by society overall. Proclaiming that she is afflicted by simply "a slight hysterical tendency" (956), John prevents himself from learning "how much I really suffer" (958). Relying

Paper now begins directly connecting theorist's ideas to specific details of the story.

on his alleged expertise as a representative of his profession, he values his own clinical precision over her vague reports of unease: "He has no patience with faith, an intense horror of superstition, and he scoffs openly at any talk of things not to be felt and seen and put down in figures" (956). Foucault might say that John wishes for his wife to discipline herself, which involves her obeying the policies that John derives from his scientific background. Indeed, at two different points in the story, she comments that he is basically focused on her achieving "self-control" (957).

It is important for the reader to note that John is not an outright monster in his treatment of the narrator. He does not physically abuse her, at least not in any dramatic way. In fact, even when he is condescending toward her, he seems to believe sincerely that he has her best interests at heart. In an article that interprets the story with Foucault's ideas in mind, John S. Bak overstates the case when he argues that the narrator's husband subjects her to "a dehumanizing imprisonment" (40) and "resembles the penal officers of the eighteenth-century psychiatric wards or penitentiaries" (42). Although he isolates her on a country estate, he does not virtually lock her up and physically torment her, as Bak implies. While much of the plot takes place in a single room, she is free to roam the estate, and it is *she* who denies *him* access to the room for a brief spell at the end. Explaining in his book how power now operates, Foucault points out that it tends to present itself not as a crude, blatant instrument of punishment but as a means of enlightened reform.

Foucault does believe, however, that agents of power like John are presumptuous in assuming that they can produce better human beings through their guidance. So, too, Gilman's narrator does not find that her husband's professional advice is helping her to grow healthier. Inwardly, she disagrees with him when he commands her to avoid physical activity, for she supposes that "congenial work, with excitement and change, would do me good" (956). Though "he hates to have me write a word" (957), she defies him by secretly writing down the story of her lingering unhappiness and tension. Similarly, she tries to conceal from him her inability to comply with his demand that she get plenty of sleep. Eventually, rather than automatically following his prescriptions, she finds herself "getting a little afraid of John" (963). She moves from believing that "he loves me so" (961) to suspecting that in his interrogations of her, he has merely "pretended to be very loving and kind" (965). Of course, the most dramatic form that her alienation from him takes is her preoccupation with the woman she sees lurking

Heads off possible misunderstanding.

Takes a position on an article that has already applied the theorist's ideas to the story.

Resumes connecting the theorist's ideas directly to the story.

behind her room's wallpaper. The narrator's effort to free the woman — including her violent tearing of the paper — vividly demonstrates that Gilman's heroine hopes to escape the forces of domination that her husband symbolizes. She is not as capable as Foucault is of coming up with a full-fledged theory of the modern disciplinary society that her husband represents, but intuitively she associates him with this kind of world, and in essence she protests against it as she strips the paper off.

While Foucault's *Discipline and Punish* provides much context for Gilman's story, it does not offer an adequate account of how lives like the narrator's are affected by their gender. In order to be complete, an analysis of "The Yellow Wallpaper" would have to acknowledge that the narrator's womanhood does matter to the plot. When she originally comes to the estate, clearly she is distressed by her society's expectation that as a mother she will be the prime nurturer of her newborn child. Then, the patriarchal authority that John enjoys in that society as her husband encourages him to tell her what is good for her. His demand that she rest instead of work is no doubt supported by their culture's belief that women of her upper-middle-class standing are not supposed to perform much physical labor in the first place. Most likely Foucault was aware that gender has usually been a key variable in modern society's power structures, and there is no reason to think he would simply ignore how it bears on Gilman's story. But because *Discipline and Punish* does not give gender much attention, its significance for Gilman's narrator is a topic that Foucault leaves other, more explicitly feminist perspectives to discover.

Points out limits of this framework, rather than simply matching it to the story.

Some feminist theorists have criticized Foucault not only for neglecting gender but also for failing to develop any model of resistance to domination. For example, Nancy C. M. Hartsock faults him for leaving people with no method of escaping "passivity and immobility," no "hope of transcendence" over "the ways humans have been subjugated" (45). Nor does Gilman offer in her story a clear notion of what resistance to unjust power would look like. One feature of "The Yellow Wallpaper" that has much been debated is whether the narrator's destruction of the wallpaper and her crawling on the floor are a truly effective challenge to disciplinary society. Readers who might otherwise agree on many elements of the story have disagreed on this issue. While Bak, for example, claims that ultimately the narrator "is successful at freeing herself from her male-imposed shackles" (40), Paula A. Treichler argues that "the surrender of patriarchy is only temporary" and that "her madness will no doubt commit her to more intense medical treatment, perhaps to the dreaded Weir Mitchell of whom her

Concluding paragraph connects the theorist to the story by briefly bringing up new topic, resistance.

husband has spoken" (67). It is possible that Gilman was being deliberately ambiguous with her ending, wishing to provoke discussion about how to define worthwhile resistance instead of attempting to settle the question herself. In any case, Foucault's *Discipline and Punish* sheds light on a lot of her story even if it keeps Gilman's readers wondering exactly what her narrator should have done.

Endnote

[1] *Discipline and Punish* is not the only text by Foucault that can help in analyzing Gilman's story. Another possible work is his book *Madness and Civilization: A History of Insanity in the Age of Reason*, which can be useful for understanding the psychological problems of Gilman's narrator. *Discipline and Punish* is especially good, however, at explaining how power relationships throughout modern societies like the narrator's involve academic and professional disciplines of various sorts.

Endnote provides additional information that is not easily incorporated into main body of the paper.

Works Cited

Bak, John S. "Escaping the Jaundiced Eye: Foucauldian Pan-
opticism in Charlotte Perkins Gilman's 'The Yellow Wallpaper.'" *Studies in Short Fiction* 31.1 (1994): 39–46.
Print.

Citation for scholarly article.

Foucault, Michel. *Discipline and Punish: The Birth of the Prison.*
Trans. Alan Sheridan. New York: Vintage, 1979. Print.
- - - . *Madness and Civilization: A History of Insanity in the Age of
Reason.* Trans. Richard Howard. New York: Vintage, 1988.
Print.

Citation for book. Note style for multiple works by same author.

Gilman, Charlotte Perkins. "The Yellow Wallpaper." *Making
Literature Matter: An Anthology for Readers and Writers.* Ed.
John Schilb and John Clifford. 5th ed. Boston: Bedford,
2012. 956–67. Print.

Citation for work in an anthology.

Hartsock, Nancy C. M. "Postmodernism and Political Change:
Issues for Feminist Theory." *Feminist Interpretations of
Michel Foucault.* Ed. Susan J. Hekman. University Park:
Pennsylvania State UP, 1996. 39–55. Print.

Treichler, Paula A. "Escaping the Sentence: Diagnosis and
Discourse in 'The Yellow Wallpaper.'" *Tulsa Studies in
Women's Literature* 3.1/2 (1984): 61–77. Print.

A PAPER THAT USES A LITERARY WORK TO EXAMINE SOCIAL ISSUES

Some research papers mention a literary work but then focus on examining a
social issue related to that work. An example of such a paper is the following
essay by student Sarah Michaels. To prepare for writing her paper, Sarah consulted numerous sources, and she turns to them during the course of her essay.
The chief danger in a project like this is that it will become a mere "data
dump" — that is, a paper in which the writer uncritically cites one source after
another without really making an original argument. In writing an essay like
Sarah's, be sure to identify your main issue and claim clearly. Present yourself
as someone who is genuinely *testing* your sources, determining the specific
ways in which they are relevant to your argument. Keep in mind that even if
you are representing a source as useful, you can indicate how its ideas need to
be further complicated. With at least some of your sources, analyze specific
terms they employ, lingering over their language. Moreover, try to relate your
sources to one another, orchestrating them into a well-organized conversation.
We think Sarah accomplishes all these objectives. Even if you disagree, aim to
practice them yourself.

Sarah Michaels
Professor Swain
English L202
21 May - - - -

"The Yellow Wallpaper" as a Guide
to Social Factors in Postpartum Depression

In 2005, actor Brooke Shields's memoir *Down Came the Rain: My Journey through Postpartum Depression* drew much public attention to the psychological problem mentioned in its subtitle.[1] But during the last couple of decades, postpartum depression has been the subject of reports by many medical institutions and media outlets. By now, lots of people other than health professionals are aware of this problem and can at least roughly define it. If asked, most of them would probably say that although it can exhibit varying degrees of severity, postpartum depression is basically a state of despair suffered by a significant number of women who have just given birth. This is, in fact, the main image of it presented in a recent document about it, an October 2010 report by Marian Earls and a committee of the American Academy of Pediatrics. Besides explaining what postpartum depression is, the report urges pediatricians and other primary care providers to screen new mothers for it. Given that many members of the public already know that the problem is widespread, the report has not sparked much disagreement. Responding to it in the online magazine *Slate*, however, Emily Anthes does challenge its almost total emphasis on mothers. She argues that the Academy's committee makes a questionable assumption in writing as if only females are traumatized by birth. In her article entitled "Dads Get Blue, Too," she criticizes the report's authors for not acknowledging at greater length that new fathers can experience postpartum depression as well.[2] More generally, her article suggests that discussions of this disorder can be skewed by ideological views that need to be recognized. But, more than a century ago, Charlotte Perkins Gilman's story "The Yellow Wallpaper" made pretty much the same point, by showing how a woman diagnosed with a label like postpartum depression is a victim of her domestic circumstances and her society's ideas about gender, not just a person who has become ill on her own. When juxtaposed with the Academy's report, Gilman's 1892 tale is a reminder that today's doctors should look beyond an individual woman's symptoms of post-birth distress, because the social arrangements in which she lives may significantly affect her health.

Calls attention to an endnote.

Quickly identifies social issue that the paper will focus on.

Introduces the literary work that the paper will relate to the social issue.

The term *postpartum depression* has for a long time appeared in analyses of "The Yellow Wallpaper" and of the personal experience that Gilman based the story on. Veronica Makowsky points out that this clinical phrase has even "become a critical commonplace" (329) in studies of the relationship between the story and Gilman's life. Gilman does not, however, actually use the term *postpartum depression* in the tale. Instead, the heroine's husband, John, declares that she suffers from "temporary nervous depression — a slight hysterical tendency" (956), and the character herself refers to her "nervous troubles" (958). Nor does Gilman bring up the term in her accounts of the real-life despair she went through when she gave birth to her daughter. In her essay "Why I Wrote 'The Yellow Wallpaper,' " she recalls being tormented much of her life by "a severe and continuous nervous breakdown tending to melancholia" (968). In her book-length autobiography *The Living of Charlotte Perkins Gilman*, she describes herself as suffering from "nervous prostration" (90). Indeed, the *Oxford English Dictionary*'s entry for *postpartum depression* indicates that the term was not recorded until 1929, when it showed up in an issue of the *American Journal of Psychiatry*.

> Concedes that the term is used by scholars rather than by the author herself.

Nevertheless, the phrase does seem to fit the condition of Gilman's narrator. According to the American Academy of Pediatrics report, the symptoms of postpartum depression can range from "crying, worrying, sadness, anxiety, and mood swings" to more disturbing signs like "paranoia, mood shifts, hallucinations, [and] delusions" (1033). Gilman's character can be said to display most of these things once her child is born. At the estate that is the story's setting, she has trouble sleeping, she comes to doubt her husband's love, and, most dramatically, she rips off the wallpaper in her bedroom to free a woman whom she imagines wanting to creep away.

> Directly connects language of the report to the story.

But simply labeling the heroine's distress as postpartum depression risks ignoring the conditions surrounding her that contribute to her suffering. Commenting on "The Yellow Wallpaper," literary critic Paula A. Treichler points out that a medical diagnosis can block understanding of "social, cultural, and economic practices" (69), even though these may support the doctor's claim to expertise, play a role in the patient's anguish, and become more important to confront than the patient's individual pain. In Gilman's story, John uses his social authority as physician and husband to control his wife. Specifically, he isolates her on the estate and makes her give up real activity, just as Gilman's real-life doctor, S. Weir Mitchell, demanded that she rest. As a result, the heroine feels obligated to surrender to the stereotypical passive female role, even

> Uses another interpreter of the story to advance this paper's argument.

though she would welcome more interaction with others and suspects that "congenial work, with excitement and change, would do me good" (956). When she proceeds to hallucinate the woman in the wallpaper, this is something that she is *driven* to do by John's assertion of masculine power, just as Mitchell's prescription for inertia drove Gilman "near the border line of utter mental ruin" ("Why" 968).

Key quote from the story.

With "The Yellow Wallpaper" in mind, readers of the American Academy of Pediatrics report might examine how it downplays what Treichler calls "social, cultural, and economic practices" in its focus on diagnosing postpartum depression in women. Although the report does note that "Paternal depression is estimated at 6%" (1032), it does not linger on this fairly significant figure. In addition, the committee mentions only in passing that while "as many as 12% of all pregnant or postpartum women experience depression in a given year," the percentage is twice as much "for low-income women" (1032). Similarly brief is the recognition that "Eighteen percent of fathers of children in Early Head Start had symptoms of depression" (1033), a distinctly high figure that again suggests one's social class can affect one's health. Nor does the report develop its brief notice that possible causes of postpartum depression include "domestic violence" (1034), which would be a serious problem in the patient's environment rather than a malfunction within the patient herself. Instead of insisting that "Treatment must address the mother-child dyad relationship" (1036), the committee might also have called for addressing the chance that the mother suffers from a lack of money or the presence of an abusive partner.

Uses the story to examine the issue raised by the report.

Paper works with specific examples and language from the report.

Juxtaposing Gilman's story with the Academy's report does not mean that readers of this recent document about postpartum depression have to declare its authors evil. The attitudes and recommendations of the committee are not as morally disturbing as those of Gilman's character John. But her story should encourage the report's readers to notice where, in its call for screening women for postpartum depression, it risks screening *out* social influences on people diagnosed with this clinical problem.

Heads off possible misunderstanding.

Endnotes

[1] Shields also discussed her postpartum depression in a *New York Times* op-ed column, in which she defended herself against actor Tom Cruise's charge that she should have relied on vitamins and exercise rather than on the prescription drug Paxil.

[2] For an article that supports Anthes's attention to fathers even though she does not mention it, see Kim and Swain.

The endnotes provide additional information not easily incorporated into the paper's main text.

Works Cited

Anthes, Emily. "Dads Get Blue, Too." *Slate.com*. Slate, 4 Nov. 2010. Web. 9 Nov. 2010.

Earls, Marian F., and the Committee on Psychosocial Aspects of Child and Family Health. "Clinical Report: Incorporating Recognition and Management of Perinatal and Postpartum Depression into Pediatric Practice." *Pediatrics.org*. Pediatrics, 25 Oct. 2010. Web. 9 Nov. 2010.

Gilman, Charlotte Perkins. *The Living of Charlotte Perkins Gilman: An Autobiography*. 1935. New York: Arno Press, 1972. Print.

- - - . "Why I Wrote 'The Yellow Wallpaper.' " 1913. Schilb and Clifford 968–69.

- - - . "The Yellow Wallpaper." 1892. Schilb and Clifford 956–67.

Kim, Pilyoung, and James E. Swain. "Sad Dads: Paternal Postpartum Depression." *Psychiatry* Feb. 2007: 36–47. Print.

Makowsky, Veronica. "Fear of Feeling and the Turn-of-the-Century Woman of Letters." *American Literary History* 5.2 (1993): 326–34. Print.

Schilb, John, and John Clifford, eds. *Making Literature Matter: An Anthology for Readers and Writers*. 5th ed. Boston: Bedford, 2012. Print.

Shields, Brooke. *Down Came the Rain: My Journey through Postpartum Depression*. New York: Hyperion, 2005. Print.

- - - . "War of Words." *New York Times* 1 July 2005, late ed.: A17. Print.

Treichler, Paula A. "Escaping the Sentence: Diagnosis and Discourse in 'The Yellow Wallpaper.' " *Tulsa Studies in Women's Literature* 3.1/2 (1984): 61–77. Print.

Citation for an online article.

Citation for a book.

Note style for multiple works by same author. Note, too, that when you cite more than one work from the same book, you give each book its own entry and cite each work from it in the shorthand form you see here.

Citation for a print article.

☰ SUMMING UP

- **Plan your research.**

  Identify an issue to pursue.

  Investigate electronic sources such as Internet Web sites *and* print sources as well.

  Take time to evaluate the materials you discover.

  Keep yourself well organized.

  Record everything that may prove useful later — do not risk plagiarism by failing to distinguish between your own ideas and those of others.

≣ SUMMING UP

- **Start composing by revisiting your tentative main claim, taking into account what you have learned through research.**

  Keep organized, and subdivide and arrange your notes in logical order.

  Focus on constructing an argument of your own, using secondary sources to support your claims and evidence.

  Follow MLA conventions for format and style.

- **Document your sources by following MLA guidelines.** (pp. 217–24)

- **For a research paper that deals with existing interpretations of a literary work, places it in a historical or social context, interprets it through the framework of a theorist, or uses it to examine social issues, be sure to make an argument of your own — identifying an issue and making a claim about it.**

Literature and
Its Issues

CHAPTER 10

≡ ——————————————————————————— ≡

Families

In the not-too-distant past, family life was the focal point of our emotional existence, the center of all our important psychological successes and failures. It was common for several generations to live together in the same town and even the same home. Grandparents, aunts, and uncles were an intimate part of daily life, not just relatives one saw during the holidays. Besides the usual emotional drama that always takes place between parents and children, there were the additional tensions that inevitably arise when the values of the old clash with those of the young. Of course, there was also the comforting emotional support available from more than just a mother and father as well as the sense of belonging and bonding with the many aunts, uncles, and cousins that usually lived nearby.

As extended families become less common, the emotional stakes of home life seem higher than ever. Since we rely on one another more in today's nuclear family, our sense of disappointment, our sense of rejection, and our sense of unworthiness can be more acute. During childhood, the drama of family life can stamp an indelible mark on our psyches, leaving psychological scars that make safe passage into adulthood difficult. Our status within the family can also offer us a sense of worth and confidence that leads to contentment and success later on. For all of us, however, family life is composed not of psychological and sociological generalities but, rather, of our one-to-one relationships with fathers, sisters, grandmothers. Writers often give us imaginative, honest, and illuminating charts of their successes and failures in negotiating both the calm and the choppy waters of our family journeys. The following clusters do not hope to be complete or representative of your experiences. We do hope, however, that in reading and discussing these poems and stories, you will find them an interesting and provocative catalyst for you to delve into the joys and sorrows of your own life in a family.

The chapter opens with contemporary writers who give autobiographical accounts of their childhood memories—of people and events that taught them valuable lessons about life and death (p. 249). Fathers are the focus of the second cluster as five poets paint memorable but not always positive portraits of their fathers (p. 270). The third cluster groups Sylvia Plath's "Daddy" with four critical commentaries on the poet's brilliant and haunting attempt to come to grips with her father's death when she was a girl (p. 279). The next cluster examines the tensions that arise between mothers and daughters as

247

they work out questions of identity and responsibility (p. 298). The fifth cluster sharply contrasts the relationships of brothers in different economic settings (p. 323). In the next cluster, you can read Tennessee Williams's classic play about a troubled family and a contemporary parody of the play by Christopher Durang (p. 361). Then a cluster of seven poets gives us loving, honest, and humorous snapshots of grandparents (p. 425). Sharon Olds meditates on her family in a cluster of four poems (p. 437). Next, Lorraine Hansberry's enduring play about an African American family is presented in its cultural context (p. 443). In another cluster, we present news stories that bear directly on the characters and themes of a fictional story about a devoted Muslim and his father (p. 532). Three short stories in the next cluster trace moments of crisis involving decisions about children (p. 551). The feelings of gays and lesbians within families are the concern of the poets in the final cluster (p. 577).

Memories of Family: Essays

BRENT STAPLES, "The Runaway Son"

RICK MOODY, "Demonology"

BELL HOOKS, From *Bone Black: Memories of Girlhood*

We all tell stories about our lives in families. Perhaps the first are those about our relationships with our parents and about our contradictory impulses for understanding and independence. When we tell these tales to others, we might be trying to give meaning to our experiences, perhaps trying to give narrative shape to what seemed confusing and random at the time. Because our childhood memories may seem a disparate series of anecdotes and snapshots, it is probably natural to order them into coherent narratives with definite beginnings and ends. But memories are puzzling. Do we really remember these events, or do we remember someone else telling us about them? Or, more mysteriously, are we remembering earlier memories? The three writers in this cluster create narratives out of their experience, giving a sense of meaning to their futures.

≡ BEFORE YOU READ

Are there members of your immediate or extended family you want to forget? Are there family members you always want to remember? Do the stories you tell about family members have a recurring theme? Why do you tell these stories? How do you feel about the stories that members of your family tell about you?

BRENT STAPLES
The Runaway Son

As an editorial writer for the New York Times, *Brent Staples (b. 1951) is an influential commentator on American politics and culture. A proponent of individual effort, Staples resists being reduced to a symbol of African American progress, remembering his childhood as economically stable until marred by his father's alcoholism. After a chaotic family life during his high-school years, he had such little hope of attending college that he did not take a college entrance exam, but a special program at Philadelphia Military College and Penn Morton College provided needed skills. He earned a B.A. with honors from Widener University (1973) and received a Danforth Fellowship for graduate study at the University of Chicago, where he earned a Ph.D. in psychology (1977). "The Runaway Son" comes from Staples's memoir,* Parallel Time: Growing Up in Black and White *(1995). In 1999, he published*

An American Love Story, *a narrative of a mixed-race couple "trying to raise color-blind children in a color-conscious world."*

The mother at the beach was supernaturally pale, speaking that blunt Canadian French with a couple on the next blanket. At the market, she wore a business suit and was lost in a dream at the cheese counter. At the museum, the mother was tan and grimly thin, wearing ink-black shades and hissing furiously into a pocket phone. I was watching when each of these women let a small child wander away. The events were years and cities apart, but basically the same each time. I shadowed the child and waited for its absence to hit home. A mother who loses her cub — even for a moment — displays a seizure of panic unique to itself. Those seizures of panic are a specialty of mine. I guess you could say I collect them.

This morning I am walking to the doctor's office, brooding about mortality and the yearly finger up the butt. Today's mother has flaming red hair and is standing on the steps, riffling her bag for keys. Her little girl is no more than four — with the same creamy face, trimmed in ringlets of red. The mother's hair is thick and shoulder length, blocking her view as she leans over the bag. The child drifts down the steps and stands on the sidewalk. Idling as children do, she crosses to the curb and stares dreamily into traffic. Three people pass her without breaking stride. A pair of teenagers with backpacks. A homeless man pushing a junk-laden shopping cart. A businessman, who glances up at the woman's legs and marches onward.

For some people a four-year-old beyond its mother's reach is invisible. For me that child is the axis of the world. Should I run to her, pull her back from the curb? Should I yell in crude Brooklynese, "Hey lady, look out for the friggin' kid!" Nearing the child, I croon in sweet falsetto, "Hey honey, let's wait for Mommy before you cross." The mention of Mommy freezes her. Up on the steps, the red mane of hair whips hysterically into the air. "Patty, get back here! I told you: Don't go near the street!" The woman thanks me and flushes with embarrassment. I smile — "No trouble at all" — and continue on my way.

Most men past forty dream of muscle tone and sex with exotic strangers. Mine is a constant fantasy of rescue, with a sobbing child as the star. What I tell now is how this came to be.

My parents were children when they married. She was eighteen. He was   5
twenty-two. The ceremony was performed in the log house where my mother was born and where she, my grandmother Mae, and my great-grandmother Luella still lived, in the foothills of the Blue Ridge Mountains. I visited the house often as a small child. The only surviving picture shows a bewildered toddler sitting in the grass, staring fixedly at an unknown something in the distance. My great-grandmother Luella was a tall, raw-boned woman with a mane of hair so long she had to move it aside to sit down. Her daughter, my Grandma Mae, wore tight dresses that showed off her bosoms and a string of dead foxes

that trailed from her shoulder. The beady eyes of the foxes were frightening when she bent to kiss me.

The log house had no running water, no electricity. At night I bathed in a metal washtub set near the big, wood-burning stove. Once washed, I got into my white dressing gown and prepared for the trip to the outhouse. My grandmother held a hurricane lamp out of the back door to light the way. The path was long and dark and went past the cornfield where all the monsters were. I could tell they were there, hidden behind the first row, by the way the corn squeaked and rustled as I passed. Most feared among them were the snakes that turned themselves into hoops and rolled after you at tremendous speed, thrashing through the corn as they came.

The outhouse itself was dank and musty. While sitting on the toilet I tried as much as possible to keep the lamp in view through cracks in the outhouse wall. The trip back to the log house was always the worst; the monsters gathered in the corn to ambush me, their groaning, growling reaching a crescendo as they prepared to spring. I ran for the light and landed in the kitchen panting and out of breath.

My father's clan, the Staples of Troutville, had an indoor toilet. My paternal great-grandparents, John Wesley and Eliza Staples, were people of substance in the Roanoke valley. In the 1920s, when folks still went about on horseback, John Wesley burst on the scene in a Model T Ford with all the extras — and let it be known that he paid for the car in cash. Though not an educated man, he could read and write. He was vain of his writing: he scribbled even grocery lists with flourish, pausing often to lick the pencil point. There was no school for black children at that time. And so John Wesley and his two immediate neighbors built one at the intersection of their three properties. Then they retained the teacher who worked in it.

The Pattersons were rich in love, but otherwise broke. This made my mother's marriage to a Staples man seem a fine idea. But domestic stability was not my father's experience, the role of husband and father not one that he could play. His own father, John Wesley's son Marshall, had routinely disappeared on payday and reappeared drunk and broke several days later. He abandoned the family at the start of the Depression, leaving Grandma Ada with four children in hand and one — my father — on the way. Ada had no choice but to place her children with relatives and go north, looking for work.

The luckiest of my uncles landed with John Wesley and Eliza. My father came to rest in hell on earth: the home of Ada's father, Tom Perdue. Three wives preceded Tom into the grave and the family lore was that he worked them to death. He hired out his sons for farmwork and collected their pay, leaving them with nothing. My father was beaten for wetting the bed and forced to sleep on a pallet under the kitchen sink. He left school at third grade and became part of Tom's dark enterprise. Birthdays went by unnoted. Christmas meant a new pair of work boots — if that. Had it not been for my father and a younger cousin, Tom would have died with no one to note his passing.

10

This childhood left its mark. My father distrusted affection and what there was of it he pushed away. He looked suspicious when you hugged or kissed him — as though doubting that affection was real. The faculty for praising us was dead in him. I could choose any number of examples from childhood, but permit me to skip ahead to college. I was obsessed with achievement and made the dean's list nearly every semester. My father was mute on the subject — and never once said "good job." Finally, I achieved the perfect semester — an A in every subject — with still not a word from him. Years later, I found that he had carried my grades in his wallet and bragged on them to strangers at truck stops.

My father worked as a truck driver; he earned a handsome salary, then tried to drink it up. My mother mishandled what was left. How could she do otherwise when money was a mystery to her? She grew up in a barter economy, where one farmer's milk bought another's eggs and the man who butchered the hogs was paid in port. She stared at dollar bills as though awaiting divine instruction on how to spend them.

I grew up in a household on the verge of collapse, the threat of eviction ever present, the utilities subject to cutoff at any moment. Gas was cheap and therefore easy to regain. The water company had pity on us and relented when we made even token efforts to pay. But the electric company had no heart to harden. We lived in darkness for weeks at a time. While our neighbors' houses were blazing with light, we ate, played, and bathed in the sepia glow of hurricane lamps. My mother made the darkness into a game. Each night before bed, she assembled us in a circle on the floor, with a hurricane lamp at the center. First she told a story, then had each of us tell one. Those too young to tell stories sang songs. I looked forward to the circle and my brothers' and sisters' faces in the lamplight. The stories I told were the first stirrings of the writer in me.

On Saturday night my father raged through the house hurling things at the walls. Sunday morning would find him placid, freshly shaven, and in his favorite chair, the air around him singing with Mennon Speed Stick and Old Spice Cologne. At his feet were stacked the Sunday papers, the *Philadelphia Bulletin* and the *Philadelphia Inquirer*. I craved his attention but I was wary of him; it was never clear who he would be.

On a table nearby was a picture of him when he was in the navy and not yet twenty years old. He was wearing dress whites, with his cap tilted snappily back on his head, his hand raised in a salute. He smiled a rich expansive smile that spread to every corner of his face. A hardness had undermined the smile and limited its radius. His lips — full and fleshy in the picture — were tense and narrow by comparison. The picture showed a carefree boy — free of terrible Tom — on the verge of a life filled with possibility. Ten years later those possibilities had all been exhausted. He was knee-deep in children, married to a woman he no longer loved but lacked the courage to leave. The children were coming fast. We were three, then five, then nine. 15

Our first neighborhood was called The Hill, a perfect place for a young mother with a large family and an unreliable husband. The men went to work at the shipyard and brought home hefty paychecks that easily supported an entire household. The women stayed home to watch and dote on the children. Not just their own, but all of us. Many of these women were no happier than my mother. They had husbands who beat them; husbands who took lovers within full view of their neighbors; husbands who drove them crazy in any number of ways. The women submerged their suffering in love for children. There was no traffic to speak of, and we played for hours in the streets. A child five years old passed easily from its mother's arms into the arms of the neighborhood. Eyes were on us at every moment. We'd be playing with broken glass when a voice rang out from nowhere: "Y'all stop that and play nice!" We'd be transfixed by the sight of wet cement, ripe for writing curse words, when the voice rang out again: "Y'all get away from that cement. Mr. Prince paid good money to have that done!" Women on errands patroled the sidewalks and made them unsafe for fighting. Every woman had license to discipline a child caught in the wrong. We feigned the deepest remorse, hopeful that the report would not reach our mothers.

Everyone on The Hill grew some kind of fruit; my gang was obsessed with stealing it. We prowled hungrily at people's fences, eyeing their apples, pears, and especially their peaches. We were crazed to get at them, even when they were tiny and bitter and green. We turned surly when there was no fruit at all. Then we raided gardens where people grew trumpet flowers, which gave a sweet nectar when you sucked them. The flowers were enormous and bright orange. When the raid was finished, the ground would be covered with them.

I lost The Hill when my family was evicted. We landed miles away in the Polish West End. The Poles and Ukrainians had once ruled much of the city. They had surrendered it street by street and were now confined to the westernmost neighborhood, their backs pressed to the city limits.

My family had crossed the color line. The people who lived in the house before us had been black as well. But they were all adults. After them, my brothers and sisters must have seemed an invading army.

The Polish and Ukrainian kids spelled their names exotically and ate unpronounceable foods. They were Catholics and on certain Wednesdays wore ashes on their foreheads. On Fridays they were forbidden to eat meat. When you walked by their churches you caught a glimpse of a priest swinging incense at the end of a chain. I wanted to know all there was to know about them. That I was their neighbor entitled me to it.

20

The Polish and Ukrainian boys did not agree. The first week was a series of fights, one after another. They despised us, as did their parents and grandparents. I gave up trying to know them and played alone. Deprived of friends, I retreated into comic books. My favorite hero was the Silver Surfer, bald and naked to his silver skin, riding a surfboard made of the same silver stuff. The comic's most perfect panels showed the seamless silver body flashing through space on the board. No words; just the long view of the Surfer hurtling past planets and stars.

My fantasies of escape centered on airplanes; I was drunk with the idea of flying. At home, I labored over model planes until the glue made me dizzy. At school, I made planes out of notebook paper and crammed them into my pockets and books. I was obsessed with movies about aerial aces and studied them carefully, prepping for the acehood that I'd been born to and that was destined to be mine. I planned to join the air force when I graduated from high school. The generals would already have heard of me; my jet would be warming up on the runway.

My favorite plane was a wooden Spitfire with British Air Force markings and a propeller powered by a rubber band. I was flying it one day when it landed in the yard of a Ukrainian boy whose nose I had bloodied. His grandfather was gardening when the plane touched down on the neatly kept lawn. He seized the plane, sputtered at me in Ukrainian, and disappeared into the house. A few minutes later one of his older grandsons delivered what was left of it. The old man had destroyed it with malevolent purpose. The wings and fuselage were broken the long way, twice. The pieces were the width of popsicle sticks and wrapped in the rubber band. This was the deepest cruelty I had known.

My mother suffered too. She missed her friends on The Hill, but we were too far west for them to reach us easily. She was learning how difficult it was to care for us on her own, especially since there were few safe places to play. The new house sat on a truck route. Forty-foot semis thundered by, spewing smoke and rattling windows. My mother lived in terror of the traffic and forbade us to roller-skate even on the sidewalk. On The Hill, she had swept off on errands confident that we would be fine. In the Polish West End, she herded us into the house and told us to stay there until she got back.

The house had become a prison. My eldest sister, Yvonne, was thirteen years old — and the first to escape. She stayed out later and later and finally disappeared for days at a time. My mother strapped her. My father threatened her with the juvenile home. But Yvonne met their anger with steeliness. When they questioned her she went dumb and stared into space. I knew the look from prisoner-of-war movies; do your worst, it said, I will tell you nothing. She lied casually and with great skill. But I was an expert listener, determined to break the code. The lie had a strained lightness, the quality of cotton candy. I recognized that sound when she said, "Mom, I'll be right back, I'm going out to the store." I followed her. She passed the store and started across town just as I thought she would. I trotted after her, firing questions. "Where do you think you're going? What is on your mind? What are you trying to do to yourself?" I was my mother's son and accepted all she told me about the dangers of the night. Girls became sluts at night. Boys got into fights and went to jail. These hazards meant nothing to Yvonne; she ignored me and walked on. I yelled "Slut! Street dog!" She lunged at me, but I dodged out of reach. "Slut" I had gotten from my mother. But "street dog" was an original, I'd made it up on the spur of the moment. I had become the child parent. I could scold and insult — but I was too young and ill-formed to instruct. I relished the role; it licensed me to be judge and disparage people I envied but lacked the courage to imitate.

Yvonne was wild to get away. You turned your back and — POOF! — she was gone. Finally she stayed away for days that stretched into weeks and then

25

months. There was no sign or word of her. My mother was beaten up with worry. By night she walked the floors, tilting at every sound in the street.

What is it like to be one of nine children, to be tangled in arms and legs in bed and at the dinner table? My brothers and sisters were part of my skin; you only notice your skin when something goes wrong with it. My youngest brother, Blake, got infections that dulled his hearing and closed his ears to the size of pinholes. Bruce broke his arm — while playing in the safety of our tree-less and boring backyard. Sherri began to sleepwalk, once leaping down a flight of stairs. Every illness and injury and visit to the hospital involved me. I was first assistant mother now, auxiliary parent in every emergency.

My five-year-old sister Christi was burned nearly to death. Her robe caught fire at the kitchen stove. I was upstairs in my room when it happened. First I heard the scream. Then came thunder of feet below me, and soon after the sound of the ambulance. The doctors did the best they could and gave the rest up to God.

The sign at the nurses' station said that no one under sixteen could visit. I was only eleven; with Yvonne missing, I was as close to sixteen as the children got. I knew that Christi had been brought back from the dead. What I saw the first day added mightily to that awareness. A domed frame had been built over the bed to keep the sheets from touching the burns. Peering under the dome, I saw her wrapped in gauze, round and round the torso, round and round each leg, like a mummy. Blood seeped through the bandages where the burns were deepest. The burns that I could see outside the bandages didn't look too bad. The skin was blackened, but bearable.

Eventually she was allowed to sit up. I would arrive to find her in her bright white gauze suit, sitting in a child's rocking chair. I got used to the gauze. Then they took it off to air out the wounds. Her body was raw from the breast to be-low the knee. The flesh was wet and bloody in places; I could see the blood puls-ing beneath what had been her skin. The room wobbled, but I kept smiling and tried to be natural. I walked in a wide circle around her that day, afraid that I would brush against her. I got past even this, because Christi smiled intermina-bly. The nerve endings were dead and she felt nothing. In time I grew accus-tomed to flesh without skin.

Christi's injuries were the worst on the ward. Next to the burns everything else was easy to look at. I was especially interested in the boy with the steel rods jutting out of his leg. He'd been hit by a car, and the bone was shattered. He didn't talk much, but the rods in his legs were fascinating. The skin clung to them like icing to the candles on a cake.

The children's ward was sparsely visited on weekdays. I cruised the room, cooing at toddlers and making jokes with frightened newcomers. On weekends the ward filled up with parents, highlighting the fact that I was eleven years old — and that my own parents were elsewhere. When real parents visited, I felt like a fraud. I clung to Christi's bedside and did not stray. I wished that the scene at Christi's bed was like the scene around the other beds: fathers, moth-ers, relatives. But that was not to be.

30

Christi's accident made the world dangerous. When left in charge, I gathered the children in the living room and imprisoned them there. Trips to the bathroom were timed and by permission only. Now and then I imagined the smell of gas and trotted into the kitchen to check the stove. I avoided looking out of windows for fear of daydreaming. Staring at the sky, I punched through it into space and roamed the galaxy with my hero, the Silver Surfer.

I was daydreaming one day when my brother Brian cried out in pain. He had taken a pee and gotten his foreskin snarled in his zipper. He had given a good yank, too, and pulled it nearly halfway up. Every step tugged at the zipper and caused him to scream. I cut off the pants and left just the zipper behind. To keep his mind off his troubles and kill time until my parents got home, I plunked out a tune on the piano. The longer they stayed away the more crazed I became.

The days were too full for an eleven-year-old who needed desperately to   35
dream. The coal-fired boiler that heated our house was part of the reason. The fire went out at night, which meant that I built a new fire in the morning: chop kindling; haul ashes; shovel coal. Then it was up from the basement, to iron shirts, polish shoes, make sandwiches, and pack the school lunches. My mother tried to sweeten the jobs by describing them as "little": "Build a little fire to throw the chill off of the house." But there was no such thing as a "little" fire. Every fire required the same backbreaking work. Chop kindling. Chop wood. Shovel coal. Haul ashes. One morning she said, "Put a little polish on the toe of your brother's shoes." I dipped the applicator into the liquid polish and dabbed the tiniest spot on the top of each shoe. Yvonne's departure had left my mother brittle and on the edge of violence. I knew this but couldn't stop myself. She was making breakfast when I presented her with the shoes, which were still scuffed and unpolished. "I told you to polish those shoes," she said. "No, you didn't," I said, "you said 'put a little polish on the toe.'" She snapped at me. I snapped back. Then she lifted the serving platter and smashed it across my head.

My father was drinking more than ever. Debt mounted in the customary pattern. We pushed credit to the limit at one store, then abandoned the bills and moved on to the next. Mine was the face of the family's debt. I romanced the shop owners into giving us food and coal on time, then tiptoed past their windows to put the bite on the next guy. When gas and electricity were cut off, I traveled across town to plead with the utility companies. The account executives were mainly women with soft spots for little boys. I conned them, knowing we would never pay. We were behind in the rent and would soon be evicted. Once settled elsewhere, we would apply for gas and electricity, under a fictitious name.

The only way to get time to myself was to steal it. During the summer, I got up early, dressed with the stealth of a burglar, and tiptoed out of the house. The idea was to get in a full day's play unencumbered by errands or housework. Most days I escaped. On other days my mother's radar was just too good, and her rich contralto came soaring out of the bedroom. "Brent, make sure you're back here in time to . . ." to go shopping, to visit Christi at the hospital, to go a thousand places on a thousand errands.

Inevitably I thought of running away — to Florida. In Florida you could sleep outside, live on fruit from the orange groves, and never have to work. I decided to do it on a snowy Saturday at the start of a blizzard. Thought and impulse were one: I took an orange from the fruit bowl, grabbed my parka from the coat rack, and ran from the house.

I did not get to Florida. In my haste, I had grabbed the coat belonging to my younger brother Brian. It was the same color as mine but too small even to zip up. The freight train I planned to take never left the rail yard. The snow thickened and began to freeze. Numb and disheartened, I headed home.

Five years later I succeeded in running away — this time to college. Wid- 40 ener University was two miles from where my family lived. For all that I visited them, two miles could have been two thousand. I lived at school year round — through holidays, semester breaks, and right through the summer. Alone in bed for the first time, I recognized how crowded my life had been. I enjoyed the campus most when it was deserted. I wandered the dormitory drinking in the space. At night I sat in the stadium, smoking pot and studying the constellations. I never slept with my brothers again.

Years later my youngest sister, Yvette, accused me of abandoning the family. But the past is never really past; what we have lived is who we are. I am still the frightened ten-year-old tending babies and waiting for my parents. The sight of a child on its own excludes everything else from view. No reading. No idle conversation. No pretending not to see. I follow and watch and intervene because I have no choice. When next you see a child beyond its mother's reach, scan the crowd for me. I am there, watching you watch the child.   *[1994]*

≣ THINKING ABOUT THE TEXT

1. If you hadn't read the first and last sections (paras. 1–4, 41), what would you say Staples's theme is? What generalizations does his narrative evidence point to?

2. Race and class figure in this essay in varying degrees. Explain. Do they figure in your experiences? In those of your friends?

3. Staples begins with three anecdotes about mothers and children and then concludes his first section with his "fantasy of rescue" (para. 4). Is his last paragraph a satisfactory conclusion to this idea?

4. Re-creating the past in nonfiction often involves the same techniques as fiction writing: using the five senses. Find examples of creative touches that you think make the essay real.

5. Do you agree that "the past is never really past" (para. 41)? Are you still somehow a ten-year-old? Is Staples's idea of having "no choice" one you identify with? Since the last paragraph cannot be literally true, what is Staples driving at?

RICK MOODY
Demonology

A winner of numerous literary awards, including a Guggenheim Fellowship in 2002, Rick Moody (b. 1961) wrote the novels Garden State *(1991) and* The Ice Storm *(1995), which were made into popular movies. His recent memoir* The Black Veil *(2002) tells of his own substance abuse and a relative who apparently wore a black veil as atonement for accidentally causing the death of a childhood friend.*

Born in Brooklyn, where he now lives, Moody grew up in suburbs much like New Canaan, Connecticut, the locale for much of his fiction. Sometimes called suburban gothic, Moody's fiction depicts, according to one critic, a world of "tidy lawns and two-car garages . . . mixed with brooding horror, melodramatic violence, extreme psychological states." A committed writer from an early age, Moody graduated from Brown University and received his M.F.A. from Columbia University. The following title piece is taken from his critically acclaimed collection of short stories, Demonology *(2001), but was first published in a collection of nonfiction,* Survival Stories: Memoirs of Crisis *(1997). The* Diviners: A Novel *was published in 2005. His latest work is* The Four Fingers of Death *(2010).*

They came in twos and threes, dressed in the fashionable Disney costumes of the year, Lion King, Pocahontas, Beauty and the Beast, or in the costumes of televised superheroes, protean, shape-shifting, thus arrayed, in twos and threes, complaining it was too hot with the mask on, Hey, I'm really hot!, lugging those orange plastic buckets, bartering, haggling with one another, Gimme your Smarties, please? as their parents tarried behind, grownups following after, grownups bantering about the schools, or about movies, about local sports, about their marriages, about the difficulties of long marriages, kids sprinting up the next driveway, kids decked out as demons or superheroes or dinosaurs or as advertisements for our multinational entertainment-providers, beating back the restless souls of the dead, in search of sweets.

They came in bursts of fertility, my sister's kids, when the bar drinking, or home-grown dope-smoking, or bed-hopping had lost its luster; they came with shrill cries and demands — little gavels, she said, instead of fists — Feed me! Change me! Pay attention to me! Now it was Halloween and the mothers in town, my sister among them, trailed after their kids, warned them away from items not fully wrapped, Just give me that, you don't even like apples, laughing at the kids hobbling in their bulky costumes — my nephew dressed as a shark, dragging a mildewed gray tail behind him. But what kind of shark? A great white? A blue? A tiger shark? A hammerhead? A nurse shark?

She took pictures of costumed urchins, my sister, as she always took pictures, e.g., my nephew on his first birthday (six years prior), blackfaced with cake and ice cream, a dozen relatives attempting in turn to read to him — about a tugboat — from a brand-new rubberized book. Toot toot! His desperate, needy expression, in the photo, all out of phase with our excitement. The first nephew!

The first grandchild! He was trying to get the cake in his mouth. Or: a later photo of my niece (his younger sister) attempting to push my nephew out of the shot — against a backdrop of autumn foliage; or a photo of my brother wearing my dad's yellow double-knit paisley trousers (with a bit of flare in the cuffs), twenty-five years after the heyday of such stylings; or my father and stepmother on their powerboat, peaceful and happy, the riotous wake behind them; or my sister's virtuoso photos of dogs — Mom's irrepressible golden retriever chasing a tennis ball across an overgrown lawn, or my dad's setter on the beach with a perspiring Lowenbrau leaning against his snout. Fifteen or twenty photo albums on the shelves in my sister's living room, a whole range of leathers and faux-leathers, no particular order, and just as many more photos loose, floating around the basement, castoffs, and files of negatives in their plastic wrappers.

She drank the demon rum, and she taught me how to do it, too, when we were kids; she taught me how to drink. We stole drinks, or we got people to steal them for us; we got reprobates of age to venture into the pristine suburban liquor stores. Later, I drank bourbon. My brother drank beer. My father drank single malt scotches. My grandmother drank half-gallons and then fell ill. My grandfather drank the finest collectibles. My sister's ex-husband drank more reasonably priced facsimiles. My brother drank until a woman lured him out of my mother's house. I drank until I was afraid to go outside. My uncle drank until the last year of his life. And I carried my sister in a blackout from a bar once — she was mumbling to herself, humming melodies, mostly unconscious. I took her arms; Peter Hunter took her legs. She slept the whole next day. On Halloween, my sister had a single gin and tonic before going out with the kids, before ambling around the condos of Kensington Court, circling from multifamily unit to multifamily unit, until my nephew's shark tail was grass-stained from the freshly mown lawns of the common areas. Then she drove her children across town to her ex-husband's house, released them into his supervision, and there they walked along empty lots, beside a brook, under the stars.

When they arrived home, these monsters, disgorged from their dad's Jeep, there was a fracas between girl and boy about which was superior (in the Aristotelian hierarchies), Milky Way, Whoppers, Slim Jim, Mike 'n Ikes, Sweet Tarts, or Pez — this bounty counted, weighed, and inventoried (on my niece's bed). Which was the Pez dispenser of greatest value? A Hanna-Barbera Pez dispenser? Or, say, a demonic totem pole Pez dispenser? And after this fracas, which my sister refereed wearily (Look, if he wants to save the Smarties, you can't make him trade.), they all slept, and this part is routine, my sister was tired as hell; she slept the sleep of the besieged, of the overworked, she fell precipitously into whorls of unconsciousness, of which no snapshot can be taken.

In one photograph, my sister is wearing a Superman outfit. This, from a prior Halloween. I think it was a Supermom outfit, actually, because she always liked these bad jokes, degraded jokes, things other people would find ridiculous. (She'd take a joke and repeat it until it was leaden, until it was funny only in its awfulness.) Jokes with the fillip of sentimentality. Anyway, in this picture her blond hair — brightened a couple of shades with the current technologies — cascades around her shoulders, disordered and impulsive. Supermom. And her expression is skeptical, as if she assumes the mantle of Supermom — raising the kids, accepting wage-slavery, growing old and contented — and thinks it's dopey at the same time.

Never any good without coffee. Never any good in the morning. Never any good until the second cup. Never any good without freshly ground Joe, because of my dad's insistence, despite advantages of class and style, on instant coffee. No way. Not for my sister. At my dad's house, where she stayed in summer, she used to grumble derisively, while staring out the kitchen windows, out the expanse of windows that gave onto the meadow there, Instant coffee! There would be horses in the meadow and the ocean just over the trees, the sound of the surf and instant coffee! Thus the morning after Halloween, with my nephew the shark (who took this opportunity to remind her, in fact, that last year he saved his Halloween candy all the way till Easter, Mommy) and my niece, the Little Mermaid, orbiting around her like a fine dream. My sister was making this coffee with the automatic grinder and the automatic drip device, and the dishes were piled in the sink behind her, and the wall calendar was staring her in the face, with its hundred urgent appointments, e.g., jury duty (the following Monday) and R & A to pediatrician; the kids whirled around the kitchen, demanding to know who got the last of the Lucky Charms, who had to settle for the Kix. My sister's eyes barely open.

Now this portrait of her cat, Pointdexter, twelve years old — he slept on my face when I stayed at her place in 1984 — Pointdexter with the brain tumor, Pointdexter with the phenobarbital habit. That morning — All Saints' Day — he stood entirely motionless before his empty dish. His need was clear. His dignity was immense. Well, except for the seizures. Pointdexter had these seizures. He was possessed. He was a demon. He would bounce off the walls, he would get up a head of steam, mouth frothing, and run straight at the wall, smack into it, shake off the ghosts, and start again. His screeches were unearthly. Phenobarbital was prescribed. My sister medicated him preemptively, before any other chore, before diplomatic initiatives on matters of cereal allocation. Hold on you guys, I'll be with you in a second. Drugging the cat, slipping him the Mickey Finn in the Science Diet, feeding the kids, then getting out the door, pecking her boyfriend on the cheek (he was stumbling sleepily down the stairs).

She printed snapshots. At this photo lab. She'd sold cameras (mnemonic devices) for years, and then she'd been kicked upstairs to the lab. Once she sold a camera to Pete Townshend, the musician. She told him — in her way both casual and rebellious — that she didn't really like The Who. Later, from her job at the lab, she used to bring home other people's pictures, e.g., an envelope of photographs of the Pope. Had she been out to Giants Stadium to use her telephoto lens to photograph John Paul II? No, she'd just printed up an extra batch of, say, Agnes Venditi's or Joey Mueller's photos. Caveat emptor. Who knew what else she'd swiped? Those Jerry Garcia pix from the show right before he died? Garcia's eyes squeezed tightly shut, as he sang in that heartbroken, exhausted voice of his? Or: somebody's trip to the Caribbean or to the Liberty Bell in Philly? Or: her neighbor's private documentations of love? Who knew? She'd get on the phone at work and gab, call up her friends, call up my family, printing pictures while gabbing, sheet after sheet of negatives, of memories. Oh, and circa Halloween, she was working in the lab with some new, exotic chemicals. She had a wicked headache.

My sister didn't pay much attention to the church calendar. Too busy. Too busy   10
to concentrate on theologies, too busy to go to the doctor, too busy to deal with her finances, her credit-card debt, etc. Too busy. (And maybe afraid, too.) She was unclear on this day set aside for God's awesome tabernacle, unclear on the feast for the departed faithful, didn't know about the church of the Middle Ages, didn't know about the particulars of the Druidic ritual of Halloween — it was a Hallmark thing, a marketing event — or how All Saints' Day emerged as an alternative to Halloween. She was not much preoccupied with nor attendant to articulations of loss, nor interested in how this feast in the church calendar was hewn into two separate holy days, one for the saints, that great cloud of witnesses, one for the dearly departed, the regular old believers. She didn't know of any attachments that bound together these constituencies, didn't know, e.g., that God would wipe away all tears from our eyes and there would be no more death, according to the evening's reading from the book of Revelation. All this academic stuff was lost on her, though she sang in the church choir, and though on All Saints' Day, a guy from the church choir happened to come into the camera store, just to say hi, a sort of an angel (let's say), and she said, Hey Bob, you know, I never asked you what you do.

To which Bob replied, I'm a designer.

My sister: What do you design?

Bob: Steel wool.

She believed him.

She was really small. She barely held down her clothes. Five feet tall. Tiny   15
hands and feet. Here's a photo from my brother's wedding (two weeks before Halloween); we were dancing on the dance floor, she and I. She liked to pogo sometimes. It was the dance we preferred when dancing together. We created mayhem on the dance floor. Scared people off. We were demons for dance, for noise and excitement. So at my brother's wedding reception I hoisted her up onto my shoulder, and she was so light, just as I remembered from years before, twenty years of dances, still tiny, and I wanted to crowd-surf her across the reception, pass her across upraised hands, I wanted to impose her on older couples, gentlemen in their cummerbunds, old guys with tennis elbow or arthritis, with red faces and gin blossoms; they would smile, passing my sister hither, to the microphone, where the wedding band was playing, where she would suddenly burst into song, into some sort of reconciliatory song, backed

by the wedding band, and there would be stills of this moment, flashbulbs popping, a spotlight on her face, a tiny bit of reverb on her microphone, she would smile and concentrate and sing. Unfortunately, the situation around us, on the dance floor, was more complicated than this. Her boyfriend was about to have back surgery. He wasn't going to do any heavy lifting. And my nephew was too little to hold her up. And my brother was preoccupied with his duties as groom. So instead I twirled her once and put her down. We were laughing, out of breath.

On All Saints' Day she had lunch with Bob the angelic designer of steel wool (maybe he had a crush on her) or with the younger guys from the lab (because she was a middle-aged free spirit), and then she printed more photos of Columbus Day parades across Jersey, or photos of other people's kids dressed as Pocahontas or as the Lion King, and then at 5:30 she started home, a commute of forty-five minutes, Morristown to Hackettstown, on two-laners. She knew every turn. Here's the local news photo that never was: my sister slumped over the wheel of her Plymouth Saturn after having run smack into a local deer. All along those roads the deer were upended, disemboweled, set upon by crows and hawks, and my sister on the way back from work, or on the way home from a bar, must have grazed an entire herd of them at one time or another, missed them narrowly, frozen in the headlights of her car, on the shoulders of the meandering back roads, pulverized.

Her boy lives on air. Disdains food. My niece, meanwhile, will eat only candy. By dinnertime, they had probably made a dent in the orange plastic bucket with the Three Musketeers, the Cadbury's, Hot Tamales, Kit Kats, Jujyfruits, Baby Ruths, Bubble Yum — at least my niece had. They had insisted on bringing a sampling of this booty to school and from there to their afterschool play group. Neither of them wanted to eat anything; they complained about the whole idea of supper, and thus my sister offered, instead, to take them to the McDonaldLand play area on the main drag in Hackettstown, where she would buy them a Happy Meal, or equivalent, a hamburger topped with American processed cheese food, and, as an afterthought, she would insist on their each trying a little bit of a salad from the brand-new McDonald's salad bar. She had to make a deal to get the kids to accept the salad. She suggested six mouthfuls of lettuce each and drew a hard line there, but then she allowed herself to be talked down to two mouthfuls each. They ate indoors at first, the three of them, and then went out to the playground, where there were slides and jungle gyms in the reds and yellows of Ray Kroc's empire. My sister made the usual conversation, How did the other kids make out on Halloween? What happened at school? and she thought of her boyfriend, fresh from spinal surgery, who had limped downstairs in the morning to give her a kiss, and then she thought about bills, bills, bills, as she caught my niece at the foot of a slide. It was time to go sing. Home by nine.

My sister as she played the guitar in the late sixties with her hair in braids; she played it before anyone else in my family, wandering around the chords, "House of the Rising Sun" or "Blackbird," on classical guitar, sticking to the open chords of guitar tablature. It never occurred to me to wonder about which instruments were used on those AM songs of the period (the Beatles with their sitars and cornets, Brian Wilson with his theremin), not until my sister started to play the guitar. (All of us sang — we used to sing and dance in the living room when my parents were married, especially to *Abbey Road* and *Bridge Over Troubled Water.*) And when she got divorced she started hanging around this bar where they had live music, this Jersey bar, and then she started hanging around at a local record label, an indy operation, and then she started managing a band (on top of everything else), and then she started to sing again. She joined the choir at St. James Church of Hackettstown and she started to sing, and after singing she started to pray — prayer and song being, I guess, styles of the same beseechment.

I don't know what songs they rehearsed at choir rehearsal, but Bob was there, as were others, Donna, Frank, Eileen, and Tim (I'm making the names up), and I know that the choir was warm and friendly, though perhaps a little bit out of tune. It was one of those Charles Ives small-town choruses that slip in and out of pitch, that misses exits and entrances. But they had a good time rehearsing, with the kids monkeying around in the pews, the kids climbing sacrilegiously over that furniture, dashing up the aisle to the altar and back, as somebody kept half an eye on them (five of the whelps in all) and after the last notes ricocheted around the choir loft, my sister offered her summation of the proceedings, Totally cool! Totally cool!, and now the intolerable part of this story begins — with joy and excitement and a church interior. My sister and her kids drove from St. James to her house, her condo, this picturesque drive home, Hackettstown as if lifted from picture postcards of autumn, the park with its streams and ponds and lighted walkways, leaves in the streetlamps, in the headlights, leaves three or four days past their peak, the sound of leaves in the breeze, the construction crane by her place (they were digging up the road), the crane swaying above a fork in the road, a left turn after the fast-food depots, and then into her parking spot in front of the condo. The porch by the front door with the Halloween pumpkins: a cat's face complete with whiskers, a clown, a jack-o'-lantern. My sister closed the front door of her house behind her. Bolted it. Her daughter reminded her to light the pumpkins. Just inside the front door, Pointdexter, on the top step, waiting.

Her keys on the kitchen table. Her coat in the closet. She sent the kids upstairs to get into their pajamas. She called up to her boyfriend, who was in bed reading a textbook, What are you doing in bed, you total slug! and then, after checking the messages on the answering machine, looking at the mail, she trudged up to my niece's room to kiss her good night. Endearments passed between them. My sister loved her kids, above all, and in spite of all the work and the hardships, in spite of my niece's reputation as a firecracker, in spite of my nephew's sometimes diabolical smarts. She loved them. There were endearments, therefore, lengthy and repetitive, as there would have been with my nephew, too. And my sister kissed her daughter multiply, because my niece is a little impish redhead, and it's hard not to kiss her. Look, it's late, so I can't read to you tonight, okay? My niece protested temporarily, and then my sister arranged the stuffed animals around her daughter (for the sake of arranging), and plumped a feather pillow, and switched off the bedside lamp on the bedside table, and she made sure the night-light underneath the table (a plug-in shaped like a ghost) was illumined, and then on the way out the door she stopped for a second. And looked back. The tableau of domesticity was what she last contemplated. Or maybe she was composing endearments for my nephew. Or maybe she wasn't looking back at my niece at all. Maybe she was lost in this next tempest.

Out of nowhere. All of a sudden. All at once. In an instant. Without warning. In no time. Helter-skelter. In the twinkling of an eye. Figurative language isn't up to the task. My sister's legs gave out, and she fell over toward my niece's desk, by the door, dislodging a pile of toys and dolls (a Barbie in evening wear, a posable Tinkerbell doll), colliding with the desk, sweeping its contents off with her, toppling onto the floor, falling heavily, her head by the door. My niece, startled, rose up from under covers.

More photos: my sister, my brother and I, back in our single digits, dressed in matching, or nearly matching outfits (there was a naval flavor to our look), playing with my aunt's basset hound — my sister grinning mischievously; or: my sister, my father, my brother and I, in my dad's Karmann-Ghia, just before she totaled it on the straightaway on Fishers Island (she skidded, she said, on antifreeze or something slippery); or: my sister, with her newborn daughter in her lap, sitting on the floor of her living room — mother and daughter with the same bemused impatience.

My sister started to seize.

The report of her fall was, of course, loud enough to stir her boyfriend from the next room. He was out of bed fast. (Despite the physical pain associated with his recent surgery.) I imagine there was a second in which other possibilities occurred to him — hoax, argument, accident, anything — but quickly the worst of these seemed most likely. You know these things somewhere. You know immediately the content of all middle-of-the-night telephone calls. He was out of bed. And my niece called out to her brother, to my nephew, next door. She called my nephew's name, plaintively, like it was a question.

My sister's hands balled up. Her heels drumming on the carpeting. Her muscles all like nautical lines, pulling tight against cleats. Her jaw clenched. Her heart rattling desperately. Fibrillating. If it was a conventional seizure, she was unconscious for this part — maybe even unconscious throughout — because of reduced blood flow to the brain, because of the fibrillation, because of her heart condition; which is to say that my sister's mitral valve prolapse — technical feature of her broken heart — was here engendering an arrhythmia, and now, if not already, she began to hemorrhage internally. Her son stood in the doorway, in his pajamas, shifting from one foot to the other (there was a draft in the hall). Her daughter knelt at the foot of the bed, staring, and my sister's boyfriend watched, as my poor sister shook, and he held her head, and then changed his mind and bolted for the phone.

After the seizure, she went slack. (Meredith's heart stopped. And her breathing. She was still.) For a second, she was alone in the room, with her children, silent. After he dialed 911, Jimmy appeared again, to try to restart her breathing. Here's how: he pressed his lips against hers. He didn't think to say, Come on, breathe, dammit, or to make similar imprecations, although he did manage to shout at the kids. Get the hell out of here, please! Go downstairs! (It was advice they followed only for a minute.) At last, my sister took a breath. Took a deep breath, a sigh, and there were two more of these. Deep resigned sighs. Five or ten seconds between each. For a few moments more, instants, she looked at Jimmy, as he pounded on her chest with his fists, thoughtless about anything but results, stopping occasionally to press his ear between her breasts. Her eyes were sad and frightened, even in the company of the people she most loved. So it seemed. More likely she was unconscious. The kids sat cross-legged on the floor in the hall, by the top of the stairs, watching. Lots of stuff was left to be accomplished in these last seconds, even if it wasn't anything unusual, people and relationships and small kindnesses, the best way to fry pumpkin seeds, what to pack for Thanksgiving, whether to make turnips or not, snapshots to be culled and arranged, photos to be taken — these possibilities spun out of my sister's grasp, torrential futures, my beloved sister, solitary with pictures taken and untaken, gone.

EMS technicians arrived and carried her body down to the living room, where they tried to start her pulse with expensive engines and devices. Her body jumped while they shocked her — she was a revenant in some corridor of simultaneities — but her heart wouldn't start. Then they put her body on the stretcher. To carry her away. Now the moment arrives when they bear her out the front door of her house and she leaves it to us, leaves to us the house and her things and her friends and her memories and the involuntary assemblage of these into language. Grief. The sound of the ambulance. The road is mostly clear on the way to the hospital; my sister's route is clear.

I should fictionalize it more, I should conceal myself. I should consider the responsibilities of characterization, I should conflate her two children into one, or reverse their genders, or otherwise alter them, I should make her boyfriend a husband, I should explicate all the tributaries of my extended family (its remarriages, its internecine politics), I should novelize the whole thing, I should make it multi-generational, I should work in my forefathers (stonemasons and newspapermen), I should let artifice create an elegant surface, I should make the events orderly, I should wait and write about it later, I should wait until I'm not angry, I shouldn't clutter a narrative with fragments, with mere recollections of good times, or with regrets, I should make Meredith's death shapely and persuasive, not blunt and disjunctive, I shouldn't have to think the unthinkable, I shouldn't have to suffer, I should address her here directly (these are the ways I miss you), I should write only of affection, I should make our travels in this earthly landscape safe and secure, I should have a better ending, I shouldn't say her life was short and often sad, I shouldn't say she had her demons, as I do too.   *[1997]*

≡ THINKING ABOUT THE TEXT

1. Among other things, this piece is a portrait of the narrator's sister, Meredith. What was she like? How does he get this across? What are the narrator's feelings about her?

2. Moody refers to photos throughout the story. What part do photos play in this piece?

3. This story/memoir is textured with specifics and concrete descriptions that help convince readers of its veracity. Which passages create the sense of "this is true, I was there"? Which passages could not have been witnessed by the narrator?

4. Do you think your response would be different if this piece were clearly labeled as either a memoir or a short story? Would the themes that Moody explores be different? What do you think are his main ideas about families and memories?

5. Read the last paragraph several times. What is your response? What do you think the narrator intends? Part of what he says suggests that he could have told this story differently. How? Why?

≡ MAKING COMPARISONS

1. Both these memoirs are narratives. Most critics believe Moody's is fictional. Do you think one is more "authentic" than the other?

2. Compare the sense of guilt in both texts.

3. Good writers go beyond a mere representation of the past. What other ideas are on these writers' minds?

BELL HOOKS

From *Bone Black: Memories of Girlhood*

Writer, professor, and social critic, bell hooks (b. 1952) adopted the name of her maternal great-grandmother, a woman known for speaking her mind. Her books reflect her position as a bold interpreter of contemporary culture in terms of race, class, and gender: Ain't I a Woman *(1981),* Talking Back: Thinking Feminist, Thinking Black *(1989),* Yearning: Race, Gender, and Cultural Politics *(1990),* Outlaw Culture: Resisting Representation *(1994), among others. She published a memoir,* Bone Black: Memories of Girlhood *(1996). Her most recent book is* When Angels Speak of Love *(2007). She has taught literature, women's studies, and African American studies at Yale University, Oberlin College, and City College of New York and continues to teach and to write poetry and social criticism at Berea College in Kentucky. The selection that follows is from* Bone Black.

53

They are concerned because she has not shown the right interest in boys. They do not talk to her about what it is about boys that she finds boring, uninteresting. She cannot talk to them. She cannot tell them how much she hates anyone to lord it over her. She cannot tell them that this is what boys often want to do. She cannot explain that she does not like to be touched, grabbed at, without agreeing to such touching. She is disgusted by the grabbing, the pleading that she let them do this and do that. Even when she is aroused, the feeling goes away when boys behave as though there is only something in this moment for them, something they are seeking that she must give. She is not ashamed to say no. She does not care that the word gets around that she will say no. She cares that she is left alone. She has no date for the senior prom. Her would-be date, someone she is talking to from out of town, someone who drives a sports car, who has a job working for a newspaper, says he will come when she asks him, then changes his mind without saying why. They will not let her go with that theater crowd she hangs out with, that group of rather wild white teenagers. They are concerned that she may be growing up funny. They watch her behavior. They think about the way a certain funny grown-up woman showed intense interest in her. They think that maybe there were wrong to allow her to accept presents, a dress, a watch with tiny diamonds. They are sure that she is not showing enough willingness to seek out boys and do what girls do. They are watching.

Every now and then they agree that she can visit with a girlfriend who lives across town, who is white, who drives a convertible. They listen to their phone conversations to hear what is being discussed, books, politics, boys. They hear that she is mainly listening to the white girl talking about the boys that interest her. They do not know that she is interested in young men but does not talk about them because they are not anybody the white girl knows. When her friend drives her home from school they sit outside and talk, sometimes for hours. They tell her this cannot happen, that she must come inside and let that white girl go home.

She does not tell them when the white girl tries to kill herself. They are just glad that she no longer comes around. She never tells anyone at home about the scars on her friend's wrists. She never tells that she and her white friend share a feeling of being outside, alone, that they comfort one another. She knows that they will think it silly, downright crazy, to want to die because some boy does not love you, does not notice even that you are alive. She understands. She takes her friend's hand. They embrace one another in the stillness of the car. They share the promise that the friend will never again act without talking about it first. They hold each other close, glad to be alive, glad to be friends.

When she enters the door her mother and father say nothing, even though they have been watching. Later in the night they keep her downstairs and want to know what is going on between her and the friend. She tells them they are friends, nothing is going on. Her daddy says, Don't lie to me. She looks at him with anger and contempt. She has no answers for them. They tell her that they will have none of this in their house, that she will have to go. She is not sure why they are so upset. She does not understand. Shaken by the fear of being told to leave, by threats of punishment, she agrees to stop seeing her friend. She does not understand why they want to take this friend from her. She does not know why they are worried that she may grow funny.

61

Loneliness brings me to the edge of what I know. My soul is dark like the inner world of the cave — bone black. I have been drowning in that blackness. Like quicksand it sucks me in and keeps me there in the space of all my pain. I never say out loud that I could die in this space of loneliness, of outsiderness. I never say out loud I want to kill myself — to go away from all this. I never tell anyone how much I want to belong. The priest I met saw me standing on the edge of a cliff about to jump off and pulled me back. It was not a real cliff, just the one inside myself. Before anyone goes to that real place where we leap to our death, the dying has to be imagined. And so he finds me there in that bone black place within myself where I am dreaming my escape. 5

He sends a student to spend time with me at the retreat. She gives me Rilke's *Letters to a Young Poet*. I am drowning and his words come to rescue me. He helps to make sense of the pain I feel. Now it is Rilke who speaks to me and urges me to go into myself and find the deeps into which my life takes rise. At last I am not alone. I have been seen.

I read poems. I write. That is my destiny. Standing on the edge of the cliff about to fall into the abyss, I remember who I am. I am a young poet, a writer. I am here to make words. I have the power to pull myself back from death — to keep myself alive.

Now when they tell me I am crazy, that if I keep reading all those books I will end up crazy, locked away in the asylum where no one will visit me — now when they tell me this I am not so afraid. Rilke gives meaning to the wilderness of spirit I am living in. His book is a world I enter and find myself. He tells me that everything terrible is really something helpless that wants help from us. I read *Letters to a Young Poet* over and over. I am drowning and it is the raft that takes me safely to the shore.

Now when I lie in bed at night thinking that it is better to die than always to be misunderstood, always to feel so much pain, I know that I am not alone. Lying in the dark I repeat the words, "Do not believe that he who would seek to comfort you lives untroubled." I still suffer. Daddy Gus says that my suffering will end. That one day I will look back on all of this and it will not matter.

I take my book to read him passages. Like Rilke, he tells me not to be afraid to look deep into everything, not to be afraid even of the pain. I can tell him, my grandfather who loves me always, that I want to belong — that it hurts to be always on the outside. He tells me there are lots of ways to belong in this world. And that it is my work to find out where I belong. 10

At night when everyone is silent and everything is still, I lie in the darkness of my windowless room, the place where they exile me from the community of their heart, and search the unmoving blackness to see if I can find my way home. I tell myself stories, write poems, record my dreams. In my journal I write — I belong in this place of words. This is my home. This dark, bone black inner cave where I am making a world for myself.   *[1996]*

■ THINKING ABOUT THE TEXT

1. Hooks seems especially sensitive to the expectations of her family. Is this a common response of contemporary teenagers?

2. How do you interpret her family's fear that she will grow up "funny"?

3. Are her parents right to always be "watching"? Are their intentions good, or are her parents simply authoritarian?

4. In the second selection, hooks finds comfort in literature. Is this common today? What other pursuits do young people use to find themselves?

5. As a respite from loneliness, hooks finds a home in words. What might have happened to her if she had grown up in a supportive, tolerant environment?

■ MAKING COMPARISONS

1. Compare hooks's relationship with her family to that of Staples and Moody.

2. Our family memories are often visual: we see in our mind's eye scenes from childhood. Which writer included in this cluster captures (or creates) the most memorable picture for you?

3. According to some psychologists, "coming to terms" with the past is a sign of good mental health. What is your sense of how well each of the writers in this cluster is doing in this regard?

■ WRITING ABOUT ISSUES

1. In a brief essay, argue that a person can or cannot get beyond the past. Use concrete examples from your own experiences and the essays in this cluster.

2. Argue that experiencing difficulties in childhood is not necessarily totally negative, using examples from two of the essays in this cluster.

3. Write a personal essay that imitates the general structure of one of the essays in this cluster.

4. In his autobiography, *All the Strange Hours* (1975), the paleontologist Loren Eiseley writes, "To grow is a gain, an enlargement of life. . . . Yet it is also a departure. There is something lost that will not return." Write an essay that argues that this is or is not true. Make reference to Staples, Moody, and hooks, as well as other texts (novels, films, memoirs) you think are appropriate. You might also want to include your own experience for support.

▤ Reconciling with Fathers: Poems

LUCILLE CLIFTON, "forgiving my father"

ROBERT HAYDEN, "Those Winter Sundays"

THEODORE ROETHKE, "My Papa's Waltz"

LI-YOUNG LEE, "My Father, in Heaven, Is Reading Out Loud"

MOLLY PEACOCK, "Say You Love Me"

In childhood, our emotions are often intense. Fears about life arise because we feel so powerless. For some of us, our fathers held all the power. Fathers may use their power in various ways — some to control or abuse, others to comfort and protect. We form perceptions about our fathers from these early memories. Often we become judgmental about their failures in the world or their failures as parents. As we grow older, we sometimes come to terms with our fathers and see them simply as human beings with strengths and weaknesses. But it is not always simple; some wounds may be too deep for us to reconcile. The five poets in this cluster approach memories of their fathers with different perspectives and purposes: to forgive their fathers and perhaps themselves, to remember fondly, to come to a closure, to relive a past that still haunts them, to come to terms with loss.

▤ BEFORE YOU READ

Make a list of four strong memories about your father from your childhood. Are the memories positive or not? Can you remember how you felt then? Is it different from how you feel now? How can you explain the difference?

LUCILLE CLIFTON
forgiving my father

Lucille Clifton (1936–2010) was born in a small town near Buffalo, New York. She attended Howard University and Fredonia State Teacher's College and taught poetry at a number of universities. Her numerous awards for writing include two creative writing fellowships from the National Endowment for the Arts (1970 and 1973), two Pulitzer Prize nominations (for Good Woman: Poems *and a Memoir and for* Next, *both in 1988), several major poetry awards, and an Emmy. The mother of six, Clifton has written fifteen children's books. She was a former poet laureate of Maryland and the Distinguished Professor of Humanities at St. Mary's College. "Forgiving my father" is from her 1980 book,* Two-Headed Woman. Voices, *her most recent book, was published in 2008.*

it is friday. we have come
to the paying of the bills.
all week you have stood in my dreams
like a ghost, asking for more time
but today is payday, payday old man,   5
my mother's hand opens in her early grave
and i hold it out like a good daughter.

there is no more time for you. there will
never be time enough daddy daddy old lecher
old liar. i wish you were rich so i could take it all   10
and give the lady what she was due
but you were the son of a needy father,
the father of a needy son,
you gave her all you had
which was nothing. you have already given her   15
all you had.

you are the pocket that was going to open
and come up empty any friday.
you were each other's bad bargain, not mine.
daddy old pauper old prisoner, old dead man   20
what am i doing here collecting?
you lie side by side in debtor's boxes
and no accounting will open them up.   *[1980]*

≡ THINKING ABOUT THE TEXT

1. How might you answer the question in line 21? Are the last two lines of the poem a kind of answer? Is there some way we can "collect" from the dead?

2. Should we bury the dead — that is, should we let the past go and let bygones be bygones? Or is it necessary to settle old scores? What do you think Clifton's answer would be?

3. How consistently does Clifton use the payday analogy? Make a list of words that reinforce her overall scheme.

4. Would you think differently about the speaker's father if Clifton had written "elderly one" instead of "old man" (line 5) or "old playboy / old fibber" instead of "old lecher / old liar" (lines 9–10)?

5. Some readers look for tensions or contradictions early in a poem, hoping they will be resolved at the end. Does this poem end in a resolution of paying up and forgiving?

ROBERT HAYDEN

Those Winter Sundays

Born in Detroit, Michigan, African American poet Robert Hayden (1913–1980)
grew up in a poor neighborhood where his natural parents left him with family friends.
He grew up with the Hayden name, not discovering his original name until he was
forty. Hayden attended Detroit City College (now Wayne State University) from
1932 to 1936, worked in the Federal Writer's Project, and later earned his M.A. at
the University of Michigan in 1944. He taught at Fisk University from 1946 to
1968 and at the University of Michigan from 1968 to 1980 and published several
collections of poetry. Although his poems sometimes contain autobiographical ele-
ments, Hayden is primarily a formalist poet who preferred that his poems not be lim-
ited to personal or ethnic interpretations. "Those Winter Sundays" is from Angle of
Ascent *(1966).*

> Sundays too my father got up early
> and put his clothes on in the blueblack cold,
> then with cracked hands that ached
> from labor in the weekday weather made
> banked fires blaze. No one ever thanked him.　　　　　　　　5
>
> I'd wake and hear the cold splintering, breaking.
> When the rooms were warm, he'd call,
> and slowly I would rise and dress,
> fearing the chronic angers of that house,
>
> Speaking indifferently to him,　　　　　　　　　　　　10
> who had driven out the cold
> and polished my good shoes as well.
> What did I know, what did I know
> of love's austere and lonely offices?　　　　　　　*[1962]*

▤ THINKING ABOUT THE TEXT

1. Is the concluding question meant rhetorically — that is, is the answer so obvious that no real reply is expected? Write a response that you think the son might give now.

2. Why did the children never thank their father? Is this common? What specific things might you thank your father (or mother) for? Do parents have basic responsibilities to their children that do not warrant thanks?

3. Is there evidence that the son loves his father now? Did he then? Why did he speak "indifferently" (line 10) to his father? Is it clear what the "chronic angers" (line 9) are? Should it be?

4. How might you fill in the gaps here? For example, how old do you think the boy is? How old is the father? What kind of a job might he have? What else can you infer?

5. What is the speaker's tone? Is he hoping for your understanding? Your sympathy? Are we responsible for the things we do in childhood? Is this speaker repentant or simply explaining?

▤ MAKING COMPARISONS

1. What degrees of forgiveness do you see in Clifton's and Hayden's poems?

2. Writing a poem for one's father seems different from writing a poem about him. Explain this statement in reference to these poems.

3. Compare the purpose of the questions in each poem. How might each poet answer the other poet's questions?

THEODORE ROETHKE
My Papa's Waltz

Born in Saginaw, Michigan, Theodore Roethke (1908–1963) was strongly influenced by childhood experiences with his father, a usually stern man who sold plants and flowers and who kept a large greenhouse, the setting for many of Roethke's poems. Roethke was educated at the University of Michigan, took courses at Harvard, and taught at several universities before becoming poet-in-residence at the University of Washington in 1948. Roethke's books include The Lost Son and Other Poems *(1949), the source for "My Papa's Waltz";* The Waking *(1953), which won a Pulitzer Prize; and* Words for the Wind *(1958), which won the National Book Award. Roethke's intensely personal style ensures his place among the most influential postmodern American poets.*

> The whiskey on your breath
> Could make a small boy dizzy;
> But I hung on like death:
> Such waltzing was not easy.
>
> We romped until the pans   5
> Slid from the kitchen shelf;
> My mother's countenance
> Could not unfrown itself.
>
> The hand that held my wrist
> Was battered on one knuckle;   10
> At every step you missed
> My right ear scraped a buckle.
>
> You beat time on my head
> With a palm caked hard by dirt,
> Then waltzed me off to bed   15
> Still clinging to your shirt.   [1948]

■ THINKING ABOUT THE TEXT

1. Is the narrator looking back at his father with fondness? Bitterness?

2. Would the poem make a different impression if we changed "romped" (line 5) to "fought" and "waltzing" (line 4) to "dancing"?

3. Why did the boy hang on and cling to his father? From fear? From affection?

4. What is the mother's role here? How would you characterize her frown?

5. Readers often have a negative view of the relationship represented here, but many change their minds, seeing some positive aspects to the father and son's waltz. How might you account for this revision?

■ MAKING COMPARISONS

1. Would you have read this poem differently if the poet had used Clifton's title "forgiving my father"?

2. How would you compare the tone of Roethke's poem with that of Hayden's? Do they miss their fathers?

3. Would you say that Roethke has more complex feelings about his father, whereas Clifton and Hayden seem clearer?

LI-YOUNG LEE

My Father, in Heaven, Is Reading Out Loud

Li-Young Lee (b. 1959) was born in Indonesia to Chinese parents. His father taught medicine and philosophy in Jakarta. During a purge of ethnic Chinese, Lee's father was imprisoned because of his Western interests. He eventually escaped, and the family finally settled in Pittsburgh, where his father became a Presbyterian minister. Lee graduated from the University of Pittsburgh in 1979. He has won many prizes for his poetry, from Rose *(1986) to* Book of My Nights *(2001). He lives in Chicago with his wife and two sons.*

My father, in heaven, is reading out loud
to himself Psalms or news. Now he ponders what
he's read. No. He is listening for the sound
of children in the yard. Was that laughing
or crying? So much depends upon the   5
answer, for either he will go on reading,
or he'll run to save a child's day from grief.
As it is in heaven, so it was on earth.

Because my father walked the earth with a grave,
determined rhythm, my shoulders ached   10

from his gaze. Because my father's shoulders
ached from the pulling of oars, my life now moves
with a powerful back-and-forth rhythm:
nostalgia, speculation. Because he
made me recite a book a month, I forget   15
everything as soon as I read it. And knowledge
never comes but while I'm mid-stride a flight
of stairs, or lost a moment on some avenue.

A remarkable disappointment to him,
I am like anyone who arrives late   20
in the millennium and is unable
to stay to the end of days. The world's
beginnings are obscure to me, its outcomes
inaccessible. I don't understand
the source of starlight, or starlight's destinations.   25
And already another year slides out
of balance. But I don't disparage scholars;
my father was one and I loved him,
who packed his books once, and all of our belongings,
then sat down to await instruction   30
from his god, yes, but also from a radio.
At the doorway, I watched, and I suddenly
knew he was one like me, who got my learning
under a lintel; he was one of the powerless,
to whom knowledge came while he sat among   35
suitcases, boxes, old newspapers, string.

He did not decide peace or war, home or exile,
escape by land or escape by sea.
He waited merely, as always someone
waits, far, near, here, hereafter, to find out: 40
is it praise or lament hidden in the next moment?   *[1990]*

≡ THINKING ABOUT THE TEXT

1. Lee begins his poem by speculating that his father is either reading or listening. What does this suggest about the narrator's view of his father?

2. What influence does Lee suggest his father had on him in stanza 2? Is it positive or negative or both?

3. When Lee says that his father awaited "instruction / from his god, yes, but also from a radio" (lines 30–31), what is he suggesting?

4. Does Lee finally identify with his father? In what way?

5. Would you interpret the last stanza as reconciliation? Be specific about the resolution that Lee comes to.

■ MAKING COMPARISONS

1. Unlike Hayden and Roethke, Lee explicitly says he loved his father. What other differences do you note?

2. Is this view of his father more or less balanced than the other three poets?

3. Which of the previous three fathers does Lee's seem most like?

MOLLY PEACOCK

Say You Love Me

Molly Peacock (b. 1947) is a multitalented poet, essayist, memoirist, and biographer. She was born in Buffalo, New York, and currently lives in both Toronto and New York City. She has published six collections of poems, the first being And Live Alone *(1980) and the last being* The Second Blush: Poems *(2008). She published her memoir,* Paradise, Piece by Piece, *in 1999. Her work has won many awards, and she was president of the Poetry Society of America from 1989 to 1995. She has taught at the University of California at Riverside, Bucknell University, and the University of Western Ontario. The following poem first appeared in her* Take Heart *(1989).*

What happened earlier I'm not sure of.
Of course he was drunk, but often he was.
His face looked like a ham on a hook above

me — I was pinned to the chair because   5
he'd hunkered over me with arms like jaws
pried open by the chair arms. "Do you love

me?" he began to sob. "Say you love me!"
I held out. I was probably fifteen.
What had happened? Had my mother — had she

said or done something? Or had he just been   10
drinking too long after work? "He'll get *mean*,"
my sister hissed, "just *tell* him." I brought my knee

up to kick him, but was too scared. Nothing
could have got the words out of me then. Rage
shut me up, yet "DO YOU?" was beginning   15

to peel, as of live layers of skin, age
from age from age from him until he gazed
through hysteria as a wet baby thing

repeating, "Do you love me? Say you do,"
in baby chokes, only loud, for they came   20
from a man. There wouldn't be a rescue

from my mother, still at work. The same
choking sobs said, "Love me, love me," and my game
was breaking down because I couldn't do

anything, not escape into my own   25
refusal, *I won't, I won't*, not fantasize
a kind, rich father, not fill the narrowed zone,

empty except for confusion until the size
of my fear ballooned as I saw his eyes,
blurred, taurean — my sister screamed — unknown,   30

unknown to me, a voice rose and leveled
off, "I love you," I said. *"Say 'I love you,
Dad!'"* "I love you, Dad," I whispered, leveled

by defeat into a cardboard image, untrue,
unbending. I was surprised I could move   35
as I did to get up, but he stayed, burled

onto the chair — my monstrous fear — she screamed,
my sister, "Dad, the phone! Go answer it!"
The phone wasn't ringing, yet he seemed

to move toward it, and I ran. He had a fit —   40
"It's not ringing!" — but I was at the edge of it
as he collapsed into the chair and blamed

both of us at a distance. No, the phone
was not ringing. There was no world out there,
so there we remained, completely alone.   *[1989]*   45

≡ THINKING ABOUT THE TEXT

1. This is an intense, narrowly focused poem about one particular scene from the poet's past. Do you think the poet means for it to stand for her whole relationship with her father?

2. What does the narrator mean by "leveled / by defeat into a cardboard image, untrue, / unbending" (lines 33–35)?

3. How do you interpret the baby imagery in stanzas 6 and 7?

4. What is the effect of similes like "ham on a hook" (line 3) and "jaws / pried open" (lines 5–6)?

5. Is there a resolution in the last stanza? Why do you think she ends with the phrase "completely alone"?

≡ MAKING COMPARISONS

1. Compare Peacock's attitude toward her father with Clifton's.

2. What do you think is Peacock's purpose in this poem? Compare it with the effects Clifton, Hayden, and Roethke are trying to achieve.

3. Compare the portraits of the fathers drawn by each of the poets in this cluster.

≣ WRITING ABOUT ISSUES

1. Choose one of the five preceding poems to argue that our feelings for our fathers are complex, not simple.

2. In *Words* (1964), Jean-Paul Sartre writes that "there is no good father, that is the rule." Use examples from the five poems to argue that this is, or is not, the case.

3. Do you think all children leave childhood or adolescence with unresolved tensions in their relationships with their fathers? Write a personal narrative that confronts this idea.

4. Locate at least three more poems that deal with memories of fathers. Write a brief report, noting the similarities to the five poems presented here.

▤ Exorcising the Dead: Critical Commentaries on a Poem

SYLVIA PLATH, "Daddy"

CRITICAL COMMENTARIES:

MARY LYNN BROE, From *Protean Poetic: The Poetry of Sylvia Plath*

LYNDA K. BUNDTZEN, From *Plath's Incarnations*

STEVEN GOULD AXELROD, From *Sylvia Plath: The Wound and the Cure of Words*

TIM KENDALL, From *Sylvia Plath: A Critical Study*

As contradictory as it might seem, we sometimes get angry when someone close to us dies. Psychologists tell us that anger is a healthy emotion in the mourning process, following sorrow and preceding acceptance: it is painful to miss loved ones, and we resent it. We might even direct the anger at them, feeling as if they are responsible for depriving us of their love. Sometimes, however, this anger lingers on long after the normal grieving process is over. Perhaps the attachment was abnormally strong, or perhaps the survivor's own life is too unstable to allow him or her to reach the final acceptance stage.

In the following poem, Sylvia Plath writes about her dead father as if he were a terrible person, even though as a young girl she seems to have adored him. Perhaps she is trying to expel his memory so she can find peace; perhaps she is using the poem as an occasion to express a deeper meaning about authority or influence from the past. Regardless, the poem is a powerful, strange, and passionate work of art. Following the poem, we include four critical essays that focus on autobiographial questions while also extending the critical discussion to include feminist issues, symbolic exorcism, and Freudian therapy.

▤ BEFORE YOU READ

Does it make sense to you that we might get angry at those who die because they have somehow deserted us? Do you think we have to "work out" the tensions between us and our parents before we can move into adulthood? Might it be healthy to exaggerate the difficulties of our childhood in poems and stories?

SYLVIA PLATH
Daddy

Born to middle-class parents in suburban New York, Sylvia Plath (1932–1963) became known as an intensely emotional "confessional" poet whose work is primarily autobiographical. Her father, a professor of biology and German, died when she was

(© Bettmann/Corbis.)

eight, the year her first poem was published. She graduated with honors from Smith College in 1950, after an internship at Mademoiselle *and a suicide attempt in her junior year, experiences described in her novel* The Bell Jar *(1963). She won a Fulbright Scholarship to study at Cambridge University, in England, where she met and married poet Ted Hughes. The couple had two children; the marriage ended the year before her suicide in 1963. "Daddy" is from* Ariel, *published posthumously in 1965.*

You do not do, you do not do
Any more, black shoe
In which I have lived like a foot
For thirty years, poor and white,
Barely daring to breathe or Achoo.   5

Daddy, I have had to kill you.
You died before I had time —
Marble-heavy, a bag full of God,
Ghastly statue with one gray toe
Big as a Frisco seal   10

And a head in the freakish Atlantic
Where it pours bean green over blue
In the waters off beautiful Nauset.°   *Cape Cod inlet*
I used to pray to recover you.
Ach, du.°   *Oh, you*   15

In the German tongue, in the Polish Town°
Scraped flat by the roller
Of wars, wars, wars.
But the name of the town is common.
My Polack friend   20

Says there are a dozen or two.
So I never could tell where you
Put your foot, your root,
I never could talk to you.
The tongue stuck in my jaw.   25

It stuck in a barb wire snare.
Ich, ich, ich, ich,°   *I, I, I, I*
I could hardly speak.
I thought every German was you.
And the language obscene   30

An engine, an engine
Chuffing me off like a Jew.
A Jew to Dachau, Auschwitz, Belsen.°
I began to talk like a Jew.
I think I may well be a Jew.   35

The snows of the Tyrol, the clear beer of Vienna
Are not very pure or true.
With my gypsy-ancestress and my weird luck
And my Taroc° pack and my Taroc pack
I may be a bit of a Jew.   40

I have always been scared of *you,*
With your Luftwaffe,° your gobbledygoo.
And your neat mustache
And your Aryan eye, bright blue.
Panzer-man, panzer-man,° O You —   45

Not God but a swastika
So black no sky could squeak through.

16 Polish Town: Plath's father was born in Granbow, Poland.   **33 Dachau . . . Belsen:**
Nazi death camps in World War II.   **39 Taroc:** Tarot cards used to tell fortunes. The practice may have originated among the early Jewish Cabalists and was then widely adopted by
European Gypsies during the Middle Ages.   **42 Luftwaffe:** World War II German air
force.   **45 panzer-man:** A member of the German armored vehicle division.

Every woman adores a Fascist,
The boot in the face, the brute
Brute heart of a brute like you.   50

You stand at the blackboard, daddy,
In the picture I have of you,
A cleft in your chin instead of your foot
But no less a devil for that, no not
Any less the black man who   55

Bit my pretty red heart in two.
I was ten when they buried you.
At twenty I tried to die
And get back, back, back to you.
I thought even the bones would do   60

But they pulled me out of the sack,
And they stuck me together with glue.
And then I knew what to do.
I made a model of you,
A man in black with a Meinkampf° look   65

And a love of the rack and the screw.
And I said I do, I do.
So daddy, I'm finally through.
The black telephone's off at the root,
The voices just can't worm through.   70

If I've killed one man, I've killed two —
The vampire who said he was you
And drank my blood for a year,
Seven years, if you want to know.
Daddy, you can lie back now.   75

There's a stake in your fat black heart
And the villagers never liked you.
They are dancing and stamping on you.
They always *knew* it was you.
Daddy, daddy, you bastard, I'm through.   [1962]   80

65 Meinkampf: Hitler's autobiography (*My Struggle*).

≣ THINKING ABOUT THE TEXT

1. Can this poem be seen as a series of arguments for why Plath has to forget her father? What complaints does the speaker seem to have against her father?

2. Some psychologists claim that we all have a love-hate relationship with our parents. Do you agree? Would Plath's speaker agree?

3. How effective is it for the speaker to compare herself to a Jew in Hitler's Germany? What other similes and metaphors are used to refer to her father? Do they work, or are they too extreme? Perhaps Plath wants them to be outrageous. Why might she?

4. Plath combines childhood rhymes and words with brutal images. What effect does this have on you? Why do you think Plath does this? What odd stylistic features can you point to here?

5. Why do you think it is necessary for the speaker to be finally "through" with her father? Is it normal young adult rebelliousness? What else might it be?

MARY LYNN BROE

From *Protean Poetic: The Poetry of Sylvia Plath*

Mary Lynn Broe (b. 1946) was educated at St. Louis University, where she received her B.A. in 1967, and the University of Connecticut, where she earned an M.A. in 1970 and a Ph.D. in 1976. She currently teaches English at Rochester Institute of Technology in Rochester, New York. She wrote Silence and Power: A Reevaluation of Djuna Barnes *(1991). She publishes and travels extensively and is an international voice in the fields of women's studies and modern literature. Her most recent book is* Black Walking: Selected Letters of Djuna Barnes to Emily Holmes Coleman, 1934–1938 *(2004).*

Among the other poems that display the performing self, "Daddy" and "Lady Lazarus" are two of the most often quoted, but most frequently misunderstood, poems in the Plath canon. The speaker in "Daddy" performs a mock poetic exorcism of an event that has already happened — the death of her father who she feels withdrew his love from her by dying prematurely: "Daddy, I have had to kill you. / You died before I had time — ."

The speaker attempts to exorcise not just the memory of her father but her own *Mein Kampf* model of him as well as her inherited behavioral traits that lead her graveward under the Freudian banner of death instinct or Thanatos's libido. But her ritual reenactment simply does not take. The event comically backfires as pure self-parody: the metaphorical murder of the father dwindles into Hollywood spectacle, while the poet is lost in the clutter of the collective unconscious.

Early in the poem, the ritual gets off on the wrong foot both literally and figuratively. A sudden rhythmic break midway through the first stanza interrupts the insistent and mesmeric chant of the poet's own freedom:

> You do not do, you do not do
> Any more, black shoe
> In which I have lived like a foot

> For thirty years, poor and white,
> Barely daring to breathe or Achoo.

The break suggests, on the one hand, that the nursery-rhyme world of contained terror is here abandoned; on the other, that the poet-exorcist's mesmeric control is superficial, founded in a shaky faith and an unsure heart — the worst possible state for the strong, disciplined exorcist.

At first, she kills her father succinctly with her own words, demythologizing him to a ludicrous piece of statuary that is hardly a Poseidon or the Colossus of Rhodes:

> Marble-heavy, a bag full of God,
> Ghastly statue with one grey toe
> Big as a Frisco seal
>
> And a head in the freakish Atlantic
> Where it pours bean green over blue
> In the waters off beautiful Nauset.
> I used to pray to recover you.
> Ach, du.

Then as she tries to patch together the narrative of him, his tribal myth (the "common" town, the "German tongue," the war-scraped culture), she begins to lose her own powers of description to a senseless Germanic prattle ("The tongue stuck in my jaw. / It stuck in a barb wire snare. / Ich, ich, ich, ich"). The individual man is absorbed by his inhuman archetype, the "panzer-man," "an engine / Chuffing me off like a Jew." Losing the exorcist's power that binds the spirit and then casts out the demon, she is the classic helpless victim of the swastika man. As she culls up her own picture of him as a devil, he refuses to adopt this stereotype. Instead he jumbles his trademark:

> A cleft in your chin instead of your foot
> But no less a devil for that, no not
> Any less the black man who
>
> Bit my pretty red heart in two.

The overt Nazi-Jew allegory throughout the poem suggests that, by a simple inversion of power, father and daughter grow more alike. But when she tries to imitate his action of dying, making all the appropriate grand gestures, she once again fails: "But they pulled me out of the sack, / And they stuck me together with glue." She retreats to a safe world of icons and replicas, but even the doll image she constructs turns out to be "the vampire who said he was you." At last, she abandons her father to the collective unconscious where it is *he* who is finally recognized ("They always *knew* it was you"). *She* is lost, impersonally absorbed by his irate persecutors, bereft of both her power and her conjurer's discipline, and possessed by the incensed villagers. The exorcist's ritual, one of purifying, cleansing, commanding silence, and then ordering the evil spirit's departure, has dwindled to a comic picture from the heart of darkness. Mad villagers stamp on the devil-vampire creation.

In the course of performing the imaginative "killing," the speaker moves through a variety of emotions, from viciousness ("a stake in your fat black heart"), to vengefulness ("you bastard, I'm through"), finally to silence ("The black telephone's off at the root"). It would seem that the real victim is the poet-performer who, despite her straining toward identification with the public events of holocaust and destruction of World War II, becomes more murderously persecuting than the "panzer-man" who smothered her, and who abandoned her with a paradoxical love, guilt, and fear. Unlike him, she kills three times: the original subject, the model to whom she said "I do, I do," and herself, the imitating victim. But each of these killings is comically inverted. Each backfires. Instead of successfully binding the spirits, commanding them to remain silent and cease doing harm, and then ordering them to an appointed place, the speaker herself is stricken dumb.

The failure of the exorcism and the emotional ambivalence are echoed in the curious rhythm. The incantatory safety of the nursery-rhyme thump (seemingly one of controlled, familiar terrors) also suggests some sinister brooding by its repetition. The poem opens with a suspiciously emphatic protest, a kind of psychological whistling-in-the-dark. As it proceeds, "Daddy"'s continuous life-rhythms—the assonance, consonance, and especially the sustained *oo* sounds—triumph over either the personal or the cultural-historical imagery. The sheer sense of organic life in the interwoven sounds carries the verse forward in boisterous spirit and communicates an underlying feeling of comedy that is also echoed in the repeated failure of the speaker to perform her exorcism.

Ultimately, "Daddy" is like an emotional, psychological, and historical autopsy, a final report. There is no real progress. The poet is in the same place in the beginning as in the end. She begins the poem as a hesitant but familiar fairy-tale daughter who parodies her attempt to reconstruct the myth of her father. Suffocating in her shoe house, she is unable to do much with that "bag full of God." She ends as a murderous member of a mythical community enacting the ritual or vampire killing, but only for a surrogate vampire, not the real thing ("The vampire who said he was you"). Although it seems that the speaker has moved from identification with the persecuted to identify as persecutor, Jew to vampire-killer, powerless to powerful, she has simply enacted a performance that allows her to live with what is unchangeable. She has used her art to stave off suffocation and performs her self-contempt with a degree of bravado.   [1980]

LYNDA K. BUNDTZEN

From *Plath's Incarnations*

Educated at the University of Minnesota, where she earned a B.A. in 1968, and the University of Chicago, where she earned a Ph.D. in 1972, Lynda Bundtzen (b. 1947) teaches at Williams College. A Renaissance scholar with a strong interest in women's issues, she teaches and writes on subjects that range from Shakespeare to

Thelma and Louise. Plath's Incarnations *was published in 1983. Her latest book is* The Other Ariel *(2001).*

In "Daddy," Plath is conscious of her complicity in creating and worshiping a father-colossus.

> You stand at the blackboard, daddy,
> In the picture I have of you,
> A cleft in your chin instead of your foot
> But no less a devil for that, no not
> Any less the black man who
>
> Bit my pretty red heart in two.
> I was ten when they buried you.
> At twenty I tried to die
> And get back, back, back to you.
> I thought even the bones would do.

The photograph is of an ordinary man, a teacher, with a cleft chin. She imaginatively transforms him into a devil who broke her heart, and she tells her audience precisely what she is doing. As Plath describes "Daddy," it is "spoken by a girl with an Electra complex. Her father died while she thought he was God. Her case is complicated by the fact that her father was also a Nazi and her mother very possibly part Jewish. In the daughter the two strains marry and paralyze each other — she has to act out the awful little allegory once over before she is free of it." The poem is a figurative drama about mourning — about the human impulse to keep a dead loved one alive emotionally. And it is about mourning gone haywire — a morbid inability to let go of the dead. The child was unready for her father's death, which is why, she says, she must kill him a second time. She resurrected Daddy and sustained his unnatural existence in her psyche as a vampire, sacrificing her own life's blood, her vitality, to a dead man. The worship of this father-god, she now realizes, is self-destructive.

There is nothing unconscious about the poem; instead it seems to force into consciousness the child's dread and love for the father, so that these feelings may be resolved. Plath skillfully evokes the child's world with her own versions of Mother Goose rhymes. Like the "old woman who lived in a shoe and had so many children she didn't know what to do," she has tried to live in the confines of the black shoe that is Daddy. Like Chicken Little, waiting for the sky to fall in, she lives under an omnipresent swastika "So black no sky could squeak through." And Daddy is a fallen giant toppled over and smothering, it seems, the entire United States. He has one grey toe (recalling Otto Plath's gangrened appendage) dangling like a Frisco seal in the Pacific and his head lies in the Atlantic.

The Mother Goose rhythms gradually build to a goose step march as the mourning process turns inward. She feels more than sorrow, now guilt, for Daddy's death and this guilt leads to feelings of inadequacy, acts of self-abasement, and finally self-murder. Nothing she can do will appease the guilt: she tries to learn his language; she tries to kill herself; she marries a man in his image. It will not do.

The self-hatred must be turned outward again into "*You* do not do" by a very self-conscious transformation of a mild-mannered professor into an active oppressor. Her emotional paralysis is acted out as a struggle between Nazi man and Jewess, and, I would argue, the Jewess wins. The poem builds toward the imaginary stake driving, the dancing and stamping and "Daddy, daddy, you bastard, I'm through." Not necessarily through with life, as many critics have read this line, but through with the paralysis, powerlessness, guilt. At last Daddy — the Nazi Daddy she frightened herself with, and not the real one, the professor — is at rest.

Plath's control over ambivalent feelings toward her father is probably the   5
result of their availability for conscious artistic manipulation. She had already written several poems about her dead father when she composed "Daddy," and we also know from a conversation recorded by Steiner that she had "worked through" her emotions in therapy. "She talked freely about her father's death when she was nine and her reactions to it. 'He was an autocrat,' she recalled. 'I adored and despised him, and I probably wished many times that he were dead. When he obliged me and died, I imagined that I had killed him.'" The result in "Daddy" is a powerful and remarkably accessible allegory about her adoration and dread, which ends in emotional catharsis.   [1983]

STEVEN GOULD AXELROD

From *Sylvia Plath: The Wound and the Cure of Words*

An expert in nineteenth- and twentieth-century American poetry, Steven Gould Axelrod (b. 1944) was educated at the University of California at Los Angeles and served as chair of the English Department at the University of California at Riverside, where he received a Distinguished Teaching Award in 1989. His publications include book-length works on modern and contemporary poets. Sylvia Plath: The Wound and the Cure of Words *was published in 1990.*

The covert protest of "The Colossus" eventually transformed itself into the overt rebellion of "Daddy." Although this poem too has traditionally been read as "personal" or "confessional," Margaret Homans has more recently suggested that it concerns a woman's dislocated relations to speech. Plath herself introduced it on the BBC as the opposite of confession, as a constructed fiction: "Here is a poem spoken by a girl with an Electra complex. Her father died while she thought he was God. Her case is complicated by the fact that her father was also a Nazi and her mother very possibly part Jewish. In the daughter the two strains marry and paralyze each other — she has to act out the awful little allegory once over before she is free of it." We might interpret this preface as an accurate retelling of the poem; or we might regard it as a case of an author's estrangement from her text, on the order of Coleridge's preface to "Kubla Khan" in which he claims to be unable to finish the poem, having forgotten what it was about. However we interpret Plath's preface, we must agree that "Daddy" is dramatic and allegorical, since its details depart freely from the facts of her biography. In this poem she again figures her unresolved conflicts with paternal authority as a textual issue. Significantly, her father was a published writer, and his successor, her husband, was also a writer. Her preface asserts that the poem concerns a young woman's paralyzing self-division, which she can defeat only through allegorical representation. Recalling that paralysis was one of Plath's main tropes for literary incapacity, we begin to see that the poem evokes the female poet's anxiety of authorship and specifically Plath's strategy of delivering herself from that anxiety by making it the topic of her discourse. Viewed from this perspective, "Daddy" enacts the woman poet's struggle with "daddy-poetry." It represents her effort to eject the "buried male muse" from her invention process and the "jealous gods" from her audience.

Plath wrote "Daddy" several months after Hughes left her, on the day she learned that he had agreed to a divorce. George Brown and Tirril Harris have shown that early loss makes one especially vulnerable to subsequent loss, and Plath seems to have defended against depression by almost literally throwing herself into her poetry. She followed "Daddy" with a host of poems that she considered her greatest achievement to date: "Medusa," "The Jailer," "Lady Lazarus," "Ariel," the bee sequence, and others. The letters she wrote to her mother and brother on the day of "Daddy," and then again four days later, brim with a sense of artistic self-discovery: "Writing like mad. . . . Terrific stuff, as if domesticity had choked me." Composing at the "still blue, almost eternal hour before the baby's cry, before the glassy music of the milkman, settling his bottles," she experienced an enormous surge in creative energy. Yet she also expressed feelings of misery: "The half year ahead seems like a lifetime, and the half behind an endless hell." She was again contemplating things German: a trip to the Austrian Alps, a renewed effort to learn the language. If "German" was Randall Jarrell's "favorite country," it was not hers, yet it returned to her discourse like clockwork at times of psychic distress. Clearly Plath was attempting to find and to evoke in her art what she could not find or communicate in her life. She wished to compensate for her fragmenting social existence by investing herself in her texts: "Hope, when free, to write myself out of this hole." Desperately eager to sacrifice her "flesh," which was "wasted," to her "mind and spirit," which were "fine," she wrote "Daddy" to demonstrate the existence of her voice, which had been silent or subservient for so long. She wrote it to prove her "genius."

Plath projected her struggle for textual identity onto the figure of a partly Jewish young woman who learns to express her anger at the patriarch and at his language of male mastery, which is as foreign to her as German, as "obscene" as murder, and as meaningless as "gobbledygoo." The patriarch's death "off beautiful Nauset" recalls Plath's journal entry in which she associated the "green seaweeded water" at "Nauset Light" with "the deadness of a being . . . who no longer creates." Daddy's deadness — suggesting Plath's unwillingness to let her father, her education, her library, or her husband inhibit her any longer — inspires the poem's speaker to her moment of illumination. At a basic level, "Daddy" concerns its own violent, transgressive birth as a text, its origin in a culture that regards it as illegitimate — a judgment the speaker hurls back on the patriarch himself when she labels *him* a bastard. Plath's unaccommodating worldview, which was validated by much in her childhood and adult experience, led her to understand literary tradition not as an expanding universe of beneficial influence . . . but as a closed universe in which every addition required a corresponding subtraction — a Spencerian agon in which only the fittest survived. If Plath's speaker was to be born as a poet, a patriarch must die.

As in "The Colossus," the father here appears as a force or an object rather than as a person. Initially he takes the form of an immense "black shoe," capable of stamping on his victim. Immediately thereafter he becomes a marble "statue," cousin to the monolith of the earlier poem. He then transforms into Nazi Germany, the archetypal totalitarian state. When the protagonist mentions Daddy's "boot in the face," she may be alluding to Orwell's comment in *1984*, "If you want a picture of the future, imagine a boot stomping on a human face — forever." Eventually the father declines in stature from God to a devil to a dying vampire. Perhaps he shrinks under the force of his victim's denunciation, which de-creates him as a power as it creates him as figure. But whatever his size, he never assumes human dimensions, aspirations, and relations — except when posing as a teacher in a photograph. Like the colossus, he remains figurative and symbolic, not individual.

Nevertheless, the male figure of "Daddy" does differ significantly from that   5
of "The Colossus." In the earlier poem, which emphasizes his lips, mouth, throat, tongue, and voice, the colossus allegorically represents the power of speech, however fragmented and resistant to the protagonist's ministrations. In the later poem Daddy remains silent, apart from the gobbledygoo attributed to him once. He uses his mouth primarily for biting and for drinking blood. The poem emphasizes his feet and, implicitly, his phallus. He is a "black shoe," a statue with "one gray toe," a "boot." The speaker, estranged from him by fear, could never tell where he put his "foot," his "root." Furthermore, she is herself silenced by his shoe: "I never could talk to you." Daddy is no "male muse," not even one in ruins, but frankly a male censor. His boot in the face of "every woman" is presumably lodged in her mouth. He stands for all the elements in the literary situation and in the female ephebe's internalization of it, that prevent her from producing any words at all, even copied or subservient ones. Appropriately, Daddy can be killed only by being stamped on: he lives and dies by force, not language. If "The Colossus" tells a tale of the patriarch's speech, his grunts and brays, "Daddy" tells a tale of the daughter's effort to speak.

Thus we are led to another important difference between the two poems. The "I" of "The Colossus" acquires her identity only through serving her "father," whereas the "I" of "Daddy" actuates her gift only through opposition to him. The latter poem precisely inscribes the plot of Plath's dream novel of

1958: "a girl's search for her dead father—for an outside authority which must be developed, instead, from the inside." As the child of a Nazi, the girl could "hardly speak," but as a Jew she begins "to talk" and to acquire an identity. In Plath's allegory, the outsider Jew corresponds to "the rebel, the artist, the odd," and particularly to the woman artist. Otto Rank's *Beyond Psychology*, which had a lasting influence on her, explicitly compares women to Jews, since "woman . . . has suffered from the very beginning a fate similar to that of the Jew, namely, suppression, slavery, confinement, and subsequent persecution." Rank, whose discourse I would consider tainted by anti-Semitism, argues that Jews speak a language of pessimistic "self-hatred" that differs essentially from the language of the majority cultures in which they find themselves. He analogously, though more sympathetically, argues that woman speaks in a language different from man's, and that as a result of man's denial of woman's world, "woman's 'native tongue' has hitherto been unknown or at least unheard." Although Rank's essentializing of woman's "nature" lapses into the sexist clichés of his time ("intuitive," "irrational"), his idea of linguistic difference based on gender and his analogy between Jewish and female speech seem to have embedded themselves in the substructure of "Daddy" (and in many of Plath's other texts as well). For Plath, as later for Adrienne Rich, the Holocaust and the patriarchy's silencing of women were linked outcomes of the masculinist interpretation of the world. Political insurrection and female self-assertion also interlaced symbolically. In "Daddy," Plath's speaker finds her voice and motive by identifying herself as antithetical to her Fascist father. Rather than getting the colossus "glued" and properly jointed, she wishes to stick herself "together with glue," an act that seems to require her father's dismemberment. Previously devoted to the patriarch—both in "The Colossus" and in memories evoked in "Daddy" of trying to "get back" to him—she now seeks only to escape from him and to see him destroyed.

Plath has unleashed the anger, normal in mourning as well as in revolt, that she suppressed in the earlier poem. But she has done so at a cost. Let us consider her childlike speaking voice. The language of "Daddy," beginning with its title, is often regressive. The "I" articulates herself by moving backward in time, using the language of nursery rhymes and fairy tales (the little old woman who lived in a shoe, the black man of the forest). Such language accords with a child's conception of the world, not an adult's. Plath's assault on the language of "daddy-poetry" has turned inward, on the language of her own poem, which teeters precariously on the edge of a preverbal abyss— represented by the eerie, keening "oo" sound with which a majority of the verses end. And then let us consider the play on "through" at the poem's conclusion. Although that last line allows for multiple readings, one interpretation is that the "I" has unconsciously carried out her father's wish: her discourse, by transforming itself into cathartic oversimplifications, has undone itself.

Yet the poem does contain its verbal violence by means more productive than silence. In a letter to her brother, Plath referred to "Daddy" as "gruesome," while on almost the same day she described it to A. Alvarez as a piece of "light verse." She later read it on the BBC in a highly ironic tone of voice. The poem's unique spell derives from its rhetorical complexity: its variegated and perhaps bizarre fusion of the horrendous and the comic. . . . [I]t both shares and remains detached from the fixation of its protagonist. The protagonist herself seems detached from her own fixation. She is "split in the most complex fashion," as Plath wrote of Ivan Karamazov in her Smith College honors thesis. Plath's speaker uses potentially self-mocking melodramatic terms to describe both her opponent ("so black no sky could squeak through") and herself ("poor and white"). While this aboriginal speaker quite literally expresses black-and-white thinking, her civilized double possesses a sensibility sophisticated enough to subject such thinking to irony. Thus the poem expresses feelings that it simultaneously parodies — it may be parodying the very idea of feeling. The tension between erudition and simplicity in the speaker's voice appears in her pairings that juxtapose adult with childlike diction: "breathe or Achoo," "your Luftwaffe, your gobbledygoo." She can expound such adult topics as Taroc packs, Viennese beer, and Tyrolean snowfall; can specify death camps by name; and can employ an adult vocabulary of "recover," "ancestress," "Aryan," "*Meinkampf*," "obscene," and "bastard." Yet she also has recourse to a more primitive lexicon that includes "chuffing," "your fat black heart," and "my pretty red heart." She proves herself capable of careful intellectual discriminations ("so I never could tell"), conventionalized description ("beautiful Nauset"), and moral analogy ("if I've killed one man, I've killed two"), while also exhibiting regressive fantasies (vampires), repetitions ("wars, wars, wars"), and inarticulateness ("panzer-man, panzer-man, O You — "). She oscillates between calm reflection ("You stand at the blackboard, daddy, / In the picture I have of you") and mad incoherence ("Ich, ich, ich, ich"). Her sophisticated language puts her wild language in an ironic perspective, removing the discourse from the control of the archaic self who understands experience only in extreme terms.

The ironies in "Daddy" proliferate in unexpected ways, however. When the speaker proclaims categorically that "every woman adores a Fascist," she is subjecting her victimization to irony by suggesting that sufferers choose, or at least accommodate themselves to, their suffering. But she is also subjecting her authority to irony, since her claim about "every woman" is transparently false. It simply parodies patriarchal commonplaces, such as those advanced . . . concerning "feminine masochism." The adult, sophisticated self seems to be speaking here: Who else would have the confidence to make a sociological generalization? Yet the content of the assertion, if taken straightforwardly, returns us to the regressive self who is dominated by extravagant emotions she cannot begin to understand. Plath's mother wished that Plath would write about "decent, courageous people," and she herself heard an inner voice demanding that she be a perfect "paragon" in her language and feeling. But in the speaker of "Daddy," she inscribed the opposite of such a paragon: a divided self whose veneer of civilization is breached and infected by unhealthy instincts.

Plath's irony cuts both ways. At the same time that the speaker's sophisti-   10
cated voice undercuts her childish voice, reducing its melodrama to comedy,
the childish or maddened voice undercuts the pretensions of the sophisticated
voice, revealing the extremity of suffering masked by its ironies. While demonstrating the inadequacy of thinking and feeling in opposites, the poem implies
that such a mode can locate truths denied more complex cognitive and affec-
tive systems. The very moderation of the normal adult intelligence, its tolerance of ambiguity, its defenses against the primal energies of the id, results in
falsification. Reflecting Schiller's idea that the creative artist experiences a
"momentary and passing madness" (quoted by Freud in a passage of *The Interpretation of Dreams* that Plath underscored), "Daddy" gives voice to that madness. Yet the poem's sophisticated awareness, its comic vision, probably wins
out in the end, since the poem concludes by curtailing the power of its extreme
discourse. . . . Furthermore, Plath distanced herself from the poem's aboriginal
voice by introducing her text as "a poem spoken by a girl with an Electra complex" — that is, as a study of the *girl's* pathology rather than her father's — and
as an allegory that will "free" her from that pathology. She also distanced herself by reading the poem in a tone that emphasized its irony. And finally, she
distanced herself by laying the poem's wild voice permanently to rest after
October. The aboriginal vision was indeed purged. "Daddy" represents not
Dickinson's madness that is divinest sense, but rather an entry into a style of
discourse and a mastery of it. The poem realizes the trope of suffering by means
of an inherent irony that both questions and validates the trope in the same
gestures, and that finally allows the speaker to conclude the discourse and to
remove herself from the trope with a sense of completion rather than wrenching, since the irony was present from the very beginning.

Plath's poetic revolt in "Daddy" liberated her pent-up creativity, but the
momentary success sustained her little more than self-sacrifice had done.
"Daddy" became another stage in her development, an unrepeatable experiment, a vocal opening that closed itself at once. The poem is not only an elegy
for the power of "daddy-poetry" but for the powers of speech Plath discovered
in composing it.

When we consider "Daddy" generically, a further range of implications
presents itself. Although we could profitably consider the poem as the dramatic
monologue Plath called it in her BBC broadcast, let us regard it instead as the
kind of poem most readers have taken it to be: a domestic poem. I have chosen
this term, rather than M. L. Rosenthal's better-known "confessional poem" or
the more neutral "autobiographical poem," because "confessional poem" implies a confession rather than a making (though Steven Hoffman and Lawrence
Kramer have recently indicated the mode's conventions) and because "autobiographical poem" is too general for our purpose. I shall define the domestic
poem as one that represents and comments on a protagonist's relationship to
one or more family members, usually a parent, child, or spouse. To focus our
discussion even further, I shall emphasize poetry that specifically concerns a
father.   *[1990]*

TIM KENDALL
From *Sylvia Plath: A Critical Study*

Tim Kendall edits Thumbscrew *and is the author of* Paul Muldoon *(2004). He received an Eric Gregory Award for his poetry in 1997 and appears in the* Oxford Poets 2000 *anthology. He was the Thomas Chatterton British Academy Lecturer for 2001 at the University of Bristol and is currently a professor of English literature at the University of Exeter. In 2005, Kendall was awarded the lucrative Philip Leverhulme Prize. This selection is from a book he published in 2001.*

Plath's journals . . . indicate that as late as December 1958, the poet was seriously considering a Ph.D. in psychology: "Awesome to confront a program of study which is so monumental: all human experience."[1] The previous day Plath had discovered in Freud's *Mourning and Melancholia* "an almost exact description of my feelings and reasons for suicide."[2] She felt creatively vindicated when she found parallels between her own life and writings and those of Freud and Jung: "All this relates in a most meaningful way my instinctive images with perfectly valid psychological analysis. However, I am the victim, rather than the analyst."[3] In these examples, experience precedes the psychoanalytical explanation; Freud and Jung confirm what Plath already knows. Despite her emphasis on victimhood, such passages show how she transforms herself into her own case history, becoming simultaneously victim and analyst. The same dual role is apparent in "Daddy," which Plath introduces for BBC radio in terms of Freudian allegory:

> Here is a poem spoken by a girl with an Electra complex. Her father died while she thought he was God. Her case is complicated by the fact that her father was also a Nazi and her mother very possibly part Jewish. In the daughter the two strains marry and paralyze each other — she has to act out the awful little allegory once over before she is free of it.

"Daddy," built on poetic repetition, is therefore a poem about a compulsion to repeat, and its psychology is characterized according to Freudian principles. Repetition necessitates performance — the speaker must "*act out* the awful little allegory once over" in order to escape it. Whether she does succeed in escaping depends on the poem's ambivalent last line: "Daddy, daddy, you bastard, I'm through." "I'm through" can mean (especially to an American ear) "I've had enough of you," but it also means "I've got away from you, I'm free of you," or "I'm done for, I'm beaten," or even "I've finished what I have to say." The speaker's ability to free herself from the urge to repeat remains in the balance.

These dilemmas and uncertainties can be traced back, as Plath suggests, to Freud's accounts of compulsive behavior. "Daddy" adopts a Freudian understanding of infantile sexuality (the Electra complex), a Freudian belief in transference (the vampire-husband "said he was you," and the father also shifts identities), and a Freudian attitude towards repetitive behavior. In a passage from *Beyond the Pleasure Principle* which might conveniently serve to diagnose the speaker of "Daddy," Freud argues that,

> The patient cannot remember the whole of what is repressed in him, and what he cannot remember may be precisely the essential part of it. Thus he acquires no sense of the conviction of the correctness of the construction that has been communicated to him. He is obliged to *repeat* the repressed material as a contemporary experience instead of, as the physician would prefer to see, *remembering* it as something belonging to the past. These reproductions, which emerge with such unwished-for exactitude, always have as their subject some portion of infantile sexual life — of the Oedipus complex, that is, and its derivatives; and they are invariably acted out in the sphere of the transference, of the patient's relation to the physician.[4]

This illuminates Plath's attempts to persuade the dead father to communicate. The refusal of the father-figure, in his various transferred roles of colossus, Nazi, teacher, and vampire, to become "something belonging to the past" is evident in the speaker's need to kill him repeatedly. He must be imaginatively disinterred in order to be killed again, and even as one of the undead, he must be destroyed with a stake in his heart. This repetitive pattern of disappearance and return represents Plath's version of the *fort-da* game as famously described in *Beyond the Pleasure Principle*, where the child's repeated and "long-drawn-out 'o-o-o-o' " is only a slight vowel modulation away from the "oo" repetitions of "Daddy." The father-figure is a "contemporary experience," not a memory; and, as Freud explains, the reason for his continuing presence lies in the speaker's "infantile sexual life." The father's early death ensures that she cannot progress, and her sense of selfhood is stutteringly confined within a compulsion to repeat:

> I never could talk to you.
> The tongue stuck in my jaw.
>
> It stuck in a barb wire snare.
> Ich, ich, ich, ich,
> I could hardly speak.

Repetition occurs when Plath's speaker gets stuck in the barb wire snare of communication with her father. She is unable to move beyond the self. This proposes a more fundamental understanding of repetitive words and phrases than those suggested by Blessing or Shapiro. "Daddy" implies that each local repetition, whatever its microcosmic effects, symptomizes a larger behavioral pattern of repetition compulsion. The poem's title, the "oo" rhymes, and the nursery-rhyme rhythms all reinforce this suggestion of a mind struggling to free itself from the need to repeat infantile trauma. Such infantilism, exhibited by an adult persona, contributes to the poem's transgressive humor: Plath read "Daddy" aloud to a friend, reports Anne Stevenson, "in a mocking, comical voice that made both women fall about with laughter."[5]

Psychoanalyzing the speaker of "Daddy" in the Freudian terms proposed by Plath herself is a valuable exercise which carries important implications for

Ariel's use of repetition, but it still does not settle the nature of the poet's complex relationship to the "girl with an Electra complex." Plath's introduction for radio seems to reverse the pattern in her journals: now Freud becomes a source as much as an explanation. Her introduction also reverses the reader's experience of the poem. "Daddy" conveys a power and an intimacy which challenge any hygienic separation of poet and poetic voice. With such contradictory evidence, the gulf between poet and persona, cold-blooded technique and blood-hot emotion, analyst and victim, seems unbridgeable. If these divisions can be successfully reconciled, it is through Plath's emphasis on performance and repetition. Freud's account of repetition compulsion shares with Plath's description of "Daddy" a crucial verb: just as Plath's persona must "act out the awful little allegory," so Freud notes that the Oedipus complex and its derivatives are "invariably acted out in the sphere of the transference." Repetition guarantees performance, and performance requires an audience. Freud notes, as if glossing "Daddy," that "the artistic play and artistic imitation carried out by adults, which, unlike children's, are aimed at an audience, do not spare the spectators (for instance, in tragedy) the most painful experiences and can yet be felt by them as highly enjoyable." Plath categorized "Daddy" as "light verse,"[6] a genre which W. H. Auden considered to be "written for performance."[7] "Daddy" may be written for performance, but it pushes the "painful experiences" and the entertainment value to extremes which many readers find intolerable. Freud's Aristotelian concern — why is tragedy pleasurable? — also seems a valid question to ask of Plath's poem: "Daddy" derives its aesthetic pleasures from incest, patricide, suicide, and the Nazi extermination camps.

These taboo-breaking juxtapositions of personal and private realms help explain the poem's notoriety. However, controversy over "Daddy" always returns eventually to Plath's relationship with her persona. Seamus Heaney's principled objection, for example, discerns no difference at all:

> A poem like "Daddy," however brilliant a *tour de force* it can be acknowledged to be, and however its violence and vindictiveness can be understood or excused in light of the poet's parental and marital relations, remains, nevertheless, so entangled in biographical circumstances and rampages so permissively in the history of other people's sorrows that it simply withdraws its rights to our sympathy.[8]

Heaney's pointed phrase "rampages so permissively" might be disputed as an unfair rhetorical flourish, especially in the context of Plath's hard-earned Emersonian desire to assimilate and her wider theological explorations. But Heaney's most revealing word is his last: "sympathy." Heaney refers to one aspect of Aristotelian catharsis — pity for the suffering of others — which he claims that "Daddy" fails to earn. It is not surprising that his critical decorum should come into conflict with a poem which is so consciously and manifestly indecorous. Heaney reads "Daddy" purely as the protest of the poet-victim, who behaves vindictively because of her difficult parental and marital relations. This fails to credit Plath with the self-awareness to be acting deliberately — to be performing. In "Daddy" Plath seeks no one's "sympathy"; she has once more become victim and analyst, the girl with the Electra complex and the physician who diagnoses her condition. Plath wonders in her journal whether "our desire to investigate psychology [is] a desire to get Beuscher's [her psychiatrist's] power and handle it ourselves."[9] "Daddy," as her introduction makes clear, represents a poetic handling of that power. Freud states that the patient must acquire "some degree of aloofness."[10] "Daddy" is the work of a poet so aloof as to render allegorical, act out, and psychoanalyze, her own mental history.   [2001]

Notes

1. Sylvia Plath, *The Journals of Sylvia Plath, 1950–1962*, ed. Karen V. Kukil (London: Faber & Faber, 2000), p. 452.
2. Ibid., p. 447.
3. Ibid., p. 514.
4. S. Freud, *Beyond the Pleasure Principle*, tr. and ed. J. Strachey (Hogarth, 1961), p. 12.
5. A. Stevenson, *Bitter Fame: A Life of Sylvia Plath* (Viking, 1989), p. 277.
6. A. Alvarez, "Sylvia Plath," in C. Newman (ed.), *The Art of Sylvia Plath* (Indiana UP, 1970), p. 66.
7. W. H. Auden (ed.), *The Oxford Book of Light Verse* (OUP, 1938), p. ix.
8. S. Heaney, "The Indefatigable Hoof-taps: Sylvia Plath," *The Government of the Tongue* (Faber, 1988), p. 165.
9. *Journals*, p. 449.
10. *Beyond the Pleasure Principle*, p. 13.

≡ MAKING COMPARISONS

1. "Daddy" seems to be a protest, but some critics see it as more than that. Which of the four commentaries makes the best case that it is more than a revolt against the speaker's father?

2. Which critic seems to answer most of the perplexing questions of this poem—for example, the father as Nazi, the father as vampire, the childlike rhythms, the speaker's vengefulness, her viciousness?

3. Do these critics make any similar points? How might you describe them? What is their most striking difference?

≡ WRITING ABOUT ISSUES

1. Choose one of the critical commentaries in this cluster and argue that the textual evidence supporting its assertions is, or is not, adequate.

2. Imagine you are Sylvia Plath. After reading these four essays, write a letter to a literary journal either attacking or praising these critics.

3. Write an essay arguing that your own reading of "Daddy" makes more sense than those of Broe, Bundtzen, Axelrod, or Kendall. Assume that the audience for the criticism is your class.

4. There are dozens of critical commentaries on Plath's "Daddy." Some were written soon after the poem's publication; others are quite recent.

Locate an early piece of criticism, and compare it to one published in the past two years. Do these critics make similar or different points? Is one more concerned with the text, with gender issues, with cultural concerns, or with what other critics say? Write a brief comparison of the two, explaining your evidence.

Mothers and Daughters: Stories

TILLIE OLSEN, "I Stand Here Ironing"

AMY TAN, "Two Kinds"

ALICE WALKER, "Everyday Use"

We all know stories of parents who want to mold their children, stories of mothers and fathers who push their reluctant children to be fashion models or beauty queens or Little League stars. Some studies of adults playing musical instruments in orchestras say the biggest factor in their success was the commitment of their parents. But we also hear about tennis prodigies who burn out at sixteen because of parental pressure. Mothers and daughters have always struggled with each other over life goals and identity. How much guidance is enough? How much is too much? What is a reasonable balance between preparing a child for life's challenges and shaping a child to act out the mother's fantasy or her internal vision of what the good life is? And no matter where parents fall on this continuum, are there childhood events so powerful that we cannot get beyond them? The following three stories chart the difficulties mothers and daughters have with each other and with the social and cultural forces that influence our destiny.

≡ BEFORE YOU READ

Are your parents responsible for your successes? Your failures? Do you wish that your parents had pushed you to succeed more insistently? Are you annoyed that your parents set unreasonable standards for you?

TILLIE OLSEN
I Stand Here Ironing

Born in Omaha, Nebraska, to Russian immigrants of Jewish descent and socialist views, Tillie Olsen (1912–2007) was an activist in social and political causes all of her life, often choosing family, work, union, feminist, or other political causes over writing. Although her publishing record is short, its quality is greatly admired. In addition to critically respected short stories, Olsen wrote a novel, Yonnondio *(1974), which paints a vivid picture of a coal-mining family during the Depression. Her essay collection,* Silences *(1978), stimulated debate about class and gender as factors in the creation of literature and led both directly and indirectly to the revived interest in works by women writers. The mother of four daughters, Olsen often wrote about generational relationships within families. "I Stand Here Ironing" is from her 1961 collection of stories,* Tell Me a Riddle.

I stand here ironing, and what you asked me moves tormented back and forth with the iron.

"I wish you would manage the time to come in and talk with me about your daughter. I'm sure you can help me understand her. She's a youngster who needs help and whom I'm deeply interested in helping."

"Who needs help." . . . Even if I came, what good would it do? You think because I am her mother I have a key, or that in some way you could use me as a key? She has lived for nineteen years. There is all that life that has happened outside of me, beyond me.

And when is there time to remember, to sift, to weigh, to estimate, to total? I will start and there will be an interruption and I will have to gather it all together again. Or I will become engulfed with all I did or did not do, with what should have been and what cannot be helped.

She was a beautiful baby. The first and only one of our five that was beauti-   5
ful at birth. You do not guess how new and uneasy her tenancy in her now-loveliness. You did not know her all those years she was thought homely, or see her poring over her baby pictures, making me tell her over and over how beautiful she had been — and would be, I would tell her — and was now, to the seeing eye. But the seeing eyes were few or nonexistent. Including mine.

I nursed her. They feel that's important nowadays. I nursed all the children, but with her, with all the fierce rigidity of first motherhood, I did like the books then said. Though her cries battered me to trembling and my breasts ached with swollenness, I waited till the clock decreed.

Why do I put that first? I do not even know if it matters, or if it explains anything.

She was a beautiful baby. She blew shining bubbles of sound. She loved motion, loved light, loved color and music and textures. She would lie on the floor in her blue overalls patting the surface so hard in ecstasy her hands and feet would blur. She was a miracle to me, but when she was eight months old I had to leave her daytimes with the woman downstairs to whom she was no miracle at all, for I worked or looked for work and for Emily's father, who "could no longer endure" (he wrote in his good-bye note) "sharing want with us."

I was nineteen. It was the pre-relief, pre-WPA world of the depression. I would start running as soon as I got off the streetcar, running up the stairs, the place smelling sour, and awake or asleep to startle awake, when she saw me she would break into a clogged weeping that could not be comforted, a weeping I can hear yet.

After a while I found a job hashing at night so I could be with her days,   10
and it was better. But it came to where I had to bring her to his family and leave her.

It took a long time to raise the money for her fare back. Then she got chicken pox and I had to wait longer. When she finally came, I hardly knew her, walking quick and nervous like her father, looking like her father, thin, and dressed in a shoddy red that yellowed her skin and glared at the pockmarks. All the baby loveliness gone.

She was two. Old enough for nursery school they said, and I did not know then what I know now — the fatigue of the long day, and the lacerations of group life in the kinds of nurseries that are only parking places for children.

Except that it would have made no difference if I had known. It was the only place there was. It was the only way we could be together, the only way I could hold a job.

And even without knowing, I knew. I knew the teacher that was evil because all these years it has curdled into my memory, the little boy hunched in the corner, her rasp, "why aren't you outside, because Alvin hits you? that's no reason, go out, scaredy." I knew Emily hated it even if she did not clutch and implore "don't go Mommy" like the other children, mornings.

She always had a reason why we should stay home. Momma, you look   15
sick. Momma, I feel sick. Momma, the teachers aren't there today, they're sick. Momma, we can't go, there was a fire there last night. Momma, it's a holiday today, no school, they told me.

But never a direct protest, never rebellion. I think of our others in their three-, four-year-oldness — the explosions, the tempers, the denunciations, the demands — and I feel suddenly ill. I put the iron down. What in me demanded that goodness in her? And what was the cost, the cost to her of such goodness?

The old man living in the back once said in his gentle way: "You should smile at Emily more when you look at her." What *was* in my face when I looked at her? I loved her. There were all the acts of love.

It was only with the others I remembered what he said, and it was the face of joy, and not of care or tightness or worry I turned to them — too late for Emily. She does not smile easily, let alone almost always as her brothers and sisters do. Her face is closed and sombre, but when she wants, how fluid. You must have seen it in her pantomimes, you spoke of her rare gift for comedy on the stage that rouses laughter out of the audience so dear they applaud and applaud and do not want to let her go.

Where does it come from, that comedy? There was none of it in her when she came back to me that second time, after I had to send her away again. She had a new daddy now to learn to love, and I think perhaps it was a better time.

Except when we left her alone nights, telling ourselves she was old enough.   20
"Can't you go some other time, Mommy, like tomorrow?" she would ask. "Will it be just a little while you'll be gone? Do you promise?"

The time we came back, the front door open, the clock on the floor in the hall. She rigid awake. "It wasn't just a little while. I didn't cry. Three times I called you, just three times, and then I ran downstairs to open the door so you could come faster. The clock talked loud. I threw it away, it scared me what it talked."

She said the clock talked loud again that night I went to the hospital to have Susan. She was delirious with the fever that comes before red measles, but she was fully conscious all the week I was gone and the week after we were home when she could not come near the new baby or me.

She did not get well. She stayed skeleton thin, not wanting to eat, and night after night she had nightmares. She would call for me, and I would rouse from exhaustion to sleepily call back: "You're all right, darling, go to sleep, it's just a dream," and if she still called, in a sterner voice, "now go to sleep, Emily, there's nothing to hurt you." Twice, only twice, when I had to get up for Susan anyhow, I went in to sit with her.

Now when it is too late (as if she would let me hold her and comfort her like I do the others) I get up and go to her at once at her moan or restless stirring. "Are you awake, Emily? Can I get you something?" And the answer is always the same: "No, I'm all right, go back to sleep, Mother." 25

They persuaded me at the clinic to send her away to a convalescent home in the country where "she can have the kind of food and care you can't manage for her, and you'll be free to concentrate on the new baby." They still send children to that place. I see pictures on the society page of sleek young women planning affairs to raise money for it, or dancing at the affairs, or decorating Easter eggs or filling Christmas stockings for the children.

They never have a picture of the children so I do not know if the girls still wear those gigantic red bows and the ravaged looks on the every other Sunday when parents can come to visit "unless otherwise notified" — as we were notified the first six weeks.

Oh it is a handsome place, green lawns and tall trees and fluted flower beds. High up on the balconies of each cottage the children stand, the girls in their red bows and white dresses, the boys in white suits and giant red ties. The parents stand below shrieking up to be heard and the children shriek down to be heard, and between them the invisible wall "Not To Be Contaminated by Parental Germs or Physical Affection."

There was a tiny girl who always stood hand in hand with Emily. Her parents never came. One visit she was gone. "They moved her to Rose Cottage," Emily shouted in explanation. "They don't like you to love anybody here."

She wrote once a week, the labored writing of a seven-year-old. "I am fine. 30 How is the baby. If I write my leter nicly I will have a star. Love." There never was a star. We wrote every other day, letters she could never hold or keep but only hear read — once. "We simply do not have room for children to keep any personal possessions," they patiently explained when we pieced one Sunday's shrieking together to plead how much it would mean to Emily, who loved so to keep things, to be allowed to keep her letters and cards.

Each visit she looked frailer. "She isn't eating," they told us.

(They had runny eggs for breakfast or mush with lumps, Emily said later, I'd hold it in my mouth and not swallow. Nothing ever tasted good, just when they had chicken.)

It took us eight months to get her released home, and only the fact that she gained back so little of her seven lost pounds convinced the social worker.

I used to try to hold and love her after she came back, but her body would stay stiff, and after a while she'd push away. She ate little. Food sickened her, and I think much of life too. Oh she had physical lightness and brightness, twinkling by on skates, bouncing like a ball up and down up and down over the jump rope, skimming over the hill; but these were momentary.

She fretted about her appearance, thin and dark and foreign-looking at a 35 time when every little girl was supposed to look or thought she should look like a chubby blonde replica of Shirley Temple. The doorbell sometimes rang for her, but no one seemed to come and play in the house or to be a best friend. Maybe because we moved so much.

There was a boy she loved painfully through two school semesters. Months later she told me how she had taken pennies from my purse to buy him candy. "Licorice was his favorite and I brought him some every day, but he still liked Jennifer better'n me. Why, Mommy?" The kind of question for which there is no answer.

School was a worry for her. She was not glib or quick in a world where glibness and quickness were easily confused with ability to learn. To her overworked and exasperated teachers she was an overconscientious "slow learner" who kept trying to catch up and was absent entirely too often.

I let her be absent, though sometimes the illness was imaginary. How different from my now-strictness about attendance with the others. I wasn't working. We had a new baby. I was home anyhow. Sometimes, after Susan grew old enough, I would keep her home from school, too, to have them all together.

Mostly Emily had asthma, and her breathing, harsh and labored, would fill the house with a curiously tranquil sound. I would bring the two old dresser mirrors and her boxes of collections to her bed. She would select beads and single earrings, bottle tops and shells, dried flowers and pebbles, old postcards and scraps, all sorts of oddments; then she and Susan would play Kingdom, setting up landscapes and furniture, peopling them with action.

Those were the only times of peaceful companionship between her and   40
Susan. I have edged away from it, that poisonous feeling between them, that terrible balancing of hurts and needs I had to do between the two, and did so badly, those earlier years.

Oh there were conflicts between the others too, each one human, needing, demanding, hurting, taking—but only between Emily and Susan, no, Emily toward Susan that corroding resentment. It seems so obvious on the surface, yet it is not obvious; Susan, the second child, Susan, golden- and curly-haired and chubby, quick and articulate and assured, everything in appearance and manner Emily was not; Susan, not able to resist Emily's precious things, losing or sometimes clumsily breaking them; Susan telling jokes and riddles to company for applause while Emily sat silent (to say to me later: that was *my* riddle, Mother, I told it to Susan); Susan, who for all the five years' difference in age was just a year behind Emily in developing physically.

I am glad for that slow physical development that widened the difference between her and her contemporaries, though she suffered over it. She was too vulnerable for that terrible world of youthful competition, of preening and parading, of constant measuring of yourself against every other, of envy, "If I had that copper hair," "If I had that skin. . . ." She tormented herself enough about not looking like the others, there was enough of unsureness, the having to be conscious of words before you speak, the constant caring—what are they thinking of me? without having it all magnified by the merciless physical drives.

Ronnie is calling. He is wet and I change him. It is rare there is such a cry now. That time of motherhood is almost behind me when the ear is not one's own but must always be racked and listening for the child cry, the child call. We sit for a while and I hold him, looking out over the city spread in charcoal with its soft aisles of light. *"Shoogily,"* he breathes and curls closer. I carry him back to bed, asleep. *Shoogily.* A funny word, a family word, inherited from Emily, invented by her to say: *comfort.*

In this and other ways she leaves her seal, I say aloud. And startle at my saying it. What do I mean? What did I start to gather together, to try and make coherent? I was at the terrible, growing years. War years. I do not remember them well. I was working, there were four smaller ones now, there was not time for her. She had to help be a mother, and housekeeper, and shopper. She had to get her seal. Mornings of crisis and near hysteria trying to get lunches packed, hair combed, coats and shoes found, everyone to school or Child Care on time, the baby ready for transportation. And always the paper scribbled on by a smaller one, the book looked at by Susan then mislaid, the homework not done. Running out to that huge school where she was one, she was lost, she was a drop; suffering over the unpreparedness, stammering and unsure in her classes.

There was so little time left at night after the kids were bedded down. She would struggle over books, always eating (it was in those years she developed her enormous appetite that is legendary in our family) and I would be ironing, or preparing food for the next day, or writing V-mail to Bill, or tending the baby. Sometimes, to make me laugh, or out of her despair, she would imitate happenings or types at school.   45

I think I said once: "Why don't you do something like this in the school amateur show?" One morning she phoned me at work, hardly understandable through the weeping: "Mother, I did it. I won, I won; they gave me first prize; they clapped and clapped and wouldn't let me go."

Now suddenly she was Somebody, and as imprisoned in her difference as she had been in anonymity.

She began to be asked to perform at other high schools, even in colleges, then at city and statewide affairs. The first one we went to, I only recognized her that first moment when thin, shy, she almost drowned herself into the curtains. Then: Was this Emily? The control, the command, the convulsing and deadly clowning, the spell, then the roaring, stamping audience, unwilling to let this rare and precious laughter out of their lives.

Afterwards: You ought to do something about her with a gift like that — but without money or knowing how, what does one do? We have left it all to her, and the gift has so often eddied inside, clogged and clotted, as been used and growing.

She is coming. She runs up the stairs two at a time with her light graceful   50 step, and I know she is happy tonight. Whatever it was that occasioned your call did not happen today.

"Aren't you ever going to finish the ironing, Mother? Whistler painted his mother in a rocker. I'd have to paint mine standing over an ironing board." This is one of her communicative nights and she tells me everything and nothing as she fixes herself a plate of food out of the icebox.

She is so lovely. Why did you want me to come in at all? Why were you concerned? She will find her way.

She starts up the stairs to bed. "Don't get me up with the rest in the morning." "But I thought you were having midterms." "Oh, those," she comes back in, kisses me, and says quite lightly, "in a couple of years when we'll all be atom-dead they won't matter a bit."

She has said it before. She *believes* it. But because I have been dredging the past, and all that compounds a human being is so heavy and meaningful in me, I cannot endure it tonight.

I will never total it all. I will never come in to say: She was a child seldom   55
smiled at. Her father left me before she was a year old. I had to work her first six years when there was work, or I sent her home and to his relatives. There were years she had care she hated. She was dark and thin and foreign-looking in a world where the prestige went to blondeness and curly hair and dimples, she was slow where glibness was prized. She was a child of anxious, not proud, love. We were poor and could not afford for her the soil of easy growth. I was a young mother, I was a distracted mother. There were other children pushing up, demanding. Her younger sister seemed all that she was not. There were years she did not want me to touch her. She kept too much in herself, her life was such she had to keep too much in herself. My wisdom came too late. She has much to her and probably little will come of it. She is a child of her age, of depression, of war, of fear.

Let her be. So all that is in her will not bloom — but in how many does it? There is still enough left to live by. Only help her to know — help make it so there is cause for her to know — that she is more than this dress on the ironing board, helpless before the iron.   [1961]

▤ THINKING ABOUT THE TEXT

1. Is Olsen's last paragraph optimistic or pessimistic about personal destiny? Is there some support in the story for both perspectives?

2. There is an old expression: "To know all is to forgive all." Does this statement apply to "I Stand Here Ironing"? Some critics want to privilege personal responsibility; others, social conditions. Do you blame Emily's mother? Or is she just a victim?

3. How might this story be different if told from Emily's perspective? From Susan's? From Emily's teacher's? What are the advantages and disadvantages of writing a story from one character's point of view?

4. How would you describe the voice or voices we hear in the story? What qualities, dimensions, or emotions can you infer? Does one dominate? Are you sympathetic to this voice? Is that what Olsen wanted?

5. Do you agree with the mother's decision not to visit the school for a conference? What are her reasons? Are they sound? What do you think the teacher wants to discuss? How involved in a child's life should a teacher be?

AMY TAN
Two Kinds

Born to Chinese immigrants in Oakland, California, Amy Tan (b. 1952) weaves in-
tricate stories about generational and intercultural relationships among women in
families, basing much of her writing on her own family history. She earned a double
B.A., in English and linguistics, and an M.A. in linguistics at San Jose State Univer-
sity. Her novels dealing with mother-daughter relationships, The Joy Luck Club
(1989) and The Kitchen God's Wife *(1991), have received awards and critical ac-*
claim. The Hundred Secret Senses *(1995) explores the relationship between sis-*
ters who grew up in different cultures. Her latest novel is The Bonesetter's Daughter
(2001), and her more recent book is a collection of nonfiction, The Opposite of Fate
(2003). "Two Kinds" is excerpted from The Joy Luck Club. *Her most recent book,*
Saving Fish from Drowning *(2005), was called a "witty parable," loosely based on*
The Canterbury Tales.

My mother believed you could be anything you wanted to be in America. You
could open a restaurant. You could work for the government and get good retirement. You could buy a house with almost no money down. You could become rich. You could become instantly famous.

"Of course you can be prodigy, too," my mother told me when I was nine.
"You can be best anything. What does Auntie Lindo know? Her daughter, she
is only best tricky."

America was where all my mother's hopes lay. She had come here in 1949
after losing everything in China: her mother and father, her family home, her
first husband, and two daughters, twin baby girls. But she never looked back
with regret. There were so many ways for things to get better.

We didn't immediately pick the right kind of prodigy. At first my mother thought
I could be a Chinese Shirley Temple. We'd watch Shirley's old movies on TV as
though they were training films. My mother would poke my arm and say, "*Ni
kan*" — You watch. And I would see Shirley tapping her feet, or singing a sailor
song, or pursing her lips into a very round O while saying, "Oh my goodness."

"*Ni kan*," said my mother as Shirley's eyes flooded with tears. "You already   5
know how. Don't need talent for crying!"

Soon after my mother got this idea about Shirley Temple, she took me to a
beauty training school in the Mission district and put me in the hands of a student who could barely hold the scissors without shaking. Instead of getting big
fat curls, I emerged with an uneven mass of crinkly black fuzz. My mother
dragged me off to the bathroom and tried to wet down my hair.

"You look like Negro Chinese," she lamented, as if I had done this on
purpose.

The instructor of the beauty training school had to lop off these soggy
clumps to make my hair even again. "Peter Pan is very popular these days," the
instructor assured my mother. I now had hair the length of a boy's, with

straight-across bangs that hung at a slant two inches above my eyebrows. I liked the haircut and it made me actually look forward to my future fame.

In fact, in the beginning, I was just as excited as my mother, maybe even more so. I pictured this prodigy part of me as many different images, trying each one on for size. I was a dainty ballerina girl standing by the curtains, waiting to hear the right music that would send me floating on my tiptoes. I was like the Christ child lifted out of the straw manger, crying with holy indignity. I was Cinderella stepping from her pumpkin carriage with sparkly cartoon music filling the air.

In all of my imaginings, I was filled with a sense that I would soon become   10
perfect. My mother and father would adore me. I would be beyond reproach. I would never feel the need to sulk for anything.

But sometimes the prodigy in me became impatient. "If you don't hurry up and get me out of here, I'm disappearing for good," it warned. "And then you'll always be nothing."

Every night after dinner, my mother and I would sit at the Formica kitchen table. She would present new tests, taking her examples from stories of amazing children she had read in *Ripley's Believe It or Not*, or *Good Housekeeping*, *Reader's Digest*, and a dozen other magazines she kept in a pile in our bathroom. My mother got these magazines from people whose houses she cleaned. And since she cleaned many houses each week, we had a great assortment. She would look through them all, searching for stories about remarkable children.

The first night she brought out a story about a three-year-old boy who knew the capitals of all the states and even most of the European countries. A teacher was quoted as saying the little boy could also pronounce the names of the foreign cities correctly.

"What's the capital of Finland?" my mother asked me, looking at the magazine story.

All I knew was the capital of California, because Sacramento was the   15
name of the street we lived on in Chinatown. "Nairobi!" I guessed, saying the most foreign word I could think of. She checked to see if that was possibly one way to pronounce "Helsinki" before showing me the answer.

The tests got harder—multiplying numbers in my head, finding the queen of hearts in a deck of cards, trying to stand on my head without using my hands, predicting the daily temperatures in Los Angeles, New York, and London.

One night I had to look at a page from the Bible for three minutes and then report everything I could remember. "Now Jehoshaphat had riches and honor in abundance and . . . that's all I remember, Ma," I said.

And after seeing my mother's disappointed face once again, something inside of me began to die. I hated the tests, the raised hopes and failed expectations. Before going to bed that night, I looked in the mirror above the bathroom sink and when I saw only my face staring back—and that it would always be this ordinary face—I began to cry. Such a sad, ugly girl! I made high-pitched noises like a crazed animal, trying to scratch out the face in the mirror.

And then I saw what seemed to be the prodigy side of me — because I had never seen that face before. I looked at my reflection, blinking so I could see more clearly. The girl staring back at me was angry, powerful. This girl and I were the same. I had new thoughts, willful thoughts, or rather thoughts filled with lots of won'ts. I won't let her change me, I promised myself. I won't be what I'm not.

So now on nights when my mother presented her tests, I performed list-   20
lessly, my head propped on one arm. I pretended to be bored. And I was. I got so bored I started counting the bellows of the foghorns out on the bay while my mother drilled me in other areas. The sound was comforting and reminded me of the cow jumping over the moon. And the next day, I played a game with myself, seeing if my mother would give up on me before eight bellows. After a while I usually counted only one, maybe two bellows at most. At last she was beginning to give up hope.

Two or three months had gone by without any mention of my being a prodigy again. And then one day my mother was watching *The Ed Sullivan Show* on TV. The TV was old and the sound kept shorting out. Every time my mother got halfway up from the sofa to adjust the set, the sound would go back on and Ed would be talking. As soon as she sat down, Ed would go silent again. She got up, the TV broke into loud piano music. She sat down. Silence. Up and down, back and forth, quiet and loud. It was like a stiff embraceless dance between her and the TV set. Finally she stood by the set with her hand on the sound dial.

She seemed entranced by the music, a little frenzied piano piece with this mesmerizing quality, sort of quick passages and then teasing lilting ones before it returned to the quick playful parts.

"*Ni kan*," my mother said, calling me over with hurried hand gestures. "Look here."

I could see why my mother was fascinated by the music. It was being pounded out by a little Chinese girl, about nine years old, with a Peter Pan haircut. The girl had the sauciness of a Shirley Temple. She was proudly modest like a proper Chinese child. And she also did this fancy sweep of a curtsy, so that the fluffy skirt of her white dress cascaded slowly to the floor like the petals of a large carnation.

In spite of these warning signs, I wasn't worried. Our family had no piano   25
and we couldn't afford to buy one, let alone reams of sheet music and piano lessons. So I could be generous in my comments when my mother bad-mouthed the little girl on TV.

"Play note right, but doesn't sound good! No singing sound," complained my mother.

"What are you picking on her for?" I said carelessly. "She's pretty good. Maybe she's not the best, but she's trying hard." I knew almost immediately I would be sorry I said that.

"Just like you," she said. "Not the best. Because you not trying." She gave a little huff as she let go of the sound dial and sat down on the sofa.

The little Chinese girl sat down also to play an encore of "Anitra's Dance" by Grieg. I remember the song, because later on I had to learn how to play it.

Three days after watching *The Ed Sullivan Show*, my mother told me what my   30
schedule would be for piano lessons and piano practice. She had talked to Mr. Chong, who lived on the first floor of our apartment building. Mr. Chong was a retired piano teacher and my mother had traded housecleaning services for weekly lessons and a piano for me to practice on every day, two hours a day, from four until six.

When my mother told me this, I felt as though I had been sent to hell. I whined and then kicked my foot a little when I couldn't stand it anymore.

"Why don't you like me the way I am? I'm *not* a genius! I can't play the piano. And even if I could, I wouldn't go on TV if you paid me a million dollars!" I cried.

My mother slapped me. "Who ask you be genius?" she shouted. "Only ask you be your best. For you sake. You think I want you be genius? Hnnh! What for! Who ask you!"

"So ungrateful," I heard her mutter in Chinese. "If she had as much talent as she has temper, she would be famous now."

Mr. Chong, whom I secretly nicknamed Old Chong, was very strange, al-   35
ways tapping his fingers to the silent music of an invisible orchestra. He looked ancient in my eyes. He had lost most of the hair on top of his head and he wore thick glasses and had eyes that always looked tired and sleepy. But he must have been younger than I thought, since he lived with his mother and was not yet married.

I met Old Lady Chong once and that was enough. She had this peculiar smell like a baby that had done something in its pants. And her fingers felt like a dead person's, like an old peach I once found in the back of the refrigerator; the skin just slid off the meat when I picked it up.

I soon found out why Old Chong had retired from teaching piano. He was deaf. "Like Beethoven!" he shouted to me. "We're both listening only in our head!" And he would start to conduct his frantic silent sonatas.

Our lessons went like this. He would open the book and point to different things, explaining their purpose: "Key! Treble! Bass! No sharps or flats! So this is C major! Listen now and play after me!"

And then he would play the C scale a few times, a simple chord, and then, as if inspired by an old, unreachable itch, he gradually added more notes and running trills and a pounding bass until the music was really something quite grand.

I would play after him, the simple scale, the simple chord, and then I just   40
played some nonsense that sounded like a cat running up and down on top of garbage cans. Old Chong smiled and applauded and then said, "Very good! But now you must learn to keep time!"

So that's how I discovered that Old Chong's eyes were too slow to keep up with the wrong notes I was playing. He went through the motions in half-time.

To help me keep rhythm, he stood behind me, pushing down on my right shoulder for every beat. He balanced pennies on top of my wrists so I would keep them still as I slowly played scales and arpeggios. He had me curve my hand around an apple and keep that shape when playing chords. He marched stiffly to show me how to make each finger dance up and down, staccato like an obedient little soldier.

He taught me all these things, and that was how I also learned I could be lazy and get away with mistakes, lots of mistakes. If I hit the wrong notes because I hadn't practiced enough, I never corrected myself. I just kept playing in rhythm. And Old Chong kept conducting his own private reverie.

So maybe I never really gave myself a fair chance. I did pick up the basics pretty quickly, and I might have become a good pianist at that young age. But I was so determined not to try, not to be anybody different that I learned to play only the most ear-splitting preludes, the most discordant hymns.

Over the next year, I practiced like this, dutifully in my own way. And then one day I heard my mother and her friend Lindo Jong both talking in a loud bragging tone of voice so others could hear. It was after church, and I was leaning against the brick wall wearing a dress with stiff white petticoats. Auntie Lindo's daughter, Waverly, who was about my age, was standing farther down the wall about five feet away. We had grown up together and shared all the closeness of two sisters squabbling over crayons and dolls. In other words, for the most part, we hated each other. I thought she was snotty. Waverly Jong had gained a certain amount of fame as "Chinatown's Littlest Chinese Chess Champion."

"She bring home too many trophy," lamented Auntie Lindo that Sunday. 45 "All day she play chess. All day I have no time do nothing but dust off her winnings." She threw a scolding look at Waverly, who pretended not to see her.

"You lucky you don't have this problem," said Auntie Lindo with a sigh to my mother.

And my mother squared her shoulders and bragged: "Our problem worser than yours. If we ask Jing-mei wash dish, she hear nothing but music. It's like you can't stop this natural talent."

And right then, I was determined to put a stop to her foolish pride.

A few weeks later, Old Chong and my mother conspired to have me play in a talent show which would be held in the church hall. By then, my parents had saved up enough to buy me a secondhand piano, a black Wurlitzer spinet with a scarred bench. It was the showpiece of our living room.

For the talent show, I was to play a piece called "Pleading Child" from 50 Schumann's *Scenes from Childhood*. It was a simple, moody piece that sounded more difficult than it was. I was supposed to memorize the whole thing, playing the repeat parts twice to make the piece sound longer. But I dawdled over it, playing a few bars and then cheating, looking up to see what notes followed. I never really listened to what I was playing. I daydreamed about being somewhere else, about being someone else.

The part I liked to practice best was the fancy curtsy: right foot out, touch the rose on the carpet with a pointed foot, sweep to the side, left leg bends, look up and smile.

My parents invited all the couples from the Joy Luck Club to witness my debut. Auntie Lindo and Uncle Tin were there. Waverly and her two older brothers had also come. The first two rows were filled with children both younger and older than I was. The littlest ones got to go first. They recited simple nursery rhymes, squawked out tunes on miniature violins, twirled Hula Hoops, pranced in pink ballet tutus, and when they bowed or curtsied, the audience would sigh in unison, "Awww," and then clap enthusiastically.

When my turn came, I was very confident. I remember my childish excitement. It was as if I knew, without a doubt, that the prodigy side of me really did exist. I had no fear whatsoever, no nervousness. I remember thinking to myself, This is it! This is it! I looked out over the audience, at my mother's blank face, my father's yawn, Auntie Lindo's stiff-lipped smile, Waverly's sulky expression. I had on a white dress layered with sheets of lace, and a pink bow in my Peter Pan haircut. As I sat down I envisioned people jumping to their feet and Ed Sullivan rushing up to introduce me to everyone on TV.

And I started to play. It was so beautiful. I was so caught up in how lovely I looked that at first I didn't worry how I would sound. So it was a surprise to me when I hit the first wrong note and I realized something didn't sound quite right. And then I hit another and another followed that. A chill started at the top of my head and began to trickle down. Yet I couldn't stop playing, as though my hands were bewitched. I kept thinking my fingers would adjust themselves back, like a train switching to the right track. I played this strange jumble through two repeats, the sour notes staying with me all the way to the end.

When I stood up, I discovered my legs were shaking. Maybe I had just been nervous and the audience, like Old Chong, had seen me go through the right motions and had not heard anything wrong at all. I swept my right foot out, went down on my knee, looked up and smiled. The room was quiet, except for Old Chong, who was beaming and shouting, "Bravo! Bravo! Well done!" But then I saw my mother's face, her stricken face. The audience clapped weakly, and as I walked back to my chair, with my whole face quivering as I tried not to cry, I heard a little boy whisper loudly to his mother, "That was awful," and the mother whispered back, "Well, she certainly tried."

And now I realized how many people were in the audience, the whole world it seemed. I was aware of eyes burning into my back. I felt the shame of my mother and father as they sat stiffly throughout the rest of the show.

We could have escaped during intermission. Pride and some strange sense of honor must have anchored my parents to their chairs. And so we watched it all: the eighteen-year-old boy with a fake mustache who did a magic show and juggled flaming hoops while riding a unicycle. The breasted girl with white makeup who sang from *Madama Butterfly* and got honorable mention. And the eleven-year-old boy who won first prize playing a tricky violin song that sounded like a busy bee.

55

After the show, the Hsus, the Jongs, and the St. Clairs from the Joy Luck Club came up to my mother and father.

"Lots of talented kids," Auntie Lindo said vaguely, smiling broadly.

"That was somethin' else," said my father, and I wondered if he was refer-   60
ring to me in a humorous way, or whether he even remembered what I had done.

Waverly looked at me and shrugged her shoulders. "You aren't a genius like me," she said matter-of-factly. And if I hadn't felt so bad, I would have pulled her braids and punched her stomach.

But my mother's expression was what devastated me: a quiet, blank look that said she had lost everything. I felt the same way, and it seemed as if every-body were now coming up, like gawkers at the scene of an accident, to see what parts were actually missing. When we got on the bus to go home, my father was humming the busy-bee tune and my mother was silent. I kept thinking she wanted to wait until we got home before shouting at me. But when my father unlocked the door to our apartment, my mother walked in and then went to the back, into the bedroom. No accusations. No blame. And in a way, I felt dis-appointed. I had been waiting for her to start shouting, so I could shout back and cry and blame her for all my misery.

I assumed my talent-show fiasco meant I never had to play the piano again. But two days later, after school, my mother came out of the kitchen and saw me watching TV.

"Four clock," she reminded me as if it were any other day. I was stunned, as though she were asking me to go through the talent-show torture again. I wedged myself more tightly in front of the TV.

"Turn off TV," she called from the kitchen five minutes later.   65

I didn't budge. And then I decided. I didn't have to do what my mother said anymore. I wasn't her slave. This wasn't China. I had listened to her before and look what happened. She was the stupid one.

She came out from the kitchen and stood in the arched entryway of the living room. "Four clock," she said once again, louder.

"I'm not going to play anymore," I said nonchalantly. "Why should I? I'm not a genius."

She walked over and stood in front of the TV. I saw her chest was heaving up and down in an angry way.

"No!" I said, and I now felt stronger, as if my true self had finally emerged.   70
So this was what had been inside me all along.

"No! I won't!" I screamed.

She yanked me by the arm, pulled me off the floor, snapped off the TV. She was frighteningly strong, half pulling, half carrying me toward the piano as I kicked the throw rugs under my feet. She lifted me up and onto the hard bench. I was sobbing by now, looking at her bitterly. Her chest was heaving even more and her mouth was open, smiling crazily as if she were pleased I was crying.

"You want me to be someone that I'm not!" I sobbed. "I'll never be the kind of daughter you want me to be!"

"Only two kinds of daughters," she shouted in Chinese. "Those who are obedient and those who follow their own mind! Only one kind of daughter can live in this house. Obedient daughter!"

"Then I wish I wasn't your daughter. I wish you weren't my mother," I   75
shouted. As I said these things I got scared. I felt like worms and toads and slimy things were crawling out of my chest, but it also felt good, as if this awful side of me had surfaced, at last.

"Too late change this," said my mother shrilly.

And I could sense her anger rising to its breaking point. I wanted to see it spill over. And that's when I remembered the babies she had lost in China, the ones we never talked about. "Then I wish I'd never been born!" I shouted. "I wish I were dead! Like them."

It was as if I had said the magic words, Alakazam! — and her face went blank, her mouth closed, her arms went slack, and she backed out of the room, stunned, as if she were blowing away like a small brown leaf, thin, brittle, lifeless.

It was not the only disappointment my mother felt in me. In the years that followed, I failed her so many times, each time asserting my own will, my right to fall short of expectations. I didn't get straight As. I didn't become class president. I didn't get into Stanford. I dropped out of college.

For unlike my mother, I did not believe I could be anything I wanted to be.   80
I could only be me.

And for all those years, we never talked about the disaster at the recital or my terrible accusations afterward at the piano bench. All that remained unchecked, like a betrayal that was now unspeakable. So I never found a way to ask her why she had hoped for something so large that failure was inevitable.

And even worse, I never asked her what frightened me the most: Why had she given up hope?

For after our struggle at the piano, she never mentioned my playing again. The lessons stopped, the lid to the piano was closed, shutting out the dust, my misery, and her dreams.

So she surprised me. A few years ago, she offered to give me the piano, for my thirtieth birthday. I had not played in all those years. I saw the offer as a sign of forgiveness, a tremendous burden removed.

"Are you sure?" I asked shyly. "I mean, won't you and Dad miss it?"   85

"No, this your piano," she said firmly. "Always your piano. You only one can play."

"Well, I probably can't play anymore," I said. "It's been years."

"You pick up fast," said my mother, as if she knew this was certain. "You have natural talent. You could been genius if you want to."

"No I couldn't."

"You just not trying," said my mother. And she was neither angry nor sad.   90
She said it as if to announce a fact that could never be disproved. "Take it," she said.

But I didn't at first. It was enough that she had offered it to me. And after that, every time I saw it in my parents' living room, standing in front of the bay windows, it made me feel proud, as if it were a shiny trophy I had won back.

Last week I sent a tuner over to my parents' apartment and had the piano reconditioned, for purely sentimental reasons. My mother had died a few months before and I had been getting things in order for my father, a little bit at a time. I put the jewelry in special silk pouches. The sweaters she had knitted in yellow, pink, bright orange — all the colors I hated — I put those in moth-proof boxes. I found some old Chinese silk dresses, the kind with little slits up the sides. I rubbed the old silk against my skin, then wrapped them in tissue and decided to take them home with me.

After I had the piano tuned, I opened the lid and touched the keys. It sounded even richer than I remembered. Really, it was a very good piano. Inside the bench were the same exercise notes with handwritten scales, the same secondhand music books with their covers held together with yellow tape.

I opened up the Schumann book to the dark little piece I had played at the recital. It was on the left-hand side of the page, "Pleading Child." It looked more difficult than I remembered. I played a few bars, surprised at how easily the notes came back to me.

And for the first time, or so it seemed, I noticed the piece on the right-hand side. It was called "Perfectly Contented." I tried to play this one as well. It had a lighter melody but the same flowing rhythm and turned out to be quite easy. "Pleading Child" was shorter but slower; "Perfectly Contented" was longer but faster. And after I played them both a few times, I realized they were two halves of the same song.

95

[1989]

≡ THINKING ABOUT THE TEXT

1. Most sons and daughters struggle to establish their own identities. Does this seem true in "Two Kinds"? Does the cultural difference between the immigrant mother and Americanized daughter intensify their struggle? Do you think you have different goals in life than your parents do?

2. Do you agree with the mother's belief that "you could be anything you wanted to be in America" (para. 1)? Does race matter? Gender? Ethnicity? Religion? Sexual orientation?

3. What do you believe each character learned from the argument at the piano bench the day after the recital?

4. How does Tan establish the differing personalities of her characters? Through details? Dialogue? Anecdotes? Do the main characters change significantly? Does she tell us or show us?

5. Do you sympathize with the mother or with the daughter? Should parents channel their children toward selected activities? Or should parents let their children choose their own paths? Can parents push their children too much? Why would they do this?

▤ MAKING COMPARISONS

1. Do you think Emily's mother in Olsen's story would want to be like the Chinese mother if given the opportunity? Which mother would you prefer to have? Why?

2. One mother seems to do too little, the other too much. Is this your reading of the two stories? Is the lesson of Olsen's and Tan's stories that mothers can't win no matter what they do? Or do you have a more optimistic interpretation?

3. Which daughter's life seems more difficult? How possible is it to say from the outside looking in?

ALICE WALKER
Everyday Use

A native of Eatonton, Georgia, Alice Walker (b. 1944) attended Spelman College and received her B.A. from Sarah Lawrence College in 1965. During the 1960s, she was active in the civil rights movement, an experience reflected in her 1976 novel Meridian *and in her autobiographical book,* The Way Forward Is with a Broken Heart *(2000). Walker is accomplished in many genres, and her essays, short stories, novels, and poems are widely read. She is perhaps best known for the novel* The Color Purple *(1976), which earned her both a Pulitzer Prize and an American Book Award and was made into a movie. Terming herself a "womanist" rather than a feminist in the essays of* In Search of Our Mothers' Gardens *(1983), Walker has confronted many issues concerning women, including abusive relationships, lesbian love, and the horrors of ritual genital mutilation in some African societies. Her daughter, Rebecca, has written her own memoir,* Black, White and Jewish, *dealing with her childhood and adolescence as the daughter of Alice Walker and activist lawyer Mel Leventhal, to whom Walker was married for nine years, after meeting him during voter registration drives in Mississippi in 1967. The short story "Everyday Use," from the collection* In Love and Trouble: Stories of Black Women *(1973), deals with definitions of history, heritage, and value in a changing world for African Americans in the mid-twentieth century. Her recent work includes a novel,* Now Is the Time to Open Your Heart *(2004);* We Are the Ones We've Been Waiting For *(2006), "a book of spiritual ruminations with a progressive political edge"; and* Hard Times Require Serious Dancing: New Poems *(2010).*

I will wait for her in the yard that Maggie and I made so clean and wavy yesterday afternoon. A yard like this is more comfortable than most people know. It is not just a yard. It is like an extended living room. When the hard clay is swept clean as a floor and the fine sand around the edges lined with tiny, irregular grooves anyone can come and sit and look up into the elm tree and wait for the breezes that never come inside the house.

Maggie will be nervous until after her sister goes: she will stand hopelessly in corners homely and ashamed of the burn scars down her arms and legs, eyeing her sister with a mixture of envy and awe. She thinks her sister has held life always in the palm of one hand, that "no" is a word the world never learned to say to her.

You've no doubt seen those TV shows where the child who has "made it" is confronted, as a surprise, by her own mother and father, tottering in weakly from backstage. (A pleasant surprise, of course: What would they do if parent and child came on the show only to curse out and insult each other?) On TV mother and child embrace and smile into each other's faces. Sometimes the mother and father weep, the child wraps them in her arms and leans across the table to tell how she would not have made it without their help. I have seen these programs.

Sometimes I dream a dream in which Dee and I are suddenly brought together on a TV program of this sort. Out of a dark and soft-seated limousine I am ushered into a bright room filled with many people. There I meet a smiling, gray, sporty man like Johnny Carson who shakes my hand and tells me what a fine girl I have. Then we are on the stage and Dee is embracing me with tears in her eyes. She pins on my dress a large orchid, even though she has told me once that she thinks orchids are tacky flowers.

In real life I am a large, big-boned woman with rough, man-working   5
hands. In the winter I wear flannel nightgowns to bed and overalls during the day. I can kill and clean a hog as mercilessly as a man. My fat keeps me hot in zero weather. I can work outside all day, breaking ice to get water for washing; I can eat pork liver cooked over the open fire minutes after it comes steaming from the hog. One winter I knocked a bull calf straight in the brain between the eyes with a sledge hammer and had the meat hung up to chill before nightfall. But of course all this does not show on television. I am the way my daughter would want me to be: a hundred pounds lighter, my skin like an uncooked barley pancake. My hair glistens in the hot bright lights. Johnny Carson has much to do to keep up with my quick and witty tongue.

But that is a mistake. I know even before I wake up. Who ever knew a Johnson with a quick tongue? Who can even imagine me looking a strange white man in the eye? It seems to me I have talked to them always with one foot raised in flight, with my head turned in whichever way is farthest from them. Dee, though. She would always look anyone in the eye. Hesitation was no part of her nature.

"How do I look, Mama?" Maggie says, showing just enough of her thin body enveloped in pink skirt and red blouse for me to know she's there, almost hidden by the door.

"Come out into the yard," I say.

Have you ever seen a lame animal, perhaps a dog run over by some careless person rich enough to own a car, sidle up to someone who is ignorant enough to be kind to him? That is the way my Maggie walks. She has been like this, chin on chest, eyes on ground, feet in shuffle, ever since the fire that burned the other house to the ground.

Dee is lighter than Maggie, with nicer hair and a fuller figure. She's a 10 woman now, though sometimes I forget. How long ago was it that the other house burned? Ten, twelve years? Sometimes I can still hear the flames and feel Maggie's arms sticking to me, her hair smoking and her dress falling off her in little black papery flakes. Her eyes seemed stretched open, blazed open by the flames reflected in them. And Dee. I see her standing off under the sweet gum tree she used to dig gum out of; a look of concentration on her face as she watched the last dingy gray board of the house fall in toward the red-hot brick chimney. Why don't you do a dance around the ashes? I'd wanted to ask her. She had hated the house that much.

I used to think she hated Maggie, too. But that was before we raised the money, the church and me, to send her to Augusta to school. She used to read to us without pity; forcing words, lies, other folks' habits, whole lives upon us two, sitting trapped and ignorant underneath her voice. She washed us in a river of make-believe, burned us with a lot of knowledge we didn't necessarily need to know. Pressed us to her with the serious way she read, to shove us away at just the moment, like dimwits, we seemed about to understand.

Dee wanted nice things. A yellow organdy dress to wear to her graduation from high school; black pumps to match a green suit she'd made from an old suit somebody gave me. She was determined to stare down any disaster in her efforts. Her eyelids would not flicker for minutes at a time. Often I fought off the temptation to shake her. At sixteen she had a style of her own: and knew what style was.

I never had an education myself. After second grade the school was closed down. Don't ask me why: in 1927 colored asked fewer questions than they do now. Sometimes Maggie reads to me. She stumbles along good-naturedly but can't see well. She knows she is not bright. Like good looks and money, quickness passed her by. She will marry John Thomas (who has mossy teeth in an earnest face) and then I'll be free to sit here and I guess just sing church songs to myself. Although I never was a good singer. Never could carry a tune. I was always better at a man's job. I used to love to milk till I was hooked in the side in '49. Cows are soothing and slow and don't bother you, unless you try to milk them the wrong way.

I have deliberately turned my back on the house. It is three rooms, just like the one that burned, except the roof is tin; they don't make shingle roofs any more. There are no real windows, just some holes cut in the sides, like the portholes in a ship, but not round and not square, with rawhide holding the shutters up on the outside. This house is in a pasture, too, like the other one. No doubt when Dee sees it she will want to tear it down. She wrote me once that no matter where we "choose" to live, she will manage to come see us. But she will never bring her friends. Maggie and I thought about this and Maggie asked me, "Mama, when did Dee ever *have* any friends?"

She had a few. Furtive boys in pink shirts hanging about on washday after   15
school. Nervous girls who never laughed. Impressed with her they worshiped
the well-turned phrase, the cute shape, the scalding humor that erupted like
bubbles in lye. She read to them.

When she was courting Jimmy T she didn't have much time to pay to us,
but turned all her faultfinding power on him. He *flew* to marry a cheap gal from
a family of ignorant flashy people. She hardly had time to recompose herself.

When she comes I will meet — but there they are!

Maggie attempts to make a dash for the house, in her shuffling way, but I
stay her with my hand. "Come back here," I say. And she stops and tries to dig
a well in the sand with her toe.

It is hard to see them clearly through the strong sun. But even the first
glimpse of leg out of the car tells me it is Dee. Her feet were always neat-looking,
as if God himself had shaped them with a certain style. From the other side of
the car comes a short, stocky man. Hair is all over his head a foot long and
hanging from his chin like a kinky mule tail. I hear Maggie suck in her breath.
"Uhnnnh," is what it sounds like. Like when you see the wriggling end of a
snake just in front of your foot on the road. "Uhnnnh."

Dee next. A dress down to the ground, in this hot weather. A dress so loud   20
it hurts my eyes. There are yellows and oranges enough to throw back the light
of the sun. I feel my whole face warming from the heat waves it throws out.
Earrings gold, too, and hanging down to her shoulders. Bracelets dangling and
making noises when she moves her arm up to shake the folds of the dress out
of her armpits. The dress is loose and flows, and as she walks closer, I like it. I
hear Maggie go "Uhnnnh" again. It is her sister's hair. It stands straight up like
the wool on a sheep. It is black as night and around the edges are two long pig-
tails that rope about like small lizards disappearing behind her ears.

"Wa-su-zo-Tean-o!" she says, coming on in that gliding way the dress
makes her move. The short stocky fellow with the hair to his navel is all grinning and he follows up with "Asalamalakim, my mother and sister!" He moves
to hug Maggie but she falls back, right up against the back of my chair. I feel
her trembling there and when I look up I see the perspiration falling off her
chin.

"Don't get up," says Dee. Since I am stout it takes something of a push. You
can see me trying to move a second or two before I make it. She turns, showing
white heels through her sandals, and goes back to the car. Out she peeks next
with a Polaroid. She stoops down quickly and lines up picture after picture of
me sitting there in front of the house with Maggie cowering behind me. She
never takes a shot without making sure the house is included. When a cow
comes nibbling around the edge of the yard she snaps it and me and Maggie
and the house. Then she puts the Polaroid in the back seat of the car, and comes
up and kisses me on the forehead.

Meanwhile Asalamalakim is going through the motions with Maggie's
hand. Maggie's hand is as limp as a fish, and probably as cold, despite the sweat,
and she keeps trying to pull it back. It looks like Asalamalakim wants to shake

hands but wants to do it fancy. Or maybe he don't know how people shake hands. Anyhow, he soon gives up on Maggie.

"Well," I say. "Dee."

"No, Mama," she says. "Not 'Dee,' Wangero Leewanika Kemanjo!"   25

"What happened to 'Dee'?" I wanted to know.

"She's dead," Wangero said. "I couldn't bear it any longer being named after the people who oppress me."

"You know as well as me you was named after your aunt Dicie," I said. Dicie is my sister. She named Dee. We called her "Big Dee" after Dee was born.

"But who was *she* named after?" asked Wangero.

"I guess after Grandma Dee," I said.   30

"And who was she named after?" asked Wangero.

"Her mother," I said, and saw Wangero was getting tired. "That's about as far back as I can trace it," I said. Though, in fact, I probably could have carried it back beyond the Civil War through the branches.

"Well," said Asalamalakim, "there you are."

"Uhnnnh," I heard Maggie say.

"There I was not," I said, "before 'Dicie' cropped up in our family, so why   35 should I try to trace it that far back?"

He just stood there grinning, looking down on me like somebody inspecting a Model A car. Every once in a while he and Wangero sent eye signals over my head.

"How do you pronounce this name?" I asked.

"You don't have to call me by it if you don't want to," said Wangero.

"Why shouldn't I?" I asked. "If that's what you want us to call you, we'll call you."

"I know it might sound awkward at first," said Wangero.   40

"I'll get used to it," I said. "Ream it out again."

Well, soon we got the name out of the way. Asalamalakim had a name twice as long and three times as hard. After I tripped over it two or three times he told me to just call him Hakim-a-barber. I wanted to ask him was he a barber, but I didn't really think he was, so I didn't ask.

"You must belong to those beef-cattle peoples down the road," I said. They said "Asalamalakim" when they met you, too, but they didn't shake hands. Always too busy: feeding the cattle, fixing the fences, putting up salt-lick shelters, throwing down hay. When the white folks poisoned some of the herd the men stayed up all night with rifles in their hands. I walked a mile and a half just to see the sight.

Hakim-a-barber said, "I accept some of their doctrines, but farming and raising cattle is not my style." (They didn't tell me, and I didn't ask, whether Wangero [Dee] had really gone and married him.)

We sat down to eat and right away he said he didn't eat collards and pork   45 was unclean. Wangero, though, went on through the chitlins and corn bread, the greens and everything else. She talked a blue streak over the sweet potatoes. Everything delighted her. Even the fact that we still used the benches her daddy made for the table when we couldn't afford to buy chairs.

"Oh, Mama!" she cried. Then turned to Hakim-a-barber. "I never knew how lovely these benches are. You can feel the rump prints," she said, running her hands underneath her and along the bench. Then she gave a sigh and her hand closed over Grandma Dee's butter dish. "That's it!" she said. "I knew there was something I wanted to ask you if I could have." She jumped up from the table and went over in the corner where the churn stood, the milk in it clabber by now. She looked at the churn and looked at it.

"This churn top is what I need," she said. "Didn't Uncle Buddy whittle it out of a tree you all used to have?"

"Yes," I said.

"Uh huh," she said happily. "And I want the dasher, too."

"Uncle Buddy whittle that, too?" asked the barber. 50

Dee (Wangero) looked up at me.

"Aunt Dee's first husband whittled the dash," said Maggie so low you almost couldn't hear her. "His name was Henry, but they called him Stash."

"Maggie's brain is like an elephant's," Wangero said, laughing. "I can use the churn top as a centerpiece for the alcove table," she said, sliding a plate over the churn, "and I'll think of something artistic to do with the dasher."

When she finished wrapping the dasher the handle stuck out. I took it for a moment in my hands. You didn't even have to look close to see where hands pushing the dasher up and down to make butter had left a kind of sink in the wood. In fact, there were a lot of small sinks; you could see where thumbs and fingers had sunk into the wood. It was beautiful light yellow wood, from a tree that grew in the yard where Big Dee and Stash had lived.

After dinner Dee (Wangero) went to the trunk at the foot of my bed and 55 started rifling through it. Maggie hung back in the kitchen over the dishpan. Out came Wangero with two quilts. They had been pieced by Grandma Dee and then Big Dee and me had hung them on the quilt frames on the front porch and quilted them. One was in the Lone Star pattern. The other was Walk Around the Mountain. In both of them were scraps of dresses Grandma Dee had worn fifty and more years ago. Bits and pieces of Grandpa Jarrell's paisley shirts. And one teeny faded blue piece, about the size of a penny matchbox, that was from Great Grandpa Ezra's uniform that he wore in the Civil War.

"Mama," Wangero said sweet as a bird. "Can I have these old quilts?"

I heard something fall in the kitchen, and a minute later the kitchen door slammed.

"Why don't you take one or two of the others?" I asked. "These old things was just done by me and Big Dee from some tops your grandma pieced before she died."

"No," said Wangero. "I don't want those. They are stitched around the borders by machine."

"That'll make them last better," I said. 60

"That's not the point," said Wangero. "These are all pieces of dresses Grandma used to wear. She did all this stitching by hand. Imagine!" She held the quilts securely in her arms, stroking them.

"Some of the pieces, like those lavender ones, come from old clothes her mother handed down to her," I said, moving up to touch the quilts. Dee (Wangero) moved back just enough so that I couldn't reach the quilts. They already belonged to her.

"Imagine!" she breathed again, clutching them closely to her bosom.

"The truth is," I said, "I promised to give them quilts to Maggie, for when she marries John Thomas."

She gasped like a bee had stung her.   65

"Maggie can't appreciate these quilts!" she said. "She'd probably be back-ward enough to put them to everyday use."

"I reckon she would," I said. "God knows I been saving 'em for long enough with nobody using 'em. I hope she will!" I didn't want to bring up how I had offered Dee (Wangero) a quilt when she went away to college. Then she had told me they were old-fashioned, out of style.

"But they're *priceless*!" she was saying now, furiously; for she has a temper. "Maggie would put them on the bed and in five years they'd be in rags. Less than that!"

"She can always make some more," I said. "Maggie knows how to quilt."

Dee (Wangero) looked at me with hatred. "You just will not understand.   70
The point is these quilts, *these* quilts!"

"Well," I said, stumped. "What would *you* do with them?"

"Hang them," she said. As if that was the only thing you *could* do with quilts.

Maggie by now was standing in the door. I could almost hear the sound her feet made as they scraped over each other.

"She can have them, Mama," she said, like somebody used to never win-ning anything, or having anything reserved for her. "I can 'member Grandma Dee without the quilts."

I looked at her hard. She had filled her bottom lip with checkerberry snuff   75
and it gave her face a kind of dopey, hangdog look. It was Grandma Dee and Big Dee who taught her how to quilt herself. She stood there with her scarred hands hidden in the folds of her skirt. She looked at her sister with something like fear but she wasn't mad at her. This was Maggie's portion. This was the way she knew God to work.

When I looked at her like that something hit me in the top of my head and ran down to the soles of my feet. Just like when I'm in church and the spirit of God touches me and I get happy and shout. I did something I never had done before: hugged Maggie to me, then dragged her on into the room, snatched the quilts out of Miss Wangero's hands and dumped them into Maggie's lap. Maggie just sat there on my bed with her mouth open.

"Take one or two of the others," I said to Dee.

But she turned without a word and went out to Hakim-a-barber.

"You just don't understand," she said, as Maggie and I came out to the car.

"What don't I understand?" I wanted to know.   80

"Your heritage," she said. And then she turned to Maggie, kissed her, and said, "You ought to try to make something of yourself, too, Maggie. It's really a new day for us. But from the way you and Mama still live you'd never know it."

She put on some sunglasses that hid everything above the tip of her nose and her chin.

Maggie smiled; maybe at the sunglasses. But a real smile, not scared. After we watched the car dust settle I asked Maggie to bring me a dip of snuff. And then the two of us sat there just enjoying, until it was time to go in the house and go to bed.   [1973]

≡ THINKING ABOUT THE TEXT

1. Be specific in arguing that Mama is more sympathetic to Maggie than to Dee. Is Mama hostile to Dee? What values are involved in the tension between Mama and Dee and Maggie?

2. Although many students seem to prefer Maggie to Dee, most would probably rather be Dee than Maggie. Is this true for you? Why?

3. Do you think Walker is against "getting back to one's roots"? Does she give a balanced characterization of Maggie? Of Dee? How might she portray Dee if she wanted to be more positive about her? Less positive?

4. Do you think it helps or hinders the social fabric to affirm ethnic differences? Do you think America is a melting pot? Is a quilt a better symbol to capture our diversity? Can you suggest another metaphor?

5. Do you think most mothers would side with daughters with whom they are more politically or culturally sympathetic? What might be the deciding factor? Are most mothers equally supportive of each of their children?

≡ MAKING COMPARISONS

1. How do you think Maggie would fare if she were the first child in "I Stand Here Ironing"? In "Two Kinds"?

2. Which relationship in the stories in this cluster is closest to your own? Explain.

3. Which one of the five daughters seems the kindest? The smartest? The most ambitious? The most troubled? The most likely to succeed? To find love? Do you think the mothers are responsible for how their daughters turn out?

≡ WRITING ABOUT ISSUES

1. After reading Olsen's story, as Emily's teacher, write a letter to Emily's mother persuading her that she should still come in for a conference. Acknowledge her excuses and her side of the issue, but offer objections.

2. Write a brief essay arguing that each of the mothers presented in Olsen's, Tan's, and Walker's stories is either a good or a bad model for parenting.

3. Write a personal-experience narrative about a time when your parents pushed you too hard or too little or wanted you to be someone you thought you were not. Conclude with your present view of the consequences of their action.

4. Ask six males and six females if they feel their parents tried to shape their personalities, behavior, choice of friends, and so forth. Were the parents' efforts successful? Do the sons and daughters resent it now? Conclude your brief report with some generalizations, including how relevant gender is.

≡ Siblings in Conflict: Stories

TOBIAS WOLFF, "The Rich Brother"

JAMES BALDWIN, "Sonny's Blues"

Although the expression "blood is thicker than water" suggests that brothers and sisters should support each other, the reality is often more complex. Children growing up together share intense emotional ties, but affection and loyalty sometimes conflict with hostility and jealousy. Children often feel they are competing for their parents' attention and love, a rivalry often played out over a lifetime and intensified as siblings choose different lifestyles. Well into adulthood, brothers and sisters often find their relationships with each other conflicted by unresolved issues of mutual responsibility and disparities in values as well as individual issues of financial success, self-esteem, and guilt. The siblings in the following two stories, separated by age and disparate occupations, engage in a psychologically complex dance that ebbs and flows over their lives. They struggle to understand each other and ultimately themselves, for, as with all of us, healthy relationships with siblings start with a healthy relationship with oneself.

≡ BEFORE YOU READ

How would you describe your relationship with your siblings? Did rivalry ever play a part? Does it now? Do you consider your siblings' futures as similar to yours? Is it important for brothers and sisters to look after each other? Or might that create more problems than it solves?

TOBIAS WOLFF
The Rich Brother

Tobias Wolff (b. 1945) is known chiefly for his short stories. The following piece comes from his second collection, Back in the World *(1985). He has produced two other volumes of stories,* In the Garden of the North American Martyrs *(1981) and* The Night in Question *(1996), and a short novel,* The Barracks Thief *(1984). His latest novel is* Old School *(2004). Wolff is also the author of two memoirs. In the first,* This Boy's Life *(1989), he recalls his parents' divorce and subsequent family dramas. These include wanderings with his mother through the West and Northwest; arguments with his abusive stepfather; occasional contact with his real father, who was a habitual liar later imprisoned for fraud; and years of separation from his brother Geoffrey, who eventually became a writer himself.* This Boy's Life *won the* Los Angeles Times Book Award *for biography and later became a movie starring Robert De Niro as the stepfather and Leonardo DiCaprio as the young Toby. Wolff's second memoir,* In Pharaoh's Army: Memories of the Lost War *(1994), deals*

mostly with his military service in Vietnam. His most recent collection is Our Story
Begins: New and Selected Stories *(2008). Today, Wolff teaches creative writing at
Stanford University.*

There were two brothers, Pete and Donald.

Pete, the older brother, was in real estate. He and his wife had a Century 21
franchise in Santa Cruz. Pete worked hard and made a lot of money, but not
any more than he thought he deserved. He had two daughters, a sailboat, a
house from which he could see a thin slice of the ocean, and friends doing well
enough in their own lives not to wish bad luck on him. Donald, the younger
brother, was still single. He lived alone, painted houses when he found the
work, and got deeper in debt to Pete when he didn't.

No one would have taken them for brothers. Where Pete was stout and
hearty and at home in the world, Donald was bony, grave, and obsessed with
the fate of his soul. Over the years Donald had worn the images of two different
Perfect Masters around his neck. Out of devotion to the second of these he
entered an ashram in Berkeley, where he nearly died of undiagnosed hepatitis.
By the time Pete finished paying the medical bills Donald had become a Christian. He drifted from church to church, then joined a pentecostal community that met somewhere in the Mission District to sing in tongues and swap
prophecies.

Pete couldn't make sense of it. Their parents were both dead, but while
they were alive neither of them had found it necessary to believe in anything.
They managed to be decent people without making fools of themselves, and
Pete had the same ambition. He thought that the whole thing was an excuse
for Donald to take himself seriously.

The trouble was that Donald couldn't content himself with worrying   5
about his own soul. He had to worry about everyone else's, and especially
Pete's. He handed down his judgments in ways that he seemed to consider
subtle: through significant silence, innuendo, looks of mild despair that said,
Brother, what have you come to? What Pete had come to, as far as he could tell,
was prosperity. That was the real issue between them. Pete prospered and
Donald did not prosper.

At the age of forty Pete took up sky diving. He made his first jump with two
friends who'd started only a few months earlier and were already doing stunts.
He never would have used the word *mystical*, but that was how Pete felt
about the experience. Later he made the mistake of trying to describe it to
Donald, who kept asking how much it cost and then acted appalled when Pete
told him.

"At least I'm trying something new," Pete said. "At least I'm breaking the
pattern."

Not long after that conversation Donald also broke the pattern, by going to
live on a farm outside Paso Robles. The farm was owned by several members of
Donald's community, who had bought it and moved there with the idea of
forming a family of faith. That was how Donald explained it in the first letter he

interesting sent. Every week Pete heard how happy Donald was, how "in the Lord." He told Pete that he was praying for him, he and the rest of Pete's brothers and sisters on the farm.

"I only have one brother," Pete wanted to answer, "and that's enough." But he kept this thought to himself.

[In November the letters stopped. Pete didn't worry about this at first, but   10 when he called Donald at Thanksgiving Donald was grim.] He tried to sound upbeat but he didn't try hard enough to make it convincing. "Now listen," Pete said, "you don't have to stay in that place if you don't want to."

"I'll be all right," Donald answered.

"That's not the point. Being all right is not the point. If you don't like what's going on up there, then get out."

"I'm all right," Donald said again, more firmly. "I'm doing fine."

But he called Pete a week later and said that he was quitting the farm. When Pete asked him where he intended to go, Donald admitted that he had no plan. His car had been repossessed just before he left the city, and he was flat broke.

"I guess you'll have to stay with us," Pete said.   15

Donald put up a show of resistance. Then he gave in. "Just until I get my feet on the ground," he said.

"Right," Pete said. "Check out your options." He told Donald he'd send him money for a bus ticket, but as they were about to hang up Pete changed his mind. He knew that Donald would try hitchhiking to save the fare. Pete didn't want him out on the road all alone where some head case would pick him up, where anything could happen to him.

"Better yet," he said, "I'll come and get you."

"You don't have to do that. I didn't expect you to do that," Donald said. He added, "It's a pretty long drive."

"Just tell me how to get there."   20

But Donald wouldn't give him directions. He said that the farm was too depressing, that Pete wouldn't like it. Instead, he insisted on meeting Pete at a service station called Jonathan's Mechanical Emporium.

"You must be kidding," Pete said.

"It's close to the highway," Donald said. "I didn't name it."

"That's one for the collection," Pete said.

The day before he left to bring Donald home, Pete received a letter from a man   25 who described himself as "head of household" at the farm where Donald had been living. [From this letter Pete learned that Donald had not quit the farm, but had been asked to leave.] The letter was written on the back of a mimeographed survey form asking people to record their response to a ceremony of some kind. The last question said:

What did you feel during the liturgy?
   a) Being
   b) Becoming
   c) Being and Becoming
   d) None of the Above
   e) All of the Above

Pete tried to forget the letter. But of course he couldn't. Each time he thought of it he felt crowded and breathless, a feeling that came over him again when he drove into the service station and saw Donald sitting against a wall with his head on his knees. It was late afternoon. A paper cup tumbled slowly past Donald's feet, pushed by the damp wind.

Pete honked and Donald raised his head. He smiled at Pete, then stood and stretched. His arms were long and thin and white. He wore a red bandanna across his forehead, a T-shirt with a couple of words on the front. Pete couldn't read them because the letters were inverted.

"Grow up," Pete yelled. "Get a Mercedes."

Donald came up to the window. He bent down and said, "Thanks for coming. You must be totally whipped."

"I'll make it." Pete pointed at Donald's T-shirt. "What's that supposed   30
to say?"

Donald looked down at his shirt front. "Try God. I guess I put it on backwards. Pete, could I borrow a couple of dollars? I owe these people for coffee and sandwiches."

Pete took five twenties from his wallet and held them out the window.

Donald stepped back as if horrified. "I don't need that much."

"I can't keep track of all these nickels and dimes," Pete said. "Just pay me back when your ship comes in." He waved the bills impatiently. "Go on — take it."

"Only for now." Donald took the money and went into the service station   35
office. He came out carrying two orange sodas, one of which he gave to Pete as he got into the car. "My treat," he said.

"No bags?"

"Wow, thanks for reminding me." Donald balanced his drink on the dashboard, but the slight rocking of the car as he got out tipped it onto the passenger's seat, where half its contents foamed over before Pete could snatch it up again. Donald looked on while Pete held the bottle out the window, soda running down his fingers.

"Wipe it up," Pete told him. "Quick!"

"With what?"

Pete stared at Donald. "That shirt. Use the shirt."   40

Donald pulled a long face but did as he was told, his pale skin puckering against the wind.

"Great, just great," Pete said. "We haven't even left the gas station yet."

Afterwards, on the highway, Donald said, "This is a new car, isn't it?"

"Yes. This is a new car."

"Is that why you're so upset about the seat?"   45

"Forget it, okay? Let's just forget about it."

"I said I was sorry."

Pete said, "I just wish you'd be more careful. These seats are made of leather. That stain won't come out, not to mention the smell. I don't see why I can't have leather seats that smell like leather instead of orange pop."

"What was wrong with the other car?"

Pete glanced over at Donald. Donald had raised the hood of the blue sweat-   50
shirt he'd put on. The peaked hood above his gaunt, watchful face gave him the
look of an inquisitor.

"There wasn't anything wrong with it," Pete said. "I just happened to like
this one better."

Donald nodded.

There was a long silence between them as Pete drove on and the day darkened toward evening. On either side of the road lay stubble-covered fields. A
line of low hills ran along the horizon, topped here and there with trees black
against the grey sky. In the approaching line of cars a driver turned on his
headlights. Pete did the same.

"So what happened?" he asked. "Farm life not your bag?"

Donald took some time to answer, and at last he said, simply, "It was my   55
fault."

"What was your fault?"

"The whole thing. Don't play dumb, Pete. I know they wrote to you."
Donald looked at Pete, then stared out the windshield again.

"I'm not playing dumb."

Donald shrugged.

"All I really know is they asked you to leave," Pete went on. "I don't know   60
any of the particulars."

"I blew it," Donald said. "Believe me, you don't want to hear the gory
details."

"Sure I do," Pete said. He added, "Everybody likes the gory details."

"You mean everybody likes to hear how someone messed up."

"Right," Pete said. "That's the way it is here on Spaceship Earth."

Donald bent one knee onto the front seat and leaned against the door so   65
that he was facing Pete instead of the windshield. Pete was aware of Donald's
scrutiny. He waited. Night was coming on in a rush now, filling the hollows of
the land. Donald's long cheeks and deep-set eyes were dark with shadow. His
brow was white. "Do you ever dream about me?" Donald asked.

"Do I ever dream about you? What kind of a question is that? Of course I
don't dream about you," Pete said, untruthfully.

"What do you dream about?"

"Sex and money. Mostly money. A nightmare is when I dream I don't
have any."

"You're just making that up," Donald said.

Pete smiled.   70

"Sometimes I wake up at night," Donald went on, "and I can tell you're
dreaming about me."

"We were talking about the farm," Pete said. "Let's finish that conversation
and then we can talk about our various out-of-body experiences and the interesting things we did during previous incarnations."

For a moment Donald looked like a grinning skull; then he turned serious
again. "There's not much to tell," he said. "I just didn't do anything right."

"That's a little vague," Pete said.

"Well, like the groceries. Whenever it was my turn to get the groceries I'd   75
blow it somehow. I'd bring the groceries home and half of them would be missing, or I'd have all the wrong things, the wrong kind of flour or the wrong kind
of chocolate or whatever. One time I gave them away. It's not funny, Pete."

Pete said, "Who did you give the groceries to?"

"Just some people I picked up on the way home. Some fieldworkers. They
had about eight kids with them and they didn't even speak English — just nodded their heads. Still, I shouldn't have given away the groceries. Not all of
them, anyway. I really learned my lesson about that. You have to be practical.
You have to be fair to yourself." Donald leaned forward, and Pete could sense
his excitement. "There's nothing actually wrong with being in business," he
said. "As long as you're fair to other people you can still be fair to yourself. I'm
thinking of going into business, Pete."

"We'll talk about it," Pete said. "So, that's the story? There isn't any more
to it than that?"

"What did they tell you?" Donald asked.

"Nothing."   80

"They must have told you something."

Pete shook his head.

"They didn't tell you about the fire?" When Pete shook his head again
Donald regarded him for a time, then folded his arms across his chest and
slumped back into the corner. "Everybody had to take turns cooking dinner. I
usually did tuna casserole or spaghetti with garlic bread. But this one night I
thought I'd do something different, something really interesting." Donald
looked sharply at Pete. "It's all a big laugh to you, isn't it?"

"I'm sorry," Pete said.

"You don't know when to quit. You just keep hitting away."   85

"Tell me about the fire, Donald."

Donald kept watching him. "You have this compulsion to make me look
foolish."

"Come off it, Donald. Don't make a big thing out of this."

"I know why you do it. It's because you don't have any purpose in life.
You're afraid to relate to people who do, so you make fun of them."

"Relate," Pete said.   90

"You're basically a very frightened individual," Donald said. "Very threatened. You've always been like that. Do you remember when you used to try to
kill me?"

"I don't have any compulsion to make you look foolish, Donald — you do it
yourself. You're doing it right now."

"You can't tell me you don't remember," Donald said. "It was after my operation. You remember that?"

"Sort of." Pete shrugged. "Not really."

"Oh yes," Donald said. "Do you want to see the scar?"   95

"I remember you had an operation. I don't remember the specifics, that's
all. And I sure as hell don't remember trying to kill you."

"Oh yes," Donald repeated, maddeningly. "You bet your life you did. All the time. The thing was, I couldn't have anything happen to me where they sewed me up because then my intestines would come apart again and poison me. That was a big issue, Pete. Mom was always in a state about me climbing trees and so on. And you used to hit me there every chance you got."

"Mom was in a state every time you burped," Pete said. "I don't know. Maybe I bumped into you accidentally once or twice. I never did it deliberately."

"Every chance you got," Donald said. "Like when the folks went out at night and left you to baby-sit. I'd hear them say good night, and then I'd hear the car start up, and when they were gone I'd lie there and listen. After a while I would hear you coming down the hall, and I would close my eyes and pretend to be asleep. There were nights when you would stand outside the door, just stand there, and then go away again. But most nights you'd open the door and I would hear you in the room with me, breathing. You'd come over and sit next to me on the bed — you remember, Pete, you have to — you'd sit next to me on the bed and pull the sheets back. If I was on my stomach you'd roll me over. Then you would lift up my pajama shirt and start hitting me on my stitches. You'd hit me as hard as you could, over and over. I was afraid that you'd get mad if you knew I was awake. Is that strange or what? I was afraid that you'd get mad if you found out that I knew you were trying to kill me." Donald laughed. "Come on, you can't tell me you don't remember that."

"It might have happened once or twice. Kids do those things. I can't get all   100
excited about something I maybe did twenty-five years ago."

"No maybe about it. You did it."

Pete said, "You're wearing me out with this stuff. We've got a long drive ahead of us and if you don't back off pretty soon we aren't going to make it. You aren't, anyway."

Donald turned away.

"I'm doing my best," Pete said. The self-pity in his own voice made the words sound like a lie. But they weren't a lie! He was doing his best.

The car topped a rise. In the distance Pete saw a cluster of lights that   105
blinked out when he started downhill. There was no moon. The sky was low and black.

"Come to think of it," Pete said, "I did have a dream about you the other night." Then he added, impatiently, as if Donald were badgering him, "A couple of other nights, too. I'm getting hungry," he said.

"The same dream?"

"Different dreams. I only remember one of them. There was something wrong with me, and you were helping out. Taking care of me. Just the two of us. I don't know where everyone else was supposed to be."

Pete left it at that. He didn't tell Donald that in this dream he was blind.

"I wonder if that was when I woke up," Donald said. He added, "I'm sorry   110
I got into that thing about my scar. I keep trying to forget it but I guess I never will. Not really. It was pretty strange, having someone around all the time who wanted to get rid of me."

"Kid stuff," Pete said. "Ancient history."

They ate dinner at a Denny's on the other side of King City. As Pete was paying the check he heard a man behind him say, "Excuse me, but I wonder if I might ask which way you're going?" and Donald answer, "Santa Cruz."

"Perfect," the man said.

Pete could see him in the fish-eye mirror above the cash register: a red blazer with some kind of crest on the pocket, little black moustache, glossy black hair combed down on his forehead like a Roman emperor's. A rug. Pete thought. Definitely a rug.

Pete got his change and turned. "Why is that perfect?" he asked.   115

The man looked at Pete. He had a soft, ruddy face that was doing its best to express pleasant surprise, as if this new wrinkle were all he could have wished for, but the eyes behind the aviator glasses showed signs of regret. His lips were moist and shiny. "I take it you're together," he said.

"You got it," Pete told him.

"All the better, then," the man went on. "It so happens I'm going to Santa Cruz myself. Had a spot of car trouble down the road. The old Caddy let me down."

"What kind of trouble?" Pete asked.

"Engine trouble," the man said. "I'm afraid it's a bit urgent. My daughter is   120
sick. Urgently sick. I've got a telegram here." He patted the breast pocket of his blazer.

Before Pete could say anything Donald got into the act again. "No problem," Donald said. "We've got tons of room."

"Not that much room," Pete said.

Donald nodded. "I'll put my things in the trunk."

"The trunk's full," Pete told him.

"It so happens I'm traveling light," the man said. "This leg of the trip any-   125
way. In fact, I don't have any luggage at this particular time."

Pete said, "Left it in the old Caddy, did you?"

"Exactly," the man said.

"No problem," Donald repeated. He walked outside and the man went with him. Together they strolled across the parking lot, Pete following at a distance. When they reached Pete's car Donald raised his face to the sky, and the man did the same. They stood there looking up. "Dark night," Donald said.

"Stygian,°" the man said.

Pete still had it in his mind to brush him off, but he didn't do that. Instead   130
he unlocked the door for him. He wanted to see what would happen. It was an adventure, but not a dangerous adventure. The man might steal Pete's ash-trays but he wouldn't kill him. If Pete got killed on the road it would be by some spiritual person in a sweatsuit, someone with his eyes on the far horizon and a wet Try God T-shirt in his duffel bag.

As soon as they left the parking lot the man lit a cigar. He blew a cloud of smoke over Pete's shoulder and sighed with pleasure. "Put it out," Pete told him.

Stygian: Unremittingly dark and frightening.

"Of course," the man said. Pete looked in the rearview mirror and saw the man take another long puff before dropping the cigar out the window. "Forgive me," he said. "I should have asked. Name's Webster, by the way."

Donald turned and looked back at him. "First name or last?"

The man hesitated. "Last," he said finally.

"I know a Webster," Donald said. "Mick Webster."   135

"There are many of us," Webster said.

"Big fellow, wooden leg," Pete said.

Donald gave Pete a look.

Webster shook his head. "Doesn't ring a bell. Still, I wouldn't deny the connection. Might be one of the cousinry."

"What's your daughter got?" Pete asked.   140

"That isn't clear," Webster answered. "It appears to be a female complaint of some nature. Then again it may be tropical." He was quiet for a moment, and added: "If indeed it *is* tropical, I will have to assume some of the blame myself. It was my own vaulting ambition that first led us to the tropics and kept us in the tropics all those many years, exposed to every evil. Truly I have much to answer for. I left my wife there."

Donald said quietly, "You mean she died?"

"I buried her with these hands. The earth will be repaid, gold for gold."

"Which tropics?" Pete asked.

"The tropics of Peru."   145

"What part of Peru are they in?"

"The lowlands," Webster said.

"What's it like down there? In the lowlands."

"Another world," Webster said. His tone was sepulchral. "A world better imagined than described."

"Far out," Pete said.   150

The three men rode in silence for a time. A line of trucks went past in the other direction, trailers festooned with running lights, engines roaring.

"Yes," Webster said at last, "I have much to answer for."

Pete smiled at Donald, but Donald had turned in his seat again and was gazing at Webster. "I'm sorry about your wife," Donald said.

"What did she die of?" Pete asked.

"A wasting illness," Webster said. "The doctors have no name for it, but I   155
do." He leaned forward and said, fiercely, "*Greed.* My greed, not hers. She wanted no part of it."

Pete bit his lip. Webster was a find and Pete didn't want to scare him off by hooting at him. In a voice low and innocent of knowingness, he asked, "What took you there?"

"It's difficult for me to talk about."

"Try," Pete told him.

"A cigar would make it easier."

Donald turned to Pete and said, "It's okay with me."   160

"All right," Pete said. "Go ahead. Just keep the window rolled down."

"Much obliged." A match flared. There were eager sucking sounds.

"Let's hear it," Pete said.

"I am by training an engineer," Webster began. "My work has exposed me to all but one of the continents, to desert and alp and forest, to every terrain and season of the earth. Some years ago I was hired by the Peruvian government to search for tungsten in the tropics. My wife and daughter accompanied me. We were the only white people for a thousand miles in any direction, and we had no choice but to live as the Indians lived — to share their food and drink and even their culture."

Pete said, "You knew the lingo, did you?"   165

"We picked it up." The ember of the cigar bobbed up and down. "We were used to learning as necessity decreed. At any rate, it became evident after a couple of years that there was no tungsten to be found. My wife had fallen ill and was pleading to be taken home. But I was deaf to her pleas, because by then I was on the trail of another metal — a metal far more valuable than tungsten."

"Let me guess," Pete said. "Gold?"

Donald looked at Pete, then back at Webster.

"Gold," Webster said. "A vein of gold greater than the Mother Lode itself. After I found the first traces of it nothing could tear me away from my search — not the sickness of my wife or anything else. I was determined to uncover the vein, and so I did — but not before I laid my wife to rest. As I say, the earth will be repaid."

Webster was quiet. Then he said, "But life must go on. In the years since my   170
wife's death I have been making the arrangements necessary to open the mine. I could have done it immediately, of course, enriching myself beyond measure, but I knew what that would mean — the exploitation of our beloved Indians, the brutal destruction of their environment. I felt I had too much to atone for already." Webster paused, and when he spoke again his voice was dull and rushed, as if he had used up all the interest he had in his own words. "Instead I drew up a program for returning the bulk of the wealth to the Indians themselves. A kind of trust fund. The interest alone will allow them to secure their ancient lands and rights in perpetuity. At the same time, our investors will be rewarded a thousandfold. Two-thousandfold. Everyone will prosper together."

"That's great," said Donald. "That's the way it ought to be."

Pete said, "I'm willing to bet that you just happen to have a few shares left. Am I right?"

Webster made no reply.

"Well?" Pete knew that Webster was on to him now, but he didn't care. The story had bored him. He'd expected something different, something original, and Webster had let him down. He hadn't even tried. Pete felt sour and stale. His eyes burned from cigar smoke and the high beams of road-hogging truckers. "Douse the stogie," he said to Webster. "I told you to keep the window down."

"Got a little nippy back here."   175

Donald said, "Hey, Pete. Lighten up."

"Douse it!"

Webster sighed. He got rid of the cigar.

"I'm a wreck," Pete said to Donald. "You want to drive for a while?"

Donald nodded.   180

Pete pulled over and they changed places.

Webster kept his counsel in the back seat. Donald hummed while he drove, until Pete told him to stop. Then everything was quiet.

Donald was humming again when Pete woke up. Pete stared sullenly at the road, at the white lines sliding past the car. After a few moments of this he turned and said, "How long have I been out?"

Donald glanced at him. "Twenty, twenty-five minutes."

Pete looked behind him and saw that Webster was gone. "Where's our   185
friend?"

"You just missed him. He got out in Soledad. He told me to say thanks and good-bye."

"Soledad? What about his sick daughter? How did he explain her away?"

"He has a brother living there. He's going to borrow a car from him and drive the rest of the way in the morning."

"I'll bet his brother's living there," Pete said. "Doing fifty concurrent life sentences. His brother and his sister and his mom and his dad."

"I kind of liked him," Donald said.   190

"I'm sure you did," Pete said wearily.

"He was interesting. He's been places."

"His cigars had been places, I'll give you that."

"Come on, Pete."

"Come on yourself. What a phony."   195

"You don't know that."

"Sure I do."

"How? How do you know?"

Pete stretched. "Brother, there are some things you're just born knowing. What's the gas situation?"

"We're a little low."   200

"Then why didn't you get some more?"

"I wish you wouldn't snap at me like that," Donald said.

"Then why don't you use your head? What if we run out?"

"We'll make it," Donald said. "I'm pretty sure we've got enough to make it. You didn't have to be so rude to him," Donald added.

Pete took a deep breath. "I don't feel like running out of gas tonight, okay?"   205

Donald pulled in at the next station they came to and filled the tank while Pete went to the men's room. When Pete came back, Donald was sitting in the passenger's seat. The attendant came up to the driver's window as Pete got in behind the wheel. He bent down and said, "Twelve fifty-five."

"You heard the man," Pete said to Donald.

Donald looked straight ahead. He didn't move.

"Cough up," Pete said. "This trip's on you."

"I can't."   210

"Sure you can. Break out that wad."

Donald glanced up at the attendant, then at Pete. "Please," he said, "Pete, I don't have it anymore."

Pete took this in. He nodded, and paid the attendant.

Donald began to speak when they left the station but Pete cut him off. He said, "I don't want to hear from you right now. You just keep quiet or I swear to God I won't be responsible."

They left the fields and entered a tunnel of tall trees. The trees went on   215
and on. "Let me get this straight," Pete said at last. "You don't have the money I gave you."

"You treated him like a bug or something," Donald said.

"You don't have the money," Pete said again.

Donald shook his head.

"Since I bought dinner, and since we didn't stop anywhere in between, I assume you gave it to Webster. Is that right? Is that what you did with it?"

"Yes."   220

Pete looked at Donald. His face was dark under the hood but he still managed to convey a sense of remove, as if none of this had anything to do with him.

"Why?" Pete asked. "Why did you give it to him?" When Donald didn't answer, Pete said, "A hundred dollars. Gone. Just like that. I *worked* for that money, Donald."

"I know, I know," Donald said.

"You don't know! How could you? You get money by holding out your hand."

"I work too," Donald said.   225

"You work too. Don't kid yourself, brother."

Donald leaned toward Pete, about to say something, but Pete cut him off again.

"You're not the only one on the payroll, Donald. I don't think you understand that. I have a family."

"Pete, I'll pay you back."

"Like hell you will. A hundred dollars!" Pete hit the steering wheel with the   230
palm of his hand. "Just because you think I hurt some goofball's feelings. Jesus, Donald."

"That's not the reason," Donald said. "And I didn't just *give* him the money."

"What do you call it, then? What do you call what you did?"

"I *invested* it. I wanted a share, Pete." When Pete looked over at him Donald nodded and said again, "I wanted a share."

Pete said, "I take it you're referring to the gold mine in Peru."

"Yes," Donald said.   235

"You believe that such a gold mine exists?"

Donald looked at Pete, and Pete could see him just beginning to catch on. "You'll believe anything," Pete said. "Won't you? You really will believe anything at all."

"I'm sorry," Donald said, and turned away.

Pete drove on between the trees and considered the truth of what he had just said—that Donald would believe anything at all. And it came to him that it would be just like this unfair life for Donald to come out ahead in the end, by believing in some outrageous promise that would turn out to be true and that he, Pete, would reject out of hand because he was too wised up to listen to anybody's pitch anymore except for laughs. What a joke. What a joke if there really was a blessing to be had, and the blessing didn't come to the one who deserved it, the one who did all the work, but to the other.

And as if this had already happened Pete felt a shadow move upon him, darkening his thoughts. After a time he said, "I can see where all this is going, Donald."

"I'll pay you back," Donald said.

"No," Pete said. "You won't pay me back. You can't. You don't know how. All you've ever done is take. All your life."

Donald shook his head.

"I see exactly where this is going," Pete went on. "You can't work, you can't take care of yourself, you believe anything anyone tells you. I'm stuck with you, aren't I?" He looked over at Donald. "I've got you on my hands for good."

Donald pressed his fingers against the dashboard as if to brace himself. "I'll get out," he said.

Pete kept driving.

"Let me out," Donald said. "I mean it, Pete."

"Do you?"

Donald hesitated. "Yes," he said.

"Be sure," Pete told him. "This is it. This is for keeps."

"I mean it."

"All right. You made the choice." Pete braked the car sharply and swung it to the shoulder of the road. He turned off the engine and got out. Trees loomed on both sides, shutting out the sky. The air was cold and musty. Pete took Donald's duffel bag from the back seat and set it down behind the car. He stood there, facing Donald in the red glow of the taillights. "It's better this way," Pete said.

Donald just looked at him.

"Better for you," Pete said.

Donald hugged himself. He was shaking. "You don't have to say all that," he told Pete. "I don't blame you."

"Blame me? What the hell are you talking about? Blame me for what?"

"For anything," Donald said.

"I want to know what you mean by blame me."

"Nothing. Nothing, Pete. You'd better get going. God bless you."

"That's it," Pete said. He dropped to one knee, searching the packed dirt with his hands. He didn't know what he was looking for, his hands would know when they found it.

Donald touched Pete's shoulder. "You'd better go," he said.

Somewhere in the trees Pete heard a branch snap. He stood up. He looked at Donald, then went back to the car and drove away. He drove fast, hunched over the wheel, conscious of the way he was hunched and the shallowness of his breathing, refusing to look in the mirror above his head until there was nothing behind him but darkness.

240

245

250

255

260

Then he said, "A hundred dollars," as if there were someone to hear.

The trees gave way to fields. Metal fences ran beside the road, plastered with windblown scraps of paper. Tule fog hung above the ditches, spilling into the road, dimming the ghostly halogen lights that burned in the yards of the farms Pete passed. The fog left beads of water rolling up the windshield.

Pete rummaged among his cassettes. He found Pachelbel's Canon and pushed it into the tape deck. When the violins began to play he leaned back and assumed an attentive expression as if he were really listening to them. He smiled to himself like a man at liberty to enjoy music, a man who has finished his work and settled his debts, done all things meet and due.

And in this way, smiling, nodding to the music, he went another mile or so and pretended that he was not already slowing down, that he was not going to turn back, that he would be able to drive on like this, alone, and have the right answer when his wife stood before him in the doorway of his home and asked, Where is he? Where is your brother?   [1985]

265

▓ THINKING ABOUT THE TEXT

1. Are you more sympathetic to Donald's side or to Pete's side in this story? Do you agree with the comment that "everybody likes to hear how someone messed up" (para. 63)? Does Donald get conned by Webster? Would you be angry with Donald for giving Webster your money? Does Pete want Donald to look foolish? Is Donald foolish?

2. How do you interpret Donald's story about Pete hitting his stitches? Was Pete trying to get rid of Donald? What could his reason have been?

3. Why doesn't Pete tell Donald he was blind in his dream? How do you interpret this dream? Is the heart of their dispute "prosperity," or is it something else?

4. In his recent book (*Our Story Begins: New and Selected Stories* [2008]), Wolff revises the end of this story. In paragraph 260, he deletes the last two sentences and adds instead, "and took a step toward Donald." Some readers were disappointed that he takes out what they see as an enigmatic action that adds mystery and complexity to the ending. Do you agree? Why do you think Wolff made this change?

5. Why would Pete turn around to get Donald? Why would he keep going? What would you do? Why?

JAMES BALDWIN

Sonny's Blues

James Baldwin (1924–1987) wanted to be a writer from the time he was a boy growing up in Harlem. He continued his writing through high school while also following in his foster father's footsteps by doing some preaching. On his own at age eighteen, Baldwin left Greenwich Village in 1948 and moved to Paris. He lived in

France for eight years before returning to New York, where he wrote widely about the civil rights movement. Indeed, Baldwin's passionate and eloquent essays, like those in Notes of a Native Son (1955) and The Fire Next Time (1963), exploring the place of African Americans in contemporary society are considered among the best nonfiction of his generation.

Being an artist and an African American were lifelong central issues for Baldwin. His fiction confronts the psychological challenges that were inevitable for black writers searching for identity in America. Themes of responsibility, pain, identity, frustration, and bitterness are woven into his fiction along with understanding, equanimity, love, and tolerance. "Sonny's Blues," from Going to Meet the Man *(1965), is one of his strongest dramatizations of the struggles and achievements of black artists.*

I read about it in the paper, in the subway, on my way to work. I read it, and I couldn't believe it, and I read it again. Then perhaps I just stared at it, at the newsprint spelling out his name, spelling out the story. I stared at it in the swinging lights of the subway car, and in the faces and bodies of the people, and in my own face, trapped in the darkness which roared outside.

It was not to be believed and I kept telling myself that, as I walked from the subway station to the high school. And at the same time I couldn't doubt it. I was scared, scared for Sonny. He became real to me again. A great block of ice got settled in my belly and kept melting there slowly all day long, while I taught my classes algebra. It was a special kind of ice. It kept melting, sending trickles of ice water all up and down my veins, but it never got less. Sometimes it hardened and seemed to expand until I felt my guts were going to come spilling out or that I was going to choke or scream. This would always be at a moment when I was remembering some specific thing Sonny had once said or done.

When he was about as old as the boys in my classes his face had been bright and open, there was a lot of copper in it; and he'd had wonderfully direct brown eyes, and great gentleness and privacy. I wondered what he looked like now. He had been picked up, the evening before, in a raid on an apartment downtown, for peddling and using heroin.

I couldn't believe it: but what I mean by that is that I couldn't find any room for it anywhere inside me. I had kept it outside me for a long time. I hadn't wanted to know. I had had suspicions, but I didn't name them, I kept putting them away. I told myself that Sonny was wild, but he wasn't crazy. And he'd always been a good boy, he hadn't ever turned hard or evil or disrespectful, the way kids can, so quick, so quick, especially in Harlem. I didn't want to believe that I'd ever see my brother going down, coming to nothing, all that light in his face gone out, in the condition I'd already seen so many others. Yet it had happened and here I was, talking about algebra to a lot of boys who might, every one of them for all I knew, be popping off needles every time they went to the head. Maybe it did more for them than algebra could.

I was sure that the first time Sonny had ever had horse,° he couldn't have been much older than these boys were now. These boys, now, were living as we'd been living then, they were growing up with a rush and their heads

horse: Name for heroin in the 1950s.

bumped abruptly against the low ceiling of their actual possibilities. They were filled with rage. All they really knew were two darknesses, the darkness of their lives, which was now closing in on them, and the darkness of the movies, which had blinded them to that other darkness, and in which they now, vindictively, dreamed, at once more together than they were at any other time, and more alone.

When the last bell rang, the last class ended, I let out my breath. It seemed I'd been holding it for all that time. My clothes were wet — I may have looked as though I'd been sitting in a steam bath, all dressed up, all afternoon. I sat alone in the classroom a long time. I listened to the boys outside, downstairs, shouting and cursing and laughing. Their laughter struck me for perhaps the first time. It was not the joyous laughter which — God knows why — one associates with children. It was mocking and insular, its intent to denigrate. It was disenchanted, and in this, also, lay the authority of their curses. Perhaps I was listening to them because I was thinking about my brother and in them I heard my brother. And myself.

One boy was whistling a tune, at once very complicated and very simple, it seemed to be pouring out of him as though he were a bird, and it sounded very cool and moving through all that harsh, bright air, only just holding its own through all those other sounds.

I stood up and walked over to the window and looked down into the courtyard. It was the beginning of the spring and the sap was rising in the boys. A teacher passed through them every now and again, quickly, as though he or she couldn't wait to get out of that courtyard, to get those boys out of their sight and off their minds. I started collecting my stuff. I thought I'd better get home and talk to Isabel.

The courtyard was almost deserted by the time I got downstairs. I saw this boy standing in the shadow of a doorway, looking just like Sonny. I almost called his name. Then I saw that it wasn't Sonny, but somebody we used to know, a boy from around our block. He'd been Sonny's friend. He'd never been mine, having been too young for me, and, anyway, I'd never liked him. And now, even though he was a grown-up man, he still hung around that block, still spent hours on the street corners, was always high and raggy. I used to run into him from time to time and he'd often work around to asking me for a quarter or fifty cents. He always had some real good excuse, too, and I always gave it to him, I don't know why.

But now, abruptly, I hated him. I couldn't stand the way he looked at me, partly like a dog, partly like a cunning child. I wanted to ask him what the hell he was doing in the school courtyard.

He sort of shuffled over to me, and he said, "I see you got the papers. So you already know about it."

"You mean about Sonny? Yes, I already know about it. How come they didn't get you?"

He grinned. It made him repulsive and it also brought to mind what he'd looked like as a kid. "I wasn't there. I stay away from them people."

"Good for you." I offered him a cigarette and I watched him through the smoke. "You come all the way down here just to tell me about Sonny?"

"That's right." He was sort of shaking his head and his eyes looked strange,   15
as though they were about to cross. The bright sun deadened his damp dark
brown skin and it made his eyes look yellow and showed up the dirt in his
kinked hair. He smelled funky. I moved a little away from him and I said, "Well,
thanks. But I already know about it and I got to get home."

"I'll walk you a little ways," he said. We started walking. There were a
couple of kids still loitering in the courtyard and one of them said goodnight to
me and looked strangely at the boy beside me.

"What're you going to do?" he asked me. "I mean, about Sonny?"

"Look. I haven't seen Sonny for over a year. I'm not sure I'm going to do
anything. Anyway, what the hell *can* I do?" **What happened?**

"That's right," he said quickly, "ain't nothing you can do. Can't much help
old Sonny no more, I guess."

It was what I was thinking and so it seemed to me he had no right to say it.   20

"I'm surprised at Sonny, though," he went on — he had a funny way of
talking, he looked straight ahead as though he were talking to himself — "I
thought Sonny was a smart boy, I thought he was too smart to get hung."

"I guess he thought so too," I said sharply, "and that's how he got hung.
And how about you? You're pretty goddamn smart, I bet."

Then he looked directly at me, just for a minute. "I ain't smart," he said. "If
I was smart, I'd have reached for a pistol a long time ago."

"Look. Don't tell *me* your sad story, if it was up to me, I'd give you one."
Then I felt guilty — guilty, probably, for never having supposed that the poor
bastard *had* a story of his own, much less a sad one, and I asked, quickly,
"What's going to happen to him now?"

He didn't answer this. He was off by himself some place. "Funny thing," he   25
said, and from his tone we might have been discussing the quickest way to get
to Brooklyn, "when I saw the papers this morning, the first thing I asked myself
was if I had anything to do with it. I felt sort of responsible."

I began to listen more carefully. The subway station was on the corner, just
before us, and I stopped. He stopped, too. We were in front of a bar and he
ducked slightly, peering in, but whoever he was looking for didn't seem to be
there. The juke box was blasting away with something black and bouncy and I
half watched the barmaid as she danced her way from the juke box to her place
behind the bar. And I watched her face as she laughingly responded to something someone said to her, still keeping time to the music. When she smiled one
saw the little girl, one sensed the doomed, still-struggling woman beneath the
battered face of the semi-whore.

"I never *give* Sonny nothing," the boy said finally, "but a long time ago I
come to school high and Sonny asked me how it felt." He paused, I couldn't
bear to watch him, I watched the barmaid, and I listened to the music which
seemed to be causing the pavement to shake. "I told him it felt great." The music stopped, the barmaid paused and watched the juke box until the music began again. "It did." — **Oh...**

All this was carrying me some place I didn't want to go. I certainly didn't
want to know how it felt. It filled everything, the people, the houses, the music,
the dark, quicksilver barmaid, with menace; and this menace was their reality.

"What's going to happen to him now?" I asked again.

"They'll send him away some place and they'll try to cure him." He shook   30
his head. "Maybe he'll even think he's kicked the habit. Then they'll let him
loose" — he gestured, throwing his cigarette into the gutter. "That's all."

"What do you mean, that's *all?*"

But I knew what he meant.

"I *mean*, that's *all.*" He turned his head and looked at me, pulling down the
corners of his mouth. "Don't you know what I mean?" he asked, softly.

"How the hell *would* I know what you mean?" I almost whispered it, I don't
know why.

"That's right," he said to the air, "how would *he* know what I mean?" He   35
turned toward me again, patient and calm, and yet I somehow felt him shaking, shaking as though he were going to fall apart. I felt that ice in my guts
again, the dread I'd felt all afternoon; and again I watched the barmaid, moving about the bar, washing glasses, and singing. "Listen. They'll let him out and
then it'll just start all over again. That's what I mean."

"You mean — they'll let him out. And then he'll just start working his way
back in again. You mean he'll never kick the habit. Is that what you mean?"

"That's right," he said, cheerfully. "*You* see what I mean."

"Tell me," I said at last, "why does he want to die? He must want to die, he's
killing himself, why does he want to die?"

He looked at me in surprise. He licked his lips. "He don't want to die. He
wants to live. Don't nobody want to die, ever."

Then I wanted to ask him — too many things. He could not have answered,   40
or if he had, I could not have borne the answers. I started walking. "Well, I
guess it's none of my business."

"It's going to be rough on old Sonny," he said. We reached the subway station. "This is your station?" he asked. I nodded. I took one step down. "Damn!"
he said, suddenly. I looked up at him. He grinned again. "Damn it if I didn't
leave all my money home. You ain't got a dollar on you, have you? Just for a
couple of days, is all."

All at once something inside gave and threatened to come pouring out of
me. I didn't hate him any more. I felt that in another moment I'd start crying
like a child.

"Sure," I said. "Don't sweat." I looked in my wallet and didn't have a dollar,
I only had a five. "Here," I said. "That hold you?"

He didn't look at it — he didn't want to look at it. A terrible closed look
came over his face, as though he were keeping the number on the bill a secret
from him and me. "Thanks," he said, and now he was dying to see me go.
"Don't worry about Sonny. Maybe I'll write him or something."

"Sure," I said. "You do that. So long."   45

"Be seeing you," he said. I went on down the steps.

And I didn't write Sonny or send him anything for a long time. When I finally
did, it was just after my little girl died, he wrote me back a letter which made me
feel like a bastard.

Here's what he said:

Dear brother,
You don't know how much I needed to hear from you. I wanted to write
you many a time but I dug how much I must have hurt you and so I didn't
write. But now I feel like a man who's been trying to climb up out of some
deep, real deep and funky hole and just saw the sun up there, outside. I got to
get outside.
    I can't tell you much about how I got here. I mean I don't know how to
tell you. I guess I was afraid of something or I was trying to escape from something and you know I have never been very strong in the head (smile). I'm glad
Mama and Daddy are dead and can't see what's happened to their son and I
swear if I'd known what I was doing I would never have hurt you so, you and
a lot of other fine people who were nice to me and who believed in me.
    I don't want you to think it had anything to do with me being a musician.
It's more than that. Or maybe less than that. I can't get anything straight in
my head down here and I try not to think about what's going to happen to me
when I get outside again. Sometime I think I'm going to flip and never get outside and sometime I think I'll come straight back. I tell you one thing, though,
I'd rather blow my brains out than go through this again. But that's what they
all say, so they tell me. If I tell you when I'm coming to New York and if you
could meet me, I sure would appreciate it. Give my love to Isabel and the kids
and I was sure sorry to hear about little Gracie. I wish I could be like Mama and
say the Lord's will be done, but I don't know it seems to me that trouble is the
one thing that never does get stopped and I don't know what good it does to
blame it on the Lord. But maybe it does some good if you believe it.

Your brother,
Sonny

That was heartbreaking.

Then I kept in constant touch with him and I sent him whatever I could
and I went to meet him when he came back to New York. When I saw him
many things I thought I had forgotten came flooding back to me. This was because I had begun, finally, to wonder about Sonny, about the life that Sonny
lived inside. This life, whatever it was, had made him older and thinner and it
had deepened the distant stillness in which he had always moved. He looked
very unlike my baby brother. Yet, when he smiled, when we shook hands, the
baby brother I'd never known looked out from the depths of his private life, like
an animal waiting to be coaxed into the light.
    "How you been keeping?" he asked me.   50
    "All right. And you?"
    "Just fine." He was smiling all over his face. "It's good to see you again."
    "It's good to see you."
    The seven years' difference in our ages lay between us like a chasm: I won-
dered if these years would ever operate between us as a bridge. I was remembering, and it made it hard to catch my breath, that I had been there when he
was born; and I had heard the first words he had ever spoken. When he started
to walk, he walked from our mother straight to me. I caught him just before he
fell when he took the first steps he ever took in this world.

"How's Isabel?"   55
"Just fine. She's dying to see you."
"And the boys?"
"They're fine, too. They're anxious to see their uncle."
"Oh, come on. You know they don't remember me."
"Are you kidding? Of course they remember you."   60
He grinned again. We got into a taxi. We had a lot to say to each other, far
too much to know how to begin.

As the taxi began to move, I asked, "You still want to go to India?"

He laughed. "You still remember that. Hell, no. This place is Indian enough
for me."

"It used to belong to them," I said.

And he laughed again. "They damn sure knew what they were doing   65
when they got rid of it."

Years ago, when he was around fourteen, he'd been all hipped on the idea
of going to India. He read books about people sitting on rocks, naked, in all
kinds of weather, but mostly bad, naturally, and walking barefoot through hot
coals and arriving at wisdom. I used to say that it sounded to me as though
they were getting away from wisdom as fast as they could. I think he sort of
looked down on me for that.

"Do you mind," he asked, "if we have the driver drive alongside the park?
On the west side — I haven't seen the city in so long."

"Of course not," I said. I was afraid that I might sound as though I were
humoring him, but I hoped he wouldn't take it that way.

So we drove along, between the green of the park and the stony, lifeless elegance of hotels and apartment buildings, toward the vivid, killing streets of our
childhood. These streets hadn't changed, though housing projects jutted up out
of them now like rocks in the middle of a boiling sea. Most of the houses in which
we had grown up had vanished, as had the stores from which we had stolen,
the basements in which we had first tried sex, the rooftops from which we had
hurled tin cans and bricks. But houses exactly like the houses of our past yet
dominated the landscape, boys exactly like the boys we once had been found
themselves smothering in these houses, came down into the streets for light
and air and found themselves encircled by disaster. Some escaped the trap, most
didn't. Those who got out always left something of themselves behind, as some
animals amputate a leg and leave it in the trap. It might be said, perhaps, that I
had escaped, after all, I was a school teacher; or that Sonny had, he hadn't lived
in Harlem for years. Yet, as the cab moved uptown through streets which seemed,
with a rush, to darken with dark people, and as I covertly studied Sonny's face,
it came to me that what we both were seeking through our separate cab windows was that part of ourselves which had been left behind. It's always at the
hour of trouble and confrontation that the missing member aches.

We hit 110th Street and started rolling up Lenox Avenue. And I'd known   70
this avenue all my life, but it seemed to me again, as it had seemed on the day
I'd first heard about Sonny's trouble, filled with a hidden menace which was its
very breath of life.

they live in Harlem?

"We almost there," said Sonny.

"Almost." We were both too nervous to say anything more.

We live in a housing project. It hasn't been up long. A few days after it was up it seemed uninhabitably new, now, of course, it's already rundown. It looks like a parody of the good, clean, faceless life — God knows the people who live in it do their best to make it a parody. The beat-looking grass lying around isn't enough to make their lives green, the hedges will never hold out the streets, and they know it. The big windows fool no one, they aren't big enough to make space out of no space. They don't bother with the windows, they watch the TV screen instead. The playground is most popular with the children who don't play at jacks, or skip rope, or roller skate, or swing, and they can be found in it after dark. We moved in partly because it's not too far from where I teach, and partly for the kids; but it's really just like the houses in which Sonny and I grew up. The same things happen, they'll have the same things to remember. The moment Sonny and I started into the house I had the feeling that I was simply bringing him back into the danger he had almost died trying to escape.

Sonny has never been talkative. So I don't know why I was sure he'd be dying to talk to me when supper was over the first night. Everything went fine, the oldest boy remembered him, and the youngest boy liked him, and Sonny had remembered to bring something for each of them; and Isabel, who is really much nicer than I am, more open and giving, had gone to a lot of trouble about dinner and was genuinely glad to see him. And she's always been able to tease Sonny in a way that I haven't. It was nice to see her face so vivid again and to hear her laugh and watch her make Sonny laugh. She wasn't, or, anyway, she didn't seem to be, at all uneasy or embarrassed. She chatted as though there were no subject which had to be avoided and she got Sonny past his first, faint stiffness. And thank God she was there, for I was filled with that icy dread again. Everything I did seemed awkward to me, and everything I said sounded freighted with hidden meaning. I was trying to remember everything I'd heard about dope addiction and I couldn't help watching Sonny for signs. I wasn't doing it out of malice. I was trying to find out something about my brother. I was dying to hear him tell me he was safe.

"Safe!" my father grunted, whenever Mama suggested trying to move to a neighborhood which might be safer for children. "Safe, hell! Ain't no place safe for kids, nor nobody."

He always went on like this, but he wasn't, ever, really as bad as he sounded, not even on weekends, when he got drunk. As a matter of fact, he was always on the lookout for "something a little better," but he died before he found it. He died suddenly, during a drunken weekend in the middle of the war, when Sonny was fifteen. He and Sonny hadn't ever got on too well. And this was partly because Sonny was the apple of his father's eye. It was because he loved Sonny so much and was frightened for him, that he was always fighting with him. It doesn't do any good to fight with Sonny. Sonny just moves back, inside himself, where he can't be reached. But the principal reason that they never hit it off is that they were so much alike. Daddy was big and rough and loud-talking, just the opposite of Sonny, but they both had — that same privacy.

75

Mama tried to tell me something about this, just after Daddy died. I was home on leave from the army.

This was the last time I ever saw my mother alive. Just the same, this picture gets all mixed up in my mind with pictures I had of her when she was younger. The way I always see her is the way she used to be on a Sunday afternoon, say, when the old folks were talking after the big Sunday dinner. I always see her wearing pale blue. She'd be sitting on the sofa. And my father would be sitting in the easy chair, not far from her. And the living room would be full of church folks and relatives. There they sit, in chairs all around the living room, and the night is creeping up outside, but nobody knows it yet. You can see the darkness growing against the windowpanes and you hear the street noises every now and again, or maybe the jangling beat of a tambourine from one of the churches close by, but it's real quiet in the room. For a moment nobody's talking, but every face looks darkening, like the sky outside. And my mother rocks a little from the waist, and my father's eyes are closed. Everyone is looking at something a child can't see. For a minute they've forgotten the children. Maybe a kid is lying on the rug, half asleep. Maybe somebody's got a kid in his lap and is absent-mindedly stroking the kid's head. Maybe there's a kid, quiet and big-eyed, curled up in a big chair in the corner. The silence, the darkness coming, and the darkness in the faces frightens the child obscurely. He hopes that the hand which strokes his forehead will never stop — will never die. He hopes that there will never come a time when the old folks won't be sitting around the living room, talking about where they've come from, and what they've seen, and what's happened to them and their kinfolk.

But something deep and watchful in the child knows that this is bound to end, is already ending. In a moment someone will get up and turn on the light. Then the old folks will remember the children and they won't talk any more that day. And when light fills the room, the child is filled with darkness. He knows that every time this happens he's moved just a little closer to that darkness outside. The darkness outside is what the old folks have been talking about. It's what they've come from. It's what they endure. The child knows that they won't talk any more because if he knows too much about what's happened to *them*, he'll know too much too soon, about what's going to happen to *him*.

The last time I talked to my mother, I remember I was restless. I wanted to   80
get out and see Isabel. We weren't married then and we had a lot to straighten out between us.

There Mama sat, in black, by the window. She was humming an old church song, *Lord, you brought me from a long ways off.* Sonny was out somewhere. Mama kept watching the streets.

"I don't know," she said, "if I'll ever see you again, after you go off from here. But I hope you'll remember the things I tried to teach you."

"Don't talk like that," I said, and smiled. "You'll be here a long time yet."

She smiled, too, but she said nothing. She was quiet for a long time. And I said, "Mama, don't you worry about nothing. I'll be writing all the time, and you be getting the checks. . . ."

"I want to talk to you about your brother," she said, suddenly. "If anything   85
happens to me he ain't going to have nobody to look out for him."

"Mama," I said, "ain't nothing going to happen to you or Sonny. Sonny's
all right. He's a good boy and he's got good sense."

"It ain't a question of his being a good boy," Mama said, "nor of his having
good sense. It ain't only the bad ones, nor yet the dumb ones that gets sucked
under." She stopped, looking at me. "Your Daddy once had a brother," she said,
and she smiled in a way that made me feel she was in pain. "You didn't never
know that, did you?"

"No," I said, "I never knew that," and I watched her face.

"Oh, yes," she said, "your Daddy had a brother." She looked out of the window again. "I know you never saw your Daddy cry. But I did — many a time,
through all these years."

I asked her, "What happened to his brother? How come nobody's ever   90
talked about him?"

This was the first time I ever saw my mother look old.

"His brother got killed," she said, "when he was just a little younger than
you are now. I knew him. He was a fine boy. He was maybe a little full of the
devil, but he didn't mean nobody no harm."

Then she stopped and the room was silent, exactly as it had sometimes
been on those Sunday afternoons. Mama kept looking out into the streets.

"He used to have a job in the mill," she said, "and, like all young folks, he
just liked to perform on Saturday nights. Saturday nights, him and your father
would drift around to different places, go to dances and things like that, or just
sit around with people they knew, and your father's brother would sing, he had
a fine voice, and play along with himself on his guitar. Well, this particular
Saturday night, him and your father was coming home from some place, and
they were both a little drunk and there was a moon that night, it was bright like
day. Your father's brother was feeling kind of good, and he was whistling to
himself, and he had his guitar slung over his shoulder. They was coming down
a hill and beneath them was a road that turned off from the highway. Well,
your father's brother, being always kind of frisky, decided to run down this hill,
and he did, with that guitar banging and clanging behind him, and he ran
across the road, and he was making water behind a tree. And your father was
sort of amused at him and he was still coming down the hill, kind of slow. Then
he heard a car motor and that same minute his brother stepped from behind
the tree, into the road, in the moonlight. And he started to cross the road. And
your father started to run down the hill, he says he don't know why. This car
was full of white men. They was all drunk, and when they seen your father's
brother they let out a great whoop and holler and they aimed the car straight
at him. They was having fun, they just wanted to scare him, the way they do
sometimes, you know. But they was drunk. And I guess the boy, being drunk,
too, and scared, kind of lost his head. By the time he jumped it was too late.
Your father says he heard his brother scream when the car rolled over him, and
he heard the wood of that guitar when it give, and he heard them strings go
flying, and he heard them white men shouting, and the car kept on a-going and

it ain't stopped till this day. And, time your father got down the hill, his brother weren't nothing but blood and pulp."

Tears were gleaming on my mother's face. There wasn't anything I   95
could say.

"He never mentioned it," she said, "because I never let him mention it before you children. Your Daddy was like a crazy man that night and for many a night thereafter. He says he never in his life seen anything as dark as that road after the lights of that car had gone away. Weren't nothing, weren't nobody on that road, just your Daddy and his brother and that busted guitar. Oh, yes. Your Daddy never did really get right again. Till the day he died he weren't sure but that every white man he saw was the man that killed his brother."

She stopped and took out her handkerchief and dried her eyes and looked at me.

"I ain't telling you all this," she said, "to make you scared or bitter or to make you hate nobody. I'm telling you this because you got a brother. And the world ain't changed."

I guess I didn't want to believe this. I guess she saw this in my face. She turned away from me, toward the window again, searching those streets.

"But I praise my Redeemer," she said at last, "that He called your Daddy   100
home before me. I ain't saying it to throw no flowers at myself, but, I declare, it keeps me from feeling too cast down to know I helped your father get safely through this world. Your father always acted like he was the roughest, strongest man on earth. And everybody took him to be like that. But if he hadn't had *me* there — to see his tears!"

She was crying again. Still, I couldn't move. I said, "Lord, Lord, Mama, I didn't know it was like that."

"Oh, honey," she said, "there's a lot that you don't know. But you are going to find it out." She stood up from the window and came over to me. "You got to hold on to your brother," she said, "and don't let him fall, no matter what it looks like is happening to him and no matter how evil you gets with him. You going to be evil with him many a time. But don't you forget what I told you, you hear?"

"I won't forget," I said. "Don't you worry, I won't forget. I won't let nothing happen to Sonny."

My mother smiled as though she were amused at something she saw in my face. Then, "You may not be able to stop nothing from happening. But you got to let him know you's *there*."

Two days later I was married, and then I was gone. And I had a lot of things on   105
my mind and I pretty well forgot my promise to Mama until I got shipped home on a special furlough for her funeral.

And, after the funeral, with just Sonny and me alone in the empty kitchen, I tried to find out something about him.

"What do you want to do?" I asked him.

"I'm going to be a musician," he said.

For he had graduated, in the time I had been away, from dancing to the juke box to finding out who was playing what, and what they were doing with it, and he had bought himself a set of drums.

"You mean, you want to be a drummer?" I somehow had the feeling that   110
being a drummer might be all right for other people but not for my brother
Sonny.

"I don't think," he said, looking at me very gravely, "that I'll ever be a good
drummer. But I think I can play a piano."

I frowned. I'd never played the role of the older brother quite so seriously
before, had scarcely ever, in fact, *asked* Sonny a damn thing. I sensed myself in
the presence of something I didn't really know how to handle, didn't understand. So I made my frown a little deeper as I asked: "What kind of musician do
you want to be?"

He grinned. "How many kinds do you think there are?"

"Be *serious*," I said.

He laughed, throwing his head back, and then looked at me. "I *am* serious."   115

"Well, then, for Christ's sake, stop kidding around and answer a serious
question. I mean, do you want to be a concert pianist, you want to play classical music and all that, or — or what?" Long before I finished he was laughing
again. "For Christ's *sake*, Sonny!"

He sobered, but with difficulty. "I'm sorry. But you sound so — *scared!*" and
he was off again.

"Well, you may think it's funny now, baby, but it's not going to be so funny
when you have to make your living at it, let me tell you *that*." I was furious because I knew he was laughing at me and I didn't know why.

"No," he said, very sober now, and afraid, perhaps, that he'd hurt me, "I
don't want to be a classical pianist. That isn't what interests me. I mean" — he
paused, looking hard at me, as though his eyes would help me to understand,
and then gestured helplessly, as though perhaps his hand would help — "I mean,
I'll have a lot of studying to do, and I'll have to study *everything*, but, I mean, I
want to play *with* — jazz musicians." He stopped. "I want to play jazz," he said.

Well, the word had never before sounded as heavy, as real, as it sounded   120
that afternoon in Sonny's mouth. I just looked at him and I was probably
frowning a real frown by this time. I simply couldn't see why on earth he'd
want to spend his time hanging around nightclubs, clowning around on band-
stands, while people pushed each other around a dance floor. It seemed —
beneath him, somehow. I had never thought about it before, had never been
forced to, but I suppose I had always put jazz musicians in a class with what
Daddy called "good-time people."

"Are you *serious*?"

"Hell, *yes*, I'm serious."

He looked more helpless than ever, and annoyed, and deeply hurt.

I suggested, helpfully: "You mean — like Louis Armstrong?"

His face closed as though I'd struck him. "No. I'm not talking about none   125
of that old-time, down home crap."

"Well, look, Sonny, I'm sorry, don't get mad. I just don't altogether get it,
that's all. Name somebody — you know, a jazz musician you admire."

"Bird."

"Who?"

"Bird! Charlie Parker! Don't they teach you nothing in the goddamn army?"

I lit a cigarette. I was surprised and then a little amused to discover that I   130
was trembling. "I've been out of touch," I said. "You'll have to be patient with
me. Now. Who's this Parker character?"

"He's just one of the greatest jazz musicians alive," said Sonny, sullenly, his
hands in his pockets, his back to me. "Maybe *the* greatest," he added, bitterly,
"that's probably why *you* never heard of him."

"All right," I said, "I'm ignorant. I'm sorry. I'll go out and buy all the cat's
records right away, all right?"

"It don't," said Sonny, with dignity, "make any difference to me. I don't
care what you listen to. Don't do me no favors."

I was beginning to realize that I'd never seen him so upset before. With
another part of my mind I was thinking that this would probably turn out to be
one of those things kids go through and that I shouldn't make it seem important by pushing it too hard. Still, I didn't think it would do any harm to ask:
"Doesn't all this take a lot of time? Can you make a living at it?"

He turned back to me and half leaned, half sat, on the kitchen table. "Ev-   135
erything takes time," he said, "and — well, yes, sure, I can make a living at it.
But what I don't seem to be able to make you understand is that it's the only
thing I want to do."

"Well, Sonny," I said, gently, "you know people can't always do exactly
what they *want* to do — "

"*No*, I don't know that," said Sonny, surprising me. "I think people *ought* to
do what they want to do, what else are they alive for?"

"You getting to be a big boy," I said desperately, "it's time you started thinking about your future."

"I'm thinking about my future," said Sonny, grimly. "I think about it all the
time."

I gave up. I decided, if he didn't change his mind, that we could always talk   140
about it later. "In the meantime," I said, "you got to finish school." We had already decided that he'd have to move in with Isabel and her folks. I knew this
wasn't the ideal arrangement because Isabel's folks are inclined to be dicty and
they hadn't especially wanted Isabel to marry me. But I didn't know what else
to do. "And we have to get you fixed up at Isabel's."

There was a long silence. He moved from the kitchen table to the window.
"That's a terrible idea. You know it yourself."

"Do you have a *better* idea?"

He just walked up and down the kitchen for a minute. He was as tall as I
was. He had started to shave. I suddenly had the feeling that I didn't know him
at all.

He stopped at the kitchen table and picked up my cigarettes. Looking at me
with a kind of mocking, amused defiance, he put one between his lips. "You
mind?"

"You smoking already?"   145

He lit the cigarette and nodded, watching me through the smoke. "I just
wanted to see if I'd have the courage to smoke in front of you." He grinned and
blew a great cloud of smoke to the ceiling. "It was easy." He looked at my face.
"Come on, now. I bet you was smoking at my age, tell the truth."

I didn't say anything but the truth was on my face, and he laughed. But now there was something very strained in his laugh. "Sure. And I bet that ain't all you was doing."

He was frightening me a little. "Cut the crap," I said. "We already decided that you was going to go and live at Isabel's. Now what's got into you all of a sudden?"

"*You* decided it," he pointed out. "*I* didn't decide nothing." He stopped in front of me, leaning against the stove, arms loosely folded. "Look, brother. I don't want to stay in Harlem no more, I really don't." He was very earnest. He looked at me, then over toward the kitchen window. There was something in his eyes I'd never seen before, some thoughtfulness, some worry all his own. He rubbed the muscle of one arm. "It's time I was getting out of here."

"Where do you want to *go*, Sonny?"   150

"I want to join the army. Or the navy, I don't care. If I say I'm old enough, they'll believe me."

Then I got mad. It was because I was so scared. "You must be crazy. You goddamn fool, what the hell do you want to go and join the *army* for?"

"I just told you. To get out of Harlem."

"Sonny, you haven't even finished *school*. And if you really want to be a musician, how do you expect to study if you're in the *army?*"

He looked at me, trapped, and in anguish. "There's ways. I might be able to   155
work out some kind of deal. Anyway, I'll have the G.I. Bill when I come out."

"*If* you come out." We stared at each other. "Sonny, please. Be reasonable. I know the setup is far from perfect. But we got to do the best we can."

"I ain't learning nothing in school," he said. "Even when I go." He turned away from me and opened the window and threw his cigarette out into the narrow alley. I watched his back. "At least, I ain't learning nothing you'd want me to learn." He slammed the window so hard I thought the glass would fly out, and turned back to me. "And I'm sick of the stink of these garbage cans!"

"Sonny," I said, "I know how you feel. But if you don't finish school now, you're going to be sorry later that you didn't." I grabbed him by the shoulders. "And you only got another year. It ain't so bad. And I'll come back and I swear I'll help you do *whatever* you want to do. Just try to put up with it till I come back. Will you please do that? For me?"

He didn't answer and he wouldn't look at me.

"Sonny. You hear me?"   160

He pulled away. "I hear you. But you never hear anything *I* say."

I didn't know what to say to that. He looked out of the window and then back at me. "OK," he said, and sighed. "I'll try."

Then I said, trying to cheer him up a little, "They got a piano at Isabel's. You can practice on it."

And as a matter of fact, it did cheer him up for a minute. "That's right," he said to himself. "I forgot that." His face relaxed a little. But the worry, the thoughtfulness, played on it still, the way shadows play on a face which is staring into the fire.

But I thought I'd never hear the end of that piano. At first, Isabel would write   165
me, saying how nice it was that Sonny was so serious about his music and how,

as soon as he came in from school, or wherever he had been when he was supposed to be at school, he went straight to that piano and stayed there until suppertime. And, after supper, he went back to that piano and stayed there until everybody went to bed. He was at the piano all day Saturday and all day Sunday. Then he bought a record player and started playing records. He'd play one record over and over again, all day long sometimes, and he'd improvise along with it on the piano. Or he'd play one section of the record, one chord, one change, one progression, then he'd do it on the piano. Then back to the record. Then back to the piano.

Well, I really don't know how they stood it. Isabel finally confessed that it wasn't like living with a person at all, it was like living with sound. And the sound didn't make any sense to her, didn't make any sense to any of them — naturally. They began, in a way, to be afflicted by this presence that was living in their home. It was as though Sonny were some sort of god, or monster. He moved in an atmosphere which wasn't like theirs at all. They fed him and he ate, he washed himself, he walked in and out of their door; he certainly wasn't nasty or unpleasant or rude, Sonny isn't any of those things; but it was as though he were all wrapped up in some cloud, some fire, some vision all his own; and there wasn't any way to reach him.

At the same time, he wasn't really a man yet, he was still a child, and they had to watch out for him in all kinds of ways. They certainly couldn't throw him out. Neither did they dare to make a great scene about that piano because even they dimly sensed, as I sensed, from so many thousands of miles away, that Sonny was at that piano playing for his life.

But he hadn't been going to school. One day a letter came from the school board and Isabel's mother got it — there had, apparently, been other letters but Sonny had torn them up. This day, when Sonny came in, Isabel's mother showed him the letter and asked where he'd been spending his time. And she finally got it out of him that he'd been down in Greenwich Village, with musicians and other characters, in a white girl's apartment. And this scared her and she started to scream at him and what came up, once she began — though she denies it to this day — was what sacrifices they were making to give Sonny a decent home and how little he appreciated it. *oh no …*

Sonny didn't play the piano that day. By evening, Isabel's mother had calmed down but then there was the old man to deal with, and Isabel herself. Isabel says she did her best to be calm but she broke down and started crying. She says she just watched Sonny's face. She could tell, by watching him, what was happening with him. And what was happening was that they penetrated his cloud, they had reached him. Even if their fingers had been a thousand times more gentle than human fingers ever are, he could hardly help feeling that they had stripped him naked and were spitting on that nakedness. For he also had to see that his presence, that music, which was life or death to him, had been torture for them and that they had endured it, not at all for his sake, but only for mine. And Sonny couldn't take that. He can take it a little better today than he could then but he's still not very good at it and, frankly, I don't know anybody who is.

The silence of the next few days must have been louder than the sound of   170
all the music ever played since time began. One morning, before she went to
work, Isabel was in his room for something and she suddenly realized that all
of his records were gone. And she knew for certain that he was gone. And he
was. He went as far as the navy would carry him. He finally sent me a postcard
from some place in Greece and that was the first I knew that Sonny was still
alive. I didn't see him any more until we were both back in New York and the
war had long been over.] Wow. how terrible.

He was a man by then, of course, but I wasn't willing to see it. He came by
the house from time to time, but we fought almost every time we met. I didn't
like the way he carried himself, loose and dreamlike all the time, and I didn't
like his friends, and his music seemed to be merely an excuse for the life he led.
It sounded just that weird and disordered.

Then we had a fight, a pretty awful fight, and I didn't see him for months.
By and by I looked him up, where he was living, in a furnished room in the Village, and I tried to make it up. But there were lots of people in the room and
Sonny just lay on his bed, and he wouldn't come downstairs with me, and he
treated these other people as though they were his family and I weren't. So I
got mad and then he got mad, and then I told him that he might just as well be
dead as live the way he was living. Then he stood up and he told me not to
worry about him any more in life, that he *was* dead as far as I was concerned.
Then he pushed me to the door and the other people looked on as though
nothing were happening, and he slammed the door behind me. I stood in
the hallway, staring at the door. I heard somebody laugh in the room and
then the tears came to my eyes. I started down the steps, whistling to keep from
crying, I kept whistling to myself, *You going to need me, baby, one of these cold,
rainy days.*] Falling out. a very bad one.

I read about Sonny's trouble in the spring. Little Grace died in the fall. She was
a beautiful little girl. But she only lived a little over two years. She died of polio
and she suffered. She had a slight fever for a couple of days, but it didn't seem
like anything and we just kept her in bed. And we would certainly have called
the doctor, but the fever dropped, she seemed to be all right. So we thought it
had just been a cold. Then, one day, she was up, playing, Isabel was in the
kitchen fixing lunch for the two boys when they'd come in from school, and she
heard Grace fall down in the living room. When you have a lot of children you
don't always start running when one of them falls, unless they start screaming
or something. And, this time, Grace was quiet. Yet, Isabel says that when she
heard that *thump* and then that silence, something happened in her to make
her afraid. And she ran to the living room and there was little Grace on the
floor, all twisted up, and the reason she hadn't screamed was that she couldn't
get her breath. And when she did scream, it was the worst sound, Isabel says,
that she'd ever heard in all her life, and she still hears it sometimes in her
dreams. Isabel will sometimes wake me up with a low, moaning, strangled
sound and I have to be quick to awaken her and hold her to me and where
Isabel is weeping against me seems a mortal wound.

I think I may have written Sonny the very day that little Grace was buried. I was sitting in the living room in the dark, by myself, and I suddenly thought of Sonny. My trouble made his real.

One Saturday afternoon, when Sonny had been living with us, or, anyway, been in our house, for nearly two weeks, I found myself wandering aimlessly about the living room, drinking from a can of beer, and trying to work up the courage to search Sonny's room. He was out, he was usually out whenever I was home, and Isabel had taken the children to see their grandparents. Suddenly I was standing still in front of the living room window, watching Seventh Avenue. The idea of searching Sonny's room made me still. I scarcely dared to admit to myself what I'd be searching for. I didn't know what I'd do if I found it. Or if I didn't.

On the sidewalk across from me, near the entrance to a barbecue joint, some people were holding an old-fashioned revival meeting. The barbecue cook, wearing a dirty white apron, his conked hair reddish and metallic in the pale sun, and a cigarette between his lips, stood in the doorway, watching them. Kids and older people paused in their errands and stood there, along with some older men and a couple of very tough-looking women who watched everything that happened on the avenue, as though they owned it, or were maybe owned by it. Well, they were watching this, too. The revival was being carried on by three sisters in black, and a brother. All they had were their voices and their Bibles and a tambourine. The brother was testifying and while he testified two of the sisters stood together, seeming to say, amen, and the third sister walked around with the tambourine outstretched and a couple of people dropped coins into it. Then the brother's testimony ended and the sister who had been taking up the collection dumped the coins into her palm and transferred them to the pocket of her long black robe. Then she raised both hands, striking the tambourine against the air, and then against one hand, and she started to sing. And the two other sisters and the brother joined in.

It was strange, suddenly, to watch, though I had been seeing these street meetings all my life. So, of course, had everybody else down there. Yet, they paused and watched and listened and I stood still at the window. "*Tis the old ship of Zion,*" they sang, and the sister with the tambourine kept a steady, jangling beat, "*it has rescued many a thousand!*" Not a soul under the sound of their voices was hearing this song for the first time, not one of them had been rescued. Nor had they seen much in the way of rescue work being done around them. Neither did they especially believe in the holiness of the three sisters and the brother, they knew too much about them, knew where they lived, and how. The woman with the tambourine, whose voice dominated the air, whose face was bright with joy, was divided by very little from the woman who stood watching her, a cigarette between her heavy, chapped lips, her hair a cuckoo's nest, her face scarred and swollen from many beatings, and her black eyes glittering like coal. Perhaps they both knew this, which was why, when, as rarely, they addressed each other, they addressed each other as Sister. As the singing filled the air the watching, listening faces underwent a change, the eyes focusing on something within; the music seemed to soothe a poison out of them;

and time seemed, nearly, to fall away from the sullen, belligerent, battered faces, as though they were fleeing back to their first condition, while dreaming of their last. The barbecue cook half shook his head and smiled, and dropped his cigarette and disappeared into his joint. A man fumbled in his pockets for change and stood holding it in his hand impatiently, as though he had just remembered a pressing appointment further up the avenue. He looked furious. Then I saw Sonny, standing on the edge of the crowd. He was carrying a wide, flat notebook with a green cover, and it made him look, from where I was standing, almost like a schoolboy. The coppery sun brought out the copper in his skin, he was very faintly smiling, standing very still. Then the singing stopped, the tambourine turned into a collection plate again. The furious man dropped in his coins and vanished, so did a couple of the women, and Sonny dropped some change in the plate, looking directly at the woman with a little smile. He started across the avenue, toward the house. He has a slow, loping walk, something like the way Harlem hipsters walk, only he's imposed on this his own half-beat. I had never really noticed it before.

I stayed at the window, both relieved and apprehensive. As Sonny disappeared from my sight, they began singing again. And they were still singing when his key turned in the lock.

"Hey," he said.

"Hey, yourself. You want some beer?"   180

"No. Well, maybe." But he came up to the window and stood beside me, looking out. "What a warm voice," he said.

They were singing *If I could only hear my mother pray again!*

"Yes," I said, "and she can sure beat that tambourine."

"But what a terrible song," he said, and laughed. He dropped his notebook on the sofa and disappeared into the kitchen. "Where's Isabel and the kids?"

"I think they went to see their grandparents. You hungry?"   185

"No." He came back into the living room with his can of beer. "You want to come some place with me tonight?"

I sensed, I don't know how, that I couldn't possibly say no. "Sure. Where?"

He sat down on the sofa and picked up his notebook and started leafing through it. "I'm going to sit in with some fellows in a joint in the Village."

"You mean, you're going to play, tonight?"

"That's right." He took a swallow of his beer and moved back to the window.   190
He gave me a sidelong look. "If you can stand it."

"I'll try," I said.

He smiled to himself and we both watched as the meeting across the way broke up. The three sisters and the brother, heads bowed, were singing *God be with you till we meet again.* The faces around them were very quiet. Then the song ended. The small crowd dispersed. We watched the three women and the lone man walk slowly up the avenue.

"When she was singing before," said Sonny, abruptly, "her voice reminded me for a minute of what heroin feels like sometimes — when it's in your veins. It makes you feel sort of warm and cool at the same time. And distant. And — and sure." He sipped his beer, very deliberately not looking at me. I watched his face. "It makes you feel — in control. Sometimes you've got to have that feeling."

"Do you?" I sat down slowly in the easy chair.

"Sometimes." He went to the sofa and picked up his notebook again. "Some people do." 195

"In order," I asked, "to play?" And my voice was very ugly, full of contempt and anger.

"Well" — he looked at me with great, troubled eyes, as though, in fact, he hoped his eyes would tell me things he could never otherwise say — "they *think* so. And *if* they think so — !"

"And what do *you* think?" I asked.

He sat on the sofa and put his can of beer on the floor. "I don't know," he said, and I couldn't be sure if he were answering my question or pursuing his thoughts. His face didn't tell me. "It's not so much to *play*. It's to *stand* it, to be able to make it at all. On any level." He frowned and smiled: "In order to keep from shaking to pieces."

"But these friends of yours," I said, "they seem to shake themselves to 200 pieces pretty goddamn fast."

"Maybe." He played with the notebook. And something told me that I should curb my tongue, that Sonny was doing his best to talk, that I should listen. "But of course you only know the ones that've gone to pieces. Some don't — or at least they haven't *yet* and that's just about all *any* of us can say." He paused. "And then there are some who just live, really, in hell, and they know it and they see what's happening and they go right on. I don't know." He sighed, dropped the notebook, folded his arms. "Some guys, you can tell from the way they play, they on something *all* the time. And you can see that, well, it makes something real for them. But of course," he picked up his beer from the floor and sipped it and put the can down again, "they *want* to, too, you've got to see that. Even some of them that say they don't — *some*, not all."

"And what about you?" I asked — I couldn't help it. "What about you? Do *you* want to?"

He stood up and walked to the window and remained silent for a long time. Then he sighed. "Me," he said. Then: "While I was downstairs before, on my way here, listening to that woman sing, it struck me all of a sudden how much suffering she must have had to go through — to sing like that. It's *repulsive* to think you have to suffer that much."

I said: "But there's no way not to suffer — is there, Sonny?"

"I believe not," he said and smiled, "but that's never stopped anyone from 205 trying." He looked at me. "Has it?" I realized, with this mocking look, that there stood between us, forever, beyond the power of time or forgiveness, the fact that I had held silence — so long! — when he had needed human speech to help him. He turned back to the window. "No, there's no way not to suffer. But you try all kinds of ways to keep from drowning in it, to keep on top of it, and to make it seem — well, like *you*. Like you did something, all right, and now you're suffering for it. You know?" I said nothing. "Well you know," he said, impatiently, "why *do* people suffer? Maybe it's better to do something to give it a reason, *any* reason."

"But we just agreed," I said, "that there's no way not to suffer. Isn't it better, then, just to — take it?"

"But nobody just takes it," Sonny cried, "that's what I'm telling you! *Everybody* tries not to. You're just hung up on the *way* some people try — it's not *your* way!"

The hair on my face began to itch, my face felt wet. "That's not true," I said, "that's not true. I don't give a damn what other people do, I don't even care how they suffer. I just care how *you* suffer." And he looked at me. "Please believe me," I said, "I don't want to see you — die — trying not to suffer."

"I won't," he said, flatly, "die trying not to suffer. At least, not any faster than anybody else."

"But there's no need," I said, trying to laugh, "is there? in killing yourself."   210

I wanted to say more, but I couldn't. I wanted to talk about will power and how life could be — well, beautiful. I wanted to say that it was all within; but was it? or, rather, wasn't that exactly the trouble? And I wanted to promise that I would never fail him again. But it would all have sounded — empty words and lies.

So I made the promise to myself and prayed that I would keep it.

"It's terrible sometimes, inside," he said, "that's what's the trouble. You walk these streets, black and funky and cold, and there's not really a living ass to talk to, and there's nothing shaking, and there's no way of getting it out — that storm inside. You can't talk it and you can't make love with it, and when you finally try to get with it and play it, you realize *nobody's* listening. So *you've* got to listen. You got to find a way to listen."

And then he walked away from the window and sat on the sofa again, as though all the wind had suddenly been knocked out of him. "Sometimes you'll do *anything* to play, even cut your mother's throat." He laughed and looked at me. "Or your brother's." Then he sobered. "Or your own." Then: "Don't worry. I'm all right now and I think I'll *be* all right. But I can't forget — where I've been. I don't mean just the physical place I've been, I mean where I've *been*. And *what* I've been."

"What have you been, Sonny?" I asked.   215

He smiled — but sat sideways on the sofa, his elbow resting on the back, his fingers playing with his mouth and chin, not looking at me. "I've been something I didn't recognize, didn't know I could be. Didn't know anybody could be." He stopped, looking inward, looking helplessly young, looking old. "I'm not talking about it now because I feel *guilty* or anything like that — maybe it would be better if I did, I don't know. Anyway, I can't really talk about it. Not to you, not to anybody," and now he turned and faced me. "Sometimes, you know, and it was actually when I was most *out* of the world, I felt that I was in it, that I was *with* it, really, and I could play or I didn't really have to *play*, it just came out of me, it was there. And I don't know how I played, thinking about it now, but I know I did awful things, those times, sometimes, to people. Or it wasn't that I *did* anything to them — it was that they weren't real." He picked up the beer can; it was empty; he rolled it between his palms: "And other times — well, I needed a fix, I needed to find a place to lean, I needed to clear a space to *listen*—and I couldn't find it, and I—went crazy, I did terrible things to *me*, I was terrible *for* me." He began pressing the beer can between his hands, I watched the metal begin to give. It glittered, as he played with it, like a knife, and I was afraid he would cut himself, but I said nothing. "Oh well. I can never tell you. I was all by myself at the bottom of something, stinking and sweating and crying and shaking, and I smelled it, you know? *my* stink, and I thought I'd die if I couldn't get away from it and yet, all the same, I knew that everything I was doing was just locking me in with it. And I didn't know," he paused, still flattening the beer can, "I didn't know, I still *don't* know, something kept telling me that maybe it was good to smell your own stink, but I didn't think that *that* was what I'd been trying to do—and—who can stand it?" and he abruptly dropped the ruined beer can, looking at me with a small, still smile, and then rose, walking to the window as though it were the lodestone rock. I watched his face, he watched the avenue. "I couldn't tell you when Mama died—but the reason I wanted to leave Harlem so bad was to get away from drugs. And then, when I ran away, that's what I was running from—really. When I came back, nothing had changed, I hadn't changed, I was just—older." And he stopped, drumming with his fingers on the windowpane. The sun had vanished, soon darkness would fall. I watched his face. "It can come again," he said, almost as though speaking to himself. Then he turned to me. "It can come again," he repeated. "I just want you to know that."

"All right," I said, at last. "So it can come again. All right."

He smiled, but the smile was sorrowful. "I had to try to tell you," he said.

"Yes," I said. "I understand that."

"You're my brother," he said, looking straight at me, and not smiling at all.   220

"Yes," I repeated, "yes. I understand that."

He turned back to the window, looking out. "All that hatred down there," he said, "all that hatred and misery and love. It's a wonder it doesn't blow the avenue apart."

We went to the only nightclub on a short, dark street, downtown. We squeezed through the narrow, chattering, jam-packed bar to the entrance of the big room, where the bandstand was. And we stood there for a moment, for the lights were very dim in this room and we couldn't see. Then, "Hello, boy," said a voice and an enormous black man, much older than Sonny or myself, erupted out of all that atmospheric lighting and put an arm around Sonny's shoulder. "I been sitting right here," he said, "waiting for you."

He had a big voice, too, and heads in the darkness turned toward us.

Sonny grinned and pulled a little away, and said, "Creole, this is my brother.   225
I told you about him."

Creole shook my hand. "I'm glad to meet you, son," he said, and it was clear that he was glad to meet me *there*, for Sonny's sake. And he smiled, "You got a real musician in *your* family," and he took his arm from Sonny's shoulder and slapped him, lightly, affectionately, with the back of his hand.

"Well. Now I've heard it all," said a voice behind us. This was another musician, and a friend of Sonny's, a coal-black, cheerful-looking man, built close to the ground. He immediately began confiding to me, at the top of his lungs, the most terrible things about Sonny, his teeth gleaming like a lighthouse and his laugh coming up out of him like the beginning of an earthquake. And it turned out that everyone at the bar knew Sonny, or almost everyone; some were musicians, working there, or nearby, or not working, some were simply hangers-on, and some were there to hear Sonny play. I was introduced to all of them and they were all very polite to me. Yet, it was clear that, for them, I was only Sonny's brother. Here, I was in Sonny's world. Or, rather: his kingdom. Here, it was not even a question that his veins bore royal blood.

They were going to play soon and Creole installed me, by myself, at a table in a dark corner. Then I watched them, Creole, and the little black man, and Sonny, and the others, while they horsed around, standing just below the bandstand. The light from the bandstand spilled just a little short of them and, watching them laughing and gesturing and moving about, I had the feeling that they, nevertheless, were being most careful not to step into that circle of light too suddenly: that if they moved into the light too suddenly, without thinking, they would perish in flame. Then, while I watched, one of them, the small, black man, moved into the light and crossed the bandstand and started fooling around with his drums. Then — being funny and being, also, extremely ceremonious — Creole took Sonny by the arm and led him to the piano. A woman's voice called Sonny's name and a few hands started clapping. And Sonny, also being funny and being ceremonious, and so touched, I think, that he could have cried, but neither hiding it nor showing it, riding it like a man, grinned, and put both hands to his heart and bowed from the waist.

Creole then went to the bass fiddle and a lean, very bright-skinned brown man jumped up on the bandstand and picked up his horn. So there they were, and the atmosphere on the bandstand and in the room began to change and tighten. Someone stepped up to the microphone and announced them. Then there were all kinds of murmurs. Some people at the bar shushed others. The waitress ran around, frantically getting in the last orders, guys and chicks got closer to each other, and the lights on the bandstand, on the quartet, turned to a kind of indigo. Then they all looked different there. Creole looked about him for the last time, as though he were making certain that all his chickens were in the coop, and then he — jumped and struck the fiddle. And there they were.

All I know about music is that not many people ever really hear it. And even then, on the rare occasions when something opens within, and the music enters, what we mainly hear, or hear corroborated, are personal, private, van-ishing evocations. But the man who creates the music is hearing something else, is dealing with the roar rising from the void and imposing order on it as it hits the air. What is evoked in him, then, is of another order, more terrible be-cause it has no words, and triumphant, too, for that same reason. And his tri-umph, when he triumphs, is ours. I just watched Sonny's face. His face was troubled, he was working hard, but he wasn't with it. And I had the feeling that, in a way, everyone on the bandstand was waiting for him, both waiting for him and pushing him along. But as I began to watch Creole, I realized that it

230

was Creole who held them all back. He had them on a short rein. Up there, keeping the beat with his whole body, wailing on the fiddle, with his eyes half closed, he was listening to everything, but he was listening to Sonny. He was having a dialogue with Sonny. He wanted Sonny to leave the shoreline and strike out for the deep water. He was Sonny's witness that deep water and drowning were not the same thing — he had been there, and he knew. And he wanted Sonny to know. He was waiting for Sonny to do the things on the keys which would let Creole know that Sonny was in the water.

And, while Creole listened, Sonny moved, deep within, exactly like someone in torment. I had never before thought of how awful the relationship must be between the musician and his instrument. He has to fill it, this instrument, with the breath of life, his own. He has to make it do what he wants it to do. And a piano is just a piano. It's made out of so much wood and wires and little hammers and big ones, and ivory. While there's only so much you can do with it, the only way to find this out is to try; to try and make it do everything.

And Sonny hadn't been near a piano for over a year. And he wasn't on much better terms with his life, not the life that stretched before him now. He and the piano stammered, started one way, got scared, stopped; started another way, panicked, marked time, started again; then seemed to have found a direction, panicked again, got stuck. And the face I saw on Sonny I'd never seen before. Everything had been burned out of it, and, at the same time, things usually hidden were being burned in, by the fire and fury of the battle which was occurring in him up there.

Yet, watching Creole's face as they neared the end of the first set, I had the feeling that something had happened, something I hadn't heard. Then they finished, there was scattered applause, and then, without an instant's warning, Creole started into something else, it was almost sardonic, it was *Am I Blue*. And, as though he commanded, Sonny began to play. Something began to happen. And Creole let out the reins. The dry, low, black man said something awful on the drums, Creole answered, and the drums talked back. Then the horn insisted, sweet and high, slightly detached perhaps, and Creole listened, commenting now and then, dry, and driving, beautiful and calm and old. Then they all came together again, and Sonny was part of the family again. I could tell this from his face. He seemed to have found, right there beneath his fingers, a damn brand-new piano. It seemed that he couldn't get over it. Then, for awhile, just being happy with Sonny, they seemed to be agreeing with him that brand-new pianos certainly were a gas.

Then Creole stepped forward to remind them that what they were playing was the blues. He hit something in all of them, he hit something in me, myself, and the music tightened and deepened, apprehension began to beat the air. Creole began to tell us what the blues were all about. They were not about anything very new. He and his boys up there were keeping it new, at the risk of ruin, destruction, madness, and death, in order to find new ways to make us listen. For, while the tale of how we suffer, and how we are delighted, and how we may triumph is never new, it always must be heard. There isn't any other tale to tell, it's the only light we've got in all this darkness.

And this tale, according to that face, that body, those strong hands on   235
those strings, has another aspect in every country, and a new depth in every
generation. Listen, Creole seemed to be saying, listen. Now these are Sonny's
blues. He made the little black man on the drums know it, and the bright,
brown man on the horn. Creole wasn't trying any longer to get Sonny in the
water. He was wishing him Godspeed. Then he stepped back, very slowly, filling
the air with the immense suggestion that Sonny speak for himself.

Then they all gathered around Sonny and Sonny played. Every now and
again one of them seemed to say, amen. Sonny's fingers filled the air with life,
his life. But that life contained so many others. And Sonny went all the way
back, he really began with the spare, flat statement of the opening phrase of
the song. Then he began to make it his. It was very beautiful because it wasn't
hurried and it was no longer a lament. I seemed to hear with what burning he
had made it his, with what burning we had yet to make it ours, how we could
cease lamenting. Freedom lurked around us and I understood, at last, that he
could help us to be free if we would listen, that he would never be free until we
did. Yet, there was no battle in his face now. I heard what he had gone through,
and would continue to go through until he came to rest in earth. He had made
it his: that long line, of which we knew only Mama and Daddy. And he was giving it back, as everything must be given back, so that, passing through death,
it can live forever. I saw my mother's face again, and felt, for the first time, how
the stones of the road she had walked on must have bruised her feet. I saw the
moonlit road where my father's brother died. And it brought something else
back to me, and carried me past it. I saw my little girl again and felt Isabel's
tears again, and I felt my own tears begin to rise. And I was yet aware that this
was only a moment, that the world waited outside, as hungry as a tiger, and
that trouble stretched above us, longer than the sky.

Then it was over. Creole and Sonny let out their breath, both soaking wet,
and grinning. There was a lot of applause and some of it was real. In the dark,
the girl came by and I asked her to take drinks to the bandstand. There was a
long pause, while they talked up there in the indigo light and after awhile I saw
the girl put a Scotch and milk on top of the piano for Sonny. He didn't seem to
notice it, but just before they started playing again, he sipped from it and looked
toward me, and nodded. Then he put it back on top of the piano. For me, then,
as they began to play again, it glowed and shook above my brother's head like
the very cup of trembling.   [1957]

This wasn't even about the events in the beginning!

■ THINKING ABOUT THE TEXT

1. Were you sympathetic to the older brother in the beginning of the story?
   Did this become more so or less so as the story progressed? Is Sonny a
   sympathetic character in the beginning? At the end?

2. In real life, what do you believe is the role of an older brother? Do you
   have a responsibility to the members of your family regardless of their
   behavior? Explain. What is Sonny's mother's view of this?

3. Baldwin refers to the "darkness outside" several times. What do you think this means for Sonny? For Sonny's mother and father? For the older brother?

4. Listening seems to play an important function for Sonny and his brother. Cite specific examples of how they do or do not listen to each other. What might be some definitions of "listening" in this context?

5. One might think that brothers would understand each other better than outsiders do. But is that the case here? In your experience? In other stories or movies? How might you account for this difficulty?

≡ MAKING COMPARISONS

1. The older brothers in "The Rich Brother" and "Sonny's Blues" struggle to understand their younger brothers. Which one seems more successful? Why?

2. Both younger brothers in these two stories seem to march to different drummers. How would you describe their variations from the norm?

3. Some critics claim that these two stories are about responsibility; others claim they are about tolerance; still others see sibling rivalry, blind faith, or ego as the focus. What do you think, and why?

≡ WRITING ABOUT ISSUES

1. Baldwin shows us the letter Sonny writes to his older brother, but we do not see any of the older brother's letters to Sonny. Based on the older brother's insights about Sonny in the closing scene, write a letter to Sonny from the older brother's point of view, explaining the substance of his new understanding of Sonny's life and music.

2. Write an essay that compares the relationship between Pete and Donald to the one between Sonny and his brother. Be sure to comment on similarities and differences.

3. Write a personal essay based on a conflict you had with a sibling, explaining how the relationship evolved. Use at least two specific incidents, and describe how they fit into a larger pattern.

4. Do some library research on birth order as it affects sibling rivalry, especially between brothers. Write a report comparing your findings to the relationships depicted in these two stories.

Family Dramas: Re-Visions of a Play

TENNESSEE WILLIAMS, *The Glass Menagerie*

CHRISTOPHER DURANG, *For Whom the Southern Belle Tolls*

Tennessee Williams's play — performed in high schools, in colleges, and on professional stages for more than sixty years — is one of the most admired dramas in American literature. *The Glass Menagerie* is based on Williams's own life, especially the time he spent working at a shoe factory. Set in a dingy apartment in a poor section of St. Louis, Missouri, the story focuses on Tom and his relationships with his sister, Laura, who walks with a slight limp, and his mother, Amanda, whose illusions about her children are thwarted by their own desires and limitations.

Williams's own sister, Rose, suffered from a variety of mental disorders. His mother's decision to have doctors perform a lobotomy on her and his decision to leave home to pursue a career as a writer inspired the central conflict in his play and haunted Williams throughout his life.

When a play is as famous as *The Glass Menagerie*, it is often imitated and sometimes parodied. In *For Whom the Southern Belle Tolls*, Christopher Durang's humor is rarely subtle and often frivolous, even slapstick. Durang is clearly having fun with Williams's masterpiece when he makes Laura, one of the most fragile characters in American literature, into a self-absorbed, unimaginative male hypochondriac. If Williams's moving play touches on such serious ideas as familial responsibility, innocence, loss, and the inescapable sadness of life, Durang's parody often delights audiences with broad humor and stand-up comic routines. Durang's play is serious fun.

▤ BEFORE YOU READ

Should your first loyalty be to yourself or to your family? What if you were expected to quit college and work in a factory to help support your mother and homebound sibling. Would you do it? Why?

TENNESSEE WILLIAMS

The Glass Menagerie

Thomas Lanier "Tennessee" Williams (1911–1983) wrote some of the most famous plays of the American stage and frankly looked at adultery, mental illness, homosexuality, and incest. The Glass Menagerie (1945), A Streetcar Named Desire (1948), Cat on a Hot Tin Roof (1955), Suddenly Last Summer (1958), and The Night of the Iguana (1961) were considered shocking when they were first staged but eventually were made into popular and acclaimed films. After a childhood

(© Bettmann/Corbis.)

that was "lonely and miserable" largely because of his domineering, alcoholic father and because of the taunts he endured for being small, sickly, and bookish, he graduated from the University of Iowa in 1939 and immediately began writing fiction and drama. With The Glass Menagerie, Williams won the first of his four New York Drama Critics' Circle Awards for the best play of the season. He received the first of two Pulitzer Prizes in 1948 for A Streetcar Named Desire. Williams struggled with depression most of his life. Addicted to prescription drugs and alcohol, he choked to death on a bottle cap at his New York City apartment at the Hotel Elysee.

> nobody, not even the rain, has such small hands
> — e. e. cummings

LIST OF CHARACTERS

AMANDA WINGFIELD, the mother. A little woman of great but confused vitality clinging frantically to another time and place. Her characterization must be carefully created, not copied from type. She is not paranoiac, but her life is paranoia. There is much to admire in Amanda, and as much to love and pity as there is to laugh at. Certainly she *has endurance and a kind of heroism, and though her foolishness makes her unwittingly cruel at times, there is tenderness in her slight person.*

LAURA WINGFIELD, *her daughter. Amanda, having failed to establish contact with reality, continues to live vitally in her illusions, but Laura's situation is even graver. A childhood illness has left her crippled, one leg slightly shorter than the other, and held in a brace. This defect need not be more than suggested on the stage. Stemming from this, Laura's separation increases till she is like a piece of her own glass collection, too exquisitely fragile to move from the shelf.*

TOM WINGFIELD, *her son. And the narrator of the play. A poet with a job in a warehouse. His nature is not remorseless, but to escape from a trap he has to act without pity.*

JIM O'CONNOR, *the gentleman caller. A nice, ordinary, young man.*

SCENE: *An alley in St. Louis.*
PART I: *Preparation for a Gentleman Caller.*
PART II: *The Gentleman Calls.*
TIME: *Now and the Past.*

Scene 1

The Wingfield apartment is in the rear of the building, one of those vast hivelike conglomerations of cellular living-units that flower as warty growths in overcrowded urban centers of lower middle-class population and are symptomatic of the impulse of this largest and fundamentally enslaved section of American society to avoid fluidity and differentiation and to exist and function as one interfused mass of automatism.

The apartment faces an alley and is entered by a fire-escape, a structure whose name is a touch of accidental poetic truth, for all of these huge buildings are always burning with the slow and implacable fires of human desperation. The fire-escape is included in the set — that is, the landing of it and steps descending from it.

The scene is memory and is therefore nonrealistic. Memory takes a lot of poetic license. It omits some details; others are exaggerated, according to the emotional value of the articles it touches, for memory is seated predominantly in the heart. The interior is therefore rather dim and poetic.

At the rise of the curtain, the audience is faced with the dark, grim rear wall of the Wingfield tenement. This building, which runs parallel to the footlights, is flanked on both sides by dark, narrow alleys which run into murky canyons of tangled clotheslines, garbage cans, and the sinister latticework of neighboring fire-escapes. It is up and down these side alleys that exterior entrances and exits are made, during the play. At the end of Tom's opening commentary, the dark tenement wall slowly reveals (by means of a transparency) the interior of the ground floor Wingfield apartment.

Downstage is the living room, which also serves as a sleeping room for Laura, the sofa unfolding to make her bed. Upstage, center, and divided by a wide arch or second proscenium with transparent faded portieres (or second curtain), is the dining room. In an old-fashioned what-not in the living room are seen scores of transparent glass animals. A blown-up photograph of the father hangs on the wall of the living room, facing the audience, to the left of the archway. It is the face of a very handsome young man in a doughboy's First World War cap. He is gallantly smiling, ineluctably smiling, as if to say, "I will be smiling forever."

The audience hears and sees the opening scene in the dining room through both the transparent fourth wall of the building and the transparent gauze portieres of the dining-room arch. It is during this revealing scene that the fourth wall slowly ascends, out of sight. This transparent exterior wall is not brought down again until the very end of the play, during Tom's final speech.

The narrator is an undisguised convention of the play. He takes whatever license with dramatic convention as is convenient to his purposes.

Tom enters dressed as a merchant sailor from alley, stage left, and strolls across the front of the stage to the fire-escape. There he stops and lights a cigarette. He addresses the audience.

TOM: Yes, I have tricks in my pocket, I have things up my sleeve. But I am the opposite of a stage magician. He gives you illusion that has the appearance of truth. I give you truth in the pleasant disguise of illusion. To begin with, I turn back time. I reverse it to that quaint period, the thirties, when the huge middle class of America was matriculating in a school for the blind. Their eyes had failed them, or they had failed their eyes, and so they were having their fingers pressed forcibly down on the fiery Braille alphabet of a dissolving economy. In Spain there was revolution. Here there was only shouting and confusion. In Spain there was Guernica.° Here there were disturbances of labor, sometimes pretty violent, in otherwise peaceful cities such as Chicago, Cleveland, Saint Louis. . . . This is the social background of the play.

(Music.)

The play is memory. Being a memory play, it is dimly lighted, it is sentimental, it is not realistic. In memory everything seems to happen to music. That explains the fiddle in the wings. I am the narrator of the play, and also a character in it. The other characters are my mother, Amanda, my sister, Laura, and a gentleman caller who appears in the final scenes. He is the most realistic character in the play, being an emissary from a world of reality that we were somehow set apart from. But since I have a poet's weakness for symbols, I am using this character also as a symbol; he is the long delayed but always expected something that we live for. There is a fifth character in the play who doesn't appear except in this larger-than-life photograph over the mantel. This is our father who left us a long time ago. He was a telephone man who fell in love with long distances; he gave up his job with the telephone company and skipped the light fantastic out of town. . . . The last we heard of him was a picture post-card from Mazatlán, on the Pacific coast of Mexico, containing a message of two words — "Hello — Good-bye!" and no address. I think the rest of the play will explain itself. . . .

Guernica: A town in northern Spain destroyed by German bombers in 1937 during the Spanish civil war.

Amanda's voice becomes audible through the portieres.

(Legend on screen: "Où sont les neiges."°)

> *He divides the portieres and enters the upstage area.*
> *Amanda and Laura are seated at a drop-leaf table. Eating is indicated by gestures without food or utensils. Amanda faces the audience.*
> *Tom and Laura are seated in profile.*
> *The interior has lit up softly and through the scrim we see Amanda and Laura seated at the table in the upstage area.*

AMANDA *(calling)*:   Tom?

TOM: Yes, Mother.

AMANDA: We can't say grace until you come to the table!

TOM: Coming, Mother. *(He bows slightly and withdraws, reappearing a few moments later in his place at the table.)*

AMANDA *(to her son)*:   Honey, don't *push* with your *fingers.* If you have to push with something, the thing to push with is a crust of bread. And chew — chew! Animals have sections in their stomachs which enable them to digest food without mastication, but human beings are supposed to chew their food before they swallow it down. Eat food leisurely, son, and really enjoy it. A well-cooked meal has lots of delicate flavors that have to be held in the mouth for appreciation. So chew your food and give your salivary glands a chance to function!

Tom deliberately lays his imaginary fork down and pushes his chair back from the table.

TOM: I haven't enjoyed one bite of this dinner because of your constant directions on how to eat it. It's you that makes me rush through meals with your hawklike attention to every bite I take. Sickening — spoils my appetite — all this discussion of animals' secretion — salivary glands — mastication!

AMANDA *(lightly)*:   Temperament like a Metropolitan star! *(He rises and crosses downstage.)* You're not excused from the table.

TOM: I am getting a cigarette.

AMANDA: You smoke too much.

Laura rises.

LAURA: I'll bring in the blanc mange.

He remains standing with his cigarette by the portieres during the following.

AMANDA *(rising)*:   No, sister, no, sister — you be the lady this time and I'll be the darky.

LAURA: I'm already up.

AMANDA: Resume your seat, little sister — I want you to stay fresh and pretty — for gentlemen callers!

LAURA: I'm not expecting any gentlemen callers.

"Où sont les neiges": Part of a line from a poem by the French medieval writer François Villon (1431–c. 1463); the full line translates, "Where are the snows of yesteryear?"

AMANDA *(crossing out to kitchenette. Airily)*:   Sometimes they come when they are least expected! Why, I remember one Sunday afternoon in Blue Mountain — *(Enters kitchenette.)*

TOM: I know what's coming!

LAURA: Yes. But let her tell it.

TOM: Again?

LAURA: She loves to tell it.

Amanda returns with bowl of dessert.

AMANDA: One Sunday afternoon in Blue Mountain — your mother received — *seventeen!* — gentlemen callers! Why, sometimes there weren't chairs enough to accommodate them all. We had to send the nigger over to bring in folding chairs from the parish house.

TOM *(remaining at portieres)*:   How did you entertain those gentlemen callers?

AMANDA: I understood the art of conversation!

TOM: I bet you could talk.

AMANDA: Girls in those days knew how to talk, I can tell you.

TOM: Yes?

(Image: Amanda as a girl on a porch greeting callers.)

AMANDA: They knew how to entertain their gentlemen callers. It wasn't enough for a girl to be possessed of a pretty face and a graceful figure — although I wasn't slighted in either respect. She also needed to have a nimble wit and a tongue to meet all occasions.

TOM: What did you talk about?

AMANDA: Things of importance going on in the world! Never anything coarse or common or vulgar. *(She addresses Tom as though he were seated in the vacant chair at the table though he remains by portieres. He plays this scene as though he held the book.)* My callers were gentlemen — all! Among my callers were some of the most prominent young planters of the Mississippi Delta — planters and sons of planters!

Tom motions for music and a spot of light on Amanda.
Her eyes lift, her face glows, her voice becomes rich and elegiac.
(Screen legend: "Où sont les neiges.")

There was young Champ Laughlin who later became vice-president of the Delta Planters Bank. Hadley Stevenson who was drowned in Moon Lake and left his widow one hundred and fifty thousand in Government bonds. There were the Cutrere brothers, Wesley and Bates. Bates was one of my bright particular beaux! He got in a quarrel with that wild Wainright boy. They shot it out on the floor of Moon Lake Casino. Bates was shot through the stomach. Died in the ambulance on his way to Memphis. His widow was also well-provided for, came into eight or ten thousand acres, that's all. She married him on the rebound — never loved her — carried my picture on him the night he died! And there was that boy that every girl in the Delta had set her cap for! That beautiful, brilliant young Fitzhugh boy from Green County!

TOM: What did he leave his widow?

AMANDA: He never married! Gracious, you talk as though all of my old admirers had turned up their toes to the daisies!

TOM: Isn't this the first you mentioned that still survives?

AMANDA: That Fitzhugh boy went North and made a fortune — came to be known as the Wolf of Wall Street! He had the Midas touch, whatever he touched turned to gold! And I could have been Mrs. Duncan J. Fitzhugh, mind you! But — I picked your *father!*

LAURA *(rising):*   Mother, let me clear the table.

AMANDA: No dear, you go in front and study your typewriter chart. Or practice your shorthand a little. Stay fresh and pretty! — It's almost time for our gentlemen callers to start arriving. *(She flounces girlishly toward the kitchenette.)* How many do you suppose we're going to entertain this afternoon?

Tom throws down the paper and jumps up with a groan.

LAURA *(alone in the dining room):*   I don't believe we're going to receive any, Mother.

AMANDA *(reappearing, airily):*   What? No one — not one? You must be joking! *(Laura nervously echoes her laugh. She slips in a fugitive manner through the half-open portieres and draws them gently behind her. A shaft of very clear light is thrown on her face against the faded tapestry of the curtains.) (Music: "The Glass Menagerie" under faintly.) (Lightly.)* Not one gentleman caller? It can't be true! There must be a flood, there must have been a tornado!

LAURA: It isn't a flood, it's not a tornado, Mother. I'm just not popular like you were in Blue Mountain. . . . *(Tom utters another groan. Laura glances at him with a faint, apologetic smile. Her voice catching a little.)* Mother's afraid I'm going to be an old maid.

(The scene dims out with "Glass Menagerie" music.)

Scene 2

"Laura, Haven't You Ever Liked Some Boy?"

On the dark stage the screen is lighted with the image of blue roses.
Gradually Laura's figure becomes apparent and the screen goes out.
The music subsides.
Laura is seated in the delicate ivory chair at the small clawfoot table.
She wears a dress of soft violet material for a kimono — her hair tied back from her forehead with a ribbon.
She is washing and polishing her collection of glass.
Amanda appears on the fire-escape steps. At the sound of her ascent, Laura catches her breath, thrusts the bowl of ornaments away, and seats herself stiffly before the diagram of the typewriter keyboard as though it held her spellbound. Something has happened to Amanda. It is written in her face as she climbs to the landing: a look that is grim and hopeless and a little absurd.

She has on one of those cheap or imitation velvety-looking cloth coats with imitation fur collar. Her hat is five or six years old, one of those dreadful cloche hats that were worn in the late twenties, and she is clasping an enormous black patent-leather pocketbook with nickel clasp and initials. This is her full-dress outfit, the one she usually wears to the D.A.R.°

Before entering she looks through the door.

She purses her lips, opens her eyes wide, rolls them upward, and shakes her head.

Then she slowly lets herself in the door. Seeing her mother's expression Laura touches her lips with a nervous gesture.

LAURA: Hello, Mother, I was— *(She makes a nervous gesture toward the chart on the wall. Amanda leans against the shut door and stares at Laura with a martyred look.)*

AMANDA: Deception? Deception? *(She slowly removes her hat and gloves, continuing the swift suffering stare. She lets the hat and gloves fall on the floor— a bit of acting.)*

LAURA *(shakily)*:   How was the D.A.R. meeting? *(Amanda slowly opens her purse and removes a dainty white handkerchief, which she shakes out delicately and delicately touches to her lips and nostrils.)* Didn't you go to the D.A.R. meeting, Mother?

AMANDA *(faintly, almost inaudibly)*:   — No. — No. *(Then more forcibly.)* I did not have the strength — to go to the D.A.R. In fact, I did not have the courage! I wanted to find a hole in the ground and hide myself in it forever! *(She crosses slowly to the wall and removes the diagram of the typewriter keyboard. She holds it in front of her for a second, staring at it sweetly and sorrowfully — then bites her lips and tears it in two pieces.)*

LAURA *(faintly)*:   Why did you do that, Mother? *(Amanda repeats the same procedure with the chart of the Gregg Alphabet.°)* Why are you—

AMANDA: Why? Why? How old are you, Laura?

LAURA: Mother, you know my age.

AMANDA: I thought that you were an adult; it seems that I was mistaken. *(She crosses slowly to the sofa and sinks down and stares at Laura.)*

LAURA: Please don't stare at me, Mother.

Amanda closes her eyes and lowers her head. Count ten.

AMANDA: What are we going to do, what is going to become of us, what is the future?

Count ten.

LAURA: Has something happened, Mother? *(Amanda draws a long breath and takes out the handkerchief again. Dabbing process.)* Mother, has — something happened?

AMANDA: I'll be all right in a minute. I'm just bewildered — *(count five)* — by life. . . .

D.A.R.: Daughters of the American Revolution; members must document that they have ancestors who served the patriots' cause in the Revolutionary War.   **Gregg Alphabet:** System of shorthand symbols invented by John Robert Gregg.

LAURA: Mother, I wish that you would tell me what's happened.

AMANDA: As you know, I was supposed to be inducted into my office at the D.A.R. this afternoon. *(Image: A swarm of typewriters.)* But I stopped off at Rubicam's Business College to speak to your teachers about your having a cold and ask them what progress they thought you were making down there.

LAURA: Oh. . . .

AMANDA: I went to the typing instructor and introduced myself as your mother. She didn't know who you were. Wingfield, she said. We don't have any such student enrolled at the school! I assured her she did, that you had been going to classes since early in January. "I wonder," she said, "if you could be talking about that terribly shy little girl who dropped out of school after only a few days' attendance?" "No," I said, "Laura, my daughter, has been going to school every day for the past six weeks!" "Excuse me," she said. She took the attendance book out and there was your name, unmistakably printed, and all the dates you were absent until they decided that you had dropped out of school. I still said, "No, there must have been some mistake! There must have been some mix-up in the records!" And she said, "No — I remember her perfectly now. Her hand shook so that she couldn't hit the right keys! The first time we gave a speed-test, she broke down completely — was sick at the stomach and almost had to be carried into the wash-room! After that morning she never showed up any more. We phoned the house but never got any answer" — while I was working at Famous and Barr, I suppose, demonstrating those — Oh! I felt so weak I could barely keep on my feet. I had to sit down while they got me a glass of water! Fifty dollars' tuition, all of our plans — my hopes and ambitions for you — just gone up the spout, just gone up the spout like that. *(Laura draws a long breath and gets awkwardly to her feet. She crosses to the Victrola, and winds it up.)* What are you doing?

LAURA: Oh! *(She releases the handle and returns to her seat.)*

AMANDA: Laura, where have you been going when you've gone out pretending that you were going to business college?

LAURA: I've just been going out walking.

AMANDA: That's not true.

LAURA: It is. I just went walking.

AMANDA: Walking? Walking? In winter? Deliberately courting pneumonia in that light coat? Where did you walk to, Laura?

LAURA: It was the lesser of two evils, Mother. *(Image: Winter scene in park.)* I couldn't go back up. I — threw up — on the floor!

AMANDA: From half past seven till after five every day you mean to tell me you walked around in the park, because you wanted to make me think that you were still going to Rubicam's Business College?

LAURA: It wasn't as bad as it sounds. I went inside places to get warmed up.

AMANDA: Inside where?

LAURA: I went in the art museum and the bird-houses at the Zoo. I visited the penguins every day! Sometimes I did without lunch and went to the movies. Lately I've been spending most of my afternoons in the Jewel-box, that big glass house where they raise the tropical flowers.

AMANDA: You did all this to deceive me, just for the deception? *(Laura looks down.)* Why?

LAURA: Mother, when you're disappointed, you get that awful suffering look on your face, like the picture of Jesus' mother in the museum!

AMANDA: Hush!

LAURA: I couldn't face it.

Pause. A whisper of strings.

(Legend: "The Crust of Humility.")

AMANDA *(hopelessly fingering the huge pocketbook)*: So what are we going to do the rest of our lives? Stay home and watch the parades go by? Amuse ourselves with the glass menagerie, darling? Eternally play those worn-out phonograph records your father left as a painful reminder of him? We won't have a business career — we've given that up because it gave us nervous indigestion! *(Laughs wearily.)* What is there left but dependency all our lives? I know so well what becomes of unmarried women who aren't prepared to occupy a position. I've seen such pitiful cases in the South — barely tolerated spinsters living upon the grudging patronage of sister's husband or brother's wife! — stuck away in some little mousetrap of a room — encouraged by one in-law to visit another — little birdlike women without any nest — eating the crust of humility all their life! Is that the future that we've mapped out for ourselves? I swear it's the only alternative I can think of! It isn't a very pleasant alternative, is it? Of course — some girls *do marry. (Laura twists her hands nervously.)* Haven't you ever liked some boy?

LAURA: Yes. I liked one once. *(Rises.)* I came across his picture a while ago.

AMANDA *(with some interest)*: He gave you his picture?

LAURA: No, it's in the year-book.

AMANDA *(disappointed)*: Oh — a high-school boy.

(Screen image: Jim as a high-school hero bearing a silver cup.)

LAURA: Yes. His name was Jim. *(Laura lifts the heavy annual from the clawfoot table.)* Here he is in *The Pirates of Penzance*.

AMANDA *(absently)*: The what?

LAURA: The operetta the senior class put on. He had a wonderful voice and we sat across the aisle from each other Mondays, Wednesdays, and Fridays in the Aud. Here he is with the silver cup for debating! See his grin?

AMANDA *(absently)*: He must have had a jolly disposition.

LAURA: He used to call me — Blue Roses.

(Image: Blue roses.)

AMANDA: Why did he call you such a name as that?

LAURA: When I had that attack of pleurosis — he asked me what was the matter when I came back. I said pleurosis — he thought that I said Blue Roses! So that's what he always called me after that. Whenever he saw me, he'd holler, "Hello, Blue Roses!" I didn't care for the girl that he went out with. Emily Meisenbach. Emily was the best-dressed girl at Soldan. She never struck me, though, as being sincere. . . . It says in the Personal Section — they're engaged. That's — six years ago! They must be married by now.

AMANDA: Girls that aren't cut out for business careers usually wind up married to some nice man. *(Gets up with a spark of revival.)* Sister, that's what you'll do!

Laura utters a startled, doubtful laugh. She reaches quickly for a piece of glass.

LAURA: But, Mother —

AMANDA: Yes? *(Crossing to photograph.)*

LAURA *(in a tone of frightened apology)*:   I'm — crippled!

(Image: Screen.)

AMANDA: Nonsense! Laura, I've told you never, never to use that word. Why, you're not crippled, you just have a little defect — hardly noticeable, even! When people have some slight disadvantage like that, they cultivate other things to make up for it — develop charm — and vivacity — and — *charm!* That's all you have to do! *(She turns again to the photograph.)* One thing your father had *plenty of* — was *charm!*

Tom motions to the fiddle in the wings.
(The scene fades out with music.)

Scene 3

(Legend on the screen: "After the Fiasco — ")
Tom speaks from the fire-escape landing.

TOM: After the fiasco at Rubicam's Business College, the idea of getting a gentleman caller for Laura began to play a more important part in Mother's calculations. It became an obsession. Like some archetype of the universal unconscious, the image of the gentleman caller haunted our small apartment. . . . *(Image: Young man at door with flowers.)* An evening at home rarely passed without some allusion to this image, this specter, this hope. . . . Even when he wasn't mentioned, his presence hung in Mother's preoccupied look and in my sister's frightened, apologetic manner — hung like a sentence passed upon the Wingfields! Mother was a woman of action as well as words. She began to take logical steps in the planned direction. Late that winter and in the early spring — realizing that extra money would be needed to properly feather the nest and plume the bird — she conducted a vigorous campaign on the telephone, roping in subscribers to one of those magazines for matrons called *The Home-maker's Companion,* the type of journal that features the serialized sublimations of ladies of letters who think in terms of delicate cuplike breasts, slim, tapering waists, rich, creamy thighs, eyes like wood-smoke in autumn, fingers that soothe and caress like strains of music, bodies as powerful as Etruscan sculpture.

(Screen image: Glamour *magazine cover.)*

Amanda enters with phone on long extension cord. She is spotted in the dim stage.

AMANDA: Ida Scott? This is Amanda Wingfield! We *missed* you at the D.A.R. last Monday! I said to myself: She's probably suffering with that sinus condition! How is that sinus condition? Horrors! Heaven have mercy! — You're a Christian martyr, yes, that's what you are, a Christian martyr! Well, I just now happened to notice that your subscription to the *Companion's* about to expire! Yes, it expires with the next issue, honey! — just when that wonderful new serial by Bessie Mae Hopper is getting off to such an exciting start. Oh, honey, it's something that you can't miss! You remember how *Gone with the Wind* took everybody by storm? You simply couldn't go out if you hadn't read it. All everybody *talked* was Scarlett O'Hara. Well, this is a book that critics already compare to *Gone with the Wind.* It's the *Gone with the Wind* of the post–World War generation! — What? — Burning? — Oh, honey, don't let them burn, go take a look in the oven and I'll hold the wire! Heavens — I think she's hung up!

(Dim out.)

(Legend on screen: "You think I'm in love with Continental Shoemakers?")

Before the stage is lighted, the violent voices of Tom and Amanda are heard. They are quarreling behind the portieres. In front of them stands Laura with clenched hands and panicky expression.

A clear pool of light on her figure throughout this scene.

TOM: What in Christ's name am I —

AMANDA *(shrilly)*:   Don't you use that —

TOM: Supposed to do!

AMANDA: Expression! Not in my —

TOM: Ohhh!

AMANDA: Presence! Have you gone out of your senses?

TOM: I have, that's true, been *driven* out!

AMANDA: What is the matter with you, you — big — big — IDIOT!

TOM: Look — I've got *no thing,* no single thing —

AMANDA: Lower your voice!

TOM: In my life here that I can call my own! Everything is —

AMANDA: Stop that shouting!

TOM: Yesterday you confiscated my books! You had the nerve to —

AMANDA: I took that horrible novel back to the library — yes! That hideous book by that insane Mr. Lawrence.° *(Tom laughs wildly.)* I cannot control the output of diseased minds or people who cater to them — *(Tom laughs*

Mr. Lawrence: D. H. Lawrence (1885–1930), English poet and novelist who advocated sexual freedom.

still more wildly.) BUT I WON'T ALLOW SUCH FILTH BROUGHT INTO MY HOUSE! No, no, no, no, no!

TOM: House, house! Who pays rent on it, who makes a slave of himself to —

AMANDA *(fairly screeching)*:   Don't you DARE to —

TOM: No, no, I mustn't say things! *I've* got to just —

AMANDA: Let me tell you —

TOM: I don't want to hear any more! *(He tears the portieres open. The upstage area is lit with a turgid smoky red glow.)*

Amanda's hair is in metal curlers and she wears a very old bathrobe, much too large for her slight figure, a relic of the faithless Mr. Wingfield.

An upright typewriter and a wild disarray of manuscripts are on the drop-leaf table. The quarrel was probably precipitated by Amanda's interruption of his creative labor. A chair lying overthrown on the floor.

Their gesticulating shadows are cast on the ceiling by the fiery glow.

AMANDA: You *will* hear more, you —

TOM: No, I won't hear more, I'm going out!

AMANDA: You come right back in —

TOM: Out, out, out! Because I'm —

AMANDA: Come back here, Tom Wingfield! I'm not through talking to you!

TOM: Oh, go —

LAURA *(desperately)*:   Tom!

AMANDA: You're going to listen, and no more insolence from you! I'm at the end of my patience! *(He comes back toward her.)*

TOM: What do you think I'm at? Aren't I supposed to have any patience to reach the end of, Mother? I know, I know. It seems unimportant to you, what I'm *doing* — what I *want* to do — having a little *difference* between them! You don't think that —

AMANDA: I think you've been doing things that you're ashamed of. That's why you act like this. I don't believe that you go every night to the movies. Nobody goes to the movies night after night. Nobody in their right minds goes to the movies as often as you pretend to. People don't go to the movies at nearly midnight, and movies don't let out at two A.M. Come in stumbling. Muttering to yourself like a maniac! You get three hours' sleep and then go to work. Oh, I can picture the way you're doing down there. Moping, doping, because you're in no condition.

TOM *(wildly)*:   No, I'm in no condition!

AMANDA: What right have you got to jeopardize your job? Jeopardize the security of us all? How do you think we'd manage if you were —

TOM: Listen! You think I'm crazy *about* the *warehouse*! *(He bends fiercely toward her slight figure.)* You think I'm in love with the Continental Shoemakers? You think I want to spend fifty-five *years* down there in that — *celotex interior*! with — *fluorescent* — *tubes*! Look! I'd rather somebody picked up a crowbar and battered out my brains — than go back mornings! I go! Every time you come in yelling that God damn *"Rise and Shine!" "Rise and Shine!"*

I say to myself "How *lucky dead* people are!" But I get up. I *go*! For sixty-five dollars a month I give up all that I dream of doing and being *ever*! And you say self — *self's* all I ever think of. Why, listen, if self is what I thought of, Mother, I'd be where he is — ! *(Pointing to father's picture.)* As far as the system of transportation reaches! *(He starts past her. She grabs his arm.)* Don't grab at me, Mother!

AMANDA: Where are you going?

TOM: I'm going to the *movies*!

AMANDA: I don't believe that lie!

TOM *(crouching toward her, overtowering her tiny figure. She backs away, gasping)*:   I'm going to opium dens! Yes, opium dens, dens of vice and criminals' hang-outs, Mother. I've joined the Hogan gang, I'm a hired assassin, I carry a tommy-gun in a violin case! I run a string of cat-houses in the Valley! They call me Killer, Killer Wingfield, I'm leading a double-life, a simple, honest warehouse worker by day, by night a dynamic *czar* of the *underworld, Mother.* I go to gambling casinos, I spin away fortunes on the roulette table! I wear a patch over one eye and a false mustache, sometimes I put on green whiskers. On those occasions they call me — *El Diablo!°* Oh, I could tell you things to make you sleepless! My enemies plan to dynamite this place. They're going to blow us all sky-high some night! I'll be glad, very happy, and so will you! You'll go up, up on a broomstick, over Blue Mountain with seventeen gentlemen callers! You ugly — babbling old — witch. . . . *(He goes through a series of violent, clumsy movements, seizing his overcoat, lunging to the door, pulling it fiercely open. The women watch him, aghast. His arm catches in the sleeve of the coat as he struggles to pull it on. For a moment he is pinioned by the bulky garment. With an outraged groan he tears the coat off again, splitting the shoulders of it, and hurls it across the room. It strikes against the shelf of Laura's glass collection, there is a tinkle of shattering glass. Laura cries out as if wounded.)*

(Music legend: "The Glass Menagerie.")

LAURA *(shrilly)*:   My glass! — menagerie. . . . *(She covers her face and turns away.)*

But Amanda is still stunned and stupefied by the "ugly witch" so that she barely notices this occurrence. Now she recovers her speech.

AMANDA *(in an awful voice)*:   I won't speak to you — until you apologize! *(She crosses through portieres and draws them together behind her. Tom is left with Laura. Laura clings weakly to the mantel with her face averted. Tom stares at her stupidly for a moment. Then he crosses to shelf. Drops awkwardly to his knees to collect the fallen glass, glancing at Laura as if he would speak but couldn't.)*

"The Glass Menagerie" steals in as
    (The scene dims out.)

El Diablo: The devil (Spanish).

Scene 4

The interior is dark. Faint light in the alley.
A deep-voiced bell in a church is tolling the hour of five as the scene commences.
Tom appears at the top of the alley. After each solemn boom of the bell in the tower, he shakes a little noise-maker or rattle as if to express the tiny spasm of man in contrast to the sustained power and dignity of the Almighty. This and the unsteadiness of his advance make it evident that he has been drinking.

As he climbs the few steps to the fire-escape landing light steals up inside. Laura appears in night-dress, observing Tom's empty bed in the front room.

Tom fishes in his pockets for the door-key, removing a motley assortment of articles in the search, including a perfect shower of movie-ticket stubs and an empty bottle. At last he finds the key, but just as he is about to insert it, it slips from his fingers. He strikes a match and crouches below the door.

TOM *(bitterly)*:   One crack — and it falls through!

Laura opens the door.

LAURA: Tom! Tom, what are you doing?
TOM: Looking for a door-key.
LAURA: Where have you been all this time?
TOM: I have been to the movies.
LAURA: All this time at the movies?
TOM: There was a very long program. There was a Garbo picture and a Mickey Mouse and a travelogue and a newsreel and a preview of coming attractions. And there was an organ solo and a collection for the milk-fund — simultaneously — which ended up in a terrible fight between a fat lady and an usher!
LAURA *(innocently)*:   Did you have to stay through everything?
TOM: Of course! And, oh, I forgot! There was a big stage show! The headliner on this stage show was Malvolio the Magician. He performed wonderful tricks, many of them, such as pouring water back and forth between pitchers. First it turned to wine and then it turned to beer and then it turned to whiskey. I know it was whiskey it finally turned into because he needed somebody to come up out of the audience to help him, and I came up — both shows! It was Kentucky Straight Bourbon. A very generous fellow, he gave souvenirs. *(He pulls from his back pocket a shimmering rainbow-colored scarf.)* He gave me this. This is his magic scarf. You can have it, Laura. You wave it over a canary cage and you get a bowl of gold-fish. You wave it over the gold-fish bowl and they fly away canaries. . . . But the wonderfullest trick of all was the coffin trick. We nailed him into a coffin and he got out of the coffin without removing one nail. *(He has come inside.)* There is a trick that would come in handy for me — get me out of this 2 by 4 situation! *(Flops onto bed and starts removing shoes.)*
LAURA: Tom — Shhh!

TOM: What you shushing me for?

LAURA: You'll wake up Mother.

TOM: Goody, goody! Pay 'er back for all those "Rise an' Shines." *(Lies down, groaning.)* You know it don't take much intelligence to get yourself into a nailed-up coffin, Laura. But who in hell ever got himself out of one without removing one nail?

As if in answer, the father's grinning photograph lights up.

(Scene dims out.)

Immediately following: The church bell is heard striking six. At the sixth stroke the alarm clock goes off in Amanda's room, and after a few moments we hear her calling: "Rise and Shine! Rise and Shine! Laura, go tell your brother to rise and shine!"

TOM *(sitting up slowly)*:   I'll rise — but I won't shine.

The light increases.

AMANDA: Laura, tell your brother his coffee is ready.

Laura slips into front room.

LAURA: Tom! it's nearly seven. Don't make Mother nervous. *(He stares at her stupidly. Beseechingly.)* Tom, speak to Mother this morning. Make up with her, apologize, speak to her!

TOM: She won't to me. It's her that started not speaking.

LAURA: If you just say you're sorry she'll start speaking.

TOM: Her not speaking — is that such a tragedy?

LAURA: Please — please!

AMANDA *(calling from kitchenette)*:   Laura, are you going to do what I asked you to do, or do I have to get dressed and go out myself?

LAURA: Going, going — soon as I get on my coat! *(She pulls on a shapeless felt hat with nervous, jerky movement, pleadingly glancing at Tom. Rushes awkwardly for coat. The coat is one of Amanda's, inaccurately made-over, the sleeves too short for Laura.)* Butter and what else?

AMANDA *(entering upstage)*:   Just butter. Tell them to charge it.

LAURA: Mother, they make such faces when I do that.

AMANDA: Sticks and stones may break my bones, but the expression on Mr. Garfinkel's face won't harm us! Tell your brother his coffee is getting cold.

LAURA *(at door)*:   Do what I asked you, will you, will you, Tom?

He looks sullenly away.

AMANDA: Laura, go now or just don't go at all!

LAURA *(rushing out)*:   Going — going! *(A second later she cries out. Tom springs up and crosses to the door. Amanda rushes anxiously in. Tom opens the door.)*

TOM: Laura?

LAURA: I'm all right. I slipped, but I'm all right.

AMANDA *(peering anxiously after her)*:   If anyone breaks a leg on those fire-escape steps, the landlord ought to be sued for every cent he possesses! *(She shuts door. Remembers she isn't speaking and returns to other room.)*

As Tom enters listlessly for his coffee, she turns her back to him and stands rigidly facing the window on the gloomy gray vault of the areaway. Its light on her face with its aged but childish features is cruelly sharp, satirical as a Daumier° print.

(Music under: "Ave Maria.")

Tom glances sheepishly but sullenly at her averted figure and slumps at the table. The coffee is scalding hot; he sips it and gasps and spits it back in the cup. At his gasp, Amanda catches her breath and half turns. Then catches herself and turns back to window.

Tom blows on his coffee, glancing sidewise at his mother. She clears her throat. Tom clears his. He starts to rise. Sinks back down again, scratches his head, clears his throat again. Amanda coughs. Tom raises his cup in both hands to blow on it, his eyes staring over the rim of it at his mother for several moments. Then he slowly sets the cup down and awkwardly and hesitantly rises from the chair.

TOM *(hoarsely)*:   Mother. I — I apologize. Mother. *(Amanda draws a quick, shuddering breath. Her face works grotesquely. She breaks into childlike tears.)* I'm sorry for what I said, for everything that I said, I didn't mean it.

AMANDA *(sobbingly)*:   My devotion has made me a witch and so I make myself hateful to my children!

TOM: No, you *don't.*

AMANDA: I worry so much, don't sleep, it makes me nervous!

TOM *(gently)*:   I understand that.

AMANDA: I've had to put up a solitary battle all these years. But you're my right-hand bower! Don't fall down, don't fail!

TOM *(gently)*:   I try, Mother.

AMANDA *(with great enthusiasm)*:   Try and you will SUCCEED! *(The notion makes her breathless.)* Why, you — you're just full of natural endowments! Both of my children — they're *unusual* children! Don't you think I know it? I'm so — proud! Happy and — feel I've — so much to be thankful for but — Promise me one thing, son!

TOM: What, Mother?

AMANDA: Promise, son, you'll — never be a drunkard!

TOM *(turns to her grinning)*:   I will never be a drunkard, Mother.

AMANDA: That's what frightened me so, that you'd be drinking! Eat a bowl of Purina!

TOM: Just coffee, Mother.

AMANDA: Shredded wheat biscuit?

TOM: No. No, Mother, just coffee.

AMANDA: You can't put in a day's work on an empty stomach. You've got ten minutes — don't gulp! Drinking too-hot liquids makes cancer of the stomach. . . . Put cream in.

TOM: No, thank you.

AMANDA: To cool it.

TOM: No! No, thank you, I want it black.

Daumier: Honoré Daumier (1808–1879), French caricaturist, lithographer, and painter who mercilessly satirized bourgeois society.

AMANDA: I know, but it's not good for you. We have to do all that we can to build ourselves up. In these trying times we live in, all that we have to cling to is — each other. . . . That's why it's so important to — Tom, I — I sent out your sister so I could discuss something with you. If you hadn't spoken I would have spoken to you. *(Sits down.)*

TOM *(gently)*:   What is it, Mother, that you want to discuss?

AMANDA: Laura!

Tom puts his cup down slowly.
   (Legend on screen: "Laura.")
   (Music: "The Glass Menagerie.")

TOM: — Oh. — Laura . . .

AMANDA *(touching his sleeve)*:   You know how Laura is. So quiet but — still water runs deep! She notices things and I think she — broods about them. *(Tom looks up.)* A few days ago I came in and she was crying.

TOM: What about?

AMANDA: You.

TOM: Me?

AMANDA: She has an idea that you're not happy here.

TOM: What gave her that idea?

AMANDA: What gives her any idea? However, you do act strangely. I — I'm not criticizing, understand *that*! I know your ambitions do not lie in the warehouse, that like everybody in the whole wide world — you've had to — make sacrifices, but — Tom — Tom — life's not easy, it calls for — Spartan endurance! There's so many things in my heart that I cannot describe to you! I've never told you but I — *loved* your father. . . .

TOM *(gently)*:   I know that, Mother.

AMANDA: And you — when I see you taking after his ways! Staying out late — and — well, you *had* been drinking the night you were in that — terrifying condition! Laura says that you hate the apartment and that you go out nights to get away from it! Is that true, Tom?

TOM: No. You say there's so much in your heart that you can't describe to me. That's true of me, too. There's so much in my heart that I can't describe to *you*! So let's respect each other's —

AMANDA: But, why — *why*, Tom — are you always so *restless*? Where do you go to, nights?

TOM: I — go to the movies.

AMANDA: Why do you go to the movies so much, Tom?

TOM: I go to the movies because — I like adventure. Adventure is something I don't have much of at work, so I go to the movies.

AMANDA: But, Tom, you go to the movies *entirely too much*!

TOM: I like a lot of adventure.

Amanda looks baffled, then hurt. As the familiar inquisition resumes he becomes hard and impatient again. Amanda slips back into her querulous attitude toward him.
   (Image on screen: Sailing vessel with Jolly Roger.)

AMANDA: Most young men find adventure in their careers.

TOM: Then most young men are not employed in a warehouse.

AMANDA: The world is full of young men employed in warehouses and offices and factories.

TOM: Do all of them find adventure in their careers?

AMANDA: They do or they do without it! Not everybody has a craze for adventure.

TOM: Man is by instinct a lover, a hunter, a fighter, and none of those instincts are given much play at the warehouse!

AMANDA: Man is by instinct! Don't quote instinct to me! Instinct is something that people have got away from! It belongs to animals! Christian adults don't want it!

TOM: What do Christian adults want, then, Mother?

AMANDA: Superior things! Things of the mind and the spirit! Only animals have to satisfy instincts! Surely your aims are somewhat higher than theirs! Than monkeys — pigs —

TOM: I reckon they're not.

AMANDA: You're joking. However, that isn't what I wanted to discuss.

TOM *(rising)*:   I haven't much time.

AMANDA *(pushing his shoulders)*:   Sit down.

TOM: You want me to punch in red° at the warehouse, Mother?

AMANDA: You have five minutes. I want to talk about Laura.

(Legend: "Plans and Provisions.")

TOM: All right! What about Laura?

AMANDA: We have to be making plans and provisions for her. She's older than you, two years, and nothing has happened. She just drifts along doing nothing. It frightens me terribly how she just drifts along.

TOM: I guess she's the type that people call home girls.

AMANDA: There's no such type, and if there is, it's a pity! That is unless the home is hers, with a husband!

TOM: What?

AMANDA: Oh, I can see the handwriting on the wall as plain as I see the nose in front of my face! It's terrifying! More and more you remind me of your father! He was out all hours without explanation — Then *left! Good-bye!* And me with the bag to hold. I saw that letter you got from the Merchant Marine. I know what you're dreaming of. I'm not standing here blindfolded. Very well, then. Then *do* it! But not till there's somebody to take your place.

TOM: What do you mean?

AMANDA: I mean that as soon as Laura has got somebody to take care of her, married, a home of her own, independent — why, then you'll be free to go wherever you please, on land, on sea, whichever way the wind blows! But until that time you've got to look out for your sister. I don't say me because

punch in red: Be late for work.

I'm old and don't matter! I say for your sister because she's young and dependent. I put her in business college — a dismal failure! Frightened her so it made her sick to her stomach. I took her over to the Young People's League at the church. Another fiasco. She spoke to nobody, nobody spoke to her. Now all she does is fool with those pieces of glass and play those worn-out records. What kind of a life is that for a girl to lead!

TOM: What can I do about it?

AMANDA: Overcome selfishness! Self, self, self is all that you ever think of! *(Tom springs up and crosses to get his coat. It is ugly and bulky. He pulls on a cap with earmuffs.)* Where is your muffler? Put your wool muffler on! *(He snatches it angrily from the closet and tosses it around his neck and pulls both ends tight.)* Tom! I haven't said what I had in mind to ask you.

TOM: I'm too late to —

AMANDA *(catching his arms — very importunately. Then shyly.):*   Down at the warehouse, aren't there some — nice young men?

TOM: No!

AMANDA: There *must* be — *some.*

TOM: Mother —

Gesture.

AMANDA: Find out one that's clean-living — doesn't drink and — ask him out for sister!

TOM: What?

AMANDA: For *sister!* To *meet!* Get *acquainted!*

TOM *(stamping to door)*:   Oh, my *go-osh!*

AMANDA: Will you? *(He opens door. Imploringly.)* Will you? *(He starts down.)* Will you? *Will* you, dear?

TOM *(calling back)*:   YES!

Amanda closes the door hesitantly and with a troubled but faintly hopeful expression.
    (Screen image: Glamour *magazine cover.)*
    Spot Amanda at phone.

AMANDA: Ella Cartwright? This is Amanda Wingfield! How are you, honey? How is that kidney condition? *(Count five.)* Horrors! *(Count five.)* You're a Christian martyr, yes, honey, that's what you are, a Christian martyr! Well, I just happened to notice in my little red book that your subscription to the *Companion* has just run out! I knew that you wouldn't want to miss out on the wonderful serial starting in this new issue. It's by Bessie Mae Hopper, the first thing she's written since *Honeymoon for Three.* Wasn't that a strange and interesting story? Well, this one is even lovelier, I believe. It has a sophisticated society background. It's all about the horsey set on Long Island!

(Fade out.)

Scene 5

(Legend on screen: "Annunciation.") Fade with music.
    It is early dusk of a spring evening. Supper has just been finished in the Wingfield apartment. Amanda and Laura in light-colored dresses are removing dishes from the table, in the upstage area, which is shadowy, their movements formalized almost as a dance or ritual, their moving forms as pale and silent as moths.
    Tom, in white shirt and trousers, rises from the table and crosses toward the fire-escape.

AMANDA *(as he passes her)*:   Son, will you do me a favor?

TOM: What?

AMANDA: Comb your hair! You look so pretty when your hair is combed! *(Tom slouches on sofa with evening paper. Enormous caption "Franco Triumphs."°)* There is only one respect in which I would like you to emulate your father.

TOM: What respect is that?

AMANDA: The care he always took of his appearance. He never allowed himself to look untidy. *(He throws down the paper and crosses to fire-escape.)* Where are you going?

TOM: I'm going out to smoke.

AMANDA: You smoke too much. A pack a day at fifteen cents a pack. How much would that amount to in a month? Thirty times fifteen is how much, Tom? Figure it out and you will be astounded at what you could save. Enough to give you a night-school course in accounting at Washington U! Just think what a wonderful thing that would be for you, son!

Tom is unmoved by the thought.

TOM: I'd rather smoke. *(He steps out on landing, letting the screen door slam.)*

AMANDA *(sharply)*:   I know! That's the tragedy of it. . . . *(Alone, she turns to look at her husband's picture.)*

(Dance music: "All the World Is Waiting for the Sunrise!")

TOM *(to the audience)*:   Across the alley from us was the Paradise Dance Hall. On evenings in spring the windows and doors were open and the music came outdoors. Sometimes the lights were turned out except for a large glass sphere that hung from the ceiling. It would turn slowly about and filter the dusk with delicate rainbow colors. Then the orchestra played a waltz or a tango, something that had a slow and sensuous rhythm. Couples would come outside, to the relative privacy of the alley. You could see them kissing behind ash-pits and telephone poles. This was the compensation for lives that passed like mine, without any change or adventure. Adventure and change were imminent in this year. They were waiting around the corner for all these kids. Suspended in the mist over the

"Franco Triumphs": In January 1939, the Republican forces of Francisco Franco (1892–1975) defeated the Loyalists, ending the Spanish civil war.

Berchtesgaden,° caught in the folds of Chamberlain's° umbrella — In Spain there was Guernica! But here there was only hot swing music and liquor, dance halls, bars, and movies, and sex that hung in the gloom like a chandelier and flooded the world with brief, deceptive rainbows. . . . All the world was waiting for bombardments!

Amanda turns from the picture and comes outside.

AMANDA *(sighing)*:   A fire-escape landing's a poor excuse for a porch. *(She spreads a newspaper on a step and sits down, gracefully and demurely as if she were settling into a swing on a Mississippi veranda.)* What are you looking at?

TOM: The moon.

AMANDA: Is there a moon this evening?

TOM: It's rising over Garfinkel's Delicatessen.

AMANDA: So it is! A little silver slipper of a moon. Have you made a wish on it yet?

TOM: Um-hum.

AMANDA: What did you wish for?

TOM: That's a secret.

AMANDA: A secret, huh? Well, I won't tell mine either. I will be just as mysterious as you.

TOM: I bet I can guess what yours is.

AMANDA: Is my head so transparent?

TOM: You're not a sphinx.

AMANDA: No, I don't have secrets. I'll tell you what I wished for on the moon. Success and happiness for my precious children! I wish for that whenever there's a moon, and when there isn't a moon, I wish for it, too.

TOM: I thought perhaps you wished for a gentleman caller.

AMANDA: Why do you say that?

TOM: Don't you remember asking me to fetch one?

AMANDA: I remember suggesting that it would be nice for your sister if you brought home some nice young man from the warehouse. I think I've made that suggestion more than once.

TOM: Yes, you have made it repeatedly.

AMANDA: Well?

TOM: We are going to have one.

AMANDA: *What?*

TOM: A gentleman caller!

(The Annunciation is celebrated with music.)
    Amanda rises.
    (Image on screen: Caller with bouquet.)

AMANDA: You mean you have asked some nice young man to come over?

TOM: Yep. I've asked him to dinner.

Berchtesgaden: A resort in the German Alps where Adolf Hitler had a heavily protected villa.   **Chamberlain:** Neville Chamberlain (1869–1940), British prime minister who sought to avoid war with Hitler through a policy of appeasement.

AMANDA: You really did?

TOM: I did!

AMANDA: You did, and did he — *accept?*

TOM: He did!

AMANDA: Well, well — well, well! That's — lovely!

TOM: I thought that you would be pleased.

AMANDA: It's definite, then?

TOM: Very definite.

AMANDA: Soon?

TOM: Very soon.

AMANDA: For heaven's sake, stop putting on and tell me some things, will you?

TOM: What things do you want me to tell you?

AMANDA: Naturally I would like to know when he's *coming!*

TOM: He's coming tomorrow.

AMANDA: *Tomorrow?*

TOM: Yep. Tomorrow.

AMANDA: But, Tom!

TOM: Yes, Mother?

AMANDA: Tomorrow gives me no time!

TOM: Time for what?

AMANDA: Preparations! Why didn't you phone me at once, as soon as you asked him, the minute that he accepted? Then, don't you see, I could have been getting ready!

TOM: You don't have to make any fuss.

AMANDA: Oh, Tom, Tom, Tom, of course I have to make a fuss! I want things nice, not sloppy! Not thrown together. I'll certainly have to do some fast thinking, won't I?

TOM: I don't see why you have to think at all.

AMANDA: You just don't know. We can't have a gentleman caller in a pig-sty! All my wedding silver has to be polished, the monogrammed table linen ought to be laundered! The windows have to be washed and fresh curtains put up. And how about clothes? We have to *wear* something, don't we?

TOM: Mother, this boy is no one to make a fuss over!

AMANDA: Do you realize he's the first young man we've introduced to your sister? It's terrible, dreadful, disgraceful that poor little sister has never received a single gentleman caller! Tom, come inside! *(She opens the screen door.)*

TOM: What for?

AMANDA: I want to ask you some things.

TOM: If you're going to make such a fuss, I'll call it off, I'll tell him not to come.

AMANDA: You certainly won't do anything of the kind. Nothing offends people worse than broken engagements. It simply means I'll have to work like a Turk! We won't be brilliant, but we'll pass inspection. Come on inside. *(Tom follows, groaning.)* Sit down.

TOM: Any particular place you would like me to sit?

AMANDA: Thank heavens I've got that new sofa! I'm also making payments on a floor lamp I'll have sent out! And put the chintz covers on, they'll brighten things up! Of course I'd hoped to have these walls re-papered. . . . What is the young man's name?

TOM: His name is O'Connor.

AMANDA: That, of course, means fish—tomorrow is Friday! I'll have that salmon loaf — with Durkee's dressing! What does he do? He works at the warehouse?

TOM: Of course! How else would I —

AMANDA: Tom, he — doesn't drink?

TOM: Why do you ask me that?

AMANDA: Your father did!

TOM: Don't get started on that!

AMANDA: He does drink, then?

TOM: Not that I know of!

AMANDA: Make sure, be certain! The last thing I want for my daughter's a boy who drinks!

TOM: Aren't you being a little premature? Mr. O'Connor has not yet appeared on the scene!

AMANDA: But will tomorrow. To meet your sister, and what do I know about his character? Nothing! Old maids are better off than wives of drunkards!

TOM: Oh, my God!

AMANDA: Be still!

TOM *(leaning forward to whisper)*:   Lots of fellows meet girls whom they don't marry!

AMANDA: Oh, talk sensibly, Tom—and don't be sarcastic! *(She has gotten a hairbrush.)*

TOM: What are you doing?

AMANDA: I'm brushing that cow-lick down! What is this young man's position at the warehouse?

TOM *(submitting grimly to the brush and the interrogation)*:   This young man's position is that of a shipping clerk, Mother.

AMANDA: Sounds to me like a fairly responsible job, the sort of a job *you* would be in if you just had more *get-up*. What is his salary? Have you got any idea?

TOM: I would judge it to be approximately eighty-five dollars a month.

AMANDA: Well—not princely, but —

TOM: Twenty more than I make.

AMANDA: Yes, how well I know! But for a family man, eighty-five dollars a month is not much more than you can just get by on. . . .

TOM: Yes, but Mr. O'Connor is not a family man.

AMANDA: He might be, mightn't he? Some time in the future?

TOM: I see. Plans and provisions.

AMANDA: You are the only young man that I know of who ignores the fact that the future becomes the present, the present the past, and the past turns into everlasting regret if you don't plan for it!

TOM: I will think that over and see what I can make of it.

AMANDA: Don't be supercilious with your mother! Tell me some more about this — what do you call him?

TOM: James D. O'Connor. The D. is for Delaney.

AMANDA: Irish on *both* sides! *Gracious!* And doesn't drink?

TOM: Shall I call him up and ask him right this minute?

AMANDA: The only way to find out about those things is to make discreet inquiries at the proper moment. When I was a girl in Blue Mountain and it was suspected that a young man drank, the girl whose attentions he had been receiving, if any girl *was*, would sometimes speak to the minister of his church, or rather her father would if her father was living, and sort of feel him out on the young man's character. That is the way such things are discreetly handled to keep a young woman from making a tragic mistake!

TOM: Then how did you happen to make a tragic mistake?

AMANDA: That innocent look of your father's had everyone fooled! He smiled — the world was *enchanted*! No girl can do worse than put herself at the mercy of a handsome appearance! I hope that Mr. O'Connor is not too good-looking.

TOM: No, he's not too good-looking. He's covered with freckles and hasn't too much of a nose.

AMANDA: He's not right-down homely, though?

TOM: Not right-down homely. Just medium homely, I'd say.

AMANDA: Character's what to look for in a man.

TOM: That's what I've always said, Mother.

AMANDA: You've never said anything of the kind and I suspect you would never give it a thought.

TOM: Don't be suspicious of me.

AMANDA: At least I hope he's the type that's up and coming.

TOM: I think he really goes in for self-improvement.

AMANDA: What reason have you to think so?

TOM: He goes to night school.

AMANDA *(beaming)*:   Splendid! What does he do, I mean study?

TOM: Radio engineering and public speaking!

AMANDA: Then he has visions of being advanced in the world! Any young man who studies public speaking is aiming to have an executive job some day! And radio engineering? A thing for the future! Both of these facts are very illuminating. Those are the sort of things that a mother should know concerning any young man who comes to call on her daughter. Seriously or — not.

TOM: One little warning. He doesn't know about Laura. I didn't let on that we had dark ulterior motives. I just said, why don't you come have dinner with us? He said okay and that was the whole conversation.

AMANDA: I bet it was! You're eloquent as an oyster. However, he'll know about Laura when he gets here. When he sees how lovely and sweet and pretty she is, he'll thank his lucky stars he was asked to dinner.

TOM: Mother, you mustn't expect too much of Laura.

AMANDA: What do you mean?

TOM: Laura seems all those things to you and me because she's ours and we love her. We don't even notice she's crippled any more.

AMANDA: Don't say crippled! You know that I never allow that word to be used!

TOM: But face facts, Mother. She is and — that's not all —

AMANDA: What do you mean "not all"?

TOM: Laura is very different from other girls.

AMANDA: I think the difference is all to her advantage.

TOM: Not quite all — in the eyes of others — strangers — she's terribly shy and lives in a world of her own and those things make her seem a little peculiar to people outside the house.

AMANDA: Don't say peculiar.

TOM: Face the facts. She is.

(The dance-hall music changes to a tango that has a minor and somewhat ominous tone.)

AMANDA: In what way is she peculiar — may I ask?

TOM *(gently)*:   She lives in a world of her own — a world of — little glass ornaments, Mother. . . . *(Gets up. Amanda remains holding brush, looking at him, troubled.)* She plays old phonograph records and — that's about all — *(He glances at himself in the mirror and crosses to door.)*

AMANDA *(sharply)*:   Where are you going?

TOM: I'm going to the movies. *(Out screen door.)*

AMANDA: Not to the movies, every night to the movies! *(Follows quickly to screen door.)* I don't believe you always go to the movies! *(He is gone. Amanda looks worriedly after him for a moment. Then vitality and optimism return and she turns from the door. Crossing to portieres.)* Laura! Laura! *(Laura answers from kitchenette.)*

LAURA: Yes, Mother.

AMANDA: Let those dishes go and come in front! *(Laura appears with dish towel. Gaily.)* Laura, come here and make a wish on the moon!

LAURA *(entering)*:   Moon — moon?

AMANDA: A little silver slipper of a moon. Look over your left shoulder, Laura, and make a wish! *(Laura looks faintly puzzled as if called out of sleep. Amanda seizes her shoulders and turns her at angle by the door.)* Now! Now, darling, wish!

LAURA: What shall I wish for, Mother?

AMANDA *(her voice trembling and her eyes suddenly filling with tears)*:   Happiness! Good Fortune!

The violin rises and the stage dims out.

Scene 6

(Image: High-school hero.)

TOM: And so the following evening I brought Jim home to dinner. I had known Jim slightly in high school. In high school Jim was a hero. He had tremendous Irish good nature and vitality with the scrubbed and polished look of white chinaware. He seemed to move in a continual spotlight. He was a star in basketball, captain of the debating club, president of the senior class and the glee club and he sang the male lead in the annual light operas. He was always running or bounding, never just walking. He seemed always at the point of defeating the law of gravity. He was shooting with such velocity through his adolescence that you would logically expect him to arrive at nothing short of the White House by the time he was thirty. But Jim apparently ran into more interference after his graduation from Soldan. His speed had definitely slowed. Six years after he left high school he was holding a job that wasn't much better than mine.

(Image: Clerk.)

He was the only one at the warehouse with whom I was on friendly terms. I was valuable to him as someone who could remember his former glory, who had seen him win basketball games and the silver cup in debating. He knew of my secret practice of retiring to a cabinet of the washroom to work on poems when business was slack in the warehouse. He called me Shakespeare. And while the other boys in the warehouse regarded me with suspicious hostility, Jim took a humorous attitude toward me. Gradually his attitude affected the others, their hostility wore off, and they also began to smile at me as people smile at an oddly fashioned dog who trots across their paths at some distance.

I knew that Jim and Laura had known each other at Soldan, and I had heard Laura speak admiringly of his voice. I didn't know if Jim remembered her or not. In high school Laura had been as unobtrusive as Jim had been astonishing. If he did remember Laura, it was not as my sister, for when I asked him to dinner, he grinned and said, "You know, Shakespeare, I never thought of you as having folks!"

He was about to discover that I did. . . .

(Light upstage.)

(Legend on screen: "The Accent of a Coming Foot.")

Friday evening. It is about five o'clock of a late spring evening which comes "scattering poems in the sky."

A delicate lemony light is in the Wingfield apartment.

Amanda has worked like a Turk in preparation for the gentleman caller. The results are astonishing. The new floor lamp with its rose-silk shade is in place, a colored paper lantern conceals the broken light fixture in the ceiling, new billowing white curtains are at the windows, chintz covers are on chairs and sofa, a pair of new sofa pillows make their initial appearance.

Open boxes and tissue paper are scattered on the floor.

Laura stands in the middle with lifted arms while Amanda crouches before her, adjusting the hem of the new dress, devout and ritualistic. The dress is colored and designed by memory. The arrangement of Laura's hair is changed; it is softer and more becoming. A fragile, unearthly prettiness has come out in Laura: she is like a piece of translucent glass touched by light, given a momentary radiance, not actual, not lasting.

AMANDA *(impatiently):*   Why are you trembling?

LAURA: Mother, you've made me so nervous!

AMANDA: How have I made you nervous?

LAURA: By all this fuss! You make it seem so important!

AMANDA: I don't understand you, Laura. You couldn't be satisfied with just sitting home, and yet whenever I try to arrange something for you, you seem to resist it. *(She gets up.)* Now take a look at yourself. No, wait! Wait just a moment — I have an idea!

LAURA: What is it now?

Amanda produces two powder puffs which she wraps in handkerchiefs and stuffs in Laura's bosom.

LAURA: Mother, what are you doing?

AMANDA: They call them "Gay Deceivers"!

LAURA: I won't wear them!

AMANDA: You will!

LAURA: Why should I?

AMANDA: Because, to be painfully honest, your chest is flat.

LAURA: You make it seem like we were setting a trap.

AMANDA: All pretty girls are a trap, a pretty trap, and men expect them to be. *(Legend: "A Pretty Trap.")* Now look at yourself, young lady. This is the prettiest you will ever be! I've got to fix myself now! You're going to be surprised by your mother's appearance! *(She crosses through portieres, humming gaily.)*

Laura moves slowly to the long mirror and stares solemnly at herself.

A wind blows the white curtains inward in a slow, graceful motion and with a faint, sorrowful sighing.

AMANDA *(offstage)*:   It isn't dark enough yet. *(She turns slowly before the mirror with a troubled look).*

(Legend on screen: "This Is My Sister: Celebrate Her with Strings!" Music.)

AMANDA *(laughing, off)*: I'm going to show you something. I'm going to make a spectacular appearance!

LAURA: What is it, Mother?

AMANDA: Possess your soul in patience — you will see! Something I've resurrected from that old trunk! Styles haven't changed so terribly much after all. . . . *(She parts the portieres.)* Now just look at your mother! *(She wears a girlish frock of yellowed voile with a blue silk sash. She carries a bunch of jonquils — the legend of her youth is nearly revived. Feverishly.)* This is the dress in which I led the cotillion. Won the cakewalk twice at Sunset Hill, wore one spring to the Governor's ball in Jackson! See how I sashayed around the ballroom, Laura? *(She raises her skirt and does a mincing step around the room.)* I wore it on Sundays for my gentlemen callers! I had it on the day I met your father — I had malaria fever all that spring. The change of climate from East Tennessee to the Delta — weakened resistance — I had a little temperature all the time — not enough to be serious — just enough to make me restless and giddy! Invitations poured in — parties all over the Delta! — "Stay in bed," said Mother, "you have fever!" — but I just wouldn't. — I took quinine but kept on going, going! — Evenings, dances! — Afternoons, long, long rides! Picnics — lovely! — So lovely, that country in May. — All lacy with dogwood, literally flooded with jonquils! — That was the spring I had the craze for jonquils. Jonquils became an absolute obsession. Mother said, "Honey, there's no more room for jonquils." And still I kept bringing in more jonquils. Whenever, wherever I saw them, I'd say, "Stop! Stop! I see jonquils!" I made the young men help me gather the jonquils! It was a joke, Amanda and her jonquils! Finally there were no more vases to hold them, every available space was filled with jonquils. No vases to hold them? All right, I'll hold them myself! And then I — *(She stops in front of the picture.) (Music.)* met your father! Malaria fever and jonquils and then — this — boy. . . . *(She switches on the rose-colored lamp.)* I hope they get here before it starts to rain. *(She crosses upstage and places the jonquils in bowl on table.)* I gave your brother a little extra change so he and Mr. O'Connor could take the service car home.

LAURA *(with altered look):*   What did you say his name was?

AMANDA: O'Connor.

LAURA: What is his first name?

AMANDA: I don't remember. Oh, yes, I do. It was — Jim!

Laura sways slightly and catches hold of a chair.
(Legend on screen: "Not Jim!")

LAURA *(faintly):*   Not — Jim!

AMANDA: Yes, that was it, it was Jim! I've never known a Jim that wasn't nice!

(Music: Ominous.)

LAURA: Are you sure his name is Jim O'Connor?

AMANDA: Yes. Why?

LAURA: Is he the one that Tom used to know in high school?

AMANDA: He didn't say so. I think he just got to know him at the warehouse.

LAURA: There was a Jim O'Connor we both knew in high school — *(Then, with effort.)* If that is the one that Tom is bringing to dinner — you'll have to excuse me, I won't come to the table.

AMANDA: What sort of nonsense is this?

LAURA: You asked me once if I'd ever liked a boy. Don't you remember I showed you this boy's picture?

AMANDA: You mean the boy you showed me in the year-book?

LAURA: Yes, that boy.

AMANDA: Laura, Laura, were you in love with that boy?

LAURA: I don't know, Mother. All I know is I couldn't sit at the table if it was him!

AMANDA: It won't be him! It isn't the least bit likely. But whether it is or not, you will come to the table. You will not be excused.

LAURA: I'll have to be, Mother.

AMANDA: I don't intend to humor your silliness, Laura. I've had too much from you and your brother, both! So just sit down and compose yourself till they come. Tom has forgotten his key so you'll have to let them in, when they arrive.

LAURA *(panicky)*:   Oh, Mother — *you* answer the door!

AMANDA *(lightly)*:   I'll be in the kitchen — busy!

LAURA: Oh, Mother, please answer the door, don't make me do it!

AMANDA *(crossing into kitchenette)*:   I've got to fix the dressing for the salmon. Fuss, fuss — silliness! — over a gentleman caller!

Door swings shut. Laura is left alone.

(Legend: "Terror!")

She utters a low moan and turns off the lamp — sits stiffly on the edge of the sofa, knotting her fingers together.

(Legend on screen: "The Opening of a Door!")

Tom and Jim appear on the fire-escape steps and climb to landing. Hearing their approach, Laura rises with a panicky gesture. She retreats to the portieres.

The doorbell. Laura catches her breath and touches her throat. Low drums.

AMANDA *(calling)*:   Laura, sweetheart! The door!

Laura stares at it without moving.

JIM: I think we just beat the rain.

TOM: Uh-huh. *(He rings again, nervously. Jim whistles and fishes for a cigarette.)*

AMANDA *(very, very gaily)*:   Laura, that is your brother and Mr. O'Connor! Will you let them in, darling?

Laura crosses toward kitchenette door.

LAURA *(breathlessly)*:   Mother — you go to the door!

Amanda steps out of kitchenette and stares furiously at Laura. She points imperiously at the door.

LAURA: Please, please!

AMANDA *(in a fierce whisper)*:   What is the matter with you, you silly thing?

LAURA *(desperately)*:   Please, you answer it, *please!*

AMANDA: I told you I wasn't going to humor you, Laura. Why have you chosen this moment to lose your mind?

LAURA: Please, please, please, you go!

AMANDA: You'll have to go to the door because I can't!

LAURA *(despairingly)*:   I can't either!

AMANDA: Why?

LAURA: I'm sick!

AMANDA: I'm sick, too — of your nonsense! Why can't you and your brother be normal people? Fantastic whims and behavior! *(Tom gives a long ring.)* Preposterous goings on! Can you give me one reason — *(Calls out lyrically.)* COMING! JUST ONE SECOND! — why should you be afraid to open a door? Now you answer it, Laura!

LAURA: Oh, oh, oh . . . *(She returns through the portieres. Darts to the Victrola and winds it frantically and turns it on.)*

AMANDA: Laura Wingfield, you march right to that door!
LAURA: Yes — yes, Mother!

A faraway, scratchy rendition of "Dardanella" softens the air and gives her strength to move through it. She slips to the door and draws it cautiously open.
    Tom enters with the caller, Jim O'Connor.

TOM: Laura, this is Jim. Jim, this is my sister, Laura.
JIM *(stepping inside)*:   I didn't know that Shakespeare had a sister!
LAURA *(retreating stiff and trembling from the door)*:   How — how do you do?
JIM *(heartily extending his hand)*:   Okay!

Laura touches it hesitantly with hers.

JIM: Your hand's *cold*, Laura!
LAURA: Yes, well — I've been playing the Victrola . . .
JIM: Must have been playing classical music on it! You ought to play a little hot swing music to warm you up!
LAURA: Excuse me — I haven't finished playing the Victrola . . .

She turns awkwardly and hurries into the front room. She pauses a second by the Victrola. Then catches her breath and darts through the portieres like a frightened deer.

JIM *(grinning)*:   What was the matter?
TOM: Oh — with Laura? Laura is — terribly shy.
JIM: Shy, huh? It's unusual to meet a shy girl nowadays. I don't believe you ever mentioned you had a sister.
TOM: Well, now you know. I have one. Here is the *Post Dispatch*. You want a piece of it?
JIM: Uh-huh.
TOM: What piece? The comics?
JIM: Sports! *(Glances at it.)* Ole Dizzy Dean is on his bad behavior.
TOM *(disinterest)*:   Yeah? *(Lights cigarette and crosses back to fire-escape door.)*
JIM: Where are *you* going?
TOM: I'm going out on the terrace.
JIM *(goes after him)*:   You know, Shakespeare — I'm going to sell you a bill of goods!
TOM: What goods?
JIM: A course I'm taking.
TOM: Huh?
JIM: In public speaking! You and me, we're not the warehouse type.
TOM: Thanks — that's good news. But what has public speaking got to do with it?
JIM: It fits you for — executive positions!
TOM: Awww.
JIM: I tell you it's done a helluva lot for me.

(Image: Executive at desk.)

TOM: In what respect?

JIM: In every! Ask yourself what is the difference between you an' me and men in the office down front? Brains? — No! — Ability? — No! Then what? Just one little thing —

TOM: What is that one little thing?

JIM: Primarily it amounts to — social poise! Being able to square up to people and hold your own on any social level!

AMANDA *(offstage)*:   Tom?

TOM: Yes, Mother?

AMANDA: Is that you and Mr. O'Connor?

TOM: Yes, Mother.

AMANDA: Well, you just make yourselves comfortable in there.

TOM: Yes, Mother.

AMANDA: Ask Mr. O'Connor if he would like to wash his hands.

JIM: Aw — no — no — thank you — I took care of that at the warehouse. Tom —

TOM: Yes?

JIM: Mr. Mendoza was speaking to me about you.

TOM: Favorably?

JIM: What do you think?

TOM: Well —

JIM: You're going to be out of a job if you don't wake up.

TOM: I am waking up —

JIM: You show no signs.

TOM: The signs are interior.

(Image on screen: The sailing vessel with Jolly Roger again.)

TOM: I'm planning to change. *(He leans over the rail speaking with quiet exhilaration. The incandescent marquees and signs of the first-run movie houses light his face from across the alley. He looks like a voyager.)* I'm right at the point of committing myself to a future that doesn't include the warehouse and Mr. Mendoza or even a night-school course in public speaking.

JIM: What are you gassing about?

TOM: I'm tired of the movies.

JIM: Movies!

TOM: Yes, movies! Look at them — *(A wave toward the marvels of Grand Avenue.)* All of those glamorous people — having adventures — hogging it all, gobbling the whole thing up! You know what happens? People go to the *movies* instead of *moving*! Hollywood characters are supposed to have all the adventures for everybody in America, while everybody in America sits in a dark room and watches them have them! Yes, until there's a war. That's when adventure becomes available to the masses! *Everyone's* dish, not only Gable's! Then the people in the dark room come out of the dark room to have some adventures themselves — Goody, goody — It's our turn now, to go to the South Sea Island — to make a safari — to be exotic, far-off — But I'm not patient. I don't want to wait till then. I'm tired of the movies and I am *about* to *move*!

JIM *(incredulously)*:   Move?
TOM: Yes.
JIM: When?
TOM: Soon!
JIM: Where? Where?

(Theme three: Music seems to answer the question, while Tom thinks it over. He searches among his pockets.)

TOM: I'm starting to boil inside. I know I seem dreamy, but inside — well, I'm boiling! Whenever I pick up a shoe, I shudder a little thinking how short life is and what I am doing! — Whatever that means. I know it doesn't mean shoes — except as something to wear on a traveler's feet! *(Finds paper.)* Look —
JIM: What?
TOM: I'm a member.
JIM *(reading)*:   The Union of Merchant Seamen.
TOM: I paid my dues this month, instead of the light bill.
JIM: You will regret it when they turn the lights off.
TOM: I won't be here.
JIM: How about your mother?
TOM: I'm like my father. The bastard son of a bastard! See how he grins? And he's been absent going on sixteen years!
JIM: You're just talking, you drip. How does your mother feel about it?
TOM: Shhh — Here comes Mother! Mother is not acquainted with my plans!
AMANDA *(enters portieres)*:   Where are you all?
TOM: On the terrace, Mother.

They start inside. She advances to them. Tom is distinctly shocked at her appearance. Even Jim blinks a little. He is making his first contact with girlish Southern vivacity and in spite of the night-school course in public speaking is somewhat thrown off the beam by the unexpected outlay of social charm.

Certain responses are attempted by Jim but are swept aside by Amanda's gay laughter and chatter. Tom is embarrassed but after the first shock Jim reacts very warmly. Grins and chuckles, is altogether won over.

(Image: Amanda as a girl.)

AMANDA *(coyly smiling, shaking her girlish ringlets)*:   Well, well, well, so this is Mr. O'Connor. Introductions entirely unnecessary. I've heard so much about you from my boy. I finally said to him, Tom — good gracious! — why don't you bring this paragon to supper? I'd like to meet this nice young man at the warehouse! — Instead of just hearing him sing your praises so much! I don't know why my son is so stand-offish — that's not Southern behavior! Let's sit down and — I think we could stand a little more air in here! Tom, leave the door open. I felt a nice fresh breeze a moment ago. Where has it gone? Mmm, so warm already! And not quite summer, even. We're going to burn up when summer really gets started. However, we're having — we're having a very light supper. I think light things are better fo' this time of year. The same as light clothes are. Light clothes an' light food are what warm weather calls fo'. You know our blood gets so thick during th' winter — it takes a while fo' us to *adjust* ou'selves! — when the season changes. . . . It's come so quick this year. I wasn't prepared. All of a sudden — heavens! Already summer! — I ran to the trunk an' pulled out this light dress — Terribly old! Historical almost! But feels so good — so good an' co-ol, y'know. . . .

TOM: Mother —

AMANDA: Yes, honey?

TOM: How about — supper?

AMANDA: Honey, you go ask Sister if supper is ready! You know that Sister is in full charge of supper! Tell her you hungry boys are waiting for it. *(To Jim.)* Have you met Laura?

JIM: She —

AMANDA: Let you in? Oh, good, you've met already! It's rare for a girl as sweet an' pretty as Laura to be domestic! But Laura is, thank heavens, not only pretty but also very domestic! I'm not at all. I never was a bit. I never could make a thing but angel-food cake. Well, in the South we had so many servants. Gone, gone, gone. All vestiges of gracious living! Gone completely! I wasn't prepared for what the future brought me. All of my gentlemen callers were sons of planters and so of course I assumed that I would be married to one and raise my family on a large piece of land with plenty of servants. But man proposes — and woman accepts the proposal! — To vary that old, old saying a little bit — I married no planter! I married a man who worked for the telephone company! — that gallantly smiling gentleman over there! *(Points to the picture.)* A telephone man who — fell in love with long distance! — Now he travels and I don't even know where! — But what am I going on for about my — tribulations! Tell me yours — I hope you don't have any! Tom?

TOM *(returning)*:   Yes, Mother?

AMANDA: Is supper nearly ready?

TOM: It looks to me like supper is on the table.

AMANDA: Let me look — *(She rises prettily and looks through portieres.)* Oh, lovely — But where is Sister?

TOM: Laura is not feeling well and she says that she thinks she'd better not come to the table.

AMANDA: What? — Nonsense! — Laura? Oh, Laura!

LAURA *(offstage, faintly)*:   Yes, Mother.

AMANDA: You really must come to the table. We won't be seated until you come to the table! Come in, Mr. O'Connor. You sit over there and I'll — Laura? Laura Wingfield! You're keeping us waiting, honey! We can't say grace until you come to the table!

The back door is pushed weakly open and Laura comes in. She is obviously quite faint, her lips trembling, her eyes wide and staring. She moves unsteadily toward the table.

(Legend: "Terror!")

Outside a summer storm is coming abruptly. The white curtains billow inward at the windows and there is a sorrowful murmur and deep blue dusk.

Laura suddenly stumbles — She catches at a chair with a faint moan.

TOM: Laura!

AMANDA: Laura! *(There is a clap of thunder.) (Legend: "Ah!") (Despairingly.)* Why, Laura, you *are* sick, darling! Tom, help your sister into the living room, dear! Sit in the living room, Laura — rest on the sofa. Well! *(To the gentleman caller.)* Standing over the hot stove made her ill! — I told her that it was just too warm this evening, but — *(Tom comes back in. Laura is on the sofa.)* Is Laura all right now?

TOM: Yes.

AMANDA: What *is* that? Rain? A nice cool rain has come up! *(She gives the gentleman caller a frightened look.)* I think we may — have grace — now . . . *(Tom looks at her stupidly.)* Tom, honey — you say grace!

TOM: Oh . . . "For these and all thy mercies — " *(They bow their heads, Amanda stealing a nervous glance at Jim. In the living room Laura, stretched on the sofa, clenches her hand to her lips, to hold back a shuddering sob.)* God's Holy Name be praised —

(The scene dims out.)

Scene 7

A Souvenir

Half an hour later. Dinner is just being finished in the upstage area, which is concealed by the drawn portieres.

As the curtain rises Laura is still huddled upon the sofa, her feet drawn under her, her head resting on a pale blue pillow, her eyes wide and mysteriously watchful. The new floor lamp with its shade of rose-colored silk gives a soft, becoming light to her face, bringing out the fragile, unearthly prettiness which usually escapes attention. There is a steady murmur of rain, but it is slackening and stops soon after the scene begins; the air outside becomes pale and luminous as the moon breaks out.

A moment after the curtain rises, the lights in both rooms flicker and go out.

JIM: Hey, there, Mr. Light Bulb!

Amanda laughs nervously.

(Legend: "Suspension of a Public Service.")

AMANDA: Where was Moses when the lights went out? Ha-ha. Do you know the answer to that one, Mr. O'Connor?

JIM: No, Ma'am, what's the answer?

AMANDA: In the dark! *(Jim laughs appreciatively.)* Everybody sit still. I'll light the candles. Isn't it lucky we have them on the table? Where's a match? Which of you gentlemen can provide a match?

JIM: Here.

AMANDA: Thank you, sir.

JIM: Not at all, Ma'am!

AMANDA: I guess the fuse has burnt out. Mr. O'Connor, can you tell a burnt-out fuse? I know I can't and Tom is a total loss when it comes to mechanics. *(Sound: Getting up: Voices recede a little to kitchenette.)* Oh, be careful you don't bump into something. We don't want our gentleman caller to break his neck. Now wouldn't that be a fine howdy-do?

JIM: Ha-ha! Where is the fuse-box?

AMANDA: Right here next to the stove. Can you see anything?

JIM: Just a minute.

AMANDA: Isn't electricity a mysterious thing? Wasn't it Benjamin Franklin who tied a key to a kite? We live in such a mysterious universe, don't we? Some people say that science clears up all the mysteries for us. In my opinion it only creates more! Have you found it yet?

JIM: No, Ma'am. All these fuses look okay to me.

AMANDA: Tom!

TOM: Yes, Mother?

AMANDA: That light bill I gave you several days ago. The one I told you we got the notices about?

TOM: Oh. — Yeah.

(Legend: "Ha!")

AMANDA: You didn't neglect to pay it by any chance?

TOM: Why, I —

AMANDA: Didn't! I might have known it!

JIM: Shakespeare probably wrote a poem on that light bill, Mrs. Wingfield.

AMANDA: I might have known better than to trust him with it! There's such a high price for negligence in this world!

JIM: Maybe the poem will win a ten-dollar prize.

AMANDA: We'll just have to spend the remainder of the evening in the nineteenth century, before Mr. Edison made the Mazda lamp!

JIM: Candlelight is my favorite kind of light.

AMANDA: That shows you're romantic! But that's no excuse for Tom. Well, we got through dinner. Very considerate of them to let us get through dinner before they plunged us into everlasting darkness, wasn't it, Mr. O'Connor?

JIM: Ha-ha!

AMANDA: Tom, as a penalty for your carelessness you can help me with the dishes.

JIM: Let me give you a hand.

AMANDA: Indeed you will not!

JIM: I ought to be good for something.

AMANDA: Good for something? *(Her tone is rhapsodic.)* You? Why, Mr. O'Connor, nobody, *nobody's* given me this much entertainment in years — as you have!

JIM: Aw, now, Mrs. Wingfield!

AMANDA: I'm not exaggerating, not one bit! But Sister is all by her lonesome. You go keep her company in the parlor! I'll give you this lovely old candelabrum that used to be on the altar at the church of the Heavenly Rest. It was melted a little out of shape when the church burnt down. Lightning struck it one spring. Gypsy Jones was holding a revival at the time and he intimated that the church was destroyed because the Episcopalians gave card parties.

JIM: Ha-ha.

AMANDA: And how about coaxing Sister to drink a little wine? I think it would be good for her! Can you carry both at once?

JIM: Sure. I'm Superman!

AMANDA: Now, Thomas, get into this apron!

The door of kitchenette swings closed on Amanda's gay laughter; the flickering light approaches the portieres.

Laura sits up nervously as he enters. Her speech at first is low and breathless from the almost intolerable strain of being alone with a stranger.

(Legend: "I Don't Suppose You Remember Me at All!")

In her first speeches in this scene, before Jim's warmth overcomes her paralyzing shyness, Laura's voice is thin and breathless as though she has run up a steep flight of stairs.

Jim's attitude is gently humorous. In playing this scene it should be stressed that while the incident is apparently unimportant, it is to Laura the climax of her secret life.

JIM: Hello, there, Laura.

LAURA *(faintly)*:   Hello. *(She clears her throat.)*

JIM: How are you feeling now? Better?

LAURA: Yes. Yes, thank you.

JIM: This is for you. A little dandelion wine. *(He extends it toward her with extravagant gallantry.)*

LAURA: Thank you.

JIM: Drink it — but don't get drunk! *(He laughs heartily. Laura takes the glass uncertainly; laughs shyly.)* Where shall I set the candles?

LAURA: Oh — oh, anywhere . . .

JIM: How about here on the floor? Any objections?

LAURA: No.

JIM: I'll spread a newspaper under to catch the drippings. I like to sit on the floor. Mind if I do?

LAURA: Oh, no.

JIM: Give me a pillow?

LAURA: What?

JIM: A pillow!

LAURA: Oh . . . *(Hands him one quickly.)*

JIM: How about you? Don't you like to sit on the floor?

LAURA: Oh — yes.

JIM: Why don't you, then?

LAURA: I—will.

JIM: Take a pillow! *(Laura does. Sits on the other side of the candelabrum. Jim crosses his legs and smiles engagingly at her.)* I can't hardly see you sitting way over there.

LAURA: I can—see you.

JIM: I know, but that's not fair, I'm in the limelight. *(Laura moves her pillow closer.)* Good! Now I can see you! Comfortable?

LAURA: Yes.

JIM: So am I. Comfortable as a cow. Will you have some gum?

LAURA: No, thank you.

JIM: I think that I will indulge, with your permission. *(Musingly unwraps it and holds it up.)* Think of the fortune made by the guy that invented the first piece of chewing gum. Amazing, huh? The Wrigley Building is one of the sights of Chicago.—I saw it summer before last when I went up to the Century of Progress. Did you take in the Century of Progress?

LAURA: No, I didn't.

JIM: Well, it was quite a wonderful exposition. What impressed me most was the Hall of Science. Gives you an idea of what the future will be in America, even more wonderful than the present time is! *(Pause. Smiling at her.)* Your brother tells me you're shy. Is that right, Laura?

LAURA: I—don't know.

JIM: I judge you to be an old-fashioned type of girl. Well, I think that's a pretty good type to be. Hope you don't think I'm being too personal—do you?

LAURA *(hastily, out of embarrassment)*:   I believe I *will* take a piece of gum, if you—don't mind. *(Clearing her throat.)* Mr. O'Connor, have you—kept up with your singing?

JIM: Singing? Me?

LAURA: Yes. I remember what a beautiful voice you had.

JIM: When did you hear me sing?

(Voice offstage in the pause.)

VOICE *(offstage)*:   O blow, ye winds, heigh-ho,
 A-roving I will go!
 I'm off to my love
 With a boxing glove—
 Ten thousand miles away!

JIM: You say you've heard me sing?

LAURA: Oh, yes! Yes, very often . . . I—don't suppose you remember me—at all?

JIM *(smiling doubtfully)*:   You know I have an idea I've seen you before. I had that idea soon as you opened the door. It seemed almost like I was about to remember your name. But the name that I started to call you—wasn't a name! And so I stopped myself before I said it.

LAURA: Wasn't it—Blue Roses?

JIM *(springs up, grinning)*:   Blue Roses! My gosh, yes — Blue Roses! That's what I had on my tongue when you opened the door! Isn't it funny what tricks your memory plays? I didn't connect you with the high school somehow or other. But that's where it was; it was high school. I didn't even know you were Shakespeare's sister! Gosh, I'm sorry.

LAURA: I didn't expect you to. You — barely knew me!

JIM: But we did have a speaking acquaintance, huh?

LAURA: Yes, we — spoke to each other.

JIM: When did you recognize me?

LAURA: Oh, right away!

JIM: Soon as I came in the door?

LAURA: When I heard your name I thought it was probably you. I knew that Tom used to know you a little in high school. So when you came in the door — Well, then I was — sure.

JIM: Why didn't you *say* something, then?

LAURA *(breathlessly)*:   I didn't know what to say, I was — too surprised!

JIM: For goodness' sakes! You know, this sure is funny!

LAURA: Yes! Yes, isn't it, though . . .

JIM: Didn't we have a class in something together?

LAURA: Yes, we did.

JIM: What class was that?

LAURA: It was — singing — Chorus!

JIM: Aw!

LAURA: I sat across the aisle from you in the Aud.

JIM: Aw.

LAURA: Mondays, Wednesdays, and Fridays.

JIM: Now I remember — you always came in late.

LAURA: Yes, it was so hard for me, getting upstairs. I had that brace on my leg — it clumped so loud!

JIM: I never heard any clumping.

LAURA *(wincing in the recollection)*:   To me it sounded like — thunder!

JIM: Well, well, well. I never even noticed.

LAURA: And everybody was seated before I came in. I had to walk in front of all those people. My seat was in the back row. I had to go clumping all the way up the aisle with everyone watching!

JIM: You shouldn't have been self-conscious.

LAURA: I know, but I was. It was always such a relief when the singing started.

JIM: Aw, yes, I've placed you now! I used to call you Blue Roses. How was it that I got started calling you that?

LAURA: I was out of school a little while with pleurosis. When I came back you asked me what was the matter. I said I had pleurosis — you thought I said Blue Roses. That's what you always called me after that!

JIM: I hope you didn't mind.

LAURA: Oh, no — I liked it. You see, I wasn't acquainted with many — people. . . .

JIM: As I remember you sort of stuck by yourself.

LAURA: I — I — never had much luck at — making friends.

JIM: I don't see why you wouldn't.

LAURA: Well, I — started out badly.

JIM: You mean being —

LAURA: Yes, it sort of — stood between me —

JIM: You shouldn't have let it!

LAURA: I know, but it did, and —

JIM: You were shy with people!

LAURA: I tried not to be but never could —

JIM: Overcome it?

LAURA: No, I — I never could!

JIM: I guess being shy is something you have to work out of kind of gradually.

LAURA *(sorrowfully)*:   Yes — I guess it —

JIM: Takes time!

LAURA: Yes —

JIM: People are not so dreadful when you know them. That's what you have to remember! And everybody has problems, not just you, but practically everybody has got some problems. You think of yourself as having the only problems, as being the only one who is disappointed. But just look around you and you will see lots of people as disappointed as you are. For instance, I hoped when I was going to high school that I would be further along at this time, six years later, than I am now — You remember that wonderful write-up I had in *The Torch?*

LAURA: Yes! *(She rises and crosses to table.)*

JIM: It said I was bound to succeed in anything I went into! *(Laura returns with the annual.)* Holy Jeez! *The Torch!* (He accepts it reverently. They smile across it with mutual wonder. Laura crouches beside him and they begin to turn through it. Laura's shyness is dissolving in his warmth.)*

LAURA: Here you are in *Pirates of Penzance!*

JIM *(wistfully)*:   I sang the baritone lead in that operetta.

LAURA *(rapidly)*:   So — *beautifully!*

JIM *(protesting)*:   Aw —

LAURA: Yes, yes — beautifully — beautifully!

JIM: You heard me?

LAURA: All three times!

JIM: No!

LAURA: Yes!

JIM: All three performances?

LAURA *(looking down)*:   Yes.

JIM: Why?

LAURA: I — wanted to ask you to — autograph my program.

JIM: Why didn't you ask me to?

LAURA: You were always surrounded by your own friends so much that I never had a chance to.

JIM: You should have just —

LAURA: Well, I — thought you might think I was —

JIM: Thought I might think you was — what?

LAURA: Oh —

JIM *(with reflective relish)*:   I was beleaguered by females in those days.

LAURA: You were terribly popular!

JIM: Yeah —

LAURA: You had such a — friendly way —

JIM: I was spoiled in high school.

LAURA: Everybody — liked you!

JIM: Including you?

LAURA: I — yes, I — I did, too — *(She gently closes the book in her lap.)*

JIM: Well, well, well! — Give me that program, Laura. *(She hands it to him. He signs it with a flourish.)* There you are — better late than never!

LAURA: Oh, I — what a — surprise!

JIM: My signature isn't worth very much right now. But someday — maybe — it will increase in value! Being disappointed is one thing and being discouraged is something else. I am disappointed but I'm not discouraged. I'm twenty-three years old. How old are you?

LAURA: I'll be twenty-four in June.

JIM: That's not old age.

LAURA: No, but —

JIM: You finished high school?

LAURA *(with difficulty)*:   I didn't go back.

JIM: You mean you dropped out?

LAURA: I made bad grades in my final examinations. *(She rises and replaces the book and the program. Her voice strained.)* How is — Emily Meisenbach getting along?

JIM: Oh, that kraut-head!

LAURA: Why do you call her that?

JIM: That's what she was.

LAURA: You're not still — going with her?

JIM: I never see her.

LAURA: It said in the Personal Section that you were — engaged!

JIM: I know, but I wasn't impressed by that — propaganda!

LAURA: It wasn't — the truth?

JIM: Only in Emily's optimistic opinion!

LAURA: Oh —

(Legend: "What Have You Done Since High School?")

Jim lights a cigarette and leans indolently back on his elbows smiling at Laura with a warmth and charm which light her inwardly with altar candles. She remains by the table and turns in her hands a piece of glass to cover her tumult.

JIM *(after several reflective puffs on a cigarette)*:   What have you done since high school? *(She seems not to hear him.)* Huh? *(Laura looks up.)* I said what have you done since high school, Laura?

LAURA: Nothing much.

JIM: You must have been doing something these six long years.

LAURA: Yes.

JIM: Well, then, such as what?

LAURA: I took a business course at business college —

JIM: How did that work out?

LAURA: Well, not very — well — I had to drop out, it gave me — indigestion —

Jim laughs gently.

JIM: What are you doing now?

LAURA: I don't do anything — much. Oh, please don't think I sit around doing nothing! My glass collection takes up a good deal of my time. Glass is something you have to take good care of.

JIM: What did you say — about glass?

LAURA: Collection I said — I have one — *(She clears her throat and turns away again, acutely shy.)*

JIM *(abruptly)*:   You know what I judge to be the trouble with you? Inferiority complex! Know what that is? That's what they call it when someone low-rates himself! I understand it because I had it, too. Although my case was not so aggravated as yours seems to be. I had it until I took up public speaking, developed my voice, and learned that I had an aptitude for science. Before that time I never thought of myself as being outstanding in any way whatsoever! Now I've never made a regular study of it, but I have a friend who says I can analyze people better than doctors that make a profession of it. I don't claim that to be necessarily true, but I can sure guess a person's psychology, Laura! *(Takes out his gum.)* Excuse me, Laura. I always take it out when the flavor is gone. I'll use this scrap of paper to wrap it in. I know how it is to get it stuck on a shoe. Yep — that's what I judge to be your principal trouble. A lack of confidence in yourself as a person. You don't have the proper amount of faith in yourself. I'm basing that fact on a number of your remarks and also on certain observations I've made. For instance that clumping you thought was so awful in high school. You say that you even dreaded to walk into class. You see what you did? You dropped out of school, you gave up an education because of a clump, which as far as I know was practically nonexistent! A little physical defect is what you have. Hardly noticeable even! Magnified thousands of times by imagination! You know what my strong advice to you is? Think of yourself as *superior* in some way!

LAURA: In what way would I think?

JIM: Why, man alive, Laura! Just look about you a little. What do you see? A world full of common people! All of 'em born and all of 'em going to die! Which of them has one-tenth of your good points! Or mine! Or anyone else's, as far as that goes — Gosh! Everybody excels in some one thing. Some in many! *(Unconsciously glances at himself in the mirror.)* All you've got to do is discover in *what*! Take me, for instance. *(He adjusts his tie at the mirror.)* My interest happened to lie in electrodynamics. I'm taking a course in radio engineering at night school, Laura, on top of a fairly responsible job at the warehouse. I'm taking that course and studying public speaking.

LAURA: Ohhhh.

JIM: Because I believe in the future of television! *(Turning back to her.)* I wish to be ready to go up right along with it. Therefore I'm planning to get in on the ground floor. In fact, I've already made the right connections and all that remains is for the industry itself to get under way! Full steam — *(His eyes are starry.)* Knowledge — Zzzzzp! Money — Zzzzzzp! — Power! That's the cycle democracy is built on! *(His attitude is convincingly dynamic. Laura stares at him, even her shyness eclipsed in her absolute wonder. He suddenly grins.)* I guess you think I think a lot of myself!

LAURA: No — o-o-o, I —

JIM: Now how about you? Isn't there something you take more interest in than anything else?

LAURA: Well, I do — as I said — have my — glass collection —

A peal of girlish laughter from the kitchen.

JIM: I'm not right sure I know what you're talking about. What kind of glass is it?

LAURA: Little articles of it, they're ornaments mostly! Most of them are little animals made out of glass, the tiniest little animals in the world. Mother calls them a glass menagerie! Here's an example of one, if you'd like to see it! This one is one of the oldest. It's nearly thirteen. *(He stretches out his hand.)* *(Music: "The Glass Menagerie.")* Oh, be careful — if you breathe, it breaks!

JIM: I'd better not take it. I'm pretty clumsy with things.

LAURA: Go on, I trust you with him! *(Places it in his palm.)* There now — you're holding him gently! Hold him over the light, he loves the light! You see how the light shines through him?

JIM: It sure does shine!

LAURA: I shouldn't be partial, but he is my favorite one.

JIM: What kind of thing is this one supposed to be?

LAURA: Haven't you noticed the single horn on his forehead?

JIM: A unicorn, huh?

LAURA: Mmm-hmmm!

JIM: Unicorns, aren't they extinct in the modern world?

LAURA: I know!

JIM: Poor little fellow, he must feel sort of lonesome.

LAURA *(smiling)*:   Well, if he does he doesn't complain about it. He stays on a shelf with some horses that don't have horns and all of them seem to get along nicely together.

JIM: How do you know?

LAURA *(lightly)*:   I haven't heard any arguments among them!

JIM *(grinning)*:   No arguments, huh? Well, that's a pretty good sign! Where shall I set him?

LAURA: Put him on the table. They all like a change of scenery once in a while!

JIM *(stretching)*:   Well, well, well, well — Look how big my shadow is when I stretch!

LAURA: Oh, oh, yes — it stretches across the ceiling!

JIM *(crossing to door)*:   I think it's stopped raining. *(Opens fire-escape door.)* Where does the music come from?

LAURA: From the Paradise Dance Hall across the alley.

JIM: How about cutting the rug a little, Miss Wingfield?

LAURA: Oh, I —

JIM: Or is your program filled up? Let me have a look at it. *(Grasps imaginary card.)* Why, every dance is taken! I'll have to scratch some out. *(Waltz music: "La Golondrina.")* Ahhh, a waltz! *(He executes some sweeping turns by himself then holds his arms toward Laura.)*

LAURA *(breathlessly)*:   I — can't dance!

JIM: There you go, that inferiority stuff!

LAURA: I've never danced in my life!

JIM: Come on, try!

LAURA: Oh, but I'd step on you!

JIM: I'm not made out of glass.

LAURA: How — how — how do we start?

JIM: Just leave it to me. You hold your arms out a little.

LAURA: Like this?

JIM: A little bit higher. Right. Now don't tighten up, that's the main thing about it — relax.

LAURA *(laughing breathlessly)*:   It's hard not to.

JIM: Okay.

LAURA: I'm afraid you can't budge me.

JIM: What do you bet I can't? *(He swings her into motion.)*

LAURA: Goodness, yes, you can!

JIM: Let yourself go, now, Laura, just let yourself go.

LAURA: I'm —

JIM: Come on!

LAURA: Trying.

JIM: Not so stiff — Easy does it!

LAURA: I know but I'm —

JIM: Loosen th' backbone! There now, that's a lot better.

LAURA: Am I?

JIM: Lots, lots better! *(He moves her about the room in a clumsy waltz.)*

LAURA: Oh, my!

JIM: Ha-ha!

LAURA: Goodness, yes you can!

JIM: Ha-ha-ha! *(They suddenly bump into the table. Jim stops.)* What did we hit on?

LAURA: Table.

JIM: Did something fall off it? I think —

LAURA: Yes.

JIM: I hope it wasn't the little glass horse with the horn!

LAURA: Yes.

JIM: Aw, aw, aw. Is it broken?

LAURA: Now it is just like all the other horses.

JIM: It's lost its —

LAURA: Horn! It doesn't matter. Maybe it's a blessing in disguise.

JIM: You'll never forgive me. I bet that that was your favorite piece of glass.

LAURA: I don't have favorites much. It's no tragedy, Freckles. Glass breaks so easily. No matter how careful you are. The traffic jars the shelves and things fall off them.

JIM: Still I'm awfully sorry that I was the cause.

LAURA *(smiling)*:   I'll just imagine he had an operation. The horn was removed to make him feel less — freakish! *(They both laugh.)* Now he will feel more at home with the other horses, the ones that don't have horns . . .

JIM: Ha-ha, that's very funny! *(Suddenly serious.)* I'm glad to see that you have a sense of humor. You know — you're — well — very different! Surprisingly different from anyone else I know! *(His voice becomes soft and hesitant with a genuine feeling.)* Do you mind me telling you that? *(Laura is abashed beyond speech.)* You make me feel sort of — I don't know how to put it! I'm usually pretty good at expressing things, but — This is something that I don't know how to say! *(Laura touches her throat and clears it — turns the broken unicorn in her hands.)* *(Even softer.)* Has anyone ever told you that you were pretty?

Pause: Music.

(Laura looks up slowly, with wonder, and shakes her head.) Well, you are! In a very different way from anyone else. And all the nicer because of the difference, too. *(His voice becomes low and husky. Laura turns away, nearly faint with the novelty of her emotions.)* I wish that you were my sister. I'd teach you to have some confidence in yourself. The different people are not like other people, but being different is nothing to be ashamed of. Because other people are not such wonderful people. They're one hundred times one thousand. You're one times one! They walk all over the earth. You just stay here. They're common as — weeds, but — you — well, you're — Blue Roses!

(Image on screen: Blue Roses.)
(Music changes.)

LAURA: But blue is wrong for — roses . . .

JIM: It's right for you — You're — pretty!

LAURA: In what respect am I pretty?

JIM: In all respects — believe me! Your eyes — your hair — are pretty! Your hands are pretty! *(He catches hold of her hand.)* You think I'm making this up because I'm invited to dinner and have to be nice. Oh, I could do that! I could put on an act for you, Laura, and say lots of things without being very sincere. But this time I am. I'm talking to you sincerely. I happened to notice you had this inferiority complex that keeps you from feeling comfortable with people. Somebody needs to build your confidence up and make you proud instead of shy and turning away and — blushing — Somebody ought to — ought to — *kiss* you, Laura! *(His hand slips slowly up her arm to her shoulder.) (Music swells tumultuously.) (He suddenly turns her about and kisses her on the lips. When he releases her Laura sinks on the sofa with a bright, dazed look. Jim backs away and fishes in his pocket for a cigarette.) (Legend on screen: "Souvenir.")* Stumble-john! *(He lights the cigarette, avoiding her look. There is a peal of girlish laughter from Amanda in the kitchen. Laura slowly raises and opens her hand. It still contains the little broken glass animal. She looks at it with a tender, bewildered expression.)* Stumble-john! I shouldn't have done that — That was way off the beam. You don't smoke, do you? *(She looks up, smiling, not hearing the question. He sits beside her a little gingerly. She looks at him speechlessly — waiting. He coughs decorously and moves a little farther aside as he considers the situation and senses her feelings, dimly, with perturbation. Gently.)* Would you — care for a — mint? *(She doesn't seem to hear him but her look grows brighter even.)* Peppermint — Life Saver? My pocket's a regular drug store — wherever I go . . . *(He pops a mint in his mouth. Then gulps and decides to make a clean breast of it. He speaks slowly and gingerly.)* Laura, you know, if I had a sister like you, I'd do the same thing as Tom. I'd bring out fellows — introduce her to them. The right type of boys of a type to — appreciate her. Only — well — he made a mistake about me. Maybe I've got no call to be saying this. That may not have been the idea in having me over. But what if it was? There's nothing wrong about that. The only trouble is that in my case — I'm not in a situation to — do the right thing. I can't take down your number and say I'll phone. I can't call up next week and — ask for a date. I thought I had better explain the situation in case you misunderstood it and — hurt your feelings. . . . *(Pause. Slowly, very slowly, Laura's look changes, her eyes returning slowly from his to the ornament in her palm.)*

Amanda utters another gay laugh in the kitchen.

LAURA *(faintly):* You — won't — call again?

JIM: No, Laura, I can't. *(He rises from the sofa.)* As I was just explaining, I've — got strings on me, Laura, I've — been going steady! I go out all the time with a girl named Betty. She's a home-girl like you, and Catholic, and Irish, and in a great many ways we — get along fine. I met her last summer on a moonlight boat trip up the river to Alton, on the *Majestic.* Well — right away from the start it was — love! *(Legend: Love!) (Laura sways slightly forward and grips the arm of the sofa. He fails to notice, now enrapt in his own comfortable being.)* Being in love has made a new man of me! *(Leaning stiffly forward, clutching the arm of the sofa, Laura struggles visibly with her storm. But Jim is oblivious, she is a long way off.)* The power of love is really pretty tremendous! Love is something that — changes the whole world, Laura! *(The storm abates a little and Laura leans back. He notices her again.)* It happened that Betty's aunt took sick, she got a wire and had to go to Centralia. So Tom — when he asked me to dinner — I naturally just accepted the invitation, not knowing that you — that he — that I — (He stops awkwardly.)* Huh — I'm a stumble-john! *(He flops back on the sofa. The holy candles in the altar of Laura's face have been snuffed out! There is a look of almost infinite* *desolation. Jim glances at her uneasily.)* I wish that you would — say something. *(She bites her lip which was trembling and then bravely smiles. She opens her hand again on the broken glass ornament. Then she gently takes his hand and raises it level with her own. She carefully places the unicorn in the palm of his hand, then pushes his fingers closed upon it.)* What are you — doing that for? You want me to have him? — Laura? *(She nods.)* What for?

LAURA: A — souvenir . . .

She rises unsteadily and crouches beside the Victrola to wind it up.

(Legend on screen: "Things Have a Way of Turning Out So Badly.")

(Or image: "Gentleman caller waving good-bye! — Gaily.")

At this moment Amanda rushes brightly back in the front room. She bears a pitcher of fruit punch in an old-fashioned cut-glass pitcher and a plate of macaroons. The plate has a gold border and poppies painted on it.

AMANDA: Well, well, well! Isn't the air delightful after the shower? I've made you children a little liquid refreshment. *(Turns gaily to the gentleman caller.)* Jim, do you know that song about lemonade?
"Lemonade, lemonade
Made in the shade and stirred with a spade —
Good enough for any old maid!"

JIM *(uneasily)*:   Ha-ha! No — I never heard it.

AMANDA: Why, Laura! You look so serious!

JIM: We were having a serious conversation.

AMANDA: Good! Now you're better acquainted!

JIM *(uncertainly)*:   Ha-ha! Yes.

AMANDA: You modern young people are much more serious-minded than my generation. I was so gay as a girl!

JIM: You haven't changed, Mrs. Wingfield.

AMANDA: Tonight I'm rejuvenated! The gaiety of the occasion, Mr. O'Connor! *(She tosses her head with a peal of laughter. Spills lemonade.)* Oooo! I'm baptizing myself!

JIM: Here — let me —

AMANDA *(setting the pitcher down)*:   There now. I discovered we had some maraschino cherries. I dumped them in, juice and all!

JIM: You shouldn't have gone to that trouble, Mrs. Wingfield.

AMANDA: Trouble, trouble? Why it was loads of fun! Didn't you hear me cutting up in the kitchen? I bet your ears were burning! I told Tom how outdone with him I was for keeping you to himself so long a time! He should have brought you over much, much sooner! Well, now that you've found your way, I want you to be a very frequent caller! Not just occasional but all the time. Oh, we're going to have a lot of gay times together! I see them coming! Mmm, just breathe that air! So fresh, and the moon's so pretty! I'll skip back out — I know where my place is when young folks are having a — serious conversation!

JIM: Oh, don't go out, Mrs. Wingfield. The fact of the matter is I've got to be going.

AMANDA: Going, now? You're joking! Why, it's only the shank of the evening, Mr. O'Connor!

JIM: Well, you know how it is.

AMANDA: You mean you're a young workingman and have to keep working-men's hours. We'll let you off early tonight. But only on the condition that next time you stay later. What's the best night for you? Isn't Saturday night the best night for you workingmen?

JIM: I have a couple of time-clocks to punch, Mrs. Wingfield. One at morning, another one at night!

AMANDA: My, but you *are* ambitious! You work at night, too?

JIM: No, Ma'am, not work but — Betty! *(He crosses deliberately to pick up his hat. The band at the Paradise Dance Hall goes into a tender waltz.)*

AMANDA: Betty? Betty? Who's — Betty! *(There is an ominous cracking sound in the sky.)*

JIM: Oh, just a girl. The girl I go steady with! *(He smiles charmingly. The sky falls.)*

(Legend: "The Sky Falls.")

AMANDA *(a long-drawn exhalation)*:   Ohhhh . . . Is it a serious romance, Mr. O'Connor?

JIM: We're going to be married the second Sunday in June.

AMANDA: Ohhhh — how nice! Tom didn't mention that you were engaged to be married.

JIM: The cat's not out of the bag at the warehouse yet. You know how they are. They call you Romeo and stuff like that. *(He stops at the oval mirror to put on his hat. He carefully shapes the brim and the crown to give a discreetly dashing effect.)* It's been a wonderful evening, Mrs. Wingfield. I guess this is what they mean by Southern hospitality.

AMANDA: It really wasn't anything at all.

JIM: I hope it don't seem like I'm rushing off. But I promised Betty I'd pick her up at the Wabash depot, an' by the time I get my jalopy down there her train'll be in. Some women are pretty upset if you keep 'em waiting.

AMANDA: Yes, I know — The tyranny of women! *(Extends her hand.)* Good-bye, Mr. O'Connor. I wish you luck — and happiness — and success! All three of them, and so does Laura — Don't you, Laura?

LAURA: Yes!

JIM *(taking her hand)*:   Good-bye, Laura. I'm certainly going to treasure that souvenir. And don't you forget the good advice I gave you. *(Raises his voice to a cheery shout.)* So long, Shakespeare! Thanks again, ladies — Good night!

He grins and ducks jauntily out.

Still bravely grimacing, Amanda closes the door on the gentleman caller. Then she turns back to the room with a puzzled expression. She and Laura don't dare to face each other. Laura crouches beside the Victrola to wind it.

AMANDA *(faintly)*:   Things have a way of turning out so badly. I don't believe that I would play the Victrola. Well, well — well — Our gentleman caller was engaged to be married! Tom!

TOM *(from back)*:   Yes, Mother?

AMANDA: Come in here a minute. I want to tell you something awfully funny.

TOM *(enters with macaroon and a glass of the lemonade)*:   Has the gentleman caller gotten away already?

AMANDA: The gentleman caller has made an early departure. What a wonderful joke you played on us!

TOM: How do you mean?

AMANDA: You didn't mention that he was engaged to be married.

TOM: Jim? Engaged?

AMANDA: That's what he just informed us.

TOM: I'll be jiggered! I didn't know about that.

AMANDA: That seems very peculiar.

TOM: What's peculiar about it?

AMANDA: Didn't you call him your best friend down at the warehouse?

TOM: He is, but how did I know?

AMANDA: It seems extremely peculiar that you wouldn't know your best friend was going to be married!

TOM: The warehouse is where I work, not where I know things about people!

AMANDA: You don't know things anywhere! You live in a dream; you manufacture illusions! *(He crosses to door.)* Where are you going?

TOM: I'm going to the movies.

AMANDA: That's right, now that you've had us make such fools of ourselves. The effort, the preparations, all the expense! The new floor lamp, the rug, the clothes for Laura! All for what? To entertain some other girl's fiancé! Go to the movies, go! Don't think about us, a mother deserted, an unmarried sister who's crippled and has no job! Don't let anything interfere with your selfish pleasure! Just go, go, go — to the movies!

TOM: All right, I will! The more you shout about my selfishness to me the quicker I'll go, and I won't go to the movies!

AMANDA: Go, then! Then go to the moon — you selfish dreamer!

Tom smashes his glass on the floor. He plunges out on the fire-escape, slamming the door. Laura screams — cut by door.

Dance-hall music up. Tom goes to the rail and grips it desperately, lifting his face in the chill white moonlight penetrating the narrow abyss of the alley.

(Legend on screen: "And So Good-Bye . . .")

Tom's closing speech is timed with the interior pantomime. The interior scene is played as though viewed through sound-proof glass. Amanda appears to be making a comforting speech to Laura who is huddled upon the sofa. Now that we cannot hear the mother's speech, her silliness is gone and she has dignity and tragic beauty. Laura's dark hair hides her face until at the end of the speech she lifts it to smile at her mother. Amanda's gestures are slow and graceful, almost dancelike, as she comforts the daughter. At the end of her speech she glances a moment at the father's picture — then withdraws through the portieres. At close of Tom's speech, Laura blows out the candles, ending the play.

TOM: I didn't go to the moon, I went much further — for time is the longest distance between two places — Not long after that I was fired for writing a poem on the lid of a shoe-box. I left Saint Louis. I descended the steps of this fire-escape for a last time and followed, from then on, in my father's footsteps, attempting to find in motion what was lost in space — I traveled around a great deal. The cities swept about me like dead leaves, leaves that were brightly colored but torn away from the branches. I would have stopped, but I was pursued by something. It always came upon me unawares, taking me altogether by surprise. Perhaps it was a familiar bit of music. Perhaps it was only a piece of transparent glass — Perhaps I am walking along a street at night, in some strange city, before I have found companions. I pass the lighted window of a shop where perfume is sold. The window is filled with pieces of colored glass, tiny transparent bottles in delicate colors, like bits of a shattered rainbow. Then all at once my sister touches my shoulder. I turn around and look into her eyes. . . . Oh, Laura, Laura, I tried to leave you behind me, but I am more faithful than I intended to be! I reach for a cigarette, I cross the street, I run into the movies or a bar, I buy a drink, I speak to the nearest stranger — anything that can blow your candles out! *(Laura bends over the candles.)* — for nowadays the world is lit by lightning! Blow out your candles, Laura — and so good-bye . . .

She blows the candles out.

(The Scene Dissolves.)   [1945]

▅ THINKING ABOUT THE TEXT

1. Is Amanda just overprotective, or does her devotion to Laura's eventual marriage suggest a more serious issue? If you were a close friend of Amanda, how would you advise her to behave toward Laura?

2. Why does Laura keep the glass menagerie? Why does she give Jim her broken unicorn? Is this a positive sign?

3. This is a play about love, guilt, pity, regret, cruelty, and self-loathing. Can you cite concrete examples of these emotions in this play? Did you notice any other emotions? Is this a realistic portrait of family life, or is it an exaggeration?

4. Critics are divided over Williams's motivation in this play. Is he trying to get rid of Laura's memory (based on his sister Rose, who went mad and whom he deserted), or is he replaying the traumatic leaving? Which makes the most sense to you? How do you read the last line, "Blow out your candles, Laura — and so good-bye . . ."?

5. Do you blame Tom for leaving? Does he abandon his responsibilities? What do you think of Tom's priorities? Does he have a duty to take the place of his absent father? What would have happened if Tom had stayed? What would you do?

CHRISTOPHER DURANG
For Whom the Southern Belle Tolls

Born in Montclair, New Jersey, in 1949, Christopher Durang graduated from Harvard University and the Yale School of Drama. He has won numerous awards, fellowships, and grants, including Obie awards for Sister Mary Ignatius Explains It All for You *(1980) and* The Marriage of Betty and Boo *(1985). The former, one of his most popular plays, focuses on a nun who is proud of the righteousness of her students. But this turns to dark comedy when her former charges appear and reveal that they despise her and her dogmatic ways. The play is insightful, violent, and hilarious. His most recent work,* Why Torture Is Wrong, and the People Who Love Them, *was published in 2009. Durang has taught playwriting at Yale and is currently co-chair of the playwriting program at the Juilliard School in New York City.*

CHARACTERS

AMANDA, *the mother*
LAWRENCE, *the son*
TOM, *the other son*
GINNY

Lights up on a fussy living room setting. Enter Amanda, the Southern belle mother.

AMANDA: Rise and shine! Rise and shine! *(Calls off.)* Lawrence, honey, come on out here and let me have a look at you!

Enter Lawrence, who limps across the room. He is very sensitive, and is wearing what are clearly his dress clothes. Amanda fiddles with his bow tie and stands back to admire him.

AMANDA: Lawrence, honey, you look lovely.

LAWRENCE: No, I don't mama. I have a pimple on the back of my neck.

AMANDA: Don't say the word "pimple," honey, it's common. Now your brother Tom is bringing home a girl from the warehouse for you to meet, and I want you to make a good impression, honey.

LAWRENCE: It upsets my stomach to meet people, mama.

AMANDA: Oh, Lawrence honey, you're so sensitive it makes me want to hit you.

LAWRENCE: I don't need to meet people, mama. I'm happy just by myself, playing with my collection of glass cocktail stirrers.

Lawrence limps over to a table on top of which sits a glass jar filled with glass swizzle sticks.

AMANDA: Lawrence, you are a caution. Only retarded people and alcoholics are interested in glass cocktail stirrers.

LAWRENCE *(picking up some of them)*:   Each one of them has a special name, mama. This one is called Stringbean because it's long and thin; and this one is called Stringbean because it's long and thin; and this one is called Blue because it's blue.

(© Chris Barth/Star
Ledger/Corbis.)

AMANDA: All my children have such imagination, why was I so blessed? Oh,
Lawrence, honey, how are you going to get on in the world if you just stay
home all day, year after year, playing with your collection of glass cocktail
stirrers?

LAWRENCE: I don't like the world, mama, I like it here in this room.

AMANDA: I know you do, Lawrence honey, that's part of your charm. Some
days. But, honey, what about making a living?

LAWRENCE: I can't work, mama. I'm crippled. *(He limps over to the couch and
sits.)*

AMANDA: There is nothing wrong with your leg, Lawrence honey, all the doctors have told you that. This limping thing is an affectation.

LAWRENCE: I only know how I feel, mama.

AMANDA: Oh, if only I had connections in the Mafia, I'd have someone come
and break both your legs.

LAWRENCE: Don't try to make me laugh, mama. You know I have asthma.

AMANDA: Your asthma, your leg, your eczema. You're just a mess, Lawrence.

LAWRENCE: I have scabs from the itching, mama.

AMANDA: That's lovely, Lawrence. You must tell us more over dinner.

LAWRENCE: Alright.

AMANDA: That was a joke, Lawrence.

LAWRENCE: Don't try to make me laugh, mama. My asthma.

AMANDA: Now, Lawrence, I don't want you talking about your ailments to the feminine caller your brother Tom is bringing home from the warehouse, honey. No nice-bred young lady likes to hear a young man discussing his eczema, Lawrence.

LAWRENCE: What else can I talk about, mama?

AMANDA: Talk about the weather. Or Red China.

LAWRENCE: Or my collection of glass cocktail stirrers?

AMANDA: I suppose so, honey, if the conversation comes to some godawful standstill. Otherwise, I'd shut up about it. Conversation is an art, Lawrence. Back at Blue Mountain, when I had seventeen gentlemen callers, I was able to converse with charm and vivacity for six hours without stop and never once mention eczema or bone cancer or vivisection. Try to emulate me, Lawrence, honey. Charm and vivacity. And charm. And vivacity. And charm.

LAWRENCE: Well, I'll try, but I doubt it.

AMANDA: Me too, honey. But we'll go through the motions anyway, won't we?

LAWRENCE: I don't know if I want to meet some girl who works in a warehouse, mama.

AMANDA: Your brother Tom says she's a lovely girl with a nice personality. And where else does he meet girls except the few who work at the warehouse? He only seems to meet men at the movies. Your brother goes to the movies entirely too much. I must speak to him about it.

LAWRENCE: It's unfeminine for a girl to work at a warehouse.

AMANDA: Lawrence, honey, if you can't go out the door without getting an upset stomach or an attack of vertigo, then we got to find some nice girl who's willing to support you. Otherwise, how am I ever going to get you out of this house and off my hands?

LAWRENCE: Why do you want to be rid of me, mama?

AMANDA: I suppose it's unmotherly of me, dear, but you really get on my nerves. Limping around the apartment, pretending to have asthma. If only some nice girl would marry you and I knew you were taken care of, then I'd feel free to start to live again. I'd join Parents Without Partners, I'd go to dinner dances, I'd have a life again. Rather than just watch you mope about this stupid apartment. I'm not bitter, dear, it's just that I hate my life.

LAWRENCE: I understand, mama.

AMANDA: Do you, dear? Oh, you're cute. Oh listen, I think I hear them.

TOM *(from offstage)*:   Mother, I forgot my key.

LAWRENCE: I'll be in the other room. *(Starts to limp away.)*

AMANDA: I want you to let them in, Lawrence.

LAWRENCE: Oh, I couldn't mama. She'd see I limp.

AMANDA: Then don't limp, damn it.

TOM *(from off)*:   Mother, are you there?

AMANDA: Just a minute, Tom, honey. Now, Lawrence, you march over to that door or I'm going to break all your swizzle sticks.

LAWRENCE: Mama, I can't.

AMANDA: Lawrence, you're a grown boy. Now you answer that door like any normal person.

LAWRENCE: I can't.

TOM: Mother, I'm going to break the door down in a minute.

AMANDA: Just be patient, Tom. Now you're causing a scene, Lawrence. I want you to answer that door.

LAWRENCE: My eczema itches.

AMANDA: I'll itch it for you in a second, Lawrence.

TOM: Alright, I'm breaking it down.

Sound of door breaking down. Enter Tom and Ginny Bennett, a vivacious girl dressed in factory clothes.

AMANDA: Oh, Tom, you got in.

TOM: Why must we go through this every night? You know the stupid fuck won't open the door, so why don't you let him alone about it? *(To Ginny.)* My kid brother has a thing about answering doors. He thinks people will notice his limp and his asthma and his eczema.

LAWRENCE: Excuse me. I think I hear someone calling me in the other room. *(Limps off, calls to imaginary person.)* Coming!

AMANDA: Now see what you've done. He's probably going to refuse to come to the table due to your insensitivity. Oh, was any woman as cursed as I? With one son who's too sensitive and another one who's this big ox. I'm sorry, how rude of me. I'm Amanda Wingvalley. You must be Virginia Bennett from the warehouse. Tom has spoken so much about you I feel you're almost one of the family, preferably a daughter-in-law. Welcome, Virginia.

GINNY *(speaking very loudly)*:   Call me Ginny or Gin. But just don't call me late for dinner! *(Roars with laughter.)*

AMANDA: Oh, how amusing. *(Whispers to Tom.)* Why is she shouting? Is she deaf?

GINNY: You're asking why I am speaking loudly. It's so that I can be heard! I am taking a course in public speaking, and so far we've covered organizing your thoughts and speaking good and loud so the people in the back of the room can hear you.

AMANDA: Public speaking. How impressive. You must be interested in improving yourself.

GINNY *(truly not having heard)*:   What?

AMANDA *(loudly)*:   YOU MUST BE INTERESTED IN IMPROVING YOURSELF.

GINNY *(loudly and happily)*:   YES I AM!

TOM: When's dinner? I want to get this over with fast if everyone's going to shout all evening.

GINNY: What?

AMANDA *(to Ginny)*:   Dinner is almost ready, Ginny.

GINNY: Who's Freddy?

AMANDA: Oh, Lord. No, dear. DINNER IS READY.

GINNY: Oh good. I'm as hungry as a bear! *(Growls enthusiastically.)*

AMANDA: You must be very popular at the warehouse, Ginny.

GINNY: No popsicle for me, ma'am, although I will take you up on some gin.

AMANDA *(confused)*:   What?

GINNY *(loudly)*:   I WOULD LIKE SOME GIN.

AMANDA: Well, fine. I think I'd like to get drunk too. Tom, why don't you go and make two Southern ladies some nice summer gin and tonics? And see if your sister would like a lemonade.

TOM: Sister?

AMANDA: I'm sorry, did I say sister? I meant brother.

TOM *(calling as he exits)*:   Hey, four eyes, you wanna lemonade?

AMANDA: Tom's so amusing. He calls Lawrence four eyes even though he doesn't wear glasses.

GINNY: And does Lawrence wear glasses?

AMANDA *(confused)*:   What?

GINNY: You said Tom called Lawrence four eyes even though he doesn't wear glasses, and I wondered if Lawrence wore glasses. Because that would, you see, explain it.

AMANDA *(looks at her with despair)*:   Ah. I don't know. I'll have to ask Lawrence someday. Speaking of Lawrence, let me go check on the supper and see if I can convince him to come out here and make conversation with you.

GINNY: No, thank you, ma'am, I'll just have the gin.

AMANDA: What?

GINNY: What?

AMANDA: Never mind. I'll be back. Or with luck I won't.

Amanda exits. Ginny looks around uncomfortably, and crosses to the table with the collection of glass cocktail stirrers.

GINNY: They must drink a lot here.

Enter Tom with a glass of gin for Ginny.

TOM: Here's some gin for Ginny.

GINNY: What?

TOM: Here's your poison.

GINNY: No, thanks, I'll just wait here.

TOM: Have you ever thought all that loud machinery at the warehouse may be affecting your hearing?

GINNY: Scenery? You mean, like trees? Yeah, I like trees.

TOM: I like trees, too.

AMANDA *(from offstage)*:   Now you get out of that bed this minute, Lawrence Wingvalley, or I'm going to give that overbearing girl your entire collection of glass gobbledygook — is that clear?

Amanda pushes in Lawrence, who is wearing a nightshirt.

AMANDA: I believe Lawrence would like to visit with you, Ginny.

GINNY *(shows her drink)*:   Tom brought me my drink already, thank you, Mrs. Wingvalley.

AMANDA: You know a hearing aid isn't really all that expensive, dear, you might look into that.

GINNY: No, if I have the gin, I don't really want any Gatorade. Never liked the stuff anyway. But you feel free.

AMANDA: Thank you, dear. I will. Come, Tom, come to the kitchen and help me prepare the dinner. And we'll let the two young people converse. Remember, Lawrence. Charm and vivacity.

TOM: I hope this dinner won't take long, mother. I don't want to get to the movies too late.

AMANDA: Oh shut up about the movies.

Amanda and Tom exit. Lawrence stands still, uncomfortable. Ginny looks at him pleasantly. Silence for a while.

GINNY: Hi.

LAWRENCE: Hi. *(Pause.)* I'd gone to bed.

GINNY: I never eat bread. It's too fattening. I have to watch my figure if I want to get ahead in the world. Why are you wearing that nightshirt?

LAWRENCE: I'd gone to bed. I wasn't feeling well. My leg hurts and I have a headache, and I have palpitations of the heart.

GINNY: I don't know. Hum a few bars, and I'll see.

LAWRENCE: We've met before, you know.

GINNY: I've never seen snow. Is it exciting?

LAWRENCE: We were in high school together. You were voted Girl Most Likely To Succeed. We sat next to one another in glee club.

GINNY: I'm sorry, I really can't hear you. You're talking too softly.

LAWRENCE *(louder)*:   You used to call me BLUE ROSES.

GINNY: Blue Roses? Oh yes, I remember, sort of. Why did I do that?

LAWRENCE: I had been absent from school for several months, and when I came back, you asked me where I'd been, and I said I'd been sick with viral pneumonia, but you thought I said "blue roses."

GINNY: I didn't get much of that, but I remember you now. You used to make a spectacle of yourself every day in glee class, clumping up the aisle with this great big noisy leg brace on your leg. God, you made a racket.

LAWRENCE: I was always so afraid people were looking at me, and pointing. But then eventually mama wouldn't let me wear the leg brace anymore. She gave it to the Salvation Army.

GINNY: I've never been in the army. How long were you in for?

LAWRENCE: I've never been in the army. I have asthma.

GINNY: You do? May I see it?

LAWRENCE *(confused)*:   See it?

GINNY: Well, sure, unless you don't want to.

LAWRENCE: Maybe you want to see my collection of glass cocktail stirrers. *(He limps to the table, and limps back to her, holding his collection.)*

LAWRENCE *(holds up a stick)*:   I call this one Stringbean, because it's long and thin.

GINNY: Thank you. *(Puts it in her glass and stirs it.)*

LAWRENCE *(fairly appalled)*:   They're not for use. *(Takes it back from her.)* They're a collection.

GINNY: Well, I guess I stirred it enough.

LAWRENCE: They're my favorite thing in the world. *(Holds up another one.)* I call this one Q-tip, because I realized it looks like a Q-tip, except it's made out of glass and doesn't have little cotton swabs at the end of it. *(She looks blank.)* Q-TIPS.

GINNY: Really? *(She takes it and puts it in her ear.)*

LAWRENCE: No! Don't put it in your ear. *(Takes it back.)* Now it's disgusting.

GINNY: Well, I didn't think it was a Q-tip, but that's what you said it was.

LAWRENCE: I call it that. I think I'm going to throw it out now. *(Holds up another one.)* I call this one Pinocchio because if you hold it perpendicular to your nose it makes your nose look long. *(He holds it to his nose.)*

GINNY: Uh huh.

LAWRENCE: And I call this one Henry Kissinger, because he wears glasses and it's made of glass.

GINNY: Uh huh. *(Takes it and stirs her drink.)*

LAWRENCE: No! They're just for looking, not for stirring. Mama, she's making a mess with my collection.

AMANDA *(from off)*:   Oh shut up about your collection, honey, you're probably driving the poor girl bananas.

GINNY: No bananas, thank you! My nutritionist says I should avoid potassium. You know what I take your trouble to be, Lawrence?

LAWRENCE: Mama says I'm retarded.

GINNY: I know you're tired, I figured that's why you put on the nightshirt, but this won't take long. I judge you to be lacking in self-confidence. Am I right?

LAWRENCE: Well, I am afraid of people and things, and I have a lot of ailments.

GINNY: But that makes you special, Lawrence.

LAWRENCE: What does?

GINNY: I don't know. Whatever you said. And that's why you should present yourself with more confidence. Throw back your shoulders, and say, "HI! HOW YA DOIN'?" Now you try it.

LAWRENCE *(unenthusiastically, softly)*:   Hello, How are you?

GINNY *(looking at watch, in response to his supposed question)*:   I don't know, it's about 8:30, but this won't take long and then you can go to bed. Alright, now try it. *(Booming.)* "HI! HOW YA DOIN'?"

LAWRENCE: Hi. How ya doin'?

GINNY: Now swagger a bit. *(Kinda butch.)* HI. HOW YA DOIN'?

LAWRENCE *(imitates her fairly successfully)*:   HI. HOW YA DOIN'?

GINNY: Good, Lawrence. That's much better, Again.

Amanda and Tom enter from behind them and watch this.

GINNY *(continued)*:   HI! HOW YA DOIN'?

LAWRENCE: HI! HOW YA DOIN'?

GINNY: THE BRAVES PLAYED A HELLUVA GAME, DON'TCHA THINK?

LAWRENCE: THE BRAVES PLAYED A HELLUVA GAME, DON'TCHA THINK?

AMANDA: Oh God I feel sorry for their children. Is this the only girl who works at the warehouse, Tom?

GINNY: HI, MRS. WINGVALLEY. YOUR SON LAWRENCE AND I ARE GETTING ON JUST FINE. AREN'T WE, LAWRENCE?

AMANDA: Please, no need to shout, I'm not deaf, even if you are.

GINNY: What?

AMANDA: I'm glad you like Lawrence.

GINNY: What?

AMANDA: I'M GLAD YOU LIKE LAWRENCE.

GINNY: What?

AMANDA: WHY DON'T YOU MARRY LAWRENCE?

GINNY *(looks shocked; has heard this)*:   Oh.

LAWRENCE: Oh, mama.

GINNY: Oh dear, I see. So that's why Shakespeare asked me here.

AMANDA *(to Tom)*:   Shakespeare?

TOM: The first day of work she asked my name, and I said Tom Wingvalley, and she thought I said Shakespeare.

GINNY: Oh dear, Mrs. Wingvalley, if I had a young brother as nice and as special as Lawrence, I'd invite girls from the warehouse home to meet him too.

AMANDA: I'm sure I don't know what you mean.

GINNY: And you're probably hoping I'll say that I'll call again.

AMANDA: Really, we haven't even had dinner yet. Tom, shouldn't you be checkin' on the roast pigs feet?

TOM: I guess so. If anything interesting happens, call me. *(Exits.)*

GINNY: But I'm afraid I won't be calling on Lawrence again.

LAWRENCE: This is so embarrassing. I told you I wanted to stay in my room.

AMANDA: Hush up, Lawrence.

GINNY: But, Lawrence, I don't want you to think that I won't be calling because I don't like you. I do like you.

LAWRENCE: You do?

GINNY: Sure. I like everybody. But I got two time clocks to punch, Mrs. Wingvalley. One at the warehouse, and one at night.

AMANDA: At night? You have a second job? That is ambitious.

GINNY: Not a second job, ma'am. Betty.

AMANDA: Pardon?

GINNY: Now who's deaf, eh what? Betty. I'm involved with a girl named Betty. We've been going together for about a year. We're saving money so that we can buy a farmhouse and a tractor together. So you *(to Lawrence)* can see why I can't visit your son, though I wish I could. No hard feelings, Lawrence. You're a good kid.

LAWRENCE *(offers her another swizzle stick)*:   I want you to keep this. It's my very favorite one. I call it Thermometer because it looks like a thermometer.

GINNY: You want me to have this?

LAWRENCE: Yes, as a souvenir.

GINNY *(offended)*:   Well, there's no need to call me a queer. Fuck you and your stupid swizzle sticks. *(Throws the offered gift upstage.)*

LAWRENCE *(very upset)*:   You've broken it!

GINNY: What?

LAWRENCE: You've broken it. YOU'VE BROKEN IT.

GINNY: So I've broken it. Big fuckin' deal. You have twenty more of them here.

AMANDA: Well, I'm so sorry you have to be going.

GINNY: What?

AMANDA: Hadn't you better be going?

GINNY: What?

AMANDA: Go away!

GINNY: Well I guess I can tell when I'm not wanted. I guess I'll go now.

AMANDA: You and Betty must come over some evening. Preferably when we're out.

GINNY: I wasn't shouting. *(Calls off.)* So long, Shakespeare. See you at the warehouse. *(To Lawrence.)* So long, Lawrence. I hope your rash gets better.

LAWRENCE *(saddened, holding the broken swizzle stick)*:   You broke Thermometer.

GINNY: What?

LAWRENCE: YOU BROKE THERMOMETER!

GINNY: Well, what was a thermometer doing in with the swizzle sticks anyway?

LAWRENCE: Its name was Thermometer, you nitwit!

AMANDA: Let it go, Lawrence. There'll be other swizzle sticks. Good-bye, Virginia.

GINNY: I sure am hungry. Any chance I might be able to take a sandwich with me?

AMANDA: Certainly you can shake hands with me, if that will make you happy.

GINNY: I said I'm hungry.

AMANDA: Really, dear? What part of Hungary are you from?

GINNY: Oh never mind. I guess I'll go.

AMANDA: That's right. You have two time clocks. It must be getting near to when you punch in Betty.

GINNY: Well, so long, everybody. I had a nice time. *(Exits.)*

AMANDA: Tom, come in here please. Lawrence, I don't believe I would play the victrola right now.

LAWRENCE: What victrola?

AMANDA: Any victrola.

Enter Tom.

TOM: Yes, mother? Where's Ginny?

AMANDA: The feminine caller made a hasty departure.

TOM: Old four eyes bored her to death, huh?

LAWRENCE: Oh, drop dead.

TOM: We should have you institutionalized.

AMANDA: That's the first helpful thing you've said all evening, but first things first. You played a little joke on us, Tom.

TOM: What are you talking about?

AMANDA: You didn't mention that your friend is already spoken for.

TOM: Really? I didn't even think she liked men.

AMANDA: Yes, well. It seems odd that you know so little about a person you see everyday at the warehouse.

TOM: The warehouse is where I work, not where I know things about people.

AMANDA: The disgrace. The expense of the pigs feet, a new tie for Lawrence. And you — bringing a lesbian into this house. We haven't had a lesbian in this house since your grandmother died, and now you have the audacity to bring in that . . . that . . .

LAWRENCE: Dyke.

AMANDA: Thank you, Lawrence. That overbearing, booming-voiced bull dyke. Into a Christian home.

TOM: Oh look, who cares? No one in their right mind would marry four eyes here.

AMANDA: You have no Christian charity, or filial devotion, or fraternal affection.

TOM: I don't want to listen to this. I'm going to the movies.

AMANDA: You go to the movies to excess, Tom. It isn't healthy.

LAWRENCE: While you're out, could you stop at the liquor store and get me some more cocktail stirrers? She broke Thermometer, and she put Q-tip in her ear.

AMANDA: Listen to your brother, Tom. He's pathetic. How are we going to support ourselves once you go? And I know you want to leave. I've seen the brochure for the merchant marines in your underwear drawer. And the application to the Air Force. And your letter of inquiry to the Ballet Trockadero. So I'm not unaware of what you're thinking. But don't leave us until you fulfill your duties here, Tom. Help brother find a wife, or a job, or a doctor. Or consider euthanasia. But don't leave me here all alone, saddled with him.

LAWRENCE: Mama, don't you like me?

AMANDA: Of course, dear. I'm just making jokes.

LAWRENCE: Be careful of my asthma.

AMANDA: I'll try, dear. Now why don't you hold your breath in case you get a case of terminal hiccups?

LAWRENCE: Alright. *(Holds his breath.)*

TOM: I'm leaving.

AMANDA: Where are you going?

TOM: I'm going to the movies.

AMANDA: I don't believe you go to the movies. What did you see last night?

TOM: Hyapatia Lee in "Beaver City."

AMANDA: And the night before that?

TOM: I don't remember. "Humpy Busboys" or something.

AMANDA: Humpy what?

TOM: Nothing. Leave me alone.

AMANDA: These are not mainstream movies, Tom. Why can't you see a normal movie like "The Philadelphia Story." Or "The Bitter Tea of General Yen"?

TOM: Those movies were made in the 1930s.

AMANDA: They're still good today.

TOM: I don't want to have this conversation. I'm going to the movies.

AMANDA: That's right, go to the movies! Don't think about us, a mother alone, an unmarried brother who thinks he's crippled, and has no job. Stop holding your breath, Lawrence, mama was kidding. *(Back to Tom.)* Don't let anything interfere with your selfish pleasure. Go see your pornographic trash that's worse than anything Mr. D. H. Lawrence ever envisioned. Just go, go, go — to the movies!

TOM: Alright, I will! And the more you shout about my selfishness and my taste in movies the quicker I'll go, and I won't just go to the movies!

AMANDA: Go then! Go to the moon — you selfish dreamer!

Tom exits.

AMANDA *(continued)*:   Oh Lawrence, honey, what's to become of us?

LAWRENCE: Tom forgot his newspaper, mama.

AMANDA: He forgot a lot more than that, Lawrence honey. He forgot his mama and brother.

Amanda and Lawrence stay in place. Tom enters down right and stands apart from them in a spot. He speaks to the audience.

TOM: I didn't go to the moon, I went to the movies. In Amsterdam. A long, lonely trip working my way on a freighter. They had good movies in Amsterdam. They weren't in English, but I didn't really care. And as for my mother and brother — well, I was adopted anyway. So I didn't miss them.

Or at least so I thought. For something pursued me. It always came upon me unawares, it always caught me by surprise. Sometimes it would be a swizzle stick in someone's vodka glass, or sometimes it would just be a jar of pigs feet. But then all of a sudden my brother touches my shoulder, and my mother puts her hands around my neck, and everywhere I look I am reminded of them. And in all the bars I go to there are those damn swizzle sticks everywhere. I find myself thinking of my brother Lawrence. And of his collection of glass. And of my mother. I begin to think that their story would maybe make a good novel, or even a play. A mother's hopes, a brother's dreams. Pathos, humor, even tragedy. But then I lose interest, I really haven't the energy. So I'll leave them both, dimly lit, in my memory. For nowadays the world is lit by lightning, and when we get those colored lights going, it feels like I'm on LSD. Or some other drug. Or maybe it's the trick of memory, and the fact that life is very, very sad. Play with your cocktail stirrers, Lawrence. And so, good-bye.

AMANDA *(calling over in Tom's direction)*:   Tom, I hear you out on the porch talking. Who are you talking to?

TOM: No one, mother. I'm just on my way to the movies.

AMANDA: Well, try not to be too late, you have to work early at the warehouse tomorrow. And please don't bring home any visitors from the movies, I'm not up to it after that awful girl. Besides, if some sailor misses his boat, that's no reason you have to put him up in your room. You're too big-hearted, son.

TOM: Yes, mother. See you later. *(Exits.)*

LAWRENCE: Look at the light through the glass, mama. *(Looks through a swizzle stick.)* Isn't it amazin'?

AMANDA: Yes, I guess it is, Lawrence. Oh, but both my children are weird. What have I done, O Lord, to deserve them?

LAWRENCE: Just lucky, mama.

AMANDA: Don't make jokes, Lawrence. Your asthma. Your eczema. My life.

LAWRENCE: Don't be sad, mama. We have each other for company and amusement.

AMANDA: That's right. It's always darkest before the dawn. Or right before a typhoon sweeps up and kills everybody.

LAWRENCE: Oh, poor mama, let me try to cheer you up with my collection. Is that a good idea?

AMANDA: It's just great, Lawrence. Thank you.

LAWRENCE: I call this one Daffodil, because its yellow, and daffodils are yellow.

AMANDA: Uh huh.

LAWRENCE *(holds up another one)*:   And I call this one Curtain Rod because it reminds me of a curtain rod.

AMANDA: Uh huh.

LAWRENCE: And I call this one Ocean, because it's blue, and the ocean is . . .

AMANDA: I THOUGHT YOU CALLED THE BLUE ONE BLUE, YOU IDIOT CHILD! DO I HAVE TO LISTEN TO THIS PATHETIC PRATTLING THE REST OF MY LIFE??? CAN'T YOU AT LEAST BE CONSISTENT???

LAWRENCE *(pause, hurt)*:   No, I guess I can't.

AMANDA: Well, try, can't you? *(Silence.)* I'm sorry, Lawrence. I'm a little short-tempered today.

LAWRENCE: That's alright.

Silence.

AMANDA *(trying to make up)*:   Do you have any other swizzle sticks with names, Lawrence?

LAWRENCE: Yes, I do. *(Holds one up.)* I call this one "Mama." *(He throws it over his shoulder onto the floor.)*

AMANDA: Well, that's lovely, Lawrence, thank you.

LAWRENCE: I guess I can be a little short-tempered too.

AMANDA: Yes, well, whatever. I think we won't kill each other this evening, alright?

LAWRENCE: Alright.

AMANDA: I'll just distract myself from my rage and despair, and read about other people's rage and despair in the newspaper, shall I? *(Picks up Tom's newspaper.)* Your brother has the worst reading and viewing taste of any living creature. This is just a piece of filth. *(Reads.)* Man Has Sex With Chicken, Then Makes Casserole. *(Closes the paper.)* Disgusting. Oh, Lawrence honey, look — it's the Evening Star. *(She holds the paper out in front of them.)* Let's make a wish on it, honey, shall we?

LAWRENCE: Alright, mama.

Amanda holds up the newspaper, and she and Lawrence close their eyes and make a wish.

AMANDA: What did you wish for, darlin'?

LAWRENCE: More swizzle sticks.
AMANDA: You're so predictable, Lawrence. It's part of your charm, I guess.
LAWRENCE: What did you wish for, mama?
AMANDA: The same thing, honey. Maybe just a little happiness, too, but mostly just some more swizzle sticks.

Sad music. Amanda and Lawrence look up at the Evening Star. Fade to black.

[1994]

≡ THINKING ABOUT THE TEXT

1. It is difficult to laugh at Laura, but why is it easy to laugh at Lawrence? What did you find amusing about Lawrence? Are there still boundaries here? That is, what changes would you suggest that would make it inappropriate to make fun of Lawrence?

2. Much of Durang's humor would be lost on those who have not read the Williams play. List some aspects of this play that rely for their effect on the context of the original.

3. Here the central symbol of the glass animals has been transformed into cocktail stirrers. Comment on this change. Do both say something about their collectors?

4. Durang keeps the basic outline of the original plot mostly intact. What changes does he make in the narrative? How do they affect your response to the parody?

5. The ending monologue by Tom in *The Glass Menagerie* is one of the most famous speeches in American theater. What makes it so, and how does Durang play off its themes, words, and emotional impact? What do you think Durang's main purpose is in this parody?

≡ MAKING COMPARISONS

1. Compare Tom's character in both plays. What makes one sympathetic and the other less so?

2. Compare Laura with Lawrence and Jim with Ginny. What changes did Durang make, and why? Are they effective changes in terms of parody?

3. What changes in Amanda's personality does Durang make, and why? Is she now more or less sympathetic?

≡ WRITING ABOUT ISSUES

1. Which play is more effective in fulfilling its purpose? Be specific in terms of character, narrative, and thematic concerns.

2. Critics claim that the following thematic strands are present in *The Glass Menagerie* — tenderness, illusions, illness, fragility, transformation,

emotion, nostalgia, and being trapped. Which seems the most important to you? Write a brief essay that explores the play's various themes.

3. Humor is often intuitive and difficult to explain, and sometimes it defies analysis. Look back on the four or five things that you found amusing in *For Whom the Southern Belle Tolls*. Then try to explain — perhaps to someone from another culture — why these things are humorous.

4. Argue either that we have a responsibility to society to develop our own talents or that we have a duty to try to meet the financial and emotional needs of our birth family.

■ Grandparents and Legacies: Poems

ELIZABETH COOK-LYNN, "Grandfather at the Indian Health Clinic"

NIKKI GIOVANNI, "Legacies"

LINDA HOGAN, "Heritage"

GARY SOTO, "Behind Grandma's House"

ALBERTO RÍOS, "Mi Abuelo"

LORNA DEE CERVANTES, "Refugee Ship"

JUDITH ORTIZ COFER, "Claims"

In contemporary middle-class America, the influence, even the presence, of our grandparents has waned. They often live elsewhere, perhaps in retirement communities or nursing homes. But this was not always the case. Grandparents in the past, and in traditional households even today, were active members of the family, exerting influence on the daily decisions of everyday life, from diet to child-rearing. Some of this was beneficial: grandparents gave children a personal understanding of their cultural traditions as well as the benefit of their accumulated wisdom. But they could also create tension in families where change and progress conflicted with the habits and attitudes of the past. The following seven poets present us with different perspectives on their grandparents, some loving and proud, others less positive, and one quite funny.

■ BEFORE YOU READ

What specific memories do you have of your grandparents? What role do you think they should play in a family's life? What effects might the segregation of the elderly have on a society?

ELIZABETH COOK-LYNN
Grandfather at the Indian Health Clinic

A member of the Crow Creek Sioux tribe, Elizabeth Cook-Lynn (b. 1930) was raised on a reservation in South Dakota by "a family of Sioux politicians and Native scholars." She received a degree in journalism in 1952 and later her doctorate from the University of Nebraska in 1978. She has been a journalist, high-school teacher, university professor, and writer-in-residence. She founded the Native American journal WICAZO Sa Review. In her autobiographical essay "I Tell You Now," she notes that anger over the absence of Native American history compelled her to write. Writing for her is "an act of defiance born of the need to survive. . . . It is the quintessential act

of optimism born of frustration." She has written a short-story collection, The
Power of Horses and Other Stories *(1990); a novel,* From the River's Edge
(1991); and a poetry collection, Seek the House of Relatives *(1983), from which
the following poem is taken.* Anti-Indianism in Modern America: A Voice from
Tatekeya's Earth *was published in 2001. She is currently professor emerita of English and Native American studies at Eastern Washington University and lives in the
Black Hills of South Dakota.*

It's cold at last and cautious winds creep
softly into coves along the riverbank. At my insistence
he wears his denim cowboy coat high on his neck; averse to
an unceremonious world, he follows me through
hallways pushing down the easy rage he always has   5
with me, a youngest child, and smiles.
This morning the lodge is closed to the dance
and he reminds me these are not the men who
raise the bag above the painted marks; for the young
intern from New Jersey he bares his chest   10
but keeps a scarf tied on his steel-gray braids
and thinks of days that have no turning: he wore
yellow chaps and went as far as Canada to ride
Mad Dog and then came home to drive the Greenwood Woman's
cattle to his brother's place,   15
two hundred miles
along the timber line
the trees were bright
he turned his hat brim down in summer rain.

Now winter's here, he says, in this white lighted place   20
where lives are sometimes saved by
throwing blankets over spaces where the leaves are brushed away
and giving brilliant gourd-shell rattles
to everyone who comes.   *[1983]*

≡ **THINKING ABOUT THE TEXT**

1. What attitude does the narrator seem to have toward her grandfather?
   Is it affectionate? Wary? Respectful? Caring?
2. How do you explain the phrase "pushing down the easy rage he always
   has / with me" (lines 5–6)?
3. What can we infer about the grandfather from the line "he turned his hat
   brim down in summer rain" (line 19)?
4. What significance do you think the grandfather places in giving out
   "gourd-shell rattles" (line 23)?

5. Indian literature is often concerned with contrasts between cultures. In this sense, how do you explain the grandfather's reaction to the young intern?

NIKKI GIOVANNI

Legacies

Raised near Cincinnati, Ohio, Nikki Giovanni (b. 1943) returned as a teenager to her birthplace and spiritual home in Knoxville, Tennessee, where she experienced the strong influence of her grandmother, Louvenia Watson. She studied at the University of Cincinnati from 1961 to 1963 and earned a B.A. at Fisk University in 1967. She also attended the University of Pennsylvania School of Social Work (1967) and Columbia University School of the Arts (1968). She has taught at a number of universities, since 1987 at Virginia Polytechnic Institute, where she is a professor of English. Her poetry, essays, and works for children reflect her commitment to African American community, family, and womanhood. Her books include Quilting the Black-Eyed Pea: Poems and Not Quite Poems *(2002). Her most recent books are* On My Journey Now: Looking at African American History through the Spirituals *(2006) and* Acolytes *(2007). "Legacies" is from Giovanni's 1972 book,* My House.

    her grandmother called her from the playground
        "yes, ma'am"
        "i want chu to learn how to make rolls," said the old
    woman proudly
    but the little girl didn't want   5
    to learn how because she knew
    even if she couldn't say it that
    that would mean when the old one died she would be less
    dependent on her spirit so
    she said   10
        "i don't want to know how to make no rolls"
    with her lips poked out
    and the old woman wiped her hands on
    her apron saying "lord
        these children"   15
    and neither of them ever
    said what they meant
    and i guess nobody ever does   *[1972]*

≡ THINKING ABOUT THE TEXT

1. Does the dialogue in Giovanni's poem reveal the true feelings of the grandmother and the girl? Be explicit about what is really going on in their minds. Is the girl superstitious?

2. Is it true that "nobody" (line 18) says what she really means? Do you? Is this an indication of honesty or something else — say, tact or convention? Are poets more likely to tell the truth?

3. What makes this piece a poem? Would you prefer more metaphors or similes, allusions, or flowery language? Is *proudly* (line 4) an important word here?

4. Change the grandmother's words to those that reflect more of what is in her heart. Might the girl respond differently if the grandmother were more forthright?

5. The title is only referred to obliquely. Why? What does it refer to? Is contemporary society concerned with legacies? Are you? Are they important or irrelevant?

LINDA HOGAN

Heritage

Born in 1947 in Denver, Colorado, Linda Hogan calls on her Chickasaw heritage to interpret environmental, antinuclear, and other spiritual and societal issues. Her published works include poems, stories, screenplays, essays, and novels. Her novel Power *(1998) has been praised for its beauty of language, mythical structure, and allegorical power. Her works include* The Woman Who Watches Over the World: A Native Memoir *(2001) and* Sightings: The Gray Whales' Mysterious Journey *(2002). Her many honors include an American Book Award for* Seeing through the Sun *(1985), a Colorado Book Award and a Pulitzer nomination for* The Book of Medicines *(1993), fellowships from the Guggenheim Foundation and the National Endowment for the Arts, and a Lannan Award. Hogan received her M.A. from the University of Colorado at Boulder, where she currently teaches creative writing. "Heritage" is from her 1978 book titled* Calling Myself Home.

From my mother, the antique mirror
where I watch my face take on her lines.
She left me the smell of baking bread
to warm fine hairs in my nostrils,
she left the large white breasts that weigh down   5
my body.

From my father I take his brown eyes,
the plague of locusts that leveled our crops,
they flew in formation like buzzards.

From my uncle the whittled wood   10
that rattles like bones
and is white
and smells like all our old houses
that are no longer there. He was the man
who sang old chants to me, the words   15
my father was told not to remember.

From my grandfather who never spoke
I learned to fear silence.
I learned to kill a snake
when you're begging for rain.   20

And Grandmother, blue-eyed woman
whose skin was brown,
she used snuff.
When her coffee can full of black saliva
spilled on me   25
it was like the brown cloud of grasshoppers
that leveled her fields.
It was the brown stain
that covered my white shirt,
my whiteness a shame.   30
That sweet black liquid like the food
she chewed up and spit into my father's mouth
when he was an infant.
It was the brown earth of Oklahoma
stained with oil.   35
She said tobacco would purge your body of poisons.
It has more medicine than stones and knives
against your enemies.
That tobacco is the dark night that covers me.

She said it is wise to eat the flesh of deer   40
so you will be swift and travel over many miles.
She told me how our tribe has always followed a stick
that pointed west
that pointed east.
From my family I have learned the secrets   45
of never having a home.   *[1978]*

≣ THINKING ABOUT THE TEXT

1. The last sentence seems to contain a contradiction. "From my family I
   have learned the secrets" might lead you to expect something positive.
   But maybe the last phrase is not meant to be positive. What is your
   reading of Hogan's conclusion?

2. What does the narrator learn from her mother? Her father? Her uncle? Her grandfather? Her grandmother? What kinds of things did you learn from your family members? Use concrete images.

3. Why does she say "my whiteness a shame" (line 30)? Is this a racial comment?

4. Examine the "black saliva" section in lines 21 to 39. Does it start off negatively? Does it change? Explain.

5. We all learn things from our families, both positive and negative. Is Hogan giving a balanced account? Should she? Would you? Do poets have any responsibility to the larger culture? Or should they just follow their own inner vision?

■ MAKING COMPARISONS

1. Compare Hogan's grandfather to Cook-Lynn's.

2. Describe the ways the tone of "Heritage" differs from Cook-Lynn's poem.

3. What indications of cultural differences do you find in these two poems?

GARY SOTO

Behind Grandma's House

Born in 1952 in Fresno, California, Gary Soto gives voice to San Joaquin Valley agricultural workers whose deprivations have been part of his experience and social awareness from an early age. After graduating with honors from California State University in 1974, Soto went on to earn an M.F.A. in creative writing from the University of California at Irvine in 1976 and to teach in the university system. He has received numerous writing awards, including the distinction of being the first writer identifying himself as Chicano to be nominated for a Pulitzer Prize. A young adult novel, The Afterlife, *was published in 2003. A book of poems,* One Kind of Faith *(2003), was cited as confirming Soto's "immense talent." His Mexican American heritage continues to be central to his work. The poem reprinted here is from Soto's 1985 book,* Black Hair.

At ten I wanted fame. I had a comb
And two Coke bottles, a tube of Bryl-creem.
I borrowed a dog, one with
Mismatched eyes and a happy tongue,
And wanted to prove I was tough   5
In the alley, kicking over trash cans,
A dull chime of tuna cans falling.
I hurled light bulbs like grenades

And men teachers held their heads,
Fingers of blood lengthening   10
On the ground. I flicked rocks at cats,
Their goofy faces spurred with foxtails.
I kicked fences. I shooed pigeons.
I broke a branch from a flowering peach
And frightened ants with a stream of piss.   15
I said "Shit," "Fuck you," and "No way
Daddy-O" to an imaginary priest
Until grandma came into the alley,
Her apron flapping in a breeze,
Her hair mussed, and said, "Let me help you,"   20
And punched me between the eyes.   *[1985]*

■ **THINKING ABOUT THE TEXT**

1. Were you glad or disturbed when the narrator's grandmother hit him?
   Does he deserve it? Are you angry or sympathetic to his attempts to be
   tough? Do you understand why he wants to appear older? Is this normal?

2. What did you want at age ten? Did your grandparents know your desires? Did they support you? Did they ever set you straight? Are our
   grandparents' values too dated to matter?

3. Are the concrete details meaningful to you? Does the profanity help
   Soto achieve authenticity, or is it unnecessary?

4. Does the speaker learn something here, or is this just a snapshot of an
   event?

5. How would you describe our culture's ideas of the different roles of
   parents and grandparents? Do grandparents in today's culture have less
   influence than in the past? Is this a good thing or not?

■ **MAKING COMPARISONS**

1. Is Soto more or less respectful of his grandparent than the writers of the
   previous two poems?

2. Is this a gendered poem? That is, could a female see herself in a comparable situation? Are the Cook-Lynn and Hogan poems gendered?

ALBERTO RÍOS
Mi Abuelo°

Alberto Ríos (b. 1952) has said that being bilingual is like going through life with a pair of binoculars; having at least two words for everything opens one's eyes to the world. Ríos is a person of the border in several ways: his father was from Chiapas, Mexico, and his mother from Lancashire, England. He grew up in the city of Nogales, Arizona, where he could stand with one foot in the United States and the other in Mexico; as a writer, he crosses the line between poetry and prose, having written seven books of poetry, three collections of short stories, and a memoir. He is an instructor of creative writing, since 1994 the Regents Professor of English at Arizona State University, where he has taught since 1982. He received his B.A. (1974) and his M.F.A. in creative writing (1979) from the University of Arizona. His work appears in 175 anthologies, including the Norton Anthology of Modern Poetry, *and his awards include fellowships from the Guggenheim Foundation and the National Endowment for the Arts and the 1982 Walt Whitman Award for* Whispering to Fool the Wind. *A recent book of poems,* The Smallest Muscle in the Human Body *(2002), was a finalist for the National Book Award. His latest work,* The Theatre of Night *(2006), was reviewed as "rhapsodic."*

Where my grandfather is is in the ground
where you can hear the future
like an Indian with his ear at the tracks.
A pipe leads down to him so that sometimes
he whispers what will happen to a man   5
in town or how he will meet the best
dressed woman tomorrow and how the best
man at her wedding will chew the ground
next to her. Mi abuelo is the man
who speaks through all the mouths in my house.   10
An echo of me hitting the pipe sometimes
to stop him from saying *my hair is a*
sieve is the only other sound. It is a phrase
that among all others is the best,
he says, and *my hair is a sieve* is sometimes   15
repeated for hours out of the ground
when I let him, which is not often.
An abuelo should be much more than a man
like you! He stops then, and speaks: *I am a man*
who has served ants with the attitude   20
of a waiter, who has made each smile as only
an ant who is fat can, and they liked me best,

Mi Abuelo: My grandfather (Spanish).

but there is nothing left. Yet I know he ground
green coffee beans as a child, and sometimes
he will talk about his wife, and sometimes   25
about when he was deaf and a man
cured him by mail and he heard groundhogs
talking, or about how he walked with a cane
he chewed on when he got hungry.
At best, mi abuelo is a liar.   30
I see an old picture of him at nani's with an
off-white yellow center mustache and sometimes
that's all I know for sure. He talks best
about these hills, *slowest waves*, and where this man
is going, and I'm convinced his hair is a sieve,   35
that his fever is cooled now underground.
Mi abuelo is an ordinary man.
I look down the pipe, sometimes, and see a
ripple-topped stream in its best suit, in the ground.   *[1990]*

▤ THINKING ABOUT THE TEXT

1. The narrator seems ambivalent about his abuelo. What specific things
   does he know about him? Can you tell his attitude toward him? How do
   you read the line "At best, mi abuelo is a liar" (line 30)? What might the
   worst be?

2. When the grandfather speaks from the grave (*"I am a man . . ."*) (lines
   19–23), he seems odd indeed. Is he a bit crazy, or do you see meaning
   in his ant speech?

3. What does Ríos mean when he writes that his abuelo "speaks through
   all the mouths in my house" (line 10)? Could this be a positive notion?

4. Ríos seems convinced that his grandfather's "fever is cooled now" (line
   36). Should we take this literally?

5. Do you agree that Ríos wants to continue conversing with his dead
   abuelo? Why? Can we see this as a metaphor?

▤ MAKING COMPARISONS

1. Compare Ríos's attitude toward his grandfather with the attitudes
   shown in the poems by Cook-Lynn, Hogan, and Soto.

2. Which of the four grandparents featured in these poems would you like
   to meet? Why?

3. Do all the poems have a sense that grandparents possess some special
   experience or knowledge?

LORNA DEE CERVANTES
Refugee Ship

Lorna Dee Cervantes (b. 1954), considered one of America's most accomplished Chicana poets, was born in San Francisco. As a child, as a way to avoid widespread racism, she was allowed to speak only English. She has won numerous awards for her poetry collections, including Drive: The First Quartet *(2005), which was nominated for a Pulitzer Prize. She was a professor at the University of Colorado. She currently lives in Boulder, Colorado. The following poem first appeared in* Emplumada *(1981).*

> Like wet cornstarch, I slide
> past my grandmother's eyes. Bible
> at her side, she removes her glasses.
> The pudding thickens.
>
> Mama raised me without language.   5
> I'm orphaned from my Spanish name.
> The words are foreign, stumbling
> on my tongue. I see in the mirror
> my reflection: bronzed skin, black hair.
>
> I feel I am captive   10
> aboard the refugee ship.
> The ship that will never dock.
> El barco que nunca atraca.°   [1981]

13 El barco que nunca atraca: The ship that never docks.

■ **THINKING ABOUT THE TEXT**

1. What does Cervantes mean when she says she is "orphaned from my Spanish name" (line 6)?

2. In what way is the poet "captive / aboard the refugee ship" (lines 10–11)?

3. What is the poet implying with the metaphor of a ship that never docks?

4. How does the poet's looking into the mirror fit into the ideas of the rest of the poem?

5. Why do you think Cervantes repeats the next-to-last line in Spanish?

■ **MAKING COMPARISONS**

1. Compare what Cervantes learns about her heritage with what Hogan and Soto learn about theirs.

2. Compare the cooking imagery in this poem with that in "Legacies" and "Heritage."

3. Compare the poet's attitude toward her grandmother with Ríos's attitude toward his grandfather.

JUDITH ORTIZ COFER
Claims

Judith Ortiz Cofer (b. 1952) was born in Puerto Rico but spent most of her childhood traveling between Paterson, New Jersey, and Hormiqueros, Puerto Rico. The constant shifting of languages and cultures influenced most of her early work, especially two volumes of poetry: Reaching for the Mainland *and* Terms of Survival, *both published in 1987. Her first novel,* The Line of the Sun *(1989), the first novel ever published by the University of Georgia Press, was widely praised and was nominated for the Pulitzer Prize. Her themes center on the pressures of migratory life and the cultural importance of male–female relationships.* Woman in Front of the Sun *was published in 2000. Her latest book is* A Love Story Beginning in Spanish *(2005). Cofer is a faculty member at the University of Georgia in Athens and is a Regents and Franklin Professor of English and Creative Writing.*

Last time I saw her, Grandmother
had grown seamed as a Bedouin tent.
She had claimed the right
to sleep alone, to own
her nights, to never bear   5
the weight of sex again nor to accept
its gift of comfort, for the luxury
of stretching her bones.
She'd carried eight children,
three had sunk in her belly, *naufragos*°   10
she called them, shipwrecked babies
drowned in her black waters.
*Children are made in the night and
steal your days
for the rest of your life, amen.* She said this   15
to each of her daughters in turn. Once she had made a pact
with man and nature and kept it. Now like the sea,
she is claiming back her territory.   *[1987]*

---

10 *naufragos*: Victims of shipwrecks (Spanish).

■ **THINKING ABOUT THE TEXT**

1. To whom does the title refer?
2. What is the pact the grandmother made with "man and nature" (line 17)?
3. Comment on the simile "like the sea" Cofer uses in the last sentence. Has the reader been prepared for that comparison? Why, or why not?
4. What parts do duty and responsibility play in the grandmother's life? Does her quote (lines 13–15) suggest a negative view of children or sex?
5. Do you think the grandmother's response is typical or unusual?

■ **MAKING COMPARISONS**

1. Is Cofer's attitude toward her grandmother more or less respectful than the other poets here?
2. Compare Cofer's grandmother with Cervantes's.
3. Which of the grandparents portrayed here might make the same decision about sex as Cofer's grandmother?

■ **WRITING ABOUT ISSUES**

1. Pick one of the seven preceding poems, and argue that it offers an appropriate view of grandparents.
2. Pick two of these poems, and argue that something of value is learned in each.
3. Which poem comes closest to your own experiences? Write a narrative that demonstrates this.
4. Do some research on over-sixty-five communities from a sociological point of view. Write a report about your findings. Include the impact of such places on the family and on the larger culture. Do you think they are a positive development or not?

■ Poetic Visions of Family: A Collection of Poems by Sharon Olds

SHARON OLDS, "I Go Back to May 1937"

SHARON OLDS, "His Stillness"

SHARON OLDS, "My Son the Man"

SHARON OLDS, "First Thanksgiving"

Although Sharon Olds is one of contemporary poetry's leading voices, she claims she is not really a deep thinker, just a commentator on the events of ordinary life, from giving birth and nursing children to dealing with an alcoholic father and, as poet Alicia Ostriker puts it, "the erotics of family love and pain." Olds's first poem is a haunting and poignant fantasy, a kind of time travel wish to prevent her mother and father from inflicting pain on each other. Olds wrote many poems about her abusive father, but the one printed here ("His Stillness") is filled more with compassion than with anger. In her poem about her son, she is stunned by the brevity of childhood, and her Houdini analogy is both clear and apt. The final poem, about her daughter's first Thanksgiving home from college, is both admiring of her daughter's maturity and bittersweet. The critic Lisel Mueller notes that Olds's poems are "believable and touching. . . . [W]e hear a proud, urgent, human voice."

■ BEFORE YOU READ

If you were to write poems about your family, what topics would interest you? Would being honest be a problem for you? Would you want your family to read these poems?

SHARON OLDS
I Go Back to May 1937

Born in 1942 in San Francisco, Sharon Olds claims she was raised as a "hellfire Calvinist." She graduated from Stanford University and earned a Ph.D. in English from Columbia University. After receiving her doctorate, she vowed that she would become a poet who wrote in her own voice, no matter what. Her second volume, The Dead and the Living, won the 1983 Lamont Poetry Prize and the National Book Award. The Father (1992) is devoted entirely to her memories of her alcoholic father, who was abusive during her childhood but who expressed his love for her on his deathbed, and her struggle to reconcile with him. Her poems are often candid and explicit, prompting a range of critical estimations, from Michael Ondaatje's "pure fire in the hands" to Helen Vendler's view that she is self-indulgent and sensationalist. Olds was the New York State poet laureate from 1998 to 2000. Her most recent collection of poems is One Sacred Thing (2009). She teaches in the graduate creative

(© 2011 David
Bartolomi.)

writing program at New York University. *"I Go Back to May 1937"* was quoted in
the popular 2007 film Into the Wild.

I see them standing at the formal gates of their colleges,
I see my father strolling out
under the ochre sandstone arch, the
red tiles glinting like bent
plates of blood behind his head, I   5
see my mother with a few light books at her hip
standing at the pillar made of tiny bricks,
the wrought-iron gate still open behind her, its
sword-tips aglow in the May air,
they are about to graduate, they are about to get married,   10
they are kids, they are dumb, all they know is they are
innocent, they would never hurt anybody.
I want to go up to them and say Stop,
don't do it — she's the wrong woman,
he's the wrong man, you are going to do things   15
you cannot imagine you would ever do,
you are going to do bad things to children,
you are going to suffer in ways you have not heard of,
you are going to want to die. I want to go
up to them there in the late May sunlight and say it,   20

her hungry pretty face turning to me,
her pitiful beautiful untouched body,
his arrogant handsome face turning to me,
his pitiful beautiful untouched body,
but I don't do it. I want to live. I   25
take them up like the male and female
paper dolls and bang them together
at the hips, like chips of flint, as if to
strike sparks from them, I say
Do what you are going to do, and I will tell about it.   *[1987]*   30

≡ THINKING ABOUT THE TEXT

1. Although this is a fanciful poem involving time travel, it has a tone of grim resignation. What does Olds decide she is not able to do? What is she able to do?

2. Have you ever looked at a photograph of your parents when they were about to get married? What was your response? Does Olds's reaction seem odd?

3. Why do you think Olds uses the phrase "pitiful beautiful untouched body" (lines 22 and 24) for both parents? Does "pitiful" seem an unusual term? How about "dumb" (line 11)?

4. What do you think Olds means by referring to her father's face as "arrogant" (line 23) and her mother's as "hungry" (line 21)?

5. How might the last line be an indication of Olds's poetic mission?

SHARON OLDS
His Stillness

In this poem, from Strike Sparks: Selected Poems, 1980–2002 *(2004), Sharon Olds recalls how experiencing her father's stillness and dignity at the news of his impending death gave her a new understanding of his life.*

The doctor said to my father, "You asked me
to tell you when nothing more could be done.
That's what I'm telling you now." My father
sat quite still, as he always did,
especially not moving his eyes. I had thought   5
he would rave if he understood he would die,
wave his arms and cry out. He sat up,
thin, and clean, in his clean gown,
like a holy man. The doctor said,
"There are things we can do which might give you time,   10
but we cannot cure you." My father said,

"Thank you." And he sat, motionless, alone,
with the dignity of a foreign leader.
I sat beside him. This was my father.
He had known he was mortal. I had feared they would have to   15
tie him down. I had not remembered
he had always held still and kept quiet to bear things,
the liquor a way to keep still. I had not
known him. My father had dignity. At the
end of his life his life began   20
to wake in me.   *[1992]*

≡ THINKING ABOUT THE TEXT

1. What is the epiphany Olds has about her father?
2. What does Olds mean by "I had not / known him" (lines 18–19)?
3. Does it seem unusual that Olds thinks liquor was "a way to keep still" (line 18)?
4. Do you think that Olds will now reevaluate her father's life?
5. Why do you think Olds thought her father would respond so differently?

≡ MAKING COMPARISONS

1. Compare Olds's attitude toward her father in this poem with that in "I Go Back to May 1937."
2. Olds wrote many poems about her alcoholic, abusive father. Are there hints of that man in these two poems?
3. Do these poems tell us something about Olds's attitude toward the role of poetry?

SHARON OLDS
My Son the Man

"My Son the Man," which appeared in The Wellspring *(1996), reveals Sharon Olds's bittersweet feelings regarding her son's sudden maturity.*

Suddenly his shoulders get a lot wider,
the way Houdini would expand his body
while people were putting him in chains. It seems
no time since I would help him to put on his sleeper,
guide his calves into the gold interior,   5
zip him up and toss him up and
catch his weight. I cannot imagine him
no longer a child, and I know I must get ready,
get over my fear of men now my son

is going to be one. This was not   10
what I had in mind when he pressed up through me like a
sealed trunk through the ice of the Hudson,
snapped the padlock, unsnaked the chains,
and appeared in my arms. Now he looks at me
the way Houdini studied a box   15
to learn the way out, then smiled and let himself be manacled.   *[1995]*

■ **THINKING ABOUT THE TEXT**

1. Explain how Olds uses the Houdini analogy to explain her feelings about her son.

2. Houdini, of course, was famous for amazing escapes. How does this idea figure in the poem?

3. Is Olds's "fear of men" (line 9) surprising? What other surprises appear in the poem?

4. What is Olds getting ready for?

5. Describe your reading of the last sentence.

■ **MAKING COMPARISONS**

1. Compare Olds's use of metaphor and simile in these three poems.

2. Critics often comment on Olds's honesty. Do you think she is being honest in these three poems?

3. Compare the sentence "I cannot imagine him / no longer a child" (lines 7–8) with "I had not remembered . . ." (lines 16–18) in "His Stillness."

SHARON OLDS

First Thanksgiving

In "First Thanksgiving," Sharon Olds uses her daughter's return home to ruminate on the joy of briefly containing something free and wild. This poem was published in Strike Sparks: Selected Poems, 1980–2002 *(2004).*

When she comes back, from college, I will see
the skin of her upper arms, cool,
matte, glossy. She will hug me, my old
soupy chest against her breasts,
I will smell her hair! She will sleep in this apartment,   5
her sleep like an untamed, good object,
like a soul in a body. She came into my life the
second great arrival, after him, fresh
from the other world — which lay, from within him,
within me. Those nights, I fed her to sleep,   10

week after week, the moon rising,
and setting, and waxing — whirling, over the months,
in a slow blur, around our planet.
Now she doesn't need love like that, she has
had it. She will walk in glowing, we will talk,   15
and then, when she's fast asleep, I'll exult
to have her in that room again,
behind that door! As a child, I caught
bees, by the wings, and held them, some seconds,
looked into their wild faces,   20
listened to them sing, then tossed them back
into the air — I remember the moment the
arc of my toss swerved, and they entered
the corrected curve of their departure.   [1999]

≡ THINKING ABOUT THE TEXT

1. Nostalgia plays an obvious part in this poem. What other emotions do you notice?

2. Poets often try to represent the complexity and the sometimes contradictory impulses of our feelings. How might that be true here?

3. Is Olds finally willing to come to peace with her daughter's departure?

4. Why does Olds use the phrase "behind that door" (line 18)?

5. Explain your understanding of the bee analogy in the last seven lines.

≡ MAKING COMPARISONS

1. Compare the effectiveness of the bee analogy in this poem with her use of Houdini in "My Son the Man."

2. What thematic similarities do you see in these two poems about her son and daughter?

3. Do you think this poem would have been different if she were talking about her son? Would the previous poem change if her daughter were the focus?

≡ WRITING ABOUT ISSUES

1. Write a personal essay involving your family that focuses on one of the emotions or insights that Olds describes in these four poems.

2. Write an essay that explores the idea that students and parents have different perceptions of their departure to and return from college.

3. Argue that Olds's insights into family life are either typical or unusual.

4. Argue that nonfiction writers, poets, and fiction writers have an artistic responsibility to describe specifically and honestly the joy and pain of family life.

▤ A Family's Dreams: Cultural Contexts for a Play

LORRAINE HANSBERRY, *A Raisin in the Sun*

CULTURAL CONTEXTS:

THE CRISIS, "The Hansberrys of Chicago: They Join Business Acumen with Social Vision"

LORRAINE HANSBERRY, *April 23, 1964, Letter to the* New York Times

ALAN EHRENHALT, From *The Lost City: Discovering the Forgotten Virtues of Community in the Chicago of the 1950s*

SIDNEY POITIER, From *The Measure of a Man: A Spiritual Autobiography*

Hansberry's title comes from the African American poet Langston Hughes's 1951 poem "Harlem," which begins by asking *"What happens to a dream deferred? / Does it dry up / Like a raisin in the sun?"* Hughes had in mind white America's continued thwarting of his own race's hopes for freedom, equality, and prosperity. This is a situation painfully familiar to the Youngers, the African American family of Hansberry's play, who live in a poor black Chicago neighborhood in the 1950s. Like many of the texts in Part One, the play deals with the topic of work. Most of the Youngers have survived by laboring for white people, though they have been stuck in near poverty all the same. Now, a large inheritance promises to fulfill their dreams at last — but these dreams conflict. Lena wants to buy a house, but her son Walter Lee wants to invest in a liquor store to escape his degrading job as a chauffeur. Much of the play's drama occurs as these two characters clash. Following the play, we include four cultural texts to help you place the drama in a specific historical moment. We hope they will help illuminate the social condition Hansberry wrote in.

▤ BEFORE YOU READ

Think of your own family or another you know well. For outsiders to get a sense of this family, what do they have to know about its social and historical background? Do you think the *phrase a dream deferred* applies to this family? Why, or why not?

LORRAINE HANSBERRY
A Raisin in the Sun

The life of Lorraine Hansberry (1930–1965) was brief. She died of cancer the day that her second play, The Sign in Sidney Brustein's Window *(1964), closed on Broadway. But by then she had been immensely productive as a writer and gained a considerable reputation for her work. In 1959, her first play,* A Raisin in the Sun, *was the first by an African American woman to be produced on Broadway. Later that*

(AP/Wide World
Photos.)

year, it became the first play by an African American to win the New York Drama Critics Circle Award. In part, the play was based on an experience that Hansberry's own family endured while she was growing up in Chicago. Her father, Carl Hansberry, a prominent real estate agent and banker, made history in 1938 when he moved his family to an all-white section of Chicago's Hyde Park neighborhood. After encountering white resistance there, he fought a series of legal battles that went all the way to the U.S. Supreme Court. In 1940, the Court ruled in his favor, but its decision largely was not enforced; housing remained basically segregated in Chicago and in most of the country. Embittered, Carl Hansberry considered moving his family permanently to Mexico, but before he could, he died of a cerebral hemorrhage there in 1946.

After attending the University of Wisconsin, Lorraine Hansberry moved to New York City. Besides plays, she wrote essays and articles on a variety of subjects, including homophobia and racism. She also wrote the screenplay for the 1961 film version of A Raisin in the Sun, *which featured the original Broadway cast (including Sidney Poitier as Walter Lee Younger). In 1969, her widower, Robert Nemiroff, combined various writings of hers into a play called* To Be Young, Gifted, and Black. *In 1970, a book version of it was published, and that same year there was a Broadway production of Hansberry's final play,* Les Blancs.

Harlem (A Dream Deferred)

What happens to a dream deferred?

Does it dry up
Like a raisin in the sun?
Or fester like a sore —
And then run?
Does it stink like rotten meat?
Or crust and sugar over —
Like a syrupy sweet?

Maybe it just sags
Like a heavy load.

Or does it explode?
                    — Langston Hughes

CHARACTERS (in order of appearance)

RUTH YOUNGER
TRAVIS YOUNGER
WALTER LEE YOUNGER, BROTHER
BENEATHA YOUNGER
LENA YOUNGER, MAMA
JOSEPH ASAGAI
GEORGE MURCHISON
MRS. JOHNSON
KARL LINDNER
BOBO
MOVING MEN

The action of the play is set in Chicago's Southside, sometime between World War II and the present.

ACT 1, Scene 1

[Friday morning.]
    The Younger living room would be a comfortable and well-ordered room if it were not for a number of indestructible contradictions to this state of being. Its furnishings are typical and undistinguished and their primary feature now is that they have clearly had to accommodate the living of too many people for too many years — and they are tired. Still, we can see that at some time, a time probably no longer remembered by the family (except perhaps for Mama), the furnishings of this room were actually selected with care and love and even hope — and brought to this apartment and arranged with taste and pride.
    That was a long time ago. Now the once loved pattern of the couch upholstery has to fight to show itself from under acres of crocheted doilies and couch covers which have themselves finally come to be more important than the upholstery. And

here a table or a chair has been moved to disguise the worn places in the carpet; but the carpet has fought back by showing its weariness, with depressing uniformity, elsewhere on its surface.

Weariness has, in fact, won in this room. Everything has been polished, washed, sat on, used, scrubbed too often. All pretenses but living itself have long since vanished from the very atmosphere of this room.

Moreover, a section of this room, for it is not really a room unto itself, though the landlord's lease would make it seem so, slopes backward to provide a small kitchen area, where the family prepares the meals that are eaten in the living room proper, which must also serve as dining room. The single window that has been provided for these "two" rooms is located in this kitchen area. The sole natural light the family may enjoy in the course of a day is only that which fights its way through this little window.

At left, a door leads to a bedroom which is shared by Mama and her daughter, Beneatha. At right, opposite, is a second room (which in the beginning of the life of this apartment was probably a breakfast room) which serves as a bedroom for Walter and his wife, Ruth.

Time: Sometime between World War II and the present.

Place: Chicago's Southside.

At rise: It is morning dark in the living room. Travis is asleep on the make-down bed at center. An alarm clock sounds from within the bedroom at right, and presently Ruth enters from that room and closes the door behind her. She crosses sleepily toward the window. As she passes her sleeping son she reaches down and shakes him a little. At the window she raises the shade and a dusky Southside morning light comes in feebly. She fills a pot with water and puts it on to boil. She calls to the boy, between yawns, in a slightly muffled voice.

Ruth is about thirty. We can see that she was a pretty girl, even exceptionally so, but now it is apparent that life has been little that she expected, and disappointment has already begun to hang in her face. In a few years, before thirty-five even, she will be known among her people as a "settled woman."

She crosses to her son and gives him a good, final, rousing shake.

RUTH: Come on now, boy, it's seven thirty! *(Her son sits up at last, in a stupor of sleepiness.)* I say hurry up, Travis! You ain't the only person in the world got to use a bathroom! *(The child, a sturdy, handsome little boy of ten or eleven, drags himself out of the bed and almost blindly takes his towels and "today's clothes" from drawers and a closet and goes out to the bathroom, which is in an outside hall and which is shared by another family or families on the same floor. Ruth crosses to the bedroom door at right and opens it and calls in to her husband.)* Walter Lee! . . . It's after seven thirty! Lemme see you do some waking up in there now! *(She waits.)* You better get up from there, man! It's after seven thirty I tell you. *(She waits again.)* All right, you just go ahead and lay there and next thing you know Travis be finished and Mr. Johnson'll be in there and you'll be fussing and cussing round here like a madman! And be late too! *(She waits, at the end of patience.)* Walter Lee — it's time for you to GET UP!

She waits another second and then starts to go into the bedroom, but is apparently satisfied that her husband has begun to get up. She stops, pulls the door to, and returns to the kitchen area. She wipes her face with a moist cloth and runs her fingers through her sleep-disheveled hair in a vain effort and ties an apron around her housecoat. The bedroom door at right opens and her husband stands in the doorway in his pajamas, which are rumpled and mismated. He is a lean, intense young man in his middle thirties, inclined to quick nervous movements and erratic speech habits — and always in his voice there is a quality of indictment.

WALTER: Is he out yet?

RUTH: What you mean *out*? He ain't hardly got in there good yet.

WALTER *(wandering in, still more oriented to sleep than to a new day)*:   Well, what was you doing all that yelling for if I can't even get in there yet? *(Stopping and thinking.)* Check coming today?

RUTH: They *said* Saturday and this is just Friday and I hopes to God you ain't going to get up here first thing this morning and start talking to me 'bout no money — 'cause I 'bout don'want to hear it.

WALTER: Something the matter with you this morning?

RUTH: No — I'm just sleepy as the devil. What kind of eggs you want?

WALTER: Not scrambled. *(Ruth starts to scramble eggs.)* Paper come? *(Ruth points impatiently to the rolled up* Tribune *on the table, and he gets it and spreads it out and vaguely reads the front page.)* Set off another bomb yesterday.

RUTH *(maximum indifference)*:   Did they?

WALTER *(looking up)*:   What's the matter with you?

RUTH: Ain't nothing the matter with me. And don't keep asking me that this morning.

WALTER: Ain't nobody bothering you. *(Reading the news of the day absently again.)* Say Colonel McCormick is sick.

RUTH *(affecting tea-party interest)*:   Is he now? Poor thing.

WALTER *(sighing and looking at his watch)*:   Oh, me. *(He waits.)* Now what is that boy doing in that bathroom all this time? He just going to have to start getting up earlier. I can't be being late to work on account of him fooling around in there.

RUTH *(turning on him)*:   Oh, no he ain't going to be getting up no earlier no such thing! It ain't his fault that he can't get to bed no earlier nights 'cause he got a bunch of crazy good-for-nothing clowns sitting up running their mouths in what is supposed to be his bedroom after ten o'clock at night . . .

WALTER: That's what you mad about, ain't it? The things I want to talk about with my friends just couldn't be important in your mind, could they?

He rises and finds a cigarette in her handbag on the table and crosses to the little window and looks out, smoking and deeply enjoying this first one.

RUTH *(almost matter of factly, a complaint too automatic to deserve emphasis)*:   Why you always got to smoke before you eat in the morning?

WALTER *(at the window)*:   Just look at 'em down there . . . Running and racing to work . . . *(He turns and faces his wife and watches her a moment at the stove, and then, suddenly.)* You look young this morning, baby.

RUTH *(indifferently)*:   Yeah?

WALTER: Just for a second — stirring them eggs. Just for a second it was — you looked real young again. *(He reaches for her; she crosses away. Then, drily.)* It's gone now — you look like yourself again!

RUTH: Man, if you don't shut up and leave me alone.

WALTER *(looking out to the street again)*:   First thing a man ought to learn in life is not to make love to no colored woman first thing in the morning. You all some eeeevil people at eight o'clock in the morning.

Travis appears in the hall doorway, almost fully dressed and quite wide awake now, his towels and pajamas across his shoulders. He opens the door and signals for his father to make the bathroom in a hurry.

TRAVIS *(watching the bathroom)*:   Daddy, come on!

Walter gets his bathroom utensils and flies out to the bathroom.

RUTH: Sit down and have your breakfast, Travis.

TRAVIS: Mama, this is Friday. *(Gleefully.)* Check coming tomorrow, huh?

RUTH: You get your mind off money and eat your breakfast.

TRAVIS *(eating)*:   This is the morning we supposed to bring the fifty cents to school.

RUTH: Well, I ain't got no fifty cents this morning.

TRAVIS: Teacher say we have to.

RUTH: I don't care what teacher say. I ain't got it. Eat your breakfast, Travis.

TRAVIS: I *am* eating.

RUTH: Hush up now and just eat!

The boy gives her an exasperated look for her lack of understanding, and eats grudgingly.

TRAVIS: You think Grandmama would have it?

RUTH: No! And I want you to stop asking your grandmother for money, you hear me?

TRAVIS *(outraged)*:   Gaaaleee! I don't ask her, she just gimme it sometimes!

RUTH: Travis Willard Younger — I got too much on me this morning to be —

TRAVIS: Maybe Daddy —

RUTH: *Travis!*

The boy hushes abruptly. They are both quiet and tense for several seconds.

TRAVIS *(presently)*:   Could I maybe go carry some groceries in front of the su-permarket for a little while after school then?

RUTH: Just hush, I said. *(Travis jabs his spoon into his cereal bowl viciously, and rests his head in anger upon his fists.)* If you through eating, you can get over there and make up your bed.

The boy obeys stiffly and crosses the room, almost mechanically, to the bed and more or less folds the bedding into a heap, then angrily gets his books and cap.

TRAVIS *(sulking and standing apart from her unnaturally)*:   I'm gone.

RUTH *(looking up from the stove to inspect him automatically)*:   Come here. *(He crosses to her and she studies his head.)* If you don't take this comb and fix this here head, you better! *(Travis puts down his books with a great sigh of oppression, and crosses to the mirror. His mother mutters under her breath about his "slubbornness.")* 'Bout to march out of here with that head looking just like chickens slept in it! I just don't know where you get your slubborn ways . . . And get your jacket, too. Looks chilly out this morning.

TRAVIS *(with conspicuously brushed hair and jacket)*:   I'm gone.

RUTH: Get carfare and milk money — *(Waving one finger.)* — and not a single penny for no caps, you hear me?

TRAVIS *(with sullen politeness)*:   Yes'm.

He turns in outrage to leave. His mother watches after him as in his frustration he approaches the door almost comically. When she speaks to him, her voice has become a very gentle tease.

RUTH *(mocking; as she thinks he would say it)*:   Oh, Mama makes me so mad sometimes, I don't know what to do! *(She waits and continues to his back as he stands stock-still in front of the door.)* I wouldn't kiss that woman good-bye for nothing in this world this morning! *(The boy finally turns around and rolls his eyes at her, knowing the mood has changed and he is vindicated; he does not, however, move toward her yet.)* Not for nothing in this world! *(She finally laughs aloud at him and holds out her arms to him and we see that it is a way between them, very old and practiced. He crosses to her and allows her to embrace him warmly but keeps his face fixed with masculine rigidity. She holds him back from her presently and looks at him and runs her fingers over the features of his face. With utter gentleness — .)* Now — whose little old angry man are you?

TRAVIS *(the masculinity and gruffness start to fade at last)*:   Aw gaalee — Mama . . .

RUTH *(mimicking)*:   Aw — gaaaaalleeeee, Mama! *(She pushes him, with rough playfulness and finality, toward the door.)* Get on out of here or you going to be late.

TRAVIS *(in the face of love, new aggressiveness)*:   Mama, could I *please* go carry groceries?

RUTH: Honey, it's starting to get so cold evenings.

WALTER *(coming in from the bathroom and drawing a make-believe gun from a make-believe holster and shooting at his son)*:   What is it he wants to do?

RUTH: Go carry groceries after school at the supermarket.

WALTER: Well, let him go . . .

TRAVIS *(quickly, to the ally)*:   I have to — she won't gimme the fifty cents . . .

WALTER *(to his wife only)*:   Why not?

RUTH *(simply, and with flavor)*:   'Cause we don't have it.

WALTER *(to Ruth only)*:   What you tell the boy things like that for? *(Reaching down into his pants with a rather important gesture.)* Here, son —

He hands the boy the coin, but his eyes are directed to his wife's. Travis takes the money happily.

TRAVIS: Thanks, Daddy.

He starts out. Ruth watches both of them with murder in her eyes. Walter stands and stares back at her with defiance, and suddenly reaches into his pocket again on an afterthought.

WALTER (*without even looking at his son, still staring hard at his wife*):   In fact, here's another fifty cents . . . Buy yourself some fruit today — or take a taxicab to school or something!

TRAVIS: Whoopee —

He leaps up and clasps his father around the middle with his legs, and they face each other in mutual appreciation; slowly Walter Lee peeks around the boy to catch the violent rays from his wife's eyes and draws his head back as if shot.

WALTER: You better get down now — and get to school, man.

TRAVIS (*at the door*):   O.K. Good-bye.

He exits.

WALTER (*after him, pointing with pride*):   That's my boy. (*She looks at him in disgust and turns back to her work.*) You know what I was thinking 'bout in the bathroom this morning?

RUTH: No.

WALTER: How come you always try to be so pleasant!

RUTH: What is there to be pleasant 'bout!

WALTER: You want to know what I was thinking bout in the bathroom or not!

RUTH: I know what you thinking 'bout.

WALTER (*ignoring her*):   'Bout what me and Willy Harris was talking about last night.

RUTH (*immediately — a refrain*):   Willy Harris is a good-for-nothing loudmouth.

WALTER: Anybody who talks to me has got to be a good-for-nothing loudmouth, ain't he? And what you know about who is just a good-for-nothing loudmouth? Charlie Atkins was just a "good-for-nothing loudmouth" too, wasn't he! When he wanted me to go in the dry-cleaning business with him. And now — he's grossing a hundred thousand a year. A hundred thousand dollars a year! You still call *him* a loudmouth!

RUTH (*bitterly*):   Oh, Walter Lee . . .

She folds her head on her arms over the table.

WALTER (*rising and coming to her and standing over her*):   You tired, ain't you? Tired of everything. Me, the boy, the way we live — this beat-up hole — everything. Ain't you? (*She doesn't look up, doesn't answer.*) So tired — moaning and groaning all the time, but you wouldn't do nothing to help, would you? You couldn't be on my side that long for nothing, could you?

RUTH: Walter, please leave me alone.

WALTER: A man needs for a woman to back him up . . .

RUTH: Walter —

WALTER: Mama would listen to you. You know she listen to you more than she do me and Bennie. She think more of you. All you have to do is just sit down with her when you drinking your coffee one morning and talking 'bout things like you do and — (*He sits down beside her and demonstrates graphically what he thinks her methods and tone should be.*) — you just sip your coffee, see, and say easy like that you been thinking 'bout that deal Walter Lee is so interested in, 'bout the store and all, and sip some more coffee, like what you saying ain't really that important to you — And the next thing you know, she be listening good and asking you questions and when I come home — I can tell her the details. This ain't no fly-by-night proposition, baby. I mean we figured it out, me and Willy and Bobo.

RUTH *(with a frown)*: Bobo?

WALTER: Yeah. You see, this little liquor store we got in mind cost seventy-five thousand and we figured the initial investment on the place be 'bout thirty thousand, see. That be ten thousand each. Course, there's a couple of hundred you got to pay so's you don't spend your life just waiting for them clowns to let your license get approved —

RUTH: You mean graft?

WALTER *(frowning impatiently)*: Don't call it that. See there, that just goes to show you what women understand about the world. Baby, don't *nothing* happen for you in the world 'less you pay *somebody* off!

RUTH: Walter, leave me alone! *(She raises her head and stares at him vigorously — then says, more quietly.)* Eat your eggs, they gonna be cold.

WALTER *(straightening up from her and looking off)*: That's it. There you are. Man say to his woman: I got me a dream. His woman say: Eat your eggs. *(Sadly, but gaining in power.)* Man say: I got to take hold of this here world, baby! And a woman will say: Eat your eggs and go to work. *(Passionately now.)* Man say: I got to change my life, I'm choking to death, baby! And his woman say — *(In utter anguish as he brings his fists down on his thighs.)* — Your eggs is getting cold!

RUTH *(softly)*: Walter, that ain't none of our money.

WALTER *(not listening at all or even looking at her)*: This morning, I was lookin' in the mirror and thinking about it . . . I'm thirty-five years old; I been married eleven years and I got a boy who sleeps in the living room — *(Very, very quietly.)* — and all I got to give him is stories about how rich white people live . . .

RUTH: Eat your eggs, Walter.

WALTER *(slams the table and jumps up)*: — DAMN MY EGGS — DAMN ALL THE EGGS THAT EVER WAS!

RUTH: Then go to work.

WALTER *(looking up at her)*: See — I'm trying to talk to you 'bout myself — *(Shaking his head with the repetition.)* — and all you can say is eat them eggs and go to work.

RUTH *(wearily)*: Honey, you never say nothing new. I listen to you every day, every night and every morning, and you never say nothing new. *(Shrugging.)* So you would rather *be* Mr. Arnold than be his chauffeur. So — I would *rather* be living in Buckingham Palace.

WALTER: That is just what is wrong with the colored woman in this world . . . Don't understand about building their men up and making 'em feel like they somebody. Like they can do something.

RUTH *(drily, but to hurt)*: There *are* colored men who do things.

WALTER: No thanks to the colored woman.

RUTH: Well, being a colored woman, I guess I can't help myself none.

She rises and gets the ironing board and sets it up and attacks a huge pile of rough-dried clothes, sprinkling them in preparation for the ironing and then rolling them into tight fat balls.

WALTER *(mumbling)*:   We one group of men tied to a race of women with small minds!

His sister Beneatha enters. She is about twenty, as slim and intense as her brother. She is not as pretty as her sister-in-law, but her lean, almost intellectual face has a handsomeness of its own. She wears a bright-red flannel nightie, and her thick hair stands wildly about her head. Her speech is a mixture of many things; it is different from the rest of the family's insofar as education has permeated her sense of English — and perhaps the Midwest rather than the South has finally — at last — won out in her inflection; but not altogether, because over all of it is a soft slurring and transformed use of vowels which is the decided influence of the Southside. She passes through the room without looking at either Ruth or Walter and goes to the outside door and looks, a little blindly, out to the bathroom. She sees that it has been lost to the Johnsons. She closes the door with a sleepy vengeance and crosses to the table and sits down a little defeated.

BENEATHA: I am going to start timing those people.

WALTER: You should get up earlier.

BENEATHA *(her face in her hands. She is still fighting the urge to go back to bed)*:   Really — would you suggest dawn? Where's the paper?

WALTER *(pushing the paper across the table to her as he studies her almost clinically, as though he has never seen her before)*:   You a horrible-looking chick at this hour.

BENEATHA *(drily)*:   Good morning, everybody.

WALTER *(senselessly)*:   How is school coming?

BENEATHA *(in the same spirit)*:   Lovely. Lovely. And you know, biology is the greatest. *(Looking up at him.)* I dissected something that looked just like you yesterday.

WALTER: I just wondered if you've made up your mind and everything.

BENEATHA *(gaining in sharpness and impatience)*:   And what did I answer yesterday morning — and the day before that?

RUTH *(from the ironing board, like someone disinterested and old)*:   Don't be so nasty, Bennie.

BENEATHA *(still to her brother)*:   And the day before that and the day before that!

WALTER *(defensively)*:   I'm interested in you. Something wrong with that? Ain't many girls who decide —

WALTER AND BENEATHA *(in unison)*:   — "to be a doctor."

Silence.

WALTER: Have we figured out yet just exactly how much medical school is going to cost?

RUTH: Walter Lee, why don't you leave that girl alone and get out of here to work?

BENEATHA *(exits to the bathroom and bangs on the door)*:   Come on out of there, please!

She comes back into the room.

WALTER *(looking at his sister intently)*:   You know the check is coming tomorrow.

BENEATHA *(turning on him with a sharpness all her own)*:   That money belongs to Mama, Walter, and it's for her to decide how she wants to use it. I don't care if she wants to buy a house or a rocket ship or just nail it up somewhere and look at it. It's hers. Not ours — *hers.*

WALTER *(bitterly)*:   Now ain't that fine! You just got your mother's interest at heart, ain't you, girl? You such a nice girl — but if Mama got that money she can always take a few thousand and help you through school too — can't she?

BENEATHA: I have never asked anyone around here to do anything for me!

WALTER: No! And the line between asking and just accepting when the time comes is big and wide — ain't it!

BENEATHA *(with fury)*:   What do you want from me, Brother — that I quit school or just drop dead, which!

WALTER: I don't want nothing but for you to stop acting holy 'round here. Me and Ruth done made some sacrifices for you — why can't you do something for the family?

RUTH: Walter, don't be dragging me in it.

WALTER: You are in it — Don't you get up and go work in somebody's kitchen for the last three years to help put clothes on her back?

RUTH: Oh, Walter — that's not fair . . .

WALTER: It ain't that nobody expects you to get on your knees and say thank you, Brother; thank you, Ruth; thank you, Mama — and thank you, Travis, for wearing the same pair of shoes for two semesters —

BENEATHA *(dropping to her knees)*:   Well — I *do* — all right? — thank everybody! And forgive me for ever wanting to be anything at all! *(Pursuing him on her knees across the floor.)* FORGIVE ME, FORGIVE ME, FORGIVE ME!

RUTH: Please stop it! Your mama'll hear you.

WALTER: Who the hell told you you had to be a doctor? If you so crazy 'bout messing 'round with sick people — then go be a nurse like other women — or just get married and be quiet . . .

BENEATHA: Well — you finally got it said . . . It took you three years but you finally got it said. Walter, give up; leave me alone — it's Mama's money.

WALTER: *He was my father, too!*

BENEATHA: So what? He was mine, too — and Travis' grandfather — but the insurance money belongs to Mama. Picking on me is not going to make her give it to you to invest in any liquor stores — *(Under breath, dropping into a chair.)* — and I for one say, God bless Mama for that!

WALTER *(to Ruth)*:   See — did you hear? Did you hear!

RUTH: Honey, please go to work.

WALTER: Nobody in this house is ever going to understand me.

BENEATHA: Because you're a nut.

WALTER: Who's a nut?

BENEATHA: You — you are a nut. Thee is mad, boy.

WALTER *(looking at his wife and his sister from the door, very sadly)*:   The world's most backward race of people, and that's a fact.

BENEATHA *(turning slowly in her chair)*:   And then there are all those prophets who would lead us out of the wilderness — *(Walter slams out of the house.)* — into the swamps!

RUTH: Bennie, why you always gotta be pickin' on your brother? Can't you be a little sweeter sometimes? *(Door opens. Walter walks in. He fumbles with his cap, starts to speak, clears throat, looks everywhere but at Ruth. Finally:)*

WALTER *(to Ruth)*:   I need some money for carfare.

RUTH *(looks at him, then warms; teasing, but tenderly)*:   Fifty cents? *(She goes to her bag and gets money.)* Here — take a taxi!

Walter exits. Mama enters. She is a woman in her early sixties, full-bodied and strong. She is one of those women of a certain grace and beauty who wear it so unobtrusively that it takes a while to notice. Her dark-brown face is surrounded by the total whiteness of her hair, and, being a woman who has adjusted to many things in life and overcome many more, her face is full of strength. She has, we can see, wit and faith of a kind that keep her eyes lit and full of interest and expectancy. She is, in a word, a beautiful woman. Her bearing is perhaps most like the noble bearing of the women of the Hereros of Southwest Africa — rather as if she imagines that as she walks she still bears a basket or a vessel upon her head. Her speech, on the other hand, is as careless as her carriage is precise — she is inclined to slur everything — but her voice is perhaps not so much quiet as simply soft.

MAMA: Who that 'round here slamming doors at this hour?

She crosses through the room, goes to the window, opens it, and brings in a feeble little plant growing doggedly in a small pot on the window sill. She feels the dirt and puts it back out.

RUTH: That was Walter Lee. He and Bennie was at it again.

MAMA: My children and they tempers. Lord, if this little old plant don't get more sun than it's been getting it ain't never going to see spring again. *(She turns from the window.)* What's the matter with you this morning, Ruth? You looks right peaked. You aiming to iron all them things? Leave some for me. I'll get to 'em this afternoon. Bennie honey, it's too drafty for you to be sitting 'round half dressed. Where's your robe?

BENEATHA: In the cleaners.

MAMA: Well, go get mine and put it on.

BENEATHA: I'm not cold, Mama, honest.

MAMA: I know — but you so thin . . .

BENEATHA *(irritably)*:   Mama, I'm not cold.

MAMA *(seeing the make-down bed as Travis has left it)*:   Lord have mercy, look at that poor bed. Bless his heart — he tries, don't he?

She moves to the bed Travis has sloppily made up.

RUTH: No — he don't half try at all 'cause he knows you going to come along behind him and fix everything. That's just how come he don't know how to do nothing right now — you done spoiled that boy so.

MAMA *(folding bedding)*:   Well — he's a little boy. Ain't supposed to know 'bout housekeeping. My baby, that's what he is. What you fix for his breakfast this morning?

RUTH *(angrily)*:   I feed my son, Lena!

MAMA: I ain't meddling — *(Under breath; busy-bodyish.)* I just noticed all last week he had cold cereal, and when it starts getting this chilly in the fall a child ought to have some hot grits or something when he goes out in the cold —

RUTH *(furious)*:   I gave him hot oats — is that all right!

MAMA: I ain't meddling. *(Pause.)* Put a lot of nice butter on it? *(Ruth shoots her an angry look and does not reply.)* He likes lots of butter.

RUTH *(exasperated)*:   Lena —

MAMA *(to Beneatha. Mama is inclined to wander conversationally sometimes)*:   What was you and your brother fussing 'bout this morning?

BENEATHA: It's not important, Mama.

She gets up and goes to look out at the bathroom, which is apparently free, and she picks up her towels and rushes out.

MAMA: What was they fighting about?

RUTH: Now you know as well as I do.

MAMA *(shaking her head)*:   Brother still worrying hisself sick about that money?

RUTH: You know he is.

MAMA: You had breakfast?

RUTH: Some coffee.

MAMA: Girl, you better start eating and looking after yourself better. You almost thin as Travis.

RUTH: Lena —

MAMA: Un-hunh?

RUTH: What are you going to do with it?

MAMA: Now don't you start, child. It's too early in the morning to be talking about money. It ain't Christian.

RUTH: It's just that he got his heart set on that store —

MAMA: You mean that liquor store that Willy Harris want him to invest in?

RUTH: Yes —

MAMA: We ain't no business people, Ruth. We just plain working folks.

RUTH: Ain't nobody business people till they go into business. Walter Lee say colored people ain't never going to start getting ahead till they start gambling on some different kinds of things in the world — investments and things.

MAMA: What done got into you, girl? Walter Lee done finally sold you on investing.

RUTH: No. Mama, something is happening between Walter and me. I don't know what it is — but he needs something — something I can't give him any more. He needs this chance, Lena.

MAMA *(frowning deeply)*:   But liquor, honey —

RUTH: Well — like Walter say — I spec people going to always be drinking themselves some liquor.

MAMA: Well — whether they drinks it or not ain't none of my business. But whether I go into business selling it to 'em *is*, and I don't want that on my ledger this late in life. *(Stopping suddenly and studying her daughter-in-law.)* Ruth Younger, what's the matter with you today? You look like you could fall over right there.

RUTH: I'm tired.

MAMA: Then you better stay home from work today.

RUTH: I can't stay home. She'd be calling up the agency and screaming at them, "My girl didn't come in today — send me somebody! My girl didn't come in!" Oh, she just have a fit . . .

MAMA: Well, let her have it. I'll just call her up and say you got the flu —

RUTH *(laughing)*:   Why the flu?

MAMA: 'Cause it sounds respectable to 'em. Something white people get, too. They know 'bout the flu. Otherwise they think you been cut up or something when you tell 'em you sick.

RUTH: I got to go in. We need the money.

MAMA: Somebody would of thought my children done all but starved to death the way they talk about money here late. Child, we got a great big old check coming tomorrow.

RUTH *(sincerely, but also self-righteously)*:   Now that's your money. It ain't got nothing to do with me. We all feel like that — Walter and Bennie and me — even Travis.

MAMA *(thoughtfully, and suddenly very far away)*:   Ten thousand dollars —

RUTH: Sure is wonderful.

MAMA: Ten thousand dollars.

RUTH: You know what you should do, Miss Lena? You should take yourself a trip somewhere. To Europe or South America or someplace —

MAMA *(throwing up her hands at the thought)*:   Oh, child!

RUTH: I'm serious. Just pack up and leave! Go on away and enjoy yourself some. Forget about the family and have yourself a ball for once in your life —

MAMA *(drily)*:   You sound like I'm just about ready to die. Who'd go with me? What I look like wandering 'round Europe by myself?

RUTH: Shoot — these here rich white women do it all the time. They don't think nothing of packing up they suitcases and piling on one of them big steamships and — swoosh! — they gone, child.

MAMA: Something always told me I wasn't no rich white woman.

RUTH: Well — what are you going to do with it then?

MAMA: I ain't rightly decided. *(Thinking. She speaks now with emphasis.)* Some of it got to be put away for Beneatha and her schoolin' — and ain't nothing going to touch that part of it. Nothing. *(She waits several seconds, trying to make up her mind about something, and looks at Ruth a little tentatively before going on.)* Been thinking that we maybe could meet the notes on a little old two-story somewhere, with a yard where Travis could play in the summertime, if we use part of the insurance for a down payment and everybody kind of pitch in. I could maybe take on a little day work again, few days a week —

RUTH *(studying her mother-in-law furtively and concentrating on her ironing, anxious to encourage without seeming to):*   Well, Lord knows, we've put enough rent into this here rat trap to pay for four houses by now . . .

MAMA *(looking up at the words "rat trap" and then looking around and leaning back and sighing — in a suddenly reflective mood —):*   "Rat trap" — yes, that's all it is. *(Smiling.)* I remember just as well the day me and Big Walter moved in here. Hadn't been married but two weeks and wasn't planning on living here no more than a year. *(She shakes her head at the dissolved dream.)* We was going to set away, little by little, don't you know, and buy a little place out in Morgan Park. We had even picked out the house. *(Chuckling a little.)* Looks right dumpy today. But Lord, child, you should know all the dreams I had 'bout buying that house and fixing it up and making me a little garden in the back — *(She waits and stops smiling.)* And didn't none of it happen.

Dropping her hands in a futile gesture.

RUTH *(keeps her head down, ironing):*   Yes, life can be a barrel of disappointments, sometimes.

MAMA: Honey, Big Walter would come in here some nights back then and slump down on that couch there and just look at the rug, and look at me and look at the rug and then back at me — and I'd know he was down then . . . really down. *(After a second very long and thoughtful pause; she is seeing back to times that only she can see.)* And then, Lord, when I lost that baby — little Claude — I almost thought I was going to lose Big Walter too. Oh, that man grieved hisself! He was one man to love his children.

RUTH: Ain't nothin' can tear at you like losin' your baby.

MAMA: I guess that's how come that man finally worked hisself to death like he done. Like he was fighting his own war with this here world that took his baby from him.

RUTH: He sure was a fine man, all right. I always liked Mr. Younger.

MAMA: Crazy 'bout his children! God knows there was plenty wrong with Walter Younger — hard-headed, mean, kind of wild with women — plenty wrong with him. But he sure loved his children. Always wanted them to have something — be something. That's where Brother gets all these notions, I reckon. Big Walter used to say, he'd get right wet in the eyes sometimes, lean his head back with the water standing in his eyes and say, "Seem like God didn't see fit to give the black man nothing but dreams — but He did give us children to make them dreams seem worthwhile." *(She smiles.)* He could talk like that, don't you know.

RUTH: Yes, he sure could. He was a good man, Mr. Younger.

MAMA: Yes, a fine man — just couldn't never catch up with his dreams, that's all.

Beneatha comes in, brushing her hair and looking up to the ceiling, where the sound of a vacuum cleaner has started up.

BENEATHA: What could be so dirty on that woman's rugs that she has to vacuum them every single day?

RUTH: I wish certain young women 'round here who I could name would take inspiration about certain rugs in a certain apartment I could also mention.

BENEATHA *(shrugging)*:   How much cleaning can a house need, for Christ's sakes.

MAMA *(not liking the Lord's name used thus)*:   Bennie!

RUTH: Just listen to her — just listen!

BENEATHA: Oh, God!

MAMA: If you use the Lord's name just one more time —

BENEATHA *(a bit of a whine)*:   Oh, Mama —

RUTH: Fresh — just fresh as salt, this girl!

BENEATHA *(drily)*:   Well — if the salt loses its savor —

MAMA: Now that will do. I just ain't going to have you 'round here reciting the scriptures in vain — you hear me?

BENEATHA: How did I manage to get on everybody's wrong side by just walking into a room?

RUTH: If you weren't so fresh —

BENEATHA: Ruth, I'm twenty years old.

MAMA: What time you be home from school today?

BENEATHA: Kind of late. *(With enthusiasm.)* Madeline is going to start my guitar lessons today.

Mama and Ruth look up with the same expression.

MAMA: Your *what* kind of lessons?

BENEATHA: Guitar.

RUTH: Oh, Father!

MAMA: How come you done taken it in your mind to learn to play the guitar?

BENEATHA: I just want to, that's all.

MAMA *(smiling)*:   Lord, child, don't you know what to do with yourself? How long it going to be before you get tired of this now — like you got tired of that little play-acting group you joined last year? *(Looking at Ruth.)* And what was it the year before that?

RUTH: The horseback-riding club for which she bought that fifty-five-dollar riding habit that's been hanging in the closet ever since!

MAMA *(to Beneatha)*:   Why you got to flit so from one thing to another, baby?

BENEATHA *(sharply)*:   I just want to learn to play the guitar. Is there anything wrong with that?

MAMA: Ain't nobody trying to stop you. I just wonders sometimes why you has to flit so from one thing to another all the time. You ain't never done nothing with all that camera equipment you brought home —

BENEATHA: I don't flit! I — I experiment with different forms of expression —

RUTH: Like riding a horse?

BENEATHA: — People have to express themselves one way or another.

MAMA: What is it you want to express?

BENEATHA *(angrily)*:   Me! *(Mama and Ruth look at each other and burst into raucous laughter.)* Don't worry — I don't expect you to understand.

MAMA *(to change the subject)*:   Who you going out with tomorrow night?

BENEATHA *(with displeasure)*:   George Murchison again.

MAMA *(pleased)*:   Oh — you getting a little sweet on him?

RUTH: You ask me, this child ain't sweet on nobody but herself — *(Under breath.)* Express herself!

They laugh.

BENEATHA: Oh — I like George all right, Mama. I mean I like him enough to go out with him and stuff, but —

RUTH *(for devilment)*:   What does *and stuff* mean?

BENEATHA: Mind your own business.

MAMA: Stop picking at her now, Ruth. *(She chuckles — then a suspicious sudden look at her daughter as she turns in her chair for emphasis.)* What DOES it mean?

BENEATHA *(wearily)*:   Oh, I just mean I couldn't ever really be serious about George. He's — he's so shallow.

RUTH: Shallow — what do you mean he's shallow? He's *rich!*

MAMA: Hush, Ruth.

BENEATHA: I know he's rich. He knows he's rich, too.

RUTH: Well — what other qualities a man got to have to satisfy you, little girl?

BENEATHA: You wouldn't even begin to understand. Anybody who married Walter could not possibly understand.

MAMA *(outraged)*:   What kind of way is that to talk about your brother?

BENEATHA: Brother is a flip — let's face it.

MAMA *(to Ruth, helplessly)*:   What's a flip?

RUTH *(glad to add kindling)*:   She's saying he's crazy.

BENEATHA: Not crazy. Brother isn't really crazy yet — he — he's an elaborate neurotic.

MAMA: Hush your mouth!

BENEATHA: As for George. Well. George looks good — he's got a beautiful car and he takes me to nice places and, as my sister-in-law says, he is probably the richest boy I will ever get to know and I even like him sometimes — but if the Youngers are sitting around waiting to see if their little Bennie is going to tie up the family with the Murchisons, they are wasting their time.

RUTH: You mean you wouldn't marry George Murchison if he asked you someday? That pretty, rich thing? Honey, I knew you was odd —

BENEATHA: No I would not marry him if all I felt for him was what I feel now. Besides, George's family wouldn't really like it.

MAMA: Why not?

BENEATHA: Oh, Mama — The Murchisons are honest-to-God-real-*live*-rich colored people, and the only people in the world who are more snobbish than rich white people are rich colored people. I thought everybody knew that. I've met Mrs. Murchison. She's a scene!

MAMA: You must not dislike people 'cause they well off, honey.

BENEATHA: Why not? It makes just as much sense as disliking people 'cause they are poor, and lots of people do that.

RUTH *(a wisdom-of-the-ages manner. To Mama)*:   Well, she'll get over some of this —

BENEATHA: Get over it? What are you talking about, Ruth? Listen, I'm going to be a doctor. I'm not worried about who I'm going to marry yet — if I ever get married.

MAMA AND RUTH: *If!*

MAMA: Now, Bennie —

BENEATHA: Oh, I probably will . . . but first I'm going to be a doctor, and George, for one, still thinks that's pretty funny. I couldn't be bothered with that. I am going to be a doctor and everybody around here better understand that!

MAMA *(kindly)*:   'Course you going to be a doctor, honey, God willing.

BENEATHA *(drily)*:   God hasn't got a thing to do with it.

MAMA: Beneatha — that just wasn't necessary.

BENEATHA: Well — neither is God. I get sick of hearing about God.

MAMA: Beneatha!

BENEATHA: I mean it! I'm just tired of hearing about God all the time. What has He got to do with anything? Does He pay tuition?

MAMA: You 'bout to get your fresh little jaw slapped!

RUTH: That's just what she needs, all right!

BENEATHA: Why? Why can't I say what I want to around here, like everybody else?

MAMA: It don't sound nice for a young girl to say things like that — you wasn't brought up that way. Me and your father went to trouble to get you and Brother to church every Sunday.

BENEATHA: Mama, you don't understand. It's all a matter of ideas, and God is just one idea I don't accept. It's not important. I am not going out and be immoral or commit crimes because I don't believe in God. I don't even think about it. It's just that I get tired of Him getting credit for all the things the human race achieves through its own stubborn effort. There simply is no blasted God — there is only man and it is *He* who makes miracles!

Mama absorbs this speech, studies her daughter, and rises slowly and crosses to Beneatha and slaps her powerfully across the face. After, there is only silence and the daughter drops her eyes from her mother's face, and Mama is very tall before her.

MAMA: Now — you say after me, in my mother's house there is still God. *(There is a long pause and Beneatha stares at the floor wordlessly. Mama repeats the phrase with precision and cool emotion.)* In my mother's house there is still God.

BENEATHA: In my mother's house there is still God.

A long pause.

MAMA *(walking away from Beneatha, too disturbed for triumphant posture. Stopping and turning back to her daughter)*:   There are some ideas we ain't going to have in this house. Not long as I am at the head of this family.

BENEATHA: Yes, ma'am.

Mama walks out of the room.

RUTH *(almost gently, with profound understanding)*:   You think you a woman, Bennie — but you still a little girl. What you did was childish — so you got treated like a child.

BENEATHA: I see. *(Quietly.)* I also see that everybody thinks it's all right for Mama to be a tyrant. But all the tyranny in the world will never put a God in the heavens!

She picks up her books and goes out. Pause.

RUTH *(goes to Mama's door)*:   She said she was sorry.

MAMA *(coming out, going to her plant)*:   They frightens me, Ruth. My children.

RUTH: You got good children, Lena. They just a little off sometimes — but they're good.

MAMA: No — there's something come down between me and them that don't let us understand each other and I don't know what it is. One done almost lost his mind thinking 'bout money all the time and the other done commence to talk about things I can't seem to understand in no form or fashion. What is it that's changing, Ruth.

RUTH *(soothingly, older than her years)*:   Now . . . you taking it all too seriously. You just got strong-willed children and it takes a strong woman like you to keep 'em in hand.

MAMA *(looking at her plant and sprinkling a little water on it)*:   They spirited all right, my children. Got to admit they got spirit — Bennie and Walter. Like this little old plant that ain't never had enough sunshine or nothing — and look at it . . .

She has her back to Ruth, who has had to stop ironing and lean against something and put the back of her hand to her forehead.

RUTH *(trying to keep Mama from noticing)*:   You . . . sure . . . loves that little old thing, don't you? . . .

MAMA: Well, I always wanted me a garden like I used to see sometimes at the back of the houses down home. This plant is close as I ever got to having one. *(She looks out of the window as she replaces the plant.)* Lord, ain't nothing as dreary as the view from this window on a dreary day, is there? Why ain't you singing this morning, Ruth? Sing that "No Ways Tired." That song always lifts me up so — *(She turns at last to see that Ruth has slipped quietly to the floor, in a state of semiconsciousness.)* Ruth! Ruth honey — what's the matter with you . . . Ruth!

Curtain.

Scene 2

It is the following morning; a Saturday morning, and house cleaning is in progress at the Youngers'. Furniture has been shoved hither and yon and Mama is giving the kitchen-area walls a washing down. Beneatha, in dungarees, with a handkerchief tied around her face, is spraying insecticide into the cracks in the walls. As they work, the radio is on and a Southside disk-jockey program is inappropriately filling the house with a rather exotic saxophone blues. Travis, the sole idle one, is leaning on his arms, looking out of the window.

TRAVIS: Grandmama, that stuff Bennie is using smells awful. Can I go downstairs, please?

MAMA: Did you get all them chores done already? I ain't seen you doing much.

TRAVIS: Yes'm — finished early. Where did Mama go this morning?

MAMA *(looking at Beneatha)*:   She had to go on a little errand.

The phone rings. Beneatha runs to answer it and reaches it before Walter, who has entered from bedroom.

TRAVIS: Where?

MAMA: To tend to her business.

BENEATHA: Haylo . . . *(Disappointed.)* Yes, he is. *(She tosses the phone to Walter, who barely catches it.)* It's Willie Harris again.

WALTER *(as privately as possible under Mama's gaze)*:   Hello, Willie. Did you get the papers from the lawyer? . . . No, not yet. I told you the mailman doesn't get here till ten-thirty . . . No, I'll come there . . . Yeah! Right away. *(He hangs up and goes for his coat.)*

BENEATHA: Brother, where did Ruth go?

WALTER *(as he exits)*:   How should I know!

TRAVIS: Aw come on, Grandma. Can I go outside?

MAMA: Oh, I guess so. You stay right in front of the house, though, and keep a good lookout for the postman.

TRAVIS: Yes'm. *(He darts into bedroom for stickball and bat, reenters, and sees Beneatha on her knees spraying under sofa with behind upraised. He edges closer to the target, takes aim, and lets her have it. She screams.)* Leave them poor little cockroaches alone, they ain't bothering you none! *(He runs as she swings the spraygun at him viciously and playfully.)* Grandma! Grandma!

MAMA: Look out there, girl, before you be spilling some of that stuff on that child!

TRAVIS *(safely behind the bastion of Mama)*:   That's right — look out, now! *(He exits.)*

BENEATHA *(drily)*:   I can't imagine that it would hurt him — it has never hurt the roaches.

MAMA: Well, little boys' hides ain't as tough as Southside roaches. You better get over there behind the bureau. I seen one marching out of there like Napoleon yesterday.

BENEATHA: There's really only one way to get rid of them, Mama —

MAMA: How?

BENEATHA: Set fire to this building! Mama, where did Ruth go?

MAMA *(looking at her with meaning)*:   To the doctor, I think.

BENEATHA: The doctor? What's the matter? *(They exchange glances.)* You don't think —

MAMA *(with her sense of drama)*:   Now I ain't saying what I think. But I ain't never been wrong 'bout a woman neither.

The phone rings.

BENEATHA *(at the phone)*:   Hay-lo . . . *(Pause, and a moment of recognition.)* Well — when did you get back! . . . And how was it? . . . Of course I've missed you — in my way . . . This morning? No . . . house cleaning and all that and Mama hates it if I let people come over when the house is like this . . . You *have?* Well, that's different . . . What is it — Oh, what the hell, come on over . . . Right, see you then. *Arrividerci.*

She hangs up.

MAMA *(who has listened vigorously, as is her habit)*:   Who is that you inviting over here with this house looking like this? You ain't got the pride you was born with!

BENEATHA: Asagai doesn't care how houses look, Mama — he's an intellectual.

MAMA: *Who?*

BENEATHA: Asagai — Joseph Asagai. He's an African boy I met on campus. He's been studying in Canada all summer.

MAMA: What's his name?

BENEATHA: Asagai, Joseph. Ah-sah-guy . . . He's from Nigeria.

MAMA: Oh, that's the little country that was founded by slaves way back . . .

BENEATHA: No, Mama — that's Liberia.

MAMA: I don't think I never met no African before.

BENEATHA: Well, do me a favor and don't ask him a whole lot of ignorant questions about Africans. I mean, do they wear clothes and all that —

MAMA: Well, now, I guess if you think we so ignorant 'round here maybe you shouldn't bring your friends here —

BENEATHA: It's just that people ask such crazy things. All anyone seems to know about when it comes to Africa is Tarzan —

MAMA *(indignantly)*:   Why should I know anything about Africa?

BENEATHA: Why do you give money at church for the missionary work?

MAMA: Well, that's to help save people.

BENEATHA: You mean save them from *heathenism* —

MAMA *(innocently)*:   Yes.

BENEATHA: I'm afraid they need more salvation from the British and the French.

Ruth comes in forlornly and pulls off her coat with dejection. They both turn to look at her.

RUTH *(dispiritedly)*:   Well, I guess from all the happy faces — everybody knows.

BENEATHA: You pregnant?

MAMA: Lord have mercy, I sure hope it's a little old girl. Travis ought to have a sister.

Beneatha and Ruth give her a hopeless look for this grandmotherly enthusiasm.

BENEATHA: How far along are you?

RUTH: Two months.

BENEATHA: Did you mean to? I mean did you plan it or was it an accident?

MAMA: What do you know about planning or not planning?

BENEATHA: Oh, Mama.

RUTH *(wearily)*:   She's twenty years old, Lena.

BENEATHA: Did you plan it, Ruth?

RUTH: Mind your own business.

BENEATHA: It is my business — where is he going to live, on the *roof? (There is silence following the remark as the three women react to the sense of it.)* Gee — I didn't mean that, Ruth, honest. Gee, I don't feel like that at all. I — I think it is wonderful.

RUTH *(dully)*:   Wonderful.

BENEATHA: Yes — really.

MAMA *(looking at Ruth, worried)*:   Doctor say everything going to be all right?

RUTH *(far away)*:   Yes — she says everything is going to be fine . . .

MAMA *(immediately suspicious)*:   "She" — What doctor you went to?

Ruth folds over, near hysteria.

MAMA *(worriedly hovering over Ruth)*:   Ruth honey — what's the matter with you — you sick?

Ruth has her fists clenched on her thighs and is fighting hard to suppress a scream that seems to be rising in her.

BENEATHA: What's the matter with her, Mama?

MAMA *(working her fingers in Ruth's shoulders to relax her)*:   She be all right. Women gets right depressed sometimes when they get her way. *(Speaking softly, expertly, rapidly.)* Now you just relax. That's right . . . just lean back, don't think 'bout nothing at all . . . nothing at all —

RUTH: I'm all right . . .

The glassy-eyed look melts and then she collapses into a fit of heavy sobbing. The bell rings.

BENEATHA: Oh, my God — that must be Asagai.

MAMA *(to Ruth)*:   Come on now, honey. You need to lie down and rest awhile . . . then have some nice hot food.

They exit, Ruth's weight on her mother-in-law. Beneatha, herself profoundly disturbed, opens the door to admit a rather dramatic-looking young man with a large package.

ASAGAI: Hello, Alaiyo —

BENEATHA *(holding the door open and regarding him with pleasure)*:   Hello . . . *(Long pause.)* Well — come in. And please excuse everything. My mother was very upset about my letting anyone come here with the place like this.

ASAGAI *(coming into the room)*:   You look disturbed too . . . Is something wrong?

BENEATHA *(still at the door, absently)*:   Yes . . . we've all got acute ghetto-itus. *(She smiles and comes toward him, finding a cigarette and sitting.)* So — sit down! No! Wait! *(She whips the spraygun off sofa where she had left it and puts the cushions back. At last perches on arm of sofa. He sits.)* So, how was Canada?

ASAGAI *(a sophisticate)*:   Canadian.

BENEATHA *(looking at him)*:   Asagai, I'm very glad you are back.

ASAGAI *(looking back at her in turn)*:   Are you really?

BENEATHA: Yes — very.

ASAGAI: Why? — you were quite glad when I went away. What happened?

BENEATHA: You went away.

ASAGAI: Ahhhhhhhh.

BENEATHA: Before — you wanted to be so serious before there was time.

ASAGAI: How much time must there be before one knows what one feels?

BENEATHA *(stalling this particular conversation. Her hands pressed together, in a deliberately childish gesture)*:   What did you bring me?

ASAGAI *(handing her the package)*:   Open it and see.

BENEATHA *(eagerly opening the package and drawing out some records and the colorful robes of a Nigerian woman)*:   Oh Asagai! . . . You got them for me! . . . How beautiful . . . and the records too! *(She lifts out the robes and runs to the mirror with them and holds the drapery up in front of herself.)*

ASAGAI *(coming to her at the mirror)*:   I shall have to teach you how to drape it properly. *(He flings the material about her for the moment and stands back to look at her.)* Ah — Oh-pay-gay-day, oh-gbah-mu-shay. *(A Yoruba exclamation for admiration.)* You wear it well . . . very well . . . mutilated hair and all.

BENEATHA *(turning suddenly)*:   My hair — what's wrong with my hair?

ASAGAI *(shrugging)*:   Were you born with it like that?

BENEATHA *(reaching up to touch it)*:   No . . . of course not.

She looks back to the mirror, disturbed.

ASAGAI *(smiling)*:   How then?

BENEATHA: You know perfectly well how . . . as crinkly as yours . . . that's how.

ASAGAI: And it is ugly to you that way?

BENEATHA *(quickly)*:   Oh, no — not ugly . . . *(More slowly, apologetically.)* But it's so hard to manage when it's, well — raw.

ASAGAI: And so to accommodate that — you mutilate it every week?

BENEATHA: It's not mutilation!

ASAGAI *(laughing aloud at her seriousness)*:   Oh . . . please! I am only teasing you because you are so very serious about these things. *(He stands back from her and folds his arms across his chest as he watches her pulling at her hair and frowning in the mirror.)* Do you remember the first time you met me at school? . . . *(He laughs.)* You came up to me and you said — and I thought you were the most serious little thing I had ever seen — you said: *(He imitates her.)* "Mr. Asagai — I want very much to talk with you. About Africa. You see, Mr. Asagai, I am looking for my *identity*!"

He laughs.

BENEATHA *(turning to him, not laughing):*   Yes —

Her face is quizzical, profoundly disturbed.

ASAGAI *(still teasing and reaching out and taking her face in his hands and turning her profile to him):*   Well . . . it is true that this is not so much a profile of a Hollywood queen as perhaps a queen of the Nile — *(A mock dismissal of the importance of the question.)* But what does it matter? Assimilationism is so popular in your country.

BENEATHA *(wheeling, passionately, sharply):*   I am not an assimilationist!

ASAGAI *(the protest hangs in the room for a moment and Asagai studies her, his laughter fading):*   Such a serious one. *(There is a pause.)* So — you like the robes? You must take excellent care of them — they are from my sister's personal wardrobe.

BENEATHA *(with incredulity):*   You — you sent all the way home — for me?

ASAGAI *(with charm):*   For you — I would do much more . . . Well, that is what I came for. I must go.

BENEATHA: Will you call me Monday?

ASAGAI: Yes . . . We have a great deal to talk about. I mean about identity and time and all that.

BENEATHA: Time?

ASAGAI: Yes. About how much time one needs to know what one feels.

BENEATHA: You see! You never understood that there is more than one kind of feeling which can exist between a man and a woman — or, at least, there should be.

ASAGAI *(shaking his head negatively but gently):*   No. Between a man and a woman there need be only one kind of feeling. I have that for you . . . Now even . . . right this moment . . .

BENEATHA: I know — and by itself — it won't do. I can find that anywhere.

ASAGAI: For a woman it should be enough.

BENEATHA: I know — because that's what it says in all the novels that men write. But it isn't. Go ahead and laugh — but I'm not interested in being someone's little episode in America or — *(With feminine vengeance.)* — one of them! *(Asagai has burst into laughter again.)* That's funny as hell, huh!

ASAGAI: It's just that every American girl I have known has said that to me. White — black — in this you are all the same. And the same speech, too!

BENEATHA *(angrily):*   Yuk, yuk, yuk!

ASAGAI: It's how you can be sure that the world's most liberated women are not liberated at all. You all talk about it too much!

Mama enters and is immediately all social charm because of the presence of a guest.

BENEATHA: Oh — Mama — this is Mr. Asagai.

MAMA: How do you do?

ASAGAI *(total politeness to an elder)*:   How do you do, Mrs. Younger. Please forgive me for coming at such an outrageous hour on a Saturday.

MAMA: Well, you are quite welcome. I just hope you understand that our house don't always look like this. *(Chatterish.)* You must come again. I would love to hear all about — *(Not sure of the name.)* — your country. I think it's so sad the way our American Negroes don't know nothing about Africa 'cept Tarzan and all that. And all that money they pour into these churches when they ought to be helping you people over there drive out them French and Englishmen done taken away your land.

The mother flashes a slightly superior look at her daughter upon completion of the recitation.

ASAGAI *(taken aback by this sudden and acutely unrelated expression of sympathy)*:   Yes . . . yes . . .

MAMA *(smiling at him suddenly and relaxing and looking him over)*:   How many miles is it from here to where you come from?

ASAGAI: Many thousands.

MAMA *(looking at him as she would Walter)*:   I bet you don't half look after yourself, being away from your mama either. I spec you better come 'round here from time to time to get yourself some decent homecooked meals . . .

ASAGAI *(moved)*:   Thank you. Thank you very much. *(They are all quiet, then —)* Well . . . I must go. I will call you Monday, Alaiyo.

MAMA: What's that he call you?

ASAGAI: Oh — "Alaiyo." I hope you don't mind. It is what you would call a nickname, I think. It is a Yoruba word. I am a Yoruba.

MAMA *(looking at Beneatha)*:   I — I thought he was from — *(Uncertain.)*

ASAGAI *(understanding)*:   Nigeria is my country. Yoruba is my tribal origin —

BENEATHA: You didn't tell us what Alaiyo means . . . for all I know, you might be calling me Little Idiot or something . . .

ASAGAI: Well . . . let me see . . . I do not know how just to explain it . . . The sense of a thing can be so different when it changes languages.

BENEATHA: You're evading.

ASAGAI: No — really it is difficult . . . *(Thinking.)* It means . . . it means One for Whom Bread — Food — Is Not Enough. *(He looks at her.)* Is that all right?

BENEATHA *(understanding, softly)*:   Thank you.

MAMA *(looking from one to the other and not understanding any of it)*:   Well . . . that's nice . . . You must come see us again — Mr. —

ASAGAI: Ah-sah-guy . . .

MAMA: Yes . . . Do come again.

ASAGAI: Good-bye.

He exits.

MAMA *(after him)*:   Lord, that's a pretty thing just went out here! *(Insinuatingly, to her daughter.)* Yes, I guess I see why we done commence to get so interested in Africa 'round here. Missionaries my aunt Jenny!

She exits.

BENEATHA: Oh, Mama! . . .

She picks up the Nigerian dress and holds it up to her in front of the mirror again. She sets the headdress on haphazardly and then notices her hair again and clutches at it and then replaces the headdress and frowns at herself. Then she starts to wriggle in front of the mirror as she thinks a Nigerian woman might. Travis enters and stands regarding her.

TRAVIS: What's the matter, girl, you cracking up?

BENEATHA: Shut up.

She pulls the headdress off and looks at herself in the mirror and clutches at her hair again and squinches her eyes as if trying to imagine something. Then, suddenly, she gets her raincoat and kerchief and hurriedly prepares for going out.

MAMA *(coming back into the room)*:   She's resting now. Travis, baby, run next door and ask Miss Johnson to please let me have a little kitchen cleanser. This here can is empty as Jacob's kettle.

TRAVIS: I just came in.

MAMA: Do as you told. *(He exits and she looks at her daughter.)* Where you going?

BENEATHA *(halting at the door)*:   To become a queen of the Nile!

She exits in a breathless blaze of glory. Ruth appears in the bedroom doorway.

MAMA: Who told you to get up?

RUTH: Ain't nothing wrong with me to be lying in no bed for. Where did Bennie go?

MAMA *(drumming her fingers)*:   Far as I could make out — to Egypt. *(Ruth just looks at her.)* What time is it getting to?

RUTH: Ten twenty. And the mailman going to ring that bell this morning just like he done every morning for the last umpteen years.

Travis comes in with the cleanser can.

TRAVIS: She say to tell you that she don't have much.

MAMA *(angrily)*:   Lord, some people I could name sure is tight-fisted! *(Directing her grandson.)* Mark two cans of cleanser on the list there. If she that hard up for kitchen cleanser, I sure don't want to forget to get her none!

RUTH: Lena — maybe the woman is just short on cleanser —

MAMA *(not listening)*:   — Much baking powder as she done borrowed from me all these years, she could of done gone into the baking business!

The bell sounds suddenly and sharply and all three are stunned — serious and silent — midspeech. In spite of all the other conversations and distractions of the morning, this is what they have been waiting for, even Travis, who looks helplessly from his mother to his grandmother. Ruth is the first to come to life again.

RUTH *(to Travis)*:   Get down them steps, boy!

Travis snaps to life and flies out to get the mail.

MAMA *(her eyes wide, her hand to her breast)*:   You mean it done really come?

RUTH *(excited)*:   Oh, Miss Lena!

MAMA *(collecting herself)*:   Well . . . I don't know what we all so excited about 'round here for. We known it was coming for months.

RUTH: That's a whole lot different from having it come and being able to hold it in your hands . . . a piece of paper worth ten thousand dollars . . . *(Travis bursts back into the room. He holds the envelope high above his head, like a little dancer, his face is radiant and he is breathless. He moves to his grandmother with sudden slow ceremony and puts the envelope into her hands. She accepts it, and then merely holds it and looks at it.)* Come on! Open it . . . Lord have mercy, I wish Walter Lee was here!

TRAVIS: Open it, Grandmama!

MAMA *(staring at it)*:   Now you all be quiet. It's just a check.

RUTH: Open it . . .

MAMA *(still staring at it)*:   Now don't act silly . . . We ain't never been no people to act silly 'bout no money —

RUTH *(swiftly)*:   We ain't never had none before — OPEN IT!

Mama finally makes a good strong tear and pulls out the thin blue slice of paper and inspects it closely. The boy and his mother study it raptly over Mama's shoulders.

MAMA: Travis! *(She is counting off with doubt.)* Is that the right number of zeros?

TRAVIS: Yes'm . . . ten thousand dollars. Gaalee, grandmama, you rich.

MAMA *(She holds the check away from her, still looking at it. Slowly her face sobers into a mask of unhappiness)*:   Ten thousand dollars. *(She hands it to Ruth.)* Put it away somewhere, Ruth. *(She does not look at Ruth; her eyes seem to be seeing something somewhere very far off.)* Ten thousand dollars they give you. Ten thousand dollars.

TRAVIS *(to his mother, sincerely)*:   What's the matter with Grandmama — don't she want to be rich?

RUTH *(distractedly)*:   You go on out and play now, baby. *(Travis exits. Mama starts wiping dishes absently, humming intently to herself. Ruth turns to her, with kind exasperation.)* You've gone and got yourself upset.

MAMA *(not looking at her)*:   I spec if it wasn't for you all . . . I would just put that money away or give it to the church or something.

RUTH: Now what kind of talk is that. Mr. Younger would just be plain mad if he could hear you talking foolish like that.

MAMA *(stopping and staring off)*:   Yes . . . he sure would. *(Sighing.)* We got enough to do with that money, all right. *(She halts then, and turns and looks at her daughter-in-law hard; Ruth avoids her eyes and Mama wipes her hands with finality and starts to speak firmly to Ruth.)* Where did you go today, girl?

RUTH: To the doctor.

MAMA *(impatiently)*:   Now, Ruth . . . you know better than that. Old Doctor Jones is strange enough in his way but there ain't nothing 'bout him make somebody slip and call him "she" — like you done this morning.

RUTH: Well, that's what happened — my tongue slipped.

MAMA: You went to see that woman, didn't you?

RUTH *(defensively, giving herself away)*:   What woman you talking about?

MAMA *(angrily)*:   That woman who —

Walter enters in great excitement.

WALTER: Did it come?

MAMA *(quietly)*:   Can't you give people a Christian greeting before you start asking about money?

WALTER *(to Ruth)*:   Did it come? *(Ruth unfolds the check and lays it quietly before him, watching him intently with thoughts of her own. Walter sits down and grasps it close and counts off the zeros.)* Ten thousand dollars — *(He turns suddenly, frantically to his mother and draws some papers out of his breast pocket.)* Mama — look. Old Willy Harris put everything on paper —

MAMA: Son — I think you ought to talk to your wife . . . I'll go on out and leave you alone if you want —

WALTER: I can talk to her later — Mama, look —

MAMA: Son —

WALTER: WILL SOMEBODY PLEASE LISTEN TO ME TODAY!

MAMA *(quietly)*:   I don't 'low no yellin' in this house, Walter Lee, and you know it — *(Walter stares at them in frustration and starts to speak several times.)* And there ain't going to be no investing in no liquor stores.

WALTER: But, Mama, you ain't even looked at it.

MAMA: I don't aim to have to speak on that again.

A long pause.

WALTER: You ain't looked at it and you don't aim to have to speak on that again? You ain't even looked at it and *you* have decided — *(Crumpling his papers.)* Well, *you* tell that to my boy tonight when you put him to sleep on the living-room couch . . . *(Turning to Mama and speaking directly to her.)* Yeah — and tell it to my wife, Mama, tomorrow when she has to go out of here to look after somebody else's kids. And tell it to *me*, Mama, every time we need a new pair of curtains and I have to watch *you* go out and work in somebody's kitchen. Yeah, you tell me then!

Walter starts out.

RUTH: Where you going?

WALTER: I'm going out!

RUTH: Where?

WALTER: Just out of this house somewhere —

RUTH *(getting her coat)*:   I'll come too.

WALTER: I don't want you to come!

RUTH: I got something to talk to you about, Walter.

WALTER: That's too bad.

MAMA *(still quietly)*:   Walter Lee — *(She waits and he finally turns and looks at her.)* Sit down.

WALTER: I'm a grown man, Mama.

MAMA: Ain't nobody said you wasn't grown. But you still in my house and my presence. And as long as you are — you'll talk to your wife civil. Now sit down.

RUTH *(suddenly)*:   Oh, let him go on out and drink himself to death! He makes me sick to my stomach! *(She flings her coat against him and exits to bedroom.)*

WALTER *(violently flinging the coat after her)*:   And you turn mine too, baby! *(The door slams behind her.)* That was my biggest mistake —

MAMA *(still quietly)*:   Walter, what is the matter with you?

WALTER: Matter with me? Ain't nothing the matter with *me*!

MAMA: Yes there is. Something eating you up like a crazy man. Something more than me not giving you this money. The past few years I been watching it happen to you. You get all nervous acting and kind of wild in the eyes — *(Walter jumps up impatiently at her words.)* I said sit there now, I'm talking to you!

WALTER: Mama — I don't need no nagging at me today.

MAMA: Seem like you getting to a place where you always tied up in some kind of knot about something. But if anybody ask you 'bout it you just yell at 'em and bust out the house and go out and drink somewheres. Walter Lee, people can't live with that. Ruth's a good, patient girl in her way — but you getting to be too much. Boy, don't make the mistake of driving that girl away from you.

WALTER: Why — what she do for me?

MAMA: She loves you.

WALTER: Mama — I'm going out. I want to go off somewhere and be by myself for a while.

MAMA: I'm sorry 'bout your liquor store, son. It just wasn't the thing for us to do. That's what I want to tell you about —

WALTER: I got to go out, Mama —

He rises.

MAMA: It's dangerous, son.

WALTER: What's dangerous?

MAMA: When a man goes outside his home to look for peace.

WALTER *(beseechingly)*:   Then why can't there never be no peace in this house then?

MAMA: You done found it in some other house?

WALTER: No — there ain't no woman! Why do women always think there's a woman somewhere when a man gets restless. *(Picks up the check.)* Do you know what this money means to me? Do you know what this money can do for us? *(Puts it back.)* Mama — Mama — I want so many things . . .

MAMA: Yes, son —

WALTER: I want so many things that they are driving me kind of crazy . . . Mama — look at me.

MAMA: I'm looking at you. You a good-looking boy. You got a job, a nice wife, a fine boy, and —

WALTER: A job. *(Looks at her.)* Mama, a job? I open and close car doors all day long. I drive a man around in his limousine and I say, "Yes, sir; no, sir; very good, sir; shall I take the Drive, sir?" Mama, that ain't no kind of job . . . that ain't nothing at all. *(Very quietly.)* Mama, I don't know if I can make you understand.

MAMA: Understand what, baby?

WALTER *(quietly)*:   Sometimes it's like I can see the future stretched out in front of me — just plain as day. The future, Mama. Hanging over there at the edge of my days. Just waiting for me — a big, looming blank space — full of *nothing.* Just waiting for *me.* But it don't have to be. *(Pause. Kneeling beside her chair.)* Mama — sometimes when I'm downtown and I pass them cool, quiet-looking restaurants where them white boys are sitting back and talking 'bout things . . . sitting there turning deals worth millions of dollars . . . sometimes I see guys don't look much older than me —

MAMA: Son — how come you talk so much 'bout money?

WALTER *(with immense passion)*:   Because it is life, Mama!

MAMA *(quietly)*:   Oh — *(Very quietly.)* So now it's life. Money is life. Once upon a time freedom used to be life — now it's money. I guess the world really do change . . .

WALTER: No — it was always money, Mama. We just didn't know about it.

MAMA: No . . . something has changed. *(She looks at him.)* You something new, boy. In my time we was worried about not being lynched and getting to the North if we could and how to stay alive and still have a pinch of dignity too . . . Now here come you and Beneatha — talking 'bout things we ain't never even thought about hardly, me and your daddy. You ain't satisfied or proud of nothing we done. I mean that you had a home; that we kept you out of trouble till you was grown; that you don't have to ride to work on the back of nobody's streetcar — You my children — but how different we done become.

WALTER *(a long beat. He pats her hand and gets up)*:   You just don't understand, Mama, you just don't understand.

MAMA: Son — do you know your wife is expecting another baby? *(Walter stands, stunned, and absorbs what his mother has said.)* That's what she wanted to talk to you about. *(Walter sinks down into a chair.)* This ain't for me to be telling — but you ought to know. *(She waits.)* I think Ruth is thinking 'bout getting rid of that child.

WALTER *(slowly understanding)*:   — No — no — Ruth wouldn't do that.

MAMA: When the world gets ugly enough — a woman will do anything for her family. *The part that's already living.*

WALTER: You don't know Ruth, Mama, if you think she would do that.

Ruth opens the bedroom door and stands there a little limp.

RUTH *(beaten)*:   Yes I would too, Walter. *(Pause.)* I gave her a five-dollar down payment.

There is total silence as the man stares at his wife and the mother stares at her son.

MAMA *(presently)*:   Well — *(Tightly.)* Well — son, I'm waiting to hear you say something . . . *(She waits.)* I'm waiting to hear how you be your father's son. Be the man he was . . . *(Pause. The silence shouts.)* Your wife say she going to destroy your child. And I'm waiting to hear you talk like him and say we a people who give children life, not who destroys them — *(She rises.)* I'm waiting to see you stand up and look like your daddy and say we done give up one baby to poverty and that we ain't going to give up nary another one . . . I'm waiting.

WALTER: Ruth — *(He can say nothing.)*

MAMA: If you a son of mine, tell her! *(Walter picks up his keys and his coat and walks out. She continues, bitterly.)* You . . . you are a disgrace to your father's memory. Somebody get me my hat!

Curtain.

ACT 2, Scene 1

Time: Later the same day.

At rise: Ruth is ironing again. She has the radio going. Presently Beneatha's bedroom door opens and Ruth's mouth falls and she puts down the iron in fascination.

RUTH: What have we got on tonight!

BENEATHA *(emerging grandly from the doorway so that we can see her thoroughly robed in the costume Asagai brought)*:   You are looking at what a well-dressed Nigerian woman wears — *(She parades for Ruth, her hair completely hidden by the headdress; she is coquettishly fanning herself with an ornate oriental fan, mistakenly more like Butterfly than any Nigerian that ever was.)* Isn't it beautiful? *(She promenades to the radio and, with an arrogant flourish, turns off the good loud blues that is playing.)* Enough of this assimilationist junk! *(Ruth follows her with her eyes as she goes to the phonograph and puts on a record and turns and waits ceremoniously for the music to come up. Then, with a shout —)* OCOMOGOSIAY!

Ruth jumps. The music comes up, a lovely Nigerian melody. Beneatha listens, enraptured, her eyes far way — "back to the past." She begins to dance. Ruth is dumfounded.

RUTH: What kind of dance is that?

BENEATHA: A folk dance.

RUTH *(Pearl Bailey)*:   What kind of folks do that, honey?

BENEATHA: It's from Nigeria. It's a dance of welcome.

RUTH: Who you welcoming?

BENEATHA: The men back to the village.

RUTH: Where they been?

BENEATHA: How should I know — out hunting or something. Anyway, they are coming back now . . .

RUTH: Well, that's good.

BENEATHA *(with the record)*:

Alundi, alundi
Alundi alunya
Jop pu a jeepua
Ang gu sooooooooooo
Ai yai yae . . .
Ayehaye —
alundi . . .

Walter comes in during this performance; he has obviously been drinking. He leans against the door heavily and watches his sister, at first with distaste. Then his eyes look off — "back to the past" — as he lifts both his fists to the roof, screaming.

WALTER: YEAH . . . AND ETHIOPIA STRETCH FORTH HER HANDS AGAIN! . . .

RUTH *(drily, looking at him):*   Yes — and Africa sure is claiming her own tonight. *(She gives them both up and starts ironing again.)*

WALTER *(all in a drunken, dramatic shout):*   Shut up! . . . I'm diggin them drums . . . them drums move me! . . . *(He makes his weaving way to his wife's face and leans in close to her.)* In my *heart of hearts* — *(He thumps his chest.)* — I am much warrior!

RUTH *(without even looking up):*   In your heart of hearts you are much drunkard.

WALTER *(coming away from her and starting to wander around the room, shouting):*   Me and Jomo . . . *(Intently, in his sister's face. She has stopped dancing to watch him in this unknown mood.)* That's my man, Kenyatta. *(Shouting and thumping his chest.)* FLAMING SPEAR! HOT DAMN! *(He is suddenly in possession of an imaginary spear and actively spearing enemies all over the room.)* OCOMOGOSIAY . . .

BENEATHA *(to encourage Walter, thoroughly caught up with this side of him):*   OCOMOGOSIAY, FLAMING SPEAR!

WALTER: THE LION IS WAKING . . . OWIMOWEH!

He pulls his shirt open and leaps up on the table and gestures with his spear.

BENEATHA: OWIMOWEH!

WALTER *(on the table, very far gone, his eyes pure glass sheets. He sees what we cannot, that he is a leader of his people, a great chief, a descendant of Chaka, and that the hour to march has come):*   Listen, my black brothers —

BENEATHA: OCOMOGOSIAY!

WALTER: — Do you hear the waters rushing against the shores of the coastlands —

BENEATHA: OCOMOGOSIAY!

WALTER: — Do you hear the screeching of the cocks in yonder hills beyond where the chiefs meet in council for the coming of the mighty war —

BENEATHA: OCOMOGOSIAY!

And now the lighting shifts subtly to suggest the world of Walter's imagination, and the mood shifts from pure comedy. It is the inner Walter speaking: the Southside chauffeur has assumed an unexpected majesty.

WALTER: — Do you hear the beating of the wings of the birds flying low over the mountains and the low places of our land —

BENEATHA: OCOMOGOSIAY!

WALTER: — Do you hear the singing of the women, singing the war songs of our fathers to the babies in the great houses? Singing the sweet war songs! *(The doorbell rings.)* OH, DO YOU HEAR, MY *BLACK* BROTHERS!

BENEATHA *(completely gone):*   We hear you, Flaming Spear —

Ruth shuts off the phonograph and opens the door. George Murchison enters.

WALTER: Telling us to prepare for the GREATNESS OF THE TIME! *(Lights back to normal. He turns and sees George.)* Black Brother!

He extends his hand for the fraternal clasp.

GEORGE: Black Brother, hell!

RUTH *(having had enough, and embarrassed for the family)*:   Beneatha, you got company — what's the matter with you? Walter Lee Younger, get down off that table and stop acting like a fool . . .

Walter comes down off the table suddenly and makes a quick exit to the bathroom.

RUTH: He's had a little to drink . . . I don't know what her excuse is.

GEORGE *(to Beneatha)*:   Look honey, we're going to the theater — we're not going to be *in* it . . . so go change, huh?

Beneatha looks at him and slowly, ceremoniously, lifts her hands and pulls off the headdress. Her hair is close-cropped and unstraightened. George freezes mid-sentence and Ruth's eyes all but fall out of her head.

GEORGE: What in the name of —

RUTH *(touching Beneatha's hair)*:   Girl, you done lost your natural mind? Look at your head!

GEORGE: What have you done to your head — I mean your hair!

BENEATHA: Nothing — except cut it off.

RUTH: Now that's the truth — it's what ain't been done to it! You expect this boy to go out with you with your head all nappy like that?

BENEATHA *(looking at George)*:   That's up to George. If he's ashamed of his heritage —

GEORGE: Oh, don't be so proud of yourself, Bennie — just because you look eccentric.

BENEATHA: How can something that's natural be eccentric?

GEORGE: That's what being eccentric means — being natural. Get dressed.

BENEATHA: I don't like that, George.

RUTH: Why must you and your brother make an argument out of everything people say?

BENEATHA: Because I hate assimilationist Negroes!

RUTH: Will somebody please tell me what assimila-whoever means!

GEORGE: Oh, it's just a college girl's way of calling people Uncle Toms — but that isn't what it means at all.

RUTH: Well, what does it mean?

BENEATHA *(cutting George off and staring at him as she replies to Ruth)*:   It means someone who is willing to give up his own culture and submerge himself completely in the dominant, and in this case *oppressive* culture!

GEORGE: Oh, dear, dear, dear! Here we go! A lecture on the African past! On our Great West African Heritage! In one second we will hear all about the great Ashanti empires; the great Songhay civilizations; and the great sculpture of Bénin — and then some poetry in the Bantu — and the whole monologue will end with the word *heritage*! *(Nastily.)* Let's face it, baby, your heritage is nothing but a bunch of raggedy-assed spirituals and some grass huts!

BENEATHA: GRASS HUTS! *(Ruth crosses to her and forcibly pushes her toward the bedroom.)* See there . . . you are standing there in your splendid ignorance talking about people who were the first to smelt iron on the face of the earth! *(Ruth is pushing her through the door.)* The Ashanti were performing surgical operations when the English — *(Ruth pulls the door to, with Beneatha on the other side, and smiles graciously at George. Beneatha opens the door and shouts the end of the sentence defiantly at George.)* — were still tatooing themselves with blue dragons! *(She goes back inside.)*

RUTH: Have a seat, George. *(They both sit. Ruth folds her hands rather primly on her lap, determined to demonstrate the civilization of the family.)* Warm, ain't it? I mean for September. *(Pause.)* Just like they always say about Chicago weather: if it's too hot or cold for you, just wait a minute and it'll change. *(She smiles happily at this cliché of clichés.)* Everybody say it's got to do with them bombs and things they keep setting off. *(Pause.)* Would you like a nice cold beer?

GEORGE: No, thank you. I don't care for beer. *(He looks at his watch.)* I hope she hurries up.

RUTH: What time is the show?

GEORGE: It's an eight-thirty curtain. That's just Chicago, though. In New York standard curtain time is eight forty.

He is rather proud of this knowledge.

RUTH *(properly appreciating it)*: You get to New York a lot?

GEORGE *(offhand)*: Few times a year.

RUTH: Oh — that's nice. I've never been to New York.

Walter enters. We feel he has relieved himself, but the edge of unreality is still with him.

WALTER: New York ain't got nothing Chicago ain't. Just a bunch of hustling people all squeezed up together — being "Eastern."

He turns his face into a screw of displeasure.

GEORGE: Oh — you've been?

WALTER: Plenty of times.

RUTH *(shocked at the lie)*: Walter Lee Younger!

WALTER *(staring her down)*: Plenty! *(Pause.)* What we got to drink in this house? Why don't you offer this man some refreshment. *(To George.)* They don't know how to entertain people in this house, man.

GEORGE: Thank you — I don't really care for anything.

WALTER *(feeling his head; sobriety coming)*: Where's Mama?

RUTH: She ain't come back yet.

WALTER *(looking Murchison over from head to toe, scrutinizing his carefully casual tweed sports jacket over cashmere V-neck sweater over soft eyelet shirt and tie, and soft slacks, finished off with white buckskin shoes)*: Why all you college boys wear them faggoty-looking white shoes?

RUTH: Walter Lee!

George Murchison ignores the remark.

WALTER *(to Ruth)*:   Well, they look crazy as hell — white shoes, cold as it is.

RUTH *(crushed)*:   You have to excuse him —

WALTER: No he don't! Excuse me for what? What you always excusing me for! I'll excuse myself when I needs to be excused! *(A pause.)* They look as funny as them black knee socks Beneatha wears out of here all the time.

RUTH: It's the college *style*, Walter.

WALTER: Style, hell. She looks like she got burnt legs or something!

RUTH: Oh, Walter —

WALTER *(an irritable mimic)*:   Oh, Walter! Oh, Walter! *(To Murchison.)* How's your old man making out? I understand you all going to buy that big hotel on the Drive? *(He finds a beer in the refrigerator, wanders over to Murchison, sipping and wiping his lips with the back of his hand, and straddling a chair backwards to talk to the other man.)* Shrewd move. Your old man is all right, man. *(Tapping his head and half winking for emphasis.)* I mean he knows how to operate. I mean he thinks *big*, you know what I mean, I mean for a *home*, you know? But I think he's kind of running out of ideas now. I'd like to talk to him. Listen, man, I got some plans that could turn this city upside down. I mean think like he does. *Big*. Invest big, gamble big, hell, lose *big* if you have to, you know what I mean. It's hard to find a man on this whole Southside who understands my kind of thinking — you dig? *(He scrutinizes Murchison again, drinks his beer, squints his eyes, and leans in close, confidential, man to man.)* Me and you ought to sit down and talk sometimes, man. Man, I got me some ideas . . .

MURCHISON *(with boredom)*:   Yeah — sometimes we'll have to do that, Walter.

WALTER *(understanding the indifference, and offended)*:   Yeah — well, when you get the time, man. I know you a busy little boy.

RUTH: Walter, please —

WALTER *(bitterly, hurt)*:   I know ain't nothing in this world as busy as you colored college boys with your fraternity pins and white shoes . . .

RUTH *(covering her face with humiliation)*:   Oh, Walter Lee —

WALTER: I see you all all the time — with the books tucked under your arms — going to your *(British A — a mimic.)* "clahsses." And for what! What the hell you learning over there? Filling up your heads — *(Counting off on his fingers.)* — with the sociology and the psychology — but they teaching you how to be a man? How to take over and run the world? They teaching you how to run a rubber plantation or a steel mill? Naw — just to talk proper and read books and wear them faggoty-looking white shoes . . .

GEORGE *(looking at him with distaste, a little above it all)*:   You're all wacked up with bitterness, man.

WALTER *(intently, almost quietly, between the teeth, glaring at the boy)*:   And you — ain't you bitter, man? Ain't you just about had it yet? Don't you see no stars gleaming that you can't reach out and grab? You happy? — You contented son-of-a-bitch — you happy? You got it made? Bitter? Man, I'm a volcano. Bitter? Here I am a giant — surrounded by ants! Ants who can't even understand what it is the giant is talking about.

RUTH *(passionately and suddenly)*:   Oh, Walter — ain't you with nobody!

WALTER *(violently)*:   No! 'Cause ain't nobody with me! Not even my own mother!

RUTH: Walter, that's a terrible thing to say!

Beneatha enters, dressed for the evening in a cocktail dress and earrings, hair natural.

GEORGE: Well — hey — *(Crosses to Beneatha; thoughtful, with emphasis, since this is a reversal.)* You look great!

WALTER *(seeing his sister's hair for the first time)*:   What's the matter with your head?

BENEATHA *(tired of the jokes now)*:   I cut it off, Brother.

WALTER *(coming close to inspect it and walking around her)*:   Well, I'll be damned. So that's what they mean by the African bush . . .

BENEATHA: Ha ha. Let's go, George.

GEORGE *(looking at her)*:   You know something? I like it. It's sharp. I mean it really is. *(Helps her into her wrap.)*

RUTH: Yes — I think so, too. *(She goes to the mirror and starts to clutch at her hair.)*

WALTER: Oh no! You leave yours alone, baby. You might turn out to have a pin-shaped head or something!

BENEATHA: See you all later.

RUTH: Have a nice time.

GEORGE: Thanks. Good night. *(Half out the door, he reopens it. To Walter.)* Good night, Prometheus!

Beneatha and George exit.

WALTER *(to Ruth)*:   Who is Prometheus?

RUTH: I don't know. Don't worry about it.

WALTER *(in fury, pointing after George)*:   See there — they get to a point where they can't insult you man to man — they got to go talk about something ain't nobody never heard of!

RUTH: How do you know it was an insult? *(To humor him.)* Maybe Prometheus is a nice fellow.

WALTER: Prometheus! I bet there ain't even no such thing! I bet that simple-minded clown —

RUTH: Walter —

She stops what she is doing and looks at him.

WALTER *(yelling)*:   Don't start!

RUTH: Start what?

WALTER: Your nagging! Where was I? Who was I with? How much money did I spend?

RUTH *(plaintively)*:   Walter Lee — why don't we just try to talk about it . . .

WALTER *(not listening)*:   I been out talking with people who understand me. People who care about the things I got on my mind.

RUTH *(wearily)*:   I guess that means people like Willy Harris.

WALTER: Yes, people like Willy Harris.

RUTH *(with a sudden flash of impatience)*:   Why don't you all just hurry up and go into the banking business and stop talking about it!

WALTER: Why? You want to know why? 'Cause we all tied up in a race of people that don't know how to do nothing but moan, pray, and have babies!

The line is too bitter even for him and he looks at her and sits down.

RUTH: Oh, Walter . . . *(Softly.)* Honey, why can't you stop fighting me?

WALTER *(without thinking)*: Who's fighting you? Who even cares about you?

This line begins the retardation of his mood.

RUTH: Well — *(She waits a long time, and then with resignation starts to put away her things.)* I guess I might as well go on to bed . . . *(More or less to herself.)* I don't know where we lost it . . . but we have . . . *(Then, to him.)* I — I'm sorry about this new baby, Walter. I guess maybe I better go on and do what I started . . . I guess I just didn't realize how bad things was with us . . . I guess I just didn't really realize — *(She starts out to the bedroom and stops.)* You want some hot milk?

WALTER: Hot milk?

RUTH: Yes — hot milk.

WALTER: Why hot milk?

RUTH: 'Cause after all that liquor you come home with you ought to have something hot in your stomach.

WALTER: I don't want no milk.

RUTH: You want some coffee then?

WALTER: No, I don't want no coffee. I don't want nothing hot to drink. *(Almost plaintively.)* Why you always trying to give me something to eat?

RUTH *(standing and looking at him helplessly)*: What *else* can I give you, Walter Lee Younger?

She stands and looks at him and presently turns to go out again. He lifts his head and watches her going away from him in a new mood which began to emerge when he asked her "Who cares about you?"

WALTER: It's been rough, ain't it, baby? *(She hears and stops but does not turn around and he continues to her back.)* I guess between two people there ain't never as much understood as folks generally thinks there is. I mean like between me and you — *(She turns to face him.)* How we gets to the place where we scared to talk softness to each other. *(He waits, thinking hard himself.)* Why you think it got to be like that? *(He is thoughtful, almost as a child would be.)* Ruth, what is it gets into people ought to be close?

RUTH: I don't know, honey. I think about it a lot.

WALTER: On account of you and me, you mean? The way things are with us. The way something done come down between us.

RUTH: There ain't so much between us, Walter . . . Not when you come to me and try to talk to me. Try to be with me . . . a little even.

WALTER *(total honesty)*: Sometimes . . . sometimes . . . I don't even know how to try.

RUTH: Walter —

WALTER: Yes?

RUTH *(coming to him, gently and with misgiving, but coming to him)*:   Honey ... life don't have to be like this. I mean sometimes people can do things so that things are better ... You remember how we used to talk when Travis was born ... about the way we were going to live ... the kind of house ... *(She is stroking his head.)* Well, it's all starting to slip away from us ...

He turns her to him and they look at each other and kiss, tenderly and hungrily. The door opens and Mama enters—Walter breaks away and jumps up. A beat.

WALTER: Mama, where have you been?

MAMA: My—them steps is longer than they used to be. Whew! *(She sits down and ignores him.)* How you feeling this evening, Ruth?

Ruth shrugs, disturbed at having been interrupted and watching her husband knowingly.

WALTER: Mama, where have you been all day?

MAMA *(still ignoring him and leaning on the table and changing to more comfortable shoes)*:   Where's Travis?

RUTH: I let him go out earlier and he ain't come back yet. Boy, is he going to get it!

WALTER: Mama!

MAMA *(as if she has heard him for the first time)*:   Yes, son?

WALTER: Where did you go this afternoon?

MAMA: I went downtown to tend to some business that I had to tend to.

WALTER: What kind of business?

MAMA: You know better than to question me like a child, Brother.

WALTER *(rising and bending over the table)*:   Where were you, Mama? *(Bringing his fists down and shouting.)* Mama, you didn't go do something with that insurance money, something crazy?

The front door opens slowly, interrupting him, and Travis peeks his head in, less than hopefully.

TRAVIS *(to his mother)*:   Mama, I—

RUTH: "Mama I" nothing! You're going to get it, boy! Get on in that bedroom and get yourself ready!

TRAVIS: But I—

MAMA: Why don't you all never let the child explain hisself.

RUTH: Keep out of it now, Lena.

Mama clamps her lips together, and Ruth advances toward her son menacingly.

RUTH: A thousand times I have told you not to go off like that—

MAMA *(holding out her arms to her grandson)*:   Well—at least let me tell him something. I want him to be the first one to hear ... Come here, Travis. *(The boy obeys, gladly.)* Travis—*(She takes him by the shoulder and looks into his face.)*—you know that money we got in the mail this morning?

TRAVIS: Yes'm—

MAMA: Well—what you think your grandmama gone and done with that money?

TRAVIS: I don't know, Grandmama.

MAMA *(putting her finger on his nose for emphasis)*:   She went out and she bought you a house! *(The explosion comes from Walter at the end of the revelation and he jumps up and turns away from all of them in a fury. Mama continues, to Travis.)* You glad about the house? It's going to be yours when you get to be a man.

TRAVIS: Yeah — I always wanted to live in a house.

MAMA: All right, gimme some sugar then — *(Travis puts his arms around her neck as she watches her son over the boy's shoulder. Then, to Travis, after the embrace.)* Now when you say your prayers tonight, you thank God and your grandfather — 'cause it was him who give you the house — in his way.

RUTH *(taking the boy from Mama and pushing him toward the bedroom)*:   Now you get out of here and get ready for your beating.

TRAVIS: Aw, Mama —

RUTH: Get on in there — *(Closing the door behind him and turning radiantly to her mother-in-law.)* So you went and did it!

MAMA *(quietly, looking at her son with pain)*:   Yes, I did.

RUTH *(raising both arms classically)*:   PRAISE GOD! *(Looks at Walter a moment, who says nothing. She crosses rapidly to her husband.)* Please, honey — let me be glad . . . you be glad too. *(She has laid her hands on his shoulders, but he shakes himself free of her roughly, without turning to face her.)* Oh, Walter . . . a home . . . a home. *(She comes back to Mama.)* Well — where is it? How big is it? How much it going to cost?

MAMA: Well —

RUTH: When we moving?

MAMA *(smiling at her)*:   First of the month.

RUTH *(throwing back her head with jubilance)*:   Praise God!

MAMA *(tentatively, still looking at her son's back turned against her and Ruth)*:   It's — it's a nice house too . . . *(She cannot help speaking directly to him. An imploring quality in her voice, her manner, makes her almost like a girl now.)* Three bedrooms — nice big one for you and Ruth . . . Me and Beneatha still have to share our room, but Travis have one of his own — and *(With difficulty.)* I figure if the — new baby — is a boy, we could get one of them double-decker outfits . . . And there's a yard with a little patch of dirt where I could maybe get to grow me a few flowers . . . And a nice big basement . . .

RUTH: Walter honey, be glad —

MAMA *(still to his back, fingering things on the table)*:   'Course I don't want to make it sound fancier than it is . . . It's just a plain little old house — but it's made good and solid — and it will be *ours*. Walter Lee — it makes a difference in a man when he can walk on floors that belong to *him* . . .

RUTH: Where is it?

MAMA *(frightened at this telling)*:   Well — well — it's out there in Clybourne Park —

Ruth's radiance fades abruptly, and Walter finally turns slowly to face his mother with incredulity and hostility.

RUTH: Where?

MAMA *(matter-of-factly)*:   Four o six Clybourne Street, Clybourne Park.

RUTH: Clybourne Park? Mama, there ain't no colored people living in Clybourne Park.

MAMA *(almost idiotically)*:   Well, I guess there's going to be some now.

WALTER *(bitterly)*:   So that's the peace and comfort you went out and bought for us today!

MAMA *(raising her eyes to meet his finally)*:   Son — I just tried to find the nicest place for the least amount of money for my family.

RUTH *(trying to recover from the shock)*:   Well — well — 'course I ain't one never been 'fraid of no crackers, mind you — but — well, wasn't there no other houses nowhere?

MAMA: Them houses they put up for colored in them areas way out all seem to cost twice as much as other houses. I did the best I could.

RUTH *(struck senseless with the news, in its various degrees of goodness and trouble, she sits a moment, her fists propping her chin in thought, and then she starts to rise, bringing her fists down with vigor, the radiance spreading from cheek to cheek again)*:   Well — well — All I can say is — if this is my time in life — MY TIME — to say good-bye — (And she builds with momentum as she starts to circle the room with an exuberant, almost tearfully happy release.) — to these Goddamned cracking walls! — (She pounds the walls.) — and these marching roaches! — (She wipes at an imaginary army of marching roaches.) — and this cramped little closet which ain't now or never was no kitchen! . . . then I say it loud and good, HALLELUJAH! AND GOOD-BYE MISERY . . . I DON'T NEVER WANT TO SEE YOUR UGLY FACE AGAIN! (She laughs joyously, having practically destroyed the apartment, and flings her arms up and lets them come down happily, slowly, reflectively, over her abdomen, aware for the first time perhaps that the life therein pulses with happiness and not despair.) Lena?

MAMA *(moved, watching her happiness)*:   Yes, honey?

RUTH *(looking off)*:   Is there — is there a whole lot of sunlight?

MAMA *(understanding)*:   Yes, child, there's a whole lot of sunlight.

Long pause.

RUTH *(collecting herself and going to the door of the room Travis is in)*:   Well — I guess I better see 'bout Travis. (To Mama.) Lord, I sure don't feel like whipping nobody today!

She exits.

MAMA *(the mother and son are left alone now and the mother waits a long time, considering deeply, before she speaks)*:   Son — you — you understand what I done, don't you? (Walter is silent and sullen.) I — I just seen my family falling apart today . . . just falling to pieces in front of my eyes . . . We couldn't of gone on like we was today. We was going backwards 'stead of for-

wards — talking 'bout killing babies and wishing each other was dead . . .
When it gets like that in life — you just got to do something different, push
on out and do something bigger . . . *(She waits.)* I wish you say something,
son . . . I wish you'd say how deep inside you you think I done the right
thing —

WALTER *(crossing slowly to his bedroom door and finally turning there and speaking
measuredly)*:   What you need me to say you done right for? You the head
of this family. You run our lives like you want to. It was your money and
you did what you wanted with it. So what you need for me to say it was all
right for? *(Bitterly, to hurt her as deeply as he knows is possible.)* So you
butchered up a dream of mine — you — who always talking 'bout your
children's dreams . . .

MAMA: Walter Lee —

He just closes the door behind him. Mama sits alone, thinking heavily.

Curtain.

Scene 2

Time: Friday night, a few weeks later.

*At rise: Packing crates mark the intention of the family to move. Beneatha and
George come in, presumably from an evening out again.*

GEORGE: O.K. . . . O.K., whatever you say . . . *(They both sit on the couch. He tries
to kiss her. She moves away.)* Look, we've had a nice evening; let's not spoil
it, huh? . . .

*He again turns her head and tries to nuzzle in and she turns away from him, not with
distaste but with momentary lack of interest; in a mood to pursue what they were
talking about.*

BENEATHA: I'm *trying* to talk to you.

GEORGE: We always talk.

BENEATHA: Yes — and I love to talk.

GEORGE *(exasperated; rising)*:   I know it and I don't mind it sometimes . . . I want
you to cut it out, see — The moody stuff, I mean. I don't like it. You're a
nice-looking girl . . . all over. That's all you need, honey, forget the atmosphere. Guys aren't going to go for the atmosphere — they're going to go
for what they see. Be glad for that. Drop the Garbo routine. It doesn't go
with you. As for myself, I want a nice — *(Groping.)* — simple *(Thoughtfully.)* — sophisticated girl . . . not a poet — O.K.?

He starts to kiss her, she rebuffs him again and he jumps up.

BENEATHA: Why are you angry, George?

GEORGE: Because this is stupid! I don't go out with you to discuss the nature of
"quiet desperation" or to hear all about your thoughts — because the
world will go on thinking what it thinks regardless —

BENEATHA: Then why read books? Why go to school?

GEORGE *(with artificial patience, counting on his fingers)*:   It's simple. You read books — to learn facts — to get grades — to pass the course — to get a degree. That's all — it has nothing to do with thoughts.

A long pause.

BENEATHA: I see. *(He starts to sit.)* Good night, George.

George looks at her a little oddly, and starts to exit. He meets Mama coming in.

GEORGE: Oh — hello, Mrs. Younger.

MAMA: Hello, George, how you feeling?

GEORGE: Fine — fine, how are you?

MAMA: Oh, a little tired. You know them steps can get you after a day's work. You all have a nice time tonight?

GEORGE: Yes — a fine time. A fine time.

MAMA: Well, good night.

GEORGE: Good night. *(He exits. Mama closes the door behind her.)* Hello, honey. What you sitting like that for?

BENEATHA: I'm just sitting.

MAMA: Didn't you have a nice time?

BENEATHA: No.

MAMA: No? What's the matter?

BENEATHA: Mama, George is a fool — honest. *(She rises.)*

MAMA *(hustling around unloading the packages she has entered with. She stops)*:   Is he, baby?

BENEATHA: Yes.

Beneatha makes up Travis's bed as she talks.

MAMA: You sure?

BENEATHA: Yes.

MAMA: Well — I guess you better not waste your time with no fools.

Beneatha looks up at her mother, watching her put groceries in the refrigerator. Finally she gathers up her things and starts into the bedroom. At the door she stops and looks back at her mother.

BENEATHA: Mama —

MAMA: Yes, baby —

BENEATHA: Thank you.

MAMA: For what?

BENEATHA: For understanding me this time.

She exits quickly and the mother stands, smiling a little, looking at the place where Beneatha just stood. Ruth enters.

RUTH: Now don't you fool with any of this stuff, Lena —

MAMA: Oh, I just thought I'd sort a few things out. Is Brother here?

RUTH: Yes.

MAMA *(with concern)*:   Is he —

RUTH *(reading her eyes)*:   Yes.

Mama is silent and someone knocks on the door. Mama and Ruth exchange weary and knowing glances and Ruth opens it to admit the neighbor, Mrs. Johnson,° who is a rather squeaky wide-eyed lady of no particular age, with a newspaper under her arm.

MAMA *(changing her expression to acute delight and a ringing cheerful greeting)*:   Oh — hello there, Johnson.

JOHNSON *(this is a woman who decided long ago to be enthusiastic about EVERYTHING in life and she is inclined to wave her wrist vigorously at the height of her exclamatory comments)*:   Hello there, yourself! H'you this evening, Ruth?

RUTH *(not much of a deceptive type)*:   Fine, Mis' Johnson, h'you?

JOHNSON: Fine. *(Reaching out quickly, playfully, and patting Ruth's stomach.)* Ain't you starting to poke out none yet! *(She mugs with delight at the over familiar remark and her eyes dart around looking at the crates and packing preparation; Mama's face is a cold sheet of endurance.)* Oh, ain't we getting ready round here, though! Yessir! Lookathere! I'm telling you the Youngers is really getting ready to "move on up a little higher!" — Bless God!

MAMA *(a little drily, doubting the total sincerity of the Blesser)*:   Bless God.

JOHNSON: He's good, ain't He?

MAMA: Oh yes, He's good.

JOHNSON: I mean sometimes He works in mysterious ways . . . but He works, don't He!

MAMA *(the same)*:   Yes, he does.

JOHNSON: I'm just soooooo happy for y'all. And this here child — *(About Ruth.)* looks like she could just pop open with happiness, don't she. Where's all the rest of the family?

MAMA: Bennie's gone to bed —

JOHNSON: Ain't no . . . *(The implication is pregnancy.)* sickness done hit you — I hope . . . ?

MAMA: No — she just tired. She was out this evening.

JOHNSON *(all is a coo, an emphatic coo)*:   Aw — ain't that lovely. She still going out with the little Murchison boy?

MAMA *(drily)*:   Ummmm huh.

JOHNSON: That's lovely. You sure got lovely children, Younger. Me and Isaiah talks all the time 'bout what fine children you was blessed with. We sure do.

MAMA: Ruth, give Mis' Johnson a piece of sweet potato pie and some milk.

JOHNSON: Oh honey, I can't stay hardly a minute — I just dropped in to see if there was anything I could do. *(Accepting the food easily.)* I guess y'all seen the news what's all over the colored paper this week . . .

MAMA: No — didn't get mine yet this week.

JOHNSON *(lifting her head and blinking with the spirit of catastrophe)*:   You mean you ain't read 'bout them colored people that was bombed out their place out there?

Mrs. Johnson: This character and the scene of her visit were cut from the original production and early editions of the play.

Ruth straightens with concern and takes the paper and reads it. Johnson notices her and feeds commentary.

JOHNSON: Ain't it something how bad these here white folks is getting here in Chicago! Lord, getting so you think you right down in Mississippi! *(With a tremendous and rather insincere sense of melodrama.)* 'Course I thinks it's wonderful how our folk keeps on pushing out. You hear some of these Negroes round here talking 'bout how they don't go where they ain't wanted and all that—but not me, honey! *(This is a lie.)* Wilhemenia Othella Johnson goes anywhere, any time she feels like it! *(With head movement for emphasis.)* Yes I do! Why if we left it up to these here crackers, the poor niggers wouldn't have nothing — *(She clasps her hand over her mouth.)* Oh, I always forgets you don't 'low that word in your house.

MAMA *(quietly, looking at her)*:   No—I don't 'low it.

JOHNSON *(vigorously again)*:   Me neither! I was just telling Isaiah yesterday when he come using it in front of me—I said, "Isaiah, it's just like Mis' Younger says all the time —"

MAMA: Don't you want some more pie?

JOHNSON: No—no thank you; this was lovely. I got to get on over home and have my midnight coffee. I hear some people say it don't let them sleep but I finds I can't close my eyes right lessen I done had that laaaast cup of coffee . . . *(She waits. A beat. Undaunted.)* My Goodnight coffee, I calls it!

MAMA *(with much eye-rolling and communication between herself and Ruth)*:   Ruth, why don't you give Mis' Johnson some coffee.

Ruth gives Mama an unpleasant look for her kindness.

JOHNSON *(accepting the coffee)*:   Where's Brother tonight?

MAMA: He's lying down.

JOHNSON: Mmmmmmm, he sure gets his beauty rest, don't he? Good-looking man. Sure is a good-looking man! *(Reaching out to pat Ruth's stomach again.)* I guess that's how come we keep on having babies around here. *(She winks at Mama.)* One thing 'bout Brother, he always know how to have a *good* time. And soooooo ambitious! I bet it was his idea y'all moving out to Clybourne Park. Lord—I bet this time next month y'all's names will have been in the papers plenty— *(Holding up her hands to mark off each word of the headline she can see in front of her.)* "NEGROES INVADE CLYBOURNE PARK—BOMBED!"

MAMA *(she and Ruth look at the woman in amazement)*:   We ain't exactly moving out there to get bombed.

JOHNSON: Oh honey—you know I'm praying to God every day that don't nothing like that happen! But you have to think of life like it is—and these here Chicago peckerwoods is some baaaad peckerwoods.

MAMA *(wearily)*:   We done thought about all that Mis' Johnson.

Beneatha comes out of the bedroom in her robe and passes through to the bathroom. Mrs. Johnson turns.

JOHNSON: Hello there, Bennie!

BENEATHA *(crisply)*:   Hello, Mrs. Johnson.

JOHNSON: How is school?

BENEATHA *(crisply)*:   Fine, thank you. *(She goes out.)*

JOHNSON *(insulted)*:   Getting so she don't have much to say to nobody.

MAMA: The child was on her way to the bathroom.

JOHNSON: I know — but sometimes she act like ain't got time to pass the time of day with nobody ain't been to college. Oh — I ain't criticizing her none. It's just — you know how some of our young people gets when they get a little education. *(Mama and Ruth say nothing, just look at her.)* Yes — well. Well, I guess I better get on home. *(Unmoving.)* 'Course I can understand how she must be proud and everything — being the only one in the family to make something of herself. I know just being a chauffeur ain't never satisfied Brother none. He shouldn't feel like that, though. Ain't nothing wrong with being a chauffeur.

MAMA: There's plenty wrong with it.

JOHNSON: What?

MAMA: Plenty. My husband always said being any kind of a servant wasn't a fit thing for a man to have to be. He always said a man's hands was made to make things, or to turn the earth with — not to drive nobody's car for 'em — or — *(She looks at her own hands.)* carry they slop jars. And my boy is just like him — he wasn't meant to wait on nobody.

JOHNSON *(rising, somewhat offended)*:   Mmmmmmmmmm. The Youngers is too much for me! *(She looks around.)* You sure one proud-acting bunch of colored folks. Well — I always thinks like Booker T. Washington said that time — "Education has spoiled many a good plow hand" —

MAMA: Is that what old Booker T. said?

JOHNSON: He sure did.

MAMA: Well, it sounds just like him. The fool.

JOHNSON *(indignantly)*:   Well — he was one of our great men.

MAMA: Who said so?

JOHNSON *(nonplussed)*:   You know, me and you ain't never agreed about some things, Lena Younger. I guess I better be going —

RUTH *(quickly)*:   Good night.

JOHNSON: Good night. Oh — *(Thrusting it at her.)* You can keep the paper! *(With a trill.)* 'Night.

MAMA: Good night, Mis' Johnson.

Mrs. Johnson exits.

RUTH: If ignorance was gold . . .

MAMA: Shush. Don't talk about folks behind their backs.

RUTH: You do.

MAMA: I'm old and corrupted. *(Beneatha enters.)* You was rude to Mis' Johnson, Beneatha, and I don't like it at all.

BENEATHA *(at her door)*:   Mama, if there are two things we, as a people, have got to overcome, one is the Klu Klux Klan — and the other is Mrs. Johnson. *(She exits.)*

MAMA: Smart aleck.

The phone rings.

RUTH: I'll get it.

MAMA: Lord, ain't this a popular place tonight.

RUTH *(at the phone):* Hello — Just a minute. *(Goes to door.)* Walter, it's Mrs. Arnold. *(Waits. Goes back to the phone. Tense.)* Hello. Yes, this is his wife speaking . . . He's lying down now. Yes . . . well, he'll be in tomorrow. He's been very sick. Yes — I know we should have called, but we were so sure he'd be able to come in today. Yes — yes, I'm very sorry. Yes . . . Thank you very much. *(She hangs up. Walter is standing in the doorway of the bedroom behind her.)* That was Mrs. Arnold.

WALTER *(indifferently):* Was it?

RUTH: She said if you don't come in tomorrow that they are getting a new man . . .

WALTER: Ain't that sad — ain't that crying sad.

RUTH: She said Mr. Arnold has had to take a cab for three days . . . Walter, you ain't been to work for three days! *(This is a revelation to her.)* Where you been, Walter Lee Younger? *(Walter looks at her and starts to laugh.)* You're going to lose your job.

WALTER: That's right . . . *(He turns on the radio.)*

RUTH: Oh, Walter, and with your mother working like a dog every day —

A steamy, deep blues pours into the room.

WALTER: That's sad too — Everything is sad.

MAMA: What you been doing for these three days, son?

WALTER: Mama — you don't know all the things a man what got leisure can find to do in this city . . . What's this — Friday night? Well — Wednesday I borrowed Willy Harris's car and I went for a drive . . . just me and myself and I drove and drove . . . Way out . . . way past South Chicago, and I parked the car and I sat and looked at the steel mills all day long. I just sat in the car and looked at them big black chimneys for hours. Then I drove back and I went to the Green Hat. *(Pause.)* And Thursday — Thursday I borrowed the car again and I got in it and I pointed it the other way and I drove the other way — for hours — way, way up to Wisconsin, and I looked at the farms. I just drove and looked at the farms. Then I drove back and I went to the Green Hat. *(Pause.)* And today — today I didn't get the car. Today I just walked. All over the Southside. And I looked at the Negroes and they looked at me and finally I just sat down on the curb at Thirty-ninth and South Parkway and I just sat there and watched the Negroes go by. And then I went to the Green Hat. You all sad? You all depressed? And you know where I am going right now —

Ruth goes out quietly.

MAMA: Oh, Big Walter, is this the harvest of our days?

WALTER: You know what I like about the Green Hat? I like this little cat they got there who blows a sax . . . He blows. He talks to me. He ain't but 'bout five feet tall and he's got a conked head and his eyes is always closed and he's all music —

MAMA *(rising and getting some papers out of her handbag)*:   Walter —

WALTER: And there's this other guy who plays the piano . . . and they got a sound. I mean they can work on some music . . . They got the best little combo in the world in the Green Hat . . . You can just sit there and drink and listen to them three men play and you realize that don't nothing matter worth a damn, but just being there —

MAMA: I've helped do it to you, haven't I, son? Walter, I been wrong.

WALTER: Naw — you ain't never been wrong about nothing, Mama.

MAMA: Listen to me, now. I say I been wrong, son. That I been doing to you what the rest of the world been doing to you. *(She turns off the radio.)* Walter — *(She stops and he looks up slowly at her and she meets his eyes pleadingly.)* What you ain't never understood is that I ain't got nothing, don't own nothing, ain't never really wanted nothing that wasn't for you. There ain't nothing as precious to me . . . There ain't nothing worth holding on to, money, dreams, nothing else — if it means — if it means it's going to destroy my boy. *(She takes an envelope out of her handbag and puts it in front of him and he watches her without speaking or moving.)* I paid the man thirty-five hundred dollars down on the house. That leaves sixty-five hundred dollars. Monday morning I want you to take this money and take three thousand dollars and put it in a savings account for Beneatha's medical schooling. The rest you put in a checking account — with your name on it. And from now on any penny that come out of it or that go in it is for you to look after. For you to decide. *(She drops her hands a little helplessly.)* It ain't much, but it's all I got in the world and I'm putting it in your hands. I'm telling you to be the head of this family from now on like you supposed to be.

WALTER *(stares at the money)*:   You trust me like that, Mama?

MAMA: I ain't never stop trusting you. Like I ain't never stop loving you.

She goes out, and Walter sits looking at the money on the table. Finally, in a decisive gesture, he gets up, and, in mingled joy and desperation, picks up the money. At the same moment, Travis enters for bed.

TRAVIS: What's the matter, Daddy? You drunk?

WALTER *(sweetly, more sweetly than we have ever known him)*:   No, Daddy ain't drunk. Daddy ain't going to never be drunk again . . .

TRAVIS: Well, good night, Daddy.

The father has come from behind the couch and leans over, embracing his son.

WALTER: Son, I feel like talking to you tonight.

TRAVIS: About what?

WALTER: Oh, about a lot of things. About you and what kind of man you going to be when you grow up . . . Son — son, what do you want to be when you grow up?

TRAVIS: A bus driver.

WALTER *(laughing a little)*:   A what? Man, that ain't nothing to want to be!

TRAVIS: Why not?

WALTER: 'Cause, man — it ain't big enough — you know what I mean.

TRAVIS: I don't know then. I can't make up my mind. Sometimes Mama asks
me that too. And sometimes when I tell her I just want to be like you — she
says she don't want me to be like that and sometimes she says she does. . . .

WALTER *(gathering him up in his arms)*:   You know what, Travis? In seven years
you going to be seventeen years old. And things is going to be very different
with us in seven years, Travis. . . . One day when you are seventeen I'll
come home — home from my office downtown somewhere —

TRAVIS: You don't work in no office, Daddy.

WALTER: No — but after tonight. After what your daddy gonna do tonight,
there's going to be offices — a whole lot of offices. . . .

TRAVIS: What you gonna do tonight, Daddy?

WALTER: You wouldn't understand yet, son, but your daddy's gonna make a
transaction . . . a business transaction that's going to change our
lives. . . . That's how come one day when you 'bout seventeen years old I'll
come home and I'll be pretty tired, you know what I mean, after a day of
conferences and secretaries getting things wrong the way they do . . . 'cause
an executive's life is hell, man — *(The more he talks the farther away he gets.)*
And I'll pull the car up on the driveway . . . just a plain black Chrysler, I
think, with white walls — no — black tires. More elegant. Rich people
don't have to be flashy . . . though I'll have to get something a little sportier
for Ruth — maybe a Cadillac convertible to do her shopping in. . . . And I'll
come up the steps to the house and the gardener will be clipping away at
the hedges and he'll say, "Good evening, Mr. Younger." And I'll say, "Hello,
Jefferson, how are you this evening?" And I'll go inside and Ruth will come
downstairs and meet me at the door and we'll kiss each other and she'll
take my arm and we'll go up to your room to see you sitting on the floor
with the catalogues of all the great schools in America around you. . . . All
the great schools in the world! And — and I'll say, all right son — it's your
seventeenth birthday, what is it you've decided? . . . Just tell me where you
want to go to school and you'll *go*. Just tell me, what it is you want to
be — and you'll *be* it. . . . Whatever you want to be — Yessir! *(He holds his
arms open for Travis.)* You just name it, son . . . *(Travis leaps into them.)* and
I hand you the world!

*Walter's voice has risen in pitch and hysterical promise and on the last line he lifts
Travis high.*

Blackout.

Scene 3

Time: Saturday, moving day, one week later.

   *Before the curtain rises, Ruth's voice, a strident, dramatic church alto, cuts
through the silence.*

   *It is, in the darkness, a triumphant surge, a penetrating statement of expecta-
tion: "Oh, Lord, I don't feel no ways tired! Children, oh, glory hallelujah!"*

As the curtain rises we see that Ruth is alone in the living room, finishing up the family's packing. It is moving day. She is nailing crates and tying cartons. Beneatha enters, carrying a guitar case, and watches her exuberant sister-in-law.

RUTH: Hey!

BENEATHA *(putting away the case)*:   Hi.

RUTH *(pointing at a package)*:   Honey — look in that package there and see what I found on sale this morning at the South Center. *(Ruth gets up and moves to the package and draws out some curtains.)* Lookahere — hand-turned hems!

BENEATHA: How do you know the window size out there?

RUTH *(who hadn't thought of that)*:   Oh — Well, they bound to fit something in the whole house. Anyhow, they was too good a bargain to pass up. *(Ruth slaps her head, suddenly remembering something.)* Oh, Bennie — I meant to put a special note on that carton over there. That's your mama's good china and she wants 'em to be very careful with it.

BENEATHA: I'll do it.

Beneatha finds a piece of paper and starts to draw large letters on it.

RUTH: You know what I'm going to do soon as I get in that new house?

BENEATHA: What?

RUTH: Honey — I'm going to run me a tub of water up to here . . . *(With her fingers practically up to her nostrils.)* And I'm going to get in it — and I am going to sit . . . and sit . . . and sit in that hot water and the first person who knocks to tell *me* to hurry up and come out —

BENEATHA: Gets shot at sunrise.

RUTH *(laughing happily)*:   You said it, sister! *(Noticing how large Beneatha is absent-mindedly making the note)*:   Honey, they ain't going to read that from no airplane.

BENEATHA *(laughing herself)*:   I guess I always think things have more emphasis if they are big, somehow.

RUTH *(looking up at her and smiling)*:   You and your brother seem to have that as a philosophy of life. Lord, that man — done changed so 'round here. You know — you know what we did last night? Me and Walter Lee?

BENEATHA: What?

RUTH *(smiling to herself)*:   We went to the movies. *(Looking at Beneatha to see if she understands.)* We went to the movies. You know the last time me and Walter went to the movies together?

BENEATHA: No.

RUTH: Me neither. That's how long it been. *(Smiling again.)* But we went last night. The picture wasn't much good, but that didn't seem to matter. We went — and we held hands.

BENEATHA: Oh, Lord!

RUTH: We held hands — and you know what?

BENEATHA: What?

RUTH: When we come out of the show it was late and dark and all the stores and things was closed up . . . and it was kind of chilly and there wasn't many people on the streets . . . and we was still holding hands, me and Walter.

BENEATHA: You're killing me.

Walter enters with a large package. His happiness is deep in him; he cannot keep still with his newfound exuberance. He is singing and wiggling and snapping his fingers. He puts his package in a corner and puts a phonograph record, which he has brought in with him, on the record player. As the music, soulful and sensuous, comes up he dances over to Ruth and tries to get her to dance with him. She gives in at last to his raunchiness and in a fit of giggling allows herself to be drawn into his mood. They dip and she melts into his arms in a classic, body-melting "slow drag."

BENEATHA *(regarding them a long time as they dance, then drawing in her breath for a deeply exaggerated comment which she does not particularly mean)*:   Talk about — olddddddddddd-fashioneddddddddd — Negroes!

WALTER *(stopping momentarily)*:   What kind of Negroes?

He says this in fun. He is not angry with her today, nor with anyone. He starts to dance with his wife again.

BENEATHA: Old-fashioned.

WALTER *(as he dances with Ruth)*:   You know, when these *New Negroes* have their convention — *(Pointing at his sister.)* — that is going to be the chairman of the Committee on Unending Agitation. *(He goes on dancing, then stops.)* Race, race, race! . . . Girl, I do believe you are the first person in the history of the entire human race to successfully brainwash yourself. *(Beneatha breaks up and he goes on dancing. He stops again, enjoying his tease.)* Damn, even the N double A C P takes a holiday sometimes! *(Beneatha and Ruth laugh. He dances with Ruth some more and starts to laugh and stops and pantomimes someone over an operating table.)* I can just see that chick someday looking down at some poor cat on an operating table and before she starts to slice him, she says . . . *(Pulling his sleeves back maliciously.)* "By the way, what are your views on civil rights down there? . . ."*

He laughs at her again and starts to dance happily. The bell sounds.

BENEATHA: Sticks and stones may break my bones but . . . words will never hurt me!

Beneatha goes to the door and opens it as Walter and Ruth go on with the clowning. Beneatha is somewhat surprised to see a quiet-looking middle-aged white man in a business suit holding his hat and a briefcase in his hand and consulting a small piece of paper.

MAN: Uh — how do you do, miss. I am looking for a Mrs. — *(He looks at the slip of paper.)* Mrs. Lena Younger? *(He stops short, struck dumb at the sight of the oblivious Walter and Ruth.)*

BENEATHA *(smoothing her hair with slight embarrassment)*:   Oh — yes, that's my mother. Excuse me. *(She closes the door and turns to quiet the other two.)* Ruth! Brother! *(Enunciating precisely but soundlessly: "There's a white man at the door!" They stop dancing, Ruth cuts off the phonograph, Beneatha opens the door. The man casts a curious quick glance at all of them.)* Uh — come in please.

MAN *(coming in)*:   Thank you.

BENEATHA: My mother isn't here just now. Is it business?

MAN: Yes . . . well, of a sort.

WALTER *(freely, the Man of the House)*:   Have a seat. I'm Mrs. Younger's son. I look after most of her business matters.

Ruth and Beneatha exchange amused glances.

MAN *(regarding Walter, and sitting)*:   Well — My name is Karl Lindner . . .

WALTER *(stretching out his hand)*:   Walter Younger. This is my wife — *(Ruth nods politely.)* — and my sister.

LINDNER: How do you do.

WALTER *(amiably, as he sits himself easily on a chair, leaning forward on his knees with interest and looking expectantly into the newcomer's face)*:   What can we do for you, Mr. Lindner!

LINDNER *(some minor shuffling of the hat and briefcase on his knees)*:   Well — I am a representative of the Clybourne Park Improvement Association —

WALTER *(pointing)*:   Why don't you sit your things on the floor?

LINDNER: Oh — yes. Thank you. *(He slides the briefcase and hat under the chair.)* And as I was saying — I am from the Clybourne Park Improvement Association and we have had it brought to our attention at the last meeting that you people — or at least your mother — has bought a piece of residential property at — *(He digs for the slip of paper again.)* — four o six Clybourne Street . . .

WALTER: That's right. Care for something to drink? Ruth, get Mr. Lindner a beer.

LINDNER *(upset for some reason)*:   Oh — no, really. I mean thank you very much, but no thank you.

RUTH *(innocently)*:   Some coffee?

LINDNER: Thank you, nothing at all.

Beneatha is watching the man carefully.

LINDNER: Well, I don't know how much you folks know about our organization. *(He is a gentle man; thoughtful and somewhat labored in his manner.)* It is one of these community organizations set up to look after — oh, you know, things like block upkeep and special projects and we also have what we call our New Neighbors Orientation Committee . . .

BENEATHA *(drily)*:   Yes — and what do they do?

LINDNER *(turning a little to her and then returning the main force to Walter)*:   Well — it's what you might call a sort of welcoming committee, I guess. I mean they, we — I'm the chairman of the committee — go around and see the new people who move into the neighborhood and sort of give them the low-down on the way we do things out in Clybourne Park.

BENEATHA *(with appreciation of the two meanings, which escape Ruth and Walter)*:   Un-huh.

LINDNER: And we also have the category of what the association calls — *(He looks elsewhere.)* — uh — special community problems . . .

BENEATHA: Yes — and what are some of those?

WALTER: Girl, let the man talk.

LINDNER *(with understated relief)*:   Thank you. I would sort of like to explain this thing in my own way. I mean I want to explain to you in a certain way.

WALTER: Go ahead.

LINDNER: Yes. Well. I'm going to try to get right to the point. I'm sure we'll all appreciate that in the long run.

BENEATHA: Yes.

WALTER: Be still now!

LINDNER: Well —

RUTH *(still innocently)*:   Would you like another chair — you don't look comfortable.

LINDNER *(more frustrated than annoyed)*:   No, thank you very much. Please. Well — to get right to the point, I — *(A great breath, and he is off at last.)* I am sure you people must be aware of some of the incidents which have happened in various parts of the city when colored people have moved into certain areas — *(Beneatha exhales heavily and starts tossing a piece of fruit up and down in the air.)* Well — because we have what I think is going to be a unique type of organization in American community life — not only do we deplore that kind of thing — but we are trying to do something about it. *(Beneatha stops tossing and turns with a new and quizzical interest to the man.)* We feel — *(gaining confidence in his mission because of the interest in the faces of the people he is talking to.)* — we feel that most of the trouble in this world, when you come right down to it — *(He hits his knee for emphasis.)* — most of the trouble exists because people just don't sit down and talk to each other.

RUTH *(nodding as she might in church, pleased with the remark)*:   You can say that again, mister.

LINDNER *(more encouraged by such affirmation)*:   That we don't try hard enough in this world to understand the other fellow's problem. The other guy's point of view.

RUTH: Now that's right.

Beneatha and Walter merely watch and listen with genuine interest.

LINDNER: Yes — that's the way we feel out in Clybourne Park. And that's why I was elected to come here this afternoon and talk to you people. Friendly like, you know, the way people should talk to each other and see if we couldn't find some way to work this thing out. As I say, the whole business is a matter of *caring* about the other fellow. Anybody can see that you are a nice family of folks, hard working and honest I'm sure. *(Beneatha frowns slightly, quizzically, her head tilted regarding him.)* Today everybody knows what it means to be on the outside of *something.* And of course, there is always somebody who is out to take advantage of people who don't always understand.

WALTER: What do you mean?

LINDNER: Well — you see our community is made up of people who've worked hard as the dickens for years to build up that little community. They're not rich and fancy people; just hard-working, honest people who don't really have much but those little homes and a dream of the kind of community they want to raise their children in. Now, I don't say we are perfect and there is a lot wrong in some of the things they want. But you've got to admit that a man, right or wrong, has the right to want to have the neighborhood he lives in a certain kind of way. And at the moment the overwhelming majority of our people out there feel that people get along better, take more of a common interest in the life of the community, when they share a common background. I want you to believe me when I tell you that race prejudice simply doesn't enter into it. It is a matter of the people of Clybourne Park believing, rightly or wrongly, as I say, that for the happiness of all concerned that our Negro families are happier when they live in their *own* communities.

BENEATHA *(with a grand and bitter gesture)*:   This, friends, is the Welcoming Committee!

WALTER *(dumfounded, looking at Lindner)*:   Is this what you came marching all the way over here to tell us?

LINDNER: Well, now we've been having a fine conversation. I hope you'll hear me all the way through.

WALTER *(tightly)*:   Go ahead, man.

LINDNER: You see — in the face of all the things I have said, we are prepared to make your family a very generous offer . . .

BENEATHA: Thirty pieces and not a coin less!

WALTER: Yeah?

LINDNER *(putting on his glasses drawing a form out of the briefcase)*:   Our association is prepared, through the collective effort of our people, to buy the house from you at a financial gain to your family.

RUTH: Lord have mercy, ain't this the living gall!

WALTER: All right, you through?

LINDNER: Well, I want to give you the exact terms of the financial arrangement —

WALTER: We don't want to hear no exact terms of no arrangements. I want to know if you got any more to tell us 'bout getting together?

LINDNER *(taking off his glasses)*:   Well — I don't suppose that you feel . . .

WALTER: Never mind how I feel — you got any more to say 'bout how people ought to sit down and talk to each other? . . . Get out of my house, man.

He turns his back and walks to the door.

LINDNER *(looking around at the hostile faces and reaching and assembling his hat and briefcase)*:   Well — I don't understand why you people are reacting this way. What do you think you are going to gain by moving into a neighborhood where you just aren't wanted and where some elements — well — people can get awful worked up when they feel that their whole way of life and everything they've ever worked for is threatened.

WALTER: Get out.

LINDNER *(at the door, holding a small card)*:   Well — I'm sorry it went like this.

WALTER: Get out.

LINDNER *(almost sadly regarding Walter)*:   You just can't force people to change their hearts, son.

He turns and puts his card on a table and exits. Walter pushes the door to with stinging hatred, and stands looking at it. Ruth just sits and Beneatha just stands. They say nothing. Mama and Travis enter.

MAMA: Well—this all the packing got done since I left out of here this morning. I testify before God that my children got all the energy of the *dead!* What time the moving men due?

BENEATHA: Four o'clock. You had a caller, Mama.

She is smiling, teasingly.

MAMA: Sure enough—who?

BENEATHA *(her arms folded saucily)*:   The Welcoming Committee.

Walter and Ruth giggle.

MAMA *(innocently)*:   Who?

BENEATHA: The Welcoming Committee. They said they're sure going to be glad to see you when you get there.

WALTER *(devilishly)*:   Yeah, they said they can't hardly wait to see your face.

Laughter.

MAMA *(sensing their facetiousness)*:   What's the matter with you all?

WALTER: Ain't nothing the matter with us. We just telling you 'bout the gentleman who came to see you this afternoon. From the Clybourne Park Improvement Association.

MAMA: What he want?

RUTH *(in the same mood as Beneatha and Walter)*:   To welcome you, honey.

WALTER: He said they can't hardly wait. He said the one thing they don't have, that they just *dying* to have out there is a fine family of fine colored people! *(To Ruth and Beneatha.)* Ain't that right!

RUTH *(mockingly)*:   Yeah! He left his card—

BENEATHA *(handing card to Mama)*:   In case.

Mama reads and throws it on the floor—understanding and looking off as she draws her chair up to the table on which she has put her plant and some sticks and some cord.

MAMA: Father, give us strength. *(Knowingly—and without fun.)* Did he threaten us?

BENEATHA: Oh—Mama—they don't do it like that any more. He talked Brotherhood. He said everybody ought to learn how to sit down and hate each other with good Christian fellowship.

She and Walter shake hands to ridicule the remark.

MAMA *(sadly)*:   Lord, protect us . . .

RUTH: You should hear the money those folks raised to buy the house from us. All we paid and then some.

BENEATHA: What they think we going to do—eat 'em?

RUTH: No, honey, marry 'em.

MAMA *(shaking her head)*:   Lord, Lord, Lord . . .

RUTH: Well — that's the way the crackers crumble. *(A beat.)* Joke.

BENEATHA *(laughingly noticing what her mother is doing)*:   Mama, what are you doing?

MAMA: Fixing my plant so it won't get hurt none on the way . . .

BENEATHA: Mama, you going to take *that* to the new house?

MAMA: Un-huh —

BENEATHA: That raggedy-looking old thing?

MAMA *(stopping and looking at her)*:   It expresses ME!

RUTH *(with delight, to Beneatha)*:   So there, Miss Thing!

Walter comes to Mama suddenly and bends down behind her and squeezes her in his arms with all his strength. She is overwhelmed by the suddenness of it and, though delighted, her manner is like that of Ruth and Travis.

MAMA: Look out now, boy! You make me mess up my thing here!

WALTER *(his face lit, he slips down on his knees beside her, his arms still about her)*:   Mama . . . you know what it means to climb up in the chariot?

MAMA *(gruffly, very happy)*:   Get on away from me now . . .

RUTH *(near the gift-wrapped package, trying to catch Walter's eye)*:   Psst —

WALTER: What the old song say, Mama . . .

RUTH: Walter — Now?

She is pointing at the package.

WALTER *(speaking the lines, sweetly, playfully, in his mother's face)*:
> I got wings . . . you got wings . . .
> All God's children got wings . . .

MAMA: Boy — get out of my face and do some work . . .

WALTER:
> When I get to heaven gonna put on my wings,
> Gonna fly all over God's heaven . . .

BENEATHA *(teasingly, from across the room)*:   Everybody talking 'bout heaven ain't going there!

WALTER *(to Ruth, who is carrying the box across to them)*:   I don't know, you think we ought to give her that . . . Seems to me she ain't been very appreciative around here.

MAMA *(eyeing the box, which is obviously a gift)*:   What is that?

WALTER *(taking it from Ruth and putting it on the table in front of Mama)*:   Well — what you all think? Should we give it to her?

RUTH: Oh — she was pretty good today.

MAMA: I'll good you —

She turns her eyes to the box again.

BENEATHA: Open it, Mama.

She stands up, looks at it, turns and looks at all of them, and then presses her hands together and does not open the package.

WALTER *(sweetly)*:   Open it, Mama. It's for you. *(Mama looks in his eyes. It is the first present in her life without its being Christmas. Slowly she opens her package and lifts out, one by one, a brand-new sparkling set of gardening tools. Walter continues, prodding.)* Ruth made up the note — read it . . .

MAMA *(picking up the card and adjusting her glasses):* "To our own Mrs. Miniver° — Love from Brother, Ruth, and Beneatha." Ain't that lovely . . .

TRAVIS *(tugging at his father's sleeve):*   Daddy, can I give her mine now?

WALTER: All right, son. *(Travis flies to get his gift.)*

MAMA: Now I don't have to use my knives and forks no more . . .

WALTER: Travis didn't want to go in with the rest of us, Mama. He got his own. *(Somewhat amused.)* We don't know what it is . . .

TRAVIS *(racing back in the room with a large hatbox and putting it in front of his grandmother):*   Here!

MAMA: Lord have mercy, baby. You done gone and bought your grandmother a hat?

TRAVIS *(very proud):*   Open it!

She does and lifts out an elaborate, but very elaborate, wide gardening hat, and all the adults break up at the sight of it.

RUTH: Travis, honey, what is that?

TRAVIS *(who thinks it is beautiful and appropriate):*   It's a gardening hat! Like the ladies always have on in the magazines when they work in their gardens.

BENEATHA *(giggling fiercely):*   Travis — we were trying to make Mama Mrs. Miniver — not Scarlett O'Hara!

MAMA *(indignantly):*   What's the matter with you all! This here is a beautiful hat! *(Absurdly.)* I always wanted me one just like it!

She pops it on her head to prove it to her grandson, and the hat is ludicrous and considerably oversized.

RUTH: Hot dog! Go, Mama!

WALTER *(doubled over with laughter):*   I'm sorry, Mama — but you look like you ready to go out and chop you some cotton sure enough!

They all laugh except Mama, out of deference to Travis's feelings.

MAMA *(gathering the boy up to her):*   Bless your heart — this is the prettiest hat I ever owned — *(Walter, Ruth, and Beneatha chime in — noisily, festively, and insincerely congratulating Travis on his gift.)* What are we all standing around here for? We ain't finished packin' yet. Bennie, you ain't packed one book.

The bell rings.

BENEATHA: That couldn't be the movers . . . it's not hardly two good yet —

Beneatha goes into her room. Mama starts for door.

WALTER *(turning, stiffening):*   Wait — wait — I'll get it.

He stands and looks at the door.

MAMA: You expecting company, son?

Mrs. Miniver: A much-admired fictional character who appeared in newspaper columns and then in a popular World War II movie (1942).

WALTER *(just looking at the door)*:   Yeah — yeah . . .

Mama looks at Ruth, and they exchange innocent and unfrightened glances.

MAMA *(not understanding)*:   Well, let them in, son.

BENEATHA *(from her room)*:   We need some more string.

MAMA: Travis — you run to the hardware and get me some string cord.

Mama goes out and Walter turns and looks at Ruth. Travis goes to a dish for money.

RUTH: Why don't you answer the door, man?

WALTER *(suddenly bounding across the floor to embrace her)*:   'Cause sometimes it
   hard to let the future begin! *(Stooping down in her face.)*
   I got wings! You got wings!
   All God's children got wings!

*He crosses to the door and throws it open. Standing there is a very slight little man in
a not-too-prosperous business suit and with haunted frightened eyes and a hat pulled
down tightly, brim up, around his forehead. Travis passes between the men and exits.
Walter leans deep in the man's face, still in his jubilance.*

   When I get to heaven gonna put on my wings,
   Gonna fly all over God's heaven . . .

The little man just stares at him.

   Heaven —

Suddenly he stops and looks past the little man into the empty hallway.

   Where's Willy, man?

BOBO: He ain't with me.

WALTER *(not disturbed)*:   Oh — come on in. You know my wife.

BOBO *(dumbly, taking off his hat)*:   Yes — h'you, Miss Ruth.

RUTH *(quietly, a mood apart from her husband already, seeing Bobo)*:   Hello, Bobo.

WALTER: You right on time today . . . Right on time. That's the way! *(He slaps
   Bobo on his back.)* Sit down . . . lemme hear.

*Ruth stands stiffly and quietly in back of them, as though somehow she senses death,
her eyes fixed on her husband.*

BOBO *(his frightened eyes on the floor, his hat in his hands)*:   Could I please get a
   drink of water, before I tell you about it, Walter Lee?

*Walter does not take his eyes off the man. Ruth goes blindly to the tap and gets a glass
of water and brings it to Bobo.*

WALTER: There ain't nothing wrong, is there?

BOBO: Lemme tell you —

WALTER: Man — didn't nothing go wrong?

BOBO: Lemme tell you — Walter Lee. *(Looking at Ruth and talking to her more
   than to Walter.)* You know how it was. I got to tell you how it was. I mean
   first I got to tell you how it was all the way . . . I mean about the money I put
   in, Walter Lee . . .

WALTER *(with taut agitation now)*:   What about the money you put in?

BOBO: Well—it wasn't much as we told you—me and Willy—*(He stops.)* I'm sorry, Walter. I got a bad feeling about it. I got a real bad feeling about it . . .

WALTER: Man, what you telling me about all this for? . . . Tell me what happened in Springfield . . .

BOBO: Springfield.

RUTH *(like a dead woman)*:   What was supposed to happen in Springfield?

BOBO *(to her)*:   This deal that me and Walter went into with Willy—Me and Willy was going to go down to Springfield and spread some money 'round so's we wouldn't have to wait so long for the liquor license . . . That's what we were going to do. Everybody said that was the way you had to do, you understand, Miss Ruth?

WALTER: Man—what happened down there?

BOBO *(a pitiful man, near tears)*:   I'm trying to tell you, Walter.

WALTER *(screaming at him suddenly)*:   THEN TELL ME, GODDAMMIT . . . WHAT'S THE MATTER WITH YOU?

BOBO: Man . . . I didn't go to no Springfield, yesterday.

WALTER *(halted, life hanging in the moment)*:   Why not?

BOBO *(the long way, the hard way to tell)*:   'Cause I didn't have no reasons to . . .

WALTER: Man, what are you talking about!

BOBO: I'm talking about the fact that when I got to the train station yesterday morning—eight o'clock like we planned . . . Man—*Willy didn't never show up.*

WALTER: Why . . . where was he . . . where is he?

BOBO: That's what I'm trying to tell you . . . I don't know . . . I waited six hours . . . I called his house . . . and I waited . . . six hours . . . I waited in that train station six hours . . . *(Breaking into tears.)* That was all the extra money I had in the world . . . *(Looking up at Walter with the tears running down his face.)* Man, *Willy is gone.*

WALTER: Gone, what you mean Willy is gone? Gone where? You mean he went by himself. You mean he went off to Springfield by himself—to take care of getting the license—*(Turns and looks anxiously at Ruth.)* You mean maybe he didn't want too many people in on the business down there? *(Looks to Ruth again, as before.)* You know Willy got his own ways. *(Looks back to Bobo.)* Maybe you was late yesterday and he just went on down there without you. Maybe—maybe—he's been callin' you at home tryin' to tell you what happened or something. Maybe—maybe—he just got sick. He's somewhere—he's got to be somewhere. We just got to find him—me and you got to find him. *(Grabs Bobo senselessly by the collar and starts to shake him.)* We got to!

BOBO *(in sudden angry, frightened agony)*:   What's the matter with you, Walter! When a cat take off with your money he don't leave you no road maps!

WALTER *(turning madly, as though he is looking for Willy in the very room)*:   Willy! . . . Willy . . . don't do it . . . Please don't do it . . . Man, not with that money . . . Man, please, not with that money . . . Oh, God . . . Don't let it be true . . . *(He is wandering around, crying out for Willy and looking for him or perhaps for help from God.) Man* . . . I trusted you . . . Man, I put my life in your hands . . . *(He starts to crumple down on the floor as Ruth just covers her face in horror. Mama opens the door and comes into the room, with Beneatha behind her.) Man* . . . *(He starts to pound the floor with his fists, sobbing wildly.)* THAT MONEY IS MADE OUT OF MY FATHER'S FLESH —

BOBO *(standing over him helplessly):*   I'm sorry, Walter . . . *(only Walter's sobs reply. Bobo puts on his hat.)* I had my life staked on this deal, too . . .

He exits.

MAMA *(to Walter):*   Son — *(She goes to him, bends down to him, talks to his bent head.)* Son . . . Is it gone? Son, I gave you sixty-five hundred dollars. Is it gone? All of it? Beneatha's money too?

WALTER *(lifting his head slowly):*   Mama . . . I never . . . went to the bank at all . . .

MAMA *(not wanting to believe him):*   You mean . . . your sister's school money . . . you used that too . . . Walter? . . .

WALTER: Yessss! All of it . . . It's all gone . . .

There is total silence. Ruth stands with her face covered with her hands; Beneatha leans forlornly against a wall, fingering a piece of red ribbon from the mother's gift. Mama stops and looks at her son without recognition and then, quite without thinking about it, starts to beat him senselessly in the face. Beneatha goes to them and stops it.

BENEATHA: Mama!

Mama stops and looks at both of her children and rises slowly and wanders vaguely, aimlessly away from them.

MAMA: I seen . . . him . . . night after night . . . come in . . . and look at that rug . . . and then look at me . . . the red showing in his eyes . . . the veins moving in his head . . . I seen him grow thin and old before he was forty . . . working and working and working like somebody's old horse . . . killing himself . . . and you — you give it all away in a day — *(She raises her arms to strike him again.)*

BENEATHA: Mama —

MAMA: Oh, God . . . *(She looks up to Him.)* Look down here — and show me the strength.

BENEATHA: Mama —

MAMA *(folding over):*   Strength . . .

BENEATHA *(plaintively):*   Mama . . .

MAMA: Strength!

Curtain.

Act 3

Time: An hour later.

At curtain, there is a sullen light of gloom in the living room, gray light not unlike that which began the first scene of Act 1. At left we can see Walter within his room, alone with himself. He is stretched out on the bed, his shirt out and open, his *arms under his head. He does not smoke, he does not cry out, he merely lies there, looking up at the ceiling, much as if he were alone in the world.*

In the living room Beneatha sits at the table, still surrounded by the now almost ominous packing crates. She sits looking off. We feel that this is a mood struck perhaps an hour before, and it lingers now, full of the empty sound of profound disappointment. We see on a line from her brother's bedroom the sameness of their attitudes. Presently the bell rings and Beneatha rises without ambition or interest in answering. It is Asagai, smiling broadly, striding into the room with energy and happy expectation and conversation.

ASAGAI: I came over . . . I had some free time. I thought I might help with the packing. Ah, I like the look of packing crates! A household in preparation for a journey! It depresses some people . . . but for me . . . it is another feeling. Something full of the flow of life, do you understand? Movement, progress . . . It makes me think of Africa.

BENEATHA: Africa!

ASAGAI: What kind of a mood is this? Have I told you how deeply you move me?

BENEATHA: He gave away the money, Asagai . . .

ASAGAI: Who gave away what money?

BENEATHA: The insurance money. My brother gave it away.

ASAGAI: Gave it away?

BENEATHA: He made an investment! With a man even Travis wouldn't have trusted with his most worn-out marbles.

ASAGAI: And it's gone?

BENEATHA: Gone!

ASAGAI: I'm very sorry . . . And you, now?

BENEATHA: Me? . . . Me? . . . Me, I'm nothing . . . Me. When I was very small . . . we used to take our sleds out in the wintertime and the only hills we had were the ice-covered stone steps of some houses down the street. And we used to fill them in with snow and make them smooth and slide down them all day . . . and it was very dangerous, you know . . . far too steep . . . and sure enough one day a kid named Rufus came down too fast and hit the sidewalk and we saw his face just split open right there in front of us . . . And I remember standing there looking at his bloody open face thinking that was the end of Rufus. But the ambulance came and they took him to the hospital and they fixed the broken bones and they sewed it all up . . . and the next time I saw Rufus he just had a little line down the middle of his face . . . I never got over that . . .

ASAGAI: What?

BENEATHA: That that was what one person could do for another, fix him up — sew up the problem, make him all right again. That was the most marvelous thing in the world . . . I wanted to do that. I always thought it was the one concrete thing in the world that a human being could do. Fix up the sick, you know — and make them whole again. This was truly being God . . .

ASAGAI: You wanted to be God?

BENEATHA: No — I wanted to cure. It used to be so important to me. I wanted to cure. It used to matter. I used to care. I mean about people and how their bodies hurt . . .

ASAGAI: And you've stopped caring?

BENEATHA: Yes — I think so.

ASAGAI: Why?

BENEATHA *(bitterly)*:   Because it doesn't seem deep enough, close enough to what ails mankind! It was a child's way of seeing things — or an idealist's.

ASAGAI: Children see things very well sometimes — and idealists even better.

BENEATHA: I know that's what you think. Because you are still where I left off. You with all your talk and dreams about Africa! You still think you can patch up the world. Cure the Great Sore of Colonialism — *(Loftily, mocking it.)* with the Penicillin of Independence — !

ASAGAI: Yes!

BENEATHA: Independence *and then what?* What about all the crooks and thieves and just plain idiots who will come into power and steal and plunder the same as before — only now they will be black and do it in the name of the new Independence — WHAT ABOUT THEM?!

ASAGAI: That will be the problem for another time. First we must get there.

BENEATHA: And where does it end?

ASAGAI: End? Who even spoke of an end? To life? To living?

BENEATHA: An end to misery! To stupidity! Don't you see there isn't any real progress, Asagai, there is only one large circle that we march in, around and around, each of us with our own little picture in front of us — our own little mirage that we think is the future.

ASAGAI: That is the mistake.

BENEATHA: What?

ASAGAI: What you just said — about the circle. It isn't a circle — it is simply a long line — as in geometry, you know, one that reaches into infinity. And because we cannot see the end — we also cannot see how it changes. And it is very odd but those who see the changes — who dream, who will not give up — are called idealists . . . and those who see only the circle — we call *them* the "realists"!

BENEATHA: Asagai, while I was sleeping in that bed in there, people went out and took the future right out of my hands! And nobody asked me, nobody consulted me — they just went out and changed my life!

ASAGAI: Was it your money?

BENEATHA: What?

ASAGAI: Was it your money he gave away?

BENEATHA: It belonged to all of us.

ASAGAI: But did you earn it? Would you have had it at all if your father had not died?

BENEATHA: No.

ASAGAI: Then isn't there something wrong in a house — in a world — where all dreams, good or bad, must depend on the death of a man? I never thought to see *you* like this, Alaiyo. You! Your brother made a mistake and you are grateful to him so that now you can give up the ailing human race on account of it! You talk about what good is struggle, what good is anything! Where are we all going and why are we bothering!

BENEATHA: AND YOU CANNOT ANSWER IT!

ASAGAI *(shouting over her)*:   *I LIVE THE ANSWER! (Pause.)* In my village at home it is the exceptional man who can even read a newspaper . . . or who ever sees a book at all. I will go home and much of what I will have to say will seem strange to the people of my village. But I will teach and work and things will happen, slowly and swiftly. At times it will seem that nothing changes at all . . . and then again the sudden dramatic events which make history leap into the future. And then quiet again. Retrogression even. Guns, murder, revolution. And I even will have moments when I wonder if the quiet was not better than all that death and hatred. But I will look about my village at the illiteracy and disease and ignorance and I will not wonder long. And perhaps . . . perhaps I will be a great man . . . I mean perhaps I will hold on to the substance of truth and find my way always with the right course . . . and perhaps for it I will be butchered in my bed some night by the servants of empire . . .

BENEATHA: *The martyr!*

ASAGAI *(he smiles)*:   . . . or perhaps I shall live to be a very old man, respected and esteemed in my new nation . . . And perhaps I shall hold office and this is what I'm trying to tell you, Alaiyo: perhaps the things I believe now for my country will be wrong and outmoded, and I will not understand and do terrible things to have things my way or merely to keep my power. Don't you see that there will be young men and women — not British soldiers then, but my own black countrymen — to step out of the shadows some evening and slit my then useless throat? Don't you see they have always been there . . . that they always will be. And that such a thing as my own death will be an advance? They who might kill me even . . . actually replenish all that I was.

BENEATHA: Oh, Asagai, I know all that.

ASAGAI: Good! Then stop moaning and groaning and tell me what you plan to do.

BENEATHA: Do?

ASAGAI: I have a bit of a suggestion.

BENEATHA: What?

ASAGAI *(rather quietly for him)*:   That when it is all over — that you come home with me —

BENEATHA *(staring at him and crossing away with exasperation)*:   Oh — Asagai — at this moment you decide to be romantic!

ASAGAI *(quickly understanding the misunderstanding)*:   My dear, young creature of the New World — I do not mean across the city — I mean across the ocean: home — to Africa.

BENEATHA *(slowly understanding and turning to him with murmured amazement)*: To Africa?

ASAGAI: Yes! . . . *(smiling and lifting his arms playfully.)* Three hundred years later the African Prince rose up out of the seas and swept the maiden back across the middle passage over which her ancestors had come —

BENEATHA *(unable to play)*:   To — to Nigeria?

ASAGAI: Nigeria. Home. *(Coming to her with genuine romantic flippancy.)* I will show you our mountains and our stars; and give you cool drinks from gourds and teach you the old songs and the ways of our people — and, in time, we will pretend that — *(Very softly.)* — you have only been away for a day. Say that you'll come — *(He swings her around and takes her full in his arms in a kiss which proceeds to passion.)*

BENEATHA *(pulling away suddenly)*:   You're getting me all mixed up —

ASAGAI: Why?

BENEATHA: Too many things — too many things have happened today. I must sit down and think. I don't know what I feel about anything right this minute.

She promptly sits down and props her chin on her fist.

ASAGAI *(charmed)*:   All right, I shall leave you. No — don't get up. *(Touching her, gently, sweetly.)* Just sit awhile and think . . . Never be afraid to sit awhile and think. *(He goes to door and looks at her.)* How often I have looked at you and said, "Ah — so this is what the New World hath finally wrought . . ."

He exits. Beneatha sits on alone. Presently Walter enters from his room and starts to rummage through things, feverishly looking for something. She looks up and turns in her seat.

BENEATHA *(hissingly)*:   Yes — just look at what the New World hath wrought! . . . Just look! *(She gestures with bitter disgust.)* There he is! *Monsieur le petit bourgeois noir*° — himself! There he is — Symbol of a Rising Class! Entrepreneur! Titan of the system! *(Walter ignores her completely and continues frantically and destructively looking for something and hurling things to floor and tearing things out of their place in his search. Beneatha ignores the eccentricity of his actions and goes on with the monologue of insult.)* Did you dream of yachts on Lake Michigan, Brother? Did you see yourself on that Great Day sitting down at the Conference Table, surrounded by all the mighty bald-headed men in America? All halted, waiting, breathless, waiting for your pronouncements on industry? Waiting for you — Chairman of the Board! *(Walter finds what he is looking for — a small piece of white paper — and pushes it in his pocket and puts on his coat and rushes out without ever having looked at her. She shouts after him.)* I look at you and I see the final triumph of stupidity in the world!

The door slams and she returns to just sitting again. Ruth comes quickly out of Mama's room.

RUTH: Who was that?

BENEATHA: Your husband.

Monsieur le petit bourgeois noir: Mr. Black Bourgeoisie (French).

RUTH: Where did he go?

BENEATHA: Who knows — maybe he has an appointment at U.S. Steel.

RUTH *(anxiously, with frightened eyes)*:   You didn't say nothing bad to him, did you?

BENEATHA: Bad? Say anything bad to him? No — I told him he was a sweet boy and full of dreams and everything is strictly peachy keen, as the ofay kids say!

Mama enters from her bedroom. She is lost, vague, trying to catch hold, to make some sense of her former command of the world, but it still eludes her. A sense of waste overwhelms her gait; a measure of apology rides on her shoulders. She goes to her plant, which has remained on the table, looks at it, picks it up and takes it to the window sill and sits it outside, and she stands and looks at it a long moment. Then she closes the window, straightens her body with effort and turns around to her children.

MAMA: Well — ain't it a mess in here, though? *(A false cheerfulness, a beginning of something.)* I guess we all better stop moping around and get some work done. All this unpacking and everything we got to do. *(Ruth raises her head slowly in response to the sense of the line; and Beneatha in similar manner turns very slowly to look at her mother.)* One of you all better call the moving people and tell 'em not to come.

RUTH: Tell 'em not to come?

MAMA: Of course, baby. Ain't no need in 'em coming all the way here and having to go back. They charges for that too. *(She sits down, fingers to her brow, thinking.)* Lord, ever since I was a little girl, I always remembers people saying, "Lena — Lena Eggleston, you aims too high all the time. You needs to slow down and see life a little more like it is. Just slow down some." That's what they always used to say down home — "Lord, that Lena Eggleston is a high-minded thing. She'll get her due one day!"

RUTH: No, Lena . . .

MAMA: Me and Big Walter just didn't never learn right.

RUTH: Lena, no! We gotta go. Bennie — tell her . . .

She rises and crosses to Beneatha with her arms outstretched. Beneatha doesn't respond.

Tell her we can still move . . . the notes ain't but a hundred and twenty-five a month. We got four grown people in this house — we can work . . .

MAMA *(to herself)*:   Just aimed too high all the time —

RUTH *(turning and going to Mama fast — the words pouring out with urgency and desperation)*:   Lena — I'll work . . . I'll work twenty hours a day in all the kitchens in Chicago . . . I'll strap my baby on my back if I have to and scrub all the floors in America and wash all the sheets in America if I have to — but we got to MOVE! We got to get OUT OF HERE!!

Mama reaches out absently and pats Ruth's hand.

MAMA: No — I sees things differently now. Been thinking 'bout some of the things we could do to fix this place up some. I seen a second-hand bureau over on Maxwell Street just the other day that could fit right there. *(She points to where the new furniture might go. Ruth wanders away from her.)* Would need some new handles on it and then a little varnish and it look like something brand-new. And — we can put up them new curtains in the kitchen . . . Why this place be looking fine. Cheer us all up so that we forget trouble ever come . . . *(To Ruth.)* And you could get some nice screens to put up in your room round the baby's bassinet . . . *(She looks at both of them pleadingly.)* Sometimes you just got to know when to give up some things . . . and hold on to what you got . . .

Walter enters from the outside, looking spent and leaning against the door, his coat hanging from him.

MAMA: Where you been, son?

WALTER *(breathing hard)*:   Made a call.

MAMA: To who, son?

WALTER: To The Man. *(He heads for his room.)*

MAMA: What man, baby?

WALTER *(stops in the door)*:   The Man, Mama. Don't you know who The Man is?

RUTH: Walter Lee?

WALTER: The Man. Like the guys in the streets say — The Man. Captain Boss — Mistuh Charley . . . Old Cap'n Please Mr. Bossman . . .

BENEATHA *(suddenly)*:   Lindner!

WALTER: That's right! That's good. I told him to come right over.

BENEATHA *(fiercely, understanding)*:   For what? What do you want to see him for!

WALTER *(looking at his sister)*:   We going to do business with him.

MAMA: What you talking 'bout, son?

WALTER: Talking 'bout life, Mama. You all always telling me to see life like it is. Well — I laid in there on my back today . . . and I figured it out. Life just like it is. Who gets and who don't get. *(He sits down with his coat on and laughs.)* Mama, you know it's all divided up. Life is. Sure enough. Between the takers and the "tooken." *(He laughs.)* I've figured it out finally. *(He looks around at them.)* Yeah. Some of us always getting "tooken." *(He laughs.)* People like Willy Harris, they don't never get "tooken." And you know why the rest of us do? 'Cause we all mixed up. Mixed up bad. We get to looking 'round for the right and the wrong; and we worry about it and cry about it and stay up nights trying to figure out 'bout the wrong and the right of things all the time . . . And all the time, man, them takers is out there operating, just taking and taking. Willy Harris? Shoot — Willy Harris don't even count. He don't even count in the big scheme of things. But I'll say one thing for old Willy Harris . . . he's taught me something. He's taught me to keep my eye on what counts in this world. Yeah — *(Shouting out a little.)* Thanks, Willy!

RUTH: What did you call that man for, Walter Lee?

WALTER: Called him to tell him to come on over to the show. Gonna put on a show for the man. Just what he wants to see. You see, Mama, the man came here today and he told us that them people out there where you want us to move — well they so upset they willing to pay us *not* to move! *(He laughs again.)* And — and oh, Mama — you would of been proud of the way me and Ruth and Bennie acted. We told him to get out . . . Lord have mercy! We told the man to get out! Oh, we was some proud folks this afternoon, yeah. *(He lights a cigarette.)* We were still full of that old-time stuff . . .

RUTH *(coming toward him slowly)*:   You talking 'bout taking them people's money to keep us from moving in that house?

WALTER: I ain't just talking 'bout it, baby — I'm telling you that's what's going to happen!

BENEATHA: Oh, God! Where is the bottom! Where is the real honest-to-God bottom so he can't go any farther!

WALTER: See — that's the old stuff. You and that boy that was here today. You all want everybody to carry a flag and a spear and sing some marching songs, huh? You wanna spend your life looking into things and trying to find the right and the wrong part, huh? Yeah. You know what's going to happen to that boy someday — he'll find himself sitting in a dungeon, locked in forever — and the takers will have the key! Forget it, baby! There ain't no causes — there ain't nothing but taking in this world, and he who takes most is smartest — and it don't make a damn bit of difference *how*.

MAMA: You making something inside me cry, son. Some awful pain inside me.

WALTER: Don't cry, Mama. Understand. That white man is going to walk in that door able to write checks for more money than we ever had. It's important to him and I'm going to help him . . . I'm going to put on the show, Mama.

MAMA: Son — I come from five generations of people who was slaves and sharecroppers — but ain't nobody in my family never let nobody pay 'em no money that was a way of telling us we wasn't fit to walk the earth. We ain't never been that poor. *(Raising her eyes and looking at him.)* We ain't never been that — dead inside.

BENEATHA: Well — we are dead now. All the talk about dreams and sunlight that goes on in this house. It's all dead now.

WALTER: What's the matter with you all! I didn't make this world! It was give to me this way! Hell, yes, I want me some yachts someday! Yes, I want to hang some real pearls 'round my wife's neck. Ain't she supposed to wear no pearls? Somebody tell me — tell me, who decides which women is suppose to wear pearls in this world. I tell you I am a *man* — and I think my wife should wear some pearls in this world!

This last line hangs a good while and Walter begins to move about the room. The word "Man" has penetrated his consciousness; he mumbles it to himself repeatedly between strange agitated pauses as he moves about.

MAMA: Baby, how you going to feel on the inside?

WALTER: Fine! . . . Going to feel fine . . . a man . . .

MAMA: You won't have nothing left then, Walter Lee.

WALTER *(coming to her):*   I'm going to feel fine, Mama. I'm going to look that son-of-a-bitch in the eyes and say — *(He falters.)* — and say, "All right, Mr. Lindner — *(He falters even more.)* — that's *your* neighborhood out there! You got the right to keep it like you want! You got the right to have it like you want! Just write the check and — the house is yours." And — and I am going to say — *(His voice almost breaks.)* "And you — you people just put the money in my hand and you won't have to live next to this bunch of stinking niggers! . . ." *(He straightens up and moves away from his mother, walking around the room.)* And maybe — maybe I'll just get down on my black knees . . . *(He does so; Ruth and Bennie and Mama watch him in frozen horror.)* "Captain, Mistuh, Bossman — *(Groveling and grinning and wringing his hands in profoundly anguished imitation of the slow-witted movie stereotype.)* A-hee-hee-hee! Oh, yassuh boss! Yassssssuh! Great white — *(Voice breaking, he forces himself to go on.)* — Father, just gi' ussen de money, fo' God's sake, and we's — we's ain't gwine come out deh and dirty up yo' white folks neighborhood . . ." *(He breaks down completely.)* And I'll feel fine! Fine! FINE! *(He gets up and goes into the bedroom.)*

BENEATHA: That is not a man. That is nothing but a toothless rat.

MAMA: Yes — death done come in this here house. *(She is nodding, slowly, reflectively.)* Done come walking in my house on the lips of my children. You what supposed to be my beginning again. You — what supposed to be my harvest. *(To Beneatha.)* You — you mourning your brother?

BENEATHA: He's no brother of mine.

MAMA: What you say?

BENEATHA: I said that that individual in that room is no brother of mine.

MAMA: That's what I thought you said. You feeling like you better than he is today? *(Beneatha does not answer.)* Yes? What you tell him a minute ago? That he wasn't a man? Yes? You give him up for me? You done wrote his epitaph too — like the rest of the world? Well, who give you the privilege?

BENEATHA: Be on my side for once! You saw what he just did, Mama! You saw him — down on his knees. Wasn't it you who taught me to despise any man who would do that? Do what he's going to do?

MAMA: Yes — I taught you that. Me and your daddy. But I thought I taught you something else too . . . I thought I taught you to love him.

BENEATHA: Love him? There is nothing left to love.

MAMA: There is *always* something left to love. And if you ain't learned that, you ain't learned nothing. *(Looking at her.)* Have you cried for that boy today? I don't mean for yourself and for the family 'cause we lost the money. I mean for him: what he been through and what it done to him. Child, when do you think is the time to love somebody the most? When they done good and made things easy for everybody? Well then, you ain't through learning — because that ain't the time at all. It's when he's at his lowest and can't believe in hisself 'cause the world done whipped him so! When you starts measuring somebody, measure him right, child, measure him right. Make sure you done taken into account what hills and valleys he come through before he got to wherever he is.

Travis bursts into the room at the end of the speech, leaving the door open.

TRAVIS: Grandmama—the moving men are downstairs! The truck just pulled up.

MAMA *(turning and looking at him)*:   Are they, baby? They downstairs?

She sighs and sits. Lindner appears in the doorway. He peers in and knocks lightly, to gain attention, and comes in. All turn to look at him.

LINDNER *(hat and briefcase in hand)*:   Uh—hello . . .

Ruth crosses mechanically to the bedroom door and opens it and lets it swing open freely and slowly as the lights come up on Walter within, still in his coat, sitting at the far corner of the room. He looks up and out through the room to Lindner.

RUTH: He's here.

A long minute passes and Walter slowly gets up.

LINDNER *(coming to the table with efficiency, putting his briefcase on the table and starting to unfold papers and unscrew fountain pens)*:   Well, I certainly was glad to hear from you people. *(Walter has begun the trek out of the room, slowly and awkwardly, rather like a small boy, passing the back of his sleeve across his mouth from time to time.)* Life can really be so much simpler than people let it be most of the time. Well—with whom do I negotiate? You, Mrs. Younger, or your son here? *(Mama sits with her hands folded on her lap and her eyes closed as Walter advances. Travis goes closer to Lindner and looks at the papers curiously.)* Just some official papers, sonny.

RUTH: Travis, you go downstairs—

MAMA *(opening her eyes and looking into Walter's)*:   No. Travis, you stay right here. And you make him understand what you doing, Walter Lee. You teach him good. Like Willy Harris taught you. You show where our five generations done come to. *(Walter looks from her to the boy, who grins at him innocently.)* Go ahead, son— *(She folds her hands and closes her eyes.)* Go ahead.

WALTER *(at last crosses to Lindner, who is reviewing the contract)*:   Well, Mr. Lindner. *(Beneatha turns away.)* We called you— *(There is a profound, simple groping quality in his speech.)* —because, well, me and my family *(He looks around and shifts from one foot to the other.)* Well—we are very plain people . . .

LINDNER: Yes—

WALTER: I mean—I have worked as a chauffeur most of my life—and my wife here, she does domestic work in people's kitchens. So does my mother. I mean—we are plain people . . .

LINDNER: Yes, Mr. Younger—

WALTER *(really like a small boy, looking down at his shoes and then up at the man)*:   And—uh—well, my father, well, he was a laborer most of his life. . . .

LINDNER *(absolutely confused)*:   Uh, yes—yes, I understand. *(He turns back to the contract.)*

WALTER *(a beat; staring at him)*:   And my father— *(With sudden intensity.)* My father almost *beat a man to death* once because this man called him a bad name or something, you know what I mean?

LINDNER *(looking up, frozen)*:   No, no, I'm afraid I don't —

WALTER *(a beat. The tension hangs; then Walter steps back from it)*:   Yeah. Well — what I mean is that we come from people who had a lot of *pride.* I mean — we are very proud people. And that's my sister over there and she's going to be a doctor — and we are very proud —

LINDNER: Well — I am sure that is very nice, but —

WALTER: What I am telling you is that we called you over here to tell you that we are very proud and that this — *(Signaling to Travis.)* Travis, come here. *(Travis crosses and Walter draws him before him facing the man.)* This is my son, and he makes the sixth generation our family in this country. And we have all thought about your offer —

LINDNER: Well, good . . . good —

WALTER: And we have decided to move into our house because my father — my father — he earned it for us brick by brick. *(Mama has her eyes closed and is rocking back and forth as though she were in church, with her head nodding the Amen yes.)* We don't want to make no trouble for nobody or fight no causes, and we will try to be good neighbors. And that's *all* we got to say about that. *(He looks the man absolutely in the eyes.)* We don't want your money. *(He turns and walks away.)*

LINDNER *(looking around at all of them)*:   I take it then — that you have decided to occupy . . .

BENEATHA: That's what the man said.

LINDNER *(to Mama in her reverie)*:   Then I would like to appeal to you, Mrs. Younger. You are older and wiser and understand things better I am sure . . .

MAMA: I am afraid you don't understand. My son said we was going to move and there ain't nothing left for me to say. *(Briskly.)* You know how these young folks is nowadays, mister. Can't do a thing with 'em! *(As he opens his mouth, she rises.)* Good-bye.

LINDNER *(folding up his materials)*:   Well — if you are that final about it . . . there is nothing left for me to say. *(He finishes, almost ignored by the family, who are concentrating on Walter Lee. At the door Lindner halts and looks around.)* I sure hope you people know what you're getting into.

He shakes his head and exits.

RUTH *(looking around and coming to life)*:   Well, for God's sake — if the moving men are here — LET'S GET THE HELL OUT OF HERE!

MAMA *(into action)*:   Ain't it the truth! Look at all this here mess. Ruth, put Travis's good jacket on him . . . Walter Lee, fix your tie and tuck your shirt in, you look like somebody's hoodlum! Lord have mercy, where is my plant? *(She flies to get it amid the general bustling of the family, who are deliberately trying to ignore the nobility of the past moment.)* You all start on down . . . Travis child, don't go empty-handed . . . Ruth, where did I put that box with my skillets in it? I want to be in charge of it myself . . . I'm going to make us the biggest dinner we ever ate tonight . . . Beneatha, what's the matter with them stockings? Pull them things up, girl . . .

The family starts to file out as two moving men appear and begin to carry out the heavier pieces of furniture, bumping into the family as they move about.

BENEATHA: Mama, Asagai asked me to marry him today and go to Africa —

MAMA *(in the middle of her getting-ready activity)*:   He did? You ain't old enough to marry nobody — *(Seeing the moving men lifting one of her chairs precariously.)* Darling, that ain't no bale of cotton, please handle it so we can sit in it again! I had that chair twenty-five years . . .

The movers sigh with exasperation and go on with their work.

BENEATHA *(girlishly and unreasonably trying to pursue the conversation)*:   To go to Africa, Mama — be a doctor in Africa . . .

MAMA *(distracted)*:   Yes, baby —

WALTER: Africa! What he want you to go to Africa for?

BENEATHA: To practice there . . .

WALTER: Girl, if you don't get all them silly ideas out your head! You better marry yourself a man with some loot . . .

BENEATHA *(angrily, precisely as in the first scene of the play)*:   What have you got to do with who I marry!

WALTER: Plenty. Now I think George Murchison —

BENEATHA: George Murchison! I wouldn't marry him if he was Adam and I was Eve!

Walter and Beneatha go out yelling at each other vigorously and the anger is loud and real till their voices diminish. Ruth stands at the door and turns to Mama and smiles knowingly.

MAMA *(fixing her hat at last)*:   Yeah — they something all right, my children . . .

RUTH: Yeah — they're something. Let's go, Lena.

MAMA *(stalling, starting to look around at the house)*:   Yes — I'm coming. Ruth —

RUTH: Yes?

MAMA *(quietly, woman to woman)*:   He finally come into his manhood today, didn't he? Kind of like a rainbow after the rain . . .

RUTH *(biting her lip lest her own pride explode in front of Mama)*:   Yes, Lena.

Walter's voice calls for them raucously.

WALTER *(offstage)*:   Y'all come on! These people charges by the hour, you know!

MAMA *(waving Ruth out vaguely)*:   All right, honey — go on down. I be down directly.

Ruth hesitates, then exits. Mama stands, at last alone in the living room, her plant on the table before her as the lights start to come down. She looks around at all the walls and ceilings and suddenly, despite herself, while the children call below, a great heaving thing rises in her and she puts her fist to her mouth to stifle it, takes a final desperate look, pulls her coat about her, pats her hat, and goes out. The lights dim down. The door opens and she comes back in, grabs her plant, and goes out for the last time.

Curtain.   [1959]

■ THINKING ABOUT THE TEXT

1. The play's main characters are Walter Lee, Mama, Ruth, and Beneatha. List three or more adjectives to describe each of these characters. What basic values does each character seem to express during the arguments that occur in their family? Do you sympathize with them equally? Why, or why not? What, evidently, was Walter Lee's father like?

2. At the end of the play, speaking to Ruth about Walter Lee, Mama says "He finally come into his manhood today, didn't he?" How does Mama appear to be defining *manhood*? What other possible definitions of *manhood* come up directly or indirectly in the play? Identify places where characteristics of *womanhood* are brought up. In general, would you say that gender is at least as important in this play as race is? Why, or why not?

3. Analyze Asagai's conversations with Beneatha and the rest of her family. What does Hansberry suggest about the relations of Africans and African Americans in the late 1950s?

4. Although there is a white character, he makes only two relatively brief appearances, and no other white characters are shown. Why do you suppose Hansberry keeps the presence of whites minimal?

5. Do you think this play is universal in its truths and concerns, or are you more inclined to see it as specifically about African Americans? Explain. In what ways is this 1959 play relevant to life in the United States today?

THE CRISIS

The Hansberrys of Chicago: They Join Business Acumen with Social Vision

The following article appeared in the April 1941 issue of The Crisis, *the journal of the National Association for the Advancement of Colored People (NAACP). The photographs to which the article refers are omitted. The NAACP was established in 1909 and* The Crisis *a year later, its founder and first editor being the noted African American intellectual W. E. B. Du Bois. This article pays tribute to Lorraine Hansberry's parents; it notes their successful real estate business, the foundation they established to get civil rights laws enforced, and their 1940 U.S. Supreme Court victory. The Court's decision was meant to erode at least some racial covenants, policies by which white neighborhoods kept out blacks. However, the decision was not enforced, and very little changed.*

Mr. and Mrs. Carl A. Hansberry of Chicago, Illinois, have the distinction not only of conducting one of the largest real estate enterprises in the country operated by Negroes but they are unique business people because they are spending much of their wealth to safeguard the civil rights of colored citizens in their city, state, and nation.

The properties shown on these pages are a part of the $250,000.00 worth of Chicago real estate from which The Hansberry Enterprises and The Hansberry Foundation receive a gross annual income of $100,000.00. The real estate firm makes available to Negroes with limited income apartments within their economic reach, while the profits from this enterprise are used to safeguard the Negro's civil rights and to make additional housing available to him. The Hansberrys played a very significant role in the recent Chicago restrictive covenant case before the United States Supreme Court whose decision opened blocks of houses and apartment buildings from which Negroes formerly had been excluded.

The Hansberry Enterprises

The Hansberry Enterprises is a real estate syndicate founded by Mr. Hansberry in 1929. From a very modest beginning, the business has grown to be one of the largest in the Mid-West. The property owned and controlled by the company is in excess of $250,000 in value and accommodates four hundred families. During the past ten years the payroll and commissions have aggregated more than $350,000.00.

The offices of the Hansberry Enterprises are located at 4247 Indiana Avenue, Chicago, Illinois.

The Hansberry Foundation

The Hansberry Foundation was established in 1936 by Mrs. N. Louise Hansberry, and her husband, Carl A. Hansberry, with substantial grants of the interest from the Hansberry Enterprises. Mr. Hansberry is the Director. The Foundation was set up as a Trust Fund and only the members of the immediate Hansberry family may contribute to this Fund. A provision of the Trust provides "That during the first ten (10) years only 60 percent of the income of the trust may be used, thereafter, both the income and the principal may be used, but at no time shall the principal be reduced to less than Ten Thousand ($10,000.00) dollars."

The purpose of the Foundation is to encourage and promote respect for all laws, and especially those laws as related to the Civil Rights of American citizens. The following paragraph taken from a letter to the Cook County Bar Association under date of April 27, 1937, gives a precise statement of the purpose and scope of the Hansberry Foundation:

> The Creators of the Hansberry Foundation believe that the Illinois Civil Rights Law represents the crystallized views of the best citizens of Illinois and were made in the best interest of the whole people of Illinois. They therefore believed, that the Civil Rights Code should be enforced; that the passiveness of any citizen should cease. Because of and in view of the foregoing premises, the Hansberry Foundation was created and now

therefore announces its desire to cooperate with sympathetic public officials, associations, or organizations, likewise interested in the active en-
forcement of the Civil Rights Laws of Illinois and throughout the Nation.
The Foundation will assume (at its discretion) a part, or all of the costs of
prosecuting violations of the law wherever, and/or whenever, the authorities willfully neglect or refuse to act; and where the victims are financially
unable to protect themselves.

[1941]

▤ THINKING ABOUT THE TEXT

1. What do you sense is the main rhetorical purpose of *The Crisis* in publishing this article? Does anyone in *A Raisin in the Sun* share the values
   expressed by the article? To what extent do you aim to "join business
   acumen with social vision"?

2. Much of the article consists of quotations from legal documents associated with the Hansberry Foundation. What do you think of this rhetorical strategy?

3. The article makes clear that when Lorraine Hansberry's family sought to
   live in an all-white part of Chicago, they were wealthier than the Youngers.
   What would you say to someone who argued that it would have been
   more honest of Hansberry to focus her play on a family as well-off as
   hers?

LORRAINE HANSBERRY
April 23, 1964, Letter to the New York Times

Here is part of a letter by Lorraine Hansberry written five years after A Raisin in the
Sun. *Once again, she quotes the poem by Langston Hughes containing her play's title.
Now, however, she is expressing approval of civil rights activists' aggressive tactics,
including attempts by the Congress of Racial Equality (CORE) to block traffic. In her
letter, Hansberry also recalls her family's fight against racial covenants and her father's subsequent death in Mexico. Although the* New York Times *never published
Hansberry's letter, some of it was included by her husband, Robert Nemiroff, in his
1969 compilation of her writings,* To Be Young, Gifted, and Black.

April 23, 1964

To the Editor,
The New York Times:
    . . . My father was typical of a generation of Negroes who believed that the
"American way" could successfully be made to work to democratize the United
States. Thus, twenty-five years ago, he spent a small personal fortune, his
considerable talents, and many years of his life fighting, in association with

NAACP attorneys, Chicago's "restrictive covenants" in one of this nation's ugliest ghettoes.

That fight also required that our family occupy the disputed property in a hellishly hostile "white neighborhood" in which, literally, howling mobs surrounded our house. One of their missiles almost took the life of the then eight-year-old signer of this letter. My memories of this "correct" way of fighting white supremacy in America include being spat at, cursed, and pummeled in the daily trek to and from school. And I also remember my desperate and courageous mother, patrolling our house all night with a loaded German luger, doggedly guarding her four children, while my father fought the respectable part of the battle in the Washington court.

The fact that my father and the NAACP "won" a Supreme Court decision, in a now famous case which bears his name in the lawbooks, is — ironically — the sort of "progress" our satisfied friends allude to when they presume to deride the more radical means of struggle. The cost, in emotional turmoil, time, and money, which led to my father's early death as a permanently embittered exile in a foreign country when he saw that after such sacrificial efforts the Negroes of Chicago were as ghetto-locked as ever, does not seem to figure in their calculations.

That is the reality that I am faced with when I now read that some Negroes my own age and younger say that we must now lie down in the streets, tie up traffic, do whatever we can — take to the hills with guns if necessary — and fight back. Fatuous people remark these days on our "bitterness." Why, of course we are bitter. The entire situation suggests that the nation be reminded of the too little noted final lines of Langston Hughes's mighty poem:

> What happens to a dream deferred?
>
> Does it dry up
> Like a raisin in the sun?
> Or fester like a sore —
> And then run?
> Does it stink like rotten meat?
> Or crust and sugar over —
> Like a syrupy sweet?
>
> Maybe it just sags
> Like a heavy load.
>
> Or does it explode?

Sincerely,
Lorraine Hansberry
[1964]

≡ THINKING ABOUT THE TEXT

1. Hansberry indicates that she is "bitter." Is *bitter* a word that you associate with the author of *A Raisin in the Sun*? Why, or why not? Do you get

the sense that the bitterness she refers to in her letter is justified? Why, or why not?

2. Does Hansberry's play give you the impression that the family in it will suffer the same kinds of things described in the second paragraph of Hansberry's letter? Support your answer with details from the play.

3. In the letter, Hansberry seems to condone acts of civil disobedience. In what kinds of cases, if any, do you think people are justified in breaking the law?

ALAN EHRENHALT

From *The Lost City: Discovering the Forgotten Virtues of Community in the Chicago of the 1950s*

Alan Ehrenhalt (b. 1947) is the executive editor of Governing *magazine and was formerly political editor of* Congressional Quarterly. *In much of his writing, he argues that Americans will achieve true democracy only if they regain the sense of community they once had. This is the basic claim of Ehrenhalt's first book,* The United States of Ambition: Politicians, Power, and the Pursuit of Office *(1991). In his second,* The Lost City: Discovering the Forgotten Virtues of Community in the Chicago of the 1950s *(1995), he extends his concern with community spirit by focusing on the role it played in Chicago during the 1950s. His latest book is* Governing *(2005). The following excerpts deal with Bronzeville, the South Side ghetto where Lorraine Hansberry grew up and where her 1959 play* A Raisin in the Sun *takes place.*

If St. Nick's parish° was a world of limited choices, a far more limited world existed five miles further east, where the bulk of Chicago's black community — hundreds of thousands of people — lived together in Bronzeville, a neighborhood they were all but prohibited from escaping.

Any discussion of the city we have lost during the past generation must eventually confront the issue of Bronzeville, and the question that may be most troublesome of all: Have we lost something important that existed even in the worst place that the Chicago of the 1950s had to offer?

Anybody who did not live in a black ghetto is bound to be leery of asking the question, with its implied assumption that segregation hid its good points. But the fact remains, long after Bronzeville's disappearance from the map, that a remarkable number of people who did live there find themselves asking it.

"Fifty-first and Dearborn was a bunch of shacks," Alice Blair wrote thirty years later, after she had become Chicago's deputy superintendent of education.

St. Nick's parish: St. Nicholas of Tolentine parish, a postimmigrant, working-class neighborhood of Chicago.

"We didn't have hot water — and the houses were torn down for slum clearance to build Robert Taylor Homes. But in those shacks, there was something different from what is there now."

What was it, exactly? Several things. "People took a great deal of pride in   5
just being where they were," says John Stroger, the first black president of the Cook County Board of Commissioners. "It was economically poor, but spiritually and socially rich. People had hope that things would be better." Stroger echoes what Vernon Jarrett, the longtime Chicago newspaper columnist, said rather hauntingly a few years ago. "The ghetto used to have something going for it. It had a beat, it had a certain rhythm, and it was all hope. I don't care how rough things were."

Then there is the bluntness of Timuel Black, a lifelong civil rights activist, looking back at age seventy-five on the South Side as it used to be and as it has become: "I would say," he declares at the end of a long conversation, "at this point in my life and experience, that we made a mistake leaving the ghetto."

These fragments prove nothing. To many who read them, they will suggest merely that nostalgia is not only powerful but dangerous, that late in life it can generate a fondness for times and places that should be properly remembered with nothing more than relief that they are gone. And yet something valuable did die with Bronzeville, and we can learn something about community and authority, faith and hope, by tracing their presence even in what was, by common agreement, an unjust and constricted corner of the world.

What Bronzeville had, and so many of its graduates continue to mourn, was a sense of posterity — a feeling that, however difficult the present might be, the future was worth thinking about and planning for in some detail. Most of the inhabitants of Bronzeville were farsighted people, able to focus on events and ideas whose outlines were hazy and whose arrival might still be very far away. They were looking forward to a time in which it would be possible to break free of the constrictions and indignities of the moment.

Forty years later, in a time-shortened world hooked on fax machines, microwave popcorn, and MTV, the word *posterity* carries far less meaning than it once did. Its gradual disappearance is one of the genuine losses of modern life. To find the concept so vibrant and well entrenched in a place as deprived as Bronzeville in the 1950s seems to mock the freer but far less anchored world that most of us inhabit today.

The indignities of life for a black person on the South Side in the 1950s are   10
unlikely to come as news to very many readers of any race, but some details are worth dredging up. They reveal the triumphs and comforts of Bronzeville society to have been that much more impressive.

It was, for example, uncommonly dangerous for a black Chicagoan to get sick. Of the seventy-seven hospitals in the metropolitan area, only six would accept black patients at all, and five of those had quotas, so that once a certain small number of beds were occupied by blacks, the next black patient would be turned away, no matter how ill he or she was. It was not unusual for blacks who could perfectly well afford private hospital care to be taken to Cook County Hospital, the spartan and overcrowded charity institution on the West Side.

Most of the time, though, even in an emergency, they would be rushed to Provident, the city's only "black" hospital, sometimes speeding past one white facility after another to get to the Provident emergency room. In 1956, Provident saw an emergency patient every nineteen minutes, five times the average for the city's other hospitals. And it was, of course, the only place where a black doctor could aspire to practice; the other hospitals did their hiring on a strict Jim Crow basis.

Getting stopped for a traffic ticket on the South Side was not the same experience for blacks that it was for whites. Until 1958, all traffic tickets in Chicago mentioned the race of the driver. The police maintained a special task force, known to just about everybody as the "flying squad," which was supposed to zero in on high-crime neighborhoods but in fact spent a good deal of its time harassing black citizens, middle-class as well as poor. It was standard practice for flying squad officers to stop black motorists for traffic violations, frisk them, and search their cars before writing the ticket, often abusing them verbally and physically in the process. The abuses nearly always took place when someone was driving alone, so there were rarely any witnesses.

The force that patrolled these neighborhoods was still mostly white, and the supervisors were essentially all white. There were 1,200 black police officers in Chicago in 1957, but only one black captain, and no lieutenants. In the Englewood district, where many of the new recruits were sent, black patrolmen were nearly always given the most tedious assignments: guard duty night after night, or a motorcycle beat in the depths of winter. The two-man teams were all segregated; blacks and whites were not allowed to work together.

Meanwhile, the public schools were not only segregated but demonstrably unequal. Most of the white elementary schools on the South Side were underused, while the black ones were jammed far beyond capacity. Some black schools in Bronzeville were handling more than 2,000 pupils a day on a double-shift basis, with one set of children in attendance from 8 A.M. to noon and another from noon to 4 P.M. At the same time, there were nearly 300 vacant classrooms elsewhere in the city and more than 1,000 classrooms being used for nonessential activities of one sort or another. But the school board did not want to adjust the district lines to permit black kids to take advantage of the space that existed beyond the racial borders.

The incidents of hospital bias, police harassment, and school inequity pointed up just how indifferent Jim Crow was to class distinctions in the 1950s: having money was simply no help in these situations. There was a fourth indignity that somehow makes this point even clearer, and it had to do with travel and vacations.

For $20 a year in 1957, a black family could join an organization called the Tourist Motor Club. What they received in return was a list of hotels and restaurants where blacks would be allowed inside the door, and a guarantee of $500 in bond money in case they found themselves being arrested for making the wrong choice. "Are you ready for any traveling emergency — even in a hostile town?" the Tourist Motor Club asked in its ads, and not unreasonably. "What would you do if you were involved in a highway accident in a hostile town—far away from home. You could lose your life savings—you could be kept in jail without adequate reason. You could lose your entire vacation fighting unjust prejudice."

Vacations were for those who could afford them. The problem that united everyone in the black community—wealthy, working class, and poor—was housing. Unlike St. Nick's or any other white community in Chicago, the ghetto was almost impossible to move out of. The rules of segregation simply made it difficult for a black family to live anywhere else, whether it could afford to or not.

By 1957, that had begun to change. Chicago's South Side black population was expanding, block by block, into what had been white working-class territory on its southern and western borders, and a new, separate black enclave had emerged a few miles west of downtown. But as a practical matter, the number of decent housing opportunities opening up for blacks was far smaller than the number needed. Thus, most of the city's black community remained where it had been since the 1920s: in a narrow strip south of Twenty-third Street, roughly eight miles long and still no more than two or three miles wide.

This ghetto had been badly overcrowded by the time of World War II, and in the years since then it had grown more crowded still. The number of black people in Chicago had increased nearly 40 percent between 1950 and 1956, while the white population was declining. And the newcomers were simply stacking up on top of one another. The Kenwood-Oakland neighborhood, centered around Forty-seventh Street, had gone from 13,000 white residents to 80,000 blacks in a matter of a few years. "A new Negro reaches this sprawling city every fifteen minutes," the young black journalist Carl Rowan wrote in 1957, seeming a little overwhelmed himself. Parts of the South Side that had once been relatively spacious and comfortable now held more people than anyone had imagined possible.

The physical world that those migrants confronted was the world of the infamous "kitchenette"—a one-room flat with an icebox, a bed, and a hotplate, typically in an ancient building that once held a few spacious apartments but had been cut up into the tiniest possible pieces to bring the landlord more money. The bathroom and stove were shared with neighbors, a dozen or more people taking turns with the same meager facilities. . . .

In Bronzeville, hope and authority tended to come out of the same package. If the ultimate authority figures were wealthy white people somewhere far away, the most familiar and important ones were right there, inside the community. They were people who had maneuvered their way through the currents of segregated life, made careers and often fortunes for themselves, and remained in the neighborhood, hammering home the message that there were victories to strive for. They were employers and entrepreneurs of all sorts: businessmen,

20

politicians, and entertainers, gambling czars and preachers of the Gospel. They were people whose moral flaws and weaknesses were no secret to those around them, and those weaknesses were a frequent topic of discussion in the community. But they were leaders nevertheless. They led by command, sometimes rather crudely, and they also led by example.

It is easy to forget, forty years later, just how many successful black-owned businesses there were in Chicago. There were black entrepreneurs all up and down the commercial streets in the 1950s, able to stay afloat because they were guaranteed a clientele. They provided services that white businesses simply did not want to provide to blacks. They ran barber shops and beauty parlors, restaurants and taverns, photography studios and small hotels. Many of them were mom-and-pop operations but quite a few evolved into sizable corporations. "Business," as Dempsey Travis says, "was the pillar of optimism."

The nation's largest black-owned bank was at Forty-seventh Street and Cottage Grove Avenue. Parker House Sausage Company, at Forty-sixth and State, called itself the "Jackie Robinson of meat-packing." At Twenty-seventh and Wabash, S. B. Fuller operated a giant cosmetics business that touted three hundred different products, maintained thirty-one branches all over the country, and employed five thousand salesmen. "Anyone can succeed," Fuller used to say, "if he has the desire."

But the great symbols of the entrepreneurial spirit in Bronzeville were the funeral parlors and the insurance companies. In many cases they were related businesses, a legacy of the burial insurance associations that had existed among black sharecroppers in Mississippi and Arkansas early in the century. Undertakers were the largest single source of advertising in the *Defender*; they were also, like their white counterparts elsewhere in the city, mainstays of every community organization: lodges, churches, social clubs. 25

The opening of a new funeral parlor was a community event in itself. In the spring of 1957, the Jackson funeral home opened a state-of-the art facility on Cottage Grove Avenue, complete, with three large chapels, slumber rooms, a powder room, and a smoking lounge. On the first day, three thousand people came to see it. The Jackson family also owned Jackson Mutual, the fifth largest insurance company in Bronzeville, employing one hundred and twenty people and writing nearly $2 million worth of policies every year.

Insurance actually was a service that white corporations were willing to provide to black customers. Thousands of Bronzeville residents had policies with Metropolitan Life, paying a dollar or two every month to an agent who came by door-to-door to collect. But this was one case where black firms could compete fairly easily. Met Life charged black families more than it charged whites for the same policies, its agents didn't like to come at night when customers were home, and they often seemed to resent having to be there at all. There were billboards all over the neighborhood urging people to buy their insurance from a Negro company.

The result was that by the mid-1950s, the five largest black-owned insurance companies in Chicago had nearly $50 million in assets and more than two thousand employees among them. "Negro life insurance companies," said

Walter Lowe, one of the leading agents, "represent the core of Negro economic life. It is the axis upon which are revolved the basic financial activities of a world constricted by the overpowering forces of discrimination."

But it was more than that. It was the underwriter of the extended time horizons that made life in Bronzeville tolerable in the first place. It was the primary symbol of hope for people burdened with a difficult present but unwilling to abandon their focus on the future. In 1954, *Ebony* magazine, published in Chicago, took a survey of its black readership and found that 42 percent owned washing machines, 44 percent owned cars, and 60 percent owned television sets. But 86 percent said they carried life insurance.

The *Defender*'s tribute to the life insurance companies was reprinted every year to coincide with National Negro Insurance Week: "I am the destroyer of poverty and the enemy of crime," it said. "I bring sunshine and happiness wherever I am given half the welcome I deserve. I do not live for the day nor for the morrow but for the unfathomable future. I am your best friend — I am life insurance." ...   30

Overcoming evil was a job at which most of Bronzeville worked very hard every Sunday, in congregations that ranged in size from tiny to immense. There were five churches whose sanctuary had a seating capacity of two thousand or more, and at least two churches had more than ten thousand people on their membership rolls. But a majority of the churches in the community, even in the late 1950s, were basically storefront operations — often a couple of dozen worshipers or even fewer than that.

In the bigger churches, Sunday worship was an all-day affair: Sunday school at nine in the morning and the main service at eleven; an evening musicale later on, with the full choir and Gospel chorus; and then, for many of the faithful, a radio sermon from one of the big-name Bronzeville preachers before retiring for the night. Music was at the heart of the experience. Most churches had choirs that accompanied the pastor when he preached as a guest in another pulpit, which all of them did. Some choirs spent considerable time traveling outside the city.

Between Sundays, the odds were that a larger congregation would be busy with some social activity every single night. All these churches had a wide variety of auxiliary organizations — youth groups, missionary societies, sewing circles — and some had as many as two dozen different ones in existence at the same time. Of all the Bronzeville social institutions of the 1950s, the churches were the most uniformly successful and self-reliant. "In their own churches in their own denominational structures," the historian C. Eric Lincoln was to write in retrospect, "black Christians had become accustomed to a sense of dignity and self-fulfillment impossible even to contemplate in the white church in America. ... To be able to say that 'I belong to Mount Nebo Baptist' or 'We go to Mason's Chapel Methodist' was the accepted way of establishing identity and status."

The storefront churches had to make do without the elaborate network of groups and social involvement. But the key distinction was not the size of the facility; it was the style of worship and particularly the level of emotion. Many of the storefronts, perhaps most, were Holiness or Pentecostal churches — Holy Rollers, as the outside world had already come to know them. The service combined shouting, faith healing, and speaking in tongues; as much as three hours of singing, accompanied by guitar, drum, and tambourine; and vivid storytelling sermons about such things as the fiery furnace or the prodigal son. Some churches employed attendants in white uniforms to calm the shouting worshipers when they became too excited. In a liturgy that devoted a great deal of its time to discussing the nature and consequences of sin — and the specific sins of alcohol, tobacco, profanity, gambling, and adultery — there was intense joy as well. "I have known the sisters and the brothers to become so happy," one woman told Horace Cayton and St. Clair Drake in *Black Metropolis*, "that persons around them are in actual danger of getting knocked in the face."

The popularity of these storefronts was something of a problem for the mainline Baptist and African Methodist Episcopal (AME) congregations that aimed for what they saw as a higher level of decorum and dignity. Some ministers used to upbraid their worshipers for becoming too emotional during the service. By the mid-1950s, however, the liturgical distinction between the storefronts and the mainline institutions was blurring. Dozens of preachers who had begun with nothing had built their churches into successful operations, all without departing significantly from the Holiness or Pentecostal script.   35

The mid-1950s were an exciting time for Bronzeville churches of all varieties. Congregations were growing, debts were being paid, and churches everywhere seemed to be moving into larger, more elaborate facilities: the shouters as well as the elite. . . .

Bronzeville no longer exists. That is not merely because no one would use such a name anymore, but because most of the buildings that comprised the neighborhood have long since been leveled. With the completion in 1962 of Robert Taylor Homes, the nation's largest public housing project and quite possibly its most squalid, the area once called Bronzeville ceased to run the gamut from worn-out but respectable apartment buildings to gruesome kitchenettes. It became a much more uniform high-rise slum, punctuated every half-mile or so by decrepit commercial strips, hosting intermittent taverns, barbecues, and convenience stores and suggesting only a remnant of the much more thriving business streets that once existed.

Bronzeville is long gone not only physically but socially; it passed out of existence as a community as soon as the middle class left, which was as soon as it was permitted to leave with the lifting of segregation. By 1960, the middle-class exodus had already begun, and by 1970, it was virtually complete. Thousands of families who had been the pillars of Bronzeville society returned at most once a week, for church on Sunday.

So much has been written about the impact of middle-class departure on the life of the ghetto that it seems unnecessary to belabor the point. Perhaps it is sufficient to say that Bronzeville was a community unique in America, that its uniqueness depended on the presence of people from all classes and with all sorts of values, living and struggling together, and that with the disappearance of that diversity, the community could not have continued to exist, even if there had been no physical changes at all.

In thinking about what has disappeared, however, there is no shortage of   40 ironies to ponder. The policy racket is legal now, run neither by local black gamblers nor by the Mafia but by the state of Illinois, which calls it a lottery. The game that was once considered an emblem of sin by much of white Chicago is now depended upon as a contributor to the financing of public education. Policy is merely a business now, managed by a colorless bureaucracy far away — it is no longer a cult or a neighborhood institution. There is no demand for dream books anymore on the South Side, no circus-like drawings in crowded basements with a light over the entrance. People play the legal numbers game with a humorless compulsiveness that has little in common with the old-fashioned emotional experience.

Legal businesses have fared almost as badly as illegal ones. Notwithstanding Earl Dickerson's prediction that Supreme Liberty Life would thrive under integration to become a billion-dollar insurance business by the end of the century, the company was simply absorbed into United of America, becoming a piece of a gigantic white institution, and a rather small and inconspicuous piece at that. Not that there was anything racist about such a consolidation; plenty of smaller white-owned insurance companies suffered the same fate. But the cumulative effect on black economic life was powerful: the old life insurance companies were the one significant engine of capital in Chicago's black community, and by 1990, not a single firm was left.

The *Chicago Defender* remains in business at the same location it occupied in the 1950s, published by the same man, John Sengstacke. But it never really found a coherent role to play as a voice of its people in an integrated city. Once the white newspapers began printing news about blacks on the South Side, the paper lost its franchise as virtually the sole source of information within the community. It played a surprisingly passive role in the civil rights confrontations of the 1960s, serving neither as a conspicuous engine of militant activism nor as a persistent critic. By the 1970s, the *Defender* had essentially been superseded as a forum for political debate by the plethora of black radio stations that had sprung up on the South Side. The Bud Billiken parade is still held each summer in Washington Park, attracting a huge contingent of Chicago politicians, white as well as black, but it is no longer the signature event of a powerful black journalistic institution: it is a reminder of the influence that institution once had.

Of all the fixtures of Bronzeville life, the churches come the closest to having survived in recognizable form. Olivet Baptist stands as an impressive edifice at Thirty-first Street and King Drive, its front lawn dominated by a statue of the Reverend J. H. Jackson, pugnacious in stone as he was in life, along with quotations from some of his sermons and praise for him from around the world. Olivet, South Park Baptist, and some of the other Bronzeville churches still turn out crowds at services on Sunday morning, attracting families who return from the far South Side and the suburbs, senior citizens who have remained in the neighborhood, and a sprinkling of children and adults from the projects nearby.

Some of the churches still maintain choirs, Sunday schools, Bible study groups, and social outreach programs, struggling rather heroically against the social disorganization that is all around them. But they have ceased to be voices of clear authority. No preacher can deliver instruction and expect compliance in the way that J. H. Jackson could in his prime. And while sin remains a familiar topic in the South Side black churches on Sundays — a more important topic than at St. Nick's or Elmhurst Presbyterian — the subject no longer has the hold over its listeners that it had a generation ago.

Only in politics can one really argue that Bronzeville has gained more than   45
it has lost. William L. Dawson was a power broker and even a role model of sorts, but he was a leader whose rewards from the white machine were disappointingly meager, somehow not commensurate with the job he did in guaranteeing the election of Richard J. Daley and other white politicians. Dawson's machine yielded in the 1980s to something truly remarkable — a citywide coalition that made possible the election of Harold Washington as the city's first black mayor. Washington's victory in 1983, in a campaign with "Our Turn" as its most conspicuous slogan, was a psychological triumph far beyond anything the old Dawson organization could possibly accomplish, perhaps beyond anything blacks had experienced in any American city. And while the extent of Washington's tangible achievements in office can be debated, the fact that he died in 1987 with his heroic status in the black community intact, and his respect growing even among whites, represented a victory comparable in its way to the first one.

Black political power in Chicago, however, seemed to disappear almost as suddenly as it emerged. Ten years after Washington's first election, Chicago was again being governed by a white mayor, Richard M. Daley, son of the old boss, and by a majority coalition in which Hispanics, not blacks, were the significant minority partner. Meanwhile, the black community was deeply divided over whom to follow and how to proceed, seemingly years away from the level of influence it had had in city politics in the mid-1980s.

In the black community, unlike the white working-class neighborhoods or white suburbia, it may seem perverse — or at least misleading — to dwell on the losses of the past generation. At the individual level, there have been so many gains — in personal freedom, in job opportunities, in income. Today's black middle class is far larger in proportional terms than the one that existed in Bronzeville in the 1950s, much of it living comfortably in neighborhoods scattered all across the Chicago metropolitan area.

When it comes to community institutions, however, the losses are no less real for Chicago's blacks than for white ethnics or for the split-level suburbanites of the 1950s generation. If anything, they are more real. Nearly all of the things that gave texture and coherence to life in Bronzeville, demeaning as that life often was, are simply not reproducible in the freer, more individualistic, more bewildering world of the 1990s.   *[1995]*

■ **THINKING ABOUT THE TEXT**

1. Does reading these passages from Ehrenhalt's book make you think differently about any of the events and characters in *A Raisin in the Sun?* Why, or why not?

2. To what extent does the neighborhood described by Ehrenhalt resemble where you grew up? Identify specific similarities and differences.

3. Note Ehrenhalt's last sentence. While he recognizes that Bronzeville was segregated, evidently he feels some regret over its passing, mourning in particular what he sees as the death of its community spirit. Does his attitude make sense to you? Explain your reasoning. What do you think he might say about the Younger family's decision to leave the neighborhood? How much does it matter to you that this historian of Bronzeville is white?

SIDNEY POITIER

From *The Measure of a Man: A Spiritual Autobiography*

Raised in the Bahamas, Sidney Poitier (b. 1927) became the leading African American film star of his generation. For his 1963 movie Lilies of the Field, *he won the Academy Award for best actor, the first African American to do so. He has also acted in such important films as* The Blackboard Jungle *(1955),* The Defiant Ones *(1958),* A Patch of Blue *(1965),* Guess Who's Coming to Dinner *(1967),* In the Heat of the Night *(1967),* To Sir, With Love *(1967), and* A Raisin in the Sun *(1961), where he again portrayed Walter Lee Younger, his role in the play's original production. In the following excerpt from his memoir,* The Measure of a Man: A Spiritual Autobiography *(2000; selected by Oprah's Book Club in 2007), Poitier recalls that first staging, especially his struggle in getting other members of the company to accept his view of the play.*

I finished a six-month run, but by the time I left the production the actress who played the mother wasn't speaking to me. She hated me. Need I tell you that this is a difficult position to find yourself in as the member of an ensemble of actors?

Claudia McNeil, a fine performer, was in complete dominance over most of the other members of the cast. Naturally enough, she perceived the play as being best when it unfolded from the mother's point of view. *I* perceived the play as being best when it unfolded from the son's point of view, however, and I argued that position. In fact, we argued constantly.

I prevailed, I guess because I was considered the principal player who was responsible for getting the piece mounted. I suppose there might have been some who didn't agree with me but simply acquiesced to my position. But I wasn't just throwing my weight around. I was not, and am not, in the habit of doing that. I genuinely felt that when tragedy fell on the family in *Raisin*, the most devastating effects were visited upon the son, because the mother was such a towering figure.

In my opinion, it was the son who carried the theatrical obligation as the force between the audience and the play. The eyes of those watching were on the son to see if the tragedy would destroy him, would blow him apart beyond recovery. And it was also my opinion that there was no such feeling between the audience and the mother. The audience witnessed the sadness that was visited on her. They saw that her family was in disarray, but they also saw her as a force beyond that kind of vulnerability. If they were to vote, they would say, "Oh, but she's going to be okay."

So where's the drama in the piece?   5

The drama asks an audience to *care*. This was my argument to the playwright and the director and the producer, all of whom were my friends. If you're going to ask that audience to care, you're going to have to take them to the place where the most damage is possible so they can feel that pain.

If you keep them focused on the mother, they're going to say, "Oh, that's too bad that happened — but listen, that family's going to be okay."

Well, I had learned in my experience as an actor and as a theater participant that wherever there's threatened destruction of a human being, that's where the focus is; and the only existence that was threatened in *Raisin* was the son's. There was simply no guarantee that he would survive. It was fifty-fifty that this boy couldn't do it, wouldn't be able to bounce back. It was highly probable that he wouldn't have the resilience, the guts, the stamina, or the determination. Or, looked at another way, it was possible that he wouldn't be able to experience the catharsis as fully as necessary for him to be reborn. That's what the audience had to see to be fully engaged: the rebirth of this person.

Now, there was no ego in that. I mean, I was a theater person. I had spent most of my early years in theater — not on Broadway necessarily, but I had done many, many off-Broadway shows. I'd seen dozens and dozens of plays, I'd *worked* in dozens of plays, so I felt comfortable in my sense of what drama is made of, both in theatrical terms and in life terms.

So that was my position, and I was fought tooth and nail on it by the director and the writer and the producer. Ruby Dee and I saw more eye to eye than did either of us with the others, so it was my intent, and she concurred, that I would play the drama on opening night the way I believed it *should* be played. That didn't require changing the words, only making a fundamental change in the attitude of the individual.   10

Now, this gets to the very core of what acting is. How do you shift the emphasis of a play when, as is the case in *A Raisin in the Sun*, there are two characters who are very forceful and quite strong? Here's how: if you see the son's need as not just personal but a need on behalf of his family, then the emotional center shifts, and it becomes a different play.

The action of the play turns on the death of the father, and the fact that the mother receives ten thousand dollars in insurance money because her husband was killed in an accident on the job. The son wants to use the money in the most constructive way he can think of, which is to start a business, to move the family in some structural way up from where they are.

The mother, on the other hand, wants to use the money to buy a house. But the son says to her, in effect, "The money used to buy a house wouldn't affect the family circumstances in that I'd still chauffeur for somebody else, my wife still works as a maid, and you'd still work as a maid. There'd be no shifting of dynamics here. But there could be, with some sweat and tears, there could be some shifting of dynamics if that money were used as down payment for a business that we could all work at. Then in two years or five years, what we'd have done would be substantial enough for us to be thinking about getting a house and, hopefully, then the business would grow and we could have two such businesses or three such businesses in ten years by the time my son is ready for college."

That's his argument, and the mother's argument runs something like, "You want to spend that money to open a liquor store?" She insists, "My husband's memory is not going to be tied in with the selling of liquor. I'm going to use that money to buy a house, to put a roof over our heads."

He says to his mother, "Isn't it better that my father's death advances the   15
family? You have a daughter who's going off to college, hopefully, but where is the money coming from? I have a son who is going to be soon a young man. What are the lessons in this for him? I am a chauffeur. Where are we going to be down the line? Am I going to be a chauffeur at the age of sixty, and is my son going to take over chauffeuring?"

So that's the heart of it. Therefore, the playing of this man has to be such that the audience believes that his need for his family is absolutely elemental, and that this is the last chance, *his* last chance. If he fails now, he'll never be able to gather the steam, gather the courage and the determination to spend himself again in a losing effort. He just won't be able to.

It's this sense of possible destruction that prepares the audience for tragedy when the mother *does* give him the money, after he really fights and struggles for it, and the money is lost. All of it.

The audience is primed to see either total destruction of this man or his resurrection, you follow? But there's no resurrection for the mother, regardless. She gives the money to her son because she finally decides to let him have his shot at being a man, his own man — and then he fucks it up. Well, sad as it might be for her as a mother, there's no great tragedy in that for her as an individual. She loses ten grand that she didn't really have in the first place.

But this young man — he's destroyed. That's what the audience assumes. But in the third act he comes out of the ashes, and that's where the real drama is, because he looks at that boy of his, and he talks to him. In fact, he's talking to the audience *through* the boy; and when he speaks, the audience just goes nuts. I mean, it's so *dramatic*.

Well, that was my position — the position I acted from. The other position,   20
as I said, was held very strongly by the actress who played the mother, as well

as by the producer, the director, and the playwright — my friends. When I left the fold to go make movies and they had to replace me, the several men who, over time, took the part had to play it the other way, the mother's way, because the continued success of the play depended on having Claudia McNeil.

Well, the audiences didn't seem to mind one bit. The play continued to work well because it had garnered such recognition by then. And the guys who took over the part were all very fine actors, all extremely fine actors, one of whom was Ruby Dee's husband, Ossie Davis.

So what was the lesson in all this?

I would say that sometimes convictions firmly held can cost more than we're willing to pay. And irrevocable change occurs when we're not up to paying, and irrevocable change occurs when we *are* up to paying. Either way, we have to live with the consequences. If I'm up to paying the price in a certain situation, I walk away from the experience with some kind of self-respect because I took the heat. And if I go the other way, feeling that the cost is too high, then however bright the situation turns out, I feel that something is missing.

For an actor to go onstage every night with the sort of hostile undercurrent we experienced with *A Raisin in the Sun* — it can only be described as being like a bad marriage. I felt that Claudia McNeil wasn't giving me what I needed. She knew where my big moments were, and she knew when to hold back and take the air out — and I lived through that opposition for months.

It was very painful for me to know the effect our disagreement was having   25
on my colleagues. If you're a producer, certainly you're irritated by dissension that threatens to interrupt the life of a hit play. Now, my friend Philip Rose, the producer, disagreed with me completely, and I believe that his disagreement was genuine, because I've known the man all these years, and today he's still one of my closest friends. But at the time, I was leaving his play. He had a play that would run, if he could hold it together and keep Claudia McNeil happy, for years and years. So he wasn't especially sympathetic to my concerns.

The playwright's sympathies were completely against me. She saw the play as weighted toward the mother; that's how she'd *written* it. She was a very intelligent young black woman, and she came from a family of achievers. Her whole family were achievers, especially the women, and she had a certain mindset about women and their potential, especially black women in America. So she wrote a play about a matriarch faced with this dilemma. But in that formulation the son is just a ne'er-do-well. He's a fuckup, not a tragic figure, not a man whose life is on the line. I simply couldn't do it that way, because in my mind the dramatic possibilities were so much greater the other way.

Then, of course, there was the director, Lloyd Richards. Again, a very close friend with whom I had very little quarrel on the question, because his first responsibility was to the work by the playwright. He had gone inside the play with her; she had taken him on an excursion into the inner selves of these characters. So he saw the play as she conceived it, and when he put it together, he put it together that way. He didn't have any conflict with it. But I did — because I had to face an audience, you know? — and I just couldn't face an audience playing it with less than the attitude I thought was necessary for this drama.

Out of town in New Haven I played it their way, but I was looking for answers. I wasn't altogether comfortable. We went on to Philadelphia. Same thing. The play was working fine, but there was something missing. It was working overall, but I wasn't really there. We went to Chicago. Same thing. So Ruby Dee and I started exploring, and in Chicago magic started to happen. Wham! And I started to play differently.

Then we went to New York, and on opening night the energy was at its apex. The director saw it, but he wouldn't characterize the added excitement he sensed as coming from the way I had played the role. The producer saw it too, but he said it was just a great night. The playwright was in the audience, and I went out and helped her up on the stage so that all the world could see this magnificent young woman, this gifted person. She assumed that the incredible night of theater we'd all just experienced was as she wrote it.

Well, I say it played well because there was something special in the conviction I held, and I carried it from Chicago to New York.   30

There's a special moment in the third act, just before the end. They had put a down payment on a house before they lost the money, but a man comes to tell them that they're not wanted in that neighborhood. My character, the son, has to stand up and talk to this man. He's talking to this man about his family. After a given point in the speech, he says, "This is my mother." Then he says, "This is my sister." And then he says. "This is my wife, — and she is" — pride, pain, and love overpower him and he's not able to get her name out. And by the time he turns to his son, his emotions are more than any words could express. The tears roll down his cheeks and he begins to cry. He gestures to the boy, but the words won't come out, and finally he forces out the words. He says, "This is my son," and the house goes nuts, you hear me?

I know from my own experience that when a guy is just afraid, and he wishes to succeed *because he's afraid of failure*, that's not much of a commitment. But there's another kind of drive to succeed. I think of my father, going from bar to bar selling his cigars, probing my arm because he's worried that I'm not getting enough to eat. Then sitting down to write a letter to his eldest son, telling him that he's no longer able to control and guide his youngest, that he needs help. You find a man like that, with a need to do something that's over and above his own ego-requirement — a need that's for his *family*, as he sees it — and you get every ounce of his energy. When a man says, "This is for my *child*," you get over and above that which he thinks he's capable of.

My father was with me every moment as I performed in *A Raisin in the Sun*. The themes, too, seemed like so many threads from my own life. The days in Nassau and Miami and New York when I seemed to be in such a downward spiral and there was no promise of resurrection. All the risks I took, all the brushes with destruction. I know how much it pained my family, but there was nothing they could do. It was this art form that saved me. Ultimately, by taking even greater risks — by going to New York and then by choosing a life in the theater — I came through. And it wasn't just for myself. It was for Reggie too.   *[2000]*

■ THINKING ABOUT THE TEXT

1. Poitier's experience with the play was very much that of an actor involved in performing it. Does his account make you aware of anything that you did not realize when you simply *read* the play? If so, what?

2. Poitier reports that even the author, Lorraine Hansberry, disagreed with his view of the play. In such cases, do you think the performer should usually defer to the playwright? Why, or why not?

3. Does Poitier succeed in persuading you that his view of the play made more sense than its rival? Specify things that affect your response to his argument.

■ WRITING ABOUT ISSUES

1. Choose a particular moment in *A Raisin in the Sun* when characters disagree. Then write an essay analyzing their disagreement. More specifically, identify the different positions they take, the warrants or assumptions that seem to underlie their positions, the outcome of their disagreement, your own evaluation of their views, and the relationship of this moment to the rest of the play. Be sure to quote from the text.

2. Imagine that Hansberry's play is being republished and that you are asked to edit it. Imagine further that the publisher asks you to introduce the play with one of the four background documents in this cluster. Write an essay stating which document you would choose and why.

3. Choose a family you know well, and write an essay comparing it with the Younger family. Above all, consider whether your chosen family, too, has conflicting dreams.

4. Spend time in the library examining newspapers and magazines from 1959, the year *A Raisin in the Sun* opened on Broadway. In particular, try to identify a variety of events and trends that might have affected an American family that year. Next, imagine a specific American family living in 1959. Finally, write an essay describing a play that might be written about your imagined family's reaction to a specific event or trend back then. Give details of the plot, the family's social background, and its members' personalities. If you wish, present some dialogue.

A Conflict of Values: A Story in the News

HANIF KUREISHI, "My Son, the Fanatic"

IN THE NEWS:
HAROON SIDDIQUI, "American Anti-Muslim Prejudice Goes Mainstream"

KNOXVILLE NEWS-SENTINEL, "Attacks on Mosque Site Pervert American Values"

ANDREW NORFOLK, "Muslim Group behind 'Mega-Mosque' Seeks to Convert All Britain"

BARBARA BRADLEY HAGERTY, "New College Teaches Young American Muslims"

Parents the world over hope that their children flourish in society. They want them to be happy, to be successful, and to lead meaningful, productive lives. And the dream of most working-class parents is that their children can move into the middle class, with all the material and cultural advantages they were not able to provide. Not only is that the American Dream; it is a universal hope. Although the following story takes place in England, it could have happened here. In fact, it has, a multitude of times. Our story, however, explores the difficulties that ensue when the child not only rejects the parent's dream but also rejects the entire culture's values and behavior. For the child, the parent's dream is a nightmare. We are familiar with the children who grew up in the 1960s in both England and America who rejected the materialism of their parents, at least for a while. But when religion is at the heart of the rebellion against the parents, the problem is more intense. The father in the following story hopes that his son will adopt Western values, but the son has recently become a devout Muslim with hostile attitudes toward all things Western. The father is baffled and frustrated and finally quite angry. There seems to be no room for compromise. And the situation today seems graver than when Hanif Kureishi wrote this story in a pre-9/11 world. Ali is not a terrorist, but he does say that becoming one is a possibility. It is a chilling and seemingly intractable situation.

■ BEFORE YOU READ

What does the word *fanatic* mean to you? Do you know people whom you would label as fanatics? What is it about their behavior that makes you think of them in this way? Are there any reasons that someone might label you a fanatic?

(© David Levenson/Getty
Images.)

HANIF KUREISHI
My Son, the Fanatic

*Of British and Pakistani descent, Hanif Kureishi was born in Kent, England, in
1954. Although he has written several plays, he is best known for his fiction and
screenplays. Much of his work deals with the struggles of South Asian immigrants
and their families as they face the tensions of Great Britain's increasingly multicultural society. Kureishi's novels include* The Buddha of Suburbia *(1990),* The
Black Album *(1995),* Intimacy *(1998),* Gabriel's Gift *(2001), and* The Body
(2004). His script for the movie My Beautiful Laundrette *(1986), which he based
on his story of the same title, was nominated for an Academy Award and won a New
York Film Critics' Award. His most recent screenplays include* Venus *(2007) and*
The Mother *(2003). His latest work,* Something to Tell You, *was published in
2008. In 2008, the* Times *(London) named Kureishi one of "The 50 Greatest British Writers since 1945." The following story first appeared in a 1994 issue of* The
New Yorker. *Kureishi then included it in his first collection of short fiction,* Love in

a Blue Time *(1997). Subsequently, he wrote a screen adaptation of the story, and this film version, also entitled* My Son, the Fanatic, *was released in 1998.*

Surreptitiously the father began going into his son's bedroom. He would sit there for hours, rousing himself only to seek clues. What bewildered him was that Ali was getting tidier. Instead of the usual tangle of clothes, books, cricket bats, video games, the room was becoming neat and ordered; spaces began appearing where before there had been only mess.

Initially Parvez had been pleased: his son was outgrowing his teenage attitudes. But one day, beside the dustbin, Parvez found a torn bag which contained not only old toys, but computer discs, video tapes, new books, and fashionable clothes the boy had bought just a few months before. Also without explanation, Ali had parted from the English girlfriend who used to come often to the house. His old friends had stopped ringing.

For reasons he didn't himself understand, Parvez wasn't able to bring up the subject of Ali's unusual behavior. He was aware that he had become slightly afraid of his son, who, alongside his silences, was developing a sharp tongue. One remark Parvez did make, "You don't play your guitar any more," elicited the mysterious but conclusive reply, "There are more important things to be done."

Yet Parvez felt his son's eccentricity as an injustice. He had always been aware of the pitfalls which other men's sons had fallen into in England. And so, for Ali he had worked long hours and spent a lot of money paying for his education as an accountant. He had bought him good suits, all the books he required, and a computer. And now the boy was throwing his possessions out!

The TV, video, and sound system followed the guitar. Soon the room was practically bare. Even the unhappy walls bore marks where Ali's pictures had been removed.   5

Parvez couldn't sleep; he went more to the whisky bottle, even when he was at work. He realized it was imperative to discuss the matter with someone sympathetic.

Parvez had been a taxi driver for twenty years. Half that time he'd worked for the same firm. Like him, most of the other drivers were Punjabis. They preferred to work at night, the roads were clearer and the money better. They slept during the day, avoiding their wives. Together they led almost a boy's life in the cabbies' office, playing cards and practical jokes, exchanging lewd stories, eating together, and discussing politics and their problems.

But Parvez had been unable to bring this subject up with his friends. He was too ashamed. And he was afraid, too, that they would blame him for the wrong turning his boy had taken, just as he had blamed other fathers whose sons had taken to running around with bad girls, truanting from school, and joining gangs.

For years Parvez had boasted to the other men about how Ali excelled at cricket, swimming, and football, and how attentive a scholar he was, getting straight A's in most subjects. Was it asking too much for Ali to get a good job now, marry the right girl, and start a family? Once this happened, Parvez would be happy. His dreams of doing well in England would have come true. Where had he gone wrong?

But one night, sitting in the taxi office on busted chairs with his two closest friends watching a Sylvester Stallone film, he broke his silence.

"I can't understand it!" he burst out. "Everything is going from his room. And I can't talk to him any more. We were not father and son — we were brothers! Where has he gone? Why is he torturing me!"

And Parvez put his head in his hands.

Even as he poured out his account the men shook their heads and gave one another knowing glances. From their grave looks Parvez realized they understood the situation. "Tell me what is happening!" he demanded.

The reply was almost triumphant. They had guessed something was going wrong. Now it was clear. Ali was taking drugs and selling his possessions to pay for them. That was why his bedroom was emptying.

"What must I do then?"

Parvez's friends instructed him to watch Ali scrupulously and then be severe with him, before the boy went mad, overdosed, or murdered someone.

Parvez staggered out into the early morning air, terrified they were right. His boy — the drug addict killer!

To his relief he found Bettina sitting in his car.

Usually the last customers of the night were local "brasses" or prostitutes. The taxi drivers knew them well, often driving them to liaisons. At the end of the girls' shifts, the men would ferry them home, though sometimes the women would join them for a drinking session in the office. Occasionally the drivers would go with the girls. "A ride in exchange for a ride," it was called.

Bettina had known Parvez for three years. She lived outside the town and on the long drive home, where she sat not in the passenger seat but beside him, Parvez had talked to her about his life and hopes, just as she talked about hers. They saw each other most nights.

He could talk to her about things he'd never be able to discuss with his own wife. Bettina, in turn, always reported on her night's activities. He liked to know where she was and with whom. Once he had rescued her from a violent client, and since then they had come to care for one another.

Though Bettina had never met the boy, she heard about Ali continually. That late night, when he told Bettina that he suspected Ali was on drugs, she judged neither the boy nor his father, but became businesslike and told him what to watch for.

"It's all in the eyes," she said. They might be bloodshot; the pupils might be dilated; he might look tired. He could be liable to sweats, or sudden mood changes. "Okay?"

Parvez began his vigil gratefully. Now he knew what the problem might be, he felt better. And surely, he figured, things couldn't have gone too far? With Bettina's help he would soon sort it out.

He watched each mouthful the boy took. He sat beside him at every opportunity and looked into his eyes. When he could he took the boy's hand, checking his temperature. If the boy wasn't at home Parvez was active, looking under the carpet, in his drawers, behind the empty wardrobe, sniffing, inspecting, probing. He knew what to look for: Bettina had drawn pictures of capsules, syringes, pills, powders, rocks.

Every night she waited to hear news of what he'd witnessed.

After a few days of constant observation, Parvez was able to report that although the boy had given up sports, he seemed healthy, with clear eyes. He didn't, as his father expected, flinch guiltily from his gaze. In fact the boy's mood was alert and steady in this sense: as well as being sullen, he was very watchful. He returned his father's long looks with more than a hint of criticism, of reproach even, so much so that Parvez began to feel that it was he who was in the wrong, and not the boy!

"And there's nothing else physically different?" Bettina asked.

"No!" Parvez thought for a moment. "But he is growing a beard."

One night, after sitting with Bettina in an all-night coffee shop, Parvez   30
came home particularly late. Reluctantly he and Bettina had abandoned their only explanation, the drug theory, for Parvez had found nothing resembling any drug in Ali's room. Besides, Ali wasn't selling his belongings. He threw them out, gave them away, or donated them to charity shops.

Standing in the hall, Parvez heard his boy's alarm clock go off. Parvez hurried into his bedroom where his wife was still awake, sewing in bed. He ordered her to sit down and keep quiet, though she had neither stood up nor said a word. From this post, and with her watching him curiously, he observed his son through the crack in the door.

The boy went into the bathroom to wash. When he returned to his room Parvez sprang across the hall and set his ear at Ali's door. A muttering sound came from within. Parvez was puzzled but relieved.

Once this clue had been established, Parvez watched him at other times. The boy was praying. Without fail, when he was at home, he prayed five times a day.

Parvez had grown up in Lahore where all the boys had been taught the Koran. To stop him falling asleep when he studied, the Moulvi° had attached a piece of string to the ceiling and tied it to Parvez's hair, so that if his head fell forward, he would instantly awake. After this indignity Parvez had avoided all religions. Not that the other taxi drivers had more respect. In fact they made jokes about the local mullahs° walking around with their caps and beards, thinking they could tell people how to live, while their eyes roved over the boys and girls in their care.

Parvez described to Bettina what he had discovered. He informed the men   35
in the taxi office. The friends, who had been so curious before, now became oddly silent. They could hardly condemn the boy for his devotions.

Moulvi: Islamic religious scholar who might perform the function of a teacher.
mullahs: Muslims with religious education, who often hold supervisory positions within Islam.

Parvez decided to take a night off and go out with the boy. They could talk things over. He wanted to hear how things were going at college; he wanted to tell him stories about their family in Pakistan. More than anything he yearned to understand how Ali had discovered the "spiritual dimension," as Bettina described it.

To Parvez's surprise, the boy refused to accompany him. He claimed he had an appointment. Parvez had to insist that no appointment could be more important than that of a son with his father.

The next day, Parvez went immediately to the street where Bettina stood in the rain wearing high heels, a short skirt, and a long mac on top, which she would open hopefully at passing cars.

"Get in, get in!" he said.

They drove out across the moors and parked at the spot where on better   40
days, with a view unimpeded for many miles by nothing but wild deer and horses, they'd lie back, with their eyes half closed, saying "This is the life." This time Parvez was trembling. Bettina put her arms around him.

"What's happened?"

"I've just had the worst experience of my life."

As Bettina rubbed his head Parvez told her that the previous evening he and Ali had gone to a restaurant. As they studied the menu, the waiter, whom Parvez knew, brought him his usual whisky and water. Parvez had been so nervous he had even prepared a question. He was going to ask Ali if he was worried about his imminent exams. But first, wanting to relax, he loosened his tie, crunched a popadom,° and took a long drink.

Before Parvez could speak, Ali made a face.

"Don't you know it's wrong to drink alcohol?" he said.   45

"He spoke to me very harshly," Parvez told Bettina. "I was about to castigate the boy for being insolent, but managed to control myself."

He had explained patiently to Ali that for years he had worked more than ten hours a day, that he had few enjoyments or hobbies and never went on holiday. Surely it wasn't a crime to have a drink when he wanted one?

"But it is forbidden," the boy said.

Parvez shrugged, "I know."

"And so is gambling, isn't it."   50

"Yes. But surely we are only human?"

Each time Parvez took a drink, the boy winced, or made a fastidious face as an accompaniment. This made Parvez drink more quickly. The waiter, wanting to please his friend, brought another glass of whisky. Parvez knew he was getting drunk, but he couldn't stop himself. Ali had a horrible look on his face, full of disgust and censure. It was as if he hated his father.

Halfway through the meal Parvez suddenly lost his temper and threw a plate on the floor. He had felt like ripping the cloth from the table, but the waiters and other customers were staring at him. Yet he wouldn't stand for his own

popadom: Unleavened bread made from lentils and shaped like a disc.

son telling him the difference between right and wrong. He knew he wasn't a
bad man. He had a conscience. There were a few things of which he was
ashamed, but on the whole he had lived a decent life.

"When have I had time to be wicked?" he asked Ali.

In a low monotonous voice the boy explained that Parvez had not, in fact,   55
lived a good life. He had broken countless rules of the Koran.

"For instance?" Parvez demanded.

Ali hadn't needed time to think. As if he had been waiting for this moment,
he asked his father if he didn't relish pork pies?

"Well . . ."

Parvez couldn't deny that he loved crispy bacon smothered with mushrooms and mustard and sandwiched between slices of fried bread. In fact he ate
this for breakfast every morning.

Ali then reminded Parvez that he had ordered his own wife to cook pork   60
sausages, saying to her, "You're not in the village now, this is England. We have
to fit in!"

Parvez was so annoyed and perplexed by this attack that he called for more
drink.

"The problem is this," the boy said. He leaned across the table. For the
first time that night his eyes were alive. "You are too implicated in Western
civilization."

Parvez burped; he thought he was going to choke. "Implicated!" he said.
"But we live here!"

"The Western materialists hate us," Ali said. "Papa, how can you love
something which hates you?"

"What is the answer then?" Parvez said miserably. "According to you."   65

Ali addressed his father fluently, as if Parvez were a rowdy crowd that had
to be quelled and convinced. The Law of Islam would rule the world; the skin of
the infidel would burn off again and again; the Jews and Christers would be
routed. The West was a sink of hypocrites, adulterers, homosexuals, drug takers, and prostitutes.

As Ali talked, Parvez looked out of the window as if to check that they were
still in London.

"My people have taken enough. If the persecution doesn't stop there will
be *jihad*. I, and millions of others, will gladly give our lives for the cause."

"But why, why?" Parvez said.

"For us the reward will be in paradise."   70

"Paradise!"

Finally, as Parvez's eyes filled with tears, the boy urged him to mend his
ways.

"How is that possible?" Parvez asked.

"Pray," Ali said. "Pray beside me."

Parvez called for the bill and ushered his boy out of the restaurant as soon   75
as he was able. He couldn't take any more. Ali sounded as if he'd swallowed
someone else's voice.

On the way home the boy sat in the back of the taxi, as if he were a customer.

"What has made you like this?" Parvez asked him, afraid that somehow he was to blame for all this. "Is there a particular event which has influenced you?"

"Living in this country."

"But I love England," Parvez said, watching his boy in the mirror. "They let you do almost anything here."

"That is the problem," he replied.   80

For the first time in years Parvez couldn't see straight. He knocked the side of the car against a lorry, ripping off the wing mirror. They were lucky not to have been stopped by the police: Parvez would have lost his license and therefore his job.

Getting out of the car back at the house, Parvez stumbled and fell in the road, scraping his hands and ripping his trousers. He managed to haul himself up. The boy didn't even offer him his hand.

Parvez told Bettina he was now willing to pray, if that was what the boy wanted, if that would dislodge the pitiless look from his eyes.

"But what I object to," he said, "is being told by my own son that I am going to hell!"

What finished Parvez off was that the boy had said he was giving up accountancy. When Parvez had asked why, Ali had said sarcastically that it was obvious.   85

"Western education cultivates an antireligious attitude."

And, according to Ali, in the world of accountants it was usual to meet women, drink alcohol, and practice usury.

"But it's well-paid work," Parvez argued. "For years you've been preparing!"

Ali said he was going to begin to work in prisons, with poor Muslims who were struggling to maintain their purity in the face of corruption. Finally, at the end of the evening, as Ali was going to bed, he had asked his father why he didn't have a beard, or at least a mustache.

"I feel as if I've lost my son," Parvez told Bettina. "I can't bear to be looked at as if I'm a criminal. I've decided what to do."   90

"What is it?"

"I'm going to tell him to pick up his prayer mat and get out of my house. It will be the hardest thing I've ever done, but tonight I'm going to do it."

"But you mustn't give up on him," said Bettina. "Many young people fall into cults and superstitious groups. It doesn't mean they'll always feel the same way."

She said Parvez had to stick by his boy, giving support, until he came through.

Parvez was persuaded that she was right, even though he didn't feel like giving his son more love when he had hardly been thanked for all he had already given.   95

Nevertheless, Parvez tried to endure his son's looks and reproaches. He attempted to make conversation about his beliefs. But if Parvez ventured any criticism, Ali always had a brusque reply. On one occasion Ali accused Parvez of "grovelling" to the whites; in contrast, he explained, he was not "inferior," there was more to the world than the West, though the West always thought it was best.

"How is it you know that?" Parvez said, "seeing as you've never left England?"

Ali replied with a look of contempt.

One night, having ensured there was no alcohol on his breath, Parvez sat down at the kitchen table with Ali. He hoped Ali would compliment him on the beard he was growing but Ali didn't appear to notice.

The previous day Parvez had been telling Bettina that he thought people in   100
the West sometimes felt inwardly empty and that people needed a philosophy to live by.

"Yes," said Bettina. "That's the answer. You must tell him what your philosophy of life is. Then he will understand that there are other beliefs."

After some fatiguing consideration, Parvez was ready to begin. The boy watched him as if he expected nothing.

Haltingly Parvez said that people had to treat one another with respect, particularly children their parents. This did seem, for a moment, to affect the boy. Heartened, Parvez continued. In his view this life was all there was and when you died you rotted in the earth. "Grass and flowers will grow out of me, but something of me will live on —"

"How?"

"In other people. I will continue — in you." At this the boy appeared a little   105
distressed. "And your grandchildren," Parvez added for good measure. "But while I am here on earth I want to make the best of it. And I want you to, as well!"

"What d'you mean by 'make the best of it'?" asked the boy.

"Well," said Parvez. "For a start . . . you should enjoy yourself. Yes. Enjoy yourself without hurting others."

Ali said that enjoyment was a "bottomless pit."

"But I don't mean enjoyment like that!" said Parvez. "I mean the beauty of living!"

"All over the world our people are oppressed," was the boy's reply.   110

"I know," Parvez replied, not entirely sure who "our people" were, "but still — life is for living!"

Ali said, "Real morality has existed for hundreds of years. Around the world millions and millions of people share my beliefs. Are you saying you are right and they are all wrong?"

Ali looked at his father with such aggressive confidence that Parvez could say no more.

One evening Bettina was sitting in Parvez's car, after visiting a client, when they passed a boy on the street.

"That's my son," Parvez said suddenly. They were on the other side of   115
town, in a poor district, where there were two mosques.

Parvez set his face hard.

Bettina turned to watch him. "Slow down then, slow down!" She said, "He's good-looking. Reminds me of you. But with a more determined face. Please, can't we stop?"

"What for?"

"I'd like to talk to him."

Parvez turned the cab round and stopped beside the boy.   120

"Coming home?" Parvez asked. "It's quite a way."

The sullen boy shrugged and got into the back seat. Bettina sat in the front. Parvez became aware of Bettina's short skirt, gaudy rings and ice-blue eyeshadow. He became conscious that the smell of her perfume, which he loved, filled the cab. He opened the window.

While Parvez drove as fast as he could, Bettina said gently to Ali, "Where have you been?"

"The mosque," he said.

"And how are you getting on at college? Are you working hard?"   125

"Who are you to ask me these questions?" he said, looking out of the window. Then they hit bad traffic and the car came to a standstill.

By now Bettina had inadvertently laid her hand on Parvez's shoulder. She said, "Your father, who is a good man, is very worried about you. You know he loves you more than his own life."

"You say he loves me," the boy said.

"Yes!" said Bettina.

"Then why is he letting a woman like you touch him like that?"   130

If Bettina looked at the boy in anger, he looked back at her with twice as much cold fury.

She said, "What kind of woman am I that deserves to be spoken to like that?"

"You know," he said. "Now let me out."

"Never," Parvez replied.

"Don't worry, I'm getting out," Bettina said.   135

"No, don't!" said Parvez. But even as the car moved she opened the door, threw herself out, and ran away across the road. Parvez shouted after her several times, but she had gone.

Parvez took Ali back to the house, saying nothing more to him. Ali went straight to his room. Parvez was unable to read the paper, watch television, or even sit down. He kept pouring himself drinks.

At last he went upstairs and paced up and down outside Ali's room. When, finally, he opened the door, Ali was praying. The boy didn't even glance his way.

Parvez kicked him over. Then he dragged the boy up by his shirt and hit him. The boy fell back. Parvez hit him again. The boy's face was bloody. Parvez was panting. He knew that the boy was unreachable, but he struck him nonetheless. The boy neither covered himself nor retaliated; there was no fear in his eyes. He only said, through his split lip: "So who's the fanatic now?"   [1994]

■ **THINKING ABOUT THE TEXT**

1. Not until a few pages into the story do we learn what is really going on with Ali. Until then, we share his father's mystification. Why do you think Kureishi does not tell us sooner about Ali's turn to religion?

2. Ali says, "The Western materialists hate us" (para. 64). Is this true? His father then asks, "What is the answer then? . . . According to you" (para. 65). How do you respond to Ali's answer?

3. What specific ideals and principles are in conflict as the father and son argue with each other? Can these differences be negotiated, or are they irreconcilable?

4. What should we conclude about Parvez's relationship with Bettina? What would you say to someone who faults Parvez for committing adultery with a prostitute? Is Parvez's relationship an individual one, or does it say something about Western values?

5. Do you approve of Parvez's behavior when he beats his son at the story's end? Why, or why not? Is Ali's response to the beating correct — that is, do you think the father has become a fanatic?

In the News

The following news items deal with cases of the fraught relationship in the years since September 11, 2001, between some Muslim groups and Western countries, specifically the United States and Britain. These conflicts test the limits of religious tolerance and free speech. The first article was written by Haroon Siddiqui, a well-known columnist for the *Toronto Star*, where the piece first appeared on August 26, 2010. Here, Siddiqui reports on anti-Muslim feelings found within American politics and media, using such conservative commentators as Rush Limbaugh and Newt Gingrich as examples.

In the second article, published on September 2, 2010, the *Knoxville News-Sentinel* voices strong opposition to those who burned the construction equipment at the site of a future Islamic center in Murfreesboro, Tennessee. The site had also been vandalized twice before the fire.

Andrew Norfolk is a journalist at the *Times* (London), where this article was published on September 10, 2007. Here, he writes about a "mega-mosque" that was to be built in east London and the potential danger it posed, mainly because of charges of anti-Western extremism against the mosque's sect, Tablighi Jamaat. Construction of the mosque, which would have held twelve thousand worshippers, was put on hold after Tablighi Jamaat failed to turn in a planning application on time.

The final piece in this cluster appeared on National Public Radio's *Morning Edition* on September 8, 2010, and was written by Barbara Bradley Hagerty, NPR's religious correspondent and author of the book *Fingerprints of God: In Search of the Science of Spirituality* (2009). Here, Hagerty reports on America's first Islamic liberal arts college, Zaytuna College, founded in 2009.

HAROON SIDDIQUI
American Anti-Muslim Prejudice Goes Mainstream

Conspiracy theorists, especially in the Muslim world, held that 9/11 was really the work of Israelis or the Americans themselves. Nine years out, it's the Americans who are singing loony tunes about Muslims.

Eighteen percent think Barack Obama is a Muslim, according to a Pew poll. That's 55 million Americans. Many use only his middle name, Hussein. Rush Limbaugh calls him Imam Obama.

Newt Gingrich believes that sharia, the Islamic law, is coming to America by stealth. The danger is so high, says a Republican state representative in Oklahoma, that "there's a war for the survival of America."

Others have called Elena Kagan, the newly appointed Supreme Court judge, "Justice Sharia" because she had been dean of Harvard Law School, which teaches Islamic jurisprudence.

Two Republican members of Congress, Sue Myrick of North Carolina and   5
Paul Broun of Georgia, believe that young Muslim interns are part of a secret Islamic infiltration into Capitol Hill.

Then there's the firestorm over the Ground Zero mosque.

"The outcry implies that Islam alone was responsible for the 9/11 attacks," writes Ron Paul, Republican member of Congress from Texas.

He says it's all part of a long and well-orchestrated campaign by those "who demand continual war in the Middle East and Central Asia" and who "never miss a chance to use hatred toward Muslims to rally support for the ill-conceived preventative wars."

Gingrich equates the proposed Islamic centre there to a Nazi display next to the Holocaust Museum in D.C. or a Japanese warrior monument at Pearl Harbor. (The analogy would be fine if Osama bin Laden was the one building a mosque at the World Trade Center and not a Manhattan couple, devoted to interfaith work, proposing a Muslim Y.)

"Gingrich is too smart to be that stupid," says John Esposito, professor   10
of Islamic Studies at Georgetown University in Washington, D.C., by way of illustrating how anti-Muslim bigotry has become so acceptable that "mainstream politicians, including two potential Republican presidential candidates [Gingrich and Sarah Palin], media commentators, hardline Christian Zionists, and a large number of Americans feel that they can say anything about Islam and Muslims with impunity.

"They are not simply members of minority anti-immigrant parties as in Europe."

Esposito's opinion, conveyed by email, contradicts mine, . . . that the anti-Muslim voices in America are marginal.

Esposito, a Catholic, is a respected public intellectual and a prolific author on contemporary Islam. His latest and 45th book, *The Future of Islam*, tackles all the controversial topics, from violent Islamists to Western Islamophobes.

That the firestorm over the Muslim centre in Manhattan reflects deeper malaise can be seen in the fact that few 9/11 families oppose the project and opposition to it is less in New York than across the United States.

Several studies show that significant percentages of Americans admit to   15
prejudice against Muslims; approve of racially profiling them and forcing them to carry identity cards; and say that Muslims should not be allowed to run for president or Congress or be appointed to the Supreme Court, etc.

All this despite the fact that American Muslims are well integrated. They are more educated and more of them are in the workforce than the average American. Muslim women report monthly household incomes more nearly equal to men's, compared with women and men in other faith groups.

Esposito: "Islamophobia is fast becoming what anti-Semitism is — rooted in hostility and intolerance toward religious and cultural beliefs and a religious or racial group. The social cancer of Islamophobia must be recognized as unacceptable as anti-Semitism."

He was sad to see that the venerable Anti-Defamation League, "devoted to fighting defamation and prejudice," decided to oppose the Manhattan Muslim centre "not because Muslims do not have a right to build it but rather to protect the feelings of those opposed! Is this a criterion the ADL has used or would subscribe to in its own struggles against anti-Semitism?"

(Fareed Zakaria, *Newsweek* columnist and CNN host, has returned an award given him by the ADL, saying its stand went against its declared aim of opposition to discrimination and bigotry.)

Esposito said that what's happening across the United States hurts the   20
country in several ways: It feeds the bin Laden theory that America is at war with Islam; it helps Al Qaeda and other militants recruit; and it erodes America itself.

"What is at stake is the very core of who and what we are as a nation and a society, the foundation of our identity, and the principles and values embodied in our constitution."   [2010]

KNOXVILLE NEWS-SENTINEL
Attacks on Mosque Site Pervert American Values

The recent arson and vandalism at the site of a proposed mosque and community center in Murfreesboro, Tennessee, is an insult to all Americans that cannot go unchallenged.

Though no one has been arrested and federal authorities are being circumspect about the burning of construction equipment at the site, the perpetrators are guilty of a hate crime at worst and of negligently spitting on our way of life at best.

The First Amendment to the Constitution affords all Americans the right to worship as they please. Individuals might disagree about religion, but each of us has the legal protection to follow his or her own path to the divine. Or opt out of any spiritual journey altogether.

The First Amendment's establishment clause is so fundamental to the concept of the United States that it seems odd even to have to invoke it. Freedom of religion is a human right that should be as natural as breathing. The poisonous cloud hanging over Murfreesboro, however, scorches the lungs and renders breathing free air impossible.

Those who oppose the right of Muslims to build a mosque in Murfreesboro   5
are either wrongheaded or bigots. Those who have broken the law in the expression of their bigotry should be considered enemies of our country. They are, quite simply, terrorists.

Muslims have been part of the Murfreesboro community for decades. They have lived in the city's neighborhoods, shopped in its stores, and supported its schools — just like their more numerous Baptist, Methodist, Presbyterian, Catholic, and atheistic neighbors.

All the Murfreesboro Muslims want to do is worship in a building that can accommodate their growing population. They want a place where Muslim families can gather for fellowship and where their children can play. The center seems not unlike the facilities common to large Christian churches in our area — First Baptist Concord or Cokesbury United Methodist, for example.

Those who oppose the mosque for religious reasons would be better served by reaching out to the Muslim community to find common ground, of which there is an abundance.

Those who oppose the mosque on technical grounds already have lost — the land has the appropriate zoning for the facility, and there's no legal barrier to its construction.

Those whose bigotry and hatred of Muslims compels them to break the   10
law should be caught and punished. They are the un-American ones, the true threats to our safety and security. They are the ones who trample on the Constitution and dishonor the flag that symbolizes our country.

Such crimes, which carry with them the implicit threat of violence, play into the hands of our true enemies — al-Qaida and the Taliban. Acts of terrorism against peaceful, moderate Muslims who are American citizens will be of great use to our enemies in cultivating extremists for their vile cause.

Attacks on mosques might seem like patriotic acts to some, but they amount to acts of treason. They strike at the very core of American values.

All people of good will should unite against them.   *[2010]*

ANDREW NORFOLK

Muslim Group behind "Mega-Mosque" Seeks to Convert All Britain

A Muslim group that wants to open a giant £100 million mosque in London has set its sights on "winning the whole of Britain to Islam."

Tablighi Jamaat aims to build an Islamic complex near to the site of the 2012 Olympic stadium, with a mosque for 12,000 people, by far the largest religious building in Britain.

The organisation, which has millions of followers worldwide, insists that it is a peaceful, apolitical revivalist movement that promotes Islamic consciousness among individual Muslims. However, intelligence agencies have cautioned that the group's ability to fire young men with a zeal for Islam acts as a staging post, for some, along a path that leads to jihadist terrorism.

Kafeel Ahmed, the Indian doctor who died from burns last month after trying to set off a car bomb at Glasgow Airport, is the latest in a line of terrorists for whose initial radicalisation Tablighi Jamaat has been blamed. The group (literally, the preaching party) belongs to the ultra-conservative Deobandi school of thought within Sunni Islam, whose adherents run more than 600 of Britain's 1,350 mosques.

In recent days the *Times* has exposed the virulently anti-Western creed of   5
some British Deobandis who preach that non-Muslims are an evil and corrupting influence. Their defensive, isolationist approach to life in Britain is shared by many British supporters of Tablighi Jamaat.

One leading advocate, Ebrahim Rangooni, has said that the movement seeks to "rescue the ummah [the global Muslim community] from the culture and civilisation of the Jews, the Christians and [other] enemies of Islam." Its aim, he wrote, is to "create such hatred for their ways as human beings have for urine and excreta."

Mr. Rangooni has also given warning to parents that non-Muslim schools "turn humans into animals" and that sending a Muslim child to a British college "is as dangerous as throwing them into hell with your own hands."

Representatives of Tablighi Jamaat refused to attend a public meeting on Friday to discuss plans for the "mega-mosque" in West Ham, even though the debate was organised by a Muslim group.

Tablighi Jamaat was founded in 1926, in India, by a Deobandi scholar, Muhammad Ilyas, who wanted to raise Islamic awareness among rural Muslims in south Asia. He promised them that by obeying Islamic laws and following the example of the Prophet Muhammad in their personal lives they would one day "dominate over non-believers" and become "masters of everything on this earth."

Ishaq Patel, Tablighi Jamaat's first amir (leader) in Britain, is said to have   10
been on pilgrimage in Mecca when Ilyas's successor gave him a long-term mission to win "the whole of Britain to Islam."

Yoginder Sikand, a Muslim expert on the movement, says that its ethos of "social and cultural separatism and insularity" seeks "to minimise contacts with people of other faiths."   *[2007]*

BARBARA BRADLEY HAGERTY
New College Teaches Young American Muslims

I don't know what I expected to find when I arrived at Zaytuna College in Berkeley, California, the country's brand new Muslim liberal arts college. Women in headscarves? Yes, for the most part. Men with heavy beards? No. A lot of prayer and fasting, since it's Ramadan? Absolutely.

What I didn't expect was 32-year-old Jamye Ford. "I grew up as an AME, African Methodist Episcopal, in a very religious Southern family," Ford says in the campus quad. "I went to church every Sunday for hours at a time, I went to Bible study, did all of those things. And from a young age, I had curiosity about religion in general and other religions."

Ford bought a Quran at a secondhand bookstore when he was 9 and memorized a few *sura*, or passages, which he always remembered. He entered Columbia University at 18 and graduated with a degree in history. But he was drawn to the poetry of the Quran, and this summer, he began studying Arabic at Zaytuna.

"That was my first opportunity to be in a Muslim environment, and within   5
a short time, a week, two weeks, I felt changed by that experience," he says.

Ford converted to Islam seven weeks ago and enrolled at Zaytuna College to cultivate his newfound faith. Is he concerned that the college is still unaccredited or that he might be making himself a target at a time when some people are furious over a proposed Islamic center in New York City?

"I think I'm looking forward to this more than I looked forward to going to Columbia, honestly," he says.

Day 1

Fifteen students settled themselves in a classroom rented from an American Baptist seminary building near the University of California, Berkeley's campus on August 23. The six men and nine women comprise Zaytuna College's inaugural class. For these students, this is their chance to study their faith with America's top Islamic scholars. For the college's founders, it's a chance to hone a new image for American Islam.

Indeed, the class looks like America's Islamic population, writ small: The largest group here is African-American. There are a few students from Middle Eastern and South Asian families, and a couple of Caucasians. All are U.S. citizens, coming from Cleveland; Denver; Brooklyn, New York; and Cape Canaveral, Florida, and there's not a foreign accent among them.

The room falls silent as Imam Zaid Shakir strides into the room. He's a tall,   10
lanky African-American and a founder of the college. The students sit rapt as he tells them that they are "pioneers," charting the future course of American Islam — which is *not* for the faint of heart.

"Literally, the whole world is looking at you," he says, as he paces in front of the room. "The whole world is listening to you. You will be put under a microscope by a lot of people, and you will have to perform."

Later, I ask student Faatimah Knight why she would come to this unaccredited Muslim college. Knight, who grew up in Brooklyn and whose parents converted to Islam, turned down seven other colleges, including the University of Chicago, Smith, and Bard.

"Zaytuna is really the only place I thought would benefit me," she says, "not just in terms of book smarts and knowledge I would gain there, but also in terms of my own character and developing myself as a person, which I'm pretty confident I couldn't get anywhere else."

Cultivating American Islam

Catholics have Notre Dame, Jews have Yeshiva University, and Evangelicals have Wheaton College — but until now, Muslim Americans didn't have their own liberal arts college. And then there's the appeal of the two founders, Imam Shakir and Sheik Hamza Yusuf, who are celebrities by preaching an Islam that resonates with young Americans.

"They're better than rock stars," Knight says, laughing, "because they're   15 real people with real morals that you should actually look up to and admire. They're like the best of us."

Knight says that "thousands, maybe millions" of teenagers around the world follow Shakir and Yusuf on YouTube, and their live speeches fill college auditoriums. Her age group relates to these two men — who were born in the United States and converted to Islam — much more than to, say, a cleric from Saudi Arabia.

"We want our American Muslim scholars because we're Americans and we're Muslims, and that's how we identify ourselves," she says. "We want to learn from people who look like us, talk like us, think like us, eat like us. It's only natural — it's just human."

And increasingly, American Islam looks and sounds, well, American. A third of all Muslims in the United States were born here, and half a million of them are converts like Jamye Ford. Ford says that as he thought about changing religions, he realized he needed to overcome a philosophical hurdle, especially challenging right now.

"So often, the way the idea is portrayed is there's a dichotomy: There's being American and there's being Muslim, and these two must necessarily be at odds with one another," he says. "And it was clear to me that these two things don't have to exist separately."

The idea that their faith can be woven into an American lifestyle rather   20 than skew it plays out in several ways at Zaytuna. Yes, most of the women wear headscarves, but that's a choice; there is no dress code. Men and women sit next to each other in class, they chat easily and share meals when they break their fast — things that would never happen in an Islamic school overseas.

"Grin and Bear It"

Yusuf says Zaytuna has a deeper motive than just making the students feel at home. He wants to tease apart the *religion* of Islam from the *customs* and *ideas* of the Middle East. He's learned this from personal experience. He says that during his 10 years studying abroad, he imbibed ideas that had nothing to do with Islam, such as anger at U.S. foreign policy.

"This idea of not liking my country, the people I come from, became problematic for me, so I had that internal struggle in my own evolution. And I think that's happened to many young converts who have gone overseas."

Consider Jose Padilla and John Walker Lindh, Americans who learned their religion under al-Qaida and the Taliban, and are now in federal prison. Yusuf says that people with shallow theology and literal interpretations of scripture—of all types—can become extremists, and he argues that having an American Islamic school is a hedge against violent Islam.

Yusuf knows some might disagree, with people threatening to burn the Quran, and others, such as Newt Gingrich, equating Muslims with terrorists and Nazis. He's bracing for some pushback, but he's not worried.

"Anybody who does even a superficial survey of who we are will, I think,   25
recognize pretty quickly that we're not radical terrorists, fundamentalists, whatever," he says.

Still, some students are a little jittery.

"You know, you can feel people's hatred," says Faatimah Knight. "It's palpable."

"It kind of makes you nervous," says another student, Adnan Alam, whose family comes from Pakistan. "You don't want to do something that is going to cause people to think, 'Wow, these guys are crazy.' The magnifying glass is so large right now. Anything can be misconstrued."

For the 15 students in the class of 2014, the opening convocation was a grand ceremony. The speakers spoke of new beginnings but warned about the hostility these students will likely face.

Knight says she knows they have a big responsibility.   30

"That's OK, we'll just have to grin and bear it," she says. "There's going to be a lot of great times and a lot of very difficult times, but we're making history, so we understand that."

The students here say that when they graduate, they hope to be teachers, business owners, public servants. Ford says that when he looks at his class-mates, he sees the next generation of Muslim leaders.

"To imagine that down the road these people will be the next imams, the next sheiks, the next senators, the next president—it's awe-inspiring," he says.

That's Zaytuna's hope, at least—a big hope for a tiny college, especially in a country now conflicted over how to treat its Muslim minority.   *[2010]*

≡ THINKING ABOUT THE TEXTS

1. What is your response to the controversies surrounding the projected Islamic cultural center near Ground Zero in New York City? What issues seem most germane?

2. What is your response to Zaytuna College in Berkeley? What aspects of Islam do you think appeal to young Americans? Do you think the comparison between Zaytuna and Notre Dame, Yeshiva University, and Wheaton College is valid?

3. Do you think the response to Muslims has historical precedents in American history?

■ WRITING ABOUT ISSUES

1. Write an argument essay that supports the idea that Parvez does his duty in regard to Ali.

2. After researching the controversy surrounding the minister who planned to burn the Quran on September 11, 2010, write an argument for or against his right to do so.

3. Find other stories about both anti-Western attitudes among Muslims and anti-Islamic attitudes among Westerners. Write a report about your findings.

4. Write an argument supporting or opposing the construction of the Islamic cultural center and mosque at Ground Zero in New York City. Be sure to carefully consider the opposition.

◼ Fateful Decisions about Parenthood: Stories

ERNEST HEMINGWAY, "Hills like White Elephants"

T. CORAGHESSAN BOYLE, "The Love of My Life"

JOHN EDGAR WIDEMAN, "Newborn Thrown in Trash and Dies"

Ambitious politicians are not the only voices extolling the virtues of family life. Millennia of images and narratives have socialized us to accept the naturalness of motherhood and fatherhood and to see parenthood as a concept that is nearly beyond critique, beyond questioning. We look askance at those who fail in their roles as loving, supportive parents — and sometimes even at couples who decide that they do not want children or at least not as a result of a particular pregnancy. Although abortion has been legal since the early 1970s, the decision to abort a fetus is often not easy to make. Some couples agonize during the decision process, especially if they are not married and especially, as in Ernest Hemingway's story, if the procedure is illegal and risky. Under these circumstances, it is not surprising if one partner sees the pressure to abort as signifying something ominous for the relationship's future.

Even though the right to terminate a pregnancy is still an emotionally contested political and ethical issue, there is almost universal condemnation — in America, at least — for parents who harm infants. Our culture does not seem to forgive such behavior, often condemning it regardless of the circumstances. But serious writers are not in the habit of shying away from the dark corners of human experience, and we can profitably turn to writers like T. Coraghessan Boyle and John Edgar Wideman to shine the artist's light on disturbing stories of family life gone awry. In his notes on "The Love of My Life," Boyle writes that at its essence the world "remains a dark and mysterious place. I write fiction to address and measure my response to that darkness and mystery." With Boyle, we can try to sort out the inevitably conflicting feelings we have about the actions of the characters in the following stories.

◼ BEFORE YOU READ

Respond to the following statement: "Neonaticide (the killing of an infant less than a day old) has been going on for centuries. Some societies have allowed the practice if done under extreme stress. Some modern philosophers also agree with this position."

ERNEST HEMINGWAY
Hills like White Elephants

One of the most influential writers of the first half of the twentieth century, Ernest Hemingway (1898–1961) was born in a suburb of Chicago but felt most alive at his parents' summer home in the woods of Michigan, where he could indulge his enthusiastic love of hunting, fishing, and camping. After high school, where he was an active and excellent student, Hemingway decided to become a journalist instead of going to college and worked successfully for the Kansas City Star. *He signed up as an ambulance driver for the Red Cross during World War I and was seriously wounded in Italy. After moving to Paris after the war, he wrote his first important book,* In Our Time *(1925). It was well received, and the next year* The Sun Also Rises, *about the "lost generation," made him a celebrity. He published several popular novels, including* For Whom the Bell Tolls *(1949) and* The Old Man and the Sea *(1952). He received the Nobel Prize for literature in 1954 and committed suicide after difficult mental and physical problems. Always full of contradictions, Hemingway was at once an inveterate sportsman and an omnivorous reader; he loved life while also being obsessed with death, especially his father's suicide. Most people think of him as a famous and intensely masculine writer of adventure tales of big game, hunting, fishing, and war. While this is true, he was also a dedicated and intricate stylist of great delicacy and power. The following story is a good example of Hemingway's technique of developing a story through dialogue. He was a believer in compression, using an analogy to an iceberg to explain his narrative method: "There is seven-eighths of it under water for every part that shows." His laconic style continues to influence today's writers.*

The hills across the valley of the Ebro were long and white. On this side there was no shade and no trees and the station was between two lines of rails in the sun. Close against the side of the station there was the warm shadow of the building and a curtain, made of strings of bamboo beads, hung across the open door into the bar, to keep out flies. The American and the girl with him sat at a table in the shade, outside the building. It was very hot and the express from Barcelona would come in forty minutes. It stopped at this junction for two minutes and went on to Madrid.

"What should we drink?" the girl asked. She had taken off her hat and put it on the table.

"It's pretty hot," the man said.

"Let's drink beer."

"*Dos cervezas*," the man said into the curtain.   5

"Big ones?" a woman asked from the doorway.

"Yes. Two big ones."

The woman brought two glasses of beer and two felt pads. She put the felt pads and the beer glasses on the table and looked at the man and the girl. The girl was looking off at the line of hills. They were white in the sun and the country was brown and dry.

"They look like white elephants," she said.

"I've never seen one," the man drank his beer.   10

"No, you wouldn't have."

"I might have," the man said. "Just because you say I wouldn't have doesn't prove anything."

The girl looked at the bead curtain. "They've painted something on it," she said. "What does it say?"

"Anis del Toro. It's a drink."

"Could we try it?" 15

The man called "Listen" through the curtain. The woman came out from the bar.

"Four reales."

"We want two Anis del Toro."

"With water?"

"Do you want it with water?" 20

"I don't know," the girl said. "Is it good with water?"

"It's all right."

"You want them with water?" asked the woman.

"Yes, with water."

"It tastes like licorice," the girl said and put the glass down. 25

"That's the way with everything."

"Yes," said the girl. "Everything tastes of licorice. Especially all the things you've waited so long for, like absinthe."

"Oh, cut it out."

"You started it," the girl said. "I was being amused. I was having a fine time."

"Well, let's try and have a fine time." 30

"All right. I was trying. I said the mountains looked like white elephants. Wasn't that bright?"

"That was bright."

"I wanted to try this new drink: That's all we do, isn't it — look at things and try new drinks?"

"I guess so."

The girl looked across at the hills. 35

"They're lovely hills," she said. "They don't really look like white elephants. I just meant the coloring of their skin through the trees."

"Should we have another drink?"

"All right."

The warm wind blew the bead curtain against the table.

"The beer's nice and cool," the man said. 40

"It's lovely," the girl said.

"It's really an awfully simple operation, Jig," the man said. "It's not really an operation at all."

The girl looked at the ground the table legs rested on.

"I know you wouldn't mind it, Jig. It's really not anything. It's just to let the air in."

The girl did not say anything. 45

"I'll go with you and I'll stay with you all the time. They just let the air in and then it's all perfectly natural."

"Then what will we do afterward?"

"We'll be fine afterward. Just like we were before."

"What makes you think so?"

"That's the only thing that bothers us. It's the only thing that's made us 50 unhappy."

The girl looked at the bead curtain, put her hand out, and took hold of two of the strings of beads.

"And you think then we'll be all right and be happy."

"I know we will. You don't have to be afraid. I've known lots of people that have done it."

"So have I," said the girl. "And afterward they were all so happy."

"Well," the man said, "if you don't want to you don't have to. I wouldn't   55
have you do it if you didn't want to. But I know it's perfectly simple."

"And you really want to?"

"I think it's the best thing to do. But I don't want you to do it if you don't really want to."

"And if I do it you'll be happy and things will be like they were and you'll love me?"

"I love you now. You know I love you."

"I know. But if I do it, then it will be nice again if I say things are like white   60
elephants, and you'll like it?"

"I'll love it. I love it now but I just can't think about it. You know how I get when I worry."

"If I do it you won't ever worry?"

"I won't worry about that because it's perfectly simple."

"Then I'll do it. Because I don't care about me."

"What do you mean?"   65

"I don't care about me."

"Well, I care about you."

"Oh, yes. But I don't care about me. And I'll do it and then everything will be fine."

"I don't want you to do it if you feel that way."

The girl stood up and walked to the end of the station. Across, on the other   70
side, were fields of grain and trees along the banks of the Ebro. Far away, beyond the river, were mountains. The shadow of a cloud moved across the field of grain and she saw the river through the trees.

"And we could have all this," she said. "And we could have everything and every day we make it more impossible."

"What did you say?"

"I said we could have everything."

"We can have everything."

"No, we can't."   75

"We can have the whole world."

"No, we can't."

"We can go everywhere."

"No, we can't. It isn't ours any more."

"It's ours."   80

"No, it isn't. And once they take it away, you never get it back."

"But they haven't taken it away."

"We'll wait and see."

"Come on back in the shade," he said. "You mustn't feel that way."

"I don't feel any way," the girl said. "I just know things."   85
"I don't want you to do anything that you don't want to do ——"
"Nor that isn't good for me," she said. "I know. Could we have another beer?"
"All right. But you've got to realize ——"
"I realize," the girl said. "Can't we maybe stop talking?"
They sat down at the table and the girl looked across at the hills on the dry   90
side of the valley and the man looked at her and at the table.
"You've got to realize," he said, "that I don't want you to do it if you don't
want to. I'm perfectly willing to go through with it if it means anything to you."
"Doesn't it mean anything to you? We could get along."
"Of course it does. But I don't want anybody but you. I don't want anyone
else. And I know it's perfectly simple."
"Yes, you know it's perfectly simple."
"It's all right for you to say that, but I do know it."   95
"Would you do something for me now?"
"I'd do anything for you."
"Would you please please please please please please please stop talking?"
He did not say anything but looked at the bags against the wall of the sta-
tion. There were labels on them from all the hotels where they had spent nights.
"But I don't want you to," he said, "I don't care anything about it."   100
"I'll scream," the girl said.
The woman came out through the curtains with two glasses of beer and put
them down on the damp felt pads. "The train comes in five minutes," she said.
"What did she say?" asked the girl.
"That the train is coming in five minutes."
The girl smiled brightly at the woman, to thank her.   105
"I'd better take the bags over to the other side of the station," the man said.
She smiled at him.
"All right. Then come back and we'll finish the beer."
He picked up the two heavy bags and carried them around the station to
the other tracks. He looked up the tracks but could not see the train. Coming
back, he walked through the barroom, where people waiting for the train were
drinking. He drank an Anis at the bar and looked at the people. They were all
waiting reasonably for the train. He went out through the bead curtain. She
was sitting at the table and smiled at him.
"Do you feel better?" he asked.
"I feel fine," she said. "There's nothing wrong with me. I feel fine."   110

[1927]

≡ **THINKING ABOUT THE TEXT**

1. At what point in the story do you sense some tension? Is it before the
   man says, "Oh, cut it out" (para. 28)? At this point, why do you think he
   says that? Do you think the tension is resolved in the last line, or is the
   relationship over?

2. Jig says, "That's all we do, isn't it—look at things and try new drinks?" (para. 33). What do you think she really means? How would you phrase this thought if you were trying to be clear and honest about your feelings?

3. Some critics see symbolic significance in the title. What might the phrase "white elephant" mean, and how might this be applied to the situation in the story?

4. When Jig asks, "Then what will we do . . . ?" (para. 47) after the operation (presumably an abortion), what do you think of the man's answer? Does she believe him? Do you? Why, or why not?

5. When Jig says, "And afterward they were all so happy" (para. 54), is she being sarcastic? How about when she says, "I don't care about me" (para. 64)? What does Jig mean by "It isn't ours any more" (para. 79)?

T. CORAGHESSAN BOYLE
The Love of My Life

T. Coraghessan Boyle (b. 1948), who says that his middle name is pronounced with the stress on the second syllable and that his friends call him Tom, has written more than twenty books of fiction, including Drop City *(2003),* The Inner Circle *(2004),* Tooth and Claw *(2005), and* Talk, Talk *(2006). His novel* The Women *(2009) focuses on the women in Frank Lloyd Wright's life.* Wild Child and Other Stories *was published in 2010. His latest novel is* When the Killing's Done *(2011). After graduating from the State University of New York, Potsdam, with a B.A. in English and history, Boyle taught for several years at the high school that he had attended as a teenager, though he continued to follow his interests in creative writing. In the early 1970s, he attended the prestigious University of Iowa Writers' Workshop and went on to receive a Ph.D. in nineteenth-century British literature from the University of Iowa in 1977. His list of awards and publications is long, and he received the O. Henry Award in 2001 for the short story reprinted here, "The Love of My Life." Boyle says that the story is based on a news event of a few years ago that "should break your heart. I know it broke mine."*

They wore each other like a pair of socks. He was at her house, she was at his. Everywhere they went—to the mall, to the game, to movies and shops and the classes that structured their days like a new kind of chronology—their fingers were entwined, their shoulders touching, their hips joined in the slow triumphant sashay of love. He drove her car, slept on the couch in the family room at her parents' house, played tennis and watched football with her father on the big, thirty-six-inch TV in the kitchen. She went shopping with his mother and hers, a triumvirate of tastes, and she would have played tennis with his father, if it came to it, but his father was dead. "I love you," he told her, because he did, because there was no feeling like this, no triumph, no high—it was like being immortal and unconquerable, like floating. And a hundred times a day she said it, too: "I love you. I love you."

They were together at his house one night when the rain froze on the streets and sheathed the trees in glass. It was her idea to take a walk and feel it in their hair and on the glistening shoulders of their parkas, an other-worldly drumming of pellets flung down out of the troposphere, alien and familiar at the same time, and they glided the length of the front walk and watched the way the power lines bellied and swayed. He built a fire when they got back, while she towelled her hair and made hot chocolate laced with Jack Daniel's. They'd rented a pair of slasher movies for the ritualized comfort of them — "Teens have sex," he said, "and then they pay for it in body parts" — and the maniac had just climbed out of the heating vent, with a meat hook dangling from the recesses of his empty sleeve, when the phone rang.

It was his mother, calling from the hotel room in Boston where she was curled up — shacked up? — for the weekend with the man she'd been dating. He tried to picture her, but he couldn't. He even closed his eyes a minute, to concentrate, but there was nothing there. Was everything all right? she wanted to know. With the storm and all? No, it hadn't hit Boston yet, but she saw on the Weather Channel that it was on its way. Two seconds after he hung up — before she could even hit the Start button on the VCR — the phone rang again, and this time it was her mother. Her mother had been drinking. She was calling from the restaurant, and China could hear a clamor of voices in the background. "Just stay put," her mother shouted into the phone. "The streets are like a skating rink. Don't you even think of getting in that car."

Well, she wasn't thinking of it. She was thinking of having Jeremy to herself, all night, in the big bed in his mother's room. They'd been having sex ever since they started going together at the end of their junior year, but it was always sex in the car or sex on a blanket or the lawn, hurried sex, nothing like she wanted it to be. She kept thinking of the way it was in the movies, where the stars ambushed each other on beds the size of small planets and then did it again and again until they lay nestled in a heap of pillows and blankets, her head on his chest, his arm flung over her shoulder, the music fading away to individual notes plucked softly on a guitar and everything in the frame glowing as if it had been sprayed with liquid gold. That was how it was supposed to be. That was how it was going to be. At least for tonight.

She'd been wandering around the kitchen as she talked, dancing with the phone in an idle slow saraband, watching the frost sketch a design on the window over the sink, no sound but the soft hiss of the ice pellets on the roof, and now she pulled open the freezer door and extracted a pint box of ice cream. She was in her socks, socks so thick they were like slippers, and a pair of black leggings under an oversize sweater. Beneath her feet, the polished floorboards were as slick as the sidewalk outside, and she liked the feel of that, skating indoors in her big socks. "Uh-huh," she said into the phone. "Uh-huh. Yeah, we're watching a movie." She dug a finger into the ice cream and stuck it in her mouth.

5

"Come on," Jeremy called from the living room, where the maniac rippled menacingly over the Pause button. "You're going to miss the best part."

"O.K., Mom, O.K.," she said into the phone, parting words, and then she hung up. "You want ice cream?" she called, licking her finger.

Jeremy's voice came back at her, a voice in the middle range, with a congenital scratch in it, the voice of a nice guy, a very nice guy who could be the star of a TV show about nice guys: "What kind?" He had a pair of shoulders and pumped-up biceps, too, a smile that jumped from his lips to his eyes, and close-cropped hair that stood up straight off the crown of his head. And he was always singing — she loved that — his voice so true he could do any song, and there was no lyric he didn't know, even on the oldies station. She scooped ice cream and saw him in a scene from last summer, one hand draped casually over the wheel of his car, the radio throbbing, his voice raised in perfect synch with Billy Corgan's, and the night standing still at the end of a long dark street overhung with maples.

"Chocolate. Swiss-chocolate almond."

"O.K.," he said, and then he was wondering if there was any whipped   10
cream, or maybe hot fudge — he was sure his mother had a jar stashed away somewhere, *Look behind the mayonnaise on the top row* — and when she turned around he was standing in the doorway.

She kissed him — they kissed whenever they met, no matter where or when, even if one of them had just stepped out of the room, because that was love, that was the way love was — and then they took two bowls of ice cream into the living room and, with a flick of the remote, set the maniac back in motion.

It was an early spring that year, the world gone green overnight, the thermometer twice hitting the low eighties in the first week of March. Teachers were holding sessions outside. The whole school, even the halls and the cafeteria, smelled of fresh-mowed grass and the unfolding blossoms of the fruit trees in the development across the street, and students — especially seniors — were cutting class to go out to the quarry or the reservoir or to just drive the backstreets with the sunroof and the windows open wide. But not China. She was hitting the books, studying late, putting everything in its place like pegs in a board, even love, even that. Jeremy didn't get it. "Look, you've already been accepted at your first-choice school, you're going to wind up in the top ten G.P.A.-wise, and you've got four years of tests and term papers ahead of you, and grad school after that. You'll only be a high-school senior once in your life. Relax. Enjoy it. Or at least *experience* it."

He'd been accepted at Brown, his father's alma mater, and his own G.P.A. would put him in the top ten percent of their graduating class, and he was content with that, skating through his final semester, no math, no science, taking art and music, the things he'd always wanted to take but never had time for — and Lit., of course, A.P. History, and Spanish 5. "*Tú eres el amor de mi vida*," he would tell her when they met at her locker or at lunch or when he picked her up for a movie on Saturday nights.

"*Y tú también,*" she would say, "or is it '*yo también*'?" — French was her language. "But I keep telling you it really matters to me, because I know I'll never catch Margery Yu or Christian Davenport, I mean they're a lock for val and salut, but it'll kill me if people like Kerry Sharp or Jalapy Seegrand finish ahead of me — you should know that, you of all people —"

It amazed him that she actually brought her books along when they went   15
backpacking over spring break. They'd planned the trip all winter and through the long wind tunnel that was February, packing away freeze-dried entrées, PowerBars, Gore-Tex windbreakers, and matching sweatshirts, weighing each item on a handheld scale with a dangling hook at the bottom of it. They were going up into the Catskills, to a lake he'd found on a map, and they were going to be together, without interruption, without telephones, automobiles, parents, teachers, friends, relatives, and pets, for five full days. They were going to cook over an open fire, they were going to read to each other and burrow into the double sleeping bag with the connubial zipper up the seam he'd found in his mother's closet, a relic of her own time in the lap of nature. It smelled of her, of his mother, a vague scent of her perfume that had lingered there dormant all these years, and maybe there was the faintest whiff of his father, too, though his father had been gone so long he didn't even remember what he looked like, let alone what he might have smelled like. Five days. And it wasn't going to rain, not a drop. He didn't even bring his fishing rod, and that was love.

When the last bell rang down the curtain on Honors Math, Jeremy was waiting at the curb in his mother's Volvo station wagon, grinning up at China through the windshield while the rest of the school swept past with no thought for anything but release. There were shouts and curses, T-shirts in motion, slashing legs, horns bleating from the seniors' lot, the school buses lined up like armored vehicles awaiting the invasion — chaos, sweet chaos — and she stood there a moment to savor it. "Your mother's car?" she said, slipping in beside him and laying both arms over his shoulders to pull him to her for a kiss. He'd brought her jeans and hiking boots along, and she was going to change as they drove, no need to go home, no more circumvention and delay, a stop at McDonald's, maybe, or Burger King, and then it was the sun and the wind and the moon and the stars. Five days. Five whole days.

"Yeah," he said, in answer to her question, "my mother said she didn't want to have to worry about us breaking down in the middle of nowhere —"

"So she's got your car? She's going to sell real estate in your car?"

He just shrugged and smiled. "Free at last," he said, pitching his voice down low till it was exactly like Martin Luther King's. "Thank God Almighty, we are free at last."

It was dark by the time they got to the trailhead, and they wound up camp-   20
ing just off the road in a rocky tumble of brush, no place on earth less likely or less comfortable, but they were together, and they held each other through the damp whispering hours of the night and hardly slept at all. They made the lake by noon the next day, the trees just coming into leaf, the air sweet with the smell of the sun in the pines. She insisted on setting up the tent, just in case — it

could rain, you never knew — but all he wanted to do was stretch out on a gray neoprene pad and feel the sun on his face. Eventually, they both fell asleep in the sun, and when they woke they made love right there, beneath the trees, and with the wide blue expanse of the lake giving back the blue of the sky. For dinner, it was étouffée and rice, out of the foil pouch, washed down with hot chocolate and a few squirts of red wine from Jeremy's bota bag.

The next day, the whole day through, they didn't bother with clothes at all. They couldn't swim, of course — the lake was too cold for that — but they could bask and explore and feel the breeze out of the south on their bare legs and the places where no breeze had touched before. She would remember that always, the feel of that, the intensity of her motions, the simple unrefined pleasure of living in the moment. Wood smoke. Duelling flashlights in the night. The look on Jeremy's face when he presented her with the bag of finger-size crayfish he'd spent all morning collecting.

What else? The rain, of course. It came midway through the third day, clouds the color of iron filings, the lake hammered to iron, too, and the storm that crashed through the trees and beat at their tent with a thousand angry fists. They huddled in the sleeping bag, sharing the wine and a bag of trail mix, reading to each other from a book of Donne's love poems (she was writing a paper for Mrs. Masterson called "Ocular Imagery in the Poetry of John Donne") and the last third of a vampire novel that weighed eighteen-point-one ounces.

And the sex. They were careful, always careful — *I will never, never be like those breeders that bring their puffed-up squalling little red-faced babies to class*, she told him, and he agreed, got adamant about it, even, until it became a running theme in their relationship, the breeders overpopulating an overpopulated world and ruining their own lives in the process — but she had forgotten to pack her pills and he had only two condoms with him, and it wasn't as if there were a drugstore around the corner.

In the fall — or the end of August, actually — they packed their cars separately and left for college, he to Providence and she to Binghamton. They were separated by three hundred miles, but there was the telephone, there was e-mail, and for the first month or so there were Saturday nights in a motel in Danbury, but that was a haul, it really was, and they both agreed that they should focus on their course work and cut back to every second or maybe third week. On the day they'd left — and no, she didn't want her parents driving her up there, she was an adult and she could take care of herself — Jeremy followed her as far as the Bear Mountain Bridge and they pulled off the road and held each other till the sun fell down into the trees. She had a poem for him, a Donne poem, the saddest thing he'd ever heard. It was something about the moon. *More than moon*, that was it, lovers parting and their tears swelling like an ocean till the girl — the woman, the female — had more power to raise the tides than the moon itself, or some such. More than moon. That's what he called her after that, because she was white and round and getting rounder, and it was no joke, and it was no term of endearment.

She was pregnant. Pregnant, they figured, since the camping trip, and it   25
was their secret, a new constant in their lives, a fact, an inescapable fact that
never varied no matter how many home-pregnancy kits they went through.
Baggy clothes, that was the key, all in black, cargo pants, flowing dresses, a
jacket even in summer. They went to a store in the city where nobody knew
them and she got a girdle, and then she went away to school in Binghamton
and he went to Providence. "You've got to get rid of it," he told her in the motel
room that had become a prison. "Go to a clinic," he told her for the hundredth
time, and outside it was raining — or, no, it was clear and cold that night, a
foretaste of winter. "I'll find the money — you know I will."

She wouldn't respond. Wouldn't even look at him. One of the *Star Wars*
movies was on TV, great flat thundering planes of metal roaring across the
screen, and she was just sitting there on the edge of the bed, her shoulders
hunched and hair hanging limp. Someone slammed a car door — two doors in
rapid succession — and a child's voice shouted, "Me! Me first!"

"China," he said. "Are you listening to me?"

"I can't," she murmured, and she was talking to her lap, to the bed, to the
floor. "I'm scared. I'm so scared." There were footsteps in the room next door,
ponderous and heavy, then the quick tattoo of the child's feet and a sudden
thump against the wall. "I don't want anyone to know," she said.

He could have held her, could have squeezed in beside her and wrapped her
in his arms, but something flared in him. He couldn't understand it. He just
couldn't. "What are you thinking? Nobody'll know. He's a doctor, for Christ's
sake, sworn to secrecy, the doctor-patient compact and all that. What are you
going to do, keep it? Huh? Just show up for English 101 with a baby on your lap
and say, 'Hi, I'm the Virgin Mary'?"

She was crying. He could see it in the way her shoulders suddenly crum-   30
pled and now he could hear it, too, a soft nasal complaint that went right
through him. She lifted her face to him and held out her arms and he was there
beside her, rocking her back and forth in his arms. He could feel the heat of her
face against the hard fibre of his chest, a wetness there, fluids, her fluids. "I
don't want a doctor," she said.

And that colored everything, that simple negative: life in the dorms, roommates, bars, bullshit sessions, the smell of burning leaves and the way the light
fell across campus in great wide smoking bands just before dinner, the unoffi-
cial skateboard club, films, lectures, pep rallies, football — none of it mattered.
He couldn't have a life. Couldn't be a freshman. Couldn't wake up in the morning and tumble into the slow steady current of the world. All he could think of
was her. Or not simply her — her and him, and what had come between them.
Because they argued now, they wrangled and fought and debated, and it was
no pleasure to see her in that motel room with the queen-size bed and the big
color TV and the soaps and shampoos they made off with as if they were treasure. She was pig-headed, stubborn, irrational. She was spoiled, he could see
that now, spoiled by her parents and their standard of living and the socioeconomic expectations of her class — of his class — and the promise of life as

you like it, an unscrolling vista of pleasure and acquisition. He loved her. He didn't want to turn his back on her. He would be there for her no matter what, but why did she have to be so *stupid*?

Big sweats, huge sweats, sweats that drowned and engulfed her, that was her campus life, sweats and the dining hall. Her dorm mates didn't know her, and so what if she was putting on weight? Everybody did. How could you shovel down all those carbohydrates, all that sugar and grease and the puddings and nachos and all the rest, without putting on ten or fifteen pounds the first semester alone? Half the girls in the dorm were waddling around like the Doughboy, their faces bloated and blotched with acne, with crusting pimples and whiteheads fed on fat. So she was putting on weight. Big deal. "There's more of me to love," she told her roommate, "and Jeremy likes it that way. And, really, he's the only one that matters." She was careful to shower alone, in the early morning, long before the light had begun to bump up against the windows.

On the night her water broke — it was mid-December, almost nine months, as best as she could figure — it was raining. Raining hard. All week she'd been having tense rasping sotto-voce debates with Jeremy on the phone — arguments, fights — and she told him that she would die, creep out into the woods like some animal and bleed to death, before she'd go to a hospital. "And what am I supposed to do?" he demanded in a high childish whine, as if he were the one who'd been knocked up, and she didn't want to hear it, she didn't.

"Do you love me?" she whispered. There was a long hesitation, a pause you could have poured all the affirmation of the world into.

"Yes," he said finally, his voice so soft and reluctant it was like the last gasp   35
of a dying old man.

"Then you're going to have to rent the motel."

"And then what?"

"Then — I don't know." The door was open, her roommate framed there in the hall, a burst of rock and roll coming at her like an assault. "I guess you'll have to get a book or something."

By eight, the rain had turned to ice and every branch of every tree was coated with it, the highway littered with glistening black sticks, no moon, no stars, the tires sliding out from under her, and she felt heavy, big as a sumo wrestler, heavy and loose at the same time. She'd taken a towel from the dorm and put it under her, on the seat, but it was a mess, everything was a mess. She was cramping. Fidgeting with her hair. She tried the radio, but it was no help, nothing but songs she hated, singers that were worse. Twenty-two miles to Danbury and the first of the contractions came like a seizure, like a knife blade thrust into her spine. Her world narrowed to what the headlights would show her.

Jeremy was waiting for her at the door to the room, the light behind him a   40
pale rinse of nothing, no smile on his face, no human expression at all. They didn't kiss — they didn't even touch — and then she was on the bed, on her back, her face clenched like a fist. She heard the rattle of the sleet at the window, the murmur of TV: *I can't let you go like this*, a man protested, and she could picture him, angular and tall, a man in a hat and overcoat in a black-and-white

world that might have been another planet, *I just can't.* "Are you —?" Jeremy's voice drifted into the mix, and then stalled. "Are you ready? I mean, is it time? Is it coming now?"

She said one thing then, one thing only, her voice as pinched and hollow as the sound of the wind in the gutters: "Get it out of me."

It took a moment, and then she could feel his hands fumbling with her sweats.

Later, hours later, when nothing had happened but pain, a parade of pain with drum majors and brass bands and penitents crawling on their hands and knees till the streets were stained with their blood, she cried out and cried out again. "It's like *Alien*," she gasped, "like that thing in *Alien* when it, it —"

"It's O.K.," he kept telling her, "it's O.K.," but his face betrayed him. He looked scared, looked as if he'd been drained of blood in some evil experiment in yet another movie, and a part of her wanted to be sorry for him, but another part, the part that was so commanding and fierce it overrode everything else, couldn't begin to be.

He was useless, and he knew it. He'd never been so purely sick at heart and   45
terrified in all his life, but he tried to be there for her, tried to do his best, and when the baby came out, the baby girl all slick with blood and mucus and the lumped white stuff that was like something spilled at the bottom of a garbage can, he was thinking of the ninth grade and how close he'd come to fainting while the teacher went around the room to prick their fingers one by one so they each could smear a drop of blood across a slide. He didn't faint now. But he was close to it, so close he could feel the room dodging away under his feet. And then her voice, the first intelligible thing she'd said in an hour: "Get rid of it. Just get rid of it."

Of the drive back to Binghamton he remembered nothing. Or practically nothing. They took towels from the motel and spread them across the seat of her car, he could remember that much . . . and the blood, how could he forget the blood? It soaked through her sweats and the towels and even the thick cotton bathmat and into the worn fabric of the seat itself. And it all came from inside her, all of it, tissue and mucus and the shining bright fluid, no end to it, as if she'd been turned inside out. He wanted to ask her about that, if that was normal, but she was asleep the minute she slid out from under his arm and dropped into the seat. If he focused, if he really concentrated, he could remember the way her head lolled against the doorframe while the engine whined and the car rocked and the slush threw a dark blanket over the windshield every time a truck shot past in the opposite direction. That and the exhaustion. He'd never been so tired, his head on a string, shoulders slumped, his arms like two pillars of concrete. And what if he'd nodded off? What if he'd gone into a skid and hurtled over an embankment into the filthy gray accumulation of the worst day of his life? What then?

She made it into the dorm under her own power, nobody even looked at her, and, no, she didn't need his help. "Call me," she whispered, and they kissed, her lips so cold it was like kissing a steak through the plastic wrap, and then he parked her car in the student lot and walked to the bus station. He made Danbury late that night, caught a ride out to the motel, and walked right through the "Do Not Disturb" sign on the door. Fifteen minutes. That was all it took. He bundled up everything, every trace, left the key in the box at the desk, and stood scraping the ice off the windshield of his car while the night opened up above him to a black glitter of sky. He never gave a thought to what lay discarded in the Dumpster out back, itself wrapped in plastic, so much meat, so much cold meat.

He was at the very pinnacle of his dream, the river dressed in its currents, the deep hole under the cutbank, and the fish like silver bullets swarming to his bait, when they woke him — when Rob woke him, Rob Greiner, his roommate, Rob with a face of crumbling stone and two policemen there at the door behind him and the roar of the dorm falling away to a whisper. And that was strange, policemen, a real anomaly in that setting, and at first — for the first thirty seconds, at least — he had no idea what they were doing there. Parking tickets? Could that be it? But then they asked him his name, just to confirm it, joined his hands together behind his back, and fitted two loops of naked metal over his wrists, and he began to understand. He saw McCaffrey and Tuttle from across the hall staring at him as if he were Jeffrey Dahmer or something, and the rest of them, all the rest, every head poking out of every door up and down the corridor, as the police led him away.

"What's all this about?" he kept saying, the cruiser nosing through the dark streets to the station house, the man at the wheel and the man beside him as incapable of speech as the seats or the wire mesh or the gleaming black dashboard that dragged them forward into the night. And then it was up the steps and into an explosion of light, more men in uniform, stand here, give me your hand, now the other one, and then the cage and the questions. Only then did he think of that thing in the garbage sack and the sound it had made — its body had made — when he flung it into the Dumpster like a sack of flour and the lid slammed down on it. He stared at the walls, and this was a movie, too. He'd never been in trouble before, never been inside a police station, but he knew his role well enough, because he'd seen it played out a thousand times on the tube: deny everything. Even as the two detectives settled in across from him at the bare wooden table in the little box of the overlit room he was telling himself just that: *Deny it, deny it all.*

The first detective leaned forward and set his hands on the table as if he'd   50
come for a manicure. He was in his thirties, or maybe his forties, a tired-looking man with the scars of the turmoil he'd witnessed gouged into the flesh under his eyes. He didn't offer a cigarette ("I don't smoke," Jeremy was prepared to say, giving them that much at least), and he didn't smile or soften his eyes. And when he spoke his voice carried no freight at all, not outrage or threat or cajolery — it was just a voice, flat and tired. "Do you know a China Berkowitz?" he said.

And she. She was in the community hospital, where the ambulance had deposited her after her roommate had called 911 in a voice that was like a bone stuck in the back of her throat, and it was raining again. Her parents were

there, her mother red-eyed and sniffling, her father looking like an actor who
has forgotten his lines, and there was another woman there, too, a policewoman. The policewoman sat in an orange plastic chair in the corner, dipping
her head to the knitting in her lap. At first, China's mother had tried to be pleasant to the woman, but pleasant wasn't what the circumstances called for, and
now she ignored her, because the very unpleasant fact was that China was being taken into custody as soon as she was released from the hospital.

For a long while no one said anything — everything had already been said,
over and over, one long flood of hurt and recrimination — and the antiseptic
silence of the hospital held them in its grip while the rain beat at the windows
and the machines at the foot of the bed counted off numbers. From down the
hall came a snatch of TV dialogue, and for a minute China opened her eyes and
thought she was back in the dorm. "Honey," her mother said, raising a purga-
torial face to her, "are you all right? Can I get you anything?"

"I need to — I think I need to pee."

"Why?" her father demanded, and it was the perfect non sequitur. He was
up out of the chair, standing over her, his eyes liked cracked porcelain. "Why
didn't you tell us, or at least tell your mother — or Dr. Fredman? Dr. Fredman,
at least. He's been — he's like a family member, you know that, and he could
have, or he would have . . . What were you *thinking*, for Christ's sake?"

Thinking? She wasn't thinking anything, not then and not now. All she   55
wanted — and she didn't care what they did to her, beat her, torture her, drag
her weeping through the streets in a dirty white dress with "Baby Killer"
stitched over her breast in scarlet letters — was to see Jeremy. Just that. Because
what really mattered was what he was thinking.

The food at the Sarah Barnes Cooper Women's Correctional Institute was exactly what they served at the dining hall in college, heavy on the sugars,
starches, and bad cholesterol, and that would have struck her as ironic if she'd
been there under other circumstances — doing community outreach, say, or
researching a paper for sociology class. But given the fact that she'd been locked
up for more than a month now, the object of the other girls' threats, scorn, and
just plain *nastiness*, given the fact that her life was ruined beyond any hope of
redemption, and every newspaper in the country had her shrunken white face
plastered across its front page under a headline that screamed "MOTEL MOM," she
didn't have much use for irony. She was scared twenty-four hours a day. Scared
of the present, scared of the future, scared of the reporters waiting for the
judge to set bail so that they could swarm all over her the minute she stepped
out the door. She couldn't concentrate on the books and magazines her mother
brought her, or even on the TV in the rec room. She sat in her room — it was a
room, just like a dorm room, except that they locked you in at night — and
stared at the walls, eating peanuts, M&M's, sunflower seeds by the handful,
chewing for the pure animal gratification of it. She was putting on more
weight, and what did it matter?

Jeremy was different. He'd lost everything — his walk, his smile, the
muscles of his upper arms and shoulders. Even his hair lay flat now, as if he

couldn't bother with a tube of gel and a comb. When she saw him at the arraignment, saw him for the first time since she'd climbed out of the car and limped into the dorm with the blood wet on her legs, he looked like a refugee, like a ghost. The room they were in — the courtroom — seemed to have grown up around them, walls, windows, benches, lights, and radiators already in place, along with the judge, the American flag, and the ready-made spectators. It was hot. People coughed into their fists and shuffled their feet, every sound magnified. The judge presided, his arms like bones twirled in a bag, his eyes searching and opaque as he peered over the top of his reading glasses.

China's lawyer didn't like Jeremy's lawyer, that much was evident, and the state prosecutor didn't like anybody. She watched him — Jeremy, only him — as the reporters held their collective breath and the judge read off the charges and her mother bowed her head and sobbed into the bucket of her hands. And Jeremy was watching her, too, his eyes locked on hers as if he defied them all, as if nothing mattered in the world but her, and when the judge said *First-degree murder* and *Murder by abuse or neglect* he never flinched.

She sent him a note that day — "I love you, will always love you no matter what, More than Moon" — and in the hallway, afterward, while their lawyers fended off the reporters and the bailiffs tugged impatiently at them, they had a minute, just a minute, to themselves. "What did you tell them?" he whispered. His voice was a rasp, almost a growl; she looked at him, inches away, and hardly recognized him.

"I told them it was dead."   60

"My lawyer — Mrs. Teagues? — she says they're saying it was alive when we, when we put it in the bag." His face was composed, but his eyes were darting like insects trapped inside his head.

"It was dead."

"It looked dead," he said, and already he was pulling away from her and some callous shit with a camera kept annihilating them with flash after flash of light, "and we certainly didn't — I mean, we didn't slap it or anything to get it breathing. . . ."

And then the last thing he said to her, just as they were pulled apart, and it was nothing she wanted to hear, nothing that had any love in it, or even the hint of love: "You told me to get rid of it."

There was no elaborate name for the place where they were keeping him. It was   65
known as Drum Hill Prison, period. No reform-minded notions here, no verbal gestures toward rehabilitation or behavior modification, no benefactors, mayors, or role models to lend the place their family names, but then who in his right mind would want a prison named after him anyway? At least they kept him separated from the other prisoners, the gangbangers and dope dealers and sexual predators and the like. He was no longer a freshman at Brown, not officially, but he had his books and his course notes and he tried to keep up as best he could. Still, when the screams echoed through the cell block at night and the walls dripped with the accumulated breath of eight and a half thousand

terminally angry sociopaths, he had to admit it wasn't the sort of college experience he'd bargained for.

And what had he done to deserve it? He still couldn't understand. That thing in the Dumpster — and he refused to call it human, let alone a baby — was nobody's business but his and China's. That's what he'd told his attorney, Mrs. Teagues, and his mother and her boyfriend, Howard, and he'd told them over and over again: *I didn't do anything wrong.* Even if it was alive, and it was, he knew in his heart that it was, even before the state prosecutor presented evidence of blunt-force trauma and death by asphyxiation and exposure, it didn't matter, or shouldn't have mattered. There was no baby. There was nothing but a mistake, a mistake clothed in blood and mucus. When he really thought about it, thought it through on its merits and dissected all his mother's pathetic arguments about where he'd be today if she'd felt as he did when she was pregnant herself, he hardened like a rock, like sand turning to stone under all the pressure the planet can bring to bear. Another unwanted child in an overpopulated world? They should have given him a medal.

It was the end of January before bail was set — three hundred and fifty thousand dollars his mother didn't have — and he was released to house arrest. He wore a plastic anklet that set off an alarm if he went out the door, and so did she, so did China, imprisoned like some fairy-tale princess at her parents' house. At first, she called him every day, but mostly what she did was cry — "I want to see it," she sobbed. "I want to see our daughter's *grave.*" That froze him inside. He tried to picture her — her now, China, the love of his life — and he couldn't. What did she look like? What was her face like, her nose, her hair, her eyes and breasts and the slit between her legs? He drew a blank. There was no way to summon her the way she used to be or even the way she was in court, because all he could remember was the thing that had come out of her, four limbs and the equipment of a female, shoulders rigid and eyes shut tight, as if she were a mummy in a tomb . . . and the breath, the shuddering long gasping rattle of a breath he could feel ringing inside her even as the black plastic bag closed over her face and the lid of the Dumpster opened like a mouth.

He was in the den, watching basketball, a drink in his hand (7UP mixed with Jack Daniel's in a ceramic mug, so no one would know he was getting shit-faced at two o'clock on a Sunday afternoon), when the phone rang. It was Sarah Teagues. "Listen, Jeremy," she said in her crisp, equitable tones, "I thought you ought to know — the Berkowitzes are filing a motion to have the case against China dropped."

His mother's voice on the portable, too loud, a blast of amplified breath and static: "On what grounds?"

"She never saw the baby, that's what they're saying. She thought she had a miscarriage." 70

"Yeah, right," his mother said.

Sarah Teagues was right there, her voice as clear and present as his mother's. "Jeremy's the one that threw it in the Dumpster, and they're saying he acted alone. She took a polygraph test day before yesterday."

He could feel his heart pounding like it used to when he plodded up that last agonizing ridge behind the school with the cross-country team, his legs sapped, no more breath left in his body. He didn't say a word. Didn't even breathe.

"She's going to testify against him."

Outside was the world, puddles of ice clinging to the lawn under a weak after-   75
noon sun, all the trees stripped bare, the grass dead, the azalea under the window reduced to an armload of dead brown twigs. She wouldn't have wanted to
go out today anyway. This was the time of year she hated most, the long interval between the holidays and spring break, when nothing grew and nothing
changed—it didn't even seem to snow much anymore. What was out there for
her anyway? They wouldn't let her see Jeremy, wouldn't even let her talk to him
on the phone or write him anymore, and she wouldn't be able to show her face
at the mall or even the movie theater without somebody shouting out her
name as if she were a freak, as if she were another Monica Lewinsky or Heidi
Fleiss. She wasn't China Berkowitz, honor student, not anymore—she was the
punch line to a joke, a footnote to history.

She wouldn't mind going for a drive, though—that was something she
missed, just following the curves out to the reservoir to watch the way the ice
cupped the shore, or up to the turnout on Route 9 to look out over the river
where it oozed through the mountains in a shimmering coil of light. Or to take
a walk in the woods, just that. She was in her room, on her bed, posters of
bands she'd outgrown staring down from the walls, her high-school books on
two shelves in the corner, the closet door flung open on all the clothes she'd
once wanted so desperately she could have died for each individual pair of
boots or the cashmere sweaters that felt so good against her skin. At the bottom of her left leg, down there at the foot of the bed, was the anklet she wore
now, the plastic anklet with the transmitter inside, no different, she supposed,
than the collars they put on wolves to track them across all those miles of barren tundra or the bears sleeping in their dens. Except that hers had an alarm
on it.

For a long while she just lay there gazing out the window, watching the
rinsed-out sun slip down into the sky that had no more color in it than a TV
tuned to an unsubscribed channel, and then she found herself picturing things
the way they were an eon ago, when everything was green. She saw the azalea
bush in bloom, the leaves knifing out of the trees, butterflies—or were they
cabbage moths?—hovering over the flowers. Deep green. That was the color of
the world. And she was remembering a night, summer before last, just after she
and Jeremy started going together, the crickets thrumming, the air thick with
humidity, and him singing along with the car radio, his voice so sweet and pure
it was as if he'd written the song himself, just for her. And when they got to
where they were going, at the end of that dark lane overhung with trees, to a
place where it was private and hushed and the night fell in on itself as if it
couldn't support the weight of the stars, he was as nervous as she was. She
moved into his arms and they kissed, his lips groping for hers in the dark, his

fingers trembling over the thin yielding silk of her blouse. He was Jeremy. He was the love of her life. And she closed her eyes and clung to him as if that were all that mattered.   [2000]

■ THINKING ABOUT THE TEXT

1. Both China and Jeremy are condemned by their peers in this story (as they were in real life). Is that your response, too? Did Boyle persuade you to see how such an event is possible? Do you want to understand how such an event is possible? Or is there no explanation for such behavior?

2. After reading the first few pages of the exposition, what do you think Boyle's purpose is in this opening scene? Is the sentence "Teens have sex . . . and then they pay for it in body parts" (para. 2) clever or perhaps even cruel?

3. Look again at the fourth paragraph. What does it tell you about China's frame of mind? Her sense of reality?

4. Is Boyle trying to make an argument about the power of the media? The obliviousness of teens? The power of first love?

5. Have China and Jeremy's lives been irreparably ruined? Boyle ends the story with China remembering a summer night shortly after she started dating Jeremy. Can this memory save the relationship, or is it proof of her blindness?

■ MAKING COMPARISONS

1. Through a brief dialogue, Hemingway indirectly sketches the relationship between Jig and the American. Boyle's description is more detailed and expansive. Can you imagine China and Jeremy having the conversation Jig and her boyfriend have? Why? Should they have?

2. If Boyle were given the task of revising "Hills like White Elephants" into his fuller style, what do you think he should include — that is, what would you want to know about Hemingway's characters?

3. Are there indications that Hemingway is sympathetic to Jig's situation? Is Boyle more sympathetic to China or to Jeremy?

JOHN EDGAR WIDEMAN
Newborn Thrown in Trash and Dies

John Edgar Wideman (b. 1941) was born in Washington, D.C., but soon moved to Homewood, an African American community in Pittsburgh, Pennsylvania, which became the setting for much of his fiction. Wideman was a star on the University of Pennsylvania's basketball team and a Rhodes Scholar at Oxford. He published his first novel, A Glance Away, *in 1967. He won the PEN/Faulkner Award for Fiction twice, for* Sent for You Yesterday *(1984) and* Philadelphia Fire *(1990). He has received many honors, including the MacArthur Award in 1993. He is a professor of English at the University of Massachusetts. The following story was published in* All Stories Are True *(1992).*

They say you see your whole life pass in review the instant before you die. How would *they* know. If you die after the instant replay, you aren't around to tell anybody anything. So much for they and what they say. So much for the wish to be a movie star for once in your life because I think that's what people are hoping, what people are pretending when they say you see your life that way at the end. Death doesn't turn your life into a five-star production. The end is the end. And what you know at the end goes down the tube with you. I can speak to you now only because I haven't reached bottom yet. I'm on my way, faster than I want to be traveling and my journey won't take long, but I'm just beginning the countdown to zero. Zero's where I started also so I know a little bit about zero. Know what they say isn't necessarily so. In fact the opposite's true. You begin and right in the eye of that instant storm your life plays itself out for you in advance. That's the theater of your fate, there's where you're granted a preview, the coming attractions of everything that must happen to you. Your life rolled into a ball so dense, so superheavy it would drag the universe down to hell if this tiny, tiny lump of whatever didn't dissipate as quickly as it formed. Quicker. The weight of it is what you recall some infinitesimal fraction of when you stumble and crawl through your worst days on earth.

Knowledge of what's coming gone as quickly as it flashes forth. Quicker. Faster. Gone before it gets here, so to speak. Any other way and nobody would stick around to play out the cards they're dealt. No future in it. You begin forgetting before the zero's entirely wiped off the clock face, before the next digit materializes. What they say is assbackwards, a saying by the way, assbackwards itself. Whether or not you're treated to a summary at the end, you get the whole thing handed to you, neatly packaged as you begin. Then you forget it. Or try to forget. Live your life as if it hasn't happened before, as if the tape has not been prepunched full of holes, the die cast.

I remember because I won't receive much of a life. A measure of justice in the world, after all. I receive a compensatory bonus. Since the time between my wake-up call and curfew is so cruelly brief, the speeded-up preview of what will come to pass, my life, my portion, my destiny, my career, slowed down just enough to let me peek. Not slow enough for me to steal much, but I know some of what it contains, its finality, the groaning, fatal weight of it around my neck.

Call it a trade-off. A standoff. Intensity for duration. I won't get much and this devastating flash isn't much either, but I get it. Zingo.

But the future remains mysterious. Even if we all put our heads together   5
and became one gigantic brain, a brain lots smarter than the sum of each of our smarts, an intelligence as great as the one that guides ants, whales or birds,

because they're smarter, they figure things out not one by one, each individual locked in the cell of its head, its mortality, but collectively, doing what the group needs to do to survive, relate to the planet. If we were smarter even than birds and bees, we'd still have only a clue about what's inside the first flash of being. I know it happened and that I receive help from it. Scattered help. Sometimes I catch on. Sometimes I don't. But stuff from it's being pumped out always. I know things I have no business knowing. Things I haven't been around long enough to learn myself. For instance, many languages. A vast palette of feelings. The names of unseen things. Nostalgia for a darkness I've never experienced, a darkness another sense I can't account for assures me I will enter again. Large matters. Small ones. Naked as I am I'm dressed so to speak for my trip. Down these ten swift flights to oblivion.

Floor Ten. Nothing under the sun, they say, is new. This time they're right. They never stop talking so percentages guarantee they'll be correct sometimes. Especially since they speak out of both sides of their mouths at once: *Birds of a feather flock together. Opposites attract.* Like the billion billion monkeys at typewriters who sooner or later will bang out this story I think is uniquely mine. Somebody else, a Russian, I believe, with a long, strange-sounding name, has already written about his life speeding past as he topples slow-motion from a window high up in a tall apartment building. But it was in another country. And alas, the Russian's dead.

Floor Nine. In this building they shoot craps. One of many forms of gambling proliferating here. Very little new wealth enters this cluster of buildings that are like high-rise covered wagons circled against the urban night, so what's here is cycled and recycled by games of chance, by murder and other violent forms of exchange. Kids do it. Adults. Birds and bees. The law here is the same one ruling the jungle, they say. They say this is a jungle of the urban asphalt concrete variety. Since I've never been to Africa or the Amazon I can't agree or disagree. But you know what I think about what they say.

Seven come eleven. Snake eyes. Boxcars. Fever in the funkhouse searching for a five. Talk to me, baby. Talk. Talk. Please. Please. Please.

They cry and sing and curse and pray all night long over these games. On one knee they chant magic formulas to summon luck. They forget luck is rigged. Some of the men carry a game called Three Card Monte downtown. They cheat tourists who are stupid enough to trust in luck. Showmen with quick hands shuffling cards to a blur, fast feet carrying them away from busy intersections when cops come to break up their scam or hit on them for a cut. Flimflam artists, con men who daily use luck as bait and hook, down on their knees in a circle of other men who also should know better, trying to sweet-talk luck into their beds. Luck is the card you wish for, the card somebody else holds. You learn luck by its absence. Luck is what separates you from what you want. Luck is always turning its back and you lose.

Like other potions and powders they sell and consume here luck creates dependency. In their rooms people sit and wait for a hit. A yearning unto death for more, more, more till the little life they've been allotted dies in a basket on the doorstep where they abandoned it.   10

The Floor of Facts. Seventeen stories in this building. The address is 2950 West 23rd Street. My mother is nineteen years old. The trash chute down which I was dropped is forty-five feet from the door of the apartment my mother was visiting. I was born and will die Monday, August 12, 1991. The small door in the yellow cinder block wall is maroon. I won't know till the last second why my mother pushes it open. In 1990 nine discarded babies were discovered in New York City's garbage. As of August this year seven have been found. 911 is the number to call if you find a baby in the trash. Ernesto Mendez, forty-four, a Housing Authority caretaker, will notice my head, shoulders and curly hair in a black plastic bag he slashes open near the square entrance of the trash compactor on the ground floor of this brown-brick public housing project called the Gerald J. Carey Gardens. Gardens are green places where seeds are planted, tended, nurtured. The headline above my story reads "Newborn Is Thrown in Trash and Dies." The headline will remind some readers of a similar story with a happy ending that appeared in March. A baby rescued and surviving after she was dropped down a trash chute by her twelve-year-old mother. The reporter, a Mr. George James who recorded many of the above facts, introduced my unhappy story in the Metro Section of the *New York Times* on Wednesday, August 14, with this paragraph: "A young Brooklyn woman gave birth on Monday afternoon in a stairwell in a Coney Island housing project and then dropped the infant down a trash chute into a compactor ten stories below, the police said yesterday." And that's about it. What's fit to print. My tale in a nutshell followed by a relation of facts obtained by interview and reading official documents. Trouble is I could not be reached for comment. No one's fault. Certainly no negligence on the reporter's part. He gave me sufficient notoriety. Many readers must have shaken their heads in dismay or sighed and blurted Jesus Christ, did you see this, handing the Metro Section across the breakfast table or passing it to somebody at work. As grateful as I am to have my story made public you should be able to understand why I feel cheated, why the newspaper account is not enough, why I want my voice to be part of the record. The awful silence is not truly broken until we speak for ourselves. One chance to speak was snatched away. Then I didn't cry out as I plunged through the darkness. I didn't know any better. Too busy thinking to myself, *This is how it is, this is how it is, how it is . . .* accustoming myself to what it seemed life brings, what life is. Spinning, tumbling, a breathless rush, terror, exhilaration, and wonder, wondering is this it, am I doing it right. I didn't know any better. The floors, the other lives packed into this building were going on their merry way as I flew past them in the darkness of my tunnel. No one waved. No one warned me. Said hello or good-bye. And of course I was too busy flailing, trying to catch my breath, trying to stop shivering in the sudden, icy air, welcoming almost the thick, pungent draft rushing up at me as if another pair of thighs were opening below to replace the ones from which I'd been ripped.

In the quiet dark of my passage I did not cry out. Now I will not be still.

A Floor of Questions. Why.

A Floor of Opinions. I believe the floor of fact should have been the ground floor, the foundation, the solid start, the place where all else is firmly rooted. I

believe there should be room on the floor of fact for what I believe, for this opinion and others I could not venture before arriving here. I believe some facts are
unnecessary and that unnecessary borders on untrue. I believe facts sometimes speak for themselves but never speak for us. They are never anyone's
voice and voices are what we must learn to listen to if we wish ever to be heard.
I believe my mother did not hate me. I believe somewhere I have a father, who
if he is reading this and listening carefully will recognize me as his daughter
and be ashamed, heartbroken. I must believe these things. What else do I have.
Who has made my acquaintance or noticed or cared or forgotten me. How
could anyone be aware of what hurtles by faster than light, blackly, in a dark
space beyond the walls of the rooms they live in, beyond the doors they lock,
shades they draw when they have rooms and the rooms have windows and the
windows have shades and the people believe they possess something worth
concealing.

In my opinion my death will serve no purpose. The streetlamps will pop on.   15
Someone will be run over by an expensive car in a narrow street and the driver
will hear a bump but consider it of no consequence. Junkies will leak out the
side doors of this gigantic mound, nodding, buzzing, greeting their kind with
hippy-dip vocalizations full of despair and irony and stylized to embrace the
very best that's being sung, played, and said around them. A young woman
will open a dresser drawer and wonder whose baby that is sleeping peaceful on
a bed of dishtowels, T-shirts, a man's ribbed sweat socks. She will feel something slither through the mud of her belly and splash into the sluggish river
that meanders through her. She hasn't eaten for days, so that isn't it. Was it a
deadly disease. Or worse, some new life she must account for. She opens and
shuts the baby's drawer, pushes and pulls, opens and shuts.

I believe all floors are not equally interesting. Less reason to notice some
than others. Equality would become boring, predictable. Though we may slight
some and rattle on about others, that does not change the fact that each floor
exists and the life on it is real, whether we pause to notice or not. As I gather
speed and weight during my plunge, each floor adds its share. When I hit bottom I will bear witness to the truth of each one.

Floor of Wishes. I will miss Christmas. They say no one likes being born on
Christmas. You lose your birthday, they say. A celebration already on December
25 and nice things happen to everyone on that day anyway, you give and receive presents, people greet you smiling and wish you peace and goodwill. The
world is decorated. Colored bulbs draped twinkling in windows and trees, doorways hung with wild berries beneath which you may kiss a handsome stranger.
Music everywhere. Even wars truced for twenty-four hours and troops served
home-cooked meals, almost. Instead of at least two special days a year, if your
birthday falls on Christmas, you lose one. Since my portion's less than a day,
less than those insects called ephemera receive, born one morning dead the
next, and I can't squeeze a complete life cycle as they do into the time allotted,
I wish today were Christmas. Once would be enough. If it's as special as they
say. And in some matters we yearn to trust them. Need to trust something,
someone, so we listen, wish what they say is true. The holiday of Christmas

seems to be the best time to be on earth, to be a child and awaken with your eyes full of dreams and expectations and believe for a while at least that all good things are possible — peace, goodwill, love, merriment, the raven-maned rocking horse you want to ride forever. No conflict of interest for me. I wouldn't lose a birthday to Christmas. Rather than this smoggy heat I wish I could see snow. The city, this building snug under a blanket of fresh snow. No footprints of men running, men on their knees, men bleeding. No women forced out into halls and streets, away from their children. I wish this city, this tower were stranded in a gentle snowstorm and Christmas happens day after day and the bright fires in every hearth never go out, and the carols ring true chorus after chorus, and the gifts given and received precipitate endless joys. The world trapped in Christmas for a day dancing on forever. I wish I could transform the ten flights of my falling into those twelve days in the Christmas song. *On the first day of Christmas my true love said to me* . . . angels, a partridge in a pear tree, ten maids a milking, five gold rings, two turtledoves. I wish those would be the sights greeting me instead of darkness, the icy winter heart of this August afternoon I have been pitched without a kiss through a maroon door.

Floor of Power. El Presidente inhabits this floor. Some say he owns the whole building. He believes he owns it, collects rent, treats the building and its occupants with contempt. He is a bold-faced man. Cheeks slotted nose to chin like a puppet's. Chicken lips. This floor is entirely white. A floury, cracked white some say used to gleam. El Presidente is white also. Except for the pink dome of his forehead. Once, long ago, his flesh was pink head to toe. Then he painted himself white to match the white floor of power. Paint ran out just after the brush stroke that permanently sealed his eyes. Since El Presidente is cheap and mean he refused to order more paint. Since El Presidente is vain and arrogant he pretended to look at his unfinished self in the mirror and proclaimed he liked what he saw, the coat of cakey white, the raw, pink dome pulsing like a bruise.

El Presidente often performs on TV. We can watch him jog, golf, fish, travel, lie, preen, mutilate the language. But these activities are not his job; his job is keeping things in the building as they are, squatting on the floor of power like a broken generator or broken furnace or broken heart, occupying the space where one that works should be.

Floor of Regrets. One thing bothers me a lot. I regret not knowing what is on the floors above the one where I began my fall. I hope it's better up there. Real gardens perhaps or even a kind of heaven for the occupants lucky enough to live above the floors I've seen. Would one of you please mount the stairs, climb slowly up from floor ten, examine carefully, one soft, warm night, the topmost floors, and sing me a lullaby of what I missed.

Floor of Love. I'm supposed to be sleeping. I could be sleeping. Early morning and my eyes don't want to open and legs don't want to push me out of bed yet. Two rooms away I can hear Mom in the kitchen. She's fixing breakfast. Daddy first, then I will slump into the kitchen Mom has made bright and smelling good already this morning. Her perkiness, the sizzling bacon, water boiling, wheat bread popping up like jack-in-the-box from the shiny toaster, the Rice Krispies crackling, fried eggs hissing, the FM's sophisticated patter and mincing

20

string trios would wake the dead. And it does. Me and Daddy slide into our places. Hi, Mom. Good morning, Dearheart. The day begins. Smells wonderful. I awaken now to his hand under the covers with me, rubbing the baby fat of my tummy where he's shoved my nightgown up past my panties. He says I shouldn't wear them. Says it ain't healthy to sleep in your drawers. Says no wonder you get those rashes. He rubs and pinches. Little nips. Then the flat of his big hand under the elastic waistband wedges my underwear down. I raise my hips a little bit to help. No reason not to. The whole thing be over with sooner. Don't do no good to try and stop him or slow him down. He said my Mama knows. He said go on fool and tell her she'll smack you for talking nasty. He was right. She beat me in the kitchen. Then took me in to their room and he stripped me butt-naked and beat me again while she watched. So I kinda hump up, wiggle, and my underwear's down below my knees, his hand's on its way back up to where I don't even understand how to grow hairs yet.

The Floor That Stands for All the Other Floors Missed or Still to Come. My step-brother Tommy was playing in the schoolyard and they shot him dead. Bang. Bang. Gang banging and poor Tommy caught a cap in his chest. People been in and out the apartment all day. Sorry. Sorry. Everybody's so sorry. Some brought cakes, pies, macaroni casseroles, lunch meat, liquor. Two Ebony Cobras laid a joint on Tommy's older brother who hadn't risen from the kitchen chair he's straddling, head down, nodding, till his boys bop through the door. They know who hit Tommy. They know tomorrow what they must do. Today one of those everybody-in-the-family-and-friends-in-dark-clothes-funeral days, the mothers, sisters, aunts, grandmothers weepy, the men motherfucking everybody from god on down. You can't see me among the mourners. My time is different from this time. You can't understand my time. Or name it. Or share it. Tommy is beginning to remember me. To join me where I am falling unseen through your veins and arteries down down to where the heart stops, the square opening through which trash passes to the compactor.   *[1992]*

■ THINKING ABOUT THE TEXT

1. Although events like this are all too real, this story is a fantasy as it imagines the thoughts of a child (if it were possible for an infant to understand its fate) on the way down the garbage chute. Is this an effective strategy?

2. Do you agree with the infant in the section "A Floor of Opinions" when she states her opinions in a series of sentences beginning with "I believe"?

3. Does Wideman attempt to place the blame for the infant's death? Where would you look for reasons that the baby was thrown down the chute?

4. What do you think Wideman hoped to achieve with this dramatic fantasy?

5. What is a possible future for the infant had she lived? Why does Wideman create this imaginary scenario?

■ MAKING COMPARISONS

1. Boyle and Wideman use different techniques to understand how such an event could happen. Is one technique more effective than the other?

2. How does the socioeconomic context of each neonaticide story affect the young mothers?

3. Compare the effect all three stories had on you. Are your sympathies engaged? Are you more disturbed by one than another?

■ WRITING ABOUT ISSUES

1. Some philosophers argue that neonaticide should not be a criminal offense. Write an argument essay that agrees or disagrees.

2. Write an essay that answers the question: What can be done to prevent such events?

3. In the conclusion of Boyle's story, Jeremy thinks: "And what had he done to deserve it? He still couldn't understand" (para. 66). Write a brief analysis of this position.

4. In *Intimate Reading*, her study of the memoir, Janet Ellerby claims that reading memoirs of women who keep secrets "will help those people who rush to damn unfortunate adolescent girls to understand why these desperate girls hide their pregnancies from their families . . . and themselves . . . and help others understand how a panicked and forsaken girl in unimaginable pain might hysterically abandon the newborn she has steadfastly denied, whether she gives birth in a delivery room or a high school bathroom . . . [and] will help our culture understand that we have not yet solved the physical and psychological obstacles that adolescent girls must brave when faced with unwanted pregnancies." Write an essay that agrees or disagrees with this position.

▰ Gays and Lesbians in Families: Poems

ESSEX HEMPHILL, "Commitments"

AUDRE LORDE, "Who Said It Was Simple"

MINNIE BRUCE PRATT, "Two Small-Sized Girls"

RANE ARROYO, "My Transvestite Uncle Is Missing"

The late Essex Hemphill was gay, as is Rane Arroyo; the late Audre Lorde was a lesbian, as is Minnie Bruce Pratt. All four writers in this cluster remind their audience that families may have gay or lesbian members, but the families depicted in most literature, films, television shows, and songs are heterosexual. Indeed, much of American society prefers this image. Throughout history, plenty of gays and lesbians have concealed their sexual identities from their families, fearing rejection. Families that do have gay or lesbian members may refuse to admit the fact, although most have grown more accepting of their loved ones' differences.

As increasing numbers of gays and lesbians "come out of the closet," many are also publicly claiming the term *family*. They seek acceptance by the families they were raised in and the right to form and raise families of their own. Some are working to get same-sex marriage legalized. In all these efforts, they have quite a few heterosexual allies, but they face heterosexual resistance too. In the 1990s, a lesbian mother, Sharon Bottoms, lost custody of her children for that reason. Also, gays and lesbians are far from winning a universal right to adopt. In 2004, Massachusetts became the first state to legalize same-sex marriage, but as arguments about it raged throughout the United States, the federal government sought to discourage it by passing the Defense of Marriage Act in 1996, and several states passed laws against it. Gays and lesbians also face difficulties with adoption and foster parenting, although there are indications that societal attitudes here are changing, albeit slowly. Consider your own position on these matters as you read the following poems. Each refers to American society's widespread assumption that families are heterosexual; each also points out the suffering that can result from this belief.

▰ BEFORE YOU READ

What, at present, is your attitude toward gays and lesbians? Try to identify specific people, experiences, and institutions that have shaped your view. If it has changed over the years, explain how. Finally, describe an occasion that made you quite conscious of the attitude you now hold.

ESSEX HEMPHILL
Commitments

Before his untimely death from AIDS-related complications, Essex Hemphill (1957–1995) explored through prose, poetry, and film what it meant to live as a black gay man. The following poem comes from his 1992 book Ceremonies: Prose and Poetry. *His other books include a collection he edited,* Brother to Brother: New Writings by Black Gay Men *(1991). Hemphill also appeared in the documentaries* Looking for Langston *and* Tongues Untied.

I will always be there.
When the silence is exhumed.
When the photographs are examined
I will be pictured smiling
among siblings, parents,   5
nieces and nephews.

In the background of the photographs
the hazy smoke of barbecue,
a checkered red-and-white tablecloth
laden with blackened chicken,   10
glistening ribs, paper plates,
bottles of beer, and pop.

In the photos
the smallest children
are held by their parents.   15
My arms are empty, or around
the shoulders of unsuspecting aunts
expecting to throw rice at me someday.

Or picture tinsel, candles,
ornamented, imitation trees,   20
or another table, this one
set for Thanksgiving,
a turkey steaming the lens.

My arms are empty
in those photos, too,   25
so empty they would break

around a lover.
I am always there
for critical emergencies,
graduations,   30
the middle of the night.

I am the invisible son.
In the family photos
nothing appears out of character.
I smile as I serve my duty.   *[1992]*   35

≡ THINKING ABOUT THE TEXT

1. The speaker begins with the announcement "I will always be there," and yet later he says "I am the invisible son" (line 32). How can these two statements be reconciled? In the second line, he uses the word *exhumed*. Look up this word in a dictionary. What do you infer from the speaker's use of it?

2. Unlike the other stanzas, the second lacks verbs. Should Hemphill have included at least one verb there for the sake of consistency? Why, or why not? Is the scene described in the second stanza characteristic of your own family? Note similarities and differences.

3. What do you think the speaker means when he describes his arms in the photographs as "so empty they would break / around a lover" (lines 26–27)?

4. In line 34, the speaker refers to "character." How does he seem to define the term? He concludes the poem by noting, "I smile as I serve my duty." Should this line be taken as an indication of how he really feels about his family commitments? Why, or why not?

5. List some commitments that you think the speaker's family should be making toward him. What overall attitude of yours toward the family does your list suggest? What is your overall attitude toward the speaker?

AUDRE LORDE
Who Said It Was Simple

Audre Lorde (1934–1992), a prolific writer and speaker, was also active in the civil rights, women's, and gay and lesbian movements. She published several books of poetry, including Cables to Rage *(1970);* From a Land Where Other People Live *(1973), where the following poem appeared;* The New York Head Shop and Museum *(1974);* Coal *(1976);* The Black Unicorn *(1978); and* Our Dead behind Us *(1986). In addition, she wrote several works of nonfiction, including a memoir,* Zami: A New Spelling of My Name *(1982); a collection of essays and speeches,* Sister Outsider *(1984); and an account of her struggle with breast cancer,* The Cancer Journals *(1980). Her last book was* The Marvelous Arithmetic of Distance *(1993). Although Lorde was a lesbian, she had two children and described herself as "black, lesbian, mother, warrior, poet." Lorde was quite controversial, as she saw a clear link among sexism, racism, and homophobia. The key issue for her*

*was mainstream culture's intolerance of difference. This issue alienated her from
many white feminists who thought solidarity was crucial. Although Lorde certainly
believed in sisterhood, for her the metaphor of family had its limits, as the following
poem suggests.*

There are so many roots to the tree of anger
that sometimes the branches shatter
before they bear.

Sitting in Nedicks
the women rally before they march   5
discussing the problematic girls
they hire to make them free.
An almost white counterman passes
a waiting brother to serve them first
and the ladies neither notice nor reject   10
the slighter pleasures of their slavery.
But I who am bound by my mirror
as well as my bed
see causes in colour
as well as sex   15

and sit here wondering
which me will survive
all these liberations.   *[1973]*

≣ THINKING ABOUT THE TEXT

1. What is the thematic focus that Lorde announces with the tree metaphor of the first three lines?
2. What does the counterman do, and why does that annoy the speaker?
3. Why does Lorde use such a strong word as *slavery* (line 11) to describe the women at the counter who are served before the "brother"?
4. What does Lorde mean by being "bound by my mirror / as well as my bed" (lines 12–13)?
5. Do you see irony in Lorde's final stanza? Do you think Lorde is using "liberations" (line 18) sarcastically?

≣ MAKING COMPARISONS

1. Explain how both Lorde and Hemphill use the idea of invisibility.
2. Lorde mentions anger. Do you think Hemphill is angry, or do you sense other emotions?
3. Lorde was the mother of two children. Do you think that gave her a different perspective when protesting for gay rights?

MINNIE BRUCE PRATT
Two Small-Sized Girls

Minnie Bruce Pratt (b. 1946) has long been active in the women's movement. Her prose writings include Rebellion: Essays, 1980–1991 *(1991) and a 1995 volume of short pieces titled* S/HE. *As a poet, she has published* The Sound of One Fork *(1981);* Crime against Nature *(1990), which won the prestigious Lamont Prize of the American Academy of Poets; and* We Say We Love Each Other *(1992). Her latest books are* Walking Back Up Depot Street *(1999) and* The Dirt She Ate *(2003). In divorce proceedings, Pratt lost custody of her two sons because she is a lesbian. Many of the poems in* Crime against Nature, *including the following, refer to this experience.*

1

Two small-sized girls, hunched in the corn crib,
skin prickly with heat and dust.   We rustle
in the corn husks and grab rough cobs gnawed
empty as bone.   We twist them with papery shreds.
Anyone passing would say we're making our dolls.   5

Almost sisters, like our mothers, we turn and shake
the shriveled beings.   We are not playing at babies.
We are doing, single-minded, what we've been watching
our grandmother do.   We are making someone.   We hunker
on splintered grey planks older than our mothers,   10
and ignore how the sun blazes across us, the straw husks,
the old door swung open for the new corn of the summer.

2

Here's the cherry spool bed from her old room,
the white bedspread crocheted by Grandma,
rough straw baskets hanging on the blank wall,   15
snapshots from her last trip home, ramshackle
houses eaten up by kudzu.   The same past
haunts us.   We have ended up in the same present

where I sit crosslegged with advice on how to keep
her children from being seized by their father   20
ten years after I lost my own.   The charge then:
crime against nature, going too far with women,
and not going back to men.   And hers?   Wanting
to have her small garden the way she wanted it,
and wanting to go her own way.   The memory: 25

  Her father's garden, immense rows of corn,
  cantaloupe and melon squiggling, us squatting,

late afternoon, cool in the four o'clocks;
waiting for them to open, making up stories,
anything might happen, waiting in the garden.   30

3

So much for the power of my ideas about oppression
and her disinterest in them.   In fact we've ended
in the same place.   Made wrong, knowing we've done
nothing wrong:
                Like the afternoon we burned up   35
the backyard, wanting to see some fire.
The match's seed opened into straw, paper,
then bushes, like enormous red and orange
lantana flowers.   We chased the abrupt power
blooming around us down to charred straw,   40
and Grandma bathed us, scorched and ashy,
never saying a word.

                Despite our raw hearts,
guilt from men who used our going to take our children,
we know we've done nothing wrong, to twist and search   45
for the kernels of fire deep in the body's shaken husk.   *[1990]*

≡ THINKING ABOUT THE TEXT

1. Do you think any behavior deserves to be called a "crime against nature" (line 22)? Explain your reasoning.

2. Ironically, one pattern in Pratt's poem is nature imagery. Do you consider some or all of this imagery to be symbolic, or do you accept the
   images simply as details of a physical scene? Refer to specific examples.

3. Compare the three sections of the poem. What are their common elements? How do they significantly differ from one another? Why does the
   speaker believe that she and her cousin have "ended / in the same
   place" (lines 32–33)?

4. How would you describe the two girls' relationship to their grandmother? Support your answer with specific details from the text.

5. Do you think this poem is an affirmation of family ties? A criticism of
   them? Both? Again, refer to specific details.

≡ MAKING COMPARISONS

1. Compare the tone of the three speakers in Hemphill's, Lorde's, and
   Pratt's poems.

2. Do you get the impression that all three speakers in this cluster are searching for Pratt's "kernels of fire deep in the body's shaken husk" (line 46)? Show how these words are or are not relevant in each case.

3. Do you sympathize with any of the three speakers more than the others? Why, or why not?

RANE ARROYO

My Transvestite Uncle Is Missing

Rane Arroyo (b. 1954) was born in Chicago to Puerto Rican parents. He received a Ph.D. in American literature from the University of Pittsburgh. Besides being a performance artist, a literary critic, and a playwright, he is currently the director of Creative Writing at the University of Toledo. He is the author of six books, including the Ciardi Prize Poetry Winner Portable Famine *(2005). Arroyo's poetic work deals with Caribbean and Latino life and his place as a gay writer in a culture that sees him as an outsider. Many of his poems deal with issues of masculinity and his relationship with his family. The following poem was published in* The Singing Shark *(1996).*

1. Questions

I remember you so Elvis Presley-thin
and ever about to join the army (now I know

the whys of that), and I remember remembering you:
before breasts, before European wigs, when

the etc. of your sexuality was a secret,   5
and you babysat me, and we danced to Aretha,°

and you taught me to scream for the joy of
a song on the radio ("Romeo requests this from

his grave!"), and I can't call you, what's
your new legal name? Is it in the phone book?   10

Are you that official? I've heard you're
dead, call me collect please, I'm on my own,

and Uncle Rachel if you were here tonight I'd . . .
I'd sing to you: "Pretty woman walking down

the street of dreams," and you could tell me   15
that story again where gold is spun out of straw

6 Aretha Franklin (b. 1942): Known as the Queen of Soul; has won eighteen Grammy Awards.

2. Answers

News of your old death, first I danced in the shower with
clothes on, cracked my green head against a corner gave you a
bloody birth in my mind, gave myself a satisfying scar,
watched an Annie Lennox° video where she has a red towel on   20
her head, I mirrored her, white towel to stop the bleeding
inside my own nest of a skull, then I screamed and screamed,
but the police never came, snow fell from the constellations,
everything was on fire, fast forward, tumbling and I stupidly
read the *Song of Solomon* for comfort, my eye filled up with   25
blood, I strapped a big bandage around my head, I'm a poor
man's Wilfred Owen,° I'm my own damnation, you're dead,
I won't sing at the funeral that took place without me, the
sun will hear my confessions, my naked body on a rooftop
cruel cock crowing as if another ordinary morning and it is,   30
I did survive, I, someone shows up to make sure I'm not in a
coma, I'm not, not with all these memories, I touch myself as
if I'm still loved, Uncle Rachel, does Death look sexy without
a fig leaf?   *[1996]*

20 Annie Lenox (b. 1954): Lead singer for British band the Erythmics; called "the greatest white soul singer alive."   **27 Wilfred Owen (1893–1914):** British poet of shockingly
realistic war verse.

≣ THINKING ABOUT THE TEXT

1. What does the unusual phrase "the etc. of your sexuality" (line 5) suggest about the way Arroyo's family and the culture dealt with Uncle
   Rachel?

2. Are you surprised that Uncle Rachel teaches Arroyo to scream at the
   song? Is this an obviously unmasculine response? What seems the response of the adult Arroyo to this?

3. Is the first half of this poem a fond remembrance? How else would you
   characterize the tone of the speaker?

4. What does the narrator's dramatic response to the news of the uncle's
   death tell you about their relationship and about the poet's feelings?

5. What significance do memories have for the narrator?

≣ MAKING COMPARISONS

1. Is the speaker here more or less sympathetic than the three speakers in
   the other poems? Why?

2. Does this poem seem more an affirmation of family ties than do the
   other poems?

3. Point to any specific lines in the four poems that give you insight into gay life.

≡ WRITING ABOUT ISSUES

1. Choose Hemphill's, Lorde's, or Pratt's poem, and write an essay arguing for or against a position held by someone in the poem. The person can be the speaker. Support your argument with specific details and examples.

2. Choose two of the poems in this cluster, and write an essay comparing how commitments figure in them. Be sure to cite specific words from each poem.

3. In the next week, observe and jot down things on your campus that you think might disturb a gay or lesbian student. (If you are a gay or lesbian student, you may have already thought about such matters.) Then write an essay addressing the issue of whether your campus is inviting to gay and lesbian students. In arguing for your position on this issue, refer to some of the observations you made. If you wish, refer as well to one or more of the poems in this cluster.

4. Increasingly, the United States is grappling with whether same-sex marriage should be legalized. Another debate is whether gays and lesbians should be allowed to become foster parents. Choose one of these issues, and read at least three articles about it. Then write an essay in which you not only put forth and support your own position on the issue but also state whether and how the articles affected your thinking. If you wish, you may refer as well to one or more of the poems in this cluster.

CHAPTER 11

Love

Our culture makes many claims about love: stories of the rejected lover who dies of a broken heart abound. Modern kings give up the throne, ancient cities go to war — all for love. Love is thought to be such a powerful emotion that its loss may even make one want to die or to kill. (In some countries, finding one's wife or husband in bed with a lover is a legal excuse for murder.) Men and women seem willing to radically change their lives to be near their beloved. These are a few examples of love's powerful influence on our behavior and our understanding of who we are.

Yet a serious discussion about the nature of love is often frustratingly difficult. We can all make a list of things we love: a cold beer in summer, a great science-fiction film, a new car, a quiet dinner with a good friend, a walk in fresh snow, a football game when our favorite team comes from behind for a dramatic victory. We love our parents, our siblings, our best friends. How can one word cover such diversity?

When we try to generalize about love, we find ourselves relying on specific incidents because giving examples is easier than giving definitions. If clarifying the essence of love seems difficult, perhaps it is because our stories, myths, and songs are filled with contradictions. Love conquers all, we say, but doesn't love fade? We profess our undying love, but divorce statistics soar. Love is complex and frustrating to pin down. Our culture even identifies different types of love: true love, platonic love, maternal love, erotic love. Yet opinions about love are strong; we all have evidence for what it is and isn't that we find persuasive.

But the evidence we find so convincing is influenced by cultural assumptions, probably more than we know. It would be naive to claim otherwise when we are bombarded with so many movies, songs, and stories about love. Indeed, some critics argue that romantic love is only a socially constructed illusion, merely an elaborate rationalization for physical desire. Once the carnal attraction fades, we get restless. At least, this is one argument, and probably not a popular one among college students in search of love. Because we know what we feel about those we love, we often grow impatient with other people's perspectives. We are likely to ignore friends who say, "He wouldn't treat you like that if he really loved you." Perhaps nothing arouses our interest more than a discussion of our hopes and dreams about love.

Our engagement with stories and poems about love is equally complex and ambivalent. Although the stories in this chapter often illuminate the sometimes dark passageways we take in our romantic journeys, there is no consensus about the final destination. Arguing about love stories engages us as much as it may also baffle us. As you read, rely on your own experience, ethical positions, and literary judgment in determining whether specific characters are indeed in love, whether they should continue their relationship, whether they need more commitment or less. The wise and the foolish seem equally perplexed in matters of the heart.

The first cluster deals with the poetic intensity of true love from eight diverse perspectives. Next, we present three stories of romantic illusions, followed by a story of arranged marriage with three essays that explore cultural difference. In the fourth cluster we present three traditional elegies followed by three essays about online memorials. The fifth cluster presents three essays about the love of wild places. The next cluster focuses on the revision of a classic poem, while the following cluster gives us three stories of love by Kate Chopin. Three love stories, by three canonical writers, are also the focus of the next cluster. *Othello*, one of Shakespeare's great tragedies, is the focus of the three critical commentaries in the penultimate cluster, and then poems by Matthew Arnold and Susan Minot conclude the chapter.

WILLIAM SHAKESPEARE, "Let me not to the marriage of true minds"

JOHN KEATS, "Bright Star"

EMILY DICKINSON, "Wild Nights — Wild Nights!"

EDNA ST. VINCENT MILLAY, "What Lips My Lips Have Kissed, and Where, and Why"

E. E. CUMMINGS, "somewhere i have never travelled"

WISLAWA SZYMBORSKA, "True Love"

MICHAEL S. HARPER, "Discovery"

WENDY ROSE, "Julia"

Think about the term *true love*. Why *true*? Does *love* need this modification? Isn't love supposed to be true? Is there a *false* love? Or is something else implied that *love* doesn't convey by itself? Might it be something like *the one-and-only*? Some writers seem committed to the idea that true love lasts forever, for better or worse, regardless of circumstances. Is this just a fantasy, something we hope will be true? Or is it a reality, delivered to those who are lucky or who work hard to make it true? See if you agree with the eight poets in this cluster, some of whom are direct and clear about the possibilities of true love, while others take a more indirect, even playfully ironic tone.

■ **BEFORE YOU READ**

Do you believe there is one perfect person in the world for you? Is it possible to love someone forever, even if both of you change over the years from young adulthood to retirement and beyond?

WILLIAM SHAKESPEARE
Let me not to the marriage of true minds

William Shakespeare (1564–1616) is best known to modern readers as a dramatist; however, there is evidence that both he and his contemporaries valued his poetry above the plays. In 1598, for example, a writer praised Shakespeare's "sugared sonnets among his private friends." As with other aspects of his life and work, questions about how much autobiographical significance to attach to Shakespeare's subject matter continue to arise. Regardless of the discussion, there can be no doubt that the sonnets attributed to Shakespeare, at times directed to a man and at others directed to a woman, address the subject of love. Sonnet 116, which was written in 1609 and proposes a "marriage of true minds," is no exception.

Let me not to the marriage of true minds,
Admit impediments. Love is not love
Which alters when it alteration finds,
Or bends with the remover to remove:
Oh, no! it is an ever-fixèd mark,   5
That looks on tempests and is never shaken;
It is the star to every wandering bark,°   *small ship*
Whose worth's unknown, although his height be taken.
Love's not Time's fool, though rosy lips and cheeks
Within his bending sickle's compass come;   10
Love alters not with his brief hours and weeks,
But bears it out even to the edge of doom.
If this be error and upon me proved,
I never writ, nor no man ever loved.   *[1609]*

☰ THINKING ABOUT THE TEXT

1. Would you be pleased if your beloved wrote you this sonnet? Is he professing his love or giving a definition of true love as unchanging?

2. What if love didn't last "even to the edge of doom" (line 12)? Would it then be ordinary?

3. Shakespeare uses images to describe true love. Which one strikes you as apt? Can you suggest an image of your own?

4. The concluding couplet seems to be saying something like "I'm absolutely right." Do you think Shakespeare is? Can you think of a situation in which love should bend or alter?

5. The world seems to demonstrate that true love seldom lasts forever. Why then do writers of all kinds profess the opposite? If you really believe that true love does not exist, would you still marry? If your beloved asked you if your love would last forever, would you truthfully answer, "Only time will tell"?

JOHN KEATS
Bright Star

John Keats (1795–1821) was born into a working-class family. He hoped to be a physician but decided that poetry was his calling. His narrative poem Endymion *(1818) received poor reviews, but he was totally committed to his work. He was stricken with tuberculosis shortly after the poem's publication and went to Italy to recover. He died in Rome at age twenty-five.*

In 2009, Jane Campion directed Bright Star, *a film based on the last three years of Keats's life. The film focuses on his intense relationship with Fanny Brawne. Lines from many of his most famous poems are recited, including "La Belle Dame Sans*

Merci" and "Ode on Melancholy," as well as lines from his poetic letters to Fanny. On
his tombstone is his own inscription: "Here lies one whose name was writ in water."
Today Keats is considered one of literature's greatest poets.

Bright star, would I were stedfast as thou art—
Not in lone splendour hung aloft the night
And watching, with eternal lids apart,
Like nature's patient, sleepless Eremite,
The moving waters at their priestlike task   5
Of pure ablution round earth's human shores,
Or gazing on the new soft-fallen mask
Of snow upon the mountains and the moors—
No—yet still stedfast, still unchangeable,
Pillow'd upon my fair love's ripening breast,   10
To feel for ever its soft fall and swell,
Awake for ever in a sweet unrest,
Still, still to hear her tender-taken breath,
And so live ever—or else swoon to death.   *[1819]*

☰ THINKING ABOUT THE TEXT

1. Discuss how the speaker wants to be like the bright star in some ways,
   but not in others.

2. Is the speaker trying to stop time (as the pop star Jim Croce sang, "If I
   could save time in a bottle"), or is he hoping that his love will never
   change?

3. "Sweet unrest" (line 12) seems to be a contradiction. Is it? What is
   Keats trying to get at?

4. Is it psychologically healthy to want to have an unchanging love for
   someone forever? Is it realistic? Is it simply a kind of ritual to say such
   things?

5. Keats was quite sickly at the end of his short life. Do you think awareness of his serious illness influenced the theme of his poem?

☰ MAKING COMPARISONS

1. Compare the images of change that both Shakespeare and Keats use.

2. Compare Shakespeare's and Keats's use of the star metaphor.

3. Do both poets have similar notions of true love?

EMILY DICKINSON

Wild Nights — Wild Nights!

Emily Dickinson (1830–1886) spent most of her life in her father's house in Am-
herst, Massachusetts. Except for a year of college and several brief excursions to
Philadelphia and Washington, D.C., Dickinson lived a quiet, reclusive life in a house
she described as "pretty much all sobriety." Although a few poems were published
during her lifetime, Dickinson wrote almost two thousand poems on love, death, im-
mortality, and nature that are universally judged to be some of the most original,
lyrical, and artistic works in American literature. Although the specific person to
whom Dickinson wrote her love poems is unclear, many critics today believe her inter-
ests were both lesbian and heterosexual. As the poem below suggests, Dickinson, al-
though outwardly retiring and isolated, lived a lively, rich, and passionate life in her
poetry.

Wild Nights — Wild Nights!
Were I with thee
Wild Nights should be
Our luxury!

Futile — the Winds —   5
To a Heart in port —
Done with the Compass —
Done with the Chart!

Rowing in Eden —
Ah, the Sea!   10
Might I but moor — Tonight —
In Thee   [c. 1861]

■ THINKING ABOUT THE TEXT

1. Many critics see this poem as an erotic fantasy, perhaps a surprising
   subject for a reclusive spinster. Are there indications that this is not a
   poem about a real sexual encounter?

2. Comment on the imagery of the ocean and port. Could the port be
   Dickinson's isolation? The ocean the actual consummation?

3. How do you read the speaker's claim that she is done with the compass
   and chart? Is she rejecting convention?

4. Comment on the images in the last stanza. Is the speaker suggesting
   that sex might bring her paradise on earth?

5. What does the image of "moor[ing] . . . In Thee" (lines 11–12) suggest
   about her erotic desire?

■ MAKING COMPARISONS

1. Compare Dickinson's final stanza with the last six lines in Keats's poem.

2. Is Dickinson's poem more erotic than Shakespeare's or Keats's?

3. Compare Dickinson's phrase "a Heart in port" (line 6) to Shakespeare's line "That looks on tempests and is never shaken" (line 6).

EDNA ST. VINCENT MILLAY

What Lips My Lips Have Kissed, and Where, and Why

Edna St. Vincent Millay (1892–1950) was born in Rockland, Maine. Her mother encouraged her to be ambitious and self-sufficient and taught her about literature at an early age. On the strength of her early poems, Millay won a scholarship to Vassar, where she became a romantic legend for breaking the "hearts of half the undergraduate class." She also soon became wildly famous for her love poetry, giving readings in large auditoriums across the country, much like a contemporary rock star. She was openly bisexual, and her fame, talent, beauty, and bohemian aura was said to have driven her many admirers to distraction. A biography by Nancy Milford, Savage Beauty *(2001), quotes from dozens of letters to Millay, whining, pleading, and groveling for her favors. Milford writes that "she gave the Jazz Age its lyric voice." In fact, we still use a phrase that Salon.com says Millay "invented to describe a life of impudent abandon":*

> My candle burns at both ends;
> It will not last the night;
> But oh, my foes, and oh, my friends —
> It gives a lovely light!

Once called "the greatest female poet since Sappho," Millay's reputation in academic circles has fallen off somewhat. Perhaps her work seems a bit obvious compared to the cerebral and allusive free verse of poets like T. S. Eliot. But some critics still think of her as America's "most illustrious love poet." The title poem of Renaissance and Other Poems *(1917) ranks as a landmark of modern literature, and the collection itself is ranked fifth on the New York Public Library's Books of the Century. The following poem is from* Collected Poems *(1956).*

What lips my lips have kissed, and where, and why,
I have forgotten, and what arms have lain
Under my head till morning; but the rain
Is full of ghosts tonight, that tap and sigh
Upon the glass and listen for reply,   5
And in my heart there stirs a quiet pain
For unremembered lads that not again

Will turn to me at midnight with a cry,
Thus in winter stands the lonely tree,
Nor knows what birds have vanished one by one,   10
Yet knows its boughs more silent than before:
I cannot say what loves have come and gone,
I only know that summer sang in me
A little while, that in me sings no more.   *[1923]*

≡ **THINKING ABOUT THE TEXT**

1. What is it the speaker misses if she can't remember who her lovers were?
2. What does Millay mean by "a quiet pain" (line 6)?
3. Is Millay the "lonely tree" in winter (line 9)? Does it surprise you that she was only thirty-one when she wrote this poem?
4. Do you read the last two lines as saying that the speaker is no longer in love?
5. How would you describe the tone of this poem? Is it wistful or nostalgic? Appropriate? Regretful or sentimental? Bittersweet or simply sad?

≡ **MAKING COMPARISONS**

1. Do you think Shakespeare and Keats would think of Millay's loves as "true"?
2. Compare the rhyme scheme of the sonnets by Shakespeare, Keats, and Millay.
3. Which of the four poems seems the most contemporary in its view of love?

E. E. CUMMINGS
somewhere i have never travelled

Edward Estlin Cummings (1894–1962) often experimented with language on every level, but he did not legally change his name to lowercase and preferred the usual uppercase. Born in Cambridge, Massachusetts, and educated at Harvard, he tried his hand at essays, plays, and other types of prose; in fact, it was a novel based on a World War I concentration camp experience in France, The Enormous Room *(1922), that first brought cummings attention. It is his poetry, however, that most readers immediately recognize for its eccentric use of typography and punctuation, its wordplay and slang usage, its jazz rhythms, and its childlike foregrounding of the concrete above the abstract. Cummings hated pretension and would agree to deliver the prestigious Eliot lectures at Harvard in 1953 only if they were called* nonlectures. *His two large volumes of* The Complete Poems, 1913–1962, *published in 1972, include humor, understated satire, and celebrations of love and sex.*

somewhere i have never travelled, gladly beyond
any experience, your eyes have their silence:
in your most frail gesture are things which enclose me,
or which i cannot touch because they are too near
your slightest look easily will unclose me   5
though i have closed myself as fingers,
you open always petal by petal myself as Spring opens
(touching skilfully, mysteriously) her first rose
or if your wish be to close me, i and
my life will shut very beautifully, suddenly,   10

as when the heart of this flower imagines
the snow carefully everywhere descending;

nothing which we are to perceive in this world equals
the power of your intense fragility: whose texture
compels me with the colour of its countries,   15
rendering death and forever with each breathing

(i do not know what it is about you that closes
and opens; only something in me understands
the voice of your eyes is deeper than all roses)
nobody, not even the rain, has such small hands   *[1931]*   20

≡ THINKING ABOUT THE TEXT

1. In your own words, what is cummings saying about the effect love has on him? Is this hyperbolic? Why?

2. Does love open us up? In what ways? Can you give a personal example of what a strong feeling did to you?

3. Is this a poem about love or obsession or romantic infatuation? What is the difference?

4. What do you think "the power of your intense fragility" (line 14) might mean? Is this a contradiction?

5. When cummings says "something in me understands" (line 18), what might he mean? Is love located inside us somewhere? In our hearts? Our brains?

≡ MAKING COMPARISONS

1. Is cummings's flower imagery more effective than the images that Shakespeare and Keats use?

2. Is this poem closer in theme to Keats's poem or to Millay's?

3. What do you imagine Shakespeare and Keats would think about cummings's sentence structure? His images?

WISLAWA SZYMBORSKA
True Love

Translated by Stanislaw Baránczak and Clare Cavanagh

Wislawa Szymborska (b. 1923) was born in Poland and has lived in Krakow since 1931, studying literature at Jagiellonian University. She worked as a poetry editor for almost twenty years for a well-known literary journal in Krakow. She has published sixteen collections of poetry, many of which have been widely translated, and has won many prizes, including, most notably, the Nobel Prize for literature in 1996 "for poetry that with ironic precision allows the historical and biological context to come to light in fragments of human reality." A recent collection, Monologue of a Dog: New Poems *(2005), was called "elegiac, personal, and often profound." The following poem is from* View with a Grain of Sand *(1995).*

True love. Is it normal,
is it serious, is it practical?
What does the world get from two people
who exist in a world of their own?

Placed on the same pedestal for no good reason,   5
drawn randomly from millions, but convinced
it had to happen this way — in reward for what?
                For nothing.
The light descends from nowhere.
Why on these two and not on others?   10
Doesn't this outrage justice? Yes it does.
Doesn't it disrupt our painstakingly erected principles,
and cast the moral from the peak? Yes on both accounts.

Look at the happy couple.
Couldn't they at least try to hide it,   15
fake a little depression for their friends' sake!
Listen to them laughing — it's an insult.
The language they use — deceptively clear.
And their little celebrations, rituals,
the elaborate mutual routines —   20
it's obviously a plot behind the human race's back!

It's hard even to guess how far things might go
if people start to follow their example.
What could religion and poetry count on?
What would be remembered? What renounced?   25
Who'd want to stay within bounds?

True love. Is it really necessary?
Tact and common sense tell us to pass over it in silence,

like a scandal in Life's highest circles.
Perfectly good children are born without its help.   30
It couldn't populate the planet in a million years,
it comes along so rarely.

Let the people who never find true love
keep saying that there's no such thing.

Their faith will make it easier for them to live and die.   *[1972]*   35

■ THINKING ABOUT THE TEXT

1. The tone of the poem seems to be crucial. Is Szymborska being ironic? Does it really matter to her if true love is practical?

2. Why does the poet ask a series of questions and then answer them? Would you have answered them in the same way she does?

3. Reading between the lines, what kind of behavior do those in "true love" exhibit? Is this true in your experience?

4. Can people just "follow their example" (line 23)? Is falling in love an act of will? Is it an accident? Does she really worry about "how far things might go" (line 22)?

5. How could this poem be seen as an argument against true love? As an argument for true love? Does the last line make you think the poet really does believe in true love? How would you explain the meaning of the last line?

■ MAKING COMPARISONS

1. How might Shakespeare, Millay, and cummings respond to this poet's tone? Would they find it amusing? Annoying?

2. How might each of the poets respond to the question, Is true love necessary?

3. Which of these four poems is the most realistic? Which is the most idealistic?

MICHAEL S. HARPER

Discovery

Born in Brooklyn, New York, in 1951 to working-class parents, Michael S. Harper and his family soon moved to a predominantly white Los Angeles neighborhood. While attending college in Los Angeles, he worked as a postal worker, where he met educated black men like his father who came of age before the civil rights movement and had not been able to advance economically. Harper received an M.F.A. from the University of Iowa's creative writing program. His first book of poems, Dear John,

Dear Coltrane *(1970), from which this selection is taken, was nominated for the*
National Book Award. He has received many writing awards, including a Guggen-
heim. Among his ten books of poetry are the recent Songlines in Michaeltree: New
and Collected Poems *(2000) and* Use Trouble *(2005). He is a professor of English*
at Brown University.

We lay together, darkness all around,
I listen to her constant breath,
and when I thought she slept,
I too fell asleep.
But something stirred me, why I . . .   5
she was staring at me with her eyes,
her breasts still sturdy,
her thigh warming mine.
And I, a little shaken as she stroked
my skin and kissed my brow,   10
reached for the light turned on,
feeling for the heat which would
reveal how long she had looked
and cared.
The bulb was hot. It burned my hand.   *[1970]*   15

≡ THINKING ABOUT THE TEXT

1. The last sentence seems literal. But how might you read it metaphorically?

2. Why do you think Harper used the ellipsis in line 5? Is this an effective device, or should he have tried to say what the "something" was?

3. Why was the speaker "a little shaken" (line 9)? Would you feel that way in a similar situation, or would your response be something else? Surprise? Satisfaction?

4. Why did he want to know "how long she had looked / and cared" (lines 13–14)? Why might it matter to him? Would it to you?

5. Would you interpret the staring as evidence of true love? Would you interpret the speaker's behavior as true love or something else?

≡ MAKING COMPARISONS

1. Does the behavior of the woman in this poem correspond to any of the definitions of true love in the other poems?

2. Compare line 4 of e. e. cummings's poem to the response of the narrator in Harper's poem.

3. Which of the poems come closest to your idea of what true love is? Why?

WENDY ROSE
Julia°

Wendy Rose (b. 1948) was born in Oakland, California, to a multiethnic family: her father was Hopi and her mother Irish, Scottish, and Native American. She was estranged from both her parents, and despite a difficult adolescence, abusive early marriage, and psychological institutionalization, she received a Ph.D. in anthropology from the University of California at Berkeley. She is currently the coordinator of the American Indian studies program at Fresno City College in California and a leading Native American poet and artist. In her first book of poems, Hopi Road Runner Dancing (1973), she sees her task as evoking ghosts to give them voice to "live in my tongue / and forget your hunger." "Julia" deals with a common theme in Rose's work: those degraded in life who must speak from death. Many of these "lush and evocative" poems are written as personal letters to the author's departed family members. Itch Like Crazy was published in 2002.

Tell me it was just a dream,
my husband, a clever trick
made by some tin-faced village god
or ghost coyote, to frighten me
with his claim that our marriage is made   5
of malice and money.
Oh tell me again
how you admire my hands,
how my jasmine tea is rich and strong,
my singing sweet, my eyes so dark   10
you would lose yourself swimming
man into fish
as you mapped the pond
you would own.
That was not all.   15
The room grew cold
as if to joke
with these warm days;
the curtains blew out
and fell back   20
against the moon-painted sill.

I rose from my bed like a spirit
and, not a spirit at all, floated slowly
to my great glass oval

Julia Pastrana (1834–1860): Was a Mexican Indian who suffered from hypertrichosis terminalis (terrible facial deformities and long black hair covering her face and body). To financially gain from her fame, she was exhibited as a monster and freak by her husband, who mistreated her. She died in childbirth; the child lived three days. Her husband then mummified and displayed them in a glass cabinet. Eventually the mummies were stolen. The remains were discovered in 1990 and are now stored in a museum in Norway.

to see myself reflected   25
as the burnished bronze woman
skin smooth and tender
I know myself to be
in the dark
above the confusion   30
of French perfumes
and I was there in the mirror
and I was not.

I had become hard
as the temple stones   35
of O'tomi,° hair grown over my ancient face
like black moss, gray as jungle fog
soaking green the tallest tree tops.
I was frail
as the breaking dry branches   40
of my winter sand canyons,
standing so still as if
to stand forever.

Oh such a small room!
No bigger than my elbows outstretched   45
and just as tall as my head.
A small room from which to sing
open the doors
with my cold graceful mouth,
my rigid lips, my silences   50
dead as yesterday,
cruel as the children
and cold as the coins
that glitter
in your pink fist.   55

And another magic
in the cold
of that small room:
in my arms
or standing near me   60
on a tall table
by my right side:
a tiny doll
that looked
like me.   65

Oh my husband
tell me again
this is only a dream

36 O'tomi: An Indian tribe in east central Mexico.

I wake from warm
and today is still today,   70
summer sun and quick rain;
tell me, husband, how you love me
for my self one more time.
It scares me so
to be with child,   75
lioness
with cub.   *[1985]*

≡ THINKING ABOUT THE TEXT

1. Since the glossnote suggests that Julia's husband saw her as a way to make money, and possibly didn't truly love her, how do you respond to Julia's tone as the dead speaker in the poem? Is she bitter? Seeking revenge? Naive? Forgiving? Incredulous?

2. From the beginning stanza (lines 1–21), what can you infer about how her husband wooed Julia?

3. Is there some indication (lines 50–55) that Julia suspects her husband's duplicity?

4. Why is Julia afraid at the poem's end? Since in reality the speaker is dead, what effect in the reader is the poet trying to produce?

5. What does Julia ask for in the poem? What does she hope to gain? Since the reader suspects her husband's motives, how do you respond to Julia's last plea to be told he loves her?

≡ MAKING COMPARISONS

1. Is Julia's commitment to her husband even after her death evidence of the kind of true love that Shakespeare, Keats, and Szymborska write of?

2. Some love poems are full of praise for the beloved; others praise the qualities of love itself. Others, like "Julia," wonder if true love was involved at all. Which of these do you respond to most favorably? Why?

3. Which speaker in these poems seems the most authentic? The most sincere? The one most likely to fall out of love? Why?

≡ WRITING ABOUT ISSUES

1. Translate the cummings poem into concrete prose. Try not to use images; just explain the individual lines as simply as you can.

2. Write a comparison of the effects these eight poems had on you.

3. Write a position paper arguing for or against the reality of true love. Make reference to three of the poems given here.

4. Find three more love poems by Emily Dickinson or Edna St. Vincent Millay and write a report about the issues of love that this poet raises.

Romantic Dreams: Stories

LESLIE MARMON SILKO, "Yellow Woman"

JAMES JOYCE, "Araby"

JOHN UPDIKE, "A & P"

Although centuries old, the cliché that the human heart is a mystery still seems valid. We still wonder if falling in love is natural: Is love our inborn impulse to seek romance, or is it simply a physical attraction spurred on by our evolutionary need to procreate? Perhaps Western culture has socialized us to believe in the power of romantic love and the often irrational behavior that follows. Might it serve some deep psychological need to find a substitute for a beloved parent? Is it a giving emotion? A selfish one? Is it a psychological malady or the one thing worth giving up everything for? Do we need to believe in it whether or not it exists? Since we are often driven to irrational behavior, delusions, and heartbreak, might we be better off without romantic love? Or might life without it be intolerably flat?

In the following cluster, three fiction writers explore the ways romantic love can sometimes cloud judgment, encouraging us to act against our best interests.

Silko shows us a woman torn between myth and reality; Joyce shows us a boy in the throes of romantic idealism; and Updike gives us a memorable picture of how an indifferent world responds to romantic gestures.

≡ BEFORE YOU READ

Can people be truly happy without being in love? Is there one person in the world who is your true love? Or are there only certain types of people you could love? If your love didn't make you "float on a cloud," would you be disappointed? Is true love unconditional? Have you ever been fooled by romantic dreams?

LESLIE MARMON SILKO
Yellow Woman

Leslie Marmon Silko (b. 1948) is a major figure in the American Indian Renaissance. Raised in "Old Laguna" on the Pueblo Reservation near Albuquerque, New Mexico, Silko weaves the mythology of her matrilineal society into stories that move freely through what she calls an "ocean of time." The Yellow Woman character appears frequently in Silko's writing, both as a traditional figure, closely connected with nature and heterosexuality, and as a female character awakening to her cultural and sexual identity. Silko writes both poetry and fiction, often synthesizing the two genres into a single text. Her novels include Storyteller *(1981), in which "Yellow Woman" appears;* Ceremony *(1977); and* Almanac of the Dead *(1991). Her latest book is* Gardens in the Dunes: A Novel *(2000). She formerly taught at the University of Arizona at Tucson.*

1

My thigh clung to his with dampness, and I watched the sun rising up through the tamaracks and willows. The small brown water birds came to the river and hopped across the mud, leaving brown scratches in the alkali-white crust. They bathed in the river silently. I could hear the water, almost at our feet where the narrow fast channel bubbled and washed green ragged moss and fern leaves. I looked at him beside me, rolled in the red blanket on the white river sand. I cleaned the sand out of the cracks between my toes, squinting because the sun was above the willow trees. I looked at him for the last time, sleeping on the white river sand.

I felt hungry and followed the river south the way we had come the afternoon before, following our footprints that were already blurred by the lizard tracks and bug trails. The horses were still lying down, and the black one whinnied when he saw me but he did not get up — maybe it was because the corral was made out of thick cedar branches and the horses had not yet felt the sun like I had. I tried to look beyond the pale red mesas to the pueblo. I knew it was there, even if I could not see it, on the sand rock hill above the river, the same river that moved past me now and had reflected the moon last night.

The horse felt warm underneath me. He shook his head and pawed the sand. The bay whinnied and leaned against the gate trying to follow, and I remembered him asleep in the red blanket beside the river. I slid off the horse and tied him close to the other horse. I walked north with the river again, and the white sand broke loose in footprints over footprints.

"Wake up."

He moved in the blanket and turned his face to me with his eyes still closed.   5
I knelt down to touch him.

"I'm leaving."

He smiled now, eyes still closed. "You are coming with me, remember?" He sat up now with his bare dark chest and belly in the sun.

"Where?"

"To my place."

"And will I come back?"   10

He pulled his pants on. I walked away from him, feeling him behind me and smelling the willows.

"Yellow Woman," he said.

I turned to face him. "Who are you?" I asked.

He laughed and knelt on the low, sandy bank, washing his face in the river. "Last night you guessed my name, and you knew why I had come."

I stared past him at the shallow moving water and tried to remember the   15
night, but I could only see the moon in the water and remember his warmth around me.

"But I only said that you were him and that I was Yellow Woman—I'm not really her—I have my own name and I come from the pueblo on the other side of the mesa. Your name is Silva and you are a stranger I met by the river yesterday afternoon."

He laughed softly. "What happened yesterday has nothing to do with what you will do today, Yellow Woman."

"I know—that's what I'm saying—the old stories about the ka'tsina spirit° and Yellow Woman can't mean us."

My old grandpa liked to tell those stories best. There is one about Badger and Coyote who went hunting and were gone all day, and when the sun was going down they found a house. There was a girl living there alone, and she had light hair and eyes and she told them that they could sleep with her. Coyote wanted to be with her all night so he sent Badger into a prairie-dog hole, telling him he thought he saw something in it. As soon as Badger crawled in, Coyote blocked up the entrance with rocks and hurried back to Yellow Woman.

"Come here," he said gently.   20

He touched my neck and I moved close to him to feel his breathing and to hear his heart. I was wondering if Yellow Woman had known who she was—if she knew that she would become part of the stories. Maybe she'd had another name that her husband and relatives called her so that only the ka'tsina from the north and the storytellers would know her as Yellow Woman. But I didn't go on; I felt him all around me, pushing me down into the white river sand.

Yellow Woman went away with the spirit from the north and lived with him and his relatives. She was gone for a long time, but then one day she came back and she brought twin boys.

"Do you know the story?"

"What story?" He smiled and pulled me close to him as he said this. I was afraid lying there on the red blanket. All I could know was the way he felt, warm, damp, his body beside me. This is the way it happens in the stories, I was thinking, with no thought beyond the moment she meets the ka'tsina spirit and they go.

"I don't have to go. What they tell in stories was real only then, back in   25
time immemorial, like they say."

He stood up and pointed at my clothes tangled in the blanket. "Let's go," he said.

I walked beside him, breathing hard because he walked fast, his hand around my wrist. I had stopped trying to pull away from him, because his hand felt cool and the sun was high, drying the river bed into alkali. I will see some-one, eventually I will see someone, and then I will be certain that he is only a man—some man from nearby—and I will be sure that I am not Yellow Woman. Because she is from out of time past and I live now and I've been to school and there are highways and pickup trucks that Yellow Woman never saw.

It was an easy ride north on horseback. I watched the change from the cottonwood trees along the river to the junipers that brushed past us in the

ka'tsina spirit: A mountain spirit of the Laguna Pueblo Indians.

foothills, and finally there were only piñons, and when I looked up at the rim of the mountain plateau I could see pine trees growing on the edge. Once I stopped to look down, but the pale sandstone had disappeared and the river was gone and the dark lava hills were all around. He touched my hand, not speaking, but always singing softly a mountain song and looking into my eyes.

I felt hungry and wondered what they were doing at home now — my mother, my grandmother, my husband, and the baby. Cooking breakfast, saying, "Where did she go? — maybe kidnapped," and Al going to the tribal police with the details: "She went walking along the river."

The house was made with black lava rock and red mud. It was high above   30 the spreading miles of arroyos and long mesas. I smelled a mountain smell of pitch and buck brush. I stood there beside the black horse, looking down on the small, dim country we had passed, and I shivered.

"Yellow Woman, come inside where it's warm."

2

He lit a fire in the stove. It was an old stove with a round belly and an enamel coffeepot on top. There was only the stove, some faded Navajo blankets, and a bedroll and cardboard box. The floor was made of smooth adobe plaster, and there was one small window facing east. He pointed at the box.

"There's some potatoes and the frying pan." He sat on the floor with his arms around his knees pulling them close to his chest and he watched me fry the potatoes. I didn't mind him watching me because he was always watching me — he had been watching me since I came upon him sitting on the river bank trimming leaves from a willow twig with his knife. We ate from the pan and he wiped the grease from his fingers on his Levis.

"Have you brought women here before?" He smiled and kept chewing, so I said, "Do you always use the same tricks?"

"What tricks?" He looked at me like he didn't understand.   35

"The story about being a ka'tsina from the mountains. The story about Yellow Woman."

Silva was silent; his face was calm.

"I don't believe it. Those stories couldn't happen now," I said.

He shook his head and said softly, "But someday they will talk about us, and they will say, 'Those two lived long ago when things like that happened.'"

He stood up and went out. I ate the rest of the potatoes and thought about   40 things — about the noise the stove was making and the sound of the mountain wind outside. I remembered yesterday and the day before, and then I went outside.

I walked past the corral to the edge where the narrow trail cut through the black rim rock. I was standing in the sky with nothing around me but the wind that came down from the blue mountain peak behind me. I could see faint mountain images in the distance miles across the vast spread of mesas and valleys and plains. I wondered who was over there to feel the mountain wind on those sheer blue edges — who walks on the pine needles in those blue mountains.

"Can you see the pueblo?" Silva was standing behind me. I shook my head. "We're too far away."

"From here I can see the world." He stepped out on the edge. "The Navajo reservation begins over there." He pointed to the east. "The Pueblo boundaries are over here." He looked below us to the south, where the narrow trail seemed to come from. "The Texans have their ranches over there, starting with that valley, the Concho Valley. The Mexicans run some cattle over there too."

"Do you ever work for them?"   45

"I steal from them," Silva answered. The sun was dropping behind us and shadows were filling the land below. I turned away from the edge that dropped forever into the valleys below.

"I'm cold," I said; "I'm going inside." I started wondering about this man who could speak the Pueblo language so well but who lived on a mountain and rustled cattle. I decided that this man Silva must be Navajo, because Pueblo men didn't do things like that.

"You must be a Navajo."

Silva shook his head gently. "Little Yellow Woman," he said, "you never give up, do you? I have told you who I am. The Navajo people know me, too." He knelt down and unrolled the bedroll and spread the extra blankets out on a piece of canvas. The sun was down, and the only light in the house came from outside — the dim orange light from sundown.

I stood there and waited for him to crawl under the blankets.   50

"What are you waiting for?" he said, and I lay down beside him. He undressed me slowly like the night before beside the river — kissing my face gently and running his hands up and down my belly and legs. He took off my pants and then he laughed.

"Why are you laughing?"

"You are breathing so hard."

I pulled away from him and turned my back to him.

He pulled me around and pinned me down with his arms and chest. "You   55 don't understand, do you, little Yellow Woman? You will do what I want."

And again he was all around me with his skin slippery against mine, and I was afraid because I understood that his strength could hurt me. I lay underneath him and I knew that he could destroy me. But later, while he slept beside me, I touched his face and I had a feeling — the kind of feeling for him that overcame me that morning along the river. I kissed him on the forehead and he reached out for me.

When I woke up in the morning he was gone. It gave me a strange feeling because for a long time I sat there on the blankets and looked around the little house for some object of his — some proof that he had been there or maybe that he was coming back. Only the blankets and the cardboard box remained. The .30–30° that had been leaning in the corner was gone, and so was the knife I had used the night before. He was gone, and I had my chance to go now. But first I had to eat, because I knew it would be a long walk home.

.30–30: A rifle.

I found some dried apricots in the cardboard box, and I sat down on a rock at the edge of the plateau rim. There was no wind and the sun warmed me. I was surrounded by silence. I drowsed with apricots in my mouth, and I didn't believe that there were highways or railroads or cattle to steal.

When I woke up, I stared down at my feet in the black mountain dirt. Little black ants were swarming over the pine needles around my foot. They must have smelled the apricots. I thought about my family far below me. They would be wondering about me, because this had never happened to me before. The tribal police would file a report. But if old Grandpa weren't dead he would tell them what happened — he would laugh and say, "Stolen by a ka'tsina, a mountain spirit. She'll come home — they usually do." There are enough of them to handle things. My mother and grandmother will raise the baby like they raised me. Al will find someone else, and they will go on like before, except that there will be a story about the day I disappeared while I was walking along the river. Silva had come for me; he said he had. I did not decide to go. I just went. Moonflowers blossom in the sand hills before dawn, just as I followed him. That's what I was thinking as I wandered along the trail through the pine trees.

It was noon when I got back. When I saw the stone house I remembered   60
that I had meant to go home. But that didn't seem important any more, maybe because there were little blue flowers growing in the meadow behind the stone house and the gray squirrels were playing in the pines next to the house. The horses were standing in the corral, and there was a beef carcass hanging on the shady side of a big pine in front of the house. Flies buzzed around the clotted blood that hung from the carcass. Silva was washing his hands in a bucket full of water. He must have heard me coming because he spoke to me without turning to face me.

"I've been waiting for you."

"I went walking in the big pine trees."

I looked into the bucket full of bloody water with brown-and-white animal hairs floating in it. Silva stood there letting his hand drip, examining me intently.

"Are you coming with me?"

"Where?" I asked him.   65

"To sell the meat in Marquez."

"If you're sure it's O.K."

"I wouldn't ask you if it wasn't," he answered.

He sloshed the water around in the bucket before he dumped it out and set the bucket upside down near the door. I followed him to the corral and watched him saddle the horses. Even beside the horses he looked tall, and I asked him again if he wasn't Navajo. He didn't say anything; he just shook his head and kept cinching up the saddle.

"But Navajos are tall."   70

"Get on the horse," he said, "and let's go."

The last thing he did before we started down the steep trail was to grab the .30–30 from the corner. He slid the rifle into the scabbard that hung from his saddle.

"Do they ever try to catch you?" I asked.

"They don't know who I am."

"Then why did you bring the rifle?" 75

"Because we are going to Marquez where the Mexicans live."

3

The trail leveled out on a narrow ridge that was steep on both sides like an animal spine. On one side I could see where the trail went around the rocky gray hills and disappeared into the southeast where the pale sandrock mesas stood in the distance near my home. On the other side was a trail that went west, and as I looked far into the distance I thought I saw the little town. But Silva said no, that I was looking in the wrong place, that I just thought I saw houses. After that I quit looking off into the distance; it was hot and the wildflowers were closing up their deep-yellow petals. Only the waxy cactus flowers bloomed in the bright sun, and I saw every color that a cactus blossom can be; the white ones and the red ones were still buds, but the purple and the yellow were blossoms, open full and the most beautiful of all.

Silva saw him before I did. The white man was riding a big gray horse, coming up the trail toward us. He was traveling fast and the gray horse's feet sent rocks rolling off the trail into the dry tumbleweeds. Silva motioned for me to stop and we watched the white man. He didn't see us right away, but finally his horse whinnied at our horses and he stopped. He looked at us briefly before he loped the gray horse across the three hundred yards that separated us. He stopped his horse in front of Silva, and his young fat face was shadowed by the brim of his hat. He didn't look mad, but his small, pale eyes moved from the blood-soaked gunny sacks hanging from my saddle to Silva's face and then back to my face.

"Where did you get the fresh meat?" the white man asked.

"I've been hunting," Silva said, and when he shifted his weight in the 80
saddle the leather creaked.

"The hell you have, Indian. You've been rustling cattle. We've been looking for the thief for a long time."

The rancher was fat, and sweat began to soak through his white cowboy shirt and the wet cloth stuck to the thick rolls of belly fat. He almost seemed to be panting from the exertion of talking, and he smelled rancid, maybe because Silva scared him.

Silva turned to me and smiled. "Go back up the mountain, Yellow Woman."

The white man got angry when he heard Silva speak in a language he couldn't understand. "Don't try anything, Indian. Just keep riding to Marquez. We'll call the state police from there."

The rancher must have been unarmed because he was very frightened and 85
if he had a gun he would have pulled it out then. I turned my horse around and the rancher yelled, "Stop!" I looked at Silva for an instant and there was something ancient and dark — something I could feel in my stomach — in his eyes, and when I glanced at his hand I saw his finger on the trigger of the .30–30

that was still in the saddle scabbard. I slapped my horse across the flank and the sacks of raw meat swung against my knees as the horse leaped up the trail. It was hard to keep my balance, and once I thought I felt the saddle slipping backward; it was because of this that I could not look back.

I didn't stop until I reached the ridge where the trail forked. The horse was breathing deep gasps and there was a dark film of sweat on its neck. I looked down in the direction I had come from, but I couldn't see the place. I waited. The wind came up and pushed warm air past me. I looked up at the sky, pale blue and full of thin clouds and fading vapor trails left by jets.

I think four shots were fired — I remember hearing four hollow explosions that reminded me of deer hunting. There could have been more shots after that, but I couldn't have heard them because my horse was running again and the loose rocks were making too much noise as they scattered around his feet.

Horses have a hard time running downhill, but I went that way instead of uphill to the mountain because I thought it was safer. I felt better with the horse running southeast past the round gray hills that were covered with cedar trees and black lava rock. When I got to the plain in the distance I could see the dark green patches of tamaracks that grew along the river; and beyond the river I could see the beginning of the pale sandrock mesas. I stopped the horse and looked back to see if anyone was coming; then I got off the horse and turned the horse around, wondering if it would go back to its corral under the pines on the mountain. It looked back at me for a moment and then plucked a mouthful of green tumbleweeds before it trotted back up the trail with its ears pointed forward, carrying its head daintily to one side to avoid stepping on the dragging reins. When the horse disappeared over the last hill, the gunny sacks full of meat were still swinging and bouncing.

4

I walked toward the river on a wood-hauler's road that I knew would eventually lead to the paved road. I was thinking about waiting beside the road for someone to drive by, but by the time I got to the pavement I had decided it wasn't very far to walk if I followed the river back the way Silva and I had come.

The river water tasted good, and I sat in the shade under a cluster of silvery 90 willows. I thought about Silva, and I felt sad at leaving him; still, there was something strange about him, and I tried to figure it out all the way back home.

I came back to the place on the river bank where he had been sitting the first time I saw him. The green willow leaves that he had trimmed from the branch were still lying there, wilted in the sand. I saw the leaves and I wanted to go back to him — to kiss him and to touch him — but the mountains were too far away now. And I told myself, because I believe it, he will come back sometime and be waiting again by the river.

I followed the path up from the river into the village. The sun was getting low, and I could smell supper cooking when I got to the screen door of my house. I could hear their voices inside — my mother was telling my grandmother how to fix the Jell-O and my husband, Al, was playing with the baby. I decided to tell them that some Navajo had kidnapped me, but I was sorry that old Grandpa wasn't alive to hear my story because it was the Yellow Woman stories he liked to tell best.   [1974]

■ THINKING ABOUT THE TEXT

1. Why does Yellow Woman run away with Silva? Does it have something to do with the coyote stories? What stories in your own culture have persuaded you to trust in romantic love?

2. How do myths and stories differ? Are they based on reality or on fantasy? What are the social or cultural purposes of stories about love?

3. Do you trust the narrator's judgment? Sincerity? On what textual evidence are you basing this evaluation? What bearing does her cultural heritage have on your analysis of her?

4. What specific details of Silko's story do you remember? Is the narrator a careful observer? Explain. What effect does the narrator's "noticing little things" have on you as a reader?

5. Has Yellow Woman learned her lesson? Do societies change their views of romantic love? How?

JAMES JOYCE

Araby

James Joyce (1882–1941) is regarded as one of the most innovative and influential writers of the modernist movement of the early twentieth century. His use of interior monologue, wordplay, complex allusions, and other techniques variously delighted, offended, or puzzled readers. Joyce's work demanded attention and was often subject to censorship during his lifetime. A Portrait of the Artist as a Young Man *(1916), set in Joyce's native Dublin, is largely autobiographical. Like his hero at the end of the novel, Joyce left Ireland at the age of twenty to spend the remainder of his life in Paris and other European cities. His long, complex novel* Ulysses *(1922), also set in Dublin, takes the reader through one day in the life of its protagonist and his city. In "Araby," published in* Dubliners *(1914), as in other stories in the collection, Joyce pictures the limited life of his character and leads him toward a sudden insight, or epiphany.*

North Richmond Street, being blind, was a quiet street except at the hour when the Christian Brothers' School set the boys free. An uninhabited house of two storeys stood at the blind end, detached from its neighbors in a square ground. The other houses of the street, conscious of decent lives within them, gazed at one another with brown imperturbable faces.

The former tenant of our house, a priest, had died in the back drawing-room. Air, musty from having been long enclosed, hung in all the rooms, and the waste room behind the kitchen was littered with old useless papers. Among these I found a few paper-covered books, the pages of which were curled and damp: *The Abbot*, by Walter Scott, *The Devout Communicant*, and *The Memoirs of Vidocq*. I liked the last best because its leaves were yellow. The wild garden behind the house contained a central apple-tree and a few straggling bushes under one of which I found the late tenant's rusty bicycle-pump. He had been a very charitable priest; in his will he had left all his money to institutions and the furniture of his house to his sister.

When the short days of winter came dusk fell before we had well eaten our dinners. When we met in the street the houses had grown sombre. The space of sky above us was the color of ever-changing violet and towards it the lamps of the street lifted their feeble lanterns. The cold air stung us and we played till our bodies glowed. Our shouts echoed in the silent street. The career of our play brought us through the dark muddy lanes behind the houses where we ran the gauntlet of the rough tribes from the cottages, to the back doors of the dark dripping gardens where odors arose from the ashpits, to the dark odorous stables where a coachman smoothed and combed the horse or shook music from the buckled harness. When we returned to the street light from the kitchen windows had filled the areas. If my uncle was seen turning the corner we hid in the shadow until we had seen him safely housed. Or if Mangan's sister came out on the doorstep to call her brother in to his tea we watched her from our shadow peer up and down the street. We waited to see whether she would remain or go in and, if she remained, we left our shadow and walked up to Mangan's steps resignedly. She was waiting for us, her figure defined by the light from the half-opened door. Her brother always teased her before he obeyed and I stood by the railings looking at her. Her dress swung as she moved her body and the soft rope of her hair tossed from side to side.

Every morning I lay on the floor in the front parlor watching her door. The blind was pulled down to within an inch of the sash so that I could not be seen. When she came out on the doorstep my heart leaped. I ran to the hall, seized my books, and followed her. I kept her brown figure always in my eye and, when we came near the point at which our ways diverged, I quickened my pace and passed her. This happened morning after morning. I had never spoken to her, except for a few casual words, and yet her name was like a summons to all my foolish blood.

Her image accompanied me even in places the most hostile to romance. On   5
Saturday evenings when my aunt went marketing I had to go to carry some of the parcels. We walked through the flaring streets, jostled by drunken men and bargaining women, amid the curses of laborers, the shrill litanies of shop-boys who stood on guard by the barrel of pigs' cheeks, the nasal chanting of street-singers, who sang a *come-all-you* about O'Donovan Rossa,° or a ballad about the troubles in our native land. These noises converged in a single sensation of

---

O'Donovan Rossa: Jeremiah O'Donovan (1831–1915) was nicknamed "Dynamite Rossa" for advocating violent means to achieve Irish independence.

life for me: I imagined that I bore my chalice safely through a throng of foes. Her name sprang to my lips at moments in strange prayers and praises which I myself did not understand. My eyes were often full of tears (I could not tell why) and at times a flood from my heart seemed to pour itself out into my bosom. I thought little of the future. I did not know whether I would ever speak to her or not or, if I spoke to her, how I could tell her of my confused adoration. But my body was like a harp and her words and gestures were like fingers running upon the wires.

One evening I went into the back drawing-room in which the priest had died. It was a dark rainy evening and there was no sound in the house. Through one of the broken panes I heard the rain impinge upon the earth, the fine incessant needles of water playing in the sodden beds. Some distant lamp or lighted window gleamed below me. I was thankful that I could see so little. All my senses seemed to desire to veil themselves and, feeling that I was about to slip from them, I pressed the palms of my hands together until they trembled, murmuring: "*O love! O love!*" many times.

At last she spoke to me. When she addressed the first words to me I was so confused that I did not know what to answer. She asked me was I going to *Araby*. I forgot whether I answered yes or no. It would be a splendid bazaar, she said she would love to go.

"And why can't you?" I asked.

While she spoke she turned a silver bracelet round and round her wrist. She could not go, she said, because there would be a retreat that week in her convent. Her brother and two other boys were fighting for their caps and I was alone at the railings. She held one of the spikes, bowing her head towards me. The light from the lamp opposite our door caught the white curve of her neck, lit up her hair that rested there and, falling, lit up the hand upon the railing. It fell over one side of her dress and caught the white border of a petticoat, just visible as she stood at ease.

"It's well for you," she said.   10

"If I go," I said, "I will bring you something."

What innumerable follies laid waste my waking and sleeping thoughts after that evening! I wished to annihilate the tedious intervening days. I chafed against the work of school. At night in my bedroom and by day in the classroom her image came between me and the page I strove to read. The syllables of the word *Araby* were called to me through the silence in which my soul luxuriated and cast an Eastern enchantment over me. I asked for leave to go to the bazaar on Saturday night. My aunt was surprised and hoped it was not some Freemason° affair. I answered few questions in class. I watched my master's face pass from amiability to sternness; he hoped I was not beginning to idle. I could not call my wandering thoughts together. I had hardly any patience with the serious work of life which, now that it stood between me and my desire, seemed to me child's play, ugly monotonous child's play.

Freemason: A Protestant fraternal society that was in the past viewed by Catholics as hostile.

On Saturday morning I reminded my uncle that I wished to go to the bazaar in the evening. He was fussing at the hallstand, looking for the hat-brush, and answered me curtly:

"Yes, boy, I know."

As he was in the hall I could not go into the front parlor and lie at the window. I left the house in bad humor and walked slowly towards the school. The air was pitilessly raw and already my heart misgave me.   15

When I came home to dinner my uncle had not yet been home. Still it was early. I sat staring at the clock for some time and, when its ticking began to irritate me, I left the room. I mounted the staircase and gained the upper part of the house. The high cold empty gloomy rooms liberated me and I went from room to room singing. From the front window I saw my companions playing below in the street. Their cries reached me weakened and indistinct and, leaning my forehead against the cool glass, I looked over at the dark house where she lived. I may have stood there for an hour, seeing nothing but the brown-clad figure cast by my imagination, touched discreetly by the lamplight at the curved neck, at the hand upon the railings, and at the border below the dress.

When I came downstairs again I found Mrs. Mercer sitting at the fire. She was an old garrulous woman, a pawnbroker's widow, who collected used stamps for some pious purpose. I had to endure the gossip of the tea-table. The meal was prolonged beyond an hour and still my uncle did not come. Mrs. Mercer stood up to go: she was sorry she couldn't wait any longer, but it was after eight o'clock and she did not like to be out late, as the night air was bad for her. When she had gone I began to walk up and down the room, clenching my fists. My aunt said:

"I'm afraid you may put off your bazaar for this night of Our Lord."

At nine o'clock I heard my uncle's latchkey in the halldoor. I heard him talking to himself and heard the hallstand rocking when it had received the weight of his overcoat. I could interpret these signs. When he was midway through his dinner I asked him to give me the money to go to the bazaar. He had forgotten.

"The people are in bed and after their first sleep now," he said.   20

I did not smile. My aunt said to him energetically:

"Can't you give him the money and let him go? You've kept him late enough as it is."

My uncle said he was very sorry he had forgotten. He said he believed in the old saying: "All work and no play makes Jack a dull boy." He asked me where I was going and, when I had told him a second time he asked me did I know *The Arab's Farewell to His Steed.* When I left the kitchen he was about to recite the opening lines of the piece to my aunt.

I held a florin° tightly in my hand as I strode down Buckingham Street towards the station. The sight of the streets thronged with buyers and glaring

---

florin: A silver coin worth two shillings.

with gas recalled to me the purpose of my journey. I took my seat in a third-class carriage of a deserted train. After an intolerable delay the train moved out of the station slowly. It crept onward among ruinous houses and over the twinkling river. At Westland Row Station a crowd of people pressed to the carriage doors; but the porters moved them back, saying that it was a special train for the bazaar. I remained alone in the bare carriage. In a few minutes the train drew up beside an improvised wooden platform. I passed out on to the road and saw by the lighted dial of a clock that it was ten minutes to ten. In front of me was a large building which displayed the magical name.

I could not find any sixpenny entrance and, fearing that the bazaar would 25 be closed, I passed in quickly through a turnstile, handing a shilling to a weary-looking man. I found myself in a big hall girdled at half its height by a gallery. Nearly all the stalls were closed and the greater part of the hall was in darkness. I recognized a silence like that which pervades a church after a service. I walked into the center of the bazaar timidly. A few people were gathered about the stalls which were still open. Before a curtain, over which the words *Café Chantant* were written in colored lamps, two men were counting money on a salver. I listened to the fall of the coins.

Remembering with difficulty why I had come I went over to one of the stalls and examined porcelain vases and flowered tea-sets. At the door of the stall a young lady was talking and laughing with two young gentlemen. I remarked their English accents and listened vaguely to their conversation.

"O, I never said such a thing!"

"O, but you did!"

"O, but I didn't!"

"Didn't she say that?" 30

"Yes. I heard her."

"O, there's a . . . fib!"

Observing me the young lady came over and asked me did I wish to buy anything. The tone of her voice was not encouraging; she seemed to have spoken to me out of a sense of duty. I looked humbly at the great jars that stood like eastern guards at either side of the dark entrance to the stall and murmured:

"No, thank you."

The young lady changed the position of one of the vases and went back to 35 the two young men. They began to talk of the same subject. Once or twice the young lady glanced at me over her shoulder.

I lingered before her stall, though I knew my stay was useless, to make my interest in her wares seem the more real. Then I turned away slowly and walked down the middle of the bazaar. I allowed the two pennies to fall against the sixpence in my pocket. I heard a voice call from one end of the gallery that the light was out. The upper part of the hall was now completely dark.

Gazing up into the darkness I saw myself as a creature driven and derided by vanity; and my eyes burned with anguish and anger.   *[1914]*

■ **THINKING ABOUT THE TEXT**

1. Why do the boy's eyes burn with anguish and anger? Has he learned something about romantic love? Was he in love with Mangan's sister? Give evidence.

2. If this story is partly autobiographical, what is Joyce's attitude toward his younger self? Are you sympathetic or critical of your own initiations into the complexities of relationships?

3. Reread the first and last paragraphs. In what ways might they be connected?

4. Find examples of religious imagery. What do you think is its purpose?

5. Do you think the boy's quest has symbolic meaning? Do you think cultures can also search for something?

■ **MAKING COMPARISONS**

1. Compare the growth of the boy with that of the wife in "Yellow Woman."

2. Make explicit the insight or epiphany the boy comes to at the end. What would be a comparable epiphany for the wife in "Yellow Woman"?

3. Is one ending more realistic than the other? Explain.

JOHN UPDIKE

A & P

John Updike (1932–2009) was born in Shillington, Pennsylvania, an only child of a father who taught high-school algebra and a mother who wrote short stories and novels. After graduating from Harvard, Updike studied art in England and later joined the staff of The New Yorker. *In 1959, he published his first novel,* The Poorhouse Fair, *and moved to Massachusetts. His many novels are notable for their lyrical and accurate depiction of the details and concerns of modern America.* Rabbit Run *(1960) and the sequels* Rabbit Redux *(1971),* Rabbit Is Rich *(1981), and* Rabbit at Rest *(1990) are considered important and insightful records of American life. His other works include the novels* Villages *(2004) and* Terrorist *(2006);* Due Considerations: Essays and Criticism *(2007);* The Maples Stories *(2009); and* Hub Fans Bid Kid Adieu: John Updike on Ted Williams *(2010). "A & P" comes from Updike's* Pigeon Feathers and Other Stories *(1962).*

In walks these three girls in nothing but bathing suits. I'm in the third checkout slot, with my back to the door, so I don't see them until they're over by the bread. The one that caught my eye first was the one in the plaid green two-piece. She was a chunky kid, with a good tan and a sweet broad soft-looking can with those two crescents of white just under it, where the sun never seems to hit, at the top of the backs of her legs. I stood there with my hand on a box of HiHo crackers trying to remember if I rang it up or not. I ring it up again and the customer starts giving me hell. She's one of these cash-register-watchers, a witch about fifty with rouge on her cheekbones and no eyebrows, and I know it made her day to trip me up. She'd been watching cash registers for fifty years and probably never seen a mistake before.

By the time I got her feathers smoothed and her goodies into a bag — she gives me a little snort in passing, if she'd been born at the right time they would have burned her over in Salem — by the time I get her on her way the girls had circled around the bread and were coming back, without a pushcart, back my way along the counters, in the aisle between the checkouts and the Special bins. They didn't even have shoes on. There was this chunky one, with the two-piece — it was bright green and the seams on the bra were still sharp and her belly was still pretty pale so I guessed she just got it (the suit) — there was this one, with one of those chubby berry-faces, the lips all bunched together under her nose, this one, and a tall one, with black hair that hadn't quite frizzed right, and one of these sunburns right across under the eyes, and a chin that was too long — you know, the kind of girl other girls think is very "striking" and "attractive" but never quite makes it, as they very well know, which is why they like her so much — and then the third one, that wasn't quite so tall. She was the queen. She kind of led them, the other two peeking around and making their shoulders round. She didn't look around, not this queen, she just walked straight on slowly, on these long white prima-donna legs. She came down a little hard on her heels, as if she didn't walk in her bare feet that much, putting down her heels and then letting the weight move along to her toes as if she was testing the floor with every step, putting a little deliberate extra action into it. You never know for sure how girls' minds work (do you really think it's a mind in there or just a little buzz like a bee in a glass jar?) but you got the idea she had talked the other two into coming in here with her, and now she was showing them how to do it, walk slow and hold yourself straight.

She had on a kind of dirty-pink — beige maybe, I don't know — bathing suit with a little nubble all over it, and what got me, the straps were down. They were off her shoulders looped loose around the cool tops of her arms, and I guess as a result the suit had slipped a little on her, so all around the top of the cloth there was this shining rim. If it hadn't been there you wouldn't have known there could have been anything whiter than those shoulders. With the straps pushed off, there was nothing between the top of the suit and the top of her head except just *her*, this clean bare plane of the top of her chest down from the shoulder bones like a dented sheet of metal tilted in the light. I mean, it was more than pretty.

She had sort of oaky hair that the sun and salt had bleached, done up in a bun that was unravelling, and a kind of prim face. Walking into the A & P with your straps down, I suppose it's the only kind of face you *can* have. She held her head so high her neck, coming up out of those white shoulders, looked kind of stretched, but I didn't mind. The longer her neck was, the more of her there was.

She must have felt in the corner of her eye me and over my shoulder   5
Stokesie in the second slot watching, but she didn't tip. Not this queen. She kept
her eyes moving across the racks, and stopped, and turned so slow it made my
stomach rub the inside of my apron, and buzzed to the other two, who kind of
huddled against her for relief, and then they all three of them went up the cat-
and-dog-food-breakfast-cereal-macaroni-rice-raisins-seasonings-spreads-
spaghetti-soft-drinks-crackers-and-cookies aisle. From the third slot I look
straight up this aisle to the meat counter, and I watched them all the way. The
fat one with the tan sort of fumbled with the cookies, but on second thought
she put the package back. The sheep pushing their carts down the aisle — the
girls were walking against the usual traffic (not that we have one-way signs or
anything) — were pretty hilarious. You could see them, when Queenie's white
shoulders dawned on them, kind of jerk, or hop, or hiccup, but their eyes
snapped back to their own baskets and on they pushed. I bet you could set off
dynamite in an A & P and the people would by and large keep reaching and
checking oatmeal off their lists and muttering "Let me see, there was a third
thing, began with A, asparagus, no, ah, yes, applesauce!" or whatever it is they
do mutter. But there was no doubt, this jiggled them. A few houseslaves in pin
curlers even looked around after pushing their carts past to make sure what
they had seen was correct.

You know, it's one thing to have a girl in a bathing suit down on the beach,
where what with the glare nobody can look at each other much anyway, and
another thing in the cool of the A & P, under the fluorescent lights, against all
those stacked packages, with her feet paddling along naked over our check-
board green-and-cream rubber-tile floor.

"Oh Daddy," Stokesie said beside me. "I feel so faint."

"Darling," I said. "Hold me tight." Stokesie's married, with two babies
chalked up on his fuselage already, but as far as I can tell that's the only difference. He's twenty-two, and I was nineteen this April.

"Is it done?" he asks, the responsible married man finding his voice. I forgot
to say he thinks he's going to be manager some sunny day, maybe in 1990 when
it's called the Great Alexandrov and Petrooshki Tea Company or something.

What he meant was, our town is five miles from a beach, with a big sum-   10
mer colony out on the Point, but we're right in the middle of town, and the
women generally put on a shirt or shorts or something before they get out of
the car into the street. And anyway these are usually women with six children
and varicose veins mapping their legs and nobody, including them, could care
less. As I say, we're right in the middle of town, and if you stand at our front
doors you can see two banks and the Congregational church and the newspaper store and three real-estate offices and about twenty-seven old freeloaders
tearing up Central Street because the sewer broke again. It's not as if we're on
the Cape; we're north of Boston and there's people in this town haven't seen
the ocean for twenty years.

The girls had reached the meat counter and were asking McMahon something. He pointed, they pointed, and they shuffled out of sight behind a pyra-
mid of Diet Delight peaches. All that was left for us to see was old McMahon

patting his mouth and looking after them sizing up their joints. Poor kids, I began to feel sorry for them, they couldn't help it.

Now here comes the sad part of the story, at least my family says it's sad, but I don't think it's so sad myself. The store's pretty empty, it being Thursday afternoon, so there was nothing much to do except lean on the register and wait for the girls to show up again. The whole store was like a pinball machine and I didn't know which tunnel they'd come out of. After a while they come around out of the far aisle, around the light bulbs, records at discount of the Caribbean Six or Tony Martin Sings or some such gunk you wonder they waste the wax on, sixpacks of candy bars, and plastic toys done up in cellophane that fall apart when a kid looks at them anyway. Around they come, Queenie still leading the way, and holding a little gray jar in her hand. Slots Three through Seven are unmanned and I could see her wondering between Stokes and me, but Stokesie with his usual luck draws an old party in baggy gray pants who stumbles up with four giant cans of pineapple juice (what do these bums *do* with all that pineapple juice? I've often asked myself) so the girls come to me. Queenie puts down the jar and I take it into my fingers icy cold. Kingfish Fancy Herring Snacks in Pure Sour Cream: 49¢. Now her hands are empty, not a ring or a bracelet, bare as God made them, and I wonder where the money's coming from. Still with that prim look she lifts a folded dollar bill out of the hollow at the center of her nubbled pink top. The jar went heavy in my hand. Really, I thought that was so cute.

Then everybody's luck begins to run out. Lengel comes in from haggling with a truck full of cabbages on the lot and is about to scuttle into that door marked manager behind which he hides all day when the girls touch his eye. Lengel's pretty dreary, teaches Sunday school and the rest, but he doesn't miss that much. He comes over and says, "Girls, this isn't the beach."

Queenie blushes, though maybe it's just a brush of sunburn I was noticing for the first time, now that she was so close. "My mother asked me to pick up a jar of herring snacks." Her voice kind of startled me, the way voices do when you see the people first, coming out so flat and dumb yet kind of tony, too, the way it ticked over "pick up" and "snacks." All of a sudden I slid right down her voice into her living room. Her father and the other men were standing around in ice-cream coats and bow ties and the women were in sandals picking up herring snacks on toothpicks off a big glass plate and they were all holding drinks the color of water with olives and sprigs of mint in them. When my parents have somebody over they get lemonade and if it's a real racy affair Schlitz in tall glasses with "They'll Do It Every Time" cartoons stencilled on.

"That's all right," Lengel said. "But this isn't the beach." His repeating this 15 struck me as funny, as if it had just occurred to him, and he had been thinking all these years the A & P was a great big sand dune and he was the head lifeguard. He didn't like my smiling — as I say he doesn't miss much — but he concentrates on giving the girls that sad Sunday-school–superintendent stare.

Queenie's blush is no sunburn now, and the plump one in plaid, that I liked better from the back — a really sweet can — pipes up, "We weren't doing any shopping. We just came in for the one thing."

"That makes no difference," Lengel tells her, and I could see from the way his eyes went that he hadn't noticed she was wearing a two-piece before. "We want you decently dressed when you come in here."

"We *are* decent," Queenie says suddenly, her lower lip pushing, getting sore now that she remembers her place, a place from which the crowd that runs the A & P must look pretty crummy. Fancy Herring Snacks flashed in her very blue eyes.

"Girls, I don't want to argue with you. After this come in here with your shoulders covered. It's our policy." He turns his back. That's policy for you. Policy is what the kingpins want. What the others want is juvenile delinquency.

All this while, the customers had been showing up with their carts but, you know, sheep, seeing a scene, they had all bunched up on Stokesie, who shook open a paper bag as gently as peeling a peach, not wanting to miss a word. I could feel in the silence everybody getting nervous, most of all Lengel, who asks me, "Sammy, have you rung up their purchase?"   20

I thought and said "No" but it wasn't about that I was thinking. I go through the punches, 4, 9, groc, tot — it's more complicated than you think, and after you do it often enough, it begins to make a little song, that you hear words to, in my case "Hello (*bing*) there, you (*gung*) hap-py *pee*-pul (*splat*)!" — the *splat* being the drawer flying out. I uncrease the bill, tenderly as you may imagine, it just having come from between the two smoothest scoops of vanilla I had ever known were there, and pass a half and a penny into her narrow pink palm, and nestle the herrings in a bag and twist its neck and hand it over, all the time thinking.

The girls, and who'd blame them, are in a hurry to get out, so I say "I quit" to Lengel enough for them to hear, hoping they'll stop and watch me, their unsuspected hero. They keep right on going, into the electric eye; the door flies open and they flicker across the lot to their car, Queenie and Plaid and Big Tall Goony-Goony (not that as raw material she was so bad), leaving me with Lengel and a kink in his eyebrow.

"Did you say something, Sammy?"

"I said I quit."

"I thought you did."   25

"You didn't have to embarrass them."

"It was they who were embarrassing us."

I started to say something that came out "Fiddle-de-doo." It's a saying of my grandmother's, and I know she would have been pleased.

"I don't think you know what you're saying," Lengel said.

"I know you don't," I said. "But I do." I pull the bow at the back of my   30 apron and start shrugging it off my shoulders. A couple customers that had been heading for my slot begin to knock against each other, like scared pigs in a chute.

Lengel sighs and begins to look very patient and old and gray. He's been a friend of my parents for years. "Sammy, you don't want to do this to your Mom and Dad," he tells me. It's true, I don't. But it seems to me that once you begin a gesture it's fatal not to go through with it. I fold the apron, "Sammy" stitched in red on the pocket, and put it on the counter, and drop the bow tie on top of it. The bow tie is theirs, if you've ever wondered. "You'll feel this for the rest of your life," Lengel says, and I know that's true, too, but remembering how he made that pretty girl blush makes me so scrunchy inside I punch the No Sale tab and the machine whirs "pee-pul" and the drawer splats out. One advantage to this scene taking place in summer, I can follow this up with a clean exit, there's no fumbling around getting your coat and galoshes, I just saunter into the electric eye in my white shirt that my mother ironed the night before, and the door heaves itself open, and outside the sunshine is skating around on the asphalt.

I look around for my girls, but they're gone, of course. There wasn't anybody but some young married screaming with her children about some candy they didn't get by the door of a powder-blue Falcon station wagon. Looking back in the big windows, over the bags of peat moss and aluminum lawn furniture stacked on the pavement, I could see Lengel in my place in the slot, checking the sheep through. His face was dark gray and his back stiff, as if he'd just had an injection of iron, and my stomach kind of fell as I felt how hard the world was going to be to me hereafter.   *[1961]*

≡ THINKING ABOUT THE TEXT

1. Why do you think Sammy quits? Make a list of several plausible answers.

2. What would you do if you were in Sammy's position? What would your priorities be in this situation?

3. When Sammy hears Queenie's voice, he imagines an elegant cocktail party that he contrasts to his parents' "real racy affair" (para. 14) with lemonade and beer. What does this scene say about Sammy's attitude toward the girls? Toward his own social status?

4. Some critics have objected to Sammy's comment in the last sentence of paragraph 2 about "girls' minds." Is this a sexist observation? Does the time frame of the story figure in your opinion? Should it?

5. Comment on the last paragraph. What is the significance of the young married woman? Why does Sammy mention "sheep"? Why does Sammy think the world will be hard on him? Do you agree? What does "hard" mean?

≡ MAKING COMPARISONS

1. Are the three main characters in this cluster wiser at each story's end? Are they happier?

2. Which character's views about romance are most compatible with yours when you were, say, thirteen? With yours presently?

3. Compare the last paragraphs of "Araby" and "A & P." What attitudes do they express?

■ WRITING ABOUT ISSUES

1. Choose either Yellow Woman, the boy in "Araby," or Sammy and argue that this character was or was not really in love. Support your argument with references to the text and your own cultural experience.

2. Write an essay that defends or denies the idea that romantic love is irrational. Use two of the stories from this cluster.

3. Would any of the characters in this cluster have been comfortable in the cultural context you were raised in? (Consider movies, books, TV, family narratives, and so forth in analyzing your culture.) Write a brief analysis of how well one or more of these characters would "fit in."

4. Look up information about Native American culture and the coyote stories referred to in "Yellow Woman." Do they help to explain her attitudes? Do the same for the culture of Joyce's Ireland, especially religion and romance. How about America in the middle of the twentieth century? In a brief essay, argue that each story is understood more fully when the cultural context is provided.

≡ The Pull of Tradition: Cultural Contexts for a Story

JHUMPA LAHIRI, "Going Ashore"

CULTURAL CONTEXTS:

JHUMPA LAHIRI, "My Two Lives"

ANITA JAIN, "Is Arranged Marriage Really Any Worse than Craigslist?"

MIGUEL HELFT, "A Decent Proposal"

Right from the start, America has been a country of immigrants. Millions have come from all over the world over the past four hundred years to become part of the fabric of American society. From Europe, Asia, Africa, Central and South America, from the Caribbean and Mexico, immigrants have brought with them myriad languages, customs, religions, and cultural assumptions about everything from food and dress to marriage and romance. Most wanted to assimilate into their new home, and most did. Of course, for many it was not easy. They were often met with resistance and overt prejudice from those already considered Americans.

But even with the goodwill of established Americans, the process of abandoning centuries-old cultural traditions is difficult. Ideas about love, romance, and marriage are part of our core identity. For example, for families socialized to think one way about whom to marry and how to conduct courtship, making significant adjustments is no small matter. These changes are made more complex when the children of immigrants are largely socialized into American norms. These children often live in two disparate worlds, the one of their parents and the other, larger world of mainstream America. This is just the conflicted universe that Jhumpa Lahiri writes about. Raised in middle-class America by Indian immigrants and highly educated, Lahiri still has to negotiate the inevitable tensions between the traditions of India, thousands of miles away, and the immediacy of a dynamically changing American cultural landscape. It is the traditional battle between parents and their children writ large.

Even for a sophisticated intellectual like Lahiri, the pull of Indian tradition is strong. Quite simply, she has been doubly socialized, first privately by her parents and then publicly by the vastness of culture beyond her home. She has both of these vital cultural expectations within her. And when confronted by such emotionally dynamic forces as love, sex, and marriage, Lahiri and her fictional heroines find themselves torn. In the following story, Lahiri creates a memorable tale of love and desire, interwoven into the overlapping cultural demands of ancient India and contemporary America.

In her collection *Unaccustomed Earth* (2008), Lahiri includes three stories about Hema and Kaushik, both Indian American children of immigrants. We first meet them when Hema is six and Kaushik is nine. Later, when Hema is thirteen, Kaushik's family temporarily moves in with her family. "Going Ashore" is the last story in this collection, and after twenty-five years Hema and Kaushik are accidentally reunited. In the interim, however, Hema, now engaged to be married, has become a professor, and Kaushik has become a globe-trotting photographer. Lahiri's tale, critics note, "details with quiet precision the divide between American born children and their Bengali parents . . . as they try to find a balance between the solace and suffocation of tradition and the terror and excitement of the future into which they're being thrust."

Following the story is an essay by Lahiri describing the difficult negotiations necessary when growing up in two different cultural traditions. This is followed by two essays on arranged marriages. The first is a personal narrative from an Indian American woman much like Hema in "Going Ashore." And the second reports on a modern couple happy that they participated in an arranged marriage, a tradition still alien to most Americans.

■ BEFORE YOU READ

Do you feel as if your dating experience has been significantly influenced by mainstream cultural norms? Do you think that you have violated these norms or would like to do so?

JHUMPA LAHIRI
Going Ashore

Jhumpa Lahiri (b. 1967) was born in London to Bengali Indian immigrants. When she was three, her family moved to America, where she grew up in Rhode Island. She received a B.A. from Barnard College in 1989 and has several degrees from Boston University, including a Ph.D. in Renaissance studies. Her debut short-story collection, Interpreter of Maladies *(1999), won a Pulitzer Prize for fiction, unusual for a book of short stories. Her first novel,* The Namesake *(2003), was made into a popular film in 2007. Lahiri's second collection,* Unaccustomed Earth *(2008), quickly went to the top of the* New York Times *best-seller list. Her work has been highly praised as "lucid and revelatory . . . in exquisitely attuned prose." A major theme in her work is personal choice in conflict with parental expectations. She lives in Brooklyn, New York, with her husband and two children.*

Again she'd lied about what had brought her to Rome. A grant had relieved her, this autumn, of teaching at Wellesley. But Hema was not in Italy in any official capacity, only to take advantage of a colleague's empty apartment in the Ghetto. She had invented something that sounded impressive, a visiting lectureship at an institute of classical studies, and neither Navin nor her parents had questioned her. Her scholarly life was a mystery to them, something at once impressive and irrelevant. It had earned her a PhD and a tenure-track job, that was the important thing. The colleague, Giovanna, had arranged for Hema to have library privileges at the American Academy and given her the numbers of a few people to call in Rome, and in October, Hema had packed her

(© Marion Ettlinger.)

laptop and clothes and flown across the ocean for an improvised leave of absence. Just before Christmas she would go to Calcutta, where her parents had returned after a lifetime in Massachusetts and where, in January, she would marry Navin.

Now it was November, the week before Thanksgiving. When Hema thought of the existence she had evaded this semester, she saw the trees on Wellesley's campus stripped of their leaves, patches of Lake Waban already freezing over, darkness descending through classroom windows as her students struggled through sentences from Wheelock's Latin: *id factum esse tum non negavit.* In Rome the leaves were also falling, untended copper piles heaped on either side of the Tiber. But the days felt languorous, warm enough to wander the streets in a cardigan, and the tables outside the restaurant where Hema went each day for lunch were still full.

The restaurant, five minutes from Giovanna's apartment, was next to the Portico di Ottavia. There were of course hundreds of other restaurants she might have tried, hundreds of versions of cacio e pepe and carbonara and deep-fried artichokes she might have eaten. But the few times she wandered into different places, she was either disappointed by the food or flustered by her broken Italian, and so she remained faithful to the one she knew, the one where she was no longer questioned. At this restaurant the waiters knew by now to bring her a bottle of acqua gassata, a half-litre of vino bianco, swiftly to clear the second place setting away. They left her alone with the book she would bring, though mostly she sat and looked at the remains of the Portico, at its chewed-up columns girded with scaffolding, its massive pediment with significant chunks missing. Well-dressed chattering Romans would pass by without a glance, while tourists would pause, gazing down at the excavations before proceeding on to the Theater of Marcellus. In front of the Portico was a little piazza where, according to the plaque Hema had managed to translate, over a thousand Jews had been deported in October 1943.

She could not take credit for discovering the restaurant on her own. She had eaten a meal there many years ago, with Julian, the other time she'd come to Rome under false pretenses. And though she had not intended to eat there again, she had found it during her first jet-lagged walk around Giovanna's neighborhood in search of food. She had accompanied Julian secretly, still confident in those days that his divorce was a matter of time. It was May, the city clogged with people, already too hot for the clothes she'd brought. She and Julian stayed together at a hotel behind the Colosseum, and he presented a paper at a conference, a recycled chapter from his study of Petronius. Under normal circumstances Hema might have presented her own paper. This was what she had told her parents she'd be doing, and they had not questioned her. But she had just defended her dissertation and was determined to take a few months off.

Before that, Hema had been to Rome only once, traveling with a girlfriend   5
after graduating from Bryn Mawr. That first visit, when she and her friend, both classics majors, earnestly walked from landmark to landmark, translating inscriptions and subsisting on panini and gelato, had left a lasting impression on Hema. But the trip with Julian was a heap of rubble that added up to nothing. She remembered breakfasts with him on the roof of the hotel, sitting among small brown birds that hopped at her feet, eating fresh ricotta and mortadella and salami under a glaring blue sky. She had been disconcerted by those salty, fleshy meats so early in the day, yet never able to resist them. She remembered the hotel room, the pink damask wallpaper, the broad bed. Every few days Julian spoke to his wife and daughters, asking them how things were in Vermont, on Lake Dunmore, where Julian and his family spent the summers. So much of their affair had taken place in hotel and motel rooms, little places Julian would seek out along the North Atlantic coast; he preferred them to the apartments Hema shared with other students throughout graduate school at CUNY. It was never possible to see each other at Julian's home in Amherst. Even their first date had taken place at a hotel, Julian inviting her back to The Mark for a drink after her department had treated him, following his lecture, to dinner.

There was no question of Navin coming to Rome. Before getting engaged they had spent just three weekends together, spaced out over as many months, Navin coming each time from Michigan to see Hema. They wandered chastely around Boston, going to museums and movies and concerts and dinners, and then, beginning on the second weekend, he kissed Hema goodnight at the door of her home and slept at a friend's. He admitted to her that he'd had lovers in the past, but he was old-fashioned when it came to a future wife. And it touched her to be treated, at thirty-seven, like a teenaged girl. She had not had a boyfriend until she was in graduate school, and by then she was too old for such measured advances from men.

In Rome, she communicated with Navin by e-mail and spoke to him a few times on the phone, conversations heavy with the weight of things to come but lacking the foundation of any lived history between them. They talked about their honeymoon in Goa, something Navin was planning, deciding together which of the resorts they preferred. She did not miss him but looked forward to Calcutta, to marrying him and returning with him on the plane in time to resume teaching at Wellesley. Navin was what her parents termed a "non-Bengali," that is, someone from any province in India other than West Bengal. His parents were Hindu-Punjabis living in Calcutta, and Navin had come to America for his PhD. Navin was also a professor, of physics, at Michigan State. But MIT had promised him a job in the fall, and so he was moving to Massachusetts to be with Hema.

She refused to think of it as an arranged marriage, but knew in her heart that that was what it was. Though she'd met Navin before her parents, they had found him for her. They had asked Hema if he might phone her, and finally, after years of refusing similar requests, after years of believing that Julian would leave his wife, she'd agreed. Her parents assumed that she was single because she was shy, too devoted to her studies to bother with men. Her mother even asked, on Hema's thirty-fifth birthday, if she preferred women. They'd had no idea, for all those years, that she was involved with anyone, never mind a married man. Even as she looked for the home her parents had helped her to buy in Newton, even as she sat signing the closing papers in the lawyer's office, putting her solitary signature where there was always space for another, she believed that eventually she would have to add Julian's name. It was her inability, ultimately, to approach middle age without a husband, without children, with her parents living now on the other side of the world, and yet to own a home and shovel the driveway when it snowed and pay her mortgage bill when it came — though she had proven to herself, to her parents, to everyone, that she was capable of all of those things — it was her unwillingness to abide that life indefinitely that led her to Navin.

From the beginning it was assumed that as long as she and Navin were attracted to each other, as long as they got along, they would marry. And after years of uncertainty with Julian, Hema found this very certainty, an attitude to love she had scorned in the past, liberating, with the power to seduce her just as Julian once had. It allowed her to find Navin physically appealing, to like his tranquil brown eyes, his long tan face, the black line of mustache that grounded it. After Navin there were no more surprise visits by Julian, no more bells ringing in the middle of the afternoon demolishing the rest of her day. No more waiting for the situation to change. After nearly a decade, a single phone conversation had ended it. "I'm engaged to be married," she told Julian the last time he wanted to arrange a weekend away, and he accused her of deceiving him, called her heartless, and then he did not call again.

Now she was free of both of them, free of her past and free of her future in   10 a place where so many different times stood cheek by jowl like guests at a crowded party. She was alone with her work, alone abroad for the first time in her life, aware that her solitary existence was about to end. In Rome she savored her isolation, immersed without effort in the silent routine of her days. At night, after a bath, she slept soundly in Giovanna's bed, in a room with meager square footage but breathtaking height, enormous shuttered windows that shielded her from the sun but let in every sound: the scooters and cars on Via Arenula, the grates of the shops being raised for business, the perpetual singsong of ambulance sirens that she found strangely soothing. Certain elements of Rome reminded her of Calcutta: the grand weathered buildings, the palm trees, the impossibility of crossing the main streets. Like Calcutta, which she'd visited throughout childhood, Rome was a city she knew on the one hand intimately and on the other hand not at all — a place that fully absorbed her and also kept her at bay. She knew the ancient language of Rome, its rulers and writers, its history from founding to collapse. But she was a tourist in everyday Italy, and apart from Giovanna, who was in Berlin on sabbatical, she did not have a single Roman friend.

In the mornings she made espresso and heated up milk and spread jam on squares of packaged toast, and by eight she was at Giovanna's desk, colonized now with the ferment of Hema's books, her notebooks, her laptop, her Latin grammar and dictionary. In spite of the hundreds of things she might be doing or seeing in the city, until one o'clock each day she maintained this routine. This was her anchor, this had been her anchor for years. She was a professor now, her dissertation on Lucretius a bound, published, quietly praised thing. And yet it was the aspect of her job that required her to sit for hours alone at a desk that still fulfilled her more than anything. Since eighth grade, reading Latin had been an addiction, every line a puzzle to coax into meaning. The knowledge she'd slowly accumulated, the ancient words and declensions and syntax that dwelled in her brain, felt sacred, enabling her to bring a dead world to life.

The Etruscans were her focus now. A few months ago she had attended a lecture in Boston about Etruscan references in Virgil, and this had ushered her headlong into that mysterious civilization prior to Rome, people who had possibly wandered from Asia Minor to central Italy and flourished for four centuries, who had ruled Rome for one hundred years before turning obsolete. Their literature was nonexistent, their language obscure. Their primary legacy was tombs and the things that were put in them: jewels, pottery, weapons to accompany the dead. She was learning about the *haruspices*, augurs who interpreted the will of the gods through the entrails of animals, lightning bolts, dreams of pregnant women, flights of birds. She wanted to put a seminar together when she returned to Wellesley, about Etruscan influence in Roman antiquity, and possibly, based on her research, a proposal for a second book. She had gone to the Vatican to see the Etruscan collection at the Gregorian Museum, and also to the Villa Giulia. She was combing through Cicero and Seneca, Livy and Pliny, reading fragments of the occultist senator Nigidius Figulus, typing notes into her laptop, marking up the many books she read.

And so Hema had not yet called anyone, not contacted any of Giovanna's friends so that they could meet her for a coffee or drive her out to Tivoli or to Ostia, as Giovanna assured her they would. She was content to spend the days alone, working, reading, and then having lunch by the Portico. In the afternoons she wandered in and out of churches, along dark cramped streets that opened into enormous light-filled squares. She walked everywhere, almost never resorting to a bus or the metro. In the evenings she retreated, preparing dinner at home, simple meals she ate while watching Italian television. It felt wrong to be out alone at night, more awkward to sit by herself at dinner than lunch. During her years with Julian, even when she was by herself, men had sensed that her heart was taken, that she would not pause to consider them, as if she were a passing taxi with its off-duty light on. But now, though she was engaged, she was aware of the Roman men who looked at her, sometimes called out. And though she was flattered by their attention, it reminded her that her heart did not belong to Navin in the same way.

Saturday mornings, instead of working, she would go to the Campo de' Fiori, watching the stylish mothers in their high heels and jewels and quilted jackets pushing strollers and buying vegetables by the kilo. These women, with their rich, loose tangles of hair, their sunglasses concealing no wrinkles, were younger than Hema, but she felt inexperienced in their company, innocent of the responsibilities of rearing children and running a household and haggling flirtatiously with vegetable vendors. She had grown used to this feeling over the years with Julian — her position as the other woman, which had felt so sophisticated when their affair began, was actually a holding pen that kept her from growing up. She had denied herself the pleasure of openly sharing life with the person she loved, denied herself even the possibility of thinking about children. But Navin had changed that, too. They were both aware of her age, and as soon as they married, Navin told her, he was eager to begin a family.

One day after lunch, feeling energetic, she walked all the way to Piazza del Popolo, and then over to the Villa Giulia for another visit. In the museum she was moved once again by the ancient cups and spoons, still intact, that had once touched people's lips; the fibulae that had fastened their clothes, the thin wands with which they had applied perfume to their skin. But this time, looking at the giant sarcophagus of the bride and groom enclosed in a box of glass, she found herself in tears. She couldn't help but think of Navin. Like the young smiling couple sitting affectionately on top of a shared casket, there was something dead about the marriage she was about to enter into. And though she knew it had every chance, over the years, of coming to life, on her way home, in the yellow light of evening, she was conscious only of its deadness. She shopped for her dinner in an *alimentari* on Via dei Giubbonari, and now she carried a bag containing lettuce, a box of spaghetti, and mushrooms and cream to turn into a sauce. She walked through the studded doorway of Giovanna's building, past a window like a ticket booth where one of two porters greeted her each day as she left and returned. In the courtyard a stone lion continually poured water from his mouth. And then up the stone steps, unlit, unyielding beneath her tired feet, three generous flights that felt like ten.

In the long hallway of Giovanna's apartment she saw the answering machine blinking. She played back the tape. It was not Navin's voice but a friend of Giovanna's. Normally these friends left messages in Italian that Giovanna retrieved from Berlin. But this message, in English, was for Hema. It was a person named Edo, a name she recognized from Giovanna's list of people to call. For weeks, Edo said in his message, he had been expecting Hema to get in touch. Was everything all right? He sounded kind, and genuinely distressed enough for Hema to return the call. She assured Edo that all was well, and because she had no other excuse, she accepted his invitation to have lunch with him and his wife the following Sunday.

Edo's wife, Paola, was a photo editor at *L'Espresso*, but Kaushik had met her in Netanya, a resort town on the Israeli coast, where they'd both gone to cover the bombing of a hotel banquet hall, the victims about to begin their Passover meal. It was only rarely that he worked in Italy, the odd photo essay about Senegalese immigrants in Brescia, or shots of the nineteen caskets containing the soldiers in Iraq being carried past the Colosseum. For most of the past five years, Rome had simply been a place from which to get to where he needed to go, and if he looked back at his pocket calendars, each with their three hundred and sixty-five sky-blue pages, and counted the days, he could have confirmed that most of them had been spent taking pictures in Gaza and the West Bank.

His life as a photojournalist had begun nearly twenty years ago. He was wandering through Latin America in 1987, living off the money his father gave him after he graduated from college. He'd gone with his friend Douglas, and they began in Tijuana, hoping to end up in Patagonia. They spent a few months in Mexico, working their way south, through Guatemala and then into El Salvador. And it was there that Douglas decided he'd had enough of Central America, enough of being harassed for looking so obviously American, and bought a ticket to Madrid. Like the Mexicans and Guatemalans, the Salvadorans were never sure what to make of Kaushik, not the soldiers who patrolled the streets with guns nearly as big as their bodies, not the children who posed eagerly for pictures when they saw him with his camera. He began to explore the country alone, a country that was smaller, he'd read in his guidebook, than Massachusetts. He took pictures of the volcano that loomed west of the capital, buildings pocked by bullets and cracked in half by the earthquake earlier that year.

He'd never been in a place so obviously at war with itself. He'd understood, in Guatemala, that the guerrillas were active, gathered from other backpackers that there were parts of the country to avoid. An overnight bus he and Douglas took to Tikal was stopped, and they and the rest of the passengers were ordered to step out and show their passports, flashlights aimed at their faces by a group of drunken checkpoint guards. One of the guards asked to see Douglas's wallet, took the cash, and tossed the wallet back in Douglas's face. In Guatemala, that had been the worst of it. But in El Salvador things were more violent, more gruesome, the tourists more scarce. In Santa Ana, Kaushik befriended a Dutch journalist named Espen and began to travel around, absorbing the history of the conflict, the stories Espen told him of the death squads, decapitated bodies strewn on highways, teenagers hanging from trees with fingernails missing and thumbs tied behind their backs. With Espen he watched air force planes dropping bombs at night on FMLN territory, went to visit a refugee camp across the Honduran border. He absorbed the fear of the place and of its people, grew used to the sound of machine-gun fire, accepted as everyone did the fact that he could at any moment, anywhere, crossing a road or asleep at night, be killed. But he'd never felt afraid, back then, for himself.

While sitting with Espen one afternoon, eating lunch in a village outside Morazán, the table began to shake, dark stew spilling from bowls. By then he'd grown used to occasional tremors, the earth's violence yielding a moment's pause. They picked up their spoons, continued eating, but then people began exclaiming, running past them through the small square. He and Espen leapt up, following the crowd, thinking perhaps a building had fallen, but the commotion had nothing to do with the tremors. They turned a corner to see a young man lying on the street. He'd been shot in the head, blood pouring like a slowly widening river away from his skull, but not a speck of blood, or even dirt, Kaushik still remembered, staining his tan shirt and trousers. He was curled on the pavement, eyes closed as if napping, the faintest sound escaping from his throat, a cheap gold watch telling the time on his wrist.

A group of people gathered around the body, calling for a doctor, while a young woman, a wife or a girlfriend in a pink sleeveless blouse, sat on the ground weeping with her fist in her mouth. Kaushik's camera was around his neck as usual, and Espen told him to take a picture. He did not have a long lens with him, had to get in close, expecting at each step for someone in the group to obstruct him, curse at him, shoo him away. But no one paid attention, and so he crept forward and lifted the camera to his face. When he thought back to that afternoon, he remembered that his hands were shaking but that otherwise he felt untouched by the situation, unmoved once he was behind the camera, shooting to the end of the roll. When he was finished, the calls for a doctor had stopped; the man was dead.

Kaushik was the only person to document what had happened. And though he had not saved the man's life he'd felt useful, aware that he had done something to mitigate the crime. Still, he never believed that the pictures would be published until Espen sent them to the right people. A week later, one ran in a Catholic newspaper published out of Amsterdam. He received a small check, and then, when the photo was picked up by a European newsmagazine, a larger one. And so he began taking pictures for a living. At first he simply woke up and followed the news, sticking close to Espen, staying in El Salvador through the elections, the transportation strike, the killing of the six Jesuit priests and their housekeepers. He photographed bodies with faces smashed and throats slit and penises hacked from between their legs, handing the images over to a human rights agency so that relatives could attempt to identify the disappeared. Thanks to a connection of Espen's he was hired as a stringer for AP, and so he remained in Latin America, first in Mexico, then Buenos Aires, working for wire services and English-language papers. When he was thirty he was hired by *The New York Times*, and they sent him to Africa and then to the Middle East. He could no longer remember all the corpses he'd photographed, their faces bloated, their mouths stuffed with dirt, their vacant eyes reflecting passing clouds over their heads.

The demands of the job allowed him permanently to avoid the United States. Occasional trips to New York to meet with an editor, to pick up equipment — this was the extent of his time in America, and there were trips when he'd not bothered to tell his father he was in the country, when he'd avoided the miserable day trip to Massachusetts to see his father's new life, though by now that life had surpassed, in years, the old. His father was in his seventies now, living off a generous pension and devoting most of his time to golf. From sporadic e-mails Kaushik learned that Rupa, the older of the girls, had married an American named Peter and taught art to elementary school students in Colorado. He had received an invitation to the wedding, but thanks to his work, his excuse for so many things, he had not gone. The little one, Piu, was in medical school at Tufts. And yet, also thanks to his work, Kaushik continued to wash up on his father's doorstep, in the form of his photo credit in one of the newsmagazines his father read, announcing that he was alive, indicating where he'd been and what he'd seen.

He kept a place in Trastevere, a tiny apartment off Piazza di San Cosimato with a generous terrace where, between assignments, he recovered. A woman had brought Kaushik to Italy. Until Franca he had preferred Latin America to Europe, and even now the Spanish he had learned all those years ago got in the way of his serviceable Italian. Franca had convinced him to follow her back to Milan. She came from a family of minor nobility, her heart-shaped face and deep-set gray eyes speaking for a refinement she had not been able to hide when he first met her working for a relief agency in Cameroon. For years he had drifted across the globe without making meaningful ties, and suddenly he was sharing an apartment with Franca, driving out to Bergamo on Sundays to eat polenta and roasted rabbit at her nonna's home, aware that her grandmother, who had spent years hand-stitching and embroidering a trousseau of nightgowns and bedjackets for Franca, approved of him. It had ended bitterly; though at the time he could never come up with a reason not to, he could not bring himself to propose. She had not taken hold of him; he could see now that that was the problem. And so he left the tears and fury in Milan and took the train down to Rome. At first he thought he'd stay a week, to see a little bit of the city, then move back to Buenos Aires. But the Second Intifada drew him back to the Middle East, and he stayed on in Europe, never telling Franca that he was living in her country, never once running into her.

He remembered Rome, of course, from the only other time he'd gone there,   25
on the way back from Bombay to Massachusetts with his parents. His mother
was dying, but at the time, apart from her thinness, there had been no signs.
She had just turned forty, Kaushik's age on his next birthday. He remembered
the look of the hotel where they stayed, the marble steps they would ascend to
go to the breakfast room. The strong shaft of light that poured through the
dome of the Pantheon, and the glances of admiration the waiters could not
conceal as his mother perused a menu. He remembered walking along the Ja-
niculum and seeing clusters of swallows like giant thumbprints swiping the
sky. And he had returned like a pilgrim to those places, recalled that the hotel
was close to the Spanish Steps and managed to find it somehow.

Last year his father and Chitra had visited him in Rome, spending four days
on their way to Calcutta. He had obliged, reserving a room for them at the Hotel d'Inghilterra and taking them everywhere. He stood in line with them to see
the Colosseum and walked with them through the Forum. He took pictures of
their stay, handing his father the rolls of film before they left as if it had been
any other job. He ordered Chitra tea with milk in every restaurant, every café,
because she did not like the taste of Italian coffee. But they had left no dent on
the place, and he never thought of their presence on the streets of Rome as he
continued to think, now and again, of his mother's.

It was in the course of those days with his father and Chitra that a faint
gray speck, smaller than the head of a pin, began floating across his left eye. He
first noticed it the afternoon they went to Testaccio, his father wanting to visit
Keats's grave. In the lush grounds of the Protestant Cemetery, Kaushik had
thought that a gnat was circling his head, and he kept swatting at it, putting
out his fingers trying to flick it away. But the speck continued to accompany
him wherever he went, quietly tormenting him, and he realized it was within
him, that it was not possible to remove it or make it stop. An optometrist explained that it was caused by vitreous gel clumping and pulling away from the
wall of his eye, that it was a harmless symptom of getting older. He was told he
would grow used to it, and he had, more or less, not bothered these days unless
he were in a bright room with white walls, or outside without his sunglasses. It
did not affect his driving, or his picture-taking. And yet it felt like an invasion of
the part of his body, the physical sense that was most precious: something that
betrayed him and also refused to abandon him.

On Sunday he set out in his Fiat for Edo and Paola's, in a suburb south of
the city. The thought of leaving the city, the streets he now navigated with ease,
made him melancholy. For he was leaving; in the new year he would be gone.
A position as a photo editor for an international newsmagazine had opened up
in Hong Kong, and he had accepted. Apart from a few visits to Tokyo, he knew
little of East Asia. It would be the first time in his life that a job would mean
waking up and going to the same place each day, the first time he would have
an office, a desk, an assistant to schedule his appointments and take his calls.
The first time he would not wake up unprepared, until he was chasing after it,
for what the day would bring. In that sense he would taste a version of the professional life his father had maintained for decades. He imagined he would hate

it. Paola told him he was making a mistake, warning him that it was death to the photographer, that since becoming an editor she hadn't taken a decent picture. The money would be better, but that wasn't what had attracted Kaushik. It was his need for a different life that was taking him to Asia. The promise, for the next few years at least, that he would be still.

The magazine was paying for his move, but apart from the Fiat, which he'd already arranged to sell to a friend, he owned little. It was nothing like the times he moved with his parents, those two colossal upheavals he had experienced as a boy, first leaving America, then returning seven years later, the furniture and paintings and tea sets his mother thought she could not live without following them slowly, both times, on cargo ships. His mother had set up households again and again in her life. It didn't matter where she was in the world, or whether or not she was dying; she had always given everything to make her homes beautiful, always drawn strength from her things, her walls. But Kaushik never fully trusted the places he'd lived, never turned to them for refuge. From childhood, he realized now, he was always happiest to be outside, away from the private detritus of life. That was the first thing he'd loved about taking pictures — it had gotten him out of the house. His earliest memories, of Cambridge, Massachusetts, where he'd been born, were all outdoors. A chain-link fence matted with forsythia. The herringbone pattern of bricks on a sidewalk. His mother's voice calling his name as he ran across the Common.

He was reminded of his family's moves every time he visited another refugee camp, every time he watched a family combing through rubble for their possessions. In the end, that was life: a few plates, a favorite comb, a pair of slippers, a child's string of beads. He wanted to believe that he was different, that in ten minutes he could be on his way to anywhere in the world. But he knew that it was impossible, wherever he landed, not to form attachments. He would miss the short, tinted wine glasses in his Trastevere cupboards, the shrinking trapezoid of sunlight cast on his bed in the afternoons. And he knew that in his own way, with his camera, he was dependent on the material world, stealing from it, hoarding it, unwilling to let it go. The move to Asia was official now. His landlord, the owner of the *gelateria* on the corner, had found a new tenant. And just yesterday he had booked his ticket, arranging for a layover in Thailand, where he planned to spend the last week of December before continuing on to Hong Kong.

Edo liked to cook, specializing in the cuisine of his native Cremona. Kaushik imagined a gathering like all the others Edo and Paola liked to organize, an international crowd of journalists and photographers and academics, always three or four languages spoken at the table. Today, Paola had mentioned, an American novelist was coming, someone homesick for Thanksgiving and bringing an apple pie. There would also be an Indian woman, Paola said — a scholar, a friend of a friend of Edo's. He pictured someone middle-aged in spectacles and a sari, an archeologist like Edo. He had so little to do with India. He had not gone back since the year his mother died, had never gone there for work. As a photographer, his origins were irrelevant. And yet, in Rome, in all of Europe, he was always regarded as an Indian first.

30

A few blocks from Edo and Paola's he parked the car and got out. The neighborhood was spectacular in its own way: broad avenues lined with cypress, concrete postwar buildings with glass entrances and protruding balconies stacked one on top of the next. He realized he would probably not return here before leaving Italy, wanted to take a picture, but he had left his camera at home. Paola and Edo lived on a high floor, in an airy apartment overlooking a park. Turning onto their street, Kaushik noticed a woman standing on the sidewalk, long hair concealing her face, staring down at a map. *"Signorina, dove deve andare?"* he asked.

The woman looked up, confused, and he realized, in spite of her dark hair and fitted leather coat, that she was not Italian. That in fact she was Indian. That he needn't have used the polite form in addressing her, that her face was one he'd known.

From the moment they arrived together at Paola and Edo's, it was assumed, by the other guests, that they were old friends. One of the guests had even assumed they were lovers, asking how long they had been together, how they had met. "Our parents," Kaushik had said lightly, but Hema thought back, saddened by those two simple words. She was aware that he had not corrected the guest's assumption. Aware, too, of the way he looked at her across the table during lunch, surprised by the allure that had come to her late. He looked the same to her, that was the astonishing thing. The sharp-faced boy who had stepped reluctantly into her parents' home. Only the eyes appeared tired, the skin surrounding them now darker, faintly bruised. He was dressed like an Italian, wearing jeans and a thin black pullover, brown-and-white sneakers with Velcro straps. She still remembered her first impression of him, a quiet teenager in a jacket and tie, refusing her mother's food. She remembered the ridiculous attraction she had felt that night, when she was thirteen years old, and that she had secretly nurtured during the weeks they lived together. It was as if no time had passed.

After lunch he drove her back, inviting her to his place, in a quiet neighborhood where laundry hung between apricot-colored houses and old men sat in folding chairs on the streets. The men watched, silently, as Kaushik unlocked the bolts and Hema waited at his side. It was unquestioned that they would not part yet, unquestioned that though they had not seen or thought of each other in decades, not sought each other out, something precious had been stumbled upon, a newborn connection that could not be left unattended, that demanded every particle of their care. The building was nothing like Giovanna's, the door easily overlooked, an enclosed staircase leading directly into his small world. The apartment was a room and a bathroom and a two-burner stove. He led her to the terrace to see the neighboring rooftops, the Romanesque belltower of the church on the piazza. "You're that way," he said, putting his hands lightly on her shoulders, orienting her. He told her that he'd returned to Rome recently, that a week before he'd been in Ramallah, covering Arafat's funeral. Twenty thousand people had turned up, he said, scaling walls and tearing down barbed wire for a glimpse of the coffin.

35

They remained on the terrace, talking into the evening. She told him about college and graduate school, learning that during her first year at Bryn Mawr he'd been close by, at Swarthmore. She told him about her years in New York, getting her PhD, her job at Wellesley. And while she mentioned nothing about Julian — that long involvement, enough to make her feel, at times, like a divorced woman, was rendered meaningless in the official chronicle of her past — eventually she told him that she was going to marry Navin.

Kaushik leaned toward her across the small metal table where they were sitting. They had long ago digested Edo's pumpkin tortelli and bollito misto with mostarda, their heads clear again after many glasses of wine, but there was no food in Kaushik's refrigerator, only a box of salted biscotti he'd put between them along with two glasses and a bottle of mineral water. He smoked a few cigarettes. She had her hands flat on the table, as if to derive heat from its surface, and he hooked one of his fingers, lightly but possessively, around the gold bangle on her wrist, causing her hand to shift slightly in his direction. "You wore this when you were a kid."

It was a gift from her grandmother, something she'd had since she was ten. It was the only piece of jewelry she never bothered to remove. She had always loved the design, small four-petaled flowers threaded along a vine, and when her wrist grew thick she'd had the bangle cut off and enlarged. "You remember."

"But you don't wear an engagement ring."   40

"I don't have one."

He studied the bangle, turning it slowly around. "What kind of man proposes without a ring?"

She explained, then, that there had not been a proposal, that she hardly knew Navin. She was looking away, at a dried-out plant on the terrace, but she felt his eyes on her, intrigued, unafraid.

"Then why are you marrying him?"

She told him the truth, a truth she had not told anybody. "I thought it   45 might fix things."

He did not question her further. Unlike her friends back in America, who either thought she was doing something outrageously stupid or thrillingly bold, Kaushik neither judged nor commended her, and the formal presentation of the facts, the declaration that she was taken, opened the door. Only his kisses, rough, aggressive kisses that were nothing like Navin's schoolboy behavior at her door, made Hema feel guilty. But the rest of what they did that night felt fresh, new, because she and Navin had never done them before, and there was nothing with which to compare. Navin had never looked at her body unclothed, never explored her with his hands, never told her she was beautiful. Hema remembered that it was Kaushik's mother who had first paid her that compliment, in a fitting room shopping for bras, and she told this to Kaushik. It was the first mention, between them, of his mother, and yet it did not cause them to grow awkward. If anything it bound them closer together, and Hema knew, without having to be told, that she was the first person he'd ever slept with who'd known his mother, who was able to remember her as he did. His bare feet were warm, surprisingly smooth against her soles as they lay afterward side by side. He slept on his back and at one point was startled awake by a nightmare, lunging forward and springing off the edge of the bed before falling asleep again. It was Hema who stayed awake, listening to him breathing, craving his touch again as light came into the sky. In the morning, looking into the small mirror over the sink in Kaushik's bathroom, she saw that the area around her lips, at the sides of her mouth, was covered with small red bumps. And she was pleased by that unbecoming proof, pleased that already he had marked her.

At first Hema tried to stick to her morning routine at Giovanna's desk. But by eleven the phone would ring, and twenty minutes later she would be crossing the Ponte Garibaldi to meet him, or he would pull up to Giovanna's building in his Fiat to take her out for the day. And so she put away her books, lowered the screen of her laptop, knowing she would not touch them again until she returned to Wellesley. At night he took her to out-of-the-way restaurants and bars, to fountains in abandoned squares where they sat like a teenaged couple, kissing. They went outside the city walls, to places she'd never been and that he wanted to see for the last time. It was Kaushik who drove her to Ostia and Tivoli, and to Cerveteri to visit the hilly tombs of the Etruscan necropolis.

Hema told him about the history of those places, who had built them and why. She told him what she was learning about the Etruscans, that it was they who taught the Romans how to build their roads and irrigate their fields. She told him about the Etruscans' love of the natural world, their belief in signs and portents, their obsession with the journey out of life. They did not speak of their own future, of where their days together would lead. Nor did they discuss the past, the months during which he had lived in her home, the friendship between their parents that was already dying, along with his mother, during that time. Their parents had liked one another only for the sake of their origins, for the sake of a time and place to which they'd lost access. Hema had never been drawn to a person for that reason, until now.

Almost always, an international news channel played without sound on the small television in Kaushik's apartment. His work depended wholly on the present, and on things yet to come. It was not the repeated resurrection of texts that had already been composed, of a time and people that had passed, and it made Hema aware of the sheltered quality not only of her life but her mind. One day, after she asked him to, he showed her his Web site. He left her alone to look at it, going out to buy food for their dinner. She sat on his bed, wrapped in a sheet, his laptop humming against her legs.

There were countless images, terrible things she'd read about in the news-   50
paper and never had to think about again. Buses blasted apart by bombs, bodies on stretchers, young boys throwing stones. He had witnessed these things, unseen and uninvolved, yet with an immediacy she had never felt. Because he had become her lover, these images upset her. Kaushik had told her about fellow photographers who were killed on the job, about the time an Israeli police officer bashed his camera in his face. And she was secretly glad, as his mother would have been, that his work would soon be different, that he would

be behind a desk in Hong Kong presiding over meetings. That he would not be constantly in harm's way.

There were also shots of dusty streets and villages, markets and homes and shop windows, arid, barren landscapes, pictures of people. An old man sat peeling an orange under a tree, a flea-bitten dog dozing at his feet. A group of women in head scarves threw back their heads, laughing. A young girl poked her head out from behind a studded metal gate, baring a gap-toothed smile. As she looked at the pictures, she began to appreciate his ability, perhaps his need, to connect to strangers in this way, and the willingness of strangers to connect to him. She began to understand his willingness — and she thought perhaps this was also a need — to disappear at any moment. He lived in a rented room with rented furniture, rented sheets and towels. In the corner his camera bags and tripods were always packed, his passport always in his pocket. Apart from a detailed map of the West Bank there was nothing on his walls. She suspected that even if it were possible to turn back the clock, to never have met Navin and wait to bump into Kaushik in Rome, it would not have made a difference. She guessed that he had casually been with many women, that she should consider herself no different. And she refused to go to that miserable place Julian had dragged her to so many times, to hope for a thing that was unchangeable.

The key turned in the lock, and then Kaushik was with her again. He set down the bags of food on a small square table set with two chairs, the only furniture, apart from the bed, in his apartment. For the first time he seemed hesitant in her presence, not kissing her first thing. He hung his coat on a hook, loosened the thin red wool scarf at his throat.

"They're amazing," she said.

"They don't all pay the bills."

"Does it affect you, seeing these things?"   55

He shrugged, opened the cupboard, took out two glasses for wine. "It doesn't help anyone if I'm affected."

They stayed in that night, eating the bread and cheese he'd bought, the sliced meats and wine. Kaushik spent a while uploading images from his camera onto his Web site, writing captions. She helped him to pack stacks of contact sheets into boxes for the movers, gather up old photo magazines for the trash. He showed her a portfolio of pictures he hoped someday might form a book. For the first time they fell asleep without sex, not for lack of desire but because a familiarity was growing. But then she felt him pressing up against her, felt his breath and his lips on the back of her neck, and she turned to face him, gave him her mouth. He could be aloof in bed as he could be in general, focusing on some part of her body to the point of seeming to forget her. But that distance no longer threatened her. It was only in bed that he uttered her name, the hot word filling her ear. It was a Saturday night, lingering voices in the piazza giving way to silence and at times the distant barking of dogs.

"It does affect me," he said afterward as they lay in the dark, awake.

"What?"

"Taking pictures. Not always, but sometimes. Sometimes in ways I don't   60
like." He lit a cigarette, and then he told her about a day last summer, when he

was driving back from Fregene and passed an accident: two cars had collided at an intersection. A crowd gathered, but the police had not yet arrived. Inside one of the cars, a child was crying. It turned out that the passengers were not badly hurt. Kaushik had pulled over, rushed out, but the first thing he'd done was take a picture. "The first thing," he told Hema. "Before even asking if they were okay."

Three weeks had passed. One evening in December as they were returning to Giovanna's, Navin called. The phone rang and then Navin left a message on the answering machine, calling to say hello as Kaushik pressed Hema against the door and began unbuttoning her jacket, the top of her blouse, uncovering her breasts and causing the keys to drop from her hands onto the terra-cotta floor. From the very beginning she had felt clear-eyed, aware that in a matter of weeks it would end. In another two weeks everything would be wiped clean — they would be in different countries, the keys to both Kaushik's and Giovanna's apartments in the hands of other people. And this knowledge allowed her once more to step out of her jeans as Navin's voice spoke into the room. Even the fact that Kaushik had to wear a condom helped to keep him in his place, reminding her, whenever he paused to rip open the little packet, that in spite of what they were about to do, they would remain separate. Such thinking was a consequence of Julian, she knew. She supposed that all those years of loving a person who was dishonest had taught her a few things.

She told Navin that she was going to travel during her last week in Italy, another lie to prevent him from contacting her again, and this gave Hema and Kaushik the idea to take a trip together. They decided to go north, to Volterra, a town founded by Etruscans, and it was in that austere, forbidding, solitary place that they spent their remaining days together. They went in Kaushik's car, up the coast into Tuscany, then cutting through the misted blue Maremma and the white chalk hills of the Cecina Valley, climbing and descending a thin slip of road. Volterra appeared in the distance, perched on a cliff high above the open countryside like an island surrounded by land. The rough, restrained architecture, the coats of arms and the hard dark walls, were something new for Hema. The medieval buildings were more recent than the Forum, yet Volterra felt more remote, impervious to tourists and time. Rome had hidden them, enabled them, their affair one of thousands, but here she felt singled out, exposed. She also sensed an indifference; they were among a handful of people who seemed not to belong to Volterra, and she felt that the people who lived there were waiting for them, politely but firmly, to pass on.

It was a nearly silent place, apart from the sharp sound of their footsteps, the insistent coupled notes of the bells, the shriek of the wind. At that great height the wind was constant, striking their faces and agitating their hair. It was the week before Christmas, the town discreetly decorated, holly draped over the antipasti tables in restaurants. They went into the workshops where alabaster was cut and polished, the translucent material quarried in Volterra for thousands of years.

It was colder than Rome, a cold that emanated from stone, and instead of her leather jacket Hema now wore a peacoat of Kaushik's, grateful for the weight over her shoulders, remembering that other coat of Kaushik's she'd so hated wearing when she was a girl, back when they were nothing but already something to each other.

They stayed in a hotel that had once been a convent, slept in the former quarters of nuns. The food was plainer, bowls of ribollita, bread without salt, bittersweet hot chocolate in the afternoons. As they ate their meals and rested their feet from walking, they, too, felt fortified, tranquil, much like the town. Kaushik took a few photographs, not many, never of Hema, less of the town itself than the spectacular views it provided, the Carrara Mountains to the north and the Ligurian Sea distantly gleaming, one cloudless afternoon, thirty miles to the west. They looked down at the ruins of a Roman amphitheatre, and over the walls at the Balze, a precipice beneath which the earth had fallen away, once claiming a church, always threatening to take more of the town. Beneath the Porta all'Arco, the Etruscan gateway, three featureless blackened heads gazed down like sentinels upon them, and upon the world they had left behind.

Mainly, because it was so cold, they took refuge in the churches and museums. They saved the Guarnacci Etruscan Museum for last, and there they saw, lined on shelves, hundreds of urns in which the ancient people of Volterra had stored the ashes of their dead. They were called urns but were more like little caskets, made of alabaster or terra-cotta, the lids topped with figures with large heads and disproportionately small bodies, grotesquely but indisputably alive. The women were veiled, held fans or pomegranates in their hands. The sides were covered with carvings showing so many migrations across land and departures in covered wagons to the underworld, so many fantastic beasts and fish-tailed gods of the sea. Hema and Kaushik were the only visitors to the museum that day, alone apart from the heat that hissed from the radiators, the guards sitting patiently in their folding chairs. In the museum there was another sarcophagus of a husband and wife. But they were nothing like the languid, loving pair Hema had seen in Rome. Here they were older, cruder, still bristling after years of marriage, ill at ease.

After the museum they went to lunch, in a restaurant on Piazza dei Priori they had already tried and liked. After eating they would drive back to Rome, and the following day Hema would fly to India. They had checked out of the hotel that morning, their bags already in the car. The padrone seated them at the table in the corner where they had sat before. They ordered bruschetta with black cabbage, soft pappardelle flecked with wild boar. Hema looked at the postcards she'd bought at the museum, lining them up on the table as they drank the first glass of wine. One thing they'd seen there had been unlike anything else: a bronze sculpture of a severely elongated boy's body, a skeleton more than flesh, standing with his arms at his sides. At the center of the restaurant, at a long messy table, a slightly raucous group was gathered, mostly men in their thirties wearing suits.

"An office holiday party," Kaushik explained, after listening for a while to the conversation. "They work in the bank." He continued listening, then said, "They have lived here, in each other's company, all their lives. They will die here."

"I envy them that," Hema said.

"Do you?" 70

"I've never belonged to any place that way."

Kaushik laughed. "You're complaining to the wrong person."

"What if you hate Hong Kong? Where will you go?"

"I don't know."

"Will you come back to Italy?" 75

"No."

"Why not?"

He poured more wine into her glass, then his. He leaned forward slightly, looking at her, then seeming to change his mind about what he wanted to say. "I've reached an end here, that's all."

The meal ended without conversation, with vin santo and a slice of chestnut cake. They stepped outside, into the first twilight, for a last look at the town. It was the hour of the *passeggiata*, the older people promenading arm-in-arm through the streets. The men were with men, women with women, segregated as Hema's and Kaushik's parents once tended to be at parties. There was a uniformity to their appearances, their faces and their clothing, the flat woolen caps on the men's heads, the straight skirts and low-heeled black and navy-blue shoes of the women. With them, alongside them, were children and grandchildren, the generations knit casually and fondly together.

"Come with me," Kaushik said. 80

"Where?"

"To Hong Kong." And then he said, "Don't marry him, Hema."

She stopped walking. They were on a street of steps, lined with cypress trees, working their way down. Those behind her in the collective procession murmured *permesso* and pressed past. She felt the lurch of a head rush. The boy who had not paid attention to her; the man who'd embarked on an affair knowing she could never be his; at the last moment he was asking for more. A piece of her was elated. But she was also struck by his selfishness, by the fact that he was telling her what to do. Unlike Navin, he was not offering to come to her.

"Don't answer now," he said, pulling her toward him, guiding her down a few more steps, his arm around her waist. "Go to India first, straighten things out. I can wait."

She moved away, upset for the first time by his touch. "It's too late, Kaushik." 85

He extended a finger toward her jaw, turned her gently to look at him, into the tired eyes she had begun to love. His face glowed with affection for her, with hope, and she knew then it was not just the wine talking, that he meant what he'd said. "In a few weeks it will be. Not yet."

He sought her hand again, and they continued walking. They entered a small piazza where she was aware everywhere of children, boys and girls of five and seven, eight and ten, swarming around them as if a school had just been dismissed. She had known Kaushik at that age, she had worn his coat, given him her bed, dreamed of him kissing her, these facts of the past haunting her and steadying her at the same time. The Italian children, eager for Christmas's approach, calling out *Buon Natale* as they greeted one another, were embracing in the cold air, their youthful excitement infectious and pure, so much so that Hema's heart leapt with theirs. In ten years, she imagined, these boys and girls would begin to fall in love with one another; in another five, their own children would be at their feet.

On the drive down from Volterra, as the landscape disappeared and they traveled through the night, she told him. She explained her reasons, reasons that had nothing to do with Navin. She told Kaushik she was not able to give up her life, not able to follow him that way. And that she didn't expect it of him. She said she didn't want to try to change him, didn't want to be accused, one day, of pinning him down.

"It doesn't mean we can't continue to see each other," she said, afraid to suggest it, more afraid not to.

"I'm not interested in any sort of arrangement," he said, in the cold tone   90
she had not heard since they were teenagers. It was the only thing he said during the drive, until he pulled up in front of Giovanna's apartment in the middle of the night. Then he said, "You're a coward." She began to cry, unable to control herself, aware that he would never forgive her for refusing him, that even if she were to change her mind he had already retracted his invitation. He had told her not to marry Navin, but he had not asked her to marry him, and Hema knew that it was not a fair trade. As she cried he sat there, unmoved, as he must have been when he took his pictures, as he'd been that morning when she was thirteen and he had uncovered graves in the snow. She realized he had nothing more to say, that he was only waiting for her to get out of the car. They spent the night apart, and she did not expect to see him again. But the next morning he called to make sure she was packed, told her that he'd be there in an hour.

He drove her to Fiumicino and accompanied her to check-in, speaking Italian on her behalf. He walked her over to Security, kissed her lightly on the mouth. And then he was gone, leaving her to wipe her tears, to take off her shoes and empty her pockets of the pretty coins that would soon buy her nothing. She navigated her way to the gate, riding an air train. She sat by a window, with a view of Alitalia jets crisscrossing slowly on the tarmac, watching other passengers, mostly Indians, fill up the seats. She sat alone, flipping through Italian fashion magazines until the flight was called.

It wasn't until she was on the ramp leading to the plane that she realized what she'd left behind. Her bangle, the one she never removed, the one Kaushik had hooked his finger through that first night, drawing her to him. She saw it now in her mind, sitting in the gray plastic tray she'd placed it in before passing through the security gate. She turned around, began walking in the opposite direction, back to the woman who had taken her boarding pass.

"Everyone is being seated now," the woman said in English. "The plane is about to take off."

"I've left something behind," Hema said. "Jewelry."

The woman looked at her, vaguely interested. "What type of jewels?"   95

"A bangle," she said. A hand went to her naked wrist.

"You would like us to check where you have been sitting?"

"No." She remembered the ride on the air train, all the shops along the way. "It's at Security. I went through this morning."

The woman shook her head. The whole time she was doing her job, taking boarding passes from the other people. "There is no way to reach Security now. If you like, we send a message."

She went back down the ramp, onto the plane, and found her seat. She 100 fastened her seat belt, her right arm feeling foreign, missing the sound the bangle would have made coming into contact with the metal buckle. It would be replaced tenfold in the course of her wedding. And yet she felt she had left a piece of her body behind. She had grown up hearing from her mother that losing gold was inauspicious, and as the plane began to climb, in those moments she was still aware of it moving, a dark thought passed through her, that it would crash or be blasted apart in the sky. Then the fear turned numb. Already on the screen at the center of the plane there was a map with a white line emerging away from Rome, creeping toward India. And this simple graphic composed her, making clear the only road available now.

He was in a place where he knew no one. He was staying at a small resort a little north of Khao Lak, in a one-room thatched bungalow on stilts. This was his third day on the beach, and already he felt drugged by the routine: getting out of bed, eating fruit and sticky rolls for breakfast, lying in his swimming trunks on the hot sand. He glanced at back issues of the magazine where he was about to work. But mainly he dozed. He had stopped shaving, an uneven beard beginning to form on his face. The food reminded him a little of his childhood: steaming rice, dense brown and yellow curries, whole red and green chilies floating in sauce. Normally he harbored no nostalgia for the particular elements of his upbringing, adapting to so many cuisines throughout his adult life. But this food caused him to feel strangely sentimental. His eye distracted him, the shifting speck visible whenever he happened to remove his sunglasses and confront the untempered brightness of the day.

The beach faced west, and each evening he ordered a beer and watched the sun set over the water. The water was calm and shallow, but he preferred swimming in the pool. There had been an occasion off the coast of Venezuela, many years ago, when the undertow caused him a genuine struggle, his throat choking on salt water to the point where he feared he would not make it back. A neighboring bather lent a hand, but since then he had not swum in the ocean, no longer trusting it, knowing that his mother, who loved water so much that she would have swum in a pool of algae, would have scoffed. Behind the beach, rubber trees rose thickly on the hills. Somewhere across the water, beyond the Andaman Sea, was the Bay of Bengal, and Calcutta, where Hema was.

On the plane from Italy his anger had dissolved, and now, in Thailand, he was left only with longing for her. He wondered if he should have brought things up earlier, wondered if he had sounded halfhearted. He regretted his surliness when she had refused. She was the only person he'd met in his adult life who had any understanding of his past, the only woman he wanted to re-main connected to. He didn't want to leave it up to chance to find her again, didn't want to share her with another man. That last day in Volterra he had searched for a way to tell her these things. She had not accused him, as Franca had, of his own cowardice, of his inability to form attachments. But Hema's refusal to accuse him made him feel worse, and without her he was lost.

There was a Swedish family in the neighboring bungalow, with a boy and a girl who both sunbathed and swam in their underpants, as if they had forgot-ten to pack their swimsuits. The children were tall for their ages; he was star-tled to learn, overhearing the mother tell one of the women who served drinks at the resort, that they were only five and seven. The mother was attractive, with a lean, freckled face and closely cropped hair, and seemed to wear a new bathing suit every few hours. In the mornings she would sit at their little round table in front of the bungalow, peeling fruit, offering pieces of coconut and pa-paya to the children, wearing a thin robe that was the color of a watermelon's flesh. While the children played and chased each other on the sand she sat in a chair and read, swatting them affectionately with a magazine when they at-tempted to involve her in their games. The woman and her husband made an incongruous couple. The husband was a large man, his skin burnt, straw-blond hair to his shoulders, hair longer than his wife's, a face like a ham. He spent most of the days sleeping in a hammock strung up between two trees, straining the knots that held him. As far as Kaushik could tell, it was just him-self and the Swedish family; the third bungalow at this end of the resort, down a path from the main hotel building, was empty.

He'd thought about moving around a bit, going down to Phuket after 105 Christmas, but for now he wasn't inspired to go anywhere else. He'd taken a few pictures, of the view from his bungalow, longtail boats on the water, the Swedish children playing on the sand. He felt no inclination to go walking through the hillside to photograph the shrines or to take a boat to the Similan Islands. In three days he left the resort only once, walking to a strip of souvenir and dive shops that bored him. He found an Internet center, considered going inside to see if Hema had written. Then he remembered that he had not given her his e-mail address. Instead, he uploaded new pictures onto his Web site: of Volterra, where Hema had been standing pressed up next to him, her hair flap-ping in the wind, strands of it sometimes intruding in front of the lens, and a few pictures of the Andaman Sea.

He spent Christmas on the beach as he had every other day. The restaurant at the resort had put up a small fake tree. He had dinner on the patio as a full moon poured its shimmering light across the water. The Swedish family occu-pied the neighboring table, conversing, laughing, eating their meal. The chil-dren's long limbs were dark from the sun. The family had ordered an array of dishes, were messily picking at a whole curried fish. Kaushik thought of Hema and anger coursed through him, thinking of her about to enter the world of marriage, of children, of taking trips and sleeping for the rest of her life with someone she did not love.

The wife stood up when they were finished, kissed the husband on the fore-head, and took the children away. "Join me for a drink?" the man called out to Kaushik after they'd gone.

They walked indoors into the air-conditioned bar and ordered whiskey. A band was setting up to play. The Swedish man, Henrik, worked as a film editor for a television station in Stockholm. They spoke about the press in Sweden and Italy, about the war in Iraq. "Our jobs, they are similar," Henrik said. "Our names, too."

Kaushik nodded.

It was the fourth Christmas the family had spent at this resort, Henrik said.   110
"The first year, Lars was just a baby."

"Your families don't mind?"

"What?"

"Your going to Thailand for Christmas?"

"My wife's parents complain. But we come anyway. They are in Stock-holm, living across the street. My parents are divorced, both remarried." Henrik shook his big head. "Too many people to see. And you, where is your family?"

"My mother's dead. My father lives in the United States."   115

"But you are Indian, no?"

"Yes."

"You live in India?"

"I don't live anywhere at the moment. I'm about to move to Hong Kong."

"Married?" Henrik asked.   120

He shook his head.

"But you are thinking of someone. My wife says so. Missing her."

He had not thought that he had been obvious, that the family had been paying attention to him. He thought about denying it. "Now and again."

"You will see her soon?"

"No."   125

Henrik shrugged. "Alone is good, too." He drained his whiskey.

Kaushik's mood darkened. As much as he'd wanted Hema to be with him now, he knew it would be easier to begin life in Hong Kong alone. He knew there was nothing for her to do there, that the move would have stripped her of her work, her world. The band started to play, the stale cover music grating. He wanted to be alone, to lie down and think. "I'm going to bed," he said.

"Goodnight," Henrik told him. He ordered another whiskey. "One last for me."

Once more the day was flawless. Kaushik got up, walked over to the restaurant for breakfast. Henrik was sitting at the bar where Kaushik had left him the night before, but he was freshly showered, dressed in swimming trunks and a Hawaiian shirt, drinking coffee, breaking apart his rolls. "You felt your bed shake this morning?"

Kaushik shook his head.   130

"They said in the hotel, a small earthquake," Henrik said. "Over now."

Whatever had happened, Kaushik had slept through it. He thought back to the day in El Salvador when he'd taken his first real picture, and the tremor that had come just before: the stew spilling from its bowls, the young man in impeccably clean tan trousers lying in a pool of blood on the street.

"There is a shallow coral reef not far from here. Like to come? My wife and the kids want to buy things in town."

Kaushik looked out at the water. "I'm not a very good swimmer."

Henrik laughed. "Someone else will be doing the swimming for us." He   135 pointed to a fishing boat resting on the shoreline. "I've arranged for a good price. When we get there, you can relax while I poke around."

After breakfast they walked over to the boat. The owner, a bare-chested teenage Thai boy wearing long red shorts, was clearing it of leaves and with-ered frangipani petals. Two small lime-colored frogs hopped out, leaping onto the sand. Henrik scooped up one in each of his large hands and brought them over to his children, who began chasing the frogs around in circles, their heads bent toward the ground. The Thai boy began to pull the boat into the water, Kaushik following, white foam like soap suds hissing around his ankles. He had brought one of his cameras, wearing it around his neck. Henrik had an extra set of snorkeling gear, in case Kaushik changed his mind.

They got into the boat, the boy taking his place at the front. On the beach Henrik's wife raised a thin arm from where she was sitting, gave a lazy wave. The children looked up briefly as Henrik and Kaushik settled themselves inside. There was plenty of room on board, and when Henrik called out to his wife and said something in Swedish, pointing to the empty seats, Kaushik guessed that it was to ask her and the children to join them. But she replied in the negative, shaking her head and retreating behind one of her magazines.

He experienced a moment's nervousness because Henrik was so large, but the boat absorbed their shared weight. The Thai boy lifted his oar and they began to move. Kaushik felt the swell of the sea beneath the hull, close to his body, not touching him but penetrating him at the same time. The resort re-treated from view, the bungalows beneath the palms and the darting forms of Henrik's children turning to specks, the familiar coastline curving away like a flat smiling beast. The boy spoke a little English, told Henrik about a school of parrotfish he'd seen the day before. The morning sun was already strong, and after a while Henrik took off his shirt. Kaushik looked at Henrik's broad pink back, glistening with sweat. They were skirting an abandoned cove. "It's get-ting hot," Henrik said. He tapped the boy on the shoulder. "I take a dip here to cool off."

The boy nodded, rested his oar. Henrik dived over the edge of the boat and started to swim, his ungainly body turning graceful as it cut through the water with swift, skillful strokes. And alongside Henrik, for a moment, Kaushik saw his mother also swimming, saw her body still vital, a brief blur that passed as effortlessly as the iridescent fish darting from time to time beneath the boat. His torso cast a shadow into the sea. He thought of the thin bronze sculp-ture of the boy he'd seen with Hema in Volterra, in the Etruscan Museum. It was called *L'Ombra della Sera:* the Shadow of Evening. But in Khao Lak it was morning, the sun burning down on Kaushik, his shadow still in proportion to his body.

When he looked up, he saw that the boy had guided them close to shore. 140 Henrik emerged from the water, waded clumsily toward the deserted cove. The white sand was spotless, limestone cliffs looming behind. Kaushik lifted the camera to his face, took a picture, and set the camera down at his feet. He dipped his hands into the water, cooling off his neck and face, not expecting its salty taste. Then he unbuttoned his shirt, felt the sun strike his skin. He wanted to swim to the cove as Henrik had, to show his mother he was not afraid. He took off his sunglasses, leaving them in the boat next to his camera. The speck in his vision rose and fell, erasing its random trail. He held on to the edge of the boat, swinging his legs over the side, lowering himself. The sea was as warm and welcoming as a bath. His feet touched the bottom, and so he let go.

All day I was oblivious. I was out with my mother and two aunts, being fitted for blouses, selecting jewels. We had spent hours on a thin futon, drinking Cokes and eating mutton rolls, as men in a sari shop unfolded the greater part of their inventory. I went along with all of it, chose a red Benarasi to wear. But the whole time I was thinking of you, fearful of the mistake I was making. I was still slightly jet-lagged, hungry for meals we were used to eating together, for the taste of good coffee and wine. On the crowded street, walking back to my parents' flat off Triangular Park, I searched foolishly for your face. "A terrible thing has happened," the gatekeeper told us when we arrived.

On television, in a pink sitting room with stark fluorescent light, I saw images of the Indian and Sri Lankan coastline, glimpses from vacationers' video cameras never intended to capture such a thing. I saw a massive surge of water moving so quickly that the tape seemed to be playing at an unnatural speed. At first it was only the damage in South India and Sri Lanka I was aware of, the fishing villages that had been obliterated, tourists stranded on Vivekananda's Rock. And then I learned that Thailand had also been hit very badly.

I did not know where you were in Thailand, only that you planned to be on a beach. I had not asked you the details, thinking, as I prepared to leave you, that such information would make it worse. The next morning I went to the newsstand and bought the papers, studying every picture, looking for your name in one of the credits, hoping you had been lucky and that you had continued to do your work. I went to an Internet center, drew up your Web site. I saw the last images you had posted. A faint sliver of the shoreline we had seen from Volterra. Three blackened faces, supposed to be Etruscan divinities, that loomed over our heads. And then, scenes of another coast. Two children playing, a gentle turquoise sea.

At the end of that week, Navin arrived to marry me. I was repulsed by the sight of him, not because I had betrayed him but because he still breathed, because he was there for me and had countless more days to live. And yet without his even realizing it, firmly but without force, Navin pulled me away from you, as the final gust of autumn wind pulls the last leaves from the trees. We were married, we were blessed, my hand was placed on top of his, and the ends of our clothing were knotted together. I felt the weight of each ritual, felt the ground once more underfoot. Our honeymoon in Goa was canceled. Navin said it didn't feel right to swim in the polluted waters that surrounded India at that time.

I returned to my existence, the existence I had chosen instead of you. It   145
was another winter in Massachusetts, thirty years after you and your parents had first gone away. In February, Giovanna got in touch to say she had heard the news from Paola. A small obituary ran in *The New York Times*. By then I needed no proof of your absence from the world; I felt it as plainly and implacably as the cells that were gathering and shaping themselves in my body. Those cold, dark days I spent in bed, unable to speak, burning with new life but mourning your death, went unquestioned by Navin, who had already begun to take a quiet pride in my condition. My mother, who called often from India to check on me, had heard, too. "Remember the Chaudhuris, the family that once stayed with us?" she began. It might have been your child but this was not the case. We had been careful, and you had left nothing behind.   *[2008]*

≡ THINKING ABOUT THE TEXT

1. Explain why it seems surprising that a thirty-seven-year-old professor raised in America would agree to an arranged marriage even though "she refused to think of it as an arranged marriage, but knew in her heart that that was what it was" (para. 8)?

2. Besides the title, the story contains a number of references to the sea and land. In fact, in the next-to-last paragraph Hema says, "I felt the weight of each ritual, felt the ground once more underfoot." Comment on the significance of this metaphor for the meaning of the story.

3. If it weren't for the deadly tsunami, do you think Hema and Kaushik had a future together? Explain.

4. Why does Hema marry Navin, considering that when visiting a museum, she observes that "like the young smiling couple sitting affectionately on top of a shared casket, there was something dead about the marriage she was about to enter into" (para. 15)?

5. Hema is a professor of antiquity, visiting an ancient city and exploring Etruscan ruins. Why is all this thematically significant?

JHUMPA LAHIRI

My Two Lives

This essay about growing up as the child of immigrants appeared in the March 6, 2006, issue of Newsweek. *Lahiri discusses how she was drawn to interpreting the "Indian-American" experience for her readers and describes her own experience of being between two cultural worlds.*

I have lived in the United States for almost thirty-seven years and anticipate growing old in this country. Therefore, with the exception of my first two years in London, "Indian-American" has been a constant way to describe me. Less constant is my relationship with the term. When I was growing up in Rhode Island in the 1970s I felt neither Indian nor American. Like many immigrant offspring I felt intense pressure to be two things, loyal to the old world and fluent in the new, approved of on either side of the hyphen. Looking back, I see that this was generally the case. But my perception as a young girl was that I fell short at both ends, shuttling between two dimensions that had nothing to do with one another.

At home I followed the customs of my parents, speaking Bengali and eating rice and dal° with my fingers. These ordinary facts seemed part of a secret, utterly alien way of life, and I took pains to hide them from my American friends. For my parents, home was not our house in Rhode Island but Calcutta, where they were raised. I was aware that the things they lived for — the Nazrul° songs they listened to on the reel-to-reel, the family they missed, the clothes my mother wore that were not available in any store in any mall — were at once as precious and as worthless as an outmoded currency.

I also entered a world my parents had little knowledge or control of: school, books, music, television, things that seeped in and became a fundamental aspect of who I am. I spoke English without an accent, comprehending the language in a way my parents still do not. And yet there was evidence that I was not entirely American. In addition to my distinguishing name and looks, I did not attend Sunday school, did not know how to ice-skate, and disappeared to India for months at a time. Many of these friends proudly called themselves Irish-American or Italian-American. But they were several generations removed from the frequently humiliating process of immigration, so that the ethnic roots they claimed had descended underground whereas mine were still tangled and green. According to my parents I was not American, nor would I ever be no matter how hard I tried. I felt doomed by their pronouncement, misunderstood and gradually defiant. In spite of the first lessons of arithmetic, one plus one did not equal two but zero, my conflicting selves always canceling each other out.

When I first started writing I was not conscious that my subject was the Indian-American experience. What drew me to my craft was the desire to force the two worlds I occupied to mingle on the page as I was not brave enough, or mature enough, to allow in life. My first book was published in 1999, and around then, on the cusp of a new century, the term "Indian-American" has become part of this country's vocabulary. I've heard it so often that these days, if asked about my background, I use the term myself, pleasantly surprised that I do not have to explain further. What a difference from my early life, when there was no such way to describe me, when the most I could do was to clumsily and ineffectually explain.

---

dal: Lentil stew.   **Nazrul:** Kazi Nazrul Islam (1899–1976), Bengali poet, musician, and revolutionary.

As I approach middle age, one plus one equals two, both in my work and in   5
my daily existence. The traditions on either side of the hyphen dwell in me like
siblings, still occasionally sparring, one outshining the other depending on the
day. But like siblings they are intimately familiar with one another, forgiving
and intertwined. When my husband and I were married five years ago in Calcutta we invited friends who had never been to India, and they came full of
enthusiasm for a place I avoided talking about in my childhood, fearful of what
people might say. Around non-Indian friends, I no longer feel compelled to hide
the fact that I speak another language. I speak Bengali to my children, even
though I lack the proficiency to teach them to read or write the language. As a
child I sought perfection and so denied myself the claim to any identity. As an
adult I accept that a bicultural upbringing is a rich but imperfect thing.

While I am American by virtue of the fact that I was raised in this country,
I am Indian thanks to the efforts of two individuals. I feel Indian not because of
the time I've spent in India or because of my genetic composition but rather because of my parents' steadfast presence in my life. They live three hours from my
home; I speak to them daily and see them about once a month. Everything will
change once they die. They will take certain things with them — conversations
in another tongue, and perceptions about the difficulties of being foreign.
Without them, the back-and-forth life my family leads, both literally and figuratively, will at last approach stillness. An anchor will drop, and a line of connection will be severed.

I have always believed that I lack the authority my parents bring to being
Indian. But as long as they live they protect me from feeling like an impostor.
Their passing will mark not only the loss of the people who created me but the
loss of a singular way of life, a singular struggle. The immigrant's journey, no
matter how ultimately rewarding, is founded on departure and deprivation,
but it secures for the subsequent generation a sense of arrival and advantage. I
can see a day coming when my American side, lacking the counterpoint India
has until now maintained, begins to gain ascendancy and weight. It is in fiction
that I will continue to interpret the term "Indian-American," calculating that
shifting equation, whatever answers it may yield.   [2006]

■ THINKING ABOUT THE TEXT

1. Consider the title: "My Two Lives." What two lives is Lahiri referring to?
   Being Indian versus American? Being a child versus an adult?

2. Lahiri draws a distinction between her Indian American experience and
   the experiences of friends who called themselves Irish American or Italian American (para. 3). What caused this distinction? Would Lahiri's
   pronouncement of the Irish American or Italian American experience
   have been different if her friends had been first-generation immigrants?
   Why, or why not?

3. Writers are often told, "Write what you know." How did writing what
   Lahiri knew influence her as she started her career (para. 4)? How does

she expect her writing will change as her knowledge grows and evolves (para. 7)? How do you think your own writing is affected by your own knowledge or point of view? Is that effect a strength or a weakness?

4. How has Lahiri's life changed as she has grown to accept her identity? Have you ever had to come to terms with something in your own life that made you feel uncomfortable? How did you do so? How has your life changed as a result?

5. Lahiri says that her Indian side will diminish with the death of her parents (paras. 6–7). How does that make you feel about her? About yourself? About the notion of identity?

ANITA JAIN

Is Arranged Marriage Really Any Worse than Craigslist?

Anita Jain (b. 1973) was born in New Delhi. Her family moved to America when she was an infant and lived initially in Baltimore and Las Vegas. She spent her childhood in Sacramento, California, and graduated from Harvard University in 1994. She has worked as a journalist in Mexico City, Singapore, London, and New York. In 2008, she published Marrying Anita: A Quest for Love in the New India, *which a reviewer for the* New York Times *found "thoughtful" and "incisive."*

Recently, I was cc'd on an e-mail addressed to my father. It read, "We liked the girl's profile. The boy is in good state job in Mississippi and cannot come to New York. The girl must relocate to Mississippi." The message was signed by Mr. Ramesh Gupta, "the boy's father."

That wasn't as bad as the time I logged on to my computer at home in Fort Greene and got a message that asked, forgoing any preamble, what the date, time, and location of my birth were. Presumably sent to determine how astrologically harmonious a match with a Hindu suitor I'd be, the e-mail was dismayingly abrupt. But I did take heart in the fact that it was addressed only to me.

I've been fielding such messages — or, rather, my father has — more and more these days, having crossed the unmarriageable threshold for an Indian woman, 30, two years ago. My parents, in a very earnest bid to secure my eternal happiness, have been trying to marry me off to, well, just about anyone lately. In my childhood home near Sacramento, my father is up at night on arranged-marriage Web sites. And the result — strange e-mails from boys' fathers and stranger dates with those boys themselves — has become so much a part of my dating life that I've lost sight of how bizarre it once seemed.

Many women, Indian or not, whose parents have had a long, healthy marriage hope we will, too, while fearing that perhaps we've made everything irreparably worse by expecting too much. Our prospective husbands have to be rich and socially conscious, hip but down-to-earth.

For some Indians, the conundrum is exacerbated by the fact that our par-   5
ents had no choice for a partner; the only choice was how hard they'd work to
be happy. My father saw my mother once before they got married. He loves to
shock Americans by recounting how he lost sight of her at a bazaar the day
after their wedding and lamented to himself that he would never find her again,
as he'd forgotten what she looked like. So while we, as modern Indian women,
eschew the idea of marrying without love, the idea that we're being too picky
tends to nag even more than it otherwise would.

Still, for years, I didn't want to get married the way my brother did. He'd
met his wife through a newspaper ad my parents had taken out. He's very happily married, with a baby daughter, but he also never had a girlfriend before his
wedding day. I was more precocious when it came to affairs of the heart, having enjoyed my first kiss with cute Matt from the football squad at 14.

Perhaps it was that same spirit of romantic adventurism that led me,
shortly after college, to go on the first of these "introductions," though I agreed
to my parents' setup mainly with an eye toward turning it into a story for
friends.

At the time, I was working as a journalist in Singapore. Vikram, "in entertainment," took me to the best restaurant in town, an Indonesian place with a
view of the skyscrapers. Before long, though, I gathered that he was of a type:
someone who prided himself on being modern and open-minded but who in
fact had horribly crusty notions passed down from his Indian parents. I was
taken aback when he told me about an Indian girl he'd liked. "I thought maybe
she was the one, but then I found out she had a Muslim boyfriend in college,"
he said. I lodged my protest against him and arranged marriage by getting rag-
ingly intoxicated and blowing smoke rings in his face. Childish? Maybe, but I
didn't want to be marriageable back then. Indeed, I rarely thought of marriage
at the time.

But for Indians, there's no way to escape thinking about marriage, eventu-
ally. It wouldn't be a stretch to say that *shaadi*, the word for marriage in many
Indian languages, is the first word a child understands after *mummy* and *papa*.
To an Indian, marriage is a matter of karmic destiny. There are many happy
unions in the pantheon of Hindu gods—Shiva and Parvati, Krishna and
Radha.

At a recent dinner party, when I was trying to explain how single-minded   10
Indian parents can be, my friend Jaidev jumped to the rescue. "Imagine you are
on a safari in Africa with your parents," he said. "A lion strolls by, and then
perhaps a tiger. Your mother turns to you and says, 'Son, when are you getting
married? You have a girl in mind? What are your intentions?'"

The pressure on me to find a husband started very early. A few days after
my 1st birthday, within months of my family's arrival in the United States, I fell
out the window of a three-story building in Baltimore. My father recalls my
mother's greatest concern, after learning that I hadn't been gravely injured:
"What boy will marry her when he finds out?" she cried, begging my father to
never mention my broken arm—from which I've enjoyed a full recovery—
to prospective suitors out of fear my dowry would be prohibitively higher. (A

middle-class family can easily spend $100,000 these days on a dowry in India.) Much savvier in the ways of his new country, my father laughed it off. "But there is no dowry in America!"

Fulfilling his parental duty, my father placed matrimonial ads for me every couple of years during my twenties in such immigrant newspapers as *India Abroad*. They read something like, "Match for Jain girl, Harvard-educated journalist, 25, fair, slim." I took it as a personal victory that they didn't include the famous Indian misnomer "homely" to mean domestically inclined.

Depending on whether my father was in a magnanimous mood, he would add "caste no bar," which meant suitors didn't have to belong to Jainism, an offshoot of Hinduism with the world's most severe dietary restrictions. Root vegetables like carrots are verboten.

Still rather prejudiced against meat-eaters, my father immediately discards responses from those with a "non-veg" diet. There is, however, a special loophole for meat-eaters who earn more than $200,000. (This is only a little shocking, since my last boyfriend was a Spanish chef who got me addicted to chorizo. Once, I was horrified to discover, he'd put a skinned rabbit in my freezer.)

This desultory casting around to see what was out there has become much more urgent now that I'm in my thirties, and in their quest, my parents have discovered a dizzying array of Web sites: shaddi.com, indiamatrimony.com, etc. Within these sites are sub-sites for Indian regions, like punjabimatrimony.com. You might be surprised at who you'd find on them: the guy in the next cubicle, your freshman-year roommate at NYU, maybe even the cute girl you tried to pick up at a Lower East Side bar last night.   15

Far from being a novel approach to matrimony, these sites are a natural extension of how things have been done in India for decades. Ever since well before the explosion of the country's famously vibrant press in the fifties, Indians were coupling up via matrimonial ads in national papers ("Match sought for Bengali Brahmin, wheatish complexion," etc.).

My father took to the Web sites like a freshly divorced 42-year-old who's just discovered Craigslist. He uploaded my profile on several, indicating that only men living in New York City need apply (nota bene, Mr. Ramesh Gupta). Unfortunately, in the world of shaddi.com, this means most of the men live in New Jersey, while working in IT departments all around New York.

My father also *wrote* my profile. This may be why dates are surprised to discover I enjoy a glass of wine or two with dinner, and another couple afterward, even though the profile says "I never drink." And he writes back to those who appear aboveboard. This is no small task, as anyone who's done any online dating can attest. As my father puts it, wagging his head, "You get a lot of useless types."

Like most Indians of their generation, my parents believe there are only two legitimate professions: doctor and engineer (not medicine and engineering, but doctor and engineer). Yes, they've heard of such newfangled professions as investment banking and law, but, oh, no, they won't be fooled. Across India can be heard the refrain, "It is good match: They found doctor," and my father expects nothing less for his little girl.

The problem is that while he wants doctor or engineer, my heart beats for   20
the diametric opposite. Take the aging but rakish foreign correspondent I was
smitten with last year. Nearing 50, he'd just seen his marriage fall apart, and
he mourned its passing by plastering his body with fresh tattoos and picking
bar fights. I found it terribly sexy that he rode a Harley, perhaps less so that his
apartment was decorated with Wonder Woman paraphernalia. He was on a
downward spiral, but perhaps my parents might appreciate that he'd won a
Pulitzer earlier in his career?

The relationship didn't go anywhere, as my father might have warned me
if I'd told him about such things. I will admit to needing a little romantic assistance. Since moving here a few years ago, I'd hardly describe my dating life
as successful. There was Sadakat, the half-Finnish, half-Pakistani barrister
from London who slept most of the day and worked most of the night writing a
book on criminal justice. Circumscribed within this schedule, our dates would
begin at midnight. Once I fell asleep on the bar during the middle of one.

Then there were the ones who simply never called again. The boy from Minnesota who imported women's leather clothing from Brazil, the Cockney song-
writer, the French dot-com millionaire. Perhaps I didn't want to marry these
men, but I certainly wanted to see them again. I began to feel baffled by Western
norms of dating, what one Indian friend calls "dating for dating's sake."

Last summer, Alex, a handsome consultant I'd met at a party, invited me to
his apartment for dinner. It was our first real date, and I was flattered — and
encouraged — that he was already cooking for me. Soon after I arrived, we
were drinking an Argentine wine I'd brought to go with his vegetarian lasagne,
hewing to my restored dietary restrictions. Then, during dessert, Alex started
talking about his long-distance Japanese girlfriend. I spat out my espresso. Not
done yet, he also sought my advice on how to ask out the cute girl from his
gym. Was it something I did? Perhaps I should have brought an old-world
wine? Dating for dating's sake indeed.

I've had greater luck attracting romantic attention (of a sort) on vacation.
It was during a trip to Argentina that I met Juan Carlos, a black-haired, green-
eyed painter — of buildings, not canvases. Within an hour of meeting me, he
said he would become a vegetarian as soon as we married, that he'd never felt
this way for any woman — "nunca en mi vida" — that I was the mother of his
children. Oddly, by the end of the night, he couldn't remember my name. Nothing fazed Juan Carlos, however. He quickly jotted off a poem explaining his
lapse: "I wrote your name in the sand, but a wave came and washed it away. I
wrote your name in a tree, but the branch fell. I have written your name in my
heart, and time will guard it."

Given such escapades, it may come as no surprise that I've started to look   25
at my father's efforts with a touch less disdain. At least the messages aren't as
mixed, right? Sometimes they're quite clear. One of the first setups I agreed to
took place a year ago. The man — I'll call him Vivek — worked in IT in New
Jersey and had lived there all his life. He took the train into the city to meet me
at a Starbucks. He was wearing pants that ended two inches before his ankles.

We spoke briefly about his work before he asked, "What are you looking for in a husband?" Since this question always leaves me flummoxed — especially when it's asked by somebody in high-waters within the first few minutes of conversation — I mumbled something along the lines of, "I don't know, a connection, I guess. What are you looking for?" Vivek responded, "Just two things. Someone who's vegetarian and doesn't smoke. That shouldn't be so hard to find, don't you think?"

It's a common online-dating complaint that people are nothing like their profiles. I've found they can be nothing but them. And in their tone-deafness, some of these men resemble the parents spurring them on. One Sunday, I was woken by a call at 9 A.M. A woman with a heavy Indian accent asked for Anita. I have a raspy voice at the best of times, but after a night of "social" smoking, my register is on par with Clint Eastwood's. So when I croaked, "This is she," the perplexed lady responded, "She or he?" before asking, "What are your qualifications?" I said I had a B.A. "B.A. only?" she responded. "What are the boy's qualifications?" I flung back in an androgynous voice. She smirked: "He is M.D. in Kentucky *only*." Still bleary-eyed, but with enough presence of mind to use the deferential term for an elder, I grumbled, "Auntie, I will speak to the boy only." Neither she, nor he, called back.

These days, I do have my limits. I'm left cold by e-mails with fresh-off-the-boat Indian English like "Hope email is finding you in pink of health" or "I am looking for life partner for share of joy of life and sorrowful time also." For the most part, though, I go and meet the men my father has screened for me. And it is much the same as I imagine it must be for any active dater.

I recall the Goldman Sachs banker who said, in the middle of dinner, which we were having steps away from Wall Street, "You know, my work will always come before my family."

Another time, I met a very sweet-seeming journalist for lunch in Chinatown. Afterward, I was planning to meet my best friend, who's gay, in a store, and I asked the guy to come in and say hello. My date became far more animated than he'd been before and even helped my friend choose a sweater. After he left, I asked my friend what he thought. He gave me a sidelong glance, and we both burst into laughter.

As with any singles Website geared toward one community, you also get 30 your interlopers. A 44-year-old Jewish doctor managed to make my dad's first cut: He *was* a doctor. Mark said he believed Indians and Jews shared similar values, like family and education. I didn't necessarily have a problem with his search for an Indian wife. (Isn't it when they dislike us for our skin color that we're supposed to get upset?) But when I met him for dinner, he seemed a decade older than he was, which made me feel like I was a decade younger.

My father's screening method is hardly foolproof. Once, he was particularly taken with a suitor who claimed to be a brain surgeon at Johns Hopkins and friends with a famous Bollywood actress, Madhuri Dixit. I was suspicious, but I agreed to speak to the fellow. Within seconds, his shaky command of English and yokel line of questioning — "You are liking dancing? I am too much liking dancing"—told me this man was as much a brain surgeon as I was Madhuri Dixit. I refused to talk to him again, even though my father persisted in thinking I was bullheaded. "Don't you think we would make sure his story checked out before marrying you off?" he said.

Sometimes, though, you get close, really close. A year ago, I was put in touch with a McKinsey consultant in Bombay whom I'll call Sameer. I liked the fact that he was Indian-American but had returned to India to work. We had great conversations on the phone—among other things, he had interesting views on how people our age were becoming more sexually liberated in Indian cities—and I began envisioning myself kept in the finest silk saris. My father kept telling me he wanted it all "wrapped up" by February—it was only Christmas! Sameer had sent a picture, and while he wasn't Shah Rukh Khan, he wasn't bad.

Back for a break in New York, Sameer kindly came to see me in Brooklyn. We went to a French bistro, where he leaned over the table and said, "You know, your father really shouldn't send out those photos of you. They don't do justice to your beauty." Sameer was generous, good-natured, engaging, seemingly besotted with me, on an expat salary—and also on the Atkins diet to lose 50 pounds. *My* Bombay dreams went up in smoke.

In this, I guess I am like every other woman in New York, complaining a man is too ambitious or not ambitious enough, too eager or not eager enough. But they are picky, too. These men, in their bid to fit in on Wall Street or on the golf course, would like a wife who is eminently presentable—to their boss, friends, and family. They would like a woman to be sophisticated enough to have a martini, and not a Diet Coke, at an office party, but, God forbid, not "sophisticated" enough to have three. Sometimes I worry that I'm a bit too sophisticated for most Indian men.

That's not to say I haven't come to appreciate what Indian men have to offer, which is a type of seriousness, a clarity of intent. I've never heard from an Indian man the New York beg-off phrase "I don't think I'm ready for a relationship right now. I have a lot of things going on in my life." 35

Indian men also seem to share my belief that Westerners have made the progression toward marriage unnecessarily agonizing. Neal, a 35-year-old Indian lawyer I know, thinks it's absurd how a couple in America can date for years and still not know if they want to get married. "I think I would only need a couple of months to get to know a girl before I married her," he says.

In more traditional arranged marriages—which are still very much alive and well in India—couples may get only one or two meetings before their wedding day. In America, and in big Indian cities, a couple may get a few months before they are expected to walk down the aisle, or around the fire, as they do seven times, in keeping with Hindu custom. By now I certainly think that would be enough time for me.

Other Indian women I know seem to be coming to the same conclusion. My friend Divya works the overnight shift at the BBC in London and stays out clubbing on her nights off. Imagine my surprise when I discovered she was on keralamatrimony.com, courtesy of her mother, who took the liberty of listing Divya's hobbies as shopping and movies. (I was under the impression her hobbies were more along the lines of trance music and international politics.) Though she's long favored pubgoing blokes, Divya, like me, doesn't discount the possibility that the urologist from Trivandrum or the IT guy could just be the one — an idea patently unthinkable to us in our twenties.

It's become second nature for women like us to straddle the two dating worlds. When I go out on a first date with an Indian man, I find myself saying things I would never utter to an American. Like, "I would expect my husband to fully share domestic chores." Undeniably, there's a lack of mystery to Indian-style dating, because both parties are fully aware of what the endgame should be. But with that also comes a certain relief.

With other forms of dating the options seem limitless. The long kiss in the   40
bar with someone I've never met before could have been just that, an exchange that has a value and meaning of its own that can't be quantified. Ditto for the one-night stand. (Try explaining that one to my parents.) The not-knowing-where-something-is-headed can be wildly exciting. It can also be a tad soul-crushing. Just ask any single woman in New York.

Indians of my mother's generation — in fact, my mother herself — like to say of arranged marriage, "It's not that there isn't love. It's just that it comes after the marriage." I'm still not sure I buy it. But after a decade of Juan Carloses and short-lived affairs with married men and Craigslist flirtations and emotionally bankrupt boyfriends and, oddly, the most painful of all, the guys who just never call, it no longer seems like the most outlandish possibility.

Some of my single friends in New York say they're still not convinced marriage is what they really want. I'm not sure I buy that, either. And no modern woman wants to close the door on any of her options — no matter how traditional — too hastily.

My friend Radhika, an unmarried 37-year-old photographer, used to hate going to her cousins' weddings, where the aunties never asked her about the famines in Africa or the political conflict in Cambodia she'd covered. Instead it was, "Why aren't you married? What are your intentions?" As much as she dreaded this, they've stopped asking, and for Radhika, that's even worse. "It's like they've written me off," she says.

On a recent trip to India, I was made to eat dinner at the children's table — they sent out for Domino's pizza and Pepsis — because as an unmarried woman, I didn't quite fit in with the adults. As much as I resented my exile, I realized that maybe I didn't want to be eating vegetable curry and drinking rum with the grown-ups. Maybe that would have meant they'd given up on me, that they'd stopped viewing me as a not-yet-married girl but as an unmarriage-able woman who'd ruined her youth by being too choosy and strong-headed.

This way, the aunties can still swing by the kids' table as I'm sucking on a   45
Pepsi and chucking a young cousin on the chin, and ask me, "When are you getting married? What are your intentions?" And I can say, "Auntie, do you have a boy in mind?"   *[2005]*

■ **THINKING ABOUT THE TEXT**

1. How do you respond to the idea that a couple should need only two months together before getting married?

2. Jain says that after years of dating failures, an arranged marriage "no longer seems like the most outlandish possibility" (para. 41). Comment on this statement.

3. In your experience, how accurate are the online self-portraits like the type found on Facebook?

MIGUEL HELFT

A Decent Proposal

Miguel Helft (b. 1963) was born in Buenos Aires, Argentina, and grew up there and in Paris, France. He graduated from Stanford University with a B.A. and an M.A. in computer science. He worked at a number of jobs, from mountain guide to software engineer. He currently covers Internet companies like Google and Yahoo for the New York Times. He has been a journalist for more than fifteen years. He lives in Oakland, California, with his wife and two sons.

When it came time to tie the knot, Rajiv Kumar was ready. His wife-to-be, Vandana, was also ready. The two had met earlier that day.

But this was no blind date. For months Rajiv and Vandana had gotten to know each other. They had seen pictures of each other and exchanged personal resumes. They had checked out credentials of one another's family members. They even spoke on the telephone. The first time they spoke, Rajiv had one pressing question. Was Vandana being forced into the marriage against her will? But before he could ask, she asked him precisely that question. "After we talked for one minute, I was completely comfortable with the whole thing," Rajiv says.

The ball had started rolling on two courts some months before. When he was 27, Rajiv, an engineer who had been in the United States for four years, called his parents in India and told them he was ready for marriage. He asked them to find a young woman who was raised in an Indian city, spoke English, was willing to live in the United States, and looked good. His parents dutifully searched the community, asking relatives and friends. They came up with more than 50 candidates whose pictures and resumes were forwarded to Rajiv. Vandana's was the first one he liked. He picked a couple more as a backup in case the attraction was not mutual.

Meanwhile in India, Vandana had finished college, and her parents were searching for a suitable groom for her. She was introduced to a few young men she rejected. She was shown candidates' pictures. She was told about their successful careers and about the distinguished members in their families. Nothing clicked until she saw Rajiv's resume and picture. He was an engineer. Their families were from the same village. They had gone to the same type of school. With similar upbringings, their values were bound to be compatible. The attraction was mutual.

Today, Rajiv and Vandana are a modern couple with two incomes and a pair of 8-year-old twins, Vishal and Tushar. Vandana is events editor at *India Currents*, a San Jose–based magazine, and Rajiv is an engineering manager in a high-technology firm. They are getting ready to celebrate their 11th anniversary of what they both call a very happy marriage. Other than how they met, they say their marriage is no different from any other. Neither was forced into an arranged marriage. Vandana's brothers and sisters had "love" marriages. Rajiv's siblings and cousins did too.

Arranged marriages in India are as old as the Holy Ganges. In the old days parents had complete control over the matchmaking, but contemporary arranged marriages are more like what Rajiv and Vandana experienced. As Rajiv puts it, "My parents were doing the legwork but I was in control." In many cases the individuals are allowed to meet before marriage. These days the institution is more like an introduction service where the children have the final say. And among immigrants the reasons for embracing — or rejecting — arranged marriages are as diverse as the 160,000-strong Indian community in California.

"Arranged marriage is not always dictatorial," says Arvind Kumar, editor of *India Currents*. "It used to be. But now, most often it is not." He says the prevailing trend among Indian immigrants is still the arranged marriage. But among their children who are brought up in the United States more and more are choosing what Arvind calls "self-arranged" marriages.

In Indian culture, marriage is the starting point of a relationship, Arvind says. Ideally, love grows out of it. Arvind tells of a conversation his parents had right after their marriage. His father asked his mother if she loved him. "No," his mother said. "I hardly know you." To which his father replied, "It doesn't matter. I'm going to win your love." Is that better than our concept of love and passion first, marriage later? Is it worse, in the United States when passion is so often seen as going downhill after the honeymoon? Arvind says, the idea is not outlandish if that's what you grew up with.

To many children of Indian immigrants raised in the United States, the idea is outlandish at first. "In theory, I'm amazed. Spending a lifetime with someone you hardly know is astounding," says Anjali Aurora, a 21-year-old senior at the University of California at Berkeley. But she is quick to add she has seen it work. "In practice it works in a lot of cases. Comparing love marriages and arranged marriages, I would never say one is better than the other." And she keeps open the door to her cultural roots. "I don't foresee an arranged marriage for myself. But I wouldn't say 'no' either. If (at the time I want to be married) I found myself lonely, I would ask my parents to introduce me to candidates. I hope that doesn't happen."

The loneliness Anjali alluded to gives a glimpse into why some immigrants choose arranged marriages. Among graduate students who had arrived from India in recent years, many spoke of the difficulties adapting to the American lifestyle. Arvind explains: "How you grow up and how you learn to socialize is very important. If you haven't learned to date, you can't deal with the dating game. It is difficult in that way to be single in America. You don't have the skills to deal with America, and you don't have the support you get in India. Arranged marriages become more of an option."

Her soft voice rising above the haunting melody of an Indian raga, Chitra Banerjee Divakaruni tells the story of Preeti and Deepak. The sounds of the sitar and tabla coming out of a tape recorder seem like a fitting backdrop for the story of the young Indian immigrant couple. As the music rises in intensity, so does the tension that is unraveling their marriage. Preeti and Deepak are torn apart by deep forces that seem alien. The chasm between Preeti's modern American values and Deepak's traditional Indian values seems to grow with every scene.

The story is fiction. In an Oakland bookstore, Chitra is reading from her new short-story anthology, *Arranged Marriage*. But while the stories are imagined, they are based on real struggles of those in the Indian immigrant community. It is about women and men coming to terms with a new identity. While not all the stories are about arranged marriages, the tensions around them seem to be a big part in the acculturation process.

Chitra grew up in India. She moved to the United States when she was 19. While in college in Ohio, she met the man who would become her husband in a marriage of their own making. It took six months to convince her mother to accept the marriage. Through her life and the experiences of those around her, Chitra has gained compassionate understanding of the struggles between the new and old values.

"Arranged marriage is seen as exotic and people fail to see why someone who was brought up in the United States would choose it. It is important for people here to understand where it is coming from, otherwise it is easy to look down on it as an exotic thing," Chitra says. "Arranged marriages come from a different concept of the family. You trust the wisdom of older relatives. Ideally, they make good decisions for you and the rest of your family. Here we are so used to make our own decisions and arranged marriage sounds so strange."

And families are very different in India, Chitra says. "In India, the needs of   15
the individual are taken care of by the family and society at large, so you can let go of your own needs. Here there is no such support and you have to take care of yourself. It makes you pull into yourself and find your own inner strength." In her stories, many of the characters find strength, usually after painful struggles.

The struggles were very real to several women who preferred not to be identified. Some spoke of women they knew in arranged marriages with abusive husbands. One woman told of her family refusing to meet her husband because she had married someone from another part of India, a foreigner, without the blessing of her family. "Women are afraid to rock the boat because it is seen as a disgrace in Indian society," she said.

Chitra knows those problems all too well, and she is working to create a safe place to give a voice to women who are afraid to speak out. She was instrumental in opening Maitri, the first help line for South Asian women in the Bay Area. But the problem, she says, is not arranged marriages themselves but the inequalities between men and women in Indian society. "In Indian culture, the man has greater freedom. Society supports what the man wants. In the old days the man ruled and had things his way. The woman made it work." Now, many women are highly educated and many have entered the workforce. And with economic empowerment comes increased control over their own destiny — and over their marriages, arranged or not.

"There are successful arranged marriages and failed ones. All marriages require a lot of work and a lot of compassion. Arranged marriages are no different," Chitra says.

Back in their San Jose home, Vandana and Rajiv sit on their couch, thumbing through a wedding photo album. "I look back at it and say, 'Oh my God! How could I have done it,'" Vandana says laughing. Rajiv laughs too. "I don't know if I'd do it again," he says. Somehow their doubts don't seem serious.

Rajiv and Vandana speak with one voice on most things that have to do   20
with relationships. They expect their impish boys will want to choose their own mates, and they have no problem with that. But if either of the kids asks them to arrange their marriage, they'll be happy to help.

"Marriage is something you have to work at all the time," Rajiv says. "Once you are married, it doesn't matter how you got together. You have to work to make it work."   [1995]

■ THINKING ABOUT THE TEXT

1. Comment on the quotation from Anjali Aurora: "Spending a lifetime with someone you hardly know is astounding. . . . But I wouldn't say 'no' either" (para. 9).

2. Would you trust in the wisdom of older relatives concerning your love life?

3. Comment on Rajiv Kumar's statement: "Once you are married, it doesn't matter how you got together. You have to work to make it work" (para. 21).

■ WRITING ABOUT ISSUES

1. Hema is in love with three men in the story. Explain the differences among the relationships, and then argue that one of them is closer to your notion of true love.

2. Argue that arranged marriages would or would not work for contemporary Americans.

3. Adopting middle-class values is difficult for many immigrants and for those in various working-class, blue-collar, and minority groups. Argue that there is or is not too much pressure in American society to conform to mainstream values.

■ Mourning a Loved One: Poems in the News

W. H. AUDEN, "Funeral Blues"

THEODORE ROETHKE, "Elegy for Jane"

ANNE SEXTON, "Sylvia's Death"

IN THE NEWS:
ADAM COHEN, "A New Kind of Memorial for the Internet Age"

LISA MILLER, "R.I.P. on Facebook: The Uses and Abuses of Virtual Grief"

SCOTT DUKE HARRIS, "Online Memorials: Internet Adds New Dimension to Grieving Process"

Public and private ways of articulating grief are, of course, historically ancient and diverse. Naturally, tears and cries of lamentation are universal and understandable when expressing grief for the loss of a loved one. But our culture has evolved more stylized and ceremonial ways of mourning. Over the centuries, priests and poets have turned our deepest feelings into words that express personal and communal sorrow. The elegy is perhaps the oldest and most common poetic form used for mourning. From the Middle Ages to the present, poetry written in English has lamented the inevitable loss that is our shared destiny. Some of these poems are among the greatest lyrics ever written. John Milton's "Lycidas," Percy Bysshe Shelley's "Adonaïs," and Walt Whitman's "When Lilacs Last in the Dooryard Bloom'd" are beloved classics that have given private consolation to generations of mourners.

In our own time, technological innovations have allowed millions to participate in the ritual of bereavement. When Diana, Princess of Wales, died in 1997, millions participated by leaving flowers and scrawling messages in cities all over the world. Songs were sung and poems written, but mostly people shared their grief by leaving tributes at impromptu funeral sites. Today those sites would be on the Internet and most probably on Facebook. For several years, people have been leaving comments on Web sites devoted to elegies, but the recent explosion of memorials on Facebook is a significant evolutionary step in the process of public mourning.

On various Web sites for W. H. Auden's "Funeral Blues," people have posted their tributes to friends and relatives, noting that they read the poem at a beloved one's funeral. Ironically, Auden's poem is technically not an elegy because the poem was written not for the deceased but for a lover who left him. But for generations, people have found in the poem a perfect form for their sadness and despair, and so it has become, along with Elton John's song "Candle in the Wind," the most embraced elegy of our time. And ever since it was read in the popular film *Four Weddings and a Funeral*, "Funeral Blues" has taken on iconic status.

We present Auden's poem along with Theodore Roethke's classic lament for one of his students and Anne Sexton's elegy for her friend and fellow poet Sylvia Plath. Today the suicide of such a beloved and famous poet as Plath would elicit thousands of comments online, especially with the phenomenal growth of Facebook memorials. While this new idea is constantly evolving, it seems a contemporary development that will last. The news stories that we present following the traditional elegies alert us to some of the emotional difficulties present in these online memorials.

≣ **BEFORE YOU READ**

How might communicating grief help people cope? Is there a difference between writing a poem, which could be private or public, and joining a community of mourners in a support group or on Facebook? In what other ways do people grieve? How do you prefer to mourn?

W. H. AUDEN
Funeral Blues

Wystan Hugh Auden (1907–1973) was born in England and is widely regarded as the finest English poet of the twentieth century. Yet he moved to the United States in 1939, became an American citizen, and spent his remaining years living alternately in this country and in Austria. Auden's reputation as a poet soared in the 1930s, especially with the publication of his second book, Poems *(1930). In this period of his career, he was much influenced by psychoanalysis and Marxism. During the late 1930s, his leftist sympathies led him to join what was ultimately a losing cause, the fight against Fascist rebels in Spain. The following poem has several titles and versions, including "Stop All the Clocks" and a text with five stanzas. Auden intended this poem to be sung by the soprano Hedli Anderson, but the lyric has taken on a life of its own and has evolved into perhaps the most frequently read elegy at funerals in English-speaking countries. From the innumerable postings online, it is clear that it beautifully and lucidly describes our deep sense of loss at the death of a loved one.*

Stop all the clocks, cut off the telephone.
Prevent the dog from barking with a juicy bone,
Silence the pianos and with muffled drum
Bring out the coffin, let the mourners come.

Let aeroplanes circle moaning overhead   5
Scribbling in the sky the message He is Dead,
Put crêpe bows round the white necks of the public doves,
Let the traffic policemen wear black cotton gloves.

(© Hulton Archive/Getty
Images.)

He was my North, my South, my East and West,
My working week and my Sunday rest   10
My noon, my midnight, my talk, my song;
I thought that love would last forever, I was wrong.

The stars are not wanted now; put out every one,
Pack up the moon and dismantle the sun.
Pour away the ocean and sweep up the wood;   15
For nothing now can ever come to any good.   *[1940]*

≡ THINKING ABOUT THE TEXT

1. What is it about this poem that makes it so universally popular?
2. What images in the poem seem most poignant to you?
3. Auden employs hyperbole throughout the poem. Is this an effective device since we are not meant to take his thoughts literally?
4. Are thoughts like those presented here normal for the grieving process?
5. Given the despair of the last line, why do you think so many people read this poem at funerals?

(Photo by James
Sneddon. University of
Washington Libraries,
Special Collections,
Neg.#UW2014z.)

THEODORE ROETHKE

Elegy for Jane

Theodore Roethke (1908–1963) was born in Saginaw, Michigan. The early deaths of Roethke's uncle and father had a profound effect on his career. Not untypically for poets of his generation, he was a heavy drinker and suffered from depression. He suffered a heart attack at age fifty-five in the swimming pool of a friend, who converted it into a public Zen rock garden on Bainbridge Island across from Seattle. The following poem and "My Papa's Waltz" (p. 273) are often thought of as his two best poems.

My Student, Thrown by a Horse

I remember the neckcurls, limp and damp as tendrils;
And her quick look, a sidelong pickerel smile;
And how, once startled into talk, the light syllables leaped for her,
And she balanced in the delight of her thought,
A wren, happy, tail into the wind,   5
Her song trembling the twigs and small branches.
The shade sang with her;
The leaves, their whispers turned to kissing;
And the mold sang in the bleached valleys under the rose.

Oh, when she was sad, she cast herself down into such a pure depth,   10
Even a father could not find her:
Scraping her cheek against straw;
Stirring the clearest water.

My sparrow, you are not here,
Waiting like a fern, making a spiny shadow.   15
The sides of wet stones cannot console me,
Nor the moss, wound with the last light.

If only I could nudge you from this sleep,
My maimed darling, my skittery pigeon.
Over this damp grave I speak the words of my love: 20
I, with no rights in this matter,
Neither father nor lover.   *[1950]*

▤ THINKING ABOUT THE TEXT

1. What does Roethke remember most about his student? Do these details surprise you?
2. Does the statement "I speak the words of my love" (line 20) surprise you? What do you think he means?
3. Do you think teachers have a complicated emotional connection to their students?
4. Most images in the poem are taken from nature. Is this an effective strategy?
5. Do you think Roethke felt the last line was necessary to prevent readers from misunderstanding his feelings?

▤ MAKING COMPARISONS

1. Compare the images used in Auden's and Roethke's poems.
2. Does the narrator in Auden's poem seem more pained than the speaker in Roethke's poem?
3. Compare the tone in both poems. Which seems more authentic?

ANNE SEXTON
Sylvia's Death

Anne Sexton (1928–1974) had a difficult childhood, growing up in an alcoholic, unstable family. Her biographers now suspect she was sexually abused by her parents. Ironically, that charge has recently been leveled against her by her own daughters. Several breakdowns caused her to be in therapy on and off her whole life, although long bouts of depression, several suicide attempts, and numerous infidelities suggest this therapy was not very successful.

She, along with Robert Lowell and Sylvia Plath, is often referred to as a confessional poet. But that is only partly true since she wrote often of sexist cultural practices and, in her last years, of her religious interests. Plath's suicide upset Sexton so

(© Ian Cook/Time Life
Pictures/Getty Images.)

*much that she also wanted to take her own life. The following poem is filled with pain
and anger. And Sexton, five years later, joined Plath in the death she "wanted so badly
and for so long."*

For Sylvia Plath

O Sylvia, Sylvia,
with a dead box of stones and spoons,

with two children, two meteors
wandering loose in the tiny playroom,

with your mouth into the sheet,   5
into the roofbeam, into the dumb prayer,

(Sylvia, Sylvia,
where did you go
after you wrote me
from Devonshire   10
about raising potatoes
and keeping bees?)

what did you stand by,
just how did you lie down into?

Thief! —   15
how did you crawl into,

crawl down alone
into the death I wanted so badly and for so long,

the death we said we both outgrew,
the one we wore on our skinny breasts,   20

the one we talked of so often each time
we downed three extra dry martinis in Boston,

the death that talked of analysts and cures,
the death that talked like brides with plots,

the death we drank to,   25
the motives and then the quiet deed?

(In Boston
the dying
ride in cabs,
yes death again,   30
that ride home
with *our* boy.)

O Sylvia, I remember the sleepy drummer
who beat on our eyes with an old story,

how we wanted to let him come   35
like a sadist or a New York fairy

to do his job,
a necessity, a window in a wall or a crib,

and since that time he waited
under our heart, our cupboard,   40

and I see now that we store him up
year after year, old suicides

and I know at the news of your death,
a terrible taste for it, like salt.

(And me,   45
me too.
And now, Sylvia,
you again
with death again,

that ride home   50
with *our* boy.)

And I say only
with my arms stretched out into that stone place,

what is your death
but an old belonging,   55

a mole that fell out
of one of your poems?

(O friend,
while the moon's bad,
and the king's gone,   60
and the queen's at her wit's end
the bar fly ought to sing!)

O tiny mother,
you too!
O funny duchess!   65
O blonde thing!   *[1964]*

■ THINKING ABOUT THE TEXT

1. Why does Sexton call Plath a "thief" (line 15)?
2. What was the apparent topic of the conversations Plath and Sexton had?
3. Who is *"our* boy" (lines 32 and 51)? Why does Sexton use such a term?
4. What does Sexton mean when she says that Plath's death is "an old belonging, / a mole that fell out / of one of your poems" (lines 55–57)?
5. Does the ending seem typical for an elegy about a friend? How do you interpret the last four lines?

■ MAKING COMPARISONS

1. How does the tone of Sexton's poem differ from the tones of the poems by Auden and Roethke?
2. If you had lost a loved one, which of these poems would you find most comforting? Least comforting? Why?
3. Does Sexton's poem seem more or less personal than Roethke's poem? Explain.

In the News

The following three stories meditate on how grieving has changed with the advent of global technologies, such as Facebook. "A New Kind of Memorial for the Internet Age," written by columnist Adam Cohen for the *New York Times* on July 25, 2009, tells a personal story in which loss and Facebook intersect. When an old friend named Luke, whom Cohen had lost touch with until Luke contacted him through Facebook, died, Cohen learned the news on Facebook. Thus followed a stream of elegies on Luke's page, which had become a memorial to the man. Here, Cohen considers what kind of community an online memorial can create, as well as its benefits and shortcomings.

Lisa Miller, whose "R.I.P. on Facebook" appeared in *Newsweek* on February 17, 2010, studies the effects of "virtual mourning" (para. 4). Miller uses disparate examples: Fan-created Web pages to mourn the death of Alexander McQueen, a British fashion designer whose clients included Sarah Jessica Parker, are discussed along with a teenager who created a page to mourn her deceased friend. Through examples like these, and the historical context of grief, Miller concludes that Web memorials are a natural way to mourn in today's technological age.

Finally, Scott Duke Harris, whose article was published on *MercuryNews .com* on October 10, 2010, profiles how companies create spaces for mourners to create online communities. Harris discusses the issues that Facebook has had to tackle when confronted with the deaths of their users and the new technologies that have been developed to fill the gap between what Facebook could do and what clients want in an Internet memorial.

ADAM COHEN

A New Kind of Memorial for the Internet Age

I got a Facebook friend request a while back from Luke Cole, who had attended law school with me. We were never close, but I liked him. He was smart and funny and he cared about important things. We had lost touch, but once I friended him back I received a steady stream of updates on his life.

After he graduated, he had co-founded a center in San Francisco that helped poor people fight environmental contamination of their communities. He had represented American Indians who were trying to protect their ancestral lands and he had worked with Alaska Inuits who were trying to stop a corporation from polluting their water supply.

Luke had a wife and son, and his Facebook photo — smiling in front of a mountain, his beard flecked with gray — suggested that he had reached his mid-40s happy and full of purpose.

It was fitting, I suppose, that I learned of Luke's death on Facebook. A mutual friend, Hillary Richard, sent an announcement out to her Facebook friends in early June, before his obituary appeared in *The Times*. Luke was killed while traveling in Uganda, when a truck veered across the road and hit his car head-on. His wife was seriously injured.

After Luke died, his Facebook page became an online gathering place   5
for his hundreds of Facebook friends. They exchanged updates on his Wall — including news about his wife's condition — reminiscences, photographs, and a poem by Rilke. There was a report on his cremation ceremony in Uganda. The post said Luke was sent off with Madagascar chocolate, root beer, and a small "environmental justice" note tucked in his pocket.

Luke's Wall remains active today. In mid-July, his friends celebrated his birthday there. "I am sure I am not alone in saying that I am so grateful that

Luke's facebook page has stayed up," Hillary wrote, adding: "I cry every single time I am on here and yet I feel I would be lost without this."

Facebook's policy is to keep members' pages up after a death unless loved ones ask that they be taken down. When the company learns that someone has died, it puts the page into a memorialized status, in which only confirmed friends can see the profile.

Until Luke's death, I had not considered what would happen as my Facebook friends began to die. Facebook allows you to de-friend dead people the same way you de-friend live ones. I suppose you could view deleting dead friends as simply routine updating of the sort people have long done with their hard-copy address books. But it seems callous to look into the eyes of an old friend and hit "remove."

There is something not entirely satisfying about an online memorial. Those of us who visit Luke's page are not physically coming together to remember him — and we are not making the effort and expending the time that it takes to gather in person.

Still, Luke's Wall works, often in ways that an offline memorial cannot. A 10
Facebook Wall is remarkably democratic — instead of a few people speaking, anyone who friended the deceased can offer a memory or a reflection. It is also long-lasting: memorial services end after an hour or two, but a Facebook page remains. It can even be, in an odd way, uniquely spiritual. It is striking how many of the comments written on Luke's Wall are addressed directly to him.

I've decided that I am going to remain Luke's Facebook friend as long as his family keeps his page up. It is a tribute to a good person gone too soon and a reminder that, as the poet said, his death diminishes me.   *[2009]*

LISA MILLER
R.I.P. on Facebook: The Uses and Abuses of Virtual Grief

Minutes after news broke that the British fashion designer Alexander McQueen was dead, a suicide at age 40, the prayers and condolences started pouring in. More than 80,000 people became "fans" of McQueen on Facebook in the first week. In the first day, messages (to the man or his memory — it's hard to know which) were being posted every second. Brief and wrenching, the messages are tiny mosaic tiles of grief: "RIP." "Genius." "It's been 5 days, I actually miss you as tho I knew you . . . sleep well."

This is how we collectively mourn: Globally. Together. Online.

The McQueen phenomenon recalls the piles of plastic-wrapped flowers laid at the stoop of John F. Kennedy Jr.'s apartment after his death, but Facebook hosts the shrines of less celebrated souls as well. One teenager started a tribute page for her murdered best friend: members are invited to write the dead girl's favorite song lyric — "Keep Breathing" — on their wrist, take a picture, and post it. In October, Facebook changed its policy regarding the pages of members who have passed away. Responding in part to urging by people at Virginia Tech who wanted after the 2007 shooting there to continue to commune with their lost friends on Facebook, the company now allows a person's page to remain active in perpetuity. (Family members may request that a loved one's page be taken down.) "When someone leaves us, they don't leave our memories or our social network," the new policy says.

One might imagine such virtual mourning is shallow, but it's not. Here is a real gathering place, where friends can grieve together — and where the deceased continues, in some sense, to exist. "You're creating something like a tombstone, but people can visit that tombstone anytime, anyplace, as long as they have Internet access," says Brian McLaren, a leader in the emerging church movement and author of *A New Kind of Christianity.* "That seems to me to be a great gain."

We live in a disjointed time. Many of us reside far from our families and   5
have grown indifferent to the habits of organized religion. More of us — 16 percent — declare ourselves "unaffiliated" with any religious denomination. Half of Americans will choose cremation over burial, and if we are buried, it will often be in a huge cemetery, among strangers, far from any place we would call home.

Yet the desire to connect with each other around death and with the dead themselves is older than the Bible. The ancient Hebrews buried their family members beneath the floors of their houses, the better to keep and care for them. The Christian ideal of "the community of saints," in which the dead rest peacefully in the churchyard, as much a part of the congregation as those singing in the nave, is something any nineteenth-century churchgoer would have instinctively understood. In the absence of that literal proximity, Facebook "keeps the person in the communal space — the way a churchyard would," says Noreen Herzfeld, professor of science and religion at St. John's University in Collegeville, Minnesota.

All of which raises tantalizing questions: the average Facebook user has aged to 33 years old. In two generations, will the pages of the dead outnumber the living? Will our unchurched children be content to memorialize us with a quip on a "wall"? Something is gained, but what is lost in this evolution from corporeal grief (the rending of garments) to grief tagged with a virtual rose?

Grief is a crucible, a physical event — and death, the loss of a physical body. Thomas Lynch, the poet, undertaker, and, as author of *The Undertaking*, chronicler of American views of death, mused in a phone call that folks today don't like to think about permanence: they are more concerned with "whether the pipes or the doves or the balloon release will go off as scheduled." Facebook memorials are fine, even good, he agrees. But then he invokes the Wallace Stevens poem "Not Ideas About the Thing but the Thing Itself," in which a man, upon waking, hears the first bird of spring — something more than a long-held hope. In "Catch and Release," the first story in his new collection, *Apparition and Late Fictions*, Lynch writes about a fishing guide's efforts to dispose of the ashes of his dead father in the rivers of northern Michigan. The story is dense with physicality — the heaviness of water, the fatness of fish, the crystalline dryness of cremated bones. It is hard to imagine Facebook muting the anguish of this mortal loss. Facebook is the idea about the thing. Celebration, desolation — that's the thing itself.   *[2010]*

SCOTT DUKE HARRIS

Online Memorials: Internet Adds New Dimension to Grieving Process

Type the word "stages" into your favorite search engine and it will quickly suggest "stages of grief" as your likely query. That's the five-step emotional process that psychiatrist Elisabeth Kübler-Ross described in her 1969 book *On Death and Dying*: denial, anger, bargaining, depression, and acceptance.

Today the Internet has added a new and sometimes unsettling dimension to those stages. Many funeral homes, for example, offer live-streaming video of memorial services to enable virtual attendance. And a new San Francisco startup called 1000 Memories, inspired in part by Facebook's difficulties with death, recently introduced a free online service that competes with the memorial sites from online obituary companies Legacy.com and Tribute.com.

Digital technology, many point out, holds the promise of providing future generations with much richer knowledge and understanding of us than we have of our forebears, which in some cases is nothing much more than words on a tombstone. But for now, much of the attention is focused on the problematic way that Facebook, as if stuck in the denial stage, conjures a kind of Twilight Zone of the digitally undead. The Palo Alto–based company also has angered users by deleting decedents' posted messages that many mourners consider precious touchstones.

Mary Alford of Florida and Val Rader of Colorado are two of many people who have lost loved ones who were active on Facebook. Both Alford's son Peter and Rader's brother Ed had used the site as a vital social outlet during their ordeals with cancer, sharing variously wry and meaningful comments with friends.

After their deaths, the families contacted Facebook to "memorialize" their   5
pages. The process would allow only friends already recognized by their Facebook pages to continue to visit and share memories and condolences.

In both instances, families and friends were stunned when Facebook removed all of Peter's and Ed's original posts without explanation. "It's nice to read what other people say about Peter, but I'd like to read what he said," explained his mother, Mary Alfrod. "It's like going back and reading his journal."

"The struggle and story of Ed's fight was all chronicled on Facebook," Val Rader said. "And it was a wonderful story to be a part of. Facebook erased that in one stroke."

In Alford's case, Facebook's algorithms didn't seem to comprehend her son's death. For a few months after Peter's page was memorialized, his friends would receive reminders from Facebook suggesting they get in touch with

Peter. If Peter's family hadn't contacted Facebook, the digital persona would, in a sense, have lived on.

With Facebook claiming more than 500 million users worldwide, it's fair to wonder how many may be apparitions. "Can you imagine what Facebook will be like in 10 years if they don't address the millions of users that will pass away?" asked Rudy Adler, co-founder of 1000 Memories.

Facebook, which developed its policy after the untimely death of an early   10
employee, says it is reviewing its approach in light of complaints. But for now, Facebook's default is denial: Unless the company is presented evidence that a user has died, such as a death certificate or newspaper obituary, the digitized persona will reside indefinitely in its system. The request for proof is understandable to minimize pranks and harassment; but despite its verification policy, Facebook reportedly once mistakenly memorialized the page of a user who was, in fact, alive.

Adler and his co-founders at 1000 Memories say their solution is a business model that aims to create a permanent online memorial that may include photos, video, audio, and testimonials. "We're ultimately interested in answering this question: How will the Internet be used to remember a person and pass the story of their life to future generations?" Adler explained.

In the near-term, 1000 Memories has an uphill challenge against incumbent online services such as Illinois-based Legacy.com, which in 1998 began partnering with more than 800 newspapers (including the *Mercury News*), and Boston-based Tributes.com, which since 2007 has partnered with funeral homes and provides obituaries for local TV station websites.

Adler, 28, had worked in advertising before teaming up with Brett Huneycutt, a childhood friend, and Jonathan Good to launch 1000 Memories with seed funding from Y Combinator, a startup incubator.

Huneycutt and Good, who became friends as Rhodes scholars at Oxford, later worked as business consultants. Determined to strike out as entrepreneurs, Adler said, they each recalled their displeasure interacting with online services after the death of a friend or relative.

For Adler, it was Facebook's ham-handed approach to a friend's death. For   15
Huneycutt, it was how Tributes.com handled his grandfather's memorial — and a sales pitch that seemed literally geared to the "bargaining" stage of grief.

It began with an e-mail: "Your free-trial Eternal Tribute . . . has expired and the photos, music, video, and templates have been disabled." But the "Eternal Tribute" could be reactivated: "If you purchase within the next 30 days, we'll offer you a 20% discount; a $30 value when you use the promotional code KEEPTHEMEMORY upon checkout." The pitch continued, suggesting that the Eternal Tribute "is a forever place for family and friends to share, enjoy, and honor their memory. Don't let it fade away."

Tributes.com president Elaine Haney says that its service — with prices ranging from $50 to $299 — is much more affordable and longer lasting than the conventional newspaper obituaries often augmented by Legacy.com's online guest book. (The *Mercury News'* basic rate is $9 per line and $108 for a photo.)

Like many Internet startups, 1000 Memories has embraced the so-called "freemium" business model, offering a basic service at no cost and charging a premium for extras, such as uploading video, which increases storage expenses. The startup also anticipates partnerships that would enable it to take a share of profits for items such as flowers ordered from the site or for the creation of physical memory books.

Meanwhile, Facebook says it is evaluating the way it deals with the inevitable fates of its users. When the company explained its policy in a blog posting — suggesting that decedents' posts are removed to protect their privacy — several baffled users reacted in tones that fell far short of acceptance.

"I want back the posts my friend made on my wall," one user said. "I hate   20
you guys, Facebook."   *[2010]*

▉ THINKING ABOUT THE TEXTS

1. To what extent are Facebook memorials a positive innovation, in your view? Explain your reasoning.

2. What rules or protocols do you think should be instituted regarding Facebook memorials?

3. Under what circumstances have you posted, or would you post, a memorial on Facebook? What, if anything, would make you reluctant to post one?

▉ WRITING ABOUT ISSUES

1. Choose one of the elegies in this cluster, and write an essay in which you analyze the extent to which it is about the speaker. Is this poem mostly about the speaker? Mostly about the person being mourned? Equally about both? Refer to specific lines in the poem.

2. Choose one of the elegies in this cluster. Then, write an essay that speculates about what one of the people mentioned in this cluster's news articles would think of how the poem's speaker mourns. Support your hypothesis with specific passages from both the poem and the news article that you have chosen.

3. Write an essay in which you analyze a memorial display that you or someone you know helped produce or maintain. This might be a memorial on the Web or a more physical one. Besides describing the memorial and your role in it, state and develop a claim about what it achieved. If you wish, refer to any of the texts in this cluster.

4. Write an essay analyzing the design of an online memorial that you have discovered through research. Choose a site that you have mixed feelings about, and use your essay to explain what specifically about the memorial leaves you with such divided emotions. If you wish, refer to any of the texts in this cluster.

▪ Places of the Heart: Essays

N. SCOTT MOMADAY, "The Way to Rainy Mountain"

BARRY LOPEZ, "Emancipation"

KEN BURNS, "Our Best Selves"

The meaning of the environment has been a lively topic for discussion in intellectual circles for decades. As the natural world becomes domesticated at an alarming rate every year, philosophers worry that we will lose a crucial connection to our own identity, to our place in history and an understanding of our planet. Some people want the land to provide, as Barry Lopez suggests, "something marketable." If it doesn't provide for us, then what good is it? But there is a backlash to this extremely utilitarian view that the land must serve us or else. Lopez claims that environmentalism has emerged "as a movement for the emancipation of land." Out of their love for wild lands, the three writers presented here understand the importance of these natural places. In an interview, the environmentalist Terry Tempest Williams echoes the thinking of our three writers when she says: "Our national parks are not only our best idea, but our highest ideal of what it means to live with an enduring grace that will survive us. . . . We remember the sacredness of life. We remember that this is the open space of democracy. And it is, as John Muir has reminded us, the beginning of creation. This is what we loved, and now they are in your hands. We entrust these sacred lands to you."

▪ BEFORE YOU READ

Do you have a special wild place that stays in your memory? What is it about that place that makes it memorable? Is there a place in your region you would like to see made into a national park? Why?

N. SCOTT MOMADAY
The Way to Rainy Mountain

Born in 1934 into a Native American family living next to Rainy Mountain in Oklahoma, N. Scott Momaday grew up on a family farm and later on several reservations. Momaday graduated from the University of New Mexico and earned his Ph.D. at Stanford University. He has taught writing at the University of California at Berkeley and at Stanford and currently teaches at the University of Arizona. Momaday is a poet and novelist as well as an accomplished essayist and painter. He won the Pulitzer Prize in 1969 for House Made of Dawn. *Momaday's work celebrates his Native American heritage, about which he writes with reverence and artistic subtlety. His more recent books include* The Man Made of Words *(1998) and* In the Bear's

House *(1999). The following essay appeared as the introduction to* The Way to Rainy Mountain *(1969), a collection of Kiowa legends.*

A single knoll rises out of the plain in Oklahoma, north and west of the Wichita range. For my people, the Kiowas, it is an old landmark, and they gave it the name Rainy Mountain. The hardest weather in the world is there. Winter brings blizzards, hot tornadic winds arise in the spring, and in summer the prairie is an anvil's edge. The grass turns brittle and brown, and it cracks beneath your feet. There are green belts along the rivers and creeks, linear groves of hickory and pecan, willow and witch hazel. At a distance in July or August the steaming foliage seems almost to writhe in fire. Great green and yellow grasshoppers are everywhere in the tall grass, popping up like corn to sting the flesh, and tortoises crawl about on the red earth, going nowhere in the plenty of time. Loneliness is an aspect of the land. All things in the plain are isolate; there is no confusion of objects in the eye, but *one* hill or *one* tree or *one* man. To look upon that landscape in the early morning, with the sun at your back, is to lose the sense of proportion. Your imagination comes to life, and this, you think, is where Creation was begun.

I returned to Rainy Mountain in July. My grandmother had died in the spring, and I wanted to be at her grave. She had lived to be very old and at last infirm. Her only living daughter was with her when she died, and I was told that in death her face was that of a child.

I like to think of her as a child. When she was born, the Kiowas were living the last great moment of their history. For more than a hundred years they had controlled the open range from the Smoky Hill River to the Red, from the headwaters of the Canadian to the fork of the Arkansas and Cimarron. In alliance with the Comanches, they had ruled the whole of the Southern Plains. War was their sacred business, and they were the finest horsemen the world has ever known. But warfare for the Kiowas was pre-eminently a matter of disposition rather than of survival, and they never understood the grim, unrelenting advance of the U.S. Cavalry. When at last, divided and ill provisioned, they were driven onto the Staked Plains in the cold of autumn, they fell into panic. In Palo Duro Canyon they abandoned their crucial stores to pillage and had nothing then but their lives. In order to save themselves, they surrendered to the soldiers at Fort Sill and were imprisoned in the old stone corral that now stands as a military museum. My grandmother was spared the humiliation of those high gray walls by eight or ten years, but she must have known from birth the affliction of defeat, the dark brooding of old warriors.

Her name was Aho, and she belonged to the last culture to evolve in North America. Her forebears came down from the high country in western Montana nearly three centuries ago. They were a mountain people, a mysterious tribe of hunters whose language has never been classified in any major group. In the late seventeenth century they began a long migration to the south and east. It was a journey toward the dawn, and it led to a golden age. Along the way the Kiowas were befriended by the Crows, who gave them the culture and religion of the Plains. They acquired horses, and their ancient nomadic spirit was suddenly free of the ground. They acquired Tai-me, the sacred sun-dance doll, from that moment the object and symbol of their worship, and so shared in the divinity of the sun. Not least, they acquired the sense of destiny, therefore courage and pride. When they entered upon the Southern Plains they had been transformed. No longer were they slaves to the simple necessity of survival; they were a lordly and dangerous society of fighters and thieves, hunters and priests of the sun. According to their origin myth, they entered the world through a hollow log. From one point of view, their migration was the fruit of an old prophecy, for indeed they emerged from a sunless world.

Though my grandmother lived out her long life in the shadow of Rainy Mountain, the immense landscape of the continental interior lay like memory in her blood. She could tell of the Crows, whom she had never seen, and of the Black Hills, where she had never been. I wanted to see in reality what she had seen more perfectly in the mind's eye, and drove fifteen hundred miles to begin my pilgrimage.   5

A dark mist lay over the Black Hills, and the land was like iron. At the top of a ridge I caught sight of Devil's Tower upthrust against the gray sky as if in the birth of time the core of the earth had broken through its crust and the motion of the world was begun. There are things in nature that engender an awful quiet in the heart of man; Devil's Tower is one of them. Two centuries ago, because of their need to explain it, the Kiowas made a legend at the base of the rock. My grandmother said:

"Eight children were there at play, seven sisters and their brother. Suddenly the boy was struck dumb; he trembled and began to run upon his hands and feet. His fingers became claws, and his body was covered with fur. There was a bear where the boy had been. The sisters were terrified; they ran, and the bear after them. They came to the stump of a great tree, and the tree spoke to them. It bade them climb upon it, and as they did so, it began to rise into the air. The bear came to kill them, but they were just beyond its reach. It reared against the tree and scored the bark all around with its claws. The seven sisters were borne into the sky, and they became the stars of the Big Dipper." From that moment, and so long as the legend lives, the Kiowas have kinsmen in the night sky. Whatever they were in the mountains, they could be no more. However tenuous their well-being, however much they had suffered and would suffer again, they had found a way out of the wilderness.

My grandmother had a reverence for the sun, a holy regard that now is all but gone out of mankind. There was a wariness in her, and an ancient awe. She was a Christian in her later years, but she had come a long way about, and she never forgot her birthright. As a child she had been to the sun dances; she had taken part in that annual rite, and by it she had learned the restoration of her people in the presence of Tai-me. She was about seven when the last Kiowa sun dance was held in 1887 on the Washita River above Rainy Mountain Creek.

The buffalo were gone. In order to consummate the ancient sacrifice — to impale the head of a buffalo bull upon the Tai-me tree — a delegation of old men journeyed into Texas, there to beg and barter for an animal from the Goodnight herd. She was ten when the Kiowas came together for the last time as a living sun-dance culture. They could find no buffalo; they had to hang an old hide from the sacred tree. Before the dance could begin, a company of soldiers rode out from Fort Sill under orders to disperse the tribe. Forbidden without cause the essential act of their faith, having seen the wild herds slaughtered and left to rot upon the ground, the Kiowas backed away forever from the tree. That was July 20, 1890, at the great bend of the Washita. My grandmother was there. Without bitterness, and for as long as she lived, she bore a vision of deicide.

Now that I can have her only in memory, I see my grandmother in the several postures that were peculiar to her: standing at the wood stove on a winter morning and turning meat in a great iron skillet; sitting at the south window, bent above her beadwork, and afterwards, when her vision failed, looking down for a long time into the fold of her hands; going out upon a cane, very slowly as she did when the weight of age came upon her; praying. I remember her most often at prayer. She made long, rambling prayers out of suffering and hope, having seen many things. I was never sure that I had the right to hear, so exclusive were they of all mere custom and company. The last time I saw her she prayed standing by the side of the bed at night, naked to the waist, the light of a kerosene lamp moving upon her dark skin. Her long black hair, always drawn and braided in the day, lay upon her shoulders and against her breasts like a shawl. I do not speak Kiowa, and I never understood her prayers, but there was something inherently sad in the sound, some merest hesitation upon the syllables of sorrow. She began in a high and descending pitch, exhausting her breath to silence; then again and again — and always the same intensity of effort, of something that is, and is not, like urgency in the human voice. Transported so in the dancing light among the shadows of her room, she seemed beyond the reach of time. But that was illusion; I think I knew then that I should not see her again.

Houses are like sentinels in the plain, old keepers of the weather watch.   10
There, in a very little while, wood takes on the appearance of great age. All colors wear soon away in the wind and rain, and then the wood is burned gray and the grain appears and the nails turn red with rust. The window panes are black and opaque; you imagine there is nothing within, and indeed there are many ghosts, bones given up to the land. They stand here and there against the sky, and you approach them for a longer time than you expect. They belong in the distance; it is their domain.

Once there was a lot of sound in my grandmother's house, a lot of coming and going, feasting and talk. The summers there were full of excitement and reunion. The Kiowas are a summer people; they abide the cold and keep to themselves, but when the season turns and the land becomes warm and vital they cannot hold still; an old love of going returns upon them. The aged visitors who came to my grandmother's house when I was a child were made of lean and leather, and they bore themselves upright. They wore great black hats and bright ample shirts that shook in the wind. They rubbed fat upon their hair and wound their braids with strips of colored cloth. Some of them painted their faces and carried the scars of old and cherished enmities. They were an old council of warlords, come to remind and be reminded of who they were. Their wives and daughters served them well. The women might indulge themselves; gossip was at once the mark and compensation of their servitude. They made loud and elaborate talk among themselves, full of jest and gesture, fright and false alarm. They went abroad in fringed and flowered shawls, bright beadwork and German silver. They were at home in the kitchen, and they prepared meals that were banquets.

There were frequent prayer meetings, and nocturnal feasts. When I was a child I played with my cousins outside, where the lamplight fell upon the ground and the singing of the old people rose up around us and carried away into the darkness. There were a lot of good things to eat, a lot of laughter and surprise. And afterwards, when the quiet returned, I lay down with my grandmother and could hear the frogs away by the river and feel the motion of the air.

Now there is a funereal silence in the rooms, the endless wake of some final word. The walls have closed in upon my grandmother's house. When I returned to it in mourning, I saw for the first time in my life how small it was. It was late at night, and there was a white moon, nearly full. I sat for a long time on the stone steps by the kitchen door. From there I could see out across the land; I could see the long row of trees by the creek, the low light upon the rolling plains, and the stars of the Big Dipper. Once I looked at the moon and caught sight of a strange thing. A cricket had perched upon the handrail, only a few inches away. My line of vision was such that the creature filled the moon like a fossil. It had gone there, I thought to live and die, for there, of all places, was its small definition made whole and eternal. A warm wind rose up and purled like the longing within me.

The next morning, I awoke at dawn and went out on the dirt road to Rainy Mountain. It was already hot and the grasshoppers began to fill the air. Still, it was early in the morning, and birds sang out of the shadows. The long yellow grass on the mountain shone in the bright light, and a scissortail hied above the land. There, where it ought to be, at the end of a long and legendary way, was my grandmother's grave. She had at last succeeded to that holy ground. Here and there on the dark stones were ancestral names. Looking back once, I saw the mountain and came away. *[1969]*

≣ THINKING ABOUT THE TEXT

1. Momaday wants to "see in reality" the things his grandmother described, so he travels "fifteen hundred miles to begin [his] pilgrimage" (para. 5). Is he successful in this quest? What does it mean to see as someone else has seen? How would you know if you had succeeded?

2. Momaday mixes memoir, folklore, myth, history, and personal reflections in this essay. Does he successfully blend these genres? What is Momaday's aim in each? How does he achieve coherence?

3. Critics claim that Momaday treats his grandmother's memory with tenderness and reverence. Can you cite specific examples of this attitude?

4. Reread the opening as well as the last two paragraphs. Why might Momaday and his ancestors think of Rainy Mountain as a holy place?

5. Can you think of a comparable place in your own family's history or in your personal experience? What makes it special to you?

BARRY LOPEZ

Emancipation

Barry Lopez (b. 1945) grew up in California and New York City. He received a B.A. (1966) and an M.A. (1968) from the University of Notre Dame. Widely regarded as one of the most important writers on the environment, Lopez won the National Book Award for Arctic Dreams *in 1986. His focus is often on the relationship between human culture and physical landscape. He has also written fiction, including the award-winning* Resistance *(2004). His highly respected essays are published in the collections* Crossing Open Ground *(1988) and* About This Life *(1998). His most recent book is* Home Ground: Language for an American Landscape *(2006), a dictionary of regional landscape terms, which he edited with Debra Gwartney. He has won many awards and fellowships and taught at Notre Dame and Texas Tech. He lives in western Oregon.*

Who can say how the break between nature and cultural man came about? Or when. Historians of the West might trace it back to the rise of agriculture among early Sumerians, 7,000 years ago in the Tigris-Euphrates valley. Anthropologists tell us, though, the breach is no neat rift, that it has no single cause; central to the separation, though, wherever and whenever it occurs, is a shift in humanity's attitude toward its place. When one's home landscape — its animals, waters, plants, and earths — comes to be regarded as a servant, a producer of wealth and surfeit, the divide has opened. When the man who once plucked a few wild berries while traveling across a landscape he belonged to, a specific place which occupied the heart of his daily prayer, evolves into a strategist for profit, the split has occurred.

In essence, one's home land, once included like a member of a family in the reciprocities of life, has become a thing, an object no longer part of the owner's moral universe. Once a part of the face of God, it is now chattel.

These breaks, of course, occurred long ago in the West. In corners of Australia and Brazil, however, in Greenland, Mongolia, and other *aboriginum refugia*, we believe the mutual obligations and courtesies that historically obtained in the human relationship with place have not been completely abrogated. We imagine we can still inquire hopefully here about our prospects.

Time is short, though. If there is wisdom to serve the billions of us in Sydney, Buenos Aires, Mumbai, and Los Angeles, if the outline of a different moral practice is to be had by listening to Navajo, Pitjantjatjara, Hadza, or Iniut tradition keepers, we need to be at it quickly.

In the meantime, we find ourselves in the Visa, CNN, AK-47 present,   5 slightly alarmed by the weather, wondering how to ensure that the last few buttons of undisturbed land remain free of their putative new owners' social and economic scheming. We must somehow counter the entrenched philosophy of the contemporary investor—corporate, individual, or governmental: the belief that every parcel of land must pay its way. If it cannot provide something marketable, they say, what's to be gained by keeping it inviolate? If it can't serve, why care for it?

Land as serf. In nineteenth-century New World terms, the land as Negro.

In the long line of emancipations that have unfolded in the West since the Enlightenment—the abolition of slavery; one man/one woman, one vote; independence thrown up in the face of colonialism—environmentalism has emerged as a movement for the emancipation of land. Wild land—"nature without an audience," as the writer Jay Griffiths calls it—is without equal as a symbol of unhindered life. Those who seek its manumission are the same women and men who once drafted the most eloquent of arguments against slavery, colonial subjugation, and corporate exploitation and thievery.

Global climate change is the great leveler in the environmental debate. Leaving our own fate out of it for the moment, it is now instructive to wonder how wild land will respond. Beautifully, one has to think. Adaptation is its history, its legacy. No matter the stress—bolide impact, monocultured forests, rerouted rivers—adaptation is its eternal answer. Wild land exists without regret, has no plan for improvement, no goal outside its own integrity. It is attractive to us partly because it has no defense against the laceration of road building, the penetration of mines, the scarifying of machinery. It is also attractive to us, strangely, because we intuit wild land is apt to meet global climate change with more equanimity than our labyrinthine cities, our drought-stricken fields.

Wild lands, of course, can give some empire builders pause. If he or she sees fresh land as more than a warehouse of goods or a mean wall between himself and other riches, the pause will do us all good. Wilderness is a warning to those who dream of controlling nature: short-term triumphs—bumper crops, fire suppression, brimming reservoirs—are no more than that. Good in the short term only. Further, untrampled land, its innate worth defended by conservationists, offers yet another sort of warning to the would-be plunderer: when strongly tempted by the promise of profit, some people will still choose to hold such ground for the next generation.

If the question remains, Why preserve these areas?, the answer can't any   10 longer be for tourism or the promise of new medicines, or for the sake of scientific discoveries, or even to preserve minerals or timber for future use. Not if we have in mind the sense of integrity we claim the work of conservation implies.

It has to be for emancipation. It has to be because every pleader for preservation knows somewhere deep in his or her psyche that the effort to protect undisturbed lands is an effort to break the stranglehold industrial man has put on the Earth. It is an effort to reduce the reach of corporate muscle, an effort to staunch the bleeding of the brutalized oceans and their continents. It's a plea to reconcile. It's a call for principles that take us beyond the adolescent urge to plunder, to overpower, to win. In defending wild lands, we reclaim our dignity.

The real work of preservation, then, is our own salvation. It is not to save nature. Nature will save itself, no matter what climatic or nuclear hell we plunge ourselves into.

One spring I took the Indian Pacific from Sydney to Perth. Most of the way I was able to ride in the locomotive's cab with the engineers, and so take in the full sweep of the countryside. Crossing the Nullarbor Plain one morning we ran into a violent storm, sheets of rain so dense there was no view forward through the windscreen and but pale views to either side. I reveled in the fury and insouciance of the storm. And then it was gone. Ahead and to the south the span of a double rainbow materialized in the mist, an entity the breadth of Perth itself. The ionized air tore through open windows on either side of us. Neither the engineers nor I spoke a word. We nodded confidently to one another. Yes, we were in it now, an apparition of the wild that lay outside any human control or language. To the north, kangaroos bounded as if in fright or glee, radiating across the Nullarbor in streaks, and the three of us in the cab knew we could sail on like this for days, with no thought of sleep or nourishment. We were feeding on the food of our ancestors, those who had not abandoned nature in order to discover man but who had gone deep into nature to discover the Eden of which man is a part.

We felt emancipated.   *[2009]*

THINKING ABOUT THE TEXT

1. What shift in our attitude toward place concerns Lopez?

2. What does Lopez think we can learn from the tradition keepers of, for example, the Navajo and Inuit?

3. What would you say is the attitude toward place in your neighborhood at home? At school? In your city?

4. What is Lopez's sense of environmentalism? What is yours?

5. How effective is Lopez's closing anecdote in advancing his argument? Do you find his claim persuasive?

MAKING COMPARISONS

1. Do you think Rainy Mountain would make Lopez feel emancipated?

2. How do think Momaday would respond to Lopez's claim that "in defending wild lands, we reclaim our dignity" (para. 10)?

3. How would Momaday respond to the next-to-last sentence of this essay, especially the idea of ancestors?

KEN BURNS

Our Best Selves

Ken Burns (b. 1953), who was born in Brooklyn, New York, is perhaps the best-known documentary producer and director in America. His nine-episode television documentary The Civil War *(1990) is considered a masterpiece. The Brooklyn Bridge* (1982) *and* The Statue of Liberty *(1986) were nominated for Academy Awards. He has won seven Emmys, mostly for* The Civil War *and* Baseball *(1994). In the following excerpt from the preface to* The National Parks: America's Best Idea *(2009), Burns explains how the beautifully illustrated book was inspired by his documentary on the parks. Both were highly praised as celebrations "of an essential expression of American democracy."*

Over the course of our film and this book, you will meet several dozen people, most of them unsung or unfamiliar, who found in the parks salvation of one kind or another. They include a talented but troubled alcoholic who fell in love with the wildwoods of western North Carolina and eastern Tennessee, reha-bilitated himself in the isolation of nature, and then sacrificed everything to see the region transformed into a park. He was aided by an equally dedicated Japanese immigrant who would with his camera help insure the preservation of the wildnerness that was so close to and so threatened by the major popula-tion centers of the east. They include a family of Colorado cowboys, Quakers, who transformed themselves into archaeologists and helped save the dwindling and often vandalized relics of ancient American cultures, and a Minnesota boy who stepped off a train in Alaska, near the nation's highest peak, and became one of the fiercest protectors of predators nearly everyone else wanted eradicated.

They include the millionaire businessman with seemingly limitless enthusiasm for the expansion of parkland in America, who would spearhead the creation of the National Park Service and then benefit from its calming and peaceful resources as perhaps no one else has; and his young assistant, who would be forced to take over during his boss's mysterious absences, and who would also help an invalid president expand the very notion of what a national park could be. They include an iconoclastic crusader from Florida, a woman with her own unique relationship to the swamp at her doorstep, who would help lead the fight to save that swamp from a relentless tide of development and commercial exploitation.

And they also include a Scottish-born wanderer who walked clear across California and into the Ahwahneechees' magical valley in the middle of the high Sierras and was utterly transformed, finding in Nature's exquisite lessons an alternative to the harsh religious discipline of his father, and who would articulate his new creed of Nature in writings so transcendent that millions of Americans are still beguiled and inspirited by the rapture flowing from his words. For John Muir, Yosemite, indeed any wild place, revealed a design and an intelligence more permanent, more valuable than anything made by man, and man would be wise to submit to that natural world. He was certain, too, that a genuine and authentic relationship with Nature would help to forge a special "kinship" between all lovers of the mountains, and this kinship, in turn, required us — each of us within ourselves — to work to become better people. For this new human evolution to take place, Muir insisted that we had to go out into nature. But by going out, he said, we were "really going in." This is the journey, the journey of self-discovery, we all can make as we embrace our national parks. "This is still," John Muir wrote assuredly, "the morning of creation."

In many ways, they are hard to get to. The siren call of civilization is nearly impossible to resist; its enervating rhythms discordant yet seductive; the promise of wealth or position too engrained a reward for most of us to ignore. Though human *beings*, we seem compelled relentlessly to *do*. Yet we are beset by discontinuity; people quarrel, get sick, die, fall away. Rarely does the momentum of things permit repair or reconciliation; rarely do we throttle back. Even in nature, even in our beloved national parks, that momentum has a way of distracting us. We are now used to and come to expect a windshield experience, a quick drive through, and anything else is a bit frightening, time-consuming, other. The intimate specificity of nature, seen in the highest of mountains or a speck of lichen on a rock, its ever-enlarging vastness, is lost in the control we seek to superimpose over the chaos, the random chaos, of events. For many of us, we just don't have the time to submit, to enroll, as it were, as students in the great classroom our natural world provides, its curriculum endless and varied, sustaining and vital. In short, we have ignored the extraordinary commonwealth that is waiting just outside the city limits, ready to end the poverty of spirit that afflicts us all from time to time.

A traveler leaving San Francisco's airport by car and heading east out of the Bay Area has to negotiate a maze of interstate highway exchanges, and it is easy to forget, despite the "progress" one sees everywhere — the random overlap and seeming endlessness of our built environment — that it was and still is a beautiful place. Unlike a walk, which makes every place infinitely big, air travel makes the country small, impersonal, a few hours to get from one side to the other. As a result, we become impatient; even in a car after a flight, the sameness of things, whether man-made or natural, can erode our precious but often squandered attention.

But civilization does relent and the highways become less crowded, the multilane swaths of the city turn into smaller two-lane ribbons that cut through rather than consume landscape. If you are heading to John Muir's Yosemite, as I was near the beginning of this project, to catch up with my partners for several days of filming, I–80, I–580, I–205, and I–5 eventually yield, west of Manteca in the vast inland valley, into California Route 120. Now the shopping centers and malls give way to smaller towns and farms and fields and orchards. The land reclaims its primacy, but all of that is just preliminary, decompression, compared to what awaits the traveler on his first visit to Yosemite. The road begins to climb, even the farms now fall away, and 120 becomes Big Oak Flat Road, and eventually California Route 140, which leads the traveler (in the car now nearly as long as in the plane) into Yosemite National Park.

There is no preparation for it. A turn in the road and suddenly the valley unfolds before you. I have never in my life felt the way I felt at that moment. The crisp air and high altitude made the mountains and waterfalls, trees and road look almost like a backdrop you could roll up and store away. But it was something more. Like Muir, though I was physically outside, I was actually going in, transforming the old generic question once again into "Who am I?" The view was an anchor and a beacon; it held me gently but firmly in its grip (a grip I don't think I have ever completely lost) and it pulled me directly into the heart of the park.

When I caught up with the rest of our crew, who had all been to Yosemite before, they grinned when they saw my face. Like the loss of one's virginity or the fresh intimacy of parenthood, I had entered a new world, one I would find hard to forget or relinquish. For the next few days, we worked dawn to dusk filming the surrounding valley floor, hiking up past Vernal and Nevada falls to spend a night outdoors, each step a further surrender to the forces that had held John Muir so closely, to the forces that were changing my life. Each of us felt it, especially my co-producer and writer Dayton Duncan (whose love of the parks had initiated this project and this journey for me), and it only took a sideways glance or a quick exchanged smile to realize that each of us felt the same, each of us was hearing the same great symphony. The Park Service sells a small booklet they call a passport to those who wish to keep a permanent record of their trips into the parks; you can get this passport stamped with the date and location of each park you enter. The symbolism then was not lost on me. I had been permitted entry into a new country, not just a country of physical space and time, but of meaning and memory. I felt born again as we walked back into the valley.

That last night before we would head back to San Francisco and our busy, compelling lives, I lay awake unable to sleep. Memories were stirring and I suddenly realized that this was not the first natural national park I had ever been to, as I had thought and as I had confessed to my friends and colleagues. And then it all rushed back, a memory so long forgotten that it had ceased to be a part of my "history." In 1959, as a six-year-old boy, my father had taken me on our first and last road trip together. My mother was slowly dying of cancer and our household was a grim and demoralized place. And he had not been the best father, either; baseball catches in the backyard were few and far between, attendance at my games nonexistent. He was moody and distracted by my mother's illness and by inner demons none of us — my mother, younger brother, or me — fully understood, demons that would consume him for most of his too-short life.

But one Friday after school, he and I drove from our home in Newark, Del-   10
aware, to my grandparents' house, the place he had grown up in, in Baltimore.
We went to bed late (I slept in his old bedroom, in his old bed under his old che-
nille comforter) and it seemed like only a second later that my father was leaning over me in the dark, gently touching my shoulder, urging me to get up
quickly. I had never been up so early in my life. It was still dark as we left the
house and I can still remember nearly fifty years later all the things we talked
about (butterflies and baseball, the route we were taking, the battlefield of the
Civil War we passed) as the sun came up and we made our way, pre–interstate
system, to Front Royal, Virginia, and the north entrance of Shenandoah National Park.

The Skyline Drive runs along the spine of the ridge that makes up the relatively small park and that morning there was still fog and mist and cloud hugging the road. I had never been in a cloud before. We went through short
tunnels carved through the mountains (!) and we saw a handful of deer standing stock-still before us on the road before my dad scattered them with his car
horn. After what seemed like hours in this new world, we turned off the drive
and checked into a small cabin just big enough for the two of us. It was chilly
and my dad insisted on my putting on a jeans jacket with red lining we had just
bought and we set off down a trail that led eventually to a waterfall. It was an
impossibly long hike for my young legs — probably all of a mile and a half — but
I held my father's hand and I can still remember his grip to this day.

We saw a bear, I think. We turned over rotting logs and caught a bright-red
salamander and my father named every butterfly and tree we saw. I don't remember what or even where we ate that night, but I do remember lying awake,
as I would do years later alone in Yosemite, thinking how great this was to be in
this magical place, with memory and emotion attached so securely, this time
with my dad. The next day we had more hikes and more adventures before we
headed home; my dad sang to me songs like "Wolverton Mountain," "Silver
Threads and Golden Needles," "Scarlet Ribbons," and other folk songs that are
permanently on my hard drive, though when I had later sung them to my children I had forgotten when I learned them. Later, after my epiphany at Yosemite,
my then thirteen-year-old middle daughter, Lilly, was dragged down the same
Skyline Drive, as I attempted to re-create what a distracted father and his desperately young son had experienced as the 1950s came to a close. This time we
most definitely saw bears.

When that memory-stirred night in Yosemite came in May of 2003, my
father had been gone for more than a year and a half, and I suppose it is reasonable to ask, confronting such an epic story as that of the national parks, what
purpose these personal stories serve. But the narrative of the parks is not just
in their spectacular scenery, the waterfalls and big trees and wildlife, or even
the complicated sagas of the charismatic individuals who saved these places. It
is also about who we see these sacred places with, whose hand we are holding
at the rim of the Grand Canyon (or in Shenandoah National Park), what intimate transmissions, as [the historian William] Cronon would say, occur between the generations as we instill this love of the parks, our parks, to our

posterity. We *are* beset by discontinuity; people do quarrel, get sick, die, fall away. Rarely does the momentum of things permit repair or reconciliation. But I have found, in places where the narrative of human lives and those of their "brotherly" rocks seem just as important, that some inexpressible something is retained, repairs are made, and we are all, as John Muir so fervently wished, kindred spirits.   *[2009]*

≣ **THINKING ABOUT THE TEXT**

1. Do you agree with John Muir that being in the wilderness inspires us to be better people? Why, or why not?

2. Explain what you think Burns means when he says that "the siren call of civilization is nearly impossible to resist" (para. 4).

3. Describe Burns's epiphany when he first sees Yosemite valley.

4. Do you think Burns's anecdote about his journey with his father is effective? Why, or why not? What purpose do his personal stories serve?

5. What does Burns mean by "kindred spirits" (para. 13)? Have you ever had such a feeling?

≣ **MAKING COMPARISONS**

1. How would Momaday and Lopez respond to John Muir's idea that by going out into nature, we are "really going in" (para. 3)?

2. Compare the effectiveness of the endings to all three essays.

3. What ideas about wild places do all three essays have in common?

≣ **WRITING ABOUT ISSUES**

1. Argue that our culture does or does not appreciate the value of wild places.

2. Write a personal narrative like Ken Burns's in which you describe an early outing in nature and what you thought then and now about that experience.

3. Write an essay that answers Lopez's question, "Why preserve these [wild] areas?" (para. 10).

4. Research the ideas of the early environmentalist John Muir, and then write a report on your findings.

▤ A Seductive Argument: Re-Visions of a Poem

ANDREW MARVELL, "To His Coy Mistress"

PETER DE VRIES, "To His Importunate Mistress"

T. S. ELIOT, "The Love Song of J. Alfred Prufrock"

Most poets are influenced by their predecessors, especially by the great canonical poets of the past. Sometimes they try to imitate the language of the great masters; sometimes, according to the critic Harold Bloom in *The Anxiety of Influence*, they misread famous poets on purpose, hoping to carve out a unique niche for themselves. But sometimes poets write parodies of well-known poems, much like Anthony Hecht's "The Dover Bitch," an amusing parody of Matthew Arnold's "Dover Beach." Parodies often make fun of the themes and language (William Carlos Williams's poem "This Is Just to Say" has been a target dozens of times), but Peter de Vries's "To His Importunate Mistress" is a more gentle parody of Andrew Marvell's "To His Coy Mistress," often cited as the greatest of the *carpe diem* poems of the seventeenth century. Marvell's work is frequently seen as a seduction poem, reflective of the attitudes of a privileged male of that time. In this context, his sexual proposal would be filled with danger since unmarried women of the time were expected to be virgins. If they weren't virgins, their marriage prospects would be severely diminished. And there were few other options for young women of that era. Although his seductive argument is not actually logical, readers have enjoyed his language and the emotions involved. De Vries updates the poem by having the male narrator reject the advances of a woman. He seems to be not so much poking fun at Marvell's poem as amusingly continuing a poetic tradition that is centuries old.

We also include here one of the most famous poems of the twentieth century, "The Love Song of J. Alfred Prufrock," not because it directly alludes to Marvell but because Prufrock's journey is often viewed as an attempt to either propose marriage or engage in a seduction. But Prufrock vacillates so much and is so uncertain about love and seems so fearful and so anxious that we wonder if he is up to the task. Prufrock is often seen as a modern antihero who reflects our own doubts and lack of self-esteem about love. Prufrock seems alienated in a meaningless world and as such is surely an ironic modern counterpoint to the confident and heedless narrator of Marvell's poem.

▤ BEFORE YOU READ

Are seduction poems (or songs or letters) effective? Is such an offer more effectively made in person? What would the difference be? Could you say some things in a letter, say, that you couldn't (or wouldn't) say in person?

ANDREW MARVELL
To His Coy Mistress

Andrew Marvell (1621–1678) was famous in his own time as an adroit politician and a writer of satire, but modern readers admire him for the style and content of his lyric, metaphysical poetry. Born into a Protestant family, Marvell was tolerant of Catholicism from a young age, and his willingness to somehow circumvent the religious prejudices of seventeenth-century England allowed his continued success. He traveled to Holland, France, Italy, and Spain—possibly to avoid the English civil war as a young man and undoubtedly to spy for England in later years. He tutored Cromwell's ward and later served on his Council of State but was influential enough during the Restoration to get his fellow poet and mentor, John Milton, released from prison. Although admired by the Romantic poets of the early nineteenth century, Marvell's poetry (much of it published after his death) was revived in the twentieth century by T. S. Eliot and has been widely read for its ironic approach to the conventions of love.

Had we but world enough, and time,
This coyness, lady, were no crime.
We would sit down, and think which way
To walk, and pass our long love's day.
Thou by the Indian Ganges'° side   5
Shouldst rubies find; I by the tide
Of Humber° would complain.° I would
Love you ten years before the Flood,
And you should, if you please, refuse
Till the conversion of the Jews.   10
My vegetable love should grow°
Vaster than empires, and more slow;
An hundred years should go to praise
Thine eyes and on thy forehead gaze,
Two hundred to adore each breast,   15
But thirty thousand to the rest:
An age at least to every part,
And the last age should show your heart.
For, lady, you deserve this state,
Nor would I love at lower rate.   20
     But at my back I always hear
Time's wingèd chariot hurrying near;
And yonder all before us lie
Deserts of vast eternity.
Thy beauty shall no more be found,   25

---

5 Ganges: A river in India sacred to the Hindus.   **7 Humber:** An estuary that flows through Marvell's native town, Hull.   **complain:** Sing love songs.   **11 My vegetable love . . . grow:** A slow, insensible growth, like that of a vegetable.

A. MARVELL

(Photo by Archive
Photos/Getty Images.)

Nor in thy marble vault shall sound
My echoing song; then worms shall try
That long preserved virginity,
And your quaint honor turn to dust,
And into ashes all my lust.   30
The grave's a fine and private place,
But none, I think, do there embrace.
     Now, therefore, while the youthful hue
Sits on thy skin like morning dew,
And while thy willing soul transpires°   35
At every pore with instant fires,
Now let us sport us while we may,

35 transpires: Breathes forth.

And now, like amorous birds of prey,
Rather at once our time devour
Than languish in his slow-chapped° power.   40
Let us roll all our strength and all
Our sweetness up into one ball,
And tear our pleasures with rough strife
Thorough° the iron gates of life.
Thus, though we cannot make our sun   45
Stand still, yet we will make him run.   *[1681]*

40 slow-chapped: Slow-jawed.   **44 Thorough:** Through.

■ THINKING ABOUT THE TEXT

1. Considered as both an intellectual and an emotional argument, what is
   the narrator's goal, and what specific claims does he make? Are they
   convincing? Do you think they were in 1681? Do you think women three
   hundred years ago worried about virginity? Why?

2. What does this poem say about the needs of Marvell's audience? What
   assumptions about women does the poem make?

3. How many sections does this poem have? What is the purpose of each?
   How is the concluding couplet in each related to that section? Is the
   rhyme scheme related to the meaning of these couplets?

4. Is the speaker passionate? Sincere? How do you make such a decision?
   Do you look at his language or at his message?

5. Some feminist readers see in the last ten lines a kind of indirect threat,
   a suggestion of force through the use of violent images. Is this a plausible reading? If this is the case, what do you now think of the narrator's
   pleading?

PETER DE VRIES
To His Importunate Mistress

*Peter de Vries (1910–1993) was born in Chicago and graduated from Calvin College
in 1931. Sometimes described as our "national humorist laureate," de Vries is noted
for his satiric jabs at our culture's shortcomings. He began a long-lasting career with*
The New Yorker *magazine in 1944 and over the years contributed numerous short
stories and poems. Because of his wit, irony, and inspired wordplay, his novels are
often compared to such critically acclaimed humorists as Evelyn Waugh and P. G.
Wodehouse. Most of his novels and poems deal with marriage and its problems and
delights. A line from* Tents of Wickedness *(1959) from a character who refuses an
affair is seen as typical of de Vries's wry style: "Thanks just the same . . . but I don't*

(Photo by Bernard
Gotfryd/Getty Images.

want any pleasures interfering with my happiness." His most famous novel, The
Blood of the Lamb *(1961), was brought back into print in 2005.*

Had we but world enough, and time,
My coyness, lady, were a crime,
But at my back I always hear
Time's winged chariot, striking fear
The hour is nigh when creditors   5
Will prove to be my predators.
As wages of our picaresque,
Bag lunches bolted at my desk
Must stand as fealty to you
For each expensive rendezvous.   10
Obeisance at your marble feet
Deserves the best-appointed suite,

And would have, lacked I not the pelf°   *money*
To pleasure also thus myself;
But amply sumptuous amorous scenes   15
Rule out the rake of modest means.

Since mistress presupposes wife,
It means a doubly costly life;
For fools by second passion fired
A second income is required,   20
The earning which consumes the hours
They'd hoped to spend in rented bowers.
To hostelries the worst of fates
That weekly raise their daily rates!
I gather, lady, from your scoffing   25
A bloke more solvent in the offing.
So revels thus to rivals go
For want of monetary flow.
How vexing that inconsistent cash
The constant suitor must abash,   30
Who with excuses vainly pled
Must rue the undishevelled bed,
And that for paltry reasons given
His conscience may remain unriven.   *[1986]*

≣ THINKING ABOUT THE TEXT

1. Morality doesn't seem to be a major factor in the narrator's apparent rejection of his demanding mistress. What is his main reason?

2. The narrator claims he is being coy, but presumably only because they don't have "world enough, and time" (line 1). What do you think he means?

3. Formulate this poetic argument into simple straightforward prose. What is gained and lost in this translation?

4. Apparently his mistress is "scoffing" (line 25) at his perhaps overly practical reasoning. Would you? Would most people? Do you think this is his real reason or just an excuse?

5. Although he claims to be remorseful for "the undishevelled bed" (line 32), he says that his reasons are paltry. Does he really think so? Since he never mentions ethical concerns, why should his conscience be of any concern to him?

≣ MAKING COMPARISONS

1. Compare the meaning of the opening two lines of each poem.

2. Marvell's argument seems more complicated and serious than de Vries's. Is this your interpretation? Why? Is de Vries's argument really serious?

What about such rhymes as "creditors" and "predators," "pelf" and "myself," "cash" and "abash"? Do they suggest a tongue-in-cheek tone?

3. What would a contemporary woman make of Marvell's seduction argument? Would de Vries's argument have been effective in Marvell's age?

T. S. ELIOT

The Love Song of J. Alfred Prufrock

One of the most respected intellectuals of his time, Thomas Stearns Eliot (1888–1965) was a poet, playwright (Murder in the Cathedral), and critic (The Sacred Wood). His poem "The Waste Land" (1922), considered a modernist masterpiece, is perhaps the last century's most influential poem. The long-running Broadway play Cats is based on some of Eliot's lighter poems. Born in America and educated at Harvard, Eliot lived his mature life in England. He was awarded the Nobel Prize for literature in 1948.

> *S'io credesse che mia risposta fosse*
> *A persona che mai tornasse al mondo,*
> *Questa fiamma staria senza più scosse.*
> *Ma perciocchè giammai di questo fondo*
> *Non tornò vivo alcun, s'i'odo il vero,*
> *Senza tema d'infamia ti rispondo.°*

Let us go then, you and I,
When the evening is spread out against the sky
Like a patient etherized upon a table;
Let us go, through certain half-deserted streets,
The muttering retreats   5
Of restless nights in one-night cheap hotels
And sawdust restaurants with oyster-shells:
Streets that follow like a tedious argument
Of insidious intent

To lead you to an overwhelming question . . .   10
Oh, do not ask, "What is it?"
Let us go and make our visit.

In the room the women come and go
Talking of Michelangelo.

The yellow fog that rubs its back upon the window panes,   15
The yellow smoke that rubs its muzzle on the window panes

EPIGRAPH: **S'io . . . rispondo:** In Dante's *Inferno,* a sufferer in hell says, "If I thought I was talking to someone who might return to earth, this flame would cease; but if what I have heard is true, no one does return; therefore, I can speak to you without fear of infamy."

(Photo by E. O. Hoppe/
Mansell/Time Life
Pictures/Getty Images.)

Licked its tongue into the corners of the evening,
Lingered upon the pools that stand in drains,
Let fall upon its back the soot that falls from chimneys,
Slipped by the terrace, made a sudden leap,   20
And seeing that it was a soft October night,
Curled once about the house, and fell asleep.

    And indeed there will be time°
For the yellow smoke that slides along the street,
Rubbing its back upon the window panes;   25
There will be time, there will be time
To prepare a face to meet the faces that you meet;
There will be time to murder and create,
And time for all the works and days° of hands

---

23 there will be time: An allusion to Ecclesiastes 3:1–8: "To everything there is a season, and a time to every purpose under heaven." **29 works and days:** Hesiod's eighth-century B.C.E. poem gave practical advice.

That lift and drop a question on your plate: 30
Time for you and time for me,
And time yet for a hundred indecisions,
And for a hundred visions and revisions,
Before the taking of a toast and tea.
In the room the women come and go   35
Talking of Michelangelo.
    And indeed there will be time
To wonder, "Do I dare?" and, "Do I dare?" —
Time to turn back and descend the stair,
With a bald spot in the middle of my hair —   40
(They will say: "How his hair is growing thin!")
My morning coat, my collar mounting firmly to the chin,
My necktie rich and modest, but asserted by a simple pin —
(They will say: "But how his arms and legs are thin!")
Do I dare   45
Disturb the universe?
In a minute there is time
For decisions and revisions which a minute will reverse.

    For I have known them all already, known them all:
Have known the evenings, mornings, afternoons,   50
I have measured out my life with coffee spoons;
I know the voices dying with a dying fall
Beneath the music from a farther room.
    So how should I presume?

    And I have known the eyes already, known them all —   55
The eyes that fix you in a formulated phrase,
And when I am formulated, sprawling on a pin,
When I am pinned and wriggling on the wall,
Then how should I begin
To spit out all the butt-ends of my days and ways?   60
    And how should I presume?

    And I have known the arms already, known them all —
Arms that are braceleted and white and bare
(But in the lamplight, downed with light brown hair!)
    Is it perfume from a dress   65
That makes me so digress?
Arms that lie along a table, or wrap about a shawl.
    And should I then presume?
    And how should I begin?

    Shall I say, I have gone at dusk through narrow streets,   70
And watched the smoke that rises from the pipes
Of lonely men in shirtsleeves, leaning out of windows? . . .

I should have been a pair of ragged claws
Scuttling across the floors of silent seas.

And the afternoon, the evening, sleeps so peacefully!   75
Smoothed by long fingers,
Asleep . . . tired . . . or it malingers,
Stretched on the floor, here beside you and me.
Should I, after tea and cakes and ices,
Have the strength to force the moment to its crisis?   80
But though I have wept and fasted, wept and prayed,
Though I have seen my head (grown slightly bald) brought in upon a
    platter,°
I am no prophet — and here's no great matter;
I have seen the moment of my greatness flicker,
And I have seen the eternal Footman hold my coat, and snicker,   85
    And in short, I was afraid.

And would it have been worth it, after all,
After the cups, the marmalade, the tea,
Among the porcelain, among some talk of you and me,
Would it have been worth while   90
To have bitten off the matter with a smile,
To have squeezed the universe into a ball°
To roll it toward some overwhelming question,
To say: "I am Lazarus,° come from the dead,
Come back to tell you all, I shall tell you all" —   95
If one, settling a pillow by her head,
    Should say: "That is not what I meant at all;
    That is not it, at all."

And would it have been worth it, after all,
Would it have been worth while,   100
After the sunsets and the dooryards and the sprinkled streets,
After the novels, after the teacups, after the skirts that trail along the
    floor —
And this, and so much more? —
It is impossible to say just what I mean!
But as if a magic lantern° threw the nerves in patterns on a screen: 105
Would it have been worth while
If one, settling a pillow or throwing off a shawl,
And turning toward the window, should say:
    "That is not it at all,
    That is not what I meant, at all."   110

82 head . . . platter: Like John the Baptist (Matt. 14:1–12).   **92 squeezed . . . ball:** See
lines 41–42 of Marvell's "To His Coy Mistress" (p. 690).   **94 "I am Lazarus":** Raised from
the dead by Jesus.   **105 magic lantern:** Precursor of the slide projector.

No! I am not Prince Hamlet, nor was meant to be;
Am an attendant lord,° one that will do
To swell a progress,° start a scene or two
Advise the prince: withal, an easy tool,
Deferential, glad to be of use,   115
Politic, cautious, and meticulous;
Full of high sentence, but a bit obtuse;
At times, indeed, almost ridiculous —
Almost, at times, the Fool.
I grow old . . . I grow old . . .   120
I shall wear the bottoms of my trowsers rolled.

    Shall I part my hair behind?° Do I dare to eat a peach°?
I shall wear white flannel trowsers, and walk upon the beach.
I have heard the mermaids singing, each to each.

I do not think that they will sing to me.   125

I have seen them riding seaward on the waves,
Combing the white hair of the waves blown back
When the wind blows the water white and black.

We have lingered in the chambers of the sea
By seagirls wreathed with seaweed red and brown,   130
Till human voices wake us, and we drown.   *[1917]*

≡ **THINKING ABOUT THE TEXT**

1. Do you think Prufrock is on a journey to propose marriage, to have a sexual rendezvous, or to do something else?

2. Is Prufrock enchanted with women (lines 62–67) or wary of them (lines 55–61)? What other lines might help to answer this question?

3. How do you interpret the questions "Do I dare" (lines 38, 45), "So how should I presume?" (line 54), "And how should I begin?" (line 69)?

4. How old do you think Prufrock is? Can you cite some evidence in the text? How might his age (young man? middle-aged man?) be a factor in the purpose for his journey toward marriage, casual sex, or something else?

5. Why do you think Prufrock ends his poem with fantasies about mermaids? Do you read this as an admission of failure?

---

112 attendant lord: Like Polonius in Shakespeare's *Hamlet*.   **113 progress:** State procession.   **121–122 trowsers rolled . . . part my hair behind:** The latest fashion; **eat a peach:** Considered a risky fruit.

≡ **MAKING COMPARISONS**

1. In what ways is Eliot's poem closer to de Vries's than to Marvell's?
2. How does the idea of conscience figure into these three poems?
3. What do you think Marvell would make of de Vries's parody and Eliot's reluctant narrator?

≡ **WRITING ABOUT ISSUES**

1. Argue that Prufrock does or does not represent contemporary concerns about romantic relationships.
2. Write a letter to Marvell explaining why contemporary readers of his poem might find his proposal objectionable.
3. Write a letter to Prufrock explaining why you think his attitude toward love is either accurate or ill founded.
4. Argue that contemporary social networks like Facebook and Twitter make verbal seduction easier or more difficult.

The Appearance of Love: A Collection of Stories by Kate Chopin

KATE CHOPIN, "The Storm"

KATE CHOPIN, "The Story of an Hour"

KATE CHOPIN, "Désirée's Baby"

People at weddings often remark how happy and in love the bridal couple looks. But people can *appear* to be in love. Indeed, psychologists tell us that someone can play a loving role for years, at times actually believing the part he or she is playing. To a limited extent, this is true for all of us. We learn what it means to be in love from watching movies, reading books, and absorbing other clues from our culture. A man proposing marriage on one knee is just one cultural notion of how we should act when we are in love.

Suppose a woman acts lovingly toward her husband and then has a passionate sexual encounter with an old boyfriend. Which is her true self? Which is the appearance and which the reality? Sometimes a society's conventions about marriage are so strong that men and women have little choice but to conform. If we were to judge the behavior of a woman toward her husband a hundred years ago, we might not get an accurate reading of how much she loved him. Likewise, people can believe their lives to be quite harmonious until they find out that one of them has a surprising past. William Shakespeare wrote of love that would not change when difficulties arose, but such is not always the case. Does that mean that one's love is not deep enough? Or when a loved one does not live up to expectations, is it natural to readjust one's heart?

The following three stories take on controversial topics. Kate Chopin was not a conformist thinker, and her stories are filled with views of desire, love, and relationships meant to provoke her late-nineteenth-century readers. Indeed, they continue to provoke audiences today.

≡ BEFORE YOU READ

Would you change your mind about loving someone if you found out he or she was having an affair? If that person lied about his or her religion or race? Is it possible to love someone and at the same time want to be free?

KATE CHOPIN

The Storm

Kate Chopin (1851–1904) is known for her evocations of the unique, multiethnic Creole and Cajun societies of late-nineteenth-century Louisiana; however, her characters transcend the limitation of regional genre writing, striking a particularly resonant note among feminist readers. Born Katherine O'Flaherty in St. Louis, Missouri,

(Missouri Historical
Society. St. Louis.
Negative Por C-146.
Kate Chopin carte de
visite photograph by
J. J. Scholten, 1869.)

she married Oscar Chopin in 1870 and went to live with him in New Orleans and on his plantation along the Mississippi River. Her short stories were collected in Bayou Folk *(1894) and* A Night in Acadie *(1897). Chopin's last novel,* The Awakening, *scandalized readers at the time of its publication in 1899 because of its frank portrayal of female sexuality in the context of an extramarital affair. Long ignored by readers and critics, her work was revived in the 1960s and continues to provoke heated discussion of her female characters: are they women who seek freedom in the only ways available to them, or are they willing participants in their own victimhood?*

"The Storm" was written about 1898, but because of its provocative content, Chopin probably did not even try to find a magazine that would risk the publicity.

1

The leaves were so still that even Bibi thought it was going to rain. Bobinôt, who was accustomed to converse on terms of perfect equality with his little son, called the child's attention to certain sombre clouds that were rolling with sinister intention from the west, accompanied by a sullen, threatening roar. They were at Friedheimer's store and decided to remain there till the storm had passed. They sat within the door on two empty kegs. Bibi was four years old and looked very wise.

"Mama'll be 'fraid, yes," he suggested with blinking eyes.

"She'll shut the house. Maybe she got Sylvie helpin' her this evenin'," Bobinôt responded reassuringly.

"No; she ent got Sylvie. Sylvie was helpin' her yistiday," piped Bibi.

Bobinôt arose and going across to the counter purchased a can of shrimps, 5
of which Calixta was very fond. Then he returned to his perch on the keg and sat stolidly holding the can of shrimps while the storm burst. It shook the wooden store and seemed to be ripping great furrows in the distant field. Bibi laid his little hand on his father's knee and was not afraid.

2

Calixta, at home, felt no uneasiness for their safety. She sat at a side window sewing furiously on a sewing machine. She was greatly occupied and did not notice the approaching storm. But she felt very warm and often stopped to mop her face on which the perspiration gathered in beads. She unfastened her white sacque at the throat. It began to grow dark, and suddenly realizing the situation she got up hurriedly and went about closing windows and doors.

Out on the small front gallery she had hung Bobinôt's Sunday clothes to air and she hastened out to gather them before the rain fell. As she stepped outside, Alcée Laballière rode in at the gate. She had not seen him very often since her marriage, and never alone. She stood there with Bobinôt's coat in her hands, and the big rain drops began to fall. Alcée rode his horse under the shelter of a side projection where the chickens had huddled and there were plows and a harrow piled up in the corner.

"May I come and wait on your gallery till the storm is over, Calixta?" he asked.

"Come 'long in, M'sieur Alcée."

His voice and her own startled her as if from a trance, and she seized 10
Bobinôt's vest. Alcée, mounting to the porch, grabbed the trousers and snatched Bibi's braided jacket that was about to be carried away by a sudden gust of wind. He expressed an intention to remain outside, but it was soon apparent that he might as well have been out in the open: the water beat in upon the boards in driving sheets, and he went inside, closing the door after him. It was even necessary to put something beneath the door to keep the water out.

"My! what a rain! It's good two years sence it rain' like that," exclaimed Calixta as she rolled up a piece of bagging and Alcée helped her to thrust it beneath the crack.

She was a little fuller of figure than five years before when she married; but she had lost nothing of her vivacity. Her blue eyes still retained their melting quality; and her yellow hair, dishevelled by the wind and rain, kinked more stubbornly than ever about her ears and temples.

The rain beat upon the low, shingled roof with a force and clatter that threatened to break an entrance and deluge them there. They were in the dining room—the sitting room—the general utility room. Adjoining was her bed room, with Bibi's couch along side her own. The door stood open, and the room with its white, monumental bed, its closed shutters, looked dim and mysterious.

Alcée flung himself into a rocker and Calixta nervously began to gather up from the floor the lengths of a cotton sheet which she had been sewing.

"If this keeps up, *Dieu sait*° if the levees goin' to stan' it!" she exclaimed.   15

"What have you got to do with the levees?"

"I got enough to do! An' there's Bobinôt with Bibi out in that storm—if he only didn' left Friedheimer's!"

"Let us hope, Calixta, that Bobinôt's got sense enough to come in out of a cyclone."

She went and stood at the window with a greatly disturbed look on her face. She wiped the frame that was clouded with moisture. It was stiflingly hot. Alcée got up and joined her at the window, looking over her shoulder. The rain was coming down in sheets obscuring the view of far-off cabins and enveloping the distant wood in a gray mist. The playing of the lightning was incessant. A bolt struck a tall chinaberry tree at the edge of the field. It filled all visible space with a blinding glare and the crash seemed to invade the very boards they stood upon.

Calixta put her hands to her eyes, and with a cry, staggered backward.   20
Alcée's arm encircled her, and for an instant he drew her close and spasmodically to him.

"*Bonté!*"° she cried, releasing herself from his encircling arm and retreating from the window, "the house'll go next! If I only knew w'ere Bibi was!" She would not compose herself; she would not be seated. Alcée clasped her shoulders and looked into her face. The contact of her warm, palpitating body when he had unthinkingly drawn her into his arm, had aroused all the old-time infatuation and desire for her flesh.

"Calixta," he said, "don't be frightened. Nothing can happen. The house is too low to be struck, with so many tall trees standing about. There! aren't you going to be quiet? say, aren't you?" He pushed her hair back from her face that was warm and steaming. Her lips were as red and moist as pomegranate seed. Her white neck and a glimpse of her full, firm bosom disturbed him powerfully. As she glanced up at him the fear in her liquid blue eyes had given place to a drowsy gleam that unconsciously betrayed a sensuous desire. He looked down into her eyes and there was nothing for him to do but to gather her lips in a kiss. It reminded him of Assumption.

"Do you remember—in Assumption, Calixta?" he asked in a low voice broken by passion. Oh! she remembered; for in Assumption he had kissed her and kissed and kissed her; until his senses would well nigh fail, and to save her he would resort to a desperate flight. If she was not an immaculate dove in those days, she was still inviolate; a passionate creature whose very defenselessness had made her defense, against which his honor forbade him to prevail.

Dieu sait: God knows.   *Bonté*: Goodness.

Now — well, now — her lips seemed in a manner free to be tasted, as well as her round, white throat and her whiter breasts.

They did not heed the crashing torrents, and the roar of the elements made her laugh as she lay in his arms. She was a revelation in that dim, mysterious chamber; as white as the couch she lay upon. Her firm, elastic flesh that was knowing for the first time its birthright, was like a creamy lily that the sun invites to contribute its breath and perfume to the undying life of the world.

The generous abundance of her passion, without guile or trickery, was like   25
a white flame which penetrated and found response in depths of his own sensuous nature that had never yet been reached.

When he touched her breasts they gave themselves up in quivering ecstasy, inviting his lips. Her mouth was a fountain of delight. And when he possessed her, they seemed to swoon together at the very borderland of life's mystery.

He stayed cushioned upon her, breathless, dazed, enervated, with his heart beating like a hammer upon her. With one hand she clasped his head, her lips lightly touching his forehead. The other hand stroked with a soothing rhythm his muscular shoulders.

The growl of the thunder was distant and passing away. The rain beat softly upon the shingles, inviting them to drowsiness and sleep. But they dared not yield.

The rain was over; and the sun was turning the glistening green world into a palace of gems. Calixta, on the gallery, watched Alcée ride away. He turned and smiled at her with a beaming face; and she lifted her pretty chin in the air and laughed aloud.

3

Bobinôt and Bibi, trudging home, stopped without at the cistern to make them-   30
selves presentable.

"My! Bibi, w'at will yo' mama say! You ought to be ashame'. You oughtn' put on those good pants. Look at 'em! An' that mud on yo' collar! How you got that mud on yo' collar, Bibi? I never saw such a boy!" Bibi was the picture of pathetic resignation. Bobinôt was the embodiment of serious solicitude as he strove to remove from his own person and his son's the signs of their tramp over heavy roads and through wet fields. He scraped the mud off Bibi's bare legs and feet with a stick and carefully removed all traces from his heavy brogans. Then, prepared for the worst — the meeting with an over-scrupulous housewife, they entered cautiously at the back door.

Calixta was preparing supper. She had set the table and was dripping coffee at the hearth. She sprang up as they came in.

"Oh, Bobinôt! You back! My! but I was uneasy. W'ere you been during the rain? An' Bibi? he ain't wet? he ain't hurt?" She had clasped Bibi and was kissing him effusively. Bobinôt's explanations and apologies which he had been composing all along the way, died on his lips as Calixta felt him to see if he were dry, and seemed to express nothing but satisfaction at their safe return.

"I brought you some shrimps, Calixta," offered Bobinôt, hauling the can from his ample side pocket and laying it on the table.

"Shrimps! Oh, Bobinôt! you too good fo' anything!" and she gave him a   35
smacking kiss on the cheek that resounded. "*J'vous réponds,*° we'll have a feas' to-night! umph-umph!"

Bobinôt and Bibi began to relax and enjoy themselves, and when the three seated themselves at table they laughed much and so loud that anyone might have heard them as far away as Laballière's.

4

Alcée Laballière wrote to his wife, Clarisse, that night. It was a loving letter, full of tender solicitude. He told her not to hurry back, but if she and the babies liked it at Biloxi, to stay a month longer. He was getting on nicely; and though he missed them, he was willing to bear the separation a while longer — realizing that their health and pleasure were the first things to be considered.

5

As for Clarisse, she was charmed upon receiving her husband's letter. She and the babies were doing well. The society was agreeable; many of her old friends and acquaintances were at the bay. And the first free breath since her marriage seemed to restore the pleasant liberty of her maiden days. Devoted as she was to her husband, their intimate conjugal life was something which she was more than willing to forego for a while.

So the storm passed and every one was happy.   [1898]

J'vous réponds: I'm telling you.

■ **THINKING ABOUT THE TEXT**

1. Does Calixta truly love Bobinôt? What explains the sudden passion of Calixta and Alcée? Are they in love?

2. Are you bothered by the happy ending? Are stories supposed to reinforce the dominant values of a society? What do you think would (or should) have happened in real life?

3. Can you recall other stories, novels, films, or television programs in which someone who is sexually transgressive is not punished?

4. Are the injured parties in this story really injured; that is, if they never find out, will they still suffer somehow?

5. Should extramarital affairs be illegal? Is Chopin suggesting that they are not so terrible, or is she simply saying something about passion?

KATE CHOPIN
The Story of an Hour

"The Story of an Hour" was first published in Bayou Folk *(1894). It is typical of Chopin's controversial works and caused a sensation among the reading public.*

Knowing that Mrs. Mallard was afflicted with a heart trouble, great care was taken to break to her as gently as possible the news of her husband's death.

It was her sister Josephine who told her, in broken sentences; veiled hints that revealed in half concealing. Her husband's friend Richards was there, too, near her. It was he who had been in the newspaper office when intelligence of the railroad disaster was received, with Brently Mallard's name leading the list of "killed." He had only taken the time to assure himself of its truth by a second telegram, and had hastened to forestall any less careful, less tender friend in bearing the sad message.

She did not hear the story as many women have heard the same, with a paralyzed inability to accept its significance. She wept at once, with sudden, wild abandonment, in her sister's arms. When the storm of grief had spent itself she went away to her room alone. She would have no one follow her.

There stood, facing the open window, a comfortable, roomy armchair. Into this she sank, pressed down by a physical exhaustion that haunted her body and seemed to reach into her soul.

She could see in the open square before her house the tops of trees that were all aquiver with the new spring life. The delicious breath of rain was in the air. In the street below a peddler was crying his wares. The notes of a distant song which some one was singing reached her faintly, and countless sparrows were twittering in the eaves.   5

There were patches of blue sky showing here and there through the clouds that had met and piled one above the other in the west facing her window.

She sat with her head thrown back upon the cushion of the chair, quite motionless, except when a sob came up into her throat and shook her, as a child who had cried itself to sleep continues to sob in its dreams.

She was young, with a fair, calm face, whose lines bespoke repression and even a certain strength. But now there was a dull stare in her eyes, whose gaze was fixed away off yonder on one of those patches of blue sky. It was not a glance of reflection, but rather indicated a suspension of intelligent thought.

There was something coming to her and she was waiting for it, fearfully. What was it? She did not know; it was too subtle and elusive to name. But she felt it, creeping out of the sky, reaching toward her through the sounds, the scents, the color that filled the air.

Now her bosom rose and fell tumultuously. She was beginning to recog-   10
nize this thing that was approaching to possess her, and she was striving to beat it back with her will — as powerless as her two white slender hands would have been.

When she abandoned herself a little whispered word escaped her slightly parted lips. She said it over and over under her breath: "free, free, free!" The vacant stare and the look of terror that had followed it went from her eyes. They stayed keen and bright. Her pulses beat fast, and the coursing blood warmed and relaxed every inch of her body.

She did not stop to ask if it were or were not a monstrous joy that held her. A clear and exalted perception enabled her to dismiss the suggestion as trivial.

She knew that she would weep again when she saw the kind, tender hands folded in death; the face that had never looked save with love upon her, fixed and gray and dead. But she saw beyond that bitter moment a long procession of years to come that would belong to her absolutely. And she opened and spread her arms out to them in welcome.

There would be no one to live for her during those coming years: she would live for herself. There would be no powerful will bending hers in that blind persistence with which men and women believe they have a right to impose a private will upon a fellow-creature. A kind intention or a cruel intention made the act seem no less a crime as she looked upon it in that brief moment of illumination.

And yet she had loved him — sometimes. Often she had not. What did it matter! What could love, the unsolved mystery, count for in face of this possession of self-assertion which she suddenly recognized as the strongest impulse of her being! 15

"Free! Body and soul free!" she kept whispering.

Josephine was kneeling before the closed door with her lips to the keyhole, imploring for admission. "Louise, open the door! I beg; open the door — you will make yourself ill. What are you doing, Louise? For heaven's sake open the door."

"Go away. I am not making myself ill." No; she was drinking in a very elixir of life through that open window.

Her fancy was running riot along those days ahead of her. Spring days, and summer days, and all sorts of days that would be her own. She breathed a quick prayer that life might be long. It was only yesterday she had thought with a shudder that life might be long.

She arose at length and opened the door to her sister's importunities. There was a feverish triumph in her eyes, and she carried herself unwittingly like a goddess of Victory. She clasped her sister's waist, and together they descended the stairs. Richards stood waiting for them at the bottom. 20

Some one was opening the front door with a latchkey. It was Brently Mallard who entered, a little travel-stained, composedly carrying his gripsack and umbrella. He had been far from the scene of accident, and did not even know there had been one. He stood amazed at Josephine's piercing cry; at Richards's quick motion to screen him from the view of his wife.

But Richards was too late.

When the doctors came they said she had died of heart disease — of joy that kills.   *[1894]*

■ THINKING ABOUT THE TEXT

1. Is Louise Mallard really in love with her husband? Regardless of your answer, would she ever leave him? Is it possible to confuse love with duty?

2. Is it possible to assign blame for this tragedy? To Mr. Mallard? Mrs. Mallard? The culture?

3. Why did Chopin keep the story so brief? What would you like to know more about?

4. What specifically do you think Mrs. Mallard was thinking about in the room?

5. Do you think this situation was common during Chopin's time? Is it today?

■ MAKING COMPARISONS

1. Compare Mrs. Mallard and Calixta. Do you think Mrs. Mallard would have an extramarital affair?

2. Is Chopin sympathetic to Mrs. Mallard and Calixta? Is she judgmental?

3. Calixta and Bobinôt seem to be on more equal terms than Mr. and Mrs. Mallard. Do you think this is the case? Explain why this might be so.

KATE CHOPIN
Désirée's Baby

"Désirée's Baby" was written in 1892 and published in Bayou Folk *(1894). The story reflects her experience among the French Creoles in Louisiana.*

As the day was pleasant, Madame Valmondé drove over to L'Abri to see Désirée and the baby.

It made her laugh to think of Désirée with a baby. Why, it seemed but yesterday that Désirée was little more than a baby herself; when Monsieur in riding through the gateway of Valmondé had found her lying asleep in the shadow of the big stone pillar.

The little one awoke in his arms and began to cry for "Dada." That was as much as she could do or say. Some people thought she might have strayed there of her own accord, for she was of the toddling age. The prevailing belief was that she had been purposely left by a party of Texans, whose canvas-covered wagon, late in the day, had crossed the ferry that Coton Maïs kept, just below the plantation. In time Madame Valmondé abandoned every speculation but the one that Désirée had been sent to her by a beneficent Providence to be the child of her affection, seeing that she was without child of the flesh. For the girl grew to be beautiful and gentle, affectionate and sincere, — the idol of Valmondé.

It was no wonder, when she stood one day against the stone pillar in whose shadow she had lain asleep, eighteen years before, that Armand Aubigny riding by and seeing her there, had fallen in love with her. That was the way all the Aubignys fell in love, as if struck by a pistol shot. The wonder was that he had not loved her before; for he had known her since his father brought him home from Paris, a boy of eight, after his mother died there. The passion that awoke in him that day, when he saw her at the gate, swept along like an avalanche, or like a prairie fire, or like anything that drives headlong over all obstacles.

Monsieur Valmondé grew practical and wanted things well considered: 5
that is, the girl's obscure origin. Armand looked into her eyes and did not care. He was reminded that she was nameless. What did it matter about a name when he could give her one of the oldest and proudest in Louisiana? He ordered the *corbeille*° from Paris, and contained himself with what patience he could until it arrived; then they were married.

Madame Valmondé had not seen Désirée and the baby for four weeks. When she reached L'Abri she shuddered at the first sight of it, as she always did. It was a sad looking place, which for many years had not known the gentle presence of a mistress, old Monsieur Aubigny having married and buried his wife in France, and she having loved her own land too well ever to leave it. The roof came down steep and black like a cowl, reaching out beyond the wide galleries that encircled the yellow stuccoed house. Big, solemn oaks grew close to it, and their thick-leaved, far-reaching branches shadowed it like a pall. Young Aubigny's rule was a strict one, too, and under it his negroes had forgotten how to be gay, as they had been during the old master's easy-going and indulgent lifetime.

The young mother was recovering slowly, and lay full length, in her soft white muslins and laces, upon a couch. The baby was beside her, upon her arm, where he had fallen sleep, at her breast. The yellow nurse woman sat beside a window fanning herself.

Madame Valmondé bent her portly figure over Désirée and kissed her, holding her an instant tenderly in her arms. Then she turned to the child.

"This is not the baby!" she exclaimed, in startled tones. French was the language spoken at Valmondé in those days.

"I knew you would be astonished," laughed Désirée, "at the way he has 10
grown. The little *cochon de lait*!° Look at his legs, mamma, and his hands and fingernails, — real fingernails. Zandrine had to cut them this morning. Isn't it true, Zandrine?"

The woman bowed her turbaned head majestically, "Mais si, Madame."

"And the way he cries," went on Désirée, "is deafening. Armand heard him the other day as far away as La Blanche's cabin."

Madame Valmondé had never removed her eyes from the child. She lifted it and walked with it over to the window that was lightest. She scanned the baby

corbeille: Double bed.   *cochon de lait*: French for "suckling pig"; an endearment.

narrowly, then looked as searchingly at Zandrine, whose face was turned to gaze across the fields.

"Yes, the child has grown, has changed," said Madame Valmondé, slowly, as she replaced it beside its mother. "What does Armand say?"

Désirée's face became suffused with a glow that was happiness itself.   15

"Oh, Armand is the proudest father in the parish, I believe, chiefly because it is a boy, to bear his name; though he says not, — that he would have loved a girl as well. But I know it isn't true. I know he says that to please me. And mamma," she added, drawing Madame Valmondé's head down to her and speaking in a whisper, "he hasn't punished one of them — not one of them — since baby is born. Even Négrillon, who pretended to have burnt his leg that he might rest from work — he only laughed, and said Négrillon was a great scamp. Oh, mamma, I'm so happy; it frightens me."

What Désirée said was true. Marriage, and later the birth of his son had softened Armand Aubigny's imperious and exacting nature greatly. This was what made the gentle Désirée so happy, for she loved him desperately. When he frowned she trembled, but loved him. When he smiled, she asked no greater blessing of God. But Armand's dark, handsome face had not often been disfigured by frowns since the day he fell in love with her.

When the baby was about three months old, Désirée awoke one day to the conviction that there was something in the air menacing her peace. It was at first too subtle to grasp. It had only been a disquieting suggestion; an air of mystery among the blacks; unexpected visits from far-off neighbors who could hardly account for their coming. Then a strange, an awful change in her husband's manner, which she dared not ask him to explain. When he spoke to her, it was with averted eyes, from which the old love-light seemed to have gone out. He absented himself from home; and when there, avoided her presence and that of her child, without excuse. And the very spirit of Satan seemed suddenly to take hold of him in his dealings with the slaves. Désirée was miserable enough to die.

She sat in her room, one hot afternoon, in her *peignoir*, listlessly drawing through her fingers the strands of her long, silky brown hair that hung about her shoulders. The baby, half naked, lay asleep upon her own great mahogany bed, that was like a sumptuous throne, with its satin-lined half-canopy. One of La Blanche's little quadroon boys — half naked too — stood fanning the child slowly with a fan of peacock feathers. Désirée's eyes had been fixed absently and sadly upon the baby, while she was striving to penetrate the threatening mist that she felt closing about her. She looked from her child to the boy who stood beside him, and back again; over and over. "Ah!" It was a cry that she could not help; which she was not conscious of having uttered. The blood turned like ice in her veins, and a clammy moisture gathered upon her face.

She tried to speak to the little quadroon boy; but no sound would come, at   20 first. When he heard his name uttered, he looked up, and his mistress was pointing to the door. He laid aside the great, soft fan, and obediently stole away, over the polished floor, on his bare tiptoes.

She stayed motionless, with gaze riveted upon her child, and her face the picture of fright.

Presently her husband entered the room, and without noticing her, went to a table and began to search among some papers which covered it.

"Armand," she called to him, in a voice which must have stabbed him, if he was human. But he did not notice. "Armand," she said again. Then she rose and tottered towards him. "Armand," she panted once more, clutching his arm, "look at our child. What does it mean? tell me."

He coldly but gently loosened her fingers from about his arm and thrust the hand away from him. "Tell me what it means!" she cried despairingly.

"It means," he answered lightly, "that the child is not white; it means that   25
you are not white."

A quick conception of all that this accusation meant for her nerved her with unwonted courage to deny it. "It is a lie; it is not true, I am white! Look at my hair, it is brown; and my eyes are gray, Armand, you know they are gray. And my skin is fair," seizing his wrist. "Look at my hand; whiter than yours, Armand," she laughed hysterically.

"As white as La Blanche's," he returned cruelly; and went away leaving her alone with their child.

When she could hold a pen in her hand, she sent a despairing letter to Madame Valmondé.

"My mother, they tell me I am not white. Armand has told me I am not white. For God's sake tell them it is not true. You must know it is not true. I shall die. I must die. I cannot be so unhappy, and live."

The answer that came was as brief: 30

"My own Désirée: Come home to Valmondé; back to your mother who loves you. Come with your child."

When the letter reached Désirée she went with it to her husband's study, and laid it open upon the desk before which he sat. She was like a stone image: silent, white, motionless after she placed it there.

In silence he ran his cold eyes over the written words. He said nothing. "Shall I go, Armand?" she asked in tones sharp with agonized suspense.

"Yes, go."

"Do you want me to go?"   35

"Yes, I want you to go."

He thought Almighty God had dealt cruelly and unjustly with him; and felt, somehow, that he was paying Him back in kind when he stabbed thus into his wife's soul. Moreover he no longer loved her, because of the unconscious injury she had brought upon his home and his name.

She turned away like one stunned by a blow, and walked slowly towards the door, hoping he would call her back.

"Good-by, Armand," she moaned.

He did not answer her. That was his last blow at fate.   40

Désirée went in search of her child. Zandrine was pacing the sombre gallery with it. She took the little one from the nurse's arms with no word of explanation, and descending the steps, walked away, under the live-oak branches.

It was an October afternoon; the sun was just sinking. Out in the still fields the negroes were picking cotton.

Désirée had not changed the thin white garment nor the slippers which she wore. Her hair was uncovered and the sun's rays brought a golden gleam from its brown meshes. She did not take the broad, beaten road which led to the far-off plantation of Valmondé. She walked across a deserted field, where the stubble bruised her tender feet, so delicately shod, and tore her thin gown to shreds.

She disappeared among the reeds and willows that grew thick along the banks of the deep, sluggish bayou; and she did not come back again.

Some weeks later there was a curious scene enacted at L'Abri. In the center of   45
the smoothly swept back yard was a great bonfire. Armand Aubigny sat in the wide hallway that commanded a view of the spectacle; and it was he who dealt out to a half dozen negroes the material which kept this fire ablaze.

A graceful cradle of willow, with all its dainty furbishings, was laid upon the pyre, which had already been fed with the richness of a priceless *layette*. Then there were silk gowns, and velvet and satin ones added to these; laces, too, and embroideries; bonnets and gloves; for the *corbeille* had been of rare quality.

The last thing to go was a tiny bundle of letters; innocent little scribblings that Désirée had sent to him during the days of their espousal. There was the remnant of one back in the drawer from which he took them. But it was not Désirée's; it was part of an old letter from his mother to his father. He read it. She was thanking God for the blessing of her husband's love: —

"But, above all," she wrote, "night and day, I thank the good God for having so arranged our lives that our dear Armand will never know that his mother, who adores him, belongs to the race that is cursed with the brand of slavery."

[1892]

≣ **THINKING ABOUT THE TEXT**

1. Does Armand really love Désirée? Explain.
2. Armand seems to have fallen in love "at first sight." Is this possible? Can love conquer all, even racial bias? Is Chopin skeptical?
3. What would you have done if you were Désirée? What will Armand do now that he knows his own racial background?
4. Are we able to break free of our cultural heritage? What are the ways society tries to keep us in line? How do some people break free? Is there a danger in disregarding societal norms? Are there benefits?
5. Could this story happen this way today?

☰ MAKING COMPARISONS

1. Which female character — Calixta, Louise, or Désirée — possesses true love for her husband? Do the husbands love their wives more? In different ways?
2. Which one of these marriages seems the strongest? Why?
3. Compare Chopin's attitude toward marriage in these three stories. Does she support all aspects of marriage? Since she wrote over a century ago, would she be pleased with the present state of marriage (including divorce)?

☰ WRITING ABOUT ISSUES

1. Which ending seems more ethically questionable? Write a brief position paper suggesting that one of Chopin's endings should be changed (or remain the same) for moral reasons before junior high students read it.
2. Compare Alcée and Armand. Write a brief justification for or refutation of the behavior of one of them.
3. Do you think Louise Mallard should have admitted her feelings for her husband and left him? Would you? Why?
4. Chopin's works shocked American audiences. Research the ways sex, love, and relationships were dealt with in the 1890s in America. Write a brief explanation of why Chopin was ahead of her time.

■ Is This Love?: Stories

WILLIAM FAULKNER, "A Rose for Emily"

RAYMOND CARVER, "What We Talk About When We Talk About Love"

ZORA NEALE HURSTON, "Sweat"

Although stories about those who die for love are not unknown, those about killing for love are much rarer. Can "killing for love" still be considered love, or is it something quite different, something dark and perverse? Can the world be so stressful, so unjust and cruel that someone batters a beloved in frustration? What if that person is looking to someone else to relieve the disappointments of the world? Is that love or just physical need? What if someone harbors violent fantasies about a person loved years before? Or what if a wife sexually betrays her loving husband so she can get for him the material possessions he desires? And can love be so worn down by cruelty that it turns to hate? These are not simple questions. Trying to understand our emotional contradictions and paradoxes never is. The following three writers grapple with these issues in creative and sometimes painful ways: Faulkner's story focuses on the interaction of tradition, madness, and love; Carver's looks at the complexity of discussing love; and Hurston's story is a folktale that vividly demonstrates how love can justifiably turn to hate as cruelty gets its just rewards. See if you can decide if the characters in these stories are motivated by love or something more dangerous.

■ BEFORE YOU READ

Have you ever hurt somebody you love? Did you mean to? Has a loved one ever hurt you? Is it possible for an emotionally disturbed person to love?

WILLIAM FAULKNER

A Rose for Emily

William Faulkner (1897–1962) is recognized as a great American novelist and storyteller and a major figure of world literature, having won the Nobel Prize in 1949. This acclaim failed to impress the people of his hometown, however, where his genteel poverty and peculiar ways earned him the title "Count No Count." Born in New Albany, Mississippi, and raised in Oxford, the home of the University of Mississippi, Faulkner briefly attended college there after World War I but was reduced to working odd jobs while continuing his writing. His fiction is most often set in Yoknapatawpha County, a created world whose history, geography, and complex genealogies parallel those of the American South. His many novels and stories blend the grotesquely comic with the appallingly tragic. The Sound and the Fury (1929) is often considered his finest work. In later years, Faulkner's "odd jobs" included script-writing for Hollywood movies, speaking at universities, and writing magazine articles. "A Rose for Emily," first published in Forum, *presents a story of love as told by citizens of Yoknapatawpha County.*

1

When Miss Emily Grierson died, our whole town went to her funeral: the men through a sort of respectful affection for a fallen monument, the women mostly out of curiosity to see the inside of her house, which no one save an old man-servant — a combined gardener and cook — had seen in at least ten years.

It was a big, squarish frame house that had once been white, decorated with cupolas and spires and scrolled balconies in the heavily lightsome style of the seventies, set on what had once been our most select street. But garages and cotton gins had encroached and obliterated even the august names of that neighborhood; only Miss Emily's house was left, lifting its stubborn and co-quettish decay above the cotton wagons and the gasoline pumps — an eyesore among eyesores. And now Miss Emily had gone to join the representatives of those august names where they lay in the cedar-bemused cemetery among the ranked and anonymous graves of Union and Confederate soldiers who fell at the battle of Jefferson.

Alive, Miss Emily had been a tradition, a duty, and a care; a sort of heredi-tary obligation upon the town, dating from that day in 1894 when Colonel Sartoris, the mayor — he who fathered the edict that no Negro woman should appear on the streets without an apron — remitted her taxes, the dispensation dating from the death of her father on into perpetuity. Not that Miss Emily would have accepted charity. Colonel Sartoris invented an involved tale to the effect that Miss Emily's father had loaned money to the town, which the town, as a matter of business, preferred this way of repaying. Only a man of Colonel Sartoris's generation and thought could have invented it, and only a woman could have believed it.

When the next generation, with its more modern ideas, became mayors and aldermen, this arrangement created some little dissatisfaction. On the first of the year they mailed her a tax notice. February came, and there was no re-ply. They wrote her a formal letter, asking her to call at the sheriff's office at her convenience. A week later the mayor wrote her himself, offering to call or to send his car for her, and received in reply a note on paper of an archaic shape, in a thin, flowing calligraphy in faded ink, to the effect that she no longer went out at all. The tax notice was also enclosed, without comment.

They called a special meeting of the Board of Aldermen. A deputation waited upon her, knocked at the door through which no visitor had passed since she ceased giving china-painting lessons eight or ten years earlier. They were admitted by the old Negro into a dim hall from which a stairway mounted into still more shadow. It smelled of dust and disuse — a close, dank smell. The Negro led them into the parlor. It was furnished in heavy, leather-covered fur-niture. When the Negro opened the blinds of one window, they could see that

5

the leather was cracked; and when they sat down, a faint dust rose sluggishly about their thighs, spinning with slow motes in the single sun-ray. On a tarnished gilt easel before the fireplace stood a crayon portrait of Miss Emily's father.

They rose when she entered — a small, fat woman in black, with a thin gold chain descending to her waist and vanishing into her belt, leaning on an ebony cane with a tarnished gold head. Her skeleton was small and spare; perhaps that was why what would have been merely plumpness in another was obesity in her. She looked bloated, like a body long submerged in motionless water, and of that pallid hue. Her eyes, lost in the fatty ridges of her face, looked like two small pieces of coal pressed into a lump of dough as they moved from one face to another while the visitors stated their errand.

She did not ask them to sit. She just stood in the door and listened quietly until the spokesman came to a stumbling halt. Then they could hear the invisible watch ticking at the end of the gold chain.

Her voice was dry and cold. "I have no taxes in Jefferson. Colonel Sartoris explained it to me. Perhaps one of you can gain access to the city records and satisfy yourselves."

"But we have. We are the city authorities, Miss Emily. Didn't you get a notice from the sheriff, signed by him?"

"I received a paper, yes," Miss Emily said. "Perhaps he considers himself   10
the sheriff. . . . I have no taxes in Jefferson."

"But there is nothing on the books to show that, you see. We must go by the —"

"See Colonel Sartoris. I have no taxes in Jefferson."

"But, Miss Emily —"

"See Colonel Sartoris." (Colonel Sartoris had been dead almost ten years.) "I have no taxes in Jefferson. Tobe!" The Negro appeared. "Show these gentlemen out."

2

So she vanquished them, horse and foot, just as she had vanquished their fa-   15
thers thirty years before about the smell. That was two years after her father's death and a short time after her sweetheart — the one we believed would marry her — had deserted her. After her father's death she went out very little; after her sweetheart went away, people hardly saw her at all. A few of the ladies had the temerity to call, but were not received, and the only sign of life about the place was the Negro man — a young man then — going in and out with a market basket.

"Just as if a man — any man — could keep a kitchen properly," the ladies said; so they were not surprised when the smell developed. It was another link between the gross, teeming world and the high and mighty Griersons.

A neighbor, a woman, complained to the mayor, Judge Stevens, eighty years old.

"But what will you have me do about it, madam?" he said.

"Why, send her word to stop it," the woman said. "Isn't there a law?"

"I'm sure that won't be necessary," Judge Stevens said. "It's probably just a   20
snake or a rat that nigger of hers killed in the yard. I'll speak to him about it."

The next day he received two more complaints, one from a man who came
in diffident deprecation. "We really must do something about it, Judge. I'd be
the last one in the world to bother Miss Emily, but we've got to do something."
That night the Board of Aldermen met — three graybeards and one younger
man, a member of the rising generation.

"It's simple enough," he said. "Send her word to have her place cleaned up.
Give her a certain time to do it in, and if she don't. . . ."

"Dammit, sir," Judge Stevens said, "will you accuse a lady to her face of
smelling bad?"

So the next night, after midnight, four men crossed Miss Emily's lawn and
slunk about the house like burglars, sniffing along the base of the brickwork
and at the cellar openings while one of them performed a regular sowing motion with his hand out of a sack slung from his shoulder. They broke open the
cellar door and sprinkled lime there, and in all the outbuildings. As they re-
crossed the lawn, a window that had been dark was lighted and Miss Emily sat
in it, the light behind her, and her upright torso motionless as that of an idol.
They crept quietly across the lawn and into the shadow of the locusts that lined
the street. After a week or two the smell went away.

That was when people had begun to feel really sorry for her. People in our   25
town, remembering how old lady Wyatt, her great-aunt, had gone completely
crazy at last, believed that the Griersons held themselves a little too high for
what they really were. None of the young men were quite good enough for
Miss Emily and such. We had long thought of them as a tableau, Miss Emily a
slender figure in white in the background, her father a spraddled silhouette in
the foreground, his back to her and clutching a horsewhip, the two of them
framed by the backflung front door. So when she got to be thirty and was still
single, we were not pleased exactly, but vindicated; even with insanity in the
family she wouldn't have turned down all of her chances if they had really
materialized.

When her father died, it got about that the house was all that was left to
her; and in a way, people were glad. At last they could pity Miss Emily. Being left
alone, and a pauper, she had become humanized. Now she too would know the
old thrill and the old despair of a penny more or less.

The day after his death all the ladies prepared to call at the house and offer
condolence and aid, as is our custom. Miss Emily met them at the door, dressed
as usual and with no trace of grief on her face. She told them that her father
was not dead. She did that for three days, with the ministers calling on her, and
the doctors, trying to persuade her to let them dispose of the body. Just as they
were about to resort to law and force, she broke down, and they buried her father quickly.

We did not say she was crazy then. We believed she had to do that. We remembered all the young men her father had driven away, and we knew that

with nothing left, she would have to cling to that which had robbed her, as people will.

3

She was sick for a long time. When we saw her again, her hair was cut short, making her look like a girl, with a vague resemblance to those angels in colored church windows — sort of tragic and serene.

The town had just let the contracts for paving the sidewalks, and in the summer after her father's death they began the work. The construction company came with niggers and mules and machinery, and a foreman named Homer Barron, a Yankee — a big, dark, ready man, with a big voice and eyes lighter than his face. The little boys would follow in groups to hear him cuss the niggers, and the niggers singing in time to the rise and fall of picks. Pretty soon he knew everybody in town. Whenever you heard a lot of laughing anywhere about the square, Homer Barron would be in the center of the group. Presently, we began to see him and Miss Emily on Sunday afternoons driving in the yellow-wheeled buggy and the matched team of bays from the livery stable. 30

At first we were glad that Miss Emily would have an interest, because the ladies all said, "Of course a Grierson would not think seriously of a Northerner, a day laborer." But there were still others, older people, who said that even grief could not cause a real lady to forget *noblesse oblige* — without calling it *noblesse oblige*. They just said, "Poor Emily. Her kinsfolk should come to her." She had some kin in Alabama; but years ago her father had fallen out with them over the estate of old lady Wyatt, the crazy woman, and there was no communication between the two families. They had not even been represented at the funeral.

And as soon as the old people said, "Poor Emily," the whispering began. "Do you suppose it's really so?" they said to one another. "Of course it is. What else could. . . ." This behind their hands; rustling of craned silk and satin behind jalousies closed upon the sun of Sunday afternoon as the thin, swift clop-clop-clop of the matched team passed: "Poor Emily."

She carried her head high enough — even when we believed that she was fallen. It was as if she demanded more than ever the recognition of her dignity as the last Grierson; as if it had wanted that touch of earthiness to reaffirm her imperviousness. Like when she bought the rat poison, the arsenic. That was over a year after they had begun to say "Poor Emily," and while the two female cousins were visiting her.

"I want some poison," she said to the druggist. She was over thirty then, still a slight woman, though thinner than usual, with cold, haughty black eyes in a face the flesh of which was strained across the temples and about the eye-sockets as you imagine a lighthouse-keeper's face ought to look. "I want some poison," she said.

"Yes, Miss Emily. What kind? For rats and such? I'd recom——" 35

"I want the best you have. I don't care what kind."

The druggist named several. "They'll kill anything up to an elephant. But what you want is —"

"Arsenic," Miss Emily said. "Is that a good one?"

"Is . . . arsenic? Yes, ma'am. But what you want —"

"I want arsenic."   40

The druggist looked down at her. She looked back at him, erect, her face like a strained flag. "Why, of course," the druggist said. "If that's what you want. But the law requires you to tell what you are going to use it for."

Miss Emily just stared at him, her head tilted back in order to look him eye for eye, until he looked away and went and got the arsenic and wrapped it up. The Negro delivery boy brought her the package; the druggist didn't come back. When she opened the package at home there was written on the box, under the skull and bones: "For rats."

4

So the next day we all said, "She will kill herself"; and we said it would be the best thing. When she had first begun to be seen with Homer Barron, we had said, "She will marry him." Then we said, "She will persuade him yet," because Homer himself had remarked — he liked men, and it was known that he drank with the younger men in the Elks' Club — that he was not a marrying man. Later we said, "Poor Emily" behind the jalousies as they passed on Sunday afternoon in the glittering buggy, Miss Emily with her head high and Homer Barron with his hat cocked and a cigar in his teeth, reins and whip in a yellow glove.

Then some of the ladies began to say that it was a disgrace to the town and a bad example to the young people. The men did not want to interfere, but at last the ladies forced the Baptist minister — Miss Emily's people were Episcopal — to call upon her. He would never divulge what happened during that interview, but he refused to go back again. The next Sunday they again drove about the streets, and the following day the minister's wife wrote to Miss Emily's relations in Alabama.

So she had blood-kin under her roof again and we sat back to watch devel-   45
opments. At first nothing happened. Then we were sure that they were to be married. We learned that Miss Emily had been to the jeweler's and ordered a man's toilet set in silver, with the letters H.B. on each piece. Two days later we learned that she had bought a complete outfit of men's clothing, including a nightshirt, and we said, "They are married." We were really glad. We were glad because the two female cousins were even more Grierson than Miss Emily had ever been.

So we were not surprised when Homer Barron — the streets had been finished some time since — was gone. We were a little disappointed that there was not a public blowing-off, but we believed that he had gone on to prepare for Miss Emily's coming, or to give her a chance to get rid of the cousins. (By that time it was a cabal, and we were all Miss Emily's allies to help circumvent the cousins.) Sure enough, after another week they departed. And, as we had expected all along, within three days Homer Barron was back in town. A neighbor saw the Negro man admit him at the kitchen door at dusk one evening.

And that was the last we saw of Homer Barron. And of Miss Emily for some time. The Negro man went in and out with the market basket, but the front door remained closed. Now and then we would see her at the window for a moment, as the men did that night when they sprinkled the lime, but for almost six months she did not appear on the streets. Then we knew that this was to be expected too; as if that quality of her father which had thwarted her woman's life so many times had been too virulent and too furious to die.

When we next saw Miss Emily, she had grown fat and her hair was turning gray. During the next few years it grew grayer and grayer until it attained an even pepper-and-salt iron-gray, when it ceased turning. Up to the day of her death at seventy-four it was still that vigorous iron-gray, like the hair of an active man.

From that time on her front door remained closed, save during a period of six or seven years, when she was about forty, during which she gave lessons in china-painting. She fitted up a studio in one of the downstairs rooms, where the daughters and granddaughters of Colonel Sartoris's contemporaries were sent to her with the same regularity and in the same spirit that they were sent to church on Sundays with a twenty-five-cent piece for the collection plate. Meanwhile her taxes had been remitted.

Then the newer generation became the backbone and the spirit of the 50 town, and the painting pupils grew up and fell away and did not send their children to her with boxes of color and tedious brushes and pictures cut from the ladies' magazines. The front door closed upon the last one and remained closed for good. When the town got free postal delivery, Miss Emily alone refused to let them fasten the metal numbers above her door and attach a mailbox to it. She would not listen to them.

Daily, monthly, yearly we watched the Negro grow grayer and more stooped, going in and out with the market basket. Each December we sent her a tax notice, which would be returned by the post office a week later, unclaimed. Now and then we would see her in one of the downstairs windows — she had evidently shut up the top floor of the house — like the carven torso of an idol in a niche, looking or not looking at us, we could never tell which. Thus she passed from generation to generation — dear, inescapable, impervious, tranquil, and perverse.

And so she died. Fell ill in the house filled with dust and shadows, with only a doddering Negro man to wait on her. We did not even know she was sick; we had long since given up trying to get any information from the Negro. He talked to no one, probably not even to her, for his voice had grown harsh and rusty, as if from disuse.

She died in one of the downstairs rooms, in a heavy walnut bed with a curtain, her gray head propped on a pillow yellow and moldy with age and lack of sunlight.

5

The Negro met the first of the ladies at the front door and let them in, with their hushed, sibilant voices and their quick, curious glances, and then he disappeared. He walked right through the house and out the back and was not seen again.

The two female cousins came at once. They held the funeral on the second   55
day, with the town coming to look at Miss Emily beneath a mass of bought flowers, with the crayon face of her father musing profoundly above the bier and the ladies sibilant and macabre; and the very old men — some in their brushed Confederate uniforms — on the porch and the lawn, talking of Miss Emily as if she had been a contemporary of theirs, believing that they had danced with her and courted her perhaps, confusing time with its mathematical progression, as the old do, to whom all the past is not a diminishing road but, instead, a huge meadow which no winter ever quite touches, divided from them now by the narrow bottleneck of the most recent decade of years.

Already we knew that there was one room in that region above stairs which no one had seen in forty years, and which would have to be forced. They waited until Miss Emily was decently in the ground before they opened it.

The violence of breaking down the door seemed to fill this room with pervading dust. A thin, acrid pall as of the tomb seemed to lie everywhere upon this room decked and furnished as for a bridal: upon the valance curtains of faded rose color, upon the rose-shaded lights, upon the dressing table, upon the delicate array of crystal and the man's toilet things backed with tarnished silver, silver so tarnished that the monogram was obscured. Among them lay a collar and tie, as if they had just been removed, which, lifted, left upon the surface a pale crescent in the dust. Upon a chair hung the suit, carefully folded; beneath it the two mute shoes and the discarded socks.

The man himself lay in the bed.

For a long while we just stood there, looking down at the profound and fleshless grin. The body had apparently once lain in the attitude of an embrace, but now the long sleep that outlasts love, that conquers even the grimace of love, had cuckolded him. What was left of him, rotted beneath what was left of the nightshirt, had become inextricable from the bed in which he lay; and upon him and upon the pillow beside him lay that even coating of the patient and biding dust.

Then we noticed that in the second pillow was the indentation of a head.   60
One of us lifted something from it, and leaning forward, that faint and invisible dust dry and acrid in the nostrils, we saw a long strand of iron-gray hair.

[1931]

■ THINKING ABOUT THE TEXT

1. Do you think some people can love another so much that they simply cannot bear for that person to leave? Is it possible Emily was like this?

2. Can a disturbed person be in love? Does love have to be healthy? Is sanity culturally defined? Can you imagine a society that would accept Emily's behavior?

3. Who do you think the narrator of "A Rose for Emily" is? Why would Faulkner tell the story from this perspective? Why not from Emily's?

4. Look at the last sentence of paragraph 51. What do you make of the five adjectives used? Are they understandable in terms of the story?

5. Some critics think this story is not a love story but a political allegory about the South. Does this make sense to you? What else does the story suggest to you?

6. Comment on the various kinds of repression — social and psychological — that occur throughout the story. What connections can you draw, and what generalizations might you make about them?

7. Reread "A Rose for Emily." How does your knowledge of the ending of the story affect your second reading? What details of the narrative tend to stand out the second time around?

RAYMOND CARVER
What We Talk About
When We Talk About Love

Raymond Carver (1938–1988) re-creates in what has been called a "stripped-down and muscular prose style" the minutiae of everyday life in mid-twentieth-century America. Brought up in the Pacific Northwest in a working-class family, Carver began writing in high school and married early. While both he and his young wife worked at low-paying jobs, Carver took college courses and struggled to find time to write. In 1958, he studied fiction writing with John Gardner and graduated in 1963 from what is now the California State University at Humboldt. He received national recognition in 1967 when a story was included in the Best American Short Stories *annual anthology. Although Carver was a National Endowment for the Arts fellow in poetry in 1971, fiction remained his primary genre, earning him numerous awards and fellowships, including O. Henry awards in 1974, 1975, and 1980. Despite his success as a writer, alcoholism plagued Carver for most of his life until with the help of Alcoholics Anonymous he stopped drinking in 1982, soon after his divorce. "What We Talk About When We Talk About Love" was the title story in his 1981 collection.*

My friend Mel McGinnis was talking. Mel McGinnis is a cardiologist, and sometimes that gives him the right.

The four of us were sitting around his kitchen table drinking gin. Sunlight filled the kitchen from the big window behind the sink. There were Mel and me and his second wife, Teresa — Terri, we called her — and my wife, Laura. We lived in Albuquerque then. But we were all from somewhere else.

There was an ice bucket on the table. The gin and the tonic water kept going around, and we somehow got on the subject of love. Mel thought real love was nothing less than spiritual love. He said he'd spent five years in a seminary before quitting to go to medical school. He said he still looked back on those years in the seminary as the most important years in his life.

Terri said the man she lived with before she lived with Mel loved her so much he tried to kill her. Then Terri said, "He beat me up one night. He dragged me around the living room by my ankles. He kept saying, 'I love you, I love you, you bitch.' He went on dragging me around the living room. My head kept knocking on things." Terri looked around the table. "What do you do with love like that?"

She was a bone-thin woman with a pretty face, dark eyes, and brown hair   5
that hung down her back. She liked necklaces made of turquoise, and long pendant earrings.

"My God, don't be silly. That's not love, and you know it," Mel said. "I don't know what you'd call it, but I sure know you wouldn't call it love."

"Say what you want to, but I know it was," Terri said. "It may sound crazy to you, but it's true just the same. People are different, Mel. Sure, sometimes he may have acted crazy. Okay. But he loved me. In his own way maybe, but he loved me. There was love there, Mel. Don't say there wasn't."

Mel let out his breath. He held his glass and turned to Laura and me. "The man threatened to kill me," Mel said. He finished his drink and reached for the gin bottle. "Terri's a romantic. Terri's of the kick-me-so-I'll-know-you-love-me school. Terri, hon, don't look that way." Mel reached across the table and touched Terri's cheek with his fingers. He grinned at her.

"Now he wants to make up," Terri said.

"Make up what?" Mel said. "What is there to make up? I know what I know.   10
That's all."

"How'd we get started on this subject, anyway?" Terri said. She raised her glass and drank from it. "Mel always has love on his mind," she said. "Don't you, honey?" She smiled, and I thought that was the last of it.

"I just wouldn't call Ed's behavior love. That's all I'm saying, honey," Mel said. "What about you guys?" Mel said to Laura and me. "Does that sound like love to you?"

"I'm the wrong person to ask," I said. "I didn't even know the man. I've only heard his name mentioned in passing. I wouldn't know. You'd have to know the particulars. But I think what you're saying is that love is an absolute."

Mel said, "The kind of love I'm talking about is. The kind of love I'm talking about, you don't try to kill people."

Laura said, "I don't know anything about Ed, or anything about the situa-   15
tion. But who can judge anyone else's situation?"

I touched the back of Laura's hand. She gave me a quick smile. I picked up Laura's hand. It was warm, the nails polished, perfectly manicured. I encircled the broad wrist with my fingers, and I held her.

"When I left, he drank rat poison," Terri said. She clasped her arms with her hands. "They took him to the hospital in Santa Fe. That's where we lived then, about ten miles out. They saved his life. But his gums went crazy from it. I mean they pulled away from his teeth. After that, his teeth stood out like fangs. My God," Terri said. She waited a minute, then let go of her arms and picked up her glass.

"What people won't do!" Laura said.

"He's out of the action now," Mel said. "He's dead."

Mel handed me the saucer of limes. I took a section, squeezed it over my drink, and stirred the ice cubes with my finger.   20

"It gets worse," Terri said. "He shot himself in the mouth. But he bungled that too. Poor Ed," she said. Terri shook her head.

"Poor Ed nothing," Mel said. "He was dangerous."

Mel was forty-five years old. He was tall and rangy with curly soft hair. His face and arms were brown from the tennis he played. When he was sober, his gestures, all his movements, were precise, very careful.

"He did love me though, Mel. Grant me that," Terri said. "That's all I'm asking. He didn't love me the way you love me. I'm not saying that. But he loved me. You can grant me that, can't you?"

"What do you mean, he bungled it?" I said.   25

Laura leaned forward with her glass. She put her elbows on the table and held her glass in both hands. She glanced from Mel to Terri and waited with a look of bewilderment on her open face, as if amazed that such things happened to people you were friendly with.

"How'd he bungle it when he killed himself?" I said.

"I'll tell you what happened," Mel said. "He took this twenty-two pistol he'd bought to threaten Terri and me with. Oh, I'm serious, the man was always threatening. You should have seen the way we lived in those days. Like fugitives. I even bought a gun myself. Can you believe it? A guy like me? But I did. I bought one for self-defense and carried it in the glove compartment. Sometimes I'd have to leave the apartment in the middle of the night. To go to the hospital, you know? Terri and I weren't married then, and my first wife had the house and kids, the dog, everything, and Terri and I were living in this apartment here. Sometimes, as I say, I'd get a call in the middle of the night and have to go in to the hospital at two or three in the morning. It'd be dark out there in the parking lot, and I'd break into a sweat before I could even get to my car. I never knew if he was going to come up out of the shrubbery or from behind a car and start shooting. I mean, the man was crazy. He was capable of wiring a bomb, anything. He used to call my service at all hours and say he needed to talk to the doctor, and when I'd return the call, he'd say, 'Son of a bitch, your days are numbered.' Little things like that. It was scary, I'm telling you."

"I still feel sorry for him," Terri said.

"It sounds like a nightmare," Laura said. "But what exactly happened after he shot himself?"   30

Laura is a legal secretary. We'd met in a professional capacity. Before we knew it, it was a courtship. She's thirty-five, three years younger than I am. In addition to being in love, we like each other and enjoy one another's company. She's easy to be with.

"What happened?" Laura said.

Mel said, "He shot himself in the mouth in his room. Someone heard the shot and told the manager. They came in with a passkey, saw what had happened, and called an ambulance. I happened to be there when they brought him in, alive but past recall. The man lived for three days. His head swelled up to twice the size of a normal head. I'd never seen anything like it, and I hope I never do again. Terri wanted to go in and sit with him when she found out about it. We had a fight over it. I didn't think she should see him like that. I didn't think she should see him, and I still don't."

"Who won the fight?" Laura said.

"I was in the room with him when he died," Terri said. "He never came up   35
out of it. But I sat with him. He didn't have anyone else."

"He was dangerous," Mel said. "If you call that love, you can have it."

"It was love," Terri said. "Sure, it's abnormal in most people's eyes. But he was willing to die for it. He did die for it."

"I sure as hell wouldn't call it love," Mel said. "I mean, no one knows what he did it for. I've seen a lot of suicides, and I couldn't say anyone ever knew what they did it for."

Mel put his hands behind his neck and tilted his chair back. "I'm not interested in that kind of love," he said. "If that's love, you can have it."

Terri said, "We were afraid. Mel even made a will out and wrote to his   40
brother in California who used to be a Green Beret. Mel told him who to look for if something happened to him."

Terri drank from her glass. She said, "But Mel's right — we lived like fugitives. We were afraid. Mel was, weren't you, honey? I even called the police at one point, but they were no help. They said they couldn't do anything until Ed actually did something. Isn't that a laugh?" Terri said.

She poured the last of the gin into her glass and waggled the bottle. Mel got up from the table and went to the cupboard. He took down another bottle.

"Well, Nick and I know what love is," Laura said. "For us, I mean," Laura said. She bumped my knee with her knee. "You're supposed to say something now," Laura said, and turned her smile on me.

For an answer, I took Laura's hand and raised it to my lips. I made a big production out of kissing her hand. Everyone was amused.

"We're lucky," I said.   45

"You guys," Terri said. "Stop that now. You're making me sick. You're still on the honeymoon, for God's sake. You're still gaga, for crying out loud. Just wait. How long have you been together now? How long has it been? A year? Longer than a year?"

"Going on a year and a half," Laura said, flushed and smiling.

"Oh, now," Terri said. "Wait awhile."

She held her drink and gazed at Laura.

"I'm only kidding," Terri said. 50
Mel opened the gin and went around the table with the bottle.
"Here, you guys," he said. "Let's have a toast. I want to propose a toast. A toast to love. To true love," Mel said.
We touched glasses.
"To love," we said.

Outside in the backyard, one of the dogs began to bark. The leaves of the aspen 55
that leaned past the window ticked against the glass. The afternoon sun was like a presence in this room, the spacious light of ease and generosity. We could have been anywhere, somewhere enchanted. We raised our glasses again and grinned at each other like children who had agreed on something forbidden.

"I'll tell you what real love is," Mel said. "I mean, I'll give you a good example. And then you can draw your own conclusions." He poured more gin into his glass. He added an ice cube and a sliver of lime. We waited and sipped our drinks. Laura and I touched knees again. I put a hand on her warm thigh and left it there.

"What do any of us really know about love?" Mel said. "It seems to me we're just beginners at love. We say we love each other and we do, I don't doubt it. I love Terri and Terri loves me, and you guys love each other too. You know the kind of love I'm talking about now. Physical love, that impulse that drives you to someone special, as well as love of the other person's being, his or her essence, as it were. Carnal love and, well, call it sentimental love, the day-to-day caring about the other person. But sometimes I have a hard time accounting for the fact that I must have loved my first wife too. But I did, I know I did. So I suppose I am like Terri in that regard. Terri and Ed." He thought about it and then he went on. "There was a time when I thought I loved my first wife more than life itself. But now I hate her guts. I do. How do you explain that? What happened to that love? What happened to it, is what I'd like to know. I wish someone could tell me. Then there's Ed. Okay, we're back to Ed. He loves Terri so much he tries to kill her and he winds up killing himself." Mel stopped talking and swallowed from his glass. "You guys have been together eighteen months and you love each other. It shows all over you. You glow with it. But you both loved other people before you met each other. You've both been married before, just like us. And you probably loved other people before that too, even. Terri and I have been together five years, been married for four. And the terrible thing, the terrible thing is, but the good thing too, the saving grace, you might say, is that if something happened to one of us — excuse me for saying this — but if something happened to one of us tomorrow I think the other one, the other person, would grieve for a while, you know, but then the surviving party would go out and love again, have someone else soon enough. All this, all of this love we're talking about, it would just be a memory. Maybe not even a memory. Am I wrong? Am I way off base? Because I want you to set me straight if you think I'm wrong. I want to know. I mean, I don't know anything, and I'm the first one to admit it."

"Mel, for God's sake," Terri said. She reached out and took hold of his wrist. "Are you getting drunk? Honey? Are you drunk?"

"Honey, I'm just talking," Mel said. "All right? I don't have to be drunk to say what I think. I mean, we're all just talking, right?" Mel said. He fixed his eyes on her.

"Sweetie, I'm not criticizing," Terri said.   60

She picked up her glass.

"I'm not on call today," Mel said. "Let me remind you of that. I am not on call," he said.

"Mel, we love you," Laura said.

Mel looked at Laura. He looked at her as if he could not place her, as if she was not the woman she was.

"Love you too, Laura," Mel said. "And you, Nick, love you too. You know   65 something?" Mel said. "You guys are our pals," Mel said.

He picked up his glass.

Mel said, "I was going to tell you about something. I mean, I was going to prove a point. You see, this happened a few months ago, but it's still going on right now, and it ought to make us feel ashamed when we talk like we know what we're talking about when we talk about love."

"Come on now," Terri said. "Don't talk like you're drunk if you're not drunk."

"Just shut up for once in your life," Mel said very quietly. "Will you do me a favor and do that for a minute? So as I was saying, there's this old couple who had this car wreck out on the interstate. A kid hit them and they were all torn to shit and nobody was giving them much chance to pull through."

Terri looked at us and then back at Mel. She seemed anxious, or maybe   70 that's too strong a word.

Mel was handing the bottle around the table.

"I was on call that night," Mel said. "It was May or maybe it was June. Terri and I had just sat down to dinner when the hospital called. There'd been this thing out on the interstate. Drunk kid, teenager, plowed his dad's pickup into this camper with this old couple in it. They were up in their midseventies, that couple. The kid—eighteen, nineteen, something—he was DOA. Taken the steering wheel through his sternum. The old couple, they were alive, you understand. I mean, just barely. But they had everything. Multiple fractures, internal injuries, hemorrhaging, contusions, lacerations, the works, and they each of them had themselves concussions. They were in a bad way, believe me. And, of course, their age was two strikes against them. I'd say she was worse off than he was. Ruptured spleen along with everything else. Both kneecaps broken. But they'd been wearing their seatbelts and, God knows, that's what saved them for the time being."

"Folks, this is an advertisement for the National Safety Council," Terri said. "This is your spokesman, Dr. Melvin R. McGinnis, talking." Terri laughed. "Mel," she said, "sometimes you're just too much. But I love you, hon," she said.

"Honey, I love you," Mel said.

He leaned across the table. Terri met him halfway. They kissed.   75
"Terri's right," Mel said as he settled himself again. "Get those seatbelts on. But seriously, they were in some shape, those oldsters. By the time I got down there, the kid was dead, as I said. He was off in a corner, laid out on a gurney. I took one look at the old couple and told the ER nurse to get me a neurologist and an orthopedic man and a couple of surgeons down there right away."

He drank from his glass. "I'll try to keep this short," he said. "So we took the two of them up to the OR and worked like fuck on them most of the night. They had these incredible reserves, those two. You see that once in a while. So we did everything that could be done, and toward morning we're giving them a fifty-fifty chance, maybe less than that for her. So here they are, still alive the next morning. So, okay, we move them into the ICU, which is where they both kept plugging away at it for two weeks, hitting it better and better on all the scopes. So we transfer them out to their own room."

Mel stopped talking. "Here," he said, "let's drink this cheapo gin the hell up. Then we're going to dinner, right? Terri and I know a new place. That's where we'll go, to this new place we know about. But we're not going until we finish up this cut-rate, lousy gin."

Terri said, "We haven't actually eaten there yet. But it looks good. From the outside, you know."

"I like food," Mel said. "If I had it to do all over again, I'd be a chef, you   80
know? Right, Terri?" Mel said.

He laughed. He fingered the ice in his glass.

"Terri knows," he said. "Terri can tell you. But let me say this. If I could come back again in a different life, a different time and all, you know what? I'd like to come back as a knight. You were pretty safe wearing all that armor. It was all right being a knight until gunpowder and muskets and pistols came along."

"Mel would like to ride a horse and carry a lance," Terri said.

"Carry a woman's scarf with you everywhere," Laura said.

"Or just a woman," Mel said.   85

"Shame on you," Laura said.

Terri said, "Suppose you came back as a serf. The serfs didn't have it so good in those days," Terri said.

"The serfs never had it good," Mel said. "But I guess even the knights were vessels to someone. Isn't that the way it worked? But then everyone is always a vessel to someone. Isn't that right? Terri? But what I liked about knights, besides their ladies, was that they had that suit of armor, you know, and they couldn't get hurt very easy. No cars in those days, you know? No drunk teenagers to tear into your ass."

"Vassals," Terri said.

"What?" Mel said.   90

"Vassals," Terri said. "They were called vassals, not vessels."

"Vassals, vessels," Mel said, "what the fuck's the difference? You knew what I meant anyway. All right," Mel said. "So I'm not educated. I learned my stuff. I'm a heart surgeon, sure, but I'm just a mechanic. I go in and I fuck around and I fix things. Shit," Mel said.

"Modesty doesn't become you," Terri said.

"He's just a humble sawbones," I said. "But sometimes they suffocated in all that armor, Mel. They'd even have heart attacks if it got too hot and they were too tired and worn out. I read somewhere that they'd fall off their horses and not be able to get up because they were too tired to stand with all that armor on them. They got trampled by their own horses sometimes."

"That's terrible," Mel said. "That's a terrible thing, Nicky. I guess they'd   95
just lay there and wait until somebody came along and made a shish kebab out of them."

"Some other vessel," Terri said.

"That's right," Mel said. "Some vassal would come along and spear the bastard in the name of love. Or whatever the fuck it was they fought over in those days."

"Same things we fight over these days," Terri said.

Laura said, "Nothing's changed."

The color was still high in Laura's cheeks. Her eyes were bright. She   100
brought her glass to her lips.

Mel poured himself another drink. He looked at the label closely as if studying a long row of numbers. Then he slowly put the bottle down on the table and slowly reached for the tonic water.

"What about the old couple?" Laura said. "You didn't finish that story you started."

Laura was having a hard time lighting her cigarette. Her matches kept going out.

The sunshine inside the room was different now, changing, getting thinner. But the leaves outside the window were still shimmering, and I stared at the pattern they made on the panes and on the Formica counter. They weren't the same patterns, of course.

"What about the old couple?" I said.   105

"Older but wiser," Terri said.

Mel stared at her.

Terri said, "Go on with your story, hon. I was only kidding. Then what happened?"

"Terri, sometimes," Mel said.

"Please, Mel," Terri said. "Don't always be so serious, sweetie. Can't you   110
take a joke?"

"Where's the joke?" Mel said.

He held his glass and gazed steadily at his wife.

"What happened?" Laura said.

Mel fastened his eyes on Laura. He said, "Laura, if I didn't have Terri and if I didn't love her so much, and if Nick wasn't my best friend, I'd fall in love with you, I'd carry you off, honey," he said.

"Tell your story," Terri said. "Then we'll go to that new place, okay?"   115

"Okay," Mel said. "Where was I?" he said. He stared at the table and then he began again.

"I dropped in to see each of them every day, sometimes twice a day if I was up doing other calls anyway. Casts and bandages, head to foot, the both of them. You know, you've seen it in the movies. That's just the way they looked, just like in the movies. Little eye-holes and nose-holes and mouth-holes. And she had to have her legs slung up on top of it. Well, the husband was very depressed for the longest while. Even after he found out that his wife was going to pull through, he was still very depressed. Not about the accident, though. I mean, the accident was one thing, but it wasn't everything. I'd get up to his mouth-hole, you know, and he'd say no, it wasn't the accident exactly but it was because he couldn't see her through his eye-holes. He said that was what was making him feel so bad. Can you imagine? I'm telling you, the man's heart was breaking because he couldn't turn his goddamn head and *see* his goddamn wife."

Mel looked around the table and shook his head at what he was going to say.

"I mean, it was killing the old fart just because he couldn't *look* at the fucking woman."

We all looked at Mel.   120

"Do you see what I'm saying?" he said.

Maybe we were a little drunk by then. I know it was hard keeping things in focus. The light was draining out of the room, going back through the window where it had come from. Yet nobody made a move to get up from the table to turn on the overhead light.

"Listen," Mel said. "Let's finish this fucking gin. There's about enough left here for one shooter all around. Then let's go eat. Let's go to the new place."

"He's depressed," Terri said. "Mel, why don't you take a pill?"

Mel shook his head. "I've taken everything there is."   125

"We all need a pill now and then," I said.

"Some people are born needing them," Terri said.

She was using her finger to rub at something on the table. Then she stopped rubbing.

"I think I want to call my kids," Mel said. "Is that all right with everybody? I'll call my kids," he said.

Terri said, "What if Marjorie answers the phone? You guys, you've heard   130
us on the subject of Marjorie? Honey, you know you don't want to talk to Marjorie. It'll make you feel even worse."

"I don't want to talk to Marjorie," Mel said. "But I want to talk to my kids."

"There isn't a day goes by that Mel doesn't say he wishes she'd get married again. Or else die," Terri said. "For one thing," Terri said, "she's bankrupting us. Mel says it's just to spite him that she won't get married again. She has a boy-friend who lives with her and the kids, so Mel is supporting the boyfriend too."

"She's allergic to bees," Mel said. "If I'm not praying she'll get married again, I'm praying she'll get herself stung to death by a swarm of fucking bees."

"Shame on you," Laura said.

"Bzzzzzzz," Mel said, turning his fingers into bees and buzzing them at   135
Terri's throat. Then he let his hands drop all the way to his sides.

"She's vicious," Mel said. "Sometimes I think I'll go up there dressed like a
beekeeper. You know, that hat that's like a helmet with the plate that comes
down over your face, the big gloves, and the padded coat? I'll knock on the door
and let loose a hive of bees in the house. But first I'd make sure the kids were
out, of course."

He crossed one leg over the other. It seemed to take him a lot of time to do
it. Then he put both feet on the floor and leaned forward, elbows on the table,
his chin cupped in his hands.

"Maybe I won't call the kids, after all. Maybe it isn't such a hot idea. Maybe
we'll just go eat. How does that sound?"

"Sounds fine to me," I said. "Eat or not eat. Or keep drinking. I could head
right on out into the sunset."

"What does that mean, honey?" Laura said.   140

"It just means what I said," I said. "It means I could just keep going. That's
all it means."

"I could eat something myself," Laura said. "I don't think I've ever been so
hungry in my life. Is there something to nibble on?"

"I'll put out some cheese and crackers," Terri said.

But Terri just sat there. She did not get up to get anything.

Mel turned his glass over. He spilled it out on the table.   145

"Gin's gone," Mel said.

Terri said, "Now what?"

I could hear my heart beating. I could hear everyone's heart. I could hear
the human noise we sat there making, not one of us moving, not even when
the room went dark.   *[1981]*

■ **THINKING ABOUT THE TEXT**

1. The argument between the couples seems to be about the nature of
   love. Which character's ideas make the most sense to you? What kinds
   of love are discussed? Are these demonstrated in the story? Do you
   think true love is an illusion?

2. Do you see similarities between Mel and Ed? Do any of the characters
   seem aware of any similarities? Is Mel a perceptive person? What are his
   problems? Is he in love with Terri? How do you interpret his fantasy with
   the bees and Marjorie?

3. Why does Mel seem so interested in knights? Is this symbolic? Are there
   other symbols here (light? dark? cardiologist?)? What do you make of
   the last paragraph? Why does it end with beating hearts and silence?

4. Is this story optimistic or pessimistic about true love? Is the old couple
   a positive or a negative example of true love? What about Nick and
   Laura? What about Ed? Could you argue that he was in love?

5. What does the title mean? Be specific, especially about the first word. Do you tell stories about love? Have you heard some recently? What lessons or information do they give about love?

≡ MAKING COMPARISONS

1. Compare Ed to Emily Grierson in Faulkner's story. What similarities do you see in their behavior?
2. Have these stories complicated your idea of love?
3. Do you see Terri and Homer Barron as victims of love? Did they do something wrong?

ZORA NEALE HURSTON
Sweat

Zora Neale Hurston (1891–1951) was born into a large family in a tiny town in Alabama. Her father, a sharecropper and a Baptist preacher, and her mother, a former schoolteacher, moved the family to Florida to the first incorporated black municipality in the country. When her mother died in 1904, Hurston was sent to care for her brother's children, but she soon grew restless and joined a traveling circus theater at sixteen and then did domestic work. She attended Howard University for a while and began to publish stories. In 1925, she moved to New York, where she became involved with the writers of the Harlem Renaissance and enrolled at Barnard College as the school's only black student. She studied with the noted anthropologist Franz Boas and received her degree in 1928. During the 1930s and 1940s, she published four novels and an autobiography. Although Hurston died a penniless recluse in Florida, her most famous novel, Their Eyes Were Watching God *(1937), about love and identity, is now considered a classic American text. Rediscovered by writers like Alice Walker, Hurston is now thought of as an important American writer.*

I

It was eleven o'clock of a Spring night in Florida. It was Sunday. Any other night, Delia Jones would have been in bed for two hours by this time. But she was a washwoman, and Monday morning meant a great deal to her. So she collected the soiled clothes on Saturday when she returned the clean things. Sunday night after church, she sorted and put the white things to soak. It saved her almost a half-day's start. A great hamper in the bedroom held the clothes that she brought home. It was so much neater than a number of bundles lying around.

She squatted on the kitchen floor beside the great pile of clothes, sorting them into small heaps according to color, and humming a song in a mournful key, but wondering through it all where Sykes, her husband, had gone with her horse and buckboard.

Just then something long, round, limp, and black fell upon her shoulders and slithered to the floor beside her. A great terror took hold of her. It softened her knees and dried her mouth so that it was a full minute before she could cry out or move. Then she saw that it was the big bull whip her husband liked to carry when he drove.

She lifted her eyes to the door and saw him standing there bent over with laughter at her fright. She screamed at him.

"Sykes, what you throw dat whip on me like dat? You know it would skeer me — looks just like a snake, an' you knows how skeered Ah is of snakes."   5

"Course Ah knowed it! That's how come Ah done it." He slapped his leg with his hand and almost rolled on the ground in his mirth. "If you such a big fool dat you got to have a fit over a earth worm or a string, Ah don't keer how bad Ah skeer you."

"You ain't got no business doing it. Gawd knows it's a sin. Some day Ah'm gointuh drop dead from some of yo' foolishness. 'Nother thing, where you been wid mah rig? Ah feeds dat pony. He ain't fuh you to be drivin' wid no bull whip."

"You sho' is one aggravatin' nigger woman!" he declared and stepped into the room. She resumed her work and did not answer him at once. "Ah done tole you time and again to keep them white folks' clothes outa dis house."

He picked up the whip and glared at her. Delia went on with her work. She went out into the yard and returned with a galvanized tub and set it on the wash-bench. She saw that Sykes had kicked all of the clothes together again, and now stood in her way truculently, his whole manner hoping, *praying*, for an argument. But she walked calmly around him and commenced to re-sort the things.

"Next time, Ah'm gointer kick 'em outdoors," he threatened as he struck a   10
match along the leg of his corduroy breeches.

Delia never looked up from her work, and her thin, stooped shoulders sagged further.

"Ah ain't for no fuss t'night, Sykes. Ah just come from taking sacrament at the church house."

He snorted scornfully. "Yeah, you just come from de church house on a Sunday night, but heah you is gone to work on them clothes. You ain't nothing but a hypocrite. One of them amen-corner Christians — sing, whoop, and shout, then come home and wash white folks' clothes on the Sabbath."

He stepped roughly upon the whitest pile of things, kicking them helter-skelter as he crossed the room. His wife gave a little scream of dismay, and quickly gathered them together again.

"Sykes, you quit grindin' dirt into these clothes! How can Ah git through   15
by Sat'day if Ah don't start on Sunday?"

"Ah don't keer if you never git through. Anyhow, Ah done promised Gawd and a couple of other men, Ah ain't gointer have it in mah house. Don't gimme no lip neither, else Ah'll throw 'em out and put mah fist up side yo' head to boot."

Delia's habitual meekness seemed to slip from her shoulders like a blown scarf. She was on her feet; her poor little body, her bare knuckly hands bravely defying the strapping hulk before her.

"Looka heah, Sykes, you done gone too fur. Ah been married to you fur fifteen years, and Ah been takin' in washin' fur fifteen years. Sweat, sweat, sweat! Work and sweat, cry and sweat, pray and sweat!"

"What's that got to do with me?" he asked brutally.

"What's it got to do with you, Sykes? Mah tub of suds is filled yo' belly with   20
vittles more times than yo' hands is filled it. Mah sweat is done paid for this house and Ah reckon Ah kin keep on sweatin' in it."

She seized the iron skillet from the stove and struck a defensive pose, which act surprised him greatly, coming from her. It cowed him and he did not strike her as he usually did.

"Naw you won't," she panted, "that ole snaggle-toothed black woman you runnin' with ain't comin' heah to pile up on *mah* sweat and blood. You ain't paid for nothin' on this place, and Ah'm gointer stay right heah till Ah'm toted out foot foremost."

"Well, you better quit gittin' me riled up, else they'll be totin' you out sooner than you expect. Ah'm so tired of you Ah don't know whut to do. Gawd! How Ah hates skinny wimmen!"

A little awed by this new Delia, he sidled out of the door and slammed the back gate after him. He did not say where he had gone, but she knew too well. She knew very well that he would not return until nearly daybreak also. Her work over, she went on to bed but not to sleep at once. Things had come to a pretty pass!

She lay awake, gazing upon the debris that cluttered their matrimonial   25
trail. Not an image left standing along the way. Anything like flowers had long ago been drowned in the salty stream that had been pressed from her heart. Her tears, her sweat, her blood. She had brought love to the union and he had brought a longing after the flesh. Two months after the wedding, he had given her the first brutal beating. She had the memory of his numerous trips to Orlando with all of his wages when he had returned to her penniless, even before the first year had passed. She was young and soft then, but now she thought of her knotty, muscled limbs, her harsh knuckly hands, and drew herself up into an unhappy little ball in the middle of the big feather bed. Too late now to hope for love, even if it were not Bertha it would be someone else. This case differed from the others only in that she was bolder than the others. Too late for everything except her little home. She had built it for her old days, and planted one by one the trees and flowers there. It was lovely to her, lovely.

Somehow, before sleep came, she found herself saying aloud: "Oh well, whatever goes over the Devil's back, is got to come under his belly. Sometime or ruther, Sykes, like everybody else, is gointer reap his sowing." After that she was able to build a spiritual earthworks against her husband. His shells could no longer reach her. AMEN. She went to sleep and slept until he announced his presence in bed by kicking her feet and rudely snatching the covers away.

"Gimme some kivah heah, an' git yo' damn foots over on yo' own side! Ah oughter mash you in yo' mouf fuh drawing dat skillet on me."

Delia went clear to the rail without answering him. A triumphant indifference to all that he was or did.

II

The week was full of work for Delia as all other weeks, and Saturday found her
behind her little pony, collecting and delivering clothes.

It was a hot, hot day near the end of July. The village men on Joe Clarke's   30
porch even chewed cane listlessly. They did not hurl the cane-knots as usual.
They let them dribble over the edge of the porch. Even conversation had collapsed under the heat.

"Heah come Delia Jones," Jim Merchant said, as the shaggy pony came
'round the bend of the road toward them. The rusty buckboard was heaped
with baskets of crisp, clean laundry.

"Yep," Joe Lindsay agreed. "Hot or col', rain or shine, jes'ez reg'lar ez de
weeks roll roun' Delia carries 'em an' fetches 'em on Sat'day."

"She better if she wanter eat," said Moss. "Syke Jones ain't wuth de shot
an' powder hit would tek tuh kill 'em. Not to *huh* he ain't."

"He sho' ain't," Walter Thomas chimed in. "It's too bad, too, cause she wuz
a right pretty li'l trick when he got huh. Ah'd uh mah'ied huh mahself if he
hadnter beat me to it."

Delia nodded briefly at the men as she drove past.   35

"Too much knockin' will ruin *any* 'oman. He done beat huh 'nough tuh
kill three women, let 'lone change they looks," said Elijah Moseley. "How Syke
kin stommuck dat big black greasy Mogul he's layin' roun' wid, gits me. Ah
swear dat eight-rock couldn't kiss a sardine can Ah done thowed out de back
do' 'way las' yeah."

"Aw, she's fat, thass how come. He's allus been crazy 'bout fat women,"
put in Merchant. "He'd a' been tied up wid one long time ago if he could a'
found one tuh have him. Did Ah tell yuh 'bout him come sidlin' roun' *mah*
wife — bringin' her a basket uh peecans outa his yard fuh a present? Yessir,
mah wife! She tol' him tuh take 'em right straight back home, 'cause Delia
works so hard ovah dat washtub she reckon everything on de place taste lak
sweat an' soapsuds. Ah jus' wisht Ah'd a' caught 'im roun' dere! Ah'd a' made
his hips ketch on fiah down dat shell road."

"Ah know he done it, too. Ah sees 'im grinnin' at every 'oman dat passes,"
Walter Thomas said. "But even so, he useter eat some mighty big hunks uh
humble pie tuh git dat li'l 'oman he got. She wuz ez pritty ez a speckled pup! Dat
wuz fifteen years ago. He useter be so skeered uh losin' huh, she could make
him do some parts of a husband's duty. Dey never wuz de same in de mind."

"There oughter be a law about him," said Lindsay. "He ain't fit tuh carry
guts tuh a bear."

Clarke spoke for the first time. "Tain't no law on earth dat kin make a man   40
be decent if it ain't in 'im. There's plenty men dat takes a wife lak dey do a joint
uh sugar-cane. It's round, juicy, an' sweet when dey gets it. But dey squeeze an'
grind, squeeze an' grind an' wring tell dey wring every drop uh pleasure dat's
in 'em out. When dey's satisfied dat dey is wrung dry, dey treats 'em jes' lak dey
do a cane-chew. Dey thows 'em away. Dey knows whut dey is doin' while dey is
at it, an' hates theirselves fuh it but they keeps on hangin' after huh tell she's
empty. Den dey hates huh fuh bein' a cane-chew an' in de way."

"We oughter take Syke an' dat stray 'oman uh his'n down in Lake Howell swamp an' lay on de rawhide till they cain't say Lawd a' mussy. He allus wuz uh ovahbearin niggah, but since dat white 'oman from up north done teached 'im how to run a automobile, he done got too beggety to live — an' we oughter kill 'im," Old Man Anderson advised.

A grunt of approval went around the porch. But the heat was melting their civic virtue and Elijah Moseley began to bait Joe Clarke.

"Come on, Joe, git a melon outa dere an' slice it up for yo' customers. We'se all sufferin' wid de heat. De bear's done got *me!*"

"Thass right, Joe, a watermelon is jes' whut Ah needs tuh cure de eppizudicks," Walter Thomas joined forces with Moseley. "Come on dere, Joe. We all is steady customers an' you ain't set us up in a long time. Ah chooses dat long, bowlegged Floridy favorite."

"A god, an' be dough. You all gimme twenty cents and slice away," Clarke retorted. "An needs a col' slice m'self. Heah, everybody chip in. Ah'll lend y'all mah meat knife." 45

The money was all quickly subscribed and the huge melon brought forth. At that moment, Sykes and Bertha arrived. A determined silence fell on the porch and the melon was put away again.

Merchant snapped down the blade of his jackknife and moved toward the store door.

"Come on in, Joe, an' gimme a slab uh sow belly an' uh pound uh coffee — almost fuhgot 'twas Sat'day. Got to git on home." Most of the men left also.

Just then Delia drove past on her way home, as Sykes was ordering magnificently for Bertha. It pleased him for Delia to see.

"Git whutsoever yo' heart desires, Honey. Wait a minute, Joe. Give huh two bottles uh strawberry soda-water, uh quart parched ground-peas, an' a block uh chewin' gum." 50

With all this they left the store, with Sykes reminding Bertha that this was his town and she could have it if she wanted it.

The men returned soon after they left, and held their watermelon feast.

"Where did Syke Jones git da 'oman from nohow?" Lindsay asked.

"Ovah Apopka. Guess dey musta been cleanin' out de town when she lef'. She don't look lak a thing but a hunk uh liver wid hair on it."

"Well, she sho' kin squall," Dave Carter contributed. "When she gits ready tuh laff, she jes' opens huh mouf an' latches it back tuh de las' notch. No ole granpa alligator down in Lake Bell ain't got nothin' on huh." 55

III

Bertha had been in town three months now. Sykes was still paying her room-rent at Della Lewis' — the only house in town that would have taken her in. Sykes took her frequently to Winter Park to "stomps." He still assured her that he was the swellest man in the state.

"Sho' you kin have dat li'l ole house soon's Ah git dat 'oman outa dere. Everything b'longs tuh me an' you sho' kin have it. Ah sho' 'bominates uh skinny 'oman. Lawdy, you sho' is got one portly shape on you! You kin git *any-thing* you wants. Dis is *mah* town an' you sho' kin have it."

Delia's work-worn knees crawled over the earth in Gethsemane° and up the rocks of Calvary many, many times during these months. She avoided the villagers and meeting places in her efforts to be blind and deaf. But Bertha nullified this to a degree, by coming to Delia's house to call Sykes out to her at the gate.

Delia and Sykes fought all the time now with no peaceful interludes. They slept and ate in silence. Two or three times Delia had attempted a timid friendliness, but she was repulsed each time. It was plain that the breaches must remain agape.

The sun had burned July to August. The heat streamed down like a million   60
hot arrows, smiting all things living upon the earth. Grass withered, leaves browned, snakes went blind in shedding, and men and dogs went mad. Dog days!

Delia came home one day and found Sykes there before her. She wondered, but started to go on into the house without speaking, even though he was standing in the kitchen door and she must either stoop under his arm or ask him to move. He made no room for her. She noticed a soap box beside the steps, but paid no particular attention to it, knowing that he must have brought it there. As she was stooping to pass under his outstretched arm, he suddenly pushed her backward, laughingly.

"Look in de box dere Delia, Ah done brung yuh somethin'!"

She nearly fell upon the box in her stumbling, and when she saw what it held, she all but fainted outright.

"Syke! Syke, mah Gawd! You take dat rattlesnake 'way from heah! You *got-tuh*. Oh, Jesus, have mussy!"

"Ah ain't got tuh do nuthin' uh de kin' — fact is Ah ain't got tuh do nothin'   65
but die. Tain't no use uh you puttin' on airs makin' out lak you skeered uh dat snake — he's gointer stay right heah tell he die. He wouldn't bite me cause Ah knows how tuh handle 'im. Nohow he wouldn't risk breakin' out his fangs 'gin *yo* skinny laigs."

"Naw, now Syke, don't keep dat thing 'round tryin' tuh skeer me tuh death. You knows Ah'm even feared uh earth worms. Thass de biggest snake Ah evah did se. Kill 'im Syke, please."

"Doan ast me tuh do nothin' fuh yuh. Goin' 'round tryin' to be so damn asterperious. Naw, Ah ain't gonna kill it. Ah think uh damn sight mo' uh him dan you! Dat's a nice snake an' anybody doan lak 'im kin jes' hit de grit."

The village soon heard that Sykes had the snake, and came to see and ask questions.

"How de hen-fire did you ketch dat six-foot rattler, Syke?" Thomas asked.

"He's full uh frogs so he cain't hardly move, thass how Ah eased up on 'm.   70
But Ah'm a snake charmer an' knows how tuh handle 'em. Shux, dat ain't nothin'. Ah could ketch one eve'y day if Ah so wanted tuh."

Gethsemane: In the Gospels, the garden where Jesus was betrayed prior to being crucified on the hill of Calvary.

"Whut he needs is a heavy hick'ry club leaned real heavy on his head. Dat's de bes' way tuh charm a rattlesnake."

"Naw, Walt, y'all jes' don't understand dese diamon' backs lak Ah do," said Sykes in a superior tone of voice.

The village agreed with Walter, but the snake stayed on. His box remained by the kitchen door with its screen wire covering. Two or three days later it had digested its meal of frogs and literally came to life. It rattled at every movement in the kitchen or the yard. One day as Delia came down the kitchen steps she saw his chalky-white fangs curved like scimitars hung in the wire meshes. This time she did not run away with averted eyes as usual. She stood for a long time in the doorway in a red fury that grew bloodier for every second that she regarded the creature that was her torment.

That night she broached the subject as soon as Sykes sat down to the table.

"Syke, Ah wants you tuh take dat snake 'way fum heah. You done starved   75
me an' Ah put up widcher, you done beat me an Ah took dat, but you don kilt all mah insides bringin' dat varmint heah."

Sykes poured out a saucer full of coffee and drank it deliberately before he answered her.

"A whole lot Ah keer 'bout how you feels inside uh out. Dat snake ain't goin' no damn wheah till Ah gits ready fuh 'im tuh go. So fur as beatin' is concerned, yuh ain't took near all dat you gointer take ef yuh stay 'round *me*."

Delia pushed back her plate and got up from the table. "Ah hates you, Sykes," she said calmly. "Ah hates you tuh de same degree dat Ah useter love yuh. Ah done took an' took till mah belly is full up tuh mah neck. Dat's de reason Ah got mah letter fum de church an' moved mah membership tuh Woodbridge — so Ah don't haftuh take no sacrament wid yuh. Ah don't wantuh see yuh 'round me atall. Lay 'round wid dat 'oman all yuh wants tuh, but gwan 'way from me an' mah house. Ah hates yuh lak uh suck-egg dog."

Syles almost let the huge wad of corn bread and collard greens he was chewing fall out of his mouth in amazement. He had a hard time whipping himself up to the proper fury to try to answer Delia.

"Well, Ah'm glad you does hate me. Ah'm sho' tiahed uh you hangin' on-   80
tuh me. Ah don't want yuh. Look at yuh stringey ole neck! Yo' rawbony laigs an' arms is enough tuh cut uh man tuh death. You looks jes' lak de devvul's doll-baby tuh *me*. You cain't hate me no worse dan Ah hates you. Ah been hatin' *you* fuh years."

"Yo' ole black hide don't look lak nothin' tuh me, but uh passle uh wrinkled up rubber, wid yo' big ole yeahs flappin' on each side lak uh paih uh buzzard wings. Don't think Ah'm gointuh be run 'way fum mah house neither. Ah'm goin' tuh de white folks 'bout *you*, mah young man, de very nex' time you lay yo' han's on me. Mah cup is done run ovah." Delia said this with no signs of fear and Sykes departed from the house, threatening her, but made not the slightest move to carry out any of them.

That night he did not return at all, and the next day being Sunday, Delia was glad she did not have to quarrel before she hitched up her pony and drove the four miles to Woodbridge.

She stayed to the night service — "love feast" — which was very warm and full of spirit. In the emotional winds her domestic trials were borne far and wide so that she sang as she drove homeward,

Jurden water, black an' col
Chills de body, not de soul
An' Ah wantah cross Jurden in uh calm time.

She came from the barn to the kitchen door and stopped.

"Whut's de mattah, ol' Satan, you ain't kicken' up yo' racket?" She addressed the snake's box. Complete silence. She went on into the house with a new hope in its birth struggles. Perhaps her threat to go to the white folks had frightened Sykes! Perhaps he was sorry! Fifteen years of misery and suppression had brought Delia to the place where she would hope *anything* that looked towards a way over or through her wall of inhibitions.

She felt in the match-safe behind the stove at once for a match. There was   85
only one there.

"Dat niggah wouldn't fetch nothin' heah tuh save his rotten neck, but he kin run thew whut Ah brings quick enough. Now he done toted off nigh on tuh haff uh box uh matches. He done had dat 'oman heah in mah house, too."

Nobody but a woman could tell how she knew this even before she struck the match. But she did and it put her into a new fury.

Presently she brought in the tubs to put the white things to soak. This time she decided she need not bring the hamper out of the bedroom; she would go in there and do the sorting. She picked up the pot-bellied lamp and went in. The room was small and the hamper stood hard by the foot of the white iron bed. She could sit and reach through the bedposts — resting as she worked.

"Ah wantah cross Jurden in uh calm time." She was singing again. The mood of the "love feast" had returned. She threw back the lid of the basket almost gaily. Then, moved by horror and terror, she sprang back toward the door. *There lay the snake in the basket!* He moved sluggishly at first, but even as she turned round and round, jumped up and down in an insanity of fear, he began to stir vigorously. She saw him pouring his awful beauty from the basket upon the bed, then she seized the lamp and ran as fast as she could to the kitchen. The wind from the open door blew out the light and the darkness added to her terror. She sped to the darkness of the yard, slamming the door after her before she thought to set down the lamp. She did not feel safe even on the ground, so she climbed up in the hay barn.

There for an hour or more she lay sprawled upon the hay a gibbering wreck.   90

Finally she grew quiet, and after that came coherent thought. With this stalked through her a cold, bloody rage. Hours of this. A period of introspection, a space of retrospection, then a mixture of both. Out of this an awful calm.

"Well, Ah done de bes' Ah could. If things ain't right, Gawd knows tain't mah fault."

She went to sleep — a twitch sleep — and woke up to a faint gray sky. There was a loud hollow sound below. She peered out. Sykes was at the wood-pile, demolishing a wire-covered box.

He hurried to the kitchen door, but hung outside there some minutes before he entered, and stood some minutes more inside before he closed it after him.

The gray in the sky was spreading. Delia descended without fear now, and crouched beneath the low bedroom window. The drawn shade shut out the dawn, shut in the night. But the thin walls held back no sound.   95

"Dat ol' scratch is woke up now!" She mused at the tremendous whirr inside, which every woodsman knows, is one of the sound illusions. The rattler is a ventriloquist. His whirr sounds to the right, to the left, straight ahead, behind, close under foot — everywhere but where it is. Woe to him who guesses wrong unless he is prepared to hold up his end of the argument! Sometimes he strikes without rattling at all.

Inside, Sykes heard nothing until he knocked a pot lid off the stove while trying to reach the match-safe in the dark. He had emptied his pockets at Bertha's.

The snake seemed to wake up under the stove and Sykes made a quick leap into the bedroom. In spite of the gin he had had, his head was clearing now.

"Mah Gawd!" he chattered, "ef Ah could on'y strack uh light!"

The rattling ceased for a moment as he stood paralyzed. He waited. It   100
seemed that the snake waited also.

"Oh, fuh de light! Ah thought he'd be too sick" — Sykes was muttering to himself when the whirr began again, closer, right underfoot this time. Long before this, Sykes' ability to think had been flattened down to primitive instinct and he leaped — onto the bed.

Outside Delia heard a cry that might have come from a maddened chimpanzee, a stricken gorilla. All the terror, all the horror, all the rage that man possibly could express, without a recognizable human sound.

A tremendous stir inside there, another series of animal screams, the intermittent whirr of the reptile. The shade torn violently down from the window, letting in the red dawn, a huge brown hand seizing the window stick, great dull blows upon the wooden floor punctuating the gibberish of sound long after the rattle of the snake had abruptly subsided. All this Delia could see and hear from her place beneath the window, and it made her ill. She crept over to the four o'clocks and stretched herself on the cool earth to recover.

She lay there. "Delia, Delia!" She could hear Sykes calling in a most despairing tone as one who expected no answer. The sun crept on up, and he called. Delia could not move — her legs had gone flabby. She never moved, he called, and the sun kept rising.

"Mah Gawd!" She heard him moan, "Mah Gawd fum Heben!" She heard   105
him stumbling about and got up from her flower-bed. The sun was growing warm. As she approached the door she heard him call out hopefully, "Delia, is dat you Ah heah?"

She saw him on his hands and knees as soon as she reached the door. He crept an inch or two toward her — all that he was able, and she saw his horribly swollen neck and his one open eye shining with hope. A surge of pity too strong to support bore her away from that eye that must, could not, fail to see the tubs. He would see the lamp. Orlando with its doctors was too far. She could scarcely reach the chinaberry tree, where she waited in the growing heat while inside she knew the cold river was creeping up and up to extinguish that eye which must know by now that she knew.   *[1926]*

≡ THINKING ABOUT THE TEXT

1. Folktales like this one are usually not subtle. Characters and values are drawn with broad strokes. How does this apply to Sykes?

2. How does the chorus of men at the store tell us something about community values?

3. Does Delia's assertion that she hates Sykes to "de same degree dat Ah useter love yuh" (para. 78) strike you as psychologically plausible? Is there a connection between the two emotions?

4. How does the beginning of the story contain the conflict and the characters and provide some foreshadowing?

5. Some readers might see the grim ending as problematic. After all, she does let her husband die a painful death. Where do you stand on Delia's decision? How does Hurston complicate the situation?

≡ MAKING COMPARISONS

1. Both Emily and Delia kill their lovers. Compare their motivations.

2. Compare the leading men in these stories: Homer, Mel, Nick, and Sykes.

3. Whose relationship in these three stories makes sense to you? Whose doesn't?

≡ WRITING ABOUT ISSUES

1. Is love or hate a stronger emotion? Use examples from these stories to support your argument.

2. What difficulties do you encounter when you try to define love? Write an essay in which you use Homer and Emily, Terri and Ed, and Delia and Sykes as examples that complicate the definition.

3. Citing evidence from these and other stories, as well as novels, films, and your own experiences, write an essay that explains your view of the necessary ingredients for a loving relationship.

4. Argue that because our culture overemphasizes romantic love, individuals feel pressured to find love, sometimes in all the wrong places.

▤ Jealous Love: Critical Commentaries on a Play

WILLIAM SHAKESPEARE, *Othello*

CRITICAL COMMENTARIES:

A. C. BRADLEY, "The Noble Othello"

MILLICENT BELL, "Othello's Jealousy"

JEFFRIE G. MURPHY, "Jealousy, Shame, and the Rival"

Of all the great tragedies of Shakespeare, *Othello* seems the closest to our own lives. Hamlet is a prince, and Lear and Macbeth are kings with the fate of their nations tied to their destiny. It is sometimes hard for contemporary readers to relate to their struggles or to regicide. But *Othello* is more domesticated, more about a relationship we can understand; few of us would claim that we have never been jealous. We know that relationships thrive on trust and openness, but even if we trust our partner, jealousy can find its way into our consciousness and might especially do so if we are prompted to doubt by a close friend.

Psychologists suggest that insecure people are prone to jealousy, perhaps because their low esteem suggests to them that they are not worthy of love. Is this the case with Othello? Although at first he seems filled with confidence and authority, he is considered a Moorish outsider in Venetian society and as such might be tempted to think that his wife, Desdemona, might find Cassio, one of her "own kind," attractive and desirable. The innocent and devoted Desdemona does not, but the seeds of distrust that are planted early on by Brabantio ("She deceived her father, and may thee") are diabolically nurtured by Iago, "an inhuman dog." The speed with which a great love is destroyed leaves the reader stunned by the potential darkness within us all.

The three essays that follow the play focus on jealousy, but they have different ideas about where that emotion comes from and how it alters our view of Othello's character and the play. A. C. Bradley develops the idea that Othello remains a noble soul and so we admire him to the end. This admiration increases our pity and the force of catharsis, which leaves us "for the moment free from pain, and exulting in the power of 'love and man's unconquerable mind.' " Millicent Bell sees jealousy as connected to philosophical ideas about truth and seeming and connects the play to ideas about skepticism in Elizabethan England and contemporary America. Jeffrie G. Murphy takes a more psychological view of jealousy as personal disintegration strongly linked to shame.

▤ BEFORE YOU READ

Do you think jealousy is a natural emotion? If you loved someone deeply, would you trust him or her? Are only insecure people jealous? Are there any positive elements to jealousy?

(© Bettmann/Corbis.)

WILLIAM SHAKESPEARE
Othello

William Shakespeare's reputation as the greatest dramatist in the English language is built on his five major tragedies: Romeo and Juliet (1594), Hamlet (1600), Othello (1604), Macbeth (1605), and King Lear (1605). But he was also a master in other genres, including comedies (As You Like It in 1599), histories (Henry IV in 1597), and romances (The Tempest in 1611). And his collection of sonnets is considered art of the highest order.

Very little is known about Shakespeare's personal life. He attended the grammar school at Stratford-upon-Avon, where he was born in 1564. He married Anne Hathaway in 1582 and had three children. Around 1590 he moved to London, where he became an actor and began writing plays. He was an astute businessperson, becoming a shareholder in London's famous Globe Theatre. After writing thirty-seven plays, he retired to Stratford in 1611. When he died in 1616, he left behind the most respected body of work in literature. Shakespeare's ability to use artistic language to convey a wide range of humor and emotion is perhaps unsurpassed.

THE NAMES OF THE ACTORS

OTHELLO, *the Moor*
BRABANTIO, *father to Desdemona*
CASSIO, *an honorable lieutenant [to Othello]*
IAGO *[Othello's ancient,] a villain*
RODERIGO, *a gulled gentleman*
DUKE OF VENICE
SENATORS OF VENICE
MONTANO, *governor of Cyprus*
LODOVICO AND GRATIANO, *[kinsmen to Brabantio,] two noble Venetians*
SAILORS
CLOWNS
DESDEMONA, *wife to Othello*
EMILIA, *wife to Iago*
BIANCA, *a courtesan*
[Messenger, Herald, Officers, Venetian Gentlemen, Musicians, Attendants
scene: Venice and Cyprus]

[ACT I, Scene I: A street in Venice.]

Enter Roderigo and Iago.

RODERIGO: Tush, never tell me! I take it much unkindly
That thou, Iago, who hast had my purse
As if the strings were thine, shouldst know of this.°
IAGO: 'Sblood,° but you'll not hear me!
If ever I did dream of such a matter,   5
Abhor me.
RODERIGO: Thou told'st me thou didst hold him in thy hate.
IAGO: Despise me if I do not. Three great ones of the city,
In personal suit to make me his lieutenant,
Off-capped to him;° and, by the faith of man,   10
I know my price; I am worth no worse a place.
But he, as loving his own pride and purposes,
Evades them with a bombast circumstance.°
Horribly stuffed with epithets of war;
[And, in conclusion,]   15
Nonsuits° my mediators; for, "Certes," says he,
"I have already chose my officer."
And what was he?
Forsooth, a great arithmetician,°

ACT I, SCENE I.   **3 this:** I.e., Desdemona's elopement.   **4 'Sblood:** By God's blood.   **10 him:** I.e., Othello.   **13 a bombast circumstance:** Pompous circumlocutions.   **16 Nonsuits:** Rejects.   **19 arithmetician:** Theoretician.

One Michael Cassio, a Florentine   20
(A fellow almost damned in a fair wife°)
That never set a squadron in the field,
Nor the division of a battle knows
More than a spinster; unless the bookish theoric,
Wherein the togèd consuls can propose   25
As masterly as he. Mere prattle without practice
Is all his soldiership. But he, sir, had th' election;
And I (of whom his eyes had seen the proof
At Rhodes, at Cyprus, and on other grounds
Christian and heathen) must be belee'd and calmed°   30
By debitor and creditor; this counter-caster,°
He, in good time, must his lieutenant be,
And I — God bless the mark! — his Moorship's ancient.°
RODERIGO: By heaven, I rather would have been his hangman.
IAGO: Why, there's no remedy; 'tis the curse of service.   35
Preferment goes by letter and affection,°
And not by old gradation, where each second
Stood heir to th' first. Now, sir, be judge yourself,
Whether I in any just term am affined°
To love the Moor.
RODERIGO: I would not follow him then.   40
IAGO: O, sir, content you;
I follow him to serve my turn upon him.
We cannot all be masters, nor all masters
Cannot be truly followed. You shall mark
Many a duteous and knee-crooking knave   45
That, doting on his own obsequious bondage,
Wears out his time, much like his master's ass,
For naught but provender; and when he's old, cashiered.°
Whip me such honest knaves! Others there are
Who, trimmed° in forms and visages of duty,   50
Keep yet their hearts attending on themselves;
And, throwing but shows of service on their lords,
Do well thrive by them, and when they have lined their coats,
Do themselves homage. These fellows have some soul;
And such a one do I profess myself. For, sir,   55
It is as sure as you are Roderigo,
Were I the Moor, I would not be Iago.
In following him, I follow but myself;
Heaven is my judge, not I for love and duty,

---

21 almost . . . wife: (An obscure allusion; Cassio is unmarried, but see IV.i.12).   **30 belee'd and calmed:** Left in the lurch.   **31 counter-caster:** Bookkeeper.   **33 ancient:** Ensign.   **36 affection:** Favoritism.   **39 affined:** Obliged.   **48 cashiered:** Turned off.   **50 trimmed:** Dressed up.

But seeming so, for my peculiar end;   60
For when my outward action doth demonstrate
The native act and figure of my heart°
In compliment extern,° 'tis not long after
But I will wear my heart upon my sleeve
For daws to peck at; I am not what I am.   65
RODERIGO: What a full fortune does the thick-lips° owe°
      If he can carry't thus!
IAGO: Call up her father,
      Rouse him. Make after him, poison his delight,
      Proclaim him in the streets. Incense her kinsmen,
      And though he in a fertile climate dwell,   70
      Plague him with flies; though that his joy be joy,
      Yet throw such changes of vexation on't
      As it may lose some color.
RODERIGO: Here is her father's house. I'll call aloud.
IAGO: Do, with like timorous° accent and dire yell   75
      As when, by night and negligence, the fire
      Is spied in populous cities.
RODERIGO: What, ho, Brabantio! Signior Brabantio, ho!
IAGO: Awake! What, ho, Brabantio! Thieves! thieves! thieves!
      Look to your house, your daughter, and your bags!   80
      Thieves! thieves!

Brabantio at a window.°

BRABANTIO *(above)*:   What is the reason of this terrible summons?
      What is the matter there?
RODERIGO: Signior, is all your family within?
IAGO: Are your doors locked?
BRABANTIO: Why, wherefore ask you this?   85
IAGO: Zounds, sir, y' are robbed! For shame, put on your gown!
      Your heart is burst; you have lost half your soul.
      Even now, now, very now, an old black ram
      Is tupping your white ewe. Arise, arise!
      Awake the snorting° citizens with the bell.   90
      Or else the devil will make a grandsire of you.
      Arise, I say!
BRABANTIO: What, have you lost your wits?
RODERIGO: Most reverend signior, do you know my voice?
BRABANTIO: Not I. What are you?   95
RODERIGO: My name is Roderigo.
BRABANTIO: The worser welcome!

62 The . . . heart: What I really believe and intend.   **63 compliment extern:** Outward appearance.   **66 thick-lips:** An Elizabethan epithet for blacks, including Moors;
owe: Own.   **75 timorous:** Terrifying.   ***Brabantio at a window:*** (added from quarto).
90 snorting: Snoring.

I have charged thee not to haunt about my doors.
In honest plainness thou hast heard me say
My daughter is not for thee; and now, in madness,
Being full of supper and distemp'ring draughts,   100
Upon malicious knavery dost thou come
To start my quiet.

RODERIGO: Sir, sir, sir —

BRABANTIO: But thou must needs be sure
My spirit and my place have in them power   105
To make this bitter to thee.

RODERIGO: Patience, good sir.

BRABANTIO: What tell'st thou me of robbing? This is Venice;
My house is not a grange.°

RODERIGO: Most grave Brabantio,
In simple and pure soul I come to you.

IAGO: Zounds, sir, you are one of those that will not serve God if the devil bid   110
you. Because we come to do you service, and you think we are ruffians,
you'll have your daughter covered with a Barbary horse; you'll have your
nephews° neigh to you; you'll have coursers for cousins, and gennets for
germans.°

BRABANTIO: What profane wretch art thou?   115

IAGO: I am one, sir, that comes to tell you your daughter and the Moor are
now making the beast with two backs.

BRABANTIO: Thou are a villain.

IAGO: You are — a senator.

BRABANTIO: This thou shalt answer. I know thee, Roderigo.

RODERIGO: Sir, I will answer anything. But I beseech you,   120
If 't be your pleasure and most wise consent,
As partly I find it is, that your fair daughter,
At this odd-even° and dull watch o' th' night,
Transported, with no worse nor better guard
But with a knave of common hire, a gondolier,   125
To the gross clasps of a lascivious Moor —
If this be known to you, and your allowance,°
We then have done you bold and saucy wrongs;
But if you know not this, my manners tell me
We have your wrong rebuke. Do not believe   130
That, from the sense° of all civility,
I thus would play and trifle with your reverence.
Your daughter, if you have not given her leave,
I say again, hath made a gross revolt,
Tying her duty, beauty, wit, and fortunes   135

108 grange: Isolated farmhouse.   **113 nephews:** I.e., grandsons.   **113–14 gen-**
nets for germans: Spanish horses for near kinsmen.   **123 odd-even:** Between night
and morning.   **127 allowance:** Approval.   **131 from the sense:** In violation.

In an extravagant and wheeling° stranger
Of here and everywhere. Straight satisfy yourself.
If she be in her chamber, or your house,
Let loose on me the justice of the state
For thus deluding you.
BRABANTIO: Strike on the tinder, ho!   140
  Give me a taper! Call up all my people!
  This accident° is not unlike my dream.
  Belief of it oppresses me already.
Light, I say! light!   *Exit [above].*
IAGO: Farewell, for I must leave you.
  It seems not meet, nor wholesome to my place,   145
  To be produced — as, if I stay, I shall —
  Against the Moor. For I do know the state,
  However this may gall him with some check,°
  Cannot with safety cast° him; for he's embarked
  With such loud reason to the Cyprus wars,   150
  Which even now stand in act,° that for their souls
  Another of his fathom° they have none
  To lead their business; in which regard,
  Though I do hate him as I do hell-pains,
  Yet, for necessity of present life,   155
  I must show out a flag and sign of love,
  Which is indeed but sign. That you shall surely find him,
  Lead to the Sagittary° the raisèd search;
  And there will I be with him. So farewell.   *Exit.*

Enter [below] Brabantio in his nightgown,° and Servants with torches.

BRABANTIO: It is too true an evil. Gone she is;   160
  And what's to come of my despisèd time
  Is naught but bitterness. Now, Roderigo,
  Where didst thou see her? — O unhappy girl! —
  With the Moor, say'st thou? — Who would be a father? —
  How didst thou know 'twas she! — O, she deceives me   165
  Past thought! — What said she to you? — Get moe° tapers!
  Raise all my kindred! — Are they married, think you?
RODERIGO: Truly I think they are.
BRABANTIO: O heaven! How got she out? O treason of the blood!
  Fathers, from hence trust not your daughters' minds   170
  By what you see them act. Is there not charms
  By which the property° of youth and maidhood

---

136 extravagant and wheeling: Expatriate and roving.   **142 accident:** Occurrence.
148 check: Reprimand.   **149 cast:** Discharge.   **151 stand in act:** Are going on.
152 fathom: Capacity.   **158 Sagittary:** An inn.   **nightgown:** Dressing gown.   **166
moe:** More.   **172 property:** Nature.

May be abused? Have you not read, Roderigo,
Of some such thing?
RODERIGO: Yes, sir, I have indeed.
BRABANTIO: Call up my brother. — O, would you had had her! —   175
Some one way, some another. — Do you know
Where we may apprehend her and the Moor?
RODERIGO: I think I can discover him, if you please
To get good guard and go along with me.
BRABANTIO: I pray you lead on. At every house I'll call;   180
I may command at most. — Get weapons, ho!
And raise some special officers of night. —
On, good Roderigo; I'll deserve° your pains.   *Exeunt.*

[Scene II: Before the lodgings of Othello.]

Enter Othello, Iago, and Attendants with torches.

IAGO: Though in the trade of war I have slain men,
Yet do I hold it very stuff o' th' conscience
To do no contrived murther. I lack iniquity
Sometimes to do me service. Nine or ten times
I had thought t' have yerked° him here under the ribs.   5
OTHELLO: 'Tis better as it is.
IAGO: Nay, but he prated,
And spoke such scurvy and provoking terms
Against your honor
That with the little godliness I have
I did full hard forbear him. But I pray you, sir,   10
Are you fast° married? Be assured of this,
That the magnifico° is much beloved,
And hath in his effect a voice potential°
As double° as the Duke's. He will divorce you,
Or put upon you what restraint and grievance   15
The law, with all his might to enforce it on,
Will give him cable.
OTHELLO: Let him do his spite.
My services which I have done the signiory°
Shall out-tongue his complaints. 'Tis yet to know° —
Which, when I know that boasting is an honor,   20
I shall promulgate — I fetch my life and being
From men of royal siege;° and my demerits°

183 deserve: Show gratitude for. SCENE II. 5 yerked: Stabbed. 11 fast: Securely.
12 magnifico: Grandee (Brabantio). 13 potential: Powerful. 14 double: Doubly influential. 18 signiory: Venetian government. 19 yet to know: Still not generally known. 22 siege: Rank; demerits: Deserts.

May speak unbonneted to as proud a fortune
As this that I have reached.° For know, Iago,
But that I love the gentle Desdemona,   25
I would not my unhousèd° free condition
Put into circumscription and confine
For the sea's worth. But look what lights come yond?
IAGO: Those are the raisèd father and his friends.
You were best go in.
OTHELLO: Not I; I must be found.   30
My parts, my title, and my perfect soul°
Shall manifest me rightly. Is it they?
IAGO: By Janus, I think no.

Enter Cassio, with torches, Officers.

OTHELLO: The servants of the Duke, and my lieutenant.
The goodness of the night upon you, friends!   35
What is the news?
CASSIO: The Duke does greet you, general;
And he requires your haste-post-haste appearance
Even on the instant.
OTHELLO: What's the matter, think you?
CASSIO: Something from Cyprus, as I may divine.
It is a business of some heat. The galleys   40
Have sent a dozen sequent° messengers
This very night at one another's heels,
And many of the consuls, raised and met,
Are at the Duke's already. You have been hotly called for;
When, being not at your lodging to be found,   45
The Senate hath sent about three several quests
To search you out.
OTHELLO: 'Tis well I am found by you.
I will but spend a word here in the house,
And go with you.   *[Exit.]*
CASSIO: Ancient, what makes he here?
IAGO: Faith, he to-night hath boarded a land carack.°   50
If it prove lawful prize, he's made for ever.
CASSIO: I do not understand.
IAGO: He's married.
CASSIO: To who?

[Enter Othello.]

IAGO: Marry, to — Come, captain, will you go?
OTHELLO: Have with you.

23–24 May speak . . . reached: Are equal, I modestly assert, to those of Desdemona's
family.   **26 unhousèd:** Unrestrained.   **31 perfect soul:** Stainless conscience.   **41
sequent:** Consecutive.   **50 carack:** Treasure ship.

CASSIO: Here comes another troop to seek for you.

Enter Brabantio, Roderigo, and others with lights and weapons.

IAGO: It is Brabantio. General, be advised.   55
    He comes to bad intent.

OTHELLO: Holla! stand there!

RODERIGO: Signior, it is the Moor.

BRABANTIO: Down with him, thief!

[They draw on both sides.]

IAGO: You, Roderigo! Come, sir, I am for you.

OTHELLO: Keep up° your bright swords, for the dew will rust them.
    Good signior, you shall more command with years   60
    Than with your weapons.

BRABANTIO: O thou foul thief, where hast thou stowed my daughter?
    Damned as thou art, thou hast enchanted her!
    For I'll refer me to all things of sense,
    If she in chains of magic were not bound,   65
    Whether a maid so tender, fair, and happy,
    So opposite to marriage that she shunned
    The wealthy curlèd darlings of our nation,
    Would ever have, t' incur a general mock,
    Run from her guardage to the sooty bosom   70
    Of such a thing as thou — to fear, not to delight.
    Judge me the world if 'tis not gross in sense°
    That thou hast practiced on her with foul charms,
    Abused her delicate youth with drugs or minerals
    That weaken motion.° I'll have't disputed on;   75
    'Tis probable, and palpable to thinking.
    I therefore apprehend and do attach° thee
    For an abuser of the world, a practicer
    Of arts inhibited and out of warrant.
    Lay hold upon him. If he do resist,   80
    Subdue him at his peril.

OTHELLO: Hold your hands,
    Both you of my inclining and the rest.
    Were it my cue to fight, I should have known it
    Without a prompter. Where will you that I go
    To answer this your charge?

BRABANTIO: To prison, till fit time   85
    Of law and course of direct session°
    Call thee to answer.

OTHELLO: What if I do obey?
    How may the Duke be therewith satisfied,

---

59 Keep up: I.e., sheath.   **72 gross in sense:** Obvious.   **75 motion:** Perception.
77 attach: Arrest.   **86 direct session:** Regular trial.

Whose messengers are here about my side
Upon some present business of the state   90
To bring me to him?
OFFICER: 'Tis true, most worthy signior.
The Duke's in council, and your noble self
I am sure is sent for.
BRABANTIO: How? The Duke in council?
In this time of the night? Bring him away.
Mine's not an idle° cause. The Duke himself,   95
Or any of my brothers of the state,
Cannot but feel this wrong as 'twere their own;
For if such actions may have passage free,
Bondslaves and pagans shall our statesmen be.   *Exeunt.*

[Scene III: The Venetian Senate Chamber.]

Enter Duke and Senators, set at a table, with lights and Attendants.

DUKE: There is no composition° in these news
That gives them credit.
1. SENATOR: Indeed they are disproportioned.
My letters say a hundred and seven galleys.
DUKE: And mine a hundred forty.
2. SENATOR: And mine two hundred.
But though they jump° not on a just account—   5
As in these cases where the aim° reports
'Tis oft with difference — yet do they all confirm
A Turkish fleet, and bearing up to Cyprus.
DUKE: Nay, it is possible enough to judgment.
I do not so secure me° in the error   10
But the main article° I do approve°
In fearful sense.
SAILOR *(within)*:   What, ho! what, ho! what, ho!
OFFICER: A messenger from the galleys.

Enter Sailor.

DUKE: Now, what's the business?
SAILOR: The Turkish preparation makes for Rhodes.
So was I bid report here to the state   15
By Signior Angelo.
DUKE: How say you by this change?
1. SENATOR: This cannot be
By no assay° of reason. 'Tis a pageant
To keep us in false gaze.° When we consider

95 idle: Trifling.   **SCENE III. 1 composition:** Consistency.   **5 jump:** Agree.
6 aim: Conjecture.   **10 so secure me:** Take such comfort.   **11 article:** Substance;
approve: Accept.   **18 assay:** Test.   **19 in false gaze:** Looking the wrong way.

Th' importancy of Cyprus to the Turk,   20
And let ourselves again but understand
That, as it more concerns the Turk than Rhodes,
So may he with more facile question bear° it,
For that it stands not in such warlike brace,°
But altogether lacks th' abilities   25
That Rhodes is dressed in — if we make thought of this,
We must not think the Turk is so unskillful
To leave that latest which concerns him first,
Neglecting an attempt of ease and gain
To wake and wage° a danger profitless.   30
DUKE: Nay, in all confidence, he's not for Rhodes.
OFFICER: Here is more news.

Enter a Messenger.

MESSENGER: The Ottomites, reverend and gracious,
Steering with due course toward the isle of Rhodes,
Have there injointed them with an after fleet.   35
1. SENATOR: Ay, so I thought. How many, as you guess?
MESSENGER: Of thirty sail; and now they do restem°
Their backward course, bearing with frank appearance
Their purposes toward Cyprus, Signior Montano,
Your trusty and most valiant servitor,   40
With his free duty recommends you thus,
And prays you to believe him.
DUKE: 'Tis certain then for Cyprus.
Marcus Luccicos,° is not he in town?
1. SENATOR: He's now in Florence.   45
DUKE: Write from us to him; post, post-haste dispatch.
1. SENATOR: Here comes Brabantio and the valiant Moor.

Enter Brabantio, Othello, Cassio, Iago, Roderigo, and Officers.

DUKE: Valiant Othello, we must straight employ you
Against the general enemy Ottoman.   *[To Brabantio.]*
I did not see you. Welcome, gentle signior.   50
We lacked your counsel and your help to-night.
BRABANTIO: So did I yours. Good your grace, pardon me.
Neither my place, nor aught I heard of business,
Hath raised me from my bed; nor doth the general care
Take hold on me; for my particular grief   55
Is of so floodgate° and o'erbearing nature
That it engluts° and swallows other sorrows,
And it is still itself.

23 with . . . bear: More easily capture.   **24 brace:** Posture of defense.   **30 wake and wage:** Rouse and risk.   **37 restem:** Steer again.   **44 Marcus Luccicos:** (Presumably a Venetian envoy).   **56 floodgate:** Torrential.   **57 engluts:** Devours.

DUKE: Why, what's the matter?
BRABANTIO: My daughter! O, my daughter!
ALL: Dead?
BRABANTIO: Ay, to me.
   She is abused, stol'n from me, and corrupted   60
   By spells and medicines bought of mountebanks;
   For nature so prepost'rously to err,
   Being not deficient,° blind, or lame of sense,
   Sans witchcraft could not.
DUKE: Whoe'er he be that in this foul proceeding   65
   Hath thus beguiled your daughter of herself,
   And you of her, the bloody book of law
   You shall yourself read in the bitter letter
   After your own sense; yea, though our proper° son
   Stood in your action.°
BRABANTIO: Humbly I thank your grace.   70
   Here is the man — this Moor, whom now, it seems,
   Your special mandate for the state affairs
   Hath hither brought.
ALL: We are very sorry for't.
DUKE [to Othello]:   What, in your own part, can you say to this?
BRABANTIO: Nothing, but this is so.   75
OTHELLO: Most potent, grave, and reverend signiors,
   My very noble, and approved° good masters,
   That I have ta'en away this old man's daughter,
   It is most true; true I have married her.
   The very head and front of my offending   80
   Hath this extent, no more. Rude° am I in my speech,
   And little blessed with the soft phrase of peace;
   For since these arms of mine had seven years' pith°
   Till now some nine moons wasted, they have used
   Their dearest action in the tented field;   85
   And little of this great world can I speak
   More than pertains to feats of broil and battle;
   And therefore little shall I grace my cause
   In speaking for myself. Yet, by your gracious patience,
   I will a round° unvarnished tale deliver   90
   Of my whole course of love — what drugs, what charms,
   What conjuration, and what mighty magic
   (For such proceeding am I charged withal)
   I won his daughter.

63 deficient: Feeble-minded. **69 our   proper:** My   own. **70 Stood   in   your action:** Were   accused   by   you. **77 approved:** Tested   by   experience. **81 Rude:** Unpolished. **83 pith:** Strength. **90 round:** Plain.

BRABANTIO: A maiden never bold;
  Of spirit so still and quiet that her motion   95
  Blushed° at herself; and she — in spite of nature,
  Of years, of country, credit, everything —
  To fall in love with what she feared to look on!
  It is a judgment maimed and most imperfect
  That will confess perfection so could err   100
  Against all rules of nature, and must be driven
  To find out practices° of cunning hell
  Why this should be. I therefore vouch° again
  That with some mixtures pow'rful o'er the blood,°
  Or with some dram, conjured to this effect,   105
  He wrought upon her.
DUKE: To vouch this is no proof,
  Without more certain and more overt test
  Than these thin habits° and poor likelihoods
  Of modern seeming° do prefer against him.
1. SENATOR: But, Othello, speak.   110
  Did you by indirect and forcèd° courses
  Subdue and poison this young maid's affections?
  Or came it by request, and such fair question°
  As soul to soul affordeth?
OTHELLO: I do beseech you,
  Send for the lady to the Sagittary   115
  And let her speak of me before her father.
  If you do find me foul in her report,
  The trust, the office, I do hold of you
  Not only take away, but let your sentence
  Even fall upon my life.
DUKE: Fetch Desdemona hither.   120
OTHELLO: Ancient, conduct them; you best know the place.

                  Exit [Iago, with] two or three [Attendants].
  And till she come, as truly as to heaven
  I do confess the vices of my blood,
  So justly to your grave ears I'll present
  How I did thrive in this fair lady's love,   125
  And she in mine.
DUKE: Say it, Othello.
OTHELLO: Her father loved me, oft invited me;
  Still° questioned me the story of my life
  From year to year — the battles, sieges, fortunes   130

95–96 her motion Blushed: Her own emotions caused her to blush.   **102 practices:** Plots.   **103 vouch:** Assert.   **104 blood:** Passions.   **108 thin habits:** Slight appearances.   **109 modern seeming:** Everyday supposition.   **111 forcèd:** Violent.   **113 question:** Conversation.   **129 Still:** Continually.

That I have passed.
I ran it through, even from my boyish days
To th' very moment that he bade me tell it.
Wherein I spoke of most disastrous chances,
Of moving accidents by flood and field;   135
Of hairbreadth scapes i' th' imminent deadly breach;
Of being taken by the insolent foe
And sold to slavery; of my redemption thence
And portance° in my travels' history;
Wherein of anters° vast and deserts idle,   140
Rough quarries, rocks, and hills whose heads touch heaven,
It was my hint° to speak — such was the process;
And of the Cannibals that each other eat,
The Anthropophagi,° and men whose heads
Do grow beneath their shoulders. This to hear   145
Would Desdemona seriously incline;
But still the house affairs would draw her thence;
Which ever as she could with haste dispatch,
She'ld come again, and with a greedy ear
Devour up my discourse. Which I observing,   150
Took once a pliant° hour, and found good means
To draw from her a prayer of earnest heart
That I would all my pilgrimage dilate,°
Whereof by parcels° she had something heard,
But not intentively.° I did consent,   155
And often did beguile her of her tears
When I did speak of some distressful stroke
That my youth suffered. My story being done,
She gave me for my pains a world of sighs.
She swore, i' faith, 'twas strange, 'twas passing strange;   160
'Twas pitiful, 'twas wondrous pitiful.
She wished she had not heard it; yet she wished
That heaven had made her such a man. She thanked me;
And bade me, if I had a friend that loved her,
I should but teach him how to tell my story,   165
And that would woo her. Upon this hint° I spake.
She loved me for the dangers I had passed,
And I loved her that she did pity them.
This only is the witchcraft I have used.
Here comes the lady. Let her witness it.   170

Enter Desdemona, Iago, Attendants.

139 portance: Behavior.   **140 anters:** Caves.   **142 hint:** Occasion.   **144
Anthropophagi:** Man-eaters.   **151 pliant:** Propitious.   **153 dilate:** Recount in full.
154 parcels: Portions.   **155 intentively:** With full attention.   **166 hint:** Opportunity.

DUKE: I think this tale would win my daughter too.
　　　　Good Brabantio,
　　　　Take up this mangled matter at the best.
　　　　Men do their broken weapons rather use
　　　　Than their bare hands.
BRABANTIO:　　　　　　　　　I pray you hear her speak.　　　175
　　　　If she confess that she was half the wooer,
　　　　Destruction on my head if my bad blame
　　　　Light on the man! Come hither, gentle mistress.
　　　　Do you perceive in all this noble company
　　　　Where most you owe obedience?
DESDEMONA:　　　　　　　　　My noble father,　　　180
　　　　I do perceive here a divided duty.
　　　　To you I am bound for life and education;°
　　　　My life and education both do learn me
　　　　How to respect you: you are the lord of duty;
　　　　I am hitherto your daughter. But here's my husband;　　　185
　　　　And so much duty as my mother showed
　　　　To you, preferring you before her father,
　　　　So much I challenge° that I may profess
　　　　Due to the Moor my lord.
BRABANTIO:　　　　　　　God be with you! I have done.
　　　　Please it your grace, on to the state affairs.　　　190
　　　　I had rather to adopt a child than get° it.
　　　　Come hither, Moor.
　　　　I here do give thee that with all my heart
　　　　Which, but thou hast already, with all my heart
　　　　I would keep from thee. For your sake,° jewel,　　　195
　　　　I am glad at soul I have no other child;
　　　　For thy escape° would teach me tyranny,
　　　　To hang clogs on them. I have done, my lord.
DUKE: Let me speak like yourself° and lay a sentence°
　　　　Which, as a grise° or step, may help these lovers　　　200
　　　　[Into your favor.]
　　　　When remedies are past, the griefs are ended
　　　　By seeing the worst, which late on hopes depended.
　　　　To mourn a mischief that is past and gone
　　　　Is the next way to draw new mischief on.　　　205
　　　　What cannot be preserved when fortune takes,
　　　　Patience her injury a mock'ry makes.
　　　　The robbed that smiles steals something from the thief;
　　　　He robs himself that spends a bootless grief.

---

182 education: Upbringing. **188 challenge:** Claim the right. **191 get:** Beget.
195 For your sake: Because of you. **197 escape:** Escapade. **199 like yourself:**
As you should; **sentence:** Maxim. **200 grise:** Step.

BRABANTIO: So let the Turk of Cyprus us beguile: 210
We lose it not so long as we can smile.
He bears the sentence well that nothing bears
But the free comfort which from thence he hears;
But he bears both the sentence and the sorrow
That to pay grief must of poor patience borrow.   215
These sentences, to sugar, or to gall,
Being strong on both sides, are equivocal.
But words are words. I never yet did hear
That the bruisèd heart was piercèd through the ear.
Beseech you, now to the affairs of state.   220

DUKE: The Turk with a most mighty preparation makes for Cyprus. Othello,
the fortitude° of the place is best known to you; and though we have there
a substitute of most allowed° sufficiency, yet opinion,° a more sovereign
mistress of effects, throws a more safer voice on you. You must therefore be
content to slubber° the gloss of your new fortunes with this more stubborn   225
and boist'rous expedition.

OTHELLO: The tyrant custom, most grave senators,
Hath made the flinty and steel couch of war
My thrice-driven bed of down. I do agnize
A natural and prompt alacrity   230
I find in hardness;° and do undertake
These present wars against the Ottomites.
Most humbly, therefore, bending to your state,
I crave fit disposition for my wife,
Due reference of place, and exhibition,°   235
With such accommodation and besort°
As levels° with her breeding.

DUKE: If you please,
Be't at her father's.

BRABANTIO: I will not have it so.

OTHELLO: Nor I.

DESDEMONA: Nor I. I would not there reside,   240
To put my father in impatient thoughts
By being in his eye. Most gracious Duke,
To my unfolding lend your prosperous° ear,
And let me find a charter in your voice,
T' assist my simpleness.°   245

DUKE: What would you, Desdemona?

DESDEMONA: That I did love the Moor to live with him,

---

222 fortitude: Fortification.   **223 allowed:** Acknowledged;   **opinion:** Public
opinion.   **225 slubber:** Sully.   **229–31 agnize . . . hardness:** Recognize in myself
a natural and easy response to hardship.   **235 exhibition:** Allowance of money.   **236
besort:** Suitable company.   **237 levels:** Corresponds.   **243 prosperous:** Favorable.
245 simpleness: Lack of skill.

My downright violence, and storm of fortunes,
May trumpet to the world. My heart's subdued
Even to the very quality of my lord.   250
I saw Othello's visage in his mind,
And to his honors and his valiant parts
Did I my soul and fortunes consecrate.
So that, dear lords, if I be left behind,
A moth of peace, and he go to the war,   255
The rites for which I love him are bereft me,
And I a heavy interim shall support
By his dear absence. Let me go with him.

OTHELLO: Let her have your voice.
Vouch with me, heaven, I therefore beg it not   260
To please the palate of my appetite,
Not to comply with heat° — the young affects°
In me defunct — and proper satisfaction;
But to be free and bounteous to her mind;
And heaven defend your good souls that you think   265
I will your serious and great business scant
When she is with me. No, when light-winged toys
Of feathered Cupid seel° with wanton dullness
My speculative and officed instruments,°
That° my disports corrupt and taint my business,   270
Let housewives make a skillet of my helm,
And all indign° and base adversities
Make head against my estimation!°

DUKE: Be it as you shall privately determine,
Either for her stay or going. Th' affair cries haste,   275
And speed must answer it.

1. SENATOR: You must away to-night.

OTHELLO: With all my heart.

DUKE: At nine i' th' morning here we'll meet again.
Othello, leave some officer behind,
And he shall our commission bring to you,   280
With such things else of quality and respect
As doth import° you.

OTHELLO: So please your grace, my ancient;
A man he is of honesty and trust
To his conveyance I assign my wife,
With what else needful your good grace shall think   285
To be sent after me.

DUKE: Let it be so.

262 **heat:** Passions; **young affects:** Tendencies of youth. **268 seel:** Blind. **269
My . . . instruments:** My perceptive and responsible faculties. **270 That:** So that.
272 indign: Unworthy. **273 estimation:** Reputation. **282 import:** Concern.

Good night to every one.
[To Brabantio.]   And, noble signior,
If virtue no delighted° beauty lack,
Your son-in-law is far more fair than black.
1. SENATOR: Adieu, brave Moor. Use Desdemona well.   290
BRABANTIO: Look to her, Moor, if thou hast eyes to see:
She has deceived her father, and may thee.
                          Exeunt [Duke, Senators, Officers, &c.].
OTHELLO: My life upon her faith!—Honest Iago,
My Desdemona must I leave to thee.
I prithee let thy wife attend on her,   295
And bring them after in the best advantage.°
Come, Desdemona. I have but an hour
Of love, of worldly matters and direction,
To spend with thee. We must obey the time.
                                   Exit Moor and Desdemona.
RODERIGO: Iago,—   300
IAGO: What say'st thou, noble heart?
RODERIGO: What will I do, think'st thou?
IAGO: Why, go to bed and sleep.
RODERIGO: I will incontinently° drown myself.
IAGO: If thou dost, I shall never love thee after. Why, thou silly gentleman!   305
RODERIGO: It is silliness to live when to live is torment; and then have we a pre-
scription to die when death is our physician.
IAGO: O villainous! I have looked upon the world for four times seven years;
and since I could distinguish betwixt a benefit and an injury, I never found
man that knew how to love himself. Ere I would say I would drown myself   310
for the love of a guinea hen, I would change my humanity with a baboon.
RODERIGO: What should I do? I confess it is my shame to be so fond, but it is not
in my virtue to amend it.
IAGO: Virtue? a fig! 'Tis in ourselves that we are thus or thus. Our bodies are
our gardens, to which our wills are gardeners; so that if we will plant   315
nettles or sow lettuce, set hyssop and weed up thyme, supply it with one
gender° of herbs or distract it with many—either to have it sterile with
idleness or manured with industry—why, the power and corrigible
authority° of this lies in our wills. If the balance of our lives had not one
scale of reason to poise° another of sensuality, the blood and baseness° of   320
our natures would conduct us to most preposterous conclusions. But we
have reason to cool our raging motions,° our carnal strings, our unbitted°
lusts; whereof I take this that you call love to be a sect or scion.°

288 delighted: Delightful.   **296 in the best advantage:** At the best opportunity.
304 incontinently: Forthwith.   **317 gender:** Species.   **318-19 corrigible
authority:** Corrective power.   **320 poise:** Counterbalance; **blood and baseness:**
Animal instincts.   **322 motions:** Appetites; **unbitted:** Uncontrolled.   **323 sect or
scion:** Offshoot, cutting.

RODERIGO: It cannot be.

IAGO: It is merely a lust of the blood and a permission of the will. Come, be a   325
man! Drown thyself? Drown cats and blind puppies! I have professed me
thy friend, and I confess me knit to thy deserving with cables of perdurable
toughness. I could never better stead thee than now. Put money in thy
purse. Follow thou the wars; defeat thy favor° with an usurped beard. I say,
put money in thy purse. It cannot be that Desdemona should long con-   330
tinue her love to the Moor — put money in thy purse — nor he his to her.
It was a violent commencement in her, and thou shalt see an answerable
sequestration° — put but money in thy purse. These Moors are change-
able in their wills — fill thy purse with money. The food that to him now is
as luscious as locusts shall be to him shortly as bitter as coloquintida.° She   335
must change for youth: when she is sated with his body, she will find the
error of her choice. [She must have change, she must.] Therefore put
money in thy purse. If thou wilt needs damn thyself, do it a more delicate
way than drowning. Make° all the money thou canst. If sanctimony and a
frail vow betwixt an erring° barbarian and a supersubtle Venetian be not   340
too hard for my wits and all the tribe of hell, thou shalt enjoy her. Therefore make money. A pox of drowning thyself! 'Tis clean out of the way.
Seek thou rather to be hanged in compassing thy joy than to be drowned
and go without her.

RODERIGO: Wilt thou be fast to my hopes, if I depend on the issue?   345

IAGO: Thou art sure of me. Go, make money. I have told thee often, and I retell
thee again and again, I hate the Moor. My cause is hearted;° thine hath no
less reason. Let us be conjunctive in our revenge against him. If thou canst
cuckold him, thou dost thyself a pleasure, me a sport. There are many
events in the womb of time, which will be delivered. Traverse,° go, provide   350
thy money! We will have more of this to-morrow. Adieu.

RODERIGO: Where shall we meet i' th' morning?

IAGO: At my lodging.

RODERIGO: I'll be with thee betimes.

IAGO: Go to, farewell — Do you hear, Roderigo?   355

RODERIGO: What say you?

IAGO: No more of drowning, do you hear?

RODERIGO: I am changed.

IAGO: Go to, farewell. Put money enough in your purse.

RODERIGO: I'll sell all my land.   *Exit.*   360

IAGO: Thus do I ever make my fool my purse;
For I mine own gained knowledge should profane
If I would time expend with such a snipe°
But for my sport and profit. I hate the Moor;

---

329 defeat thy favor: Spoil thy appearance.   **333 sequestration:** Estrangement.
335 coloquintida: A medicine.   **339 Make:** Raise.   **340 erring:** Wandering.
347 My cause is hearted: My heart is in it.   **350 Traverse:** Forward march.   **363
snipe:** Fool.

And it is thought abroad that 'twixt my sheets   365
H'as done my office. I know not if 't be true;
But I, for mere suspicion in that kind,
Will do as if for surety. He holds me well;°
The better shall my purpose work on him.
Cassio's a proper man. Let me see now: 370
To get his place, and to plume up° my will
In double knavery — How, how? — Let's see: —
After some time, to abuse Othello's ears
That he is too familiar with his wife.
He hath a person and a smooth dispose°   375
To be suspected — framed to make women false.
The Moor is of a free° and open nature
That thinks men honest that but seem to be so;
And will as tenderly be led by th' nose
As asses are.   380
I have 't! It is engend'red! Hell and night
Must bring this monstrous birth to the world's light.   *Exit.*

[ACT II, Scene I: An open place in Cyprus, near the harbor.]

Enter Montano and two Gentlemen.
MONTANO: What from the cape can you discern at sea?
1. GENTLEMAN: Nothing at all: it is a high-wrought flood.
  I cannot 'twixt the heaven and the main
  Descry a sail.
MONTANO: Methinks the wind hath spoke aloud at land;   5
  A fuller blast ne'er shook our battlements.
  If it hath ruffianed so upon the sea,
  What ribs of oak, when mountains melt on them,
  Can hold the mortise?° What shall we hear of this?
2. GENTLEMAN: A segregation° of the Turkish fleet.   10
  For do but stand upon the foaming shore,
  The chidden billow seems to pelt the clouds;
  The wind-shaked surge, with high and monstrous mane,
  Seems to cast water on the burning Bear
  And quench the Guards° of th' ever-fixèd pole.°   15
  I never did like molestation° view
  On the enchafèd flood.
MONTANO: If that the Turkish fleet

---

368 well: In high regard. **371 plume up:** Gratify. **375 dispose:** Manner. **377 free:** Frank. ACT II, SCENE I. **9 hold the mortise:** Hold their joints together. **10 segregation:** Scattering. **15 Guards:** Stars near the North Star; **pole:** Polestar. **16 molestation:** Tumult.

Be not ensheltered and embayed, they are drowned;
It is impossible to bear it out.

Enter a third Gentleman.

3. GENTLEMAN: News, lads! Our wars are done.   20
The desperate tempest hath so banged the Turks
That their designment halts.° A noble ship of Venice
Hath seen a grievous wrack and sufferance°
On most part of their fleet.

MONTANO: How? Is this true?

3. GENTLEMAN: The ship is here put in,   25
A Veronesa;° Michael Cassio,
Lieutenant to the warlike Moor Othello,
Is come on shore; the Moor himself at sea,
And is in full commission here for Cyprus.

MONTANO: I am glad on't. 'Tis a worthy governor.   30

3. GENTLEMAN: But his same Cassio, though he speak of comfort
Touching the Turkish loss, yet he looks sadly
And prays the Moor be safe, for they were parted
With foul and violent tempest.

MONTANO: Pray heaven he be;
For I have served him, and the man commands   35
Like a full soldier. Let's to the seaside, ho!
As well to see the vessel that's come in
As to throw out our eyes for brave Othello,
Even till we make the main and th' aerial blue
An indistinct regard.°   40

3. GENTLEMAN: Come, let's do so;
For every minute is expectancy
Of more arrivance.

Enter Cassio.

CASSIO: Thanks, you the valiant of this warlike isle,
That so approve the Moor! O, let the heavens
Give him defense against the elements,   45
For I have lost him on a dangerous sea!

MONTANO: Is he well shipped?

CASSIO: His bark is stoutly timbered, and his pilot
Of very expert and approved allowance;
Therefore my hopes, not surfeited to death,°   50
Stand in bold cure.°

    (Within.)   A sail, a sail, a sail!   *Enter a messenger.*

CASSIO: What noise?

---

22 designment halts: Plan is crippled.   **23 sufferance:** Disaster.   **26 Veronesa:**
Ship furnished by Verona.   **40 An indistinct regard:** Indistinguishable.   **50 surfeited
to death:** Overindulged.   **51 in bold cure:** A good chance of fulfillment.

MESSENGER: The town is empty; on the brow o' th' sea
Stand ranks of people, and they cry "A sail!"
CASSIO: My hopes do shape him for the governor.   55

A shot.

2. GENTLEMAN: They do discharge their shot of courtesy:
Our friends at least.
CASSIO: I pray you, sir, go forth
And give us truth who 'tis that is arrived.
2. GENTLEMAN: I shall.   *Exit.*
MONTANO: But, good lieutenant, is your general wived?   60
CASSIO: Most fortunately. He hath achieved a maid
That paragons° description and wild fame;
One that excels the quirks° of blazoning° pens,
And in th' essential vesture of creation
Does tire the ingener.°

Enter Second Gentleman.

                          How now? Who has put in?   65
2. GENTLEMAN: 'Tis one Iago, ancient to the general.
CASSIO: H'as had most favorable and happy speed:
Tempests themselves, high seas, and howling winds,
The guttered° rocks and congregated sands,
Traitors ensteeped° to clog the guiltless keel,   70
As having sense of beauty, do omit
Their mortal° natures, letting go safely by
The divine Desdemona.
MONTANO: What is she?
CASSIO: She that I spake of, our great captain's captain,
Left in the conduct of the bold Iago,   75
Whose footing° here anticipates our thoughts
A se'nnight's° speed. Great Jove, Othello guard,
And swell his sail with thine own pow'rful breath,
That he may bless this bay with his tall ship,
Make love's quick pants in Desdemona's arms,   80
Give renewed fire to our extincted spirits,
[And bring all Cyprus comfort!]

Enter Desdemona, Iago, Roderigo, and Emilia [with Attendants].

                          O, behold!
The riches of the ship is come on shore!
You men of Cyprus, let her have your knees.°

---

62 paragons: Surpasses.   **63 quirks:** Ingenuities;   **blazoning:** Describing.
64–65 And . . . ingener: Merely to describe her as God made her exhaust her praiser.
69 guttered: Jagged.   **70 ensteeped:** Submerged.   **72 mortal:** Deadly.   **76
footing:** Landing.   **77 se'nnight's:** Week's.   **84 knees:** I.e., kneeling.

Hail to thee, lady! and the grace of heaven,   85
Before, behind thee, and on every hand,
Enwheel thee round!

DESDEMONA: I thank you, valiant Cassio.
What tidings can you tell me of my lord?

CASSIO: He is not yet arrived; nor know I aught
But that he's well and will be shortly here.   90

DESDEMONA: O but I fear! How lost you company?

CASSIO: The great contention of the sea and skies
Parted our fellowship.
    (Within.)   A sail, a sail! *[A shot.]*
                                        But hark. A sail!

2. GENTLEMAN: They give their greeting to the citadel;
This likewise is a friend.

CASSIO: See for the news.   95

                                            [Exit Gentleman.]

Good ancient, you are welcome.
[To Emilia.]   Welcome, mistress. —
Let it not gall your patience, good Iago,
That I extend my manners. 'Tis my breeding
That gives me this bold show of courtesy.

[Kisses Emilia.°]

IAGO: Sir, would she give you so much of her lips   100
As of her tongue she oft bestows on me,
You would have enough.

DESDEMONA: Alas, she has no speech!

IAGO: In faith, too much.
I find it still when I have list to sleep.
Marry, before your ladyship, I grant,   105
She puts her tongue a little in her heart
And chides with thinking.

EMILIA: You have little cause to say so.

IAGO: Come on, come on! You are pictures out of doors,
Bells in your parlors, wildcats in your kitchens,   110
Saints in your injuries, devils being offended,
Players in your housewifery,° and housewives° in your beds.

DESDEMONA: O, fie upon thee, slanderer!

IAGO: Nay, it is true, or else I am a Turk:
You rise to play, and go to bed to work.   115

EMILIA: You shall not write my praise.

IAGO: No, let me not.

Kisses Emilia: (Kissing was a common Elizabethan form of social courtesy).   **112 house-**
wifery: Housekeeping;   **housewives**: Hussies.

DESDEMONA: What wouldst thou write of me, if thou shouldst praise me?
IAGO: O gentle lady, do not put me to't,
   For I am nothing if not critical.
DESDEMONA: Come on, assay.° — There's one gone to the harbor?   120
IAGO: Ay, madam.
DESDEMONA: I am not merry; but I do beguile
   The thing I am by seeming otherwise. —
   Come, how wouldst thou praise me?
IAGO: I am about it; but indeed my invention   125
   Comes from my pate as birdlime° does from frieze° —
   It plucks out brains and all. But my Muse labors,
   And thus she is delivered:
   If she be fair and wise, fairness and wit —
   The one's for use, the other useth it.   130
DESDEMONA: Well praised! How if she be black° and witty?
IAGO: If she be black, and thereto have a wit,
   She'll find a white that shall her blackness fit.
DESDEMONA: Worse and worse!
EMILIA: How if fair and foolish?   135
IAGO: She never yet was foolish that was fair,
   For even her folly° helped her to an heir.
DESDEMONA: These are old fond° paradoxes to make fools laugh i' th' alehouse.
   What miserable praise hast thou for her that's foul° and foolish?
IAGO: There's none so foul, and foolish thereunto,   140
   But does foul pranks which fair and wise ones do.
DESDEMONA: O heavy ignorance! Thou praisest the worst best. But what praise
   couldst thou bestow on a deserving woman indeed — one that in the
   authority of her merit did justly put on the vouch° of very malice itself?
IAGO: She that was ever fair, and never proud;   145
   Had tongue at will, and yet was never loud;
   Never lacked gold, and yet went never gay;
   Fled from her wish, and yet said "Now I may";
   She that, being ang'red, her revenge being nigh,
   Bade her wrong stay, and her displeasure fly;   150
   She that in wisdom never was so frail
   To change the cod's head for the salmon's tail;°
   She that could think, and ne'er disclose her mind;
   See suitors following, and not look behind:
   She was a wight (if ever such wight were) —   155
DESDEMONA: To do what?
IAGO: To suckle fools and chronicle small beer.°

120 **assay:** Try.   126 **birdlime:** A sticky paste;   **frieze:** Rough cloth.   131 **black:**
Brunette.   137 **folly:** Wantonness.   138 **fond:** Foolish.   139 **foul:** Ugly.   144 **put
on the vouch:** Compel the approval.   152 **To . . . tail:** I.e., to exchange the good for
the poor but expensive.   157 **chronicle small beer:** Keep petty household accounts.

DESDEMONA:　O most lame and impotent conclusion! Do not learn of him, Emilia, though he be thy husband. How say you, Cassio? Is he not a most profane and liberal° counsellor?　　160

CASSIO:　He speaks home,° madam. You may relish him more in the soldier than in the scholar.

IAGO *[aside]*:　He takes her by the palm. Ay, well said, whisper! With as little a web as this will I ensnare as great a fly as Cassio. Ay, smile upon her, do! I will gyve thee in thine own courtship.° — You say true; 'tis so, indeed! — If　165 such tricks as these strip you out of your lieutenantry, it had been better you had not kissed your three fingers so oft — which now again you are most apt to play the sir° in. Very good! well kissed! an excellent courtesy! 'Tis so, indeed. Yet again your fingers to your lips? Would they were clyster pipes° for your sake! (Trumpet within.)　　170
The Moor! I know his trumpet.

CASSIO:　'Tis truly so.

DESDEMONA:　Let's meet him and receive him.

CASSIO:　Lo, where he comes.

Enter Othello and Attendants.

OTHELLO:　O my fair warrior!

DESDEMONA:　　　　　　　　My dear Othello!　　175

OTHELLO:　It gives me wonder great as my content
To see you here before me. O my soul's joy!
If after every tempest come such calms,
May the winds blow till they have wakened death!
And let the laboring bark climb hills of seas　　180
Olympus-high, and duck again as low
As hell's from heaven! If it were now to die,
'Twere now to be most happy;° for I fear
My soul hath her content so absolute
That not another comfort like to this　　185
Succeeds in unknown fate.

DESDEMONA:　　　　　　　　The heavens forbid
But that our loves and comforts should increase
Even as our days do grow.

OTHELLO:　　　　　　　　Amen to that, sweet powers!
I cannot speak enough of this content;
It stops me here; it is too much of joy.　　190
And this, and this, the greatest discords be

They kiss.

That e'er our hearts shall make!

IAGO *[aside]*:　　　　　　　　O, you are well tuned now!

---

160 profane and liberal: Worldly and licentious. **161 home:** Bluntly. **165 gyve . . . courtship:** Manacle you by means of your courtly manners. **168 sir:** Courtly gentleman. **169–70 clyster pipes:** Syringes. **183 happy:** Fortunate.

But I'll set down° the pegs that make this music,
As honest as I am.
OTHELLO: Come, let us to the castle.
News, friends! Our wars are done; the Turks are drowned.   195
How does my old acquaintance of this isle? —
Honey, you shall be well desired° in Cyprus;
I have found great love amongst them. O my sweet,
I prattle out of fashion, and I dote
In mine own comforts. I prithee, good Iago,   200
Go to the bay and disembark my coffers.
Bring thou the master° to the citadel;
He is a good one, and his worthiness
Does challenge° much respect. — Come, Desdemona,
Once more well met at Cyprus.   205

            Exit Othello [with all but Iago and Roderigo].

IAGO [to an Attendant, who goes out]:   Do thou meet me presently at the harbor.
    [To Roderigo.] Come hither. If thou be'st valiant (as they say base men
    being in love have then a nobility in their natures more than is native to
    them), list me. The lieutenant to-night watches on the court of guard.°
    First, I must tell thee this: Desdemona is directly in love with him.   210
RODERIGO: With him? Why, 'tis not possible.
IAGO: Lay thy finger thus,° and let thy soul be instructed. Mark me with
    what violence she first loved the Moor, but for bragging and telling her
    fantastical lies; and will she love him still for prating? Let not thy discreet
    heart think it. Her eye must be fed; and what delight shall she have to look   215
    on the devil? When the blood is made dull with the act of sport, there
    should be, again to inflame it and to give satiety a fresh appetite, loveliness
    in favor, sympathy in years, manners, and beauties; all which the Moor is
    defective in. Now for want of these required conveniences,° her delicate
    tenderness will find itself abused, begin to heave the gorge,° disrelish and   220
    abhor the Moor. Very nature will instruct her in it and compel her to some
    second choice. Now, sir, this granted — as it is a most pregnant° and
    unforced position — who stands so eminent in the degree of this fortune as
    Cassio does? A knave very voluble; no further conscionable° than in
    putting on the mere form of civil and humane° seeming for the better   225
    compassing of his salt° and most hidden loose affection? Why, none! why,
    none! A slipper° and subtle knave; a finder-out of occasions; that has an
    eye can stamp and counterfeit advantages, though true advantage never
    present itself; a devilish knave! Besides, the knave is handsome, young, and

---

193 **set down:** Loosen.   197 **well desired:** Warmly welcomed.   202 **master:** Ship
captain.   204 **challenge:** Deserve.   209 **court of   guard:** Headquarters.   212
thus: I.e., on your lips.   219 **conveniences:** Compatibilities.   220 **heave the gorge:**
Be nauseated.   222 **pregnant:** Evident.   224 **conscionable:** Conscientious.   225
humane: Polite.   226 **salt:** Lecherous.   227 **slipper:** Slippery.

hath all those requisites in him that folly and green minds look after. A   230
pestilent complete knave! and the woman hath found him already.

RODERIGO: I cannot believe that in her; she's full of most blessed condition.°

IAGO: Blessed fig's-end! The wine she drinks is made of grapes. If she had been
blessed, she would never have loved the Moor. Blessed pudding! Didst thou
not see her paddle with the palm of his hand? Didst not mark that?   235

RODERIGO: Yes, that I did; but that was but courtesy.

IAGO: Lechery, by this hand! an index and obscure prologue to the history of
lust and foul thoughts. They met so near with their lips that their breaths
embraced together. Villainous thoughts, Roderigo! When these mutuali-
ties° so marshal the way, hard at hand comes the master and main exer-   240
cise, th' incorporate° conclusion. Pish! But, sir, be you ruled by me: I have
brought you from Venice. Watch you to-night; for the command, I'll lay't
upon you. Cassio knows you not. I'll not be far from you: do you find some
occasion to anger Cassio, either by speaking too loud, or tainting° his discipline, or from what other course you please which the time shall more fa-   245
vorably minister.

RODERIGO: Well.

IAGO: Sir, he's rash and very sudden in choler,° and haply with his truncheon
may strike at you. Provoke him that he may; for even out of that will I
cause these of Cyprus to mutiny; whose qualification° shall come into no   250
true taste° again but by the displanting of Cassio. So shall you have a
shorter journey to your desires by the means I shall then have to prefer°
them; and the impediment most profitably removed with-out the which
there were no expectation of our prosperity.

RODERIGO: I will do this if you can bring it to any opportunity.   255

IAGO: I warrant thee. Meet me by and by at the citadel; I must fetch his neces-
saries ashore. Farewell.

RODERIGO: Adieu.   *Exit.*

IAGO: That Cassio loves her, I do well believe't;
That she loves him, 'tis apt° and of great credit.   260
The Moor, howbeit that I endure him not,
Is of a constant, loving, noble nature,
And I dare think he'll prove to Desdemona
A most dear husband. Now I do love her too;
Not out of absolute lust, though peradventure   265
I stand accountant° for as great a sin,
But partly led to diet° my revenge,
For that I do suspect the lusty Moor
Hath leaped into my seat; the thought whereof
Doth, like a poisonous mineral, gnaw my inwards;   270

---

232 condition: Character.   **239–240 mutualities:** Exchanges.   **241 incorporate:** Carnal.   **244 tainting:** Discrediting.   **248 sudden in choler:** Violent in anger.
250 qualification: Appeasement.   **251 true taste:** Satisfactory state.   **252 prefer:**
Advance.   **260 apt:** Probable.   **266 accountant:** Accountable.   **267 diet:** Feed.

And nothing can or shall content my soul
Till I am evened with him, wife for wife;
Or failing so, yet that I put the Moor
At least into a jealousy so strong
That judgment cannot cure. Which thing to do, 275
If this poor trash of Venice, whom I trash°
For° his quick hunting, stand the putting on,°
I'll have our Michael Cassio on the hip,°
Abuse him to the Moor in the rank garb°
(For I fear Cassio with my nightcap too), 280
Make the Moor thank me, love me, and reward me
For making him egregiously an ass
And practicing upon° his peace and quiet
Even to madness. 'Tis here, but yet confused:
Knavery's plain face is never seen till used.   *Exit.* 285

[Scene II: A street in Cyprus.]

Enter Othello's Herald, with a proclamation.

HERALD: It is Othello's pleasure, our noble and valiant general, that, upon certain tidings now arrived, importing the mere perdition° of the Turkish fleet,
every man put himself into triumph; some to dance, some to make bonfires,
each man to what sport and revels his addiction leads him. For, besides
these beneficial news, it is the celebration of his nuptial. So much was his   5
pleasure should be proclaimed. All offices° are open, and there is full liberty
of feasting from the present hour of five till the bell have told eleven. Heaven
bless the isle of Cyprus and our noble general Othello!   *Exit.*

[Scene III: The Cyprian Castle.]

Enter Othello, Desdemona, Cassio, and Attendants.

OTHELLO: Good Michael, look you to the guard to-night.
Let's teach ourselves that honorable stop,
Not to outsport discretion.
CASSIO: Iago hath direction what to do;
But not withstanding, with my personal eye   5
Will I look to 't.
OTHELLO: Iago is most honest.
Michael, good night. To-morrow with your earliest
Let me have speech with you.

---

276 I trash: I weight down (in order to keep under control).   **277 For:** In order to
develop;   **stand the putting on:** Responds to my inciting.   **278 on the hip:** At my
mercy.   **279 rank garb:** Gross manner.   **283 practicing upon:** Plotting against.
SCENE II. **2 mere perdition:** Complete destruction.   **6 offices:** Kitchens and storerooms.

[To Desdemona.]   Come, my dear love.
The purchase made, the fruits are to ensue;
That profit 's yet to come 'tween me and you. —   10
Good night.

                               Exit [Othello with Desdemona and Attendants].

Enter Iago.

CASSIO: Welcome, Iago. We must to the watch.

IAGO: Not this hour, lieutenant; 'tis not yet ten o' th' clock. Our general cast°
us thus early for the love of his Desdemona; who let us not therefore
blame. He hath not yet made wanton the night with her, and she is sport   15
for Jove.

CASSIO: She's a most exquisite lady.

IAGO: And, I'll warrant her, full of game.

CASSIO: Indeed, she's a most fresh and delicate creature.

IAGO: What an eye she has! Methinks it sounds a parley to provocation.   20

CASSIO: An inviting eye; and yet methinks right modest.

IAGO: And when she speaks, is it not an alarum to love?

CASSIO: She is indeed perfection.

IAGO: Well, happiness to their sheets! Come, lieutenant, I have a stoup° of
wine, and here without are a brace of Cyprus gallants that would fain have   25
a measure to the health of black Othello.

CASSIO: Not to-night, good Iago. I have very poor and unhappy brains for
drinking; I could well wish courtesy would invent some other custom of
entertainment.

IAGO: O, they are our friends. But one cup! I'll drink for you.   30

CASSIO: I have drunk but one cup to-night, and that was craftily qualified° too;
and behold what innovation° it makes here. I am unfortunate in the infir-
mity and dare not task my weakness with any more.

IAGO: What, man! 'Tis a night of revels: the gallants desire it.

CASSIO: Where are they?   35

IAGO: Here at the door; I pray you call them in.

CASSIO: I'll do't, but it dislikes me.   *Exit.*

IAGO: If I can fasten but one cup upon him
With that which he hath drunk to-night already,
He'll be as full of quarrel and offense   40
As my young mistress' dog. Now my sick fool Roderigo,
Whom love hath turned almost the wrong side out,
To Desdemona hath to-night caroused
Potations pottle-deep;° and he's to watch.
Three lads of Cyprus — noble swelling spirits,   45
That hold their honors in a wary distance,°
The very elements° of this warlike isle —

SCENE III. **14 cast:** Dismissed.   **24 stoup:** Two-quart tankard.   **31 qualified:** Diluted.
32 innovation: Disturbance.   **44 pottle-deep:** Bottoms up.   **46 That . . . distance:**
Very sensitive about their honor.   **47 very elements:** True representatives.

Have I to-night flustered with flowing cups,
And they watch too. Now, 'mongst this flock of drunkards
Am I to put our Cassio in some action   50
That may offend the isle.

Enter Cassio, Montano, and Gentlemen [; Servants following with wine].

But here they come.
If consequence do but approve my dream,
My boat sails freely, both with wind and stream.

CASSIO: 'Fore God, they have given me a rouse° already.
MONTANO: Good faith, a little one; not past a pint, as I am a soldier.   55
IAGO: Some wine, ho!

  [Sings.]   And let me the canakin clink, clink;
                 And let me the canakin clink
                    A soldier's a man;
                    A life's but a span,   60
                    Why then, let a soldier drink.

Some wine, boys!

CASSIO: 'Fore God, an excellent song!
IAGO: I learned it in England, where indeed they are most potent in potting.
    Your Dane, your German, and your swag-bellied Hollander — Drink,   65
    ho! — are nothing to your English.
CASSIO: Is your Englishman so expert in his drinking?
IAGO: Why, he drinks you with facility your Dane dead drunk; he sweats not
    to overthrow your Almain; he gives your Hollander a vomit ere the next
    pottle can be filled.   70
CASSIO: To the health of our general!
MONTANO: I am for it, lieutenant, and I'll do you justice.
IAGO: O sweet England!

  [Sings.]   King Stephen was a worthy peer;
                 His breeches cost him but a crown;   75
                 He held 'em sixpence all too dear,
                    With that he called the tailor lown.°
                 He was a wight of high renown,
                    And thou art but of low degree.
                 'Tis pride that pulls the country down;   80
                    Then take thine auld cloak about thee.

Some wine, ho!

CASSIO: 'Fore God, this is a more exquisite song than the other.
IAGO: Will you hear't again?
CASSIO: No, for I hold him to be unworthy of his place that does those things.°   85
    Well, God's above all; and there be souls must be saved, and there be souls
    must not be saved.
IAGO: It's true, good lieutenant.

54 rouse: Bumper.   **77 lown:** Rascal.   **85 does...things:** I.e., behaves in this fashion.

CASSIO: For mine own part — no offense to the general, nor any man of qual
    ity — I hope to be saved.   90
IAGO: And so do I too, lieutenant.
CASSIO: Ay, but, by your leave, not before me. The lieutenant is to be saved
    before the ancient. Let's have no more of this; let's to our affairs. — God for-
    give us our sins! — Gentlemen, let's look to our business. Do not think, gen-
    tlemen, I am drunk. This is my ancient; this is my right hand, and this is my
    left. I am not drunk now. I can stand well enough, and I speak well enough.
ALL: Excellent well!
CASSIO: Why, very well then. You must not think then that I am drunk.

                                                            Exit.

MONTANO: To th' platform, masters. Come, let's set the watch.
IAGO: You see this fellow that is gone before.   100
    He's a soldier fit to stand by Caesar
    And give direction; and do but see his vice.
    'Tis to his virtue a just equinox,°
    The one as long as th' other. 'Tis pity of him.
    I fear the trust Othello puts him in,   105
    On some odd time of his infirmity,
    Will shake this island.
MONTANO: But is he often thus?
IAGO: 'Tis evermore his prologue to his sleep:
    He'll watch the horologe a double set°
    If drink rock not his cradle.
MONTANO: It were well   110
    The general were put in mind of it.
    Perhaps he sees it not, or his good nature
    Prizes the virtue that appears in Cassio
    And looks not on his evils. Is not this true?

Enter Roderigo.

IAGO *[aside to him]*:   How now, Roderigo?   115
    I pray you after the lieutenant, go!   *Exit Roderigo.*
MONTANO: And 'tis great pity that the noble Moor
    Should hazard such a place as his own second
    With one of an ingraft° infirmity.
    It were an honest action to say   120
    So to the Moor.
IAGO: Not I, for this fair island!
    I do love Cassio well and would do much
    To cure him of this evil.
        (Within.) Help! help!
                But hark! What noise?

---

103 just equinox: Exact equivalent.   **109 watch . . . set:** Stay awake twice around
the clock.   **119 ingraft:** I.e., ingrained.

Enter Cassio, driving in Roderigo.

CASSIO: Zounds, you rogue! you rascal!   125
MONTANO: What's the matter, lieutenant?
CASSIO: A knave to teach me my duty?
   I'll beat the knave into a twiggen° bottle.
RODERIGO: Beat me?
CASSIO: Dost thou prate, rogue? *[Strikes him.]*
MONTANO: Nay, good lieutenant!

                                                    [Stays him.]

   I pray you, sir, hold your hand.
CASSIO: Let me go, sir,
   Or I'll knock you o'er the mazzard.°
MONTANO: Come, come, you're drunk!   130
CASSIO: Drunk?

They fight.

IAGO *[aside to Roderigo]:*   Away, I say! Go out and cry a mutiny!

                                                    Exit Roderigo.

   Nay, good lieutenant. God's will, gentlemen!
   Help, ho! — lieutenant — sir — Montano — sir —
   Help, masters! — Here's a goodly watch indeed!   135

A bell rung.

   Who's that which rings the bell? Diablo, ho!
   The town will rise.° God's will, lieutenant, hold!
   You'll be shamed for ever.

Enter Othello and Gentlemen with weapons.

OTHELLO: What is the matter here?
MONTANO: Zounds, I bleed still. I am hurt to th' death.
   He dies!   140
OTHELLO: Hold for your lives!
IAGO: Hold, hold! Lieutenant — sir — Montano — gentlemen!
   Have you forgot all sense of place and duty?
   Hold! The general speaks to you. Hold, for shame!
OTHELLO: Why, how now ho? From whence ariseth this?   145
   Are we turned Turks, and to ourselves do that
   Which heaven hath forbid the Ottomites?
   For Christian shame put by this barbarous brawl!
   He that stirs next to carve for° his own rage.
   Holds his soul light; he dies upon his motion.   150
   Silence that dreadful bell! It frights the isle
   From her propriety.° What is the matter, masters?
   Honest Iago, that looks dead with grieving,

---

127 twiggen: Wicker-covered.   **130 mazzard:** Head.   **137 rise:** Grow riotous.
149 carve for: Indulge.   **152 propriety:** Proper self.

Speak. Who began this? On thy love, I charge thee.

IAGO: I do not know. Friends all, but now, even now,   155
In quarter,° and in terms like bride and groom
Devesting them for bed; and then, but now —
As if some planet had unwitted men —
Swords out, and tilting one at other's breast
In opposition bloody. I cannot speak   160
Any beginning to this peevish odds,°
And would in action glorious I had lost
Those legs that brought me to a part of it!

OTHELLO: How comes it, Michael, you are thus forgot?

CASSIO: I pray you pardon me; I cannot speak.   165

OTHELLO: Worthy Montano, you were wont to be civil;
The gravity and stillness of your youth
The world hath noted, and your name is great
In months of wisest censure.° What's the matter
That you unlace° your reputation thus   170
And spend your rich opinion° for the name
Of a night-brawler? Give me answer to it.

MONTANO: Worthy Othello, I am hurt to danger.
Your officer, Iago, can inform you,
While I spare speech, which something now offends° me,   175
Of all that I do know; nor know I aught
By me that's said or done amiss this night,
Unless self-charity be sometimes a vice,
And to defend ourselves it be a sin
When violence assails us.

OTHELLO: Now, by heaven,   180
My blood° begins my safer guides to rule,
And passion, having my best judgment collied,°
Assays° to lead the way. If I once stir
Or do but lift this arm, the best of you
Shall sink in my rebuke. Give me to know   185
How this foul rout began, who set it on;
And he that is approved in° this offense,
Though he had twinned with me, both at a birth,
Shall lose me. What! in a town of war,
Yet wild, the people's hearts brimful of fear,   190
To manage° private and domestic quarrel?
In night, and on the court and guard of safety?
'Tis monstrous. Iago, who began't?

---

156 quarter: Friendliness.   **161 peevish odds:** Childish quarrel.   **169 censure:** Judgment.   **170 unlace:** Undo.   **171 rich   opinion:** High   reputation.   **175 offends:** Pains.   **181 blood:** Passion.   **182 collied:** Darkened.   **183 Assays:** Tries.   **187 approved in:** Proved guilty of.   **191 manage:** Carry on.

MONTANO: If partially affined, or leagued in office,°
    Thou dost deliver more or less than truth,   195
    Thou art no soldier.
IAGO: Touch me not so near.
    I had rather have this tongue cut from my mouth
    Than it should do offense to Michael Cassio;
    Yet I persuade myself, to speak the truth
    Shall nothing wrong him. This it is, general.   200
    Montano and myself being in speech,
    There comes a fellow crying out for help,
    And Cassio following him with determined sword
    To execute° upon him. Sir, this gentleman
    Steps in to Cassio and entreats his pause.   205
    Myself the crying fellow did pursue,
    Lest by his clamor — as it so fell out —
    The town might fall in fright. He, swift of foot,
    Outran my purpose; and I returned then rather
    For that I heard the clink and fall of swords,   210
    And Cassio high in oath;° which till to-night
    I ne'er might say before. When I came back —
    For this was brief — I found them close together
    At blow and thrust, even as again they were
    When you yourself did part them.   215
    More of this matter cannot I report;
    But men are men; the best sometimes forget.
    Though Cassio did some little wrong to him,
    As men in rage strike those that wish them best,
    Yet surely Cassio I believe received   220
    From him that fled some strange indignity,
    Which patience could not pass.°
OTHELLO: I know, Iago,
    Thy honesty and love doth mince this matter,
    Making it light to Cassio. Cassio, I love thee;
    But never more be officer of mine.   225

Enter Desdemona, attended.

    Look if my gentle love be not raised up!
    I'll make thee an example.
DESDEMONA: What's the matter?
OTHELLO: All's well now, sweeting; come away to bed.
    [To Montano.]
    Sir, for your hurts, myself will be your surgeon.
    Lead him off.   230

---

194 partially . . . office: Prejudiced by comradeship or official relations.   **204 execute:** Work his will.   **211 high in oath:** Cursing.   **222 pass:** Pass over, ignore.

[Montano is led off.]

> Iago, look with care about the town
> And silence those whom this vile brawl distracted.°
> Come, Desdemona; 'tis the soldiers' life
> To have their balmy slumbers waked with strife.

Exit [with all but Iago and Cassio].

IAGO: What, are you hurt, lieutenant?   235

CASSIO: Ay, past all surgery.

IAGO: Marry, God forbid!

CASSIO: Reputation, reputation, reputation! O, I have lost my reputation! I have lost the immortal part of myself, and what remains is bestial. My reputation, Iago, my reputation!   240

IAGO: As I am an honest man, I thought you had received some bodily wound. There is more sense in that than in reputation. Reputation is an idle and most false imposition; oft got without merit and lost without deserving. You have lost no reputation at all unless you repute yourself such a loser. What, man! there are ways to recover° the general again. You are but now   245 cast in his mood° — a punishment more in policy than in malice, even so as one would beat his offenseless dog to affright an imperious lion. Sue to him again, and he's yours.

CASSIO: I will rather sue to be despised than to deceive so good a commander with so slight, so drunken, and so indiscreet an officer. Drunk! and speak   250 parrot!° and squabble! swagger! swear! and discourse fustian° with one's own shadow! O thou invisible spirit of wine, if thou hast no name to be known by, let us call thee devil!

IAGO: What was he that you followed with your sword? What had he done to you?   255

CASSIO: I know not.

IAGO: Is't possible?

CASSIO: I remember a mass of things, but nothing distinctly; a quarrel, but nothing wherefore. O God, that men should put an enemy in their mouths to steal away their brains! that we should with joy, pleasance, revel, and   260 applause° transform ourselves into beasts!

IAGO: Why, but you are now well enough. How came you thus recovered?

CASSIO: It hath pleased the devil drunkenness to give place to the devil wrath. One unperfectness shows me another, to make me frankly despise myself.

IAGO: Come, you are too severe a moraler. As the time, the place, and the con-   265 dition of this country stands, I could heartily wish this had not so befall'n; but since it is as it is, mend it for your own good.

CASSIO: I will ask him for my place again: he shall tell me I am a drunkard! Had I as many mouths as Hydra,° such an answer would stop them all. To

---

232 distracted: Excited.   **245 recover:** Regain favor with.   **246 in his mood:** Dismissed because of his anger.   **251 parrot:** Meaningless phrases.   **fustian:** Bombastic nonsense.   **261 applause:** Desire to please.   **269 Hydra:** Monster with many heads.

be now a sensible man, by and by a fool, and presently a beast! O strange!   270
Every inordinate cup is unblest, and the ingredient° is a devil.

IAGO: Come, come, good wine is a good familiar creature if it be well used.
Exclaim no more against it. And, good lieutenant, I think you think I
love you.

CASSIO: I have well approved° it, sir. I drunk!   275

IAGO: You or any man living may be drunk at some time, man. I'll tell you
what you shall do. Our general's wife is now the general. I may say so in
this respect, for that he hath devoted and given up himself to the contemplation, mark, and denotement of her parts and graces. Confess yourself
freely to her; importune her help to put you in your place again. She is of so   280
free,° so kind, so apt, so blessed a disposition she holds it a vice in her goodness not to do more than she is requested. This broken joint between you
and her husband entreat her to splinter;° and my fortunes against any lay°
worth naming, this crack of your love shall grow stronger than it was
before.   285

CASSIO: You advise me well.

IAGO: I protest, in the sincerity of love and honest kindness.

CASSIO: I think it freely; and betimes in the morning will I beseech the virtuous Desdemona to undertake for me. I am desperate of my fortunes if they
check me here.   290

IAGO: You are in the right. Good night, lieutenant; I must to the watch.

CASSIO: Good night, honest Iago.   *Exit Cassio.*

IAGO: And what's he then that says I play the villain,
When this advice is free I give and honest,
Probal° to thinking, and indeed the course   295
To win the Moor again? For 'tis most easy
Th' inclining Desdemona to subdue°
In an honest suit; she's framed as fruitful
As the free elements. And then for her
To win the Moor — were't to renounce his baptism,   300
All seals and symbols of redeemèd sin —
His soul is so enfettered to her love
That she may make, unmake, do what she list,
Even as her appetite shall play the god
With his weak function. How am I then a villain   305
To counsel Cassio to this parallel° course,
Directly to his good? Divinity° of hell!
When devils will the blackest sins put on,°
They do suggest at first with heavenly shows,
As I do now. For whiles this honest fool   310
Plies Desdemona to repair his fortunes,

271 ingredient: Contents. **275 approved:** Proved. **281 free:** Bounteous.
283 splinter: Bind up with splints; **lay:** Wager. **295 Probal:** Probable. **297 subdue:** Persuade. **306 parallel:** Corresponding. **307 Divinity:** Theology. **308
put on:** Incite.

And she for him pleads strongly to the Moor,
I'll pour this pestilence into his ear,
That she repeals him° for her body's lust;
And by how much she strives to do him good,   315
She shall undo her credit with the Moor.
So will I turn her virtue into pitch,
And out of her own goodness make the net
That shall enmesh them all.

Enter Roderigo.

                                    How, now, Roderigo?
RODERIGO: I do follow here in the chase, not like a hound that hunts, but one   320
    that fills up the cry.° My money is almost spent; I have been to-night
    exceedingly well cudgelled; and I think the issue will be — I shall have so
    much experience for my pains; and so, with no money at all, and a little
    more wit, return again to Venice.
IAGO: How poor are they that have not patience!   325
    What wound did ever heal but by degrees?
    Thou know'st we work by wit, and not by witchcraft;
    And wit depends on dilatory time.
    Does't not go well? Cassio hath beaten thee,
    And thou by that small hurt hast cashiered Cassio.°   330
    Though other things grow fair against the sun,
    Yet fruits that blossom first will first be ripe.
    Content thyself awhile. By the mass, 'tis morning!
    Pleasure and action make the hours seem short.
    Retire thee; go where thou art billeted.   335
    Away, I say! Thou shalt know more hereafter.
    Nay, get thee gone!   *Exit Roderigo.*
                        Two things are to be done:
    My wife must move for Cassio to her mistress;
    I'll set her on;
    Myself the while to draw the Moor apart   340
    And bring him jump° when he may Cassio find
    Soliciting his wife. Ay, that's the way!
    Dull no device by coldness and delay.   *Exit.*

[ACT III, Scene I: Before the chamber of Othello and Desdemona.]

Enter Cassio, with Musicians and the Clown.

CASSIO: Masters, play here, I will content° your pains:
    Something that's brief; and bid "Good morrow, general."

314 repeals him: Seeks his recall.   **321 cry:** Pack.   **330 cashiered Cassio:**
Maneuvered Cassio's discharge.   **341 jump:** At the exact moment.   ACT III, SCENE I. 1
content: Reward.

[They play.]

CLOWN: Why, masters, ha' your instruments been in Naples,° that they speak
i' th' nose thus?

MUSICIAN: How, sir, how?   5

CLOWN: Are these, I pray you, called wind instruments?

MUSICIAN: Ay, marry, are they, sir.

CLOWN: O, thereby hangs a tail.

MUSICIAN: Whereby hangs a tail, sir?

CLOWN: Marry, sir, by many a wind instrument that I know. But, masters,   10
here's money for you; and the general so likes your music that he desires
you, for love's sake, to make no more noise with it.

MUSICIAN: Well, sir, we will not.

CLOWN: If you have any music that may not be heard, to't again: but, as they
say, to hear music the general does not greatly care.   15

MUSICIAN: We have none such, sir.

CLOWN: Then put up your pipes in your bag, for I'll away. Go, vanish into air,
away!   *Exit Musician [with his fellows].*

CASSIO: Dost thou hear, my honest friend?

CLOWN: No, I hear not your honest friend. I hear you.   20

CASSIO: Prithee keep up thy quillets.° There's a poor piece of gold for thee. If
the gentlewoman that attends the general's wife be stirring, tell her there's
one Cassio entreats her a little favor of speech. Wilt thou do this?

CLOWN: She is stirring sir. If she will stir hither, I shall seem to notify unto her.

CASSIO: [Do, good my friend.]   *Exit Clown.*

Enter Iago.

                                        In happy time,° Iago.   25

IAGO: You have not been abed then?

CASSIO: Why, no; the day had broke
Before we parted. I have made bold, Iago,
To send in to your wife: my suit to her
Is that she will to virtuous Desdemona   30
Procure me some access.

IAGO: I'll send her to you presently;
And I'll devise a mean to draw the Moor
Out of the way, that your converse and business
May be more free.

CASSIO: I humbly thank you for't.   *Exit [Iago].*
                                        I never knew   35
A Florentine° more kind and honest.

Enter Emilia.

EMILIA: Good morrow, good lieutenant. I am sorry

---

3 Naples: (Notorious for its association with venereal disease). **21 quillets:** Quips.
25 In happy time: Well met. **36 Florentine:** I.e., even a Florentine (like Cassio; Iago
was a Venetian).

For your displeasure: but all will sure be well.
The general and his wife are talking of it,
And she speaks for you stoutly. The Moor replied   40
That he you hurt is of great fame in Cyprus
And great affinity,° and that in wholesome wisdom
He might not but refuse you; but he protests he loves you,
And needs no other suitor but his likings
[To take the safest occasion° by the front°]   45
To bring you in again.
CASSIO: Yet I beseech you,
If you think fit, or that it may be done,
Give me advantage of some brief discourse
With Desdemona alone.
EMILIA: Pray you come in.
I will bestow you where you shall have time   50
To speak your bosom° freely.
CASSIO: I am much bound to you.   *Exeunt.*

[Scene II: The castle.]

Enter Othello, Iago, and Gentlemen.

OTHELLO: These letters give, Iago, to the pilot
And by him do my duties to the Senate.
That done, I will be walking on the works;°
Repair there to me.
IAGO: Well, my good lord, I'll do't.
OTHELLO: This fortification, gentlemen, shall we see't?   5
GENTLEMEN: We'll wait upon your lordship.   *Exeunt.*

[Scene III: The castle grounds.]

Enter Desdemona, Cassio, and Emilia.

DESDEMONA: Be thou assured, good Cassio, I will do
All my abilities in thy behalf.
EMILIA: Good madam, do. I warrant it grieves my husband
As if the cause were his.
DESDEMONA: O, that's an honest fellow. Do not doubt, Cassio,   5
But I will have my lord and you again
As friendly as you were.
CASSIO: Bounteous madam,
Whatever shall become of Michael Cassio,
He's never anything but your true servant.
DESDEMONA: I know't; I thank you. You do love my lord;   10

42 affinity: Family   connections.   **45 occasion:** Opportunity;   **front:** Forelock.   **51 your bosom:** Your inmost thoughts.   SCENE II.   **3 works:** Fortifications.

You have known him long; and be you well assured
He shall in strangeness° stand no farther off
Than in a politic distance.°
CASSIO: Ay, but, lady,
  That policy may either last so long,
  Or feed upon such nice and waterish diet,°   15
  Or breed itself so out of circumstance,
  That, I being absent, and my place supplied,
  My general will forget my love and service.
DESDEMONA: Do not doubt° that; before Emilia here
  I give thee warrant of thy place. Assure thee,   20
  If I do vow a friendship, I'll perform it
  To the last article. My lord shall never rest;
  I'll watch him tame° and talk him out of patience;
  His bed shall seem a school, his board a shrift;°
  I'll intermingle everything he does   25
  With Cassio's suit. Therefore be merry, Cassio,
  For thy solicitor shall rather die
  Than give thy cause away.

Enter Othello and Iago [at a distance].

EMILIA: Madam, here comes my lord.
CASSIO: Madam, I'll take my leave.   30
DESDEMONA: Why, stay, and hear me speak.
CASSIO: Madam, not now: I am very ill at ease,
  Unfit for mine own purposes.
DESDEMONA: Well, do your discretion.   *Exit Cassio.*
IAGO: Ha! I like not that.
OTHELLO: What dost thou say?   35
IAGO: Nothing, my lord; or if — I know not what.
OTHELLO: Was not that Cassio parted from my wife?
IAGO: Cassio, my lord? No, sure, I cannot think it,
  That he would steal away so guilty-like,
  Seeing your coming.
OTHELLO: I do believe 'twas he.   40
DESDEMONA: How now, my lord?
  I have been talking with a suitor here,
  A man that languishes in your displeasure.
OTHELLO: What is't you mean?
DESDEMONA: Why, your lieutenant, Cassio. Good my lord,   45
  If I have any grace or power to move you,
  His present° reconciliation take;
  For if he be not one that truly loves you,

SCENE III. **12 strangeness:** Aloofness. **13 Than . . . distance:** Than wise policy
requires. **15 Or . . . diet:** Or be continued for such slight reasons. **19 doubt:** Fear.
23 watch him tame: Keep him awake until he gives in. **24 shrift:** Confessional. **47
present:** Immediate.

That errs in ignorance, and not in cunning,
I have no judgment in an honest face,   50
I prithee call him back.
OTHELLO: Went he hence now?
DESDEMONA: Yes, faith; so humbled
That he hath left part of his grief with me
To suffer with him. Good love, call him back.
OTHELLO: Not now, sweet Desdemon; some other time.   55
DESDEMONA: But shall't be shortly?
OTHELLO: The sooner, sweet, for you.
DESDEMONA: Shall't be to-night at supper?
OTHELLO: No, not to-night.
DESDEMONA: To-morrow dinner then?
OTHELLO: I shall not dine at home;
I meet the captains at the citadel.
DESDEMONA: Why then, to-morrow night, or Tuesday morn,   60
On Tuesday noon or night, or Wednesday morn.
I prithee name the time, but let it not
Exceed three days. I' faith, he's penitent;
And yet his trespass, in our common reason
(Save that, they say, the wars must make examples   65
Out of their best), is not almost° a fault
T' incur a private check.° When shall he come?
Tell me, Othello. I wonder in my soul
What you could ask me that I should deny
Or stand so mamm'ring on.° What? Michael Cassio,   70
That came a-wooing with you, and so many a time,
When I have spoke of you dispraisingly,
Hath ta'en your part—to have so much to do
To bring him in? By'r Lady, I could do much—
OTHELLO: Prithee no more. Let him come when he will!   75
I will deny thee nothing.
DESDEMONA: Why, this is not a boon;
'Tis as I should entreat you wear your gloves,
Or feed on nourishing dishes, or keep you warm,
Or sue to you to do a peculiar profit
To your own person. Nay, when I have a suit   80
Wherein I mean to touch your love indeed,
It shall be full of poise and difficult weight,
And fearful° to be granted.
OTHELLO: I will deny thee nothing!
Whereon I do beseech thee grant me this,
To leave me but a little to myself.   85

66 not almost: Hardly.   **67 a private check:** Even a private reprimand.   **70 mamm'ring on:** Hesitating about.   **83 fearful:** Dangerous.

DESDEMONA: Shall I deny you? No. Farewell, my lord.
OTHELLO: Farewell, my Desdemon: I'll come to thee straight.
DESDEMONA: Emilia, come. — Be as your fancies teach you;
   Whate'er you be, I am obedient.   *Exit [with Emilia].*
OTHELLO: Excellent wretch!° Perdition catch my soul   90
   But I do love thee! and when I love thee not,
   Chaos is come again.
IAGO: My noble lord —
OTHELLO: What dost thou say, Iago?
IAGO: Did Michael Cassio, when you wooed my lady,
   Know of your love?   95
OTHELLO: He did, from first to last. Why dost thou ask?
IAGO: But for a satisfaction of my thought;
   No further harm.
OTHELLO: Why of thy thought, Iago?
IAGO: I did not think he had been acquainted with her.
OTHELLO: O, yes, and went between us° very oft.   100
IAGO: Indeed?
OTHELLO: Indeed? Ay, indeed! Discern'st thou aught in that?
   Is he not honest?
IAGO: Honest, my lord?
OTHELLO: Honest. Ay, honest.
IAGO: My lord, for aught I know.
OTHELLO: What dost thou think?
IAGO: Think, my lord?
OTHELLO: Think, my lord?   105
   By heaven, he echoes me,
   As if there were some monster in his thought
   Too hideous to be shown. Thou dost mean something:
   I heard thee say even now, thou lik'st not that,
   When Cassio left my wife. What didst not like?   110
   And when I told thee he was of my counsel
   In my whole course of wooing, thou cried'st "Indeed?"
   And didst contract and purse thy brow together,
   As if thou then hadst shut up in thy brain
   Some horrible conceit.° If thou dost love me,   115
   Show me thy thought
IAGO: My lord, you know I love you.
OTHELLO: I think thou dost;
   And, for I know thou'rt full of love and honesty
   And weigh'st thy words before thou giv'st them breath,
   Therefore these stops of thine fright me the more;   120
   For such things in a false disloyal knave

---

90 wretch: (A term of endearment). **100 went . . . us:** (I.e., as messenger). **115 conceit:** Fancy.

Are tricks of custom; but in a man that's just
They are close dilations, working from the heart
That passion cannot rule.°
IAGO: For Michael Cassio,
I dare be sworn I think that he is honest.   125
OTHELLO: I think so too.
IAGO: Men should be what they seem;
Or those that be not, would they might seem none!°
OTHELLO: Certain, men should be what they seem.
IAGO: Why then, I think Cassio's an honest man.
OTHELLO: Nay, yet there's more in this.   130
I prithee speak to me as to thy thinkings,
As thou dost ruminate, and give thy worst of thoughts
The worst of words.
IAGO: Good my lord, pardon me:
Though I am bound to every act of duty,
I am not bound to that all slaves are free to.°   135
Utter my thoughts? Why, say they are vile and false,
As where's that palace whereinto foul things
Sometimes intrude not? Who has a breast so pure
But some uncleanly apprehensions
Keep leets and law days,° and in Sessions sit   140
With meditations lawful?
OTHELLO: Thou dost conspire against thy friend, Iago,
If thou but think'st him wronged, and mak'st his ear
A stranger to thy thoughts.
IAGO: I do beseech you —
Though I perchance am vicious in my guess   145
(As I confess it is my nature's plague
To spy into abuses, and oft my jealousy°
Shapes faults that are not), that your wisdom yet
From one that so imperfectly conjects°
Would take no notice, nor build yourself a trouble   150
Out of his scattering and unsure observance.
It were not for your quiet nor your good,
Nor for my manhood, honesty, and wisdom,
To let you know my thoughts.
OTHELLO: What dost thou mean?
IAGO: Good name in man and woman, dear my lord,   155
Is the immediate° jewel of their souls.

123–24 close dilations . . . rule: Secret emotions that well up in spite of restraint.
127 seem none: I.e., not pretend to be men when they are really monsters.   **135
bound . . . free to:** Bound to tell that which even slaves are allowed to keep to themselves.
140 leets and law days: Sittings of the courts.   **147 jealousy:** Suspicion.   **149
conjects:** Conjectures.   **156 immediate:** Nearest the heart.

Who steals my purse steals trash; 'tis something, nothing;
'Twas mine, 'tis his, and has been slave to thousands;
But he that filches from me my good name
Robs me of that which not enriches him   160
And makes me poor indeed.
OTHELLO: By heaven, I'll know thy thoughts!
IAGO: You cannot, if my heart were in your hand;
Nor shall not whilst 'tis in my custody.
OTHELLO: Ha!
IAGO: O, beware, my lord, of jealousy!   165
It is the green-eyed monster, which doth mock°
The meat it feeds on. That cuckold lives in bliss
Who, certain of his fate, loves not his wronger;
But O, what damnèd minutes tells he o'er
Who dotes, yet doubts — suspects, yet strongly loves!   170
OTHELLO: O misery!
IAGO: Poor and content is rich, and rich enough;
But riches fineless° is as poor as winter
To him that ever fears he shall be poor.
Good God, the souls of all my tribe defend
From jealousy!   175
OTHELLO: Why, why is this?
Think'st thou I'ld make a life of jealousy,
To follow still the changes of the moon
With fresh suspicions? No! To be once in doubt
Is once to be resolved. Exchange me for a goat   180
When I shall turn the business of my soul
To such exsufflicate and blown° surmises,
Matching this inference. 'Tis not to make me jealous
To say my wife is fair, feeds well, loves company,
Is free of speech, sings, plays, and dances;   185
Where virtue is, these are more virtuous.
Nor from mine own weak merits will I draw
The smallest fear or doubt of her revolt,°
For she had eyes, and chose me. No, Iago;
I'll see before I doubt; when I doubt, prove;   190
And on the proof there is no more but this —
Away at once with love or jealousy!
IAGO: I am glad of this; for now I shall have reason
To show the love and duty that I bear you
With franker spirit. Therefore, as I am bound,   195
Receive it from me. I speak not yet of proof.
Look at your wife; observe her well with Cassio;

166 mock: Play with, like a cat with a mouse.   **173 fineless:** Unlimited.   **182
exsufflicate and blown:** Spat out and flyblown.   **188 revolt:** Unfaithfulness.

Wear your eyes thus, not jealous nor secure:°
I would not have your free and noble nature,
Out of self-bounty,° be abused. Look to't.   200
I know our country disposition well:
In Venice they do let God see the pranks
They dare not show their husbands; their best conscience
Is not to leave't undone, but keep't unknown.
OTHELLO: Dost thou say so?   205
IAGO: She did deceive her father, marrying you;
And when she seemed to shake and fear your looks,
She loved them most.
OTHELLO: And so she did.
IAGO: Why, go to then!
She that, so young, could give out such a seeming
To seel° her father's eyes up close as oak°—   210
He thought 'twas witchcraft — but I am much to blame.
I humbly do beseech you of your pardon
For too much loving you.
OTHELLO: I am bound to thee for ever.
IAGO: I see this hath a little dashed your spirits.
OTHELLO: Not a jot, not a jot.   215
IAGO: I' faith, I fear it has.
I hope you will consider what is spoke
Comes from my love. But I do see y' are moved.
I am to pray you not to strain my speech
To grosser issues° nor to larger reach
Than to suspicion.   220
OTHELLO: I will not.
IAGO: Should you do so, my lord,
My speech should fall into such vile success°
As my thoughts aim not at. Cassio's my worthy friend—
My lord, I see y' are moved.
OTHELLO: No, not much moved:
I do not think but Desdemona's honest.°   225
IAGO: Long live she so! and long live you to think so!
OTHELLO: And yet, how nature erring from itself—
IAGO: Ay, there's the point! as (to be bold with you)
Not to affect many proposèd matches
Of her own clime, complexion, and degree,   230
Whereto we see in all things nature tends—
Foh! one may smell in such a will most rank,
Foul disproportions, thought unnatural—

198 **secure:** Overconfident.   200 **self-bounty:** Natural goodness.   210 **seel:** Close;
oak: Oak grain.   219 **To grosser issues:** To mean something more monstrous.   222
vile success: Evil outcome.   225 **honest:** Chaste.

But pardon me — I do not in position°
Distinctly speak of her; though I may fear   235
Her will, recoiling° to her better judgment,
May fall to match° you with her country forms,
And happily° repent.
OTHELLO: Farewell, farewell!
If more thou dost perceive, let me know more.
Set on thy wife to observe. Leave me, Iago.   240
IAGO: My lord, I take my leave.   *[Going.]*
OTHELLO: Why did I marry? This honest creature doubtless
Sees and knows more, much more, than he unfolds.
IAGO *[returns]*:   My lord, I would I might entreat your honor
To scan this thing no further: leave it to time.   245
Although 'tis fit that Cassio have his place,
For sure he fills it up with great ability,
Yet, if you please to hold off a while,
You shall by that perceive him and his means.
Note if your lady strain his entertainment°   250
With any strong or vehement importunity;
Much will be seen in that. In the mean time
Let me be thought too busy° in my fears
(As worthy cause I have to fear I am)
And hold her free,° I do beseech your honor.   255
OTHELLO: Fear not my government.°
IAGO: I once more take my leave.   *Exit.*
OTHELLO: This fellow's of exceeding honesty,
And knows all qualities,° with a learned spirit
Of° human dealings. If I do prove her haggard,°   260
Though that her jesses° were my dear heartstrings,
I'd whistle her off and let her down the wind
To prey at fortune.° Haply, for I am black
And have not those soft parts of conversation°
That chamberers° have, or for I am declined   265
Into the vale of years — yet that's not much —
She's gone. I am abused, and my relief
Must be to loathe her. O curse of marriage,
That we can call these delicate creatures ours,
And not their appetites! I had rather be a toad   270

---

234 position: Definite assertion.   **236 recoiling:** Reverting.   **237 fall to match:** Happen to compare.   **238 happily:** Haply, perhaps.   **250 strain his entertainment:** Urge his recall.   **253 busy:** Meddlesome.   **255 hold her free:** Consider her guiltless.   **256 government:** Self-control.   **259 qualities:** Natures.   **259–60 learned spirit Of:** Mind informed about.   **260 haggard:** A wild hawk.   **261 jesses:** Thongs for controlling a hawk.   **262–63 whistle . . . fortune:** Turn her out and let her take care of herself.   **264 soft . . . conversation:** Ingratiating manners.   **265 chamberers:** Courtiers.

And live upon the vapor of a dungeon
Than keep a corner in the thing I love
For others' uses. Yet 'tis the plague of great ones;°
Prerogatived° are they less than the base.
'Tis destiny unshunnable, like death.   275
Even then this forkèd plague° is fated to us
When we do quicken.° Look where she comes.

Enter Desdemona and Emilia.

If she be false, O, then heaven mocks itself!
I'll not believe't.
DESDEMONA: How now, my dear Othello?
Your dinner, and the generous° islanders   280
By you invited, do attend your presence.
OTHELLO: I am to blame.
DESDEMONA: Why do you speak so faintly?
Are you not well?
OTHELLO: I have a pain upon my forehead, here.
DESDEMONA: Faith, that's with watching;° 'twill away again.   285
Let me but bind it hard, within this hour
It will be well.
OTHELLO: Your napkin° is too little;

[He pushes the handkerchief from him, and it falls unnoticed.]

Let it° alone. Come, I'll go in with you.
DESDEMONA: I am very sorry that you are not well.   *Exit [with Othello].*
EMILIA: I am glad I have found this napkin;   290
This was her first remembrance from the Moor,
My wayward husband hath a hundred times
Wooed me to steal it; but she so loves the token
(For he conjured her she should ever keep it)
That she reserves it evermore about her   295
To kiss and talk to. I'll have the work ta'en out°
And give't Iago.
What he will do with it heaven knows, not I;
I nothing but to please his fantasy.°

Enter Iago.

IAGO: How now? What do you here alone?   300
EMILIA: Do not you chide; I have a thing for you.
IAGO: A thing for me? It is a common thing —
EMILIA: Ha?
IAGO: To have a foolish wife.

273 great   ones: Prominent   men.   **274 Prerogatived:** Privileged.   **276 forkèd
plague:** I.e., horns of a cuckold.   **277 do quicken:** Are born.   **280 generous:**
Noble.   **285 watching:** Working late.   **287 napkin:** Handkerchief.   **288 it:** I.e., his
forehead.   **296 work ta'en out:** Pattern copied.   **299 fantasy:** Whim.

EMILIA: O, is that all? What will you give me now   305
   For that same handkerchief?
IAGO: What handkerchief?
EMILIA: What handkerchief!
   Why, that the Moor first gave to Desdemona;
   That which so often you did bid me steal.
IAGO: Hast stol'n it from her?   210
EMILIA: No, faith; she let it drop by negligence,
   And to th' advantage,° I, being here, took't up.
   Look, here it is.
IAGO: A good wench! Give it me.
EMILIA: What will you do with't, that you have been so earnest
   To have me filch it?
IAGO: Why, what is that to you?   315
[Snatches it.]
EMILIA: If it be not for some purpose of import,°
   Give't me again. Poor lady, she'll run mad
   When she shall lack it.
IAGO: Be not acknown on't;° I have use for it.
   Go, leave me.   *Exit Emilia.*   320
   I will in Cassio's lodgings lose this napkin
   And let him find it. Trifles light as air
   Are to the jealous confirmations strong
   As proofs of holy writ. This may do something.
   The Moor already changes with my poison: 325
   Dangerous conceits° are in their nature poisons,
   Which at the first are scarce found to distaste,
   But with a little act upon the blood
   Burn like the mines of sulphur.
Enter Othello.
                 I did say so.
   Look where he comes! Not poppy nor mandragora,°   330
   Nor all the drowsy syrups of the world,
   Shall ever med'cine thee to that sweet sleep
   Which thou owedst yesterday.
OTHELLO: Ha! ha! false to me?
IAGO: Why, how now, general? No more of that!
OTHELLO: Avaunt! be gone! Thou hast set me on the rack.   335
   I swear 'tis better to be much abused
   Than but to know't a little.
IAGO: How now, my lord?
OTHELLO: What sense had I of her stol'n hours of lust?

312 to th' advantage: Opportunely.   **316 import:** Importance.   **319 Be . . . on't:**
Do not acknowledge it.   **326 conceits:** Ideas.   **330 mandragora:** A narcotic.

I saw't not, thought it not, it harmed not me;
I slept the next night well, fed well, was free° and merry;   340
I found not Cassio's kisses on her lips
He that is robbed, not wanting° what is stol'n,
Let him not know't, and he's not robbed at all.

IAGO: I am sorry to hear this.

OTHELLO: I had been happy if the general camp,   345
Pioneers° and all, had tasted her sweet body,
So I had nothing known. O, now for ever
Farewell the tranquil mind! farewell content!
Farewell the plumèd troop, and the big° wars
That make ambition virtue! O, farewell!   350
Farewell the neighing steed and the shrill trump,
The spirit-stirring drum, th' ear-piercing fife,
The royal banner, and all quality,
Pride, pomp, and circumstance° of glorious war!
And O you mortal engines° whose rude throats   355
Th' immortal Jove's dread clamors counterfeit,°
Farewell! Othello's occupation's gone!

IAGO: Is't possible, my lord?

OTHELLO: Villain, be sure thou prove my love a whore!
Be sure of it; give me the ocular proof;   360
Or, by the worth of mine eternal soul,
Thou hadst been better have been born a dog
Than answer my waked wrath!

IAGO: Is't come to this?

OTHELLO: Make me to see't; or at the least so prove it
That the probation° bear no hinge nor loop   365
To hang a doubt on — or woe upon thy life!

IAGO: My noble lord —

OTHELLO: If thou dost slander her and torture me,
Never pray more; abandon all remorse;
On horror's head horrors accumulate;   370
Do deeds to make heaven weep, all earth amazed;
For nothing canst thou to damnation add
Greater than that.

IAGO: O grace! O heaven forgive me!
Are you a man? Have you a soul or sense? —
God b' wi' you! take mine office. O wretched fool,   375
That liv'st to make thine honesty a vice!
O monstrous world! Take note, take note, O world,
To be direct and honest is not safe.

---

340 free: Carefree. **342 wanting:** Missing. **346 Pioneers:** Sappers, laborers.
349 big: Stately. **354 circumstance:** Pageantry. **355 mortal   engines:** Deadly
artillery. **356 counterfeit:** Imitate. **365 probation:** Proof.

I thank you for this profit;° and from hence
I'll love no friend, sith love breeds such offense.   380
OTHELLO: Nay, stay. Thou shouldst be honest.
IAGO: I should be wise; for honesty's a fool
   And loses that it works for.
OTHELLO: By the world,
   I think my wife be honest, and think she is not;
   I think that thou art just, and think thou art not.   385
   I'll have some proof. Her name, that was as fresh
   As Dian's visage, is now begrimed and black
   As mine own face. If there be cords, or knives,
   Poison, or fire, or suffocating streams,
   I'll not endure it. Would I were satisfied!°   390
IAGO: I see, sir, you are eaten up with passion:
   I do repent me that I put it to you.
   You would be satisfied?
OTHELLO: Would? Nay, I will.
IAGO: And may; but how? how satisfied, my lord?
   Would you, the supervisor,° grossly gape on?   395
   Behold her topped?
OTHELLO: Death and damnation! O!
IAGO: It were a tedious difficulty, I think,
   To bring them to that prospect. Damn them then,
   If ever mortal eyes do see them bolster°
   More than their own! What then? How then?   400
   What shall I say? Where's satisfaction?
   It is impossible you should see this,
   Were they as prime° as goats, as hot as monkeys,
   As salt° as wolves in pride,° and fools as gross
   As ignorance made drunk. But yet, I say,   405
   If imputation and strong circumstances
   Which lead directly to the door of truth
   Will give you satisfaction, you may have't.
OTHELLO: Give me a living reason she's disloyal.
IAGO: I do not like the office.   410
   But sith I am ent'red in this cause so far,
   Pricked to't by foolish honesty and love,
   I will go on. I lay with Cassio lately,
   And being troubled with a raging tooth,
   I could not sleep.   415
   There are a kind of men so loose of soul
   That in their sleeps will mutter their affairs.

---

379 profit: Profitable lesson.   **390 satisfied:** Completely informed.   **395 supervisor:** Spectator.   **399 bolster:** Lie together.   **403 prime:** Lustful.   **404 salt:** Lecherous; **pride:** Heat.

One of this kind is Cassio.
In sleep I heard him say, "Sweet Desdemona,
Let us be wary, let us hide our loves!"   420
And then, sir, would he gripe and wring my hand,
Cry "O sweet creature!" and then kiss me hard,
As if he plucked up kisses by the roots
That grew upon my lips; then laid his leg
Over my thigh, and sighed, and kissed, and then   425
Cried "Cursèd fate that gave thee to the Moor!"

OTHELLO: O monstrous! monstrous!

IAGO: Nay, this was but his dream.

OTHELLO: But this denoted a foregone conclusion;°
'Tis a shrewd doubt,° though it be but a dream.

IAGO: And this may help to thicken other proofs   430
That do demonstrate thinly.

OTHELLO: I'll tear her all to pieces!

IAGO: Nay, but be wise. Yet we see nothing done;
She may be honest yet. Tell me but this —
Have you not sometimes seen a handkerchief
Spotted with strawberries in your wife's hand?   435

OTHELLO: I gave her such a one; 'twas my first gift.

IAGO: I know not that; but such a handkerchief —
I am sure it was your wife's — did I to-day
See Cassio wipe his beard with.

OTHELLO: If it be that —

IAGO: If it be that, or any that was hers,   440
It speaks against her with the other proofs.

OTHELLO: O, that the slave had forty thousand lives!
One is too poor, too weak for my revenge.
Now do I see 'tis true. Look here, Iago:
All my fond love thus do I blow to heaven.   445
'Tis gone.
Arise, black vengeance, from the hollow hell!
Yield up, O love, thy crown and hearted throne
To tyrannous hate! Swell, bosom, with thy fraught,°
For 'tis of aspics'° tongues!

IAGO: Yet be content.   450

OTHELLO: O, blood, blood, blood!

IAGO: Patience, I say. Your mind perhaps may change.

OTHELLO: Never, Iago. Like to the Pontic sea,°
Whose icy current and compulsive course
Ne'er feels retiring ebb, but keeps due on   455

---

428 foregone conclusion: Previous experience. **429 a shrewd doubt:** Cursedly
suspicious. **449 fraught:** Burden. **450 aspics:** Deadly poisonous snakes. **453
Pontic sea:** Black Sea.

To the Propontic and the Hellespont,
Even so my bloody thoughts, with violent pace,
Shall ne'er look back, ne'er ebb to humble love,
Till that a capable° and wide revenge
Swallow them up.
   (He kneels.)   Now, by yond marble heaven,   460
In the due reverence of a sacred vow
I here engage my words.
IAGO: Do not rise yet.

(Iago kneels.)

Witness, you ever-burning lights above,
You elements that clip° us round about,
Witness that here Iago doth give up   465
The execution° of his wit,° hands, heart
To wronged Othello's service! Let him command,
And to obey shall be in me remorse,°
What bloody business ever.

[They rise.]

OTHELLO: I greet thy love,
Not with vain thanks but with acceptance bounteous,   470
And will upon the instant put thee to't.
Within these three days let me hear thee say
That Cassio's not alive.
IAGO: My friend is dead; 'tis done at your request.
But let her live.   475
OTHELLO: Damn her, lewd minx! O, damn her! damn her!
Come, go with me apart. I will withdraw
To furnish me with some swift means of death
For the fair devil. Now art thou my lieutenant.
IAGO: I am your own forever.   *Exeunt.* 480

[Scene IV: The environs of the castle.]

Enter Desdemona, Emilia, and Clown.

DESDEMONA: Do you know, sirrah, where Lieutenant Cassio lies?°
CLOWN: I dare not say he lies anywhere.
DESDEMONA: Why, man?
CLOWN: He's a soldier, and for me to say a soldier lies is stabbing.
DESDEMONA: Go to. Where lodges he?   5
CLOWN: To tell you where he lodges is to tell you where I lie.
DESDEMONA: Can anything be made of this?

---

459 capable: All-embracing.   **464 clip:** Encompass.   **466 execution:** Activities;
wit: Mind.   **468 remorse:** Pity.   **SCENE IV. 1 lies:** Lives, lodges.

CLOWN: I know not where he lodges; and for me to devise a lodging, and say he
lies here or he lies there, were to lie in mine own throat.

DESDEMONA: Can you enquire him out, and be edified by report?   10

CLOWN: I will catechize the world for him; that is, make questions, and by
them answer.

DESDEMONA: Seek him, bid him come hither. Tell him I have moved° my lord on
his behalf and hope all will be well.

CLOWN: To do this is within the compass of man's wit, and therefore I'll   15
attempt the doing of it.   *Exit.*

DESDEMONA: Where should I lose that handkerchief, Emilia?

EMILIA: I know not, madam.

DESDEMONA: Believe me, I had rather have lost my purse
Full of crusadoes;° and but my noble Moor
Is true of mind, and made of no such baseness   20
As jealous creatures are, it were enough
To put him to ill thinking.

EMILIA: Is he not jealous?

DESDEMONA: Who? he? I think the sun where he was born
Drew all such humors° from him.

Enter Othello.

EMILIA: Look where he comes.   25

DESDEMONA: I will not leave him now till Cassio
Be called to him — How is't with you, my lord?

OTHELLO: Well, my good lady. [Aside.] O, hardness to dissemble! —
How do you, Desdemona?

DESDEMONA: Well, my good lord.

OTHELLO: Give me your hand. This hand is moist, my lady.   30

DESDEMONA: It yet hath felt no age nor known no sorrow.

OTHELLO: This argues fruitfulness and liberal heart.
Hot, hot, and moist. This hand of yours requires
A sequester° from liberty, fasting and prayer,
Much castigation, exercise devout;   35
For here's a young and sweating devil here
That commonly rebels. 'Tis a good hand,
A frank one.

DESDEMONA: You may, indeed, say so;
For 'twas that hand that gave away my heart.   40

OTHELLO: A liberal hand! The hearts of old gave hands;
But our new heraldry° is hands, not hearts.

DESDEMONA: I cannot speak of this. Come now, your promise!

OTHELLO: What promise, chuck?

DESDEMONA: I have sent to bid Cassio come speak with you.   45

---

13 moved: Made proposals to.   **20 crusadoes:** Portuguese gold coins.   **25 humors:**
Inclinations.   **34 sequester:** Removal.   **42 heraldry:** Heraldic symbolism.

OTHELLO: I have a salt and sorry rheum° offends me.
Lend me thy handkerchief.
DESDEMONA: Here, my lord.
OTHELLO: That which I gave you.
DESDEMONA: I have it not about me.
OTHELLO: Not?
DESDEMONA: No, faith, my lord.
OTHELLO: That's a fault.
That handkerchief   50
Did an Egyptian° to my mother give.
She was a charmer,° and could almost read
The thoughts of people. She told her, while she kept it,
'Twould make her amiable° and subdue my father
Entirely to her love; but if she lost it   55
Or made a gift of it, my father's eye
Should hold her loathèd, and his spirits should hunt
After new fancies. She, dying, gave it me,
And bid me, when my fate would have me wive;
To give it her. I did so; and take heed on't;   60
Make it a darling like your precious eye.
To lose't or give't away were such perdition°
As nothing else could match.
DESDEMONA: Is't possible?
OTHELLO: 'Tis true. There's magic in the web of it.
A sibyl that had numb'red in the world   65
The sun to course two hundred compasses,°
In her prophetic fury sewed the work;
The worms were hallowed that did breed the silk;
And it was dyed in mummy° which the skillful
Conserved of maidens' hearts.
DESDEMONA: I' faith? Is't true?   70
OTHELLO: Most veritable. Therefore look to't well.
DESDEMONA: Then would to God that I had never seen't!
OTHELLO: Ha! Wherefore?
DESDEMONA: Why do you speak so startingly and rash?
OTHELLO: Is't lost? Is't gone? Speak, is it out o' th' way?   75
DESDEMONA: Heaven bless us!
OTHELLO: Say you?
DESDEMONA: It is not lost. But what an if it were?
OTHELLO: How?
DESDEMONA: I say it is not lost.
OTHELLO: Fetch't, let me see't!   80

46 salt . . . rheum: Distressing head cold.   51 Egyptian: Gypsy.   52 charmer:
Sorceress.   54 amiable: Lovable.   62 perdition: Disaster.   66 compasses:
Annual rounds.   69 mummy: A drug made from mummies.

DESDEMONA: Why, so I can, sir; but I will not now.
 This is a trick to put° me from my suit:
 Pray you let Cassio be received again.
OTHELLO: Fetch me the handkerchief! My mind misgives.
DESDEMONA: Come, come!   85
 You'll never meet a more sufficient man.
OTHELLO: The handkerchief!
DESDEMONA: I pray talk me of Cassio.
OTHELLO: The handkerchief!
DESDEMONA: A man that all his time°
 Hath founded his good fortunes on your love,
 Shared dangers with you —   90
OTHELLO: The handkerchief!
DESDEMONA: I' faith, you are to blame.
OTHELLO: Zounds!   *Exit Othello.*
EMILIA: Is not this man jealous?
DESDEMONA: I ne'er saw this before.   95
 Sure there's some wonder in this handkerchief;
 I am most unhappy in the loss of it.
EMILIA: 'Tis not a year or two shows us a man.
 They are all but stomachs, and we all but food;
 They eat us hungerly, and when they are full,   100
 They belch us.

Enter Iago and Cassio.

    Look you — Cassio and my husband!
IAGO: There is no other way; 'tis she must do't.
 And lo the happiness!° Go and importune her.
DESDEMONA: How now, good Cassio? What's the news with you?
CASSIO: Madam, my former suit. I do beseech you   105
 That by your virtuous means I may again
 Exist, and be a member of his love
 Whom I with all the office of my heart
 Entirely honor. I would not be delayed.
 If my offense be of such mortal kind   110
 That neither service past, nor present sorrows,
 Nor purposed merit in futurity,
 Can ransom me into his love again,
 But to know so must be my benefit.
 So shall I clothe me in a forced content,   115
 And shut myself up in° some other course,
 To fortune's alms.
DESDEMONA: Alas, thrice-gentle Cassio!

82 put: Divert.   **88 all . . . time:** During his whole career.   **103 happiness:** Good
luck.   **116 shut myself up in:** Confine myself to.

My advocation° is not now in tune.
My lord is not my lord; nor should I know him,
Were he in favor° as in humor altered.   120
So help me every spirit sanctified
As I have spoken for you all my best
And stood within the blank° of his displeasure
For my free speech! You must a while be patient.
What I can do I will; and more I will   125
Than for myself I dare. Let that suffice you.
IAGO: Is my lord angry?
EMILIA: He went hence but now,
And certainly in strange unquietness.
IAGO: Can he be angry? I have seen the cannon
When it hath blown his ranks into the air   130
And, like the devil, from his very arm
Puffed his own brother — and is he angry?
Something of moment then. I will go meet him.
There's matter in't indeed if he be angry.
DESDEMONA: I prithee do so.   *Exit [Iago].*
                      Something sure of state,°   135
Either from Venice or some unhatched practice°
Made demonstrable here in Cyprus to him,
Hath puddled° his clear spirit; and in such cases
Men's natures wrangle with inferior things,
Though great ones are their object. 'Tis even so;   140
For let our finger ache, and it endues°
Our other, healthful members even to a sense
Of pain. Nay, we must think men are not gods,
Nor of them look for such observancy
As fits the bridal. Beshrew me much, Emilia,   145
I was, unhandsome warrior° as I am,
Arraigning his unkindness with my soul;°
But now I find I had suborned the witness,
And he's indicted falsely.
EMILIA: Pray heaven it be state matters, as you think,   150
And no conception nor no jealous toy°
Concerning you.
DESDEMONA: Alas the day! I never gave him cause.
EMILIA: But jealous souls will not be answered so;
They are not ever jealous for the cause,   155

---

118 advocation: Advocacy.   **120 favor:** Appearance.   **123 blank:** Bull's-eye of the
target.   **135 state:** Public affairs.   **136 unhatched practice:** Budding plot.   **138
puddled:** Muddied.   **141 endues:** Brings.   **146 unhandsome warrior:** Inadequate
soldier.   **147 Arraigning . . . soul:** Indicting his unkindness before the bar of my soul.
151 toy: Fancy.

But jealous for they're jealous. 'Tis a monster
Begot upon itself,° born on itself.
DESDEMONA: Heaven keep that monster from Othello's mind!
EMILIA: Lady, amen.
DESDEMONA: I will go seek him. Cassio, walk here about: 160
If I do find him fit, I'll move your suit
And seek to effect it to my uttermost.
CASSIO: I humbly thank your ladyship.

                                        Exeunt Desdemona and Emilia.

Enter Bianca.

BIANCA: Save you, friend Cassio!
CASSIO: What make you from home?
How is't with you, my most fair Bianca?   165
I' faith, sweet love, I was coming to your house.
BIANCA: And I was going to your lodging, Cassio.
What, keep a week away? seven days and nights?
Eightscore eight hours? and lovers' absent hours,
More tedious than the dial° eightscore times?   170
O weary reck'ning!
CASSIO: Pardon me, Bianca:
I have this while with leaden thoughts been pressed;
But I shall in a more continuate° time
Strike off this score of absence. Sweet Bianca,

[Gives her Desdemona's handkerchief.]

Take me this work out.°
BIANCA: O Cassio, whence came this?   175
This is some token from a newer friend.
To the felt absence now I feel a cause.
Is't come to this? Well, well.
CASSIO: Go to, woman!
Throw your vile guesses in the devil's teeth,
From whence you have them. You are jealous now   180
That this is from some mistress, some remembrance.
No, by my faith, Bianca.
BIANCA: Why, whose is it?
CASSIO: I know not, sweet; I found it in my chamber.
I like the work° well; ere it be demanded,
As like enough it will, I'd have it copied.   185
Take it and do't, and leave me for this time.
BIANCA: Leave you? Wherefore?
CASSIO: I do attend here on the general

---

157 Begot . . . itself: Self-engendered.   **170 dial:** Clock.   **173 continuate:** Uninterrupted.   **175 Take . . . out:** Copy this embroidery for me.   **184 work:** Needlework.

And think it no addition, nor my wish,
To have him see me womaned.
BIANCA: Why, I pray you?   190
CASSIO: Not that I love you not.
BIANCA: But that you do not love me!
I pray you bring me on the way a little,
And say if I shall see you soon at night.
CASSIO: 'Tis but a little way that I can bring you,
For I attend here; but I'll see you soon.   195
BIANCA: 'Tis very good. I must be circumstanced.°   *Exeunt.*

[ACT IV, Scene I: The environs of the castle.]

Enter Othello and Iago.

IAGO: Will you think so?
OTHELLO: Think so, Iago?
IAGO: What,
To kiss in private?
OTHELLO: An unauthorized kiss.
IAGO: Or to be naked with her friend in bed
An hour or more, not meaning any harm?
OTHELLO: Naked in bed, Iago, and not mean harm?   5
It is hypocrisy against the devil.°
They that mean virtuously, and yet do so,
The devil their virtue tempts, and they tempt heaven.
IAGO: So they do nothing, 'tis a venial slip.
But if I give my wife a handkerchief —   10
OTHELLO: What then?
IAGO: Why, then 'tis hers, my lord; and being hers,
She may, I think, bestow't on any man.
OTHELLO: She is protectress of her honor too;
May she give that?   15
IAGO: Her honor is an essence that's not seen;
They have it very oft that have it not.
But for the handkerchief —
OTHELLO: By heaven, I would most gladly have forgot it!
Thou said'st — O, it comes o'er my memory   20
As doth the raven o'er the infected° house,
Boding to all! — he had my handkerchief.
IAGO: Ay, what of that?
OTHELLO: That's not so good now.
IAGO: What

---

196 circumstanced: Governed by circumstances. **ACT IV, SCENE I. 6 hypocrisy . . . devil:** I.e., feigned sin instead of feigned virtue. **21 infected:** Plague-stricken.

If I had said I had seen him do you wrong?
Or heard him say — as knaves be such abroad   25
Who having, by their own importunate suit,
Or voluntary dotage of some mistress,
Convincèd or supplied° them, cannot choose
But they must blab —
OTHELLO: Hath he said anything?
IAGO: He hath, my lord; but be you well assured,   30
No more than he'll unswear.
OTHELLO: What hath he said?
IAGO: Faith, that he did — I know not what he did.
OTHELLO: What? what?
IAGO: Lie —
OTHELLO: With her?
IAGO: With her, on her; what you will.   35
OTHELLO: Lie with her? lie on her? — We say lie on her when they belie her. —
Lie with her! Zounds, that's fulsome. — Handkerchief — confessions —
handkerchief! — To confess, and be hanged for his labor — first to be
hanged, and then to confess! I tremble at it. Nature would not invest herself
in such shadowing passion without some instruction.° It is not words that   40
shakes me thus. — Pish! Noses, ears, and lips? Is't possible? — Confess? —
Handkerchief? — O devil!

(Falls in a trance.)

IAGO: Work on,
My med'cine, work! Thus credulous fools are caught,
And many worthy and chaste dames even thus,   45
All guiltless, meet reproach. — What, ho! my lord!
My lord, I say! Othello!
Enter Cassio.   How now, Cassio?
CASSIO: What's the matter?
IAGO: My lord is fall'n into an epilepsy.
This is his second fit; he had one yesterday.   50
CASSIO: Rub him about the temples.
IAGO: No, forbear.
The lethargy° must have his quiet course.
If not, he foams at mouth, and by and by
Breaks out to savage madness. Look, he stirs.
Do you withdraw yourself a little while.   55
He will recover straight. When he is gone,
I would on great occasion speak with you.   *[Exit Cassio.]*
How is it, general? Have you not hurt your head?
OTHELLO: Dost thou mock me?

28 Convincèd or supplied: Overcome or gratified.   **39–40 Nature . . . instruction:**
My natural faculties would not be so overcome by passion without reason.   **52 lethargy:**
Coma.

IAGO: I mock you? No, by heaven.
Would you would bear your fortune like a man!   60
OTHELLO: A hornèd man's° a monster and a beast.
IAGO: There's many a beast then in a populous city,
And many a civil monster.
OTHELLO: Did he confess it?
IAGO: Good sir, be a man.
Think every bearded fellow that's but yoked   65
May draw with you. There's millions now alive
That nightly lie in those unproper° beds
Which they dare swear peculiar:° your case is better.
O, 'tis the spite of hell, the fiend's arch-mock,
To lip a wanton in a secure° couch,   70
And to suppose her chaste! No, let me know;
And knowing what I am, I know what she shall be.
OTHELLO: O, thou art wise! 'Tis certain.
IAGO: Stand you awhile apart;
Confine yourself but in a patient list.°
Whilst you were here, o'erwhelmèd with your grief —   75
A passion most unsuiting such a man —
Cassio came hither. I shifted him away
And laid good 'scuse upon your ecstasy;°
Bade him anon return, and here speak with me;
The which he promised. Do but encave° yourself   80
And mark the fleers, the gibes, and notable scorns
That dwell in every region of his face;
For I will make him tell the tale anew —
Where, how, how oft, how long ago, and when
He hath, and is again to cope° your wife.   85
I say, but mark his gesture. Marry, patience!
Or I shall say y'are all in all in spleen,°
And nothing of a man.
OTHELLO: Dost thou hear, Iago?
I will be found most cunning in my patience;
But — dost thou hear? — most bloody.
IAGO: That's not amiss: 90
But yet keep time in all. Will you withdraw?

[Othello retires.]

Now will I question Cassio of Bianca,
A huswife° that by selling her desires
Buys herself bread and clothes. It is a creature

---

61 hornèd man: Cuckold.   **67 unproper:** Not exclusively their own.   **68 peculiar:**
Exclusively their own.   **70 secure:** Free from fear of rivalry.   **74 in a patient list:** With-
in the limits of self-control.   **78 ecstasy:** Trance.   **80 encave:** Conceal.   **85 cope:**
Meet.   **87 all in all in spleen:** Wholly overcome by your passion.   **93 huswife:** Hussy.

That dotes on Cassio, as 'tis the strumpet's plague   95
To beguile many and be beguiled by one.
He, when he hears of her, cannot refrain
From the excess of laughter. Here he comes.

Enter Cassio.

As he shall smile, Othello shall go mad;
And his unbookish° jealousy must conster°   100
Poor Cassio's smiles, gestures, and light behavior
Quite in the wrong. How do you now, lieutenant?
CASSIO: The worser that you give me the addition°
Whose want even kills me.
IAGO: Ply Desdemona well, and you are sure on't.   105
Now, if this suit lay in Bianca's power,
How quickly should you speed!
CASSIO: Alas, poor caitiff!°
OTHELLO: Look how he laughs already!
IAGO: I never knew a woman love man so.
CASSIO: Alas, poor rogue! I think, i' faith, she loves me.   110
OTHELLO: Now he denies it faintly, and laughs it out.
IAGO: Do you hear, Cassio?
OTHELLO: Now he importunes him
To tell it o'er. Go to! Well said, well said!
IAGO: She gives out that you shall marry her.
Do you intend it?   115
CASSIO: Ha, ha, ha!
OTHELLO: Do you triumph, Roman? Do you triumph?
CASSIO: I marry her? What, a customer?° Prithee bear some charity to my wit;
do not think it so unwholesome. Ha, ha, ha!
OTHELLO: So, so, so, so! They laugh that win!   120
IAGO: Faith, the cry goes that you shall marry her.
CASSIO: Prithee say true.
IAGO: I am a very villain else.
OTHELLO: Have you scored me?° Well.
CASSIO: This is the monkey's own giving out. She is persuaded I will marry   125
her out of her own love and flattery, not out of my promise.
OTHELLO: Iago beckons° me; now he begins the story.
CASSIO: She was here even now; she haunts me in every place. I was t' other
day talking on the sea bank with certain Venetians, and thither comes the
bauble,° and, by this hand, she falls me thus about my neck —   130
OTHELLO: Crying "O dear Cassio!" as it were. His gesture imports it.
CASSIO: So hangs, and lolls, and weeps upon me; so shakes and pulls me! Ha,
ha, ha!

---

100 unbookish: Uninstructed;   **conster:** Construe, interpret.   **103 addition:** Title.
107 caitiff: Wretch.   **118 customer:** Prostitute.   **124 scored   me:** Settled   my
account (?).   **127 beckons:** Signals.   **130 bauble:** Plaything.

OTHELLO: Now he tells how she plucked him to my chamber. O, I see that nose
   of yours, but not that dog I shall throw it to.   135
CASSIO: Well, I must leave her company.

Enter Bianca.

IAGO: Before me! Look where she comes.
CASSIO: 'Tis such another fitchew!° marry, a perfumed one. What do you
   mean by this haunting of me?
BIANCA: Let the devil and his dam haunt you! What did you mean by that   140
   same handkerchief you gave me even now? I was a fine fool to take it. I
   must take out the whole work? A likely piece of work that you should find it
   in your chamber and know not who left it there! This is some minx's token,
   and I must take out the work? There! Give it your hobby-horse.° Whereso-
   ever you had it, I'll take out no work on't.   145
CASSIO: How now, my sweet Bianca? How now? how now?
OTHELLO: By heaven, that should be my handkerchief!
BIANCA: An you'll come to supper to-night, you may; an you will not, come
   when you are next prepared for.   *Exit.*
IAGO: After her, after her!   150
CASSIO: Faith, I must; she'll rail in the street else.
IAGO: Will you sup there?
CASSIO: Yes, I intend so.
IAGO: Well, I may chance to see you; for I would very fain speak with you.
CASSIO: Prithee come. Will you?   155
IAGO: Go to! say no more.   *Exit Cassio.*
OTHELLO *[comes forward]*:   How shall I murder him, Iago?
IAGO: Did you perceive how he laughed at his vice?°
OTHELLO: O Iago!
IAGO: And did you see the handkerchief?   160
OTHELLO: Was that mine?
IAGO: Your, by this hand! And to see how he prizes° the foolish woman your
   wife! She gave it him, and he hath giv'n it his whore.
OTHELLO: I would have him nine years a-killing — A fine woman! a fair
   woman! a sweet woman!   165
IAGO: Nay, you must forget that.
OTHELLO: Ay, let her rot, and perish, and be damned to-night; for she shall not
   live. No, my heart is turned to stone; I strike it, and it hurts my hand. O, the
   world hath not a sweeter creature! She might lie by an emperor's side and
   command him tasks.   170
IAGO: Nay, that's not your way.
OTHELLO: Hang her! I do but say what she is. So delicate with her needle! an
   admirable musician! O, she will sing the savageness out of a bear! Of so
   high and plenteous wit and invention° —

---

138 fitchew: Polecat (slang for whore).   **144 hobby-horse:** Harlot.   **158 vice:**
I.e., vicious conduct.   **162 prizes:** Values.   **174 invention:** Imagination.

IAGO: She's the worse for all this.   175
OTHELLO: O, a thousand thousand times! And then, of so gentle a condition!°
IAGO: Ay, too gentle.
OTHELLO: Nay, that's certain. But yet the pity of it, Iago! O Iago, the pity of it,
Iago!
IAGO: If you are so fond over her iniquity, give her patent° to offend; for if it   180
touch not you, it comes near nobody.
OTHELLO: I will chop her into messes! Cuckold me!
IAGO: O, 'tis foul in her.
OTHELLO: With mine officer!
IAGO: That's fouler.   185
OTHELLO: Get me some poison, Iago, this night. I'll not expostulate with her,
lest her body and beauty unprovide° my mind again. This night, Iago!
IAGO: Do it not with poison. Strangle her in her bed, even the bed she hath
contaminated.
OTHELLO: Good, good! The justice of it pleases. Very good!   190
IAGO: And for Cassio, let me be his undertaker;° you shall hear more by
midnight.
OTHELLO: Excellent good!

A trumpet.

What trumpet is that same?
IAGO: I warrant something from Venice.

Enter Lodovico, Desdemona, and Attendants.

                                                              'Tis Lodovico.   195
This comes from the Duke; and see, your wife is with him.
LODOVICO: God save you, worthy general!
OTHELLO: With all my heart, sir.
LODOVICO: The Duke and senators of Venice greet you.

[Gives him a letter.]

OTHELLO: I kiss the instrument of their pleasures.

[Opens the letter and reads.]

DESDEMONA: And what's the news, good cousin Lodovico?   200
IAGO: I am very glad to see you, signior.
Welcome to Cyprus.
LODOVICO: I thank you. How does Lieutenant Cassio?
IAGO: Lives, sir.
DESDEMONA: Cousin, there's fall'n between him and my lord
An unkind breach; but you shall make all well.   205
OTHELLO: Are you sure of that?
DESDEMONA: My lord?
OTHELLO *[reads]*:   "This fail you not to do, as you will—"

176 condition: Disposition.   **180 patent:** License.   **187 unprovide:** Disarm.
191 be his undertaker: Undertake to deal with him.

LODOVICO:He did not call; he's busy in the paper.
    Is there division 'twixt thy lord and Cassio?   210
DESDEMONA: A most unhappy one. I would do much
    T' atone° them, for the love I bear to Cassio.
OTHELLO: Fire and brimstone!
DESDEMONA: My lord?
OTHELLO: Are you wise?
DESDEMONA: What, is he angry?
LODOVICO: May be the letter moved him;
    For, as I think, they do command him home,   215
    Deputing Cassio in his government.
DESDEMONA: By my troth, I am glad on't.
OTHELLO: Indeed?
DESDEMONA: My lord?
OTHELLO: I am glad to see you mad.°
DESDEMONA: Why, sweet Othello—
OTHELLO: Devil!

[Strikes her.]

DESDEMONA: I have not deserved this.   220
LODOVICO: My lord, this would not be believed in Venice,
    Though I should swear I saw't. 'Tis very much.
    Make her amends; she weeps.
OTHELLO: O devil, devil!
    If that the earth could teem° with woman's tears,
    Each drop she falls would prove a crocodile.°   225
    Out of my sight!
DESDEMONA: I will not stay to offend you.   *[Going.]*
LODOVICO: Truly, an obedient lady.
    I do beseech your lordship call her back.
OTHELLO: Mistress!
DESDEMONA: My lord?
OTHELLO: What would you with her, sir?   230
LODOVICO: Who? I, my lord?
OTHELLO: Ay! You did wish that I would make her turn.
    Sir, she can turn, and turn, and yet go on
    And turn again; and she can weep, sir, weep;
    And she's obedient; as you say, obedient,   235
    Very obedient. — Proceed you in your tears. —
    Concerning this, sir — O well-painted passion!° —
    I am commanded home. — Get you away;
    I'll send for you anon. — Sir, I obey the mandate
    And will return to Venice. — Hence, avaunt!   240

212 atone: Reconcile. **218 mad:** I.e.,   waggish. **224 teem:** Breed. **225 croco-dile:** Crocodiles were supposed to shed hypocritical tears to lure men to destruction.
237 passion: Grief.

806	CHAPTER 11	Love

Cassio shall have my place. And, sir, to-night
I do entreat that we may sup together.
You are welcome, sir, to Cyprus — Goats and monkeys!

Exit.

LODOVICO:	Is this the noble Moor whom our full Senate
Call all in all sufficient? Is this the nature   245
Whom passion could not shake? whose solid virtue
The shot of accident nor dart of chance
Could neither graze nor pierce?
IAGO: He is much changed.
LODOVICO:	Are his wits safe? Is he not light of brain?
IAGO:	He's that he is; I may not breathe my censure. 250
What he might be — if what he might he is not —
I would to heaven he were!
LODOVICO: What, strike his wife?
IAGO:	Faith, that was not so well; yet would I knew
That stroke would prove the worst!
LODOVICO: Is it his use?°
Or did the letters work upon his blood   255
And new-create this fault?
IAGO: Alas, alas!
It is not honesty in me to speak
What I have seen and known. You shall observe him,
And his own courses will denote him so
That I may save my speech. Do but go after   260
And mark how he continues.
LODOVICO:	I am sorry that I am deceived in him. *Exeunt.*

[Scene II: Within the castle.]

Enter Othello and Emilia.

OTHELLO:	You have seen nothing then?
EMILIA:	Nor ever heard, nor ever did suspect.
OTHELLO:	Yes, you have seen Cassio and she together.
EMILIA:	But then I saw no harm, and then I heard
Each syllable that breath made up between them.   5
OTHELLO:	What, did they never whisper?
EMILIA: Never, my lord.
OTHELLO:	Nor send you out o' th' way?
EMILIA:	Never.
OTHELLO:	To fetch her fan, her gloves, her mask, nor nothing?

254 use: Custom.

EMILIA: Never, my lord.   10
OTHELLO: That's strange.
EMILIA: I durst, my lord, to wager she is honest,
   Lay down my soul at stake. If you think other,
   Remove your thought; it doth abuse your bosom.°
   If any wretch have put this in your head,   15
   Let heaven requite it with the serpent's curse!°
   For if she be not honest, chaste, and true,
   There's no man happy; the purest of their wives
   Is foul as slander.
OTHELLO: Bid her come hither. Go.   *Exit Emilia.*
   She says enough; yet she's a simple bawd   20
   That cannot say as much. This is a subtle whore,
   A closet lock and key of villainous secrets;
   And yet she'll kneel and pray; I have seen her do't.

Enter Desdemona and Emilia.

DESDEMONA: My lord, what is your will?
OTHELLO: Pray, chuck, come hither.
DESDEMONA: What is your pleasure?
OTHELLO: Let me see your eyes.   25
   Look in my face.
DESDEMONA: What horrible fancy's this?
OTHELLO *[to Emilia]*:   Some of your function, mistress.
   Leave procreants° alone and shut the door;
   Cough or cry hem if anybody come.
   Your mystery, your mystery!° Nay, dispatch!   30

                                                       Exit Emilia.

DESDEMONA: Upon my knees, what doth your speech import?
   I understand a fury in your words,
   [But not the words.]
OTHELLO: Why, what art thou?
DESDEMONA: Your wife, my lord; your true
   And loyal wife.
OTHELLO: Come, swear it, damn thyself;   35
   Lest, being like one of heaven,° the devils themselves
   Should fear to seize thee. Therefore be double-damned —
   Swear thou art honest.°
DESDEMONA: Heaven doth truly know it.
OTHELLO: Heaven truly knows that thou art false as hell.
DESDEMONA: To whom, my lord? With whom? How am I false?   40
OTHELLO: Ah, Desdemona! away! away! away!

SCENE II. **14 abuse . . . bosom:** Deceive your heart. **16 serpent's curse:** (cf. Genesis 3:14). **28 procreants:** Mating couples. **30 mystery:** Trade, occupation. **36 being . . . heaven:** Looking like an angel. **38 honest:** Chaste.

DESDEMONA: Alas the heavy day! Why do you weep?
   Am I the motive of these tears, my lord?
   If haply you my father do suspect
   An instrument° of this your calling back,   45
   Lay not your blame on me. If you have lost him,
   Why, I have lost him too.
OTHELLO: Had it pleased heaven
   To try me with affliction, had they rained
   All kinds of sores and shames on my bare head,
   Steeped me in poverty to the very lips,   50
   Given to captivity me and my utmost hopes,
   I should have found in some place of my soul
   A drop of patience. But, alas, to make me
   A fixèd figure for the time of scorn°
   To point his slow unmoving finger at!   55
   Yet could I bear that too; well, very well.
   But there where I have garnered up my heart,
   Where either I must live or bear no life,
   The fountain from the which my current runs
   Or else dries up — to be discarded thence,   60
   Or keep it as a cistern for foul toads
   To knot and gender in — turn thy complexion there,°
   Patience, thou young and rose-lipped cherubin!
   Ay, there look grim as hell!
DESDEMONA: I hope my noble lord esteems me honest.   65
OTHELLO: O, ay; as summer flies are in the shambles,°
   That quicken° even with blowing. O thou weed,
   Who art so lovely fair, and smell'st so sweet,
   That the sense aches at thee, would thou hadst ne'er been born!
DESDEMONA: Alas, what ignorant sin have I committed?   70
OTHELLO: Was this fair paper, this most goodly book,
   Made to write "whore" upon? What committed?
   Committed? O thou public commoner!°
   I should make very forges of my cheeks
   That would to cinders burn up modesty,   75
   Did I but speak thy deeds. What committed?
   Heaven stops the nose at it, and the moon winks;°
   The bawdy wind, that kisses all it meets,
   Is hushed within the hollow mine of earth
   And will not hear it. What committed?   80
   Impudent strumpet!
DESDEMONA: By heaven, you do me wrong!

---

45 An instrument: To be the cause.   **54 time of scorn:** Scornful world.   **62 turn thy complexion there:** Change thy color at that point.   **66 shambles:** Slaughterhouse. **67 quicken:** Come to life.   **73 commoner:** Harlot.   **77 winks:** Closes her eyes.

OTHELLO: Are not you a strumpet?

DESDEMONA: No, as I am a Christian!
 If to preserve this vessel for my lord
 From any other foul unlawful touch
 Be not to be a strumpet, I am none.   85

OTHELLO: What, not a whore?

DESDEMONA: No, as I shall be saved!

OTHELLO: Is't possible?

DESDEMONA: O, heaven forgive us!

OTHELLO: I cry you mercy° then.
 I took you for that cunning whore of Venice
 That married with Othello. — *[Calling.]* You, mistress,   90
 That have the office opposite to Saint Peter
 And keep the gate of hell!

Enter Emilia.

                          You, you, ay, you!
 We have done our course; there's money for your pains:
 I pray you turn the key, and keep our counsel.   *Exit.*

EMILIA: Alas, what does this gentleman conceive?   95
 How do you, madam? How do you, my good lady?

DESDEMONA: Faith, half asleep.°

EMILIA: Good madam, what's the matter with my lord?

DESDEMONA: With who?

EMILIA: Why, with my lord, madam.   100

DESDEMONA: Who is thy lord?

EMILIA: He that is yours, sweet lady.

DESDEMONA: I have none. Do not talk to me, Emilia.
 I cannot weep; nor answer have I none
 But what should go by water. Prithee to-night
 Lay on my bed my wedding sheets, remember;   105
 And call thy husband hither.

EMILIA: Here's a change indeed!   *Exit.*

DESDEMONA: 'Tis meet I should be used so, very meet.
 How have I been behaved, that he might stick
 The small'st opinion° on my least misuse?°

Enter Iago and Emilia.

IAGO: What is your pleasure, madam? How is't with you?   110

DESDEMONA: I cannot tell. Those that do teach young babes
 Do it with gentle means and easy tasks:
 He might have chid me so; for, in good faith,
 I am a child to chiding.

IAGO: What is the matter, lady?

88 cry you mercy: Beg your pardon.   **97 half asleep:** I.e., stunned.   **109 small'st opinion:** Least suspicion;   **least misuse:** Slightest misconduct.

EMILIA: Alas, Iago, my lord hath so bewhored her,   115
    Thrown such despite and heavy terms upon her
    As true hearts cannot bear.
DESDEMONA: Am I that name, Iago?
IAGO: What name, fair lady?
DESDEMONA: Such as she said my lord did say I was.
EMILIA: He called her whore. A beggar in his drink   120
    Could not have laid such terms upon his callet.°
IAGO: Why did he so?
DESDEMONA: I do not know; I am sure I am none such.
IAGO: Do not weep, do not weep. Alas the day!
EMILIA: Hath she forsook so many noble matches,   125
    Her father and her country, and her friends,
    To be called whore? Would it not make one weep?
DESDEMONA: It is my wretched fortune.
IAGO: Beshrew him for't!
    How comes this trick° upon him?
DESDEMONA: Nay, heaven doth know.
EMILIA: I will be hanged if some eternal villain,   130
    Some busy and insinuating rogue,
    Some cogging, cozening° slave, to get some office,
    Have not devised this slander. I'll be hanged else.
IAGO: Fie, there is no such man! It is impossible.
DESDEMONA: If any such there be, heaven pardon him!   135
EMILIA: A halter pardon him! and hell gnaw his bones!
    Why should he call her whore? Who keeps her company?
    What place? what time? what form? what likelihood?
    The Moor 's abused by some most villainous knave,
    Some base notorious knave, some scurvy fellow.   140
    O heaven, that such companions° thou 'dst unfold,°
    And put in every honest hand a whip
    To lash the rascals naked through the world
    Even from the east to th' west!
IAGO: Speak within door.°
EMILIA: O, fie upon them! Some such squire he was   145
    That turned your wit the seamy side without
    And made you to suspect me with the Moor.
IAGO: You are a fool. Go to.
DESDEMONA: Alas, Iago,
    What shall I do to win my lord again?
    Good friend, go to him; for, by this light of heaven,   150
    I know not how I lost him. Here I kneel:

---

121 callet: Whore.   **129 trick:** Freakish behavior.   **132 cogging, cozening:** Cheating, defrauding.   **141 companions:** Rogues;   **unfold:** Expose.   **144 within door:** With restraint.

If e'er my will did trespass 'gainst his love
Either in discourse° of thought or actual deed,
Or that mine eyes, mine ears, or any sense
Delighted them in any other form,   155
Or that I do not yet, and ever did,
And ever will (though he do shake me off
To beggarly divorcement) love him dearly,
Comfort forswear° me! Unkindness may do much;
And his unkindness may defeat° my life,   160
But never taint my love. I cannot say "whore."
It does abhor me now I speak the word;
To do the act that might the addition earn
Not the world's mass of vanity could make me.

IAGO: I pray you be content. 'Tis but his humor.   165
The business of the state does him offense,
[And he does chide with you.]

DESDEMONA: If 'twere no other —

IAGO: 'Tis but so, I warrant.

[Trumpets within.]

Hark how these instruments summon you to supper.
The messengers of Venice stay the meat: 170
Go in, and weep not. All things shall be well.

                              Exeunt Desdemona and Emilia.

Enter Roderigo.

        How now, Roderigo?

RODERIGO: I do not find that thou deal'st justly with me.

IAGO: What in the contrary?

RODERIGO: Every day thou daff'st me with some device,° Iago, and rather, as it   175
seems to me now, keep'st from me all conveniency° than suppliest me with
the least advantage of hope. I will indeed no longer endure it; nor am I yet
persuaded to put up in peace what already I have foolishly suffered.

IAGO: Will you hear me, Roderigo?

RODERIGO: Faith, I have heard too much; for your words and performances are   180
no kin together.

IAGO: You charge me most unjustly.

RODERIGO: With naught° but truth. I have wasted myself out of my means. The
jewels you have had from me to deliver to Desdemona would half have
corrupted a votarist.° You have told me she hath received them, and   185
returned me expectations and comforts of sudden respect° and acquaintance; but I find none.

---

153 discourse: Course.   **159 Comfort forswear:** Happiness forsake.   **160 defeat:**
Destroy.   **175 thou . . . device:** You put me off with some trick.   **176 conveniency:**
Favorable   opportunities.   **185 votarist:** Nun.   **186 sudden   respect:** Immediate
notice.

IAGO: Well, go to; very well.

RODERIGO: Very well! go to! I cannot go to, man; nor 'tis not very well. By this hand, I say 'tis very scurvy, and begin to find myself fopped° in it.   190

IAGO: Very well.

RODERIGO: I tell you 'tis not very well. I will make myself known to Desdemona. If she will return me my jewels, I will give over my suit and repent my unlawful solicitation; if not, assure yourself I will seek satisfaction of you.

IAGO: You have said now.   195

RODERIGO: Ay, and said nothing but what I protest intendment of doing.

IAGO: Why, now I see there's mettle in thee; and even from this instant do build on thee a better opinion than ever before. Give me thy hand, Roderigo. Thou has taken against me a most just exception; but yet I protest I have dealt most directly° in thy affair.   200

RODERIGO: It hath not appeared.

IAGO: I grant indeed it hath not appeared, and your suspicion is not without wit and judgment. But, Roderigo, if thou hast that in thee indeed which I have greater reason to believe now than ever, I mean purpose, courage, and valor, this night show it. If thou the next night following enjoy not   205 Desdemona, take me from this world with treachery and devise engines for° my life.

RODERIGO: Well, what is it? Is it within reason and compass?

IAGO: Sir, there is especial commission come from Venice to depute Cassio in Othello's place.   210

RODERIGO: Is that true? Why, then Othello and Desdemona return again to Venice.

IAGO: O, no; he goes into Mauritania and takes away with him the fair Desdemona, unless his abode be lingered here° by some accident; wherein none can be so determinate° as the removing of Cassio.   215

RODERIGO: How do you mean removing of him?

IAGO: Why, by making him uncapable of Othello's place—knocking out his brains.

RODERIGO: And that you would have me to do?

IAGO: Ay, if you dare do yourself a profit and a right. He sups to-night with a   220 harlotry, and thither will I go to him. He knows not yet of his honorable fortune. If you will watch his going thence, which I will fashion to fall out between twelve and one, you may take him at your pleasure. I will be near to second your attempt, and he shall fall between us. Come, stand not amazed at it, but go along with me. I will show you such a necessity in his   225 death that you shall think yourself bound to put it on him. It is now high supper time, and the night grows to waste. About it!

RODERIGO: I will hear further reason for this.

IAGO: And you shall be satisfied.   *Exeunt.*

190 fopped: Duped.   **200 directly:** Straightforwardly.   **207 engines for:** Plots against. **214 abode . . . here:** Stay here be extended.   **215 determinate:** Effective.

[Scene III: Within the castle.]

Enter Othello, Lodovico, Desdemona, Emilia, and Attendants.

LODOVICO: I do beseech you, sir, trouble yourself no further.
OTHELLO: O, pardon me; 'twill do me good to walk.
LODOVICO: Madam, good night. I humbly thank your ladyship.
DESDEMONA: Your honor is most welcome.
OTHELLO: Will you walk, sir?
O, Desdemona —   5
DESDEMONA: My lord?
OTHELLO: Get you to bed on th' instant; I will be returned forthwith. Dismiss
your attendant there. Look't be done.
DESDEMONA: I will, my lord.

                              Exit [Othello, with Lodovico and Attendants].

EMILIA: How goes it now? He looks gentler than he did.   10
DESDEMONA: He says he will return incontinent.°
He hath commanded me to go to bed,
And bade me to dismiss you.
EMILIA: Dismiss me?
DESDEMONA: It was his bidding; therefore, good Emilia,
Give me my nightly wearing, and adieu.   15
We must not now displease him.
EMILIA: I would you had never seen him!
DESDEMONA: So would not I. My love doth so approve him
That even his stubbornness,° his checks,° his frowns —
Prithee unpin me — have grace and favor in them.   20
EMILIA: I have laid those sheets you bade me on the bed.
DESDEMONA: All's one. Good faith, how foolish are our minds!
If I do die before thee, prithee shroud me
In one of those same sheets.
EMILIA: Come, come! You talk.
DESDEMONA: My mother had a maid called Barbary.   25
She was in love; and he she loved proved mad°
And did forsake her. She had a song of "Willow";
An old thing 'twas; but it expressed her fortune,
And she died singing it. That song to-night
Will not go from my mind; I have much to do   30
But to go hang my head all at one side
And sing it like poor Barbary. Prithee dispatch.
EMILIA: Shall I go fetch your nightgown?°
DESDEMONA: No, unpin me here.
This Lodovico is a proper man.

SCENE III.   **11 incontinent:** At once.   **19 stubbornness:** Roughness;   **checks:** Rebukes.   **26 mad:** Wild, faithless.   **33 nightgown:** Dressing gown.

EMILIA: A very handsome man.   35
DESDEMONA: He speaks well.
EMILIA: I know a lady in Venice would have walked barefoot to Palestine for a
touch of his nether lip.
DESDEMONA *(sings)*:   "The poor soul sat sighing by a sycamore tree
                                   Sing all a green willow;   40
                        Her hand on her bosom, her head on her knee,
                                   Sing willow, willow, willow.
                        The fresh streams ran by her and murmured her moans;
                                   Sing willow, willow, willow;
                        Her salt tears fell from her, and soft'ned the stones" —   45
Lay by these.

                        "Sing willow, willow, willow" —
                        Prithee hie thee;° he'll come anon.
                        "Sing all a green willow must be my garland.
                        Let nobody blame him; his scorn I approve" —   50
Nay, that's not next. Hark! who is't that knocks?
EMILIA: It's the wind.
DESDEMONA *(sings)*:   "I call my love false love; but what said he then?
                        "Sing willow, willow, willow" —
                        If I court moe women, you'll couch with moe men."   55
So get thee gone; good night. Mine eyes do itch.
Doth that bode weeping?
EMILIA: 'Tis neither here nor there.
DESDEMONA: I have heard it said so. O, these men, these men!
Dost thou in conscience think — tell me, Emilia —
That there be women do abuse their husbands   60
In such gross kind?
EMILIA: There be some such, no question.
DESDEMONA: Wouldst thou do such a deed for all the world?
EMILIA: Why, would not you?
DESDEMONA: No, by this heavenly light!
EMILIA: Nor I neither by this heavenly light.
I might do't as well i' th' dark.   65
DESDEMONA: Wouldst thou do such a deed for all the world?
EMILIA: The world's a huge thing; it is a great price for a small vice.
DESDEMONA: In troth, I think thou wouldst not.
EMILIA: In troth, I think I should; and undo't when I had done it. Marry, I
would not do such a thing for a joint-ring,° nor for measures of lawn, nor   70
for gowns, petticoats, nor caps, nor any petty exhibition;° but, for all the
whole world — 'Ud's pity! who would not make her husband a cuckold to
make him a monarch? I should venture purgatory for't.
DESDEMONA: Beshrew me if I would do such a wrong

48 hie thee: Hurry.   **70 joint-ring:** Ring made in separable halves.   **71 exhibition:** Gift.

For the whole world.   75

EMILIA: Why, the wrong is but a wrong i' th' world; and having the world
for your labor, 'tis a wrong in your own world, and you might quickly make
it right.

DESDEMONA: I do not think there is any such woman.

EMILIA: Yes, a dozen; and as many to th' vantage° as   80
would store° the world they played for.
But I do think it is their husbands' faults
If wives do fall. Say that they slack their duties
And pour our treasures into foreign laps;
Or else break out in peevish° jealousies,   85
Throwing restraint upon us; or say they strike us,
Or scant our former having° in despite —
Why, we have galls;° and though we have some grace,
Yet have we some revenge. Let husbands know
Their wives have sense like them. They see, and smell,   90
And have their palates both for sweet and sour,
As husbands have. What is it that they do
When they change us for others? Is it sport?
I think it is. And doth affection breed it?
I think it doth. Is't frailty that thus errs?   95
It is so too. And have not we affections,
Desires for sport, and frailty, as men have?
Then let them use us well; else let them know,
The ills we do, their ills instruct us so.

DESDEMONA: Good night, good night. God me such usage° send,   100
Not to pick bad from bad, but by bad mend!   *Exeunt.*

[ACT V, Scene I: A street in Cyprus]

Enter Iago and Roderigo.

IAGO: Here, stand behind this bulk;° straight will he come.
Wear thy good rapier bare, and put it home.
Quick, quick! Fear nothing; I'll be at thy elbow.
It makes us, or it mars us — think on that,
And fix most firm thy resolution.   5

RODERIGO: Be near at hand; I may miscarry in't.

IAGO: Here, at thy hand. Be bold, and take thy stand.

[Stands aside.]

RODERIGO: I have no great devotion to the deed,
And yet he hath given me satisfying reasons.

80 to   th'   vantage: Besides.   **81 store:** Populate.   **85 peevish:** Senseless.   **87
having:** Allowance.   **88 galls:** Spirits to resent.   **100 usage:** Habits.   ACT V, SCENE I.
1 bulk: Projecting shop-front.

'Tis but a man gone. Forth my sword! He dies!   10
IAGO: I have rubbed this young quat° almost to the sense,°
       And he grows angry. Now whether he kill Cassio,
       Or Cassio him, or each do kill the other,
       Every way makes my gain. Live Roderigo,
       He calls me to a restitution large   15
       Of gold and jewels that I bobbed° from him
       As gifts to Desdemona.
       It must not be. If Cassio do remain,
       He hath a daily beauty in his life
       That makes me ugly; and besides, the Moor   20
       May unfold me to him; there stand I in much peril.
       No, he must die. Be't so! I hear him coming.

Enter Cassio.

RODERIGO: I know his gait. 'Tis he. Villain, thou diest!

[Makes a pass at Cassio.]

CASSIO: That thrust had been mine enemy indeed
       But that my coat° is better than thou know'st.   25
       I will make proof of thine.

[Draws, and wounds Roderigo.]

RODERIGO: O, I am slain!

[Iago darts from concealment behind Cassio, wounds him in the leg, and exit.]

CASSIO: I am maimed for ever. Help, ho! Murder! murder!

[Falls.]

Enter Othello.

OTHELLO: The voice of Cassio. Iago keeps his word.
RODERIGO: O, villain that I am!
OTHELLO: It is even so.
CASSIO: O, help, ho! light! a surgeon!   30
OTHELLO: 'Tis he. O brave Iago, honest and just,
       That hast such noble sense of thy friend's wrong!
       Thou teachest me. Minion,° your dear lies dead,
       And your unblest fate hies.° Strumpet, I come.
       Forth of my heart those charms, thine eyes, are blotted.   35
       Thy bed, lust-stained, shall with lust's blood be spotted.

                                                    Exit Othello.

Enter Lodovico and Gratiano.

CASSIO: What, ho? No watch? No passage?° Murder! murder!
GRATIANO: 'Tis some mischance. The cry is very direful.

---

11 quat: Pimple;   **sense:** Quick.   **16 bobbed:** Swindled.   **25 coat:** Undershirt of
mail.   **33 Minion:** Mistress.   **34 hies:** Hurries on.   **37 passage:** Passersby.

CASSIO: O, help!

LODOVICO: Hark!   40

RODERIGO: O wretched villain!

LODOVICO: Two or three groan. It is a heavy° night.
These may be counterfeits. Let's think't unsafe
To come in to the cry without more help.

RODERIGO: Nobody come? Then shall I bleed to death.   45

LODOVICO: Hark!

Enter Iago, with a light.

GRATIANO: Here's one comes in his shirt, with light and weapons.

IAGO: Who's there? Whose noise is this that cries on° murder?

LODOVICO: We do not know.

IAGO: Did not you hear a cry?

CASSIO: Here, here! For heaven's sake, help me!

IAGO: What's the matter?   50

GRATIANO: This is Othello's ancient, as I take it.

LODOVICO: The same indeed, a very valiant fellow.

IAGO: What are you here that cry so grievously?

CASSIO: Iago? O, I am spoiled, undone by villains!
Give me some help.   55

IAGO: O me, lieutenant! What villains have done this?

CASSIO: I think that one of them is hereabout
And cannot make° away.

IAGO: O treacherous villains!

[To Lodovico and Gratiano.]

What are you there? Come in, and give some help.

RODERIGO: O, help me here!   60

CASSIO: That's one of them.

IAGO: O murd'rous slave! O villain!

[Stabs Roderigo.]

RODERIGO: O damned Iago! O inhuman dog!

IAGO: Kill men i' th' dark? — Where be these bloody thieves? —
How silent is this town! — Ho! murder! murder! —
What may you be? Are you of good or evil?   65

LODOVICO: As you shall prove us, praise us.

IAGO: Signior Lodovico?

LODOVICO: He, sir.

IAGO: I cry you mercy. Here's Cassio hurt by villains.

GRATIANO: Cassio?   70

IAGO: How is't, brother?

CASSIO: My leg is cut in two.

IAGO: Marry,° heaven forbid!
Light, gentlemen. I'll bind it with my shirt.

42 heavy: Cloudy, dark. **48 cries on:** Raises the cry of. **58 make:** Get. **72 Marry:** (From "By Mary").

Enter Bianca.

BIANCA: What is the matter, ho? Who is't that cried?

IAGO: Who is't that cried?   75

BIANCA: O my dear Cassio! my sweet Cassio!
    O Cassio, Cassio, Cassio!

IAGO: O notable strumpet! — Cassio, may you suspect
    Who they should be that have thus mangled you?

CASSIO: No.   80

GRATIANO: I am sorry to find you thus. I have been to seek you.

IAGO: Lend me a garter. So. O for a chair°
    To bear him easily hence!

BIANCA: Alas, he faints! O Cassio, Cassio, Cassio!

IAGO: Gentlemen all, I do suspect this trash   85
    To be a party in this injury. —
    Patience a while, good Cassio. — Come, come!
    Lend me a light. Know we this face or no?
    Alas, my friend and my dear countryman
    Roderigo? No — Yes, sure. — O heaven, Roderigo!   90

GRATIANO: What, of Venice?

IAGO: Even he, sir. Did you know him?

GRATIANO: Know him? Ay.

IAGO: Signior Gratiano? I cry your gentle pardon.
    These bloody accidents must excuse my manners
    That so neglected you.

GRATIANO: I am glad to see you.   95

IAGO: How do you, Cassio? — O, a chair, a chair!

GRATIANO: Roderigo?

IAGO: He, he, 'tis he!

[A chair brought in.]

    O, that's well said;° the chair.
    Some good man bear him carefully from hence.   100
    I'll fetch the general's surgeon. *[To Bianca.]* For you, mistress,
    Save you your labor. — He that lies slain here, Cassio,
    Was my dear friend. What malice was between you?

CASSIO: None in the world; nor do I know the man.

IAGO *[to Bianca]*:   What, look you pale? — O, bear him out o' th' air.   105

                        [Cassio and Roderigo are borne off.]

    Stay you, good gentlemen. — Look you pale, mistress? —
    Do you perceive the gastness° of her eye? —
    Nay, if you stare, we shall hear more anon.
    Behold her well; I pray you look upon her.
    Do you see, gentlemen? Nay, guiltiness will speak.   110
    Though tongues were out of use.

---

82 chair: Litter.   **99 well said:** Well done.   **107 gastness:** Terror.

Enter Emilia.

EMILIA: 'Las, what's the matter? What's the matter, husband?
IAGO: Cassio hath here been set on in the dark
   By Roderigo, and fellows that are scaped.
   He's almost slain, and Roderigo dead.   115
EMILIA: Alas, good gentlemen! alas, good Cassio!
IAGO: This is the fruits of whoring. Prithee, Emilia,
   Go know of Cassio where he supped to-night.

[To Bianca.]

What, do you shake at that?
BIANCA: He supped at my house; but I therefore shake not.   120
IAGO: O, did he so? I charge you go with me.
EMILIA: Fie, fie upon thee, strumpet!
BIANCA: I am no strumpet, but of life as honest°
   As you that thus abuse me.
EMILIA: As I? Foh! fie upon thee!
IAGO: Kind gentlemen, let's go see poor Cassio dressed.   125

[To Bianca.]

Come, mistress, you must tell 's another tale.
   Emilia, run you to the citadel
   And tell my lord and lady what hath happed.

[Exit Emilia.]

Will you go on afore?   *Exeunt [all but Iago].*
   This is the night
   That either makes me or fordoes° me quite.   *[Exit.]* 130

[Scene II: A bedchamber in the castle.]

Desdemona [asleep] in her bed. Enter Othello with a light.

OTHELLO: It is the cause, it is the cause,° my soul.
   Let me not name it to you, you chaste stars!
   It is the cause. Yet I'll not shed her blood,
   Nor scar that whiter skin of hers than snow,
   And smooth as monumental alabaster.   5
   Yet she must die, else she'll betray more men.
   Put out the light, and then put out the light.
   If I quench thee, thou flaming minister,°
   I can again thy former light restore,
   Should I repent me; but once put out thy light,   10
   Thou cunning'st pattern of excelling nature,
   I know not where is that Promethean heat°

---

123 honest: Chaste.   **130 fordoes:** Destroys.   **SCENE II. 1 cause:** Cause of justice.
8 minister: Servant.   **12 Promethean heat:** Divine fire.

That can thy light relume.° When I have plucked the rose,
I cannot give it vital growth again;
It needs must wither. I'll smell thee on the tree.   15

(He kisses her.)

O balmy breath, that dost almost persuade
   Justice to break her sword! One more, one more!
   Be thus when thou art dead, and I will kill thee,
   And love thee after. One more, and that's the last!
   So sweet was ne'er so fatal. I must weep,   20
   But they are cruel tears. This sorrow's heavenly;
   It strikes where it doth love. She wakes.

DESDEMONA: Who's there? Othello?

OTHELLO: Ay, Desdemona.

DESDEMONA: Will you come to bed, my lord?

OTHELLO: Have you prayed to-night, Desdemona?

DESDEMONA: Ay, my lord.   25

OTHELLO: If you bethink yourself of any crime°
   Unreconciled as yet to heaven and grace,
   Solicit for it straight.

DESDEMONA: Alack, my lord, what may you mean by that?

OTHELLO: Well, do it, and be brief; I will walk by.   30
   I would not kill thy unprepared spirit.
   No, heaven forfend!° I would not kill thy soul.

DESDEMONA: Talk you of killing?

OTHELLO: Ay, I do.

DESDEMONA: Then heaven
   Have mercy on me!

OTHELLO: Amen, with all my heart!

DESDEMONA: If you say so, I hope you will not kill me.   35

OTHELLO: Hum!

DESDEMONA: And yet I fear you; for you're fatal then
   When your eyes roll so. Why I should fear I know not,
   Since guiltiness I know not; but yet I feel I fear.

OTHELLO: Think on thy sins.

DESDEMONA: They are loves I bear to you.   40

OTHELLO: Ay, and for that thou diest.

DESDEMONA: That death 's unnatural that kills for loving.
   Alas, why gnaw you so your nether lip?
   Some bloody passion shakes your very frame.
   These are portents,° but yet I hope, I hope,   45
   They do not point on me.

OTHELLO: Peace and be still!

DESDEMONA: I will so. What's the matter?

---

13 relume: Relight. **26 crime:** Sin. **32 forfend:** Forbid. **45 portents:** Signs of
impending violence.

OTHELLO: That handkerchief which I so loved and gave thee
   Thou gav'st to Cassio.
DESDEMONA: No, by my life and soul!
   Send for the man and ask him.
OTHELLO: Sweet soul, take heed,   50
   Take heed of perjury; thou art on thy deathbed.
DESDEMONA: Ay, but not yet to die.
OTHELLO: Yes, presently.°
   Therefore confess thee freely of thy sin;
   For to deny each article with oath
   Cannot remove nor choke the strong conception°   55
   That I do groan withal. Thou art to die.
DESDEMONA: Then Lord have mercy on me!
OTHELLO: I say amen.
DESDEMONA: And have you mercy too! I never did
   Offend° you in my life; never loved Cassio
   But with such general warranty of heaven   60
   As I might love. I never gave him token.
OTHELLO: By heaven, I saw my handkerchief in's hand!
   O perjured woman! thou dost stone my heart,°
   And mak'st me call what I intend to do
   A murder, which I thought a sacrifice.   65
   I saw the handkerchief.
DESDEMONA: He found it then.
   I never gave it him. Send for him hither.
   Let him confess a truth.
OTHELLO: He hath confessed.
DESDEMONA: What, my lord?
OTHELLO: That he hath used thee.
DESDEMONA: How? Unlawfully?
OTHELLO: Ay.   70
DESDEMONA: He will not say so.
OTHELLO: No, his mouth is stopped.
   Honest Iago hath ta'en order° for't.
DESDEMONA: O, my fear interprets. What, is he dead?
OTHELLO: Had all his hairs been lives, my great revenge
   Had stomach for them all.   75
DESDEMONA: Alas, he is betrayed, and I undone!
OTHELLO: Out, strumpet! Weep'st thou for him to my face?
DESDEMONA: O, banish me, my lord, but kill me not!
OTHELLO: Down, strumpet!
DESDEMONA: Kill me to-morrow; let me live to-night!   80
OTHELLO: Nay, if you strive —

52 presently: At   once.   **55 conception:** Belief.   **59 Offend:** Wrong.   **63 stone
my heart:** Turn my heart to stone.   **72 ta'en order:** Taken measures.

DESDEMONA: But half an hour!
OTHELLO: Being done, there is no pause.
DESDEMONA: But while I say one prayer!
OTHELLO: It is too late.

                                              (Smothers her.)
DESDEMONA: [O Lord, Lord, Lord!]
Emilia at the door.

EMILIA *(calls within):*   My lord, my lord! What, ho! my lord, my lord!   85
OTHELLO: What noise is this? Not dead? not yet quite dead?
       I that am cruel am yet merciful;
       I would not have thee linger in thy pain.
       So, so.
EMILIA *(within):*   What, ho! my lord, my lord!
OTHELLO: Who's there?   90
EMILIA *(within):*   O, good my lord, I would speak a word with you!
OTHELLO: Yes, 'tis Emilia. — By and by.° — She's dead. —
       'Tis like she comes to speak of Cassio's death.
       The noise was here. Ha! no more moving?
       Still as the grave. — Shall she come in? Were't good! —   95
       I think she stirs again. No. — What's best to do?
       If she come in, she'll sure speak to my wife.
       My wife! my wife! what wife? I have no wife.
       O, insupportable! O heavy hour!
       Methinks it should be now a huge eclipse   100
       Of sun and moon, and that th' affrighted globe
       Should yawn° at alteration.
EMILIA *(within):*   I do beseech you
       That I may speak with you, O good my lord!
OTHELLO: I had forgot thee. O, come in, Emilia.
       Soft, by and by. — Let me the curtains draw. —   105
[Closes the bed-curtains.]
       Where art thou?
[Opens the door.]

Enter Emilia.
                      What's the matter with thee now?
EMILIA: O my good lord, yonder's foul murder done!
OTHELLO: What? Now?
EMILIA: But now, my lord.
OTHELLO: It is the very error° of the moon.   110
       She comes more nearer earth than she was wont
       And makes men mad.

92 By and by: Just a moment (addressed to Emilia).   **102 yawn:** Open, as in an earthquake.   **110 error:** Straying off course.

EMILIA: Cassio, my lord, hath killed a young Venetian
Called Roderigo.

OTHELLO: Roderigo killed?
And Cassio killed?

EMILIA: No, Cassio is not killed.   115

OTHELLO: Not Cassio killed? Then murder's out of tune,
And sweet revenge grows harsh.

DESDEMONA: O, falsely, falsely murdered?

EMILIA: O, Lord! what cry is that?

OTHELLO: That? What?

EMILIA: Out and alas! that was my lady's voice.   120
Help! help, ho! help! O lady, speak again!
Sweet Desdemona! O sweet mistress, speak!

DESDEMONA: A guiltless death I die.

EMILIA: O, who hath done this deed?

DESDEMONA: Nobody — I myself. Farewell.   125
Commend° me to my kind lord. O, farewell!

(She dies.)

OTHELLO: Why, how should she be murd'red?

EMILIA: Alas, who knows?

OTHELLO: You heard her say herself, it was not I.

EMILIA: She said so. I must needs report the truth.

OTHELLO: She's like a liar gone to burning hell!   130
'Twas I that killed her.

EMILIA: O, the more angel she,
And you the blacker devil!

OTHELLO: She turned to folly, and she was a whore.

EMILIA: Thou dost belie her, and thou art a devil.

OTHELLO: She was false as water.°

EMILIA: Thou art rash as fire to say   135
That she was false. O, she was heavenly true!

OTHELLO: Cassio did top her. Ask thy husband else.
O, I were damned beneath all depth in hell
But that I did proceed upon just grounds
To this extremity. Thy husband knew it all.   140

EMILIA: My husband?

OTHELLO: Thy husband.

EMILIA: That she was false to wedlock?

OTHELLO: Ay, with Cassio. Nay, had she been true,
If heaven would make me such another world
Of one entire and perfect chrysolite,°   145
I'ld not have sold her for it.

EMILIA: My husband?

126 Commend: Remember. **135 water:** (Which   is   yielding). **146 chrysolite:**
(Precious topaz).

OTHELLO: Ay 'twas he that told me first.
   An honest man he is, and hates the slime
   That sticks on filthy deeds.
EMILIA: My husband?   150
OTHELLO: What needs this iterance,° woman? I say thy husband.
EMILIA: O mistress, villainy hath made mocks with love!
   My husband say that she was false?
OTHELLO: He, woman.
   I say, thy husband. Dost understand the word?
   My friend, thy husband; honest, honest Iago.   155
EMILIA: If he say so, may his pernicious soul
   Rot half a grain a day! he lies to th' heart.
   She was too fond of her most filthy bargain.
OTHELLO: Ha!
EMILIA: Do thy worst.   160
   This deed of thine is no more worthy heaven
   Than thou wast worthy her.
OTHELLO: Peace, you were best.
EMILIA: Thou hast not half the power to do me harm
   As I have to be hurt.° O gull! O dolt!
   As ignorant as dirt! thou hast done a deed —   165
   I care not for thy sword; I'll make thee known,
   Though I lost twenty lives. Help! help! Ho! help!
   The Moor hath killed my mistress! Murder! murder!

Enter Montano, Gratiano, Iago, and others.

MONTANO: What is the matter? How now, general?
EMILIA: O, are you come, Iago? You have done well,   170
   That men must lay their murders on your neck.
GRATIANO: What is the matter?
EMILIA: Disprove this villain, if thou be'st a man.
   He says thou told'st him that his wife was false.
   I know thou didst not; thou'rt not such a villain.   175
   Speak, for my heart is full.
IAGO: I told him what I thought, and told no more
   Than what he found himself was apt and true.
EMILIA: But did you ever tell him she was false?
IAGO: I did.   180
EMILIA: You told a lie, an odious damnèd lie!
   Upon my soul, a lie! a wicked lie!
   She false with Cassio? Did you say with Cassio?
IAGO: With Cassio, mistress. Go to, charm° your tongue.

---

151 iterance: Repetition.   **164 to be hurt:** To endure hurt.   **184 charm:** Cast a
spell on.

EMILIA: I will not charm my tongue; I am bound to speak: 185
   My mistress here lies murdered in her bed —
ALL: O heavens forfend!
EMILIA: And your reports have set the murder on.
OTHELLO: Nay, stare not, masters. It is true indeed.
GRATIANO: 'Tis a strange truth.   190
MONTANO: O monstrous act!
EMILIA: Villainy, villainy, villainy!
   I think upon't — I think I smell't! — O villainy!
   I thought so then. — I'll kill myself for grief. —
   O villainy, villainy!
IAGO: What, are you mad? I charge you get you home.   195
EMILIA: Good gentlemen, let me have leave to speak.
   'Tis proper I obey him, but not now.
   Perchance, Iago, I will ne'er go home.
OTHELLO: O! O! O!   *(Falls on the bed.)*
EMILIA: Nay, lay thee down and roar!
   For thou hast killed the sweetest innocent   200
   That e'er did lift up eye.
OTHELLO: O, she was foul!
[Rises.]
   I scarce did know you, uncle. There lies your niece,
   Whose breath, indeed, these hands have newly stopped.
   I know this act shows° horrible and grim.
GRATIANO: Poor Desdemon! I am glad thy father's dead.   205
   Thy match was mortal to him, and pure grief
   Shore his old thread in twain. Did he live now,
   This sight would make him do a desperate turn;°
   Yea, curse his better angel from his side,
   And fall to reprobation.°   210
OTHELLO: 'Tis pitiful; but yet Iago knows
   That she with Cassio hath the act of shame
   A thousand times committed. Cassio confessed it;
   And she did gratify° his amorous works
   With that recognizance° and pledge of love   215
   Which I first gave her. I saw it in his hand.
   It was a handkerchief, an antique token
   My father gave my mother.
EMILIA: O God! O heavenly God!
IAGO: Zounds, hold your peace!
EMILIA: 'Twill out, 'twill out! I peace?   220

---

204 shows: Appears.   **208 turn:** Act.   **210 reprobation:** Rejection by God, damnation.   **214 gratify:** Reward.   **215 recognizance:** Token.

No, I will speak as liberal as the north,°
Let heaven and men and devils, let them all,
All, all, cry shame against me, yet I'll speak.
IAGO: Be wise, and get you home.
EMILIA: I will not.

[Iago draws and threatens Emilia.]

GRATIANO: Fie!
    Your sword upon a woman?   225
EMILIA: O thou dull Moor, that handkerchief thou speak'st of
    I found by fortune, and did give my husband;
    For often with a solemn earnestness —
    More than indeed belonged to such a trifle —
    He begged of me to steal't.
IAGO: Villainous whore!   230
EMILIA: She give it Cassio? No, alas, I found it,
    And I did give't my husband.
IAGO: Filth, thou liest!
EMILIA: By heaven, I do not, I do not, gentlemen.
    O murd'rous coxcomb! what should such a fool
    Do with so good a wife?
OTHELLO: Are there no stones° in heaven   235
    But what serves for the thunder? Precious villain!

The Moor runs at Iago [but is disarmed by Montano].
Iago kills his wife.

GRATIANO: The woman falls. Sure he hath killed his wife.
EMILIA: Ay, ay. O, lay me by my mistress' side.   *Exit Iago.*
GRATIANO: He's gone, but his wife's killed.
MONTANO: 'Tis a notorious° villain. Take you this weapon,   240
    Which I have here recovered from the Moor.
    Come, guard the door without. Let him not pass,
    But kill him rather. I'll after that same villain,
    For 'tis a damnèd slave.

                     Exit [Montano, with all but Othello and Emilia].

OTHELLO: I am not valiant neither;
    But every puny whipster° gets my sword.   245
    But why should honor outlive honesty?
    Let it go all.
EMILIA: What did thy song bode, lady?
    Hark, canst thou hear me? I will play the swan,
    And die in music. *[Sings.]* "Willow, willow, willow."

---

221 liberal as the north: Unchecked as the north wind blows.   **235 stones:** Bolts like those used for thunderbolts.   **240 notorious:** Notable.   **245 puny whipster:** Whippersnapper.

Moor, she was chaste. She loved thee, cruel Moor: 250
So come my soul to bliss as I speak true.
So speaking as I think, alas, I die.

(She dies.)

OTHELLO: I have another weapon in this chamber;
It is a sword of Spain, the ice brook's° temper.
O, here it is. — Uncle, I must come forth.   255
GRATIANO *(within)*:   If thou attempt it, it will cost thee dear.
Thou hast no weapon, and perforce must suffer.
OTHELLO: Look in upon me then and speak with me,
Or, naked° as I am, I will assault thee.

[Enter Gratiano.]

GRATIANO: What is the matter?
OTHELLO: Behold, I have a weapon;   260
A better never did itself sustain
Upon a soldier's thigh. I have seen the day
That with this little arm and this good sword
I have made my way through more impediments
Than twenty times your stop.° But O vain boast!   265
Who can control his fate? 'Tis not so now.
Be not afraid, though you do see me weaponed.
Here is my journey's end, here is my butt,°
And very seamark° of my utmost sail:
Do you go back dismayed? 'Tis a lost° fear.   270
Man but a rush° against Othello's breast,
And he retires. Where should Othello go?
Now, how dost thou look now? O ill-starred wench!
Pale as thy smock! When we shall meet at compt,°
This look of thine will hurl my soul from heaven,   275
And fiends will snatch at it. Cold, cold, my girl?
Even like thy chastity.
O cursèd, cursèd slave! Whip me, ye devils,
From the possession of this heavenly sight!
Blow me about in winds! roast me in sulphur!   280
Wash me in steep-down gulfs of liquid fire!
Oh Desdemon! dead Desdemon! dead! Oh! Oh!

Enter Lodovico, Montano, Iago [as prisoner], and Officers; Cassio in a chair.

LODOVICO: Where is this rash and most unfortunate man?
OTHELLO: That's he that was Othello. Here I am.

---

254 ice brook: I.e., a Spanish blade, tempered in cold running water. **259 naked:**
Disarmed. **265 stop:** Power to stop. **268 butt:** Limit. **269 seamark:** Beacon,
destination. **270 lost:** Wasted. **271 Man but a rush:** Wield only a reed. **274
compt:** Final accounting, Last Judgment.

LODOVICO: Where is that viper? Bring the villain forth.   285
OTHELLO: I look down towards his feet° — but that's a fable.
If that thou be'st a devil, I cannot kill thee.

[Wounds Iago.]

LODOVICO: Wrench his sword from him.

[Othello is disarmed.]

IAGO: I bleed, sir, but not killed.
OTHELLO: I am not sorry neither. I'ld have thee live;
For in my sense, 'tis happiness to die.   290
LODOVICO: O thou Othello that wert once so good,
Fall'n in the practice° of a damnèd slave,
What shall be said to thee?
OTHELLO: Why, anything;
An honorable murderer, if you will;
For naught did I in hate, but all in honor.   295
LODOVICO: This wretch hath part confessed his villainy.
Did you and he consent in° Cassio's death?
OTHELLO: Ay.
CASSIO: Dear general, I never gave you cause.
OTHELLO: I do believe it, and I ask your pardon.   300
Will you, I pray, demand that demi-devil
Why he hath thus ensnared my soul and body?
IAGO: Demand me nothing. What you know, you know.
From this time forth I never will speak word.
LODOVICO: What, not to pray?
GRATIANO: Torments will ope your lips.   305
OTHELLO: Well, thou dost best.
LODOVICO: Sir, you shall understand what hath befall'n,
Which, as I think, you know not. Here is a letter
Found in the pocket of the slain Roderigo;
And here another. The one of them imports   310
The death of Cassio to be undertook
By Roderigo.
OTHELLO: O villain!
CASSIO: Most heathenish and most gross!
LODOVICO: Now here's another discontented paper
Found in the pocket too; and this, it seems,   315
Roderigo meant t' have sent this damnèd villain;
But that, belike, Iago in the nick°
Came in and satisfied him.
OTHELLO: O thou pernicious caitiff! —

286 I . . . feet: I.e., to see if they are cloven, like the Devil's.   **292 practice:** Plot.
297 consent in: Agree upon.   **317 nick:** Nick of time.

How came you, Cassio, by that handkerchief
That was my wife's?
CASSIO: I found it in my chamber;   320
And he himself confessed but even now
That there he dropped it for a special purpose
Which wrought to his desire.
OTHELLO: O fool! fool! fool!
CASSIO: There is besides in Roderigo's letter,
How he upbraids Iago that he made him   325
Brave me upon the watch; whereon it came
That I was cast;° and even but now he spake,
After long seeming dead — Iago hurt him,
Iago set him on.
LODOVICO: You must forsake this room and go with us.   330
Your power and your command is taken off,
And Cassio rules in Cyprus. For this slave,
If there be any cunning cruelty
That can torment him much and hold him long,
It shall be his. You shall close prisoner rest   335
Till that the nature of your fault be known
To the Venetian state. Come, bring away.
OTHELLO: Soft you! a word or two before you go.
I have done the state some service, and they know't.
No more of that. I pray you, in your letters,   340
When you shall these unlucky° deeds relate,
Speak of me as I am. Nothing extenuate,
Nor set down aught in malice. Then must you speak
Of one that loved not wisely, but too well;
Of one not easily jealous, but, being wrought,   345
Perplexed° in the extreme; of one whose hand,
Like the base Judean,° threw a pearl away
Richer than all his tribe; of one whose subdued° eyes,
Albeit unusèd to the melting mood,
Drop tears as fast as the Arabian trees   350
Their med'cinable gum. Set you down this.
And say besides that in Aleppo once,
Where a malignant and a turbaned Turk
Beat a Venetian and traduced the state,
I took by th' throat the circumcisèd dog   355
And smote him — thus.
(He stabs himself.)

---

327 cast: Dismissed.   **341 unlucky:** Fatal.   **346 Perplexed:** Distracted.   **347 Judean:** Judas Iscariot (?) (quarto reads "Indian").   **348 subdued:** I.e., conquered by grief.

LODOVICO: O bloody period!°
GRATIANO: All that's spoke is marred.
OTHELLO: I kissed thee ere I killed thee. No way but this,
    Killing myself, to die upon a kiss.

(He [falls upon the bed and] dies.)

CASSIO: This did I fear, but thought he had no weapon;   360
    For he was great of heart.
LODOVICO *[to Iago]:*   O Spartan dog,
    More fell° than anguish, hunger, or the sea!
    Look on the tragic loading of this bed.
    This is thy work. The object poisons sight;
    Let it be hid.° Gratiano, keep the house,   365
    And seize upon° the fortunes of the Moor,
    For they succeed on you. To you, lord governor,
    Remains the censure° of this hellish villain,
    The time, the place, the torture. O, enforce it!
    Myself will straight aboard, and to the state   370
    This heavy act with heavy heart relate.

                                                            Exeunt.

357 period: Ending.   **362 fell:** Cruel.   **365 Let it be hid:** I.e., draw the bed curtains.   **366 seize upon:** Take legal possession of.   **368 censure:** Judicial sentence.

☰ THINKING ABOUT THE TEXT

1. Jealousy is one of the central motifs in this play. What characters are jealous and for what reasons?

2. Is Iago diabolically devious and clever, or is Othello especially gullible? How would you respond if a trusted friend made similar accusations against someone whom you cared for deeply?

3. Is Othello's tragic flaw — the quality that leads to his downfall — jealousy or something else, perhaps credulity?

4. Is it possible for Othello's love to turn so quickly into hate?

5. How might the end of the play and the final resolution of the characters' fates be seen as Shakespeare's commentary on jealousy?

A. C. BRADLEY
The Noble Othello

A. C. Bradley (1851–1935), a British literary critic and highly influential Shakespearean scholar, was the youngest boy among twenty-one children. His father was a well-regarded preacher. Bradley attended Balliol College at Oxford University and later was a professor at the University of Liverpool and at Oxford. His books include

Oxford Lectures on Poetry *(1909) and* Shakespearean Tragedy *(1904), where
"The Noble Othello" appeared. The essays published in both books were originally
lectures delivered by Bradley. Upon his death, Bradley's will established a fellowship
for English literary scholars. Here, Bradley refutes the common notion that Othello
was unjustifiably and easily jealous by considering how Othello's character diminishes only in light of the evidence Iago provides regarding Desdemona's supposed
affair.*

This character is so noble, Othello's feelings and actions follow so inevitably
from it and from the forces brought to bear on it, and his sufferings are so
heart-rending, that he stirs, I believe, in most readers a passion of mingled love
and pity which they feel for no other hero in Shakespeare, and to which not
even Mr. Swinburne can do more than justice. Yet there are some critics and
not a few readers who cherish a grudge against him. They do not merely think
that in the later stages of his temptation he showed a certain obtuseness, and
that, to speak pedantically, he acted with unjustifiable precipitation and violence; no one, I suppose, denies that. But, even when they admit that he was
not of a jealous temper, they consider that he *was* "easily jealous"; they seem to
think that it was inexcusable in him to feel any suspicion of his wife at all; and
they blame him for never suspecting Iago or asking him for evidence. I refer to
this attitude of mind chiefly in order to draw attention to certain points in the
story. It comes partly from mere inattention (for Othello did suspect Iago and
did ask him for evidence); partly from a misconstruction of the text which
makes Othello appear jealous long before he really is so; and partly from failure
to realise certain essential facts. I will begin with these.

(1) Othello, we have seen, was trustful, and thorough in his trust. He put
entire confidence in the honesty of Iago, who had not only been his companion
in arms, but, as he believed, had just proved his faithfulness in the matter of the
marriage. This confidence was misplaced, and we happen to know it; but it was
no sign of stupidity in Othello. For his opinion of Iago was the opinion of practically everyone who knew him: and that opinion was that Iago was before all
things "honest," his very faults being those of excess in honesty. This being so,
even if Othello had not been trustful and simple, it would have been quite unnatural in him to be unmoved by the warnings of so honest a friend, warnings
offered with extreme reluctance and manifestly from a sense of a friend's duty.
Any husband would have been troubled by them.

(2) Iago does not bring these warnings to a husband who had lived with a
wife for months and years and knew her like his sister or his bosom-friend. Nor
is there any ground in Othello's character for supposing that, if he had been
such a man, he would have felt and acted as he does in the play. But he was
newly married; in the circumstances he cannot have known much of Desdemona
before his marriage; and further he was conscious of being under the spell of a
feeling which can give glory to the truth but can also give it to a dream.

(3) This consciousness in any imaginative man is enough, in such circumstances, to destroy his confidence in his powers of perception. In Othello's case,

after a long and most artful preparation, there now comes, to reinforce its effect, the suggestions that he is not an Italian, nor even a European; that he is totally ignorant of the thoughts and the customary morality of Venetian women; that he had himself seen in Desdemona's deception of her father how perfect an actress she could be. As he listens in horror, for a moment at least the past is revealed to him in a new and dreadful light, and the ground seems to sink under his feet. These suggestions are followed by a tentative but hideous and humiliating insinuation of what his honest and much-experienced friend fears may be the true explanation of Desdemona's rejection of acceptable suitors, and of her strange, and naturally temporary, preference for a black man. Here Iago goes too far. He sees something in Othello's face that frightens him, and he breaks off. Nor does this idea take any hold of Othello's mind. But it is not surprising that his utter powerlessness to repel it on the ground of knowledge of his wife, or even of that instinctive interpretation of character which is possible between persons of the same race, should complete his misery, so that he feels he can bear no more, and abruptly dismisses his friend (III. iii. 238).

Now I repeat that *any* man situated as Othello was would have been disturbed by Iago's communications, and I add that many men would have been made wildly jealous. But up to this point, where Iago is dismissed, Othello, I must maintain, does not show jealousy. His confidence is shaken, he is confused and deeply troubled, he feels even horror; but he is not yet jealous in the proper sense of that word. In his soliloquy (III. iii. 258ff.) the beginning of this passion may be traced; but it is only after an interval of solitude, when he has had time to dwell on the idea presented to him, and especially after statements of fact, not mere general grounds of suspicion, are offered, that the passion lays hold of him. Even then, however, and indeed to the very end, he is quite unlike the essentially jealous man, quite unlike Leontes. No doubt the thought of another man's possessing the woman he loves is intolerable to him; no doubt the sense of insult and the impulse of revenge are at times most violent; and these are the feelings of jealousy proper. But these are not the chief or the deepest source of Othello's suffering. It is the wreck of his faith and his love. It is the feeling,

If she be false, oh then Heaven mocks itself;

the feeling,

O Iago, the pity of it, Iago!

the feeling,

But there where I have garner'd up my heart,
Where either I must live, or bear no life;
The fountain from the which my current runs,
Or else dries up — to be discarded thence. . . .

You will find nothing like this in Leontes.

Up to this point, it appears to me, there is not a syllable to be said against Othello. But the play is a tragedy, and from this point we may abandon the un-

5

grateful and undramatic task of awarding praise and blame. When Othello, after a brief interval, re-enters (III. iii. 329), we see at once that the poison has been at work, and "burns like the mines of sulphur."

> Look where he comes! Not poppy, nor mandragora,
> Nor all the drowsy syrups of the world,
> Shall ever medicine thee to that sweet sleep
> Which thou owedst yesterday.

He is "on the rack," in an agony so unbearable that he cannot endure the sight of Iago. Anticipating the probability that Iago has spared him the whole truth, he feels that in that case his life is over and his "occupation gone" with all its glories. But he has not abandoned hope. The bare possibility that his friend is deliberately deceiving him — though such a deception would be a thing so monstrously wicked that he can hardly conceive it credible — is a kind of hope. He furiously demands proof, ocular proof. And when he is compelled to see that he is demanding an impossibility he still demands evidence. He forces it from the unwilling witness, and hears the maddening tale of Cassio's dream. It is enough. And if it were not enough, has he not sometimes seen a handkerchief spotted with strawberries in his wife's hand? Yes, it was his first gift to her.

> I know not that; but such a handkerchief —
> I am sure it was your wife's — did I to-day
> See Cassio wipe his beard with.

"If it be that," he answers — but what need to test the fact? The "madness of revenge" is in his blood, and hesitation is a thing he never knew. He passes judgment, and controls himself only to make his sentence a solemn vow.

The Othello of the Fourth Act is Othello in his fall. His fall is never complete, but he is much changed. Towards the close of the Temptation-scene he becomes at times most terrible, but his grandeur remains almost undiminished. Even in the following scene (III. iv.), where he goes to test Desdemona in the matter of the handkerchief, and receives a fatal confirmation of her guilt, our sympathy with him is hardly touched by any feeling of humiliation. But in the Fourth Act "Chaos has come." A slight interval of time may be admitted here. It is but slight; for it was necessary for Iago to hurry on, and terribly dangerous to leave a chance for a meeting of Cassio with Othello; and his insight into Othello's nature taught him that his plan was to deliver blow on blow, and never to allow his victim to recover from the confusion of the first shock. Still there is a slight interval; and when Othello reappears we see at a glance that he is a changed man. He is physically exhausted, and his mind is dazed. He sees everything blurred through a mist of blood and tears. He has actually forgotten the incident of the handkerchief, and has to be reminded of it. When Iago, perceiving that he can now risk almost any lie, tells him that Cassio has confessed his guilt, Othello, the hero who has seemed to us only second to Coriolanus in physical power, trembles all over; he mutters disjointed words; a blackness suddenly intervenes between his eyes and the world; he takes it for the shuddering testimony of nature to the horror he has just heard, and he falls senseless to the ground. When he recovers it is to watch Cassio, as he imagines, laughing over his shame. It is an imposition so gross, and should have been one so perilous, that Iago would never have ventured it before. But he is safe now. The sight only adds to the confusion of intellect the madness of rage; and a ravenous thirst for revenge, contending with motions of infinite longing and regret, conquers them. The delay till night-fall is torture to him. His self-control has wholly deserted him, and he strikes his wife in the presence of the Venetian envoy. He is so lost to all sense of reality that he never asks himself what will follow the deaths of Cassio and his wife. An ineradicable instinct of justice, rather than any last quiver of hope, leads him to question Emilia; but nothing could convince him now, and there follows the dreadful scene of accusation; and then, to allow us the relief of burning hatred and burning tears, the interview of Desdemona with Iago, and that last talk of hers with Emilia, and her last song.

But before the end there is again a change. The supposed death of Cassio (V. i.) satiates the thirst for vengeance. The Othello who enters the bed-chamber with the words,

> It is the cause, it is the cause, my soul,

is not the man of the Fourth Act. The deed he is bound to do is no murder, but a sacrifice. He is to save Desdemona from herself, not in hate but in honour; in honour, and also in love. His anger has passed; a boundless sorrow has taken its place; and

> this sorrow's heavenly:
> It strikes where it doth love.

Even when, at the sight of her apparent obduracy, and at the hearing of words which by a crowning fatality can only reconvince him of her guilt, these feelings give way to others, it is to righteous indignation they give way, not to rage; and, terribly painful as this scene is, there is almost nothing here to diminish the admiration and love which heighten pity. And pity itself vanishes, and love and admiration alone remain, in the majestic dignity and sovereign ascendancy of the close. Chaos has come and gone; and the Othello of the Council-chamber and the quay of Cyprus has returned, or a greater and nobler Othello still. As he speaks those final words in which all the glory and agony of his life — long ago in India and Arabia and Aleppo, and afterwards in Venice, and now in Cyprus — seem to pass before us, like the pictures that flash before the eyes of a drowning man, a triumphant scorn for the fetters of the flesh and the littleness of all the lives that must survive him sweeps our grief away, and when he dies upon a kiss the most painful of all tragedies leaves us for the moment free from pain, and exulting in the power of "love and man's unconquerable mind."   *[1904]*

MILLICENT BELL
Othello's Jealousy

Millicent Bell is a professor emerita in the English department at Boston University and a frequent contributor to The New York Review of Books. *She is the author of the books* Marquand: An American Life *(1979),* Meaning in Henry James *(1993), and* Shakespeare's Tragic Skepticism *(2002), where this essay appeared after first publication in the* Yale Review *(1997). In "Othello's Jealousy," Bell delves into how the notion of "seeing is believing" drives Othello to madness as what he sees in life and what he sees in his imagination are used by Iago to disturb his trust in Desdemona.*

Oh, yes, the chief subject of *Othello* is sexual jealousy. Most dramatic representations seize upon and emphasize the way this condition, like a fatal disease, grows on the hero and destroys him until the recovery of sanity and dignity arrives at the tragic end. The more directly we see and hear him the more we almost share the madness that mounts in his mind until it reaches a point in which he appears to hallucinate, seeing what is not there, writhing before the inner vision of his wife's betrayal. In the recent Kenneth Branagh film this inner vision reaches the screen and the viewer is briefly unable to distinguish between what is and what is imagined as he or she sees — for a terrifying moment, like a clip from a porn film — Cassio's lips meeting Desdemona's, their naked bodies twining together. Film's hallucinatory power, its ability to make virtual what words have only suggested, its ability to make us voyeurs who desire to witness the last detail of a scene, particularly an erotic scene, adds something that goes beyond stage presentation. The movie's powerful language of the visible provides — delusively even to us, though we know Othello is deluded — that ultimate visibility which goes beyond the evidence Iago has manipulated to "prove" Othello's love a whore.

But the greater reserve of the play as we read it, and even the reserve of stage presentation, which works such tricks awkwardly if at all, reminds us that jealousy feeds, precisely, upon what is *not* witnessed but only imagined. Othello, desperately swinging between belief in his wife's innocence and conviction of her guilt, pleads for visible proof: "I'll see before I doubt," he cries. He thinks he can trust Desdemona, "for she had eyes and chose me," he tells Iago, who responds, "Look to your wife. Observe her well with Cassio; wear your eyes thus: not jealous, nor secure. . . . Look to't. . . . In Venice they do let God see the pranks / They dare not show their husbands." "Make me to see't," Othello pleads.

He groans, "Would I were satisfied!" but his tormentor observes — in an age before hidden video cameras and paparazzi — "but how? How satisfied, my Lord? / Would you the supervisor, grossly gape on? / Behold her topped?" and summons into inner view the dreadful vision, after all. But Iago says, at the same time,

It is impossible you should see this,
Were they as prime as goats, as hot as monkeys,
As salt as wolves in pride, and fools as gross
As Ignorance made drunk.

Iago will continue throughout the travail of Othello's jealousy to induce such hallucinations, to make Othello's own imagination set them forth on his inner stage. By the time we have reached the opening of the fourth act, the process is complete, and inner and outer vision are indistinguishable.

IAGO: Will you think so?
OTHELLO: Think so, Iago!
IAGO: What!
     To kiss in private?
OTHELLO: An unauthorized kiss!
IAGO: Or to be naked with her friend in bed
     An hour or more, not meaning any harm?
OTHELLO: Naked in bed, Iago, and not mean harm?

Othello is driven mad by what, by the force of suggestion, he *inwardly* sees, and yet he craves a certainty that can be satisfied only by outward sight — the sense that most convincingly assures us that we know what is before us. The central utterance in the play is, surely, Othello's anguished "Give me the ocular proof." But he craves confirmation of suspicion to end the agony aroused by what he cannot really see. For, as Iago says, "Her honor is an essence that's not seen." If he could witness the pair in bed together it might still not be enough. He is plagued by the realization that truth cannot be directly known; what we perceive is only *seeming*. "Seeing" and "seeming" are significantly repeated words that underline this problem throughout the play.

Othello, I want to argue against many of the play's critics, is the *most* intel-   5
lectual of all Shakespeare's tragedies, including *Hamlet*, despite its concern with elementary personal emotion. In a genuine sense, the play is a "domestic tragedy," as it is frequently termed. But this is not at all to say that it simply shows the evolution of wife-murder, a version of the O. J. Simpson case. Harley Granville-Barker said it was "a tragedy without meaning," and A. C. Bradley thought it inferior to Shakespeare's other tragedies for lacking "the power of dilating the imagination by vague suggestions of huge universal powers working in the world of individual fate and passion." The editor of the New Cambridge Shakespeare edition, Norman Sanders, calls it "the most private of the great tragedies," though he insists that "to complain of its lack of supernatural reference or its limited metaphysical range is to miss the point." "The object poisons sight; / Let it be hid," says Lodovico when Othello and Desdemona lie dead together on their bed. Sanders says this "is the only possible end, because the arena for the struggle the protagonists have lived through is best symbolized by the curtained bed." But I shall insist that the play is not the less philosophical for that. "Sight" is indeed "poisoned" — yet not merely because of the

spectacle of a love that has made such horror, but because this ending has shown the inadequacy of human vision.

Shakespeare, as is his habit, is always telling us a number of things at once. The power of the theme of sexual jealousy obscures other subjects in the play. Race and the divisive role of prejudice seem much more central than used to be conceded by critics who could not imagine how the Elizabethan world provided Shakespeare with so strong a sense of the most acute social problem of modern societies — expressed by the symbolic fantasy of miscegenation, the monstrous union of the socially separated. Shakespeare's treatment of marital violence also contains much that we respond to with recognition, seeing this problem rooted, then as now, in false notions of the differentiations of gender. Jealousy is also rooted in the unnaturalness of *any* love inordinate in its expectations, because each of us is just one and no more, and the single "beast with two backs" — that frightening visibility with which Iago arouses the rage of Brabantio — is a monster created only in an instant of sensual joy. Jealousy is evidence of the doubt that lies at the bottom of love's desire for knowledge of another, the doubt beneath love's refusal to accept the difference between one's perception and another's reality. The torment of Othello is epistemological, a condition of doubt of which sexual jealousy is only a specific illustration or consequence.

That Othello is so vulnerable to suggestion, passing so readily from hypothesis to certainty, has bothered those who have complained that he does not connect, as a character, with what happens; his noble strength, the slowness to anger that rules his early responses to Brabantio and to the drunken scuffle that awakens him from his wedded bliss in Cyprus, the majesty of his language — none of this prepares us for the speed with which he casts reason and refinement aside and becomes brutal and coarse. But it is precisely because jealousy cannot be satisfied by any degree of proof that it is a representation of the effect of skepticism, the specter that haunted the Renaissance imagination.

At the end of the sixteenth century, natural science was becoming more empirical. The view the educated person took of human history and of an individual life was apt to distinguish more consciously between certainty and probability, to discriminate among different kinds of evidence, whereas what "truth" was had become problematic. Though the truth of received religion was still a matter of faith, only a few kinds of certainty — like the certainty of mathematical proofs — were practically attainable. Shakespeare's great contemporary, Sir Francis Bacon, aspired with his grand inductive program to the ultimate restitution of "moral certainty," a concept borrowed from theology by which one might be sure about most things after observing and evaluating the facts. Bacon's effort was directed against the devastating view expressed by Montaigne that nothing could be known. A response to the problem of Montaigne's radical disbelief has been noted in Shakespeare's best writing — the sonnets and the great tragedies. Florio's translation into English of Montaigne's *Essais* was published in 1603, the year before *Othello* appeared on the stage. Perhaps, even, as Stanley Cavell argues, Shakespeare intuitively anticipated the terrifying culmination of Renaissance skepticism in René Descartes, who would make the issue "no longer, or not alone, as with earlier skepticism, how to conduct oneself in an uncertain world; the issue suggested is how to live at all in a groundless world."

In *Othello*, Iago is the source of skepticism; his nihilism links him in Shakespeare's works with Thersites and Edmund. But Othello's mind is the theater in which faith in the unseen and unseeable contends with the doubt that demands physical seeing and yet is never convinced it sees enough. Because Othello becomes the victim of his desire to know by seeing, his almost unbelievable collapse, his too-swift descent from composure and confidence to panic and disbelief, can be understood. But we are not meant to view him altogether in terms of realistic psychology — though nothing seems more real than his actual feelings when they overtake him.

If we do try to explain his fall realistically, we find ourselves in the crossfire   10
of critical tradition. F. R. Leavis was able to make a devastating case against Bradley's view that Othello's perfect nature — noble, strong-minded, self-disciplined — is destroyed by Iago's inhuman malice and intellect. Leavis discovered grounds for seeing Othello as a man infatuated with his own ideal view of himself, and *self*-destroyed. More recent psychological views suggest that Othello's great love, expressed in majestic, romantic hyperbole, may be the bluster of the untried bridegroom whose fear of inadequacy already rouses him from his nuptial bed along with the shouts of Iago and Roderigo in the opening scene. But neither a completely heroic nor a fatuous or secretly vulnerable Othello accounts adequately for the way this hero affects us. Perhaps Othello's improbable gullibility and precipitate fall depends, then, as E. E. Stoll claimed, on the literary convention of the "calumniator believed." We need to remember how commonplace and even farcical are some of the delusionary tricks that destroy Othello's faith in Desdemona; in Shakespeare's own *Much Ado About Nothing*, another ex-soldier, Claudio, is tricked by similar means into believing in the wantonness of his innocent betrothed. But Othello, unlike the lightweight Claudio, is really undone by an idea, though he is hardly philosopher enough himself to formulate it. Shakespeare makes us experience — through Othello's trauma — the absolute difference between a trust in appearances and the loss of that trust. . . .

Throughout *Othello*, Shakespeare's strong interest in the law is also evident in language full of legal terms drawn from the procedures of court trials that those who have hoped to detect more about his life from such elusive traces can suppose that he had had some training in the law. But English court trials were open to the public, forms of entertainment like the theater, and the audience for both was likely to contain persons who were amateur experts, like recent viewers of televised trials. Iago complains that Othello turned a deaf ear to those who urged his advancement; he "non-suites my Mediators," he says — that is, he rules their case out of court. When he refuses to tell Othello his private thoughts, he asks if anyone has "a breast so pure, / But some uncleanly apprehensions / Keep leets and law-days, and in sessions sit / With meditations lawful," "leets and law-days" being court sessions to certify the good behavior of a community. Pleading Cassio's case with Othello, Desdemona insists that the handkerchief business is but "a trick to put me from my suit." She chides herself for "Arraigning his unkindness with my soul; / But now I find I had suborned the witness / And he's indicted falsely," a reference to the crime of subornation of perjury. What is important to note, among these obscurities, is the way words that have a common usage as well as a specific legal sense seem to reverberate with a courtroom meaning — as when Othello's handkerchief, the central symbolic object that is the mark of the troth between him and Desdemona, is called "the recognizance and pledge of love," where "recognizance" is the *legal* word for a binding bond.

It is appropriate to the preoccupation of the play with a general epistemological crisis that the issue of proof is expressed as a legal question. The general evolution of thought in the sixteenth and seventeenth centuries is connected with the fact that English common law established in this period a foundation of rules of evidence that persists to this day. Brabantio's charges and Othello's refutation reflect current controversy over trials for witchcraft. In 1597, James I of England[1] had felt called upon to attempt in his *Demonologie* to refute Reginald Scott's attack (*Discoverie of Witchcraft*, 1584) on the procedures for trying those accused of witchcraft. Yet James I soon developed doubts and censured judges who rushed to judgment without adequate proof. A general movement had begun in the courts to develop proper modes of establishing this crime. Along with that skeptical doubt that caused some, like Montaigne, to doubt the existence of witchcraft altogether, the trial of witches was changing from the search for a hidden character — established only by confession, formerly extracted by torture, if necessary — to a weighing of visible effects, testified to by witnesses. The shift is epistemological.

The courtroom, like the stage, was for the Elizabethans a place where the dynamics of changing concepts of the self were being enacted, being tried. How might one argue from crime to criminal — or reverse the process? By what evidence might the play connect plot and character? In the courtroom it was not enough to argue from "reputation" in deciding probable guilt — as it is not enough for Iago to convict Desdemona by referring to her "Venetian" character — but the prosecution might add plausibility to its case by presenting, as Iago does, a narrative of events leading to her crime, by "imputation." Beyond this, how might guilt be proven? Circumstantial evidence in criminal cases was becoming the most usual basis of conviction. Iago protests that he cannot enable Othello to see his wife in her lover's arms, but adds,

> If imputation and strong circumstances,
> Which lead directly to the door of truth,
> Will give you satisfaction, you might have't.

[1] Before becoming James I of England in 1603, he was James VI of Scotland from 1567–1603. [Eds.]

The paradigm of a trial of law, invoked at the start by an actual trial, is replicated in the structure of the play, a trial of Desdemona that ends in her execution. In a terrible parody of judicial sentence, in the second scene of the last act, Othello enters with a speech of deliberate dignity:

> It is the cause, it is the cause, my soul:
> Let me not name it to you, you chaste stars.
> It is the cause. Yet I'll not shed her blood,
> Nor scar that whiter skin of hers than snow,
> And smooth as monumental alabaster —
> Yet she must die, else she'll betray more men.

"Cause" is a legal term in addition to meaning simply a reason for an occurrence. To seek a cause is to seek a motive to increase the probability of guilt, while the accused may claim for his deed that he had *just* cause. Iago has begun by telling Roderigo, "I hate the Moor. My cause is hearted; thine hath no less reason." He has begun the motive-hunting that Coleridge deemed motiveless; his search for his own motive is a legal procedure to reinforce belief. A cause may be a general purpose, even a high principle to which one is attached; the cause of a heavenly ideal of chastity for which, Othello declares, Desdemona must die. But a cause is also, simply, a suit, as Desdemona called her effort to win pardon for Cassio, acting as his "solicitor." And Othello's charge against Desdemona is a suit in which he becomes prosecutor, judge, and, finally, executioner under a rule of human law aimed not only at punishment but to protect society from further crimes by the criminal ("else she'll betray more men").

Proof as in a law court is what Othello so mistakenly has asked Iago to produce. When Othello says, "I'll see before I doubt; when I doubt prove," Iago says, "I speak not yet of proof," but urges him to watch Desdemona for some self-betrayal and sets forth, meanwhile, her record as a practiced deceiver who has known how to make seeing her directly impossible: "She that so young could give out such a seeming / To seal her father's eyes up close as oak." Perhaps this would not be enough — though Othello is already frantic — but prompt to his purpose, Desdemona reappears to drop the handkerchief that Iago will seize and enter into evidence. "Trifles light as air / Are to the jealous confirmations strong / As proofs of holy writ" — though a just judge and dispassionate jury might not take them so. The handkerchief, for Othello, is the exhibit brought into the courtroom, a piece of the accused's clothing found at the scene of the crime, "ocular proof" — not of the unseeable act but circumstantial evidence, so that "the probation [or determining test] bear no hinge nor loop to hang a doubt on."

Feebly, Othello clings to his faith that Desdemona is honest and asks for presumptive motive: "Give me a living reason she's disloyal," but Iago ignores this. He testifies that he has observed Cassio relive in sleep his secret moments with Desdemona. And when Othello protests that this was but a dream, Iago says, "this may help to thicken other proofs / That do demonstrate thinly." And what are these? Iago saw Cassio wipe his beard with the handkerchief. "It speaks against her with the other proofs."

15

So, as the fourth act opens, Iago provokingly drives the question of proof to its most paradoxical extreme — with the assurance that, although absolute knowledge is impossible, circumstances will convict. There is no direct witness to adultery between Cassio and Desdemona — but after all, how could there be? What if you found them naked and kissing in bed together for an hour or more? Would it *prove* they were "meaning any harm? . . . if they do nothing, 'tis a venial slip." As though the case would be similar, Iago asks if giving a hand-kerchief away need convict a woman of much — knowing that Othello will conclude that it is as circumstantially damning as a sight of the lovers fla-grantly embracing. But the time has come for Iago to offer the confirming proof of confession, though, of course, it is confession reported at second hand — Cassio has supposedly confessed to *him*. It is not quite enough, and Iago will repair the defect in his case, or appear to; Othello will think he witnesses Cassio boasting how "he hath and is again to cope" Desdemona when Cassio really is talking about his mistress, who appears on cue, handkerchief in hand.

It is no use for Desdemona to defend herself. Or for Emilia to protest in a logical way, "Who keeps her company? What place, what time, what form, what likelihood?" But Emilia as defense witness arrives too late, discovering her husband's perfidy only after the death of her mistress. Before Othello executes his sentence, he asks Desdemona if she has repented of crime, as condemned criminals generally were asked, for the rescue of her soul and also to confirm the sentence by the strongest of proofs: "Take heed of perjury: thou art on thy death bed."

She maintains her innocence, having nothing to confess. Iago, who has everything to tell, withholds *his* confession, but Emilia will dispose of the false evidence of the handkerchief by revealing that she stole it for him, and docu-mentary proof, letters from Iago found on Roderigo, close the case — unneces-sarily for the audience but in keeping with the judicial process that governs the play.

20

But if the legal conceptualization of *Othello* relates it to the whole issue of the nature of truth, it is really an ironic parody of real legal inquiry. The search for evidentiary proof is, in fact, constantly mocked despite all the talk of proofs and making the wronged husband "see." Iago's pseudo-legal demonstration of Cassio's and Desdemona's guilt is conducted in the Cyprus world ruled by "seeming" — a world that makes such deceptions possible by demonic magic. Emilia's "what place, what time, what form, what likelihood" reminds us of the sleights that the playwright has himself exercised, not the least by that famous deception of "double time" that allows no time or opportunity — though we fail to notice it — for an affair between Cassio and Desdemona. Iago has merely to repeat Brabantio's charges that there was something "unnatural" in Desdemona's love to get Othello's assent to an idea he had serenely rejected in the Venetian court. He says Cassio's declarations, in sleep, of his love for Desdemona, reported by Iago, "denoted a foregone conclusion," and it is enough for him to have heard that Cassio has the handkerchief to be convinced that she would betray him sexually, accepting the false analogy: may she not just as freely give away her invisible honor? Othello does not have to hear Cassio's actual conversation with Iago about Bianca to assume that his wife is the subject.

There is a subtle slippage that merges supposition with ascertained fact. When Iago says, "What if I had said I had seen him do you wrong?" or heard Cassio "blab" of his conquest, the "what if" glides by as though never uttered. Othello reaches vainly for his sanity: "Hath he said anything?" *Then*, Iago slips in the knife — "He hath my lord" — only to assure Othello that Cassio would deny it. When Othello asks, "What hath he said?" he receives the riddling answer "what he did — I know not what he did," and to Othello's "with her?" the reply is a verbal quibble that throws his victim into his swoon, "With her, on her, what you will."

As we attend this collapse of logic, the difference between the world of illusion and the real world in which fact and appearance are distinguishable dissolves, for we are ourselves swept along by the play's hypnotic persuasion to jealousy, which banishes such distinctions. When Desdemona wonders at the "cause" for Othello's rage, Emilia rightly says,

> . . . jealous souls will not be answered so.
> They are not ever jealous for the cause,
> But jealous for they're jealous. 'Tis a monster
> Begot upon itself, born on itself.

But as I have been suggesting, jealousy becomes, in this extraordinary play, just a way of exhibiting a change of mind that equalizes the effect of all impressions. Othello may well say that contentedness in deception is best; it annihilates the reality that gives pain: "He that is robbed, not wanting what is stolen, / Let him not know't and he's not robbed at all."

It is often pointed out that the play exhibits contrasted viewpoints in the language of Othello and Iago — there is the poetic "Othello music," as L. C. Knights called it, sounded in words that seem to arise from a sense of the ordered cosmos and the hero's place in it. And there is the language of Iago, prosaically intelligent without any element of the ideal. Only Leavis and a few others have felt that Iago had some right to complain of Othello as "loving his own pride and purposes" and apt to employ "bombast circumstance" and "stuff'd" epithets. But it must be said that Othello's is the half of language most vulnerable to skepticism. Iago's version of Othello's tragedy is not the one most readers and viewers of the play embrace — he sees it as comedy, the leveling of preposterous presumption. His view goes down in defeat, we assume, as we listen to Othello's last grand speech as he prepares to kill himself — even though one suspects that T. S. Eliot was right in pointing out that the "honorable murderer" whom Emilia has called a "gull" and a "dolt" is simply trying to cheer himself up. Where Shakespeare stood is, as usual, not evident.

But if we see Othello's fall as a telescoped representation of the mind overtaken by its own epistemological distrust of appearances — and the paradoxical trust *only* in appearances — we can see that what overcomes Othello, or   25 rather what is represented *through* Othello's mad jealousy, is a trembling of the universal spheres, a perturbation from which recovery comes only at the cost of deadly anguish. It is not mere hyperbole that causes him to tell Desdemona, out of her hearing, "When I love thee not, / Chaos is come again," to exclaim, "If she be false, O then heaven mocks itself," or to say, in later confirmation of this prediction,

> O heavy hour!
> Methinks it should be now a huge eclipse
> Of sun and moon, and that th'affrighted globe
> Should yawn at alteration. [1997]

JEFFRIE G. MURPHY
Jealousy, Shame, and the Rival

Jeffrie G. Murphy (b. 1941) is a distinguished legal and moral philosopher. He has published a number of books, including Getting Even: Forgiveness and Mercy *(2004) and most recently* Retribution Reconsidered: More Essays in the Philosophy of Law *(2010). His essay, "Jealousy, Shame, and the Rival," which appeared in the journal* Philosophical Studies, *is essentially a critique of Jerome Neu's work on jealousy in* A Tear Is an Intellectual Thing *(2000). Murphy maintains that Othello's acts of jealousy stem not from a fear of loss of love (as Neu's definition of jealousy requires) but from a fear of the shame brought on by that loss.*

When Jerome Neu's essay "Jealous Thoughts" was published in 1980, jealousy was widely regarded — at least in leftist intellectual and cultural circles — as an irrational and even evil "bourgeois" passion — one tied to a capitalistic market conception of human relations. The jealous person — according to this view — regards the loved person as a kind of object — as owned property over which the lover has rights. Jealousy is thus a kind of property fear — analogous to the fear of theft. The fear intrinsically involves the belief that one risks losing a possessed loved object to whose love one has a right.

Neu — rightly in my judgment — rejects this account of jealousy as psychologically shallow. He argues — in "Jealous Thoughts" and in the later "Jealous Afterthoughts" — that psychoanalytic theory teaches us that love gets its initial life and draws its basic character from the Oedipal situation. The child so needs and depends upon the mother that loss of the mother's love would appear both as biological and psychological annihilation — psychological because the very self of the child is identified with that of the mother. Any perceived rival for the mother's affections (initially the father) is seen as a threat to security and thus provokes in the child a fear of loss of love. It is here that love and jealousy begin, develop through what Winnicott calls "transitional objects," and assume forms that will persist in adult life. To love is, at least in part, to be so identified with another person that the loss of that person's love will be perceived as loss or annihilation of one's very self or personality. Jealousy, then, is simply the fear that one will lose the love of a person with whom one is psychologically identified — an instance of the fear of annihilation. "If others do not love us," Neu writes, "we will disintegrate."

This fear is not, according to Neu, grounded in a bourgeois or possessive model of human relations, for one can fear the loss of love without believing that one owns the loved person or that one has a right to that person's love. All that is required is that one has the love. Love, then, in part involves self identification — when we lose it we lose ourselves, having our vulnerabilities open and unsupported. All human beings, regardless of social setting — bourgeois or communitarian — fear the exposure of vulnerabilities and the resulting loss of self. According to Neu, this fear is jealousy. Thus jealousy and love are necessarily connected — we cannot get rid of the former without losing the latter.

There are some questions that I immediately want to raise about this analysis. First, what about unrequited love? There are surely intense cases of jealousy where the jealous person knows full well that the love he feels is not returned. Not having it, he cannot fear its loss. Thus it cannot be literally true to say, as Neu does in the first essay, that "to be jealous over someone, you must believe that they love you or have loved you."

Unrequited love thus presents a problem for Neu's original analysis, but I think that the problem can be rather easily fixed. One might draw on some of the instructive things that Neu has to say in the later essay about the role of illusion and projection in erotic love, or one might suggest (think of the John Hinckley/Jodie Foster case) that what the jealous unrequited lover fears is not the loss of love (which he clearly does not have) but the loss of the *possibility* of love (which he may still hope for).

There is also, of course, the problem of jealousy over love that one believes is already hopelessly lost. Othello — often presented (as he is by Neu) as a paradigm of a jealous person — is frequently thought to be most jealous *after* he believes that he has lost Desdemona's love to Cassio. But surely this cannot be understood simply as the fear of loss of love, for how can one fear to lose what one has already lost?

In keeping with the spirit — if not the exact letter — of Neu's analysis, one might try to deal with the Othello case in this way: The fear that constitutes Othello's jealousy should not be seen as the fear of the loss of love (it is simply too late for *that* fear) but rather as the fear of the personal disintegration that may result from that loss.

Perhaps killing or other acts of revenge against the lost lover are strategies to defend against this possible consequence. Perhaps they are preventive strategies that seek the prevention, not of the loss of love, but rather of the dire consequences that — according to Neu — may flow from that loss. Or perhaps they are *retributive* strategies — seeking to inflict punishment on the person who has caused such personal disruption and pain at the core of one's very self. Thus it is possible that the jealous person who inflicts pain over love lost is somewhat like the lover of a murder victim who believes (sometimes rightly, sometimes wrongly) that a kind of closure will result from the execution of the killer.

We are all, alas, familiar with newspaper reports that read "He killed her in a jealous rage." Such a phrase might well describe Othello, but I am not sure. He was surely jealous when he suspected Desdemona of infidelity, but was he jealous at the time he murdered her? Perhaps he was simply vindictive. However, if such murderous rage is properly to be identified as "jealous," it surely cannot be motivated by the fear of losing love since the surest way permanently to lose love is to kill the lover. Dead people cannot love. So what goes on in these cases is either not jealousy at all but rather something else — vengeance perhaps — or it is jealousy motivated by something other than the fear of losing love. Perhaps it is motivated by a deep aversion to certain *consequences* of losing love. Neu would stress the consequence of annihilation or disintegration — since that is so integral to his analysis of love — but I shall later argue that one of these consequences may be *shame.* . . .

It is a perhaps sad but surely true claim that, to a substantial degree, people   10
derive their sense of self worth from the judgments of others. If we love a person, we tend to take that person's judgments in these matters quite seriously — i.e., we take them in some sense to be accurate judges of our own worth. (The mentally healthy among us — if there are any — would not follow Groucho Marx in contemptuously refusing to join any club that would have us for members; nor would we deeply mistrust the judgment of any person who could love us.) If we add to this the fact that non-moral judgments of worth are generally comparative, then the fact that a judge whom we trust prefers someone over us may make us doubt our own worth or value. So jealousy may stand as testimony, not merely to our need for love and attention, but also to our need for validation by another. We are thus shamed by rejection.

It is, of course, not merely the judgment of the loved person who matters. The judgment of a wider circle of people matters as well, for even the strongest of us needs validation from some relevant reference group. Consider Achilles. His rage over the loss of Briseis to Agamemnon is to a substantial degree based on his loss of honor — face and standing — in the eyes of his fellow warriors. He has been shamed by having the girl taken from him.

I think that similar shame may be found in many contemporary cases of jealousy and loss. The jilted lover is often ashamed to report this to others — thinking that it casts some bad reflection on his or her worth or standing. (Sometimes — for similar reasons I suspect — people are reluctant even to admit that they are divorced.) Being a victim of infidelity is, among other unpleasant things, shameful and embarrassing. Perhaps this in part explains the rage that is often found in those who have been jilted — a rage that may provoke expensive and vicious lawsuits, small or even major acts of retribution, and sometimes even murder. Why do people do these things? These acts will not get the love back, but they may go a long way — at least in the eyes of the perpetrator — toward saving face, restoring lost status and honor, and thus overcoming the shame of it all. If one believes that he has been brought down by another, he may find it therapeutic — or think he will find it therapeutic — to bring that person down as well. I am not, of course, saying that such a response is justified, only that it is — unfortunately — not unusual (particularly among men). As Norman Mailer (who ought to know) has asked: "Isn't human nature depressing?"

To summarize and conclude: I think that Neu has provided us with many profound insights on jealousy and its relation to love. Indeed, if I were asked to recommend just one philosophical essay on jealousy, it would be Neu's. It is, I think, the best place to start — for its insights, the framework it provides, and the provocative questions it forces us to raise.

In raising these questions, however, I have come to think that Neu's account of jealousy needs to be supplemented in certain ways. In particular, I have suggested that *shame* needs to be stressed in order fully to account for the role of the rival in jealousy.   *[2002]*

■ **MAKING COMPARISONS**

1. Murphy focuses on jealousy as having a psychological basis, arguing that jealousy is "the fear that one will lose the love of a person with whom one is psychologically identified" (para. 2) and later adds shame into the mix of jealousy. Bell, however, seems to think jealousy has more to do with philosophy, with appearances and reality, with the distinction "between seeming and true seeing" — indeed, with the very nature of truth itself. Explain why one of these interpretations helps you understand *Othello* better.

2. Bradley claims that the true source of Othello's suffering is "the wreck of his faith and love" (para. 5). Do you think Bell and Murphy agree?

3. From each essay, choose a sentence or two that impresses you as offering an interesting insight into the play. How did each one deepen your understanding of *Othello*?

■ **WRITING ABOUT ISSUES**

1. Write an argument that Bradley's last paragraph captures your feelings as you read the last scene.

2. In a brief essay, agree or disagree with Bell's comment that "the power of the theme of sexual jealousy obscures other subjects in the play" (para. 6).

3. Most critics think of Othello as noble in thought and action, and he is often seen as authoritative, disciplined, human, and eloquent. But if we heard the outline of this play on today's news — "General kills wife suspected of adultery, then kills self" — we might not think highly of him. Write an essay that explores this disparity. You might want to take into consideration the nature and purpose of tragedy.

4. Write an essay about your response to *Othello* that focuses on the familiar idea "There, but for the grace of God, go I." That is, is the tragedy of the Moor and "the green-eyed monster" one we could all succumb to?

MATTHEW ARNOLD, "Dover Beach"

SUSAN MINOT, "My Husband's Back"

Part of our cultural narrative about romance — circulating for centuries in novels, poems, and films — is that love will save us from the disappointments and frustrations of the world. If our society sometimes seems cruel or unfair, if our jobs are tedious, if the economy fails, if war, injustice, and racism persist, we can always find solace in the arms of our beloved. It is here in a loving relationship that one can escape the world's duplicity, finding instead loyalty, acceptance, intimacy, and comfort. It is a popular and widespread scenario. Is romantic love enough to keep the world at bay? Can it help us suffer, with Hamlet, the "slings and arrows of outrageous fortune" or endure "the heart-ache and the thousand natural shocks that flesh is heir to"? Is that perhaps putting too much pressure on romance?

Both poems in this cluster seem to have a fairly dark view of existence, although Minot's woes are more domestic frustrations than Arnold's cosmic angst. Arnold's famous concluding stanza employs the chilling metaphor "Where ignorant armies clash by night" to characterize his pessimistic view of life. Minot begins more locally: "Sunday evening. / Breakdown hour." Both poets are filled with gloomy thoughts, and both hope love will cure what ails them.

≡ BEFORE YOU READ

Do you expect love to be a buffer against the world? To protect you from life's disappointments?

MATTHEW ARNOLD
Dover Beach

Victorian poet Matthew Arnold (1822–1889) was the eldest son of Thomas Arnold, an influential clergyman and historian and headmaster of Rugby, one of England's most prestigious college preparatory schools. He grew up in an educational milieu in which religious, political, and social issues were discussed in depth. He went on to Oxford, where he eventually achieved success despite his irreverence and eccentricity. In 1851, he became an inspector of schools and served in this capacity for thirty-five years. He drew on his experiences with people of diverse social classes to become a keen critic of British education and culture, and he expressed his views of society in critical essays on literary, social, and religious issues as well as in poems. Living during an age in which Charles Darwin published On the Origin of Species *(1859) and religious dogma was being questioned in many ways, Arnold suggests in "Dover Beach" that human love becomes especially important in such a world. The poem may have been written during the months just before or just after Arnold's marriage and honeymoon, which included a ferry ride from Dover, England, to Calais, France.*

The sea is calm tonight.
The tide is full, the moon lies fair
Upon the straits; — on the French coast the light
Gleams and is gone; the cliffs of England stand,
Glimmering and vast, out in the tranquil bay.   5
Come to the window, sweet is the night-air!
Only, from the long line of spray
Where the sea meets the moon-blanched land,
Listen! you hear the grating roar
Of pebbles which the waves draw back, and fling,   10
At their return, up the high strand,
Begin, and cease, and then again begin,
With tremulous cadence slow, and bring
The eternal note of sadness in.

Sophocles long ago   15
Heard it on the Aegean, and it brought
Into his mind the turbid ebb and flow
Of human misery;° we
Find also in the sound a thought,
Hearing it by this distant northern sea.   20

The Sea of Faith
Was once, too, at the full, and round earth's shore
Lay like the folds of a bright girdle furled.
But now I only hear
Its melancholy, long, withdrawing roar,   25
Retreating, to the breath
Of the night-wind, down the vast edges drear
And naked shingles° of the world.

Ah, love, let us be true
To one another! for the world, which seems   30
To lie before us like a land of dreams,
So various, so beautiful, so new,
Hath really neither joy, nor love, nor light,
Nor certitude, nor peace, nor help for pain;
And we are here as on a darkling plain   35
Swept with confused alarms of struggle and flight,
Where ignorant armies clash by night.   *[1867]*

15–18 Sophocles . . . misery: In *Antigone*, Sophocles compares the disasters that beset the house of Oedipus to a mounting tide.   **28 shingles:** Pebble beach.

≡ THINKING ABOUT THE TEXT

1. In trying to re-create this scene — say, for a movie script — what would you have the lovers look like? Where would the couple be positioned? If you were the director, how would you explain the scene to the actors — that is, what is the speaker saying? Put another way, what argument is being made?

2. Arnold uses the sea as a metaphor. What do you think it represents? What other metaphors and similes are used? Are they effective in making his point?

3. Some feminist readers see this poem as yet another example of a man who hopes to escape temporarily from the troubles of the world by finding comfort and support from a woman. Is there some validity to this point? Why, for example, doesn't the woman speak?

4. In the film *The Anniversary Party*, Kevin Kline's character reads the last stanza of this poem to a couple celebrating their sixth wedding anniversary. Some critics saw it as an ironic joke, others as a parody of a "sweet" love poem. What is it about the poem that seems to make it inappropriate for such an occasion? Would you send it to your beloved? Why, or why not?

5. What specific reasons does the speaker give for the lovers to be true to each other, beginning with "for the world" (line 30)? Is this an attitude you share? Do you know others who agree? Is this an extreme position? What would the opposite view be? Is this extreme, as well?

SUSAN MINOT

My Husband's Back

Susan Minot (b. 1956) was born in Boston and grew up in Manchester-by-the-Sea, Massachusetts. She studied writing and painting at Brown University and received an M.F.A. from Columbia University. Minot was an editor of the literary journal Grant Street. *Her first book,* Monkeys *(1986), is a collection of nine stories about a large New England family. Minot's female protagonists are searching for love, usually unsuccessfully. Her best-selling collection* Lust and Other Stories *(1989) focuses on romantic love, although one critic cautions readers not to "look for a happy, mutual, heterosexual relationship in Minot. You will not find it." Her novel* Evening *(1998) was made into a popular film in 2007 starring Vanessa Redgrave, Meryl Streep, and Claire Danes. A volume of her verse,* Poems 4am, *was published in 2002. The women in these poems seem more optimistic about love than do those in her fiction.*

Sunday evening.
Breakdown hour. Weeping into
a pot of burnt rice. Sun dimmed

like a light bulb gone out
behind a gray lawn of snow.   5
The baby flushed with the flu
asleep on a pillow.
The fire won't catch.
The wet wood's caked
with ice. Sitting   10
on the couch my spine
collides with all its bones
and I watch my husband
peer past the glass grate
and blow.   15
His back in a snug plaid shirt
gray and white
leaning into the woodstove
is firm and compact
like a young man's back.   20

And the giant world which swirls
in my head
stopping most thought
suddenly ceases
to spin. It sits   25
right there, the back I love,
animal and gamine,° leaning
on one arm.
I could crawl on it forever
the one point in the world   30
turns out
I have traveled everywhere
to get to.   [2005]

gamine: Untamed and mischievous.

≡ THINKING ABOUT THE TEXT

1. Why is the speaker "Weeping" (line 2)? Is she unhappy? Frustrated? Overwhelmed?

2. Why does "the giant world" (line 21) cease to spin?

3. What do you think the speaker means in the last two lines when she says she has "traveled everywhere / to get to" (lines 32–33)?

4. Do you think being in love can help a person deal with global tragedies? Domestic frustration? Cosmic gloom?

5. Do you think Minot's feelings of love are momentary, caused by the "Breakdown hour"?

≡ MAKING COMPARISONS

1. Would you agree with some critics who see the speakers in these two poems as stereotypically male and female? Why?

2. Does Minot seem more in love than Arnold? Is Arnold declaring his love or his loyalty?

3. Is it dangerous to put too many expectations on love? Do these poets?

≡ WRITING ABOUT ISSUES

1. Argue that Arnold's last stanza is or is not an appropriate metaphor for contemporary life.

2. The poet Percy Bysshe Shelley noted that our "sweetest songs are of saddest thought," perhaps commenting on the often melancholy nature of some of our best literature. Argue that this is or is not the case with these two poems. Try to include other favorite texts as examples to support your claim.

3. Argue that people put too much or too little emphasis on love in their lives. Use the works of Arnold and Minot or other poets or songwriters as part of your support.

4. Do you think that one's outlook on life is directly related to age? Do middle-aged writers tend to have a darker vision and younger writers a sunnier perspective? You might examine several early and recent songs by well-established singers or bands that you know and like. Write a report in which you compare the early songs with the later songs and also analyze these songs as either typical or atypical of youth's optimistic view of life.

CHAPTER 12

Freedom and Confinement

Like most abstract and frequently used terms, *freedom* means many things to many people. In countries in the West, freedom is usually associated with political and religious choice, with the ability to dissent publicly from government policy, and even with an ability to dye our hair orange and paint our lips black. Indeed, freedom involves the right not to conform to conventional ideas about who we are and how we should behave as well as the right not to be stereotyped by a culture's demeaning, limiting, and distorted images and assumptions.

Readers of nineteenth-century fiction by women are familiar with the rigid cultural expectations that constricted the lives of most women. Excluded from public life and confined almost exclusively to domestic spaces, many women felt trapped in helping roles constructed for them by men. The consequences for the mental and physical health of thousands of would-be writers, artists, scientists, and intellectuals were often severe. Today many minorities in America also feel limited by the confining legacies of both racial and gender stereotypes. Children, who are especially vulnerable to the negative images that adults from the dominant culture have of them, have few defenses against internalizing damaging stereotypes that can adversely affect them well into adulthood. And when an entire culture constructs invidious stereotypes, as German Nazis did about European Jews, the consequences can be deadly. Although cultural prejudices against ethnic, religious, sexual, and gender minorities can be devastating, actual physical confinement can sorely test the limits of mind and body. Too often, minorities suffer from both prejudice and confinement when, like Martin Luther King Jr., they are jailed for protesting their lack of freedom. This chapter brings together diverse literary texts that explore some of these issues of freedom and confinement, both physical and ideological—from the American internment of Japanese Americans during World War II to Langston Hughes's dreams of freedom, from Nora's refusal in *A Doll House* to a bizarre torture on a remote penal colony, and an amazing fantasy of girls raised by wolves. We hope you will be engaged by these imaginative and insightful writers as they explore the complex and moving ways that freedom is crucial in all our lives.

The chapter opens with a cluster of five poems focusing on animal stereotypes, followed by responses to a famous story about the dangers of unreflective traditions. The third cluster pairs two plays about marriage, and then we present a disturbing tale of confinement, along with cultural contexts. A memoir about the social and familial problems of learning a second language, along with two responses to it, is followed by seven poems about the painful consequences of stereotyping. Five harrowing poems about the Holocaust make up the seventh cluster. Then we present three stories about flawed masculinity. Four poems by Langston Hughes comprise the ninth cluster. The next cluster includes a tale of vampires, along with associated news stories. The chapter concludes with a contemporary re-visioning of the classic story of Little Red Riding Hood.

≡ Freedom for Animals: Poems

WILLIAM BLAKE, "The Tyger"

D. H. LAWRENCE, "Snake"

ELIZABETH BISHOP, "The Fish"

THOMAS LUX, "To Help the Monkey Cross the River"

DEAN YOUNG, "Clam Ode"

Since before the Greeks, writers have used animals as symbols. The temptation to see in animal behavior human traits such as evil, sneakiness, tranquility, kindness, or cruelty seems too great for us to resist. The term *anthropomorphize* is used to describe how we superimpose human motives and attitudes on animals. But we are curtailing their freedom when we confine their lives to our assumptions and expectations. When we symbolize animals, we are almost always talking about ourselves. Although it is usually harmless and often insightful when poets anthropomorphize animals, the practice has nevertheless brought grievous harm to wolves, snakes, sharks, and other creatures that have been tortured for centuries by those who see them as irredeemably evil.

Certainly William Blake is talking about our own "deadly terrors" when he writes about tigers. And surely no one really thinks that snakes are inherently evil, even though D. H. Lawrence uses a biblical narrative to talk about temptation. When Elizabeth Bishop writes of the noble fish, or Thomas Lux the cute monkey, or Dean Young the calm clam, they are confining the freedom of these animals but giving us interesting and insightful comments on the human condition.

≡ BEFORE YOU READ

Describe at least one encounter you have had with wildlife, noting how you behaved at the time and what influenced your conduct. What is your attitude toward people who like to hunt or fish? What forms of wildlife, if any, do you think people are justified in fearing or despising? Do you think the notion of animal rights has merit? Identify particular values that your answers reflect.

WILLIAM BLAKE
The Tyger

William Blake (1757–1827) is today considered the major visionary poet, painter, and printmaker in Western culture, although his contemporaries thought him highly eccentric, even mad. A thinker and artist well ahead of his time, Blake is often cited as a forerunner of contemporary secular liberalism, feminism, and even birth control and divorce. He was a philosophical anti-authoritarian, perhaps even an anarchist. He did brilliant paintings for many of his collections, including Marriage of Heaven and Hell. *"The Tyger," one of the most well-known poems in literature, has engaged critics and ordinary readers alike with its compelling imagery and its deep, mysterious questions.*

Tyger! Tyger! burning bright
In the forests of the night,
What immortal hand or eye
Could frame thy fearful symmetry?

In what distant deeps or skies   5
Burnt the fire of thine eyes?
On what wings dare he aspire?
What the hand, dare seize the fire?

And what shoulder, & what art,
Could twist the sinews of thy heart?   10
And when thy heart began to beat,
What dread hand? & what dread feet?

What the hammer? what the chain?
In what furnace was thy brain?
What the anvil? what dread grasp   15
Dare its deadly terrors clasp?

When the stars threw down their spears,
And water'd heaven with their tears,
Did he smile his work to see?
Did he who made the Lamb make thee?   20

Tyger! Tyger! burning bright
In the forests of the night,
What immortal hand or eye
Dare frame thy fearful symmetry?   [1794]

≡ THINKING ABOUT THE TEXT

1. What do you think Blake means in the first stanza by "fearful symmetry"?
2. What images does the poet use to describe the creation of the tiger? What is his purpose?
3. Why does the poet ask if the tiger's creator also made the lamb?
4. Why does Blake change the "could" of stanza 1 to "dare" in the last stanza?
5. Critics have argued over the meaning of this poem for centuries. How do you interpret Blake's question about the creation of the tiger? Is he really asking a more philosophical question?

D. H. LAWRENCE

Snake

David Herbert Lawrence (1885–1930) was a leading novelist and short-story writer in the first half of the twentieth century. The son of a coal miner and a former schoolteacher, he describes his English working-class upbringing in his autobiographical novel Sons and Lovers *(1913). Probably he remains best known for his 1928 novel* Lady Chatterley's Lover. *For many years, it was banned in England and the United States because it explicitly described the sexual relationship between an aristocratic woman and her husband's gamekeeper. In most of his work, Lawrence endorses human passion, although he argued that people needed to exist in harmony with nature as well as with one another. Besides writing fiction, he painted and wrote poetry. "Snake," published in 1913, is based on Lawrence's stay in Sicily, one of the many places he went as he searched for a land friendly to his ideals.*

A snake came to my water-trough
On a hot, hot day, and I in pyjamas for the heat,
To drink there.

In the deep, strange-scented shade of the great dark carob-tree
I came down the steps with my pitcher   5
And must wait, must stand and wait, for there he was at the trough
    before me.

He reached down from a fissure in the earth-wall in the gloom
And trailed his yellow-brown slackness soft-bellied down, over the edge
    of the stone trough
And rested his throat upon the stone bottom,
And where the water had dripped from the tap, in a small clearness,   10
He sipped with his straight mouth,
Softly drank through his straight gums, into his slack long body,
Silently.

Someone was before me at my water-trough,
And I, like a second comer, waiting.   15

He lifted his head from his drinking, as cattle do,
And looked at me vaguely, as drinking cattle do,
And flickered his two-forked tongue from his lips, and mused a moment,
And stooped and drank a little more,
Being earth-brown, earth-golden from the burning bowels of the earth   20
On the day of Sicilian July, with Etna smoking.

The voice of my education said to me
He must be killed,
For in Sicily the black, black snakes are innocent, the gold are
    venomous.

And voices in me said, If you were a man   25
You would take a stick and break him now, and finish him off.

But must I confess how I liked him,
How glad I was he had come like a guest in quiet, to drink at my
        water-trough
And depart peaceful, pacified, and thankless,
Into the burning bowels of this earth?   30

Was it cowardice, that I dared not kill him?
Was it perversity, that I longed to talk to him?
Was it humility, to feel so honoured?
I felt so honoured.

And yet those voices: 35
If you were not afraid, you would kill him!

And truly I was afraid, I was most afraid,
But even so, honoured still more
That he should seek my hospitality
From out the dark door of the secret earth.   40

He drank enough
And lifted his head, dreamily, as one who has drunken,
And flickered his tongue like a forked night on the air, so black;
Seeming to lick his lips,
And looked around like a god, unseeing, into the air,   45
And slowly turned his head,
And slowly, very slowly, as if thrice adream,
Proceeded to draw his slow length curving round
And climb again the broken bank of my wall-face.

And as he put his head into that dreadful hole,   50
And as he slowly drew up, snake-easing his shoulders, and entered
        farther,
A sort of horror, a sort of protest against his withdrawing into that
        horrid black hole,
Deliberately going into the blackness, and slowly drawing himself after,
Overcame me now his back was turned.

I looked round, I put down my pitcher,   55
I picked up a clumsy log
And threw it at the water-trough with a clatter.

I think it did not hit him,
But suddenly that part of him that was left behind convulsed in
        undignified haste,
Writhed like lightning, and was gone   60
Into the black hole, the earth-lipped fissure in the wall-front,
At which, in the intense still noon, I stared with fascination.

And immediately I regretted it.
I thought how paltry, how vulgar, what a mean act!
I despised myself and the voices of my accursed human education.   65

And I thought of the albatross,°
And I wished he would come back, my snake.

For he seemed to me again like a king,
Like a king in exile, uncrowned in the underworld,
Now due to be crowned again.   70

And so, I missed my chance with one of the lords
Of life.
And I have something to expiate;
A pettiness.   *[1913]*

66 albatross: In Samuel Taylor Coleridge's "Rime of the Ancient Mariner," a seaman brings misfortune to the crew of his ship by killing an albatross, an ocean bird.

≡ THINKING ABOUT THE TEXT

1. What did you associate with snakes before reading this poem? Does Lawrence push you to look at snakes differently, or does his poem endorse the view you already had? Develop your answer by referring to specific lines.

2. Discuss the poem as an argument involving various "voices." How do you think you would have reacted to the snake if you had been the speaker? What "voices" might you have heard inside your own mind? What people or institutions would these "voices" have come from?

3. Why does the speaker throw the log just as the snake is leaving? Note the explanation the speaker gives as well as the judgment he then makes about his act. Do both make sense to you? Why, or why not?

4. Lawrence begins many lines with the word *and*. What is the effect of his doing so?

5. In "Snake," Lawrence writes positively about an animal that is often feared. Think of a similar poem that you might write. What often-feared animal would you choose? What positive qualities would you point out or suggest in describing this animal? If you wish, try actually writing such a poem.

≡ MAKING COMPARISONS

1. Both tigers and snakes are feared. How do Blake and Lawrence use this idea?

2. Does Lawrence seem more self-conscious about his attitude toward his animal than Blake?

3. What assumptions about these poets' animals would you question?

ELIZABETH BISHOP

The Fish

Although she also wrote short stories, Elizabeth Bishop (1911–1979) is primarily
known for her poetry, winning both the Pulitzer Prize and the National Book Award
for it. Born in Worcester, Massachusetts, she spent much of her youth in Nova Scotia.
As an adult, she lived in various places, including New York City, Florida, Mexico,
and Brazil. Much of her poetry observes and reflects on a particular object or figure.
Such is the case with "The Fish," which Bishop wrote in 1940 and then included in
her 1946 book North and South.

I caught a tremendous fish
and held him beside the boat
half out of water, with my hook
fast in a corner of his mouth.
He didn't fight.   5
He hadn't fought at all.
He hung a grunting weight,
battered and venerable
and homely. Here and there
his brown skin hung in strips   10
like ancient wall-paper,
and its pattern of darker brown
was like wall-paper:
shapes like full-blown roses
stained and lost through age.   15
He was speckled with barnacles,
fine rosettes of lime,
and infested
with tiny white sea-lice,
and underneath two or three   20
rags of green weed hung down.
While his gills were breathing in
the terrible oxygen
— the frightening gills,
fresh and crisp with blood,   25
that can cut so badly —
I thought of the coarse white flesh
packed in like feathers,
the big bones and the little bones,
the dramatic reds and blacks   30
of his shiny entrails,
and the pink swim-bladder
like a big peony.
I looked into his eyes

which were far larger than mine   35
but shallower, and yellowed,
the irises backed and packed
with tarnished tinfoil
seen through the lenses
of old scratched isinglass.°   40
They shifted a little, but not
to return my stare.
— It was more like the tipping
of an object toward the light.
I admired his sullen face,   45
the mechanism of his jaw,
and then I saw
that from his lower lip
— if you could call it a lip —
grim, wet, and weapon-like,   50
hung five old pieces of fish-line,
or four and a wire leader
with the swivel still attached,
with all their five big hooks
grown firmly in his mouth.   55
A green line, frayed at the end
where he broke it, two heavier lines,
and a fine black thread
still crimped from the strain and snap
when it broke and he got away.   60
Like medals with their ribbons
frayed and wavering,
a five-haired beard of wisdom
trailing from his aching jaw.
I stared and stared   65
and victory filled up
the little rented boat,
from the pool of bilge
where oil had spread a rainbow
around the rusted engine   70
to the bailer rusted orange,
the sun-cracked thwarts,
the oarlocks on their strings,
the gunnels — until everything
was rainbow, rainbow, rainbow!   75
And I let the fish go.   [1946]

40 **isinglass:** A substitute for glass made from mica.

■ THINKING ABOUT THE TEXT

1. Does the speaker change her attitude toward the fish, or does it stay pretty much the same? Support your reasoning by referring to specific lines. Are you surprised that the speaker lets the fish go? Why, or why not? How effective a conclusion is her release of the fish?

2. To what extent is the 'speaker describing the fish objectively? In what ways, if any, does her description of him seem to reflect her own particular values? Refer to specific lines.

3. The speaker reports that "victory filled up / the little rented boat" (lines 66–67). Whose victory might she have in mind? Why might she use this word? Often, a victory for one is a defeat for another. Is that the case here?

4. Where does the poem refer to acts and instruments of seeing? What conclusions might be drawn from these references?

5. How significant is it that the fish is male?

■ MAKING COMPARISONS

1. What would you say to someone who argues that Bishop's speaker is more admirable than Lawrence's speaker because she lets the animal go free?

2. With each of these three poems, consider what you learn about the speaker's own state of mind. Does one of these poems tell you more about its speaker's thoughts than the other poems do? Support your answer by referring to specific lines.

3. Bishop's poem is one long, continuous stanza, whereas Blake and Lawrence divide theirs into several stanzas. Does this difference in strategy lead to a significant difference in effect? Do you consider one of these strategies better than the other? Explain your reasoning.

THOMAS LUX

To Help the Monkey Cross the River

Thomas Lux (b. 1946) was born in Northampton, Massachusetts, and attended Emerson College in Boston. He is the author of numerous volumes of poetry, including The Street of Clocks *(2001) and* The Cradle Place: Poems *(2004), as well as the recipient of prestigious grants and prizes. His latest collection is* God Particles *(2008). He has taught at Sarah Lawrence College; the University of California, Irvine; and Emerson College. He currently holds the Bourne Chair in poetry at*

Georgia Tech in Atlanta, where he lives. The following poem is from The Cradle
Place: Poems.

which he must
cross, by swimming, for fruits and nuts,
to help him
I sit with my rifle on a platform
high in a tree, same side of the river   5
as the hungry monkey. How does this assist
him? When he swims for it
I look first upriver: predators move faster with
the current than against it.
If a crocodile is aimed from upriver to eat the monkey   10
and an anaconda from downriver burns
with the same ambition, I do
the math, algebra, angles, rate-of-monkey,
croc- and snake-speed, and if, if
it looks as though the anaconda or the croc   15
will reach the monkey
before he attains the river's far bank,
I raise my rifle and fire
one, two, three, even four times into the river
just behind the monkey   20
to hurry him up a little.
Shoot the snake, the crocodile?
They're just doing their jobs,
but the monkey, the monkey
has little hands like a child's,   25
and the smart ones, in a cage, can be taught to smile.   *[2004]*

≣ THINKING ABOUT THE TEXT

1. Perhaps irony is not a strong enough notion for the juxtaposition between the title and the last line. Explain what, in fact, appears to be the
   speaker's intention for the monkey. How would you define the speaker's
   use of *help*?

2. Why might the speaker be sympathetic to the snake and the croc? Are
   you sympathetic to the speaker?

3. What is the effect of the repeated "if" in line 14 and "monkey" in line 24?

4. Lux plays with the reader's expectations. What did you assume Lux was
   going to do "to help" after you read the first nineteen lines (up to ". . . into
   the river")?

5. What is the effect of the phrase "in a cage" (line 26)? Does this change
   the meaning of the entire poem?

■ MAKING COMPARISONS

1. Perhaps the speaker in Lux's poem is not what he appears to be at first. Which speaker in the three other poems does he most closely resemble? Why?

2. Do you think the speaker in Lawrence's poem would approve of a cute monkey in a cage?

3. Would the speaker in Bishop's poem be upset by Lux's speaker's tone and attitude toward the monkey?

DEAN YOUNG

Clam Ode

Dean Young (b. 1955) was born in Columbia, Pennsylvania. He is the author of ten books of poetry and poetics, most recently 7 Poets, 4 Days, 1 Book *(2009) and* The Art of Recklessness *(2010). He currently holds an endowed chair in poetry at the University of Texas at Austin. The following poem appeared in* The Best American Poetry 2006. *Somewhat tongue-in-cheek, Young writes, "One of the biggest challenges this poem presented was how not to confuse the spelling of* clam *and* calm."

One attempts to be significant on a grand scale
in the knock-down battle of life
but settles.
I love the expression "happy as a clam,"
how it imparts buoyant emotion   5
to a rather, when you get down to it,
nonexpressive creature: In piles of ice
it awaits its doom pretty much the same
as on the ocean's floor it awaits
life's banquet and bouquet and sexual joys.   10
Some barnacles we know are eggs dropped from outer space
but clams, who has a clue how they reproduce?
By trading clouds?
The Chinese thought them capable of prolonging life
while clams doubtlessly considered   15
the Chinese the opposite.
I remember the jawbreakers my dad would buy me
on the wharf at Stone Harbor,
every thirty seconds you'd take out
the one you were working on   20
to check what color it turned.

What does this have to do with clams?
A feeling.
States of feeling, unlike states of the upper Midwest,
are difficult to name.   25
That is why music was invented,
which caused a whole new slue of feelings
and is why ever since
people have had more feelings than they know what to do with
so you can see music sorta backfired   30
like a fire extinguisher that turns out to be a flame thrower.
They look somewhat alike, don't they?
If you're buying one be sure
you don't get the other,
the boys in the stockroom are stoners   35
who like to wear their pants falling down
and deserve their own island in *Gulliver's Travels.*
The clam however remains calm.
Green is the color of the kelp it rests on,
having a helluva wingding calm.   40
I am going to kill you in butter and white wine
so forgive me, great clam spirit,
join yourself to me through the emissary
of this al dente fettuccini
so I may be qualmless and happy as you.   *[2005]*   45

≡ THINKING ABOUT THE TEXT

1. Although the poem has a serious theme, the poet, not surprisingly in a poem about clams, uses humor. Point out some amusing lines.

2. What do you think the common expression "happy as a clam" means?

3. Why does the narrator start talking about feelings and music?

4. What does the poet mean when he says: "The clam however remains calm" (line 38)? Is this a positive response? Why does he use "however"?

5. Were you surprised by the word "qualmless" in the last line? Were you expecting "calmness" or perhaps "clamness"? What does he mean by this term?

≡ MAKING COMPARISONS

1. Why do you think there is humor in this poem and not in the others?

2. Young eats the clam. Does this make a significant difference in evaluating the poem?

3. Compare the theme of this poem with that of Bishop's poem.

▦ WRITING ABOUT ISSUES

1. Choose one of the poems in this cluster, and write an essay describing and evaluating its speaker. As you develop your judgment, acknowledge and address at least one other possible way of looking at this person: that is, a different judgment that someone might make of him or her.

2. Write an essay suggesting what one of the speakers in these poems might say about another. What, for example, might Bishop's speaker say about Lawrence's? Support your conjecture with details from both texts.

3. Write an essay arguing for or against how you treated a certain animal in a certain situation. Choose a situation in which you did, in fact, consider acting differently at the time. If you wish, you can draw analogies between your experience and any of those depicted in this cluster.

4. Argue that each of these poets is talking about human behavior, not animal behavior.

Can Tradition Be a Trap?: Critical Commentaries on a Story

SHIRLEY JACKSON, "The Lottery"

CRITICAL COMMENTARIES:

SHIRLEY JACKSON, "The Morning of June 28, 1948, and 'The Lottery'"

NICK CRAWFORD, "Learning from 'The Lottery': How Jackson's Story Might Help Us Rethink Tradition"

JON SCHNEIDERMAN, "Tradition, Justice, and Bloodlust in American Society"

AIMEE WILSON, "Under the Guise of Tradition: 'The Lottery' and Female Circumcision"

"The Lottery" was published in *The New Yorker* on June 28, 1948, and caused a furor. Hundreds of readers canceled their subscriptions, and the magazine received bags of hate mail. For years the collection containing the story was listed among the top twenty most banned books. Shirley Jackson's biographer Judy Oppenheimer wrote that "nothing in the magazine before or since would prove to be such a huge outpouring of fury, horror, rage, disgust, and intense fascination." Even Jackson's parents wrote her a letter disapproving of her story. Perhaps in the years following World War II, readers wanted to return to optimism and didn't want to be reminded about what Jackson later characterized as "the pointless violence and general inhumanity in their own lives." Many readers wanted to know what the story meant, and critics have supplied a multitude of answers from feminist, Marxist, psychological, and anthropological perspectives. During the Vietnam War, the story was read quite literally as a critique of the draft lottery, but usually this tale is seen as an allegory. And an allegory of *what* usually depends on who is reading the story and from what historical perspective. We asked three students to use a reader-response perspective in writing a brief critical essay about their reading of "The Lottery" in December 2007. Their responses follow the story and might also inspire you to see contemporary connections to this most suggestive of stories and make you ponder if tradition can be liberating or ensnaring. We also include a brief essay Jackson wrote about the amazing response to her story.

≡ BEFORE YOU READ

What do you think of when you hear the word *lottery*? Have you ever played a lottery? Are they fair? Do you expect a prize? In another vein, might there be a dark side to a tradition? To rituals?

SHIRLEY JACKSON
The Lottery

Shirley Jackson (1916–1965) was born in San Francisco and grew up in the affluent suburb of Burlingame. Her family moved to Rochester, New York, in 1939, and she graduated from Syracuse University in 1940. Jackson wrote of her life: "I was married in 1940 to Stanley Edgar Hyman, critic and numismatist, and we live in Vermont, in a quiet rural community with fine scenery and comfortably away from city life. Our major export are books and children, both of which we produce in abundance." She received a National Book Award nomination for The Haunting of Hill House *(1959), which was adapted for film twice (1963 and 1999); this popular book is often cited as one of the best horror novels of the twentieth century and as an influence on contemporary masters of that genre such as Stephen King.*

The morning of June 27th was clear and sunny, with the fresh warmth of a full-summer day; the flowers were blossoming profusely and the grass was richly green. The people of the village began to gather in the square, between the post office and the bank, around ten o'clock; in some towns there were so many people that the lottery took two days and had to be started on June 26th, but in this village, where there were only about three hundred people, the whole lottery took less than two hours, so it could begin at ten o'clock in the morning and still be through in time to allow the villagers to get home for noon dinner.

The children assembled first, of course. School was recently over for the summer, and the feeling of liberty sat uneasily on most of them; they tended to gather together quietly for a while before they broke into boisterous play, and their talk was still of the classroom and teacher, of books and reprimands. Bobby Martin had already stuffed his pockets full of stones, and the other boys soon followed his example, selecting the smoothest and roundest stones; Bobby and Harry Jones and Dickie Delacroix — the villagers pronounced this name "Dellacroy" — eventually made a great pile of stones in one corner of the square and guarded it against the raids of the other boys. The girls stood aside, talking among themselves, looking over their shoulders at the boys, and the very small children rolled in the dust or clung to the hands of their older brothers or sisters.

Soon the men began to gather, surveying their own children, speaking of planting and rain, tractors and taxes. They stood together, away from the pile of stones in the corner, and their jokes were quiet and they smiled rather than laughed. The women, wearing faded house dresses and sweaters, came shortly after their menfolk. They greeted one another and exchanged bits of gossip as they went to join their husbands. Soon the women, standing by their husbands, began to call to their children, and the children came reluctantly, having to be called four or five times. Bobby Martin ducked under his mother's grasping hand and ran, laughing, back to the pile of stones. His father spoke up sharply,

(AP/Wide World Photos.)

and Bobby came quickly and took his place between his father and his oldest brother.

The lottery was conducted — as were the square dances, the teenage club, the Halloween program — by Mr. Summers, who had time and energy to devote to civic activities. He was a round-faced, jovial man and he ran the coal business, and people were sorry for him, because he had no children and his wife was a scold. When he arrived in the square, carrying the black wooden box, there was a murmur of conversation among the villagers, and he waved and called, "Little late today, folks." The postmaster, Mr. Graves, followed him, carrying a three-legged stool, and the stool was put in the center of the square and Mr. Summers set the black box down on it. The villagers kept their distance, leaving a space between themselves and the stool, and when Mr. Summers said, "Some of you fellows want to give me a hand?" there was a hesitation before two men, Mr. Martin and his oldest son, Baxter, came forward to hold the box steady on the stool while Mr. Summers stirred up the papers inside it.

The original paraphernalia for the lottery had been lost long ago, and the black box now resting on the stool had been put into use even before Old Man Warner, the oldest man in town, was born. Mr. Summers spoke frequently to

5

the villagers about making a new box, but no one liked to upset even as much tradition as was represented by the black box. There was a story that the present box had been made with some pieces of the box that had preceded it, the one that had been constructed when the first people settled down to make a village here. Every year, after the lottery, Mr. Summers began talking again about a new box, but every year the subject was allowed to fade off without anything's being done. The black box grew shabbier each year; by now it was no longer completely black but splintered badly along one side to show the original wood color, and in some places faded or stained.

Mr. Martin and his oldest son, Baxter, held the black box securely on the stool until Mr. Summers had stirred the papers thoroughly with his hand. Because so much of the ritual had been forgotten or discarded, Mr. Summers had been successful in having slips of paper substituted for the chips of wood that had been used for generations. Chips of wood, Mr. Summers had argued, had been all very well when the village was tiny, but now that the population was more than three hundred and likely to keep on growing, it was necessary to use something that would fit more easily into the black box. The night before the lottery, Mr. Summers and Mr. Graves made up the slips of paper and put them in the box, and it was then taken to the safe of Mr. Summers's coal company and locked up until Mr. Summers was ready to take it to the square next morning. The rest of the year, the box was put away, sometimes one place, sometimes another; it had spent one year in Mr. Graves's barn and another year underfoot in the post office, and sometimes it was set on a shelf in the Martin grocery and left there.

There was a great deal of fussing to be done before Mr. Summers declared the lottery open. There were the lists to make up — of heads of families, heads of households in each family, members of each household in each family. There was the proper swearing-in of Mr. Summers by the postmaster, as the official of the lottery; at one time, some people remembered, there had been a recital of some sort, performed by the official of the lottery, a perfunctory, tuneless chant that had been rattled off duly each year; some people believed that the official of the lottery used to stand just so when he said or sang it, others believed that he was supposed to walk among the people, but years and years ago this part of the ritual had been allowed to lapse. There had been, also, a ritual salute, which the official of the lottery had had to use in addressing each person who came up to draw from the box, but this also had changed with time, until now it was felt necessary only for the official to speak to each person approaching. Mr. Summers was very good at all this; in his clean white shirt and blue jeans, with one hand resting carelessly on the black box, he seemed very proper and important as he talked interminably to Mr. Graves and the Martins.

Just as Mr. Summers finally left off talking and turned to the assembled villagers, Mrs. Hutchinson came hurriedly along the path to the square, her sweater thrown over her shoulders, and slid into place in the back of the crowd. "Clean forgot what day it was," she said to Mrs. Delacroix, who stood next to her, and they both laughed softly. "Thought my old man was out back stacking wood," Mrs. Hutchinson went on, "and then I looked out the window and the kids was gone, and then I remembered it was the twenty-seventh and came a-running." She dried her hands on her apron, and Mrs. Delacroix said, "You're in time, though. They're still talking away up there."

Mrs. Hutchinson craned her neck to see through the crowd and found her husband and children standing near the front. She tapped Mrs. Delacroix on the arm as a farewell and began to make her way through the crowd. The people separated good-humoredly to let her through; two or three people said, in voices just loud enough to be heard across the crowd, "Here comes your Missus, Hutchinson," and "Bill, she made it after all." Mrs. Hutchinson reached her husband, and Mr. Summers, who had been waiting, said cheerfully, "Thought we were going to have to get on without you, Tessie." Mrs. Hutchinson said, grinning, "Wouldn't have me leave m'dishes in the sink, now, would you, Joe?" and soft laughter ran through the crowd as the people stirred back into position after Mrs. Hutchinson's arrival.

"Well, now," Mr. Summers said soberly, "guess we better get started, get   10
this over with, so's we can go back to work. Anybody ain't here?"

"Dunbar," several people said. "Dunbar; Dunbar."

Mr. Summers consulted his list. "Clyde Dunbar," he said. "That's right. He's broke his leg, hasn't he? Who's drawing for him?"

"Me, I guess," a woman said, and Mr. Summers turned to look at her. "Wife draws for her husband," Mr. Summers said. "Don't you have a grown boy to do it for you, Janey?" Although Mr. Summers and everyone else in the village knew the answer perfectly well, it was the business of the official of the lottery to ask such questions formally. Mr. Summers waited with an expression of polite interest while Mrs. Dunbar answered.

"Horace's not but sixteen yet," Mrs. Dunbar said regretfully. "Guess I gotta fill in for the old man this year."

"Right," Mr. Summers said. He made a note on the list he was holding.   15
Then he asked, "Watson boy drawing this year?"

A tall boy in the crowd raised his hand. "Here," he said. "I'm drawing for m'mother and me." He blinked his eyes nervously and ducked his head as several voices in the crowd said things like "Good fellow, Jack," and "Glad to see your mother's got a man to do it."

"Well," Mr. Summers said, "guess that's everyone. Old Man Warner make it?"

"Here," a voice said, and Mr. Summers nodded.

A sudden hush fell on the crowd as Mr. Summers cleared his throat and looked at the list. "All ready?" he called. "Now, I'll read the names — heads of families first — and the men come up and take a paper out of the box. Keep the paper folded in your hand without looking at it until everyone has had a turn. Everything clear?"

The people had done it so many times that they only half listened to the   20
directions; most of them were quiet, wetting their lips, not looking around. Then Mr. Summers raised one hand high and said, "Adams." A man disengaged himself from the crowd and came forward. "Hi, Steve," Mr. Summers said, and Mr. Adams said, "Hi, Joe." They grinned at one another humorlessly

and nervously. Then Mr. Adams reached into the black box and took out a folded paper. He held it firmly by one corner as he turned and went hastily back to his place in the crowd, where he stood a little apart from his family, not looking down at his hand.

"Allen," Mr. Summers said, "Anderson. . . . Bentham."

"Seems like there's no time at all between lotteries any more," Mrs. Delacroix said to Mrs. Graves in the back row. "Seems like we got through with the last one only last week."

"Time sure goes fast," Mrs. Graves said.

"Clark. . . . Delacroix."

"There goes my old man," Mrs. Delacroix said. She held her breath while   25
her husband went forward.

"Dunbar," Mr. Summers said, and Mrs. Dunbar went steadily to the box while one of the women said, "Go on, Janey," and another said, "There she goes."

"We're next," Mrs. Graves said. She watched while Mr. Graves came around from the side of the box, greeted Mr. Summers gravely, and selected a slip of paper from the box. By now, all through the crowd there were men holding the small folded papers in their large hands, turning them over and over nervously. Mrs. Dunbar and her two sons stood together, Mrs. Dunbar holding the slip of paper.

"Harburt. . . . Hutchinson."

"Get up there, Bill," Mrs. Hutchinson said, and the people near her laughed.

"Jones."   30

"They do say," Mr. Adams said to Old Man Warner, who stood next to him, "that over in the north village they're talking of giving up the lottery."

Old Man Warner snorted. "Pack of crazy fools," he said. "Listening to the young folks, nothing's good enough for *them.* Next thing you know, they'll be wanting to go back to living in caves, nobody work any more, live *that* way for a while. Used to be a saying about 'Lottery in June, corn be heavy soon.' First thing you know, we'd all be eating stewed chickweed and acorns. There's *always* been a lottery," he added petulantly. "Bad enough to see young Joe Summers up there joking with everybody."

"Some places have already quit lotteries," Mrs. Adams said.

"Nothing but trouble in *that,*" Old Man Warner said stoutly. "Pack of young fools."

"Martin." And Bobby Martin watched his father go forward. "Overdyke. . . .   35
Percy."

"I wish they'd hurry," Mrs. Dunbar said to her older son. "I wish they'd hurry."

"They're almost through," her son said.

"You get ready to run tell Dad," Mrs. Dunbar said.

Mr. Summers called his own name and then stepped forward precisely and selected a slip from the box. Then he called, "Warner."

"Seventy-seventh year I been in the lottery," Old Man Warner said as he   40
went through the crowd. "Seventy-seventh time."

"Watson." The tall boy came awkwardly through the crowd. Someone said, "Don't be nervous, Jack," and Mr. Summers said, "Take your time, son."

"Zanini."

After that, there was a long pause, a breathless pause, until Mr. Summers, holding his slip of paper in the air, said, "All right, fellows." For a minute, no one moved, and then all the slips of paper were opened. Suddenly, all the women began to speak at once, saying, "Who is it?" "Who's got it?" "Is it the Dunbars?" "Is it the Watsons?" Then the voices began to say, "It's Hutchinson. It's Bill," "Bill Hutchinson's got it."

"Go tell your father," Mrs. Dunbar said to her older son.

People began to look around to see the Hutchinsons. Bill Hutchinson was standing quiet, staring down at the paper in his hand. Suddenly, Tessie Hutchinson shouted to Mr. Summers, "You didn't give him time enough to take any paper he wanted. I saw you. It wasn't fair!"   45

"Be a good sport, Tessie," Mrs. Delacroix called, and Mrs. Graves said, "All of us took the same chance."

"Shut up, Tessie," Bill Hutchinson said.

"Well, everyone," Mr. Summers said, "that was done pretty fast, and now we've got to be hurrying a little more to get done in time." He consulted his next list. "Bill," he said, "you draw for the Hutchinson family. You got any other households in the Hutchinsons?"

"There's Don and Eva," Mrs. Hutchinson yelled. "Make *them* take their chance!"

"Daughters drew with their husbands' families, Tessie," Mr. Summers said gently. "You know that as well as anyone else."   50

"It wasn't *fair*," Tessie said.

"I guess not, Joe," Bill Hutchinson said regretfully. "My daughter draws with her husband's family, that's only fair. And I've got no other family except the kids."

"Then, as far as drawing for families is concerned, it's you," Mr. Summers said in explanation, "and as far as drawing for households is concerned, that's you, too. Right?"

"Right," Bill Hutchinson said.

"How many kids, Bill?" Mr. Summers asked formally.   55

"Three," Bill Hutchinson said. "There's Bill Jr., and Nancy, and little Dave. And Tessie and me."

"All right, then," Mr. Summers said. "Harry, you got their tickets back?"

Mr. Graves nodded and held up the slips of paper. "Put them in the box, then," Mr. Summers directed. "Take Bill's and put it in."

"I think we ought to start over," Mrs. Hutchinson said, as quietly as she could. "I tell you it wasn't *fair*. You didn't give him time enough to choose. *Every*body saw that."

Mr. Graves had selected the five slips and put them in the box, and he dropped all the papers but those onto the ground, where the breeze caught them and lifted them off.   60

"Listen, everybody," Mrs. Hutchinson was saying to the people around her.

"Ready, Bill?" Mr. Summers asked, and Bill Hutchinson, with one quick glance around at his wife and children, nodded.

"Remember," Mr. Summers said, "take the slips and keep them folded until each person has taken one. Harry, you help little Dave." Mr. Graves took the hand of the little boy, who came willingly with him up to the box. "Take a paper out of the box, Davy," Mr. Summers said. Davy put his hand into the box and laughed. "Take just *one* paper," Mr. Summers said. "Harry, you hold it for him." Mr. Graves took the child's hand and removed the folded paper from the tight fist and held it while little Dave stood next to him and looked up at him wonderingly.

"Nancy next," Mr. Summers said. Nancy was twelve, and her school friends breathed heavily as she went forward, switching her skirt, and took a slip daintily from the box. "Bill Jr.," Mr. Summers said, and Billy, his face red and his feet overlarge, nearly knocked the box over as he got a paper out. "Tessie," Mr. Summers said. She hesitated for a minute, looking around defiantly, and then set her lips and went up to the box. She snatched a paper out and held it behind her.

"Bill," Mr. Summers said, and Bill Hutchinson reached into the box and felt   65
around, bringing his hand out at last with the slip of paper in it.

The crowd was quiet. A girl whispered, "I hope it's not Nancy," and the sound of the whisper reached the edges of the crowd.

"It's not the way it used to be," Old Man Warner said clearly. "People ain't the way they used to be."

"All right," Mr. Summers said. "Open the papers. Harry, you open little Dave's."

Mr. Graves opened the slip of paper and there was a general sigh through the crowd as he held it up and everyone could see that it was blank. Nancy and Bill Jr. opened theirs at the same time, and both beamed and laughed, turning around to the crowd and holding their slips of paper above their heads.

"Tessie," Mr. Summers said. There was a pause, and then Mr. Summers   70
looked at Bill Hutchinson, and Bill unfolded his paper and showed it. It was blank.

"It's Tessie," Mr. Summers said, and his voice was hushed. "Show us her paper, Bill."

Bill Hutchinson went over to his wife and forced the slip of paper out of her hand. It had a black spot on it, the black spot Mr. Summers had made the night before with the heavy pencil in the coal-company office. Bill Hutchinson held it up and there was a stir in the crowd.

"All right, folks," Mr. Summers said. "Let's finish quickly."

Although the villagers had forgotten the ritual and lost the original black box, they still remembered to use stones. The pile of stones the boys had made earlier was ready; there were stones on the ground with the blowing scraps of paper that had come out of the box. Mrs. Delacroix selected a stone so large she had to pick it up with both hands and turned to Mrs. Dunbar. "Come on," she said. "Hurry up."

Mrs. Dunbar had small stones in both hands, and she said, gasping for   75
breath, "I can't run at all. You'll have to go ahead and I'll catch up with you."

The children had stones already, and someone gave little Davy Hutchinson
a few pebbles.

Tessie Hutchinson was in the center of a cleared space by now, and she
held her hands out desperately as the villagers moved in on her. "It isn't fair,"
she said. A stone hit her on the side of the head.

Old Man Warner was saying, "Come on, come on, everyone." Steve Adams
was in the front of the crowd of villagers, with Mrs. Graves beside him.

"It isn't fair, it isn't right," Mrs. Hutchinson screamed and then they were
upon her.   *[1948]*

■ **THINKING ABOUT THE TEXT**

1. At what point in the story did you suspect that something was amiss in
   this bucolic village? How does Jackson both prepare you for and surprise you with her ending?

2. Make a list of the characters' names in the story. What symbolic significance might they have?

3. What do the phrase "Lottery in June, corn be heavy soon" and the pile
   of stones suggest about the origins of the lottery?

4. Critics often mention scapegoating, man's inherent evil, and the destructive consequence of hanging on to ancient and outdated rituals as
   the principal themes of this story. Do you agree? What are some other
   themes suggested by the story?

5. What contemporary issues does "The Lottery" bring to mind?

SHIRLEY JACKSON

The Morning of June 28, 1948, and "The Lottery"

Shirley Jackson wrote this essay a dozen years after her story appeared in The
New Yorker. *It explains the bizarre and disturbing reaction to what many readers
took to be a literal account instead of a fictional allegory of arbitrary violence in our
culture.*

On the morning of June 28, 1948, I walked down to the post office in our little
Vermont town to pick up the mail. I was quite casual about it, as I recall —
I opened the box, took out a couple of bills and a letter or two, talked to the
postmaster for a few minutes, and left, never supposing that it was the last time
for months that I was to pick up the mail without an active feeling of panic.
By the next week I had had to change my mailbox to the largest one in the
post office, and casual conversation with the postmaster was out of the question, because he wasn't speaking to me. June 28, 1948, was the day *The New*

Yorker came out with a story of mine in it. It was not my first published story, not my last, but I have been assured over and over that if it had been the only story I ever wrote or published, there would be people who would not forget my name.

I had written the story three weeks before, on a bright June morning when summer seemed to have come at last, with blue skies and warm sun and no heavenly signs to warn me that my morning's work was anything but just another story. The idea had come to me while I was pushing my daughter up the hill in her stroller—it was, as I say, a warm morning, and the hill was steep, and beside my daughter the stroller held the day's groceries—and perhaps the effort of that last fifty yards up the hill put an edge to the story; at any rate, I had the idea fairly clearly in my mind when I put my daughter in her playpen and the frozen vegetables in the refrigerator, and, writing the story, I found that it went quickly and easily, moving from beginning to end without pause. As a matter of fact, when I read it over later I decided that except for one or two minor corrections, it needed no changes, and the story I finally typed up and sent off to my agent the next day was almost word for word the original draft. This, as any writer of stories can tell you, is not a usual thing. All I know is that when I came to read the story over I felt strongly that I didn't want to fuss with it. I didn't think it was perfect, but I didn't want to fuss with it. It was, I thought, a serious, straightforward story, and I was pleased and a little surprised at the ease with which it had been written; I was reasonably proud of it, and hoped that my agent would sell it to some magazine and I would have the gratification of seeing it in print.

My agent did not care for the story, but—as she said in her note at the time—her job was to sell it, not to like it. She sent it at once to *The New Yorker,* and about a week after the story had been written I received a telephone call from the fiction editor of *The New Yorker;* it was quite clear that he did not really care for the story, either, but *The New Yorker* was going to buy it. He asked for one change—that the date mentioned in the story be changed to coincide with the date of the issue of the magazine in which the story would appear, and I said of course. He then asked, hesitantly, if I had any particular interpretation of my own for the story; Mr. Harold Ross, then the editor of *The New Yorker,* was not altogether sure that he understood the story, and wondered if I cared to enlarge upon its meaning. I said no. Mr. Ross, he said, thought that the story might be puzzling to some people, and in case anyone telephoned the magazine, as sometimes happened, or wrote in asking about the story, was there anything in particular I wanted them to say? No, I said, nothing in particular; it was just a story I wrote.

I had no more preparation than that. I went on picking up the mail every morning, pushing my daughter up and down the hill in her stroller, anticipating pleasurably the check from *The New Yorker,* and shopping for groceries. The weather stayed nice and it looked as though it was going to be a good summer. Then, on June 28, *The New Yorker* came out with my story.

Things began mildly enough with a note from a friend at *The New Yorker:* "Your story has kicked up quite a fuss around the office," he wrote. I was flattered; it's nice to think that your friends notice what you write. Later that day there was a call from one of the magazine's editors; they had had a couple of people phone in about my story, he said, and was there anything I particularly wanted him to say if there were any more calls? No, I said, nothing particular; anything he chose to say was perfectly all right with me; it was just a story.

I was further puzzled by a cryptic note from another friend: "Heard a man talking about a story of yours on the bus this morning," she wrote. "Very exciting. I wanted to tell him I knew the author, but after I heard what he was saying I decided I'd better not."

One of the most terrifying aspects of publishing stories and books is the realization that they are going to be read, and read by strangers. I had never fully realized this before, although I had of course in my imagination dwelt lovingly upon the thought of the millions and millions of people who were going to be uplifted and enriched and delighted by the stories I wrote. It had simply never occurred to me that these millions and millions of people might be so far from being uplifted that they would sit down and write me letters I was downright scared to open; of the three-hundred-odd letters that I received that summer I can count only thirteen that spoke kindly to me, and they were mostly from friends. Even my mother scolded me: "Dad and I did not care at all for your story in *The New Yorker*," she wrote sternly, "it does seem, dear, that this gloomy kind of story is what all you young people think about these days. Why don't you write something to cheer people up?"

By mid-July I had begun to perceive that I was very lucky indeed to be safely in Vermont, where no one in our small town had ever heard of *The New Yorker*, much less read my story. Millions of people, and my mother, had taken a pronounced dislike to me.

The magazine kept no track of telephone calls, but all letters addressed to me care of the magazine were forwarded directly to me for answering, and all letters addressed to the magazine — some of them addressed to Harold Ross personally; these were the most vehement — were answered at the magazine and then the letters were sent me in great batches, along with carbons of the answers written at the magazine. I have all the letters still, and if they could be considered to give any accurate cross section of the reading public, or the reading public of *The New Yorker*, or even the reading public of one issue of *The New Yorker*, I would stop writing now.

Judging from these letters, people who read stories are gullible, rude, frequently illiterate, and horribly afraid of being laughed at. Many of the writers were positive that *The New Yorker* was going to ridicule them in print, and the most cautious letters were headed, in capital letters: NOT FOR PUBLICATION or PLEASE DO NOT PRINT THIS LETTER, or, at best, THIS LETTER MAY BE PUBLISHED AT YOUR USUAL RATES OF PAYMENT. Anonymous letters, of which there were a few, were destroyed. *The New Yorker* never published any comment of any kind about the story in the magazine, but did issue one publicity release saying that the story had received more mail than any piece of fiction they had ever published; this was after the newspapers had gotten into the act, in midsummer, with a front-

10

page story in the San Francisco *Chronicle* begging to know what the story meant, and a series of columns in New York and Chicago papers pointing out that *New Yorker* subscriptions were being canceled right and left.

Curiously, there are three main themes which dominate the letters of that first summer — three themes which might be identified as bewilderment, speculation, and plain old-fashioned abuse. In the years since then, during which the story has been anthologized, dramatized, televised, and even — in one completely mystifying transformation — made into a ballet, the tenor of letters I receive has changed. I am addressed more politely, as a rule, and the letters largely confine themselves to questions like what does this story mean? The general tone of the early letters, however, was a kind of wide-eyed, shocked innocence. People at first were not so much concerned with what the story meant; what they wanted to know was where these lotteries were held, and whether they could go there and watch.   *[1960]*

NICK CRAWFORD

Learning from "The Lottery": How Jackson's Story Might Help Us Rethink Tradition

Nick Crawford (b. 1983) was born in Dublin, Ireland. He grew up on the island of Trinidad, and in North and South Carolina in the United States. He is a graduate of the University of North Carolina, Wilmington, and has interests in literature and popular culture.

In "The Lottery," Shirley Jackson tells the story of a small American town and the cruel and unusual tradition to which the inhabitants of the town blindly adhere. First-time readers are no doubt shocked to discover that the ritual taking place on a "clear and sunny" June morning ultimately leads to the brutal and tragic death of one of the villagers. The most disturbing thing about Tessie Hutchinson's unexpected demise is its sheer pointlessness. At best, Old Man Warner's axiomatic recital of the saying "Lottery in June, corn be heavy soon" seems like a shaky reason for ceremonially stoning another human being to death. Yet this appears to be the central point of the story: once people are used to a way of doing things, it's hard for them to break with that tradition, no matter how pointless and destructive it might be.

Reading Jackson's story in this way sheds light on a number of real-life practices that, despite their harmful consequences, are still performed because they are rooted in tradition. In the 1980s, for example, Edna Bogert likened the villagers who take part in the lottery to the South African voters who were continually electing an apartheid government (47). However, the destructive consequences of traditions like these are not always easily recognizable to the people situated within those traditions. Far removed from the lottery or a racist apartheid government, it is easy for us to condemn such practices. Still, the undeniably American setting of Jackson's story compels us to examine some of the (self-) destructive traditions that we, as Americans, might take part in. One parallel to "The Lottery," then, might be the obstinacy displayed by so many Americans who continue to drive large, impractical, gas-guzzling vehicles, despite the fact that these automobiles have proven to be directly detrimental to our economic and environmental well-being.

Tradition is a key component of "The Lottery." We learn, for instance, that the lottery has been conducted dutifully since "the first people settled down to make a village." The continuation of that tradition is a link to the village's past, which explains why the townspeople are so reluctant to replace the black box, ignoring Mr. Summers's frequent suggestion that they build a new one. Furthermore, we might also infer that this tradition initially served some sort of (possibly practical) agricultural purpose. Thus, Old Man Warner scoffs at the idea of abandoning the lottery, noting that the villagers would be reduced to "eating stewed chickweed and acorns" without it.

Much like the lottery, Americans' love for impractical vehicles is rooted in tradition. Our nation's love affair with sport-utility vehicles and other large automobiles denotes a uniquely American experience. David E. Shi writes that the automobile is "an integral part of the American dream" and that "the romantic mythology associated with the frontier experience has been transferred to the car culture." This transference is particularly evident in the marketing of SUVs and large trucks, and it is not uncommon to see these vehicles advertised driving in rugged, uncultivated landscapes. Like the lottery, automobiles once served a more practical function too. As Shi explains, cars were initially a cleaner alternative to the horse and buggy because they helped do away with the waste the animals produced.

But in spite of their practical origins, over time the use values of both the   5
lottery and American car culture have become purely symbolic. Mrs. Adams, one of the villagers, informs us that " '[s]ome places have already quit lotteries,' " indicating the lottery's increasing purposelessness. Likewise, Edna Bogert confirms that "[t]here *is* no reason for the lottery, except that of tradition" (46; Bogert's emphasis). Similarly, as our environmental awareness increases and more fuel-efficient technologies are being developed, enormous gas-guzzling automobiles are no longer a practical choice for transportation. Yet, as David Shi writes, "The automobile retains its firm hold over our psyche because it continues to represent a metaphor for what Americans have always prized: the seductive ideal of private freedom, personal mobility, and empowered spontaneity." They might theoretically allow us to brave a vast and untouched frontier just like our ancestors, but like Jackson's fictional lottery, driving an SUV or a truck is more symbolic than it is practical. The biggest adventure many of these large vehicles undertake is a trip to and from soccer practice.

That's not to say that all traditions should have a concrete use value. Certainly, there would be nothing wrong with carrying on a purely symbolic tradition if it were essentially harmless. The problem with both the lottery and

Americans' obsession with oversized vehicles is that they do cause harm. Indeed, the outcome of these traditions is anything but "clear and sunny." As I mentioned before, the detrimental effects of a tradition are easier to see when we are not part of that tradition ourselves. Thus, it is easy for us to condemn the lottery and its ritualistic murder of innocent victims. But what about our own distinctly American car culture?

"Almost everything Americans do uses energy," writes Matthew L. Wald, "making the earth warmer and purses thinner, and often raising demand for oil from unstable places." This is especially true of American driving habits. Yet Wald admits that the cost of our enormous energy consumption "is not always evident." But while this may be the case, it doesn't disprove the fact that the vast number of SUVs and trucks on the roads today play a major part in global warming. A 2003 article from the Sierra Club notes that SUVs and trucks produce 43 percent more global-warming pollution and 47 percent more air pollution than an average car. Much like Jackson's deadly lottery, these negative results are harmful to the same people who are responsible for bringing them about. The global warming perpetuated by these emissions is linked to wildfires, deadly heat waves, and infectious-disease outbreaks that are already occurring. As I'm writing this essay, in fact, wildfires in Southern California are causing hundreds of thousands of residents to flee their homes. Furthermore, Wald suggests, large inefficient vehicles cost their owners more money at the gas pump and put a strain on dwindling natural resources that perpetuates our reliance on foreign oil from unstable regions. America's thirst for oil has also led us to the sacrifice of already-dwindling natural resources. In an article that details the significant lack of funding for the research of alternative energy, Clifford Krauss describes this disturbing trend, noting that "energy companies are stepping up research and investments into oil sands, deep-ocean oil and gas drilling, and gasifying and liquefying coal — all with significant environmental consequences."

That's not to say we shouldn't do anything about this destructive tradition. Edna Bogert writes that "The adherence of people to unconsidered traditions and unchallenged controls is held up to examination in 'The Lottery' in such a way as to suggest that traditions *ought* to be re-examined from time to time" (47; Bogert's emphasis). In fact, if there's any purpose in drawing parallels between "The Lottery" and our country's driving habits, it's to compel us to reexamine one of our long-standing traditions. Reconsidering our poor transportation choices in light of the negative consequences would surely be the first step to improving those habits. Krauss writes that the "growing love affair" that Americans have with renewable energy and energy conservation "is a fickle one." But surely if more people would take a step back and examine the human costs, this might change. According to Matthew Wald, this is essential to lessening the negative ecological impact of our country's long-standing tradition of environmentally unfriendly driving habits, and he writes that "changing how we travel would make by far the biggest difference." And disturbing narratives like "The Lottery" help us to see just how dangerous not examining tradition can be.

Works Cited

Bogert, Edna. "Censorship and 'The Lottery.'" *The English Journal* 74.1 (Jan. 1985): 45–47. Print.

Krauss, Clifford. "Energy Research on a Shoestring." *New York Times* 25 Jan. 2007. Web. 21 Oct. 2007.

Shi, David E. "Well, America: Is the Car Culture Working?" *Philadelphia Inquirer* 9 July 2000. Web. 23 Oct. 2007.

Sierra Club. "Sport Utility Vehicles Contribute to Global Warming." *Opposing Viewpoints Resource Center*. Gale, 2003. Web. 18 Oct. 2007.

Ward, Matthew L. "Travel Habits Must Change to Make a Big Difference in Energy Consumption." *New York Times* 30 Dec. 2006. Web. 23 Oct. 2007.

JON SCHNEIDERMAN

Tradition, Justice, and Bloodlust in American Society

Jon Schneiderman (b. 1962) was born in Bloomington, Indiana. He was a dive instructor and boat captain for fifteen years before returning to school to pursue his B.A. from Florida Atlantic University. Schneiderman is currently teaching high school English in Ohio.

The pastoral setting of Shirley Jackson's story "The Lottery" is sharply contrasted with the innate and ritual violence perpetuated within the village's society. Jackson's short story is a disturbing portrayal of a society in which the village inhabitants tenaciously cling to a ritual with obscure origins, even though this ritual has deleterious effects on the society as a whole. While many readers might be inclined to write off "The Lottery" as far-fetched fiction, the story provides some disturbing parallels with contemporary American society. While James M. Gibson explored some of the similarities between "The Lottery" and the Old Testament in his critical essay "An Old Testament Analogue for 'The Lottery,'" this essay will focus on some of the comparisons between Jackson's short story and the contemporary issue of the death penalty within the United States.

In examining these comparisons, it is essential to explore the origins of the lottery ritual as well as the origins of capital punishment within American society. It is also necessary to compare the negative consequences of both Jackson's lottery and capital punishment. Finally, it is important to determine why the citizens of the village blindly cling to the lottery ritual and why the majority in America steadfastly cling to the ritual of executing its citizens. After examining these comparisons, Jackson's short story can be interpreted as delivering a scathing indictment of American penal practices.

The origins of the ritual stoning conducted in "The Lottery" appear to have been obscured over time. While the specific origins may be unclear, Old Man Warner provides a possible clue when he claims, "'Used to be a saying about "Lottery in June, corn be heavy soon." ' " It can be inferred that the origins of the lottery may be tied to some ancient fertility rite. The fact that Old Man Warner claims that there " '[u]sed to be a saying' " implies that the saying is no longer popularly used, indicating that the villagers no longer believe there is a need for this fertility rite. Regardless of the true origin, Old Man Warner maintains " 'There's *always* been a lottery.' " As a village elder, Old Man Warner suggests that while the original need for the lottery may no longer exist, the fact that there has " '*always*' " been a lottery is justification for continuing the ritual. The lottery is a ritual that has become a tradition, and Warner suggests that because there has always been this ritual, the tradition should be continued.

In many respects, this need to embrace tradition is mirrored in contemporary society by Americans' need to embrace the death penalty. While the origins of the villagers' ritual have been obscured over time and may no longer be relevant, the origins of capital punishment within this country can be traced back to the Old Testament (Exodus 21:23–27), which calls for retributive justice ("an eye for an eye, tooth for a tooth"). Many in this country believe that if a person commits murder, the murderer should be put to death. Regina Sass reported on October 13, 2007, that a recent Gallup poll found that 69 percent of Americans favor the death penalty for those convicted of murder. The origins of the need to inflict retributive justice have led to the majority of Americans supporting a tradition for tradition's sake.

There can be little doubt that the lottery does not serve the collective interest of the village. Jackson provides no observable benefit provided to the village by the stoning of its inhabitants. In fact, it can be argued that the lottery has a negative impact on the village. It is intuitively obvious that the ritual killing of innocent men, women, and children has negative consequences for village inhabitants. In addition, Mr. Summers hints at other negative consequences of the lottery when he says, " 'guess we better get started, get this over with, so's we can go back to work.' " The lottery ritual contributes nothing to the village, it only serves as a distraction from everyday village life. Tessie Hutchinson even goes as far as to claim that the administration of the lottery " 'wasn't fair.' " Jackson portrays the lottery as a ritual that serves no purpose. The lottery detracts from village life; its administration can be considered capricious.

In many respects, the death penalty in America is similar to Jackson's lottery. Just as the ritual in "The Lottery" has been carried out for generations, the execution of American citizens has continued throughout our nation's history, despite substantial evidence that capital punishment does not deter crime, is often administered unfairly, and runs a substantial risk of executing the innocent. Hugo Bedau claims that there is no evidence that the death penalty provides deterrent value (22). Clearly, the majority of Americans support a tradition that is ineffective in preventing crime. Variables such as where the crime is committed (some states practice the death penalty while others do not), quality of legal representation, gender and race of the defendant, race of the victim, and even political expediency can determine whether a defendant is charged with a capital crime and/or executed. Berk, Weiss, and Boger's aptly

5

entitled essay "Chance and the Death Penalty," in fact, likened the death penalty to a lottery, in which murderers' names were placed in an urn (versus
Jackson's black box) and the risk of execution was statistically compared to the
risk of drawing an offender's name from the urn. The authors conclude that
"From the point of view of that unlucky offender, the charging system must
seem very capricious indeed!" (106). Tessie Hutchinson claims that the lottery
is administered unfairly, and it can be argued that the death penalty in America is also applied unfairly. Sadly, Americans cling to this tradition of executing
criminals in the same way that the villagers cling to the ritualistic stoning of
their fellow citizens.

Perhaps the most shocking aspect of "The Lottery" is the fact that innocent men, women, and children are brutally stoned to death. Many readers
react to the stoning of the innocent in Jackson's story on a visceral level,
shocked at these horrible acts carried out in the name of tradition.

Michael Radelet and Hugo Bedau report in their essay "The Execution of
the Innocent" that they have "published accounts of more than four hundred
cases where persons were wrongfully convicted in capital (or potentially capital) cases" (105). While readers of "The Lottery" find the ritual taking of innocent lives shocking, the American public has come to accept the risk of
executing the innocent in contemporary society. Radelet and Bedau note that
"for the immediate future it appears that most Americans will either ignore the
risk of executing the innocent or simply accept its inevitability" (123). Americans' acceptance of executing the innocent appears no different than Jackson's
villagers' acceptance of their macabre lottery.

When comparing Shirley Jackson's "The Lottery" and capital punishment
in America, it is clear that both the fictional villagers and American citizens
cling fiercely to obscure traditions which no longer serve the interests of their
respective societies. Readers must ask themselves, Why this unyielding support for these traditions? The answer to this question may lie in the darkest
part of the human psyche. While we are loath to admit it, human history is
replete with examples of a grotesque bloodlust. This can best be observed in the
readers' responses to Jackson's story. Jackson received over 450 letters in response to "The Lottery," and these responses were indeed unsettling. Jackson
writes in her essay "The Biography of a Story" that "People at first were not so
much concerned with what the story meant; what they wanted to know was
where these lotteries were held, and whether they could go there and watch"
(214). The only rationale for blindly clinging to these rituals is pure and simple
bloodlust.

Works Cited

Bedau, Hugo. "The Case Against the Death Penalty." *ACLU Publications.* ACLU,
    1997. Web. 19 Oct. 2007.
Berk, Richard A., Robert Weiss, and Jack Boger. "Chance and the Death Pen-
    alty." *Law & Society Review* 27.1 (1993): 89–110. Print.

Gibson, James M. "An Old Testament Analogue for 'The Lottery.' " *Journal of Modern Literature* 11.1 (1984): 193–95. Print.

Jackson, Shirley. "Biography of a Story." *Come Along with Me*. Ed. Stanley Edgar Hyman. New York: Viking, 1968. 211–24. Print.

Radelet, Michael L., and Hugo Adam Bedau. "The Execution of the Innocent." *Law and Contemporary Problems* 61.4 (1998): 105–24. Print.

Sass, Regina. "Poll: 69% of Americans Favor Death Penalty." *Associated Content: The People's Media Company*. AC Media, 13 Oct. 2007. Web. 20 Oct. 2007.

AIMEE WILSON
Under the Guise of Tradition: "The Lottery" and Female Circumcision

Aimee Wilson (b. 1982) was born in Detroit, Michigan, and grew up in the mountains of North Carolina. She is a graduate of the University of North Carolina, Chapel Hill, and a doctoral candidate in English at Florida State University.

Ask a friend about traditions and you're likely to hear stories about the pumpkin pie grandma always makes for Thanksgiving, the fireworks Uncle Bill always shoots off on the Fourth of July, or the Easter-egg hunt for grown-ups that always results in broken knick-knacks (and one time a broken finger). But ask why these things are repeated every year and you're likely to encounter a lot of *I don't knows*. These muddy or lost origins are unproblematic when the negative outcome of a tradition is nothing more than the occasional broken finger. But while traditions are not inherently bad, our adherence to them should be examined when they result in more serious, negative outcomes (as some indeed do).

Shirley Jackson's "The Lottery" depicts one such meaningless tradition, the result of which is death by stoning. Though Jackson's story was written nearly sixty years ago, her depiction of a ritual can help us see clearly when problematic following of tradition takes place in our modern world. For example, it is worth comparing the ritual in "The Lottery" to the often misunderstood practice of female genital mutilation, an operation more commonly known as female circumcision, because Jackson's story highlights the need to reconsider blind adherence to tradition when that tradition leads to needless violence. As Alice Walker, a prominent author and opponent of female circumcision, points out, "[r]ecent articles in the media have reported on the growing practice of 'female circumcision' in the United States and Europe" (281). Thus the issue, and the need to reexamine it, hits closer to home than we might like to acknowledge.

In Egypt, at least 70 percent of women who are married or have been married undergo female circumcision. This number, according to NPR's Melissa

Block, might be significantly lower than the 96 percent reported by a 2003 UNICEF study, but it is still shockingly high. Female circumcision involves removal of all or part of the clitoris and is usually done between the ages of seven and thirteen. The procedure has been in practice for centuries; indeed, researchers found female mummies with evidence of genital mutilation from the sixteenth century B.C.E., "long before either Christianity or Islam arrived on the scene" ("Egypt Reinforces"). Though many proponents of female circumcision cite religious justifications for the procedure, most major Egyptian religious officials denounce or prohibit female genital mutilation. The *New York Times*'s Michael Slackman states, "[Egypt] is conservative, religious, and, for many, guided largely by traditions, even when those traditions do not adhere to the tenets of their faith, be it Christianity or Islam" (A1). Most proponents of female circumcision today believe that a family's honor and the girl's marriage prospects depend on her being circumcised, though religious justifications for why honor and marriage are tied to the practice have been all but invalidated by religious officials.

Jackson's fictional lottery rests on a similarly shaky foundation. The original significance of the ritual has been either grossly misconstrued or entirely forgotten. The black box is a replacement, the three-legged stool is an addition, paper slips are used instead of wood chips, and only Old Man Warner seems to still believe that the ritual will produce a tangible outcome (" 'Lottery in June, corn be heavy soon' "). Nevertheless, Jackson tells us that "[a]lthough the villagers had forgotten the ritual and lost the original black box, they still remembered to use stones." We are to understand that the second, violent half of the ritual has become more important, more worthy of remembrance, than the reason for the violence in the first place.

For girls in Egypt and boys in "The Lottery," these violent rituals function   5
as a rite of passage. Jody Joseph of Egypt's Better Life Association explains that Egyptian families will often encourage a girl to have the procedure done by offering her food or new clothes: "[i]t's like the girl is a bride. They sort of prepare her psychologically that she's going to be purified" ("Egypt Reinforces"). The older men in Jackson's story also play to adolescent males' sense of honor and pride. As critic Gail Whittier points out, Jack Watson's experience demonstrates this rite of passage. He participates in the drawing this year for the first time (we assume because he is newly of age) and is encouraged by the crowd with sayings such as " 'Glad to see your mother's got a man to do it.' " In other words, Jack is considered an adult now that he is old enough to draw slips for his mother; the villagers respond to Jack's willingness to draw by verbally granting him manhood.

Though Jackson's central village continues to blindly follow the tradition (and even heighten its significance by making a rite of passage out of it), we are told that a neighboring village is contemplating ending the ritual. Similarly, the Egyptian government is taking steps to erase the practice of female circumcision. In 1996, the government issued a ministerial decree banning hospitals from performing the operation. Moreover, both the government and Jackson's fictional community seem to recognize the importance of a name in the perception of both practices. In the government's efforts to stop the operation, a push is being made to rename *female circumcision* as *female genital mutilation*. The difference between *circumcision* and *mutilation* is enormous: *circumcision* likens the procedure to the more common male circumcision, which is widely acceptable in the Western world. *Mutilation,* conversely, highlights the cruelty and brings with it associations of wrongdoing.

Similarly, the community in Jackson's story refers to its ritual as a "lottery" rather than a "stoning," which places the emphasis on the first half of the event rather than the second and serves to obscure the brutality and deaden the emotional impact of the act. This obfuscation is apparently necessary as the villagers seem generally hesitant to go through with the ritual. We're even told that they "kept their distance, leaving a space between themselves and the stool" — a physical representation of the moral distance the villagers want to keep between themselves and the ritual. Naming the ritual for the more benign part of it allows a further buffer between themselves and the brutality of what the ritual necessitates.

The men in Jackson's fictional village are largely able to maintain this desired distance throughout the event. Mr. Summers performs a "civic activity" by preparing the box and slips of paper, a job that entails using a heavy pencil in the coal company office to make a black mark on the fatal slip; his civic duty is thus to literally and symbolically get his hands dirty so others don't have to. Then, when the ritual stoning begins, it is the women who instigate the physical action. Whittier interestingly notes that "*no* man is seen as holding stones or actually stoning Tessie, though two women are presented as armed" (356). Likewise in Egypt, the circumcision procedure is usually arranged for by the girl's mother, grandmother, or other female relative (Ross).

The familiarity of tradition in both "The Lottery" and in the case of female circumcision allows malice to hide unexamined under the guise of tradition. Drawing parallels between "The Lottery" and the world in which we live helps clear away the dust that the idea of tradition allows to settle and encourages us to turn a critical eye on those traditions in our lives that might otherwise evade much-needed scrutiny.

Works Cited

"Egypt Reinforces Ban on Female Circumcision." Narr. Melissa Block and Peter Kenyon. *All Things Considered.* Natl. Public Radio. 6 July 2007. Radio.

Ross, Oakland. "Egypt Holds Fast to Centuries-Old Tradition." *Toronto Star* 25 June 2007: AA01. Print.

Slackman, Michael. "In Egypt, Shielding Girls from an Old Practice." *New York Times* 20 Sept. 2007, natl. ed.: A1+. Print.

Walker, Alice. *Possessing the Secret of Joy.* New York: Harcourt, 1992. Print.

Whittier, Gail. " 'The Lottery' as Misogynist Parable." *Women's Studies* 18 (1991): 353–66. Print.

≡ **MAKING COMPARISONS**

1. Which one of the student essays makes the most persuasive connection between "The Lottery" and contemporary events?
2. Which student essay makes the most effective use of specific details from the story?
3. Which student essay do you imagine Jackson would think comes closest to her own meaning?

≡ **WRITING ABOUT ISSUES**

1. Write an essay that argues that "The Lottery" is an allegory. Be specific about the characters and details of the story.
2. Write an essay in which you argue that certain traditional rituals do, or do not, serve a useful purpose.
3. Write an essay that describes contemporary traditions/rituals that Jackson might have had in mind when she wrote "The Lottery."
4. When Jackson found out that South Africa banned her story in 1948, she said, "Well at least they understand it." Write an essay that explains what you think she meant by that statement. Use specific references to the story.

■ The Marriage Trap: Plays

HENRIK IBSEN, *A Doll House*

SUSAN GLASPELL, *Trifles*

The writer and scientist Loren Eiseley notes that "to grow is a gain, an enlargement of life. . . . Yet it is also a departure." Eiseley's seems a more sophisticated idea than one portraying personal and social progress as only positive. Life is more complicated than that. Most of us eagerly anticipate becoming adults and embracing adult responsibilities and privileges. But our literature is filled with nostalgia for the innocence and wonder of childhood. We have a sense that we have lost something as our culture, technology, and lifestyles have advanced. There is no going back, but to some the old ways sometimes seem simpler. Our grandparents longed to leave the limitations of small-town life, but fifty years later their urban grandchildren idealize small communities. Women agonized over the legal and personal restrictions of Victorian marriages, but contemporary women understand that divorce is often painful and difficult. No reasonable thinker would want women to return to the childlike position that wives were expected to inhabit a hundred years ago, but that does not mean we cannot acknowledge that divorce often comes with a steep emotional and practical price.

It appears that Henrik Ibsen understood this when he wrote *A Doll House* in 1879. It was an era of great political and social change, and Ibsen believed that writers could be instrumental in affecting the way people thought about the great issues of the day. His realistic problem plays confronted topical and controversial issues. Among the most debated was the status of women in society, especially their legal and emotional subjugation within marriage. To a contemporary audience, Nora, the main character of *A Doll House*, is treated like a child. Although that disturbs most women today, Ibsen's female audience tended not to sympathize with Nora. The play's unsettling conclusion outraged most men. Changes in accepted thinking are always contested. But although most critics today see Ibsen as a social visionary who championed equality in marriage, he was not naive enough to think that great sacrifice and pain would not also accompany freedom and equality. The solution of one problem often creates new problems. When Nora begins to question the old ways, her future starts to grow uncertain. Knowing what she knows, can she really remain in a marriage that seems to her a cruel and unjust trap?

Written almost forty years later, Susan Glaspell's *Trifles* explores similar feelings of confinement but in a different geographical context. Although the scene shifts from a comfortable middle-class home in Ibsen's Norway to rural America and the gloomy, abandoned kitchen of Minnie Wright, readers quickly get the feeling that the marriage of John and Minnie was also one of emotional domination. As the details surrounding John's death are cleverly and subtly revealed to us, we also get the clear impression that we cannot look to the men in the play for insight and understanding of Minnie's situation. They are too concerned with a search for physical evidence to see the devastating emotional truth of this marriage that is in plain sight.

≡ **BEFORE YOU READ**

Do you think a woman is ever justified in leaving her children? Do you think absolute equality is necessary for love to exist in a marriage? Do you think an abused wife who takes revenge on her husband deserves punishment?

HENRIK IBSEN
A Doll House

Translated by Rolf Fjelde

Henrik Ibsen (1828–1906) was born into a family with money in a small town in Norway, but his father soon went bankrupt. Ibsen later remembered this genteel poverty by writing about issues of social injustice that he experienced firsthand. At fifteen Ibsen was apprenticed to a pharmacist, a profession he had no interest in. He soon was drawn to the theater, working to establish a Norwegian national theater. But this led to frustration, and Ibsen spent almost thirty years in a self-imposed exile in Italy and Germany, where he wrote some of his most famous plays. Ibsen's plays are often performed today and still provoke controversy. They include Ghosts *(1881),* An Enemy of the People *(1882),* Hedda Gabler *(1890), and* When We Dead Awaken *(1899).*

THE CHARACTERS

TORVALD HELMER, *a lawyer*
NORA, *his wife*
DR. RANK
MRS. LINDE
NILS KROGSTAD, *a bank clerk*
THE HELMERS' THREE SMALL CHILDREN
ANNE-MARIE, *their nurse*
HELENE, *a maid*
A DELIVERY BOY

SCENE: *The action takes place in Helmer's residence.*

Act 1

A comfortable room, tastefully but not expensively furnished. A door to the right in the back wall leads to the entryway; another to the left leads to Helmer's study. Be-

tween these doors, a piano. Midway in the left-hand wall a door, and further back a window. Near the window a round table with an armchair and a small sofa. In the right-hand wall, toward the rear, a door, and nearer the foreground a porcelain stove with two armchairs and a rocking chair beside it. Between the stove and the side door, a small table. Engravings on the walls. An etagère with china figures and other small art objects; a small bookcase with richly bound books; the floor carpeted; a fire burning in the stove. It is a winter day.

A bell rings in the entryway; shortly after we hear the door being unlocked. Nora comes into the room, humming happily to herself; she is wearing street clothes and carries an armload of packages, which she puts down on the table to the right. She has left the hall door open; and through it a Delivery Boy is seen, holding a Christmas tree and a basket, which he gives to the Maid who let them in.

NORA: Hide the tree well, Helene. The children mustn't get a glimpse of it till this evening, after it's trimmed. *(To the Delivery Boy, taking out her purse.)* How much?

DELIVERY BOY: Fifty, ma'am.

NORA: There's a crown. No, keep the change. *(The Boy thanks her and leaves. Nora shuts the door. She laughs softly to herself while taking off her street things. Drawing a bag of macaroons from her pocket, she eats a couple, then steals over and listens at her husband's study door.)* Yes, he's home. *(Hums again as she moves to the table right.)*

HELMER *(from the study)*: Is that my little lark twittering out there?

NORA *(busy opening some packages)*: Yes, it is.

HELMER: Is that my squirrel rummaging around?

NORA: Yes!

HELMER: When did my squirrel get in?

NORA: Just now. *(Putting the macaroon bag in her pocket and wiping her mouth.)* Do come in, Torvald, and see what I've bought.

HELMER: Can't be disturbed. *(After a moment he opens the door and peers in, pen in hand.)* Bought, you say? All that there? Has the little spendthrift been out throwing money around again?

NORA: Oh, but Torvald, this year we really should let ourselves go a bit. It's the first Christmas we haven't had to economize.

HELMER: But you know we can't go squandering.

NORA: Oh yes, Torvald, we can squander a little now. Can't we? Just a tiny, wee bit. Now that you've got a big salary and are going to make piles and piles of money.

HELMER: Yes — starting New Year's. But then it's a full three months till the raise comes through.

NORA: Pooh! We can borrow that long.

HELMER: Nora! *(Goes over and playfully takes her by the ear.)* Are your scatter-brains off again? What if today I borrowed a thousand crowns, and you squandered them over Christmas week, and then on New Year's Eve a roof tile fell on my head and I lay there —

NORA *(putting her hand on his mouth)*: Oh! Don't say such things!

HELMER: Yes, but what if it happened—then what?

NORA: If anything so awful happened, then it just wouldn't matter if I had debts or not.

HELMER: Well, but the people I'd borrowed from?

NORA: Them? Who cares about them! They're strangers.

HELMER: Nora, Nora, how like a woman! No, but seriously, Nora, you know what I think about that. No debts! Never borrow! Something of freedom's lost—and something of beauty, too—from a home that's founded on borrowing and debt. We've made a brave stand up to now, the two of us; and we'll go right on like that the little while we have to.

NORA *(going toward the stove)*:   Yes, whatever you say, Torvald.

HELMER *(following her)*:   Now, now, the little lark's wings mustn't droop. Come on, don't be a sulky squirrel. *(Taking out his wallet.)* Nora, guess what I have here.

NORA *(turning quickly)*:   Money!

HELMER: There, see. *(Hands her some notes.)* Good grief, I know how costs go up in a house at Christmastime.

NORA: Ten—twenty—thirty—forty. Oh, thank you, Torvald; I can manage no end on this.

HELMER: You really will have to.

NORA: Oh yes, I promise I will! But come here so I can show you everything I bought. And so cheap! Look, new clothes for Ivar here—and a sword. Here a horse and a trumpet for Bob. And a doll and a doll's bed here for Emmy; they're nothing much, but she'll tear them to bits in no time anyway. And here I have dress material and handkerchiefs for the maids. Old Anne-Marie really deserves something more.

HELMER: And what's in that package there?

NORA *(with a cry)*:   Torvald, no! You can't see that till tonight!

HELMER: I see. But tell me now, you little prodigal, what have you thought of for yourself?

NORA: For myself? Oh, I don't want anything at all.

HELMER: Of course you do. Tell me just what—within reason—you'd most like to have.

NORA: I honestly don't know. Oh, listen, Torvald—

HELMER: Well?

NORA *(fumbling at his coat buttons, without looking at him)*:   If you want to give me something, then maybe you could—you could—

HELMER: Come on, out with it.

NORA *(hurriedly)*:   You could give me money, Torvald. No more than you think you can spare; then one of these days I'll buy something with it.

HELMER: But Nora—

NORA: Oh please, Torvald darling, do that! I beg you, please. Then I could hang the bills in pretty gilt paper on the Christmas tree. Wouldn't that be fun?

HELMER: What are those little birds called that always fly through their fortunes?

NORA: Oh yes, spendthrifts: I know all that. But let's do as I say, Torvald; then I'll have time to decide what I really need most. That's very sensible, isn't it?

HELMER *(smiling)*:   Yes, very — that is, if you actually hung onto the money I give you, and you actually used it to buy yourself something. But it goes for the house and for all sorts of foolish things, and then I only have to lay out some more.

NORA: Oh, but Torvald —

HELMER: Don't deny it, my dear little Nora. *(Putting his arm around her waist.)* Spendthrifts are sweet, but they use up a frightful amount of money. It's incredible what it costs a man to feed such birds.

NORA: Oh, how can you say that! Really, I save everything I can.

HELMER *(laughing)*:   Yes, that's the truth. Everything you can. But that's nothing at all.

NORA *(humming, with a smile of quiet satisfaction)*:   Hm, if you only knew what expenses we larks and squirrels have, Torvald.

HELMER: You're an odd little one. Exactly the way your father was. You're never at a loss for scaring up money; but the moment you have it, it runs right out through your fingers; you never know what you've done with it. Well, one takes you as you are. It's deep in your blood. Yes, these things are hereditary, Nora.

NORA: Ah, I could wish I'd inherited many of Papa's qualities.

HELMER: And I couldn't wish you anything but just what you are, my sweet little lark. But wait; it seems to me you have a very — what should I call it? — a very suspicious look today —

NORA: I do?

HELMER: You certainly do. Look me straight in the eye.

NORA *(looking at him)*:   Well?

HELMER *(shaking an admonitory finger)*:   Surely my sweet tooth hasn't been running riot in town today, has she?

NORA: No. Why do you imagine that?

HELMER: My sweet tooth really didn't make a little detour through the confectioner's?

NORA: No, I assure you, Torvald —

HELMER: Hasn't nibbled some pastry?

NORA: No, not at all.

HELMER: Not even munched a macaroon or two?

NORA: No, Torvald, I assure you, really —

HELMER: There, there now. Of course I'm only joking.

NORA *(going to the table, right)*:   You know I could never think of going against you.

HELMER: No, I understand that; and you *have* given me your word. *(Going over to her.)* Well, you keep your little Christmas secrets to yourself, Nora darling. I expect they'll come to light this evening, when the tree is lit.

NORA: Did you remember to ask Dr. Rank?

HELMER: No. But there's no need for that: it's assumed he'll be dining with us. All the same, I'll ask him when he stops by here this morning. I've ordered some fine wine. Nora, you can't imagine how I'm looking forward to this evening.

NORA: So am I. And what fun for the children, Torvald!

HELMER: Ah, it's so gratifying to know that one's gotten a safe, secure job, and with a comfortable salary. It's a great satisfaction, isn't it?

NORA: Oh, it's wonderful!

HELMER: Remember last Christmas? Three whole weeks before, you shut yourself in every evening till long after midnight, making flowers for the Christmas tree, and all the other decorations to surprise us. Ugh, that was the dullest time I've ever lived through.

NORA: It wasn't at all dull for me.

HELMER *(smiling)*:   But the outcome *was* pretty sorry, Nora.

NORA: Oh, don't tease me with that again. How could I help it that the cat came in and tore everything to shreds.

HELMER: No, poor thing, you certainly couldn't. You wanted so much to please us all, and that's what counts. But it's just as well that the hard times are past.

NORA: Yes, it's really wonderful.

HELMER: Now I don't have to sit here alone, boring myself, and you don't have to tire your precious eyes and your fair little delicate hands —

NORA *(clapping her hands)*:   No, is it really true, Torvald, I don't have to? Oh, how wonderfully lovely to hear! *(Taking his arm.)* Now I'll tell you just how I've thought we should plan things. Right after Christmas — *(The doorbell rings.)* Oh, the bell. *(Straightening the room up a bit.)* Somebody would have to come. What a bore!

HELMER: I'm not home to visitors, don't forget.

MAID *(from the hall doorway)*:   Ma'am, a lady to see you —

NORA: All right, let her come in.

MAID *(to Helmer)*:   And the doctor's just come too.

HELMER: Did he go right to my study?

MAID: Yes, he did.

Helmer goes into his room. The Maid shows in Mrs. Linde, dressed in traveling clothes, and shuts the door after her.

MRS. LINDE *(in a dispirited and somewhat hesitant voice)*   Hello, Nora.

NORA *(uncertain)*:   Hello —

MRS. LINDE: You don't recognize me.

NORA: No, I don't know — but wait, I think — *(Exclaiming.)* What! Kristine! Is it really you?

MRS. LINDE: Yes, it's me.

NORA: Kristine! To think I didn't recognize you. But then, how could I? *(More quietly.)* How you've changed, Kristine!

MRS. LINDE: Yes, no doubt I have. In nine — ten long years.

NORA: Is it so long since we met! Yes, it's all of that. Oh, these last eight years have been a happy time, believe me. And so now you've come in to town, too. Made the long trip in the winter. That took courage.

MRS. LINDE: I just got here by ship this morning.

NORA: To enjoy yourself over Christmas, of course. Oh, how lovely! Yes, enjoy ourselves, we'll do that. But take your coat off. You're not still cold? *(Helping her.)* There now, let's get cozy here by the stove. No, the easy chair there! I'll take the rocker here. *(Seizing her hands.)* Yes, now you have your old look again; it was only in that first moment. You're a bit more pale, Kristine — and maybe a bit thinner.

MRS. LINDE: And much, much older, Nora.

NORA: Yes, perhaps a bit older: a tiny, tiny bit; not much at all. *(Stopping short; suddenly serious.)* Oh, but thoughtless me, to sit here, chattering away. Sweet, good Kristine, can you forgive me?

MRS. LINDE: What do you mean, Nora?

NORA *(softly)*:   Poor Kristine, you've become a widow.

MRS. LINDE: Yes, three years ago.

NORA: Oh, I knew it, of course: I read it in the papers. Oh, Kristine, you must believe me; I often thought of writing you then, but I kept postponing it, and something always interfered.

MRS. LINDE: Nora dear, I understand completely.

NORA: No, it was awful of me, Kristine. You poor thing, how much you must have gone through. And he left you nothing?

MRS. LINDE: No.

NORA: And no children?

MRS. LINDE: No.

NORA: Nothing at all, then?

MRS. LINDE: Not even a sense of loss to feed on.

NORA *(looking incredulously at her)*:   But Kristine, how could that be?

MRS. LINDE *(smiling wearily and smoothing her hair)*:   Oh, sometimes it happens, Nora.

NORA: So completely alone. How terribly hard that must be for you. I have three lovely children. You can't see them now; they're out with the maid. But now you must tell me everything —

MRS. LINDE: No, no, no, tell me about yourself.

NORA: No, you begin. Today I don't want to be selfish. I want to think only of you today. But there *is* something I must tell you. Did you hear of the wonderful luck we had recently?

MRS. LINDE: No, what's that?

NORA: My husband's been made manager in the bank, just think!

MRS. LINDE: Your husband? How marvelous!

NORA: Isn't it? Being a lawyer is such an uncertain living, you know, especially if one won't touch any cases that aren't clean and decent. And of course Torvald would never do that, and I'm with him completely there. Oh, we're simply delighted, believe me! He'll join the bank right after New Year's and start getting a huge salary and lots of commissions. From now on we can live quite differently — just as we want. Oh, Kristine, I feel so light and happy! Won't it be lovely to have stacks of money and not a care in the world?

MRS. LINDE: Well, anyway, it would be lovely to have enough for necessities.

NORA: No, not just for necessities, but stacks and stacks of money!

MRS. LINDE *(smiling)*:   Nora, Nora, aren't you sensible yet? Back in school you were such a free spender.

NORA *(with a quiet laugh)*:   Yes, that's what Torvald still says. *(Shaking her finger.)* But "Nora, Nora" isn't as silly as you all think. Really, we've been in no position for me to go squandering. We've had to work, both of us.

MRS. LINDE   You too?

NORA: Yes, at odd jobs — needlework, crocheting, embroidery, and such — *(Casually.)* and other things too. You remember that Torvald left the department when we were married? There was no chance of promotion in his office, and of course he needed to earn more money. But that first year he drove himself terribly. He took on all kinds of extra work that kept him going morning and night. It wore him down, and then he fell deathly ill. The doctors said it was essential for him to travel south.

MRS. LINDE: Yes, didn't you spend a whole year in Italy?

NORA: That's right. It wasn't easy to get away, you know. Ivar had just been born. But of course we had to go. Oh, that was a beautiful trip, and it saved Torvald's life. But it cost a frightful sum, Kristine.

MRS. LINDE: I can well imagine.

NORA: Four thousand, eight hundred crowns it cost. That's really a lot of money.

MRS. LINDE: But it's lucky you had it when you needed it.

NORA: Well, as it was, we got it from Papa.

MRS. LINDE: I see. It was just about the time your father died.

NORA: Yes, just about then. And, you know, I couldn't make that trip out to nurse him. I had to stay here, expecting Ivar any moment, and with my poor sick Torvald to care for. Dearest Papa, I never saw him again, Kristine. Oh, that was the worst time I've known in all my marriage.

MRS. LINDE: I know how you loved him. And then you went off to Italy?

NORA: Yes. We had the means now, and the doctors urged us. So we left a month after.

MRS. LINDE: And your husband came back completely cured?

NORA: Sound as a drum!

MRS. LINDE: But — the doctor?

NORA: Who?

MRS. LINDE: I thought the maid said he was a doctor, the man who came in with me.

NORA: Yes, that was Dr. Rank — but he's not making a sick call. He's our closest friend, and he stops by at least once a day. No, Torvald hasn't had a sick moment since, and the children are fit and strong, and I am, too. *(Jumping up and clapping her hands.)* Oh, dear God, Kristine, what a lovely thing to live and be happy! But how disgusting of me — I'm talking of nothing but my own affairs. *(Sits on a stool close by Kristine, arms resting across her knees.)* Oh, don't be angry with me! Tell me, is it really true that you weren't in love with your husband? Why did you marry him, then?

MRS. LINDE: My mother was still alive, but bedridden and helpless — and I had my two younger brothers to look after. In all conscience, I didn't think I could turn him down.

NORA: No, you were right there. But was he rich at the time?

MRS. LINDE: He was very well off, I'd say. But the business was shaky, Nora. When he died, it all fell apart, and nothing was left.

NORA: And then — ?

MRS. LINDE: Yes, so I had to scrape up a living with a little shop and a little teaching and whatever else I could find. The last three years have been like one endless workday without a rest for me. Now it's over, Nora. My poor mother doesn't need me, for she's passed on. Nor the boys, either; they're working now and can take care of themselves.

NORA: How free you must feel —

MRS. LINDE: No — only unspeakably empty. Nothing to live for now. *(Standing up anxiously.)* That's why I couldn't take it any longer out in that desolate hole. Maybe here it'll be easier to find something to do and keep my mind occupied. If I could only be lucky enough to get a steady job, some office work —

NORA: Oh, but Kristine, that's so dreadfully tiring, and you already look so tired. It would be much better for you if you could go off to a bathing resort.

MRS. LINDE *(going toward the window)*:   I have no father to give me travel money, Nora.

NORA *(rising)*:   Oh, don't be angry with me.

MRS. LINDE *(going to her)*:   Nora dear, don't you be angry with me. The worst of my kind of situation is all the bitterness that's stored away. No one to work for, and yet you're always having to snap up your opportunities. You have to live; and so you grow selfish. When you told me the happy change in your lot, do you know I was delighted less for your sakes than for mine?

NORA: How so? Oh, I see. You think maybe Torvald could do something for you.

MRS. LINDE: Yes, that's what I thought.

NORA: And he will, Kristine! Just leave it to me; I'll bring it up so delicately — find something attractive to humor him with. Oh, I'm so eager to help you.

MRS. LINDE: How very kind of you, Nora, to be so concerned over me — doubly kind, considering you really know so little of life's burdens yourself.

NORA: I — ? I know so little — ?

MRS. LINDE *(smiling)*:   Well, my heavens — a little needlework and such — Nora, you're just a child.

NORA *(tossing her head and pacing the floor)*:   You don't have to act so superior.

MRS. LINDE: Oh?

NORA: You're just like the others. You all think I'm incapable of anything serious —

MRS. LINDE: Come now —

NORA: That I've never had to face the raw world.

MRS. LINDE: Nora dear, you've just been telling me all your troubles.

NORA: Hm! Trivia! *(Quietly.)* I haven't told you the big thing.

MRS. LINDE: Big thing? What do you mean?

NORA: You look down on me so, Kristine, but you shouldn't. You're proud that you worked so long and hard for your mother.

MRS. LINDE: I don't look down on a soul. But it *is* true: I'm proud — and happy, too — to think it was given to me to make my mother's last days almost free of care.

NORA: And you're also proud thinking of what you've done for your brothers.

MRS. LINDE: I feel I've a right to be.

NORA: I agree. But listen to this, Kristine — I've also got something to be proud and happy for.

MRS. LINDE: I don't doubt it. But whatever do you mean?

NORA: Not so loud. What if Torvald heard! He mustn't, not for anything in the world. Nobody must know, Kristine. No one but you.

MRS. LINDE: But what is it, then?

NORA: Come here. *(Drawing her down beside her on the sofa.)* It's true — I've also got something to be proud and happy for. I'm the one who saved Torvald's life.

MRS. LINDE: Saved — ? Saved how?

NORA: I told you about the trip to Italy. Torvald never would have lived if he hadn't gone south —

MRS. LINDE: Of course; your father gave you the means —

NORA *(smiling)*:   That's what Torvald and all the rest think, but —

MRS. LINDE: But — ?

NORA: Papa didn't give us a pin. I was the one who raised the money.

MRS. LINDE: You? That whole amount?

NORA: Four thousand, eight hundred crowns. What do you say to that?

MRS. LINDE: But Nora, how was it possible? Did you win the lottery?

NORA *(disdainfully)*:   The lottery? Pooh! No art to that.

MRS. LINDE: But where did you get it from then?

NORA *(humming, with a mysterious smile)*:   Hmm, tra-la-la-la.

MRS. LINDE: Because you couldn't have borrowed it.

NORA: No? Why not?

MRS. LINDE: A wife can't borrow without her husband's consent.

NORA *(tossing her head)*:   Oh, but a wife with a little business sense, a wife who knows how to manage —

MRS. LINDE: Nora, I simply don't understand —

NORA: You don't have to. Whoever said I *borrowed* the money? I could have gotten it other ways. *(Throwing herself back on the sofa.)* I could have gotten it from some admirer or other. After all, a girl with my ravishing appeal —

MRS. LINDE: You lunatic.

NORA: I'll bet you're eaten up with curiosity, Kristine.

MRS. LINDE: Now listen here, Nora — you haven't done something indiscreet?

NORA *(sitting up again)*:   Is it indiscreet to save your husband's life?

MRS. LINDE: I think it's indiscreet that without his knowledge you —

NORA: But that's the point: he mustn't know! My Lord, can't you understand? He mustn't ever know the close call he had. It was to *me* the doctors came to say his life was in danger — that nothing could save him but a stay in the south. Didn't I try strategy then! I began talking about how lovely it would be for me to travel abroad like other young wives; I begged and I cried; I told him please to remember my condition, to be kind and indulge me; and then I dropped a hint that he could easily take out a loan. But at that, Kristine, he nearly exploded. He said I was frivolous, and it was his duty as man of the house not to indulge me in whims and fancies — as I think he called them. Aha, I thought, now you'll just have to be saved — and that's when I saw my chance.

MRS. LINDE: And your father never told Torvald the money wasn't from him?

NORA: No, never. Papa died right about then. I'd considered bringing him into my secret and begging him never to tell. But he was too sick at the time — and then, sadly, it didn't matter.

MRS. LINDE: And you've never confided in your husband since?

NORA: For heaven's sake, no! Are you serious? He's so strict on that subject. Besides — Torvald, with all his masculine pride — how painfully humiliating for him if he ever found out he was in debt to me. That would just ruin our relationship. Our beautiful, happy home would never be the same.

MRS. LINDE: Won't you ever tell him?

NORA *(thoughtfully, half smiling)*:   Yes — maybe sometime, years from now, when I'm no longer so attractive. Don't laugh! I only mean when Torvald loves me less than now, when he stops enjoying my dancing and dressing up and reciting for him. Then it might be wise to have something in reserve — *(Breaking off.)* How ridiculous! That'll never happen — Well, Kristine, what do you think of my big secret? I'm capable of something too, hm? You can imagine, of course, how this thing hangs over me. It really hasn't been easy meeting the payments on time. In the business world there's what they call quarterly interest and what they call amortization, and these are always so terribly hard to manage. I've had to skimp a little here and there, wherever I could, you know. I could hardly spare anything from my house allowance, because Torvald has to live well. I couldn't let the children go poorly dressed; whatever I got for them, I felt I had to use up completely — the darlings!

MRS. LINDE: Poor Nora, so it had to come out of your own budget, then?

NORA: Yes, of course. But I was the one most responsible, too. Every time Torvald gave me money for new clothes and such, I never used more than half; always bought the simplest, cheapest outfits. It was a godsend that everything looks so well on me that Torvald never noticed. But it did weigh me down at times, Kristine. It *is* such a joy to wear fine things. You understand.

MRS. LINDE: Oh, of course.

NORA: And then I found other ways of making money. Last winter I was lucky enough to get a lot of copying to do. I locked myself in and sat writing every evening till late in the night. Ah, I was tired so often, dead tired. But still it was wonderful fun, sitting and working like that, earning money. It was almost like being a man.

MRS. LINDE: But how much have you paid off this way so far?

NORA: That's hard to say, exactly. These accounts, you know, aren't easy to figure. I only know that I've paid out all I could scrape together. Time and again I haven't known where to turn. *(Smiling.)* Then I'd sit here dreaming of a rich old gentleman who had fallen in love with me —

MRS. LINDE: What! Who is he?

NORA: Oh, really! And that he'd died, and when his will was opened, there in big letters it said, "All my fortune shall be paid over in cash, immediately, to that enchanting Mrs. Nora Helmer."

MRS. LINDE: But Nora dear — who *was* this gentleman?

NORA: Good grief, can't you understand? The old man never existed; that was only something I'd dream up time and again whenever I was at my wits' end for money. But it makes no difference now; the old fossil can go where he pleases for all I care; I don't need him or his will — because now I'm free. *(Jumping up.)* Oh, how lovely to think of that, Kristine! Carefree! To know you're carefree, utterly carefree; to be able to romp and play with the children, and to keep up a beautiful, charming home — everything just the way Torvald likes it! And think, spring is coming, with big blue skies. Maybe we can travel a little then. Maybe I'll see the ocean again. Oh yes, it *is* so marvelous to live and be happy!

The front doorbell rings.

MRS. LINDE *(rising)*:   There's the bell. It's probably best that I go.

NORA: No, stay. No one's expected. It must be for Torvald.

MAID *(from the hall doorway)*:   Excuse me, ma'am — there's a gentleman here to see Mr. Helmer, but I didn't know — since the doctor's with him —

NORA: Who is the gentleman?

KROGSTAD *(from the doorway)*:   It's me, Mrs. Helmer.

Mrs. Linde starts and turns away toward the window.

NORA *(stepping toward him, tense, her voice a whisper)*:   You? What is it? Why do you want to speak to my husband?

KROGSTAD: Bank business — after a fashion. I have a small job in the investment bank, and I hear now your husband is going to be our chief —

NORA: In other words, it's —

KROGSTAD: Just dry business, Mrs. Helmer. Nothing but that.

NORA: Yes, then please be good enough to step into the study. *(She nods indifferently as she sees him out by the hall door, then returns and begins stirring up the stove.)*

MRS. LINDE: Nora — who was that man?

NORA: That was a Mr. Krogstad — a lawyer.

MRS. LINDE: Then it really was him.

NORA: Do you know that person?

MRS. LINDE: I did once — many years ago. For a time he was a law clerk in our town.

NORA: Yes, he's been that.

MRS. LINDE: How he's changed.

NORA: I understand he had a very unhappy marriage.

MRS. LINDE: He's a widower now.

NORA: With a number of children. There now, it's burning. *(She closes the stove door and moves the rocker a bit to one side.)*

MRS. LINDE: They say he has a hand in all kinds of business.

NORA: Oh? That may be true; I wouldn't know. But let's not think about business. It's so dull.

Dr. Rank enters from Helmer's study.

RANK *(still in the doorway)*:   No, no really — I don't want to intrude, I'd just as soon talk a little while with your wife. *(Shuts the door, then notices Mrs. Linde.)* Oh, beg pardon. I'm intruding here too.

NORA: No, not at all. *(Introducing him.)* Dr. Rank, Mrs. Linde.

RANK: Well now, that's a name much heard in this house. I believe I passed the lady on the stairs as I came.

MRS. LINDE: Yes, I take the stairs very slowly. They're rather hard on me.

RANK: Uh-hm, some touch of internal weakness?

MRS. LINDE: More overexertion, I'd say.

RANK: Nothing else? Then you're probably here in town to rest up in a round of parties?

MRS. LINDE: I'm here to look for work.

RANK: Is that the best cure for overexertion?

MRS. LINDE: One has to live, Doctor.

RANK: Yes, there's a common prejudice to that effect.

NORA: Oh, come on, Dr. Rank — you really do want to live yourself.

RANK: Yes, I really do. Wretched as I am, I'll gladly prolong my torment indefinitely. All my patients feel like that. And it's quite the same, too, with the morally sick. Right at this moment there's one of those moral invalids in there with Helmer —

MRS. LINDE *(softly)*:   Ah!

NORA: Who do you mean?

RANK: Oh, it's a lawyer, Krogstad, a type you wouldn't know. His character is rotten to the root — but even he began chattering all-importantly about how he had to *live*.

NORA: Oh? What did he want to talk to Torvald about?

RANK: I really don't know. I only heard something about the bank.

NORA: I didn't know that Krog — that this man Krogstad had anything to do with the bank.

RANK: Yes, he's gotten some kind of berth down there. *(To Mrs. Linde.)* I don't know if you also have, in your neck of the woods, a type of person who scuttles about breathlessly, sniffing out hints of moral corruption, and then maneuvers his victim into some sort of key position where he can keep an eye on him. It's the healthy these days that are out in the cold.

MRS. LINDE: All the same, it's the sick who most need to be taken in.

RANK *(with a shrug)*:   Yes, there we have it. That's the concept that's turning society into a sanatorium.

Nora, lost in her thoughts, breaks out into quiet laughter and claps her hands.

RANK: Why do you laugh at that? Do you have any real idea of what society is?

NORA: What do I care about dreary old society? I was laughing at something quite different — something terribly funny. Tell me, Doctor — is everyone who works in the bank dependent now on Torvald?

RANK: Is that what you find so terribly funny?

NORA *(smiling and humming)*:   Never mind, never mind! *(Pacing the floor.)* Yes, that's really immensely amusing: that we — that Torvald has so much power now over all those people. *(Taking the bag out of her pocket.)* Dr. Rank, a little macaroon on that?

RANK: See here, macaroons! I thought they were contraband here.

NORA: Yes, but these are some that Kristine gave me.

MRS. LINDE: What? I — ?

NORA: Now, now, don't be afraid. You couldn't possibly know that Torvald had forbidden them. You see, he's worried they'll ruin my teeth. But hmp! Just this once! Isn't that so, Dr. Rank? Help yourself! *(Puts a macaroon in his mouth.)* And you too, Kristine. And I'll also have one, only a little one — or two, at the most. *(Walking about again.)* Now I'm really tremendously happy. Now there's just one last thing in the world that I have an enormous desire to do.

RANK: Well! And what's that?

NORA: It's something I have such a consuming desire to say so Torvald could hear.

RANK: And why can't you say it?

NORA: I don't dare. It's quite shocking.

MRS. LINDE: Shocking?

RANK: Well, then it isn't advisable. But in front of us you certainly can. What do you have such a desire to say so Torvald could hear?

NORA: I have such a huge desire to say — to hell and be damned!

RANK: Are you crazy?

MRS. LINDE: My goodness, Nora!

RANK: Go on, say it. Here he is.

NORA *(hiding the macaroon bag)*:   Shh, shh, shh!

Helmer comes in from his study, hat in hand, overcoat over his arm.

NORA *(going toward him)*:   Well, Torvald dear, are you through with him?

HELMER: Yes, he just left.

NORA: Let me introduce you — this is Kristine, who's arrived here in town.

HELMER: Kristine — ? I'm sorry, but I don't know —

NORA: Mrs. Linde, Torvald dear. Mrs. Kristine Linde.

HELMER: Of course. A childhood friend of my wife's, no doubt?

MRS. LINDE: Yes, we knew each other in those days.

NORA: And just think, she made the long trip down here in order to talk with you.

HELMER: What's this?

MRS. LINDE: Well, not exactly —

NORA: You see, Kristine is remarkably clever in office work, and so she's terribly eager to come under a capable man's supervision and add more to what she already knows —

HELMER: Very wise, Mrs. Linde.

NORA: And then when she heard that you'd become a bank manager — the story was wired out to the papers — then she came in as fast as she could and — Really, Torvald, for my sake you can do a little something for Kristine, can't you?

HELMER: Yes, it's not at all impossible. Mrs. Linde, I suppose you're a widow?

MRS. LINDE: Yes.

HELMER: Any experience in office work?

MRS. LINDE: Yes, a good deal.

HELMER: Well, it's quite likely that I can make an opening for you —

NORA (clapping her hands):   You see, you see!

HELMER: You've come at a lucky moment, Mrs. Linde.

MRS. LINDE: Oh, how can I thank you?

HELMER: Not necessary. (Putting his overcoat on.) But today you'll have to excuse me —

RANK: Wait, I'll go with you. (He fetches his coat from the hall and warms it at the stove.)

NORA: Don't stay out long, dear.

HELMER: An hour; no more.

NORA: Are you going too, Kristine?

MRS. LINDE (putting on her winter garments):   Yes, I have to see about a room now.

HELMER: Then perhaps we can all walk together.

NORA (helping her):   What a shame we're so cramped here, but it's quite impossible for us to —

MRS. LINDE: Oh, don't even think of it! Good-bye, Nora dear, and thanks for everything.

NORA: Good-bye for now. Of course you'll be back this evening. And you too, Dr. Rank. What? If you're well enough? Oh, you've got to be! Wrap up tight now.

In a ripple of small talk the company moves out into the hall; children's voices are heard outside on the steps.

NORA: There they are! There they are! (She runs to open the door. The children come in with their nurse, Anne-Marie.) Come in, come in! (Bends down and kisses them.) Oh, you darlings—! Look at them, Kristine. Aren't they lovely!

RANK: No loitering in the draft here.

HELMER: Come, Mrs. Linde — this place is unbearable now for anyone but mothers.

Dr. Rank, Helmer, and Mrs. Linde go down the stairs. Anne-Marie goes into the living room with the children. Nora follows, after closing the hall door.

NORA: How fresh and strong you look. Oh, such red cheeks you have! Like apples and roses. *(The children interrupt her throughout the following.)* And it was so much fun? That's wonderful. Really? You pulled both Emmy and Bob on the sled? Imagine, all together! Yes, you're a clever boy, Ivar. Oh, let me hold her a bit, Anne-Marie. My sweet little doll baby! *(Takes the smallest from the nurse and dances with her.)* Yes, yes, Mama will dance with Bob as well. What? Did you throw snowballs? Oh, if I'd only been there! No, don't bother, Anne-Marie — I'll undress them myself. Oh yes, let me. It's such fun. Go in and rest; you look half frozen. There's hot coffee waiting for you on the stove. *(The nurse goes into the room to the left. Nora takes the children's winter things off, throwing them about, while the children talk to her all at once.)* Is that so? A big dog chased you? But it didn't bite? No, dogs never bite little, lovely doll babies. Don't peek in the packages, Ivar! What is it? Yes, wouldn't you like to know. No, no, it's an ugly something. Well? Shall we play? What shall we play? Hide-and-seek? Yes, let's play hide-and-seek. Bob must hide first. I must? Yes, let me hide first. *(Laughing and shouting, she and the children play in and out of the living room and the adjoining room to the right. At last Nora hides under the table. The children come storming in, search, but cannot find her, then hear her muffled laughter, dash over to the table, lift the cloth up, and find her. Wild shouting. She creeps forward as if to scare them. More shouts. Meanwhile, a knock at the hall door; no one has noticed it. Now the door half opens, and Krogstad appears. He waits a moment; the game goes on.)*

KROGSTAD: Beg pardon, Mrs. Helmer —

NORA *(with a strangled cry, turning and scrambling to her knees)*:   Oh! What do you want?

KROGSTAD: Excuse me. The outer door was ajar; it must be someone forgot to shut it —

NORA *(rising)*:   My husband isn't home, Mr. Krogstad.

KROGSTAD: I know that.

NORA: Yes — then what do you want here?

KROGSTAD: A word with you.

NORA: With —? *(To the children, quietly.)* Go in to Anne-Marie. What? No, the strange man won't hurt Mama. When he's gone, we'll play some more. *(She leads the children into the room to the left and shuts the door after them. Then, tense and nervous:)* You want to speak to me?

KROGSTAD: Yes, I want to.

NORA: Today? But it's not yet the first of the month —

KROGSTAD: No, it's Christmas Eve. It's going to be up to you how merry a Christmas you have.

NORA: What is it you want? Today I absolutely can't —

KROGSTAD: We won't talk about that till later. This is something else. You do have a moment to spare, I suppose?

NORA: Oh yes, of course — I do, except —

KROGSTAD: Good. I was sitting over at Olsen's Restaurant when I saw your husband go down the street —

NORA: Yes?

KROGSTAD: With a lady.

NORA: Yes. So?

KROGSTAD: If you'll pardon my asking: wasn't that lady a Mrs. Linde?

NORA: Yes.

KROGSTAD: Just now come into town?

NORA: Yes, today.

KROGSTAD: She's a good friend of yours?

NORA: Yes, she is. But I don't see —

KROGSTAD: I also knew her once.

NORA: I'm aware of that.

KROGSTAD: Oh? You know all about it. I thought so. Well, then let me ask you short and sweet: is Mrs. Linde getting a job in the bank?

NORA: What makes you think you can cross-examine me, Mr. Krogstad — you, one of my husband's employees? But since you ask, you might as well know — yes, Mrs. Linde's going to be taken on at the bank. And I'm the one who spoke for her, Mr. Krogstad. Now you know.

KROGSTAD: So I guessed right.

NORA *(pacing up and down)*:   Oh, one does have a tiny bit of influence, I should hope. Just because I am a woman, don't think it means that — When one has a subordinate position, Mr. Krogstad, one really ought to be careful about pushing somebody who — hm —

KROGSTAD: Who has influence?

NORA: That's right.

KROGSTAD *(in a different tone)*:   Mrs. Helmer, would you be good enough to use your influence on my behalf?

NORA: What? What do you mean?

KROGSTAD: Would you please make sure that I keep my subordinate position in the bank?

NORA: What does that mean? Who's thinking of taking away your position?

KROGSTAD: Oh, don't play the innocent with me. I'm quite aware that your friend would hardly relish the chance of running into me again; and I'm also aware now whom I can thank for being turned out.

NORA: But I promise you —

KROGSTAD: Yes, yes, yes, to the point: there's still time, and I'm advising you to use your influence to prevent it.

NORA: But Mr. Krogstad, I have absolutely no influence.

KROGSTAD: You haven't? I thought you were just saying —

NORA: You shouldn't take me so literally. I! How can you believe that I have any such influence over my husband?

KROGSTAD: Oh, I've known your husband from our student days. I don't think the great bank manager's more steadfast than any other married man.

NORA: You speak insolently about my husband, and I'll show you the door.

KROGSTAD: The lady has spirit.

NORA: I'm not afraid of you any longer. After New Year's, I'll soon be done with the whole business.

KROGSTAD *(restraining himself)*:   Now listen to me, Mrs. Helmer. If necessary, I'll fight for my little job in the bank as if it were life itself.

NORA: Yes, so it seems.

KROGSTAD: It's not just a matter of income; that's the least of it. It's something else — All right, out with it! Look, this is the thing. You know, just like all the others, of course, that once, a good many years ago, I did something rather rash.

NORA: I've heard rumors to that effect.

KROGSTAD: The case never got into court; but all the same, every door was closed in my face from then on. So I took up those various activities you know about. I had to grab hold somewhere; and I dare say I haven't been among the worst. But now I want to drop all that. My boys are growing up. For their sakes, I'll have to win back as much respect as possible here in town. That job in the bank was like the first rung in my ladder. And now your husband wants to kick me right back down in the mud again.

NORA: But for heaven's sake, Mr. Krogstad, it's simply not in my power to help you.

KROGSTAD: That's because you haven't the will to — but I have the means to make you.

NORA: You certainly won't tell my husband that I owe you money?

KROGSTAD: Hm — what if I told him that?

NORA: That would be shameful of you. *(Nearly in tears.)* This secret — my joy and my pride — that he should learn it in such a crude and disgusting way — learn it from you. You'd expose me to the most horrible unpleasantness —

KROGSTAD: Only unpleasantness?

NORA *(vehemently)*:   But go on and try. It'll turn out the worse for you, because then my husband will really see what a crook you are, and then you'll *never* be able to hold your job.

KROGSTAD: I asked if it was just domestic unpleasantness you were afraid of?

NORA: If my husband finds out, then of course he'll pay what I owe at once, and then we'd be through with you for good.

KROGSTAD *(a step closer)*:   Listen, Mrs. Helmer — you've either got a very bad memory, or else no head at all for business. I'd better put you a little more in touch with the facts.

NORA: What do you mean?

KROGSTAD: When your husband was sick, you came to me for a loan of four thousand, eight hundred crowns.

NORA: Where else could I go?

KROGSTAD: I promised to get you that sum —

NORA: And you got it.

KROGSTAD: I promised to get you that sum, on certain conditions. You were so involved in your husband's illness, and so eager to finance your trip, that I guess you didn't think out all the details. It might just be a good idea to remind you. I promised you the money on the strength of a note I drew up.

NORA: Yes, and that I signed.

KROGSTAD: Right. But at the bottom I added some lines for your father to guarantee the loan. He was supposed to sign down there.

NORA: Supposed to? He did sign.

KROGSTAD: I left the date blank. In other words, your father would have dated his signature himself. Do you remember that?

NORA: Yes, I think —

KROGSTAD: Then I gave you the note for you to mail to your father. Isn't that so?

NORA: Yes.

KROGSTAD: And naturally you sent it at once — because only some five, six days later you brought me the note, properly signed. And with that, the money was yours.

NORA: Well, then; I've made my payments regularly, haven't I?

KROGSTAD: More or less. But — getting back to the point — those were hard times for you then, Mrs. Helmer.

NORA: Yes, they were.

KROGSTAD: Your father was very ill, I believe.

NORA: He was near the end.

KROGSTAD: He died soon after?

NORA: Yes.

KROGSTAD: Tell me, Mrs. Helmer, do you happen to recall the date of your father's death? The day of the month, I mean.

NORA: Papa died the twenty-ninth of September.

KROGSTAD: That's quite correct; I've already looked into that. And now we come to a curious thing — *(Taking out a paper.)* which I simply cannot comprehend.

NORA: Curious thing? I don't know —

KROGSTAD: This is the curious thing: that your father cosigned the note for your loan three days after his death.

NORA: How —? I don't understand.

KROGSTAD: Your father died the twenty-ninth of September. But look. Here your father dated his signature October second. Isn't that curious, Mrs. Helmer? *(Nora is silent.)* Can you explain it to me? *(Nora remains silent.)* It's also remarkable that the words "October second" and the year aren't written in your father's hand, but rather in one that I think I know. Well, it's easy to understand. Your father forgot perhaps to date his signature, and then someone or other added it, a bit sloppily, before anyone knew of his death. There's nothing wrong in that. It all comes down to the signature. And there's no question about *that*, Mrs. Helmer. It really *was* your father who signed his own name here, wasn't it?

NORA (*after a short silence, throwing her head back and looking squarely at him*):   No, it wasn't. *I* signed Papa's name.

KROGSTAD: Wait, now — are you fully aware that this is a dangerous confession?

NORA: Why? You'll soon get your money.

KROGSTAD: Let me ask you a question — why didn't you send the paper to your father?

NORA: That was impossible. Papa was so sick. If I'd asked him for his signature, I also would have had to tell him what the money was for. But I couldn't tell him, sick as he was, that my husband's life was in danger. That was just impossible.

KROGSTAD: Then it would have been better if you'd given up the trip abroad.

NORA: I couldn't possibly. The trip was to save my husband's life. I couldn't give that up.

KROGSTAD: But didn't you ever consider that this was a fraud against me?

NORA: I couldn't let myself be bothered by that. You weren't any concern of mine. I couldn't stand you, with all those cold complications you made, even though you knew how badly off my husband was.

KROGSTAD: Mrs. Helmer, obviously you haven't the vaguest idea of what you've involved yourself in. But I can tell you this: it was nothing more and nothing worse than I once did — and it wrecked my whole reputation.

NORA: You? Do you expect me to believe that you ever acted bravely to save your wife's life?

KROGSTAD: Laws don't inquire into motives.

NORA: Then they must be very poor laws.

KROGSTAD: Poor or not — if I introduce this paper in court, you'll be judged according to law.

NORA: This I refuse to believe. A daughter hasn't a right to protect her dying father from anxiety and care? A wife hasn't a right to save her husband's life? I don't know much about laws, but I'm sure that somewhere in the books these things are allowed. And you don't know anything about it — you who practice the law? You must be an awful lawyer, Mr. Krogstad.

KROGSTAD: Could be. But business — the kind of business we two are mixed up in — don't you think I know about that? All right. Do what you want now. But I'm telling you *this*: if I get shoved down a second time, you're going to keep me company. (*He bows and goes out through the hall.*)

NORA (*pensive for a moment, then tossing her head*):   Oh, really! Trying to frighten me! I'm not so silly as all that. (*Begins gathering up the children's clothes, but soon stops.*) But — ? No, but that's impossible! I did it out of love.

THE CHILDREN (*in the doorway, left*):   Mama, that strange man's gone out the door.

NORA: Yes, yes, I know it. But don't tell anyone about the strange man. Do you hear? Not even Papa!

THE CHILDREN: No, Mama. But now will you play again?

NORA: No, not now.

THE CHILDREN: Oh, but Mama, you promised.

NORA: Yes, but I can't now. Go inside; I have too much to do. Go in, go in, my sweet darlings. *(She herds them gently back in the room and shuts the door after them. Settling on the sofa, she takes up a piece of embroidery and makes some stitches, but soon stops abruptly.)* No! *(Throws the work aside, rises, goes to the hall door, and calls out.)* Helene! Let me have the tree in here. *(Goes to the table, left, opens the table drawer, and stops again.)* No, but that's utterly impossible!

MAID *(with the Christmas tree)*:   Where should I put it, ma'am?

NORA: There. The middle of the floor.

MAID: Should I bring anything else?

NORA: No, thanks. I have what I need.

The Maid, who has set the tree down, goes out.

NORA *(absorbed in trimming the tree)*:   Candles here — and flowers here. That terrible creature! Talk, talk, talk! There's nothing to it at all. The tree's going to be lovely. I'll do anything to please you, Torvald. I'll sing for you, dance for you —

Helmer comes in from the hall, with a sheaf of papers under his arm.

NORA: Oh! You're back so soon?

HELMER: Yes. Has anyone been here?

NORA: Here? No.

HELMER: That's odd. I saw Krogstad leaving the front door.

NORA: So? Oh yes, that's true. Krogstad was here a moment.

HELMER: Nora, I can see by your face that he's been here, begging you to put in a good word for him.

NORA: Yes.

HELMER: And it was supposed to seem like your own idea? You were to hide it from me that he'd been here. He asked you that, too, didn't he?

NORA: Yes, Torvald, but —

HELMER: Nora, Nora, and you could fall for that? Talk with that sort of person and promise him anything? And then in the bargain, tell me an untruth?

NORA: An untruth —?

HELMER: Didn't you say that no one had been here? *(Wagging his finger.)* My little songbird must never do that again. A songbird needs a clean beak to warble with. No false notes. *(Putting his arm about her waist.)* That's the way it should be, isn't it? Yes, I'm sure of it. *(Releasing her.)* And so, enough of that. *(Sitting by the stove.)* Ah, how snug and cozy it is here. *(Leafing among his papers.)*

NORA *(busy with the tree, after a short pause)*:   Torvald!

HELMER: Yes.

NORA: I'm so much looking forward to the Stenborgs' costume party, day after tomorrow.

HELMER: And I can't wait to see what you'll surprise me with.

NORA: Oh, that stupid business!

HELMER: What?

NORA: I can't find anything that's right. Everything seems so ridiculous, so inane.

HELMER: So my little Nora's come to *that* recognition?

NORA *(going behind his chair, her arms resting on its back)*:   Are you very busy, Torvald?

HELMER: Oh —

NORA: What papers are those?

HELMER: Bank matters.

NORA: Already?

HELMER: I've gotten full authority from the retiring management to make all necessary changes in personnel and procedure. I'll need Christmas week for that. I want to have everything in order by New Year's.

NORA: So that was the reason this poor Krogstad —

HELMER: Hm.

NORA *(still leaning on the chair and slowly stroking the nape of his neck)*:   If you weren't so very busy, I would have asked you an enormous favor, Torvald.

HELMER: Let's hear. What is it?

NORA: You know, there isn't anyone who has your good taste — and I want so much to look well at the costume party. Torvald, couldn't you take over and decide what I should be and plan my costume?

HELMER: Ah, is my stubborn little creature calling for a lifeguard?

NORA: Yes, Torvald, I can't get anywhere without your help.

HELMER: All right — I'll think it over. We'll hit on something.

NORA: Oh, how sweet of you. *(Goes to the tree again. Pause.)* Aren't the red flowers pretty — ? But tell me, was it really such a crime that this Krogstad committed?

HELMER: Forgery. Do you have any idea what that means?

NORA: Couldn't he have done it out of need?

HELMER: Yes, or thoughtlessness, like so many others. I'm not so heartless that I'd condemn a man categorically for just one mistake.

NORA: No, of course not, Torvald!

HELMER: Plenty of men have redeemed themselves by openly confessing their crimes and taking their punishment.

NORA: Punishment — ?

HELMER: But now Krogstad didn't go that way. He got himself out by sharp practices, and that's the real cause of his moral breakdown.

NORA: Do you really think that would — ?

HELMER: Just imagine how a man with that sort of guilt in him has to lie and cheat and deceive on all sides, has to wear a mask even with the nearest and dearest he has, even with his own wife and children. And with the children, Nora — that's where it's most horrible.

NORA: Why?

HELMER: Because that kind of atmosphere of lies infects the whole life of a home. Every breath the children take in is filled with the germs of something degenerate.

NORA *(coming closer behind him)*:   Are you sure of that?

HELMER: Oh, I've seen it often enough as a lawyer. Almost everyone who goes bad early in life has a mother who's a chronic liar.

NORA: Why just — the mother?

HELMER: It's usually the mother's influence that's dominant, but the father's works in the same way, of course. Every lawyer is quite familiar with it. And still this Krogstad's been going home year in, year out, poisoning his own children with lies and pretense; that's why I call him morally lost. *(Reaching his hands out toward her.)* So my sweet little Nora must promise me never to plead his cause. Your hand on it. Come, come, what's this? Give me your hand. There, now. All settled. I can tell you it'd be impossible for me to work alongside of him. I literally feel physically revolted when I'm anywhere near such a person.

NORA *(withdraws her hand and goes to the other side of the Christmas tree)*:   How hot it is here! And I've got so much to do.

HELMER *(getting up and gathering his papers)*:   Yes, and I have to think about getting some of these read through before dinner. I'll think about your costume, too. And something to hang on the tree in gilt paper, I may even see about that. *(Putting his hand on her head.)* Oh you, my darling little songbird. *(He goes into his study and closes the door after him.)*

NORA *(softly, after a silence)*:   Oh, really! It isn't so. It's impossible. It must be impossible.

ANNE-MARIE *(in the doorway, left)*:   The children are begging so hard to come in to Mama.

NORA: No, no, no, don't let them in to me! You stay with them, Anne-Marie.

ANNE-MARIE: Of course, ma'am. *(Closes the door.)*

NORA *(pale with terror)*:   Hurt my children — ! Poison my home? *(A moment's pause; then she tosses her head.)* That's not true. Never. Never in all the world.

Act 2

Same room. Beside the piano the Christmas tree now stands stripped of ornament, burned-down candle stubs on its ragged branches. Nora's street clothes lie on the sofa. Nora, alone in the room, moves restlessly about; at last she stops at the sofa and picks up her coat.

NORA *(dropping the coat again)*:   Someone's coming! *(Goes toward the door, listens.)* No — there's no one. Of course — nobody's coming today, Christmas Day — or tomorrow, either. But maybe — *(Opens the door and looks out.)* No, nothing in the mailbox. Quite empty. *(Coming forward.)* What nonsense! He won't do anything serious. Nothing terrible could happen. It's impossible. Why, I have three small children.

Anne-Marie, with a large carton, comes in from the room to the left.

ANNE-MARIE: Well, at last I found the box with the masquerade clothes.

NORA: Thanks. Put it on the table.

ANNE-MARIE *(does so)*:   But they're all pretty much of a mess.

NORA: Ahh! I'd love to rip them in a million pieces!

ANNE-MARIE: Oh, mercy, they can be fixed right up. Just a little patience.

NORA: Yes, I'll go get Mrs. Linde to help me.

ANNE-MARIE: Out again now? In this nasty weather? Miss Nora will catch cold — get sick.

NORA: Oh, worse things could happen. How are the children?

ANNE-MARIE: The poor mites are playing with their Christmas presents, but —

NORA: Do they ask for me much?

ANNE-MARIE: They're so used to having Mama around, you know.

NORA: Yes, but Anne-Marie, I *can't* be together with them as much as I was.

ANNE-MARIE: Well, small children get used to anything.

NORA: You think so? Do you think they'd forget their mother if she was gone for good?

ANNE-MARIE: Oh, mercy — gone for good!

NORA: Wait, tell me, Anne-Marie — I've wondered so often — how could you ever have the heart to give your child over to strangers?

ANNE-MARIE: But I had to, you know, to become little Nora's nurse.

NORA: Yes, but how could you *do* it?

ANNE-MARIE: When I could get such a good place? A girl who's poor and who's gotten in trouble is glad enough for that. Because that slippery fish, he didn't do a thing for me, you know.

NORA: But your daughter's surely forgotten you.

ANNE-MARIE: Oh, she certainly has not. She's written to me, both when she was confirmed and when she was married.

NORA *(clasping her about the neck)*:   You old Anne-Marie, you were a good mother for me when I was little.

ANNE-MARIE: Poor little Nora, with no other mother but me.

NORA: And if the babies didn't have one, then I know that you'd — What silly talk! *(Opening the carton.)* Go in to them. Now I'll have to — Tomorrow you can see how lovely I'll look.

ANNE-MARIE: Oh, there won't be anyone at the party as lovely as Miss Nora. *(She goes off into the room, left.)*

NORA *(begins unpacking the box, but soon throws it aside)*:   Oh, if I dared to go out. If only nobody would come. If only nothing would happen here while I'm out. What craziness — nobody's coming. Just don't think. This muff — needs a brushing. Beautiful gloves, beautiful gloves. Let it go. Let it go! One, two, three, four, five, six — *(With a cry.)* Oh, there they are! (Poises to move toward the door, but remains irresolutely standing. Mrs. Linde enters from the hall, where she has removed her street clothes.)

NORA: Oh, it's you, Kristine. There's no one else out there? How good that you've come.

MRS. LINDE: I hear you were up asking for me.

NORA: Yes, I just stopped by. There's something you really can help me with. Let's get settled on the sofa. Look, there's going to be a costume party tomorrow evening at the Stenborgs' right above us, and now Torvald wants me to go as a Neapolitan peasant girl and dance the tarantella that I learned in Capri.

MRS. LINDE: Really, are you giving a whole performance?

NORA: Torvald says yes, I should. See, here's the dress. Torvald had it made for me down there; but now it's all so tattered that I just don't know —

MRS. LINDE: Oh, we'll fix that up in no time. It's nothing more than the trimmings — they're a bit loose here and there. Needle and thread? Good, now we have what we need.

NORA: Oh, how sweet of you!

MRS. LINDE *(sewing)*:   So you'll be in disguise tomorrow, Nora. You know what? I'll stop by then for a moment and have a look at you all dressed up. But listen, I've absolutely forgotten to thank you for that pleasant evening yesterday.

NORA *(getting up and walking about)*:   I don't think it was as pleasant as usual yesterday. You should have come to town a bit sooner, Kristine — Yes, Torvald really knows how to give a home elegance and charm.

MRS. LINDE: And you do, too, if you ask me. You're not your father's daughter for nothing. But tell me, is Dr. Rank always so down in the mouth as yesterday?

NORA: No, that was quite an exception. But he goes around critically ill all the time — tuberculosis of the spine, poor man. You know, his father was a disgusting thing who kept mistresses and so on — and that's why the son's been sickly from birth.

MRS. LINDE *(lets her sewing fall to her lap)*:   But my dearest Nora, how do you know about such things?

NORA *(walking more jauntily)*:   Hmp! When you've had three children, then you've had a few visits from — from women who know something of medicine, and they tell you this and that.

MRS. LINDE *(resumes sewing; a short pause)*:   Does Dr. Rank come here every day?

NORA: Every blessed day. He's Torvald's best friend from childhood, and *my* good friend, too. Dr. Rank almost belongs to this house.

MRS. LINDE: But tell me — is he quite sincere? I mean, doesn't he rather enjoy flattering people?

NORA: Just the opposite. Why do you think that?

MRS. LINDE: When you introduced us yesterday, he was proclaiming that he'd often heard my name in this house; but later I noticed that your husband hadn't the slightest idea who I really was. So how could Dr. Rank — ?

NORA: But it's all true, Kristine. You see, Torvald loves me beyond words, and, as he puts it, he'd like to keep me all to himself. For a long time he'd almost be jealous if I even mentioned any of my old friends back home. So of course I dropped that. But with Dr. Rank I talk a lot about such things, because he likes hearing about them.

MRS. LINDE: Now listen, Nora; in many ways you're still like a child. I'm a good deal older than you, with a little more experience. I'll tell you something: you ought to put an end to all this with Dr. Rank.

NORA: What should I put an end to?

MRS. LINDE: Both parts of it, I think. Yesterday you said something about a rich admirer who'd provide you with money —

NORA: Yes, one who doesn't exist — worse luck. So?

MRS. LINDE: Is Dr. Rank well off?

NORA: Yes, he is.

MRS. LINDE: With no dependents?

NORA: No, no one. But —

MRS. LINDE: And he's over here every day?

NORA: Yes, I told you that.

MRS. LINDE: How can a man of such refinement be so grasping?

NORA: I don't follow you at all.

MRS. LINDE: Now don't try to hide it, Nora. You think I can't guess who loaned you the forty-eight hundred crowns?

NORA: Are you out of your mind? How could you think such a thing! A friend of ours, who comes here every single day. What an intolerable situation that would have been!

MRS. LINDE: Then it really wasn't him.

NORA: No, absolutely not. It never even crossed my mind for a moment — And he had nothing to lend in those days; his inheritance came later.

MRS. LINDE: Well, I think that was a stroke of luck for you, Nora dear.

NORA: No, it never would have occurred to me to ask Dr. Rank — Still, I'm quite sure that if I had asked him —

MRS. LINDE: Which you won't, of course.

NORA: No, of course not. I can't see that I'd ever need to. But I'm quite positive that if I talked to Dr. Rank —

MRS. LINDE: Behind your husband's back?

NORA: I've got to clear up this other thing; *that's* also behind his back. I've *got* to clear it all up.

MRS. LINDE: Yes, I was saying that yesterday, but —

NORA *(pacing up and down)*:   A man handles these problems so much better than a woman —

MRS. LINDE: One's husband does, yes.

NORA: Nonsense. *(Stopping.)* When you pay everything you owe, then you get your note back, right?

MRS. LINDE: Yes, naturally.

NORA: And can rip it into a million pieces and burn it up — that filthy scrap of paper!

MRS. LINDE *(looking hard at her, laying her sewing aside, and rising slowly)*:   Nora, you're hiding something from me.

NORA: You can see it in my face?

MRS. LINDE: Something's happened to you since yesterday morning. Nora, what is it?

NORA *(hurrying toward her)*:   Kristine! *(Listening.)* Shh! Torvald's home. Look, go in with the children a while. Torvald can't bear all this snipping and stitching. Let Anne-Marie help you.

MRS. LINDE *(gathering up some of the things)*:   All right, but I'm not leaving here until we've talked this out. *(She disappears into the room, left, as Torvald enters from the hall.)*

NORA: Oh, how I've been waiting for you, Torvald dear.

HELMER: Was that the dressmaker?

NORA: No, that was Kristine. She's helping me fix up my costume. You know, it's going to be quite attractive.

HELMER: Yes, wasn't that a bright idea I had?

NORA: Brilliant! But then wasn't I good as well to give in to you?

HELMER: Good — because you give in to your husband's judgment? All right, you little goose, I know you didn't mean it like that. But I won't disturb you. You'll want to have a fitting, I suppose.

NORA: And you'll be working?

HELMER: Yes. *(Indicating a bundle of papers.)* See. I've been down to the bank. *(Starts toward his study.)*

NORA: Torvald.

HELMER *(stops)*:   Yes.

NORA: If your little squirrel begged you, with all her heart and soul, for something — ?

HELMER: What's that?

NORA: Then would you do it?

HELMER: First, naturally, I'd have to know what it was.

NORA: Your squirrel would scamper about and do tricks, if you'd only be sweet and give in.

HELMER: Out with it.

NORA: Your lark would be singing high and low in every room —

HELMER: Come on, she does that anyway.

NORA: I'd be a wood nymph and dance for you in the moonlight.

HELMER: Nora — don't tell me it's that same business from this morning?

NORA *(coming closer)*:   Yes, Torvald, I beg you, please!

HELMER: And you actually have the nerve to drag that up again?

NORA: Yes, yes, you've got to give in to me; you *have* to let Krogstad keep his job in the bank.

HELMER: My dear Nora, I've slated his job for Mrs. Linde.

NORA: That's awfully kind of you. But you could just fire another clerk instead of Krogstad.

HELMER: This is the most incredible stubbornness! Because you go and give an impulsive promise to speak up for him, I'm expected to —

NORA: That's not the reason, Torvald. It's for your own sake. That man does writing for the worst papers; you said it yourself. He could do you any amount of harm. I'm scared to death of him —

HELMER: Ah, I understand. It's the old memories haunting you.

NORA: What do you mean by that?

HELMER: Of course, you're thinking about your father.

NORA: Yes, all right. Just remember how those nasty gossips wrote in the papers about Papa and slandered him so cruelly. I think they'd have had him dismissed if the department hadn't sent you up to investigate, and if you hadn't been so kind and open-minded toward him.

HELMER: My dear Nora, there's a notable difference between your father and me. Your father's official career was hardly above reproach. But mine is; and I hope it'll stay that way as long as I hold my position.

NORA: Oh, who can ever tell what vicious minds can invent? We could be so snug and happy now in our quiet, carefree home — you and I and the children, Torvald! That's why I'm pleading with you so —

HELMER: And just by pleading for him you make it impossible for me to keep him on. It's already known at the bank that I'm firing Krogstad. What if it's rumored around now that the new bank manager was vetoed by his wife —

NORA: Yes, what then — ?

HELMER: Oh yes — as long as our little bundle of stubbornness gets her way — ! I should go and make myself ridiculous in front of the whole office — give people the idea I can be swayed by all kinds of outside pressure. Oh, you can bet I'd feel the effects of that soon enough! Besides — there's something that rules Krogstad right out at the bank as long as I'm the manager.

NORA: What's that?

HELMER: His moral failings I could maybe overlook if I had to —

NORA: Yes, Torvald, why not?

HELMER: And I hear he's quite efficient on the job. But he was a crony of mine back in my teens — one of those rash friendships that crop up again and again to embarrass you later in life. Well, I might as well say it straight out: we're on a first-name basis. And that tactless fool makes no effort at all to hide it in front of others. Quite the contrary — he thinks that entitles him to take a familiar air around me, and so every other second he comes booming out with his "Yes, Torvald!" and "Sure thing, Torvald!" I tell you, it's been excruciating for me. He's out to make my place in the bank unbearable.

NORA: Torvald, you can't be serious about all this.

HELMER: Oh no? Why not?

NORA: Because these are such petty considerations.

HELMER: What are you saying? Petty? You think I'm petty!

NORA: No, just the opposite, Torvald dear. That's exactly why —

HELMER: Never mind. You call my motives petty; then I might as well be just that. Petty! All right! We'll put a stop to this for good. *(Goes to the hall door and calls.)* Helene!

NORA: What do you want?

HELMER *(searching among his papers)*:   A decision. *(The maid comes in.)* Look here; take this letter; go out with it at once. Get hold of a messenger and have him deliver it. Quick now. It's already addressed. Wait, here's some money.

MAID: Yes, sir. *(She leaves with the letter.)*

HELMER *(straightening his papers)*:   There, now, little Miss Willful.

NORA *(breathlessly)*:   Torvald, what was that letter?

HELMER: Krogstad's notice.

NORA: Call it back, Torvald! There's still time. Oh, Torvald, call it back! Do it for my sake — for your sake, for the children's sake! Do you hear, Torvald; do it! You don't know how this can harm us.

HELMER: Too late.

NORA: Yes, too late.

HELMER: Nora dear, I can forgive you this panic, even though basically you're insulting me. Yes, you are! Or isn't it an insult to think that *I* should be afraid of a courtroom hack's revenge? But I forgive you anyway, because this shows so beautifully how much you love me. *(Takes her in his arms.)* This is the way it should be, my darling Nora. Whatever comes, you'll see; when it really counts, I have strength and courage enough as a man to take on the whole weight myself.

NORA *(terrified)*:   What do you mean by that?

HELMER: The whole weight, I said.

NORA *(resolutely)*:   No, never in all the world.

HELMER: Good. So we'll share it, Nora, as man and wife. That's as it should be. *(Fondling her.)* Are you happy now? There, there, there — not these frightened dove's eyes. It's nothing at all but empty fantasies — Now you should run through your tarantella and practice your tambourine. I'll go to the inner office and shut both doors, so I won't hear a thing; you can make all the noise you like. *(Turning in the doorway.)* And when Rank comes, just tell him where he can find me. *(He nods to her and goes with his papers into the study, closing the door.)*

NORA *(standing as though rooted, dazed with fright, in a whisper)*:   He really could do it. He will do it. He'll do it in spite of everything. No, not that, never, never! Anything but that! Escape! A way out — *(The doorbell rings.)* Dr. Rank! Anything but that! *Anything,* whatever it is! *(Her hands pass over her face, smoothing it; she pulls herself together, goes over and opens the hall door. Dr. Rank stands outside, hanging his fur coat up. During the following scene, it begins getting dark.)*

NORA: Hello, Dr. Rank. I recognized your ring. But you mustn't go in to Torvald yet; I believe he's working.

RANK: And you?

NORA: For you, I always have an hour to spare — you know that. *(He has entered, and she shuts the door after him.)*

RANK: Many thanks. I'll make use of these hours while I can.

NORA: What do you mean by that? While you can?

RANK: Does that disturb you?

NORA: Well, it's such an odd phrase. Is anything going to happen?

RANK: What's going to happen is what I've been expecting so long — but I honestly didn't think it would come so soon.

NORA *(gripping his arm)*:   What is it you've found out? Dr. Rank, you have to tell me!

RANK *(sitting by the stove)*:   It's all over for me. There's nothing to be done about it.

NORA *(breathing easier)*:   Is it you — then — ?

RANK: Who else? There's no point in lying to one's self. I'm the most miserable of all my patients, Mrs. Helmer. These past few days I've been auditing my internal accounts. Bankrupt! Within a month I'll probably be laid out and rotting in the churchyard.

NORA: Oh, what a horrible thing to say.

RANK: The thing itself is horrible. But the worst of it is all the other horror before it's over. There's only one final examination left; when I'm finished with that, I'll know about when my disintegration will begin. There's something I want to say. Helmer with his sensitivity has such a sharp distaste for anything ugly. I don't want him near my sickroom.

NORA: Oh, but Dr. Rank —

RANK: I won't have him in there. Under no condition. I'll lock my door to him — As soon as I'm completely sure of the worst, I'll send you my calling card marked with a black cross, and you'll know then the wreck has started to come apart.

NORA: No, today you're completely unreasonable. And I wanted you so much to be in a really good humor.

RANK: With death up my sleeve? And then to suffer this way for somebody else's sins. Is there any justice in that? And in every single family, in some way or another, this inevitable retribution of nature goes on —

NORA (her hands pressed over her ears):   Oh, stuff! Cheer up! Please — be gay!

RANK: Yes, I'd just as soon laugh at it all. My poor, innocent spine, serving time for my father's gay army days.

NORA (by the table, left):   He was so infatuated with asparagus tips and pâté de foie gras, wasn't that it?

RANK: Yes — and with truffles.

NORA: Truffles, yes. And then with oysters, I suppose?

RANK: Yes, tons of oysters, naturally.

NORA: And then the port and champagne to go with it. It's so sad that all these delectable things have to strike at our bones.

RANK: Especially when they strike at the unhappy bones that never shared in the fun.

NORA: Ah, that's the saddest of all.

RANK (looks searchingly at her):   Hm.

NORA (after a moment):   Why did you smile?

RANK: No, it was you who laughed.

NORA: No, it was you who smiled, Dr. Rank!

RANK (getting up):   You're even a bigger tease than I'd thought.

NORA: I'm full of wild ideas today.

RANK: That's obvious.

NORA (putting both hands on his shoulders):   Dear, dear Dr. Rank, you'll never die for Torvald and me.

RANK: Oh, that loss you'll easily get over. Those who go away are soon forgotten.

NORA (looks fearfully at him):   You believe that?

RANK: One makes new connections, and then —

NORA: Who makes new connections?

RANK: Both you and Torvald will when I'm gone. I'd say you're well under way already. What was that Mrs. Linde doing here last evening?

NORA: Oh, come — you can't be jealous of poor Kristine?

RANK: Oh yes, I am. She'll be my successor here in the house. When I'm down under, that woman will probably —

NORA: Shh! Not so loud. She's right in there.

RANK: Today as well. So you see.

NORA: Only to sew on my dress. Good gracious, how unreasonable you are. *(Sitting on the sofa.)* Be nice now, Dr. Rank. Tomorrow you'll see how beautifully I'll dance; and you can imagine then that I'm dancing only for you — yes, and of course for Torvald, too — that's understood. *(Takes various items out of the carton.)* Dr. Rank, sit over here and I'll show you something.

RANK *(sitting)*:   What's that?

NORA: Look here. Look.

RANK: Silk Stockings.

NORA: Flesh-colored. Aren't they lovely? Now it's so dark here, but tomorrow — No, no, no, just look at the feet. Oh well, you might as well look at the rest.

RANK: Hm —

NORA: Why do you look so critical? Don't you believe they'll fit?

RANK: I've never had any chance to form an opinion on that.

NORA *(glancing at him a moment)*:   Shame on you. *(Hits him lightly on the ear with the stockings.)* That's for you. *(Puts them away again.)*

RANK: And what other splendors am I going to see now?

NORA: Not the least bit more, because you've been naughty. *(She hums a little and rummages among her things.)*

RANK *(after a short silence)*:   When I sit here together with you like this, completely easy and open, then I don't know — I simply can't imagine — whatever would have become of me if I'd never come into this house.

NORA *(smiling)*:   Yes, I really think you feel completely at ease with us.

RANK *(more quietly, staring straight ahead)*:   And then to have to go away from it all —

NORA: Nonsense, you're not going away.

RANK *(his voice unchanged)*:   — and not even be able to leave some poor show of gratitude behind, scarcely a fleeting regret — no more than a vacant place that anyone can fill.

NORA: And if I asked you now for — ? No —

RANK: For what?

NORA: For a great proof of your friendship —

RANK: Yes, yes?

NORA: No, I mean — for an exceptionally big favor —

RANK: Would you really, for once, make me so happy?

NORA: Oh, you haven't the vaguest idea what it is.

RANK: All right, then tell me.

NORA: No, but I can't, Dr. Rank — it's all out of reason. It's advice and help, too — and a favor —

RANK: So much the better. I can't fathom what you're hinting at. Just speak out. Don't you trust me?

NORA: Of course. More than anyone else. You're my best and truest friend, I'm
sure. That's why I want to talk to you. All right, then, Dr. Rank: there's
something you can help me prevent. You know how deeply, how inexpress-
ibly dearly Torvald loves me; he'd never hesitate a second to give up his life
for me.

RANK *(leaning close to her)*:   Nora — do you think he's the only one —

NORA *(with a slight start)*:   Who — ?

RANK: Who'd gladly give up his life for you.

NORA *(heavily)*:   I see.

RANK: I swore to myself you should know this before I'm gone. I'll never find a
better chance. Yes, Nora, now you know. And also you know now that you
can trust me beyond anyone else.

NORA *(rising, natural and calm)*:   Let me by.

RANK *(making room for her, but still sitting)*:   Nora —

NORA *(in the hall doorway)*:   Helene, bring the lamp in. *(Goes over to the stove.)*
Ah, dear Dr. Rank, that was really mean of you.

RANK *(getting up)*:   That I've loved you just as deeply as somebody else? Was
that mean?

NORA: No, but that you came out and told me. That was quite unnecessary —

RANK: What do you mean? Have you known — ?

The Maid comes in with the lamp, sets it on the table, and goes out again.

RANK: Nora — Mrs. Helmer — I'm asking you: have you known about it?

NORA: Oh, how can I tell what I know or don't know? Really, I don't know
what to say — Why did you have to be so clumsy, Dr. Rank! Everything was
so good.

RANK: Well, in any case, you now have the knowledge that my body and soul
are at your command. So won't you speak out?

NORA *(looking at him)*:   After that?

RANK: Please, just let me know what it is.

NORA: You can't know anything now.

RANK: I have to. You mustn't punish me like this. Give me the chance to do
whatever is humanly possible for you.

NORA: Now there's nothing you can do for me. Besides, actually, I don't need
any help. You'll see — it's only my fantasies. That's what it is. Of course!
(Sits in the rocker, looks at him, and smiles.) What a nice one you are, Dr.
Rank. Aren't you a little bit ashamed, now that the lamp is here?

RANK: No, not exactly. But perhaps I'd better go — for good?

NORA: No, you certainly can't do that. You must come here just as you always
have. You know Torvald can't do without you.

RANK: Yes, but *you?*

NORA: You know how much I enjoy it when you're here.

RANK: That's precisely what threw me off. You're a mystery to me. So many
times I've felt you'd almost rather be with me than with Helmer.

NORA: Yes — you see, there are some people that one loves most and other
people that one would almost prefer being with.

RANK: Yes, there's something to that.

NORA: When I was back home, of course I loved Papa most. But I always thought it was so much fun when I could sneak down to the maids' quarters, because they never tried to improve me, and it was always so amusing, the way they talked to each other.

RANK: Aha, so it's *their* place that I've filled.

NORA *(jumping up and going to him)*:   Oh, dear, sweet Dr. Rank, that's not what I meant at all. But you can understand that with Torvald it's just the same as with Papa—

The Maid enters from the hall.

MAID: Ma'am—please! *(She whispers to Nora and hands her a calling card.)*

NORA *(glancing at the card)*:   Ah! *(Slips it into her pocket.)*

RANK: Anything wrong?

NORA: No, no, not at all. It's only some—it's my new dress—

RANK: Really? But—there's your dress.

NORA: Oh, that. But this is another one—I ordered it—Torvald mustn't know—

RANK: Ah, now we have the big secret.

NORA: That's right. Just go in with him—he's back in the inner study. Keep him there as long as—

RANK: Don't worry. He won't get away. *(Goes into the study.)*

NORA *(to the Maid)*:   And he's standing waiting in the kitchen?

MAID: Yes, he came up by the back stairs.

NORA: But didn't you tell him somebody was here?

MAID: Yes, but that didn't do any good.

NORA: He won't leave?

MAID: No, he won't go till he's talked with you, ma'am.

NORA: Let him come in, then—but quietly. Helene, don't breathe a word about this. It's a surprise for my husband.

MAID: Yes, yes, I understand— *(Goes out.)*

NORA: This horror—it's going to happen. No, no, no, it can't happen, it mustn't. *(She goes and bolts Helmer's door. The Maid opens the hall door for Krogstad and shuts it behind him. He is dressed for travel in a fur coat, boots, and a fur cap.)*

NORA *(going toward him)*:   Talk softly. My husband's home.

KROGSTAD: Well, good for him.

NORA: What do you want?

KROGSTAD: Some information.

NORA: Hurry up, then. What is it?

KROGSTAD: You know, of course, that I got my notice.

NORA: I couldn't prevent it, Mr. Krogstad. I fought for you to the bitter end, but nothing worked.

KROGSTAD: Does your husband's love for you run so thin? He knows everything I can expose you to, and all the same he dares to—

NORA: How can you imagine he knows anything about this?

KROGSTAD: Ah, no — I can't imagine it either, now. It's not at all like my fine Torvald Helmer to have so much guts —

NORA: Mr. Krogstad, I demand respect for my husband!

KROGSTAD: Why, of course — all due respect. But since the lady's keeping it so carefully hidden, may I presume to ask if you're also a bit better informed than yesterday about what you've actually done?

NORA: More than you could ever teach me.

KROGSTAD: Yes, I *am* such an awful lawyer.

NORA: What is it you want from me?

KROGSTAD: Just a glimpse of how you are, Mrs. Helmer. I've been thinking about you all day long. A cashier, a night-court scribbler, a — well, a type like me also has a little of what they call a heart, you know.

NORA: Then show it. Think of my children.

KROGSTAD: Did you or your husband ever think of mine? But never mind. I simply wanted to tell you that you don't need to take this thing too seriously. For the present, I'm not proceeding with any action.

NORA: Oh no, really! Well — I knew that.

KROGSTAD: Everything can be settled in a friendly spirit. It doesn't have to get around town at all; it can stay just among us three.

NORA: My husband must never know anything of this.

KROGSTAD: How can you manage that? Perhaps you can pay me the balance?

NORA: No, not right now.

KROGSTAD: Or you know some way of raising the money in a day or two?

NORA: No way that I'm willing to use.

KROGSTAD: Well, it wouldn't have done you any good, anyway. If you stood in front of me with a fistful of bills, you still couldn't buy your signature back.

NORA: Then tell me what you're going to do with it.

KROGSTAD: I'll just hold onto it — keep it on file. There's no outsider who'll even get wind of it. So if you've been thinking of taking some desperate step —

NORA: I have.

KROGSTAD: Been thinking of running away from home —

NORA: I have!

KROGSTAD: Or even of something worse —

NORA: How could you guess that?

KROGSTAD: You can drop those thoughts.

NORA: How could you guess I was thinking of *that*?

KROGSTAD: Most of us think about *that* at first. I thought about it too, but I discovered I hadn't the courage —

NORA *(lifelessly)*:   I don't either.

KROGSTAD *(relieved)*:   That's true, you haven't the courage? You too?

NORA: I don't have it — I don't have it.

KROGSTAD: It would be terribly stupid, anyway. After that first storm at home blows out, why, then — I have here in my pocket a letter for your husband —

NORA: Telling everything?

KROGSTAD: As charitably as possible.

NORA *(quickly)*:   He mustn't ever get that letter. Tear it up. I'll find some way to get money.

KROGSTAD: Beg pardon, Mrs. Helmer, but I think I just told you —

NORA: Oh, I don't mean the money I owe you. Let me know how much you want from my husband, and I'll manage it.

KROGSTAD: I don't want money from your husband.

NORA: What do you want, then?

KROGSTAD: I'll tell you what. I want to recoup, Mrs. Helmer; I want to get on in the world — and there's where your husband can help me. For a year and a half I've kept myself clean of anything disreputable — all that time struggling with the worst conditions; but I was satisfied, working my way up step by step. Now I've been written right off, and I'm just not in the mood to come crawling back. I tell you, I want to move on. I want to get back in the bank — in a better position. Your husband can set up a job for me —

NORA: He'll never do that!

KROGSTAD: He'll do it. I know him. He won't dare breathe a word of protest. And once I'm in there together with him, you just wait and see! Inside of a year, I'll be the manager's right-hand man. It'll be Nils Krogstad, not Torvald Helmer, who runs the bank.

NORA: You'll never see the day!

KROGSTAD: Maybe you think you can —

NORA: I have the courage now — for *that.*

KROGSTAD: Oh, you don't scare me. A smart, spoiled lady like you —

NORA: You'll see; you'll see!

KROGSTAD: Under the ice, maybe? Down in the freezing coal-black water? There, till you float up in the spring, ugly, unrecognizable, with your hair falling out —

NORA: You don't frighten me.

KROGSTAD: Nor do you frighten me. One doesn't do these things, Mrs. Helmer. Besides, what good would it be? I'd still have him safe in my pocket.

NORA: Afterwards? When I'm no longer — ?

KROGSTAD: Are you forgetting that *I'll* be in control then over your final reputation? *(Nora stands speechless, staring at him.)* Good; now I've warned you. Don't do anything stupid. When Helmer's read my letter, I'll be waiting for his reply. And bear in mind that it's your husband himself who's forced me back to my old ways. I'll never forgive him for that. Good-bye, Mrs. Helmer. *(He goes out through the hall.)*

NORA *(goes to the hall door, opens it a crack, and listens)*:   He's gone. Didn't leave the letter. Oh no, no, that's impossible too! *(Opening the door more and more.)* What's that? He's standing outside — not going downstairs. He's thinking it over? Maybe he'll — ? *(A letter falls in the mailbox; then Krogstad's footsteps are heard, dying away down a flight of stairs. Nora gives a muffled cry and runs over toward the sofa table. A short pause.)* In the mailbox. *(Slips warily over to the hall door.)* It's lying there. Torvald, Torvald — now we're lost!

MRS. LINDE *(entering with costume from the room, left)*:   There now, I can't see anything else to mend. Perhaps you'd like to try —

NORA *(in a hoarse whisper)*:   Kristine, come here.

MRS. LINDE *(tossing the dress on the sofa)*:   What's wrong? You look upset.

NORA: Come here. See that letter? *There!* Look — through the glass in the mailbox.

MRS. LINDE: Yes, yes, I see it.

NORA: That letter's from Krogstad —

MRS. LINDE: Nora — it's Krogstad who loaned you the money!

NORA: Yes, and now Torvald will find out everything.

MRS. LINDE: Believe me, Nora, it's best for both of you.

NORA: There's more you don't know. I forged a name.

MRS. LINDE: But for heaven's sake — ?

NORA: I only want to tell you that, Kristine, so that you can be my witness.

MRS. LINDE: Witness? Why should I — ?

NORA: If I should go out of my mind — it could easily happen —

MRS. LINDE: Nora!

NORA: Or anything else occurred — so I couldn't be present here —

MRS. LINDE: Nora, Nora, you aren't yourself at all!

NORA: And someone should try to take on the whole weight, all of the guilt, you follow me —

MRS. LINDE: Yes, of course, but why do you think — ?

NORA: Then you're the witness that it isn't true, Kristine. I'm very much myself; my mind right now is perfectly clear; and I'm telling you: nobody else has known about this; I alone did everything. Remember that.

MRS. LINDE: I will. But I don't understand all this.

NORA: Oh, how could you ever understand it? It's the miracle now that's going to take place.

MRS. LINDE: The miracle?

NORA: Yes, the miracle. But it's so awful, Kristine. It mustn't take place, not for anything in the world.

MRS. LINDE: I'm going right over and talk with Krogstad.

NORA: Don't go near him; he'll do you some terrible harm!

MRS. LINDE: There was a time once when he'd gladly have done anything for me.

NORA: He?

MRS. LINDE: Where does he live?

NORA: Oh, how do I know? Yes. *(Searches in her pocket.)* Here's his card. But the letter, the letter — !

HELMER *(from the study, knocking on the door)*:   Nora!

NORA *(with a cry of fear)*:   Oh! What is it? What do you want?

HELMER: Now, now, don't be so frightened. We're not coming in. You locked the door — are you trying on the dress?

NORA: Yes, I'm trying it. I'll look just beautiful, Torvald.

MRS. LINDE *(who has read the card)*:   He's living right around the corner.

NORA: Yes, but what's the use? We're lost. The letter's in the box.

MRS. LINDE: And your husband has the key?

NORA: Yes, always.

MRS. LINDE: Krogstad can ask for his letter back unread; he can find some excuse —

NORA: But it's just this time that Torvald usually —

MRS. LINDE: Stall him. Keep him in there. I'll be back as quick as I can. *(She hurries out through the hall entrance.)*

NORA *(goes to Helmer's door, opens it, and peers in)*:   Torvald!

HELMER *(from the inner study)*:   Well — does one dare set foot in one's own living room at last? Come on, Rank, now we'll get a look — *(In the doorway.)* But what's this?

NORA: What, Torvald dear?

HELMER: Rank had me expecting some grand masquerade.

RANK *(in the doorway)*:   That was my impression, but I must have been wrong.

NORA: No one can admire me in my splendor — not till tomorrow.

HELMER: But Nora dear, you look so exhausted. Have you practiced too hard?

NORA: No, I haven't practiced at all yet.

HELMER: You know, it's necessary —

NORA: Oh, it's absolutely necessary, Torvald. But I can't get anywhere without your help. I've forgotten the whole thing completely.

HELMER: Ah, we'll soon take care of that.

NORA: Yes, take care of me, Torvald, please! Promise me that? Oh, I'm so nervous. That big party — You must give up everything this evening for me. No business — don't even touch your pen. Yes? Dear Torvald, promise?

HELMER: It's a promise. Tonight I'm totally at your service — you little helpless thing. Hm — but first there's one thing I want to — *(Goes toward the hall door.)*

NORA: What are you looking for?

HELMER: Just to see if there's any mail.

NORA: No, no, don't do that, Torvald!

HELMER: Now what?

NORA: Torvald, please. There isn't any.

HELMER: Let me look, though. *(Starts out. Nora, at the piano, strikes the first notes of the tarantella. Helmer, at the door, stops.)* Aha!

NORA: I can't dance tomorrow if I don't practice with you.

HELMER *(going over to her)*:   Nora dear, are you really so frightened?

NORA: Yes, so terribly frightened. Let me practice right now; there's still time before dinner. Oh, sit down and play for me, Torvald. Direct me. Teach me, the way you always have.

HELMER: Gladly, if it's what you want. *(Sits at the piano.)*

NORA *(snatches the tambourine up from the box, then a long, varicolored shawl, which she throws around herself, whereupon she springs forward and cries out)*:   Play for me now! Now I'll dance!

Helmer plays and Nora dances. Rank stands behind Helmer at the piano and looks on.

HELMER *(as he plays)*:   Slower. Slow down.

NORA: Can't change it.

HELMER: Not so violent, Nora!

NORA: Has to be just like this.

HELMER *(stopping)*:   No, no, that won't do at all.

NORA *(laughing and swinging her tambourine)*:   Isn't that what I told you?

RANK: Let me play for her.

HELMER *(getting up)*:   Yes, go on. I can teach her more easily then.

Rank sits at the piano and plays; Nora dances more and more wildly. Helmer has stationed himself by the stove and repeatedly gives her directions; she seems not to hear them; her hair loosens and falls over her shoulders; she does not notice, but goes on dancing. Mrs. Linde enters.

MRS. LINDE *(standing dumbfounded at the door)*:   Ah—!

NORA *(still dancing)*:   See what fun, Kristine!

HELMER: But Nora darling, you dance as if your life were at stake.

NORA: And it is.

HELMER: Rank, stop! This is pure madness. Stop it, I say!

Rank breaks off playing, and Nora halts abruptly.

HELMER *(going over to her)*:   I never would have believed it. You've forgotten everything I taught you.

NORA *(throwing away the tambourine)*:   You see for yourself.

HELMER: Well, there's certainly room for instruction here.

NORA: Yes, you see how important it is. You've got to teach me to the very last minute. Promise me that, Torvald?

HELMER: You can bet on it.

NORA: You mustn't, either today or tomorrow, think about anything else but me; you mustn't open any letters—or the mailbox—

HELMER: Ah, it's still the fear of that man—

NORA: Oh yes, yes, that too.

HELMER: Nora, it's written all over you—there's already a letter from him out there.

NORA: I don't know. I guess so. But you mustn't read such things now; there mustn't be anything ugly between us before it's all over.

RANK *(quietly to Helmer)*:   You shouldn't deny her.

HELMER *(putting his arms around her)*:   The child can have her way. But tomorrow night, after you've danced—

NORA: Then you'll be free.

MAID *(in the doorway, right)*:   Ma'am, dinner is served.

NORA: We'll be wanting champagne, Helene.

MAID: Very good, ma'am. *(Goes out.)*

HELMER: So—a regular banquet, hm?

NORA: Yes, a banquet—champagne till daybreak! *(Calling out.)* And some macaroons, Helene. Heaps of them—just this once.

HELMER *(taking her hands)*:   Now, now, now—no hysterics. Be my own little lark again.

NORA: Oh, I will soon enough. But go on in — and you, Dr. Rank. Kristine, help me put up my hair.

RANK *(whispering, as they go)*:   There's nothing wrong — really wrong, is there?

HELMER: Oh, of course not. It's nothing more than this childish anxiety I was telling you about. *(They go out, right.)*

NORA: Well?

MRS. LINDE: Left town.

NORA: I could see by your face.

MRS. LINDE: He'll be home tomorrow evening. I wrote him a note.

NORA: You shouldn't have. Don't try to stop anything now. After all, it's a wonderful joy, this waiting here for the miracle.

MRS. LINDE: What is it you're waiting for?

NORA: Oh, you can't understand that. Go in to them; I'll be along in a moment.

Mrs. Linde goes into the dining room. Nora stands a short while as if composing herself; then she looks at her watch.

NORA: Five. Seven hours to midnight. Twenty-four hours to the midnight after, and then the tarantella's done. Seven and twenty-four? Thirty-one hours to live.

HELMER *(in the doorway, right)*:   What's become of the little lark?

NORA *(going toward him with open arms)*:   Here's your lark!

Act 3

Same scene. The table, with chairs around it, has been moved to the center of the room. A lamp on the table is lit. The hall door stands open. Dance music drifts down from the floor above. Mrs. Linde sits at the table, absently paging through a book, trying to read, but apparently unable to focus her thoughts. Once or twice she pauses, tensely listening for a sound at the outer entrance.

MRS. LINDE *(glancing at her watch)*:   Not yet — and there's hardly any time left. If only he's not — *(Listening again.)* Ah, there he is. *(She goes out in the hall and cautiously opens the outer door. Quiet footsteps are heard on the stairs. She whispers:)* Come in. Nobody's here.

KROGSTAD *(in the doorway)*:   I found a note from you at home. What's back of all this?

MRS. LINDE: I just *had* to talk to you.

KROGSTAD: Oh? And it just *had* to be here in this house?

MRS. LINDE: At my place it was impossible; my room hasn't a private entrance. Come in; we're all alone. The maid's asleep, and the Helmers are at the dance upstairs.

KROGSTAD *(entering the room)*:   Well, well, the Helmers are dancing tonight? Really?

MRS. LINDE: Yes, why not?

KROGSTAD: How true — why not?

MRS. LINDE: All right, Krogstad, let's talk.

KROGSTAD: Do we two have anything more to talk about?

MRS. LINDE: We have a great deal to talk about.

KROGSTAD: I wouldn't have thought so.

MRS. LINDE: No, because you've never understood me, really.

KROGSTAD: Was there anything more to understand — except what's all too common in life? A calculating woman throws over a man the moment a better catch comes by.

MRS. LINDE: You think I'm so thoroughly calculating? You think I broke it off lightly?

KROGSTAD: Didn't you?

MRS. LINDE: Nils — is that what you really thought?

KROGSTAD: If you cared, then why did you write me the way you did?

MRS. LINDE: What else could I do? If I had to break off with you, then it was my job as well to root out everything you felt for me.

KROGSTAD *(wringing his hands)*:   So that was it. And this — all this, simply for money!

MRS. LINDE: Don't forget I had a helpless mother and two small brothers. We couldn't wait for you, Nils; you had such a long road ahead of you then.

KROGSTAD: That may be; but you still hadn't the right to abandon me for somebody else's sake.

MRS. LINDE: Yes — I don't know. So many, many times I've asked myself if I did have that right.

KROGSTAD *(more softly)*:   When I lost you, it was as if all the solid ground dissolved from under my feet. Look at me; I'm a half-drowned man now, hanging onto a wreck.

MRS. LINDE: Help may be near.

KROGSTAD: It was near — but then you came and blocked it off.

MRS. LINDE: Without my knowing it, Nils. Today for the first time I learned that it's you I'm replacing at the bank.

KROGSTAD: All right — I believe you. But now that you know, will you step aside?

MRS. LINDE: No, because that wouldn't benefit you in the slightest.

KROGSTAD: Not "benefit" me, hm! I'd step aside anyway.

MRS. LINDE: I've learned to be realistic. Life and hard, bitter necessity have taught me that.

KROGSTAD: And life's taught me never to trust fine phrases.

MRS. LINDE: Then life's taught you a very sound thing. But you do have to trust in actions, don't you?

KROGSTAD: What does that mean?

MRS. LINDE: You said you were hanging on like a half-drowned man to a wreck.

KROGSTAD: I've good reason to say that.

MRS. LINDE: I'm also like a half-drowned woman on a wreck. No one to suffer with; no one to care for.

KROGSTAD: You made your choice.

MRS. LINDE: There wasn't any choice then.

KROGSTAD: So — what of it?

MRS. LINDE: Nils, if only we two shipwrecked people could reach across to each other.

KROGSTAD: What are you saying?

MRS. LINDE: Two on one wreck are at least better off than each on his own.

KROGSTAD: Kristine!

MRS. LINDE: Why do you think I came into town?

KROGSTAD: Did you really have some thought of me?

MRS. LINDE: I have to work to go on living. All my born days, as long as I can remember, I've worked, and it's been my best and my only joy. But now I'm completely alone in the world; it frightens me to be so empty and lost. To work for yourself — there's no joy in that. Nils, give me something — someone to work for.

KROGSTAD: I don't believe all this. It's just some hysterical feminine urge to go out and make a noble sacrifice.

MRS. LINDE: Have you ever found me to be hysterical?

KROGSTAD: Can you honestly mean this? Tell me — do you know everything about my past?

MRS. LINDE: Yes.

KROGSTAD: And you know what they think I'm worth around here.

MRS. LINDE: From what you were saying before, it would seem that with me you could have been another person.

KROGSTAD: I'm positive of that.

MRS. LINDE: Couldn't it happen still?

KROGSTAD: Kristine — you're saying this in all seriousness? Yes, you are! I can see it in you. And do you really have the courage, then — ?

MRS. LINDE: I need to have someone to care for; and your children need a mother. We both need each other. Nils, I have faith that you're good at heart — I'll risk everything together with you.

KROGSTAD *(gripping her hands)*:   Kristine, thank you, thank you — Now I know I can win back a place in their eyes. Yes — but I forgot —

MRS. LINDE *(listening)*:   Shh! The tarantella. Go now! Go on!

KROGSTAD: Why? What is it?

MRS. LINDE: Hear the dance up there? When that's over, they'll be coming down.

KROGSTAD: Oh, then I'll go. But — it's all pointless. Of course, you don't know the move I made against the Helmers.

MRS. LINDE: Yes, Nils, I know.

KROGSTAD: And all the same, you have the courage to — ?

MRS. LINDE: I know how far despair can drive a man like you.

KROGSTAD: Oh, if I only could take it all back.

MRS. LINDE: You easily could — your letter's still lying in the mailbox.

KROGSTAD: Are you sure of that?

MRS. LINDE: Positive. But —

KROGSTAD *(looks at her searchingly)*:   Is that the meaning of it, then? You'll save your friend at any price. Tell me straight out. Is that it?

MRS. LINDE: Nils—anyone who's sold herself for somebody else once isn't going to do it again.

KROGSTAD: I'll demand my letter back.

MRS. LINDE: No, no.

KROGSTAD: Yes, of course. I'll stay here till Helmer comes down; I'll tell him to give me my letter again—that it only involves my dismissal—that he shouldn't read it—

MRS. LINDE: No, Nils, don't call the letter back.

KROGSTAD: But wasn't that exactly why you wrote me to come here?

MRS. LINDE: Yes, in that first panic. But it's been a whole day and night since then, and in that time I've seen such incredible things in this house. Helmer's got to learn everything; this dreadful secret has to be aired; those two have to come to a full understanding; all these lies and evasions can't go on.

KROGSTAD: Well, then, if you want to chance it. But at least there's one thing I can do, and do right away—

MRS. LINDE *(listening)*:   Go now, go quick! The dance is over. We're not safe another second.

KROGSTAD: I'll wait for you downstairs.

MRS. LINDE: Yes, please do; take me home.

KROGSTAD: I can't believe it; I've never been so happy. *(He leaves by way of the outer door; the door between the room and the hall stays open.)*

MRS. LINDE *(straightening up a bit and getting together her street clothes)*:   How different now! How different! Someone to work for, to live for—a home to build. Well, it is worth the try! Oh, if they'd only come! *(Listening.)* Ah, there they are. Bundle up. *(She picks up her hat and coat. Nora's and Helmer's voices can be heard outside; a key turns in the lock, and Helmer brings Nora into the hall almost by force. She is wearing the Italian costume with a large black shawl about her; he has on evening dress, with a black domino open over it.)*

NORA *(struggling in the doorway)*:   No, no, no, not inside! I'm going up again. I don't want to leave so soon.

HELMER: But Nora dear—

NORA: Oh, I beg you, please, Torvald. From the bottom of my heart, *please*—only an hour more!

HELMER: Not a single minute, Nora darling. You know our agreement. Come on, in we go; you'll catch cold out here. *(In spite of her resistance, he gently draws her into the room.)*

MRS. LINDE: Good evening.

NORA: Kristine!

HELMER: Why, Mrs. Linde—are you here so late?

MRS. LINDE: Yes, I'm sorry, but I did want to see Nora in costume.

NORA: Have you been sitting here, waiting for me?

MRS. LINDE: Yes. I didn't come early enough; you were all upstairs; and then I thought I really couldn't leave without seeing you.

HELMER *(removing Nora's shawl)*:   Yes, take a good look. She's worth looking at, I can tell you that, Mrs. Linde. Isn't she lovely?

MRS. LINDE: Yes, I should say —

HELMER: A dream of loveliness, isn't she? That's what everyone thought at the party, too. But she's horribly stubborn — this sweet little thing. What's to be done with her? Can you imagine, I almost had to use force to pry her away.

NORA: Oh, Torvald, you're going to regret you didn't indulge me, even for just a half hour more.

HELMER: There, you see. She danced her tarantella and got a tumultuous hand — which was well earned, although the performance may have been a bit too naturalistic — I mean it rather overstepped the proprieties of art. But never mind — what's important is, she made a success, an overwhelming success. You think I could let her stay on after that and spoil the effect? Oh no; I took my lovely little Capri girl — my capricious little Capri girl, I should say — took her under my arm; one quick tour of the ballroom, a curtsy to every side, and then — as they say in novels — the beautiful vision disappeared. An exit should always be effective, Mrs. Linde, but that's what I can't get Nora to grasp. Phew, it's hot in here. *(Flings the domino on a chair and opens the door to his room.)* Why's it dark in here? Oh yes, of course. Excuse me. *(He goes in and lights a couple of candles.)*

NORA *(in a sharp, breathless whisper)*:   So?

MRS. LINDE *(quietly)*:   I talked with him.

NORA: And — ?

MRS. LINDE: Nora — you must tell your husband everything.

NORA *(dully)*:   I knew it.

MRS. LINDE: You've got nothing to fear from Krogstad, but you have to speak out.

NORA: I won't tell.

MRS. LINDE: Then the letter will.

NORA: Thanks, Kristine. I know now what's to be done. Shh!

HELMER *(reentering)*:   Well, then, Mrs. Linde — have you admired her?

MRS. LINDE: Yes, and now I'll say good night.

HELMER: Oh, come, so soon? Is this yours, this knitting?

MRS. LINDE: Yes, thanks. I nearly forgot it.

HELMER: Do you knit, then?

MRS. LINDE: Oh yes.

HELMER: You know what? You should embroider instead.

MRS. LINDE: Really? Why?

HELMER: Yes, because it's a lot prettier. See here, one holds the embroidery so, in the left hand, and then one guides the needle with the right — so — in an easy, sweeping curve — right?

MRS. LINDE: Yes, I guess that's —

HELMER: But, on the other hand, knitting — it can never be anything but ugly. Look, see here, the arms tucked in, the knitting needles going up and down — there's something Chinese about it. Ah, that was really a glorious champagne they served.

MRS. LINDE: Yes, good night, Nora, and don't be stubborn anymore.

HELMER: Well put, Mrs. Linde!

MRS. LINDE: Good night, Mr. Helmer.

HELMER *(accompanying her to the door)*:   Good night, good night. I hope you get home all right. I'd be very happy to — but you don't have far to go. Good night, good night. *(She leaves. He shuts the door after her and returns.)* There, now, at last we got her out the door. She's a deadly bore, that creature.

NORA: Aren't you pretty tired, Torvald?

HELMER: No, not a bit.

NORA: You're not sleepy?

HELMER: Not at all. On the contrary, I'm feeling quite exhilarated. But you? Yes, you really look tired and sleepy.

NORA: Yes, I'm very tired. Soon now I'll sleep.

HELMER: See! You see! I was right all along that we shouldn't stay longer.

NORA: Whatever you do is always right.

HELMER *(kissing her brow)*:   Now my little lark talks sense. Say, did you notice what a time Rank was having tonight?

NORA: Oh, was he? I didn't get to speak with him.

HELMER: I scarcely did either, but it's a long time since I've seen him in such high spirits. *(Gazes at her a moment, then comes nearer her.)* Hm — it's marvelous, though, to be back home again — to be completely alone with you. Oh, you bewitchingly lovely young woman!

NORA: Torvald, don't look at me like that!

HELMER: Can't I look at my richest treasure? At all that beauty that's mine, mine alone — completely and utterly.

NORA *(moving around to the other side of the table)*:   You mustn't talk to me that way tonight.

HELMER *(following her)*:   The tarantella is still in your blood, I can see — and it makes you even more enticing. Listen. The guests are beginning to go. *(Dropping his voice.)* Nora — it'll soon be quiet through this whole house.

NORA: Yes, I hope so.

HELMER: You do, don't you, my love? Do you realize — when I'm out at a party like this with you — do you know why I talk to you so little, and keep such a distance away; just send you a stolen look now and then — you know why I do it? It's because I'm imagining then that you're my secret darling, my secret bride-to-be, and that no one suspects there's anything between us.

NORA: Yes, yes; oh, yes, I know you're always thinking of me.

HELMER: And then when we leave and I place the shawl over those fine young rounded shoulders — over that wonderful curving neck — then I pretend that you're my young bride, that we're just coming from the wedding, that for the first time I'm bringing you into my house — that for the first time I'm alone with you — completely alone with you, your trembling young beauty! All this evening I've longed for nothing but you. When I saw you turn and sway in the tarantella — my blood was pounding till I couldn't stand it — that's why I brought you down here so early —

NORA: Go away, Torvald! Leave me alone. I don't want all this.

HELMER: What do you mean? Nora, you're teasing me. You will, won't you? Aren't I your husband — ?

A knock at the outside door.

NORA *(startled)*:   What's that?

HELMER *(going toward the hall)*:   Who is it?

RANK *(outside)*:   It's me. May I come in a moment?

HELMER *(with quiet irritation)*:   Oh, what does he want now? *(Aloud.)* Hold on. *(Goes and opens the door.)* Oh, how nice that you didn't just pass us by!

RANK: I thought I heard your voice, and then I wanted so badly to have a look in. *(Lightly glancing about.)* Ah, me, these old familiar haunts. You have it snug and cozy in here, you two.

HELMER: You seemed to be having it pretty cozy upstairs, too.

RANK: Absolutely. Why shouldn't I? Why not take in everything in life? As much as you can, anyway, and as long as you can. The wine was superb —

HELMER: The champagne especially.

RANK: You noticed that too? It's amazing how much I could guzzle down.

NORA: Torvald also drank a lot of champagne this evening.

RANK: Oh?

NORA: Yes, and that always makes him so entertaining.

RANK: Well, why shouldn't one have a pleasant evening after a well-spent day?

HELMER: Well spent? I'm afraid I can't claim that.

RANK *(slapping him on the back)*:   But I can, you see!

NORA: Dr. Rank, you must have done some scientific research today.

RANK: Quite so.

HELMER: Come now — little Nora talking about scientific research!

NORA: And can I congratulate you on the results?

RANK: Indeed you may.

NORA: Then they were good?

RANK: The best possible for both doctor and patient — certainty.

NORA *(quickly and searchingly)*:   Certainty?

RANK: Complete certainty. So don't I owe myself a gay evening afterwards?

NORA: Yes, you're right, Dr. Rank.

HELMER: I'm with you — just so long as you don't have to suffer for it in the morning.

RANK: Well, one never gets something for nothing in life.

NORA: Dr. Rank — are you very fond of masquerade parties?

RANK: Yes, if there's a good array of odd disguises —

NORA: Tell me, what should we two go as at the next masquerade?

HELMER: You little featherhead — already thinking of the next!

RANK: We two? I'll tell you what: you must go as Charmed Life —

HELMER: Yes, but find a costume for *that!*

RANK: Your wife can appear just as she looks every day.

HELMER: That was nicely put. But don't you know what you're going to be?

RANK: Yes, Helmer, I've made up my mind.

HELMER: Well?

RANK: At the next masquerade I'm going to be invisible.

HELMER: That's a funny idea.

RANK: They say there's a hat—black, huge—have you never heard of the hat that makes you invisible? You put it on, and then no one on earth can see you.

HELMER *(suppressing a smile):*   Ah, of course.

RANK: But I'm quite forgetting what I came for. Helmer, give me a cigar, one of the dark Havanas.

HELMER: With the greatest pleasure. *(Holds out his case.)*

RANK: Thanks. *(Takes one and cuts off the tip.)*

NORA *(striking a match):*   Let me give you a light.

RANK: Thank you. *(She holds the match for him; he lights the cigar.)* And now good-bye.

HELMER: Good-bye, good-bye, old friend.

NORA: Sleep well, Doctor.

RANK: Thanks for that wish.

NORA: Wish me the same.

RANK: You? All right, if you like—Sleep well. And thanks for the light. *(He nods to them both and leaves.)*

HELMER *(his voice subdued):*   He's been drinking heavily.

NORA *(absently):*   Could be. *(Helmer takes his keys from his pocket and goes out in the hall.)* Torvald—what are you after?

HELMER: Got to empty the mailbox; it's nearly full. There won't be room for the morning papers.

NORA: Are you working tonight?

HELMER: You know I'm not. Why—what's this? Someone's been at the lock.

NORA: At the lock—?

HELMER: Yes, I'm positive. What do you suppose—? I can't imagine one of the maids—? Here's a broken hairpin. Nora, it's yours—

NORA *(quickly):*   Then it must be the children—

HELMER: You'd better break them of that. Hm, hm—well, opened it after all. *(Takes the contents out and calls into the kitchen.)* Helene! Helene, would you put out the lamp in the hall. *(He returns to the room shutting the hall door, then displays the handful of mail.)* Look how it's piled up. *(Sorting through them.)* Now what's this?

NORA *(at the window):*   The letter! Oh, Torvald, no!

HELMER: Two calling cards—from Rank.

NORA: From Dr. Rank?

HELMER *(examining them):*   "Dr. Rank, Consulting Physician." They were on top. He must have dropped them in as he left.

NORA: Is there anything on them?

HELMER: There's a black cross over the name. See? That's a gruesome notion. He could almost be announcing his own death.

NORA: That's just what he's doing.

HELMER: What! You've heard something? Something he's told you?

NORA: Yes. That when those cards came, he'd be taking his leave of us. He'll shut himself in now and die.

HELMER: Ah, my poor friend! Of course I knew he wouldn't be here much longer. But so soon — And then to hide himself away like a wounded animal.

NORA: If it has to happen, then it's best it happens in silence — don't you think so, Torvald?

HELMER *(pacing up and down)*:   He'd grown right into our lives. I simply can't imagine him gone. He with his suffering and loneliness — like a dark cloud setting off our sunlit happiness. Well, maybe it's best this way. For him, at least. *(Standing still.)* And maybe for us too, Nora. Now we're thrown back on each other, completely. *(Embracing her.)* Oh you, my darling wife, how can I hold you close enough? You know what, Nora — time and again I've wished you were in some terrible danger, just so I could stake my life and soul and everything, for your sake.

NORA *(tearing herself away, her voice firm and decisive)*:   Now you must read your mail, Torvald.

HELMER: No, no, not tonight. I want to stay with you, dearest.

NORA: With a dying friend on your mind?

HELMER: You're right. We've both had a shock. There's ugliness between us — these thoughts of death and corruption. We'll have to get free of them first. Until then — we'll stay apart.

NORA *(clinging about his neck)*:   Torvald — good night! Good night!

HELMER *(kissing her on the cheek)*:   Good night, little songbird. Sleep well, Nora. I'll be reading my mail now. *(He takes the letters into his room and shuts the door after him.)*

NORA *(with bewildered glances, groping about, seizing Helmer's domino, throwing it around her, and speaking in short, hoarse, broken whispers)*:   Never see him again. Never, never. *(Putting her shawl over her head.)* Never see the children either — them, too. Never, never. Oh, the freezing black water! The depths — down — Oh, I wish it were over — He has it now; he's reading it — now. Oh no, no, not yet. Torvald, good-bye, you and the children — *(She starts for the hall; as she does, Helmer throws open his door and stands with an open letter in his hand.)*

HELMER: Nora!

NORA *(screams)*:   Oh — !

HELMER: What is this? You know what's in this letter?

NORA: Yes, I know. Let me go! Let me out!

HELMER *(holding her back)*:   Where are you going?

NORA *(struggling to break loose)*:   You can't save me, Torvald!

HELMER *(slumping back)*:   True! Then it's true what he writes? How horrible! No, no, it's impossible — it can't be true.

NORA: It *is* true. I've loved you more than all this world.

HELMER: Ah, none of your slippery tricks.

NORA *(taking one step toward him)*:   Torvald — !

HELMER: What *is* this you've blundered into!

NORA:　Just let me loose. You're not going to suffer for my sake. You're not going to take on my guilt.

HELMER:　No more play-acting. *(Locks the hall door.)* You stay right here and give me a reckoning. You understand what you've done? Answer! You understand?

NORA *(looking squarely at him, her face hardening)*:　Yes. I'm beginning to understand everything now.

HELMER *(striding about)*:　Oh, what an awful awakening! In all these eight years—she who was my pride and joy—a hypocrite, a liar—worse, worse—a criminal! How infinitely disgusting it all is! The shame! *(Nora says nothing and goes on looking straight at him. He stops in front of her.)* I should have suspected something of the kind. I should have known. All your father's flimsy values—Be still! All your father's flimsy values have come out in you. No religion, no morals, no sense of duty—Oh, how I'm punished for letting him off! I did it for your sake, and you repay me like this.

NORA:　Yes, like this.

HELMER:　Now you've wrecked all my happiness—ruined my whole future. Oh, it's awful to think of. I'm in a cheap little grafter's hands; he can do anything he wants with me, ask for anything, play with me like a puppet—and I can't breathe a word. I'll be swept down miserably into the depths on account of a featherbrained woman.

NORA:　When I'm gone from this world, you'll be free.

HELMER:　Oh, quit posing. Your father had a mess of those speeches too. What good would that ever do me if you were gone from this world, as you say? Not the slightest. He can still make the whole thing known; and if he does, I could be falsely suspected as your accomplice. They might even think that I was behind it—that I put you up to it. And all that I can thank you for—you that I've coddled the whole of our marriage. Can you see now what you've done to me?

NORA *(icily calm)*:　Yes.

HELMER:　It's so incredible, I just can't grasp it. But we'll have to patch up whatever we can. Take off the shawl. I said, take if off! I've got to appease him somehow or other. The thing has to be hushed up at any cost. And as for you and me, it's got to seem like everything between us is just as it was—to the outside world, that is. You'll go right on living in this house, of course. But you can't be allowed to bring up the children; I don't dare trust you with them—Oh, to have to say this to someone I've loved so much! Well, that's done with. From now on happiness doesn't matter; all that matters is saving the bits and pieces, the appearance— *(The doorbell rings. Helmer starts.)* What's that? And so late. Maybe the worst—? You think he'd—? Hide, Nora! Say you're sick. *(Nora remains standing motionless. Helmer goes and opens the door.)*

MAID *(half dressed, in the hall)*:　A letter for Mrs. Helmer.

HELMER:　I'll take it. *(Snatches the letter and shuts the door.)* Yes, it's from him. You don't get it; I'm reading it myself.

NORA: Then read it.

HELMER *(by the lamp)*:   I hardly dare. We may be ruined, you and I. But—I've got to know. *(Rips open the letter, skims through a few lines, glances at an enclosure, then cries out joyfully.)* Nora! *(Nora looks inquiringly at him.)* Nora! Wait—better check it again—Yes, yes, it's true. I'm saved. Nora, I'm saved!

NORA: And I?

HELMER: You too, of course. We're both saved, both of us. Look. He's sent back your note. He says he's sorry and ashamed—that a happy development in his life—oh, who cares what he says! Nora, we're saved! No one can hurt you. Oh, Nora, Nora—but first, this ugliness all has to go. Let me see— *(Takes a look at the note.)* No, I don't want to see it; I want the whole thing to fade like a dream. *(Tears the note and both letters to pieces, throws them into the stove, and watches them burn.)* There—now there's nothing left—He wrote that since Christmas Eve you—Oh, they must have been three terrible days for you, Nora.

NORA: I fought a hard fight.

HELMER: And suffered pain and saw no escape but—No, we're not going to dwell on anything unpleasant. We'll just be grateful and keep on repeating: it's over now, it's over! You hear me, Nora? You don't seem to realize—it's over. What's it mean—that frozen look? Oh, poor little Nora, I understand. You can't believe I've forgiven you. But I have, Nora; I swear I have. I know that what you did, you did out of love for me.

NORA: That's true.

HELMER: You loved me the way a wife ought to love her husband. It's simply the means that you couldn't judge. But you think I love you any the less for not knowing how to handle your affairs? No, no—just lean on me; I'll guide you and teach you. I wouldn't be a man if this feminine helplessness didn't make you twice as attractive to me. You mustn't mind those sharp words I said—that was all in the first confusion of thinking my world had collapsed. I've forgiven you, Nora; I swear I've forgiven you.

NORA: My thanks for your forgiveness. *(She goes out through the door, right.)*

HELMER: No, wait— *(Peers in.)* What are you doing in there?

NORA *(inside)*:   Getting out of my costume.

HELMER *(by the open door)*:   Yes, do that. Try to calm yourself and collect your thoughts again, my frightened little songbird. You can rest easy now; I've got wide wings to shelter you with. *(Walking about close by the door.)* How snug and nice our home is, Nora. You're safe here; I'll keep you like a hunted dove I've rescued out of a hawk's claws. I'll bring peace to your poor, shuddering heart. Gradually it'll happen, Nora; you'll see. Tomorrow all this will look different to you; then everything will be as it was. I won't have to go on repeating I forgive you; you'll feel it for yourself. How can you imagine I'd ever conceivably want to disown you—or even blame you in any way? Ah, you don't know a man's heart, Nora. For a man there's something indescribably sweet and satisfying in knowing he's forgiven his wife—and forgiven her out of a full and open heart. It's as if she belongs to him in two ways now: in a sense he's given her fresh into the world again, and she's become his wife and his child as well. From now on that's what you'll be to me — you little, bewildered, helpless thing. Don't be afraid of anything, Nora; just open your heart to me, and I'll be conscience and will to you both — *(Nora enters in her regular clothes.)* What's this? Not in bed? You've changed your dress?

NORA: Yes, Torvald, I've changed my dress.

HELMER: But why now, so late?

NORA: Tonight I'm not sleeping.

HELMER: But Nora dear —

NORA *(looking at her watch)*:   It's still not so very late. Sit down, Torvald; we have a lot to talk over. *(She sits at one side of the table.)*

HELMER: Nora — what is this? That hard expression —

NORA: Sit down. This'll take some time. I have a lot to say.

HELMER *(sitting at the table directly opposite her)*:   You worry me, Nora. And I don't understand you.

NORA: No, that's exactly it. You don't understand me. And I've never understood you either — until tonight. No, don't interrupt. You can just listen to what I say. We're closing out accounts, Torvald.

HELMER: How do you mean that?

NORA *(after a short pause)*:   Doesn't anything strike you about our sitting here like this?

HELMER: What's that?

NORA: We've been married now eight years. Doesn't it occur to you that this is the first time we two, you and I, man and wife, have ever talked seriously together?

HELMER: What do you mean — seriously?

NORA: In eight whole years — longer even — right from our first acquaintance, we've never exchanged a serious word on any serious thing.

HELMER: You mean I should constantly go and involve you in problems you couldn't possibly help me with?

NORA: I'm not talking of problems. I'm saying that we've never sat down seriously together and tried to get to the bottom of anything.

HELMER: But dearest, what good would that ever do you?

NORA: That's the point right there: you've never understood me. I've been wronged greatly, Torvald — first by Papa, and then by you.

HELMER: What! By us — the two people who've loved you more than anyone else?

NORA *(shaking her head)*:   You never loved me. You've thought it fun to be in love with me, that's all.

HELMER: Nora, what a thing to say!

NORA: Yes, it's true now, Torvald. When I lived at home with Papa, he told me all his opinions, so I had the same ones too; or if they were different I hid them, since he wouldn't have cared for that. He used to call me his doll-child, and he played with me the way I played with my dolls. Then I came into your house —

HELMER: How can you speak of our marriage like that?

NORA *(unperturbed)*:   I mean, then I went from Papa's hands into yours. You arranged everything to your own taste, and so I got the same taste as you — or I pretended to; I can't remember. I guess a little of both, first one, then the other. Now when I look back, it seems as if I'd lived here like a beggar — just from hand to mouth. I've lived by doing tricks for you, Torvald. But that's the way you wanted it. It's a great sin what you and Papa did to me. You're to blame that nothing's become of me.

HELMER: Nora, how unfair and ungrateful you are! Haven't you been happy here?

NORA: No, never. I thought so — but I never have.

HELMER: Not — not happy!

NORA: No, only lighthearted. And you've always been so kind to me. But our home's been nothing but a playpen. I've been your doll-wife here, just as at home I was Papa's doll-child. And in turn the children have been my dolls. I thought it was fun when you played with me, just as they thought it fun when I played with them. That's been our marriage, Torvald.

HELMER: There's some truth in what you're saying — under all the raving exaggeration. But it'll all be different after this. Playtime's over; now for the schooling.

NORA: Whose schooling — mine or the children's?

HELMER: Both yours and the children's, dearest.

NORA: Oh, Torvald, you're not the man to teach me to be a good wife to you.

HELMER: And you can say that?

NORA: And I — how am I equipped to bring up children?

HELMER: Nora!

NORA: Didn't you say a moment ago that that was no job to trust me with?

HELMER: In a flare of temper! Why fasten on that?

NORA: Yes, but you were so very right. I'm not up to the job. There's another job I have to do first. I have to try to educate myself. You can't help me with that. I've got to do it alone. And that's why I'm leaving you now.

HELMER *(jumping up)*:   What's that?

NORA: I have to stand completely alone, if I'm ever going to discover myself and the world out there. So I can't go on living with you.

HELMER: Nora, Nora!

NORA: I want to leave right away. Kristine should put me up for the night —

HELMER: You're insane! You've no right! I forbid you!

NORA: From here on, there's no use forbidding me anything. I'll take with me whatever is mine. I don't want a thing from you, either now or later.

HELMER: What kind of madness is this!

NORA: Tomorrow I'm going home — I mean, home where I came from. It'll be easier up there to find something to do.

HELMER: Oh, you blind, incompetent child!

NORA: I must learn to be competent, Torvald.

HELMER: Abandon your home, your husband, your children! And you're not even thinking what people will say.

NORA: I can't be concerned about that. I only know how essential this is.

HELMER: Oh, it's outrageous. So you'll run out like this on your most sacred vows.

NORA: What do you think are my most sacred vows?

HELMER: And I have to tell you that! Aren't they your duties to your husband and children?

NORA: I have other duties equally sacred.

HELMER: That isn't true. What duties are they?

NORA: Duties to myself.

HELMER: Before all else, you're a wife and mother.

NORA: I don't believe in that anymore. I believe that, before all else, I'm a human being, no less than you — or anyway, I ought to try to become one. I know the majority thinks you're right, Torvald, and plenty of books agree with you, too. But I can't go on believing what the majority says, or what's written in books. I have to think over these things myself and try to understand them.

HELMER: Why can't you understand your place in your own home? On a point like that, isn't there one everlasting guide you can turn to? Where's your religion?

NORA: Oh, Torvald, I'm really not sure what religion is.

HELMER: What — ?

NORA: I only know what the minister said when I was confirmed. He told me religion was this thing and that. When I get clear and away by myself, I'll go into that problem too. I'll see if what the minister said was right, or, in any case, if it's right for me.

HELMER: A young woman your age shouldn't talk like that. If religion can't move you, I can try to rouse your conscience. You do have some moral feeling? Or, tell me — has that gone too?

NORA: It's not easy to answer that, Torvald. I simply don't know. I'm all confused about these things. I just know I see them so differently from you. I find out, for one thing, that the law's not at all what I'd thought — but I can't get it through my head that the law is fair. A woman hasn't a right to protect her dying father or save her husband's life! I can't believe that.

HELMER: You talk like a child. You don't know anything of the world you live in.

NORA: No, I don't. But now I'll begin to learn for myself. I'll try to discover who's right, the world or I.

HELMER: Nora, you're sick; you've got a fever. I almost think you're out of your head.

NORA: I've never felt more clearheaded and sure in my life.

HELMER: And — clearheaded and sure — you're leaving your husband and children?

NORA: Yes.

HELMER: Then there's only one possible reason.

NORA: What?

HELMER: You no longer love me.

NORA: No. That's exactly it.

HELMER: Nora! You can't be serious!

NORA: Oh, this is so hard, Torvald — you've been so kind to me always. But I can't help it. I don't love you anymore.

HELMER *(struggling for composure)*:   Are you also clearheaded and sure about that?

NORA: Yes, completely. That's why I can't go on staying here.

HELMER: Can you tell me what I did to lose your love?

NORA: Yes, I can tell you. It was this evening when the miraculous thing didn't come — then I knew you weren't the man I'd imagined.

HELMER: Be more explicit; I don't follow you.

NORA: I've waited now so patiently eight long years — for, my Lord, I know miracles don't come every day. Then this crisis broke over me, and such a certainty filled me: *now* the miraculous event would occur. While Krogstad's letter was lying out there, I never for an instant dreamed that you could give in to his terms. I was so utterly sure you'd say to him: go on, tell your tale to the whole wide world. And when he'd done that —

HELMER: Yes, what then? When I'd delivered my own wife into shame and disgrace —

NORA: When he'd done that, I was so utterly sure that you'd step forward, take the blame on yourself and say: I am the guilty one.

HELMER: Nora — !

NORA: You're thinking I'd never accept such a sacrifice from you? No, of course not. But what good would my protests be against you? That was the miracle I was waiting for, in terror and hope. And to stave that off, I would have taken my life.

HELMER: I'd gladly work for you day and night, Nora — and take on pain and deprivation. But there's no one who gives up honor for love.

NORA: Millions of women have done just that.

HELMER: Oh, you think and talk like a silly child.

NORA: Perhaps. But you neither think nor talk like the man I could join myself to. When your big fright was over — and it wasn't from any threat against me, only for what might damage you — when all the danger was past, for you it was just as if nothing had happened. I was exactly the same, your little lark, your doll, that you'd have to handle with double care now that I'd turned out so brittle and frail. *(Gets up.)* Torvald — in that instant it dawned on me that for eight years I've been living here with a stranger, and that I've even conceived three children — oh, I can't stand the thought of it! I could tear myself to bits.

HELMER *(heavily)*:   I see. There a gulf that's opened between us — that's clear. Oh, but Nora, can't we bridge it somehow?

NORA: The way I am now, I'm no wife for you.

HELMER: I have the strength to make myself over.

NORA: Maybe — if your doll gets taken away.

HELMER: But to part! To part from you! No, Nora no — I can't imagine it.

NORA *(going out, right)*:   All the more reason why it has to be. *(She reenters with her coat and a small overnight bag, which she puts on a chair by the table.)*

HELMER: Nora, Nora, not now! Wait till tomorrow.

NORA: I can't spend the night in a strange man's room.

HELMER: But couldn't we live here like brother and sister —

NORA: You know very well how long that would last. *(Throws her shawl about her.)* Good-bye, Torvald. I won't look in on the children. I know they're in better hands than mine. The way I am now, I'm no use to them.

HELMER: But someday, Nora — someday — ?

NORA: How can I tell? I haven't the least idea what'll become of me.

HELMER: But you're my wife, now and wherever you go.

NORA: Listen, Torvald — I've heard that when a wife deserts her husband's house just as I'm doing, then the law frees him from all responsibility. In any case, I'm freeing you from being responsible. Don't feel yourself bound, any more than I will. There has to be absolute freedom for us both. Here, take your ring back. Give me mine.

HELMER: That too?

NORA: That too.

HELMER: There it is.

NORA: Good. Well, now it's all over. I'm putting the keys here. The maids know all about keeping up the house — better than I do. Tomorrow, after I've left town, Kristine will stop by to pack up everything that's mine from home. I'd like those things shipped up to me.

HELMER: Over! All over! Nora, won't you ever think about me?

NORA: I'm sure I'll think of you often, and about the children and the house here.

HELMER: May I write you?

NORA: No — never. You're not to do that.

HELMER: Oh, but let me send you —

NORA: Nothing. Nothing.

HELMER: Or help you if you need it.

NORA: No. I accept nothing from strangers.

HELMER: Nora — can I never be more than a stranger to you?

NORA *(picking up her overnight bag)*: Ah, Torvald — it would take the greatest miracle of all —

HELMER: Tell me the greatest miracle!

NORA: You and I both would have to transform ourselves to the point that — Oh, Torvald, I've stopped believing in miracles.

HELMER: But I'll believe. Tell me! Transform ourselves to the point that — ?

NORA: That our living together could be a true marriage. *(She goes out down the hall.)*

HELMER *(sinks down on a chair by the door, face buried in his hands)*: Nora! Nora! *(Looking about and rising.)* Empty. She's gone. *(A sudden hope leaps in him.)* The greatest miracle — ?

From below, the sound of a door slamming shut. [1879]

▤ THINKING ABOUT THE TEXT

1. Critics disagree about the necessity for Nora's leaving. What would your advice to her be? One critic thinks she has to leave because Torvald is impossible. What do you think?

2. Do you find credible the change in Nora's character from the first scene to the last? Do you know people who have transformed themselves?

3. Is Torvald in love with Nora in the first act? Explain. Is Nora in love with him in the first act? What is your idea of love in a marriage?

4. An early critic of the play claims that it is a comedy. Is this possible? How would you characterize it? Is it an optimistic or a pessimistic play? Is it tragic?

5. A few critics think Nora will return. Do you think this is possible? Under what conditions would you counsel her to do so? Do you think the "door heard 'round the world" had a positive or a negative effect on marriage?

SUSAN GLASPELL
Trifles

Susan Glaspell (1876–1948) is best known for the frequently anthologized play Trifles *and its short-story version, "A Jury of Her Peers." Surprisingly modern, Glaspell's work is in harmony with contemporary feminist concerns of identity, the difficulty of female expression in a patriarchal culture, the disillusionment of marriage for gifted women, and the necessity for female support and understanding.*

Glaspell graduated from Drake University in 1899 and first worked as a journalist in Des Moines, Iowa. She soon began to publish short stories in prestigious magazines like Harper's *and* The American. *After she married novelist and playwright George Cram Cook, they moved to Greenwich Village, where they felt more comfortable with its freethinking attitudes. Glaspell continued to publish both stories and novels. She also began writing plays, and in 1916 she and her husband founded the Provincetown Players, an important source for innovative American drama. During the 1920s and 1930s, Glaspell published a number of best-selling novels, including* Brook Evans *(1928), which was turned into a successful movie. Her play* Alison's House *won the Pulitzer Prize in 1931, and her novel* The Morning Is Near *(1939) sold more than one hundred thousand copies. Today her significant successes in two genres, drama and fiction, are considered remarkable.*

CHARACTERS

GEORGE HENDERSON, *county attorney*
HENRY PETERS, *sheriff*
LEWIS HALE, *a neighboring farmer*
MRS. PETERS
MRS. HALE

SCENE: *The kitchen in the now-abandoned farmhouse of John Wright, a gloomy kitchen, and left without having been put in order— the walls covered with a faded wallpaper. Down right is a door leading to the parlor. On the right wall above this door is a built-in kitchen cupboard with shelves in the upper portion and drawers below. In the rear wall at right, up two steps is a door opening onto stairs leading to the second floor. In the rear wall at left is a door to the shed and from there to the outside. Between these two doors is an old-fashioned black iron stove. Running along the left wall from the shed door is an old iron sink and sink shelf, in which is set a hand pump. Downstage of the sink is an uncurtained window. Near the window is an old wooden rocker. Center stage is an unpainted wooden kitchen table with straight chairs on either side. There is a small chair down right. Unwashed pans under the sink, a loaf of bread outside the breadbox, a dish towel on the table— other signs of incompleted work. At the rear the shed door opens and the Sheriff comes in followed by the County Attorney and Hale. The Sheriff and Hale are men in middle life, the County Attorney is a young man; all are much bundled up and go at once to the stove. They are followed by the two women— the Sheriff's wife, Mrs. Peters, first; she is a slight wiry woman, a thin nervous face. Mrs. Hale is larger and would ordinarily be called more comfortable looking, but she is disturbed now and looks fearfully about as she enters. The women have come in slowly, and stand close together near the door.*

COUNTY ATTORNEY *(at stove rubbing his hands)*:   This feels good. Come up to the fire, ladies.

MRS. PETERS *(after taking a step forward)*:   I'm not—cold.

SHERIFF *(unbuttoning his overcoat and stepping away from the stove to right of table as if to mark the beginning of official business)*:   Now, Mr. Hale, before we move things about, you explain to Mr. Henderson just what you saw when you came here yesterday morning.

COUNTY ATTORNEY *(crossing down to left of the table)*:   By the way, has anything been moved? Are things just as you left them yesterday?

SHERIFF *(looking about)*:   It's just about the same. When it dropped below zero last night I thought I'd better send Frank out this morning to make a fire for us— *(sits right of center table)* no use getting pneumonia with a big case on, but I told him not to touch anything except the stove— and you know Frank.

COUNTY ATTORNEY: Somebody should have been left here yesterday.

SHERIFF: Oh— yesterday. When I had to send Frank to Morris Center for that man who went crazy— I want you to know I had my hands full yesterday.

I knew you could get back from Omaha by today and as long as I went over everything here myself ——

COUNTY ATTORNEY: Well, Mr. Hale, tell just what happened when you came here yesterday morning.

HALE *(crossing down to above table)*:   Harry and I had started to town with a load of potatoes. We came along the road from my place and as I got here I said, "I'm going to see if I can't get John Wright to go in with me on a party telephone." I spoke to Wright about it once before and he put me off, saying folks talked too much anyway, and all he asked was peace and quiet—I guess you know about how much he talked himself; but I thought maybe if I went to the house and talked about it before his wife, though I said to Harry that I didn't know as what his wife wanted made much difference to John ——

COUNTY ATTORNEY: Let's talk about that later, Mr. Hale. I do want to talk about that, but tell now just what happened when you got to the house.

HALE: I didn't hear or see anything; I knocked at the door, and still it was all quiet inside. I knew they must be up, it was past eight o'clock. So I knocked again, and I thought I heard somebody say, "Come in." I wasn't sure, I'm not sure yet, but I opened the door—this door *(indicating the door by which the two women are still standing)* and there in that rocker— *(pointing to it)* sat Mrs. Wright. *(They all look at the rocker down left.)*

COUNTY ATTORNEY: What—was she doing?

HALE: She was rockin' back and forth. She had her apron in her hand and was kind of—pleating it.

COUNTY ATTORNEY: And how did she—look?

HALE: Well, she looked queer.

COUNTY ATTORNEY: How do you mean—queer?

HALE: Well, as if she didn't know what she was going to do next. And kind of done up.

COUNTY ATTORNEY *(takes out notebook and pencil and sits left of center table)*:   How did she seem to feel about your coming?

HALE: Why, I don't think she minded—one way or other. She didn't pay much attention. I said, "How do, Mrs. Wright, it's cold, ain't it?" And she said, "Is it?"—and went on kind of pleating at her apron. Well, I was surprised; she didn't ask me to come up to the stove, or to set down, but just sat there, not even looking at me, so I said, "I want to see John." And then she—laughed. I guess you would call it a laugh. I thought of Harry and the team outside, so I said a little sharp: "Can't I see John?" "No," she says, kind o' dull like. "Ain't he home?" says I. "Yes," says she, "he's home." "Then why can't I see him?" I asked her, out of patience. " 'Cause he's dead," says she. *"Dead?"* says I. She just nodded her head, not getting a bit excited, but rockin' back and forth. "Why—where is he?" says I, not knowing what to say. She just pointed upstairs—like that. *(Himself pointing to the room above.)* I started for the stairs, with the idea of going up there. I walked from there to here—then I says, "Why, what did he die of?" "He died of a rope round his neck," says she, and just went on pleatin' at her apron. Well, I went out and called Harry. I thought I might — need help. We went upstairs and there he was lyin' ——

COUNTY ATTORNEY: I think I'd rather have you go into that upstairs, where you can point it all out. Just go on now with the rest of the story.

HALE: Well, my first thought was to get that rope off. It looked . . . *(stops; his face twitches)* . . . but Harry, he went up to him, and he said, "No, he's dead all right, and we'd better not touch anything." So we went back downstairs. She was still sitting that same way. "Has anybody been notified?" I asked. "No," says she, unconcerned. "Who did this, Mrs. Wright?" said Harry. He said it businesslike — and she stopped pleatin' of her apron. "I don't know," she says. "You don't *know?*" says Harry. "No," says she. "Weren't you sleepin' in the bed with him?" says Harry. "Yes," says she, "but I was on the inside." "Somebody slipped a rope round his neck and strangled him and you didn't wake up?" says Harry. "I didn't wake up," she said after him. We must 'a' looked as if we didn't see how that could be, for after a minute she said, "I sleep sound." Harry was going to ask her more questions but I said maybe we ought to let her tell her story first to the coroner, or the sheriff, so Harry went fast as he could to Rivers's place, where there's a telephone.

COUNTY ATTORNEY: And what did Mrs. Wright do when she knew that you had gone for the coroner?

HALE: She moved from the rocker to that chair over there *(pointing to a small chair in the down right corner)* and just sat there with her hands held together and looking down. I got a feeling that I ought to make some conversation, so I said I had come in to see if John wanted to put in a telephone, and at that she started to laugh, and then she stopped and looked at me — scared. *(The County Attorney, who has had his notebook out, makes a note.)* I dunno, maybe it wasn't scared. I wouldn't like to say it was. Soon Harry got back, and then Dr. Lloyd came and you, Mr. Peters, and so I guess that's all I know that you don't.

COUNTY ATTORNEY *(rising and looking around)*:   I guess we'll go upstairs first — and then out to the barn and around there. *(To the Sheriff.)* You're convinced that there was nothing important here — nothing that would point to any motive?

SHERIFF: Nothing here but kitchen things. *(The County Attorney, after again looking around the kitchen, opens the door of a cupboard closet in right wall. He brings a small chair from right — gets on it and looks on a shelf. Pulls his hand away, sticky.)*

COUNTY ATTORNEY: Here's a nice mess. *(The women draw nearer up center.)*

MRS. PETERS *(to the other woman)*:   Oh, her fruit; it did freeze. *(To the Lawyer.)* She worried about that when it turned so cold. She said the fire'd go out and her jars would break.

SHERIFF *(rises)*:   Well, can you beat the woman! Held for murder and worryin' about her preserves.

COUNTY ATTORNEY *(getting down from chair)*:   I guess before we're through she may have something more serious than preserves to worry about. *(Crosses down right center.)*

HALE: — Well, women are used to worrying over trifles. *(The two women move a little closer together.)*

COUNTY ATTORNEY *(with the gallantry of a young politician)*:   And yet, for all their worries, what would we do without the ladies? *(The women do not unbend. He goes below the center table to the sink, takes a dipperful of water from the pail, and pouring it into a basin, washes his hands. While he is doing this the Sheriff and Hale cross to cupboard, which they inspect. The County Attorney starts to wipe his hands on the roller towel, turns it for a cleaner place.)* Dirty towels! *(Kicks his foot against the pans under the sink.)* Not much of a housekeeper, would you say, ladies?

MRS. HALE *(stiffly)*:   There's a great deal of work to be done on a farm.

COUNTY ATTORNEY: To be sure. And yet *(with a little bow to her)* I know there are some Dickson County farmhouses which do not have such roller towels. *(He gives it a pull to expose its full-length again.)*

MRS. HALE: Those towels get dirty awful quick. Men's hands aren't always as clean as they might be.

COUNTY ATTORNEY: Ah, loyal to your sex, I see. But you and Mrs. Wright were neighbors. I suppose you were friends, too.

MRS. HALE *(shaking her head)*:   I've not seen much of her of late years. I've not been in this house — it's more than a year.

COUNTY ATTORNEY *(crossing to women up center)*:   And why was that? You didn't like her?

MRS. HALE: I liked her all well enough. Farmers' wives have their hands full, Mr. Henderson. And then ——

COUNTY ATTORNEY: Yes —— ?

MRS. HALE *(looking about)*:   It never seemed a very cheerful place.

COUNTY ATTORNEY: No — it's not cheerful. I shouldn't say she had the home-making instinct.

MRS. HALE: Well, I don't know as Wright had, either.

COUNTY ATTORNEY: You mean that they didn't get on very well?

MRS. HALE: No, I don't mean anything. But I don't think a place'd be any cheerfuller for John Wright's being in it.

COUNTY ATTORNEY: I'd like to talk more of that a little later. I want to get the lay of things upstairs now. *(He goes past the women to up right where steps lead to a stair door.)*

SHERIFF: I suppose anything Mrs. Peters does'll be all right. She was to take in some clothes for her, you know, and a few little things. We left in such a hurry yesterday.

COUNTY ATTORNEY: Yes, but I would like to see what you take, Mrs. Peters, and keep an eye out for anything that might be of use to us.

MRS. PETERS: Yes, Mr. Henderson. *(The men leave by up right door to stairs. The women listen to the men's steps on the stairs, then look about the kitchen.)*

MRS. HALE *(crossing left to sink)*:   I'd hate to have men coming into my kitchen, snooping around and criticizing. *(She arranges the pans under sink which the lawyer had shoved out of place.)*

MRS. PETERS: Of course it's no more than their duty. *(Crosses to cupboard up right.)*

MRS. HALE: Duty's all right, but I guess that deputy sheriff that came out to make the fire might have got a little of this on. *(Gives the roller towel a pull.)* Wish I'd thought of that sooner. Seems mean to talk about her for not having things slicked up when she had to come away in such a hurry. *(Crosses right to Mrs. Peters at cupboard.)*

MRS. PETERS *(who has been looking through cupboard, lifts one end of towel that covers a pan)*:   She had bread set. *(Stands still.)*

MRS. HALE *(eyes fixed on a loaf of bread beside the breadbox, which is on a low shelf of the cupboard)*:   She was going to put this in there. *(Picks up loaf, abruptly drops it. In a manner of returning to familiar things.)* It's a shame about her fruit. I wonder if it's all gone. *(Gets up on the chair and looks.)* I think there's some here that's all right, Mrs. Peters. Yes — here; *(holding it toward the window)* this is cherries, too. *(Looking again.)* I declare I believe that's the only one. *(Gets down, jar in her hand. Goes to the sink and wipes it off on the outside.)* She'll feel awful bad after all her hard work in the hot weather. I remember the afternoon I put up my cherries last summer. *(She puts the jar on the big kitchen table, center of the room. With a sigh, is about to sit down in the rocking chair. Before she is seated realizes what chair it is; with a slow look at it, steps back. The chair which she has touched rocks back and forth. Mrs. Peters moves to center table and they both watch the chair rock for a moment or two.)*

MRS. PETERS *(shaking off the mood which the empty rocking chair has evoked. Now in a businesslike manner she speaks)*:   Well I must get those things from the front room closet. *(She goes to the door at the right but, after looking into the other room, steps back.)* You coming with me, Mrs. Hale? You could help me carry them. *(They go in the other room; reappear, Mrs. Peters carrying a dress, petticoat, and skirt, Mrs. Hale following with a pair of shoes.)* My, it's cold in there. *(She puts the clothes on the big table and hurries to the stove.)*

MRS. HALE *(right of center table examining the skirt)*:   Wright was close. I think maybe that's why she kept so much to herself. She didn't even belong to the Ladies' Aid. I suppose she felt she couldn't do her part, and then you don't enjoy things when you feel shabby. I heard she used to wear pretty clothes and be lively, when she was Minnie Foster, one of the town girls singing in the choir. But that — oh, that was thirty years ago. This all you want to take in?

MRS. PETERS: She said she wanted an apron. Funny thing to want, for there isn't much to get you dirty in jail, goodness knows. But I suppose just to make her feel more natural. *(Crosses to cupboard.)* She said they was in the top drawer in this cupboard. Yes, here. And then her little shawl that always hung behind the door. *(Opens stair door and looks.)* Yes, here it is. *(Quickly shuts door leading upstairs.)*

MRS. HALE *(abruptly moving toward her)*:   Mrs. Peters?

MRS. PETERS: Yes, Mrs. Hale? *(At up right door.)*

MRS. HALE: Do you think she did it?

MRS. PETERS *(in a frightened voice)*:   Oh, I don't know.

MRS. HALE: Well, I don't think she did. Asking for an apron and her little shawl. Worrying about her fruit.

MRS. PETERS *(starts to speak, glances up, where footsteps are heard in the room above. In a low voice)*:   Mr. Peters says it looks bad for her. Mr. Henderson is awful sarcastic in a speech and he'll make fun of her sayin' she didn't wake up.

MRS. HALE: Well, I guess John Wright didn't wake when they was slipping that rope under his neck.

MRS. PETERS *(crossing slowly to table and placing shawl and apron on table with other clothing)*:   No, it's strange. It must have been done awful crafty and still. They say it was such a — funny way to kill a man, rigging it all up like that.

MRS. HALE *(crossing to left of Mrs. Peters at table)*:   That's just what Mr. Hale said. There was a gun in the house. He says that's what he can't understand.

MRS. PETERS: Mr. Henderson said coming out that what was needed for the case was a motive; something to show anger, or — sudden feeling.

MRS. HALE *(who is standing by the table)*:   Well, I don't see any signs of anger around here. *(She puts her hand on the dish towel, which lies on the table, stands looking down at table, one-half of which is clean, the other half messy.)* It's wiped to here. *(Makes a move as if to finish work, then turns and looks at loaf of bread outside the breadbox. Drops towel. In that voice of coming back to familiar things.)* Wonder how they are finding things upstairs. *(Crossing below table to down right.)* I hope she had it a little more red-up° up there. You know, it seems kind of *sneaking.* Locking her up in town and then coming out here and trying to get her own house to turn against her!

MRS. PETERS: But, Mrs. Hale, the law is the law.

MRS. HALE: I s'pose 'tis. *(Unbuttoning her coat.)* Better loosen up your things, Mrs. Peters. You won't feel them when you go out. *(Mrs. Peters takes off her fur tippet, goes to hang it on chair back left of table, stands looking at the work basket on floor near down left window.)*

MRS. PETERS: She was piecing a quilt. *(She brings the large sewing basket to the center table and they look at the bright pieces, Mrs. Hale above the table and Mrs. Peters left of it.)*

MRS. HALE: It's a log cabin pattern. Pretty, isn't it? I wonder if she was goin' to quilt it or just knot it? *(Footsteps have been heard coming down the stairs. The Sheriff enters followed by Hale and the County Attorney.)*

SHERIFF: They wonder if she was going to quilt it or just knot it! *(The men laugh, the women look abashed.)*

COUNTY ATTORNEY *(rubbing his hands over the stove)*:   Frank's fire didn't do much up there, did it? Well, let's go out to the barn and get that cleared up. *(The men go outside by up left door.)*

MRS. HALE *(resentfully)*:   I don't know as there's anything so strange, our takin' up our time with little things while we're waiting for them to get the

---

red-up: To get ready or clean up.

evidence. *(She sits in chair right of table smoothing out a block with decision.)* I don't see as it's anything to laugh about.

MRS. PETERS *(apologetically):*   Of course they've got awful important things on their minds. *(Pulls up a chair and joins Mrs. Hale at the left of the table.)*

MRS. HALE *(examining another block):*   Mrs. Peters, look at this one. Here, this is the one she was working on, and look at the sewing! All the rest of it has been so nice and even. And look at this! It's all over the place! Why, it looks as if she didn't know what she was about! *(After she has said this they look at each other, then start to glance back at the door. After an instant Mrs. Hale has pulled at a knot and ripped the sewing.)*

MRS. PETERS: Oh, what are you doing, Mrs. Hale?

MRS. HALE *(mildly):*   Just pulling out a stitch or two that's not sewed very good. *(Threading a needle.)* Bad sewing always made me fidgety.

MRS. PETERS *(with a glance at door, nervously):*   I don't think we ought to touch things.

MRS. HALE: I'll just finish up this end. *(Suddenly stopping and leaning forward.)* Mrs. Peters?

MRS. PETERS: Yes, Mrs. Hale?

MRS. HALE: What do you suppose she was so nervous about?

MRS. PETERS: Oh — I don't know. I don't know as she was nervous. I sometimes sew awful queer when I'm just tired. *(Mrs. Hale starts to say something, looks at Mrs. Peters, then goes on sewing.)* Well, I must get these things wrapped up. They may be through sooner than we think. *(Putting apron and other things together.)* I wonder where I can find a piece of paper, and string. *(Rises.)*

MRS. HALE: In that cupboard, maybe.

MRS. PETERS *(crosses right looking in cupboard):*   Why, here's a bird-cage. *(Holds it up.)* Did she have a bird, Mrs. Hale?

MRS. HALE: Why, I don't know whether she did or not — I've not been here for so long. There was a man around last year selling canaries cheap, but I don't know as she took one; maybe she did. She used to sing real pretty herself.

MRS. PETERS *(glancing around):*   Seems funny to think of a bird here. But she must have had one, or why would she have a cage? I wonder what happened to it?

MRS. HALE: I s'pose maybe the cat got it.

MRS. PETERS: No, she didn't have a cat. She's got that feeling some people have about cats — being afraid of them. My cat got in her room and she was real upset and asked me to take it out.

MRS. HALE: My sister Bessie was like that. Queer, ain't it?

MRS. PETERS *(examining the cage):*   Why, look at this door. It's broke. One hinge is pulled apart. *(Takes a step down to Mrs. Hale's right.)*

MRS. HALE *(looking too):*   Looks as if someone must have been rough with it.

MRS. PETERS: Why, yes. *(She brings the cage forward and puts it on the table.)*

MRS. HALE *(glancing toward up left door):*   I wish if they're going to find any evidence they'd be about it. I don't like this place.

MRS. PETERS: But I'm awful glad you came with me, Mrs. Hale. It would be lonesome for me sitting here alone.

MRS. HALE: It would, wouldn't it? *(Dropping her sewing.)* But I tell you what I do wish, Mrs. Peters. I wish I had come over sometimes when *she* was here. I — *(looking around the room)* — wish I had.

MRS. PETERS: But of course you were awful busy, Mrs. Hale — your house and your children.

MRS. HALE *(rises and crosses left)*:   I could've come. I stayed away because it weren't cheerful — and that's why I ought to have come. I — *(looking out left window)* — I've never liked this place. Maybe because it's down in a hollow and you don't see the road. I dunno what it is, but it's a lonesome place and always was. I wish I had come over to see Minnie Foster sometimes. I can see now — *(Shakes her head.)*

MRS. PETERS *(left of table and above it)*:   Well, you mustn't reproach yourself, Mrs. Hale. Somehow we just don't see how it is with other folks until — something turns up.

MRS. HALE: Not having children makes less work — but it makes a quiet house, and Wright out to work all day, and no company when he did come in. *(Turning from window.)* Did you know John Wright, Mrs. Peters?

MRS. PETERS: Not to know him; I've seen him in town. They say he was a good man.

MRS. HALE: Yes — good; he didn't drink, and kept his word as well as most, I guess, and paid his debts. But he was a hard man, Mrs. Peters. Just to pass the time of day with him — *(Shivers.)* Like a raw wind that gets to the bone. *(Pauses, her eye falling on the cage.)* I should think she would 'a' wanted a bird. But what do you suppose went with it?

MRS. PETERS: I don't know, unless it got sick and died. *(She reaches over and swings the broken door, swings it again, both women watch it.)*

MRS. HALE: You weren't raised round here, were you? *(Mrs. Peters shakes her head.)* You didn't know — her?

MRS. PETERS: Not till they brought her yesterday.

MRS. HALE: She — come to think of it, she was kind of like a bird herself — real sweet and pretty, but kind of timid and — fluttery. How — she — did — change. *(Silence: then as if struck by a happy thought and relieved to get back to everyday things. Crosses right above Mrs. Peters to cupboard, replaces small chair used to stand on to its original place down right.)* Tell you what, Mrs. Peters, why don't you take the quilt in with you? It might take up her mind.

MRS. PETERS: Why, I think that's a real nice idea, Mrs. Hale. There couldn't possibly be any objection to it could there? Now, just what would I take? I wonder if her patches are in here — and her things. *(They look in the sewing basket.)*

MRS. HALE *(crosses to right of table)*:   Here's some red. I expect this has got sewing things in it. *(Brings out a fancy box.)* What a pretty box. Looks like something somebody would give you. Maybe her scissors are in here. *(Opens box. Suddenly puts her hand to her nose.)* Why —— *(Mrs. Peters bends nearer, then turns her face away.)* There's something wrapped up in this piece of silk.

MRS. PETERS: Why, this isn't her scissors.

MRS. HALE *(lifting the silk)*:   Oh, Mrs. Peters — it's —— *(Mrs. Peters bends closer.)*

MRS. PETERS: It's the bird.

MRS. HALE: But, Mrs. Peters — look at it! Its neck! Look at its neck! It's all — other side *to.*

MRS. PETERS: Somebody — wrung — its — neck. *(Their eyes meet. A look of growing comprehension, of horror. Steps are heard outside. Mrs. Hale slips box under quilt pieces, and sinks into her chair. Enter Sheriff and County Attorney. Mrs. Peters steps down left and stands looking out of window.)*

COUNTY ATTORNEY *(as one turning from serious things to little pleasantries)*:   Well, ladies, have you decided whether she was going to quilt it or knot it? *(Crosses to center above table.)*

MRS. PETERS: We think she was going to — knot it. *(Sheriff crosses to right of stove, lifts stove lid, and glances at fire, then stands warming hands at stove.)*

COUNTY ATTORNEY: Well, that's interesting, I'm sure. *(Seeing the bird-cage.)* Has the bird flown?

MRS. HALE *(putting more quilt pieces over the box)*:   We think the — cat got it.

COUNTY ATTORNEY *(preoccupied)*:   Is there a cat? *(Mrs. Hale glances in a quick covert way at Mrs. Peters.)*

MRS. PETERS *(turning from window takes a step in)*:   Well, not *now.* They're superstitious, you know. They leave.

COUNTY ATTORNEY *(to Sheriff Peters, continuing an interrupted conversation)*:   No sign at all of anyone having come from the outside. Their own rope. Now let's go up again and go over it piece by piece. *(They start upstairs.)* It would have to have been someone who knew just the —— *(Mrs. Peters sits down left of table. The two women sit there not looking at one another, but as if peering into something and at the same time holding back. When they talk now it is in the manner of feeling their way over strange ground, as if afraid of what they are saying, but as if they cannot help saying it.)*

MRS. HALE *(hesitatively and in hushed voice)*:   She liked the bird. She was going to bury it in that pretty box.

MRS. PETERS *(in a whisper)*:   When I was a girl — my kitten — there was a boy took a hatchet, and before my eyes — and before I could get there —— *(Covers her face an instant.)* If they hadn't held me back I would have — *(catches herself, looks upstairs where steps are heard, falters weakly)* — hurt him.

MRS. HALE *(with a slow look around her)*:   I wonder how it would seem never to have had any children around. *(Pause.)* No, Wright wouldn't like the bird — a thing that sang. She used to sing. He killed that, too.

MRS. PETERS *(moving uneasily)*:   We don't know who killed the bird.

MRS. HALE: I knew John Wright.

MRS. PETERS: It was an awful thing was done in this house that night, Mrs. Hale. Killing a man while he slept, slipping a rope around his neck that choked the life out of him.

MRS. HALE: His neck. Choked the life out of him. *(Her hand goes out and rests on the bird-cage.)*

MRS. PETERS *(with rising voice)*: We don't know who killed him. We don't *know.*

MRS. HALE *(her own feeling not interrupted)*: If there'd been years and years of nothing, then a bird to sing to you, it would be awful — still, after the bird was still.

MRS. PETERS *(something within her speaking)*: I know what stillness is. When we homesteaded in Dakota, and my first baby died — after he was two years old, and me with no other then ——

MRS. HALE *(moving)*: How soon do you suppose they'll be through looking for the evidence?

MRS. PETERS: I know what stillness is. *(Pulling herself back.)* The law has got to punish crime, Mrs. Hale.

MRS. HALE *(not as if answering that)*: I wish you'd seen Minnie Foster when she wore a white dress with blue ribbons and stood up there in the choir and sang. *(A look around the room.)* Oh, I *wish* I'd come over here once in a while! That was a crime! That was a crime! Who's going to punish that?

MRS. PETERS *(looking upstairs)*: We mustn't — take on.

MRS. HALE: I might have known she needed help! I know how things can be — for women. I tell you, it's queer, Mrs. Peters. We live close together and we live far apart. We all go through the same things — it's all just a different kind of the same thing. *(Brushes her eyes, noticing the jar of fruit, reaches out for it.)* If I was you I wouldn't tell her her fruit was gone. Tell her it *ain't.* Tell her it's all right. Take this in to prove it to her. She — she may never know whether it was broke or not.

MRS. PETERS *(takes the jar, looks about for something to wrap it in; takes petticoat from the clothes brought from the other room, very nervously begins winding this around the jar. In a false voice)*: My, it's a good thing the men couldn't hear us. Wouldn't they just laugh! Getting all stirred up over a little thing like a — dead canary. As if that could have anything to do with — with — wouldn't they *laugh!* *(The men are heard coming downstairs.)*

MRS. HALE *(under her breath)*: Maybe they would — maybe they wouldn't.

COUNTY ATTORNEY: No, Peters, it's all perfectly clear except a reason for doing it. But you know juries when it comes to women. If there was some definite thing. *(Crosses slowly to above table. Sheriff crosses down right. Mrs. Hale and Mrs. Peters remain seated at either side of table.)* Something to show — something to make a story about — a thing that would connect up with this strange way of doing it —— *(The women's eyes meet for an instant. Enter Hale from outer door.)*

HALE *(remaining by door)*: Well, I've got the team around. Pretty cold out there.

COUNTY ATTORNEY: I'm going to stay awhile by myself. *(To the Sheriff.)* You can send Frank out for me, can't you? I want to go over everything. I'm not satisfied that we can't do better.

SHERIFF: Do you want to see what Mrs. Peters is going to take in? *(The Lawyer picks up the apron, laughs.)*

COUNTY ATTORNEY: Oh, I guess they're not very dangerous things the ladies have picked out. *(Moves a few things about, disturbing the quilt pieces which cover the box. Steps back.)* No, Mrs. Peters doesn't need supervising. For that matter a sheriff's wife is married to the law. Ever think of it that way, Mrs. Peters?

MRS. PETERS: Not — just that way.

SHERIFF *(chuckling)*:   Married to the law. *(Moves to down right door to the other room.)* I just want you to come in here a minute, George. We ought to take a look at these windows.

COUNTY ATTORNEY *(scoffingly)*:   Oh, windows!

SHERIFF: We'll be right out, Mr. Hale. *(Hale goes outside. The Sheriff follows the County Attorney into the room. Then Mrs. Hale rises, hands tight together, looking intensely at Mrs. Peters, whose eyes make a slow turn, finally meeting Mrs. Hale's. A moment Mrs. Hale holds her, then her own eyes point the way to where the box is concealed. Suddenly Mrs. Peters throws back quilt pieces and tries to put the box in the bag she is carrying. It is too big. She opens box, starts to take bird out, cannot touch it, goes to pieces, stands there helpless. Sound of a knob turning in the other room. Mrs. Hale snatches the box and puts it in the pocket of her big coat. Enter County Attorney and Sheriff, who remains down right.)*

COUNTY ATTORNEY *(crosses to up left door facetiously)*:   Well, Henry, at least we found out that she was not going to quilt it. She was going to — what is it you call it, ladies?

MRS. HALE *(standing center below table facing front, her hand against her pocket)*:   We call it — knot it, Mr. Henderson.

Curtain.   [1916]

■ THINKING ABOUT THE TEXT

1. Although much of this play is about Minnie Wright, Glaspell keeps her offstage. Why, do you think?

2. What does Glaspell imply about differences between men and women? Support your inference with details from the text.

3. What do Mrs. Hale and Mrs. Peters realize about themselves during the course of the play? To what extent should they feel guilty about their own past behavior?

4. Ultimately, Mrs. Hale and Mrs. Peters cover up evidence to protect Minnie Wright. They seem to act out of loyalty to their sex. How sympathetic are you to their stand? Do you feel there are times when you should be someone's ally because that person is of the same gender as you?

5. Is this play about freedom and confinement? About the injustice of male domination? About the bonds that hold women together? Or something else? Explain your answer.

■ MAKING COMPARISONS

1. Does class or socioeconomic level play a significant role in the freedom of the women in these two plays?

2. Compare Torvald and John Wright.

3. Both endings were controversial in their day. Would they be today? Why, or why not?

■ WRITING ABOUT ISSUES

1. Write an argument that claims justice was done in either *A Doll House* or *Trifles.*

2. Write a comparison of the problems in both marriages. Note whether these issues exist in contemporary marriages.

3. Write a personal reflection on the endings of these plays. Can you condone the actions of these women?

4. After doing research about the status of women in America in 1879 and 1916, write a brief report. Were there differences? What were they? Was marriage a more flexible institution in 1916? Did geography matter? Did class?

■ Confined for Her Own Good: Cultural Contexts for a Story

CHARLOTTE PERKINS GILMAN, "The Yellow Wallpaper"

CULTURAL CONTEXTS:
CHARLOTTE PERKINS GILMAN, "Why I Wrote 'The Yellow Wallpaper' "

S. WEIR MITCHELL, From "The Evolution of the Rest Treatment"

JOHN HARVEY KELLOGG, From *The Ladies' Guide in Health and Disease*

When doctors make a medical or psychiatric diagnosis, they pinpoint their patient's condition but also often accept or reject their society's definition of *health*. The social context of diagnoses seems especially worth considering when a particular condition afflicts one gender much more than the other. Today, many more women than men appear to suffer from depression, anorexia, bulimia, and dissociative identity disorder. Why? Perhaps traditional female roles encourage these illnesses; perhaps gender bias affects how doctors label and treat them. Charlotte Perkins Gilman raised both these possibilities in her 1892 short story "The Yellow Wallpaper." In her own life, the consequences from her egregious treatment were not as serious as she depicts in her story. But Gilman was the exception. Many women suffered terribly from doctors who ignored the cultural causes of depression. Besides Gilman's story, we include her account of why she wrote it, an excerpt from a lecture by Mitchell about his cure, and some advice about motherhood from John Kellogg, another influential doctor of the time.

■ BEFORE YOU READ

How is mental illness depicted in movies and television shows you have seen? Which representations of mental illness have you appreciated the most? Which have you especially disliked? State your criteria for these judgments.

CHARLOTTE PERKINS GILMAN
The Yellow Wallpaper

Charlotte Perkins Gilman (1860–1935) was a major activist and theorist in America's first wave of feminism. During her lifetime, she was chiefly known for her 1898 book Women and Economics. *In it she argued that women should not be confined to the household and made economically dependent on men. Gilman also advanced such ideas through her many public-speaking appearances and her magazine* The Forerunner, *which she edited from 1909 to 1916. Gilman wrote many articles and*

(Charlotte Perkins
Gilman. The Granger
Collection. New York.)

works of fiction for The Forerunner, including a tale called Herland (1915) in
which she envisioned an all-female utopia. Today, however, Gilman is best known for
her short story "The Yellow Wallpaper," which she published first in an 1892 issue of
the New England Magazine. The story is based on Gilman's struggle with depression after the birth of her daughter Katharine in 1885. Seeking help for emotional
turmoil, Gilman consulted the eminent neurologist Silas Weir Mitchell, who prescribed his famous "rest cure." This treatment, which forbade Gilman to work, actually worsened her distress. She improved only after she moved to California, divorced
her husband, let him raise Katharine with his new wife, married someone else, and
plunged fully into a literary and political career. As Gilman noted in her posthumously
published autobiography, The Living of Charlotte Perkins Gilman (1935), she
never fully recovered from the debilitation that had led her to Dr. Mitchell, but she
ultimately managed to be enormously productive. Although "The Yellow Wallpaper"
is a work of fiction rather than a factual account of her experience with Mitchell,
Gilman used the story to criticize the doctor's patriarchal approach as well as society's efforts to keep women passive.

It is very seldom that mere ordinary people like John and myself secure ancestral halls for the summer.

A colonial mansion, a hereditary estate, I would say a haunted house and
reach the height of romantic felicity — but that would be asking too much of fate!

Still I will proudly declare that there is something queer about it.

Else, why should it be let so cheaply? And why have stood so long untenanted?

John laughs at me, of course, but one expects that in marriage.   5

John is practical in the extreme. He has no patience with faith, an intense
horror of superstition, and he scoffs openly at any talk of things not to be felt
and seen and put down in figures.

John is a physician, and *perhaps* — (I would not say it to a living soul, of
course, but this is dead paper and a great relief to my mind) — *perhaps* that is
one reason I do not get well faster.

You see, he does not believe I am sick!

And what can one do?

If a physician of high standing, and one's own husband, assures friends   10
and relatives that there is really nothing the matter with one but temporary
nervous depression — a slight hysterical tendency° — what is one to do?

My brother is also a physician, and also of high standing, and he says the
same thing.

So I take phosphates or phosphites — whichever it is, and tonics, and journeys, and air, and exercise, and am absolutely forbidden to "work" until I am
well again.

Personally, I disagree with their ideas.

Personally, I believe that congenial work, with excitement and change,
would do me good.

But what is one to do?   15

I did write for a while in spite of them; but it *does* exhaust me a good
deal — having to be so sly about it, or else meet with heavy opposition.

I sometimes fancy that in my condition if I had less opposition and more
society and stimulus — but John says the very worst thing I can do is to think
about my condition, and I confess it always makes me feel bad.

So I will let it alone and talk about the house.

The most beautiful place! It is quite alone, standing well back from the
road, quite three miles from the village. It makes me think of English places
that you read about, for there are hedges and walls and gates that lock, and lots
of separate little houses for the gardeners and people.

There is a *delicious* garden! I never saw such a garden — large and shady,   20
full of box-bordered paths, and lined with long grape-covered arbors with seats
under them.

There were greenhouses, too, but they are all broken now.

There was some legal trouble, I believe, something about the heirs and co-
heirs; anyhow, the place has been empty for years.

hysterical tendency: It was common among Victorian doctors to believe women had an
innate tendency to be overly emotional; now a discredited assumption.

That spoils my ghostliness, I am afraid, but I don't care—there is something strange about the house—I can feel it.

I even said so to John one moonlight evening, but he said what I felt was a *draught*, and shut the window.

I get unreasonably angry with John sometimes. I'm sure I never used to be 25
so sensitive. I think it is due to this nervous condition.

But John says if I feel so, I shall neglect proper self-control; so I take pains to control myself — before him, at least, and that makes me very tired.

I don't like our room a bit. I wanted one downstairs that opened on the piazza and had roses all over the window, and such pretty old-fashioned chintz hangings! but John would not hear of it.

He said there was only one window and not room for two beds, and no near room for him if he took another.

He is very careful and loving, and hardly lets me stir without special direction.

I have a schedule prescription for each hour in the day; he takes all care 30
from me, and so I feel basely ungrateful not to value it more.

He said we came here solely on my account, that I was to have perfect rest and all the air I could get. "Your exercise depends on your strength, my dear," said he, "and your food somewhat on your appetite; but air you can absorb all the time." So we took the nursery at the top of the house.

It is a big, airy room, the whole floor nearly, with windows that look all ways, and air and sunshine galore. It was nursery first and then playroom and gymnasium, I should judge; for the windows are barred for little children, and there are rings and things in the walls.

The paint and paper look as if a boys' school had used it. It is stripped off — the paper — in great patches all around the head of my bed, about as far as I can reach, and in a great place on the other side of the room low down. I never saw a worse paper in my life.

One of those sprawling flamboyant patterns committing every artistic sin.

It is dull enough to confuse the eye in following, pronounced enough to 35
constantly irritate and provoke study, and when you follow the lame uncertain curves for a little distance they suddenly commit suicide—plunge off at outrageous angles, destroy themselves in unheard of contradictions.

The color is repellant, almost revolting; a smouldering unclean yellow, strangely faded by the slow-turning sunlight.

It is a dull yet lurid orange in some places, a sickly sulphur tint in others.

No wonder the children hated it! I should hate it myself if I had to live in this room long.

There comes John, and I must put this away, — he hates to have me write a word.

We have been here two weeks, and I haven't felt like writing before, since that 40
first day.

I am sitting by the window now, up in this atrocious nursery, and there is nothing to hinder my writing as much as I please, save lack of strength.

John is away all day, and even some nights when his cases are serious.

I am glad my case is not serious!

But these nervous troubles are dreadfully depressing.

John does not know how much I really suffer. He knows there is no *reason*   45
to suffer, and that satisfies him.

Of course it is only nervousness. It does weigh on me so not to do my duty
in any way!

I meant to be such a help to John, such a real rest and comfort, and here I
am a comparative burden already!

Nobody would believe what an effort it is to do what little I am able, — to
dress and entertain, and order things.

It is fortunate Mary is so good with the baby. Such a dear baby!

And yet I *cannot* be with him, it makes me so nervous.   50

I suppose John never was nervous in his life. He laughs at me so about this
wallpaper!

At first he meant to repaper the room, but afterward he said that I was letting it get the better of me, and that nothing was worse for a nervous patient
than to give way to such fancies.

He said that after the wallpaper was changed it would be the heavy bedstead, and then the barred windows, and then that gate at the head of the
stairs, and so on.

"You know the place is doing you good," he said, "and really, dear, I don't
care to renovate the house just for a three months' rental."

"Then do let us go downstairs," I said, "there are such pretty rooms there."   55

Then he took me in his arms and called me a blessed little goose, and said
he would go down cellar, if I wished, and have it whitewashed into the bargain.

But he is right enough about the beds and windows and things.

It is an airy and comfortable room as anyone need wish, and, of course, I
would not be so silly as to make him uncomfortable just for a whim.

I'm really getting quite fond of the big room, all but that horrid paper.

Out of one window I can see the garden, those mysterious deep-shaded   60
arbors, the riotous old-fashioned flowers, and bushes and gnarly trees.

Out of another I get a lovely view of the bay and a little private wharf belonging to the estate. There is a beautiful shaded lane that runs down there
from the house. I always fancy I see people walking in these numerous paths
and arbors, but John has cautioned me not to give way to fancy in the least. He
says that with my imaginative power and habit of story-making, a nervous
weakness like mine is sure to lead to all manner of excited fancies, and that I
ought to use my will and good sense to check the tendency. So I try.

I think sometimes that if I were only well enough to write a little it would
relieve the press of ideas and rest me.

But I find I get pretty tired when I try.

It is so discouraging not to have any advice and companionship about my
work. When I get really well, John says we will ask Cousin Henry and Julia
down for a long visit; but he says he would as soon put fireworks in my pillow-
case as to let me have those stimulating people about now.

I wish I could get well faster.   65

But I must not think about that. This paper looks to me as if it *knew* what a vicious influence it had!

There is a recurrent spot where the pattern lolls like a broken neck and two bulbous eyes stare at you upside down.

I get positively angry with the impertinence of it and the everlastingness. Up and down and sideways they crawl, and those absurd, unblinking eyes are everywhere. There is one place where two breadths didn't match, and the eyes go all up and down the line, one a little higher than the other.

I never saw so much expression in an inanimate thing before, and we all know how much expression they have! I used to lie awake as a child and get more entertainment and terror out of blank walls and plain furniture than most children could find in a toy-store.

I remember what a kindly wink the knobs of our big, old bureau used to   70
have, and there was one chair that always seemed like a strong friend.

I used to feel that if any of the other things looked too fierce I could always hop into that chair and be safe.

The furniture in this room is no worse than inharmonious, however, for we had to bring it all from downstairs. I suppose when this was used as a play-room they had to take the nursery things out, and no wonder! I never saw such ravages as the children have made here.

The wallpaper, as I said before, is torn off in spots, and it sticketh closer than a brother — they must have had perseverance as well as hatred.

Then the floor is scratched and gouged and splintered, the plaster itself is dug out here and there, and this great heavy bed, which is all we found in the room, looks as if it had been through the wars.

But I don't mind it a bit — only the paper.   75

There comes John's sister. Such a dear girl as she is, and so careful of me! I must not let her find me writing.

She is a perfect and enthusiastic housekeeper, and hopes for no better profession. I verily believe she thinks it is the writing which made me sick!

But I can write when she is out, and see her a long way off from these windows.

There is one that commands the road, a lovely shaded winding road, and one that just looks off over the country. A lovely country, too, full of great elms and velvet meadows.

This wallpaper has a kind of sub-pattern in a different shade, a particularly   80
irritating one, for you can only see it in certain lights, and not clearly then.

But in the places where it isn't faded and where the sun is just so — I can see a strange, provoking, formless sort of figure, that seems to skulk about behind that silly and conspicuous front design.

There's sister on the stairs!

Well, the Fourth of July is over! The people are all gone and I am tired out. John thought it might do me good to see a little company, so we just had mother and Nellie and the children down for a week.

Of course I didn't do a thing. Jennie sees to everything now.

But it tired me all the same.   85

John says if I don't pick up faster he shall send me to Weir Mitchell° in the fall.

But I don't want to go there at all. I had a friend who was in his hands once, and she says he is just like John and my brother, only more so!

Besides, it is such an undertaking to go so far.

I don't feel as if it was worthwhile to turn my hand over for anything, and I'm getting dreadfully fretful and querulous.

I cry at nothing, and cry most of the time.   90

Of course I don't when John is here, or anybody else, but when I am alone.

And I am alone a good deal just now. John is kept in town very often by serious cases, and Jennie is good and lets me alone when I want her to.

So I walk a little in the garden or down that lovely lane, sit on the porch under the roses, and lie down up here a good deal.

I'm getting really fond of the room in spite of the wallpaper. Perhaps *because* of the wallpaper.

It dwells in my mind so!   95

I lie here on this great immovable bed — it is nailed down, I believe — and follow that pattern about by the hour. It is as good as gymnastics, I assure you. I start, we'll say, at the bottom, down in the corner over there where it has not been touched, and I determine for the thousandth time that I *will* follow that pointless pattern to some sort of a conclusion.

I know a little of the principle of design, and I know this thing was not arranged on any laws of radiation, or alternation, or repetition, or symmetry, or anything else that I ever heard of.

It is repeated, of course, by the breadths, but not otherwise.

Looked at in one way each breadth stands alone, the bloated curves and flourishes — a kind of "debased Romanesque" with *delirium tremens* — go waddling up and down in isolated columns of fatuity.

But, on the other hand, they connect diagonally, and the sprawling out-   100
lines run off in great slanting waves of optic horror, like a lot of wallowing seaweeds in full chase.

The whole thing goes horizontally, too, at least it seems so, and I exhaust myself in trying to distinguish the order of its going in that direction.

They have used a horizontal breadth for a frieze, and that adds wonderfully to the confusion.

There is one end of the room where it is almost intact, and there, when the crosslights fade and the low sun shines directly upon it, I can almost fancy radiation after all, — the interminable grotesques seem to form around a common center and rush off in headlong plunges of equal distraction.

It makes me tired to follow it. I will take a nap I guess.

I don't know why I should write this.   105
     I don't want to.

Weir Mitchell: Dr. S. Weir Mitchell (1829–1914) was an eminent Philadelphia neurologist who advocated "rest cures" for nervous disorders. He was the author of *Diseases of the Nervous System, Especially of Women* (1881).

I don't feel able.

And I know John would think it absurd. But I *must* say what I feel and think in some way — it is such a relief!

But the effort is getting to be greater than the relief.

Half the time now I am awfully lazy, and lie down ever so much.   110

John says I mustn't lose my strength, and has me take cod liver oil and lots of tonics and things, to say nothing of ale and wine and rare meat.

Dear John! He loves me very dearly, and hates to have me sick. I tried to have a real earnest reasonable talk with him the other day, and tell him how I wish he would let me go and make a visit to Cousin Henry and Julia.

But he said I wasn't able to go, nor able to stand it after I got there; and I did not make out a very good case for myself, for I was crying before I had finished.

It is getting to be a great effort for me to think straight. Just this nervous weakness I suppose.

And dear John gathered me up in his arms, and just carried me upstairs   115
and laid me on the bed, and sat by me and read to me till it tired my head.

He said I was his darling and his comfort and all he had, and that I must take care of myself for his sake, and keep well.

He says no one but myself can help me out of it, that I must use my will and self-control and not let any silly fancies run away with me.

There's one comfort, the baby is well and happy, and does not have to occupy this nursery with the horrid wallpaper.

If we had not used it, that blessed child would have! What a fortunate escape! Why, I wouldn't have a child of mine, an impressionable little thing, live in such a room for worlds.

I never thought of it before, but it is lucky that John kept me here after all,   120
I can stand it so much easier than a baby, you see.

Of course I never mention it to them any more — I am too wise, but I keep watch of it all the same.

There are things in the wallpaper that nobody knows but me, or ever will.

Behind that outside pattern the dim shapes get clearer every day.

It is always the same shape, only very numerous.

And it is like a woman stooping down and creeping about behind that pat-   125
tern. I don't like it a bit. I wonder — I begin to think — I wish John would take me away from here!

It is so hard to talk with John about my case, because he is so wise, and because he loves me so.

But I tried it last night.

It was moonlight. The moon shines in all around just as the sun does.

I hate to see it sometimes, it creeps so slowly, and always comes in by one window or another.

John was asleep and I hated to waken him, so I kept still and watched the   130
moonlight on that undulating wallpaper till I felt creepy.

The faint figure behind seemed to shake the pattern, just as if she wanted to get out.

I got up softly and went to feel and see if the paper *did* move, and when I came back John was awake.

"What is it, little girl?" he said. "Don't go walking about like that — you'll get cold."

I thought it was a good time to talk, so I told him that I really was not gaining here, and that I wished he would take me away.

"Why, darling!" said he, "our lease will be up in three weeks, and I can't see   135 how to leave before.

"The repairs are not done at home, and I cannot possibly leave town just now. Of course if you were in any danger, I could and would, but you really are better, dear, whether you can see it or not. I am a doctor, dear, and I know. You are gaining flesh and color, your appetite is better, I feel really much easier about you."

"I don't weigh a bit more," said I, "nor as much; and my appetite may be better in the evening when you are here but it is worse in the morning when you are away!"

"Bless her little heart!" said he with a big hug, "she shall be as sick as she pleases! But now let's improve the shining hours by going to sleep, and talk about it in the morning!"

"And you won't go away?" I asked gloomily.

"Why, how can I, dear? It is only three weeks more and then we will take a   140 nice little trip of a few days while Jennie is getting the house ready. Really dear you are better!"

"Better in body perhaps —" I began, and stopped short, for he sat up straight and looked at me with such a stern, reproachful look that I could not say another word.

"My darling," said he, "I beg you, for my sake and for our child's sake, as well as for your own, that you will never for one instant let that idea enter your mind! There is nothing so dangerous, so fascinating, to a temperament like yours. It is a false and foolish fancy. Can you trust me as a physician when I tell you so?"

So of course I said no more on that score, and we went to sleep before long. He thought I was asleep first, but I wasn't, and lay there for hours trying to decide whether that front pattern and the back pattern really did move together or separately.

On a pattern like this, by daylight, there is a lack of sequence, a defiance of law, that is a constant irritant to a normal mind.

The color is hideous enough, and unreliable enough, and infuriating   145 enough, but the pattern is torturing.

You think you have mastered it, but just as you get well underway in following, it turns a back-somersault and there you are. It slaps you in the face, knocks you down, and tramples upon you. It is like a bad dream.

The outside pattern is a florid arabesque, reminding one of a fungus. If you can imagine a toadstool in joints, an interminable string of toadstools, budding and sprouting in endless convolutions—why, that is something like it.

That is, sometimes!

There is one marked peculiarity about this paper, a thing nobody seems to notice but myself, and that is that it changes as the light changes.

When the sun shoots in through the east window—I always watch for   150
that first long, straight ray—it changes so quickly that I never can quite believe it.

That is why I watch it always.

By moonlight—the moon shines in all night when there is a moon—I wouldn't know it was the same paper.

At night in any kind of light, in twilight, candlelight, lamplight, and worst of all by moonlight, it becomes bars! The outside pattern I mean, and the woman behind it is as plain as can be.

I didn't realize for a long time what the thing was that showed behind, that dim sub-pattern, but now I am quite sure it is a woman.

By daylight she is subdued, quiet. I fancy it is the pattern that keeps her so   155
still. It is so puzzling. It keeps me quiet by the hour.

I lie down ever so much now. John says it is good for me, and to sleep all I can.

Indeed he started the habit by making me lie down for an hour after each meal.

It is a very bad habit I am convinced, for you see I don't sleep.

And that cultivates deceit, for I don't tell them I'm awake—O, no!

The fact is I am getting a little afraid of John.   160

He seems very queer sometimes, and even Jennie has an inexplicable look.

It strikes me occasionally, just as a scientific hypothesis,—that perhaps it is the paper!

I have watched John when he did not know I was looking, and come into the room suddenly on the most innocent excuses, and I've caught him several times *looking at the paper*! And Jennie too. I caught Jennie with her hand on it once.

She didn't know I was in the room, and when I asked her in a quiet, a very quiet voice, with the most restrained manner possible, what she was doing with the paper—she turned around as if she had been caught stealing, and looked quite angry—asked me why I should frighten her so!

Then she said that the paper stained everything it touched, that she had   165
found yellow smooches on all my clothes and John's, and she wished we would be more careful!

Did not that sound innocent? But I know she was studying that pattern, and I am determined that nobody shall find it out but myself!

Life is very much more exciting now than it used to be. You see I have something more to expect, to look forward to, to watch. I really do eat better, and am more quiet than I was.

John is so pleased to see me improve! He laughed a little the other day, and said I seemed to be flourishing in spite of my wallpaper.

I turned it off with a laugh. I had no intention of telling him it was *because* of the wallpaper — he would make fun of me. He might even want to take me away.

I don't want to leave now until I have found it out. There is a week more, 170 and I think that will be enough.

I'm feeling ever so much better! I don't sleep much at night, for it is so interesting to watch developments; but I sleep a good deal in the daytime.

In the daytime it is tiresome and perplexing.

There are always new shoots on the fungus, and new shades of yellow all over it. I cannot keep count of them, though I have tried conscientiously.

It is the strangest yellow, that wallpaper! It makes me think of all the yellow things I ever saw — not beautiful ones like buttercups, but old foul, bad yellow things.

But there is something else about that paper — the smell! I noticed it the 175 moment we came into the room, but with so much air and sun it was not bad. Now we have had a week of fog and rain, and whether the windows are open or not, the smell is here.

It creeps all over the house.

I find it hovering in the dining-room, skulking in the parlor, hiding in the hall, lying in wait for me on the stairs.

It gets into my hair.

Even when I go to ride, if I turn my head suddenly and surprise it — there is that smell!

Such a peculiar odor, too! I have spent hours in trying to analyze it, to find 180 what it smelled like.

It is not bad — at first, and very gentle, but quite the subtlest, most enduring odor I ever met.

In this damp weather it is awful, I wake up in the night and find it hanging over me.

It used to disturb me at first. I thought seriously of burning the house — to reach the smell.

But now I am used to it. The only thing I can think of that it is like is the *color* of the paper! A yellow smell.

There is a very funny mark on this wall, low down, near the mopboard. 185 A streak that runs round the room. It goes behind every piece of furniture, except the bed, a long, straight, even *smooch*, as if it had been rubbed over and over.

I wonder how it was done and who did it, and what they did it for. Round and round and round — round and round and round — it makes me dizzy!

I really have discovered something at last.

Through watching so much at night, when it changes so, I have finally found out.

The front pattern *does* move—and no wonder! The woman behind shakes it!

Sometimes I think there are a great many women behind, and sometimes only one, and she crawls around fast, and her crawling shakes it all over. 190

Then in the very bright spots she keeps still, and in the very shady spots she just takes hold of the bars and shakes them hard.

And she is all the time trying to climb through. But nobody could climb through that pattern—it strangles so; I think that is why it has so many heads.

They get through, and then the pattern strangles them off and turns them upside down, and makes their eyes white!

If those heads were covered or taken off it would not be half so bad.

I think that woman gets out in the daytime! 195

And I'll tell you why—privately—I've seen her!

I can see her out of every one of my windows!

It is the same woman, I know, for she is always creeping, and most women do not creep by daylight.

I see her in that long shaded lane, creeping up and down. I see her in those dark grape arbors, creeping all around the garden.

I see her on that long road under the trees, creeping along, and when a 200 carriage comes she hides under the blackberry vines.

I don't blame her a bit. It must be very humiliating to be caught creeping by daylight!

I always lock the door when I creep by daylight. I can't do it at night, for I know John would suspect something at once.

And John is so queer now, that I don't want to irritate him. I wish he would take another room! Besides, I don't want anybody to get that woman out at night but myself.

I often wonder if I could see her out of all the windows at once.

But, turn as fast as I can, I can only see out of one at one time. 205

And though I always see her, she *may* be able to creep faster than I can turn!

I have watched her sometimes away off in the open country, creeping as fast as a cloud shadow in a high wind.

If only that top pattern could be gotten off from the under one! I mean to try it, little by little.

I have found out another funny thing, but I shan't tell it this time! It does not do to trust people too much.

There are only two more days to get this paper off, and I believe John is 210 beginning to notice. I don't like the look in his eyes.

And I heard him ask Jennie a lot of professional questions, about me. She had a very good report to give.

She said I slept a good deal in the daytime.

John knows I don't sleep very well at night, for all I'm so quiet!

He asked me all sorts of questions too, and pretended to be very loving and kind.

As if I couldn't see through him!   215

Still, I don't wonder he acts so, sleeping under this paper for three months.

It only interests me, but I feel sure John and Jennie are secretly affected by it.

Hurrah! This is the last day, but it is enough. John to stay in town over night, and won't be out until this evening.

Jennie wanted to sleep with me — the sly thing! But I told her I should undoubtedly rest better for a night all alone.

That was clever, for really I wasn't alone a bit! As soon as it was moonlight and   220
that poor thing began to crawl and shake the pattern, I got up and ran to help her.

I pulled and she shook, I shook and she pulled, and before morning we had peeled off yards of that paper.

A strip about as high as my head and half around the room.

And then when the sun came and that awful pattern began to laugh at me, I declared I would finish it to-day!

We go away to-morrow, and they are moving all my furniture down again to leave things as they were before.

Jennie looked at the wall in amazement, but I told her merrily that I did it   225
out of pure spite at the vicious thing.

She laughed and said she wouldn't mind doing it herself, but I must not get tired.

How she betrayed herself that time!

But I am here, and no person touches this paper but me, — not *alive*!

She tried to get me out of the room — it was too patent! But I said it was so quiet and empty and clean now that I believed I would lie down again and sleep all I could, and not to wake me even for dinner — I would call when I woke.

So now she is gone, and the servants are gone, and the things are gone,   230
and there is nothing left but that great bedstead nailed down, with the canvas mattress we found on it.

We shall sleep downstairs to-night, and take the boat home to-morrow.

I quite enjoy the room, now it is bare again.

How those children did tear about here!

This bedstead is fairly gnawed!

But I must get to work.   235

I have locked the door and thrown the key down into the front path.

I don't want to go out, and I don't want to have anybody come in, till John comes.

I want to astonish him.

I've got a rope up here that even Jennie did not find. If that woman does get out, and tries to get away, I can tie her!

But I forgot I could not reach far without anything to stand on!   240

This bed will *not* move!

I tried to lift and push it until I was lame, and then I got so angry I bit off a little piece at one corner — but it hurt my teeth.

Then I peeled off all the paper I could reach standing on the floor. It sticks horribly and the pattern just enjoys it! All those strangled heads and bulbous eyes and waddling fungus growths just shriek with derision!

I am getting angry enough to do something desperate. To jump out of the window would be admirable exercise, but the bars are too strong even to try.

Besides I wouldn't do it. Of course not. I know well enough that a step like that is improper and might be misconstrued.   245

I don't like to *look* out of the windows even — there are so many of those creeping women, and they creep so fast.

I wonder if they all come out of that wallpaper as I did?

But I am securely fastened now by my well-hidden rope — you don't get *me* out in the road there!

I suppose I shall have to get back behind the pattern when it comes night, and that is hard!

It is so pleasant to be out in this great room and creep around as I please!   250

I don't want to go outside. I won't, even if Jennie asks me to.

For outside you have to creep on the ground, and everything is green instead of yellow.

But here I can creep smoothly on the floor, and my shoulder just fits in that long smooch around the wall, so I cannot lose my way.

Why, there's John at the door!

It is no use, young man, you can't open it!   255

How he does call and pound!

Now he's crying for an axe.

It would be a shame to break down that beautiful door!

"John dear!" said I in the gentlest voice, "the key is down by the front steps, under a plantain leaf!"

That silenced him for a few moments.   260

Then he said — very quietly indeed, "Open the door, my darling!"

"I can't," said I. "The key is down by the front door under a plantain leaf!"

And then I said it again, several times, very gently and slowly, and said it so often that he had to go and see, and he got it of course, and came in. He stopped short by the door.

"What is the matter?" he cried. "For God's sake, what are you doing!"

I kept on creeping just the same, but I looked at him over my shoulder.   265

"I've got out at last," said I, "in spite of you and Jane. And I've pulled off most of the paper, so you can't put me back!"

Now why should that man have fainted? But he did, and right across my path by the wall, so that I had to creep over him every time!   [1892]

≡ THINKING ABOUT THE TEXT

1. What psychological stages does the narrator go through as the story progresses?

2. How does the wallpaper function as a symbol in this story? What do you conclude about the narrator when she becomes increasingly interested in the woman she finds there?

3. Explain your ultimate view of the narrator, by using specific details of the story and by identifying some of the warrants or assumptions behind your opinion. Do you admire her? Sympathize with her? Recoil from her? What would you say to someone who simply dismisses her as crazy?

4. The story is narrated in the present tense. Would its effect be different if it were narrated in the past tense? Why, or why not?

5. In real life, Gilman's husband and her doctor were two separate people. In the story, the narrator's husband is her doctor as well. Why do you think Gilman made this change? What is the effect of her combining husband and doctor?

CHARLOTTE PERKINS GILMAN

Why I Wrote "The Yellow Wallpaper"

Gilman published the following piece in the October 1913 issue of her magazine, The Forerunner.

Many and many a reader has asked that. When the story first came out, in the *New England Magazine* about 1891, a Boston physician made protest in *The Transcript.* Such a story ought not to be written, he said; it was enough to drive anyone mad to read it.

Another physician, in Kansas I think, wrote to say that it was the best description of incipient insanity he had ever seen, and — begging my pardon — had I been there?

Now the story of the story is this:

For many years I suffered from a severe and continuous nervous breakdown tending to melancholia — and beyond. During about the third year of this trouble I went, in devout faith and some faint stir of hope, to a noted specialist in nervous diseases, the best known in the country. This wise man put me to bed and applied the rest cure, to which a still good physique responded so promptly that, he concluded there was nothing much the matter with me, and sent me home with solemn advice to "live as domestic a life as far as possible," to "have but two hours' intellectual life a day," and "never to touch pen, brush, or pencil again as long as I lived." This was in 1887.

I went home and obeyed those directions for some three months, and came so near the border line of utter mental ruin that I could see over.   5

Then, using the remnants of intelligence that remained, and helped by a wise friend, I cast the noted specialist's advice to the winds and went to work again — work, the normal life of every human being; work, in which is joy and growth and service, without which one is a pauper and a parasite; ultimately recovering some measure of power.

Being naturally moved to rejoicing by this narrow escape, I wrote *The Yellow Wallpaper*, with its embellishments and additions to carry out the ideal (I never had hallucinations or objections to my mural decorations) and sent a copy to the physician who so nearly drove me mad. He never acknowledged it.

The little book is valued by alienists° and as a good specimen of one kind of literature. It has to my knowledge saved one woman from a similar fate — so terrifying her family that they let her out into normal activity and she recovered.

But the best result is this. Many years later I was told that the great specialist had admitted to friends of his that he had altered his treatment of neurasthenia since reading *The Yellow Wallpaper.*

It was not intended to drive people crazy, but to save people from being driven crazy, and it worked.   10

[*1913*]

alienists: Nineteenth-century term for psychiatrists.

≡ THINKING ABOUT THE TEXT

1. S. Weir Mitchell was the "noted specialist in nervous diseases" (para. 4) whom Gilman mentions. Yet she does not identify him by name. Why not, do you think? Some historians argue that, contrary to Gilman's claim here, Mitchell continued to believe his "rest cure" valid. Does this issue of fact matter to your judgment of her piece? Why, or why not?

2. Look again at Gilman's last sentence. Do you believe that her story could indeed "save people from being driven crazy"? Why, or why not?

3. Does this piece as a whole affect your interpretation and opinion of Gilman's story? Why, or why not? In general, how much do you think readers of a story should know about its author's life?

S. WEIR MITCHELL

From The Evolution of the Rest Treatment

Charlotte Perkins Gilman sought help from Silas Weir Mitchell (1829–1914) because he was a well-known and highly respected physician who had treated many women's mental problems. Mitchell developed his "rest cure" while serving as an army surgeon during the Civil War. Ironically, like Gilman he was also a writer. Besides producing numerous monographs on medical subjects, he published many short stories and novels. The following is an excerpt from a lecture that Mitchell gave to the Philadelphia Neurological Society in 1904, twelve years after "The Yellow Wallpaper" appeared. As you will see, Mitchell was still enthusiastic about his "rest cure," although he had changed it in certain respects since devising it.

I have been asked to come here to-night to speak to you on some subject connected with nervous disease. I had hoped to have had ready a fitting paper for so notable an occasion, but have been prevented by public engagements and private business so as to make it quite impossible. I have, therefore, been driven to ask whether it would be agreeable if I should speak in regard to the mode in which the treatment of disease by rest was evolved. This being favorably received, I am here this evening to say a few words on that subject.

You all know full well that the art of cure rests upon a number of sciences, and that what we do in medicine, we cannot always explain, and that our methods are far from having the accuracy involved in the term scientific. Very often, however, it is found that what comes to us through some accident or popular use and proves of value, is defensible in the end by scientific explanatory research. This was the case as regards the treatment I shall briefly consider for you to-night.

The first indication I ever had of the great value of mere rest in disease, was during the Civil War, when there fell into the hands of Doctors Morehouse, Keen, and myself, a great many cases of what we called acute exhaustion. These were men, who, being tired by much marching, gave out suddenly at the end of some unusual exertion, and remained for weeks, perhaps months, in a pitiable state of what we should call today, Neurasthenia. In these war cases, it came on with strange abruptness. It was more extreme and also more certainly curable than are most of the graver male cases which now we are called on to treat.

I have seen nothing exactly like it in civil experience, but the combination of malaria, excessive exertion, and exposure provided cases such as no one sees today. Complete rest and plentiful diet usually brought these men up again and in many instances enabled them to return to the front.

In 1872 I had charge of a man who had locomotor ataxia° with extreme pain in the extremities, and while making some unusual exertion, he broke his right thigh. This confined him to his bed for three months, and the day he got up, he broke his left thigh. This involved another three months of rest. At the end of that time he confessed with satisfaction that his ataxia was better, and that he was, as he remained thereafter, free from pain. I learned from this, and two other cases, that in ataxia the bones are brittle, and I learned also that rest in bed is valuable in a proportion of such cases. You may perceive that my attention was thus twice drawn towards the fact that mere rest had certain therapeutic values.

In 1874 Mrs. G., of B ——, Maine, came to see me in the month of January. I have described her case elsewhere, so that it is needless to go into detail here, except to say that she was a lady of ample means, with no special troubles or annoyances, but completely exhausted by having had children in rapid succession and from having undertaken to do charitable and other work to an extent far beyond her strength. When first I saw this tall woman, large, gaunt,

5

---

ataxia: An inability to control muscular movements that is symptomatic of some nervous diseases.

weighing under a hundred pounds, her complexion pale and acneous, and heard her story, I was for a time in a state of such therapeutic despair as usually fell upon physicians of that day when called upon to treat such cases. She had been to Spas, to physicians of the utmost eminence, passed through the hands of gynecologists, worn spinal supporters, and taken every tonic known to the books. When I saw her she was unable to walk up stairs. Her exercise was limited to moving feebly up and down her room, a dozen times a day. She slept little and, being very intelligent, felt deeply her inability to read or write. Any such use of the eyes caused headache and nausea. Conversation tired her, and she had by degrees accepted a life of isolation. She was able partially to digest and retain her meals if she lay down in a noiseless and darkened room. Any disturbance or the least excitement, in short, any effort, caused nausea and immediate rejection of her meal. With care she could retain enough food to preserve her life and hardly to do more. Anemia, which we had then no accurate means of measuring, had been met by half a dozen forms of iron, all of which were said to produce headache, and generally to disagree with her. Naturally enough, her case had been pronounced to be hysteria, but calling names may relieve a doctor and comfort him in failure, but does not always assist the patient, and to my mind there was more of a general condition of nervous excitability due to the extreme of weakness than I should have been satisfied to label with the apologetic label hysteria.

I sat beside this woman day after day, hearing her pitiful story, and distressed that a woman, young, once handsome, and with every means of enjoyment in life should be condemned to what she had been told was a state of hopeless invalidism. After my third or fourth visit, with a deep sense that everything had been done for her that able men could with reason suggest, and many things which reason never could have suggested, she said to me that I appeared to have nothing to offer which had not been tried over and over again. I asked her for another day before she gave up the hope which had brought her to me. The night brought counsel. The following morning I said to her, if you are at rest you appear to digest your meals better. "Yes," she said. "I have been told that on that account I ought to lie in bed. It has been tried, but when I remain in bed for a few days, I lose all appetite, have intense constipation, and get up feeling weaker than when I went to bed. Please do not ask me to go to bed." Nevertheless, I did, and a week in bed justified her statements. She threw up her meals undigested, and was manifestly worse for my experiment. Sometimes the emesis° was mere regurgitation, sometimes there was nausea and violent straining, with consequent extreme exhaustion. She declared that unless she had the small exercise of walking up and down her room, she was infallibly worse. I was here between two difficulties. That she needed rest I saw, that she required some form of exercise I also saw. How could I unite the two?

As I sat beside her, with a keen sense of defeat, it suddenly occurred to me that some time before, I had seen a man, known as a layer on of hands, use very rough rubbing for a gentleman who was in a state of general paresis.°

emesis: Vomiting.   **paresis:** Brain syphilis.

Mr. S. had asked me if I objected to this man rubbing him. I said no, and that I should like to see him do so, as he had relieved, to my knowledge, cases of rheumatic stiffness. I was present at two sittings and saw this man rub my patient. He kept him sitting in a chair at the time and was very rough and violent like the quacks now known as osteopaths. I told him he had injured my patient by his extreme roughness, and that if he rubbed him at all he must be more gentle. He took the hint and as a result there was every time a notable but temporary gain. Struck with this, I tried to have rubbing used on spinal cases, but those who tried to do the work were inefficient, and I made no constant use of it. It remained, however, on my mind, and recurred to me as I sat beside this wreck of a useful and once vigorous woman. The thought was fertile. I asked myself why rubbing might not prove competent to do for the muscles and tardy circulation what voluntary exercise does. I said to myself, this may be exercise without exertion, and wondered why I had not long before had this pregnant view of the matter.

Suffice it to say that I brought a young woman to Mrs. G.'s bedside and told her how I thought she ought to be rubbed. The girl was clever, and developed talent in that direction, and afterwards became the first of that great number of people who have since made a livelihood by massage. I watched the rubbing two or three times, giving instructions, in fact developing out of the clumsy massage I had seen, the manual of a therapeutic means, at that time entirely new to me. A few days later I fell upon the idea of giving electric passive exercise and cautiously added this second agency. Meanwhile, as she had always done best when secluded, I insisted on entire rest and shut out friends, relatives, books, and letters. I had some faith that I should succeed. In ten days I was sure the woman had found a new tonic, hope, and blossomed like a rose. Her symptoms passed away one by one. I was soon able to add to her diet, to feed her between meals, to give her malt daily, and, after a time, to conceal in it full doses of pyro-phosphates of iron. First, then, I had found two means which enabled me to use rest in bed without causing the injurious effects of unassisted rest; secondly, I had discovered that massage was a tonic of extraordinary value; thirdly, I had learned that with this combination of seclusion, massage, and electricity, I could overfeed the patient until I had brought her into a state of entire health. I learned later the care which had to be exercised in getting these patients out of bed. But this does not concern us now. In two months she gained forty pounds and was a cheerful, blooming woman, fit to do as she pleased. She has remained, save for time's ravage, what I made her.

It may strike you as interesting that for a while I was not fully aware of the   10
enormous value of a therapeutic discovery which employed no new agents, but owed its usefulness to a combination of means more or less well known.

Simple rest as a treatment had been suggested, but not in this class of cases. Massage has a long history. Used, I think, as a luxury by the Orientals for ages, it was employed by Ling in 1813. It never attained perfection in the hands of the Swedes, nor do they to-day understand the proper use of this agent. It was over and over recognized in Germany, but never generally accepted. In France, at a later period, Dreyfus, in 1841, wrote upon it and advised its use, as did Recamier and Lainé in 1868. Two at least of these authors thought it useful as a general agent, but no one seems to have accepted their views, nor was its value as a tonic spoken of in the books on therapeutics or recommended on any text-book as a powerful toning agent. It was used here in the Rest Treatment, and this, I think, gave it vogue and caused the familiar use of this invaluable therapeutic measure.

A word before I close. My first case left me in May, 1874, and shortly afterwards I began to employ the same method in other cases, being careful to choose only those which seemed best suited to it. My first mention in print of the treatment was in 1875, in the Sequin Lectures, Vol. 1., No. 4, "Rest in the Treatment of Disease." In that paper I first described Mrs. G.'s case. My second paper was in 1877, an address before the Medico-Chirurgical faculty of Maryland, and the same year I printed my book on "Rest Treatment." The one mistake in the book was the title. I was, however, so impressed at the time by the extraordinary gain in flesh and blood under this treatment that I made it too prominent in the title of the book. Let me say that for a long time the new treatment was received with the utmost incredulity. When I spoke in my papers of the people who had gained half a pound a day or more, my results were questioned and ridiculed in this city as approaching charlatanism. At a later date in England some physicians were equally wanting in foresight and courtesy. It seems incredible that any man who was a member of the British Medical Association could have said that he would rather see his patients not get well than have them cured by such a method as that. It was several years before it was taken up by Professor Goodell, and it was a longer time in making its way in Europe when by mere accident it came to be first used by Professor William Playfair.

I suffered keenly at that time from this unfair criticism, as any sensitive man must have done, for some who were eminent in the profession said of it and of me things which were most inconsiderate. Over and over in consultation I was rejected with ill-concealed scorn. I made no reply to my critics. I knew that time would justify me: I have added a long since accepted means of helping those whom before my day few helped. This is a sufficient reward for silence, patience, and self-faith. I fancy that there are in this room many who have profited for themselves and their patients by the thought which evolved the Rest Treatment as I sat by the bedside of my first rest case in 1874. Playfair said of it at the British Association that he had nothing to add to it and nothing to omit, and to this day no one has differed as to his verdict.

How fully the use of massage has been justified by the later scientific studies of Lauder Brunton, myself, and others you all know. It is one of the most scientific of remedial methods.   *[1904]*

■ THINKING ABOUT THE TEXT

1. How would you describe Mitchell's tone in this lecture? What self-image does he seem to cultivate? Support your answers by referring to specific words in the text.

2. Why does Mitchell consider Mrs. G.'s case significant? In what ways does she resemble Gilman and the narrator of Gilman's story?

3. Mitchell indicates that his patients have included male as well as female hysterics. Are we therefore justified in concluding that gender did not matter much in his application of the "rest cure"? Why, or why not?

JOHN HARVEY KELLOGG

From *The Ladies' Guide in Health and Disease*

John Harvey Kellogg (1852–1943) was an American physician who wrote much advice about how to discipline one's sexual desires and, in the case of women, how to be a good mother. As founder and superintendent of the Battle Creek Sanitarium in Michigan, Dr. Kellogg urged that his patients eat cereals as part of their treatment, and eventually his brother established the cereal company that bears their family name. Dr. Kellogg's keen interest in cereals and health foods is satirized in T. Coraghessan Boyle's 1993 novel, The Road to Wellville, *and the film based on that book. The following piece is an excerpt from Kellogg's 1882* Ladies' Guide in Health and Disease: Girlhood, Maidenhood, Wifehood, Motherhood. *In this selection, he virtually equates womanhood with motherhood and discusses what a woman must do to produce outstanding children. Kellogg's advice reflects the view that much of his society held about women — or at least about middle- and upper-class white women. His discussion of "puerperal mania" is especially relevant to Gilman's story.*

The special influence of the mother begins with the moment of conception. In fact it is possible that the mental condition at the time of the generative act has much to do with determining the character of the child, though it is generally conceded that at this time the influence of the father is greater than that of the mother. Any number of instances have occurred in which a drunken father has impressed upon his child the condition of his nervous system to such a degree as to render permanent in the child the staggering gait and maudlin manner which in his own case was a transient condition induced by the poisonous influence of alcohol. A child born as the result of a union in which both parents were in a state of beastly intoxication was idiotic.

Another fact might be added to impress the importance that the new being should be supplied from the very beginning of its existence with the very best conditions possible. Indeed, it is desirable to go back still further, and secure a proper preparation for the important function of maternity. The qualities which go to make up individuality of character are the result of the summing up of a long line of influences, too subtle and too varied to admit of full control, but still, to some degree at least, subject to management. The dominance of law is nowhere more evident than in the relation of ante-natal influences to character.

The hap-hazard way in which human beings are generated leaves no room for surprise that the race should deteriorate. No stock-breeder would expect anything but ruin should he allow his animals to propagate with no attention to their physical conditions or previous preparation.

Finding herself in a pregnant condition, the mother should not yield to the depressing influences which often crowd upon her. The anxieties and fears which women sometimes yield themselves to, grow with encouragement, until they become so absorbed as to be capable of producing a profoundly evil impression on the child. The true mother who is prepared for the functions of maternity, will welcome the evidence of pregnancy, and joyfully enter upon the Heaven-given task of molding a human character, of bringing into the world a new being whose life-history may involve the destinies of nations, or change the current of human thought for generations to come.

The pregnant mother should cultivate cheerfulness of mind and calmness of temper, but should avoid excitements of all kinds, such as theatrical performances, public contests of various descriptions, etc. Anger, envy, irritability of temper, and, in fact, all the passions and propensities should be held in check. The fickleness of desire and the constantly varying whims which characterize the pregnant state in some women should not be regarded as uncontrollable, and to be yielded to as the only means of appeasing them. The mother should be gently encouraged to resist such tendencies when they become at all marked, and to assist her in the effort, her husband should endeavor to engage her mind by interesting conversation, reading, and various harmless and pleasant diversions.

If it is desired that the child should possess a special aptitude for any particular art or pursuit, during the period of pregnancy the mother's mind should be constantly directed in this channel. If artistic taste or skill is the trait desired, the mother should be surrounded by works of art of a high order of merit. She should read art, think art, talk, and write about art, and if possible, herself engage in the close practical study of some one or more branches of art, as painting, drawing, etching, or modeling. If ability for authorship is desired, then the mother should devote herself assiduously to literature. It is not claimed that by following these suggestions any mother can make of her children great artists or authors at will; but it is certain that by this means the greatest possibilities in individual cases can be attained; and it is certain that decided results have been secured by close attention to the principles laid down. It should be understood, however, that not merely a formal and desultory effort on the part of the mother is what is required. The theme selected must completely absorb her mind. It must be the one idea of her waking thoughts and the model on which is formed the dreams of her sleeping hours.

The question of diet during pregnancy as before stated is a vitally important one as regards the interests of the child. A diet into which enters largely such unwholesome articles as mustard, pepper, hot sauces, spices, and other stimulating condiments, engenders a love for stimulants in the disposition of the infant. Tea and coffee, especially if used to excess, undoubtedly tend in the same direction. We firmly believe that we have, in the facts first stated, the key to the constant increase in the consumption of ardent spirits. The children of the present generation inherit from their condiment-consuming, tea-, coffee-, and liquor-drinking, and tobacco-using parents, not simply a readiness for the acquirement of the habits mentioned, but a propensity for the use of stimulants which in persons of weak will-power and those whose circumstances are not the most favorable, becomes irresistible.

The present generation is also suffering in consequence of the impoverished diet of its parents. The modern custom of bolting the flour from the different grains has deprived millions of infants and children of the necessary supply of bone-making material, thus giving rise to a greatly increased frequency of the various diseases which arise from imperfect bony structure, as rickets, caries, premature decay of the teeth, etc. The proper remedy is the disuse of fine-flour bread and all other bolted grain preparations. Graham-flour bread, oatmeal, cracked wheat, and similar preparations, should be relied upon as the leading articles of diet. Supplemented by milk, the whole-grain preparations constitute a complete form of nourishment, and render a large amount of animal food not only unnecessary but really harmful on account of its stimulating character. It is by no means so necessary as is generally supposed that meat, fish, fowl, and flesh in various forms should constitute a large element of the dietary of the pregnant or nursing mother in order to furnish adequate nourishment for the developing child. We have seen the happiest results follow the employment of a strictly vegetarian dietary, and do not hesitate to advise moderation in the use of flesh food, though we do not recommend the entire discontinuance of its use by the pregnant mother who has been accustomed to use it freely.

A nursing mother should at once suspend nursing if she discovers that pregnancy has again occurred. The continuance of nursing under such circumstances is to the disadvantage of three individuals, the mother, the infant at the breast, and the developing child.

Sexual indulgence during pregnancy may be suspended with decided ben-   10
efit to both mother and child. The most ancient medical writers call attention to the fact that by the practice of continence° during gestation, the pains of childbirth are greatly mitigated. The injurious influences upon the child of the gratification of the passions during the period when its character is being formed, is undoubtedly much greater than is usually supposed. We have no doubt that this is a common cause of the transmission of libidinous tendencies to the child; and that the tendency to abortion is induced by sexual indulgence has long been a well-established fact. The females of most animals resolutely resist the advances of the males during this period, being guided in harmony with natural law by their natural instincts which have been less perverted in them than in human beings. The practice of continence during pregnancy is also enforced in the harems of the East, which fact leads to the practice of abor-

---

continence: Chastity, abstinence, or restraint.

tion among women of this class who are desirous of remaining the special favorites of the common husband.

The general health of the mother must be kept up in every way. It is especially important that the regularity of the bowels should be maintained. Proper diet and as much physical exercise as can be taken are the best means for accomplishing this. When constipation is allowed to exist, the infant as well as the mother suffers. The effete products which should be promptly removed from the body, being long retained, are certain to find their way back into the system again, poisoning not only the blood of the mother but that of the developing fetus. . . .

Puerperal Mania. — This form of mental disease is most apt to show itself about two weeks after delivery. Although, fortunately, of not very frequent occurrence, it is a most serious disorder when it does occur, and hence we may with propriety introduce the following somewhat lengthy, but most graphic description of the disease from the pen of Dr. Ramsbotham, an eminent English physician: —

"In mania there is almost always, at the very commencement, a troubled, agitated, and hurried manner, a restless eye, an unnaturally anxious, suspicious, and unpleasing expression of face; — sometimes it is pallid, at others more flushed than usual; — an unaccustomed irritability of temper, and impatience of control or contradiction; a vacillation of purpose, or loss of memory; sometimes a rapid succession of contradictory orders are issued, or a paroxysm of excessive anger is excited about the merest trifle. Occasionally, one of the first indications will be a sullen obstinacy, or listlessness and stubborn silence. The patient lies on her back, and can by no means be persuaded to reply to the questions of her attendants, or she will repeat them, as an echo, until, all at once, without any apparent cause, she will break out into a torrent of language more or less incoherent, and her words will follow each other with surprising rapidity. These symptoms will sometimes show themselves rather suddenly, on the patient's awakening from a disturbed and unrefreshing sleep, or they may supervene more slowly when she has been harassed with wakefulness for three or four previous nights in succession, or perhaps ever since her delivery. She will very likely then become impressed with the idea that some evil has befallen her husband, or, what is still more usual, her child; that it is dead or stolen; and if it be brought to her, nothing can persuade her it is her own; she supposes it to belong to somebody else; or she will fancy that her husband is unfaithful to her, or that he and those about her have conspired to poison her. Those persons who are naturally the objects of her deepest and most devout affection, are regarded by her with jealousy, suspicion, and hatred. This is particularly remarkable with regard to her newly born infant; and I have known many instances where attempts have been made to destroy it when it has been incautiously left within her power. Sometimes, though rarely, may be observed a great anxiety regarding the termination of her own case, or a firm conviction that she is speedily about to die. I have observed upon occasions a constant movement of the lips, while the mouth was shut; or the patient is incessantly rubbing the inside of her lips with her fingers, or thrusting them far back into her mouth; and if questions are asked, particularly if she be desired to put out her tongue, she will often compress the lips forcibly together, as if with an obstinate determination of resistance. One peculiarity attending some cases of puerperal mania is the immorality and obscenity of the expressions uttered; they are often such, indeed, as to excite our astonishment that women in a respectable station of society could ever have become acquainted with such language."

The insanity of childbirth differs from that of pregnancy in that in the latter cases the patient is almost always melancholy,° while in the former there is active mania. Derangement of the digestive organs is a constant accompaniment of the disease.

If the patient has no previous or hereditary tendency to insanity, the prospect of a quite speedy recovery is good. The result is seldom immediately fatal, but the patient not infrequently remains in a condition of mental unsoundness for months or even years, and sometimes permanently.   15

Treatment: When there is reason to suspect a liability to puerperal mania from previous mental disease or from hereditary influence, much can be done to ward off an attack. Special attention must be paid to the digestive organs, which should be regulated by proper food and simple means to aid digestion. The tendency to sleeplessness must be combatted by careful nursing, light massage at night, rubbing of the spine, alternate hot and cold applications to the spine, cooling the head by cloths wrung out of cold water, and the use of the warm bath at bed time. These measures are often successful in securing sleep when all other measures fail.

The patient must be kept very quiet. Visitors, even if near relatives, must not be allowed when the patient is at all nervous or disturbed, and it is best to exclude nearly every one from the sick-room with the exception of the nurse, who should be a competent and experienced person.

When the attack has really begun, the patient must have the most vigilant watchcare, not being left alone for a moment. It is much better to care for the patient at home, when possible to do so efficiently, than to take her to an asylum.

When evidences of returning rationality appear, the greatest care must be exercised to prevent too great excitement. Sometimes a change of air, if the patient is sufficiently strong, physically, will at this period prove eminently beneficial. A visit from a dear friend will sometimes afford a needed stimulus to the dormant faculties. Such cases as these of course require intelligent medical supervision.   [1882]

melancholy: Mental state characterized by severe depression, somatic problems, and hallucinations or delusions.

≡ THINKING ABOUT THE TEXT

1. What specific responsibilities does Kellogg assign to women? What are some key assumptions he makes about them?

2. Quite possibly Kellogg would have said that the narrator of Gilman's story suffers from puerperal mania. What details of the story would support this diagnosis? What significant details of the narrator's life, if any, would Kellogg be ignoring if he saw her as *merely* a case of puerperal mania?

3. If Kellogg's advice were published today, what parts of it do you think readers would accept? What parts do you think many readers would reject?

≡ **WRITING ABOUT ISSUES**

1. "The Yellow Wallpaper" ends with the narrator creeping. Write an essay explaining how you think this act should be judged. What should readers take into consideration as they seek to put this act in context?

2. Write an essay discussing "The Yellow Wallpaper" as a response to the kind of thinking expressed in Mitchell's or Kellogg's selection. Refer to specific details of both texts. If you wish, you may refer as well to Gilman's "Why I Wrote 'The Yellow Wallpaper.' "

3. Write an essay about an occasion when you, or someone you know, tried to challenge a medical or psychiatric diagnosis. Above all, analyze how doctor and patient behaved toward each other. (There may have been more than one doctor involved.) If you wish, imagine what Gilman would have said about this experience.

4. As we said in the introduction to this cluster, today many more women than men seek treatment for depression, anorexia, bulimia, and dissociative identity disorder. Research one of these conditions, and then write an essay in which you try to explain why it seems to afflict mostly women. If you wish, refer to any of the texts in this cluster.

Hobbled by Language: Essays

RICHARD RODRIGUEZ, "Aria"

TOMÁS RIVERA, "On Richard Rodriguez's *Hunger of Memory*"

VICTOR VILLANUEVA JR., "Reflecting on Richard Rodriguez"

For many American children, the culture of school differs greatly from the one they know at home. Children of immigrants to America may sense such a cultural divide, especially if their teachers speak English in the classroom while their parents speak another language at home. In his 1982 memoir, *Hunger of Memory*, Richard Rodriguez recalls how he faced exactly this situation as the child of Mexican immigrants. Rodriguez uses his own experiences to argue that if the children of immigrants are to succeed in the United States, they must separate themselves from their home culture and immerse themselves in the English-oriented atmosphere of the American school. In making this argument, Rodriguez comes out against bilingual education and affirmative action. When it was first published, many people praised his book for its eloquence, honesty, and realism. Subsequently, however, the book received strong criticism, especially from Hispanic American educators. Several of them disagree with the positions it takes; moreover, they worry that Rodriguez will be seen as the authoritative guide to Hispanic American life. Here we include an excerpt from Rodriguez's book along with comments by two of his Hispanic critics. Although these texts are from the 1980s, the issues they examine are still very much alive. In the twenty-first century, people continue to debate how American immigrants and their children should be educated, arguing over such things as California's Proposition 209 (which outlawed racial preferences) and the English Only movement (which wants laws requiring government business to be conducted entirely in English).

≣ BEFORE YOU READ

The following excerpt from Richard Rodriguez's *Hunger of Memory* ends with his claim that "the day I raised my hand in class and spoke loudly to an entire roomful of faces, my childhood started to end." When do you think your childhood started to end? Think of a particular moment or set of experiences.

RICHARD RODRIGUEZ
Aria

A native of San Francisco, California, Richard Rodriguez (b. 1944) is the son of Mexican immigrants. Until he entered school at the age of six, he spoke primarily Spanish. His 1982 memoir, Hunger of Memory, *describes how English-language instruction distanced him from his parents' native culture. Rodriguez went on to attend Stanford University and the University of California at Berkeley, where he earned a doctorate in English Renaissance literature.* He is also the author of Days of Obligation: An Argument with My Mexican Father *(1992) and* Brown: The Last Discovery of America *(2003). His essay "The God of the Desert" was published in* Best American Essays 2009. *Currently Rodriguez is a contributing editor for* Harper's *magazine and a commentator on public television's* NewsHour.

1

I remember to start with that day in Sacramento — a California now nearly thirty years past — when I first entered a classroom, able to understand some fifty stray English words.

The third of four children, I had been preceded to a neighborhood Roman Catholic school by an older brother and sister. But neither of them had revealed very much about their classroom experiences. Each afternoon they returned, as they left in the morning, always together, speaking in Spanish as they climbed the five steps of the porch. And their mysterious books, wrapped in shopping-bag paper, remained on the table next to the door, closed firmly behind them.

An accident of geography sent me to a school where all my classmates were white, many the children of doctors and lawyers and business executives. All my classmates certainly must have been uneasy on that first day of school — as most children are uneasy — to find themselves apart from their families in the first institution of their lives. But I was astonished.

The nun said, in a friendly but oddly impersonal voice, "Boys and girls, this is Richard Rodriguez." (I heard her sound out: *Rich-heard Road-ree-guess.*) It was the first time I had heard anyone name me in English. "Richard," the nun repeated more slowly, writing my name down in her black leather book. Quickly I turned to see my mother's face dissolve in a watery blur behind the pebbled glass door.

Many years later there is something called bilingual education — a scheme proposed in the late 1960s by Hispanic-American social activists, later endorsed by a congressional vote. It is a program that seeks to permit non-English-speaking children, many from lower-class homes, to use their family language as the language of school. (Such is the goal its supporters announce.) I hear them and am forced to say no: it is not possible for a child — any child — ever to use his family's language in school. Not to understand this is to misunderstand the public uses of schooling and to trivialize the nature of intimate life — a family's "language."

Memory teaches me what I know of these matters; the boy reminds the adult. I was a bilingual child, a certain kind — socially disadvantaged — the son of working-class parents, both Mexican immigrants.

In the early years of my boyhood, my parents coped very well in America. My father had steady work. My mother managed at home. They were nobody's

5

victims. Optimism and ambition led them to a house (our home) many blocks from the Mexican south side of town. We lived among *gringos* and only a block from the biggest, whitest houses. It never occurred to my parents that they couldn't live wherever they chose. Nor was the Sacramento of the fifties bent on teaching them a contrary lesson. My mother and father were more annoyed than intimidated by those two or three neighbors who tried initially to make us unwelcome. ("Keep your brats away from my sidewalk!") But despite all they achieved, perhaps because they had so much to achieve, any deep feeling of ease, the confidence of "belonging" in public was withheld from them both. They regarded the people at work, the faces in crowds, as very distant from us. They were the others, *los gringos*. That term was interchangeable in their speech with another, even more telling, *los americanos*.

I grew up in a house where the only regular guests were my relations. For one day, enormous families of relatives would visit and there would be so many people that the noise and the bodies would spill out to the backyard and front porch. Then, for weeks, no one came by. (It was usually a salesman who rang the doorbell.) Our house stood apart. A gaudy yellow in a row of white bungalows. We were the people with the noisy dog. The people who raised pigeons and chickens. We were the foreigners on the block. A few neighbors smiled and waved. We waved back. But no one in the family knew the names of the old couple who lived next door; until I was seven years old, I did not know the names of the kids who lived across the street.

In public, my father and mother spoke a hesitant, accented, not always grammatical English. And they would have to strain — their bodies tense — to catch the sense of what was rapidly said by *los gringos*. At home they spoke Spanish. The language of their Mexican past sounded in counterpoint to the English of public society. The words would come quickly, with ease. Conveyed through those sounds was the pleasing, soothing, consoling reminder of being at home.

During those years when I was first conscious of hearing, my mother and   10
father addressed me only in Spanish; in Spanish I learned to reply. By contrast, English (*inglés*), rarely heard in the house, was the language I came to associate with *gringos*. I learned my first words of English overhearing my parents speak to strangers. At five years of age, I knew just enough English for my mother to trust me on errands to stores one block away. No more.

I was a listening child, careful to hear the very different sounds of Spanish and English. Wide-eyed with hearing, I'd listen to sounds more than words. First, there were English (*gringo*) sounds. So many words were still unknown that when the butcher or the lady at the drugstore said something to me, exotic polysyllabic sounds would bloom in the midst of their sentences. Often, the speech of people in public seemed to me very loud, booming with confidence. The man behind the counter would literally ask, "What can I do for you?" But by being so firm and so clear, the sound of his voice said that he was a *gringo*; he belonged in public society.

I would also hear then the high nasal notes of middle-class American speech. The air stirred with sound. Sometimes, even now, when I have been traveling abroad for several weeks, I will hear what I heard as a boy. In hotel lobbies or airports, in Turkey or Brazil, some Americans will pass, and suddenly I will hear it again — the high sound of American voices. For a few seconds I will hear it with pleasure, for it is now the sound of *my* society — a reminder of home. But inevitably — already on the flight headed for home — the sound fades with repetition. I will be unable to hear it anymore.

When I was a boy, things were different. The accent of *los gringos* was never pleasing nor was it hard to hear. Crowds at Safeway or at bus stops would be noisy with sound. And I would be forced to edge away from the chirping chatter above me.

I was unable to hear my own sounds, but I knew very well that I spoke English poorly. My words could not stretch far enough to form complete thoughts. And the words I did speak I didn't know well enough to make into distinct sounds. (Listeners would usually lower their heads, better to hear what I was trying to say.) But it was one thing for *me* to speak English with difficulty. It was more troubling for me to hear my parents speak in public: their high-whining vowels and guttural consonants; their sentences that got stuck with "eh" and "ah" sounds; the confused syntax; the hesitant rhythm of sounds so different from the way *gringos* spoke. I'd notice, moreover, that my parents' voices were softer than those of *gringos* we'd meet.

I am tempted now to say that none of this mattered. In adulthood I am embarrassed by childhood fears. And in a way, it didn't matter very much that my parents could not speak English with ease. Their linguistic difficulties had no serious consequences. My mother and father made themselves understood at the county hospital clinic and at government offices. And yet, in another way, it mattered very much — it was unsettling to hear my parents struggle with English. Hearing them, I'd grow nervous, my clutching trust in their protection and power weakened.

There were many times like the night at a brightly lit gasoline station (a blaring white memory) when I stood uneasily, hearing my father. He was talking to a teenaged attendant. I do not recall what they were saying, but I cannot forget the sounds my father made as he spoke. At one point his words slid together to form one word — sounds as confused as the threads of blue and green oil in the puddle next to my shoes. His voice rushed through what he had left to say. And, toward the end, reached falsetto notes, appealing to his listener's understanding. I looked away to the lights of passing automobiles. I tried not to hear anymore. But I heard only too well the calm, easy tones in the attendant's reply. Shortly afterward, walking toward home with my father, I shivered when he put his hand on my shoulder. The very first chance that I got, I evaded his grasp and ran on ahead into the dark, skipping with feigned boyish exuberance.

But then there was Spanish. *Español*: my family's language. *Español*: the language that seemed to me a private language. I'd hear strangers on the radio and in the Mexican Catholic church across town speaking in Spanish, but I couldn't really believe that Spanish was a public language, like English. Spanish speakers, rather, seemed related to me, for I sensed that we shared — through our language — the experience of feeling apart from *los gringos*. It was thus a

15

ghetto Spanish that I heard and I spoke. Like those whose lives are bound by a barrio, I was reminded by Spanish of my separateness from *los otros, los gringos* in power. But more intensely than for most barrio children — because I did not live in a barrio — Spanish seemed to me the language of home. (Most days it was only at home that I'd hear it.) It became the language of joyful return.

A family member would say something to me and I would feel myself specially recognized. My parents would say something to me and I would feel embraced by the sounds of their words. Those sounds said: *I am speaking with ease in Spanish. I am addressing you in words I never use with* los gringos. *I recognize you as someone special, close, like no one outside. You belong with us. In the family.* (*Ricardo.*)

At the age of five, six, well past the time when most other children no longer easily notice the difference between sounds uttered at home and words spoken in public, I had a different experience. I lived in a world magically compounded of sounds. I remained a child longer than most; I lingered too long, poised at the edge of language — often frightened by the sounds of *los gringos,* delighted by the sounds of Spanish at home. I shared with my family a language that was startlingly different from that used in the great city around us,   20

For me there were none of the gradations between public and private society so normal to a maturing child. Outside the house was public society; inside the house was private. Just opening or closing the screen door behind me was an important experience. I'd rarely leave home all alone or without reluctance. Walking down the sidewalk, under the canopy of tall trees, I'd warily notice the — suddenly — silent neighborhood kids who stood warily watching me. Nervously, I'd arrive at the grocery store to hear there the sounds of the *gringo* — foreign to me — reminding me that in this world so big, I was a foreigner. But then I'd return. Walking back toward our house, climbing the steps from the sidewalk, when the front door was open in summer, I'd hear voices beyond the screen door talking in Spanish. For a second or two, I'd stay, linger there, listening. Smiling, I'd hear my mother call out, saying in Spanish (words): "Is that you, Richard?" All the while her sounds would assure me: *You are home now; come closer; inside. With us.*

"*Sí,*" I'd reply.

Once more inside the house I would resume (assume) my place in the family. The sounds would dim, grow harder to hear. Once more at home, I would grow less aware of that fact. It required, however, no more than the blurt of the doorbell to alert me to listen to sounds all over again. The house would turn instantly still while my mother went to the door. I'd hear her hard English sounds. I'd wait to hear her voice return to soft-sounding Spanish, which assured me, as surely as did the clicking tongue of the lock on the door, that the stranger was gone.

Plainly, it is not healthy to hear such sounds so often. It is not healthy to distinguish public words from private sounds so easily. I remained cloistered by sounds, timid and shy in public, too dependent on voices at home. And yet it needs to be emphasized: I was an extremely happy child at home. I remember many nights when my father would come back from work, and I'd hear him call out to my mother in Spanish, sounding relieved. In Spanish, he'd sound light and free notes he never could manage in English. Some nights I'd jump up just at hearing his voice. With *mis hermanos* I would come running into the room where he was with my mother. Our laughing (so deep was the pleasure!) became screaming. Like others who know the pain of public alienation, we transformed the knowledge of our public separateness and made it consoling — the reminder of intimacy. Excited, we joined our voices in a celebration of sounds. *We are speaking now the way we never speak out in public. We are alone — together,* voices sounded, surrounded to tell me. Some nights, no one seemed willing to loosen the hold sounds had on us. At dinner, we invented new words. (Ours sounded Spanish, but made sense only to us.) We pieced together new words by taking, say, an English verb and giving it Spanish endings. My mother's instructions at bedtime would be lacquered with mock-urgent tones. Or a word like *sí* would become, in several notes, able to convey added measures of feeling. Tongues explored the edges of words, especially the fat vowels. And we happily sounded that military drum roll, the twirling roar of the Spanish *r.* Family language: my family's sounds. The voices of my parents and sisters and brother. Their voices insisting: *You belong here. We are family members. Related. Special to one another. Listen!* Voices singing and sighing, rising, straining, then surging, teeming with pleasure that burst syllables into fragments of laughter. At times it seemed there was steady quiet only when, from another room, the rustling whispers of my parents faded and I moved closer to sleep.

2

Supporters of bilingual education today imply that students like me miss a great   25
deal by not being taught in their family's language. What they seem not to recognize is that, as a socially disadvantaged child, I considered Spanish to be a private language. What I needed to learn in school was that I had the right — and the obligation — to speak the public language of *los gringos.* The odd truth is that my first-grade classmates could have become bilingual, in the conventional sense of that word, more easily than I. Had they been taught (as upper-middle-class children are often taught early) a second language like Spanish or French, they could have regarded it simply as that: another public language. In my case such bilingualism could not have been so quickly achieved. What I did not believe was that I could speak a single public language.

Without question, it would have pleased me to hear my teachers address me in Spanish when I entered the classroom. I would have felt much less afraid. I would have trusted them and responded with ease. But I would have delayed — for how long postponed? — having to learn the language of public society. I would have evaded — and for how long could I have afforded to delay? — learning the great lesson of school, that I had a public identity.

Fortunately, my teachers were unsentimental about their responsibility. What they understood was that I needed to speak a public language. So their voices would search me out, asking me questions. Each time I'd hear them, I'd look up in surprise to see a nun's face frowning at me. I'd mumble, not really meaning to answer. The nun would persist, "Richard, stand up. Don't look at the floor. Speak up. Speak to the entire class, not just to me!" But I couldn't believe that the English language was mine to use. (In part, I did not want to believe it.) I continued to mumble. I resisted the teacher's demands. (Did I somehow suspect that once I learned public language my pleasing family life would be changed?) Silent, waiting for the bell to sound, I remained dazed, diffident, afraid.

Because I wrongly imagined that English was intrinsically a public language and Spanish an intrinsically private one, I easily noted the difference between classroom language and the language of home. At school, words were directed to a general audience of listeners. ("Boys and girls.") Words were meaningfully ordered. And the point was not self-expression alone but to make oneself understood by many others. The teacher quizzed: "Boys and girls, why do we use that word in this sentence? Could we think of a better word to use there? Would the sentence change its meaning if the words were differently arranged? And wasn't there a better way of saying much the same thing?" (I couldn't say. I wouldn't try to say.)

Three months. Five. Half a year passed. Unsmiling, ever watchful, my teachers noted my silence. They began to connect my behavior with the difficult progress my older sister and brother were making. Until one Saturday morning three nuns arrived at the house to talk to our parents. Stiffly, they sat on the blue living room sofa. From the doorway of another room, spying the visitors, I noted the incongruity—the clash of two worlds, the faces and voices of school intruding upon the familiar setting of home. I overheard one voice gently wondering, "Do your children speak only Spanish at home, Mrs. Rodriguez?" While another voice added, "That Richard especially seems so timid and shy."

That Rich-heard!   30

With great tact the visitors continued, "Is it possible for you and your husband to encourage your children to practice their English when they are home?" Of course, my parents complied. What would they not do for their children's well-being? And how could they have questioned the Church's authority which those women represented? In an instant, they agreed to give up the language (the sounds) that had revealed and accentuated our family's closeness. The moment after the visitors left, the change was observed. "*Ahora,* speak to us *en inglés,*" my father and mother united to tell us.

At first, it seemed a kind of game. After dinner each night, the family gathered to practice "our" English. (It was still then *inglés,* a language foreign to us, so we felt drawn as strangers to it.) Laughing, we would try to define words we could not pronounce. We played with strange English sounds, often overanglicizing our pronunciations. And we filled the smiling gaps of our sentences with familiar Spanish sounds. But that was cheating, somebody shouted. Everyone laughed. In school, meanwhile, like my brother and sister, I was required to attend a daily tutoring session. I needed a full year of special attention. I also needed my teachers to keep my attention from straying in class by calling out,

Rich-heard—their English voices slowly prying loose my ties to my other name, its three notes, *Ri-car-do*. Most of all I needed to hear my mother and father speak to me in a moment of seriousness in broken—suddenly heartbreaking—English. The scene was inevitable: one Saturday morning I entered the kitchen where my parents were talking in Spanish. I did not realize that they were talking in Spanish however until, at the moment they saw me, I heard their voices change to speak English. Those *gringo* sounds they uttered startled me. Pushed me away. In that moment of trivial misunderstanding and profound insight, I felt my throat twisted by unsounded grief. I turned quickly and left the room. But I had no place to escape to with Spanish. (The spell was broken.) My brother and sisters were speaking English in another part of the house.

Again and again in the days following, increasingly angry, I was obliged to hear my mother and father: "Speak to us *en inglés*." (*Speak*.) Only then did I determine to learn classroom English. Weeks after, it happened: one day in school I raised my hand to volunteer an answer. I spoke out in a loud voice. And I did not think it remarkable when the entire class understood. That day, I moved very far from the disadvantaged child I had been only days earlier. The belief, the calming assurance that I belonged in public, had at last taken hold.

Shortly after, I stopped hearing the high and loud sounds of *los gringos*. A more and more confident speaker of English, I didn't trouble to listen to *how* strangers sounded, speaking to me. And there simply were too many English-speaking people in my day for me to hear American accents anymore. Conversations quickened. Listening to persons who sounded eccentrically pitched voices, I usually noted their sounds for an initial few seconds before I concentrated on *what* they were saying. Conversations became content-full. Transparent. Hearing someone's *tone* of voice—angry or questioning or sarcastic or happy or sad—I didn't distinguish it from the words it expressed. Sound and word were thus tightly wedded. At the end of a day, I was often bemused, always relieved, to realize how "silent," though crowded with words, my day in public had been. (This public silence measured and quickened the change in my life.)

At last, seven years old, I came to believe what had been technically true since my birth: I was an American citizen.   35

But the special feeling of closeness at home was diminished by then. Gone was the desperate, urgent, intense feeling of being at home; rare was the experience of feeling myself individualized by family intimates. We remained a loving family, but one greatly changed. No longer so close; no longer bound tight by the pleasing and troubling knowledge of our public separateness. Neither my older brother nor sister rushed home after school anymore. Nor did I. When I arrived home there would often be neighborhood kids in the house. Or the house would be empty of sounds.

Following the dramatic Americanization of their children, even my parents grew more publicly confident. Especially my mother. She learned the names of all the people on our block. And she decided we needed to have a telephone installed in the house. My father continued to use the word *gringo*. But it was no longer charged with the old bitterness or distrust. (Stripped of any emotional content, the word simply became a name for those Americans not of Hispanic descent.) Hearing him, sometimes, I wasn't sure if he was pronouncing the Spanish word *gringo* or saying gringo in English.

Matching the silence I started hearing in public was a new quiet at home. The family's quiet was partly due to the fact that, as we children learned more and more English, we shared fewer and fewer words with our parents. Sentences needed to be spoken slowly when a child addressed his mother or father. (Often the parent wouldn't understand.) The child would need to repeat himself. (Still the parent misunderstood.) The young voice, frustrated, would end up saying, "Never mind" — the subject was closed. Dinners would be noisy with the clinking of knives and forks against dishes. My mother would smile softly between her remarks; my father at the other end of the table would chew and chew at his food, while he stared over the heads of his children.

My *mother*! My *father*! After English became my primary language, I no longer knew what words to use in addressing my parents. The old Spanish words (those tender accents of sound) I had used earlier — *mamá* and *papá* — I couldn't use anymore. They would have been too painful reminders of how much had changed in my life. On the other hand, the words I heard neighborhood kids call *their* parents seemed equally unsatisfactory. *Mother* and *Father*; *Ma, Papa, Pa, Dad, Pop* (how I hated the all-American sound of that last word especially) — all these terms I felt were unsuitable, not really terms of address for *my* parents. As a result, I never used them at home. Whenever I'd speak to my parents, I would try to get their attention with eye contact alone. In public conversations, I'd refer to "my parents" or "my mother and father."

My mother and father, for their part, responded differently, as their children spoke to them less. She grew restless, seemed troubled and anxious at the scarcity of words exchanged in the house. It was she who would question me about my day when I came home from school. She smiled at small talk. She pried at the edges of my sentences to get me to say something more. (What?) She'd join conversations she overheard, but her intrusions often stopped her children's talking. By contrast, my father seemed reconciled to the new quiet. Though his English improved somewhat, he retired into silence. At dinner he spoke very little. One night his children and even his wife helplessly giggled at his garbled English pronunciation of the Catholic Grace before Meals. Thereafter he made his wife recite the prayer at the start of each meal, even on formal occasions, when there were guests in the house. Hers became the public voice of the family. On official business, it was she, not my father, one would usually hear on the phone or in stores, talking to strangers. His children grew so accustomed to his silence that, years later, they would speak routinely of his shyness. (My mother would often try to explain: both his parents died when he was eight. He was raised by an uncle who treated him like little more than a menial servant. He was never encouraged to speak. He grew up alone. A man of few words.) But my father was not shy, I realized, when I'd watch him speaking Spanish with relatives. Using Spanish, he was quickly effusive. Especially when talking with other men, his voice would spark, flicker, flare alive with sounds. In Spanish, he expressed ideas and feelings he rarely revealed in En-

40

glish. With firm Spanish sounds, he conveyed confidence and authority English would never allow him.

The silence at home, however, was finally more than a literal silence. Fewer words passed between parent and child, but more profound was the silence that resulted from my inattention to sounds. At about the time I no longer bothered to listen with care to the sounds of English in public, I grew careless about listening to the sounds family members made when they spoke. Most of the time I heard someone speaking at home and didn't distinguish his sounds from the words people uttered in public. I didn't even pay much attention to my parents' accented and ungrammatical speech. At least not at home. Only when I was with them in public would I grow alert to their accents. Though, even then, their sounds caused me less and less concern. For I was increasingly confident of my own public identity.

I would have been happier about my public success had I not sometimes recalled what it had been like earlier, when my family had conveyed its intimacy through a set of conveniently private sounds. Sometimes in public, hearing a stranger, I'd hark back to my past. A Mexican farmworker approached me downtown to ask directions to somewhere. "¿Hijito . . . ?" he said. And his voice summoned deep longing. Another time, standing beside my mother in the visiting room of a Carmelite convent, before the dense screen which rendered the nuns shadowy figures, I heard several Spanish-speaking nuns—their busy, singsong overlapping voices—assure us that yes, yes, we were remembered, all our family was remembered in their prayers. (Their voices echoed faraway family sounds.) Another day, a dark-faced old woman—her hand light on my shoulder—steadied herself against me as she boarded a bus. She murmured something I couldn't quite comprehend. Her Spanish voice came near, like the face of a never-before-seen relative in the instant before I was kissed. Her voice, like so many of the Spanish voices I'd hear in public, recalled the golden age of my youth. Hearing Spanish then, I continued to be a careful, if sad, listener to sounds. Hearing a Spanish-speaking family walking behind me, I turned to look. I smiled for an instant, before my glance found the Hispanic-looking faces of strangers in the crowd going by.

Today I hear bilingual educators say that children lose a degree of "individuality" by becoming assimilated into public society. (Bilingual schooling was popularized in the seventies, that decade when middle-class ethnics began to resist the process of assimilation—the American melting pot.) But the bilingualists simplistically scorn the value and necessity of assimilation. They do not seem to realize that there are *two* ways a person is individualized. So they do not realize that while one suffers a diminished sense of *private* individuality by becoming assimilated into public society, such assimilation makes possible the achievement of *public* individuality.

The bilingualists insist that a student should be reminded of his difference from others in mass society, his heritage. But they equate mere separateness with individuality. The fact is that only in private—with intimates—is separateness from the crowd a prerequisite for individuality. (An intimate draws me apart, tells me that I am unique, unlike all others.) In public, by contrast, full individuality is achieved, paradoxically, by those who are able to consider themselves members of the crowd. Thus it happened for me: only when I was able to think of myself as an American, no longer an alien in *gringo* society, could I seek the rights and opportunities necessary for full public individuality. The social and political advantages I enjoy as a man result from the day that I came to believe that my name, indeed, is *Rich-heard Road-ree-guess*. It is true that my public society today is often impersonal. (My public society is usually mass society.) Yet despite the anonymity of the crowd and despite the fact that the individuality I achieve in public is often tenuous — because it depends on my being one in a crowd — I celebrate the day I acquired my new name. Those middle-class ethnics who scorn assimilation seem to me filled with decadent self-pity, obsessed by the burden of public life. Dangerously, they romanticize public separateness and they trivialize the dilemma of the socially disadvantaged.

My awkward childhood does not prove the necessity of bilingual educa-   45
tion. My story discloses instead an essential myth of childhood — inevitable pain. If I rehearse here the changes in my private life after my Americanization, it is finally to emphasize the public gain. The loss implies the gain: the house I returned to each afternoon was quiet. Intimate sounds no longer rushed to the door to greet me. There were other noises inside. The telephone rang. Neighborhood kids ran past the door of the bedroom where I was reading my schoolbooks — covered with shopping-bag paper. Once I learned public language, it would never again be easy for me to hear intimate family voices. More and more of my day was spent hearing words. But that may only be a way of saying that the day I raised my hand in class and spoke loudly to an entire roomful of faces, my childhood started to end.   *[1982]*

≣ THINKING ABOUT THE TEXT

1. What distinctions does Rodriguez make between the "private" and "public" worlds of his childhood? Ultimately, he brings up the possibility of "*public* individuality" (para. 43). What does he mean by this? Does this concept make sense to you?

2. What, according to Rodriguez, were the changes he experienced? With what tone does he recall these changes? Consider in particular the way he describes his changing relationship to his parents.

3. Do you agree with Rodriguez that the changes he went through were necessary? To what extent is your answer influenced by your own social position?

4. Rodriguez declares, "Those middle-class ethnics who scorn assimilation seem to me filled with decadent self-pity, obsessed by the burden of public life. Dangerously, they romanticize public separateness and they trivialize the dilemma of the socially disadvantaged" (para. 44). Evalu-

ate this claim. Would you say that you are a "middle-class ethnic"? Why, or why not?

5. Rodriguez suggests that a student must speak up in class to succeed in school. Do you agree? Rodriguez indicates that matters of language play a crucial role in a child's education. Have you found this true? Be specific.

TOMÁS RIVERA

On Richard Rodriguez's *Hunger of Memory*

Tomás Rivera (1935–1984) was chancellor of the University of California at the time he wrote the following comments. They appear in his article "Richard Rodriguez's Hunger of Memory *as Humanistic Antithesis," which was published posthumously in a 1984 issue of the journal* Melus.

[Rodriguez's] search for life and form in the literary form of autobiography has as a premise the basic core of family life. But then Richard Rodriguez struggles with the sense of dissociation from that basic culture. Clearly, he opts to dissociate, and, as a scholar, attempts to rationalize that only through dissociation from a native culture was he to gain and thus has gained the "other," that is, the "public" world. Without wisdom he almost forgets the original passions of human life. Is he well educated in literature? For literature above all gives and inculcates in the student and scholar the fundamental original elements of humanistic endeavor without regard to race or language, much less with regards to a public voice. The most important ideas that the study of the humanities relates are the fundamental values and elements of human beings, regardless of race and nationality. Ultimately, the study of the humanities teaches the idea that life is a relationship with the totality of people within its circumstance.

Then we come to the question of place and being. In Spanish there are two verbs meaning "to be," *ser* and *estar.* This is quite important to *Hunger of Memory.* Being born into a family is equal to being, *ser.* Education and instruction teaches us to be, *estar.* Both are fundamental verbs. *Ser* is an interior stage, and *estar* is an exterior one. To leave the *ser* only for the *estar* is a grievous error. Richard Rodriguez implies, at times explicitly, that the authentic being is and can be only in the *estar* (public voice) and only there is he/she complete. And further, he states that authenticity can only come by being an exterior being in English in the English-speaking world. In the Hispanic world, the interior world of *ser* is ultimately more important than the world of *estar. Honra,* honesty, emanates from and is important to the *ser.* Richard Rodriguez opts for the *estar* world as the more important and does not give due importance to the world of *ser.* He has problems, in short, with the world from which he came. Surely this is an antithesis to a humanistic development.

As with memory, the centrality of language is a constant pattern in the book. For the Hispanic reader the struggle quickly becomes English versus Spanish. His parents do not know the grand development of the Spanish language and its importance beyond their immediate family. However, Richard Rodriguez should, as an educated person, recognize this grand development. Surely, he could have given credit to the development of a language that has existed over six hundred years, which has elaborated a world literature, which has mixed with the many languages of the American continents, which is perhaps the most analytical of the romance languages, and which will be of such importance in the twenty-first century. Instead Richard Rodriguez flees, as a young man, from this previous human achievement. This fleeing is understandable as a symbol of the pressures of the Americanization process. Yet, as a formally educated scholar, reflecting upon that flight, he does not dare to signal the importance that the language has. Instead he sees it as an activity that has no redeeming value. He gives no value to the Hispanic language, its culture, its arts. It is difficult to believe that as an educated humanist he doesn't recognize the most important element of Hispanic culture — the context of the development of the distinct religions in the Spanish peninsula — the Judaic, the Christian, and the Moorish. These distinct cultures reached their apogees and clearly influenced Spanish. As a humanist, surely he must know this. The Hispanic world has elaborated and developed much in the history of ideas. Richard Rodriguez seems to indicate that the personal Spanish voice lacks the intelligence and ability to communicate beyond the sensibilities of the personal interactions of personal family life. This is intolerable. Hispanic culture has a historical tradition of great intellectual development.   *[1984]*

≡ THINKING ABOUT THE TEXT

1. What does Rivera find "intolerable" about Rodriguez's position?

2. What distinctions does Rivera make about the Spanish verbs for "to be"? Are such distinctions possible in English?

3. Do you agree with the idea Rivera asserts in the last sentence of the first paragraph? Is this a lesson you learned in literature courses?

4. Do you see the home and neighborhood you came from as a plus or a minus or a combination of both positive and negative influences?

5. Did you think of the language you used as a child at home as private and your school voice as public? Do you now? Is this a matter of class or ethnicity?

≡ MAKING COMPARISONS

1. What do you think about the effectiveness of Rivera's assertion that "[w]ithout wisdom [Rodriguez] almost forgets the original passions of human life"?

2. Is it true that, as Rivera asserts, Rodriguez "does not give due importance to the world of *ser*"?

3. What other arguments in the last paragraph does Rivera have with Rodriguez? Which seems the most effective?

VICTOR VILLANUEVA JR.
Reflecting on Richard Rodriguez

Of Puerto Rican descent, Victor Villanueva Jr. (b. 1948) grew up in New York City. Currently he is a professor of English at Washington State University in Pullman, Washington. In 1993, he published an autobiography entitled Bootstraps: The Autobiography of an Academic of Color. *In 2003, he edited a widely read text in composition studies,* Cross-Talk in Comp Theory: A Reader, *and in 2004 he co-edited* Latino/a Discourses. *The following remarks come from his article "Whose Voice Is It Anyway? Rodriguez's Speech in Retrospect," which appeared in a 1987 issue of* English Journal. *As its title implies, Villanueva's article concerns not only* Hunger of Memory *but also a speech that Richard Rodriguez gave at a convention of English teachers.*

[Rodriguez] is a fine writer; of that there can be no doubt. But it is his message that has brought him fame, a message that states that the minority is no different than any other immigrant who came to this country not knowing its culture or its language, leaving much of the old country behind to become part of this new one, and in becoming part of America subtly changing what it means to be American. . . .

But choice hardly entered into most minorities' decisions to become American. Most of us recognize this when it comes to Blacks or American Indians. Slavery, forcible displacement, and genocide are fairly clear-cut. Yet the circumstances by which most minorities became Americans are no less clear-cut. The minority became an American almost by default, as part of the goods in big-time real-estate deals or as some of the spoils of war. What is true for the Native American applies to the Alaska Native, the Pacific Islander (including the Asian), Mexican Americans, Puerto Ricans. Puerto Rico was part of Christopher Columbus's great discovery, Arawaks and Boriquens among his "Indians," a real-estate coup for the Queen of Spain. Then one day in 1898, the Puerto Ricans who had for nearly four hundred years been made proud to be the offspring of Spain, so much so that their native Arawak and Boricua languages and ways were virtually gone, found themselves the property of the United States, property without the rights and privileges of citizenship until — conveniently — World War I. But citizenship notwithstanding, Puerto Rico remains essentially a colony today.

One day in 1845 and in 1848 other descendants of Spain who had all but lost their Indian identities found themselves Americans. These were the longtime residents and landowners of the Republic of Texas and the California Republic: the area from Texas to New Mexico, Arizona, Utah, and California. Residents in the newly established U.S. territories were given the option to relocate to Mexico or to remain on their native lands, with the understanding that should they remain they would be guaranteed American constitutional rights. Those who stayed home saw their rights not very scrupulously guarded, falling victim over time to displacement, dislocation, and forced expatriation. There is something tragic in losing a long-established birthright, tragic but not heroic — especially not heroic to those whose ancestors had fled their homelands rather than acknowledge external rule.

The immigrant gave up much in the name of freedom — and for the sake of dignity. For the Spanish-speaking minority in particular, the freedom to be American without once again relinquishing one's ancestry is also a matter of dignity. . . .

Today I sport a doctorate in English from a major university, study and   5
teach rhetoric at another university, do research in and teach composition, continue to enjoy and teach English literature. I live in an all-American city in the heart of America. And I know I am not quite assimilated. In one weekend I was asked if I was Iranian one day and East Indian the next. "No," I said. "You have an accent," I was told. Yet tape recordings and passing comments throughout the years have told me that though there is a "Back East" quality to my voice, there isn't much of New York to it anymore, never mind the Black English of my younger years or the Spanish of my youngest. My "accent" was in my not sounding Midwestern, which does have a discernible, though not usually a pronounced, regional quality. And my "accent," I would guess, was in my "foreign" features (which pale alongside the brown skin of Richard Rodriguez).

Friends think I make too much of such incidents. Minority hypersensitivity, they say. They desensitize me (and display their liberal attitudes) with playful jabs at Puerto Ricans: greasy-hair jokes, knife-in-pocket jokes, spicy-food jokes (and Puerto Ricans don't even eat hot foods, unless we're eating Mexican or East Indian foods). If language alone were the secret to assimilation, the rate of Puerto Rican and Mexican success would be greater, I think. So many Mexican Americans and Puerto Ricans remain in the barrios — even those who are monolingual, who have never known Spanish. If language alone were the secret, wouldn't the secret have gotten out long before Richard Rodriguez recorded his memoirs?   [1987]

≡ THINKING ABOUT THE TEXT

1. Do you agree with Villanueva that the problems of assimilation for minority immigrants are as difficult as those for Native Americans and African Americans?

2. What historical connection between Puerto Ricans and Mexican Americans does Villanueva make? Do you think it's valid?

3. Do you think Villanueva's anecdote in the last two paragraphs is typical? Do you have any experiences with similar incidents, either on the giving end or on the receiving end?

4. Villanueva notes that some of his friends think he is hypersensitive. Do you think so? Is there a best way to deal with these issues?

5. What, finally, is Villaneuva's point about the connections between assimilation and language?

≡ MAKING COMPARISONS

1. Which of the three Hispanic voices here seems the most balanced, judicious, and reasonable? Is that an important consideration in judging their arguments?

2. Villanueva uses both public and private history to refute Rodriguez. Are they equally effective?

3. Which argument, Villanueva's or Rivera's, is more effective in disputing Rodriguez?

≡ WRITING ABOUT ISSUES

1. Write an essay arguing for a particular characterization of the older Rodriguez, focusing on particular words that he uses as he recalls his childhood.

2. Should the young Rodriguez's school have been more respectful toward his home language and culture? Write an essay stating and arguing for your answer to this question. Refer to at least one of the critics quoted here. (Keep in mind that you don't have to agree with any of them.)

3. Write an essay recalling an experience that made you aware of the extent to which school had distanced you from the values and habits you knew at home. Perhaps you came to see the distance as vast; then again, perhaps you decided that it was minimal or nonexistent. Describe the experience with specific details and identify the conclusions it led you to. Also indicate whether you feel the same way as you look back on the experience now.

4. Write an essay arguing for your position on bilingual education or the English Only movement. Refer to at least two articles on your chosen topic. If you wish, refer to one or more of the selections in this cluster.

≡ Trapped in Stereotypes: Poems

CHRYSTOS, "Today Was a Bad Day like TB"

LOUISE ERDRICH, "Dear John Wayne"

DWIGHT OKITA, "In Response to Executive Order 9066"

DAVID HERNANDEZ, "Pigeons"

PAT MORA, "Legal Alien"

TOI DERRICOTTE, "Black Boys Play the Classics"

NAOMI SHIHAB NYE, "Blood"

When pressed, thoughtful people would agree that each of us has an individual personality and attributes that make us different from others. No one is an exact duplicate: even identical twins have both subtle and significant differences. Even so, cultures tend to lump together whole groups under dubious but convenient generalizations: used car dealers are dishonest, surfers are laid-back slackers, and computer geniuses are geeks. Usually based on limited, anecdotal, and often highly contextual historical and cultural evidence, these generalizations have a way of taking hold in a society long after the original context has disappeared (if there ever was one). Does anyone really think that dumb-blond jokes had any original validity? Is considering each person on his or her own merits too complicated?

When ethnic groups are stereotyped, their members may suffer consequences that are significantly more severe than those endured by, say, absent-minded professors. Some stereotypes are benign: as children growing up in New York, we routinely heard about industrious Chinese or hardworking Germans. But we also heard many negative generalizations that went hand in hand with racial discrimination and psychological damage. Members of the dominant groups in America are often oblivious to the ways that members of minority groups internalize destructive and distorted images of themselves, often seeing themselves as inferior to the dominant group and irredeemably other. They become trapped in images rampant in the culture and struggle daily to overcome the limited reality these stereotypes portray. The following seven poems represent aspects of this struggle in various ways — some with anger, resentment, and despair, others with thoughtful reflection, but all with an awareness of the pain that thoughtless stereotypes have on millions of Americans.

≡ BEFORE YOU READ

Do you think of yourself as an ethnic American? Have you ever seen the term *English American* or *Dutch American*? What's the difference between those terms and *African American* or *Irish American*? Do you think ethnic traditions should be preserved, or should they be replaced with American traditions? Can these traditions coexist?

CHRYSTOS
Today Was a Bad Day like TB

Born in San Francisco of a Lithuanian/Alsace-Lorraine mother and a Native American father of the Menominee tribe, Chrystos (b. 1946) writes in the outsider traditions of her ancestry, her lesbian perspective, and her geographical position on Bainbridge Island off the coast of the Pacific Northwest. She is a women's and native rights advocate, a working artist, and a poet. Her poetry collections include Not Vanishing *(1988),* Dream On *(1991),* In Her I Am *(1993),* Fire Power *(1995), and the 1994 winner of the Audre Lorde International Poetry Competition,* Fugitive Colors. *In 2007, she published* Some Poems by People I Like. *She is a Lannan Foundation fellow and the 1995 recipient of the Sappho Award of Distinction. The poem reprinted here is from* Not Vanishing.

> For Amanda White
>
> Saw whites clap during a sacred dance
> Saw young blond hippie boy with a red stone pipe°
>   My eyes burned him up
> He smiled   *This is a Sioux pipe* he said from his sportscar
>   *Yes*   I hiss   *I'm wondering how you got it*   5
>   *& the name is Lakota not Sioux*
> *I'll tell you* he said all friendly & liberal as only
>   those with no pain can be
>   I turned away   Can't charm me   can't bear to know
> thinking of the medicine bundle I saw opened up in a glass case   10
>   with a small white card beside it
>   naming the rich whites who say they
>   "own" it
> Maybe they have an old Indian grandma back in time
>   to excuse themselves   15
> Today was a day I wanted to beat up the smirking man wearing
> a pack with a Haida design from Moe's bookstore
> Listen Moe's   How many Indians do you have working there?
> How much money are you sending the Haida people
> to use their sacred Raven design?   20
>   You probably have an Indian grandma too
>   whose name you don't know
>   Today was a day like TB
>   you cough & cough trying to get it out
>   all that comes   25
>   is blood & spit   *[1988]*

---

2 red stone pipe: Traditionally, sacred peace pipes were made of red catlinite, a fine-grained stone.

■ THINKING ABOUT THE TEXT

1. What argument about the ways whites relate to Native Americans is Chrystos making? What assumptions about whites does Chrystos seem to have? What stereotypes does she seem to harbor?

2. Might you have clapped during a Lakota dance? During a Catholic Mass? What is the "it" in line 24 that the poet is trying to get out? Do you think she is angry with her readers?

3. Is the ending too stark or perhaps too crude? Might the language have been more indirect and subtle, or is it appropriate to the theme?

4. Americans who are part of the "mainstream" — that is, white, male, middle class, or heterosexual — sometimes get annoyed when those who are not complain about bias, probably because the offense was inadvertent. (Think of Atlanta Braves fans doing "the tomahawk chop.") The young man in this poem, for example, seems quite oblivious of giving offense. Who determines who is right in these situations?

LOUISE ERDRICH

Dear John Wayne

Born in Little Falls, Minnesota, Louise Erdrich (b. 1954) is a member of the Turtle Mountain Band of the Chippewa tribe. Her parents taught at the Bureau of Indian Affairs Boarding School in North Dakota, where Erdrich worked as a beet weeder, waitress, and teacher. She earned a B.A. from Dartmouth College in 1976 and an M.A. from the writing program at Johns Hopkins University in 1979 and has won many awards and fellowships for her writing, including the National Book Critics Circle Award in 1984 for her first novel, Love Medicine. *Although she writes both poetry and nonfiction, she has received the most acclaim for her novels, which include* The Beet Queen *(1986),* Tracks *(1988),* The Bingo Palace *(1994), and* Tales of Burning Love *(1996). Some recent novels are* The Master Butchers Singing Club *(2003),* Four Souls *(2004), and* Shadow Fog *(2010).* The Game of Silence, *a children's book, was published in 2005. "Dear John Wayne" is taken from* Jacklight, *her 1984 collection of poems.*

August and the drive-in picture is packed.
We lounge on the hood of the Pontiac
surrounded by the slow-burning spirals they sell
at the window, to vanquish the hordes of mosquitoes.
Nothing works. They break through the smoke-screen for blood.   5

Always the look-out spots the Indians first,
spread north to south, barring progress.
The Sioux, or Cheyenne, or some bunch

in spectacular columns, arranged like SAC° missiles,   10
their feathers bristling in the meaningful sunset.

The drum breaks. There will be no parlance.
Only the arrows whining, a death-cloud of nerves
swarming down on the settlers
who die beautifully, tumbling like dust weeds
into the history that brought us all here   15
together: this wide screen beneath the sign of the bear.

The sky fills, acres of blue squint and eye
that the crowd cheers. His face moves over us,
a thick cloud of vengeance, pitted
like the land that was once flesh. Each rut,   20
each scar makes a promise: It is
not over, this fight, not as long as you resist.

Everything we see belongs to us.
A few laughing Indians fall over the hood
slipping in the hot spilled butter.   25
The eye sees a lot, John, but the heart is so blind.
How will you know what you own?

He smiles, a horizon of teeth
the credits reel over, and then the white fields
again blowing in the true-to-life dark.   30
The dark films over everything.
We get into the car
scratching our mosquito bites, speechless and small
as people are when the movie is done.
We are back in ourselves.   35

How can we help but keep hearing his voice,
the flip side of the sound-track, still playing:
Come on, boys, we've got them
where we want them, drunk, running.
They will give us what we want, what we need: 40
The heart is a strange wood inside of everything
we see, burning, doubling, splitting out of its skin.   [1984]

9 **SAC:** The Strategic Air Command was part of America's nuclear deterrent.

■ **THINKING ABOUT THE TEXT**

1. While watching John Wayne fighting the Sioux or Cheyenne, Erdrich realizes she is not the intended audience for this mid-twentieth-century
   Western. Why not? Who is? What are the traditional assumptions about
   the Native Americans in the movies from this era?

2. When John Wayne and other movie heroes defeat "our" enemies, do you ever doubt that you are on the same side? Would Native Americans see these films differently than a mainstream audience? Have you seen recent films about Native Americans in which the conventional us-versus-them plot was disrupted in some way?

3. What do you think of Erdrich's transition from "hordes of mosquitoes" (line 4) to "Always the look-out spots the Indians first" (line 6)? What does "laughing Indians" mean in line 24?

4. Why does Erdrich say that "the heart is so blind" (line 26)? What does "They will give us what we want, what we need" refer to in line 40? Is that what John Wayne actually thought?

5. Movies give us a powerful sense of our history and our identity as Americans. Historical films about wars and heroes seem especially influential. Do you think Erdrich is overly sensitive? Do you think filmmakers have a responsibility to portray the ethnic diversity of America positively?

≣ MAKING COMPARISONS

1. If Chrystos's tone is bitter and angry, how might you characterize Erdrich's?

2. Compare the arguments both poets make about how whites perceive Native Americans. Which is more persuasive? Why?

3. How do you imagine Chrystos would respond to the movie? Erdrich to the dance?

DWIGHT OKITA
In Response to Executive Order 9066

A third-generation Japanese American, poet and playwright Dwight Okita (b. 1958) won an Illinois Art Council Fellowship for poetry in 1988. Although Crossing with the Light *(1992), from which this poem is taken, is his first book of poetry, Okita has been more active in promoting the performance of poetry than the printing of it, and he is well known as a "slam" poet at open-mike readings in Chicago. A member of the large Japanese American community that developed in Chicago as a result of the migration from the West after the bitter experience of the internment camps during World War II, Okita expresses his family history in his poetry and plays. His dramas include* The Rainy Season *(1992) and* The Salad Bowl Dance *(1993). His book* The Prospect of My Arrival *(2008) was nominated for the Amazon Breakthrough Novel Award.*

All Americans of Japanese Descent
Must Report to Relocation Centers

Dear Sirs:
Of course I'll come. I've packed my galoshes
and three packets of tomato seeds. Denise calls them
love apples. My father says where we're going
they won't grow.   5

I am a fourteen-year-old girl with bad spelling
and a messy room. If it helps any, I will tell you
I have always felt funny using chopsticks
and my favorite food is hot dogs.
My best friend is a white girl named Denise —   10
we look at boys together. She sat in front of me
all through grade school because of our names:
O'Connor, Ozawa. I know the back of Denise's head very well.

I tell her she's going bald. She tells me I copy on tests.
We're best friends.   15

I saw Denise today in Geography class.
She was sitting on the other side of the room.
"You're trying to start a war," she said, "giving secrets
away to the Enemy. Why can't you keep your big
mouth shut?"   20

I didn't know what to say.
I gave her a packet of tomato seeds
and asked her to plant them for me, told her
when the first tomato ripened
she'd miss me.   *[1992]*   25

■ THINKING ABOUT THE TEXT

1. What claim is Okita making in the last stanza? On what assumption
   about friendship is it based?
2. During the U.S. government's internment of Japanese American citizens, thousands were told to leave their homes to live in relocation centers for the duration of the war. To represent this complex historical
   event, do you think it effective to have a young girl writing a letter about
   being shunned by her best friend?
3. Explain Okita's use of the tomato seeds throughout the poem (lines 3,
   22). What about other concrete words: *galoshes* (line 2), *chopsticks*
   (line 8), *hot dogs* (line 9)?

4. Since there was no evidence that Japanese American citizens ever gave any "secrets / away to the Enemy" (lines 18–19) during World War II, why do you think Denise and millions of other Americans made that assumption?

≣ MAKING COMPARISONS

1. Compare the tone of Okita's poem with that of Chrystos's. What emotions do you see in each?
2. Okita creates a young female narrator to speak for him. Does this make his poem less direct than Chrystos's and Erdrich's? Who might be appropriate narrators in their poems?
3. Is the alienation described by Okita more or less painful than that described by Chrystos and Erdrich?

DAVID HERNANDEZ
Pigeons

An active member of Chicago's arts community, David Hernandez (b. 1946) has published several books of poetry, including Despertando / Waking Up *(1991),* Satin City Lullaby *(1986), and* Rooftop Piper *(1991), from which this poem is taken. He has written, recited, and taught poetry for more than thirty years and was commissioned to write a poem for Chicago's 150th anniversary in 1987. In addition to his own publications, Hernandez has edited three poetry anthologies. His recent work includes the poetry collections* Always Danger *(2006) and* Hoodwinked *(2011), and a young adult novel,* A House Waiting for Music *(2003).*

Pigeons are the spiks of Birdland.
   They are survivors of blood, fire and stone.
      They can't afford to fly south
         or a Florida winter home.

Most everybody passing up a pigeon pack   5
tries to break it up because they move funny
and seem to be dancing like young street thugs
with an 18-foot, 10-speaker Sanyo book box radio
on a 2-foot red shoulder strap.
                  Pigeons have feathers of a different color.   10
                  They are too bright to be dull
                  and too dull to be bright
                  so they are not accepted anywhere.

Nobody wants to give pigeons a job.
Parakeets, canaries and parrots   15
have the market sewn up as far as that goes.
They live in fancy cages, get 3 meals a day
for a song and dance routine.
When was the last time you saw a pigeon
in someone's home?   20
Unless they bleach their feathers white
and try to pass off as doves,
you will never see pet pigeons.
Besides, their accents give them away
when they start cooing.   25

Once in a while, some creature will treat them decent.
    They are known as pigeon ladies, renegades,
        or bleeding-heart Liberals.
                        What they do is build these wooden cages
                            on rooftops that look like huge   30
                        pigeon housing projects
                    where they freeze during the winters
                and get their little claws stuck in tar
            on hot summer days
No wonder they are pigeon-toed.   35
I tell you,
        Pigeons are the spiks of Birdland.   *[1991]*

≡ THINKING ABOUT THE TEXT

1. Hernandez uses the pigeon simile to comment on the place of Latinos in Birdland/America. What specific comparisons does he make? What is his larger argument?

2. Is this poem a complaint or an accusation of Birdland/America? Do you see some validity in what Hernandez says?

3. Does he press the bird comparison too far? Not far enough? What about attempts to eradicate pigeons or their reputation as disease carriers? How far should a poet carry such similes or metaphors? How far should the reader?

4. Is *spiks* an appropriate word to use in a poem? What if a white person (a dove?) used the term? What does Hernandez mean by "pigeon-toed" (line 35)?

5. Is the poet being ironic about those who try to treat the pigeons decently? What would he have preferred?

▤ MAKING COMPARISONS

1. How would you compare Hernandez's complaint against the liberals with Chrystos's against the hippie?

2. Hernandez's poem seems more ambitious than some of the other poems. Do you think he is trying to paint a fuller picture of discrimination?

3. Which of the poetic devices in these first four poems strikes you as the most effective? The least? Why?

PAT MORA
Legal Alien

Pat Mora (b. 1942) was born in El Paso, Texas. She earned a B.A. from Texas Western College in 1963 and an M.A. from the University of Texas, El Paso, in 1967. She is a versatile writer of many children's books, essays, and poems. Her poems are, according to the New York Times, *"proudly bilingual." Her sixth collection,* Adobe Odes *(2006), was praised for turning its back on hopelessness, "finding a way to delight in the sensual world as well as its people," and a "must-have for libraries serving Latino communities." Her latest collection is* Dizzy in Your Eyes *(2010). Mora lives in Santa Fe, New Mexico. "Legal Alien" is from* Chants *(1984) and focuses on a common Chicana theme: the difficulties of living in two cultures simultaneously.*

Bi-lingual, Bi-cultural,
able to slip from "How's life?"
to *"Me'stan volviendo loca,"*°
able to sit in a paneled office
drafting memos in smooth English,   5
able to order in fluent Spanish
at a Mexican restaurant,
American but hyphenated,
viewed by Anglos as perhaps exotic,
perhaps inferior, definitely different,   10
viewed by Mexicans as alien,
(their eyes say, "You may speak
Spanish but you're not like me")
an American to Mexicans
a Mexican to Americans   15
a handy token
sliding back and forth
between the fringes of both worlds

---

3 *"Me'stan volviendo loca"*: They're driving me crazy (Spanish).

by smiling
by masking the discomfort   20
of being pre-judged
Bi-laterally.   *[1984]*

≡ THINKING ABOUT THE TEXT

1. Was your first response to the opening line to think that such a situation is an advantage? Is that Mora's intent?
2. What advantages does being bicultural have? What disadvantages?
3. What other Americans are referred to as "hyphenated"? Do you think the same pluses and minuses apply?
4. Is the title appropriate? Explain.
5. Explain the significance of the "token" metaphor in line 16.

≡ MAKING COMPARISONS

1. Mora sees some advantage to being bicultural. Do any of the other poets?
2. Compare Mora's tone with Chrystos's.
3. Which of the stereotypes in these poems seems the most psychologically damaging? Why?

TOI DERRICOTTE
Black Boys Play the Classics

Toi Derricotte (b. 1941) was born in Louisiana and was influenced as a child by her Creole and Catholic background. She graduated from Wayne State University in 1965. The first of her six books, The Empress of the Death House, *was published in 1978. Her latest collection of poems and stories,* Gathering Ground, *was published in 2006. Often compared to Sylvia Plath and Anne Sexton, Derricotte writes poems that, according to the poet and critic Marilyn Hacker, are "honest, fine-boned, deceptively simple . . . and deadly accurate." She is currently a professor of English at the University of Pittsburgh. The following poem is from* Tender *(1997).*

The most popular "act" in
Penn Station
is the three black kids in ratty
sneakers & T-shirts playing
two violins and a cello — Brahms.   5
White men in business suits

have already dug into their pockets
as they pass and they toss in
a dollar or two without stopping.
Brown men in work-soiled khakis   10
stand with their mouths open,
arms crossed on their bellies
as if they themselves have always
wanted to attempt those bars.
One white boy, three, sits   15
cross-legged in front of his
idols — in ecstasy —
their slick, dark faces,
their thin, wiry arms,
who must begin to look   20
like angels!
Why does this trembling
pull us?
A: *Beneath the surface we are one.*
B: *Amazing! I did not think that they could speak this tongue.*   [1997]   25

≡ **THINKING ABOUT THE TEXT**

1. Why do the "brown men" (line 10) respond as they do? Why do the "white men" (line 6)?

2. Why does the poet offer a description of the boys' clothes? Does it have to do with our stereotyped expectations?

3. What are some possible meanings for "pull us" (line 23)?

4. Explain what you think Derricotte means by the last line.

5. How would you state the theme of this poem? Do you agree with it? Who is the "we" in the next-to-last line?

≡ **MAKING COMPARISONS**

1. How does Derricotte's tone differ from Chrystos's tone? From Hernandez's?

2. How does the end of this poem differ from the ends of the other poems in this cluster? Is it more effective or less effective?

3. If you were to rewrite "Black Boys Play the Classics" as a first-person poem (as Okita's poem demonstrates), which character from this poem would you choose, and why? How would a different point of view change the poem?

NAOMI SHIHAB NYE
Blood

Naomi Shihab Nye (b. 1952) was born to a Lutheran German American mother and a Muslim Palestinian American father in St. Louis. Her parents moved to the Middle East near Jerusalem, where her father edited the Jerusalem Times, *for which Nye, at fourteen, wrote a weekly column. Eventually turmoil forced their return to America. They settled in Texas, and Nye graduated from Trinity University in San Antonio in 1974. She has published books for children and adolescents with subject matter she hopes will dispel stereotypes and foster an understanding of "difference." Her poetic focus is often on the Palestinian Diaspora and on themes of our common humanity. Her books include* 19 Varieties of Gazelle *(2002) and* You and Yours: Poems *(2005). "Blood" is from* Yellow Glove *(1986).*

"A true Arab knows how to catch a fly in his hands,"
my father would say. And he'd prove it,
cupping the buzzer instantly
while the host with the swatter stared.

In the spring our palms peeled like snakes.   5
True Arabs believed watermelon could heal fifty ways.
I changed these to fit the occasion.

Years before, a girl knocked,
wanted to see the Arab.
I said we didn't have one.   10
After that, my father told me who he was,
"Shihab" — "shooting star" —
a good name, borrowed from the sky.
Once I said, "When we die, we give it back?"
He said that's what a true Arab would say.   15

Today the headlines clot in my blood.
A little Palestinian dangles a truck on the front page.
Homeless fig, this tragedy with a terrible root
is too big for us. What flag can we wave?
I wave the flag of stone and seed,   20
table mat stitched in blue.

I call my father, we talk around the news.
It is too much for him,
neither of his two languages can reach it.
I drive into the country to find sheep, cows,   25
to plead with the air:
Who calls anyone *civilized*?
Where can the crying heart graze?
What does a true Arab do now?   *[1986]*

■ **THINKING ABOUT THE TEXT**

1. What is your response to the girl who comes looking "to see the Arab" (line 9)? What is the speaker's response?

2. What do you think the father means by "a true Arab"? Is there a true American? A true man? Woman? Texan?

3. What is the father's response to the news about the Middle East? What is the speaker's? What is yours?

4. What is the purpose of the speaker's drive into the country?

5. How would you answer the questions the speaker asks in the last stanza?

■ **MAKING COMPARISONS**

1. Compare Nye's bicultural perspective to Mora's. Is Nye's status more precarious than Mora's in contemporary America?

2. Which of the speakers in all these poems seems angriest? Saddest? The most understanding?

3. What seems to be the most common theme among the poems?

■ **WRITING ABOUT ISSUES**

1. Write a journal entry from either Chrystos's or Erdrich's perspective that comments on the writing of the poem, what you (as the author) were trying to do, how you feel about stereotyping, and what response you are hoping for from readers.

2. Write an essay that compares the stereotyping that occurs in "Pigeons" and "Dear John Wayne." Comment on its origins, consequences, and possible solutions.

3. Write an essay that explores the kind of stereotyping you were exposed to as a child and an adolescent in your family, in your peer group, or in the larger culture.

4. After doing research on an ethnic group not represented here, locate a poet from that group and write a brief report on his or her work.

■ Remembering the Death Camps: Poems

MARTIN NIEMÖLLER, "First They Came for the Jews"

NELLY SACHS, "Chorus of the Rescued"

MARIANNE COHN, "I Shall Betray Tomorrow"

KAREN GERSHON, "Race"

ANNE SEXTON, "After Auschwitz"

Being shunned by neighbors because of religion, race, gender, or ethnicity creates painful psychological alienation for victims of such treatment. But what if your religion, cultural heritage, or sexual orientation were deemed dangerous to the well-being of your country? What if the powerful so dehumanized you that you were thought of as vermin to be disposed of? This would be more than alienation; this would be putting respect for human life beyond normal moral restraints. As in war, the different ones become the enemy who is less than human and who can be destroyed with impunity.

Of course, this describes exactly what happened during the Holocaust when the Nazis murdered millions of Jews. Thousands of eyewitness accounts have been written about this tragedy, but writers who were not there feel equally compelled to write about the events of the Holocaust. It is impossible to adequately represent such horrors: some writers are furious; others are disciplined and controlled. It is one of a writer's challenges to try to express in words what is truly beyond description.

■ BEFORE YOU READ

Have you seen photographs of Holocaust survivors? Have you seem films, read books, or heard stories about these events? What are your feelings? Can you explain how systematic genocide is possible? Do such things still happen in the world?

MARTIN NIEMÖLLER
First They Came for the Jews

A German Protestant theologian and pastor, Martin Niemöller (1892–1984), who won the Iron Cross as a submarine commander in World War I, is best known as an outspoken critic of Adolf Hitler and Nazism preceding and during World War II. As the pastor of the Berlin congregation of the Evangelical Church from 1931, Niemöller led a group of clergy working to counter Nazism and earned Hitler's hatred. From 1937 to 1945, he was interned at the Dachau and Sachsenhausen concentration camps. After the war, he focused his efforts on international disarmament and the recovery of the German church. He served as president of the World Council of Churches from 1961 to 1968.

First they came for the Jews
and I did not speak out
because I was not a Jew.
Then they came for the Communists
and I did not speak out   5
because I was not a Communist.
Then they came for the trade unionists
and I did not speak out
because I was not a trade unionist.
Then they came for me   10
and there was no one left
to speak out for me.   *[1945]*

≡ THINKING ABOUT THE TEXT

1. The poem seems to merely narrate a sequence of events, but is there an implicit argument here? Should the writer have been more explicit?

2. As you read this poem, do you think, "He's talking to me"? Do you think that might be Niemöller's intention?

3. Many poems are lyrical, filled with beautiful images and imaginative phrases. Would this poem be improved by moving in this direction?

4. Often in poetry, people and situations can be taken both literally and as symbols for something else. Do you think that is the case here with the Jews and Communists?

5. Most societies, even democracies, have insiders and outsiders, those with power and privilege and those with no influence. In your experience, does literature relate the feelings and experiences of both equally? Should this anthology balance the poems in this cluster with the experience of insiders?

NELLY SACHS

Chorus of the Rescued

Translated by Ruth and Matthew Mead

A poet and playwright born in Berlin of Jewish parents, Nelly Sachs (1891–1970) escaped from Nazi Germany in 1940 to Stockholm, where she became a Swedish citizen and eventually won the Nobel Prize for literature in 1966. First published as a poet in Germany in 1921, she later used biblical forms and motifs and empathized with the millions who suffered in the Holocaust. Her best-known play, Eli: A Mystery Play of the Sufferings of Israel, *epitomizes this style, as does the following poem, which uses pathos to evoke sympathy.*

We, the rescued,
From whose hollow bones death had begun to whittle his flutes,
And on whose sinews he had already stroked his bow —
Our bodies continue to lament
With their mutilated music.   5
We, the rescued,
The nooses would for our necks still dangle
Before us in the blue air —
Hourglasses still fill with our dripping blood.
We, the rescued,   10
The worms of fear still feed on us.
Our constellation is buried in dust.
We, the rescued,
Beg you:
Show us your sun, but gradually.   15
Lead us from star to star, step by step.
Be gentle when you teach us to live again.
Lest the song of a bird,
Or a pail being filled at the well,
Let our badly sealed pain burst forth again   20
And carry us away —
We beg you:
Do not show us an angry dog, not yet —
It could be, it could be
That we will dissolve into dust —   25
Dissolve into dust before your eyes.
For what binds our fabric together?
We whose breath vacated us,
Whose soul fled to Him out of that midnight?
Long before our bodies were rescued   30
Into the arc of the moment.
We, the rescued,
We press your hand
We look into your eye —
But all that binds us together now is leave-taking.   35
The leave-taking in the dust
Binds us together with you.   *[1967]*

≡ THINKING ABOUT THE TEXT

1. What is your reading of "Show us your sun" (line 15)?
2. What is meant by "Do not show us an angry dog, not yet" (line 23)?
3. How would you describe the emotional state of the narrator?

4. The poet uses metaphors throughout the poem, but particularly in the first twelve lines. How would you paraphrase the poet's descriptions?

5. According to the last three lines, what finally binds the poet to the reader?

≡ MAKING COMPARISONS

1. Even though both Niemöller's and Sachs's poems are about the Holocaust, are you able to relate to them from your own experiences?

2. With its metaphors, Sachs's poem seems more typically poetic. Would Niemöller's poem have been improved with more poetic devices? Might Sachs's poem have been improved with fewer?

3. One might argue that these two poems are causally connected. Explain.

MARIANNE COHN
I Shall Betray Tomorrow

Marianne Cohn (1922–1944) was born in Mannheim, Germany. Her family went into exile in Spain in 1934. Marianne joined the Resistance in France, taking Jewish children to territories outside Nazi control. In 1943, she was imprisoned for three months in Nice, where she wrote this poem. She was arrested again in 1944 with a group of twenty-eight children and tortured. Then, in July, she was murdered by the Gestapo. The children were eventually saved.

I shall betray tomorrow, not today.
Today, pull out my fingernails,
I shall not betray.
You do not know the limits of my courage,
I, I do.   5
You are five hands, harsh and full of rings,
Wearing hob-nailed boots.
I shall betray tomorrow, not today.
I need the night to make up my mind.
I need at least one night,   10
To disown, to abjure, to betray.
To disown my friends,
To abjure bread and wine,
To betray life,
To die.   15
I shall betray tomorrow, not today.
The file is under the window-pane.
The file is not [meant] for the window-bars,
The file is not [meant] for the executioner,
The file is for my own wrists.   20

Today, I have nothing to say,
I shall betray tomorrow.   *[1943]*

▰ THINKING ABOUT THE TEXT

1. Is the title meant ironically? How do you know?
2. What seems to be the most pronounced attitude of the narrator?
3. Does anything suggest that she is contemplating suicide?
4. The narrator seems quite confident about her ability to resist torture. Do you think she really is? Would you be able to resist torture?
5. Do you think other prisoners would be inspired or dispirited by this poem?

▰ MAKING COMPARISONS

1. Compare your response to the attitude of the speakers in Sachs's and Cohn's poems.
2. What do you think is the purpose of each of the three poems?
3. Do you think Cohn might have written a poem like "Chorus of the Rescued" had she survived?

KAREN GERSHON
Race

Later known by her married name, Karen Tripp, Gershon (1923–1993) escaped from Nazi Germany in 1939 as a teenager. Sent to England without her family, she wrote in her poetry of this experience and the loss of her parents, who died in the Holocaust. Gershon published eight books, contributed to numerous periodicals, and won much recognition, including the British Arts Council Award in 1967. Her poetry was widely read in the 1960s and later, perhaps influencing contemporaries Anne Sexton and Sylvia Plath, who borrowed the imagery of Holocaust survivors to describe family conflict and inner turmoil. "Race" is from Selected Poems *(1966).*

When I returned to my home town
believing that no one would care
who I was and what I thought
it was as if the people caught
an echo of me everywhere   5
they knew my story by my face
and I who am always alone
became a symbol of my race

Like every living Jew I have
in imagination seen   10

the gas-chamber the mass-grave
the unknown body which was mine
and found in every German face
behind the mask the mark of Cain
I will not make their thoughts my own   15
by hating people for their race.   *[1966]*

▤ THINKING ABOUT THE TEXT

1. Is Gershon imagining or actually describing her reception? How can you tell?
2. Do you mind the poet speaking for "every living Jew" (line 9)? Do you think this is accurate? Can someone be a symbol of their race?
3. Does the title refer to Jews or to Germans? Why is neither group mentioned in the title?
4. Gershon writes fairly straightforward poetry, letting her content speak for itself. What specific poetic devices does she employ? Should she use more?
5. Do you find the last four lines ambiguous? Does she see Germans as murderers, or does she reject such invidious generalizations? Should Germans be held accountable for the Holocaust? Should Americans be held accountable for slavery? Are only the people who specifically partake in evil deeds responsible, or is the whole culture that "allowed" it guilty as well?

▤ MAKING COMPARISONS

1. Compare Gershon's attitude in the last two lines of her poem with Sachs's attitude in the last three lines of her poem.
2. Had Cohn lived, might she have written "Chorus of the Rescued" or "Race"?
3. Describe the emotions you find in all four poems.

ANNE SEXTON
After Auschwitz

Growing up in New England and attending elite boarding and finishing schools during the years of World War II, Anne Sexton (1928–1974) had an emotional connection with the Holocaust rather than a firsthand one: her obsession with images of death and degradation and her "confessional" poetic stance blend seamlessly with such a theme. "After Auschwitz" is from The Awful Rowing toward God *(1977).*

Anger,
as black as a hook,
overtakes me.
Each day,
each Nazi   5
took, at 8.00 a.m., a baby
and sautéed him for breakfast
in his frying pan.

And death looks on with a casual eye
and picks at the dirt under his fingernail.   10

Man is evil,
I say aloud.
Man is a flower
that should be burnt,
I say aloud.   15
Man
is a bird full of mud,
I say aloud.

And death looks on with a casual eye
and scratches his anus.   20

Man with his small pink toes,
with his miraculous fingers
is not a temple
but an outhouse,
I say aloud.   25
Let man never again raise his teacup.
Let man never again write a book.
Let man never again put on his shoe.
Let man never again raise his eyes,
on a soft July night.   30
Never. Never. Never. Never. Never.
I say these things aloud.

I beg the Lord not to hear.   *[1977]*

≡ THINKING ABOUT THE TEXT

1. What is Sexton's purpose here if she really does not want God to listen?
2. What is your response to the image of Nazi cannibalism in lines 4–8?
   What about her inclusive accusation that "Man is evil" (line 11)?
3. As Sexton's editor, would you suggest that she change any specific
   words or phrases? Should she control the generally angry tone?
4. Sexton personifies death. Why? Why do you think she refers to man's
   "pink toes" and "miraculous fingers" in lines 21 and 22?

5. Sexton sees the Holocaust as an indictment of everyone. Do you agree with her?

≡ MAKING COMPARISONS

1. Compare the ambivalence at the end of Sexton's poem with the last sentence in Sachs's poem.

2. Do you think Gershon's poem would be improved by Sexton's explicit anger?

3. Which of these five poets comes closest to expressing your feelings about the Holocaust?

≡ WRITING ABOUT ISSUES

1. Argue that Sexton's indictment of humankind is either hyperbolic or accurate.

2. Make a case in a brief essay that "First They Came for the Jews" leads to "I Shall Betray Tomorrow."

3. Write a brief personal response explaining your feelings about the Holocaust or suggesting what such an event tells us about human nature, if anything.

4. Rent a film about the Holocaust such as Steven Spielberg's *Schindler's List* or Roman Polanski's *The Pianist*. Write a review expressing your feelings and thoughts about its contents and its representation of the Holocaust. Include a comparison to the poems you read.

≡ Prisoners of Masculinity: Stories

ANN BEATTIE, "The Four-Night Fight"

OLAF OLAFSSON, "On the Lake"

HARUKI MURAKAMI, "Another Way to Die"

Although the long-standing debate about the influence of nature versus nurture on our behavior remains unresolved, most current observers of culture put a good deal of emphasis on context, on where and when we were born, on our class, gender, and race. And most serious commentators believe that our behavior as males and females is mostly learned — not completely, of course, but our ideas about what's masculine and what's feminine seem clearly linked to specific cultural, not universal, norms.

In subtle and obvious ways, we are taught to be masculine or feminine, to be assertive or passive, to be physically aggressive or not. As children, we are usually the enforcers of this behavior, taunting boys on the schoolyard who are not up to physical play and shunning "tomboy" girls who want to be included in just that kind of roughhousing.

Psychologists tell us that these learned, culturally specific traits become a crucial part of who we are as adults. That is exactly how societies pass on their cultural values. As adults, we often feel guilty when we don't live up to these arbitrary standards. To compensate for our shame, we often compound the problem with flawed behavior that makes us feel even guiltier. Because socialization is such a powerful and pervasive influence, we are never really sure which behaviors are the result of nurture and which are the result of nature.

The three stories in this cluster all involve men caught in various stereotypically masculine behaviors that they don't seem able to escape from. It might be boorish and threatening behavior, reckless competitiveness, or military rigidity. These behaviors make the men prisoners of a certain kind of masculinity. Henry, in Ann Beattie's story, seems adolescent and a bully. Because of a foolish competitiveness, Oskar, in "On the Lake," tries to hide a shameful secret. Finally, the lieutenant in Haruki Murakami's tale is bound to authoritarian rules at the expense of his humanity.

≡ BEFORE YOU READ

Have you consciously tried to act in a stereotypically masculine or feminine way? Did you enforce gender roles with your childhood friends? Do you think you are different from your proscribed gender role?

ANN BEATTIE
The Four-Night Fight

Ann Beattie (b. 1947) was born in Washington, D.C., and grew up in the Chevy Chase suburbs. She graduated from American University and received a master's degree from the University of Connecticut. In 1976, she published her first collection of stories, Distortions, *and her first novel,* Chilly Scenes of Winter, *which was made into a well-received film. Her reputation was built on her perceptive and ironic narration of the lives of what the critic Christopher Lehman-Haupt called "disaffected post-countercultural yuppies." Her stories have been selected four times by the O. Henry Award Collections, and in 2005 she received the Rea Award for the Short Story. She lives with the painter Lincoln Perry in Charlottesville, where she is the Edgar Allan Poe Professor of Literature and Creative Writing at the University of Virginia. Her recent work includes* Walks with Men *(2010) and* The New Yorker Stories *(2010). The following story is from* Park City *(1998).*

The four-night fight began on Father's Day, June 20, but had nothing to do with the day. Her father had been dead for almost fifteen years; his father had left his mother and moved to Santa Barbara to spend his remaining years — so far, twelve had passed — golfing. Henry was not himself a father.

It had been a beautiful, sunny day. Lavender geraniums were in bloom, bordering the back porch. Inside the porch, yellow and red begonias blossomed, their flowers as large as their leaves. In one of the pots, a plastic parrot's one moving wing rotated as the wind blew. The summer before, Henry had gotten the other wing going, but this year he'd done nothing. Neither had he brought home plants for the porch, nor helped weed the geranium bed, to which he had added, against her objections, a dozen blue-black tulips, planting the bulbs the previous fall as she slept. First he refused to enlarge the flower bed. Then, when she did that, he "borrowed" bricks from the border to brace a rickety bookshelf. Then he ordered red tulips, was sent the bruise-colored ones instead, shrugged, ignored her dismay, and planted them while she was asleep. None of these things had anything to do with the fight.

The fight began in early evening, so that properly speaking, it was a four-night, three-day fight. The fight reminded her of hotel package deals: four nights, five days, in sunny Bermuda — but after you struggled to the hotel the pleasure of the first day would inevitably be shot: plane late; luggage delayed; rainstorm slowing the car to the hotel; a long line for check-in. They had taken a trip to Bermuda in October, to celebrate their anniversary. She had wanted to stay in a small hotel, he had insisted on staying at a sprawling resort. Like his father, he loved to golf. She had gone around on her moped alone, while he golfed, and though that might have made her feel bad, it had not, so why pretend to hold a grudge when actually she had quite enjoyed her freedom? She didn't pretend to hold a grudge. Nothing that happened in Bermuda had anything to do with the fight.

In fact, the reason the fight was so bad was that it snuck up on her. In the seconds preceding the fight, she had been perfectly happy, scooping the center out of a cantaloupe. Henry had become diabetic, so they no longer had cookies for dessert, only fruit. She kept a package of Chips Ahoy hidden behind boxes of Tide in the laundry room, but she'd lost her taste for sweets, suddenly. Or maybe not so suddenly: she'd lost it when the cookies somehow absorbed, like a sponge, the smell of Tide. When she was a child, her mother had put milk of magnesia in chocolate milk to disguise the taste, but all it had done was make her cringe at the thought of plain chocolate milk, and also chocolate ice cream, or chocolate milk shakes. She was even wary of chocolate cake, and sniffed skeptically at Hershey bars. No matter: cookies and chocolate could easily be done without, and a person would be healthier because of it. So there she had been, scooping out the melon, looking forward to a made-for-TV movie the listing had said would be good, when suddenly Henry was standing in the kitchen doorway, looking at her in a peculiar way, contributing nothing toward fixing their dessert, having said not a word about the dinner she had just served. . . . Well: the thing was, the fight, in his mind, had already begun, but she had been slow to understand his sulking, mistaking it for simple fatigue, since before dinner he'd hauled out the trash and sprayed the lid with Clorox so that during the night the raccoon couldn't simply saunter up to the can and with a swipe of its paw crash the top of the trash can to the ground. Also, he had sawed off the broken limb of the lilac and dragged it into the woods, then gone inside and called his mother to give her some information she needed to pay her taxes. His mother was not the world's most pleasant person. Also, since it was Father's Day, she was in a bleaker mood than usual, despising Henry's father for leaving her and spending his retirement golfing in California. Maybe his mother's bad mood was contagious. Maybe Henry had done one too many chores. Maybe he harbored a grudge that she had made him spray the trash can with Clorox, which he continued to call "ridiculous," though it was the one thing that had ever deterred the tenacious, fat, garbage-can-toppling raccoon.

Standing in the kitchen doorway, he had said to her: "Sometimes I think   5
this is all a huge fucking joke. Sometimes I think we're ants, and here in our anthill we scurry around, moving the dirt, building the anthill higher, eating our food, shitting it out, doing our humble chores for the fucking Queen Ant, foraging and accumulating, bringing things in, piling things up, moving the piles around, and all the while, in our little specks of ant brain, we hope a big rainstorm doesn't come and pound the whole fucking anthill into the ground, that we don't get washed down the hill, that we don't drown in the flood, but what would it matter if we did? What the fuck would it matter?"

It was so unexpected. So typical of Henry, though, who while having finally admitted, one night in Bermuda, as the sky was brightening from rose to crimson, that his obsessing about the deterioration of the ozone layer was really a way of not focusing on more immediate, personal problems that he might do something about . . . well: going on with this line of thought would give the mistaken impression that she had been assessing the situation, seeing in it the seeds of similar situations — Christ! Did he think she'd gone to college to scoop the insides of melons into a garbage disposal? Could he really have thought that she would appreciate such a barrage of adolescent, ridiculous despair . . . had he been standing in the doorway with his weight thrown on one hip, in his loafers with their mashed-down backs, and his thumb hooked through a belt loop . . . was this miserable sight, this person she'd for some un-fathomable reason married, so stupid as to think she'd appreciate being com-pared to an ant as she stood scooping pulp and seeds and fiber into the sink so that his diabetes wouldn't rage out of control . . . had they had what they agreed would be their last discussion of the ozone layer only to have him recast everything in terms of their pointless life inside an anthill?

"You're really insane," she said.

"I'm insane?" he said. And then he said something she didn't get — something about the Clorox. That didn't surprise her at all, because whenever she gave him a helpful hint he derided her or ignored it. The use of Clorox as a repellent hadn't been her own epiphany, by the way: it was something she'd read flipping through a tabloid in the supermarket, which was where she spent half her life, half of her pointless ant life, gathering food for Henry, because maybe Henry himself was the Ant King? After all, who was standing in the doorway, the picture of casualness, while her hair had fallen from her barrette to tickle her nose as she peered down into the messy abortion of melon pulp in the sink. . . .

She had apparently thrown the phone book at him. She saw that she had, because his hands flew up to protect his head, and certainly the phone book had not just animated itself to join in the fracas, surely she must have thrown it, accelerating the fight, which by that time had been going on for perhaps five minutes, of screaming and accusations, suspended only for troubled sleep, to resume the next morning.

The day after the fight he did not go to work, which did trouble her. If he   10
had called to say he would not be at work, he would have had to do it while she slept — he didn't mind planting ugly tulips while she slept, for all she knew he had a complete private life. He told her about deficiencies in her character as he toasted an English muffin — one only; none for her — blaming her for try-ing to infantilize him with her air of superiority, banging his fist on the kitchen island and sending the nondairy creamer crashing to the floor, whatever he was saying about Clorox drowned out by the crashing glass. Then, insanely, completely insanely, as the muffin lodged in the toaster and began to burn, though it would be a cold day in hell if she ever again rescued any of his food, let him forage for it himself, ant that he was . . . Henry began to pick up the shards of glass and throw them, claiming the bits of glass were ants, or like ants — whatever he was saying. He was saying that he was scattering the ant-hill. Really, he was just a bully, uncivilized and out of control, wanting to lash out at who knew what, who could know who the designated Queen Ant was that morning, in his paranoia and rage. Black smoke poured from the toaster, and again the telephone book was animated, sailing through the air, smeared with cantaloupe juice, crashing way off course into the wall. She had wanted

to paint the kitchen walls green; Henry had wanted them yellow. They had compromised on peach, which was good, considering the melon juice that was now smeared on the wall, though she resolutely did not care about that, did not care if the whole toaster erupted, did not care what he did with the rest of his day, did not care if he stood forever making analogies between broken glass and anthills, because he was cynical and unbalanced, she was not, she was — he was saying again — superior. Then he kicked the phone book as if he were making a final goal and looked around crazily, as if she represented a whole team who would cheer him. Looking over his shoulder, he asked if she had ever had a kind thought about his mother in her life. It did not deserve an answer.

The next day, he was gone when she woke up, but he was so agitated that he had left a message — a rant, really — on the answering machine. At the beginning, he taunted her by daring her to listen to the message all the way through, which she did intend to do, sitting at the kitchen counter, the air still redolent with the smell of burned bread, bits of glass scattered underfoot. "I did what the raccoon couldn't do," he screamed on the tape. "I turned over your fucking garbage can that the fucking garbage truck neglected to empty because they do not give a flying fuck if the whole world festers and deteriorates, if they can shorten their working day by ignoring the cans on the route. I turned it over and I was within one second, one millionth of an inch, of taking the lid and ramming it through the side window of your car. . . ."

At this, she got slowly off the stool and went out to the driveway, his voice fading in the background. She walked as if in a trance, but she was not really in a trance, she was just practicing being in a trance. What if he had really traumatized her, so that she had become a zombie? What if at this moment she was a zombie, looking at chicken bones, food-stained newspapers, all the detritus of their lives scattered in the street — not by the raccoon, but by the wild beast that was her husband? No: she would not let him drive her crazy. It was reasonable to be superior, and not a zombie. She could shuffle along, traumatized, and become what he would like her to become, but it was better simply to sidestep his expectations, just as she sidestepped the garbage. That night, a neighbor's boy would stuff most of it back in the can. She would see that from the bathroom window, getting up from the closed toilet seat where she was reading a mystery, preferring to be locked in the bathroom rather than downstairs, where Henry was silently watching the long-ago resignation of Richard Nixon on TV. It was not true that all teenagers were destructive and self-absorbed. The boy picked up almost everything, including soup cans with jagged edges and soggy coffee filters, then put the lid firmly on the trash can again. He could have been Sir Lancelot, he shone so in her imagination as what a man could be. Downstairs, she heard gunshots, and for a horrifying second she was so on edge that she had rewritten history and imagined Nixon being shot, then realized that Henry must have begun shooting at the teenager! Henry having a gun. Did he have a gun? Of course he didn't have a gun. And if he did have a gun, then she hoped he would use it on himself.

No, she didn't. She tried thinking that, to see how it would feel. It felt wrong. She was afraid she was beginning to forgive him. In saying she wanted him shot when she did not want him shot, she had begun to forgive him. And she might have, too, if he hadn't glared at her so coldly before pulling off the comforter and going to sleep on the sofa. Such histrionics, when there was a guest room. He was really out of control. Maybe he was actually cracking up. She tossed in bed half the night, and when she went down in the morning he was still there, the cover over the top of his body, including his head, his bare legs sticking out, one on the sofa arm, one on the floor. It was like finding the Elephant Man in a casual moment. She stood in the doorway, so fatigued she decided to forgive him, to try to get things back on track. If nothing else, he would certainly have to go back to his job soon. Perhaps he hadn't gone back yesterday. Perhaps she had assumed, incorrectly, that the hysterical message of the day before had been left from work — but how likely was that? He had probably not sat at his desk and simply raged, spitting his irrational thoughts into a telephone. He had probably called from . . . "Henry," she said, trying to keep her voice calm, "were you at work yesterday when you left that ridiculous message?"

He jumped up, tossing off the comforter with such force that she jumped back. He stood there, glowering at her, the comforter puddled around him like a collapsed parachute. His wild eyes made her think of someone who had just crashed into a dangerous jungle. He might have been wondering: Could this native be friendly? She tried to look friendlier by smiling, but the attempt to alter the expression of her mouth, she could tell, was only resulting in narrowed eyes. She could not smile. She did manage to unknot the frown that creased between her eyes. They stood there that way, gazing at each other, she barefoot in her long nightgown patterned with blue morning glories, he wearing a white sleeveless undershirt and nothing else, his knock-knees pathetic, his penis curved like a tiny fountain spout, and — she had been blocking it out because she really did not want to focus on it — on his arm, on his biceps, a terrible bruise, a terrible swelling: from doing battle with the trash can? From . . . God, it was a tattoo. It was a tattoo, and he saw that she saw it. Even the fountain spout seemed to recoil in dismay. Henry was standing there, staring at her with the We Are Ants expression on his face, and on his upper arm, the part of his arm she had clasped so many times as they made love, was MOM in red-inked script, and a circle inscribing it, a circle, she saw, upon closer inspection, that was not a conglomerate of ants, but swirls of small hearts and flowers, interspersed with skin puckered into scabs, an outer rim of flesh around the circle swollen and flecked with what seemed to be broken veins.

"Hurts," he said.   15

"Hurts?" she echoed. She was becoming the zombie whose role she had tried on for size. Numb. Unblinking. Who could blink looking at such a thing?

"I went drinking with Jim Cavalli, made a bet, guy couldn't pay up, we went to his tattoo studio, I got to choose from the fifty-dollar possibilities."

"Henry," she said, "what is this about your mother?"

"Cavalli chose."

"Cavalli had your arm tattooed MOM?"   20

"Cavalli wanted to beat him up. I was the one who agreed to settle on a tattoo."

"Cavalli . . . ," she said, searching her mind for a visual image of the man. The new, gawky kid from Princeton? Pink shirt, drank a lot of Dos Equis at the company picnic? Though she was not aware she'd been speaking, Henry began to respond to her sharpening mental image of Cavalli. "Went off the wagon himself because his Princeton girlfriend left him for her analyst," Henry said.

"So . . . what?" she said. "You and Cavalli went to a bar, and he told you his girlfriend had left him, you told him the human race, or you and I, how should I know? You told him we were ants, and then some guy who worked at a tattoo parlor sat down and you bet him . . . you bet what?"

"That the guy on TV would miss the shot."

"You bet that a guy would miss a shot, he said the guy would make it, the guy missed, and you ended up with MOM in majesty on your arm?"

"Hurts," he said quietly.

"Well, Jesus," she said. "I think we should go to the doctor and see if he can treat it, because I think your arm is infected." A headache came up inside her like rolling thunderclouds spreading across the sky. By the time she finished her sentence, electricity was crackling through her brain, a tooth-chattering wind had begun.

It was as if her pain made her transparent. Suddenly, he looked at her as if he could see the rain clouds inside. The pain piercings sinking into her jaw like lightning. "Your name is Angelina," he said. Her head hurt so much that she didn't mind this simple, neutral observation at all. Indeed she was Angelina. So true. He continued: "While I admit I hated you in that moment, it did occur to me that if I hadn't been angry, if I hadn't been angry when I was getting the tattoo, I could have had a tattoo of my wife's name, except that only three letters could be had for fifty dollars, because Cavalli was insisting on scrollwork. The part around the word is called scrolling. It's generic hearts and flowers and stuff."

This was too much to take in. Her head was pounding.

"They do it the way people doodle on a notepad when they're on the telephone, I guess." He had sunk into the sofa, pulling the comforter over himself. He looked like an ill, miserable child. He looked at her expectantly.

"I think we should go to the doctor," she said. She had begun to worry about the tattooist's needles. Why would Henry have done such a thing, when everyone was so worried about AIDS? How could he have been sure the needles were clean? Needles — Jesus Christ. He had let someone take needles and scratch dye into his flesh. He had gone with some self-pitying moron named Cavalli. And yet, she was on the sofa beside him, snuggled under his good arm, the comforter around them both feeling soft and sheltering. At that moment, the last thing she was thinking about was the fight. He had become, in her mind, a victim. Someone who had received far worse punishment than he deserved. Someone who needed medical attention, understanding, forgiveness. She envisioned herself driving him to the doctor's office — never mind that the doctor was sure to be horrified — going there, getting a prescription for antibiotics, perhaps topical creams, perhaps . . . perhaps the doctor would see that Henry was unbalanced and think of something to do. Though the more she

25

30

thought about it, the more she disbelieved it. Unless she could walk right into the doctor's office with him, he would probably present it as regrettable, drunken madness. She would have to go in and be a Greek chorus: *No, no, he was comparing life to being in an anthill; he's never cared if flowers are atrocious colors, he just plants them anyway, like flowers that would bloom in hell; his mother upsets him, complaining about his father; our fight began on Father's Day, which can't be insignificant — either it's resentment of his own father spilling over into our life, or he's angry that people are procreating: he sees all these things as a personal affront, whether it's the holes in the ozone layer or clear-cutting the forest or people giving birth to a child. He's in a state of madness and despair, I tell you. He doesn't go to work anymore. Come to think of it, for days I haven't seen him eat.* She would have to say those things; no sitting in the waiting room reading *Good Housekeeping*. No information, today, about Kathie Lee's thoughts on how to parent. Cheese dips be damned.

The fight began again when, to her complete surprise, he refused to see the doctor. It was feeling better already, he suddenly said. He thought he had a bit of a fever though, so he would — if she did not mind — nap for a bit.

"You're going to the doctor," she said.

"No," he said. "I am not."

Thus began a new day of fighting, which she had not been prepared for at all, having begun to forgive him. And, like anyone dragged into something unexpectedly, her reactions were not the best. Instead of focusing on his obviously infected arm, she found herself demanding an explanation of how, exactly, he would keep the raccoon out of the trash if he did not want to use her method. She twisted up her mouth and marched like a martinet, imitating his expression and his quick exit from the living room when the phone rang. The phone: news from the outside world. The doctor, by telepathic message having realized he should call? When she picked it up, it was Cavalli. The nerve! What did he want, she asked: to know if Henry would meet him for more drinks and then go out to a whorehouse? "No," Cavalli said evenly. "To know if he's coming to work." She hung up on him. Then the fight really swung into full gear. She was emasculating him again, it appeared. Again, he threatened her car windows. Couldn't he think of anything more original than that? Or, at the very least, admit that he wanted to hit *her*? "You'd like that, wouldn't you?" he said. It was not until three in the afternoon that she looked and realized that neither of them had brought in the paper.

That night, he ate nothing. He sat with the remote control, flipping through channels, sentence fragments and incomplete sounds no doubt echoing the chaos of his brain. Once, he ran out the front door with the still-rolled newspaper, threatening a cat digging near a bush. He could have been heard miles away. If he did become violent, no one in the neighborhood would be surprised. Yes, they'd say, that guy was really nuts. Nuts but wounded. She couldn't get the image of his infected arm out of her mind. It was as if the pain throbbed in her own head. Of course, it was next to impossible to sleep. And when she was at last almost asleep, what did he do but tear off in the car, going

35

who knew where, dressed — as she later found out — in the only clothes he could find downstairs: a pair of madras bermudas with a ripped zipper he'd taken from her sewing room and his flip-flops with the thongs he'd glued back together in the basement, and her blouse. The nice navy-blue blouse she'd ironed before the fight began and never taken upstairs. He had left after cramming his body into her navy-blue blouse.

She went downstairs and turned off the answering machine because she did not want to hear whatever vicious message he might leave. She did, though, make sure the ringer on the phone was on, so that if he — or the police, God forbid — needed to reach her, they could. The only phone call came from his mother, who had no sense of time, wanting him to install a new bathroom sink for her at what she called "your convenience." Wait until she saw the MOM tattoo. Let the two of them discuss that.

Was he, in fact, headed for his mother's — and should she have warned the woman that might be the case? Or to Cavalli's? Back to the bar? Who knew where. Who knew how this was going to end, if it ever did end. It was the longest fight she had ever been involved in, and it was exhausting her and making her feel crazy herself. She took aspirin and went back to bed.

In the morning, when she awoke, he was lying next to her. It was not a dream, he was really there. The blue blouse was on the floor, the madras bermudas discarded amid the thongs, his eyes squeezed shut so tightly she wondered if he was only pretending to sleep. At first, barely distinguishable in the tangle of white sheets, she didn't realize there was a large gauze bandage on his arm. It was a thick pad of gauze, wrapped entirely around his arm, and near the top were black stitches — no: there was writing. On the gauze bandage, he had written, as best he could, left-handed, because the tattoo was on his right arm, the scratchy letters S O R R Y. There it was: the white flag of surrender, and an added apology lest she mistake it. Propped on one elbow, she frowned as she considered it: the wobbly O like bubble being blown from a bubble wand; the Y like a sprouting seed. It seemed to her the sweetest thing he had ever done. Though he had done so many sweet things in the time they'd been together. The four-night fight must have been worse for him than for her, because he hated to carry a grudge. "Let him golf. Forget him if you can't forgive him," he always said to his mother. "Buy more flowers if that's what you want, honey," he had said to her when the garden bloomed that spring with its strange blossoms. She stared at the bandage. It was professionally done. He must have gone to the emergency room. On the night table she saw a glass of water and a bottle of medicine. It seemed to her a real salvation: the antibiotics that would cure the wound's infection, protecting his precious arm, that arm that had curled around her so many times, guiding her through crowds, protectively placed when he introduced her to a stranger. She stayed there, propped up, observing him, the way a person will look out a window and study the land after a storm, everything seeming greener, lighter, suddenly distinct. The familiar landscape was all there: from chin stubble to chest hair, from navel to knee, it was Henry, slumbering after the great storm. Henry, simply, no scrollwork needed to establish his importance, because when she saw him small hearts and flowers invisibly surrounded him always, an embellished border around the valentine of affection that was her love. What couple does not occasionally fight?   [1998]

■ THINKING ABOUT THE TEXT

1. When Henry calls the Cloroxing of the trash can "ridiculous," what does this say about him?

2. What seems to be Henry's purpose in ranting to his wife about ants? Why does his wife think this is typical of Henry?

3. Angelina accuses Henry of deriding or ignoring her "whenever she gave him a helpful hint" (para. 8). Is this a stereotypically masculine behavior? What about his actions during the toast-burning episode?

4. We hear about Henry through his wife's point of view. Do any of her behaviors make you somewhat skeptical that Henry is a "wild beast" (para. 12), or do you think she is accurate?

5. What causes Angelina to change her perspective about her husband? Would you be convinced by the "SORRY" bandage? Is this story's last question rhetorical? How would you answer it?

OLAF OLAFSSON
On the Lake

Olaf Olafsson (b. 1962) was born in Reykjavik, Iceland, and received a degree in physics from Brandeis University. He is currently the executive vice president of Time Warner. *He is the author of several novels, including* Absolution *(1994),* The Journey Home *(2003), and* Walking into the Night *(2003). He lives in New York City with his wife and three children. The following story appeared in* The O'Henry Prize Stories, 2008.

They sat in the living room drinking coffee, looking out at the lake. Margret got up every now and then to check on their son. He had fallen asleep in her arms in the living room, and she had taken him into his bedroom and laid him down. He was sleeping peacefully, but she kept looking in on him every few minutes to listen to his breathing. When she couldn't hear it, she put her ear to his nose and mouth. Only then could she relax.

They had started using the summer cabin just over a year before. Margret's parents had a cabin farther up the hillside and had given them a piece of their land for a wedding present. Oskar had built the cabin himself. It had taken a long time, since he was busy with so many other things. The cabin wasn't large, but it was well situated, with an uninterrupted view of the lake. A hollow cut by a stream and some tall trees, mostly fir and birch, separated them from

Margret's parents. Although Oskar got on well with his in-laws, he liked having the stream and the hollow between them.

They had come down after work on Friday. The weather forecast had been uncertain, but Margret paid no attention, knowing from experience that it could seldom be relied on. She had spent her childhood summers by the lake with her mother and her siblings, her father coming out as often as he could. She had hoped it would be the same for her and Oskar. Until this evening, she had been confident that it would.

They were drinking their coffee. Oskar had his back to the window; the men who had rescued him and their son, Jonas, sat facing him across the coffee table. Margret was sitting beside Oskar. When she got up yet again to check on the boy, Oskar said: "Leave it. He's all right."

She gave him a sharp glance but said nothing. Once she had left the room, Oskar said: "How about some scotch? A man can't live on coffee alone."   5

He was filling their glasses when she returned.

"Scotch?" he asked.

She shook her head.

He added a little water and an ice cube to each of their glasses. The water came from the spring below the hollow. It was delicious and cold, even on hot days, he told the rescuers while mixing their drinks. He also told them that he had built the cabin with his own hands, as well as installed the electricity and piped the water from the spring.

"The water at Margret's parents' place always had a muddy taste," he said.   10
"But now they get their water from our spring."

Easter was behind them; it was the end of April. The earth was gray and the air raw, but one could sense that spring wasn't far away. It was light past nine and then dusky for a while before it got dark. The snow was gone.

"Not a breath of wind now," said Oskar. "Cheers!"

Margret studied the men. One of them had bought the cabin next door to her parents' place earlier that year. She had seen him in the distance but had not spoken to him until now. Her parents often complained of his noisy boat, which roared around the lake while they were trying to appreciate the silence and sound of the Great Northern Divers.

"A banker," said her father. "Nouveau riche."

From time to time the new neighbor held parties — with the barbecues   15
pouring out smoke and people swilling beer and wine on the veranda, according to Margret's father, who spied on them with the binoculars that Oskar and Margret had given him for his sixtieth birthday. Margret had the same kind of binoculars. Her father reported that his neighbor had two barbecues: one coal, one gas. "He'll end up setting the whole place on fire," he predicted.

The rescuers introduced themselves after the boy had fallen asleep. There hadn't been time before. The banker's name was Vilhelm, his friend's, Bjorn. Still frantic, Margret flung her arms round them. Oskar stood to one side, watching.

"All right, all right," he had said. "No need to make such a big deal out of it."

The look she gave him did not escape Vilhelm or Bjorn, who exchanged glances. Vilhelm said: "Glad we could help."

It had been after dinner when Oskar suggested to the boy that they go out on the lake. He and Margret had eaten salad and lamb, drinking white wine with the salad and red with the meat. They were content.

Jonas was their only child, just turned six. He was named after Margret's father and was thought to have his features. His grandparents had given him a fishing rod for Christmas, and a couple of times Oskar had taken him out on the water to fish from their boat. Jonas had caught his first fish the prior weekend, a small trout that Margret fried for lunch. He had been very proud of it.   20

"Wouldn't it be better to go tomorrow morning?" she asked. "It's already eight thirty."

"We won't be long," answered Oskar. "I promised him."

She did the dishes, and Oskar finished his wine as he cleared the table. It had been a rule when Margret was growing up that people shouldn't go out on the lake when they had been drinking, but she decided not to bring that up now. She had mentioned it before, and Oskar hadn't hidden his opinion that her father's rules had no place in their home. He was far from drunk, anyway, and Margret made sure that Jonas's life jacket was securely fastened before father and son went down to the shore. She had been waiting for a moment to herself; as soon as they were gone, she took a seat by the window with a crime novel and a bowl of raisins. By the time they reached the lake, she was already immersed.

There was a breeze, and the boat rocked a little as they fished. They had no luck in the first spot and motored farther out. They got nothing there either. When the wind picked up, Oskar told Jonas they should be getting home. Jonas begged to stay just a little longer. Oskar agreed, but the trout still weren't biting. "The fish have gone to bed," he said, "and so should we."

Jonas hung his head, disappointed.   25

"I never catch any fish with you," he said, "and you never do anything fun like the man in the white boat. You never spin around or anything."

The man in the white boat was Vilhelm. He sometimes amused himself by making tight turns on the lake, and Jonas would watch him, enthralled. "Bloody fool," said Margret's father, but this had no effect on Jonas, who saw the white boat sending big waves up the beach.

"Shall we do a few turns?" Oskar asked.

"You never do," said Jonas. "You never do turns like the man in the white boat."

"Right," said Oskar. "Hold tight."   30

They weren't far from land when Oskar turned round, headed out into the lake, and increased his speed. Keeping within what he thought a safe limit, he swerved to the left and right before slowing down again.

"Wasn't that fun?" he asked.

"No," said Jonas, "not like the man in the white boat. It was boring."

Oskar sped up again, heading for land this time. He was feeling irritable and wanted to go home. He opened the throttle as far as he could, then thrust the tiller hard right. The boat capsized.

They went under. Oskar surfaced and then gasped. He couldn't see Jonas   35
anywhere. Oskar splashed round the boat and found Jonas, coughing up water. Oskar gripped the gunwale with one hand and pulled Jonas to him with the other. The water was too cold for them to swim to land. The boy was crying and kept choking on water every time a wave washed over them.

Margret didn't see the boat capsize. The murderer had struck again, this time with good reason. She felt more sympathy for him than for the victim. Eventually she stretched, put down the book, and looked out.

She screamed, snatched up the binoculars, and dashed out to the veranda. First Oskar appeared, then Jonas. There was nothing she could do, but she set off down to the lakeside anyway. Trying to run despite the steepness of the slope, she quickly lost her footing. When she got up again, she noticed the white boat. She reached for the binoculars.

After nearly ten minutes in the water Oskar was losing strength. He had tried to hoist Jonas up on the side of the boat but couldn't manage it, his grip on the boy loosening. Jonas was no longer whimpering, and Oskar was afraid he was losing consciousness. The water was glacial. One wouldn't last long in it.

Vilhelm cut the boat's engines a short distance from Oskar and Jonas, careful not to bump against them. He and Bjorn leaned over the side, holding out their hands. Oskar set off with Jonas; but, unable to hold on to his son, he used the last of his strength to get to the rescuers himself. They quickly hauled him aboard, then peered around for Jonas, who vanished briefly beneath a wave before reappearing. Vilhelm jumped into the water, grabbed the boy, and swam back. Then they returned to land, towing the capsized boat.

Without waiting for the boat to dock, Margret waded into the water and   40
took Jonas in her arms. Speechless, she briefly collapsed on the shore. As the men disembarked, she rose and set off up the slope with the boy. Bjorn and Vilhelm followed her, with Oskar between them. He was still weak and couldn't walk without help. When Margret reached the steepest pitch, she stopped to gather her strength. Vilhelm let go of Oskar and helped her up the last stretch.

There was a hot tub by the cabin, and Margret stripped off Jonas's wet clothes and held him in the hot water. Vilhelm and Bjorn borrowed some old swimming trunks from Oskar, and they all got into the tub with Jonas. They didn't say much. Oskar just stared out at the lake. From a distance the waves looked insignificant, and when the setting sun broke through the clouds they were struck with gold.

Oskar loaned Vilhelm some dry clothes. The jeans were too big, so Oskar fetched some rope from the toolshed. In an attempt to put a good face on things, he joked: "We'll make a country boy of you yet."

Oskar drained his glass. Bjorn and Vilhelm were taking their time, and Oskar decided not to have another until they had finished. He started talking about the fishing in the lake, keeping an eye on their glasses as he talked. As soon as Bjorn took his last mouthful, Oskar leaped to his feet and fetched the bottle and some ice.

"Another drop?" he asked.

Bjorn nodded, but Vilhelm declined.   45

"We haven't eaten," he said. "The steak was on the barbecue when you capsized."

Margret, who had been silent until now, looked up.

"You didn't see it happen?" Vilhelm asked her.

"No," she said. "I didn't see."

Oskar interrupted: "I bought this whiskey in London last spring. We were   50
there on a weekend trip. Glenlivet. Sixteen years old."

"It's good," said Bjorn.

"We had the steak on the grill," said Vilhelm. "I can't remember if we turned it off."

"Neither can I," said Bjorn.

"Filet mignon," continued Vilhelm. "A beautiful cut."

"We've got some leftovers from dinner," said Oskar. "Why don't we heat   55
them up for you?"

"We ran out the moment you capsized," said Vilhelm. "The steak's proba-bly burnt to a cinder."

"I'll heat up the lamb," said Oskar.

"What happened?" asked Margret.

The men looked at each other.

"I didn't see," said Bjorn. "I was inside."   60

Margret stared at Oskar, waiting for an answer. She had not spoken to him since they had come in. He twisted the glass in his hands.

"I don't really know," he said. "I turned and must have been hit broadside by a wave. That sort of thing shouldn't happen. The boat's supposed to be stable."

He glanced at Vilhelm, who was silent. Margret got up.

"I'll fetch the lamb," she said.

She checked on Jonas before putting the meat in the pan. She heated the   65
gravy too and divided the rest of the salad onto the plates along with the lamb.

"Here you go," she said.

Oskar refilled his and Bjorn's glasses. Vilhelm was still nursing his first.

"People have died of hypothermia in a shorter time than you were in the water," Vilhelm said.

"I tried to hold Jonas out of the water," said Oskar. "That's probably what saved him. I was pretty cold myself by then."

He looked at Margret. She looked away.   70

"We must have been in the water for at least twenty minutes," he con-tinued.

"It was less than ten," said Vilhelm. "I'd been watching you."

"Really," said Oskar.

"I was watching you while the barbecue heated up."

"We watch you too sometimes when you're out in your boat," said Oskar.   75
"My father-in-law thinks you set a bad example."

Vilhelm smiled.

"He's got a good set of binoculars, your father-in-law. He doesn't seem
to have much else to do but look through them. Do you know what make
they are?"

Oskar glanced around. "Where are the binoculars?" he asked.

"Down by the lake," said Margret.

"Down by the lake? What are they doing there?"   80

She said nothing.

"It turned out all right," said Vilhelm. "Everybody's safe. Perhaps I will
have another whiskey."

Oskar filled his glass.

"How about a game of cards?" he asked.

"Yes, why not?" said Bjorn.   85

"I'm not playing," said Margret.

"Oh, come on," said Oskar.

"You can play," she said.

"Perhaps we should be going anyway," said Vilhelm, handing Margret his
empty plate. "Thank you. I was starving."

Their hands touched briefly and she said quietly: "All right, perhaps for a   90
little while."

"Good," said Oskar. "Whist?"

"Sure," said Bjorn.

"Of course we could play bridge, but that wouldn't be fair," said Oskar.

"Why not?" said Bjorn.

"I'm two-time Icelandic champion."   95

He began to shuffle.

"Then this should be a walk in the park for you," said Vilhelm.

Margret sat down diagonally opposite Vilhelm, making them partners in
the game. Oskar shuffled showily, unaware of his wife's look of contempt.
Vilhelm stood up and splashed some water in his glass.

"Are you sure you won't have any?" he asked Margret.

Oskar looked up.   100

"Well," she said, "why not?"

"How about that," said Oskar.

"Ice?" asked Vilhelm.

She nodded.

Vilhelm handed her the glass and sat down. Oskar dealt, then suddenly   105
looked up.

"What were you doing while we were on the lake?" he asked.

Margret didn't answer.

"It was just luck that I happened to be watching you," said Vilhelm.

"She must have been reading," said Oskar. "Give her a book and she won't
notice if the house is burning down."

He laughed. Margret looked away.   110

Bjorn and Oskar won the first couple of games. Vilhelm noticed that Margret forgot herself every now and then, her eyes straying to the window. Dusk had fallen, but the lake was still visible.

"You've got better hands than we do," said Oskar, "yet you still manage to lose."

Getting up, he fetched the whiskey bottle and filled Bjorn's and Vilhelm's glasses. There wasn't much left, but he took care to save a few drops for Margret. When he went to top off her glass she snatched it from the table and said quietly: "No."

"Right," he said, "in that case I'll finish it myself."

He and Bjorn kept winning. Oskar couldn't contain himself and pointed   115
out Vilhelm's mistakes as he made them. Oskar didn't usually behave like this. Vilhelm listened with a half smile on his lips.

"Are you sure the engine didn't cut out?" he asked suddenly.

Oskar waited without answering.

"Just a thought," said Vilhelm.

"There's nothing wrong with the engine," said Oskar.

"What made you think that?" asked Margret.   120

"The boat slewed round so oddly," said Vilhelm. "I thought perhaps something had come loose. A screw, maybe."

Margret looked at them both in turn. Oskar stared at his cards. Vilhelm smiled.

"Let's finish this," said Oskar. "Who's out?"

"I'm out," said Bjorn. "Don't you have any more scotch?"

"No," said Oskar. "It's finished."   125

He saw that he was losing control of the evening. "It's nearly midnight anyway," he added, hoping to get rid of them.

"There's whiskey at my parents' place," said Margret. "You could go and get it."

"I don't want any more whiskey," said Oskar.

"I do," said Margret.

"I'll go with you," Bjorn told Oskar. "I could do with some fresh air."   130

Oskar thought for a moment. He didn't see a way out.

"All right," he said. "Let's go."

Margret and Vilhelm stayed in their seats.

"We'll practice while you're gone," said Vilhelm. "We need it."

They walked quickly. Bjorn had trouble keeping up with Oskar. The tem-   135
perature had dropped, and the wind was blowing off the lake, swaying the trees in the hollow.

"Where's the spring?" asked Bjorn.

"What?" said Oskar.

"The water supply you set up," said Bjorn.

"Over there," said Oskar, gesturing down the hollow without slowing his pace. From time to time he looked back to their cabin, though he could see nothing from this distance but a faint light in the living room window.

His in-laws were in the Canaries, so Oskar fetched a key from their toolshed   140
and opened the door to the cabin, which held the usual smell of damp. He
headed straight for the cupboard where the liquor was kept and found half a
bottle of Johnnie Walker. After locking up in a hurry, he returned the key to the
shed.

"That should do," said Bjorn.

They walked back the same way. When they came to the stream, Bjorn
remembered the binoculars.

"Shouldn't we go down to the lake and get them?" he asked. "It won't take
us a minute."

They stepped over the stream, and Oskar quickened his stride even more.
After a short search of the shore they found the binoculars lying among the
rushes where Margret had sat down with Jonas. They had just started for the
cabin when Oskar stopped abruptly. Bjorn stopped too and waited.

Oskar hesitated, then raised the binoculars to his eyes. There was no one in   145
the living room. He searched outside the cabin but found no one there either.

"Is everything all right?" asked Bjorn.

"Let's go," said Oskar, setting off at a run.

Reaching the cabin before Bjorn, he opened the door. He stopped short in
the doorway, sweating and out of breath. Vilhelm and Margret were in the living room, still in their seats. But Oskar was sure they had only just sat down; he
thought he could see the change in them. Margret looked at him, then away.

"You didn't take long," said Vilhelm.

"We ran," said Bjorn. "Oskar was in a hurry to get back."   150

"It's late," said Vilhelm, looking at his watch. "We really should be going.
The whiskey can wait till another time."

He stood up. The door was still open.

"Thanks for the lamb," said Vilhelm. "I'll return your clothes tomorrow."

As they left, Margret remained in her seat, staring out at the lake. Oskar
still hadn't moved. When he opened his mouth he had difficulty talking.

"What happened?" he said. "Tell me what happened."   155

She was trembling and didn't answer immediately. Then she buried her
face in her hands.

"You let go of him," she said in a low voice. "That's what happened. You let
go of him."

[2007]

■ THINKING ABOUT THE TEXT

1. Why does Oskar let his son's pleading govern his actions? Can you sympathize with him, or was he simply being reckless?

2. Comment on the line "he used the last of his strength to get to the rescuers himself" (para. 39). Is this what his wife sees?

3. Why does Oskar want to play cards? Point out the various ways in which
   Oskar brags.

4. Why does Oskar run back to the house? Why does he suspect his wife? What masculine expectations does Oskar violate?

5. When Oskar asks "Tell me what happened" his wife lets him know what she saw. Is this response actually an answer to Oskar's suspicions?

≡ MAKING COMPARISONS

1. Compare Oskar and Henry.

2. Compare the impact of guilt in both stories.

3. Compare Angelina's response to Henry with Margret's reaction to Oskar.

HARUKI MURAKAMI
Another Way to Die

Translated by Jay Rubin

Haruki Murakami (b. 1949) was born in Kobe, Japan, and for many Japanese readers he is now their country's leading fiction writer. As more of his works have been translated, he is becoming better known in the United States and other countries. Murakami has translated into Japanese the works of several American writers, and during the first half of the 1990s he taught at Princeton University. Recently, Murakami has studied terrorism. For his book Underground *(published in English in 2000), he interviewed survivors of a religious cult's 1995 poison gas attack on the Tokyo subway system. His latest novels are* Sputnik Sweetheart *(2002),* Kafka on the Shore *(2005), and* After Dark *(2007). But political concerns are evident as well in the following story, a chapter from Murakami's novel* The Wind-Up Bird Chronicle *(published in English in 1997). The novel deals with the Japanese occupation of Manchuria, an area of China, beginning in the 1930s. The Japanese established a nation called Manchukuo, which was nominally headed by the former emperor of China until 1945, when Russian forces moved in and World War II ended overall. "Another Way to Die" takes place during this period.*

The Japanese veterinarian woke before 6 A.M. Most of the animals in the Hsinching zoo were already awake. The open window let in their cries and the breeze that carried their smells, which told him the weather without his having to look outside. This was part of his routine here in Manchuria: he would listen, then inhale the morning air, and so ready himself for each new day.

Today, however, should have been different from the day before. It *had* to be different. So many voices and smells had been lost! The tigers, the leopards, the wolves, the bears: all had been liquidated — eliminated — by a Japanese squad the previous afternoon to avoid the animals' escaping as the city came under Russian attack. Now, after some hours of sleep, those events seemed to him like part of a sluggish nightmare he had had long ago. But he knew they had actually happened. His ears still felt a dull ache from the roar of the soldiers' rifles; that could not be a dream. It was August now, the year 1945, and he was here in the city of Hsin-ching, in Japanese-held Manchuria; Soviet troops had burst across the border and were pressing closer every hour. This was reality — as real as the sink and toothbrush he saw in front of him.

The sound of the elephants' trumpeting gave him some sense of relief. Ah, yes — the elephants had survived. Fortunately, the young lieutenant in charge of yesterday's action had had enough normal human sensitivity to remove the elephants from the list, the veterinarian thought as he washed his face. Since coming to Manchuria, he had met any number of stiff-necked, fanatical young officers from his homeland, and the experience always left him shaken. Most of them were farmers' sons who had spent their youthful years in the depressed nineteen-thirties, steeped in the tragedies of poverty while a megalomaniac nationalism was hammered into their skulls. They would follow the orders of a superior without a second thought, no matter how outlandish. If they were commanded, in the name of the Emperor, to dig a hole through the earth to Brazil, they would grab a shovel and set to work. Some people called this "purity," but the veterinarian had other words for it. As an urban doctor's son, educated in the relatively liberal atmosphere of Japan in the twenties, the veterinarian could never understand those young officers. Shooting a couple of elephants should have been a simpler assignment than digging through the earth to Brazil, but yesterday's lieutenant, though he spoke with a slight country accent, seemed to be a more normal human being than other officers were — better educated and more reasonable. The veterinarian could sense this from the way the young man spoke and handled himself.

In any case, the elephants had not been killed, and the veterinarian told himself that he should probably be grateful. The soldiers, too, must have been glad to be spared the task. The Chinese workers may have regretted the omission — they had missed out on a lot of meat and ivory.

The veterinarian boiled water in a kettle, soaked his beard in a hot towel, and shaved. Then he ate breakfast alone: tea, toast, and butter. The food rations in Manchuria were far from sufficient, but compared with those elsewhere they were still fairly generous. This was good news both for him and for the animals. The animals showed resentment at their reduced allotments of feed, but the situation here was better than in zoos back in the Japanese homeland, where food supplies had already bottomed out. No one could predict the future, but for now, at least, both animals and humans were spared the pain of extreme hunger.

He wondered how his wife and daughter were doing. They had left for Japan a few days earlier, and if all went according to plan their train should have reached the Korean coast by now. There they would board the transport ship that would carry them home to Japan. The doctor missed seeing them when he woke up in the morning. He missed hearing their lively voices as they prepared breakfast. A hollow quiet ruled the house. This was no longer the home he loved, the place where he belonged. And yet, at the same time, he could not help feeling a certain strange joy at being left alone in this empty official residence; now he was able to sense the implacable power of fate in his very bones and flesh.

Fate itself was the veterinarian's own fatal disease. From his youngest days, he had had a weirdly lucid awareness that "I, as an individual, am living under the control of some outside force." Most of the time, the power of fate played on like a quiet and monotonous ground bass, coloring only the edges of his life. Rarely was he reminded of its existence. But every once in a while the balance would shift and the force would increase, plunging him into a state of near-paralytic resignation. He knew from experience that nothing he could do or think would ever change the situation.

Not that he was a passive creature; indeed, he was more decisive than most, and he always saw his decisions through. In his profession, too, he was outstanding: a veterinarian of exceptional skill, a tireless educator. He was certainly no fatalist, as most people use the word. And yet never had he experienced the unshakable certainty that he had arrived at a decision entirely on his own. He always had the sense that fate had forced him to decide things to suit its own convenience. On occasion, after the momentary satisfaction of having decided something of his own free will, he would see that things had been decided beforehand by an external power cleverly camouflaged as free will, mere bait thrown in his path to lure him into behaving as he was meant to. He felt like a titular head of state who did nothing more than impress the royal seal on documents at the behest of a regent who wielded all true power in the realm — like the Emperor of this puppet empire of Manchukuo.

Now, left behind in his residence at the zoo, the veterinarian was alone with his fate. And it was fate above all, the gigantic power of fate, that held sway here — not the Kwantung Army, not the Soviet Army, not the troops of the Chinese Communists or of the Kuomintang.° Anyone could see that fate was the ruler here, and that individual will counted for nothing. It was fate that had spared the elephants and buried the tigers and leopards and wolves and bears the day before. What would it bury now, and what would it spare? These were questions that no one could answer.

The veterinarian left his residence to prepare for the morning feeding. He assumed that no one would show up for work anymore, but he found two Chinese boys waiting for him in his office. He did not know them. They were thirteen or fourteen years old, dark-complexioned and skinny, with roving animal eyes. "They told us to help you," one boy said. The doctor nodded. He asked their names, but they made no reply. Their faces remained blank, as if they had not heard the question. These boys had obviously been sent by the Chinese people who had worked here until the day before. Those people had probably ended all contact with the Japanese now, in anticipation of a new regime, but

10

---

not the . . . the Kuomintang: The Kwantung Army was the Japanese-controlled military force in Manchukuo. In August 1945, when Murakami's story takes place, the Soviet Army was on the verge of defeating this force. The Kuomintang, led by General Chiang Kai-shek, was the controlling party in the overall Chinese government. The Chinese Communists managed to take over China in 1948, forcing Chiang Kai-shek and his allies to flee to Taiwan.

assumed that children would not be held accountable. The boys had been sent as a sign of good will — the workers knew that he could not care for the animals alone.

The veterinarian gave each boy two cookies, then put them to work helping him feed the animals. They led a mule-drawn cart from cage to cage, providing each animal with its particular feed and changing its water. Cleaning the cages was out of the question. The best they could manage was a quick hose-down, to wash away the droppings.

They started the work at eight o'clock and finished after ten. The boys then disappeared without a word. The veterinarian felt exhausted from the hard physical labor. He went back to the office and reported to the zoo director that the animals had been fed.

Just before noon, the young lieutenant came back to the zoo leading the same eight soldiers he had brought the day before. Fully armed again, they walked with a metallic clinking that could be heard far in advance of their arrival. Their shirts were blackened with sweat. Cicadas were screaming in the trees, as they had been yesterday. Today, however, the soldiers had not come to kill animals. The lieutenant saluted the director and said, "We need to know the current status of the zoo's usable carts and draft animals." The director informed him that the zoo had exactly one mule and one wagon. "We contributed our only truck and two horses two weeks ago," he noted. The lieutenant nodded and announced that he would immediately commandeer the mule and wagon, as per orders of Kwantung Army Headquarters.

"Wait just a minute," the veterinarian interjected. "We need those to feed the animals twice a day. All our local people have disappeared. Without that mule and wagon, our animals will starve to death. Even with them, we can barely keep up."

"We're all just barely keeping up, sir," said the lieutenant, whose eyes were red and whose face was covered with stubble. "Our first priority is to defend the city. You can always let the animals out of their cages if need be. We've taken care of the dangerous carnivores. The others pose no security risk. These are military orders, sir. You'll just have to manage as you see fit."   15

Cutting the discussion short, the lieutenant had his men take the mule and wagon. When they were gone, the veterinarian and the director looked at each other. The director sipped his tea, shook his head, and said nothing.

Four hours later, the soldiers were back with the mule and wagon, a filthy canvas tarpaulin covering the mounded contents of the wagon. The mule was panting, its hide foaming with the afternoon heat and the weight of the load. The eight soldiers marched four Chinese men ahead of them at bayonet point — young men, perhaps twenty years old, wearing baseball uniforms and with their hands tied behind their backs. Black-and-blue marks on their faces made it obvious that they had been severely beaten. The right eye of one man was swollen almost shut, and the bleeding lips of another had stained his baseball shirt bright red. The shirtfronts had nothing written on them, but there were small rectangles where the name patches had been torn off. The numbers on their backs were 1, 4, 7, and 9. The veterinarian could not begin to imagine why, at such a time of crisis, four young Chinese men would be wearing baseball uniforms or why they had been so badly beaten and dragged here by Japanese troops. The scene looked like something not of this world — a painting by a mental patient.

The lieutenant asked the zoo director if he had any picks and shovels he could let them use. The young officer looked even more pale and haggard than he had before. The veterinarian led him and his men to a toolshed behind the office. The lieutenant chose two picks and two shovels for his men. Then he asked the veterinarian to come with him and, leaving his men there, walked into a thicket beyond the road. The veterinarian followed. Wherever the lieutenant walked, huge grasshoppers scattered. The smell of summer grass hung in the air. Mixed in with the deafening screams of cicadas, the sharp trumpeting of elephants now and then seemed to sound a distant warning.

The lieutenant went on among the trees without speaking, until he found a kind of opening in the woods. The area had been slated for construction of a plaza for small animals that children could play with. The plan had been postponed indefinitely, however, when the worsening military situation made construction materials scarce. The trees had been cleared away to make a circle of bare ground, and the sun illuminated this one part of the woods like stage lighting. The lieutenant stood in the center of the circle and scanned the area. Then he dug at the ground with the heel of his boot.

"We're going to bivouac here for a while," he said, kneeling down and   20
scooping up a handful of dirt.

The veterinarian nodded in response. He had no idea why they had to bivouac in a zoo, but he decided not to ask. Here in Hsin-ching, experience had taught him never to question military men. Questions did nothing but make them angry, and they never gave you a straight answer in any case.

"First we dig a big hole here," the lieutenant said, speaking as if to himself. He stood up and took a pack of cigarettes from his shirt pocket. Putting a cigarette between his lips, he offered one to the doctor, then lit both with a match. The two concentrated on their smoking to fill the silence. Again the lieutenant began digging at the ground with his boot. He drew a kind of diagram in the earth, then rubbed it out. Finally, he asked the veterinarian, "Where were you born?"

"In Kanagawa," the doctor said. "In a town called Ofuna, near the sea, an hour or two from Tokyo."

The lieutenant nodded.

"And where were you born?" the veterinarian asked.   25

Instead of answering, the lieutenant narrowed his eyes and watched the smoke rising from between his fingers. No, it never pays to ask a military man questions, the veterinarian told himself again. They like to ask questions, but they'll never give you an answer. They wouldn't give you the time of day — literally.

"There's a movie studio there," the lieutenant said.

It took the veterinarian a few seconds to realize the lieutenant was talking about Ofuna. "That's right. A big studio. I've never been inside, though."

The lieutenant dropped what was left of his cigarette on the ground and crushed it out. "I hope you make it back there," he said. "Of course, there's an ocean to cross between here and Japan. We'll probably all die over here." He kept his eyes on the ground as he spoke. "Tell me, Doctor, are you afraid of death?"

"I guess it depends on how you die," the veterinarian said after a moment's thought.   30

The lieutenant raised his eyes and looked at the veterinarian as if his curiosity had been aroused. He had apparently been expecting another answer. "You're right," he said. "It does depend on how you die."

The two remained silent for a time. The lieutenant looked as if he might just fall asleep there standing up. He was obviously exhausted. An especially large grasshopper flew over them like a bird and disappeared into a distant clump of grass with a noisy beating of wings. The lieutenant glanced at his watch.

"Time to get started," he said to no one in particular. Then he spoke to the veterinarian. "I'd like you to stay around for a while. I might have to ask you to do me a favor."

The veterinarian nodded.

The soldiers led the Chinese prisoners to the opening in the woods and untied   35
their hands. The corporal drew a large circle on the ground using a baseball bat—why a soldier would have a bat the veterinarian found another mystery—and ordered the prisoners, in Japanese, to dig a deep hole the size of the circle. With the picks and shovels, the four men in baseball uniforms started digging in silence. Half the Japanese squad stood guard over them while the other half stretched out beneath the trees. They seemed to be in desperate need of sleep; no sooner had they hit the ground in full gear than they began snoring. The four soldiers who remained awake kept watch over the digging nearby, rifles resting on their hips, bayonets fixed, ready for immediate use. The lieutenant and the corporal took turns overseeing the work and napping under the trees.

It took less than an hour for the four Chinese prisoners to dig a hole some twelve feet across and deep enough to come up to their necks. One of the men asked for water, speaking in Japanese. The lieutenant nodded, and a soldier brought a bucket full of water. The four Chinese took turns ladling water from the bucket and gulping it down with obvious relish. They drank almost the entire bucketful. Their uniforms were smeared black with blood, mud, and sweat.

The lieutenant had two of the soldiers pull the wagon over to the hole. The corporal yanked the tarpaulin off, to reveal four dead men piled in the wagon. They wore the same baseball uniforms as the prisoners, and they, too, were obviously Chinese. They appeared to have been shot, and their uniforms were covered with black bloodstains. Large flies were beginning to swarm over the corpses. Judging from the way the blood had dried, the doctor guessed that they had been dead for close to twenty-four hours.

The lieutenant ordered the four Chinese who had dug the hole to throw the bodies into it. Without a word, faces blank, the men took the bodies out of the wagon and threw them, one at a time, into the hole. Each corpse landed with a dull thud. The numbers on the dead men's uniforms were 2, 5, 6, and 8. The veterinarian committed them to memory.

When the four Chinese had finished throwing the bodies into the hole, the soldiers tied each man to a nearby tree. The lieutenant held up his wrist and studied his watch with a grim expression. Then he looked up toward a spot in the sky for a while, as if searching for something there. He looked like a stationmaster standing on the platform and waiting for a hopelessly overdue train. But in fact he was looking at nothing at all. He was just allowing a certain amount of time to go by. Once he had accomplished that, he turned to the corporal and gave him curt orders to bayonet three of the four prisoners — Nos. 1, 7, and 9.

Three soldiers were chosen and took up their positions in front of the three   40
Chinese. The soldiers looked paler than the men they were about to kill. The Chinese looked too tired to hope for anything. The corporal offered each of them a smoke, but they refused. He put his cigarettes back into his shirt pocket.

Taking the veterinarian with him, the lieutenant went to stand somewhat apart from the other soldiers. "You'd better watch this," he said. "This is another way to die."

The veterinarian nodded. The lieutenant is not saying this to me, he thought. He's saying it to himself.

In a gentle voice, the lieutenant explained, "Shooting them would be the simplest and most efficient way to kill them, but we have orders not to waste a single bullet — and certainly not to waste bullets killing Chinese. We're supposed to save our ammunition for the Russians. We'll just bayonet them, I suppose, but that's not as easy as it sounds. By the way, Doctor, did they teach you how to use a bayonet in the Army?"

The doctor explained that, as a cavalry veterinarian, he had not been trained to use a bayonet.

"Well, the proper way to kill a man with a bayonet is this: First, you thrust   45
it in under the ribs — here." The lieutenant pointed to his own torso just above the stomach. "Then you drag the point in a big, deep circle inside him to scramble the organs. Then you thrust upward to puncture the heart. You can't just stick it in and expect him to die. We soldiers have this drummed into us. Hand-to-hand combat using bayonets ranks right up there along with night assaults as the pride of the Imperial Army — though mainly it's a lot cheaper than tanks and planes and cannons. Of course, you can train all you want, but finally what you're stabbing is a straw doll, not a live human being. It doesn't bleed or scream or spill its guts on the ground. These soldiers have never actually killed a human being that way. And neither have I."

The lieutenant looked at the corporal and gave him a nod. The corporal barked his order to the three soldiers, who snapped to attention. Then they took a half step back and thrust out their bayonets, each man aiming his blade at his prisoner. One of the young men (No. 7) growled something in Chinese that sounded like a curse and gave a defiant spit — which never reached the ground but dribbled down the front of his baseball uniform.

At the sound of the next order, the three soldiers thrust their bayonets into the Chinese men with tremendous force. Then, as the lieutenant had said, they twisted the blades so as to rip the men's internal organs, and thrust the tips upward. The cries of the Chinese men were not very loud — more like deep sobs than like screams, as if they were heaving out the breath left in their bodies all at once through a single opening. The soldiers pulled out their bayonets and stepped back. The corporal barked his order again, and the men repeated the procedure exactly as before — stabbing, twisting, thrusting upward, withdrawing. The veterinarian watched in numbed silence, overtaken by the sense that he was beginning to split in two. He became simultaneously the stabber and the stabbed. He could feel both the impact of the bayonet as it entered his victim's body and the pain of having his internal organs slashed to bits.

It took much longer than he would have imagined for the Chinese men to die. Their sliced-up bodies poured prodigious amounts of blood on the ground, but, even with their organs shredded, they went on twitching slightly for quite some time. The corporal used his own bayonet to cut the ropes that bound the men to the trees, and then he had the soldiers who had not participated in the killing help drag the fallen bodies to the hole and throw them in. These corpses also made a dull thud on impact, but the doctor couldn't help feeling that the sound was different from that made by the earlier corpses — probably because these were not entirely dead yet.

Now only the young Chinese prisoner with the number 4 on his shirt was left. The three pale-faced soldiers tore broad leaves from plants at their feet and proceeded to wipe their bloody bayonets. Not only blood but strange-colored body fluids and chunks of flesh adhered to the blades. The men had to use many leaves to return the bayonets to their original bare-metal shine.

The veterinarian wondered why only the one man, No. 4, had been left 50 alive, but he was not going to ask questions. The lieutenant took out another cigarette and lit up. He then offered a smoke to the veterinarian, who accepted it in silence and, after putting it between his lips, struck his own match. His hand did not tremble, but it seemed to have lost all feeling, as if he were wearing thick gloves.

"These men were cadets in the Manchukuo Army Officer Candidate School," the lieutenant said. "They refused to participate in the defense of Hsin-ching. They killed two of their Japanese instructors last night and tried to run away. We caught them during night patrol, killed four of them on the spot, and captured the other four. Two more escaped in the dark." The lieutenant rubbed his beard with the palm of his hand. "They were trying to make their getaway in baseball uniforms. I guess they figured they'd be arrested as deserters if they wore their military uniforms. Or maybe they were afraid of what Communist troops would do to them if they were caught in their Manchukuo uniforms. Anyway, all they had in their barracks to wear besides their cadet outfits were uniforms of the O.C.S. baseball team. So they tore off the names and tried to get away wearing these. I don't know if you know, but the school had a great team. They used to go to Taiwan and Korea for friendship games. That guy" — and here the lieutenant motioned toward the man tied to the tree — "was captain of the team and batted cleanup. We think he was the one who organized the getaway, too. He killed the two instructors with a bat. The instructors knew there was trouble in the barracks and weren't going to distribute weapons to the cadets until it was an absolute emergency. But they forgot about the baseball bats. Both of them had their skulls cracked open. They probably died instantly. Two perfect home runs. This is the bat."

The lieutenant had the corporal bring the bat to him. He passed the bat to the veterinarian. The doctor took it in both hands and held it up in front of his face, the way a player stepping into the batter's box does. It was just an ordinary bat, not very well made, with a rough finish and an uneven grain. It was heavy, though, and well broken in. The handle was black with sweat. It didn't look like a bat that had been used recently to kill two human beings. After getting a feel for its weight, the veterinarian handed it back to the lieutenant, who gave it a few easy swings, handling it like an expert.

"Do you play baseball?" the lieutenant asked the veterinarian.

"All the time when I was a kid."

"Too grown up now?"

55

"No more baseball for me," the veterinarian said, and he was on the verge of asking "How about you, lieutenant?" but he swallowed the words.

"I've been ordered to beat this guy to death with the same bat he used," the lieutenant said in a dry voice as he tapped the ground with the tip of the bat. "An eye for an eye, a tooth for a tooth. Just between you and me, I think the order stinks. What the hell good is it going to do to kill these guys? We don't have any planes left, we don't have any warships, our best troops are dead. Just the other day some kind of special new bomb wiped out the whole city of Hiroshima in a split second. Either we're going to be swept out of Manchuria or we'll all be killed, and China will belong to the Chinese again. We've already killed a lot of Chinese, and adding a few bodies to the count isn't going to make any difference. But orders are orders. I'm a soldier and I have to follow orders. We killed the tigers and leopards yesterday, and today we have to kill these guys. So take a good look, Doctor. This is another way for people to die. You're a doctor, so you're probably used to knives and blood and guts, but you've probably never seen anyone beaten to death with a baseball bat."

The lieutenant ordered the corporal to bring player No. 4, the cleanup batter, to the edge of the hole. Once again they tied his hands behind his back, then blindfolded him and had him kneel down on the ground. He was a tall, strongly built young man with massive arms the size of most people's thighs. The lieutenant called over one young soldier and handed him the bat. "Kill him with this," he said. The young soldier stood at attention and saluted before taking the bat, but having taken it in his hands he just went on standing there as if stupefied. He seemed unable to grasp the concept of beating a Chinese man to death with a baseball bat.

"Have you ever played baseball?" the lieutenant asked the young soldier.

"No, sir, never," the soldier replied in a loud voice. Both the village in Hok-   60
kaido where he was born and the village in Manchuria where he grew up had been so poor that no family in either place could have afforded the luxury of a baseball or a bat. He had spent his boyhood running around the fields, catching dragonflies and playing at sword fighting with sticks. He had never in his life played baseball, or even seen a game. This was the first time he had ever held a bat.

The lieutenant showed him how to hold the bat and taught him the basics of the swing, demonstrating a few times himself. "See? It's all in the hips," he grunted through clenched teeth. "Starting from the backswing, you twist from the waist down. The tip of the bat follows through naturally. Understand? If you concentrate too much on swinging the bat, your arms do all the work and you lose power. Swing from the hips."

The soldier didn't seem fully to comprehend the lieutenant's instructions, but he took off his heavy gear as ordered and practiced his swing for a while. Everyone was watching him. The lieutenant placed his hands over the soldier's to help him adjust his grip. He was a good teacher. Before long, the soldier's swing, though somewhat awkward, was swishing through the air. What the young soldier lacked in skill he made up for in muscle power, having spent his days working on the farm.

"That's good enough," the lieutenant said, using his hat to wipe the sweat from his brow. "O.K., now try to do it in one good, clean swing. Don't let him suffer."

What he really wanted to say was "I don't want to do this any more than you do. Who the hell could have thought of anything so stupid? Killing a guy with a baseball bat . . ." But an officer could never say such a thing to an en-listed man.

The soldier stepped up behind the blindfolded Chinese man where he knelt   65
on the ground. When the soldier raised the bat, the strong rays of the setting sun cast its long, thick shadow on the earth. This is so weird, the veterinarian thought. The lieutenant's right: I've never seen a man killed with a baseball bat. The young soldier held the bat aloft for a long time. The veterinarian saw its tip shaking.

The lieutenant nodded to the soldier. With a deep breath, the soldier took a backswing, then smashed the bat with all his strength into the back of the Chinese cadet's head. He did it amazingly well. He swung his hips exactly as the lieutenant had taught him to, the brand of the bat made a direct hit behind the man's ear, and the bat followed through perfectly. There was a dull crush-ing sound as the skull shattered. The man himself made no sound. His body hung in the air for a moment in a strange pose, then flopped forward. He lay with his cheek on the ground, blood flowing from one ear. He did not move. The lieutenant looked at his watch. Still gripping the bat, the young soldier stared off into space, his mouth agape.

The lieutenant was a person who did things with great care. He waited for a full minute. When he was certain that the Chinese man was not moving at all, he said to the veterinarian, "Could you do me a favor and check to see that he's really dead?"

The veterinarian nodded, walked over to where the young Chinese lay, and knelt down and removed his blindfold. The man's eyes were open wide, the pupils turned upward, and bright-red blood was flowing from his ear. His half-opened mouth revealed the tongue lying tangled inside. The impact had left his neck twisted at a strange angle. The man's nostrils had expelled thick gobs of blood, making black stains on the dry ground. One particularly alert — and large — fly had already burrowed its way into a nostril to lay eggs. Just to make sure, the veterinarian took the man's wrist and felt for a pulse. There was no pulse — certainly not where there was supposed to be one. The young soldier had ended this burly man's life with a single swing of a bat — indeed, his first-ever swing of a bat. The veterinarian glanced toward the lieutenant and nodded, to signal that the man was, without a doubt, dead. Having completed his assigned task, he was beginning slowly to rise to his full height when it seemed to him that the sun shining on his back suddenly increased in intensity.

At that very moment, the young Chinese batter in uniform No. 4 rose up into a sitting position as if he had just come fully awake. Without the slightest uncertainty or hesitation — or so it seemed to those watching — he grabbed the doctor's wrist. It all happened in a split second. The veterinarian could not understand; this man was dead, he was sure of it. But now, thanks to one last drop of life that seemed to well up out of nowhere, the man was gripping the veterinarian's wrist with the strength of a steel vise. Eyelids stretched open to the limit, pupils still glaring upward, the man fell forward into the hole, dragging the doctor in after him. The doctor fell in on top of him and heard the man's ribs crack as his weight came down. Still the Chinese ballplayer continued to grip his wrist. The soldiers saw all this happening, but they were too stunned to do anything more than stand and watch. The lieutenant recovered first and leaped into the hole. He drew his pistol from his holster, set the muzzle against the Chinese man's head, and pulled the trigger twice. Two sharp, over-lapping cracks rang out, and a large black hole opened in the man's temple. Now his life was completely gone, but still he refused to release the doctor's wrist. The lieutenant knelt down and, pistol in one hand, began the pains-taking process of prying open the corpse's fingers one at a time. The veterinarian lay there in the hole, surrounded by eight silent Chinese corpses in baseball uniforms. Down in the hole, the screeching of cicadas sounded very different from the way it sounded above ground.

Once the veterinarian had been freed from the dead man's grasp, the soldiers pulled him and the lieutenant out of the grave. The veterinarian squatted down on the grass and took several deep breaths. Then he looked at his wrist. The man's fingers had left five bright-red marks. On this hot August afternoon, the veterinarian felt chilled to the core of his body. I'll never get rid of this coldness again, he thought. That man was truly, seriously trying to take me with him wherever he was going.

The lieutenant reset the pistol's safety and carefully slipped the gun into its holster. This was the first time he had ever fired a gun at a human being. But he tried not to think about it. The war would continue for a little while at least, and people would continue to die. He could leave the deep thinking for later. He wiped his sweaty right palm on his pants, then ordered the soldiers who had not participated in the execution to fill in the hole. A huge swarm of flies had already taken custody of the pile of corpses.

The young soldier went on standing where he was, stupefied, gripping the bat. He couldn't seem to make his hands let go. The lieutenant and the corporal left him alone. He had seemed to be watching the whole bizarre series of events — the "dead" Chinese suddenly grabbing the veterinarian by the wrist, their falling into the grave, the lieutenant's leaping in and finishing him off, and now the other soldiers' filling in the hole. But in fact he had not been watching any of it. He had been listening to a bird in a tree somewhere making a *"Creeeak! Creeeak!"* sound as if winding a spring. The soldier looked up, trying to pinpoint the direction of the cries, but he could see no sign of the windup bird. He felt a slight sense of nausea at the back of his throat.

As he listened to the winding of the spring, the young soldier saw one fragmentary image after another rise up before him and fade away. After the Japanese were disarmed by the Soviets, the lieutenant would be handed over to the Chinese and hanged for his responsibility in these executions. The corporal would die of the plague in a Siberian concentration camp: he would be thrown into a quarantine shed and left there until dead, though in fact he had merely collapsed from malnutrition and had not contracted the plague — not, at least, until he was thrown into the shed. The veterinarian would die in an accident a year later: a civilian, he would be taken by the Soviets for cooperating with the military and sent to another Siberian camp to do hard labor; he would be working in a deep shaft of a Siberian coal mine when a flood would drown him along with many soldiers. And I, thought the young soldier with the bat in his hands — but he could not see his own future. He could not even see as real the events that were happening before his very eyes. He closed his eyes now and listened to the call of the windup bird.

Then, all at once, he thought of the ocean — the ocean he had seen from the deck of the ship bringing him from Japan to Manchuria eight years earlier. He had never seen the ocean before, nor had he seen it since. He could still remember the smell of the salt air. The ocean was one of the greatest things he had ever seen in his life — bigger and deeper than anything he had imagined. It changed its color and shape and expression according to time and place and weather. It aroused a deep sadness in his heart, and at the same time it brought his heart peace and comfort. Would he ever see it again? He loosened his grip and let the bat fall to the ground. It made a dry sound as it struck the earth. After the bat left his hands, he felt a slight increase in his nausea.

The windup bird went on crying, but no one else could hear its call.   75

[1997]

≣ **THINKING ABOUT THE TEXT**

1. The veterinarian knows enough not to ask questions of the lieutenant. Why is this?
2. What is another way of saying "orders are orders"?
3. What is the young soldier doing after he hits the prisoner with the bat? Does this suggest his feeling about having to execute the prisoner?
4. What is the point of so much graphic violence in the story?
5. Can you give an example of how the lieutenant is a prisoner of masculinity?

≣ **MAKING COMPARISONS**

1. Which man — Henry, Oskar, or the lieutenant — seems most ensnared by the codes of masculinity?
2. Are the authors' opinions about these men clear?
3. Which of the masculine values the men are upholding are most familiar in our present cultural landscape, including movies and television?

≣ **WRITING ABOUT ISSUES**

1. Write an argument defending or opposing the idea that Henry and Oskar are prisoners of masculinity.
2. Write an entry in Angelina's diary about her confrontation with Henry. Write another one in Margret's diary after the incidents in her story.
3. Write an essay that argues that Henry and Oskar are or are not typical men.
4. These three stories focus on the negative aspects of excessive masculinity. Write an essay that explains the negative aspects of excessive femininity.

▦ A Dream of Freedom: A Collection of Poems by Langston Hughes

LANGSTON HUGHES, "Let America Be America Again"

LANGSTON HUGHES, "Open Letter to the South"

LANGSTON HUGHES, "Theme for English B"

LANGSTON HUGHES, "Harlem"

Inspired by two of the great poetic voices of American life, Walt Whitman and Carl Sandburg, Langston Hughes is often thought of as the African American poet laureate, a writer who is able to sing eloquently about the reality and idealism of democracy in America. He was committed to telling the truth about the lives of black people. In the introduction to *The Collected Poems of Langston Hughes*, it is noted that Hughes wrote of "the joys and sorrows, the trials and triumphs, of ordinary black folk, in the language of their typical speech and composed out of a genuine love of these people."

In response to the Depression of the 1930s, Hughes became radicalized by the poverty and injustice he saw everywhere in black America. His poems from this period are radical, indeed. "Open Letter to the South" calls for a socialist solidarity against oppression, and "Let America Be America Again" poignantly laments the wide gulf that often existed between the idealistic rhetoric of democracy and the appalling social reality of segregation. Although he later became less radical in his poetry, "Theme for English B" and "Harlem" still reflect his belief that poetry is a form of social action. At the heart of all Hughes's poetry was the deferred dream of African Americans to achieve the freedom and equality promised to all in America.

▦ BEFORE YOU READ

Can you imagine what would have happened to your personality if a dream of yours (perhaps going to college, playing a sport, or marrying someone you loved deeply) were denied? What would you do if America was not living up to its stated ideals or if those ideals were suddenly altered significantly? Would you express your disappointment publicly or only privately?

LANGSTON HUGHES
Let America Be America Again

Langston Hughes (1902–1967) has long been regarded as a major African American writer and is increasingly seen as an important contributor to American literature in general. Like Countee Cullen, Hughes was actively involved in the 1920s

(© Corbis)

movement called the Harlem Renaissance. Then and later, he worked in various genres, including fiction, drama, and autobiography. Nevertheless, he is primarily known for his poems. "Let America Be America Again" appeared in a 1938 pamphlet by Hughes entitled A New Song, which was published by a socialist organization named the International Worker Order. At this point in his career, Hughes was critical of capitalism and sympathetic toward Communism, as were many other writers during the Great Depression. During the late 1930s, Communism in the United States entered a phase called the Popular Front, which linked Marxist principles to traditional American ideas and values. The title of Hughes's poem reflects this attempt at connection. Note, too, that within the poem Hughes sees African Americans as part of a larger population suffering from poverty and powerlessness. Indeed, the Depression led many writers to connect racism with other kinds of oppression, especially inequalities of class.

Let America be America again.
Let it be the dream it used to be.
Let it be the pioneer on the plain

Seeking a home where he himself is free.
(America never was America to me.)   5

Let America be the dream the dreamers dreamed —
Let it be that great strong land of love
Where never kings connive nor tyrants scheme
That any man be crushed by one above.
(It never was America to me.)   10

O, let my land be a land where Liberty
Is crowned with no false patriotic wreath,
But opportunity is real, and life is free,
Equality is in the air we breathe.

(There's never been equality for me,   15
Nor freedom in this "homeland of the free.")

Say, who are you that mumbles in the dark?
And who are you that draws your veil across the stars?

I am the poor white, fooled and pushed apart,
I am the Negro bearing slavery's scars.   20
I am the red man driven from the land,
I am the immigrant clutching the hope I seek —
And finding only the same old stupid plan
Of dog eat dog, of mighty crush the weak.

I am the young man, full of strength and hope,   25
Tangled in that ancient endless chain
Of profit, power, gain, of grab the land!
Of grab the gold! Of grab the ways of satisfying need!
Of work the men! Of take the pay!
Of owning everything for one's own greed!   30

I am the farmer, bondsman to the soil.
I am the worker sold to the machine.
I am the Negro, servant to you all.
I am the people, humble, hungry, mean —
Hungry yet today despite the dream.   35
Beaten yet today — O, Pioneers!
I am the man who never got ahead,
The poorest worker bartered through the years.

Yet I'm the one who dreamt our basic dream
In that Old World while still a serf of kings,   40
Who dreamt a dream so strong, so brave, so true,
That even yet its mighty daring sings
In every brick and stone, in every furrow turned

That's made America the land it has become.
O, I'm the man who sailed those early seas   45
In search of what I meant to be my home —
For I'm the one who left dark Ireland's shore,
And Poland's plain, and England's grassy lea,
And torn from Black Africa's strand I came
To build a "homeland of the free."   50

The free?

Who said the free? Not me?
Surely not me? The millions on relief today?
The millions shot down when we strike?
The millions who have nothing for our pay?   55
For all the dreams we've dreamed
And all the songs we've sung
And all the hopes we've held
And all the flags we've hung,
The millions who have nothing for our pay —   60
Except the dream that's almost dead today.

O, let America be America again —
The land that never has been yet —
And yet must be — the land where *every* man is free.
The land that's mine — the poor man's, Indian's, Negro's, ME —   65
Who made America,
Whose sweat and blood, whose faith and pain,
Whose hand at the foundry, whose plow in the rain,
Must bring back our mighty dream again.

Sure, call me any ugly name you choose —   70
The steel of freedom does not stain.
From those who live like leeches on the people's lives,
We must take back our land again,
America!

O, yes,   75
I say it plain,
America never was America to me,
And yet I swear this oath —
America will be!

Out of the rack and ruin of our gangster death,   80
The rape and rot of graft, and stealth, and lies,
We, the people, must redeem
The land, the mines, the plants, the rivers.
The mountains and the endless plain —
All, all the stretch of these great green states —   85
And make America again!   *[1938]*

▤ THINKING ABOUT THE TEXT

1. In the title and in the first line comes the plea "Let America be America again." At several points in the poem, however, the speaker indicates that America has never lived up to its ideals, especially about freedom and equality. Identify these points. How can we reconcile them with the opening plea?

2. When this poem was written in 1938, what do you think the response to the poem would have been among poor blacks? Poor whites? Members of Congress? Intellectuals? Religious groups in the South? The North? How would you answer this question in today's America?

3. What other oppressed peoples does the speaker refer to besides African Americans? Does he succeed in convincing you that all these groups belong together in the poem? What significant differences among them, if any, do you think he overlooks?

4. Although the speaker uses "I" a lot, sometimes he refers to "we." What is the effect of this shift? Should he have used one of these pronouns more than he does? Explain.

5. What lines of this poem seem to reflect the specific period of the Depression? What lines, if any, strike you as still relevant today?

LANGSTON HUGHES

Open Letter to the South

This poem was originally published in New Masses *in 1932 as "Red Flag over Tuskegee." It clearly reflected the feeling among many working-class intellectuals and artists in the 1930s that solidarity among the workers of the world was the only sure path toward freedom and equality.*

White workers of the South
    Miners,
    Farmers,
    Mechanics,
    Mill hands,   5
    Shop girls,
    Railway men,
    Servants,
    Tobacco workers,
    Sharecroppers,   10
    GREETINGS!

I am the black worker,
    Listen:
That the land might be ours,

And the mines and the factories and the office towers   15
At Harlan, Richmond, Gastonia, Atlanta, New Orleans;
That the plants and the roads and the tools of power
Be ours:

Let us forget what Booker T. said,
"Separate as the fingers."   20

Let us become instead, you and I,
One single hand
That can united rise
To smash the old dead dogmas of the past —
To kill the lies of color   25
That keep the rich enthroned
And drive us to the time-clock and the plow
Helpless, stupid, scattered, and alone — as now —
Race against race,
Because one is black,   30
Another white of face.

Let us new lessons learn,
All workers,
New life-ways make,
One union form: 35
Until the future burns out
Every past mistake
Let us together, say:
"You are my brother, black or white,
You my sister — now — today!"   40
For me, no more, the great migration to the North.

Instead: migration into force and power —
Tuskegee with a new flag on the tower!
On every lynching tree, a poster crying FREE
Because, O poor white workers,   45
You have linked your hands with me.

We did not know that we were brothers.
Now we know!
Out of that brotherhood
Let power grow!   50
We did not know
That we were strong.
Now we see
In union lies our strength.
Let union be   55
The force that breaks the time-clock,

Smashes misery,
Takes land,
Takes factories,
Takes office towers,   60
Takes tools and banks and mines.
Railroads, ships and dams,
Until the forces of the world
Are ours!

White worker,   65
Here is my hand.

Today,
We're Man to Man.   *[1932]*

≣ **THINKING ABOUT THE TEXT**

1. Who does Hughes blame for "the lies of color" (line 25) that divide black from white? Do you agree?

2. Booker T. Washington (1856–1915), the most prominent African American of his day, is now often seen as an accommodationist who urged only gradual progress toward equality between blacks and whites. Why do you think Hughes tells his readers to "forget what Booker T. said" (line 19)?

3. If you think of this poem as an argument, what would be Hughes's claim? Who is his audience, and what is his evidence? Do you think he made the right choices for his argument?

4. What do you think Hughes meant by the following lines: "We did not know that we were brothers. / Now we know!" (lines 47–48).

5. Hughes is hoping that class solidarity is stronger than racial divisions. Was this the case in 1932? Is it the case today?

≣ **MAKING COMPARISONS**

1. "Open Letter to the South" was written six years earlier than "Let America Be America Again," yet it seems more optimistic. Was this your feeling? How might you account for this?

2. Compare the arguments of both poems. Is "Let America Be America Again" more ambitious? Less focused? More or less persuasive in terms of audience?

3. Is there a comparable line in "Open Letter to the South" to "We must take back our land again, / America!" (lines 73–74)?

LANGSTON HUGHES
Theme for English B

Langston Hughes wrote "Theme for English B" in 1949, when he was twenty-five years older than the poem's speaker. As a young man, he had attended a "college on the hill above Harlem": Columbia University.

The instructor said,
> Go home and write
> a page tonight.
> And let that page come out of you —
> Then, it will be true.   5

I wonder if it's that simple?
I am twenty-two, colored, born in Winston-Salem.
I went to school there, then Durham, then here
to this college on the hill above Harlem.
I am the only colored student in my class.   10
The steps from the hill lead down into Harlem,
through a park, then I cross St. Nicholas,
Eighth Avenue, Seventh, and I come to the Y,
the Harlem Branch Y, where I take the elevator
up to my room, sit down, and write this page: 15

It's not easy to know what is true for you or me
at twenty-two, my age. But I guess I'm what
I feel and see and hear, Harlem, I hear you:
hear you, hear me — we two — you, me, talk on this page.
(I hear New York, too.) Me — who?   20
Well, I like to eat, sleep, drink, and be in love.
I like to work, read, learn, and understand life.
I like a pipe for a Christmas present,
or records — Bessie,° bop, or Bach.
I guess being colored doesn't make me *not* like   25
the same things other folks like who are other races.
So will my page be colored that I write?
Being me, it will not be white.
But it will be
a part of you, instructor.   30
You are white —
yet a part of me, as I am part of you.
That's American.
Sometimes perhaps you don't want to be a part of me.
Nor do I often want to be a part of you.   35

---

24 Bessie: Bessie Smith (1898?–1937), the famous American blues singer.

But we are, that's true!
As I learn from you,
I guess you learn from me —
although you're older — and white —
and somewhat more free.   40
This is my page for English B.   *[1949]*

▰ THINKING ABOUT THE TEXT

1. What do you think the instructor's response to "my page" (line 41) would be? What would yours be?

2. What do you think the instructor was hoping for? On what basis does the narrator seem to critique the assignment?

3. What do you think the narrator means by "American" in line 33? After more than sixty years, does it mean something different?

4. What do you think he means by the line "It's not easy to know what is true for you or me / at twenty-two" (lines 16–17)? Do you agree?

5. The emphasis on freedom here seems more indirect than in the previous two poems. What do you think Hughes means by "free" in the next-to-last line? Would you agree with him then (1949)? Now?

▰ MAKING COMPARISONS

1. Although this poem, like the previous two, seems written to a white audience, its tone seems less aggressive. Is this your reading? What lines seem particularly diplomatic in contrast to "Let America Be America Again"?

2. Is there a line in this poem that might be comparable to "(America was never America to me)" (line 5) from "Let America Be America Again"?

3. Is "Today, / We're Man to Man" (lines 67–68) from "Open Letter to the South" the most hopeful (or naive) line in the three poems?

LANGSTON HUGHES

Harlem

Sometimes called "A Dream Deferred," "Harlem" is Hughes's most anthologized poem and has become synonymous with African Americans' long struggle for freedom and equality.

What happens to a dream deferred?

　　Does it dry up
　　like a raisin in the sun?

Or fester like a sore —
And then run?   5
Does it stink like rotten meat?
Or crust and sugar over —
like a syrupy sweet?

Maybe it just sags
like a heavy load.   10

Or does it explode?   [1951]

≡ THINKING ABOUT THE TEXT

1. The inspiration for Lorraine Hansberry's famous play, *A Raisin in the Sun* (p. 443), Hughes's brief poem asks a question and then answers it with more questions. Is this effective? Should he have been more explicit?

2. What is the "dream deferred" (line 1)?

3. The alternatives given are specific and concrete metaphors presumably embodied in people. What kind of person would be "like a raisin in the sun" (line 3)?

4. How would you imagine a person who stank "like rotten meat" (line 6) would behave? One who "sags / like a heavy load" (lines 9–10)? One who is "like a syrupy sweet" (line 8)?

5. How do you read the last line?

≡ MAKING COMPARISONS

1. Why do you think "Harlem" is the most popular of the four poems presented here?

2. Are there hints in the previous three poems of the ideas developed in "Harlem"?

3. Which poem would you recommend to someone from another country who is trying to understand our racial history? Why?

≡ WRITING ABOUT ISSUES

1. Arguments are made in both "Let America Be America Again" and "Open Letter to the South." Choose one to analyze in terms of issue, claim, evidence, audience, and persuasion. (See the section on "Looking at Literature as Argument," p. 69.)

2. Write an essay that agrees or disagrees with Hughes's accusation in line 24 of "Let America Be America Again" that life in capitalist America is one of "dog eat dog, of mighty crush the weak."

3. Write an essay about your personal responses to these four poems. Include what you think the poems mean, whether you agree or not with the writer's points, and what emotions the poems provoked.

4. Both "Let America Be America Again" and "Open Letter to the South" were written in the 1930s, and we know that the civil rights movement didn't gain serious national attention until the mid-1960s. Since many other voices besides Hughes's were addressing the lack of freedom among America's minorities, especially African Americans, how can you account for the length of time it took for freedom and equality to become serious issues among white voters? Write an essay that addresses this issue.

■ Vampires Unleashed: A Story in the News

KAREN RUSSELL, "Vampires in the Lemon Grove"

IN THE NEWS:
JASON ZINOMAN, "Necking: *True Blood* Reinvents Vampire Sex"

KIM HONE-McMAHAN, "Vampire Fad Really Bites When Teens
Leave Marks"

THE DOMINION POST, " 'Vampire' Victim in Hospital
for a Week"

Vampire folklore has been pervasive for hundreds of years, well before medieval times. The stereotypes are familiar even to most children: fangs, blood sucking, coffins, aversion to sunlight, stakes in the heart, and so forth. Narratives of the undead exist as myths in popular cultures in all Western societies.

Inspired by legends from the Baltic, Bram Stoker's *Dracula* (1897) has been the prototype for most recent vampire novels, films, and television shows. Although most educated societies consider the vampire a fictitious entity, mobs in Malawi stoned to death a suspected vampire and accused the government of being in league with vampires. And purported vampire sightings and the burning of corpses are not so rare in contemporary Romania.

The psychoanalyst Ernest Jones in *On the Nightmare* (1931) claims that vampires can symbolize several issues, such as our obvious anxieties about dying, our longing to be reunited with loved ones, and a critique of aristocrats. Sexual implications have never been far from the vampire mythology. Richard Matheson's *I Am Legend* (1954) has been turned into three films, most recently in 2007. Anne Rice's *Vampire Chronicles* (1976–2003) were extremely popular and influential. And, of course, the best-selling *Twilight* series alters some of the traditional apparatus of the vampire myth to focus on the tension of teenage desire in a surprisingly chaste and romantic fashion.

In contrast to *Twilight*, the popular cable television series *True Blood* is explicitly sexual and graphically violent. In fact, a line in the theme song of *True Blood* is "I want to do bad things to you." In perhaps an obvious allegory concerning gays and lesbians, the vampires in this critically acclaimed show are out of the closet (coffin?) and demanding equal rights. This is probably because a synthetic drink called "Tru Blood" allows them to forgo their usual diet of warm human blood.

Surely vampires stand in for all those "others" that our society marginalizes, including, in a surprising twist on vampire lore, the movie *Let Me In* (2010), about a twelve-year-old vampire who epitomizes the myriad difficulties real teens have adjusting to the cruelties of their peer group. With our current pervasive fear of terrorists and a fervent anti-immigration sentiment, the vampire's symbolism has become even richer and more complex. In a world where anger and fear are widespread, the vampire stands in nicely for everything from an all-purpose whipping boy to a romantic antihero.

So influential has the vampire craze become among young viewers that the boundaries between fiction and reality have sometimes become disturbingly foggy. Some recent news stories have reported on teenagers who bite each other in imitation of vampire lore. Movies and books have always had some influence on adolescent behavior, but the following story and news accounts seem to be a more serious commentary either on the appeal of the vampire or on the increasing recklessness of young teenagers.

≡ **BEFORE YOU READ**

With the widespread popularity of the movie and book series *Twilight* and the TV show *True Blood*, vampire stories have moved from the horror genre into mainstream culture. Why are people so enthralled by vampires? Does any other fantastical monster attract as much attention from such a wide audience? Why, or why not?

KAREN RUSSELL
Vampires in the Lemon Grove

Karen Russell (b. 1981) was born in Miami and received her M.F.A. from Columbia University. She was named one of the "best young American novelists" in 2007, before she had even published a novel. The recognition was given on the strength of her critically acclaimed collection of stories, St. Lucy's Home for Girls Raised by Wolves *(2006). Her stories have recently appeared in* Conjunctions, Granta, *and* Zoetrope. The New Yorker *debut fiction issue also featured her work. Her novel* Swamplandia *(2011) concerns alligator wrestlers. The story that follows was selected for* The Best American Short Stories 2008 *and originally appeared in* Zoetrope *in 2007.*

In October, the men and women of Sorrento harvest the *primofiore*, or "first fruit," the most succulent lemons; in March, the yellow *bianchetti* ripen, followed in June by the green *verdelli*. In every season you can find me sitting at my bench, watching them fall. Only one or two lemons tumble from the branches each hour, but I've been sitting here so long, their falling seems contiguous, close as raindrops. My wife has no patience for this sort of meditation. "Jesus Christ, Clyde," she says. "You need a hobby."

Most people mistake me for a small, kindly Italian grandfather, a *nonno*. I have an old *nonno*'s coloring, the dark walnut stain peculiar to southern Italians, a tan that won't fade until I die (which I never will). I wear a neat periwinkle shirt, a canvas sunhat, black suspenders that sag at my chest. My loafers are battered but always polished. The few visitors to the lemon grove who notice me smile blankly into my raisin face and catch the whiff of some sort of tragedy; they whisper that I am a widower, or an old man who has survived his children. They never guess that I am a vampire.

(© Joanne Chan.)

Santa Francesca's Lemon Grove, where I spend my days and nights, was part of a Jesuit convent in the 1800s. Now it's privately owned by the Alberti family, the prices are excessive, and the locals know to buy their lemons elsewhere. In summers a teenage girl named Fila mans a wooden stall at the back of the grove. She's painfully thin, with heavy, black bangs. I can tell by the careful way she saves the best lemons for me, slyly kicking them under my bench, that she knows I am a monster. Sometimes she'll smile vacantly in my direction, but she never gives me any trouble. And because of her benevolent indifference to me, I feel a swell of love for the girl.

Fila makes the lemonade and monitors the hot dog machine, watching the meat rotate on wire spigots. I'm fascinated by this machine. The Italian name for it translates as "carousel of beef." Who would have guessed at such a device two hundred years ago? Back then we were all preoccupied with visions of apocalypse; Santa Francesca, the foundress of this very grove, gouged out her eyes while dictating premonitions of fire. What a shame, I often think, that she foresaw only the end times, never hot dogs.

A sign posted just outside the grove reads: 5

CIGARETTE PIE
HEAT DOGS
GRANITE DRINKS
Santa Francesca's Limonata —
THE MOST REFRESHING DRANK ON THE PLENET!!

Every day, tourists from Wales and Germany and America are ferried over from cruise ships to the base of these cliffs. They ride the funicular up here to visit the grove, to eat "heat dogs" with speckly brown mustard and sip lemon ices. They snap photographs of the Alberti brothers, Benny and Luciano, teenage twins who cling to the trees' wooden supports and make a grudging show of harvesting lemons, who spear each other with trowels and refer to the tourist women as "vaginas" in Italian slang. "*Buona sera*, vaginas!" they cry from the trees. I think the tourists are getting stupider. None of them speak Italian anymore, and these new women seem deaf to aggression. Often I fantasize about flashing my fangs at the brothers, just to keep them in line.

As I said, the tourists usually ignore me; perhaps it's the dominoes. A few years back, I bought a battered red set from Benny, a prop piece, and this makes me invisible, sufficiently banal to be hidden in plain sight. I have no real interest in the game; I mostly stack the pieces into little houses and corrals.

At sunset, the tourists all around begin to shout. "Look! Up there!" It's time for the path of *I Pipistrelli Impazziti* — the descent of the bats.

They flow from cliffs that glow like pale chalk, expelled from caves seemingly in billions. Their drop is steep and vertical, a black hail. Sometimes a change in weather sucks a bat beyond the lemon trees and into the turquoise sea. It's three hundred feet to the lemon grove, six hundred feet to the churning foam of the Tyrrhenian. At the precipice, they soar upward and crash around the green tops of the trees.

"Oh!" the tourists shriek, delighted, ducking their heads.   10

Up close, the bats' spread wings are an alien membrane — fragile, like something internal flipped out. The waning sun washes their bodies a dusky red. They have wrinkled black faces, these bats, tiny, like gargoyles or angry grandfathers. They have teeth like mine.

Tonight, one of the tourists, a Texan lady with a big strawberry-red updo, has successfully captured a bat in her hair, simultaneously crying real tears and howling: "TAKE THE GODDAMN PICTURE, Sarah!"

I stare ahead at a fixed point above the trees and light a cigarette. My bent spine goes rigid. Mortal terror always trips some old wire that leaves me sad and irritable. It will be whole minutes now before everybody stops screaming.

The moon is a muted shade of orange. Twin discs of light burn in the sky and the sea. I scan the darker indents in the skyline, the cloudless spots that I know to be caves. I check my watch again. It's eight o'clock, and all the bats have disappeared into the interior branches. Where is Magreb? My fangs are throbbing, but I won't start without her.

I once pictured time as a black magnifying glass and myself as a micro-   15
scopic, flightless insect trapped in that circle of night. But then Magreb came along, and eternity ceased to frighten me. Suddenly each moment followed its antecedent in a neat chain, moments we filled with each other.

I watch a single bat falling from the cliffs, dropping like a stone: headfirst, motionless, dizzying to witness.

Pull up.

I close my eyes. I press my palms flat against the picnic table and tense the muscles of my neck.

Pull UP. I tense up until my temples pulse, until little black and red stars flutter behind my eyelids.

"You can look now."   20

Magreb is sitting on the bench, blinking her bright pumpkin eyes. "You weren't even *watching.* If you saw me coming down, you'd know you have nothing to worry about." I try to smile at her and find I can't. My own eyes feel like ice cubes.

"It's stupid to go so fast." I don't look at her. "That easterly could knock you over the rocks."

"Don't be ridiculous. I'm an excellent flier."

She's right. Magreb can shape-shift midair, much more smoothly than I ever could. Even back in the 1850s when I used to transmute into a bat two, three times a night, my metamorphosis was a shy, halting process.

"Look!" she says, triumphant, mocking. "You're still trembling!"   25

I look down at my hands, angry to realize it's true.

Magreb roots through the tall, black blades of grass. "It's late, Clyde; where's my lemon?"

I pluck a soft, round lemon from the grass, a summer moon, and hand it to her. The *verdelli* I have chosen is perfect, flawless. She looks at it with distaste and makes a big show of brushing off a marching ribbon of ants.

"A toast!" I say.

"A toast," Magreb replies, with the rote enthusiasm of a Christian saying   30
grace. We left the lemons and swing them to our faces. We plunge our fangs, piercing the skin, and emit a long, united hiss: *"Aaah!"*

Over the years, Magreb and I have tried everything — fangs in apples, fangs in rubber balls. We have lived everywhere: Tunis, Laos, Cincinnati, Salamanca. We spent our honeymoon hopping continents, haunting liquid chimeras: mint tea in Fez, coconut slurries in Oahu, jet black coffee in Bogotá, jackal's milk in Dakar, cherry Coke floats in rural Alabama, a thousand beverages that purported to have magical quenching properties. We went thirsty in every region of the globe before finding our oasis here, in the blue boot of Italy, at this dead nun's lemonade stand. It's only these lemons that give us any relief.

When we first landed in Sorrento I was skeptical. The pitcher of lemon-ade we ordered looked cloudy and adulterated. Sugar clumped at the bottom. I took a gulp, and a whole small lemon lodged in my mouth; there is no word sufficiently lovely for the first taste, the first feeling of my fangs in that lemon. It was bracingly sour, with a delicate hint of ocean salt. After an initial prick-ling — a sort of chemical effervescence along my gums — a soothing blankness traveled from the tip of each fang to my fevered brain. These lemons are a vam-pire's analgesic. If you have been thirsty for a long time, if you have been suffer-ing, then the absence of those two feelings — however brief — becomes a kind of heaven. I breathed deeply through my nostrils. My throbbing fangs were still.

By daybreak, the numbness had begun to wear off. The lemons relieve our thirst without ending it, like a drink we can hold in our mouths but never swallow. Eventually the original hunger returns. I have tried to be very good, very correct and conscientious about not confusing this original hunger with the thing I feel for Magreb.

I can't joke about my early years on the blood, can't even think about them without guilt and acidic embarrassment. Unlike Magreb, who has never had a sip of the stuff, I listened to the village gossips and believed every rumor, internalized every report of corrupted bodies and boiled blood. Vampires were the favorite undead of the Enlightenment, and as a young boy I aped the diction and mannerisms I read about in books: Vlad the Impaler, Count Heinrich the Despoiler, Goethe's blood-sucking bride of Corinth. I eavesdropped on the terrified prayers of an old woman in a cemetery, begging God to protect her from . . . me. I felt a dislocation then, a spreading numbness, as if I were invisible or already dead. After that, I did only what the stories suggested, beginning with that old woman's blood. I slept in coffins, in black cedar boxes, and woke every night with a fierce headache. I was famished, perennially dizzy. I had unspeakable dreams about the sun.

In practice I was no suave viscount, just a teenager in a red velvet cape, awkward and voracious. I wanted to touch the edges of my life. The same instinct, I think, that inspires young mortals to flip tractors and enlist in foreign wars. One night I skulked into a late Mass with some vague plan to defeat eternity. At the back of the nave, I tossed my mousy curls, rolled my eyes heavenward, and then plunged my entire arm into the bronze pail of holy water. Death would be painful, probably, but I didn't care about pain. I wanted to overturn my sentence. It was working; I could feel the burn beginning to spread. Actually, it was more like an itch, but I was sure the burning would start any second. I slid into a pew, snug in my misery, and waited for my body to turn to ash.

By sunrise, I'd developed a rash between my eyebrows, a little late-flowering acne, but was otherwise fine, and I understood I truly was immortal. At that moment I yielded all discrimination; I bit anyone kind or slow enough to let me get close: men, women, even some older boys and girls. The littlest children I left alone, very proud at the time of this one scruple. I'd read stories about Hungarian *vampirs* who drank the blood of orphan girls and mentioned this to Magreb early on, hoping to impress her with my decency. Not *children!* she wept. She wept for a day and a half.

Our first date was in Cementerio de Colón, if I can call a chance meeting between headstones a date. I had been stalking her, following her swishing hips as she took a shortcut through the cemetery grass. She wore her hair in a low, snaky braid that was coming unraveled. When I was near enough to touch her trailing ribbon, she whipped around. "Are you following me?" she asked, annoyed, not scared. She regarded my face with the contempt of a woman confronting the town drunk. "Oh," she said, "your teeth . . ."

And then she grinned. Magreb was the first and only other vampire I'd ever met. We bared our fangs over a tombstone and recognized each other. There is a loneliness that must be particular to monsters, I think, the feeling that each is the only child of a species. And now that loneliness was over.

35

Our first date lasted all night. Magreb's talk seemed to lunge forward like a train without a conductor; I suspect even she didn't know what she was saying. I certainly wasn't paying attention, staring dopily at her fangs, and then I heard her ask: "So, when did you figure out that the blood does nothing?"

At the time of this conversation, I was edging on 130. I had never gone a   40 day since early childhood without drinking several pints of blood. *The blood does nothing?* My forehead burned and burned.

"Didn't you think it suspicious that you had a heartbeat?" she asked me. "That you had a reflection in water?"

When I didn't answer, Magreb went on. "Every time I saw my own face in a mirror, I knew I wasn't any of those ridiculous things, a blood-sucker, a *sanguina.* You know?"

"Sure," I said, nodding. For me, mirrors had the opposite effect: I saw a mouth ringed in black blood. I saw the pale son of the villagers' fears.

Those initial days with Magreb nearly undid me. At first my euphoria was sharp and blinding, all my thoughts spooling into a single blue thread of relief — *The blood does nothing! I don't have to drink the blood!* — but when that subsided, I found I had nothing left. If we didn't have to drink the blood, then what on earth were these fangs for?

Sometimes I think she preferred me then: I was like her own child, raw and   45 amazed. We smashed my coffin with an ax and spent the night at a hotel. I lay there wide-eyed in the big bed, my heart thudding like a fishtail against the floor of a boat.

"You're really sure?" I whispered to her. "I don't have to sleep in a coffin? I don't have to sleep through the day?" She had already drifted off.

A few months later, she suggested a picnic.

"But the sun."

Magreb shook her head. "You poor thing, believing all that garbage."

By this time we'd found a dirt cellar in which to live in Western Australia,   50 where the sun burned through the clouds like dining lace. That sun ate lakes, rising out of dead volcanoes at dawn, triple the size of a harvest moon and skull-white, a grass-scorcher. Go ahead, try to walk into that sun when you've been told your bones are tinder.

I stared at the warped planks of the trapdoor above us, the copper ladder that led rung by rung to the bright world beyond. Time fell away from me and I was a child again, afraid, afraid. Magreb rested her hand on the small of my back. "You can do it," she said, nudging me gently. I took a deep breath and hunched my shoulders, my scalp grazing the cellar door, my hair soaked through with sweat. I focused my thoughts to still the tremors, lest my fangs slice the inside of my mouth, and turned my face away from Magreb.

"Go on."

I pushed up and felt the wood give way. Light exploded through the cellar. My pupils shrank to dots.

Outside, the whole world was on fire. Mute explosions rocked the scrubby forest, motes of light burning like silent rockets. The sun fell through the eucalyptus and Australian pines in bright red bars. I pulled myself out onto my belly, balled up in the soil, and screamed for mercy until I'd exhausted myself. Then I opened one watery eye and took a long look around. The sun wasn't fatal! It was just uncomfortable, making my eyes itch and water and inducing a sneezing attack.

After that, and for the whole of our next thirty years together, I watched   55
the auroral colors and waited to feel anything but terror. Fingers of light spread across the gray sea toward me, and I couldn't see these colors as beautiful. The sky I lived under was a hideous, lethal mix of orange and pink, a physical deformity. By the 1950s we were living in a Cincinnati suburb; and as a day's first light hit the kitchen windows, I'd press my face against the linoleum and gibber my terror into the cracks.

"So-o," Magreb would say, "I can tell you're not a morning person." Then she'd sit on the porch swing and rock with me, patting my hand.

"What's wrong, Clyde?"

I shook my head. This was a new sadness, difficult to express. My bloodlust was undiminished but now the blood wouldn't fix it.

"It never fixed it," Magreb reminded me, and I wished she would please stop talking.

That cluster of years was a very confusing period. Mostly I felt grateful,   60
above-ground feelings. I was in love. For a vampire, my life was very normal. Instead of stalking prostitutes, I went on long bicycle rides with Magreb. We visited botanical gardens and rowed in boats. In a short time, my face had gone from lithium white to the color of milky coffee. Yet sometimes, especially at high noon, I'd study Magreb's face with a hot, illogical hatred, each pore opening up to swallow me. *You've ruined my life*, I'd think. To correct for her power over my mind I tried to fantasize about mortal women, their wild eyes and bare swan necks; I couldn't do it, not anymore — an eternity of vague female smiles eclipsed by Magreb's tiny razor fangs. Two gray tabs against her lower lip.

But like I said, I was mostly happy. I was making a kind of progress.

One night, children wearing necklaces of garlic bulbs arrived giggling at our door. It was Halloween; they were vampire hunters. The smell of garlic blasted through the mail slot, along with their voices: "Trick or treat!" In the old days, I would have cowered from these children. I would have run downstairs to barricade myself in my coffin. But that night, I pulled on an undershirt and opened the door. I stood in a square of green light in my boxer shorts hefting a bag of Tootsie Roll Pops, a small victory over the old fear.

"Mister, you okay?"

I blinked down at a little blond child and then saw that my two hands were shaking violently, soundlessly, like old friends wishing not to burden me with their troubles. I dropped the candies into the children's bags, thinking: *You small mortals don't realize the power of your stories.*

We were downing strawberry velvet cocktails on the Seine when something   65
inside me changed. Thirty years. Eleven thousand dawns. That's how long it took for me to believe the sun wouldn't kill me.

"Want to go see a museum or something? We're in Paris, after all."

"Okay."

We walked over a busy pedestrian bridge in a flood of light, and my heart was in my throat. Without any discussion, I understood that Magreb was my wife.

Because I love her, my hunger pangs gradually mellowed into a comfortable despair. Sometimes I think of us as two holes cleaved together, two twin hungers. Our bellies growl at each other like companionable dogs. I love the sound, assuring me we're equals in our thirst. We bump our fangs and feel like we're coming up against the same hard truth.

Human marriages amuse me: the brevity of the commitment and all the   70
ceremony that surrounds it, the calla lilies, the veiled mother-in-laws like lilac spiders, the tears and earnest toasts. Till death do us part! Easy. These mortal couples need only keep each other in sight for fifty, sixty years.

Often I wonder to what extent a mortal's love grows from the bedrock of his or her foreknowledge of death, love coiling like a green stem out of that blankness in a way I'll never quite understand. And lately I've been having a terrible thought: *Our love affair will end before the world does.*

One day, without any preamble, Magreb flew up to the caves. She called over her furry, muscled shoulder that she just wanted to sleep for a while.

"What? Wait! What's wrong?"

I'd caught her midshift, halfway between a wife and a bat.

"Don't be so sensitive, Clyde! I'm just tired of this century, so very tired,   75
maybe it's the heat? I think I need a little rest . . ."

I assumed this was an experiment, like my cape, an old habit to which she was returning; and from the clumsy, ambivalent way she crashed around on the wind I understood I was supposed to follow her. Well, too bad. Magreb likes to say she freed me, disabused me of the old stories; but I gave up more than I intended: I can't shudder myself out of this old man's body. I can't fly anymore.

Fila and I are alone. I press my dry lips together and shove dominoes around the table; they buckle like the cars of a tiny train.

"More lemonade, *nonno?*" She smiles. She leans from her waist and boldly touches my right fang, a thin string of hanging drool. "Looks like you're thirsty."

"Please." I gesture at the bench. "Have a seat."

Fila is seventeen now and has known about me for some time. She's toying   80
with the idea of telling her boss, weighing the sentence within her like a bullet in a gun: *There is a vampire in our grove.*

"You don't believe me, signore Alberti?" she'll say, before taking him by the wrist and leading him to this bench, and I'll choose that moment to rise up and bite him in his hog-thick neck. "Right through his stupid tie!" she says with a grin.

But this is just idle fantasy, she assures me. Fila is content to let me alone. "You remind me of my *nonno,*" she says approvingly. "You look very Italian."

In fact, she wants to help me hide here. It gives her a warm feeling to do so, like helping her own fierce *nonno* do up the small buttons of his trousers, now too intricate a maneuver for his palsied hands. She worries about me too. And she should: lately I've gotten sloppy, incontinent about my secrets. I've stopped polishing my shoes; I let the tip of one fang hang over my pink lip. "You must be more careful," she reprimands. "There are tourists *everywhere.*"

I study her neck as she says this, her head rolling with the natural expressiveness of a girl. She checks to see if I am watching her collarbone, and I let her see that I am. I feel like a threat again.

Last night I went on a rampage. On my seventh lemon I found with a sort of   85
drowsy despair that I couldn't stop. I crawled around on all fours, looking for the last *bianchettis* in the dewy grass: soft with rot, mildewed, sun-shriveled, blackened. Lemon skin bulging with tiny cellophane-green worms. Dirt smells, rain smells, all swirled through with the tart sting of decay.

In the morning, Magreb steps around the wreckage and doesn't say a word.

"I came up with a new name," I say, hoping to distract her. "*Brandolino.* What do you think?"

I have spent the last several years trying to choose an Italian name, and every day that I remain Clyde feels like a defeat. Our names are relics of the places we've been. "Clyde" is a souvenir from the California Gold Rush. I was callow and blood-crazed back then, and I saw my echo in the freckly youths panning along the Sacramento River. I used the name as a kind of bait. It sounded innocuous, like someone a boy might get a malt beer with or follow into the woods.

Magreb chose her name in the Atlas Mountains for its etymology, the root word *ghuroob,* which means "to set" or "to be hidden." "That's what we're looking for," she tells me. "The setting place. Some final answer." She won't change her name until we find it.

She takes a lemon from her mouth, slides it down the length of her fangs,   90
and places its shriveled core on the picnic table. When she finally speaks, her voice is so low, the words are almost unintelligible.

"The lemons aren't working, Clyde."

But the lemons have never worked. At best, they give us eight hours of peace. We aren't talking about the lemons.

"How long?"

"Longer than I've let on. I'm sorry."

"Well, maybe it's this crop. Those Alberti boys haven't been fertilizing   95
properly, maybe the *primofiore* will turn out better."

Magreb fixes me with one fish-bright eye. "Clyde, I think it's time for us to go."

Wind blows the leaves apart. Lemons wink like a firmament of yellow stars, slowly ripening, and I can see the other, truer night behind them.

"Go where?" Our marriage, as I conceive it, is a commitment to starve together.

"We've been resting here for decades. I think it's time . . . what is that thing?"

I have been preparing a present for Magreb, for our anniversary, a "cave"   100
of scavenged materials—newspaper and bottle glass and wooden beams

from the lemon tree supports—so that she can sleep down here with me.
I've smashed dozens of bottles of fruity beer to make stalactites. Looking at it
now, though, I see the cave is very small. It looks like an umbrella mauled by
a dog.

"That thing?" I say. "That's nothing. I think it's part of the hot dog
machine."

"Jesus. Did it catch on fire?"

"Yes. The girl threw it out yesterday."

"Clyde." Magreb shakes her head. "We never meant to stay here forever,
did we? That was never the plan."

"I didn't know we had a plan," I snap. "What if we've outlived our food   105
supply? What if there's nothing left for us to find?"

"You don't really believe that."

"Why can't you just be grateful? Why can't you be happy and admit defeat? Look at what we've found here!" I grab a lemon and wave it in her face.

"Good night, Clyde."

I watch my wife fly up into the watery dawn, and again I feel the awful tension. In the flats of my feet, in my knobbed spine. Love has infected me with a
muscular superstition that one body can do the work of another.

I consider taking the funicular, the ultimate degradation—worse than the   110
dominoes, worse than an eternity of sucking cut lemons. All day I watch the
cars ascend, and I'm reminded of those American fools who accompany their
wives to the beach but refuse to wear bathing suits. I've seen them by the harbor, sulking in their trousers, panting through menthol cigarettes and pacing
the dock while the women sea-bathe. They pretend they don't mind when
sweat darkens the armpits of their suits. When their wives swim out and leave
them. When their wives are just a splash in the distance.

Tickets for the funicular are twenty lire. I sit at the bench and count as the
cars go by.

That evening, I take Magreb on a date. I haven't left the lemon grove in up-
wards of two years, and blood roars in my ears as I stand and clutch at her like
an old man. We're going to the Thursday night show, an antique theater in a
castle in the center of town. I want her to see that I'm happy to travel with her,
so long as our destination is within walking distance.

A teenage usher in a vintage red jacket with puffed sleeves escorts us to our
seats, his biceps manacled in clouds, threads loosening from the badge on his
chest. I am jealous of the name there: GUGLIELMO.

The movie's title is already scrolling across the black screen: *Something
Clandestine Is Happening in the Corn!*

Magreb snorts. "That's a pretty lousy name for a horror movie. It sounds   115
like a student film."

"Here's your ticket," I say. "I didn't make the title up."

It's a vampire movie set in the Dust Bowl. Magreb expects a comedy, but
the Dracula actor fills me with the sadness of an old photo album. An Okie has

unwittingly fallen in love with the monster, whom she's mistaken for a rich European creditor eager to pay off the mortgage on her family's farm.

"That Okie," says Magreb, "is an idiot."

I turn my head miserably and there's Fila, sitting two rows in front of us with a greasy young man. Benny Alberti. Her white neck is bent to the left, Benny's lips affixed to it as she impassively sips a soda.

"Poor thing," Magreb whispers, indicating the pig-tailed actress. "She   120
thinks he's going to save her."

Dracula shows his fangs, and the Okie flees through a cornfield. Cornstalks smack her face. "Help!" she screams to a sky full of crows. "He's not actually from Europe!"

There is no music, only the girl's breath and the *fwap-fwap-fwap* of the off-screen fan blades. Dracula's mouth hangs wide as a sewer grate. His cape is curiously still.

The movie picture is frozen. The *fwap*ing is emanating from the projection booth; it rises to a grinding *r-r-r*, followed by lyrical Italian cussing and silence and finally a tidal sigh. Magreb shifts in her seat.

"Let's wait," I say, seized with an empathy for these two still figures on the screen, mutely waiting for repair. "They'll fix it."

People begin to file out of the theater, first in twos and threes and then in   125
droves.

"I'm tired, Clyde."

"Don't you want to know what happens?" My voice is more frantic than I intend it to be.

"I already know what happens."

"Don't you leave now, Magreb. I'm telling you, they're going to fix it. If you leave now, that's it for us, I'll never . . ."

Her voice is beautiful, like gravel underfoot: "I'm going to the caves."   130

I'm alone in the theater. When I turn to exit, the picture is still frozen, the Okie's blue dress floating over windless corn, Dracula's mouth a hole in his white greasepaint.

Outside I see Fila standing in a clot of her friends, lit by the marquee. These kids wear too much makeup, and clothes that move like colored oils. They all looked rained on. I scowl at them and they scowl back; and then Fila crosses to me.

"Hey, you." She grins, breathless, so very close to my face. "Are you stalking somebody?"

My throat tightens.

"Guys!" Her eyes gleam. "Guys, come over and meet the *vampire*."   135

But the kids are gone.

"Well! Some friends," she says, then winks. "Leaving me alone, defenseless . . ."

"You want the old vampire to bite you, eh?" I hiss. "You want a story for your friends?"

Fila laughs. Her horror is a round, genuine thing, bouncing in both her black eyes. She smells like hard water and glycerin. The hum of her young life all around me makes it difficult to think. A bat filters my thoughts, opens its trembling lampshade wings.

Magreb. She'll want to hear about this. How ridiculous, at my age, to find   140 myself down this alley with a young girl: Fila powdering her neck, doing her hair up with little temptress pins, yanking me behind this Dumpster. "Can you imagine," Magreb will laugh, "a teenager goading you to attack her! You're still a menace, Clyde."

I stare vacantly at a pale mole above the girl's collarbone. *Magreb,* I think again, and I smile; and the smile feels like a muzzle. It seems my hand has tightened on the girl's wrist, and I realize with surprise, as if from a great distance, that she is twisting away.

"Hey, *nonno,* come on now, what are you —"

The girl's head lolls against my shoulder like that of a sleepy child, then swings forward in a rag-doll circle. The starlight is white mercury compared to her blotted-out eyes. There's a dark stain on my periwinkle shirt, and one suspender has snapped. I sit Fila's body against the alley wall, watch it dim and stiffen. Spidery graffiti weaves over the brick behind her, and I scan for some answer contained there: GIOVANNA & FABIANO. VAFFANCULO! VAI IN CULO.

A scabby-furred creature, our only witness, arches its orange back against the Dumpster. If not for the lock I would ease the girl inside. I would climb in with her and let the red stench fill my nostrils, let the flies crawl into the red corners of my eyes. I am a monster again.

I ransack Fila's pockets and find the key to the funicular office, careful not   145 to look at her face. Then I'm walking, running for the lemon grove. I jimmy my way into the control room and turn the silver key, relieved to hear the engine roar to life. Locked, locked, every car is locked, but then I find one with thick tape in X's over a busted door. I dash after it and pull myself onto the cushion, quickly, because the cars are already moving. The box jounces and trembles. The chain pulls me into the heavens link by link.

My lips are soon chapped; I stare through a crack in the glass window. The box swings wildly in the wind. The sky is a deep blue vacuum. I can still smell the girl in the folds of my clothes.

The cave system is vaster than I expected; and with their grandfather faces tucked away, the bats are anonymous as stones. I walk beneath a chandelier of furry bodies, heartbeats wrapped in wings the color of rose petals or corn silk. Breath ripples through each of them, a tiny life in its translucent envelope.

"Magreb?"

Is she up here?

Has she left me?   150

(I will never find another vampire.)

I double back to the moonlit entrance, the funicular cars. When I find Magreb, I'll beg her to tell me what she dreams up here. I'll tell her my waking dreams in the lemon grove: the mortal men and women floating serenely by in balloons freighted with the ballast of their deaths. Millions of balloons ride over a wide ocean, lives darkening the sky. Death is a dense powder cinched inside tiny sandbags, and in the dream I am given to understand that instead of a sandbag I have Magreb.

I make the bats' descent in a cable car with no wings to spread, knocked around by the wind with a force that feels personal. I struggle to hold the door shut and look for the green speck of our grove.

The box is plunging now, far too quickly. It swings wide, and the igneous surface of the mountain fills the left window. The tufa shines like water, like a black, heat-bubbled river. For a disorienting moment I expect the rock to seep through the glass.

Each swing takes me higher than the last, a grinding pendulum that ap-   155
proaches a full revolution around the cable. I'm on my hands and knees on the car floor, seasick in the high air, pressing my face against the floor grate. I can see stars or boats burning there, and also a ribbon of white, a widening fissure. Air gushes through the cracks in the glass box.

What does Magreb see, if she can see? Is she waking from a nightmare to watch the line snap, the glass box plummet? From her inverted vantage, dangling from the roof of the cave, does the car seem to be sucked upward, rushing not toward the sea but to another sort of sky? To a black mouth open and foaming with stars?

I like to picture my wife like this: Magreb shuts her thin eyelids tighter. She digs her claws into the rock. Little clouds of dust rise around her toes as she swings upside-down. She feels something growing inside her, unstoppable as a dreadful suspicion. It is solid, this new thing, it is the opposite of hunger. She's emerging from a dream of distant thunder, rumbling and loose. Something has happened tonight that she thought impossible. In the morning, she will want to tell me about it.   *[2007]*

☰ THINKING ABOUT THE TEXT

1. Were you surprised that Clyde attacks Fila? Why does he?

2. Why did Clyde sleep in coffins and fear the sun?

3. What does Clyde mean when he says, "I wanted to touch the edges of my life" (para. 35)?

4. When Magreb says, "You poor thing, believing all that garbage" (para. 49), what does she mean? How might this be connected to the themes of the story?

5. Stereotypes figure significantly in this story. Explain how the tale both conforms to and goes against traditional ideas about vampires.

In the News

The following three articles delve into the recent vampire craze. The first selection, published on *Slate* on June 28, 2010, reviews season 3, episode 3, of the popular HBO television show *True Blood*. *True Blood*, which has been on the air since 2008, follows the story of Sookie Stackhouse, a waitress in the fictional bayou town of Bon Temps, Louisiana, where vampires have recently integrated into society. Sookie falls in love with a vampire named Bill Compton (also called "Vampire Bill"), a circumstance with life-changing consequences. *True Blood* is known for being sexually and violently graphic, and this review focuses on that intersection.

The second piece was written by Kim Hone-McMahan, a staff writer for the *Akron Beacon Journal*, where this piece was published on August 8, 2010. McMahan reports on a new trend teenagers seem to be engaging in: biting. She believes that this trend is caused by teens' fascination with shows like *True Blood* and the book and movie series *Twilight*. Hone-McMahan interviews teenagers and medical experts in the Akron community.

The final piece, from New Zealand newspaper *The Dominion Post*'s May 7, 2010, edition, brings Hone-McMahan's reporting to life. This story reports on a teenager who was hospitalized after allegedly being bitten in a "vampire-type attack" (para. 1). The attackers, who range in age from nineteen to twenty-two, have been arrested under the charge of "wounding with intent to render a person unconscious" (para. 6).

JASON ZINOMAN
Necking: *True Blood* Reinvents Vampire Sex

Sleeping with a vampire is basically necrophilia and can even suggest incest (you're sleeping with your "maker"), and since you are dealing with an immortal, the age differences between partners can be positively vast. But the most troublingly taboo aspect of the sex lives of vampires concerns the question of consent. Rape is as dominant a subtext in vampire stories as mindless conformity is in zombie stories. No less an authority than Stephen King has said that the re-enactment of the primal rape scene is part of the vampire's enduring success.

Stephen Moyer, whose Vampire Bill is the romantic center of *True Blood*, took some criticism last year for suggesting in a magazine interview that one plot twist was built on a rape fantasy, but the allure of forbidden sex has long been a part of the vampire story since Bram Stoker's *Dracula*.

True Blood is such supremely dirty fun because it doesn't just tap into the dark sexual kinks of the vampire myth. It refines and experiments on them, giving old taboos a fresh spin. For one thing, the traditional vampire is a man preying on women; here, women are the predators just as often. Rape has become something of a vampire cliché. The sick genius of Episode 3, which returns the series strongly to form, is that it finds other creatively perverse ways to mingle sex and violence.

The show starts with Sookie titillated by the spectacle of Eric straddling and devouring a nude man recently transformed from a wolf. His mouth dripping blood, he looks up at the breathless Sookie and delivers this purple double-entendre: "I got your rug all wet." That's soon followed by a second violent and sexual act in which the charmingly devilish British vampire Franklin (played with sleepy-eyed menace by British stage and screen star James Frain) has his way with Tara, who appears terrified and ecstatic at the same time.

But the real radical innovation in vampire sex arrives in the startling final   5
scene. It discovers a potent variation on sexual violence: hate sex. For those unfamiliar with the concept, it's when you sleep with someone not out of love — or even desire, exactly — but out of passionate contempt. As far as I know, this spin on sexual violence has never been tried in vampire programming until, in an animalistic rage, Bill threw Lorena down last night and forced himself on her. This angry assault looks like rape but isn't, exactly. It preserves the excitement of the taboo while also making it less morally problematic. As the woman who turned him into a vampire, Lorena has a tortured history with Bill, and she has repeatedly told him that love with a human is futile. He assaults her, but she doesn't seem to mind. In fact, while she seems to enjoy being handled roughly, *he* is clearly in pain as he violates his own sense of carefully maintained restraint and fidelity.

This upsetting scene is a masterstroke of dramatic perversion, pushing sadistic *and* masochistic buttons. For an idea so fittingly twisted, someone deserves an Emmy or at least a congratulatory slap in the face. The execution is as inventive as the concept, since at the end, Bill grabs her neck and just when you think you know where this is going — wait a second, what the hell? — he turns her neck completely around. Somewhere, Linda Blair is smiling.

The other highlight of this eventful episode, in which Sookie sets out to find Bill, who cuts a deal with the Vampire King of Mississippi to save her, is a visit to a werewolf bar (or barn, as it's called), Lon Pines. Since we've already seen Fangtasia, the sleek vampire bar, this gives us another metric in the eternally raging vampire-vs.-werewolf debate. Let's compare. Vampire style means leather, nose rings, fish-nets, all black, while werewolves prefer flannel, blue jeans, and tank tops. Vampires listen to techno and metal; werewolves rock out to blues licks. A vampire sees Sookie and says "How sweet it is," while werewolves are more direct: "You look like dinner," the bouncer says. In terms of décor, it's the difference between a goth bar in downtown Manhattan and a dive in the Pacific Northwest. It's a question of taste, but even with its dungeon downstairs, Fangtasia has my vote.

The gradual softening up of Eric continues as he adopts a gentler approach with Lafayette and confesses to Sookie that a werewolf who has sucked on vampire blood poses a challenge to his strength. *True Blood*'s writers are masters at compression, and that they have made us care about a ferocious, cold-blooded character who seemed like an unsmiling cult leader one season ago is an accomplishment. I have taken a firm anti-Sookie stance — earning responses evenly divided between *Amen!* and *Hell, no* — but if some vampire must have her, I'd like it to be Eric.

As for the new theater stars from last week, I am getting more optimistic. The casting of the elegant J. Smith Cameron as Sam's redneck mother remains bizarre — look at her manicured eyebrows! — but since it's perhaps suggested that she might not be what she seems, this might be an elaborate trick. I hope so. And Denis O'Hare's turn as the vampire king is growing into a very canny performance of a master manipulator and power player who fakes everyone out with a tone of weary reasonableness. He truly seems like an ancient gentleman when he sighs out lines such as "It's like Armageddon here every time someone chips a dessert glass."   *[2010]*

KIM HONE-McMAHAN

Vampire Fad Really Bites When Teens Leave Marks

Hickeys are still popular with teens, but there's a trend bleeding to the surface — biting. Sometimes it's a superficial wound, other times it draws blood, just like a bite from the creatures many teens have come to love.

The popularity of the *Twilight* series, both the books and movies, and television hits like HBO's *True Blood* might be causing some kids to imitate the behavior of their favorite vampires, according to *ABC News* and other outlets. Teens are even using Internet sites like YouTube to post videos of their bites — usually involving the arm, face, or neck.

"I have occasionally noticed the crescent-shaped marks on their necks," Carly Cundiff, a Wadsworth 14-year-old, said of her classmates. "The biting just doesn't seem right. If you bite hard enough to draw blood, I think you would be dumped faster than a rabid raccoon."

Akron Children's Hospital isn't reporting an increase in human bites, though it's unlikely kids would voluntarily squeal on their pals or sweethearts for sinking canines into flesh.

Carly and other adolescents who are members of the *Beacon Journal*'s   5
young readers' group agreed that biting is unsafe, though one gal admitted that she still thinks "hickeys have their place."

Dr. Nneka Holder, an adolescent medicine specialist at Akron Children's Hospital, warns that a human bite is not something to trivialize.

"Human mouths are not much cleaner than a dog's mouth," said Holder, who added that bites that cause infection could land a child in the hospital.

Hickeys, which are created by sucking, not biting, have been around for generations, are unsightly, and cause bruising, but they aren't likely to cause serious harm.

Some people bite or give hickeys as a sign of possession, warning others to keep away from the victim.

"Anything done like that to show ownership is not a healthy relationship," said Dr. Joseph Salwan, a psychologist with the Akron Family Institute.   10

If the idea is to brand someone, Holder said, a hickey is just a hickey — no one's name is attached to it. No one will know who the sucker is, unless the suckee shares that information. Same goes for a bite.

Maddie Winer, a student at St. Vincent–St. Mary High School, doesn't understand why someone would want to mark a person in such a manner.

"It is very animalistic," Carly added. "In nature, animals bite to show possession, but I don't know. Somehow the biting just doesn't seem right."

Teens' attraction to vampire tales is nothing new.

Many of us were exposed to vampires as toddlers. The Count, an adorable vampire on *Sesame Street* who was modeled after Bela Lugosi's Count Dracula, has been teaching youngsters about numbers for nearly four decades.   15

And baby boomers may recall rushing home from school to watch *Dark Shadows*. The weekday television show had a huge following of teenagers, both boys and girls.

Unlike the *Twilight* movies, in which mostly 'tween and teenage girls swoon over a good-looking vampire and a hunky werewolf, Barnabas Collins was a homely supernatural character. While the acting was melodramatic, fans still loved the show, which ranked 19th in *TV Guide*'s list of the "25 Top Cult Shows Ever!"

The *Twilight* movies were spawned from a series of four vampire-romance novels by Stephenie Meyer. Fans have embraced the books, and other tales of preternatural beings, with great hunger.

"Vampires lure us into our dark side, and for some of us, that is a thrilling literary adventure," said 18-year-old Maddie.

In the *Twilight* books, it isn't until the final book, *Breaking Dawn*, that vampire Edward and human Bella have sex — and only after they are married.   20

But then the descriptions become too dicey for some parents.

"People told my mom that it wasn't for young kids, like me," said 10-year-old Macie Mathews of Brimfield Township. "My mom stopped me from reading any more when I was halfway through the third book, *Eclipse*."

Macie's mother, Valerie, said while parents are excited that their children are immersed in reading, they need to keep a close eye on a book's content — even if it means disappointing their youngster partway through a series.

But for the older, more mature fans, their journey to the underworld is just a page or scene away.

"I think vampire movies . . . are popular because they are so exotic, especially in *Twilight*'s case," Maddie said. "You have unconventional vampires that don't eat humans, but rather are 'vegetarians' that eat animal blood." And fans so rabid, they like to chew on each other.   25

Bon appetit.

THE DOMINION POST

"Vampire" Victim in Hospital for a Week

The teenager bitten in an alleged vampire-type attack spent days in hospital afterwards fighting infection and fever.

The last of the three people charged over the Wellington assault has now been arrested. James Eric Orr, 19, appeared in Napier District Court yesterday in relation to the attack.

On his Facebook page, he refers to himself as "the.vampire.marius" — after a character in Anne Rice's *The Vampire Chronicles* novels. His lawyer said he denied any involvement in the attack.

The two other alleged attackers — James Phillip Brooks, 22, and Xenia Gregoriana Borichevsky, 19 — appeared in Wellington District Court on Wednesday.

It is alleged that the three all bit their teenage victim on Mt. Victoria in February and some of them drank his blood. It is understood the victim passed out after being bitten.   5

The trio have been charged with wounding with intent to render a person unconscious. The charge carries a maximum penalty of 14 years' jail.

A source with ties to the victim's family told *The Dominion Post* that he suffered serious bites on his body during the "disgraceful physical assault."

Some of the bites were on his neck and chest, and one of them soon became infected, leaving the feverish teen in hospital for a week.

"It is a disgrace the [alleged] perpetrators are making this out to be something minor that has been exaggerated," the source said.

Both Wellington Hospital and police had photos of the "deep bites," he said.   10

Neither the hospital nor police would confirm that the victim had been in hospital, or that photos of the wounds had been taken.

Cases of people biting others to drink their blood are rare and dangerous, as the human mouth harbours more bacteria than that of a cat or dog. Infected bites can lead to sepsis, which can be fatal.

After his appearance in court yesterday, Orr, who appeared thin and pale, told *The Dominion Post*: "What? Do I look like a vampire?" when asked for comment on the case. He then drew his jacket over his head and said: "No comment, no comment."

In court, duty solicitor Michael McAleer told Judge Bridget Mackintosh that Orr "denies any involvement."

On Wednesday, James Brooks told *The Dominion Post* he had bitten the victim but did not think he had drawn blood.   15

Judge Mackintosh gave *The Dominion Post* permission to photograph Orr in court but later banned publication of photos after Mr. McAleer asked for a suppression order.

Orr was also charged with possession of a knife, possession of prescription drugs, and failing to appear in court. A warrant for his arrest had been issued after he failed to appear in Wellington on charges not connected with the assault.

Orr, who did not speak during the brief appearance, was remanded on bail and will reappear in Wellington District Court with his co-accused on June 3 for a pre-committal hearing.   [2010]

≡ THINKING ABOUT THE TEXTS

1. Is the vampire craze much ado about not too much? Is it just a harmless trend that will pass?

2. Smoking, speeding, binge drinking, and unprotected sex are dangerous behaviors. Is vampire-style biting analogous to these behaviors? Explain.

3. Are there other "vampire behaviors" that have the potential to be imitated?

≡ WRITING ABOUT ISSUES

1. Write an argument essay about Russell's story that focuses on stereotypes in the story and in our culture.

2. Write an essay that focuses on Russell's tale as a love story.

3. What vampire movies have you seen? Do they seem to have a subtext about sexuality or the "other"? Write an essay that focuses on subtexts in vampire movies or television shows.

4. Watch the film Let Me In (a remake of the Swedish vampire film Let the Right One In) and write a review for your college newspaper, noting the unconventional twist on the vampire legend.

▤ Variations on a Stereotype: Re-Visions of a Story

CHARLES PERRAULT, "Little Red Riding Hood"

JACOB AND WILHELM GRIMM, "Little Red Cap"

ANGELA CARTER, "The Company of Wolves"

The story of Little Red Riding Hood is still told to children throughout the world. Her adventure in facing mortal danger is part of their education. What, though, do they learn from this narrative? Scholars have suggested various interpretations, many of which hold that the tale helps its young readers face their own childhood fears. Among the best-known and most provocative interpreters of the story is the psychoanalyst Bruno Bettelheim, who sees it as a symbolic treatment of a girl's effort to understand her sexual development. In this view, the story teaches girls to work through adolescent anxieties. But whatever decoding the tale receives, two aspects of it remain important. First, it depicts a child's journey from innocence to experience, however these terms are defined. Little Red Riding Hood learns something from her encounters with the murderous wolf, and she does so largely on her own. Several versions of her story exist. Because this tale of a perilous journey is so popular and has circulated in various forms, we invite you to compare three versions of it: Charles Perrault's from the seventeenth century, the Brothers Grimm's from the nineteenth century, and Angela Carter's modern variation. Note that the Grimms' tale does not stray too far from Perrault's, at least not in representing Little Red Riding Hood as an innocent in need of male protection. Under the influence of contemporary feminism, however, Carter feels no need to conform to the fairy-tale tradition. As a result, Little Red Riding Hood is freed not only from genre conventions but also from a centuries-old stereotype about passive females.

▤ BEFORE YOU READ

Write down what you remember about the story of Little Red Riding Hood, and then compare your version with those of your classmates. What elements of the story do your class's various renditions of it have in common? What differences, if any, emerge? Why do you think the story has been so popular?

CHARLES PERRAULT
Little Red Riding Hood

Along with the Brothers Grimm, Charles Perrault (1628–1703) was the most influential teller of the fairy tales many of us learned as children. Born in Paris to a fairly wealthy family, Perrault was trained as a lawyer. For his literary and philo-

(Jacob and Wilhelm Grimm. Culver Pictures, Inc.)

(Charles Perrault. The Granger Collection, New York.)

(Angela Carter. Miriam Berkley.)

sophical achievements, however, Perrault was elected to the prestigious Académie Française in 1671. During his lifetime, he and others were involved in a major cultural dispute over the relative merits of ancient authors and modern ones, with Perrault favoring the more up-to-date group. Later generations remember him best, though, for his 1697 book Stories or Tales from Times Past, with Morals: Tales of Mother Goose. This collection included "Le Petit Chaperon Rouge," which English-speaking readers have come to know as "Little Red Riding Hood." This story did not completely originate with Perrault; probably he had heard folktales containing some of its narrative elements. Nevertheless, his version became popular on publication and has remained so ever since.

Once upon a time there lived in a certain village a little country girl, the prettiest creature who was ever seen. Her mother was excessively fond of her, and her grandmother doted on her still more. This good woman had a little red riding hood made for her. It suited the girl so extremely well that everybody called her Little Red Riding Hood.

One day her mother, having made some cakes, said to her, "Go, my dear, and see how your grandmother is doing, for I hear she has been very ill. Take her a cake, and this little pot of butter."

Little Red Riding Hood set out immediately to go to her grandmother, who lived in another village.

As she was going through the wood, she met with a wolf, who had a very great mind to eat her up, but he dared not, because of some woodcutters working nearby in the forest. He asked her where she was going. The poor child, who did not know that it was dangerous to stay and talk to a wolf, said to him, "I am going to see my grandmother and carry her a cake and a little pot of butter from my mother."

Does she live far off?" said the wolf.   5

"Oh I say," answered Little Red Riding Hood. "It is beyond that mill you see there, at the first house in the village."

"Well," said the wolf, "and I'll go and see her too. I'll go this way and go you that, and we shall see who will be there first."

The wolf ran as fast as he could, taking the shortest path, and the little girl took a roundabout way, entertaining herself by gathering nuts, running after butterflies, and gathering bouquets of little flowers. It was not long before the wolf arrived at the old woman's house. He knocked at the door: tap, tap.

"Who's there?"

"Your grandchild, Little Red Riding Hood," replied the wolf, counterfeiting   10
her voice, "who has brought you a cake and a little pot of butter sent you by Mother."

The good grandmother, who was in bed because she was somewhat ill, cried out, "Pull the bobbin, and the latch will go up."

The wolf pulled the bobbin, and the door opened, and then he immediately fell upon the good woman and ate her up in a moment, for it had been more than three days since he had eaten. He then shut the door and got into the grandmother's bed, expecting Little Red Riding Hood, who came some time afterwards and knocked at the door: tap, tap.

"Who's there?"

Little Red Riding Hood, hearing the big voice of the wolf, was at first afraid but, believing her grandmother had a cold and was hoarse, answered, "It is your grandchild Little Red Riding Hood, who has brought you a cake and a little pot of butter Mother sends you."

The wolf cried out to her, softening his voice as much as he could, "Pull the   15
bobbin, and the latch will go up."

Little Red Riding Hood pulled the bobbin, and the door opened.

The wolf, seeing her come in, said to her, hiding himself under the bed-clothes, "Put the cake and the little pot of butter upon the stool, and come get into bed with me."

Little Red Riding Hood took off her clothes and got into bed. She was greatly amazed to see how her grandmother looked in her nightclothes and said to her, "Grandmother, what big arms you have!"

"All the better to hug you with, my dear."

"Grandmother, what big legs you have!"   20
"All the better to run with, my child."
"Grandmother, what big ears you have!"
"All the better to hear with, my child."
"Grandmother, what big eyes you have!"
"All the better to see with, my child."   25
"Grandmother, what big teeth you have got!"
"All the better to eat you up with."
And saying these words, this wicked wolf fell upon Little Red Riding Hood,
and ate her all up.

Moral: Children, especially attractive, well bred young ladies, should never talk
to strangers, for if they should do so, they may well provide dinner for a wolf. I
say "wolf," but there are various kinds of wolves. There are also those who
are charming, quiet, polite, unassuming, complacent, and sweet, who pursue
young women at home and in the streets. And unfortunately, it is these gentle
wolves who are the most dangerous ones of all.   *[1697]*

☰ THINKING ABOUT THE TEXT

1. To what extent does it matter to the story that Little Red Riding Hood is
   pretty? Would your reaction be the same if you learned she was homely
   or if you did not know how she looked? Explain.

2. The two main female characters are Little Red Riding Hood and her
   grandmother. Although the girl's mother appears briefly at the start,
   she then disappears from the narrative. What purposes are served by
   Perrault's leaving her out?

3. How would you describe Little Red Riding Hood as Perrault depicts her?
   Refer to specific details of the text.

4. In this version, Little Red Riding Hood dies. Would you draw different
   ideas from the text if she had lived? If so, what?

5. Does Perrault's moral seem well connected to the preceding story? Why,
   or why not? What metaphoric wolves might this moral apply to?

JACOB AND WILHELM GRIMM
Little Red Cap

*Jacob Grimm (1785–1863) and Wilhelm Grimm (1786–1859) were born in
Hanau, Germany, and studied law at Marburg University. They served as linguistics
professors at Göttingen University and made major contributions to the historical
study of language. The Grimms began to collect folktales from various oral European
traditions for their friends but later published their efforts for both children and
adults. Their methods became a model for the scientific collection of folktales and folk*

songs. Today they are known best for their volume Children's and Household Tales, *which was first published in 1812 and went through six more editions, the last in 1857. Their book included their version of the Little Red Riding Hood story, although their title for it was (in English translation) "Little Red Cap."*

Once upon a time there was a sweet little girl. Everyone who saw her liked her, but most of all her grandmother, who did not know what to give the child next. Once she gave her a little cap made of red velvet. Because it suited her so well, and she wanted to wear it all the time, she came to be known as Little Red Cap.

One day her mother said to her, "Come Little Red Cap. Here is a piece of cake and a bottle of wine. Take them to your grandmother. She is sick and weak, and they will do her well. Mind your manners, and give her my greetings. Behave yourself on the way, and do not leave the path, or you might fall down and break the glass, and then there will be nothing for your grandmother. And when you enter her parlor, don't forget to say 'Good morning,' and don't peer into all the corners first."

"I'll do everything just right," said Little Red Cap, shaking her mother's hand.

The grandmother lived out in the woods, a half hour from the village. When Little Red Cap entered the woods, a wolf came up to her. She did not know what a wicked animal he was and was not afraid of him.

"Good day to you, Little Red Cap."   5

"Thank you, wolf."

"Where are you going so early, Little Red Cap?"

"To Grandmother's."

"And what are you carrying under your apron?"

"Grandmother is sick and weak, and I am taking her some cake and wine.   10
We baked yesterday, and they should be good for her and give her strength."

"Little Red Cap, just where does your grandmother live?"

"Her house is a good quarter hour from here in the woods, under the three large oak trees. There's a hedge of hazel bushes there. You must know the place," said Little Red Cap.

The wolf thought to himself, "Now that sweet young thing is a tasty bite for me. She will taste even better than the old woman. You must be sly, and you can catch them both."

He walked along a little while with Little Red Cap. Then he said, "Little Red Cap, just look at the beautiful flowers that are all around us. Why don't you go and take a look? And I don't believe you can hear how beautifully the birds are singing. You are walking along as though you were on your way to school. It is very beautiful in the woods."

Little Red Cap opened her eyes, and when she saw the sunbeams dancing   15
to and fro through the trees and how the ground was covered with beautiful flowers, she thought, "If I take a fresh bouquet to Grandmother, she will be very pleased. Anyway, it is still early, and I'll be home on time." And she ran off the path into the woods looking for flowers. Each time she picked one, she

thought that she could see an even more beautiful one a little way off, and she ran after it, going farther and farther into the woods. But the wolf ran straight to the grandmother's house and knocked on the door.

"Who's there?"

"Little Red Cap. I'm bringing you some cake and wine. Open the door."

"Just press the latch," called out the grandmother. "I'm too weak to get up."

The wolf pressed the latch, and the door opened. He stepped inside, went straight to the grandmother's bed, and ate her up. Then he put on her clothes, put her cap on his head, got into her bed, and pulled the curtains shut.

Little Red Cap had run after the flowers. After she had gathered so many   20
that she could not carry any more, she remembered her grandmother and then continued on her way to her house. She found, to her surprise, that the door was open. She walked into the parlor, and everything looked so strange that she thought, "Oh, my God, why am I so afraid? I usually like it at Grandmother's."

She called out, "Good morning!" but received no answer.

Then she went to the bed and pulled back the curtains. Grandmother was lying there with her cap pulled down over her face and looking very strange.

"Oh, Grandmother, what big ears you have!"

"All the better to hear you with."

"Oh, Grandmother, what big eyes you have!"   25

"All the better to see you with."

"Oh, Grandmother, what big hands you have!"

"All the better to grab you with!"

"Oh, Grandmother, what a horribly big mouth you have!"

"All the better to eat you with!"   30

The wolf had scarcely finished speaking when he jumped from the bed with a single leap and ate up poor Little Red Cap. As soon as the wolf had satisfied his desires, he climbed back into bed, fell asleep, and began to snore very loudly.

A huntsman was just passing by. He thought, "The old woman is snoring so loudly. You had better see if something is wrong with her."

He stepped into the parlor, and when he approached the bed, he saw the wolf lying there. "So here I find you, you old sinner," he said. "I have been hunting for you a long time."

He was about to aim his rifle when it occurred to him that the wolf might have eaten the grandmother and that she still might be rescued. So instead of shooting, he took a pair of scissors and began to cut open the wolf's belly. After a few cuts he saw the red cap shining through, and after a few more cuts the girl jumped out, crying, "Oh, I was so frightened! It was so dark inside the wolf's body!"

And then the grandmother came out as well, alive but hardly able to   35
breathe. Then Little Red Cap fetched some large stones. She filled the wolf's body with them, and when he woke up and tried to run away, the stones were so heavy that he immediately fell down dead.

The three of them were happy. The huntsman skinned the wolf and went home with the pelt. The grandmother ate the cake and drank the wine that

Little Red Cap had brought. And Little Red Cap thought, "As long as I live, I will never leave the path and run off into the woods by myself if Mother tells me not to."

They also tell how Little Red Cap was taking some baked things to her grandmother another time, when another wolf spoke to her and wanted her to leave the path. But Little Red Cap took care and went straight to Grandmother's. She told her that she had seen the wolf and that he had wished her a good day but had stared at her in a wicked manner. "If we hadn't been on a public road, he would have eaten me up," she said.

"Come," said the grandmother. "Let's lock the door, so he can't get in."

Soon afterward the wolf knocked on the door and called out, "Open up, Grandmother. It's Little Red Cap, and I'm bringing you some baked things."

They remained silent and did not open the door. Gray-Head crept around   40
the house several times and finally jumped onto the roof. He wanted to wait until Little Red Cap went home that evening and then follow her and eat her up in the darkness. But the grandmother saw what he was up to. There was a large stone trough in front of the house.

"Fetch a bucket, Little Red Cap," she said to the child. "Yesterday I cooked some sausage. Carry the water that I boiled them with to the trough." Little Red Cap carried water until the large, large trough was clear full. The smell of sausage arose into the wolf's nose. He sniffed and looked down, stretching his neck so long that he could no longer hold himself, and he began to slide. He slid off the roof, fell into the trough, and drowned. And Little Red Cap returned home happily, and no one harmed her.   *[1857]*

≡ THINKING ABOUT THE TEXT

1. Why do you think that, at the beginning of the tale, the Grimms emphasize how sweet and likable Little Red Cap is?

2. To what extent do you blame Little Red Cap for being distracted by the beauty of nature? Explain your reasoning.

3. The Grimms have Little Red Cap and her grandmother rescued by a hunter. What would you say to someone who sees the Grimms as implying that women always need help from a man?

4. The wolf dies because Little Red Cap has filled his body with stones. Why do you think the Grimms did not have the huntsman simply shoot the wolf after freeing Little Red Cap and her grandmother?

5. Why do you think the Grimms added the second story? What is its effect?

≡ MAKING COMPARISONS

1. Does Little Red Riding Hood seem basically the same in both Perrault's version and the Grimms' version? Refer to specific details from both texts.

2. In Perrault's tale, the wolf persuades Little Red Riding Hood to take off her clothes and get into bed with him. In the Grimms' account, the wolf jumps up from the bed and eats her. How significant is this difference between the two versions?

3. In Perrault's version, Little Red Riding Hood and her grandmother die. In the Grimms' tale, on the other hand, they are rescued. Do you therefore see these two versions as putting forth different views of life? Explain.

ANGELA CARTER

The Company of Wolves

A native of Sussex, England, Angela Carter (1940–1991) worked in various genres, writing novels, short stories, screenplays, essays, and newspaper articles. Her fiction is most known for imaginatively refashioning classic tales of fantasy, including supernatural and gothic thrillers as well as fairy tales. Often, Carter rewrote these narratives from a distinctly female point of view, challenging what she saw as their patriarchal values and using them to explore the psychology of both genders. "The Company of Wolves," her version of the Little Red Riding Hood tale, was first published in the journal Bananas *in 1977. It then appeared in Carter's short-story volume* The Bloody Chamber *(1979) and was reprinted in* Burning Our Boats *(1995), a posthumous collection of all her stories. This tale also served as the basis for a 1984 film of the same title, which Carter wrote with director Neil Jordan.*

One beast and only one howls in the woods by night.

The wolf is carnivore incarnate, and he's as cunning as he is ferocious; once he's had a taste of flesh then nothing else will do.

At night, the eyes of wolves shine like candle flames, yellowish, reddish, but that is because the pupils of their eyes fatten on darkness and catch the light from your lantern to flash it back to you — red for danger; if a wolf's eyes reflect only moonlight, then they gleam a cold and unnatural green, a mineral, a piercing color. If the benighted traveler spies those luminous, terrible sequins stitched suddenly on the black thickets, then he knows he must run, if fear has not struck him stock-still.

But those eyes are all you will be able to glimpse of the forest assassins as they cluster invisibly round your smell of meat as you go through the wood unwisely late. They will be like shadows, they will be like wraiths, gray members of a congregation of nightmare; hark! his long, wavering howl . . . an aria of fear made audible.

The wolfsong is the sound of the rending you will suffer, in itself a murdering. 5

It is winter and cold weather. In this region of mountain and forest, there is now nothing for the wolves to eat. Goats and sheep are locked up in the

byre,° the deer departed for the remaining pasturage on the southern slopes — wolves grow lean and famished. There is so little flesh on them that you could count the starveling ribs through their pelts, if they gave you time before they pounced. Those slavering jaws; the lolling tongue; the rime of saliva on the grizzled chops — of all the teeming perils of the night and the forest, ghosts, hobgoblins, ogres that grill babies upon gridirons, witches that fatten their captives in cages for cannibal tables, the wolf is worst for he cannot listen to reason.

You are always in danger in the forest, where no people are. Step between the portals of the great pines where the shaggy branches tangle about you, trapping the unwary traveler in nets as if the vegetation itself were in a plot with the wolves who live there, as though the wicked trees go fishing on behalf of their friends — step between the gateposts of the forest with the greatest trepidation and infinite precautions, for if you stray from the path for one instant, the wolves will eat you. They are gray as famine, they are as unkind as plague.

The grave-eyed children of the sparse villages always carry knives with them when they go out to tend the little flocks of goats that provide the homesteads with acrid milk and rank, maggoty cheeses. Their knives are half as big as they are, the blades are sharpened daily.

But the wolves have ways of arriving at your own hearthside. We try and try but sometimes we cannot keep them out. There is no winter's night the cottager does not fear to see a lean, gray, famished snout questing under the door, and there was a woman once bitten in her own kitchen as she was straining the macaroni.

Fear and flee the wolf; for, worst of all, the wolf may be more than he   10
seems.

There was a hunter once, near here, that trapped a wolf in a pit. This wolf had massacred the sheep and goats; eaten up a mad old man who used to live by himself in a hut halfway up the mountain and sing to Jesus all day; pounced on a girl looking after the sheep, but she made such a commotion that men came with rifles and scared him away and tried to track him into the forest but he was cunning and easily gave them the slip. So this hunter dug a pit and put a duck in it, for bait, all alive-oh; and he covered the pit with straw smeared with wolf dung. Quack, quack! went the duck and a wolf came slinking out of the forest, a big one, a heavy one, he weighed as much as a grown man, and the straw gave way beneath him — into the pit he tumbled. The hunter jumped down after him, slit his throat, cut off all his paws for a trophy.

And then no wolf at all lay in front of the hunter but the bloody trunk of a man, headless, footless, dying, dead.

A witch from up the valley once turned an entire wedding party into wolves because the groom had settled on another girl. She used to order them to visit her, at night, from spite, and they would sit and howl around her cottage for her, serenading her with their misery.

byre: Barn or shed.

Not so very long ago, a young woman in our village married a man who vanished clean away on her wedding night. The bed was made with new sheets and the bride lay down in it; the groom said, he was going out to relieve himself, insisted on it, for the sake of decency, and she drew the coverlet up to her chin and she lay there. And she waited and she waited and then she waited again — surely he's been gone a long time? Until she jumps up in bed and shrieks to hear a howling, coming on the wind from the forest.

That long-drawn, wavering howl has, for all its fearful resonance, some   15
inherent sadness in it, as if the beasts would love to be less beastly if only they knew how and never cease to mourn their own condition. There is a vast melancholy in the canticles° of the wolves, melancholy infinite as the forest, endless as these long nights of winter and yet that ghastly sadness, that mourning for their own, irremediable appetites, can never move the heart for not one phrase in it hints at the possibility of redemption; grace could not come to the wolf from its own despair, only through some external mediator, so that, sometimes, the beast will look as if he half welcomes the knife that dispatches him.

The young woman's brothers searched the outhouses and the haystacks but never found any remains, so the sensible girl dried her eyes and found herself another husband not too shy to piss into a pot who spent the nights indoors. She gave him a pair of bonny babies and all went right as a trivet until, one freezing night, the night of the solstice, the hinge of the year when things do not fit together as well as they should, the longest night, her first good man came home again.

A great thump on the door announced him as she was stirring the soup for the father of her children, and she knew him the moment she lifted the latch to him although it was years since she'd worn black for him and now he was in rags and his hair hung down his back and never saw a comb, alive with lice.

"Here I am again, missus," he said. "Get me my bowl of cabbage and be quick about it."

Then her second husband came in with wood for the fire and when the first one saw she'd slept with another man and, worse, clapped his red eyes on her little children who'd crept into the kitchen to see what all the din was about, he shouted: "I wish I were a wolf again, to teach this whore a lesson!" So a wolf he instantly became and tore off the eldest boy's left foot before he was chopped up with the hatchet they used for chopping logs. But when the wolf lay bleeding and gasping its last, the pelt peeled off again and he was just as he had been, years ago, when he ran away from his marriage bed, so that she wept and her second husband beat her.

They say there's an ointment the Devil gives you that turns you into a wolf the   20
minute you rub it on. Or that he was born feet first and had a wolf for his father and his torso is a man's but his legs and genitals are a wolf's. And he has a wolf's heart.

canticles: Songs or chants.

Seven years is a werewolf's natural span but if you burn his human clothing you condemn him to wolfishness for the rest of his life, so old wives hereabouts think it some protection to throw a hat or an apron at the werewolf, as if clothes made the man. Yet by the eyes, those phosphorescent eyes, you know him in all his shapes; the eyes alone unchanged by metamorphosis.

Before he can become a wolf, the lycanthrope° strips stark naked. If you spy a naked man among the pines, you must run as if the Devil were after you.

It is midwinter and the robin, the friend of man, sits on the handle of the gardener's spade and sings. It is the worst time in all the year for wolves, but this strong-minded child insists she will go off through the wood. She is quite sure the wild beasts cannot harm her although, well-warned, she lays a carving knife in the basket her mother has packed with cheeses. There is a bottle of harsh liquor distilled from brambles; a batch of flat oatcakes baked on the hearthstone; a pot or two of jam. The flaxen-haired girl will take these delicious gifts to a reclusive grandmother so old the burden of her years is crushing her to death. Granny lives two hours' trudge through the winter woods; the child wraps herself up in her thick shawl, draws it over her head. She steps into her stout wooden shoes; she is dressed and ready and it is Christmas Eve. The malign door of the solstice still swings upon its hinges, but she has been too much loved ever to feel scared.

Children do not stay young for long in this savage country. There are no toys for them to play with, so they work hard and grow wise, but this one, so pretty and the youngest of her family, a little late-comer, had been indulged by her mother and the grandmother who'd knitted her the red shawl that, today, has the ominous if brilliant look of blood on snow. Her breasts have just begun to swell; her hair is like lint, so fair it hardly makes a shadow on her pale forehead; her cheeks are an emblematic scarlet and white and she has just started her woman's bleeding, the clock inside her that will strike, henceforward, once a month.

She stands and moves within the invisible pentacle° of her own virginity.   25
She is an unbroken egg; she is a sealed vessel; she has inside her a magic space the entrance to which is shut tight with a plug of membrane; she is a closed system; she does not know how to shiver. She has her knife and she is afraid of nothing.

Her father might forbid her, if he were home, but he is away in the forest, gathering wood, and her mother cannot deny her.

The forest closed upon her like a pair of jaws.

There is always something to look at in the forest, even in the middle of winter — the huddled mounds of birds, succumbed to the lethargy of the season, heaped on the creaking boughs and too forlorn to sing; the bright frills of the winter fungi on the blotched trunks of the trees; the cuneiform° slots of rabbits and deer, the herringbone tracks of the birds, a hare as lean as a rasher of bacon streaking across the path where the thin sunlight dapples the russet brakes of last year's bracken.

---

lycanthrope: Werewolf.   **pentacle:** Five-pointed star; also called a pentagram.   **cuneiform:** Wedge-shaped.

When she heard the freezing howl of a distant wolf, her practiced hand sprang to the handle of her knife, but she saw no sign of a wolf at all, nor of a naked man, neither, but then she heard a clattering among the brushwood and there sprang on to the path a fully clothed one, a very handsome young one, in the green coat and wide-awake hat of a hunter, laden with carcasses of game birds. She had her hand on her knife at the first rustle of twigs, but he laughed with a flash of white teeth when he saw her and made her a comic yet flattering little bow; she'd never seen such a fine fellow before, not among the rustic clowns of her native village. So on they went together, through the thickening light of the afternoon.

Soon they were laughing and joking like old friends. When he offered to   30
carry her basket, she gave it to him although her knife was in it because he told her his rifle would protect them. As the day darkened, it began to snow again; she felt the first flakes settle on her eyelashes, but now there was only half a mile to go and there would be a fire, and hot tea, and a welcome, a warm one, surely, for the dashing huntsman as well as for herself.

This young man had a remarkable object in his pocket. It was a compass. She looked at the little round glass face in the palm of his hand and watched the wavering needle with a vague wonder. He assured her this compass had taken him safely through the wood on his hunting trip because the needle always told him with perfect accuracy where the north was. She did not believe it; she knew she should never leave the path on the way through the wood or else she would be lost instantly. He laughed at her again; gleaming trails of spittle clung to his teeth. He said, if he plunged off the path into the forest that surrounded them, he could guarantee to arrive at her grandmother's house a good quarter of an hour before she did, plotting his way through the undergrowth with his compass, while she trudged the long way, along the winding path.

I don't believe you. Besides, aren't you afraid of the wolves?

He only tapped the gleaming butt of his rifle and grinned.

Is it a bet? he asked her. Shall we make a game of it? What will you give me if I get to your grandmother's house before you?

What would you like? she asked disingenuously.   35

A kiss.

Commonplaces of a rustic seduction; she lowered her eyes and blushed.

He went through the undergrowth and took her basket with him but she forgot to be afraid of the beasts, although now the moon was rising, for she wanted to dawdle on her way to make sure the handsome gentleman would win his wager.

Grandmother's house stood by itself a little way out of the village. The freshly falling snow blew in eddies about the kitchen garden, and the young man stepped delicately up the snowy path to the door as if he were reluctant to get his feet wet, swinging his bundle of game and the girl's basket and humming a little tune to himself.

There is a faint trace of blood on his chin; he has been snacking on his catch.   40

He rapped upon the panels with his knuckles.

Aged and frail, granny is three-quarters succumbed to the mortality the ache in her bones promises her and almost ready to give in entirely. A boy came out from the village to build up her hearth for the night an hour ago and the kitchen crackles with busy firelight. She has her Bible for company, she is a pious old woman. She is propped up on several pillows in the bed set into the wall peasant-fashion, wrapped up in the patchwork quilt she made before she was married, more years ago than she cares to remember. Two china spaniels with liver-colored blotches on their coats and black noses sit on either side of the fireplace. There is a bright rug of woven rags on the pantiles. The grandfather clock ticks away her eroding time.

We keep the wolves outside by living well.

He rapped upon the panels with his hairy knuckles.

It is your granddaughter, he mimicked in a high soprano.   45

Lift up the latch and walk in, my darling.

You can tell them by their eyes, eyes of a beast of prey, nocturnal, devastating eyes as red as a wound; you can hurl your Bible at him and your apron after, granny, you thought that was a sure prophylactic against these infernal vermin . . . now call on Christ and his mother and all the angels in heaven to protect you but it won't do you any good.

His feral muzzle is sharp as a knife; he drops his golden burden of gnawed pheasant on the table and puts down your dear girl's basket, too. Oh, my God, what have you done with her?

Off with his disguise, that coat of forest-colored cloth, the hat with the feather tucked into the ribbon; his matted hair streams down his white shirt and she can see the lice moving in it. The sticks in the hearth shift and hiss; night and the forest has come into the kitchen with darkness tangled in its hair.

He strips off his shirt. His skin is the color and texture of vellum. A crisp   50
stripe of hair runs down his belly, his nipples are ripe and dark as poison fruit, but he's so thin you could count the ribs under his skin if only he gave you the time. He strips off his trousers and she can see how hairy his legs are. His genitals, huge. Ah! huge.

The last thing the old lady saw in all this world was a young man, eyes like cinders, naked as a stone, approaching her bed.

The wolf is carnivore incarnate.

When he had finished with her, he licked his chops and quickly dressed himself again, until he was just as he had been when he came through her door. He burned the inedible hair in the fireplace and wrapped the bones up in a napkin that he hid away under the bed in the wooden chest in which he found a clean pair of sheets. These he carefully put on the bed instead of the tell-tale stained ones he stowed away in the laundry basket. He plumped up the pillows and shook out the patchwork quilt, he picked up the Bible from the floor, closed it and laid it on the table. All was as it had been before except that grandmother was gone. The sticks twitched in the grate, the clock ticked and the young man sat patiently, deceitfully beside the bed in granny's nightcap.

Rat-a-tap-tap.

Who's there, he quavers in granny's antique falsetto.   55

Only your granddaughter.

So she came in, bringing with her a flurry of snow that melted in tears on the tiles, and perhaps she was a little disappointed to see only her grandmother sitting beside the fire. But then he flung off the blanket and sprang to the door, pressing his back against it so that she could not get out again.

The girl looked round the room and saw there was not even the indentation of a head on the smooth cheek of the pillow and how, for the first time she'd seen it so, the Bible lay closed on the table. The tick of the clock cracked like a whip. She wanted her knife from her basket, but she did not dare reach for it because his eyes were fixed upon her — huge eyes that now seemed to shine with a unique, interior light, eyes the size of saucers, saucers full of Greek fire, diabolic phosphorescence.

What big eyes you have.

All the better to see you with.   60

No trace at all of the old woman except for a tuft of white hair that had caught in the bark of an unburned log. When the girl saw that, she knew she was in danger of death.

Where is my grandmother?

There's nobody here but we two, my darling.

Now a great howling rose up all around them, near, very near, as close as the kitchen garden, the howling of a multitude of wolves; she knew the worst wolves are hairy on the inside and she shivered, in spite of the scarlet shawl she pulled more closely round herself as if it could protect her although it was as red as the blood she must spill.

Who has come to sing us carols, she said.   65

Those are the voices of my brothers, darling; I love the company of wolves. Look out of the window and you'll see them.

Snow half-caked the lattice and she opened it to look into the garden. It was a white night of moon and snow; the blizzard whirled round the gaunt, grey beasts who squatted on their haunches among the rows of winter cabbage, pointing their sharp snouts to the moon and howling as if their hearts would break. Ten wolves; twenty wolves — so many wolves she could not count them, howling in concert as if demented or deranged. Their eyes reflected the light from the kitchen and shone like a hundred candles.

It is very cold, poor things, she said; no wonder they howl so.

She closed the window on the wolves' threnody° and took off her scarlet shawl, the color of poppies, the color of sacrifices, the color of her menses, and, since her fear did her no good, she ceased to be afraid.

What shall I do with my shawl?   70

Throw it on the fire, dear one. You won't need it again.

She bundled up her shawl and threw it on the blaze, which instantly consumed it. Then she drew her blouse over her head; her small breasts gleamed as if the snow had invaded the room.

What shall I do with my blouse?

---

threnody: Lament or dirge.

Into the fire with it, too, my pet.

The thin muslin went flaring up the chimney like a magic bird and now   75
off came her skirt, her woolen stockings, her shoes, and on to the fire they went,
too, and were gone for good. The firelight shone through the edges of her skin;
now she was clothed only in her untouched integument° of flesh. This dazzling,
naked she combed out her hair with her fingers; her hair looked white as the snow
outside. Then went directly to the man with red eyes in whose unkempt mane the
lice moved; she stood up on tiptoe and unbuttoned the collar of his shirt.

What big arms you have.

All the better to hug you with.

Every wolf in the world now howled a prothalamion° outside the window
as she freely gave the kiss she owed him.

What big teeth you have!

She saw how his jaw began to slaver and the room was full of the clamor of   80
the forest's Liebestod° but the wise child never flinched, even when he answered:

All the better to eat you with.

The girl burst out laughing; she knew she was nobody's meat. She laughed
at him full in the face, she ripped off his shirt for him and flung it into the fire,
in the fiery wake of her own discarded clothing. The flames danced like dead
souls on Walpurgisnacht,° and the old bones under the bed set up a terrible
clattering, but she did not pay them any heed.

Carnivore incarnate, only immaculate flesh appeases him.

She will lay his fearful head on her lap and she will pick out the lice from
his pelt and perhaps she will put the lice into her mouth and eat them, as he
will bid her, as she would do in a savage marriage ceremony.

The blizzard will die down.   85

The blizzard died down, leaving the mountains as randomly covered with
snow as if a blind woman had thrown a sheet over them, the upper branches of
the forest pines limed, creaking, swollen with the fall.

Snowlight, moonlight, a confusion of paw-prints.

All silent, all still.

Midnight; and the clock strikes. It is Christmas Day, the werewolves' birthday, the door of the solstice stands wide open; let them all sink through.

See! sweet and sound she sleeps in granny's bed, between the paws of the   90
tender wolf.   [1977]

integument: Outer covering, such as animal skin or seed coat.   **prothalamion:** Wed-
ding song.   **Liebestod:** Final aria in Richard Wagner's opera *Tristan und Isolde,* in which
Isolde sings over Tristan's dead body and ultimately dies herself.   **Walpurgisnacht:** May
Day eve, the medieval witches' sabbath.

≡ THINKING ABOUT THE TEXT

1. The story begins with a section about wolves before it gets to the Little
   Red Riding Hood narrative. What image of wolves does this prologue
   convey? What in particular seems the purpose of the extended anecdote
   about the wife with two husbands?

2. Point out various places where Carter diverges from the conventions of the fairy tale.

3. Do you find it surprising that the girl does not get to her grandmother's house first? Do you suspect that the girl is not so innocent?

4. Obviously this is not a story for children. What traditional ideas about females and sexuality is Carter revising?

5. What do you conclude about the girl from her behavior at the end of the story? To what extent is "savage marriage ceremony" (para. 84) indeed an apt term for what occurs?

≡ MAKING COMPARISONS

1. To what extent is Carter's image of wolves different from Perrault's and the Grimms'? Refer to details from all three texts.

2. Several critics have described Carter's versions of fairy tales as feminist. To what extent can this term be applied to Perrault's and the Grimms' narratives as well as to hers? Define what you mean by *feminist*.

3. Would you say Carter's writing style is more realistic than that of Perrault and the Grimms? Or is the term *realism* completely irrelevant in the case of fairy tales? Explain.

≡ WRITING ABOUT ISSUES

1. Choose one of these versions of the Little Red Riding Hood story, and write an essay in which you elaborate a moral that modern *adults* might learn from it. Or write an essay in which you explain what an adolescent might learn from Carter's version.

2. Does Carter's version radically depart from Perrault's and the Grimms', or does it basically resemble them? Write an essay that addresses this question by focusing on Carter's story and one of the other two.

3. Write an essay explaining what you think you learned from a fairy tale or other fictional story that you heard as a child. If you want to contrast your thinking about the story now with your thinking about it then, do so. Feel free to compare the story you focus on with any of the versions of Little Red Riding Hood in this cluster.

4. Write your own version of the story of Little Red Riding Hood, and on a separate piece of paper write the moral you think should be drawn from your text. Then give your version to a classmate, and see if he or she can guess your moral.

CHAPTER 13

Doing Justice

Thinking about literature involves people making judgments about other people's views. Throughout your course, you have been making judgments as you interpret and evaluate written works, including the texts in this book and those produced by the class. You have been deciding also how you feel about positions expressed by your teacher and classmates. In all these acts of judgment, you have considered where you stand on general issues of aesthetics, ethics, politics, religion, and law.

Outside school, you judge things all the time, though you may not always be aware that you are doing so. You may be more conscious of your judgments when other people disagree with you, when you face multiple options, when you are trying to understand something complex, when your decisions will have significant consequences, or when you must review an act you have already committed. Some people are quite conscious that they make judgments because they have the political, professional, or institutional authority to enforce their will. Of course, these people may wind up being judged by whomever they dominate, and they may even face active revolt.

A term closely related to *judgment* is *justice*, which many people associate with judgments that are wise, fair, and sensitive to the parties involved. In this sense, justice is an ideal, which may not always be achieved in real life. Indeed, though communities hope their police departments and courts will act soundly, sometimes representatives of our legal institutions are accused of violating justice instead of upholding it. Much, of course, depends on how *justice* is defined in any particular case, and equally crucial is who defines it. Many works of literature have challenged laws of the society in which they were written, while others have at least questioned or complicated the notions of justice prevailing in their culture. Often, literature has probed the complexities of situations that in real life are resolved as clear victories for one particular party. In this respect, literature draws attention to issues that we may normally oversimplify or overlook.

The opening cluster in this chapter treats the issue of what people should do when faced with laws they consider unjust. Henry David Thoreau's classic essay "Civil Disobedience," Rebecca Solnit's commentary on his text, and Martin Luther King Jr.'s well-known "Letter from Birmingham Jail" argue for nonviolent defiance. The next set of works—which puts together Nathaniel Hawthorne's famous tale "Young Goodman Brown" with modern-day stories by Toni Cade Bambara and Alice Walker — probes the psychological changes that youths may experience when they sense great injustice for the first time. Then come four poems that examine the responsibilities of people who inflict, witness, or learn about punishments. These texts are followed by a trio of essays that ponder the social standards involved when a person moves through a legal system from judgment to conviction and punishment. Next come two clusters focused on revenge — that is, the personal pursuit of justice. In Robert Browning's classic poem "My Last Duchess," the speaker takes revenge against his wife; we add Gabriel Spera's contemporary poem "My Ex-Husband," which presents the reverse perspective. Stories by Andre Dubus and Ha Jin then both chronicle how a man avenges wrongdoing against him by turning murderous himself.

Even people who unscrupulously murder someone may come to feel remorse over their act. In many of his stories, master of horror Edgar Allan Poe raises the possibility of a killer's developing a guilty conscience, whereas other Poe tales focus on a character who does not seem to regret committing murder. Both kinds of narratives are featured in a section devoted to Poe's fiction. The next several clusters in this chapter, though, all deal with people who evidently feel that they themselves are victims of injustice. The centerpiece of the first grouping is Ida Fink's play *The Table*, in which Holocaust survivors must endure stern, relentless questioning as they prepare for a trial of their Nazi persecutors. To help you analyze this work and put it in a larger context, we include Wladyslaw Szpilman's account of his own escape from deportation to the Nazi death camps, and we offer as well Dori Laub's reflection of Holocaust survivors' capacity to recall historical facts. After this unit comes one centered on Flannery O'Connor's short story "A Good Man Is Hard to Find," in which a figure called The Misfit becomes homicidal in an effort to achieve a sense of cosmic justice. We include O'Connor's explanation of this story and comments by three critics who seek to complicate her analysis. In the subsequent cluster, we turn to Sophocles' ancient Greek tragedy *Antigone*, a classic conflict between an individual's and a state's visions of justice. We accompany this drama with two newspaper accounts of contemporary women who can be seen as present-day Antigones insofar as they, too, challenge governments they deem oppressive. In the next section, poems by Countee Cullen and Natasha Trethewey — both entitled "Incident" — present speakers confronted by racial injustice.

We end the chapter with two clusters that broaden its considerations. Stories by Sherwood Anderson, Rebecca Makkai, and Linh Dinh examine what a "criminal" is in the first place, focusing on characters who try to outmaneuver authorities by assuming false identities. Finally, poems by William Blake, Martin Espada, and Mark Jarman imagine what a world of ideal justice would be like.

▤ Civil Disobedience: Essays

HENRY DAVID THOREAU, "Civil Disobedience"

REBECCA SOLNIT, "The Thoreau Problem"

MARTIN LUTHER KING JR., "Letter from Birmingham Jail"

Many people assume that the legal systems they live under are fair and moral. At various times and places, however, individuals and social movements have objected to certain laws, declaring them unethical and perhaps even condemning the entire government behind them. History has seen numerous occasions when such criticism has turned violent, even becoming outright revolt. At other moments, though, the protest has taken the form of civil disobedience. This is usually defined as the use of relatively *non*violent means to defy a law, on behalf of what the protesters claim is a higher principle. Contemporary examples in the United States have included mass demonstrations by foes of capitalism at economic summits, as well as the blocking of abortion clinics by right-to-life groups. Of course, civil disobedience has also occurred in other countries. Mahatma Gandhi famously practiced it in working for the independence of India. More recently, rallies have defied oppressive regimes in Myanmar (Burma) and Iran, while smaller circles of dissidents continue to challenge the leaders of Communist China.

Featured in this cluster are two of the most well-known and inspirational arguments for civil disobedience, Henry David Thoreau's essay of that title and Martin Luther King Jr.'s "Letter from Birmingham Jail." Also here is a commentary by Rebecca Solnit that ponders the implications of Thoreau's text. All three pieces leave you, the reader, having to decide how *you* would identify and deal with the differences between "just" and "unjust" laws.

▤ BEFORE YOU READ

Civil disobedience is usually defined as a form of protest: specifically, the use of nonviolent means to defy a law on behalf of a supposedly higher moral principle. In Thoreau's classic essay on this subject, for example, he relates that he refused to pay taxes because he opposed the U.S. government's tolerance of slavery and also its war against Mexico. Under what circumstances, if any, do you think civil disobedience is justified? What particular historical and contemporary events come to your mind when you consider this issue?

HENRY DAVID THOREAU
Civil Disobedience

Henry David Thoreau (1817–1862) spent his life in the area of Concord, Massachusetts. But since his death, he has been acclaimed worldwide as a major contributor to American thought and literature. His writings on ecology, philosophy, theology, and agriculture inspire many people even today. His most well-known text is his book Walden *(1854). A classic argument for plain, simple living in harmony with nature, it grew out of the journal that Thoreau kept during the two years he spent in a cabin at Walden Pond, on land owned by his friend Ralph Waldo Emerson. Also renowned, however, is the following essay, which has influenced such important civic activists as Mahatma Gandhi and Martin Luther King Jr. It was first a public lecture that Thoreau gave locally on January 26, 1848. With the title "Resistance to Civil Government," it was then published in May 1849 in* Aesthetic Papers, *a periodical that lasted for only one issue. "Civil Disobedience" acquired its present title in an 1866 volume of Thoreau's works. Although the essay expresses a theory of law and politics that he held throughout his life, in part Thoreau was moved to write it by hatred of two then-current U.S. government policies. One was the system of slavery, which federal law permitted to exist in the southern states. The other was the Mexican-American War, which to Thoreau was an immoral conflict sparked by his nation's lust for territory. The chief form of civil disobedience that Thoreau discusses in the essay is his own refusal to pay taxes. As he recalls, this once resulted in his being jailed for a night.*

I heartily accept the motto, "That government is best which governs least"; and I should like to see it acted up to more rapidly and systematically. Carried out, it finally amounts to this, which also I believe — "That government is best which governs not at all"; and when men are prepared for it, that will be the kind of government which they will have. Government is at best but an expedient; but most governments are usually, and all governments are sometimes, inexpedient. The objections which have been brought against a standing army, and they are many and weighty, and deserve to prevail, may also at last be brought against a standing government. The standing army is only an arm of the standing government. The government itself, which is only the mode which the people have chosen to execute their will, is equally liable to be abused and perverted before the people can act through it. Witness the present Mexican war, the work of comparatively a few individuals using the standing government as their tool; for, in the outset, the people would not have consented to this measure.

   This American government — what is it but a tradition, though a recent one, endeavoring to transmit itself unimpaired to posterity, but each instant losing some of its integrity? It has not the vitality and force of a single living man; for a single man can bend it to his will. It is a sort of wooden gun to the people themselves. But it is not the less necessary for this; for the people must have some complicated machinery or other, and hear its din, to satisfy that idea of government which they have. Governments show thus how successfully men can be imposed on, even impose on themselves, for their own advantage. It is excellent, we must all allow. Yet this government never of itself furthered any enterprise, but by the alacrity with which it got out of its way. It does not keep the country free. It does not settle the West. It does not educate. The character inherent in the American people has done all that has been accomplished; and it would have done somewhat more, if the government had not sometimes got in its way. For government is an expedient by which men would fain succeed in letting one another alone; and, as has been said, when it is most expedient, the governed are most let alone by it. Trade and commerce, if they were not made of india-rubber, would never manage to bounce over the obstacles which legislators are continually putting in their way; and, if one were to judge these men wholly by the effects of their actions and not partly by their intentions, they would deserve to be classed and punished with those mischievous persons who put obstructions on the railroads.

But, to speak practically and as a citizen, unlike those who call themselves no-government men, I ask for, not at once no government, but at once a better government. Let every man make known what kind of government would command his respect, and that will be one step toward obtaining it.

After all, the practical reason why, when the power is once in the hands of the people, a majority are permitted, and for a long period continue, to rule is not because they are most likely to be in the right, nor because this seems fairest to the minority, but because they are physically the strongest. But a government in which the majority rule in all cases cannot be based on justice, even as far as men understand it. Can there not be a government in which majorities do not virtually decide right and wrong, but conscience? — in which majorities decide only those questions to which the rule of expediency is applicable? Must the citizen ever for a moment, or in the least degree, resign his conscience to the legislation? Why has every man a conscience, then? I think that we should be men first, and subjects afterward. It is not desirable to cultivate a respect for the law, so much as for the right. The only obligation which I have a right to assume is to do at any time what I think right. It is truly enough said that a corporation has no conscience; but a corporation of conscientious men is a corporation with a conscience. Law never made men a whit more just; and, by means of their respect for it, even the well-disposed are daily made the agents of injustice. A common and natural result of an undue respect for law is, that you may see a file of soldiers, colonel, captain, corporal, privates, powder-monkeys, and all, marching in admirable order over hill and dale to the wars, against their wills, ay, against their common sense and consciences, which makes it very steep marching indeed, and produces a palpitation of the heart. They have no doubt that it is a damnable business in which they are concerned; they are all peaceably inclined. Now, what are they? Men at all? or small movable forts and magazines, at the service of some unscrupulous man in power? Visit the Navy-Yard, and behold a marine, such a man as an American government can make, or such as it can make a man with its black arts —

a mere shadow and reminiscence of humanity, a man laid out alive and standing, and already, as one may say, buried under arms with funeral accompaniments, though it may be,

> "Not a drum was heard, not a funeral note,
>   As his corse to the rampart we hurried;
> Not a soldier discharged his farewell shot
>   O'er the grave where our hero we buried."

The mass of men serve the state thus, not as men mainly, but as machines, with their bodies. They are the standing army, and the militia, jailers, constables, posse comitatus, etc. In most cases there is no free exercise whatever of the judgment or of the moral sense; but they put themselves on a level with wood and earth and stones; and wooden men can perhaps be manufactured that will serve the purpose as well. Such command no more respect than men of straw or a lump of dirt. They have the same sort of worth only as horses and dogs. Yet such as these even are commonly esteemed good citizens. Others — as most legislators, politicians, lawyers, ministers, and office-holders — serve the state chiefly with their heads; and, as they rarely make any moral distinctions, they are as likely to serve the devil, without intending it, as God. A very few — as heroes, patriots, martyrs, reformers in the great sense, and men — serve the state with their consciences also, and so necessarily resist it for the most part; and they are commonly treated as enemies by it. A wise man will only be useful as a man, and will not submit to be "clay," and "stop a hole to keep the wind away," but leave that office to his dust at least:

> "I am too high-born to be propertied,
>   To be a secondary at control,
> Or useful serving-man and instrument
> To any sovereign state throughout the world."

He who gives himself entirely to his fellow-men appears to them useless and selfish; but he who gives himself partially to them is pronounced a benefactor and philanthropist.

How does it become a man to behave toward this American government today? I answer, that he cannot without disgrace be associated with it. I cannot for an instant recognize that political organization as my government which is the slave's government also.

All men recognize the right of revolution; that is, the right to refuse allegiance to, and to resist, the government, when its tyranny or its inefficiency are great and unendurable. But almost all say that such is not the case now. But such was the case, they think, in the Revolution of '75. If one were to tell me that this was a bad government because it taxed certain foreign commodities brought to its ports, it is most probable that I should not make an ado about it, for I can do without them. All machines have their friction; and possibly this does enough good to counterbalance the evil. At any rate, it is a great evil to make a stir about it. But when the friction comes to have its machine, and oppression and robbery are organized, I say, let us not have such a machine any

5

longer. In other words, when a sixth of the population of a nation which has undertaken to be the refuge of liberty are slaves, and a whole country is unjustly overrun and conquered by a foreign army, and subjected to military law, I think that it is not too soon for honest men to rebel and revolutionize. What makes this duty the more urgent is the fact that the country so overrun is not our own, but ours is the invading army.

Paley, a common authority with many on moral questions, in his chapter on the "Duty of Submission to Civil Government," resolves all civil obligation into expediency; and he proceeds to say that "so long as the interest of the whole society requires it, that is, so long as the established government cannot be resisted or changed without public inconveniency, it is the will of God . . . that the established government be obeyed — and no longer. This principle being admitted, the justice of every particular case of resistance is reduced to a computation of the quantity of the danger and grievance on the one side, and of the probability and expense of redressing it on the other." Of this, he says, every man shall judge for himself. But Paley appears never to have contemplated those cases to which the rule of expediency does not apply, in which a people, as well as an individual, must do justice, cost what it may. If I have unjustly wrested a plank from a drowning man, I must restore it to him though I drown myself. This, according to Paley, would be inconvenient. But he that would save his life, in such a case, shall lose it. This people must cease to hold slaves, and to make war on Mexico, though it cost them their existence as a people.

In their practice, nations agree with Paley; but does any one think that   10
Massachusetts does exactly what is right at the present crisis?

"A drab of state, a cloth-o'-silver slut,
To have her train borne up, and her soul trail in the dirt."

Practically speaking, the opponents to a reform in Massachusetts are not a hundred thousand politicians at the South, but a hundred thousand merchants and farmers here, who are more interested in commerce and agriculture than they are in humanity, and are not prepared to do justice to the slave and to Mexico, cost what it may. I quarrel not with far-off foes, but with those who, near at home, cooperate with, and do the bidding of those far away, and without whom the latter would be harmless. We are accustomed to say, that the mass of men are unprepared; but improvement is slow, because the few are not materially wiser or better than the many. It is not so important that many should be as good as you, as that there be some absolute goodness somewhere; for that will leaven the whole lump. There are thousands who are in opinion opposed to slavery and to the war, who yet in effect do nothing to put an end to them; who, esteeming themselves children of Washington and Franklin, sit down with their hands in their pockets, and say that they know not what to do, and do nothing; who even postpone the question of freedom to the question of free trade, and quietly read the prices-current along with the latest advices from Mexico, after dinner, and, it may be, fall asleep over them both. What is the price-current of an honest man and patriot today? They hesitate, and they regret, and sometimes they petition; but they do nothing in earnest and with effect. They will wait, well disposed, for others to remedy the evil, that they may no longer have it to regret. At most, they give only a cheap vote, and a feeble countenance and God-speed, to the right, as it goes by them. There are nine hundred and ninety-nine patrons of virtue to one virtuous man. But it is easier to deal with the real possessor of a thing than with the temporary guardian of it.

All voting is a sort of gaming, like checkers or backgammon, with a slight moral tinge to it, a playing with right and wrong, with moral questions; and betting naturally accompanies it. The character of the voters is not staked. I cast my vote, perchance, as I think right; but I am not vitally concerned that that right should prevail. I am willing to leave it to the majority. Its obligation, therefore, never exceeds that of expediency. Even voting for the right is doing nothing for it. It is only expressing to men feebly your desire that it should prevail. A wise man will not leave the right to the mercy of chance, nor wish it to prevail through the power of the majority. There is but little virtue in the action of masses of men. When the majority shall at length vote for the abolition of slavery, it will be because they are indifferent to slavery, or because there is but little slavery left to be abolished by their vote. They will then be the only slaves. Only his vote can hasten the abolition of slavery who asserts his own freedom by his vote.

I hear of a convention to be held at Baltimore, or elsewhere, for the selection of a candidate for the Presidency, made up chiefly of editors, and men who are politicians by profession; but I think, what is it to any independent, intelligent, and respectable man what decision they may come to? Shall we not have the advantage of his wisdom and honesty, nevertheless? Can we not count upon some independent votes? Are there not many individuals in the country who do not attend conventions? But no: I find that the respectable man, so called, has immediately drifted from his position, and despairs of his country, when his country has more reason to despair of him. He forthwith adopts one of the candidates thus selected as the only available one, thus proving that he is himself available for any purposes of the demagogue. His vote is of no more worth than that of any unprincipled foreigner or hireling native, who may have been bought. O for a man who is a man, and, as my neighbor says, has a bone in his back which you cannot pass your hand through! Our statistics are at fault: the population has been returned too large. How many men are there to a square thousand miles in this country? Hardly one. Does not America offer any inducement for men to settle here? The American has dwindled into an Odd Fellow — one who may be known by the development of his organ of gregariousness, and a manifest lack of intellect and cheerful self-reliance; whose first and chief concern, on coming into the world, is to see that the almshouses are in good repair; and, before yet he has lawfully donned the virile garb, to collect a fund for the support of the widows and orphans that may be; who, in short, ventures to live only by the aid of the Mutual Insurance company, which has promised to bury him decently.

It is not a man's duty, as a matter of course, to devote himself to the eradication of any, even the most enormous, wrong; he may still properly have other concerns to engage him; but it is his duty, at least, to wash his hands of it, and, if he gives it no thought longer, not to give it practically his support. If I devote myself to other pursuits and contemplations, I must first see, at least, that I do not pursue them sitting upon another man's shoulders. I must get off him first, that he may pursue his contemplations too. See what gross inconsistency is tolerated. I have heard some of my townsmen say, "I should like to have them order me out to help put down an insurrection of the slaves, or to march to Mexico; — see if I would go"; and yet these very men have each, directly by their allegiance, and so indirectly, at least, by their money, furnished a substitute. The soldier is applauded who refuses to serve in an unjust war by those who do not refuse to sustain the unjust government which makes the war; is applauded by those whose own act and authority he disregards and sets at naught; as if the state were penitent to that degree that it differed one to scourge it while it sinned, but not to that degree that it left off sinning for a moment. Thus, under the name of Order and Civil Government, we are all made at last to pay homage to and support our own meanness. After the first blush of sin comes its indifference; and from immoral it becomes, as it were, unmoral, and not quite unnecessary to that life which we have made.

The broadest and most prevalent error requires the most disinterested   15
virtue to sustain it. The slight reproach to which the virtue of patriotism is commonly liable, the noble are most likely to incur. Those who, while they disapprove of the character and measures of a government, yield to it their allegiance and support are undoubtedly its most conscientious supporters, and so frequently the most serious obstacles to reform. Some are petitioning the State to dissolve the Union, to disregard the requisitions of the President. Why do they not dissolve it themselves — the union between themselves and the State — and refuse to pay their quota into its treasury? Do not they stand in the same relation to the State that the State does to the Union? And have not the same reasons prevented the State from resisting the Union which have prevented them from resisting the State?

How can a man be satisfied to entertain an opinion merely, and enjoy it? Is there any enjoyment in it, if his opinion is that he is aggrieved? If you are cheated out of a single dollar by your neighbor, you do not rest satisfied with knowing that you are cheated, or with saying that you are cheated, or even with petitioning him to pay you your due; but you take effectual steps at once to obtain the full amount, and see that you are never cheated again. Action from principle, the perception and the performance of right, changes things and relations; it is essentially revolutionary, and does not consist wholly with anything which was. It not only divides States and churches, it divides families; ay, it divides the individual, separating the diabolical in him from the divine.

Unjust laws exist: shall we be content to obey them, or shall we endeavor to amend them, and obey them until we have succeeded, or shall we transgress them at once? Men generally, under such a government as this, think that they ought to wait until they have persuaded the majority to alter them. They think that, if they should resist, the remedy would be worse than the evil. But it is the fault of the government itself that the remedy is worse than the evil. It makes it worse. Why is it not more apt to anticipate and provide for reform? Why does it not cherish its wise minority? Why does it cry and resist before it is hurt? Why does it not encourage its citizens to be on the alert to point out its faults, and do better than it would have them? Why does it always crucify Christ, and excommunicate Copernicus and Luther, and pronounce Washington and Franklin rebels?

One would think, that a deliberate and practical denial of its authority was the only offence never contemplated by government; else, why has it not assigned its definite, its suitable and proportionate, penalty? If a man who has no property refuses but once to earn nine shillings for the State, he is put in prison for a period unlimited by any law that I know, and determined only by the discretion of those who placed him there; but if he should steal ninety times nine shillings from the State, he is soon permitted to go at large again.

If the injustice is part of the necessary friction of the machine of government, let it go, let it go: perchance it will wear smooth — certainly the machine will wear out. If the injustice has a spring, or a pulley, or a rope, or a crank, exclusively for itself, then perhaps you may consider whether the remedy will not be worse than the evil; but if it is of such a nature that it requires you to be the agent of injustice to another, then, I say, break the law. Let your life be a counter-friction to stop the machine. What I have to do is to see, at any rate, that I do not lend myself to the wrong which I condemn.

As for adopting the ways which the State has provided for remedying the   20
evil, I know not of such ways. They take too much time, and a man's life will be gone. I have other affairs to attend to. I came into this world, not chiefly to make this a good place to live in, but to live in it, be it good or bad. A man has not everything to do, but something; and because he cannot do everything, it is not necessary that he should do something wrong. It is not my business to be petitioning the Governor or the Legislature any more than it is theirs to petition me; and if they should not bear my petition, what should I do then? But in this case the State has provided no way: its very Constitution is the evil. This may seem to be harsh and stubborn and unconciliatory; but it is to treat with the utmost kindness and consideration the only spirit that can appreciate or deserves it. So is all change for the better, like birth and death, which convulse the body.

I do not hesitate to say, that those who call themselves Abolitionists should at once effectually withdraw their support, both in person and property, from the government of Massachusetts, and not wait till they constitute a majority of one, before they suffer the right to prevail through them. I think that it is enough if they have God on their side, without waiting for that other one. Moreover, any man more right than his neighbors constitutes a majority of one already.

I meet this American government, or its representative, the State government, directly, and face to face, once a year — no more — in the person of its tax-gatherer; this is the only mode in which a man situated as I am necessarily meets it; and it then says distinctly, Recognize me; and the simplest, the most effectual, and, in the present posture of affairs, the indispensablest mode of treating with it on this head, of expressing your little satisfaction with and love for it, is to deny it then. My civil neighbor, the tax-gatherer, is the very man I have to deal with — for it is, after all, with men and not with parchment that I quarrel — and he has voluntarily chosen to be an agent of the government. How shall he ever know well what he is and does as an officer of the government, or as a man, until he is obliged to consider whether he shall treat me, his neighbor, for whom he has respect, as a neighbor and well-disposed man, or as a maniac and disturber of the peace, and see if he can get over this obstruction to his neighborliness without a ruder and more impetuous thought or speech corresponding with his action. I know this well, that if one thousand, if one hundred, if ten men whom I could name — if ten honest men only — ay, if one HONEST man, in this State of Massachusetts, ceasing to hold slaves, were actually to withdraw from this copartnership, and be locked up in the county jail therefor, it would be the abolition of slavery in America. For it matters not how small the beginning may seem to be: what is once well done is done forever. But we love better to talk about it: that we say is our mission. Reform keeps many scores of newspapers in its service, but not one man. If my esteemed neighbor, the State's ambassador, who will devote his days to the settlement of the question of human rights in the Council Chamber, instead of being threatened with the prisons of Carolina, were to sit down the prisoner of Massachusetts, that State which is so anxious to foist the sin of slavery upon her sister — though at present she can discover only an act of inhospitality to be the ground of a quarrel with her — the Legislature would not wholly waive the subject the following winter.

Under a government which imprisons any unjustly, the true place for a just man is also a prison. The proper place today, the only place which Massachusetts has provided for her freer and less desponding spirits, is in her prisons, to be put out and locked out of the State by her own act, as they have already put themselves out by their principles. It is there that the fugitive slave, and the Mexican prisoner on parole, and the Indian come to plead the wrongs of his race should find them; on that separate, but more free and honorable, ground, where the State places those who are not with her, but against her — the only house in a slave State in which a free man can abide with honor. If any think that their influence would be lost there, and their voices no longer afflict the ear of the State, that they would not be as an enemy within its walls, they do not know by how much truth is stronger than error, nor how much more eloquently and effectively he can combat injustice who has experienced a little in his own person. Cast your whole vote, not a strip of paper merely, but your whole influence. A minority is powerless while it conforms to the majority; it is not even a minority then; but it is irresistible when it clogs by its whole weight. If the alternative is to keep all just men in prison, or give up war and slavery, the State will not hesitate which to choose. If a thousand men were not to pay their tax-bills this year, that would not be a violent and bloody measure, as it would be to pay them, and enable the State to commit violence and shed innocent blood. This is, in fact, the definition of a peaceable revolution, if any such is possible. If the tax-gatherer, or any other public officer, asks me, as one has done, "But what shall I do?" my answer is, "If you really wish to do anything, resign your office." When the subject has refused allegiance, and the officer has resigned his office, then the revolution is accomplished. But even suppose blood should flow. Is there not a sort of blood shed when the conscience is wounded? Through this wound a man's real manhood and immortality flow out, and he bleeds to an everlasting death. I see this blood flowing now.

I have contemplated the imprisonment of the offender, rather than the seizure of his goods — though both will serve the same purpose — because they who assert the purest right, and consequently are most dangerous to a corrupt State, commonly have not spent much time in accumulating property. To such the State renders comparatively small service, and a slight tax is wont to appear exorbitant, particularly if they are obliged to earn it by special labor with their hands. If there were one who lived wholly without the use of money, the State itself would hesitate to demand it of him. But the rich man — not to make any invidious comparison — is always sold to the institution which makes him rich. Absolutely speaking, the more money, the less virtue; for money comes between a man and his objects, and obtains them for him; and it was certainly no great virtue to obtain it. It puts to rest many questions which he would otherwise be taxed to answer; while the only new question which it puts is the hard but superfluous one, how to spend it. Thus his moral ground is taken from under his feet. The opportunities of living are diminished in proportion as what are called the "means" are increased. The best thing a man can do for his culture when he is rich is to endeavor to carry out those schemes which he entertained when he was poor. Christ answered the Herodians according to their condition. "Show me the tribute-money," said he; — and one took a penny out of his pocket; — if you use money which has the image of Caesar on it, and which he has made current and valuable, that is, if you are men of the State, and gladly enjoy the advantages of Caesar's government, then pay him back some of his own when he demands it. "Render therefore to Caesar that which is Caesar's, and to God those things which are God's" — leaving them no wiser than before as to which was which; for they did not wish to know.

When I converse with the freest of my neighbors, I perceive that, whatever they may say about the magnitude and seriousness of the question, and their regard for the public tranquility, the long and the short of the matter is, that they cannot spare the protection of the existing government, and they dread the consequences to their property and families of disobedience to it. For my own part, I should not like to think that I ever rely on the protection of the State. But, if I deny the authority of the State when it presents its tax-bill, it will soon take and waste all my property, and so harass me and my children without end. This is hard. This makes it impossible for a man to live honestly, and at the same time comfortably, in outward respects. It will not be worth the while to accumulate property; that would be sure to go again. You must hire or squat somewhere, and raise but a small crop, and eat that soon. You must live within yourself, and depend upon yourself always tucked up and ready for a start, and not have many affairs. A man may grow rich in Turkey even, if he will be in all respects a good subject of the Turkish government. Confucius said: "If a state is governed by the principles of reason, poverty and misery are subjects of shame; if a state is not governed by the principles of reason, riches and honors are the subjects of shame." No: until I want the protection of Massachusetts to be extended to me in some distant Southern port, where my liberty is endangered, or until I am bent solely on building up an estate at home by peaceful enterprise, I can afford to refuse allegiance to Massachusetts, and her right to my property and life. It costs me less in every sense to incur the penalty of disobedience to the State than it would to obey. I should feel as if I were worth less in that case.

Some years ago, the State met me in behalf of the Church, and commanded me to pay a certain sum toward the support of a clergyman whose preaching my father attended, but never I myself. "Pay," it said, "or be locked up in the jail." I declined to pay. But, unfortunately, another man saw fit to pay it. I did not see why the schoolmaster should be taxed to support the priest, and not the priest the schoolmaster; for I was not the State's schoolmaster, but I supported myself by voluntary subscription. I did not see why the lyceum should not present its tax-bill, and have the State to back its demand, as well as the Church. However, at the request of the selectmen, I condescended to make some such statement as this in writing: — "Know all men by these presents, that I, Henry Thoreau, do not wish to be regarded as a member of any incorporated society which I have not joined." This I gave to the town clerk; and he has it. The State, having thus learned that I did not wish to be regarded as a member of that church, has never made a like demand on me since; though it said that it must adhere to its original presumption that time. If I had known how to name them, I should then have signed off in detail from all the societies which I never signed on to; but I did not know where to find a complete list.

I have paid no poll-tax for six years. I was put into a jail once on this account, for one night; and, as I stood considering the walls of solid stone, two or three feet thick, the door of wood and iron, a foot thick, and the iron grating which strained the light, I could not help being struck with the foolishness of that institution which treated me as if I were mere flesh and blood and bones, to be locked up. I wondered that it should have concluded at length that this was the best use it could put me to, and had never thought to avail itself of my services in some way. I saw that, if there was a wall of stone between me and my townsmen, there was a still more difficult one to climb or break through before they could get to be as free as I was. I did not for a moment feel confined, and the walls seemed a great waste of stone and mortar. I felt as if I alone of all my townsmen had paid my tax. They plainly did not know how to treat me, but behaved like persons who are underbred. In every threat and in every compliment there was a blunder; for they thought that my chief desire was to stand the other side of that stone wall. I could not but smile to see how industriously they locked the door on my meditations, which followed them out again without let or hindrance, and they were really all that was dangerous. As they could not reach me, they had resolved to punish my body; just as boys, if they cannot come at some person against whom they have a spite, will abuse his dog. I saw that the State was half-witted, that it was timid as a lone woman with her silver spoons, and that it did not know its friends from its foes, and I lost all my remaining respect for it, and pitied it.

Thus the State never intentionally confronts a man's sense, intellectual or moral, but only his body, his senses. It is not armed with superior wit or honesty, but with superior physical strength. I was not born to be forced. I will breathe after my own fashion. Let us see who is the strongest. What force has a multitude? They only can force me who obey a higher law than I. They force me to become like themselves. I do not hear of men being forced to have this way or that by masses of men. What sort of life were that to live? When I meet a government which says to me, "Your money or your life," why should I be in haste to give it my money? It may be in a great strait, and not know what to do: I cannot help that. It must help itself; do as I do. It is not worth the while to snivel about it. I am not responsible for the successful working of the machinery of society. I am not the son of the engineer. I perceive that, when an acorn and a chestnut fall side by side, the one does not remain inert to make way for the other, but both obey their own laws, and spring and grow and flourish as best they can, till one, perchance, overshadows and destroys the other. If a plant cannot live according to its nature, it dies; and so a man.

The night in prison was novel and interesting enough. The prisoners in their shirt-sleeves were enjoying a chat and the evening air in the doorway, when I entered. But the jailer said, "Come, boys, it is time to lock up"; and so they dispersed, and I heard the sound of their steps returning into the hollow apartments. My room-mate was introduced to me by the jailer as "a first-rate fellow and a clever man." When the door was locked, he showed me where to hang my hat, and how he managed matters there. The rooms were whitewashed once a month; and this one, at least, was the whitest, most simply furnished, and probably the neatest apartment in the town. He naturally wanted to know where I came from, and what brought me there; and, when I had told him, I asked him in my turn how he came there, presuming him to be an honest man, of course; and, as the world goes, I believe he was. "Why," said he, "they accuse me of burning a barn; but I never did it." As near as I could discover, he had probably gone to bed in a barn when drunk, and smoked his pipe there; and so a barn was burnt. He had the reputation of being a clever man, had been there some three months waiting for his trial to come on, and would have to wait as much longer; but he was quite domesticated and contented, since he got his board for nothing, and thought that he was well treated.

He occupied one window, and I the other; and I saw that if one stayed there long, his principal business would be to look out the window. I had soon read all the tracts that were left there, and examined where former prisoners had broken out, and where a grate had been sawed off, and heard the history of the various occupants of that room; for I found that even here there was a history and a gossip which never circulated beyond the walls of the jail. Probably this is the only house in the town where verses are composed, which are afterward printed in a circular form, but not published. I was shown quite a long list of

30

verses which were composed by some young men who had been detected in an attempt to escape, who avenged themselves by singing them.

I pumped my fellow-prisoner as dry as I could, for fear I should never see him again; but at length he showed me which was my bed, and left me to blow out the lamp.

It was like travelling into a far country, such as I had never expected to behold, to lie there for one night. It seemed to me that I never had heard the town clock strike before, nor the evening sounds of the village; for we slept with the windows open, which were inside the grating. It was to see my native village in the light of the Middle Ages, and our Concord was turned into a Rhine stream, and visions of knights and castles passed before me. They were the voices of old burghers that I heard in the streets. I was an involuntary spectator and auditor of whatever was done and said in the kitchen of the adjacent village inn — a wholly new and rare experience to me. It was a closer view of my native town. I was fairly inside of it. I never had seen its institutions before. This is one of its peculiar institutions; for it is a shire town. I began to comprehend what its inhabitants were about.

In the morning, our breakfasts were put through the hole in the door, in small oblong-square tin pans, made to fit, and holding a pint of chocolate, with brown bread, and an iron spoon. When they called for the vessels again, I was green enough to return what bread I had left; but my comrade seized it, and said that I should lay that up for lunch or dinner. Soon after he was let out to work at haying in a neighboring field, whither he went every day, and would not be back till noon; so he bade me good-day, saying that he doubted if he should see me again.

When I came out of prison — for some one interfered, and paid that tax — I did not perceive that great changes had taken place on the common, such as he observed who went in a youth and emerged a tottering and gray-headed man; and yet a change had to my eyes come over the scene — the town, and State, and country — greater than any that mere time could effect. I saw yet more distinctly the State in which I lived. I saw to what extent the people among whom I lived could be trusted as good neighbors and friends; that their friendship was for summer weather only; that they did not greatly propose to do right; that they were a distinct race from me by their prejudices and superstitions, as the Chinamen and Malays are; that in their sacrifices to humanity they ran no risks, not even to their property; that after all they were not so noble but they treated the thief as he had treated them, and hoped, by a certain outward observance and a few prayers, and by walking in a particular straight though useless path from time to time, to save their souls. This may be to judge my neighbors harshly; for I believe that many of them are not aware that they have such an institution as the jail in their village.

It was formerly the custom in our village, when a poor debtor came out of jail, for his acquaintances to salute him, looking through their fingers, which were crossed to represent the grating of a jail window, "How do ye do?" My neighbors did not thus salute me, but first looked at me, and then at one another, as if I had returned from a long journey. I was put into jail as I was going

35

to the shoemaker's to get a shoe which was mended. When I was let out the next morning, I proceeded to finish my errand, and, having put on my mended shoe, joined a huckleberry party, who were impatient to put themselves under my conduct; and in half an hour—for the horse was soon tackled—was in the midst of a huckleberry field, on one of our highest hills, two miles off, and then the State was nowhere to be seen.

This is the whole history of "My Prisons."

I have never declined paying the highway tax, because I am as desirous of being a good neighbor as I am of being a bad subject; and as for supporting schools, I am doing my part to educate my fellow-countrymen now. It is for no particular item in the tax-bill that I refuse to pay it. I simply wish to refuse allegiance to the State, to withdraw and stand aloof from it effectually. I do not care to trace the course of my dollar, if I could, till it buys a man or a musket to shoot one with—the dollar is innocent—but I am concerned to trace the effects of my allegiance. In fact, I quietly declare war with the State, after my fashion, though I will still make what use and get what advantage of her I can, as is usual in such cases.

If others pay the tax which is demanded of me, from a sympathy with the State, they do but what they have already done in their own case, or rather they abet injustice to a greater extent than the State requires. If they pay the tax from a mistaken interest in the individual taxed, to save his property, or prevent his going to jail, it is because they have not considered wisely how far they let their private feelings interfere with the public good.

This, then, is my position at present. But one cannot be too much on his guard in such a case, lest his action be biased by obstinacy or an undue regard for the opinions of men. Let him see that he does only what belongs to himself and to the hour.

I think sometimes, Why, this people mean well, they are only ignorant; they would do better if they knew how: why give your neighbors this pain to treat you as they are not inclined to? But I think again, This is no reason why I should do as they do, or permit others to suffer much greater pain of a different kind. Again, I sometimes say to myself, When many millions of men, without heat, without ill will, without personal feeling of any kind, demand of you a few shillings only, without the possibility, such is their constitution, of retracting or altering their present demand, and without the possibility, on your side, of appeal to any other millions, why expose yourself to this overwhelming brute force? You do not resist cold and hunger, the winds and the waves, thus obstinately; you quietly submit to a thousand similar necessities. You do not put your head into the fire. But just in proportion as I regard this as not wholly a brute force, but partly a human force, and consider that I have relations to those millions as to so many millions of men, and not of mere brute or inanimate things, I see that appeal is possible, first and instantaneously, from them to the Maker of them, and, secondly, from them to themselves. But if I put my head deliberately into the fire, there is no appeal to fire or to the Maker of fire, and I have only myself to blame. If I could convince myself that I have any right to be satisfied with men as they are, and to treat them accordingly, and

40

not according, in some respects, to my requisitions and expectations of what they and I ought to be, then, like a good Mussulman° and fatalist, I should endeavor to be satisfied with things as they are, and say it is the will of God. And, above all, there is this difference between resisting this and a purely brute or natural force, that I can resist this with some effect; but I cannot expect, like Orpheus, to change the nature of the rocks and trees and beasts.

I do not wish to quarrel with any man or nation. I do not wish to split hairs, to make fine distinctions, or set myself up as better than my neighbors. I seek rather, I may say, even an excuse for conforming to the laws of the land. I am but too ready to conform to them. Indeed, I have reason to suspect myself on this head; and each year, as the tax-gatherer comes round, I find myself disposed to review the acts and position of the general and State governments, and the spirit of the people, to discover a pretext for conformity.

> "We must affect our country as our parents,
>   And if at any time we alienate
> Our love or industry from doing it honor,
> We must respect effects and teach the soul
>   Matter of conscience and religion,
>   And not desire of rule or benefit."

I believe that the State will soon be able to take all my work of this sort out of my hands, and then I shall be no better a patriot than my fellow-countrymen. Seen from a lower point of view, the Constitution, with all its faults, is very good; the law and the courts are very respectable; even this State and this American government are, in many respects, very admirable, and rare things, to be thankful for, such as a great many have described them; but seen from a point of view a little higher, they are what I have described them; seen from a higher still, and the highest, who shall say what they are, or that they are worth looking at or thinking of at all? However, the government does not concern me much, and I shall bestow the fewest possible thoughts on it. It is not many moments that I live under a government, even in this world. If a man is thought-free, fancy-free, imagination-free, that which is not never for a long time appearing to be to him, unwise rulers or reformers cannot fatally interrupt him.

I know that most men think differently from myself; but those whose lives are by profession devoted to the study of these or kindred subjects content me as little as any. Statesmen and legislators, standing so completely within the institution, never distinctly and nakedly behold it. They speak of moving society, but have no resting-place without it. They may be men of a certain experience and discrimination, and have no doubt invented ingenious and even useful systems, for which we sincerely thank them; but all their wit and usefulness lie within certain not very wide limits. They are wont to forget that the world is not governed by policy and expediency. Webster° never goes behind government, and so cannot speak with authority about it. His words are wisdom to those legislators who contemplate no essential reform in the existing

---

Mussulman: Muslim.   **Daniel Webster (1782–1852):** Celebrated U.S. Senator and Secretary of State who advocated compromise between slave and free states.

government; but for thinkers, and those who legislate for all time, he never once glances at the subject. I know of those whose serene and wise speculations on this theme would soon reveal the limits of his mind's range and hospitality. Yet, compared with the cheap professions of most reformers, and the still cheaper wisdom and eloquence of politicians in general, his are almost the only sensible and valuable words, and we thank Heaven for him. Comparatively, he is always strong, original, and, above all, practical. Still, his quality is not wisdom, but prudence. The lawyer's truth is not Truth, but consistency or a consistent expediency. Truth is always in harmony with herself, and is not concerned chiefly to reveal the justice that may consist with wrong-doing. He well deserves to be called, as he has been called, the Defender of the Constitution. There are really no blows to be given by him but defensive ones. He is not a leader, but a follower. His leaders are the men of '87 — "I have never made an effort," he says, "and never propose to make an effort; I have never countenanced an effort, and never mean to countenance an effort, to disturb the arrangement as originally made, by which the various States came into the Union." Still thinking of the sanction which the Constitution gives to slavery, he says, "Because it was a part of the original compact — let it stand." Notwithstanding his special acuteness and ability, he is unable to take a fact out of its merely political relations, and behold it as it lies absolutely to be disposed of by the intellect — what, for instance, it behooves a man to do here in America today with regard to slavery — but ventures, or is driven, to make some such desperate answer as the following, while professing to speak absolutely, and as a private man — from which what new and singular code of social duties might be inferred? "The manner," says he, "in which the governments of those States where slavery exists are to regulate it is for their own consideration, under their responsibility to their constituents, to the general laws of propriety, humanity, and justice, and to God. Associations formed elsewhere, springing from a feeling of humanity, or any other cause, have nothing whatever to do with it. They have never received any encouragement from me, and they never will."

They who know of no purer sources of truth, who have traced up its stream no higher, stand, and wisely stand, by the Bible and the Constitution, and drink at it there with reverence and humility; but they who behold where it comes trickling into this lake or that pool, gird up their loins once more, and continue their pilgrimage toward its fountain-head.

No man with a genius for legislation has appeared in America. They are rare in the history of the world. There are orators, politicians, and eloquent men, by the thousand; but the speaker has not yet opened his mouth to speak who is capable of settling the much-vexed questions of the day. We love eloquence for its own sake, and not for any truth which it may utter, or any heroism it may inspire. Our legislators have not yet learned the comparative value of free trade and of freedom, of union, and of rectitude, to a nation. They have no genius or talent for comparatively humble questions of taxation and finance, commerce and manufactures and agriculture. If we were left solely to the wordy wit of legislators in Congress for our guidance, uncorrected by the seasonable experience and the effectual complaints of the people, America would not long retain her rank among the nations. For eighteen hundred years, though perchance I have no right to say it, the New Testament has been written; yet where is the legislator who has wisdom and practical talent enough to avail himself of the light which it sheds on the science of legislation?

The authority of government, even such as I am willing to submit to — for I will cheerfully obey those who know and can do better than I, and in many things even those who neither know nor can do so well — is still an impure one: to be strictly just, it must have the sanction and consent of the governed. It can have no pure right over my person and property but what I concede to it. The progress from an absolute to a limited monarchy, from a limited monarchy to a democracy, is a progress toward a true respect for the individual. Even the Chinese philosopher was wise enough to regard the individual as the basis of the empire. Is a democracy, such as we know it, the last improvement possible in government? Is it not possible to take a step further towards recognizing and organizing the rights of man? There will never be a really free and enlightened State until the State comes to recognize the individual as a higher and independent power, from which all its own power and authority are derived, and treats him accordingly. I please myself with imagining a State at least which can afford to be just to all men, and to treat the individual with respect as a neighbor; which even would not think it inconsistent with its own repose if a few were to live aloof from it, not meddling with it, nor embraced by it, who fulfilled all the duties of neighbors and fellow-men. A State which bore this kind of fruit, and suffered it to drop off as fast as it ripened, would prepare the way for a still more perfect and glorious State, which also I have imagined, but not yet anywhere seen.   *[1849]*

≣ THINKING ABOUT THE TEXT

1. What is Thoreau's view of government in general? Identify specific passages that relate his major points about it. Do any groups or individuals put forth this view today? Consider the theories of government expressed by various public figures, political parties, and personal relatives or friends.

2. What would you say to someone who argues that Thoreau is encouraging anyone who disagrees with a law to break it? Identify specific passages that support this inference or complicate it.

3. Two words that Thoreau repeats in various forms are *machine* and *expediency*. What ideas is he emphasizing by using these words multiple times? Note the specific passages where *machine* or *expediency* appear.

4. Note where Thoreau refers to "man." Writers of his time often used this word in a generic sense, intending it to mean women as well as men. Do you assume that this is always Thoreau's intent, or are there moments when you think that he has only the male gender in mind? Explain.

5. What specific points does Thoreau seem most concerned to make as he describes his night in jail? Why do you suppose he held off describing it until near the end of the essay?

REBECCA SOLNIT

The Thoreau Problem

Rebecca Solnit (b. 1961) writes chiefly about politics, ecology, human rights, and the visual arts. Her dozen books include As Eve Said to the Serpent: On Landscape, Gender, and Art *(2001);* River of Shadows: Eadweard Muybridge and the Technological Wild West *(2003), for which she won a National Book Critics Circle Award; and* A Paradise Built in Hell: The Extraordinary Communities That Arise in Disaster *(2009), a study of people's resilience in the wake of calamities like Hurricane Katrina. Solnit regularly contributes commentaries to the Web site* Tomdispatch.com *and to* Orion, *an environmental magazine, which published the following essay in its May/June 2007 issue.*

Thoreau was emphatic about the huckleberries. In one of his two most famous pieces of writing, "Civil Disobedience," he concluded his account of a night in Concord's jail with, "I was put in jail as I was going to the shoemaker's to get a shoe which was mended. When I was let out the next morning, I proceeded to finish my errand, and having put on my mended shoe, joined a huckleberry party." He told the same story again in *Walden,* this time saying that he "returned to the woods in season to get my dinner of huckleberries on Fair-Haven Hill." That he told it twice suggests that he considered the conjunction of prisons and berry parties, of the landscape of incarceration and of pastoral pleasure, significant. But why?

The famous night in jail took place about halfway through his stay on Emerson's woodlot at Walden Pond. His two-year stint in the small cabin he built himself is often portrayed as a monastic retreat from the world of human affairs into the world of nature, though he went back to town to eat and talk with friends and family and to pick up money doing odd jobs that didn't fit into *Walden's* narrative. He went to jail not only because he felt passionately enough about national affairs — slavery and the war on Mexico — to refuse to pay his tax, but also because the town jailer ran into him while he was getting his shoe mended.

Says the introduction to my paperback edition of *Walden* and "Civil Disobedience": "As much as Thoreau wanted to disentangle himself from other people's problems so he could get on with his own life, he sometimes found that the issue of black slavery spoiled his country walks. His social conscience impinged on his consciousness, even though he believed that his duty was not to eradicate social evils but to live his life independently." To believe this is to believe that the woods were far from Concord jail not merely by foot but by thought. To believe that conscience is an imposition upon consciousness is to regard engagement as a hijacker rather than a rudder, interference with one's true purpose rather than perhaps at least part of that purpose.

Thoreau did not believe so or wish that it were so, and he contradicted this isolationist statement explicitly in "Civil Disobedience" (completed, unlike *Walden*, shortly after those years in the woods), but many who have charge of his reputation do. These scholars and critics permit no conversation, let alone any unity, between Thoreau the rebel, intransigent muse to Gandhi and Martin Luther King, and that other Thoreau who wrote about autumnal tints, ice, light, color, grasses, woodchucks, and other natural histories, essays easily and often defanged and diced up into inspiring extracts. But for Thoreau, any subject was a good enough starting point to travel any distance, toward any destination.

This compartmentalizing of Thoreau is a microcosm of a larger partition   5
in American thought, a fence built in the belief that places in the imagination can be contained. Those who deny that nature and culture, landscape and politics, the city and the country are inextricably interfused have undermined the connections for all of us (so few have been able to find Thoreau's short, direct route between them since). This makes politics dreary and landscape trivial, a vacation site. It banishes certain thoughts, including the thought that much of what the environmental movement dubbed wilderness was or is indigenous homeland — a very social and political space indeed, then and now — and especially the thought that Thoreau in jail must have contemplated the following day's huckleberry party, and Thoreau among the huckleberries must have ruminated on his stay in jail.

If "black slavery spoiled his country walks," it spoiled the slaves' country walks even more. Thus the unresisting walk to jail. "Eastward, I go only by force; but westward I go free," Thoreau wrote. His thoughts on the matter might be summed up this way: You head for the hills to enjoy the best of what the world is at this moment; you head for confrontation, for resistance, for picket lines to protect it, to liberate it. Thus it is that the road to paradise often runs through prison, thus it is that Thoreau went to jail to enjoy a better country, and thus it is that one of his greatest students, Martin Luther King Jr., found himself in jail and eventually in the way of a bullet on what got called the long road to freedom, whose goal he spoke of as the mountaintop.

Conventional environmental writing has often maintained a strict silence on or even an animosity toward the city, despite its importance as a lower-impact place for the majority to live, its intricate relations to the rural, and the direct routes between the two. Imagining the woods or any untrammeled landscape as an unsocial place, an outside, also depends on erasing those who dwelt and sometimes still dwell there, the original Americans — and one more thing that can be said in favor of Thoreau is that he spent a lot of time imaginatively repopulating with Indians the woods around Concord, and even prepared quantities of notes for a never-attempted history of Native America.

Not that those woods were unsocial even after the aboriginal population was driven out. "Visitors" was one of the chapters of *Walden*, and in it he describes meeting in the woods and guiding farther on the road to freedom run-away slaves. Rather than ruining his country walks, some slaves joined him on them, or perhaps he joined them in the act of becoming free. Some of those he guided were on the Underground Railroad, in which his mother and sisters in Concord were deeply involved, and a few months after that famous night in jail Thoreau hosted a meeting of Concord's most important abolitionist group, the Concord Female Anti-Slavery Society, at his Walden Pond hut. What kind of a forest was this, with slaves, rebels, and the ghosts of the original inhabitants all moving through the trees?

If he went to jail to demonstrate his commitment to the freedom of others, he went to the berries to exercise his own recovered freedom, the liberty to do whatever he wished, and the evidence in all his writing is that he very often wished to pick berries. There's a widespread belief, among both activists and those who cluck disapprovingly over insufficiently austere activists, that ideal-ists should not enjoy any pleasure denied to others, that beauty, sensuality, de-light all ought to be stalled behind some dam that only the imagined revolution will break. This schism creates, as the alternative to a life of selfless devotion, a life of flight from engagement, which seems to be one way those years at Walden Pond are sometimes portrayed. But change is not always by revolution, the deprived don't generally wish that the rest of us would join them in depri-vation, and a passion for justice and pleasure in small things are not incompat-ible. That's part of what the short jaunt from jail to hill says.

Perhaps prison is anything that severs and alienates, paradise is the re-   10
claimed commons with the fences thrown down, and so any step toward con-nection and communion is a step toward paradise, even if the route detours through jail. Thoreau was demonstrating on that one day in Concord in June of 1847 both what dedication to freedom was and what enjoyment of freedom might look like — free association, free roaming, the picking of the fruits of the Earth for free, free choice of commitments. That is the direct route to paradise, the one road worth traveling.   *[2007]*

■ THINKING ABOUT THE TEXT

1. What, according to Solnit, *is* "the Thoreau problem," and for whom does it exist? What larger problem in American thinking does she think it illustrates?

2. What does Solnit emphasize about the woods surrounding Thoreau? How is this emphasis part of her effort to solve "the Thoreau problem"?

3. How do prisons and journeys function as metaphors in Solnit's argu-ment? Trace the passages where these references appear.

4. Solnit wrote this essay for *Orion*, a magazine whose readers are gener-ally interested in environmental issues and are likely to be fond of Thoreau's *Walden* as well as other writings of his about nature. At what moments does she seem to have this specific audience very much in mind?

5. To what extent do you agree with Solnit's claim that "a passion for justice and pleasure in small things are not incompatible" (para. 9)? Whom, if anyone, do you see combining such "passion" and "pleasure" today?

■ **MAKING COMPARISONS**

1. As an analysis of Thoreau's essay, Solnit's is rather brief. What major points of his does she *not* touch on? Should she have referred to any of these? Why, or why not?

2. What aspects of Thoreau's life and world does Solnit discuss *more* than he does in "Civil Disobedience"?

3. Should Solnit have told us about how she personally tries to implement the values and ideas of Thoreau's that she admires? Explain.

MARTIN LUTHER KING JR.
Letter from Birmingham Jail°

A native of Atlanta, Martin Luther King Jr. (1929–1968) was the son of a Baptist minister and a schoolteacher. After graduating from Morehouse College in Atlanta, he studied at several universities before receiving a Ph.D. in theology from Boston University. He married Coretta Scott in 1955 and had four children. In 1959, he resigned his position as pastor of a church in Alabama to move back to Atlanta to direct the activities of the Southern Christian Leadership Conference. From 1960 until his death, he was copastor with his father at Ebenezer Baptist Church in Atlanta.

Dr. King was a central figure in the civil rights movement. Pivotal in the successful Montgomery bus boycott in 1956, he was arrested more than thirty times for his participation in nonviolent demonstrations. His charismatic leadership and eloquent speeches stirred and inspired the conscience of a generation. Dr. King's idea of "somebodiness" gave black and poor people a new sense of worth and dignity, and his philosophy of nonviolent direct action helped change the nation's attitudes and priorities. His famous "I have a dream" speech at the Lincoln Memorial in 1963 and the classic "Letter" printed here are among the most important documents in American history. At thirty-five, he was the youngest person to win the Nobel Prize for peace. His assassination in 1968 set off riots in more than a hundred cities. Today the nation honors his birthday as a holiday.

Letter from Birmingham Jail: This response to a published statement by eight fellow clergymen from Alabama (Bishop C. C. J. Carpenter, Bishop Joseph A. Durick, Rabbi Hilton L. Grafman, Bishop Paul Hardin, Bishop Holan B. Harmon, the Reverend George M. Murray, the Reverend Edward V. Ramage, and the Reverend Earl Stallings) was composed under somewhat constricting circumstances. Begun on the margins of the newspaper in which the statement appeared while I was in jail, the letter was continued on scraps of writing paper supplied by a friendly Negro trusty, and concluded on a pad my attorneys were eventually permitted to leave me. Although the text remains in substance unaltered, I have indulged in the author's prerogative of polishing it for publication. [King's note.]

My Dear Fellow Clergymen:
   While confined here in the Birmingham city jail, I came across your recent statement calling my present activities "unwise and untimely." Seldom do I pause to answer criticism of my work and ideas. If I sought to answer all the criticisms that cross my desk, my secretaries would have little time for anything other than such correspondence in the course of the day, and I would have no time for constructive work. But since I feel that you are men of genuine good will and that your criticisms are sincerely set forth, I want to try to answer your statement in what I hope will be patient and reasonable terms.
   I think I should indicate why I am here in Birmingham, since you have been influenced by the view which argues against "outsiders coming in." I have the honor of serving as president of the Southern Christian Leadership Conference, an organization operating in every southern state, with headquarters in Atlanta, Georgia. We have some eighty-five affiliated organizations across the South, and one of them is the Alabama Christian Movement for Human Rights. Frequently we share staff, educational, and financial resources with our affiliates. Several months ago the affiliate here in Birmingham asked us to be on call to engage in a nonviolent direct-action program if such were deemed necessary. We readily consented, and when the hour came we lived up to our promise. So I, along with several members of my staff, am here because I was invited here. I am here because I have organizational ties here.
   But more basically, I am in Birmingham because injustice is here. Just as the prophets of the eighth century B.C. left their villages and carried their "thus saith the Lord" far beyond the boundaries of their home towns, and just as the Apostle Paul left his village of Tarsus° and carried the gospel of Jesus Christ to the far corners of the Greco-Roman world, so am I compelled to carry the gospel of freedom beyond my own home town. Like Paul, I must constantly respond to the Macedonian call for aid.°
   Moreover, I am cognizant of the interrelatedness of all communities and states. I cannot sit idly by in Atlanta and not be concerned about what happens in Birmingham. Injustice anywhere is a threat to justice everywhere. We are caught in an inescapable network of mutuality, tied in a single garment of destiny. Whatever affects one directly, affects all indirectly. Never again can we afford to live with the narrow, provincial "outside agitator" idea. Anyone who lives inside the United States can never be considered an outsider anywhere within its bounds.
   You deplore the demonstrations taking place in Birmingham. But your statement, I am sorry to say, fails to express a similar concern for the conditions that brought about the demonstrations. I am sure that none of you would want to rest content with the superficial kind of social analysis that deals merely with effects and does not grapple with the underlying causes. It is unfortunate that demonstrations are taking place in Birmingham, but it is even more unfortunate that the city's white power structure left the Negro community with no alternative.

5

Tarsus: Present-day Turkey, birthplace of St. Paul.   **Macedonian . . . aid:** The Christian community in Macedonia often called on Paul for aid.

In any nonviolent campaign there are four basic steps: collection of the facts to determine whether injustices exist; negotiation; self-purification; and direct action. We have gone through all these steps in Birmingham. There can be no gainsaying the fact that racial injustice engulfs this community. Birmingham is probably the most thoroughly segregated city in the United States. Its ugly record of brutality is widely known. Negroes have experienced grossly unjust treatment in the courts. There have been more unsolved bombings of Negro homes and churches in Birmingham than in any other city in the nation. These are the hard, brutal facts of the case. On the basis of these conditions, Negro leaders sought to negotiate with the city fathers. But the latter consistently refused to engage in good-faith negotiation.

Then, last September, came the opportunity to talk with leaders of Birmingham's economic community. In the course of the negotiations, certain promises were made by the merchants — for example, to remove the stores' humiliating racial signs. On the basis of these promises, the Reverend Fred Shuttlesworth and the leaders of the Alabama Christian Movement for Human Rights agreed to a moratorium on all demonstrations. As the weeks and months went by, we realized that we were the victims of a broken promise. A few signs, briefly removed, returned; the others remained.

As in so many past experiences, our hopes had been blasted, and the shadow of deep disappointment settled upon us. We had no alternative except to prepare for direct action, whereby we would present our very bodies as a means of laying our case before the conscience of the local and the national community. Mindful of the difficulties involved, we decided to undertake a process of self-purification. We began a series of workshops on nonviolence, and we repeatedly asked ourselves: "Are you able to accept blows without retaliating?" "Are you able to endure the ordeal of jail?" We decided to schedule our direct-action program for the Easter season, realizing that except for Christmas, this is the main shopping period of the year. Knowing that a strong economic-withdrawal program would be the by-product of direct action, we felt that this would be the best time to bring pressure to bear on the merchants for the needed change.

Then it occurred to us that Birmingham's mayoral election was coming up in March, and we speedily decided to postpone action until after election-day. When we discovered that the Commissioner of Public Safety, Eugene "Bull" Connor, had piled up enough votes to be in the run-off, we decided again to postpone action until the day after the run-off so that the demonstrations could not be used to cloud the issues. Like many others, we waited to see Mr. Connor defeated, and to this end we endured postponement after postponement. Having aided in this community need, we felt that our direct-action program could be delayed no longer.

You may well ask, "Why direct action? Why sit-ins, marches, and so forth? Isn't negotiation a better path?" You are quite right in calling for negotiation. Indeed, this is the very purpose of direct action. Nonviolent direct action seeks to create such a crisis and foster such a tension that a community which has constantly refused to negotiate is forced to confront the issue. It seeks so to dra-   10 matize the issue that it can no longer be ignored. My citing the creation of tension as part of the work of the nonviolent-resister may sound rather shocking. But I must confess that I am not afraid of the word "tension." I have earnestly opposed violent tension, but there is a type of constructive, nonviolent tension which is necessary for growth. Just as Socrates° felt that it was necessary to create a tension in the mind so that individuals could rise from the bondage of myths and half-truths to the unfettered realm of creative analysis and objective appraisal, so must we see the need for nonviolent gadflies to create the kind of tension in society that will help men rise from the dark depths of prejudice and racism to the majestic heights of understanding and brotherhood.

The purpose of our direct-action program is to create a situation so crisis-packed that it will inevitably open the door to negotiation. I therefore concur with you in your call for negotiation. Too long has our beloved Southland been bogged down in a tragic effort to live in monologue rather than dialogue.

One of the basic points in your statement is that the action that I and my associates have taken in Birmingham is untimely. Some have asked: "Why didn't you give the new city administration time to act?" The only answer that I can give to this query is that the new Birmingham administration must be prodded about as much as the outgoing one, before it will act. We are sadly mistaken if we feel that the election of Albert Boutwell as mayor will bring the millennium to Birmingham. While Mr. Boutwell is a much more gentle person than Mr. Connor, they are both segregationists, dedicated to maintenance of the status quo. I have hoped that Mr. Boutwell will be reasonable enough to see the futility of massive resistance to desegregation. But he will not see this without pressure from devotees of civil rights. My friends, I must say to you that we have not made a single gain in civil rights without determined legal and nonviolent pressure. Lamentably, it is an historical fact that privileged groups seldom give up their privileges voluntarily. Individuals may see the moral light and voluntarily give up their unjust posture; but, as Reinhold Niebuhr° has reminded us, groups tend to be more immoral than individuals.

We know through painful experience that freedom is never voluntarily given by the oppressor; it must be demanded by the oppressed. Frankly, I have yet to engage in a direct-action campaign that was "well timed" in the view of those who have not suffered unduly from the disease of segregation. For years now I have heard the word "Wait!" It rings in the ear of every Negro with piercing familiarity. This "Wait" has almost always meant "Never." We must come to see, with one of our distinguished jurists, that "justice too long delayed is justice denied."

We have waited for more than 340 years for our constitutional and God-given rights. The nations of Asia and Africa are moving with jetlike speed toward gaining political independence, but we still creep at horse-and-buggy pace toward gaining a cup of coffee at a lunch counter. Perhaps it is easy for

---

Socrates (469–399 B.C.E.): The Greek philosopher would feign ignorance to expose the errors in his opponent's arguments. **Reinhold Niebuhr (1892–1971):** American theologian.

those who have never felt the stinging darts of segregation to say, "Wait." But when you have seen vicious mobs lynch your mothers and fathers at will and drown your sisters and brothers at whim; when you have seen hate-filled policemen curse, kick, and even kill your black brothers and sisters; when you see the vast majority of your twenty million Negro brothers smothering in an airtight cage of poverty in the midst of an affluent society; when you suddenly find your tongue twisted and your speech stammering as you seek to explain to your six-year-old daughter why she can't go to the public amusement park that has just been advertised on television, and see tears welling up in her eyes when she is told that Funtown is closed to colored children, and see ominous clouds of inferiority beginning to form in her little mental sky, and see her beginning to distort her personality by developing an unconscious bitterness toward white people; when you have to concoct an answer for a five-year-old son who is asking, "Daddy, why do white people treat colored people so mean?"; when you take a cross-country drive and find it necessary to sleep night after night in the uncomfortable corners of your automobile because no motel will accept you; when you are humiliated day in and day out by nagging signs reading "white" and "colored"; when your first name becomes "nigger," your middle name becomes "boy" (however old you are), and your last name becomes "John," and your wife and mother are never given the respected title "Mrs."; when you are harried by day and haunted by night by the fact that you are a Negro, living constantly at tiptoe stance, never quite knowing what to expect next, and are plagued with inner fears and outer resentments; when you are forever fighting a degenerating sense of "nobodiness" — then you will understand why we find it difficult to wait. There comes a time when the cup of endurance runs over, and men are no longer willing to be plunged into the abyss of despair. I hope, sirs, you can understand our legitimate and unavoidable impatience.

You express a great deal of anxiety over our willingness to break laws. This   15
is certainly a legitimate concern. Since we so diligently urge people to obey the Supreme Court's decision of 1954 outlawing segregation in the public schools, at first glance it may seem rather paradoxical for us consciously to break laws. One may well ask: "How can you advocate breaking some laws and obeying others?" The answer lies in the fact that there are two types of laws: just and unjust. I would be the first to advocate obeying just laws. One has not only a legal but a moral responsibility to obey just laws. Conversely, one has a moral responsibility to disobey unjust laws. I would agree with St. Augustine that "an unjust law is no law at all."

Now, what is the difference between the two? How does one determine whether a law is just or unjust? A just law is a man-made code that squares with the moral law or the law of God. An unjust law is a code that is out of harmony with the moral law. To put it in the terms of St. Thomas Aquinas: An unjust law is a human law that is not rooted in eternal law and natural law. Any law that uplifts human personality is just. Any law that degrades human personality is unjust. All segregation statutes are unjust because segregation distorts the soul and damages the personality. It gives the segregator a false sense of superiority and the segregated a false sense of inferiority. Segregation, to use the terminology of the Jewish philosopher Martin Buber, substitutes an "I-it" relationship for an "I-thou" relationship and ends up relegating persons to the status of things. Hence segregation is not only politically, economically, and sociologically unsound, it is morally wrong and sinful. Paul Tillich has said that sin is separation. Is not segregation an existential expression of man's tragic separation, his awful estrangement, his terrible sinfulness? Thus it is that I can urge men to obey the 1954 decision of the Supreme Court, for it is morally right; and I can urge them to disobey segregation ordinances, for they are morally wrong.

Let us consider a more concrete example of just and unjust laws. An unjust law is a code that a numerical or power majority group compels a minority group to obey but does not make binding on itself. This is *difference* made legal. By the same token, a just law is a code that a majority compels a minority to follow and that it is willing to follow itself. This is *sameness* made legal.

Let me give another explanation. A law is unjust if it is inflicted on a minority that, as a result of being denied the right to vote, had no part in enacting or devising the law. Who can say that the legislature of Alabama which set up that state's segregation laws was democratically elected? Throughout Alabama all sorts of devious methods are used to prevent Negroes from becoming registered voters, and there are some counties in which, even though Negroes constitute a majority of the population, not a single Negro is registered. Can any law enacted under such circumstances be considered democratically structured?

Sometimes a law is just on its face and unjust in its application. For instance, I have been arrested on a charge of parading without a permit. Now, there is nothing wrong in having an ordinance which requires a permit for a parade. But such an ordinance becomes unjust when it is used to maintain segregation and to deny citizens the First-Amendment privilege of peaceful assembly and protest.

I hope you are able to see the distinction I am trying to point out. In no sense   20
do I advocate evading or defying the law, as would the rabid segregationist. That would lead to anarchy. One who breaks an unjust law must do so openly, lovingly, and with a willingness to accept the penalty. I submit that an individual who breaks a law that conscience tells him is unjust, and who willingly accepts the penalty of imprisonment in order to arouse the conscience of the community over its injustice, is in reality expressing the highest respect for law.

Of course, there is nothing new about this kind of civil disobedience. It was evidenced sublimely in the refusal of Shadrach, Meshach, and Abednego to obey the laws of Nebuchadnezzar, on the ground that a higher moral law was at stake.° It was practiced superbly by the early Christians, who were willing to face hungry lions and the excruciating pain of chopping blocks rather than submit to certain unjust laws of the Roman Empire. To a degree, academic freedom is a reality today because Socrates practiced civil disobedience. In our own nation, the Boston Tea Party represented a massive act of civil disobedience.

Shadrach . . . : See the book of Daniel in the Hebrew Scriptures (1:7–3:30).

We should never forget that everything Adolf Hitler did in Germany was "legal" and everything the Hungarian freedom fighters did in Hungary was "illegal." It was "illegal" to aid and comfort a Jew in Hitler's Germany. Even so, I am sure that, had I lived in Germany at the time, I would have aided and comforted my Jewish brothers. If today I lived in a Communist country where certain principles dear to the Christian faith are suppressed, I would openly advocate disobeying that country's anti-religious laws.

I must make two honest confessions to you, my Christian and Jewish brothers. First, I must confess that over the past few years I have been gravely disappointed with the white moderate. I have almost reached the regrettable conclusion that the Negro's great stumbling block in his stride toward freedom is not the white Citizen's Counciler° or the Ku Klux Klanner, but the white moderate, who is more devoted to "order" than to justice; who prefers a negative peace which is the absence of tension to a positive peace which is the presence of justice; who constantly says, "I agree with you in the goal you seek, but I cannot agree with your methods of direct action"; who paternalistically believes he can set the timetable for another man's freedom; who lives by a mythical concept of time and who constantly advises the Negro to wait for a "more convenient season." Shallow understanding from people of good will is more frustrating than absolute misunderstanding from people of ill will. Lukewarm acceptance is much more bewildering than outright rejection.

I had hoped that the white moderate would understand that law and order exist for the purpose of establishing justice and that when they fail in this purpose they become the dangerously structured dams that block the flow of social progress. I had hoped that the white moderate would understand that the present tension in the South is a necessary phase of the transition from an obnoxious negative peace, in which the Negro passively accepted his unjust plight, to a substantive and positive peace, in which all men will respect the dignity and worth of human personality. Actually, we who engage in nonviolent direct action are not the creators of tension. We merely bring to the surface the hidden tension that is already alive. We bring it out in the open, where it can be seen and dealt with. Like a boil that can never be cured so long as it is covered up but must be opened with all its ugliness to the natural medicines of air and light, injustice must be exposed, with all the tension its exposure creates, to the light of human conscience and the air of national opinion, before it can be cured.

In your statement you assert that our actions, even though peaceful, must   25
be condemned because they precipitate violence. But is this a logical assertion? Isn't this like condemning a robbed man because his possession of money precipitated the evil act of robbery? Isn't this like condemning Socrates because his unswerving commitment to truth and his philosophical inquiries precipitated the act by the misguided populace in which they made him drink hemlock? Isn't this like condemning Jesus because his unique God-consciousness

---

White Citizen's Councils: Resisted desegregation after the U.S. Supreme Court declared segregated education unconstitutional in 1954.

and never-ceasing devotion to God's will precipitated the evil act of crucifixion? We must come to see that, as the federal courts have consistently affirmed, it is wrong to urge an individual to cease his efforts to gain his basic constitutional rights because the quest may precipitate violence. Society must protect the robbed and punish the robber.

I had also hoped that the white moderate would reject the myth concerning time in relation to the struggle for freedom. I have just received a letter from a white brother in Texas. He writes: "All Christians know that the colored people will receive greater equal rights eventually, but it is possible that you are in too great a religious hurry. It has taken Christianity almost two thousand years to accomplish what it has. The teachings of Christ take time to come to earth." Such an attitude stems from a tragic misconception of time, from the strangely irrational notion that there is something in the very flow of time that will inevitably cure all ills. Actually, time itself is neutral; it can be used either destructively or constructively. More and more I feel that the people of ill will have used time much more effectively than have the people of good will. We will have to repent in this generation not merely for the hateful words and actions of the bad people, but for the appalling silence of the good people. Human progress never rolls in on wheels of inevitability; it comes through the tireless efforts of men willing to be co-workers with God, and without this hard work, time itself becomes an ally of the forces of social stagnation. We must use time creatively, in the knowledge that the time is always ripe to do right. Now is the time to make real the promise of democracy and transform our pending national elegy into a creative psalm of brotherhood. Now is the time to lift our national policy from the quicksand of racial injustice to the solid rock of human dignity.

You speak of our activity in Birmingham as extreme. At first I was rather disappointed that fellow clergymen would see my nonviolent efforts as those of an extremist. I began thinking about the fact that I stand in the middle of two opposing forces in the Negro community. One is a force of complacency, made up in part of Negroes, who, as a result of long years of oppression, are so drained of self-respect and a sense of "somebodiness" that they have adjusted to segregation; and in part of a few middle-class Negroes who, because of a degree of academic and economic security and because in some ways they profit by segregation, have become insensitive to the problems of the masses. The other force is one of bitterness and hatred, and it comes perilously close to advocating violence. It is expressed in the various black nationalist groups that are springing up across the nation, the largest and best-known being Elijah Muhammad's Muslim movement.° Nourished by the Negro's frustration over the continued existence of racial discrimination, this movement is made up of people who have lost faith in America, who have absolutely repudiated Christianity, and who have concluded that the white man is an incorrigible "devil."

Elijah Muhammad (1897–1975): Leader of the Nation of Islam, a Muslim religious group that called on African Americans to reject integration and establish their own nation.

I have tried to stand between these two forces, saying that we need emulate neither the "do-nothingism" of the complacent nor the hatred and despair of the black nationalist. For there is the more excellent way of love and nonviolent protest. I am grateful to God that, through the influence of the Negro church, the way of nonviolence became an integral part of our struggle.

If this philosophy had not emerged, by now many streets of the South would, I am convinced, be flowing with blood. And I am further convinced that if our white brothers dismiss as "rabble-rousers" and "outside agitators" those of us who employ nonviolent direct action, and if they refuse to support our nonviolent efforts, millions of Negroes will, out of frustration and despair, seek solace and security in black-nationalist ideologies — a development that would inevitably lead to a frightening racial nightmare.

Oppressed people cannot remain oppressed forever. The yearning for free-   30
dom eventually manifests itself, and that is what has happened to the American Negro. Something within has reminded him of his birthright of freedom, and something without has reminded him that it can be gained. Consciously or unconsciously, he has been caught up by the *Zeitgeist*,° and with his black brothers of Africa and his brown and yellow brothers of Asia, South America, and the Caribbean, the United States Negro is moving with a sense of great urgency toward the promised land of racial justice. If one recognizes this vital urge that has engulfed the Negro community, one should readily understand why public demonstrations are taking place. The Negro has many pent-up resentments and latent frustrations, and he must release them. So let him march; let him make prayer pilgrimages to the city hall; let him go on freedom rides° — and try to understand why he must do so. If his repressed emotions are not released in nonviolent ways, they will seek expression through violence; this is not a threat but a fact of history. So I have not said to my people, "Get rid of your discontent." Rather, I have tried to say that this normal and healthy discontent can be channeled into the creative outlet of nonviolent direct action. And now this approach is being termed extremist.

But though I was initially disappointed at being categorized as an extremist, as I continued to think about the matter I gradually gained a measure of satisfaction from the label. Was not Jesus an extremist for love: "Love your enemies, bless them that curse you, do good to them that hate you, and pray for them that despitefully use you, and persecute you." Was not Amos an extremist for justice: "Let justice roll down like waters and righteousness like an ever-flowing stream." Was not Paul an extremist for the Christian gospel: "I bear in my body the marks of the Lord Jesus." Was not Martin Luther an extremist: "Here I stand; I cannot do otherwise, so help me God." And John Bunyan: "I will stay in jail to the end of my days before I make a butchery of my conscience." And Abraham Lincoln: "This nation cannot survive half slave and half free." And Thomas Jefferson: "We hold these truths to be self-evident, that

Zeitgeist: The spirit of the age (German).   **freedom rides:** In 1961, the Congress of Racial Equality (CORE) directed activists to flout race laws in the South that mandated segregation in buses and bus terminals.

all men are created equal. . . ." So the question is not whether we will be extremists, but what kind of extremists we will be. Will we be extremists for the preservation of injustice or for the extension of justice? In that dramatic scene on Calvary's hill three men were crucified. We must never forget that all three were crucified for the same crime — the crime of extremism. Two were extremists for immorality, and thus fell below their environment. The other, Jesus Christ, was an extremist for love, truth, and goodness, and thereby rose above his environment. Perhaps the South, the nation, and the world are in dire need of creative extremists.

I had hoped that the white moderate would see this need. Perhaps I was too optimistic; perhaps I expected too much. I suppose I should have realized that few members of the oppressor race can understand the deep groans and passionate yearnings of the oppressed race, and still fewer have the vision to see that injustice must be rooted out by strong, persistent, and determined action. I am thankful, however, that some of our white brothers in the South have grasped the meaning of this social revolution and committed themselves to it. They are still all too few in quantity, but they are big in quality. Some — such as Ralph McGill, Lillian Smith, Harry Golden, James McBride Dabbs, Ann Braden, and Sarah Patton Boyle — have written about our struggle in eloquent and prophetic terms. Others have marched with us down nameless streets of the South. They have languished in filthy, roach-infested jails, suffering the abuse and brutality of policemen who view them as "dirty nigger-lovers." Unlike so many of their moderate brothers and sisters, they have recognized the urgency of the moment and sensed the need for powerful "action" antidotes to combat the disease of segregation.

Let me take note of my other major disappointment. I have been so greatly disappointed with the white church and its leadership. Of course, there are some notable exceptions. I am not unmindful of the fact that each of you has taken some significant stands on this issue. I commend you, Reverend Stallings, for your Christian stand on this past Sunday, in welcoming Negroes to your worship service on a nonsegregated basis. I commend the Catholic leaders of this state for integrating Spring Hill College several years ago.

But despite these notable exceptions, I must honestly reiterate that I have been disappointed with the church. I do not say this as one of those negative critics who can always find something wrong with the church. I say this as a minister of the gospel, who loves the church; who was nurtured in its bosom; who has been sustained by its spiritual blessings and who will remain true to it as long as the cord of life shall lengthen.

When I was suddenly catapulted into the leadership of the bus protest in   35
Montgomery, Alabama, a few years ago, I felt we would be supported by the white church. I felt that the white ministers, priests, and rabbis of the South would be among our strongest allies. Instead, some have been outright opponents, refusing to understand the freedom movement and misrepresenting its leaders; all too many others have been more cautious than courageous and have remained silent behind the anesthetizing security of stained-glass windows.

In spite of my shattered dreams, I came to Birmingham with the hope that the white religious leadership of this community would see the justice of our cause and, with deep moral concern, would serve as the channel through which our just grievances could reach the power structure. I had hoped that each of you would understand. But again I have been disappointed.

I have heard numerous southern religious leaders admonish their worshipers to comply with a desegregation decision because it is the law, but I have longed to hear white ministers declare: "Follow this decree because integration is morally right and because the Negro is your brother." In the midst of blatant injustices inflicted upon the Negro, I have watched white churchmen stand on the sideline and mouth pious irrelevancies and sanctimonious trivialities. In the midst of a mighty struggle to rid our nation of racial and economic injustice, I have heard many ministers say: "Those are social issues, with which the gospel has no real concern." And I have watched many churches commit themselves to a completely otherworldly religion which makes a strange, unbiblical distinction between body and soul, between the sacred and the secular.

I have traveled the length and breadth of Alabama, Mississippi, and all the other southern states. On sweltering summer days and crisp autumn mornings I have looked at the South's beautiful churches with their lofty spires pointing heavenward. I have beheld the impressive outlines of her massive religious-education buildings. Over and over I have found myself asking: "What kind of people worship here? Who is their God? Where were their voices when the lips of Governor Barnett dripped with words of interposition and nullification? Where were they when Governor Wallace gave a clarion call for defiance and hatred? Where were their voices of support when bruised and weary Negro men and women decided to rise from the dark dungeons of complacency to the bright hills of creative protest?"

Yes, these questions are still in mind. In deep disappointment I have wept over the laxity of the church. But be assured that my tears have been tears of love. There can be no deep disappointment where there is not deep love. Yes, I love the church. How could I do otherwise? I am in the rather unique position of being the son, the grandson, and the great-grandson of preachers. Yes, I see the church as the body of Christ. But, oh! How we have blemished and scarred the body through social neglect and through fear of being nonconformists.

There was a time when the church was very powerful — in the time when the early Christians rejoiced at being deemed worthy to suffer for what they believed. In those days the church was not merely a thermometer that transformed the mores of society. Whenever the early Christians entered a town, the people in power became disturbed and immediately sought to convict the Christians for being "disturbers of the peace" and "outside agitators." But the Christians pressed on, in the conviction that they were "a colony of heaven," called to obey God rather than man. Small in number, they were big in commitment. They were too God-intoxicated to be "astronomically intimidated." By their effort and example they brought an end to such ancient evils as infanticide and gladiatorial contests.

40

Things are different now. So often the contemporary church is a weak, ineffectual voice with an uncertain sound. So often it is an archdefender of the status quo. Far from being disturbed by the presence of the church, the power structure of the average community is consoled by the church's silent — and often even vocal — sanction of things as they are.

But the judgment of God is upon the church as never before. If today's church does not recapture the sacrificial spirit of the early church, it will lose its authenticity, forfeit the loyalty of millions, and be dismissed as an irrelevant social club with no meaning for the twentieth century. Every day I meet young people whose disappointment with the church has turned into outright disgust.

Perhaps I have once again been too optimistic. Is organized religion too inextricably bound to the status quo to save our nation and the world? Perhaps I must turn my faith to the inner spiritual church, the church within the church, as the true *ekklesia*° and the hope of the world. But again I am thankful to God that some noble souls from the ranks of organized religion have broken loose from the paralyzing chains of conformity and joined us as active partners in the struggle for freedom. They have left their secure congregations and walked the streets of Albany, Georgia, with us. They have gone down the highways of the South on tortuous rides for freedom. Yes, they have gone to jail with us. Some have been dismissed from their churches, have lost the support of their bishops and fellow ministers. But they have acted in the faith that right defeated is stronger than evil triumphant. Their witness has been the spiritual salt that has preserved the true meaning of the gospel in these troubled times. They have carved a tunnel of hope through the dark mountain of disappointment.

I hope that the church as a whole will meet the challenge of this decisive hour. But even if the church does not come to the aid of justice, I have no despair about the future. I have no fear about the outcome of our struggle in Birmingham, even if our motives are at present misunderstood. We will reach the goal of freedom in Birmingham and all over the nation, because the goal of America is freedom. Abused and scorned though we may be, our destiny is tied up with America's destiny. Before the pilgrims landed at Plymouth, we were here. Before the pen of Jefferson etched the majestic words of the Declaration of Independence across the pages of history, we were here. For more than two centuries our forebears labored in this country without wages; they made cotton king; they built the homes of their masters while suffering gross injustice and shameful humiliation — and yet out of a bottomless vitality they continued to thrive and develop. If the inexpressible cruelties of slavery could not stop us, the opposition we now face will surely fail. We will win our freedom because the sacred heritage of our nation and the eternal will of God are embodied in our echoing demands.

Before closing I feel impelled to mention one other point in your statement   45
that has troubled me profoundly. You warmly commended the Birmingham police force for keeping "order" and "preventing violence." I doubt that you

---

ekklesia: The ancient Greek term for "people's assembly." It was chosen by early Christians to describe their gatherings or church.

would have so warmly commended the police force if you had seen its dogs sinking their teeth into unarmed, nonviolent Negroes. I doubt that you would so quickly commend the policemen if you were to observe their ugly and inhumane treatment of Negroes here in the city jail; if you were to watch them push and curse old Negro women and young Negro girls; if you were to see them slap and kick old Negro men and young boys; if you were to observe them, as they did on two occasions, refuse to give us food because we wanted to sing our grace together. I cannot join you in your praise of the Birmingham police department.

It is true that the police have exercised a degree of discipline in handling the demonstrators. In this sense they have conducted themselves rather "nonviolently" in public. But for what purpose? To preserve the evil system of segregation. Over the past few years I have consistently preached that nonviolence demands that the means we use must be as pure as the ends we seek. I have tried to make clear that it is wrong to use immoral means to attain moral ends. But now I must affirm that it is just as wrong, or perhaps even more so, to use moral means to preserve immoral ends. Perhaps Mr. Connor and his policemen have been rather nonviolent in public, as was Chief Pritchett in Albany, Georgia, but they have used the moral means of nonviolence to maintain the immoral end of racial injustice. As T. S. Eliot° has said, "The last temptation is the greatest treason: to do the right deed for the wrong reason."

I wish you had commended the Negro sit-inners and demonstrators of Birmingham for their sublime courage, their willingness to suffer, and their amazing discipline in the midst of great provocation. One day the South will recognize its real heroes. They will be the James Merediths,° with the noble sense of purpose that enables them to face jeering and hostile mobs, and with the agonizing loneliness that characterizes the life of the pioneer. They will be old, oppressed, battered Negro women, symbolized in a seventy-two-year-old woman in Montgomery, Alabama, who rose up with a sense of dignity and with her people decided not to ride segregated buses, and who responded with ungrammatical profundity to one who inquired about her weariness: "My feets is tired, but my soul is at rest." They will be the young high school and college students, the young ministers of the gospel and a host of their elders, courageously and nonviolently sitting in at lunch counters and willingly going to jail for conscience' sake. One day the South will know that when these disinherited children of God sat down at lunch counters, they were in reality standing up for what is best in the American dream and for the most sacred values in our Judaeo-Christian heritage, thereby bringing our nation back to those great wells of democracy which were dug deep by the founding fathers in their formulation of the Constitution and the Declaration of Independence.

Never before have I written so long a letter. I'm afraid it is much too long to take your precious time. I can assure you that it would have been much shorter

Thomas Stearns Eliot (1888–1965): American-born poet and literary critic. **James Meredith (b. 1933):** The first African American student to be admitted to the University of Mississippi.

if I had been writing from a comfortable desk, but what else can one do when he is alone in a narrow jail cell, other than write long letters, think long thoughts, and pray long prayers?

If I have said anything in this letter that overstates the truth and indicates an unreasonable impatience, I beg you to forgive me. If I have said anything that understates the truth and indicates my having a patience that allows me to settle for anything less than brotherhood, I beg God to forgive me.

I hope this letter finds you strong in the faith. I hope that circumstances will soon make it possible for me to meet each of you, not as an integrationist or a civil-rights leader but as a fellow clergyman and a Christian brother. Let us all hope that the dark clouds of a racial prejudice will soon pass away and the deep fog of misunderstanding will be lifted from our fear-drenched communities, and in some not too distant tomorrow the radiant stars of love and brotherhood will shine over our great nation with all their scintillating beauty. 50

Yours for the cause of Peace and Brotherhood,
Martin Luther King Jr.   *[1963]*

≡ THINKING ABOUT THE TEXT

1. King wrote his letter in response to a published statement by eight clergymen from Alabama, who — as he points out in his first sentence — felt that his actions in Birmingham were "unwise and untimely." In what passages does he seem to be addressing this particular audience of religious leaders, referring to their specific accusation as well as to other ideas and texts that they would be especially familiar with? What are some passages where he seems to be addressing a larger audience, perhaps American society as a whole?

2. In one of the letter's most famous sections, King distinguishes between just and unjust laws (paras. 16–22). How does he define each of these two caregories? To what extent do you find helpful the differences he draws between them?

3. In the middle of his letter (beginning in para. 23), King criticizes at length "the white moderate." What are his main observations about this kind of person? Why, apparently, does he devote his central section to *this* figure rather than to the extreme segregationist, who many people would think is his biggest enemy?

4. How would you describe King's tone? What impression of himself does he evidently seek to convey with it? Identify specific passages where you are especially conscious of his tone, perhaps because you are aware that another writer in his situation might have used a different one.

5. Among the rhetorical devices that King employs is anaphora, a pattern of repetition in which consecutive sentences all start with the same word or words. For example, in paragraph 25, King begins three sentences in a row with the words "Isn't this." Where else in his letter does he use the technique? How effective do you find it?

≡ **MAKING COMPARISONS**

1. How do Thoreau, Solnit, and King refer to prison not just as a physical structure but also as a psychological condition?

2. In her paragraph 4, Solnit suggests that despite what certain "scholars and critics" have said, the Thoreau who inspired King is connected to "that other Thoreau who wrote about autumnal tints, ice, light, color, grasses, woodchucks, and other natural histories." After reading King's letter, do you think that he might see himself as resembling "that other Thoreau"? Explain.

3. King's text is more overtly religious in its references than Thoreau's and Solnit's are. Do you think this is a significant difference? Why, or why not?

≡ **WRITING ABOUT ISSUES**

1. Choose one of the texts in this cluster and write an essay in which you explain how it attempts to solve a conceptual problem, which in Solnit's case might be what her title refers to as "the Thoreau problem." Whatever the problem you choose to discuss, phrase it as a question to which there could be more than one answer. For example, you might ask: How can one determine when civil disobedience is justified? or How can one make the best use of one's time? At some point in your essay, you may want to evaluate the writer's approach to solving the problem, but focus for the most part on identifying what the approach and the problem are in the first place.

2. Is civic disobedience for King a more active, dramatic, and sustained process than it seems to be for Thoreau and Solnit? Write an essay that addresses this question by comparing King's letter to at least one of the other two texts.

3. Write an essay in which you recall and analyze an occasion when you were inclined to disobey a law, rule, or regulation that you thought was unjust. Perhaps you did engage in disobedience; then again, perhaps you ultimately decided not to. Besides giving details of the incident, explain what criteria you used in determining the "right" thing to do. If you wish, refer to one or more texts in this cluster. Especially helpful may be the distinctions they draw between "just" and "unjust" government politics.

4. Choose a recent case of civil disobedience that the media have reported on, and read some opinion columns that have been published about it. Then, write an essay in which you analyze and evaluate at least two of these arguments. If you wish, refer to one or more texts in this cluster. Again, you may want to consider the distinctions they draw between "just" and "unjust" government policies.

▤ Discovering Injustice: Stories

NATHANIEL HAWTHORNE, "Young Goodman Brown"

TONI CADE BAMBARA, "The Lesson"

ALICE WALKER, "The Flowers"

Much fiction depicts characters learning about injustice they had not been aware of before. They move from relative innocence to knowledge of corruption. Moreover, they must now figure out what to do about the wrongdoing they have found. They must also decide how, in general, they will live in a world where virtue mixes with vice. The title character of Nathaniel Hawthorne's classic tale "Young Goodman Brown" comes to believe that his New England community is satanic, and therefore he grows alienated from it. But does he thereby become excessively self-righteous? In Toni Cade Bambara's modern-day story "The Lesson," the narrator is an African American girl who must decide what to think when a woman of her race tries to teach her that whites monopolize society's wealth. Meanwhile, the ten-year-old heroine of Alice Walker's very brief story "The Flowers," published close in time to Bambara's, finds herself suddenly having to cope with signs of a lynching. On issues of justice, the protagonists of all three stories undergo discovery and reflection. Readers of their narratives are encouraged to do the same.

▤ BEFORE YOU READ

In his memoir *Fatheralong* (1994), John Edgar Wideman notes that his father's attitude toward society differs from that of his late mother. "The first rule of my father's world," Wideman writes, "is that you stand alone. Alone, alone, alone. . . . Accept the bottom line, icy clarity, of the one thing you can rely on: nothing" (50). On the other hand, "My mother's first rule was love. She refused to believe she was alone. *Be not dismayed, what e'er betides / God will take care of you*" (51). What were you taught about society as you were growing up? What specific messages were you given about it by your parents or the people who raised you? How did they convey these messages to you?

NATHANIEL HAWTHORNE
Young Goodman Brown

Nathaniel Hawthorne (1804–1864) was born in Salem, Massachusetts, into a family that was founded by New England's Puritan colonists. This lineage troubled Hawthorne, especially because his ancestor John Hathorne was involved as a judge in the Salem witch trials. After graduating from Maine's Bowdoin College in 1825,

Hawthorne returned to Salem and began his career as a writer. In 1832, he self-published his first novel, Fanshawe, but considered it an artistic as well as a commercial failure and tried to destroy all unsold copies of it. He was more successful with his 1832 short-story collection Twice-Told Tales (reprinted and enlarged in 1842). In the early 1840s, Hawthorne worked as a surveyor in the Boston Custom House, briefly joined the Utopian community of Brook Farm, and then moved to Concord. There he published several children's books and lived with his wife, Sophia, in writer Ralph Waldo Emerson's former home, the Old Manse. In 1846, he produced a second collection of short stories, Mosses from an Old Manse. For the next three years, Hawthorne worked in a custom house in his hometown of Salem before publishing his most famous analysis of Puritan culture, The Scarlet Letter (1850). Later novels included The House of the Seven Gables (1851), The Blithedale Romance (an 1852 satire on Brook Farm), and The Marble Faun (1860). When his friend Franklin Pierce became president of the United States, Hawthorne served as American consul in Liverpool, England, for four years and then traveled in Italy for two more. At his death in 1864, he was already highly respected as a writer. Much of his fiction deals with conflicted characters whose hearts and souls are torn by sin, guilt, pride, and isolation. Indeed, his good friend Herman Melville, author of Moby-Dick, praised "the power of blackness" he found in Hawthorne's works. The allegorical story "Young Goodman Brown" is an especially memorable example of this power. Hawthorne wrote the tale in 1835 and later included it in Mosses from an Old Manse.

Young Goodman Brown came forth at sunset into the street at Salem village; but put his head back, after crossing the threshold, to exchange a parting kiss with his young wife. And Faith, as the wife was aptly named, thrust her own pretty head into the street, letting the wind play with the pink ribbons of her cap while she called to Goodman Brown.

"Dearest heart," whispered she, softly and rather sadly, when her lips were close to his ear, "prithee put off your journey until sunrise and sleep in your own bed to-night. A lone woman is troubled with such dreams and such thoughts that she's afeared of herself sometimes. Pray tarry with me this night, dear husband, of all nights in the year."

"My love and my Faith," replied young Goodman Brown, "of all nights in the year, this one night must I tarry away from thee. My journey, as thou callest it, forth and back again, must needs be done 'twixt now and sunrise. What, my sweet, pretty wife, dost thou doubt me already, and we but three months married?"

"Then God bless you!" said Faith, with the pink ribbons; "and may you find all well when you come back."

"Amen!" cried Goodman Brown. "Say thy prayers, dear Faith, and go to bed at dusk, and no harm will come to thee."   5

So they parted; and the young man pursued his way until, being about to turn the corner by the meeting-house, he looked back and saw the head of Faith still peeping after him with a melancholy air, in spite of her pink ribbons.

"Poor little Faith!" thought he, for his heart smote him. "What a wretch am I to leave her on such an errand! She talks of dreams, too. Methought as she spoke there was trouble in her face, as if a dream had warned her what work is to be done to-night. But no, no; 't would kill her to think it. Well, she's a blessed angel on earth, and after this one night I'll cling to her skirts and follow her to heaven."

With this excellent resolve for the future, Goodman Brown felt himself justified in making more haste on his present evil purpose. He had taken a dreary road, darkened by all the gloomiest trees of the forest, which barely stood aside to let the narrow path creep through, and closed immediately behind. It was all as lonely as could be; and there is this peculiarity in such a solitude, that the traveller knows not who may be concealed by the innumerable trunks and the thick boughs overhead; so that with lonely footsteps he may yet be passing through an unseen multitude.

"There may be a devilish Indian behind every tree," said Goodman Brown to himself; and he glanced fearfully behind him as he added, "What if the devil himself should be at my very elbow!"

His head being turned back, he passed a crook of the road, and, looking   10
forward again, beheld the figure of a man, in grave and decent attire, seated at the foot of an old tree. He arose at Goodman Brown's approach and walked onward side by side with him.

"You are late, Goodman Brown," said he. "The clock of the Old South was striking as I came through Boston, and that is full fifteen minutes agone."

"Faith kept me back a while," replied the young man, with a tremor in his voice, caused by the sudden appearance of his companion, though not wholly unexpected.

It was now deep dusk in the forest, and deepest in that part of it where these two were journeying. As nearly as could be discerned, the second traveller was about fifty years old, apparently in the same rank of life as Goodman Brown, and bearing a considerable resemblance to him, though perhaps more in expression than features. Still they might have been taken for father and son. And yet, though the elder person was as simply clad as the younger, and as simple in manner too, he had an indescribable air of one who knew the world, and who would not have felt abashed at the governor's dinner table or in King William's court, were it possible that his affairs should call him thither. But the only thing about him that could be fixed upon as remarkable was his staff, which bore the likeness of a great black snake, so curiously wrought that it might almost be seen to twist and wriggle itself like a living serpent. This, of course, must have been an ocular deception, assisted by the uncertain light.

"Come, Goodman Brown," cried his fellow-traveller, "this is a dull pace for the beginning of a journey. Take my staff, if you are so soon weary."

"Friend," said the other, exchanging his slow pace for a full stop, "having   15
kept covenant by meeting thee here, it is my purpose now to return whence I came. I have scruples touching the matter thou wot'st of."

"Sayest thou so?" replied he of the serpent, smiling apart. "Let us walk on, nevertheless, reasoning as we go; and if I convince thee not thou shalt turn back. We are but a little way in the forest yet."

"Too far! too far!" exclaimed the goodman, unconsciously resuming his walk. "My father never went into the woods on such an errand, nor his father before him. We have been a race of honest men and good Christians since the days of the martyrs; and shall I be the first of the name of Brown that ever took this path and kept" —

"Such company, thou wouldst say," observed the elder person, interpreting his pause. "Well said, Goodman Brown! I have been as well acquainted with your family as with ever a one among the Puritans; and that's no trifle to say. I helped your grandfather, the constable, when he lashed the Quaker woman so smartly through the streets of Salem; and it was I that brought your father a pitch-pine knot, kindled at my own hearth, to set fire to an Indian village, in King Philip's war.° They were my good friends, both; and many a pleasant walk have we had along this path, and returned merrily after midnight. I would fain be friends with you for their sake."

"If it be as thou sayest," replied Goodman Brown, "I marvel they never spoke of these matters; or, verily, I marvel not, seeing that the least rumor of the sort would have driven them from New England. We are a people of prayer, and good works to boot, and abide no such wickedness."

"Wickedness or not," said the traveller with the twisted staff, "I have a very   20
general acquaintance here in New England. The deacons of many a church have drunk the communion wine with me; the selectmen of divers towns make me their chairman; and a majority of the Great and General Court are firm supporters of my interest. The governor and I, too — But these are state secrets."

"Can this be so?" cried Goodman Brown, with a stare of amazement at his undisturbed companion. "Howbeit, I have nothing to do with the governor and council; they have their own ways, and are no rule for a simple husbandman like me. But, were I to go on with thee, how should I meet the eye of that good old man, our minister, at Salem village? Oh, his voice would make me tremble both Sabbath day and lecture day."

Thus far the elder traveller had listened with due gravity; but now burst into a fit of irrepressible mirth, shaking himself so violently that his snake-like staff actually seemed to wriggle in sympathy.

"Ha! ha! ha!" shouted he again and again; then composing himself, "Well, go on, Goodman Brown, go on; but, prithee, don't kill me with laughing."

"Well, then, to end the matter at once," said Goodman Brown, considerably nettled, "there is my wife, Faith. It would break her dear little heart; and I'd rather break my own."

"Nay, if that be the case," answered the other, "e'en go thy ways, Goodman   25
Brown. I would not for twenty old women like the one hobbling before us that Faith should come to any harm."

King Philip's war: King Philip, a Wampanoag chief, waged a bloody war against the New England colonists from 1675 to 1676.

As he spoke he pointed his staff at a female figure on the path, in whom Goodman Brown recognized a very pious and exemplary dame, who had taught him his catechism in youth, and was still his moral and spiritual adviser, jointly with the minister and Deacon Gookin.

"A marvel, truly that Goody Cloyse should be so far in the wilderness at nightfall," said he. "But with your leave, friend, I shall take a cut through the woods until we have left this Christian woman behind. Being a stranger to you, she might ask whom I was consorting with and whither I was going."

"Be it so," said his fellow-traveller. "Betake you to the woods, and let me keep the path."

Accordingly the young man turned aside, but took care to watch his companion, who advanced softly along the road until he had come within a staff's length of the old dame. She, meanwhile, was making the best of her way, with singular speed for so aged a woman, and mumbling some indistinct words — a prayer, doubtless — as she went. The traveller put forth his staff and touched her withered neck with what seemed the serpent's tail.

"The devil!" screamed the pious old lady.   30

"Then Goody Cloyse knows her old friend?" observed the traveller, confronting her and leaning on his writhing stick.

"Ah, forsooth, and is it your worship indeed?" cried the good dame. "Yea, truly is it, and in the very image of my old gossip, Goodman Brown, the grandfather of the silly fellow that now is. But — would your worship believe it? — my broomstick hath strangely disappeared, stolen, as I suspect, by that unhanged witch, Goody Cory, and that, too, when I was all anointed with the juice of smallage, and cinquefoil, and wolf's bane" —

"Mingled with fine wheat and the fat of a new-born babe," said the shape of old Goodman Brown.

"Ah, your worship knows the recipe," cried the old lady, cackling aloud. "So, as I was saying, being all ready for the meeting, and no horse to ride on, I made up my mind to foot it; for they tell me there is a nice young man to be taken into communion to-night. But now your good worship will lend me your arm, and we shall be there in a twinkling."

"That can hardly be," answered her friend. "I may not spare you my arm,   35 Goody Cloyse; but here is my staff, if you will."

So saying, he threw it down at her feet, where, perhaps, it assumed life, being one of the rods which its owner had formerly lent to the Egyptian magi. Of this fact, however, Goodman Brown could not take cognizance. He had cast up his eyes in astonishment, and, looking down again, beheld neither Goody Cloyse nor the serpentine staff, but his fellow-traveller alone, who waited for him as calmly as if nothing had happened.

"That old woman taught me my catechism," said the young man; and there was a world of meaning in this simple comment.

They continued to walk onward, while the elder traveller exhorted his companion to make good speed and persevere in the path, discoursing so aptly that his arguments seemed rather to spring up in the bosom of his auditor than to be suggested by himself. As they went, he plucked a branch of maple to serve for a walking stick, and began to strip it of the twigs and little boughs, which were wet with evening dew. The moment his fingers touched them they became strangely withered and dried up as with a week's sunshine. Thus the pair proceeded, at a good free pace, until suddenly, in a gloomy hollow of the road, Goodman Brown sat himself down on the stump of a tree and refused to go any farther.

"Friend," he said, stubbornly, "my mind is made up. Not another step will I budge on this errand. What if a wretched old woman do choose to go to the devil when I thought she was going to heaven: is that any reason why I should quit my dear Faith and go after her?"

"You will think better of this by and by," said his acquaintance, compos-   40
edly. "Sit here and rest yourself a while; and when you feel like moving again, there is my staff to help you along."

Without more words, he threw his companion the maple stick, and was as speedily out of sight as if he had vanished into the deepening gloom. The young man sat a few moments by the roadside, applauding himself greatly, and thinking with how clear a conscience he should meet the minister in his morning walk, nor shrink from the eye of good old Deacon Gookin. And what calm sleep would be his that very night, which was to have been spent so wickedly, but so purely and sweetly now, in the arms of Faith! Amidst these pleasant and praiseworthy meditations, Goodman Brown heard the tramp of horses along the road, and deemed it advisable to conceal himself within the verge of the forest, conscious of the guilty purpose that had brought him thither, though now so happily turned from it.

On came the hoof tramps and the voices of the riders, two grave old voices, conversing soberly as they drew near. These mingled sounds appeared to pass along the road, within a few yards of the young man's hiding-place; but, owing doubtless to the depth of the gloom at that particular spot, neither the travellers nor their steeds were visible. Though their figures brushed the small boughs by the wayside, it could not be seen that they intercepted, even for a moment, the faint gleam from the strip of bright sky athwart which they must have passed. Goodman Brown alternately crouched and stood on tiptoe, pulling aside the branches and thrusting forth his head as far as he durst without discerning so much as a shadow. It vexed him the more, because he could have sworn, were such a thing possible, that he recognized the voices of the minister and Deacon Gookin, jogging along quietly, as they were wont to do, when bound to some ordination or ecclesiastical council. While yet within hearing, one of the riders stopped to pluck a switch.

"Of the two, reverend sir," said the voice like the deacon's, "I had rather miss an ordination dinner than to-night's meeting. They tell me that some of our community are to be here from Falmouth and beyond, and others from Connecticut and Rhode Island, besides several of the Indian powwows, who, after their fashion, know almost as much deviltry as the best of us. Moreover, there is a goodly young woman to be taken into communion."

"Mighty well, Deacon Gookin!" replied the solemn old tones of the minister. "Spur up, or we shall be late. Nothing can be done, you know, until I get on the ground."

The hoofs clattered again; and the voices, talking so strangely in the empty 45
air, passed on through the forest, where no church had ever been gathered or
solitary Christian prayed. Whither, then, could these holy men be journeying
so deep into the heathen wilderness? Young Goodman Brown caught hold of a
tree for support, being ready to sink down on the ground, faint and overbur-
dened with the heavy sickness of his heart. He looked up to the sky, doubting
whether there really was a heaven above him. Yet there was the blue arch, and
the stars brightening in it.

"With heaven above and Faith below, I will yet stand firm against the
devil!" cried Goodman Brown.

While he still gazed upward into the deep arch of the firmament and had
lifted his hands to pray, a cloud, though no wind was stirring, hurried across
the zenith and hid the brightening stars. The blue sky was still visible, except
directly overhead, where this black mass of cloud was sweeping swiftly north-
ward. Aloft in the air, as if from the depths of the cloud, came a confused and
doubtful sound of voices. Once the listener fancied that he could distinguish
the accents of towns-people of his own, men and women, both pious and un-
godly, many of whom he had met at the communion table, and had seen others
rioting at the tavern. The next moment, so indistinct were the sounds, he
doubted whether he had heard aught but the murmur of the old forest, whispering without a wind. Then came a stronger swell of those familiar tones,
heard daily in the sunshine at Salem village, but never until now from a cloud
of night. There was one voice, of a young woman, uttering lamentations, yet
with an uncertain sorrow, and entreating for some favor, which, perhaps, it
would grieve her to obtain; and all the unseen multitude, both saints and sinners, seemed to encourage her onward.

"Faith!" shouted Goodman Brown, in a voice of agony and desperation;
and the echoes of the forest mocked him, crying, "Faith! Faith!" as if bewildered wretches were seeking her all through the wilderness.

The cry of grief, rage, and terror was yet piercing the night, when the unhappy husband held his breath for a response. There was a scream, drowned
immediately in a louder murmur of voices, fading into far-off laughter, as the
dark cloud swept away, leaving the clear and silent sky above Goodman Brown.
But something fluttered lightly down through the air and caught on the branch
of a tree. The young man seized it, and beheld a pink ribbon.

"My Faith is gone!" cried he after one stupefied moment. "There is no good 50
on earth; and sin is but a name. Come, devil; for to thee is this world given."

And, maddened with despair, so that he laughed loud and long, did Goodman
Brown grasp his staff and set forth again, at such a rate that he seemed to fly
along the forest path rather than to walk or run. The road grew wilder and drea-
rier and more faintly traced, and vanished at length, leaving him in the heart
of the dark wilderness, still rushing onward with the instinct that guides mortal
man to evil. The whole forest was peopled with frightful sounds — the creaking
of the trees, the howling of wild beasts, and the yell of Indians; while sometimes
the wind tolled like a distant church bell, and sometimes gave a broad roar
around the traveller, as if all Nature were laughing him to scorn. But he was
himself the chief horror of the scene, and shrank not from its other horrors.

"Ha! ha! ha!" roared Goodman Brown when the wind laughed at him. "Let us hear which will laugh loudest. Think not to frighten me with your deviltry. Come witch, come wizard, come Indian powwow, come devil himself, and here comes Goodman Brown. You may as well fear him as he fear you."

In truth, all through the haunted forest there could be nothing more frightful than the figure of Goodman Brown. On he flew among the black pines, brandishing his staff with frenzied gestures, now giving vent to an inspiration of horrid blasphemy, and now shouting forth such laughter as set all the echoes of the forest laughing like demons around him. The fiend in his own shape is less hideous than when he rages in the breast of man. Thus sped the demoniac on his course, until, quivering among the trees, he saw a red light before him, as when the felled trunks and branches of a clearing have been set on fire, and throw up their lurid blaze against the sky, at the hour of midnight. He paused, in a lull of the tempest that had driven him onward, and heard the swell of what seemed a hymn, rolling solemnly from a distance with the weight of many voices. He knew the tune; it was a familiar one in the choir of the village meeting-house. The verse died heavily away, and was lengthened by a chorus, not of human voices, but of all the sounds of the benighted wilderness pealing in awful harmony together. Goodman Brown cried out, and his cry was lost to his own ear by its unison with the cry of the desert.

In the interval of silence he stole forward until the light glared full upon his eyes. At one extremity of an open space, hemmed in by the dark wall of the forest, arose a rock, bearing some rude, natural resemblance either to an altar or a pulpit, and surrounded by four blazing pines, their tops aflame, their stems untouched, like candles at an evening meeting. The mass of foliage that had overgrown the summit of the rock was all on fire, blazing high into the night and fitfully illuminating the whole field. Each pendent twig and leafy festoon was in a blaze. As the red light arose and fell, a numerous congregation alternately shone forth, then disappeared in shadow, and again grew, as it were, out of the darkness, peopling the heart of the solitary woods at once.

"A grave and dark-clad company," quoth Goodman Brown.   55

In truth they were such. Among them, quivering to and fro between gloom and splendor, appeared faces that would be seen next day at the council board of the province, and others which, Sabbath after Sabbath, looked devoutly heavenward, and benignantly over the crowded pews, from the holiest pulpits in the land. Some affirm that the lady of the governor was there. At least there were high dames well known to her, and wives of honored husbands, and widows, a great multitude, and ancient maidens, all of excellent repute, and fair young girls, who trembled lest their mothers should espy them. Either the sudden gleams of light flashing over the obscure field bedazzled Goodman Brown, or he recognized a score of the church members of Salem village famous for their especial sanctity. Good old Deacon Gookin had arrived, and waited at the skirts of that venerable saint, his revered pastor. But, irreverently consorting with these grave, reputable, and pious people, these elders of the church, these chaste dames and dewy virgins, there were men of dissolute lives and women of spotted fame, wretches given over to all mean and filthy vice, and suspected even of horrid crimes. It was strange to see that the good shrank not from the wicked, nor were the sinners abashed by the saints. Scattered also among their pale-faced enemies were the Indian priests, or powwows, who had often scared their native forest with more hideous incantations than any known to English witchcraft.

"But where is Faith?" thought Goodman Brown; and, as hope came into his heart, he trembled.

Another verse of the hymn arose, a slow and mournful strain, such as the pious love, but joined to words which expressed all that our nature can conceive of sin, and darkly hinted at far more. Unfathomable to mere mortals is the lore of fiends. Verse after verse was sung; and still the chorus of the desert swelled between like the deepest tone of a mighty organ; and with the final peal of that dreadful anthem there came a sound, as if the roaring wind, the rushing streams, the howling beasts, and every other voice of the unconcerted wilderness were mingling and according with the voice of guilty man in homage to the prince of all. The four blazing pines threw up a loftier flame, and obscurely discovered shapes and visages of horror on the smoke wreaths above the impious assembly. At the same moment the fire on the rock shot redly forth and formed a flowing arch above its base, where now appeared a figure. With reverence be it spoken, the figure bore no slight similitude, both in garb and manner, to some grave divine of the New England churches.

"Bring forth the converts!" cried a voice that echoed through the field and rolled into the forest.

At the word, Goodman Brown stepped forth from the shadow of the trees and approached the congregation, with whom he felt a loathful brotherhood by the sympathy of all that was wicked in his heart. He could have well-nigh sworn that the shape of his own dead father beckoned him to advance, looking downward from a smoke wreath, while a woman, with dim features of despair, threw out her hand to warn him back. Was it his mother? But he had no power to retreat one step, nor to resist, even in thought, when the minister and good old Deacon Gookin seized his arms and led him to the blazing rock. Thither came also the slender form of a veiled female, led between Goody Cloyse, that pious teacher of the catechism, and Martha Carrier, who had received the devil's promise to be queen of hell. A rampant hag was she. And there stood the proselytes beneath the canopy of fire.

"Welcome, my children," said the dark figure, "to the communion of your race. Ye have found thus young your nature and your destiny. My children, look behind you!"

They turned; and flashing forth, as it were, in a sheet of flame, the fiend worshippers were seen; the smile of welcome gleamed darkly on every visage.

"There," resumed the sable form, "are all whom ye have reverenced from youth. Ye deemed them holier than yourselves and shrank from your own sin, contrasting it with their lives of righteousness and prayerful aspirations heavenward. Yet here are they all in my worshipping assembly. This night it shall be granted you to know their secret deeds: how hoary-bearded elders of the church have whispered wanton words to the young maids of their households;

how many a woman, eager for widows' weeds, has given her husband a drink at bedtime and let him sleep his last sleep in her bosom; how beardless youths have made haste to inherit their fathers' wealth; and how fair damsels — blush not, sweet ones — have dug little graves in the garden, and bidden me, the sole guest, to an infant's funeral. By the sympathy of your human hearts for sin ye shall scent out all the places — whether in church, bedchamber, street, field, or forest — where crime has been committed, and shall exult to behold the whole earth one stain of guilt, one mighty blood spot. Far more than this. It shall be yours to penetrate, in every bosom, the deep mystery of sin, the fountain of all wicked arts, and which inexhaustibly supplies more evil impulses than human power — than my power at its utmost — can make manifest in deeds. And now, my children, look upon each other."

They did so; and, by the blaze of the hell-kindled torches, the wretched man beheld his Faith, and the wife her husband, trembling before that unhallowed altar.

"Lo, there ye stand, my children," said the figure, in a deep and solemn   65
tone, almost sad with its despairing awfulness, as if his once angelic nature could yet mourn for our miserable race. "Depending upon one another's hearts, ye had still hoped that virtue were not all a dream. Now are ye undeceived. Evil is the nature of mankind. Evil must be your only happiness. Welcome again, my children, to the communion of your race."

"Welcome," repeated the fiend worshippers, in one cry of despair and triumph.

And there they stood, the only pair, as it seemed, who were yet hesitating on the verge of wickedness in this dark world. A basin was hallowed, naturally, in the rock. Did it contain water, reddened by the lurid light? or was it blood? or, perchance, a liquid flame? Herein did the shape of evil dip his hand and prepare to lay the mark of baptism upon their foreheads, that they might be partakers of the mystery of sin, more conscious of the secret guilt of others, both in deed and thought, than they could now be of their own. The husband cast one look at his pale wife, and Faith at him. What polluted wretches would the next glance show them to each other, shuddering alike at what they disclosed and what they saw!

"Faith! Faith!" cried the husband, "look up to heaven, and resist the wicked one."

Whether Faith obeyed he knew not. Hardly had he spoken when he found himself amid calm night and solitude, listening to a roar of the wind which died heavily away through the forest. He staggered against the rock, and felt it chill and damp; while a hanging twig, that had been all on fire, besprinkled his cheek with the coldest dew.

The next morning young Goodman Brown came slowly into the street   70
of Salem village, staring around him like a bewildered man. The good old minister was taking a walk along the graveyard to get an appetite for breakfast and meditate his sermon, and bestowed a blessing, as he passed, on Goodman Brown. He shrank from the venerable saint as if to avoid an anathema. Old Deacon Gookin was at domestic worship, and the holy words of his prayer were

heard through the open window. "What God doth the wizard pray to?" quoth Goodman Brown. Goody Cloyse, that excellent old Christian, stood in the early sunshine at her own lattice, catechizing a little girl who had brought her a pint of morning's milk. Goodman Brown snatched away the child as from the grasp of the fiend himself. Turning the corner by the meeting-house, he spied the head of Faith, with the pink ribbons, gazing anxiously forth, and bursting into such joy at sight of him that she skipped along the street and almost kissed her husband before the whole village. But Goodman Brown looked sternly and sadly into her face, and passed on without a greeting.

Had Goodman Brown fallen asleep in the forest and only dreamed a wild dream of a witch-meeting?

Be it so if you will; but, alas! it was a dream of evil omen for young Goodman Brown. A stern, a sad, a darkly meditative, a distrustful, if not a desperate man did he become from the night of that fearful dream. On the Sabbath day, when the congregation were singing a holy psalm, he could not listen because an anthem of sin rushed loudly upon his ear and drowned all the blessed strain. When the minister spoke from the pulpit with power and fervid eloquence, and, with his hand on the open Bible, of the sacred truths of our religion, and of saint-like lives and triumphant deaths, and of future bliss or misery unutterable, then did Goodman Brown turn pale, dreading lest the roof should thunder down upon the gray blasphemer and his hearers. Often, awaking suddenly at midnight, he shrank from the bosom of Faith; and at morning or eventide, when the family knelt down at prayer, he scowled and muttered to himself, and gazed sternly at his wife, and turned away. And when he had lived long, and was borne to his grave a hoary corpse, followed by Faith, an aged woman, and children and grandchildren, a goodly procession, besides neighbors not a few, they carved no hopeful verse upon his tombstone, for his dying hour was gloom.   *[1835]*

≡ **THINKING ABOUT THE TEXT**

1. "Young Goodman Brown" seems quite allegorical, with journeys in the night woods and statements like "My Faith is gone!" (para. 50). How would you explain this allegorical story? What is Brown looking for? What does he find out? How does he deal with his discoveries?

2. If you were a good friend of Brown's, what might you tell him to try to save him from a life of gloom?

3. The devil suggests that there is more evil in the human heart "than my power at its utmost" (para. 63). Do you agree? If so, is this a message to despair about?

4. The devil says he is well acquainted with Brown's family. What has his family done? Is Brown innocent and naive, or perhaps stubborn and arrogant, in his refusal to admit that evil exists all around us?

5. Do you suspect that Brown merely dreamed or imagined his experience in the woods? Or do you think it really took place? Refer to specific details of the text.

TONI CADE BAMBARA

The Lesson

Toni Cade Bambara (1939–1995) taught at various colleges and worked as a community activist. She edited The Black Woman *(1970), a collection of essays that became a landmark of contemporary black feminism. Bambara wrote two novels:* The Salt Eaters *(1980), which won the American Book Award, and* These Bones Are Not My Child *(2000), a posthumously published work about the murders of several African American children in late 1970s Atlanta. She also produced several collections of short stories. "The Lesson" comes from her first,* Gorilla, My Love *(1972).*

Back in the days when everyone was old and stupid or young and foolish and me and Sugar were the only ones just right, this lady moved on our block with nappy hair and proper speech and no makeup. And quite naturally we laughed at her, laughed the way we did at the junk man who went about his business like he was some big-time president and his sorry-ass horse his secretary. And we kinda hated her too, hated the way we did the winos who cluttered up our parks and pissed on our handball walls and stank up our hallways and stairs so you couldn't halfway play hide-and-seek without a goddamn gas mask. Miss Moore was her name. The only woman on the block with no first name. And she was black as hell, cept for her feet, which were fish-white and spooky. And she was always planning these boring-ass things for us to do, us being my cousin, mostly, who lived on the block cause we all moved North the same time and to the same apartment then spread out gradual to breathe. And our parents would yank our heads into some kinda shape and crisp up our clothes so we'd be presentable for travel with Miss Moore, who always looked like she was going to church, though she never did. Which is just one of the things the grownups talked about when they talked behind her back like a dog. But when she came calling with some sachet she'd sewed up or some gingerbread she'd made or some book, why then they'd all be too embarrassed to turn her down and we'd get handed over all spruced up. She'd been to college and said it was only right that she should take responsibility for the young ones' education, and she not even related by marriage or blood. So they'd go for it. Specially Aunt Gretchen. She was the main gofer in the family. You got some ole dumb shit foolishness you want somebody to go for, you send for Aunt Gretchen. She been screwed into the go-along for so long, it's a blood-deep natural thing with her. Which is how she got saddled with me and Sugar and Junior in the first place while our mothers were in a la-de-da apartment up the block having a good ole time.

So this one day, Miss Moore rounds us all up at the mailbox and it's puredee hot and she's knockin herself out about arithmetic. And school suppose to let up in summer I heard, but she don't never let up. And the starch in my pinafore scratching the shit outta me and I'm really hating this nappy-head bitch and her goddamn college degree. I'd much rather go to the pool or to the show where it's cool. So me and Sugar leaning on the mailbox being surly, which is a Miss Moore word. And Flyboy checking out what everybody brought for lunch. And Fat Butt already wasting his peanut-butter-and-jelly sandwich like the pig he is. And Junebug punchin on Q.T.'s arm for potato chips. And Rosie Giraffe shifting from one hip to the other waiting for somebody to step on her foot or ask her if she from Georgia so she can kick ass, preferably Mercedes's. And Miss Moore asking us do we know what money is, like we a bunch of retards. I mean real money, she say, like it's only poker chips or monopoly papers we lay on the grocer. So right away I'm tired of this and say so. And would much rather snatch Sugar and go to the Sunset and terrorize the West Indian kids and take their hair ribbons and their money too. And Miss Moore files that remark away for next week's lesson on brotherhood, I can tell. And finally I say we oughta get to the subway cause it's cooler and besides we might meet some cute boys. Sugar done swiped her mama's lipstick, so we ready.

So we heading down the street and she's boring us silly about what things cost and what our parents make and how much goes for rent and how money ain't divided up right in this country. And then she gets to the part about we all poor and live in the slums, which I don't feature. And I'm ready to speak on that, but she steps out in the street and hails two cabs just like that. Then she hustles half the crew in with her and hands me a five-dollar bill and tells me to calculate 10 percent tip for the driver. And we're off. Me and Sugar and Junebug and Flyboy hangin out the window and hollering to everybody, putting lipstick on each other cause Flyboy a faggot anyway, and making farts with our sweaty armpits. But I'm mostly trying to figure how to spend this money. But they all fascinated with the meter ticking and Junebug starts laying bets as to how much it'll read when Flyboy can't hold his breath no more. Then Sugar lays bets as to how much it'll be when we get there. So I'm stuck. Don't nobody want to go for my plan, which is to jump out at the next light and run off to the first bar-b-que we can find. Then the driver tells us to get the hell out cause we there already. And the meter reads eighty-five cents. And I'm stalling to figure out the tip and Sugar say give him a dime. And I decide he don't need it bad as I do, so later for him. But then he tries to take off with Junebug foot still in the door so we talk about his mama something ferocious. Then we check out that we on Fifth Avenue and everybody dressed up in stockings. One lady in a fur coat, hot as it is. White folks crazy.

"This is the place," Miss Moore say, presenting it to us in the voice she uses at the museum. "Let's look in the windows before we go in."

"Can we steal?" Sugar asks very serious like she's getting the ground rules squared away before she plays. "I beg your pardon," say Miss Moore, and we fall out. So she leads us around the windows of the toy store and me and Sugar screamin, "This is mine, that's mine, I gotta have that, that was made for me, I was born for that," till Big Butt drowns us out.

"Hey, I'm goin to buy that there."

"That there? You don't even know what it is, stupid."

5

"I do so," he say punchin on Rosie Giraffe. "It's a microscope."

"Whatcha gonna do with a microscope, fool?"

"Look at things."   10

"Like what, Ronald?" ask Miss Moore. And Big Butt ain't got the first notion. So here go Miss Moore gabbing about the thousands of bacteria in a drop
of water and the somethinorother in a speck of blood and the million and one
living things in the air around us is invisible to the naked eye. And what she say
that for? Junebug go to town on that "naked" and we rolling. Then Miss Moore
ask what it cost. So we all jam into the window smudgin it up and the price tag
say $300. So then she ask how long'd take for Big Butt and Junebug to save
up their allowances. "Too long," I say. "Yeh," adds Sugar, "outgrown it by that
time." And Miss Moore say no, you never outgrow learning instruments. "Why,
even medical students and interns and," blah, blah, blah. And we ready to
choke Big Butt for bringing it up in the first damn place.

"This here costs four hundred eighty dollars," says Rosie Giraffe. So we
pile up all over her to see what she pointin out. My eyes tell me it's a chunk of
glass cracked with something heavy, and different-color inks dripped into the
splits, then the whole thing put into a oven or something. But for $480 it don't
make sense.

"That's a paperweight made of semi-precious stones fused together under
tremendous pressure," she explains slowly, with her hands doing the mining
and all the factory work.

"So what's a paperweight?" asks Rosie Giraffe.

"To weigh paper with, dumbbell," say Flyboy, the wise man from the East.   15

"Not exactly," say Miss Moore, which is what she say when you warm or
way off too. "It's to weigh paper down so it won't scatter and make your desk
untidy." So right away me and Sugar curtsy to each other and then to Mercedes
who is more the tidy type.

"We don't keep paper on top of the desk in my class," say Junebug, figuring
Miss Moore crazy or lyin one.

"At home, then," she say. "Don't you have a calendar and pencil case and a
blotter and a letter-opener on your desk at home where you do your homework?" And she know damn well what our homes look like cause she nosys
around in them every chance she gets.

"I don't even have a desk," say Junebug. "Do we?"

"No. And I don't get no homework neither," says Big Butt.   20

"And I don't even have a home," say Flyboy like he do at school to keep the
white folks off his back and sorry for him. Send this poor kid to camp posters, is
his specialty.

"I do," says Mercedes. "I have a box of stationery on my desk and a picture
of my cat. My godmother bought the stationery and the desk. There's a big rose
on each sheet and the envelopes smell like roses."

"Who wants to know about your smelly-ass stationery," say Rosie Giraffe
fore I can get my two cents in.

"It's important to have a work area all your own so that . . ."

"Will you look at this sailboat, please," say Flyboy, cuttin her off and   25
pointin to the thing like it was his. So once again we tumble all over each other
to gaze at this magnificent thing in the toy store which is just big enough to
maybe sail two kittens across the pond if you strap them to the posts tight. We
all start reciting the price tag like we in assembly. "Handcrafted sailboat of fi-
berglass at one thousand one hundred ninety-five dollars."

"Unbelievable," I hear myself say and am really stunned. I read it again for
myself just in case the group recitation put me in a trance. Same thing. For
some reason this pisses me off. We look at Miss Moore and she lookin at us,
waiting for I dunno what.

"Who'd pay all that when you can buy a sailboat set for a quarter at Pop's,
a tube of glue for a dime, and a ball of string for eight cents? It must have a motor and a whole lot else besides," I say. "My sailboat cost me about fifty cents."

"But will it take water?" say Mercedes with her smart ass.

"Took mine to Alley Pond Park once," say Flyboy. "String broke. Lost it.
Pity."

"Sailed mine in Central Park and it keeled over and sank. Had to ask my   30
father for another dollar."

"And you got the strap," laugh Big Butt. "The jerk didn't even have a string
on it. My old man wailed on his behind."

Little Q.T. was staring hard at the sailboat and you could see he wanted it
bad. But he too little and somebody'd just take it from him. So what the hell.
"This boat for kids, Miss Moore?"

"Parents silly to buy something like that just to get all broke up," say Rosie
Giraffe.

"That much money it should last forever," I figure.

"My father'd buy it for me if I wanted it."   35

"Your father, my ass," say Rosie Giraffe getting a chance to finally push
Mercedes.

"Must be rich people shop here," say Q.T.

"You are a very bright boy," say Flyboy. "What was your first clue?" And he
rap him on the head with the back of his knuckles, since Q.T. the only one he
could get away with. Though Q.T. liable to come up behind you years later and
get his licks in when you half expect it.

"What I want to know is," I says to Miss Moore though I never talk to her,
I wouldn't give the bitch that satisfaction, "is how much a real boat costs? I
figure a thousand'd get you a yacht any day."

"Why don't you check that out," she says, "and report back to the group?"   40
Which really pains my ass. If you gonna mess up a perfectly good swim day
least you could do is have some answers. "Let's go in," she say like she got something up her sleeve. Only she don't lead the way. So me and Sugar turn the
corner to where the entrance is, but when we get there I kinda hang back. Not
that I'm scared, what's there to be afraid of, just a toy store. But I feel funny,
shame. But what I got to be shamed about? Got as much right to go in as anybody. But somehow I can't seem to get hold of the door, so I step away from

Sugar to lead. But she hangs back too. And I look at her and she looks at me and this is ridiculous. I mean, damn, I have never ever been shy about doing nothing or going nowhere. But then Mercedes steps up and then Rosie Giraffe and Big Butt crowd in behind and shove, and next thing we all stuffed into the doorway with only Mercedes squeezing past us, smoothing out her jumper and walking right down the aisle. Then the rest of us tumble in like a glued-together jigsaw done all wrong. And people lookin at us. And it's like the time me and Sugar crashed into the Catholic church on a dare. But once we got in there and everything so hushed and holy and the candles and the bowin and the hand-kerchiefs on all the drooping heads, I just couldn't go through with the plan. Which was for me to run up to the altar and do a tap dance while Sugar played the nose flute and messed around in the holy water. And Sugar kept givin me the elbow. Then later teased me so bad I tied her up in the shower and turned it on and locked her in. And she'd be there till this day if Aunt Gretchen hadn't finally figured I was lying about the boarder takin a shower.

Same thing in the store. We all walkin on tiptoe and hardly touchin the games and puzzles and things. And I watched Miss Moore who is steady watchin us like she waitin for a sign. Like Mama Drewery watches the sky and sniffs the air and takes note of just how much slant is in the bird formation. Then me and Sugar bump smack into each other, so busy gazing at the toys, 'specially the sailboat. But we don't laugh and go into our fat-lady bump-stomach routine. We just stare at that price tag. Then Sugar run a finger over the whole boat. And I'm jealous and want to hit her. Maybe not her, but I sure want to punch somebody in the mouth.

"Watcha bring us here for, Miss Moore?"

"You sound angry, Sylvia. Are you mad about something?" Givin me one of them grins like she tellin a grown-up joke that never turns out to be funny. And she's lookin very closely at me like maybe she plannin to do my portrait from memory. I'm mad, but I won't give her that satisfaction. So I slouch around the store bein very bored and say, "Let's go."

Me and Sugar at the back of the train watchin the tracks whizzin by large then small then getting gobbled up in the dark. I'm thinkin about this tricky toy I saw in the store. A clown that somersaults on a bar then does chin-ups just cause you yank lightly at his leg. Cost $35. I could see me askin my mother for a $35 birthday clown. "You wanna who that costs what?" she'd say, cocking her head to the side to get a better view of the hole in my head. Thirty-five dollars could buy new bunk beds for Junior and Gretchen's boy. Thirty-five dollars and the whole household could go visit Grand-daddy Nelson in the country. Thirty-five dollars would pay for the rent and the piano bill too. Who are these people that spend that much for performing clowns and $1000 for toy sail-boats? What kinda work they do and how they live and how come we ain't in on it? Where we are is who we are, Miss Moore always pointin out. But it don't necessarily have to be that way, she always adds then waits for somebody to say that poor people have to wake up and demand their share of the pie and don't none of us know what kind of pie she talking about in the first damn place. But she ain't so smart cause I still got her four dollars from the taxi and she sure ain't gettin it. Messin up my day with this shit. Sugar nudges me in my pocket and winks.

Miss Moore lines us up in front of the mailbox where we started from, seem   45
like years ago, and I got a headache for thinkin so hard. And we lean all over each other so we can hold up under the draggy-ass lecture she always finishes us off with at the end before we thank her for borin us to tears. But she just looks at us like she readin tea leaves. Finally she say, "Well, what did you think of F. A. O. Schwarz?"

Rosie Giraffe mumbles, "White folks crazy."

"I'd like to go there again when I get my birthday money," says Mercedes, and we shove her out the pack so she has to lean on the mailbox by herself.

"I'd like a shower. Tiring day," say Flyboy.

Then Sugar surprises me by sayin, "You know, Miss Moore, I don't think all of us here put together eat in a year what that sailboat costs." And Miss Moore lights up like somebody goosed her. "And?" she say, urging Sugar on. Only I'm standin on her foot so she don't continue.

"Imagine for a minute what kind of society it is in which some people   50
can spend on a toy what it would cost to feed a family of six or seven. What do you think?"

"I think," say Sugar pushing me off her feet like she never done before, cause I whip her ass in a minute, "that this is not much of a democracy if you ask me. Equal chance to pursue happiness means an equal crack at the dough, don't it?" Miss Moore is beside herself and I am disgusted with Sugar's treachery. So I stand on her foot one more time to see if she'll shove me. She shuts up, and Miss Moore looks at me, sorrowfully I'm thinkin. And somethin weird is goin on, I can feel it in my chest.

"Anybody else learn anything today?" lookin dead at me. I walk away and Sugar has to run to catch up and don't even seem to notice when I shrug her arm off my shoulder.

"Well, we got four dollars anyway," she says.

"Uh hunh."

"We could go to Hascombs and get half a chocolate layer and then go to   55
the Sunset and still have plenty money for potato chips and ice cream sodas."

"Un hunh."

"Race you to Hascombs," she say.

We start down the block and she gets ahead which is O.K. by me cause I'm going to the West End and then over to the Drive to think this day through. She can run if she want to and even run faster. But ain't nobody gonna beat me at nuthin.   *[1972]*

■ **THINKING ABOUT THE TEXT**

1. Bambara's story begins with "Back in the days," which suggests that Sylvia is significantly older now than she was then. How much time do you think has passed since the events she recalls? Does it matter to you how old she is now? Why, or why not?

2. Miss Moore is not officially a teacher. Nor is she a relative of the children she instructs. Is it right, then, for her to "take responsibility for the young ones' education" (para. 1)? Make arguments for and against her doing so.

3. Consider Miss Moore herself as making an argument. What are her claims? Which of her strategies, if any, seem effective in persuading her audience? Which, if any, seem ineffective?

4. What statements by the children articulate the lesson that Miss Moore teaches? Are all these statements saying pretty much the same thing? At the end of the story, is Sylvia ready to agree with all of them? Explain.

5. Do class and race seem equally important in this story, or does one seem more important than the other? Elaborate your reasoning.

■ MAKING COMPARISONS

1. "The Lesson" is more humorous than "Young Goodman Brown." Does its humor lead you to take Bambara's story of injustice less seriously than you do Hawthorne's? Why, or why not?

2. Whereas "Young Goodman Brown" has an omniscient narrator, "The Lesson" is narrated in the first person, by Sylvia herself. To what extent does this difference matter as you read the two stories together?

3. Sylvia is younger in age than Goodman Brown is. How significant is this difference to you as you consider their responses to injustice?

ALICE WALKER
The Flowers

A native of Eatonton, Georgia, Alice Walker (b. 1944) attended Spelman College and received her B.A. from Sarah Lawrence College in 1965. During the 1960s, she was active in the civil rights movement, an experience reflected in her 1976 novel Meridian *and in her autobiographical book,* The Way Forward Is with a Broken Heart *(2000). Walker is accomplished in many genres, and her essays, short stories, novels, and poems are widely read. She is perhaps best known for the novel* The Color Purple *(1976), which earned her both a Pulitzer Prize and an American Book Award and was made into a movie. Terming herself a "womanist" rather than a feminist in the essays of* In Search of Our Mothers' Gardens *(1983), Walker has confronted many issues concerning women, including abusive relationships, lesbian love, and the horrors of ritual genital mutilation in some African societies. Her daughter, Rebecca, has written her own memoir,* Black, White, and Jewish, *dealing with her childhood and adolescence as the daughter of Alice Walker and activist lawyer Mel Leventhal, to whom Walker was married for nine years, after meeting him during voter registration drives in Mississippi in 1967. The short story "The Flowers" is from Walker's collection* In Love and Trouble: Stories of Black Women

(1973). Her latest novel is Now Is the Time to Open Your Heart *(2004). Her most recent books are a collection of poems,* Hard Times Require Furious Dancing *(2010), and two works of nonfiction:* We Are the Ones We Have Been Waiting For *(2007) and* Overcoming Speechlessness *(2010).*

It seemed to Myop as she skipped lightly from hen house to pigpen to smokehouse that the days had never been as beautiful as these. The air held a keenness that made her nose twitch. The harvesting of the corn and cotton, peanuts and squash, made each day a golden surprise that caused excited little tremors to run up her jaws.

Myop carried a short, knobby stick. She struck out at random at chickens she liked, and worked out the beat of a song on the fence around the pigpen. She felt light and good in the warm sun. She was ten, and nothing existed for her but her song, the stick clutched in her dark brown hand, and the tat-de-ta-ta-ta of accompaniment.

Turning her back on the rusty boards of her family's sharecropper cabin, Myop walked along the fence till it ran into the stream made by the spring. Around the spring, where the family got drinking water, silver ferns and wildflowers grew. Along the shallow banks pigs rooted. Myop watched the tiny white bubbles disrupt the thin black scale of soil and the water that silently rose and slid away down the stream.

She had explored the woods behind the house many times. Often, in late autumn, her mother took her to gather nuts among the fallen leaves. Today she made her own path, bouncing this way and that way, vaguely keeping an eye out for snakes. She found, in addition to various common but pretty ferns and leaves, an armful of strange blue flowers with velvety ridges and a sweet-suds bush full of the brown, fragrant buds.

By twelve o'clock, her arms laden with sprigs of her findings, she was a mile or more from home. She had often been as far before, but the strangeness of the land made it not as pleasant as her usual haunts. It seemed gloomy in the little cove in which she found herself. The air was damp, the silence close and deep.

Myop began to circle back to the house, back to the peacefulness of the morning. It was then she stepped smack into his eyes. Her heel became lodged in the broken ridge between brow and nose, and she reached down quickly, unafraid, to free herself. It was only when she saw his naked grin that she gave a little yelp of surprise.

He had been a tall man. From feet to neck covered a long space. His head lay beside him. When she pushed back the leaves and layers of earth and debris Myop saw that he'd had large white teeth, all of them cracked or broken, long fingers, and very big bones. All his clothes had rotted away except some threads of blue denim from his overalls. The buckles of the overalls had turned green.

Myop gazed around the spot with interest. Very near where she'd stepped into the head was a wild pink rose. As she picked it to add to her bundle she

5

noticed a raised mound, a ring, around the rose's root. It was the rotted remains of a noose, a bit of shredding plowline, now blending benignly into the soil. Around an overhanging limb of a great spreading oak clung another piece. Frayed, rotted, bleached, and frazzled — barely there — but spinning restlessly in the breeze. Myop laid down her flowers.

And the summer was over.   [1973]

■ **THINKING ABOUT THE TEXT**

1. The story centers on Myop, but it is not told by her. How close do you sense that the narrator is to her thoughts?

2. Do you assume that Myop and the dead man are African American? Why, or why not?

3. Upon discovering the decomposing body, "Myop gazed around the spot with interest" (para. 8). What would you say to someone bothered that the child is first "interested" rather than horrified?

4. Why do you think Walker chose to focus the story so much on flowers, even putting them in her title? What should we infer from the next-to-last sentence, "Myop laid down her flowers" (para. 8)?

5. What is your interpretation of the last sentence? What does it suggest to you about Myop's thinking at this point? Why do you think Walker chose to have the story take place at the end of summer, rather than at the end of some other season? Why do you suppose she decided to keep the story quite brief?

■ **MAKING COMPARISONS**

1. Is it helpful to think that Myop discovers in the wilderness pretty much the same thing that Goodman Brown finds there? Why, or why not? Is there a counterpart to the wilderness in Bambara's story?

2. What might Goodman Brown and Sylvia each say to Myop now that she has discovered a lynched body? What would be *their* perspective on it?

3. How can each of these three stories be seen as a journey narrative, in addition to being a narrative about the discovery of injustice?

■ **WRITING ABOUT ISSUES**

1. Choose "Young Goodman Brown," "The Lesson," or "The Flowers," and write an essay in which you identify the extent to which the protagonist changes over the course of the story. What signs of change, if any, does this character show? In what ways might he or she remain the same?

2. About Myop, Walker writes, "Today she made her own path" (para. 4). Write an essay in which you analyze how, metaphorically speaking, this

statement can apply to the protagonists of two stories in this cluster. Compare the degrees to which they "make their own paths."

3. Write an essay recalling an occasion when someone you knew or read about was intent on branding someone else a sinner or wrongdoer. Moreover, let this occasion be one that left you with mixed feelings. Then write an essay that identifies the issues you thought were at stake and also expresses and supports your view of the outcome. If you wish, refer to one or two of the stories in this cluster.

4. Imagine that you are giving a brief speech about "Young Goodman Brown" to a college class studying issues of religion, or a brief speech about "The Lesson" or "The Flowers" to a group of elementary-school teachers. Write this speech, making clear the main point that you are using the story to illustrate.

≡ Punishments: Poems

Acts of punishment may be just or unjust: in any case, a punishment reflects the decisions and values of the person ordering it and the ethics of the person willing to carry it out. Even people who merely learn about a punishment wind up judging it. Consciously or unconsciously, they choose to praise it, criticize it, or passively tolerate it. Each of these four poems deals with judgments made by punishers and by those who are, in some sense, their audience. Think about the actions you are taking and the principles you are expressing as you judge the people you encounter here.

≡ BEFORE YOU READ

Recall a particular punishment that you considered unjust. What were the circumstances? What experiences, values, and reasoning led you to disapprove of the punishment? Could you have done anything to prevent it or to see that similarly unfair punishments did not recur? If so, what?

SEAMUS HEANEY
Punishment

For his distinguished career as a poet, Seamus Heaney (b. 1939) won the Nobel Prize for literature in 1995. He was raised as a Catholic in Northern Ireland, where Protestants remained in the majority and frequently conflicted with Catholics. Until the Peace Accord of 1997, the region was controlled by the British government, whereas now it is ruled by a mixed body representing both religions. Several of Heaney's poems deal with Catholic resistance to the longtime British domination of his native land. Heaney moved to Dublin, in the Republic of Ireland, in the early 1970s, but he has often visited the United States, even holding an appointment as Boylston Professor of Rhetoric at Harvard University. The following poem appears in Heaney's 1975 book North. *It is part of a whole sequence of poems based on P. V. Glob's 1969 book* The Bog People. *Heaney was drawn to Glob's photographs of Iron Age people whose preserved bodies were discovered in bogs of Denmark and other European countries.*

I can feel the tug
of the halter at the nape
of her neck, the wind
on her naked front.

It blows her nipples   5
to amber beads,
it shakes the frail rigging
of her ribs.

I can see her drowned
body in the bog,   10
the weighing stone,
the floating rods and boughs.

Under which at first
she was a barked sapling
that is dug up   15
oak-bone, brain-firkin:

her shaved head
like a stubble of black corn,
her blindfold a soiled bandage,
her noose a ring   20

to store
the memories of love.
Little adulteress,
before they punished you

you were flaxen-haired,   25
undernourished, and your
tar-black face was beautiful.
My poor scapegoat,

I almost love you
but would have cast, I know,   30
the stones of silence.°
I am the artful voyeur

of your brain's exposed
and darkened combs,
your muscles' webbing   35
and all your numbered bones:

I who have stood dumb
when your betraying sisters,

30–31 would have cast . . . of silence: In John 8:7–9, Jesus confronts a mob about to stone
an adulterous woman and makes the famous statement "He that is without sin among you,
let him first cast a stone at her." The crowd retreats, "being convicted by their own conscience."

cauled in tar,
wept by the railings,°   40

who would connive
in civilized outrage
yet understand the exact
and tribal, intimate revenge.   *[1975]*

37–40 I who . . . by the railings: In 1969, the British army became highly visible occupiers of Northern Ireland. In Heaney's native city of Belfast, the Irish Republican Army
retaliated against Irish Catholic women who dated British soldiers. Punishments included
shaving the women's heads, stripping and tarring them, and handcuffing them to the city's
railings.

■ THINKING ABOUT THE TEXT

1. Summarize your impression of the bog woman. Where does the speaker
   begin addressing her directly? Why do you suppose Heaney has him
   refrain from addressing her right away?

2. Who is the main subject of this poem? The bog woman? The "betraying
   sisters" (line 38)? The speaker? Some combination of these people?

3. The speaker refers to himself as a "voyeur" (line 32). Consult a dictionary definition of this word. How might it apply to the speaker? Do you
   think it is ultimately the best label for him? Explain. Do you feel like a
   voyeur reading this poem? Why, or why not?

4. What are the speaker's thoughts in the last stanza? What connotation
   do you attach to the word *connive?* (You might want to consult a dictionary definition of it.) What is the speaker's attitude toward "the exact /
   and tribal, intimate revenge"? Do you see him as tolerating violence?

5. What words in this poem, if any, are unfamiliar to you? What is their effect on you? Each stanza has four lines. Does this pattern create a steady
   rhythm or one more fragmented than harmonious? Try reading it aloud.

CAROLYN FORCHÉ
The Colonel

*In her poetry, Carolyn Forché (b. 1950) often addresses contemporary abuses of
power. Her first book of poems,* Gathering the Tribes *(1976), won the Yale Series
of Younger Poets competition. The following poem is from her second,* The Country
between Us *(1981), which won the Lamont Award from the Academy of American
Poets. Much of this book is based on Forché's experiences during her stay in
El Salvador, which at the time was beset by civil war. She has edited a collection entitled* Against Forgetting: Twentieth-Century Poetry of Witness *(1993), and her
latest book of poetry is* The Blue Hour *(2003). She is currently a professor of English at Georgetown University in Washington, D.C.*

What you have heard is true. I was in his house. His wife carried a tray of coffee and sugar. His daughter filed her nails, his son went out for the night. There were daily papers, pet dogs, a pistol on the cushion beside him. The moon swung bare on its black cord over the house. On the television was a cop show. It was in English. Broken bottles were embedded in the walls around the house   5
to scoop the kneecaps from a man's legs or cut his hands to lace. On the windows there were gratings like those in liquor stores. We had dinner, rack of lamb, good wine, a gold bell was on the table for calling the maid. The maid brought green mangoes, salt, a type of bread. I was asked how I enjoyed the country. There was a brief commercial in Spanish. His wife took everything   10
away. There was some talk then of how difficult it had become to govern. The parrot said hello on the terrace. The colonel told it to shut up, and pushed himself from the table. My friend said to me with his eyes: say nothing. The colonel returned with a sack used to bring groceries home. He spilled many human ears on the table. They were like dried peach halves. There is no other way to   15
say this. He took one of them in his hands, shook it in our faces, dropped it into a water glass. It came alive there. I am tired of fooling around he said. As for the rights of anyone, tell your people they can go fuck themselves. He swept the ears to the floor with his arm and held the last of his wine in the air. Something for your poetry, no? he said. Some of the ears on the floor caught this scrap of   20
his voice. Some of the ears on the floor were pressed to the ground.   *[1978]*

▤ THINKING ABOUT THE TEXT

1. How do you characterize the colonel? List a number of specific adjectives and supporting details. Does your impression of him change as you read, or does it stay pretty much the same? Explain.

2. Forché calls this text a poem, and yet it seems to consist of one long prose paragraph. Here is an issue of genre: Is it *really* a poem? Support your answer by identifying what you think are characteristics of poetry. What is the effect of Forché's presenting the text as a poem? Note what the colonel says about poetry. How might this text be considered a response to him?

3. Forché uses many short sentences here. What is the effect of this strategy? Even though she quotes the colonel, she does not use quotation marks. What is the effect of this choice?

4. The poem begins, "What you have heard is true." Do you think the situation it describes really occurred? Identify some warrants or assumptions that influence your answer. Where else does the poem refer to hearing? How might it be seen as being about audiences and their responses?

5. Forché wrote "The Colonel" after a stay in El Salvador, and so it is reasonable for her audience to conclude that the poem is set in that country. Yet she does not actually specify the setting. Should she have done so? Why, or why not?

■ MAKING COMPARISONS

1. Do you find the punishments alluded to in Heaney's and Forché's poems equally disturbing? Note specific details that influence your impressions.

2. To what extent does each of these two poems seem an effort to imagine the mind of someone who inflicts punishment?

3. Which, if any, of the situations referred to in these two poems could happen in the contemporary United States?

C. K. WILLIAMS
The Nail

Originally from Newark, New Jersey, C. K. Williams (b. 1936) has taught for many years at Princeton University while also spending much time in France. His most recent books include his Collected Poems *(2006) and* On Whitman *(2010), a study of Walt Whitman. During his long career as a poet, he has won several major prizes, including the National Book Award for* The Singing *(2003), the National Book Critics Circle Award for* Flesh and Blood *(1987), and the Pulitzer Prize for* Repair *(1999), which includes the following selection.*

Some dictator or other had gone into exile, and now reports were coming
  about his regime,
the usual crimes, torture, false imprisonment, cruelty and corruption,
  but then a detail:
that the way his henchmen had disposed of enemies was by hammering
  nails into their skulls.
Horror, then, what mind does after horror, after that first feeling that
  you'll never catch your breath,
mind imagines — how not be annihilated by it? — the preliminary tap,   5
  feels it in the tendons of the hand,
feels the way you do with *your* nail when you're fixing something,
  making something, shelves, a bed;
the first light tap to set the slant, and then the slightly harder tap, to
  embed the tip a little more . . .

No, no more: this should be happening in myth, in stone, or paint, not in
  reality, not here;
it should be an emblem of itself, not itself, something that would *mean*,
  not really have to happen,
something to go out, expand in implication from that unmoved mass of   10
  matter in the breast;
as in the image of an anguished face, in grief for us, not us as us, us as in
  a myth, a moral tale,

a way to tell the truth that grief is limitless, a way to tell us we must
    always understand
it's we who do such things, we who set the slant, embed the tip, lift the
    sledge and drive the nail,
drive the nail which is the axis upon which turns the brutal human world
    upon the world.   *[1999]*

▦ THINKING ABOUT THE TEXT

1. If not for the "detail" of the nailing, do you think the speaker would have been greatly bothered by what he refers to as "the usual crimes, torture, false imprisonment, cruelty and corruption" (line 2)? Explain your reasoning.

2. Although the first stanza begins by referring to people other than the speaker ("Some dictator or other," "his henchmen"), it then refers to "you." What is the effect of this shift? The second stanza then brings up "we" and "us." Why does Williams make this change in pronouns, do you think?

3. In line 5, the speaker suggests that the mind can be "annihilated." In what sense might this be so?

4. The speaker seems to compare the dictator's punishment of his foes — his "hammering nails into their skulls" (line 3) — to ordinary carpentry that the poem's readers might perform. What would you say to a reader who argues that this comparison trivializes the barbarity of the dictator's act?

5. At the beginning of the second stanza, the speaker understandably expresses a wish that the dictator's act take place "not in reality, not here." Explain the alternative he imagines. What does he mean when he says that "this should be happening in myth, in stone, or paint" (line 8) — that "it should be an emblem of itself, not itself, something that would *mean*" (line 9)?

6. What would you say to a reader who sees references to Christ's crucifixion in the last few lines? How helpful do you find this association for an understanding of the poem? How should non-Christian readers feel about it?

▦ MAKING COMPARISONS

1. Williams's title, "The Nail," suggests that his poem depends heavily on imagery. Does imagery play as big a role in Heaney's and Forché's poems as it does in Williams's? Explain by referring to specific lines in each.

2. Are Williams's and Heaney's poems more about the speaker's *reaction* to punishment than Forché's is? Refer to specific lines in all three texts.

3. In what ways does each of the three poems turn the physical punishment it focuses on into a metaphor? What would you say to someone who argues that a poem should never do this — that making punishment metaphorical is insensitive to the pain of those it actually hurts?

SHERMAN ALEXIE

Capital Punishment

Born in Spokane, Washington, Sherman Alexie (b. 1966) is a member of the Spokane/ Coeur d'Alene tribe. His fiction includes the novels Reservation Blues *(1996),* Indian Killer *(1997),* Flight *(2007), and* The Absolutely True Diary of a Part-Time Indian *(2007). He has also produced three collections of short stories:* The Toughest Indian in the World *(2001),* Ten Little Indians *(2003), and* The Lone Ranger and Tonto Fistfight in Heaven *(1994), which he adapted for the acclaimed 1998 film* Smoke Signals. *Alexie is a poet, too, with his collections of verse including* The Business of Fancy Dancing *(1992),* Old Shirts and New Skins *(1993),* First Indian on the Moon *(1993),* Drums like This *(1996), and* One Stick Song *(2000). "Capital Punishment" appeared in a 1996 issue of* Indiana Review *and, that same year, in Alexie's collection* The Summer of Black Widows. *It was also selected for the 1996 edition of the volume* Best American Poetry. *Alexie wrote the poem after reading media coverage of an actual execution in the state of Washington.*

I prepare the last meal
for the Indian man to be executed

but this killer doesn't want much:
baked potato, salad, tall glass of ice water.

(I am not a witness)   5

It's mostly the dark ones
who are forced to sit in the chair

especially when white people die.
It's true, you can look it up

and this Indian killer pushed   10
his fists all the way down

a white man's throat, just to win a bet
about the size of his heart.

Those Indians are always gambling.
Still, I season this last meal   15

with all I have. I don't have much
but I send it down the line

with the handsome guard
who has fallen in love

with the Indian killer.   20
I don't care who loves whom.

(I am not a witness)

I don't care if I add too much
salt or pepper to the warden's stew.

He can eat what I put in front of him.   25
I just cook for the boss

but I cook just right
for the Indian man to be executed.

The temperature is the thing.
I once heard a story   30

about a black man who was electrocuted
in that chair and lived to tell about it

before the court decided to sit him back down
an hour later and kill him all over again.

I have an extra sandwich hidden away   35
in the back of the refrigerator

in case this Indian killer survives
that first slow flip of the switch

and gets hungry while he waits
for the engineers to debate the flaws.   40

(I am not a witness)

I prepare the last meal for free
just like I signed up for the last war.

I learned how to cook
by lasting longer than any of the others.   45

Tonight, I'm just the last one left
after the handsome guard takes the meal away.

I turn off the kitchen lights
and sit alone in the dark

because the whole damn prison dims   50
when the chair is switched on.

You can watch a light bulb flicker
on a night like this

and remember it too clearly
like it was your first kiss   55

or the first hard kick to your groin.
It's all the same

when I am huddled down here
trying not to look at the clock

look at the clock, no, don't   60
look at the clock, when all of it stops

making sense: a salad, a potato
a drink of water all taste like heat.

(I am not a witness)

I want you to know I tasted a little   65
of that last meal before I sent it away.

It's the cook's job, to make sure
and I was sure I ate from the same plate

and ate with the same fork and spoon
that the Indian killer used later   70

in his cell. Maybe a little bit of me
lodged in his stomach, wedged between

his front teeth, his incisors, his molars
when he chewed down on the bit

and his body arced like modern art   75
curving organically, smoke rising

from his joints, wispy flames decorating
the crown of his head, the balls of his feet.

(I am not a witness)

I sit here in the dark kitchen   80
when they do it, meaning

when they kill him, kill
and add another definition of the word

to the dictionary. American fills
its dictionary. We write down *kill* and everybody   85

in the audience shouts out exactly how
they spell it, what it means to them

and all of the answers are taken down
by the pollsters and secretaries

who take care of the small details: 90
time of death, pulse rate, press release.

I heard a story once about some reporters
at a hanging who wanted the hood removed

from the condemned's head, so they could look
into his eyes and tell their readers   95

what they saw there. What did they expect?
All of the stories should be simple.

1 death + 1 death = 2 deaths.
But we throw the killers in one grave

and victims in another. We form sides   100
and have two separate feasts.

(I am a witness)

I prepared the last meal
for the Indian man who was executed

and have learned this: If any of us   105
stood for days on top of a barren hill

during an electrical storm
then lightning would eventually strike us

and we'd have no idea for which of our sins
we were reduced to headlines and ash.   *[1996]*   110

▤ THINKING ABOUT THE TEXT

1. Alexie reports that in writing this poem, he aimed "to call for the abolition of the death penalty." In reading the poem, do you sense that this
   is his aim? Why, or why not? In what respects might the poem be seen
   as arguing against the death penalty? State how you viewed capital punishment before and after you read it. Did Alexie affect your attitude? If
   so, how?

2. Why do you think Alexie cast the speaker as the condemned man's
   cook? How do you explain the speaker's shift from denying that he is a
   witness to acknowledging that he is one? Identify how he seems to define the term *witness*. What would you say to someone who argues that
   the speaker is unreasonably stretching the meaning of this word because apparently he didn't directly observe the execution?

3. How does race figure in this poem? Should people consider race when
   discussing capital punishment? If so, what about race should they especially ponder? In examining Alexie's poem, should readers bear in mind
   that the author is Native American? Why, or why not?

4. The film *Dead Man Walking* (1995), which deals with arguments about capital punishment, shows in chilling detail an execution by injection. Yet at the moment the condemned man dies, the film also shows the faces of his two victims. By contrast, Alexie doesn't refer to the victim of the executed man after line 12. Should he have mentioned this victim again? Identify some of the values reflected in your answer.

5. Summarize and evaluate the lesson delivered by the speaker at the end of the poem. What do you think headlines might say about you if you were killed in the manner he describes?

≡ MAKING COMPARISONS

1. Forché's first sentence is "What you have heard is true." After noting that "It's mostly the dark ones / who are forced to sit in the chair / especially when white people die" (lines 6–8), Alexie's speaker declares, "It's true, you can look it up" (line 9). What do these lines imply about each poem's readers?

2. In his last three lines, Alexie's speaker refers to "us." Williams's last stanza also uses this pronoun and goes so far as to say, "it's we who do such things" (line 13). Do you take both speakers, as well as Forché's and Heaney's, to be making the same observation about their society in general? Why, or why not?

3. Of all the punishments mentioned in these four poems, only the one discussed in Alexie's — capital punishment — is currently authorized by law in the United States. Should this fact make his poem the most relevant to American readers? Why, or why not?

≡ WRITING ABOUT ISSUES

1. Choose one of the poems in this cluster. Then write an essay explaining how it can be seen as a poem about witnessing *or* about how people may be somehow involved with events that they haven't directly observed. If your essay refers to witnessing, make clear your definition of the term.

2. Even when people are not literally guilty of a crime or an atrocity, they may still *feel* guilty in a psychological sense. Choose two of the poems in this cluster, and write an essay arguing that one poem's main speaker evidently feels more guilt than the other poem's main speaker does. Refer to specific lines in both texts.

3. Write an essay in which you discuss whether the phrase "cruel and unusual punishment" applies to the event described in this paragraph from the March 26, 1997, issue of the *Washington Post*:

> Moments after convicted killer Pedro Medina was strapped into Florida's electric chair and 2,000 volts of electricity surged into his body

this morning, flames leapt from the inmate's head, filling the death chamber with smoke and horrifying two dozen witnesses.

Does Medina's execution amount to "cruel and unusual punishment"? If you need additional information before firmly deciding, what do you need to know?

4. Today, Amnesty International and PEN International, a writers' organization, regularly bring to the American public's attention cases of what they deem unjust punishment. In fact, Amnesty International has criticized all instances of capital punishment in the United States. Research one of the cases reported by these organizations. Then write an article for your school newspaper in which you (a) present the basic facts of the case, (b) identify values and principles you think your audience should apply to it, and (c) point out anything you believe can and should be done about it. If you wish, refer to any of the poems in this cluster.

SCOTT RUSSELL SANDERS, "Doing Time in the Thirteenth Chair"

MAXINE HONG KINGSTON, "No Name Woman"

ATUL GAWANDE, "Hellhole"

A system of justice is a series of activities. Typically they include investigation of a crime, arrest of the most likely culprit, a trial, and some form of punishment if the person is found guilty. Of course, such acts need not involve official laws, police, and courts. Many a community has regulated itself through informal codes and customs. Whether institutional or traditional, no justice system is perfect, and writers of literature have often raised questions about the handling of a particular case. In the first essay in this cluster, Scott Russell Sanders reflects on the human drama of a criminal trial that took place in a small American city. You will see that he sympathizes with the jurors but also with the defendant they judged. In the second essay, Maxine Hong Kingston ponders the suicide of an aunt in China, who was driven to kill herself when her village condemned her adulterous pregnancy. Finally, through specific case histories, Atul Gawande argues against the U.S. penal system's use of solitary confinement.

■ **BEFORE YOU READ**

Have you ever served on a jury? If so, what was the experience like? If not, would you like to be on a jury? Why, or why not? In general, do you have faith in the jury system? What specifically comes to mind as you consider this question?

SCOTT RUSSELL SANDERS
Doing Time in the Thirteenth Chair

Scott Russell Sanders (b. 1945) spent much of his youth at a military munitions base, where his father worked. He describes this experience in the title essay of his 1987 book The Paradise of Bombs, *which also includes the following piece. Today, Sanders is a professor emeritus of English at Indiana University in Bloomington. Besides essays, he has published fiction; a study of the writer D. H. Lawrence; and book-length nonfictional works, including* Staying Put: Making a Home in a Restless World *(1993);* Hunting for Hope: A Father's Journeys *(1998); a memoir of his spiritual experiences entitled* A Private History of Awe *(2007); and* A Conservationist Manifesto *(2009), which reflects Sanders's long-standing interest in the environment.*

1164

The courtroom is filled with the ticking of a clock and the smell of mold. Listening to the minutes click away, I imagine bombs or mechanical hearts sealed behind the limestone walls. Forty of us have been yanked out of our usual orbits and called to appear for jury duty in this ominous room, beneath the stained-glass dome of the county courthouse. We sit in rows like strangers in a theater, coats rumpled in our laps, crossing and uncrossing our legs, waiting for the show to start.

I feel sulky and rebellious, the way I used to feel when a grade-school teacher made me stay inside during recess. This was supposed to have been the first day of my Christmas vacation, and the plain, uncitizenly fact is that I don't want to be here. I want to be home hammering together some bookshelves for my wife. I want to be out tromping the shores of Lake Monroe with my eye cocked skyward for bald eagles and sharp-shinned hawks.

But the computer-printed letter said to report today for jury duty, and so here I sit. The judge beams down at us from his bench. Tortoise-shell glasses, twenty-dollar haircut, square boyish face: although probably in his early forties, he could pass for a student-body president. He reminds me of an owlish television know-it-all named Mr. Wizard who used to conduct scientific experiments (Magnetism! Litmus tests! Sulphur dioxide!) on a kids' show in the 1950s. Like Mr. Wizard, he lectures us in slow, pedantic speech: trial by one's peers, tradition stretching back centuries to England, defendant innocent until proven guilty beyond a reasonable doubt, and so abundantly on. I spy around for the clock. It must be overhead, I figure, up in the cupola above the dome, raining its ticktocks down on us.

When the lecture is finished, the judge orders us to rise, lift our hands, and swear to uphold the truth. There is a cracking of winter-stiff knees as we stand and again as we sit down. Then he introduces the principal actors: the sleek young prosecutor, who peacocks around like a politician on the hustings; the married pair of brooding, elegantly dressed defense lawyers; and the defendant. I don't want to look at this man who is charged with crimes against the "peace and dignity" of the State of Indiana. I don't want anything to do with his troubles. But I grab an image anyway, of a squat, slit-eyed man about my age, mid-thirties, stringy black hair parted in the middle and dangling like curtains across his face, sparse black beard. The chin whiskers and squinted-up eyes make him look faintly Chinese, and faintly grimacing.

Next the judge reads a list of twelve names, none of them mine, and twelve   5
sworn citizens shuffle into the jury box. The lawyers have at them, darting questions. How do you feel about drugs? Would you say the defendant there looks guilty because he has a beard? Are you related to any police officers? Are you pregnant? When these twelve have finished answering, the attorneys scribble names on sheets of paper which they hand to the judge, and eight of the first bunch are sent packing. The judge reads eight more names, the jury box fills up with fresh bodies, the questioning resumes. Six of these get the heave-ho. And so the lawyers cull through the potential jurors, testing and chucking them like two men picking over apples in the supermarket. At length they agree on a dozen, and still my name has not been called. Hooray, I think. I can build those bookshelves after all, can watch those hawks.

Before setting the rest of us free, however, the judge consults his list. "I am calling alternate juror number one," he says, and then he pronounces my name.

Groans echo down my inmost corridors. For the first time I notice a thirteenth chair beside the jury box, and that is where the judge orders me to go.

"Yours is the most frustrating job," the judge advises me soothingly. "Unless someone else falls ill or gets called away, you will have to listen to all the proceedings without taking part in the jury's final deliberations or decisions."

I feel as though I have been invited to watch the first four acts of a five-act play. Never mind, I console myself: the lawyers will throw me out. I'm the only one in the courtroom besides the defendant who sports a beard or long hair. A backpack decorated with NO NUKES and PEACE NOW and SAVE THE WHALES buttons leans against my boots. How can they expect me, a fiction writer, to confine myself to facts? I am unreliable, a confessed fabulist, a marginal Quaker and Wobbly socialist, a man so out of phase with my community that I am thrown into fits of rage by the local newspaper. The lawyers will take a good look at me and race one another to the bench for the privilege of having the judge boot me out.

But neither Mr. Defense nor Mr. Prosecution quite brings himself to focus   10
on my shady features. Each asks me a perfunctory question, the way vacationers will press a casual thumb against the spare tire before hopping into the car for a trip. If there's air in the tire, you don't bother about blemishes. And that is all I am, a spare juror stashed away in the trunk of the court, in case one of the twelve originals gives out during the trial.

Ticktock. The judge assures us that we should be finished in five days, just in time for Christmas. The real jurors exchange forlorn glances. Here I sit, number thirteen, and nobody looks my way. Knowing I am stuck here for the duration, I perk up, blink my eyes. Like the bear going over the mountain, I might as well see what I can see.

What I see is a parade of mangled souls. Some of them sit on the witness stand and reveal their wounds; some of them remain offstage, summoned up only by the words of those who testify. The case has to do with the alleged sale, earlier this year, of hashish and cocaine to a confidential informer. First the prosecutor stands at a podium in front of the jury and tells us how it all happened, detail by criminal detail, and promises to prove every fact to our utter satisfaction. Next, one of the defense attorneys has a fling at us. It is the husband of the Mr.-and-Mrs. team, a melancholy-looking man with bald pate and mutton-chop sideburns, deep creases in the chocolate skin of his forehead. Leaning on the podium, he vows that he will raise a flock of doubts in our minds — grave doubts, reasonable doubts — particularly regarding the seedy character of the confidential informer. They both speak well, without hemming and hawing, without stumbling over syntactic cliffs, better than senators at a press conference. Thus, like rival suitors, they begin to woo the jury.

At mid-morning, before hearing from the first witness, we take a recess. (It sounds more and more like school.) Thirteen of us with peel-away JUROR tags stuck to our shirts and sweaters retreat to the jury room. We drink coffee and make polite chat. Since the only thing we have in common is this trial, and since the judge has just forbidden us to talk about that, we grind our gears trying to get a conversation started. I find out what everybody does in the way of work: a bar waitress, a TV repairman (losing customers while he sits here), a department store security guard, a dentist's assistant, an accountant, a nursing-home nurse, a cleaning woman, a caterer, a mason, a boisterous old lady retired from rearing children (and married, she tells us, to a school-crossing guard), a meek college student with the demeanor of a groundhog, a teacher. Three of them right now are unemployed. Six men, six women, with ages ranging from twenty-one to somewhere above seventy. Chaucer could gather this bunch together for a literary pilgrimage, and he would not have a bad sampling of smalltown America.

Presently the bailiff looks in to see what we're up to. She is a jowly woman, fiftyish, with short hair the color and texture of buffed aluminum. She wears silvery half-glasses of the sort favored by librarians; in the courtroom she peers at us above the frames with a librarian's skeptical glance, as if to make sure we are awake. To each of us she now gives a small yellow pad and a ballpoint pen. We are to write our names on the back, take notes on them during the trial, and surrender them to her whenever we leave the courtroom. (School again.) Without saying so directly, she lets us know that we are her flock and she is our shepherd. Anything we need, any yen we get for traveling, we should let her know.

I ask her whether I can go downstairs for a breath of air, and the bailiff answers "sure." On the stairway I pass a teenage boy who is listlessly polishing with a rag the wrought-iron filigree that supports the banister. Old men sheltering from December slouch on benches just inside the ground-floor entrance of the courthouse. Their faces have been caved in by disappointment and the loss of teeth. Two-dollar cotton work gloves, the cheapest winter hand-covers, stick out of their back pockets. They are veterans of this place; so when they see me coming with the blue JUROR label pasted on my chest, they look away. Don't tamper with jurors, especially under the very nose of the law. I want to tell them I'm not a real juror, only a spare, number thirteen. I want to pry old stories out of them, gossip about hunting and dogs, about their favorite pickup trucks, their worst jobs. I want to ask them when and how it all started to go wrong for them. Did they hear a snap when the seams of their life began to come apart? But they will not be fooled into looking at me, not these wily old men with the crumpled faces. They believe the label on my chest and stare down at their unlaced shoes.

I stick my head out the door and swallow some air. The lighted thermometer on the bank reads twenty-eight degrees. Schmaltzy Christmas organ music rebounds from the brick-and-limestone shopfronts of the town square. The Salvation Army bell rings and rings. Delivery trucks hustling through yellow lights blare their horns at jaywalkers.

The bailiff must finally come fetch me, and I feel like a wayward sheep. On my way back upstairs, I notice the boy dusting the same square foot of iron

15

filigree, and realize that he is doing this as a penance. Some judge ordered him to clean the metalwork. I'd like to ask the kid what mischief he's done, but the bailiff, looking very dour, is at my heels.

In the hallway she lines us up in our proper order, me last. Everybody stands up when we enter the courtroom, and then, as if we have rehearsed these routines, we all sit down at once. Now come the facts.

The facts are a mess. They are full of gaps, chuckholes, switchbacks, and dead ends — just like life.

At the outset we are shown three small plastic bags. Inside the first is a   20
wad of aluminum foil about the size of an earlobe; the second contains two white pills; the third holds a pair of stamp-sized, squarish packets of folded brown paper. A chemist from the state police lab testifies that he examined these items and found cocaine inside the brown packets, hashish inside the wad of aluminum foil. As for the white pills, they are counterfeits of a popular barbiturate, one favored by politicians and movie stars. They're depressants — downers — but they contain no "controlled substances."

There follows half a day's worth of testimony about how the bags were sealed, who locked them in the narcotics safe at the Bloomington police station, which officer drove them up to the lab in Indianapolis and which drove them back again, who carried them in his coat pocket and who carried them in his briefcase. Even the judge grows bored during this tedious business. He yawns, tips back in his chair, sips coffee from a mug, folds and unfolds with deft thumbs a square of paper about the size of the cocaine packets. The wheels of justice grind slowly. We hear from police officers in uniform, their handcuffs clanking, and from mustachioed officers in civvies, revolvers bulging under their suitcoats. From across the courtroom, the bailiff glares at us above her librarian's glasses, alert to catch us napping. She must be an expert at judging the degrees of tedium.

"Do you have to go back and be in the jail again tomorrow?" my little boy asks me at supper.

"Not jail," I correct him. "*Jury.* I'm in the jury."

"With real police?"

"Yes."   25

"And guns?"

"Yes, real guns."

On the second day there is much shifting of limbs in the jury box when the confidential informer, whom the police call 190, takes the stand. Curly-haired, thirty-three years old, bear-built and muscular like a middle-range wrestler, slow of eye, calm under the crossfire of questions, 190 works — when he works — as a drywall finisher. (In other words, he gets plasterboard ready for painting. It's a dusty, blinding job; you go home powdered white as a ghost, and you taste the joint-filler all night.) Like roughly one-quarter of the construction workers in the county, right now he's unemployed.

The story he tells is essentially this: just under a year ago, two cops showed up at his house. They'd been tipped off that he had a mess of stolen goods in his basement, stuff he'd swiped from over in a neighboring county. "Now look here," the cops said to him, "you help us out with some cases we've got going, and we'll see what we can do to help you when this here burglary business comes to court." "Like how?" he said. "Like tell us what you know about hot property, and maybe finger a drug dealer or so." He said yes to that, with the two cops sitting at his kitchen table, and — zap! — he was transformed into 190. (Hearing of this miraculous conversion, I am reminded of Saul on the road to Damascus, the devil's agent suddenly seeing the light and joining the angels.) In this new guise he gave information that led to several arrests and some prison terms, including one for his cousin and two or three for other buddies.

In this particular case, his story goes on, he asked a good friend of his   30
where a guy could buy some, you know, drugs. The friend's brother led him to Bennie's trailer, where Bennie offered to sell 190 about any kind of drug a man's heart could desire. "All I want's some hash," 190 told him, "but I got to go get some money off my old lady first." "Then go get it," said Bennie.

Where 190 went was to the police station. There they fixed him up to make a "controlled buy": searched him, searched his car; strapped a radio transmitter around his waist; took his money and gave him twenty police dollars to make the deal. Back 190 drove to Bennie's place, and on his tail in an unmarked police car drove Officer B., listening over the radio to every burp and glitch sent out by 190's secret transmitter. On the way, 190 picked up a six-pack of Budweiser. ("If you walk into a suspect's house drinking a can of beer," Officer B. later tells us, "usually nobody'll guess you're working for the police.") Inside the trailer, the woman Bennie lives with was now fixing supper, and her three young daughters were playing cards on the linoleum floor. 190 bought a gram of blond Lebanese hashish from Bennie for six dollars. Then 190 said that his old lady was on him bad to get her some downers, and Bennie obliged by selling him a couple of 714s (the white pills favored by movie stars and politicians) at seven dollars for the pair. They shot the bull awhile, Bennie bragging about how big a dealer he used to be (ten pounds of hash and five hundred hits of acid a week), 190 jawing along like an old customer. After about twenty minutes in the trailer, 190 drove to a secluded spot near the L & N railroad depot, and there he handed over the hash and pills to Officer B., who milked the details out of him.

Four days later, 190 went through the same routine, this time buying two packets of cocaine — two "dimes'" worth — from Bennie for twenty dollars. Inside the trailer were half a dozen or so of Bennie's friends, drinking whiskey and smoking pot and watching TV and playing backgammon and generally getting the most out of a Friday night. Again Officer B. tailed 190, listened to the secret radio transmission, and took it all down in a debriefing afterwards behind the Colonial Bakery.

The lawyers burn up a full day leading 190 through this story, dropping questions like breadcrumbs to lure him on, Mr. Prosecutor trying to guide him out of the labyrinth of memory and Mr. Defense trying to get him lost. 190 refuses to get lost. He tells and retells his story without stumbling, intent as a wrestler on a dangerous hold.

On the radio news I hear that U.S. ships have intercepted freighters bound out from Beirut carrying tons and tons of Lebanese hashish, the very same prize strain of hash that 190 claims he bought from Bennie. Not wanting to irk the Lebanese government, the radio says, our ships let the freighters through. Tons and tons sailing across the Mediterranean — into how many one-gram slugs could that cargo be divided?

Out of jail the defense lawyers subpoena one of 190's brothers, who is await-   35
ing his own trial on felony charges. He has a rabbity look about him, face pinched with fear, ready to bolt for the nearest exit. His canary yellow T-shirt is emblazoned with a scarlet silhouette of the Golden Gate Bridge. The shirt and the fear make looking at him painful. He is one of seven brothers and four sisters. Hearing that total of eleven children — the same number as in my father's family — I wonder if the parents were ever booked for burglary or other gestures of despair.

This skittish gent tells us that he always buys his drugs from his brother, good old 190. And good old 190, he tells us further, has a special fondness for snorting cocaine. Glowing there on the witness stand in his yellow shirt, dear brother gives the lie to one after another of 190's claims. But just when I'm about ready, hearing all of this fraternal gossip, to consign 190 to the level of hell reserved by Dante for liars, the prosecutor takes over the questioning. He soon draws out a confession that there has been a bitter feud recently between the two brothers. "And haven't you been found on three occasions to be mentally incompetent to stand trial?" the prosecutor demands.

"Yessir," mutters the brother.

"And haven't you spent most of the past year in and out of mental institutions?"

"Yessir."

This second admission is so faint, like a wheeze, that I must lean forward to   40
hear it, even though I am less than two yards away. While the prosecutor lets this damning confession sink into the jury, the rabbity brother just sits there, as if exposed on a rock while the hawks dive, his eyes pinched closed.

By day three of the trial, we jurors are no longer strangers to one another. Awaiting our entry into court, we exhibit wallet photos of our children, of nieces and nephews. We moan in chorus about our Christmas shopping lists. The caterer tells about serving 3,000 people at a basketball banquet. The boisterous old lady, to whom we have all taken a liking, explains how the long hairs on her white cats used to get on her husband's black suit pants until she put the cats out in the garage with heating pads in their boxes.

"Where do you leave your car?" the accountant asks.

"On the street," explains the lady. "I don't want to crowd those cats. They're particular as all get-out."

People compare their bowling scores, their insurance rates, their diets. The mason, who now weighs about 300 pounds, recounts how he once lost 129 pounds in nine months. His blood pressure got so bad he had to give up dieting, and inside of a year he'd gained all his weight back and then some. The nurse, who wrestles the bloated or shriveled bodies of elderly paupers at the city's old folks' home, complains about her leg joints, and we all sympathize. The security guard entertains us with sagas about shoplifters. We compare notes on car wrecks, on where to get a transmission overhauled, on the outgoing college football coach and the incoming city mayor. We talk, in fact, about everything under the sun except the trial.

In the hall, where we line up for our reentry into the courtroom, a sullen   45
boy sits at a table scrawling on a legal pad. Line after line he copies the same sentence: "I never will steal anything ever again." More penance. He's balancing on the first rung of a ladder that leads up — or down — to the electric chair. Somewhere in the middle of the ladder is a good long prison sentence, and that, I calculate, is what is at stake in our little drug-dealing case.

On the third day of testimony, we learn that 190 has been hidden away overnight by police. After he stepped down from the witness stand yesterday, Bennie's mate, Rebecca, greeted the informant outside in the lobby and threatened to pull a bread knife out of her purse and carve him into mincemeat. I look with new interest at the stolid, bulky, black-haired woman who has been sitting since the beginning of the trial right behind the defendant. From time to time she has leaned forward, touched Bennie on the shoulder, and bent close to whisper something in his good ear. She reminds me of the Amish farm wives of my Ohio childhood — stern, unpainted, built stoutly for heavy chores, her face a fortress against outsiders.

When Rebecca takes the stand, just half a dozen feet from where I sit in chair thirteen, I sense a tigerish fierceness beneath her numb surface. She plods along behind the prosecutor's questions until he asks her, rhetorically, whether she would like to see Bennie X put in jail; then she lashes out. God no, she doesn't want him locked away. Didn't he take her in when she had two kids already and a third in the oven, and her first husband run off, and the cupboards empty? And haven't they been living together just as good as married for eight years, except while he was in jail, and don't her three little girls call him Daddy? And hasn't he been working on the city garbage trucks, getting up at four in the morning, coming home smelling like other people's trash, and hasn't she been bagging groceries at the supermarket, her hands slashed with paper cuts, and her mother looking after the girls, all so they can keep off the welfare? Damn right she doesn't want him going to any prison.

What's more, Rebecca declares, Bennie don't deserve prison because he's clean. Ever since he got out of the slammer a year ago, he's quit dealing. He's done his time and he's mended his ways and he's gone straight. What about that sale of cocaine? the prosecutor wants to know. It never happened, Rebecca vows. She was there in the trailer the whole blessed night, and she never saw Bennie sell nobody nothing, least of all cocaine, which he never used because it's too expensive — it'll run you seventy-five dollars a day — and which he never sold even when he was dealing. The prosecutor needles her: How can she remember that particular night so confidently? She can remember, she flares at him, because early that evening she got a call saying her sister's ten-year-old crippled boy was fixing to die, and all the family was going to the children's hospital in Indianapolis to watch him pass away. That was a night she'll never forget as long as she lives.

When I was a boy, my friends and I believed that if you killed a snake, the mate would hunt you out in your very bed and strangle or gnaw or smother you. We held a similar belief regarding bears, wolves, and mountain lions, although we were much less likely to run into any of those particular beasts. I have gone years without remembering that bit of child's lore, until today, when Rebecca's tigerish turn on the witness stand revives it. I can well imagine her stashing a bread knife in her purse. And if she loses her man for years and stony years, and has to rear those three girls alone, the cupboards empty again, she might well jerk that knife out of her purse one night and use it on something other than bread.

During recess, we thirteen sit in the jury room and pointedly avoid talking   50
about the bread knife. The mason tells how a neighbor kid's Ford Pinto skidded across his lawn and onto his front porch, blocking the door and nosing against the picture window. "I took the wheels off and chained the bumper to my maple tree until his daddy paid for fixing my porch."

Everyone, it seems, has been assaulted by a car or truck. Our vehicular yarns wind closer and closer about the courthouse. Finally, two of the women jurors — the cigarillo-smoking caterer and the elderly cat lady — laugh nervously. The two of them were standing just inside the plate-glass door of the courthouse last night, the caterer says, when along came a pickup truck, out poked an arm from the window, up flew a smoking beer can, and then BAM! the can exploded. "We jumped a yard in the air!" cries the old woman. "We thought it was some of Bennie's mean-looking friends," the caterer admits. Everybody laughs at the tableau of speeding truck, smoking can, exploding cherry bomb, leaping jurors. Then we choke into sudden silence, as if someone has grabbed each of us by the throat.

Four of Bennie's friends — looking not so much mean as broken, like shell-shocked refugees — testify on his behalf during the afternoon of day three. Two of them are out-of-work men in their twenties, with greasy hair to their shoulders, fatigue jackets, and clodhopper boots: their outfits and world-weary expressions are borrowed from record jackets. They are younger versions of the old men with caved-in faces who crouch on benches downstairs, sheltering from December. The other two witnesses are young women with reputations to keep up, neater than the scruffy men; gold crosses dangle over their sweaters, and gum cracks between crooked teeth. All four speak in muttered monosyllables and orphaned phrases, as if they are breaking a long vow of silence and must fetch bits and pieces of language from the archives of memory. They were all at Bennie's place on the night of the alleged cocaine sale, and they swear in unison that no such sale took place.

Officer B., the puppetmaster who pulled the strings on 190, swears just as adamantly that both the sales, of cocaine and of hash, *did* take place, for he listened to the proceedings over the radio in his unmarked blue Buick. He is a sleepy-eyed man in his mid-thirties, about the age of the informant and the defendant, a law-upholding alter ego for those skewed souls.

Double-chinned, padded with the considerable paunch that seems to be issued along with the police badge, Officer B. answers Mr. Prosecutor and Mr. Defense in a flat, walkie-talkie drawl, consulting a sheaf of notes in his lap, never contradicting himself. Yes, he neglected to tape the opening few minutes of the first buy, the minutes when the exchange of hashish and money actually took place. Why? "I had a suspicion my batteries were weak, and I wanted to hold off." And, yes, he did erase the tape of the debriefing that followed buy number one. Why? "It's policy to reuse the old cassettes. Saves the taxpayers' money." And, yes, the tape of the second buy is raw, indecipherable noise, because a blaring TV in the background drowns out all human voices. (Listening to the tape, we can understand nothing in the scrawking except an ad for the American Express Card.) The tapes, in other words, don't prove a thing. What it all boils down to is the word of the law and of the unsavory informer versus the word of the many-times-convicted defendant, his mate, and his friends.

Toward the end of Officer B.'s testimony, there is a resounding clunk, like a   55
muffled explosion, at the base of the witness stand. We all jump — witness, judge, jury, onlookers — and only relax when the prosecutor squats down and discovers that a pair of handcuffs has fallen out of Officer B.'s belt. Just a little reminder of the law's muscle. All of us were envisioning bombs. When Officer B. steps down, the tail of his sportcoat is hitched up over the butt of his gun.

The arrest: a squad car pulls up to the front of the trailer, and out the trailer's back door jumps Bennie, barefooted, wearing T-shirt and cut-off jeans. He dashes away between tarpaper shacks, through dog yards, over a stubbled field (his bare feet bleeding), through a patch of woods to a railroad cut. Behind him puffs a skinny cop (who recounts this scene in court), shouting, "Halt! Police!" But Bennie never slows down until he reaches that railroad cut, where he stumbles, falls, rolls down to the tracks like the sorriest hobo. The officer draws his gun. Bennie lifts his hands for the familiar steel cuffs. The two of them trudge back to the squad car, where Officer B. reads the arrest warrant and Bennie blisters everybody with curses.

The judge later instructs us that flight from arrest may be regarded as evidence, not of guilt but of *consciousness* of guilt. Oh ho! A fine distinction! Guilt for what! Selling drugs? Playing hooky? Original sin? Losing his job at Coca-Cola? I think of those bleeding feet, the sad chase. I remember a drunken uncle who stumbled down a railroad cut, fell asleep between the tracks, and died of fear when a train passed over.

On day four of the trial, Bennie himself takes the stand. He is shorter than I thought, and fatter — too many months of starchy jail food and no exercise. With exceedingly long thumbnails he scratches his jaw. When asked a question, he rolls his eyes, stares at the ceiling, then answers in a gravelly country voice, the voice of a late-night disk jockey. At first he is gruffly polite, brief in his replies, but soon he gets cranked up and rants in a grating monologue about his painful history.

He graduated from high school in 1968, worked eight months at RCA and Coca-Cola, had a good start, had a sweetheart, then the army got him, made him a cook, shipped him to Vietnam. After a few weeks in the kitchen, he was transferred to the infantry because the fodder-machine was short of foot soldiers. "Hey, listen, man, I ain't nothing but a cook," he told them. "I ain't been trained for combat." And they said, "Don't you worry; you'll get on-the-job training. Learn or die." The artillery ruined his hearing. (Throughout the trial he has held a hand cupped behind one ear, and has followed the proceedings like a grandfather.) Some of his buddies got shot up. He learned to kill people. "We didn't even know what we was there for." To relieve his constant terror, he started doing drugs: marijuana, opium, just about anything that would ease a man's mind. Came home from Vietnam in 1971 a wreck, got treated like dirt, like a baby killer, like a murdering scumbag, and found no jobs. His sweetheart married an insurance salesman.

Within a year after his return he was convicted of shoplifting and burglary. He was framed on the second charge by a friend, but couldn't use his only alibi because he had spent the day of the robbery in bed with a sixteen-year-old girl, whose father would have put him away for statutory rape. As it was, he paid out two years in the pen, where he sank deeper into drugs than ever before. "If you got anything to buy or trade with, you can score more stuff in the state prisons than on the streets of Indianapolis." After prison, he still couldn't find work, couldn't get any help for his drug-thing from the Veterans' Administration, moved in with Rebecca and her three girls, eventually started selling marijuana and LSD. "Everytime I went to somebody for drugs, I got ripped off. That's how I got into dealing. If you're a user, you're always looking for a better deal."

In 1979 he was busted for selling hash, in 1980 for possessing acid, betrayed in both cases by the man from whom he had bought his stock. "He's a snitch, just a filthy snitch. You can't trust nobody." Back to prison for a year, back out again in December 1981. No jobs, no jobs, no damn jobs; then part-time on the city garbage truck, up at four in the morning, minus five degrees and the wind blowing and the streets so cold his gloves stuck to the trash cans. Then March came, and this 190 guy showed up, wanted to buy some drugs, and "I told him I wasn't dealing any more. I done my time and gone straight. I told him he didn't have enough money to pay me for no thirty years in the can." (The prosecutor bristles, the judge leans meaningfully forward: we jurors are not supposed to have any notion of the sentence that might follow a conviction on this drug charge.)

In his disk-jockey voice, Bennie denies ever selling anything to this 190 snitch. (He keeps using the word "snitch": I think of tattle-tales, not this adult betrayal.) It was 190, he swears, who tried to sell *him* the hash. Now the pills, why, those he had lying around for a friend who never picked them up, and so he just gave them to 190. "They was give to me, and so I couldn't charge him nothing. They wasn't for me anyway. Downers I do not use. To me, life is a downer. Just to cope with every day, that is way down low enough for me." And as for the cocaine, he never laid eyes on it until the man produced that little plastic bag in court. "I don't use coke. It's too expensive. That's for the bigwigs and the upstanding citizens, as got the money."

Sure, he admits, he ran when the police showed up at his trailer. "I'm flat scared of cops. I don't like talking to them about anything. Since I got back from Vietnam, every time they cross my path they put bracelets on me." (He holds up his wrists. They are bare now, but earlier this morning, when I saw a deputy escorting him into the courthouse, they were handcuffed.) He refuses to concede that he is a drug addict, but agrees he has a terrible habit, "a gift from my country in exchange for me going overseas and killing a bunch of strangers."

After the arrest, forced to go cold turkey on his dope, he begged the jail doctor — "He's no kind of doctor, just one of them that fixes babies" — to zonk him out on something. And so, until the trial, he has spent eight months drowsing under Valium and Thorazine. "You can look down your nose at me for that if you want, but last month another vet hung himself two cells down from me." (The other guy was a scoutmaster, awaiting trial for sexually molesting one of his boys. He had a record of severe depression dating from the war, and used his belt for the suicide.)

"The problem with my life," says Bennie, "is Vietnam." For awhile after   65 coming home, he slept with a knife under his pillow. Once, wakened suddenly, thinking he was still in Vietnam, he nearly killed his best friend. During the week of our trial, another Vietnam vet up in Indianapolis shot his wife in the head, imagining she was a gook. Neighbors got to him before he could pull out her teeth, as he used to pull out the teeth of the enemies he bagged over in Vietnam.

When I look at Bennie, I see a double image. He was drafted during the same month in which I, studying in England, gave Uncle Sam the slip. I hated that war, and feared it, for exactly the reasons he describes — because it was foul slaughter, shameful, sinful, pointless butchery. While he was over there killing and dodging, sinking into the quicksand of drugs, losing his hearing, storing up a lifetime's worth of nightmares, I was snug in England, filling my head with words. We both came home to America in the same year, I to job and family, he to nothing. Ten years after that homecoming, we stare across the courtroom at one another as into a funhouse mirror.

As the twelve jurors file past me into the room where they will decide on Bennie's guilt or innocence, three of them pat my arm in a comradely way. They withdraw beyond a brass-barred gate; I sit down to wait on a deacon's bench in the hallway outside the courtroom. I feel stymied, as if I have rocketed to the moon only to be left riding the ship round and round in idle orbit while my fellow astronauts descend to the moon's surface. At the same time I feel profoundly relieved, because, after the four days of testimony, I still cannot decide whether Bennie truly sold those drugs, or whether 190, to cut down on his own prison time, set up this ill-starred Bennie for yet another fall. Time, time — it always comes down to time: in jail, job, and jury box we are spending and hoarding our only wealth, the currency of days.

Even through the closed door of the courtroom, I still hear the ticking of the clock. The sound reminds me of listening to my daughter's pulse through a stethoscope when she was still riding, curled up like a stowaway, in my wife's womb. Ask not for whom this heart ticks, whispered my unborn daughter through the stethoscope: it ticks for thee. So does the courtroom clock. It grabs me by the ear and makes me fret about time — about how little there is of it, about how we are forever bumming it from one another as if it were cups of sugar or pints of blood ("You got a minute?" "Sorry, have to run, not a second to spare"). Seize the day, we shout, to cheer ourselves; but the day has seized us and flings us forward pell-mell toward the end of all days.

Now and again there is a burst of laughter from the jury room, but it is always squelched in a hurry. They are tense, and laugh to relieve the tension, and then feel ashamed of their giddiness. Lawyers traipse past me — the men smoking, striking poses, their faces like lollipops atop their ties; the women teetering on high heels. The bailiff walks into our judge's office carrying a bread knife. To slice her lunch? As evidence against Rebecca? A moment later she emerges bearing a piece of cake and licking her fingers. Christmas parties are breaking out all over the courthouse.

Rebecca herself paces back and forth at the far end of my hallway, her steps as regular as the clock's tick, killing time. Her bearded and cross-wearing friends sidle up to comfort her, but she shrugs them away. Once she paces down my way, glances at the barred door of the jury room, hears muffled shouts. This she must take for good news, because she throws me a rueful smile before turning back.   70

Evidently the other twelve are as muddled by the blurred and contradictory "facts" of the case as I am, for they spend from noon until five reaching their decision. They ask for lunch. They ask for a dictionary. They listen again to the tapes. Sullen teenagers, following in the footsteps of Bennie and 190, slouch into the misdemeanor office across the hall from me; by and by they slouch back out again, looking unrepentant. At length the 300-pound mason lumbers up to the gate of the jury room and calls the bailiff. "We're ready as we're going to be." He looks bone-weary, unhappy, and dignified. Raising his eyebrows at me, he shrugs. Comrades in uncertainty.

The cast reassembles in the courtroom, the judge asks the jury for its decision, and the mason stands up to pronounce Bennie guilty. I stare at my boots. Finally I glance up, not at Bennie or Rebecca or the lawyers, but at my fellow jurors. They look distraught, wrung-out and despairing, as if they have just crawled out of a mine after an explosion and have left some of their buddies behind. Before quitting the jury room, they composed and signed a letter to the judge pleading with him to get some help — drug help, mind help, any help — for Bennie.

The ticking of the clock sounds louder in my ears than the judge's closing recital. But I do, with astonishment, hear him say that we must all come back tomorrow for one last piece of business. He is sorry, he knows we are worn out, but the law has prevented him from warning us ahead of time that we might have to decide on one more question of guilt.

The legal question posed for us on the morning of day five is simple: Has Bennie been convicted, prior to this case, of two or more unrelated felonies? If so, then he is defined by Indiana state law as a "habitual offender," and we must declare him to be such. We are shown affidavits for those earlier convictions — burglary, sale of marijuana, possession of LSD — and so the answer to the legal question is clear.

But the moral and psychological questions are tangled, and they occupy   75
the jury for nearly five more hours on this last day of the trial. Is it fair to sentence a person again, after he has already served time for his earlier offenses? How does the prosecutor decide when to apply the habitual offender statute, and does its use in this case have anything to do with the political ambitions of the sleek young attorney? Did Bennie really steal that $150 stereo, for which he was convicted a decade ago, or did he really spend the day in bed with his sixteen-year-old girlfriend? Did Vietnam poison his mind and blight his life?

Two sheriff's deputies guard the jury today; another guards me in my own little cell. The bailiff would not let me stay out on the deacon's bench in the hall, and so, while a plainclothes detective occupies my old seat, I sit in a room lined with file cabinets and stare out like a prisoner through the glass door. "I have concluded," wrote Pascal, "that the whole misfortune of men comes from a single thing, and that is their inability to remain at rest in a room." I agree with him; nothing but that cruising deputy would keep me here.

This time, when the verdict is announced, Rebecca has her daughters with her, three little girls frightened into unchildlike stillness by the courtroom. Their lank hair and washed-out eyes remind me of my childhood playmates, the children of dead-end, used-up West Virginia coal miners who'd moved to Ohio in search of work. The mother and daughter are surrounded by half a dozen rough customers, guys my age with hair down over their shoulders and rings in their ears, with flannel shirts, unfocused eyes. Doubtless they are the reason so many holstered deputies and upholstered detectives are patrolling the courthouse, and the reason I was locked safely away in a cell while the jury deliberated.

When the mason stands to pronounce another verdict of guilty, I glimpse what I do not want to glimpse: Bennie flinging his head back, Rebecca snapping hers forward into her palms, the girls wailing.

The judge accompanies all thirteen of us into the jury room, where he keeps us for an hour while the deputies clear the rough customers from the courthouse.

We are not to be alarmed, he reassures us; he is simply being cautious, since so much was at stake for the defendant. "How much?" the mason asks. "Up to twenty-four years for the drug convictions, plus a mandatory thirty years for the habitual offender charges," the judge replies. The cleaning woman, the nurse, and the TV repairman begin crying. I swallow carefully. For whatever it's worth, the judge declares comfortingly, he agrees with our decisions. If we knew as much about this Bennie as he knows, we would not be troubled. And that is just the splinter in the brain, the fact that we know so little — about Bennie, about Vietnam, about drugs, about ourselves — and yet we must grope along in our ignorance, pronouncing people guilty or innocent, squeezing out of one another that precious fluid, time.

And so I do my five days in the thirteenth chair. Bennie may do as many as   80
fifty-four years in prison, buying his drugs from meaner dealers, dreaming of land mines and of his adopted girls, checking the date on his watch, wondering at what precise moment the hinges of his future slammed shut.   *[1987]*

■ THINKING ABOUT THE TEXT

1. Trace the references to time in this essay. In what ways does Sanders make it a central subject? Note his references to bombs. What is the effect of his emphasis on them?

2. On the whole, is your impression of the jury positive? Negative? Somewhere in between? Identify some things that influence your opinion. Is there any other information about the jury that you wish Sanders had provided? If so, what sort of information?

3. Rather than being a full-fledged juror, Sanders was an alternate, occupying the thirteenth chair. What, if any, were the advantages of this position for him as an observer? What, if any, were the disadvantages?

4. At one point in his essay, Sanders compares himself to Bennie. Does this comparison make sense to you? Why, or why not? Throughout the essay, Sanders emphasizes the sense of community that developed among the jurors. To what extent does he call attention to Bennie's community — that is, Bennie's friends and family? Does he treat this community in a way you think appropriate? Explain.

5. Are you inclined to believe that justice was served in Bennie's case? Why, or why not? What additional sort of information, if any, would you need to be sure?

MAXINE HONG KINGSTON
No Name Woman

Born in Stockton, California, to Chinese immigrants, Maxine Hong Kingston's (b. 1940) first language was Say Yup, a dialect of Cantonese. As a member of a close-knit community, many of whose members came from the same village in China, she was immersed in the storytelling tradition of her particular Chinese culture and soon became a gifted writer in her second language, English. Winning eleven scholarships, Kingston began her education at the University of California at Berkeley as an engineering major but soon moved into English literature, receiving her B.A. in 1962 and her teaching certificate in 1965. After teaching in Hawaii for ten years, Kingston published her first book, The Woman Warrior: Memoirs of a Girlhood among Ghosts *(1976), from which the following selection comes. This volume won the National Book Critics Circle Award for nonfiction. Kingston's reinterpretation of oral traditions is continued in her later works, including* Tripmaster Monkey: His Fake Book *(1989),* Hawai'i One Summer *(1998),* To Be a Poet *(2003),* The Fifth Book of Peace *(2003), an edited volume of contemporary soldiers' memoirs entitled* Veterans of War, Veterans of Peace *(2006), and* I Love a Broad Margin to My Life *(2011), a book of poems.*

"You must not tell anyone," my mother said, "what I am about to tell you. In China your father had a sister who killed herself. She jumped into the family well. We say that your father has all brothers because it is as if she had never been born.

"In 1924 just a few days after our village celebrated seventeen hurry-up weddings — to make sure that every young man who went 'out on the road' would responsibly come home — your father and his brothers and your grandfather and his brothers and your aunt's new husband sailed for America, the Gold Mountain. It was your grandfather's last trip. Those lucky enough to get contracts waved good-bye from the decks. They fed and guarded the stowaways and helped them off in Cuba, New York, Bali, Hawaii. 'We'll meet in California next year,' they said. All of them sent money home.

"I remember looking at your aunt one day when she and I were dressing; I had not noticed before that she had such a protruding melon of a stomach. But I did not think, 'She's pregnant,' until she began to look like other pregnant women, her shirt pulling and the white tops of her black pants showing. She could not have been pregnant, you see, because her husband had been gone for years. No one said anything. We did not discuss it. In early summer she was ready to have the child, long after the time when it could have been possible.

"The village had also been counting. On the night the baby was to be born the villagers raided our house. Some were crying. Like a great saw, teeth strung with lights, files of people walked zigzag across our land, tearing the rice. Their lanterns doubled in the disturbed black water, which drained away through the broken bunds. As the villagers closed in, we could see that some of them,

probably men and women we knew well, wore white masks. The people with
long hair hung it over their faces. Women with short hair made it stand up on
end. Some had tied white bands around their foreheads, arms, and legs.

"At first they threw mud and rocks at the house. Then they threw eggs   5
and began slaughtering our stock. We could hear the animals scream their
deaths — the roosters, the pigs, a last great roar from the ox. Familiar wild
heads flared in our night windows; the villagers encircled us. Some of the faces
stopped to peer at us, their eyes rushing like searchlights. The hands flattened
against the panes, framed heads, and left red prints.

"The villagers broke in the front and the back doors at the same time, even
though we had not locked the doors against them. Their knives dripped with the
blood of our animals. They smeared blood on the doors and walls. One woman
swung a chicken, whose throat she had slit, splattering blood in red arcs about
her. We stood together in the middle of our house, in the family hall with the
pictures and tables of the ancestors around us, and looked straight ahead.

"At that time the house had only two wings. When the men came back, we
would build two more to enclose our courtyard and a third one to begin a second courtyard. The villagers pushed through both wings, even your grandparents' rooms, to find your aunt's, which was also mine until the men returned.
From this room a new wing for one of the younger families would grow. They
ripped up her clothes and shoes and broke her combs, grinding them underfoot. They tore her work from the loom. They scattered the cooking fire and
rolled the new weaving in it. We could hear them in the kitchen breaking our
bowls and banging the pots. They overturned the great waist-high earthen-
ware jugs; duck eggs, pickled fruits, vegetables burst out and mixed in acrid
torrents. The old woman from the next field swept a broom through the air and
loosed the spirits-of-the-broom over our heads. 'Pig.' 'Ghost.' 'Pig,' they sobbed
and scolded while they ruined our house.

"When they left, they took sugar and oranges to bless themselves. They cut
pieces from the dead animals. Some of them took bowls that were not broken
and clothes that were not torn. Afterward we swept up the rice and sewed it
back up into sacks. But the smells from the spilled preserves lasted. Your aunt
gave birth in the pigsty that night. The next morning when I went for the water,
I found her and the baby plugging up the family well.

"Don't let your father know that I told you. He denies her. Now that you
have started to menstruate, what happened to her could happen to you. Don't
humiliate us. You wouldn't like to be forgotten as if you had never been born.
The villagers are watchful."

Whenever she had to warn us about life, my mother told stories that ran   10
like this one, a story to grow up on. She tested our strength to establish realities. Those in the emigrant generations who could not reassert brute survival
died young and far from home. Those of us in the first American generations
have had to figure out how the invisible world the emigrants built around our
childhoods fits in solid America.

The emigrants confused the gods by diverting their curses, misleading
them with crooked streets and false names. They must try to confuse their off-

spring as well, who, I suppose, threaten them in similar ways — always trying to get things straight, always trying to name the unspeakable. The Chinese I know hide their names; sojourners take new names when their lives change and guard their real names with silence.

Chinese-Americans, when you try to understand what things in you are Chinese, how do you separate what is peculiar to childhood, to poverty, insanities, one family, your mother who marked your growing with stories, from what is Chinese? What is Chinese tradition and what is the movies?

If I want to learn what clothes my aunt wore, whether flashy or ordinary, I would have to begin, "Remember Father's drowned-in-the-well sister?" I cannot ask that. My mother has told me once and for all the useful parts. She will add nothing unless powered by Necessity, a riverbank that guides her life. She plants vegetable gardens rather than lawns; she carries the odd-shaped tomatoes home from the fields and eats food left for the gods.

Whenever we did frivolous things, we used up energy; we flew high kites. We children came up off the ground over the melting cones our parents brought home from work and the American movie on New Year's Day — *Oh, You Beautiful Doll* with Betty Grable one year, and *She Wore a Yellow Ribbon* with John Wayne another year. After the one carnival ride each, we paid in guilt; our tired father counted his change on the dark walk home.

Adultery is extravagance. Could people who hatch their own chicks and eat the embryos and the heads for delicacies and boil the feet in vinegar for party food, leaving only the gravel, eating even the gizzard lining — could such people engender a prodigal aunt? To be a woman, to have a daughter in starvation time was a waste enough. My aunt could not have been the lone romantic who gave up everything for sex. Women in the old China did not choose. Some man had commanded her to lie with him and be his secret evil. I wonder whether he masked himself when he joined the raid on her family. 15

Perhaps she had encountered him in the fields or on the mountain where the daughters-in-law collected fuel. Or perhaps he first noticed her in the marketplace. He was not a stranger because the village housed no strangers. She had to have dealings with him other than sex. Perhaps he worked an adjoining field, or he sold her the cloth for the dress she sewed and wore. His demand must have surprised, then terrified her. She obeyed him; she always did as she was told.

When the family found a young man in the next village to be her husband, she had stood tractably beside the best rooster, his proxy, and promised before they met that she would be his forever. She was lucky that he was her age and she would be the first wife, an advantage secure now. The night she first saw him, he had sex with her. Then he left for America. She had almost forgotten what he looked like. When she tried to envision him, she only saw the black and white face in the group photograph the men had had taken before leaving.

The other man was not, after all, much different from her husband. They both gave orders: she followed. "If you tell your family, I'll beat you. I'll kill you. Be here again next week." No one talked sex, ever. And she might have separated the rapes from the rest of living if only she did not have to buy her oil from him or gather wood in the same forest. I want her fear to have lasted just as long as rape lasted so that the fear could have been contained. No drawn-out fear. But women at sex hazarded birth and hence lifetimes. The fear did not stop but permeated everywhere. She told the man, "I think I'm pregnant." He organized the raid against her.

On nights when my mother and father talked about their life back home, sometimes they mentioned an "outcast table" whose business they still seemed to be settling, their voices tight. In a commensal tradition, where food is precious, the powerful older people made wrongdoers eat alone. Instead of letting them start separate new lives like the Japanese, who could become samurais and geishas, the Chinese family, faces averted but eyes glowering sideways, hung on to the offenders and fed them leftovers. My aunt must have lived in the same house as my parents and eaten at an outcast table. My mother spoke about the raid as if she had seen it, when she and my aunt, a daughter-in-law to a different household, should not have been living together at all. Daughters-in-law lived with their husbands' parents, not their own; a synonym for marriage in Chinese is "taking a daughter-in-law." Her husband's parents could have sold her, mortgaged her, stoned her. But they had sent her back to her own mother and father, a mysterious act hinting at disgraces not told me. Perhaps they had thrown her out to deflect the avengers.

She was the only daughter; her four brothers went with her father, husband, and uncles "out on the road" and for some years became Western men. When the goods were divided among the family, three of the brothers took land, and the youngest, my father, chose an education. After my grandparents gave their daughter away to her husband's family, they had dispensed all the adventure and all the property. They expected her alone to keep the traditional ways, which her brothers, now among the barbarians, could fumble without detection. The heavy, deep-rooted women were to maintain the past against the flood, safe for returning. But the rare urge west had fixed upon our family, and so my aunt crossed boundaries not delineated in space.

The work of preservation demands that the feelings playing about in one's guts not be turned into action. Just watch their passing like cherry blossoms. But perhaps my aunt, my forerunner, caught in a slow life, let dreams grow and fade and after some months or years went toward what persisted. Fear at the enormities of the forbidden kept her desires delicate, wire and bone. She looked at a man because she liked the way the hair was tucked behind his ears, or she liked the question-mark line of a long torso curving at the shoulder and straight at the hip. For warm eyes or a soft voice or a slow walk — that's all — a few hairs, a line, a brightness, a sound, a pace, she gave up family. She offered us up for a charm that vanished with tiredness, a pigtail that didn't toss when the wind died. Why, the wrong lighting could erase the dearest thing about him.

It could very well have been, however, that my aunt did not take subtle enjoyment of her friend, but, a wild woman, kept rollicking company. Imagining her free with sex doesn't fit, though. I don't know any women like that, or men either. Unless I see her life branching into mine, she gives me no ancestral help.

20

To sustain her being in love, she often worked at herself in the mirror, guessing at the colors and shapes that would interest him, changing them frequently in order to hit on the right combination. She wanted him to look back.

On a farm near the sea, a woman who tended her appearance reaped a reputation for eccentricity. All the married women blunt-cut their hair in flaps about their ears or pulled it back in tight buns. No nonsense. Neither style blew easily into heart-catching tangles. And at their weddings they displayed themselves in their long hair for the last time. "It brushed the backs of my knees," my mother tells me. "It was braided, and even so, it brushed the backs of my knees."

At the mirror my aunt combined individuality into her bob. A bun could have been contrived to escape into black streamers blowing in the wind or in quiet wisps about her face, but only the older women in our picture album wear buns. She brushed her hair back from her forehead, tucking the flaps behind her ears. She looped a piece of thread, knotted into a circle between her index fingers and thumbs, and ran the double strand across her forehead. When she closed her fingers as if she were making a pair of shadow geese bite, the string twisted together catching the little hairs. Then she pulled the thread away from her skin, ripping the hairs out neatly, her eyes watering from the needles of pain. Opening her fingers, she cleaned the thread, then rolled it along her hairline and the tops of her eyebrows. My mother did the same to me and my sisters and herself. I used to believe that the expression "caught by the short hairs" meant a captive held with a depilatory string. It especially hurt at the temples, but my mother said we were lucky we didn't have to have our feet bound when we were seven. Sisters used to sit on their beds and cry together, she said, as their mothers or their slave removed the bandages for a few minutes each night and let the blood gush back into their veins. I hope that the man my aunt loved appreciated a smooth brow, that he wasn't just a tits-and-ass man.

Once my aunt found a freckle on her chin, at a spot that the almanac said predestined her for unhappiness. She dug it out with a hot needle and washed the wound with peroxide.

More attention to her looks than these pullings of hairs and pickings at spots would have caused gossip among the villagers. They owned work clothes and good clothes, and they wore good clothes for feasting the new seasons. But since a woman combing her hair hexes beginnings, my aunt rarely found an occasion to look her best. Women looked like great sea snails — the corded wood, babies, and laundry they carried were the whorls on their backs. The Chinese did not admire a bent back; goddesses and warriors stood straight. Still there must have been a marvelous freeing of beauty when a worker laid down her burden and stretched and arched.

Such commonplace loveliness, however, was not enough for my aunt. She dreamed of a lover for the fifteen days of New Year's, the time for families to exchange visits, money, and food. She plied her secret comb. And sure enough she cursed the year, the family, the village, and herself.

Even as her hair lured her imminent lover, many other men looked at her. Uncles, cousins, nephews, brothers would have looked, too, had they been

25

home between journeys. Perhaps they had already been restraining their curiosity, and they left, fearful that their glances, like a field of nesting birds, might be startled and caught. Poverty hurt, and that was their first reason for leaving. But another, final reason for leaving the crowded house was the never-said.

She may have been unusually beloved, the precious only daughter, spoiled   30
and mirror gazing because of the affection the family lavished on her. When her husband left, they welcomed the chance to take her back from the in-laws; she could live like the little daughter for just a while longer. There are stories that my grandfather was different from other people, "crazy ever since the little Jap bayoneted him in the head." He used to put his naked penis on the dinner table, laughing. And one day he brought home a baby girl, wrapped up inside his brown Western-style greatcoat. He had traded one of his sons, probably my father, the youngest, for her. My grandmother made him trade back. When he finally got a daughter of his own, he doted on her. They must have all loved her, except perhaps my father, the only brother who never went back to China, having once been traded for a girl.

Brothers and sisters, newly men and women, had to efface their sexual color and present plain miens. Disturbing hair and eyes, a smile like no other, threatened the ideal of five generations living under one roof. To focus blurs, people shouted face to face and yelled from room to room. The immigrants I know have loud voices, unmodulated to American tones even after years away from the village where they called their friendships out across the fields. I have not been able to stop my mother's screams in public libraries or over telephones. Walking erect (knees straight, toes pointed forward, not pigeon-toed, which is Chinese-feminine) and speaking in an inaudible voice, I have tried to turn myself American-feminine. Chinese communication was loud, public. Only sick people had to whisper. But at the dinner table, where the family members came nearest one another, no one could talk, not the outcasts nor any eaters. Every word that falls from the mouth is a coin lost. Silently they gave and accepted food with both hands. A preoccupied child who took his bowl with one hand got a sideways glare. A complete moment of total attention is due everyone alike. Children and lovers have no singularity here, but my aunt used a secret voice, a separate attentiveness.

She kept the man's name to herself throughout her labor and dying; she did not accuse him that he be punished with her. To save her inseminator's name she gave silent birth.

He may have been somebody in her own household, but intercourse with a man outside the family would have been no less abhorrent. All the village were kinsmen, and the titles shouted in loud country voices never let kinship be forgotten. Any man within visiting distance would have been neutralized as a lover — "brother," "younger brother," "older brother" — one hundred and fifteen relationship titles. Parents researched birth charts probably not so much to assure good fortune as to circumvent incest in a population that has but one hundred surnames. Everybody has eight million relatives. How useless then sexual mannerisms, how dangerous.

As if it came from an atavism deeper than fear, I used to add "brother" silently to boys' names. It hexed the boys, who would or would not ask me to dance, and made them less scary and as familiar and deserving of benevolence as girls.

But, of course, I hexed myself also—no dates. I should have stood up, both   35
arms waving, and shouted out across libraries, "Hey, you! Love me back." I had no idea, though, how to make attraction selective, how to control its direction and magnitude. If I made myself American-pretty so that the five or six Chinese boys in the class fell in love with me, everyone else — the Caucasian, Negro, and Japanese boys — would too. Sisterliness, dignified and honorable, made much more sense.

Attraction eludes control so stubbornly that whole societies designed to organize relationships among people cannot keep order, not even when they bind people to one another from childhood and raise them together. Among the very poor and the wealthy, brothers married their adopted sisters, like doves. Our family allowed some romance, paying adult brides' prices and providing dowries so that their sons and daughters could marry strangers. Marriage promises to turn strangers into friendly relatives — a nation of siblings.

In the village structure, spirits shimmered among the live creatures, balanced and held in equilibrium by time and land. But one human being flaring up into violence could open up a black hole, a maelstrom that pulled in the sky. The frightened villagers, who depended on one another to maintain the real, went to my aunt to show her a personal, physical representation of the break she had made in the "roundness." Misallying couples snapped off the future, which was to be embodied in true offspring. The villagers punished her for acting as if she could have a private life, secret and apart from them.

If my aunt had betrayed the family at a time of large grain yields and peace, when many boys were born, and wings were being built on many houses, perhaps, she might have escaped such severe punishment. But the men — hungry, greedy, tired of planting in dry soil — had been forced to leave the village in order to send food-money home. There were ghost plagues, bandit plagues, wars with the Japanese, floods. My Chinese brother and sister had died of an unknown sickness. Adultery, perhaps only a mistake during good times, became a crime when the village needed food.

The round moon cakes and round doorways, the round tables of graduated size that fit one roundness inside another, round windows and rice bowls — these talismans had lost their power to warn this family of the law: a family must be whole, faithfully keeping the descent line by having sons to feed the old and the dead, who in turn look after the family. The villagers came to show my aunt and her lover-in-hiding a broken house. The villagers were speeding up the circling of events because she was too shortsighted to see that her infidelity had already harmed the village, that waves of consequences would return unpredictably, sometimes in disguise, as now, to hurt her. This roundness had to be made coin-sized so that she would see its circumference: punish her at the birth of her baby. Awaken her to the inexorable. People who refused fatalism because they could invent small resources insisted on culpability. Deny accidents and wrest fault from the stars.

After the villagers left, their lanterns now scattering in various directions   40
toward home, the family broke their silence and cursed her. "Aiaa, we're going
to die. Death is coming. Death is coming. Look what you've done. You've killed
us. Ghost! Dead ghost! Ghost! You've never been born." She ran out into the
fields, far enough from the house so that she could no longer hear their voices,
and pressed herself against the earth, her own land no more. When she felt the
birth coming, she thought that she had been hurt. Her body seized together.
"They've hurt me too much," she thought. "This is gall, and it will kill me."
With forehead and knees against the earth, her body convulsed and then relaxed. She turned on her back, lay on the ground. The black well of sky and
stars went out and out and out forever; her body and her complexity seemed to
disappear. She was one of the stars, a bright dot in blackness, without home,
without a companion, in eternal cold and silence. An agoraphobia rose in her,
speeding higher and higher, bigger and bigger; she would not be able to contain
it; there would be no end to fear.

Flayed, unprotected against space, she felt pain return, focusing her body.
This pain chilled her — a cold, steady kind of surface pain. Inside, spasmodically, the other pain, the pain of the child, heated her. For hours she lay on the
ground, alternately body and space. Sometimes a vision of normal comfort
obliterated reality: she saw the family in the evening gambling at the dinner
table, the young people massaging their elders' backs. She saw them congratulating one another, high joy on the mornings the rice shoots came up. When
these pictures burst, the stars drew yet further apart. Black space opened.

She got to her feet to fight better and remembered that old-fashioned
women gave birth in their pigsties to fool the jealous, pain-dealing gods, who do
not snatch piglets. Before the next spasms could stop her, she ran to the pigsty,
each step a rushing out into emptiness. She climbed over the fence and knelt in
the dirt. It was good to have a fence enclosing her, a tribal person alone.

Laboring, this woman who had carried her child as a foreign growth that
sickened her every day, expelled it at last. She reached down to touch the hot,
wet, moving mass, surely smaller than anything human, and could feel that
it was human after all — fingers, toes, nails, nose. She pulled it up on to her
belly, and it lay curled there, butt in the air, feet precisely tucked one under the
other. She opened her loose shirt and buttoned the child inside. After resting,
it squirmed and thrashed and she pushed it up to her breast. It turned its
head this way and that until it found her nipple. There, it made little snuffling
noises. She clenched her teeth at its preciousness, lovely as a young calf, a pig-
let, a little dog.

She may have gone to the pigsty as a last act of responsibility: she would
protect this child as she had protected its father. It would look after her soul,
leaving supplies on her grave. But how would this tiny child without family find
her grave when there would be no marker for her anywhere, neither in the
earth nor the family hall? No one would give her a family hall name. She had

taken the child with her into the wastes. At its birth the two of them had felt the same raw pain of separation, a wound that only the family pressing tight could close. A child with no descent line would not soften her life but only trail after her, ghostlike, begging her to give it purpose. At dawn the villagers on their way to the fields would stand around the fence and look.

Full of milk, the little ghost slept. When it awoke, she hardened her breasts   45
against the milk that crying loosens. Toward morning she picked up the baby and walked to the well.

Carrying the baby to the well shows loving. Otherwise abandon it. Turn its face into the mud. Mothers who love their children take them along. It was probably a girl; there is some hope of forgiveness for boys.

"Don't tell anyone you had an aunt. Your father does not want to hear her name. She has never been born." I have believed that sex was unspeakable and words so strong and fathers so frail that "aunt" would do my father mysterious harm. I have thought that my family, having settled among immigrants who had also been their neighbors in the ancestral land, needed to clean their name, and a wrong word would incite the kinspeople even here. But there is more to this silence: they want me to participate in her punishment. And I have.

In the twenty years since I heard this story I have not asked for details nor said my aunt's name; I do not know it. People who can comfort the dead can also chase after them to hurt them further — a reverse ancestor worship. The real punishment was not the raid swiftly inflicted by the villagers, but the family's deliberately forgetting her. Her betrayal so maddened them, they saw to it that she would suffer forever, even after death. Always hungry, always needing, she would have to beg food from other ghosts, snatch and steal it from those whose living descendants give them gifts. She would have to fight the ghosts massed at crossroads for the buns a few thoughtful citizens leave to decoy her away from village and home so that the ancestral spirits could feast unharassed. At peace, they could act like gods, not ghosts, their descent lines providing them with paper suits and dresses, spirit money, paper houses, paper automobiles, chicken, meat, and rice into eternity — essences delivered up in smoke and flames, steam and incense rising from each rice bowl. In an attempt to make the Chinese care for people outside the family, Chairman Mao encourages us now to give our paper replicas to the spirits of outstanding soldiers and workers, no matter whose ancestors they may be. My aunt remains forever hungry. Goods are not distributed evenly among the dead.

My aunt haunts me — her ghost drawn to me because now, after fifty years of neglect, I alone devote pages of paper to her, though not origamied into houses and clothes. I do not think she always means me well. I am telling on her, and she was a spite suicide, drowning herself in the drinking water. The Chinese are always very frightened of the drowned one, whose weeping ghost, wet hair hanging and skin bloated, waits silently by the water to pull down a substitute.   *[1976]*

≡ THINKING ABOUT THE TEXT

1. This cautionary tale is meant to persuade Kingston to conform to her parents' values. What is the argument behind the narrative the mother tells? Does it make sense to you? What might be a contemporary argument in a middle-class American family?

2. Were you ever put at an "outcast table" (para. 19) or anything comparable in your house or school? Have you ever heard of such a ritual? What did happen when you were punished? What kinds of things were you punished for? Why do you think these specific things were chosen?

3. Is this also a tale about gender inequality? How does Kingston suggest this? How are relations between men and women portrayed here?

4. How do ghosts and spirits function in this essay? Which parts of this piece seem true to you, and which seem fictional? Why do you suppose Kingston blends these elements?

5. Sexual mores change over time and from country to country. What specifically about the aunt's context made her transgression so severe? How would her "crime" be viewed in contemporary America? Why? What do you think an ideal response would be?

≡ MAKING COMPARISONS

1. Whereas Sanders was involved in the case he reports on, Kingston is pretty distant from the one she discusses. In what ways, if any, is this difference relevant?

2. Do the defendant in Sanders's essay and the aunt in Kingston's essay both seem rational? Define what you mean by *rational*.

3. To what extent is each of these two essays, Sanders's and Kingston's, about *injustice*? Define what you mean by the term.

ATUL GAWANDE

Hellhole

Atul Gawande (b. 1965) is a surgeon and also a professor of medicine and public health at Harvard University. Moreover, he has written much about his work and on topics related to it. His books include Complications: A Surgeon's Notes on an Imperfect Science *(2002),* Better: A Surgeon's Notes on Performance *(2007), and* The Checklist Manifesto *(2010). Gawande contributes regularly to* The New Yorker *magazine, which published the following essay in its March 30, 2009, issue.*

Human beings are social creatures. We are social not just in the trivial sense that we like company, and not just in the obvious sense that we each depend on others. We are social in a more elemental way: simply to exist as a normal human being requires interaction with other people.

Children provide the clearest demonstration of this fact, although it was slow to be accepted. Well into the nineteen-fifties, psychologists were encouraging parents to give children *less* attention and affection, in order to encourage independence. Then Harry Harlow, a professor of psychology at the University of Wisconsin at Madison, produced a series of influential studies involving baby rhesus monkeys.

He happened upon the findings in the mid-fifties, when he decided to save money for his primate-research laboratory by breeding his own lab monkeys instead of importing them from India. Because he didn't know how to raise infant monkeys, he cared for them the way hospitals of the era cared for human infants — in nurseries, with plenty of food, warm blankets, some toys, and in isolation from other infants to prevent the spread of infection. The monkeys grew up sturdy, disease-free, and larger than those from the wild. Yet they were also profoundly disturbed, given to staring blankly and rocking in place for long periods, circling their cages repetitively, and mutilating themselves.

At first, Harlow and his graduate students couldn't figure out what the problem was. They considered factors such as diet, patterns of light exposure, even the antibiotics they used. Then, as Deborah Blum recounts in a fascinating biography of Harlow, *Love at Goon Park*, one of his researchers noticed how tightly the monkeys clung to their soft blankets. Harlow wondered whether what the monkeys were missing in their Isolettes was a mother. So, in an odd experiment, he gave them an artificial one.

In the studies, one artificial mother was a doll made of terry cloth; the   5
other was made of wire. He placed a warming device inside the dolls to make them seem more comforting. The babies, Harlow discovered, largely ignored the wire mother. But they became deeply attached to the cloth mother. They caressed it. They slept curled up on it. They ran to it when frightened. They refused replacements: they wanted only "their" mother. If sharp spikes were made to randomly thrust out of the mother's body when the rhesus babies held it, they waited patiently for the spikes to recede and returned to clutching it. No matter how tightly they clung to the surrogate mothers, however, the monkeys remained psychologically abnormal.

In a later study on the effect of total isolation from birth, the researchers found that the test monkeys, upon being released into a group of ordinary monkeys, "usually go into a state of emotional shock, characterized by . . . autistic self-clutching and rocking." Harlow noted, "One of six monkeys isolated for three months refused to eat after release and died five days later." After several weeks in the company of other monkeys, most of them adjusted — but not those who had been isolated for longer periods. "Twelve months of isolation almost obliterated the animals socially," Harlow wrote. They became permanently withdrawn, and they lived as outcasts — regularly set upon, as if inviting abuse.

The research made Harlow famous (and infamous, too — revulsion at his work helped spur the animal-rights movement). Other psychologists produced evidence of similarly deep and sustained damage in neglected and orphaned children. Hospitals were made to open up their nurseries to parents. And it became widely accepted that children require nurturing human beings not just for food and protection but also for the normal functioning of their brains.

We have been hesitant to apply these lessons to adults. Adults, after all, are fully formed, independent beings, with internal strengths and knowledge to draw upon. We wouldn't have anything like a child's dependence on other people, right? Yet it seems that we do. We don't have a lot of monkey experiments to call upon here. But mankind has produced tens of thousands of human ones, including in our prison system. And the picture that has emerged is profoundly unsettling.

Among our most benign experiments are those with people who voluntarily isolate themselves for extended periods. Long-distance solo sailors, for instance, commit themselves to months at sea. They face all manner of physical terrors: thrashing storms, fifty-foot waves, leaks, illness. Yet, for many, the single most overwhelming difficulty they report is the "soul-destroying loneliness," as one sailor called it. Astronauts have to be screened for their ability to tolerate long stretches in tightly confined isolation, and they come to depend on radio and video communications for social contact.

The problem of isolation goes beyond ordinary loneliness, however. Consider what we've learned from hostages who have been held in solitary confinement — from the journalist Terry Anderson, for example, whose extraordinary memoir, *Den of Lions*, recounts his seven years as a hostage of Hezbollah in Lebanon.   10

Anderson was the chief Middle East correspondent for the Associated Press when, on March 16, 1985, three bearded men forced him from his car in Beirut at gunpoint. He was pushed into a Mercedes sedan, covered head to toe with a heavy blanket, and made to crouch head down in the footwell behind the front seat. His captors drove him to a garage, pulled him out of the car, put a hood over his head, and bound his wrists and ankles with tape. For half an hour, they grilled him for the names of other Americans in Beirut, but he gave no names and they did not beat him or press him further. They threw him in the trunk of the car, drove him to another building, and put him in what would be the first of a succession of cells across Lebanon. He was soon placed in what seemed to be a dusty closet, large enough for only a mattress. Blindfolded, he could make out the distant sounds of other hostages. (One was William Buckley, the C.I.A. station chief who was kidnapped and tortured repeatedly until he weakened and died.) Peering around his blindfold, Anderson could see a bare light bulb dangling from the ceiling. He received three unpalatable meals a day — usually a sandwich of bread and cheese, or cold rice with canned vegetables, or soup. He had a bottle to urinate in and was allotted one five- to ten-minute trip each day to a rotting bathroom to empty his bowels and wash with water at a dirty sink. Otherwise, the only reprieve from isolation came when the guards made short visits to bark at him for breaking a rule or to threaten him, sometimes with a gun at his temple.

He missed people terribly, especially his fiancée and his family. He was despondent and depressed. Then, with time, he began to feel something more. He felt himself disintegrating. It was as if his brain were grinding down. A month into his confinement, he recalled in his memoir, "The mind is a blank. Jesus, I always thought I was smart. Where are all the things I learned, the books I read, the poems I memorized? There's nothing there, just a formless, gray-black misery. My mind's gone dead. God, help me."

He was stiff from lying in bed day and night, yet tired all the time. He dozed off and on constantly, sleeping twelve hours a day. He craved activity of almost any kind. He would watch the daylight wax and wane on the ceiling, or roaches creep slowly up the wall. He had a Bible and tried to read, but he often found that he lacked the concentration to do so. He observed himself becoming neurotically possessive about his little space, at times putting his life in jeopardy by flying into a rage if a guard happened to step on his bed. He brooded incessantly, thinking back on all the mistakes he'd made in life, his regrets, his offenses against God and family.

His captors moved him every few months. For unpredictable stretches of time, he was granted the salvation of a companion — sometimes he shared a cell with as many as four other hostages — and he noticed that his thinking recovered rapidly when this occurred. He could read and concentrate longer, avoid hallucinations, and better control his emotions. "I would rather have had the worst companion than no companion at all," he noted.

In September 1986, after several months of sharing a cell with another hostage, Anderson was, for no apparent reason, returned to solitary confinement, this time in a six-by-six-foot cell, with no windows, and light from only a flickering fluorescent lamp in an outside corridor. The guards refused to say how long he would be there. After a few weeks, he felt his mind slipping away again.

"I find myself trembling sometimes for no reason," he wrote. "I'm afraid I'm beginning to lose my mind, to lose control completely."

One day, three years into his ordeal, he snapped. He walked over to a wall and began beating his forehead against it, dozens of times. His head was smashed and bleeding before the guards were able to stop him.

Some hostages fared worse. Anderson told the story of Frank Reed, a fifty-four-year-old American private-school director who was taken hostage and held in solitary confinement for four months before being put in with Anderson. By then, Reed had become severely withdrawn. He lay motionless for hours facing a wall, semi-catatonic. He could not follow the guards' simplest instructions. This invited abuse from them, in much the same way that once isolated rhesus monkeys seemed to invite abuse from the colony. Released after three and a half years, Reed ultimately required admission to a psychiatric hospital.

"It's an awful thing, solitary," John McCain wrote of his five and a half years as a prisoner of war in Vietnam — more than two years of it spent in isolation in a fifteen-by-fifteen-foot cell, unable to communicate with other P.O.W.s except by tap code, secreted notes, or by speaking into an enamel cup

15

pressed against the wall. "It crushes your spirit and weakens your resistance more effectively than any other form of mistreatment." And this comes from a man who was beaten regularly; denied adequate medical treatment for two broken arms, a broken leg, and chronic dysentery; and tortured to the point of having an arm broken again. A U.S. military study of almost a hundred and fifty naval aviators returned from imprisonment in Vietnam, many of whom were treated even worse than McCain, reported that they found social isolation to be as torturous and agonizing as any physical abuse they suffered.

And what happened to them *was* physical. EEG studies going back to the   20
nineteen-sixties have shown diffuse slowing of brain waves in prisoners after a week or more of solitary confinement. In 1992, fifty-seven prisoners of war, released after an average of six months in detention camps in the former Yugoslavia, were examined using EEG-like tests. The recordings revealed brain abnormalities months afterward; the most severe were found in prisoners who had endured either head trauma sufficient to render them unconscious or, yes, solitary confinement. Without sustained social interaction, the human brain may become as impaired as one that has incurred a traumatic injury.

On December 4, 1991, Terry Anderson was released from captivity. He had been the last and the longest-held American hostage in Lebanon. I spoke to Keron Fletcher, a former British military psychiatrist who had been on the receiving team for Anderson and many other hostages, and followed them for years afterward. Initially, Fletcher said, everyone experiences the pure elation of being able to see and talk to people again, especially family and friends. They can't get enough of other people, and talk almost non-stop for hours. They are optimistic and hopeful. But, afterward, normal sleeping and eating patterns prove difficult to reestablish. Some have lost their sense of time. For weeks, they have trouble managing the sensations and emotional complexities of their freedom.

For the first few months after his release, Anderson said when I reached him by phone recently, "it was just kind of a fog." He had done many television interviews at the time. "And if you look at me in the pictures? Look at my eyes. You can tell. I look drugged."

Most hostages survived their ordeal, Fletcher said, although relationships, marriages, and careers were often lost. Some found, as John McCain did, that the experience even strengthened them. Yet none saw solitary confinement as anything less than torture. This presents us with an awkward question: If prolonged isolation is — as research and experience have confirmed for decades — so objectively horrifying, so intrinsically cruel, how did we end up with a prison system that may subject more of our own citizens to it than any other country in history has?

Recently, I met a man who had spent more than five years in isolation at a prison in the Boston suburb of Walpole, Massachusetts, not far from my home. Bobby Dellelo was, to say the least, no Terry Anderson or John McCain. Brought up in the run-down neighborhoods of Boston's West End, in the nineteen-forties, he was caught burglarizing a shoe store at the age of ten. At thirteen, he recalls, he was nabbed while robbing a Jordan Marsh department store. (He and his friends learned to hide out in stores at closing time, steal their merchandise, and then break out during the night.) The remainder of his childhood was spent mostly in the state reform school. That was where he learned how to fight, how to hot-wire a car with a piece of foil, how to pick locks, and how to make a zip gun using a snapped-off automobile radio antenna, which, in those days, was just thick enough to barrel a .22-calibre bullet. Released upon turning eighteen, Dellelo returned to stealing. Usually, he stole from office buildings at night. But some of the people he hung out with did stickups, and, together with one of them, he held up a liquor store in Dorchester.

"What a disaster that thing was," he recalls, laughing. They put the store's   25
owner and the customers in a walk-in refrigerator at gunpoint, took their wallets, and went to rob the register. But more customers came in. So they robbed them and put them in the refrigerator, too. Then still more customers arrived, the refrigerator got full, and the whole thing turned into a circus. Dellelo and his partner finally escaped. But one of the customers identified him to the police. By the time he was caught, Dellelo had been fingered for robbing the Commander Hotel in Cambridge as well. He served a year for the first conviction and two and a half years for the second.

Three months after his release, in 1963, at the age of twenty, he and a friend tried to rob the Kopelman jewelry store in downtown Boston. But an alarm went off before they got their hands on anything. They separated and ran. The friend shot and killed an off-duty policeman while trying to escape, then killed himself. Dellelo was convicted of first-degree murder and sentenced to life in prison. He ended up serving forty years. Five years and one month were spent in isolation.

The criteria for the isolation of prisoners vary by state but typically include not only violent infractions but also violation of prison rules or association with gang members. The imposition of long-term isolation — which can be for months or years — is ultimately at the discretion of prison administrators. One former prisoner I spoke to, for example, recalled being put in solitary confinement for petty annoyances like refusing to get out of the shower quickly enough. Bobby Dellelo was put there for escaping.

It was an elaborate scheme. He had a partner, who picked the lock to a supervisor's office and got hold of the information manual for the microwave-detection system that patrolled a grassy no man's land between the prison and the road. They studied the manual long enough to learn how to circumvent the system and returned it. On Halloween Sunday, 1993, they had friends stage a fight in the prison yard. With all the guards in the towers looking at the fight through binoculars, the two men tipped a picnic table up against a twelve-foot wall and climbed it like a ladder. Beyond it, they scaled a sixteen-foot fence. To get over the razor wire on top, they used a Z-shaped tool they'd improvised from locker handles. They dropped down into the no man's land and followed an invisible path that they'd calculated the microwave system would not detect. No alarm sounded. They went over one more fence, walked around a parking lot, picked their way through some woods, and emerged onto a four-lane road.

After a short walk to a convenience store, they called a taxi from a telephone booth and rolled away before anyone knew they were gone.

They lasted twenty-four days on the outside. Eventually, somebody ratted them out, and the police captured them on the day before Thanksgiving, at the house of a friend in Cambridge. The prison administration gave Dellelo five years in the Departmental Disciplinary Unit of the Walpole prison, its hundred-and-twenty-four-cell super-maximum segregation unit.

Wearing ankle bracelets, handcuffs, and a belly chain, Dellelo was marched   30
into a thirteen-by-eight-foot off-white cell. A four-inch-thick concrete bed slab jutted out from the wall opposite the door. A smaller slab protruding from a side wall provided a desk. A cylindrical concrete block in the floor served as a seat. On the remaining wall was a toilet and a metal sink. He was given four sheets, four towels, a blanket, a bedroll, a toothbrush, toilet paper, a tall clear plastic cup, a bar of soap, seven white T-shirts, seven pairs of boxer shorts, seven pairs of socks, plastic slippers, a pad of paper, and a ballpoint pen. A speaker with a microphone was mounted on the door. Cells used for solitary confinement are often windowless, but this one had a ribbonlike window that was seven inches wide and five feet tall. The electrically controlled door was solid steel, with a seven-inch-by-twenty-eight-inch aperture and two wickets — little door slots, one at ankle height and one at waist height, for shackling him whenever he was let out and for passing him meal trays.

As in other supermaxes — facilities designed to isolate prisoners from so-cial contact — Dellelo was confined to his cell for at least twenty-three hours a day and permitted out only for a shower or for recreation in an outdoor cage that he estimated to be fifty feet long and five feet wide, known as "the dog ken-nel." He could talk to other prisoners through the steel door of his cell, and during recreation if a prisoner was in an adjacent cage. He made a kind of fish-ing line for passing notes to adjacent cells by unwinding the elastic from his boxer shorts, though it was contraband and would be confiscated. Prisoners could receive mail and as many as ten reading items. They were allowed one phone call the first month and could earn up to four calls and four visits per month if they followed the rules, but there could be no physical contact with anyone, except when guards forcibly restrained them. Some supermaxes even use food as punishment, serving the prisoners nutra-loaf, an unpalatable food brick that contains just enough nutrition for survival. Dellelo was spared this. The rules also permitted him to have a radio after thirty days, and, after sixty days, a thirteen-inch black-and-white television.

"This is going to be a piece of cake," Dellelo recalls thinking when the door closed behind him. Whereas many American supermax prisoners — and most P.O.W.s and hostages — have no idea when they might get out, he knew exactly how long he was going to be there. He drew a calendar on his pad of paper to start counting down the days. He would get a radio and a TV. He could read. No one was going to bother him. And, as his elaborate escape plan showed, he could be patient. "This is their sophisticated security?" he said to himself. "They don't know what they're doing."

After a few months without regular social contact, however, his experi-ence proved no different from that of the P.O.W.s or hostages, or the majority of isolated prisoners whom researchers have studied: he started to lose his mind. He talked to himself. He paced back and forth compulsively, shuffling along the same six-foot path for hours on end. Soon, he was having panic attacks, screaming for help. He hallucinated that the colors on the walls were changing. He became enraged by routine noises — the sound of doors opening as the guards made their hourly checks, the sounds of inmates in nearby cells. After a year or so, he was hearing voices on the television talking directly to him. He put the television under his bed, and rarely took it out again.

One of the paradoxes of solitary confinement is that, as starved as people become for companionship, the experience typically leaves them unfit for social interaction. Once, Dellelo was allowed to have an in-person meeting with his lawyer, and he simply couldn't handle it. After so many months in which his primary human contact had been an occasional phone call or brief conversations with an inmate down the tier, shouted through steel doors at the top of their lungs, he found himself unable to carry on a face-to-face conversation. He had trouble following both words and hand gestures and couldn't generate them himself. When he realized this, he succumbed to a full-blown panic attack.

Craig Haney, a psychology professor at the University of California at Santa Cruz, received rare permission to study a hundred randomly selected inmates at California's Pelican Bay supermax, and noted a number of phenomena. First, after months or years of complete isolation, many prisoners "begin to lose the ability to initiate behavior of any kind — to organize their own lives around activity and purpose," he writes. "Chronic apathy, lethargy, depression, and despair often result. . . . In extreme cases, prisoners may literally stop behaving," becoming essentially catatonic.

35

Second, almost ninety percent of these prisoners had difficulties with "irrational anger," compared with just three percent of the general population. Haney attributed this to the extreme restriction, the totality of control, and the extended absence of any opportunity for happiness or joy. Many prisoners in solitary become consumed with revenge fantasies.

"There were some guards in D.D.U. who were decent guys," Dellelo told me. They didn't trash his room when he was let out for a shower, or try to trip him when escorting him in chains, or write him up for contraband if he kept food or a salt packet from a meal in his cell. "But some of them were evil, evil pricks." One correctional officer became a particular obsession. Dellelo spent hours imagining cutting his head off and rolling it down the tier. "I mean, I know this is insane thinking," he says now. Even at the time, he added, "I had a fear in the background — like how much of this am I going to be able to let go? How much is this going to affect who I am?"

He was right to worry. Everyone's identity is socially created: it's through your relationships that you understand yourself as a mother or a father, a teacher or an accountant, a hero or a villain. But, after years of isolation, many prisoners change in another way that Haney observed. They begin to see themselves primarily as combatants in the world, people whose identity is rooted in thwarting prison control.

As a matter of self-preservation, this may not be a bad thing. According to the Navy P.O.W. researchers, the instinct to fight back against the enemy constituted the most important coping mechanism for the prisoners they studied. Resistance was often their sole means of maintaining a sense of purpose, and so their sanity. Yet resistance is precisely what we wish to destroy in our supermax prisoners. As Haney observed in a review of research findings, prisoners in solitary confinement must be able to withstand the experience in order to be allowed to return to the highly social world of mainline prison or free society. Perversely, then, the prisoners who can't handle profound isolation are the ones who are forced to remain in it. "And those who have adapted," Haney writes, "are prime candidates for release to a social world to which they may be incapable of ever fully readjusting."

Dellelo eventually found a way to resist that would not prolong his ordeal.   40
He fought his battle through the courts, filing motion after motion in an effort to get his conviction overturned. He became so good at submitting his claims that he obtained a paralegal certificate along the way. And, after forty years in prison, and more than five years in solitary, he got his first-degree-homicide conviction reduced to manslaughter. On November 19, 2003, he was freed.

Bobby Dellelo is sixty-seven years old now. He lives on Social Security in a Cambridge efficiency apartment that is about four times larger than his cell. He still seems to be adjusting to the world outside. He lives alone. To the extent that he is out in society, it is, in large measure, as a combatant. He works for prisoners' rights at the American Friends Service Committee. He also does occasional work assisting prisoners with their legal cases. Sitting at his kitchen table, he showed me how to pick a padlock — you know, just in case I ever find myself in trouble.

But it was impossible to talk to him about his time in isolation without seeing that it was fundamentally no different from the isolation that Terry Anderson and John McCain had endured. Whether in Walpole or Beirut or Hanoi, all human beings experience isolation as torture.

The main argument for using long-term isolation in prisons is that it provides discipline and prevents violence. When inmates refuse to follow the rules — when they escape, deal drugs, or attack other inmates and corrections officers — wardens must be able to punish and contain the misconduct. Presumably, less stringent measures haven't worked, or the behavior would not have occurred. And it's legitimate to incapacitate violent aggressors for the safety of others. So, advocates say, isolation is a necessary evil, and those who don't recognize this are dangerously naïve.

The argument makes intuitive sense. If the worst of the worst are removed from the general prison population and put in isolation, you'd expect there to be markedly fewer inmate shankings and attacks on corrections officers. But the evidence doesn't bear this out. Perhaps the most careful inquiry into whether supermax prisons decrease violence and disorder was a 2003 analysis examining the experience in three states — Arizona, Illinois, and Minnesota — following the opening of their supermax prisons. The study found that levels of inmate-on-inmate violence were unchanged, and that levels of inmate-on-staff violence changed unpredictably, rising in Arizona, falling in Illinois, and holding steady in Minnesota.

Prison violence, it turns out, is not simply an issue of a few belligerents. In   45
the past thirty years, the United States has quadrupled its incarceration rate
but not its prison space. Work and education programs have been cancelled,
out of a belief that the pursuit of rehabilitation is pointless. The result has been
unprecedented overcrowding, along with unprecedented idleness — a nice formula for violence. Remove a few prisoners to solitary confinement, and the violence doesn't change. So you remove some more, and still nothing happens.
Before long, you find yourself in the position we are in today. The United States
now has five percent of the world's population, twenty-five percent of its prisoners, and probably the vast majority of prisoners who are in long-term solitary confinement.

It wasn't always like this. The wide-scale use of isolation is, almost exclusively, a phenomenon of the past twenty years. In 1890, the United States Supreme Court came close to declaring the punishment to be unconstitutional.
Writing for the majority in the case of a Colorado murderer who had been held
in isolation for a month, Justice Samuel Miller noted that experience had revealed "serious objections" to solitary confinement:

> A considerable number of the prisoners fell, after even a short confine-
> ment, into a semi-fatuous condition, from which it was next to impossible
> to arouse them, and others became violently insane; others, still, commit-
> ted suicide; while those who stood the ordeal better were not generally
> reformed, and in most cases did not recover sufficient mental activity to be
> of any subsequent service to the community.

Prolonged isolation was used sparingly, if at all, by most American prisons
for almost a century. Our first supermax — our first institution specifically designed for mass solitary confinement — was not established until 1983, in
Marion, Illinois. In 1995, a federal court reviewing California's first supermax
admitted that the conditions "hover on the edge of what is humanly tolerable
for those with normal resilience." But it did not rule them to be unconstitution-
ally cruel or unusual, except in cases of mental illness. The prison's supermax
conditions, the court stated, did not pose "a sufficiently high risk to all inmates
of incurring a serious mental illness." In other words, there could be no legal
objection to its routine use, given that the isolation didn't make *everyone* crazy.
The ruling seemed to fit the public mood. By the end of the nineteen-nineties,
some sixty supermax institutions had opened across the country. And new
solitary-confinement units were established within nearly all of our ordinary
maximum-security prisons.

The number of prisoners in these facilities has since risen to extraordinary
levels. America now holds at least twenty-five thousand inmates in isolation in
supermax prisons. An additional fifty to eighty thousand are kept in restrictive
segregation units, many of them in isolation, too, although the government
does not release these figures. By 1999, the practice had grown to the point
that Arizona, Colorado, Maine, Nebraska, Nevada, Rhode Island, and Virginia
kept between five and eight percent of their prison population in isolation, and,
by 2003, New York had joined them as well. Mississippi alone held eighteen
hundred prisoners in supermax — twelve percent of its prisoners overall. At

the same time, other states had just a tiny fraction of their inmates in solitary confinement. In 1999, for example, Indiana had eighty-five supermax beds; Georgia had only ten. Neither of these two states can be described as being soft on crime.

Advocates of solitary confinement are left with a single argument for subjecting thousands of people to years of isolation: What else are we supposed to do? How else are we to deal with the violent, the disruptive, the prisoners who are just too dangerous to be housed with others?

As it happens, only a subset of prisoners currently locked away for long   50
periods of isolation would be considered truly dangerous. Many are escapees or suspected gang members; many others are in solitary for nonviolent breaches of prison rules. Still, there are some highly dangerous and violent prisoners who pose a serious challenge to prison discipline and safety. In August, I met a man named Robert Felton, who had spent fourteen and a half years in isolation in the Illinois state correctional system. He is now thirty-six years old. He grew up in the predominantly black housing projects of Danville, Illinois, and had been a force of mayhem from the time he was a child.

His crimes were mainly impulsive, rather than planned. The first time he was arrested was at the age of eleven, when he and a relative broke into a house to steal some Atari video games. A year later, he was sent to state reform school after he and a friend broke into an abandoned building and made off with paint cans, irons, and other property that they hardly knew what to do with. In reform school, he got into fights and screamed obscenities at the staff. When the staff tried to discipline him by taking away his recreation or his television privileges, his behavior worsened. He tore a pillar out of the ceiling, a sink and mirrors off the wall, doors off their hinges. He was put in a special cell, stripped of nearly everything. When he began attacking counsellors, the authorities transferred him to the maximum-security juvenile facility at Joliet, where he continued to misbehave.

Felton wasn't a sociopath. He made friends easily. He was close to his family, and missed them deeply. He took no pleasure in hurting others. Psychiatric evaluations turned up little more than attention-deficit disorder. But he had a terrible temper, a tendency to escalate rather than to defuse confrontations, and, by the time he was released, just before turning eighteen, he had achieved only a ninth-grade education.

Within months of returning home, he was arrested again. He had walked into a Danville sports bar and ordered a beer. The barman took his ten-dollar bill.

"Then he says, 'Naw, man, you can't get no beer. You're underage,' " Felton recounts. "I says, 'Well, give me my ten dollars back.' He says, 'You ain't getting shit. Get the hell out of here.' "

Felton stood his ground. The bartender had a pocket knife on the counter.   55
"And, when he went for it, I went for it," Felton told me. "When I grabbed the knife first, I turned around and spinned on him. I said, 'You think you're gonna cut me, man? You gotta be fucked up.' "

The barman had put the ten-dollar bill in a Royal Crown bag behind the counter. Felton grabbed the bag and ran out the back door. He forgot his car keys on the counter, though. So he went back to get the keys — "the stupid keys," he now says ruefully — and in the fight that ensued he left the barman severely injured and bleeding. The police caught Felton fleeing in his car. He was convicted of armed robbery, aggravated unlawful restraint, and aggravated battery, and served fifteen years in prison.

He was eventually sent to the Stateville Correctional Center, a maximum-security facility in Joliet. Inside the overflowing prison, he got into vicious fights over insults and the like. About three months into his term, during a shakedown following the murder of an inmate, prison officials turned up a makeshift knife in his cell. (He denies that it was his.) They gave him a year in isolation. He was a danger, and he had to be taught a lesson. But it was a lesson that he seemed incapable of learning.

Felton's Stateville isolation cell had gray walls, a solid steel door, no window, no clock, and a light that was kept on twenty-four hours a day. As soon as he was shut in, he became claustrophobic and had a panic attack. Like Dellelo, Anderson, and McCain, he was soon pacing back and forth, talking to himself, studying the insects crawling around his cell, reliving past events from childhood, sleeping for as much as sixteen hours a day. But, unlike them, he lacked the inner resources to cope with his situation.

Many prisoners find survival in physical exercise, prayer, or plans for escape. Many carry out elaborate mental exercises, building entire houses in their heads, board by board, nail by nail, from the ground up, or memorizing team rosters for a baseball season. McCain recreated in his mind movies he'd seen. Anderson reconstructed complete novels from memory. Yuri Nosenko, a K.G.B. defector whom the C.I.A. wrongly accused of being a double agent and held for three years in total isolation (no reading material, no news, no human contact except with interrogators) in a closet-size concrete cell near Williamsburg, Virginia, made chess sets from threads and a calendar from lint (only to have them discovered and swept away).

But Felton would just yell, "Guard! Guard! Guard! Guard! Guard!," or bang his cup on the toilet, for hours. He could spend whole days hallucinating that he was in another world, that he was a child at home in Danville, playing in the streets, having conversations with imaginary people. Small cruelties that others somehow bore in quiet fury — getting no meal tray, for example — sent him into a rage. Despite being restrained with handcuffs, ankle shackles, and a belly chain whenever he was taken out, he managed to assault the staff at least three times. He threw his food through the door slot. He set his cell on fire by tearing his mattress apart, wrapping the stuffing in a sheet, popping his light bulb, and using the exposed wires to set the whole thing ablaze. He did this so many times that the walls of his cell were black with soot.

After each offense, prison officials extended his sentence in isolation. Still, he wouldn't stop. He began flooding his cell, by stuffing the door crack with socks, plugging the toilet, and flushing until the water was a couple of feet deep. Then he'd pull out the socks and the whole wing would flood with wastewater.

"Flooding the cell was the last option for me," Felton told me. "It was when I had nothing else I could do. You know, they took everything out of my cell,

60

and all I had left was toilet water. I'd sit there and I'd say, 'Well, let me see what I can do with this toilet water.' "

Felton was not allowed out again for fourteen and a half years. He spent almost his entire prison term, from 1990 to 2005, in isolation. In March, 1998, he was among the first inmates to be moved to Tamms, a new, high-tech supermax facility in southern Illinois.

"At Tamms, man, it was like a lab," he says. Contact even with guards was tightly reduced. Cutoff valves meant that he couldn't flood his cell. He had little ability to force a response — negative or positive — from a human being. And, with that gone, he began to deteriorate further. He ceased showering, changing his clothes, brushing his teeth. His teeth rotted and ten had to be pulled. He began throwing his feces around his cell. He became psychotic.

It is unclear how many prisoners in solitary confinement become psy-   65
chotic. Stuart Grassian, a Boston psychiatrist, has interviewed more than two hundred prisoners in solitary confinement. In one in-depth study, prepared for a legal challenge of prisoner-isolation practices, he concluded that about a third developed acute psychosis with hallucinations. The markers of vulnerability that he observed in his interviews were signs of cognitive dysfunction — a history of seizures, serious mental illness, mental retardation, illiteracy, or, as in Felton's case, a diagnosis such as attention-deficit hyperactivity disorder, signalling difficulty with impulse control. In the prisoners Grassian saw, about a third had these vulnerabilities, and these were the prisoners whom solitary confinement had made psychotic. They were simply not cognitively equipped to endure it without mental breakdowns.

A psychiatrist tried giving Felton anti-psychotic medication. Mostly, it made him sleep — sometimes twenty-four hours at a stretch, he said. Twice he attempted suicide. The first time, he hanged himself in a noose made from a sheet. The second time, he took a single staple from a legal newspaper and managed to slash the radial artery in his left wrist with it. In both instances, he was taken to a local emergency room for a few hours, patched up, and sent back to prison.

Is there an alternative? Consider what other countries do. Britain, for example, has had its share of serial killers, homicidal rapists, and prisoners who have taken hostages and repeatedly assaulted staff. The British also fought a seemingly unending war in Northern Ireland, which brought them hundreds of Irish Republican Army prisoners committed to violent resistance. The authorities resorted to a harshly punitive approach to control, including, in the mid-seventies, extensive use of solitary confinement. But the violence in prisons remained unchanged, the costs were phenomenal (in the United States, they reach more than fifty thousand dollars a year per inmate), and the public outcry became intolerable. British authorities therefore looked for another approach.

Beginning in the nineteen-eighties, they gradually adopted a strategy that focussed on preventing prison violence rather than on delivering an ever more brutal series of punishments for it. The approach starts with the simple observation that prisoners who are unmanageable in one setting often behave perfectly reasonably in another. This suggested that violence might, to a critical extent, be a function of the conditions of incarceration. The British noticed that problem prisoners were usually people for whom avoiding humiliation and saving face were fundamental and instinctive. When conditions maximized humiliation and confrontation, every interaction escalated into a trial of strength. Violence became a predictable consequence.

So the British decided to give their most dangerous prisoners more control, rather than less. They reduced isolation and offered them opportunities for work, education, and special programming to increase social ties and skills. The prisoners were housed in small, stable units of fewer than ten people in individual cells, to avoid conditions of social chaos and unpredictability. In these reformed "Close Supervision Centres," prisoners could receive mental-health treatment and earn rights for more exercise, more phone calls, "contact visits," and even access to cooking facilities. They were allowed to air grievances. And the government set up an independent body of inspectors to track the results and enable adjustments based on the data.

The results have been impressive. The use of long-term isolation in England is now negligible. In all of England, there are now fewer prisoners in "extreme custody" than there are in the state of Maine. And the other countries of Europe have, with a similar focus on small units and violence prevention, achieved a similar outcome.

In this country, in June of 2006, a bipartisan national task force, the Commission on Safety and Abuse in America's Prisons, released its recommendations after a yearlong investigation. It called for ending long-term isolation of prisoners. Beyond about ten days, the report noted, practically no benefits can be found and the harm is clear — not just for inmates but for the public as well. Most prisoners in long-term isolation are returned to society, after all. And evidence from a number of studies has shown that supermax conditions — in which prisoners have virtually no social interactions and are given no programmatic support — make it highly likely that they will commit more crimes when they are released. Instead, the report said, we should follow the preventive approaches used in European countries.

The recommendations went nowhere, of course. Whatever the evidence in its favor, people simply did not believe in the treatment.

I spoke to a state-prison commissioner who wished to remain unidentified. He was a veteran of the system, having been either a prison warden or a commissioner in several states across the country for more than twenty years. He has publicly defended the use of long-term isolation everywhere that he has worked. Nonetheless, he said, he would remove most prisoners from long-term isolation units if he could and provide programming for the mental illnesses that many of them have.

"Prolonged isolation is not going to serve anyone's best interest," he told me. He still thought that prisons needed the option of isolation. "A bad violation should, I think, land you there for about ninety days, but it should not go beyond that."

He is apparently not alone among prison officials. Over the years, he has　75
come to know commissioners in nearly every state in the country. "I believe
that today you'll probably find that two-thirds or three-fourths of the heads of
correctional agencies will largely share the position that I articulated with
you," he said.

Commissioners are not powerless. They could eliminate prolonged isolation with the stroke of a pen. So, I asked, why haven't they? He told me what
happened when he tried to move just one prisoner out of isolation. Legislators
called for him to be fired and threatened to withhold basic funding. Corrections
officers called members of the crime victim's family and told them that he'd
gone soft on crime. Hostile stories appeared in the tabloids. It is pointless for
commissioners to act unilaterally, he said, without a change in public opinion.

This past year, both the Republican and the Democratic Presidential candidates came out firmly for banning torture and closing the facility in Guantá-
namo Bay, where hundreds of prisoners have been held in years-long isolation.
Neither Barack Obama nor John McCain, however, addressed the question of
whether prolonged solitary confinement is torture. For a Presidential candidate, no less than for the prison commissioner, this would have been political
suicide. The simple truth is that public sentiment in America is the reason that
solitary confinement has exploded in this country, even as other Western nations have taken steps to reduce it. This is the dark side of American exception-
alism. With little concern or demurral, we have consigned tens of thousands of
our own citizens to conditions that horrified our highest court a century ago.
Our willingness to discard these standards for American prisoners made it easy
to discard the Geneva Conventions prohibiting similar treatment of foreign
prisoners of war, to the detriment of America's moral stature in the world. In
much the same way that a previous generation of Americans countenanced
legalized segregation, ours has countenanced legalized torture. And there is no
clearer manifestation of this than our routine use of solitary confinement—
on our own people, in our own communities, in a supermax prison, for example, that is a thirty-minute drive from my door.

Robert Felton drifted in and out of acute psychosis for much of his solitary
confinement. Eventually, however, he found an unexpected resource. One day,
while he was at Tamms, he was given a new defense lawyer, and, whatever expertise this lawyer provided, the more important thing was genuine human
contact. He visited regularly, and sent Felton books. Although some were rejected by the authorities and Felton was restricted to a few at a time, he devoured those he was permitted. "I liked political books," he says. "*From Beirut
to Jerusalem*, Winston Churchill, Noam Chomsky."

That small amount of contact was a lifeline. Felton corresponded with the
lawyer about what he was reading. The lawyer helped him get his G.E.D. and a
paralegal certificate through a correspondence course, and he taught Felton
how to advocate for himself. Felton began writing letters to politicians and
prison officials explaining the misery of his situation, opposing supermax isolation, and asking for a chance to return to the general prison population. (The

Illinois Department of Corrections would not comment on Felton's case, but a spokesman stated that "Tamms houses the most disruptive, violent, and problematic inmates.") Felton was persuasive enough that Senator Paul Simon, of Illinois, wrote him back and, one day, even visited him. Simon asked the director of the State Department of Corrections, Donald Snyder, Jr., to give consideration to Felton's objections. But Snyder didn't budge. If there was anyone whom Felton fantasized about taking revenge upon, it was Snyder. Felton continued to file request after request. But the answer was always no.

On July 12, 2005, at the age of thirty-three, Felton was finally released. He   80 hadn't socialized with another person since entering Tamms, at the age of twenty-five. Before his release, he was given one month in the general prison population to get used to people. It wasn't enough. Upon returning to society, he found that he had trouble in crowds. At a party of well-wishers, the volume of social stimulation overwhelmed him and he panicked, headed for a bathroom, and locked himself in. He stayed at his mother's house and kept mostly to himself.

For the first year, he had to wear an ankle bracelet and was allowed to leave home only for work. His first job was at a Papa John's restaurant, delivering pizzas. He next found work at the Model Star Laundry Service, doing pressing. This was a steady job, and he began to settle down. He fell in love with a waitress named Brittany. They moved into a three-room house that her grandmother lent them, and got engaged. Brittany became pregnant.

This is not a story with a happy ending. Felton lost his job with the laundry service. He went to work for a tree-cutting business; a few months later, it went under. Meanwhile, he and Brittany had had a second child. She had found work as a certified nursing assistant, but her income wasn't nearly enough. So he took a job forty miles away, at Plastipak, the plastics manufacturer, where he made seven-fifty an hour inspecting Gatorade bottles and Crisco containers as they came out of the stamping machines. Then his twenty-year-old Firebird died. The bus he had to take ran erratically, and he was fired for repeated tardiness.

When I visited Felton in Danville last August, he and Brittany were upbeat about their prospects. She was working extra shifts at a nursing home, and he was taking care of their children, ages one and two. He had also applied to a six-month training program for heating and air-conditioning technicians.

"I could make twenty dollars an hour after graduation," he said.

"He's a good man," Brittany told me, taking his arm and giving him a kiss.   85

But he was out of work. They were chronically short of money. It was hard to be optimistic about Felton's prospects. And, indeed, six weeks after we met, he was arrested for breaking into a car dealership and stealing a Dodge Charger. He pleaded guilty and, in January, began serving a seven-year sentence.

Before I left town — when there was still a glimmer of hope for him — we went out for lunch at his favorite place, a Mexican restaurant called La Potosina. Over enchiladas and Cokes, we talked about his family, Danville, the economy, and, of course, his time in prison. The strangest story had turned up in the news, he said. Donald Snyder, Jr., the state prison director who had refused to let him out of solitary confinement, had been arrested, convicted, and sentenced to two years in prison for taking fifty thousand dollars in payoffs from lobbyists.

"Two years in prison," Felton marvelled. "He could end up right where I used to be."

I asked him, "If he wrote to you, asking if you would release him from solitary, what would you do?"

Felton didn't hesitate for a second. "If he wrote to me to let him out, I'd let   90
him out," he said.

This surprised me. I expected anger, vindictiveness, a desire for retribution. "You'd let him out?" I said.

"I'd let him out," he said, and he put his fork down to make the point. "I wouldn't wish solitary confinement on anybody. Not even him."   [2009]

■ THINKING ABOUT THE TEXT

1. Gawande's essay becomes chiefly an argument against the use of solitary confinement in American prisons. He does not begin to criticize this specific policy, however, until he brings up the case of Bobby Dellelo (para. 24). Why do you think he delays? What are some ways that he builds support for his criticism before he actually raises it?

2. How would you characterize Gawande's attitude toward Bobby Dellelo and Robert Felton? How complex is his view of each? Refer to specific statements in his accounts of them. What particular details about them does he evidently hope will lead you to share his disapproval of solitary confinement?

3. Besides his stories about particular individuals, what evidence does Gawande use to strengthen his argument against solitary confinement?

4. As a surgeon, Gawande spends much of his time repairing *physical* damage. Yet apparently he thinks that *psychological* damage can be at least as awful. How reasonable does this view seem to you?

5. Do you think Gawande adequately confronts all of the things that might be said on behalf of keeping solitary confinement as a punishment in American prisons? Explain.

■ MAKING COMPARISONS

1. Do you suspect that Sanders and Kingston would agree with Gawande's stand against solitary confinement in the U.S. prison system? Why, or why not?

2. In their essays, Sanders and Kingston say a great deal about the psychological impact on them of certain people and events. Do you find Gawande less revealing in this regard, or do you sense that he, too, conveys much about his own psychological reactions? Refer to specific passages in his text.

3. To what extent can Gawande's title, "Hellhole," be applied to the defendant's circumstances in Sanders's essay and to the aunt's circumstances in Kingston's piece?

≡ **WRITING ABOUT ISSUES**

1. Choose one of the essays in this cluster. What should readers mainly consider in evaluating the behavior of the defendant (or one of the defendants) it analyzes? Write an essay of your own answering this question. If necessary, distinguish your views from those you think the author holds.

2. Choose Kingston's or Gawande's piece, and then write an essay in which you hypothesize how she or he would behave as a juror judging the case that Sanders discusses. Support your hypothesis by referring to specific details from Sanders's essay and from the one by your chosen author.

3. In 1991, four white police officers went on trial for various offenses related to their videotaped beating of an African American man, Rodney King, who was resisting arrest. The judge believed that the officers could not receive a fair trial in southeast Los Angeles, where the beating occurred. Therefore, the trial was moved to a suburb, Simi Valley. The jury's ten whites, one Hispanic, and one Asian reflected the predominantly white middle-class makeup of the town. Critics argued that a Los Angeles jury probably would have been partially or even predominantly black. The Simi Valley jurors proceeded to acquit the officers of almost every charge. Many Americans protested the outcome, believing that a more racially diverse jury would have reached more responsible verdicts and that the trial should have taken place where the complaint was filed. In the *Washington Post*, however, a letter writer disagreed: "As for the change of venue, the Constitution guarantees us a jury of our peers. The Simi Valley jury was surely more representative of the officers' peers than a southeast Los Angeles jury would have been." Write an essay in which you identify and defend what you think should be meant by the phrase "a jury of one's peers." In arguing for your definition, refer to at least one actual case. Possibilities include the King case; a case described in this cluster; the two O. J. Simpson trials; and recent cases in the local, national, or international news.

4. Write an essay analyzing and evaluating the behavior of a particular jury. It might be a jury that you sat on or observed. Then again, it might be a jury that someone told you about or that you read about. Feel free to compare your chosen jury with any of the judging groups in this cluster's essays.

☰ He Said/She Said: Re-Visions of a Poem

ROBERT BROWNING, "My Last Duchess"

GABRIEL SPERA, "My Ex-Husband"

Although the terms *justice* and *injustice* are most often applied to developments that affect entire groups, these words can also prove relevant to personal relationships. In particular, two people may quit being a couple because at least one of them feels that the other has done an injustice to him or her. Of course, the two parties may define *justice* differently, and they may disagree as well about which of them is in the wrong. Together, the following poems illustrate such a conflict of views. Indeed, they present a he said/she said scenario. In the first poem, Robert Browning's famous "My Last Duchess," the speaker explains how his wife's allegedly unjust behavior forced him to get rid of her. In the second poem, Gabriel Spera's more recent "My Ex-Husband," the speaker recalls how her former spouse's injustices drove her to divorce him. Notice the specific ways that Spera's re-vision of Browning's poem forces us to consider differences in perspective.

☰ BEFORE YOU READ

Think of two people you know who have broken off a relationship they had with each other. To what extent do these people see the breakup the same way? How, if at all, do their views of it differ?

ROBERT BROWNING
My Last Duchess

Today, Robert Browning (1812–1889) is regarded as one of the greatest poets of ✦
nineteenth-century England, but in his own time he was not nearly as celebrated as his wife, the poet Elizabeth Barrett Browning. He is chiefly known for his achievements with the dramatic monologue, *a genre of poetry that emphasizes the speaker's own distinct personality. Often Browning's speakers are his imaginative re-creations of people who once existed in real life. He was especially interested in religious, political, and artistic figures from the Renaissance. The following poem, perhaps Browning's most famous, was written in 1842, and its speaker, the Duke of Ferrara, was an actual man.*

(© Bettmann/Corbis.)

Ferrara°

That's my last Duchess painted on the wall,
Looking as if she were alive. I call
That piece a wonder, now: Frà Pandolf's° hands
Worked busily a day, and there she stands.
Will't please you sit and look at her? I said   5
"Frà Pandolf" by design, for never read
Strangers like you that pictured countenance,
The depth and passion of its earnest glance,
But to myself they turned (since none puts by
The curtain I have drawn for you, but I)   10
And seemed as they would ask me, if they durst,
How such a glance came there; so, not the first
Are you to turn and ask thus. Sir, 'twas not
Her husband's presence only, called that spot
Of joy into the Duchess' cheek: perhaps   15

EPIGRAPH **Ferrara:** In the sixteenth century, the duke of this Italian city arranged to marry a second time after the mysterious death of his very young first wife. **3 Frà Pandolf:** A fictitious artist.

Frà Pandolf chanced to say "Her mantle laps
Over my lady's wrist too much," or "Paint
Must never hope to reproduce the faint
Half-flush that dies along her throat": such stuff
Was courtesy, she thought, and cause enough   20
For calling up that spot of joy. She had
A heart — how shall I say? — too soon made glad,
Too easily impressed; she liked whate'er
She looked on, and her looks went everywhere.
Sir, 'twas all one! My favor at her breast,   25
The dropping of the daylight in the West,
The bough of cherries some officious fool
Broke in the orchard for her, the white mule
She rode with round the terrace — all and each
Would draw from her alike the approving speech,   30
Or blush, at least. She thanked men, — good! but thanked
Somehow — I know not how — as if she ranked
My gift of a nine-hundred-years-old name
With anybody's gift. Who'd stoop to blame
This sort of trifling? Even had you skill   35
In speech — which I have not — to make your will
Quite clear to such an one, and say, "Just this
Or that in you disgusts me; here you miss,
Or there exceed the mark" — and if she let
Herself be lessoned so, nor plainly set   40
Her wits to yours, forsooth, and made excuse,
— E'en then would be some stooping; and I choose
Never to stoop. Oh sir, she smiled, no doubt,
Whene'er I passed her; but who passed without
Much the same smile? This grew; I gave commands;   45
Then all smiles stopped together. There she stands
As if alive. Will 't please you rise? We'll meet
The company below, then. I repeat,
The Count your master's known munificence
Is ample warrant that no just pretense   50
Of mine for dowry will be disallowed;
Though his fair daughter's self, as I avowed
At starting, is my object. Nay, we'll go
Together down, sir. Notice Neptune, though,
Taming a sea-horse, thought a rarity,   55
Which Claus of Innsbruck° cast in bronze for me!   *[1842]*

---

56 Claus of Innsbruck: A fictitious artist.

≡ THINKING ABOUT THE TEXT

1. The duke offers a history of his first marriage. Summarize his story in your own words, including the reasons he gives for his behavior. How would you describe him? Do you admire anything about him? If so, what?

2. Try to reconstruct the rhetorical situation in which the duke is making his remarks. Who might be his audience? What might be his goals? What strategies is he using to accomplish them? Cite details that support your conjectures.

3. When you read the poem aloud, how conscious are you of its rhymes? What is its rhyme scheme? What is the effect of Browning's using just one stanza rather than breaking the poem into several?

4. Going by this example of the genre, what are the advantages of writing a poem as a dramatic monologue? What are the disadvantages?

5. Browning suggests that the setting of this poem is Renaissance Italy. What relevance might his poem have had for readers in mid-nineteenth-century England? What relevance might it have for audiences in the United States today?

GABRIEL SPERA
My Ex-Husband

Raised in New Jersey, Gabriel Spera (b. 1966) graduated from Cornell University and earned an M.F.A. from the University of North Carolina at Greensboro. He has worked as a technical writer for several years, most recently for a California aerospace firm. At the same time, he has published many poems, including the following one, which first appeared in the journal Poetry *in 1992. It also appears in his book* The Standing Wave *(2003), which was chosen for the National Poetry Series and also won the PEN-USA West Literary Book Award for Poetry.*

That's my ex-husband pictured on the shelf,
Smiling as if in love. I took it myself
With his Leica, and stuck it in that frame
We got for our wedding. Kind of a shame
To waste it on him, but what could I do?   5
(Since I haven't got a photograph of you.)
I know what's on your mind — you want to know
Whatever could have made me let him go —
He seems like any woman's perfect catch,
What with his ruddy cheeks, the thin mustache,   10
Those close-set, baggy eyes, that tilted grin.

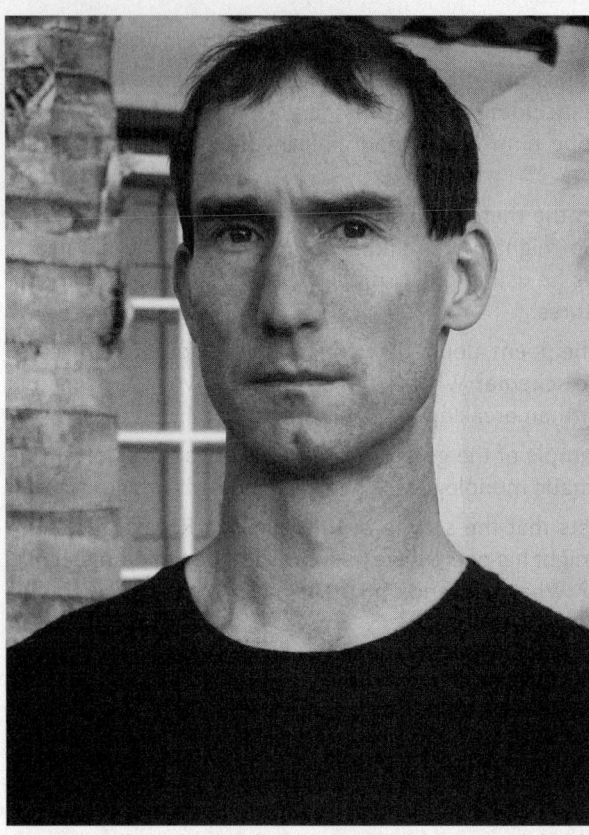

(Photo by Rachel Lee.)

But snapshots don't show what's beneath the skin!
He had a certain charm, charisma, style,
That passionate, earnest glance he struck, meanwhile
Whispering the sweetest things, like "Your lips   15
Are like plump rubies, eyes like diamond chips,"
Could flush the throat of any woman, not
Just mine. He blew the most romantic spots
In town, where waiters, who all knew his face,
Reserved an intimately dim-lit place   20
Half-hidden in a corner nook. Such stuff
Was all too well rehearsed, I soon enough
Found out. He had an attitude — how should
I put it — smooth, self-satisfied, too good
For the rest of the world, too easily   25
Impressed with his officious self. And he
flirted — fine! but flirted somehow a bit
Too ardently, too blatantly, as if,

If someone ever noticed, no one cared
How slobbishly he carried on affairs.   30
Who'd lower herself to put up with shit
Like that? Even if you'd the patience — which
I have not — to go and see some counsellor
And say, "My life's a living hell," or
"Everything he does disgusts, the lout!" —   35
And even if you'd somehow worked things out,
Took a long trip together, made amends,
Let things get back to normal, even then
You'd still be on the short end of the stick;
And I choose never ever to get stuck.   40
Oh, no doubt, it always made my limbs go
Woozy when he kissed me, but what bimbo
In the steno pool went without the same
Such kisses? So, I made some calls, filed some claims,
All kisses stopped together. There he grins,   45
Almost lovable. Shall we go? I'm in
The mood for Chez Pierre's, perhaps, tonight,
Though anything you'd like would be all right
As well, of course, though I'd prefer not to go
To any place with checkered tables. No,   50
We'll take my car. By the way, have I shown
You yet these lovely champagne flutes, hand blown,
Imported from Murano, Italy,
Which Claus got in the settlement for me!   [1992]

≡ **THINKING ABOUT THE TEXT**

1. Why, evidently, did the speaker get divorced? What would you say to someone who argues that because she still thinks about her former husband, keeps his photograph on the shelf, and clearly has not forgiven him, she remains "stuck" (line 40) in that relationship?

2. How reliable do you think the speaker's account of her former husband is?

3. Where does the speaker shift the kind of language she's been using? Do you think her feelings are consistent despite this shifting? Explain.

4. Who do you think the "you" (line 6) in this poem is? In what ways, if any, does the presence of this "you" seem to influence what the speaker says and how she says it?

5. Although the speaker is a woman, poet Gabriel Spera is a man. Does this poem lead you to believe that a man can, in fact, write from a woman's point of view? Why, or why not?

■ MAKING COMPARISONS

1. Where in his poem does Spera closely echo Browning's poem? Refer to specific lines in both texts. What is the effect of the changes in wording that Spera makes?

2. Do you sympathize more with Spera's speaker than with Browning's? Why, or why not? Explain.

3. Do the listeners in these two poems both seem passive? Refer to specific details of both texts.

■ WRITING ABOUT ISSUES

1. Choose either of the poems in this cluster, and write an essay analyzing what you consider to be its most significant line. Be sure to explain why you find your chosen line important.

2. To what extent and in what ways does Spera's poem seem more "modern" than Browning's? Write an essay in which you answer this question. Refer to specific details from both poems, and define clearly what you mean by *modern*.

3. Write an essay analyzing a relationship that you broke off because you thought the other person had acted unjustly. To what extent do you still brood about this relationship? How much have you forgiven the other person? What meaning of the term *justice* seems applicable here?

4. Write a dialogue between the speakers of these two poems, or write a dialogue between the listeners in them. Shape the dialogue so that it emphasizes ideas and principles that the two people have in common. Then write a brief essay in which you analyze the conversation you have constructed. What do you want your readers to conclude from it?

▤ Taking Revenge: Stories

ANDRE DUBUS, "Killings"

HA JIN, "Saboteur"

Many people consider revenge abhorrent. They hold that wrongdoers should be forgiven, left to the judgment of God ("Vengeance is mine, saith the Lord"), or dealt with through the supposedly fair and rational processes of the judicial system. Yet others believe in getting even. They may tolerate or encourage revenge taken by others or retaliate themselves against perceived offenders, in effect following the ancient biblical principle of "an eye for an eye, a tooth for a tooth." In the first story in this cluster, a man takes revenge for the killing of his son, while the protagonist of the second story attempts to punish an entire city for the humiliation that its police have inflicted on him. As you read each of these works, consider the logic, morality, context, and effects of the vengeance described.

▤ BEFORE YOU READ

Do you believe it is ever justifiable for someone to avenge a crime or wrong-doing by going outside the law? What specific cases do you think about as you address this issue?

ANDRE DUBUS

Killings

Andre Dubus (1936–1999) served five years in the Marine Corps, attaining the rank of captain before becoming a full-time writer of short stories. Dubus lived in Haverhill, Massachusetts, and much of his fiction is set in the Merrimack Valley north of Boston. This is true of the following story, which appeared in his collection Finding a Girl in America *(1980) and was reprinted in his* Selected Stories *(1988). In 1991, Dubus also published a collection of essays,* Broken Vessels. *In part, the book deals with a 1986 accident that changed his life. Getting out of his car to aid stranded motorists, he was struck by another car; he eventually lost most of one leg and power over the other. Though confined to a wheelchair, Dubus continued to work actively. In 1996, he published his last collection of stories,* Dancing After Hours, *and in 1998, another volume of essays entitled* Meditations from a Moveable Chair. *Two years after he died came a much-acclaimed film adaptation of "Killings," entitled* In the Bedroom *(2001).*

On the August morning when Matt Fowler buried his youngest son, Frank, who had lived for twenty-one years, eight months, and four days, Matt's older son, Steve, turned to him as the family left the grave and walked between their friends, and said: "I should kill him." He was twenty-eight, his brown hair starting to thin in front where he used to have a cowlick. He bit his lower lip, wiped his eyes, then said it again. Ruth's arm, linked with Matt's, tightened; he looked at her. Beneath her eyes there was swelling from the three days she had suffered. At the limousine Matt stopped and looked back at the grave, the casket, and the Congregationalist minister who he thought had probably had a difficult job with the eulogy though he hadn't seemed to, and the old funeral director who was saying something to the six young pallbearers. The grave was on a hill and overlooked the Merrimack, which he could not see from where he stood; he looked at the opposite bank, at the apple orchard with its symmetrically planted trees going up a hill.

Next day Steve drove with his wife back to Baltimore where he managed the branch office of a bank, and Cathleen, the middle child, drove with her husband back to Syracuse. They had left the grandchildren with friends. A month after the funeral Matt played poker at Willis Trottier's because Ruth, who knew this was the second time he had been invited, told him to go, he couldn't sit home with her for the rest of her life, she was all right. After the game Willis went outside to tell everyone good night and, when the others had driven away, he walked with Matt to his car. Willis was a short, silver-haired man who had opened a diner after World War II, his trade then mostly very early breakfast, which he cooked, and then lunch for the men who worked at the leather and shoe factories. He now owned a large restaurant.

"He walks the Goddamn streets," Matt said.

"I know. He was in my place last night, at the bar. With a girl."

"I don't see him. I'm in the store all the time. Ruth sees him. She sees him too much. She was at Sunnyhurst today getting cigarettes and aspirin, and there he was. She can't even go out for cigarettes and aspirin. It's killing her."

"Come back in for a drink."

Matt looked at his watch. Ruth would be asleep. He walked with Willis back into the house, pausing at the steps to look at the starlit sky. It was a cool summer night; he thought vaguely of the Red Sox, did not even know if they were at home tonight; since it happened he had not been able to think about any of the small pleasures he believed he had earned, as he had earned also what was shattered now forever: the quietly harried and quietly pleasurable days of fatherhood. They went inside. Willis's wife, Martha, had gone to bed hours ago, in the rear of the large house which was rigged with burglar and fire alarms. They went downstairs to the game room: the television set suspended from the ceiling, the pool table, the poker table with beer cans, cards, chips, filled ashtrays, and the six chairs where Matt and his friends had sat, the friends picking up the old banter as though he had only been away on vacation; but he could see the affection and courtesy in their eyes. Willis went behind the bar and mixed them each a Scotch and soda; he stayed behind the bar and looked at Matt sitting on the stool.

"How often have you thought about it?" Willis said.

"Every day since he got out. I didn't think about bail. I thought I wouldn't have to worry about him for years. She sees him all the time. It makes her cry."

"He was in my place a long time last night. He'll be back."   10
"Maybe he won't."
"The band. He likes the band."
"What's he doing now?"
"He's tending bar up to Hampton Beach. For a friend. Ever notice even the worst bastard always has friends? He couldn't get work in town. It's just tourists and kids up to Hampton. Nobody knows him. If they do, they don't care. They drink what he mixes."
"Nobody tells me about him."   15
"I hate him, Matt. My boys went to school with him. He was the same then. Know what he'll do? Five at the most. Remember that woman about seven years ago? Shot her husband and dropped him off the bridge in the Merrimack with a hundred-pound sack of cement and said all the way through it that nobody helped her. Know where she is now? She's in Lawrence now, a secretary. And whoever helped her, where the hell is he?"
"I've got a .38 I've had for years, I take it to the store now. I tell Ruth it's for the night deposits. I tell her things have changed: we got junkies here now too. Lots of people without jobs. She knows though."
"What does she know?"
"She knows I started carrying it after the first time she saw him in town. She knows it's in case I see him, and there's some kind of a situation — "
He stopped, looked at Willis, and finished his drink. Willis mixed him   20
another.
"What kind of situation?"
"Where he did something to me. Where I could get away with it."
"How does Ruth feel about that?"
"She doesn't know."
"You said she does, she's got it figured out."   25
He thought of her that afternoon: when she went into Sunnyhurst, Strout was waiting at the counter while the clerk bagged the things he had bought; she turned down an aisle and looked at soup cans until he left.
"Ruth would shoot him herself, if she thought she could hit him."
"You got a permit?"
"No."
"I do. You could get a year for that."   30
"Maybe I'll get one. Or maybe I won't. Maybe I'll just stop bringing it to the store."

Richard Strout was twenty-six years old, a high school athlete, football scholarship to the University of Massachusetts where he lasted for almost two semesters before quitting in advance of the final grades that would have forced him not to return. People then said: Dickie can do the work; he just doesn't want to. He came home and did construction work for his father but refused his father's offer to learn the business; his two older brothers had learned it, so that Strout and Sons trucks going about town, and signs on construction sites, now slashed wounds into Matt Fowler's life. Then Richard married a young girl and became a bartender, his salary and tips augmented and perhaps sometimes matched by his father, who also posted his bond. So his friends, his enemies (he had those: fist fights or, more often, boys and then young men who had not fought him when they thought they should have), and those who simply knew him by face and name, had a series of images of him which they recalled when they heard of the killing: the high school running back, the young drunk in bars, the oblivious hard-hatted young man eating lunch at a counter, the bartender who could perhaps be called courteous but not more than that: as he tended bar, his dark eyes and dark, wide-jawed face appeared less sullen, near blank.

One night he beat Frank. Frank was living at home and waiting for September, for graduate school in economics, and working as a lifeguard at Salisbury Beach, where he met Mary Ann Strout, in her first month of separation. She spent most days at the beach with her two sons. Before ten o'clock one night Frank came home; he had driven to the hospital first, and he walked into the living room with stitches over his right eye and both lips bright and swollen.

"I'm all right," he said, when Matt and Ruth stood up, and Matt turned off the television, letting Ruth get to him first: the tall, muscled but slender sun-tanned boy. Frank tried to smile at them but couldn't because of his lips.

"It was her husband, wasn't it?" Ruth said.   35

"Ex," Frank said. "He dropped in."

Matt gently held Frank's jaw and turned his face to the light, looked at the stitches, the blood under the white of the eye, the bruised flesh.

"Press charges," Matt said.

"No."

"What's to stop him from doing it again? Did you hit him at all? Enough so   40
he won't want to next time?"

"I don't think I touched him."

"So what are you going to do?"

"Take karate," Frank said, and tried again to smile.

"That's not the problem," Ruth said.

"You know you like her," Frank said.   45

"I like a lot of people. What about the boys? Did they see it?"

"They were asleep."

"Did you leave her alone with him?"

"He left first. She was yelling at him. I believe she had a skillet in her hand."

"Oh for God's sake," Ruth said.   50

Matt had been dealing with that too: at the dinner table on evenings when Frank wasn't home, was eating with Mary Ann; or, on the other nights — and Frank was with her every night — he talked with Ruth while they watched television, or lay in bed with the windows open and he smelled the night air and imagined, with both pride and muted sorrow, Frank in Mary Ann's arms. Ruth didn't like it because Mary Ann was in the process of divorce, because she had two children, because she was four years older than Frank, and finally — she told this in bed, where she had during all of their marriage told him of her deepest feelings: of love, of passion, of fears about one of the children, of pain

Matt had caused her or she had caused him — she was against it because of what she had heard: that the marriage had gone bad early, and for most of it Richard and Mary Ann had both played around.

"That can't be true," Matt said. "Strout wouldn't have stood for it."

"Maybe he loves her."

"He's too hot-tempered. He couldn't have taken that."

But Matt knew Strout had taken it, for he had heard the stories too. He 55 wondered who had told them to Ruth; and he felt vaguely annoyed and isolated: living with her for thirty-one years and still not knowing what she talked about with her friends. On these summer nights he did not so much argue with her as try to comfort her, but finally there was no difference between the two: she had concrete objections, which he tried to overcome. And in his attempt to do this, he neglected his own objections, which were the same as hers, so that as he spoke to her he felt as disembodied as he sometimes did in the store when he helped a man choose a blouse or dress or piece of costume jewelry for his wife.

"The divorce doesn't mean anything," he said. "She was young and maybe she liked his looks and then after a while she realized she was living with a bastard. I see it as a positive thing."

"She's not divorced yet."

"It's the same thing. Massachusetts has crazy laws, that's all. Her age is no problem. What's it matter when she was born? And that other business: even if it's true, which it probably isn't, it's got nothing to do with Frank, and it's in the past. And the kids are no problem. She's been married six years; she ought to have kids. Frank likes them. He plays with them. And he's not going to marry her anyway, so it's not a problem of money."

"Then what's he doing with her?"

"She probably loves him, Ruth. Girls always have. Why can't we just leave 60 it at that?"

"He got home at six o'clock Tuesday morning."

"I didn't know you knew. I've already talked to him about it."

Which he had: since he believed almost nothing he told Ruth, he went to Frank with what he believed. The night before, he had followed Frank to the car after dinner.

"You wouldn't make much of a burglar," he said.

"How's that?" 65

Matt was looking up at him; Frank was six feet tall, an inch and a half taller than Matt, who had been proud when Frank at seventeen outgrew him; he had only felt uncomfortable when he had to reprimand or caution him. He touched Frank's bicep, thought of the young taut passionate body, believed he could sense the desire, and again he felt the pride and sorrow and envy too, not knowing whether he was envious of Frank or Mary Ann.

"When you came in yesterday morning, I woke up. One of these mornings your mother will. And I'm the one who'll have to talk to her. She won't interfere with you. Okay? I know it means —" But he stopped, thinking: I know it means getting up and leaving that suntanned girl and going sleepy to the car, I know —

"Okay," Frank said, and touched Matt's shoulder and got into the car.

There had been other talks, but the only long one was their first one: a night driving to Fenway Park, Matt having ordered the tickets so they could talk, and knowing when Frank said yes, he would go, that he knew the talk was coming too. It took them forty minutes to get to Boston, and they talked about Mary Ann until they joined the city traffic along the Charles River, blue in the late sun. Frank told him all the things that Matt would later pretend to believe when he told them to Ruth.

"It seems like a lot for a young guy to take on," Matt finally said.   70

"Sometimes it is. But she's worth it."

"Are you thinking about getting married?"

"We haven't talked about it. She can't for over a year. I've got school."

"I *do* like her," Matt said.

He did. Some evenings, when the long summer sun was still low in the sky,   75
Frank brought her home; they came into the house smelling of suntan lotion and the sea, and Matt gave them gin and tonics and started the charcoal in the backyard, and looked at Mary Ann in the lawn chair: long and very light brown hair (Matt thinking that twenty years ago she would have dyed it blonde), and the long brown legs he loved to look at; her face was pretty; she had probably never in her adult life gone unnoticed into a public place. It was in her wide brown eyes that she looked older than Frank; after a few drinks Matt thought what he saw in her eyes was something erotic, testament to the rumors about her; but he knew it wasn't that, or all that: she had, very young, been through a sort of pain that his children, and he and Ruth, had been spared. In the moments of his recognizing that pain, he wanted to tenderly touch her hair, wanted with some gesture to give her solace and hope. And he would glance at Frank, and hope they would love each other, hope Frank would soothe that pain in her heart, take it from her eyes; and her divorce, her age, and her children did not matter at all. On the first two evenings she did not bring her boys, and then Ruth asked her to bring them the next time. In bed that night Ruth said, "She hasn't brought them because she's embarrassed. She shouldn't feel embarrassed."

Richard Strout shot Frank in front of the boys. They were sitting on the living room floor watching television, Frank sitting on the couch, and Mary Ann just returning from the kitchen with a tray of sandwiches. Strout came in the front door and shot Frank twice in the chest and once in the face with a 9 mm automatic. Then he looked at the boys and Mary Ann, and went home to wait for the police.

It seemed to Matt that from the time Mary Ann called weeping to tell him until now, a Saturday night in September, sitting in the car with Willis, parked beside Strout's car, waiting for the bar to close, that he had not so much moved through his life as wandered through it, his spirits like a dazed body bumping into furniture and corners. He had always been a fearful father: when his children were young, at the start of each summer he thought of them drowning in a pond or the sea, and he was relieved when he came home in the evenings and they were there; usually that relief was his only acknowledgment of his fear, which he never spoke of, and which he controlled within his heart. As he had when they were very young and all of them in turn, Cathleen too, were drawn to the high oak in the backyard, and had to climb it. Smiling, he watched them, imagining the fall: and he was poised to catch the small body before it hit the earth. Or his legs were poised; his hands were in his pockets or his arms were folded and, for the child looking down, he appeared relaxed and confident while his heart beat with the two words he wanted to call out but did not: *Don't fall.* In winter he was less afraid: he made sure the ice would hold him before they skated, and he brought or sent them to places where they could sled without ending in the street. So he and his children had survived their childhood, and he only worried about them when he knew they were driving a long distance, and then he lost Frank in a way no father expected to lose his son, and he felt that all the fears he had borne while they were growing up, and all the grief he had been afraid of, had backed up like a huge wave and struck him on the beach and swept him out to sea. Each day he felt the same and when he was able to forget how he felt, when he was able to force himself not to feel that way, the eyes of his clerks and customers defeated him. He wished those eyes were oblivious, even cold; he felt he was withering in their tenderness. And beneath his listless wandering, every day in his soul he shot Richard Strout in the face; while Ruth, going about town on errands, kept seeing him. And at night in bed she would hold Matt and cry, or sometimes she was silent and Matt would touch her tightening arm, her clenched fist.

As his own right fist was now, squeezing the butt of the revolver, the last of the drinkers having left the bar, talking to each other, going to their separate cars which were in the lot in front of the bar, out of Matt's vision. He heard their voices, their cars, and then the ocean again, across the street. The tide was in and sometimes it smacked the sea wall. Through the windshield he looked at the dark red side wall of the bar, and then to his left, past Willis, at Strout's car, and through its windows he could see the now-emptied parking lot, the road, the sea wall. He could smell the sea.

The front door of the bar opened and closed again and Willis looked at Matt then at the corner of the building; when Strout came around it alone Matt got out of the car, giving up the hope he had kept all night (and for the past week) that Strout would come out with friends, and Willis would simply drive away; thinking: *All right then. All right*; and he went around the front of Willis's car, and at Strout's he stopped and aimed over the hood at Strout's blue shirt ten feet away. Willis was aiming too, crouched on Matt's left, his elbow resting on the hood.

"Mr. Fowler," Strout said. He looked at each of them, and at the guns. 80 "Mr. Trottier."

Then Matt, watching the parking lot and the road, walked quickly between the car and the building and stood behind Strout. He took one leather glove from his pocket and put it on his left hand.

What is happening?

this seems well planned and thought out...

"Don't talk [...] in."

Strout unlo[...] unlocked the back, then got in, and Matt sli[...] r with his gloved hand, and touched Strout'[...]

"It's cocked [...]

When Stro[...] k the car, Matt aimed at his 85
temple and did [...]

"Drive slow..," he said. "Don't try to get stopped."

They drove across the empty front lot and onto the road, Willis's headlights shining into the car; then back through town, the sea wall on the left

Mistake hiding the beach, though far out Matt could see the ocean; he uncocked the
revolver; on the right were the places, most with their neon signs off, that did so
much business in summer: the lounges and cafés and pizza houses, the street
itself empty of traffic, the way he and Willis had known it would be when they
decided to take Strout at the bar rather than knock on his door at two o'clock
one morning and risk that one insomniac neighbor. Matt had not told Willis he
was afraid he could not be alone with Strout for very long, smell his smells, feel
the presence of his flesh, hear his voice, and then shoot him. They left the beach
town and then were on the high bridge over the channel: to the left the smacking curling white at the breakwater and beyond that the dark sea and the full
moon, and down to his right the small fishing boats bobbing at anchor in the
cove. When they left the bridge, the sea was blocked by abandoned beach cottages, and Matt's left hand was sweating in the glove. Out here in the dark in
the car he believed Ruth knew. Willis had come to his house at eleven and asked

What is with this preparation

if he wanted a nightcap; Matt went to the bedroom for his wallet, put the gloves
in one trouser pocket and the .38 in the other and went back to the living room,
his hand in his pocket covering the bulge of the cool cylinder pressed against
his fingers, the butt against his palm. When Ruth said good night she looked
at his face, and he felt she could see in his eyes the gun, and the night he was
going to. But he knew he couldn't trust what he saw. Willis's wife had taken her
sleeping pill, which gave her eight hours — the reason, Willis had told Matt, he
had the alarms installed, for nights when he was late at the restaurant — and
when it was all done and Willis got home he would leave ice and a trace of
Scotch and soda in two glasses in the game room and tell Martha in the morning that he had left the restaurant early and brought Matt home for a drink.

ex wife, right

"He was making it with my wife." Strout's voice was careful, not pleading.
Matt pressed the muzzle against Strout's head, pressed it harder than he
wanted to, feeling through the gun Strout's head flinching and moving forward; then he lowered the gun to his lap.

"Don't talk," he said. 90

Strout did not speak again. They turned west, drove past the Dairy Queen
closed until spring, and the two lobster restaurants that faced each other and
were crowded all summer and were now also closed, onto the short bridge
crossing the tidal stream, and over the engine Matt could hear through his
open window the water rushing inland under the bridge; looking to his left he
saw its swift moonlit current going back into the marsh which, leaving the

bridge, they entered: the salt marsh stretching out on both sides, the grass tall in patches but mostly low and leaning earthward as though windblown, a large dark rock sitting as though it rested on nothing but itself, and shallow pools reflecting the bright moon.

Beyond the marsh they drove through woods, Matt thinking now of the hole he and Willis had dug last Sunday afternoon after telling their wives they were going to Fenway Park. They listened to the game on a transistor radio, but heard none of it as they dug into the soft earth on the knoll they had chosen because elms and maples sheltered it. Already some leaves had fallen. When the hole was deep enough they covered it and the piled earth with dead branches, then cleaned their shoes and pants and went to a restaurant farther up in New Hampshire where they ate sandwiches and drank beer and watched the rest of the game on television. Looking at the back of Strout's head he thought of Frank's grave; he had not been back to it; but he would go before winter, and its second burial of snow.

He thought of Frank sitting on the couch and perhaps talking to the children as they watched television, imagined him feeling young and strong, still warmed from the sun at the beach, and feeling loved, hearing Mary Ann moving about in the kitchen, hearing her walking into the living room; maybe he looked up at her and maybe she said something, looking at him over the tray of sandwiches, smiling at him, saying something the way women do when they offer food as a gift, then the front door opening and this son of a bitch coming in and Frank seeing that he meant the gun in his hand, this son of a bitch and his gun the last person and thing Frank saw on earth.

When they drove into town the streets were nearly empty: a few slow cars, a policeman walking his beat past the darkened fronts of stores. Strout and Matt both glanced at him as they drove by. They were on the main street, and all the stoplights were blinking yellow. Willis and Matt had talked about that too: the lights changed at midnight, so there would be no place Strout had to stop and where he might try to run. Strout turned down the block where he lived and Willis's headlights were no longer with Matt in the back seat. They had planned that too, had decided it was best for just the one car to go to the house, and again Matt had said nothing about his fear of being alone with Strout, especially in his house: a duplex, dark as all the houses on the street were, the street itself lit at the corner of each block. As Strout turned into the driveway Matt thought of the one insomniac neighbor, thought of some man or woman sitting alone in the dark living room, watching the all-night channel from Boston. When Strout stopped the car near the front of the house, Matt said: "Drive it to the back."

He touched Strout's head with the muzzle.

"You wouldn't have it cocked, would you? For when I put on the brakes."

Matt cocked it, and said: "It is now."

Strout waited a moment; then he eased the car forward, the engine doing little more than idling, and as they approached the garage he gently braked. Matt opened the door, then took off the glove and put it in his pocket. He stepped out and shut the door with his hip and said: "All right."

95

Strout looked at the gun, then got out, and Matt followed him across the grass, and as Strout unlocked the door Matt looked quickly at the row of small backyards on either side, and scattered tall trees, some evergreens, others not, and he thought of the red and yellow leaves on the trees over the hole, saw them falling soon, probably in two weeks, dropping slowly, covering. Strout stepped into the kitchen.

"Turn on the light."   100

Strout reached to the wall switch, and in the light Matt looked at his wide back, the dark blue shirt, the white belt, the red plaid pants.

"Where's your suitcase?"

"My suitcase?"

"Where is it?"

"In the bedroom closet."   105

"That's where we're going then. When we get to a door you stop and turn on the light."

They crossed the kitchen, Matt glancing at the sink and stove and refrigerator: no dishes in the sink or even the dish rack beside it, no grease splashings on the stove, the refrigerator door clean and white. He did not want to look at any more but he looked quickly at all he could see: in the living room magazines and newspapers in a wicker basket, clean ashtrays, a record player, the records shelved next to it, then down the hall where, near the bedroom door, hung a color photograph of Mary Ann and the two boys sitting on a lawn — there was no house in the picture — Mary Ann smiling at the camera or Strout or whoever held the camera, smiling as she had on Matt's lawn this summer while he waited for the charcoal and they all talked and he looked at her brown legs and at Frank touching her arm, her shoulder, her hair; he moved down the hall with her smile in his mind, wondering: was that when they were both playing around and she was smiling like that at him and they were happy, even sometimes, making it worth it? He recalled her eyes, the pain in them, and he was conscious of the circles of love he was touching with the hand that held the revolver so tightly now as Strout stopped at the door at the end of the hall.

"There's no wall switch."

"Where's the light?"

"By the bed."   110

"Let's go."

Matt stayed a pace behind, then Strout leaned over and the room was lighted: the bed, a double one, was neatly made; the ashtray on the bedside table clean, the bureau top dustless, and no photographs; probably so the girl — who _was_ she? — would not have to see Mary Ann in the bedroom she believed was theirs. But because Matt was a father and a husband, though never an ex-husband, he knew (and did not want to know) that this bedroom had never been theirs alone. Strout turned around; Matt looked at his lips, his wide jaw, and thought of Frank's doomed and fearful eyes looking up from the couch.

"Where's Mr. Trottier?"

"He's waiting. Pack clothes for warm weather."

"What's going on?"   115

"You're jumping bail."

"Mr. Fowler — "

He pointed the cocked revolver at Strout's face. The barrel trembled but not much, not as much as he had expected. Strout went to the closet and got the suitcase from the floor and opened it on the bed. As he went to the bureau, he said: "He was making it with my wife. I'd go pick up my kids and he'd be there. Sometimes he spent the night. My boys told me." *➔ not married, right?*

He did not look at Matt as he spoke. He opened the top drawer and Matt stepped closer so he could see Strout's hands: underwear and socks, the socks rolled, the underwear folded and stacked. He took them back to the bed, arranged them neatly in the suitcase, then from the closet he was taking shirts and trousers and a jacket; he laid them on the bed and Matt followed him to the bathroom and watched from the door while he packed those things a person accumulated and that became part of him so that at times in the store Matt felt he was selling more than clothes.

"I wanted to try to get together with her again." He was bent over the suit-   120
case. "I couldn't even talk to her. He was always with her. I'm going to jail for it; if I ever get out I'll be an old man. Isn't that enough?"

"You're not going to jail."

Strout closed the suitcase and faced Matt, looking at the gun. Matt went to his rear, so Strout was between him and the lighted hall; then using his handkerchief he turned off the lamp and said: "Let's go."

They went down the hall, Matt looking again at the photograph, and through the living room and kitchen, Matt turning off the lights and talking, frightened that he was talking, that he was telling this lie he had not planned: "It's the trial. We can't go through that, my wife and me. So you're leaving. We've got you a ticket, and a job. A friend of Mr. Trottier's. Out west. My wife keeps seeing you. We can't have that anymore."

Matt turned out the kitchen light and put the handkerchief in his pocket, and they went down the two brick steps and across the lawn. Strout put the suitcase on the floor of the back seat, then got into the front seat and Matt got in the back and put on his glove and shut the door.

"They'll catch me. They'll check passenger lists."   125

"We didn't use your name."

"They'll figure that out too. You think I wouldn't have done it myself if it was that easy?"

He backed into the street, Matt looking down the gun barrel but not at the profiled face beyond it.

"You were alone," Matt said. "We've got it worked out."

"There's no planes this time of night, Mr. Fowler."   130

"Go back through town. Then north on 125."

They came to the corner and turned, and now Willis's headlights were in the car with Matt.

"Why north, Mr. Fow[...]

"Somebody's going t[...] [...]ou to the airport."

He uncocked the hamme[...] [...] and said wearily: "No more talking."

As they drove back t[...] [...]oing limp with his   135
spirit and its new and fal[...] [...] had given Strout.
He had grown up in this [...]laces of apprehension and pain for Ruth as [...] she had to do; and
for him too, if only in his [...] [...] days a week in his
store; he wondered now if his lie would have worked, if sending Strout away
would have been enough; but then he knew that just thinking of Strout in
Montana or whatever place lay at the end of the lie he had told, thinking of
him walking the streets there, loving a girl there (who *was* she?) would be
enough to slowly rot the rest of his days. And Ruth's. Again he was certain that
she knew, that she was waiting for him.

They were in New Hampshire now, on the narrow highway, passing the
shopping center at the state line, and then houses and small stores and sandwich shops. There were few cars on the road. After ten minutes he raised his
trembling hand, touched Strout's neck with the gun, and said: "Turn in up
here. At the dirt road."

Strout flicked on the indicator and slowed.

"Mr. Fowler?"

"They're waiting here."

Strout turned very slowly, easing his neck away from the gun. In the   140
moonlight the road was light brown, lighter and yellowed where the headlights
shone; weeds and a few trees grew on either side of it, and ahead of them were
the woods.

"There's nothing back here, Mr. Fowler."

"It's for your car. You don't think we'd leave it at the airport, do you?"

He watched Strout's large, big-knuckled hands tighten on the wheel, saw
Frank's face that night: not the stitches and bruised eye and swollen lips, but
his own hand gently touching Frank's jaw, turning his wounds to the light.
They rounded a bend in the road and were out of sight of the highway: tall
trees all around them now, hiding the moon. When they reached the abandoned gravel pit on the left, the bare flat earth and steep pale embankment behind it, and the black crowns of trees at its top, Matt said: "Stop here."

Strout stopped but did not turn off the engine. Matt pressed the gun hard
against his neck, and he straightened in the seat and looked in the rearview
mirror, Matt's eyes meeting his in the glass for an instant before looking at the
hair at the end of the gun barrel.

"Turn it off."   145

Strout did, then held the wheel with two hands, and looked in the mirror.

"I'll do twenty years, Mr. Fowler; at least. I'll be forty-six years old."

"That's nine years younger than I am," Matt said, and got out and took off
the glove and kicked the door shut. He aimed at Strout's ear and pulled back the
hammer. Willis's headlights were off and Matt heard him walking on the soft

thin layer of dust, the hard earth beneath it. Strout opened the door, sat for a moment in the interior light, then stepped out onto the road. Now his face was pleading. Matt did not look at his eyes, but he could see it in the lips.

"Just get the suitcase. They're right up the road."

Willis was beside him now, to his left. Strout looked at both guns. Then he 150 opened the back door, leaned in, and with a jerk brought the suitcase out. He was turning to face them when Matt said: "Just walk up the road. Just ahead."

Strout turned to walk, the suitcase in his right hand, and Matt and Willis followed; as Strout cleared the front of his car he dropped the suitcase and, ducking, took one step that was the beginning of a sprint to his right. The gun kicked in Matt's hand, and the explosion of the shot surrounded him, isolated him in a nimbus of sound that cut him off from all his time, all his history, isolated him standing absolutely still on the dirt road with the gun in his hand, looking down at Richard Strout squirming on his belly, kicking one leg behind him, pushing himself forward, toward the woods. Then Matt went to him and shot him once in the back of the head.

Driving south to Boston, wearing both gloves now, staying in the middle lane and looking often in the rearview mirror at Willis's headlights, he relived the suitcase dropping, the quick dip and turn of Strout's back, and the kick of the gun, the sound of the shot. When he walked to Strout, he still existed within the first shot, still trembled and breathed with it. The second shot and the burial seemed to be happening to someone else, someone he was watching. He and Willis each held an arm and pulled Strout face-down off the road and into the woods, his bouncing sliding belt white under the trees where it was so dark that when they stopped at the top of the knoll, panting and sweating, Matt could not see where Strout's blue shirt ended and the earth began. They pulled off the branches then dragged Strout to the edge of the hole and went behind him and lifted his legs and pushed him in. They stood still for a moment. The woods were quiet save for their breathing, and Matt remembered hearing the movements of birds and small animals after the first shot. Or maybe he had not heard them. Willis went down to the road. Matt could see him clearly out on the tan dirt, could see the glint of Strout's car and, beyond the road, the gravel pit. Willis came back up the knoll with the suitcase. He dropped it in the hole and took off his gloves and they went down to his car for the spades. They worked quietly. Sometimes they paused to listen to the woods. When they were finished Willis turned on his flashlight and they covered the earth with leaves and branches and then went down to the spot in front of the car, and while Matt held the light Willis crouched and sprinkled dust on the blood, backing up till he reached the grass and leaves, then he used leaves until they had worked up to the grave again. They did not stop. They walked around the grave and through the woods, using the light on the ground, looking up through the trees to where they ended at the lake. Neither of them spoke above the sounds of their heavy and clumsy strides through low brush and over fallen branches. Then they reached it: wide and dark, lapping softly at the bank, pine needles smooth under Matt's feet, moonlight on the lake, a small island near its middle, with black, tall evergreens. He took out the gun and threw for the island: taking two steps back on the pine needles, striding with the throw and going to one knee as he followed through, looking up to see the dark shapeless object arcing downward, splashing.

They left Strout's car in Boston, in front of an apartment building on Commonwealth Avenue. When they got back to town Willis drove slowly over the bridge and Matt threw the keys into the Merrimack. The sky was turning light. Willis let him out a block from his house, and walking home he listened for sounds from the houses he passed. They were quiet. A light was on in his living room. He turned it off and undressed in there, and went softly toward the bedroom; in the hall he smelled the smoke, and he stood in the bedroom doorway and looked at the orange of her cigarette in the dark. The curtains were closed. He went to the closet and put his shoes on the floor and felt for a hanger.

"Did you do it?" she said. → so she did know

He went down the hall to the bathroom and in the dark he washed his   155
hands and face. Then he went to her, lay on his back, and pulled the sheet up to his throat.

"Are you all right?" she said.

"I think so."

Now she touched him, lying on her side, her hand on his belly, his thigh.

"Tell me," she said.

He started from the beginning, in the parking lot at the bar; but soon with   160
his eyes closed and Ruth petting him, he spoke of Strout's house: the order, the woman presence, the picture on the wall.

"The way she was smiling," he said.

"What about it?"

"I don't know. Did you ever see Strout's girl? When you saw him in town?"

"No."

"I wonder who she was."   165

Then he thought: *not was: is. Sleeping now she is his girl.* He opened his eyes, then closed them again. There was more light beyond the curtains. With Ruth now he left Strout's house and told again his lie to Strout, gave him again that hope that Strout must have for a while believed, else he would have to believe only the gun pointed at him for the last two hours of his life. And with Ruth he saw again the dropping suitcase, the darting move to the right: and he told of the first shot, feeling her hand on him but his heart isolated still, beating on the road still in that explosion like thunder. He told her the rest, but the words had no images for him, he did not see himself doing what the words said he had done; he only saw himself on that road.

"We can't tell the other kids," she said. "It'll hurt them, thinking he got away. But we mustn't."

"No."

She was holding him, wanting him, and he wished he could make love with her but he could not. He saw Frank and Mary Ann making love in her bed, their eyes closed, their bodies brown and smelling of the sea; the other girl was faceless, bodiless, but he felt her sleeping now; and he saw Frank and Strout, their faces alive; he saw red and yellow leaves falling on the earth, then snow: falling and freezing and falling; and holding Ruth, his cheek touching her breast, he shuddered with a sob that he kept silent in his heart. *[1979]*

▤ THINKING ABOUT THE TEXT

1. Here is an issue of cause and effect: Why, evidently, does Matt kill Richard Strout? Consider the possibility that he has more than one reason. Here is an issue of evaluation: To what extent should the reader sympathize with Matt? Identify some things that readers should especially consider in addressing this question.

2. Identify the argument that Richard Strout makes as he tries to keep Matt from killing him. What warrants or assumptions does Strout use? How common is his way of thinking?

3. Why does Willis help Matt take revenge? To what extent does Ruth's thinking resemble her husband's?

4. What is Matt's view of Mary Ann, his late son's girlfriend?

5. After beginning with Frank's funeral, the story features several flashbacks. Only gradually does Dubus provide certain seemingly important facts, such as exactly how Matt's son died. ("Richard Strout shot Frank in front of the boys" [para. 76].) What do you think might have been Dubus's purpose(s) in refusing to be more straightforward? In the last several pages, the story is pretty straightforward, moving step-by-step through the night of Matt's revenge. Why do you suppose Dubus changed his method of storytelling?

HA JIN
Saboteur

Although originally from China, Ha Jin (b. 1956) writes fiction in English. He served in the People's Liberation Army during his native country's Cultural Revolution, a period during the 1960s and 1970s when militant followers of leader Mao Zedong brutalized China's intellectuals and other segments of its population. After undergraduate and graduate education in China, Ha Jin was studying at Brandeis University in Massachusetts when, in 1989, the Chinese government attacked protesters in Tiananmen Square. He has written about this event in his novel The Crazed *(2002), and it played a role in his deciding to settle in the United States. Currently a professor at Boston University, he is the author of several books. His other novels include* A Free Life *(2007),* War Trash *(2004), and* Waiting *(1999), for which he won the National Book Award. The following story first appeared in a 1996 issue of* The Antioch Review *and was then reprinted in his 2001 collection* The Bridegroom: Stories.*

Mr. Chiu and his bride were having lunch in the square before Muji Train Station. On the table between them were two bottles of soda spewing out brown foam and two paper boxes of rice and sautéed cucumber and pork. "Let's eat," he said to her, and broke the connected ends of the chopsticks. He picked up a slice of streaky pork and put it into his mouth. As he was chewing, a few crinkles appeared on his thin jaw.

To his right, at another table, two railroad policemen were drinking tea and laughing; it seemed that the stout, middle-aged man was telling a joke to his young comrade, who was tall and of athletic build. Now and again they would steal a glance at Mr. Chiu's table.

The air smelled of rotten melon. A few flies kept buzzing above the couple's lunch. Hundreds of people were rushing around to get on the platform or to catch buses to downtown. Food and fruit vendors were crying for customers in lazy voices. About a dozen young women, representing the local hotels, held up placards which displayed the daily prices and words as large as a palm, like FREE MEALS, AIR-CONDITIONING, and ON THE RIVER. In the center of the square stood a concrete statue of Chairman Mao, at whose feet peasants were napping, their backs on the warm granite and their faces toward the sunny sky. A flock of pigeons perched on the Chairman's raised hand and forearm.

The rice and cucumber tasted good, and Mr. Chiu was eating unhurriedly. His sallow face showed exhaustion. He was glad that the honeymoon was finally over and that he and his bride were heading back for Harbin. During the two weeks' vacation, he had been worried about his liver, because three months ago he had suffered from acute hepatitis; he was afraid he might have a relapse. But he had had no severe symptoms, despite his liver being still big and tender. On the whole he was pleased with his health, which could endure even the strain of a honeymoon; indeed, he was on the course of recovery. He looked at his bride, who took off her wire glasses, kneading the root of her nose with her fingertips. Beads of sweat coated her pale cheeks.

"Are you all right, sweetheart?" he asked.   5

"I have a headache. I didn't sleep well last night."

"Take an aspirin, will you?"

"It's not that serious. Tomorrow is Sunday and I can sleep in. Don't worry."

As they were talking, the stout policeman at the next table stood up and threw a bowl of tea in their direction. Both Mr. Chiu's and his bride's sandals were wet instantly.

"Hooligan!" she said in a low voice.   10

Mr. Chiu got to his feet and said out loud, "Comrade Policeman, why did you do this?" He stretched out his right foot to show the wet sandal.

"Do what?" the stout man asked huskily, glaring at Mr. Chiu while the young fellow was whistling.

"See, you dumped tea on our feet."

"You're lying. You wet your shoes yourself."

"Comrade Policemen, your duty is to keep order, but you purposely tor-   15
tured us common citizens. Why violate the law you are supposed to enforce?"

As Mr. Chiu was speaking, dozens of people began gathering around.

With a wave of his hand, the man said to the young fellow, "Let's get hold of him!"

They grabbed Mr. Chiu and clamped handcuffs around his wrists. He cried, "You can't do this to me. This is utterly unreasonable."

"Shut up!" The man pulled out his pistol. "You can use your tongue at our headquarters."

The young fellow added, "You're a saboteur, you know that? You're disrupting public order."

The bride was too petrified to say anything coherent. She was a recent college graduate, had majored in fine arts, and had never seen the police make an arrest. All she could say was, "Oh, please, please!"   20

The policemen were pulling Mr. Chiu, but he refused to go with them, holding the corner of the table and shouting, "We have a train to catch. We already bought the tickets."

The stout man punched him in the chest. "Shut up. Let your ticket expire." With the pistol butt he chopped Mr. Chiu's hands, which at once released the table. Together the two men were dragging him away to the police station.

Realizing he had to go with them, Mr. Chiu turned his head and shouted to his bride, "Don't wait for me here. Take the train. If I'm not back by tomorrow morning, send someone over to get me out."

She nodded, covering her sobbing mouth with her palm.

After removing his belt, they locked Mr. Chiu into a cell in the back of the Railroad Police Station. The single window in the room was blocked by six steel bars; it faced a spacious yard, in which stood a few pines. Beyond the trees, two swings hung from an iron frame, swaying gently in the breeze. Somewhere in the building a cleaver was chopping rhythmically. There must be a kitchen upstairs, Mr. Chiu thought.   25

He was too exhausted to worry about what they would do to him, so he lay down on the narrow bed and shut his eyes. He wasn't afraid. The Cultural Revolution was over already, and recently the Party had been propagating the idea that all citizens were equal before the law. The police ought to be a law-abiding model for common people. As long as he remained coolheaded and reasoned with them, they probably wouldn't harm him.

Late in the afternoon he was taken to the Interrogation Bureau on the second floor. On his way there, in the stairwell, he ran into the middle-aged policeman who had manhandled him. The man grinned, rolling his bulgy eyes and pointing his fingers at him as if firing a pistol. Egg of a tortoise! Mr. Chiu cursed mentally.

The moment he sat down in the office, he burped, his palm shielding his mouth. In front of him, across a long desk, sat the chief of the bureau and a donkey-faced man. On the glass desktop was a folder containing information on his case. He felt it bizarre that in just a matter of hours they had accumulated a small pile of writing about him. On second thought he began to wonder whether they had kept a file on him all the time. How could this have happened?

He lived and worked in Harbin, more than three hundred miles away, and this was his first time in Muji City.

The chief of the bureau was a thin, bald man who looked serene and intelligent. His slim hands handled the written pages in the folder in the manner of a lecturing scholar. To Mr. Chiu's left sat a young scribe, with a clipboard on his knee and a black fountain pen in his hand.

"Your name?" the chief asked, apparently reading out the question from a form.   30

"Chiu Maguang."

"Age?"

"Thirty-four."

"Profession?"

"Lecturer."   35

"Work unit?"

"Harbin University."

"Political status?"

"Communist Party member."

The chief put down the paper and began to speak. "Your crime is sabotage,   40
although it hasn't induced serious consequences yet. Because you are a Party member, you should be punished more. You have failed to be a model for the masses and you —"

"Excuse me, sir," Mr. Chiu cut him off.

"What?"

"I didn't do anything. Your men are the saboteurs of our social order. They threw hot tea on my feet and on my wife's feet. Logically speaking, you should criticize them, if not punish them."

"That statement is groundless. You have no witness. Why should I believe you?" the chief said matter-of-factly.

"This is my evidence." He raised his right hand. "Your man hit my fingers   45
with a pistol."

"That doesn't prove how your feet got wet. Besides, you could have hurt your fingers yourself."

"But I am telling the truth!" Anger flared up in Mr. Chiu. "Your police station owes me an apology. My train ticket has expired, my new leather sandals are ruined, and I am late for a conference in the provincial capital. You must compensate me for the damage and losses. Don't mistake me for a common citizen who would tremble when you sneeze. I'm a scholar, a philosopher, and an expert in dialectical materialism. If necessary, we will argue about this in *The Northeastern Daily*, or we will go to the highest People's Court in Beijing. Tell me, what's your name?" He got carried away with his harangue, which was by no means trivial and had worked to his advantage on numerous occasions.

"Stop bluffing us," the donkey-faced man broke in. "We have seen a lot of your kind. We can easily prove you are guilty. Here are some of the statements given by eyewitnesses." He pushed a few sheets of paper toward Mr. Chiu.

Mr. Chiu was dazed to see the different handwritings, which all stated that he had shouted in the square to attract attention and refused to obey the police.

One of the witnesses had identified herself as a purchasing agent from a ship-yard in Shanghai. Something stirred in Mr. Chiu's stomach, a pain rising to his rib. He gave out a faint moan.

"Now you have to admit you are guilty," the chief said. "Although it's a serious crime, we won't punish you severely, provided you write out a self-criticism and promise that you won't disrupt the public order again. In other words, your release will depend on your attitude toward this crime." 50

"You're daydreaming!" Mr. Chiu cried. "I won't write a word, because I'm innocent. I demand that you provide me with a letter of apology so I can ex-plain to my university why I'm late."

Both the interrogators smiled contemptuously. "Well, we've never done that," said the chief, taking a puff of his cigarette.

"Then make this a precedent."

"That's unnecessary. We are pretty certain that you will comply with our wishes." The chief blew a column of smoke toward Mr. Chiu's face.

At the tilt of the chief's head, two guards stepped forward and grabbed the criminal by the arms. Mr. Chiu meanwhile went on saying, "I shall report you to the Provincial Administration. You'll have to pay for this! You are worse than the Japanese military police." 55

They dragged him out of the room.

After dinner, which consisted of a bowl of millet porridge, a corn bun, and a piece of pickled turnip, Mr. Chiu began to have a fever, shaking with a chill and sweating profusely. He knew that the fire of anger had gotten into his liver and that he was probably having a relapse. No medicine was available, because his briefcase had been left with his bride. At home it would have been time for him to sit in front of their color TV, drinking jasmine tea and watching the evening news. It was so lonesome in here. The orange bulb above the single bed was the only source of light, which enabled the guards to keep him under surveillance at night. A moment ago he had asked them for a newspaper or a magazine to read, but they turned him down.

Through the small opening on the door noises came in. It seemed that the police on duty were playing cards or chess in a nearby office; shouts and laugh-ter could be heard now and then. Meanwhile, an accordion kept coughing from a remote corner in the building. Looking at the ballpoint and the letter paper left for him by the guards when they took him back from the Interroga-tion Bureau, Mr. Chiu remembered the old saying, "When a scholar runs into soldiers, the more he argues, the muddier his point becomes." How ridiculous this whole thing was. He ruffled his thick hair with his fingers.

He felt miserable, massaging his stomach continually. To tell the truth, he was more upset than frightened, because he would have to catch up with his work once he was back home — a paper that was due at the printers next week, and two dozen books he ought to read for the courses he was going to teach in the fall.

A human shadow flitted across the opening. Mr. Chiu rushed to the door and shouted through the hole, "Comrade Guard, Comrade Guard!" 60

"What do you want?" a voice rasped.

"I want you to inform your leaders that I'm very sick. I have heart disease and hepatitis. I may die here if you keep me like this without medication."

"No leader is on duty on the weekend. You have to wait till Monday."

"What? You mean I'll stay in here tomorrow?"

"Yes."   65

"Your station will be held responsible if anything happens to me."

"We know that. Take it easy, you won't die."

It seemed illogical that Mr. Chiu slept quite well that night, though the light above his head had been on all the time and the straw mattress was hard and infested with fleas. He was afraid of ticks, mosquitoes, cockroaches — any kind of insect but fleas and bedbugs. Once, in the countryside, where his school's faculty and staff had helped the peasants harvest crops for a week, his colleagues had joked about his flesh, which they said must have tasted nonhuman to fleas. Except for him, they were all afflicted with hundreds of bites.

More amazing now, he didn't miss his bride a lot. He even enjoyed sleeping alone, perhaps because the honeymoon had tired him out and he needed more rest.

The backyard was quiet on Sunday morning. Pale sunlight streamed   70
through the pine branches. A few sparrows were jumping on the ground, catching caterpillars and ladybugs. Holding the steel bars, Mr. Chiu inhaled the morning air, which smelled meaty. There must have been an eatery or a cooked-meat stand nearby. He reminded himself that he should take this detention with ease. A sentence that Chairman Mao had written to a hospitalized friend rose in his mind: "Since you are already in here, you may as well stay and make the best of it."

His desire for peace of mind originated in his fear that this hepatitis might get worse. He tried to remain unperturbed. However, he was sure that his liver was swelling up, since the fever still persisted. For a whole day he lay in bed, thinking about his paper on the nature of contradictions. Time and again he was overwhelmed by anger, cursing aloud, "A bunch of thugs!" He swore that once he was out, he would write an article about this experience. He had better find out some of the policemen's names.

It turned out to be a restful day for the most part; he was certain that his university would send somebody to his rescue. All he should do now was remain calm and wait patiently. Sooner or later the police would have to release him, although they had no idea that he might refuse to leave unless they wrote him an apology. Damn those hoodlums, they had ordered more than they could eat!

When he woke up on Monday morning, it was already light. Somewhere a man was moaning; the sound came from the backyard. After a long yawn, and kicking off the tattered blanket, Mr. Chiu climbed out of bed and went to the window. In the middle of the yard, a young man was fastened to a pine, his wrists handcuffed around the trunk from behind. He was wriggling and swearing loudly, but there was no sight of anyone else in the yard. He looked familiar to Mr. Chiu.

Mr. Chiu squinted his eyes to see who it was. To his astonishment, he recognized the man, who was Fenjin, a recent graduate from the Law Department at Harbin University. Two years ago Mr. Chiu had taught a course in Marxist materialism, in which Fenjin had enrolled. Now, how on earth had this young devil landed here?

Then it dawned on him that Fenjin must have been sent over by his bride. What a stupid woman! A bookworm, who only knew how to read foreign novels! He had expected that she would contact the school's Security Section, which would for sure send a cadre here. Fenjin held no official position; he merely worked in a private law firm that had just two lawyers; in fact, they had little business except for some detective work for men and women who suspected their spouses of having extramarital affairs. Mr. Chiu was overcome with a wave of nausea.

Should he call out to let his student know he was nearby? He decided not to because he didn't know what had happened. Fenjin must have quarreled with the police to incur such a punishment. Yet this could never have occurred if Fenjin hadn't come to his rescue. So no matter what, Mr. Chiu had to do something. But what could he do?

It was going to be a scorcher. He could see purple steam shimmering and rising from the ground among the pines. Poor devil, he thought, as he raised a bowl of corn glue to his mouth, sipped, and took a bite of a piece of salted celery.

When a guard came to collect the bowl and the chopsticks, Mr. Chiu asked him what had happened to the man in the backyard. "He called our boss 'bandit,' " the guard said. "He claimed he was a lawyer or something. An arrogant son of a rabbit."

Now it was obvious to Mr. Chiu that he had to do something to help his rescuer. Before he could figure out a way, a scream broke out in the backyard. He rushed to the window and saw a tall policeman standing before Fenjin, an iron bucket on the ground. It was the same young fellow who had arrested Mr. Chiu in the square two days before. The man pinched Fenjin's nose, then raised his hand, which stayed in the air for a few seconds, then slapped the lawyer across the face. As Fenjin was groaning, the man lifted up the bucket and poured water on his head.

"This will keep you from getting sunstroke, boy. I'll give you some more every hour," the man said loudly.

Fenjin kept his eyes shut, yet his wry face showed that he was struggling to hold back from cursing the policeman, or, more likely, that he was sobbing in silence. He sneezed, then raised his face and shouted, "Let me go take a piss."

"Oh, yeah?" the man bawled. "Pee in your pants."

Still Mr. Chiu didn't make any noise, gripping the steel bars with both hands, his fingers white. The policeman turned and glanced at the cell's window; his pistol, partly holstered, glittered in the sun. With a snort he spat his cigarette butt to the ground and stamped it into the dust.

Then the door opened and the guards motioned Mr. Chiu to come out.
Again they took him upstairs to the Interrogation Bureau.

The same men were in the office, though this time the scribe was sitting   85
there empty-handed. At the sight of Mr. Chiu the chief said, "Ah, here you are.
Please be seated."

After Mr. Chiu sat down, the chief waved a white silk fan and said to him,
"You may have seen your lawyer. He's a young man without manners, so our
director had him taught a crash course in the backyard."

"It's illegal to do that. Aren't you afraid to appear in a newspaper?"

"No, we are not, not even on TV. What else can you do? We are not afraid
of any story you make up. We call it fiction. What we do care about is that you
cooperate with us. That is to say, you must admit your crime."

"What if I refuse to cooperate?"

"Then your lawyer will continue his education in the sunshine."   90

A swoon swayed Mr. Chiu, and he held the arms of the chair to steady
himself. A numb pain stung him in the upper stomach and nauseated him, and
his head was throbbing. He was sure that the hepatitis was finally attacking
him. Anger was flaming up in his chest; his throat was tight and clogged.

The chief resumed, "As a matter of fact, you don't even have to write out
your self-criticism. We have your crime described clearly here. All we need is
your signature."

Holding back his rage, Mr. Chiu said, "Let me look at that."

With a smirk the donkey-faced man handed him a sheet which carried
these words:

> I hereby admit that on July 13 I disrupted public order at Muji Train Sta-
> tion, and that I refused to listen to reason when the railroad police issued
> their warning. Thus I myself am responsible for my arrest. After two days'
> detention, I have realized the reactionary nature of my crime. From now
> on, I shall continue to educate myself with all my effort and shall never
> commit this kind of crime again.

A voice started screaming in Mr. Chiu's ears, "Lie, lie!" But he shook his   95
head and forced the voice away. He asked the chief, "If I sign this, will you release both my lawyer and me?"

"Of course, we'll do that." The chief was drumming his fingers on the blue
folder — their file on him.

Mr. Chiu signed his name and put his thumbprint under his signature.

"Now you are free to go," the chief said with a smile, and handed him a
piece of paper to wipe his thumb with.

Mr. Chiu was so sick that he couldn't stand up from the chair at first try.
Then he doubled his effort and rose to his feet. He staggered out of the building
to meet his lawyer in the backyard, having forgotten to ask for his belt back. In
his chest he felt as though there were a bomb. If he were able to, he would have
razed the entire police station and eliminated all their families. Though he
knew he could do nothing like that, he made up his mind to do something.

"I'm sorry about this torture, Fenjin," Mr. Chiu said when they met.   100
   "It doesn't matter. They are savages." The lawyer brushed a patch of dirt
off his jacket with trembling fingers. Water was still dribbling from the bottoms
of his trouser legs.
   "Let's go now," the teacher said.
   The moment they came out of the police station, Mr. Chiu caught sight of
a tea stand. He grabbed Fenjin's arm and walked over to the old woman at the
table. "Two bowls of black tea," he said and handed her a one-yuan note.
   After the first bowl, they each had another one. Then they set out for the
train station. But before they walked fifty yards, Mr. Chiu insisted on eating a
bowl of tree-ear soup at a food stand. Fenjin agreed. He told his teacher, "You
mustn't treat me like a guest."
   "No, I want to eat something myself."   105
   As if dying of hunger, Mr. Chiu dragged his lawyer from restaurant to restaurant near the police station, but at each place he ordered no more than two
bowls of food. Fenjin wondered why his teacher wouldn't stay at one place and
eat his fill.
   Mr. Chiu bought noodles, wonton, eight-grain porridge, and chicken soup,
respectively, at four restaurants. While eating, he kept saying through his teeth,
"If only I could kill all the bastards!" At the last place he merely took a few sips
of the soup without tasting the chicken cubes and mushrooms.
   Fenjin was baffled by his teacher, who looked ferocious and muttered to
himself mysteriously, and whose jaundiced face was covered with dark puck-
ets. For the first time Fenjin thought of Mr. Chiu as an ugly man.
   Within a month over eight hundred people contracted acute hepatitis in
Muji. Six died of the disease, including two children. Nobody knew how the
epidemic had started.   [2000]

≡ THINKING ABOUT THE TEXT

1. In what places in the story is its title especially relevant? Who can be
   considered a "saboteur," and what acts of "sabotage" does the story
   deal with? Define what these terms mean to you.

2. What evidence is there that Mr. Chiu is not used to being treated the way
   that the police treat him? Identify specific passages. Do you find him
   unreasonably naive? Why, or why not?

3. Why, apparently, do the police arrest Mr. Chiu and demand a confession from him before they are willing to release him? How might the
   author be using their behavior to comment on Chinese authorities in
   general?

4. In his fiction, Ha Jin typically mentions small physical details that may
   appear trivial at first but can eventually be thought of as significant.
   Identify some moments in "Saboteur" when he uses such details, and
   explain what their actual importance might be.

5. How sympathetic were you toward Mr. Chiu until the story's end? Was your degree of sympathy affected by what he ultimately did? What do you conclude about him from his final action?

■ MAKING COMPARISONS

1. Whereas Matt Fowler's son is murdered, Mr. Chiu does not suffer something that obviously horrible. Does Matt therefore have a more understandable case for revenge? Explain.

2. Do you think that Matt Fowler has more of a conscience than Mr. Chiu does? Why, or why not? Define what you mean by *conscience*.

3. Could the police's abusive behavior in the Chinese city of "Saboteur" occur in Matt Fowler's New England community? What features of American society come to your mind as you answer this question?

■ WRITING ABOUT ISSUES

1. Choose one of the two stories in this cluster, and write an essay identifying the extent to which its author encourages readers to take a complex view of the story's protagonist. Argue for your position by citing specific details of the text.

2. In her book *Bird by Bird: Some Instructions on Writing and Life*, Anne Lamott advises would-be fiction writers that a story must culminate in "a killing or a healing or a domination." She goes on to explain:

   It can be a real killing, a murder, or it can be a killing of the spirit, or of something terrible inside one's soul, or it can be a killing of a deadness within, after which the person becomes alive again. The healing may be about union, reclamation, the rescue of a fragile prize. But whatever happens, we need to feel that it was inevitable, that even though we may be amazed, it feels absolutely right, that of course things would come to this, of course they would shake down in this way.

   Write an essay discussing the extent to which Dubus and Jin obey this advice. Refer to specific words in the passage from Lamott, as well as to specific details of the stories. If you wish, feel free to evaluate Lamott's advice. Do you think fiction writers ought to follow it?

3. Gerald Murphy, a famous socialite of the 1920s, once said that "living well is the best revenge." Murphy did not identify whom it was revenge against. Still, his statement is thought provoking in its suggestion that revenge is not always recognizable as such. "Living well" may be revenge in disguise. Write an essay showing how a specific action you are familiar with can be seen as an act of revenge, even though many people wouldn't realize this. In your essay, also evaluate the action. Do you approve of this act of revenge? Why, or why not?

4. Write an essay examining how at least three movie critics have responded to a particular film about revenge, such as *In the Bedroom* (the movie adaptation of "Killings"), *Kill Bill I* or *II*, *Mystic River*, *Cape Fear* (old or new version), *Collateral Damage*, *Being Julia*, *Spider-Man*, *The Lion King*, or *Fatal Attraction*. To learn critics' responses, you will have to do research. A good Web site to consult is the Internet Movie Database at imdb.com. In your essay, point out a key issue that your chosen critics have raised, identify their positions on this issue, and develop a case for your own position.

People who commit despicable acts, such as murder, lead us to think that they lack the principles of justice that society requires. Yet it is possible that sooner or later they will conclude that they have perpetrated a monstrous injustice. Even so, we may have trouble determining whether a criminal has developed a guilty conscience and whether there are extenuating circumstances for the crime. Many of the stories of Edgar Allan Poe explore such issues of guilt. They push readers to consider, for example, the nature of evil; the role of justice in acts of revenge; and wrongdoers' capacity for remorse. As you read the following stories by Poe, notice how these subjects come up, and think about your own views on them.

EDGAR ALLAN POE
The Cask of Amontillado

The life of Edgar Allan Poe (1809–1849) was relatively brief, its end tragically hastened by his alcohol and drug abuse, but his contributions to literature were unique. As a book reviewer, he produced pieces of literary criticism and theory that are still widely respected. As a poet, he wrote such classics as "The Raven" (1845), "The Bells" (1849), and "Annabel Lee" (1849). Moreover, his short fiction was groundbreaking and continues to be popular, a source for many films and television shows. With works such as "The Murders in the Rue Morgue" (1841), "The Gold Bug" (1843), and "The Purloined Letter" (1844), he pioneered the modern detective story. Some of Poe's other tales are masterpieces of horror, including "The Fall of the House of Usher" (1842), "The Pit and the Pendulum" (1842), and the following story, one of Poe's most famous. It was first published in an 1846 issue of Godey's Lady's Book *and was then included in a posthumous 1850 collection of Poe's writings.*

The thousand injuries of Fortunato I had borne as I best could; but when he ventured upon insult, I vowed revenge. You, who so well know the nature of my soul, will not suppose, however, that I gave utterance to a threat. *At length* I would be avenged; this was a point definitely settled — but the very definitiveness with which it was resolved precluded the idea of risk. I must not only punish, but punish with impunity. A wrong is unredressed when retribution overtakes its redresser. It is equally unredressed when the avenger fails to make himself felt as such to him who has done the wrong.

(Library of Congress.)

It must be understood, that neither by word nor deed had I given Fortunato cause to doubt my good-will. I continued, as was my wont, to smile in his face, and he did not perceive that my smile *now* was at the thought of his immolation.

He had a weak point — this Fortunato — although in other regards he was a man to be respected and even feared. He prided himself on his connoisseurship in wine. Few Italians have the true virtuoso spirit. For the most part their enthusiasm is adopted to suit the time and opportunity — to practice imposture upon the British and Austrian *millionnaires*. In painting and gemmary Fortunato, like his countrymen, was a quack — but in the matter of old wines he was sincere. In this respect I did not differ from him materially: I was skillful in the Italian vintages myself, and bought largely whenever I could.

It was about dusk, one evening during the supreme madness of the carnival season, that I encountered my friend. He accosted me with excessive warmth, for he had been drinking much. The man wore motley. He had on a tight-fitting parti-striped dress, and his head was surmounted by the conical cap and bells. I was so pleased to see him, that I thought I should never have done wringing his hand.

I said to him: "My dear Fortunato, you are luckily met. How remarkably   5
well you are looking to-day! But I have received a pipe° of what passes for
Amontillado, and I have my doubts."

"How?" said he. "Amontillado? A pipe? Impossible! And in the middle of
the carnival!"

"I have my doubts," I replied; "and I was silly enough to pay the full Amontillado price without consulting you in the matter. You were not to be found,
and I was fearful of losing a bargain."

"Amontillado!"

"I have my doubts."

"Amontillado!"   10

"And I must satisfy them."

"Amontillado!"

"As you are engaged, I am on my way to Luchesi. If any one has a critical
turn, it is he. He will tell me ——"

"Luchesi cannot tell Amontillado from Sherry."

"And yet some fools will have it that his taste is a match for your own."   15

"Come, let us go."

"Whither?"

"To your vaults."

"My friend, no; I will not impose upon your good nature. I perceive you
have an engagement. Luchesi ——"

"I have no engagement; — come."   20

"My friend, no. It is not the engagement, but the severe cold with which I
perceive you are afflicted. The vaults are insufferably damp. They are encrusted
with nitre."

"Let us go, nevertheless. The cold is merely nothing. Amontillado! You
have been imposed upon. And as for Luchesi, he cannot distinguish Sherry
from Amontillado."

Thus speaking, Fortunato possessed himself of my arm. Putting on a mask
of black silk, and drawing a *roquelaire*° closely about my person, I suffered him
to hurry me to my palazzo.

There were no attendants at home; they had absconded to make merry in
honor of the time. I had told them that I should not return until the morning,
and had given them explicit orders not to stir from the house. These orders
were sufficient, I well knew, to insure their immediate disappearance, one and
all, as soon as my back was turned.

I took from their sconces two flambeaux, and giving one to Fortunato,   25
bowed him through several suites of rooms to the archway that led into the
vaults. I passed down a long and winding staircase, requesting him to be cautious as he followed. We came at length to the foot of the descent, and stood
together on the damp ground of the catacombs of the Montresors.

The gait of my friend was unsteady, and the bells upon his cap jingled as he
strode.

pipe: A large cask.   ***roqueclaire*:** A short cloak.

"The pipe?" said he.

"It is farther on," said I; "but observe the white web-work which gleams from these cavern walls."

He turned toward me, and looked into my eyes with two filmy orbs that distilled the rheum of intoxication.

"Nitre?" he asked, at length.   30

"Nitre," I replied. "How long have you had that cough?"

"Ugh! ugh! ugh! — ugh! ugh! ugh! — ugh! ugh! ugh! — ugh! ugh! ugh! — ugh! ugh! ugh!"

My poor friend found it impossible to reply for many minutes.

"It is nothing," he said, at last.

"Come," I said, with decision, "we will go back; your health is precious.   35
You are rich, respected, admired, beloved; you are happy, as once I was. You are a man to be missed. For me it is no matter. We will go back; you will be ill, and I cannot be responsible. Besides, there is Luchesi ——"

"Enough," he said; "the cough is a mere nothing; it will not kill me. I shall not die of a cough."

"True — true," I replied; "and, indeed, I had no intention of alarming you unnecessarily; but you should use all proper caution. A draught of this Medoc will defend us from the damps."

Here I knocked off the neck of a bottle which I drew from a long row of its fellows that lay upon the mold.

"Drink," I said, presenting him the wine.

He raised it to his lips with a leer. He paused and nodded to me familiarly,   40
while his bells jingled.

"I drink," he said, "to the buried that repose around us."

"And I to your long life."

He again took my arm, and we proceeded.

"These vaults," he said, "are extensive."

"The Montresors," I replied, "were a great and numerous family."   45

"I forget your arms."

"A huge human foot d'or,° in a field azure; the foot crushes a serpent rampant whose fangs are imbedded in the heel."

"And the motto?"

"*Nemo me impune lacessit.*"°

"Good!" he said.   50

The wine sparkled in his eyes and the bells jingled. My own fancy grew warm with the Medoc. We had passed through walls of piled bones, with casks and puncheons intermingling into the inmost recesses of the catacombs. I paused again, and this time I made bold to seize Fortunato by an arm above the elbow.

"The nitre!" I said; "see, it increases. It hangs like moss upon the vaults. We are below the river's bed. The drops of moisture trickle among the bones. Come, we will go back ere it is too late. Your cough ——"

---

d'or: Of gold.   ***nemo me impune lacessit:*** "No one wounds me with impunity" is the motto on the royal arms of Scotland.

"It is nothing," he said; "let us go on. But first, another draught of the Medoc."

I broke and reached him a flagon of De Grâve. He emptied it at a breath. His eyes flashed with a fierce light. He laughed and threw the bottle upward with a gesticulation I did not understand.

I looked at him in surprise. He repeated the movement — a grotesque one.   55
"You do not comprehend?" he said.
"Not I," I replied.
"Then you are not of the brotherhood."
"How?"
"You are not of the masons."   60
"Yes, yes," I said; "yes, yes."
"You? Impossible! A mason?"
"A mason," I replied.
"A sign," he said.
"It is this," I answered, producing a trowel from beneath the folds of my   65
roquelaire.
"You jest," he exclaimed, recoiling a few paces. "But let us proceed to the Amontillado."

"Be it so," I said, replacing the tool beneath the cloak, and again offering him my arm. He leaned upon it heavily. We continued our route in search of the Amontillado. We passed through a range of low arches, descended, passed on, and descending again, arrived at a deep crypt, in which the foulness of the air caused our flambeaux rather to glow than flame.

At the most remote end of the crypt there appeared another less spacious. Its walls had been lined with human remains, piled to the vault overhead, in the fashion of the great catacombs of Paris. Three sides of this interior crypt were still ornamented in this manner. From the fourth the bones had been thrown down, and lay promiscuously upon the earth, forming at one point a mound of some size. Within the wall thus exposed by the displacing of the bones, we perceived a still interior recess, in depth about four feet, in width three, in height six or seven. It seemed to have been constructed for no especial use within itself, but formed merely the interval between two of the colossal supports of the roof of the catacombs, and was backed by one of their circumscribing walls of solid granite.

It was in vain that Fortunato, uplifting his dull torch, endeavored to pry into the depth of the recess. Its termination the feeble light did not enable us to see.

"Proceed," I said; "herein is the Amontillado. As for Luchesi ——"   70
"He is an ignoramus," interrupted my friend, as he stepped unsteadily forward, while I followed immediately at his heels. In an instant he had reached the extremity of the niche, and finding his progress arrested by the rock, stood stupidly bewildered. A moment more and I had fettered him to the granite. In its surface were two iron staples, distant from each other about two feet, horizontally. From one of these depended a short chain, from the other a padlock. Throwing the links about his waist, it was but the work of a few seconds to se-

cure it. He was too much astounded to resist. Withdrawing the key I stepped back from the recess.

"Pass your hand," I said, "over the wall; you cannot help feeling the nitre. Indeed it is *very* damp. Once more let me *implore* you to return. No? Then I must positively leave you. But I must first render you all the little attentions in my power."

"The Amontillado!" ejaculated my friend, not yet recovered from his astonishment.

"True," I replied; "the Amontillado."

As I said these words I busied myself among the pile of bones of which I have before spoken. Throwing them aside, I soon uncovered a quantity of building stone and mortar. With these materials and with the aid of my trowel, I began vigorously to wall up the entrance of the niche.

I had scarcely laid the first tier of the masonry when I discovered that the intoxication of Fortunato had in a great measure worn off. The earliest indication I had of this was a low moaning cry from the depth of the recess. It was *not* the cry of a drunken man. There was then a long and obstinate silence. I laid the second tier, and the third, and the fourth; and then I heard the furious vibrations of the chain. The noise lasted for several minutes, during which, that I might hearken to it with the more satisfaction, I ceased my labors and sat down upon the bones. When at last the clanking subsided, I resumed the trowel, and finished without interruption the fifth, the sixth, and the seventh tier. The wall was now nearly upon a level with my breast. I again paused, and holding the flambeaux over the masonwork, threw a few feeble rays upon the figure within.

A succession of loud and shrill screams, bursting suddenly from the throat of the chained form, seemed to thrust me violently back. For a brief moment I hesitated — I trembled. Unsheathing my rapier, I began to grope with it about the recess; but the thought of an instant reassured me. I placed my hand upon the solid fabric of the catacombs, and felt satisfied. I reapproached the wall. I replied to the yells of him who clamored. I reechoed — I aided — I surpassed them in volume and in strength. I did this, and the clamorer grew still.

It was now midnight, and my task was drawing to a close. I had completed the eighth, the ninth, and the tenth tier. I had finished a portion of the last and the eleventh; there remained but a single stone to be fitted and plastered in. I struggled with its weight; I placed it partially in its destined position. But now there came from out the niche a low laugh that erected the hairs upon my head. It was succeeded by a sad voice, which I had difficulty in recognizing as that of the noble Fortunato. The voice said —

"Ha! ha! ha! — he! he! — a very good joke indeed — an excellent jest. We will have many a rich laugh about it at the palazzo — he! he! he! — over our wine — he! he! he!"

"The Amontillado!" I said.

"He! he! he! — he! he! he! — yes, the Amontillado. But is it not getting late? Will not they be awaiting us at the palazzo, the Lady Fortunato and the rest? Let us be gone."

75

80

"Yes," I said, "let us be gone."

"*For the love of God, Montresor!*"

"Yes," I said, "for the love of God!"

But to these words I hearkened in vain for a reply. I grew impatient. I called   85
aloud:

"Fortunato!"

No answer. I called again:

"Fortunato!"

No answer still, I thrust a torch through the remaining aperture and let it fall within. There came forth in return only a jingling of the bells. My heart grew sick — on account of the dampness of the catacombs. I hastened to make an end of my labor. I forced the last stone into its position; I plastered it up. Against the new masonry I re-erected the old rampart of bones. For the half of a century no mortal has disturbed them. *In pace requiescat!°*   [1846]

In pace requiescat: In peace may he rest (Latin).

▤ THINKING ABOUT THE TEXT

1. Evidently Montresor is recounting the story of his revenge fifty years after it took place. To whom might he be speaking? With what purposes?

2. Montresor does not describe in detail any of the offenses that Fortunato has supposedly committed against him. In considering how to judge Montresor, do you need such information? Why, or why not? State in your own words the principles of revenge he lays out in the first paragraph.

3. What, if anything, does Poe achieve by having this story take place during a carnival? By repeating the word *amontillado* so much?

4. What does Montresor mean when he echoes Fortunato's words "for the love of God" (para. 84)? What might Fortunato be attempting to communicate with his final "jingling of the bells" (para. 89)?

5. Do you sympathize with Montresor? With Fortunato? Explain. What emotion did you mainly feel as you read the story? Identify specific features of it that led to this emotion.

EDGAR ALLAN POE
The Tell-Tale Heart

The following tale, also one of Poe's best known, appeared in an 1843 issue of the periodical The Pioneer *and an 1845 issue of* The Broadway Journal *before being included in the 1850 collection of Poe's writings published after his death. The story has been adapted for film, television, and radio numerous times.*

True! — nervous — very, very dreadfully nervous I had been and am; but why *will* you say that I am mad? The disease had sharpened my senses — not destroyed — not dulled them. Above all was the sense of hearing acute. I heard all things in the heaven and in the earth. I heard many things in hell. How, then, am I mad? Hearken! and observe how healthily — how calmly I can tell you the whole story.

It is impossible to say how first the idea entered my brain; but once conceived, it haunted me day and night. Object there was none. Passion there was none. I loved the old man. He had never wronged me. He had never given me insult. For his gold I had no desire. I think it was his eye! yes, it was this! One of his eyes resembled that of a vulture — a pale blue eye, with a film over it. Whenever it fell upon me, my blood ran cold; and so by degrees — very gradually — I made up my mind to take the life of the old man, and thus rid myself of the eye for ever.

Now this is the point. You fancy me mad. Madmen know nothing. But you should have seen *me*. You should have seen how wisely I proceeded — with what caution — with what foresight — with what dissimulation I went to work! I was never kinder to the old man than during the whole week before I killed him. And every night, about midnight, I turned the latch of his door and opened it — oh, so gently! And then, when I had made an opening sufficient for my head, I put in a dark lantern, all closed, closed, so that no light shone out, and then I thrust in my head. Oh, you would have laughed to see how cunningly I thrust it in! I moved it slowly — very, very slowly, so that I might not disturb the old man's sleep. It took me an hour to place my whole head within the opening so far that I could see him as he lay upon his bed. Ha — would a madman have been so wise as this? And then, when my head was well in the room, I undid the lantern cautiously — oh, so cautiously — cautiously (for the hinges creaked) — I undid it just so much that a single thin ray fell upon the vulture eye. And this I did for seven long nights — every night just after midnight — but I found the eye always closed; and so it was impossible to do the work; for it was not the old man who vexed me, but his Evil Eye. And every morning, when the day broke, I went boldly into the chamber, and spoke courageously to him, calling him by name in a hearty tone, and inquiring how he had passed the night. So you see he would have been a very profound old man, indeed, to suspect that every night, just at twelve, I looked in upon him while he slept.

Upon the eighth night I was more than usually cautious in opening the door. A watch's minute hand moves more quickly than did mine. Never before that night had I *felt* the extent of my own powers — of my sagacity. I could scarcely contain my feelings of triumph. To think that there I was, opening the door, little by little, and he not even to dream of my secret deeds or thoughts. I fairly chuckled at the idea; and perhaps he heard me; for he moved on the bed suddenly, as if startled. Now you may think that I drew back — but no. His room was as black as pitch with the thick darkness (for the shutters were close fastened, through fear of robbers), and so I knew that he could not see the opening of the door, and I kept pushing it on steadily, steadily.

I had my head in, and was about to open the lantern, when my thumb   5
slipped upon the tin fastening, and the old man sprang up in the bed, crying
out — "Who's there?"

I kept quite still and said nothing. For a whole hour I did not move a muscle,
and in the meantime I did not hear him lie down. He was still sitting up in the
bed listening; — just as I have done, night after night, hearkening to the death
watches in the wall.

Presently I heard a slight groan, and I knew it was the groan of mortal terror. It was not a groan of pain or of grief — oh, no! — it was the low stifled
sound that arises from the bottom of the soul when overcharged with awe.
I knew the sound well. Many a night, just at midnight, when all the world slept,
it has welled up from my own bosom, deepening with its dreadful echo, the terrors that distracted me. I say I knew it well. I knew what the old man felt, and
pitied him, although I chuckled at heart. I knew that he had been lying awake
ever since the first slight noise, when he had turned in the bed. His fears had
been ever since growing upon him. He had been trying to fancy them cause-
less, but could not. He had been saying to himself — "It is nothing but the wind
in the chimney — it is only a mouse crossing the floor," or "it is merely a cricket
which has made a single chirp." Yes, he has been trying to comfort himself
with these suppositions; but he had found all in vain. *All in vain;* because Death,
in approaching him, had stalked with his black shadow before him, and enveloped the victim. And it was the mournful influence of the unperceived shadow
that caused him to feel — although he neither saw nor heard — to *feel* the presence of my head within the room.

When I had waited a long time, very patiently, without hearing him lie
down, I resolved to open a little — a very, very little crevice in the lantern. So
I opened it — you cannot imagine how stealthily, stealthily — until, at length,
a single dim ray, like the thread of the spider, shot from out the crevice and full
upon the vulture eye.

It was open — wide, wide open — and I grew furious as I gazed upon it.
I saw it with perfect distinctness — all a dull blue, with a hideous veil over it
that chilled the very marrow in my bones, but I could see nothing else of the old
man's face or person: for I had directed the ray as if by instinct, precisely upon
the damned spot.

And now have I not told you that what you mistake for madness is but   10
overacuteness of the senses? — now, I say, there came to my ears a low, dull,
quick sound, such as a watch makes when enveloped in cotton. I knew *that*
sound well too. It was the beating of the old man's heart. It increased my fury,
as the beating of a drum stimulates the soldier into courage.

But even yet I refrained and kept still. I scarcely breathed. I held the lantern
motionless. I tried how steadily I could maintain the ray upon the eye. Meantime the hellish tattoo of the heart increased. It grew quicker and quicker, and
louder and louder every instant. The old man's terror *must* have been extreme!
It grew louder, I say, louder every moment — do you mark me well? I have told
you that I am nervous: so I am. And now at the dead hour of the night, amid
the dreadful silence of that old house, so strange a noise as this excited me to

uncontrollable terror. Yet, for some minutes longer I refrained and stood still. But the beating grew louder, louder! I thought the heart must burst. And now a new anxiety seized me — the sound would be heard by a neighbor! The old man's hour had come! With a loud yell, I threw open the lantern and leaped into the room. He shrieked once — once only. In an instant I dragged him to the floor, and pulled the heavy bed over him. I then smiled gaily, to find the deed so far done. But, for many minutes, the heart beat on with a muffled sound. This, however, did not vex me; it would not be heard through the wall. At length it ceased. The old man was dead. I removed the bed and examined the corpse. Yes, he was stone, stone dead. I placed my hand upon the heart and held it there many minutes. There was no pulsation. He was stone dead. His eye would trouble me no more.

If still you think me mad, you will think so no longer when I describe the wise precautions I took for the concealment of the body. The night waned, and I worked hastily, but in silence. First of all I dismembered the corpse. I cut off the head and the arms and the legs.

I then took up three planks from the flooring of the chamber, and deposited all between the scantlings. I then replaced the boards so cleverly, so cunningly, that no human eye — not even *his* — could have detected anything wrong. There was nothing to wash out — no stain of any kind — no blood-spot whatever. I had been too wary for that. A tub had caught all — ha! ha!

When I had made an end of these labors, it was four o'clock — still dark as midnight. As the bell sounded the hour, there came a knocking at the street door. I went down to open it with a light heart — for what had I *now* to fear? There entered three men, who introduced themselves, with perfect suavity, as officers of the police. A shriek had been heard by a neighbor during the night; suspicion of foul play had been aroused; information had been lodged at the police office, and they (the officers) had been deputed to search the premises.

I smiled — for *what* had I to fear? I bade the gentlemen welcome. The shriek, I said, was my own in a dream. The old man, I mentioned, was absent in the country. I took my visitor all over the house. I bade them search — search well. I led them, at length, to *his* chamber. I showed them his treasures, secure, undisturbed. In the enthusiasm of my confidence, I brought chairs into the room, and desired them *here* to rest from their fatigues, while I myself, in the wild audacity of my perfect triumph, placed my own seat upon the very spot beneath which reposed the corpse of the victim.

The officers were satisfied. My *manner* had convinced them. I was singularly at ease. They sat, and while I answered cheerily, they chatted familiar things. But, ere long, I felt myself getting pale and wished them gone. My head ached, and I fancied a ringing in my ears: but still they sat and still chatted. The ringing became more distinct: — it continued and became more distinct: I talked more freely to get rid of the feeling: but it continued and gained definitiveness — until, at length, I found that the noise was *not* within my ears.

No doubt I now grew *very* pale; — but I talked more fluently, and with a heightened voice. Yet the sound increased — and what could I do? It was a *low,*

15

dull, quick sound — much such a sound as a watch makes when enveloped in cotton. I gasped for breath — and yet the officers heard it not. I talked more quickly — more vehemently; but the noise steadily increased. I arose and argued about trifles, in a high key and with violent gesticulations, but the noise steadily increased. Why would they not be gone? I paced the floor to and fro with heavy strides, as if excited to fury by the observation of the men — but the noise steadily increased. Oh God! what could I do? I foamed — I raved — I swore! I swung the chair upon which I had been sitting, and grated it upon the boards, but the noise arose over all and continually increased. It grew louder — louder — louder! And still the men chatted pleasantly, and smiled. Was it possible they heard not? Almighty God! — no, no! They heard! — they suspected! — they knew! — they were making a mockery of my horror! — this I thought, and this I think. But any thing was better than this agony! Any thing was more tolerable than this derision! I could bear those hypocritical smiles no longer! I felt that I must scream or die! — and now — again! — hark! louder! louder! louder! louder! —

"Villains!" I shrieked, "dissemble no more! I admit the deed! — tear up the planks! — here, here! — it is the beating of his hideous heart!"   [1843]

≡ THINKING ABOUT THE TEXT

1. Why do you think the narrator killed the old man? Was he simply "mad," or do you gather that he had a particular reason? Explain.

2. Why do you think Poe spends as much time as he does on the narrator's observations of the old man prior to the killing?

3. Of the various senses, hearing seems to be the one emphasized in this story. Where does it come up in the text? Why do you think Poe chose to focus his tale on this particular sense? What other senses are also referred to here?

4. Other than his hearing, what features of the narrator's behavior and thinking shape your view of him?

5. Would you say this is a supernatural story? Why, or why not?

≡ MAKING COMPARISONS

1. The two main characters of "The Cask of Amontillado" have names: Montresor and Fortunato. In "The Tell-Tale Heart," however, Poe leaves the two main characters nameless. They are merely "I" and "the old man." Does this approach produce a significant difference in effect? Why, or why not?

2. Does the narrator of this story seem to know the old man as well as Montresor knows Fortunato? Define what you mean by know in this instance.

3. Does the narrator of "The Tell-Tale Heart" strike you as more "mad" than Montresor is? Explain, making clear your definition of mad.

EDGAR ALLAN POE
Hop-Frog

The following story isn't as well known as "The Cask of Amontillado" and "The Tell-Tale Heart," but it deserves attention as one of Poe's final stories and as one of his most horrifying tales of revenge. It first appeared in 1849 in The Flag of Our Union, *a Boston newspaper, and it was then included in the collection of Poe's writings published in 1850, the year after his death.*

I never knew any one so keenly alive to a joke as the king was. He seemed to live only for joking. To tell a good story of the joke kind, and to tell it well, was the surest road to his favor. Thus it happened that his seven ministers were all noted for their accomplishments as jokers. They all took after the king, too, in being large, corpulent, oily men, as well as inimitable jokers. Whether people grow fat by joking, or whether there is something in fat itself which predisposes to a joke, I have never been quite able to determine; but certain it is that a lean joker is a *rara avis in terris.*°

About the refinements, or, as he called them, the "ghosts" of wit, the king troubled himself very little. He had an especial admiration for *breadth* in a jest, and would often put up with *length*, for the sake of it. Overniceties wearied him. He would have preferred Rabelais's "Gargantua" to the "Zadig" of Voltaire: and, upon the whole, practical jokes suited his taste far better than verbal ones.

At the date of my narrative, professing jesters had not altogether gone out of fashion at court. Several of the great Continental "powers" still retained their "fools," who wore motley, with caps and bells, and who were expected to be always ready with sharp witticisms, at a moment's notice, in consideration of the crumbs that fell from the royal table.

Our king, as a matter of course, retained his "fool." The fact is, he *required* something in the way of folly — if only to counterbalance the heavy wisdom of the seven wise men who were his ministers — not to mention himself.

His fool, or professional jester, was not *only* a fool, however. His value was trebled in the eyes of the king, by the fact of his being also a dwarf and a cripple. Dwarfs were as common at court, in those days, as fools; and many monarchs would have found it difficult to get through their days (days are rather longer at court than elsewhere) without both a jester to laugh *with*, and a dwarf to laugh *at*. But, as I have already observed, your jesters, in ninety-nine cases out of a hundred, are fat, round, and unwieldy — so that it was no small source of self-gratulation with our king that, in Hop-Frog (this was the fool's name), he possessed a triplicate treasure in one person.

I believe the name "Hop-Frog" was *not* that given to the dwarf by his sponsors at baptism, but it was conferred upon him, by general consent of the seven ministers, on account of his inability to walk as other men do. In fact, Hop-Frog could only get along by a sort of interjectional gait — something between a leap and a wriggle, — a movement that afforded illimitable amusement, and of

5

rara avis in terris: Rare bird.

course consolation, to the king, for (notwithstanding the protuberance of his stomach and a constitutional swelling of the head) the king, by his whole court, was accounted a capital figure.

But although Hop-Frog, through the distortion of his legs, could move only with great pain and difficulty along a road or floor, the prodigious muscular power which nature seemed to have bestowed upon his arms, by way of compensation for deficiency in the lower limbs, enabled him to perform many feats of wonderful dexterity, where trees or ropes were in question, or anything else to climb. At such exercises he certainly much more resembled a squirrel, or a small monkey, than a frog.

I am not able to say, with precision, from what country Hop-Frog originally came. It was from some barbarous region, however, that no person ever heard of — a vast distance from the court of our king. Hop-Frog, and a young girl very little less dwarfish than himself (although of exquisite proportions, and a marvelous dancer), had been forcibly carried off from their respective homes in adjoining provinces, and sent as presents to the king, by one of his ever-victorious generals.

Under these circumstances, it is not to be wondered at that a close intimacy arose between the two little captives. Indeed, they soon became sworn friends. Hop-Frog, who, although he made a great deal of sport, was by no means popular, had it not in his power to render Trippetta many services; but *she*, on account of her grace and exquisite beauty (although a dwarf), was universally admired and petted; so she possessed much influence; and never failed to use it, whenever she could, for the benefit of Hop-Frog.

On some grand state occasion — I forget what — the king determined   10
to have a masquerade; and whenever a masquerade, or any thing of that kind, occurred at our court, then the talents both of Hop-Frog and Trippetta were sure to be called into play. Hop-Frog, in especial, was so inventive in the way of getting up pageants, suggesting novel characters, and arranging costume, for masked balls, that nothing could be done, it seems, without his assistance.

The night appointed for the *fête* had arrived. A gorgeous hall had been fitted up, under Trippetta's eye, with every kind of device which could possibly give *éclat* to a masquerade. The whole court was in a fever of expectation. As for costumes and characters, it might well be supposed that everybody had come to a decision on such points. Many had made up their minds (as to what *rôles* they should assume) a week, or even a month, in advance; and, in fact, there was not a particle of indecision anywhere — except in the case of the king and his seven ministers. Why *they* hesitated I never could tell, unless they did it by way of a joke. More probably, they found it difficult, on account of being so fat, to make up their minds. At all events, time flew; and, as a last resort, they sent for Trippetta and Hop-Frog.

When the two little friends obeyed the summons of the king, they found him sitting at his wine with the seven members of his cabinet council; but the monarch appeared to be in a very ill humor. He knew that Hop-Frog was not fond of wine; for it excited the poor cripple almost to madness; and madness is no comfortable feeling. But the king loved his practical jokes, and took pleasure in forcing Hop-Frog to drink and (as the king called it) "to be merry."

"Come here, Hop-Frog," said he, as the jester and his friend entered the room; "swallow this bumper to the health of your absent friends [here Hop-Frog sighed] and then let us have the benefit of your invention. We want characters — *characters*, man, — something novel — out of the way. We are wearied with this everlasting sameness. Come, drink! the wine will brighten your wits."

Hop-Frog endeavored, as usual, to get up a jest in reply to these advances from the king; but the effort was too much. It happened to be the poor dwarf's birthday, and the command to drink to his "absent friends" forced the tears to his eyes. Many large, bitter drops fell into the goblet as he took it, humbly, from the hand of the tyrant.

"Ah! ha! ha! ha!" roared the latter, as the dwarf reluctantly drained the 15 beaker. "See what a glass of good wine can do! Why, your eyes are shining already!"

Poor fellow! his large eyes *gleamed*, rather than shone; for the effect of wine on his excitable brain was not more powerful than instantaneous. He placed the goblet nervously on the table, and looked round upon the company with a half-insane stare. They all seemed highly amused at the success of the king's "*joke*."

"And now to business," said the prime minister, a *very* fat man.

"Yes," said the king. "Come, Hop-Frog, lend us your assistance. Characters, my fine fellow; we stand in need of characters — all of us — ha! ha! ha!" and as this was seriously meant for a joke, his laugh was chorused by the seven.

Hop-Frog also laughed, although feebly and somewhat vacantly.

"Come, come," said the king, impatiently, "have you nothing to suggest?" 20

"I am endeavoring to think of something *novel*," replied the dwarf, abstractedly, for he was quite bewildered by the wine.

"Endeavoring!" cried the tyrant, fiercely; "what do you mean by *that*? Ah, I perceive. You are sulky, and want more wine. Here, drink this!" and he poured out another goblet full and offered it to the cripple, who merely gazed at it, gasping for breath.

"Drink, I say!" shouted the monster, "or by the fiends ——"

The dwarf hesitated. The king grew purple with rage. The courtiers smirked. Trippetta, pale as a corpse, advanced to the monarch's seat, and, falling on her knees before him, implored him to spare her friend.

The tyrant regarded her, for some moments, in evident wonder at her au- 25 dacity. He seemed quite at a loss what to do or say — how most becomingly to express his indignation. At last, without uttering a syllable, he pushed her violently from him, and threw the contents of the brimming goblet in her face.

The poor girl got up as best she could, and, not daring even to sigh, resumed her position at the foot of the table.

There was a dead silence for about half a minute, during which the falling of a leaf, or of a feather, might have been heard. It was interrupted by a low, but harsh and protracted *grating* sound which seemed to come at once from every corner of the room.

"What — what — *what* are you making that noise for?" demanded the king, turning furiously to the dwarf.

The latter seemed to have recovered, in great measure, from his intoxication, and looking fixedly but quietly into the tyrant's face, merely ejaculated:

"I — I? How could it have been me?"   30

"The sound appeared to come from without," observed one of the courtiers. "I fancy it was the parrot at the window, whetting his bill upon his cage-wires."

"True," replied the monarch, as if much relieved by the suggestion; "but, on the honor of a knight, I could have sworn that it was the gritting of this vagabond's teeth."

Hereupon the dwarf laughed (the king was too confirmed a joker to object to any one's laughing), and displayed a set of large, powerful, and very repulsive teeth. Moreover, he avowed his perfect willingness to swallow as much wine as desired. The monarch was pacified; and having drained another bumper with no very perceptible ill effect, Hop-Frog entered at once, and with spirit, into the plans for the masquerade.

"I cannot tell what was the association of idea," observed he, very tranquilly, and as if he had never tasted wine in his life, "but *just after* your majesty had struck the girl and thrown the wine in her face — *just after* your majesty had done this, and while the parrot was making that odd noise outside the window, there came into my mind a capital diversion — one of my own country frolics — often enacted among us, at our masquerades: but here it will be new altogether. Unfortunately, however, it requires a company of eight persons, and ——"

"Here we *are*!" cried the king, laughing at his acute discovery of the coin-   35
cidence; "eight to a fraction — I and my seven ministers. Come! what is the diversion?"

"We call it," replied the cripple, "the Eight Chained Ourang-Outangs, and it really is excellent sport if well enacted."

"*We* will enact it," remarked the king, drawing himself up, and lowering his eyelids.

"The beauty of the game," continued Hop-Frog, "lies in the fright it occasions among the women."

"Capital!" roared in chorus the monarch and his ministry.

"I will equip you as ourang-outangs," proceeded the dwarf; "leave all that   40
to me. The resemblance shall be so striking, that the company of masqueraders will take you for real beasts — and of course, they will be as much terrified as astonished."

"Oh, this is exquisite!" exclaimed the king. "Hop-Frog! I will make a man of you."

"The chains are for the purpose of increasing the confusion by their jangling. You are supposed to have escaped, *en masse*, from your keepers. Your majesty cannot conceive the *effect* produced, at a masquerade, by eight chained ourang-outangs, imagined to be real ones by most of the company; and rushing in with savage cries, among the crowd of delicately and gorgeously habited men and women. The *contrast* is inimitable."

"It *must* be," said the king: and the council arose hurriedly (as it was growing late), to put in execution the scheme of Hop-Frog.

His mode of equipping the party as ourang-outangs was very simple, but effective enough for his purposes. The animals in question had, at the epoch of my story, very rarely been seen in any part of the civilized world; and as the imitations made by the dwarf were sufficiently beast-like and more than sufficiently hideous, their truthfulness to nature was thus thought to be secured.

The king and his ministers were first encased in tight-fitting stockinet   45
shirts and drawers. They were then saturated with tar. At this stage of the process, some one of the party suggested feathers; but the suggestion was at once overruled by the dwarf, who soon convinced the eight, by ocular demonstration, that the hair of such a brute as the ourang-outang was much more efficiently represented by *flax*. A thick coating of the latter was accordingly plastered upon the coating of tar. A long chain was now procured. First, it was passed about the waist of the king, *and tied*; then about another of the party, and also tied; then about all successively, in the same manner. When this chaining arrangement was complete, and the party stood as far apart from each other as possible, they formed a circle; and to make all things appear natural, Hop-Frog passed the residue of the chain, in two diameters, at right angles, across the circle, after the fashion adopted, at the present day, by those who capture chimpanzees, or other large apes, in Borneo.

The grand saloon in which the masquerade was to take place, was a circular room, very lofty, and receiving the light of the sun only through a single window at top. At night (the season for which the apartment was especially designed) it was illuminated principally by a large chandelier, depending by a chain from the center of the skylight, and lowered, or elevated, by means of a counterbalance as usual; but (in order not to look unsightly) this latter passed outside the cupola and over the roof.

The arrangements of the room had been left to Trippetta's superintendence; but, in some particulars, it seems, she had been guided by the calmer judgment of her friend the dwarf. At his suggestion it was that, on this occasion, the chandelier was removed. Its waxen drippings (which, in weather so warm, it was quite impossible to prevent) would have been seriously detrimental to the rich dresses of the guests, who, on account of the crowded state of the saloon, could not *all* be expected to keep from out its center — that is to say, from under the chandelier. Additional sconces were set in various parts of the hall, out of the way; and a flambeau, emitting sweet odor, was placed in the right hand of each of the Caryatides° that stood against the wall — some fifty or sixty all together.

The eight ourang-outangs, taking Hop-Frog's advice, waited patiently until midnight (when the room was thoroughly filled with masqueraders) before making their appearance. No sooner had the clock ceased striking,

Caryatides: Sculptures in the form of a woman with a table-like structure on her head; used instead of columns to support an overhead building structure.

however, than they rushed, or rather rolled in, all together — for the impediments of their chains caused most of the party to fall, and all to stumble as they entered.

The excitement among the masqueraders was prodigious, and filled the heart of the king with glee. As had been anticipated, there were not a few of the guests who supposed the ferocious-looking creatures to be beasts of *some* kind in reality, if not precisely ourang-outangs. Many of the women swooned with affright; and had not the king taken the precaution to exclude all weapons from the saloon, his party might soon have expiated their frolic in their blood. As it was, a general rush was made for the doors; but the king had ordered them to be locked immediately upon his entrance; and, at the dwarf's suggestion, the keys had been deposited with *him*.

While the tumult was at its height, and each masquerader attentive only to   50
his own safety (for, in fact, there was much *real* danger from the pressure of the excited crowd), the chain by which the chandelier ordinarily hung, and which had been drawn up on its removal, might have been seen very gradually to descend, until its hooked extremity came within three feet of the floor.

Soon after this, the king and his seven friends having reeled about the hall in all directions, found themselves, at length, in its center, and, of course, in immediate contact with the chain. While they were thus situated, the dwarf, who had followed noiselessly at their heels, inciting them to keep up the commotion, took hold of their own chain at the intersection of the two portions which crossed the circle diametrically and at right angles. Here, with the rapidity of thought, he inserted the hook from which the chandelier had been wont to depend; and, in an instant, by some unseen agency, the chandelier-chain was drawn so far upward as to take the hook out of reach, and, as an inevitable consequence, to drag the ourang-outangs together in close connection, and face to face.

The masqueraders, by this time, had recovered, in some measure, from their alarm; and, beginning to regard the whole matter as a well-contrived pleasantry, set up a loud shout of laughter at the predicament of the apes.

"Leave them to *me!*" now screamed Hop-Frog, his shrill voice making itself easily heard through all the din. "Leave them to *me*. I fancy *I* know them. If I can only get a good look at them, *I* can soon tell who they are."

Here, scrambling over the heads of the crowd, he managed to get to the wall; when, seizing a flambeau from one of the Caryatides, he returned, as he went, to the center of the room — leaped, with the agility of a monkey, upon the king's head — and thence clambered a few feet up the chain — holding down the torch to examine the group of ourang-outangs, and still screaming: "*I* shall soon find out who they are!"

And now, while the whole assembly (the apes included) were convulsed   55
with laughter, the jester suddenly uttered a shrill whistle; when the chain flew violently up for about thirty feet — dragging with it the dismayed and struggling ourang-outangs, and leaving them suspended in midair between the skylight and the floor. Hop-Frog, clinging to the chain as it rose, still maintained his relative position in respect to the eight maskers, and still (as if nothing were

the matter) continued to thrust his torch down toward them, as though endeavoring to discover who they were.

So thoroughly astonished was the whole company at this ascent, that a dead silence, of about a minute's duration, ensued. It was broken by just such a low, harsh, *grating* sound, as had before attracted the attention of the king and his councillors when the former threw the wine in the face of Trippetta. But, on the present occasion, there could be no question as to *whence* the sound issued. It came from the fang-like teeth of the dwarf, who ground them and gnashed them as he foamed at the mouth, and glared, with an expression of maniacal rage, into the upturned countenances of the king and his seven companions.

"Ah, ha!" said at length the infuriated jester. "Ah, ha! I begin to see who these people *are*, now!" Here, pretending to scrutinize the king more closely, he held the flambeau to the flaxen coat which enveloped him, and which instantly burst into a sheet of vivid flame. In less than half a minute the whole eight ourang-outangs were blazing fiercely, amid the shrieks of the multitude who gazed at them from below, horror-stricken, and without the power to render them the slightest assistance.

At length the flames, suddenly increasing in virulence, forced the jester to climb higher up the chain, to be out of their reach; and, as he made this movement, the crowd again sank, for a brief instant, into silence. The dwarf seized his opportunity, and once more spoke:

"I now see *distinctly,*" he said, "what manner of people these maskers are. They are a great king and his seven privy-councillors, — a king who does not scruple to strike a defenseless girl, and his seven councillors who abet him in the outrage. As for myself, I am simply Hop-Frog, the jester — and *this is my last jest.*"

Owing to the high combustibility of both the flax and the tar to which it adhered, the dwarf had scarcely made an end of his brief speech before the work of vengeance was complete. The eight corpses swung in their chains, a fetid, blackened, hideous, and indistinguishable mass. The cripple hurled his torch at them, clambered leisurely to the ceiling, and disappeared through the skylight.   60

It is supposed that Trippetta, stationed on the roof of the saloon, had been the accomplice of her friend in his fiery revenge, and that, together, they effected their escape to their own country; for neither was seen again.   *[1849]*

▤ THINKING ABOUT THE TEXT

1. The first paragraph of the story focuses on the concepts of "a joke" and "joking." Do these concepts cease to play a role in the story by the end? Can the story itself be considered a "joke"? Make clear your own definitions of the terms.

2. During your reading of this story, how predictable did you find it? At what points, if any, did the plot go in a direction you didn't foresee?

3. What does Poe do to encourage readers to sympathize with Hop-Frog? Do you find his final act of revenge so awful that you lose all sympathy for him? Why, or why not?

4. When Poe wrote this story, African American slavery still existed in the American South, his home region. Indeed, some interpreters of "Hop-Frog" have seen it as being really about this institution. Assuming for the moment that they might be right, what features of the story do you see as related to slavery, and what do you infer as Poe's beliefs about it? Does the story seem to reflect Poe's hostility toward the abolition movement, which he expressed clearly in various essays?

5. What would you say to someone who worries that Poe's depiction of Hop-Frog will give readers a bad impression of people with disabilities?

■ MAKING COMPARISONS

1. This story brings in several more characters than the other two Poe stories do. In fact, we learn about an entire community. Would you say, therefore, that this story has more social implications than the other two do? Why, or why not?

2. Both "Hop-Frog" and "The Cask of Amontillado" are about revenge, but "The Tell-Tale Heart" is not. Should we therefore conclude that the murderer in "The Tell-Tale Heart" is less justified in his killing than his counterparts in the other stories are? Why, or why not?

3. Though "The Cask of Amontillado" and "The Tell-Tale Heart" are told in the first person, "Hop-Frog" is not. Why do you think Poe changed strategies? Refer to specific details of all three stories.

■ WRITING ABOUT ISSUES

1. Choose one of these three stories, and write an essay in which you explain a way in which the story *doesn't* clearly resolve an issue related to guilt.

2. Choose two of these Poe stories, and write an essay in which you consider whether and how one is more realistic than the other. Make clear how you are defining *realism*.

3. Write an essay in which you analyze how someone you have known, read about, or heard about displayed a guilty conscience. Refer to specific things this person did that suggested he or she felt guilty about something. If you wish, feel free to mention any of the Poe stories in this cluster.

4. How much and in what ways should society punish a criminal who has confessed? Address this question by writing an essay about a particular case that you have researched.

Eyewitness Testimony: Cultural Contexts for a Play

IDA FINK, *The Table*

CULTURAL CONTEXTS:

WLADYSLAW SZPILMAN, "The *Umschlagplatz*"

DORI LAUB AND SHOSHANA FELMAN, "Testimony and Historical Truth"

Most people from the Western world would say that among the worst injustices of the twentieth century were the mass killings of Jews and other groups perpetrated by Nazi Germany and its collaborators during World War II. Indeed, many of the people responsible for this genocide were eventually found guilty of war crimes. Nevertheless, several of the murderers eluded efforts to track them down. Moreover, others were not arrested and tried in court until decades after the war. Even when they were brought to trial, their conviction was by no means assured. On various occasions, Holocaust survivors who testified against them could not remember exact details of the atrocities the perpetrators had committed. Inevitably, these eyewitnesses had to rely on fading and tormented memories, which defense lawyers were quick to criticize. Ida Fink's short play *The Table* explores the limits, as well as the strengths, of such recollections by showing a prosecutor for one of the trials interrogating his own team of witnesses. To help you think about the play and the issues it raises, we provide background texts. The first — a chapter from Wladyslaw Szpilman's celebrated memoir, *The Pianist* — is an eyewitness account of a deadly Nazi roundup in Warsaw. Then, we present Dori Laub's analysis of a Holocaust survivor's testimony.

BEFORE YOU READ

Think of an occasion when your memory of an event conflicted with someone else's memory of it. What, if anything, about the event were the two of you able to agree on? What did you disagree about, and what do you think produced this disagreement? Do you now believe that one of you remembered the event more accurately? If so, why do you believe this?

IDA FINK

The Table

A Play for Four Voices and Basso Ostinato
Translated by Francine Prose and Madeline G. Levine

Originally from Zbaraz, Poland (now part of the Ukraine), Ida Fink (b. 1921) writes in Polish about the Holocaust. During the Nazi occupation of her country, she was confined along with other Jews to a ghetto in her hometown but then escaped to its

(Yad Vashem–The Archive.)

"Aryan" section and hid there using false identity papers. In 1957, she moved to Israel, where she still lives. Her works of fiction include a novel, The Journey (1990), as well as the short-story collections Traces (1997) and A Scrap of Time (1987), a book that also contains the following play. Fink wrote The Table for Israeli radio in 1970. "At that time," she reports, "I was working as an interpreter and a clerk of the court during hearings of witnesses at the trials of Nazi criminals." Eleven years later, the play was performed on German television. Fink identifies it as being "for four voices and basso ostinato," a term that literally means "obstinate bass" and that in music refers to a continuously repeating bass line. Here, Fink evidently associates the term with the prosecutor's voice.

CHARACTERS:

FIRST MAN, 50 years old
FIRST WOMAN, 45 years old
SECOND MAN, 60 years old
SECOND WOMAN, 38 years old
PROSECUTOR, 35–40 years old

The stage is empty and dark. Spotlights only on the witness, seated in a chair, and the prosecutor, seated at a desk.

PROSECUTOR: Have you recovered, Mr. Grumbach? Can we go on? Where did we stop? . . . Oh, yes. So you remember precisely that there was a table there.
FIRST MAN: Yes. A small table.
PROSECUTOR: A *small* table? How small? How many people could sit at a table that size?
FIRST MAN: Do I know? It's hard for me to say now.
PROSECUTOR: How long was it? A meter? Eight centimeters? Fifty centimeters?

FIRST MAN: A table. A regular table — not too small, not too big. It's been so many years . . . And at a time like that, who was thinking about a table?

PROSECUTOR: Yes, of course, I understand. But you have to understand me, too, Mr. Grumbach: every detail is crucial. You must understand that it's for a good purpose that I'm tormenting you with such details.

FIRST MAN: *(resigned)* All right, let it be eighty centimeters. Maybe ninety.

PROSECUTOR: Where did that table — that small table — stand? On the right side or the left side of the marketplace as you face the town hall?

FIRST MAN: On the left. Yes.

PROSECUTOR: Are you certain?

FIRST MAN: Yes . . . I saw them carry it out.

PROSECUTOR: That means that at the moment you arrived at the marketplace the table was not there yet.

FIRST MAN: No . . . Or maybe it was. You know, I don't remember. Maybe I saw them carrying it from one place to another. But is it so important if they were bringing it out or just moving it?

PROSECUTOR: Please concentrate.

FIRST MAN: How many years has it been? Twenty-five? And you want me to remember such details? I haven't thought about that table once in twenty-five years.

PROSECUTOR: And yet today, while you were telling your story, on your own, without prompting, you said, "He was sitting at a table." Please concentrate and tell me what you saw as you entered the square.

FIRST MAN: What did I see? I was coming from Rozana Street, from the opposite direction, because Rozana is on the other side of the market. I was struck by the silence. That was my first thought: so many people, and so quiet. I noticed a group of people I knew; among them was the druggist, Mr. Weidel, and I asked Weidel, "What do you think, Doctor, what will they do with us?" And he answered me, "My dear Mr. Grumbach . . ."

PROSECUTOR: You already mentioned that, please stick to the point. What did you see in the square?

FIRST MAN: The square was black with people.

PROSECUTOR: Earlier you said that the people assembled in the marketplace were standing at the rear of the square, facing the town hall, and that there was an empty space between the people and the town hall.

FIRST MAN: That's right.

PROSECUTOR: In other words, to say, "The square was black with people," is not completely accurate. That empty space was, shall we say, white — especially since, as you've mentioned, fresh snow had fallen during the night.

FIRST MAN: Yes, that's right.

PROSECUTOR: Now please think, Mr. Grumbach. Did you notice anything or anyone in that empty white space?

FIRST MAN: Kiper was sitting in a chair and striking his boots with a riding crop.

PROSECUTOR: I would like to call your attention to the fact that none of the witnesses until now has mentioned that Kiper was walking around with a riding crop. Are you certain that Kiper was striking his boots with a riding crop?

FIRST MAN: Maybe it was a stick or a branch. In any case, he was striking his boots — *that* I remember. Sometimes you remember such tiny details. Hamke and Bondke were standing next to him, smoking cigarettes. There were policemen and Ukrainians standing all around the square — a lot of them, one next to the other.

PROSECUTOR: Yes, we know that already. So, you remember that Kiper was sitting in a chair.

FIRST MAN: Absolutely.

PROSECUTOR: So if there was a chair in the marketplace, wouldn't there have been a table as well?

FIRST MAN: A table . . . just a minute . . . a table . . . no. Because that chair seemed so . . . wait a minute . . . No, there wasn't any table there. But they carried out a small table later. Now I remember exactly. Two policemen brought a small table out from the town hall.

PROSECUTOR: *(relieved)* Well, something concrete at last. What time would that have been?

FIRST MAN: *(reproachfully)* Really, I . . .

PROSECUTOR: Please, think about it.

FIRST MAN: The time? . . . God knows, I have no idea. I left the house at 6:15, that I know. I stopped in at my aunt's on Poprzeczna Street, that took ten minutes, then I walked down Miodna, Krotka, Okolna, and Mickiewicza streets. On Mickiewicza I hid for a few minutes inside the gate of one of the houses because I heard shots. It must have taken me about half an hour to walk there.

PROSECUTOR: How much time elapsed from the moment you arrived in the square to the moment when you noticed the policemen carrying the table out from the town hall?

FIRST MAN: Not a long time. Let's say half an hour.

PROSECUTOR: In other words, the policemen carried a table into the marketplace around 7:15. A small table.

FIRST MAN: That's right. Now I recall that Kiper pointed with his riding crop to the place where they were supposed to set the table down.

PROSECUTOR: Please indicate on the map you drew for us the exact place where the policemen set the table down. With a cross or a circle. Thank you. *(satisfied)* Excellent. Kiper is sitting in a chair, the policemen carry in the table, the length of the table is about eighty centimeters. How was the table placed? I mean, in front of Kiper? Next to him?

FIRST MAN: I don't know. That I couldn't see.

PROSECUTOR: If you could see them carrying in the table you could see that, too — perhaps you just don't remember. But maybe you can remember where Kiper sat? At the table? Beside it? In front of it?

FIRST MAN: Obviously, at the table. When someone waits for a table, it's so he can sit at it. He was sitting at the table. Of course. That's what people do.

PROSECUTOR: Alone?

FIRST MAN: In the beginning? I don't know. I wasn't looking that way the whole time. But later — this I know — they were all there: Kiper, Hamke, Bondke, Rossel, Kuntz, and Wittelmann.

PROSECUTOR: *(slowly)* Kiper, Hamke, Bondke, Rossel, Kuntz, and Wittelmann. When you testified a year ago you didn't mention either Rossel or Wittelmann.

FIRST MAN: I must have forgotten about them then. Now I remember that they were there, too.

PROSECUTOR: Were they all sitting at the table?

FIRST MAN: No. Not all of them. Some of them were standing next to it.

PROSECUTOR: Who was sitting?

FIRST MAN: What I saw was that Kiper, Hamke, Bondke, and Kuntz were sitting. The rest were standing. There were more than a dozen of them, I don't remember all the names.

PROSECUTOR: How were they seated, one beside the other?

FIRST MAN: Yes.

PROSECUTOR: Is it possible that four grown men could sit one beside the other at a table that is eighty centimeters long?

FIRST MAN: I don't know. Maybe the table was longer than that; or maybe it wasn't big enough for all of them. In any event, they were sitting in a row.

PROSECUTOR: Who read the names from the list?

FIRST MAN: Hamke or Bondke.

PROSECUTOR: How did they do it?

FIRST MAN: People walked up to the table, showed their *Arbeitskarten*,° and Kiper looked them over and pointed either to the right or to the left. The people who had good *Arbeitskarten* went to the right, and those whose work wasn't considered important, or who didn't have any *Arbeitskarten*, they went to the left.

PROSECUTOR: Was Kiper the one who conducted the selection?

FIRST MAN: Yes, I'm positive about that.

PROSECUTOR: Did Kiper stay in that spot during the whole time the names were read? Or did he get up from the table?

FIRST MAN: I don't know. Maybe he got up. I wasn't looking at him every minute. It took a very long time. And anyway, is it that important?

PROSECUTOR: I'm sorry to be tormenting you with these seemingly unimportant details . . . In other words, is it possible that Kiper got up and walked away from the table, or even left the square?

FIRST MAN: I can't give a definite answer. I wasn't watching Kiper every minute. It's possible that he did get up from the table. That's not out of the question. Still, he was the one in charge at the marketplace. Kiper — and no one else. And he was the one who shot the mother and child.

PROSECUTOR: Did you see this with your own eyes?

FIRST MAN: Yes.

PROSECUTOR: Please describe the incident.

FIRST MAN: The woman wasn't from our town, so I don't know her name. She was young, she worked in the brickworks. She had a ten-year-old daughter, Mala. I remember the child's name; she was a pretty little girl. When this woman's name was called she walked up to the table with her daughter.

Arbeitskarten: Identity cards.

She was holding the child by the hand. Kiper gave her back her *Arbeitskarte* and ordered her to go to the right. But he ordered the child to go to the left. The mother started begging him to leave the child with her, but he wouldn't agree. Then she placed her *Arbeitskarte* on the table and walked to the left side with the child. Kiper called her back and asked her if she knew the penalty for disobeying an order, and then he shot them — first the girl, and then the mother.

PROSECUTOR: Did you actually see Kiper shoot?

FIRST MAN: I saw the woman approach the table with the child. I saw them standing in front of Kiper. A moment later I heard two shots.

PROSECUTOR: Where were you standing at that moment? Please mark it on the map. With a cross or a circle. Thank you. So, you were standing near the pharmacy. How far was it from the table to the pharmacy?

FIRST MAN: Thirty meters, maybe fifty.

PROSECUTOR: Then you couldn't have heard the conversation between Kiper and the mother.

FIRST MAN: No, obviously. I didn't hear what they said, but I saw that the mother exchanged several sentences with Kiper. It was perfectly clear what they were talking about. Everyone understood what the mother was asking. Then I saw the mother place her *Arbeitskarte* on the table and go to the left with the child. I heard Kiper call her back. They went back.

PROSECUTOR: They went back and stood in front of the table, correct?

FIRST MAN: That's correct.

PROSECUTOR: In other words, they were blocking your view of the men who were sitting at the table, or at least of some of the men sitting at the table.

FIRST MAN: It's possible. I don't remember exactly. In any case, I saw them come back to the table, and a moment later there were two shots, and then I saw them lying on the ground. People who stood closer to them clearly heard Kiper ask her if she knew the penalty for disobeying an order.

PROSECUTOR: Was Kiper standing or sitting at that moment?

FIRST MAN: I don't remember.

PROSECUTOR: So, you didn't see him at the exact moment you heard the shots. Did you see a gun in his hand? What kind of gun? A pistol? A machine gun?

FIRST MAN: He must have shot them with a pistol. Those were pistol shots.

PROSECUTOR: Did you see a pistol in Kiper's hand?

FIRST MAN: No . . . perhaps the mother and child were blocking my view; or maybe I was looking at the victims and not at the murderer. I don't know. But in any case, I did see something that told me it was Kiper who shot them, and no one else.

PROSECUTOR: Namely?

FIRST MAN: Namely . . . immediately after the shots, when the mother and child were lying on the ground, I saw with my own eyes how Kiper rubbed his hands together with a disgusted gesture, as if to cleanse them of filth. I won't forget that gesture.

PROSECUTOR: (*summarizing*) And so, Mr. Grumbach, you saw Kiper sitting at a table in the company of Hamke, Bondke, Rossel, and Kuntz. Then you saw

Kiper carrying out the selection and Kiper brushing off his hands immediately after you heard the shots that killed the mother and child. But you didn't see a gun in Kiper's hand nor the shooting itself. Is that correct?

FIRST MAN: Still, I assert with absolute confidence that the murderer of the mother and child was Kiper.

PROSECUTOR: Was Kiper sitting behind the table when your name was called?

FIRST MAN: (hesitating) I was one of the last to be called. My *Arbeitskarte* was taken and returned by Bondke. I don't remember if Kiper was present or not. By then I was already half dead.

PROSECUTOR: Of course. What time would it have been when your name was called?

FIRST MAN: What time? My God, I don't know, it was already past noon.

PROSECUTOR: Did you witness any other murders committed that day?

FIRST MAN: That day more than four hundred people were shot in the town. Another eight hundred at the cemetery.

PROSECUTOR: Did you see any member of the Gestapo shoot someone?

FIRST MAN: No.

PROSECUTOR: Were you one of the group that buried the victims in the cemetery?

FIRST MAN: No.

PROSECUTOR: Is there anything else that you would like to say in connection with that day?

FIRST MAN: Yes.

PROSECUTOR: Please, go ahead.

FIRST MAN: It was a sunny, cold day. There was snow in the streets. The snow was red.

FIRST WOMAN: It was a Sunday. I remember it perfectly. As I was walking to the square, the church bells were ringing. It was a Sunday. Black Sunday.

PROSECUTOR: Is that what the day was called afterwards?

FIRST WOMAN: Yes.

PROSECUTOR: Some of the witnesses have testified that the day was called Bloody Sunday.

FIRST WOMAN: (dryly) I should think the name would be unimportant. It was certainly bloody. Four hundred corpses on the streets of the town.

PROSECUTOR: How do you know the exact figure?

FIRST WOMAN: From those who buried the victims. The *Ordnungsdienst°* did that. Later they told us, four hundred murdered in the town alone. A hard, packed snow lay on the streets; it was red with blood. The worst one was Kiper.

PROSECUTOR: Slow down. Please describe the events in the square as they occurred.

FIRST WOMAN: At six they ordered us to leave our houses and go to the marketplace. First I decided not to go, and I ran up to the attic. There was a window there, so I looked out. I saw people pouring down Rozana, Kwiatowa,

Ordnungsdienst: Jewish police forces controlled by the Nazis.

Piekna, and Mickiewicza streets towards the square. Suddenly I noticed two SS entering the house next door. They stayed inside for a moment, then came out leading an elderly couple, the Weintals. Mrs. Weintal was crying. I saw that. They were elderly people. They owned a paper goods store. The SS-men ordered them to stand facing the wall of the house, and then they shot them.

PROSECUTOR: Do you know the names of the two SS-men?

FIRST WOMAN: No. One was tall and thin. He had a terrifying face. I might be able to recognize him in a photograph. You don't forget such a face. But they were local SS, because there were no outside SS in town that day. *They* did it, the locals. Four hundred murdered on the spot, twice that number in the cemetery.

PROSECUTOR: Let's take it slowly now. So, you saw two SS leading the Weintal couple out of the building and putting them against the wall. You lived on Kwiatowa Street. Was their house also located on Kwiatowa?

FIRST WOMAN: I lived on Kwiatowa at number 1; it was the corner building. The Weintals lived in a building on Rozana.

PROSECUTOR: What number?

FIRST WOMAN: I don't know, I don't remember . . .

PROSECUTOR: Did you see which of the two SS shot them? The tall one or the other one?

FIRST WOMAN: That I didn't see, because when they ordered them to stand facing the wall, I knew what would happen next and I couldn't watch. I was afraid. I moved away from the window. I was terribly afraid.

PROSECUTOR: Afterwards, did you see the Weintal couple lying on the ground dead?

FIRST WOMAN: They shot them from a distance of two meters; I assume they knew how to aim.

PROSECUTOR: Did you see the bodies afterwards?

FIRST WOMAN: No, I ran downstairs from the attic, I was afraid — with good reason — I was afraid that they would search the houses for people who were trying to hide, but I didn't go out into the street, I took the back exit to the garden and made my way to the marketplace by a roundabout route.

PROSECUTOR: Would you recognize those two SS in photos?

FIRST WOMAN: Perhaps. I'm fairly certain I could recognize the tall thin one. You don't forget such a face.

PROSECUTOR: Please look through this album. It contains photographs of members of the Gestapo who were in your town; but there are also photographs here of people who were never there.

FIRST WOMAN: *(she turns the pages; a pause)* Oh, that's him.

PROSECUTOR: Is that one of the men you saw from the window?

FIRST WOMAN: No, it's that awful murderer. It's Kiper. Yes, I remember, it's definitely him.

PROSECUTOR: Please look through all the photographs.

FIRST WOMAN: *(a pause)* No, I can't find that face. Unfortunately.

PROSECUTOR: You said "awful murderer." Did you ever witness a murder committed by Kiper?

FIRST WOMAN: *(laughs)* Witness? You're joking. The witnesses to his murders aren't alive.

PROSECUTOR: But there are people who saw him shoot.

FIRST WOMAN: I did, too. Sure — in the square, he fired into the crowd. Just like that.

PROSECUTOR: Do you know who he killed then?

FIRST WOMAN: I don't know. There were fifteen hundred of us in the square. But I saw him rushing around like a wild man and shooting. Not just him, others, too. Bendke, for example.

PROSECUTOR: When was that?

FIRST WOMAN: In the morning. Before the selection. But it's possible it also went on during the selection. I don't remember. I know that they fired into the crowd. Just like that.

PROSECUTOR: Who read the names from the list?

FIRST WOMAN: An SS-man. I don't know his name.

PROSECUTOR: How did they do it?

FIRST WOMAN: Very simply. Names were called out, some people went to the right and others to the left. The left meant death.

PROSECUTOR: Who conducted the selection?

FIRST WOMAN: They were all there: Kiper, Bendke, Hamm, Rosse.

PROSECUTOR: Which one of them reviewed the *Arbeitskarten?*

FIRST WOMAN: I don't remember.

PROSECUTOR: Who ordered you to go to the right? Kiper? Bendke? Hamm? Rosse?

FIRST WOMAN: I don't remember. At such a time, you know . . . at such a time, when you don't know . . . life or death . . . I didn't look at their faces. To me, they all had the same face. All of them! What difference does it make whether it was Kiper or Bendke or Hamm or Rosse? They were all there. There were ten or maybe fifteen of those murderers. They stood in a semi-circle, with their machine guns across their chests. What difference does it make which one? They all gave orders, they all shot! All of them!

PROSECUTOR: Please calm yourself. I am terribly sorry that I have to provoke you with such questions. But you see, we can only convict people if we can *prove* that they committed murder. You say that all the members of the local Gestapo were there. But it could be that one of them was on leave, or possibly on duty in the *Dienststelle.*° And didn't shoot.

FIRST WOMAN: Every one of them shot. If not that day, then another. During the second or third action, during the liquidation.

PROSECUTOR: The law requires proof. And I, as the prosecuting attorney, am asking you for proof. I am asking for the names of the murderers, the names of the victims, the circumstances in which they were murdered. Otherwise, I can do nothing.

FIRST WOMAN: *(quietly)* My God . . .

PROSECUTOR: Excuse me?

FIRST WOMAN: Nothing, nothing.

Dienststelle: Police station.

PROSECUTOR: Please think: which one of them was in charge of the selection in the square?

FIRST WOMAN: They all participated in the selection. Kiper, Bendke, Hamm, Rosse. They were standing in a semicircle.

PROSECUTOR: Standing? Were all of them standing? Or perhaps some of them were seated?

FIRST WOMAN: No, they were standing. Is it that important?

PROSECUTOR: It's very important. Do you remember seeing a table in the marketplace at which several Gestapo men were seated? The others were standing near the table.

FIRST WOMAN: A table? I don't remember. There was no table there.

SECOND MAN: Here's the map. The marketplace was shaped like a trapezoid. At the top was the town hall, a beautiful old building that had been built by a Polish nobleman in the seventeenth century. The jewel of the town. The square sloped down towards the actual market where the stores were, as if the town hall reigned over the place. On the left, by the ruins of the old ramparts, stood those whose *Arbeitskarten* were taken away and also those who did not have *Arbeitskarten*. Note that the streets radiate out like a star. Here's Rozana, then Sienkiewicza, then Piekna, then Male Targi, then Nadrzeczna. There was no river in the town, but maybe once upon a time there was one, and that's why it was called Nadrzeczna — Riverside. Then came Zamkowa Street. All the streets I've named were later included in the ghetto, with the exception of Piekna. Beyond Male Targi there was a cemetery. Yes. That's where they were shot. Nadrzeczna was adjacent to the cemetery. Most of the people who lived on Nadrzeczna were Poles, but it was incorporated into the ghetto nonetheless, because of the cemetery. Because the cemetery played a major role in our life then. Between Rozana and Sienkiewicza there were shops. First, Weidel's pharmacy — he was killed in the camp; then Rosenzweig's iron shop — he was shot during the second action. Then Kreitz's dry goods store, the Haubers' restaurant and hotel — they were the wealthiest people among us, their daughter lives in Canada — and then two groceries, one beside the other, Blumenthal's and Hochwald's. They were rivals all their lives, and now they're lying in the same grave. Oh yes, I can draw every single stone for you, describe every single person. Do you know how many of us survived?

PROSECUTOR: Forty.

SECOND MAN: How do you know?

PROSECUTOR: They are my witnesses.

SECOND MAN: And have you found all of them? And taken their testimony?

PROSECUTOR: I have found almost all of them, but I still haven't taken testimony from everyone. Several witnesses live in America; they will be questioned by our consular officials, and if necessary, subpoenaed for the trial. Two live in Australia, one in Venezuela. Now I would like to ask you about the details of the selection that took place during the first action. When was it, do you remember?

SECOND MAN: Of course. It was a Sunday, in December, towards the end of the month. It was a sunny, cold day. Nature, you see, was also against us. She was mocking us. Yes, indeed. If it had rained, or if there had been a storm, who knows, perhaps they wouldn't have kept shooting from morning till night. Darkness was already falling when they led those people to the cemetery. Oh, you want proof, don't you? The snow on the town's streets was red. Red! Does that satisfy you?

PROSECUTOR: Unfortunately, Mr. Zachwacki, snow doesn't constitute proof for judges, especially snow that melted twenty-five years ago.

SECOND MAN: The snow was red. Bloody Sunday. Four hundred fifty corpses on the streets. That's not proof? Then go there and dig up the mass graves.

PROSECUTOR: I'm interested in the selection. Who was in charge of it?

SECOND MAN: Kiper. A thug, a murderer. The worst sort. I can't talk about this calmly. No. Do you mind if I smoke? These are things . . . I'm sixty, my blood pressure shoots right up. A cutthroat like that . . .

PROSECUTOR: How do you know that Kiper was in charge of the selection?

SECOND MAN: What do you mean, how? I gave him my *Arbeitskarte* myself. He peered at me from under his brows and snarled, "*Rechts!*" I went to the right. Saved. Saved until the next time.

PROSECUTOR: Please describe the scene in more detail.

SECOND MAN: I was standing some distance away. We all tried to stand as far away from them as possible, as if that could have helped. I was standing near the Haubers' hotel. It was one in the afternoon. The church bell struck one, and since it was quiet in the square, you could hear the bell clearly even though the church was in a different part of town, near Waly Ksiazece. By then they had been calling out names for about an hour. Suddenly I hear, "Zachwacki!"

PROSECUTOR: Who called your name?

SECOND MAN: One of the Gestapo, but I don't know which one.

PROSECUTOR: Didn't you notice which of them was holding the list?

SECOND MAN: No, you're asking too much. There was a list, because they read the names from a list, but I didn't see it. If a person saw a scene like that in the theater, maybe he could describe it in detail. This here, that there, and so on. But when a tragedy like this is being played in real life? You expect me to look at a list when my life is hanging by a thread? I was standing there with my wife. She had an *Arbeitskarte* from the sawmill — that was a good place to work — and I had one from the cement works. Also a good place. When they called my name, my wife grabbed my arm. "Let's stay together!" she cried. Dr. Gluck was standing nearby, a kind old doctor. He told my wife, "Mrs. Zachwacki, calm down, your husband has a good *Arbeitskarte*, you have a good *Arbeitskarte*, get a grip on yourself." But she kept saying, "I want to stay together, if we don't we won't see each other ever again. Albert," she said, "I'm afraid." I literally had to tear myself away, she was holding on to me so tight. There, you see, so much for instinct, intuition . . . I never saw her again. All the women who worked in the sawmill were sent to the left. (*he clears his throat*)

PROSECUTOR: *(a short pause)* Then what happened?

SECOND MAN: I dashed through the crowd. There was an empty space between us and them, you had to walk about thirty meters to cross the empty square. First — I remember this — someone kicked me, who I don't know. I took a deep breath and ran as hard as I could to get to the town hall as fast as possible. When I handed them my *Arbeitskarte* my hand was trembling like an aspen leaf, although I'm not a coward. Not at all!

PROSECUTOR: To whom did you hand your *Arbeitskarte?*

SECOND MAN: I already told you, to Kiper. He opened it, read it, handed it back to me and snarled, *"Rechts!"* I was young, tall, strong. He gave me a reprieve.

PROSECUTOR: At the moment that you handed him your *Arbeitskarte*, was Kiper standing or sitting?

SECOND MAN: He was standing with his legs apart, his machine gun across his chest. His face was swollen, red.

PROSECUTOR: And the rest of the Gestapo?

SECOND MAN: I didn't see. I don't remember if any of them were standing next to Kiper.

PROSECUTOR: Did you see a table?

SECOND MAN: Yes, there was a table, but it was further to the right, as if it had nothing to do with what was happening there.

PROSECUTOR: A small table?

SECOND MAN: No, not at all. It was a big, long oak table, like one of those trestle tables you see in monasteries. It was probably one of those antique tables from the old town hall.

PROSECUTOR: Long, you say. What were its dimensions, more or less?

SECOND MAN: How should I know? Two, three meters. The Gestapo sat in a row on one side of the table; and there was quite a large group of them sitting there. Bondke was sitting, Rossel was sitting — them I remember. And there were at least six others.

PROSECUTOR: Did you by any chance notice whether Kiper was sitting at the table earlier and whether the reviewing of the *Arbeitskarten* took place at the table?

SECOND MAN: I didn't notice. When I was called, Kiper was standing several meters from the table.

PROSECUTOR: Who do you think was in charge of the action?

SECOND MAN: Kuntze. He had the highest rank.

PROSECUTOR: Did you see him in the square?

SECOND MAN: I don't remember if I saw Kuntze. Presumably he was sitting at the table. But I only remember Bondke and Rossel.

PROSECUTOR: Was the table already there when you got to the square?

SECOND MAN: Yes.

PROSECUTOR: Who was seated at it?

SECOND MAN: No one.

PROSECUTOR: Some people claim that Kiper was sitting in a chair even before the table was brought out and that afterwards he sat at the head of the table. That he took the *Arbeitskarten* while he was sitting.

SECOND MAN: It's possible. Everything is possible. When I was called, Kiper was standing.

PROSECUTOR: Mr. Zachwacki, do you recall an incident with a mother and child who were shot in the square?

SECOND MAN: Yes, I do. It was Rosa Rubinstein and her daughter Ala. They were from another town and had lived in our town only since the beginning of the war. I knew them.

PROSECUTOR: Who shot them, and under what circumstances?

SECOND MAN: I was standing in the group of workers on the right side of the square, beside the well.

PROSECUTOR: Please indicate the place on the map. With a circle or a cross. Thank you. There was a well there, you say. No one has yet mentioned that well.

SECOND MAN: It was an old well, wooden, with a wooden fence around it. All around it, in a semicircle, there were trees, poplars. At one moment I heard a shot, and people who were standing somewhat closer said that Rosa Rubinstein and her daughter had been shot. It seems that both of them had been sent to the left, but they went to the right. People said that Kiper ran after them and shot them.

PROSECUTOR: You said, "I heard a shot." Do you mean you heard a single shot?

SECOND MAN: Those were my words, but it's hard for me to say if I heard one shot, or two, or three. No doubt he fired at least twice.

PROSECUTOR: Did you see the shooting with your own eyes?

SECOND MAN: No. I saw the bodies lying on the ground. They were lying next to each other. Then the *Ordnungsdienst* picked them up. A red stain was left on the snow.

PROSECUTOR: You were part of the group that helped to bury the victims afterwards?

SECOND MAN: That's correct. There were so many victims that the *Ordnungsdienst* had to take twenty men to help. Four hundred and fifty people were killed in the town — in the square and in the house searches — and eight hundred and forty were shot in the cemetery. My wife was one of them.

PROSECUTOR: *(pause)* But you didn't see any murders with your own eyes? Can you say, "I saw with my own eyes that this one or that one shot so-and-so or so-and-so?"

SECOND MAN: I saw thirteen hundred victims. The mass grave was thirty meters long, three meters wide, five meters deep.

SECOND WOMAN: No, I wasn't in the square. Because I worked as a cleaning woman for the Gestapo, and in the morning, when everyone was going to the marketplace, Mama said to me, "See if they'll let you stay at work." I took my pail and a rag and a brush and said goodbye to my parents on the corner of Mickiewicza and Rozana. We lived on Mickiewicza Street. My parents kept going straight, and I turned onto Rozana. I had gone a few steps when suddenly I caught sight of Rossel and Hamke; they were walking towards me and I got terribly frightened, so I ran into the first gate, and they passed by, they didn't notice me. Later I saw them entering the building at number 13. I kept going.

PROSECUTOR: Who lived in the house?

SECOND WOMAN: I don't know, I was young, I was thirteen years old, but I said I was sixteen because children, you know, were killed. I was well developed, so I said I was sixteen and they let me work for them. That was good luck. That day the Gestapo were going around to all the houses looking for people who hadn't gone to the square, and if they found someone, they shot him either in his apartment or on the street.

PROSECUTOR: Was there a family named Weintal in the house at number 13?

SECOND WOMAN: Weintal? No, I never heard of anyone with that name. I stayed at the Gestapo all day long, hiding. I knew the building, I knew where I could hide. Well, I must say, I certainly was lucky.

PROSECUTOR: Which Gestapo members were in the building that day?

SECOND WOMAN: I don't know. I was hiding in an alcove next to the stairway to the cellar, at the very end of the corridor. Once I thought I heard Wittelmann's voice; he seemed to be on the telephone and was yelling something awful.

PROSECUTOR: Did you ever witness an execution while you worked there?

SECOND WOMAN: I know that they took place, and I know where. But I never saw them shoot anyone. I was afraid, and as soon as they brought someone in, I would hide, get out of their way. I was afraid that they might shoot me, too. They killed them against the fence.

PROSECUTOR: Which fence?

SECOND WOMAN: There was a courtyard at the back surrounded by a fence, and behind the fence there was a trench. That's where they were shot. I know, because afterwards the *Ordnungsdienst* would come and collect the bodies. Once I saw them carrying a doctor whom they had killed. His name was Gluck. But that was after the first action, in the spring. Another time I saw a group of Gestapo men walk out into the courtyard and immediately afterwards I heard a burst of machine-gun fire.

PROSECUTOR: Who did you see then?

SECOND WOMAN: Bondke, Rossel, Hamke, and Wittelmann.

PROSECUTOR: All together?

SECOND WOMAN: Yes. All together. I was washing the stairs to the cellar then.

PROSECUTOR: Were they all armed? Did each of them have a weapon?

SECOND WOMAN: Yes.

PROSECUTOR: Those shots you heard then, were they from a single machine gun or from several?

SECOND WOMAN: I don't know. I didn't pay attention. I wasn't thinking that someday someone would ask me about that. Maybe one of them shot, maybe two. Maybe they took turns. How should I know?

PROSECUTOR: When was that?

SECOND WOMAN: That was even before the first action, probably in the fall.

PROSECUTOR: Do you know how many people were shot then? Do you know their names?

SECOND WOMAN: I don't. I didn't see their bodies being taken away. I saw them collect the dead only once or twice. I don't know who was killed then.

PROSECUTOR: And you never saw a Gestapo man fire a gun?

SECOND WOMAN: No. I only worked there until the second action. I couldn't stand it any longer, I preferred to go to a camp. In general they were nice to me and never did anything bad. Once Bondke gave me cigarettes. The best-mannered was Kiper. He was an educated man, like Kuntze. But the others, no. Kiper had a lot of books in his room. He wanted fresh flowers in a vase every day. Once, when I didn't bring flowers, he yelled at me. Once he broke the vase because the flowers were wilted. On the desk in his room was a photograph of an elegant woman with a dog. But it was Hamke who had a dog. I used to prepare food for the dog. His name was Roosevelt. A wolfhound, very well trained. He tore the druggist Weidel's child to pieces. I heard Hamke boasting about him: "*Roosevelt hat heute ein Jüdlein zum Frühstück bekommen*" — Roosevelt had a little Jew for breakfast today. He said that to Kiper, and Kiper screwed up his face in disgust. Kiper couldn't stand Hamke and used to quarrel with Bondke. In general, he kept to himself. He didn't drink. That Sunday he was the first to come back from the marketplace.

PROSECUTOR: How do you know it was Kiper? Did you see him?

SECOND WOMAN: I heard his voice.

PROSECUTOR: Who was he talking to?

SECOND WOMAN: He was talking to himself. I thought he was reciting a poem. Anyway, that's what it sounded like. Then he went to his room and played his violin — I forgot to say that he was a trained musician. Bondke used to make fun of him and call him *Gestapogeiger* — Gestapo-fiddler. I don't know much about music, but I think he played very well. I heard him play several times. Always the same thing. I don't know what melody it was, I don't know much about music.

PROSECUTOR: Did you see him that day?

SECOND WOMAN: No, I only heard him playing.

PROSECUTOR: What time would that have been?

SECOND WOMAN: I don't know. It was growing dark.

PROSECUTOR: Could you hear the shots from the cemetery inside the Gestapo building?

SECOND WOMAN: I don't know. Maybe not. The cemetery is on Male Targi, and the Gestapo headquarters was on St. Jerzy Square. That's quite a distance. But maybe in the silence, in the clear air . . .

PROSECUTOR: Did you hear any shots when Kiper returned?

SECOND WOMAN: I can't say. Because the way I felt that Sunday and for several days afterwards, I was hearing shots all the time, and my parents thought I had lost my mind. I kept saying, "Listen, they're shooting . . . ," and I'd run and hide. Mama took me to Gluck, who gave me a powder, but it didn't help. I kept on hearing shots for a week. It was my nerves.

PROSECUTOR: When did the other Gestapo men come back?

SECOND WOMAN: I don't know. When it got dark, I sneaked out through the courtyard and returned home. The city was empty, as if no one was left

alive. I was astonished: the snow was black. That was the blood. The most
blood was on Sienkiewicza Street, and on Rozana. I didn't meet anyone in
the marketplace either. It was empty. In the center of the square, lying on
its back with its legs in the air, was a small, broken table.   *[1970]*

▤ THINKING ABOUT THE TEXT

1. Is the prosecutor being reasonable when he seeks to know facts about
   the table? In general, how fair is he in his questioning of the witnesses?
   Why do you think Fink decided to focus on a prosecutor as the interro-
   gator, rather than confronting them with the defense attorney for the
   person or persons they are testifying against?

2. What sorts of details do the witnesses recall?

3. How much does the order of the witnesses matter in this play? Would
   the play have the same effect if their testimonies appeared in a different
   order? Why, or why not?

4. This play was originally written for radio, which is evidently the reason
   that Fink does not provide any description of the set. Describe the kind
   of set you would use if you were staging the play in a theater. What props
   and pieces of furniture, if any, would you employ?

5. Fink herself has stated that this play "is a protest against the law which
   tries genocide according to the code intended for trivial crimes." What
   do you think she means? Refer to specific lines in the script.

WLADYSLAW SZPILMAN
The *Umschlagplatz*

Translated by Anthea Bell

*Born in Sosnowiec, Poland, Wladyslaw Szpilman (1911–2000) became one of his
nation's leading pianists and composers, especially celebrated for his performances on
Polish radio. As Jews living in Warsaw, he and his family were forced into the ghetto
of that city during its Nazi occupation. Indeed, his parents and siblings ultimately
perished in the death camps, while he himself was rescued from deportation to them
and managed to hide in Warsaw for the rest of the war. Afterward, Szpilman returned
to his musical career. He also wrote a memoir of his wartime experience,* Death of a
City. *Published in Poland in 1946, it was quickly withdrawn by the country's Communist leaders, who were disturbed by its references to Poles and members of the
Soviet army who helped the Nazi cause. In 1999, the book was republished in Poland
as* The Pianist, *and with the same title it was made into an Oscar-winning film in
2002. In the following chapter from the book, Szpilman recollects a scene similar to
the one recalled by the witnesses in Fink's play. It is set in a big public area of Warsaw
called the* Umschlagplatz, *where the Nazis assembled the city's Jews for shipment to
extinction.*

The *Umschlagplatz* lay on the border of the ghetto. A compound by the railway sidings, it was surrounded by a network of dirty streets, alleys, and pathways. Despite its unprepossessing appearance, it had contained riches before the war. One of the sidings had been the destination of large quantities of goods from all over the world. Jewish businessmen bargained over them, later supplying them to the Warsaw shops from depots in Nalewki Street and Simon Passage. The place was a huge oval, partly surrounded by buildings, partly fenced, with a number of roads running into it like streams into a lake, useful links with the city. The area had been closed off with gates where the streets reached it, and could now contain up to eight thousand people.

When we arrived it was still quite empty. People were walking up and down, searching in vain for water. It was a hot, fine day in late summer. The sky was blue-grey, as if it would turn to ashes in the heat rising from the trodden ground and the dazzling walls of the buildings, and the blazing sun squeezed the last drops of sweat from exhausted bodies.

At the edge of the compound, where one of the streets ran into it, there was an unoccupied space. Everyone was giving this spot a wide berth, never lingering there but casting glances of horror at it. Bodies lay there: the bodies of those killed yesterday for some crime or other, perhaps even for attempting to escape. Among the bodies of men were the corpses of a young woman and two girls with their skulls smashed to pieces. The wall under which the corpses lay showed clear traces of bloodstains and brain tissue. The children had been murdered by a favorite German method: seized by the legs, their heads swung violently against the wall. Large black flies were walking over the dead and the pools of spilt blood on the ground, and the bodies were almost visibly bloating and decaying in the heat.

We had settled down reasonably comfortably, waiting for the train. Mother was sitting on the bundle of our things, Regina was on the ground beside her, I was standing, and Father was walking nervously up and down, his hands behind his back, four steps one way, four steps back. Only now, in the glaring sunlight, when there was no point in worrying about any useless plans to save us any more, did I have time to examine Mother closely. She looked dreadful, although she was apparently fully in control of herself. Her hair, once beautiful and always carefully tended, had hardly any color left in it and was hanging down in strands over her careworn, wrinkled face. The light in her bright black eyes seemed to have gone out, and a nervous twitch ran down from her right temple and over her cheek to the corner of her mouth. I had never noticed it before, and it showed how distressed Mother was by the scene around us. Regina was weeping, with her hands in front of her face, the tears running through her fingers.

At intervals vehicles drove up to the gates of the *Umschlagplatz* and crowds   5
of people destined for resettlement were herded in. These new arrivals did not conceal their despair. The men were talking in raised voices, and women whose children had been taken away from them were wailing and sobbing convulsively. But soon the atmosphere of leaden apathy reigning over the compound began to affect them too. They quietened down, and only occasionally was there a brief outbreak of panic when it entered the head of a passing SS man to

shoot someone who did not get out of his way quickly enough, or whose expression was not sufficiently humble.

A young woman sat on the ground not far away from us. Her dress was torn and her hair disheveled, as if she had been fighting someone. Now, however, she sat there quite calmly, her face like death, her eyes fixed on some point in space. Her fingers spread wide, clutching her throat, and from time to time she asked, with monotonous regularity, "Why did I do it? Why did I do it?"

A young man standing beside her, obviously her husband, was trying to comfort her and convince her of something, speaking softly, but it did not seem to penetrate her mind.

We kept meeting acquaintances among the people driven into the compound. They came over to us, greeted us, and out of sheer habit tried to make some kind of conversation, but it was not long before these conversations broke off. They moved away, preferring to try to master their anxiety alone.

The sun rose higher and higher, blazing down, and we suffered increasing torments of hunger and thirst. We had eaten the last of our bread and soup the evening before. It was difficult to stay put in one place, and I decided to walk about; that might be an improvement.

As more and more people arrived the place became increasingly crowded,   10
and you had to avoid groups of people standing and lying around. They were all discussing the same subject: where we would be taken, and if we were really going to be sent to do labor, as the Jewish police tried to convince everyone.

I saw a group of old people lying down in one part of the compound, men and women probably evacuated from an old people's home. They were dreadfully thin, exhausted by hunger and the heat, and obviously at the very limit of their strength. Some of them were lying there with their eyes closed, and you could not tell if they were already dead or just dying. If we were going to be a labor force, then what were these old people doing here?

Women carrying children dragged themselves from group to group, begging for a drop of water. The Germans had turned off the water supply to the *Umschlagplatz* on purpose. The children's eyes were lifeless, their lids already drooping over them: their little heads nodded on thin necks, and their dry lips were open like the mouths of small fish discarded on the bank by the fishermen.

When I came back to my family they were not alone. A friend of Mother's was sitting beside her, and her husband, once the owner of a large shop, had joined my father and another acquaintance of theirs. The businessman was in quite good spirits. However, their other companion, a dentist who used to practice in Śliska Street not far from our flat, saw everything in very dark hues. He was nervous and bitter.

"It's a disgrace to us all!" he almost screamed. "We're letting them take us to our death like sheep to the slaughter! If we attacked the Germans, half a million of us, we could break out of the ghetto, or at least die honorably, not as a stain on the face of history!"

Father listened. Rather embarrassed, but with a kindly smile, he shrugged   15
his shoulders slightly and asked, "How can you be absolutely certain they're sending us to our death?"

The dentist clasped his hands. "Well, of course I don't know for certain. How could I? Are they about to tell us? But you can be ninety percent sure they plan to wipe us all out!"

Father smiled again, as if he were even more sure of himself after this reply. "Look," he said, indicating the crowd at the *Umschlagplatz*. "We're not heroes! We're perfectly ordinary people, which is why we prefer to risk hoping for that ten percent chance of living."

The businessman agreed with Father. His opinion too was diametrically opposite to the dentist's: the Germans couldn't be so stupid as to squander the huge potential labor force represented by the Jews. He thought we were going to labor camps, perhaps very strictly run labor camps, but surely they would not kill us.

Meanwhile the businessman's wife was telling Mother and Regina how she had left her silverware walled up in the cellar. It was beautiful, valuable silver, and she expected to find it again on her return from deportation.

It was already afternoon when we saw a new group for resettlement being 20 herded into the compound. We were horrified to see Halina and Henryk among them. So they were to share our fate too — and it had been such a comfort to think that at least the two of them would be safe.

I hurried to meet Henryk, certain that his idiotically upright attitude was to blame for bringing him and Halina here. I bombarded him with questions and reproaches before he could get a word of explanation in, but he was not going to deign to answer me anyway. He shrugged his shoulders, took a small Oxford edition of Shakespeare out of his pocket, moved over to one side of us and began to read.

It was Halina who told us what had happened. They heard at work that we had been taken away, and they simply volunteered to go to the *Umschlagplatz* because they wanted to be with us.

What a stupid emotional reaction on their part! I decided to get them away from here at any price. After all, they were not on the list for resettlement. They could stay in Warsaw.

The Jewish policeman who had brought them knew me from the Sztuka café, and I was counting on being able to soften his heart quite easily, particularly as there was no formal reason for the two of them to be here. Unfortunately I had miscalculated: he wouldn't hear of letting them go. Like every policeman, he was duty bound to deliver five people to the *Umschlagplatz* every day personally, on pain of being resettled himself if he did not comply. Halina and Henryk made up today's quota of five. He was tired and had no intention of letting them go and setting out to chase up two more people, God knew where. In his opinion these hunts were not an easy assignment, since people would not come when the police called them but hid instead, and anyway he was sick of the whole thing.

I went back to my family empty-handed. Even this last attempt to save at 25 least a couple of us had failed, like all my earlier attempts. I sat down beside Mother in a very downcast mood.

It was now five in the afternoon, but as hot as ever, and the crowd grew greater with every passing hour. People got lost in the crush and called to one another in vain. We heard the shots and shouting which meant raids were going on in the nearby streets. Agitation grew as the hour approached at which the train was supposed to come.

The woman next to us who kept asking, "Why did I do it?" got on our nerves more than anyone else. We knew what she was talking about by now. Our friend the businessman had found out. When everyone was told to leave their building this woman, her husband, and their child had hidden in a place prepared in advance. As the police were passing it the baby began crying, and in her fear the mother smothered it with her own hands. Unfortunately even that did not help. The baby's crying and then its death rattle were heard, and the hiding place was discovered.

At one point a boy made his way through the crowd in our direction with a box of sweets on a string round his neck. He was selling them at ridiculous prices, although heaven knows what he thought he was going to do with the money. Scraping together the last of our small change, we bought a single cream caramel. Father divided it into six parts with his penknife. That was our last meal together.

Around six o'clock a sense of nervous tension came over the compound. Several German cars had driven up, and the police were inspecting those destined to be taken away, picking out the young and strong. These lucky ones were obviously to be used for other purposes. A crowd of many thousands began pressing that way; people were shouting, trying to drown each other out, get to the front and display their physical advantages. The Germans responded by firing. The dentist, still with our group, could scarcely contain his indignation. He snapped furiously at my father, as if it were all his fault. "So now do you believe me when I say they're going to kill us all? People fit for work will stay here. Death lies that way!"

His voice broke as he tried to shout this above the noise of the crowd and   30
the shooting, pointing the way the transports were to go.

Downcast and grief-stricken, Father did not reply. The businessman shrugged his shoulders and smiled ironically; he was still in good spirits. He did not think the selection of a few hundred people meant anything.

The Germans had finally picked their labor force and now drove off, but the crowd's agitation did not die down. Soon afterwards we heard the whistle of a locomotive in the distance and the sound of trucks rattling over the rails as they came closer. A few more minutes, and the train came into sight: more than a dozen cattle trucks and goods trucks rolling slowly towards us. The evening breeze, blowing in the same direction, wafted a suffocating wave of chlorine our way.

At the same time the cordon of Jewish police and SS men surrounding the compound became denser and began making its way towards its center. Once again we heard shots fired to frighten us. Loud wailing from the women and the sound of children weeping rose from the close-packed crowd.

We got ready to leave. Why wait? The sooner we were in the trucks the better. A line of police was stationed a few paces away from the train, leaving a broad path open for the crowd. The path led to the open doors of the chlorinated trucks.

By the time we had made our way to the train the first trucks were already 35
full. People were standing in them pressed close to each other. SS men were still pushing with their rifle butts, although there were loud cries from inside and complaints about the lack of air. And indeed the smell of chlorine made breathing difficult, even some distance from the trucks. What went on in there if the floors had to be so heavily chlorinated? We had gone about halfway down the train when I suddenly heard someone shout, "Here! Here, Szpilman!" A hand grabbed me by the collar, and I was flung back and out of the police cordon.

Who dared do such a thing? I didn't want to be parted from my family. I wanted to stay with them!

My view was now of the closed ranks of the policemen's backs. I threw myself against them, but they did not give way. Peering past the policemen's heads I could see Mother and Regina, helped by Halina and Henryk, clambering into the trucks, while Father was looking around for me.

"Papa!" I shouted.

He saw me and took a couple of steps my way, but then hesitated and stopped. He was pale, and his lips trembled nervously. He tried to smile, helplessly, painfully, raised his hand and waved goodbye, as if I were setting out into life and he was already greeting me from beyond the grave. Then he turned and went towards the trucks.

I flung myself at the policemen's shoulders again with all my might. 40

"Papa! Henryk! Halina!"

I shouted like someone possessed, terrified to think that now, at the last vital moment, I might not get to them and we would be parted for ever.

One of the policemen turned and looked angrily at me.

"What the hell do you think you're doing? Go on, save yourself!"

Save myself? From what? In a flash I realized what awaited the people in 45
the cattle trucks. My hair stood on end. I glanced behind me. I saw the open compound, the railway lines and platforms, and beyond them the streets. Driven by compulsive animal fear, I ran for the streets, slipped in among a column of Council workers just leaving the place, and got through the gate that way.

When I could think straight again, I was on a pavement among buildings. An SS man came out of one of the houses with a Jewish policeman. The SS man had an impassive, arrogant face; the policeman was positively crawling to him, smiling, dancing attendance. He pointed to the train standing at the *Umschlagplatz* and said to the German, with comradely familiarity and in a sarcastic tone, "Well, off they go for meltdown!"

I looked the way he was pointing. The doors of the trucks had been closed, and the train was starting off, slowly and laboriously.

I turned away and staggered down the empty street, weeping out loud, pursued by the fading cries of the people shut up in those trucks. It sounded like the twittering of caged birds in deadly peril. *[1946]*

■ THINKING ABOUT THE TEXT

1. Imagine Szpilman's being interrogated about this scene by Fink's prosecutor. What would this dialogue be like? Try writing it. How credible do
   you find Szpilman's recollection? Refer to specific details of his account.

2. Should Szpilman have felt guilty that he was rescued from the train
   while his family was not? Why, or why not?

3. The last sentence of this chapter in Szpilman's memoir refers to "the
   twittering of caged birds in deadly peril." To what extent, and in what
   ways, can these words be applied to the roundup described by the witnesses in Fink's play?

DORI LAUB AND SHOSHANA FELMAN
Testimony and Historical Truth

Originally from Czernowitz, Romania, Dori Laub (b. 1937) is a clinical professor of
psychiatry at the Yale University School of Medicine and a private psychoanalyst.
A specialist in psychological trauma, he cofounded the Holocaust Survivors Film
Project in 1979. Eventually, this turned into Yale's Fortunoff Video Archive for Ho-
locaust Testimonies, many of which Laub participated in gathering. The following is
a section from a book he wrote with literary critic Shoshana Felman, Testimony:
Crises of Witnessing in Literature, Psychoanalysis, and History *(1992). He is*
concerned here with the relationship between personal memory and historical truth.

A woman in her late sixties was narrating her Auschwitz experience to interviewers from the Video Archive for Holocaust Testimonies at Yale. She was
slight, self-effacing, almost talking in whispers, mostly to herself. Her presence
was indeed barely noteworthy in spite of the overwhelming magnitude of the
catastrophe she was addressing. She tread lightly, leaving hardly a trace.

She was relating her memories as an eyewitness of the Auschwitz uprising; a sudden intensity, passion, and color were infused into the narrative. She
was fully there. "All of sudden," she said, "we saw four chimneys going up in
flames, exploding. The flames shot into the sky, people were running. It was
unbelievable." There was a silence in the room, a fixed silence against which
the woman's words reverberated loudly, as though carrying along an echo of
the jubilant sounds exploding from behind barbed wires, a stampede of people
breaking loose, screams, shots, battle cries, explosions. It was no longer the
deadly timelessness of Auschwitz. A dazzling, brilliant moment from the past
swept through the frozen stillness of the muted, grave-like landscape with dashing meteoric speed, exploding it into a shower of sights and sounds. Yet the
meteor from the past kept moving on. The woman fell silent and the tumults of
the moment faded. She became subdued again and her voice resumed the un-
eventful, almost monotonous and lamenting tone. The gates of Auschwitz

closed and the veil of obliteration and of silence, at once oppressive and repressive, descended once again. The comet of intensity and of aliveness, the explosion of vitality and of resistance faded and receded into the distance.

Many months later, a conference of historians, psychoanalysts, and artists, gathered to reflect on the relation of education to the Holocaust, watched the videotaped testimony of the woman, in an attempt to better understand the era. A lively debate ensued. The testimony was not accurate, historians claimed. The number of chimneys was misrepresented. Historically, only one chimney was blown up, not all four. Since the memory of the testifying woman turned out to be, in this way, fallible, one could not accept — nor give credence to — her whole account of the events. It was utterly important to remain accurate, lest the revisionists in history discredit everything.

A psychoanalyst who had been one of the interviewers of this woman, profoundly disagreed. "The woman was testifying," he insisted, "not to the number of the chimneys blown up, but to something else, more radical, more crucial: the reality of an unimaginable occurrence. One chimney blown up in Auschwitz was as incredible as four. The number mattered less than the fact of the occurrence. The event itself was almost inconceivable. The woman testified to an event that broke the all-compelling frame of Auschwitz, where Jewish armed revolts just did not happen, and had no place. She testified to the breakage of a framework. That was historical truth."

The psychoanalyst who had interviewed that woman happened to have   5
been myself, and though my attitude vis-à-vis her testimony was different than the attitude of the historians, I had myself the opportunity of encountering — during the very process of the interviewing — questions similar in nature to those that the historians were now raising. And yet I had to deal with those objections and those questions in a different manner.

I figured from the woman's testimony that in Auschwitz she had been a member of what is known as "the Canada commando," a group of inmates chosen to sort out the belongings of those who had been gassed, so that those belongings could be recuperated by the Nazis and sent back to Germany. The testifying woman spoke indeed at length of her work in a commando that would leave each morning, separately from the others, and return every night with various items of clothes and shoes in excellent condition. She emphasized with pride the way in which, upon returning, she would supply these items to her fellow inmates, thus saving the lives of some of them who literally had no shoes to walk in and no clothes to protect them from the frost. She was perking up again as she described these almost breathtaking exploits of rescue. I asked her if she knew of the name of the commando she was serving on. She did not. Does the term "Canada commando" mean anything to her? I followed up. "No," she said, taken aback, as though startled by my question. I asked nothing more about her work. I had probed the limits of her knowledge and decided to back off; to respect, that is, the silence out of which this testimony spoke. We did not talk of the sorting out of the belongings of the dead. She did not think of them as the remainings of the thousands who were gassed. She did not ask herself where they had come from. The presents she brought back to her fellow inmates, the better, newer clothes and shoes, had for her no origin.

My attempt as interviewer and as listener was precisely to respect — not to upset, not to trespass — the subtle balance between what the woman *knew* and what she *did not*, or *could not, know*. It was only at the price of this respect, I felt, this respect of the constraints and of the boundaries of silence, that what the woman *did know* in a way that none of us did — what she came to testify about — could come forth and could receive, indeed, a hearing. The historians' stance, however, differed from my way of listening, in their firm conviction that the limits of the woman's knowledge in effect called into question the validity of her whole testimony.

"Don't you see," one historian passionately exclaimed, "that the woman's eyewitness account of the uprising that took place at Auschwitz is hopelessly misleading in its incompleteness? She had no idea what was going on. She ascribes importance to an attempt that, historically, made no difference. Not only was the revolt put down and all the inmates executed; the Jewish underground was, furthermore, betrayed by the Polish resistance, which had promised to assist in the rebellion, but failed to do so. When the attempt to break out of the camps began, the Jewish inmates found themselves completely alone. No one joined their ranks. They flung themselves into their death, alone and in desperation."

When I interviewed the woman, I knew, of course, that the Auschwitz uprising was put down, but I myself did not know the specific contribution of the Polish underground to the defeat: I did not know of the extent of the betrayal.

Had I known, however, would I have questioned her about it? Probably   10
not, since such questions might have in effect suppressed her message, suppressed what she was there to tell me.

Had I known, moreover, I might have had an agenda of my own that might have interfered with my ability to listen, and to hear. I might have felt driven to confirm my knowledge, by asking questions that could have derailed the testimony, and by proceeding to hear everything she had to say in light of what I knew already. And whether my agenda would have been historical or psychoanalytical, it might unwittingly have interfered with the process of the testimony. In this respect, it might be useful, sometimes, not to know too much.

Of course, it is by no means ignorance that I espouse. The listener must be quite well informed if he is to be able to hear — to be able to pick up the cues. Yet knowledge should not hinder or obstruct the listening with foregone conclusions and preconceived dismissals, should not be an obstacle or a foreclosure to new, diverging, unexpected information.

In the process of the testimony to a trauma, as in psychoanalytic practice, in effect, you often do not want to know anything except what the patient tells you, because what is important is the situation of *discovery* of knowledge — its evolution, and its very *happening*. Knowledge in the testimony is, in other words, not simply a factual given that is reproduced and replicated by the testifier, but a genuine advent, an event in its own right. In a case such as this witness, for example, I had to be particularly careful that what I knew would not affect — would not obstruct, coerce, or overshadow — what she was there to tell me. I had, in fact, to be all the more cautious because this testifying woman did not simply come to convey knowledge that was already safely, and exhaustively, in her possession. On the contrary, it was her very talk to me, the very process of her bearing witness to the trauma she had lived through, that helped her now to come to know of the event. And it was through my listening to her that I in turn came to understand not merely her subjective truth, but the very historicity of the event, in an entirely new dimension.

She was testifying not simply to empirical historical facts, but to the very secret of survival and of resistance to extermination. The historians could not hear, I thought, the way in which her silence was itself part of her testimony, an essential part of the historical truth she was precisely bearing witness to. She saw four chimneys blowing up in Auschwitz: she saw, in other words, the unimaginable taking place right in front of her own eyes. And she came to testify to the unbelievability, precisely, of what she had eyewitnessed — this bursting open of the very frame of Auschwitz. The historians' testifying to the fact that only one chimney was blown up in Auschwitz, as well as to the fact of the betrayal of the Polish underground, does not break the frame. The woman's testimony, on the other hand, is breaking the frame of the concentration camp by and through her very testimony: she is breaking out of Auschwitz even by her very talking. She had come, indeed, to testify, not to the empirical number of the chimneys, but to resistance, to the affirmation of survival, to the breakage of the frame of death; in the same way, she had come to testify not to betrayal, nor to her actual removal of the belongings of the dead, but to her vital memory of helping people, to her effective rescuing of lives. This was her way of being, of surviving, of resisting. It is not merely her speech, but the very boundaries of silence which surround it, which attest, today as well as in the past, to this assertion of resistance.

There is thus a subtle dialectic between what the survivor did not know   15
and what she knew; between what I as interviewer did not know and what I knew; between what the historians knew and what they did not know. Because the testifier did not know the number of the chimneys that blew up; because she did not know of the betrayal of the Polish underground and of the violent and desperate defeat of the rebellion of the Auschwitz inmates, the historians said that she knew nothing. I thought that she knew more, since she knew about the breakage of the frame, that her very testimony was now reenacting.   *[1992]*

≡ THINKING ABOUT THE TEXT

1. In part, Laub writes about what it means to be a "good" listener for a Holocaust survivor. Would Fink's prosecutor meet Laub's standards? Why, or why not?

2. How might the responsibility of a prosecutor or judge listening to a Holocaust survivor differ from that of a psychoanalyst? Refer to details of both Fink's play and Laub's text.

3. Do any of the witnesses in Fink's play seem to go through the "breakage of the frame" that Laub refers to? Explain.

▤ WRITING ABOUT ISSUES

1. Write an essay in which you explain what must happen in the trial depicted by Fink if justice is to be done. In particular, discuss the relationship of the witnesses' testimonies to the issue of justice, making sure to be clear about what you mean by *justice* in this case.

2. Write an essay in which you compare the reliability of a witness in Fink's play with that of Wladyslaw Szpilman or the woman discussed by Laub. Do these two people seem equally reliable, or do you find yourself accepting the testimony of one more than that of the other?

3. Write an essay about a time when *your* testimony about an event was challenged. What did you do to make your account more persuasive?

4. Write an essay that you imagine will be included in the program for a production of *The Table* on your campus. More specifically, your essay is to create a context for Fink's play by relating it to at least one of the other texts in this cluster *and* to at least one recent event or trend.

Misfit Justice: Critical Commentaries on a Story

FLANNERY O'CONNOR, "A Good Man Is Hard to Find"

CRITICAL COMMENTARIES:

FLANNERY O'CONNOR, From *Mystery and Manners*

MARTHA STEPHENS, From *The Question of Flannery O'Connor*

STEPHEN BANDY, From " 'One of My Babies': The Misfit and the Grandmother"

JOHN DESMOND, From "Flannery O'Connor's Misfit and the Mystery of Evil"

Most of us are social beings; we long to fit in. The communities we form sustain us, giving us our moral compasses and our psychological bearings. But sometimes people voluntarily remove themselves from all traditional communities. Indeed, literature is filled with misfits. Their decisions may intrigue us but also perplex and trouble us, perhaps because they represent antisocial impulses in all of us. Especially interesting are those literary misfits who demand that their own sense of justice be satisfied. Probably the most notable example in post–World War II American fiction is a character in Flannery O'Connor's 1953 short story "A Good Man Is Hard to Find." This man actually calls himself The Misfit, and he turns violent as he challenges Christianity's belief in Jesus' ability to raise the dead. O'Connor's story has been widely read, in part because it is subject to various interpretations. Here, in addition to the story and O'Connor's own remarks about it, we present three critical commentaries that respond to her analysis.

■ BEFORE YOU READ

What do you think you might find in a story by a practicing Roman Catholic author? What topics, themes, characters, and events might she write about?

FLANNERY O'CONNOR

A Good Man Is Hard to Find

Flannery O'Connor (1925–1964) spent most of her life in Millidgeville, Georgia, where she raised peacocks on a farm with her mother. She died of lupus at the age of thirty-nine, when she was at the peak of her creative powers. All of her fiction reflects her Roman Catholic faith and Southern heritage, as do her nonfiction writings, which were collected after her death in Mystery and Manners *(1969). Critics have often seen in her work Christian parables of grace and redemption in the face of random violence. Like other Southern writers such as William Faulkner and Carson McCullers, she uses grotesque characters to suggest our own morally flawed humanity. O'Connor's*

(Flannery O'Connor
Collection. Ina Dillard
Russell Library. Georgia
College and State
University.)

early stories won her a scholarship to the University of Iowa, where she received an
M.F.A. She went on to produce two novels, Wise Blood *(1952) and* The Violent
Bear It Away *(1960), but she is known and admired mostly for her short fiction. The*
following story was first published in the volume Modern Writing 1 *in 1953.*
O'Connor then included it in her 1955 collection entitled A Good Man Is Hard to
Find and Other Stories. *The book won her national acclaim, as did a later collection,*
the posthumously published Everything That Rises Must Converge *(1965). These*
two volumes were combined in 1979 as The Complete Stories of Flannery
O'Connor, *which won the National Book Award for fiction.*

> The dragon is by the side of the road, watching those who pass. Beware
> lest he devour you. We go to the Father of Souls, but it is necessary to pass
> by the dragon.
> — St. Cyril of Jerusalem

The grandmother didn't want to go to Florida. She wanted to visit some of her
connections in east Tennessee and she was seizing at every chance to change
Bailey's mind. Bailey was the son she lived with, her only boy. He was sitting on
the edge of his chair at the table, bent over the orange sports section of the

Journal. "Now look here, Bailey," she said, "see here, read this," and she stood with one hand on her thin hip and the other rattling the newspaper at his bald head. "Here this fellow that calls himself The Misfit is aloose from the Federal Pen and headed toward Florida and you read here what it says he did to these people. Just you read it. I wouldn't take my children in any direction with a criminal like that aloose in it. I couldn't answer to my conscience if I did."

Bailey didn't look up from his reading so she wheeled around then and faced the children's mother, a young woman in slacks, whose face was as broad and innocent as a cabbage and was tied around with a green head-kerchief that had two points on the top like rabbit's ears. She was sitting on the sofa, feeding the baby his apricots out of a jar. "The children have been to Florida before," the old lady said. "You all ought to take them somewhere else for a change so they would see different parts of the world and be broad. They never have been to east Tennessee."

The children's mother didn't seem to hear her but the eight-year-old boy, John Wesley, a stocky child with glasses, said, "If you don't want to go to Florida, why dontcha stay at home?" He and the little girl, June Star, were reading the funny papers on the floor.

"She wouldn't stay at home to be queen for a day," June Star said without raising her yellow head.

"Yes and what would you do if this fellow, The Misfit, caught you?" the grandmother asked.   5

"I'd smack his face," John Wesley said.

"She wouldn't stay at home for a million bucks," June Star said. "Afraid she'd miss something. She has to go everywhere we go."

"All right, Miss," the grandmother said. "Just remember that the next time you want me to curl your hair."

June Star said her hair was naturally curly.

The next morning the grandmother was the first one in the car, ready to go. She had her big black valise that looked like the head of a hippopotamus in one corner, and underneath it she was hiding a basket with Pitty Sing, the cat, in it. She didn't intend for the cat to be left alone in the house for three days because he would miss her too much and she was afraid he might brush against one of the gas burners and accidentally asphyxiate himself. Her son, Bailey, didn't like to arrive at a motel with a cat.   10

She sat in the middle of the back seat with John Wesley and June Star on either side of her. Bailey and the children's mother and the baby sat in front and they left Atlanta at eight forty-five with the mileage on the car at 55890. The grandmother wrote this down because she thought it would be interesting to say how many miles they had been when they got back. It took them twenty minutes to reach the outskirts of the city.

The old lady settled herself comfortably, removing her white cotton gloves and putting them up with her purse on the shelf in front of the back window. The children's mother still had on slacks and still had her head tied up in a green kerchief, but the grandmother had on a navy blue straw sailor hat with a bunch of white violets on the brim and a navy blue dress with a small white dot in the print. Her collars and cuffs were white organdy trimmed with lace and at her neckline she had pinned a purple spray of cloth violets containing a sachet. In case of an accident, anyone seeing her dead on the highway would know at once that she was a lady.

She said she thought it was going to be a good day for driving, neither too hot nor too cold, and she cautioned Bailey that the speed limit was fifty-five miles an hour and that the patrolmen hid themselves behind billboards and small clumps of trees and sped out after you before you had a chance to slow down. She pointed out interesting details of the scenery: Stone Mountain; the blue granite that in some places came up to both sides of the highway; the brilliant red clay banks slightly streaked with purple; and the various crops that made rows of green lace-work on the ground. The trees were full of silver-white sunlight and the meanest of them sparkled. The children were reading comic magazines and their mother had gone back to sleep.

"Let's go through Georgia fast so we won't have to look at it much," John Wesley said.

"If I were a little boy," said the grandmother, "I wouldn't talk about my   15
native state that way. Tennessee has the mountains and Georgia has the hills."

"Tennessee is just a hillbilly dumping ground," John Wesley said, "and Georgia is a lousy state too."

"You said it," June Star said.

"In my time," said the grandmother, folding her thin veined fingers, "children were more respectful of their native states and their parents and everything else. People did right then. Oh look at the cute little pickaninny!" she said and pointed to a Negro child standing in the door of a shack. "Wouldn't that make a picture, now?" she asked and they all turned and looked at the little Negro out of the back window. He waved.

"He didn't have any britches on," June Star said.

"He probably didn't have any," the grandmother explained. "Little niggers   20
in the country don't have things like we do. If I could paint, I'd paint that picture," she said.

The children exchanged comic books.

The grandmother offered to hold the baby and the children's mother passed him over the front seat to her. She set him on her knee and bounced him and told him about the things they were passing. She rolled her eyes and screwed up her mouth and stuck her leathery thin face into his smooth bland one. Occasionally he gave her a faraway smile. They passed a large cotton field with five or six graves fenced in the middle of it, like a small island. "Look at the graveyard!" the grandmother said, pointing it out. "That was the old family burying ground. That belonged to the plantation."

"Where's the plantation?" John Wesley asked.

"Gone with the Wind," said the grandmother. "Ha. Ha."

When the children finished all the comic books they had brought, they   25
opened the lunch and ate it. The grandmother ate a peanut butter sandwich and an olive and would not let the children throw the box and the paper napkins out the window. When there was nothing else to do they played a game by

choosing a cloud and making the other two guess what shape it suggested. John Wesley took one the shape of a cow and June Star guessed a cow and John Wesley said, no, an automobile, and June Star said he didn't play fair, and they began to slap each other over the grandmother.

The grandmother said she would tell them a story if they would keep quiet. When she told a story, she rolled her eyes and waved her head and was very dramatic. She said once when she was a maiden lady she had been courted by a Mr. Edgar Atkins Teagarden from Jasper, Georgia. She said he was a very good-looking man and a gentleman and that he brought her a watermelon every Saturday afternoon with his initials cut in it, E. A. T. Well, one Saturday, she said, Mr. Teagarden brought the watermelon and there was nobody at home and he left it on the front porch and returned in his buggy to Jasper, but she never got the watermelon, she said, because a nigger boy ate it when he saw the initials, E. A. T.! This story tickled John Wesley's funny bone and he giggled and giggled but June Star didn't think it was any good. She said she wouldn't marry a man that just brought her a watermelon on Saturday. The grandmother said she would have done well to marry Mr. Teagarden because he was a gentleman and had bought Coca-Cola stock when it first came out and that he had died only a few years ago, a very wealthy man.

They stopped at The Tower for barbecued sandwiches. The Tower was a part stucco and part wood filling station and dance hall set in a clearing outside of Timothy. A fat man named Red Sammy Butts ran it and there were signs stuck here and there on the building and for miles up and down the highway saying, TRY RED SAMMY'S FAMOUS BARBECUE. NONE LIKE FAMOUS RED SAMMY'S! RED SAM! THE FAT BOY WITH THE HAPPY LAUGH. A VETERAN! RED SAMMY'S YOUR MAN!

Red Sammy was lying on the bare ground outside The Tower with his head under a truck while a gray monkey about a foot high, chained to a small chinaberry tree, chattered nearby. The monkey sprang back into the tree and got on the highest limb as soon as he saw the children jump out of the car and run toward him.

Inside, The Tower was a long dark room with a counter at one end and tables at the other and dancing space in the middle. They all sat down at a board table next to the nickelodeon and Red Sam's wife, a tall burnt-brown woman with hair and eyes lighter than her skin, came and took their order. The children's mother put a dime in the machine and played "The Tennessee Waltz," and the grandmother said that tune always made her want to dance. She asked Bailey if he would like to dance but he only glared at her. He didn't have a naturally sunny disposition like she did and trips made him nervous. The grandmother's brown eyes were very bright. She swayed her head from side to side and pretended she was dancing in her chair. June Star said play something she could tap to so the children's mother put in another dime and played a fast number and June Star stepped out onto the dance floor and did her tap routine.

"Ain't she cute?" Red Sam's wife said, leaning over the counter. "Would you like to come be my little girl?"   30

"No I certainly wouldn't," June Star said. "I wouldn't live in a broken-down place like this for a million bucks!" and she ran back to the table.

"Ain't she cute?" the woman repeated, stretching her mouth politely.

"Aren't you ashamed?" hissed the grandmother.

Red Sam came in and told his wife to quit lounging on the counter and hurry up with these people's order. His khaki trousers reached just to his hip bones and his stomach hung over them like a sack of meal swaying under his shirt. He came over and sat down at a table nearby and let out a combination sigh and yodel. "You can't win," he said. "You can't win," and he wiped his sweating red face off with a gray handkerchief. "These days you don't know who to trust," he said. "Ain't that the truth?"

"People are certainly not nice like they used to be," said the grandmother.   35

"Two fellers come in here last week," Red Sammy said, "driving a Chrysler. It was a old beat-up car but it was a good one and these boys looked all right to me. Said they worked at the mill and you know I let them fellers charge the gas they bought? Now why did I do that?"

"Because you're a good man!" the grandmother said at once.

"Yes'm, I suppose so," Red Sam said as if he were struck with this answer.

His wife brought the orders, carrying the five plates all at once without a tray, two in each hand and one balanced on her arm. "It isn't a soul in this green world of God's that you can trust," she said. "And I don't count nobody out of that, not nobody," she repeated, looking at Red Sammy.

"Did you read about that criminal, The Misfit, that's escaped?" asked the   40
grandmother.

"I wouldn't be a bit surprised if he didn't attack this place right here," said the woman. "If he hears about it being here, I wouldn't be none surprised to see him. If he hears it's two cent in the cash register, I wouldn't be a tall surprised if he . . ."

"That'll do," Red Sam said. "Go bring these people their Co'-Colas," and the woman went off to get the rest of the order.

"A good man is hard to find," Red Sammy said. "Everything is getting terrible. I remember the day you could go off and leave your screen door unlatched. Not no more."

He and the grandmother discussed better times. The old lady said that in her opinion Europe was entirely to blame for the way things were now. She said the way Europe acted you would think we were made of money and Red Sam said it was no use talking about it, she was exactly right. The children ran outside into the white sunlight and looked at the monkey in the lacy chinaberry tree. He was busy catching fleas on himself and biting each one carefully between his teeth as if it were a delicacy.

They drove off again into the hot afternoon. The grandmother took cat   45
naps and woke up every few minutes with her own snoring. Outside of Toombsboro she woke up and recalled an old plantation that she had visited in this neighborhood once when she was a young lady. She said the house had six white columns across the front and that there was an avenue of oaks leading up to it and two little wooden trellis arbors on either side in front where you sat

down with your suitor after a stroll in the garden. She recalled exactly which road to turn off to get to it. She knew that Bailey would not be willing to lose any time looking at an old house, but the more she talked about it, the more she wanted to see it once again and find out if the little twin arbors were still standing. "There was a secret panel in this house," she said craftily, not telling the truth but wishing that she were, "and the story went that all the family silver was hidden in it when Sherman came through but it was never found . . ."

"Hey!" John Wesley said. "Let's go see it! We'll find it! We'll poke all the woodwork and find it! Who lives there? Where do you turn off at? Hey Pop, can't we turn off there?"

"We never have seen a house with a secret panel!" June Star shrieked. "Let's go to the house with the secret panel! Hey Pop, can't we go see the house with the secret panel!"

"It's not far from here, I know," the grandmother said. "It wouldn't take over twenty minutes."

Bailey was looking straight ahead. His jaw was as rigid as a horseshoe. "No," he said.

The children began to yell and scream that they wanted to see the house   50 with the secret panel. John Wesley kicked the back of the front seat and June Star hung over her mother's shoulder and whined desperately into her ear that they never had any fun even on their vacation, that they could never do what THEY wanted to do. The baby began to scream and John Wesley kicked the back of the seat so hard that his father could feel the blows in his kidney.

"All right!" he shouted and drew the car to a stop at the side of the road. "Will you all shut up? Will you all just shut up for one second? If you don't shut up, we won't go anywhere."

"It would be very educational for them," the grandmother murmured.

"All right," Bailey said, "but get this: this is the only time we're going to stop for anything like this. This is the one and only time."

"The dirt road that you have to turn down is about a mile back," the grandmother directed. "I marked it when we passed."

"A dirt road," Bailey groaned.   55

After they had turned around and were headed toward the dirt road, the grandmother recalled other points about the house, the beautiful glass over the front doorway and the candle-lamp in the hall. John Wesley said that the secret panel was probably in the fireplace.

"You can't go inside this house," Bailey said. "You don't know who lives there."

"While you all talk to the people in front, I'll run around behind and get in a window," John Wesley suggested.

"We'll all stay in the car," his mother said.

They turned onto the dirt road and the car raced roughly along in a swirl   60 of pink dust. The grandmother recalled the times when there were no paved roads and thirty miles was a day's journey. The dirt road was hilly and there were sudden washes in it and sharp curves on dangerous embankments. All at once they would be on a hill, looking down over the blue tops of trees for miles around, then the next minute, they would be in a red depression with the dust-coated trees looking down on them.

"This place had better turn up in a minute," Bailey said, "or I'm going to turn around."

The road looked as if no one had traveled on it in months.

"It's not much farther," the grandmother said and just as she said it, a horrible thought came to her. The thought was so embarrassing that she turned red in the face and her eyes dilated and her feet jumped up, upsetting her valise in the corner. The instant the valise moved, the newspaper top she had over the basket under it rose with a snarl and Pitty Sing, the cat, sprang onto Bailey's shoulder.

The children were thrown to the floor and their mother, clutching the baby, was thrown out the door onto the ground; the old lady was thrown into the front seat. The car turned over once and landed right-side-up in a gulch off the side of the road. Bailey remained in the driver's seat with the cat — gray-striped with a broad white face and an orange nose — clinging to his neck like a caterpillar.

As soon as the children saw they could move their arms and legs, they scrambled out of the car, shouting, "We've had an ACCIDENT!" The grandmother was curled up under the dashboard, hoping she was injured so that Bailey's wrath would not come down on her all at once. The horrible thought she had had before the accident was that the house she had remembered so vividly was not in Georgia but in Tennessee.

Bailey removed the cat from his neck with both hands and flung it out the window against the side of a pine tree. Then he got out of the car and started looking for the children's mother. She was sitting against the side of the red gutted ditch, holding the screaming baby, but she only had a cut down her face and a broken shoulder. "We've had an ACCIDENT!" the children screamed in a frenzy of delight.

"But nobody's killed," June Star said with disappointment as the grandmother limped out of the car, her hat still pinned to her head but the broken front brim standing up at a jaunty angle and the violet spray hanging off the side. They all sat down in the ditch, except the children, to recover from the shock. They were all shaking.

"Maybe a car will come along," said the children's mother hoarsely.

"I believe I have injured an organ," said the grandmother, pressing her side, but no one answered her. Bailey's teeth were clattering. He had on a yellow sport shirt with bright blue parrots designed in it and his face was as yellow as the shirt. The grandmother decided that she would not mention that the house was in Tennessee.

The road was about ten feet above and they could only see the tops of the trees on the other side of it. Behind the ditch they were sitting in there were more woods, tall and dark and deep. In a few minutes they saw a car some distance away on top of a hill, coming slowly as if the occupants were watching them. The grandmother stood up and waved both arms dramatically to attract their attention. The car continued to come on slowly, disappeared around

65

70

a bend and appeared again, moving even slower, on top of the hill they had gone over. It was a big black battered hearse-like automobile. There were three men in it.

It came to a stop just over them and for some minutes, the driver looked down with a steady expressionless gaze to where they were sitting, and didn't speak. Then he turned his head and muttered something to the other two and they got out. One was a fat boy in black trousers and a red sweat shirt with a silver stallion embossed on the front of it. He moved around on the right side of them and stood staring, his mouth partly open in a kind of loose grin. The other had on khaki pants and a blue striped coat and a gray hat pulled very low, hiding most of his face. He came around slowly on the left side. Neither spoke.

The driver got out of the car and stood by the side of it, looking down at them. He was an older man than the other two. His hair was just beginning to gray and he wore silver-rimmed spectacles that gave him a scholarly look. He had a long creased face and didn't have on any shirt or undershirt. He had on blue jeans that were too tight for him and was holding a black hat and a gun. The two boys also had guns.

"We've had an ACCIDENT!" the children screamed.

The grandmother had the peculiar feeling that the bespectacled man was someone she knew. His face was as familiar to her as if she had known him all her life but she could not recall who he was. He moved away from the car and began to come down the embankment, placing his feet carefully so that he wouldn't slip. He had on tan and white shoes and no socks, and his ankles were red and thin. "Good afternoon," he said. "I see you all had you a little spill."

"We turned over twice!" said the grandmother.   75

"Oncet," he corrected. "We seen it happen. Try their car and see will it run, Hiram," he said quietly to the boy with the gray hat.

"What you got that gun for?" John Wesley asked. "Whatcha gonna do with that gun?"

"Lady," the man said to the children's mother, "would you mind calling them children to sit down by you? Children make me nervous. I want all you all to sit down right together there where you're at."

"What are you telling US what to do for?" June Star asked.

Behind them the line of woods gaped like a dark open mouth. "Come here,"   80
said the mother.

"Look here now," Bailey began suddenly, "we're in a predicament! We're in . . ."

The grandmother shrieked. She scrambled to her feet and stood staring. "You're The Misfit!" she said. "I recognized you at once!"

"Yes'm," the man said, smiling slightly as if he were pleased in spite of himself to be known, "but it would have been better for all of you, lady, if you hadn't of reckernized me."

Bailey turned his head sharply and said something to his mother that shocked even the children. The old lady began to cry and The Misfit reddened.

"Lady," he said, "don't you get upset. Sometimes a man says things he   85
don't mean. I don't reckon he meant to talk to you thataway."

"You wouldn't shoot a lady, would you?" the grandmother said and removed a clean handkerchief from her cuff and began to slap at her eyes with it.

The Misfit pointed the toe of his shoe into the ground and made a little hole and then covered it up again. "I would hate to have to," he said.

"Listen," the grandmother almost screamed, "I know you're a good man. You don't look a bit like you have common blood. I know you must come from nice people!"

"Yes mam," he said, "finest people in the world." When he smiled he showed a row of strong white teeth. "God never made a finer woman than my mother and my daddy's heart was pure gold," he said. The boy with the red sweat shirt had come around behind them and was standing with his gun at his hip. The Misfit squatted down on the ground. "Watch them children, Bobby Lee," he said. "You know they make me nervous." He looked at the six of them huddled together in front of him and he seemed to be embarrassed as if he couldn't think of anything to say. "Ain't a cloud in the sky," he remarked, looking up at it. "Don't see no sun but don't see no cloud neither."

"Yes, it's a beautiful day," said the grandmother. "Listen," she said, "you   90
shouldn't call yourself The Misfit because I know you're a good man at heart. I can just look at you and tell."

"Hush!" Bailey yelled. "Hush! Everybody shut up and let me handle this!" He was squatting in the position of a runner about to sprint forward but he didn't move.

"I pre-chate that, lady," The Misfit said and drew a little circle in the ground with the butt of his gun.

"It'll take a half a hour to fix this here car," Hiram called, looking over the raised hood of it.

"Well, first you and Bobby Lee get him and that little boy to step over yonder with you," The Misfit said, pointing to Bailey and John Wesley. "The boys want to ast you something," he said to Bailey. "Would you mind stepping back in them woods there with them?"

"Listen," Bailey began, "we're in a terrible predicament! Nobody realizes   95
what this is," and his voice cracked. His eyes were as blue and intense as the parrots in his shirt and he remained perfectly still.

The grandmother reached up to adjust her hat brim as if she were going to the woods with him but it came off in her hand. She stood staring at it and after a second she let it fall on the ground. Hiram pulled Bailey up by the arm as if he were assisting an old man. John Wesley caught hold of his father's hand and Bobby Lee followed. They went off toward the woods and just as they reached the dark edge, Bailey turned and supporting himself against a gray naked pine trunk, he shouted, "I'll be back in a minute, Mamma, wait on me!"

"Come back this instant!" his mother shrilled but they all disappeared into the woods.

"Bailey Boy!" the grandmother called in a tragic voice but she found she was looking at The Misfit squatting on the ground in front of her. "I just know you're a good man," she said desperately. "You're not a bit common!"

"Nome, I ain't a good man," The Misfit said after a second as if he had considered her statement carefully, "but I ain't the worst in the world neither. My daddy said I was a different breed of dog from my brothers and sisters. 'You know,' Daddy said, 'it's some that can live their whole life out without asking about it and it's others has to know why it is, and this boy is one of the latters. He's going to be into everything!' " He put on his black hat and looked up suddenly and then away deep into the woods as if he were embarrassed again. "I'm sorry I don't have on a shirt before you ladies," he said, hunching his shoulders slightly. "We buried our clothes that we had on when we escaped and we're just making do until we can get better. We borrowed these from some folks we met," he explained.

"That's perfectly all right," the grandmother said. "Maybe Bailey has an 100
extra shirt in his suitcase."

"I'll look and see terrectly," The Misfit said.

"Where are they taking him?" the children's mother screamed.

"Daddy was a card himself," The Misfit said. "You couldn't put anything over on him. He never got in trouble with the Authorities though. Just had the knack of handling them."

"You could be honest too if you'd only try," said the grandmother. "Think how wonderful it would be to settle down and live a comfortable life and not have to think about somebody chasing you all the time."

The Misfit kept scratching in the ground with the butt of his gun as if he 105
were thinking about it. "Yes'm, somebody is always after you," he murmured.

The grandmother noticed how thin his shoulder blades were just behind his hat because she was standing up looking down at him. "Do you ever pray?" she asked.

He shook his head. All she saw was the black hat wiggle between his shoulder blades. "Nome," he said.

There was a pistol shot from the woods, followed closely by another. Then silence. The old lady's head jerked around. She could hear the wind move through the tree tops like a long satisfied insuck of breath. "Bailey Boy!" she called.

"I was a gospel singer for a while," The Misfit said. "I been most everything. Been in the arm service, both land and sea, at home and abroad, been twict married, been an undertaker, been with the railroads, plowed Mother Earth, been in a tornado, seen a man burnt alive oncet," and he looked up at the children's mother and the little girl who were sitting close together, their faces white and their eyes glassy; "I even seen a woman flogged," he said.

"Pray, pray," the grandmother began, "pray, pray . . ." 110

"I never was a bad boy that I remember of," The Misfit said in an almost dreamy voice, "but somewheres along the line I done something wrong and got sent to the penitentiary. I was buried alive," and he looked up and held her attention to him by a steady stare.

"That's when you should have started to pray," she said. "What did you do to get sent to the penitentiary, that first time?"

"Turn to the right, it was a wall," The Misfit said, looking up again at the cloudless sky. "Turn to the left, it was a wall. Look up it was a ceiling, look down it was a floor. I forgot what I done, lady. I set there and set there, trying to remember what it was I done and I ain't recalled it to this day. Oncet in a while, I would think it was coming to me, but it never come."

"Maybe they put you in by mistake," the old lady said vaguely.

"Nome," he said. "It wasn't no mistake. They had the papers on me."   115

"You must have stolen something," she said.

The Misfit sneered slightly. "Nobody had nothing I wanted," he said. "It was a head-doctor at the penitentiary said what I had done was kill my daddy but I known that for a lie. My daddy died in nineteen ought nineteen of the epidemic flu and I never had a thing to do with it. He was buried in the Mount Hopewell Baptist churchyard and you can go there and see for yourself."

"If you would pray," the old lady said, "Jesus would help you."

"That's right," The Misfit said.

"Well then, why don't you pray?" she asked trembling with delight   120 suddenly.

"I don't want no hep," he said. "I'm doing all right by myself."

Bobby Lee and Hiram came ambling back from the woods. Bobby Lee was dragging a yellow shirt with bright blue parrots in it.

"Thow me that shirt, Bobby Lee," The Misfit said. The shirt came flying at him and landed on his shoulder and he put it on. The grandmother couldn't name what the shirt reminded her of. "No, lady," The Misfit said while he was buttoning it up, "I found out the crime don't matter. You can do one thing or you can do another, kill a man or take a tire off his car, because sooner or later you're going to forget what it was you done and just be punished for it."

The children's mother had begun to make heaving noises as if she couldn't get her breath. "Lady," he asked, "would you and that little girl like to step off yonder with Bobby Lee and Hiram and join your husband?"

"Yes, thank you," the mother said faintly. Her left arm dangled helplessly   125 and she was holding the baby, who had gone to sleep, in the other. "Hep that lady up, Hiram," The Misfit said as she struggled to climb out of the ditch, "and Bobby Lee, you hold onto that little girl's hand."

"I don't want to hold hands with him," June Star said. "He reminds me of a pig."

The fat boy blushed and laughed and caught her by the arm and pulled her off into the woods after Hiram and her mother.

Alone with The Misfit, the grandmother found that she had lost her voice. There was not a cloud in the sky nor any sun. There was nothing around her but woods. She wanted to tell him that he must pray. She opened and closed her mouth several times before anything came out. Finally she found herself saying, "Jesus. Jesus," meaning, Jesus will help you, but the way she was saying it, it sounded as if she might be cursing.

"Yes'm," The Misfit said as if he agreed. "Jesus thown everything off balance. It was the same case with Him as with me except He hadn't committed any crime and they could prove I had committed one because they had the papers on me. Of course," he said, "they never shown me my papers. That's why I sign myself now. I said long ago, you get you a signature and sign everything you do and keep a copy of it. Then you'll know what you done and you can hold up the crime to the punishment and see do they match and in the end you'll have something to prove you ain't been treated right. I call myself The Misfit," he said, "because I can't make what all I done wrong fit what all I gone through in punishment."

There was a piercing scream from the woods, followed closely by a pistol report. "Does it seem right to you, lady, that one is punished a heap and another ain't punished at all?"   130

"Jesus!" the old lady cried. "You've got good blood! I know you wouldn't shoot a lady! I know you come from nice people! Pray! Jesus, you ought not to shoot a lady. I'll give you all the money I've got!"

"Lady," The Misfit said, looking beyond her far into the woods, "there never was a body that give the undertaker a tip."

There were two more pistol reports and the grandmother raised her head like a parched old turkey hen crying for water and called, "Bailey Boy, Bailey Boy!" as if her heart would break.

"Jesus was the only One that ever raised the dead," The Misfit continued, "and He shouldn't have done it. He thown everything off balance. If He did what He said, then it's nothing for you to do but thow away everything and follow Him, and if He didn't, then it's nothing for you to do but enjoy the few minutes you got left the best you can — by killing somebody or burning down his house or doing some other meanness to him. No pleasure but meanness," he said and his voice had become almost a snarl.

"Maybe He didn't raise the dead," the old lady mumbled, not knowing what she was saying and feeling so dizzy that she sank down in the ditch with her legs twisted under her.   135

"I wasn't there so I can't say He didn't," The Misfit said. "I wisht I had of been there," he said, hitting the ground with his fist. "It ain't right I wasn't there because if I had of been there I would of known. Listen lady," he said in a high voice, "if I had of been there I would of known and I wouldn't be like I am now." His voice seemed about to crack and the grandmother's head cleared for an instant. She saw the man's face twisted close to her own as if he were going to cry and she murmured, "Why you're one of my babies. You're one of my own children!" She reached out and touched him on the shoulder. The Misfit sprang back as if a snake had bitten him and shot her three times through the chest. Then he put his gun down on the ground and took off his glasses and began to clean them.

Hiram and Bobby Lee returned from the woods and stood over the ditch, looking down at the grandmother who half sat and half lay in a puddle of blood with her legs crossed under her like a child's and her face smiling up at the cloudless sky.

Without his glasses, The Misfit's eyes were red-rimmed and pale and defenseless-looking. "Take her off and thow her where you thown the others," he said, picking up the cat that was rubbing itself against his leg.

"She was a talker, wasn't she?" Bobby Lee said, sliding down the ditch with a yodel.

"She would of been a good woman," The Misfit said, "if it had been some-   140
body there to shoot her every minute of her life."

"Some fun!" Bobby Lee said.

"Shut up, Bobby Lee," The Misfit said. "It's no real pleasure in life."

[1955]

▦ THINKING ABOUT THE TEXT

1. Although this story begins with comedy, ultimately it shocks many readers. Did it shock you? Why, or why not? What would you say to someone who argues that the shift in tone is a flaw in the story?

2. Note places where the word *good* comes up in this story. How is it defined? Do the definitions change? Do you think the author has in mind a definition that does not occur to the characters? If so, what might that definition be?

3. What in his life history is The Misfit unsure about? Why do you think he is hazy about these matters? Should O'Connor have resolved for us all the issues of fact that bother him? Why, or why not?

4. Does The Misfit have any redeeming qualities? Does the grandmother? Explain. What do you think the grandmother means when she murmurs, "Why you're one of my babies. You're one of my own children!" (para. 136)? Why do you think The Misfit responds as he does?

5. There is much talk about Jesus and Christianity in this story. Should O'Connor have done more to help non-Christian readers see the story as relevant to them? Explain your reasoning.

FLANNERY O'CONNOR
From *Mystery and Manners*

For public presentations at colleges and other places, Flannery O'Connor often chose to read and comment on "A Good Man Is Hard to Find." The following remarks come from her introduction to the story when she read it at Hollins College in Virginia in 1963. After her death, the introduction was published as "On Her Own Work" in Mystery and Manners, *a 1969 collection of O'Connor's nonfiction pieces. Her comments on "A Good Man Is Hard to Find" encourage a religious analysis of it. How helpful, though, is her own interpretation? Many critics who have subsequently written about the story have raised and addressed this issue.*

It is true that the old lady is a hypocritical old soul; her wits are no match for the Misfit's, nor is her capacity for grace equal to his; yet I think the unprejudiced reader will feel that the Grandmother has a special kind of triumph in this story which instinctively we do not allow to someone altogether bad.

I often ask myself what makes a story work and what makes it hold up as a story, and I have decided that it is probably some action, some gesture of a character that is unlike any other in the story, one which indicates where the real heart of the story lies. This would have to be an action or a gesture which was both totally right and totally unexpected; it would have to be one that was both in character and beyond character; it would have to suggest both the world and eternity. The action or gesture I'm talking about would have to be on the anagogical level, that is, the level which has to do with the Divine life and our participation in it. It would be a gesture that transcended any neat allegory that might have been intended or any pat moral categories a reader could make. It would be a gesture which somehow made contact with mystery.

There is a point in this story where such a gesture occurs. The Grandmother is at last alone, facing the Misfit. Her head clears for an instant and she realizes, even in her limited way, that she is responsible for the man before her and joined to him by ties of kinship which have their roots deep in the mystery she has been merely prattling about so far. And at this point, she does the right thing, she makes the right gesture.

I find that students are often puzzled by what she says and does here, but I think myself that if I took out this gesture and what she says with it, I would have no story. What was left would not be worth your attention. Our age not only does not have a very sharp eye for the almost imperceptible intrusions of grace, it no longer has much feeling for the nature of the violences which precede and follow them. The devil's greatest wile, Baudelaire has said, is to convince us that he does not exist.

I suppose the reasons for the use of so much violence in modern fiction will differ with each writer who uses it, but in my own stories I have found that violence is strangely capable of returning my characters to reality and preparing them to accept their moment of grace. Their heads are so hard that almost nothing else will do the work. This idea, that reality is something to which we must be returned at considerable cost, is one which is seldom understood by the casual reader, but it is one which is implicit in the Christian view of the world.

I don't want to equate the Misfit with the devil. I prefer to think that, however unlikely this may seem, the old lady's gesture, like the mustard-seed, will grow to be a great crow-filled tree in the Misfit's heart and will be enough of a pain to him there to turn him into the prophet he was meant to become. But that's another story.

This story has been called grotesque, but I prefer to call it literal. A good story is literal in the same sense that a child's drawing is literal. When a child draws, he doesn't intend to distort but to set down exactly what he sees, and as his gaze is direct, he sees the lines that create motion. Now the lines of motion that interest the writer are usually invisible. They are lines of spiritual motion. And in this story you should be on the lookout for such things as the action of grace in the Grandmother's soul, and not for the dead bodies.   [*1963*]

MARTHA STEPHENS

From *The Question of Flannery O'Connor*

Martha Stephens is professor emeritus of English and comparative literature at the University of Cincinnati. After Flannery O'Connor's religious explanation of "A Good Man Is Hard to Find" was published in the 1969 volume Mystery and Manners, *other readers of the story began responding to her comments. Stephens's 1973 book* The Question of Flannery O'Connor *includes one of the earliest attempts to gauge the helpfulness of O'Connor's analysis. Stephens is disturbed by the story's apparent shift of tone as it moves from farce to violent tragedy. O'Connor's remarks clarify this shift, Stephens thinks, but the religious doctrine reflected in them is severe.*

An ordinary and undistinguished family, a family even comical in its dullness, ill-naturedness, and triviality, sets out on a trip to Florida and on an ordinary summer day meets with a terrible fate. In what would the interest of such a story normally lie? Perhaps, one might think, in something that is revealed about the family in the way it meets its death, in some ironical or interesting truth about the nature of those people or those relationships — something we had been prepared unbeknownst to see, at the end plainly dramatized by their final common travail and death. But obviously, as regards the family as a whole, no such thing happens. The family is shown to be in death just as ordinary and ridiculous as before. With the possible exception of the grandmother, we know them no better; nothing about them of particular significance is brought forth.

The grandmother, being as we have seen the last to die, suffers the deaths of all her family while carrying on the intermittent conversation with the Misfit, and any reader will have some dim sense that it is through this encounter that the story is trying to transform and justify itself. One senses that this conversation — even though our attention is in reality fastened upon the horrible acts that are taking place in the background (and apparently against the thrust of the story) — is meant to be the real center of the story and the part in which the "point," as it were, of the whole tale lies.

But what is the burden of that queer conversation between the Misfit and the grandmother; what power does it have, even when we retrospectively sift and weigh it line by line, to transform our attitude towards the seemingly gratuitous — in terms of the art of the tale — horror of the massacre? The uninitiated reader will not, most likely, be able to unravel the strange complaint of the killer without some difficulty, but when we see the convict's peculiar dilemma in the context of O'Connor's whole work and what is known of her religious thought, it is not difficult to explain.

The Misfit's most intriguing statement — the line that seemingly the reader must ponder, set as it is as the final pronouncement on the grandmother after her death — is from the final passage . . . . : "She would of been a good woman if it had been somebody there to shoot her every minute of her life." Certainly we know from the first half of the story that the grandmother has seen herself as a good woman — and a good woman in a day when good men and women are hard to find, when people are disrespectful and dishonest, when they are not nice like they used to be. The grandmother is not common but a lady; and at the end of the story we know that she will be found dead just as we know she wanted to be — in the costume of a lady. She was not common, and the Misfit, with his "scholarly spectacles," his courtly apology for not wearing a shirt, his yes ma'ams and no ma'ams, was not common either — she had believed, wanted to believe, or pretended to believe. "Why I can see you come from good people," she said, "not common at all." Yet the Misfit says of her that she *would* have been a good woman if somebody had been there to shoot her all her life. And if we take the Misfit's statement as the right one about the grandmother, how was she a good woman in her death?

A good woman, perhaps we are given to believe, is one who understands   5
the worthlessness and emptiness of being or not being a "lady," of having or not having Coca-Cola stock, of "being broad" and seeing the world, of good manners and genteel attire. "Woe to them," said Isaiah, "that are wise in their own eyes, and prudent in their own sight." The futility of all the grandmother's values, the story strives to encapsulate in this image of her disarray after the car has overturned and she has recognized the Misfit: "The grandmother reached up to adjust her hat brim as if she were going to the woods with him but it came off in her hand. She stood staring at it and after a second she let it fall on the ground."

The Misfit is a figure that seems, one must say to the story's credit, to have fascinated more readers than any other single O'Connor character, and it is by contrast with the tormented spiritual state of this seeming monster that the nature of the grandmother's futile values becomes evident. We learn that the center of the Misfit's thought has always been Jesus Christ, and what becomes clear as we study over the final scene is that the Misfit has, in the eyes of the author, the enormous distinction of having at least faced up to the problem of Christian belief. And everything he has done — everything he so monstrously does here — proceeds from his inability to accept Christ, to truly believe. This is the speech which opens the narrow and emotionally difficult route into the meaning of the story:

> "Jesus was the only One that ever raised the dead," The Misfit continued, "and He shouldn't have done it. He thown everything off balance. If He did what He said, then it's nothing for you to do but thow away everything and follow Him, and if He didn't, then it's nothing for you to do but enjoy the few minutes you got left the best way you can — by killing somebody or burning down his house or doing some other meanness to him. No pleasure but meanness," he said and his voice had become almost a snarl.

The Misfit has chosen, at least, whom he would serve — has followed the injunction of the prophet in I Kings 18:21: "And Elijah came unto all the people, and said, How long halt ye between two opinions? if the Lord be God, follow him: but if Baal, then follow him." The crucial modern text for the authorial view here, which belongs to a tradition in religio-literary thought sometimes referred to as the sanctification of the sinner, is T. S. Eliot's essay on Baudelaire, in which he states: "So far as we are human, what we do must be either evil or good; so far as we do evil or good, we are human; and it is better, in a paradoxical way, to do evil than to do nothing; at least, we exist. It is true that the glory of man is his capacity for salvation; it is also true to say that his glory is his capacity for damnation."

Thus observe how, in the context of these statements, "A Good Man Is Hard to Find" begins to yield its meaning. What O'Connor has done is to take, in effect, Eliot's maxim — "It is better, in a paradoxical way, to do evil than to do nothing" — and to stretch our tolerance of this idea to its limits. The conclusion that one cannot avoid is that the story depends, for its final effect, on our being able to appreciate — even to be startled by, to be pleasurably struck with — the notion of the essential moral superiority of the Misfit over his victims, who have lived without choice or commitment of any kind, who have in effect not "lived" at all.

But again, in what sense is the grandmother a "good woman" in her death, as the Misfit claims? Here even exegesis falters. Because in her terror she calls on the name of Jesus, because she exhorts the Misfit to pray? Is she "good" because as the old lady sinks fainting into the ditch, after the Misfit's Jesus speech recorded above, she mumbles, "Maybe he didn't raise the dead"? Are we to see her as at last beginning to face the central question of human existence: did God send his son to save the world? Perhaps there is a clue in the dead grandmother's final image: she is said to half lie and half sit "in a puddle of blood with her legs crossed under her like a child's and her face smiling up at the cloudless sky." For Christ said, after all, that "whosoever shall not receive the kingdom of God as a little child shall in no wise enter herein."

To see that the Misfit is really the one courageous and admirable figure in the story; that the grandmother was perhaps — even as he said — a better woman in her death than she had ever been; to see that the pain of the other members of the family, that any godless pain or pleasure that human beings may experience is, beside the one great question of existence, *unimportant* — to see all these things is to enter fully into the experience of the story. Not to see them is to find oneself pitted not only against the forces that torture and destroy the wretched subjects of the story, but against the story itself and its attitude of indifference to and contempt for human pain.

Now as it happens, "A Good Man Is Hard to Find" was a favorite story of 10 O'Connor's. It was the story she chose to read whenever she was asked to read from her work, and clearly it held a meaning for her that was particularly important. Whenever she read the story, she closed by reading a statement giving her own explanation of it. (One version of that statement can now be read in the collection of O'Connor's incidental prose edited by Robert and Sally Fitzgerald titled *Mystery and Manners*.) She had come to realize that it was a story that readers found difficult, and she said in her statement that she felt that the reason the story was misunderstood was that the present age "not only does not have a very sharp eye for the almost imperceptible intrusions of grace, it no longer has much feeling for the nature of the violences which precede and follow them." The intrusion of grace in "A Good Man Is Hard to Find" comes, Miss O'Connor said, in that much-discussed passage in which the grandmother, her head suddenly clearing for a moment, murmurs to the Misfit, "Why, you're one of my babies. You're one of my own children!" and is shot just as she reaches out to touch him. The grandmother's gesture here is what, according to O'Connor, makes the story work; it shows that the grandmother realizes that "she is responsible for the man before her and joined to him by ties of kinship which have their roots deep in the mystery she has been merely prattling about so far," and it affords the grandmother "a special kind of triumph . . . which we instinctively do not allow to someone altogether bad."

This explanation does solve, in a sense, one of the riddles of this odd story — although, of course, one must say that while it is interesting to know the intent of the author, speaking outside the story and after the fact, such knowledge does not change the fact that the intent of the narrator manifested strictly within the story is damagingly unclear on this important point. And what is even more important here is that O'Connor's statement about the story, taken as a whole, only further confirms the fact that the only problem in this tale is really a function of our difficulty with O'Connor's formidable doctrine. About the Misfit, O'Connor says that while he is not to be seen as the hero of the story, yet his capacity for grace is far greater than the grandmother's and that the author herself prefers to think "that the old lady's gesture, like the mustard-seed, will grow to be a great crow-filled tree in the Misfit's heart, and will be enough of a pain to him there to turn him into the prophet he was meant to become." The capacity for grace of the other members of the family is apparently zero, and hence — Christian grace in O'Connor, one cannot help noting, is rather an expensive process — it is proper that their deaths should have no spiritual context whatever.   [1973]

STEPHEN BANDY

From "One of My Babies":
The Misfit and the Grandmother

In an article published in a 1996 issue of Studies in Short Fiction, *Stephen Bandy strongly disagrees with O'Connor's interpretation of "A Good Man Is Hard to Find." In particular, he thinks that the grandmother is sentimental and vindictive, whereas O'Connor is sympathetic to the character and believes that she manifests grace. Following are excerpts from Bandy's analysis.*

Grasping at any appeal, and hardly aware of what she is saying, the Grandmother declares to the Misfit: " 'Why you're one of my babies. You're one of my own children!' " As she utters these shocking words, "She reached out and touched him on the shoulder. The Misfit sprang back as if a snake had bitten him and shot her three times through the chest" (p. 1295).

Noting that some squeamish readers had found this ending too strong, O'Connor defended the scene in this way: "If I took out this gesture and what she says with it, I would have no story. What was left would not be worth your attention" (*Mystery and Manners* 112).[1] Certainly the scene is crucial to the story, and most readers, I think, grant its dramatic "rightness" as a conclusion. What is arguable is the meaning to the Grandmother's final words to the Misfit, as well as her "gesture," which seemed equally important to O'Connor. One's interpretation depends on one's opinion of the Grandmother.

What *are* we to think of this woman? At the story's beginning, she seems a harmless busybody, utterly self-absorbed but also amusing, in her way. And, in her way, she provides a sort of human Rorschach test of her readers. We readily forgive her so much, including her mindless racism — she points at the "cute little pickaninny" by the roadside, and entertains her grandchildren with a story in which a watermelon is devoured by "a nigger boy." She is filled with the prejudices of her class and her time. And so, some readers conclude, she is in spite of it all a "good" person. Somewhat more ominously, the Misfit — after he has fired three bullets into her chest — pronounces that she might have been " 'a good woman . . . if it had been somebody there to shoot her every minute of her life' " (p. 1296). We surmise that in the universe of this story, the quality of what is "good" (which is after all the key word of the story's title) depends greatly on who is using the term. I do not think the Misfit is capable of irony — he truly means what he says about her, even though he finds it necessary to kill her. Indeed, the opposing categories of "good" and "evil" are very much in the air throughout this story. But like most supposed opposites, they have an alarming tendency to merge. It is probably worth noting that the second line of the once-popular song that gave O'Connor her title is "You always get the other kind."

Much criticism of the story appears to take a sentimental view of the Grandmother largely because she *is* a grandmother. Flannery O'Connor herself, as we shall see shortly, found little to blame in this woman, choosing to wrap her in the comfortable mantle of elderly Southern womanhood. O'Connor applies this generalization so uncritically that we half suspect she is pulling our leg. In any case, we can be sure that such sentimentality (in the mind of either the writer or her character) is fatal to clear thinking. If the Grandmother is old (although she does not seem to be *that* old), grey-haired, and "respectable," it follows that she must be weak, gentle, and benevolent — precisely the Grandmother's opinion of herself, and she is not shy of letting others know it. Intentionally or not, O'Connor has etched the Grandmother's character with wicked irony, which makes it all the more surprising to read the author's response to a frustrated teacher whose (Southern) students persisted in favoring the Grandmother, despite his strenuous efforts to point out her flaws. O'Connor said,

> I had to tell him that they resisted . . . because they all had grandmothers
> or great-aunts just like her at home, and they knew, from personal experi-

---

[1] Flannery O'Connor, *Mystery and Manners: Occasional Prose*. Selected and Edited by Sally and Robert Fitzgerald (New York: Farrar, Straus, and Giroux, 1969).

ence, that the old lady lacked comprehension, but that she had a good heart.

O'Connor continued,

> The Southerner is usually tolerant of those weaknesses that proceed from innocence, and he knows that a taste for self-preservation can be readily combined with the missionary spirit. (*Mystery and Manners* 110)

What is most disappointing in this moral summary of the Grandmother, and her ilk, is its disservice to the spiky, vindictive woman of the story. There may be a purpose to O'Connor's betrayal of her own character: her phrase "missionary spirit" gives the game away. O'Connor is determined that the Grandmother shall be the Misfit's savior, even though she may not seem so in the story.

The Grandmother's role as grace-bringer is by now a received idea, largely because the author said it is so. But one must question the propriety of such tinkering with the character, after the fact. It reduces the fire-breathing woman who animates this story to nothing much more than a cranky maiden aunt. On the contrary, the Grandmother is a fierce fighter, never more so than in her final moments, nose-to-nose with the Misfit.

Granted, the Grandmother is not a homicidal monster like the Misfit, and she certainly does not deserve to die for her minor sins. And yet, does she quite earn absolution from any moral weakness beyond that of "a hypocritical old soul" (111)? For every reader who sees the image of his or her own grandmother printed on this character's cold face, as O'Connor suggested we might do, there are surely many others who can only be appalled by a calculating opportunist who is capable of embracing her family's murderer, to save her own skin. Where indeed is the "good heart" which unites this unprincipled woman with all those "grandmothers or great-aunts just like her at home"? The answer to that question can only be an affirmation of the "banality of evil," to use Hannah Arendt's well-known phrase. . . .

What does in fact happen in this part of the story is quite straightforward: the Grandmother, having exhausted all other appeals to the Misfit, resorts to her only remaining (though certainly imperfect) weapon: motherhood. Declaring to the Misfit that he is one of her babies, she sets out to conquer him. Perhaps she hopes that this ultimate flattery will melt his heart, and he will collapse in her comforting motherly embrace. Such are the stratagems of sentimentality. The moral shoddiness of her action is almost beyond description. If we had not already guessed the depths to which the Grandmother might sink, now we know. It is not easy to say who is the more evil, the Misfit or the Grandmother, and indeed that is the point. Her behavior is the manifest of her character.

It has been said that no action is without its redeeming aspect. Could this unspeakable act of selfishness carry within it the seeds of grace, acting, as it were, above the Grandmother? So Flannery O'Connor believed. But what is the precise movement of grace in this scene? It is surely straining the text to propose that the Grandmother has in this moment "seen the light." Are we to regard her as the unwitting agent of divine grace whose selfish intentions are somehow transfigured into a blessing? Such seems to have been O'Connor's opinion:

> ... however unlikely this may seem, the old lady's gesture, like the mustard-seed, will grow to be a great crow-filled tree in the Misfit's heart, and will be enough of a pain to him there to turn him into the prophet he was meant to become. (*Mystery and Manners* 113)

We are almost persuaded to forget that none of this happens in the story itself. If this can be so, then we can just as easily attribute any interpretation we like to the scene. But in fact he is in no way changed. There is no "later on" in fiction. We do not, and will not, see "created grace" in the spirit of the Misfit.

But more important, this is not the way grace works. As we read in the   10 *New Catholic Encyclopedia*:

> ... the spiritual creature must respond to this divine self-donation freely. Hence, the doctrine of grace supposes a creature already constituted in its own being in such wise that it has the possibility of entering into a free and personal relationship with the Divine Persons or of rejecting that relationship. (6:661)

If grace was extended to the Misfit, he refused it and that is the end. There can be no crow-filled tree, nor can there be the "lines of spiritual motion" leading to that tree, however attractive the image may be. Prudently, O'Connor added, "But that's another story" (*Mystery and Manners* 113)   [1996]

JOHN DESMOND
From Flannery O'Connor's Misfit and the Mystery of Evil

In an article published in a 2004 issue of Renascence, *a journal that examines religious issues in literature, John Desmond tends to support O'Connor's interpretation of "A Good Man Is Hard to Find." For help in understanding the climactic scene between The Misfit and the grandmother, he turns to the late French Catholic philosopher Simone Weil. The following is an excerpt from his analysis.*

This climactic scene, full of ambiguity, has occasioned a wealth of critical comment. O'Connor herself argued that the grandmother's final words and actions represent the mysterious action of grace (5). Some readers have viewed it more skeptically, even arguing that the grandmother's gesture may be a final desperate attempt to save her own life. Other critics have argued a middle ground, granting O'Connor's right to her theological view, while judging the scene as satisfactory or not on the basis of strictly literary criteria. My focus here is on what this climactic scene suggests about the mysterious interpenetration of good and evil.

What initially strikes the reader about the scene is the enormous gap or lacuna between the grandmother's statement of doubt — "Maybe He didn't raise the dead . . ." — and her reaching out fatally to touch the Misfit and embrace him as "one of my babies . . . ," one of "my own children." O'Connor explains nothing of what happens in the grandmother's mind and heart to bring her to this touch of kinship with the criminal, except to say that "her head cleared for an instant." The gap is mysterious, perhaps supernatural, yet also exactly right in the human sense. Such acts of metanoia,° while inexplicable, are totally within the range of human behavior. What is significant about her calling him "one of my babies . . . ," one of "my own children," and "touching him" is that her actions threaten to undermine his self-designation of himself as the Misfit, the name he chose to signify his difference from ordinary humanity. The Misfit rejects the communal world, just as his sense of "justice" is individualistic rather than communal. Significantly, he remarked earlier in that story that "children make me nervous." The grandmother's claim of kinship rejects his solitary identity, and instead places him within the community as a child of man, like any other. So also, her touching him threatens his proud, isolated self-created role as the Misfit, a threat he cannot tolerate. After all, if he is not the Misfit, what is he? An ordinary, frail, suffering creature. So what we view from the grandmother's perspective as a good act — her recognition of her own bond with an evil man, her complicity, yet also her compassion for his suffering — is viewed by the Misfit as evil: he springs back from her touch "as if a snake had bitten him. . . ."

Why does the Misfit regard the touch as evil, and then answer it with evil? We recall Simone Weil's maxim: "Evil is to love, what mystery is to the intelligence." The grandmother's touch brings the Misfit into direct contact with the good of charity. The touch of charity measures the gap between him and the good. He cannot abide such threatening contact because it would mean opening himself to an admission of failure, and more importantly, to the possibility of good within the human community. Instead, he chooses the "hell" of isolation and despair. The truth of compassion, and being named a child of the human community, is for the Misfit an "evil" he must escape. Once again, Weil's comments are insightful:

> The sin against the Spirit consists of knowing a thing to be good, and hating it because it is good. We experience the equivalent of it in the form of resistance every time we set our faces in the direction of good. For every contact with good leads to a knowledge of the distance between good and evil and the commencement of a painful effort of assimilation. It is something which hurts and we are afraid. This fear is perhaps the sign of the reality of the contact. The corresponding sin cannot come about unless a lack of hope makes the consciousness of the distance intolerable and changes the pain into hatred. (*Gravity and Grace* 67)

metanoia: A Greek term meaning repentance or spiritual conversion.

The Misfit's pain at the grandmother's touch is instantly transformed into a hatred of the gratuitous act of charity, which he then answers with a brutal execution. What the Misfit fears is the mystery of love, the demands of love which the grandmother mysteriously responded to when faced with the criminal's suffering, and her own impending death. In her case, evil issued finally in good, or as Weil expressed it, evil exposed the good. But if the encounter with evil exposed the good in the grandmother, the final predicament of the Misfit is more complicated, more mysterious.

As I noted earlier, the Misfit acts under the delusion that his actions are somehow good, i.e., good for him. Since he cannot make sense of his spiritual condition, he now tries to reduce ethical mystery to a perverse pleasure-pain principle. Initially he told the grandmother: "No pleasure but meanness." Yet his encounter with her touch has exposed his need, his human vulnerability. In his crucial final remark, he shifts from the earlier "No pleasure but meanness" to "It's no real pleasure in life." He has again failed to liberate himself from his predicament through violence, failed to "balance out" his deeds and find the meaning of his life. He himself is his own deepest mystery, a profoundly human condition which he can neither fathom nor abide. His last statement, that there is no "real pleasure" in life, shows that what he thought might bring pleasure, i.e., acts of meanness, has also proven to be bankrupt, a hollow illusion.

In the end, the Misfit's spiritual and mental suffering continues and intensifies, for with the failure of his code, his awareness of the gap between good and evil has widened. His violence is projected back onto himself as self-hatred. Perhaps at some future time his knowledge of this interior chasm will bring about the collapse of his self-begotten identity as a "Misfit," and an acceptance of his broken humanity. O'Connor suggested the possibility that he might ultimately be brought to such a conversion. She called the Misfit a "prophet gone wrong," and referred to the grandmother's touching him as "like the mustard-seed," which "will grow to be a great crow-filled tree in the Misfit's heart, and will be enough of a pain to him there to turn him into the prophet he was meant to become" (*Mystery and Manners* 110, 112–13). The grandmother's touch may bring him to the point where the mystery of good and evil is finally subsumed in the mystery of love. For the Misfit, evil may, in the end, through the grace of charity, bring about his ultimate good.

≡ MAKING COMPARISONS

1. Stephens believes that her interpretation of "A Good Man Is Hard to Find" is compatible with O'Connor's. Do you accept both? Why, or why not?

2. In what ways, if any, does Desmond's use of Simone Weil go beyond O'Connor's view of her story or complicate it? Do the other two critics, Stephens and Bandy, make you hesitate to accept O'Connor's account? In general, do you think readers should accept an author's interpretation of his or her work? Explain your reasoning.

3. All of these commentaries on the story focus on religious aspects of it, though not all of them agree on how much of a role, and what kind of a role, religion plays in it. Are you similarly inclined to put the story in a religious framework? Why, or why not?

≣ WRITING ABOUT ISSUES

1. The Misfit says that the grandmother " 'would of been a good woman . . . if it had been somebody there to shoot her every minute of her life' " (para. 140). Write an essay in which you argue for your own understanding of this claim. Is The Misfit right or just cruel? How should we define *good* in this context?

2. Choose one of the critics' interpretations featured in this cluster, and write an essay in which you imagine how O'Connor would respond to its points. Feel free to express and support your own views, too.

3. The man in O'Connor's story calls himself The Misfit " 'because I can't make what all I done wrong fit what all I gone through in punishment' " (para. 129). But plainly he is also a misfit in the sense that he has become alienated from society. Write an essay recalling someone you knew who seemed to be a misfit in this sense. More specifically, speculate on and try to describe this person's own perspective — what the person believed, how the person viewed the world, why he or she acted in certain ways. If you wish, your essay can be in the form of a letter to this person.

4. O'Connor promoted her version of Christianity in "A Good Man Is Hard to Find" and in her commentary on the story. On the basis of both texts, list various principles and concepts that she associates with her religion. Then do research on another religion, perhaps by reading two or three articles on it. Write an essay in which you compare O'Connor's theology with the religion you have researched. If you wish, you can focus your comparison by imagining what adherents to the other religion would say about "A Good Man Is Hard to Find."

▓ Women Resisting Injustice: A Play in the News

SOPHOCLES, *Antigone*

IN THE NEWS:
PETER BEAUMONT AND SAEED KAMALI DEHGHAN, "Iran: Women on the Frontline of the Fight for Rights"

ISABEL HILTON, "A Triumph for Moral Authority"

We began this chapter with the topic of civil disobedience, nonviolent dissent that assumes that moral law can require violation of human law. For recent examples, we pointed to Myanmar, Iran, and China, where advocates of democracy dare to resist dictators. For most Americans, these are distant places. By studying the protests in them, however, you can better understand how literature has depicted similar acts. The reverse is true as well: literary works about such defiance can shed light on its current role in these nations. So, here we connect Sophocles' ancient tragedy *Antigone* with accounts of protests in these countries.

Think in particular about how the following texts center on women, shown as fighting unjust rule. Of course, history has seen countless women oppose their governments, whether through peaceful or violent means. In the United States, for example, Harriet Tubman helped slaves escape their owners. American and British suffragists militantly campaigned to win the vote. Later, Algerian women joined in their country's revolt against French control. In the Philippines, Corazon Aquino led a revolt against the corrupt Marcos government. And when the regime of Argentina arrested alleged subversives — often proceeding to torture and kill them — mothers of "the disappeared" protested through daily marches. Nevertheless, many people still feel that politics has been — and should be — the domain of men. The texts we feature here challenge this belief, even as their heroines emerge as complex and perhaps even flawed in fighting oppressive leaders.

▓ BEFORE YOU READ

Around the world today, many female protesters — and many male ones, too — claim to be working on behalf of "human rights," a term that was the subject of a United Nations declaration in 1948. What does this term mean to you? What specific "rights" do you associate with it?

SOPHOCLES
Antigone

Translated by Robert Fagles

Antigone was first produced in 441 B.C.E., more than a decade before Oedipus the King was first produced. Just before the action of Antigone begins, the heroine's two brothers have killed each other in battle. One, Eteocles, was defending Thebes; the other, Polynices, was leading an army against it. The current ruler of Thebes, Antigone's uncle Creon, now forbids burial of Polynices — a command that Antigone will defy.

CHARACTERS

ANTIGONE, *daughter of Oedipus and Jocasta*
ISMENE, *sister of Antigone*
A CHORUS *of old Theban citizens and their* LEADER
CREON, *king of Thebes, uncle of Antigone and Ismene*
A SENTRY
HAEMON, *son of Creon and Eurydice*
TIRESIAS, *a blind prophet*
A MESSENGER
EURYDICE, *wife of Creon*
GUARDS, ATTENDANTS, AND A BOY

TIME AND SCENE: *The royal house of Thebes. It is still night, and the invading armies of Argos have just been driven from the city. Fighting on opposite sides, the sons of Oedipus, Eteocles and Polynices, have killed each other in combat. Their uncle, Creon, is now king of Thebes.*

    Enter Antigone, slipping through the central doors of the palace. She motions to her sister, Ismene, who follows her cautiously toward an altar at the center of the stage.

ANTIGONE: My own flesh and blood — dear sister, dear Ismene,
   how many griefs our father Oedipus handed down!
   Do you know one, I ask you, one grief
   that Zeus° will not perfect for the two of us
   while we still live and breathe? There's nothing,   5
   no pain — our lives are pain — no private shame,
   no public disgrace, nothing I haven't seen
   in your griefs and mine. And now this:
   an emergency decree, they say, the Commander
   has just declared for all of Thebes.   10

4 Zeus: The highest Olympian deity.

(© Bettmann/Corbis.)

What, haven't you heard? Don't you see?
The doom reserved for enemies
marches on the ones we love the most.

ISMENE: Not I, I haven't heard a word, Antigone.
Nothing of loved ones,   15
no joy or pain has come my way, not since
the two of us were robbed of our two brothers,
both gone in a day, a double blow —
not since the armies of Argos vanished,
just this very night. I know nothing more,   20
whether our luck's improved or ruin's still to come.

ANTIGONE: I thought so. That's why I brought you out here,
past the gates, so you could hear in private.

ISMENE: What's the matter? Trouble, clearly . . .
you sound so dark, so grim.   25

ANTIGONE: Why not? Our own brothers' burial!

Hasn't Creon graced one with all the rites,
disgraced the other? Eteocles, they say,
has been given full military honors,
rightly so — Creon's laid him in the earth   30
and he goes with glory down among the dead.
But the body of Polynices, who died miserably —
why, a city-wide proclamation, rumor has it,
forbids anyone to bury him, even mourn him.
He's to be left unwept, unburied, a lovely treasure   35
for birds that scan the field and feast to their heart's content.

Such, I hear, is the martial law our good Creon
lays down for you and me — yes, me, I tell you —
and he's coming here to alert the uninformed
in no uncertain terms,   40
and he won't treat the matter lightly. Whoever
disobeys in the least will die, his doom is sealed:
stoning to death inside the city walls!

There you have it. You'll soon show what you are,
worth your breeding, Ismene, or a coward —   45
for all your royal blood.
ISMENE: My poor sister, if things have come to this,
who am I to make or mend them, tell me,
what good am I to you?
ANTIGONE: Decide.
Will you share the labor, share the work?   50
ISMENE: What work, what's the risk? What do you mean?
ANTIGONE:

Raising her hands.

Will you lift up his body with these bare hands
and lower it with me?
ISMENE: What? You'd bury him —
when a law forbids the city?
ANTIGONE: Yes!
He is my brother and — deny it as you will —   55
your brother too.
No one will ever convict me for a traitor.
ISMENE: So desperate, and Creon has expressly —
ANTIGONE: No,
he has no right to keep me from my own.
ISMENE: Oh my sister, think —   60
think how our own father died, hated,
his reputation in ruins, driven on
by the crimes he brought to light himself
to gouge out his eyes with his own hands —

then mother . . . his mother and wife, both in one,   65
mutilating her life in the twisted noose —
and last, our two brothers dead in a single day,
both shedding their own blood, poor suffering boys,
battling out their common destiny hand-to-hand.
Now look at the two of us, left so alone . . .   70
think what a death we'll die, the worst of all
if we violate the laws and override
the fixed decree of the throne, its power —
we must be sensible. Remember we are women,
we're not born to contend with men. Then too,   75
we're underlings, ruled by much stronger hands,
so we must submit in this, and things still worse.

I, for one, I'll beg the dead to forgive me —
I'm forced, I have no choice — I must obey
the ones who stand in power. Why rush to extremes?   80
It's madness, madness.
ANTIGONE: I won't insist,
no, even if you should have a change of heart,
I'd never welcome you in the labor, not with me.
So, do as you like, whatever suits you best —
I'll bury him myself.   85
And even if I die in the act, that death will be a glory.
I'll lie with the one I love and loved by him —
an outrage sacred to the gods! I have longer
to please the dead than please the living here:
in the kingdom down below I'll lie forever.   90
Do as you like, dishonor the laws
the gods hold in honor.
ISMENE: I'd do them no dishonor . . .
but defy the city? I have no strength for that.
ANTIGONE: You have your excuses. I am on my way,
I'll raise a mound for him, for my dear brother.   95
ISMENE: Oh Antigone, you're so rash — I'm so afraid for you!
ANTIGONE: Don't fear for me. Set your own life in order.
ISMENE: Then don't, at least, blurt this out to anyone.
Keep it a secret. I'll join you in that, I promise.
ANTIGONE: Dear god, shout it from the rooftops. I'll hate you   100
all the more for silence — tell the world!
ISMENE: So fiery — and it ought to chill your heart.
ANTIGONE: I know I please where I must please the most.
ISMENE: Yes, if you can, but you're in love with impossibility.
ANTIGONE: Very well then, once my strength gives out   105
I will be done at last.
ISMENE: You're wrong from the start,

you're off on a hopeless quest.
ANTIGONE: If you say so, you will make me hate you,
and the hatred of the dead, by all rights,
will haunt you night and day.   110
But leave me to my own absurdity, leave me
to suffer this — dreadful thing. I'll suffer
nothing as great as death without glory.

Exit to the side.

ISMENE: Then go if you must, but rest assured,
wild, irrational as you are, my sister,   115
you are truly dear to the ones who love you.

*Withdrawing to the palace. Enter a Chorus, the old citizens of Thebes, chanting as
the sun begins to rise.*

CHORUS: Glory! — great beam of sun, brightest of all
that ever rose on the seven gates of Thebes,
you burn through night at last!
            Great eye of the golden day,   120
mounting the Dirce's° banks you throw him back —
the enemy out of Argos, the white shield, the man of bronze —
he's flying headlong now
            the bridle of fate stampeding him with pain!

And he had driven against our borders,   125
launched by the warring claims of Polynices —
like an eagle screaming, winging havoc
over the land, wings of armor
shielded white as snow,
a huge army massing,   130
crested helmets bristling for assault.

He hovered above our roofs, his vast maw gaping
closing down around our seven gates,
his spears thirsting for the kill
            but now he's gone, look,   135
before he could glut his jaws with Theban blood
or the god of fire put our crown of towers to the torch.

He grappled the Dragon none can master — Thebes —
            the clang of our arms like thunder at his back!

Zeus hates with a vengeance all bravado,   140
the mighty boasts of men. He watched them
coming on in a rising flood, the pride
of their golden armor ringing shrill —

121 the Dirce: A river near Thebes.

and brandishing his lightning
blasted the fighter just at the goal,   145
rushing to shout his triumph from our walls.

Down from the heights he crashed, pounding down on the earth!
And a moment ago, blazing torch in hand —
        mad for attack, ecstatic
he breathed his rage, the storm   150
    of his fury hurling at our heads!
But now his high hopes have laid him low
and down the enemy ranks the iron god of war
        deals his rewards, his stunning blows — Ares°
        rapture of battle, our right arm in the crisis.   155

        Seven captains marshaled at seven gates
        seven against their equals, gave
        their brazen trophies up to Zeus,
        god of the breaking rout of battle,
        all but two: those blood brothers,   160
        one father, one mother — matched in rage,
        spears matched for the twin conquest —
        clashed and won the common prize of death.

But now for Victory! Glorious in the morning,
joy in her eyes to meet our joy   165
        she is winging down to Thebes,
our fleets of chariots wheeling in her wake —
        Now let us win oblivion from the wars,
thronging the temples of the gods
in singing, dancing choirs through the night!   170
        Lord Dionysus,° god of the dance
        that shakes the land of Thebes, now lead the way!

Enter Creon from the palace, attended by his guard.

        But look, the king of the realm is coming,
        Creon, the new man for the new day,
        whatever the gods are sending now . . .   175
        what new plan will he launch?
        Why this, this special session?
        Why this sudden call to the old men
        summoned at one command?
CREON: My countrymen,
    the ship of state is safe. The gods who rocked her,   180
    after a long, merciless pounding in the storm,
    have righted her once more.

---

154 Ares: God of war.   **171 Dionysus:** God of fertility and wine.

Out of the whole city
I have called you here alone. Well I know,
first, your undeviating respect
for the throne and royal power of King Laius.   185
Next, while Oedipus steered the land of Thebes,
and even after he died, your loyalty was unshakable,
you still stood by their children. Now then,
since the two sons are dead — two blows of fate
in the same day, cut down by each other's hands,   190
both killers, both brothers stained with blood —
as I am next in kin to the dead,
I now possess the throne and all its powers.

Of course you cannot know a man completely,
his character, his principles, sense of judgment,   195
not till he's shown his colors, ruling the people,
making laws. Experience, there's the test.
As I see it, whoever assumes the task,
the awesome task of setting the city's course,
and refuses to adopt the soundest policies   200
but fearing someone, keeps his lips locked tight,
he's utterly worthless. So I rate him now,
I always have. And whoever places a friend
above the good of his own country, he is nothing:
I have no use for him. Zeus my witness,   205
Zeus who sees all things, always —
I could never stand by silent, watching destruction
march against our city, putting safety to rout,
nor could I ever make that man a friend of mine
who menaces our country. Remember this: 210
our country *is* our safety.
Only while she voyages true on course
can we establish friendships, truer than blood itself.
Such are my standards. They make our city great.

Closely akin to them I have proclaimed,   215
just now, the following decree to our people
concerning the two sons of Oedipus.
Eteocles, who died fighting for Thebes,
excelling all in arms: he shall be buried,
crowned with a hero's honors, the cups we pour   220
to soak the earth and reach the famous dead.

But as for his blood brother, Polynices,
who returned from exile, home to his father-city
and the gods of his race, consumed with one desire —

to burn them roof to roots — who thirsted to drink   225
his kinsmen's blood and sell the rest to slavery:
that man — a proclamation has forbidden the city
to dignify him with burial, mourn him at all.
No, he must be left unburied, his corpse
carrion for the birds and dogs to tear,   230
an obscenity for the citizens to behold!
These are my principles. Never at my hands
will the traitor be honored above the patriot.
But whoever proves his loyalty to the state:
I'll prize that man in death as well as life.   235

LEADER: If this is your pleasure, Creon, treating
our city's enemy and our friend this way . . .
The power is yours, I suppose, to enforce it
with the laws, both for the dead and all of us,
the living.

CREON: Follow my orders closely then,   240
be on your guard.

LEADER: We're too old.
Lay that burden on younger shoulders.

CREON: No, no,
I don't mean the body — I've posted guards already.

LEADER: What commands for us then? What other service?

CREON: See that you never side with those who break my orders.   245

LEADER: Never. Only a fool could be in love with death.

CREON: Death is the price — you're right. But all too often
the mere hope of money has ruined many men.

A Sentry enters from the side.

SENTRY: My lord,
I can't say I'm winded from running, or set out
with any spring in my legs either — no sir,   250
I was lost in thought, and it made me stop, often,
dead in my tracks, wheeling, turning back,
and all the time a voice inside me muttering,
"Idiot, why? You're going straight to your death."
Then muttering, "Stopped again, poor fool?   255
If somebody gets the news to Creon first,
what's to save your neck?"
                            And so,
mulling it over, on I trudged, dragging my feet,
you can make a short road take forever . . .
but at last, look, common sense won out,   260
I'm here, and I'm all yours,
and even though I come empty-handed
I'll tell my story just the same, because

I've come with a good grip on one hope,
what will come will come, whatever fate —   265
CREON: Come to the point!
   What's wrong — why so afraid?
SENTRY: First, myself, I've got to tell you,
   I didn't do it, didn't see who did —
   Be fair, don't take it out on me.   270
CREON: You're playing it safe, soldier,
   barricading yourself from any trouble.
   It's obvious, you've something strange to tell.
SENTRY: Dangerous too, and danger makes you delay
   for all you're worth.   275
CREON: Out with it — then dismiss!
SENTRY: All right, here it comes. The body —
   someone's just buried it, then run off . . .
   sprinkled some dry dust on the flesh,
   given it proper rites.
CREON: What?   280
   What man alive would dare —
SENTRY: I've no idea, I swear it.
   There was no mark of a spade, no pickaxe there,
   no earth turned up, the ground packed hard and dry,
   unbroken, no tracks, no wheelruts, nothing,
   the workman left no trace. Just at sunup   285
   the first watch of the day points it out —
   it was a wonder! We were stunned . . .
   a terrific burden too, for all of us, listen:
   you can't see the corpse, not that it's buried,
   really, just a light cover of road-dust on it,   290
   as if someone meant to lay the dead to rest
   and keep from getting cursed.
   Not a sign in sight that dogs or wild beasts
   had worried the body, even torn the skin.

But what came next! Rough talk flew thick and fast,   295
   guard grilling guard — we'd have come to blows
   at last, nothing to stop it; each man for himself
   and each the culprit, no one caught red-handed,
   all of us pleading ignorance, dodging the charges,
   ready to take up red-hot iron in our fists,   300
   go through fire, swear oaths to the gods —
   "I didn't do it, I had no hand in it either,
   not in the plotting, not in the work itself!"

Finally, after all this wrangling came to nothing,
   one man spoke out and made us stare at the ground,   305

hanging our heads in fear. No way to counter him,
no way to take his advice and come through
safe and sound. Here's what he said:
"Look, we've got to report the facts to Creon,
we can't keep this hidden." Well, that won out,   310
and the lot fell on me, condemned me,
unlucky as ever, I got the prize. So here I am,
against my will and yours too, well I know —
no one wants the man who brings bad news.

LEADER: My king,
ever since he began I've been debating in my mind,   315
could this possibly be the work of the gods?

CREON: Stop —
before you make me choke with anger — the gods!
You, you're senile, must you be insane?
You say — why it's intolerable — say the gods
could have the slightest concern for that corpse?   320
Tell me, was it for meritorious service
they proceeded to bury him, prized him so? The hero
who came to burn their temples ringed with pillars,
their golden treasures — scorch their hallowed earth
and fling their laws to the winds.   325
Exactly when did you last see the gods
celebrating traitors? Inconceivable!

No, from the first there were certain citizens
who could hardly stand the spirit of my regime,
grumbling against me in the dark, heads together,   330
tossing wildly, never keeping their necks beneath
the yoke, loyally submitting to their king.
These are the instigators, I'm convinced —
they've perverted my own guard, bribed them
to do their work.

                    Money! Nothing worse   335
in our lives, so current, rampant, so corrupting.
Money — you demolish cities, root men from their homes,
you train and twist good minds and set them on
to the most atrocious schemes. No limit,
you make them adept at every kind of outrage,   340
every godless crime — money!

                        Everyone —
the whole crew bribed to commit this crime,
they've made one thing sure at least:
sooner or later they will pay the price.

Wheeling on the Sentry.

You —   345
I swear to Zeus as I still believe in Zeus,
if you don't find the man who buried that corpse,
the very man, and produce him before my eyes,
simple death won't be enough for you,
not till we string you up alive   350
and wring the immorality out of you.
Then you can steal the rest of your days,
better informed about where to make a killing.
You'll have learned, at last, it doesn't pay
to itch for rewards from every hand that beckons.   355
Filthy profits wreck most men, you'll see —
they'll never save your life.

SENTRY: Please,
   may I say a word or two, or just turn and go?

CREON: Can't you tell? Everything you say offends me.

SENTRY: Where does it hurt you, in the ears or in the heart?   360

CREON: And who are you to pinpoint my displeasure?

SENTRY: The culprit grates on your feelings,
   I just annoy your ears.

CREON: Still talking?
   You talk too much! A born nuisance —

SENTRY: Maybe so,
   but I never did this thing, so help me!

CREON: Yes you did —   365
   what's more, you squandered your life for silver!

SENTRY: Oh it's terrible when the one who does the judging
   judges things all wrong.

CREON: Well now,
   you just be clever about your judgments —
   if you fail to produce the criminals for me,   370
   you'll swear your dirty money brought you pain.

Turning sharply, reentering the palace.

SENTRY: I hope he's found. Best thing by far.
   But caught or not, that's in the lap of fortune;
   I'll never come back, you've seen the last of me.
   I'm saved, even now, and I never thought,   375
   I never hoped —
   dear gods, I owe you all my thanks!

Rushing out.

CHORUS: Numberless wonders
   terrible wonders walk the world but none the match for man —
   that great wonder crossing the heaving gray sea,
      driven on by the blasts of winter   380

on through breakers crashing left and right,
    holds his steady course
and the oldest of the gods he wears away —
the Earth, the immortal, the inexhaustible —
as his plows go back and forth, year in, year out   385
    with the breed of stallions turning up the furrows.
And the blithe, lightheaded race of birds he snares,
the tribes of savage beasts, the life that swarms the depths —
        with one fling of his nets
woven and coiled tight, he takes them all,   390
    man the skilled, the brilliant!
He conquers all, taming with his techniques
the prey that roams the cliffs and wild lairs,
training the stallion, clamping the yoke across
    his shaggy neck, and the tireless mountain bull.   395
And speech and thought, quick as the wind
and the mood and mind for law that rules the city —
    all these he has taught himself
and shelter from the arrows of the frost
when there's rough lodging under the cold clear sky   400
and the shafts of lashing rain —
        ready, resourceful man!
            Never without resources
never an impasse as he marches on the future —
only Death, from Death alone he will find no rescue   405
but from desperate plagues he has plotted his escapes.

Man the master, ingenious past all measure
past all dreams, the skills within his grasp —
    he forges on, now to destruction
now again to greatness. When he weaves in   410
the laws of the land, and the justice of the gods
that binds his oaths together
    he and his city rise high —
        but the city casts out
that man who weds himself to inhumanity   415
thanks to reckless daring. Never share my hearth
never think my thoughts, whoever does such things.

Enter Antigone from the side, accompanied by the Sentry.

    Here is a dark sign from the gods —
    what to make of this? I know her,
    how can I deny it? That young girl's Antigone!   420
    Wretched, child of a wretched father,
    Oedipus. Look, is it possible?
    They bring you in like a prisoner —

why? did you break the king's laws?
Did they take you in some act of mad defiance?   425
SENTRY: She's the one, she did it single-handed —
we caught her burying the body. Where's Creon?

Enter Creon from the palace.

LEADER: Back again, just in time when you need him.
CREON: In time for what? What is it?
SENTRY: My king,
there's nothing you can swear you'll never do —   430
second thoughts make liars of us all.
I could have sworn I wouldn't hurry back
(what with your threats, the buffeting I just took),
but a stroke of luck beyond our wildest hopes,
what a joy, there's nothing like it. So,   435
back I've come, breaking my oath, who cares?
I'm bringing in our prisoner — this young girl —
we took her giving the dead the last rites.
But no casting lots this time; this is *my* luck,
my prize, no one else's.
                              Now, my lord,   440
here she is. Take her, question her,
cross-examine her to your heart's content.
But set me free, it's only right —
I'm rid of this dreadful business once for all.
CREON: Prisoner! Her? You took her — where, doing what?   445
SENTRY: Burying the man. That's the whole story.
CREON: What?
You mean what you say, you're telling me the truth?
SENTRY: She's the one. With my own eyes I saw her
bury the body, just what you've forbidden.
There. Is that plain and clear?   450
CREON: What did you see? Did you catch her in the act?
SENTRY: Here's what happened. We went back to our post,
those threats of yours breathing down our necks —
we brushed the corpse clean of the dust that covered it,
stripped it bare . . . it was slimy, going soft,   455
and we took to high ground, backs to the wind
so the stink of him couldn't hit us;
jostling, baiting each other to keep awake,
shouting back and forth — no napping on the job,
not this time. And so the hours dragged by   460
until the sun stood dead above our heads,
a huge white ball in the noon sky, beating,
blazing down, and then it happened —
suddenly, a whirlwind!

Twisting a great dust-storm up from the earth,   465
a black plague of the heavens, filling the plain,
ripping the leaves off every tree in sight,
choking the air and sky. We squinted hard
and took our whipping from the gods.

And after the storm passed — it seemed endless —   470
there, we saw the girl!
And she cried out a sharp, piercing cry,
like a bird come back to an empty nest,
peering into its bed, and all the babies gone . . .
Just so, when she sees the corpse bare   475
she bursts into a long, shattering wail
and calls down withering curses on the heads
of all who did the work. And she scoops up dry dust,
handfuls, quickly, and lifting a fine bronze urn,
lifting it high and pouring, she crowns the dead   480
with three full libations.
                              Soon as we saw
we rushed her, closed on the kill like hunters,
and she, she didn't flinch. We interrogated her,
charging her with offenses past and present —
she stood up to it all, denied nothing. I tell you,   485
it made me ache and laugh in the same breath.
It's pure joy to escape the worst yourself,
it hurts a man to bring down his friends.
But all that, I'm afraid, means less to me
than my own skin. That's the way I'm made.

CREON:

Wheeling on Antigone.

                                         You,   490
with your eyes fixed on the ground — speak up.
Do you deny you did this, yes or no?
ANTIGONE: I did it. I don't deny a thing.

CREON:

To the Sentry.

You, get out, wherever you please —
you're clear of a very heavy charge.   495

He leaves; Creon turns back to Antigone.

You, tell me briefly, no long speeches —
were you aware a decree had forbidden this?
ANTIGONE: Well aware. How could I avoid it? It was public.
CREON: And still you had the gall to break this law?

ANTIGONE: Of course I did. It wasn't Zeus, not in the least,   500
who made this proclamation — not to me.
Nor did that Justice, dwelling with the gods
beneath the earth, ordain such laws for men.
Nor did I think your edict had such force
that you, a mere mortal, could override the gods,   505
the great unwritten, unshakable traditions.
They are alive, not just today or yesterday:
they live forever, from the first of time,
and no one knows when they first saw the light.

These laws — I was not about to break them,   510
not out of fear of some man's wounded pride,
and face the retribution of the gods.
Die I must, I've known it all my life —
how could I keep from knowing? — even without
your death-sentence ringing in my ears.   515
And if I am to die before my time
I consider that a gain. Who on earth,
alive in the midst of so much grief as I,
could fail to find his death a rich reward?
So for me, at least, to meet this doom of yours   520
is precious little pain. But if I had allowed
my own mother's son to rot, an unburied corpse —
that would have been an agony! This is nothing.
And if my present actions strike you as foolish,
let's just say I've been accused of folly   525
by a fool.
LEADER: Like father like daughter,
passionate, wild . . .
she hasn't learned to bend before adversity.
CREON: No? Believe me, the stiffest stubborn wills
fall the hardest; the toughest iron,   530
tempered strong in the white-hot fire,
you'll see it crack and shatter first of all.
And I've known spirited horses you can break
with a light bit — proud, rebellious horses.
There's no room for pride, not in a slave,   535
not with the lord and master standing by.

This girl was an old hand at insolence
when she overrode the edicts we made public.
But once she'd done it — the insolence,
twice over — to glory in it, laughing,   540
mocking us to our face with what she'd done.

I'm not the man, not now: she is the man
if this victory goes to her and she goes free.

Never! Sister's child or closer in blood
than all my family clustered at my altar   545
worshiping Guardian Zeus — she'll never escape,
she and her blood sister, the most barbaric death.
Yes, I accuse her sister of an equal part
in scheming this, this burial.

To his attendants.

                              Bring her here!
I just saw her inside, hysterical, gone to pieces.   550
It never fails: the mind convicts itself
in advance, when scoundrels are up to no good,
plotting in the dark. Oh but I hate it more
when a traitor, caught red-handed,
tries to glorify his crimes.   555
ANTIGONE: Creon, what more do you want
than my arrest and execution?
CREON: Nothing. Then I have it all.
ANTIGONE: Then why delay? Your moralizing repels me,
every word you say — pray god it always will.   560
So naturally all I say repels you too.
                              Enough.
Give me glory! What greater glory could I win
than to give my own brother decent burial?
These citizens here would all agree,

To the Chorus.

they'd praise me too   565
if their lips weren't locked in fear.

Pointing to Creon.

Lucky tyrants — the perquisites of power!
Ruthless power to do and say whatever pleases *them.*
CREON: You alone, of all the people in Thebes,
see things that way.
ANTIGONE: They see it just that way   570
but defer to you and keep their tongues in leash.
CREON: And you, aren't you ashamed to differ so from them?
So disloyal!
ANTIGONE: Not ashamed for a moment,
not to honor my brother, my own flesh and blood.
CREON: Wasn't Eteocles a brother too — cut down, facing him?   575
ANTIGONE: Brother, yes, by the same mother, the same father.
CREON: Then how can you render his enemy such honors,

such impieties in his eyes?
ANTIGONE: He'll never testify to that,
    Eteocles dead and buried.
CREON: He will —   580
    if you honor the traitor just as much as him.
ANTIGONE: But it was his brother, not some slave that died —
CREON: Ravaging our country! —
    but Eteocles died fighting in our behalf.
ANTIGONE: No matter — Death longs for the same rites for all.   585
CREON: Never the same for the patriot and the traitor.
ANTIGONE: Who, Creon, who on earth can say the ones below
    don't find this pure and uncorrupt?
CREON: Never. Once an enemy, never a friend,
    not even after death.   590
ANTIGONE: I was born to join in love, not hate —
    that is my nature.
CREON: Go down below and love,
    if love you must — love the dead! While I'm alive,
    no woman is going to lord it over me.

Enter Ismene from the palace, under guard.

CHORUS: Look,
    Ismene's coming, weeping a sister's tears,   595
    loving sister, under a cloud . . .
    her face is flushed, her cheeks streaming.
    Sorrow puts her lovely radiance in the dark.
CREON: You —
    in my house, you viper, slinking undetected,
    sucking my life-blood! I never knew   600
    I was breeding twin disasters, the two of you
    rising up against my throne. Come, tell me,
    will you confess your part in the crime or not?
    Answer me. Swear to me.
ISMENE: I did it, yes —
    if only she consents — I share the guilt,   605
    the consequences too.
ANTIGONE: No,
    Justice will never suffer that — not you,
    you were unwilling. I never brought you in.
ISMENE: But now you face such dangers . . . I'm not ashamed
    to sail through trouble with you,   610
    make your troubles mine.
ANTIGONE: Who did the work?
    Let the dead and the god of death bear witness!
    I've no love for a friend who loves in words alone.
ISMENE: Oh no, my sister, don't reject me, please,

let me die beside you, consecrating   615
the dead together.
ANTIGONE: Never share my dying,
don't lay claim to what you never touched.
My death will be enough.
ISMENE: What do I care for life, cut off from you?
ANTIGONE: Ask Creon. Your concern is all for him.   620
ISMENE: Why abuse me so? It doesn't help you now.
ANTIGONE: You're right —
if I mock you, I get no pleasure from it,
only pain.
ISMENE: Tell me, dear one,
what can I do to help you, even now?
ANTIGONE: Save yourself. I don't grudge you your survival.   625
ISMENE: Oh no, no, denied my portion in your death?
ANTIGONE: You chose to live, I chose to die.
ISMENE: Not, at least,
without every kind of caution I could voice.
ANTIGONE: Your wisdom appealed to one world — mine, another.
ISMENE: But look, we're both guilty, both condemned to death.   630
ANTIGONE: Courage! Live your life. I gave myself to death,
long ago, so I might serve the dead.
CREON: They're both mad, I tell you, the two of them.
One's just shown it, the other's been that way
since she was born.
ISMENE: True, my king,   635
the sense we were born with cannot last forever . . .
commit cruelty on a person long enough
and the mind begins to go.
CREON: Yours did,
when you chose to commit your crimes with her.
ISMENE: How can I live alone, without her?
CREON: Her?   640
Don't even mention her — she no longer exists.
ISMENE: What? You'd kill your own son's bride?
CREON: Absolutely:
there are other fields for him to plow.
ISMENE: Perhaps,
but never as true, as close a bond as theirs.
CREON: A worthless woman for my son? It repels me.   645
ISMENE: Dearest Haemon, your father wrongs you so!
CREON: Enough, enough — you and your talk of marriage!
ISMENE: Creon — you're really going to rob your son of Antigone?
CREON: Death will do it for me — break their marriage off.
LEADER: So, it's settled then? Antigone must die?   650
CREON: Settled, yes — we both know that.

To the guards.

> Stop wasting time. Take them in.
> From now on they'll act like women.
> Tie them up, no more running loose;
> even the bravest will cut and run,   655
> once they see Death coming for their lives.

The guards escort Antigone and Ismene into the palace. Creon remains while the old citizens form their chorus.

CHORUS: Blest, they are the truly blest who all their lives
    have never tasted devastation. For others, once
    the gods have rocked a house to its foundations
       the ruin will never cease, cresting on and on   660
    from one generation on throughout the race —
    like a great mounting tide
    driven on by savage northern gales,
       surging over the dead black depths
    roiling up from the bottom dark heaves of sand   665
    and the headlands, taking the storm's onslaught full-force,
    roar, and the low moaning
              echoes on and on
                and now
    as in ancient times I see the sorrows of the house,
    the living heirs of the old ancestral kings,
    piling on the sorrows of the dead   670
       and one generation cannot free the next —
    some god will bring them crashing down,
    the race finds no release.
    And now the light, the hope
       springing up from the late last root   675
    in the house of Oedipus, that hope's cut down in turn
    by the long, bloody knife swung by the gods of death
    by a senseless word
          by fury at the heart.
                  Zeus,
    yours is the power, Zeus, what man on earth
    can override it, who can hold it back?   680
    Power that neither Sleep, the all-ensnaring
       no, nor the tireless months of heaven
    can ever overmaster — young through all time,
    mighty lord of power, you hold fast
       the dazzling crystal mansions of Olympus.   685
    And throughout the future, late and soon
    as through the past, your law prevails:
    no towering form of greatness
       enters into the lives of mortals

              free and clear of ruin.
                                      True,   690
our dreams, our high hopes voyaging far and wide
bring sheer delight to many, to many others
    delusion, blithe, mindless lusts
and the fraud steals on one slowly . . . unaware
till he trips and puts his foot into the fire.   695
    He was a wise old man who coined
the famous saying: "Sooner or later
foul is fair, fair is foul
to the man the gods will ruin" —
    He goes his way for a moment only   700
              free of blinding ruin.

Enter Haemon from the palace.

    Here's Haemon now, the last of all your sons.
    Does he come in tears for his bride,
    his doomed bride, Antigone —
    bitter at being cheated of their marriage?   705
CREON: We'll soon know, better than seers could tell us.

Turning to Haemon.

    Son, you've heard the final verdict on your bride?
    Are you coming now, raving against your father?
    Or do you love me, no matter what I do?
HAEMON: Father, I'm your *son* . . . you in your wisdom   710
set my bearings for me — I obey you.
No marriage could ever mean more to me than you,
whatever good direction you may offer.
CREON: Fine, Haemon.
That's how you ought to feel within your heart,
subordinate to your father's will in every way.   715
That's what a man prays for: to produce good sons —
households full of them, dutiful and attentive,
so they can pay his enemy back with interest
and match the respect their father shows his friend.
But the man who rears a brood of useless children,   720
what has he brought into the world, I ask you?
Nothing but trouble for himself, and mockery
from his enemies laughing in his face.
                          Oh Haemon,
never lose your sense of judgment over a woman.
The warmth, the rush of pleasure, it all goes cold   725
in your arms, I warn you . . . a worthless woman
in your house, a misery in your bed.
What wound cuts deeper than a loved one

turned against you? Spit her out,
like a mortal enemy — let the girl go.   730
Let her find a husband down among the dead.

Imagine it: I caught her in naked rebellion,
the traitor, the only one in the whole city.
I'm not about to prove myself a liar,
not to my people, no, I'm going to kill her!   735
That's right — so let her cry for mercy, sing her hymns
to Zeus who defends all bonds of kindred blood.
Why, if I bring up my own kin to be rebels,
think what I'd suffer from the world at large.
Show me the man who rules his household well: 740
I'll show you someone fit to rule the state.
That good man, my son,
I have every confidence he and he alone
can give commands and take them too. Staunch
in the storm of spears he'll stand his ground,   745
a loyal, unflinching comrade at your side.

But whoever steps out of line, violates the laws
or presumes to hand out orders to his superiors,
he'll win no praise from me. But that man
the city places in authority, his orders   750
must be obeyed, large and small,
right and wrong.
                    Anarchy —
show me a greater crime in all the earth!
She, she destroys cities, rips up houses,
breaks the ranks of spearmen into headlong rout.   755
But the ones who last it out, the great mass of them
owe their lives to discipline. Therefore
we must defend the men who live by law,
never let some woman triumph over us.
Better to fall from power, if fall we must,   760
at the hands of a man — never be rated
inferior to a woman, never.
LEADER: To us,
unless old age has robbed us of our wits,
you seem to say what you have to say with sense.
HAEMON: Father, only the gods endow a man with reason,   765
the finest of all their gifts, a treasure.
Far be it from me — I haven't the skill,
and certainly no desire, to tell you when,
if ever, you make a slip in speech . . . though
someone else might have a good suggestion.   770

Of course it's not for you,
in the normal run of things, to watch
whatever men say or do, or find to criticize.
The man in the street, you know, dreads your glance,
he'd never say anything displeasing to your face.   775
But it's for me to catch the murmurs in the dark,
the way the city mourns for this young girl.
"No woman," they say, "ever deserved death less,
and such a brutal death for such a glorious action.
She, with her own dear brother lying in his blood —   780
she couldn't bear to leave him dead, unburied,
food for the wild dogs or wheeling vultures.
Death? She deserves a glowing crown of gold!"
So they say, and the rumor spreads in secret,
darkly . . .
           I rejoice in your success, father —   785
nothing more precious to me in the world.
What medal of honor brighter to his children
than a father's growing glory? Or a child's
to his proud father? Now don't, please,
be quite so single-minded, self-involved,   790
or assume the world is wrong and you are right.
Whoever thinks that he alone possesses intelligence,
the gift of eloquence, he and no one else,
and character too . . . such men, I tell you,
spread them open — you will find them empty.
                       No,   795
it's no disgrace for a man, even a wise man,
to learn many things and not to be too rigid.
You've seen trees by a raging winter torrent,
how many sway with the flood and salvage every twig,
but not the stubborn — they're ripped out, roots and all.   800
Bend or break. The same when a man is sailing:
haul your sheets too taut, never give an inch,
you'll capsize, go the rest of the voyage
keel up and the rowing-benches under.

Oh give way. Relax your anger — change!   805
I'm young, I know, but let me offer this:
it would be best by far, I admit,
if a man were born infallible, right by nature.
If not — and things don't often go that way,
it's best to learn from those with good advice.   810
LEADER: You'd do well, my lord, if he's speaking to the point,
to learn from him,

Turning to Haemon.

and you, my boy, from him.
You both are talking sense.
CREON: So,
    men our age, we're to be lectured, are we? —
    schooled by a boy his age?   815
HAEMON: Only in what is right. But if I seem young,
    look less to my years and more to what I do.
CREON: Do? Is admiring rebels an achievement?
HAEMON: I'd never suggest that you admire treason.
CREON: Oh? —
    isn't that just the sickness that's attacked her?   820
HAEMON: The whole city of Thebes denies it, to a man.
CREON: And is Thebes about to tell me how to rule?
HAEMON: Now, you see? Who's talking like a child?
CREON: Am I to rule this land for others — or myself?
HAEMON: It's no city at all, owned by one man alone.   825
CREON: What? The city *is* the king's — that's the law!
HAEMON: What a splendid king you'd make of a desert island —
    you and you alone.
CREON:

To the Chorus.

                        This boy, I do believe,
    is fighting on her side, the woman's side.
HAEMON: If you are a woman, yes;   830
    my concern is all for you.
CREON: Why, you degenerate — bandying accusations,
    threatening me with justice, your own father!
HAEMON: I see my father offending justice — wrong.
CREON: Wrong?
    To protect my royal rights?
HAEMON: Protect your rights?   835
    When you trample down the honors of the gods?
CREON: You, you soul of corruption, rotten through —
    woman's accomplice!
HAEMON: That may be,
    but you'll never find me accomplice to a criminal.
CREON: That's what *she* is,   840
    and every word you say is a blatant appeal for her —
HAEMON: And you, and me, and the gods beneath the earth.
CREON: You'll never marry her, not while she's alive.
HAEMON: Then she'll die . . . but her death will kill another.
CREON: What, brazen threats? You go too far!
HAEMON: What threat?   845
    Combating your empty, mindless judgments with a word?
CREON: You'll suffer for your sermons, you and your empty wisdom!

HAEMON: If you weren't my father, I'd say you were insane.
CREON: Don't flatter me with Father — you woman's slave!
HAEMON: You really expect to fling abuse at me   850
        and not receive the same?
CREON: Is that so!
    Now, by heaven, I promise you, you'll pay —
    taunting, insulting me! Bring her out,
    that hateful — she'll die now, here,
    in front of his eyes, beside her groom!   855
HAEMON: No, no, she will never die beside me —
    don't delude yourself. And you will never
    see me, never set eyes on my face again.
    Rage your heart out, rage with friends
    who can stand the sight of you.   860

Rushing out.

LEADER: Gone, my king, in a burst of anger.
    A temper young as his . . . hurt him once,
    he may do something violent.
CREON: Let him do —
    dream up something desperate, past all human limit!
    Good riddance. Rest assured,   865
    he'll never save those two young girls from death.
LEADER: Both of them, you really intend to kill them both?
CREON: No, not her, the one whose hands are clean;
    you're quite right.
LEADER: But Antigone —
    what sort of death do you have in mind for her?   870
CREON: I'll take her down some wild, desolate path
    never trod by men, and wall her up alive
    in a rocky vault, and set out short rations,
    just a gesture of piety
    to keep the entire city free of defilement.   875
    There let her pray to the one god she worships:
    Death — who knows? — may just reprieve her from death.
    Or she may learn at last, better late than never,
    what a waste of breath it is to worship Death.

Exit to the palace.

CHORUS: Love, never conquered in battle   880
    Love the plunderer laying waste the rich!
    Love standing the night-watch
                        guarding a girl's soft cheek,
    you range the seas, the shepherds' steadings off in the wilds —
    not even the deathless gods can flee your onset,   885
    nothing human born for a day —

whoever feels your grip is driven mad.
Love
you wrench the minds of the righteous into outrage,
swerve them to their ruin — you have ignited this,
this kindred strife, father and son at war   890
and Love alone the victor —
warm glance of the bride triumphant, burning with desire!
Throned in power, side-by-side with the mighty laws!
Irresistible Aphrodite,° never conquered —
Love, you mock us for your sport.   895

Antigone is brought from the palace under guard.

But now, even I'd rebel against the king,
I'd break all bounds when I see this —
I fill with tears, can't hold them back,
not any more . . . I see Antigone make her way
to the bridal vault where all are laid to rest.   900

ANTIGONE: Look at me, men of my fatherland,
setting out on the last road
looking into the last light of day
the last I'll ever see . . .
the god of death who puts us all to bed   905
takes me down to the banks of Acheron° alive —
denied my part in the wedding-songs,
no wedding-song in the dusk has crowned my marriage —
I go to wed the lord of the dark waters.

CHORUS: Not crowned with glory, crowned with a dirge,   910
you leave for the deep pit of the dead.
No withering illness laid you low,
no strokes of the sword — a law to yourself,
alone, no mortal like you, ever, you go down
to the halls of Death alive and breathing.   915

ANTIGONE: But think of Niobe° — well I know her story —
think what a living death she died,
Tantalus's daughter, stranger queen from the east:
there on the mountain heights, growing stone
binding as ivy, slowly walled her round   920
and the rains will never cease, the legends say
the snows will never leave her . . .
wasting away, under her brows the tears
showering down her breasting ridge and slopes —
a rocky death like hers puts me to sleep.   925

894 Aphrodite: Goddess of love. **906 Acheron:** A river in the underworld, to which the dead go. **916 Niobe:** A queen of Thebes who was punished by the gods for her pride and was turned into stone.

CHORUS: But she was a god, born of gods,
          and we are only mortals born to die.
          And yet, of course, it's a great thing
          for a dying girl to hear, just hear
          she shares a destiny equal to the gods,   930
          during life and later, once she's dead.
ANTIGONE: O you mock me!
     Why, in the name of all my fathers' gods
     why can't you wait till I am gone —
          must you abuse me to my face?
     O my city, all your fine rich sons!   935
     And you, you springs of the Dirce,
     holy grove of Thebes where the chariots gather,
               you at least, you'll bear me witness, look,
     unmourned by friends and forced by such crude laws
     I go to my rockbound prison, strange new tomb —   940
          always a stranger, O dear god,
     I have no home on earth and none below,
          not with the living, not with the breathless dead.
CHORUS: You went too far, the last limits of daring —
          smashing against the high throne of Justice!   945
               Your life's in ruins, child — I wonder . . .
          do you pay for your father's terrible ordeal?
ANTIGONE: There — at last you've touched it, the worst pain
     the worst anguish! Raking up the grief for father
          three times over, for all the doom   950
     that's struck us down, the brilliant house of Laius.
     O mother, your marriage-bed
     the coiling horrors, the coupling there —
          you with your own son, my father — doomstruck mother!
     Such, such were my parents, and I their wretched child. 955
     I go to them now, cursed, unwed, to share their home —
          I am a stranger! O dear brother, doomed
          in your marriage — your marriage murders mine,
               your dying drags me down to death alive!

Enter Creon.

CHORUS: Reverence asks some reverence in return —   960
          but attacks on power never go unchecked,
               not by the man who holds the reins of power.
          Your own blind will, your passion has destroyed you.
ANTIGONE: No one to weep for me, my friends,
          no wedding-song — they take me away   965
          in all my pain . . . the road lies open, waiting.
          Never again, the law forbids me to see
          the sacred eye of day. I am agony!

No tears for the destiny that's mine,
no loved one mourns my death.
CREON: Can't you see?   970
If a man could wail his own dirge *before* he dies,
he'd never finish.
To the guards.
                            Take her away, quickly!
Wall her up in the tomb, you have your orders.
Abandon her there, alone, and let her choose —
death or a buried life with a good roof for shelter.   975
As for myself, my hands are clean. This young girl —
dead or alive, she will be stripped of her rights,
her stranger's rights, here in the world above.
ANTIGONE: O tomb, my bridal-bed — my house, my prison
cut in the hollow rock, my everlasting watch!   980
I'll soon be there, soon embrace my own,
the great growing family of our dead
Persephone° has received among her ghosts.
                                                  I,
the last of them all, the most reviled by far,
go down before my destined time's run out.   985
But still I go, cherishing one good hope:
my arrival may be dear to father,
dear to you, my mother,
dear to you, my loving brother, Eteocles —
When you died I washed you with my hands,   990
I dressed you all, I poured the cups
across your tombs. But now, Polynices,
because I laid your body out as well,
this, this is my reward. Nevertheless
I honored you — the decent will admit it —   995
well and wisely too.
                          Never, I tell you,
if I had been the mother of children
or if my husband died, exposed and rotting —
I'd never have taken this ordeal upon myself,
never defied our people's will. What law,   1000
you ask, do I satisfy with what I say?
A husband dead, there might have been another.
A child by another too, if I had lost the first.
But mother and father both lost in the halls of Death,
no brother could ever spring to light again.   1005
For this law alone I held you first in honor.
For this, Creon, the king, judges me a criminal

983 Persephone: Queen of the underworld.

guilty of dreadful outrage, my dear brother!
And now he leads me off, a captive in his hands,
with no part in the bridal-song, the bridal-bed,   1010
denied all joy of marriage, raising children —
deserted so by loved ones, struck by fate,
I descend alive to the caverns of the dead.
What law of the mighty gods have I transgressed?
Why look to the heavens any more, tormented as I am?   1015
Whom to call, what comrades now? Just think,
my reverence only brands me for irreverence!
Very well: if this is the pleasure of the gods,
once I suffer I will know that I was wrong.
But if these men are wrong, let them suffer   1020
nothing worse than they mete out to me —
these masters of injustice!
LEADER: Still the same rough winds, the wild passion
    raging through the girl.
CREON:

To the guards.

                    Take her away.
    You're wasting time — you'll pay for it too.   1025
ANTIGONE: Oh god, the voice of death. It's come, it's here.
CREON: True. Not a word of hope — your doom is sealed.
ANTIGONE: Land of Thebes, city of all my fathers —
        O you gods, the first gods of the race!
        They drag me away, now, no more delay.   1030
        Look on me, you noble sons of Thebes —
        the last of a great line of kings,
        I alone, see what I suffer now
        at the hands of what breed of men —
        all for reverence, my reverence for the gods!   1035

She leaves under guard; the Chorus gathers.

CHORUS: Danaë, Danaë° —
    even she endured a fate like yours,
        in all her lovely strength she traded
    the light of day for the bolted brazen vault —
    buried within her tomb, her bridal-chamber,   1040
    wed to the yoke and broken.
        But she was of glorious birth
                my child, my child
    and treasured the seed of Zeus within her womb,
    the cloudburst streaming gold!   1045

1036 Danaë: Locked in a cell by her father because it was prophesied that her son would kill him, but visited by Zeus in the form of a shower of gold. Their son was Perseus.

The power of fate is a wonder,
dark, terrible wonder —
neither wealth nor armies
towered walls nor ships
black hulls lashed by the salt   1050
can save us from that force.
The yoke tamed him too
    young Lycurgus° flaming in anger
king of Edonia, all for his mad taunts
Dionysus clamped him down, encased   1055
in the chain-mail of rock
    and there his rage
                his terrible flowering rage burst —
sobbing, dying away . . . at last that madman
came to know his god —   1060
    the power he mocked, the power
    he taunted in all his frenzy
    trying to stamp out
    the women strong with the god —
    the torch, the raving sacred cries —   1065
    enraging the Muses° who adore the flute.

And far north where the Black Rocks
    cut the sea in half
and murderous straits
split the coast of Thrace   1070
    a forbidding city stands
where once, hard by the walls
the savage Ares thrilled to watch
a king's new queen, a Fury rearing in rage
    against his two royal sons —   1075
    her bloody hands, her dagger-shuttle
stabbing out their eyes — cursed, blinding wounds —
their eyes blind sockets screaming for revenge!

They wailed in agony, cries echoing cries
    the princes doomed at birth . . .   1080
and their mother doomed to chains,
walled off in a tomb of stone —
    but she traced her own birth back
to a proud Athenian line and the high gods
and off in caverns half the world away,   1085
born of the wild North Wind
    she sprang on her father's gales,

1053 Lycurgus: Punished by Dionysus because he would not worship him.   **1066 Muses:** Goddesses of the arts.

racing stallions up the leaping cliffs —
child of the heavens. But even on her the Fates
the gray everlasting Fates rode hard   1090
my child, my child.

Enter Tiresias, the blind prophet, led by a boy.

TIRESIAS: Lords of Thebes,
I and the boy have come together,
hand in hand. Two see with the eyes of one . . .
so the blind must go, with a guide to lead the way.
CREON: What is it, old Tiresias? What news now?   1095
TIRESIAS: I will teach you. And you obey the seer.
CREON: I will,
I've never wavered from your advice before.
TIRESIAS: And so you kept the city straight on course.
CREON: I owe you a great deal, I swear to that.
TIRESIAS: Then reflect, my son: you are poised,   1100
once more, on the razor-edge of fate.
CREON: What is it? I shudder to hear you.
TIRESIAS: •   You will learn
when you listen to the warnings of my craft.
As I sat on the ancient seat of augury,°
in the sanctuary where every bird I know   1105
will hover at my hands — suddenly I heard it,
a strange voice in the wingbeats, unintelligible,
barbaric, a mad scream! Talons flashing, ripping,
they were killing each other — that much I knew —
the murderous fury whirring in those wings   1110
made that much clear!
                        I was afraid,
I turned quickly, tested the burnt-sacrifice,
ignited the altar at all points — but no fire,
the god in the fire never blazed.
Not from those offerings . . . over the embers   1115
slid a heavy ooze from the long thighbones,
smoking, sputtering out, and the bladder
puffed and burst — spraying gall into the air —
and the fat wrapping the bones slithered off
and left them glistening white. No fire!   1120
The rites failed that might have blazed the future
with a sign. So I learned from the boy here;
he is my guide, as I am guide to others.
                        And it's you —
your high resolve that sets this plague on Thebes.
The public altars and sacred hearths are fouled,   1125

1104 seat of augury: Where Tiresias looked for omens among birds.

one and all, by the birds and dogs with carrion
torn from the corpse, the doomstruck son of Oedipus!
And so the gods are deaf to our prayers, they spurn
the offerings in our hands, the flame of holy flesh.
No birds cry out an omen clear and true — 1130
they're gorged with the murdered victim's blood and fat.
Take these things to heart, my son, I warn you.
All men make mistakes, it is only human.
But once the wrong is done, a man
can turn his back on folly, misfortune too, 1135
if he tries to make amends, however low he's fallen,
and stops his bullnecked ways. Stubbornness
brands you for stupidity — pride is a crime.
No, yield to the dead!
Never stab the fighter when he's down. 1140
Where's the glory, killing the dead twice over?

I mean you well. I give you sound advice.
It's best to learn from a good adviser
when he speaks for your own good:
it's pure gain.
CREON: Old man — all of you! So, 1145
you shoot your arrows at my head like archers at the target —
I even have *him* loosed on me, this fortune-teller.
Oh his ilk has tried to sell me short
and ship me off for years. Well,
drive your bargains, traffic — much as you like — 1150
in the gold of India, silver-gold of Sardis.
You'll never bury that body in the grave,
not even if Zeus's eagles rip the corpse
and wing their rotten pickings off to the throne of god!
Never, not even in fear of such defilement 1155
will I tolerate his burial, that traitor.
Well I know, we can't defile the gods —
no mortal has the power.
                           No,
reverend old Tiresias, all men fall,
it's only human, but the wisest fall obscenely 1160
when they glorify obscene advice with rhetoric —
all for their own gain.
TIRESIAS: Oh god, is there a man alive
who knows, who actually believes . . .
CREON: What now?
What earth-shattering truth are you about to utter? 1165
TIRESIAS: . . . just how much a sense of judgment, wisdom
is the greatest gift we have?

CREON: Just as much, I'd say,
    as a twisted mind is the worst affliction going.
TIRESIAS: You are the one who's sick, Creon, sick to death.
CREON: I am in no mood to trade insults with a seer.   1170
TIRESIAS: You have already, calling my prophecies a lie.
CREON: Why not?
    You and the whole breed of seers are mad for money!
TIRESIAS: And the whole race of tyrants lusts to rake it in.
CREON: This slander of yours —
    are you aware you're speaking to the king?   1175
TIRESIAS: Well aware. Who helped you save the city?
CREON: You —
    you have your skills, old seer, but you lust for injustice!
TIRESIAS: You will drive me to utter the dreadful secret in my heart.
CREON: Spit it out! Just don't speak it out for profit.
TIRESIAS: Profit? No, not a bit of profit, not for you.   1180
CREON: Know full well, you'll never buy off my resolve.
TIRESIAS: Then know this too, learn this by heart!
    The chariot of the sun will not race through
    so many circuits more, before you have surrendered
    one born of your own loins, your own flesh and blood,   1185
    a corpse for corpses given in return, since you have thrust
    to the world below a child sprung for the world above,
    ruthlessly lodged a living soul within the grave —
    then you've robbed the gods below the earth,
    keeping a dead body here in the bright air,   1190
    unburied, unsung, unhallowed by the rites.

    You, you have no business with the dead,
    nor do the gods above — this is violence
    you have forced upon the heavens.
    And so the avengers, the dark destroyers late   1195
    but true to the mark, now lie in wait for you,
    the Furies sent by the gods and the god of death
    to strike you down with the pains that you perfected!

    There. Reflect on that, tell me I've been bribed.
    The day comes soon, no long test of time, not now,   1200
    that wakes the wails for men and women in your halls.
    Great hatred rises against you —
    cities in tumult, all whose mutilated sons
    the dogs have graced with burial, or the wild beasts,
    some wheeling crow that wings the ungodly stench of carrion   1205
    back to each city, each warrior's hearth and home.

    These arrows for your heart! Since you've raked me
    I loose them like an archer in my anger,

arrows deadly true. You'll never escape
their burning, searing force.   1210

Motioning to his escort.

Come, boy, take me home.
So he can vent his rage on younger men,
and learn to keep a gentler tongue in his head
and better sense than what he carries now.

Exit to the side.

LEADER: The old man's gone, my king —   1215
terrible prophecies. Well I know,
since the hair on this old head went gray,
he's never lied to Thebes.
CREON: I know it myself — I'm shaken, torn.
It's a dreadful thing to yield . . . but resist now?   1220
Lay my pride bare to the blows of ruin?
That's dreadful too.
LEADER: But good advice,
Creon, take it now, you must.
CREON: What should I do? Tell me . . . I'll obey.
LEADER: Go! Free the girl from the rocky vault   1225
and raise a mound for the body you exposed.
CREON: That's your advice? You think I should give in?
LEADER: Yes, my king, quickly. Disasters sent by the gods
cut short our follies in a flash.
CREON: Oh it's hard.
giving up the heart's desire . . . but I will do it —   1230
no more fighting a losing battle with necessity.
LEADER: Do it now, go, don't leave it to others.
CREON: Now — I'm on my way! Come, each of you,
take up axes, make for the high ground,
over there, quickly! I and my better judgment   1235
have come round to this — I shackled her,
I'll set her free myself. I am afraid . . .
it's best to keep the established laws
to the very day we die.

Rushing out, followed by his entourage. The Chorus clusters around the altar.

CHORUS: God of a hundred names!
                        Great Dionysus —   1240
        Son and glory of Semele! Pride of Thebes —
Child of Zeus whose thunder rocks the clouds —
Lord of the famous lands of evening —
King of the Mysteries!
                King of Eleusis, Demeter's plain°

1244 Demeter's plain: The goddess of grain was worshipped at Eleusis, near Athens.

her breasting hills that welcome in the world —   1245
Great Dionysus!
                    Bacchus,° living in Thebes
the mother-city of all your frenzied women —
                                              Bacchus
          living along the Ismenus's° rippling waters
standing over the field sown with the Dragon's teeth!

You — we have seen you through the flaring smoky fires,   1250
     your torches blazing over the twin peaks
where nymphs of the hallowed cave climb onward
                    fired with you, your sacred rage —
we have seen you at Castalia's running spring°
and down from the heights of Nysa° crowned with ivy   1255
the greening shore rioting vines and grapes
          down you come in your storm of wild women
          ecstatic, mystic cries —
                              Dionysus —
down to watch and ward the roads of Thebes!

First of all cities, Thebes you honor first   1260
you and your mother, bride of the lightning —
come, Dionysus! now your people lie
in the iron grip of plague,
come in your racing, healing stride
                    down Parnassus's° slopes   1265
or across the moaning straits.
                              Lord of the dancing —
dance, dance the constellations breathing fire!
Great master of the voices of the night!
Child of Zeus, God's offspring, come, come forth!
Lord, king, dance with your nymphs, swirling, raving   1270
arm-in-arm in frenzy through the night
          they dance you, Iacchus° —
                              Dance, Dionysus
giver of all good things!

Enter a Messenger from the side.

MESSENGER: Neighbors,
friends of the house of Cadmus° and the kings,
there's not a thing in this life of ours   1275

1246 Bacchus: Another name for Dionysus.   **1248 Ismenus:** A river near Thebes
where the founders of the city were said to have sprung from a dragon's teeth.
1254 Castalia's running spring: The sacred spring of Apollo's oracle at Delphi.
1255 Nysa: A mountain where Dionysus was worshipped.   **1265 Parnassus:** A
mountain in Greece that was sacred to Dionysus as well as other gods and goddesses.
1272 Iacchus: Dionysus.   **1274 Cadmus:** The legendary founder of Thebes.

I'd praise or blame as settled once for all.
Fortune lifts and Fortune fells the lucky
and unlucky every day. No prophet on earth
can tell a man his fate. Take Creon:
there was a man to rouse your envy once,   1280
as I see it. He saved the realm from enemies;
taking power, he alone, the lord of the fatherland,
he set us true on course — flourished like a tree
with the noble line of sons he bred and reared . . .
and now it's lost, all gone.
                              Believe me,   1285
when a man has squandered his true joys,
he's good as dead, I tell you, a living corpse.
Pile up riches in your house, as much as you like —
live like a king with a huge show of pomp,
but if real delight is missing from the lot,   1290
I wouldn't give you a wisp of smoke for it,
not compared with joy.
LEADER: What now?
What new grief do you bring the house of kings?
MESSENGER: Dead, dead — and the living are guilty of their death!
LEADER: Who's the murderer? Who is dead? Tell us.   1295
MESSENGER: Haemon's gone, his blood spilled by the very hand —
LEADER: His father's or his own?
MESSENGER: His own . . .
raging mad with his father for the death —
LEADER: Oh great seer,
you saw it all, you brought your word to birth!
MESSENGER: Those are the facts. Deal with them as you will.   1300

As he turns to go, Eurydice enters from the palace.

LEADER: Look, Eurydice. Poor woman, Creon's wife,
so close at hand. By chance perhaps,
unless she's heard the news about her son.
EURYDICE: My countrymen,
all of you — I caught the sound of your words
as I was leaving to do my part,   1305
to appeal to queen Athena° with my prayers.
I was just loosing the bolts, opening the doors,
when a voice filled with sorrow, family sorrow,
struck my ears, and I fell back, terrified,
into the women's arms — everything went black.   1310
Tell me the news, again, whatever it is . . .
sorrow and I are hardly strangers;
I can bear the worst.

1306 Athena: Goddess of wisdom and protector of Greek cities.

MESSENGER: I — dear lady,
I'll speak as an eye-witness. I was there.
And I won't pass over one word of the truth.   1315
Why should I try to soothe you with a story,
only to prove a liar in a moment?
Truth is always best.
                          So,
I escorted your lord, I guided him
to the edge of the plain where the body lay,   1320
Polynices, torn by the dogs and still unmourned.
And saying a prayer to Hecate of the Crossroads,
Pluto° too, to hold their anger and be kind,
we washed the dead in a bath of holy water
and plucking some fresh branches, gathering . . .   1325
what was left of him, we burned them all together
and raised a high mound of native earth, and then
we turned and made for that rocky vault of hers,
the hollow, empty bed of the bride of Death.
And far off, one of us heard a voice,   1330
a long wail rising, echoing
out of that unhallowed wedding-chamber;
he ran to alert the master and Creon pressed on,
closer — the strange, inscrutable cry came sharper,
throbbing around him now, and he let loose   1335
a cry of his own, enough to wrench the heart,
"Oh god, am I the prophet now? going down
the darkest road I've ever gone? My son —
it's *his* dear voice, he greets me! Go, men,
closer, quickly! Go through the gap,   1340
the rocks are dragged back —
right to the tomb's very mouth — and look,
see if it's Haemon's voice I think I hear,
or the gods have robbed me of my senses."

The king was shattered. We took his orders,   1345
went and searched, and there in the deepest,
dark recesses of the tomb we found her . . .
hanged by the neck in a fine linen noose,
strangled in her veils — and the boy,
his arms flung around her waist,   1350
clinging to her, wailing for his bride,
dead and down below, for his father's crimes
and the bed of his marriage blighted by misfortune.
When Creon saw him, he gave a deep sob,

1322–23 Hecate, Pluto: Gods of the underworld.

he ran in, shouting, crying out to him,   1355
"Oh my child — what have you done? what seized you,
what insanity? what disaster drove you mad?
Come out, my son! I beg you on my knees!"
But the boy gave him a wild burning glance,
spat in his face, not a word in reply,   1360
he drew his sword — his father rushed out,
running as Haemon lunged and missed! —
and then, doomed, desperate with himself,
suddenly leaning his full weight on the blade,
he buried it in his body, halfway to the hilt.   1365
And still in his senses, pouring his arms around her,
he embraced the girl and breathing hard,
released a quick rush of blood,
bright red on her cheek glistening white.
And there he lies, body enfolding body . . .   1370
he has won his bride at last, poor boy,
not here but in the houses of the dead.

Creon shows the world that of all the ills
afflicting men the worst is lack of judgment.

Eurydice turns and reenters the palace.

LEADER: What do you make of that? The lady's gone,   1375
      without a word, good or bad.
MESSENGER: I'm alarmed too
      but here's my hope — faced with her son's death,
      she finds it unbecoming to mourn in public.
      Inside, under her roof, she'll set her women
      to the task and wail the sorrow of the house.   1380
      She's too discreet. She won't do something rash.
LEADER: I'm not so sure. To me, at least,
      a long heavy silence promises danger,
      just as much as a lot of empty outcries.
MESSENGER: We'll see if she's holding something back,   1385
      hiding some passion in her heart.
      I'm going in. You may be right — who knows?
      Even too much silence has its dangers.

Exit to the palace. Enter Creon from the side, escorted by attendants carrying
Haemon's body on a bier.

LEADER: The king himself! Coming toward us,
           look, holding the boy's head in his hands.   1390
           Clear, damning proof, if it's right to say so —
           proof of his own madness, no one else's,
                 no, his own blind wrongs.
CREON: Ohhh,

so senseless, so insane . . . my crimes,
my stubborn, deadly —   1395
Look at us, the killer, the killed,
father and son, the same blood — the misery!
My plans, my mad fanatic heart,
my son, cut off so young!
Ai, dead, lost to the world,   1400
not through your stupidity, no, my own.

LEADER: Too late,
too late, you see what justice means.

CREON: Oh I've learned
through blood and tears! Then, it was then,
when the god came down and struck me — a great weight
shattering, driving me down that wild savage path,   1405
ruining, trampling down my joy. Oh the agony,
the heartbreaking agonies of our lives.

Enter the Messenger from the palace.

MESSENGER: Master,
what a hoard of grief you have, and you'll have more.
The grief that lies to hand you've brought yourself —

Pointing to Haemon's body.

the rest, in the house, you'll see it all too soon.   1410

CREON: What now? What's worse than this?

MESSENGER: The queen is dead.
The mother of this dead boy . . . mother to the end —
poor thing, her wounds are fresh.

CREON: No, no,
harbor of Death, so choked, so hard to cleanse! —
why me? why are you killing me?   1415
Herald of pain, more words, more grief?
I died once, you kill me again and again!
What's the report, boy . . . some news for me?
My wife dead? O dear god!
Slaughter heaped on slaughter?

The doors open; the body of Eurydice is brought out on her bier.

MESSENGER: See for yourself: 1420
now they bring her body from the palace.

CREON: Oh no,
another, a second loss to break the heart.
What next, what fate still waits for me?
I just held my son in my arms and now,
look, a new corpse rising before my eyes —   1425
wretched, helpless mother — O my son!

MESSENGER: She stabbed herself at the altar,
   then her eyes went dark, after she'd raised
   a cry for the noble fate of Megareus,° the hero
   killed in the first assault, then for Haemon,   1430
   then with her dying breath she called down
   torments on your head — you killed her sons.
CREON: Oh the dread,
   I shudder with dread! Why not kill me too? —
   run me through with a good sharp sword?
   Oh god, the misery, anguish —   1435
   I, I'm churning with it, going under.
MESSENGER: Yes, and the dead, the woman lying there,
   piles the guilt of all their deaths on you.
CREON: How did she end her life, what bloody stroke?
MESSENGER: She drove home to the heart with her own hand,   1440
   once she learned her son was dead . . . that agony.
CREON: And the guilt is all mine —
   can never be fixed on another man,
   no escape for me. I killed you,
   I, god help me, I admit it all!   1445

To his attendants.

   Take me away, quickly, out of sight.
   I don't even exist — I'm no one. Nothing.
LEADER: Good advice, if there's any good in suffering.
   Quickest is best when troubles block the way.
CREON:

Kneeling in prayer.

   Come, let it come! — that best of fates for me   1450
   that brings the final day, best fate of all.
   Oh quickly, now —
   so I never have to see another sunrise.
LEADER: That will come when it comes;
   we must deal with all that lies before us.   1455
   The future rests with the ones who tend the future.
CREON: That prayer — I poured my heart into that prayer!
LEADER: No more prayers now. For mortal men
   there is no escape from the doom we must endure.
CREON: Take me away, I beg you, out of sight.   1460
   A rash, indiscriminate fool!
   I murdered you, my son, against my will —
   you too, my wife . . .

1429 Megareus: A son of Creon and Eurydice; he died when Thebes was attacked.

Wailing wreck of a man,
whom to look to? where to lean for support?

Desperately turning from Haemon to Eurydice on their biers.

Whatever I touch goes wrong — once more   1465
a crushing fate's come down upon my head.

The Messenger and attendants lead Creon into the palace.

CHORUS: Wisdom is by far the greatest part of joy,
and reverence toward the gods must be safeguarded.
The mighty words of the proud are paid in full
with mighty blows of fate, and at long last   1470
those blows will teach us wisdom.

The old citizens exit to the side.   [c. 441 B.C.E.]

■ THINKING ABOUT THE TEXT

1. Describe Antigone with at least three adjectives of your own. How much do you sympathize with her? Do you consider her morally superior to Creon? Identify specific things that influence your view of her. Do your feelings about her shift during the course of the play? If so, when and how?

2. Do you feel any sympathy for Creon? For Ismene? Explain your reasoning. What values seem to be in conflict as Antigone argues with each?

3. Where, if anywhere, do you see the chorus as expressing wisdom? Where, if anywhere, do the members of the chorus strike you as imperfect people?

4. Here is an issue of genre: Ever since the ancient Greek philosopher Aristotle analyzed tragedy in his *Poetics*, a common definition of this kind of play is that its central character has a fatal flaw. How well does this definition fit *Antigone*? Must it be altered to accommodate Sophocles' play? Explain. Here is another issue of genre: In the *Poetics*, Aristotle also argued that a tragedy ends in catharsis. After arousing pity and fear in the audience, a tragedy relieves the audience of these feelings. How well does Aristotle's observation apply in the case of *Antigone*?

5. As was customary in Greek tragedy, the violent events in this play occur offstage and are merely reported. Had they occurred onstage, how might the audience's reaction have been different? Today, many films and television shows directly confront their audience with violence. Do you prefer this directness to Greek tragedy's way of dealing with violence? Support your answer by comparing some contemporary presentations of violence with *Antigone*'s.

In the News

The following two articles, drawn from London-based newspapers, examine present-day fights by women against governmental injustice. The first piece, which appeared in the September 12, 2010, issue of the *Observer*, reports on female activists and judicial victims in Iran. Since the deposing of the shah of Iran in 1979, the country has been ruled by Islamic clerics (ayatollahs), although its citizens supposedly choose the president and other officials. Notable opponents of the regime have included Shirin Ebadi, whose campaign for human rights in her nation won her the Nobel Peace Prize in 2003. Women also figured prominently in the mass demonstrations against the government that broke out in June 2009, when the highly conservative president Mahmoud Ahmadinejad won reelection in a vote that was clearly rigged. This large-scale protest is sometimes called the "Green Movement," a term that the authors of the article use.

The second piece, essentially an opinion column, was published in the November 15, 2010, issue of the *Independent*. Author Isabel Hilton is responding to the appearance in public of Aung San Suu Kyi, another female winner of the Nobel Peace Prize. She had recently been freed after several years of house arrest in her native country of Myanmar, formerly known as Burma. Basically, she had been sentenced for demanding more democracy from the military officers who now rule her nation. Hilton uses the occasion of her release to consider whether an individual protester's moral authority can lead to significant political change. In pondering this issue, she refers to other famous activists, including Corazon Aquino (who led a movement that overthrew the dictator Ferdinand Marcos in the Philippines), Nelson Mandela (who became prime minister of South Africa after a long imprisonment by its formerly white-supremacist regime), Václav Havel (a Czech playwright who became president of his country after helping to topple its Communist leaders), the Dalai Lama (who still fights for the liberation of Tibet from Chinese control), and Liu Xiabo, a jailed pro-democracy activist in China who had won the Nobel Peace Prize just before Hilton wrote this article.

PETER BEAUMONT AND SAEED KAMALI DEHGHAN

Iran: Women on the Frontline of the Fight for Rights

When Shahrzad Kariman finally saw her imprisoned daughter Shiva Nazar Ahari earlier this month, it was for a brief moment outside the Tehran courtroom where the 26-year-old human rights campaigner had been brought. "We could see her for a few minutes," Kariman told the International Campaign for Human Rights in Iran last week. "Just enough to hug her. But we couldn't ask her how the court session went. . . . We didn't know what the charges were prior to the court session."

The charges against Nazar Ahari are among the most serious that can be levelled in Iran: *muharebeh* (enmity against God), a crime, in theory punishable by death, originally intended to be used against armed gangs and pirates, not dissidents.

Nazar Ahari is also charged with assembly and collusion aiming to commit a crime, propagating against the regime, and disrupting public order. But perhaps most dangerous among the allegations — strongly denied both by her family and her organisation, the Committee for Human Rights Reporters — is of "relations" with the banned Mojahedin e-Khalq group, which is accused by the Iranian regime of terrorist activities. Her family says that she deplores the organisation.

Arrested twice since the disputed Iranian elections in June 2009 and held in the notorious Evin prison, in north-west Tehran, Nazar Ahari has been kept largely incommunicado since December, when she was arrested with several other women activists on her way to the funeral of Grand Ayatollah Hossein Ali Montazeri in the city of Qom. Also detained was Mahboubeh Abbasgholizadeh, another prominent women's rights activist and film-maker, who has since left Iran and was sentenced in absentia to two-and-a-half years in jail and 30 lashes for her part in a 2007 protest.

For the 15 months since Iran's stolen elections, the faces of these women   5
and others like them have been visible from Paris to New York, in London, Berlin, Sydney, and the Hague.

Their pictures have been held aloft at demonstrations, appeared on human rights websites, and are plastered almost daily across newspapers and television screens. They have joined the faces of other Iranian women who, through their activism or by dint of becoming victims of the regime, have come to be the most visible symbols in the west of the wider political and social oppression in Iran under its conservative president, Mahmoud Ahmadinejad.

Then there are the images of the dead, such as Neda Agha Soltan, shot on 20 June 2009 while attending an opposition demonstration to protest at the theft of the Iranian election by Ahmadinejad and his supporters.

If female activists have been prominent, so too have women threatened with death, such as Sakineh Mohammadi Ashtiani, the 43-year-old mother-of-two thrust to international attention after she was sentenced to being stoned to death for adultery.

And if Mohammadi Ashtiani is not an activist but a victim, her shocking case has become a lightning rod for activism for Iranian human rights, an example of how women are treated in the Islamic republic and the failure of its judicial system. This has been seized on by film stars and celebrities such as Colin Firth, Emma Thompson, and Carla Bruni, the wife of France's president, Nicolas Sarkozy, by politicians such as foreign secretary William Hague, and by institutions such as the European parliament and the Vatican.

The consequence has been that some names and pictures have become as   10
recognisable as those Iranian women internationally renowned before 2009, such as Shirin Ebadi, the Nobel Prize–winning human rights activist.

There is a simple reason why the cases of those women being persecuted for their activism and the case of Mohammadi Ashtiani are connected. Their stories reflect different aspects of the same confrontation in Iran: the place of women — and how women who fall foul of the regime can be accused and charged with anything, with no guarantee of a fair trial.

While the existence of this faultline long predates the events surrounding the 2009 election and the rise of the Green Movement, what is true is that Iran's opposition, for a while at least, has amplified the calls for women's rights which have come to define both the international anxiety about and protest against Ahmadinejad's regime.

Dr Ziba Mir-Hosseini, a Cambridge-based activist and scholar, argues that the current thrusting of women to the fore of the struggle between "despotism and democracy," as she calls it, has been inevitable given the history of women's rights in Iran.

It is a tension, she argues, that has been exacerbated by the contradictory attitude of the 1979 Islamic revolution towards women's political rights. For while the family protection law, introduced by the shah to give women equal rights in issues such as divorce, was quickly revoked after his downfall, the Islamic revolution allowed women to continue voting — a political right, ironically, that was invested with more meaning after the revolution, even as women's human rights were being eroded again under the pretence of the revolution's "protection of women's honour."

The reformists also opened up political space for women to operate, according to Mir-Hosseini. "Mohammad Khatami, during the eight years of his reformist presidency, set up a Centre for Women's Participation that saw the number of women's NGOs in Iran increase from around 45 to over 500."   15

The consequence, she believes, was that feminism — a word that could not even be uttered in the early 1980s — and a feminism linked strongly to notions of wider human rights, took hold in a new generation of Iranian women.

But even during the period when the country's women were actively encouraged to participate, conservative elements of the regime were working to silence them.

With the birth of the One Million Signature campaign, set up by veteran women's rights activists in 2006, a year after the election of Ahmadinejad for the first time, the scene was set for a confrontation.

And while the campaign was successful in forcing the temporary shelving of Ahmadinejad's own new family protection law, which would have made polygamy easier for men and divorce more difficult for women, the emerging power of women activists, who became leaders of the street protests against the 2009 election result, set them on a collision course with the increasingly hardline regime.

"I think part of the reason there has been so much focus on women's rights   20 since the election is the important role women had in the protests [in 2009]," says Maryam Namazie of the international support group Iran Solidarity.

"They were at the very forefront, leading the chanting of the slogans. It is also a fact that women's rights are very much the target of this government."

If the face of that activism went largely unnoticed in the international media before the 2009 election protests, confined to the figure of Shirin Ebadi, the violent sweeping up of those protests catapulted a wider group of women to global attention, both as prisoners of conscience and campaigners on an international stage.

This was partly due to the Neda effect, which drew attention to the role of women activists after Neda Agha Soltan was gunned down, with her death recorded on video and viewed around the world.

But if that event created a climate of intense interest in the often young women protestors, the response of the Ahmadinejad regime in clamping down on female campaigners drew even more attention.

A final component is the global attention paid to the stoning sentence delivered against Sakineh Mohammadi Ashtiani, which has served to underline what the women activists had long been saying about the broader attempt to dismantle women's rights.

Another prominent case is that of Shadi Sadr, who ran Rahai, a women's   25
legal advice centre, campaigning against stoning, and acted as defence lawyer for Nazar Ahari.

Arrested in July last year walking to Tehran University, where she had been planning to attend the Friday prayers led by the reformist former president Ayatollah Akbar Hashemi Rafsanjani, Shadi Sadr was bundled into an unmarked car and taken to Evin prison. Here she was held in solitary confinement and interrogated about other women's rights activists and the election, before being informed that she would be charged with endangering national security by causing riots.

In court, she was named as a leader of a women's rights movement accused of attempting to overthrow the Islamic republic. Shadi Sadr fled to Turkey two days later.

Describing her attempts to defend Nazar Ahari last week, Shadi Sadr said: "I was never given the permission to meet Shiva [Nazar Ahari] until the day I myself was arrested and, ironically, taken to the same cell Shiva was kept in until the day before I was taken in.

"On the wall of the cell she had written her stories and the charges she thought she was facing. Can you imagine that? The lawyer and her client both kept in one cell within a day? I was not allowed to meet her to hear what she had to say in her defence but that day I read it all on a cell wall.

"Shiva's arrest and especially charging her with *muharebeh*, which is pun-   30
ishable by death, is a clear message to all women's rights activists in Iran and the message is that they face execution if they continue."

The fate of Shadi Sadr, Shiva Nazar Ahari, and Mahboubeh Abbasgholizadeh since 2009 is deeply instructive. Their cases, as the Iran Human Rights Documentation Centre (IHRDC) argued last month in a report entitled "Silencing the Women's Rights Movement in Iran," have been used to attempt to dismantle the women's rights movement, and to cow it into silence under the cover of national security concerns.

That has included claims of links with "terrorism," as in Nazar Ahari's case, or collaboration with foreign countries, which was the explicit claim made by the Iranian authorities last year when they identified the women's rights movement as being one of six groups behind an attempted "velvet revolution."

Whether the regime really believes that or not, the aim since then, says Parisa Kakaee, a veteran women's rights activist quoted in the IHRDC report, is to present women activists with three options: "to become inactive, to go to prison, or to leave the country."

There is no indication that the campaign against women activists is letting up. Last month it was the turn of Nasrin Sotoudeh, 45, an outspoken lawyer and colleague of Shirin Ebadi who has defended a number of opposition activists and protesters. A member of the One Million Signatures campaign, she had been threatened by intelligence service officials that she would be arrested if she continued representing Shirin Ebadi, who left Iran a day before the election for a conference in Spain and didn't return for fear of harassment.

Ebadi said of Sotoudeh's arrest: "The only reason she was arrested is be-   35
cause of her human rights activities, because of defending her clients without any fear. Since the election last summer, a new move of intimidating and putting pressures on lawyers and especially women lawyers has emerged.

"Many have been forced to leave Iran and some are in jail. In this situation, Sotoudeh was one of the very few lawyers and women's right activists who was still working in Iran."

Ebadi is certain why the present Iranian regime is so afraid of women. In an article in the Guardian, she declared: "Mark my words, it will be women who bring democracy to Iran."

That socially potent coincidence of women's rights and democratic reform is something Ahmadinejad and his supporters are determined should not be permitted to arise.

It had been hoped that US citizen Sarah Shourd would be released to mark the end of Ramadan, but she remains in custody. Shourd is one of three American hikers who crossed into Iran from Iraq's northern Kurdish region in July 2009.

Iran has threatened to put Shourd and her two male companions on trial   40
for spying. Their families say they were hiking in the largely peaceful region of Iraq and that, if they did cross the border, it was accidental.

Clotilde Reiss, a French teaching assistant, was released earlier this year after being initially accused, like Shourd and her companions, of espionage. Reiss was arrested during the mass protests in 2009, when she was 24, and given two five-year jail sentences. Two Iranian men tried on the same day were hanged.

Found to have attended a demonstration and sent photographs of Iran to contacts at home, Reiss was put on trial with more than 100 others accused of

trying to topple the regime and spent a month and a half in Evin prison before
she was freed on bail and transferred to the French embassy.   *[2010]*

ISABEL HILTON

A Triumph for Moral Authority

All who watched Aung San Suu Kyi's short walk to freedom on Saturday had
waited a long time for a moment that was full of both joy and uncertainty
about the future.

As millions around the world caught their first glimpse of this resolute and
courageous woman, who has borne her nearly two decades of confinement
with dignity and integrity of purpose, other moments in recent history inevitably came to mind: would her release signal that change is coming to Burma, as
that of Nelson Mandela did in South Africa? Would she be able to lead a people-
power revolution, as Corazon Aquino did in the Philippines in 1986, or Vaclav
Havel in Czechoslovakia in 1989? Would her return to public life in Burma
bring the first rays of a political dawn, or will darkness return?

There are as many reasons to hope as to fear a new disappointment, but
whatever the final impact of her release, there is no questioning the power of
her presence. However we marshal the many arguments against the likelihood
of a restoration of democracy to Burma, the mesmerizing impact of those first
images reminds us of the exemplary catalyzing force of personal courage and
moral purpose.

It is not a good time for politics: In America, politics has descended into a
destructive, dysfunctional condition in which popular frustration is channeled
into a corporate-funded, poisonous populism. The conduct of the wars in Iraq
and Afghanistan has fatally damaged the West's ability to argue for human
rights elsewhere: how can Washington lecture Beijing or Burma on human
rights when it has itself embraced torture and imprisonment without trial?
Western governments still wave their rhetorical moral flags, but they are too
tarnished to be convincing.

Yet the desire to believe that political leaders can embody the moral values   5
essential to fair, equitable, and tolerant societies refuses to die. We continue to
hope for a politics that upholds humanity and justice against greed and violence. For many, the prospects of such a leadership seem unbearably distant.
Most of us struggle to match the moral claims of our leaders with political reality. Out of this disappointment comes the extraordinary power of those individuals who display personal courage against overwhelming odds.

The government of Burma's giant neighbor, China, has spent more than
two decades hoping the world — and its own citizens — will forget the devastating brutality of its suppression of the student demonstrators in Tiananmen
Square in 1989. But the unforgettable image of that tragic episode is one unidentified man in a white shirt and dark trousers, a shopping bag in one hand,
facing down an advancing column of tanks and bringing it to a standstill with

nothing more than unshakeable individual courage. To this day, Chinese contemporary art works are scrutinised by the security forces for images that might be read as coded references to that iconic moment.

We measure political power in material terms: how strong is the party, how big the army, how full the coffers, how secure the grip on the levers of state? By those measures, the Burmese generals hold all the cards, just as the apartheid regime did in South Africa when Nelson Mandela made his walk to freedom. But that assessment leaves out of account the unmeasurable power of moral authority, a power that derives from the ability not to coerce or to marshal fear, but to inspire citizens to acts of individual and collective courage, to keep hope alive, and to engender actions that may bring tragedy to the individual but that can create an unstoppable collective force.

Who would have predicted that an unarmed Czech playwright would catalyse a peaceful revolution against the armed might of the Soviet Union, or that an Indian campaigner for non-violence would drive the British from India? Such symbols take root in our memories and endure, long after the tanks have rusted. Does anyone doubt that the Dalai Lama is able to inspire — or that Hu Jintao° is not? How many citizens would shout for joy at the sight of one of Burma's military dictators? Would any real tears be shed if they were never seen again?

No doubt the Burmese regime does not seek to be loved, as long as it is sufficiently feared. Nevertheless, it has shown that it is not immune to the need to pretend that its mission is the general good. The election that the generals staged last month was an empty attempt to paint a coat of popular assent on coercion. That a regime that holds all the material cards needs to indulge in such pretence reveals both the limits of force and the fragility of a power that must suspect subversion everywhere. By every conventional measure, Aung San Suu Kyi is weak: a 65-year-old widow with no troops, few funds, and, formally at least, no party. When strong regimes show their fear of weak individuals their own vulnerability stands revealed.

Aung San Suu Kyi's release is one of those universal moments that resonate far beyond the borders of her suffering country. When she won the Nobel Peace Prize in 1991, she was already in detention. Her late husband, Michael Aris, and her two sons accepted the prize on her behalf. A photograph of the imprisoned laureate sat in the centre of the stage, a reminder to all of the regime's brutal intransigence.   10

On 10 December, China will undergo a similar moral rebuke when the Nobel Peace Prize is awarded to Liu Xiaobo, the Chinese public intellectual currently imprisoned for calling, amongst other things, for the Chinese government to respect its own constitution and to respect its own laws.

China is both Burma's neighbor and economic mainstay. China's official news agency, Xinhua, reported Aung San Suu Kyi's release in a few short paragraphs that led with her willingness to work for "national reconciliation." China's state television news led their report with the Burmese government's

Hu Jintao: Leader of the People's Republic of China.

announcement of her release. Neither mentioned that she, like Liu Xiaobo, is a Nobel Peace Prize laureate.

Liu is not someone who inspires a mass following in China as Aung San Suu Kyi does in Burma, but his moral courage, like hers, serves as a mirror that magnifies the lack of it in his jailers. Ever since the Nobel announcement in October, Beijing has been on the horns of a painful dilemma: they cannot release Liu to attend the ceremony without acknowledging the injustice of his imprisonment, but his absence at a ceremony makes the case against them even more powerfully.

Beijing has been attempting to coerce other countries into boycotting the ceremony, while detaining, or restricting the travel, of an ever wider circle of friends and sympathizers who might be suspected of planning to represent him in Oslo. The greater the effort to limit the impact of the Nobel prize, the worse the Chinese government looks; their impotence eats away at the one thing that no regime can enforce — the abstract but potent qualities of credibility and legitimacy.

Without the legitimacy of popular consent, even a lone, unarmed, impris-   15
oned individual is a potential threat. Their example shows us that we can decline to believe in a lie and that fear can be conquered. Once a people conquers its fears, the outcome is no longer in doubt. It is only a matter of time.   *[2010]*

≣ THINKING ABOUT THE TEXTS

1. In the first of these two articles, authors Beaumont and Dehghan suggest it makes sense to connect female activists with female victims of the Iranian justice system who are not necessarily protesting the overall government. To what extent do you accept the authors' linking of the two groups? Do you see Antigone as both activist *and* victim, or are you more inclined to give her just one of these labels? Explain.

2. In the second article, Hilton argues that Aung San Suu Kyi and other protesters she discusses carry "moral authority." How would *you* define this term? Do you see it as applicable to Antigone? Why, or why not?

3. Do you see Antigone as more flawed than the main women mentioned in the news articles? Why, or why not?

≣ WRITING ABOUT ISSUES

1. Write an essay that analyzes a character in Sophocles' play *other* than Antigone or Creon: examples include the chorus (which you can treat as one character), Ismene, Haemon, Tiresias, and Eurydice. Concentrate on explaining the relation between your chosen character and an issue that Antigone must deal with, too. (Remember that it's useful to phrase an issue as a question with more than one possible answer.)

2. Imagine that you are producing a contemporary staging of *Antigone* and must advertise it with a poster depicting one of the women mentioned

in the news articles. Write an essay explaining your selection of the particular woman you choose. Feel free to do further research on her if necessary.

3. Write an essay about a woman you know, directly or indirectly, whom you see as a fighter against injustice. Although you can use some of the essay to praise her, spend most of it explaining how she has had to confront at least one difficult issue — that is, a question with more than one possible answer. If you wish, refer to any of the texts in this cluster.

4. Write an essay or a script in which you imagine how Antigone would behave if she were transported to contemporary Iran, Myanmar, or China. If you wish, refer to one or both of the news articles in this cluster.

≣ Racial Injustice: Poems

COUNTEE CULLEN, "Incident"

NATASHA TRETHEWEY, "Incident"

Throughout literary history, writers have called attention to the injustices of racial oppression. The following pair of poems, both entitled "Incident," remind us that racial prejudice could be blatant and vicious both early in the twentieth century and toward its end. Indeed, the subject is not likely to die out even now, when laws blatantly permitting slavery or segregation have ceased to exist. Racism continues in various forms, though perhaps subtler ones. As you read these poems, consider what recent "incidents" might be topics of similar texts.

≣ BEFORE YOU READ

How do you define *racism*? What, for you, are possible signs of it?

COUNTEE CULLEN
Incident

Countee Cullen (1903–1946) was one of the leading writers of the Harlem Renaissance, a New York–based movement of African American authors, artists, and intellectuals that flourished from World War I to the Great Depression. Cullen's place of birth may have been Baltimore, Louisville, or New York, but by 1918 he was living in New York as the adopted son of a Methodist minister. Cullen wrote poetry and received prizes for it even as he attended New York University. In 1925, while pursuing a master's degree from Harvard, he published his first book of poems, Color, *which contained "Incident." His later books include* Copper Sun *(1927),* The Black Christ and Other Poems *(1929), a translation of Euripides' play* Medea *(1935), and a children's book,* The Lost Zoo *(1940). Cullen gained much attention when, in 1928, he wed the daughter of famed African American writer and scholar W. E. B. DuBois, but their marriage ended just two years later. During the 1930s, Cullen's writing did not earn him enough to live on, so he taught English and French at Frederick Douglass High School. At the time of his death in 1946, he was collaborating on the Broadway musical* St. Louis Woman. *In part because he died relatively young, Cullen's reputation faded. Langston Hughes became much better known as a Harlem Renaissance figure. "Incident," however, has been consistently anthologized, and today Cullen is being rediscovered along with other contributors to African American literature.*

Once riding in old Baltimore
    Heart-filled, head-filled with glee,
I saw a Baltimorean
    Keep looking straight at me.

Now I was eight and very small,   5
    And he was no whit bigger,
And so I smiled, but he poked out
    His tongue and called me, "Nigger."

I saw the whole of Baltimore
    From May until December: 10
Of all the things that happened there
    That's all that I remember.   *[1925]*

■ THINKING ABOUT THE TEXT

1. Why do you think the speaker calls attention to his heart *and* his head in the second line? Might referring to just one of these things have been enough?

2. "Baltimorean" (line 3) seems a rather unusual and abstract term for the boy that the speaker encountered. How do you explain its presence in the poem? How important is it that the speaker name the city where the incident occurred?

3. Although the incident that the speaker recalls must have been painful for him, why do you think he does not state his feelings about it more explicitly? What is the effect of his relative reticence about it?

4. The rhythm of this poem is rather singsongy. Why do you think Cullen made it so?

5. The speaker states that he was eight at the time of the incident. How old might he be now? How important is his age?

NATASHA TRETHEWEY

Incident

The child of an interracial marriage, Natasha Trethewey (b. 1966) graduated from the University of Georgia and earned a master's degree at Hollins College in Virginia. Now she teaches creative writing at Emory University in Atlanta, Georgia. She is the author of three volumes of poetry: Domestic Work *(2000),* Bellocq's Ophelia *(2002), and* Native Guard *(2006), which won the Pulitzer Prize and includes the following poem. Her latest book,* Beyond Katrina: A Meditation on the Mississippi Gulf Coast *(2010), is a combination of memoir and reportage that also mixes prose with verse.*

We tell the story every year —
how we peered from the windows, shades drawn —
though nothing really happened,
the charred grass now green again.

We peered from the windows, shade drawn,   5
at the cross trussed like a Christmas tree,
the charred grass still green. Then
we darkened our rooms, lit the hurricane lamps.

At the cross trussed like a Christmas tree,
a few men gathered, white as angels in their gowns.   10
We darkened our room and lit hurricane lamps,
the wicks trembling in their fonts of oil.

It seemed the angels had gathered, white men in their gowns.
When they were done, they left quietly. No one came.
The wicks trembled all night in their fonts of oil;   15
by morning the flames had all dimmed.

When they were done, the men left quietly. No one came.
Nothing really happened.
By morning all the flames had dimmed.
We tell the story every year.   [2006]   20

≡ THINKING ABOUT THE TEXT

1. Trethewey has acknowledged that this poem is a *pantoum*. This form of
   verse consists of *quatrains* (stanzas of four lines each); also, the second
   and fourth lines of a quatrain are repeated as the first and third lines of
   the following quatrain, with the final line of the entire poem repeating its
   very first line. It's a difficult type of poem to write. Why do you think
   Trethewey attempted it here?

2. How does the poem use religious imagery?

3. What information does the poet leave out? Why do you think she
   omits it?

4. Why do you think the "we" of the poem "tell[s] the story every year"?
   Why tell the story at all? Why not tell it more often?

5. Twice, the speaker claims that "nothing really happened." Do you agree
   with her? Why, or why not?

≡ MAKING COMPARISONS

1. In giving her poem the title "Incident," Trethewey is surely aware of
   Cullen's poem. What other connections between these two texts do you
   feel encouraged by her to make?

2. Which of the two poems, Cullen's or Trethewey's, strikes you as more abstract? Does this difference lead to a difference in effect? Why, or why not?

3. Do the speakers in these two poems strike you as using pretty much the same tone? Refer to specific lines in each work.

≡ WRITING ABOUT ISSUES

1. Choose either Cullen's poem or Trethewey's, and write an essay in which you examine what the poem suggests about the act of *remembering* an incident of race-related injustice.

2. Cullen's poem is famous; does Trethewey's deserve to be equally well known? Write an essay addressing this question for your audience, making clear your criteria for artistic success.

3. Take a line from either Cullen's poem or Trethewey's, and write an essay showing how the line is applicable to an "incident" that you recently witnessed or saw being reported in the media.

4. Find and read at least three articles on racial discrimination in early twentieth-century Baltimore or on American laws against interracial marriage. Then write an essay explaining how these articles illuminate the "incident" described in Cullen's or Trethewey's poem.

☰ What Is a Criminal?: Stories

SHERWOOD ANDERSON, "Hands"

REBECCA MAKKAI, "The Briefcase"

LINH DINH, "!"

Many of the literary works in this chapter focus on characters whose society brands them as criminals. In literature and in real life, however, the term *criminal* has proved controversial. People have argued that in certain cases it has been misapplied. They have claimed that a particular person labeled a criminal is guiltless of wrongdoing or has engaged in conduct that should not concern officers of the law. Among the issues in this debate is a basic one: What *is* a criminal? That is, how should the term be defined in the first place? This question is raised, in effect, by the three stories in this cluster. Their main characters are, fairly or unfairly, stigmatized as criminals, and each copes by clinging to a false identity. When the protagonist of Sherwood Anderson's "Hands" is banished from his hometown, he tries to lead a new life and adopts a new name along with it. Seized as a rebel, the chef in Rebecca Makkai's "The Briefcase" escapes and then survives by impersonating someone else. In Linh Dinh's "!," a North Vietnamese man continues to pose as an expert on the English language even after authorities have punished him for imposture. All of the stories suggest that determining what the word *criminal* should mean involves more than consulting dictionaries. It's an issue that requires complex thought — reflection that these stories provoke.

☰ BEFORE YOU READ

Who are some people that not everyone would consider "criminals" even though they have been labeled as such by an official system of law or by the general public?

SHERWOOD ANDERSON
Hands

Sherwood Anderson (1876–1941) was a major writer in the first half of the twentieth century. Even now, he is regarded as a leading figure in American literary naturalism, a movement that produced realistic and often pessimistic works about ordinary people. Although he also wrote novels, Anderson achieved his greatest impact with his short-story collection Winesburg, Ohio *(1919). Through interrelated episodes, this book focuses on a single town, depicting the stifled lives within it. George Willard, reminiscent of Anderson himself, is a recurring character in the stories. In "Hands," he hesitates to learn the secret history of another man, curiously named Wing Biddlebaum.*

Upon the half decayed veranda of a small frame house that stood near the edge of a ravine near the town of Winesburg, Ohio, a fat little old man walked nervously up and down. Across a long field that had been seeded for clover but that had produced only a dense crop of yellow mustard weeds, he could see the public highway along which went a wagon filled with berry pickers returning from the fields. The berry pickers, youths and maidens, laughed and shouted boisterously. A boy clad in a blue shirt leaped from the wagon and attempted to drag after him one of the maidens who screamed and protested shrilly. The feet of the boy in the road kicked up a cloud of dust that floated across the face of the departing sun. Over the long field came a thin girlish voice. "Oh, you Wing Biddlebaum, comb your hair, it's falling into your eyes," commanded the voice to the man, who was bald and whose nervous little hands fiddled about the bare white forehead as though arranging a mass of tangled locks.

Wing Biddlebaum, forever frightened and beset by a ghostly band of doubts, did not think of himself as in any way a part of the life of the town where he had lived for twenty years. Among all the people of Winesburg but one had come close to him. With George Willard, son of Tom Willard, the proprietor of the new Willard House, he had formed something like a friendship. George Willard was the reporter on the *Winesburg Eagle* and sometimes in the evenings he walked out along the highway to Wing Biddlebaum's house. Now as the old man walked up and down on the veranda, his hands moving nervously about, he was hoping that George Willard would come and spend the evening with him. After the wagon containing the berry pickers had passed, he went across the field through the tall mustard weeds and climbing a rail fence peered anxiously along the road to the town. For a moment he stood thus, rubbing his hands together and looking up and down the road, and then, fear overcoming him, ran back to walk again upon the porch of his own house.

In the presence of George Willard, Wing Biddlebaum, who for twenty years had been the town mystery, lost something of his timidity, and his shadowy personality, submerged in a sea of doubts, came forth to look at the world. With the young reporter at his side, he ventured in the light of day into Main Street or strode up and down on the rickety front porch of his own house, talking excitedly. The voice that had been low and trembling became shrill and loud. The bent figure straightened. With a kind of wriggle, like a fish returned to the brook by the fisherman, Biddlebaum the silent began to talk, striving to put into words the ideas that had been accumulated by his mind during long years of silence.

Wing Biddlebaum talked much with his hands. The slender expressive fingers, forever active, forever striving to conceal themselves in his pockets or behind his back, came forth and became the piston rods of his machinery of expression.

The story of Wing Biddlebaum is a story of hands. Their restless activity, like unto the beating of the wings of an imprisoned bird, had given him his name. Some obscure poet of the town had thought of it. The hands alarmed their owner. He wanted to keep them hidden away and looked with amazement at the quiet inexpressive hands of other men who worked beside him in the fields, or passed, driving sleepy teams on country roads.

When he talked to George Willard, Wing Biddlebaum closed his fists and beat with them upon a table or on the walls of his house. The action made him more comfortable. If the desire to talk came to him when the two were walking in the fields, he sought out a stump or the top board of a fence and with his hands pounding busily talked with renewed ease.

The story of Wing Biddlebaum's hands is worth a book itself. Sympathetically set forth it would tap many strange, beautiful qualities in obscure men. It is a job for a poet. In Winesburg the hands had attracted attention merely because of their activity. With them Wing Biddlebaum had picked as high as a hundred and forty quarts of strawberries in a day. They became his distinguishing feature, the source of his fame. Also they made more grotesque an already grotesque and elusive individuality. Winesburg was proud of the hands of Wing Biddlebaum in the same spirit in which it was proud of Banker White's new stone house and Wesley Moyer's bay stallion, Tony Tip, that had won the two-fifteen trot at the fall races in Cleveland.

As for George Willard, he had many times wanted to ask about the hands. At times an almost overwhelming curiosity had taken hold of him. He felt that there must be a reason for their strange activity and their inclination to keep hidden away and only a growing respect for Wing Biddlebaum kept him from blurting out the questions that were often in his mind.

Once he had been on the point of asking. The two were walking in the fields on a summer afternoon and had stopped to sit upon a grassy bank. All afternoon Wing Biddlebaum had talked as one inspired. By a fence he had stopped and beating like a giant woodpecker upon the top board had shouted at George Willard, condemning his tendency to be too much influenced by the people about him. "You are destroying yourself," he cried.

"You have the inclination to be alone and to dream and you are afraid of dreams. You want to be like others in town here. You hear them talk and you try to imitate them."   10

On the grassy bank Wing Biddlebaum had tried again to drive his point home. His voice became soft and reminiscent, and with a sigh of contentment he launched into a long rambling talk, speaking as one lost in a dream.

Out of the dream Wing Biddlebaum made a picture for George Willard. In the picture men lived again in a kind of pastoral golden age. Across a green open country came clean-limbed young men, some afoot, some mounted upon horses. In crowds the young men came to gather about the feet of an old man who sat beneath a tree in a tiny garden and who talked to them.

Wing Biddlebaum became wholly inspired. For once he forgot the hands. Slowly they stole forth and lay upon George Willard's shoulders. Something new and bold came into the voice that talked. "You must try to forget all you have learned," said the old man. "You must begin to dream. From this time on you must shut your ears to the roaring of the voices."

Pausing in his speech, Wing Biddlebaum looked long and earnestly at George Willard. His eyes glowed. Again he raised the hands to caress the boy and then a look of horror swept over his face.

With a convulsive movement of his body, Wing Biddlebaum sprang to   15
his feet and thrust his hands deep into his trousers pockets. Tears came to

his eyes. "I must be getting along home. I can talk no more with you," he said nervously.

Without looking back, the old man had hurried down the hillside and across a meadow, leaving George Willard perplexed and frightened upon the grassy slope. With a shiver of dread the boy arose and went along the road toward town. "I'll not ask him about his hands," he thought, touched by the memory of the terror he had seen in the man's eyes. "There's something wrong, but I don't want to know what it is. His hands have something to do with his fear of me and of everyone."

And George Willard was right. Let us look briefly into the story of the hands. Perhaps our talking of them will arouse the poet who will tell the hidden wonder story of the influence for which the hands were but fluttering pennants of promise.

In his youth Wing Biddlebaum had been a school teacher in a town in Pennsylvania. He was not then known as Wing Biddlebaum, but went by the less euphoric name of Adolph Myers. As Adolph Myers he was much loved by the boys of his school.

Adolph Myers was meant by nature to be a rare teacher of youth. He was one of those rare, little-understood men who rule by a power so gentle that it passes as a lovable weakness. In their feeling for the boys under their charge such men are not unlike the finer sort of women in their love of men.

And yet that is but crudely stated. It needs the poet there. With the boys of his school, Adolph Myers had walked in the evening or had sat talking until dusk upon the schoolhouse steps lost in a kind of dream. Here and there went his hands, caressing the shoulders of the boys, playing about the tousled heads. As he talked his voice became soft and musical. There was a caress in that also. In a way the voice and the hands, the stroking of the shoulders and the touching of the hair was a part of the schoolmaster's effort to carry a dream into the young minds. By the caress that was in his fingers he expressed himself. He was one of those men in whom the force that creates life is diffused, not centralized. Under the caress of his hands doubt and disbelief went out of the minds of the boys and they began also to dream. 20

And then the tragedy. A half-witted boy of the school became enamored of the young master. In his bed at night he imagined unspeakable things and in the morning went forth to tell his dreams as facts. Strange, hideous accusations fell from his loose-hung lips. Through the Pennsylvania town went a shiver. Hidden, shadowy doubts that had been in men's minds concerning Adolph Myers were galvanized into beliefs.

The tragedy did not linger. Trembling lads were jerked out of bed and questioned. "He put his arms about me," said one. "His fingers were always playing in my hair," said another.

One afternoon a man of the town, Henry Bradford, who kept a saloon, came to the schoolhouse door. Calling Adolph Myers into the school yard he began to beat him with his fists. As his hard knuckles beat down into the frightened face of the schoolmaster, his wrath became more and more terrible. Screaming with dismay, the children ran here and there like disturbed insects. "I'll teach you to put your hands on my boy, you beast," roared the saloon keeper, who, tired of beating the master, had begun to kick him about the yard.

Adolph Myers was driven from the Pennsylvania town in the night. With lanterns in their hands a dozen men came to the door of the house where he lived alone and commanded that he dress and come forth. It was raining and one of the men had a rope in his hands. They had intended to hang the schoolmaster, but something in his figure, so small, white, and pitiful, touched their hearts and they let him escape. As he ran away into the darkness they repented of their weakness and ran after him, swearing and throwing sticks and great balls of soft mud at the figure that screamed and ran faster and faster into the darkness.

For twenty years Adolph Myers had lived alone in Winesburg. He was but   25
forty but looked sixty-five. The name Biddlebaum he got from a box of goods seen at a freight station as he hurried through an eastern Ohio town. He had an aunt in Winesburg, a black-toothed old woman who raised chickens, and with her he lived until she died. He had been ill for a year after the experience in Pennsylvania, and after his recovery worked as a day laborer in the fields, going timidly about and striving to conceal his hands. Although he did not understand what had happened he felt that the hands must be to blame. Again and again the fathers of the boys had talked of the hands. "Keep your hands to yourself," the saloon keeper had roared, dancing with fury in the schoolhouse yard.

Upon the veranda of his house by the ravine, Wing Biddlebaum continued to walk up and down until the sun had disappeared and the road beyond the field was lost in the grey shadows. Going into his house he cut slices of bread and spread honey upon them. When the rumble of the evening train that took away the express cars loaded with the day's harvest of berries had passed and restored the silence of the summer night, he went again to walk upon the veranda. In the darkness he could not see the hands and they became quiet. Although he still hungered for the presence of the boy, who was the medium through which he expressed his love of man, the hunger became again a part of his loneliness and his waiting. Lighting a lamp, Wing Biddlebaum washed the few dishes soiled by his simple meal and, setting up a folding cot by the screen door that led to the porch, prepared to undress for the night. A few stray white bread crumbs lay on the cleanly washed floor by the table; putting the lamp upon a low stool he began to pick up the crumbs, carrying them to his mouth one by one with unbelievable rapidity. In the dense blotch of light beneath the table, the kneeling figure looked like a priest engaged in some service of his church. The nervous expressive fingers, flashing in and out of the light, might well have been mistaken for the fingers of the devotee going swiftly through decade after decade of his rosary.   *[1919]*

■ **THINKING ABOUT THE TEXT**

1. "The story of Wing Biddlebaum is a story of hands," announces the narrator (para. 5). In what ways is this so? Refer to specific passages that mention various things that Biddlebaum's hands do. How do you interpret his inability to control them? The narrator says that "George Willard

was right" (para. 17) to believe that "[Biddlebaum's] hands have something to do with his fear of me and of everyone" (para. 16). How can this
be so?

2. Telling Biddlebaum's story "is a job for a poet," the narrator observes in
   paragraph 7, an idea echoed in paragraph 17. How is the term *poet* apparently being defined in these two places?

3. Do you assume that Anderson agrees with Biddlebaum's advice to
   George in paragraph 13? Why, or why not?

4. What seems to be Biddlebaum's attitude toward the people who drove
   him out of his town? Toward the boy whose accusation ruined him?
   What does the story's last sentence suggest to you about the degree of
   guilt that Biddlebaum feels?

5. What would you say to someone who argues that Biddlebaum is gay?
   Identify specific passages that would influence your response, as well as
   any other factors you think relevant to this question.

REBECCA MAKKAI

The Briefcase

*Rebecca Makkai (b. 1978) graduated from Washington and Lee University in Vir-
ginia and then earned a master's degree at the Bread Loaf School of English in Vermont. Her first novel,* The Borrower, *is scheduled for publication in 2011.
Meanwhile, she has received much acclaim for her short fiction. After appearing in a
2008 issue of* New England Review, *"The Briefcase" was selected for* The Best
American Stories 2009 *and* The Best American Nonrequired Reading 2009.
Other stories of hers have been chosen for the 2008 and 2010 editions of the Best
American Stories *series, as well as for* Real Unreal: Best American Fantasy 3
(2010).

He thought how strange that a political prisoner, marched through town in a
line, chained to the man behind and chained to the man ahead, should take
comfort in the fact that this had all happened before. He thought of other
chains of men on other islands of the Earth, and he thought how since there
have been men there have been prisoners. He thought of mankind as a line of
miserable monkeys chained at the wrist, dragging each other back into the
ground.

In the early morning of December first, the sun was finally warming them all,
enough to walk faster. With his left hand, he adjusted the loop of steel that
cuffed his right hand to the line of doomed men. His hand was starved, his
wrist was thin, his body was cold: the cuff slipped off. In one beat of the heart
he looked back to the man behind him and forward to the man limping ahead,
and knew that neither saw his naked red wrist; each saw only his own mother
weeping in a kitchen, his own love lying on a bed in white sheets and sunlight.

He walked in step with them to the end of the block.

Before the war this man had been a chef, and his one crime was feeding the people who sat at his tables in small clouds of smoke and talked politics. He served them the wine that fueled their underground newspaper, their aborted revolution. And after the night his restaurant disappeared in fire, he had run and hidden and gone without food — he who had roasted ducks until the meat jumped from the bone, he who had evaporated three bottles of wine into one pot of cream soup, he who had peeled the skin from small pumpkins with a twist of his hand.

And here was his hand, twisted free of the chain, and here he was running   5
and crawling, until he was through a doorway. It was a building of empty classrooms — part of the university he had never attended. He watched from the bottom corner of a second-story window as the young soldiers stopped the line, counted 199 men, shouted to each other, shouted at the men in the panicked voices of children who barely filled the shoulders of their uniforms. One soldier, a bigger one, a louder one, stopped a man walking by. A man in a suit, with a briefcase, a beard — some sort of professor. The soldiers stripped him of his coat, his shirt, his leather case, cuffed him to the chain. They marched again. And as soon as they were past — no, not that soon; many minutes later, when he had the stomach — the chef ran down to the street and collected the man's briefcase, coat, and shirt.

In the alley, the chef sat against a wall and buttoned the professor's shirt over his own ribs. When he opened the briefcase, papers flew out, a thousand doves flailing against the walls of the alley. The chef ran after them all, stopped them with his feet and arms, herded them back into the case. Pages of numbers, of arrows and notes and hand-drawn star maps. Here were business cards: a professor of physics. Envelopes showed his name and address — information that might have been useful in some other lifetime, one where the chef could ring the bell of this man's house and explain to his wife about empty chains, empty wrists, empty classrooms. Here were graded papers, a fall syllabus, the typed draft of an exam. The question at the end, a good one: "Using modern astronomical data, construct, to the best of your ability, a proof that the Sun revolves around the Earth."

The chef knew nothing of physics. He understood chemistry only insofar as it related to the baking time of bread at various elevations or the evaporation rate of alcohol. His knowledge of biology was limited to the deboning of chickens and the behavior of *Saccharomyces cerevisiae*, common bread yeast. And what did he know at all of moving bodies and gravity? He knew this: he had moved from his line of men, creating a vacuum — one that had sucked the good professor in to fill the void.

The chef sat on his bed in the widow K——'s basement and felt, in the cool leather of the briefcase, a second vacuum: here was a vacated life. Here were salary receipts, travel records, train tickets, a small address book. And these belonged to a man whose name was not blackened like his own, a man whose life was not hunted. If he wanted to live through the next year, the chef would have to learn this life and fill it — and oddly, this felt not like a robbery but an apology, a way to put the world back in balance. The professor would not die, because he himself would become the professor, and he would live.

Surely he could not teach at the university; surely he could not slip into the man's bed unnoticed. But what was in this leather case, it seemed, had been left for him to use. These addresses of friends; this card of identification; this riddle about the inversion of the universe.

Five cities east, he now gave his name as the professor's, and grew out his beard   10
so it would match the photograph on the card he now carried in his pocket. They did not, anymore, look entirely dissimilar. To the first man in the address book, the chef had written a typed letter: "Am in trouble and have fled the city . . . Tell my dear wife I am safe, but for her safety do not tell her where I am . . . If you are able to help a poor old man, send money to the following post box . . . I hope to remain your friend, Professor T———."

He had to write this about the wife; how could he ask these men for money if she held a funeral? And what of it, if she kept her happiness another few months, another year?

The next twenty-six letters were similar in nature, and money arrived now in brown envelopes and white ones. The bills came wrapped in notes — was his life in danger? did he have his health? — and with the money he paid another widow for another basement, and he bought weak cigarettes. He sat on café chairs and drew pictures of the universe, showed stars and planets looping each other in light. He felt, perhaps, that if he used the other papers in the briefcase, he must also make use of this question. Or perhaps he felt that if he could answer it, he could put the universe back together. Or perhaps it was something to do with his empty days.

He wrote in his small notebook: "The light of my cigarette is a fire like the Sun. From where I sit, all the universe is equidistant from my cigarette. Ergo, my cigarette is the center of the universe. My cigarette is on Earth. Ergo, the Earth is the center of the universe. If all heavenly bodies move, they must therefore move in relation to the Earth, and in relation to my cigarette."

His hand ached; these words were the most he had written since school, which had ended for him at age sixteen. He had been a smart boy, even talented in languages and mathematics, but his mother knew these were no way to make a living. He was not blessed, like the professor, with years of scholarship and quiet offices and leather books. He was blessed instead with chicken stocks and herbs and sherry. Thirty years had passed since his last day of school, and his hand was accustomed now to wooden spoon, mandolin, peeling knife, rolling pin.

Today, his hands smelled of ink, when for thirty years they had smelled of   15
leeks. They were the hands of the professor; ergo, he was now the professor.

He had written to friends A through L, and now he saved the rest and wrote instead to students. Here in the briefcase's outermost pocket were class rosters from the past two years; letters addressed to those young men care of the university were sure to reach them. The amounts they sent were smaller, the notes that accompanied them more inquisitive. What exactly had transpired? Could they come to the city and meet him?

The post box, of course, was in a city different from the one where he stayed. He arrived at the post office just before closing, and came only once every two or three weeks. He always looked through the window first to check that the lobby was empty. If it was not, he would leave and come again another day. Surely, one of these days a friend of the professor would be waiting there for him. He prepared a story, that he was the honored professor's assistant, that he could not reveal the man's location but would certainly pass on your kindest regards, sir.

If the Earth moved, all it would take for a man to travel its distance would be a strong balloon. Rise twenty feet above, and wait for the Earth to turn under you; you would be home again in a day. But this was not true, and a man could not escape his spot on the Earth but to run along the surface. Ergo, the Earth was still. Ergo, the Sun was the moving body of the two.

No, he did not believe it. He wanted only to know who this professor was, this man who would, instead of teaching his students the laws of the universe, ask them to prove as true what was false.

On the wall of the café: plate-sized canvas, delicate oils of an apple, half-peeled.   20
Signed, below, by a girl he had known in school. The price was more than three weeks of groceries, and so he did not buy it, but for weeks he read his news under the apple and drank his coffee. Staining his fingers in cheap black ink were the signal fires of the world, the distress sirens, the dispatches from the trenches and hospitals and abattoirs of the war; but here, on the wall, a sign from another world. He had known this girl as well as any other: had spoken with her every day, but had not made love to her; had gone to her home one winter holiday, but knew nothing of her life since then. And here, a clue, perfect and round and unfathomable. After all this time: apple.

After he finished the news, he worked at the proof and saw in the coil of green-edged skin some model of spiraling, of expansion. The stars were at one time part of the Earth, until the hand of God peeled them away, leaving us in the dark. They do not revolve around us: they escape in widening circles. The Milky Way is the edge of this peel.

After eight months in the new city, the chef stopped buying his newspapers on the street by the café and began instead to read the year-old news the widow gave him for his fires. Here, fourteen months ago: Minister P—— of the Interior predicts war. One day he found that in a box near the widow's furnace were papers three, four, five years old. Pages were missing, edges eaten. He took his fragments of yellowed paper to the café and read the beginnings and ends of opinions and letters. He read reports from what used to be his country's borders.

When he had finished the last paper of the box, he began to read the widow's history books. The Americas, before Columbus; the oceans, before the British; the Romans, before their fall.

History was safer than the news, because there was no question of how it would end.

He took a lover in the city and told her he was a professor of physics. He showed   25
her the stars in the sky and explained that they circled the Earth, along with the Sun.

That's not true at all, she said. You tease me because you think I'm a silly girl.

No, he said and touched her neck. You are the only one who might understand. The universe has been folded inside out.

A full year had passed, and he paid the widow in coins. He wrote to friends M through Z. I have been in hiding for a year, he wrote. Tell my dear wife I have my health. May time and history forgive us all.

A year had passed, but so had many years passed for many men. And after all what was a year, if the Earth did not circle the Sun?

The Earth does not circle the Sun, he wrote. Ergo, the years do not pass.   30
The Earth, being stationary, does not erase the past nor escape toward the future. Rather, the years pile on like blankets, existing all at once. The year is 1848; the year is 1789; the year is 1956.

If the Earth hangs still in space, does it spin? If the Earth were to spin, the space I occupy I will therefore vacate in an instant. This city will leave its spot, and the city to the west will usurp its place. Ergo, this city is all cities at all times. This is Kabul; this is Dresden; this is Johannesburg.

I run by standing still.

At the post office, he collects his envelopes of money. He has learned from the notes of concerned colleagues and students and friends that the professor suffered from infections of the inner ear that often threw his balance. He has learned of the professor's wife, A——, whose father died the year they married. He has learned that he has a young son. Rather, the professor has a son.

At each visit to the post office, he fears he will forget the combination. It is an old lock, and complicated: F1, clockwise to B3, back to A6, forward again to J3. He must shake the little latch before it opens. More than forgetting, perhaps what he fears is that he will be denied access — that the little box will one day recognize him behind his thick and convincing beard, will decide he has no right of entry.

One night, asleep with his head on his lover's leg, he dreams that a letter   35
has arrived from the professor himself. They freed me at the end of the march, it says, and I crawled my way home. My hands are bloody and my knees are worn through, and I want my briefcase back.

In his dream, the chef takes the case and runs west. If the professor takes it back, there will be no name left for the chef, no place on the Earth. The moment his fingers leave the leather loop of the handle, he will fall off the planet.

He sits in a wooden chair on the lawn behind the widow's house. Inside, he hears her washing dishes. In exchange for the room, he cooks all her meals. It is March, and the cold makes the hairs rise from his arms, but the sun warms the arm beneath them. He thinks, The tragedy of a moving Sun is that it leaves us each day. Hence the Aztec sacrifices, the ancient rites of the eclipse. If the Sun so willingly leaves us, each morning it returns is a stay of execution, an undeserved gift.

Whereas: if it is we who turn, how can we so flagrantly leave behind that which has warmed us and given us light? If we are moving, then each turn is a turn away. Each revolution a revolt.

The money comes less often, and even old friends who used to write monthly now send only rare, apologetic notes, a few small bills. Things are more difficult now, their letters say. No one understood when he first ran away, but now it is clear: after they finished with the artists, the journalists, the fighters, they came for the professors. How wise he was to leave when he did. Some letters come back unopened, with a black stamp.

Life is harder here, too. Half the shops are closed. His lover has left him. The little café is filled with soldiers.   40

One afternoon, he enters the post office two minutes before closing. The lobby is empty but for the postman and his broom.

The mailbox is empty as well, and he turns to leave but hears the voice of the postman behind him. You are the good Professor T——, no? I have something for you in the back.

Yes, he says, I am the professor. And it feels as if this is true, and he will have no guilt over the professor's signature when the box is brought out. He is even wearing the professor's shirt, as loose again over his hungry ribs as it was the day he slipped it on in the alley.

From behind the counter, the postman brings no box, but a woman in a long gray dress, a white handkerchief in her fingers.

She moves toward him, looks at his hands and his shoes and his face. Forgive me for coming, she says, and the postman pulls the cover down over his window and disappears. She says, No one would tell me anything, only that my husband had his health. And then a student gave me the number of the box and the name of the city.   45

He begins to say, You are the widow. But why would he say this? What proof is there that the professor is dead? Only that it must be; that it follows logically.

She says, I don't understand what has happened.

He begins to say, I am the good professor's assistant, madam — but then what next? She would ask questions he had no way to answer.

I don't understand, she says again.

All he can say is, This is his shirt. He holds out an arm so she can see the   50
gaping sleeve.

She says, What have you done with him? She has a calm voice and wet,
brown eyes. He feels he has seen her before, in the streets of the old city. Perhaps he served her a meal, a bottle of wine. Perhaps, in another lifetime, she
was the center of his universe.

This is his beard, he says.

She begins to cry into the handkerchief. She says, Then he is dead. He sees
now from the quiet of her voice that she must have known this long ago. She
has come here only to confirm.

He feels the floor of the post office move beneath him, and he tries to turn
his eyes from her, to ground his gaze in something solid: postbox, ceiling tile,
window. He finds he cannot turn away. She is a force of gravity in her long gray
dress.

No, he says. No, no, no, no, no, I am right here.   55

No, he does not believe it, but he knows that if he had time, he could prove
it. And he must, because he is the only piece of the professor left alive. The
woman does not see how she is murdering her husband, right here in the post
office lobby. He whispers to her: Let me go home with you. I'll be a father to your
son, and I'll warm your bed, and I'll keep you safe.

He wraps his hands around her small, cold wrists, but she pulls loose. She
might be the most beautiful woman he has ever seen.

As if from far away, he hears her call to the postmaster to send for the
police.

His head is light, and he feels he might float away from the post office forever. It is an act of will not to fly off, but instead to hold tight to the Earth and
wait. If the police aren't too busy to come, he feels confident he can prove to
them that he is the professor. He has the papers, after all, and in the havoc of
war, what else will they have the time to look for?

She is backing away from him on steady feet, and he feels it like a peeling   60
off of skin.

If not the police, perhaps he'll convince a city judge. The witnesses who
would denounce him are mostly gone or killed, and the others would fear to
come before the law. If the city judge will not listen, he can prove it to the high
court. One day he might try to convince the professor's own child. He feels certain that somewhere down the line, someone will believe him.   [2008]

■ THINKING ABOUT THE TEXT

1. Why do you suppose Makkai resisted naming any of the characters or
   even the country where the story takes place?

2. The narrator says, "Before the war this man had been a chef, and his one
   crime was feeding the people who sat at his tables in small clouds of

smoke and talked politics" (para. 4). Where, if anywhere, does the story show the chef committing what you consider to be additional crimes? Does the amount of sympathy you feel toward him change over the course of the story? Why, or why not? Do you think he could have survived *without* taking the professor's identity?

3. At various moments, the chef wrestles with the science problem he has found in the professor's briefcase. How do these particular passages represent stages in the chef's thinking? In paragraph 38, he thinks that "if we are moving, then each turn is a turn away," yet in paragraph 54, "he finds he cannot turn away." What is the relation between these two sentences?

4. Characterize the chef's thinking in the last sentence. Why is he now "certain that somewhere down the line, someone will believe him"?

5. Makkai begins the story in the past tense and stays in that tense for a while. But, from paragraph 32 to the end, she uses present tense. Why do you think she shifts tenses?

■ MAKING COMPARISONS

1. Does the chef in "The Briefcase" have more control over what happens than Wing Biddlebaum does? Identify passages in both stories that influence your answer.

2. Does one of these characters feel guiltier than the other? Explain.

3. "The Briefcase" has a consistent point of view, being told basically from the perspective of the chef. "Hands," however, features shifting points of view. Though it begins with Biddlebaum's, it eventually moves to George Willard's, and even the narrator becomes a conspicuous presence when we learn Biddlebaum's past. Does this difference lead to a significant difference in effect?

LINH DINH
"!"

Born in Saigon in 1963, Linh Dinh moved to the United States in 1975. At times he has returned to his native country, and he has also lived for a few years in Italy, but Philadelphia is now his home. Besides being a photographer, he has written in various genres, producing translations and political commentary as well as his own literary texts. He has published five volumes of his poetry, examples of which have been selected for the 2000, 2004, and 2007 editions of The Best American Poetry. *His first novel,* Love Like Hate, *came out in 2010. His two collections of short fiction are* Fake House *(2000) and* Blood and Soap *(2004), which includes the following story. Although a work of prose, it first appeared in a 2001 issue of* American Poetry Review. *Ho Muoi, its protagonist, becomes a soldier for Communist North Vietnam during that country's war with the United States, a conflict in which the North Vietnamese were aided by Russian military advisers. As you will see, however, Ho Muoi aspires to master the English language and comes to assume that he can teach it to others, even if his notion of it is largely his own invention.*

In *The Workers* newspaper of October 10, 2000, there was a curious item about a fake doctor. A certain Ngo Thi Nghe had been practicing medicine for over ten years on a false degree, which she procured, it is speculated, by killing its original owner. She had all the accoutrements of medicine, a white suit, a thermometer, a bedpan, a syringe, many bottles of pills, but no formal knowledge of medicine. In fact, she had never gotten out of the eighth grade. The mortality rate of her patients, however, was no higher than usual, and she was even defended by some of her clients, after all the facts had come out, for saving their lives. "A most compassionate doctor," said one elderly gentleman.

There are so many scams nowadays that this case drew no special attention. Every day there are news reports of fake lawyers, fake architects, fake professors, and fake politicians doing business without the proper license or training. A most curious case in recent memory, however, is that of Ho Muoi, who was accused of being a fake English teacher. From perusing innumerable newspaper accounts, I was able to piece together the following:

Ho Muoi was born in 1952 in Ky Dong village. His family made firecrackers until they were banned because of the war. Thereafter the father became an alcoholic and left the family. Although Ho Muoi was only six at the time, he knew enough to swear that he would never mention or even think of his father's name again. His mother supported the children, all five of them, by carrying water and night soil for hire, a backbreaking labor that made her shorter by several inches. She also made meat dumplings that she sold on special occasions.

Ky Dong Village is known for a festival, held every January 5th, in honor of a legendary general of a mythical king who fought against a real enemy two or three thousand years ago. The festival features a duck-catching demonstration, a wrestling tournament for the boys, a meat dumpling making contest for the girls, and, until it was banned because of the war, a procession of firecrackers.

Those who've witnessed this procession of firecrackers describe a scene   5
where boys and girls and gay men jiggle papier-mâché animals and genitals strung from bamboo sticks amid the smoke and din of a million firecrackers.

But the excitement from the festival only came once a year. For the rest of the time, the villagers were preoccupied with the tedium and anxieties of daily life. Most of the young men were drafted into the army, sent away and never came back, but the war never came directly to Ky Dong Village.

When Ho Muoi was ten, his mother enrolled him in school for the first time. He was slow and it took him a year to learn the alphabet. He could never figure out how to add or subtract. His worst subject, however, was geography.

It was inconceivable to him that there are hundreds of countries in the world, each with a different spoken language. Every single word of his own language felt so inevitable that he thought it would be a crime against nature to call a cow or a bird anything different.

Ho Muoi could not even conceive of *two* countries sharing this same earth. "Countries" in the plural sounds like either a tautology or an oxymoron. "Country," "earth," and "universe" were all synonymous in his mind.

Ho Muoi's teacher was a very sophisticated young man from Hanoi. He was the only one within a fifty-mile radius who had ever read a newspaper or who owned even a single book. He even fancied himself a poet in his spare time. He did not mind teaching a bunch of village idiots, however, because it spared him from the bombs and landmines that were the fate of his contemporaries. In the evening he could be found in his dark room reading a Russian novel. The teacher was short and scrawny and had a habit of shutting his eyes tight and sticking his lips out when concentrating. Still, it was odd that he managed to attract no women in a village almost entirely emptied of its young men.

Whenever this teacher was exasperated with his charge he would shout   10
"!" but no one knew what the word meant or what language it was in so it was dismissed as a sort of a sneeze or a clearing of the throat.

At twelve, something happened to Ho Muoi that would change his whole outlook on life. He was walking home from school when he saw a crowd gathering around three men who were at least two heads taller than the average person. The men had a pink, almost red complexion and their hair varied from a bright orange to a whitish yellow. They were not unfriendly and allowed people to tug at the abundant hair growing on their arms. "Wonderful creatures," Ho Muoi thought as he stared at them, transfixed. One of the men noticed Ho Muoi and started to say something. The words were rapid, like curses, but the man was smiling as he was saying them. All eyes turned to look at Ho Muoi. Some people started to laugh and he wanted to laugh along with them but he could not. Suddenly his face flushed and he felt an intense hatred against these foreign men. If he had a gun he would have shot them already. Without premeditation he blurted out "!" then ran away.

When Ho Muoi got home his heart was still beating wildly. The excitement of blurting out a magical word, a word he did not know the meaning of, was overwhelming. He also remembered the look of shock on the man's face after the word had left his mouth. He repeated "!" several times and felt its power each time.

Ho Muoi would think about this incident for years afterward. He recalled how he was initially enraged by a series of foreign words, and that he had retaliated with a foreign word of his own. In his mind, foreign words became equated with a terrible power. The fact that his own language would be foreign to a foreigner never occurred to him.

The incident also turned Ho Muoi into a celebrity. The villagers would recall with relish how one of their own, a twelve-year-old boy, had "stood up to a foreigner" by hurling a curse at him in his own language. Many marveled at the boy's intelligence for knowing how to use a foreign word, heard maybe once or twice in passing, on just the right occasion and with authority. They even suggested to the schoolteacher that he teach "the boy genius" all the foreign words from his Russian novels.

The schoolteacher never got around to doing this. He was drafted soon after, sent south, and was never heard from again. As for Ho Muoi, he became convinced that, given the opportunity, he could quickly learn any foreign language. This opportunity came after Ho Muoi himself was drafted into the army.   15

His battalion served in the Central Highlands, along the Truong Son Mountain, guarding supply lines. They rarely made contact with the enemy but whenever they did, Ho Muoi acquitted himself miserably. He often froze and had to be literally kicked into action. What was perceived by his comrades as cowardice, however, was not so much a fear of physical pain as the dread that he would not be allowed to fulfill his destiny.

The war was an outrage, Ho Muoi thought, not because it was wiping out thousands of people a day, the young, the old, and the unborn, but that it could exterminate a man of destiny like himself. And yet he understood that wars also provide many lessons to those who survived them. A war is a working man's university. Knowing that, he almost felt grateful.

Ho Muoi also had the superstition (or the inspiration) that if the war eliminates a single book from this earth, then that would be a greater loss than all the lives wasted. The death of a man affects three or four other individuals, at most. Its significance is symbolic and sentimental, but the loss of a single book is tangible, a disaster which should be mourned forever by all of mankind. The worth of a society is measured by how many books it has produced. This, from a man who had never actually read a book. Ho Muoi had seen so few books, he could not tell one from another; they were all equal in his mind. He never suspected that war is the chief generator of books. A war is a thinking man's university.

In 1970 or 1971, after a brief skirmish, they caught an American soldier whom they kept for about thirty days. The prisoner was made to march along with Ho Muoi's battalion until he fell ill and died (he was not badly injured). This man was given the same ration as the others but the food did not agree with him. Once, they even gave him an extra helping of orangutan meat, thinking it would restore his health.

As the prisoner sank into delirium, the color drained from his face but his eyes lit up. He would blather for hours on end. No one paid him any attention but Ho Muoi. In his tiny notebook he would record as much of the man's rambling as possible. These phonetic notations became the source for Ho Muoi's English lessons after the war. I've seen pages from the notebook. Its lines often ran diagonally from one corner to another. A typical run-on sentence: "hoo he hoo ah utta ma nut m pap m home."   20

The notebook also includes numerous sketches of the American. Each portrait was meant as a visual clue to the words swarming around it. Ho Muoi's skills as an artist were so poor, however, that the face depicted always appeared the same, that of a young man, any man, really, who has lost all touch with the world.

Ho Muoi was hoping his unit would catch at least one more American so he could continue his English lesson, but this tutor never materialized, unfortunately.

Though all the English he had was contained within a single notebook, Ho Muoi was not discouraged. The American must have spoken just about every word there was in his native language, he reasoned, through all those nights of raving. And the invisible words can be inferred from the visible ones.

Words are like numbers, he further reasoned, a closed system with a small set of self-generated rules. And words arranged on a page resemble a dull, monotonous painting. If one could look at the weirdest picture and decipher, sooner or later, its organizing principle, why can't one do the same with words?

Everything seems chaotic at first, but nothing is chaotic. One can read 25 anything: ants crawling on the ground; pimples on a face; trees in a forest. Fools will argue with you about this, but any surface can be deciphered. The entire world, as seen from an airplane, is just a warped surface.

A man may fancy he's making an abstract painting, but there is no such thing as an abstract painting, only abstracted ones. Every horizontal surface is a landscape because it features a horizon (thus implying a journey, escape from the self, and the unreachable). Every vertical surface is either a door or a portrait (thus implying a house, another being, yourself as another being, and the unreachable). And all colors have shared and private associations. Red may inspire horror in one culture, elation in another, but it is still red, is still blood. Green always evokes trees and a pretty green dress.

Ho Muoi also believed that anything made by man can be duplicated: a chair, a gun, a language, provided one has the raw materials, as he did, with his one notebook of phonetic notations. If one can break apart a clock and reassemble it, one can scramble up phonetic notations and rearrange them in newer combinations, thus ending up with not just a language, but a literature.

At the time of his arrest, Ho Muoi was teaching hundreds of students beginning, intermediate, and advanced English three nights a week. For twenty-five years, he had taught his students millions of vocabulary words. He had patiently explained to them the intricacies of English grammar, complete with built-in inconsistencies. He had even given them English poems and short stories (written by himself and the more advanced students) to read. When interrogated at the police station, however, our English teacher proved ignorant of the most basic knowledge of the language. He did not know the verb "to be" or "to do." He did not know there is a past tense in English. He had never heard of Shakespeare and was not even aware that Australians and Englishmen also speak English.

In Ho Muoi's made-up English, there are not five but twenty-four vowels. The new nuances in pronunciation force each student to fine-tune his ear to the level of the finest musician. There is a vast vocabulary for pain and bamboo but no equivalent for cheese. Any adjective can be used as a verb. *I will hot you*, for example, or, *Don't red me*. There are so many personal pronouns, each one denoting an exact relationship between speaker and subject, that even the most brilliant student cannot master them all.

By sheer coincidence, some of Ho Muoi's made-up English words corre-   30
spond exactly with actual English. In his system, a cat is also called a cat; a
tractor, a tractor; and a rose, inevitably, perhaps, a rose.

Some of his more curious inventions include *blanket,* to denote a husband.
Basin, to denote a wife. *Pin prick:* a son. *A leaky faucet:* a daughter.

Ho Muoi's delusion was so absolute, however, that after he was sentenced
to twenty-five years for "defrauding the people," he asked to be allowed to take
to prison a *Dictionary of the English Language* and a *Dictionary of English Slang,*
two volumes he himself had compiled, so that "I can continue my life studies."

It is rumored that many of his former students have banded together to
continue their English lessons. Harassed by the police, they must hold their
nightly meetings in underground bunkers, lit by oil lamps. Their strange syllables, carried by the erratic winds, crosshatch the surrounding countryside.

But why are they doing this? You ask. Don't they know they are studying a
false language?

As the universal language—for now—English represents to these stu-   35
dents the rest of the world. English *is* the world. These students also know that
Vietnam, as it exists, is not of this world. To cling even to a false English is to
insist on another reality.

A bogus English is better than no English, is better, in fact, than actual
English, since it corresponds to no English or American reality.

Hoo he hoo ah utta ma nut m pap m home.   *[2004]*

▤ THINKING ABOUT THE TEXT

1. The story does not begin by moving right away to details of Ho Muoi's
   life. What do you see as the function of the two paragraphs that come
   before such details?

2. The title of this story is just an exclamation mark. As readers, we never
   actually learn the word used by Ho Muoi's teacher and later by Ho Muoi
   himself. Why do you suppose Dinh withholds this word from us?

3. As the story proceeds through the years, what strike you as key aspects
   of Ho Muoi's thinking? Refer to specific passages.

4. The narrator reports that Ho Muoi was arrested and sentenced for "defrauding the people" (para. 32). Are the Communist authorities completely unfair in declaring him a criminal? In the same paragraph, Ho
   Muoi's belief that he knows English is referred to as a "delusion." How
   fair is this label? Does his concept of the English language seem to you
   completely illogical? Explain.

5. After Ho Muoi's imprisonment, rumor has it, students of his "have
   banded together to continue their English lessons" (para. 33). The story's remaining paragraphs offer a rationale for their behavior. Paraphrase this in your own words. What, ultimately, do you think Dinh is
   suggesting about the role of the English language in today's world?

■ MAKING COMPARISONS

1. Obviously a major subject of Dinh's story is language. To what extent, and in what ways, can Makkai's story be seen as dealing with this topic?

2. Do you feel equally negative toward the people of Wing Biddlebaum's hometown, the government in Makkai's story, and the Communist authorities in Dinh's story? Why, or why not?

3. What would you say to someone who argues that *criminal* is not a fair term for any of the protagonists in these three stories, regardless of how they are labeled by other characters?

■ WRITING ABOUT ISSUES

1. Choose one of the stories in this cluster, and write an essay in which you defend what you consider to be the most appropriate term for the story's main character. This term might be a word you come up with, rather than one you find in the story itself. Be sure to make clear what you mean by the term and which passages in the story support your use of it.

2. Besides considering what a *criminal* is, these three stories consider what a *teacher* is, or what a teacher should be. Write an essay comparing how two of the stories deal with the role of teacher. Be clear with your definitions, and support your analyses by referring to specific passages in both stories.

3. Write an essay about a time when someone you know was called a criminal or given a similar label. More specifically, argue that this term obscured the complexity of the person's mind-set, behavior, or circumstances. If you wish, refer to any of the stories in this cluster.

4. When, if ever, is it acceptable for people to conceal their real identities on Facebook or elsewhere on the Internet? Write an essay in which you argue for your position on this topic. Imagine that the essay has been solicited by your campus newspaper as an op-ed column, so that your main audience is students at your college. If you wish, mention to these readers that you have been studying one or more of the stories in this cluster.

We conclude this chapter with three poems that invite their readers to imagine what a more just world than the current one would be like. Such a vision involves defining what *justice* means in the first place. It also involves identifying what the leading examples of present injustice are. Directly or indirectly, each poem in this cluster points to moral blights that its speaker hopes to cure. Whether or not utopia can ever be achieved, these literary works encourage their audiences to identify and challenge existing social ills.

≣ BEFORE YOU READ

When you think about major types of injustice today, what specifically comes to your mind?

WILLIAM BLAKE
The Chimney Sweeper

His contemporaries largely dismissed him as eccentric, even mad, but William Blake (1757–1827) is now regarded as a major figure in British Romanticism. In part, Blake was a printer and an engraver, lavishly illustrating his own editions of his poems. Through both his visual and his verbal art, Blake promoted his own self-devised religion, which incorporated stories and characters from the Bible. The following poem appears in his 1789 collection Songs of Innocence. *In 1794, he produced a counterpart volume,* Songs of Experience.

When my mother died I was very young,
And my father sold me while yet my tongue
Could scarcely cry "'weep! 'weep! 'weep! 'weep!"
So your chimneys I sweep & in soot I sleep.

There's little Tom Dacre, who cried when his head   5
That curled like a lamb's back, was shaved, so I said,
"Hush, Tom! never mind it, for when your head's bare,
You know that the soot cannot spoil your white hair."

And so he was quiet, & that very night,
As Tom was a-sleeping he had such a sight!   10
That thousands of sweepers, Dick, Joe, Ned, & Jack,
Were all of them locked up in coffins of black;

And by came an Angel who had a bright key,
And he opened the coffins & set them all free;
Then down a green plain, leaping, laughing they run,   15
And wash in a river and shine in the Sun.

Then naked & white, all their bags left behind,
They rise upon clouds, and sport in the wind.
And the Angel told Tom, if he'd be a good boy,
He'd have God for his father & never want joy.   20

And so Tom awoke; and we rose in the dark
And got with our bags & our brushes to work.
Though the morning was cold, Tom was happy & warm;
So if all do their duty, they need not fear harm.   *[1789]*

≡ THINKING ABOUT THE TEXT

1. How do colors matter in this poem?
2. What is the effect of the poem's obvious rhyming?
3. Why do you think that Blake made the dream Tom's rather than the speaker's?
4. As an imaginative vision of a better world, how unusual does Tom's dream strike you?
5. Do you assume that the author himself agrees with the last line? Why, or why not? In general, how much of what the speaker says do you think Blake wants his readers to accept? Explain.

MARTIN ESPADA
Imagine the Angels of Bread

Originally from Brooklyn, New York, Martin Espada (b. 1957) is a widely published poet, essayist, and translator whose work often reflects on his Puerto Rican heritage. Though currently a professor of English at the University of Massachusetts–Amherst, he has also practiced as a tenant lawyer. His collections of verse include The Trouble Ball *(2011),* The Republic of Poetry *(2006),* A Mayan Astronomer in Hell's Kitchen *(2000), and* City of Coughing and Dead Radiators *(1993). The following is the title poem of his book* Imagine the Angels of Bread *(1996), which won the American Book Award.*

This is the year that squatters evict landlords,
gazing like admirals from the rail
of the roofdeck
or levitating hands in praise
of steam in the shower;   5
this is the year

that shawled refugees deport judges
who stare at the floor
and their swollen feet
as files are stamped   10
with their destination;
this is the year that police revolvers,
stove-hot, blister the fingers
of raging cops,
and nightsticks splinter   15
in their palms;
this is the year
that darkskinned men
lynched a century ago
return to sip coffee quietly   20
with the apologizing descendants
of their executioners.

This is the year that those
who swim the border's undertow
and shiver in boxcars   25
are greeted with trumpets and drums
at the first railroad crossing
on the other side;
this is the year that the hands
pulling tomatoes from the vine   30
uproot the deed to the earth that sprouts the vine,
the hands canning tomatoes
are named in the will
that owns the bedlam of the cannery;
this is the year that the eyes   35
stinging from the poison that purifies toilets
awaken at last to the sight
of a rooster-loud hillside,
pilgrimage of immigrant birth;
this is the year that cockroaches   40
become extinct, that no doctor
finds a roach embedded
in the ear of an infant;
this is the year that the food stamps
of adolescent mothers   45
are auctioned like gold doubloons,
and no coin is given to buy machetes
for the next bouquet of severed heads
in coffee plantation country.

If the abolition of slave-manacles   50
began as a vision of hands without manacles,
then this is the year;

if the shutdown of extermination camps
began as imagination of a land
without barbed wire or the crematorium,   55
then this is the year;
if every rebellion begins with the idea
that conquerors on horseback
are not many-legged gods, that they too drown
if plunged in the river,   60
then this is the year.

So may every humiliated mouth,
teeth like desecrated headstones,
fill with the angels of bread.   [1997]

≡ THINKING ABOUT THE TEXT

1. Identify the patterns of repetition in this poem. What is their effect?
2. The poem is divided into four stanzas. What is the function of each?
3. What are the specific types of injustice that the speaker seems concerned about?
4. What are the various kinds of actions that the speaker envisions the victims of injustice performing? To what extent does he imagine them taking revenge?
5. What action does the speaker encourage the poem's readers to take?

≡ MAKING COMPARISONS

1. Angels figure in both Espada's poem and Blake's. Do they play the same role in these poems, however? Refer to specific lines in each text.
2. Espada's poem refers to a greater number of injustices than Blake's does. Does this difference produce a significant difference in effect? Explain.
3. What do you think Espada's speaker would say about the last line uttered by Blake's speaker?

MARK JARMAN

If I Were Paul

Mark Jarman (b. 1952) is Centennial Professor of English at Vanderbilt University in Nashville, Tennessee. The author of two essay collections, The Secret of Poetry *(2001) and* Body and Soul *(2002), he has also produced several books of verse, including* Questions for Ecclesiastes *(1998),* Unholy Sonnets *(2000),* To the Green Man *(2004), and* Epistles *(2007), which begins with the following poem. In the Bible, the genre of the epistle is associated with Paul of Tarsus. It is a type of letter that he supposedly wrote to the people of various cities, urging them to become Christians. Martin Luther King Jr.'s "Letter from Birmingham Jail" (see this chapter's "Civil Disobedience" cluster) has been viewed as a modern-day Pauline epistle.*

Consider how you were made.

Consider the loving geometry that sketched your bones, the passionate symmetry that sewed flesh to your skeleton, and the cloudy zenith whence your soul descended in shimmering rivulets across pure granite to pour as a single braided stream into the skull's cup.

Consider the first time you conceived of justice, engendered mercy, brought parity into being, coaxed liberty like a marten from its den to uncoil its limber spine in a sunny clearing, how you understood the inheritance of first principles, the legacy of noble thought, and built a city like a forest in the forest, and erected temples like thunderheads.

Consider, as if it were penicillin or the speed of light, the discovery of another's hands, his oval field of vision, her muscular back and hips, his nerve-jarred neck and shoulders, her bleeding gums and dry elbows and knees, his baldness and cauterized skin cancers, her lucid and forgiving gaze, his healing touch, her mind like a prairie. Consider the first knowledge of otherness. How it felt.

Consider what you were meant to be in the egg, in your parents' arms, under a sky full of stars.   5

Now imagine what I have to say when I learn of your enterprising viciousness, the discipline with which one of you turns another into a robot or a parasite or a maniac or a body strapped to a chair. Imagine what I have to say.

Do the impossible. Restore life to those you have killed, wholeness to those you have maimed, goodness to what you have poisoned, trust to those you have betrayed.

Bless each other with the heart and soul, the hand and eye, the head and foot, the lips, tongue, and teeth, the inner ear and the outer ear, the flesh and spirit, the brain and bowels, the blood and lymph, the heel and toe, the muscle and bone, the waist and hips, the chest and shoulders, the whole body, clothed and naked, young and old, aging and growing up.

I sent you this not knowing if you will receive it, or if having received it, you will read it, or if having read it, you will know that it contains my blessing.   *[2008]*

≡ **THINKING ABOUT THE TEXT**

1. Paul was an early Christian. Do you see Jarman's poem as addressed primarily to people of this faith? Why, or why not?

2. Note the first line. Why, in order to correct injustice, might it be important to "Consider how you were made"?

3. The next three stanzas are pretty dense in their language. Try to express in your own words the main ideas they convey. Should Jarman have used much simpler wording than he does? Why, or why not?

4. In the sixth stanza, the speaker accuses his audience of "enterprising viciousness." In the next stanza, he says that they have "killed," "maimed," "poisoned," and "betrayed" people. What would you say to someone who argues that language like this would merely offend readers rather than persuade them to share the speaker's ideals?

5. What, in general, does the speaker emphasize in his next-to-last stanza when he calls for things to be blessed?

≡ MAKING COMPARISONS

1. Both Espada's poem and Jarman's use the word *imagine*. Do you think that the poems are inviting their readers to imagine the same sorts of things? Refer to specific lines in each text.

2. Does Jarman's speaker seem angrier than Espada's? Do you detect any anger in Blake's speaker? Explain.

3. Can Espada's poem and Blake's also be considered epistles? Why, or why not?

≡ WRITING ABOUT ISSUES

1. Choose one of the poems in this cluster, and write an essay in which you identify what are, in general, the injustice(s) that the poem considers. Refer to specific lines.

2. The three poems in this cluster differ markedly in the number and kinds of stanzas they use. Choose two of the poems, and write an essay in which you explain how the different ways they use stanzas produce major differences in effect.

3. Write your own epistle, in prose or verse, to a specific group of people who in your view have committed a particular injustice. In your letter, do not simply accuse your readers of a moral failing and demand that they correct it; explain *why* you are disturbed by something they have done, as well as *how* it amounts to an injustice in your definition of the term. If you wish, refer to any of the poems in this cluster.

4. Choose a recent speech, editorial, or blog entry that you see as identifying an injustice and as imagining a world in which it no longer exists. Write an essay analyzing the strategies of persuasion the speaker or writer uses. If you wish, refer to any of the poems in this cluster.

CHAPTER 14

Journeys

Perhaps no impulse is as ancient and as natural as the desire to leave one's home, to journey out of the village to unknown lands. Ancient epics like the *Iliad* and the *Odyssey* and more modern tales like Mark Twain's *Adventures of Huckleberry Finn* and Jack Kerouac's *On the Road* are narratives of wandering, encountering the strange and the wondrous. Sometimes the journey has a specific goal, a quest for riches, for fame, or for adventure. Sometimes the journey is simply for escape, for curiosity's sake, for an understanding of the wider world. Of course the idea of the journey easily lends itself to both the literal and the metaphorical, to quests external and internal. We all take journeys of self-discovery from childhood to adolescence to adulthood and eventually to death. Life as a journey is a notion deeply woven into our cultural understanding from Greek mythology, epics, novels, religious beliefs, and popular culture.

It is no surprise then that writers for thousands of years have written about their perilous journeys to dangerous places, their contemplative journeys to self-reflection and wisdom, as well as their imaginative treks to dystopic futures. Our selections in this chapter work with an expansive idea of the journey, featuring work from Eudora Welty's classic short story "A Worn Path" to Kurt Vonnegut's journey to a harrowing future. For some the journey is quite literal; for others the path is decidedly metaphorical. Like the dancers in the Eagles' song "Hotel California," some writers journey to remember, others to forget. Whether the journey is the writer's own or a fictional one a character takes, the creative leap is always thoughtful, illuminating, and moving.

The arduous journey of Phoenix Jackson to help her grandson in Welty's "A Worn Path" is clearly both a literal and a symbolic quest and a favorite of critics who see mythic significance in her odyssey. We also include three critical commentaries on this classic story to demonstrate some of the tale's interpretative challenges. Jill McCorkle, Joyce Carol Oates, and Sherman Alexie also have their main characters take journeys, and like Phoenix Jackson's these trips can be dangerous, even deadly. Robert Frost's poetry is filled with journeys on roads not taken and those lingered on. The three poems reprinted here are typical of his poetry's ability to seem simple and straightforward on first reading but complex and ambiguous on reflection. Three disturbing accounts of addiction are followed by perhaps the most famous story about the Vietnam War and a magazine piece on going to war. Ralph Ellison's first chapter of *Invisible Man*, "Battle Royal," is a terrifying tale of a young man's initiation into a racist society that wants him to leave. It is the focus of the cultural context cluster that presents three selections that illuminate the racial issues Ellison deals with. Sometimes imagined futures are more disturbing than the present. Ray Bradbury, Octavia Butler, Ursula Le Guin, and Kurt Vonnegut paint a picture of a future we hope will never happen. The next cluster presents poems that in one way or another have been influenced by William Stafford's classic poem "Traveling through the Dark." Some of these poems suggest an obvious narrative and verbal allusion to Stafford while one, quite amazingly, gives us Stafford's entire poem with just one word changed. Marsha Norman's acclaimed play about the end of a journey is followed by a brief play with a character who doesn't speak. The five poems that follow also focus on the journey to death but take imaginatively different perspectives, from an iconic poem by John Donne to Wislawa Szymborska's lyric perspective. And the final cluster of three poems deals with ferry trips, an experience that poets from Walt Whitman onward have seen as much more than a pleasant ride. Each of these clusters offers an opportunity to ponder the beauty and significance of journeys of various kinds. We believe the trip will be worthwhile.

An Errand of Love?: Critical Commentaries on a Story

EUDORA WELTY, "A Worn Path"

CRITICAL COMMENTARIES:

ROLAND BARTEL, "Life and Death in Eudora Welty's 'A Worn Path'"

NEIL D. ISAACS, "Life for Phoenix"

EUDORA WELTY, "Is Phoenix Jackson's Grandson Really Dead?"

Countless writers from Homer to Mark Twain to Jack Kerouac have used journeys in symbolic ways to suggest quests for meaning, the pursuit of understanding, and simply as metaphors for the narrative shape of our lives from birth through innocence to experience and death. Eudora Welty quite explicitly uses this device in "A Worn Path" to narrate Phoenix Jackson's journey at Christmastime from her home to Natchez. She endures her difficult trek apparently to buy medicine for her grandson and then slowly begins the arduous journey home.

Critics have seen many things in this journey, from religious pilgrimage to civil rights allegory, and there is still debate as to whether the grandson is even alive. Roland Bartel believes he is dead; Neil D. Isaacs does not. Interestingly, in our third critical essay, the author herself suggests it may not matter, as the story's meaning lies elsewhere.

▤ BEFORE YOU READ

Have you ever thought of your life as a journey, as a narrative with a beginning, a middle, and an end? Can your life be considered a quest? Does it have goals?

EUDORA WELTY

A Worn Path

Eudora Welty (1909–2001) — who was born, raised, and died in Jackson, Mississippi — is considered one of the twentieth century's most gifted short-story writers. She studied at the University of Wisconsin and Columbia University and worked for the New York Times Book Review *during World War II. During this time, she began writing stories for the* Southern Review. *Soon after one of her stories appeared in the* Atlantic Monthly, *she published her first collection in 1941,* A Curtain of Green, *which was followed by* The Wide Net and Other Stories *(1943). Her first novel was* Delta Wedding *(1946). Another novel,* The Optimist's Daughter *(1972), won the Pulitzer Prize. Although Welty herself admitted that she led a*

(© Eudora Welty/
Corbis.)

sheltered life, her critics have always been impressed by her lyrical portrayal of the
complexities of the heart's emotional truths. "A Worn Path" received an O. Henry
Award in 1941.

It was December — a bright frozen day in the early morning. Far out in the
country there was an old Negro woman with her head tied in a red rag, coming
along a path through the pinewoods. Her name was Phoenix Jackson. She was
very old and small and she walked slowly in the dark pine shadows, moving a
little from side to side in her steps, with the balanced heaviness and lightness of
a pendulum in a grandfather clock. She carried a thin, small cane made from
an umbrella, and with this she kept tapping the frozen earth in front of her.
This made a grave and persistent noise in the still air, that seemed meditative
like the chirping of a solitary little bird.

   She wore a dark striped dress reaching down to her shoe tops, and an
equally long apron of bleached sugar sacks, with a full pocket: all neat and tidy,
but every time she took a step she might have fallen over her shoelaces, which
dragged from her unlaced shoes. She looked straight ahead. Her eyes were blue
with age. Her skin had a pattern all its own of numberless branching wrinkles
and as though a whole little tree stood in the middle of her forehead, but a
golden color ran underneath, and the two knobs of her cheeks were illumined
by a yellow burning under the dark. Under the red rag her hair came down on
her neck in the frailest of ringlets, still black, and with an odor like copper.

Now and then there was a quivering in the thicket. Old Phoenix said, "Out of my way, all you foxes, owls, beetles, jack rabbits, coons, and wild animals! . . . Keep out from under these feet, little bobwhites. . . . Keep the big wild hogs out of my path. Don't let none of those come running my direction. I got a long way." Under her small black-freckled hand her cane, limber as a buggy whip, would switch at the brush as if to rouse up any hiding things.

On she went. The woods were deep and still. The sun made the pine needles almost too bright to look at, up where the wind rocked. The cones dropped as light as feathers. Down in the hollow was the mourning dove — it was not too late for him.

The path ran up a hill. "Seem like there is chains about my feet, time I   5
get this far," she said, in the voice of argument old people keep to use with themselves. "Something always take a hold of me on this hill — pleads I should stay."

After she got to the top she turned and gave a full, severe look behind her where she had come. "Up through pines," she said at length. "Now down through oaks."

Her eyes opened their widest, and she started down gently. But before she got to the bottom of the hill a bush caught her dress.

Her fingers were busy and intent, but her skirts were full and long, so that before she could pull them free in one place they were caught in another. It was not possible to allow the dress to tear. "I in the thorny bush," she said. "Thorns, you doing your appointed work. Never want to let folks pass, no sir. Old eyes thought you was a pretty little *green* bush."

Finally, trembling all over, she stood free, and after a moment dared to stoop for her cane.

"Sun so high!" she cried, leaning back and looking, while the thick tears   10
went over her eyes. "The time getting all gone here."

At the foot of this hill was a place where a log was laid across the creek.

"Now comes the trial," said Phoenix.

Putting her right foot out, she mounted the log and shut her eyes. Lifting her skirt, leveling her cane fiercely before her, like a festival figure in some parade, she began to march across. Then she opened her eyes and she was safe on the other side.

"I wasn't as old as I thought," she said.

But she sat down to rest. She spread her skirts on the bank around her and   15
folded her hands over her knees. Up above her was a tree in a pearly cloud of mistletoe. She did not dare to close her eyes, and when a little boy brought her a plate with a slice of marble-cake on it she spoke to him. "That would be acceptable," she said. But when she went to take it there was just her own hand in the air.

So she left that tree, and had to go through a barbed-wire fence. There she had to creep and crawl, spreading her knees and stretching her fingers like a baby trying to climb the steps. But she talked loudly to herself: she could not let her dress be torn now, so late in the day, and she could not pay for having her arm or her leg sawed off if she got caught fast where she was.

At last she was safe through the fence and risen up out in the clearing. Big dead trees, like black men with one arm, were standing in the purple stalks of the withered cotton field. There sat a buzzard.

"Who you watching?"

In the furrow she made her way along.

"Glad this not the season for bulls," she said, looking sideways, "and the   20 good Lord made his snakes to curl up and sleep in the winter. A pleasure I don't see no two-headed snake coming around that tree, where it come once. It took a while to get by him, back in the summer."

She passed through the old cotton and went into a field of dead corn. It whispered and shook and was taller than her head. "Through the maze now," she said, for there was no path.

Then there was something tall, black, and skinny there, moving before her.

At first she took it for a man. It could have been a man dancing in the field. But she stood still and listened, and it did not make a sound. It was as silent as a ghost.

"Ghost," she said sharply, "who be you the ghost of? For I have heard of nary death close by."

But there was no answer — only the ragged dancing in the wind.   25

She shut her eyes, reached out her hand, and touched a sleeve. She found a coat and inside that an emptiness, cold as ice.

"You scarecrow," she said. Her face lighted. "I ought to be shut up for good," she said with laughter. "My senses is gone. I too old. I the oldest people I ever know. Dance, old scarecrow," she said, "while I dancing with you."

She kicked her foot over the furrow, and with mouth drawn down, shook her head once or twice in a little strutting way. Some husks blew down and whirled in streamers about her skirts.

Then she went on, parting her way from side to side with the cane, through the whispering field. At last she came to the end, to a wagon track where the silver grass blew between the red ruts. The quail were walking around like pullets, seeming all dainty and unseen.

"Walk pretty," she said. "This the easy place. This the easy going."   30

She followed the track, swaying through the quiet bare fields, through the little strings of trees silver in their dead leaves, past cabins silver from weather, with the doors and windows boarded shut, all like old women under a spell sitting there. "I walking in their sleep," she said, nodding her head vigorously.

In a ravine she went where a spring was silently flowing through a hollow log. Old Phoenix bent and drank. "Sweet-gum makes the water sweet," she said, and drank more. "Nobody know who made this well, for it was here when I was born."

The track crossed a swampy part where the moss hung as white as lace from every limb. "Sleep on, alligators, and blow your bubbles." Then the track went into the road.

Deep, deep the road went down between the high green-colored banks. Overhead the live-oaks met, and it was as dark as a cave.

A black dog with a lolling tongue came up out of the weeds by the ditch. 35
She was meditating, and not ready, and when he came at her she only hit him
a little with her cane. Over she went in the ditch, like a little puff of milkweed.

Down there, her senses drifted away. A dream visited her, and she reached
her hand up, but nothing reached down and gave her a pull. So she lay there
and presently went to talking. "Old woman," she said to herself, "that black dog
come up out of the weeds to stall you off, and now there he sitting on his fine
tail, smiling at you."

A white man finally came along and found her — a hunter, a young man,
with his dog on a chain.

"Well, Granny!" he laughed. "What are you doing there?"

"Lying on my back like a June-bug waiting to be turned over, mister," she
said, reaching up her hand.

He lifted her up, gave her a swing in the air, and set her down. "Anything 40
broken, Granny?"

"No sir, them old dead weeds is springy enough," said Phoenix, when she
had got her breath. "I thank you for your trouble."

"Where do you live, Granny?" he asked, while the two dogs were growling
at each other.

"Away back yonder, sir, behind the ridge. You can't even see it from here."

"On your way home?"

"No sir, I going to town." 45

"Why, that's too far! That's as far as I walk when I come out myself, and
I get something for my trouble." He patted the stuffed bag he carried, and there
hung down a little closed claw. It was one of the bobwhites, with its beak
hooked bitterly to show it was dead. "Now you go on home, Granny!"

"I bound to go to town, mister," said Phoenix. "The time come around."

He gave another laugh, filling the whole landscape. "I know you old colored people! Wouldn't miss going to town to see Santa Claus!"

But something held old Phoenix very still. The deep lines in her face went
into a fierce and different radiation. Without warning, she had seen with her
own eyes a flashing nickel fall out of the man's pocket onto the ground.

"How old are you, Granny?" he was saying. 50

"There is no telling, mister," she said, "no telling."

Then she gave a little cry and clapped her hands and said, "Git on away
from here, dog! Look! Look at that dog!" She laughed as if in admiration. "He
ain't scared of nobody. He a big black dog." She whispered, "Sic him!"

"Watch me get rid of that cur," said the man. "Sic him, Pete! Sic him!"

Phoenix heard the dogs fighting, and heard the man running and throwing sticks. She even heard a gunshot. But she was slowly bending forward by
that time, further and further forward, the lid stretched down over her eyes,
as if she were doing this in her sleep. Her chin was lowered almost to her
knees. The yellow palm of her hand came out from the fold of her apron. Her
fingers slid down and along the ground under the piece of money with the
grace and care they would have in lifting an egg from under a setting hen. Then

she slowly straightened up, she stood erect, and the nickel was in her apron pocket. A bird flew by. Her lips moved. "God watching me the whole time. I come to stealing."

The man came back, and his own dog panted about them. "Well, I scared him off that time," he said, and then he laughed and lifted his gun and pointed it at Phoenix.   55

She stood straight and faced him.

"Doesn't the gun scare you?" he said, still pointing it.

"No, sir, I seen plenty go off closer by, in my day, and for less than what I done," she said, holding utterly still.

He smiled, and shouldered the gun. "Well, Granny," he said, "you must be a hundred years old, and scared of nothing. I'd give you a dime if I had any money with me. But you take my advice and stay home, and nothing will happen to you."

"I bound to go on my way, mister," said Phoenix. She inclined her head in the red rag. Then they went in different directions, but she could hear the gun shooting again and again over the hill.   60

She walked on. The shadows hung from the oak trees to the road like curtains. Then she smelled wood-smoke, and smelled the river, and she saw a steeple and the cabins on their steep steps. Dozens of little black children whirled around her. There ahead was Natchez shining. Bells were ringing. She walked on.

In the paved city it was Christmas time. There were red and green electric lights strung and crisscrossed everywhere, and all turned on in the daytime. Old Phoenix would have been lost if she had not distrusted her eyesight and depended on her feet to know where to take her.

She paused quietly on the sidewalk where people were passing by. A lady came along in the crowd, carrying an armful of red-, green-, and silver-wrapped presents; she gave off perfume like the red roses in hot summer, and Phoenix stopped her.

"Please, missy, will you lace up my shoe?" She held up her foot.

"What do you want, Grandma?"   65

"See my shoe," said Phoenix. "Do all right for out in the country, but wouldn't look right to go in a big building."

"Stand still then, Grandma," said the lady. She put her packages down on the sidewalk beside her and laced and tied both shoes tightly.

"Can't lace 'em with a cane," said Phoenix. "Thank you, missy. I doesn't mind asking a nice lady to tie up my shoe, when I gets out on the street."

Moving slowly and from side to side, she went into the big building, and into a tower of steps, where she walked up and around and around until her feet knew to stop.

She entered a door, and there she saw nailed up on the wall the document that had been stamped with the gold seal and framed in the gold frame, which matched the dream that was hung up in her head.   70

"Here I be," she said. There was a fixed and ceremonial stiffness over her body.

"A charity case, I suppose," said an attendant who sat at the desk before her.

But Phoenix only looked above her head. There was sweat on her face, the wrinkles in her skin shone like a bright net.

"Speak up, Grandma," the woman said. "What's your name? We must have your history, you know. Have you been here before? What seems to be the trouble with you?"

Old Phoenix only gave a twitch to her face as if a fly were bothering her.   75

"Are you deaf?" cried the attendant.

But then the nurse came in.

"Oh, that's just old Aunt Phoenix," she said. "She doesn't come for herself — she has a little grandson. She makes these trips just as regular as clockwork. She lives away back off the Old Natchez Trace." She bent down. "Well, Aunt Phoenix, why don't you just take a seat? We won't keep you standing after your long trip." She pointed.

The old woman sat down, bolt upright in the chair.

"Now, how is the boy?" asked the nurse.   80

Old Phoenix did not speak.

"I said, how is the boy?"

But Phoenix only waited and stared straight ahead, her face very solemn and withdrawn into rigidity.

"Is his throat any better?" asked the nurse. "Aunt Phoenix, don't you hear me? Is your grandson's throat any better since the last time you came for the medicine?"

With her hands on her knees, the old woman waited, silent, erect, and motionless, just as if she were in armor.   85

"You mustn't take up our time this way, Aunt Phoenix," the nurse said. "Tell us quickly about your grandson, and get it over. He isn't dead, is he?"

At last there came a flicker and then a flame of comprehension across her face, and she spoke.

"My grandson. It was my memory had left me. There I sat and forgot why I made my long trip."

"Forgot?" The nurse frowned. "After you came so far?"

Then Phoenix was like an old woman begging a dignified forgiveness for   90
waking up frightened in the night. "I never did go to school, I was too old at the Surrender,° " she said in a soft voice. "I'm an old woman without an education. It was my memory fail me. My little grandson, he is just the same, and I forgot it in the coming."

"Throat never heals, does it?" said the nurse, speaking in a loud, sure voice to old Phoenix. By now she had a card with something written on it, a little list. "Yes. Swallowed lye. When was it? — January — two, three years ago —"

Phoenix spoke unasked now. "No, missy, he not dead, he just the same. Every little while his throat began to close up again, and he not able to swallow.

the Surrender: On April 9, 1865, General Robert E. Lee surrendered to General Ulysses S. Grant, at Appomattox, Virginia, ending the Civil War.

He not get his breath. He not able to help himself. So the time come around, and I go on another trip for the soothing medicine."

"All right. The doctor said as long as you came to get it, you could have it," said the nurse. "But it's an obstinate case."

"My little grandson, he sit up there in the house all wrapped up, waiting by himself," Phoenix went on. "We is the only two left in the world. He suffer and it don't seem to put him back at all. He got a sweet look. He going to last. He wear a little patch quilt and peep out holding his mouth open like a little bird. I remembers so plain now. I not going to forget him again, no, the whole enduring time. I could tell him from all the others in creation."

"All right." The nurse was trying to hush her now. She brought her a bottle   95
of medicine. "Charity," she said, making a check mark in a book.

Old Phoenix held the bottle close to her eyes, and then carefully put it into her pocket.

"I thank you," she said.

"It's Christmas time, Grandma," said the attendant. "Could I give you a few pennies out of my purse?"

"Five pennies is a nickel," said Phoenix stiffly.

"Here's a nickel," said the attendant.   100

Phoenix rose carefully and held out her hand. She received the nickel and then fished the other nickel out of her pocket and laid it beside the new one. She stared at her palm closely, with her head on one side.

Then she gave a tap with her cane on the floor.

"This is what come to me to do," she said. "I going to the store and buy my child a little windmill they sells, made out of paper. He going to find it hard to believe there such a thing in the world. I'll march myself back where he waiting, holding it straight up in this hand."

She lifted her free hand, gave a little nod, turned around, and walked out of the doctor's office. Then her slow step began on the stairs, going down.

[1941]

■ THINKING ABOUT THE TEXT

1. Comment on the old woman's name; in a tale about a journey, it seems to have allegorical significance.

2. Phoenix meets a hunter on her trek. Comment on the significant details of their encounter.

3. Phoenix speaks directly to a number of things. What are they, and what allegorical significance might they have?

4. Welty ends her essay on this story (p. 1403) by saying that Phoenix's journey might serve as a parallel to young writers. What might she mean?

5. Welty has claimed that the most frequent question she was asked about this story was whether Phoenix's grandson is really dead. Her answer is that, either way, the meaning of this story would not be affected. What do you think she means?

ROLAND BARTEL
Life and Death in Eudora Welty's "A Worn Path"

Roland Bartel (b. 1927) is professor emeritus at the University of Oregon, where he was department head from 1968 to 1976. He received his Ph.D. from Indiana University in 1957. He has published articles and reviews in such journals as English Journal, College Composition and Communication, *and* Comparative Literature.

As most critics have noted, Phoenix Jackson's first name links her to the Egyptian myth of the bird that renews itself periodically from its own ashes. Equally obvious is the quest motif associated with her annual journey to Natchez. What concerns me about these discussions is that they treat Phoenix Jackson as a stereotype and allow the obvious archetypal significance of her name and her journey to overshadow the uniqueness of one of the most memorable women in short fiction.

Phoenix Jackson is a very old woman who walks from the Old Natchez Trace into Natchez at Christmastime to get medicine for her grandson. Previous critics have noted the many ways in which the renewal myth applies to the frail grandmother and to the grandson for whom she undertakes the hazardous journey each year. I want to add the suggestion that the story operates on the psychological level also, that Phoenix Jackson must make the journey to sustain her own life, that her character becomes unusually poignant if we consider seriously the possibility that her grandson is, in fact, dead. The journey to Natchez then becomes a psychological necessity for Phoenix, her only way of coping with her loss and her isolation. As she says to the white hunter who twice urges her to give up the journey: "I bound to go to town, mister, the time come around" and "I bound to go on my way, mister." Having at first made the journey to save the life of her grandson, she now follows the worn path each Christmas season to save herself. Her survival depends on her going through a ritual that symbolically brings her grandson back to life.

The assumption that the grandson is dead helps to explain Phoenix Jackson's stoical behavior in the doctor's office. She displays a "ceremonial stiffness" as she sits "bolt upright" staring "straight ahead, her face solemn and withdrawn into rigidity." This passiveness suggests her psychological dilemma — she cannot explain why she made the journey. Her attempt to blame her lapse of memory on her illiteracy is unconvincing. Her lack of education is hardly an excuse for forgetting her grandson, but it goes a long way toward explaining her inability to articulate her subconscious motives for her journey.

When the nurse asks whether the grandson is dead, Phoenix suddenly remembers and then overcompensates. In her imagination she brings him back to life, her concluding comment sounding very much like the language of a person trying to revive the image of someone who has died: "I remember so plain now. I not going to forget him again, no, the whole enduring time. I could tell him from all others in creation."

The story ends with Phoenix going down the stairs. Ascending a stairway   5
is associated in folklore and religion with entering a new level of life, with
achieving one's destination. Descending a stairway has the opposite implication and has, since Dante's *Inferno*, often been associated with a descent into
hell. When Phoenix ascends the stairs she knows she has reached her destination when she sees hanging on the wall the gold seal in the gold frame, "which
matched the dream that was hung up in her head." After she gets the medicine
from the nurse and the nickel from the attendant, she talks briefly about a paper windmill for her grandson, but then the story ends abruptly with her going
down the stairs, a fact that suggests the end of her hope, possibly the end of her
life. This interpretation strengthens the thematic unity and symmetry of the
story by beginning and ending with references to death. At the beginning of
the story Phoenix taps the frozen ground with her cane. At the end of the story,
just before she goes down the stairs, she taps the wooden floor with her cane,
an action reminiscent of the old man in Chaucer's *Pardoner's Tale*, who taps the
earth with his cane seeking death.

Phoenix has to make herself and others believe that her grandson lives so
that she can endure her hardships and her subconscious awareness of the im-
minence of her own death. Literally she seeks the city to give life to her grandson, but symbolically she needs the city to support her own life. Carl Jung has
interpreted the city as the feminine principle in general and more specifically as
a woman who cares for the inhabitants as if they were her children. When
Phoenix enters the city she cannot trust her eyes, so she relies on her feet to
take her to [her] destination, another indication of the subconscious element
of her journey.

If the journey is as much a necessity for the grandmother as for the grandson, then the episodes along the way take on added significance. After she
crosses the creek with her eyes closed, she has a vision of a boy offering her a
cake, quite possibly her deceased grandson. Her desperate need for companionship is demonstrated not only by this vision but also by her practice of talking
to animals and objects, most of which she imagines rather than sees.

Phoenix Jackson thus emerges from the story as a distinctive person, a feeble
old woman whose active imagination rescues her from the harshest aspects of
her existence. She is driven to the necessity of inventing such details as make the
last portion of her life bearable. If her grandson is dead, then the rebirth implied
in her name is doubly pathetic: she unwittingly makes the journey to meet her
own needs rather than her grandson's, and what begins as a life-sustaining journey seems to end in a journey of death. If the white hunter was right in saying
that she hardly had enough time to return home if she started back immediately,
she certainly will not make it back, literally or symbolically, after the passing of
the additional time required to get to the city and the doctor's office. During the
first part of the journey we get flashes of her sense of humor, but by the end of
the story her senility seems to overcome her. The second sentence of the story,
"Her name was Phoenix Jackson," seems to suggest by its brevity that all she has
left in life is her name and all it implies. At the end of the story the impression
prevails that she has risen from the ashes for the last time.   *[1977]*

NEIL D. ISAACS
Life for Phoenix

Neil D. Isaacs (b. 1931) is a professor of English at the University of Maryland, and he is also a family therapist in Colesville, Maryland. He has written widely on baseball as well as authored scholarly publications on J. R. R. Tolkien, Grace Paley, and Eudora Welty. Isaacs is also the author of The Miller Masks — A Novel in Stories *(2000).*

The first four sentences of "A Worn Path"[1] contain simple declarative statements using the simple past of the verb "to be": "It was December . . . ," ". . . there was an old Negro woman . . . ," "Her name was Phoenix Jackson," "She was very old and small. . . ." The note of simplicity thus struck is the keynote of Eudora Welty's artistic design in the story. For it is a simple story (a common reaction is "simply beautiful"). But it is also a story which employs many of the devices which can make of the modern short story an intricate and densely complex form. It uses them, however, in such a way that it demonstrates how a single meaning may be enriched through the use of various techniques. Thus, instead of various levels of meaning, we have here a single meaning reinforced on several levels of perception. Moreover, there is no muddying of levels and techniques; they are neatly arranged, straightforwardly presented, and simply perceived.

The plotline follows Phoenix Jackson, who is graphically described in the second paragraph, on her long walk into Natchez where she has to get medicine for her grandson. The trek is especially difficult because of her age, and in the process of struggling on she forgets the reason for the struggle. At the end she has remembered, received the medicine, and decided to buy the child a Christmas present with the ten cents she has acquired during the day.

What makes this a story? It barely appears to fulfill even Sidney Cox's generous criterion of "turning a corner or at least a hair."[2] But it does belong to a specific story-teller's genre familiar from Homer to Fielding to Kerouac — "road" literature. This form provides a ready-made plot pattern with some inherent weaknesses. The story concerns the struggle to achieve a goal, the completion of the journey; and the story's beginning, middle, and end are the same as those of the road. The primary weakness of this structure is its susceptibility to too much middle.

A traditional concept of road literature, whether the mythical journey of the sun across the heavens or a boy's trip down the Mississippi or any other variation, is its implicit equation with life: the road of life, life's journey, ups and downs, the straight and narrow, and a host of other clichés reflect the universality of this primitive metaphor. "A Worn Path" makes explicit, beginning

---

[1] References are to Eudora Welty, *A Curtain of Green*, Garden City, N.Y. (Doubleday, Doran and Company), 1943. [Isaacs's note.]

[2] Familiar words to a generation of students at Dartmouth College. [Isaacs's note.]

with the very title, Eudora Welty's acceptance of the traditional equation as a basic aspect of the story. In fact, the whole meaning of "A Worn Path" will rely on an immediate recognition of the equation — the worn path equals the path of life — which is probably why it is so explicit. But we needn't start with a concept which is metaphorical or perhaps primitively allegorical. It will probably be best for us to begin with the other literal elements in the story: they will lead us back to the sub- or supraliteral eventually anyway.

An important part of the setting is the time element, that is, the specific   5
time of the year. We learn immediately that it is "a bright frozen day" in December, and there are several subsequent, direct statements which mark it more precisely as Christmastime. The hunter talks about Santa Claus and the attendant at the hospital says that "It's Christmas time," echoing what the author has said earlier. There are several other references and images forming a pattern to underline the idea of Christmastime, such as "Up above her was a tree in a pearly cloud of *mistletoe.*" [Italics in this paragraph all mine.] Notice especially the elaborate color pattern of red, green, and silver, the traditional colors of Christmas. It begins with Phoenix's head "in a *red* rag, coming along a path through the pinewoods" (which are green as well as Christmas trees). Later she sees "a wagon track, where the *silver grass* blew between the *red* ruts" and "little strings of trees *silver* in their dead leaves" (reddish brown?). This pattern comes to a climax in the description of the city and the lady's packages, which also serves to make explicit its purpose, return it to the literal: "There were red and green electric lights strung and crisscrossed everywhere. . . . an armful of red-, green-, and silver-wrapped presents."

From the plotline alone the idea of Christmas doesn't seem to be more than incidental, but it is obvious from the persistent references that Christmas is going to play an important part in the total effect of the story. Besides the direct statements already mentioned, there proliferates around the pattern throughout the story a dense cluster of allusions to and suggestions of the Christmas myth at large and to the *meanings* of Christmas in particular. For instance, as Phoenix rests under a tree, she has a vision of a little boy offering her a slice of marble-cake on a little plate, and she says, "That would be acceptable." The allusion here is to Communion and church ritual. Later, when a bird flies by, Phoenix says, "God watching me the whole time." Then there are references to the Eden story (the ordering of the species, the snake in summer to be avoided), to the parting of the Red Sea (Phoenix walking through the field of corn), to a sequence of temptations, to the River Jordan and the City of Heaven (when Phoenix gets to the river, sees the city shining, and hears the bells ringing; then there is the angel who waits on her, tying her shoes), to the Christ-child in the manger (Phoenix describing her grandson as "all wrapped up" in "a little patch quilt . . . like a little bird" with "a sweet look"). In addition, the whole story is suggestive of a religious pilgrimage, while the conclusion implies that the return trip will be like the journey of the Magi, with Phoenix following a star (the marvelous windmill) to bring a gift to the child (medicine, also windmill). Moreover, there's the hunter who is, in part, a Santa Claus figure himself (he carries a big sack over his shoulder, he is always laughing, he brings Phoenix a gift of a nickel).

The richness of all this evocation of a Christianity-Christmas frame of reference heightens the specific points about the meanings of Christmas. The Christmas spirit, of course, is the Christian ethic in its simplest terms; giving, doing for others, charity. This concept is made explicit when the nurse says of Phoenix, "She doesn't come for herself." But it had already been presented in a brilliant piece of ironic juxtaposition [italics mine]:

> She entered a door, and there she saw *nailed up on the wall* the document that had been stamped with the *gold seal* and framed in the *gold frame* which *matched the dream that was hung up in her head.*
>
> "*Here I be,*" she said. There was a *fixed and ceremonial stiffness* over her body.
>
> "A *charity* case, I suppose," said an attendant. . . .

Amid the Christmas season and the dense Christmas imagery, Phoenix, with an abiding intuitive faith, arrives at the shrine of her pilgrimage, beholds a symbolic crucifixion, presents herself as a celebrant in the faith, and is recognized as an embodiment of the message of the faith. This entire scene, however, with its gold trimming and the attitude of the attendant, is turned ironically to suggest greed, corruption, cynicism — the very opposite of the word used, charity. Yet the episode, which is Phoenix's final and most severe trial, also results in her final emergence as a redeemer and might be called her Calvary.

Perhaps a better way to get at the meaning of Christmas and the meaning of "A Worn Path" is to talk about life and death. In a sense, the meaning of Christmas and that of Easter are the same — a celebration of life out of death. (Notice that Phoenix refers to herself as a *June* bug and that the woman with the packages "gave off perfume like the *red roses in hot summer.*") [Italics mine.] Christ is born in the death of the year and in a near-dead nature-society situation in order to rejuvenate life itself, naturally and spiritually. He dies in order that the life of others may be saved. He is reborn out of death, and so are nature, love, and the spirit of man. All this is the potent Christian explanation of the central irony of human existence, that life means death and death is life. One might state the meaning of "A Worn Path" in similar terms, where Phoenix endures a long, agonizing dying in order to redeem her grandson's life. So the medicine, which the nurse calls charity as she makes a check in her book, is a symbol of love and life. The windmill represents the same duality, but lighter sides of both aspects. If the path is the path of life, then its end is death and the purpose of that death is new life.

It would be misleading, however, to suggest that the story is merely a paralleling of the Christian nature-myth. It is, rather, a miniature nature-myth of its own which uses elements of many traditions. The most obvious example is the name Phoenix from the mythological Egyptian bird, symbol of immortality and resurrection, which dies so that a new Phoenix may emerge from its ashes. There is a reference to the Daedalus labyrinth myth° when Phoenix walks

Daedalus labyrinth myth: In Greek mythology, Daedalus was a famous architect who built an elaborate maze to contain the monstrous minotaur.

through the corn field and Miss Welty puns: " 'Through the maze now,' she said, for there was no path." That ambivalent figure of the hunter comes into play here as both a death figure (killer, bag full of slain quail) and a life figure (unconscious giver of life with the nickel, banisher of Cerberus°-like black dog who is attacking Phoenix), but in any case a folk-legend figure who can fill "the whole landscape" with his laugh. And there are several references to the course of the sun across the sky which gives a new dimension to the life-road equation; e.g., "Sun so high! . . . The time getting all gone here."

The most impressive extra-Christian elements are the patterns that iden-   10
tify Phoenix as a creature of nature herself and as a ritual-magic figure. Thus, Phoenix makes a sound "like the chirping of a solitary little bird," her hair has "an odor like copper," and at one point "with [her] mouth drawn down, [she] shook her head once or twice in a little strutting way." Even more remarkable is the "fixed and ceremonial stiffness" of her body, which moves "like a festival figure in some parade." The cane she carries, made from an umbrella, is tapped on the ground like a magic wand, and she uses it to "switch at the brush as if to rouse up any hiding things." At the same time she utters little spells:

> Out of my way, all you foxes, owls, beetles, jack rabbits, coons, and wild animals! . . . Keep out from under these feet, little bobwhites. . . . Keep the big wild hogs out of my path. Don't let none of those come running my direction. . . . Ghost, . . . who be you the ghost of? . . . Sweetgum makes the water sweet. . . . Nobody know who made this well for it was here when I was born. . . . Sleep on, alligators, and blow your bubbles.

Other suggestions of magic appear in the whirling of cornhusks in streamers about her skirts, when she parts "her way from side to side with the cane, through the whispering field," when the quail seem "unseen," and when the cabins are "all like old women under a spell sitting there." Finally, ironically, when Phoenix swings at the black dog, she goes over "in the ditch, like a little puff of milk-weed."

More or less remote, more or less direct, all these allusions are used for the same effect as are the references to Christianity, to reinforce a statement of the meaning of life. This brings us back to the basic life-road equation of the story, and there are numerous indications that the path is life and that the end of the road is death and renewal of life. These suggestions are of three types; statements which relate the road, the trip, or Phoenix to time: Phoenix walks "with the balanced heaviness and lightness of a pendulum in a grandfather clock"; she tells the hunter, "I bound to go. . . . The time come around"; and the nurse says "She makes these trips just as regular as clockwork." Second (the most frequent type), there are descriptions of the road or episodes along the way which are suggestive of life, usually in a simple metaphorical way: "I got a long way" (ambiguously referring to past and future); "I in the thorny bush"; "Up through pines. . . . Now down through oaks"; "This the easy place. This the easy going." Third, there are direct references to death, age, and life: Phoenix

---

Cerberus: Monstrous three-headed dog who guards the gates of Hades.

says to a buzzard, "Who you watching?" and to a scarecrow, "Who be you the ghost of? For I have heard of nary death close by"; then she performs a little dance of death with the scarecrow after she says, "My senses is gone. I too old. I the oldest people I ever know."

This brings us full circle in an examination of the design of the story, and it should be possible now to say something about the total meaning of "A Worn Path." The path is the path of life, and the story is an attempt to probe the meaning of life in its simplest, most elementary terms. Through the story we arrive at a definition of life, albeit a teleological one. When the hunter tells Phoenix to "take my advice and stay home, and nothing will happen to you," the irony is obvious and so is the metaphor: don't live and you can't die. When Phoenix forgets why she has made the arduous trek to Natchez,[3] we understand that it is only a rare person who knows the meaning of his life, that living does not imply knowing. When Phoenix describes the Christ-like child waiting for her and says, "I not going to forget him again, no, the whole enduring time. I could tell him from all the others in creation," we understand several things about it: her life is almost over, she sees clearly the meaning of life, she has an abiding faith in that meaning, and she will share with her grandson this great revelation just as together they embody its significance. And when Phoenix's "slow step began on the stairs, going down," as she starts back to bring the boy the medicine and the windmill, we see a composite symbol of life itself, dying so that life may continue. Life is a journey toward death, because one must die in order that life may go on.   [1963]

---

[3] p. 283: "It was my memory had left me. . . . I forgot it in the coming." [Isaacs's note.]

EUDORA WELTY
Is Phoenix Jackson's Grandson Really Dead?

Because of her many prizes, including the Pulitzer, Welty is best known as a fiction writer, but she is also the respected author of two collections of photographs, a children's book, and three works of nonfiction. The following discussion of her short story is from The Eye of the Storm *(1977).*

A story writer is more than happy to be read by students; the fact that these serious readers think and feel something in response to his work he finds life-giving. At the same time he may not always be able to reply to their specific questions in kind. I wondered if it might clarify something, for both the questioners and myself, if I set down a general reply to the question that comes to me most often in the mail, from both students and their teachers, after some classroom discussion. The unrivaled favorite is this: "Is Phoenix Jackson's grandson really *dead?*"

It refers to a short story I wrote years ago called "A Worn Path," which tells of a day's journey an old woman makes on foot from deep in the country into town and into a doctor's office on behalf of her little grandson; he is at home, periodically ill, and periodically she comes for his medicine; they give it to her as usual, she receives it and starts the journey back.

I had not meant to mystify readers by withholding any fact; it is not a writer's business to tease. The story is told through Phoenix's mind as she undertakes her errand. As the author at one with the character as I tell it, I must assume that the boy is alive. As the reader, you are free to think as you like, of course: the story invites you to believe that no matter what happens, Phoenix for as long as she is able to walk and can hold to her purpose will make her journey. The *possibility* that she would keep on even if he were dead is there in her devotion and its single-minded, single-track errand. Certainly the *artistic* truth, which should be good enough for the fact, lies in Phoenix's own answer to that question. When the nurse asks, " 'He isn't dead, is he?' " she speaks for herself: " 'He still the same. He going to last.' "

The grandchild is the incentive. But it is the journey, the going of the errand, that is the story, and the question is not whether the grandchild is in reality alive or dead. It doesn't affect the outcome of the story or its meaning from start to finish. But it is not the question itself that has struck me as much as the idea, almost without exception implied in the asking, that for Phoenix's grandson to be dead would somehow make the story "better."

It's *all right*, I want to say to the students who write to me, for things to be 5
what they appear to be, and for words to mean what they say. It's all right, too, for words and appearances to mean more than one thing — ambiguity is a fact of life. A fiction writer's responsibility covers not only what he presents as the facts of a given story but what he chooses to stir up as their implications; in the end, these implications, too, become facts, in the larger, fictional sense. But it is not all right, not in good faith, for things *not* to mean what they say.

The grandson's plight was real and it made the truth of the story, which is the story of an errand of love carried out. If the child no longer lived, the truth would persist in the "wornness" of the path. But his being dead can't increase the truth of the story, can't affect it one way or the other. I think I signal this, because the end of the story has been reached before old Phoenix gets home again: she simply starts back. To the question "Is the grandson really dead?" I could reply that it doesn't make any difference. I could also say that I did not make him up in order to let him play a trick on Phoenix. But my best answer would be: "*Phoenix* is alive."

The origin of a story is sometimes a trustworthy clue to the author — or can provide him with the clue — to its key image; maybe in this case it will do the same for the reader. One day I saw a solitary old woman like Phoenix. She was walking; I saw her, at middle distance, in a winter country landscape, and watched her slowly make her way across my line of vision. That sight of her made me write the story. I invented an errand for her, but that only seemed a living part of the figure she was herself: what errand other than for someone else could be making her go? And her going was the first thing, her persisting in her landscape was the real thing, and the first and the real were what I wanted and worked to keep. I brought her up close enough, by imagination, to describe her face, make her present to the eyes, but the full-length figure moving across the winter fields was the indelible one and the image to keep, and the perspective extending into the vanishing distance the true one to hold in mind.

I invented for my character, as I wrote, some passing adventures — some dreams and harassments and a small triumph or two, some jolts to her pride, some flights of fancy to console her, one or two encounters to scare her, a moment that gave her cause to feel ashamed, a moment to dance and preen — for it had to be a *journey*, and all these things belonged to that, parts of life's uncertainty.

A narrative line is in its deeper sense, of course, the tracing out of a meaning, and the real continuity of a story lies in this probing forward. The real dramatic force of a story depends on the strength of the emotion that has set it going. The emotional value is the measure of the reach of the story. What gives any such content to "A Worn Path" is not its circumstances but its *subject*: the deep-grained habit of love.

What I hoped would come clear was that in the whole surround of this   10
story, the world it threads through, the only certain thing at all is the worn path. The habit of love cuts through confusion and stumbles or contrives its way out of difficulty, it remembers the way even when it forgets, for a dumbfounded moment, its reason for being. The path is the thing that matters.

Her victory — old Phoenix's — is when she sees the diploma in the doctor's office, when she finds "nailed up on the wall the document that had been stamped with the gold seal and framed in the gold frame, which matched the dream that was hung up in her head." The return with the medicine is just a matter of retracing her own footsteps. It is the part of the journey, and of the story, that can now go without saying.

In the matter of function, old Phoenix's way might even do as a sort of parallel to your way of work if you are a writer of stories. The way to get there is the all-important, all-absorbing problem, and this problem is your reason for undertaking the story. Your only guide, too, is your sureness about your subject, about what this subject is. Like Phoenix, you work all your life to find your way, through all the obstructions and the false appearances and the upsets you may have brought on yourself, to reach a meaning — using inventions of your imagination, perhaps helped out by your dreams and bits of good luck. And finally too, like Phoenix, you have to assume that what you are working in aid of is life, not death.

But you would make the trip anyway — wouldn't you? — just on hope.

                                                                    [1974]

■ MAKING COMPARISONS

1. Bartel suggests the grandson is dead, Isaacs doesn't, and Welty claims it does not really matter. Which is closest to your position?

2. Bartel suggests that Phoenix makes the journey for herself. Does this jibe with the positions of Isaacs and Welty?

3. In your opinion, which critic offers the best evidence?

■ **WRITING ABOUT ISSUES**

1. Write an argument that takes issue with Bartel's thesis that Phoenix takes the journey for her own survival.

2. Write a brief essay that answers the question Welty asks in the last sentence of her essay.

3. Write a personal essay about a trip/journey/pilgrimage/errand that you took that had significance for you either at the time or in retrospect.

4. Assuming that Phoenix's journey is an extended allegory, write an essay that incorporates as many of the details of the story as you can into your analysis.

▇ Going on Uncertain Journeys: Stories

JOYCE CAROL OATES, "Where Are You Going, Where Have You Been?"

JILL McCORKLE, "Magic Words"

SHERMAN ALEXIE, "What You Pawn I Will Redeem"

The harrowing ending of Joyce Carol Oates's much-anthologized initiation tale of innocence versus evil can still shock readers. The fifteen-year-old Connie, focused on boys and pop music, seems defenseless against her bizarre stalker. The journey she is about to take is chilling to contemplate. Negotiating the desires and impulses of adolescence has never been an easy journey, but Jill McCorkle puts an interesting spin on Oates's iconic story by having the mother, not the daughter, succumb to desire and begin a potentially perilous quest for adventure. The mothers and daughters in these two tales have interesting similarities and differences. Jackson's quest in Alexie's narrative is also fraught with danger, but somehow he seems to end up the most satisfied. These three stories do not underestimate the perils of our journeys in an uncertain and precarious world.

JOYCE CAROL OATES
Where Are You Going, Where Have You Been?

Joyce Carol Oates (b. 1938) is perhaps the most prolific of major American writers, publishing about two books a year for more than forty years. Always cited as a favorite to win the Nobel Prize for literature, Oates has won numerous awards, including a National Book Award for fiction (1970).

Oates grew up in the countryside of upstate New York. She started writing early and won a scholarship to Syracuse University, where she was valedictorian in 1960. She received her M.A. from the University of Wisconsin a year later. She taught at the University of Detroit and the University of Windsor before joining the faculty at Princeton, where she has taught since 1978. Like Flannery O'Connor and William Faulkner, her work is usually referred to as gothic, probably because of her violent characters, many of whom are filled with enigmatic malice and tormented emotions. Working in the realistic tradition, the "Dark Lady of American Literature" writes compelling narratives about seemingly ordinary people who beneath the surface live in a nightmare world of unconscious forces and sometimes sensational events.

Oates claims the story printed here was written after listening to Bob Dylan's "It's All Over Now, Baby Blue." The story was inspired by the serial killer Charles Schmid, also known as "The Pied Piper of Tucson." Her recent books are the novels The Gravedigger's Daughter *(2007) and* Fair Maiden *(2010) and the short-story collections* The Museum of Dr. Moses: Tales of Mystery and Suspense *(2007) and* Sourland: Stories *(2010).*

For Bob Dylan

Her name was Connie. She was fifteen and she had a quick nervous giggling habit of craning her neck to glance into mirrors, or checking other people's faces to make sure her own was all right. Her mother, who noticed everything and knew everything and who hadn't much reason any longer to look at her own face, always scolded Connie about it. "Stop gawking at yourself, who are you? You think you're so pretty?" she would say. Connie would raise her eyebrows at these familiar complaints and look right through her mother, into a shadowy vision of herself as she was right at that moment: she knew she was pretty and that was everything. Her mother had been pretty once too, if you could believe those old snapshots in the album, but now her looks were gone and that was why she was always after Connie.

"Why don't you keep your room clean like your sister? How've you got your hair fixed — what the hell stinks? Hair spray? You don't see your sister using that junk."

Her sister June was twenty-four and still lived at home. She was a secretary in the high school Connie attended, and if that wasn't bad enough — with her in the same building — she was so plain and chunky and steady that Connie had to hear her praised all the time by her mother and her mother's sisters. June did this, June did that, she saved money and helped clean the house and cooked and Connie couldn't do a thing, her mind was all filled with trashy daydreams. Their father was away at work most of the time and when he came home he wanted supper and he read the newspaper at supper and after supper he went to bed. He didn't bother talking much to them, but around his bent head Connie's mother kept picking at her until Connie wished her mother was dead and she herself was dead and it was all over. "She makes me want to throw up sometimes," she complained to her friends. She had a high, breathless, amused voice which made everything she said a little forced, whether it was sincere or not.

There was one good thing: June went places with girl friends of hers, girls who were just as plain and steady as she, and so when Connie wanted to do that her mother had no objections. The father of Connie's best girl friend drove the girls the three miles to town and left them off at a shopping plaza, so that they could walk through the stores or go to a movie, and when he came to pick them up again at eleven he never bothered to ask what they had done.

They must have been familiar sights, walking around that shopping plaza in their shorts and flat ballerina slippers that always scuffed the sidewalk, with charm bracelets jingling on their thin wrists; they would lean together to whisper and laugh secretly if someone passed by who amused or interested them. Connie had long dark blond hair that drew anyone's eye to it, and she wore part of it pulled up on her head and puffed out and the rest of it she let fall down her back. She wore a pullover jersey blouse that looked one way when she was at home and another way when she was away from home. Everything about her had two sides to it, one for home and one for anywhere that was not home: her walk that could be childlike and bobbing, or languid enough to make any-

5

one think she was hearing music in her head, her mouth which was pale and smirking most of the time, but bright and pink on these evenings out, her laugh which was cynical and drawling at home — "Ha, ha, very funny" — but high-pitched and nervous anywhere else, like the jingling of the charms on her bracelet.

Sometimes they did go shopping or to a movie, but sometimes they went across the highway, ducking fast across the busy road, to a drive-in restaurant where older kids hung out. The restaurant was shaped like a big bottle, though squatter than a real bottle, and on its cap was a revolving figure of a grinning boy who held a hamburger aloft. One night in midsummer they ran across, breathless with daring, and right away someone leaned out a car window and invited them over, but it was just a boy from high school they didn't like. It made them feel good to be able to ignore him. They went up through the maze of parked and cruising cars to the bright-lit, fly-infested restaurant, their faces pleased and expectant as if they were entering a sacred building that loomed out of the night to give them what haven and what blessing they yearned for. They sat at the counter and crossed their legs at the ankles, their thin shoulders rigid with excitement and listened to the music that made everything so good: the music was always in the background like music at a church service, it was something to depend upon.

A boy named Eddie came in to talk with them. He sat backwards on his stool, turning himself jerkily around in semi-circles and then stopping and turning again, and after a while he asked Connie if she would like something to eat. She said she did and so she tapped her friend's arm on her way out — her friend pulled her face up into a brave droll look — and Connie said she would meet her at eleven, across the way. "I just hate to leave her like that," Connie said earnestly, but the boy said that she wouldn't be alone for long. So they went out to his car and on the way Connie couldn't help but let her eyes wander over the windshields and faces all around her, her face gleaming with the joy that had nothing to do with Eddie or even this place; it might have been the music. She drew her shoulders up and sucked in her breath with the pure pleasure of being alive, and just at that moment she happened to glance at a face just a few feet from hers. It was a boy with shaggy black hair, in a convertible jalopy painted gold. He stared at her and then his lips widened into a grin. Connie slit her eyes at him and turned away, but she couldn't help glancing back and there he was still watching her. He wagged a finger and laughed and said. "Gonna get you, baby," and Connie turned away again without Eddie noticing anything.

She spent three hours with him, at the restaurant where they ate hamburgers and drank Cokes in wax cups that were always sweating, and then down an alley a mile or so away, and when he left her off at five to eleven only the movie house was still open at the plaza. Her girl friend was there, talking with a boy. When Connie came up the two girls smiled at each other and Connie said, "How was the movie?" and the girl said, "*You* should know." They rode off with the girl's father, sleepy and pleased, and Connie couldn't help but look at the darkened shopping plaza with its big empty parking lot and its signs that were faded and ghostly now, and over at the drive-in restaurant where cars were still circling tirelessly. She couldn't hear the music at this distance.

Next morning June asked her how the movie was and Connie said, "So-so."

She and that girl and occasionally another girl went out several times a week that way, and the rest of the time Connie spent around the house — it was summer vacation — getting in her mother's way and thinking, dreaming, about the boys she met. But all the boys fell back and dissolved into a single face that was not even a face, but an idea, a feeling, mixed up with the urgent insistent pounding of the music and the humid night air of July. Connie's mother kept dragging her back to the daylight by finding things for her to do or saying suddenly, "What's this about the Pettinger girl?"

And Connie would say nervously, "Oh, her. That dope." She always drew thick clear lines between herself and such girls, and her mother was simple and kindly enough to believe her. Her mother was so simple, Connie thought, that it was maybe cruel to fool her so much. Her mother went scuffling around the house in old bedroom slippers and complained over the telephone to one sister about the other, then the other called up and the two of them complained about the third one. If June's name was mentioned her mother's tone was approving, and if Connie's name was mentioned it was disapproving. This did not really mean she disliked Connie and actually Connie thought that her mother preferred her to June because she was prettier, but the two of them kept up a pretense of exasperation, a sense that they were tugging and struggling over something of little value to either of them. Sometimes, over coffee, they were almost friends, but something would come up — some vexation that was like a fly buzzing suddenly around their heads — and their faces went hard with contempt.

One Sunday Connie got up at eleven — none of them bothered with church — and washed her hair so that it could dry all day long, in the sun. Her parents and sister were going to a barbecue at an aunt's house and Connie said no, she wasn't interested, rolling her eyes, to let mother know just what she thought of it. "Stay home alone then," her mother said sharply. Connie sat out back in a lawn chair and watched them drive away, her father quiet and bald, hunched around so that he could back the car out, her mother with a look that was still angry and not at all softened through the windshield, and in the back seat poor old June all dressed up as if she didn't know what a barbecue was, with all the running yelling kids and the flies. Connie sat with her eyes closed in the sun, dreaming and dazed with the warmth about her as if this were a kind of love, the caresses of love, and her mind slipped over onto thoughts of the boy she had been with the night before and how nice he had been, how sweet it always was, not the way someone like June would suppose but sweet, gentle, the way it was in movies and promised in songs; and when she opened her eyes she hardly knew where she was, the back yard ran off into weeds and a fenceline of trees and behind it the sky was perfectly blue and still. The asbestos "ranch house" that was now three years old startled her — it looked small. She shook her head as if to get awake.

It was too hot. She went inside the house and turned on the radio to drown out the quiet. She sat on the edge of her bed, barefoot, and listened for an hour and a half to a program called XYZ Sunday Jamboree, record after record of hard, fast, shrieking songs she sang along with, interspersed by exclamations from "Bobby King": "An' look here you girls at Napoleon's — Son and Charley want you to pay real close attention to this song coming up!"

And Connie paid close attention herself, bathed in a glow of slow-pulsed joy that seemed to rise mysteriously out of the music itself and lay languidly about the airless little room, breathed in and breathed out with each gentle rise and fall of her chest.

After a while she heard a car coming up the drive. She sat up at once, star- 15
tled, because it couldn't be her father so soon. The gravel kept crunching all the way in from the road — the driveway was long — and Connie ran to the window. It was a car she didn't know. It was an open jalopy, painted a bright gold that caught the sun opaquely. Her heart began to pound and her fingers snatched at her hair, checking it, and she whispered "Christ. Christ," wondering how bad she looked. The car came to a stop at the side door and the horn sounded four short taps as if this were a signal Connie knew.

She went into the kitchen and approached the door slowly, then hung out the screen door, her bare toes curling down off the step. There were two boys in the car and now she recognized the driver: he had shaggy, shabby black hair that looked crazy as a wig and he was grinning at her.

"I ain't late, am I?" he said.

"Who the hell do you think you are?" Connie said.

"Toldja I'd be out, didn't I?"

"I don't even know who you are." 20

She spoke sullenly, careful to show no interest or pleasure, and he spoke in a fast bright monotone. Connie looked past him to the other boy, taking her time. He had fair brown hair, with a lock that fell onto his forehead. His sideburns gave him a fierce, embarrassed look, but so far he hadn't even bothered to glance at her. Both boys wore sunglasses. The driver's glasses were metallic and mirrored everything in miniature.

"You wanta come for a ride?" he said.

Connie smirked and let her hair fall loose over one shoulder.

"Don'tcha like my car? New paint job," he said. "Hey."

"What?" 25

"You're cute."

She pretended to fidget, chasing flies away from the door.

"Don'tcha believe me, or what?" he said.

"Look, I don't even know who you are," Connie said in disgust.

"Hey, Ellie's got a radio, see. Mine's broke down." He lifted his friend's arm 30
and showed her the little transistor the boy was holding, and now Connie began to hear the music. It was the same program that was playing inside the house.

"Bobby King?" she said.

"I listen to him all the time. I think he's great."

"He's kind of great," Connie said reluctantly.

"Listen, that guy's *great*. He knows where the action is."

Connie blushed a little, because the glasses made it impossible for her to see   35
just what this boy was looking at. She couldn't decide if she liked him or if he
was just a jerk, and so she dawdled in the doorway and wouldn't come down or
go back inside. She said, "What's all that stuff painted on your car?"

"Can'tcha read it?" He opened the door very carefully, as if he was afraid it
might fall off. He slid out just as carefully, planting his feet firmly on the ground,
the tiny metallic world in his glasses slowing down like gelatine hardening and
in the midst of it Connie's bright green blouse. "This here is my name, to begin
with," he said. ARNOLD FRIEND was written in tar-like black letters on the side,
with a drawing of a round grinning face that reminded Connie of a pumpkin,
except it wore sunglasses. "I wanta introduce myself, I'm Arnold Friend and
that's my real name and I'm gonna be your friend, honey, and inside the car's
Ellie Oscar, he's kinda shy." Ellie brought his transistor up to his shoulder and
balanced it there. "Now these numbers are a secret code, honey," Arnold Friend
explained. He read off the numbers 33, 19, 17 and raised his eyebrows at her
to see what she thought of that, but she didn't think much of it. The left rear
fender had been smashed and around it was written, on the gleaming gold
background: DONE BY CRAZY WOMAN DRIVER. Connie had to laugh at that. Arnold
Friend was pleased at her laughter and looked up at her. "Around the other
side's a lot more — you wanta come and see them?"

"No."

"Why not?"

"Why should I?"

"Don'tcha wanta see what's on the car? Don'tcha wanta go for a ride?"   40

"I don't know."

"Why not?"

"I got things to do."

"Like what?"

"Things."   45

He laughed as if she had said something funny. He slapped his thighs. He
was standing in a strange way, leaning back against the car as if he were balancing himself. He wasn't tall, only an inch or so taller than she would be if she
came down to him. Connie liked the way he was dressed, which was the way all
of them dressed: tight faded jeans stuffed into black, scuffed boots, a belt that
pulled his waist in and showed how lean he was, and a white pullover shirt that
was a little soiled and showed the hard small muscles of his arms and shoulders. He looked as if he probably did hard work, lifting and carrying things.
Even his neck looked muscular. And his face was a familiar face, somehow: the
jaw and chin and cheeks slightly darkened, because he hadn't shaved for a day
or two, and the nose long and hawk-like, sniffing as if she were a treat he was
going to gobble up and it was all a joke.

"Connie, you ain't telling the truth. This is your day set aside for a ride with
me and you know it," he said, still laughing. The way he straightened and recovered from his fit of laughing showed that it had been all fake.

"How do you know what my name is?" she said suspiciously.

"It's Connie."

"Maybe and maybe not."   50

"I know my Connie," he said, wagging his finger. Now she remembered him even better, back at the restaurant, and her cheeks warmed at the thought of how she sucked in her breath just at the moment she passed him — how she must have looked to him. And he had remembered her. "Ellie and I come out here especially for you." he said. "Ellie can sit in back. How about it?"

"Where?"

"Where what?"

"Where're we going?"

He looked at her. He took off the sunglasses and she saw how pale the skin   55
around his eyes was, like holes that were not in shadow but instead in light. His eyes were like chips of broken glass that catch the light in an amiable way. He smiled. It was as if the idea of going for a ride somewhere, to some place, was a new idea to him.

"Just for a ride, Connie sweetheart."

"I never said my name was Connie," she said.

"But I know what it is. I know your name and all about you, lots of things," Arnold Friend said. He had not moved yet but stood still leaning back against the side of his jalopy. "I took a special interest in you, such a pretty girl, and found out all about you like I know your parents and sister are gone some-wheres and I know where and how long they're going to be gone, and I know who you were with last night, and your best friend's name is Betty. Right?"

He spoke in a simple lilting voice, exactly as if he were reciting the words to a song. His smile assured her that everything was fine. In the car Ellie turned up the volume on his radio and did not bother to look around at them.

"Ellie can sit in the back seat," Arnold Friend said. He indicated his friend   60
with a casual jerk of his chin, as if Ellie did not count and she could not bother with him.

"How'd you find out all that stuff?" Connie said.

"Listen: Betty Schultz and Tony Fitch and Jimmy Pettinger and Nancy Pettinger," he said, in a chant. "Raymond Stanley and Bob Hutter —"

"Do you know all those kids?"

"I know everybody."

"Look, you're kidding. You're not from around here."   65

"Sure."

"But — how come we never saw you before?"

"Sure you saw me before," he said. He looked down at his boots, as if he were a little offended. "You just don't remember."

"I guess I'd remember you," Connie said.

"Yeah?" He looked up at this, beaming. He was pleased. He began to mark   70
time with the music from Ellie's radio, tapping his fists lightly together. Connie looked away from his smile to the car, which was painted so bright it almost hurt her eyes to look at it. She looked at that name, ARNOLD FRIEND. And up at the front fender was an expression that was familiar — MAN THE FLYING SAUCERS. It was

an expression kids had used the year before, but didn't use this year. She looked at it for a while as if the words meant something to her that she did not yet know.

"What're you thinking about? Huh?" Arnold Friend demanded. "Not worried about your hair blowing around in the car, are you?"

"No."

"Think I maybe can't drive good?"

"How do I know?"

"You're a hard girl to handle. How come?" he said. "Don't you know I'm   75
your friend? Didn't you see me put my sign in the air when you walked by?"

"What sign?"

"My sign." And he drew an X in the air, leaning out toward her. They were maybe ten feet apart. After his hand fell back to his side the X was still in the air, almost visible. Connie let the screen door close and stood perfectly still inside it, listening to the music from her radio and the boy's blend together. She stared at Arnold Friend. He stood there so stiffly relaxed, pretending to be relaxed, with one hand idly on the door handle as if be were keeping himself up that way and had no intention of ever moving again. She recognized most things about him, the tight jeans that showed his thighs and buttocks and the greasy leather boots and the tight shirt, and even that slippery friendly smile of his, that sleepy dreamy smile that all the boys used to get across ideas they didn't want to put into words. She recognized all this and also the singsong way he talked, slightly mocking, kidding, but serious and a little melancholy, and she recognized the way he tapped one fist against the other in homage to the perpetual music behind him. But all these things did not come together.

She said suddenly, "Hey, how old are you?"

His smile faded. She could see then that he wasn't a kid, he was much older — thirty, maybe more. At this knowledge her heart began to pound faster.

"That's a crazy thing to ask. Can'tcha see I'm your own age?"   80

"Like hell you are."

"Or maybe a coupla years older, I'm eighteen."

"Eighteen?" she said doubtfully.

He grinned to reassure her and lines appeared at the corners of his mouth. His teeth were big and white. He grinned so broadly his eyes became slits and she saw how thick the lashes were, thick and black as if painted with a black tar-like material. Then he seemed to become embarrassed, abruptly, and looked over his shoulder at Ellie. "*Him*, he's crazy," he said. "Ain't he a riot, he's a nut, a real character." Ellie was still listening to the music. His sunglasses told nothing about what he was thinking. He wore a bright orange shirt unbuttoned halfway to show his chest, which was a pale, bluish chest and not muscular like Arnold Friend's. His shirt collar was turned up all around and the very tips of the collar pointed out past his chin as if they were protecting him. He was pressing the transistor radio up against his ear and sat there in a kind of daze, right in the sun.

"He's kinda strange," Connie said.   85

"Hey, she says you're kinda strange! Kinda strange!" Arnold Friend cried. He pounded on the car to get Ellie's attention. Ellie turned for the first time and

Connie saw with shock that he wasn't a kid either — he had a fair, hairless face, cheeks reddened slightly as if the veins grew too close to the surface of his skin, the face of a forty-year-old baby. Connie felt a wave of dizziness rise in her at this sight and she stared at him as if waiting for something to change the shock of the moment, make it all right again. Ellie's lips kept shaping words, mumbling along with the words blasting his ear.

"Maybe you two better go away," Connie said faintly.

"What? How come?" Arnold Friend cried. "We come out here to take you for a ride. It's Sunday." He had the voice of the man on the radio now. It was the same voice, Connie thought. "Don'tcha know it's Sunday all day and honey, no matter who you were with last night today you're with Arnold Friend and don't you forget it! — Maybe you better step out here," he said, and this last was in a different voice. It was a little flatter, as if the heat was finally getting to him.

"No. I got things to do."

"Hey." 90

"You two better leave."

"We ain't leaving until you come with us."

"Like hell I am —"

"Connie, don't fool around with me. I mean — I mean, don't fool *around*," he said, shaking his head. He laughed incredulously. He placed his sunglasses on top of his head, carefully, as if he were indeed wearing a wig, and brought the stems down behind his ears. Connie stared at him, another wave of dizziness and fear rising in her so that for a moment he wasn't even in focus but was just a blur; standing there against his gold car, and she had the idea that he had driven up the driveway all right but had come from nowhere before that and belonged nowhere and that everything about him and even the music that was so familiar to her was only half real.

"If my father comes and sees you —" 95

"He ain't coming. He's at a barbecue."

"How do you know that?"

"Aunt Tillie's. Right now they're — uh — they're drinking. Sitting around," he said vaguely, squinting as if he were staring all the way to town and over to Aunt Tillie's back yard. Then the vision seemed to clear and he nodded energetically. "Yeah. Sitting around. There's your sister in a blue dress, huh? And high heels, the poor sad bitch — nothing like you, sweetheart! And your mother's helping some fat woman with the corn, they're cleaning the corn — husking the corn —"

"What fat woman?" Connie cried.

"How do I know what fat woman. I don't know every goddamn fat woman 100 in the world!" Arnold Friend laughed.

"Oh, that's Mrs. Hornby. . . . Who invited her?" Connie said. She felt a little light-headed. Her breath was coming quickly.

"She's too fat. I don't like them fat. I like them the way you are, honey," he said, smiling sleepily at her. They stared at each other for a while, through the screen door. He said softly, "Now what you're going to do is this: you're going to come out that door. You're going to sit up front with me and Ellie's going to sit in the back, the hell with Ellie, right? This isn't Ellie's date. You're my date. I'm your lover, honey."

"What? You're crazy —"

"Yes, I'm your lover. You don't know what that is but you will," he said. "I know that too. I know all about you. But look: it's real nice and you couldn't ask for nobody better than me, or more polite. I always keep my word. I'll tell you how it is, I'm always nice at first, the first time. I'll hold you so tight you won't think you have to try to get away or pretend anything because you'll know you can't. And I'll come inside you where it's all secret and you'll give in to me and you'll love me —"

"Shut up! You're crazy!" Connie said. She backed away from the door. She   105
put her hands against her ears as if she'd heard something terrible, something not meant for her. "People don't talk like that, you're crazy," she muttered. Her heart was almost too big now for her chest and its pumping made sweat break out all over her. She looked out to see Arnold Friend pause and then take a step toward the porch lurching. He almost fell. But, like a clever drunken man, he managed to catch his balance. He wobbled in his high boots and grabbed hold of one of the porch posts.

"Honey?" he said. "You still listening?"

"Get the hell out of here!"

"Be nice, honey. Listen."

"I'm going to call the police —"

He wobbled again and out of the side of his mouth came a fast spat curse,   110
an aside not meant for her to hear. But even this "Christ!" sounded forced. Then he began to smile again. She watched this smile come, awkward as if he were smiling from inside a mask. His whole face was a mask, she thought wildly, tanned down onto his throat but then running out as if he had plastered make-up on his face but had forgotten about his throat.

"Honey —? Listen, here's how it is. I always tell the truth and I promise you this: I ain't coming in that house after you."

"You better not! I'm going to call the police if you — if you don't —"

"Honey," he said, talking right through her voice, "honey, I'm not coming in there but you are coming out here. You know why?"

She was panting. The kitchen looked like a place she had never seen before, some room she had run inside but which wasn't good enough, wasn't going to help her. The kitchen window had never had a curtain, after three years, and there were dishes in the sink for her to do — probably — and if you ran your hand across the table you'd probably feel something sticky there.

"You listening, honey? Hey?"   115

"— going to call the police —"

"Soon as you touch the phone I don't need to keep my promise and can come inside. You won't want that."

She rushed forward and tried to lock the door. Her fingers were shaking. "But why lock it," Arnold Friend said gently, talking right into her face. "It's just a screen door. It's just nothing." One of his boots was at a strange angle, as if his foot wasn't in it. It pointed out to the left, bent at the ankle. "I mean, anybody can break through a screen door and glass and wood and iron or anything else if he needs to, anybody at all and specially Arnold Friend. If the place got lit up with a fire, honey, you'd come runnin' out into my arms, right into my arms an' safe at home — like you knew I was your lover and'd stopped fooling around, I don't mind a nice shy girl but I don't like no fooling around." Part of those words were spoken with a slight rhythmic lilt, and Connie somehow recognized them — the echo of a song from last year, about a girl rushing into her boy friend's arms and coming home again —

Connie stood barefoot on the linoleum floor, staring at him. "What do you want?" she whispered.

"I want you," he said.   120

"What?"

"Seen you that night and thought, that's the one, yes sir. I never needed to look any more."

"But my father's coming back. He's coming to get me. I had to wash my hair first —" She spoke in a dry, rapid voice, hardly raising it for him to hear.

"No, your daddy is not coming and yes, you had to wash your hair and you washed it for me. It's nice and shining and all for me. I thank you, sweetheart," he said, with a mock bow, but again he almost lost his balance. He had to bend and adjust his boots. Evidently his feet did not go all the way down; the boots must have been stuffed with something so that he would seem taller. Connie stared out at him and behind him at Ellie in the car, who seemed to be looking off toward Connie's right, into nothing. Then Ellie said, pulling the words out of the air one after another as if he were just discovering them, "You want me to pull out the phone?"

"Shut your mouth and keep it shut," Arnold Friend said, his face red from   125
bending over or maybe from embarrassment because Connie had seen his boots. "This ain't none of your business."

"What — what are you doing? What do you want?" Connie said. "If I call the police they'll get you, they'll arrest you —"

"Promise was not to come in unless you touch that phone, and I'll keep that promise," he said. He resumed his erect position and tried to force his shoulders back. He sounded like a hero in a movie, declaring something important. He spoke too loudly and it was as if he were speaking to someone behind Connie. "I ain't made plans for coming in that house where I don't belong but just for you to come out to me, the way you should. Don't you know who I am?"

"You're crazy," she whispered. She backed away from the door but did not want to go into another part of the house, as if this would give him permission to come through the door. "What do you . . . You're crazy, you. . . ."

"Huh? What're you saying, honey?"

Her eyes darted everywhere in the kitchen. She could not remember what   130
it was, this room.

"This is how it is, honey: you come out and we'll drive away, have a nice ride. But if you don't come out we're gonna wait till your people come home and then they're all going to get it."

"You want that telephone pulled out?" Ellie said. He held the radio away from his ear and grimaced, as if without the radio the air was too much for him.

"I toldja shut up, Ellie," Arnold Friend said, "you're deaf, get a hearing aid, right? Fix yourself up. This little girl's no trouble and's gonna be nice to me, so Ellie keep to yourself, this ain't your date — right? Don't hem in on me, don't hog, don't crush, don't bird dog, don't trail me," he said in a rapid, meaningless voice, as if he were running through all the expressions he'd learned but was no longer sure which one of them was in style, then rushing on to new ones, making them up with his eyes closed. "Don't crawl under my fence, don't squeeze in my chipmunk hole, don't sniff my glue, suck my popsicle, keep your own greasy fingers on yourself!" He shaded his eyes and peered in at Connie, who was backed against the kitchen table. "Don't mind him, honey, he's just a creep. He's a dope. Right? I'm the boy for you and like I said, you come out here nice like a lady and give me your hand, and nobody else gets hurt, I mean, your nice old bald-headed daddy and your mummy and your sister in her high heels. Because listen: why bring them in this?"

"Leave me alone," Connie whispered.

"Hey, you know that old woman down the road, the one with the chickens   135
and stuff — you know her?"

"She's dead!"

"Dead? What? You know her?" Arnold Friend said.

"She's dead —"

"Don't you like her?"

"She's dead — she's — she isn't here any more —"   140

"But don't you like her, I mean, you got something against her? Some grudge or something?" Then his voice dipped as if he were conscious of rudeness. He touched the sunglasses on top of his head as if to make sure they were still there. "Now you be a good girl."

"What are you going to do?"

"Just two things, or maybe three," Arnold Friend said. "But I promise it won't last long and you'll like me that way you get to like people you're close to. You will. It's all over for you here, so come on out. You don't want your people in any trouble, do you?"

She turned and bumped against a chair or something, hurting her leg, but she ran into the back room and picked up the telephone. Something roared in her ear, a tiny roaring, and she was so sick with fear that she could do nothing but listen to it — the telephone was clammy and very heavy and her fingers groped down to the dial but were too weak to touch it. She began to scream into the phone, into the roaring. She cried out, she cried for her mother, she felt her breath start jerking back and forth in her lungs as if it were something Arnold Friend was stabbing her with again and again with no tenderness. A noisy sorrowful wailing rose all about her and she was locked inside it the way she was locked inside this house.

After a while she could hear again. She was sitting on the floor, with her   145
wet back against the wall.

Arnold Friend was saying from the door, "That's a good girl. Put the phone back."

She kicked the phone away from her.

"No, honey. Pick it up. Put it back right."

She picked it up and put it back. The dial tone stopped.

"That's a good girl. Now you come outside."   150

She was hollow with what had been fear but what was now just an emptiness. All that screaming had blasted it out of her. She sat, one leg cramped under her, and deep inside her brain was something like a pinpoint of light that kept going and would not let her relax. She thought, I'm not going to see my mother again. She thought, I'm not going to sleep in my bed again. Her bright green blouse was all wet.

Arnold Friend said, in a gentle-loud voice that was like a stage voice, "The place where you came from ain't there any more, and where you had in mind to go is cancelled out. This place you are now — inside your daddy's house — is nothing but a cardboard box I can knock down any time. You know that and always did know it. You hear me?"

She thought, I have got to think. I have got to know what to do.

"We'll go out to a nice field, out in the country here where it smells so nice and it's sunny," Arnold Friend said. "I'll have my arms tight around you so you won't need to try to get away and I'll show you what love is like, what it does. The hell with this house! It looks solid all right," he said. He ran a fingernail down the screen and the noise did not make Connie shiver, as it would have the day before. "Now put your hand on your heart, honey. Feel that? That feels solid too but we know better. Be nice to me, be sweet like you can because what else is there for a girl like you but to be sweet and pretty and give in? — and get away before her people get back?"

She felt her pounding heart. Her hand seemed to enclose it. She thought   155 for the first time in her life that it was nothing that was hers, that belonged to her, but just a pounding, living thing inside this body that wasn't really hers either.

"You don't want them to get hurt," Arnold Friend went on. "Now get up, honey. Get up all by yourself."

She stood.

"Now turn this way. That's right. Come over to me — Ellie, put that away, didn't I tell you? You dope. You miserable creepy dope," Arnold Friend said. His words were not angry but only part of an incantation. The incantation was kindly. "Now come out through the kitchen to me honey and let's see a smile, try it, you're a brave sweet little girl and now they're eating corn and hotdogs cooked to bursting over an outdoor fire, and they don't know one thing about you and never did and honey you're better than them because not a one of them would have done this for you."

Connie felt the linoleum under her feet; it was cool. She brushed her hair back out of her eyes. Arnold Friend let go of the post tentatively and opened his arms for her, his elbows pointing in toward each other and his wrists limp, to show that this was an embarrassed embrace and a little mocking, he didn't want to make her self-conscious.

She put out her hand against the screen. She watched herself push the   160
door slowly open as if she were back safe somewhere in the other doorway, watching this body and this head of long hair moving out into the sunlight where Arnold Friend waited.

"My sweet little blue-eyed girl," he said in a half-sung sigh that had nothing to do with her brown eyes but was taken up just the same by the vast sunlit reaches of the land behind him and on all sides of him — so much land that Connie had never seen before and did not recognize except to know that she was going to it.   [1966]

■ THINKING ABOUT THE TEXT

1. This story was first published in 1966. What still seems typical of fifteen-year-old Connie's behavior? What seems dated about her?

2. Is Oates making a comment about the effect music has on Connie? Should popular music be accountable for the behavior of its listeners? Can popular culture make us oblivious to the real dangers of the world? Can it make us suspicious and cynical?

3. The suggestions about what will happen to Connie when she leaves the protection of her home are not so subtle. What is your view of her future? What does Connie mean when she says, " 'People don't talk like that, you're crazy' "? What is your reading of her response? Is Arnold Friend crazy?

4. A common response to this story is frustration with Connie's hesitation and her inability to take appropriate action in the face of serious danger. Was this your response? Why isn't she more assertive?

5. Could Connie have been better prepared for this encounter with evil? What evidence does the author give to show how prepared she is or isn't? What is her relationship with her parents? Is her social awareness primarily her parents' responsibility? If not, whose is it?

JILL McCORKLE
Magic Words

Jill McCorkle (b. 1958) was born in Lumberton, North Carolina; graduated from the University of North Carolina at Chapel Hill; and received a master's degree at Hollins College. She has published five novels, including The Cheer Leader *(1984) and* Carolina Moon *(1997). Her latest of four short-story collections,* Going Away Shoes, *was published in 2009. She is the recipient of numerous literary prizes and has taught at Chapel Hill, Tufts University, Harvard University, and Bennington College.*

She is currently on the faculty at North Carolina State University. "Magic Words" was included in The Best American Short Stories, 2009. *The story imaginatively weaves three different but intimately connected narratives.*

Because Paula Blake is planning something secret, she feels she must account for her every move and action, overcompensating in her daily chores and agreeing to whatever her husband and children demand. *Of course I'll pick up the dry cleaning, drive the kids, swing by the drugstore.* This is where the murderer always screws up in a movie, way too accommodating, too much information. The guilty one always has trouble maintaining direct eye contact.

"Of course I will take you and your friends to the movies," she tells Erin late one afternoon. "But do you think her mom can drive you home? I'm taking your brother to a sleepover too." She is doing it again, talking too much.

"Where are *you* going?" Erin asks, mouth sullen and sarcastic as it has been since her thirteenth birthday two years ago.

"Out with a friend," Paula says, forcing herself to make eye contact, the rest of the story she has practiced for days ready to roll. *She's someone I work with, someone going through a really hard time, someone brand-new to the area, knows no one, really needs a friend.*

But her daughter never looks up from the glossy magazine spread before her, engrossed in yet another drama about a teen star lost to drugs and wild nights. Her husband doesn't even ask her new friend's name or where she moved from, yet the answer is poised and waiting on her tongue. *Tonya Matthews from Phoenix, Arizona.* He is glued to the latest issue of *Our Domestic Wildlife*, his own newsletter to the neighborhood about various sightings of wild and possibly dangerous creatures — coyotes, raccoons, bats. Their message box is regularly filled with detailed sightings of raccoons acting funny in daylight or reports of missing cats. Then there's the occasional giggling kid faking a deep voice to report a kangaroo or rhino. She married a reserved and responsible banker who now fancies himself a kind of watchdog Crocodile Dundee. They are both seeking interests outside their lackluster marriage. His are all about threat and encroachment, being on the defense, and hers are about human contact, a craving for warmth like one of the bats her husband fears might find its way into their attic.

Her silky legs burn as if shamed where she has slathered lavender body lotion whipped as light as something you might eat. And the new silk panties, bought earlier in the day, feel heavy around her hips. But it is not enough to thwart the thought of what lies ahead, the consummation of all those notes and looks exchanged with the sales rep on the second floor during weeks at work, that one time in the stairwell — hard thrust of a kiss interrupted by the heavy door and footsteps two floors up — when the fantasy became enough of a reality to lead to this date. They have been careful, and the paper trail is slight — unsigned suggestive notes with penciled times and places, all neatly rolled like tiny scrolls and saved in the toe of the heavy wool ski socks

5

in the far corner of her underwear drawer, where heavier, far more substantial pairs of underwear than what she is wearing cover the surface. It all feels as safe as it can be because he has a family too. He has just as much to lose as she does.

And now she looks around to see the table filled with cartons of Chinese food from last night and cereal boxes from the morning, and the television blares from the other room. Her son is anxious to get to his sleepover; her daughter has painted her toenails, and the fumes of the purple enamel fill the air. Her husband is studying a map showing the progression of killer bees up the coast. He speaks of them like hated relatives who are determined to drop in, whether you want them to or not. Their arrival is as inevitable as all the other predicted disasters that will wreak havoc on human life.

"Where did you say you've got to go?" her husband asks, and she immediately jumps to her creation. Tonya Matthews, Phoenix, Arizona, new to the area, just divorced. Her palms are sweating, and she is glad she is wearing a turtleneck to hide the nervous splotches on her chest. She won't be wearing it later. She will slip it off in the darkness of the car after she takes Gregory to the sleepover and Erin and her friend to the cinema. Under the turtleneck she is wearing a thin silk camisole, also purchased that afternoon at a pricey boutique she had never been in before, a place the size of a closet where individual lingerie items hang separately on the wall like art. A young girl, sleek, pierced, and polished, gave a cool nod of approval when she leaned in to look at the camisole. Paula finally chose the black one after debating between it and the peacock blue. Maybe she will get the blue next time, already hoping that this new part of her life will remain. Instead of the turtleneck, she will wear a loose cashmere cardigan that slides from one shoulder when she inclines her head inquisitively. It will come off easily, leaving only the camisole between them in those first awkward seconds. She tilts her head as she has practiced, and with that thought all others disappear, and now she doesn't know what has even been asked of her. Her heart beats a little too fast. She once failed a polygraph test for this reason. She had never — would never — shoot heroin, but her pulse had raced with the memory of someone she knew who had. Did she do drugs? Her answer was no, but her mind had taken her elsewhere, panicked when she remembered the boy who gave her a ride home from a high school party with his head thrown back and teeth gritted, arm tied off with a large rubber band while a friend loomed overhead to inject him, one bloody needle already on the littered floor.

You can't afford to let your mind wander in a polygraph test — or in life, as now, when once again she finds herself looking at her husband with no idea of what he has just said. Her ability to hold eye contact is waning, the light out the window waning, but the desire that has built all these weeks is determined to linger, flickering like a candle under labored breath. Somewhere, her husband says, between their house and the interstate are several packs of coyotes, their little dens tucked away in brush and fallen trees. The coyote is a creature that often remains monogamous. The big bumbling mouthful of a word lingers there, a pause that lasts too long before he continues with his report. He heard the coyotes last night, so this is a good time to get the newsletter out, a good time to remind people to bring their pets indoors. Dusk is when they come out, same as the bats, most likely rabid.

The kids are doing what they call creepy crawling. Their leader picked the term   10 up from the book *Helter Skelter*. They slip in and out behind trees and bushes, surveying houses, peeping in windows, finding windows and doors ajar or unlocked. Their leader is a badly wounded boy in need of wounding others, and so he frightens them, holds them enthralled with his stories of violence or murder. They might not believe all he says, but they believe enough to know he is capable of bad things. As frightening as it is to be with him, it is more frightening not to be — to be on the outside and thus a potential victim.

To the kids he looks tough with his tongue ring and tattoos, his mouth tight and drawn by a bitterness rarely seen on such a young face, some vicious word always coiled on his tongue and ready to strike those who least expect it — though he has to be careful when bagging groceries at Food Lion; he has been reprimanded twice for making sarcastic remarks to elderly shoppers, things like *You sure you need these cookies, fat granny?* He has been told he will be fired the next time he is disrespectful, which is fine with him. He doesn't give a shit what any of them says. Dirt cakes the soles of his feet, like callused hooves, as he stands on the asphalt in front of the bowling alley, smoking, guzzling, or ingesting whatever gifts his flock of disciples brings to him. He likes to make and hold eye contact until people grow nervous.

When Agnes Hayes sees the boy bagging groceries in the market, her heart surges with pity, his complexion blotched and infected, hair long and oily. "Don't I know you?" she asks, but he doesn't even look up, his arms all inked with reptiles and knives and what looks like a religious symbol. Now she has spent the day trying to place him. She taught so many of them, but their names and faces run together. In the three years since retirement, she has missed them more than she ever dreamed. Some days she even drives her car and parks near the high school to watch them, to catch a glimpse of all that energy and to once again feel it in her own pulse. She still drives Edwin's copper-colored Electra and has since he died almost two years ago. She would never have retired had she seen his death coming, and with it an end to all their plans about where they would go and what they would do. One day she was complaining about plastic golf balls strewn all over the living room, and the next she was calling 911, knowing even as she dialed and begged for someone to *please help* that it was too late.

The school is built on the same land where she went to school. She once practiced there, her clarinet held in young hands while she stepped high with the marching band. Edwin's cigar is there in the ashtray, stinking as always, only now she loves the stink, can't get enough of it, wishes that she had never complained and made him go out to the garage or down to the basement to smoke. She wishes he were sitting there beside her, ringed in smoke. Their son, Preston, is clear across the country, barely in touch.

Sometimes creepy crawling involves only the car, cruising slowly through a driveway, headlights turned off, gravel crunching. There are lots of dogs. Lots of sensor lights. Lots of security systems, or at least signs *saying* there are systems. The boy trusts nothing and no one. He believes in jiggling knobs and trying windows. When asked one time, by a guidance counselor feigning compassion and concern, what he believed in, he said, "Not a goddamn thing," but of course he did. Anyone drawing breath believes in something, even if it is only that life sucks and there's no reason to live. Tonight he has announced that it is Lauren's turn to prove herself. She is a pretty girl behind the wall of heavy black makeup and black studded clothing. She wants out of the car, but she owes him fifty dollars. He makes it sound like if she doesn't pay it back soon he'll take it out in sex. She is only here to get back at the boy she loved enough to do everything he asked. She wants him to worry about her, to want her, to think about that night at the campground the way she does.

The leader reminds her often that he was there for her when no one else   15
was. He listened to her story about the squeaky-clean asshole boyfriend, feeding her sips of cheap wine and stroking her dyed black hair the whole time she cried and talked and later reeled and heaved on all fours in a roadside ditch.

"He's an asswipe," the boy had said. "He used you." And then later when she woke just before dawn with her head pounding and her body filled with the sick knowledge that she had to go home and face her parents, he reminded her again how much she needed him, couldn't survive without him. "I didn't leave you," he said. "Could've easily fucked you and didn't."

And now she is here, and the boy who broke her heart is out with someone else or maybe just eating dinner with his parents and talking about where he might choose to go to school. He is a boy who always smells clean, even right off the track where he runs long-distance, his thigh muscles like hard ropes, his lungs healthy and strong. He might be at the movies, and she wishes she were there too — the darkness, the popcorn. She wishes she were anywhere else. She had wanted her parents to restrict her after that night, to say she couldn't go anywhere for weeks and weeks, but they did something so much worse; they said how disappointed they were, that they had given up, how she would have to work really hard to regain their trust, and by *trust* it seems they meant love.

The leader is talking about how he hates their old math teacher. "And I know where she lives too." He circles the block, drives slowly past a neat gray colonial with a bright red door, the big Electra parked in the drive. "What's the magic word?" he mimics in a high southern voice and reaches over to grab Lauren's thigh, then inches up, gripping harder as if daring her to move. He motions for her to unzip her jeans, wanting her to just sit there that way, silver chain from her navel grazing the thin strip of nylon that covers her. Lower, he says, even though there is a boy in the back seat hearing every word. She feels cold but doesn't say a word. Her shoes and jacket and purse are locked in the trunk of the car. "For safekeeping," he said. She is about to readjust the V of denim when he swings the car off the side of the road behind a tall hedge of lagustrum, where they are partially hidden but can still see the house. "Like this," he says and tugs, a seam ripping, and then he slides across the seat toward her, his mouth hard on hers as he forces her hand to his own zipper. The boy in the back seat lights a cigarette, and she focuses on that, the sound, the smell; she can hear the paper burn.

Erin and her friend, Tina, sit in the back seat, and Gregory is in front with his Power Ranger sleeping bag rolled up at his feet. Paula will drop him off at the party and then go to the cinema, and then she will still have time to sit and collect herself before driving seven miles down the interstate to the Days Inn, where he will be waiting. The children have said that this car — their dad's — smells like old farts and jelly beans. They say he saves up all day at the bank and then rips all the way home. Gregory acts this out, and with each "Ewww" and laugh from the girls, he gets a little more confident and louder. He says their grandmother smells like diarrhea dipped in peppermint and their grandfather is chocolate vomick. They are having a wonderful time, mainly because it's daring, the way he is testing Paula, the way they all are waiting for her to intervene and reprimand, but she is so distracted she forgets to be a good mother. When he turns and scrutinizes her with a mischievous look, she snaps back.

"Not acceptable, young man, and you know it," she says, but really she is   20
worried that they are right and that *she* will smell like old farts and jelly beans when she arrives at the motel. Her cell phone buzzes against her hip, and she knows that he is calling to see if they are on schedule, calling to make sure that she doesn't stand him up again.

"Aren't you going to answer that?" Erin says. "Who is it, Dad looking for underwear? Some lame friend in need of a heart-to-heart?" The laughing continues as Paula turns onto the street where a crowd of eight-year-olds and sleeping bags are gathered in the front yard of a small brick ranch.

"One of my lame friends, I'm sure," she answers, but with the words pictures him there in the room, maybe already undressed, a glass of wine poured. They have already said so much in their little notes that it feels not only like they have already made love but like they have done so for so long that they are already needing to think up new things to do. Her pulse races, and she slams on the brakes when Gregory screams, "Stop!"

"Pay attention, Mom," Gregory says. "See, they're everywhere," and she thinks he means her lame friends, or kids at the party, but he picks up one of those little gourmet jelly beans, tosses it at his sister, and then jumps from the car. "Thanks, Mom," he says, and Paula waves to the already frazzled-looking mother who has taken this on. Thank you, Ronald Reagan. That's when jelly bean frenzy started, and then after her husband said something cute and trite about sharing the desires of the president since he was now a vice president at the bank, all his workers gave him jelly beans because what else can you give someone you don't know at all who has power and authority over you? He got all kinds of jelly beans. And now if people hear about the neighborhood wildlife, it means many more years of useless presents — coyote and raccoon and bat figurines and mugs and mugs and more mugs. She will write and send all those thank-you notes. She will take all the crap to Goodwill.

Sometimes Agnes watches television in the dark. She likes a lot of these new shows that are all about humiliating people until they confess that they are fat and need to lose weight or that they are inept workers who need to be fired or bad members of a team who need to be rejected and banished from the island. Her pug, Oliver, died not long after Edwin did, and she misses the way he used to paw and tug and make a little nest at the foot of her bed. She misses the sounds of his little snorts in the night. How could there have been a moment in life when she wished for this — the quiet, the lack of activity and noise? The clock ticks, the refrigerator hums. She could call Preston. She could give him an apology, whether or not she owes it. What she could say is that she is so sorry they misunderstood each other. Or she could call him and pretend nothing ever happened. She keeps thinking of the boy at the grocery, trying to place what year she taught him. Who were his parents? What is his name? Some children she gave things to over the years — her son's outgrown clothes and shoes — but then she stopped, dumping it all at the church instead, because the children never acted the same afterward, and that bothered her. They never said thank you, and they never looked her in the eye, as if she had never made a difference in their lives, and that was what hurt so much when she thought of Preston, how easily he had let a few things make him forget all that she had done for him in his life. She stated the truth, is all. When Preston planned to marry Amy, she told him how people might talk about them, might call their children names.

Right after Edwin's funeral, he called her Miss Christian Ethics, Miss Righteous Soul. He told her he wished he could stay and dig into all that ham and Jell-O but that Amy was at the Holiday Inn waiting for him. "They let dogs stay there too," he said and lingered over the prize rod and reel of his father's she had handed to him, only to put it back and leave. She hasn't seen him since. Now her chest is heavy with the memory, and her head and arm and side ache.

The parking lot stretches for miles, it seems, kids everywhere in packs, snuggly couples, the occasional middle-aged, settled-looking couple Paula envies more than all the others. The Cinema Fourteen Plex looms up ahead like Oz, like a big bright fake city offering anything and everything, a smorgasbord of action and emotion as varied as the jelly bean connoisseur basket her husband's secretary sent at Christmas, a woman Paula has so often wished would become something more. Wouldn't that be easier?

"He's here," Tina says, and points to where a tall skinny kid in a letter jacket is pacing along the curb. "Oh, my God. Oh, my God."

"Puhleeze," Erin says, sounding way too old. "Chill out. He's *just a boy.*" And then they collapse in another round of laughter and are out of the car and gone. Paula's hip is buzzing again. Buzzing and buzzing. What if it's Gregory and the sleepover is canceled? Or he fell on the skate ramp and broke something or needs stitches and her husband can't be found because he's out in the woods with a flashlight looking for wildlife? Or maybe her husband really does need her. He just got a call that his mother died. Does she know where he put the Havahart trap? And when is the last time she saw *their* cat?

Lauren is feeling frightened. The other boy, the one from the back seat who is always quiet and refuses to talk about the bruises on his face and arms, has announced he's leaving. He can't do this anymore. The leader slams on the brakes and calls him a pussy. The leader says that if he leaves that's it, no more rides, no more pot, no more anything except he'll catch him some dark night and beat the shit out of him. "I'll beat you worse than whatever goes on in that trash house of yours," he says, but the boy keeps walking, and Lauren feels herself wanting to yell out for him to wait for her. She has always found him scary and disgusting, but now she admires his ability to put one foot in front of the other. He says he's bored with it all — lame amateur shit — but she sees a fear in him as recognizable as her own. "Let him go," she whispers. She is watching the flicker of television light in the teacher's upstairs window. "Please. Can't we just ride around or something?"

"Afraid you won't get any more tonight?" he asks, and leans in so close she   30
can smell his breath, oddly sweet with Dentyne. The lost possibility of his features makes her sad, eyes you might otherwise think a beautiful shade of blue, dimple in the left cheek. He pulls a coiled rope from under the seat. "You gonna stay put, or do I need to tie you up?" She forces herself to laugh, assure him that she will stay put, but she makes the mistake of glancing at the key in the ignition, and he reaches and takes it.

She cautions herself to keep breathing, to act like she's with him. "Next one," she says. "I need to collect myself."

"Well, you just collect," he says. "I'll be back to deal with you in a minute." She doesn't ask what he plans to do. His outlines of all the ways such an event might go are lengthy and varied, some of them tame and pointless and others not pretty at all. He has already said he wants to scare the hell out of the old woman, let *her* know what it feels like to have someone make you say *please* and *thank you* every goddamn day. The girl watches him move into the darkness, numb fingers struggling to finally zip her pants back up, to pretend that his rough fingertips never touched her there. She will get out and run. She will leave the door open and crawl through the hedge until she reaches the main road. She will call her parents, beg for their forgiveness. There is no way now to get her shoes or phone, but she moves and keeps moving. She thinks of her bed and how good it will feel to crawl between clean sheets, to stare at the faces of all the dolls collected before everything in her life seemed to go so bad. Now all the things she has been so upset about mean nothing. So what if she let the handsome, clean-smelling track star do everything he wanted to do? She liked it too, didn't she? Not making the soccer team last year, being told on college day that she had no prayer of getting into any of the schools she had listed, most of them ones he was considering if he could run track. But losing or getting rejected — that happens to a lot of people, doesn't it? She can still find something she's good at, go *somewhere*. Right now she just wants to get home, to shower herself clean with the hottest water she can stand, to soap and scrub and wrap up in a flannel robe. She once watched her uncle skin a catfish, tearing the tight skin from the meat like an elastic suit, and she keeps thinking of the sound it made, a sound that made her want to pull her jacket close, to hide and protect her own skin. She feels that way now, only there's nothing to pull around her, the night air much cooler than she'd thought — and she keeps thinking she hears him behind her, so she moves faster. She is almost to the main road, the busy intersection, the rows of cars heading toward the cinema. Her foot is bleeding, a sliver of glass, and she is pinned at a corner, lines upon lines of cars waiting for the light to change.

Paula's cell phone buzzes again, and she takes a deep breath and answers. "Where are you?" he asks. She can hear the impatience, perhaps a twinge of anger, and his voice does not match the way she remembers him sounding in the stairwell. When she pictures his face or reads his tiny penciled scrawl, it's a different voice, like it's been dubbed.

"Almost there," she says and tries to sound flirtatious, leaving him a promise of making up for lost time. Then she glances out her window and sees a girl she thinks she recognizes. Shirt torn and barefooted. They certainly won't let her in the theater that way. The girl is so familiar, and then she remembers — her daughter's school, story time in the library. But that was years ago, when the girl's hair was light brown and pulled up in a high ponytail. She knows exactly who she is. This is a girl parents caution their *good* girls against. She is rumored to be bulimic. She locks herself in the school bathroom and cuts her arms. She once tried to overdose on vodka and aspirin and had to have her stomach pumped. She gives blow jobs in the stairwell of the high school in exchange for drugs. She has blackened ghoulish eyes and jet-black hair, silver safety pins through her eyebrows and lip. Paula has heard parents whispering about her at various school functions. They say, "Last year she was perfectly normal, and now this. She was a B student with some artistic talent and a pretty face, and now this." She is the "Don't" poster child of this town, the local object lesson in how quickly a child can go bad.

Agnes is trying to remember what exactly it was she said to anger Preston so. She had tried to make it complimentary, something about skin like café au lait. She had often seen black people described that way in stories, coffee and chocolates, conjuring delicious smells instead of those like the bus station or fish market across the river, which is what a lot of people might associate with black people. Her maid once used a pomade so powerful-smelling Agnes had to ask that she please stop wearing it, but certainly Agnes never held that against the woman; she couldn't help being born into a culture that thought that was the thing to do.

"Sometimes it's not even *what* stupid thing you say," Preston shouted, the vein in his forehead throbbing like it might burst. "It's *how* you say it. So, so goddamned *godlike*." He spit the word and shook all over, hands clenched into fists. But now she wants him to come back and be with her. She didn't know coffee would be insulting. She is going through her phone numbers, she has it somewhere. That same day she reminded him that even the president of the United States said things like that. The president had once referred to his grandchildren as "the little brown ones," and why is that okay and chocolate and coffee are not?

It's your mom, she practices now. *Please talk to me, Preston.* She is dialing when she hears something down on her front porch. The wind? Her cat? There was a flyer in her mailbox just this evening saying how she should not leave the cat outside.

Lauren shivers as she stands there on the corner. She expects to hear his car roar up any second and wonders what she will do when that happens. She will have to tell her parents that she lost her purse, that it got stolen, and her shoes and jacket. She shudders with the thought of the boy pawing through her personal things, a picture of the track star cut from the school newspaper, a poem she was writing about the ocean, a pale pink rabbit's foot she has carried since sixth grade when she won the school math bee with it in her pocket. The light is about to change, and she concentrates on that instead of imagining her parents' reaction. Just once she wishes one of them would pull her close and say, "Please, tell me what's wrong," and then she would. She would start talking and not stop, like a dam breaking; she would tell them so many things if there were really such a thing as unconditional love. But instead they will say, "What is wrong with you? Why are you doing this to us? Do you know what people are saying about you?"

"Do you need a ride?" A woman in an old black Audi leans out the window and motions her to hurry. "I know you from school."

She does know the woman, the mother of a girl in her class, a girl who 40
makes good grades and doesn't get into trouble. Not a popular girl, just a normal girl. A nice girl who smiles shyly and will let you copy her notes if you get behind. Erin from Algebra I freshman year. This is Erin's mother.

She hears a car slowing in the lane beside her and runs to get in with the woman just as the light changes. "Thank you."

"My daughter goes to your school," the woman says. She is wearing a low-cut camisole with a pretty silver necklace. Her black sweater is soft and loose around her shoulders. The car smells like crayons and the woman's cologne. "I'm sorry my car is so messy. My husband's car, that is." Her cell phone buzzes in the cup holder, but she ignores it. "Where are you going, sweetheart?" she asks. "It's too chilly to be out without shoes and long sleeves." Something in her voice brings tears to the girl's eyes, and then her crying is uncontrollable. The woman just keeps driving, circling first the cinema and then many of the neighborhoods around the area. The girl sinks low in her seat when they pass the teacher's house, that old Pontiac still parked behind the hedge. She can't allow herself to imagine what he is doing, what he will do when he finds her gone. They drive out to the interstate and make a big loop, the woman patting her shoulder from time to time, telling her it's okay, that nothing can be that bad. Every third or fourth time the woman asks for her address, but for now the girl just wants to be here in this car riding. The woman's cell phone keeps buzzing and buzzing. Once she answers it to the loud voice of her daughter from the movie lobby saying she will need a ride home after all. "Are you mad, Mom?" the girl screams. "Is that okay?" And the woman assures her that it is okay. It is fine. She will be there. Then she answers to say she saw their cat early this morning. And then, apologizing when it rings again, she answers and says little at all, except that so much has happened, she just might not get there at all. "In fact," she whispers, "I know I can't get there." And Lauren knows there is a good chance that she is part of what has happened, but the heat is blowing on her cold feet and the woman has the radio turned down low with classical music, and her eyelids are so heavy she can barely keep them open. When she was little and couldn't sleep, her parents would sometimes put her in a warm car and drive her around. Her dad called it a "get lost" drive, and he let her make all the choices, turn here, turn there, turn there again, and then she would relax while he untangled the route and led them back home, by which time she would be nearly or already asleep. There was never any doubt that he could find the way home and that she would wake to find herself already tucked in her bed or in his arms being taken there.

Preston's answering machine comes on, and Agnes is about to speak, but then she hears the noise again and puts down the phone. She wishes she would find Preston there—Preston and Amy, waiting to embrace her and start all over again. Preston in his letter jacket like he was all those nights she waited up for him and said, "Where have you been, young man?" And Edwin would be in the basement smoking, and Oliver would be rooting around at the foot of her bed.

Her chest is tight with the worry of it all. She swallows and opens the door. Nothing.

"Here, kitty," she calls in a faint voice. She steps out on the stoop into the chilly air. The sky is clear overhead, a sliver of a moon. There is a car parked way down at the end of her drive, just the front bumper showing beyond the hedge. It wasn't there when she came home. Perhaps someone had a flat or ran out of gas. She calls the cat again and hears leaves crunching around the side of the house. She waits, expecting to see it slink around the corner, but then nothing. There is more noise beyond the darkness, where she can't see. And it is coming closer, short quick sounds, footsteps in the leaves. She is backing into the house when she thinks she sees something much larger than the cat slip around the corner near her kitchen door. She pulls her sweater close and pushes the door to, turns the dead bolt. The flyer talked about coyotes and how they have been spotted all over town.

The girl finally tells Paula where she lives, a neighborhood out of town and in the opposite direction from the motel. Paula's cell phone beeps with yet another message, but now she ignores it. She doesn't want to hear what he has to say now that he has had time to shape an answer to her standing him up yet again. She parks in front of a small brick ranch. The front porch is lit with a yellow bulb, all the drapes pulled closed.

"I'm happy to walk you up," Paula says, but the girl shakes her head. She says thank you without making eye contact and then gets out, making her way across the yard in slow, careful steps. Paula waits to see if a parent comes out, but the girl slips in and recloses the door without a trace.

Paula sits there in the dark as if expecting something to happen. And then she slips off the cardigan and pulls her turtleneck over her head. The message is waiting. He might be saying this is the last time he will do this, he has wasted too much time on her already. "Why are you fucking with me?" he might ask. Or, "Who do you think you are?" The chances of him saying he understands completely and they will try again some other, better time are slim. She imagines him there in the room, bare-chested and waiting, already thinking about his other options, his better options. And she imagines her own house and her return, sink full of dirty dishes, purple nail polish and Power Ranger figures everywhere. A litter box that needs scooping and clothes that need washing and an empty pantry that would have been filled had she not been out buying lingerie all day.

She saw a coyote just last week, but she didn't report it. She was standing at the kitchen window and glanced out to see a tall, skinny shepherd mix — except just as her mind was shaping the thought about someone letting a dog run loose in the neighborhood, it came to her that this was not a dog. It was wild and fearful-looking, thin and hungry, and she felt a kinship as they stood frozen, staring at each other. Everyone wants something.

The leader can see her in there, old bat, holding her chest and shaking. She   50
looks like a puppet, her old bitch of a body jerking in time with his jiggling the knob. "I wore your fucking boy's shirt," he will say. "Thank you so much. That little polo fucker really helped turn my life around." She lifts the phone and pulls the cord around the corner where he can't see her, so he jiggles harder, leans the weight of his body against the door. "Loafers! Neckties! F in fucking math." He creeps around and climbs high enough on a trellis to see that she is slumped down in a chair with the receiver clutched against her chest. "Say the magic word," he says and covers his fist with his shirt before punching out the window. "Say it."

When Paula pulls up to the theater, Erin and Tina are waiting. A tall, thin boy in a letter jacket trails alongside Tina, his hand in her hip pocket in a familiar way, and then they kiss before the girls get in the car. Paula is about to mention the girl she picked up but then thinks better of it. She wants to say things like, "Don't you ever . . ." but the sound of her daughter's laughter makes her think better of it.

"I can't believe you, like, ate face in front of my mom," Erin says, and Tina blushes and grins. She is a girl with cleavage and braces, betwixt and between.

"Jesus, Mom, let some air in this stinkhole car," Erin laughs, and then the two girls talk over the movie and everyone they saw there as if Paula were not even present. Paula can't stop thinking about the girl and how she came to be on that busy corner with no shoes, how she looks so different from that clean-faced little girl in a library chair, and yet she is one and the same. And what will she write and slip to her coworker on Monday, or will she avoid him altogether and pretend nothing ever happened, that she never ventured from her own darkened den in search of excitement? She imagines the coyotes living as her husband has described, little nests under piles of brush, helpless cubs curled there waiting for the return of their mother.

"I'm sorry if I messed up your time with your lame friend," Erin says sarcastically, and then leans in close. "Really, Momsy, I am." She air-kisses Paula and smiles a sincere thanks before turning back to her friend with a shriek of something she can't believe she forgot to tell, something about cheating, someone getting caught with a teacher's grade book. She has licorice twists braided and tied around her throat like a necklace, and her breath is sweet with Milk Duds.

The old woman is dead or acting dead, the recorded voice from the receiver on her chest telling her to please hang up and try her call again. It's one of those houses where everything is in place, little useless bullshit glass things nobody wants. She looks as miserable dead as she did alive. It makes him want to trash the place, but why bother now? He didn't kill her. He didn't do a thing but pop out a pane of glass. He searches around and then carefully, using his shirt so as not to leave a print, takes a golf ball from the basket beside the fireplace and places it down in the broken glass. Television is too big to lift, no purse in sight, not even a liquor cabinet. She gives him the creeps, and so do all the people looking out from portraits and photographs. He'll tell the girl that he just scared the old bitch, threatened to tie her up and put a bullet in her head until she cried and begged for his mercy and forgiveness. He'll say he left her alive and grateful.   55

The moon is high in the bright clear sky when Paula ventures outside to look for their cat. She pulls her sweater close and steps away from the light of the house, the woods around her spreading into darkness. Her husband is sleeping, and Erin is on the phone. There were no messages other than the one on her cell phone, still trapped there and waiting. She hears a distant siren, the wind in the trees, the bass beat from a passing car. *Please,* she thinks. *Please.* She is about to go inside for a flashlight when she hears the familiar bell and then sees the cat slinking up from the dark woods, her manner cool and unaffected.

■ THINKING ABOUT THE TEXT

1. Describe the various ways McCorkle stitches together the three narratives of Paula, Lauren, and Agnes.

2. Describe the various meanings the word *please* has in the story.

3. How is the recurring motif of "eye contact" used in the story?

4. The last sentence of paragraph 49 is "Everyone wants something." How does this statement apply to Paula, Lauren, Erin, and the leader?

5. At first, it seems as if Paula's husband seems overly concerned about menacing animals; however, the world of the story does seem filled with danger. How do you think McCorkle is commenting on how we should conduct ourselves in such an environment?

■ MAKING COMPARISONS

1. Compare Erin in McCorkle's 2009 story to Connie in Oates's 1966 story. Compare the fathers in both stories.

2. Compare the leader in "Magic Words" to Arnold Friend in Oates's story.

3. Lauren escapes the leader, whereas Connie cannot evade Arnold Friend. Would Lauren have done better than Connie in that situation? How about Erin?

SHERMAN ALEXIE
What You Pawn I Will Redeem

Sherman Alexie's (b. 1966) novel for young adults, The Absolutely True Diary of a Part-Time Indian, *won the 2007 National Book Award for the category. The multitalented Alexie once opened for the Indigo Girls, performing songs from his album* Reservation Blues. *He won the World Heavyweight Poetry Bout four consecutive times (defeating Jimmy Santiago Baca) and continues to appear on the comedy circuit as well as on PBS as a serious commentator on politics and race. The story printed here was selected by the editor, Ann Patchett, as her favorite work in the 2005* O'Henry Prize Stories.

— Wow. Very charged statement

Noon

[One day you have a home and the next you don't, but I'm not going to tell you my particular reasons for being homeless, because it's my secret story, and Indians have to work hard to keep secrets from hungry white folks.]

I'm a Spokane Indian boy, an Interior Salish, and my people have lived within a hundred-mile radius of Spokane, Washington, for at least ten thousand years. [I grew up in Spokane, moved to Seattle twenty-three years ago for college, flunked out after two semesters, worked various blue- and bluer-collar jobs, married two or three times, fathered two or three kids, and then went crazy. Of course, crazy is not the official definition of my mental problem, but I don't think asocial disorder fits it, either, because that makes me sound like I'm a serial killer or something.] I've never hurt another human being, or, at least, not physically. [I've broken a few hearts in my time, but we've all done that, so

wow. we got issues.

I'm nothing special in that regard. I'm a boring heartbreaker, too. I never dated or married more than one woman at a time. I didn't break hearts into pieces overnight. I broke them slowly and carefully. And I didn't set any land-speed records running out the door. Piece by piece, I disappeared. I've been disappearing ever since.

I've been homeless for six years now. If there's such a thing as an effective homeless man, then I suppose I'm effective. Being homeless is probably the only thing I've ever been good at. I know to get the best free food. I've made friends with restaurant and convenience-store managers who let me use their bathrooms. And I don't mean the public bathrooms, either. I mean the employees' bathrooms, the clean ones hidden behind the kitchen or the pantry or the cooler. I know it sounds strange to be proud of this, but it means a lot to me, being trustworthy enough to piss in somebody else's clean bathroom. Maybe you don't understand the value of a clean bathroom, but I do.

Probably none of this interests you. Homeless Indians are everywhere in Seattle. We're common and boring, and you walk right on by us, with maybe a look of anger or disgust or even sadness at the terrible fate of the noble savage. But we have dreams and families. I'm friends with a homeless Plains Indian man whose son is the editor of a big-time newspaper back East. Of course, that's his story, but we Indians are great storytellers and liars and mythmakers, so maybe that Plains Indian hobo is just a plain old everyday Indian. I'm kind of suspicious of him, because he identifies himself only as Plains Indian, a generic term, and not by a specific tribe. When I asked him why he wouldn't tell me exactly what he is, he said, "Do any of us know exactly what we are?" Yeah, great, a philosophizing Indian. "Hey," I said, "you got to have a home to be that homely." He just laughed and flipped me the eagle and walked away.

I wander the streets with a regular crew — my teammates, my defenders, my posse. It's Rose of Sharon, Junior, and me. We matter to each other if we don't matter to anybody else. Rose of Sharon is a big woman, about seven feet tall if you're measuring over-all effect and about five feet tall if you're only talking about the physical. She's a Yakama Indian of the Wishram variety. Junior is a Colville, but there are about a hundred and ninety-nine tribes that make up the Colville, so he could be anything. He's good-looking, though, like he just stepped out of some "Don't Litter the Earth" public-service advertisement. He's got those great big cheekbones that are like planets, you know, with little moons orbiting them. He gets me jealous, jealous, and jealous. If you put Junior and me next to each other, he's the Before Columbus Arrived Indian and I'm the After Columbus Arrived Indian. I am living proof of the horrible damage that colonialism has done to us Skins. But I'm not going to let you know how scared I sometimes get of history and its ways. I'm a strong man, and I know that silence is the best method of dealing with white folks.

This whole story really started at lunchtime, when Rose of Sharon, Junior, and I were panning the handle down at Pike Place Market. After about two hours of negotiating, we earned five dollars — good enough for a bottle of fortified courage from the most beautiful 7-Eleven in the world. So we headed over

5

that way, feeling like warrior drunks, and we walked past this pawnshop I'd never noticed before. And that was strange, because we Indians have built-in pawnshop radar. But the strangest thing of all was the old powwow-dance regalia I saw hanging in the window.

"That's my grandmother's regalia," I said to Rose of Sharon and Junior.

"How you know for sure?" Junior asked.

I didn't know for sure, because I hadn't seen that regalia in person ever. I'd only seen photographs of my grandmother dancing in it. And those were taken before somebody stole it from her, fifty years ago. But it sure looked like my memory of it, and it had all the same color feathers and beads that my family sewed into our powwow regalia.

"There's only one way to know for sure," I said.   10

So Rose of Sharon, Junior, and I walked into the pawnshop and greeted the old white man working behind the counter.

"How can I help you?" he asked.

"That's my grandmother's powwow regalia in your window," I said. "Somebody stole it from her fifty years ago, and my family has been searching for it ever since."

The pawnbroker looked at me like I was a liar. I understood. Pawnshops are filled with liars.

"I'm not lying," I said. "Ask my friends here. They'll tell you."   15

"He's the most honest Indian I know," Rose of Sharon said.

"All right, honest Indian," the pawnbroker said. "I'll give you the benefit of the doubt. Can you prove it's your grandmother's regalia?"

Because they don't want to be perfect, because only God is perfect, Indian people sew flaws into their powwow regalia. My family always sewed one yellow bead somewhere on our regalia. But we always hid it so that you had to search really hard to find it.

"If it really is my grandmother's," I said, "there will be one yellow bead hidden somewhere on it."

"All right, then," the pawnbroker said, "Let's take a look."   20

He pulled the regalia out of the window, laid it down on the glass counter, and we searched for that yellow bead and found it hidden beneath the armpit.

"There it is," the pawnbroker said. He didn't sound surprised. "You were right. This is your grandmother's regalia."

"It's been missing for fifty years," Junior said.

"Hey, Junior," I said. "It's my family's story. Let me tell it."

"All right," he said. "I apologize. You go ahead."   25

"It's been missing for fifty years," I said.

"That's his family's sad story," Rose of Sharon said. "Are you going to give it back to him?"

"That would be the right thing to do," the pawnbroker said. "But I can't afford to do the right thing. I paid a thousand dollars for this. I can't just give away a thousand dollars."

"We could go to the cops and tell them it was stolen," Rose of Sharon said.

"Hey," I said to her. "Don't go threatening people."   30

The pawnbroker sighed. He was thinking about the possibilities.

"Well, I suppose you could go to the cops," he said. "But I don't think they'd believe a word you said."

He sounded sad about that. As if he was sorry for taking advantage of our disadvantages.

"What's your name?" the pawnbroker asked me.

"Jackson," I said.   35

"Is that first or last?"

"Both," I said.

"Are you serious?"

"Yes, it's true. My mother and father named me Jackson Jackson. My family nickname is Jackson Squared. My family is funny."

"All right, Jackson Jackson," the pawnbroker said. "You wouldn't happen   40
to have a thousand dollars, would you?"

"We've got five dollars total," I said.

"That's too bad," he said, and thought hard about the possibilities. "I'd sell it to you for a thousand dollars if you had it. Heck, to make it fair, I'd sell it to you for nine hundred and ninety-nine dollars. I'd lose a dollar. That would be the moral thing to do in this case. To lose a dollar would be the right thing."

"We've got five dollars total," I said again.

"That's too bad," he said once more, and thought harder about the possibilities. "How about this? I'll give you twenty-four hours to come up with nine hundred and ninety-nine dollars. You come back here at lunchtime tomorrow with the money and I'll sell it back to you. How does that sound?"

"It sounds all right," I said.   45

"All right, then," he said. "We have a deal. And I'll get you started. Here's twenty bucks."

He opened up his wallet and pulled out a crisp twenty-dollar bill and gave it to me. And Rose of Sharon, Junior, and I walked out into the daylight to search for nine hundred and seventy-four more dollars.

wow. How can three homeless Indians accomplish this?

1 P.M.

Rose of Sharon, Junior, and I carried our twenty-dollar bill and our five dollars in loose change over to the 7-Eleven and bought three bottles of imagination. We needed to figure out how to raise all that money in only one day. Thinking hard, we huddled in an alley beneath the Alaska Way Viaduct and finished off those bottles — one, two, and three.

2 P.M.

Rose of Sharon was gone when I woke up. I heard later that she had hitchhiked back to Toppenish and was living with her sister on the reservation.

Junior had passed out beside me and was covered in his own vomit, or   50
maybe somebody else's vomit, and my head hurt from thinking, so I left him

alone and walked down to the water. I love the smell of ocean water. Salt always smells like memory.

When I got to the wharf, I ran into three Aleut cousins, who sat on a wooden bench and stared out at the bay and cried. Most of the homeless Indians in Seattle come from Alaska. One by one, each of them hopped a big working boat in Anchorage or Barrow or Juneau, fished his way south to Seattle, jumped off the boat with a pocketful of cash to party hard at one of the highly sacred and traditional Indian bars, went broke and broker, and has been trying to find his way back to the boat and the frozen North ever since.

These Aleuts smelled like salmon, I thought, and they told me they were going to sit on that wooden bench until their boat came back.

"How long has your boat been gone?" I asked.

"Eleven years," the elder Aleut said.

I cried with them for a while.   55

"Hey," I said. "Do you guys have any money I can borrow?"

They didn't.

3 P.M.

I walked back to Junior. He was still out cold. I put my face down near his mouth to make sure he was breathing. He was alive, so I dug around in his blue-jeans pockets and found half a cigarette. I smoked it all the way down and thought about my grandmother.

Her name was Agnes, and she died of breast cancer when I was fourteen. My father always thought Agnes caught her tumors from the uranium mine on the reservation. But my mother said the disease started when Agnes was walking back from a powwow one night and got run over by a motorcycle. She broke three ribs, and my mother always said those ribs never healed right, and tumors take over when you don't heal right.

Sitting beside Junior, smelling the smoke and the salt and the vomit, I won-   60
dered if my grandmother's cancer started when somebody stole her powwow regalia. Maybe the cancer started in her broken heart and then leaked out into her breasts. I know it's crazy, but I wondered whether I could bring my grandmother back to life if I bought back her regalia.

I needed money, big money, so I left Junior and walked over to the Real Change office.

4 P.M.

Real Change is a multifaceted organization that publishes a newspaper, supports cultural projects that empower the poor and the homeless, and mobilizes the public around poverty issues. Real Change's mission is to organize, educate, and build alliances to create solutions to homelessness and poverty. It exists to provide a voice for poor people in our community.

I memorized Real Change's mission statement because I sometimes sell the newspaper on the streets. But you have to stay sober to sell it, and I'm not always good at staying sober. Anybody can sell the paper. You buy each copy for thirty cents and sell it for a dollar, and you keep the profit.

"I need one thousand four hundred and thirty papers," I said to the Big Boss.

"That's a strange number," he said. "And that's a lot of papers."   65

"I need them."

The Big Boss pulled out his calculator and did the math.

"It will cost you four hundred and twenty-nine dollars for that many," he said.

"If I had that kind of money, I wouldn't need to sell the papers."

"What's going on, Jackson-to-the-Second-Power?" he asked. He is the only   70
person who calls me that. He's a funny and kind man.

I told him about my grandmother's powwow regalia and how much money I needed in order to buy it back.

"We should call the police," he said.

"I don't want to do that," I said. "It's a quest now, I need to win it back by myself."

"I understand," he said. "And, to be honest, I'd give you the papers to sell if I thought it would work. But the record for the most papers sold in one day by one vendor is only three hundred and two."

"That would net me about two hundred bucks," I said.   75

The Big Boss used his calculator. "Two hundred and eleven dollars and forty cents," he said.

"That's not enough," I said.

"And the most money anybody has made in one day is five hundred and twenty-five. And that's because somebody gave Old Blue five hundred-dollar bills for some dang reason. The average daily net is about thirty dollars."

"This isn't going to work."

"No."   80

"Can you lend me some money?"

"I can't do that," he said. "If I lend you money, I have to lend money to everybody."

"What can you do?"

"I'll give you fifty papers for free. But don't tell anybody I did it."

"O.K.," I said.   85

He gathered up the newspapers and handed them to me. I held them to my chest. He hugged me. I carried the newspapers back toward the water.

5 P.M.

Back on the wharf, I stood near the Bainbridge Island Terminal and tried to sell papers to business commuters boarding the ferry.

I sold five in one hour, dumped the other forty-five in a garbage can, and walked into McDonald's, ordered four cheeseburgers for a dollar each, and slowly ate them.

After eating, I walked outside and vomited on the sidewalk. I hated to lose my food so soon after eating it. As an alcoholic Indian with a busted stomach, I always hope I can keep enough food in me to stay alive.

6 P.M.

With one dollar in my pocket, I walked back to Junior. He was still passed out, and I put my ear to his chest and listened for his heartbeat. He was alive, so I took off his shoes and socks and found one dollar in his left sock and fifty cents in his right sock.   90

With two dollars and fifty cents in my hand, I sat beside Junior and thought about my grandmother and her stories.

When I was thirteen, my grandmother told me a story about the Second World War. She was a nurse at a military hospital in Sydney, Australia. For two years, she healed and comforted American and Australian soldiers.

One day she tended to a wounded Maori soldier, who had lost his legs to an artillery attack. He was very dark-skinned. His hair was black and curly and his eyes were black and warm. His face was covered with bright tattoos.

"Are you Maori?" he asked my grandmother.

"No," she said. "I'm Spokane Indian. From the United States."   95

"Ah, yes," he said. "I have heard of your tribes. But you are the first American Indian I have ever met."

"There's a lot of Indian soldiers fighting for the United States," she said. "I have a brother fighting in Germany, and I lost another brother on Okinawa."

"I am sorry," he said. "I was on Okinawa as well. It was terrible."

"I am sorry about your legs," my grandmother said.

"It's funny, isn't it?" he said.   100

"What's funny?"

"How we brown people are killing other brown people so white people will remain free."

"I hadn't thought of it that way."

"Well, sometimes I think of it that way. And other times I think of it the way they want me to think of it. I get confused."

She fed him morphine.   105

"Do you believe in Heaven?" he asked.

"Which Heaven?" she asked.

"I'm talking about the Heaven where my legs are waiting for me."

They laughed.

"Of course," he said, "my legs will probably run away from me when I get to Heaven. And how will I ever catch them?"   110

"You have to get your arms strong," my grandmother said. "So you can run on your hands."

They laughed again.

Sitting beside Junior, I laughed at the memory of my grandmother's story. I put my hand close to Junior's mouth to make sure he was still breathing. Yes, Junior was alive, so I took my two dollars and fifty cents and walked to the Korean grocery store in Pioneer Square.

7 P.M.

At the Korean grocery store, I bought a fifty-cent cigar and two scratch lottery tickets for a dollar each. The maximum cash prize was five hundred dollars a ticket. If I won both, I would have enough money to buy back the regalia.

I loved Mary, the young Korean woman who worked the register. She was   115
the daughter of the owners, and she sang all day.

"I love you," I said when I handed her the money.

"You always say you love me," she said.

"That's because I will always love you."

"You are a sentimental fool."

"I'm a romantic old man."   120

"Too old for me."

"I know I'm too old for you, but I can dream."

"O.K.," she said. "I agree to be a part of your dreams, but I will only hold your hand in your dreams. No kissing and no sex. Not even in your dreams."

"O.K.," I said. "No sex. Just romance."

"Good-bye, Jackson Jackson, my love. I will see you soon."   125

I left the store, walked over to Occidental Park, sat on a bench, and smoked my cigar all the way down.

Ten minutes after I finished the cigar, I scratched my first lottery ticket and won nothing. I could only win five hundred dollars now, and that would only be half of what I needed.

Ten minutes after I lost, I scratched the other ticket and won a free ticket — a small consolation and one more chance to win some money.

I walked back to Mary.

"Jackson Jackson," she said. "Have you come back to claim my heart?"   130

"I won a free ticket," I said.

"Just like a man," she said. "You love money and power more than you love me."

"It's true," I said. "And I'm sorry it's true."

She gave me another scratch ticket, and I took it outside. I like to scratch my tickets in private. Hopeful and sad, I scratched that third ticket and won real money. I carried it back inside to Mary.

"I won a hundred dollars," I said.   135

She examined the ticket and laughed.

"That's a fortune," she said, and counted out five twenties. Our fingertips touched as she handed me the money. I felt electric and constant.

"Thank you," I said, and gave her one of the bills.

"I can't take that," she said. "It's your money."

"No, it's tribal. It's an Indian thing. When you win, you're supposed to   140
share with your family."

"I'm not your family."

"Yes, you are."

She smiled. She kept the money. With eighty dollars in my pocket, I said good-bye to my dear Mary and walked out into the cold night air.

8 P.M.

⌈I wanted to share the good news with Junior. I walked back to him, but he was gone. I heard later that he had hitchhiked down to Portland, Oregon, and died of exposure in an alley behind the Hilton Hotel.⌉

9 P.M.

Lonesome for Indians, I carried my eighty dollars over to Big Heart's in South   145
Downtown. Big Heart's is an all-Indian bar. Nobody knows how or why Indians migrate to one bar and turn it into an official Indian bar. But Big Heart's has been an Indian bar for twenty-three years. It used to be way up on Aurora Avenue, but a crazy Lummi Indian burned that one down, and the owners moved to the new location, a few blocks south of Safeco Field.

I walked into Big Heart's and counted fifteen Indians — eight men and seven women. I didn't know any of them, but Indians like to belong, so we all pretended to be cousins.

"How much for whiskey shots?" I asked the bartender, a fat white guy.

"You want the bad stuff or the badder stuff?"

"As bad as you got."

"One dollar a shot."   150

I laid my eighty dollars on the bar top.

"All right," I said. "Me and all my cousins here are going to be drinking eighty shots. How many is that apiece?"

"Counting you," a woman shouted from behind me, "that's five shots for everybody."

I turned to look at her. She was a chubby and pale Indian woman, sitting with a tall and skinny Indian man.

"All right, math genius," I said to her, and then shouted for the whole bar   155
to hear. "Five drinks for everybody!"

All the other Indians rushed the bar, but I sat with the mathematician and her skinny friend. We took our time with our whiskey shots.

"What's your tribe?" I asked.

"I'm Duwamish," she said. "And he's Crow."

"You're a long way from Montana," I said to him.

"I'm Crow," he said. "I flew here."   160

"What's your name?" I asked them.

"I'm Irene Muse," she said. "And this is Honey Boy."

She shook my hand hard, but he offered his hand as if I was supposed to kiss it. So I did. He giggled and blushed, as much as a dark-skinned Crow can blush.

"You're one of them two-spirits, aren't you?" I asked him.

"I love women," he said. "And I love men."   165

"Sometimes both at the same time," Irene said.

We laughed.

"Man," I said to Honey Boy. "So you must have about eight or nine spirits going on inside you, enit?"

"Sweetie," he said. "I'll be whatever you want me to be."

"Oh, no," Irene said. "Honey Boy is falling in love."   170

"It has nothing to do with love," he said.

We laughed.

"Wow," I said. "I'm flattered, Honey Boy, but I don't play on your team."

"Never say never," he said.

"You better be careful," Irene said. "Honey Boy knows all sorts of magic."   175

"Honey Boy," I said, "you can try to seduce me, but my heart belongs to a woman named Mary."

"Is your Mary a virgin?" Honey Boy asked.

We laughed.

And we drank our whiskey shots until they were gone. But the other Indians bought me more whiskey shots, because I'd been so generous with my money. And Honey Boy pulled out his credit card, and I drank and sailed on that plastic boat.

After a dozen shots, I asked Irene to dance. She refused. But Honey Boy   180
shuffled over to the jukebox, dropped in a quarter, and selected Willie Nelson's "Help Me Make It Through the Night." As Irene and I sat at the table and laughed and drank more whiskey, Honey Boy danced a slow circle around us and sang along with Willie.

"Are you serenading me?" I asked him.

He kept singing and dancing.

"Are you serenading me?" I asked him again.

"He's going to put a spell on you," Irene said.

I leaned over the table, spilling a few drinks, and kissed Irene hard. She   185
kissed me back.

10 P.M.

Irene pushed me into the women's bathroom, into a stall, shut the door behind us, and shoved her hand down my pants. She was short, so I had to lean over to kiss her. I grabbed and squeezed her everywhere I could reach, and she was wonderfully fat, and every part of her body felt like a large, warm, soft breast.

Midnight

Nearly blind with alcohol, I stood alone at the bar and swore I had been standing in the bathroom with Irene only a minute ago.

"One more shot!" I yelled at the bartender.

"You've got no more money!" he yelled back.

"Somebody buy me a drink!" I shouted.   190

"They've got no more money!"

"Where are Irene and Honey Boy?"

"Long gone!"

2 A.M.

"Closing time!" the bartender shouted at the three or four Indians who were still drinking hard after a long, hard day of drinking. Indian alcoholics are either sprinters or marathoners.

    "Where are Irene and Honey Boy?" I asked.   195

    "They've been gone for hours," the bartender said.

    "Where'd they go?"

    "I told you a hundred times, I don't know."

    "What am I supposed to do?"

    "It's closing time. I don't care where you go, but you're not staying here."   200

    "You are an ungrateful bastard. I've been good to you."

    "You don't leave right now, I'm going to kick your ass."

    "Come on, I know how to fight."

    He came at me. I don't remember what happened after that.

4 A.M.

I emerged from the blackness and discovered myself walking behind a big   205
warehouse. I didn't know where I was. My face hurt. I felt my nose and decided that it might be broken. Exhausted and cold, I pulled a plastic tarp from a truck bed, wrapped it around me like a faithful lover, and fell asleep in the dirt.

6 A.M.

Somebody kicked me in the ribs. I opened my eyes and looked up at a white cop.

    "Jackson," the cop said. "Is that you?"

    "Officer Williams," I said. He was a good cop with a sweet tooth. He'd given me hundreds of candy bars over the years. I wonder if he knew I was diabetic.

    "What the hell are you doing here?" he asked.

    "I was cold and sleepy," I said. "So I lay down."   210

    "You dumb-ass, you passed out on the railroad tracks."

    I sat up and looked around. I was lying on the railroad tracks. Dockworkers stared at me. I should have been a railroad-track pizza, a double Indian pepperoni with extra cheese. Sick and scared, I leaned over and puked whiskey.

    "What the hell's wrong with you?" Officer Williams asked. "You've never been this stupid."

    "It's my grandmother," I said. "She died."

    "I'm sorry, man. When did she die?"   215

    "Nineteen seventy-two."

    "And you're killing yourself now?"

    "I've been killing myself ever since she died."

    He shook his head. He was sad for me. Like I said, he was a good cop.

    "And somebody beat the hell out of you," he said. "You remember who?"   220

    "Mr. Grief and I went a few rounds."

    "It looks like Mr. Grief knocked you out."

"Mr. Grief always wins."

"Come on," he said. "Let's get you out of here."

He helped me up and led me over to his squad car. He put me in the back.   225
"You throw up in there and you're cleaning it up," he said.

"That's fair."

He walked around the car and sat in the driver's seat. "I'm taking you over
to detox," he said.

"No, man, that place is awful," I said. "It's full of drunk Indians."

We laughed. He drove away from the docks.

"I don't know how you guys do it," he said.   230

"What guys?" I asked.

"You Indians. How the hell do you laugh so much? I just picked your ass
off the railroad tracks, and you're making jokes. Why the hell do you do that?"

⌈"The two funniest tribes I've ever been around are Indians and Jews, so
I guess that says something about the inherent humor of genocide."⌉

We laughed.

"Listen to you, Jackson. You're so smart. Why the hell are you on the   235
street?"

"Give me a thousand dollars and I'll tell you."

"You bet I'd give you a thousand dollars if I knew you'd straighten up
your life."

He meant it. He was the second-best cop I'd ever known.

"You're a good cop," I said.

"Come on, Jackson," he said. "Don't blow smoke up my ass."   240

"No, really, you remind me of my grandfather."

"Yeah, that's what you Indians always tell me."

"No, man, my grandfather was a tribal cop. He was a good cop. He never
arrested people. He took care of them. Just like you."

"I've arrested hundreds of scumbags, Jackson. And I've shot a couple in
the ass."

"It don't matter. You're not a killer."   245

"I didn't kill them. I killed their asses. I'm an ass-killer."

We drove through downtown. The missions and shelters had already released their overnighters. Sleepy homeless men and women stood on street
corners and stared up at a gray sky. It was the morning after the night of the
living dead.

"Do you ever get scared?" I asked Officer Williams.

"What do you mean?"

"I mean, being a cop, is it scary?"   250

He thought about that for a while. He contemplated it. I liked that
about him.

"I guess I try not to think too much about being afraid," he said. "If you
think about fear, then you'll be afraid. The job is boring most of the time. Just
driving and looking into dark corners, you know, and seeing nothing. But then
things get heavy. You're chasing somebody, or fighting them or walking around

a dark house, and you just know some crazy guy is hiding around a corner, and hell, yes, it's scary."

"My grandfather was killed in the line of duty," I said.

"I'm sorry. How'd it happen?"

I knew he'd listen closely to my story.   255

"He worked on the reservation. Everybody knew everybody. It was safe. We aren't like those crazy Sioux or Apache or any of those other warrior tribes. There've only been three murders on my reservation in the last hundred years."

"That is safe."

"Yeah, we Spokane, we're passive, you know. We're mean with words. And we'll cuss out anybody. But we don't shoot people. Or stab them. Not much, anyway."

"So what happened to your grandfather?"

"This man and his girlfriend were fighting down by Little Falls."   260

"Domestic dispute. Those are the worst."

"Yeah, but this guy was my grandfather's brother. My great-uncle."

"Oh, no."

"Yeah, it was awful. My grandfather just strolled into the house. He'd been there a thousand times. And his brother and his girlfriend were drunk and beating on each other. And my grandfather stepped between them, just as he'd done a hundred times before. And the girlfriend tripped or something. She fell down and hit her head and started crying. And my grandfather kneeled down beside her to make sure she was all right. And for some reason my great-uncle reached down, pulled my grandfather's pistol out of the holster, and shot him in the head."

"That's terrible. I'm sorry."   265

"Yeah, my great-uncle could never figure out why he did it. He went to prison forever, you know, and he always wrote these long letters. Like fifty pages of tiny little handwriting. And he was always trying to figure out why he did it. He'd write and write and write and try to figure it out. He never did. It's a great big mystery."

"Do you remember your grandfather?"

"A little bit. I remember the funeral. My grandmother wouldn't let them bury him. My father had to drag her away from the grave."

"I don't know what to say."

"I don't, either."   270

We stopped in front of the detox center.

"We're here," Officer Williams said.

"I can't go in there," I said.

"You have to."

"Please, no. They'll keep me for twenty-four hours. And then it will be   275
too late."

"Too late for what?"

I told him about my grandmother's regalia and the deadline for buying it back.

"If it was stolen, you need to file a report," he said. "I'll investigate it myself. If that thing is really your grandmother's, I'll get it back for you. Legally."

"No," I said. "That's not fair. The pawnbroker didn't know it was stolen. And, besides, I'm on a mission here. I want to be a hero, you know? I want to win it back, like a knight."

"That's romantic crap."　　280

"That may be. But I care about it. It's been a long time since I really cared about something."

Officer Williams turned around in his seat and stared at me. He studied me. "I'll give you some money," he said. "I don't have much. Only thirty bucks. I'm short until payday. And it's not enough to get back the regalia. But it's something."

"I'll take it," I said.

"I'm giving it to you because I believe in what you believe. I'm hoping and　285 I don't know why I'm hoping it, but I hope you can turn thirty bucks into a thousand somehow."

"I believe in magic."

"I believe you'll take my money and get drunk on it."

"Then why are you giving it to me?"

"There ain't no such thing as an atheist cop."

"Sure, there is."　　290

"Yeah, well, I'm not an atheist cop."

He let me out of the car, handed me two fivers and a twenty, and shook my hand.

"Take care of yourself, Jackson," he said. "Stay off the railroad tracks."

"I'll try," I said.

He drove away. Carrying my money, I headed back toward the water.　295

8 A.M.

On the wharf, those three Aleuts still waited on the wooden bench.

"Have you seen your ship?" I asked.

"Seen a lot of ships," the elder Aleut said. "But not our ship."

I sat on the bench with them. We sat in silence for a long time. I wondered if we would fossilize if we sat there long enough.

I thought about my grandmother. I'd never seen her dance in her regalia.　300 And, more than anything, I wished I'd seen her dance at a powwow.

"Do you guys know any songs?" I asked the Aleuts.

"I know all of Hank Williams," the elder Aleut said.

"How about Indian songs?"

"Hank Williams is Indian."

"How about sacred songs?"　305

"Hank Williams is sacred."

"I'm talking about ceremonial songs. You know, religious ones. The songs you sing back home when you're wishing and hoping."

"What are you wishing and hoping for?"

"I'm wishing my grandmother was still alive."

"Every song I know is about that."   310

"Well, sing me as many as you can."

The Aleuts sang their strange and beautiful songs. I listened. They sang about my grandmother and about their grandmothers. They were lonesome for the cold and the snow. I was lonesome for everything.

10 A.M.

After the Aleuts finished their last song, we sat in silence for a while. Indians are good at silence.

"Was that the last song?" I asked.

"We sang all the ones we could," the elder Aleut said. "The others are just   315 for our people."

I understood. We Indians have to keep our secrets. And these Aleuts were so secretive they didn't refer to themselves as Indians.

"Are you guys hungry?" I asked.

They looked at one another and communicated without talking.

"We could eat," the elder Aleut said.

11 A.M.

The Aleuts and I walked over to the Big Kitchen, a greasy diner in the Inter-   320 national District. I knew they served homeless Indians who'd lucked into money.

"Four for breakfast?" the waitress asked when we stepped inside.

"Yes, we're very hungry," the elder Aleut said.

She took us to a booth near the kitchen. I could smell the food cooking. My stomach growled.

"You guys want separate checks?" the waitress asked.

"No, I'm paying," I said.   325

"Aren't you the generous one," she said.

"Don't do that," I said.

"Do what?" she asked.

"Don't ask me rhetorical questions. They scare me."

She looked puzzled, and then she laughed.   330

"O.K., Professor," she said. "I'll only ask you real questions from now on."

"Thank you."

"What do you guys want to eat?"

"That's the best question anybody can ask anybody," I said. "What have you got?"

"How much money you got?" she asked.   335

"Another good question," I said. "I've got twenty-five dollars I can spend. Bring us all the breakfast you can, plus your tip."

She knew the math.

"All right, that's four specials and four coffees and fifteen percent for me."

The Aleuts and I waited in silence. Soon enough, the waitress returned and poured us four coffees, and we sipped at them until she returned again, with four plates of food. Eggs, bacon, toast, hash-brown potatoes. It's amazing how much food you can buy for so little money.

Grateful, we feasted.   340

Noon

[I said farewell to the Aleuts and walked toward the pawnshop. I heard later that the Aleuts had waded into the salt water near Dock 47 and disappeared. Some Indians swore they had walked on the water and headed north. Other Indians saw the Aleuts drown. I don't know what happened to them.]

I looked for the pawnshop and couldn't find it. I swear it wasn't in the place where it had been before. I walked twenty or thirty blocks looking for the pawnshop, turned corners and bisected intersections and looked up its name in the phone books and asked people walking past me if they'd ever heard of it. But that pawnshop seemed to have sailed away like a ghost ship. I wanted to cry. And just when I'd given up, when I turned one last corner and thought I might die if I didn't find that pawnshop, there it was in a space I swear it hadn't occupied a few minutes ago.

I walked inside and greeted the pawnbroker, who looked a little younger than he had before.

"It's you," he said.

"Yes, it's me," I said.   345

"Jackson Jackson."

"That is my name."

"Where are your friends?"

"They went traveling. But it's O.K. Indians are everywhere."

"Do you have the money?"   350

"How much do you need again?" I asked, and hoped the price had changed.

"Nine hundred and ninety-nine dollars."

It was still the same price. Of course, it was the same price. Why would it change?

"I don't have that," I said.

"What do you have?"   355

"Five dollars."

I set the crumpled Lincoln on the countertop. The pawnbroker studied it.

"Is that the same five dollars from yesterday?"

"No, it's different."

He thought about the possibilities.   360

"Did you work hard for this money?" he asked.

"Yes," I said.

He closed his eyes and thought harder about the possibilities. Then he stepped into the back room and returned with my grandmother's regalia.

"Take it," he said, and held it out to me.

"I don't have the money."   365

"I don't want your money."

"But I wanted to win it."

"You did win it. Now take it before I change my mind."

Do you know how many good men live in this world? Too many to count!

I took my grandmother's regalia and walked outside. I knew that solitary   370
yellow bead was part of me. I knew I was that yellow bead in part. Outside, I
wrapped myself in my grandmother's regalia and breathed her in. I stepped off
the sidewalk and into the intersection. Pedestrians stopped. Cars stopped. The
city stopped. They all watched me dance with my grandmother. I was my
grandmother, dancing.

■ THINKING ABOUT THE TEXT

1. Jackson's quest seems quite fanciful. At what time exactly does it begin?
   What does he hope to do? What are the imagined consequences of his
   quest? What does he tell the policeman about his quest?

2. What is Junior's fate? What about the Aleuts'? What does this suggest
   about Jackson's quest?

3. What did you learn about Indians from the various comments Jackson
   makes about them? Are you aware of stereotypical views of Indians? Do
   you share any? Does this story disabuse you of them?

4. Jackson seems unfazed by the dangers of his quest. What are some of
   them? As on most quests, Jackson also meets good people. Do you
   agree with his assessment that there are too many good people to count?

5. Unexpectedly, Jackson's quest for the regalia ends successfully. Did this
   surprise you? How do you interpret the last paragraph, especially the
   last two sentences about dancing with his grandmother?

■ MAKING COMPARISONS

1. Speculate about the futures of Connie, Paula, and Jackson.

2. Which story conveys the darkest view of human nature? Which is the
   most hopeful?

3. Compare the contrast between innocence and experience in all three
   stories.

■ WRITING ABOUT ISSUES

1. In a brief essay, argue that Oates's story is more or less pessimistic than
   McCorkle's.

2. Using Connie as an example, argue that our culture does or does not
   prepare adolescents for the dangers of the world.

3. Argue that the leader is a more or less realistic character than Arnold
   Friend.

4. Read two other stories by Sherman Alexie, and write a brief report on the
   issues the author raises about contemporary Indian life.

▬ Roads Taken: A Collection of Poems by Robert Frost

ROBERT FROST, "Stopping by Woods on a Snowy Evening"

ROBERT FROST, "The Road Not Taken"

ROBERT FROST, "Acquainted with the Night"

Critic Randall Jarrell saw Robert Frost as "the subtlest and saddest of poets." Although many readers thought of this esteemed, pastoral poet as the optimistic voice of the common man, his lyrical vision is actually quite tragic, a quality President Kennedy thought helped strengthen his own presidential character. Alert readers should be careful about equating Frost's simple language and rural settings with lack of depth. The three poems assembled here (and "Mending Wall," p. 72) use the common motif of an external journey to comment on the internal burdens of adult responsibility, the anxiety inherent in making choices, and the loneliness of the human heart. The language of these journeys is beautifully crafted and evocative, able to be read profitably by both schoolchildren and sophisticated critics.

▬ BEFORE YOU READ

Do you remember reading a Frost poem in high school? What is your memory of that reading and discussion in class?

ROBERT FROST

Stopping by Woods on a Snowy Evening

Robert Frost (1874–1963) was perhaps the best-known poet of the twentieth century: winning four Pulitzer Prizes, garnering more than forty honorary degrees, and being widely anthologized throughout the world. His popular image, perhaps forever fixed by his reading at John Kennedy's inauguration, is of a white-haired New Englander fond of simple, homey descriptions of nature. Actually, Frost was born in San Francisco, and most critics think his poetry is anything but simple.

Frost spent his childhood in California and later moved with his mother to eastern Massachusetts, where he grew up in the small city of Lawrence. He briefly attended Dartmouth College and married in 1895. Frost and his wife taught school together, but they soon moved to a farm in New Hampshire, where he worked and wrote poetry. In 1912, he moved to a town outside London and soon published his first book of poetry, A Boy's Will, in 1913. The book was well received, and a few years later Frost moved to Franconia, New Hampshire, and began a lifelong career of writing and teaching. For more than twenty years, he was a professor at Amherst College and for decades taught summers at the Bread Loaf School in Vermont.

(© Bettmann/Corbis.)

Frost's most popular poems — "Mending Wall," "After Apple-Picking," "Birches,"
and "Fire and Ice" — and those printed here deal with complex social issues in a
seemingly natural manner. But even a casual search of essays interpreting "Mending
Wall," for example, demonstrates that critics see in Frost's poems a sophisticated,
searching, and often dark commentary on the human condition.

Whose woods these are I think I know.
His house is in the village, though;
He will not see me stopping here
To watch his woods fill up with snow.

My little horse must think it queer
To stop without a farmhouse near   5
Between the woods and frozen lake
The darkest evening of the year.

He gives his harness bells a shake
To ask if there is some mistake   10

The only other sound's the sweep
Of easy wind and downy flake.

The woods are lovely, dark and deep,
But I have promises to keep,
And miles to go before I sleep,   15
And miles to go before I sleep.   *[1923]*

■ **THINKING ABOUT THE TEXT**

1. Why does the narrator seem so concerned that someone will notice him watching "woods fill up with snow" (line 4)?

2. Is the "darkest evening" (line 8) meant literally or metaphorically or both?

3. Notice the alliteration in lines 11–12. What effect is Frost trying to achieve with this poetic device?

4. Some critics see the narrator's pause and the lure of woods that "are lovely, dark and deep" (line 13) as something like a death wish. Do you agree?

5. How do you interpret the last lines? Are they a literal or a figurative statement? Why the repetition?

ROBERT FROST

The Road Not Taken

Two roads diverged in a yellow wood,
And sorry I could not travel both
And be one traveler, long I stood
And looked down one as far as I could
To where it bent in the undergrowth;   5

Then took the other, as just as fair,
And having perhaps the better claim,
Because it was grassy and wanted wear;
Though as for that the passing there
Had worn them really about the same,   10

And both that morning equally lay
In leaves no step had trodden black.
Oh, I kept the first for another day!
Yet knowing how way leads on to way,
I doubted if I should ever come back.   15

I shall be telling this with a sigh
Somewhere ages and ages hence:

Two roads diverged in a wood, and I —
I took the one less traveled by,
And that has made all the difference.   *[1916]*   20

▤ THINKING ABOUT THE TEXT

1. Is it odd that the title would refer to a road *not* taken?
2. This is clearly a poem about a journey. Did you ever think of your life as a journey on a particular path? How far can you see your future on this path?
3. Critics have noticed that although the narrator says he has taken the path less traveled, he also says the paths were worn about the same. How might you account for this?
4. The conventional interpretation of this poem is that it is about nonconformity. Does this make sense? Why? Given the issue in the previous question, might there be other interpretations?
5. Why does the narrator "sigh" in the last stanza? Is it due to boredom? Regret? Resignation? Nostalgia?

▤ MAKING COMPARISONS

1. Compare the moods of the speakers in both poems.
2. Both poems touch on the future. In what ways?
3. Is the focus of "Stopping by Woods on a Snowy Evening" more pessimistic than that of "The Road Not Taken"?

ROBERT FROST

Acquainted with the Night

I have been one acquainted with the night.
I have walked out in rain — and back in rain.
I have outwalked the furthest city light.

I have looked down the saddest city lane.
I have passed by the watchman on his beat   5
And dropped my eyes, unwilling to explain.

I have stood still and stopped the sound of feet
When far away an interrupted cry
Came over houses from another street,

But not to call me back or say good-by;   10
And further still at an unearthly height
One luminary clock against the sky

Proclaimed the time was neither wrong nor right.
I have been one acquainted with the night.   *[1928]*

■ THINKING ABOUT THE TEXT

1. When the narrator passes the watchman, he drops his eyes (lines 5–6). Why?

2. It seems that the cry (line 8) has nothing to do with the narrator. Is this detail a key to his psychological and emotional state?

3. The narrator says the "time was neither wrong nor right" (line 13). What is he trying to suggest? What might the "time was right" suggest?

4. Why does the narrator choose the night for his walks? Why not walk during the day?

5. Although the first and last lines are identical, do you sense a difference in meaning?

■ MAKING COMPARISONS

1. Which of these three journeys in Frost's poems seems the most hopeful?

2. Is the speaker in "Acquainted with the Night" more honest than the other speakers? Why?

3. Which line in the three poems seems the most enigmatic? Why?

■ WRITING ABOUT ISSUES

1. Write an essay about a decision you made that you assumed would make a difference in your life.

2. All three poems involve journeys. Write an essay that compares the three journeys in terms of purpose, mood, and meaning.

3. Write an essay about a significant and recent journey that you have taken. Did you learn something about yourself? Did you change?

4. Another Frost poem, "Mending Wall," appears in the first part of this book (p. 72). Write an essay that compares the attitude of that speaker with the three speakers in this cluster.

▤ Journeys to Addiction: Nonfiction

RICHARD WRIGHT, From *Black Boy*

CAROLINE KNAPP, "Love"

SUSAN CHEEVER, "Drinking with Daddy"

Susan Cheever's father, John Cheever, wrote a famous story called "The Swimmer" in which the main character hopes to swim home using swimming pools. It appears to the reader that his journey takes all day, but toward the end we realize that years have passed. He seems oblivious to the reality that his family has long ago abandoned their home and him because of his chronic alcoholism. This fictional story is allegorical, of course, but it makes a depressing point about addicts' ability to deny what is happening to them. Serious drinking rarely begins immediately. It is usually a gradual process from casual social drinking to obsessive, isolated addiction. It might take years, and the symptoms are probably obvious to all but the drinker. The reasons for such behavior are both environmental and deeply psychological. For many, awareness comes too late, but for some the stunning realization of their addiction and looming demise is enough to begin the difficult journey back to sobriety.

The three selections in this cluster all deal with excessive drinking, but from different ages, races, genders, and social classes. Richard Wright's childhood experience is bizarre. Caroline Knapp's memoir is more typical but nevertheless harrowing. Like Wright, Susan Cheever also begins her drinking education at the age of six, although it takes some years before a serious problem arises.

▤ BEFORE YOU READ

What stereotypes do you have of an alcoholic? How do you think a person develops alcoholism? What would your definition of an alcoholic be? Could you become one?

RICHARD WRIGHT
From *Black Boy*

Richard Wright (1908–1960) was born on a plantation in Roxie, Mississippi. His grandparents were slaves. When his mother suffered a stroke, he went to live with his strict, religious aunt and maternal grandmother, an experience that Wright remembers as emotionally traumatic, souring him forever toward religion. Wright eventually moved to Chicago and became involved in leftist politics. In 1937, Wright moved to New York, where he became friends with the novelist Ralph Ellison. Wright's novel Native Son *(1940) was the first book by an African American to be selected by the*

Book of the Month Club. Black Boy was published in 1945, and Wright soon moved to Paris and became a permanent expatriate. He was friends with Jean-Paul Sartre and Albert Camus. Wright's The Outsider *(1953) is considered the first existential American novel. His realistic portrayal of African Americans is today considered masterly and a significant literary achievement. The following excerpt is from the first chapter of* Black Boy.

Hunger stole upon me so slowly that at first I was not aware of what hunger really meant. Hunger had always been more or less at my elbow when I played, but now I began to wake up at night to find hunger standing at my bedside, staring at me gauntly. The hunger I had known before this had been no grim, hostile stranger; it had been a normal hunger that had made me beg constantly for bread, and when I ate a crust or two I was satisfied. But this new hunger baffled me, scared me, made me angry and insistent. Whenever I begged for food now my mother would pour me a cup of tea which would still the clamor in my stomach for a moment or two; but a little later I would feel hunger nudging my ribs, twisting my empty guts until they ached. I would grow dizzy and my vision would dim. I became less active in my play, and for the first time in my life I had to pause and think of what was happening to me.

"Mama, I'm hungry," I complained one afternoon.

"Jump up and catch a kungry," she said, trying to make me laugh and forget.

"What's a *kungry?*"

"It's what little boys eat when they get hungry," she said.   5

"What does it taste like?"

"I don't know."

"Then why do you tell me to catch one?"

"Because you said that you were hungry," she said, smiling.

I sensed that she was teasing me and it made me angry.   10

"But I'm hungry. I want to eat."

"You'll have to wait."

"But I want to eat now."

"But there's nothing to eat," she told me.

"Why?"   15

"Just because there's none," she explained.

"But I want to eat," I said, beginning to cry.

"You'll just have to wait," she said again.

"But why?"

"For God to send some food."   20

"When is He going to send it?"

"I don't know."

"But I'm hungry!"

She was ironing and she paused and looked at me with tears in her eyes.

"Where's your father?" she asked me.   25

I stared in bewilderment. Yes, it was true that my father had not come home to sleep for many days now and I could make as much noise as I wanted. Though I had not known why he was absent, I had been glad that he was not there to shout his restrictions at me. But it had never occurred to me that his absence would mean that there would be no food.

"I don't know," I said.

"Who brings food into the house?" my mother asked me.

"Papa," I said. "He always brought food."

"Well, your father isn't here now," she said.   30

"Where is he?"

"I don't know," she said.

"But I'm hungry," I whimpered, stomping my feet.

"You'll have to wait until I get a job and buy food," she said.

As the days slid past the image of my father became associated with my   35
pangs of hunger, and whenever I felt hunger I thought of him with a deep biological bitterness.

My mother finally went to work as a cook and left me and my brother alone in the flat each day with a loaf of bread and a pot of tea. When she returned at evening she would be tired and dispirited and would cry a lot. Sometimes, when she was in despair, she would call us to her and talk to us for hours, telling us that we now had no father, that our lives would be different from those of other children, that we must learn as soon as possible to take care of ourselves, to dress ourselves, to prepare our own food; that we must take upon ourselves the responsibility of the flat while she worked. Half frightened, we would promise solemnly. We did not understand what had happened between our father and our mother and the most that these long talks did to us was to make us feel a vague dread. Whenever we asked why father had left, she would tell us that we were too young to know.

One evening my mother told me that thereafter I would have to do the shopping for food. She took me to the corner store to show me the way. I was proud; I felt like a grownup. The next afternoon I looped the basket over my arm and went down the pavement toward the store. When I reached the corner, a gang of boys grabbed me, knocked me down, snatched the basket, took the money, and sent me running home in panic. That evening I told my mother what had happened, but she made no comment; she sat down at once, wrote another note, gave me more money, and sent me out to the grocery again. I crept down the steps and saw the same gang of boys playing down the street. I ran back into the house.

"What's the matter?" my mother asked.

"It's those same boys," I said. "They'll beat me."

"You've got to get over that," she said. "Now, go on."   40

"I'm scared," I said.

"Go on and don't pay any attention to them," she said.

I went out of the door and walked briskly down the sidewalk, praying that the gang would not molest me. But when I came abreast of them someone shouted.

"There he is!"

They came toward me and I broke into a wild run toward home. They over-   45
took me and flung me to the pavement. I yelled, pleaded, kicked, but they
wrenched the money out of my hand. They yanked me to my feet, gave me a
few slaps, and sent me home sobbing. My mother met me at the door.

"They b-beat m-me," I gasped. "They t-t-took the m-money."

I started up the steps, seeking the shelter of the house.

"Don't you come in here," my mother warned me.

I froze in my tracks and stared at her.

"But they're coming after me," I said.   50

"You just stay right where you are," she said in a deadly tone. "I'm going to
teach you this night to stand up and fight for yourself."

She went into the house and I waited, terrified, wondering what she was
about. Presently she returned with more money and another note; she also
had a long heavy stick.

"Take this money, this note, and this stick," she said. "Go to the store and
buy those groceries. If those boys bother you, then fight."

I was baffled. My mother was telling me to fight, a thing that she had never
done before.

"But I'm scared," I said.   55

"Don't you come into this house until you've gotten those groceries,"
she said.

"They'll beat me; they'll beat me," I said.

"Then stay in the streets; don't come back here!"

I ran up the steps and tried to force my way past her into the house. A
stinging slap came on my jaw. I stood on the sidewalk, crying.

"Please, let me wait until tomorrow," I begged.   60

"No," she said. "Go now! If you come back into this house without those
groceries, I'll whip you!"

She slammed the door and I heard the key turn in the lock. I shook with
fright. I was alone upon the dark, hostile streets and gangs were after me. I had
the choice of being beaten at home or away from home. I clutched the stick,
crying, trying to reason. If I were beaten at home, there was absolutely nothing
that I could do about it; but if I were beaten in the streets, I had a chance to
fight and defend myself. I walked slowly down the sidewalk, coming closer to
the gang of boys, holding the stick tightly. I was so full of fear that I could
scarcely breathe. I was almost upon them now.

"There he is again!" the cry went up.

They surrounded me quickly and began to grab for my hand.

"I'll kill you!" I threatened.   65

They closed in. In blind fear I let the stick fly, feeling it crack against a boy's
skull. I swung again, lamming another skull, then another. Realizing that they
would retaliate if I let up for but a second, I fought to lay them low, to knock
them cold, to kill them so that they could not strike back at me. I flayed with
tears in my eyes, teeth clenched, stark fear making me throw every ounce of
my strength behind each blow. I hit again and again, dropping the money and

the grocery list. The boys scattered, yelling, nursing their heads, staring at me in utter disbelief. They had never seen such frenzy. I stood panting, egging them on, taunting them to come on and fight. When they refused, I ran after them and they tore out for their homes, screaming. The parents of the boys rushed into the streets and threatened me, and for the first time in my life I shouted at grownups, telling them that I would give them the same if they bothered me. I finally found my grocery list and the money and went to the store. On my way back I kept my stick poised for instant use, but there was not a single boy in sight. That night I won the right to the streets of Memphis.

Of a summer morning, when my mother had gone to work, I would follow a crowd of black children—abandoned for the day by their working parents—to the bottom of a sloping hill whose top held a long row of ramshackle, wooden outdoor privies whose opened rear ends provided a raw and startling view. We would crouch at the foot of the slope and look up—a distance of twenty-five feet or more—at the secret and fantastic anatomies of black, brown, yellow, and ivory men and women. For hours we would laugh, point, whisper, joke, and identify our neighbors by the signs of their physiological oddities, commenting upon the difficulty or projectile force of their excretions. Finally some grownup would see us and drive us away with disgusted shouts. Occasionally children of two and three years of age would emerge from behind the hill with their faces smeared and their breath reeking. At last a white policeman was stationed behind the privies to keep the children away and our course in human anatomy was postponed.

To keep us out of mischief, my mother often took my brother and me with her to her cooking job. Standing hungrily and silently in a corner of the kitchen, we would watch her go from the stove to the sink, from the cabinet to the table. I always loved to stand in the white folks' kitchen when my mother cooked, for it meant that I got occasional scraps of bread and meat; but many times I regretted having come, for my nostrils would be assailed with the scent of food that did not belong to me and which I was forbidden to eat. Toward evening my mother would take the hot dishes into the dining room where the white people were seated, and I would stand as near the dining-room door as possible to get a quick glimpse of the white faces gathered around the loaded table, eating, laughing, talking. If the white people left anything, my brother and I would eat well; but if they did not, we would have our usual bread and tea.

Watching the white people eat would make my empty stomach churn and I would grow vaguely angry. Why could I not eat when I was hungry? Why did I always have to wait until others were through? I could not understand why some people had enough food and others did not.

I now found it irresistible to roam during the day while my mother was cooking in the kitchens of the white folks. A block away from our flat was a saloon in front of which I used to loiter all day long. Its interior was an enchanting place that both lured and frightened me. I would beg for pennies, then peer under the swinging doors to watch the men and women drink. When some neighbor would chase me away from the door, I would follow the drunks about the streets, trying to understand their mysterious mumblings, pointing

70

at them, teasing them, laughing at them, imitating them, jeering, mocking, and taunting them about their lurching antics. For me the most amusing spectacle was a drunken woman stumbling and urinating, the dampness seeping down her stockinged legs. Or I would stare in horror at a man retching. Somebody informed my mother about my fondness for the saloon and she beat me, but it did not keep me from peering under the swinging doors and listening to the wild talk of drunks when she was at work.

One summer afternoon — in my sixth year — while peering under the swinging doors of the neighborhood saloon, a black man caught hold of my arm and dragged me into its smoky and noisy depths. The odor of alcohol stung my nostrils. I yelled and struggled, trying to break free of him, afraid of the staring crowd of men and women, but he would not let me go. He lifted me and sat me upon the counter, put his hat upon my head and ordered a drink for me. The tipsy men and women yelled with delight. Somebody tried to jam a cigar into my mouth, but I twisted out of the way.

"How do you feel, setting there like a man, boy?" a man asked.

"Make 'im drunk and he'll stop peeping in here," somebody said.

"Let's buy 'im drinks," somebody said.

Some of my fright left as I stared about. Whisky was set before me.   75

"Drink it, boy," somebody said.

I shook my head. The man who had dragged me in urged me to drink it, telling me that it would not hurt me. I refused.

"Drink it; it'll make you feel good," he said.

I took a sip and coughed. The men and women laughed. The entire crowd in the saloon gathered about me now, urging me to drink. I took another sip. Then another. My head spun and I laughed. I was put on the floor and I ran giggling and shouting among the yelling crowd. As I would pass each man, I would take a sip from an offered glass. Soon I was drunk.

A man called me to him and whispered some words into my ear and told   80
me that he would give me a nickel if I went to a woman and repeated them to her. I told him that I would say them; he gave me the nickel and I ran to the woman and shouted the words. A gale of laughter went up in the saloon.

"Don't teach that boy that," someone said.

"He doesn't know what it is," another said.

From then on, for a penny or a nickel, I would repeat to anyone whatever was whispered to me. In my foggy, tipsy state the reaction of the men and women to my mysterious words enthralled me. I ran from person to person, laughing, hiccoughing, spewing out filth that made them bend double with glee.

"Let that boy alone now," someone said.

"It ain't going to hurt 'im," another said.   85

"It's a shame," a woman said, giggling.

"Go home, boy," somebody yelled at me.

Toward early evening they let me go. I staggered along the pavements, drunk, repeating obscenities to the horror of the women I passed and to the amusement of the men en route to their homes from work.

To beg drinks in the saloon became an obsession. Many evenings my mother would find me wandering in a daze and take me home and beat me; but the next morning, no sooner had she gone to her job than I would run to the saloon and wait for someone to take me in and buy me a drink. My mother protested tearfully to the proprietor of the saloon, who ordered me to keep out of his place. But the men — reluctant to surrender their sport — would buy me drinks anyway, letting me drink out of their flasks on the streets, urging me to repeat obscenities.

I was a drunkard in my sixth year, before I had begun school. With a gang   90 of children, I roamed the streets, begging pennies from passers-by, haunting the doors of saloons, wandering farther and farther away from home each day. I saw more than I could understand and heard more than I could remember. The point of life became for me the times when I could beg drinks. My mother was in despair. She beat me; then she prayed and wept over me, imploring me to be good, telling me that she had to work, all of which carried no weight to my wayward mind. Finally she placed me and my brother in the keeping of an old black woman who watched me every moment to keep me from running to the doors of the saloons to beg for whisky. The craving for alcohol finally left me and I forgot the taste of it.   *[1945]*

≣ THINKING ABOUT THE TEXT

1. How might it be possible for any six-year-old you know to have Wright's experiences?

2. Do Wright's experiences with hunger prepare the reader for his drinking?

3. Comment on Wright's mother's decision to keep him going to the store.

4. Do any of Wright's reminiscences seem unrealistic for a six-year-old? Which memories seem the most appropriate?

5. Do you think any of these events will have a lasting effect on Wright? In what way?

CAROLINE KNAPP
Love

Caroline Knapp (1959–2002) grew up in Cambridge, Massachusetts, and gradu-
ated from Brown University in 1981. As a columnist for the Boston Phoenix *for*
seven years, she wrote essays that were collected in her first book, Alice K's Guide to
Life: One Woman's Quest for Survival, Sanity, and the Perfect New Shoes
(1994). In 1996, she published the best-selling memoir Drinking: A Love Story
(1996) to critical acclaim and financial success. It describes her twenty-year obses-
sion with alcohol, even as she functioned as a skilled professional writer. The selection
printed here is from that book. She is also the author of the best-selling Pack of Two

(1998), an account of her relationship with her dog, Lucille. Her work has been praised as "eloquent, sophisticated, and painfully honest."

Prologue

It happened this way: I fell in love and then, because the love was ruining everything I cared about, I had to fall out.

This didn't happen easily, or simply, but if I had to pinpoint it, I'd say the relationship started to fall apart the night I nearly killed my oldest friend's two daughters.

I'd been visiting my friend Jennifer over Thanksgiving weekend a few years ago, and we'd all gone for a walk after dinner, she and her husband and the two daughters and me. The kids were five and nine years old, beautiful little blue-eyed girls with freckles and wide grins, and I'd been playing Rambunctious Friend of Mom's. I chased them around, and hoisted them into the air, and then, in a blur of supremely bad judgment, I dreamed up the Double Marsupial Hold.

I put the older girl, Elizabeth, on my back, piggyback, and then I picked up the younger one, Julia, and held her facing me, so that her arms were around my neck and her legs around my waist. I was sandwiched between them, holding 130 pounds of kid. Then I started running across the street, shouting like a sportscaster: "It's the Double Marsupial Hold! They've accomplished the Double Marsupial Hold!" And then I lost my balance.

I flew forward and came crashing down and I still believe it's a miracle that   5
Julia's tiny, five-year-old skull wasn't the first thing to hit the pavement. Somehow, I kept her in my arms and allowed my right leg to take the fall, and I remember hitting the ground and feeling something like a minor explosion in my knee. The kids were okay, but I ended up in the emergency room with a gash on my knee so deep the nurses could see my kneecap.

This is the truth: I was extremely drunk that night and I put those kids in serious jeopardy.

Three months later I quit drinking, beginning the long, slow process of disentangling myself from a deeply passionate, profoundly complex, twenty-year relationship with alcohol.

Love

I drank.

I drank Fumé Blanc at the Ritz-Carlton Hotel, and I drank double shots of Johnnie Walker Black on the rocks at a dingy Chinese restaurant across the street from my office, and I drank at home. For a long time I drank expensive red wine, and I learned to appreciate the subtle differences between a silky Merlot and a tart Cabernet Sauvignon and a soft, earthy Beaucastel from the south of France, but I never really cared about those nuances because, honestly, they were beside the point. Toward the end I kept two bottles of

Cognac in my house: the bottle for show, which I kept on the counter, and the real bottle, which I kept in the back of a cupboard beside an old toaster. The level of liquid in the show bottle was fairly consistent, decreasing by an inch or so, perhaps less, each week. The liquid in the real bottle disappeared quickly, sometimes within days. I was living alone at the time, when I did this, but I did it anyway and it didn't occur to me not to: it was always important to maintain appearances.

I drank when I was happy and I drank when I was anxious and I drank when I was bored and I drank when I was depressed, which was often. I started to raid my parents' liquor cabinet the year my father was dying. He'd be in the back of their house in Cambridge, lying in the hospital bed in their bedroom, and I'd steal into the front hall bathroom and pull out a bottle of Old Grand-Dad that I'd hidden behind the toilet. It tasted vile — the bottle must have been fifteen years old — but my father was dying, dying very slowly and gradually from a brain tumor, so I drank it anyway and it helped.

My mother found that bottle, empty, that April, the day of my father's funeral. I'd thrown most of the others away but I must have forgotten that one, and she'd discovered it stashed behind the toilet as she was cleaning the front bathroom for guests. I was sitting at the dining-room table and as she walked through the room, the bottle in her hand, she glared at me, a look of profound disappointment. So I lied.

"That was *before*," I said, referring to a promise I'd made her nine months before my father died. "Two drinks a day," I'd said. "No more than that. I promise I'll cut down."

I'd made the promise on a Sunday the previous July, in the midst of a pounding hangover. I'd been visiting my parents at their summerhouse on Martha's Vineyard and I'd gotten so drunk the night before, I almost passed out on the sofa, sitting right there next to my mother. I'd done the drinking in secret, of course, stealing off to my bedroom every thirty minutes or so to take a slug off a bottle of Scotch I'd stashed in my bag, and I vaguely remember the end of the night, my words slurring when I tried to talk, my eyelids so droopy I had to strain to keep them open. I was usually more careful than that, careful to walk the line between being drunk enough and too drunk, careful to do most of the serious drinking at the very end of the night, after everyone else had gone to bed. But I slipped up that time and my mother caught me. The next day she asked me to take a walk with her on the beach, an unusual move for my mother, who requested a private audience only when she had something very serious to say. I remember it was a sunny morning, mid-July, with a stiff breeze and hot light, and I remember a feeling of dread and contrition; I was hoping she wouldn't be mad at me.

We made our way down the dirt path that led from our house to Menemsha Pond, a blue arc of water at the bottom of the hill, and then we walked for a while in silence. Finally she said, "I need to talk to you. I'm very worried about your drinking."

I said, "I know." I walked beside her, keeping my eyes on my feet in the sand, afraid that if I looked up I'd bump too abruptly into a truth I didn't really want to see. I added, softly, "I am too." I could tell from her tone that she wasn't angry, just worried, and I had to admit to her: I was too. Sort of.

We walked some more. She said, "This is very serious. It's more serious than smoking."

My mother was the sort of person who chose her words with the utmost care, and I understood that a wealth of meanings ran beneath that simple phrase: *more serious than smoking.* Smoking caused cancer, a disease that was killing my father, that had killed several women in her family, that would kill her just a few years later. She understood that drinking was more dangerous and she understood why: smoking could ruin my body; drinking could ruin my mind and my future. It could eat its way through my life in exactly the same way a physical cancer eats its way through bones and blood and tissue, destroying everything.

"It *really* is serious," she said.

I kept my head lowered. "I know."

And I meant it, at least just then. There are moments as an active alcoholic   20 where you *do* know, where in a flash of clarity you grasp that alcohol is the central problem, a kind of liquid glue that gums up all the internal gears and keeps you stuck. The pond was beautiful that day, rippled and sparkling, turning the sand a deep sienna where it lapped against the shore, and for an instant, I did know, I could see it: I was thirty-three and I was drinking way too much and I was miserable, and there had to be a connection.

My mother was such a gentle woman. She said, "What can I do to help you? I'll do anything I can," and that's when I made the promise.

I looked out across the pond, not wanting to look her in the eyes. "I don't know," I said. "I know I have to deal with it." I told her I'd look into Alcoholics Anonymous. I said, "In the meantime I'll cut down. Two drinks a day. No more than that. I promise."

I'd meant it. That afternoon I took the ferry from Martha's Vineyard to Woods Hole, en route back to Boston where I lived, and I remember sitting there on the boat, vaguely nauseated, my head still aching from the night before. I wanted a beer, just one beer to help ease the headache, and I debated with myself about that for several long minutes: Shouldn't I prove to myself that I could go a day — just one simple day — without a drink? Shouldn't I? The ninety-minute ride to Boston loomed ahead. The sky was clear, with the sharp light of late afternoon, and people wearing windbreakers and sweatshirts and sunglasses lolled on the deck in canvas chairs, sipping Budweiser and Michelob Light from tall plastic cups.

I had the beer. And then, when I got back to my apartment, I had a little wine with dinner. Just a little: two glasses, but they were small ones, so I considered them half-glasses and counted them as one. From that point on, though, I was always very careful around my mother — careful not to drink more than two glasses of anything in front of her, careful never to call her when I was drunk — but I didn't keep the promise.

And that's how it works. Active alcoholics try and active alcoholics fail. We   25 make the promises and we really do try to stick with them and we keep ignoring the fact that we can't do it, keep rationalizing the third drink, or the fourth or fifth. *Just today. Bad day. I deserve a reward. I'll deal with it tomorrow.*

A few weeks after the walk with my mother, I read a book that mentioned a test people could take in order to determine whether or not they're alcoholics. The test involved setting limits: three drinks a day for six months, no more, no less, and no variation no matter what the circumstances. Someone dies, you still don't have more than three. You get fired from your job, just three. Weddings, funerals, celebrations, disasters — it doesn't matter. I can't even remember how many times I took that test — dozens of times. I also can't remember consciously deciding to stray from the rule or to cheat, to have the fourth glass of wine, or to pour the three glasses in such enormous goblets that I might as well have had six.

I just couldn't do it. Alcohol had become too important. By the end it was the single most important relationship in my life.

A love story. Yes: this is a love story.

It's about passion, sensual pleasure, deep pulls, lust, fears, yearning hungers. It's about needs so strong they're crippling. It's about saying good-bye to something you can't fathom living without.

I loved the way drink made me feel, and I loved its special power of deflec-   30
tion, its ability to shift my focus away from my own awareness of self and onto something else, something less painful than my own feelings. I loved the sounds of drink: the slide of a cork as it eased out of a wine bottle, the distinct glug-glug of booze pouring into a glass, the clatter of ice cubes in a tumbler. I loved the rituals, the camaraderie of drinking with others, the warming, melting feelings of ease and courage it gave me.

Our introduction was not dramatic; it wasn't love at first sight, I don't even remember my first taste of alcohol. The relationship developed gradually, over many years, time punctuated by separations and reunions. Anyone who's ever shifted from general affection and enthusiasm for a lover to outright obsession knows what I mean: the relationship is just there, occupying a small corner of your heart, and then you wake up one morning and some indefinable tide has turned forever and you can't go back. You *need* it; it's a central part of who you are.

I used to drink with a woman named Elaine, a next-door neighbor of mine. I was in my twenties when we met and she was in her late forties, divorced and involved with a married man whom she could not give up. Elaine drank a lot, more than I did, and she drank especially hard when the relationship with the married man got rocky, which was often. She drank beer and vodka, and she'd call me up on bad nights and ask me to come over. The beer made her over-weight and the vodka made her sloppy, and she'd sit on her sofa with a bottle and cry, her face stained with tears and mascara. I used to sit there and think, *Whoa.* I'd sympathize and listen and say all the things girlfriends are supposed to say, but inside I'd be shaking my head, knowing she was a wreck and know-ing on some level that the booze made her that way, that the liquor fueled her obsession for the married man, fueled her tears, fueled her hopelessness and inability to change.

But some small part of me (it got larger over the years) was always secretly relieved to see Elaine that way: a messy drunk's an ugly thing, particularly when the messy drunk's a woman, and I could compare myself to her and feel superiority and relief. I wasn't *that* bad; no way I was *that* bad.

And I wasn't that bad. I had lots of rules. I never drank in the morning and I never drank at work, and except for an occasional mimosa or Bloody Mary at a weekend brunch, except for a glass of white wine (maybe two) with lunch on days when I didn't have to do too much in the afternoon, except for an occasional zip across the street from work to the Chinese restaurant with a colleague, I always abided by them.

For a long time I didn't even need rules. The drink was there, always just 35 there, the way food's in the refrigerator and ice is in the freezer. In high school the beer just appeared at parties, lugged over in cases by boys in denim jackets and Levi's corduroys. In my parents' house the Scotch and the gin sat in a liquor cabinet, to the left of the fireplace in the living room, and it just emerged, every evening at cocktail hour. I never saw it run out and I never saw it replenished either: it was just there. In college, of course, it was there all the time — in small, squat refrigerators in dorm rooms, in kegs at parties, in chilled draft glasses on tavern tabletops — and by the time I graduated, by the time I was free to buy alcohol and consume it where and when I wanted, drinking seemed as natural as breathing, an ordinary part of social convention, a simple prop.

Still, I look in the mirror sometimes and think, What happened? I have the CV of a model citizen or a gifted child, not a common drunk. Hometown: Cambridge, Massachusetts, backyard of Harvard University. Education: Brown University, class of '81, magna cum laude. Parents: esteemed psychoanalyst (dad) and artist (mom), both devoted and insightful and keenly intelligent.

In other words, nice person, from a good, upper-middle-class family. I look and I think, What *happened*?

Of course, there is no simple answer. Trying to describe the process of becoming an alcoholic is like trying to describe air. It's too big and mysterious and pervasive to be defined. Alcohol is everywhere in your life, omnipresent, and you're both aware and unaware of it almost all the time; all you know is you'd die without it, and there is no simple reason why this happens, no single moment, no physiological event that pushes a heavy drinker across a concrete line into alcoholism. It's a slow, gradual, insidious, elusive *becoming*.

My parents' house on Martha's Vineyard is in the town of Gay Head, on the westernmost side of the island, in a dry town, a forty-minute drive from the nearest liquor store or bar. When I was a teenager, our lack of proximity to alcohol was fine, a fact, something I didn't notice. Then, in my twenties, it became slightly questionable. I'd come for a weekend to visit my parents, and I'd assume my father would have gin for martinis and wine for dinner, and he would, and I'd be somewhat relieved, without really knowing it. And then, after I turned thirty, it became more than questionable; it became a problem, this dry town on Martha's Vineyard, a forty-minute drive from the nearest liquor store.

Somewhere inside I acknowledged that this made me nervous. Somewhere   40
inside I'd become desperately aware that the last time I was at the house, there
was only one bottle of wine for dinner—one bottle to share between four or
five people—and that the level of liquid in the gin bottle was dangerously low
by the end of the weekend. I'd remember, very clearly, that I'd had to compensate for the lack of wine by returning to that gin bottle several times, surreptitiously, sneaking into the kitchen to top off my drink while the rest of the family
sat outside on the porch. In some dark place an anxiety about this festered: I
didn't want to be trapped there again with an insufficient supply, but I didn't
want to let on that I was anxious about the supply either.

So I'd debate, without even noticing the arguments and counterargu-
ments circling in the back of my mind. Should I show up for the weekend with
a case of wine, on the pretext that I'd brought it there "just to have it in the
house"? Should I forget about the whole thing and just hope someone else had
restocked the liquor cabinet? Should I borrow the car and drive the forty minutes to the liquor store, pretending to be off for a solo trek at the beach? In a
back corner of my mind I'd notice that this question of what there was to drink
in the house had become a big deal, and that fact would nag at me just a little
bit, raising a tiny flag, a question about how much I seemed to need the alcohol. The questions would continue: what to do, how to do it, who'd notice, why
didn't anyone else drink the way I did? And after a while these voices would
start to feel too big and too confusing and too overwhelming, and in the briefest
instant I'd just do it: I'd mentally wash my hands of the whole business, and I'd
pick up a bottle of Scotch the day before the drip, and I'd stash it in my weekend bag.

There. Problem solved.

That, of course, is how an alcoholic starts *not* to notice it. *Just this one time.*
That's how you put it to yourself: I'll just do it this one time, the same way a
jealous woman might pick up the phone at midnight to see if her lover is home,
or cruise slowly past his house to check his lights, promising herself that this is
the last time. *I know this is insane, but I'll only do it this once.* I'll just bring the
Scotch this one time because I'm particularly stressed out this week and I just
want to be able to have a Scotch where and when I want it, okay? It's no big
deal: just a little glass in my room before dinner so I don't have to steal into the
kitchen and sneak one there. Just a little glass so I don't drink up any more of
Dad's liquor. No big deal; it makes *sense.*

And it *would* make sense, in a certain perverse way. There I'd be, out on the
porch on Martha's Vineyard with my family, and I'd excuse myself for just a
minute—just a minute, to go to the bathroom. Then, on the way to the bathroom, I'd make a quick detour to my bedroom, and I'd pull the Scotch out from
the bag, and I'd unscrew the cap and take a long slug off the bottle and swallow.
The liquor would burn going down, and the burn would feel good: it would feel
warming and protective; it would feel like insurance.

Yes: insurance: the Scotch in my bag gave me a measure of safety. It let me   45
sit at the table during dinner and not obsess through the whole meal about
whether there was enough wine, whether anyone would notice how fast I
slammed down my first glass, whether or how I could reach for the bottle to

refill my glass without calling too much attention to myself. It let me know I'd be taken care of when the need became too strong.

When you love somebody, or something, it's amazing how willing you are to overlook the flaws. Around that same time, in my thirties, I started to notice that tiny blood vessels had burst all along my nose and cheeks. I started to dry-heave in the mornings, driving to work in my car. A tremor in my hands developed, then grew worse, then persisted for longer periods, all day sometimes.

I did my best to ignore all this. I struggled to ignore it, the way a woman hears coldness in a lover's voice and struggles, mightily and knowingly, to misread it.

Coda

A few months after my one-year anniversary[1] I went to the meeting I usually go to on Wednesday nights, on the ground floor of a church outside of Boston. It's a big meeting — about fifty people each week — and it's oriented toward alcoholics in their first year of sobriety. One person tells his or her story for the first half hour, and then the meeting opens up, first to those in their first month of sobriety, then to those with three months or less, then six months or less, and so on.

A dozen people must have spoken that night. I heard a woman named Megan, sober for about six months, talk about being in incredible pain — losing both her job and custody of her son — but getting through it, managing to get through it without a drink. I heard a guy named Bill talk about living with fear — he'd lost his job, too, and he was terrified of looking for another, and he had to keep reminding himself that there's a big difference between walking through fears, which you do in sobriety, and escaping them, which you do through drink. I heard people talk about being angry and hopeless, and about being grateful and relieved, and about just getting through the day.

At the end of the meeting there was a presentation for a young guy named John, who was celebrating one year without a drink. He's a model AA citizen, the kind of guy who goes to tons of meetings and sits in the front row at every one and always raises his hand, and I'd watched him work all year, work really hard to live with his own feelings one day after the next and just keep coming. He was so happy that evening, so grateful to get that one-year medallion, and so moved by the amount of support he'd gotten over the year, that his eyes welled up and his voice kept cracking.   50

"I can't thank you all enough," he said, and his face was the picture of hope.

I sat near the back and looked out over the room. Familiar faces, unfamiliar faces, all of us more or less like John, pulling in the same direction. Then I had an image of every person in that room climbing into bed that night, all fifty of us getting into our beds clean and sober, another day without a drink behind us. It was a simple image but it filled me with a range of complicated feelings:

[1] Refers to her decision to stop drinking one year ago. [Eds.]

appreciation for the simple presence of all those people; admiration for their courage and strength; a tinge of melancholy for the amount of pain it must have taken each and every one of them to put down the drink; affection for their humanity.

I didn't realize until hours later that there was a name for that feeling. It's called love.   *[1996]*

▤ THINKING ABOUT THE TEXT

1. Are you disturbed by Knapp's opening narrative in the prologue? What would your response be to the girls' parents?

2. What do you think of Knapp's strategy of calling her addiction a love relationship? In what ways does this seem both accurate and inaccurate?

3. What details do you find particularly honest? Which seem less so?

4. Comment on Knapp's excuse: "I know this is insane, but I'll only do it this once" (para. 43).

5. Compare Knapp's "love" of alcohol with the "love" of the last sentence.

▤ MAKING COMPARISONS

1. Compare the environments in which Wright and Knapp live.

2. Is there something in the personality of these two writers that makes alcohol addiction possible?

3. Does each writer give enough specific detail to create a sense of authority?

SUSAN CHEEVER

Drinking with Daddy

Susan Cheever (b. 1945) was born in New York City and graduated from Brown University in 1965. Her biography Home before Dark *(1994), about her father, the celebrated writer John Cheever, was well received and controversial. She has written five novels and a number of nonfiction books, including* American Bloomsbury: The Lives of Louisa May Alcott, Ralph Waldo Emerson, Margaret Fuller, Nathaniel Hawthorne, and Henry David Thoreau in Concord, Massachusetts, from 1840–1860 *(2008). The selection printed here is from* Note Found in a Bottle: My Life as a Drinker *(1999). About her thirteenth book,* Desire: Where Sex Meets Addiction *(2008), Cheever says, "In 1999 when I wrote about alcoholism, I had no idea there was such a thing as sex addiction. It's only through writing this book that I've come to see that all addictions are one addiction."*

My grandmother Cheever taught me how to embroider, how to say the Lord's Prayer, and how to make a perfect dry martini. She showed me how to tilt the gin bottle into the tumbler with the ice, strain the iced liquid into the long-stemmed martini glass, and add the vermouth. "Just pass the bottle over the gin," she explained in the genteel Yankee voice that had made her gift shop such a success that she was able to support her sons and husband. I watched enthralled as she twisted the lemon peel with her tiny white hands and its oil spread across the shimmery surface. I was six.

New York City in the 1940s was a postwar paradise. Soldiers brought back wonderful, exotic war souvenirs: bamboo hats from the Philippines and delicate lacquered boxes from Japan. It was all sunlight and promise and hope in those days. The streets were safe; the shopkeepers knew everyone who lived on the block. The women wore dresses and high-heeled shoes, and the men all wore brimmed felt hats trimmed with grosgrain ribbon.

Outside our windows the Queensboro Bridge rumbled with traffic. The avenues around our apartment building filled up with the rounded shapes of Buicks and Chevrolets. My father bought a secondhand Dodge for trips to the country, and he parked it across Fifty-ninth Street, right next to the bridge, so that we could admire it from the windows of our apartment. It was that car, I always thought, that wrecked our golden New York City life. In that car my parents started taking us out to visit friends who had moved from the city to the suburbs. These friends were always telling my parents how great the suburbs were. In the suburbs there were wonderful public schools. In the suburbs a young family could have their own house. In the suburbs there was plenty of outdoors for children to run around in, and a community of like-minded parents. In 1951 we moved.

Every evening at six o'clock, right on schedule — because almost everything in those days was right on schedule — the grown-ups in the suburbs would prepare for what they called their preprandial libation. They twisted open the caps of the clinking, golden bottles and filled the opalescent ice bucket, brought out the silver martini shaker and the heart-shaped strainer and the frosted glasses, and the entire mood would change. I loved those mood changes even then.

I loved the paraphernalia of drinking, the slippery ice trays that I was allowed to refill and the pungent olives, which were my first childhood treat, and I loved the way the adults got loose and happy and forgot that I was just a child. I loved the way the great men would sit down so close to me that I smelled their smell of tweed and cigarette smoke and whiskey and tell me their best stories about hiding in a tree at Roosevelt's inauguration, or dodging German bullets in France, or meeting Henry James as a doddering old man in a London club; and the way the women would let me play with their lipsticks and mirrors and would show off the mysterious lacy underwear that held up their silky stockings and held in their tiny waists.

I knew that, like them, I would grow up and get married. My husband would have a job in the city, and I would iron his Brooks shirts; I would learn to cook pork chops in cream sauce and to bake a Lady Baltimore cake, and I would serve cheese and crackers and nuts at parties and take care of my children. We would have a little house, just like my parents', and on vacations we would take

5

our children to visit them just as they took us to visit Bamie in Quincy and Binney and Gram in New Haven and New Hampshire. In the evenings, I would greet my homecoming hubby with the ice bucket and the martini shaker. On Sunday mornings we would have Bloody Marys. In the summer we would stay cool with gin and tonics. In the winter we would drink Manhattans. In good times we would break out champagne, in bad times we would dull the pain with stingers. I was already well acquainted with the miraculous medicinal powers of alcohol. My mother dispensed two fingers of whiskey for stomach pain and beer for other digestive problems. Gin was an all-purpose anesthetic.

Drinking was part of our heritage, I understood. My earliest memories were of my father playing backgammon with my grandmother over a pitcher of martinis. The Cheevers had come over in 1630 on the *Arbella*, the flagship of the Winthrop fleet. The trash came over on the *Mayflower*, my father always said. The best Puritans, the Puritans like us waited until it was clear that the New World was a place worthy of our attention. I learned that the *Arbella* set sail with three times as much beer as water, along with ten thousand gallons of wine. Hemingway had called rum "liquid alchemy." Jack London and John Berryman and Dylan Thomas had written about the wonders of drinking. Brendan Behan came to visit and, with a drink in his hand, sang to me. "The bells of hell go ting-a-ling-a-ling for you but not for me," he sang. "O death where is thy sting-a-ling-a-ling, O grave thy victory?"

I found out about divorce at around the same time that I learned that the Russians, who lived on the other side of the world, had enough atomic power to blow us all up. These two ways in which my life could be shattered by outside forces wielded by irrational adults seemed equally terrifying. From what I saw around me in those idyllic suburbs, marriage was not a happy state. Often when there were parties at our house, the merriment of the first cocktails became sparring and loud arguing before the dessert was served.

By the time we had lived in the suburbs a few years, my father's suburban stories were appearing regularly in *The New Yorker*. Although we couldn't afford to join a country club, or buy a new car — all our cars were secondhand — as a family we had a status conferred on us by my father's success. My father liked to tell divorce stories: he loved the story of how Gert Simon had left her husband while he was at work in his office in New York City — taking the children, the furniture, and even the pets and leaving nothing at all — so that he came back at nightfall to an empty house where he thought his home was.

Divorce was still pretty rare though. If you ask me, the grown-ups were too   10
dressed up for the indignities of divorce court. They still had their hats on every time they went out. When they got clinically depressed, when their adulteries caught up with them, when all the martinis in the world weren't enough to blot out the pain of their humanness, they killed themselves quietly. No one talked about it. They hanged themselves with their hats on. . . .

I grew up with a secret. My family did have a skeleton in the closet. Nothing was as it seemed. In his journals, as early as the early 1960s, my father is in agony over his desire for men and his affairs with men. This private agony took a tremendous amount of his moral and emotional energy. My father was often distracted, and no wonder. His focus was on saving his marriage — a marriage continually threatened by his hidden sexual life. To hide the reality, he created a potent myth, the myth of the shabby country squire — the myth of the family whose beauty and talents would win them entrée into the society from which they had been banned. We had the lost Eden, the world of the Boston Brahmins, we had our own glorious past — and we had our marching orders. We grew up in a weird kind of incubator in which the parts we were assigned to play were much more important than anything else.

But the real family secret was not my father's bisexuality, it was the drinking. My father's fear of exposure, his terrified reaction to others' exposure — in those years other men were discredited for things he did — his intense, life-or-death desire to appear to be something he wasn't: that was nothing. That was a secret that could be discovered in an instant. It *was* discovered in an instant. I read my father's journals and I knew and that was that. The drinking was a different kind of secret and a more dangerous one. It wasn't hidden, it was completely visible. Because it was completely visible, the drinking was a secret that we kept from ourselves.

There was no private agony about hiding the fact that we drank or even that my father drank. What alcohol does is hidden until the very end, and even when it's exposed it hides. I don't think my father ever knew — even after seven years of being sober and going to AA meetings and courting rigorous honesty — I don't think he ever knew how much drinking had distorted our family life. I am just now beginning to know.

The recovery people say that alcoholism is like an elephant in the living room, and that living with alcoholism induces insanity because everyone has to pretend that the elephant isn't there. Pretending that things are not as they seem — that you don't see what you do see, that you don't hear what you do hear — makes children crazy. We had the elephant of alcoholism, but it was completely invisible. The way we drank was entirely normal, and the proof of that was that everyone we knew drank that way. It never dawned on me, or any of us, that the people my family knew were chosen *because* they drank that way — anymore than I realized that in choosing Warren° I disguised my own alcoholism.

Even these days, when everyone thinks they know about alcoholism, it still   15
hides. No one imagines that their own drinking is a problem. No one guesses that young people, people whose faces aren't red, whose bodies aren't bloated, who don't stumble and slur, might still be completely controlled by their drinking. Alcohol warps the mind long before it even begins on the body — that's why we love it so. Alcoholism is still invisible, even now.

Even when my father took me to AA meetings I never dreamed I might be an alcoholic. If you had told me that the problems in my life came from my breathing, it would have made as much sense to me as if you said the problems in my life came from my drinking. Alcohol was already controlling me in its

Warren: Cheever's alcoholic ex-husband.

powerful, cunning ways. When there were things I didn't want to face, I took a drink. It worked. If it was the feelings of a woman whose husband I was sleeping with, or his children, or if it was the problem of what to wear to a party, or if it was the politics of *Newsweek* magazine, the cure was the same. I had a glass or two of wine, or a scotch; that was what everyone did. The next morning the things I didn't want to face didn't loom so large. I thought that was part of being a grown-up, and in the world where I was a child, I wasn't wrong.

And somehow, I spent all those years searching, searching for someplace where I did belong, and I finally found it by making my own family, and I couldn't even do that right, but I finally found it anyway. I accept what happened to me as just what happened. My family was aberrant, but aberrant from what? We were who we were, just as my children and I are who we are. Last night I dreamt that I lost my son. I looked around and he wasn't there. This is my worst fear, but even my worst fears are not so bad anymore. I have a kind of jerry-built faith that I've been able to cobble together a little bit at a time. My faith has a Rube Goldberg aspect to it — there are plenty of places where I lift a weight and a marble goes down a chute and hits a lever that activates a cog wheel, which turns a crank.

It seems as though my belief in God should take up more space in this book, but it is intensely private and truly beyond my ability to describe. I don't understand God; I just believe in God. I have faith that there is a benevolent force at large in the universe, and my life has reflected that faith. I have experienced God's grace in abundance, and I am grateful for that. Most of all, though, I don't hope to persuade anyone else to believe in God. Although magazine and newspaper polls show that most Americans believe in God and that most of us pray regularly, this is not true in my community here in New York City. Many people I know think that they are too smart for God, and they are very smart. God is for people who are uneducated, they think, or not too smart, or weak and needy. Maybe they're right. It's not something I argue about; if I did I'd be happy to lose.

Faith in God is hard to maintain these days, but I do feel that it's taken me fifty years to discover what centuries of civilized people already knew, and that we, in our time, somehow forgot. I wouldn't be able to believe in a God I could describe in mere words. I do believe, though, that the answer to life's questions is a faith in something outside of life; belief in God.

My last drink was a glass of white wine, poured and sipped in the floor-through living and dining room of the frame house on Ninety-second Street. Warren was on the telephone. The children were asleep downstairs — Q in his crib, Sarah in the bunk bed. After they slept, I went upstairs, curled up with a book or a magazine, and tried to stay awake until Warren was ready for bed. I couldn't. Instead I drank the white wine, and read until my eyelids drooped, and I went downstairs to bed alone. I didn't even know what the trouble was.

I didn't know I had to stop drinking, and I didn't know I could stop drinking. I didn't know that I had to leave Warren, and I didn't know that I could leave Warren.

20

At night now, when my children Quad and Sarah have gone to bed and I have read for a while, I walk down the hall to turn out the kitchen lights. The dog is curled up on a chair in the living room, and I shoo her off. On the way back to bed, I look into my children's rooms. My daughter is nestled under the covers; my son has thrown off his quilt and is already sprawled across the bed. I take a sweet, deep breath. I watch my children sleeping safely and rejoice.

[1999]

≣ THINKING ABOUT THE TEXT

1. Comment on Cheever's observation that "the entire mood would change. I loved those mood changes even then" (para. 4).

2. As a young girl, is Cheever the victim of her privileged environment? In other words, did the adults in her world prepare the way for her to become a serious drinker?

3. Is drinking part of your family heritage? Of the community you came from? Of the one you are part of now? Can serious drinking be part of one's cultural heritage?

4. Comment on Cheever's final sentence in paragraph 10: "They hanged themselves with their hats on."

5. What do you think Cheever means by her insight that "the drinking was a secret that we kept from ourselves" (para. 12)? Is this common among alcoholics?

≣ MAKING COMPARISONS

1. Are all the narrators in this cluster sufficiently honest?

2. How much does the environment influence these three drinkers?

3. Does anything in these passages suggest that the writers will stop drinking?

≣ WRITING ABOUT ISSUES

1. Write a focused personal narrative about your observations and experiences with excessive drinking.

2. Write an argument that people become alcoholics only in a certain environment.

3. Write an argument that colleges should or should not do more to control drinking on campus.

4. Research the causes of alcoholism, and in a report apply your finding to the Cheever and Knapp selections.

≡ A Journey to War: A Story in the News

TIM O'BRIEN, "The Things They Carried"

IN THE NEWS:
VALERIE SEILING JACOBS, "Packing for the Ineffable"

Throughout history, soldiers have had to defend their native regions against invaders. Just as commonly, armies have journeyed far from home, to wage war in distant countries. And upon arriving there, they have wandered even farther, their sites of battle shifting as they engage their enemy. During these various physical treks, many of them have displayed incredible endurance and bravery. But some have become mentally dislocated, finding themselves on a confusing and unpredictable journey of the mind. This can be especially true when the soldier is barely mature and the war's aim is unclear. Such was the case for many Americans who fought in Vietnam, as Tim O'Brien suggests in his now-classic story "The Things They Carried." Its characters risk becoming psychologically lost as they roam a land strange and dangerous to them, serving missions whose aims are vague. Decades later, Americans sent to fight in Iraq and Afghanistan have often faced similar stress. To help you compare *their* journeys with the ones that O'Brien depicts, we pair his story with a 2007 newspaper column in which the author reflects on the things her stepson carried off to war.

≡ BEFORE YOU READ

What do you associate with the United States' war in Vietnam? List specific details that come to mind. To what extent do the present wars in Iraq and Afghanistan strike you as similar to that one?

TIM O'BRIEN
The Things They Carried

A native of Minnesota, Tim O'Brien (b. 1946) was drafted after he graduated from Macalester College. Subsequently, he served in the Vietnam War, during which he received a Purple Heart. In one way or another, practically all of his fiction deals with the war, although he has been repeatedly ambiguous about how and when his work incorporates his own Vietnam experiences. O'Brien's novels include If I Die in a Combat Zone *(1973),* Going After Cacciato *(which won the National Book Award in 1978),* In the Lake of the Woods *(a 1994 book that touches on the massacre at My Lai),* Tomcat in Love *(1998), and* July *(2002). Originally published in Es-quire* magazine, the following story was reprinted in The Best American Short Stories 1987. *It then appeared along with related stories by O'Brien in a 1990 book also entitled* The Things They Carried.

(Bill Giduz Photo.)

First Lieutenant Jimmy Cross carried letters from a girl named Martha, a junior at Mount Sebastian College in New Jersey. They were not love letters, but Lieutenant Cross was hoping, so he kept them folded in plastic at the bottom of his rucksack. In the late afternoon, after a day's march, he would dig his foxhole, wash his hands under a canteen, unwrap the letters, hold them with the tips of his fingers, and spend the last hour of light pretending. He would imagine romantic camping trips into the White Mountains in New Hampshire. He would sometimes taste the envelope flaps, knowing her tongue had been there. More than anything, he wanted Martha to love him as he loved her, but the letters were mostly chatty, elusive on the matter of love. She was a virgin, he was almost sure. She was an English major at Mount Sebastian, and she wrote beautifully about her professors and roommates and midterm exams, about her respect for Chaucer and her great affection for Virginia Woolf. She often quoted lines of poetry; she never mentioned the war, except to say, Jimmy, take care of yourself. The letters weighed ten ounces. They were signed "Love, Martha," but Lieutenant Cross understood that "Love" was only a way of signing and did not mean what he sometimes pretended it meant. At dusk, he would carefully return the letters to his rucksack. Slowly, a bit distracted, he would get up and move among his men, checking the perimeter, then at full dark he would return to his hole and watch the night and wonder if Martha was a virgin.

The things they carried were largely determined by necessity. Among the necessities or near necessities were P-38 can openers, pocket knives, heat tabs, wrist watches, dog tags, mosquito repellant, chewing gum, candy, cigarettes,

salt tablets, packets of Kool-Aid, lighters, matches, sewing kits, Military Payment Certificates, C rations, and two or three canteens of water. Together, these
items weighed between fifteen and twenty pounds, depending upon a man's
habits or rate of metabolism. Henry Dobbins, who was a big man, carried extra
rations; he was especially fond of canned peaches in heavy syrup over pound
cake. Dave Jensen, who practiced field hygiene, carried a toothbrush, dental
floss, and several hotel-size bars of soap he'd stolen on R&R in Sydney, Australia. Ted Lavender, who was scared, carried tranquilizers until he was shot in the
head outside the village of Than Khe in mid-April. By necessity and because it
was SOP,° they all carried steel helmets that weighed five pounds including the
liner and camouflage cover. They carried the standard fatigue jackets and trousers. Very few carried underwear. On their feet they carried jungle boots — 2.1
pounds — and Dave Jensen carried three pairs of socks and a can of Dr. Scholl's
foot powder as a precaution against trench foot. Until he was shot, Ted Lavender
carried six or seven ounces of premium dope, which for him was a necessity.
Mitchell Sanders, the RTO,° carried condoms. Norman Bowker carried a diary.
Rat Kiley carried comic books. Kiowa, a devout Baptist, carried an illustrated
New Testament that had been presented to him by his father, who taught Sunday school in Oklahoma City, Oklahoma. As a hedge against bad times, however, Kiowa also carried his grandmother's distrust of the white man, his
grandfather's old hunting hatchet. Necessity dictated. Because the land was
mined and booby-trapped, it was SOP for each man to carry a steel-centered,
nylon-covered flak jacket, which weighed 6.7 pounds, but which on hot days
seemed much heavier. Because you could die so quickly, each man carried at
least one large compress bandage, usually in the helmet band for easy access.
Because the nights were cold, and because the monsoons were wet, each carried a green plastic poncho that could be used as a raincoat or ground sheet or
makeshift tent. With its quilted liner, the poncho weighed almost two pounds,
but it was worth every ounce. In April, for instance, when Ted Lavender was
shot, they used his poncho to wrap him up, then to carry him across the paddy,
then to lift him into the chopper that took him away.

They were called legs or grunts.

To carry something was to "hump" it, as when Lieutenant Jimmy Cross
humped his love for Martha up the hills and through the swamps. In its intransitive form, "to hump" meant "to walk," or "to march," but it implied burdens
far beyond the intransitive.

Almost everyone humped photographs. In his wallet, Lieutenant Cross   5
carried two photographs of Martha. The first was a Kodachrome snapshot
signed "Love," though he knew better. She stood against a brick wall. Her eyes
were gray and neutral, her lips slightly open as she stared straight-on at the
camera. At night, sometimes, Lieutenant Cross wondered who had taken the
picture, because he knew she had boyfriends, because he loved her so much,
and because he could see the shadow of the picture taker spreading out against

---

SOP: Standard operating procedure.   **RTO:** Radiotelephone operator.

the brick wall. The second photograph had been clipped from the 1968 Mount Sebastian yearbook. It was an action shot — women's volleyball — and Martha was bent horizontal to the floor, reaching, the palms of her hands in sharp focus, the tongue taut, the expression frank and competitive. There was no visible sweat. She wore white gym shorts. Her legs, he thought, were almost certainly the legs of a virgin, dry and without hair, the left knee cocked and carrying her entire weight, which was just over one hundred pounds. Lieutenant Cross remembered touching that left knee. A dark theater, he remembered, and the movie was *Bonnie and Clyde*, and Martha wore a tweed skirt, and during the final scene, when he touched her knee, she turned and looked at him in a sad, sober way that made him pull his hand back, but he would always remember the feel of the tweed skirt and the knee beneath it and the sound of the gunfire that killed Bonnie and Clyde, how embarrassing it was, how slow and oppressive. He remembered kissing her good night at the dorm door. Right then, he thought, he should've done something brave. He should've carried her up the stairs to her room and tied her to the bed and touched that left knee all night long. He should've risked it. Whenever he looked at the photographs, he thought of new things he should've done.

What they carried was partly a function of rank, partly of field specialty.

As a first lieutenant and platoon leader, Jimmy Cross carried a compass, maps, code books, binoculars, and a .45-caliber pistol that weighed 2.9 pounds fully loaded. He carried a strobe light and the responsibility for the lives of his men.

As an RTO, Mitchell Sanders carried the PRC-25 radio, a killer, twenty-six pounds with its battery.

As a medic, Rat Kiley carried a canvas satchel filled with morphine and plasma and malaria tablets and surgical tape and comic books and all the things a medic must carry, including M&M's for especially bad wounds, for a total weight of nearly twenty pounds.

As a big man, therefore a machine gunner, Henry Dobbins carried the M-60, which weighed twenty-three pounds unloaded, but which was almost always loaded. In addition, Dobbins carried between ten and fifteen pounds of ammunition draped in belts across his chest and shoulders.

10

As PFCs or Spec 4s, most of them were common grunts and carried the standard M-16 gas-operated assault rifle. The weapon weighed 7.5 pounds unloaded, 8.2 pounds with its full twenty-round magazine. Depending on numerous factors, such as topography and psychology, the riflemen carried anywhere from twelve to twenty magazines, usually in cloth bandoliers, adding on another 8.4 pounds at minimum, fourteen pounds at maximum. When it was available, they also carried M-16 maintenance gear — rods and steel brushes and swabs and tubes of LSA on — all of which weighed about a pound. Among the grunts, some carried the M-79 grenade launcher, 5.9 pounds unloaded, a reasonably light weapon except for the ammunition, which was heavy. A single round weighed ten ounces. The typical load was twenty-five rounds. But Ted Lavender, who was scared, carried thirty-four rounds when he was shot and killed outside Than Khe, and he went down under an exceptional burden, more than twenty pounds of ammunition, plus the flak jacket and helmet and rations and water and toilet paper and tranquilizers and all the rest, plus the unweighed fear. He was dead weight. There was no twitching or flopping. Kiowa, who saw it happen, said it was like watching a rock fall, or a big sandbag or something — just boom, then down — not like the movies where the dead guy rolls around and does fancy spins and goes ass over teakettle — not like that, Kiowa said, the poor bastard just flats fuck fell Boom. Down. Nothing else. It was a bright morning in mid-April Lieutenant Cross felt the pain. He blamed himself. They stripped off Lavender's canteens and ammo, all the heavy things, and Rat Kiley said the obvious, the guy's dead, and Mitchell Sanders used his radio to report one U.S. KIA° and to request a chopper. Then they wrapped Lavender in his poncho. They carried him out to a dry paddy, established security, and sat smoking the dead man's dope until the chopper came. Lieutenant Cross kept to himself. He pictured Martha's smooth young face, thinking he loved her more than anything, more than his men, and now Ted Lavender was dead because he loved her so much and could not stop thinking about her. When the dust-off arrived, they carried Lavender aboard. Afterward they burned Than Khe. They marched until dusk, then dug their holes, and that night Kiowa kept explaining how you had to be there, how fast it was, how the poor guy just dropped like so much concrete. Boom-down, he said. Like cement.

In addition to the three standard weapons — the M-60, M-16, and M-79 — they carried whatever presented itself, or whatever seemed appropriate as a means of killing or staying alive. They carried catch-as-catch-can. At various times, in various situations, they carried M-14s and CAR-15s and Swedish Ks and grease guns and captured AK-47s and Chi-Coms and RPGs and Simonov carbines and black-market Uzis and .38-caliber Smith & Wesson handguns and 66 mm LAWs and shotguns and silencers and blackjacks and bayonets and C-4 plastic explosives. Lee Strunk carried a slingshot; a weapon of last resort, he called it. Mitchell Sanders carried brass knuckles. Kiowa carried his grandfather's feathered hatchet. Every third or fourth man carried a Claymore antipersonnel mine — 3.5 pounds with its firing device. They all carried fragmentation grenades — fourteen ounces each. They all carried at least one M-18 colored smoke grenade — twenty-four ounces. Some carried CS or tear-gas grenades. Some carried white-phosphorus grenades. They carried all they could bear, and then some, including a silent awe for the terrible power of the things they carried.

In the first week of April, before Lavender died, Lieutenant Jimmy Cross received a good-luck charm from Martha. It was a simple pebble, an ounce at most. Smooth to the touch, it was a milky-white color with flecks of orange and violet, oval-shaped, like a miniature egg. In the accompanying letter, Martha wrote that she had found the pebble on the Jersey shoreline, precisely where the land touched water at high tide, where things came together but also separated.

KIA: Killed in action.

It was this separate-but-together quality, she wrote, that had inspired her to pick up the pebble and to carry it in her breast pocket for several days, where it seemed weightless, and then to send it through the mail, by air, as a token of her truest feelings for him. Lieutenant Cross found this romantic. But he wondered what her truest feelings were, exactly, and what she meant by separate-but-together. He wondered how the tides and waves had come into play on that afternoon along the Jersey shoreline when Martha saw the pebble and bent down to rescue it from geology. He imagined bare feet. Martha was a poet, with the poet's sensibilities, and her feet would be brown and bare, the toenails unpainted, the eyes chilly and somber like the ocean in March, and though it was painful, he wondered who had been with her that afternoon. He imagined a pair of shadows moving along the strip of sand where things came together but also separated. It was phantom jealousy, he knew, but he couldn't help himself. He loved her so much. On the march, through the hot days of early April, he carried the pebble in his mouth, turning it with his tongue, tasting sea salts and moisture. His mind wandered. He had difficulty keeping his attention on the war. On occasion he would yell at his men to spread out the column, to keep their eyes open, but then he would slip away into daydreams, just pretending, walking barefoot along the Jersey shore, with Martha, carrying nothing. He would feel himself rising. Sun and waves and gentle winds, all love and lightness.

What they carried varied by mission.

When a mission took them to the mountains, they carried mosquito netting, machetes, canvas tarps, and extra bug juice.   15

If a mission seemed especially hazardous, or if it involved a place they knew to be bad, they carried everything they could. In certain heavily mined AOs,° where the land was dense with Toe Poppers and Bouncing Betties, they took turns humping a twenty-eight-pound mine detector. With its headphones and big sensing plate, the equipment was a stress on the lower back and shoulders, awkward to handle, often useless because of the shrapnel in the earth, but they carried it anyway, partly for safety, partly for the illusion of safety.

On ambush, or other night missions, they carried peculiar little odds and ends. Kiowa always took along his New Testament and a pair of moccasins for silence. Dave Jensen carried night-sight vitamins high in carotin. Lee Strunk carried his slingshot; ammo, he claimed, would never be a problem. Rat Kiley carried brandy and M&M's. Until he was shot, Ted Lavender carried the starlight scope, which weighed 6.3 pounds with its aluminum carrying case. Henry Dobbins carried his girlfriend's pantyhose wrapped around his neck as a comforter. They all carried ghosts. When dark came, they would move out single file across the meadows and paddies to their ambush coordinates, where they would quietly set up the Claymores and lie down and spend the night waiting.

Other missions were more complicated and required special equipment. In mid-April, it was their mission to search out and destroy the elaborate tunnel

AOs: Areas of operations.

complexes in the Than Khe area south of Chu Lai. To blow the tunnels, they carried one-pound blocks of pentrite high explosives, four blocks to a man, sixty-eight pounds in all. They carried wiring, detonators, and battery-powered clackers. Dave Jensen carried earplugs. Most often, before blowing the tunnels, they were ordered by higher command to search them, which was considered bad news, but by and large they just shrugged and carried out orders. Because he was a big man, Henry Dobbins was excused from tunnel duty. The others would draw numbers. Before Lavender died there were seventeen men in the platoon, and whoever drew the number seventeen would strip off his gear and crawl in head first with a flashlight and Lieutenant Cross's .45-caliber pistol. The rest of them would fan out as security. They would sit down or kneel, not facing the hole, listening to the ground beneath them, imagining cobwebs and ghosts, whatever was down there — the tunnel walls squeezing in — how the flashlight seemed impossibly heavy in the hand and how it was tunnel vision in the very strictest sense, compression in all ways, even time, and how you had to wiggle in — ass and elbows — a swallowed-up feeling — and how you found yourself worrying about odd things — will your flashlight go dead? Do rats carry rabies? If you screamed, how far would the sound carry? Would your buddies hear it? Would they have the courage to drag you out? In some respects, though not many, the waiting was worse than the tunnel itself. Imagination was a killer.] ~ oh yes it is...

On April 16, when Lee Strunk drew the number seventeen, he laughed and muttered something and went down quickly. The morning was hot and very still. Not good, Kiowa said. He looked at the tunnel opening, then out across a dry paddy toward the village of Than Khe. Nothing moved. No clouds or birds or people. As they waited, the men smoked and drank Kool-Aid, not talking much, feeling sympathy for Lee Strunk but also feeling the luck of the draw. You win some, you lose some, said Mitchell Sanders, and sometimes you settle for a rain check. It was a tired line and no one laughed.

Henry Dobbins ate a tropical chocolate bar. Ted Lavender popped a tran-   20
quilizer and went off to pee.

After five minutes, Lieutenant Jimmy Cross moved to the tunnel, leaned down, and examined the darkness. Trouble, he thought — a cave-in maybe. And then suddenly, without willing it, he was thinking about Martha. The stresses and fractures, the quick collapse, the two of them buried alive under all that weight. Dense, crushing love. Kneeling, watching the hole, he tried to concentrate on Lee Strunk and the war, all the dangers, but his love was too much for him, he felt paralyzed, he wanted to sleep inside her lungs and breathe her blood and be smothered. He wanted her to be a virgin and not a virgin, all at once. He wanted to know her. Intimate secrets — why poetry? Why so sad? Why the grayness in her eyes? Why so alone? Not lonely, just alone — riding her bike across campus or sitting off by herself in the cafeteria. Even dancing, she danced alone — and it was the aloneness that filled him with love. He remembered telling her that one evening. How she nodded and looked away. And how, later, when he kissed her, she received the kiss without returning it, her eyes wide open, not afraid, not a virgin's eyes, just flat and uninvolved.

Lieutenant Cross gazed at the tunnel. But he was not there. He was buried with Martha under the white sand at the Jersey shore. They were pressed together, and the pebble in his mouth was her tongue. He was smiling. Vaguely, he was aware of how quiet the day was, the sullen paddies, yet he could not bring himself to worry about matters of security. He was beyond that. He was just a kid at war, in love. He was twenty-two years old. He couldn't help it.

A few moments later Lee Strunk crawled out of the tunnel. He came up grinning, filthy but alive. Lieutenant Cross nodded and closed his eyes while the others clapped Strunk on the back and made jokes about rising from the dead.

Worms, Rat Kiley said. Right out of the grave. Fuckin' zombie.

The men laughed. They all felt great relief.   25

Spook City, said Mitchell Sanders.

Lee Strunk made a funny ghost sound, a kind of moaning, yet very happy, and right then, when Strunk made that high happy moaning sound, when he went *Ahhooooo*, right then Ted Lavender was shot in the head on his way back from peeing. He lay with his mouth open. The teeth were broken. There was a swollen black bruise under his left eye. The cheekbone was gone. Oh shit, Rat Kiley said, the guy's dead. The guy's dead, he kept saying, which seemed profound—the guy's dead. I mean really.

The things they carried were determined to some extent by superstition. Lieutenant Cross carried his good-luck pebble. Dave Jensen carried a rabbit's foot. Norman Bowker, otherwise a very gentle person, carried a thumb that had been presented to him as a gift by Mitchell Sanders. The thumb was dark brown, rubbery to the touch, and weighed four ounces at most. It had been cut from a VC corpse, a boy of fifteen or sixteen. They'd found him at the bottom of an irrigation ditch, badly burned, flies in his mouth and eyes. The boy wore black shorts and sandals. At the time of his death he had been carrying a pouch of rice, a rifle, and three magazines of ammunition.

You want my opinion, Mitchell Sanders said, there's a definite moral here.

He put his hand on the dead boy's wrist. He was quiet for a time, as if   30
counting a pulse, then he patted the stomach, almost affectionately, and used Kiowa's hunting hatchet to remove the thumb.

Henry Dobbins asked what the moral was.

Moral?

You know. *Moral.*

Sanders wrapped the thumb in toilet paper and handed it across to Norman Bowker. There was no blood. Smiling, he kicked the boy's head, watched the flies scatter, and said, It's like with that old TV show—Paladin. Have gun, will travel.

Henry Dobbins thought about it.   35

Yeah, well, he finally said. I don't see no moral.

There it *is*, man.

Fuck off.

They carried USO stationery and pencils and pens. They carried Sterno, safety pins, trip flares, signal flares, spools of wire, razor blades, chewing tobacco, liberated joss sticks and statuettes of the smiling Buddha, candles, grease pencils, *The Stars and Stripes*, fingernail clippers, Psy Ops° leaflets, bush hats, bolos, and much more. Twice a week, when the resupply choppers came in, they carried hot chow in green Mermite cans and large canvas bags filled with iced beer and soda pop. They carried plastic water containers, each with a two-gallon capacity. Mitchell Sanders carried a set of starched tiger fatigues for special occasions. Henry Dobbins carried Black Flag insecticide. Dave Jensen carried empty sandbags that could be filled at night for added protection. Lee Strunk carried tanning lotion. Some things they carried in common. Taking turns, they carried the big PRC-77 scrambler radio, which weighed thirty pounds with its battery. They shared the weight of memory. They took up what others could no longer bear. Often, they carried each other, the wounded or weak. They carried infections. They carried chess sets, basketballs, Vietnamese-English dictionaries, insignia of rank, Bronze Stars and Purple Hearts, plastic cards imprinted with the Code of Conduct. They carried diseases, among them malaria and dysentery. They carried lice and ringworm and leeches and paddy algae and various rots and molds. They carried the land itself — Vietnam, the place, the soil — a powdery orange-red dust that covered their boots and fatigues and faces. They carried the sky. The whole atmosphere, they carried it, the humidity, the monsoons, the stink of fungus and decay, all of it, they carried gravity. They moved like mules. By daylight they took sniper fire, at night they were mortared, but it was not battle, it was just the endless march, village to village, without purpose, nothing won or lost. They marched for the sake of the march. They plodded along slowly, dumbly, leaning forward against the heat, unthinking, all blood and bone, simple grunts, soldiering with their legs, toiling up the hills and down into the paddies and across the rivers and up again and down, just humping, one step and then the next and then another, but no volition, no will, because it was automatic, it was anatomy, and the war was entirely a matter of posture and carriage, the hump was everything, a kind of inertia, a kind of emptiness, a dullness of desire and intellect and conscience and hope and human sensibility. Their principles were in their feet. Their calculations were biological. They had no sense of strategy or mission. They searched the villages without knowing what to look for, not caring, kicking over jars of rice, frisking children and old men, blowing tunnels, sometimes setting fires and sometimes not, then forming up and moving on to the next village, then other villages, where it would always be the same. They carried their own lives. The pressures were enormous. In the heat of early afternoon, they would remove their helmets and flak jackets, walking bare, which was dangerous but which helped ease the strain. They would often discard things along the route of march. Purely for comfort, they would throw away rations, blow their Claymores and grenades, no matter, because by nightfall the resupply choppers would arrive with more of the same, then a day or two later still more, fresh watermelons and crates of ammunition and sunglasses and woolen sweaters — the resources were stunning — sparklers for the Fourth of July, colored eggs for Easter. It was the great American war chest — the fruits of science, the

Psy Ops: Psychological operations.

smokestacks, the canneries, the arsenals at Hartford, the Minnesota forests, the machine shops, the vast fields of corn and wheat — they carried like freight trains, they carried it on their backs and shoulders — and for all the ambiguities of Vietnam, all the mysteries and unknowns, there was at least the single abiding certainty that they would never be at a loss for things to carry.

After the chopper took Lavender away, Lieutenant Jimmy Cross led his men   40
into the village of Than Khe. They burned everything. They shot chickens and dogs, they trashed the village well, they called in artillery and watched the wreckage, then they marched for several hours through the hot afternoon, and then at dusk, while Kiowa explained how Lavender died, Lieutenant Cross found himself trembling.

He tried not to cry. With his entrenching tool, which weighed five pounds, he began digging a hole in the earth.

He felt shame. He hated himself. He had loved Martha more than his men, and as a consequence Lavender was now dead, and this was something he would have to carry like a stone in his stomach for the rest of the war.

All he could do was dig. He used his entrenching tool like an ax, slashing, feeling both love and hate, and then later, when it was full dark, he sat at the bottom of his foxhole and wept. It went on for a long while. In part, he was grieving for Ted Lavender, but mostly it was for Martha, and for himself, because she belonged to another world, which was not quite real, and because she was a junior at Mount Sebastian College in New Jersey, a poet and a virgin and uninvolved, and because he realized she did not love him and never would.

Like cement, Kiowa whispered in the dark. I swear to God — boom-down. Not a word.

I've heard this, said Norman Bowker.   45

A pisser, you know? Still zipping himself up. Zapped while zipping.

All right, fine. That's enough.

Yeah, but you had to see it, the guy just —

I *heard*, man. Cement. So why not shut the fuck *up?*

Kiowa shook his head sadly and glanced over at the hole where Lieutenant   50
Jimmy Cross sat watching the night. The air was thick and wet. A warm, dense fog had settled over the paddies and there was the stillness that precedes rain.

After a time Kiowa sighed.

One thing for sure, he said. The Lieutenant's in some deep hurt. I mean that crying jag — the way he was carrying on — it wasn't fake or anything, it was real heavy-duty hurt. The man cares.

Sure, Norman Bowker said.

Say what you want, the man does care.

We all got problems.   55

Not Lavender.

No, I guess not, Bowker said. Do me a favor, though.

Shut up?

That's a smart Indian. Shut up.

Shrugging, Kiowa pulled off his boots. He wanted to say more, just to   60
lighten up his sleep, but instead he opened his New Testament and arranged it
beneath his head as a pillow. The fog made things seem hollow and unattached.
He tried not to think about Ted Lavender, but then he was thinking how fast it
was, no drama, down and dead, and how it was hard to feel anything except
surprise. It seemed un-Christian. He wished he could find some great sadness,
or even anger, but the emotion wasn't there and he couldn't make it happen.
Mostly he felt pleased to be alive. He liked the smell of the New Testament under
his cheek, the leather and ink and paper and glue, whatever the chemicals
were. He liked hearing the sounds of night. Even his fatigue, it felt fine, the stiff
muscles and the prickly awareness of his own body, a floating feeling. He enjoyed not being dead. Lying there, Kiowa admired Lieutenant Jimmy Cross's
capacity for grief. He wanted to share the man's pain, he wanted to care as
Jimmy Cross cared. And yet when he closed his eyes, all he could think was
Boom-down, and all he could feel was the pleasure of having his boots off and
the fog curling in around him and the damp soil and the Bible smells and the
plush comfort of night.

After a moment Norman Bowker sat up in the dark.

What the hell, he said. You want to talk, *talk*. Tell it to me.

Forget it.

No, man, go on. One thing I hate, it's a silent Indian.

For the most part they carried themselves with poise, a kind of dignity. Now   65
and then, however, there were times of panic, when they squealed or wanted to
squeal but couldn't, when they twitched and made moaning sounds and covered their heads and said Dear Jesus and flopped around on the earth and fired
their weapons blindly and cringed and sobbed and begged for the noise to stop
and went wild and made stupid promises to themselves and to God and to their
mothers and fathers, hoping not to die. In different ways, it happened to all of
them. Afterward, when the firing ended, they would blink and peek up. They
would touch their bodies, feeling shame, then quickly hiding it. They would
force themselves to stand. As if in slow motion, frame by frame, the world
would take on the old logic — absolute silence, then the wind, then sunlight,
then voices. It was the burden of being alive. Awkwardly, the men would reassemble themselves, first in private, then in groups, becoming soldiers again.
They would repair the leaks in their eyes. They would check for casualties, call
in dust-offs, light cigarettes, try to smile, clear their throats and spit and begin
cleaning their weapons. After a time someone would shake his head and say,
No lie, I almost shit my pants, and someone else would laugh, which meant it
was bad, yes, but the guy had obviously not shit his pants, it wasn't that bad,
and in any case nobody would ever do such a thing and then go ahead and talk
about it. They would squint into the dense, oppressive sunlight. For a few moments, perhaps, they would fall silent, lighting a joint and tracking its passage
from man to man, inhaling, holding in the humiliation. Scary stuff, one of
them might say. But then someone else would grin or flick his eyebrows and
say, Roger-dodger, almost cut me a new asshole, *almost*.

There were numerous such poses. Some carried themselves with a sort of wistful resignation, others with pride or stiff soldierly discipline or good humor or macho zeal. They were afraid of dying but they were even more afraid to show it.

They found jokes to tell.

They used a hard vocabulary to contain the terrible softness. *Greased,* they'd say. *Offed, lit up, zapped while zipping.* It wasn't cruelty, just stage presence. They were actors and the war came at them in 3-D. When someone died, it wasn't quite dying, because in a curious way it seemed scripted, and because they had their lines mostly memorized, irony mixed with tragedy, and because they called it by other names, as if to encyst and destroy the reality of death itself. They kicked corpses. They cut off thumbs. They talked grunt lingo. They told stories about Ted Lavender's supply of tranquilizers, how the poor guy didn't feel a thing, how incredibly tranquil he was.

There's a moral here, said Mitchell Sanders.

They were waiting for Lavender's chopper, smoking the dead man's dope.   70

The moral's pretty obvious, Sanders said, and winked. Stay away from drugs. No joke, they'll ruin your day every time.

Cute, said Henry Dobbins.

Mind-blower, get it? Talk about wiggy — nothing left, just blood and brains. They made themselves laugh.

There it is, they'd say, over and over, as if the repetition itself were an act of   75 poise, a balance between crazy and almost crazy, knowing without going. There it is, which meant be cool, let it ride, because oh yeah, man, you can't change what can't be changed, there it is, there it absolutely and positively and fucking well *is.*

They were tough.

They carried all the emotional baggage of men who might die. Grief, terror, love, longing — these were intangibles, but the intangibles had their own mass and specific gravity, they had tangible weight. They carried shameful memories. They carried the common secret of cowardice barely restrained, the instinct to run or freeze or hide, and in many respects this was the heaviest burden of all, for it could never be put down, it required perfect balance and perfect posture. They carried their reputations. They carried the soldier's greatest fear, which was the fear of blushing. Men killed, and died, because they were embarrassed not to. It was what had brought them to the war in the first place, nothing positive, no dreams of glory or honor, just to avoid the blush of dishonor. They died so as not to die of embarrassment. They crawled into tunnels and walked point and advanced under fire. Each morning, despite the unknowns, they made their legs move. They endured. They kept humping. They did not submit to the obvious alternative, which was simply to close the eyes and fall. So easy, really. Go limp and tumble to the ground and let the muscles unwind and not speak and not budge until your buddies picked you up and lifted you into the chopper that would roar and dip its nose and carry you off to the world. A mere matter of falling, yet no one ever fell. It was not courage, exactly; the object was not valor. Rather, they were too frightened to be cowards.

By and large they carried these things inside, maintaining the masks of composure. They sneered at sick call. They spoke bitterly about guys who had found release by shooting off their own toes or fingers. Pussies, they'd say. Candyasses. It was fierce, mocking talk, with only a trace of envy or awe, but even so, the image played itself out behind their eyes.

They imagined the muzzle against flesh. They imagined the quick, sweet pain, then the evacuation to Japan, then a hospital with warm beds and cute geisha nurses.

They dreamed of freedom birds.   80

At night, on guard, staring into the dark, they were carried away by jumbo jets. They felt the rush of takeoff. *Gone!* they yelled. And then velocity, wings and engines, a smiling stewardess — but it was more than a plane, it was a real bird, a big sleek silver bird with feathers and talons and high screeching. They were flying. The weights fell off, there was nothing to bear. They laughed and held on tight, feeling the cold slap of wind and altitude, soaring, thinking *It's over, I'm gone!* — they were naked, they were light and free — it was all lightness, bright and fast and buoyant, light as light, a helium buzz in the brain, a giddy bubbling in the lungs as they were taken up over the clouds and the war, beyond duty, beyond gravity and mortification and global entanglements — *Sin loi!*° they yelled, *I'm sorry, motherfuckers, but I'm out of it. I'm goofed, I'm on a space cruise, I'm gone!* — and it was a restful, disencumbered sensation, just riding the light waves, sailing that big silver freedom bird over the mountains and oceans, over America, over the farms and great sleeping cities and cemeteries and highways and the golden arches of McDonald's. It was flight, a kind of fleeing, a kind of falling, falling higher and higher, spinning off the edge of the earth and beyond the sun and through the vast, silent vacuum where there were no burdens and where everything weighed exactly nothing. *Gone!* they screamed, *I'm sorry but I'm gone!* And so at night, not quite dreaming, they gave themselves over to lightness, they were carried, they were purely borne.

On the morning after Ted Lavender died, First Lieutenant Jimmy Cross crouched at the bottom of his foxhole and burned Martha's letters. Then he burned the two photographs. There was a steady rain falling, which made it difficult, but he used heat tabs and Sterno to build a small fire, screening it with his body, holding the photographs over the tight blue flame with the tips of his fingers.

He realized it was only a gesture. Stupid, he thought. Sentimental, too, but mostly just stupid.

Lavender was dead. You couldn't burn the blame.

Besides, the letters were in his head. And even now, without photographs,   85
Lieutenant Cross could see Martha playing volleyball in her white gym shorts and yellow T-shirt. He could see her moving in the rain.

When the fire died out, Lieutenant Cross pulled his poncho over his shoulders and ate breakfast from a can.

There was no great mystery, he decided.

Sin loi!: "Sorry about that."

In those burned letters Martha had never mentioned the war, except to say, Jimmy, take care of yourself. She wasn't involved. She signed the letters "Love," but it wasn't love, and all the fine lines and technicalities did not matter.

The morning came up wet and blurry. Everything seemed part of everything else, the fog and Martha and the deepening rain.

It was a war, after all.   90

Half smiling, Lieutenant Jimmy Cross took out his maps. He shook his head hard, as if to clear it, then bent forward and began planning the day's march. In ten minutes, or maybe twenty, he would rouse the men and they would pack up and head west, where the maps showed the country to be green and inviting. They would do what they had always done. The rain might add some weight, but otherwise it would be one more day layered upon all the other days.

He was realistic about it. There was that new hardness in his stomach.

No more fantasies, he told himself.

Henceforth, when he thought about Martha, it would be only to think that she belonged elsewhere. He would shut down the day dreams. This was not Mount Sebastian, it was another world, where there were no pretty poems or midterm exams, a place where men died because of carelessness and gross stupidity. Kiowa was right. Boom-down, and you were dead, never partly dead.

Briefly, in the rain, Lieutenant Cross saw Martha's gray eyes gazing back   95
at him.

He understood.

It was very sad, he thought. The things men carried inside. The things men did or felt they had to do.

He almost nodded at her, but didn't.

Instead he went back to his maps. He was now determined to perform his duties firmly and without negligence. It wouldn't help Lavender, he knew that, but from this point on he would comport himself as a soldier. He would dispose of his good-luck pebble. Swallow it, maybe, or use Lee Strunk's slingshot, or just drop it along the trail. On the march he would impose strict field discipline. He would be careful to send out flank security, to prevent straggling or bunching up, to keep his troops moving at the proper pace and at the proper interval. He would insist on clean weapons. He would confiscate the remainder of Lavender's dope. Later in the day, perhaps, he would call the men together and speak to them plainly. He would accept the blame for what had happened to Ted Lavender. He would be a man about it. He would look them in the eyes, keeping his chin level, and he would issue the new SOPs in a calm, impersonal tone of voice, an officer's voice, leaving no room for argument or discussion. Commencing immediately, he'd tell them, they would no longer abandon equipment along the route of march. They would police up their acts. They would get their shit together, and keep it together, and maintain it neatly and in good working order.

He would not tolerate laxity. He would show strength, distancing himself.   100

Among the men there would be grumbling, of course, and maybe worse, because their days would seem longer and their loads heavier, but Lieutenant

Cross reminded himself that his obligation was not to be loved but to lead. He would dispense with love; it was not now a factor. And if anyone quarreled or complained, he would simply tighten his lips and arrange his shoulders in the correct command posture. He might give a curt little nod. Or he might not. He might just shrug and say Carry on, then they would saddle up and form into a column and move out toward the villages of Than Khe.   *[1986]*

end vs. beginning - very different

■ THINKING ABOUT THE TEXT

1. This story does not depict events in chronological order. Instead, it moves around in time. Why do you think O'Brien structured the story this way?

2. In various places, the narrator refers to things that the men carried. In each of these sections, what *kind* of things does the narrator focus on? Does the order of these sections matter? Why, or why not?

3. What are some significant differences, if any, among the soldiers under Jimmy Cross's command?

4. What is your attitude toward Jimmy Cross's apparent obsession with Martha?

5. Jimmy Cross seems to feel guilty about Ted Lavender's death. To what extent does his feeling seem rational? *Should* he feel guilty, in your view? Why, or why not? In the final two paragraphs, he makes a number of resolutions. Which, if any, do you think that he is capable of keeping?

In the News

The following piece appeared as an op-ed column in the April 11, 2007, issue of the *New York Times*. Its author, Valerie Seiling Jacobs, was a practicing attorney for many years. She has published several essays and is pursuing an M.F.A. degree at Columbia University in New York. She also leads workshops on legal writing. "Packing for the Ineffable" is part of a memoir that she is working on, *Waiting for Greg*, which is about her family's life during her stepson's service in Iraq.

VALERIE SEILING JACOBS
Packing for the Ineffable

I have a photograph of the guns he packed. Apparently, it is true that a rifle is a marine's best friend. Greg will travel, indeed sleep, with his weapons. My husband snapped the photo and e-mailed it from North Carolina, right after he put Greg on the bus that took him to the airstrip where he began his journey to Iraq.

We are 48 hours into a 210-day tour. I write "we," though it is Greg, our 19-year-old son, who will actually serve the time. And I include myself in the equation, although I am not related to Greg by blood, having met and married his father only six years ago.

Each soldier is limited to a knapsack and two sea bags — what civilians would call duffels. Space is tight. Once Greg packed his firearms, there was hardly room for any of the other paraphernalia that might make seven months in Iraq bearable, assuming that such a thing is possible.

I am not there for the send-off, but confident that he made room for his iPod. "I would lose my mind without it," he told me during his last visit home. "What makes you think you won't lose your mind anyway?" I wanted to ask. But that is exactly the kind of thing I can never say.

My husband reports that Greg took a stack of DVDs to play on his laptop,   5 another piece of electronic equipment that he presumably managed to cram into his bags. But I have few details. I do not know, for example, whether he chose comedies or combat films to while away the downtime, if such a thing exists.

And I know precious little about what else he stuffed into his bags. Just as well, I think. It would be all too reminiscent of Tim O'Brien's *The Things They Carried*, a book that I picked up and then put down somewhere around page 10. Right after the nervous guy who carried the tranquilizers took a bullet in the head. Besides, if he doesn't make it, we'll know soon enough what he carried. Don't they send the stuff home?

Sometimes, however, curiosity gets the better of me. And then I wonder if the three items I sent made the cut.

Choosing those articles was tricky. What do you give to a young man who has decided to put himself in harm's way? It must be small, it must be light, and it must be thoughtful. And because I am only his stepmother, it cannot be overly sentimental. Technically speaking, I do not have a place card at this party. I would be wise to tread lightly. So I opt for a prayer, a book, and a journal, which, in a lighter moment, my husband predicts will come home still encased in its shrink wrap. I accept the teasing with good humor, and laugh. That's O.K., as long as Greg doesn't come home wrapped in anything.

At Christmas, Greg casually mentioned that when this is all over, he wants to climb Mount Everest. "Sounds like a good plan," my husband replied. Sounds like another ridiculously dangerous decision.

But I keep quiet, switch lenses, and focus on my stepson's optimism and on   10 his unspoken assumption that he will come home in one piece. Healthy enough to undertake such an arduous expedition. And that premise makes selecting a book easy.

"Great choice," says the cashier at the bookstore, when I plunk down a paperback copy of Jon Krakauer's *Into Thin Air*.°

But Ari, my 17-year-old daughter, is cautious. "Do they all make it?" she asks, examining the book jacket.

"Of course," I answer.

___

Into Thin Air: A 1999 nonfiction best-seller about a disastrous 1996 climbing expedition on Mount Everest in which five people died when a blizzard hit.

But later, I am not so sure. After the book is gift-wrapped, and it's too late to retrieve it from my husband's luggage, I suddenly recall the image of empty oxygen bottles and frozen corpses littering the path to the summit. But then, that little voice in my brain — the one that excuses bad behavior and stupid decisions — begins to rationalize: "Oh, well, better that he knows the risks up front. Besides, it's a page-turner. It will help to kill time in Iraq." Assuming of course, that Iraq doesn't kill him.

The prayer I pick is neither Christian, Jewish, nor Muslim. Perfect for a   15
member of this hodgepodge of a family, a patchwork of people, faiths, and traditions. It is an old Celtic blessing, famous for its entreaty for the safekeeping of a loved one. An ideal choice. If anyone needs to be held in the hollow of God's hand, then it is this sweet boy, who by some combination of fate and ill luck has pulled the short straw. The one that requires him to man the machine gun in the Humvee. Isn't that the most dangerous job? Do they know that he is 6-foot-4? How will he be able to keep his head down? But that is exactly the kind of thing I can never say.

Instead, I type and retype the prayer, playing with the format and font until it is the size of a small card. Tiny enough to fit in a pocket — or hold in a private moment of panic. And then, at the last minute, I decide to laminate the slip of paper. I remember how my children loved that wonder film when they were young. How they coated everything they could lay their hands on. I still carry their shiny library cards in my wallet, tangible proof of their enthusiasm and wobbly beginner signatures. So I dig out the roll of plastic from the closet. This way, it won't get torn. And he can still read the prayer if it gets wet, in case anybody spills anything on it. "Like blood," a scary voice whispers.

By now, Greg is halfway around the world. Most likely in Kuwait, cooling his heels and waiting for transport to the real action. Already, he is lucky not to have been on that helicopter that was shot down by a missile. The one I read about in the morning while I sipped my coffee — and did not mention to my husband.

But my efforts to shield my spouse proved futile. Of course he spotted that headline. How could he miss it? We are now on red alert. No detail about Iraq goes unnoticed. We listen to the evening news like bloodhounds, thirsty for the scent of our beloved son.

"Don't worry," I tell my husband. "Bad news travels on wings. We will know soon enough if there is a problem."

But silently, I worry. What if I am wrong? What if, in our upper-middle-   20
class complacency, we assume the best and suffer the worst? What if the death notification squad arrives late, after we have read the newspaper? How will we bear it? But that is exactly the kind of thing I can never say.

Two hundred and eight days to go.   *[2007]*

■ **THINKING ABOUT THE TEXTS**

1. Jacobs reports that she could read only a little of O'Brien's *The Things They Carried*, a book of interrelated short stories that includes the one

you have just read. What, if anything, about that story might conceivably have helped her cope at home with her stepson's dangerous service in the Middle East?

2. Do any of O'Brien's characters rely on items similar to Greg's iPod and DVD collection (entertainment technology that developed well after the Vietnam War)? Explain.

3. Although Jacobs spends two paragraphs discussing the prayer she sent along with her stepson, she does not actually reveal what it is. Should she have done so? Why, or why not? What, if anything, are significant details that O'Brien withholds from his story?

▤ WRITING ABOUT ISSUES

1. Write an essay analyzing "The Things They Carried" as a depiction of a *psychological* journey. Feel free to concentrate for the most part on just one or two characters. Be sure to make clear what the term *psychological journey* means to you — the specific sorts of changes it involves.

2. Take a word from Jacobs's article, and write an essay in which you explain how it does or does not apply to a specific character in O'Brien's story. Be sure to make clear how Jacobs and you define the term (your definitions might differ). Some possible words of hers include "thoughtful" (para. 8), "sentimental" (para. 8), "ridiculously" (para. 9), "optimism" (para. 10), "rationalize" (para. 14), and "complacency" (para. 20).

3. Write an essay in which you show how a particular book, movie, or television show about war includes at least one physical journey that is not *just* physical. Support your claims with specific details of the work, and be sure to specify the other kind(s) of journey that it depicts. If you wish, refer to one or both of the texts in this cluster.

4. Write an essay about the journey *back* from war taken by a recent combat veteran whom you know or have read about. More specifically, explain how this person's return home and subsequent life need to be placed in a particular context in order to be understood. The assignment might include research, such as reading various general accounts of the conditions that today's veterans face. If you wish, refer to one or both of the texts in this cluster.

Keep This Boy Running: Cultural Contexts for a Story

RALPH ELLISON, "Battle Royal"

CULTURAL CONTEXTS:

BOOKER T. WASHINGTON, "Atlanta Exposition Address (The Atlanta Compromise)"

W. E. B. DU BOIS, "Of Mr. Booker T. Washington"

GUNNAR MYRDAL, "Social Equality"

More than forty years after the civil rights movement of the 1960s, our national awareness of how brutal discrimination was against African Americans is diminished. Although educational and economic equality has not been completely attained, progress has been made, especially in eliminating official policies and gestures of bias. Before World War II, however, overt discrimination was common, especially in the small towns of the segregated South and the rural Midwest. African Americans were rarely allowed to hold anything other than menial jobs in small towns, and most middle-class whites knew African Americans only as maids, gardeners, and servants. African Americans were completely outside the established power structure and rarely able to complain about or obtain justice for their many grievances. Public protest was out of the question. Many African Americans even avoided private protest against their outsider status because they feared that it would worsen their situation. Among African American intellectuals and ordinary citizens, debates raged about which strategy to pursue: to cooperate with the white establishment, hoping to modify hostility, or to agitate for change. Generations of blacks followed the first course until the 1960s, when the nonviolent sit-ins of the civil rights movement ushered in the public protests that ended state-sanctioned segregation. Ralph Ellison's story takes place in the era of segregation and graphically portrays how marginalized African Americans were and how difficult they found it to decide on an effective strategy for progress. At the story's end, the main character, like Ellison himself, begins a lifelong journey from racism toward social justice.

≣ BEFORE YOU READ

Have you ever been in a situation in which you felt discriminated against because of your race, religion, gender, sexual orientation, or age? Did you ever see someone else suffer discrimination? Did you feel powerless? What was your strategy for dealing with this feeling?

(National Archives.)

RALPH ELLISON

Battle Royal

Born in Oklahoma to an activist mother and an intellectual father, Ralph Ellison (1914–1994) was well grounded in literary and social matters by the time he entered Tuskegee Institute to study music in 1933. Finding the conservatism and accommodationism of Tuskegee limiting, Ellison read modernist poets like T. S. Eliot and in 1936 moved to New York, where he met writers Langston Hughes and Richard Wright. Inspired by Wright and by the works of Conrad, Dostoyevsky, and other writers of fiction, Ellison began drafting his novel Invisible Man *(1952) while he was serving in the merchant marine during World War II. Published as a short story in 1947, "Battle Royal" became the first chapter of this National Book Award–winning novel.*

It goes a long way back, some twenty years. All my life I had been looking for something, and everywhere I turned someone tried to tell me what it was. I accepted their answers too, though they were often in contradiction and even self-contradictory. I was naive. I was looking for myself and asking everyone except myself questions which I, and only I, could answer. It took me a long time and much painful boomeranging of my expectations to achieve a realization everyone else appears to have been born with: that I am nobody but myself. But first I had to discover that I am an invisible man!

And yet I am no freak of nature, not of history. I was in the cards, other things having been equal (or unequal) eighty-five years ago. I am not ashamed of my grandparents for having been slaves. I am only ashamed of myself for having at one time been ashamed. About eighty-five years ago they were told that they were free, united with others of our country in everything pertaining to the common good, and, in everything social, separate like the fingers of the hand. And they believed it. They exulted in it. They stayed in their place, worked hard, and brought up my father to do the same. But my grandfather is the one. He was an odd old guy, my grandfather, and I am told I take after him. It was he who caused the trouble. On his deathbed he called my father to him and said, "Son, after I'm gone I want you to keep up the good fight. I never told you, but our life is a war and I have been a traitor all my born days, a spy in the enemy's country ever since I give up my gun back in the Reconstruction. Live with your head in the lion's mouth. I want you to overcome 'em with yeses, undermine 'em with grins, agree 'em to death and destruction, let 'em swoller you till they vomit or bust wide open." They thought the old man had gone out of his mind. He had been the meekest of men. The younger children were rushed from the room, the shades drawn and the flame of the lamp turned so low that it sputtered on the wick like the old man's breathing. "Learn it to the younguns," he whispered fiercely; then he died.

But my folks were more alarmed over his last words than over his dying. It was as though he had not died at all, his words caused so much anxiety. I was warned emphatically to forget what he had said and, indeed, this is the first time it has been mentioned outside the family circle. It had a tremendous effect upon me, however. I could never be sure of what he meant. Grandfather had been a quiet old man who never made any trouble, yet on his deathbed he had called himself a traitor and a spy, and he had spoken of his meekness as a dangerous activity. It became a constant puzzle which lay unanswered in the back of my mind. And whenever things went well for me I remembered my grandfather and felt guilty and uncomfortable. It was as though I was carrying out his advice in spite of myself. And to make it worse, everyone loved me for it. I was praised by the most lily-white men of the town. I was considered an example of desirable conduct — just as my grandfather had been. And what puzzled me was that the old man had defined it as *treachery*. When I was praised for my conduct I felt a guilt that in some way I was doing something that was really against the wishes of the white folks, that if they had understood they would have desired me to act just the opposite, that I should have been sulky and mean, and that that really would have been what they wanted, even though they were fooled and thought they wanted me to act as I did. It made me afraid that some day they would look upon me as a traitor and I would be lost. Still I was more afraid to act any other way because they didn't like that at all. The old man's words were like a curse. On my graduation day I delivered an oration in which I showed that humility was the secret, indeed, the very essence of progress.

(Not that I believed this — how could I, remembering my grandfather? — I only believed that it worked.) It was a great success. Everyone praised me and I was invited to give the speech at a gathering of the town's leading white citizens. It was a triumph for our whole community.

It was in the main ballroom of the leading hotel. When I got there I discovered that it was on the occasion of a smoker, and I was told that since I was to be there anyway I might as well take part in the battle royal to be fought by some of my schoolmates as part of the entertainment. The battle royal came first.

All of the town's big shots were there in their tuxedoes, wolfing down the   5
buffet foods, drinking beer and whiskey and smoking black cigars. It was a large room with a high ceiling. Chairs were arranged in neat rows around three sides of a portable boxing ring. The fourth side was clear, revealing a gleaming space of polished floor. I had some misgivings over the battle royal, by the way. Not from a distaste for fighting, but because I didn't care too much for the other fellows who were to take part. They were tough guys who seemed to have no grandfather's curse worrying their minds. No one could mistake their toughness. And besides, I suspected that fighting a battle royal might detract from the dignity of my speech. In those pre-invisible days I visualized myself as a potential Booker T. Washington. But the other fellows didn't care too much for me either, and there were nine of them. I felt superior to them in my way, and I didn't like the manner in which we were all crowded together into the servants' elevator. Nor did they like my being there. In fact, as the warmly lighted floors flashed past the elevator we had words over the fact that I, by taking part in the fight, had knocked one of their friends out of a night's work.

We were led out of the elevator through a rococo hall into an anteroom and told to get into our fighting togs. Each of us was issued a pair of boxing gloves and ushered out into the big mirrored hall, which we entered looking cautiously about us and whispering, lest we might accidentally be heard above the noise of the room. It was foggy with cigar smoke. And already the whiskey was taking effect. I was shocked to see some of the most important men of the town quite tipsy. They were all there — bankers, lawyers, judges, doctors, fire chiefs, teachers, merchants. Even one of the more fashionable pastors. Something we could not see was going on up front. A clarinet was vibrating sensuously and the men were standing up and moving eagerly forward. We were a small tight group, clustered together, our bare upper bodies touching and shining with anticipatory sweat; while up front the big shots were becoming increasingly excited over something we still could not see. Suddenly I heard the school superintendent, who had told me to come, yell, "Bring up the shines, gentlemen! Bring up the little shines!"

We were rushed up to the front of the ballroom, where it smelled even more strongly of tobacco and whiskey. Then we were pushed into place. I almost wet my pants. A sea of faces, some hostile, some amused, ringed around us, and in the center, facing us, stood a magnificent blonde — stark naked. There was dead silence. I felt a blast of cold air chill me. I tried to back away, but they were behind me and around me. Some of the boys stood with lowered heads, trembling. I felt a wave of irrational guilt and fear. My teeth chattered, my skin turned to goose flesh, my knees knocked. Yet I was strongly attracted and looked in spite of myself. Had the price of looking been blindness, I would have looked. The hair was yellow like that of a circus kewpie doll, the face heavily powdered and rouged, as though to form an abstract mask, the eyes hollow and smeared a cool blue, the color of a baboon's butt. I felt a desire to spit upon her as my eyes brushed slowly over her body. Her breasts were firm and round as the domes of East Indian temples, and I stood so close as to see the fine skin texture and beads of pearly perspiration glistening like dew around the pink and erected buds of her nipples. I wanted at one and the same time to run from the room, to sink through the floor, or go to her and cover her from my eyes and the eyes of the others with my body; to feel the soft thighs, to caress her and destroy her, to love her and murder her, to hide from her, and yet to stroke where below the small American flag tattooed upon her belly her thighs formed a capital V. I had a notion that of all in the room she saw only me with her impersonal eyes.

And then she began to dance, a slow sensuous movement; the smoke of a hundred cigars clinging to her like the thinnest of veils. She seemed like a fair bird-girl girdled in veils calling to me from the angry surface of some gray and threatening sea. I was transported. Then I became aware of the clarinet playing and the big shots yelling at us. Some threatened us if we looked and others if we did not. On my right I saw one boy faint. And now a man grabbed a silver pitcher from a table and stepped close as he dashed ice water upon him and stood him up and forced two of us to support him as his head hung and moans issued from his thick bluish lips. Another boy began to plead to go home. He was the largest of the group, wearing dark red fighting trunks much too small to conceal the erection which projected from him as though in answer to the insinuating low-registered moaning of the clarinet. He tried to hide himself with his boxing gloves.

And all the while the blonde continued dancing, smiling faintly at the big shots who watched her with fascination, and faintly smiling at our fear. I noticed a certain merchant who followed her hungrily, his lips loose and drooling. He was a large man who wore diamond studs in a shirtfront which swelled with the ample paunch underneath, and each time the blonde swayed her undulating hips he ran his hand through the thin hair of his bald head and, with his arms upheld, his posture clumsy like that of an intoxicated panda, wound his belly in a slow and obscene grind. This creature was completely hypnotized. The music had quickened. As the dancer flung herself about with a detached expression on her face, the men began reaching out to touch her. I could see their beefy fingers sink into the soft flesh. Some of the others tried to stop them as she began to move around the floor in graceful circles, as they gave chase, slipping and sliding over the polished floor. It was mad. Chairs went crashing, drinks were spilt, as they ran laughing and howling after her. They caught her just as she reached a door, raised her from the floor, and tossed her as college boys are tossed at a hazing, and above her red, fixed-smiling lips I saw the terror and disgust in her eyes, almost like my own terror and that which I saw in some of the other boys. As I watched, they tossed her twice and her soft breasts seemed to flatten against the air and her legs flung wildly as she spun. Some of the more sober ones helped her to escape. And I started off the floor, heading for the anteroom with the rest of the boys.

Some were still crying in hysteria. But as we tried to leave we were stopped and ordered to get into the ring. There was nothing to do but what we were told. All ten of us climbed under the ropes and allowed ourselves to be blindfolded with broad bands of white cloth. One of the men seemed to feel a bit sympathetic and tried to cheer us up as we stood with our backs against the ropes. Some of us tried to grin. "See that boy over there?" one of the men said. "I want you to run across at the bell and give it to him right in the belly. If you don't get him, I'm going to get you. I don't like his looks." Each of us was told the same. The blindfolds were put on. Yet even then I had been going over my speech. In my mind each word was as bright as flame. I felt the cloth pressed into place, and frowned so that it would be loosened when I relaxed.

But now I felt a sudden fit of blind terror. I was unused to darkness. It was as though I had suddenly found myself in a dark room filled with poisonous cotton-mouths. I could hear the bleary voices yelling insistently for the battle royal to begin.

"Get going in there!"

"Let me at that big nigger!"

I strained to pick up the school superintendent's voice, as though to squeeze some security out of that slightly more familiar sound.

"Let me at those black sonsabitches!" someone yelled.

"No, Jackson, no!" another voice yelled. "Here, somebody, help me hold Jack."

"I want to get at that ginger-colored nigger. Tear him limb from limb," the first voice yelled.

I stood against the ropes trembling. For in those days I was what they called ginger-colored, and he sounded as though he might crunch me between his teeth like a crisp ginger cookie.

Quite a struggle was going on. Chairs were being kicked about and I could hear voices grunting as with a terrific effort. I wanted to see, to see more desperately than ever before. But the blindfold was tight as a thick skin-puckering scab and when I raised my gloved hands to push the layers of white aside a voice yelled, "Oh, no you don't, black bastard! Leave that alone!"

"Ring the bell before Jackson kills him a coon!" someone boomed in the sudden silence. And I heard the bell clang and the sound of the feet scuffling forward.

A glove smacked against my head. I pivoted, striking out stiffly as someone went past, and felt the jar ripple along the length of my arm to my shoulder. Then it seemed as though all nine of the boys had turned upon me at once. Blows pounded me from all sides while I struck out as best I could. So many blows landed upon me that I wondered if I were not the only blindfolded fighter in the ring, or if the man called Jackson hadn't succeeded in getting me after all.

Blindfolded, I could no longer control my motions. I had no dignity. I stumbled about like a baby or a drunken man. The smoke had become thicker and with each new blow it seemed to sear and further restrict my lungs. My saliva became like hot bitter glue. A glove connected with my head, filling my mouth with warm blood. It was everywhere. I could not tell if the moisture I felt upon my body was sweat or blood. A blow landed hard against the nape of my neck. I felt myself going over, my head hitting the floor. Streaks of blue light filled the black world behind the blindfold. I lay prone, pretending that I was knocked out, but felt myself seized by hands and yanked to my feet. "Get going, black boy! Mix it up!" My arms were like lead, my head smarting from blows. I managed to feel my way to the ropes and held on, trying to catch my breath. A glove landed in my mid-section and I went over again, feeling as though the smoke had become a knife jabbed into my guts. Pushed this way and that by the legs milling around me, I finally pulled erect and discovered that I could see the black, sweat-washed forms weaving in the smoky-blue atmosphere like drunken dancers weaving to the rapid drumlike thuds of blows.

Everyone fought hysterically. It was complete anarchy. Everybody fought everybody else. No group fought together for long. Two, three, four, fought one, then turned to fight each other, were themselves attacked. Blows landed below the belt and in the kidney, with the gloves open as well as closed, and with my eye partly opened now there was not so much terror. I moved carefully, avoiding blows, although not too many to attract attention, fighting from group to group. The boys groped about like blind, cautious crabs crouching to protect their mid-sections, their heads pulled in short against their shoulders, their arms stretched nervously before them, with their fists testing the smoke-filled air like the knobbed feelers of hypersensitive snails. In one corner I glimpsed a boy violently punching the air and heard him scream in pain as he smashed his hand against a ring post. For a second I saw him bent over holding his hand, then going down as a blow caught his unprotected head. I played one group against the other, slipping in and throwing a punch then stepping out of range while pushing the others into the melee to take the blows blindly aimed at me. The smoke was agonizing and there were no rounds, no bells at three minute intervals to relieve our exhaustion. The room spun round me, a swirl of lights, smoke, sweating bodies surrounded by tense white faces. I bled from both nose and mouth, the blood spattering upon my chest.

The men kept yelling, "Slug him, black boy! Knock his guts out!"

"Uppercut him! Kill him! Kill that big boy!"   25

Taking a fake fall, I saw a boy going down heavily beside me as though we were felled by a single blow, saw a sneaker-clad foot shoot into his groin as the two who had knocked him down stumbled upon him. I rolled out of range, feeling a twinge of nausea.

The harder we fought the more threatening the men became. And yet, I had begun to worry about my speech again. How would it go? Would they recognize my ability? What would they give me?

I was fighting automatically when suddenly I noticed that one after another of the boys was leaving the ring. I was surprised, filled with panic, as though I had been left alone with an unknown danger. Then I understood. The boys had arranged it among themselves. It was the custom for the two men left in the ring to slug it out for the winner's prize. I discovered this too late. When the bell sounded two men in tuxedoes leaped into the ring and removed the blindfold. I found myself facing Tatlock, the biggest of the gang. I felt sick at my stomach. Hardly had the bell stopped ringing in my ears than it clanged again and I saw him moving swiftly toward me. Thinking of nothing else to do I hit him smash on the nose. He kept coming, bringing the rank sharp violence of stale sweat. His face was a black blank of a face, only his eyes alive — with hate of me and aglow with a feverish terror from what had happened to us all. I became anxious. I wanted to deliver my speech and he came at me as though he meant to beat it out of me. I smashed him again and again, taking his blows as they came. Then on a sudden impulse I struck him lightly and as we clinched, I whispered, "Fake like I knocked you out, you can have the prize."

"I'll break your behind," he whispered hoarsely.

"For *them?*"   30

"For *me*, sonofabitch!"

They were yelling for us to break it up and Tatlock spun me half around with a blow, and as a joggled camera sweeps in a reeling scene, I saw the howling red faces crouching tense beneath the cloud of blue-gray smoke. For a moment the world wavered, unraveled, flowed, then my head cleared and Tatlock bounced before me. That fluttering shadow before my eyes was his jabbing left hand. Then falling forward, my head against his damp shoulder, I whispered,

"I'll make it five dollars more."

"Go to hell!"

But his muscles relaxed a trifle beneath my pressure and I breathed, "Seven?"   35

"Give it to your ma," he said, ripping me beneath the heart.

And while I still held him I butted him and moved away. I felt myself bombarded with punches. I fought back with hopeless desperation. I wanted to deliver my speech more than anything else in the world, because I felt that only these men could judge truly my ability, and now this stupid clown was ruining my chances. I began fighting carefully now, moving in to punch him and out again with my greater speed. A lucky blow to his chin and I had him going too — until I heard a loud voice yell, "I got my money on the big boy."

Hearing this, I almost dropped my guard. I was confused: Should I try to win against the voice out there? Would not this go against my speech, and was not this a moment for humility, for nonresistance? A blow to my head as I danced about sent my right eye popping like a jack-in-the-box and settled my dilemma. The room went red as I fell. It was a dream fall, my body languid and fastidious as to where to land, until the floor became impatient and smashed up to meet me. A moment later I came to. An hypnotic voice said FIVE, emphatically. And I lay there, hazily watching a dark red spot of my own blood shaping itself into a butterfly, glistening and soaking into the soiled gray world of the canvas.

When the voice drawled TEN I was lifted up and dragged to a chair. I sat dazed. My eye pained and swelled with each throb of my pounding heart and I wondered if now I would be allowed to speak, I was wringing wet, my mouth still bleeding. We were grouped along the wall now. The other boys ignored me as they congratulated Tatlock and speculated as to how much they would be paid. One boy whimpered over his smashed hand. Looking up front, I saw attendants in white jackets rolling the portable ring away and placing a small square rug in the vacant space surrounded by chairs. Perhaps, I thought, I will stand on the rug to deliver my speech.

Then the M.C. called to us, "Come on up here boys and get your money." 40
We ran forward to where the men laughed and talked in their chairs, waiting. Everyone seemed friendly now.

"There it is on the rug," the man said. I saw the rug covered with coins of all dimensions and a few crumpled bills. But what excited me, scattered here and there, were the gold pieces.

"Boys, it's all yours," the man said. "You get all you grab."

"That's right, Sambo," a blond man said, winking at me confidentially.

I trembled with excitement, forgetting my pain. I would get the gold and the bills, I thought. I would use both hands. I would throw my body against the boys nearest me to block them from the gold.

"Get down around the rug now," the man commanded, "and don't anyone 45
touch it until I give the signal."

"This ought to be good," I heard.

As told, we got around the square rug on our knees. Slowly the man raised his freckled hand as we followed it upward with our eyes.

I heard, "These niggers look like they're about to pray!"

Then, "Ready," the man said. "Go!"

I lunged for a yellow coin lying on the blue design of the carpet, touching 50
it and sending a surprised shriek to join those rising around me. I tried frantically to remove my hand but could not let go. A hot, violent force tore through my body, shaking me like a wet rat. The rug was electrified. The hair bristled up on my head as I shook myself free. My muscles jumped, my nerves jangled, writhed. But I saw that this was not stopping the other boys. Laughing in fear and embarrassment, some were holding back and scooping up the coins knocked off by the painful contortions of the others. The men roared above us as we struggled.

"Pick it up, goddamnit, pick it up!" someone called like a bass-voiced parrot. "Go on, get it!"

I crawled rapidly around the floor, picking up the coins, trying to avoid the coppers and to get greenbacks and the gold. Ignoring the shock by laughing, as I brushed the coins off quickly, I discovered that I could contain the electricity — a contradiction, but it works. Then the men began to push us onto the rug. Laughing embarrassedly, we struggled out of their hands and kept after the coins. We were all wet and slippery and hard to hold. Suddenly I saw a boy lifted into the air, glistening with sweat like a circus seal, and dropped, his wet back landing flush upon the charged rug, heard him yell and saw him literally dance upon his back, his elbows beating a frenzied tattoo upon the floor, his muscles twitching like the flesh of a horse stung by many flies. When he finally rolled off, his face was gray and no one stopped him when he ran from the floor amid booming laughter.

"Get the money," the M.C. called. "That's good hard American cash!"

And we snatched and grabbed, snatched and grabbed. I was careful not to come too close to the rug now, and when I felt the hot whiskey breath descend upon me like a cloud of foul air I reached out and grabbed the leg of a chair. It was occupied and I held on desperately.

"Leggo, nigger! Leggo!"   55

The huge face wavered down to mine as he tried to push me free. But my body was slippery and he was too drunk. It was Mr. Colcord, who owned a chain of movie houses and "entertainment palaces." Each time he grabbed me I slipped out of his hands. It became a real struggle. I feared the rug more than I did the drunk, so I held on, surprising myself for a moment by trying to topple *him* upon the rug. It was such an enormous idea that I found myself actually carrying it out. I tried not to be obvious, yet when I grabbed his leg, trying to tumble him out of the chair, he raised up roaring with laughter, and, looking at me with soberness dead in the eye, kicked me viciously in the chest. The chair leg flew out of my hand and I felt myself going and rolled. It was as though I had rolled through a bed of hot coals. It seemed a whole century would pass before I would roll free, a century in which I was seared through the deepest levels of my body to the fearful breath within me and the breath seared and heated to the point of explosion. It'll all be over in a flash, I thought as I rolled clear. It'll all be over in a flash.

But not yet, the men on the other side were waiting, red faces swollen as though from apoplexy as they bent forward in their chairs. Seeing their fingers coming toward me I rolled away as a fumbled football rolls off the receiver's fingertips, back into the coals. That time I luckily sent the rug sliding out of place and heard the coins ringing against the floor and the boys scuffling to pick them up and the M.C. calling, "All right, boys, that's all. Go get dressed and get your money."

I was limp as a dish rag. My back felt as though it had been beaten with wires.

When we had dressed the M.C. came in and gave us each five dollars, except Tatlock, who got ten for being last in the ring. Then he told us to leave. I was not to get a chance to deliver my speech, I thought. I was going out into the dim alley in despair when I was stopped and told to go back. I returned to the ballroom, where the men were pushing back their chairs and gathering in groups to talk.

The M.C. knocked on a table for quiet. "Gentlemen," he said, "we almost   60
forgot an important part of the program. A most serious part, gentlemen. This boy was brought here to deliver a speech which he made at his graduation yesterday . . ."

"Bravo!"

"I'm told that he is the smartest boy we've got out there in Greenwood. I'm told that he knows more big words than a pocket-sized dictionary."

Much applause and laughter.

"So now, gentlemen, I want you to give him your attention."

There was still laughter as I faced them, my mouth dry, my eye throbbing. 65
I began slowly, but evidently my throat was tense, because they began shouting, "Louder! Louder!"

"We of the younger generation extol the wisdom of that great leader and
educator," I shouted, "who first spoke these flaming words of wisdom: 'A ship
lost at sea for many days suddenly sighted a friendly vessel. From the mast of
the unfortunate vessel was seen a signal: "Water, water; we die of thirst!" The
answer from the friendly vessel came back: "Cast down your bucket where you
are." The captain of the distressed vessel, at last heeding the injunction, cast
down his bucket, and it came up full of fresh sparkling water from the mouth
of the Amazon River.' And like him I say, and in his words, 'To those of my race
who depend upon bettering their condition in a foreign land, or who underestimate the importance of cultivating friendly relations with the Southern white
man, who is his next-door neighbor, I would say: "Cast down your bucket
where you are" — cast it down in making friends in every manly way of the
people of all races by whom we are surrounded . . .' "

I spoke automatically and with such fervor that I did not realize that the
men were still talking and laughing until my dry mouth, filling up with blood
from the cut, almost strangled me. I coughed, wanting to stop and go to one of
the tall brass, sand-filled spittoons to relieve myself, but a few of the men, especially the superintendent, were listening and I was afraid. So I gulped it down,
blood, saliva, and all, and continued. (What powers of endurance I had during
those days! What enthusiasm! What a belief in the rightness of things!) I spoke
even louder in spite of the pain. But still they talked and still they laughed, as
though deaf with cotton in dirty ears. So I spoke with greater emotional emphasis. I closed my ears and swallowed blood until I was nauseated. The speech
seemed a hundred times as long as before, but I could not leave out a single
word. All had to be said, each memorized nuance considered, rendered. Nor
was that all. Whenever I uttered a word of three or more syllables a group of
voices would yell for me to repeat it. I used the phrase "social responsibility"
and they yelled:

"What's that word you say, boy?"
"Social responsibility," I said.
"What?" 70
"Social . . ."
"Louder."
". . . responsibility."
"More!"
"Respon —" 75
"Repeat!"
"— sibility."

The room filled with the uproar of laughter until, no doubt, distracted by
having to gulp down my blood, I made a mistake and yelled a phrase I had often
seen denounced in newspaper editorials, heard debated in private.

"Social . . ."

"What?" they yelled.   80

". . . equality —"

The laughter hung smokelike in the sudden stillness. I opened my eyes, puzzled. Sounds of displeasure filled the room. The M.C. rushed forward. They shouted hostile phrases at me. But I did not understand.

A small dry mustached man in the front row blared out, "Say that slowly, son!"

"What, sir?"

"What you just said!"   85

"Social responsibility, sir," I said.

"You weren't being smart, were you, boy?" he said, not unkindly.

"No, sir!"

"You sure that about 'equality' was a mistake?"

"Oh, yes, sir," I said. "I was swallowing blood."   90

"Well, you had better speak more slowly so we can understand. We mean to do right by you, but you've got to know your place at all times. All right, now, go on with your speech."

I was afraid. I wanted to leave but I wanted also to speak and I was afraid they'd snatch me down.

"Thank you, sir," I said, beginning where I had left off, and having them ignore me as before.

Yet when I finished there was a thunderous applause. I was surprised to see the superintendent come forth with a package wrapped in white tissue paper, and, gesturing for quiet, address the men.

"Gentlemen, you see that I did not overpraise this boy. He makes a good   95
speech and some day he'll lead his people in the proper paths. And I don't have to tell you that that is important in these days and times. This is a good, smart boy, and so to encourage him in the right direction, in the name of the Board of Education I wish to present him a prize in the form of this . . ."

He paused, removing the tissue paper and revealing a gleaming calfskin brief case.

". . . in the form of this first-class article from Shad Whitmore's shop."

"Boy," he said, addressing me, "take this prize and keep it well. Consider it a badge of office. Prize it. Keep developing as you are and some day it will be filled with important papers that will help shape the destiny of your people."

I was so moved that I could hardly express my thanks. A rope of bloody saliva forming a shape like an undiscovered continent drooled upon the leather and I wiped it quickly away. I felt an importance that I had never dreamed.

"Open it and see what's inside," I was told.   100

My fingers a-tremble, I complied, smelling the fresh leather and finding an official-looking document inside. It was a scholarship to the state college for Negroes. My eyes filled with tears and I ran awkwardly off the floor.

I was overjoyed; I did not even mind when I discovered that the gold pieces I had scrambled for were brass pocket tokens advertising a certain make of automobile.

When I reached home everyone was excited. Next day the neighbors came to congratulate me. I even felt safe from grandfather, whose deathbed curse usually spoiled my triumphs. I stood beneath his photograph with my brief case in hand and smiled triumphantly into his stolid black peasant's face. It was a face that fascinated me. The eyes seemed to follow everywhere I went.

That night I dreamed I was at a circus with him and that he refused to laugh at the clowns no matter what they did. Then later he told me to open my brief case and read what was inside and I did, finding an official envelope stamped with the state seal; and inside the envelope I found another and another, endlessly, and I thought I would fall of weariness. "Them's years," he said. "Now open that one." And I did and in it I found an engraved document containing a short message in letters of gold. "Read it," my grandfather said. "Out loud!"

"To Whom It May Concern," I intoned. "Keep This Nigger-Boy Running."   105

I awoke with the old man's laughter ringing in my ears.

(It was a dream I was to remember and dream again for many years after. But at that time I had no insight into its meaning. First I had to attend college.)   [1947]

■ THINKING ABOUT THE TEXT

1. Some critics have seen the events at the smoker as symbolic or perhaps as an allegory of the plight of African Americans in the segregated South. Pick at least two specific events from the story. How are they meant to explain certain aspects of the African American experience before the civil rights movement of the 1960s?

2. Some readers are surprised by the bizarre and cruel behavior of the town's leaders. Are you? How do you explain what goes on there?

3. How do you interpret the narrator's dream (paras. 104–06)? Why would his grandfather be laughing?

4. Reread paragraphs 1 through 3. How is this opening section connected to the story? To the last paragraph? What might Ellison's narrator mean when he says in paragraph 1 that he is "an invisible man"?

5. The grandfather's deathbed advice in paragraph 2 causes quite a stir. In your own words, what is his advice? Why are his relatives surprised? What might be some alternatives for dealing with oppression? Which "solution" sounds like the one you would have promoted for our society during Ellison's boyhood?

BOOKER T. WASHINGTON
Atlanta Exposition Address (The Atlanta Compromise)

Recognized in his time as the major spokesman for his race, Booker T. Washington (1856–1915) is often seen today as an accommodationist whose insistence on gradual progress and vocational rather than intellectual education played into the hands of the white power structure, delaying racial equality. He founded and served as president of Tuskegee Institute, wrote twelve books (including the autobiographical Up from Slavery in 1901), controlled much of the Negro press, and spoke in cities throughout the nation. His speech at the Atlanta Cotton States and International Exposition in 1895, in which he praised the South, condoned segregation and the glory of "common labor" for his race, and called for harmony and cooperation between the races, is often called "The Atlanta Compromise."

One-third of the population of the South is of the Negro race. No enterprise seeking the material, civil, or moral welfare of this section can disregard this element of our population and reach the highest success. I but convey to you, Mr. President and Directors, the sentiment of the masses of my race when I say that in no way have the value and manhood of the American Negro been more fittingly and generously recognized than by the managers of this magnificent Exposition at every stage of its progress. It is a recognition that will do more to cement the friendship of the two races than any occurrence since the dawn of our freedom.

Not only this, but the opportunity here afforded will awaken among us a new era of industrial progress. Ignorant and inexperienced, it is not strange that in the first years of our new life we began at the top instead of at the bottom; that a seat in Congress or the state legislature was more sought than real estate or industrial skill; that the political convention or stump speaking had more attractions than starting a dairy farm or truck garden.

A ship lost at sea for many days suddenly sighted a friendly vessel. From the mast of the unfortunate vessel was seen a signal, "Water, water; we die of thirst!" The answer from the friendly vessel at once came back, "Cast down your bucket where you are." A second time the signal, "Water, water, send us water!" ran up from the distressed vessel, and was answered, "Cast down your bucket where you are." And a third and fourth signal for water was answered, "Cast down your bucket where you are." The captain of the distressed vessel, at last heeding the injunction, cast down his bucket, and it came up full of fresh, sparkling water from the mouth of the Amazon River. To those of my race who depend on bettering their condition in a foreign land or who underestimate the importance of cultivating friendly relations with the Southern white man, who is their next-door neighbor, I would say: "Cast down your bucket where you are" — cast it down in making friends in every manly way of the people of all races by whom we are surrounded.

Cast it down in agriculture, mechanics, in commerce, in domestic service, and in the professions. And in this connection it is well to bear in mind that whatever other sins the South may be called to bear, when it comes to business, pure and simple, it is in the South that the Negro is given a man's chance in the commercial world, and in nothing is this Exposition more eloquent than in emphasizing this chance. Our greatest danger is that in the great leap from slavery to freedom we may overlook the fact that the masses of us are to live by the productions of our hands, and fail to keep in mind that we shall prosper in proportion as we learn to dignify and glorify common labor and put brains and skill into the common occupations of life; shall prosper in proportion as we learn to draw the line between the superficial and the substantial, the ornamental gewgaws of life and the useful. No race can prosper till it learns that there is as much dignity in tilling a field as in writing a poem. It is at the bottom of life we must begin, and not at the top. Nor should we permit our grievances to overshadow our opportunities.

To those of the white race who look to the incoming of those of foreign   5
birth and strange tongue and habits for the prosperity of the South, were I permitted I would repeat what I say to my own race, "Cast down your bucket where you are." Cast it down among the eight millions of Negroes whose habits you know, whose fidelity and love you have tested in days when to have proved treacherous meant the ruin of your firesides. Cast down your bucket among these people who have, without strikes and labor wars, tilled your fields, cleared your forests, builded your railroads and cities, and brought forth treasures from the bowels of the earth, and helped make possible this magnificent representation of the progress of the South. Casting down your bucket among my people, helping and encouraging them as you are doing on these grounds, and to education of head, hand, and heart, you will find that they will buy your surplus land, make blossom the waste places in your fields, and run your factories. While doing this, you can be sure in the future, as in the past, that you and your families will be surrounded by the most patient, faithful, law-abiding, and unresentful people that the world has seen. As we have proved our loyalty to you in the past, in nursing your children, watching by the sick-bed of your mothers and fathers, and often following them with tear-dimmed eyes to their graves, so in the future, in our humble way, we shall stand by you with a devotion that no foreigner can approach, ready to lay down our lives, if need be, in defense of yours, interlacing our industrial, commercial, civil, and religious life with yours in a way that shall make the interests of both races one. In all things that are purely social we can be as separate as the fingers, yet one as the hand in all things essential to mutual progress.

There is no defense or security for any of us except in the highest intelligence and development of all. If anywhere there are efforts tending to curtail the fullest growth of the Negro, let these efforts be turned into stimulating, encouraging, and making him the most useful and intelligent citizen. Effort or means so invested will pay a thousand per cent interest. These efforts will be twice blessed — "blessing him that gives and him that takes."

There is no escape through law of man or God from the inevitable: —

The laws of changeless justice bind
Oppressor with oppressed;

And close as sin and suffering joined
We march to fate abreast.

Nearly sixteen millions of hands will aid you in pulling the load upward, or they will pull against you the load downward. We shall constitute one-third and more of the ignorance and crime of the South, or one-third its intelligence and progress; we shall contribute one-third to the business and industrial prosperity of the South, or we shall prove a veritable body of death, stagnating, depressing, retarding every effort to advance the body politic.

Gentlemen of the Exposition, as we present to you our humble effort at an exhibition of our progress, you must not expect overmuch. Starting thirty years ago with ownership here and there in a few quilts and pumpkins and chickens (gathered from miscellaneous sources), remember the path that has led from these to the inventions and production of agricultural implements, buggies, steam-engines, newspapers, books, statuary, carving, paintings, the management of drug-stores and banks, has not been trodden without contact with thorns and thistles. While we take pride in what we exhibit as a result of our independent efforts, we do not for a moment forget that our part in this exhibition would fall far short of your expectations but for the constant help that has come to our educational life, not only from the Southern states, but especially from Northern philanthropists who have made their gifts a constant stream of blessing and encouragement.

The wisest among my race understand that the agitation of questions of   10
social equality is the extremest folly, and that progress in the enjoyment of all the privileges that will come to us must be the result of severe and constant struggle rather than of artificial forcing. No race that has anything to contribute to the markets of the world is long in any degree ostracized. It is important and right that all privileges of the law be ours, but it is vastly more important that we be prepared for the exercises of these privileges. The opportunity to earn a dollar in a factory just now is worth infinitely more than the opportunity to spend a dollar in an opera-house.

In conclusion, may I repeat that nothing in thirty years has given us more hope and encouragement, and drawn us so near to you of the white race, as this opportunity offered by the Exposition; and here bending, as it were, over the altar that represents the results of the struggles of your race and mine, both starting practically empty-handed three decades ago, I pledge that in your effort to work out the great and intricate problem which God has laid at the doors of the South, you shall have at all times the patient, sympathetic help of my race; only let this be constantly in mind, that, while from representations in these buildings of the product of field, of forest, of mine, of factory, letters, and art, much good will come, yet far above and beyond material benefits will be that higher good, that, let us pray God, will come, in a blotting out of sectional differences and racial animosities and suspicions, in a determination to administer absolute justice, in a willing obedience among all classes to the mandates of law. This, this, coupled with our material prosperity, will bring into our beloved South a new heaven and a new earth.   [1895]

■ **THINKING ABOUT THE TEXT**

1. Cite two passages from Washington's speech that would probably have had an impact on the African American characters in "Battle Royal."

2. Do you think Washington is right in saying, "No race can prosper till it learns that there is as much dignity in tilling a field as in writing a poem" (para. 4)?

3. Are you surprised that Washington pledges "the patient, sympathetic help of my race" as those whites in power "work out the great and intricate problem which God has laid at the doors of the South" (para. 11)? What might contemporary black leaders think of this attitude?

W. E. B. DU BOIS
Of Mr. Booker T. Washington

W. E. B. Du Bois (1868–1963) was a driving force in the movement for equality for people of color in America and throughout the world well into his nineties. He was born in Massachusetts soon after the Civil War, and his death in Africa coincided with the March on Washington in 1963. Du Bois was educated at Fisk, Berlin, and Harvard universities, receiving a Ph.D. from Harvard in 1895 for his dissertation on the history of the slave trade. He is best known for his work with the National Association for the Advancement of Colored People (NAACP), serving as editor of The Crisis *from 1910 to 1932. As a scholar, writer, and intellectual, Du Bois openly opposed policies such as those supported by Booker T. Washington that kept social, political, and educational opportunities from most African Americans.* The Souls of Black Folk *(1903), from which our reading is taken, is perhaps the most influential of his many writings.*

Easily the most striking thing in the history of the American Negro since 1876 is the ascendancy of Mr. Booker T. Washington. It began at the time when war memories and ideals were rapidly passing; a day of astonishing commercial development was dawning; a sense of doubt and hesitation overtook the freedmen's sons, — then it was that his leading began. Mr. Washington came, with a simple definite programme, at the psychological moment when the nation was a little ashamed of having bestowed so much sentiment on Negroes, and was concentrating its energies on Dollars. His programme of industrial education, conciliation of the South, and submission and silence as to civil and political rights, was not wholly original; the Free Negroes from 1830 up to wartime had striven to build industrial schools, and the American Missionary Association had from the first taught various trades; and Price° and others had sought a way of honorable alliance with the best of the Southerners. But

Price: Joseph C. Price (1854–1893), founder of Zion Wesley College and Livingstone College, was a prominent African American educator and championed liberal-arts education.

Mr. Washington first indissolubly linked these things; he put enthusiasm, un-limited energy, and perfect faith into this programme, and changed it from a by-path into a veritable Way of Life. And the tale of the methods by which he did this is a fascinating study of human life.

It startled the nation to hear a Negro advocating such a programme after many decades of bitter complaint; it startled and won the applause of the South, it interested and won the admiration of the North; and after a confused murmur of protest, it silenced if it did not convert the Negroes themselves.

To gain the sympathy and cooperation of the various elements comprising the white South was Mr. Washington's first task; and this, at the time Tuskegee was founded, seemed, for a black man, well-nigh impossible. And yet ten years later it was done in the word spoken at Atlanta: "In all things purely social we can be as separate as the five fingers, and yet one as the hand in all things essential to mutual progress." This "Atlanta Compromise" is by all odds the most notable thing in Mr. Washington's career. The South interpreted it in different ways: the radicals received it as a complete surrender of the demand for civil and political equality; the conservatives, as a generously conceived working basis for mutual understanding. So both approved it, and today its author is certainly the most distinguished Southerner since Jefferson Davis, and the one with the largest personal following. . . .

Mr. Washington represents in Negro thought the old attitude of adjust-ment and submission; but adjustment at such a peculiar time as to make his programme unique. This is an age of unusual economic development, and Mr. Washington's programme naturally takes an economic cast, becoming a gospel of Work and Money to such an extent as apparently almost completely to over-shadow the higher aims of life. Moreover, this is an age when the more advanced races are coming in closer contact with the less developed races, and the race-feeling is therefore intensified; and Mr. Washington's programme practically accepts the alleged inferiority of the Negro races. Again, in our own land, the reaction from the sentiment of war time has given impetus to race-prejudice against Negroes, and Mr. Washington withdraws many of the high demands of Negroes as men and American citizens. In other periods of intensi-fied prejudice all the Negro's tendency to self-assertion has been called forth; at this period a policy of submission is advocated. In the history of nearly all other races and people the doctrine preached at such crises has been that manly self-respect is worth more than lands and houses, and that a people who volun-tarily surrender such respect, or cease striving for it, are not worth civilizing.

In answer to this, it has been claimed that the Negro can survive only   5 through submission. Mr. Washington distinctly asks that black people give up, at least for the present, three things —

First, political power,

Second, insistence on civil rights,

Third, higher education of Negro youth, —

and concentrate all their energies on industrial education, the accumulation of wealth, and the conciliation of the South. This policy has been courageously and insistently advocated for over fifteen years, and has been triumphant for perhaps ten years. As a result of this tender of the palm-branch, what has been the return? In these years there have occurred:

1. The disfranchisement of the Negro.
2. The legal creation of a distinct status of civil inferiority for the Negro.
3. The steady withdrawal of aid from institutions for the higher training of the Negro.

These movements are not, to be sure, direct results of Mr. Washington's teachings; but his propaganda has, without a shadow of doubt, helped their speedier accomplishment. The question then comes: Is it possible, and probable, that nine millions of men can make effective progress in economic lines if they are deprived of political rights, made a servile caste, and allowed only the most meager chance for developing their exceptional men? If history and reason give any distinct answer to these questions, it is an emphatic *No*. . . .

In failing thus to state plainly and unequivocally the legitimate demands of their people, even at the cost of opposing an honored leader the thinking classes of American Negroes would shirk a heavy responsibility, — a responsibility to themselves, a responsibility to struggling masses, a responsibility to the darker races of men whose future depends so largely on this American experiment, but especially a responsibility to this nation, — this common Fatherland. It is wrong to encourage a man or a people in evil-doing; it is wrong to aid and abet a national crime simply because it is unpopular not to do so. The growing spirit of kindliness and reconciliation between the North and South after the frightful differences of a generation ago ought to be a source of deep congratulation to all, and especially to those whose mistreatment caused the war; but if that reconciliation is to be marked by the industrial slavery and civic death of those same black men, with permanent legislation into a position of inferiority, then those black men, if they are really men, are called upon by every consideration of patriotism and loyalty to oppose such a course by all civilized methods, even though such opposition involves disagreement with Mr. Booker T. Washington. We have no right to sit silently by while the inevitable seeds are sown for a harvest of disaster to our children, black and white.

First, it is the duty of black men to judge the South discriminatingly. The present generation of Southerners are not responsible for the past, and they should not be blindly hated or blamed for it. Furthermore, to no class is the indiscriminate endorsement of the recent course of the South toward Negroes more nauseating than to the best thought of the South. The South is not "solid"; it is a land in the ferment of social change, wherein forces of all kinds are fighting for supremacy; and to praise the ill the South is today perpetrating is just as wrong as to condemn the good. Discriminating and broad-minded criticism is what the South needs, — needs it for the sake of her own white sons and daughters, and for the insurance of robust, healthy mental and moral development.

Today even the attitude of the Southern whites toward the blacks is not, as so many assume, in all cases the same; the ignorant Southerner hates the

Negro, the workingmen fear his competition, the money-makers wish to use him as a laborer, some of the educated see a menace in his upward development, while others, — usually the sons of the masters — wish to help him to rise. National opinion has enabled this last class to maintain the Negro common schools, and to protect the Negro partially in property, life, and limb. Through the pressure of the money-makers, the Negro is in danger of being reduced to semi-slavery, especially in the country districts; the workingmen, and those of the educated who fear the Negro, have united to disfranchise him, and some have urged his deportation; while the passions of the ignorant are easily aroused to lynch and abuse any black man. To praise this intricate whirl of thought and prejudice is nonsense, to inveigh indiscriminately against "the South" is unjust; but to use the same breath in praising Governor Aycock, exposing Senator Morgan, arguing with Mr. Thomas Nelson Page, and denouncing Senator Ben Tillman, is not only sane, but the imperative duty of thinking black men.

It would be unjust to Mr. Washington not to acknowledge that in several   10
instances he has opposed movements in the South which were unjust to the Negro; he sent memorials to the Louisiana and Alabama constitutional conventions, he has spoken against lynching, and in other ways has openly or silently set his influence against sinister schemes and unfortunate happenings. Notwithstanding this, it is equally true to assert that on the whole the distinct impression left by Mr. Washington's propaganda is, first, that the South is justified in its present attitude toward the Negro because of the Negro's degradation; secondly, that the prime cause of the Negro's failure to rise more quickly is his wrong education in the past; and, thirdly, that his future rise depends primarily on his own efforts. Each of these propositions is a dangerous half-truth. The supplementary truths must never be lost sight of: first, slavery and race-prejudice are potent if not sufficient causes of the Negro's position; second, industrial and common-school training were necessarily slow in planting because they had to await the black teachers trained by higher institutions, — it being extremely doubtful if any essentially different development was possible, and certainly a Tuskegee was unthinkable before 1880; and, third, while it is a great truth to say that the Negro must strive and strive mightily to help himself, it is equally true that unless his striving be not simply seconded, but rather aroused and encouraged, by the initiative of the richer and wiser environing group, he cannot hope for great success.

In his failure to realize and impress this last point, Mr. Washington is especially to be criticized. His doctrine has tended to make the whites, North and South, shift the burden of the Negro problem to the Negro's shoulders and stand aside as critical and rather pessimistic spectators; when in fact the burden belongs to the nation, and the hands of none of us are clean if we bend not our energies to righting these great wrongs.

The South ought to be led, by candid and honest criticism, to assert her better self and do her full duty to the race she has cruelly wronged and is still wronging. The North — her copartner in guilt — cannot salve her conscience by plastering it with gold. We cannot settle this problem by diplomacy and suaveness, by "policy" alone. If worse come to worst, can the moral fiber of this country survive the slow throttling and murder of nine millions of men?

The black men of America have a duty to perform, a duty stern and delicate, — a forward movement to oppose a part of the work of their greatest leader. So far as Mr. Washington preaches Thrift, Patience, and Industrial Training for the masses, we must hold up his hands and strive with him, rejoicing in his honors and glorying in the strength of this Joshua called of God and of man to lead the headless host. But so far as Mr. Washington apologizes for injustice, North or South, does not rightly value the privilege and duty of voting, belittles the emasculating effects of caste distinctions, and opposes the higher training and ambition of our brighter minds, — so far as he, the South, or the Nation, does this, — we must unceasingly and firmly oppose them. By every civilized and peaceful method we must strive for the rights which the world accords to men, clinging unwaveringly to those great words which the sons of the Fathers would fain forget: "We hold these truths to be self-evident: that all men are created equal; that they are endowed by their Creator with certain unalienable rights; that among these are life, liberty, and the pursuit of happiness."   [1903]

■ THINKING ABOUT THE TEXT

1. Du Bois is clearly upset with Washington. What is his main objection to the Atlanta Compromise? Do you agree with him?

2. Is the narrator of "Battle Royal" still under Washington's influence, or has the thinking of Du Bois made some inroads?

3. What might the grandfather in "Battle Royal" think of Du Bois's last paragraph?

GUNNAR MYRDAL

Social Equality

A Swedish economist who with his wife, Alva Myrdal (winner of the 1982 Nobel Peace Prize), established a model social-welfare system for Sweden in the 1930s, Gunnar Myrdal (1898–1987) was asked by the Carnegie Foundation in 1938 to study racism in the United States. "Social Equality" is an excerpt from the book that elaborated on the results of his study, An American Dilemma: The Negro Problem and Modern Democracy *(1944). In* Cultural Contexts for Ralph Ellison's "Invisible Man," *historian Eric Sundquist points out that for the white men in "Battle Royal," the term social equality would have included sexual relations and marriage between black men and white women, which was then an important cultural taboo.*

In his first encounter with the American Negro problem, perhaps nothing perplexes the outside observer more than the popular term and the popular theory of "no social equality." He will be made to feel from the start that it has concrete implications and a central importance for the Negro problem in America. But, nevertheless, the term is kept vague and elusive, and the theory loose and ambiguous. One moment it will be stretched to cover and justify every form of social segregation and discrimination, and, in addition, all the inequalities in justice, politics, and breadwinning. The next moment it will be narrowed to express only the denial of close personal intimacies and intermarriage. The very lack of precision allows the notion of "no social equality" to rationalize the rather illogical and wavering system of color caste in America.

The kernel of the popular theory of "no social equality" will, when pursued, be presented as a firm determination on the part of the whites to block amalgamation and preserve "the purity of the white race." The white man identifies himself with "the white race" and feels that he has a stake in resisting the dissipation of its racial identity. Important in this identification is the notion of "the absolute and unchangeable superiority of the white race." From this racial dogma will often be drawn the *direct* inference that the white man shall dominate in all spheres. But when the logic of this inference is inquired about, the inference will be made *indirect* and will be made to lead over to the danger of amalgamation, or, as it is popularly expressed, "intermarriage."

It is further found that the ban on intermarriage is focused on white women. For them it covers both formal marriage and illicit intercourse. In regard to white men it is taken more or less for granted that they would not stoop to marry Negro women, and that illicit intercourse does not fall under the same intense taboo. Their offspring, under the popular doctrine that maternity is more certain than paternity, become Negroes anyway, and the white race easily avoids pollution with Negro blood. To prevent "intermarriage" in this specific sense of sex relations between white women and Negro men, it is not enough to apply legal and social sanctions against it — so the popular theory runs. In using the danger of intermarriage as a defense for the whole caste system, it is assumed both that Negro men have a strong desire for "intermarriage," and that white women would be open to proposals from Negro men, *if* they are not guarded from even meeting them on an equal plane. The latter assumption, of course, is never openly expressed, but is logically implicit in the popular theory. The conclusion follows that the whole system of segregation and discrimination is justified. Every single measure is defended as necessary to block "social equality" which in its turn is held necessary to prevent "intermarriage."

The basic role of the fear of amalgamation in white attitudes to the race problem is indicated by the popular magical concept of "blood." Educated white Southerners, who know everything about modern genetic and biological research, confess readily that they actually feel an irrational or "instinctive" repugnance in thinking of "intermarriage." These measures of segregation and discrimination are often of the type found in the true taboos, and in the notion "not to be touched" of primitive religion. The specific taboos are characterized, further, by a different degree of excitement which attends their violation and a different degree of punishment to the violator: the closer the act to sexual association, the more furious is the public reaction. Sexual association itself is punished by death and is accompanied by tremendous public excitement; the other social relations meet decreasing degrees of public fury. Sex becomes in this popular theory the principle around which the whole structure of segregation of the Negroes — down to disfranchisement and denial of equal opportunities on the labor market — is organized. The reasoning is this: "For, say what we will, may not all the equalities be ultimately based on potential social equality, and that in turn on intermarriage? Here we reach the real *crux* of the question." In cruder language, but with the same logic, the Southern man on the street responds to any plea for social equality: "Would you like to have your daughter marry a Negro?"

This theory of color caste centering around the aversion to amalgamation   5
determines, as we have just observed, the white man's rather definite rank order of the various measures of segregation and discrimination against Negroes. The relative significance attached to each of those measures is dependent upon their degree of expediency or necessity — in the view of white people — as means of upholding the ban on "intermarriage." In this rank order, (1) the ban on intermarriage and other sex relations involving white women and colored men takes precedence before everything else. It is the end for which the other restrictions are arranged as means. Thereafter follow: (2) all sorts of taboos and etiquettes in personal contacts; (3) segregation in schools and churches; (4) segregation in hotels, restaurants, and theaters, and other public places where people meet socially; (5) segregation in public conveyances; (6) discrimination in public services; and, finally, inequality in (7) politics, (8) justice, and (9) breadwinning and relief.

The degree of liberalism on racial matters in the white South can be designated mainly by the point on this rank order where a man stops because he believes further segregation and discrimination are not necessary to prevent "intermarriage." We have seen that white liberals in the South of the present day, as a matter of principle, rather unanimously stand up against inequality in breadwinning, relief, justice, and politics. These fields of discrimination form the chief battleground and considerable changes in them are, as we have seen, on the way. When we ascend to the higher ranks which concern social relations in the narrow sense, we find the Southern liberals less prepared to split off from the majority opinion of the region. Hardly anybody in the South is prepared to go the whole way and argue that even the ban on intermarriage should be lifted. Practically all agree, not only upon the high desirability of preventing "intermarriage," but also that a certain amount of separation between the two groups is expedient and necessary to prevent it. Even the one who has his philosophical doubts on the point must, if he is reasonable, abstain from ever voicing them. The social pressure is so strong that it would be foolish not to conform. Conformity is a political necessity for having any hope of influence; it is, in addition, a personal necessity for not meeting social ostracism. . . .

The fixation on the purity of white womanhood, and also part of the intensity of emotion surrounding the whole sphere of segregation and discrimination, are to be understood as the backwashes of the sore conscience on the part of white men for their own or their compeers' relations with, or desires for, Negro women. These psychological effects are greatly magnified because of the puritan *milieu* of America and especially of the South. The upper class men in a less puritanical people could probably have indulged in sex relations with, and sexual day-dreams of, lower caste women in a more matter-of-course way and without generating so much pathos about white womanhood. The Negro people have to carry the burden not only of the white men's sins but also of their virtues. The virtues of the honest, democratic, puritan white Americans in the South are great, and the burden upon the Negroes becomes ponderous.

Our practical conclusion is that it would have cleansing effects on race relations in America, and particularly in the South, to have an open and sober discussion in rational terms of this ever present popular theory of "intermarriage" and "social equality," giving matters their factual ground, true proportions and logical relations. Because it is, to a great extent, an opportunistic rationalization, and because it refers directly and indirectly to the most touchy spots in American life and American morals, tremendous inhibitions have been built up against a detached and critical discussion of this theory. But such inhibitions are gradually overcome when, in the course of secularized education, people become rational about their life problems. It must never be forgotten that in our increasingly intellectualized civilization even the plain citizen feels an urge for truth and objectivity, and that this rationalistic urge is increasingly competing with the opportunistic demands for rationalization and escape.

There are reasons to believe that a slow but steady cleansing of the American mind is proceeding as the cultural level is raised. The basic racial inferiority doctrine is being undermined by research and education. For a white man to have illicit relations with Negro women is increasingly meeting disapproval. Negroes themselves are more and more frowning upon such relations. This all must tend to dampen the emotional fires around "social equality." Sex and race fears are, however, even today the main defense for segregation and, in fact, for the whole caste order. The question shot at the interviewer touching any point of this order is still: "Would you like to have your daughter (sister) marry a Negro?"   *[1944]*

≡ **THINKING ABOUT THE TEXT**

1. Look back at the smoker section in "Battle Royal," especially when the narrator during his speech says "social equality" instead of "social responsibility." Why do you think there was a "sudden stillness" in the room?

2. Based on his ideas about white sexual fears, how might Myrdal read the part of the smoker dealing with the naked dancer?

3. Myrdal writes that "conformity is a political necessity for having any hope of influence; it is, in addition, a personal necessity for not meeting social ostracism" (para. 6). Does this insight help your understanding of the world of the smoker?

■ WRITING ABOUT ISSUES

1. Argue that the episode at the smoker is or is not evidence that the grand-father's advice in "Battle Royal" to " 'overcome 'em with yeses, undermine 'em with grins, agree 'em to death and destruction' " (para. 2) will not work.

2. Analyze the arguments of Washington and Du Bois in terms of the claims they both make, the assumptions they base their claims on, the evidence they use as support for their assumptions, and the effectiveness of their claims with the intended audience. Which writer do you find more persuasive?

3. Write a personal narrative detailing an experience either when you were the victim of bias because of your race, sex, age, religion, ethnicity, sexual preference, or any other personal dynamic or when you were part of a group that held biased views. Be specific about what happened, how you felt then, how you feel now, and what you learned from the experience.

≡ Journeys to a Dark Future: Stories

RAY BRADBURY, "Mars Is Heaven!"

OCTAVIA BUTLER, "Bloodchild"

URSULA K. LE GUIN, "The Ones Who Walk Away from Omelas"

KURT VONNEGUT, "Harrison Bergeron"

Ever since H. G. Wells and through the golden age of Ray Bradbury, Isaac Asimov, Robert Heinlein, and Kurt Vonnegut to recent masters like William Gibson and Philip K. Dick, literary science fiction has been used to make serious and critical observations about society. Aldous Huxley in his famous *Brave New World* (1932), for example, was fearful of government's power to control all aspects of our lives, even determining at birth who would collect garbage and who would be future bureaucrats. Indeed, the depiction of Big Brother in George Orwell's *1984* (1948) is still a chilling image of governing authority taken to the extreme.

Much of science fiction uses satire's technique of exaggerating a contemporary concern and transporting it to the future. Because of this, most science fiction is seen as a warning. If this trend continues, it cautions, this is where we might end up. And here science fiction joins with another popular genre — the utopian vision. A utopia is an ideal society, a kind of earthly paradise. Famous examples are Plato's *Republic* and the book that coined the term, Thomas More's *Utopia*. Often initiated by idealism, historical attempts to create perfect societies, such as the French and Russian revolutions, have turned repressive and authoritarian. Perhaps this is why science fiction, like the four stories here, more often than not depict the flip side of utopia — a fictional dystopian world. Ray Bradbury's story creates a seemingly idealized vision of childhood memories, but the illusion has serious consequences. In Octavia Butler's chilling allegory, humans in the future are involved in an eerie parasitic union. And although Ursula K. Le Guin and Kurt Vonnegut plunge us into future dystopias, their real focus is our own culture and its dangerous inclinations.

≡ BEFORE YOU READ

What would be some features of your perfect utopian world? What are some aspects of our present culture that could develop into a future dystopian society?

RAY BRADBURY
Mars Is Heaven!

Ray Bradbury (b. 1920), perhaps the most well-known American science fiction writer, was born in Waukegan, Illinois, a beloved town often represented in his fiction as a comforting metaphor for safety, especially in his dangerous fictional dystopias. Although he did not go to college, Bradbury was well read. His professional career began in 1941 with the publication of "Pendulum" in Super Science Stories. *In 1945, his first collection of stories,* Dark Carnival, *appeared. His reputation as a literary science fiction writer was assured in 1950 with the publication of* The Martian Chronicles. *This masterpiece uses a fictional attempt to colonize Mars to comment on American society and its racial, political, and psychological struggles in the 1950s.* Fahrenheit 451 *(1953), another widely praised novel, is set in a dystopic future where books are burned by a totalitarian regime. His best work is characterized by a vivid imagination and the psychological complexity and depth of his characters. He has won numerous awards, including the Nebula Grand Master Award in 1989. The haunting story printed here, from* The Martian Chronicles, *builds its suspense from a masterful blend of hope and suspicion. We want the nostalgic and sentimental vision of the astronauts to be true, but we wisely fear the worst.*

The ship came down from space. It came from the stars and the black velocities, and the shining movements, and the silent gulfs of space. It was a new ship; it had fire in its body and men in its metal cells, and it moved with a clean silence, fiery and warm. In it were seventeen men, including a captain. The crowd at the Ohio field had shouted and waved their hands up into the sunlight, and the rocket had bloomed out great flowers of heat and color and run away into space on the *third* voyage to Mars!

Now it was decelerating with metal efficiency in the upper Martian atmospheres. It was still a thing of beauty and strength. It had moved in the midnight waters of space like a pale sea leviathan; it had passed the ancient moon and thrown itself onward into one nothingness following another. The men within it had been battered, thrown about, sickened, made well again, each in his turn. One man had died, but now the remaining sixteen, with their eyes clear in their heads and their faces pressed to the thick glass ports, watched Mars swing up under them.

"Mars! Mars! Good old Mars, here we are!" cried Navigator Lustig.

"Good old Mars!" said Samuel Hinkston, archaeologist.

"Well," said Captain John Black.   5

The ship landed softly on a lawn of green grass. Outside, upon the lawn, stood an iron deer. Further up the lawn, a tall brown Victorian house sat in the quiet sunlight, all covered with scrolls and rococo, its windows made of blue and pink and yellow and green colored glass. Upon the porch were hairy geraniums and an old swing which was hooked into the porch ceiling and which now swung back and forth, back and forth, in a little breeze. At the top of the house was a cupola with diamond, leaded-glass windows, and a dunce-cap roof! Through the front window you could see an ancient piano with yellow keys and a piece of music titled *Beautiful Ohio* sitting on the music rest.

Around the rocket in four directions spread the little town, green and motionless in the Martian spring. There were white houses and red brick ones, and tall elm trees blowing in the wind, and tall maples and horse chestnuts. And church steeples with golden bells silent in them.

The men in the rocket looked out and saw this. Then they looked at one another and then they looked out again. They held on to each other's elbows, suddenly unable to breathe, it seemed. Their faces grew pale and they blinked constantly, running from glass port to glass port of the ship.

"I'll be damned," whispered Lustig, rubbing his face with his numb fingers, his eyes wet. "I'll be damned, damned, damned."

"It can't be, it just can't be," said Samuel Hinkston.   10

"Lord," said Captain John Black.

There was a call from the chemist. "Sir, the atmosphere is fine for breathing, sir."

Black turned slowly. "Are you sure?"

"No doubt of it, sir."

"Then we'll go out," said Lustig.   15

"Lord, yes," said Samuel Hinkston.

"Hold on," said Captain John Black. "Just a moment. Nobody gave any orders."

"But, sir —"

"Sir, nothing. How do we know what this is?"

"We know what it is, sir," said the chemist. "It's a small town with good air   20
in it, sir."

"And it's a small town the like of Earth towns," said Samuel Hinkston, the archaeologist. "Incredible. It can't be, but it is."

Captain John Black looked at him, idly. "Do you think that the civilizations of two planets can progress at the same rate and evolve in the same way, Hinkston?"

"I wouldn't have thought so, sir."

Captain Black stood by the port. "Look out there. The geraniums. A specialized plant. That specific variety has only been known on Earth for fifty years. Think of the thousands of years of time it takes to evolve plants. Then tell me if it is logical that the Martians should have: one, leaded glass windows; two, cupolas; three, porch swings; four, an instrument that looks like a piano and probably is a piano; and, five, if you look closely, if a Martian composer would have published a piece of music titled, strangely enough, *Beautiful Ohio*. All of which means that we have an Ohio River here on Mars!"

"It is quite strange, sir."   25

"Strange, hell, it's absolutely impossible, and I suspect the whole bloody shooting setup. Something's wrong here, and I'm not leaving the ship until I know what it is."

"Oh, sir," said Lustig.

"Darn it," said Samuel Hinkston. "Sir, I want to investigate this at first hand. It may be that there are similar patterns of thought, movement, civilization on *every* planet in our system. We may be on the threshold of the great psychological and metaphysical discovery in our time, sir, don't you think?"

"I'm willing to wait a moment," said Captain John Black.

"It may be, sir, that we are looking upon a phenomenon that, for the first time, would absolutely prove the existence of a God, sir." 30

"There are many people who are of good faith without such proof, Mr. Hinkston."

"I'm one myself, sir. But certainly a thing like this, out there," said Hinkston, "could not occur without divine intervention, sir. It fills me with such terror and elation I don't know whether to laugh or cry, sir."

"Do neither, then, until we know what we're up against."

"Up against, sir?" inquired Lustig. "I see that we're up against nothing. It's a good quiet, green town, much like the one I was born in, and I like the looks of it."

"When were you born, Lustig?" 35

"In 1910, sir."

"That makes you fifty years old, now, doesn't it?"

"This being 1960, yes, sir."

"And you, Hinkston?"

"1920, sir. In Illinois. And this looks swell to me, sir." 40

"This couldn't be Heaven," said the captain, ironically. "Though, I must admit, it looks peaceful and cool, and pretty much like Green Bluff, where I was born, in 1915." He looked at the chemist. "The air's all right, is it?"

"Yes, sir."

"Well, then, tell you what we'll do. Lustig, you and Hinkston and I will fetch ourselves out to look this town over. The other 14 men will stay aboard ship. If anything untoward happens, lift the ship and get the hell out, do you hear what I say, Craner?"

"Yes, sir. The hell out we'll go, sir. Leaving *you?*"

"A loss of three men's better than a whole ship. If something bad happens 45 get back to Earth and warn the next Rocket, that's Lingle's Rocket, I think, which will be completed and ready to take off some time around next Christmas, what he has to meet up with. If there's something hostile about Mars we certainly want the next expedition to be well armed."

"So are we, sir. We've got a regular arsenal with us."

"Tell the men to stand by the guns, then, as Lustig and Hinkston and I go out."

"Right, sir."

"Come along, Lustig, Hinkston."

The three men walked together, down through the levels of the ship. 50

It was a beautiful spring day. A robin sat on a blossoming apple tree and sang continuously. Showers of petal snow sifted down when the wind touched the apple tree, and the blossom smell drifted upon the air. Somewhere in the town, somebody was playing the piano and the music came and went, came and went, softly, drowsily. The song was *Beautiful Dreamer.* Somewhere else, a phonograph, scratchy and faded, was hissing out a record of *Roamin' in the Gloamin'*, sung by Harry Lauder.

The three men stood outside the ship. The port closed behind them. At every window, a face pressed, looking out. The large metal guns pointed this way and that, ready.

Now the phonograph record being played was:

"Oh give me a June night
The moonlight and you — "

Lustig began to tremble. Samuel Hinkston did likewise.

Hinkston's voice was so feeble and uneven that the captain had to ask him   55
to repeat what he had said. "I said, sir, that I think I have solved this, all of this, sir!"

"And what is the solution, Hinkston?"

The soft wind blew. The sky was serene and quiet and somewhere a stream of water ran through the cool caverns and tree-shadings of a ravine. Somewhere a horse and wagon trotted and rolled by, bumping.

"Sir, it must be, it has to be, this is the *only* solution! Rocket travel began to Mars in the years before the first World War, sir!"

The captain stared at his archaeologist. "No!"

"But, yes, sir! You must admit, look at all of this! How else to explain it, the   60
houses, the lawns, the iron deer, the flowers, the pianos, the music!"

"Hinkston, Hinkston, oh," and the captain put his hand to his face, shaking his head, his hand shaking now, his lips blue.

"Sir, listen to me." Hinkston took his elbow persuasively and looked up into the captain's face, pleading. "Say that there were some people in the year 1905, perhaps, who hated wars and wanted to get away from Earth and they got together, some scientists, in secret, and built a rocket and came out here to Mars."

"No, no, Hinkston."

"Why not? The world was a different place in 1905, they could have kept it a secret much more easily."

"But the work, Hinkston, the work of building a complex thing like a   65
rocket, oh, no, no." The captain looked at his shoes, looked at his hands, looked at the houses, and then at Hinkston.

"And they came up here, and naturally the houses they built were similar to Earth houses because they brought the cultural architecture with them, and here it is!"

"And they've lived here all these years?" said the captain.

"In peace and quiet, sir, yes. Maybe they made a few trips, to bring enough people here for one small town, and then stopped, for fear of being discovered. That's why the town seems so old-fashioned. I don't see a thing, myself, that is older than the year 1927, do you?"

"No frankly, I don't, Hinkston."

"These are *our* people, sir. This is an American city; it's definitely not   70
European!"

"That — that's right, too, Hinkston."

"Or maybe, just maybe, sir, rocket travel is older than we think. Perhaps it
started in some part of the world hundreds of years ago, was discovered and
kept secret by a small number of men, and they came to Mars, with only occasional visits to Earth over the centuries."

"You make it sound almost reasonable."

"It is, sir. It has to be. We have the proof here before us, all we have to do
now, is find some people and verify it!"

"You're right there, of course. We can't just stand here and talk. Did you   75
bring your gun?"

"Yes, but we won't need it."

"We'll see about it. Come along, we'll ring that doorbell and see if anyone
is home."

Their boots were deadened of all sound in the thick green grass. It smelled
from a fresh mowing. In spite of himself, Captain John Black felt a great peace
come over him. It had been thirty years since he had been in a small town, and
the buzzing of spring bees on the air lulled and quieted him, and the fresh look
of things was a balm to the soul.

Hollow echoes sounded from under the boards as they walked across the porch
and stood before the screen door. Inside, they could see a bead curtain hung
across the hall entry, and a crystal chandelier and a Maxfield Parrish painting
framed on one wall over a comfortable Morris Chair. The house smelled old,
and of the attic, and infinitely comfortable. You could hear the tinkle of ice rattling in a lemonade pitcher. In a distant kitchen, because of the heat of the day,
someone was preparing a soft, lemon drink.

Captain John Black rang the bell.   80

Footsteps, dainty and thin, came along the hall and a kind faced lady of
some forty years, dressed in the sort of dress you might expect in the year 1909,
peered out at them.

"Can I help you?" she asked.

"Beg your pardon," said Captain Black, uncertainly. "But we're looking for,
that is, could you help us, I mean." He stopped. She looked out at him with dark
wondering eyes.

"If you're selling something," she said, "I'm much too busy and I haven't
time." She turned to go.

"No, *wait*," he cried, bewilderedly. "What town is this?"   85

She looked him up and down as if he were crazy. "What do you mean, what
town is it? How could you be in a town and not know what town it was?"

The captain looked as if he wanted to go sit under a shady apple tree. "I beg
your pardon," he said. "But we're strangers here. We're from Earth, and we
want to know how this town got here and you got here."

"Are you census takers?" she asked.

"No," he said.

"What do you want then?" she demanded.   90

"Well," said the captain.

"Well?" she asked.

"How long has this town been here?" he wondered.

"It was built in 1868," she snapped at them. "Is this a game?"

"No, not a game," cried the captain. "Oh, God," he said. "Look here. We're   95
from Earth!"

"From *where?*" she said.

"From Earth!" he said.

"Where's that?" she said.

"From Earth," he cried.

"Out of the ground, do you mean?"   100

"No, from the planet Earth!" he almost shouted. "Here," he insisted, "come
out on the porch and I'll show you."

"No," she said. "I won't come out there, you are all evidently quite mad
from the sun."

Lustig and Hinkston stood behind the captain. Hinkston now spoke up.
"Mrs.," he said. "We came in a flying ship across space, among the stars. We
came from the third planet from the sun, Earth, to this planet, which is Mars.
Now do you understand, Mrs.?"

"Mad from the sun," she said, taking hold of the door. "Go away now, before I call my husband who's upstairs taking a nap, and he'll beat you all with
his fists."

"But — " said Hinkston. "This is Mars, is it not?"   105

"This," explained the woman, as if she were addressing a child, "is Green
Lake, Wisconsin, on the continent of America, surrounded by the Pacific and
Atlantic Oceans, on a place called the world, or sometimes, the Earth. Go away
now. Good-bye!"

She slammed the door.

The three men stood before the door with their hands up in the air toward
it, as if pleading with her to open it once more.

They looked at one another.

"Let's knock the door down," said Lustig.   110

"We can't," sighed the captain.

"Why not?"

"She didn't do anything bad, did she? We're the strangers here. This is private property. Good God, Hinkston!" He went and sat down on the porchstep.

"What, sir?"

"Did it ever strike you, that maybe we got ourselves, somehow, some way,   115
fouled up. And, by accident, came back and landed on Earth!"

"Oh, sir, oh, sir, oh oh, sir." And Hinkston sat down numbly and thought
about it.

Lustig stood up in the sunlight. "How could we have done that?"

"I don't know, just let me think."

Hinkston said, "But we checked every mile of the way, and we saw Mars and our chronometers said so many miles gone, and we went past the moon and out into space and here we are, on Mars. I'm sure we're on Mars, sir."

Lustig said, "But, suppose, just suppose that, by accident, in space, in time, 120 or something, we landed on a planet in space, in another time. Suppose this is Earth, thirty or fifty years ago? Maybe we got lost in the dimensions, do you think?"

"Oh, go away, Lustig."

"Are the men in the ship keeping an eye on us, Hinkston?"

"At their guns, sir."

Lustig went to the door, rang the bell. When the door opened again, he asked, "What year is this?"

"1926, of course!" cried the woman, furiously, and slammed the door 125 again.

"Did you hear that?" Lustig ran back to them, wildly. "She said 1926! We *have* gone back in time! This *is* Earth!"

Lustig sat down and the three men let the wonder and terror of the thought afflict them. Their hands stirred fitfully on their knees. The wind blew, nodding the locks of hair on their heads.

The captain stood up, brushing off his pants. "I never thought it would be like this. It scares the hell out of me. How can a thing like this happen?"

"Will anybody in the whole town believe us?" wondered Hinkston. "Are we playing around with something dangerous? Time, I mean. Shouldn't we just take off and go home?"

"No. We'll try another house." 130

They walked three houses down to a little white cottage under an oak tree. "I like to be as logical as I can get," said the captain. He nodded at the town. "How does this sound to you, Hinkston? Suppose, as you said originally, that rocket travel occurred years ago. And when the Earth people had lived here a number of years they began to get homesick for Earth. First a mild neurosis about it, then a full fledged psychosis. Then, threatened insanity. What would you do, as a psychiatrist, if faced with such a problem?"

Hinkston thought. "Well, I think I'd re-arrange the civilization on Mars so it resembled Earth more and more each day. If there was any way of reproducing every plant, every road and every lake, and even an ocean, I would do so. Then I would, by some vast crowd hypnosis, theoretically anyway, convince everyone in a town this size that this really *was* Earth, not Mars at all."

"Good enough, Hinkston. I think we're on the right track now. That woman in that house back there, just *thinks* she's living on Earth. It protects her sanity. She and all the others in this town are the patients of the greatest experiment in migration and hypnosis you will ever lay your eyes on in your life."

"That's it, sir!" cried Lustig.

"Well," the captain sighed. "Now we're getting somewhere. I feel better. It 135 all sounds a bit more logical now. This talk about time and going back and forth and traveling in time turns my stomach upside down. But, *this* way—" He actually smiled for the first time in a month. "Well. It looks as if we'll be fairly welcome here."

"Or, will we, sir?" said Lustig. "After all, like the Pilgrims, these people came here to escape Earth. Maybe they won't be too happy to see us, sir. Maybe they'll try to drive us out or kill us?"

"We have superior weapons if that should happen. Anyway, all we can do is try. This next house now. Up we go."

But they had hardly crossed the lawn when Lustig stopped and looked off across the town, down the quiet, dreaming afternoon street. "Sir," he said.

"What is it, Lustig?" asked the captain.

"Oh, sir, *sir*, what I see, what I do see now before me, oh, oh — " said Lustig,   140
and he began to cry. His fingers came up, twisting and trembling, and his face was all wonder and joy and incredulity. He sounded as if any moment he might go quite insane with happiness. He looked down the street and he began to run, stumbling, awkwardly, falling, picking himself up, and running on. "Oh, God, God, thank you, God! Thank you!"

"Don't let him get away!" The captain broke into a run.

Now Lustig was running at full speed, shouting. He turned into a yard half way down the little shady side street and leaped up upon the porch of a large green house with an iron rooster on the roof.

He was beating upon the door, shouting and hollering and crying when Hinkston and the captain ran up and stood in the yard.

The door opened. Lustig yanked the screen wide and in a high wail of discovery and happiness, cried out, "Grandma! Grandpa!"

Two old people stood in the doorway, their faces lighting up.   145

"Albert!" Their voices piped and they rushed out to embrace and pat him on the back and move around him. "Albert, oh, Albert, it's been so many years! How you've grown, boy, how big you are, boy, oh, Albert boy, how are you!"

"Grandma, Grandpa!" sobbed Albert Lustig. "Good to see you! You look fine, fine! Oh, fine!" He held them, turned them, kissed them, hugged them, cried on them, held them out again, blinked at the little old people. The sun was in the sky, the wind blew, the grass was green, the screen door stood open.

"Come in, lad, come in, there's lemonade for you, fresh, lots of it!"

"Grandma, Grandpa, good to see you! I've got friends down here! Here!" Lustig turned and waved wildly at the captain and Hinkston, who, all during the adventure on the porch, had stood in the shade of a tree, holding onto each other. "Captain, captain, come up, come up, I want you to meet my grandfolks!"

"Howdy," said the folks. "Any friend of Albert's is ours, too! Don't stand   150
there with your mouths open! Come on!"

In the living room of the old house it was cool and a grandfather clock ticked high and long and bronzed in one corner. There were soft pillows on large couches and walls filled with books and a rug cut in a thick rose pattern and antimacassars pinned to furniture, and lemonade in the hand, sweating, and cool on the thirsty tongue.

"Here's to our health." Grandma tipped her glass to her porcelain teeth.

"How long have you *been* here, Grandma?" said Lustig.

"A good many years," she said, tartly. "Ever since we died."

"Ever since you what?" asked Captain John Black, putting his drink down. 155
"Oh, yes," Lustig looked at his captain. "They've been dead thirty years."

"And you *sit* there, calmly!" cried the captain.

"Tush," said the old woman, and winked glitteringly at John Black. "Who are we to question what happens? Here we are. What's life, anyways? Who does what for why and where? All we know is here we are, alive again, and no questions asked. A second chance." She toddled over and held out her thin wrist to Captain John Black. "Feel." He felt. "Solid, ain't I?" she asked. He nodded. "You hear my voice don't you?" she inquired. Yes, he did. "Well, then," she said in triumph, "why go around questioning?"

"Well," said the captain, "it's simply that we never thought we'd find a thing like this on Mars."

"And now you've found it. I dare say there's lots on every planet that'll 160
show you God's infinite ways."

"Is this Heaven?" asked Hinkston.

"Nonsense, no. It's a world and we get a second chance. Nobody told us why. But then nobody told us why we were on Earth, either. That *other* Earth, I mean. The one you came from. How do we know there wasn't *another* before *that* one?"

"A good question," said the captain.

The captain stood up and slapped his hand on his leg in an off-hand fashion. "We've got to be going. It's been nice. Thank you for the drinks."

He stopped. He turned and looked toward the door, startled. 165

Far away, in the sunlight, there was a sound of voices, a crowd, a shouting and a great hello.

"What's that?" asked Hinkston.

"We'll soon find out!" And Captain John Black was out the front door abruptly, jolting across the green lawn and into the street of the Martian town.

He stood looking at the ship. The ports were open and his crew were streaming out, waving their hands. A crowd of people had gathered and in and through and among these people the members of the crew were running, talking, laughing, shaking hands. People did little dances. People swarmed. The rocket lay empty and abandoned.

A brass band exploded in the sunlight, flinging off a gay tune from up- 170
raised tubas and trumpets. There was a bang of drums and a shrill of fifes. Little girls with golden hair jumped up and down. Little boys shouted, "Hooray!" And fat men passed around ten-cent cigars. The mayor of the town made a speech. Then, each member of the crew with a mother on one arm, a father or sister on the other, was spirited off down the street, into little cottages or big mansions and doors slammed shut.

The wind rose in the clear spring sky and all was silent. The brass band had banged off around a corner leaving the rocket to shine and dazzle alone in the sunlight.

"Abandoned!" cried the captain. "Abandoned the ship, they did! I'll have their skins, by God! They had orders!"

"Sir," said Lustig. "Don't be too hard on them. Those were all old relatives and friends."

"That's no excuse!"

"Think how they felt, captain, seeing familiar faces outside the ship!"   175

"I would have obeyed orders! I would have—" The captain's mouth remained open.

Striding along the sidewalk under the Martian sun, tall, smiling, eyes blue, face tan, came a young man of some twenty-six years.

"John!" the man cried, and broke into a run.

"What?" said Captain John Black. He swayed.

"John, you old beggar, you!"   180

The man ran up and gripped his hand and slapped him on the back.

"It's you," said John Black.

"Of course, who'd you *think* it was!"

"Edward!" The captain appealed now to Lustig and Hinkston, holding the stranger's hand. "This is my brother Edward. Ed, meet my men, Lustig, Hinkston! My brother!"

They tugged at each other's hands and arms and then finally embraced.   185
"Ed!" "John, you old bum, you!" "You're looking fine, Ed, but, Ed, what is this? You haven't changed over the years. You died, I remember, when you were twenty-six, and I was nineteen, oh God, so many years ago, and here you are, and, Lord, what goes on, what goes on?"

Edward Black gave him a brotherly knock on the chin. "Mom's waiting," he said.

"Mom?"

"And Dad, too."

"And Dad?" The captain almost fell to earth as if hit upon the chest with a mighty weapon. He walked stiffly and awkwardly, out of coordination. He stuttered and whispered and talked only one or two words at a time. "Mom alive? Dad? Where?"

"At the old house on Oak Knoll Avenue."   190

"The old house." The captain stared in delighted amazement. "Did you *hear* that, Lustig, Hinkston?"

"I know it's hard for you to believe."

"But alive. Real."

"Don't I *feel* real?" The strong aim, the firm grip, the white smile. The light, curling hair.

Hinkston was gone. He had seen his own house down the street and was   195
running for it. Lustig was grinning. "Now you understand, sir, what happened to everybody on the ship. They couldn't help themselves."

"Yes. Yes," said the captain, eyes shut. "Yes." He put out his hand. "When I open my eyes, you'll be gone." He opened his eyes. "You're still here. God, Edward, you look fine!"

"Come along, lunch is waiting for you. I told Mom."

Lustig said, "Sir, I'll be with my grandfolks if you want me."

"What? Oh, fine, Lustig. Later, then."

Edward grabbed his arm and marched him. "You need support." 200

"I do. My knees, all funny. My stomach, loose. God."

"There's the house. Remember it?"

"Remember it? Hell! I can beat you to the front porch!"

They ran. The wind roared over Captain John Black's ears. The earth roared under his feet. He saw the golden figure of Edward Black pull ahead of him in the amazing dream of reality. He saw the house rush forward, the door open, the screen swing back. "Beat you!" cried Edward, bounding up the steps. "I'm an old man," panted the captain, "and you're still young. But, then, you *always* beat me, I remember!"

In the doorway, Mom, pink and plump and bright. And behind her, pepper 205 grey, Dad, with his pipe in his hand.

"Mom, Dad!"

He ran up the steps like a child, to meet them.

It was a fine long afternoon. They finished lunch and they sat in the living room and he told them all about his rocket and his being captain and they nodded and smiled upon him and Mother was just the same, and Dad bit the end off a cigar and lighted it in his old fashion. Mom brought in some iced tea in the middle of the afternoon. Then, there was a big turkey dinner at night and time flowing on. When the drumsticks were sucked clean and lay brittle upon the plates, the captain leaned back in his chair and exhaled his deep contentment. Dad poured him a small glass of dry sherry. It was seven-thirty in the evening. Night was in all the trees and coloring the sky, and the lamps were halos of dim light in the gentle house. From all the other houses down the streets came sounds of music, pianos playing, laughter.

Mom put a record on the victrola and she and Captain John Black had a dance. She was wearing the same perfume he remembered from the summer when she and Dad had been killed in the train accident. She was very real in his arms as they danced lightly to the music.

"I'll wake in the morning," said the captain. "And I'll be in my rocket in 210 space, and all this will be gone."

"No, no, don't think that," she cried, softly, pleadingly. "We're here. Don't question. God is good to us. Let's be happy."

The record ended with a circular hissing.

"You're tired, son," said Dad. He waved his pipe. "You and Ed go on upstairs. Your old bedroom is waiting for you."

"The old one?"

"The brass bed and all," laughed Edward. 215

"But I should report my men in."

"Why?" Mother was logical.

"Why? Well, I don't know. No reason, I guess. No, none at all. What's the difference?" He shook his head. "I'm not being very logical these days."

"Good night, son." She kissed his cheek.

"'Night, Mom." 220

"Sleep tight, son." Dad shook his hand.

"Same to you, Pop."

"It's good to have you home."

"It's good to *be* home."

He left the land of cigar smoke and perfume and books and gentle light 225
and ascended the stairs, talking, talking with Edward. Edward pushed a door
open and there was the yellow brass bed and the old semaphore banners from
college days and a very musty raccoon coat which he petted with strange,
muted affection. "It's too much," he said faintly. "Like being in a thunder
shower without an umbrella. I'm soaked to the skin with emotion. I'm numb.
I'm tired."

"A night's sleep between cool clean sheets for you, my bucko." Edward
slapped wide the snowy linens and flounced the pillows. Then he put up a window and let the night blooming jasmine float in. There was moonlight and the
sound of distant dancing and whispering.

"So this is Mars," said the captain undressing.

"So this is Mars," Edward undressed in idle, leisurely moves, drawing his
shirt off over his head, revealing golden shoulders and the good muscular neck.

The lights were out, they were into bed, side by side, as in the days, how
many decades ago? The captain lolled and was nourished by the night wind
pushing the lace curtains out upon the dark room air. Among the trees, upon
a lawn, someone had cranked up a portable phonograph and now it was playing softly. "I'll be loving you, always, with a love that's true, always."

The thought of Anna came to his mind. "Is Anna here?" 230

His brother, lying straight out in the moonlight from the window, waited
and then said, "Yes. She's out of town. But she'll be here in the morning."

The captain shut his eyes. "I want to see Anna very much."

The room was square and quiet except for their breathing. "Good
night, Ed."

A pause. "Good night, John."

He lay peacefully, letting his thoughts float. For the first time the stress of 235
the day was moved aside, all of the excitement was calmed. He could think
logically now. It had all been emotion. The bands playing, the sight of familiar
faces, the sick pounding of your heart. But — now . . .

How? He thought. How was all this made? And why? For what purpose?
Out of the goodness of some kind God? Was God, then, really that fine and
thoughtful of his children? How and why and what for?

He thought of the various theories advanced in the first heat of the afternoon by Hinkston and Lustig. He let all kinds of new theories drop in lazy
pebbles down through his mind, as through a dark water, now, turning, throwing out dull flashes of white light. Mars. Earth. Mom. Dad. Edward. Mars.
Martians.

Who had lived here a thousand years ago on Mars? Martians? Or had this
always been like this? Martians. He repeated the word quietly, inwardly.

He laughed out loud, almost. He had the most ridiculous theory, all of a sudden. It gave him a kind of chilled feeling. It was really nothing to think of, of course. Highly improbable. Silly. Forget it. Ridiculous.

But, he thought, just suppose. Just *suppose* now, that there were Martians living   240
on Mars and they saw our ship coming and saw us inside our ship and hated us. Suppose, now, just for the hell of it, that they wanted to destroy us, as invaders, as unwanted ones, and they wanted to do it in a very clever way, so that we would be taken off guard. Well, what would the best weapon be that a Martian could use against Earth-men with atom weapons?

The answer was interesting. Telepathy, hypnosis, memory, and imagination.

Suppose all these houses weren't real at all, this bed not real, but only figments of my own imagination, given substance by telepathy and hypnosis by the Martians.

Suppose these houses are really some other shape, a Martian shape, but, by playing on my desires and wants, these Martians have made this seem like my old home town, my old house, to lull me out of my suspicions? What better way to fool a man, by his own emotions.

And suppose those two people in the next room, asleep, are not my mother and father at all. But two Martians, incredibly brilliant, with the ability to keep me under this dreaming hypnosis all of the time?

And that brass band, today? What a clever plan it would be. First, fool   245
Lustig, then fool Hinkston, then gather a crowd around the rocket ship and wave. And all the men in the ship, seeing mothers, aunts, uncles, sweethearts dead ten, twenty years ago, naturally, disregarding orders, would rush out and abandon the ship. What more natural? What more unsuspecting? What more simple? A man doesn't ask too many questions when his mother is suddenly brought back to life; he's much too happy. And the brass band played and everybody was taken off to private homes. And here we all are, tonight, in various houses, in various beds, with no weapons to protect us, and the rocket lies in the moonlight, empty. And wouldn't it be horrible and terrifying to discover that all of this was part of some great clever plan by the Martians to divide and conquer us, and kill us. Some time during the night, perhaps, my brother on this bed, will change form, melt, shift, and become a one-eyed, green and yellow-toothed Martian. It would be very simple for him just to turn over in bed and put a knife into my heart. And in all those other houses down the street a dozen other brothers or fathers suddenly melting away and taking out knives and doing things to the unsuspecting, sleeping men of Earth.

His hands were shaking under the covers. His body was cold. Suddenly it was not a theory. Suddenly he was very afraid. He lifted himself in bed and listened. The night was very quiet. The music had stopped. The wind had died. His brother (?) lay sleeping beside him.

Very carefully he lifted the sheets, rolled them back. He slipped from bed and was walking softly across the room when his brother's voice said, "Where are you going?"

"What?"

His brother's voice was quite cold. "I said, where do you think you're going?"

"For a drink of water."   250

"But you're not thirsty."

"Yes, yes, I am."

"No, you're not."

Captain John Black broke and ran across the room. He screamed. He screamed twice.

He never reached the door.   255

In the morning, the brass band played a mournful dirge. From every house in the street came little solemn processions bearing long boxes and along the sun-filled street, weeping and changing, came the grandmas and grandfathers and mothers and sisters and brothers, walking to the churchyard, where there were open holes dug freshly and new tombstones installed. Seventeen holes in all, and seventeen tombstones. Three of the tombstones said, CAPTAIN JOHN BLACK, ALBERT LUSTIG, and SAMUEL HINKSTON.

The mayor made a little sad speech, his face sometimes looking like the mayor, sometimes looking like something else.

Mother and Father Black were there, with Brother Edward, and they cried, their faces melting now from a familiar face into something else.

Grandpa and Grandma Lustig were there, weeping, their faces also shifting like wax, shivering as a thing does in waves of heat on a summer day.

The coffins were lowered. Somebody murmured about "the unexpected   260 and sudden deaths of seventeen fine men during the night — "

Earth was shoveled in on the coffin tops.

After the funeral the brass band slammed and banged back into town and the crowd stood around and waved and shouted as the rocket was torn to pieces and strewn about and blown up.   *[1948]*

≡ THINKING ABOUT THE TEXT

1. What was your first response to the Victorian town? The captain says that "it's absolutely impossible" (para. 26). Did you think he is right?

2. What was your response to the attempted explanations for the town's appearance? Isn't seeing believing? Did you think that perhaps time travel is involved?

3. Comment on the thematic significance of the line "the buzzing of spring bees on the air lulled and quieted him, and the fresh look of things was a balm to the soul" (para. 78).

4. After Captain Black recovers from being "soaked to the skin with emotion" (para. 225), he begins thinking logically. At this point, as you sense the ending is near, what logical explanation did you suspect was coming — something about illusion, or perhaps delusion? What is ironic about the astronauts' coming armed with atomic weapons?

5. Readers are often puzzled by the ending. Indeed, it is strange that the Martians would hold a human funeral. After all, if the men are dead, why continue the charade? Why do you think they perform the ritual?

OCTAVIA BUTLER
Bloodchild

Octavia Butler (1947–2006), one of the few prominent African American science fiction writers, won numerous prizes for her work, including the prestigious Hugo and Nebula Awards. In 1995, she became the first science fiction writer to receive a MacArthur Foundation "genius" grant. Butler was born in Pasadena, California, where, as an introspective child, she began reading and writing science fiction at a young age. Her first novel, Master Pattern, *was published in 1976. Her most popular novel,* Kindred *(1979), transports an African American protagonist from the present to the time of slavery in the antebellum South. It has sold well over two hundred thousand copies. "Bloodchild" is one of Butler's most chilling and disturbing tales. Although her plot of alien oppression and dominance sounds horrible, at least to humans, it also involves tenderness, even love. In this psychologically complex story, there are implications for the issues of slavery and rape on Earth. This unsettling story might remind you of the* Alien *films, although here the aliens are clearly going to flourish. The second edition of* Bloodchild and Other Stories *was published posthumously in 2006.*

My last night of childhood began with a visit home. T'Gatoi's sister had given us two sterile eggs. T'Gatoi gave one to my mother, brother, and sisters. She insisted that I eat the other one alone. It didn't matter. There was still enough to leave everyone feeling good. Almost everyone. My mother wouldn't take any. She sat, watching everyone drifting and dreaming without her. Most of the time she watched me.

I lay against T'Gatoi's long, velvet underside, sipping from my egg now and then, wondering why my mother denied herself such a harmless pleasure. Less of her hair would be gray if she indulged now and then. The eggs prolonged life, prolonged vigor. My father, who had never refused one in his life, had lived more than twice as long as he should have. And toward the end of his life, when he should have been slowing down, he had married my mother and fathered four children.

But my mother seemed content to age before she had to. I saw her turn away as several of T'Gatoi's limbs secured me closer. T'Gatoi liked our body heat and took advantage of it whenever she could. When I was little and at home more, my mother used to try to tell me how to behave with T'Gatoi — how to be respectful and always obedient because T'Gatoi was the Tlic government official in charge of the Preserve, and thus the most important of her kind to deal directly with Terrans. It was an honor, my mother said, that such a person had chosen to come into the family. My mother was at her most formal and severe when she was lying.

I had no idea why she was lying, or even what she was lying about. It *was* an honor to have T'Gatoi in the family, but it was hardly a novelty. T'Gatoi and my mother had been friends all my mother's life, and T'Gatoi was not interested in being honored in the house she considered her second home. She simply came in, climbed onto one of her special couches, and called me over to keep her warm. It was impossible to be formal with her while lying against her and hearing her complain as usual that I was too skinny.

"You're better," she said this time, probing me with six or seven of her   5
limbs. "You're gaining weight finally. Thinness is dangerous." The probing changed subtly, became a series of caresses.

"He's still too thin," my mother said sharply.

T'Gatoi lifted her head and perhaps a meter of her body off the couch as though she was sitting up. She looked at my mother, and my mother, her face lined and old looking, turned away.

"Lien, I would like you to have what's left of Gan's egg."

"The eggs are for the children," my mother said.

"They are for the family. Please take it."   10

Unwillingly obedient, my mother took it from me and put it to her mouth. There were only a few drops left in the now-shrunken, elastic shell, but she squeezed them out, swallowed them, and after a few moments some of the lines of tension began to smooth from her face.

"It's good," she whispered. "Sometimes I forget how good it is."

"You should take more," T'Gatoi said. "Why are you in such a hurry to be old?"

My mother said nothing.

"I like being able to come here," T'Gatoi said. "This place is a refuge be-   15
cause of you, yet you won't take care of yourself."

T'Gatoi was hounded on the outside. Her people wanted more of us made available. Only she and her political faction stood between us and the hordes who did not understand why there was a Preserve — why any Terran could not be courted, paid, drafted, in some way made available to them. Or they did understand, but in their desperation, they did not care. She parceled us out to the desperate and sold us to the rich and powerful for their political support. Thus, we were necessities, status symbols, and an independent people. She oversaw the joining of families, putting an end to the final remnants of the earlier system of breaking up Terran families to suit impatient Tlic. I had lived outside with her. I had seen the desperate eagerness in the way some people looked at me. It was a little frightening to know that only she stood between us and that desperation that could so easily swallow us. My mother would look at her sometimes and say to me, "Take care of her." And I would remember that she too had been outside, had seen.

Now T'Gatoi used four of her limbs to push me away from her onto the floor. "Go on, Gan," she said. "Sit down there with your sisters and enjoy not being sober. You had most of the egg. Lien, come warm me."

My mother hesitated for no reason that I could see. One of my earliest memories is of my mother stretched alongside T'Gatoi, talking about things I could not understand, picking me up from the floor and laughing as she sat me on one of T'Gatoi's segments. She ate her share of eggs then. I wondered when she had stopped, and why.

She lay down now against T'Gatoi, and the whole left row of T'Gatoi's limbs closed around her, holding her loosely, but securely. I had always found it comfortable to lie that way, but except for my older sister, no one else in the family liked it. They said it made them feel caged.

T'Gatoi meant to cage my mother. Once she had, she moved her tail slightly, then spoke. "Not enough egg, Lien. You should have taken it when it was passed to you. You need it badly now." 20

T'Gatoi's tail moved once more, its whip motion so swift I wouldn't have seen it if I hadn't been watching for it. Her sting drew only a single drop of blood from my mother's bare leg.

My mother cried out — probably in surprise. Being stung doesn't hurt. Then she sighed and I could see her body relax. She moved languidly into a more comfortable position within the cage of T'Gatoi's limbs. "Why did you do that?" she asked, sounding half asleep.

"I could not watch you sitting and suffering any longer."

My mother managed to move her shoulders in a small shrug. "Tomorrow," she said.

"Yes. Tomorrow you will resume your suffering — if you must. But just now, just for now, lie here and warm me and let me ease your way a little." 25

"He's still mine, you know," my mother said suddenly.

"Nothing can buy him from me." Sober, she would not have permitted herself to refer to such things.

"Nothing," T'Gatoi agreed, humoring her.

"Did you think I would sell him for eggs? For long life? My son?"

"Not for anything," T'Gatoi said, stroking my mother's shoulders, toying with her long, graying hair. 30

I would like to have touched my mother, shared that moment with her. She would take my hand if I touched her now. Freed by the egg and the sting, she would smile and perhaps say things long held in. But tomorrow, she would remember all this as a humiliation. I did not want to be part of a remembered humiliation. Best just be still and know she loved me under all the duty and pride and pain.

"Xuan Hoa, take off her shoes," T'Gatoi said. "In a little while I'll sting her again and she can sleep."

My older sister obeyed, swaying drunkenly as she stood up. When she had finished, she sat down beside me and took my hand. We had always been a unit, she and I.

My mother put the back of her head against T'Gatoi's underside and tried from that impossible angle to look up into the broad, round face. "You're going to sting me again?"

"Yes, Lien." 35

"I'll sleep until tomorrow noon."

"Good. You need it. When did you sleep last?"

My mother made a wordless sound of annoyance. "I should have stepped on you when you were small enough," she muttered.

It was an old joke between them. They had grown up together, sort of, though T'Gatoi had not, in my mother's lifetime, been small enough for any Terran to step on. She was nearly three times my mother's present age, yet would still be young when my mother died of age. But T'Gatoi and my mother had met as T'Gatoi was coming into a period of rapid development — a kind of Tlic adolescence. My mother was only a child, but for a while they developed at the same rate and had no better friends than each other.

T'Gatoi had even introduced my mother to the man who became my fa-   40
ther. My parents, pleased with each other in spite of their different ages, married as T'Gatoi was going into her family's business — politics. She and my mother saw each other less. But sometime before my older sister was born, my mother promised T'Gatoi one of her children. She would have to give one of us to someone, and she preferred T'Gatoi to some stranger.

Years passed. T'Gatoi traveled and increased her influence. The Preserve was hers by the time she came back to my mother to collect what she probably saw as her just reward for her hard work. My older sister took an instant liking to her and wanted to be chosen, but my mother was just coming to term with me and T'Gatoi liked the idea of choosing an infant and watching and taking part in all the phases of development. I'm told I was first caged within T'Gatoi's many limbs only three minutes after my birth. A few days later, I was given my first taste of egg. I tell Terrans that when they ask whether I was ever afraid of her. And I tell it to Tlic when T'Gatoi suggests a young Terran child for them and they, anxious and ignorant, demand an adolescent. Even my brother who had somehow grown up to fear and distrust the Tlic could probably have gone smoothly into one of their families if he had been adopted early enough. Sometimes, I think for his sake he should have been. I looked at him, stretched out on the floor across the room, his eyes open, but glazed as he dreamed his egg dream. No matter what he felt toward the Tlic, he always demanded his share of egg.

"Lien, can you stand up?" T'Gatoi asked suddenly.

"Stand?" my mother said. "I thought I was going to sleep."

"Later. Something sounds wrong outside." The cage was abruptly gone.

"What?"   45

"Up, Lien!"

My mother recognized her tone and got up just in time to avoid being dumped on the floor. T'Gatoi whipped her three meters of body off her couch, toward the door, and out at full speed. She had bones — ribs, a long spine, a skull, four sets of limb bones per segment. But when she moved that way, twisting, hurling herself into controlled falls, landing running, she seemed not only boneless, but aquatic — something swimming through the air as though it were water. I loved watching her move.

I left my sister and started to follow her out the door, though I wasn't very steady on my own feet. It would have been better to sit and dream, better yet to find a girl and share a waking dream with her. Back when the Tlic saw us as not much more than convenient, big, warm-blooded animals, they would pen several of us together, male and female, and feed us only eggs. That way they could be sure of getting another generation of us no matter how we tried to hold out. We were lucky that didn't go on long. A few generations of it and we would have *been* little more than convenient, big animals.

"Hold the door open, Gan," T'Gatoi said. "And tell the family to stay back."

"What is it?" I asked. 50

"N'Tlic."

I shrank back against the door. "Here? Alone?"

"He was trying to reach a call box, I suppose." She carried the man past me, unconscious, folded like a coat over some of her limbs. He looked young — my brother's age perhaps — and he was thinner than he should have been. What T'Gatoi would have called dangerously thin.

"Gan, go to the call box," she said. She put the man on the floor and began stripping off his clothing.

I did not move. 55

After a moment, she looked up at me, her sudden stillness a sign of deep impatience.

"Send Qui," I told her. "I'll stay here. Maybe I can help."

She let her limbs begin to move again, lifting the man and pulling his shirt over his head. "You don't want to see this," she said. "It will be hard. I can't help this man the way his Tlic could."

"I know. But send Qui. He won't want to be of any help here. I'm at least willing to try."

She looked at my brother — older, bigger, stronger, certainly more able to help her here. He was sitting up now, braced against the wall, staring at the man on the floor with undisguised fear and revulsion. Even she could see that he would be useless. 60

"Qui, go!" she said.

He didn't argue. He stood up, swayed briefly, then steadied, frightened sober.

"This man's name is Bram Lomas," she told him, reading from the man's armband. I fingered my own armband in sympathy. "He needs T'Khotgif Teh. Do you hear?"

"Bram Lomas, T'Khotgif Teh," my brother said. "I'm going." He edged around Lomas and ran out the door.

Lomas began to regain consciousness. He only moaned at first and clutched spasmodically at a pair of T'Gatoi's limbs. My younger sister, finally awake from her egg dream, came close to look at him, until my mother pulled her back. 65

T'Gatoi removed the man's shoes, then his pants, all the while leaving him two of her limbs to grip. Except for the final few, all her limbs were equally dexterous. "I want no argument from you this time, Gan," she said.

I straightened. "What shall I do?"

"Go out and slaughter an animal that is at least half your size."

"Slaughter? But I've never —"

She knocked me across the room. Her tail was an efficient weapon whether   70
she exposed the sting or not.

I got up, feeling stupid for having ignored her warning, and went into the
kitchen. Maybe I could kill something with a knife or an ax. My mother raised
a few Terran animals for the table and several thousand local ones for their fur.
T'Gatoi would probably prefer something local. An achti, perhaps. Some of
those were the right size, though they had about three times as many teeth as I
did and a real love of using them. My mother, Hoa, and Qui could kill them
with knives. I had never killed one at all, had never slaughtered any animal. I
had spent most of my time with T'Gatoi while my brother and sisters were
learning the family business. T'Gatoi had been right. I should have been the
one to go to the call box. At least I could do that.

I went to the corner cabinet where my mother kept her large house and
garden tools. At the back of the cabinet there was a pipe that carried off waste
water from the kitchen — except that it didn't anymore. My father had rerouted the waste water below before I was born. Now the pipe could be turned
so that one half slid around the other and a rifle could be stored inside. This
wasn't our only gun, but it was our most easily accessible one. I would have to
use it to shoot one of the biggest of the achti. Then T'Gatoi would probably
confiscate it. Firearms were illegal in the Preserve. There had been incidents
right after the Preserve was established — Terrans shooting Tlic, shooting
N'Tlic. This was before the joining of families began, before everyone had a
personal stake in keeping the peace. No one had shot a Tlic in my lifetime or my
mother's, but the law still stood — for our protection, we were told. There were
stories of whole Terran families wiped out in reprisal back during the assas-
sinations.

I went out to the cages and shot the biggest achti I could find. It was a
handsome breeding male, and my mother would not be pleased to see me bring
it in. But it was the right size, and I was in a hurry.

I put the achti's long, warm body over my shoulder — glad that some of
the weight I'd gained was muscle — and took it to the kitchen. There, I put the
gun back in its hiding place. If T'Gatoi noticed the achti's wounds and demanded the gun, I would give it to her. Otherwise, let it stay where my father
wanted it.

I turned to take the achti to her, then hesitated. For several seconds, I stood   75
in front of the closed door wondering why I was suddenly afraid. I knew what
was going to happen. I hadn't seen it before but T'Gatoi had shown me dia-
grams and drawings. She had made sure I knew the truth as soon as I was old
enough to understand it.

Yet I did not want to go into that room. I wasted a little time choosing a
knife from the carved, wooden box in which my mother kept them. T'Gatoi
might want one, I told myself, for the tough, heavily furred hide of the achti.

"Gan!" T'Gatoi called, her voice harsh with urgency.

I swallowed. I had not imagined a single moving of the feet could be so difficult. I realized I was trembling and that shamed me. Shame impelled me
through the door.

I put the achti down near T'Gatoi and saw that Lomas was unconscious again. She, Lomas, and I were alone in the room — my mother and sisters probably sent out so they would not have to watch. I envied them.

But my mother came back into the room as T'Gatoi seized the achti. Ignoring the knife I offered her, she extended claws from several of her limbs and slit the achti from throat to anus. She looked at me, her yellow eyes intent. "Hold this man's shoulders, Gan."

I stared at Lomas in panic, realizing that I did not want to touch him, let alone hold him. This would not be like shooting an animal. Not as quick, not as merciful, and, I hoped, not as final, but there was nothing I wanted less than to be part of it.

My mother came forward, "Gan, you hold his right side," she said. "I'll hold his left." And if he came to, he would throw her off without realizing he had done it. She was a tiny woman. She often wondered aloud how she had produced, as she said, such "huge" children.

"Never mind," I told her, taking the man's shoulders. "I'll do it." She hovered nearby.

"Don't worry," I said. "I won't shame you. You don't have to stay and watch."

She looked at me uncertainly, then touched my face in a rare caress. Finally, she went back to her bedroom.

T'Gatoi lowered her head in relief. "Thank you, Gan," she said with courtesy more Terran than Tlic. "That one . . . she is always finding new ways for me to make her suffer."

Lomas began to groan and make choked sounds. I had hoped he would stay unconscious. T'Gatoi put her face near his so that he focused on her.

"I've stung you as much as I dare for now," she told him. "When this is over, I'll sting you to sleep and you won't hurt anymore."

"Please," the man begged. "Wait . . ."

"There's no more time, Bram. I'll sting you as soon as it's over. When T'Khotgif arrives she'll give you eggs to help you heal. It will be over soon."

"T'Khotgif!" the man shouted, straining against my hands.

"Soon, Bram." T'Gatoi glanced at me, then placed a claw against his abdomen slightly to the right of the middle, just below the left rib. There was movement on the right side — tiny, seemingly random pulsations moving his brown flesh, creating a concavity here, a convexity there, over and over until I could see the rhythm of it and knew where the next pulse would be.

Lomas's entire body stiffened under T'Gatoi's claw, though she merely rested it against him as she wound the rear section of her body around his legs. He might break my grip, but he would not break hers. He wept helplessly as she used his pants to tie his hands, then pushed his hands above his head so that I could kneel on the cloth between them and pin them in place. She rolled up his shirt and gave it to him to bite down on.

And she opened him.

His body convulsed with the first cut. He almost tore himself away from me. The sound he made . . . I had never heard such sounds come from anything human. T'Gatoi seemed to pay no attention as she lengthened and deepened the cut, now and then pausing to lick away blood. His blood vessels contracted, reacting to the chemistry of her saliva, and the bleeding slowed.

I felt as though I were helping her torture him, helping her consume him. I knew I would vomit soon, didn't know why I hadn't already. I couldn't possibly last until she was finished.

She found the first grub. It was fat and deep red with his blood — both inside and out. It had already eaten its own egg case but apparently had not yet begun to eat its host. At this stage, it would eat any flesh except its mother's. Let alone, it would have gone on excreting the poisons that had both sickened and alerted Lomas. Eventually it would have begun to eat. By the time it ate its way out of Lomas's flesh, Lomas would be dead or dying — and unable to take revenge on the thing that was killing him. There was always a grace period between the time the host sickened and the time the grubs began to eat him.

T'Gatoi picked up the writhing grub carefully and looked at it, somehow ignoring the terrible groans of the man.

Abruptly, the man lost consciousness.

"Good," T'Gatoi looked down at him. "I wish you Terrans could do that at   100
will." She felt nothing. And the thing she held . . .

It was limbless and boneless at this stage, perhaps fifteen centimeters long and two thick, blind and slimy with blood. It was like a large worm. T'Gatoi put it into the belly of the achti, and it began at once to burrow. It would stay there and eat as long as there was anything to eat.

Probing through Lomas's flesh, she found two more, one of them smaller and more vigorous. "A male!" she said happily. He would be dead before I would. He would be through his metamorphosis and screwing everything that would hold still before his sisters even had limbs. He was the only one to make a serious effort to bite T'Gatoi as she placed him in the achti.

Paler worms oozed to visibility in Lomas's flesh. I closed my eyes. It was worse than finding something dead, rotting, and filled with tiny animal grubs. And it was far worse than any drawing or diagram.

"Ah, there are more," T'Gatoi said, plucking out two long, thick grubs. You may have to kill another animal, Gan. Everything lives inside you Terrans."

I had been told all my life that this was a good and necessary thing Tlic and   105
Terran did together — a kind of birth. I had believed it until now. I knew birth was painful and bloody, no matter what. But this was something else, something worse. And I wasn't ready to see it. Maybe I never would be. Yet I couldn't not see it. Closing my eyes didn't help.

T'Gatoi found a grub still eating its egg case. The remains of the case were still wired into a blood vessel by their own little tube or hook or whatever. That was the way the grubs were anchored and the way they fed. They took only blood until they were ready to emerge. Then they ate their stretched, elastic egg cases. Then they ate their hosts.

T'Gatoi bit away the egg case, licked away the blood. Did she like the taste? Did childhood habits die hard — or not die at all?

The whole procedure was wrong, alien. I wouldn't have thought anything about her could seem alien to me.

"One more, I think," she said. "Perhaps two. A good family. In a host animal these days, we would be happy to find one or two alive." She glanced at me. "Go outside, Gan, and empty your stomach. Go now while the man is unconscious."

I staggered out, barely made it. Beneath the tree just beyond the front door, I vomited until there was nothing left to bring up. Finally, I stood shaking, tears streaming down my face. I did not know why I was crying, but I could not stop. I went further from the house to avoid being seen. Every time I closed my eyes I saw red worms crawling over redder human flesh.

There was a car coming toward the house. Since Terrans were forbidden motorized vehicles except for certain farm equipment, I knew this must be Lomas's Tlic with Qui and perhaps a Terran doctor. I wiped my face on my shirt, struggled for control.

"Gan," Qui called as the car stopped. "What happened?" He crawled out of the low, round, Tlic-convenient car door. Another Terran crawled out the other side and went into the house without speaking to me. The doctor. With his help and a few eggs, Lomas might make it.

"T'Khotgif Teh?" I said.

The Tlic driver surged out of the car, reared up half her length before me. She was paler and smaller than T'Gatoi—probably born from the body of an animal. Tlic from Terran bodies were always larger as well as more numerous.

"Six young," I told her. "Maybe seven, all alive. At least one male."

"Lomas?" she said harshly. I liked her for the question and the concern in her voice when she asked it. The last coherent thing he had said was her name.

"He's alive," I said.

She surged away to the house without another word.

"She's been sick," my brother said, watching her go. "When I called, I could hear people telling her she wasn't well enough to go out even for this."

I said nothing. I had extended courtesy to the Tlic. Now I didn't want to talk to anyone. I hoped he would go in — out of curiosity if nothing else.

"Finally found out more than you wanted to know, eh?"

I looked at him.

"Don't give me one of her looks," he said. "You're not her. You're just her property."

One of her looks. Had I picked up even an ability to imitate her expressions?

"What'd you do, puke?" He sniffed the air. "So now you know what you're in for."

I walked away from him. He and I had been close when we were kids. He would let me follow him around when I was home, and sometimes T'Gatoi would let me bring him along when she took me into the city. But something had happened when he reached adolescence. I never knew what. He began keeping out of T'Gatoi's way. Then he began running away — until he realized there was no "away." Not in the Preserve. Certainly not outside. After that he concentrated on getting his share of every egg that came into the house and on looking out for me in a way that made me all but hate him — a way that clearly said, as long as I was all right, he was safe from the Tlic.

"How was it, really?" he demanded, following me.

"I killed an achti. The young ate it."

"You didn't run out of the house and puke because they ate an achti."

"I had . . . never seen a person cut open before." That was true, and enough 130 for him to know. I couldn't talk about the other. Not with him.

"Oh," he said. He glanced at me as though he wanted to say more, but he kept quiet.

We walked, not really headed anywhere. Toward the back, toward the cages, toward the fields.

"Did he say anything?" Qui asked. "Lomas, I mean."

Who else would he mean? "He said 'T'Khotgif.' "

Qui shuddered. "If she had done that to me, she'd be the last person I'd 135 call for."

"You'd call for her. Her sting would ease your pain without killing the grubs in you."

"You think I'd care if they died?"

No. Of course he wouldn't. Would I?

"Shit!" He drew a deep breath. "I've seen what they do. You think this thing with Lomas was bad? It was nothing."

I didn't argue. He didn't know what he was talking about.   140

"I saw them eat a man," he said.

I turned to face him. "You're lying!"

"I saw them eat a man." He paused. "It was when I was little. I had been to the Hartmund house and I was on my way home. Halfway here, I saw a man and a Tlic and the man was N'Tlic. The ground was hilly. I was able to hide from them and watch. The Tlic wouldn't open the man because she had nothing to feed the grubs. The man couldn't go any further and there were no houses around. He was in so much pain, he told her to kill him. He begged her to kill him. Finally, she did. She cut his throat. One swipe of one claw. I saw the grubs eat their way out, then burrow in again, still eating."

His words made me see Lomas's flesh again, parasitized, crawling. "Why didn't you tell me that?" I whispered.

He looked startled as though he'd forgotten I was listening. "I don't know." 145

"You started to run away not long after that, didn't you?"

"Yeah. Stupid. Running inside the Preserve. Running in a cage."

I shook my head, said what I should have said to him long ago. "She wouldn't take you, Qui. You don't have to worry."

"She would . . . if anything happened to you."

"No. She'd take Xuan Hoa. Hoa . . . wants it." She wouldn't if she had 150 stayed to watch Lomas.

"They don't take women," he said with contempt.

"They do sometimes." I glanced at him. "Actually, they prefer women. You should be around them when they talk among themselves. They say women have more body fat to protect the grubs. But they usually take men to leave the women free to bear their own young."

"To provide the next generation of host animals," he said, switching from contempt to bitterness.

"It's more than that!" I countered. Was it?

"If it were going to happen to me, I'd want to believe it was more, too." 155

"It *is* more!" I felt like a kid. Stupid argument.

"Did you think so while T'Gatoi was picking worms out of that guy's guts?"

"It's not supposed to happen that way."

"Sure it is. You weren't supposed to see it, that's all. And his Tlic was supposed to do it. She could sting him unconscious and the operation wouldn't have been as painful. But she'd still open him, pick out the grubs, and if she missed even one, it would poison him and eat him from the inside out."

There was actually a time when my mother told me to show respect for Qui 160
because he was my older brother. I walked away, hating him. In his way, he was gloating. He was safe and I wasn't. I could have hit him, but I didn't think I would be able to stand it when he refused to hit back, when he looked at me with contempt and pity.

He wouldn't let me get away. Longer legged, he swung ahead of me and made me feel as though I were following him.

"I'm sorry," he said.

I strode on, sick and furious.

"Look, it probably won't be that bad with you. T'Gatoi likes you. She'll be careful."

I turned back toward the house, almost running from him. 165

"Has she done it to you yet?" he asked, keeping up easily. "I mean, you're about the right age for implantation. Has she —"

I hit him. I didn't know I was going to do it, but I think I meant to kill him. If he hadn't been bigger and stronger, I think I would have.

He tried to hold me off, but in the end, had to defend himself. He only hit me a couple of times. That was plenty. I don't remember going down, but when I came to, he was gone. It was worth the pain to be rid of him.

I got up and walked slowly toward the house. The back was dark. No one was in the kitchen. My mother and sisters were sleeping in their bedrooms — or pretending to.

Once I was in the kitchen, I could hear voices — Tlic and Terran from the 170
next room. I couldn't make out what they were saying — didn't want to make it out.

I sat down at my mother's table, waiting for quiet. The table was smooth and worn, heavy and well crafted. My father had made it for her just before he died. I remembered hanging around underfoot when he built it. He didn't mind. Now I sat leaning on it, missing him. I could have talked to him. He had done it three times in his long life. Three clutches of eggs, three times being opened up and sewed up. How had he done it? How did anyone do it?

I got up, took the rifle from its hiding place, and sat down again with it. It needed cleaning, oiling.

All I did was load it.

"Gan?"

She made a lot of little clicking sounds when she walked on bare floor, each   175
limb clicking in succession as it touched down. Waves of little clicks.

She came to the table, raised the front half of her body above it, and surged
onto it. Sometimes she moved so smoothly she seemed to flow like water itself. She coiled herself into a small hill in the middle of the table and looked
at me.

"That was bad," she said softly. "You should not have seen it. It need not be
that way."

"I know."

"T'Khotgif — Ch'Khotgif now — she will die of her disease. She will not
live to raise her children. But her sister will provide for them, and for Bram
Lomas." Sterile sister. One fertile female in every lot. One to keep the family going. That sister owed Lomas more than she could ever repay.

"He'll live then?"   180

"Yes."

"I wonder if he would do it again."

"No one would ask him to do that again."

I looked into the yellow eyes, wondering how much I saw and understood
there, and how much I only imagined. "No one ever asks us," I said. "You never
asked me."

She moved her head slightly. "What's the matter with your face?"   185

"Nothing. Nothing important." Human eyes probably wouldn't have noticed the swelling in the darkness. The only light was from one of the moons,
shining through a window across the room.

"Did you use the rifle to shoot the achti?"

"Yes."

"And do you mean to use it to shoot me?"

I stared at her, outlined in the moonlight — coiled, graceful body. "What   190
does Terran blood taste like to you?"

She said nothing.

"What are you?" I whispered. "What are we to you?"

She lay still, rested her head on her topmost coil. "You know me as no
other does," she said softly. "You must decide."

"That's what happened to my face," I told her.

"What?"   195

"Qui goaded me into deciding to do something. It didn't turn out very
well." I moved the gun slightly, brought the barrel up diagonally under my own
chin. "At least it was a decision I made."

"As this will be."

"Ask me, Gatoi."

"For my children's lives?"

She would say something like that. She knew how to manipulate people,   200
Terran and Tlic. But not this time.

"I don't want to be a host animal," I said. "Not even yours."

It took her a long time to answer. "We use almost no host animals these days," she said. "You know that."

"You use us."

"We do. We wait long years for you and teach you and join our families to yours." She moved restlessly. "You know you aren't animals to us."

I stared at her, saying nothing.   205

"The animals we once used began killing most of our eggs after implantation long before your ancestors arrived," she said softly. "You know these things, Gan. Because your people arrived, we are relearning what it means to be a healthy, thriving people. And your ancestors, fleeing from their homeworld, from their own kind who would have killed or enslaved them — they survived because of us. We saw them as people and gave them the Preserve when they still tried to kill us as worms."

At the word "worms," I jumped. I couldn't help it, and she couldn't help noticing it.

"I see," she said quietly. "Would you really rather die than bear my young, Gan?"

I didn't answer.

"Shall I go to Xuan Hoa?"   210

"Yes!" Hoa wanted it. Let her have it. She hadn't had to watch Lomas. She'd be proud . . . . Not terrified.

T'Gatoi flowed off the table onto the floor, startling me almost too much.

"I'll sleep in Hoa's room tonight," she said. "And sometime tonight or in the morning, I'll tell her."

This was going too fast. My sister Hoa had had almost as much to do with raising me as my mother. I was still close to her — not like Qui. She could want T'Gatoi and still love me.

"Wait! Gatoi!"   215

She looked back, then raised nearly half her length off the floor and turned to face me. "These are adult things, Gan. This is my life, my family!"

"But she's . . . my sister."

"I have done what you demanded. I have asked you!"

"But — "

"It will be easier for Hoa. She has always expected to carry other lives in-   220
side her."

Human lives. Human young who should someday drink at her breasts, not at her veins.

I shook my head. "Don't do it to her, Gatoi." I was not Qui. It seemed I could become him, though, with no effort at all. I could make Xuan Hoa my shield. Would it be easier to know that red worms were growing in her flesh instead of mine?

"Don't do it to Hoa," I repeated.

She stared at me, utterly still.

I looked away, then back at her. "Do it to me."   225

I lowered the gun from my throat and she leaned forward to take it.

"No," I told her.

"It's the law," she said.

"Leave it for the family. One of them might use it to save my life someday."

She grasped the rifle barrel, but I wouldn't let go. I was pulled into a stand-   230
ing position over her.

"Leave it here!" I repeated. "If we're not your animals, if these are adult
things, accept the risk. There is risk, Gatoi, in dealing with a partner."

It was clearly hard for her to let go of the rifle. A shudder went through her
and she made a hissing sound of distress. It occurred to me that she was afraid.
She was old enough to have seen what guns could do to people. Now her young
and this gun would be together in the same house. She did not know about the
other guns. In this dispute, they did not matter.

"I will implant the first egg tonight," she said as I put the gun away. "Do
you hear, Gan?"

Why else had I been given a whole egg to eat while the rest of the family
was left to share one? Why else had my mother kept looking at me as though I
were going away from her, going where she could not follow? Did T'Gatoi imagine I hadn't known?

"I hear."   235

"Now!" I let her push me out of the kitchen, then walked ahead of her
toward my bedroom. The sudden urgency in her voice sounded real. "You
would have done it to Hoa tonight!" I accused.

"I must do it to someone tonight."

I stopped in spite of her urgency and stood in her way. "Don't you
care who?"

She flowed around me and into my bedroom. I found her waiting on the
couch we shared. There was nothing in Hoa's room that she could have used.
She would have done it to Hoa on the floor. The thought of her doing it to Hoa
at all disturbed me in a different way now, and I was suddenly angry.

Yet I undressed and lay down beside her. I knew what to do, what to expect.   240
I had been told all my life. I felt the familiar sting, narcotic, mildly pleasant.
Then the blind probing of her ovipositor. The puncture was painless, easy. So
easy going in. She undulated slowly against me, her muscles forcing the egg
from her body into mine. I held on to a pair of her limbs until I remembered
Lomas holding her that way. Then I let go, moved inadvertently, and hurt her.
She gave a low cry of pain and I expected to be caged at once within her limbs.
When I wasn't, I held on to her again, feeling oddly ashamed.

"I'm sorry," I whispered.

She rubbed my shoulders with four of her limbs.

"Do you care?" I asked. "Do you care that it's me?"

She did not answer for some time. Finally, "You were the one making the
choices tonight, Gan. I made mine long ago."

"Would you have gone to Hoa?"   245

"Yes. How could I put my children into the care of one who hates them?"

"It wasn't . . . hate."

"I know what it was."

"I was afraid."

Silence.   250

"I still am." I could admit it to her here, now.

"But you came to me . . . to save Hoa."

"Yes." I leaned my forehead against her. She was cool velvet, deceptively soft. "And to keep you for myself," I said. It was so. I didn't understand it, but it was so.

She made a soft hum of contentment. "I couldn't believe I had made such a mistake with you," she said. "I chose you. I believed you had grown to choose me."

"I had, but . . ."   255

"Lomas."

"Yes."

"I had never known a Terran to see a birth and take it well. Qui has seen one, hasn't he?"

"Yes."

"Terrans should be protected from seeing."   260

I didn't like the sound of that — and I doubted that it was possible. "Not protected," I said. "Shown. Shown when we're young kids, and shown more than once. Gatoi, no Terran ever sees a birth that goes right. All we see is N'Tlic — pain and terror and maybe death."

She looked down at me. "It is a private thing. It has always been a private thing."

Her tone kept me from insisting — that and the knowledge that if she changed her mind, I might be the first public example. But I had planted the thought in her mind. Chances were it would grow, and eventually she would experiment.

"You won't see it again," she said. "I don't want you thinking any more about shooting me."

The small amount of fluid that came into me with her egg relaxed me as   265
completely as a sterile egg would have, so that I could remember the rifle in my hands and my feelings of fear and revulsion, anger and despair. I could remember the feelings without reviving them. I could talk about them.

"I wouldn't have shot you," I said. "Not you." She had been taken from my father's flesh when he was my age.

"You could have," she insisted.

"Not you." She stood between us and her own people, protecting, interweaving.

"Would you have destroyed yourself?"

I moved carefully; uncomfortable. "I could have done that. I nearly did.   270
That's Qui's 'away.' I wonder if he knows."

"What?"

I did not answer.

"You will live now."

"Yes." *Take care of her,* my mother used to say. Yes.

"I'm healthy and young," she said. "I won't leave you as Lomas was left —   275
alone, N'Tlic. I'll take care of you."   *[1984]*

≡ THINKING ABOUT THE TEXT

1. This is a difficult story to be neutral about. What parts of the narrative disturbed you the most? Did your reaction change over the course of the tale?

2. Butler builds up the suspense about what is to happen to Gan, the narrator. When did you suspect the truth?

3. This tale is filled with complicated, even contradictory, emotions. Describe some of Gan's ambivalent feelings. How do they differ from Qui's feelings?

4. Comment on Gan's reason for allowing the implantation: "And to keep you for myself" (para. 253).

5. Think of the Tlic as Southern plantation owners and the Terrans as black slaves. Comment on the story's details from this allegorical perspective.

≡ MAKING COMPARISONS

1. What is the most disturbing element of Bradbury's and Butler's alien worlds?

2. What are some familiar psychological aspects in these science fiction tales?

3. If you were in either of these situations, how might you respond?

URSULA K. LE GUIN

The Ones Who Walk Away from Omelas

Ursula K. Le Guin (b. 1929) was born and raised in Berkeley, California, where she began writing at eleven, unsuccessfully submitting a story to Astounding Science Fiction. *She graduated from Radcliffe College (Phi Beta Kappa) in 1951 and received her M.A. from Columbia University a year later. She became famous with the publication of* The Left Hand of Darkness *(1969), an exploration of a hermaphroditic race that most critics see as a comment on contemporary gender politics. The novel won science fiction's highest awards: the Hugo and the Nebula.* The Farthest Shore *(1972) won the National Book Award, and* Tehanu: The Last Book of Earthsea *(1990) won the prestigious Nebula Award. More recently,* Powers *won the Nebula Award for 2008, and* Lavinia *won the 2009 Locus Award for Best Fantasy Novel. Besides her twenty novels, Le Guin has also published scores of short stories, books for children, nonfiction, and six volumes of poems. In 2000, Le Guin received the Library of Congress Living Legends award for her "significant contribution to America's heritage."*

With a clamor of bells that set the swallows soaring, the Festival of Summer came to the city Omelas, bright-towered by the sea. The rigging of the boats in harbor sparkled with flags. In the streets between houses with red roofs and painted walls, between old moss-grown gardens and under avenues of trees, past great parks and public buildings, processions moved. Some were decorous: old people in long stiff robes of mauve and gray, grave master workmen, quiet, merry women carrying their babies and chatting as they walked. In other streets the music beat faster, a shimmering of gong and tambourine, and the people went dancing, the procession was a dance. Children dodged in and out, their high calls rising like the swallows' crossing flights over the music and the singing. All the processions wound towards the north side of the city, where on the great water-meadow called the Green Fields boys and girls, naked in the bright air, with mudstained feet and ankles and long, lithe arms, exercised their restive horses before the race. The horses wore no gear at all but a halter without bit. Their manes were braided with streamers of silver, gold, and green. They flared their nostrils and pranced and boasted to one another; they were vastly excited, the horse being the only animal who has adopted our ceremonies as his own. Far off to the north and west the mountains stood up half encircling Omelas on her bay. The air of morning was so clear that the snow still crowning the Eighteen Peaks burned with white-gold fire across the miles of sunlit air, under the dark blue of the sky. There was just enough wind to make the banners that marked the racecourse snap and flutter now and then. In the silence of the broad green meadows one could hear the music winding through the city streets, farther and nearer and ever approaching, a cheerful faint sweetness of the air that from time to time trembled and gathered together and broke out into the great joyous clanging of the bells.

Joyous! How is one to tell about joy? How describe the citizens of Omelas?

They were not simple folk, you see, though they were happy. But we do not say the words of cheer much any more. All smiles have become archaic. Given a description such as this one tends to make certain assumptions. Given a description such as this one tends to look next for the King, mounted on a splendid stallion and surrounded by his noble knights, or perhaps in a golden litter borne by great-muscled slaves. But there was no king. They did not use swords, or keep slaves. They were not barbarians. I do not know the rules and laws of their society, but I suspect that they were singularly few. As they did without monarchy and slavery, so they also got on without the stock exchange, the advertisement, the secret police, and the bomb. Yet I repeat that these were not simple folk, not dulcet shepherds, noble savages, bland utopians. They were not less complex than us. The trouble is that we have a bad habit, encouraged by pedants and sophisticates, of considering happiness as something rather stupid. Only pain is intellectual, only evil interesting. This is the treason of the artist: a refusal to admit the banality of evil and the terrible boredom of pain. If you can't lick 'em, join 'em. If it hurts, repeat it. But to praise despair is to condemn delight, to embrace violence is to lose hold of everything else. We have almost lost hold, we can no longer describe a happy man, nor make any celebration of joy. How can I tell you about the people of Omelas? They were not naive and happy children — though their children were, in fact, happy. They were mature, intelligent, passionate adults whose lives were not wretched.

O miracle! But I wish I could describe it better. I wish I could convince you. Omelas sounds in my words like a city in a fairy tale, long ago and far away, once upon a time. Perhaps it would be best if you imagined it as your own fancy bids, assuming it will rise to the occasion, for certainly I cannot suit you all. For instance, how about technology? I think that there would be no cars or helicopters in and above the streets; this follows from the fact that the people of Omelas are happy people. Happiness is based on a just discrimination of what is necessary, what is neither necessary nor destructive, and what is destructive. In the middle category, however — that of the unnecessary but undestructive, that of comfort, luxury, exuberance, etc. — they could perfectly well have central heating, subway trains, washing machines, and all kinds of marvelous devices not yet invented here, floating light-sources, fuelless power, a cure for the common cold. Or they could have none of that: it doesn't matter. As you like it. I incline to think that people from towns up and down the coast have been coming in to Omelas during the last days before the Festival on very fast little trains and double-decked trams, and that the train station of Omelas is actually the handsomest building in town, though plainer than the magnificent Farmers' Market. But even granted trains, I fear that Omelas so far strikes some of you as goody-goody. Smiles, bells, parades, horses, bleh. If so, please add an orgy. If an orgy would help, don't hesitate. Let us not, however, have temples from which issue beautiful nude priests and priestesses already half in ecstasy and ready to copulate with any man or woman, lover or stranger, who desires union with the deep godhead of the blood, although that was my first idea. But really it would be better not to have any temples in Omelas — at least, not manned temples. Religion yes, clergy no. Surely the beautiful nudes can just wander about, offering themselves like divine soufflés to the hunger of the needy and the rapture of the flesh. Let them join the processions. Let tambourines be struck above the copulations, and the glory of desire be proclaimed upon the gongs, and (a not unimportant point) let the offspring of these delightful rituals be beloved and looked after by all. One thing I know there is none of in Omelas is guilt. But what else should there be? I thought that first there were no drugs, but that is puritanical. For those who like it, the faint insistent sweetness of *drooz* may perfume the ways of the city, *drooz* which first brings a great lightness and brilliance to the mind and limbs, and then after some hours a dreamy languor, and wonderful visions at last of the very arcana and inmost secrets of the Universe, as well as exciting the pleasure of sex beyond all belief; and it is not habit-forming. For more modest tastes I think there ought to be beer. What else, what else belongs in the joyous city? The sense of victory, surely, the celebration of courage. But as we did without clergy, let us do without soldiers. The joy built upon successful slaughter is not the right kind of joy; it will not do; it is fearful and it is trivial. A boundless and generous contentment, a magnanimous triumph felt not against some outer enemy but in communion with the finest and fairest in the souls of all men everywhere and the splendor of the world's summer: this is what swells the hearts of the people of Omelas, and the victory they celebrate is that of life. I really don't think many of them need to take *drooz*.

Most of the processions have reached the Green Fields by now. A marvelous smell of cooking goes forth from the red and blue tents of the provisioners. The faces of small children are amiably sticky; in the benign grey beard of a man a couple of crumbs of rich pastry are entangled. The youths and girls have mounted their horses and are beginning to group around the starting line of the course. An old woman, small, fat, and laughing, is passing out flowers from a basket, and tall young men wear her flowers in their shining hair. A child of nine or ten sits at the edge of the crowd, alone, playing on a wooden flute. People pause to listen, and they smile, but they do not speak to him, for he never ceases playing and never sees them, his dark eyes wholly rapt in the sweet, thin magic of the tune.

He finishes, and slowly lowers his hands holding the wooden flute.   5

As if that little private silence were the signal, all at once a trumpet sounds from the pavilion near the starting line: imperious, melancholy, piercing. The horses rear on their slender legs, and some of them neigh in answer. Sober-faced, the young riders stroke the horses' necks and soothe them, whispering, "Quiet, quiet, there my beauty, my hope. . . ." They begin to form in rank along the starting line. The crowds along the racecourse are like a field of grass and flowers in the wind. The Festival of Summer has begun.

Do you believe? Do you accept the festival, the city, the joy? No? Then let me describe one more thing.

In a basement under one of the beautiful public buildings of Omelas, or perhaps in the cellar of one of its spacious private homes, there is a room. It has one locked door, and no window. A little light seeps in dustily between cracks in the boards, secondhand from a cobwebbed window somewhere across the cellar. In one corner of the little room a couple of mops, with stiff, clotted, foul-smelling heads, stand near a rusty bucket. The floor is dirt, a little damp to the touch, as cellar dirt usually is. The room is about three paces long and two wide: a mere broom closet or disused tool room. In the room a child is sitting. It could be a boy or a girl. It looks about six, but actually is nearly ten. It is feeble-minded. Perhaps it was born defective, or perhaps it has become imbecile through fear, malnutrition, and neglect. It picks its nose and occasionally fumbles vaguely with its toes or genitals, as it sits hunched in the corner farthest from the bucket and the two mops. It is afraid of the mops. It finds them horrible. It shuts its eyes, but it knows the mops are still standing there; and the door is locked; and nobody will come. The door is always locked; and nobody ever comes, except that sometimes — the child has no understanding of time or interval — sometimes the door rattles terribly and opens, and a person, or several people, are there. One of them may come in and kick the child to make it stand up. The others never come close, but peer in at it with frightened, disgusted eyes. The food bowl and the water jug are hastily filled, the door is locked, the eyes disappear. The people at the door never say anything, but the child, who has not always lived in the tool room, and can remember sunlight and its mother's voice, sometimes speaks. "I will be good," it says. "Please let me out. I will be good!" They never answer. The child used to scream for help at night, and cry a good deal, but now it only makes a kind of whining, "eh-haa, eh-haa," and it speaks less and less often. It is so thin there are no calves to its legs; its belly protrudes; it lives on a half-bowl of corn meal and grease a day. It is naked. Its buttocks and thighs are a mass of festered sores, as it sits in its own excrement continually.

They all know it is there, all the people of Omelas. Some of them have come to see it, others are content merely to know it is there. They all know that it has to be there. Some of them understand why, and some do not, but they all understand that their happiness, the beauty of their city, the tenderness of their friendships, the health of their children, the wisdom of their scholars, the skill of their makers, even the abundance of their harvest and the kindly weathers of their skies, depend wholly on this child's abominable misery.

This is usually explained to children when they are between eight and twelve, whenever they seem capable of understanding; and most of those who come to see the child are young people, though often enough an adult comes, or comes back, to see the child. No matter how well the matter has been explained to them, these young spectators are always shocked and sickened at the sight. They feel disgust, which they had thought themselves superior to. They feel anger, outrage, impotence, despite all the explanations. They would like to do something for the child. But there is nothing they can do. If the child were brought up into the sunlight out of that vile place, if it were cleaned and fed and comforted, that would be a good thing, indeed; but if it were done, in that day and hour all the prosperity and beauty and delight of Omelas would wither and be destroyed. Those are the terms. To exchange all the goodness and grace of every life in Omelas for that single, small improvement: to throw away the happiness of thousands for the chance of the happiness of one: that would be to let guilt within the walls indeed.

The terms are strict and absolute; there may not even be a kind word spoken to the child.

Often the young people go home in tears, or in a tearless rage, when they have seen the child and faced this terrible paradox. They may brood over it for weeks or years. But as time goes on they begin to realize that even if the child could be released, it would not get much good of its freedom: a little vague pleasure of warmth and food, no doubt, but little more. It is too degraded and imbecile to know any real joy. It has been afraid too long ever to be free of fear. Its habits are too uncouth for it to respond to humane treatment. Indeed, after so long it would probably be wretched without walls about it to protect it, and darkness for its eyes, and its own excrement to sit in. Their tears at the bitter injustice dry when they begin to perceive the terrible justice of reality, and to accept it. Yet it is their tears and anger, the trying of their generosity and the acceptance of their helplessness, which are perhaps the true source of the splendor of their lives. Theirs is no vapid, irresponsible happiness. They know that they, like the child, are not free. They know compassion. It is the existence of the child, and their knowledge of its existence, that makes possible the nobility of their architecture, the poignancy of their music, the profundity of their science. It is because of the child that they are so gentle with children. They

10

know that if the wretched one were not there snivelling in the dark, the other one, the flute-player, could make no joyful music as the young riders line up in their beauty for the race in the sunlight of the first morning of summer.

Now do you believe in them? Are they not more credible? But there is one more thing to tell, and this is quite incredible.

At times one of the adolescent girls or boys who go to see the child does not go home to weep or rage, does not, in fact, go home at all. Sometimes also a man or woman much older falls silent for a day or two, and then leaves home. These people go out into the street, and walk down the street alone. They keep walking, and walk straight out of the city of Omelas, through the beautiful gates. They keep walking across the farmlands of Omelas. Each one goes alone, youth or girl, man or woman. Night falls; the traveler must pass down village streets, between the houses with yellow-lit windows, and on out into the darkness of the fields. Each alone, they go west or north, towards the mountains. They go on. They leave Omelas, they walk ahead into the darkness, and they do not come back. The place they go towards is a place even less imaginable to most of us than the city of happiness. I cannot describe it at all. It is possible that it does not exist. But they seem to know where they are going, the ones who walk away from Omelas.   *[1973]*

≣ THINKING ABOUT THE TEXT

1. The opening three paragraphs make Omelas sound idyllic. Would some-place like this be your idea of utopia? What would you add? Subtract? Is such a world possible?

2. Is life inherently unfair? Are some destined to prosper and be happy and others destined for a life of toil and hardship? Does this tale touch on this idea?

3. Is Le Guin trying, in this dark fairy tale/allegory, to say something about our own culture? Is our happiness and comfort based on the pain or inconvenience of others?

4. What would your response be to the suffering outcast? Would you be outraged? Would you, like most of those in Omelas, come to accept the necessity of the solution?

5. Speculate on the reasons why some walk away from Omelas. Where are they going? How come they seem so resolute?

≣ MAKING COMPARISONS

1. Compare Qui in "Bloodchild" with the people who leave Omelas.

2. Compare ideas of right and wrong in "Bloodchild" and "The Ones Who Walk Away from Omelas."

3. Describe how morality is affected by our emotions in these three stories.

KURT VONNEGUT
Harrison Bergeron

Kurt Vonnegut (1922–2007), one of the best-known science fiction writers in America, was widely popular in the 1960s and 1970s, mostly for his darkly ironic, antiwar novel Slaughterhouse-Five *(1969), a tale based on Vonnegut's own experiences as a prisoner of war in Dresden. Vonnegut survived the massive Allied firebombing that killed more than 130,000 people, mostly civilians. The mental anguish he suffered there haunted him for years. His novel of these events became a best-seller, and Vonnegut became a hero of the anti–Vietnam War movement.*

Vonnegut was born in Indianapolis and attended Cornell University before entering World War II. His other works include the novel The Breakfast of Champions *(1973) and his short-story collection* Welcome to the Monkey House *(1968), which solidified his iconic status in America's counterculture as a comic genius with an urgent moral vision. In his last book,* A Man without a Country *(2005), he focuses his bitter satire on the Bush administration, the Iraq War, and conformist Americans. The novel was a best-seller.*

The year was 2081, and everybody was finally equal. They weren't only equal before God and the law. They were equal every which way. Nobody was smarter than anybody else. Nobody was better looking than anybody else. Nobody was stronger or quicker than anybody else. All this equality was due to the 211th, 212th, and 213th Amendments to the Constitution, and to the unceasing vigilance of agents of the United States Handicapper General.

Some things about living still weren't quite right, though. April, for instance, still drove people crazy by not being springtime. And it was in that clammy month that the H-G men took George and Hazel Bergeron's fourteen-year-old son, Harrison, away.

It was tragic, all right, but George and Hazel couldn't think about it very hard. Hazel had a perfectly average intelligence, which meant she couldn't think about anything except in short bursts. And George, while his intelligence was way above normal, had a little mental handicap radio in his ear. He was required by law to wear it at all times. It was tuned to a government transmitter. Every twenty seconds or so, the transmitter would send out some sharp noise to keep people like George from taking unfair advantage of their brains.

George and Hazel were watching television. There were tears on Hazel's cheeks, but she'd forgotten for the moment what they were about.

On the television screen were ballerinas.   5

A buzzer sounded in George's head. His thoughts fled in panic, like bandits from a burglar alarm.

"That was a real pretty dance, that dance they just did," said Hazel.

"Huh?" said George.

"That dance — it was nice," said Hazel.

"Yup," said George. He tried to think a little about the ballerinas. They   10
weren't really very good — no better than anybody else would have been,

anyway. They were burdened with sash-weights and bags of birdshot, and their faces were masked, so that no one, seeing a free and graceful gesture or a pretty face, would feel like something the cat dragged in. George was toying with the vague notion that maybe dancers shouldn't be handicapped. But he didn't get very far with it before another noise in his ear radio scattered his thoughts.

George winced. So did two out of the eight ballerinas.

Hazel saw him wince. Having no mental handicap herself, she had to ask George what the latest sound had been.

"Sounded like somebody hitting a milk bottle with a ball peen hammer," said George.

"I'd think it would be real interesting, hearing all the different sounds," said Hazel, a little envious. "All the things they think up."

"Um," said George.   15

"Only, if I was Handicapper General, you know what I would do?" said Hazel. Hazel, as a matter of fact, bore a strong resemblance to the Handicapper General, a woman named Diana Moon Glampers. "If I was Diana Moon Glampers," said Hazel, "I'd have chimes on Sunday — just chimes. Kind of in honor of religion."

"I could think, if it was just chimes," said George.

"Well — maybe make 'em real loud," said Hazel. "I think I'd make a good Handicapper General."

"Good as anybody else," said George.

"Who knows better'n I do what normal is?" said Hazel.   20

"Right," said George. He began to think glimmeringly about his abnormal son who was now in jail, about Harrison, but a twenty-one-gun salute in his head stopped that.

"Boy!" said Hazel, "that was a doozy, wasn't it?"

It was such a doozy that George was white and trembling, and tears stood on the rims of his red eyes. Two of the eight ballerinas had collapsed to the studio floor, were holding their temples.

"All of a sudden you look so tired," said Hazel. "Why don't you stretch out on the sofa, so's you can rest your handicap bag on the pillows, honeybunch." She was referring to the forty-seven pounds of birdshot in a canvas bag, which was padlocked around George's neck. "Go on and rest the bag for a little while," she said. "I don't care if you're not equal to me for a while."

George weighed the bag with his hands. "I don't mind it," he said. "I don't notice it any more. It's just a part of me."   25

"You been so tired lately — kind of wore out," said Hazel. "If there was just some way we could make a little hole in the bottom of the bag, and just take out a few of them lead balls. Just a few."

"Two years in prison and two thousand dollars fine for every ball I took out," said George. "I don't call that a bargain."

"If you could just take a few out when you came home from work," said Hazel, "I mean — you don't compete with anybody around here. You just set around."

"If I tried to get away with it," said George, "then other people'd get away with it — and pretty soon we'd be right back to the dark ages again, with everybody competing against everybody else. You wouldn't like that, would you?"

"I'd hate it," said Hazel.   30

"There you are," said George. "The minute people start cheating on laws, what do you think happens to society?"

If Hazel hadn't been able to come up with an answer to this question, George couldn't have supplied one. A siren was going off in his head.

"Reckon it'd fall all apart," said Hazel.

"What would?" said George blankly.

"Society," said Hazel uncertainly. "Wasn't that what you just said?"   35

"Who knows?" said George.

The television program was suddenly interrupted for a news bulletin. It wasn't clear at first as to what the bulletin was about, since the announcer, like all announcers, had a serious speech impediment. For about half a minute, and in a state of high excitement, the announcer tried to say, "Ladies and gentlemen —"

He finally gave up, handed the bulletin to a ballerina to read.

"That's all right —" Hazel said of the announcer, "he tried. That's the big thing. He tried to do the best he could with what God gave him. He should get a nice raise for trying so hard."

"Ladies and gentlemen —" said the ballerina, reading the bulletin. She   40
must have been extraordinarily beautiful, because the mask she wore was hideous. And it was easy to see that she was the strongest and most graceful of all the dancers, for her handicap bags were as big as those worn by two-hundred-pound men.

And she had to apologize at once for her voice, which was a very unfair voice for a woman to use. Her voice was a warm, luminous, timeless melody. "Excuse me —" she said, and she began again, making her voice absolutely uncompetitive.

"Harrison Bergeron, age fourteen," she said in a grackle squawk, "has just escaped from jail, where he was held on suspicion of plotting to overthrow the government. He is a genius and an athlete, is under-handicapped, and should be regarded as extremely dangerous."

A police photograph of Harrison Bergeron was flashed on the screen — upside down, then sideways, upside down again, then right side up. The picture showed the full length of Harrison against a background calibrated in feet and inches. He was exactly seven feet tall.

The rest of Harrison's appearance was Halloween and hardware. Nobody had ever borne heavier handicaps. He had outgrown hindrances faster than the H-G men could think them up. Instead of a little ear radio for a mental handicap, he wore a tremendous pair of earphones, and spectacles with thick wavy lenses. The spectacles were intended to make him not only half blind, but to give him whanging headaches besides.

Scrap metal was hung all over him. Ordinarily, there was a certain   45
symmetry, a military neatness to the handicaps issued to strong people, but

Harrison looked like a walking junkyard. In the race of life, Harrison carried three hundred pounds.

And to offset his good looks, the H-G men required that he wear at all times a red rubber ball for a nose, keep his eyebrows shaved off, and cover his even white teeth with black caps at snaggle-tooth random.

"If you see this boy," said the ballerina, "do not — I repeat, do not — try to reason with him."

There was the shriek of a door being torn from its hinges.

Screams and barking cries of consternation came from the television set. The photograph of Harrison Bergeron on the screen jumped again and again, as though dancing to the tune of an earthquake.

George Bergeron correctly identified the earthquake, and well he might   50
have — for many was the time his own home had danced to the same crashing tune. "My God —" said George, "that must be Harrison!"

The realization was blasted from his mind instantly by the sound of an automobile collision in his head.

When George could open his eyes again, the photograph of Harrison was gone. A living, breathing Harrison filled the screen.

Clanking, clownish, and huge, Harrison stood in the center of the studio. The knob of the uprooted studio door was still in his hand. Ballerinas, technicians, musicians, and announcers cowered on their knees before him, expecting to die.

"I am the Emperor!" cried Harrison. "Do you hear? I am the Emperor! Everybody must do what I say at once!" He stamped his foot and the studio shook.

"Even as I stand here —" he bellowed, "crippled, hobbled, sickened — I am   55
a greater ruler than any man who ever lived! Now watch me become what I *can* become!"

Harrison tore the straps of his handicap harness like wet tissue paper, tore straps guaranteed to support five thousand pounds.

Harrison's scrap-iron handicaps crashed to the floor.

Harrison thrust his thumbs under the bar of the padlock that secured his head harness. The bar snapped like celery. Harrison smashed his headphones and spectacles against the wall.

He flung away his rubber-ball nose, revealed a man that would have awed Thor, the god of thunder.

"I shall now select my Empress!" he said, looking down on the cowering   60
people. "Let the first woman who dares rise to her feet claim her mate and her throne!"

A moment passed, and then a ballerina arose, swaying like a willow.

Harrison plucked the mental handicap from her ear, snapped off her physical handicaps with marvellous delicacy. Last of all, he removed her mask.

She was blindingly beautiful.

"Now —" said Harrison, taking her hand, "shall we show the people the meaning of the word dance? Music!" he commanded.

The musicians scrambled back into their chairs, and Harrison stripped   65
them of their handicaps, too. "Play your best," he told them, "and I'll make you barons and dukes and earls."

The music began. It was normal at first — cheap, silly, false. But Harrison snatched two musicians from their chairs, waved them like batons as he sang the music as he wanted it played. He slammed them back into their chairs.

The music began again and was much improved.

Harrison and his Empress merely listened to the music for a while — listened gravely, as though synchronizing their heartbeats with it.

They shifted their weights to their toes.

Harrison placed his big hands on the girl's tiny waist, letting her sense the   70
weightlessness that would soon be hers.

And then, in an explosion of joy and grace, into the air they sprang!

Not only were the laws of the land abandoned, but the law of gravity and the laws of motion as well.

They reeled, whirled, swiveled, flounced, capered, gamboled, and spun.

They leaped like deer on the moon.

The studio ceiling was thirty feet high, but each leap brought the dancers   75
nearer to it.

It became their obvious intention to kiss the ceiling.

They kissed it.

And then, neutralizing gravity with love and pure will, they remained suspended in air inches below the ceiling, and they kissed each other for a long, long time.

It was then that Diana Moon Glampers, the Handicapper General, came into the studio with a double-barreled ten-gauge shotgun. She fired twice, and the Emperor and the Empress were dead before they hit the floor.

Diana Moon Glampers loaded the gun again. She aimed it at the musicians   80
and told them they had ten seconds to get their handicaps back on.

It was then that the Bergerons' television tube burned out.

Hazel turned to comment about the blackout to George. But George had gone out into the kitchen for a can of beer.

George came back in with the beer, paused while a handicap signal shook him up. And then he sat down again. "You been crying?" he said to Hazel.

"Yup," she said.

"What about?" he said.   85

"I forget," she said. "Something real sad on television."

"What was it?" he said.

"It's all kind of mixed up in my mind," said Hazel.

"Forget sad things," said George.

"I always do," said Hazel.   90

"That's my girl," said George. He winced. There was the sound of a riveting gun in his head.

"Gee — I could tell that one was a doozy," said Hazel.

"You can say that again," said George.

"Gee —" said Hazel, "I could tell that one was a doozy."   [1961]

▤ THINKING ABOUT THE TEXT

1. The famous nineteenth-century French historian Alexis de Tocqueville was impressed by American democracy but worried about its tendency to gravitate toward centrism, especially in small towns. Is this story a satire or a parody of that pressure to conform?

2. Does our culture have difficulty with difference, with those, say, with a very low or a very high IQ or with rebels, saints, and eccentrics?

3. If you read just the first sentence, would you assume that this is a story about a utopia? Since it is not, what is being satirized? Affirmative action? Authoritarian governments? Fear of difference?

4. What does "all men are created equal" mean? Do you think the meaning of this statement has changed over time?

5. What impulse does Harrison demonstrate when he rebels? Why does Glampers kill him?

▤ MAKING COMPARISONS

1. Compare Harrison with Qui.

2. What prevents rebellion in all four stories?

3. What elements of Vonnegut's story do you find present in contemporary society? How about Le Guin's story?

▤ WRITING ABOUT ISSUES

1. Argue that one of these satires is still, or even more, relevant to contemporary concerns.

2. Compare the theme of escape in at least three of the stories.

3. Write a personal response explaining why one of the stories speaks most directly to your concerns about contemporary society.

4. Do research on one of the writers in this cluster, and write a brief report focusing on his or her characteristic themes and concerns.

☰ Travels through the Dark: Re-Visions of a Poem

WILLIAM STAFFORD, "Traveling through the Dark"

JOHN BURNSIDE, "Penitence"

ROBERT WRIGLEY, "Highway 12, Just East of Paradise, Idaho"

LOREN GOODMAN, "Traveling through the Dark (2005)"

One of life's more disturbing events is hitting an animal as you drive alone on a dark night. Perhaps not in the city, but unfortunately in many suburban and rural sections of the country, it is an all too familiar occurrence. Depending on the context, it can test our ethical and social responsibility. Perhaps the temptation to flee is too great for many. But others will do more, seeing their predicament as a call to action, however ineffective. Given our cultural inclinations, hurting a deer seems particularly horrific. A surprising number of writers have dealt with just this situation, none more famously than William Stafford in "Traveling through the Dark." It seems reasonable to assume that the three poets in this cluster are familiar with Stafford's poignant and ethically resonant poem. But as with many iconic texts, some writers will treat it satirically and others seriously. And perhaps others — like Wrigley — want to parody the darkness of Stafford's ethical dilemma. Certainly the controversy surrounding the publication of Goodman's almost identical poem testifies to the esteemed place Stafford's text has in the literary canon.

☰ **BEFORE YOU READ**

Do you believe our interactions with animals should be influenced by ethical concerns? Do you see contradictions in our culture's treatment of animals?

WILLIAM STAFFORD
Traveling through the Dark

Besides being a poet himself, William Stafford (1914–1995) was a mentor to many others. During World War II, he was a conscientious objector. Later, he wrote and taught poetry at a variety of places in the United States, eventually settling in Oregon. The following poem was written in 1960 and subsequently appeared in a 1962 collection of Stafford's poems, also entitled Traveling through the Dark, *which won the National Book Award in 1963. He went on to publish over fifty more volumes of poetry and prose. He taught at Lewis and Clark College until his retirement in 1980. Like those of Robert Frost, to whom Stafford is often compared, his poems are deceptively simple. On closer examination, however, they reveal themselves to be complex and highly suggestive of deeper concerns.*

(Photo by Kim Stafford.)

(© Ulf Andersen/Getty Images.)

(Photo by Matt Valentine. Courtesy Robert Wrigley.)

(Courtesy Loren Goodman.)

Traveling through the dark I found a deer
dead on the edge of the Wilson River road.
It is usually best to roll them into the canyon:
that road is narrow; to swerve might make more dead.

By glow of the tail-light I stumbled back of the car   5
and stood by the heap, a doe, a recent killing;
she had stiffened already, almost cold.
I dragged her off; she was large in the belly.

My fingers touching her side brought me the reason —
her side was warm; her fawn lay there waiting,   10
alive, still, never to be born.
Beside that mountain road I hesitated.

The car aimed ahead its lowered parking lights;
under the hood purred the steady engine.
I stood in the glare of the warm exhaust turning red;   15
around our group I could hear the wilderness listen.

I thought hard for us all — my only swerving —
then pushed her over the edge into the river.   *[1962]*

■ THINKING ABOUT THE TEXT

1. Depending on where readers have grown up, the narrative of this poem might seem exotic or routine. Some readers have, in fact, faced exactly this situation. Have you any experience with such an event? Have you ever hit an animal with your car? What was your response?

2. How do you read "I could hear the wilderness listen" (line 16)? Why do you think the speaker uses "purred" in line 14?

3. What are some possible readings of the title? Of the word *dark*?

4. Why do you think the narrator "hesitated"? How would you define "swerve" as used in line 4? How about as it is used in the penultimate line?

5. This is, in part, a poem about decisions. Do you agree with the narrator's choice at the end? Would you have wanted to do otherwise?

JOHN BURNSIDE
Penitence

John Burnside (b. 1955) grew up in Dunfermline, Scotland. He studied English at Cambridge College and worked as a computer-software engineer. He currently teaches at the University of St. Andrews. His books of poetry have won numerous awards, including the Whitbread Poetry Award for Asylum Dance *(2000). The Light Trap was also short-listed for the T. S. Eliot Prize. He recently published his memoir,* A Lie about My Father *(2006), and* Gift Songs *(2007). He published a novel,* Glister, *in 2008 and a book of poems,* The Hunt in the Forest, *in 2009. The critic George Szirtes has said that Burnside's "antennae are tuned to the buzz and flow of nature."*

I was driving into the wind
on a northern road,
the redwoods swaying around me like a black
ocean.
     I'd drifted off: I didn't see the deer   5
till it bounced away,
the back legs swinging outwards as I braked
and swerved into the tinder
of the verge.
     Soon as I stopped   10
the headlamps filled with moths
and something beyond the trees was tuning in,
a hard attention
boring through my flesh
to stroke the bone.   15
     That shudder took so long

to end, I thought the animal had slipped
beneath the wheels, and lay there
quivering.
       I left the engine running; stepped outside;   20
away, at the edge of the light, a body
shifted amongst the leaves
and I wanted to go, to help, to make it well,
but every step I took
pushed it away.   25
       Or — no; that's not the truth,
or all the truth:
now I admit my own fear held me back,
not fear of the dark or that presence
bending the trees;   30
not even fear, exactly, but the dread
of touching, of colliding with that pain.
I stood there, in the river of the wind,
for minutes; then I walked back to the car
and drove away.   35
       I want to think that deer
survived; or, if it died,
it slipped into the blackness unawares.
But now and then I drive out to the woods
and park the car: the headlamps fill with moths;   40
the woods tune in; I listen to the night
and hear an echo, fading through the trees,
my own flesh in the body of the deer
still resonant, remembered through the fender.   *[1997]*

■ THINKING ABOUT THE TEXT

1. The narrator is more responsible for the deer's death than the speaker in the previous poem. Do you think this affects his behavior?

2. What specific words echo those in Stafford's poem?

3. This narrator says "the woods tune in" (line 41). Is this different from "I could hear the wilderness listen" in Stafford's poem?

4. Like Stafford's narrator, the driver here leaves the engine running and steps outside. Describe the differences in their subsequent behaviors.

5. This narrator walks away from the deer. Can you understand why? What would you have done?

■ MAKING COMPARISONS

1. Compare the narrators of both poems. Does one seem more ethical than the other?

2. What are the similarities and differences in these two poems?

3. What seems the strongest first evidence that Burnside was thinking of the Stafford poem?

ROBERT WRIGLEY

Highway 12, Just East of Paradise, Idaho

Robert Wrigley (b. 1951) is the director of the M.F.A. program in creative writing at the University of Idaho. He received his M.A. from the University of Utah and has written six volumes of poetry, including Lives of Animals *(2003). He has won numerous awards, including a Guggenheim Fellowship and a National Endowment of the Arts Fellowship. Wrigley lives in Moscow, Idaho, with the writer Kim Barnes. His most recent book is* Early Meditations: New and Selected Poems *(2006).*

The doe, at a dead run, was dead
the instant the truck hit her.
In the headlights I saw her tongue
extend and her eyes go shocked and vacant.
Launched at a sudden right angle — say   5
from twenty miles per hour south to fifty
miles per hour east — she skated
many yards on the slightest toe-edge tips
of her dainty deer hooves, then fell
slowly, inside the speed of her new trajectory,   10
not pole-axed but stunned, away
from me and the truck's decelerating pitch.
She skidded along the right lane's
fog line true as a cue ball,
until her neck caught a sign post   15
that spun her across both lanes and out of sight
beyond the edge. For which, I admit, I was grateful,
the road there being dark, narrow, and shoulderless,
and home, with its lights, not far away.   *[2003]*

≡ THINKING ABOUT THE TEXT

1. Does the narrator seem too matter-of-fact or perhaps too indifferent to the deer's death? What are some other ways he might have responded? How would you?

2. Are you surprised that most of this poem is a quite detailed account of the deer's demise? What effect do you think the poet is after? Is it effective?

3. Does the phrase "her dainty deer hooves" (line 9) seem a bit odd with respect to the general tone and language of the poem? Are there other words or phrases that caught your attention?

4. Were you surprised by the term "grateful" (line 17)? Do you think the speaker is insensitive, honest, or simply practical and unsentimental?

5. Do you think Wrigley wrote this poem with "Traveling through the Dark" in the background; that is, is this yet another way of dealing with the death of a deer on a dark road?

▤ MAKING COMPARISONS

1. What specific similarities do you see among the poems?

2. Is Wrigley more practical or less heartless than Stafford and Burnside?

3. Which response to hitting a deer do you imagine would be closest to yours? Why?

LOREN GOODMAN
Traveling through the Dark (2005)

Loren Goodman (b. 1969) was raised in Wichita, Kansas, and graduated from Columbia University in 1991. He later received an M.A. from SUNY-Buffalo. Critics see his book of poems, Famous Americans *(2006), which was published in the prestigious Yale Younger Poets Series, as sophisticated comic art. His most recent work is* Suppository Writing *(2008). The poet W. S. Merwin notes that Goodman seems to love nonsense for its own sake but that his work is also clever, spontaneous, playful, and surreal. Others are not so sure. When the controversial poem presented here appeared in the prestigious journal* Poetry *(July/August 2005), some readers were surprised, some outraged. Others saw this poem, an intriguing and surprising reworking of William Stafford's classic verse, as provocative and serious.*

Traveling through the dark I found a deer
dead on the edge of the Wilson River road.
It is usually best to roll them into the canyon:
that road is narrow; to swerve might make more dead.

By glow of the tail-light I stumbled back of the car   5
and stood by the heap, a doe, a recent killing;
she had stiffened already, almost cold.
I dragged her off; she was large in the belly.

My fingers touching her side brought me the reason —
her side was warm; her fawn lay there waiting,   10
alive, still, never to be born.
Beside that mountain road I hesitated.

The car aimed ahead its lowered parking lights;
under the hood purred the steady engine.
I stood in the glare of the warm exhaust turning red;   15
around our group I could hear the wilderness listen.

I thought hard for us all — my only swerving —,
then pushed myself over the edge into the river.   *[2005]*

≣ THINKING ABOUT THE TEXT

1. Assuming this parody is also meant to be serious, how does "myself" change the meaning of the poem?
2. If this were the first time you were reading this poem, might you be surprised by the last line? Why?
3. Is it possible to read the poem as leading logically to "myself"? Why?
4. Goodman is probably trying for multiple effects. What might they be?
5. Can you think of other plausible ways to change the last lines? What effect does your change make on the meaning of the poem? What would be the effect if you changed "deer" to a person — say, a friend, a lover, or an enemy?

≣ MAKING COMPARISONS

1. Both the Wrigley and Goodman poems can be seen as parodies. Which do you prefer?
2. Of the four "takes" on accidents with animals, which seems the most insightful? Why?
3. Which of the three poems do you think Stafford would be most impressed by? The most surprised by?

≣ WRITING ABOUT ISSUES

1. Argue that the title of Stafford's poem is the key to understanding the verse's meaning.
2. Argue that Goodman's poem is not plagiarism.
3. Write a brief critique of these poems, choosing one as the response to hitting a deer that you feel most resembles your own.
4. Argue that there are or are not ethical issues in the situation Stafford and the others deal with.

▤ End of the Journey: Plays

MARSHA NORMAN, *'night, Mother*

TERRENCE McNALLY, *Andre's Mother*

Metaphors about life being a journey or a quest are as old as literature itself. Naturally writers have often compared death to the end of the journey. Sometimes, of course, the end is expected, as the elderly succumb to the inexorable force of time. But most literary tales of the end of the journey gain their poignancy because the end of the journey comes too soon. We usually understand how disease and accident can interrupt a life in mid-journey, but we are stunned and dismayed when the traveler voluntarily cuts short a life's journey through suicide. In fact, in the drama *'night Mother* by Pulitzer Prize–winning Marsha Norman, the daughter, Jessie, tells her mother that for her it is simply time to get off the bus. The play unpacks the drama of the decision in honest and unsettling ways. Terrence McNally's *Andre's Mother*, on the other hand, tells the very brief story of a talented actor cut down in his prime by AIDS. This sketch says a good deal about our culture's response to this epidemic by having Andre's mother remain silent at his funeral.

▤ BEFORE YOU READ

What influences your view of suicide? Would you ever approve of someone's committing suicide? If so, under what circumstances? Are there people today who blame AIDS patients for their illness? Why do they do so?

MARSHA NORMAN
'night, Mother

Marsha Norman (b. 1947) grew up in Louisville, Kentucky, and has long been associated with the Actors Theatre there. Her plays include Getting Out *(1977),* Traveler in the Dark *(1984), and, most recently,* Last Dance *(2003). She wrote the book for the 2005 Broadway adaptation of Alice Walker's* The Color Purple. *In 1991, her script for the musical* The Secret Garden *won her a Tony Award. The play* 'night, Mother, *for which Norman won the Pulitzer Prize, premiered at the American Repertory Theatre in Cambridge, Massachusetts, in January 1983. In March of that year, it was produced on Broadway. Both of these productions featured Kathy Bates as Jessie and Anne Pitoniak as Thelma; in the 1986 film version, the roles were played by Sissy Spacek and Anne Bancroft. In 2004, the play was revived on Broadway, with Edie Falco of the television series* The Sopranos *as Jessie and film actress Brenda Blethlyn as Thelma. As a theater piece,* 'night, Mother *has aroused a lot of attention for its treatment of suicide. It is also distinctive in its time span. With plays and movies, hardly ever does the time span represented coincide with the work's* actual running time. This play covers about ninety minutes in the lives of its characters and takes the same amount of time to perform. Indeed, in most productions of the play, the time shown by the clocks on the set is the same as the actual time when the play is performed in the evening.

CHARACTERS

JESSIE CATES, *in her late thirties or early forties, is pale and vaguely unsteady physically. It is only in the last year that Jessie has gained control of her mind and body, and tonight she is determined to hold on to that control. She wears pants and a long black sweater with deep pockets, which contain scraps of paper, and there may be a pencil behind her ear or a pen clipped to one of the pockets of the sweater.*

> *As a rule, Jessie doesn't feel much like talking. Other people have rarely found her quirky sense of humor amusing. She has a peaceful energy on this night, a sense of purpose, but is clearly aware of the time passing moment by moment. Oddly enough, Jessie has never been as communicative or as enjoyable as she is on this evening, but we must know she has not always been this way. There is a familiarity between these two women that comes from having lived together for a long time. There is a shorthand to the talk and a sense of routine comfort in the way they relate to each other physically. Naturally, there are also routine aggravations.*

THELMA CATES, MAMA, *is Jessie's mother, in her late fifties or early sixties. She has begun to feel her age and so takes it easy when she can, or when it serves her purpose to let someone help her. But she speaks quickly and enjoys talking. She believes that things are what she says they are. Her sturdiness is more a mental quality than a physical one, finally. She is chatty and nosy, and this is her house.*

The play takes place in a relatively new house built way out on a country road, with a living room and connecting kitchen, and a center hall that leads off to the bedrooms. A pull cord in the hall ceiling releases a ladder which leads to the attic. One of these bedrooms opens directly onto the hall, and its entry should be visible to everyone in the audience. It should be, in fact, the focal point of the entire set, and the lighting should make it disappear completely at times and draw the entire set into it at others. It is a point of both threat and promise. It is an ordinary door that opens onto absolute nothingness. That door is the point of all the action, and the utmost care should be given to its design and construction.

The living room is cluttered with magazines and needlework catalogs, ashtrays and candy dishes. Examples of Mama's needlework are everywhere — pillows, afghans, and quilts, doilies and rugs, and they are quite nice examples. The house is more comfortable than messy, but there is quite a lot to keep in place here. It is more personal than charming. It is not quaint. Under no circumstances should the set and its dressing make a judgment about the intelligence or taste of Jessie and Mama. It should simply indicate that they are very specific real people who happen to live in a particular part of the country. Heavy accents, which would further distance the audience from Jessie and Mama, are also wrong.

The time is the present, with the action beginning about 8:15. Clocks onstage in the kitchen and on a table in the living room should run throughout the performance and be visible to the audience.

There will be no intermission.

Mama stretches to reach the cupcakes in a cabinet in the kitchen. She can't see them, but she can feel around for them, and she's eager to have one, so she's working pretty hard at it. This may be the most serious exercise Mama ever gets. She finds a cupcake, the coconut-covered, raspberry-and-marshmallow-filled kind known as a snowball, but sees that there's one missing from the package. She calls to Jessie, who is apparently somewhere else in the house.

MAMA *(unwrapping the cupcake)*:   Jessie, it's the last snowball, sugar. Put it on the list, O.K.? And we're out of Hershey bars, and where's that peanut brittle? I think maybe Dawson's been in it again. I ought to put a big mirror on the refrigerator door. That'll keep him out of my treats, won't it? You hear me, honey? *(Then more to herself.)* I hate it when the coconut falls off. Why does the coconut fall off?

Jessie enters from her bedroom, carrying a stack of newspapers.

JESSIE: We got any old towels?

MAMA: There you are!

JESSIE *(holding a towel that was on the stack of newspapers)*:   Towels you don't want anymore. *(Picking up Mama's snowball wrapper.)* How about this swimming towel Loretta gave us? Beach towel, that's the name of it. You want it? *(Mama shakes her head no.)*

MAMA: What have you been doing in there?

JESSIE: And a big piece of plastic like a rubber sheet or something. Garbage bags would do if there's enough.

MAMA: Don't go making a big mess, Jessie. It's eight o'clock already.

JESSIE: Maybe an old blanket or towels we got in a soap box sometime?

MAMA: I said don't make a mess. Your hair is black enough, hon.

JESSIE *(continuing to search the kitchen cabinets, finding two or three more towels to add to her stack)*:   It's not for my hair, Mama. What about some old pillows anywhere, or a foam cushion out of a yard chair would be real good.

MAMA: You haven't forgot what night it is, have you? *(Holding up her fingernails.)* They're all chipped, see? I've been waiting all week, Jess. It's Saturday night, sugar.

JESSIE: I know. I got it on the schedule.

MAMA *(crossing to the living room)*:   You want me to wash 'em now or are you making your mess first? *(Looking at the snowball.)* We're out of these. Did I say that already?

JESSIE: There's more coming tomorrow. I ordered you a whole case.

MAMA *(checking the TV Guide)*:   A whole case will go stale, Jessie.

JESSIE: They can go in the freezer till you're ready for them. Where's Daddy's gun?

MAMA: In the attic.

JESSIE: Where in the attic? I looked your whole nap and couldn't find it anywhere.

MAMA: One of his shoeboxes, I think.

JESSIE: Full of shoes. I looked already.

MAMA: Well, you didn't look good enough, then. There's that box from the
ones he wore to the hospital. When he died, they told me I could have them
back, but I never did like those shoes.

JESSIE *(pulling them out of her pocket)*:   I found the bullets. They were in an old
milk can.

MAMA *(as Jessie starts for the hall)*:   Dawson took the shotgun, didn't he? Hand
me that basket, hon.

JESSIE *(getting the basket for her)*:   Dawson better not've taken that pistol.

MAMA *(stopping her again)*:   Now my glasses, please. *(Jessie returns to get the
glasses.)* I told him to take those rubber boots, too, but he said they were for
fishing. I told him to take up fishing.

Jessie reaches for the cleaning spray and cleans Mama's glasses for her.

JESSIE: He's just too lazy to climb up there, Mama. Or maybe he's just being
smart. That floor's not very steady.

MAMA *(getting out a piece of knitting)*:   It's not a floor at all, hon, it's a board
now and then. Measure this for me. I need six inches.

JESSIE *(as she measures)*:   Dawson could probably use some of those clothes up
there. Somebody should have them. You ought to call the Salvation Army
before the whole thing falls in on you. Six inches exactly.

MAMA: It's plenty safe! As long as you don't go up there.

JESSIE *(turning to go again)*:   I'm careful.

MAMA: What do you want the gun for, Jess?

JESSIE *(not returning this time. Opening the ladder in the hall.)*:   Protection. *(She
steadies the ladder as Mama talks.)*

MAMA: You take the TV way too serious, hon. I've never seen a criminal in
my life. This is way too far to come for what's out here to steal. Never seen
a one.

JESSIE *(taking her first step up)*:   Except for Ricky.

MAMA: Ricky is mixed up. That's not a crime.

JESSIE: Get your hands washed. I'll be right back. And get 'em real dry. You dry
your hands till I get back or it's no go, all right?

MAMA: I thought Dawson told you not to go up those stairs.

JESSIE *(going up)*:   He did.

MAMA: I don't like the idea of a gun, Jess.

JESSIE *(calling down from the attic)*:   Which shoebox, do you remember?

MAMA: Black.

JESSIE: The box was black?

MAMA: The shoes were black.

JESSIE: That doesn't help much, Mother.

MAMA: I'm not trying to help, sugar. *(No answer.)* We don't have anything
anybody'd want, Jessie. I mean, I don't even want what we got, Jessie.

JESSIE: Neither do I. Wash your hands. *(Mama gets up and crosses to stand under the ladder.)*

MAMA: You come down from there before you have a fit. I can't come up and get you, you know.

JESSIE: I know.

MAMA: We'll just hand it over to them when they come, how's that? Whatever they want, the criminals.

JESSIE: That's a good idea, Mama.

MAMA: Ricky will grow out of this and be a real fine boy, Jess. But I have to tell you, I wouldn't want Ricky to know we had a gun in the house.

JESSIE: Here it is. I found it.

MAMA: It's just something Ricky's going through. Maybe he's in with some bad people. He just needs some time, sugar. He'll get back in school or get a job or one day you'll get a call and he'll say he's sorry for all the trouble he's caused and invite you out for supper someplace dress-up.

JESSIE *(coming back down the steps)*:   Don't worry. It's not for him, it's for me.

MAMA: I didn't think you would shoot your own boy, Jessie. I know you've felt like it, well, we've all felt like shooting somebody, but we don't do it. I just don't think we need . . .

JESSIE *(interrupting)*:   Your hands aren't washed. Do you want a manicure or not?

MAMA: Yes, I do, but . . .

JESSIE *(crossing to the chair)*:   Then wash your hands and don't talk to me anymore about Ricky. Those two rings he took were the last valuable things *I* had, so now he's started in on other people, door to door. I hope they put him away sometime. I'd turn him in myself if I knew where he was.

MAMA: You don't mean that.

JESSIE: Every word. Wash your hands and that's the last time I'm telling you.

Jessie sits down with the gun and starts cleaning it, pushing the cylinder out, checking to see that the chambers and barrel are empty, then putting some oil on a small patch of cloth and pushing it through the barrel with the push rod that was in the box. Mama goes to the kitchen and washes her hands, as instructed, trying not to show her concern about the gun.

MAMA: I shoulda got you to bring down that milk can. Agnes Fletcher sold hers to somebody with a flea market for forty dollars apiece.

JESSIE: I'll go back and get it in a minute. There's a wagon wheel up there, too. There's even a churn. I'll get it all if you want.

MAMA *(coming over, now, taking over now)*:   What are you doing?

JESSIE: The barrel has to be clean, Mama. Old powder, dust gets in it . . .

MAMA: What for?

JESSIE: I told you.

MAMA *(reaching for the gun)*:   And I told you, we don't get criminals out here.

JESSIE *(quickly pulling it to her)*:   And I told you . . . *(Then trying to be calm.)* The gun is for me.

MAMA: Well, you can have it if you want. When I die, you'll get it all, anyway.

JESSIE: I'm going to kill myself, Mama.

MAMA *(returning to the sofa)*:   Very funny. Very funny.

JESSIE: I am.

MAMA: You are not! Don't even say such a thing, Jessie.

JESSIE: How would you know if I didn't say it? You want it to be a surprise? You're lying there in your bed or maybe you're just brushing your teeth and you hear this . . . noise down the hall?

MAMA: Kill yourself.

JESSIE: Shoot myself. In a couple of hours.

MAMA: It must be time for your medicine.

JESSIE: Took it already.

MAMA: What's the matter with you?

JESSIE: Not a thing. Feel fine.

MAMA: You feel fine. You're just going to kill yourself.

JESSIE: Waited until I felt good enough, in fact.

MAMA: Don't make jokes, Jessie. I'm too old for jokes.

JESSIE: It's not a joke, Mama.

Mama watches for a moment in silence.

MAMA: That gun's no good, you know. He broke it right before he died. He dropped it in the mud one day.

JESSIE: Seems O.K. *(She spins the chamber, cocks the pistol, and pulls the trigger. The gun is not yet loaded, so all we hear is the click, but it will definitely work. It's also obvious that Jessie knows her way around a gun. Mama cannot speak.)* I had Cecil's all ready in there, just in case I couldn't find this one, but I'd rather use Daddy's.

MAMA: Those bullets are at least fifteen years old.

JESSIE *(pulling out another box)*:   These are from last week.

MAMA: Where did you get those?

JESSIE: Feed store Dawson told me about.

MAMA: Dawson!

JESSIE: I told him I was worried about prowlers. He said he thought it was a good idea. He told me what kind to ask for.

MAMA: If he had any idea . . .

JESSIE: He took it as a compliment. He thought I might be taking an interest in things. He got through telling me all about the bullets and then he said we ought to talk like this more often.

MAMA: And where was I while this was going on?

JESSIE: On the phone with Agnes. About the milk can, I guess. Anyway, I asked Dawson if he thought they'd send me some bullets and he said he'd just call for me, because he knew they'd send them if he told them to. And he was absolutely right. Here they are.

MAMA: How could he do that?

JESSIE: Just trying to help, Mama.

MAMA: And then I told you where the gun was.

JESSIE *(smiling, enjoying this joke)*:   See? Everybody's doing what they can.

MAMA: You told me it was for protection!

JESSIE: It *is*! I'm still doing your nails, though. Want to try that new Chinaberry color?

MAMA: Well, I'm calling Dawson right now. We'll just see what he has to say about this little stunt.

JESSIE: Dawson doesn't have any more to do with this.

MAMA: He's your brother.

JESSIE: And that's all.

MAMA *(stands up, moves toward the phone)*: Dawson will put a stop to this. Yes he will. He'll take the gun away.

JESSIE: If you call him, I'll just have to do it before he gets here. Soon as you hang up the phone, I'll just walk in the bedroom and lock the door. Dawson will get here just in time to help you clean up. Go ahead, call him. Then call the police. Then call the funeral home. Then call Loretta and see if *she'll* do your nails.

MAMA: You will not! This is crazy talk, Jessie!

Mama goes directly to the telephone and starts to dial, but Jessie is fast, coming up behind her and taking the receiver out of her hand, putting it back down.

JESSIE *(firm and quiet)*: I said no. This is private. Dawson is not invited.

MAMA: Just me.

JESSIE: I don't want anybody else over here. Just you and me. If Dawson comes over, it'll make me feel stupid for not doing it ten years ago.

MAMA: I think we better call the doctor. Or how about the ambulance. You like that one driver, I know. What's his name, Timmy? Get you somebody to talk to.

JESSIE *(going back to her chair)*: I'm through talking, Mama. You're it. No more.

MAMA: We're just going to sit around like every other night in the world and then you're going to kill yourself? *(Jessie doesn't answer.)* You'll miss. *(Again there is no response.)* You'll just wind up a vegetable. How would you like that? Shoot your ear off? You know what the doctor said about getting excited. You'll cock the pistol and have a fit.

JESSIE: I think I can kill myself, Mama.

MAMA: You're not going to kill yourself, Jessie. You're not even upset! *(Jessie smiles, or laughs quietly, and Mama tries a different approach.)* People don't really kill themselves, Jessie. No, mam, doesn't make sense, unless you're retarded or deranged, and you're as normal as they come, Jessie, for the most part. We're all *afraid* to die.

JESSIE: I'm not, Mama. I'm cold all the time, anyway.

MAMA: That's ridiculous.

JESSIE: It's exactly what I want. It's dark and quiet.

MAMA: So is the back yard, Jessie! Close your eyes. Stuff cotton in your ears. Take a nap! It's quiet in your room. I'll leave the TV off all night.

JESSIE: So quiet I don't know it's quiet. So nobody can get me.

MAMA: You don't know what dead is like. It might not be quiet at all. What if it's like an alarm clock and you can't wake up so you can't shut it off. Ever.

JESSIE: Dead is everybody and everything I ever knew, gone. Dead is dead quiet.

MAMA: It's a sin. You'll go to hell.

JESSIE: Uh-huh.

MAMA: You will!

JESSIE: Jesus was a suicide, if you ask me.

MAMA: You'll go to hell just for saying that. Jessie!

JESSIE *(with genuine surprise)*:   I didn't know I thought that.

MAMA: Jessie!

Jessie doesn't answer. She puts the now-loaded gun back in the box and crosses to the kitchen. But Mama is afraid she's headed for the bedroom.

MAMA *(in a panic)*:   You can't use my towels! They're my towels. I've had them for a long time. I like my towels.

JESSIE: I asked you if you wanted that swimming towel and you said you didn't.

MAMA: And you can't use your father's gun, either. It's mine now, too. And you can't do it in my house.

JESSIE: Oh, come on.

MAMA: No. You can't do it. I won't let you. The house is in my name.

JESSIE: I have to go in the bedroom and lock the door behind me so they won't arrest you for killing me. They'll probably test your hands for gunpowder, anyway, but you'll pass.

MAMA: Not in my house!

JESSIE: If I'd known you were going to act like this, I wouldn't have told you.

MAMA: How am I supposed to act? Tell you to go ahead? O.K. by me, sugar? Might try it myself. What took you so long?

JESSIE: There's just no point in fighting me over it, that's all. Want some coffee?

MAMA: Your birthday's coming up, Jessie. Don't you want to know what we got you?

JESSIE: You got me dusting powder, Loretta got me a new housecoat, pink probably, and Dawson got me new slippers, too small, but they go with the robe, he'll say. *(Mama cannot speak.)* Right? *(Apparently Jessie is right.)* Be back in a minute.

Jessie takes the gun box, puts it on top of the stack of towels and garbage bags, and takes them into her bedroom. Mama, alone for a moment, goes to the phone, picks up the receiver, looks toward the bedroom, starts to dial, and then replaces the receiver in its cradle as Jessie walks back into the room. Jessie wonders, silently. They have lived together for so long there is very rarely any reason for one to ask what the other was about to do.

MAMA: I started to, but I didn't. I didn't call him.

JESSIE: Good. Thank you.

MAMA *(starting over, a new approach)*:   What's this all about, Jessie?

JESSIE: About?

Jessie now begins the next task she had "on the schedule," which is refilling all the candy jars, taking the empty papers out of the boxes of chocolates, etc. Mama generally snitches when Jessie does this. Not tonight, though. Nevertheless, Jessie offers.

MAMA: What did I do?

JESSIE: Nothing. Want a caramel?

MAMA *(ignoring the candy)*:   You're mad at me.

JESSIE: Not a bit. I am worried about you, but I'm going to do what I can before I go. We're not just going to sit around tonight. I made a list of things.

MAMA: What things?

JESSIE: How the washer works. Things like that.

MAMA: I know how the washer works. You put the clothes in. You put the soap in. You turn it on. You wait.

JESSIE: You do something else. You don't just wait.

MAMA: Whatever else you find to do, you're still mainly waiting. The waiting's the worst part of it. The waiting's what you pay somebody else to do, if you can.

JESSIE *(nodding)*:   O.K. Where do we keep the soap?

MAMA: I could find it.

JESSIE: See?

MAMA: If you're mad about doing the wash, we can get Loretta to do it.

JESSIE: Oh now, that might be worth staying to see.

MAMA: She'd never in her life, would she?

JESSIE: Nope.

MAMA: What's the matter with her?

JESSIE: She thinks she's better than we are. She's not.

MAMA: Maybe if she didn't wear that yellow all the time.

JESSIE: The washer repair number is on a little card taped to the side of the machine.

MAMA: Loretta doesn't ever have to come over here again. Dawson can just leave her at home when he comes. And we don't ever have to see Dawson either if he bothers you. Does he bother you?

JESSIE: Sure he does. Be sure you clean out the lint tray every time you use the dryer. But don't ever put your house shoes in, it'll melt the soles.

MAMA: What does Dawson do, that bothers you?

JESSIE: He just calls me Jess like he knows who he's talking to. He's always wondering what I do all day. I mean, I wonder that myself, but it's my day, so it's mine to wonder about, not his.

MAMA: Family is just accident, Jessie. It's nothing personal, hon. They don't mean to get on your nerves. They don't even mean to be your family, they just are.

JESSIE: They know too much.

MAMA: About what?

JESSIE: They know things about you, and they learned it before you had a chance to say whether you wanted them to know it or not. They were there when it happened and it don't belong to them, it belongs to you, only they got it. Like my mail-order bra got delivered to their house.

MAMA: By accident!

JESSIE: All the same . . . they opened it. They saw the little rosebuds on it. *(Offering her another candy.)* Chewy mint?

MAMA *(shaking her head no)*:   What do they know about you? I'll tell them never to talk about it again. Is it Ricky or Cecil or your fits or your hair is falling out or you drink too much coffee or you never go out of the house or what?

JESSIE: I just don't like their talk. The account at the grocery is in Dawson's name when you call. The number's on a whole list of numbers on the back cover of the phone book.

MAMA: Well! Now we're getting somewhere. They're none of them ever setting foot in this house again.

JESSIE: It's not them, Mother. I wouldn't kill myself just to get away from them.

MAMA: You leave the room when they come over, anyway.

JESSIE: I stay as long as I can. Besides, it's you they come to see.

MAMA: That's because I stay in the room when they come.

JESSIE: It's not them.

MAMA: Then what is it?

JESSIE *(checking the list on her note pad)*:   The grocery won't deliver on Saturday anymore. And if you want your order the same day, you have to call before ten. And they won't deliver less than fifteen dollars' worth. What I do is tell them what we need and tell them to add on cigarettes until it gets to fifteen dollars.

MAMA: It's Ricky. You're trying to get through to him.

JESSIE: If I thought I could do that, I would stay.

MAMA: Make him sorry he hurt you, then. That's it, isn't it?

JESSIE: He's hurt me, I've hurt him. We're about even.

MAMA: You'll be telling him killing is O.K. with you, you know. Want him to start killing next? Nothing wrong with it. Mom did it.

JESSIE: Only a matter of time, anyway, Mama. When the call comes, you let Dawson handle it.

MAMA: Honey, nothing says those calls are always going to be some new trouble he's into. You could get one that he's got a job, that he's getting married, or how about he's joined the army, wouldn't that be nice?

JESSIE: If you call the Sweet Tooth before you call the grocery, that Susie will take your fudge next door to the grocery and it'll all come out together. Be sure you talk to Susie, though. She won't let them put it in the bottom of a sack like that one time, remember?

MAMA: Ricky could come over, you know. What if he calls us?

JESSIE: It's not Ricky, Mama.

MAMA: Or anybody could call us, Jessie.

JESSIE: Not on Saturday night, Mama.

MAMA: Then what is it? Are you sick? If your gums are swelling again, we can get you to the dentist in the morning.

JESSIE: No. Can you order your medicine or do you want Dawson to? I've got a note to him. I'll add that to it if you want.

MAMA: Your eyes don't look right. I thought so yesterday.

JESSIE: That was just the ragweed. I'm not sick.

MAMA: Epilepsy is sick, Jessie.

JESSIE: It won't kill me. *(A pause.)* If it would, I wouldn't have to.

MAMA: You don't *have* to.

JESSIE: No, I don't. That's what I like about it.

MAMA: Well, I won't let you!

JESSIE: It's not up to you.

MAMA: Jessie!

JESSIE: I want to hang a big sign around my neck, like Daddy's on the barn. GONE FISHING.

MAMA: You don't like it here.

JESSIE *(smiling)*:   Exactly.

MAMA: I meant here in my house.

JESSIE: I know you did.

MAMA: You never should have moved back in here with me. If you'd kept your little house or found another place when Cecil left you, you'd have made some new friends at least. Had a life to lead. Had your own things around you. Give Ricky a place to come see you. You never should've come here.

JESSIE: Maybe.

MAMA: But I didn't force you, did I?

JESSIE: If it was a mistake, we made it together. You took me in. I appreciate that.

MAMA: You didn't have any business being by yourself right then, but I can see how you might want a place of your own. A grown woman should . . .

JESSIE: Mama . . . I'm just not having a very good time and I don't have any reason to think it'll get anything but worse. I'm tired. I'm hurt. I'm sad. I feel used.

MAMA: Tired of what?

JESSIE: It all.

MAMA: What does that mean?

JESSIE: I can't say it any better.

MAMA: Well, you'll have to say it better because I'm not letting you alone till you do. What were those other things? Hurt . . . *(Before Jessie can answer.)* You had this all ready to say to me, didn't you? Did you write this down? How long have you been thinking about this?

JESSIE: Off and on, ten years. On all the time, since Christmas.

MAMA: What happened at Christmas?

JESSIE: Nothing.

MAMA: So why Christmas?

JESSIE: That's it. On the nose.

A pause. Mama knows exactly what Jessie means. She was there, too, after all.

JESSIE *(putting the candy sacks away)*:   See where all this is? Red hots up front, sour balls and horehound mixed together in this one sack. New packages of toffee and licorice right in back there.

MAMA: Go back to your list. You're hurt by what?

JESSIE *(Mama knows perfectly well)*:   Mama . . .

MAMA: O.K. Sad about what? There's nothing real sad going on right now. If it was after your divorce or something, that would make sense.

JESSIE *(looking at her list, then opening the drawer)*:   Now, this drawer has every-thing in it that there's no better place for. Extension cords, batteries for the radio, extra lighters, sandpaper, masking tape, Elmer's glue, thumbtacks, that kind of stuff. The mousetraps are under the sink, but you call Dawson if you've got one and let him do it.

MAMA: Sad about what?

JESSIE: The way things are.

MAMA: Not good enough. What things?

JESSIE: Oh, everything from you and me to Red China.

MAMA: I think we can leave the Chinese out of this.

JESSIE *(crosses back into the living room)*:   There's extra light bulbs in a box in the hall closet. And we've got a couple of packages of fuses in the fuse box. There's candles and matches in the top of the broom closet, but if the lights go out, just call Dawson and sit tight. But don't open the refrigerator door. Things will stay cool in there as long as you keep the door shut.

MAMA: I asked you a question.

JESSIE: I read the paper. I don't like how things are. And they're not any better out there than they are in here.

MAMA: If you're doing this because of the newspapers, I can sure fix that!

JESSIE: There's just more of it on TV.

MAMA *(kicking the television set)*:   Take it out, then!

JESSIE: You wouldn't do that.

MAMA: Watch me.

JESSIE: What would you do all day?

MAMA *(desperately)*:   Sing. *(Jessie laughs.)* I would, too. You want to watch? I'll sing till morning to keep you alive, Jessie, please!

JESSIE: No. *(Then affectionately.)* It's a funny idea, though. What do you sing?

MAMA *(has no idea how to answer this)*:   We've got a good life here!

JESSIE *(going back into the kitchen)*:   I called this morning and canceled the pa-pers, except for Sunday, for your puzzles; you'll still get that one.

MAMA: Let's get another dog, Jessie! You liked a big dog, now, didn't you? That King dog, didn't you?

JESSIE *(washing her hands)*:   I did like that King dog, yes.

MAMA: I'm so dumb. He's the one run under the tractor.

JESSIE: That makes him dumb, not you.

MAMA: For bringing it up.

JESSIE: It's O.K. Handi-Wipes and sponges under the sink.

MAMA: We could get a new dog and keep him in the house. Dogs are cheap!

JESSIE *(getting big pill jars out of the cabinet)*:   No.

MAMA: Something for you to take care of.

JESSIE: I've had you, Mama.

MAMA *(frantically starting to fill pill bottles)*:   You do too much for me. I can fill pill bottles all day, Jessie, and change the shelf paper and wash the floor when I get through. You just watch me. You don't have to do another thing in this house if you don't want to. You don't have to take care of me, Jessie.

JESSIE: I know that. You've just been letting me do it so I'll have something to do, haven't you?

MAMA *(realizing this was a mistake)*:   I don't do it as well as you. I just meant if it tires you out or makes you feel used . . .

JESSIE: Mama, I know you used to ride the bus. Riding the bus and it's hot and bumpy and crowded and too noisy and more than anything in the world you want to get off and the only reason in the world you don't get off is it's still fifty blocks from where you're going? Well, I can get off right now if I want to, because even if I ride fifty more years and get off then, it's the same place when I step down to it. Whenever I feel like it, I can get off. As soon as I've had enough, it's my stop. I've had enough.

MAMA: You're feeling sorry for yourself!

JESSIE: The plumber's helper is under the sink, too.

MAMA: You're not having a good time! Whoever promised you a good time? Do you think I've had a good time?

JESSIE: I think you're pretty happy, yeah. You have things you like to do.

MAMA: Like what?

JESSIE: Like crochet.

MAMA: I'll teach you to crochet.

JESSIE: I can't do any of that nice work, Mama.

MAMA: Good time don't come looking for you, Jessie. You could work some puzzles or put in a garden or go to the store. Let's call a taxi and go to the A & P!

JESSIE: I shopped you up for about two weeks already. You're not going to need toilet paper till Thanksgiving.

MAMA *(interrupting)*:   You're acting like some little brat, Jessie. You're mad and everybody's boring and you don't have anything to do and you don't like me and you don't like going out and you don't like staying in and you never talk on the phone and you don't watch TV and you're miserable and it's your own sweet fault.

JESSIE: And it's time I did something about it.

MAMA: Not something like killing yourself. Something like . . . buying us all new dishes! I'd like that. Or maybe the doctor would let you get a driver's license now, or I know what let's do right this minute, let's rearrange the furniture.

JESSIE: I'll do that. If you want. I always thought if the TV was somewhere else, you wouldn't get such a glare on it during the day. I'll do whatever you want before I go.

MAMA *(badly frightened by those words)*:   You could get a job!

JESSIE: I took that telephone sales job and I didn't even make enough money to pay the phone bill, and I tried to work at the gift shop at the hospital and they said I made people real uncomfortable smiling at them the way I did.

MAMA: You could keep books. You kept your dad's books.

JESSIE: But nobody ever checked them.

MAMA: When he died, they checked them.

JESSIE: And that's when they took the books away from me.

MAMA: That's because without him there wasn't any business, Jessie!

JESSIE *(putting the pill bottles away)*:   You know I couldn't work. I can't do anything. I've never been around people my whole life except when I went to
the hospital. I could have a seizure any time. What good would a job do?
The kind of job I could get would make me feel worse.

MAMA: Jessie!

JESSIE: It's true!

MAMA: It's what you think is true!

JESSIE *(struck by the clarity of that)*:   That's right. It's what I think is true.

MAMA *(hysterically)*:   But I can't do anything about that!

JESSIE *(quietly)*:   No. You can't. *(Mama slumps, if not physically, at least emotionally.)* And I can't do anything either, about my life, to change it, make it
better, make me feel better about it. Like it better, make it work. But I can
stop it. Shut it down, turn it off like the radio when there's nothing on I
want to listen to. It's all I really have that belongs to me and I'm going to
say what happens to it. And it's going to stop. And I'm going to stop it. So.
Let's just have a good time.

MAMA: Have a good time.

JESSIE: We can't go on fussing all night. I mean, I could ask you things I always
wanted to know and you could make me some hot chocolate. The old way.

MAMA *(in despair)*:   It takes cocoa, Jessie.

JESSIE *(gets it out of the cabinet)*:   I bought cocoa, Mama. And I'd like to have a
caramel apple and do your nails.

MAMA: You didn't eat a bite of supper.

JESSIE: Does that mean I can't have a caramel apple?

MAMA: Of course not. I mean . . . *(Smiling a little.)* Of course you can have a
caramel apple.

JESSIE: I thought I could.

MAMA: I make the best caramel apples in the world.

JESSIE: I know you do.

MAMA: Or used to. And you don't get cocoa like mine anywhere anymore.

JESSIE: It takes time, I know, but . . .

MAMA: The salt is the trick.

JESSIE: Trouble and everything.

MAMA *(backing away toward the stove)*:   It's no trouble. What trouble? You put it
in the pan and stir it up. All right. Fine. Caramel apples. Cocoa. O.K.

*Jessie walks to the counter to retrieve her cigarettes as Mama looks for the right pan.
There are brief near-smiles, and maybe Mama clears her throat. We have a truce, for
the moment. A genuine but nevertheless uneasy one. Jessie, who has been in constant
motion since the beginning, now seems content to sit.*

*Mama starts looking for a pan to make the cocoa, getting out all the pans in the
cabinets in the process. It looks like she's making a mess on purpose so Jessie will have
to put them all away again. Mama is buying time, or trying to, and entertaining.*

JESSIE: You talk to Agnes today?

MAMA: She's calling me from a pay phone this week. God only knows why. She has a perfectly good Trimline at home.

JESSIE *(laughing)*:   Well, how is she?

MAMA: How is she every day, Jessie? Nuts.

JESSIE: Is she really crazy or just silly?

MAMA: No, she's really crazy. She was probably using the pay phone because she had another little fire problem at home.

JESSIE: Mother . . .

MAMA: I'm serious! Agnes Fletcher's burned down every house she ever lived in. Eight fires, and she's due for a new one any day now.

JESSIE *(laughing)*:   No!

MAMA: Wouldn't surprise me a bit.

JESSIE *(laughing)*:   Why didn't you tell me this before? Why isn't she locked up somewhere?

MAMA: 'Cause nobody ever got hurt, I guess. Agnes woke everybody up to watch the fires as soon as she set 'em. One time she set out porch chairs and served lemonade.

JESSIE *(shaking her head)*:   Real lemonade?

MAMA: The houses they lived in, you knew they were going to fall down anyway, so why wait for it, is all I could ever make out about it. Agnes likes a feeling of accomplishment.

JESSIE: Good for her.

MAMA *(finding the pan she wants)*:   Why are you asking about Agnes? One cup or two?

JESSIE: One. She's your friend. No marshmallows.

MAMA *(getting the milk, etc.)*:   You have to have marshmallows. That's the old way, Jess. Two or three? Three is better.

JESSIE: Three, then. Her whole house burns up? Her clothes and pillows and everything? I'm not sure I believe this.

MAMA: When she was a girl, Jess, not now. Long time ago. But she's still got it in her, I'm sure of it.

JESSIE: She wouldn't burn her house down now. Where would she go? She can't get Buster to build her a new one, he's dead. How could she burn it up?

MAMA: Be exciting, though, if she did. You never know.

JESSIE: You do too know, Mama. She wouldn't do it.

MAMA *(forced to admit, but reluctant)*:   I guess not.

JESSIE: What else? Why does she wear all those whistles around her neck?

MAMA: Why does she have a house full of birds?

JESSIE: I didn't know she had a house full of birds!

MAMA: Well, she does. And she says they just follow her home. Well, I know for a fact she's still paying on the last parrot she bought. You gotta keep your life filled up, she says. She says a lot of stupid things. *(Jessie laughs, Mama continues, convinced she's getting somewhere.)* It's all that okra she eats. You can't just willy-nilly eat okra two meals a day and expect to get away with it. Made her crazy.

JESSIE: She really eats okra twice a day? Where does she get it in the winter?

MAMA: Well, she eats it a lot. Maybe not two meals, but . . .

JESSIE: More than the average person.

MAMA *(beginning to get irritated)*:   I don't know how much okra the average person eats.

JESSIE: Do you know how much okra Agnes eats?

MAMA: No.

JESSIE: How many birds does she have?

MAMA: Two.

JESSIE: Then what are the whistles for?

MAMA: They're not real whistles. Just little plastic ones on a necklace she won playing Bingo, and I only told you about it because I thought I might get a laugh out of you for once even if it wasn't the truth, Jessie. Things don't have to be true to talk about 'em, you know.

JESSIE: Why won't she come over here?

Mama is suddenly quiet, but the cocoa and milk are in the pan now, so she lights the stove and starts stirring.

MAMA: Well now, what a good idea. We should've had more cocoa. Cocoa is perfect.

JESSIE: Except you don't like milk.

MAMA *(another attempt, but not as energetic)*:   I hate milk. Coats your throat as bad as okra. Something just downright disgusting about it.

JESSIE: It's because of me, isn't it?

MAMA: No, Jess.

JESSIE: Yes, Mama.

MAMA: O.K. Yes, then, but she's crazy. She's as crazy as they come. She's a lunatic.

JESSIE: What is it exactly? Did I say something, sometime? Or did she see me have a fit and's afraid I might have another one if she came over, or what?

MAMA: I guess.

JESSIE: You guess what? What's she ever said? She must've given you some reason.

MAMA: Your hands are cold.

JESSIE: What difference does that make?

MAMA: "Like a corpse," she says, "and I'm gonna be one soon enough as it is."

JESSIE: That's crazy.

MAMA: That's Agnes. "Jessie's shook the hand of death and I can't take the chance it's catching, Thelma, so I ain't comin' over, and you can understand or no, but I ain't comin'. I'll come up the driveway, but that's as far as I go."

JESSIE *(laughing, relieved)*:   I thought she didn't like me! She's scared of me! How about that! Scared of me.

MAMA: I could make her come over here, Jessie. I could call her up right now and she could bring the birds and come visit. I didn't know you ever thought about her at all. I'll tell her she just has to come and she'll come, all right. She owes me one.

JESSIE: No, that's all right. I just wondered about it. When I'm in the hospital, does she come over here?

MAMA: Her kitchen is just a tiny thing. When she comes over here, she feels like . . . *(Toning it down a little.)* Well, we all like a change of scene, don't we?

JESSIE *(playing along)*: Sure we do. Plus there's no birds diving around.

MAMA: I hate those birds. She says I don't understand them. What's there to understand about birds?

JESSIE: Why Agnes likes them, for one thing. Why they stay with her when they could be outside with the other birds. What their singing means. How they fly. What they think Agnes is.

MAMA: Why do you have to know so much about things, Jessie? There's just not that much *to* things that I could ever see.

JESSIE: That you could ever *tell,* you mean. You didn't have to lie to me about Agnes.

MAMA: I didn't lie. You never asked before!

JESSIE: You lied about setting fire to all those houses and about how many birds she has and how much okra she eats and why she won't come over here. If I have to keep dragging the truth out of you, this is going to take all night.

MAMA: That's fine with me. I'm not a bit sleepy.

JESSIE: Mama . . .

MAMA: All right. Ask me whatever you want. Here.

They come to an awkward stop, as the cocoa is ready and Mama pours it into the cups Jessie has set on the table.

JESSIE *(as Mama takes her first sip)*: Did you love Daddy?

MAMA: No.

JESSIE *(pleased that Mama understands the rules better now)*: I didn't think so. Were you really fifteen when you married him?

MAMA: The way he told it? I'm sitting in the mud, he comes along, drags me in the kitchen, "She's been there ever since"?

JESSIE: Yes.

MAMA: No. It was a big fat lie, the whole thing. He just thought it was funnier that way. God, this milk in here.

JESSIE: The cocoa helps.

MAMA *(pleased that they agree on this, at least)*: Not enough, though, does it? You can still taste it, can't you?

JESSIE: Yeah, it's pretty bad. I thought it was my memory that was bad, but it's not. It's the milk, all right.

MAMA: It's a real waste of chocolate. You don't have to finish it.

JESSIE *(putting her cup down)*: Thanks, though.

MAMA: I should've known not to make it. I knew you wouldn't like it. You never did like it.

JESSIE: You didn't ever love him, or he did something and you stopped loving him, or what?

MAMA: He felt sorry for me. He wanted a plain country woman and that's what he married, and then he held it against me the rest of my life like I was supposed to change and surprise him somehow. Like I remember this one day he was standing on the porch and I told him to get a shirt on and he went in and got one and then he said, real peaceful, but to the point, "You're right, Thelma. If God had meant for people to go around without any clothes on, they'd have been born that way."

JESSIE *(sees Mama's hurt)*:   He didn't mean anything by that, Mama.

MAMA: He never said a word he didn't have to, Jessie. That was probably all he'd said to me all day, Jessie. So if he said it, there was something to it, but I never did figure that one out. What did that mean?

JESSIE: I don't know. I liked him better than you did, but I didn't know him any better.

MAMA: How could I love him, Jessie. I didn't have a thing he wanted. *(Jessie doesn't answer.)* He got his share, though. You loved him enough for both of us. You followed him around like some . . . Jessie, all the man ever did was farm and sit . . . and try to think of somebody to sell the farm to.

JESSIE: Or make me a boyfriend out of pipe cleaners and sit back and smile like the stick man was about to dance and wasn't I going to get a kick out of that. Or sit up with a sick cow all night and leave me a chain of sleepy stick elephants on my bed in the morning.

MAMA: Or just sit.

JESSIE: I liked him sitting. Big old faded blue man in the chair. Quiet.

MAMA: Agnes gets more talk out of her birds than I got from the two of you. He could've had that GONE FISHING sign around his neck in that chair. I saw him stare off at the water. I saw him look at the weather rolling in. I got where I could practically see the boat myself. But you, you knew what he was thinking about and you're going to tell me.

JESSIE: I don't know, Mama! His life, I guess. His corn. His boots. Us. Things. You know.

MAMA: No, I don't know, Jessie! You had those quiet little conversations after supper every night. What were you whispering about?

JESSIE: We weren't whispering, you were just across the room.

MAMA: What did you talk about?

JESSIE: We talked about why black socks are warmer than blue socks. Is that something to go tell Mother? You were just jealous because I'd rather talk to him than wash the dishes with you.

MAMA: I was jealous because you'd rather talk to him than anything! *(Jessie reaches across the table for the small clock and starts to wind it.)* If I had died instead of him, he wouldn't have taken you in like I did.

JESSIE: I wouldn't have expected him to.

MAMA: Then what would you have done?

JESSIE: Come visit.

MAMA: Oh, I see. He died and left you stuck with me and you're mad about it.

JESSIE *(getting up from the table)*:   Not anymore. He didn't mean to. I didn't have to come here. We've been through this.

MAMA: He felt sorry for you, too, Jessie, don't kid yourself about that. He said you were a runt and he said it from the day you were born and he said you didn't have a chance.

JESSIE *(getting the canister of sugar and starting to refill the sugar bowl)*:   I know he loved me.

MAMA: What if he did? It didn't change anything.

JESSIE: It didn't have to. I miss him.

MAMA: He never really went fishing, you know. Never once. His tackle box was full of chewing tobacco and all he ever did was drive out to the lake and sit in his car. Dawson told me. And Bennie at the bait shop, he told Dawson. They all laughed about it. And he'd come back from fishing and all he'd have to show for it was . . . a whole pipe-cleaner *family* — chickens, pigs, a dog with a bad leg — it was creepy strange. It made me sick to look at them and I hid his pipe cleaners a couple of times but he always had more somewhere.

JESSIE: I thought it might be better for you after he died. You'd get interested in things. Breathe better. Change somehow.

MAMA: Into what? The Queen? A clerk in a shoe store? Why should I? Because he said to? Because you said to? *(Jessie shakes her head.)* Well I wasn't here for his entertainment and I'm not here for yours either, Jessie. I don't know what I'm here for, but then I don't think about it. *(Realizing what all this means.)* But I bet you wouldn't be killing yourself if he were still alive. That's a fine thing to figure out, isn't it?

JESSIE *(filling the honey jar now)*:   That's not true.

MAMA: Oh no? Then what were you asking about him for? Why did you want to know if I loved him?

JESSIE: I didn't think you did, that's all.

MAMA: Fine then. You were right. Do you feel better now?

JESSIE *(cleaning the honey jar carefully)*:   It feels good to be right about it.

MAMA: It didn't matter whether I loved him. It didn't matter to me and it didn't matter to him. And it didn't mean we didn't get along. It wasn't important. We didn't talk about it. *(Sweeping the pots off the cabinet.)* Take all these pots out to the porch!

JESSIE: What for?

MAMA: Just leave me this one pan. *(She jerks the silverware drawer open.)* Get me one knife, one fork, one big spoon, and the can opener, and put them out where I can get them. *(Starts throwing knives and forks in one of the pans.)*

JESSIE: Don't do that! I just straightened that drawer!

MAMA *(throwing the pan in the sink)*:   And throw out all the plates and cups. I'll use paper. Loretta can have what she wants and Dawson can sell the rest.

JESSIE *(calmly)*:   What are you doing?

MAMA: I'm not going to cook. I never liked it, anyway. I like candy. Wrapped in plastic or coming in sacks. And tuna. I like tuna. I'll eat tuna, thank you.

JESSIE *(taking the pan out of the sink)*:   What if you want to make apple butter? You can't make apple butter in that little pan. What if you leave carrots on cooking and burn up that pan?

MAMA: I don't like carrots.

JESSIE: What if the strawberries are good this year and you want to go picking with Agnes.

MAMA: I'll tell her to bring a pan. You said you would do whatever I wanted! I don't want a bunch of pans cluttering up my cabinets I can't get down to, anyway. Throw them out. Every last one.

JESSIE *(gathering up the pots)*:   I'm putting them all back in. I'm not taking them to the porch. If you want them, they'll be here. You'll bend down and get them, like you got the one for the cocoa. And if somebody else comes over here to cook, they'll have something to cook in, and that's the end of it!

MAMA: Who's going to come cook here?

JESSIE: Agnes.

MAMA: In my pots. Not on your life.

JESSIE: There's no reason why the two of you couldn't just live here together. Be cheaper for both of you and somebody to talk to. And if the birds bothered you, well, one day when Agnes is out getting her hair done, you could take them all for a walk!

MAMA *(as Jessie straightens the silverware)*:   So that's why you're pestering me about Agnes. You think you can rest easy if you get me a new babysitter? Well, I don't want to live with Agnes. I barely want to talk with Agnes. She's just around. We go back, that's all. I'm not letting Agnes near this place. You don't get off as easy as that, child.

JESSIE: O.K., then. It's just something to think about.

MAMA: I don't like things to think about. I like things to go on.

JESSIE *(closing the silverware drawer)*:   I want to know what Daddy said to you the night he died. You came storming out of his room and said I could wait it out with him if I wanted to, but you were going to watch *Gunsmoke*. What did he say to you?

MAMA: He didn't have *anything* to say to me, Jessie. That's why I left. He didn't say a thing. It was his last chance not to talk to me and he took full advantage of it.

JESSIE *(after a moment)*:   I'm sorry you didn't love him. Sorry for you, I mean. He seemed like a nice man.

MAMA *(as Jessie walks to the refrigerator)*:   Ready for your apple now?

JESSIE: Soon as I'm through here, Mama.

MAMA: You won't like the apple, either. It'll be just like the cocoa. You never liked eating at all, did you? Any of it! What have you been living on all these years, toothpaste?

JESSIE *(as she starts to clean out the refrigerator)*:   Now, you know the milkman comes on Wednesdays and Saturdays, and he leaves the order blank in an egg box, and you give the bills to Dawson once a month.

MAMA: Do they still make that orangeade?

JESSIE: It's not orangeade, it's just orange.

MAMA: I'm going to get some. I thought they stopped making it. You just stopped ordering it.

JESSIE: You should drink milk.

MAMA: Not anymore, I'm not. That hot chocolate was the last. Hooray.

JESSIE *(getting the garbage can from under the sink)*:   I told them to keep delivering a quart a week no matter what you said. I told them you'd run out of Cokes and you'd have to drink it. I told them I knew you wouldn't pour it on the ground . . .

MAMA *(finishing her sentence)*:   And you told them you weren't going to be ordering anymore?

JESSIE: I told them I was taking a little holiday and to look after you.

MAMA: And they didn't think something was funny about that? You who doesn't go to the front steps? You, who only sees the driveway looking down from a stretcher passed out cold?

JESSIE *(enjoying this, but not laughing)*:   They said it was about time, but why didn't I take you with me? And I said I didn't think you'd want to go, and they said, "Yeah, everybody's got their own idea of vacation."

MAMA: I guess you think that's funny.

JESSIE *(pulling jars out of the refrigerator)*:   You know there never was any reason to call the ambulance for me. All they ever did for me in the emergency room was let me wake up. I could've done that here. Now, I'll just call them out and you say yes or no. I know you like pickles. Ketchup?

MAMA: Keep it.

JESSIE: We've had this since last Fourth of July.

MAMA: Keep the ketchup. Keep it all.

JESSIE: Are you going to drink ketchup from the bottle or what? How can you want your food and not want your pots to cook it in? This stuff will all spoil in here, Mother.

MAMA: Nothing I ever did was good enough for you and I want to know why.

JESSIE: That's not true.

MAMA: And I want to know why you've lived here this long feeling the way you do.

JESSIE: You have no earthly idea how I feel.

MAMA: Well, how could I? You're real far back there, Jessie.

JESSIE: Back where?

MAMA: What's it like over there, where you are? Do people always say the right thing or get whatever they want, or what?

JESSIE: What are you talking about?

MAMA: Why do you read the newspaper? Why don't you wear that sweater I made for you? Do you remember how I used to look, or am I just any old woman now? When you have a fit, do you see stars or what? How did you fall off the horse, really? Why did Cecil leave you? Where did you put my old glasses?

JESSIE *(stunned by Mama's intensity)*:   They're in the bottom drawer of your dresser in an old Milk of Magnesia box. Cecil left me because he made me choose between him and smoking.

MAMA: Jessie, I know he wasn't that dumb.

JESSIE: I never understood why he hated it so much when it's so good. Smoking is the only thing I know that's always just what you think it's going to be. Just like it was the last time, right there when you want it and real quiet.

MAMA: Your fits made him sick and you know it.

JESSIE: Say seizures, not fits. Seizures.

MAMA: It's the same thing. A seizure in the hospital is a fit at home.

JESSIE: They didn't bother him at all. Except he did feel responsible for it. It *was* his idea to go horseback riding that day. It was his idea I could do *anything* if I just made up my mind to. I fell off the horse because I didn't know how to hold on. Cecil left for pretty much the same reason.

MAMA: He had a girl, Jessie. I walked right in on them in the toolshed.

JESSIE *(after a moment)*:   O.K. That's fair. *(Lighting another cigarette.)* Was she very pretty?

MAMA: She was Agnes's girl, Carlene. Judge for yourself.

JESSIE *(as she walks to the living room)*:   I guess you and Agnes had a good talk about that, huh?

MAMA: I never thought he was good enough for you. They moved here from Tennessee, you know.

JESSIE: What are you talking about? You liked him better than I did. You flirted him out here to build your porch or I'd never even met him at all. You thought maybe he'd help you out around the place, come in and get some coffee and talk to you. God knows what you thought. All that curly hair.

MAMA: He's the best carpenter I ever saw. That little house of yours will still be standing at the end of the world, Jessie.

JESSIE: You didn't need a porch, Mama.

MAMA: All right! I wanted you to have a husband.

JESSIE: And I couldn't get one on my own, of course.

MAMA: How were you going to get a husband never opening your mouth to a living soul?

JESSIE: So I was quiet about it, so what?

MAMA: So I should have let you just sit here? Sit like your daddy? Sit here?

JESSIE: Maybe.

MAMA: Well, I didn't think so.

JESSIE: Well, what did you know?

MAMA: I never said I knew much. How was I supposed to learn anything living out here? I didn't know enough to do half the things I did in my life. Things happen. You do what you can about them and you see what happens next. I married you off to the wrong man, I admit that. So I took you in when he left. I'm sorry.

JESSIE: He wasn't the wrong man.

MAMA: He didn't love you, Jessie, or he wouldn't have left.

JESSIE: He wasn't the wrong man, Mama. I loved Cecil so much. And I tried to get more exercise and I tried to stay awake. I tried to learn to ride a horse. And I tried to stay outside with him, but he always knew I was trying, so it didn't work.

MAMA: He was a selfish man. He told me once he hated to see people move into his houses after he built them. He knew they'd mess them up.

JESSIE: I loved that bridge he built over the creek in back of the house. It didn't have to be anything special, a couple of boards would have been just fine, but he used that yellow pine and rubbed it so smooth . . .

MAMA: He had responsibilities here. He had a wife and son here and he failed you.

JESSIE: Or that baby bed he built for Ricky. I told him he didn't have to spend so much time on it, but he said it had to last, and the thing ended up weighing two hundred pounds and I couldn't move it. I said, "How long does a baby bed have to last, anyway?" But maybe he thought if it was strong enough, it might keep Ricky a baby.

MAMA: Ricky is too much like Cecil.

JESSIE: He is not. Ricky is as much like me as it's possible for any human to be. We even wear the same size pants. These are his, I think.

MAMA: That's just the same size. That's not you're the same person.

JESSIE: I see it on his face. I hear it when he talks. We look out at the world and we see the same thing: not fair. And the only difference between us is Ricky's out there trying to get even. And he knows not to trust anybody and he got it straight from me. And he knows not to try to get work, and guess where he got that. He walks around like there's loose boards in the floor, and you know who laid that floor, I did.

MAMA: Ricky isn't through yet. You don't know how he'll turn out!

JESSIE (going back to the kitchen):   Yes I do and so did Cecil. Ricky is the two of us together for all time in too small a space. And we're tearing each other apart, like always, inside that boy, and if you don't see it, then you're just blind.

MAMA: Give him time, Jess.

JESSIE: Oh, he'll have plenty of that. Five years for forgery, ten years for armed assault . . .

MAMA (furious):   Stop that! (Then pleading.) Jessie, Cecil might be ready to try it again, honey, that happens sometimes. Go downtown. Find him. Talk to him. He didn't know what he had in you. Maybe he sees things different now, but you're not going to know that till you go see him. Or call him up! Right now! He might be home.

JESSIE: And say what? Nothing's changed, Cecil, I'd just like to look at you, if you don't mind? No. He loved me, Mama. He just didn't know how things fall down around me like they do. I think he did the right thing. He gave himself another chance, that's all. But I did beg him to take me with him. I did tell him I would leave Ricky and you and everything I loved out here if only he would take me with him, but he couldn't and I understood that. (Pause.) I wrote that note I showed you. I wrote it. Not Cecil. I said "I'm sorry, Jessie, I can't fix it all for you." I said I'd always love me, not Cecil. But that's how he felt.

MAMA: Then he should've taken you with him!

JESSIE (picking up the garbage bag she has filled):   Mama, you don't pack your garbage when you move.

MAMA: You will not call yourself garbage, Jessie.

JESSIE *(taking the bag to the big garbage can near the back door)*:   Just a way of say-
    ing it, Mama. Thinking about my list, that's all. *(Opening the can, putting the
    garbage in, then securing the lid.)* Well, a little more than that. I was trying to
    say it's all right that Cecil left. It was . . . a relief in a way. I never was what
    he wanted to see, so it was better when he wasn't looking at me all the
    time.

MAMA: I'll make your apple now.

JESSIE: No thanks. You get the manicure stuff and I'll be right there.

*Jessie ties up the big garbage bag in the can and replaces the small garbage bag under
the sink, all the time trying desperately to regain her calm. Mama watches, from a
distance, her hand reaching unconsciously for the phone. Then she has a better idea.
Or rather she thinks of the only other thing left and is willing to try it. Maybe she is
even convinced it will work.*

MAMA: Jessie, I think your daddy had little . . .

JESSIE *(interrupting her)*:   Garbage night is Tuesday. Put it out as late as you
    can. The Davis's dogs get in it if you don't. *(Replacing the garbage bag in the
    can under the sink.)* And keep ordering the heavy black bags. It doesn't pay
    to buy the cheap ones. And I've got all the ties here with the hammers and
    all. Take them out of the box as soon as you open a new one and put them
    in this drawer. They'll get lost if you don't, and rubber bands or something
    else won't work.

MAMA: I think your daddy had fits, too. I think he sat in his chair and had little
    fits. I read this a long time ago in a magazine, how little fits go, just little
    blackouts where maybe their eyes don't even close and people just call
    them "thinking spells."

JESSIE *(getting the slipcover out of the laundry basket)*:   I don't think you want
    this manicure we've been looking forward to. I washed this cover for the
    sofa, but it'll take both of us to get it back on.

MAMA: I watched his eyes. I know that's what it was. The magazine said some
    people don't even know they've had one.

JESSIE: Daddy would've known if he'd had fits, Mama.

MAMA: The lady in this story had kept track of hers and she'd had eighty thou-
    sand of them in the last eleven years.

JESSIE: Next time you wash this cover, it'll dry better if you put it on wet.

MAMA: Jessie, listen to what I'm telling you. This lady had anywhere between
    five and five hundred fits a day and they lasted maybe fifteen seconds
    apiece, so that out of her life, she'd only lost about two weeks altogether,
    and she had a full-time secretary job and an IQ of 120.

JESSIE *(amused by Mama's approach)*:   You want to talk about fits, is that it?

MAMA: Yes. I do. I want to say . . .

JESSIE *(interrupting)*:   Most of the time I wouldn't even know I'd had one, ex-
    cept I wake up with different clothes on, feeling like I've been run over.
    Sometimes I feel my head start to turn around or hear myself scream. And

sometimes there *is* this dizzy stupid feeling a little before it, but if the TV's on, well, it's easy to miss.

As Jessie and Mama replace the slipcover on the sofa and the afghan on the chair, the physical struggle somehow mirrors the emotional one in the conversation.

MAMA: I can tell when you're about to have one. Your eyes get this big! But, Jessie, you haven't . . .

JESSIE *(taking charge of this)*: What do they look like? The seizures.

MAMA *(reluctant)*: Different each time, Jess.

JESSIE: O.K. Pick one, then. A good one. I think I want to know now.

MAMA: There's not much to tell. You just . . . crumple, in a heap, like a puppet and somebody cut the strings all at once, or like the firing squad in some Mexican movie, you just slide down the wall, you know. You don't know what happens? How can you not know what happens?

JESSIE: I'm busy.

MAMA: That's not funny.

JESSIE: I'm not laughing. My head turns around and I fall down and then what?

MAMA: Well, your chest squeezes in and out, and you sound like you're gagging, sucking air in and out like you can't breathe.

JESSIE: Do it for me. Make the sound for me.

MAMA: I will not. It's awful-sounding.

JESSIE: Yeah. It felt like it might be. What's next?

MAMA: Your mouth bites down and I have to get your tongue out of the way fast, so you don't bite yourself.

JESSIE: Or you. I bite you, too, don't I?

MAMA: You got me once real good. I had to get a tetanus! But I know what to watch for now. And then you turn blue and the jerks start up. Like I'm standing there poking you with a cattle prod or you're sticking your finger in a light socket as fast as you can . . .

JESSIE: Foaming like a mad dog the whole time.

MAMA: It's bubbling, Jess, not foam like the washer overflowed, for God's sake; it's bubbling like a baby spitting up. I go get a wet washcloth, that's all. And then the jerks slow down and you wet yourself and it's over. Two minutes tops.

JESSIE: How do I get to the bed?

MAMA: How do you think?

JESSIE: I'm too heavy for you now. How do you do it?

MAMA: I call Dawson. But I get you cleaned up before he gets here and I make him leave before you wake up.

JESSIE: You could just leave me on the floor.

MAMA: I want you to wake up someplace nice, O.K.? *(Then making a real effort.)* But, Jessie, and this is the reason I even brought this up! You haven't had a seizure for a solid year. A whole year, do you realize that?

JESSIE: Yeah, the phenobarb's about right now, I guess.

MAMA: You bet it is. You might never have another one, ever! You might be through with it for all time!

JESSIE: Could be.

MAMA: You are. I know you are!

JESSIE: I sure am feeling good. I really am. The double vision's gone and my gums aren't swelling. No rashes or anything. I'm feeling as good as I ever felt in my life. I'm even feeling like worrying or getting mad and I'm not afraid it will start a fit if I do, I just go ahead.

MAMA: Of course you do! You can even scream at me, if you want to. I can take it. You don't have to act like you're just visiting here, Jessie. This is your house, too.

JESSIE: The best part is, my memory's back.

MAMA: Your memory's always been good. When couldn't you remember things? You're always reminding me what . . .

JESSIE: Because I've made lists for everything. But now I remember what things mean on my lists. I see "dish towels," and I used to wonder whether I was supposed to wash them, buy them, or look for them because I wouldn't remember where I put them after I washed them, but now I know it means wrap them up, they're a present for Loretta's birthday.

MAMA *(finished with the sofa now)*:   You used to go looking for your lists, too, I've noticed that. You always know where they are now! *(Then suddenly worried.)* Loretta's birthday isn't coming up, is it?

JESSIE: I made a list of all the birthdays for you. I even put yours on it. *(A small smile.)* So you can call Loretta and remind her.

MAMA: Let's take Loretta to Howard Johnson's and have those fried clams. I *know* you love that clam roll.

JESSIE *(slight pause)*:   I won't be here, Mama.

MAMA: What have we just been talking about? You'll be here. You're well, Jessie. You're starting all over. You said it yourself. You're remembering things and . . .

JESSIE: I won't be here. If I'd ever had a year like this, to think straight and all, before now, I'd be gone already.

MAMA *(not pleading, commanding)*:   No, Jessie.

JESSIE *(folding the rest of the laundry)*:   Yes, Mama. Once I started remembering, I could see what it all added up to.

MAMA: The fits are over!

JESSIE: It's not the fits, Mama.

MAMA: Then it's me for giving them to you, but I didn't do it!

JESSIE: It's not the fits! You said it yourself, the medicine takes care of the fits.

MAMA *(interrupting)*:   Your daddy gave you those fits, Jessie. He passed it down to you like your green eyes and your straight hair. It's not my fault!

JESSIE: So what if he had little fits? It's not inherited. I fell off the horse. It was an accident.

MAMA: The horse wasn't the first time, Jessie. You had a fit when you were five years old.

JESSIE: I did not.

MAMA: You did! You were eating a popsicle and down you went. He gave it to you. It's *his* fault, not mine.

JESSIE: Well, you took your time telling me.

MAMA: How do you tell that to a five-year-old?

JESSIE: What did the doctor say?

MAMA: He said kids have them all the time. He said there wasn't anything to do but wait for another one.

JESSIE: But I didn't have another one.

Now there is a real silence.

JESSIE: You mean to tell me I had fits all the time as a kid and you just told me I fell down or something and it wasn't till I had the fit when Cecil was looking that anybody bothered to find out what was the matter with me?

MAMA: It wasn't *all the time*, Jessie. And they changed when you started to school. More like your daddy's. Oh, that was some swell time, sitting here with the two of you turning off and on like light bulbs some nights.

JESSIE: How many fits did I have?

MAMA: You never hurt yourself. I never let you out of my sight. I caught you every time.

JESSIE: But you didn't tell anybody.

MAMA: It was none of their business.

JESSIE: You were ashamed.

MAMA: I didn't want anybody to know. Least of all you.

JESSIE: Least of all me. Oh, right. That was mine to know, Mama, not yours. Did Daddy know?

MAMA: He thought you were . . . you fell down a lot. That's what he thought. You were careless. Or maybe he thought I beat you. I don't know what he thought. He didn't think about it.

JESSIE: Because you didn't tell him!

MAMA: If I told him about you, I'd have to tell him about him!

JESSIE: I don't like this. I don't like this one bit.

MAMA: I didn't think you'd like it. That's why I didn't tell you.

JESSIE: If I'd known I was an epileptic, Mama, I wouldn't have ridden any horses.

MAMA: Make you feel like a freak, is that what I should have done?

JESSIE: Just get the manicure tray and sit down!

MAMA *(throwing it to the floor)*: I don't want a manicure!

JESSIE: Doesn't look like you do, no.

MAMA: Maybe I did drop you, you don't know.

JESSIE: If you say you didn't, you didn't.

MAMA *(beginning to break down)*: Maybe I fed you the wrong thing. Maybe you had a fever sometime and I didn't know it soon enough. Maybe it's a punishment.

JESSIE: For what?

MAMA: I don't know. Because of how I felt about your father. Because I didn't want any more children. Because I smoked too much or didn't eat right when I was carrying you. It has to be something I did.

JESSIE: It does not. It's just a sickness, not a curse. Epilepsy doesn't mean any-thing. It just is.

MAMA: I'm not talking about the fits here, Jessie! I'm talking about this killing yourself. It has to be me that's the matter here. You wouldn't be doing this if it wasn't. I didn't tell you things or I married you off to the wrong man or I took you in and let your life get away from you or all of it put together. I don't know what I did, but I did it, I know. This is all my fault, Jessie, but I don't know what to do about it now!

JESSIE *(exasperated at having to say this again)*:   It doesn't have anything to do with you!

MAMA: Everything you do has to do with me, Jessie. You can't do *anything*, wash your face or cut your finger, without doing it to me. That's right! You might as well kill me as you, Jessie, it's the same thing. This has to do with me, Jessie.

JESSIE: Then what if it does! What if it has everything to do with you! What if you are all I have and you're not enough? What if I could take all the rest of it if only I didn't have you here? What if the only way I can get away from you for good is to kill myself? What if it is? I can *still* do it!

MAMA *(in desperate tears)*:   Don't leave me, Jessie! *(Jessie stands for a moment, then turns for the bedroom.)* No! *(She grabs Jessie's arm.)*

JESSIE *(carefully taking her arm away)*:   I have a box of things I want people to have. I'm just going to go get it for you. You . . . just rest a minute.

Jessie is gone. Mama heads for the telephone, but she can't even pick up the receiver this time and, instead, stoops to clean up the bottles that have spilled out of the man-icure tray.

Jessie returns, carrying a box that groceries were delivered in. It probably says Hershey Kisses or Starkist Tuna. Mama is still down on the floor cleaning up, hoping that maybe if she just makes it look nice enough, Jessie will stay.

MAMA: Jessie, how can I live here without you? I need you! You're supposed to tell me to stand up straight and say how nice I look in my pink dress, and drink my milk. You're supposed to go around and lock up so I know we're safe for the night, and when I wake up, you're supposed to be out there making the coffee and watching me get older every day, and you're sup-posed to help me die when the time comes. I can't do that by myself, Jessie. I'm not like you, Jessie. I hate the quiet and I don't want to die and I don't want you to go, Jessie. How can I . . . *(Has to stop a moment.)* How can I get up every day knowing you had to kill yourself to make it stop hurting and I was here all the time and I never even saw it. And then you gave me this chance to make it better, convince you to stay alive, and I couldn't do it. How can I live with myself after this, Jessie?

JESSIE: I only told you so I could explain it, so you wouldn't blame yourself, so you wouldn't feel bad. There wasn't anything you could say to change my mind. I didn't want you to save me. I just wanted you to know.

MAMA: Stay with me just a little longer. Just a few more years. I don't have that many more to go, Jessie. And as soon as I'm dead, you can do whatever you want. Maybe with me gone, you'll have all the quiet you want, right here in the house. And maybe one day you'll put in some begonias up the walk and get just the right rain for them all summer. And Ricky will be married by then and he'll bring your grandbabies over and you can sneak them a piece of candy when their daddy's not looking and then be real glad when they've gone home and left you to your quiet again.

JESSIE: Don't you see, Mama, everything I do winds up like this. How could I think you would understand? How could I think you would want a manicure? We could hold hands for an hour and then I could go shoot myself? I'm sorry about tonight, Mama, but it's exactly why I'm doing it.

MAMA: If you've got the guts to kill yourself, Jessie, you've got the guts to stay alive.

JESSIE: I know that. So it's really just a matter of where I'd rather be.

MAMA: Look, maybe I can't think of what you should do, but that doesn't mean there isn't something that would help. *You* find it. *You* think of it. You can keep trying. You can get brave and try some more. You don't have to give up!

JESSIE: I'm *not* giving up! This *is* the other thing I'm trying. And I'm sure there are some other things that might work, but *might* work isn't good enough anymore. I need something that *will* work. *This* will work. That's why I picked it.

MAMA: But something might happen. Something that could change everything. Who knows what it might be, but it might be worth waiting for! *(Jessie doesn't respond.)* Try it for two more weeks. We could have more talks like tonight.

JESSIE: No, Mama.

MAMA: I'll pay more attention to you. Tell the truth when you ask me. Let you have your say.

JESSIE: No, Mama! We wouldn't have more talks like tonight, because it's this next part that's made this last part so good, Mama. No, Mama. *This* is how I have my say. This is how I say what I thought about it *all* and I say no. To Dawson and Loretta and the Red Chinese and epilepsy and Ricky and Cecil and you. And me. And hope. I say no! *(Then going to Mama on the sofa.)* Just let me go easy, Mama.

MAMA: How can I let you go?

JESSIE: You can because you have to. It's what you've always done.

MAMA: You are my child!

JESSIE: I am what became of your child. *(Mama cannot answer.)* I found an old baby picture of me. And it was somebody else, not me. It was somebody pink and fat who never heard of sick or lonely, somebody who cried and got fed, and reached up and got held and kicked but didn't hurt anybody, and slept whenever she wanted to, just by closing her eyes. Somebody who mainly just laid there and laughed at the colors waving around over her head and chewed on a polka-dot whale and woke up knowing some new trick nearly every day, and rolled over and drooled on the sheet and felt your hand pulling my quilt back up over me. That's who I started out and this is who is left. *(There is no self-pity here.)* That's what this is about. It's somebody I lost, all right, it's my own self. Who I never was. Or who I tried to be and never got there. Somebody I waited for who never came. And never will. So, see, it doesn't much matter what else happens in the world or in this house, even. I'm what was worth waiting for and I didn't make it. Me . . . who might have made a difference to me . . . I'm not going to show up, so there's no reason to stay, except to keep you company, and that's . . . not reason enough because I'm not . . . very good company. *(Pause.)* Am I.

MAMA *(knowing she must tell the truth)*:   No. And neither am I.

JESSIE: I had this strange little thought, well, maybe it's not so strange. Anyway, after Christmas, after I decided to do this, I would wonder, sometimes, what might keep me here, what might be worth staying for, and you know what it was? It was maybe if there was something I really liked, like maybe if I really liked rice pudding or cornflakes for breakfast or something, that might be enough.

MAMA: Rice pudding is good.

JESSIE: Not to me.

MAMA: And you're not afraid?

JESSIE: Afraid of what?

MAMA: I'm afraid of it, for me, I mean. When my time comes. I know it's coming, but . . .

JESSIE: You don't know when. Like in a scary movie.

MAMA: Yeah, sneaking up on me like some killer on the loose, hiding out in the back yard just waiting for me to have my hands full someday and how am I supposed to protect myself anyhow when I don't know what he looks like and I don't know how he sounds coming up behind me like that or if it will hurt or take very long or what I don't get done before it happens.

JESSIE: You've got plenty of time left.

MAMA: I forget what for, right now.

JESSIE: For whatever happens, I don't know. For the rest of your life. For Agnes burning down one more house or Dawson losing his hair or . . .

MAMA *(quickly)*:   Jessie, I can't just sit here and say O.K., kill yourself if you want to.

JESSIE: Sure you can. You just did. Say it again.

MAMA *(really startled)*:   Jessie! *(Quiet horror.)* How dare you! *(Furious.)* How dare you! You think you can just leave whenever you want, like you're watching television here? No, you can't, Jessie. You make me feel like a fool for being alive, child, and you are so wrong! I like it here, and I will stay here until they make me go, until they drag me screaming and I mean screeching into my grave, and you're real smart to get away before then because, I mean, honey, you've never heard noise like that in your life. *(Jessie turns away.)* Who am I talking to? You're gone already, aren't you? I'm looking right through you! I can't stop you because you're already gone! I guess you think they'll all have to talk about you now! I guess you think this will really confuse them. Oh yes, ever since Christmas you've been laughing to yourself and thinking, "Boy, are they all in for a surprise." Well, nobody's going to be a bit surprised, sweetheart. This is just like you. Do it the hard way, that's my girl, all right. *(Jessie gets up and goes into the kitchen, but Mama follows her.)* You know who they're going to feel sorry for? Me! How about that! Not you, me! They're going to be *ashamed* of you. Yes. *Ashamed!* If somebody asks Dawson about it, he'll change the subject as fast as he can. He'll talk about how much he has to pay to park his car these days.

JESSIE: Leave me alone.

MAMA: It's the truth!

JESSIE: I should've just left you a note!

MAMA *(screaming)*: Yes! *(Then suddenly understanding what she has said, nearly paralyzed by the thought of it, she turns slowly to face Jessie, nearly whispering.)* No. No. I . . . might not have thought of all the things you've said.

JESSIE: It's O.K., Mama.

Mama is nearly unconscious from the emotional devastation of these last few moments. She sits down at the kitchen table, hurt and angry and desperately afraid. But she looks almost numb. She is so far beyond what is known as pain that she is virtually unreachable and Jessie knows this, and talks quietly, watching for signs of recovery.

JESSIE *(washes her hands in the sink)*: I remember you liked that preacher who did Daddy's, so if you want to ask him to do the service, that's O.K. with me.

MAMA *(not an answer, just a word)*: What.

JESSIE *(putting on hand lotion as she talks)*: And pick some songs you like or let Agnes pick, she'll know exactly which ones. Oh, and I had your dress cleaned that you wore to Daddy's. You looked real good in that.

MAMA: I don't remember, hon.

JESSIE: And it won't be so bad once your friends start coming to the funeral home. You'll probably see people you haven't seen for years, but I thought about what you should say to get you over that nervous part when they first come in.

MAMA *(simply repeating)*: Come in.

JESSIE: Take them up to see their flowers, they'd like that. And when they say, "I'm so sorry, Thelma," you just say, "I appreciate your coming, Connie." And then ask how their garden was this summer or what they're doing for Thanksgiving or how their children . . .

MAMA: I don't think I should ask about their children. I'll talk about what they have on, that's always good. And I'll have some crochet work with me.

JESSIE: And Agnes will be there, so you might not have to talk at all.

MAMA: Maybe if Connie Richards does come, I can get her to tell me where she gets that Irish yarn, she calls it. I know it doesn't come from Ireland. I think it just comes with a green wrapper.

JESSIE: And be sure to invite enough people home afterward so you get enough food to feed them all and have some left for you. But don't let anybody take anything home, especially Loretta.

MAMA: Loretta will get all the food set up, honey. It's only fair to let her have
some macaroni or something.

JESSIE: No, Mama. You have to be more selfish from now on. *(Sitting at the table
with Mama.)* Now, somebody's bound to ask you why I did it and you just
say you don't know. That you loved me and you know I loved you and we
just sat around tonight like every other night of our lives, and then I came
over and kissed you and said, " 'night, Mother," and you heard me close my
bedroom door and the next thing you heard was the shot. And whatever
reasons I had, well, you guess I just took them with me.

MAMA *(quietly)*:   It was something personal.

JESSIE: Good. That's good, Mama.

MAMA: That's what I'll say, then.

JESSIE: Personal. Yeah.

MAMA: Is that what I tell Dawson and Loretta, too? We sat around, you kissed
me, " 'night, Mother"? They'll want to know more, Jessie. They won't believe it.

JESSIE: Well, then, tell them what we did. I filled up the candy jars. I cleaned
out the refrigerator. We made some hot chocolate and put the cover back
on the sofa. You had no idea. All right? I really think it's better that way.
If they know we talked about it, they really won't understand how you let
me go.

MAMA: I guess not.

JESSIE: It's private. Tonight is private, yours and mine, and I don't want anybody else to have any of it.

MAMA: O.K., then.

JESSIE *(standing behind Mama now, holding her shoulders)*:   Now, when you hear
the shot, I don't want you to come in. First of all, you won't be able to get
in by yourself, but I don't want you trying. Call Dawson, then call the police, and then call Agnes. And then you'll need something to do till somebody gets here, so wash the hot-chocolate pan. You wash that pan till you
hear the doorbell ring and I don't care if it's an hour, you keep washing
that pan.

MAMA: I'll make my calls and then I'll just sit. I won't need something to do.
What will the police say?

JESSIE: They'll do that gunpowder test, I guess, and ask you what happened,
and by that time, the ambulance will be here and they'll come in and get
me and you know how that goes. You stay out here with Dawson and
Loretta. You keep Dawson out here. I want the police in the room first, not
Dawson, O.K.?

MAMA: What if Dawson and Loretta want me to go home with them?

JESSIE *(returning to the living room)*:   That's up to you.

MAMA: I think I'll stay here. All they've got is Sanka.

JESSIE: Maybe Agnes could come stay with you for a few days.

MAMA *(standing up, looking into the living room)*:   I'd rather be by myself, I think.
(Walking toward the box Jessie brought in earlier.) You want me to give people
those things?

JESSIE *(they sit down on the sofa, Jessie holding the box on her lap)*:   I want Loretta to have my little calculator. Dawson bought it for himself, you know, but then he saw one he liked better and he couldn't bring both of them home with Loretta counting every penny the way she does, so he gave the first one to me. Be funny for her to have it now, don't you think? And all my house slippers are in a sack for her in my closet. Tell her I know they'll fit and I've never worn any of them, and make sure Dawson hears you tell her that. I'm glad he loves Loretta so much, but I wish he knew not everybody has her size feet.

MAMA *(taking the calculator)*:   O.K.

JESSIE *(reaching into the box again)*:   This letter is for Dawson, but it's mostly about you, so read it if you want. There's a list of presents for you for at least twenty more Christmases and birthdays, so if you want anything special you better add it to this list before you give it to him. Or if you want to be surprised, just don't read that page. This Christmas, you're getting mostly stuff for the house, like a new rug in your bathroom and needlework, but next Christmas, you're really going to cost him next Christmas. I think you'll like it a lot and you'd never think of it.

MAMA: And you think he'll go for it?

JESSIE: I think he'll feel like a real jerk if he doesn't. Me telling him to, like this and all. Now, this number's where you call Cecil. I called it last week and he answered, so I know he still lives there.

MAMA: What do you want me to tell him?

JESSIE: Tell him we talked about him and I only had good things to say about him, but mainly tell him to find Ricky and tell him what I did, and tell Ricky you have something for him, out here, from me, and to come get it. *(Pulls a sack out of the box.)*

MAMA *(the sack feels empty)*:   What is it?

JESSIE *(taking it off)*:   My watch. *(Putting it in the sack and taking a ribbon out of the sack to tie around the top of it.)*

MAMA: He'll sell it!

JESSIE: That's the idea. I appreciate him not stealing it already. I'd like to buy him a good meal.

MAMA: He'll buy dope with it!

JESSIE: Well, then, I hope he gets some good dope with it, Mama. And the rest of this is for you. *(Handing Mama the box now. Mama picks up the things and looks at them.)*

MAMA *(surprised and pleased)*:   When did you do all this? During my naps, I guess.

JESSIE: I guess. I tried to be quiet about it. *(As Mama is puzzled by the presents.)* Those are just little presents. For whenever you need one. They're not bought presents, just things I thought you might like to look at, pictures or things you think you've lost. Things you didn't know you had, even. You'll see.

MAMA: I'm not sure I want them. They'll make me think of you.

JESSIE: No they won't. They're just things, like a free tube of toothpaste I found hanging on the door one day.

MAMA: Oh. All right, then.

JESSIE: Well, maybe there's one present in there somewhere. It's Granny's ring she gave me and I thought you might like to have it, but I didn't think you'd wear it if I gave it to you right now.

MAMA *(taking the box to a table nearby)*:   No. Probably not. *(Turning back to face her.)* I'm ready for my manicure, I guess. Want me to wash my hands again?

JESSIE *(standing up)*:   It's time for me to go, Mama.

MAMA *(starting for her)*:   No, Jessie, you've got all night!

JESSIE *(as Mama grabs her)*:   No, Mama.

MAMA: It's not even ten o'clock.

JESSIE *(very calm)*:   Let me go, Mama.

MAMA: I can't. You can't go. You can't do this. You didn't say it would be so soon, Jessie. I'm scared. I love you.

JESSIE *(takes her hands away)*:   Let go of me, Mama. I've said everything I had to say.

MAMA *(standing still a minute)*:   You said you wanted to do my nails.

JESSIE *(taking a small step backward)*:   I can't. It's too late.

MAMA: It's not too late!

JESSIE: I don't want you to wake Dawson and Loretta when you call. I want them to still be up and dressed so they can get right over.

MAMA *(as Jessie backs up, Mama moves in on her, but carefully)*:   They wake up fast, Jessie, if they have to. They don't matter here, Jessie. You do. I do. We're not through yet. We've got a lot of things to take care of here. I don't know where my prescriptions are and you didn't tell me what to tell Dr. Davis when he calls or how much you want me to tell Ricky or who I call to rake the leaves or . . .

JESSIE: Don't try and stop me, Mama, you can't do it.

MAMA *(grabbing her again, this time hard)*:   I can too! I'll stand in front of this hall and you can't get past me. *(They struggle.)* You'll have to knock me down to get away from me, Jessie. I'm not about to let you . . .

Mama struggles with Jessie at the door and in the struggle Jessie gets away from her and —

JESSIE *(almost a whisper)*:   'Night, Mother. *(She vanishes into her bedroom and we hear the door lock just as Mama gets to it.)*

MAMA *(screams)*:   Jessie! *(Pounding on the door.)* Jessie, you let me in there. Don't you do this, Jessie. I'm not going to stop screaming until you open this door, Jessie. Jessie! Jessie! What if I don't do any of the things you told me to do! I'll tell Cecil what a miserable man he was to make you feel the way he did and I'll give Ricky's watch to Dawson if I feel like it and the only way you can make sure I do what you want is you come out here and make me, Jessie! *(Pounding again.)* Jessie! Stop this! I didn't know! I was here with you all the time. How could I know you were so alone?

And Mama stops for a moment, breathless and frantic, putting her ear to the door, and when she doesn't hear anything, she stands up straight again and screams once more.

Jessie! Please!

And we hear the shot, and it sounds like an answer, it sounds like No.

Mama collapses against the door, tears streaming down her face, but not scream-ing anymore. In shock now.

Jessie, Jessie, child . . . Forgive me. *(Pause.)* I thought you were mine.

And she leaves the door and makes her way through the living room, around the fur-niture, as though she didn't know where it was, not knowing what to do. Finally, she goes to the stove in the kitchen and picks up the hot-chocolate pan and carries it with her to the telephone and holds on to it while she dials the number. She looks down at the pan, holding it tight like her life depended on it. She hears Loretta answer.

MAMA: Loretta, let me talk to Dawson, honey.   [1983]

■ THINKING ABOUT THE TEXT

1. Does Thelma understand her daughter? Does Jessie understand her mother? Is it Jessie's death that helps Thelma to say, "Forgive me. I thought you were mine"?

2. What are Thelma's main arguments against Jessie's committing sui-cide? What are Jessie's main arguments in return? Do you side with one character more than the other? Why, or why not?

3. What are the advantages and disadvantages for the playwright in re-stricting the time span covered by the play to the length of its perfor-mance? How surprised were you by the play's ending? In the course of your reading, what elements in the text did you especially consider as you thought about how it might end?

4. Jessie and Thelma refer to several absent characters. Do any of them seem more important than others? If so, which and why? Evaluate Norman's decision to keep all of these characters offstage. Should she have brought any of them onstage?

5. What would you say to people worried that Norman's play will encour-age suicide?

TERRENCE McNALLY
Andre's Mother

Terrence McNally (b. 1939) was born in Florida and raised in Texas. He graduated in 1960 from Columbia University, where he majored in English, and was granted membership in the prestigious honor society Phi Beta Kappa. He became famous with the off-Broadway play Frankie and Johnny in the Claire de Lune *(1982). Most of his work deals with the lives of gays and the response of the straight world. His most controversial play,* Corpus Christi *(1998), portrays Christ and his disciples as homosexuals. He has won numerous awards for his plays, films, and television* productions. *The following brief play was expanded for television and won an Emmy. His musical* Ganesha, A Perfect God *was produced in 2010.*

CHARACTERS

CAL, *a young man*
ARTHUR, *his father*
PENNY, *his sister*
ANDRÉ'S MOTHER

TIME: *Now*
PLACE: *New York City, Central Park*

Four people—Cal, Arthur, Penny, and Andre's Mother—enter: They are nicely dressed and each carries a white helium-filled balloon on a string.

CAL: You know what's really terrible? I can't think of anything terrific to say. Goodbye. I love you. I'll miss you. And I'm supposed to be so great with words!

PENNY: What's that over there?

ARTHUR: Ask your brother.

CAL: It's a theatre. An outdoor theatre. They do plays there in the summer. Shakespeare's plays. *(To Andre's Mother.)* God, how much he wanted to play Hamlet again. He would have gone to Timbuktu to have another go at that part. The summer he did it in Boston, he was so happy!

PENNY: Cal, I don't think she . . . ! It's not the time. Later.

ARTHUR: Your son was a . . . the Jews have a word for it . . .

PENNY *(quietly appalled)*:   Oh my God!

ARTHUR: Mensch, I believe it is, and I think I'm using it right. It means warm, solid, the real thing. Correct me if I'm wrong.

PENNY: Fine, Dad, fine. Just quit while you're ahead.

ARTHUR: I won't say he was like a son to me. Even my son isn't always like a son to me. I mean . . . ! In my clumsy way, I'm trying to say how much I liked Andre. And how much he helped me to know my own boy. Cal was always two handsful but Andre and I could talk about anything under the sun. My wife was very fond of him, too.

PENNY: Cal, I don't understand about the balloons.

CAL: They represent the soul. When you let go, it means you're letting his soul ascend to Heaven. That you're willing to let go. Breaking the last earthly ties.

PENNY: Does the Pope know about this?

ARTHUR: Penny!

PENNY: Andre loved my sense of humor. Listen, you can hear him laughing. *(She lets go of her white balloon.)* So long, you glorious, wonderful, I-know-what-Cal-means-about-words . . . *man!* God forgive me for wishing you were straight every time I laid eyes on you. But if any man was going to have you, I'm glad it was my brother! Look how fast it went up. I bet that means something. Something terrific.

ARTHUR *(Lets his balloon go)*:   Goodbye. God speed.

PENNY: Cal?

CAL: I'm not ready yet.

PENNY: Okay. We'll be over there. Come on, Pop, you can buy your little girl a Good Humor.

ARTHUR: They still make Good Humor?

PENNY: Only now they're called Dove Bars and they cost twelve dollars.

(Penny takes Arthur off. Cal and Andre's Mother stand with their balloons.)

CAL: I wish I knew what you were thinking. I think it would help me. You know almost nothing about me and I only know what Andre told me about you. I'd always had it in my mind that one day we would be friends, you and me. But if you didn't know about Andre and me . . . If this hadn't happened, I wonder if he would have ever told you. When he was sick, if I asked him once I asked him a thousand times, tell her. She's your mother. She won't mind. But he was so afraid of hurting you and of your disapproval. I don't know which was worse. *(No response. He sighs.)* God, how many of us live in this city because we don't want to hurt our mothers and live in mortal terror of their disapproval. We lose ourselves here. Our lives aren't furtive, just our feelings toward people like you are! A city of fugitives from our parents' scorn or heartbreak. Sometimes he'd seem a little down and I'd say, "What's the matter, babe?" and this funny sweet, sad smile would cross his face and he'd say, "Just a little homesick, Cal, just a little bit." I always accused him of being a country boy just playing at being a hotshot, sophisticated New Yorker. *(He sighs.)*

It's bullshit. It's all bullshit. *(Still no response.)*

Do you remember the comic strip *Little Lulu?* Her mother had no name, she was so remote, so formidable to all the children. She was just Lulu's mother. "Hello, Lulu's Mother," Lulu's friends would say. She was almost anonymous in her remoteness. You remind me of her, Andre's Mother. Let me answer the questions you can't ask and then I'll leave you alone and you won't ever have to see me again. Andre died of AIDS. I don't know how he got it. I tested negative. He died bravely. You would have been proud of him. The only thing that frightened him was you. I'll have everything that was his sent to you. I'll pay for it. There isn't much. You should have come up the summer he played Hamlet. He was magnificent. Yes, I'm bitter. I'm bitter I've lost him. I'm bitter what's happening. I'm bitter even now, after all this, I can't reach you. I'm beginning to feel your disapproval and it's making me ill. *(He looks at his balloon.)* Sorry, old friend. I blew it. *(He lets go of the balloon.)*

Good night, sweet prince, and flights of angels sing thee to thy rest.

(Beat.)

Goodbye, Andre's Mother.

(He goes. Andre's Mother stands alone holding her white balloon. Her lips tremble. She looks on the verge of breaking down. She is about to let go of the balloon when she pulls it down to her. She looks at it awhile before she gently kisses it. She lets go of the

balloon. She follows it with her eyes as it rises and rises. The lights are beginning to fade. Andre's Mother's eyes are still on the balloon. The lights fade.)   *[1988]*

≡ **THINKING ABOUT THE TEXT**

1. Although this play begins with a death while *'night, Mother* ends with one, does Andre's mother also come to an insight?

2. What is the point of the allusion to *Little Lulu*?

3. Even though the mother does not speak, what do you think her feelings were toward her son?

4. After Cal says, "Goodbye, Andre's Mother," what does she do, and how does that affect your view of her?

5. Why is this play about someone who doesn't speak called *Andre's Mother*? Can you think of other possible titles?

≡ **MAKING COMPARISONS**

1. Compare Andre's mother with Jessie's mother.

2. Do your feelings about both mothers change because of their actions at the end of each play?

3. Do you think *'night, Mother* would be effective if it were as short as McNally's play? Might *Andre's Mother* be effective if it were as long as Norman's play?

≡ **WRITING ABOUT ISSUES**

1. Shortly before *'night, Mother* was revived on Broadway in 2004, author Marsha Norman said, "I no longer think that the play is about the right to die or about death at all." Instead, she claimed, "It's about secrets, about what hasn't been said during life." Write an essay about whether Norman's claim is true for both plays, or only one, or neither.

2. Write an essay that argues that our culture does or does not have an appropriate perspective on suicide or homosexuality.

3. Write a personal narrative, supported by examples, about the responsibility of parents and children to be honest with each other.

4. Argue that Thelma's and Andre's mothers are or are not more sinned against than sinners.

▤ A Journey to Death: Poems

MARY OLIVER, "When Death Comes"

JOHN DONNE, "Death Be Not Proud"

DYLAN THOMAS, "Do Not Go Gentle into That Good Night"

WISLAWA SZYMBORSKA, "On Death, without Exaggeration"

EMILY DICKINSON, "I heard a Fly buzz — when I died"

For many cultures, death seems more than a metaphorical journey. This is especially true of the Greeks, in whose mythology Charon, the ferryman of the underworld, is literally charged with taking the dead across the river Styx, where they will continue their trek for better or worse. Contemporary poets tend to see death's journey differently than the ancients did, but their appreciation of the mysteries and power of death is enduring. And poets reflect on death's presence in our lives in lyrical and illuminating ways.

Mary Oliver uses a series of interesting similes both to describe death's arrival ("like the hungry bear") and to prepare herself for its inevitability. John Donne sneers at death, perhaps to demonstrate its power. Dylan Thomas wants to resist that power, and Wislawa Szymborska describes death in terms that considerably reduce its significance. Something like this was probably on Emily Dickinson's mind when she ironically has a lowly fly appear instead of the king. Death has intrigued and puzzled poets for centuries perhaps because, as Shakespeare reminds us, it is a country from which no traveler returns.

▤ BEFORE YOU READ

Does our society have a particular attitude toward death? Can you point to films that might reveal such a cultural inclination? Does your religion have a specific take on death? What is your general attitude toward death, and where does it come from?

MARY OLIVER
When Death Comes

Mary Oliver (b. 1935) was born in Maple Heights, Ohio, and briefly attended Ohio State University. She was strongly influenced by the poet Edna St. Vincent Millay. Her collection No Voyage and Other Poems *(1963) was the first of numerous volumes, including* New and Selected Poems *(1992), which won the National Book Award, and* American Primitive *(1984), which won the Pulitzer Prize for poetry. She has taught at Bucknell University and Sweet Briar College. Her most recent volume of poetry is* Thirst *(2006), a volume of forty-three poems that confirm Diane*

Ackerman's judgment of Oliver as an "earth ecstatic." The poet Maxine Kumin calls Oliver "an undefatigable guide to the natural world."

When death comes
like the hungry bear in autumn;
when death comes and takes all the bright coins from his purse

to buy me, and snaps the purse shut;
when death comes   5
like the measles-pox;

when death comes
like an iceberg between the shoulder blades,

I want to step through the door full of curiosity, wondering:
what is it going to be like, that cottage of darkness?   10

And therefore I look upon everything
as a brotherhood and a sisterhood,
and I look upon time as no more than an idea,
and I consider eternity as another possibility,

and I think of each life as a flower, as common   15
as a field daisy, and as singular,
and each name a comfortable music in the mouth
tending as all music does, toward silence,

and each body a lion of courage, and something
precious to the earth.   20

When it's over, I want to say: all my life
I was a bride married to amazement.
I was the bridegroom, taking the world into my arms.

When it is over, I don't want to wonder
if I have made of my life something particular, and real.   25
I don't want to find myself sighing and frightened,
or full of argument.

I don't want to end up simply having visited this world.   *[1992]*

▤ THINKING ABOUT THE TEXT

1. How would you describe what the narrator wants to avoid when death comes?

2. The poet uses a number of similes to describe death's coming. Explain why any one of these seems particularly apt.

3. How does Oliver's view of death influence the way she lives her life?

4. Unpack "visited" in the last line.

5. Does our culture have a particular view of death? What might that be? Does your religion have an attitude toward death that may have influenced you? Is there evidence for a cultural view of death in movies? In popular songs? On TV shows?

JOHN DONNE

Death Be Not Proud

Long regarded as a major English writer, John Donne (1572–1631) was also trained as a lawyer and clergyman. Around 1594, he converted from Catholicism to Anglicanism; in 1615, he was ordained; and in 1621, he was appointed to the prestigious position of dean of St. Paul's Cathedral in London. Today, his sermons continue to be studied as literature, yet he is more known for his poetry. When he was a young man, he often wrote about love, but later he focused on religious themes. The following poem, one of Donne's "holy sonnets," is from 1611.

Death be not proud, though some have callèd thee
Mighty and dreadful, for thou art not so;
For those whom thou think'st thou dost overthrow
Die not, poor Death, nor yet canst thou kill me.
From rest and sleep, which but thy pictures° be,   *images*   5
Much pleasure; then from thee much more must flow,
And soonest our best men with thee do go,
Rest of their bones, and soul's delivery.°   *deliverance*
Thou art slave to Fate, Chance, kings, and desperate men,
And dost with Poison, War, and Sickness dwell;   10
And poppy or channs can make us sleep as well,
And better than thy stroke; why swell'st° thou then?   *swell with pride*
One short sleep past, we wake eternally
And death shall be no more; Death, thou shalt die.   *[1611]*

≡ THINKING ABOUT THE TEXT

1. In a sense, Death is the speaker's audience. But presumably Donne expected the living to read his poem. What reaction might he have wanted from this audience?

2. Is the speaker proud? Define what you mean by the term.

3. Evidently the speaker believes in an afterlife. What would you say to people who consider the speaker naive and the poem irrelevant because they don't believe that "we wake eternally" (line 13)? How significant is this warrant or assumption? Do you share it?

4. What are the arguments the narrator uses to diminish Death?

5. Imagine Death writing a sonnet in response to the speaker. Perhaps it would be entitled "Life Be Not Proud." What might Death say in it?

■ MAKING COMPARISONS

1. Is death more or less fearsome in Donne's poem than in Oliver's?
2. Do both speakers refuse to be afraid of death?
3. What optimistic note do both speakers take?

DYLAN THOMAS

Do Not Go Gentle into That Good Night

Dylan Thomas (1914–1953) was a Welsh poet, short-story writer, and playwright. Among his most enduring works are his radio dramas Under Milk Wood *(1954) and* A Child's Christmas in Wales *(1955). A frequent visitor to the United States, Thomas built a devoted audience in this country through his electrifying public readings. Unfortunately, he was also well known for his alcoholism, which killed him at a relatively young age. He wrote the following poem in 1952, not long before his own death. It takes the form of a* villanelle, *which consists of nineteen lines: five tercets (three-line stanzas) followed by a quatrain (four-line stanza). The first and third lines of the opening tercet are used alternately to conclude each succeeding tercet, and they are joined to form a rhyme at the poem's end.*

Do not go gentle into that good night,
Old age should burn and rave at close of day;
Rage, rage against the dying of the light.

Though wise men at their end know dark is right,
Because their words had forked no lightning they   5
Do not go gentle into that good night.

Good men, the last wave by, crying how bright
Their frail deeds might have danced in a green bay,
Rage, rage against the dying of the light.

Wild men who caught and sang the sun in flight,   10
And learn, too late, they grieved it on its way,
Do not go gentle into that good night.

Grave men, near death, who see with blinding sight
Blind eyes could blaze like meteors and be gay,
Rage, rage against the dying of the light.   15

And you, my father, there on the sad height,
Curse, bless, me now with your fierce tears, I pray.

Do not go gentle into that good night.
Rage, rage against the dying of the light.   *[1952]*

■ THINKING ABOUT THE TEXT

1. In what sense could the night possibly be "good," given that people are supposed to "rage" at it?

2. Why do you think Thomas has his speaker refer to "the dying of the light" instead of simply to "dying"? What other parts of the poem relate to the word *light?*

3. The speaker refers to four kinds of "men." Restate in your own words the description given of each. Should Thomas's language about them have been less abstract? Why, or why not?

4. What is the effect of climaxing the poem with a reference to "you, my father" (line 16)? If the father had been introduced in the first or second stanzas, would the effect have been quite different? If so, how?

5. What is the effect of the villanelle form? Judging by Thomas's poem, do you think it is worthwhile for a poet to write in this way, despite the technical challenges of the form? Should teachers of poetry writing push their students to write a villanelle? Explain your reasoning.

■ MAKING COMPARISONS

1. Is this poem an affirmation of life? Could Oliver's or Donne's poem be considered as such?

2. Compare the speaker's attitude in this poem to that in Oliver's.

3. Which poet seems most at peace with death?

WISLAWA SZYMBORSKA

On Death, without Exaggeration

Translated by Stanislaw Baranczak and Clare Cavanagh

Although she has written several volumes of poetry, Wislawa Szymborska (b. 1923) was little known outside of her native Poland until she won the Nobel Prize for literature in 1996. Since then, readers in various countries have come to admire the blend of simplicity, wit, and wisdom in her writing. The Polish version of the following poem appeared in Szymborska's 1986 book The People on the Bridge. *Subsequently, Stanislaw Baranczak and Clare Cavanagh included it in their 1995 English collection of Szymborska's poems,* View with a Grain of Sand. *We present their translation of the text.*

It can't take a joke,
find a star, make a bridge.
It knows nothing about weaving, mining, farming,
building ships, or baking cakes.

In our planning for tomorrow,   5
it has the final word,
which is always beside the point.

It can't even get the things done
that are part of its trade:
dig a grave,   10
make a coffin,
clean up after itself.

Preoccupied with killing,
it does the job awkwardly,
without system or skill.   15
As though each of us were its first kill.

Oh, it has its triumphs,
but look at its countless defeats,
missed blows,
and repeat attempts!   20

Sometimes it isn't strong enough
to swat a fly from the air.
Many are the caterpillars
that have outcrawled it.

All those bulbs, pods,   25
tentacles, fins, tracheae,
nuptial plumage, and winter fur
show that it has fallen behind
with its halfhearted work.

Ill will won't help   30
and even our lending a hand with wars and coups d'état
is so far not enough.

Hearts beat inside eggs.
Babies' skeletons grow.
Seeds, hard at work, sprout their first tiny pair of leaves   35
and sometimes even tall trees fall away.

Whoever claims that it's omnipotent
is himself living proof
that it's not.

There's no life   40
that couldn't be immortal
if only for a moment.

Death
always arrives by that very moment too late.

In vain it tugs at the knob   45
of the invisible door.
As far as you've come
can't be undone.   *[1986]*

≣ THINKING ABOUT THE TEXT

1. Although the word *death* appears in the title, it doesn't appear in the text of the poem until the next-to-last stanza. Up to that point, death is repeatedly referred to as "it." What is the effect of this pronoun? What might be the effect had Szymborska referred to death more explicitly throughout the text?

2. Evidently the speaker is trying not to exaggerate death. What sorts of remarks about death might the speaker see as an exaggeration of it? Define what you mean by *exaggeration*.

3. What images of death does the speaker create? Refer to specific lines.

4. In the eighth stanza, the speaker mentions that human beings are "lending a hand" to death. Do you take the speaker to be criticizing humanity at this point? Why, or why not?

5. Does the order of the stanzas matter? Could the speaker's observations about death appear in any order and have the same effect? Explain your reasoning.

≣ MAKING COMPARISONS

1. Do all four poems speak of death "without exaggeration"? Define what you mean by the phrase.

2. Does Szymborska's poem strike you as lighter, less serious than Donne's and Thomas's? Refer to specific lines in each text.

3. If you didn't know the authors of the four poems, could you guess which two were written by women? What evidence supports your position?

EMILY DICKINSON

I heard a Fly buzz — when I died

Although Emily Dickinson (1830–1886) was considered an eccentric recluse by many of her provincial neighbors, history has interpreted Emily Dickinson's life in various ways, according to the thinking of the times. Once considered isolated, she is now seen by many critics as connected to the issues and literature of her age. And feminist and queer studies scholars now see the once shy figure as an active champion of defying gender stereotypes. Although she has often been described as a nunlike, passive figure, critics today see her as a nonconformist mistrustful of power and dogma and as someone who questioned any kind of received opinion, even popular views on religion and the afterlife.

I heard a Fly buzz — when I died —
The Stillness in the Room
Was like the Stillness in the Air —
Between the Heaves of Storm —

The Eyes around — had wrung them dry —   5
And Breaths were gathering firm
For that last Onset — when the King
Be witnessed — in the Room —

I willed my Keepsakes — Signed away
What portion of me be   10
Assignable — and then it was
There interposed a Fly —

With Blue — uncertain stumbling Buzz —
Between the light — and me —
And then the Windows failed — and then   15
I could not see to see —   *[1896]*

■ THINKING ABOUT THE TEXT

1. Dickinson's famous opening line ends with the strange "when I died." How is this possible? What are some possible interpretations?

2. What are some possible meanings for "the King" (line 7)?

3. What are possible interpretations of the phrase "Between the Heaves of Storm" (line 4)?

4. Satan is sometimes called the "lord of the flies." Might this figure into the poem's meaning?

5. The juxtaposition between the momentousness of death and the insignificance of the fly seems to be at the heart of Dickinson's meaning here. Comment on this idea.

■ MAKING COMPARISONS

1. Do the three poems by women have a different tone from those by Donne and Thomas?

2. Using just a word or phrase, how would you characterize the attitude of these five poems about death?

3. Why do you think Donne would like (or dislike) Dickinson's poem?

≡ WRITING ABOUT ISSUES

1. Choose one of the five poems about death, and write an essay analyzing it as an argument for a certain position on death. Specify the main claim and the evidence given in support of it. Feel free to evaluate the argument you discuss, although keep in mind that the artistic success of the poem may or may not depend on whether its argument is fully developed.

2. Write an essay comparing two of the poems in this cluster, focusing on the issue of whether they are basically similar or significantly different in the ideas and feelings they express. Refer to specific lines from each text.

3. Write an essay recalling a specific occasion when you had difficulty deciding whether to accept something as inevitable. In your essay, give details of the occasion, the difficulty, and your ultimate reasoning. Indicate as well what your final decision revealed about you. Perhaps you will want to distinguish between the self you were then and the self you are now. If you wish, refer to any of the poems in this cluster.

4. Imagine that you are on the staff of a nursing home. At a staff meeting, the chief administrator asks you and your colleagues to consider framing and hanging one of these five poems in the recreation room. Write a letter to the administrator in which you favor one of these poems or reject them all as inappropriate. Be sure to give reasons for your view.

Crossing the Waters: Poems

For some reason, journeys on ferries seem to put us in a wistful, meditative frame of mind. Especially for a writer, this trip seems more symbolic than those in cars or on planes. It often brings to mind previous outings, perhaps from childhood, or sometimes it might remind us that "all life," as Arthur Miller wrote, is a "leave taking." And, of course, there is the larger metaphor that our life is a kind of ferry ride between the shores of life and death. The three poets included here take advantage of these notions, adding their own lyrical perspectives. Katia Kapovich, for example, muses on time passing, Linda Pastan on rituals repeated, and Mark Doty on mysteries as deep as the seas. As Pastan writes, "The ferry is no simple pleasure boat."

≡ BEFORE YOU READ

Why do you think ferries evoke meditative responses that planes or cars usually do not elicit? Have you ever taken a ferry ride? What was your response?

KATIA KAPOVICH

The Ferry

Katia Kapovich (b. 1960) was born in Moldova in the former Soviet Union, where as a young intellectual artist she was under considerable pressure to conform. As a member of an underground literary dissident movement, she was in constant conflict with an oppressive government. During a demonstration for intellectual freedom at a university in Leningrad, she was arrested after clashing with police. She was briefly confined and later immigrated to America. For the past nearly twenty years, she has lived in Boston, where she teaches Russian literature and writes in both Russian and English. Her poems have been described as exquisitely crafted and quite complex. She and her husband edit the journal Fulcrum. *Her latest book of poems is* Cossacks and Bandits *(2008). The following poem is from* Best American Poetry 2006.

I'm jotting down these lines,
having borrowed a pen from a waitress
in this roadside restaurant. Three rusty pines

prod up the sky in the windows.
My soup gets cold, which implies   5

I'll eat it cold. Soon I too
will leave a tip on the table, merge
into the beehive of travelers
and board one of the ferries,
where there's always a line to the loo   10
and no one knows where the captain is.

Slightly seasick, I keep on writing
of the wind rose and lobster traps,
seagulls, if any — and there always are.
Check the air and you'll see them   15
above straw hats and caps.
The sun at noon glides like a monstrous star-

fish through clouds. Others drink iced tea,
training binoculars on a tugboat.
When I finish this letter, I'll take a gulp   20
from the flask you gave me for the road
in days when I was too young to care about
those on the pier who waved goodbye.

I miss them now: cousins in linen dresses,
my mother, you, boys in light summer shirts.   25
Life is too long. The compass needle dances.
Everything passes by. The ferry passes
by ragged yellow shores.   *[2006]*

■ **THINKING ABOUT THE TEXT**

1. Who might the "you" referred to in lines 21 and 25 be? Is there a difference between missing one's mother and missing "cousins in linen
   dresses" (line 24) and "boys in light summer shirts" (line 25)?

2. How do the details in the first three stanzas (rusty pines, cold soup,
   long lines, seasickness) suggest the narrator's mood?

3. The poem shifts from the present to the past in stanza 4. What thought
   comes first to the narrator's mind? How old do you think the narrator is?

4. Is the claim that "[l]ife is too long" (line 26) surprising? Are the following
   two sentences (lines 26–27) evidence of this?

5. Do ferry rides (as opposed to bridge crossings or tunnel passages)
   seem to make you reflective or nostalgic? Why?

LINDA PASTAN
Leaving the Island

Linda Pastan (b. 1932) was born in the Bronx and graduated from Radcliffe College; she later received her M.A. from Brandeis University. The recipient of numerous prestigious awards and nominations for the National Book Award, Pastan has published several volumes of poetry, including Cardinal Evening: New and Selected Poems 1968–1998 *(1998) and* Queen of a Rainy Country *(2006).* Traveling Light, *a book of poems, is to be published in 2011. The poet May Sarton has praised Pastan for her integrity, noting her "unsentimental acceptance of hard work." Pastan was poet laureate of Maryland (1991–1995) and for twenty years taught at the noted Bread Loaf Writers Conference sponsored by Middlebury College in Vermont.*

We roll up rugs and strip the beds by rote,
summer expires as it has done before.
The ferry is no simple pleasure boat

nor are we simply cargo, though we'll float
alongside heavy trucks — their stink and roar.   5
We roll up rugs and strip the beds by rote.

This bit of land whose lines the glaciers wrote
becomes the muse of memory once more;
the ferry is no simple pleasure boat.

I'll trade my swimsuit for a woolen coat;   10
the torch of autumn has but small allure.

We roll up rugs and strip the beds by rote.

The absences these empty shells denote
suggest the losses winter has in store.
The ferry is no simple pleasure boat.   15

The songs of summer dwindle to one note:
the fog horn's blast (which drowns this closing door).
We rolled up rugs and stripped the beds by rote.
The ferry is no simple pleasure boat.   *[2004]*

≡ THINKING ABOUT THE TEXT

1. How would you describe the narrator's mood? Is it temporary? What effects does the repetition of "We roll up rugs and strip the beds by rote" and "The ferry is no simple pleasure boat" have on the reader?

2. Is this a poem about summer's passing or about something more general — say, time passing or aging?

3. Why does summer seem the best of times for the narrator? Is it for you? Do losses happen mostly in the winter?

4. Do you remember a childhood vacation? Is your memory positive? Were you sad when it ended?

5. How would you expand on the refrain "The ferry is no simple pleasure boat"? Is "simple" the key idea?

≣ MAKING COMPARISONS

1. Compare the mood or the tone of the speakers in these two poems.

2. Is nostalgia part of the poems? How does a poet avoid being too sentimental about the past? Do these poets succeed in that regard?

3. Note the rhyme scheme in both poems. Does the pattern work better in Pastan's poem than in Kapovich's? Why?

MARK DOTY
Night Ferry

Mark Doty (b. 1953) was born in Tennessee, but his father, who was a builder working for the Army Corps of Engineers, was a man who could not get along with supervisors and often moved the family. In the autobiographical Firebird *(1999), Doty describes growing up as "a sissy" in a Southern Gothic family. He attended high school in Tucson, Arizona, where he first developed an interest in writing. Then he briefly attended the University of Tucson, but dropped out and married when he was eighteen. In the 1970s, he attended Drake University in Iowa, where he and his wife published chapbooks of poetry together. In 1981, he dissolved his marriage when he acknowledged his homosexuality. He received his M.F.A. at Goddard College in Vermont and taught there, eventually moving with his partner to Provincetown, Massachusetts. After his partner died from complications of AIDS in 1984, Doty's poetry took on a new intensity and significance. Doty has taught at several universities and now teaches at Rutgers University. He has published five poetry collections and two memoirs. His awards and fellowships include the National Book Critics Award and the T. S. Eliot Prize in 1993 for* My Alexandria. *His recent books include* School of the Arts: Poems *(2005),* Dog Years: A Memoir *(2007), and* Theories and Apparitions *(2008).*

> We're launched into the darkness,
> half a load of late passengers
>   gliding onto the indefinite
>   black surface, a few lights vague
>
> and shimmering on the island shore.   5
> Behind us, between the landing's twin flanks

(wooden pylons strapped with old tires),
          the docklights shatter in our twin,

     folding wakes, their colors
on the roughened surface combed   10
     like the patterns of Italian bookpaper,
          lustrous and promising. The narrative

     of the ferry begins and ends brilliantly,
and its text is this moving out
     into what is soon before us   15
          and behind: the night going forward,

     sentence by sentence, as if on faith,
into whatever takes place.
     It's strange how we say things *take place*,
          as if occurrence were a location —   20

     the dark between two shores,
for instance, where for a little while
     we're on no solid ground. Twelve minutes,
          precisely, the night ferry hurries

     across the lake. And what happens   25
is always the body of water,
     its skin like the wrong side of satin.
          I love to stand like this,

     where the prow pushes blunt into the future,
knowing, more than seeing, how   30
     the surface rushes and doesn't even break
          but simply slides under us.

     Lake melds into shoreline,
one continuous black moiré;°
     the boatmen follow the one course they know   35
          toward a dock nearly the mirror

     of the first, mercury lamps vaporing
over the few late birds
     attending the pier. Even the bored men
          at the landing, who wave   40

     their flashlights for the last travelers,
steering us toward the road, will seem
     the engineers of our welcome,
          their red-sheathed lights marking

     the completion of our, or anyone's, crossing.   45
Twelve dark minutes. Love,

34 *moiré*: Wavy pattern.

we are between worlds, between
        unfathomed water and I don't know how much

    light-flecked black sky, the fogged circles
of island lamps. I am almost not afraid   50
        on this good boat, breathing its good smell
            of grease and kerosene,

    warm wind rising up the stairwell
from the engine's serious study.
        There's no beautiful binding   55
            for this story, only the temporary,

    liquid endpapers of the hurried water,
shot with random color. But in the gliding forward's
        a scent so quick and startling
            it might as well be blowing   60

    off the stars. Now, just before we arrive,
the wind carries a signal and a comfort,
        lovely, though not really meant for us:
            woodsmoke risen from the chilly shore.   *[1993]*

≡ THINKING ABOUT THE TEXT

1. The poem seems to be a sustained metaphor for life's journey. In
   what ways does this comparison make sense? What other significant
   metaphor is developed?

2. As symbols, what do the following images suggest — "a few lights
   vague / and shimmering" (lines 4–5), "like the patterns of Italian book-
   paper, / lustrous and promising" (lines 11–12), "no beautiful binding /
   for this story, only the temporary, / liquid endpapers of the hurried water, / shot with random color" (lines 55–58)?

3. How did you evaluate the speaker's attitude when he says, "I am almost not afraid / on this good boat, breathing its good smell" (lines
   50–51)?

4. Does the image of "a scent ... / ... blowing / off the stars" (lines 59–61)
   seem more mysterious than Doty's other images? What idea might the
   poet be after with such imagery?

5. Can we sustain the journey-of-life metaphor into the last stanza? Where
   might the passengers be arriving? What is the signal "not really meant
   for us" (line 63)? Why woodsmoke? Why "the chilly shore" (line 64)?

≡ MAKING COMPARISONS

1. Is Doty's poem more melancholy than the other poems? Why?

2. Is Doty's poem more metaphorical than the others? Why?

3. Which line or lines in these four poems do you find the most lyrical? The most mysterious? The most suggestive?

≡ WRITING ABOUT ISSUES

1. Which of these three poems most closely reflects your own sense of what life's journey is like? Write an essay in which you make the case for your poem in comparison with one or both of the other poems.

2. Write a brief essay defending the idea that ferry rides in literature often have symbolic value. Use the poems here as evidence.

3. Write a brief personal essay about a ferry trip you took, noting your thoughts about it.

4. Read Walt Whitman's famous poem "Crossing Brooklyn Ferry," and write a brief analysis of Whitman's response to his ride.

APPENDIX

Critical Approaches to Literature

Exploring the topics of literary criticism can help readers understand the various ways literature can matter. One popular way to investigate critical approaches to literature is to group critics into schools. Critics who are concerned primarily with equality for women, for example, are often classified as feminist critics, and those concerned with the responses of readers are classified as reader-response critics. Likewise, critics who focus on the unconscious are said to belong to the psychoanalytic school, and those who analyze class conflicts belong to the Marxist school.

Classifying critics in this way is probably more convenient than precise. Few critics like to be pigeonholed or thought predictable, and many professional readers tend to be eclectic — that is, they use ideas from various schools to help them illuminate the text. Nevertheless, knowing something about contemporary schools of criticism can make you a more informed reader and help literature matter to you even more.

There is a commonsense belief that words mean just what they say — that to understand a certain passage in a text a reader simply needs to know what the words mean. But meaning is rarely straightforward. Scholars have been arguing over the meaning of passages in the Bible, in the Constitution, and in Shakespeare's plays for centuries without reaching agreement. Pinning down the exact meaning of words like *sin, justice,* and *love* is almost impossible, but even more daunting is the unacknowledged theory of reading that each person brings to any text, including literature. Some people who read the Bible or the Constitution, for example, believe in the literal meaning of the words, and some think the real meaning lies in the original intention of the writer, while others believe that the only meaning we can be sure of is our own perspective. For these latter readers, there is no objective meaning, and no absolutely true meaning is possible.

Indeed, a good deal of what a text means depends on the perspective that readers bring with them. Passages can be read effectively from numerous points of view. A generation ago most English professors taught their students to pay attention to the internal aspects of a poem and not to the poem's larger social and political contexts. So oppositions, irony, paradox, and coherence — not gender equality or social justice — were topics of discussion. Proponents of this approach were said to belong to the New Critical school. In the last twenty-five years or so, however, professors have put much more emphasis on the external aspects of interpretation, stressing social, political, cultural, sexual, and gender-based perspectives. Each one of these perspectives can give us a valuable window on a text, helping us see the rich possibilities of literature. Even though each approach can provide insights into a text, it can also be blind to other textual elements. When we read in too focused a way, we can sometimes miss the opportunity to see what others see.

In this appendix, however, we want to present our interpretation in a clear, logical, and reflective manner as we take a position and try to persuade others of its reasonableness. Since there are many possible lenses to see a text through, you can be sure your classmates will see things differently. Part of the excitement and challenge of making arguments that matter is your ability to analyze and clarify your ideas, gather and organize your evidence, and present your claim in carefully revised and edited prose.

Contemporary Schools of Criticism

The following eight approaches are just a few of the many different literary schools or perspectives a reader can use in engaging a text. Think of them as intellectual tools or informed lenses that you can employ to enhance your interpretation of a particular literary text:

- New Criticism
- Feminist criticism
- Psychoanalytic criticism
- Marxist criticism
- Deconstruction
- Reader-response criticism
- Postcolonial criticism
- New Historicism

NEW CRITICISM

New Criticism was developed about seventy years ago as a way to focus on "the text itself." Although it is no longer as popular as it once was, some of its principles are still widely accepted, especially the use of specific examples from the text as evidence for a particular interpretation. Sometimes called *close reading*, this approach does not see either the writer's intention or the reader's personal response as relevant. It is also uninterested in the text's social context, the spirit of the age, or its relevance to issues of gender, social justice, or oppression. These critics are interested, for example, in a poem's internal structure, images, symbols, metaphors, point of view, plot, and characterizations. Emphasis is placed on literary language — on the ways connotation, ambiguity, irony, and paradox all reinforce the meaning. In fact, *how* a poem means is inseparable from *what* it means. The primary method for judging the worth of a piece of literature is its organic unity or the complex way all the elements of a text contribute to the poem's meaning.

Critics often argue that their interpretations are the most consistent with textual evidence. A popular approach is to note the oppositions in the text and to focus on tensions, ironies, and paradoxes. Typically a paradox early in the text is shown at the end not to be that contradictory after all. The critic then argues that all the elements of the text can be seen as contributing to this resolution.

FEMINIST CRITICISM

Feminist criticism developed during the 1970s as an outgrowth of a resurgent women's movement. The goals of the feminist critic and the feminist political activist are similar — to contest the patriarchal point of view as the standard for all moral, aesthetic, political, and intellectual judgments and to assert that gender roles are primarily learned, not universal. They hope to uncover and challenge essentialist attitudes that hold it is normal for women to be kept in domestic, secondary, and subservient roles, and they affirm the value of a woman's experiences and perspectives in understanding the world. Recently both female and male critics have become interested in gender studies, a branch of theory concerned with the ways cultural practices socialize us to act in certain ways because of our gender. Focused primarily on issues of identity, gender criticism looks at the ways characters in literary texts are represented, or how they are constructed in a particular culture as feminine or masculine. Like the broader area of feminism, many gender specialists hope that studying the arbitrary ways we are expected to dress, walk, talk, and behave can help us widen the conventional notions of gender.

PSYCHOANALYTIC CRITICISM

Psychoanalytic criticism began with Sigmund Freud's theories of the unconscious, especially the numerous repressed wounds, fears, unresolved conflicts, and guilty desires from childhood that can significantly affect behavior and mental health in our adult lives. Freud developed the tripart division of the mind into the ego (the conscious self), the superego (the site of what our culture has taught us about good and bad), and the id (the primitive unconscious and source of our sexual drive). Psychoanalytic critics often see literature as a kind of dream filled with symbolic elements that often mask their real meaning. Freud also theorized that young males were threatened by their fathers in the competition for the affection of their mothers. Critics are alert to the complex ways this Oedipal drama unfolds in literature.

MARXIST CRITICISM

Marxist criticism is based on the political and economic theories of Karl Marx. Marxists think that a society is propelled by its economy, which is manipulated by a class system. Most people, especially blue-collar workers (the proletariat), do not understand the complex ways their lives are subject to economic forces beyond their control. This false consciousness about history and material well-being prevents workers from seeing that their values have been socially constructed to keep them in their place. What most interests contemporary Marxists is the way ideology shapes our consciousness. And since literature both represents and projects ideology, Marxist critics see it as a way to unmask our limited view of society's structures.

DECONSTRUCTION

Deconstruction is really more a philosophical movement than a school of literary criticism, but many of its techniques have been used by Marxist and feminist literary critics to uncover important concepts they believe are hidden in texts. Made famous by the French philosopher Jacques Derrida, deconstruction's main tenet is that Western thought has divided the world into binary opposites. To gain a semblance of control over the complexity of human experience, we have constructed a worldview in which good is clearly at one end of a continuum and bad at the other. Additional examples of binary opposites include masculine and feminine, freedom and slavery, objective and subjective, mind and body, and presence and absence. According to Derrida, however, this arbitrary and illusory construct simply reflects the specific ideology of one culture. Far from being opposed to each other, masculinity and femininity, for example, are intimately interconnected, and traces of the feminine are to be found within the masculine. The concepts need each other for meaning to occur, an idea referred to as *différance*. Derrida also notes that language, far from being a neutral medium of communication, is infused with our biases, assumptions, and values—which leads some of us to refer to sexually active women as "sluts" and to sexually active men as "studs." One term ("sluts") is marginalized, and the other ("studs") is privileged because our culture grants men more power than women in shaping the language that benefits them.

Thus, language filters, distorts, and alters our perception of the world. For deconstructors or deconstructive critics, language is not stable or reliable, and when closely scrutinized, it becomes slippery and ambiguous, constantly overflowing with implications, associations, and contradictions. For Derrida, this endless freeplay of meaning suggests that language is always changing, always in flux — especially so when we understand that words can be viewed from almost endless points of view or contexts. That is why deconstructionists claim that texts (or individuals or systems of thought) have no fixed definition, no center, no absolute meaning. And so one way to deconstruct or lay bare the arbitrary construction of a text is to show that the oppositions in the text are not really absolutely opposed, that outsiders can be seen to be insiders, and that words that seem to mean one thing can mean many things.

READER-RESPONSE CRITICISM

Reader-response criticism is often misunderstood to be simply giving one's opinion about a text: "I liked it," "I hate happy endings," "I think the characters were unrealistic." But reader-response criticism is actually more interested in why readers have certain responses. The central assumption is that texts do not come alive and do not mean anything until active readers engage them with specific assumptions about what reading is. New Critics think a reader's response is irrelevant because a text's meaning is timeless. But response critics, including feminists and Marxists, maintain that what a text means cannot be separated from the reading process used by readers as they draw on personal and literary experiences to make meaning. In other words, the text is not an object but an event that occurs in readers over time.

Response criticism includes critics who think that the reader's contribution to the making of meaning is quite small as well as critics who think that readers play a primary role in the process. Louise Rosenblatt is a moderate response critic since she thinks the contributions are about equal. Her transactive theory claims that the text guides our response, like a printed musical score that we adjust as we move through the text. She allows for a range of acceptable meanings as long as she can find reasonable textual support in the writing.

Response critics like Stanley Fish downplay individual responses, focusing instead on how communities influence our responses to texts. We probably all belong to a number of these interpretive communities (such as churches, universities, neighborhoods, political parties, and social class) and have internalized their interpretive strategies, their discourse, or their way of reading texts of all kinds. Fish's point is that we all come to texts already predisposed to read them in a certain way: we do not interpret stories, but we create them by using the reading tools and cultural assumptions we bring with us. Our reading then reveals what is in us more than what is in the text. We find what we expect to see.

POSTCOLONIAL CRITICISM

Postcolonial criticism, like feminist criticism, has developed because of the dramatic shrinking of the world and the increasing multicultural cast of our own country. It is mainly interested in the ways nineteenth-century European political domination affects the lives of people living in former colonies, especially the way the dominant culture becomes the norm and those without power are portrayed as inferior. Postcolonial critics often look for stereotypes in texts as well as in characters whose self-image has been damaged by being forced to see themselves as Other, as less than. As oppressed people try to negotiate life in both the dominant and the oppressed cultures, they can develop a double consciousness that leads to feelings of alienation and deep conflicts.

Literary critics often argue that being caught between the demands of two cultures — one dominant and privileged, the other marginalized and scorned — causes a character to be "unhomed," a psychological refugee who is uncomfortable everywhere.

NEW HISTORICISM

New Historicism was developed because critics were dissatisfied with the old historicism, a long-standing traditional approach that viewed history simply as a background for understanding the literary text. History was thought to be an accurate record of what happened because the professional historian used objective and proven methods. But most literary critics no longer hold to this view of history. Instead, history is now thought to be just one perspective among many possibilities, inevitably subjective and biased. Influenced by the theorist Michel Foucault, history is seen as one of many discourses that can shed light on the past. But the dominant view is that all of us, including historians, writers, and critics, live in a particular culture and cannot escape its influences. And since these social, cultural, literary, economic, and political influences are all interrelated, all texts can tell us something important. Stories, histories, diaries, laws, speeches, newspapers, and magazines are all relevant. Culture permeates all texts, influencing everyone to see society's view of reality, of what's right and wrong and which values, assumptions, and truths are acceptable. Critics and historians try to interpret a vast web of interconnected discourses and forces in order to understand an era. Naturally, since many of these forces are competing for power, critics are always looking for power struggles among discourses. Think of the present struggle over the amount of influence religion should have in politics or who has the right to marry. Literature is one of the texts in a culture that shapes our views and which critics investigate to unearth these competing ideas.

Working with the Critical Approaches

Keep these brief descriptions of the critical approaches in mind as you read the following story by James Joyce, one of the most important writers of the twentieth century. Joyce (1882–1941) was born in Ireland, although he spent most of his life in self-imposed exile on the European continent. "Counterparts" is from *Dubliners* (1914), a collection of stories set in the Irish city of his childhood years. (For more on James Joyce, see his story "Araby," on p. 609.)

JAMES JOYCE

Counterparts

The bell rang furiously and, when Miss Parker went to the tube, a furious voice called out in a piercing North of Ireland accent:
— Send Farrington here!
    Miss Parker returned to her machine, saying to a man who was writing at a desk:
— Mr Alleyne wants you upstairs.
    The man muttered *Blast him!* under his breath and pushed back his chair   5
to stand up. When he stood up he was tall and of great bulk. He had a hanging face, dark wine-coloured, with fair eyebrows and moustache: his eyes bulged forward slightly and the whites of them were dirty. He lifted up the counter and, passing by the clients, went out of the office with a heavy step.

He went heavily upstairs until he came to the second landing, where a door bore a brass plate with the inscription *Mr Alleyne*. Here he halted, puffing with labor and vexation, and knocked. The shrill voice cried:

— Come in!

The man entered Mr Alleyne's room. Simultaneously Mr Alleyne, a little man wearing gold-rimmed glasses on a cleanshaven face, shot his head up over a pile of documents. The head itself was so pink and hairless that it seemed like a large egg reposing on the papers. Mr Alleyne did not lose a moment:

— Farrington? What is the meaning of this? Why have I always to complain of you? May I ask you why you haven't made a copy of that contract between Bodley and Kirwan? I told you it must be ready by four o'clock.

— But Mr Shelley said, sir —

— *Mr Shelley said, sir.* . . . Kindly attend to what I say and not to what *Mr Shelley says, sir.* You have always some excuse or another for shirking work. Let me tell you that if the contract is not copied before this evening I'll lay the matter before Mr Crosbie. . . . Do you hear me now?

— Yes, sir.

— Do you hear me now? . . . Ay and another little matter! I might as well be talking to the wall as talking to you. Understand once for all that you get a half an hour for your lunch and not an hour and a half. How many courses do you want, I'd like to know. . . . Do you mind me, now?

— Yes, sir.

Mr Alleyne bent his head again upon his pile of papers. The man stared fixedly at the polished skull which directed the affairs of Crosbie & Alleyne, gauging its fragility. A spasm of rage gripped his throat for a few moments and then passed, leaving after it a sharp sensation of thirst. The man recognized the sensation and felt that he must have a good night's drinking. The middle of the month was passed and, if he could get the copy done in time, Mr Alleyne might give him an order on the cashier. He stood still, gazing fixedly at the head upon the pile of papers. Suddenly Mr Alleyne began to upset all the papers, searching for something. Then, as if he had been unaware of the man's presence till that moment, he shot up his head again, saying:

— Eh? Are you going to stand there all day? Upon my word, Farrington, you take things easy!

— I was waiting to see . . .

— Very good, you needn't wait to see. Go downstairs and do your work.

The man walked heavily towards the door and, as he went out of the room, he heard Mr Alleyne cry after him that if the contract was not copied by evening Mr Crosbie would hear of the matter.

He returned to his desk in the lower office and counted the sheets which remained to be copied. He took up his pen and dipped it in the ink but he continued to stare stupidly at the last words he had written: *In no case shall the said Bernard Bodley be.* . . . The evening was falling and in a few minutes they would be lighting the gas: then he could write. He felt that he must slake the thirst in his throat. He stood up from his desk and, lifting the counter as before, passed out of the office. As he was passing out the chief clerk looked at him inquiringly.

10

15

20

— It's all right, Mr Shelley, said the man, pointing with his finger to indicate the objective of his journey.

The chief clerk glanced at the hat-rack but, seeing the row complete, offered no remark. As soon as he was on the landing the man pulled a shepherd's
plaid cap out of his pocket, put it on his head and ran quickly down the rickety
stairs. From the street door he walked on furtively on the inner side of the path
towards the corner and all at once dived into a doorway. He was now safe in the
dark snug of O'Neill's shop, and, filling up the little window that looked into the
bar with his inflamed face, the color of dark wine or dark meat, he called out:

— Here, Pat, give us a g.p., like a good fellow.

The curate brought him a glass of plain porter. The man drank it at a gulp
and asked for a caraway seed. He put his penny on the counter and, leaving the
curate to grope for it in the gloom, retreated out of the snug as furtively as he
had entered it.

Darkness, accompanied by a thick fog, was gaining upon the dusk of   25
February and the lamps in Eustace Street had been lit. The man went up by the
houses until he reached the door of the office, wondering whether he could
finish his copy in time. On the stairs a moist pungent odor of perfumes saluted
his nose: evidently Miss Delacour had come while he was out in O'Neill's. He
crammed his cap back again into his pocket and re-entered the office assuming
an air of absent-mindedness.

— Mr Alleyne has been calling for you, said the chief clerk severely. Where
were you?

The man glanced at the two clients who were standing at the counter as if
to intimate that their presence prevented him from answering. As the clients
were both male the chief clerk allowed himself a laugh.

— I know that game, he said. Five times in one day is a little bit. . . . Well,
you better look sharp and get a copy of our correspondence in the Delacour
case for Mr Alleyne.

This address in the presence of the public, his run upstairs, and the porter
he had gulped down so hastily confused the man and, as he sat down at his
desk to get what was required, he realized how hopeless was the task of finishing his copy of the contract before half past five. The dark damp night was
coming and he longed to spend it in the bars, drinking with his friends amid the
glare of gas and the clatter of glasses. He got out the Delacour correspondence
and passed out of the office. He hoped Mr Alleyne would not discover that the
last two letters were missing.

The moist pungent perfume lay all the way up to Mr Alleyne's room. Miss   30
Delacour was a middle-aged woman of Jewish appearance. Mr Alleyne was
said to be sweet on her or on her money. She came to the office often and stayed
a long time when she came. She was sitting beside his desk now in an aroma
of perfumes, smoothing the handle of her umbrella, and nodding the great
black feather in her hat. Mr Alleyne had swivelled his chair round to face her
and thrown his right foot jauntily upon his left knee. The man put the correspondence on the desk and bowed respectfully but neither Mr Alleyne nor

Miss Delacour took any notice of his bow. Mr Alleyne tapped a finger on the correspondence and then flicked it towards him as if to say: *That's all right: you can go.*

The man returned to the lower office and sat down again at his desk. He stared intently at the incomplete phrase: *In no case shall the said Bernard Bodley be* . . . and thought how strange it was that the last three words began with the same letter. The chief clerk began to hurry Miss Parker, saying she would never have the letters typed in time for post. The man listened to the clicking of the machine for a few minutes and then set to work to finish his copy. But his head was not clear and his mind wandered away to the glare and rattle of the public-house. It was a night for hot punches. He struggled on with his copy, but when the clock struck five he had still fourteen pages to write. Blast it! He couldn't finish it in time. He longed to execrate aloud, to bring his fist down on something violently. He was so enraged that he wrote *Bernard Bernard* instead of *Bernard Bodley* and had to begin again on a clean sheet.

He felt strong enough to clear out the whole office singlehanded. His body ached to do something, to rush out and revel in violence. All the indignities of his life enraged him. . . . Could he ask the cashier privately for an advance? No, the cashier was no good, no damn good: he wouldn't give an advance. . . . He knew where he would meet the boys: Leonard and O'Halloran and Nosey Flynn. The barometer of his emotional nature was set for a spell of riot.

His imagination had so abstracted him that his name was called twice before he answered. Mr Alleyne and Miss Delacour were standing outside the counter and all the clerks had turned round in anticipation of something. The man got up from his desk. Mr Alleyne began a tirade of abuse, saying that two letters were missing. The man answered that he knew nothing about them, that he had made a faithful copy. The tirade continued: it was so bitter and violent that the man could hardly restrain his fist from descending upon the head of the manikin before him.

— I know nothing about any other two letters, he said stupidly.

— *You — know — nothing.* Of course you know nothing, said Mr Alleyne. 35 Tell me, he added, glancing first for approval to the lady beside him, do you take me for a fool? Do you think me an utter fool?

The man glanced from the lady's face to the little egg-shaped head and back again; and, almost before he was aware of it, his tongue had found a felicitous moment:

— I don't think, sir, he said, that that's a fair question to put to me.

There was a pause in the very breathing of the clerks. Everyone was astounded (the author of the witticism no less than his neighbors) and Miss Delacour, who was a stout amiable person, began to smile broadly. Mr Alleyne flushed to the hue of a wild rose and his mouth twitched with a dwarf's passion. He shook his fist in the man's face till it seemed to vibrate like the knob of some electric machine:

— You impertinent ruffian! You impertinent ruffian! I'll make short work of you! Wait till you see! You'll apologize to me for your impertinence or you'll quit the office instanter! You'll quit this, I'm telling you, or you'll apologize to me!

He stood in a doorway opposite the office watching to see if the cashier would   40
come out alone. All the clerks passed out and finally the cashier came out with the chief clerk. It was no use trying to say a word to him when he was with the chief clerk. The man felt that his position was bad enough. He had been obliged to offer an abject apology to Mr Alleyne for his impertinence but he knew what a hornet's nest the office would be for him. He could remember the way in which Mr Alleyne had hounded little Peake out of the office in order to make room for his own nephew. He felt savage and thirsty and revengeful, annoyed with himself and with everyone else. Mr Alleyne would never give him an hour's rest; his life would be a hell to him. He had made a proper fool of himself this time. Could he not keep his tongue in his cheek? But they had never pulled together from the first, he and Mr Alleyne, ever since the day Mr Alleyne had overheard him mimicking his North of Ireland accent to amuse Higgins and Miss Parker: that had been the beginning of it. He might have tried Higgins for the money, but sure Higgins never had anything for himself. A man with two establishments to keep up, of course he couldn't. . . .

He felt his great body again aching for the comfort of the public-house. The fog had begun to chill him and he wondered could he touch Pat in O'Neill's. He could not touch him for more than a bob — and a bob was no use. Yet he must get money somewhere or other: he had spent his last penny for the g.p. and soon it would be too late for getting money anywhere. Suddenly, as he was fingering his watch-chain, he thought of Terry Kelly's pawn-office in Fleet Street. That was the dart! Why didn't he think of it sooner?

He went through the narrow alley of Temple Bar quickly, muttering to himself that they could all go to hell because he was going to have a good night of it. The clerk in Terry Kelly's said *A crown!* but the consignor held out for six shillings; and in the end the six shillings was allowed him literally. He came out of the pawn-office joyfully, making a little cylinder of the coins between his thumb and fingers. In Westmoreland Street the footpaths were crowded with young men and women returning from business and ragged urchins ran here and there yelling out the names of the evening editions. The man passed through the crowd, looking on the spectacle generally with proud satisfaction and staring masterfully at the office-girls. His head was full of the noises of tram-gongs and swishing trolleys and his nose already sniffed the curling fumes of punch. As he walked on he preconsidered the terms in which he would narrate the incident to the boys:

— So, I just looked at him — coolly, you know, and looked at her. Then I looked back at him again — taking my time, you know. *I don't think that that's a fair question to put to me*, says I.

Nosey Flynn was sitting up in his usual corner of Davy Byrne's and, when he heard the story, he stood Farrington a half-one, saying it was as smart a thing as ever he heard. Farrington stood a drink in his turn. After a while O'Halloran and Paddy Leonard came in and the story was repeated to them.

O'Halloran stood tailors of malt, hot, all round and told the story of the retort he had made to the chief clerk when he was in Callan's of Fownes's Street; but, as the retort was after the manner of the liberal shepherds in the eclogues, he had to admit that it was not so clever as Farrington's retort. At this Farrington told the boys to polish off that and have another.

Just as they were naming their poisons who should come in but Higgins! 45 Of course he had to join in with the others. The men asked him to give his version of it, and he did so with great vivacity for the sight of five small hot whiskies was very exhilarating. Everyone roared laughing when he showed the way in which Mr Alleyne shook his fist in Farrington's face. Then he imitated Farrington, saying, *And here was my nabs, as cool as you please*, while Farrington looked at the company out of his heavy dirty eyes, smiling and at times drawing forth stray drops of liquor from his moustache with the aid of his lower lip.

When that round was over there was a pause. O'Halloran had money but neither of the other two seemed to have any; so the whole party left the shop somewhat regretfully. At the corner of Duke Street Higgins and Nosey Flynn bevelled off to the left while the other three turned back towards the city. Rain was drizzling down on the cold streets and, when they reached the Ballast Office, Farrington suggested the Scotch House. The bar was full of men and loud with the noise of tongues and glasses. The three men pushed past the whining match-sellers at the door and formed a little party at the corner of the counter. They began to exchange stories. Leonard introduced them to a young fellow named Weathers who was performing at the Tivoli as an acrobat and knockabout *artiste*. Farrington stood a drink all round. Weathers said he would take a small Irish and Apollinaris. Farrington, who had definite notions of what was what, asked the boys would they have an Apollinaris too; but the boys told Tim to make theirs hot. The talk became theatrical. O'Halloran stood a round and then Farrington stood another round, Weathers protesting that the hospitality was too Irish. He promised to get them in behind the scenes and introduce them to some nice girls. O'Halloran said that he and Leonard would go but that Farrington wouldn't go because he was a married man; and Farrington's heavy dirty eyes leered at the company in token that he understood he was being chaffed. Weathers made them all have just one little tincture at his expense and promised to meet them later on at Mulligan's in Poolbeg Street.

When the Scotch House closed they went round to Mulligan's. They went into the parlor at the back and O'Halloran ordered small hot specials all round. They were all beginning to feel mellow. Farrington was just standing another round when Weathers came back. Much to Farrington's relief he drank a glass of bitter this time. Funds were running low but they had enough to keep them going. Presently two young women with big hats and a young man in a check suit came in and sat at a table close by. Weathers saluted them and told the company that they were out of the Tivoli. Farrington's eyes wandered at every moment in the direction of one of the young women. There was something striking in her appearance. An immense scarf of peacock-blue muslin was wound round her hat and knotted in a great bow under her chin; and she wore bright yellow gloves, reaching to the elbow. Farrington gazed admiringly at the plump arm which she moved very often and with much grace; and when, after a little time, she answered his gaze he admired still more her large dark brown eyes. The oblique staring expression in them fascinated him. She glanced at him once or twice and, when the party was leaving the room, she brushed against his chair and said *O, pardon!* in a London accent. He watched her leave the room in the hope that she would look back at him, but he was disappointed. He cursed his want of money and cursed all the rounds he had stood, particularly all the whiskies and Apollinaris which he had stood to Weathers. If there was one thing that he hated it was a sponge. He was so angry that he lost count of the conversation of his friends.

When Paddy Leonard called him he found that they were talking about feats of strength. Weathers was showing his biceps muscle to the company and boasting so much that the other two had called on Farrington to uphold the national honor. Farrington pulled up his sleeve accordingly and showed his biceps muscle to the company. The two arms were examined and compared and finally it was agreed to have a trial of strength. The table was cleared and the two men rested their elbows on it, clasping hands. When Paddy Leonard said *Go!* each was to try to bring down the other's hand on to the table. Farrington looked very serious and determined.

The trial began. After about thirty seconds Weathers brought his opponent's hand slowly down on to the table. Farrington's dark wine-coloured face flushed darker still with anger and humiliation at having been defeated by such a stripling.

— You're not to put the weight of your body behind it. Play fair, he said.   50

— Who's not playing fair? said the other.

— Come on again. The two best out of three.

The trial began again. The veins stood out on Farrington's forehead, and the pallor of Weathers' complexion changed to peony. Their hands and arms trembled under the stress. After a long struggle Weathers again brought his opponent's hand slowly on to the table. There was a murmur of applause from the spectators. The curate, who was standing beside the table, nodded his red head towards the victor and said with loutish familiarity:

— Ah! that's the knack!

— What the hell do you know about it? said Farrington fiercely, turning on   55
the man. What do you put in your gab for?

— Sh, sh! said O'Halloran, observing the violent expression of Farrington's face. Pony up, boys. We'll have just one little smahan more and then we'll be off.

A very sullen-faced man stood at the corner of O'Connell Bridge waiting for the little Sandymount tram to take him home. He was full of smouldering anger and revengefulness. He felt humiliated and discontented; he did not even feel drunk; and he had only twopence in his pocket. He cursed everything. He had done for himself in the office, pawned his watch, spent all his money; and he had not even got drunk. He began to feel thirsty again and he longed to be back again in the hot reeking public-house. He had lost his reputation as a strong man, having been defeated twice by a mere boy. His heart swelled with fury and, when he thought of the woman in the big hat who had brushed against him and said *Pardon!* his fury nearly choked him.

His tram let him down at Shelbourne Road and he steered his great body along in the shadow of the wall of the barracks. He loathed returning to his home. When he went in by the side-door he found the kitchen empty and the kitchen fire nearly out. He bawled upstairs:

— Ada! Ada!

His wife was a little sharp-faced woman who bullied her husband when he 60
was sober and was bullied by him when he was drunk. They had five children. A little boy came running down the stairs.

— Who is that? said the man, peering through the darkness.

— Me, pa.

— Who are you? Charlie?

— No, pa. Tom.

— Where's your mother? 65

— She's out at the chapel.

— That's right. . . . Did she think of leaving any dinner for me?

— Yes, pa. I —

— Light the lamp. What do you mean by having the place in darkness? Are the other children in bed?

The man sat down heavily on one of the chairs while the little boy lit the 70
lamp. He began to mimic his son's flat accent, saying half to himself: *At the chapel. At the chapel, if you please!* When the lamp was lit he banged his fist on the table and shouted:

— What's for my dinner?

— I'm going . . . to cook it, pa, said the little boy.

The man jumped up furiously and pointed to the fire.

— On that fire! You let the fire out! By God, I'll teach you to do that again!

He took a step to the door and seized the walking-stick which was standing 75
behind it.

— I'll teach you to let the fire out! he said, rolling up his sleeve in order to give his arm free play.

The little boy cried *O, pa!* and ran whimpering round the table, but the man followed him and caught him by the coat. The little boy looked about him wildly but, seeing no way of escape fell upon his knees.

— Now, you'll let the fire out the next time! said the man, striking at him viciously with the stick. Take that, you little whelp!

The boy uttered a squeal of pain as the stick cut his thigh. He clasped his hands together in the air and his voice shook with fright.

— O, pa! he cried. Don't beat me, pa! And I'll . . . I'll say a *Hail Mary* for 80
you. . . . I'll say a *Hail Mary* for you, pa, if you don't beat me. . . . I'll say a *Hail Mary*. . . .   [1914]

A thorough critical analysis of "Counterparts" using any one of these approaches would take dozens of pages. The following are brief suggestions for how such a reading might proceed.

1634   APPENDIX   Critical Approaches to Literature

NEW CRITICISM

A New Critic might want to demonstrate the multiple ways the title holds the narrative together, giving it unity and coherence — for example, Farrington and his son Tom are counterparts since Tom is the victim of his father's bullying just as Farrington is bullied by Mr. Alleyne at work. You can also probably spot other counterparts: Farrington and his wife, for example, trade off bullying each other, and their means of escaping from the drudgery of their lives, the bar and the church, are also parallel. And naturally when Weathers, the acrobat, defeats the much larger Farrington in arm wrestling, we are reminded of the verbal beating Farrington must endure from his equally diminutive boss, Mr. Alleyne. New Critics are fond of finding the ways all the elements of a text reinforce one another.

A New Critic might argue that these counterparts or oppositions introduce tensions into the story from the first few lines when the "bell rang furiously" for Farrington to report to Mr. Alleyne for a dressing-down. The irony is that Farrington is big and Alleyne is small, that Farrington is powerful and Alleyne is fragile as an egg. But it is Mr. Alleyne who breaks Farrington; it is Farrington who is weak. Throughout the story, tensions, oppositions, and ironies continue, for example, when Farrington is defeated by the smaller Weathers. In the last scene, the tension is finally resolved when the larger Farrington beats his small son, making him a counterpart to both Alleyne and Weathers in oppressing the weak. The final evidence that Farrington is ethically powerless is cruelly obvious as the son promises to pray for his abusing father.

FEMINIST CRITICISM

Feminist critics and their first cousins, gender critics, would naturally be struck by the violent masculinity of Farrington, his fantasies of riot and abuse, his savage feelings of revenge, and his "smouldering anger" (para. 57). Farrington is depicted not only as crude and brutish but also as a kind of perverse stereotype of male vanity, self-centeredness, and irresponsibility. His obsession with obtaining money for drinking completely disregards his role as the provider for a large family, and, of course, the beatings of his son are a cruel parody of his role as paternal protector. And if he had not wasted his money on drink, Farrington would also be a womanizer ("Farrington's eyes wandered at every moment in the direction of one of the young women," para. 47). Gender critics would be interested in the social and cultural mechanisms that could construct such primitive masculinity.

A reasonable argument might focus on the representation of women in the story. Miss Parker, Miss Delacour, Farrington's wife, and the performer Farrington sees in the bar are marginal characters. One student made the following claim: "The women in Farrington's world, and Irish society in general, have no agency: they are prevented from taking an active part in determining their lives and futures." Another student argued differently, saying, "While women in general are oppressed by the raw and brutal masculinity represented by Farrington, the women in this story do hold a degree of power over men." Based on their own analysis and interpretations, these students demonstrated that there was reasonable textual evidence to support their claims.

PSYCHOANALYTIC CRITICISM

A psychoanalytic critic would first notice the extreme pattern of behavior Farrington exhibits, as he repeatedly withdraws from his adult work responsibilities and as he fantasizes about being physically violent against his supervisors. Critics would argue that such behavior is typical of Farrington's repressed wounds and his unresolved conflicts with his own father. Farrington seems to be playing out painful childhood experiences. Given the violent displacement (taking it out on someone else) visited on Tom, we can imagine that Farrington is beating not only his boss, Mr. Alleyne, but also perhaps his own abusive father. The fantasies at work in Farrington also suggest the psychological defense of projection, since Farrington is blaming his problems on Mr. Alleyne and his job. Although his tasks do seem to be tedious, they certainly cannot account for his "spasm of rage" (para. 15) or his desire "to clear out the whole office single-handed" (para. 32). When Farrington feels "humiliated and discontented" (para. 57), it is only in part because of his immediate context. It is the return of the repressed that plagues Farrington, a resurfacing of a buried pain. These ideas should also be tied to Farrington's death wish, especially his stunningly self-destructive behavior at work. Freudian critics would also argue that these specific actions are related to other core issues that would include intense loss of self-esteem, fear of intimacy, and betrayal.

MARXIST CRITICISM

A Marxist critic would be interested in focusing on the specific historical moment of "Counterparts" and not on Farrington's individual psyche, which can only distract us from the real force that affects human experience — the economic system in which Farrington is trapped. Economic power — not the Oedipal drama or gender — is the crucial human motivator. Farrington's material circumstances and not timeless values are the key to understanding his behavior. The real battle lines are drawn between Crosbie and Alleyne (the "haves") and Farrington (a "have-not") — that is, between the bourgeoisie and the proletariat, between those who control economic resources and those who perform the labor that fills the coffers of the rich. In a Marxist analysis, critics would argue that Farrington is a victim of class warfare. His desperation, his humiliation, his rage, his cruel violence are all traceable to classism — an ideology that determines people's worth according to their economic class. Although Farrington does appear shiftless and irresponsible, it is not because of his class; it is because of the meaninglessness of his work and the demeaning hierarchy that keeps him at the bottom. In his alienation, he reverts to a primitive physical masculinity, a false consciousness that only further diminishes his sense of his worth.

Marxists are often interested in what lies beneath the text in its political unconscious. To get at the unconscious, Marxists, like psychoanalytic critics, look for symptoms on the surface that suggest problems beneath. Typically, such symptomatic readings reveal class conflicts that authors are sometimes unaware of themselves. Marxist critics might debate whether Joyce himself understood that the root cause of Farrington's aberrant behavior was economic and not psychological. This makes sense since for Marxists both reader and writer are under the sway of the same ideological system that they see as natural.

One student made the following claim: "Farrington's role as proletarian results in his feelings of inferiority, resentment over lack of entitlement, and an expectation of disappointment." This same student, like many Marxist critics who see the function of literature through a pragmatic lens, concluded her essay with an appeal toward change, arguing that "The remedy does not lie in changing Farrington's consciousness, but rather in changing the economic and political discourse of power that has constituted him."

DECONSTRUCTION

One of many possible deconstructions of "Counterparts" would involve focusing on a troubling or puzzling point called an *aporia*. Some deconstructive critics have looked at the incomplete phrase that Farrington copies, "*In no case shall the said Bernard Bodley be . . .*" as an aporia, an ambiguous and not completely understandable textual puzzle but one that might be a way into the story's meaning. The oppositions that are being deconstructed or laid bare here are *presence* and *absence, word* and *reality.* Working off the implications of the title "Counterparts," Bernard Bodley can be seen as a double or counterpart for Farrington, a character like Bodley whose existence is in doubt. Although Farrington's size suggests that he is very much physically present, his behavior might suggest otherwise. He spends his time copying other people's words and has a compelling need to repeat the narrative of his encounter with Mr. Alleyne, as if he must demonstrate his own existence through repetition. He does not have a viable inner life, an authentic identity. Farrington's essence is not present but absent. His identity is insubstantial. He tries to fill the emptiness at the center of his being with camaraderie and potency, but his efforts produce the opposite — escape, loneliness, and weakness. In other words, the said Farrington does not really exist and cannot be. In this way, we can deconstruct "Counterparts" as a story in which presence is absence, strength is weakness, Farrington's actions lead only to paralysis and repetition, and Farrington's frustration with his impotence makes his oppressors more powerful.

One student working with similar interpretations of "Counterparts" noted other oppositions, especially between male and female, escape and confinement. She argued that Farrington spends most of his time trying to avoid being thought of as stereotypically feminine. However, the more exaggerated his masculine aggression, drinking, violence, and irresponsibility become, the weaker, the more stereotypically feminine he becomes. Similarly, the more Farrington tries to escape, the more ensnared he is. In this way, the student argued, our conventional understandings of these opposing terms are deconstructed, so that we are no longer confident about the meaning of escape, masculinity, or strength.

READER-RESPONSE CRITICISM

Willa Ervinman, a student, was asked to respond to the story by using Stanley Fish's ideas and noting the conflicts between the interpretive or discourse communities Willa belonged to and those depicted in the story. The following are excerpts from her response journal:

> I was upset by Farrington's lack of responsibility at work. He is completely unreliable and demonstrates very little self-esteem. He must know that the people he works with consider him a slacker and a fake. I was raised in a middle-class home where both my parents worked hard in a bank from 9 to 5. Just the idea that they would sneak out of work to drink in dark bars is absurd. My belief in the discourse of middle-class responsibility or perhaps the Protestant work ethic makes it almost impossible for me to see Farrington with sympathy even though I can see that his work is probably completely mechanical and unfulfilling. . . .
>
> Farrington's domestic violence against his son is such a violation of the discourse of domesticity that it is hard to understand any other response. Someone in my response group thought that Farrington was a victim of his working-class discourse of masculinity. I can see how he was humiliated by the smaller men, Mr. Alleyne and Weathers, but beating his innocent son as a kind of revenge cannot be forgiven. My grandmother tells me that it was common for children to be physically punished in her day, but in the interpretive community I was raised in, there is no excuse for domestic violence. It is more than a character flaw; it is criminal behavior, and I judge Farrington to be a social menace, beyond compassion.

Willa went on to argue that Farrington's violent behavior is inexcusable, interpreting our current understandings of domestic violence and responsible masculinity as evidence. She blended this personal view with textual support. Her warrant for her claim was that historical circumstances and norms should not be used to excuse reprehensible behavior.

POSTCOLONIAL CRITICISM

"Counterparts" was written in the early twentieth century at a time when the Ireland Joyce writes about was still a colony of the British Empire. Farrington is, then, a colonial subject and subject to political domination. At the story's opening, Farrington, a Catholic from the south of Ireland, is summoned by a "furious voice" from Northern Ireland, a stronghold of British sympathy and Protestant domination. The tension is announced early because it is crucial to Farrington's behavior and his internalized and colonized mindset. Many colonials have a negative self-image because they are alienated from their own indigenous culture. Indeed, Farrington seems completely ill suited to the office copying task he is relegated to. He seems more suited to some physical endeavor, but given the difficult economics of Dublin, he probably has few career options.

Farrington is the Other in the discourse of colonialism, and he is made to seem inferior at every turn, from the verbal lashing of Mr. Alleyne to the physical defeat by Weathers, who is probably British. Symbolically, Farrington tries to resist his subjugation by the British establishment but fails. He is what postcolonial theorists refer to as *unhomed* or *displaced*. He is uncomfortable at work, in the bars where he seeks solace, and finally in his ultimate refuge, a place unprepared even to feed him. Indeed, in an act likely to perpetuate abuse upon future generations, Farrington turns on his own family, becoming, through his enraged attack on his child Tom, a metaphor for the conflicted, tormented, and defeated Ireland. When a colonial is not "at home" even in his own home, he is truly in psychological agony and exile. Joyce represents the trauma of British domination through one subject's self-destructive and self-hating journey, a journey made even more cruelly ironic by Farrington's attack — in a mimicry of British aggression and injustice — on his own subjected son.

NEW HISTORICISM

A critic influenced by Foucault and New Historicism might argue that Farrington is a victim of an inflexible discourse of masculinity, that he has been socialized by working-class norms of how a man should behave to such an extent that he cannot change. Growing up in a working-class culture, Farrington would have received high marks among his peers for his size and strength, just as Mr. Alleyne would be diminished in status for his. And in another context, say, on a construction site, Farrington's sense of masculinity might be a plus. But in an office, his aggressive masculinity is a liability. In all cultures, people are subject to multiple discourses that pull them one way then another. Farrington's sarcasm, his drinking, his longing for camaraderie, and his resorting to violence to solve problems are the results of being too enmeshed in a discourse of masculinity from working-class Dublin and not enough in the middle-class business assumptions about discipline, responsibility, and concentration. Farrington is defeated at work, in the pubs, and at home because he is unable to move from one discourse to another. He is stuck in a subject position that only reinforces his powerlessness. His self-esteem is so damaged by the end of the story that he even violates his own code of masculinity by beating a defenseless child.

Sample Student Essay

The following essay was written by a first-year student using a postcolonial perspective.

Molly Frye
Prof. Christine Hardee
English 102
10 May - - - -

A Refugee at Home

It is difficult to argue that Farrington, the main character in James Joyce's "Counterparts," should be seen in a sympathetic light. After all, he seems an extreme stereotype of an aggressive, irresponsible drinker. Although his character traits certainly do not conform to our modern standards of mature masculinity, I want to argue that although we do not want to condone Farrington's brutal behavior, we can find it understandable. As an Irish subject in the British Empire, Farrington is more sinned against than sinner, more victim than victimizer. Farrington is not simply an obnoxious male since his actions can be understood as stemming from his colonial consciousness in struggling vainly against his powerlessness. His frustrations are especially clear in the three spaces Farrington inhabits: his office, the bars, and his home.

Farrington's first appearance is telling. Because of his poor job performance, his boss demands to see him: "Send Farrington here!" Farrington, who most often is referred to as "the man," mutters his first words, "Blast him!" This typical antagonistic relationship in a colonial context foreshadows the rest of the story. Farrington is the working-class subject caught in a menial and unsatisfying job he can never complete under a boss who has social and cultural power. This counterpart relationship is similar to the positions of Ireland and England where the colony is disparaged and oppressed by the empire. In his office run by Protestants loyal to the British, Farrington is ironically "tall and of great bulk," while his boss, Mr. Alleyne, is "a little man" whose head, "pink and hairless," resembles a "large egg." Farrington's only asset, his size and strength, is irrelevant because he is so economically and socially weak. This disparity only increases Farrington's frustration and precipitates fantasies of violence against his oppressor. When Mr. Alleyne rebukes him, "Do you mind me now," Farrington is sent into a "spasm of rage." He cannot, of course, act on his aggressive urges, so he represses these feelings by rationalizing that he must have a "good night's drinking." Thus begins a pattern of self-destructive behavior that only increases Farrington's marginal position in society.

Farrington is so uncomfortable at work, a postcolonial condition known as being unhomed, that he cannot concentrate on anything but drinking. He seems quite unsuited for the tedious task of copying legal documents, staring "stupidly at the last words he has written," knowing he will never finish his task, never advance, never get anywhere. Farrington is paralyzed by his alienation. He feels his only recourse is sneaking out to drink, which only exacerbates his poverty and powerlessness. When he attempts to cover up his inability to concentrate and finish copying letters for Mr. Alleyne, he is caught and confronted. Instead of acknowledging his underling position, he attempts a witticism which, of course, backfires. Even though he is forced to apologize, his job now seems in jeopardy. Mr. Alleyne humiliates him by calling him an "impertinent ruffian," a status that seems to him the most he can hope for. As a colonial subject, Farrington is plagued by a double consciousness. He longs for the masculine status his physical strength should give him in his working-class culture, but he must suffer indignities at the hands of Mr. Alleyne because of his inability to perform a simple task a competent child could do. Farrington should probably be working in construction as a laborer, not an office worker where discipline, patience, and mental concentration are necessary.

When Farrington finally leaves work, he expects to find some solace in the Dublin pubs. He has hocked his watch for drinking money, a clear indication of how desperate he is to escape the confines of regimented office work. The camaraderie of Paddy Leonard and Nosey Flynn is temporary, and Farrington is not at home in these public spaces either. He runs out of money he would have spent drinking and womanizing, and he is finally humiliated by another small British man. Called on to "uphold the national honor," Farrington's loss in an arm-wrestling contest with Weathers leaves him "full of smouldering anger and revengefulness. He is humiliated and discontented . . . His heart swelled with fury. . . ." His longing for escape from the confinement and disappointment of work has taken a disastrous turn. Farrington's already damaged self-esteem is degraded, and his repressed anger at his oppressor is near the breaking point. Perhaps his self-destructive behavior can be redirected at his home, his last possibility for comfort and acceptance.

For the unhomed colonized, however, this is not to be. Farrington enters the kitchen to find it symbolically empty, "the fire nearly out." His wife is at chapel, his five children in bed, and his dinner is cold. His agonies continue. Having internalized the humiliations suffered at work and in the pubs, Farrington has no resources left. And so in a bitter irony, he beats his son for not attending to the fire, "striking at him viciously with a stick. 'Take that, you little whelp!'" Farrington the oppressed becomes Farrington the oppressor. His role as provider and protector is cruelly turned upside-down. Farrington compensates for his defeats at the hands of Mr. Alleyne and Weathers by beating his son, and in doing so, mimics the cycle of oppression prevalent in countries dominated by the empire. Farrington is not only a cog in the bureaucratic wheel at work; he is also a pathetic, but understandable cog crushed by the wheel of power even in his own home.

≡ FOR THINKING AND WRITING

1. Using a feminist critique of Joyce, one student claimed that "Joyce's text indulges dominance over submission." Do you think there is textual evidence to support this assertion?

2. How might various critics (postcolonial, feminist, Marxist, psychoanalytical) interpret these lines from "Counterparts":

   - "The man passed through the crowd, looking on the spectacle generally with proud satisfaction and staring masterfully at the office-girls" (para. 42).

   - "His heart swelled with fury and, when he thought of the woman in the big hat who had brushed against him and said *Pardon!* his fury nearly choked him" (para. 57).

   - "What's for my dinner?" (para. 71).

3. Influenced by New Critical ideas, one student wrote, "'Counterparts' is filled with parallel scenes and emotions that reflect one another." What textual evidence would help support this notion?

4. Engaging in a Marxist critique, one student wrote, "His unfair work conditions so distract him that he does not even know the names of his children." What is the warrant behind such an assertion? What work conditions might the student think "fair"?

5. Using a New Historicist approach, what might you learn about this story from doing research on the elementary-school curriculum in Dublin, the pay scale in a law office, the legal rights of women, the laws on domestic violence, the unemployment rate? What other practices and texts do you think would illuminate the story?

≡ A WRITING EXERCISE

Now you try. After reading the following story, construct an argument influenced by one or more of the following critical approaches: postcolonial, Marxist, reader-response, or feminist.

JAMES JOYCE
Eveline

Like "Counterparts," "Eveline" is from Dubliners *(1914). For more on James Joyce,*
see his story "Araby" on page 609.

She sat at the window watching the evening invade the avenue. Her head was
leaned against the window curtains and in her nostrils was the odor of dusty
cretonne. She was tired.

Few people passed. The man out of the last house passed on his way home;
she heard his footsteps clacking along the concrete pavement and afterwards
crunching on the cinder path before the new red houses. One time there used
to be a field there in which they used to play every evening with other people's
children. Then a man from Belfast bought the field and built houses in it — not
like their little brown houses but bright brick houses with shining roofs. The
children of the avenue used to play together in that field — the Devines, the
Waters, the Dunns, little Keogh the cripple, she and her brothers and sisters.
Ernest, however, never played: he was too grown up. Her father used often to
hunt them in out of the field with his blackthorn stick; but usually little Keogh
used to keep *nix* and call out when he saw her father coming. Still they seemed
to have been rather happy then. Her father was not so bad then; and besides,
her mother was alive. That was a long time ago; she and her brothers and sisters were all grown up; her mother was dead. Tizzie Dunn was dead, too, and
the Waters had gone back to England. Everything changes. Now she was going
to go away like the others, to leave her home.

Home! She looked round the room, reviewing all its familiar objects which
she had dusted once a week for so many years, wondering where on earth all
the dust came from. Perhaps she would never see again those familiar objects
from which she had never dreamed of being divided. And yet during all those
years she had never found out the name of the priest whose yellowing photograph hung on the wall above the broken harmonium beside the colored print
of the promises made to Blessed Margaret Mary Alacoque. He had been a
school friend of her father. Whenever he showed the photograph to a visitor
her father used to pass it with a casual word:

— He is in Melbourne now.

She had consented to go away, to leave her home. Was that wise? She tried   5
to weigh each side of the question. In her home anyway she had shelter and
food; she had those whom she had known all her life about her. Of course she
had to work hard both in the house and at business. What would they say of
her in the Stores when they found out that she had run away with a fellow? Say
she was a fool, perhaps; and her place would be filled up by advertisement. Miss
Gavan would be glad. She had always had an edge on her, especially whenever
there were people listening.

— Miss Hill, don't you see these ladies are waiting?

— Look lively, Miss Hill, please.

She would not cry many tears at leaving the Stores.

But in her new home, in a distant unknown country, it would not be like that. Then she would be married — she, Eveline. People would treat her with respect then. She would not be treated as her mother had been. Even now, though she was over nineteen, she sometimes felt herself in danger of her father's violence. She knew it was that that had given her the palpitations. When they were growing up he had never gone for her, like he used to go for Harry and Ernest, because she was a girl; but latterly he had begun to threaten her and say what he would do to her only for her dead mother's sake. And now she had nobody to protect her. Ernest was dead and Harry, who was in the church decorating business, was nearly always down somewhere in the country. Besides, the invariable squabble for money on Saturday nights had begun to weary her unspeakably. She always gave her entire wages — seven shillings — and Harry always sent up what he could but the trouble was to get any money from her father. He said she used to squander the money, that she had no head, that he wasn't going to give her his hard-earned money to throw about the streets, and much more, for he was usually fairly bad of a Saturday night. In the end he would give her the money and ask her had she any intention of buying Sunday's dinner. Then she had to rush out as quickly as she could and do her marketing, holding her black leather purse tightly in her hand as she elbowed her way through the crowds and returning home late under her load of provisions. She had hard work to keep the house together and to see that the two young children who had been left to her charge went to school regularly and got their meals regularly. It was hard work — a hard life — but now that she was about to leave it she did not find it a wholly undesirable life.

She was about to explore another life with Frank. Frank was very kind, manly, open-hearted. She was to go away with him by the night-boat to be his wife and to live with him in Buenos Aires where he had a home waiting for her. How well she remembered the first time she had seen him; he was lodging in a house on the main road where she used to visit. It seemed a few weeks ago. He was standing at the gate, his peaked cap pushed back on his head and his hair tumbled forward over a face of bronze. Then they had come to know each other. He used to meet her outside the Stores every evening and see her home. He took her to see *The Bohemian Girl* and she felt elated as she sat in an unaccustomed part of the theater with him. He was awfully fond of music and sang a little. People knew that they were courting and, when he sang about the lass that loves a sailor, she always felt pleasantly confused. He used to call her Poppens out of fun. First of all it had been an excitement for her to have a fellow and then she had begun to like him. He had tales of distant countries. He had started as a deck boy at a pound a month on a ship of the Allan Line going out to Canada. He told her the names of the ships he had been on and the names of the different services. He had sailed through the Straits of Magellan and he told her stories of the terrible Patagonians. He had fallen on his feet in Buenos Aires, he said, and had come over to the old country just for a holiday. Of course, her father had found out the affair and had forbidden her to have anything to say to him.

10

— I know these sailor chaps, he said.

One day he had quarreled with Frank and after that she had to meet her lover secretly.

The evening deepened in the avenue. The white of two letters in her lap grew indistinct. One was to Harry; the other was to her father. Ernest had been her favorite but she liked Harry too. Her father was becoming old lately, she noticed; he would miss her. Sometimes he could be very nice. Not long before, when she had been laid up for a day, he had read her out a ghost story and made toast for her at the fire. Another day, when their mother was alive, they had all gone for a picnic to the Hill of Howth. She remembered her father putting on her mother's bonnet to make the children laugh.

Her time was running out but she continued to sit by the window, leaning her head against the window curtain, inhaling the odor of dusty cretonne. Down far in the avenue she could hear a street organ playing. She knew the air. Strange that it should come that very night to remind her of the promise to her mother, her promise to keep the home together as long as she could. She remembered the last night of her mother's illness; she was again in the close dark room at the other side of the hall and outside she heard a melancholy air of Italy. The organ-player had been ordered to go away and given sixpence. She remembered her father strutting back into the sickroom saying:

— Damned Italians! coming over here!   15

As she mused the pitiful vision of her mother's life laid its spell on the very quick of her being — that life of commonplace sacrifices closing in final craziness. She trembled as she heard again her mother's voice saying constantly with foolish insistence:

— Derevaun Seraun! Derevaun Seraun!°

She stood up in a sudden impulse of terror. Escape! She must escape! Frank would save her. He would give her life, perhaps love, too. But she wanted to live. Why should she be unhappy? She had a right to happiness. Frank would take her in his arms, fold her in his arms. He would save her.

She stood among the swaying crowd in the station at the North Wall. He held her hand and she knew that he was speaking to her, saying something about the passage over and over again. The station was full of soldiers with brown baggages. Through the wide doors of the sheds she caught a glimpse of the black mass of the boat, lying in beside the quay wall, with illumined portholes. She answered nothing. She felt her cheek pale and cold and, out of a maze of distress, she prayed to God to direct her, to show her what was her duty. The boat blew a long mournful whistle into the mist. If she went, tomorrow she would be on the sea with Frank, steaming toward Buenos Aires. Their passage had been booked. Could she still draw back after all he had done for her? Her distress awoke a nausea in her body and she kept moving her lips in silent fervent prayer.

A bell clanged upon her heart. She felt him seize her hand: 20

Derevaun Seraun!: Gaelic for "The end of pleasure is pain."

—Come!

All the seas of the world tumbled about her heart. He was drawing her into them: he would drown her. She gripped with both hands at the iron railing.

—Come!

No! No! No! It was impossible. Her hands clutched the iron in frenzy. Amid the seas she sent a cry of anguish!

—Eveline! Evvy!   25

He rushed beyond the barrier and called to her to follow. He was shouted at to go on but he still called to her. She set her white face to him, passive, like a helpless animal. Her eyes gave him no sign of love or farewell or recognition.

≣ FOR THINKING AND WRITING

1. There is a French expression that says to understand all is to forgive all. Given the ending of "Eveline," argue for or against this idea.

2. Compare "Counterparts" and "Eveline" (see "Strategies for Writing a Comparative Paper," p. 98), arguing that Joyce has or has not prepared us for the endings.

Toi Derricotte. "Black Boys Play the Classics" from *Tender* by Toi Derricotte. © 1997. Reprinted by permission of the University of Pittsburgh Press.

John Desmond. "Flannery O'Connor's Misfit and the Mystery of Evil" by John Desmond from *Renascence*, 2004, pages 129–130.

Emily Dickinson. "Wild Nights—Wild Nights!" and "I heard a Fly buzz—when I died" from *The Poems of Emily Dickinson*, Thomas H. Johnson, ed. Copyright © 1951, 1955, 1979, 1983 by the President and Fellows of Harvard College. Reprinted by permission of the publishers and the Trustees of Amherst College, Cambridge, Mass.: The Belknap Press of Harvard University Press.

Linh Dinh. "!" from *Blood and Soap: Stories*. Copyright © 2004 by Linh Dinh. Reprinted with permission of Seven Stories Press, www.sevenstories.com.

Mark Doty. "Night Ferry" from *My Alexandria*. Copyright 1993 by Mark Doty. Used with permission of the poet and the University of Illinois Press.

W. E. B. Du Bois. "Of Mr. Booker T. Washington" from *The Souls of Black Folk* (1903). Reprinted by permission of the David Graham Du Bois Trust.

Andre Dubus."Killings" from *Finding a Girl in America* by Andre Dubus. Copyright © 1980 by Andre Dubus. Reprinted by permission of David R. Godine, Publisher, Inc.

Christopher Durang. "For Whom the Southern Belle Tolls." Copyright © 1995 by Christopher Durang. Reprinted by permission of International Creative Management, Inc.

Alan Ehrenhalt. From *The Lost City: Discovering the Forgotten Virtues of Community in the Chicago of the 1950s* by Alan Ehrenhalt. Copyright © 1995 by Alan Ehrenhalt. Reprinted by permission of the author.

T. S. Eliot. "The Love Song of J. Alfred Prufrock" from *Collected Poems 1909–1962* by T. S. Eliot. Reprinted by permission of Faber and Faber Ltd.

Ralph Ellison. "Battle Royal" from *Invisible Man* by Ralph Ellison. Copyright © 1948 by Ralph Ellison. Used by permission of Random House, Inc.

Louise Erdrich. "The Lady in the Pink Mustang" and "Dear John Wayne" from *Jacklight* by Louise Erdrich. Copyright © 1984 by Louise Erdrich. Used with permission of The Wylie Agency LLC.

Martin Espada. "Imagine the Angels of Bread" from *Imagine the Angels of Bread* by Martin Espada. Copyright © 1996 by Martin Espada. Used by permission of W. W. Norton & Company, Inc.

William Faulkner. "A Rose for Emily" from *Collected Stories of William Faulkner* by William Faulkner. Copyright 1930 and renewed 1958 by William Faulkner. Used by permission of Random House, Inc.

Lawrence Ferlinghetti. "Short Story on a Painting of Gustav Klimt" from *Endless Life*. Copyright © 1976 by Lawrence Ferlinghetti. Reprinted by permission of New Directions Publishing Corp.

Ida Fink. "The Table" from *A Scrap of Time and Other Stories*, translated by Madeline Levine and Francine Prose. Copyright © 1983 by Ida Fink. Evanston: Northwestern University Press, 1995, pp. 139–165. Reprinted by permission of Northwestern University Press.

Carolyn Forché. All lines from "The Colonel" from *The Country Between Us* by Carolyn Forché. Originally appeared in *Women's International Resource Exchange*. Copyright © 1981 by Carolyn Forché. Reprinted by permission of HarperCollins Publishers.

Charles Fort. "We Did Not Fear the Father" originally appeared in *The Georgia Review*, Volume LIII, Number 2 (Summer 1999). © 1999 by The University of Georgia. Reprinted by permission of *The Georgia Review* and Charles Fort.

Robert Frost. "Stopping by Woods on a Snowy Evening," "The Road Not Taken," and "Acquainted with the Night" from *The Poetry of Robert Frost*, edited by Edward Connery Lathem. Copyright © 1923, 1928, 1969 by Henry Holt and Company, copyright © 1944, 1951, 1956 by Robert Frost. Reprinted by permission of Henry Holt and Company, LLC.

Deborah Garrison. "I Saw You Walking" from *The Second Child* by Deborah Garrison. Copyright © 2006 by Deborah Garrison. Used by permission of Random House, Inc.

Atul Gawande. "Hellhole" originally published in *The New Yorker*, March 30, 2009.

Karen Gershon. "Race" from *Selected Poems* by Karen Gershon. Copyright © C. V. M. Tripp. Reprinted with the permission of C. V. M. Tripp.

Nikki Giovanni. "Legacies" from *My House* by Nikki Giovanni. Copyright © 1972 by Nikki Giovanni, renewed 2000 by Nikki Giovanni. Reprinted by permission of HarperCollins Publishers.

Loren Goodman. "Traveling through the Dark (2005)" first published in the journal *Poetry*, July/August 2005, vol. CLXXXVL: 4. Reprinted by permission of the author.

Barbara Bradley Hagerty. "New College Teaches Young American Muslims." © 2010 National Public Radio, Inc. NPR® news report titled "New College Teaches Young American Muslims" by NPR's Barbara Bradley Hagerty was originally broadcast on NPR's Morning Edition® September 8, 2010, and is used with the permission of NPR. Any unauthorized duplication is strictly prohibited.

Ha Jin. "Saboteur" from *The Bridegroom* by Ha Jin. Copyright © 2000 by Ha Jin. Used by permission of Pantheon Books, a division of Random House, Inc.

Lorraine Hansberry. *A Raisin in the Sun* by Lorraine Hansberry. Copyright © 1958 by Robert Nemiroff, as an unpublished work. Copyright © 1959, 1966, 1984 by Robert Nemiroff. Copyright renewed 1986, 1987 by Robert Nemiroff. Used by permission of Random House, Inc. "April 23, 1964, Letter to the *New York Times*" by Lorraine Hansberry from *To Be Young, Gifted and Black: Lorraine Hansberry in Her Own Words* by Robert Nemiroff. Copyright © 1969 by Robert Nemiroff and Robert Nemiroff as Executor of the Estate of Lorraine Hansberry. All rights reserved. Reprinted with the permission of Simon & Schuster, Inc.

Michael S. Harper. "Discovery" from *Songlines in Michaeltree: New and Collected Poems*. Copyright 2000 by Michael S. Harper. Used with permission of the poet and the University of Illinois Press.

Scott Duke Harris. "Online Memorials: Internet Adds New Dimension to Grieving Process" from *Mercury News*, October 10, 2010. Copyright © 2010. Used with permission of *San Jose Mercury News*. All rights reserved.

Robert Hayden. "Those Winter Sundays" from *Collected Poems of Robert Hayden* by Robert Hayden, edited by Frederick Glaysher. Copyright © 1966 by Robert Hayden. Used by permission of Liveright Publishing Corporation.

Seamus Heaney. "Punishment" from *Opened Ground: Selected Poems 1966–1996* by Seamus Heaney. Copyright © 1998 by Seamus Heaney. Reprinted by permission of Farrar, Straus and Giroux, LLC and Faber and Faber Ltd.

Miguel Helft. "A Decent Proposal" from *Prism*, November 1995. Reprinted by permission of the author.

Ernest Hemingway. "Hills like White Elephants" from *The Complete Short Stories of Ernest Hemingway* by Ernest Hemingway. Copyright © 1927 by Charles Scribner's Sons. Copyright renewed © 1955 by Ernest Hemingway. All rights reserved. Reprinted with the permission of Scribner, a division of Simon & Schuster, Inc.

Essex Hemphill. "Commitments" from *Ceremonies* by Essex Hemphill. Copyright © 1992 by Essex Hemphill. Used by permission of Plume, a division of Penguin Group (USA) Inc.

David Hernandez. "Pigeons." Copyright © David Hernandez. Reprinted by permission of the author.

Isabel Hilton. "A Triumph for Moral Authority" by Isabel Hilton from *The Independent*, November 15, 2010. Copyright © 2010 by *The Independent*.

Edward Hirsch. "Execution" from *The Night Parade* by Edward Hirsch. Copyright © 1989 by Edward Hirsch. Used by permission of Alfred A. Knopf, a division of Random House, Inc.

Linda Hogan. "Heritage" from *Calling Myself Home* by Linda Hogan. First appeared in *Red Clay* by Linda Hogan. Copyright © 1991 by Linda Hogan. Reprinted by permission of The Greenfield Review Press.

bell hooks. Excerpt taken from the book *Bone Black* by bell hooks. Copyright © 1996 by Gloria Watkins. Reprinted by permission of Henry Holt and Company, LLC.

Yusef Komunyakaa. "Blackberries" from *Pleasure Dome: New and Collected Poems*. © 2001 by Yusef Komunyakaa. Reprinted by permission of Wesleyan University Press.

Maxine Kumin. "Woodchucks" from *Selected Poems 1960–1990* by Maxine Kumin. Copyright © 1972, 1997 by Maxine Kumin. Used by permission of W. W. Norton & Company, Inc.

Hanif Kureishi. "My Son, the Fanatic." Copyright © Hanif Kureishi 1998. Reproduced by permission of the author c/o Rogers, Coleridge & White Ltd., 20 Powis Mews, London W11 1JN.

Jhumpa Lahiri. "Going Ashore" from *Unaccustomed Earth* by Jhumpa Lahiri. Copyright © 2008 by Jhumpa Lahiri. Used by permission of Alfred A. Knopf, a division of Random House, Inc. "My Two Lives" by Jhumpa Lahiri. Originally published in *Newsweek*. Copyright © 2006 by Jhumpa Lahiri. Reprinted by permission of the author.

Dori Laub and Shoshana Felman. "Testimony and Historical Truth" from *Testimony: Crises of Witnessing in Literature, Psychoanalysis, and History* by Dori Laub and Shoshana Felman. Copyright 1991. Reproduced by permission of Routledge, Inc. via Copyright Clearance Center.

Ursula K. Le Guin. "The Ones Who Talk Away from Omelas" from *The Wind's Twelve Quarters*. First appeared in *New Dimensions* 3. Copyright © 1973, 2001 by Ursula K. Le Guin. Reprinted by permission of the author and the author's agent, the Virginia Kidd Agency, Inc.

Philip Levine. "What Work Is" from *What Work Is* by Philip Levine. Copyright © 1991 by Philip Levine. "A Story" from *News of the World: Poems* by Philip Levine. Copyright © 2009 by Philip Levine. Used by permission of Alfred A. Knopf, a division of Random House, Inc.

Paul Lisicky. "What Might Life Be Like in the 21st Century?" Reprinted from *Prairie Schooner* Vol. 83, No. 3 by permission of the University of Nebraska Press. Copyright 2009 by the University of Nebraska Press.

Li-Young Lee. "My Father, in Heaven, Is Reading Out Loud" from *The City in Which I Love You*. Copyright © 1990 by Li-Young Lee. Reprinted with the permission of BOA Editions, Ltd., www.boaeditions.org.

Barry Lopez. "Emancipation." Reprinted by permission of SLL/Sterling Lord Literistic, Inc. Copyright by Barry Holstun Lopez.

Audre Lorde. "Who Said It Was Simple" from *The Collected Poems of Audre Lorde* by Audre Lorde. Copyright © 1973 by Audre Lorde. Used by permission of W. W. Norton & Company, Inc.

Thomas Lux. "To Help the Monkey Cross the River" from *The Cradle Place: Poems* by Thomas Lux. Copyright © 2004 by Thomas Lux. Reprinted by permission of Houghton Mifflin Harcourt Publishing Company. All rights reserved.

Rebecca Makkai. "The Briefcase." First published in *The New England Review*, Vol. 29, No. 2, 2008. Reprinted by permission of Rebecca Makkai and Aragi Inc.

Jill McCorkle. "Magic Words" from *Going Away Shoes* by Jill McCorkle. © 2009 by Jill McCorkle. Reprinted by permission of Algonquin Books of Chapel Hill. All rights reserved.

Terrence McNally. *Andre's Mother*. Copyright © 1995 by Terrence McNally. All rights reserved. CAUTION: Professionals and amateurs are hereby warned that "Andre's Mother" is subject to a royalty. It is fully protected under the copyright laws of the United States of America and of all countries covered by the International Copyright Union (including the Dominion of Canada and the rest of the British Commonwealth), the Berne Convention, the Pan-American Copyright Convention and the Universal Copyright Convention as well as all countries with which the United States has reciprocal copyright relations. All rights, including professional/amateur stage rights, motion picture, recitation, lecturing, public reading, radio broadcasting, television, video or sound recording, all other forms of mechanical or electronic reproduction, such as CD-ROM, CD-I, information storage and retrieval systems and photocopying, and the rights of translation into foreign languages, are strictly reserved. Particular emphasis is laid upon the matter of readings, permission for which must be secured from the Author's agent in writing. Inquiries concerning rights should be addressed to: William Morris Endeavor Entertainment, LLC, 1325 Avenue of the Americas, New York, New York 10019, Attn: Jonathan Lomma. Originally Produced by The Manhattan Theatre Club.

John Updike. "A & P" from *Pigeon Feathers and Other Stories* by John Updike. Copyright © 1962 and renewed 1990 by John Updike. Used by permission of Alfred A. Knopf, a division of Random House, Inc.

"'Vampire' Victim in Hospital for a Week." *The Dominion Post*, May 7, 2010. Reprinted courtesy of *The Dominion Post*.

Victor Villanueva Jr. "Reflecting on Richard Rodriguez." Copyright 1987 by the National Council of Teachers of English. Reprinted with permission.

Kurt Vonnegut Jr. "Harrison Bergeron" from *Welcome to the Monkey House* by Kurt Vonnegut Jr. Copyright © 1961 by Kurt Vonnegut Jr. Used by permission of Dell Publishing, a division of Random House, Inc.

Peter de Vries. "To His Importunate Mistress." Reprinted by permission of Jon and Derek de Vries.

Joyce Wadler. "Peter Rabbit Must Die" from *The New York Times*, June 5, 2008. © 2008 *The New York Times*. All rights reserved. Used by permission and protected by the Copyright Laws of the United States. The printing, copying, redistribution, or retransmission of this Content without express written permission is prohibited.

Alice Walker. "In Search of Our Mothers' Gardens" from *In Search of Our Mothers' Gardens: Womanist Prose*. Copyright © 1974 by Alice Walker. "Women" from *Revolutionary Petunias & Other Poems*. Copyright © 1970 and renewed 1998 by Alice Walker. "Everyday Use" and "The Flowers" from *In Love & Trouble: Stories of Black Women*. Copyright © 1973 by Alice Walker. Reprinted by permission of Houghton Mifflin Harcourt Publishing Company.

Eudora Welty. "A Visit of Charity" and "A Worn Path" from *A Curtain of Green and Other Stories*. Copyright © 1941 and renewed 1969 by Eudora Welty. Reprinted by permission of Houghton Mifflin Harcourt Publishing Company. "Is Phoenix Jackson's Grandson Really Dead?" from *The Eye of the Story* by Eudora Welty. Copyright © 1978 by Eudora Welty. Used by permission of Random House, Inc.

John Edgar Wideman. "Newborn Thrown in Trash and Dies" from *The Stories of John Edgar Wideman* by John Edgar Wideman. Copyright © 1981, 1992 by John Edgar Wideman. Used by permission of Pantheon Books, a division of Random House, Inc.

C. K. Williams. "The Nail" from *Repair* by C. K. Williams. Copyright © 1999 by C. K. Williams. Reprinted by permission of Farrar, Straus and Giroux, LLC.

Tennessee Williams. *The Glass Menagerie* by Tennessee Williams. Copyright © 1945, renewed 1973 by The University of the South. Reprinted by permission of Georges Borchardt, Inc., for The Estate of Tennessee Williams.

William Carlos Williams. "The Use of Force" from *The Collected Stories of William Carlos Williams*. Copyright © 1938 by William Carlos Williams. Reprinted by permission of New Directions Publishing Corp.

Tobias Wolff. "The Rich Brother." Copyright © 1985 by Tobias Wolff. Reprinted by permission of International Creative Management, Inc.

James Wright. "Lying in a Hammock at William Duffy's Farm in Pine Island, Minnesota" from *Collected Poems*. © 1971 by James Wright. Reprinted by permission of Wesleyan University Press.

Richard Wright. Pp. 14–22 from *Black Boy* by Richard Wright. Copyright 1937, 1942, 1944, 1945 by Richard Wright; renewed © 1973 by Ellen Wright. Reprinted by permission of HarperCollins Publishers.

Robert Wrigley. "Highway 12, Just East of Paradise, Idaho" from *Lives of the Animals* by Robert Wrigley. Copyright © 2003 by Robert Wrigley. Used by permission of Penguin, a division of Penguin Group (USA) Inc.

Dean Young. "Clam Ode" from *Embryoyo* by Dean Young. Reprinted by permission of the author.

Jason Zinoman. "Necking: *True Blood* Reinvents Vampire Sex" from *Slate*, June 28, 2010. © 2010 The Slate Group. All rights reserved. Used by permission and protected by the Copyright Laws of the United States. The printing, copying, redistribution, or retransmission of the Material without express written permission is prohibited.

Index of Authors, Titles, First Lines, and Key Terms

Key terms page numbers are in bold.